T
Oxford–Hachette
French Dictionary

Second Edition

French ⟶ English
English ⟶ French

Edited by
Marianne Chalmers
Martine Pierquin

WITHDRAWN

OXFORD
UNIVERSITY PRESS

OXFORD
UNIVERSITY PRESS

Great Clarendon Street, Oxford OX2 6DP

Oxford University Press is a department of the University of Oxford.
It furthers the University's objective of excellence in research, scholarship,
and education by publishing worldwide in

Oxford New York

Auckland Bangkok Buenos Aires Cape Town Chennai
Dar es Salaam Delhi Hong Kong Istanbul Karachi Kolkata
Kuala Lumpur Madrid Melbourne Mexico City Mumbai Nairobi
São Paulo Shanghai Singapore Taipei Tokyo Toronto

and an associated company in Berlin

Oxford is a registered trade mark of Oxford University Press
in the UK and in certain other countries

Published in the United States
by Oxford University Press Inc., New York

© Oxford University Press, Hachette Livre 1996, 2000

The moral rights of the author have been asserted

Database right Oxford University Press (maker)

First published 1996
Second edition 2000

British Library Cataloguing in Publication Data

Data available

Library of Congress Cataloging in Publication Data

Data available

ISBN 0-19-860279-0

10 9 8 7 6

Designed by Information Design Unit, Newport Pagnell
Typeset in Nimrod, Arial and Meta by Tradespools
Printed in Great Britain by Clays Ltd, Bungay, Suffolk

Preface

This major new edition of the *Pocket Oxford-Hachette French Dictionary* has been expanded and extensively updated to reflect recent additions to both the French and English languages, with the needs of both the general and school user in mind. The dictionary provides comprehensive coverage of core vocabulary across a broad spectrum of contemporary written and spoken language, incorporating many idiomatic phrases and expressions. The wordlist is further enhanced by the addition of new words and phrases generated by recent developments in information technology, science, and popular culture, for effective and up-to-date communication.

Essential information on grammar, style, and pronunciation is provided in a convenient and accessible format, making the dictionary an ideal reference tool and study aid. The user is guided in selecting appropriate translations by clear examples of usage and construction and by information on the register of language, where required.

All grammatical terms used are explained in a glossary at the back of the dictionary, and French verbs are cross-referenced to a set of verb tables.

New features of the dictionary include an A – Z of French life and culture, providing information on contemporary French society, a calendar of traditions, festivals, and holidays in France, and a practical guide to writing letters in French. A series of sample letters illustrates the differences between French and English usage, highlighting important features of style and format in a variety of situations.

Designed to meet the needs of a wide range of users, from the student at intermediate level and above to the enthusiastic traveller or business professional, the *Pocket Oxford-Hachette Dictionary* is an invaluable practical resource for learners of contemporary, idiomatic French at the start of the twenty-first century.

The Editors

Editors and contributors

Second edition

Chief Editors
Marianne Chalmers
Martine Pierquin

Data Capture
Anne McConnell
Anna Cotgreave
Marianne Selby-Smith

A-Z of French Life and Culture
Calendar of French traditions, festivals, and holidays
Ella Associates
Valerie Grundy

First edition

Chief Editor
Marie-Hélène Corréard

Editors
Frances Illingworth
Natalie Pomier

Associate Editor
Mary O'Neill

Proofreading
Genevieve Hawkins

Note on proprietary status

This dictionary includes some words which have, or are asserted to have, proprietary status as trademarks or otherwise. Their inclusion does not imply that they have acquired for legal purposes a non-proprietary or general significance, nor any other judgement concerning their legal status.

In cases where the editorial staff have some evidence that a word has proprietary status this is indicated in the entry for that word by the symbol ®, but no judgement concerning the legal status of such words is made or implied thereby.

v

Contents

The structure of French-English entries

headword •————— **délice** /delis/ *nm* delight
délicieusement /delisjøzmɑ̃/ *adv* **(a)** deliciously

délicieux, -ieuse /delisjø, øz/ *adj* **(a)** ————— • feminine form of delicious — the headword

demandeur¹, -euse /dəmɑ̃dœʀ, øz/ *nm,f* applicant
compounds in •——— ■ ~ **d'asile** asylum-seeker; ~ **d'emploi** job-seeker
block at end of entry

épaule /epol/ *nf* shoulder
IDIOMS changer son fusil d'~ to change one's ————— • idioms in block at tactics; **avoir la tête sur les** ~**s** to have one's — end of entry head screwed on (colloq)

pronunciation •——— **épicier, -ière** /episje, ɛʀ/ *nm,f* grocer
in IPA

francophone /fʀɑ̃kɔfɔn/ **1** *adj* French- ————— • grammatical speaking; ‹*literature*› in the French language — categories **2** *nmf* French speaker

part of speech •——— **free-lance** /fʀilɑ̃s/ *nmf* freelance, freelancer;
plus gender

juguler /ʒygyle/ [1] *vtr* to stamp out ‹*epidemic,* ————— • number of verb group referring to sense categories •——— **liquider** /likide/ [1] *vtr* **(a)** to settle ‹*accounts*›; — the French verb to liquidate ‹*company, business*› — tables at the end of **(b)** to clear ‹*goods, stock*› — the dictionary

lot /lo/ *nm* **(a)** (of inheritance) share; (of land) plot ————— • sense indicators **(b)** (in lottery) prize; **gagner le gros** ~ to hit the jackpot

field labels for •——— **luth** /lyt/ *nm* **(a)** (Mus) lute
specialist terms **(b)** (Zool) leatherback

magner: se magner /maɲe/ [1] *v refl* ————— • style labels
(+ *v être*) (slang) to get a move on (colloq)

pomponner: se pomponner /pɔ̃pɔne/ [1]
grammatical •——— *v refl* (+ *v être*) to get dolled up
information

précédent, ~**e** /pʀesedɑ̃, ɑ̃t/ **1** *adj* ————— • translations
previous
2 *nm,f* **le** ~, **la** ~**e** the previous one

profaner /pʀɔfane/ [1] *vtr* to desecrate
typical collocates •——— ‹*temple*›; to defile ‹*memory*›; to debase
– words used with ‹*institution*›
the headword, shown to help select **RN** /ɛʀɛn/ *nf* (*abbr* = **route nationale**) ≈ A ————— • approximate the right translation road (GB), highway (US) — translation

examples, with •——— **souci** /susi/ *nm* **(a) se faire du** ~ to worry
a swung dash **(b)** problem; **j'ai d'autres** ~**s** (**en tête**) I've got
representing the other things to worry about
headword

transfusé, ~**e** /tʀɑ̃sfyze/ **1** *pp* ▶ ————— • cross-reference
TRANSFUSER

The structure of English-French entries

headword • —— **battery** n pile f; (in car) batterie f

battery charger n chargeur m de batteries • separate entries for compounds
battery farming n élevage m en batterie

beat 1 n (a) (of drum, heart) battement m ...
phrasal verbs • ■ **beat back** repousser ⟨group, flames⟩
■ **beat down** ⟨rain⟩ tomber à verse (on sur)

cat n (domestic) chat m; (female) chatte f; **the big ~s** les grands félins mpl
IDIOMS **to let the ~ out of the bag** vendre la mèche; **to rain ~s and dogs** pleuvoir des cordes • idioms in block at end of entry

grammatical • **clutter** 1 n désordre m
categories 2 vtr (also ~ **up**) encombrer
and parts of speech

edge 1 n (a) (outer limit) bord m; (of wood, clearing) lisière f; **the film had us on the ~ of our seats** le film nous a tenus en haleine • sense categories
(b) (of blade) tranchant m

sense indicators • **especially** adv (a) (above all) surtout, en particulier; **him ~** lui en particulier; **~ as it's so hot** d'autant plus qu'il fait si chaud
(b) (on purpose) exprès, spécialement

fishy adj (a) ⟨smell, taste⟩ de poisson
(b) (colloq) (suspect) louche (colloq) • style labels

field labels for • **message window** n (Comput) feuille f de specialist terms message
mushroom n (a) (Bot, Culin) champignon

non-smoking adj non fumeur inv • grammatical information

translations • **nuisance** n (gen) embêtement m; (Law) nuisance f; **what a ~!** que c'est agaçant!

official 1 n fonctionnaire mf; (of party, union) officiel/-ielle m/f; (at town hall) employé/-e m/f • feminine ending in translation

typical collocates • **plump** adj ⟨person, arm, leg⟩ potelé/-e;
– words used with ⟨cheek, face⟩ rond/-e, plein/-e
the headword, shown **plunge** 1 vtr plonger (**into** dans)
to help select the 2 vi ⟨road, cliff, waterfall⟩ plonger; ⟨bird, right translation plane⟩ piquer

secondary school n ≈ école f secondaire • approximate translation equivalent

examples, with • **shut** 1 adj fermé/-e; **her eyes were ~** elle
a swung dash avait les yeux fermés; **to slam the door ~**
representing the claquer la porte (pour bien la fermer); **to**
headword **keep one's mouth ~** (colloq) se taire

these ▶ THIS • cross-reference

The pronunciation of French

Vowels

a	*as in*	*patte*	/pat/
ɑ		*pâte*	/pɑt/
ɑ̃		*clan*	/klɑ̃/
e		*dé*	/de/
ɛ		*belle*	/bɛl/
ɛ̃		*lin*	/lɛ̃/
ə		*demain*	/dəmɛ̃/
i		*gris*	/ɡʀi/
o		*gros*	/ɡʀo/
ɔ		*corps*	/kɔʀ/
ɔ̃		*long*	/lɔ̃/
œ		*leur*	/lœʀ/
œ̃		*brun*	/bʀœ̃/
ø		*deux*	/dø/
u		*fou*	/fu/
y		*pur*	/pyʀ/

Semi-vowels

j	*as in*	*fille*	/fij/
ɥ		*huit*	/ɥit/
w		*oui*	/wi/

Consonants

b	*as in*	*bal*	/bal/
d		*dent*	/dɑ̃/
f		*foire*	/fwaʀ/
ɡ		*gomme*	/ɡɔm/
k		*clé*	/kle/
l		*lien*	/ljɛ̃/
m		*mer*	/mɛʀ/
n		*nage*	/naʒ/
ɲ		*gnon*	/ɲɔ̃/
ŋ		*dancing*	/dɑ̃siŋ/
p		*porte*	/pɔʀt/
ʀ		*rire*	/ʀiʀ/
s		*sang*	/sɑ̃/
ʃ		*chien*	/ʃjɛ̃/
t		*train*	/tʀɛ̃/
v		*voile*	/vwal/
z		*zèbre*	/zɛbʀ/
ʒ		*jeune*	/ʒœn/

The symbols used in this dictionary for the pronunciation of French are those of the IPA (International Phonetic Alphabet). Certain differences in pronunciation are shown in the phonetic transcription, although many speakers do not observe them—e.g. the long 'a' /ɑ/ in *pâte* and the short 'a' /a/ in *patte*, or the difference between the nasal vowels 'un' /œ̃/ as in *brun* and 'in' /ɛ̃/ as in *brin*.

Transcription

Each entry is followed by its phonetic transcription between slashes, with a few exceptions.

Morphological variations

The phonetic transcription of the plural and feminine forms of certain nouns and adjectives does not repeat the root, but shows only the change in ending. Therefore, in certain cases, the presentation of the entry does not correspond to that of the phonetic transcripton e.g. *électricien, -ienne* /elɛktʀisjɛ̃, ɛn/.

Phrases

Full phonetic transcription is given for adverbial or prepositional phrases which are shown in alphabetical order within the main headword e.g. *emblée, d'emblée* /dɑ̃ble/, *plain-pied, de plain-pied* /d(ə)plɛ̃pje/.

Consonants

Aspiration of 'h'

Where it is impossible to make a liaison this is indicated by /'/ immediately after the slash e.g. *haine* /'ɛn/.

Assimilation

A voiced consonant can become unvoiced when it is followed by an unvoiced consonant within a word e.g. *absorber* /apsɔʀbe/.

Vowels

Open 'e' and closed 'e'

A clear distinction is made at the end of a word between a closed 'e' and an open 'e' e.g. *pré* /pʀe/ and *près* /pʀɛ/, *complet* /kɔ̃plɛ/ and *combler* /kɔ̃ble/.

Within a word the following rules apply:
• 'e' is always open in a syllable followed by a syllable containing a mute 'e' e.g. *règle* /ʀɛgl/, *réglementaire* /ʀɛgləmɑ̃tɛʀ/

• in careful speech 'e' is pronounced as a closed 'e' when it is followed by a syllable containing a closed vowel (y, i, e) e.g. *pressé* /pʀese/
• 'e' is pronounced as an open 'e' when it is followed by a syllable containing an open vowel e.g. *pressant* /pʀɛsɑ̃/.

Mute 'e'

The pronunciation of mute 'e' varies considerably depending on the level of language used and on the region from which the speaker originates. As a general rule it is only pronounced at the end of a word in the South of France or in poetry and it is, therefore, not shown. In an isolated word the mute 'e' preceded by a single consonant is dropped e.g. *parfaitement* /paʀfɛtmɑ̃/, but *probablement* /pʀɔbabləmɑ̃/. In many cases the pronunciation of the mute 'e' depends on the surrounding context. Thus one would say *une reconnaissance de dette* /ynʀəkɔnɛsɑ̃sdədɛt/, but, *ma reconnaissance est éternelle* /maʀkɔnɛsɑ̃sɛtetɛʀnɛl/. The mute 'e' is shown in brackets in order to account for this phenomenon.

Stress

There is no real stress as such in French. In normal unemphasized speech a slight stress falls on the final syllable of a word or group of words, providing that it does not contain a mute 'e'. This is not shown in the phonetic transcription of individual entries.

Abbreviations

abbr	abbreviation	phr	phrase
adj	adjective	pl	plural
adv	adverb	Pol	politics
Anat	anatomy	pp	past participle
Aut	automobile	pp adj	past participle adjective
aux	auxiliary	pr n	proper noun
Bot	botany	pref	prefix
colloq	colloquial	prep	preposition
Comput	computing	pres p adj	present participle adjective
conj	conjunction	pron	pronoun
Culin	culinary	qch	quelque chose (something)
dem pron	demonstrative pronoun	qn	quelqu'un (somebody)
det	determiner	quantif	quantifier
Econ	economy	®	registered trademark
excl	exclamation	rel pron	relative pronoun
f	feminine	sb	somebody
Fr	French	Sch	school
GB	British English	sg	singular
gen	generally	sth	something
indic	indicative	subj	subjunctive
inv	invariable	Tech	technology
m	masculine	Univ	university
Med	medicine	US	American English
Mil	military	v	verb
Mus	music	v aux	auxiliary verb
n	noun	vi	intransitive verb
nf	feminine noun	v impers	impersonal verb
nm	masculine noun	v refl	reflexive verb
nmf	masculine and feminine noun	vtr	transitive verb
nm,f	masculine and feminine noun	Zool	zoology
Naut	nautical		

a¹, A /a, ɑ/ **1** *nm inv* a, A; **démontrer qch à qn par A plus B** to demonstrate sth conclusively to sb
2 A *nf* (*abbr* = **autoroute**) motorway (GB), freeway (US)

a² /a/ ▶ AVOIR¹

à /a/ *prep*

■ **Note** You will find translations for expressions such as *machine à écrire*, *aller à la pêche* etc, at the entries MACHINE, PÊCHE etc.
– For the uses of *à* with the verbs *aller, être, avoir, penser* etc, see the entries for these verbs.

(a) to; **aller ~ Paris** to go to Paris; **se rendre au travail** to go to work
(b) at; in; **~ la maison** at home; **être ~ Paris** to be in Paris; **au printemps** in (the) spring; **~ midi** at midday; **~ quatre kilomètres d'ici** four kilometres (GB) from here; **~ 100 kilomètres-heure** at 100 kilometres (GB) per *or* an hour; **un timbre ~ trois francs** a three-franc stamp; **(de) huit ~ dix heures par jour** between eight and ten hours a day
(c) with; **le garçon aux cheveux bruns** the boy with dark hair
(d) **~ qui est cette montre?** whose is this watch?; **elle est ~ elle** it's hers; **je suis ~ vous tout de suite** I'll be with you in a minute; **c'est ~ qui de jouer?** whose turn is it?
(e) **il est ~ plaindre** he's to be pitied
(f) **~ nous tous on devrait y arriver** between all of us we should be able to manage; **~ trois on est serrés** with three people it's a squash
(g) **~ ce qu'il paraît** apparently; **~ ta santé**, **~ la tienne!** cheers!; **~ tes souhaits!** bless you!

abaisser /abese/ [1] **1** *vtr* to pull down ‹*lever*›; to lower ‹*safety curtain, window*›
2 s'abaisser *v refl* (+ *v être*) **(a)** ‹*stage curtain*› to fall
(b) **s'~ à faire** to stoop to doing

abandon /abɑ̃dɔ̃/ *nm* **(a)** **être à l'~** ‹*house*› to be abandoned; ‹*garden*› to be neglected
(b) (of project, method) abandonment; (of right) relinquishment
(c) (from race, competition) withdrawal

abandonné, **~e** /abɑ̃dɔne/ **1** *pp* ▶ ABANDONNER
2 *pp adj* **(a)** ‹*spouse, friend, cause*› deserted; ‹*vehicle, house, nation*› abandoned
(b) ‹*path, factory*› disused

abandonner /abɑ̃dɔne/ [1] *vtr* **(a)** (gen) to give up; (in school) to drop ‹*subject*›
(b) (from game, tournament) to withdraw; to retire
(c) to leave ‹*person, place*›; to abandon ‹*car, object*›
(d) to abandon ‹*child, animal*›; to desert ‹*home, post, cause*›
(e) ‹*courage, chance*› to fail ‹*person*›

abat-jour /abaʒuʀ/ *nm inv* lampshade

abats /aba/ *nm pl* offal; (of poultry) giblets

abattement /abatmɑ̃/ *nm*
(a) despondency
(b) **~ fiscal** tax allowance (GB) *or* deduction (US)

abattoir /abatwaʀ/ *nm* abattoir, slaughterhouse

abattre /abatʀ/ [61] **1** *vtr* **(a)** to shoot [sb] down ‹*person*›; to shoot ‹*animal*›; to slaughter ‹*cattle, sheep*›
(b) to pull down ‹*building*›; to knock down ‹*wall*›; ‹*person*› to fell ‹*tree*›; ‹*storm*› to bring down ‹*tree*›
(c) to show ‹*card, hand*›
(d) to demoralize
(e) **~ de la besogne** to get through a lot of work
2 s'abattre *v refl* (+ *v être*) **s'~ sur** ‹*storm*› to break over; ‹*rain*› to beat down on; ‹*bird of prey*› to swoop down on

abbaye /abei/ *nf* abbey

abbé /abe/ *nm* **(a)** priest
(b) abbot

abc /abese/ *nm* ABC, rudiments

abcès /apsɛ/ *nm inv* abscess; **crever l'~** to resolve a crisis

abdication /abdikasjɔ̃/ *nf* abdication

abdiquer /abdike/ [1] *vi* ‹*sovereign*› to abdicate

abdomen /abdɔmɛn/ *nm* abdomen, stomach

abdominal, **~e**, *mpl* **-aux** /abdɔminal, o/ **1** *adj* abdominal
2 abdominaux *nm pl* abdominal muscles

abeille /abɛj/ *nf* bee

aberrant, **~e** /abɛʀɑ̃, ɑ̃t/ *adj* **(a)** absurd
(b) aberrant

aberration /abɛʀasjɔ̃/ *nf* aberration

abêtir /abetiʀ/ [3]: **s'abêtir** *v refl* (+ *v être*) to become stupid

abêtissant, **~e** /abetisɑ̃, ɑ̃t/ *adj* mindless

abîme /abim/ *nm* **(a)** abyss
(b) (figurative) gulf

abîmer /abime/ [1] **1** *vtr* to damage
2 s'abîmer *v refl* (+ *v être*) ‹*object*› to get damaged; ‹*fruit*› to spoil

abject, **~e** /abʒɛkt/ *adj* despicable, abject

ablation /ablasjɔ̃/ *nf* excision, removal

abnégation /abnegasjɔ̃/ *nf* self-sacrifice

aboiement /abwamã/ nm barking

abolir /abɔliʀ/ [3] vtr to abolish

abominable /abɔminabl/ adj abominable

abomination /abɔminasjɔ̃/ nf abomination

abondamment /abɔ̃damã/ adv ⟨drink⟩ a lot; ⟨illustrate⟩ amply; **rincer** ∼ rinse thoroughly

abondance /abɔ̃dɑ̃s/ nf (a) (of information) wealth; (of resources) abundance
(b) affluence

abondant, ∼**e** /abɔ̃dã, ãt/ adj ⟨food⟩ plentiful; ⟨illustrations⟩ numerous; ⟨vegetation⟩ lush

abonder /abɔ̃de/ [1] vi to be plentiful; to abound

IDIOMS ∼ **dans le sens de qn** to agree wholeheartedly with sb

abonné, ∼**e** /abɔne/ **1** pp ▶ ABONNER
2 nm,f (a) subscriber
(b) season ticket holder

abonnement /abɔnmã/ nm
(a) subscription
(b) (**carte d'**)∼ season ticket

abonner /abɔne/ [1] **1** vtr ∼ **qn à qch** (to magazine) to take out a subscription to sth for sb; (for theatre) to buy sb a season ticket for sth
2 s'abonner v refl (+ v être) to subscribe (à to); to buy a season ticket (à for)

abord /abɔʀ/ **1** nm (a) **elle est d'un** ∼ **difficile** she is rather unapproachable
(b) **être d'un** ∼ **aisé** ⟨subject, book⟩ to be accessible
(c) **au premier** ∼ at first sight
2 d'abord phr first; **tout d'**∼ first of all
3 abords nm pl surrounding area, area around

abordable /abɔʀdabl/ adj ⟨product, price⟩ affordable; ⟨text⟩ accessible

abordage /abɔʀdaʒ/ nm (by pirates) boarding

aborder /abɔʀde/ [1] **1** vtr (a) to tackle ⟨problem⟩
(b) to approach ⟨person⟩
(c) to reach ⟨place, shore⟩
2 vi ⟨traveller, ship⟩ to land

aboutir /abutiʀ/ [3] **1 aboutir à** v+prep to lead to
2 vi ⟨negotiations, project⟩ to succeed

aboutissants /abutisã/ nm pl **les tenants et les** ∼ **de qch** the ins and outs of sth

aboutissement /abutismã/ nm
(a) culmination
(b) (successful) outcome

aboyer /abwaje/ [23] vi ⟨dog⟩ to bark (**après** at)

abracadabrant, ∼**e** /abʀakadabʀã, ãt/ adj bizarre

abrasif, **-ive** /abʀazif, iv/ adj abrasive

abrégé /abʀeʒe/ nm (book) concise guide

abréger /abʀeʒe/ [15] vtr (a) to shorten ⟨word, expression⟩
(b) to cut short ⟨visit, career⟩

abreuver: s'abreuver /abʀøve/ [1] v refl (+ v être) ⟨animal⟩ to drink

abreuvoir /abʀøvwaʀ/ nm drinking trough

abréviation /abʀevjasjɔ̃/ nf abbreviation

abri /abʀi/ nm (a) shelter; **à l'**∼ **de** sheltered from; (figurative) safe from
(b) shed

abricot /abʀiko/ nm apricot

abricotier /abʀikɔtje/ nm apricot tree

abriter /abʀite/ [1] **1** vtr (a) ⟨building⟩ to shelter ⟨people, animals⟩
(b) ⟨country, region⟩ to provide a habitat for ⟨animals, plant life⟩
2 s'abriter v refl (+ v être) to take shelter

abrogation /abʀɔgasjɔ̃/ nf repeal

abroger /abʀɔʒe/ [13] vtr to repeal

abrupt, ∼**e** /abʀypt/ adj (a) ⟨hill, road⟩ steep; ⟨cliff⟩ sheer
(b) ⟨person, tone⟩ abrupt

abruti, ∼**e** /abʀyti/ nm,f (offensive) moron (colloq)

abrutir /abʀytiʀ/ [3] **1** vtr ⟨noise⟩ to deafen; ⟨alcohol, medication, fatigue⟩ to have a numbing effect on; ⟨blow⟩ to stun
2 s'abrutir v refl (+ v être) (a) to become dull-witted
(b) **s'**∼ **de travail** to wear oneself out with work

abrutissant, ∼**e** /abʀytisã, ãt/ adj ⟨music, noise⟩ deafening; ⟨job⟩ mind-numbing

absence /apsɑ̃s/ nf (a) absence
(b) lack; **l'**∼ **de pluie** the lack of rain

absent, ∼**e** /apsã, ãt/ **1** adj (a) **être** ∼ to be away; (for brief spell) to be out
(b) ⟨pupil, employee⟩ absent
(c) (missing) absent (**de** from)
(d) absent-minded
2 nm,f absentee

absentéisme /apsãteism/ nm absenteeism

absenter: s'absenter /apsãte/ [1] v refl (+ v être) to go away; to go out

absolu, ∼**e** /apsɔly/ adj absolute; ⟨rule⟩ hard and fast

absolument /apsɔlymã/ adv absolutely

absolution /apsɔlysjɔ̃/ nf absolution

absolutisme /apsɔlytism/ nm absolutism

absorbant, ∼**e** /apsɔʀbã, ãt/ adj
(a) ⟨substance⟩ absorbent
(b) ⟨job, work⟩ absorbing

absorber /apsɔʀbe/ [1] vtr (a) ⟨material, plant⟩ to absorb
(b) to take ⟨food, medicine⟩
(c) to occupy ⟨mind⟩

absorption /apsɔʀpsjɔ̃/ nf (a) (of liquid) absorption
(b) (of food, medicine) taking

abstenir: s'abstenir /apstəniʀ/ [36] v refl (+ v être) (a) (from voting) to abstain
(b) **s'**∼ **de faire** to refrain from doing

abstention /apstɑ̃sjɔ̃/ nf abstention

abstinence /apstinãs/ nf abstinence

abstraction /apstʀaksjɔ̃/ nf abstraction;
faire ~ de to set aside

abstrait, ~e /apstʀɛ, ɛt/ **1** adj abstract
2 nm (gen) abstract; (art) abstract art

absurde /apsyʀd/ adj, nm absurd

absurdité /apsyʀdite/ nf absurdity

abus /aby/ nm inv abuse

abuser /abyze/ [1] **1** vtr to fool
2 abuser de v+prep (a) ~ **de l'alcool** to
drink to excess
(b) ~ **de** to exploit ⟨situation, credibility⟩
(c) ~ **de qn** to sexually abuse sb
3 vi to go too far; **je ne voudrais pas** ~ I
don't want to impose
4 s'abuser v refl (+ v être) **si je ne
m'abuse** if I'm not mistaken

abusif, -ive /abyzif, iv/ adj (a) excessive
(b) unfair
(c) improper
(d) over-possessive

acabit /akabi/ nm **du même** ~ of that sort

acacia /akasja/ nm (a) (European) **(faux)** ~
locust tree
(b) (tropical) acacia

académicien, -ienne /akademisjɛ̃, ɛn/
nm,f academician

académie /akademi/ nf (Sch) ≈ local
education authority (GB), school district (US)

académique /akademik/ adj (a) (gen)
academic; of the Académie française
(b) (Sch, Univ) ≈ of the local education
authority (GB) or school district (US)
(c) (in art) academic

acajou /akaʒu/ nm mahogany

acariâtre /akaʀjɑtʀ/ adj cantankerous

accablant, ~e /akablɑ̃, ɑ̃t/ adj (a) ⟨heat,
silence⟩ oppressive
(b) ⟨evidence, testimony⟩ damning

accabler /akable/ [1] vtr (a) ⟨bad news⟩ to
devastate; **être accablé par** to be overcome
by ⟨heat, grief⟩
(b) ⟨testimony, person⟩ to condemn

accalmie /akalmi/ nf (a) lull
(b) slack period

accaparant, ~e /akapaʀɑ̃, ɑ̃t/ adj very
demanding

accaparer /akapaʀe/ [1] vtr to corner
⟨market⟩; to monopolize ⟨person, power⟩

accédant, ~e /aksedɑ̃, ɑ̃t/ nm,f ~ **à la
propriété** home-buyer

accéder /aksede/ [14] v+prep (a) ~ **à** to
reach ⟨place⟩
(b) ~ **à** to achieve ⟨fame, glory⟩; to obtain
⟨job⟩; to rise to ⟨high office⟩

accélérateur /akseleʀatœʀ/ nm
accelerator

accélération /akseleʀasjɔ̃/ nf
acceleration; (of consumption) sharp increase
(de in)

accélérer /akseleʀe/ [14] **1** vtr to speed
up ⟨rhythm, process⟩; ~ **le pas** to quicken
one's step
2 vi ⟨driver⟩ to accelerate

3 s'accélérer v refl (+ v être) ⟨pulse,
movement⟩ to become faster; ⟨phenomenon⟩
to accelerate

accent /aksɑ̃/ nm (a) (of person, region)
accent
(b) (on a letter) accent
(c) (on a syllable) ~ **tonique** stress; **mettre l'**~
sur qch to emphasize sth, to put the
emphasis on sth
(d) ~ **de sincérité** hint of sincerity

accentuer /aksɑ̃tɥe/ [1] **1** vtr (a) (gen) to
emphasize, to accentuate
(b) to heighten ⟨tension⟩; to increase
⟨tendency⟩
(c) (in pronouncing) to stress ⟨syllable⟩
2 s'accentuer v refl (+ v être) to become
more marked

acceptable /aksɛptabl/ adj (a) acceptable
(b) passable; satisfactory

acceptation /aksɛptasjɔ̃/ nf acceptance

accepter /aksɛpte/ [1] vtr to accept; to
agree to

acception /aksɛpsjɔ̃/ nf sense; **dans toute
l'**~ **du terme** or **mot** in every sense of the
word

accès /aksɛ/ nm inv (a) access; **d'un** ~
facile ⟨place⟩ easy to get to; '~ **aux quais**' 'to
the trains'; '~ **interdit**' 'no entry'; **l'**~ **à**
access to ⟨profession, course⟩; admission to
⟨club, school⟩
(b) ~ **de colère** fit of anger; ~ **de fièvre** bout
of fever; **par** ~ by fits and starts
(c) (Comput) access

accessible /aksesibl/ adj (a) ⟨place,
book, information⟩ accessible
(b) ~ **à** ⟨job⟩ open to
(c) ⟨price, fare⟩ affordable

accession /aksesjɔ̃/ nf ~ **à** accession to
⟨throne, power⟩; attainment of
⟨independence⟩

accessoire /akseswaʀ/ **1** adj incidental
2 nm (a) accessory; attachment; ~**s de
toilette** toilet requisites
(b) (in the theatre) ~**s** props

accessoirement /akseswaʀmɑ̃/ adv
(a) incidentally, as it happens
(b) if desired

accessoiriste /akseswaʀist/ nm,f props
man/woman

accident /aksidɑ̃/ nm (a) accident
(b) hitch; mishap; ~ **de parcours** (colloq)
hitch
■ ~ **domestique** accident in the home

accidenté, ~e /aksidɑ̃te/ **1** adj
(a) ⟨person⟩ injured; ⟨car⟩ involved in an
accident
(b) ⟨road, ground⟩ uneven
2 nm,f accident victim

accidentel, -elle /aksidɑ̃tɛl/ adj
accidental

accidentellement /aksidɑ̃tɛlmɑ̃/ adv
(a) in an accident
(b) by accident, accidentally

acclamation /aklamasjɔ̃/ nf cheering

acclamer /aklame/ [1] *vtr* to cheer, to acclaim

acclimater /aklimate/ [1] **1** *vtr* to acclimatize
2 s'acclimater *v refl* (+ *v être*) to become acclimatized; to adapt

accointances /akwɛ̃tɑ̃s/ *nf pl* contacts

accolade /akɔlad/ *nf* embrace

accommoder /akɔmɔde/ [1] **1** *vtr* to prepare
2 *vi* ‹eyes› to focus
3 s'accommoder *v refl* (+ *v être*) **s'~ de qch** to make the best of sth; to put up with sth

accompagnateur, -trice /akɔ̃paɲatœʀ, tʀis/ *nm,f* **(a)** (Mus) accompanist
(b) (with children) accompanying adult; (with tourists) courier

accompagnement /akɔ̃paɲmɑ̃/ *nm* accompaniment

accompagner /akɔ̃paɲe/ [1] *vtr*
(a) ‹person› to accompany, to go with, to come with
(b) to accompany ‹phenomenon, event›
(c) (Mus) to accompany
(d) ‹wine› to be served with

accomplir /akɔ̃pliʀ/ [3] **1** *vtr* to accomplish ‹task›; to fulfil (GB) ‹obligation›
2 s'accomplir *v refl* (+ *v être*) to be fulfilled

accomplissement /akɔ̃plismɑ̃/ *nm* (of mission) accomplishment, fulfilment (GB); (of ambition, aim) realization, achievement

accord /akɔʀ/ *nm* **(a)** agreement; (tacit) understanding; **d'~** all right, OK (colloq); **je suis d'~** I agree (**avec** with); **se mettre** *or* **tomber d'~** to come to an agreement
(b) harmony
(c) (in grammar) **~ en genre/en nombre** gender/number agreement
(d) (Mus) chord

accordéon /akɔʀdeɔ̃/ *nm* accordion

accorder /akɔʀde/ [1] **1** *vtr* **(a)** **~ qch à qn** to grant sb sth ‹favour, loan, interview, permission, right›; to give sb sth ‹grant, reduction, chance›; **il n'a pas entièrement tort, je te l'accorde** he's not entirely wrong, I'll give you that
(b) to attach ‹importance, value› (**à** to); to pay ‹attention›
(c) (Mus) to tune ‹instrument›
(d) to make [sth] agree ‹word, adjective›
2 s'accorder *v refl* (+ *v être*) **(a)** to give oneself ‹rest, time off›
(b) to agree (**sur** about, on)
(c) ‹colours, clothes› to go (together) well
(d) ‹adjective, verb› to agree (**avec** with)

accordeur /akɔʀdœʀ/ *nm* tuner

accostage /akɔstaʒ/ *nm* docking

accoster /akɔste/ [1] **1** *vtr* to accost ‹person›
2 *vi* ‹ship› to dock

accotement /akɔtmɑ̃/ *nm* verge

accouchement /akuʃmɑ̃/ *nm* delivery

accoucher /akuʃe/ [1] *vi* to give birth (**de** to)

accoucheur /akuʃœʀ/ *nm* obstetrician

accouder: s'accouder /akude/ [1] *v refl* (+ *v être*) to lean on one's elbows

accoudoir /akudwaʀ/ *nm* arm-rest

accouplement /akupləmɑ̃/ *nm* mating

accourir /akuʀiʀ/ [26] *vi* to run up

accoutrement /akutʀəmɑ̃/ *nm* get-up (colloq)

accoutrer: s'accoutrer /akutʀe/ [1] *v refl* (+ *v être*) to get oneself up (**de** in)

accoutumance /akutymɑ̃s/ *nf* addiction

accoutumer /akutyme/ [1] **1** *vtr* to accustom (**à** to)
2 s'accoutumer *v refl* (+ *v être*) to grow accustomed (**à** to)

accrédité, ~e /akʀedite/ *adj* authorized; accredited

accréditer /akʀedite/ [1] *vtr* **(a)** to give credence to ‹rumour›
(b) to accredit ‹ambassador›

accro /akʀo/ *adj* (colloq) hooked (colloq) (**à** on)

accroc /akʀo/ *nm* tear (**à** in)

accrochage /akʀɔʃaʒ/ *nm* (between people) clash; (between vehicles) collision

accrocher /akʀɔʃe/ [1] **1** *vtr* **(a)** to hang (**à** from)
(b) to hook [sth] on (**à** to)
(c) to catch ‹stocking, sweater› (**à** on)
(d) to catch ‹eye, attention›
2 s'accrocher *v refl* (+ *v être*) **(a)** (to ledge) to hang on; (to post) to cling (on) (**à** to)
(b) ‹person› **s'~ à qn** to cling to sb
(c) **l'hameçon s'est accroché à ma veste** the hook got caught in my jacket
(d) (colloq) **s'~ pour faire** to try hard to do
IDIOMS avoir le cœur *or* **l'estomac bien accroché** to have a strong stomach

accrocheur, -euse /akʀɔʃœʀ, øz/ *adj* ‹song, tune› catchy; ‹picture, title› eye-catching

accroissement /akʀwasmɑ̃/ *nm* growth

accroître /akʀwatʀ/ [72] *vtr*, **s'accroître** *v refl* (+ *v être*) to increase

accroupir: s'accroupir /akʀupiʀ/ [3] *v refl* (+ *v être*) to squat (down); to crouch (down)

accru, ~e /akʀy/ ▶ ACCROÎTRE

accueil /akœj/ *nm* **(a)** welcome
(b) reception desk

accueillant, ~e /akœjɑ̃, ɑ̃t/ *adj*
(a) hospitable, welcoming
(b) homely (GB), homey (US)

accueillir /akœjiʀ/ [27] *vtr* **(a)** to welcome
(b) to receive, to greet
(c) ‹room, hotel› to accommodate
(d) ‹hospital, organization› to cater for

accumulation /akymylasjɔ̃/ *nf*
(a) accumulation
(b) storage

accumuler /akymyle/ [1] **1** *vtr* **(a)** to store (up) ‹things›; to accumulate ‹capital›; to make a succession of ‹mistakes›

(b) to store (up) ⟨*energy*⟩

2 **s'accumuler** *v refl* (+ *v être*) ⟨*snow, rubbish*⟩ to pile up; ⟨*stocks, debts*⟩ to accrue

accusateur, -trice /akyzatœʀ, tʀis/
1 *adj* ⟨*silence, finger*⟩ accusing; ⟨*presence, speech*⟩ accusatory
2 *nm,f* accuser; ~ **public** public prosecutor

accusation /akyzasjɔ̃/ *nf* **(a)** accusation; (Law) charge
(b) l'~ the prosecution

accusé, ~e /akyze/ **1** *pp* ▶ ACCUSER
2 *pp adj* ⟨*wrinkles*⟩ deep; ⟨*relief*⟩ marked
3 *nm,f* defendant; **les** ~**s** the accused
■ ~ **de réception** acknowledgement (of receipt)

accuser /akyze/ [1] **1** *vtr* **(a)** to accuse ⟨*person*⟩; to blame ⟨*fate*⟩; ⟨*evidence*⟩ to point to ⟨*person*⟩; ⟨*judge*⟩ to charge ⟨*defendant*⟩ (**de** with)
(b) to show, to register ⟨*fall, deficit*⟩
2 **s'accuser** *v refl* (+ *v être*) **(a)** ⟨*person*⟩ to take the blame
(b) to become more marked
IDIOMS ~ **le coup** to be visibly shaken

acerbe /asɛʀb/ *adj* acerbic

acéré, ~e /aseʀe/ *adj* sharp

acharné, ~e /aʃaʀne/ *adj* ⟨*supporter*⟩ passionate; ⟨*work*⟩ unremitting; ⟨*struggle*⟩ fierce

acharnement /aʃaʀnəmɑ̃/ *nm* furious energy

acharner: s'acharner /aʃaʀne/ [1] *v refl* (+ *v être*) **(a)** to persevere; **s'**~ **contre** to fight against ⟨*project*⟩
(b) **s'**~ **sur** ⟨*person, animal*⟩ to keep going at ⟨*victim, prey*⟩; (figurative) to hound ⟨*person*⟩; **la malchance s'acharne contre lui** he is dogged by bad luck

achat /aʃa/ *nm* purchase

acheminement /aʃ(ə)minmɑ̃/ *nm* transportation

acheminer /aʃ(ə)mine/ [1] **1** *vtr* to transport
2 **s'acheminer** *v refl* (+ *v être*) **s'**~ **vers** to make one's way toward(s); to move toward(s)

acheter /aʃte/ [18] **1** *vtr* to buy; ~ **qch à qn** to buy sth from sb; to buy sth for sb
2 **s'acheter** *v refl* (+ *v être*) **(a)** **s'**~ **qch** to buy oneself sth
(b) **cela s'achète où?** where can you get it?

acheteur, -euse /aʃtœʀ, øz/ *nm,f* buyer

achever /aʃve/ [16] **1** *vtr* **(a)** to finish ⟨*work*⟩; to conclude ⟨*discussions*⟩; to complete ⟨*project, inquiry*⟩; to end ⟨*life*⟩
(b) to destroy ⟨*animal*⟩; to finish off ⟨*person*⟩
2 **s'achever** *v refl* (+ *v être*) to end

achoppement /aʃɔpmɑ̃/ *nm* **pierre d'**~ stumbling block

acide /asid/ *adj, nm* acid

acidité /asidite/ *nf* acidity, tartness, sharpness

acidulé, ~e /asidyle/ *adj* slightly acid; tangy

acier /asje/ **1** *adj inv* steel(y)
2 *nm* steel; **d'**~ ⟨*girder, column*⟩ steel; ⟨*nerves*⟩ of steel

aciérie /asjeʀi/ *nf* steelworks

acné /akne/ *nf* acne; ~ **juvénile** teenage acne

acolyte /akɔlit/ *nmf* henchman, acolyte

acompte /akɔ̃t/ *nm* **(a)** deposit
(b) part payment

acoquiner: s'acoquiner /akɔkine/ [1] *v refl* (+ *v être*) **s'**~ **avec qn** to get thick (colloq) with sb

à-côté, *pl* ~**s** /akote/ *nm* **(a)** perk
(b) extra expense
(c) extra profit

à-coup, *pl* ~**s** /aku/ *nm* jolt; **par** ~**s** by fits and starts

acoustique /akustik/ **1** *adj* acoustic
2 *nf* acoustics

acquéreur /akeʀœʀ/ *nm* buyer, purchaser

acquérir /akeʀiʀ/ [35] *vtr* **(a)** to acquire; (by buying) to purchase
(b) to acquire ⟨*reputation*⟩

acquiescement /akjɛsmɑ̃/ *nm* **donner son** ~ **à** to acquiesce to

acquiescer /akjese/ [12] *vi* to acquiesce

acquis, ~e /aki, iz/ **1** *pp* ▶ ACQUÉRIR
2 *pp adj* **(a)** ⟨*skills*⟩ acquired
(b) ⟨*principle, right*⟩ accepted, established; **les avantages** ~ the gains made; **tenir qch pour** ~ to take sth for granted
3 *nm inv* **(a)** acquired knowledge
(b) ~ **sociaux** social benefits
IDIOMS **bien mal** ~ **ne profite jamais** (Proverb) ill-gotten gains never prosper

acquisition /akizisjɔ̃/ *nf* **(a)** purchase
(b) acquisition

acquit /aki/ *nm* **je le ferai par** ~ **de conscience** I'll do it to put my mind at rest

acquittement /akitmɑ̃/ *nm* (Law) acquittal

acquitter /akite/ [1] **1** *vtr* (Law) to acquit
2 **s'acquitter** *v refl* (+ *v être*) **s'**~ **de son devoir** to do one's duty; **s'**~ **d'une dette** to pay off a debt

acre /akʀ/ *nf* acre

âcre /akʀ/ *adj* ⟨*taste*⟩ sharp; ⟨*smell*⟩ acrid

acrobate /akʀɔbat/ *nmf* acrobat

acrobatie /akʀɔbasi/ *nf* acrobatics

acronyme /akʀɔnim/ *nm* acronym

acrylique /akʀilik/ *adj, nm* acrylic

acte /akt/ *nm* **(a)** act; ~ **manqué** Freudian slip; **être libre de ses** ~**s** to do as one wishes; **faire** ~ **de candidature** to put oneself forward as a candidate
(b) (Law) deed; ~ **de naissance** birth certificate
(c) (in play) act

acteur, -trice /aktœʀ, tʀis/ *nm,f*
(a) actor/actress
(b) protagonist

actif, -ive /aktif, iv/ **1** *adj* (gen) active; ⟨*market*⟩ buoyant; **la vie active** working life **2** *nm* **(a)** l'∼ the assets
(b) à l'∼ de qn in sb's favour (GB)

action /aksjɔ̃/ *nf* **(a)** action, act; **une bonne** ∼ a good deed
(b) l'∼ action; **moyens d'**∼ courses of action; **en** ∼ in operation
(c) effect; l'∼ **de qn sur** sb's influence on
(d) ∼ **en justice** legal action
(e) (in finance) share

actionnaire /aksjɔnɛʀ/ *nmf* shareholder

actionner /aksjɔne/ [1] *vtr* to activate

activement /aktivmɑ̃/ *adv* actively

activer /aktive/ [1] **1** *vtr* **(a)** to speed up ⟨*work*⟩; to stimulate ⟨*digestion*⟩
(b) ⟨*wind*⟩ to stir up ⟨*flames*⟩
(c) to stoke ⟨*fire*⟩
2 s'activer *v refl* (+ *v être*) (colloq) to hurry up

activiste /aktivist/ *adj, nmf* activist

activité /aktivite/ *nf* **(a)** activity; ∼ **professionnelle** occupation
(b) **être en pleine** ∼ ⟨*street*⟩ to be bustling with activity; ⟨*person*⟩ to be very busy; **volcan en** ∼ active volcano

actrice *nf* ▶ ACTEUR

actualisation /aktɥalizasjɔ̃/ *nf* (process) updating; (result) update

actualiser /aktɥalize/ [1] *vtr* to update

actualité /aktɥalite/ **1** *nf* **(a)** current affairs; l'∼ **culturelle** cultural events
(b) **d'**∼ topical; **toujours d'**∼ still relevant today
2 actualités *nf pl* **(a)** news
(b) newsreel

actuel, -elle /aktɥɛl/ *adj* **(a)** present, current
(b) ⟨*film, discussion*⟩ topical

actuellement /aktɥɛlmɑ̃/ *adv* **(a)** at the moment
(b) currently

acuité /akɥite/ *nf* **(a)** acuity
(b) shrillness
(c) (of pain) intensity

acupuncteur, -trice /akypɔ̃ktœʀ, tʀis/ *nmf* acupuncturist

acupuncture /akypɔ̃ktyʀ/ *nf* acupuncture

adage /adaʒ/ *nm* saying, adage

adaptable /adaptabl/ *adj* **(a)** (flexible) adaptable (à to)
(b) ⟨*height, pressure*⟩ adjustable; ∼ **à toutes les circonstances** *or* **tous les besoins** all-purpose

adaptateur, -trice /adaptatœʀ, tʀis/ **1** *nm,f* (for cinema, theatre) (Théât) adapter
2 *nm* (Tech) adapter

adaptation /adaptasjɔ̃/ *nf* adaptation

adapté, ∼e /adapte/ *adj* **(a)** suitable
(b) ∼ **à** ⟨*solution*⟩ suited to
(c) (for TV, stage) adapted

adapter /adapte/ [1] **1** *vtr* **(a)** to fit (à to)
(b) to adapt ⟨*equipment*⟩
(c) to adapt ⟨*novel*⟩

2 s'adapter *v refl* (+ *v être*) **(a)** ⟨*tool, part*⟩ to fit
(b) to adapt, to adjust (à to)

addition /adisjɔ̃/ *nf* **(a)** addition
(b) bill, check (US)

additionner /adisjɔne/ [1] *vtr* to add up

adduction /adyksjɔ̃/ *nf* adduction; ∼ **d'eau** water conveyance

adepte /adɛpt/ *nmf* **(a)** (of theory) supporter; (of person) disciple
(b) enthusiast

adéquat, ∼e /adekwa, at/ *adj*
(a) appropriate, suitable
(b) adequate

adéquation /adekwasjɔ̃/ *nf*
(a) (correspondence) appropriateness (à, **avec** to)
(b) (of model) adequacy (à to)

adhérence /adeʀɑ̃s/ *nf* (of tyre, sole) grip

adhérent, ∼e /adeʀɑ̃, ɑ̃t/ *nm,f* member

adhérer /adeʀe/ [14] *v+prep* **(a)** ∼ **à** ⟨*glue*⟩ to stick to; ⟨*tyre*⟩ to grip
(b) ∼ **à** to join

adhésif, -ive /adezif, iv/ *adj* adhesive

adhésion /adezjɔ̃/ *nf* **(a)** membership
(b) support

adieu, *pl* ∼**x** /adjø/ *nm* goodbye, farewell

adipeux, -euse /adipø, øz/ *adj* fatty

adjectif /adʒɛktif/ *nm* adjective

adjoint, ∼e /adʒwɛ̃, ɛ̃t/ *nm,f* assistant; deputy; ∼ **au maire** deputy mayor

adjudant /adʒydɑ̃/ *nm* ≈ warrant officer

adjudication /adʒydikasjɔ̃/ *nf* auction; ∼ **judiciaire** sale by order of the court

adjuger /adʒyʒe/ [13] *vtr* to auction; **une fois, deux fois, adjugé!** going, going, gone!

adjuvant /adʒyvɑ̃/ *nm* additive

admettre /admɛtʀ/ [60] *vtr* **(a)** to accept, to admit ⟨*fact*⟩
(b) to admit ⟨*person, student*⟩; **être admis à un examen** to pass an exam
(c) ∼ **que** to suppose (that)

administrateur, -trice /administʀatœʀ, tʀis/ *nm,f* **(a)** administrator
(b) director
(c) trustee

administratif, -ive /administʀatif, iv/ *adj* **(a)** ⟨*staff, building*⟩ administrative
(b) ⟨*report*⟩ official

administration /administʀasjɔ̃/ *nf*
(a) administration
(b) civil service
(c) **être placé sous** ∼ **judiciaire** to go into receivership
(d) management
(e) (of medicine, sacrament) administration, giving

administrer /administʀe/ [1] *vtr* **(a)** to administer ⟨*funds*⟩; to run ⟨*company, country*⟩
(b) to administer, to give ⟨*drug, sacrament*⟩

admirable /admiʀabl/ *adj* admirable

admirablement /admiʀabləmɑ̃/ *adv* ⟨*do*⟩ admirably; ⟨*done*⟩ superbly

admirateur, -trice /admiRatœR, tRis/ *nm,f* admirer

admiration /admiRasjɔ̃/ *nf* admiration

admirer /admiRe/ [1] *vtr* to admire

admis, ~e /admi, iz/ **1** *pp* ▶ ADMETTRE **2** *pp adj* accepted; ⟨candidate⟩ successful

admissible /admisibl/ *adj* **(a)** acceptable **(b)** eligible

admission /admisjɔ̃/ *nf* admission; **service des ~s** reception

ado /ado/ *nmf* (colloq) teenager

adolescence /adɔlesɑ̃s/ *nf* adolescence

adolescent, ~e /adɔlesɑ̃, ɑ̃t/ **1** *adj* teenage **2** *nm,f* teenager, adolescent

adonner: s'adonner /adɔne/ [1] *v refl* (+ *v être*) **s'~ à** to devote all one's time to; **il s'adonne à la boisson** he drinks too much

adopter /adɔpte/ [1] *vtr* to adopt ⟨child, method⟩; to pass ⟨law⟩

adoptif, -ive /adɔptif, iv/ *adj* **(a)** ⟨child, country⟩ adopted **(b)** ⟨parent⟩ adoptive

adoption /adɔpsjɔ̃/ *nf* **(a)** adoption **(b)** passing

adorable /adɔRabl/ *adj* adorable

adorateur, -trice /adɔRatœR, tRis/ *nm,f* worshipper (GB)

adoration /adɔRasjɔ̃/ *nf* worship, adoration

adorer /adɔRe/ [1] *vtr* to adore, to worship

adosser: s'adosser /adose/ [1] *v refl* (+ *v être*) **s'~ à** to lean back on

adoucir /adusiR/ [3] **1** *vtr* to soften ⟨skin, water⟩; to moderate ⟨tone of voice⟩; to soothe ⟨throat⟩; to ease ⟨suffering⟩ **2 s'adoucir** *v refl* (+ *v être*) ⟨temperature⟩ to become milder; ⟨slope⟩ to become more gentle

adoucissant, ~e /adusisɑ̃, ɑ̃t/ **1** *adj* soothing **2** *nm* softener

adrénaline /adRenalin/ *nf* adrenalin

adresse /adRɛs/ *nf* **(a)** address; **se tromper d'~** to get the wrong address; (figurative) to pick the wrong person; **remarque lancée à l'~ de qn** remark directed at sb **(b)** dexterity **(c)** skill

adresser /adRese/ [1] **1** *vtr* **(a)** to direct ⟨criticism⟩ (à at); to make ⟨request, declaration, appeal⟩; to deliver ⟨ultimatum⟩; to present ⟨petition⟩; to aim ⟨blow⟩; **~ la parole à qn** to speak to sb **(b)** to send ⟨letter⟩ **(c)** to refer [sb] (à to) **2 s'adresser** *v refl* (+ *v être*) **(a) s'~ à qn** to speak to sb **(b) s'~ à** to contact ⟨embassy⟩; **s'~ au guichet 8** to go to window 8 **(c) s'~ à** ⟨measure⟩ to be aimed at

adroit, ~e /adRwa, at/ *adj* skilful (GB); clever

adulte /adylt/ *adj, nmf* adult

adultère /adyltɛR/ **1** *adj* adulterous **2** *nm* adultery

advenir /advəniR/ [36] *v impers* **(a)** to happen; **advienne que pourra** come what may **(b) ~ de** to become of

adverbe /advɛRb/ *nm* adverb

adversaire /advɛRsɛR/ *nmf* (gen) opponent; (Mil) adversary

adverse /advɛRs/ *adj* **(a)** opposing **(b)** opposite

adversité /advɛRsite/ *nf* adversity

aérer /aeRe/ [14] **1** *vtr* **(a)** to air **(b)** to space out **2 s'aérer** *v refl* (+ *v être*) to get some fresh air

aérien, -ienne /aeRjɛ̃, ɛn/ *adj* ⟨transport⟩ air; ⟨photography⟩ aerial; **métro ~** elevated section of the underground (GB), elevated railroad (US)

aéro-club, *pl* **~s** /aeRoklœb/ *nm* flying club

aérodrome /aeRodRom/ *nm* aerodrome (GB), (small) airfield

aérodynamique /aeRodinamik/ *adj* aerodynamic

aérogare /aeRogaR/ *nf* air terminal

aéroglisseur /aeRoglisœR/ *nm* hovercraft

aéronautique /aeRonotik/ *nf* aeronautics

aérophagie /aeRofaʒi/ *nf* aerophagia

aéroport /aeRopɔR/ *nm* airport

aéroporté, ~e /aeRopɔRte/ *adj* ⟨troops⟩ airborne; ⟨equipment⟩ transported by air

aérosol /aeRosɔl/ *nm* **(a)** aerosol **(b)** spray

aérospatiale /aeRospasjal/ *nf* aerospace industry

affabulation /afabylasjɔ̃/ *nf* fabrication

affaiblir /afɛbliR/ [3] **1** *vtr* to weaken **2 s'affaiblir** *v refl* (+ *v être*) to get weaker

affaiblissement /afɛblismɑ̃/ *nm* **(a)** weakening **(b)** weakened state

affaire /afɛR/ **1** *nf* **(a)** affair; (political) crisis, affair; (moral) scandal; (legal) case **(b)** affair, matter; **une ~ délicate** a delicate matter; **c'est l'~ de quelques jours** it'll only take a few days; **j'en fais mon ~** I'll deal with it; **c'est une autre ~** that's another matter; **c'est une ~ d'argent** there's money involved; **et voilà toute l'~** and that's that; **c'est toute une ~, ce n'est pas une petite ~** it's quite a business **(c)** (skill, trade) **il connaît bien son ~** he knows his job; **la mécanique, c'est leur ~** mechanics is their thing **(d)** deal; **faire ~ avec** to do a deal with; **avoir ~ à** to be dealing with **(e)** bargain; **la belle ~!** (colloq) big deal!; (colloq) **ça fera l'~** that'll do **(f)** business, concern **(g)** (difficulty) **être tiré d'~** to be out of danger **2 affaires** *nf pl* **(a)** business ····⟩

(b) (personal) business affairs; **occupe-toi de tes ∼s!** mind your own business!
(c) things, belongings
■ **∼s courantes** daily business

affairer: s'affairer /afeʀe/ [1] *v refl*
(+ *v être*) to bustle about (**à faire** doing)

affairisme /afeʀism/ *nm* wheeling and dealing (colloq)

affaisser: s'affaisser /afese/ [1] *v refl*
(+ *v être*) **(a)** to subside
(b) ⟨shoulders, roof⟩ to sag
(c) ⟨person⟩ to collapse

affaler: s'affaler /afale/ [1] *v refl* (+ *v être*)
(a) to collapse
(b) (colloq) to fall

affamé, ∼e /afame/ ① *pp* ▶ AFFAMER
② *pp adj* **(a)** starving
(b) ∼ **de** hungry for

affamer /afame/ [1] *vtr* to starve

affectation /afɛktasjɔ̃/ *nf* **(a)** allocation
(à to)
(b) appointment (à to); posting (à to)
(c) affectation

affecter /afɛkte/ [1] *vtr* **(a)** to feign, to affect ⟨interest⟩; to affect ⟨behaviour⟩; ∼ **de faire/d'être** to pretend to do/to be
(b) to allocate ⟨funds⟩ (à to)
(c) to appoint (à to); to post (à, en to)
(d) to affect ⟨market, person⟩

affectif, -ive /afɛktif, iv/ *adj* **(a)** emotional
(b) affective

affection /afɛksjɔ̃/ *nf* **(a)** affection; **prendre qn en** ∼ to become fond of sb
(b) (Med) disease

affectionner /afɛksjɔne/ [1] *vtr* to be fond of

affectivité /afɛktivite/ *nf* feelings

affectueusement /afɛktɥøzmɑ̃/ *adv* affectionately, fondly

affectueux, -euse /afɛktɥø, øz/ *adj* affectionate

affermir /afɛʀmiʀ/ [3] ① *vtr* to strengthen ⟨will⟩; to consolidate ⟨power⟩; to firm up ⟨muscles⟩
② **s'affermir** *v refl* (+ *v être*) ⟨power⟩ to be consolidated; ⟨voice⟩ to become stronger; ⟨muscles⟩ to firm up; ⟨ground⟩ to become firmer

affermissement /afɛʀmismɑ̃/ *nm*
(of power, recovery) consolidation; (of will, muscles, voice) strengthening; (economic) improvement (**de** in)

affichage /afiʃaʒ/ *nm* **(a)** billsticking; **campagne d'**∼ poster campaign
(b) (Comput) display
■ ∼ **à cristaux liquides** liquid crystal display, LCD

affiche /afiʃ/ *nf* poster; (official) notice; **à l'**∼ ⟨film⟩ now showing; ⟨play⟩ on; **quitter l'**∼ to come off
■ ∼ **de théâtre** playbill

affiché, ∼e /afiʃe/ ① *pp* ▶ AFFICHER
② *pp adj* **(a)** ⟨ad, picture⟩ (put) up; ⟨information⟩ posted (up)

(b) ⟨result⟩ published
(c) ⟨optimism, opinion⟩ declared
(d) (Comput) ⟨data⟩ displayed

afficher /afiʃe/ [1] ① *vtr* **(a)** to put up ⟨poster, notice⟩
(b) to display ⟨prices, result⟩; ∼ **complet** ⟨film, play⟩ to be sold out; ⟨hotel⟩ to be fully booked
(c) ⟨market⟩ to show ⟨rise⟩
(d) to declare ⟨ambitions⟩; to display ⟨scorn⟩; to flaunt ⟨opinions, liaison⟩
② **s'afficher** *v refl* (+ *v être*) **(a)** to flaunt oneself
(b) ⟨smile⟩ to appear (**sur** on)

afficheur /afiʃœʀ/ *nm* **(a)** poster (GB) *or* billboard (US) sticker
(b) (Comput) visual display unit, VDU

affichiste /afiʃist/ *nmf* poster artist

affilé, ∼e¹ /afile/ *adj* ⟨blade⟩ sharpened

affilée²: d'affilée /dafile/ *phr* in a row

affiler /afile/ [1] *vtr* to sharpen

affilier: s'affilier /afilje/ [2] *v refl* (+ *v être*) to become affiliated

affiner /afine/ [1] ① *vtr* **(a)** to hone ⟨style⟩
(b) to slim down ⟨waistline⟩
② **s'affiner** *v refl* (+ *v être*) **(a)** ⟨style, taste⟩ to become (more) refined
(b) ⟨waistline⟩ to slim down

affinité /afinite/ *nf* affinity

affirmatif, -ive¹ /afiʀmatif, iv/ *adj* affirmative; **faire un signe de tête** ∼ to nod agreement

affirmation /afiʀmasjɔ̃/ *nf* assertion; **l'**∼ **de soi** assertiveness

affirmative² /afiʀmativ/ ① *adj f* ▶ AFFIRMATIF
② *nf* affirmative

affirmer /afiʀme/ [1] ① *vtr* **(a)** to maintain; ∼ **faire** to claim to do
(b) to assert ⟨talent, authority⟩
(c) to declare, to affirm ⟨will⟩
② **s'affirmer** *v refl* (+ *v être*) ⟨tendency⟩ to become apparent; ⟨personality⟩ to assert itself

affleurer /aflœʀe/ [1] *vi* ⟨reef⟩ to show on the surface; ⟨rock⟩ to come through the soil

affligeant, ∼e /afliʒɑ̃, ɑ̃t/ *adj* pathetic

affliger /afliʒe/ [13] *vtr* **(a)** to afflict (**de** with)
(b) to distress

affluence /aflyɑ̃s/ *nf* crowd(s)

affluent /aflyɑ̃/ *nm* tributary

affluer /aflye/ [1] *vi* ⟨people⟩ to flock (**à, vers** to); ⟨letters⟩ to pour in

affolant, ∼e /afɔlɑ̃, ɑ̃t/ *adj* (colloq) frightening

affolement /afɔlmɑ̃/ *nm* panic

affoler /afɔle/ [1] ① *vtr* to throw [sb] into a panic
② **s'affoler** *v refl* (+ *v être*) to panic

affranchi, ∼e /afʀɑ̃ʃi/ *nm,f* emancipated slave

affranchir /afʀɑ̃ʃiʀ/ [3] ① *vtr* **(a)** to stamp ⟨letter⟩

a

(b) to free ⟨*slave, country*⟩

2 **s'affranchir** *v refl* (+ *v être*) to free oneself

affranchissement /afʀɑ̃ʃismɑ̃/ *nm*
(a) stamping; (cost) postage
(b) liberation; freeing

affres /afʀ/ *nf pl* (of pain) agony; (of hunger) pangs; (of jealousy) throes; **les ~ de la mort** death throes

affréter /afʀete/ [14] *vtr* to charter

affréteur /afʀetœʀ/ *nm* charter company

affreusement /afʀøzmɑ̃/ *adv* (colloq) terribly

affreux, -euse /afʀø, øz/ *adj* **(a)** hideous
(b) awful, dreadful

affront /afʀɔ̃/ *nm* affront

affrontement /afʀɔ̃tmɑ̃/ *nm* confrontation

affronter /afʀɔ̃te/ [1] *vtr* to face ⟨*situation*⟩; to brave ⟨*weather*⟩

affubler /afyble/ [1] *vtr* ~ **qn de** to deck sb out in ⟨*clothes*⟩; to saddle sb with ⟨*nickname*⟩

affût /afy/ *nm* **se tenir** or **être à l'~** to lie in wait; (figurative) to be on the lookout (**de** for)

affûter /afyte/ [1] *vtr* **(a)** to sharpen
(b) to grind

afin /afɛ̃/ **1** **afin de** *phr* ~ **de faire** in order to do
2 **afin que** *phr* so that

AFP /aɛfpe/ *nf* (*abbr* = **Agence France-Presse**) AFP (*French news agency*)

africain, ~e /afʀikɛ̃, ɛn/ *adj* African

Afrique /afʀik/ *pr nf* Africa

AG /aʒe/ *nf*: *abbr* ▶ **ASSEMBLÉE**

agaçant, ~e /agasɑ̃, ɑ̃t/ *adj* annoying

agacement /agasmɑ̃/ *nm* irritation

agacer /agase/ [12] *vtr* to annoy, to irritate

agapes /agap/ *nf pl* feast, banquet

agate /agat/ *nf* **(a)** agate
(b) marble

âge /aʒ/ *nm* **(a)** age; **faire son ~** to look one's age; **un homme d'un certain ~** a middle-aged man
(b) old age; **avec l'~** as one gets older; **prendre de l'~** to grow old
(c) age, era
■ **l'~ bête** or **ingrat** the awkward or difficult age; **l'~ mûr** maturity

âgé, ~e /aʒe/ *adj* old

agence /aʒɑ̃s/ *nf* **(a)** agency
(b) (of bank) branch
■ ~ **immobilière** estate agents (GB), real-estate agency (US;) ~ **de placement** employment agency; **Agence nationale pour l'emploi, ANPE** *French employment agency*

agencer /aʒɑ̃se/ [12] *vtr* to lay out ⟨*room*⟩

agenda /aʒɛ̃da/ *nm* diary

agenouiller: s'agenouiller /aʒnuje/ [1] *v refl* (+ *v être*) to kneel (down)

agent /aʒɑ̃/ *nm* **(a)** officer, official
(b) agent
(c) employee

■ ~ **de change** stockbroker; ~ **de la circulation** traffic policeman; ~ **commercial** sales representative; ~ **de police** policeman

agglomération /aglɔmeʀasjɔ̃/ *nf* town; village; **l'~ lyonnaise** Lyons and its suburbs

aggloméré /aglɔmeʀe/ *nm* chipboard

agglomérer /aglɔmeʀe/ [14] **1** *vtr* to agglomerate
2 **s'agglomérer** *v refl* (+ *v être*) ⟨*people*⟩ to gather together; ⟨*houses*⟩ to be grouped together

agglutiner: s'agglutiner /aglytine/ [1] *v refl* (+ *v être*) ⟨*onlookers*⟩ to crowd together (**à** at); ⟨*insects*⟩ to cluster together

aggravation /agʀavasjɔ̃/ *nf* (of situation) worsening; (in debt) increase

aggraver /agʀave/ [1] **1** *vtr* to aggravate, to make [sth] worse
2 **s'aggraver** *v refl* (+ *v être*) to get worse

agile /aʒil/ *adj* agile, nimble

agilité /aʒilite/ *nf* agility

agios /aʒjo/ *nm pl* bank charges

agir /aʒiʀ/ [3] **1** *vi* **(a)** to act
(b) to behave; ~ **en lâche** to act like a coward
(c) ⟨*medicine*⟩ to take effect, to work
2 **s'agir de** *v impers* (+ *v être*) **de quoi s'agit-il?** what is it about?; **il s'agit de votre mari** it's about your husband; **mais il ne s'agit pas de ça!** but that's not the point!; **il s'agit de faire vite** we must act quickly

âgisme /aʒism/ *nm* ageism

agissements /aʒismɑ̃/ *nm pl* activities

agitateur, -trice /aʒitatœʀ, tʀis/ *nm,f* agitator

agitation /aʒitasjɔ̃/ *nf* **(a)** restlessness
(b) bustle (**de** in); activity
(c) unrest

agité, ~e /aʒite/ *adj* ⟨*sea*⟩ rough, choppy; ⟨*sleep*⟩ troubled; ⟨*period*⟩ turbulent; ⟨*night*⟩ restless
(b) ⟨*street*⟩ bustling; ⟨*life*⟩ hectic

agiter /aʒite/ [1] **1** *vtr* to wave ⟨*hand*⟩; to shake ⟨*can*⟩; to shake up ⟨*liquid*⟩
2 **s'agiter** *v refl* (+ *v être*) **(a)** to fidget; (in bed) to toss and turn
(b) to sway (in the wind)
(c) to bustle about
(d) to become restless

agneau, *pl* ~**x** /aɲo/ *nm* **(a)** lamb
(b) lambskin

agonie /agɔni/ *nf* death throes

agonir /agɔniʀ/ [3] *vtr* ~ **qn d'injures** to hurl insults at sb; **en rentrant, il s'est fait ~** when he got home he was told off soundly

agoniser /agɔnize/ [1] *vi* to be dying

agrafe /agʀaf/ *nf* **(a)** (for paper) staple
(b) (on waistband, bra) hook
(c) (Med) skin clip

agrafer /agʀafe/ [1] *vtr* **(a)** to staple [sth] (together)
(b) to fasten

agrafeuse /agʀaføz/ *nf* stapler

agraire /agʀɛʀ/ *adj* agrarian; **réforme ~** land reform

agrandir /agʀɑ̃diʀ/ [3] **①** *vtr* **(a)** to enlarge ‹*town, photo*›; to extend ‹*house*› **(b)** to expand ‹*organization*› **② s'agrandir** *v refl* (+ *v être*) ‹*hole*› to get bigger; ‹*town, family*› to expand; ‹*eyes*› to widen

agrandissement /agʀɑ̃dismɑ̃/ *nm* enlargement

agréable /agʀeabl/ *adj* nice, pleasant; **~ à vivre** ‹*person*› pleasant to be with

agréer /agʀee/ [11] *vtr* **(a)** to agree to ‹*request*›; **veuillez ~ mes salutations distinguées** yours faithfully; yours sincerely **(b)** to register ‹*taxi, doctor*›; **agent agréé** authorized dealer

agrégat /agʀega/ *nm* aggregate; (figurative) jumble

agrégation /agʀegasjɔ̃/ *nf*: high-level competitive examination for the recruitment of teachers

agrément /agʀemɑ̃/ *nm* **(a)** charm; **plein d'~** very pleasant; **full of charm; sans ~** dull; unattractive; cheerless; **voyage d'~** pleasure trip **(b)** (by official body) approval

agrémenter /agʀemɑ̃te/ [1] *vtr* to liven up ‹*story*›; to brighten up ‹*garden*›

agrès /agʀɛ/ *nm pl* (Sport) apparatus

agresser /agʀese/ [1] *vtr* **(a)** to attack **(b)** to mug **(c)** to be aggressive with

agresseur /agʀesœʀ/ *nm* **(a)** attacker **(b)** (in war) aggressor

agressif, -ive /agʀesif, iv/ *adj* **(a)** aggressive **(b)** violent; ear-splitting; harsh

agression /agʀesjɔ̃/ *nf* **(a)** attack **(b)** mugging **(c)** act of aggression

agressivité /agʀesivite/ *nf* aggressiveness, aggression

agricole /agʀikɔl/ *adj* **produit ~** farm produce; **coopérative ~** farming cooperative

agriculteur, -trice /agʀikyltœʀ, tʀis/ *nm,f* farmer

agriculture /agʀikyltyʀ/ *nf* farming

agripper /agʀipe/ [1] **①** *vtr* to grab **②s'agripper** *v refl* (+ *v être*) to cling (to)

agro-alimentaire, *pl* **~s** /agʀoalimɑ̃tɛʀ/ *adj* food-processing

agrochimie /agʀoʃimi/ *nf* agro-chemistry

agronomie /agʀɔnɔmi/ *nf* agronomy

agrume /agʀym/ *nm* citrus fruit

aguerrir /ageʀiʀ/ [3] **①** *vtr* to harden ‹*person*› **②s'aguerrir** *v refl* (+ *v être*) to become hardened

aguets: **aux aguets** /ozagɛ/ *phr* **être aux ~** to be on one's guard

aguicher /agiʃe/ [1] *vtr* to lead [sb] on

aguicheur, -euse /agiʃœʀ, øz/ *adj* alluring

ah /a/ *excl* oh!; **~ oui?**, **~ bon?** really?

ahuri, ~e /ayʀi/ *adj* **(a)** dazed **(b)** stunned

ahurissant, ~e /ayʀisɑ̃, ɑ̃t/ *adj* ‹*news, strength*› incredible; ‹*figure*› staggering

ai /ɛ/ ▶ AVOIR¹

aide¹ /ɛd/ **①** *nmf* assistant **②aide-** (*combining form*) **~-soignant** nursing auxiliary (GB), nurse's aide (US)

aide² /ɛd/ *nf* **(a)** (from individual, group) help, assistance; (from state) assistance; **apporter son ~ à qn** to help sb **(b)** (financial) aid; **~ au développement** foreign aid; **~ judiciaire** legal aid

aider /ede/ [1] **①** *vtr* **(a)** to help (**à faire** to do) **(b)** to aid; to give aid to **②aider à** *v+prep* to help toward(s) ‹*understanding, funding*› **③s'aider** *v refl* (+ *v être*) **(a) s'~ de** to use ‹*dictionary, tool*› **(b)** to help each other

aie /ɛ/ ▶ AVOIR¹

aïe /aj/ *excl* (in pain) ouch!; (in concern) **~ (~ ~), que se passe-t-il?** oh dear, what's going on?; (in anticipation) **~ ~ ~!...** oh NO!...

aient /ɛ/ ▶ AVOIR¹

aies /ɛ/ ▶ AVOIR¹

aïeul, ~e /ajœl/ *nm,f* grandfather/grandmother

aïeux /ajø/ *nm pl* ancestors

aigle /ɛgl/ *nm, nf* eagle

aiglefin /ɛgləfɛ̃/ *nm* haddock

aigre /ɛgʀ/ *adj* ‹*smell, taste*› sour

aigre-doux, -douce, *pl* **aigres-doux, aigres-douces** /ɛgʀədu, dus/ *adj* (Culin) ‹*fruit,taste*› bitter-sweet; ‹*sauce*› sweet and sour

aigrette /ɛgʀɛt/ *nf* (Zool) (bird) egret; (plumes) crest

aigreur /ɛgʀœʀ/ *nf* **(a)** sourness; sharpness **(b) ~s d'estomac** heartburn **(c)** (figurative) bitterness

aigrir /egʀiʀ/ [3] *vtr* to embitter

aigu, aiguë /egy/ **①** *adj* **(a)** ‹*sound, voice*› high-pitched **(b)** ‹*pain, symptom*› acute **(c)** ‹*sense*› keen **②** *nm* (Mus) treble; high notes

aigue-marine, *pl* **aigues-marines** /ɛgmaʀin/ *nf* aquamarine

aiguillage /egɥijaʒ/ *nm* (for trains) points (GB), switch (US); **une erreur d'~** a signalling (GB) error

aiguille /egɥij/ *nf* **(a)** needle; **~ à coudre** sewing needle **(b)** (of watch, chronometer) hand; (of gauge) needle; (of weighing scales) pointer; **dans le sens des ~s d'une montre** clockwise

aiguiller /egɥije/ [1] *vtr* **(a)** to direct ‹*person*›; to send ‹*mail*› **(b)** (towards career) to guide ‹*person*›

aiguilleur /egɥijœʀ/ *nm* ~ du ciel air traffic controller

aiguillonner /egɥijɔne/ [1] *vtr* (a) to spur ⟨*person*⟩; to stimulate ⟨*ambition*⟩; la faim m'aiguillonnant... driven by hunger... (b) to goad ⟨*ox*⟩

aiguiser /egize/ [1] *vtr* (a) to sharpen ⟨*knife*⟩
(b) to whet ⟨*appetite*⟩; to arouse ⟨*curiosity*⟩

aiguiseur /egizœʀ/ *nm* knife grinder

ail, *pl* ~**s** *or* **aulx** /aj, o/ *nm* garlic

aile /ɛl/ *nf* (gen) wing; (of windmill) sail; (of car) wing (GB), fender (US); (of army) flank
IDIOMS battre de l'~ to be in a bad way; se sentir pousser des ~s to feel exhilarated; prendre un coup dans l'~ to suffer a setback; voler de ses propres ~s to stand on one's own two feet

aileron /ɛlʀɔ̃/ *nm* (of bird) wing tip; (of shark) fin; (of plane) aileron; (of ship) fin

ailier /elje/ *nm* (in football) winger; (in rugby) wing three-quarter

ailleurs /ajœʀ/ 1 *adv* elsewhere
2 **d'ailleurs** *phr* besides, moreover
3 **par ailleurs** *phr* ils se sont par ~ engagés à faire they have also undertaken to do
IDIOMS être ~ to be miles away

aimable /ɛmabl/ *adj* (a) ⟨*word*⟩ kind
(b) ⟨*remark*⟩ polite

aimablement /ɛmabləmã/ *adv* politely; kindly

aimant, ~**e** /ɛmã, ãt/ 1 *pp* ▶ AIMER
2 *pp adj* affectionate
3 *nm* magnet

aimé, ~**e** /eme/ ▶ AIMER

aimer /eme/ [1] 1 *vtr* (a) to love ⟨*person*⟩; ~ qn à la folie to adore sb
(b) to like, to be fond of ⟨*person, activity, thing*⟩; ~ faire to like doing; il aime autant le vin que la bière he likes wine as much as he likes beer; ~ mieux to prefer; il n'a rien de cassé? j'aime mieux ça! (in relief) nothing's broken? thank goodness!; j'aime mieux ça! (threateningly) that's more like it!
2 **s'aimer** *v refl* (+ *v être*) (a) to love each other
(b) to like each other

aine /ɛn/ *nf* groin

aîné, ~**e** /ene/ 1 *adj* elder; eldest
2 *nm,f* (a) elder son/daughter, elder child
(b) eldest son/daughter, eldest child
(c) elder brother/sister
(d) elder; oldest

ainsi /ɛ̃si/ 1 *adv* (a) thus; le mélange ~ obtenu the mixture obtained in this way; Charlotte, c'est ~ qu'on m'appelait Charlotte, that's what they used to call me; s'il en est ~ if that's the way it is; le jury se compose ~ the panel is made up as follows; ~ soit-il amen
(b) thus, so
2 **ainsi que** *phr* (a) as well as

(b) as; ~ que nous en avions convenu as we had agreed

air /ɛʀ/ *nm* (a) air; le bon ~ clean air; concert en plein ~ open-air concert; activités de plein ~ outdoor activities; aller prendre l'~ to go and get some fresh air; on manque d'~ ici it's stuffy in here; être dans l'~ ⟨*reform, idea*⟩ to be in the air; regarder en l'~ to look up; avoir le nez en l'~ to daydream; en l'~ ⟨*threat, words*⟩ empty; ⟨*plan, idea*⟩ vague; tout mettre en l'~ (colloq) to make a dreadful mess; de l'~! (colloq) get lost! (colloq)
(b) il y a de l'~ (in room) there's a draught (GB) *or* draft (US); (outside) there's a breeze; il n'y a pas d'~ there's no wind; un courant d'~ a draught (GB) *or* draft (US)
(c) manner; expression; avoir un drôle d'~ to look odd; d'un ~ fâché angrily; il y a un ~ de famille entre vous deux you two share a family likeness; cela m'en a tout l'~ it seems like it to me; j'aurais l'~ de quoi? I'd look a right idiot!; cela a l'~ d'être une usine it looks like a factory; il a l'~ de vouloir faire beau it looks as if it's going to be fine
(d) tune; un ~ d'opéra an aria
IDIOMS il ne manque pas d'~! (colloq) he's got a nerve!; se donner de grands ~s to put on airs; j'ai besoin de changer d'~ I need a change of scene

aire /ɛʀ/ *nf* (a) (surface) area
(b) eyrie
■ ~ d'atterrissage (for plane) landing strip; (for helicopter) landing pad; ~ de jeu playground; ~ de services motorway (GB) *or* freeway (US) service station; ~ de stationnement parking area

airelle /ɛʀɛl/ *nf* (a) bilberry
(b) cranberry

aisance /ɛzãs/ *nf* (a) ease
(b) affluence, comfort

aise /ɛz/ 1 **aises** *nf pl* aimer ses ~s to like one's creature comforts; il prenait ses ~s sur le canapé he was stretched out on the sofa
2 **à l'aise** *phr* être à l'~ *or* à son ~ (physically) to be comfortable; (financially) to be comfortably off; (psychologically) to be at ease; mal à l'~ ill at ease; à votre ~! as you wish *or* like!

aisé, ~**e** /eze/ *adj* (a) easy
(b) wealthy

aisément /ezemã/ *adv* easily

aisselle /ɛsɛl/ *nf* armpit

ait /ɛ/ ▶ AVOIR[1]

Aix-la-Chapelle /ɛkslaʃapɛl/ *pr n* Aachen

ajonc /aʒɔ̃/ *nm* gorse bush

ajouré, ~**e** /aʒuʀe/ *adj* ⟨*tablecloth*⟩ openwork; ⟨*edge, border*⟩ hemstitched

ajournement /aʒuʀnəmã/ *nm* (of decision) postponement; (of trial) adjournment

ajourner /aʒuʀne/ [1] *vtr* to postpone ⟨*decision, plan*⟩; to adjourn ⟨*debate, trial*⟩

ajout /aʒu/ *nm* addition
■ (Comput) ∼ **de mémoire** memory upgrade
ajouter /aʒute/ [1] **1** *vtr* to add (**à** to)
2 s'ajouter *v refl* (+ *v être*) **s'**∼ **à** to be added to
ajustement /aʒystəmɑ̃/ *nm* **(a)** (Tech) fit
(b) adjustment; ∼ **des prix** price adjustment
ajuster /aʒyste/ [1] *vtr* **(a)** to adjust ‹*strap, price, timetable*›; to alter ‹*garment*› (**à** to); to calibrate ‹*weighing scales*›; ∼ **qch à** *or* **sur qch** to make sth fit sth; **corsage ajusté** close-fitting bodice
(b) to arrange ‹*hair*›; to straighten ‹*hat, tie*›
(c) ∼ **son tir** to adjust one's aim
ajusteur /aʒystœʀ/ *nm* fitter
alaise = ALÈSE
alambic /alɑ̃bik/ *nm* still
alambiqué, ∼**e** /alɑ̃bike/ *adj* ‹*expression, style*› convoluted; ‹*explanation*› tortuous
alangui, ∼**e** /alɑ̃gi/ *adj* **(a)** languid
(b) listless
alarmant, ∼**e** /alaʀmɑ̃, ɑ̃t/ *adj* alarming
alarme /alaʀm/ *nf* alarm
alarmer /alaʀme/ [1] **1** *vtr* to alarm
2 s'alarmer *v refl* (+ *v être*) to become alarmed (**de qch** about sth)
albanais, ∼**e** /albanɛ, ɛz/ **1** *adj* Albanian
2 *nm* (language) Albanian
Albanie /albani/ *pr nf* Albania
albâtre /albɑtʀ/ *nm* alabaster
albatros /albatʀos/ *nm inv* albatross
albinos /albinos/ *adj inv*, *nmf inv* albino
album /albɔm/ *nm* **(a)** illustrated book; ∼ **de bandes dessinées** comic strip book
(b) album
■ ∼ **à colorier** colouring (GB) book
albumine /albymin/ *nf* albumin
alchimie /alʃimi/ *nf* alchemy
alcool /alkɔl/ *nm* **(a)** alcohol; ∼ **de poire** pear brandy; **teneur en** ∼ alcohol content
(b) drink; **l'**∼ **au volant** drink-driving
(c) **un** ∼ a spirit
■ ∼ **à brûler** methylated spirits; ∼ **à 90°** ≈ surgical spirit (GB), rubbing alcohol (US)
alcoolémie /alkɔlemi/ *nf* presence of alcohol in the blood
alcoolique /alkɔlik/ *adj*, *nmf* alcoholic
alcoolisé, ∼**e** /alkɔlize/ *adj* alcoholic
alcoolisme /alkɔlism/ *nm* alcoholism
alcootest /alkɔtɛst/ *nm* **(a)** Breathalyzer®
(b) breath test
alcôve /alkov/ *nf* alcove
aléas /alea/ *nm pl* vagaries; (financial) hazards
aléatoire /aleatwaʀ/ *adj* **(a)** ‹*events*› unpredictable; ‹*profession*› insecure
(b) ‹*number*› random
alentours /alɑ̃tuʀ/ *nm pl* surrounding area
alerte /alɛʀt/ **1** *adj* alert; lively
2 *nf* alert; **donner l'**∼ to raise the alarm; ∼ **générale** full alert

■ ∼ **à la bombe** bomb scare
alerter /alɛʀte/ [1] *vtr* to alert (**sur** to)
alèse /alɛz/ *nf* undersheet, mattress protector
alexandrin /alɛksɑ̃dʀɛ̃/ *adj m*, *nm* alexandrine
algèbre /alʒɛbʀ/ *nf* algebra
Algérie /alʒeʀi/ *pr nf* Algeria
algérien, **-ienne** /alʒeʀjɛ̃, ɛn/ *adj* Algerian
algue /alg/ *nf* **(a)** **des** ∼**s** algae
(b) seaweed
alias /aljas/ *adv* alias
alibi /alibi/ *nm* **(a)** (Law) alibi
(b) excuse
aliénation /aljenasjɔ̃/ *nf* alienation
aliéné, ∼**e** /aljene/ *nm,f* insane person
alignement /aliɲ(ə)mɑ̃/ *nm* **(a)** row, line
(b) alignment
(c) ∼ **de qch sur qch** ‹*currency, salaries*› bringing into line of sth with sth
aligner /aliɲe/ [1] **1** *vtr* **(a)** to line [sth] up
(b) ∼ **qch sur qch** to bring sth into line with sth
(c) to give a list of ‹*figures*›
(d) to line up ‹*players*›
2 s'aligner *v refl* (+ *v être*) **(a)** ‹*houses, trees*› to be in a line
(b) ‹*people*› to line up
(c) **s'**∼ **sur** to align oneself with ‹*country, party, ideas*›
aliment /alimɑ̃/ *nm* (gen) food; (for farm animals) feed; (for plants) nutrient
alimentaire /alimɑ̃tɛʀ/ *adj* ‹*needs, habits*› dietary; ‹*industry, shortage*› food; **régime** ∼ diet
alimentation /alimɑ̃tasjɔ̃/ *nf* **(a)** diet
(b) feeding
(c) food; **magasin d'**∼ food shop
(d) food industry
(e) supply, feeding; **l'**∼ **en eau** the water supply
alimenter /alimɑ̃te/ [1] **1** *vtr* **(a)** to feed ‹*person, animal*›
(b) to feed, to supply ‹*engine, boiler*›
(c) to fuel ‹*conversation, hostility*›
2 s'alimenter *v refl* (+ *v être*) **(a)** ‹*person*› to eat; ‹*animal*› to feed
(b) (with water, gas) **s'**∼ **en** to be supplied with
alinéa /alinea/ *nm* **(a)** indentation
(b) indented line
(c) paragraph
alité, ∼**e** /alite/ *adj* **être** ∼ to be confined to bed
alla /ala/ ▶ ALLER[1]
allai /alɛ/ ▶ ALLER[1]
allaient /alɛ/ ▶ ALLER[1]
allais /alɛ/ ▶ ALLER[1]
allait /alɛ/ ▶ ALLER[1]
allaitement /alɛtmɑ̃/ *nm* **(a)** breast-feeding
(b) suckling
allaiter /alete/ [1] *vtr* **(a)** to breast-feed

(b) to suckle

allâmes /alɑm/ ▶ ALLER¹

allant, **~e** /alɑ̃, ɑ̃t/ **1** *pp* ▶ ALLER¹
2 *adj* active, lively
3 *nm* drive, bounce; **avoir de l'~, être plein d'~** to have plenty of drive, to be full of bounce; **perdre son ~** to run out of steam

allâtes /alɑt/ ▶ ALLER¹

allé, **~e** /ale/ ▶ ALLER¹

allécher /aleʃe/ [14] *vtr* to tempt (**avec** with)

allée /ale/ **1** *nf* **(a)** (in garden, wood) path; (leading to house) drive; (in town) avenue
(b) aisle
2 **allées** *nf pl* **~s et venues** comings and goings

allégé, **~e** /aleʒe/ **1** *pp* ▶ ALLÉGER
2 *pp adj* low-fat; ‹*chocolate*› diet

allégeance /aleʒɑ̃s/ *nf* allegiance

allégement /aleʒmɑ̃/ *nm* (of charges) reduction; (of restrictions, controls) relaxing; **~ fiscal** tax relief

alléger /aleʒe/ [15] **1** *vtr* **(a)** to lighten ‹*load, weight*›
(b) to reduce ‹*debt*› (**de** by); to cut ‹*taxes*›; to relax ‹*control, restrictions*›
2 **s'alléger** *v refl* (+ *v être*) **(a)** ‹*load*› to get lighter
(b) ‹*debt, taxation*› to be reduced; ‹*embargo*› to be relaxed

allégorie /alegɔʀi/ *nf* allegory

allègre /alɛgʀ/ *adj* ‹*style*› light; ‹*tone*› light-hearted; ‹*step, mood*› buoyant

allégrement /alegʀəmɑ̃/ *adv* joyfully; (ironic) blithely

allégresse /alegʀɛs/ *nf* joy

allegro /alegʀo/ *adv* allegro

alléguer /alege/ [14] *vtr* **(a)** to invoke
(b) to allege

Allemagne /almaɲ/ *pr nf* Germany

allemand, **~e** /almɑ̃, ɑ̃d/ **1** *adj* German
2 *nm* (language) German

aller¹ /ale/ [9] **1** *v aux* **je vais apprendre l'italien** I'm going to learn Italian; **j'allais partir quand il est arrivé** I was about to leave when he arrived; **il est allé voir l'exposition** he went to see the exhibition; **va leur parler** go and speak to them
2 *vi* (+ *v être*) **(a)** **comment vas-tu, comment ça va?** how are you?; **ça va (bien)** I'm fine; **~ beaucoup mieux** to be much better; **bois ça, ça ira mieux** drink this, you'll feel better; **les affaires vont bien** business is good; **qu'est-ce qui ne va pas?** what's the matter?; **ne pas ~ sans peine** *or* **mal** not to be easy; **ça devrait ~ de soi** it should be obvious; **ça va pas non?** (colloq), **ça va pas la tête?** (colloq) are you crazy? (colloq)
(b) to go; **où vas-tu?** where are you going?; **~ nager/au travail** to go swimming/to work; **vas-y, demande-leur!** go on, ask them!; **allons-y!** let's go!; **allons!, allez!** come on!; **~ et venir** to pace up and down; to run in and out; **les nouvelles vont vite** news travels

fast; **j'y vais** (answering phone, door) I'll get it; (when leaving) (colloq) I'm off (colloq); **~ contre la loi** to break the law; to be against the law
(c) **ça va, ça ira** (colloq), **ça peut aller** (colloq) that'll do; it'll do; **ça va comme ça** it's all right as it is; **ça ne va pas du tout** that's no good at all; **lundi ça (te) va?** would Monday suit you?
(d) **~ à qn** to fit sb
(e) **~ à qn** to suit sb; **ta cravate ne va pas avec ta chemise** your tie doesn't go with your shirt
(f) **~ jusqu'à tuer** to go as far as to kill; **la voiture peut ~ jusqu'à 200 km/h** the car can do up to 200 km/h; **la période qui va de 1918 à 1939** the period between 1918 and 1939; **~ sur ses 17 ans** to be going on 17
(g) **y ~ de sa petite larme** to shed a little tear
3 **s'en aller** *v refl* (+ *v être*) **(a)** **s'en aller** to go, to leave, to be off; to go away
(b) **la tache ne s'en va pas** the stain won't come out
(c) (formal) to pass away, to die
4 *v impers* **(a)** **il y va de ma réputation** my reputation is at stake
(b) **il en va de même pour toi** that goes for you too

aller² /ale/ *nm* **(a)** **j'ai pris le bus à l'~** I took the bus there; I took the bus here; **il n'arrête pas de faire des ~s et retours entre chez lui et son bureau** he's always going to and fro between the house and the office
(b) **~ (simple)** single (ticket) (GB), one-way ticket (**pour** to); **~ retour** return ticket, round trip (US)
(c) (Sport) (**match**) **~** first leg

allèrent /alɛʀ/ ▶ ALLER¹

allergie /alɛʀʒi/ *nf* (Med) allergy

allergique /alɛʀʒik/ *adj* allergic (**à** to)

allergologue /alɛʀgɔlɔg/ *nmf* allergist

allez /ale/ ▶ ALLER¹

alliage /aljaʒ/ *nm* **(a)** alloy
(b) (figurative) combination

alliance /aljɑ̃s/ *nf* **(a)** wedding ring
(b) alliance

allié, **~e** /alje/ **1** *pp* ▶ ALLIER
2 *pp adj* allied
3 *nm,f* **(a)** ally; **les ~s** the Allies
(b) relative

allier /alje/ [2] **1** *vtr* **(a)** to combine (**et, à** with)
(b) (Tech) to alloy ‹*metals*› (**à, avec** with)
2 **s'allier** *v refl* (+ *v être*) to form an alliance

alliez /alje/ ▶ ALLER¹

alligator /aligatɔʀ/ *nm* alligator

allions /aljɔ̃/ ▶ ALLER¹

allô /alo/ *excl* hello!, hallo!

allocation /al(l)ɔkasjɔ̃/ *nf* **(a)** allocation, granting
(b) benefit (GB), benefits (US)
■ **~ chômage** unemployment benefit (GB) *or* benefits (US); **~s familiales** family allowance

allocution /al(l)ɔkysjɔ̃/ *nf* address

a

allongé, **∼e** /alɔ̃ʒe/ adj (a) être ∼ ⟨person⟩ to be lying down; to be reclining; (b) elongated

allonger /alɔ̃ʒe/ [13] **1** vtr (a) to lay [sb] down
(b) to extend ⟨list, holiday⟩; **cette coiffure t'allonge le visage** that hairstyle makes your face look longer
(c) to water [sth] down ⟨coffee⟩
2 **s'allonger** v refl (+ v être) (a) to lie down
(b) to get longer

allons /alɔ̃/ ▶ ALLER¹

allouer /alwe/ [1] vtr to allocate ⟨sum, allowance, budget⟩; to grant ⟨loan⟩; to allot ⟨time⟩

allumage /alymaʒ/ nm (Aut) ignition

allumé, **∼e** /alyme/ adj (colloq) (a) mad (colloq)
(b) tipsy (colloq)

allume-gaz /alymgaz/ nm inv gas lighter

allumer /alyme/ [1] **1** vtr (a) to light ⟨candle, gas⟩; to start ⟨fire⟩
(b) to switch [sth] on, to turn [sth] on; **laisser ses phares allumés** to leave one's headlights on
2 **s'allumer** v refl (+ v être) (a) ⟨heating, radio, lighting⟩ to come on
(b) **son regard s'alluma** his face lit up

allumette /alymɛt/ nf match, matchstick

allumeur, -euse /alymœʀ, øz/ nm,f (colloq) tease

allure /alyʀ/ nf (a) (of walker) pace; (of vehicle) speed; **ralentir son ∼** to slow down; **à toute ∼** at top speed; **à cette ∼** at this rate
(b) (of animal) gait
(c) (of person) appearance
(d) style; **avoir de l'∼** to have style

allusif, -ive /alyzif, iv/ adj ⟨remark⟩ allusive; ⟨person⟩ indirect

allusion /alyzjɔ̃/ nf allusion (à to); **faire ∼ à** to allude to

alluvial, **∼e**, mpl **-iaux** /alyvjal, o/ adj alluvial

alluvion /alyvjɔ̃/ nf alluvium; **des ∼s** alluvia

almanach /almana(k)/ nm almanac

aloi /alwa/ nm **un succès de bon ∼** a well-deserved success; **une plaisanterie de mauvais ∼** a tasteless joke; **une gaieté de bon ∼** a simple cheerfulness

alors /alɔʀ/ **1** adv (a) then; **il avait ∼ 18 ans** he was 18 at the time; **la mode d'∼** the fashion in those days; **jusqu'∼** until then
(b) then; (mais) ∼ **cela change tout!** but that changes everything!; **et (puis) ∼?** so what?
(c) so; **il y avait une grève des trains, ∼ j'ai pris l'autobus** there was a train strike, so I took the bus
(d) **ou ∼** or else
(e) (colloq) so; ∼ **il me dit…** so he said to me…
(f) **non mais ∼!** honestly!
2 **alors que** phr (a) while
(b) when

3 **alors même que** phr even though

alouette /alwɛt/ nf lark

alourdir /aluʀdiʀ/ [3] **1** vtr (a) to weigh [sb] down ⟨person⟩; to make [sth] tense ⟨atmosphere⟩
(b) to increase ⟨tax, charges⟩
2 **s'alourdir** v refl (+ v être) ⟨eyelids⟩ to begin to droop; ⟨air⟩ to grow heavy

alourdissement /aluʀdismɑ̃/ nm (of tax, deduction) increase (de in)

alpestre /alpɛstʀ/ adj alpine

alphabet /alfabe/ nm alphabet

alphabétique /alfabetik/ adj alphabetical

alphabétiser /alfabetize/ [1] vtr to teach [sb] to read and write

alpin, **∼e** /alpɛ̃, in/ adj alpine

alpinisme /alpinism/ nm mountaineering

alpiniste /alpinist/ nmf mountaineer, climber

altération /alteʀasjɔ̃/ nf (of faculties) impairment (de of); (of foodstuff) spoiling (de of); (in environment) deterioration (de in)

altérer /alteʀe/ [14] vtr (a) to affect ⟨taste, health⟩
(b) to spoil ⟨foodstuff⟩; to fade ⟨colour⟩
(c) to distort ⟨text⟩; to adulterate ⟨substance⟩

alternance /altɛʀnɑ̃s/ nf alternation; **en ∼ avec** alternately with

alternateur /altɛʀnatœʀ/ nm alternator

alternatif, -ive¹ /altɛʀnatif, iv/ adj
(a) (gen) alternate
(b) ⟨current⟩ alternating
(c) ⟨culture, theatre⟩ alternative

alternative² /altɛʀnativ/ **1** adj f ▶ ALTERNATIF
2 nf alternative

alterner /altɛʀne/ [1] **1** vtr to alternate
2 vi (a) to alternate
(b) ∼ **avec qn pour faire** to take turns with sb (at) doing

altesse /altɛs/ nf (a) highness
(b) prince/princess

altier, -ière /altje, ɛʀ/ adj haughty

altitude /altityd/ nf altitude; **en ∼** high up (in the mountains)

alto /alto/ **1** adj alto
2 nm (a) (instrument) viola
(b) viola player (GB), violin (US)
(c) (voice) alto

altruiste /altʀɥist/ adj altruistic

alu /aly/ (colloq), **aluminium** /alyminjɔm/ nm aluminium (GB), aluminum (US)

alvéole /alveɔl/ nf (a) (in honeycomb) cell
(b) (in rock) cavity

alvéolé, **∼e** /alveɔle/ adj honeycombed

amabilité /amabilite/ nf (a) kindness
(b) courtesy

amadouer /amadwe/ [1] vtr to coax, to cajole

amaigrir /amegʀiʀ/ [3] vtr to make [sb] thinner

amaigrissant, **∼e** /amegʀisɑ̃, ɑ̃t/ adj slimming

amalgame /amalgam/ *nm* **(a)** (gen) mixture
(b) (in dentistry, chemistry) amalgam

amalgamer /amalgame/ [1] *vtr* **(a)** to lump together ‹*problems*›; to mix ‹*feelings, people*›
(b) to blend, to amalgamate ‹*ingredients*›

amande /amɑ̃d/ *nf* **(a)** almond
(b) kernel

amanite /amanit/ *nf* amanita; **~ phalloïde** death cap

amant /amɑ̃/ *nm* lover

amarre /amaʀ/ *nf* rope; **les ~s** moorings

amarrer /amaʀe/ [1] *vtr* **(a)** to moor ‹*boat*›
(b) to tie (**à, sur** to)

amas /ama/ *nm inv* pile; heap

amasser /amase/ [1] **1** *vtr* to amass, to accumulate ‹*fortune, books*›; to collect ‹*proof*›
2 **s'amasser** *v refl* (+ *v être*) ‹*snow, objects*› to pile up; ‹*proof, evidence*› to build up

amateur /amatœʀ/ **1** *adj inv* amateur
2 *nm* **(a)** (non-professional) amateur
(b) (of sport, photography) enthusiast; (of wine) connoisseur
(c) il vend sa voiture, vous êtes ~? he's selling his car, are you interested?

amazone /amazon/ *nf* **en ~** sidesaddle

ambassade /ɑ̃basad/ *nf* embassy

ambassadeur /ɑ̃basadœʀ/ *nm* ambassador

ambassadrice /ɑ̃basadʀis/ *nf*
(a) ambassador
(b) ambassador's wife

ambiance /ɑ̃bjɑ̃s/ *nf* atmosphere

ambiant, ~e /ɑ̃bjɑ̃, ɑ̃t/ *adj* ‹*air*› surrounding; **à température ~e** at room temperature
(b) prevailing

ambigu, ambiguë /ɑ̃bigy/ *adj* ‹*remark, situation*› ambiguous; ‹*feeling, attitude*› ambivalent

ambiguïté /ɑ̃biguite/ *nf* ambiguity; enigmatic nature; ambivalence

ambitieux, -ieuse /ɑ̃bisjø, øz/ *adj* ambitious

ambition /ɑ̃bisjɔ̃/ *nf* ambition

ambitionner /ɑ̃bisjone/ [1] *vtr* to aspire to

ambivalent, ~e /ɑ̃bivalɑ̃, ɑ̃t/ *adj* ambivalent

ambre /ɑ̃bʀ/ *nm* **(a)** **~ (jaune)** amber
(b) **~ (gris)** ambergris

ambulance /ɑ̃bylɑ̃s/ *nf* ambulance

ambulancier, -ière /ɑ̃bylɑ̃sje, ɛʀ/ *nmf* ambulance driver

ambulant, ~e /ɑ̃bylɑ̃, ɑ̃t/ *adj* ‹*circus*› travelling (GB); **vendeur ~** (in station) snack trolley man; **un cadavre ~** (colloq) a walking skeleton (colloq)

âme /ɑm/ *nf* soul; **Dieu ait son ~** God rest his/her soul; **socialiste dans l'~** a socialist to the core; **en mon ~ et conscience** in all honesty; **pas ~ qui vive** not a (single) soul; **~ sœur** soul mate

amélioration /ameljɔʀasjɔ̃/ *nf* improvement

améliorer /ameljɔʀe/ [1] *vtr*, **s'améliorer** *v refl* (+ *v être*) to improve

amen /amɛn/ *nm inv* amen

aménagé, ~e /amenaʒe/ **1** *pp* ▶ AMÉNAGER
2 *pp adj* **(a)** converted
(b) equipped

aménagement /amenaʒmɑ̃/ *nm*
(a) (of region, town) development
(b) (of roads) construction; (of parks, green spaces) creation
(c) (of house, boat) fitting
(d) (of timetable) adjustment; **l'~ du temps de travail** flexible working hours

aménager /amenaʒe/ [13] *vtr* **(a)** to convert; to do up ‹*house, attic*›
(b) to equip ‹*kitchen*›; to develop ‹*region*›
(c) to create ‹*parks, green spaces*›; to build ‹*road*›; to lay out ‹*garden*›
(d) to arrange ‹*timetable*›; to adjust ‹*regulations*›

amende /amɑ̃d/ *nf* fine

amendement /amɑ̃dmɑ̃/ *nm* **(a)** (in law) amendment (**à** to; **sur** on)
(b) (of soil) enrichment

amener /amne/ [16] *vtr* **(a)** **~ qn quelque part** to take sb somewhere
(b) (accompany) **~ qn (quelque part)** to bring sb (somewhere)
(c) (controversial) **~ qch (à qn)** to bring (sb) sth
(d) to cause ‹*problems, illness*›; to bring ‹*rain, fame*›
(e) to bring up ‹*issue, subject*›; **être bien amené** ‹*conclusion*› to be well-presented
(f) **~ qn à qch/faire** to lead sb to sth/to do

amenuiser: s'amenuiser /amənɥize/ [1] *v refl* (+ *v être*) ‹*supplies*› to dwindle; ‹*risk*› to lessen

amer, -ère /amɛʀ/ *adj* bitter

américain, ~e /ameʀikɛ̃, ɛn/ **1** *adj* American; **à l'~e** (gen) in the American style; (Culin) à l'américaine
2 *nm* American English

Amérindien, -ienne /ameʀɛ̃djɛ̃, ɛn/ *nm,f* Amerindian, American Indian

Amérique /ameʀik/ *pr nf* America

amerrir /ameʀiʀ/ [3] *vi* ‹*hydroplane*› to land (on water); ‹*spacecraft*› to splash down

amertume /amɛʀtym/ *nf* bitterness

ameublement /amœbləmɑ̃/ *nm*
(a) furniture
(b) furniture trade
(c) (of room, house) furnishing

ameuter /amøte/ [1] *vtr* **(a)** ‹*person, noise*› to bring [sb] out
(b) to stir [sb] up

ami, ~e /ami/ **1** *adj* friendly

2 *nm,f* friend; en ∼ as a friend; un ∼ des bêtes an animal lover; ▶ FAUX¹
IDIOMS les bons comptes font les bons ∼s (*Proverb*) a debt paid is a friend kept

amiable: à l'amiable /alamjabl/ *phr* ⟨*separate*⟩ on friendly terms; ⟨*separation*⟩ amicable; ⟨*divorce*⟩ by mutual consent; ▶ CONSTAT

amiante /amjãt/ *nm* asbestos

amical, ∼e¹, *pl* **-aux** /amikal, o/ *adj* friendly

amicale² /amikal/ *nf* association

amicalement /amikalmã/ *adv* (a) ⟨*greet, receive*⟩ warmly; ⟨*compete*⟩ in a friendly way
(b) (*at end of letter*) (**bien**) ∼ best wishes

amidon /amidõ/ *nm* starch

amincir /amɛ̃siR/ [3] *vtr* to make [sb] look slimmer

amiral, *mpl* **-aux** /amiral, o/ *nm* admiral

amitié /amitje/ **1** *nf* friendship; **se lier d'**∼ **avec qn** to strike up a friendship with sb
2 amitiés *nf pl* (*at end of letter*) kindest regards

ammoniac /amɔnjak/ *nm* (gas) ammonia

ammoniaque /amɔnjak/ *nf* ammonia

amnésie /amnezi/ *nf* amnesia

amnésique /amnezik/ *adj* amnesic

amnistie /amnisti/ *nf* amnesty

amocher /amɔʃe/ (*colloq*) [1] **1** *vtr* to bash (*colloq*) [sb/sth] up ⟨*person, car*⟩
2 s'amocher *v refl* (+ *v être*) to bash oneself up (*colloq*); **s'**∼ **le nez** to bash up (*colloq*) one's nose

amoindrir /amwɛ̃driR/ [3] *vtr* to reduce ⟨*resistance*⟩; to weaken ⟨*person*⟩

amonceler /amõsle/ [19] **1** *vtr* to pile up
2 s'amonceler *v refl* (+ *v être*) ⟨*clouds, snow*⟩ to build up; ⟨*evidence, problems*⟩ to pile up

amoncellement /amõsɛlmã/ *nm* pile; mass

amont /amõ/ *nm* (*of river*) upper reaches; **en** ∼ upstream (**de** from); **naviguer d'**∼ **en aval** to sail downstream

amoral, ∼e, *mpl* **-aux** /amɔral, o/ *adj* amoral

amorce /amɔRs/ *nf* (a) (*of discussion*) initiation
(b) bait
(c) (*of explosive*) cap, primer; (*of gun*) cap

amorcer /amɔRse/ [12] *vtr* (a) to begin
(b) to prime

amorphe /amɔRf/ *adj* apathetic

amortir /amɔRtiR/ [3] *vtr* (a) to deaden ⟨*noise*⟩; to absorb ⟨*shock, impact*⟩; to break ⟨*fall*⟩
(b) to pay off ⟨*debt*⟩
(c) **j'ai amorti mon ordinateur en quelques mois** my computer paid for itself in a few months

amortissement /amɔRtismã/ *nm*
(a) (*of noise*) deadening; (*of shock*) absorption; (*of fall*) cushioning
(b) (*of debt*) paying off

(c) (*of equipment*) depreciation

amortisseur /amɔRtisœR/ *nm* shock absorber

amour /amuR/ **1** *nm* love; **pour l'**∼ **de** for the sake of; out of love for; **c'était un** ∼ **de jeunesse** it was a youthful romance
2 amours *nm pl or nf pl* (a) (Zool) mating
(b) love affairs; **à tes** ∼**s!** (*to somebody sneezing*) bless you!

amouracher: s'amouracher /amuRaʃe/ [1] *v refl* (+ *v être*) **s'**∼ **de** to become infatuated with

amourette /amuRɛt/ *nf* passing infatuation

amoureux, -euse /amuRø, øz/ *adj* in love

amour-propre /amuRpRɔpR/ *nm* self-esteem; pride

amovible /amɔvibl/ *adj* detachable; removable

ampère /ɑ̃pɛR/ *nm* amp, ampère

amphibie /ɑ̃fibi/ *adj* (Zool, Aut) amphibious

amphithéâtre /ɑ̃fiteatR/ *nm* (a) (natural, ancient) amphitheatre (GB)
(b) (*at university*) lecture hall

amphore /ɑ̃fɔR/ *nf* amphora

ample /ɑ̃pl/ *adj* (a) ⟨*coat, dress*⟩ loose-fitting; ⟨*skirt, sleeve*⟩ full; ⟨*gesture*⟩ sweeping
(b) ⟨*quantity*⟩ ample; ⟨*harvest*⟩ abundant; ⟨*details*⟩ full

amplement /ɑ̃pləmã/ *adv* fully; **c'est** ∼ **suffisant** that's more than enough!

ampleur /ɑ̃plœR/ *nf* (*of problem*) size; (*of project, subject, survey*) scope; (*of event, disaster, task*) scale; (*of damage, reaction*) extent

amplificateur /ɑ̃plifikatœR/ *nm* amplifier

amplification /ɑ̃plifikasjõ/ *nf* (a) (*in physics*) amplification
(b) (extension) (*of relations*) development; (*of strike*) escalation; (*of debate*) expansion

amplifier /ɑ̃plifje/ [2] **1** *vtr* to amplify ⟨*sound, current*⟩; to magnify ⟨*rumour*⟩
2 s'amplifier *v refl* (+ *v être*) ⟨*sound*⟩ to grow louder; ⟨*trade*⟩ to increase; ⟨*strike*⟩ to intensify

ampoule /ɑ̃pul/ *nf* (a) ∼ (**électrique**) (light) bulb
(b) (Med) (drinkable) phial; (injectable) ampoule
(c) blister

ampoulé, ∼e /ɑ̃pule/ *adj* bombastic

amputation /ɑ̃pytasjõ/ *nf* amputation

amputer /ɑ̃pyte/ [1] *vtr* (a) (Med) to amputate ⟨*limb*⟩; to perform an amputation on ⟨*person*⟩
(b) to cut [sth] drastically ⟨*budget*⟩

amusant, ∼e /amyzã, ãt/ *adj*
(a) entertaining
(b) funny

amuse-gueule /amyzgœl/ *nm inv* cocktail snack (GB), munchies (US)

amusement /amyzmã/ *nm* entertainment

amuser /amyze/ [1] **1** *vtr* (a) to entertain; to amuse
(b) to distract

② **s'amuser** *v refl* (+ *v être*) **(a)** to play; **pour s'~** for fun
(b) **bien s'~** to have a good time
amuseur, -euse /amyzœʀ, øz/ *nm,f* entertainer
amygdale /amidal/ *nf* tonsil
an /ɑ̃/ *nm* year; **avoir huit ~s** to be eight (years old); **en l'~ deux mille** in the year two thousand; **l'~ 55 avant J.-C./après J.-C.** 55 BC/AD
IDIOMS **bon ~, mal ~** year in, year out
anabolisant /anabolizɑ̃/ *nm* anabolic steroid
anachronique /anakʀɔnik/ *adj* anachronistic
anachronisme /anakʀɔnism/ *nm* anachronism
anal, ~e, *mpl* **-aux** /anal, o/ *adj* anal
analogie /analɔʒi/ *nf* analogy
analogue /analɔg/ *adj* similar (**à** to)
analphabète /analfabɛt/ *adj, nmf* illiterate
analphabétisme /analfabetism/ *nm* illiteracy
analyse /analiz/ *nf* **(a)** analysis; **faire l'~ de qch** to analyse (GB) sth
(b) (Med) test
(c) psychoanalysis
analyser /analize/ [1] *vtr* **(a)** (gen) to analyse (GB)
(b) (Med) to test ⟨*blood, urine*⟩
ananas /anana(s)/ *nm inv* pineapple
anarchie /anaʀʃi/ *nf* anarchy
anarchiste /anaʀʃist/ **①** *adj* anarchistic
② *nmf* anarchist
anatomie /anatɔmi/ *nf* anatomy
ancêtre /ɑ̃sɛtʀ/ *nmf* ancestor
anchois /ɑ̃ʃwa/ *nm inv* anchovy
ancien, -ienne¹ /ɑ̃sjɛ̃, ɛn/ **①** *adj*
(a) ⟨*champion, president, capital*⟩ former
(b) ⟨*history, language*⟩ ancient
(c) ⟨*style, book, building*⟩ old; ⟨*car*⟩ vintage; ⟨*piece of furniture*⟩ antique
(d) **c'est lui le plus ~** (in job) he's been here longest
② *nm* **(a)** (in tribe, congregation) elder; (in company) senior member; **les ~s** the older people
(b) old member; former student
(c) **l'~** older property; (furniture) antiques
■ **~ combattant** veteran
ancienne²: à l'ancienne /alɑ̃sjɛn/ *phr* ⟨*jam, piece of furniture*⟩ traditional-style
anciennement /ɑ̃sjɛnmɑ̃/ *adv* formerly
ancienneté /ɑ̃sjɛnte/ *nf* **(a)** (of person) seniority; **trois ans d'~** three years' service
(b) (of tradition, relic) antiquity; (of building) age
ancre /ɑ̃kʀ/ *nf* (Naut) anchor
ancrer /ɑ̃kʀe/ [1] **①** *vtr* **(a)** to anchor ⟨*ship*⟩
(b) to fix ⟨*idea*⟩; to establish ⟨*custom*⟩
② **s'ancrer** *v refl* (+ *v être*) **(a)** to anchor
(b) ⟨*idea*⟩ to become fixed; ⟨*custom*⟩ to become established

Andorre /ɑ̃dɔʀ/ *pr nf* Andorra
andouille /ɑ̃duj/ *nf* **(a)** (Culin) andouille
(b) (colloq)fool
âne /ɑn/ *nm* **(a)** (Zool) donkey, ass
(b) (colloq) dimwit (colloq)
IDIOMS **faire l'~ pour avoir du son** to act dumb to find out more
anéantir /aneɑ̃tiʀ/ [3] *vtr* **(a)** to ruin ⟨*crops, harvest*⟩; to lay waste to ⟨*town*⟩; to shatter ⟨*hopes*⟩
(b) ⟨*news*⟩ to crush; ⟨*strain*⟩ to exhaust
anéantissement /aneɑ̃tismɑ̃/ *nm*
(a) destruction, devastation
(b) (of hope) shattering
(c) (of person) total collapse
anecdote /anɛkdɔt/ *nf* anecdote
anémie /anemi/ *nf* **(a)** anaemia
(b) weakness
anémier /anemje/ [2] **①** *vtr* **(a)** (Med) to make [sb] anaemic ⟨*person*⟩
(b) (figurative) to weaken
② **s'anémier** *v refl* (+ *v être*) **(a)** (Med) to become anaemic
(b) (figurative) to grow feeble
anémique /anemik/ *adj* **(a)** anaemic
(b) weak
anémone /anemɔn/ *nf* anemone
ânerie /ɑnʀi/ *nf* **(a)** silly remark
(b) silly blunder
ânesse /ɑnɛs/ *nf* she-ass, female donkey
anesthésie /anɛstezi/ *nf* anaesthesia
aneth /anɛt/ *nm* dill
anfractuosité /ɑ̃fʀaktyozite/ *nf* crevice
ange /ɑ̃ʒ/ *nm* angel
IDIOMS **être aux ~s** to be in (one's) seventh heaven
angélique¹ /ɑ̃ʒelik/ *adj* angelic
angélique² /ɑ̃ʒelik/ *nf* angelica
angelot /ɑ̃ʒlo/ *nm* cherub
angine /ɑ̃ʒin/ *nf* throat infection
anglais, ~e¹ /ɑ̃glɛ, ɛz/ **①** *adj* English
② *nm* (language) English
Anglais, ~e /ɑ̃glɛ, ɛz/ *nm,f* Englishman/Englishwoman
anglaise² /ɑ̃glɛz/ **①** *adj f* ▶ ANGLAIS 1
② *nf* ringlet
angle /ɑ̃gl/ *nm* **(a)** angle
(b) corner
Angleterre /ɑ̃glətɛʀ/ *pr nf* England
anglo-américain, ~e, *mpl* **~s** /ɑ̃gloameʀikɛ̃, ɛn/ **①** *adj* **(a)** Anglo-American
(b) American English
② *nm* (language) American English
anglo-normand, ~e, *mpl* **~s** /ɑ̃glonɔʀmɑ̃, ɑ̃d/ *adj* Anglo-Norman
Anglo-Normande /ɑ̃glonɔʀmɑ̃d/ *adj f* **les îles ~s** the Channel Islands
anglophone /ɑ̃glɔfɔn/ **①** *adj* English-speaking
② *nmf* English speaker; Anglophone
anglo-saxon, -onne, *mpl* **~s** /ɑ̃glosaksɔ̃, ɔn/ *adj* Anglo-Saxon

angoissant, **∼e** /ɑ̃gwasɑ̃, ɑ̃t/ adj
⟨prospect⟩ alarming; ⟨film, silence⟩
frightening

angoisse /ɑ̃gwas/ nf anxiety

angoissé, **∼e** /ɑ̃gwase/ adj anxious

angoisser /ɑ̃gwase/ [1] **1** vtr to worry
2 vi (colloq) to be anxious, to be nervous

anguille /ɑ̃gij/ nf eel

angulaire /ɑ̃gylɛʀ/ adj angular

anicroche /anikʀɔʃ/ nf hitch; **sans ∼(s)**
without a hitch

animal, **∼e**, mpl **-aux** /animal, o/ **1** adj
animal
2 nm animal; **∼ familier** pet; **∼ domestique**
domestic animal; **∼ nuisible** pest

animalier, **-ière** /animalje, ɛʀ/ **1** adj
wildlife
2 nm,f (in a lab) animal keeper
3 nm wildlife artist

animateur, **-trice** /animatœʀ, tʀis/ nm,f
(a) (of group of holidaymakers, club) coordinator;
(of association) leader; (of festival) organizer
(b) presenter

animation /animasjɔ̃/ nf **(a)** (of group,
exhibition, festival) organization; (of sales)
coordination
(b) life, liveliness; **ville qui manque d'∼** dull
town
(c) (of street, market) hustle and bustle;
(of people) excitement

animé, **∼e** /anime/ adj **(a)** animated;
lively; busy
(b) **∼ de mauvaises intentions** spurred on by
bad intentions

animer /anime/ [1] **1** vtr **(a)** to lead
⟨discussion, group⟩; to run ⟨course, show⟩; to
present ⟨programme⟩
(b) to liven up ⟨town, story, meeting⟩
2 **s'animer** v refl (+ v être)
(a) ⟨conversation⟩ to become lively; ⟨meeting⟩
to liven up; ⟨face⟩ to light up
(b) ⟨statue⟩ to come to life

animosité /animozite/ nf animosity
(envers toward(s); entre between)

anis /ani/ nm inv **(a)** anise
(b) aniseed

ankyloser: **s'ankyloser** /ɑ̃kiloze/ [1]
v refl (+ v être) to get stiff

annales /anal/ nf pl **(a)** annals
(b) (of exams) (book of) past papers

anneau, pl **∼x** /ano/ nm ring

année /ane/ nf year; **l'∼ en cours** this year,
the current year; **avec les ∼s** over the years;
d'∼ en ∼ year by year; **ces dix dernières ∼s**
over the last ten years; **souhaiter la bonne ∼**
à qn to wish sb a happy new year; **(dans) les
∼s 80** (in) the eighties; **location à l'∼** annual
rent
■ **∼ bissextile** leap year; **∼ civile** calendar
year; **∼ universitaire** academic year

année-lumière, pl **années-lumière**
/anelymjɛʀ/ nf light-year

annexe¹ /anɛks/ adj **(a)** ⟨room⟩ adjoining

(b) ⟨questions⟩ additional; ⟨file, document⟩
attached

annexe² /anɛks/ nf **(a)** (building) annexe
(GB), annex (US)
(b) (document) appendix

annexer /anɛkse/ [1] vtr to annex

annihiler /aniile/ [1] vtr to destroy ⟨efforts,
hopes⟩; to cancel out ⟨effect, results⟩

anniversaire /anivɛʀsɛʀ/ **1** adj **date** or
jour ∼ de anniversary of
2 nm **(a)** birthday
(b) anniversary

annonce /anɔ̃s/ nf **(a)** announcement
(b) advertisement, ad (colloq); **petite ∼**
classified advertisement
(c) declaration; **faire une ∼** (in bridge) to bid
(d) sign

annoncer /anɔ̃se/ [12] **1** vtr **(a)** to
announce
(b) to forecast ⟨rain, event⟩
(c) ⟨event, signal⟩ to herald
2 **s'annoncer** v refl (+ v être) **(a)** ⟨crisis,
storm⟩ to be brewing
(b) **la récolte 92 s'annonce excellente** the '92
harvest promises to be very good

annonciateur, **-trice** /anɔ̃sjatœʀ, tʀis/
adj ⟨sign, signal⟩ warning

annoter /anɔte/ [1] vtr to annotate ⟨work⟩;
to write notes on ⟨worksheet, homework⟩

annuaire /anɥɛʀ/ nm **(a)** directory
(b) yearbook

annuel, **-elle** /anɥɛl/ adj ⟨gen⟩ annual,
yearly; ⟨contract⟩ one-year

annulaire /anylɛʀ/ nm ring finger

annulation /anylasjɔ̃/ nf **(a)** (gen)
cancellation; (of law) repeal
(b) (Law) (of verdict) quashing; (of elections)
cancellation (GB); (of marriage) annulment

annuler /anyle/ [1] **1** vtr **(a)** to cancel
⟨appointment, trip⟩; to write off ⟨debt⟩; to
discount ⟨result of match⟩
(b) (Law) to declare [sth] void ⟨elections⟩; to
quash ⟨verdict⟩
2 **s'annuler** v refl (+ v être) to cancel each
other out

anodin, **∼e** /anɔdɛ̃, in/ adj ⟨subject⟩ safe,
neutral; ⟨question, joke⟩ innocent

anomalie /anɔmali/ nf **(a)** anomaly
(b) fault

anonymat /anɔnima/ nm **(a)** anonymity
(b) confidentiality

anonyme /anɔnim/ adj anonymous

anorexie /anɔʀɛksi/ nf anorexia

anormal, **∼e**, mpl **-aux** /anɔʀmal, o/ adj
abnormal

ANPE /aɛnpeœ/ nf ⟨abbr = **Agence
nationale pour l'emploi**⟩ French
national employment agency

anse /ɑ̃s/ nf (of cup, basket) handle

antagoniste /ɑ̃tagɔnist/ adj ⟨groups⟩
opposing; ⟨interests⟩ conflicting

antan: **d'antan** /dɑ̃tɑ̃/ phr ⟨wars, festivals⟩

of old; ⟨*prestige*⟩ former; **les métiers d'~** the old trades; **le Lyon d'~** the Lyons of yesteryear

antarctique /ɑ̃taʀktik/ *adj* Antarctic

Antarctique /ɑ̃taʀktik/ *pr nm*
(a) Antarctic; **océan ~** Antarctic Ocean
(b) Antarctica

antécédent, ~e /ɑ̃tesedɑ̃, ɑ̃t/ **1** *adj* previous
2 *nm* **(a)** past history
(b) medical history
(c) (in grammar, mathematics) antecedent

antenne /ɑ̃tɛn/ *nf* **(a)** (of radio, television) aerial; (of radar, satellite) antenna; **passer à l'~** ⟨*programme, person*⟩ to go on the air
(b) (of organization, service) branch
(c) (of insect, shrimp) antenna; **avoir des ~s** (figurative) to have a sixth sense

antérieur, ~e /ɑ̃teʀjœʀ/ *adj*
(a) ⟨*situation, work*⟩ previous
(b) ⟨*limb, ligament*⟩ anterior

anthracite /ɑ̃tʀasit/ *adj inv* charcoal grey (GB), charcoal gray (US)

anthropologie /ɑ̃tʀɔpɔlɔʒi/ *nf* anthropology

anthropophage /ɑ̃tʀɔpɔfaʒ/ *nmf* cannibal

antiaérien, -ienne /ɑ̃tiaeʀjɛ̃, ɛn/ *adj* anti-aircraft

antiatomique /ɑ̃tiatɔmik/ *adj* (anti-) radiation; **abri ~** nuclear shelter

antibiotique /ɑ̃tibjɔtik/ *adj, nm* antibiotic

antibrouillard /ɑ̃tibʀujaʀ/ *adj inv* **phare ~** fog light

antibruit /ɑ̃tibʀɥi/ *adj inv* soundproof

antichambre /ɑ̃tiʃɑ̃bʀ/ *nf* anteroom

antichoc /ɑ̃tiʃɔk/ *adj inv* **(a)** **casque ~** crash helmet
(b) ⟨*watch*⟩ shockproof

anticipation /ɑ̃tisipasjɔ̃/ *nf* anticipation; **roman d'~** science fiction novel

anticipé, ~e /ɑ̃tisipe/ *adj* early

anticiper /ɑ̃tisipe/ [1] **1** *vtr* to anticipate ⟨*reaction, change, movement*⟩
2 *vi* **(a)** to get ahead of oneself
(b) to think ahead

anticonformiste /ɑ̃tikɔ̃fɔʀmist/ *adj, nmf* nonconformist

anticorps /ɑ̃tikɔʀ/ *nm inv* antibody

antidater /ɑ̃tidate/ [1] *vtr* to backdate

antidémocratique /ɑ̃tidemɔkʀatik/ *adj* undemocratic

antidérapant, ~e /ɑ̃tideʀapɑ̃, ɑ̃t/ *adj* ⟨*tyre*⟩ nonskid; ⟨*sole*⟩ nonslip

antidopage /ɑ̃tidɔpaʒ/ *adj* ⟨*measure*⟩ anti-doping; **contrôle ~** dope test

antidote /ɑ̃tidɔt/ *nm* antidote

antigang /ɑ̃tigɑ̃g/ *adj inv* **brigade ~** crime squad

antigel /ɑ̃tiʒɛl/ *adj inv, nm* antifreeze

anti-inflammatoire, *pl* **~s** /ɑ̃tiɛ̃flamatwaʀ/ *adj, nm* anti-inflammatory

antillais, ~e /ɑ̃tijɛ, ɛz/ *adj* West Indian

Antilles /ɑ̃tij/ *pr nf pl* **les ~** the West Indies; **les Petites/Grandes ~** the Lesser/ Greater Antilles

antilope /ɑ̃tilɔp/ *nf* antelope

antimite /ɑ̃timit/ *adj, nm* moth-repellent

antipathie /ɑ̃tipati/ *nf* antipathy

antipathique /ɑ̃tipatik/ *adj* unpleasant

antipelliculaire /ɑ̃tipɛlikylɛʀ/ *adj* antidandruff

antipode /ɑ̃tipɔd/ *nm* antipodes

antipoison /ɑ̃tipwazɔ̃/ *adj inv* **centre ~** poisons unit

antiquaire /ɑ̃tikɛʀ/ *nmf* antique dealer

antique /ɑ̃tik/ *adj* ancient

antiquité /ɑ̃tikite/ **1** *nf* antique
2 **antiquités** *nf pl* antiquities

Antiquité /ɑ̃tikite/ *nf* antiquity

antireflet /ɑ̃tiʀəflɛ/ *adj inv* nonreflective; (in photography) antiglare

antirouille /ɑ̃tiʀuj/ *adj inv* **(a)** rust-proofing
(b) rust-removing

antisèche /ɑ̃tisɛʃ/ *nf* (colloq) (students' slang) crib (colloq)

antisémite /ɑ̃tisemit/ **1** *adj* anti-Semitic
2 *nmf* anti-Semite

antitabac /ɑ̃titaba/ *adj inv* antismoking

antiterroriste /ɑ̃titeʀɔʀist/ *adj* **lutte ~** fight against terrorism

antithèse /ɑ̃titɛz/ *nf* antithesis

antituberculeux, -euse /ɑ̃titybɛʀkylø, øz/ *adj* **vaccin ~** tuberculosis vaccine

antivol /ɑ̃tivɔl/ *nm* (of bicycle, motorbike) lock; (of car) anti-theft device

anus /anys/ *nm inv* anus

Anvers /ɑ̃vɛʀ/ *pr n* Antwerp

anxiété /ɑ̃ksjete/ *nf* anxiety

anxieux, -ieuse /ɑ̃ksjø, øz/ *adj* ⟨*person*⟩ anxious; ⟨*attitude*⟩ concerned

aorte /aɔʀt/ *nf* aorta

août /u(t)/ *nm* August

apaisant, ~e /apɛzɑ̃, ɑ̃t/ *adj* **(a)** soothing
(b) calming

apaiser /apeze/ [1] **1** *vtr* **(a)** to pacify, to appease
(b) to ease ⟨*conflict*⟩
(c) to calm ⟨*rage*⟩
2 **s'apaiser** *v refl* (+ *v être*) **(a)** to die down
(b) to calm down

apanage /apanaʒ/ *nm* **être l'~ de qch/qn** to be the prerogative of sth/sb

aparté /apaʀte/ *nm* **en ~** in private; (in a play) in an aside

apathie /apati/ *nf* **(a)** apathy
(b) stagnation

apatride /apatʀid/ *adj* stateless

APEC /apɛk/ *nf* (*abbr* = **Agence pour l'emploi des cadres**) *executive employment agency*

apercevoir /apɛʀsəvwaʀ/ [5] **1** *vtr* **(a)** to make out
(b) to catch sight of
2 s'apercevoir *v refl* (+ *v être*) **(a)** s'~ que to realize that; s'~ de to notice ⟨*mistake*⟩
(b) to catch sight of each other
(c) to meet briefly

aperçu /apɛʀsy/ **1** *pp* ▸ APERCEVOIR
2 *nm* **(a)** glimpse
(b) outline
(c) insight

apéritif /apeʀitif/ *nm* drink

apesanteur /apəzɑ̃tœʀ/ *nf* weightlessness

à-peu-près /apøpʀɛ/ *nm inv* vague approximation

apeuré, **~e** /apœʀe/ *adj* (scared) frightened; (shy) timid

aphone /afɔn/ *adj* être ~ to have lost one's voice

aphte /aft/ *nm* mouth ulcer

apiculture /apikyltyʀ/ *nf* beekeeping

apitoiement /apitwamɑ̃/ *nm* pity (sur for)

apitoyer /apitwaje/ [23] **1** *vtr* to move [sb] to pity
2 s'apitoyer *v refl* (+ *v être*) s'~ sur (le sort de) qn to feel sorry for sb

aplanir /aplaniʀ/ [3] *vtr* to level

aplati, **~e** /aplati/ **1** *pp* ▸ APLATIR
2 *pp adj* **(a)** flattened
(b) ⟨*nose*⟩ flat

aplatir /aplatiʀ/ [3] *vtr* **(a)** to flatten
(b) to smooth out ⟨*cushion*⟩; to smooth down ⟨*hair*⟩
(c) to press ⟨*seams*⟩

aplomb /aplɔ̃/ **1** *nm* **(a)** confidence; vous ne manquez pas d'~! you've got a nerve!
(b) plumb, perpendicularity
2 d'aplomb *phr* **(a)** être d'~ to be straight, to be plumb vertical
(b) (colloq) ça va te remettre d'~ it will put you back on your feet

apocalypse /apɔkalips/ *nf* apocalypse

apogée /apɔʒe/ *nm* **(a)** (of moon, satellite) apogee
(b) (of career, empire) peak

apologie /apɔlɔʒi/ *nf* panegyric; apologia; faire l'~ de to justify; to praise

a posteriori /apɔsteʀjɔʀi/ *phr* after the event

apostolat /apɔstɔla/ *nm* **(a)** apostolate
(b) (figurative) apostolic mission

apostrophe /apɔstʀɔf/ *nf* apostrophe

apostropher /apɔstʀɔfe/ [1] *vtr* to heckle

apothéose /apɔteoz/ *nf* **(a)** (of show) high point
(b) (of career, work) culmination

apôtre /apotʀ/ *nm* apostle

apparaître /apaʀɛtʀ/ [73] **1** *vi* (+ *v être*)
(a) ⟨*person, problem*⟩ to appear; ⟨*sun, moon*⟩ to come out
(b) laisser *or* faire ~ to show
(c) to seem

2 *v impers* il apparaît que it appears that

apparat /apaʀa/ *nm* grandeur; d'~ ceremonial

appareil /apaʀɛj/ *nm* **(a)** device
(b) appliance
(c) telephone; qui est à l'~? who's calling please?
(d) aircraft
(e) system; l'~ digestif the digestive system
(f) apparatus; l'~ du parti the party apparatus
■ ~ auditif hearing aid; ~ (dentaire) brace (GB), braces (US); ~ à sous slot machine; ~ photo camera
IDIOMS être dans son plus simple ~ to be in one's birthday suit

appareiller /apaʀeje/ [1] *vi* to cast off

apparemment /apaʀamɑ̃/ *adv*
(a) apparently
(b) seemingly

apparence /apaʀɑ̃s/ *nf* appearance

apparent, **~e** /apaʀɑ̃, ɑ̃t/ *adj* **(a)** visible
(b) ⟨*embarrassment*⟩ apparent
(c) seeming, apparent

apparenté, **~e** /apaʀɑ̃te/ *adj* **(a)** ⟨*person*⟩ related (à to)
(b) ⟨*company*⟩ allied

apparenter: s'apparenter /apaʀɑ̃te/ [1] *v refl* (+ *v être*) s'~ à to resemble

apparition /apaʀisjɔ̃/ *nf* **(a)** (of product) appearance; (of problem) emergence
(b) apparition

appartement /apaʀtəmɑ̃/ *nm* flat (GB), apartment; ~ témoin show flat (GB), show apartment (US)

appartenance /apaʀtənɑ̃s/ *nf* membership (à of)

appartenir /apaʀtəniʀ/ [36]
1 appartenir *à v+prep* **(a)** ~ à to belong to
(b) ~ à to be a member of
2 *v impers* il appartient à qn de faire it is up to sb to do

appât /apa/ *nm* **(a)** bait
(b) lure

appâter /apate/ [1] *vtr* **(a)** to bait
(b) to lure

appauvrir /apovʀiʀ/ [3] **1** *vtr* to impoverish
2 s'appauvrir *v refl* (+ *v être*) to become impoverished

appel /apɛl/ *nm* **(a)** call; (urgent) appeal; ~ à call for ⟨*solidarity*⟩; appeal for ⟨*calm*⟩; ~ au secours call for help; cry for help; faire ~ à to appeal to ⟨*person*⟩; to call ⟨*fire brigade*⟩; ⟨*task*⟩ to call for ⟨*skills*⟩
(b) roll call; (Sch) registration
(c) (Mil) call up (GB), draft (US)
(d) (Law) appeal; faire ~ to appeal
(e) (Sport) take off
■ ~ d'air draught (GB), draft (US); ~ de phares flash of headlights (GB) *or* high beams (US)

appelé, **~e** /aple/ **1** *pp* ▸ APPELER

2 *pp adj* ∼ à qch/à faire destined for sth/to do

3 *nm* (Mil) conscript, draftee (US)

appeler /aple/ [19] **1** *vtr* **(a)** to call; ∼ (qn) à l'aide to call (to sb) for help
(b) to phone (GB), to call
(c) to call ⟨doctor, taxi⟩; to send for ⟨pupil⟩; ∼ qn sous les drapeaux (Mil) to call sb up
(d) ∼ qn à faire to call on sb to do; ∼ à la grève to call for strike action
(e) mon travail m'appelle à beaucoup voyager my work involves a lot of travel
2 en appeler à *v+prep* to appeal to
3 s'appeler *v refl* (+ *v être*) to be called; comment t'appelles-tu? what's your name?; je m'appelle Vladimir my name is Vladimir; voilà ce qui s'appelle une belle voiture! now, that's what you call a nice car!
IDIOMS ∼ les choses par leur nom, ∼ un chat un chat to call a spade a spade

appellation /apɛlɑsjɔ̃/ *nf* name, appellation

appendice /apɛ̃dis/ *nm* (Anat) appendix

appendicite /apɛ̃disit/ *nf* appendicitis

appesantir: s'appesantir /apəzɑ̃tiʀ/ [3] *v refl* (+ *v être*) s'∼ sur to dwell on

appétissant, **∼e** /apetisɑ̃, ɑ̃t/ *adj* appetizing

appétit /apeti/ *nm* appetite

applaudir /aplodiʀ/ [3] **1** *vtr* to applaud
2 *vi* **(a)** to applaud, to clap
(b) (figurative) to approve; ∼ des deux mains to approve heartily

applaudissement /aplodismɑ̃/ *nm*
(a) applause
(b) acclaim

applicateur /aplikatœʀ/ *nm* applicator

application /aplikasjɔ̃/ *nf* **(a)** care; il manque d'∼ he doesn't apply himself
(b) implementation, enforcement; mettre en ∼ to apply ⟨theory⟩; to implement ⟨law⟩
(c) (of device, program) ∼s applications
(d) (of ointment) application
(e) (Comput) application program

applique /aplik/ *nf* wall light

appliqué, **∼e** /aplike/ *adj*
(a) hardworking
(b) ⟨work⟩ careful
(c) ⟨science⟩ applied

appliquer /aplike/ [1] **1** *vtr* **(a)** to apply ⟨ointment⟩ (sur to); to put ⟨stamp⟩ (sur on)
(b) to implement ⟨policy, law⟩
(c) to apply ⟨technique⟩ (à to)
2 s'appliquer *v refl* (+ *v être*) **(a)** to take great care (à faire to do)
(b) s'∼ à qn/qch ⟨law, remark⟩ to apply to sb/sth

appoint /apwɛ̃/ *nm* **(a)** exact change; faire l'∼ to give the exact change
(b) d'∼ ⟨salary⟩ supplementary; ⟨heating⟩ additional

appointements /apwɛ̃tmɑ̃/ *nm pl* salary

apport /apɔʀ/ *nm* **(a)** provision
(b) contribution

apporter /apɔʀte/ [1] *vtr* **(a)** to bring

⟨improvement, news⟩; to bring in ⟨revenue⟩; to bring about ⟨change⟩; ∼ qch à qn to bring sb sth, to take sb sth
(b) to give ⟨support, explanation⟩

apposer /apoze/ [1] *vtr* to affix (sur on)

apposition /apozisjɔ̃/ *nf* apposition

appréciable /apʀesjabl/ *adj*
(a) substantial
(b) c'est ∼ it's nice

appréciatif, **-ive** /apʀesjatif, iv/ *adj*
(a) appreciative
(b) appraising

appréciation /apʀesjɑsjɔ̃/ *nf* **(a)** (of quantity) estimate
(b) (financial) evaluation
(c) (of quality) assessment; être laissé à l'∼ de qn to be left to sb's discretion

apprécier /apʀesje/ [2] *vtr* **(a)** to appreciate ⟨art⟩; to like ⟨person⟩
(b) (financially) to value
(c) to estimate ⟨distance⟩
(d) to assess ⟨situation⟩

appréhender /apʀeɑ̃de/ [1] *vtr* **(a)** to arrest
(b) to dread
(c) to comprehend, to understand

appréhension /apʀeɑ̃sjɔ̃/ *nf* apprehension

apprendre /apʀɑ̃dʀ/ [52] *vtr* **(a)** to learn (à faire to do)
(b) to learn ⟨truth⟩; to hear (about) ⟨news⟩
(c) to teach
(d) ∼ qch à qn to tell sb sth

apprenti, **∼e** /apʀɑ̃ti/ *nm,f* **(a)** apprentice, trainee
(b) novice; ∼ poète novice poet

apprentissage /apʀɑ̃tisaʒ/ *nm*
(a) training, apprenticeship
(b) learning

apprêté, **∼e** /apʀɛte/ **1** *pp* ▶ APPRÊTER
2 *pp adj* **(a)** affected
(b) ⟨hairstyle⟩ fussy

apprêter: s'apprêter /apʀɛte/ [1] *v refl* (+ *v être*) s'∼ à faire to get ready to do

apprivoiser /apʀivwaze/ [1] *vtr* to tame

approbateur, **-trice** /apʀɔbatœʀ, tʀis/ *adj* sourire ∼ smile of approval

approbation /apʀɔbasjɔ̃/ *nf* approval

approche /apʀɔʃ/ *nf* approach

approcher /apʀɔʃe/ [1] **1** *vtr* **(a)** ∼ qch de la fenêtre to move sth near to the window
(b) to go up to; to come up to
(c) to come into contact with
2 approcher de *v+prep* to be (getting) close to
3 *vi* to approach
4 s'approcher *v refl* (+ *v être*) s'∼ de to go near; to come near

approfondi, **∼e** /apʀɔfɔ̃di/ **1** *pp* ▶ APPROFONDIR
2 *pp adj* detailed, in-depth

approfondir /apʀɔfɔ̃diʀ/ [3] *vtr* **(a)** to go into [sth] in depth ⋯✦

(b) ~ ses connaissances en français to improve one's knowledge of French
(c) to make [sth] deeper

approprié, **~e** /apʁɔpʁije/ adj appropriate

approprier: s'approprier /apʁɔpʁije/ [2] v refl (+ v être) **(a)** to take, to appropriate ⟨object, idea⟩
(b) to seize ⟨power⟩

approuver /apʁuve/ [1] vtr **(a)** to approve of; je t'approuve d'avoir accepté I think you were right to accept
(b) to approve ⟨budget⟩

approvisionnement /apʁɔvizjɔnmɑ̃/ nm supply (en of)

approvisionner /apʁɔvizjɔne/ [1] **1** vtr
(a) to supply (en with); mal approvisionné ⟨shop⟩ badly stocked
(b) to pay money into ⟨account⟩
2 s'approvisionner v refl (+ v être)
(a) s'~ en to get one's supplies of (auprès de from)
(b) to stock up (en on, with)

approximatif, **-ive** /apʁɔksimatif, iv/ adj ⟨estimate, translation⟩ rough

approximation /apʁɔksimasjɔ̃/ nf
(a) rough estimate
(b) approximation

appui /apɥi/ nm support; à l'~ de in support of ⟨theory⟩; prendre ~ sur to lean on

appui-tête, pl **appuis-tête** /apɥitɛt/ nm headrest

appuyé, **~e** /apɥije/ **1** pp ▶ APPUYER
2 pp adj **(a)** ⟨look⟩ intent
(b) ⟨joke⟩ laboured (GB)

appuyer /apɥije/ [22] **1** vtr **(a)** to rest (sur on); to lean (sur on)
(b) to press (contre against)
(c) to support, to back (up)
2 vi **(a)** ~ sur to press ⟨switch⟩; to put one's foot on ⟨brake⟩
(b) ~ sur to stress ⟨word⟩
3 s'appuyer v refl (+ v être) **(a)** to lean (sur on; contre against)
(b) s'~ sur to rely on ⟨theory⟩; to draw on ⟨report⟩

âpre /ɑpʁ/ adj **(a)** ⟨taste, cold⟩ bitter
(b) ⟨voice⟩ harsh
(c) ⟨struggle⟩ fierce; ⟨argument⟩ bitter

après /apʁɛ/ **1** adv afterward(s), after; later; peu/bien ~ shortly/long afterward(s); une heure ~ one hour later; peu ~ il y a un lac a bit further on there's a lake; et ~? and then what?; so what? (colloq)
2 prep after; ~ mon départ after I leave; ~ coup afterward(s); il est toujours ~ son fils (colloq) he's always on at his son (colloq)
3 d'après phr **(a)** d'~ moi in my opinion; d'~ lui/la météo according to him/the weather forecast; d'~ ma montre by my watch
(b) from; based on; d'~ un dessin de Gauguin from a drawing by Gauguin

(c) l'année d'~ the year after; la fois d'~ the next time
4 après que phr after; ~ qu'il a parlé after he had spoken
5 après- (combining form) l'~-guerre the postwar years

après-demain /apʁɛdmɛ̃/ adv the day after tomorrow

après-midi /apʁɛmidi/ nm inv or nf inv afternoon

après-rasage, pl **~s** /apʁɛʁazaʒ/ adj inv, nm after-shave

après-ski /apʁɛski/ nm inv snowboot

après-vente /apʁɛvɑ̃t/ adj inv after-sales

a priori /apʁijɔʁi/ **1** phr a priori
2 phr ~, ça ne devrait pas poser de problèmes on the face of it there shouldn't be any problems

à-propos /apʁɔpo/ nm inv intervenir avec ~ to make an apposite remark; agir avec ~ to do the right thing

apte /apt/ adj ~ à qch/à faire capable of sth/of doing; fit for sth/to do

aptitude /aptityd/ nf aptitude; fitness

aquarelle /akwaʁɛl/ nf **(a)** watercolours (GB)
(b) watercolour (GB)

aquarium /akwaʁjɔm/ nm aquarium, fish tank

aquatique /akwatik/ adj **(a)** aquatic
(b) sport ~ water sport

aqueduc /akdyk/ nm aqueduct

aquilin /akilɛ̃/ adj m aquiline

aquitain, **~e** /akitɛ̃, ɛn/ adj of Aquitaine; le bassin ~ the Aquitaine Basin

arabe /aʁab/ **1** adj **(a)** Arab
(b) Arabic
2 nm (language) Arabic

Arabe /aʁab/ nmf Arab

arabesque /aʁabɛsk/ nf arabesque

Arabie /aʁabi/ pr nf Arabia
■ ~ Saoudite Saudi Arabia

arabique /aʁabik/ adj Arabian

arachide /aʁaʃid/ nf groundnut, peanut

araignée /aʁeɲe/ nf spider
■ ~ de mer spider crab
IDIOMS avoir une ~ au plafond (colloq) to have a screw loose (colloq)

arbalète /aʁbalɛt/ nf crossbow

arbitraire /aʁbitʁɛʁ/ adj arbitrary

arbitrairement /aʁbitʁɛʁmɑ̃/ adv arbitrarily

arbitre /aʁbitʁ/ nm **(a)** referee, umpire
(b) arbitrator

arbitrer /aʁbitʁe/ [1] **1** vtr **(a)** to referee, to umpire
(b) to arbitrate in
2 vi to arbitrate (entre between)

arborer /aʁbɔʁe/ [1] vtr **(a)** to wear ⟨smile⟩; to sport ⟨badge⟩
(b) to bear ⟨banner⟩; to fly ⟨flag⟩

arboriculture /aʁbɔʁikyltyʁ/ nf arboriculture

arbre /aʀbʀ/ *nm* (a) tree
  (b) (Tech) shaft
  ■ ∼ généalogique family tree

arbrisseau, *pl* ∼**x** /aʀbʀiso/ *nm* small tree

arbuste /aʀbyst/ *nm* shrub

arc /aʀk/ *nm* (a) (Sport) bow
  (b) arc
  (c) arch

arcade /aʀkad/ *nf* arcade; ∼s archways.
  ■ ∼ sourcilière arch of the eyebrow

arc-bouter: s'arc-bouter /aʀkbute/ [1] *v refl* (+ *v être*) to brace oneself

arceau, *pl* ∼**x** /aʀso/ *nm* (a) arch
  (b) (in croquet) hoop
  (c) (in car) roll bar

arc-en-ciel, *pl* **arcs-en-ciel** /aʀkɑ̃sjɛl/ *nm* rainbow

archaïque /aʀkaik/ *adj* archaic

archange /aʀkɑ̃ʒ/ *nm* archangel

arche /aʀʃ/ *nf* arch; ∼ de Noé Noah's Ark

archéologie /aʀkeɔlɔʒi/ *nf* archaeology

archéologique /aʀkeɔlɔʒik/ *adj* archaeological

archet /aʀʃɛ/ *nm* (Mus) bow

archétype /aʀketip/ *nm* archetype

archevêché /aʀʃəveʃe/ *nm*
  (a) archdiocese
  (b) archbishop's palace

archevêque /aʀʃəvɛk/ *nm* archbishop

archi /aʀʃi/ *pref* (colloq) ∼connu really well-known

archipel /aʀʃipɛl/ *nm* archipelago

architecte /aʀʃitɛkt/ *nmf* architect

architecture /aʀʃitɛktyʀ/ *nf*
  (a) architecture
  (b) structure

archives /aʀʃiv/ *nf pl* archives, records

arctique /aʀktik/ *adj* arctic

Arctique /aʀktik/ *pr nm* Arctic

ardemment /aʀdamɑ̃/ *adv* passionately

ardent, ∼**e** /aʀdɑ̃, ɑ̃t/ *adj* (a) ⟨ember⟩ glowing; ⟨sun⟩ blazing
  (b) ⟨faith⟩ burning; ⟨patriot⟩ fervent; ⟨speech⟩ impassioned; ⟨nature⟩ passionate

ardeur /aʀdœʀ/ *nf* (of person) ardour (GB); (of beliefs) fervour; (of beginner) enthusiasm

ardoise /aʀdwaz/ *nf* (a) slate
  (b) (colloq) account

ardu, ∼**e** /aʀdy/ *adj* (a) arduous
  (b) taxing

arène /aʀɛn/ *nf* (a) arena
  (b) bullring
  (c) ∼s amphitheatre (GB)

arête /aʀɛt/ *nf* (a) fishbone
  (b) (of roof, mountain) ridge; (of prism) edge; (of nose) bridge

argent /aʀʒɑ̃/ *nm* (a) money
  (b) silver
  ■ ∼ liquide cash
  IDIOMS prendre qch pour ∼ comptant to take sth at face value

argenté, ∼**e** /aʀʒɑ̃te/ *adj* (a) silver-plated
  (b) (in colour) silvery

argenterie /aʀʒɑ̃tʀi/ *nf* silverware, silver

Argentine /aʀʒɑ̃tin/ *pr nf* Argentina

argile /aʀʒil/ *nf* clay

argot /aʀgo/ *nm* slang

arguer /aʀge/ [1] **1** *vtr* ∼ que to claim that
  2 arguer de *v+prep* to give [sth] as a reason

argument /aʀgymɑ̃/ *nm* argument

argumentation /aʀgymɑ̃tasjɔ̃/ *nf* line of argument

argumenter /aʀgymɑ̃te/ [1] *vi* to argue

argus /aʀgys/ *nm inv*: used car prices guide

aride /aʀid/ *adj* arid

aridité /aʀidite/ *nf* aridity

aristocratie /aʀistɔkrasi/ *nf* aristocracy

aristocratique /aʀistɔkratik/ *adj* aristocratic

arithmétique /aʀitmetik/ **1** *adj* arithmetical
  2 *nf* arithmetic

arlequin /aʀləkɛ̃/ *nm* harlequin

armateur /aʀmatœʀ/ *nm* shipowner

armature /aʀmatyʀ/ *nf* (a) (of tent) frame
  (b) (in construction) framework

arme /aʀm/ **1** *nf* (a) weapon; charger une ∼ to load a gun; rendre les ∼s to surrender; en ∼s armed; à ∼s égales on equal terms; faire ses premières ∼s dans l'enseignement to start out as a teacher
  (b) branch of the armed services
  2 armes *nf pl* coat of arms
  ■ ∼ blanche *weapon with a blade*; ∼ à feu firearm

armé, ∼**e**[1] /aʀme/ **1** *pp* ▶ ARMER
  2 *pp adj* (a) armed; vol à main ∼e armed robbery
  (b) equipped (de with; contre against)

armée[2] /aʀme/ *nf* army
  ■ ∼ de l'air air force; l'∼ de réserve the reserves; l'∼ de terre the army

armement /aʀməmɑ̃/ *nm* (a) armament; arming
  (b) arms, weapons
  (c) (of rifle) cocking; (of camera) winding on
  (d) (of ship) fitting out

armer /aʀme/ [1] **1** *vtr* (a) to arm (de with; contre against)
  (b) to fit out ⟨ship⟩
  (c) to wind on ⟨camera⟩; to cock ⟨rifle⟩
  2 s'armer *v refl* (+ *v être*) to arm oneself

armistice /aʀmistis/ *nm* armistice

armoire /aʀmwaʀ/ *nf* (a) cupboard
  (b) wardrobe
  ■ ∼ à glace wardrobe with a full length mirror; c'est une ∼ à glace (colloq) he/she is built like a tank (colloq); ∼ métallique metal locker; ∼ à pharmacie medicine cabinet; ∼ de toilette bathroom cabinet

armoiries /aʀmwaʀi/ *nf pl* arms

armure /aʀmyʀ/ *nf* armour (GB)

armurier /aʀmyʀje/ nm **(a)** gunsmith
(b) armourer (GB)

aromates /aʀɔmat/ nm pl herbs and spices

aromatique /aʀɔmatik/ adj aromatic

aromatiser /aʀɔmatize/ [1] vtr to flavour (GB)

arôme /aʀom/ nm **(a)** aroma
(b) flavouring (GB)

arpège /aʀpɛʒ/ nm arpeggio

arpenter /aʀpɑ̃te/ [1] vtr **(a)** to stride along
(b) to pace up and down
(c) to survey ⟨piece of land⟩

arqué, **~e** /aʀke/ adj ⟨brows⟩ arched; ⟨nose⟩ hooked; ⟨legs⟩ bandy

arquebuse /aʀkəbyz/ nf arquebus

arquer /aʀke/ [1] **1** vtr to bend ⟨bar⟩
2 **s'arquer** v refl (+ v être) to become bowed

arrachage /aʀaʃaʒ/ nm (of crop) picking; (of tooth, post) pulling out; (of scrub, root) digging out; **~ des mauvaises herbes** weeding

arraché /aʀaʃe/ nm snatch; **obtenir à l'~** to snatch ⟨victory⟩; **vol à l'~** bag snatching

arrache-pied: **d'arrache-pied** /daʀaʃpje/ phr ⟨work⟩ flat out

arracher /aʀaʃe/ [1] **1** vtr **(a)** to pull up or dig up ⟨weeds⟩; to pull out ⟨tooth⟩; to tear down ⟨poster⟩; to rip out ⟨page⟩; to tear off ⟨mask⟩; to uproot ⟨tree⟩; to blow off ⟨tiles⟩
(b) **~ à qn** to snatch [sth] from sb ⟨bag, victory⟩; to extract [sth] from sb ⟨promise⟩; to get [sth] from sb ⟨smile⟩
(c) **~ qn à** to uproot sb from ⟨home⟩; to drag sb away from ⟨work⟩; to rouse sb from ⟨thoughts⟩; to rescue sb from ⟨poverty⟩
2 **s'arracher** v refl (+ v être) **(a)** **~ qch** to fight over sth
(b) **s'~ à** to rouse oneself from ⟨thoughts⟩; to tear oneself away from ⟨work⟩
IDIOMS **c'est à s'~ les cheveux!** (colloq) it's enough to make you tear your hair out!; **~ les yeux à qn** to scratch sb's eyes out

arracheur /aʀaʃœʀ/ nm **mentir comme un ~ de dents** to be a born liar

arraisonner /aʀɛzɔne/ [1] vtr to board and inspect

arrangeant, **~e** /aʀɑ̃ʒɑ̃, ɑ̃t/ adj obliging

arrangement /aʀɑ̃ʒmɑ̃/ nm arrangement

arranger /aʀɑ̃ʒe/ [13] **1** vtr **(a)** to arrange, to organize
(b) to sort out; **pour ne rien ~, pour tout ~** to make matters worse
(c) to arrange ⟨flowers⟩
(d) to tidy ⟨hair⟩; to straighten ⟨skirt⟩
(e) (Mus) to arrange
(f) ⟨events⟩ to suit ⟨person⟩
2 **s'arranger** v refl (+ v être) **(a)** to get better, to improve
(b) **s'~ avec qn** to arrange it with sb
(c) to manage
(d) **on s'arrangera après** we'll sort it out later

(e) (colloq) **elle ne sait pas s'~** she doesn't know how to make the most of herself

arrangeur, **-euse** /aʀɑ̃ʒœʀ, øz/ nm,f (Mus) arranger

arrestation /aʀɛstasjɔ̃/ nf arrest

arrêt /aʀɛ/ nm **(a)** (gen) stopping; (of conflict) cessation; (of delivery) cancellation; (in production) halt
(b) stop; **sans ~** ⟨travel⟩ nonstop; ⟨interrupt⟩ constantly; **à l'~** ⟨vehicle⟩ stationary; ⟨machine⟩ idle; ⟨electrical appliance⟩ off; **marquer un temps d'~** to pause; **être aux ~s** (Mil) to be under arrest
(c) stop; **un ~ de bus** a bus stop
(d) (Law) ruling
■ **~ du cœur** heart failure; **~ sur image** freeze-frame, still; **~ de jeu** stoppage time; **~ de mort** death sentence; **~ de travail** stoppage of work; sick leave; sick note

arrêté, **~e** /aʀete/ **1** pp ▶ ARRÊTER
2 pp adj **(a)** ⟨matter⟩ settled
(b) ⟨ideas⟩ fixed
3 nm order, decree

arrêter /aʀete/ [1] **1** vtr **(a)** to stop (de faire doing); **être arrêté pour trois semaines** to be given a sick note for three weeks
(b) to switch off ⟨machine⟩; to halt ⟨process⟩
(c) to give up (de faire doing)
(d) to arrest
(e) to decide on ⟨plan⟩
2 vi to stop; **arrête!** stop it!
3 **s'arrêter** v refl (+ v être) **(a)** to stop
(b) to give up (de faire doing)
(c) to end
(d) **s'~ sur** to dwell on; **s'~ à** to focus on

arrhes /aʀ/ nf pl deposit

arriéré, **~e** /aʀjere/ **1** adj **(a)** outdated
(b) backward
(c) behind the times
(d) retarded
2 nm arrears

arrière /aʀjɛʀ/ **1** adj inv back; rear
2 nm **(a)** rear; **à l'~** (in car) in the back; (on plane, train, ship) at the rear; **en ~** backward(s); (position) behind; **pencher la tête en ~** to tilt one's head back; **revenir en ~** ⟨person⟩ to turn back; (figurative) to take a backward step; (on tape) to rewind
(b) (Sport) fullback

arrière-cour, pl **~s** /aʀjɛʀkuʀ/ nf backyard

arrière-goût, pl **~s** /aʀjɛʀgu/ nm aftertaste

arrière-grand-mère, pl **arrière-grands-mères** /aʀjɛʀgʀɑ̃mɛʀ/ nf great-grandmother

arrière-grand-père, pl **arrière-grands-pères** /aʀjɛʀgʀɑ̃pɛʀ/ nm great-grandfather

arrière-grands-parents /aʀjɛʀgʀɑ̃paʀɑ̃/ nm pl great-grandparents

arrière-pays /aʀjɛʀpei/ nm inv hinterland

arrière-pensée, pl **~s** /aʀjɛʀpɑ̃se/ nf
(a) ulterior motive
(b) **sans ~** without reservation

arrière-petits-enfants /aʀjɛʀpətizɑ̃fɑ̃/ *nm pl* great-grandchildren

arrière-plan, *pl* ~**s** /aʀjɛʀplɑ̃/ *nm* (of picture) background

arrière-saison, *pl* ~**s** /aʀjɛʀsɛzɔ̃/ *nf* late autumn (GB), late fall (US)

arrière-train, *pl* ~**s** /aʀjɛʀtʀɛ̃/ *nm* hindquarters

arrimer /aʀime/ [1] *vtr* (a) to fasten
(b) (Naut) to stow

arrivage /aʀivaʒ/ *nm* delivery, consignment

arrivant, ~**e** /aʀivɑ̃, ɑ̃t/ *nm,f* un nouvel ~ a newcomer

arrivé, ~**e**[1] /aʀive/ [1] *pp* ▶ ARRIVER
[2] *pp adj* (a) le premier ~ the first person to arrive
(b) être ~ to have made it (socially)

arrivée[2] /aʀive/ *nf* (a) arrival; trains à l'~ arrivals
(b) (in race) finish
(c) (Tech) inlet

arriver /aʀive/ [1] (+ *v être*) [1] *vi* (a) (gen) to arrive; (Sport) to finish; ~ à/de Paris to arrive in/from Paris
(b) to come; ~ en courant to come running up
(c) ~ à to reach ⟨*level, agreement*⟩; to find ⟨*solution*⟩; ~ (jusqu')à qn to reach sb
(d) ~ à faire to manage to do; je n'y arrive pas I can't do it; ~ à ses fins to achieve one's ends
(e) en ~ à to come to
(f) to happen
[2] *v impers* qu'est-il arrivé? what happened? (à to); il m'arrive d'y aller, il arrive que j'y aille I sometimes go there

arrivisme /aʀivism/ *nm* ruthless ambition

arrogance /aʀɔgɑ̃s/ *nf* arrogance

arrogant, ~**e** /aʀɔgɑ̃, ɑ̃t/ *adj* arrogant

arroger: s'arroger /aʀɔʒe/ [13] *v refl* (+ *v être*) to appropriate ⟨*title*⟩; to assume ⟨*right, role*⟩

arrondi, ~**e** /aʀɔ̃di/ [1] *adj* rounded; round
[2] *nm* (of face) roundness; (of shoulder) curve

arrondir /aʀɔ̃diʀ/ [3] [1] *vtr* (a) to round off ⟨*edge*⟩; coiffure qui arrondit le visage hairstyle that makes one's face look round
(b) to open wide ⟨*eyes*⟩
(c) to round off ⟨*figure*⟩ (à to)
[2] **s'arrondir** *v refl* (+ *v être*) (a) ⟨*object*⟩ to become round(ed); ⟨*eyes*⟩ to widen
(b) ⟨*face*⟩ to fill out
(c) ⟨*fortune*⟩ to be growing
IDIOMS ~ les angles to smooth the rough edges

arrondissement /aʀɔ̃dismɑ̃/ *nm*
(a) (in city) arrondissement
(b) (region) *administrative division in France*

arrosage /aʀozaʒ/ *nm* watering

arroser /aʀoze/ [1] [1] *vtr* (a) to water, to spray; on va se faire ~! (colloq) we're going to get soaked!
(b) to baste ⟨*meat*⟩; to sprinkle ⟨*cake*⟩

(c) to drink to
(d) repas arrosé au bourgogne meal washed down with Burgundy
[2] **s'arroser** *v refl* (+ *v être*) (colloq) ça s'arrose that calls for a drink

arroseur /aʀozœʀ/ *nm* sprinkler

arrosoir /aʀozwaʀ/ *nm* watering can

arsenal, *pl* **-aux** /aʀsənal, o/ *nm* (a) naval shipyard
(b) arsenal
(c) (colloq) gear

art /aʀ/ *nm* (a) art
(b) art, skill; avoir l'~ de faire to have a knack of doing
■ ~ dramatique drama; ~ lyrique opera; ~ de vivre art of living; ~s ménagers home economics; ~s plastiques plastic arts

Artaban /aʀtabɑ̃/ *n pr* fier comme ~ proud as a peacock

artère /aʀtɛʀ/ *nf* (a) (Anat) artery
(b) arterial road
(c) main street

artériel, -ielle /aʀteʀjɛl/ *adj* arterial

arthrite /aʀtʀit/ *nf* arthritis

arthrose /aʀtʀoz/ *nf* osteoarthritis

artichaut /aʀtiʃo/ *nm* (globe) artichoke.
IDIOMS avoir un cœur d'~ to be fickle (*in love*)

article /aʀtikl/ *nm* (a) (in paper, law) article; (in contract) clause
(b) (in grammar) article
(c) item; ~s de consommation courante basic consumer goods; faire l'~ à qn to give sb the sales pitch
IDIOMS être à l'~ de la mort to be at death's door

articulaire /aʀtikylɛʀ/ *adj* articular

articulation /aʀtikylasjɔ̃/ *nf* (a) (Anat) joint
(b) (of lamp, sunshade) mobile joint
(c) (in phonetics) articulation
(d) (in sentence) link
(e) (of speech, essay) structure

articuler /aʀtikyle/ [1] [1] *vtr* (a) to articulate; articule! speak clearly!
(b) to utter
(c) to structure ⟨*ideas*⟩
[2] **s'articuler** *v refl* (+ *v être*) s'~ autour de to be based on, to hinge on

artifice /aʀtifis/ *nm* (a) trick
(b) device; les ~s du style stylistic devices
(c) sans ~ unpretentious

artificiel, -ielle /aʀtifisjɛl/ *adj*
(a) artificial; man-made
(b) superficial; forced

artificier /aʀtifisje/ *nm* (a) bomb disposal expert
(b) explosives manufacturer
(c) fireworks manufacturer

artillerie /aʀtijʀi/ *nf* artillery

artisan /aʀtizɑ̃/ *nm* (a) artisan, craftsman
(b) architect, author

artisanal, ∼**e**, *mpl* **-aux** /ʀrtizanal, o/ *adj* ⟨*method*⟩ traditional; **de fabrication** ∼**e** hand-crafted; home-made

artisanat /ʀrtizana/ *nm* **(a)** craft industry, cottage industry
(b) artisans
■ ∼ **d'art** arts and crafts

artiste /ʀrtist/ **1** *adj* **(a)** artistic
(b) il est un peu ∼ he's a bit of a dreamer
2 *nmf* **(a)** artist; ∼ **peintre** painter
(b) (on stage) performer; (in music hall) artiste; ∼ **lyrique** opera singer

artistique /ʀrtistik/ *adj* artistic

as¹ /a/ ▶ AVOIR¹

as² /as/ *nm inv* ace
IDIOMS **être plein aux** ∼ (colloq) to be loaded (colloq); **passer à l'**∼ (colloq) ⟨*money*⟩ to go down the drain; ⟨*holidays*⟩ to go by the board; **être fagoté comme l'**∼ **de pique** (colloq) to look a mess

ascendance /asɑ̃dɑ̃s/ *nf* descent, ancestry

ascendant, ∼**e** /asɑ̃dɑ̃, ɑ̃t/ **1** *adj* ⟨*curve*⟩ rising; ⟨*movement*⟩ upward; ⟨*star*⟩ ascending
2 *nm* **(a)** influence (**sur** over)
(b) (Law) ascendant

ascenseur /asɑ̃sœʀ/ *nm* lift (GB), elevator (US)
IDIOMS **renvoyer l'**∼ to return the favour (GB)

ascension /asɑ̃sjɔ̃/ *nf* **(a)** ascent; **faire l'**∼ **de** to climb
(b) (figurative) rise

ascensionnel, -elle /asɑ̃sjɔnɛl/ *adj* ⟨*movement*⟩ upward; **parachute** ∼ parascending

ascète /asɛt/ *nmf* ascetic

ascétisme /asetism/ *nm* asceticism

aseptique /asɛptik/ *adj* aseptic

aseptisé, ∼**e** /asɛptize/ *adj* ⟨*art*⟩ sanitized; ⟨*world*⟩ sterile; ⟨*decor*⟩ impersonal

aseptiser /asɛptize/ [1] *vtr* to disinfect ⟨*wound*⟩; to sterilize ⟨*instrument*⟩

asexué, ∼**e** /asɛksɥe/ *adj* asexual

asiatique /azjatik/ *adj* Asian

Asie /azi/ *pr nf* Asia; ∼ **Mineure** Asia Minor

asile /azil/ *nm* **(a)** refuge; **chercher** ∼ to seek refuge
(b) (political) asylum
(c) ∼ **de vieillards** old people's home; ∼ **de nuit** night shelter

asocial, ∼**e**, *mpl* **-iaux** /asɔsjal, o/
1 *adj* antisocial
2 *nmf* social misfit

aspect /aspɛ/ *nm* **(a)** side; **voir qch sous son** ∼ **positif** to see the good side of sth
(b) ⟨*campaign*⟩; **par bien des** ∼**s** in many respects
(c) appearance

asperge /aspɛʀʒ/ *nf* **(a)** asparagus
(b) (colloq) beanpole (colloq), string bean (US)

asperger /aspɛʀʒe/ [13] *vtr* to spray; to splash

aspérité /asperite/ *nf* (in terrain) bump

asphalte /asfalt/ *nm* asphalt

asphyxiant, ∼**e** /asfiksjɑ̃, ɑ̃t/ *adj* asphyxiating

asphyxie /asfiksi/ *nf* asphyxiation

asphyxier /asfiksje/ [2] **1** *vtr* **(a)** to asphyxiate ⟨*person*⟩
(b) to paralyse ⟨*network, company*⟩
2 s'asphyxier *v refl* (+ *v être*) **(a)** to suffocate to death
(b) to gas oneself
(c) ⟨*network, company*⟩ to become paralysed

aspirateur /aspiʀatœʀ/ *nm* vacuum cleaner, hoover® (GB)

aspiration /aspiʀasjɔ̃/ *nf* **(a)** aspiration (à for)
(b) sucking up, drawing up
(c) inhalation

aspirer /aspiʀe/ [1] **1** *vtr* **(a)** to breathe in, to inhale
(b) to suck [sth] up
(c) consonne aspirée aspirated consonant
2 aspirer à *v+prep* to yearn for; to aspire to

aspirne® /aspiʀin/ *nf* aspirin
IDIOMS **être blanc comme un cachet d'**∼ to be lily white

assagir: s'assagir /asaʒiʀ/ [3] *v refl* (+ *v être*) to quieten down (GB), to quiet down (US)

assaillant, ∼**e** /asajɑ̃, ɑ̃t/ *nm,f*
(a) attacker
(b) (Mil) **les** ∼**s** the attacking forces

assaillir /asajiʀ/ [28] *vtr* **(a)** to attack
(b) to plague; ∼ **qn de questions** to bombard sb with questions

assainir /aseniʀ/ [3] *vtr* **(a)** to clean up
(b) to stabilize ⟨*economy*⟩; to streamline ⟨*company*⟩

assainissement /asenismɑ̃/ *nm*
(a) cleaning up
(b) (of economy) stabilization; (of company) streamlining

assaisonnement /asɛzɔnmɑ̃/ *nm* (Culin) seasoning; (on salad) dressing

assaisonner /asɛzɔne/ [1] *vtr* to season ⟨*dish*⟩; to dress ⟨*salad*⟩

assassin, ∼**e** /asasɛ̃, in/ **1** *adj*
(a) murderous
(b) ⟨*campaign*⟩ vicious
2 *nm* **(a)** murderer
(b) assassin

assassinat /asasina/ *nm* **(a)** murder
(b) assassination

assassiner /asasine/ [1] *vtr* **(a)** to murder
(b) to assassinate
(c) (colloq) to slate (colloq)

assaut /aso/ *nm* attack, assault; **se lancer** *or* **monter à l'**∼ **de** to launch an attack on; **prendre d'**∼ to storm; **les** ∼**s du froid** the onslaught of cold weather

assécher /aseʃe/ [14] *vtr* **(a)** to drain
(b) ⟨*heat*⟩ to dry up

ASSEDIC /asedik/ *nf* (*abbr* = **Association pour l'emploi dans**

l'industrie et le commerce)
organization managing unemployment contributions and payments
assemblage /asɑ̃blaʒ/ *nm* **(a)** (of motor) assembly (de of)
(b) (of ideas) assemblage; (of objects) collection; (of colours) combination
assemblée /asɑ̃ble/ *nf* **(a)** gathering
(b) meeting
(c) assembly
■ ∼ **générale, AG** general meeting; **l'Assemblée nationale** the French National Assembly
assembler /asɑ̃ble/ [1] **1** *vtr* to assemble, to put together
2 s'assembler *v refl* (+ *v être*) ⟨crowd⟩ to gather; ⟨ministers⟩ to assemble
IDIOMS **qui se ressemble s'assemble** (Proverb) birds of a feather flock together
asséner /asene/ [14] *vtr* ∼ **un coup à qn/ qch** to deal sb/sth a blow
assentiment /asɑ̃timɑ̃/ *nm* assent, consent
asseoir /aswaʀ/ [41] **1** *vtr* **(a)** to sit [sb] down; (in bed) to sit [sb] up; **faire** ∼ **qn** to make sb sit down; (politely) to offer a seat to sb
(b) to establish ⟨reputation⟩
(c) (colloq) to stagger, to astound
2 s'asseoir *v refl* (+ *v être*) to sit (down); (in bed) to sit up
assermenté, ∼e /asɛʀmɑ̃te/ *adj* sworn, on oath
assertion /asɛʀsjɔ̃/ *nf* assertion
asservir /asɛʀviʀ/ [3] *vtr* **(a)** to enslave ⟨person⟩
(b) to subjugate ⟨country⟩
asservissement /asɛʀvismɑ̃/ *nm*
(a) (of country, people) subjugation
(b) subjection
(c) subservience
assesseur /asesœʀ/ *nm* magistrate's assistant
assez /ase/ *adv* **(a)** enough; ∼ **fort** strong enough; **j'en ai** ∼ I've got enough; I'm fed up (colloq)
(b) quite; **je suis** ∼ **pressé** I'm in rather a hurry; **je suis** ∼ **d'accord** I tend to agree
assidu, ∼e /asidy/ *adj* **(a)** diligent
(b) ⟨care⟩ constant
(c) ⟨presence, visits⟩ regular
(d) devoted
assiduité /asidɥite/ *nf* **(a)** diligence; **avec** ∼ ⟨work⟩ diligently; ⟨train⟩ assiduously; ⟨read⟩ regularly
(b) regular attendance
(c) ∼**s** assiduities
assiégeant, ∼e /asjeʒɑ̃, ɑ̃t/ *nm,f* besieger
assiéger /asjeʒe/ [15] *vtr* to besiege
assiette /asjɛt/ *nf* **(a)** (for food) plate
(b) ∼ **(fiscale)** tax base
■ ∼ **anglaise** assorted cold meats; ∼ **en carton** paper plate; ∼ **creuse** soup plate; ∼ **à dessert** dessert plate

IDIOMS **ne pas être dans son** ∼ to be out of sorts
assignation /asiɲasjɔ̃/ *nf* **(a)** allocation
(b) (Law) summons
assigner /asiɲe/ [1] *vtr* **(a)** to assign ⟨task⟩
(b) to set ⟨objective⟩
(c) to ascribe ⟨value, role⟩ (à to)
(d) (Law) ∼ **à comparaître** to summons; ∼ **à résidence** to put sb under house arrest
assimilation /asimilasjɔ̃/ *nf*
(a) comparison
(b) assimilation
assimilé, ∼e /asimile/ *adj* similar
assimiler /asimile/ [1] **1** *vtr* **(a)** to assimilate; **être assimilé cadre** to have executive status
(b) ∼ **qn/qch à** to liken sb/sth to
2 s'assimiler *v refl* (+ *v être*) **(a) s'**∼ **à** ⟨method⟩ to be comparable to; ⟨person⟩ to compare oneself to
(b) ⟨minority⟩ to become assimilated; ⟨substances⟩ to be assimilated
assis, ∼e[1] /asi, iz/ **1** *pp* ▶ ASSEOIR
2 *pp adj* **(a)** seated; **être** ∼ to be sitting down; (in bed) to be sitting up; **reste** ∼ don't get up; (as reprimand) sit still
(b) ⟨reputation⟩ well-established
(c) (colloq) staggered
assise[2] /asiz/ *nf* basis, foundation
assises /asiz/ *nf pl* **(a)** meeting
(b) (Law) assizes
assistanat /asistana/ *nm* **(a)** (Univ) assistantship
(b) (state aid) (pej) charity
assistance /asistɑ̃s/ *nf* **(a)** assistance; aid
(b) audience
(c) attendance (à at)
■ ∼ **respiratoire** artificial respiration; **l'Assistance publique** ≈ welfare services
assistant, ∼e /asistɑ̃, ɑ̃t/ *nm,f* assistant
■ ∼**e sociale** social worker
assisté, ∼e /asiste/ **1** *pp* ▶ ASSISTER
2 *pp adj* **(a)** assisted (de by)
(b) receiving benefit (GB), on welfare (US)
(c) ∼ **par ordinateur** computer-aided
(d) **direction** ∼**e** power steering
3 *nm,f:* person receiving benefit (GB) or welfare (US)
assister /asiste/ [1] **1** *vtr* to assist; to aid
2 assister à *v+prep* **(a)** ∼ **à** to be at, to attend
(b) ∼ **à** to witness
associatif, -ive /asɔsjatif, iv/ *adj*
(a) ⟨memory⟩ associative
(b) **vie associative** community life
association /asɔsjasjɔ̃/ *nf* **(a)** association
(b) combination
associé, ∼e /asɔsje/ **1** *adj* ⟨member⟩ associate; ⟨companies⟩ associated
2 *nm,f* associate, partner
associer /asɔsje/ [2] **1** *vtr* **(a)** ∼ **qn à** to include sb in ⟨success⟩; to make sb a partner in ⟨business⟩; to give sb a share of ⟨profits⟩ ···⋗

(b) ~ **qch à** to combine sth with; to associate sth with

2 s'associer *v refl* (+ *v être*) **(a)** to go into partnership, to link up; **s'~ pour faire** to join forces to do

(b) s'~ à to join ⟨*movement*⟩; to share in ⟨*grief*⟩

(c) to combine

assoiffé, ~e /aswafe/ *adj* **(a)** thirsty

(b) ~ **de** thirsting for

assombrir /asɔ̃bʀiʀ/ [3] **1** *vtr* **(a)** to make [sth] dark, to darken

(b) to spoil; **la tristesse assombrit son visage** his/her face clouded

2 s'assombrir *v refl* (+ *v être*) **(a)** ⟨*sky*⟩ to darken

(b) ⟨*face*⟩ to become gloomy

assommant, ~e /asɔmɑ̃, ɑ̃t/ *adj* (colloq)

(a) (dull) deadly boring (colloq)

(b) (irritating) **tu es ~ avec tes questions** you're a real pain (colloq) with your questions

assommer /asɔme/ [1] *vtr* **(a)** to knock [sb] senseless

(b) (colloq) ~ **qn** to get on sb's nerves

(c) (colloq) ⟨*news*⟩ to stagger; ⟨*heat*⟩ to overcome

assorti, ~e /asɔʀti/ *adj* **(a)** matching

(b) assorted

assortiment /asɔʀtimɑ̃/ *nm* **(a)** set

(b) assortment, selection

(c) (in shop) stock

assortir /asɔʀtiʀ/ [3] **1** *vtr* **(a)** to match (à to; avec with)

(b) ~ **qch de qch** to add sth to sth

2 s'assortir *v refl* (+ *v être*) **(a) s'~ à** *or* **avec** to match

(b) s'~ de to come with

assoupir /asupiʀ/ [3] **1** *vtr* **(a)** to make [sb] drowsy

(b) to dull ⟨*senses, passion*⟩

2 s'assoupir *v refl* (+ *v être*) to doze off

assoupissement /asupismɑ̃/ *nm* drowsiness; (sleep) doze

assouplir /asupliʀ/ [3] **1** *vtr* **(a)** to soften ⟨*washing*⟩

(b) to make [sth] more supple ⟨*body, leather*⟩

(c) to relax ⟨*rule*⟩

2 s'assouplir *v refl* (+ *v être*) **(a)** to get softer

(b) to become more supple

(c) ⟨*person, rule*⟩ to become more flexible

assouplissant /asuplisɑ̃/ *nm* fabric softener

assouplissement /asuplismɑ̃/ *nm*

(a) (of leather, woollens) softening; (of washing) conditioning

(b) (sport) **faire des ~s** *or* **des exercices d'~** to limber up

(c) (of rules, policy, attitude) relaxing

assouplisseur /asuplisœʀ/ *nm* fabric conditioner

assourdir /asuʀdiʀ/ [3] *vtr* **(a)** to deafen

(b) to muffle

assouvir /asuviʀ/ [3] *vtr* to satisfy ⟨*hunger*⟩; to assuage ⟨*anger*⟩

assouvissement /asuvismɑ̃/ *nm*

(a) (of hunger) satisfying; (of anger) assuaging

(b) satisfaction

assujetti, ~e /asyʒeti/ *adj* ~ **à** liable for ⟨*tax*⟩; subject to ⟨*rule*⟩

assujettir /asyʒetiʀ/ [3] **1** *vtr* **(a)** to subject (à to)

(b) to subjugate, to subdue

(c) to secure

2 s'assujettir *v refl* (+ *v être*) ⟨*person*⟩ to submit (à to)

assumer /asyme/ [1] **1** *vtr* **(a)** to take ⟨*responsibility*⟩; to hold ⟨*post*⟩; to meet ⟨*costs*⟩

(b) to come to terms with ⟨*conditions, identity, past*⟩; to accept ⟨*consequences*⟩

2 s'assumer *v refl* (+ *v être*) **(a)** to take responsibility for oneself

(b) to come to terms with oneself

assurable /asyʀabl/ *adj* insurable

assurance /asyʀɑ̃s/ *nf* **(a)** (self-) confidence, assurance; **avec ~** confidently

(b) assurance; **donner à qn l'~ que** to assure sb that

(c) insurance (policy)

(d) insurance company

(e) insurance (premium)

(f) insurance (sector)

(g) benefit (GB), benefits (US)

■ ~ **au tiers** third-party insurance; ~ **maladie** health insurance; sickness benefit (GB) *or* benefits (US); ~ **tous risques** comprehensive insurance; ~**s sociales** social insurance

assurance-crédit, *pl* **assurances-crédit** /asyʀɑ̃skʀedi/ *nf* credit insurance

assurance-vie, *pl* **assurances-vie** /asyʀɑ̃svi/ *nf* life insurance

assuré, ~e /asyʀe/ **1** *pp* ▶ ASSURER

2 *pp adj* **(a)** sure, certain (**de faire** of doing); **soyez ~ de ma reconnaissance** I am very grateful to you

(b) insured

3 *adj* **(a)** ⟨*step, air*⟩ confident; ⟨*hand*⟩ steady; **mal ~** ⟨*step, voice*⟩ faltering; ⟨*gesture*⟩ nervous

(b) certain, assured

4 *nm,f* insured party

■ ~ **social** social insurance contributor

assurément /asyʀemɑ̃/ *adv* **(a)** definitely

(b) most certainly

assurer /asyʀe/ [1] **1** *vtr* **(a)** ~ **à qn que** to assure sb that; **ce n'est pas drôle, je t'assure** believe me, it's no joke

(b) ~ **qn de** to assure sb of ⟨*support*⟩

(c) to insure ⟨*property, goods*⟩

(d) to carry out ⟨*maintenance*⟩; to provide ⟨*service*⟩; ~ **la liaison entre** ⟨*train, bus, ferry*⟩ to operate between; ~ **la gestion de** to manage

(e) to ensure ⟨*victory*⟩; to secure ⟨*right, post*⟩ (à qn for sb); to assure ⟨*future*⟩; ~ **un revenu à qn** to give sb an income; ~ **ses vieux jours** to provide for one's old age

(f) to secure ⟨*rope*⟩; to belay ⟨*climber*⟩

2 s'assurer *v refl* (+ *v être*) **(a)** s'∼ de qch to make sure of sth
(b) to secure ⟨*advantage, help*⟩
(c) to take out insurance
(d) (figurative) s'∼ **contre** to insure against ⟨*eventuality, risk*⟩

assureur /asyRœR/ *nm* **(a)** insurance agent
(b) insurance company

astérisque /asteRisk/ *nm* asterisk

asthmatique /asmatik/ *adj, nmf* asthmatic

asthme /asm/ *nm* asthma

asticot /astiko/ *nm* maggot

astigmate /astigmat/ *adj* astigmatic

astiquer /astike/ [1] *vtr* to polish

astral, ∼**e**, *mpl* **-aux** /astRal, o/ *adj* astral

astre /astR/ *nm* star

astreindre /astRɛ̃dR/ [55] **1** *vtr* ∼ qn à qch ⟨*person*⟩ to force sth upon sb; ⟨*rule*⟩ to bind sb to sth; ∼ qn à **faire** to compel sb to do
2 s'astreindre *v refl* (+ *v être*) s'∼ à qch to subject oneself to sth

astringent, ∼**e** /astRɛ̃ʒɑ̃, ɑ̃t/ *adj* astringent

astrologie /astRɔlɔʒi/ *nf* astrology

astrologique /astRɔlɔʒik/ *adj* astrological

astrologue /astRɔlɔg/ *nmf* astrologer

astronaute /astRonot/ *nmf* astronaut

astronautique /astRonotik/ *nf* astronautics

astronomie /astRɔnɔmi/ *nf* astronomy

astronomique /astRɔnɔmik/ *adj* astronomical

astrophysique /astRofizik/ *nf* astrophysics

astuce /astys/ *nf* **(a)** cleverness
(b) shrewdness, astuteness
(c) trick
(d) pun; joke

astucieux, -ieuse /astysjø, øz/ *adj*
(a) clever
(b) shrewd, sharp

asymétrique /asimetRik/ *adj* asymmetrical

atchoum /atʃum/ *nm* atishoo

atelier /atəlje/ *nm* **(a)** (place) workshop; (artist's) studio
(b) working group
(c) (seminar) workshop

atermoyer /atɛRmwaje/ [23] *vi* to procrastinate

athée /ate/ **1** *adj* atheistic
2 *nmf* atheist

athéisme /ateism/ *nm* atheism

athénien, -ienne /atenjɛ̃, ɛn/ *adj* Athenian

athlète /atlɛt/ *nmf* athlete

athlétique /atletik/ *adj* athletic

athlétisme /atletism/ *nm* athletics (GB), track and field events

Atlantique /atlɑ̃tik/ *pr nm* l'∼ the Atlantic

atlas /atlas/ *nm inv* atlas

atmosphère /atmɔsfɛR/ *nf* atmosphere

atoll /atɔl/ *nm* atoll

atome /atom/ *nm* atom
IDIOMS avoir des ∼s crochus avec qn (colloq) to get on well with sb

atomique /atɔmik/ *adj* atomic

atomiseur /atɔmizœR/ *nm* spray, atomizer

atone /atɔn/ *adj* **(a)** lifeless, apathetic
(b) ⟨*syllable*⟩ unstressed

atours /atuR/ *nm pl* finery

atout /atu/ *nm* **(a)** trump (card); trumps
(b) (figurative) asset; trump card; **mettre tous les ∼s dans son jeu** to leave nothing to chance

âtre /atR/ *nm* hearth

atroce /atRɔs/ *adj* atrocious, dreadful, terrible

atrocité /atRɔsite/ *nf* **(a)** atrocity
(b) monstrosity

atrophie /atRɔfi/ *nf* atrophy

atrophier: s'atrophier /atRɔfje/ [2] *v refl* (+ *v être*) to atrophy; **bras atrophié** wasted arm

attabler: s'attabler /atable/ [1] *v refl* (+ *v être*) to sit down at (the) table

attachant, ∼e /ataʃɑ̃, ɑ̃t/ *adj* engaging

attache /ataʃ/ *nf* **(a)** tie; string; rope; strap; ∼s **familiales** family ties
(b) avoir des ∼s **fines** to have delicate ankles and wrists

attaché, ∼e /ataʃe/ *nm,f* attaché
■ ∼ **de presse** press attaché

attachement /ataʃmɑ̃/ *nm* **(a)** (to person) attachment
(b) (to principle, cause) commitment

attacher /ataʃe/ [1] **1** *vtr* **(a)** to tie ⟨*person, hands, laces*⟩ (à to); to tether ⟨*horse, goat*⟩; to chain ⟨*dog*⟩ (à to); to lock ⟨*bicycle*⟩ (à to); to tie up ⟨*person, parcel*⟩
(b) to fasten ⟨*belt*⟩
(c) to attach ⟨*importance*⟩
(d) les privilèges attachés à un poste the privileges attached to a post
2 s'attacher *v refl* (+ *v être*) **(a)** to fasten
(b) s'∼ à qn/qch to become attached to sb/ sth

attaquable /atakabl/ *adj* **(a)** ⟨*place*⟩ facilement ∼ easy to attack
(b) ⟨*theory, position*⟩ shaky
(c) ⟨*will*⟩ contestable

attaquant, ∼e /atakɑ̃, ɑ̃t/ *nm,f* attacker

attaque /atak/ **1** *nf* **(a)** attack; (on bank) raid; **passer à l'∼** to move into the attack; (figurative) to go on the attack; ∼ **à main armée** armed raid
(b) (Med) stroke; ∼ **cardiaque** heart attack
2 d'attaque *phr* (colloq) on (GB) *or* in (US) form; **être d'∼ pour faire** to feel up to doing

attaquer /atake/ [1] **1** *vtr* **(a)** to attack; to raid ⟨*bank*⟩
(b) (Law) to contest ⟨*contract, will*⟩; ∼ **qn en justice** to bring a lawsuit against sb
(c) to tackle ⟨*problem*⟩
2 *vi* **(a)** (in tennis, golf) to drive
(b) ⟨*speaker*⟩ to begin (brusquely)
3 **s'attaquer** *v refl* (+ *v être*) **s'**∼ **à** to attack ⟨*person, policy*⟩; to tackle ⟨*problem*⟩

attardé, ∼**e** /atarde/ **1** *adj* retarded
2 *nm,f* mentally retarded person

attarder: **s'attarder** /atarde/ [1] *v refl* (+ *v être*) **(a)** to stay until late; to linger
(b) **s'**∼ **sur** to dwell on ⟨*point*⟩

atteindre /atɛdʀ/ [55] **1** *vtr* **(a)** to reach ⟨*place, age, level, target*⟩; to achieve ⟨*aim*⟩
(b) ⟨*projectile, marksman*⟩ to hit ⟨*target*⟩
(c) ⟨*illness*⟩ to affect
2 **atteindre à** *v+prep* to reach; to achieve

atteint, ∼**e¹** /atɛ̃, ɛ̃t/ **1** *pp* ▶ ATTEINDRE
2 *pp adj* **(a)** affected (**de, par** by); **être** ∼ **de** to be suffering from ⟨*illness*⟩
(b) hit (**de, par** by)

atteinte² /atɛ̃t/ **1** *nf* ∼ **à** attack on; **porter** ∼ **à** to undermine ⟨*prestige*⟩; to damage ⟨*reputation*⟩; to endanger ⟨*security*⟩; to infringe ⟨*rights*⟩; ∼ **à la vie privée** breach of privacy
2 **hors d'atteinte** *phr* **hors d'**∼ ⟨*person*⟩ beyond reach; ⟨*target*⟩ out of range

attelage /atlaʒ/ *nm* **(a)** (of horse) harness; (of oxen) yoke; (of wagon) coupling; (of trailer) towing attachment
(b) (animals) team; (of oxen) yoke
(c) horse-drawn carriage

atteler /atle/ [19] **1** *vtr* to harness ⟨*horse*⟩; to yoke ⟨*oxen*⟩; to couple ⟨*wagon*⟩
2 **s'atteler** *v refl* (+ *v être*) **s'**∼ **à une tâche** to get down to a job

attelle /atɛl/ *nf* (Med) splint

attenant, ∼**e** /atnɑ̃, ɑ̃t/ *adj* adjacent

attendre /atɑ̃dʀ/ [6] **1** *vtr* **(a)** to wait for ⟨*person, event*⟩; **j'attends de voir pour le croire** I'll believe it when I see it; **se faire** ∼ to keep people waiting; **la réaction ne se fit pas** ∼ the reaction was instantaneous; ∼ **son jour** *or* **heure** to bide one's time; **en attendant mieux** until something better turns up; **on ne t'attendait plus!** we'd given up on you!
(b) to await, to be in store for ⟨*person*⟩
(c) to expect; ∼ **qch de qn/qch** to expect sth from sb/sth; **elle attend un bébé** she's expecting a baby
2 *vi* to wait; (on phone) to hold; **faire** ∼ **qn** to keep sb waiting; **en attendant** in the meantime; all the same, nonetheless; **tu ne perds rien pour** ∼**!** (colloq) I'll get you (colloq), just you wait!
3 **s'attendre** *v refl* (+ *v être*) **s'**∼ **à qch** to expect sth; **s'**∼ **à ce que qn fasse** to expect sb to do

attendrir /atɑ̃dʀiʀ/ [3] **1** *vtr* to touch, to move ⟨*person*⟩; **se laisser** ∼ to soften
2 **s'attendrir** *v refl* (+ *v être*) to feel moved

attendrissant, ∼**e** /atɑ̃dʀisɑ̃, ɑ̃t/ *adj* touching, moving; ⟨*innocence*⟩ endearing

attendrissement /atɑ̃dʀismɑ̃/ *nm* emotion

attendu¹: **attendu que** /atɑ̃dy/ *phr* **(a)** given *or* considering that
(b) (Law) whereas

attendu², ∼**e** /atɑ̃dy/ *adj* **(a)** expected
(b) **le jour (tant)** ∼ the long-awaited day

attentat /atɑ̃ta/ *nm* assassination attempt, attack; ∼ **à la bombe** bomb attack.
■ ∼ **à la pudeur** (Law) indecent assault

attente /atɑ̃t/ *nf* **(a)** waiting; wait; **mon** ∼ **a été vaine** I waited in vain; **dans l'**∼ **de vous lire** looking forward to hearing from you; **en** ∼ ⟨*passenger*⟩ waiting; ⟨*file*⟩ pending; ⟨*call*⟩ on hold
(b) expectation; **répondre à l'**∼ **de qn** to come up to sb's expectations

attenter /atɑ̃te/ [1] *v+prep* ∼ **à ses jours** to attempt suicide; ∼ **à la vie de qn** to make an attempt on sb's life

attentif, **-ive** /atɑ̃tif, iv/ *adj* attentive; **sous l'œil** ∼ **de leur mère** under the watchful eye of their mother

attention /atɑ̃sjɔ̃/ **1** *nf* **(a)** attention; **faire** ∼ **à qch** to mind ⟨*cars, step*⟩; to watch out for ⟨*black ice*⟩; to take care of ⟨*clothes, belongings*⟩; to watch ⟨*diet, health*⟩; to pay attention to ⟨*fashion, details*⟩; **faire** ∼ **à qn** to pay attention to sb; to keep an eye on sb; to take notice of sb
(b) kind gesture; **être plein d'**∼**s pour qn** to be very attentive to sb
2 *excl* **(a)** (cry) look out!, watch out!; (written) attention!; (in case of danger) warning!; (on road sign) caution!
(b) ∼, **je ne veux pas dire…** don't get me wrong, I don't mean…

attentionné, ∼**e** /atɑ̃sjɔne/ *adj* attentive, considerate

attentisme /atɑ̃tism/ *nm* wait-and-see attitude

attentivement /atɑ̃tivmɑ̃/ *adv* **(a)** attentively
(b) carefully

atténuantes /atenɥɑ̃t/ *adj f pl* **circonstances** ∼ (Law) mitigating circumstances

atténuer /atenɥe/ [1] **1** *vtr* to ease ⟨*pain, distress*⟩; to lessen ⟨*impact*⟩; to smooth over ⟨*differences*⟩; to weaken ⟨*effect*⟩; to soften ⟨*blow*⟩; to reduce ⟨*inequalities*⟩; to dim ⟨*light*⟩; to make [sth] less strong ⟨*smell, taste*⟩
2 **s'atténuer** *v refl* (+ *v être*) ⟨*pain*⟩ to ease; ⟨*anger, grief*⟩ to subside; ⟨*corruption, pessimism*⟩ to lessen; ⟨*gaps*⟩ to be reduced; ⟨*wrinkles, colour*⟩ to fade; ⟨*storm, noise*⟩ to die down

atterrant, ∼**e** /ateʀɑ̃, ɑ̃t/ *adj* **(a)** appalling
(b) shattering

atterré, ∼**e** /ateʀe/ *adj* **(a)** appalled
(b) shattered

atterrir /ateʀiʀ/ [3] *vi* to land

atterrissage /ateʀisaʒ/ *nm* landing

attestation /atɛstasjɔ̃/ *nf* (a) attestation
(b) certificate

attester /atɛste/ [1] *vtr* (a) to vouch for; to testify to
(b) to prove, to attest to

attirail /atiʀaj/ *nm* gear, equipment

attirance /atiʀɑ̃s/ *nf* attraction

attirant, ~**e** /atiʀɑ̃, ɑ̃t/ *adj* attractive

attirer /atiʀe/ [1] **1** *vtr* (a) to attract ⟨person, capital⟩; to draw ⟨crowd, attention⟩; ~ qn dans un coin to take sb into a corner; ~ qn dans un piège to lure sb into a trap
(b) ⟨country, profession⟩ to appeal to
(c) to bring ⟨shame, anger⟩; ~ des ennuis à qn to cause sb problems
2 **s'attirer** *v refl* (+ *v être*) s'~ le soutien de qn to win sb's support; s'~ des ennuis to get into trouble

attiser /atize/ [1] *vtr* (a) to kindle ⟨feeling⟩; to fuel ⟨discord⟩; to stir up ⟨hatred⟩
(b) to fan ⟨fire⟩

attitré, ~**e** /atitʀe/ *adj* (a) ⟨chauffeur⟩ official
(b) ⟨customer⟩ regular

attitude /atityd/ *nf* (a) bearing; posture
(b) attitude

attouchement /atuʃmɑ̃/ *nm*
(a) molesting
(b) fondling
(c) (by healer) laying on of hands

attractif, -ive /atʀaktif, iv/ *adj* attractive

attraction /atʀaksjɔ̃/ *nf* attraction
■ ~ terrestre earth's gravity; ~ universelle gravitation

attrait /atʀɛ/ *nm* (a) appeal, attraction; lure
(b) l'~ de qn pour qn/qch sb's liking for sb/sth

attraper /atʀape/ [1] *vtr* (a) to catch; se faire ~ to get caught; attrapez-le! stop him!
(b) to catch hold of ⟨rope, hand, leg⟩
(c) (colloq) to catch ⟨cold, illness⟩
(d) (colloq) to tell [sb] off

attrayant, ~**e** /atʀɛjɑ̃, ɑ̃t/ *adj*
(a) attractive
(b) pleasant

attribuer /atʀibɥe/ [1] **1** *vtr* (a) to allocate ⟨seat, task⟩; to grant ⟨right⟩; to award ⟨prize⟩; to lend ⟨importance⟩; ~ qch à la fatigue to put sth down to tiredness
(b) ~ qch à qn to credit sb with sth ⟨quality⟩; to attribute sth to sb ⟨work⟩
2 **s'attribuer** *v refl* (+ *v être*) s'~ la meilleure part to give oneself the largest share; s'~ tout le mérite to take all the credit

attribut /atʀiby/ *nm* (a) (quality, symbol) attribute
(b) (in grammar) complement; adjectif ~ predicative adjective; nom ~ complement

attribution /atʀibysjɔ̃/ **1** *nf* (a) allocation
(b) awarding
2 **attributions** *nf pl* (of individual) remit; (of court) competence

attristant, ~**e** /atʀistɑ̃, ɑ̃t/ *adj*
(a) distressing, upsetting
(b) depressing; d'une bêtise ~e depressingly stupid

attrister /atʀiste/ [1] *vtr* to sadden; j'ai été attristé d'apprendre I was sorry to hear

attroupement /atʀupmɑ̃/ *nm* gathering

attrouper: **s'attrouper** /atʀupe/ [1] *v refl* (+ *v être*) to gather

au /o/ *prep* (= à le) ▶ À

aubade /obad/ *nf* dawn serenade

aubaine /obɛn/ *nf* (a) godsend
(b) bargain

aube /ob/ *nf* (a) dawn
(b) alb; cassock

aubépine /obepin/ *nf* hawthorn

auberge /obɛʀʒ/ *nf* inn; ~ de jeunesse youth hostel
IDIOMS tu n'es pas sorti de l'~! (colloq) you're not out of the woods yet!

aubergine /obɛʀʒin/ *nf* aubergine, eggplant

aubergiste /obɛʀʒist/ *nmf* innkeeper

aucun, ~**e** /okœ̃, yn/ **1** *adj* no, not any; en ~ cas under no circumstances
2 *pron* none; je n'ai lu ~ de vos livres I haven't read any of your books; ~ de ses arguments n'est convaincant none of his arguments are convincing

aucunement /okynmɑ̃/ *adv* in no way

audace /odas/ *nf* (a) boldness
(b) daring
(c) audacity, nerve (colloq); impudence

audacieux, -ieuse /odasjø, øz/ *adj*
(a) bold
(b) audacious, daring

au-delà /od(ə)la/ **1** *nm* l'~ the hereafter
2 *adv* beyond; jusqu'à 1 000 francs mais pas ~ up to 1,000 francs but no more
3 **au-delà de** *phr* beyond; over

au-dessous /odəsu/ **1** *adv* (a) below
(b) under; les enfants de dix ans et ~ children of ten years and under
2 **au-dessous de** *phr* below; être ~ de tout (colloq) to be absolutely useless

au-dessus /odəsy/ **1** *adv* above; les enfants de 10 ans et ~ children of 10 and over; la taille ~ the next size up
2 **au-dessus de** *phr* above; ~ de chez moi in the apartment above mine; un pont ~ de la rivière a bridge over the river; se pencher ~ de la table to lean across the table

au-devant: **au-devant de** /odəvɑ̃də/ *phr* aller ~ de qn to go to meet sb; aller ~ des ennuis to let oneself in for trouble

audible /odibl/ *adj* audible

audience /odjɑ̃s/ *nf* (a) (Law) hearing; salle d'~ courtroom
(b) (interview) audience
(c) ⟨public⟩ audience

Audimat® /odimat/ *nm* audience ratings

audiovisuel, -elle /odjovisɥel/ **1** *adj*
(a) broadcasting ····>

a

(b) audiovisual
2 *nm* **(a)** broadcasting
(b) audiovisual equipment
(c) audiovisual methods

audit /odit/ *nm* audit

auditeur, -trice /oditœr, tris/ *nm,f* listener

auditif, -ive /oditif, iv/ *adj* ⟨*nerve*⟩ auditory; ⟨*problems*⟩ hearing; ⟨*memory*⟩ aural

audition /odisjɔ̃/ *nf* **(a)** (sense) hearing
(b) audition
(c) (Law) hearing, examination

auditionner /odisjɔne/ [1] *vtr, vi* to audition

auditoire /oditwar/ *nm* audience

auge /oʒ/ *nf* (for animal feed) trough

augmentation /ogmɑ̃tasjɔ̃/ *nf* increase; **une ∼ (de salaire)** a pay rise (GB) *or* raise (US)

augmenter /ogmɑ̃te/ [1] **1** *vtr* to raise, to increase; to extend; **∼ le loyer de qn** to put sb's rent up
2 *vi* to increase, to go up, to rise

augure /ogyr/ *nm* **(a)** omen
(b) augury

augurer /ogyre/ [1] *vtr* **que peut-on ∼ de cette attitude?** what should we expect from this attitude?

auguste /ogyst/ *adj* august, noble

aujourd'hui /oʒurdɥi/ *adv* **(a)** today
(b) nowadays, today; **la France d'∼** present-day France

aulne /on/ *nm* alder

aumône /omon/ *nf* hand-out, alms; **demander l'∼** to ask for charity

aumônerie /omonri/ *nf* chaplaincy

aumônier /omonje/ *nm* chaplain

aune /on/ *nm* = AULNE

auparavant /oparavɑ̃/ *adv* before; beforehand; previously; formerly

auprès: auprès de /opredə/ *phr* **(a)** next to, beside; **il s'est rendu ∼ de sa tante** he went to see his aunt
(b) compared with
(c) **s'excuser ∼ de qn** to apologize to sb; **renseigne-toi ∼ de la mairie** ask for information at the town hall; **représentant ∼ de l'ONU** representative to the UN

auquel ▸ LEQUEL

aura /ora/ ▸ AVOIR[1]

aurai /ore/ ▸ AVOIR[1]

auras /ora/ ▸ AVOIR[1]

auréole /oreol/ *nf* **(a)** (stain) ring
(b) halo

auréolé, ∼e /oreole/ *adj* **∼ de** basking in the glow of

aurez /ore/ ▸ AVOIR[1]

auriculaire /orikyler/ **1** *adj* auricular
2 *nm* little finger, pinkie

aurifère /orifer/ *adj* **(a)** ⟨*mineral*⟩ auriferous
(b) **valeurs ∼s** gold stocks

aurons /orɔ̃/ ▸ AVOIR[1]

auront /orɔ̃/ ▸ AVOIR[1]

aurore /oror/ *nf* dawn; **∼ boréale** Northern Lights, aurora borealis

auscultation /oskyltasjɔ̃/ *nf* examination

ausculter /oskylte/ [1] *vtr* (Med) to examine

auspices /ospis/ *nm pl* auspices

aussi /osi/ **1** *adv* **(a)** too, as well, also; **il sera absent et moi ∼** he'll be away and so will I
(b) **∼ bien que** as well as; **∼ âgé que** as old as
(c) so; **je ne savais pas qu'il était ∼ vieux** I didn't know he was so old; **dans une ∼ belle maison** in such a nice house
2 *conj* so, consequently

aussitôt /osito/ **1** *adv* **(a)** immediately, straight away
(b) **∼ arrivé** as soon as he arrived; **∼ dit ∼ fait** no sooner said than done
2 **aussitôt que** *phr* as soon as

austère /oster, ɔster/ *adj* austere; severe

austérité /osterite/ *nf* austerity; severity

austral, ∼e, *mpl* **∼s** /ostral/ *adj* southern, south

Australie /ostrali/ *pr nf* Australia

australien, -ienne /ostraljɛ̃, ɛn/ *adj* Australian

autant /otɑ̃/ **1** *adv* **il n'a jamais ∼ neigé** it has never snowed so much; **je t'aime toujours ∼** I still love you as much; **essaie d'en faire ∼** try and do the same; **je les hais tous ∼ qu'ils sont** I hate every single one of them; **j'aime ∼ partir tout de suite** I'd rather leave straight away; **∼ dire que la réunion est annulée** in other words the meeting is cancelled (GB); **∼ parler à un mur** you might as well be talking to the wall; **∼ que je sache** as far as I know; **∼ que tu peux** as much as you can
2 **autant de** *quantif* **(a)** **∼ de cadeaux** so many presents; **il y a ∼ de femmes que d'hommes** there are as many women as (there are) men
(b) **∼ de gentillesse** such kindness; **je n'ai pas eu ∼ de chance que lui** I haven't had as much luck as he has
3 **d'autant** *phr* **cela va permettre de réduire d'∼ les coûts de production** this will allow an equivalent reduction in production costs; **d'∼ plus!** all the more reason!; **d'∼ moins** even less, all the less; **d'∼ que** all the more so as
4 **pour autant** *phr* for all that; **sans pour ∼ tout modifier** without necessarily changing everything; **pour ∼ que je sache** as far as I know

autarcie /otarsi/ *nf* autarky; **vivre en ∼** to be self-sufficient

autel /otel/ *nm* altar

auteur /otœr/ *nm* **(a)** author
(b) creator; (of song) composer; (of crime) perpetrator
■ **∼ dramatique** playwright

auteur-compositeur, pl **auteurs-compositeurs** /otœʀkɔ̃pozitœʀ/ nm songwriter

authenticité /otɑ̃tisite/ nf authenticity

authentifier /otɑ̃tifje/ [2] vtr to authenticate

authentique /otɑ̃tik/ adj ⟨story⟩ true; ⟨painting, document⟩ authentic; ⟨feeling⟩ genuine

autiste /otist/ nm,f autistic person

auto /oto/ nf car, automobile (US)
■ ~ tamponneuse bumper car, dodgem

autobiographie /otobjɔgʀafi/ nf autobiography

autobus /otɔbys/ nm inv bus

autocar /otɔkaʀ/ nm coach (GB), bus (US)

autochtone /otɔkton/ adj, nmf native

autocollant, ~e /otɔkɔlɑ̃, ɑ̃t/ [1] adj self-adhesive
[2] nm sticker

autocuiseur /otokɥizœʀ/ nm pressure cooker

autodéfense /otodefɑ̃s/ nf self-defence (GB)

autodestructeur, -trice /otodɛstʀyktœʀ, tʀis/ adj self-destructive

autodestruction /otodɛstʀyksjɔ̃/ nf self-destruction

autodétruire: s'autodétruire /otodetʀɥiʀ/ [69] v refl (+ v être) ⟨person⟩ to destroy oneself; ⟨tape⟩ to self-destruct; ⟨missile⟩ to autodestruct

autodidacte /otodidakt/ nmf self-educated person

auto-école, pl ~s /otoekɔl/ nf driving school

autogérer: s'autogérer /otoʒeʀe/ [14] v refl (+ v être) ⟨company⟩ to be run on a cooperative basis

autographe /otɔgʀaf/ adj, nm autograph

automate /otɔmat/ nm robot, automaton

automatique /otɔmatik/ [1] adj
(a) automatic
(b) inevitable
[2] nm (a) automatic (revolver)
(b) automatic camera

automatiquement /otɔmatikmɑ̃/ adv
(a) automatically
(b) (colloq) inevitably

automatiser /otɔmatize/ [1] vtr to automate

automatisme /otɔmatism/ nm automatism; automatic functioning; **acquérir des ~s** to acquire automatic reflexes

automne /otɔn/ nm autumn (GB), fall (US)

automobile /otɔmɔbil/ [1] adj (a) car
(b) (Sport) ⟨racing⟩ motor; ⟨circuit⟩ motor racing
[2] nf (a) (motor) car, automobile (US)
(b) the motor (GB) or automobile (US) industry

automobiliste /otɔmɔbilist/ nmf motorist

autonome /otɔnɔm/ adj autonomous; independent; self-sufficient

autonomie /otɔnɔmi/ nf (a) autonomy
(b) (of car, plane) range; ~ **de vol** flight range

autonomiste /otɔnɔmist/ adj, nmf separatist

autoportrait /otopɔʀtʀɛ/ nm self-portrait

autopsie /otɔpsi/ nf postmortem (examination)

autoradio /otoʀadjo/ nm car radio

autorisation /otɔʀizasjɔ̃/ nf
(a) permission; authorization
(b) permit

autorisé, ~e /otɔʀize/ adj authorized; legal; accredited; permitted

autoriser /otɔʀize/ [1] vtr (a) to allow, to authorize
(b) ~ **qn à faire** to entitle sb to do
(c) to make [sth] possible

autoritaire /otɔʀitɛʀ/ adj, nmf authoritarian

autorité /otɔʀite/ nf (a) authority; **faire qch d'~** to do sth without consultation; **il n'a aucune ~ sur ses enfants** he has no control over his children; **faire ~** ⟨person⟩ to be an authority; ⟨work⟩ to be authoritative
(b) (person) authority, expert

autoroute /otoʀut/ nf motorway (GB), freeway (US); ~ **à péage** toll motorway
■ ~ **de l'information** information highway

autoroutier, -ière /otoʀutje, ɛʀ/ adj motorway (GB), freeway (US)

auto-stop /otostɔp/ nm hitchhiking

auto-stoppeur, -euse, mpl ~s /otostɔpœʀ, øz/ nm,f hitchhiker

autour /otuʀ/ [1] adv **un parterre de fleurs avec des pierres ~** a flower bed with stones around it; **tout ~** all around
[2] **autour de** phr (a) around, round (GB); ~ **de la table** around the table
(b) around, about; ~ **de 10 heures** around 10 o'clock
(c) about; on; **un débat ~ du thème du pouvoir** a debate on the theme of power

autre /otʀ/ [1] det (a) other; **une ~ histoire** another story; **rien d'~** nothing else; **l'effet obtenu est tout ~** the effect produced is completely different
(b) (colloq) **nous ~s professeurs/Français** we teachers/French
[2] pron (a) **où sont les ~s?** where are the other ones?; where are the others?; **je t'ai pris pour un ~** I mistook you for someone else; **ils se respectent les uns les ~s** they respect each other; **chez lui c'est tout l'un ou tout l'~** with him it's all or nothing; **à d'~s!** (colloq) pull the other one! (colloq)
(b) **prends-en un ~** have another one; **si je peux je t'en apporterai d'~s** if I can I'll bring you some more
[3] **autre part** phr somewhere else

autrefois /otʀəfwa/ adv in the past; before, formerly; in the old days; ~, **quand** ···⟩

Paris s'appelait Lutèce long ago, when Paris was called Lutetia; **les légendes d'~** old legends

autrement /otʀəmɑ̃/ *adv* **(a)** differently, in a different way; **c'est comme ça, et pas ~** that's just the way it is; **je n'ai pas pu faire ~ que de les inviter** I had no alternative but to invite them; **on ne peut y accéder ~ que par bateau** you can only get there by boat; **je ne l'ai jamais vue ~ qu'en jean** I've never seen her in anything but jeans; **~ dit** in other words
(b) otherwise
(c) (colloq) **~ grave** (much) more serious; **il n'était pas ~ impressionné** he wasn't particularly impressed

Autriche /otʀiʃ/ *pr nf* Austria

autrichien, -ienne /otʀiʃjɛ̃, ɛn/ *adj* Austrian

autruche /otʀyʃ/ *nf* ostrich
IDIOMS **pratiquer la politique de l'~** to bury one's head in the sand

autrui /otʀɥi/ *pron* others, other people

auvent /ovɑ̃/ *nm* **(a)** canopy
(b) awning

aux /o/ *prep* (= **à les**) ▶ À

auxiliaire /oksiljɛʀ/ ① *adj* **(a)** ⟨verb⟩ auxiliary
(b) ⟨equipment, service⟩ auxiliary; ⟨motor⟩ back-up
(c) **maître ~** assistant teacher; **infirmier ~** nursing auxiliary (GB), nurse's aide (US)
② *nmf* assistant, helper
③ *nm* auxiliary (verb)

auxquels, auxquelles ▶ LEQUEL

avachir: s'avachir /avaʃiʀ/ [3] *v refl* (+ *v être*) **(a)** ⟨chair⟩ to sag
(b) ⟨person⟩ to let oneself go

avaient /avɛ/ ▶ AVOIR[1]

avais /avɛ/ ▶ AVOIR[1]

avait /avɛ/ ▶ AVOIR[1]

aval /aval/ *nm* **(a)** (of river) lower reaches; **en ~** downstream
(b) approval

avalanche /avalɑ̃ʃ/ *nf* avalanche

avaler /avale/ [1] *vtr* **(a)** to swallow; '**ne pas ~**' (Med) 'not to be taken internally'
(b) to inhale ⟨smoke, fumes⟩

avaleur /avalœʀ/ *nm* **~ de sabres** sword swallower

à-valoir /avalwaʀ/ *nm inv* instalment (GB)

avance /avɑ̃s/ ① *nf* **(a)** advance
(b) lead; **avoir/prendre de l'~ sur** to be/pull ahead of
(c) **une ~ (sur salaire)** an advance (on one's salary)
② **à l'avance** *phr* in advance
③ **d'avance** *phr* in advance; **avoir cinq minutes d'~** to be five minutes early
④ **en avance** *phr* **(a)** early
(b) **être en ~ sur qn** to be ahead of sb
(c) **il est en ~ pour son âge** he's advanced for his age
⑤ **avances** *nf pl* advances

avancé, ~e[1] /avɑ̃se/ ① *pp* ▶ AVANCER
② *pp adj* ⟨ideas⟩ progressive; **la saison est bien ~e** it's late in the season; **te voilà bien ~!** that's done you a lot of good!

avancée[2] /avɑ̃se/ *nf* (of roof, rock) overhang

avancement /avɑ̃smɑ̃/ *nm* **(a)** promotion
(b) progress
(c) **~ de l'âge de la retraite** lowering of the retirement age

avancer /avɑ̃se/ [12] ① *vtr* **(a)** to move [sth] forward ⟨object⟩; to push [sth] forward ⟨plate⟩
(b) to bring forward ⟨trip, meeting⟩
(c) **~ sa montre de cinq minutes** to put one's watch forward (by) five minutes
(d) to get ahead with ⟨work⟩; **cela ne nous avance à rien** that doesn't get us anywhere
(e) **~ de l'argent à qn** ⟨bank⟩ to advance money to sb
(f) to put forward ⟨argument, theory⟩; to propose ⟨figure⟩
② *vi* **(a)** ⟨person, vehicle⟩ to move (forward); ⟨army⟩ to advance; **elle avança vers le guichet** she went up to the ticket office
(b) to make progress, to progress; **faire ~ la science** to further science
(c) **ma montre avance de deux minutes** my watch is two minutes fast
(d) ⟨teeth, chin⟩ to stick out; ⟨peninsula⟩ to jut out
③ **s'avancer** *v refl* (+ *v être*) **(a)** **s'~ vers qch** to move toward(s) sth; **s'~ vers qn** to go toward(s) sb; to come up to sb
(b) to get ahead
(c) to jut out, to protrude
(d) **je me suis un peu avancé en lui promettant le dossier pour demain** I shouldn't have committed myself by promising him/her I'd have the file ready for tomorrow

avant[1] /avɑ̃/ ① *adv* before; first; **bien ~** long before; **il l'a mentionné ~ dans l'introduction** he mentioned it earlier in the introduction
② *prep* before; **~ mon retour** before I get back; **before I got back**; **~ le 1er juillet** by 1 July; **~ peu** shortly; **~ tout, ~ toute chose** above all; first and foremost
③ **d'avant** *phr* **la séance d'~** the previous performance; **la fois d'~ nous nous étions déjà perdus** we got lost the last time as well
④ **avant de ~ de faire** before doing
⑤ **avant que** *phr* before
⑥ **en avant** *phr* forward(s); **en ~ toute!** full steam ahead!; **mettre en ~ le fait que** to point out the fact that; **se mettre en ~** to push oneself forward
⑦ **en avant de** *phr* ahead of ⟨group⟩

avant[2] /avɑ̃/ ① *adj inv* ⟨wheel, seat, paw⟩ front
② *nm* **(a)** **l'~** the front; **aller de l'~** to forge ahead
(b) (Sport) forward
③ **avant-** (combining form) **l'~-Thatcher** the pre-Thatcher era

avantage /avɑ̃taʒ/ *nm* **(a)** advantage; **tirer ∼ de qch** to take advantage of sth; **paraître à son ∼** to look one's best **(b)** benefit; **∼ fiscaux** tax benefits

avantager /avɑ̃taʒe/ [13] *vtr* **(a)** ⟨person⟩ to favour (GB); ⟨situation⟩ to be to the advantage of **(b)** ⟨clothes⟩ to show [sb/sth] off to advantage

avantageusement /avɑ̃taʒøzmɑ̃/ *adv* favourably (GB)

avantageux, -euse /avɑ̃taʒø, øz/ *adj* **(a)** ⟨conditions, offer⟩ favourable (GB), advantageous; ⟨rate, price⟩ attractive; **tirer un parti ∼ de qch** to use sth to one's advantage **(b)** ⟨description, outfit⟩ flattering

avant-bras /avɑ̃bʀa/ *nm inv* forearm

avant-centre, *pl* **avants-centres** /avɑ̃sɑ̃tʀ/ *nm* centre (GB) forward; **jouer ∼** to play centre (GB) forward

avant-coureur, *pl* **∼s** /avɑ̃kuʀœʀ/ *adj* **signes ∼s** early warning signs

avant-dernier, -ière, *pl* **∼s** /avɑ̃dɛʀnje, ɛʀ/ **1** *adj* penultimate; **l'∼ jour** the last day but one **2** *nm,f* the last but one; **l'∼ d'une famille de cinq** the second youngest of five children

avant-garde, *pl* **∼s** /avɑ̃gaʀd/ *nf* **(a)** avant-garde **(b)** vanguard; **à l'∼** in the vanguard

avant-goût, *pl* **∼s** /avɑ̃gu/ *nm* foretaste

avant-guerre, *pl* **∼s** /avɑ̃gɛʀ/ *nm or f* **l'∼** the prewar period; **l'Espagne d'∼** prewar Spain

avant-hier /avɑ̃tjɛʀ/ *adv* the day before yesterday

avant-poste, *pl* **∼s** /avɑ̃pɔst/ *nm* (Mil) outpost; **être aux ∼s** to be in the vanguard

avant-première, *pl* **∼s** /avɑ̃pʀəmjɛʀ/ *nf* preview

avant-propos /avɑ̃pʀɔpo/ *nm inv* foreword

avant-veille, *pl* **∼s** /avɑ̃vɛj/ *nf* two days before

avare /avaʀ/ **1** *adj* mean, miserly; **∼ de** sparing with **2** *nm,f* miser

avarice /avaʀis/ *nf* meanness (GB), miserliness

avarier: s'avarier /avaʀje/ [2] *v refl* (+ *v être*) ⟨meat, fish⟩ to go rotten

avatar /avataʀ/ *nm* **(a)** mishap **(b)** change

avec /avɛk/ **1** *adv* (colloq) **elle est partie ∼** she went off with it **2** *prep* with; **∼ attention** carefully; **et ∼ cela, que désirez-vous?** what else would you like?; **je fais tout son travail et ∼ ça il n'est pas content!** I do all his work and he's still not happy!; **sa séparation d'∼ sa femme** his separation from his wife

avenant, -e /avnɑ̃, ɑ̃t/ **1** *adj* pleasant **2** **à l'avenant** *phr* in keeping

avènement /avɛnmɑ̃/ *nm* **(a)** (of monarch) accession; (of politician, era) advent; **∼ au trône** accession to the throne **(b)** Advent

avenir /avniʀ/ *nm* future; **d'∼** ⟨job⟩ with a future; ⟨technique, science⟩ of the future

aventure /avɑ̃tyʀ/ *nf* **(a)** adventure **(b)** **il m'est arrivé une drôle d'∼** something strange happened to me **(c)** venture **(d)** (love) affair **IDIOMS dire la bonne ∼ à qn** to tell sb's fortune

aventurer: s'aventurer /avɑ̃tyʀe/ [1] *v refl* (+ *v être*) to venture

aventurier, -ière /avɑ̃tyʀje, ɛʀ/ *nm,f* adventurer/adventuress

avenue /avny/ *nf* avenue

avérer: s'avérer /aveʀe/ [14] *v refl* (+ *v être*) **s'∼ utile** to prove useful; **il s'avère que** it turns out that

averse /avɛʀs/ *nf* shower

aversion /avɛʀsjɔ̃/ *nf* aversion; **avoir qn/ qch en ∼** to loathe sb/sth

averti, ∼e /avɛʀti/ **1** *pp* ▶ AVERTIR **2** *pp adj* **(a)** ⟨reader⟩ informed **(b)** experienced

avertir /avɛʀtiʀ/ [3] *vtr* **(a)** to inform **(b)** to warn

avertissement /avɛʀtismɑ̃/ *nm* **(a)** warning **(b)** (Sport) caution **(c)** (in book) foreword

avertisseur /avɛʀtisœʀ/ *nm* **(a)** alarm **(b)** (of car) horn

aveu, *pl* **∼x** /avø/ *nm* confession; admission

aveuglant, ∼e /avœglɑ̃, ɑ̃t/ *adj* blinding

aveugle /avœgl/ **1** *adj* **(a)** blind **(b)** ⟨faith, love⟩ blind; ⟨violence⟩ indiscriminate **2** *nmf* blind person; **les ∼s** the blind

aveuglement /avœgləmɑ̃/ *nm* blindness

aveuglément /avœglemɑ̃/ *adv* blindly

aveugler /avœgle/ [1] *vtr* to blind

aveuglette: à l'aveuglette /alavœglɛt/ *phr* **(a)** blindly **(b)** at random

avez /ave/ ▶ AVOIR[1]

aviateur /avjatœʀ/ *nm* airman

aviation /avjasjɔ̃/ *nf* **(a)** aviation **(b)** aircraft industry **(c)** **l'∼** the air force

aviatrice /avjatʀis/ *nf* woman pilot

aviculteur, -trice /avikyltœʀ, tʀis/ *nm,f* **(a)** (of fowl) poultry farmer **(b)** (of birds) aviculturist

aviculture /avikyltyʀ/ *nf* **(a)** (of fowl) poultry farming **(b)** (of birds) aviculture

avide /avid/ *adj* **(a)** greedy **(b)** **∼ de** avid for, eager for

a

avidement /avidmɑ̃/ adv ⟨eat⟩ greedily; ⟨read⟩ avidly; ⟨look, search⟩ eagerly

avidité /avidite/ nf **(a)** greed
(b) eagerness

aviez /avje/ ▶ AVOIR¹

avilir /aviliʀ/ [3] vtr to demean

avilissant, ⁓**e** /avilisɑ̃, ɑ̃t/ adj demeaning

avilissement /avilismɑ̃/ nm degradation

aviné, ⁓**e** /avine/ adj ⟨person⟩ inebriated; ⟨look, face⟩ drunken

avion /avjɔ̃/ nm **(a)** (aero)plane (GB), airplane (US), aircraft; **aller à Rome en ⁓** to fly to Rome; **'par ⁓'** 'by air mail'
(b) flight
■ ⁓ **de chasse** fighter; ⁓ **à réaction** jet; ⁓ **de tourisme** light passenger aircraft

avions /avjɔ̃/ ▶ AVOIR¹

aviron /aviʀɔ̃/ nm **(a)** rowing
(b) oar

avis /avi/ nm inv **(a)** opinion; **je suis de ton ⁓** I agree with you; **changer d'⁓** to change one's mind
(b) advice; **sauf ⁓ contraire** unless otherwise informed
(c) (of jury, commission) recommendation
(d) notice; **lancer un ⁓ de recherche** to issue a description of a missing person/wanted person
■ ⁓ **au lecteur** foreword; ⁓ **de passage** calling card (left by postman etc)

avisé, ⁓**e** /avize/ adj sensible; **être bien/mal ⁓** to be well-/ill-advised

aviser /avize/ [1] **1** vtr to notify
2 vi to decide
3 s'aviser v refl (+ v être) **ne t'avise pas de recommencer** don't dare do that again

aviver /avive/ [1] **1** vtr **(a)** to intensify ⟨feeling⟩; to stir up ⟨quarrel⟩; to make [sth] more acute ⟨pain⟩
(b) to liven up ⟨colour⟩
(c) to kindle ⟨fire⟩
2 s'aviver v refl (+ v être) ⟨desire, anger⟩ to grow; ⟨pain, grief⟩ to become more acute

avocat /avɔka/ nm **(a)** lawyer, solicitor (GB), attorney (at law) (US)
(b) barrister (GB), (trial) lawyer (US); ⁓ **de l'accusation** counsel for the prosecution
(c) (of idea) advocate; (of cause, person) champion
(d) avocado (pear)

avocate /avɔkat/ nf woman lawyer

avoine /avwan/ nf oats

avoir¹ /avwaʀ/ [8]

■ **Note** You will find translations for expressions such as avoir raison, avoir beau, en avoir marre etc, at the entries RAISON, BEAU, MARRE etc.

1 v aux to have; **j'ai perdu mon briquet** I've lost my lighter; **il aurait aimé te parler** he would have liked to speak to her
2 vtr **(a)** to have (got) ⟨child, book, room, time⟩; **elle avait les larmes aux yeux** there were tears in her eyes

(b) to get ⟨object, job⟩; to catch ⟨train, plane⟩; (on the phone) **j'ai réussi à l'⁓** I managed to get through to him
(c) to wear, to have [sth] on
(d) to feel; ⁓ **du chagrin** to feel sad; **qu'est-ce que tu as?** what's wrong with you?
(e) avoir faim/froid/20 ans to be hungry/cold/20 years old
(f) to beat; to have (colloq); to con (colloq); **j'ai été eu** I've been had

3 avoir à v+prep to have to; **tu n'as pas à le critiquer** you shouldn't criticize him; **j'ai beaucoup à faire** I have a lot to do; **tu n'as qu'à leur écrire** all you have to do is write to them

4 en avoir pour v+prep **(a)** **vous en avez pour combien de temps?** how long will it take you?; how long are you going to be?
(b) **j'en ai eu pour 500 francs** it cost me 500 francs

5 il y a v impers **(a)** there is/there are; **qu'est-ce qu'il y a?** what's wrong?; what's going on?; **il y a qu'elle m'énerve** she's getting on my nerves, that's what's wrong; **il y a à manger pour quatre** there's enough food for four; **il y en a toujours qui se plaignent** there's always someone who complains; **il n'y en a que pour leur chien** their dog comes first
(b) **il y a longtemps** a long time ago; **il n'y a que cinq ans que j'habite ici** I have only been living here for five years
(c) **combien y a-t-il jusqu'à la gare?** how far is it to the station?; **il y a au moins 15 kilomètres** it's at least 15 kilometres (GB) away

avoir² /avwaʀ/ nm **(a)** credit
(b) credit note
(c) assets, holdings

avoisinant, ⁓**e** /avwazinɑ̃, ɑ̃t/ adj neighbouring (GB)

avoisiner /avwazine/ [1] vtr **(a)** ⟨cost, sum⟩ to be close to, to be about
(b) ⟨place⟩ to be near

avons /avɔ̃/ ▶ AVOIR¹

avortement /avɔʀtəmɑ̃/ nm (Med) abortion

avorter /avɔʀte/ [1] vi **(a)** (Med) to have an abortion
(b) ⟨cow, ewe⟩ to abort, to miscarry
(c) ⟨plan⟩ to be aborted; ⟨uprising⟩ to fail

avorton /avɔʀtɔ̃/ nm runt

avouable /avwabl/ adj worthy; respectable

avoué, ⁓**e** /avwe/ **1** pp ▶ AVOUER
2 pp adj ⟨enemy⟩ declared; ⟨intention⟩ avowed
3 nm ≈ solicitor (GB), attorney(-at-law) (US)

avouer /avwe/ [1] **1** vtr to confess, to admit
2 vi to confess; to own up
3 s'avouer v refl (+ v être) **s'⁓ rassuré** to say one feels reassured; **s'⁓ vaincu** to admit defeat

avril /avʀil/ nm April

axe /aks/ nm **(a)** axis

(b) (Tech) axle
(c) major road
(d) dans l'~ du bâtiment in a line with the building; la cible est dans l'~ du viseur the target is lined up in the sights

axer /akse/ [1] *vtr* **(a)** to centre (GB) ‹*screw*›; to line up ‹*part*›
(b) to base, to centre (GB) (sur on)

axiome /aksjom/ *nm* axiom

ayant /ɛjɑ̃/ ▶ AVOIR[1]

ayant droit, *pl* **ayants droit** /ɛyɑ̃dʀwa/ *nm* **(a)** legal claimant, beneficiary
(b) assignee

ayez /aje/ ▶ AVOIR[1]

ayons /ajɔ̃/ ▶ AVOIR[1]

azalée /azale/ *nf* azalea

Azerbaïdjan /azɛʀbajdʒɑ̃/ *pr nm* Azerbaijan

azimut /azimyt/ *nm* **(a)** (in astronomy) azimuth
(b) (figurative) une offensive tous ~s an all-out offensive; dans tous les ~s everywhere

azote /azɔt/ *nm* nitrogen

aztèque /astɛk/ *adj* Aztec

azur /azyʀ/ *nm* azure

azyme /azim/ *adj* unleavened

· ·

Bb

· ·

b, B /be/ *nm inv* b, B; le b a ba the rudiments

baba /baba/ *adj inv* (colloq) en être *or* rester ~ to be flabbergasted (colloq)

babillage /babijaʒ/ *nm* babbling

babiller /babije/ [1] *vi* to babble, to chatter

babines /babin/ *nf pl* lips; retrousser les ~ ‹*dog*› to bare its teeth; se lécher les ~ to lick one's chops

babiole /babjɔl/ *nf* **(a)** trinket
(b) trifle

bâbord /babɔʀ/ *nm* port (side)

babouche /babuʃ/ *nf* oriental slipper

babouin /babwɛ̃/ *nm* baboon

baby-foot /babifut/ *nm inv* table football (GB), table soccer

bac /bak/ *nm* **(a)** (colloq) *abbr* = **baccalauréat**
(b) ferry
(c) tub; évier à deux ~s double sink
■ ~ à sable sandpit (GB), sandbox (US)

baccalauréat /bakalɔʀea/ *nm* baccalaureate (*school-leaving certificate taken at 17–18*); ~ professionnel vocational baccalaureate (*vocationally-oriented school-leaving certificate*)

bâche /baʃ/ *nf* tarpaulin

bachelier, -ière /baʃəlje, ɛʀ/ *nm,f:* holder of the baccalaureate

bâcher /baʃe/ [1] *vtr* to cover [sth] with tarpaulin ‹*vehicle*›; un camion bâché a covered truck

bachotage /baʃɔtaʒ/ *nm* (Sch) (colloq) cramming

bâcler /bakle/ [1] *vtr* to dash [sth] off ‹*piece of work*›; to rush through ‹*ceremony*›

bactérie /bakteʀi/ *nf* bacterium

badaud, ~e /bado, od/ *nm,f* **(a)** passerby
(b) onlooker

badigeonner /badiʒɔne/ [1] *vtr* **(a)** to paint
(b) to daub (de with)
(c) (Culin) to brush (de with)

badin, ~e /badɛ̃, in/ *adj* ‹*tone*› bantering

baffe /baf/ *nf* (colloq) clout, slap

baffle /bafl/ *nm* **(a)** speaker
(b) baffle

bafouille /bafuj/ *nf* (colloq) letter

bafouiller /bafuje/ [1] *vtr, vi* to mumble

bagage /bagaʒ/ *nm* piece of luggage; faire ses ~s to pack
IDIOMS plier ~ (colloq) to pack up and go

bagagiste /bagaʒist/ *nm* baggage handler

bagarre /bagaʀ/ *nf* fight, scuffle

bagarrer: se bagarrer /bagaʀe/ *v refl* (+ *v être*) (colloq) to fight

bagarreur, -euse /bagaʀœʀ, øz/ *adj* (colloq) aggressive

bagatelle /bagatɛl/ *nf* **(a)** trifle, triviality
(b) pour la ~ de (ironic) for the trifling sum of

bagne /baɲ/ *nm* penal colony

bagou(t) /bagu/ *nm* (colloq) avoir du ~ to have the gift of the gab

bague /bag/ *nf* **(a)** ring
(b) (around pipe) collar

baguette /bagɛt/ *nf* **(a)** baguette, French stick
(b) stick; mener qn à la ~ to rule sb with a rod of iron; ~ de chef d'orchestre conductor's baton
(c) drumstick
(d) chopstick
■ ~ magique magic wand

bahut /bay/ *nm* **(a)** sideboard
(b) (students' slang) school
(c) (colloq) truck

bai, ~e /bɛ/ *adj* bay

baie /bɛ/ *nf* **(a)** bay ·····›

(b) berry
(c) ~ (vitrée) picture window
baignade /bɛɲad/ *nf* swimming
baigner /beɲe/ [1] **1** *vtr* **(a)** to give [sb] a bath
(b) to bathe ‹wound›
2 *vi* ~ **dans l'huile** to be swimming in grease
3 se baigner *v refl* (+ *v être*) to go swimming
IDIOMS **ça baigne** (colloq) things are going fine
baigneur, -euse /bɛɲœʀ, øz/ *nm,f* swimmer
baignoire /bɛɲwaʀ/ *nf* bathtub; ~ **sabot** hip bath
bail, *pl* **baux** /baj, bo/ *nm* lease; **ça fait un ~** (colloq) it's been ages **(que since)**
bâiller /baje/ [1] *vi* **(a)** to yawn
(b) to gape (open)
bailleur, bailleresse /bajœʀ, bajʀɛs/ *nm,f* lessor
■ ~ **de fonds** backer, silent partner
bâillon /bɑjɔ̃/ *nm* gag
bain /bɛ̃/ *nm* **(a)** bath
(b) swim
(c) **grand/petit ~** deep/shallow pool
■ ~ **de bouche** mouthwash; ~ **de foule** walkabout; **prendre un ~ de soleil** to sunbathe
IDIOMS **se remettre dans le ~** to get back into the swing of things
baïonnette /bajɔnɛt/ *nf* bayonet
baiser /beze/ *nm* kiss
baisse /bɛs/ *nf* **(a)** fall; **en ~** falling
(b) fading
(c) decline
(d) cut; **la ~ du dollar** the fall in the value of the dollar; **une ~ des loyers de 2%** a 2% drop in rents; **être en ~** ‹rates, stocks, shares› to be going down; ‹results› to be decreasing; **le marché est à la ~** (Econ) the market is bearish; **revoir des prévisions à la ~** to revise estimates downward(s); **spéculations à la ~** bear speculations
baisser /bese/ [1] **1** *vtr* **(a)** to lower ‹blind›; to wind [sth] down ‹window›; to turn down ‹collar›; ~ **les bras** (figurative) to give up; ~ **le nez** (figurative) to hang one's head
(b) to turn down ‹volume›; to dim ‹light›; to cut ‹prices›
2 *vi* to go down, to fall, to drop **(à** to; **de** by); (drop in value) ‹price, profit, rates, production› to fall; ‹wages, shares› to go down; ‹purchasing power, unemployment› decrease; ‹productivity, market› to decline; ‹budget› to be cut; ‹currency› to slide; ‹water› to subside; ‹sight› to fail; ‹hearing› to deteriorate; ~ **d'un ton** (colloq) ‹person› to calm down
3 se baisser *v refl* (+ *v être*) **(a)** to bend down
(b) to duck
(c) to go down
baissier, -ière /besje, ɛʀ/ **1** *adj* bearish

2 *nm* (on stock exchange) bear
bajoue /baʒu/ *nf* cheek
bal /bal/ *nm* **(a)** ball, dance
(b) dancehall
balade /balad/ *nf* walk; ride
balader /balade/ [1] (colloq) **1** *vtr* **(a)** to take [sb] for a walk/drive
(b) to carry [sth] around
2 se balader *v refl* (+ *v être*) to go for a walk/ride/drive
IDIOMS **envoyer qn ~** (colloq) to send sb packing (colloq)
baladeur /baladœʀ/ *nm* walkman®, personal stereo
balafre /balafʀ/ *nf* **(a)** scar
(b) slash, gash
balai /balɛ/ *nm* broom; **passer le ~** to sweep the floor; **du ~** (colloq)! go away!
balance /balɑ̃s/ *nf* **(a)** (weighing) scales; **faire pencher la ~** (figurative) to tip the scales
(b) (Econ) balance; ~ **commerciale** balance of trade; ~ **des comptes**, ~ **des paiements** balance of payments
Balance /balɑ̃s/ *pr nf* Libra
balancelle /balɑ̃sɛl/ *nf* swing seat
balancement /balɑ̃smɑ̃/ *nm* swaying; swinging
balancer /balɑ̃se/ [12] **1** *vtr* **(a)** to sway; to swing
(b) (colloq) to chuck (colloq) **(sur** at); to chuck out (colloq) ‹old clothes, junk›
(c) (colloq) to squeal on (colloq)
2 *vi* **(a)** to sway
(b) to hesitate
3 se balancer *v refl* (+ *v être*) **(a)** ‹person› to sway; ‹boat› to rock
(b) (colloq) **je m'en balance** I couldn't care less
balancier /balɑ̃sje/ *nm* pendulum
balançoire /balɑ̃swaʀ/ *nf* swing
balayer /baleje/ [21] *vtr* **(a)** to sweep (up); ~ **le sol** ‹coat› to brush the ground
(b) to brush [sth] aside ‹objections›
(c) ‹radar› to scan
balayette /balɛjɛt/ *nf* (short-handled) brush
balayeur, -euse /balɛjœʀ, øz/ *nm,f* roadsweeper
balbutiement /balbysimɑ̃/ *nm* **les ~s du cinéma** the early days of the cinema
balbutier /balbysje/ [2] *vtr, vi* to mumble
balcon /balkɔ̃/ *nm* **(a)** balcony
(b) (in theatre, cinema) balcony, circle
Bâle /bɑl/ *pr n* Basel
baleine /balɛn/ *nf* **(a)** whale
(b) whalebone; stay; rib
balisage /balizaʒ/ *nm* (in port, channel) beaconing; (on airstrip) runway lighting; (on road) signposting; (on path) marking; (of text) tagging
balise /baliz/ *nf* **(a)** beacon
(b) signpost, waymark
(c) (Comput) tag

baliser /balize/ [1] *vtr* (a) to mark [sth] out with beacons
(b) to signpost, to waymark
(c) (Comput) to tag ⟨*text*⟩

balistique /balistik/ *nf* ballistics

baliverne /balivɛʀn/ *nf* nonsense

ballade /balad/ *nf* ballad; ballade

balle /bal/ *nf* (a) ball; renvoyer la ∼ (à qn) (figurative) to retort (to sb); se renvoyer la ∼ to keep up an animated discussion; to keep passing the buck
(b) (in ball games) shot; faire des ∼s to knock the ball around; ∼ de jeu game point
(c) bullet
(d) (colloq) franc

ballerine /balʀin/ *nf* (a) ballerina
(b) ballet pump

ballet /balɛ/ *nm* ballet

ballon /balɔ̃/ *nm* (a) ball
(b) balloon
(c) wine glass
(d) ∼ (alcootest) Breathalyzer®
∎ ∼ dirigeable airship (GB), blimp (US); ∼ d'eau chaude hot water tank; ∼ ovale rugby ball; ∼ rond soccer ball

ballonnement /balɔnmɑ̃/ *nm* bloating

ballot /balo/ *nm* (colloq) nerd (colloq), fool

ballottage /balɔtaʒ/ *nm*: *absence of an absolute majority in the first round of an election*

ballotter /balɔte/ [1] *vtr* (a) ⟨*sea*⟩ to toss [sb/sth] around; ⟨*movement*⟩ to jolt
(b) être ballotté entre sa famille et son travail to be torn between one's family and one's job

balluchon = BALUCHON

balnéaire /balneɛʀ/ *adj* ⟨*resort*⟩ seaside

balte /balt/ *adj* Baltic; les pays ∼s the Baltic States

baluchon /balyʃɔ̃/ *nm* bundle

balustrade /balystʀad/ *nf* (a) parapet
(b) railing
(c) balustrade

bambin, ∼e /bɑ̃bɛ̃, in/ *nm,f* kid (colloq), child

bambou /bɑ̃bu/ *nm* bamboo

ban /bɑ̃/ ①*nm* round of applause
②**bans** *nm pl* banns
IDIOMS mettre qn au ∼ de la société to ostracize sb

banal, ∼e /banal/ *adj* (a) commonplace, ordinary; peu ∼ unusual
(b) trivial, trite

banalisation /banalizasjɔ̃/ *nf* la ∼ de l'informatique the way in which computing has become part of everyday life

banaliser /banalize/ [1] *vtr* (a) to make [sth] commonplace
(b) voiture banalisée unmarked car

banalité /banalite/ *nf* (a) ordinariness
(b) triteness
(c) trite remark

banane /banan/ *nf* (a) banana
(b) quiff

(c) bumbag (GB), fanny pack (US)

banc /bɑ̃/ *nm* (a) bench
(b) (of fish) shoal
∎ ∼ des accusés dock; ∼ d'essai test bench; testing ground; ∼ de sable sandbank

bancaire /bɑ̃kɛʀ/ *adj* (a) ⟨*business*⟩ banking
(b) ⟨*card*⟩ bank

bancal, ∼e /bɑ̃kal/ *adj* (a) ⟨*chair*⟩ rickety
(b) ⟨*solution*⟩ unsatisfactory

bande /bɑ̃d/ *nf* (a) gang; group; ∼ de crétins! you bunch of idiots!; ils font ∼ à part they don't join in
(b) (of animals) pack
(c) (of material, paper) strip; band
(d) bandage
(e) broad stripe
(f) (for recording) tape
∎ ∼ d'arrêt d'urgence, BAU hard shoulder; ∼ dessinée, BD (colloq) comic strip; comic book; ∼ de fréquences waveband; ∼ originale (of film) original soundtrack

bande-annonce, *pl* **bandes-annonces** /bɑ̃dɑnɔ̃s/ *nf* trailer

bandeau, *pl* ∼**x** /bɑ̃do/ *nm* (a) blindfold
(b) eye patch
(c) headband

bandelette /bɑ̃dlɛt/ *nf* bandage

bander /bɑ̃de/ [1] *vtr* (a) to bandage
(b) ∼ les yeux à qn to blindfold sb

banderole /bɑ̃dʀɔl/ *nf* banner

bande-son, *pl* **bandes-son** /bɑ̃dsɔ̃/ *nm* soundtrack

bandit /bɑ̃di/ *nm* (a) bandit; ∼ de grand chemin highwayman
(b) crook
(c) rascal

banditisme /bɑ̃ditism/ *nm* le (grand) ∼ (organized) crime

bandoulière /bɑ̃duljɛʀ/ *nf* shoulder strap

bang /bɑ̃g/ *nm* sonic boom

banlieue /bɑ̃ljø/ *nf* (a) suburbs; de ∼ suburban
(b) suburb

banlieusard, ∼e /bɑ̃ljøzaʀ, aʀd/ *nm,f* suburbanite

bannière /banjɛʀ/ *nf* banner; la ∼ étoilée the star-spangled banner.
IDIOMS c'est la croix et la ∼ it's hell (pour faire doing)

bannir /baniʀ/ [3] *vtr* (a) to banish (de from)
(b) to ban

bannissement /banismɑ̃/ *nm* banishment (de from)

banque /bɑ̃k/ *nf* (a) bank
(b) banking
∎ ∼ de données data bank

banqueroute /bɑ̃kʀut/ *nf* bankruptcy

banquet /bɑ̃kɛ/ *nm* (a) banquet
(b) feast

banquette /bɑ̃kɛt/ *nf* (in café) wall seat; (in car, train) seat

banquier /bɑ̃kje/ *nm* banker

banquise /bɑ̃kiz/ *nf* ice floe
baptême /batɛm/ *nm* (a) baptism, christening
(b) (of ship) christening; (of bell) blessing
■ ~ **de l'air** first flight
baptiser /batize/ [1] *vtr* (a) to baptize, to christen
(b) to call, to name; to nickname
(c) to christen ⟨*ship*⟩; to bless ⟨*bell*⟩
bar /baʀ/ *nm* (a) bar
(b) (Zool) sea bass
baragouiner /baʀagwine/ [1] *vtr* (colloq) to gabble ⟨*sentence*⟩; to speak [sth] badly ⟨*language*⟩
baraka /baʀaka/ *nf* (colloq) luck
baraque /baʀak/ *nf* (a) shack
(b) (colloq) pad (colloq), house
baraqué, ~**e** /baʀake/ *adj* (colloq) hefty
baraquement /baʀakmɑ̃/ *nm* (a) group of huts
(b) hut
(c) army camp
baratin /baʀatɛ̃/ *nm* (colloq) (a) sales pitch
(b) sweet-talk; smooth talk (GB) (colloq)
baratiner /baʀatine/ [1] *vtr* (colloq) (a) to give [sb] the spiel (colloq)
(b) to chat [sb] up (colloq)
(c) to try to persuade
baratineur, -euse /baʀatinœʀ, øz/ *nm,f* (colloq) smooth talker (colloq); (dishonest) liar
barbant, ~**e** /baʀbɑ̃, ɑ̃t/ *adj* (colloq) boring
barbare /baʀbaʀ/ ① *adj* barbaric; barbarian
② *nmf* barbarian
barbarie /baʀbaʀi/ *nf* barbarity, barbarism
barbe /baʀb/ ① *nf* beard; ~ **naissante** stubble
② *excl* (colloq) **la** ~! I've had enough!; **la** ~ **avec leurs consignes!** to hell with their orders! (colloq)
■ ~ **à papa** candyfloss (GB), cotton candy (US)
IDIOMS **à la** ~ **de qn** under sb's nose
barbelé /baʀbəle/ *nm* barbed wire (GB), barbwire (US)
barbiche /baʀbiʃ/ *nf* (a) goatee (beard)
(b) (on goat) (small) beard
barbier /baʀbje/ *nm* barber
barbiturique /baʀbityʀik/ *nm* barbiturate
barboteuse /baʀbɔtøz/ *nf* romper suit
barbouiller /baʀbuje/ [1] ① *vtr* (a) to smear (**de** with)
(b) to daub (**de** with)
(c) ~ **des toiles** to do daubs; ~ **du papier** to write drivel
(d) **être barbouillé** to feel queasy
② **se barbouiller** *v refl* (+ *v être*) **se** ~ **le visage de qch** to get one's face all covered in sth
barbu, ~**e** /baʀby/ *adj* bearded; **il est** ~ he has a beard
barde /baʀd/ *nf* thin slice of bacon, bard
bardé, ~**e** /baʀde/ *adj* covered (**de** in)
barème /baʀɛm/ *nm* scale; ~ **des prix** price list; ~ **d'imposition** tax schedule *or* scale

baril /baʀil/ *nm* barrel, cask; keg; drum
barillet /baʀijɛ/ *nm* cylinder
bariolé, ~**e** /baʀjɔle/ *adj* multicoloured (GB)
baromètre /baʀɔmɛtʀ/ *nm* barometer
baron /baʀɔ̃/ *nm* baron
baronne /baʀɔn/ *nf* baroness
baroque /baʀɔk/ *adj* (a) baroque
(b) bizarre
baroudeur /baʀudœʀ/ *nm* (a) fighter, warrior
(b) adventurer
barque /baʀk/ *nf* (small) boat
barquette /baʀkɛt/ *nf* punnet (GB), basket (US); tub; container
barrage /baʀaʒ/ *nm* (a) dam
(b) roadblock; barricade; **faire** ~ **à** to block
barre /baʀ/ *nf* (a) bar, rod
(b) (of chocolate) piece
(c) tiller, helm
(d) band, stripe
(e) stroke; **la** ~ **du t** the cross on the t
(f) (of goal) crossbar; (in high jump) bar
(g) (in ballet practice) barre
(h) (Law) bar; ≈ witness box (GB), witness stand (US)
(i) mark; **franchir la** ~ **des 13%** to go over the 13% mark
■ ~ **fixe** horizontal bar; ~ **oblique** slash
IDIOMS **avoir un coup de** ~ (colloq) to feel drained all of a sudden
barreau, *pl* ~**x** /baʀo/ *nm* (a) (of cage) bar
(b) rung
(c) (Law) **le** ~ the Bar
barrer /baʀe/ [1] *vtr* (a) to block ⟨*way*⟩; **'route barrée'** 'road closed'
(b) to cross out
barrette /baʀɛt/ *nf* (hair) slide (GB), barrette (US)
barreur, -euse /baʀœʀ, øz/ *nm,f* (gen) helmsman; (in rowing) cox; **avec** ~ coxed; **sans** ~ coxless
barricade /baʀikad/ *nf* barricade
barrière /baʀjɛʀ/ *nf* (a) fence
(b) gate
(c) barrier
barrique /baʀik/ *nf* barrel
barrir /baʀiʀ/ [3] *vi* ⟨*elephant*⟩ to trumpet
bar-tabac, *pl* **bars-tabac** /baʀtaba/ *nm* café ⟨*selling stamps and cigarettes*⟩
baryton /baʀitɔ̃/ *adj*, *nm* baritone
bas, basse¹ /bɑ, bas/ ① *adj* low; ⟨*room*⟩ low-ceilinged; ⟨*land*⟩ low-lying; **le ciel est** ~ the sky is overcast; **un enfant en** ~ **âge** a very young child; **être au plus** ~ ⟨*prices*⟩ to have reached rock bottom; **les cours sont au plus** ~ (en Bourse) prices have reached rock bottom
② *adv* (a) low; **comment peut-on tomber si** ~! how can one sink so low!
(b) **voir plus** ~ see below
(c) quietly; **tout** ~ ⟨*speak*⟩ in a whisper; ⟨*sing*⟩ softly

(d) être au plus ~ to be extremely weak; to be at one's lowest

3 *nm inv* **(a)** bottom; **le ~ du visage** the lower part of the face; **les pièces du ~** the downstairs rooms

(b) stocking

4 en bas *phr* downstairs; down below; at the bottom

■ **~ de gamme** *adj* low-quality; *nm* lower end of the market; **~ morceaux** (Culin) cheap cuts; **basse saison** low season

IDIOMS **avoir des hauts et des ~** to have one's ups and downs; **à ~ les tyrans!** down with tyranny!

basané, **~e** /bazane/ *adj* swarthy

bas-côté, *pl* **~s** /bɑkote/ *nm* **(a)** verge (GB), shoulder (US)

(b) (side) aisle

basculant, **~e** /baskylɑ̃, ɑ̃t/ *adj* **pont ~** bascule bridge; **camion à benne ~e** dump truck

bascule /baskyl/ *nf* **fauteuil à ~** rocking chair

basculer /baskyle/ [1] **1** *vtr* to transfer ⟨call⟩

2 *vi* **(a)** to topple over; **faire ~** to tip up ⟨skip⟩; to tip out ⟨load⟩; to knock [sb] off balance ⟨person⟩

(b) (figurative) to change radically

base /bɑz/ *nf* **(a)** base; **le riz forme la ~ de leur alimentation** rice is their staple diet

(b) basis; **reposer sur des ~s solides** to rest on a firm foundation; **à la ~ de qch** at the root *or* heart of sth; **salaire de ~** basic salary; **repartir sur de nouvelles ~s** to make a fresh start

(c) (in politics) **la ~** the rank and file

■ **~ de données** database; **~ de lancement** launching site

baser /bɑze/ [1] **1** *vtr* to base (**sur** on)

2 se baser *v refl* (*+ v être*) **se ~ sur qch** to go by sth

bas-fond, *pl* **~s** /bɑfɔ̃/ **1** *nm* **(a)** shallows

(b) dip

2 bas-fonds *nm pl* seedy areas

basilic /bazilik/ *nm* basil

basilique /bazilik/ *nf* basilica

basket /basket/ *nm* **(a)** basketball

(b) trainer (GB), sneaker (US)

IDIOMS **être bien** *or* **à l'aise dans ses ~s** (colloq) to be very together (colloq)

basque /bask/ *adj, nm* Basque

basse² /bɑs/ **1** *adj* ▶ BAS 1

2 *nf* (Mus) bass

basse-cour, *pl* **basses-cours** /bɑskur/ *nf* **(a)** poultry-yard

(b) poultry

bassement /bɑsmɑ̃/ *adv* basely

bassesse /bɑsɛs/ *nf* **(a)** baseness

(b) base act

bassin /bɑsɛ̃/ *nm* **(a)** pond; fountain; pool

(b) (in geography) basin

(c) pelvis

(d) bedpan

■ **~ houiller** coal field

bassine /basin/ *nf* bowl; basin

bassiste /basist/ *nmf* bass player

bastingage /bastɛ̃gaʒ/ *nm* ship's rail

bas-ventre, *pl* **~s** /bɑvɑ̃tʀ/ *nm* lower abdomen

bât /bɑ/ *nm* pack-saddle

IDIOMS **c'est là que le ~ blesse** that's where the shoe pinches

bataille /bataj/ **1** *nf* **(a)** battle

(b) fight

2 en bataille *phr* ⟨hair⟩ dishevelled (GB); ⟨eyebrows⟩ bushy

batailler /bataje/ [1] *vi* to fight, to battle

bataillon /batajɔ̃/ *nm* battalion; **Dupont?, inconnu au ~** Dupont?, never heard of him

bâtard, **~e** /bɑtaʀ, aʀd/ **1** *adj* **(a)** ⟨dog⟩ mongrel

(b) ⟨work, style⟩ hybrid

(c) (offensive) ⟨child⟩ bastard

2 *nm,f* **(a)** mongrel

(b) (offensive) bastard

bateau, *pl* **~x** /bato/ **1** *adj inv* hackneyed

2 *nm:* **(a)** boat, ship; **~ à voile/moteur/ vapeur** sailing/motor/steam boat; **faire du ~** to go boating; to go sailing

(b) dropped kerb (GB) *or* curb (US)

■ **~ amiral** flagship; **~ pneumatique** rubber dinghy; **~ de sauvetage** lifeboat

bateau-école, *pl* **bateaux-écoles** /batoekɔl/ *nm* training boat

bateau-mouche, *pl* **bateaux-mouches** /batomuʃ/ *nm:* *large river boat for sightseeing*

bateleur, **-euse** /batlœʀ, øz/ *nm,f* tumbler, juggler

batelier, **-ière** /batəlje, ɛʀ/ *nm,f* boatman/boatwoman

bâti, **~e** /bɑti/ **1** *pp* ▶ BÂTIR

2 *pp adj* **(a)** built; **terrain ~** developed site

(b) **un homme bien ~** a well-built man

batifoler /batifɔle/ [1] *vi* **(a)** to romp about

(b) to flirt

bâtiment /bɑtimɑ̃/ *nm* **(a)** building

(b) building trade

(c) ship

bâtir /bɑtiʀ/ [3] *vtr* **(a)** to build

(b) to tack ⟨hem⟩

bâtisse /bɑtis/ *nf* (dwelling) house; (structure) building

bâtisseur, **-euse** /bɑtisœʀ, øz/ *nm, f* master-builder; (figurative) builder

bâton /bɑtɔ̃/ *nm* **(a)** stick

(b) vertical stroke

(c) (colloq) ten thousand francs

■ **~ de rouge (à lèvres)** lipstick

IDIOMS **discuter à ~s rompus** to talk about this and that; **mettre des ~s dans les roues de qn** to put a spoke in sb's wheel

bâtonnet /bɑtɔne/ *nm* stick

■ **~ de poisson** fish finger (GB), fish stick (US)

batracien /batʀasjɛ̃/ *nm* batrachian

b

battage /bataʒ/ nm (colloq) publicity, hype (colloq)

battant, **~e** /batɑ̃, ɑ̃t/ **1** adj le cœur ~ with a beating heart
2 nm,f fighter
3 nm porte à deux ~s double door

batte /bat/ nf (Sport) bat (GB), paddle (US)

battement /batmɑ̃/ nm (a) beating; beat; fluttering; flutter
(b) break, gap; wait

batterie /batRi/ nf (a) percussion section
(b) drum kit
(c) battery
■ ~ de cuisine pots and pans

batteur /batœR/ nm (a) percussionist
(b) drummer
(c) whisk

battre /batR/ [61] **1** vtr (a) (defeat) to beat ⟨opponent⟩; to break ⟨record⟩
(b) (hit) to beat ⟨person, animal, carpet⟩; to thresh ⟨corn⟩
(c) ⟨rain, sea⟩ to beat against
(d) to whisk ⟨eggs⟩; to whip ⟨cream⟩
(e) to shuffle ⟨cards⟩
(f) (Mus) ~ la mesure to beat time
(g) to scour ⟨countryside⟩
2 battre de v+prep ~ des ailes to flap its wings; ~ des cils to flutter one's eyelashes; ~ des mains to clap (one's hands)
3 vi (a) ⟨heart, pulse⟩ to beat
(b) ⟨door⟩ to bang
4 se battre v refl (+ v être) to fight
IDIOMS ~ en retraite devant qch to retreat before sth; ~ son plein to be in full swing

battu, **~e** /baty/ **1** pp ▶ BATTRE
2 pp adj ⟨child, wife⟩ battered

BAU /beay/ nf: abbr ▶ BANDE

baudet /bodɛ/ nm (colloq) donkey, ass

baume /bom/ nm balm, balsam

baux /bo/ nm pl ▶ BAIL

bavard, **~e** /bavaR, aRd/ **1** adj
(a) talkative
(b) indiscreet
(c) long-winded
2 nm,f (a) chatterbox
(b) blabbermouth (colloq)

bavardage /bavaRdaʒ/ nm (a) gossip
(b) idle chatter

bavarder /bavaRde/ [1] vi (a) to talk, to chatter
(b) to chat
(c) to gossip (sur about)

bavarois, **~e** /bavaRwa, az/ **1** adj Bavarian
2 nm (Culin) Bavarian cream, bavarois

bave /bav/ nf dribble; spittle; slaver; slime

baver /bave/ [1] vi (a) ⟨person⟩ to dribble; ⟨animal⟩ to slaver
(b) ⟨pen⟩ to leak; ⟨brush⟩ to drip; ⟨ink, paint⟩ to run
IDIOMS il leur en a fait ~ (colloq) he gave them a hard time

bavette /bavet/ nf (a) bib
(b) (Culin) flank

bavoir /bavwaR/ nm bib

bavure /bavyR/ nf (a) smudge
(b) blunder

bazar /bazaR/ nm (a) general store
(b) (colloq) mess
(c) (colloq) clutter
(d) bazaar

bazarder /bazaRde/ [1] vi (colloq) to throw out

BCBG /besebeʒe/ adj (colloq) (abbr = **bon chic bon genre**) chic and conservative, Sloaney (GB)

BCG /beseʒe/ nm (abbr = **bacille bilié de Calmette et Guérin**) BCG

BD /bede/ nf (colloq): abbr ▶ BANDE

béant, **~e** /beɑ̃, ɑ̃t/ adj gaping

béat, **~e** /bea, at/ adj ⟨person⟩ blissfully happy; ⟨smile⟩ blissful, beatific

beau (**bel** before vowel or mute h), **belle¹**, mpl **~x** /bo, bɛl/ **1** adj
(a) beautiful; handsome; **se faire ~** to do oneself up; **ce n'est pas ~ à voir** (colloq)! it's not a pretty sight!
(b) good; fine; nice; lovely; **un ~ geste** a noble gesture; **fais de ~x rêves!** sweet dreams!; **au ~ milieu de** right in the middle of; **c'est bien ~ tout ça, mais...** (colloq) that's all well and good, but...
(c) ⟨sum⟩ tidy; ⟨salary⟩ very nice
2 nm **qu'est-ce que tu as fait de ~?** done anything interesting?
3 avoir beau phr **j'ai ~ essayer, je n'y arrive pas** it's no good my trying, I can't do it
4 bel et bien phr (a) well and truly
(b) definitely
■ ~ **fixe** fine weather; **~x jours** fine weather; palmy days, good days
IDIOMS **faire le ~** ⟨dog⟩ to sit up and beg; **c'est du ~!** (colloq) (ironic) lovely!

beaucoup /boku/ **1** adv (a) a lot; much; **c'est ~ dire** that's going a bit far; **c'est déjà ~ qu'elle soit venue** it's already quite something that she came; **~ moins de livres** far fewer books; **c'est ~ trop** it's far too much; **~ trop longtemps** far too long, much too long
(b) **~ de** a lot of, a great deal of; much; many; **il ne reste plus ~ de pain** there isn't much bread left; **avec ~ de soin** very carefully; **~ d'entre eux** many of them
2 de beaucoup phr by far
3 pour beaucoup phr **être pour ~ dans** to have a lot to do with

beauf /bof/ nm (colloq) (a) (abbr = **beau-frère**) brother-in-law
(b) (yokel) boor (colloq)

beau-fils, pl **beaux-fils** /bofis/ nm
(a) son-in-law
(b) stepson

beau-frère, pl **beaux-frères** /bofRɛR/ nm brother-in-law

beau-père, pl **beaux-pères** /bopɛR/ nm (a) father-in-law
(b) stepfather

beauté /bote/ *nf* beauty; **se faire une ~** to do oneself up; **finir en ~** to end with a flourish

beaux-arts /bozaʀ/ *nm pl* fine arts and architecture

bébé /bebe/ *nm* baby

bec /bɛk/ *nm* (a) beak; **donner des coups de ~** to peck; **il a toujours la cigarette au ~** (colloq) he's always got a cigarette stuck in his mouth
(b) (of jug) lip; (of teapot) spout; (of wind instrument) mouthpiece; **~ verseur** pourer(-spout)
IDIOMS **clouer le ~ à qn** (colloq) to shut sb up (colloq); **tomber sur un ~** (colloq) to come across a snag

bécane /bekan/ *nf* (colloq) bike, bicycle

bécasse /bekas/ *nf* woodcock

bec-de-lièvre, *pl* **becs-de-lièvre** /bɛkdəljɛvʀ/ *nm* harelip

bêche /bɛʃ/ *nf* (a) spade
(b) garden fork

bêcher /beʃe/ [1] *vtr* to dig (with a spade)

becquée /beke/ *nf* beakful; **donner la ~ à** to feed ‹fledgling›

bedaine /bədɛn/ *nf* (colloq) paunch

bedonnant, ~e /bədɔnɑ̃, ɑ̃t/ *adj* (colloq) ‹person› paunchy

bée /be/ *adj f* **être bouche ~** to stand open-mouthed *or* gaping

beffroi /befʀwa/ *nm* belfry

bégaiement /begɛmɑ̃/ *nm* stammer, stutter

bégayer /begeje/ [21] *vtr*, *vi* to stammer

bègue /bɛg/ *adj* **être ~** to stammer

béguin /begɛ̃/ *nm* (colloq) **avoir le ~ pour qn** to have a crush on sb

beige /bɛʒ/ *adj*, *nm* beige

beignet /bɛɲɛ/ *nm* (a) fritter
(b) doughnut, donut (US) (colloq)

bel *adj m* ▶ BEAU 1, 4

bêler /bɛle/ [1] *vi* to bleat

belette /bəlɛt/ *nf* weasel

belge /bɛlʒ/ *adj* Belgian

Belgique /bɛlʒik/ *pr nf* Belgium

bélier /belje/ *nm* (a) ram
(b) battering ram

Bélier /belje/ *pr nm* Aries

belle² /bɛl/ **1** *adj f* ▶ BEAU 1
2 *nf* decider, deciding game
3 **de plus belle** *phr* with renewed vigour (GB)
IDIOMS **(se) faire la ~** (colloq) to do a bunk (GB) (colloq), to take a powder (US) (colloq); **en faire voir de ~s à qn** (colloq) to give sb a hard time

belle-famille, *pl* **belles-familles** /bɛlfamij/ *nf* in-laws

belle-fille, *pl* **belles-filles** /bɛlfij/ *nf*
(a) daughter-in-law
(b) stepdaughter

belle-mère, *pl* **belles-mères** /bɛlmɛʀ/ *nf* (a) mother-in-law
(b) stepmother

belle-sœur, *pl* **belles-sœurs** /bɛlsœʀ/ *nf* sister-in-law

belligérant /bɛliʒeʀɑ̃/ *nm* (a) belligerent, warring party
(b) combatant

belliqueux, -euse /bɛlikø, øz/ *adj* aggressive

bémol /bemɔl/ *nm* (Mus) flat; **mi ~** E flat

bénédiction /benediksjɔ̃/ *nf* blessing

bénéfice /benefis/ *nm* (a) profit
(b) benefit, beneficial effect
(c) advantage

bénéficiaire /benefisjɛʀ/ *nmf* beneficiary

bénéficier /benefisje/ [2] *v+prep* **~ de** to receive ‹help›; to enjoy ‹immunity›; to get ‹special treatment›

bénéfique /benefik/ *adj* beneficial

Bénélux /benelyks/ *pr nm* Benelux

benêt /bənɛ/ *nm* half-wit

bénévolat /benevɔla/ *nm* voluntary work

bénévole /benevɔl/ **1** *adj* voluntary
2 *nmf* voluntary worker

bénévolement /benevɔlmɑ̃/ *adv* on a voluntary basis

bénin, -igne /benɛ̃, iɲ/ *adj* minor; benign

béni-oui-oui /beniwiwi/ *nm inv* (colloq) yes-man

bénir /beniʀ/ [3] *vtr* to bless

bénit, ~e /beni, it/ *adj* blessed; holy

bénitier /benitje/ *nm* holy water font

benjamin, ~e /bɛ̃ʒamɛ̃, in/ *nm,f* youngest child

benne /bɛn/ *nf* (a) skip (GB), dumpster® (US)
(b) (colliery) wagon
(c) (cable) car

BEPC /beapese, bɛps/ *nm* (*abbr* = **Brevet d'études du premier cycle**) *former examination at the end of the first stage of secondary education*

béquille /bekij/ *nf* (a) crutch
(b) kickstand

bercail /bɛʀkaj/ *nm* (colloq) home

berceau, *pl* **~x** /bɛʀso/ *nm* cradle

bercer /bɛʀse/ [12] **1** *vtr* to rock ‹baby›
2 **se bercer** *v refl* (+ *v être*) **se ~ d'illusions** to delude oneself

berceuse /bɛʀsøz/ *nf* lullaby

béret /beʀɛ/ *nm* beret

bergamote /bɛʀgamɔt/ *nf* bergamot

berge /bɛʀʒ/ *nf* (of river, canal) bank

berger, -ère /bɛʀʒe, ɛʀ/ *nm,f* shepherd/ shepherdess
■ **~ allemand** Alsatian (GB), German shepherd

bergerie /bɛʀʒəʀi/ *nf* sheepfold

berlue /bɛʀly/ *nf* (colloq) **avoir la ~** to be seeing things

bermuda /bɛʀmyda/ *nm* bermudas

Bermudes /bɛʀmyd/ *pr nf pl* **les ~s** Bermuda

b

berner /bɛʀne/ [1] *vtr* to fool, to deceive

besace /bəzas/ *nf* pouch

besogne /bəzɔɲ/ *nf* job

besoin /bəzwɛ̃/ **1** *nm* need (de for; de faire to do); avoir ~ de to need; répondre à un ~ to meet a need; au ~ if need be; pour les ~s de la cause for the good of the cause; être dans le ~ to be in need

2 besoins *nm pl* needs; subvenir aux ~s de qn to provide for sb

IDIOMS faire ses ~s (colloq) ⟨person⟩ to relieve oneself; ⟨animal⟩ to do its business

bestial, ~e, *mpl* -**iaux** /bɛstjal, o/ *adj* brutish, bestial

bestiaux /bɛstjo/ *nm pl* (a) livestock
(b) cattle

bestiole /bɛstjɔl/ *nf* (colloq) (a) creepy-crawly (colloq), bug
(b) animal

bétail /betaj/ *nm* livestock; cattle

bête /bɛt/ **1** *adj* stupid, silly; je suis restée toute ~ I was dumbfounded

2 *nf* creature; animal

■ ~ à bon Dieu ladybird (GB), ladybug (US); ~ noire bête noire (GB), pet hate

IDIOMS il est ~ comme ses pieds (colloq) he's as dumb as can be; chercher la petite ~ (colloq) to nit-pick (colloq); reprendre du poil de la ~ (colloq) to perk up; travailler comme une ~ (colloq) to work like crazy (colloq)

bêtement /bɛtmɑ̃/ *adv* stupidly; il suffit (tout) ~ de faire you simply need to do

bêtise /betiz/ *nf* la ~ stupidity; faire une ~ to do something stupid; dire des ~s to talk nonsense; surtout pas de ~s! be good now!

bêtisier /betizje/ *nm* collection of howlers (colloq)

béton /betɔ̃/ *nm* concrete; (figurative) watertight

■ ~ armé reinforced concrete

bétonnière /betɔnjɛʀ/ *nf* concrete mixer

betterave /bɛtʀav/ *nf* beet; ~ rouge beetroot; ~ sucrière sugar beet

beugler /bøgle/ [1] *vi* to moo; to bellow

beur /bœʀ/ *nmf* (colloq) second-generation North African (*living in France*)

beurette /bœʀɛt/ *nf* second-generation North African girl

beurre /bœʀ/ *nm* butter; ~ doux unsalted butter

■ ~ d'escargot garlic and parsley butter; ~ noir black butter; œil au ~ noir (colloq) black eye

IDIOMS faire son ~ (colloq) to make a packet (colloq); compter pour du ~ (colloq) to count for nothing; vouloir le ~ et l'argent du ~ (colloq) to want to have one's cake and eat it

beurré, ~e /bœʀe/ *adj* (colloq) drunk, plastered (colloq)

beurrer /bœʀe/ [1] *vtr* to butter

beurrier /bœʀje/ *nm* butter dish

beuverie /bœvʀi/ *nf* drinking session

biais /bjɛ/ **1** *nm inv* (a) (of material) bias

(b) way; par le ~ de qn through sb; par le ~ de qch by means of sth

2 de biais, en biais *phr* couper une étoffe en ~ to cut material on the cross

biaiser /bjɛze/ [1] *vi* to hedge

bibelot /biblo/ *nm* ornament

biberon /bibʀɔ̃/ *nm* (baby's) bottle (GB), (nursing) bottle (US)

bible /bibl/ *nf* bible; la Bible the Bible

bibliographie /biblijɔgʀafi/ *nf* bibliography

bibliographique /biblijɔgʀafik/ *adj* bibliographical

bibliothécaire /biblijɔtekɛʀ/ *nmf* librarian

bibliothèque /biblijɔtɛk/ *nf* (a) library
(b) bookcase

biblique /biblik/ *adj* biblical

bic® /bik/ *nm* biro®

bicarbonate /bikaʀbɔnat/ *nm* bicarbonate

bicentenaire /bisɑ̃tnɛʀ/ *nm* bicentenary, bicentennial

biceps /bisɛps/ *nm inv* biceps

biche /biʃ/ *nf* doe

bichonner /biʃɔne/ [1] *vtr* (colloq) to pamper

bicolore /bikɔlɔʀ/ *adj* ⟨flag⟩ two-coloured (GB); ⟨fabric⟩ two-tone

bicoque /bikɔk/ *nf* (colloq) dump (colloq), house

bicyclette /bisiklɛt/ *nf* (a) bicycle
(b) cycling

bidasse /bidas/ *nm* (colloq) soldier

bidet /bidɛ/ *nm* bidet

bidon /bidɔ̃/ **1** *adj inv* (colloq) bogus; phoney (colloq)

2 *nm* (a) can; drum; flask
(b) (colloq) stomach, paunch
(c) (colloq) c'est du ~ it is a load of hogwash (colloq)

bidonner: se bidonner /bidɔne/ [1] *v refl* (+ *v être*) (colloq) to laugh, to fall about (colloq)

bidonville /bidɔ̃vil/ *nm* shanty town

bidule /bidyl/ *nm* (colloq) thingy (GB) (colloq), thingamajig (colloq)

bielle /bjɛl/ *nf* connecting rod

bien /bjɛ̃/ **1** *adj inv* (a) être ~ dans un rôle to be good in a part; être ~ de sa personne to be good-looking; ce n'est pas ~ de mentir it's not nice to lie; ça fait ~ d'aller à l'opéra (colloq) it's the done thing to go to the opera
(b) well; ne pas se sentir ~ not to feel well; t'es pas ~ (colloq)! you're out of your mind (colloq)!
(c) je suis ~ dans ces bottes these boots are comfortable; on est ~ au soleil! isn't it nice in the sun!
(d) ⟨place⟩ un quartier ~ a nice district; des gens ~ respectable people

2 *adv* (a) well; ⟨function⟩ properly; ⟨interpret⟩ correctly; ~ joué! well done!; aller ~ ⟨person⟩ to be well; ⟨business⟩ to go well;

ni ~ ni mal so-so; **j'ai cru ~ faire** I thought I was doing the right thing; **c'est ~ fait pour elle!** it serves her right!; **tu ferais ~ d'y aller** it would be a good idea for you to go
(b) ⟨*mix*⟩ thoroughly; ⟨*fill*⟩ completely; ⟨*listen*⟩ carefully
(c) ⟨*presented*⟩ well; ⟨*furnished*⟩ tastefully; ⟨*live*⟩ comfortably; **femme ~ faite** shapely woman; **aller ~ ensemble** to go well together; **aller ~ à qn** to suit sb; **~ prendre une remarque** to take a remark in good part
(d) ⟨*nice, sad*⟩ very; ⟨*fear, enjoy*⟩ very much; ⟨*simple, true*⟩ quite; **il y a ~ longtemps** a very long time ago; **merci ~** thank you very much; **~ rire** to have a good laugh; **c'est ~ compris?** is that clear?; **~ au contraire** on the contrary; **~ mieux** much *or* far better; **~ sûr** of course; **~ entendu** *or* **évidemment** naturally; **il y a ~ des années** a good many years ago; **~ des fois** often, many a time
(e) je veux ~ t'aider I don't mind helping you; **j'aimerais ~ essayer** I would love to try
(f) il faut ~ que ça finisse it has just got to come to an end
(g) ça montre ~ que it just goes to show that; **je sais ~ que** I know that; **insiste ~** make sure you insist; **on verra ~** well, we'll see; **il le fait ~ lui, pourquoi pas moi?** if he can do it, why can't I?; **tu peux très ~ le faire toi-même** you can easily do it yourself; **que peut-il ~ faire à Paris?** what on earth can he be doing in Paris?
(h) definitely; **c'est ~ ce qu'il a dit** that's exactly what he said; **tu as ~ pris les clés?** are you sure you've got the keys?; **c'est ~ de lui!** it's just like him!; **c'est ~ le moment!** (ironic) great timing!; **c'est ~ le moment de partir!** (ironic) what a time to leave!
(i) at least; **elle a ~ 40 ans** she's at least 40
3 *nm* **(a)** good; **le ~ et le mal** good and evil; **ça fait du ~ aux enfants** it's good for the children; **vouloir le ~ de qn** to have sb's best interests at heart; **vouloir du ~ à qn** to wish sb well; **dire du ~/le plus grand ~ de qn** to speak well/very highly of sb
(b) possession; **des ~s considérables** substantial assets
4 bien que *phr* although
■ **~s de consommation** consumer goods; **~s immobiliers** real estate; **~s mobiliers** personal property; **~s personnels** private property

bien-être /bjɛ̃nɛtʀ/ *nm* **(a)** well-being
(b) welfare
(c) comforts

bienfaisance /bjɛ̃fəzɑ̃s/ *nf* charity

bienfaisant, ~e /bjɛ̃fəzɑ̃, ɑ̃t/ *adj* beneficial, beneficent

bienfait /bjɛ̃fɛ/ *nm* **(a)** kind deed; **~ du ciel** godsend
(b) beneficial effect

bienfaiteur, -trice /bjɛ̃fɛtœʀ, tʀis/ *nm,f* benefactor/benefactress

bien-fondé /bjɛ̃fɔ̃de/ *nm* (of idea) validity; (of claim) legitimacy

bien-pensant, ~e, *mpl* **~s** /bjɛ̃pɑ̃sɑ̃, ɑ̃t/ *adj* **(a)** right-thinking
(b) self-righteous

bienséance /bjɛ̃seɑ̃s/ *nf* propriety; **les règles de la ~** the rules of polite society

bientôt /bjɛ̃to/ *adv* soon; **à ~** see you soon

bienveillant, ~e /bjɛ̃vɛjɑ̃, ɑ̃t/ *adj* benevolent

bienvenu, ~e¹ /bjɛ̃vəny/ *adj* welcome

bienvenue² /bjɛ̃vəny/ *nf* welcome

bière /bjɛʀ/ *nf* **(a)** beer; **~ (à la) pression** draught (GB) *or* draft (US) beer
(b) coffin, casket (US)
■ **~ blonde** lager; **~ brune** ≈ stout; **~ rousse** brown ale

bifteck /biftɛk/ *nm* steak
IDIOMS **gagner son ~** (colloq) to earn a living

bifurcation /bifyʀkasjɔ̃/ *nf* (in road) fork

bifurquer /bifyʀke/ [1] *vi* **(a)** ⟨*road*⟩ to fork
(b) ⟨*driver*⟩ to turn off
(c) (in career) to change tack

bigame /bigam/ *adj* bigamous

bigamie /bigami/ *nf* bigamy

bigarré, ~e /bigaʀe/ *adj* **(a)** multicoloured (GB)
(b) ⟨*crowd*⟩ colourful (GB)

bigleux, -euse /biglø, øz/ *adj* (pej) (colloq) poor-sighted; **complètement ~** as blind as a bat (colloq)

bigorneau, *pl* **~x** /bigɔʀno/ *nm* winkle

bigot, ~e /bigo, ɔt/ *nm,f* religious zealot

bigoudi /bigudi/ *nm* roller, curler

bijou, *pl* **~x** /biʒu/ *nm* **(a)** piece of jewellery (GB) *or* jewelry (US)
(b) jewel; (figurative) gem

bijouterie /biʒutʀi/ *nf* (shop) jeweller's (GB), jewelry store (US)

bilan /bilɑ̃/ *nm* **(a)** balance sheet; **déposer son ~** to file a petition in bankruptcy
(b) outcome
(c) (after disaster) toll
(d) assessment; **~ de santé** check-up
(e) report

bilatéral, ~e, *mpl* **-aux** /bilateʀal, o/ *adj* bilateral

bile /bil/ *nf* bile
IDIOMS **se faire de la ~** (colloq) to worry

bilingue /bilɛ̃g/ *adj* bilingual

billard /bijaʀ/ *nm* **(a)** billiards
(b) billiard table
■ **~ américain** pool; **~ anglais** snooker
IDIOMS **passer sur le ~** (colloq) to have an operation

bille /bij/ *nf* **(a)** marble
(b) (billiard) ball

billet /bije/ *nm* **(a)** (bank)note, bill (US)
(b) ticket
■ **~ doux** love letter

billetterie /bijetʀi/ *nf* cash dispenser

billion /biljɔ̃/ *nm* billion (GB), trillion (US)

bimensuel /bimɑ̃sɥɛl/ *nm* fortnightly magazine (GB), semimonthly (US)

bimoteur /bimɔtœʀ/ nm twin-engined plane

binaire /binɛʀ/ adj binary

biniou /binju/ nm Breton bagpipes

binocles /binɔkl/ nf pl (colloq) specs (colloq), glasses

bio /bjo/ [1] adj inv (natural) **aliments ~** health foods; **produits ~** organic produce; **yaourt ~** bio yoghurt
[2] nf (colloq) biography

biochimie /bjoʃimi/ nf biochemistry

biodégradable /bjodegʀadabl/ adj biodegradable

biographie /bjɔgʀafi/ nf biography

biologie /bjɔlɔʒi/ nf biology

biophysique /bjofisik/ nf biophysics

bip /bip/ nm beep; **~ sonore** tone

bipède /bipɛd/ nm biped

biplace /biplas/ adj, nm two-seater

bique /bik/ nf (colloq) **une vieille ~** an old bag (colloq)

biréacteur /biʀeaktœʀ/ nm twin-engined jet

bis¹ /bis/ adv (a) (in address) bis; **33 ~ rue Juliette Lamber** 33 bis rue Juliette Lamber
(b) (at show, concert) encore

bis², ~e¹ /bi, biz/ adj greyish (GB) or grayish (US) brown

bisannuel, -elle /bizanɥɛl/ adj biennial

biscornu, ~e /biskɔʀny/ adj quirky

biscotte /biskɔt/ nf continental toast

biscuit /biskɥi/ nm biscuit (GB), cookie (US)
■ **~ à la cuillère** sponge finger (GB), ladyfinger (US); **~ salé** cracker

bise² /biz/ [1] adj f ▸ BIS²
[2] nf (a) (colloq) kiss; **faire la ~ à qn** to kiss sb on the cheeks
(b) North wind

biseau, pl ~x /bizo/ nm (a) bevel (edge); **tailler en ~** to bevel
(b) (tool) bevel

bison /bizɔ̃/ nm (a) bison
(b) buffalo

bissextile /bisɛkstil/ adj **année ~** leap year

bistouri /bistuʀi/ nm (Med) bistoury

bistro(t) /bistʀo/ nm (colloq) bistro, café

bit /bit/ nm bit

BIT /beit/ nm (abbr = **Bureau international du travail**) ILO

bitume /bitym/ nm (on road) asphalt

bivouac /bivwak/ nm bivouac

bizarre /bizaʀ/ adj odd, strange

blafard, ~e /blafaʀ, aʀd/ adj pale

blague /blag/ nf (colloq) (a) joke; **~ à part** seriously
(b) fib (colloq)
(c) trick; **faire une ~ à qn** to play a trick on sb

blaguer /blage/ [1] vi (colloq) to joke

blagueur, -euse /blagœʀ, øz/ nm,f (colloq) joker

blaireau, pl ~x /blɛʀo/ nm (a) badger
(b) shaving brush

blâmer /blɑme/ [1] vtr to criticize; to blame

blanc, blanche¹ /blɑ̃, blɑ̃ʃ/ [1] adj (gen) white; ⟨page⟩ blank; **~ cassé** off-white
[2] nm (a) white; **habillé/peint en ~** dressed in/painted white
(b) household linen
(c) white meat
(d) (egg) white
(e) blank; gap; **j'ai eu un ~** my mind went blank
(f) (colloq) correction fluid
(g) **tirer à ~** to fire blanks
[3] **blancs** nm pl (in chess, draughts) white

Blanc, Blanche /blɑ̃, blɑ̃ʃ/ nm,f white man/woman

blanc-bec, pl blancs-becs /blɑ̃bɛk/ nm greenhorn

blanchâtre /blɑ̃ʃɑtʀ/ adj whitish

blanche² /blɑ̃ʃ/ [1] adj f ▸ BLANCHE 1
[2] nf (Mus) minim (GB), half note (US)

blanchiment /blɑ̃ʃimɑ̃/ nm (a) (of money) laundering
(b) (of fabric, paper, pulp) bleaching

blanchir /blɑ̃ʃiʀ/ [3] [1] vtr (a) to whiten ⟨shoes⟩
(b) to clear ⟨name⟩
(c) to launder ⟨money⟩
[2] vi (a) to turn grey (GB) or gray (US)
(b) **faire ~** to blanch ⟨vegetables⟩
[3] **se blanchir** v refl (+ v être) to clear oneself

blanchisserie /blɑ̃ʃisʀi/ nf laundry

blanchisseur /blɑ̃ʃisœʀ/ nm (shop) laundry

blanchisseuse /blɑ̃ʃisøz/ nf laundress

blasé, ~e /blaze/ adj blasé

blason /blazɔ̃/ nm coat of arms
IDIOMS **redorer son ~** to restore one's reputation

blasphème /blasfɛm/ nm blasphemy

blasphémer /blasfeme/ [14] vi to blaspheme

blatte /blat/ nf cockroach

blé /ble/ nm wheat; **~ noir** buckwheat

bled /blɛd/ nm (colloq) village

blême /blɛm/ adj pale

blessant, ~e /blesɑ̃, ɑ̃t/ adj ⟨remark⟩ cutting

blessé, ~e /blese/ nm,f injured or wounded man/woman; casualty

blesser /blese/ [1] [1] vtr (a) to injure, to hurt; to wound; **il a été blessé à la tête** he sustained head injuries
(b) to hurt ⟨person, feelings⟩; to wound ⟨pride⟩
[2] **se blesser** v refl (+ v être) to hurt oneself

blessure /blesyʀ/ nf injury; wound

blet, blette /blɛ, blɛt/ adj overripe

bleu, ~**e** /blø/ **1** adj **(a)** blue
(b) ‹steak› very rare
2 nm **(a)** blue
(b) bruise
(c) ~ **de travail** overalls
(d) blue cheese
IDIOMS **avoir une peur** ~**e de qch** to be
scared stiff (colloq) of sth

bleuâtre /bløɑtʀ/ adj bluish

bleuet /bløɛ/ nm (Bot) cornflower

blindé, ~**e** /blɛ̃de/ adj armoured (GB)

blinder /blɛ̃de/ [1] vtr to put security
fittings on ‹door›; to armour-plate (GB) ‹car›

blizzard /blizaʀ/ nm blizzard

bloc /blɔk/ **1** nm **(a)** block; **faire** ~ **avec/
contre qn** to side with/unite against sb
(b) notepad; ~ **de papier à lettres** writing
pad
(c) (Comput) block
2 **à bloc** phr ‹screw› tightly; ‹inflate› fully
3 **en bloc** phr ‹deny› outright
■ ~ **opératoire** surgical unit

blocage /blɔkaʒ/ nm blocking; ~ **des
salaires** wage freeze

blockhaus /blɔkos/ nm inv blockhouse

bloc-notes, pl **blocs-notes** /blɔknɔt/
nm notepad

blocus /blɔkys/ nm inv blockade

blond, ~**e** /blɔ̃, ɔ̃d/ **1** adj **(a)** blonde (GB),
blond (US)
(b) ‹wheat› golden; ‹tobacco› light
2 nm,f (female) blonde (GB), blond (US);
(male) blond

bloqué, ~**e** /blɔke/ **1** pp ▶ BLOQUER
2 pp adj **(a)** blocked
(b) ‹mechanism, door› jammed; **elle/la
voiture est** ~**e** she/the car is stuck
(c) être ~ ‹activity› to be at a standstill;
‹situation› to be deadlocked

bloquer /blɔke/ [1] **1** vtr **(a)** to block
‹road›
(b) to lock ‹steering wheel›; to wedge ‹door›;
(accidentally) to jam ‹mechanism, door›
(c) to stop ‹vehicle, traveller›
(d) to freeze ‹prices›
(e) to stop ‹project›
(f) to lump [sth] together ‹days›
2 **se bloquer** v refl (+ v être) **(a)** ‹brakes,
door› to jam; ‹wheel› to lock
(b) to retreat

blottir: se blottir /blɔtiʀ/ [3] v refl
(+ v être) **se** ~ **contre** to huddle up against;
to snuggle up against

blouse /bluz/ nf **(a)** overall
(b) coat; ~ **blanche** white coat
(c) blouse

blouson /bluzɔ̃/ nm **(a)** blouson;
~ **d'aviateur** bomber jacket
(b) ~ **noir** ≈ rocker

blue-jean, pl ~**s** /bludʒin/ nm jeans

bluffer /blœfe/ [1] vtr, vi (colloq) to bluff

BN /been/ nf (abbr = **Bibliothèque
nationale**) national library in Paris

boa /bɔa/ nm boa

bobard /bɔbaʀ/ nm (colloq) fib (colloq), tall
story

bobine /bɔbin/ nf (of film, cable) reel

bobo /bobo/ nm (colloq) (baby talk) **(a)** pain
(b) scratch

bocage /bɔkaʒ/ nm hedged farmland

bocal, pl -**aux** /bɔkal, o/ nm jar; bowl

bœuf, pl **bœ** /bœf, pl bø/ nm **(a)** bullock (GB), steer
(US)
(b) ox
(c) beef
IDIOMS **faire un effet** ~ (colloq) to make a
fantastic (colloq) impression

bof /bɔf/ excl (colloq) 'tu préfères la mer ou la
montagne?'—'~!' 'which do you prefer, the
sea or the mountains?'—'I don't mind'

bogue /bɔg/ nf or m (Comput) bug; ~ **de l'an
2000** millennium bug

bohème /bɔɛm/ **1** adj bohemian
2 nf **la** ~ bohemia

bohémien, -ienne /bɔemjɛ̃, ɛn/ nm,f
Romany, gypsy

boire /bwaʀ/ [70] **1** vtr **(a)** to drink
(b) ‹paper› to soak up
2 **se boire** v refl (+ v être) **ce vin se boit
frais** this wine should be drunk chilled
IDIOMS ~ **comme un trou** (colloq) to drink
like a fish (colloq); **il y a à** ~ **et à manger
dans leur théorie** there's both good and bad
in their theory

bois /bwa/ **1** nm inv wood; **en** ~ ‹chair›
wooden; ‹cheque› dud (colloq); ~ **mort**
firewood
2 nm pl **(a)** antlers
(b) woodwind section
IDIOMS **être de** ~ to be insensitive; **il va voir
de quel** ~ **je me chauffe** (colloq) I'll show him

boisé, ~**e** /bwaze/ adj wooded

boiserie /bwazʀi/ nf ~(s) panelling (GB)

boisson /bwasɔ̃/ nf drink

boîte /bwat/ nf **(a)** (container) box
(b) (for food) tin (GB), can; **petits pois en** ~
canned peas
(c) (club) ~ **(de nuit)** nightclub
(d) (colloq) (company) firm; office
■ ~ **crânienne** cranium; ~ **à gants** glove
compartment; ~ **à** or **aux lettres** post box
(GB), mailbox (US); ~ **à** or **aux lettres
électronique** (Comput) electronic mailbox; ~ **à
musique** musical box (GB), music box (US);
~ **à outils** toolbox; ~ **postale, BP** PO Box;
~ **de vitesses** gearbox
IDIOMS **mettre qn en** ~ (colloq) to tease sb

boiter /bwate/ [1] vi to limp

boiteux, -euse /bwatø, øz/ **1** adj
(a) lame
(b) ‹chair› wobbly
(c) ‹argument, alliance› shaky
2 nm,f lame person

boîtier /bwatje/ nm (gen) case; (of camera)
body

boitiller /bwatije/ [1] vi to limp slightly

bol /bɔl/ nm **(a)** bowl; ~ **d'air** breath of
fresh air ····•·

(b) (colloq) luck; **coup de** ~ stroke of luck

bolée /bɔle/ *nf* ~ **de cidre** bowl of cider

bolide /bɔlid/ *nm* high-powered car

bombage /bɔ̃baʒ/ *nm* (action) graffiti spraying; (result) (sprayed) graffiti

bombardement /bɔ̃baʀdəmɑ̃/ *nm* (Mil) bombardment; bombing; shelling; ~ **aérien** air raid

bombarder /bɔ̃baʀde/ [1] *vtr* (a) to bombard; to bomb; to shell
(b) ~ **qn de questions** to bombard sb with questions
(c) (colloq) ~ **qn à un poste** to catapult sb into a job

bombardier /bɔ̃baʀdje/ *nm* (a) bomber
(b) bombardier

bombe /bɔ̃b/ *nf* (a) bomb; **faire l'effet d'une** ~ to come as a bombshell
(b) ~ (**aérosol**) spray
(c) riding hat
IDIOMS **partir à toute** ~ (colloq) to rush off

bombé, ~**e** /bɔ̃be/ *adj* (a) ⟨forehead⟩ domed; ⟨shape⟩ rounded
(b) ⟨road⟩ cambered

bomber /bɔ̃be/ [1] **1** *vtr* ~ **le torse** to thrust out one's chest; (figurative) to swell with pride
2 *vi* (a) ⟨plank⟩ to bulge out
(b) (colloq) to belt along (colloq)

bon, bonne[1] /bɔ̃, bɔn/ **1** *adj* (a) good; **prends un** ~ **pull** take a warm jumper; **elle est (bien) bonne** (colloq)! that's a good one!; (indignantly) I like that!; **voilà une bonne chose de faite!** that's that out of the way!; **nous sommes** ~**s derniers** we're well and truly last; **il n'est pas** ~ **à grand-chose** he's pretty useless; **il serait** ~ **qu'elle le sache** she ought to know; **à quoi** ~? what's the point?
(b) ⟨person, words⟩ kind; ⟨smile⟩ nice; **avoir** ~ **cœur** to be good-hearted
(c) ⟨time, answer⟩ right; **c'est** ~, **vous pouvez y aller** it's OK, you can go
(d) ⟨ticket⟩ valid; **tu es** ~ **pour la vaisselle, ce soir!** you're in line for the dishes tonight!
(e) **bonne nuit/chance** good night/luck
2 *nm,f* **les** ~**s et les méchants** good people and bad people; (in films) the good guys and the bad guys (colloq)
3 *nm* (a) coupon; voucher
(b) **il y a du** ~ **dans cet article** there are some good things in this article
4 *adv* **ça sent** ~! that smells good!; **il fait** ~ the weather's mild; **il fait** ~ **dans ta chambre** it's nice and warm in your room
5 pour de bon *phr* (a) really; **tu dis ça pour de** ~? are you serious?
(b) for good
■ ~ **de commande** order form; ~ **enfant** good-natured; ~ **de garantie** guarantee slip; ~ **marché** cheap; ~ **mot** witticism; ~ **à rien** good-for-nothing; ~ **sens** common sense; ~ **du Trésor** Treasury bond; ~ **vivant** bon viveur; **bonne action** good deed; **bonne femme** (derogatory) (colloq) woman, dame (US) (colloq); wife, old lady (colloq); **bonne pâte** good sort; **bonne sœur** (colloq) nun

bonbon /bɔ̃bɔ̃/ *nm* sweet (GB), candy (US)

bonbonne /bɔ̃bɔn/ *nf* (a) demijohn; (bigger) carboy
(b) (for gas) cylinder

bond /bɔ̃/ *nm* (a) leap; **se lever d'un** ~ to leap to one's feet
(b) (in time) jump
(c) (in profits, exports) leap; (in prices) jump (**de** in); **la médecine a fait un** ~ **en avant avec cette découverte** this discovery was a medical breakthrough
IDIOMS **saisir la balle au** ~ to seize the opportunity; **faire faux** ~ **à qn** to let sb down

bonde /bɔ̃d/ *nf* (a) (of swimming pool) outlet; (of sink) plughole
(b) (stopper) (in pool) outlet cover; (in sink) plug

bondé, ~**e** /bɔ̃de/ *adj* packed (**de** with)

bondir /bɔ̃diʀ/ [3] *vi* (a) to leap; ~ **de joie** to jump for joy
(b) ~ **sur qn/qch** to pounce on sb/sth
(c) ⟨animal⟩ to leap about
(d) **ça m'a fait** ~ I was absolutely furious (about it)

bonheur /bɔnœʀ/ *nm* (a) happiness
(b) pleasure; **faire le** ~ **de qn** ⟨present⟩ to make sb happy; ⟨event, exhibition⟩ to delight sb
(c) **par** ~ fortunately; **au petit** ~ (**la chance**) at random; **tu ne connais pas ton** ~! you don't realize how lucky you are!
IDIOMS **alors, tu as trouvé ton** ~? (colloq) did you find what you wanted?

bonhomie /bɔnɔmi/ *nf* good-nature

bonhomme, *pl* ~**s, bonshommes** /bɔnɔm, bɔzɔm/ **1** *adj* good-natured
2 *nm* (colloq) (a) fellow, chap (colloq)
(b) husband, old man (colloq)
■ ~ **de neige** snowman
IDIOMS **aller** *or* **suivre son petit** ~ **de chemin** to go peacefully along

bonification /bɔnifikasjɔ̃/ *nf* (a) (in sport) bonus points
(b) (financial) bonus

boniments /bɔnimɑ̃/ *nm pl* stories; **raconter des** ~ **à qn** to give sb some story (colloq) (**à propos de** about); to smooth-talk sb

bonjour /bɔ̃ʒuʀ/ *nm, excl* hello
IDIOMS **être simple comme** ~ (colloq) to be very easy

bonne[2] /bɔn/ **1** *adj f* ▶ **BON** 1
2 *nf* (a) maid, servant
(b) **tu en as de** ~**s, toi!** you must be joking!
■ ~ **d'enfants** nanny

bonnement /bɔnmɑ̃/ *adv* **tout** ~ (quite) simply

bonnet /bɔnε/ *nm* (a) hat; (for baby) bonnet
(b) (on bra) cup
■ ~ **de nuit** nightcap; (figurative) wet blanket (colloq)

bonneterie /bɔnεtʀi/ *nf* hosiery

bonshommes ▶ **BONHOMME**

bonsoir /bɔ̃swaʀ/ *nm, excl* good evening, good night

bonté /bɔ̃te/ *nf* (a) kindness
(b) (of God) goodness

bonus /bɔnys/ *nm inv* no-claims bonus

boom /bum/ *nm* boom; **en plein ~** booming

bord /bɔʀ/ *nm* **(a)** (of plate, bed) edge; (of road) side; (of river) bank; **au ~ de** on *or* at the edge of ‹lake, road›; (figurative) on the verge of; **au ~ de la mer** at the seaside; by the sea; **~ à ~** edge-to-edge
(b) (of cup) rim; (of hat) brim
(c) à ~ ‹work› on board; **de ~** ‹instruments, staff› on board; **on fera** (colloq) **avec les moyens du ~** we'll make do with what we've got
(d) side; **être du même ~** to be on the same side

bordeaux /bɔʀdo/ **1** *adj inv* burgundy
2 *nm* Bordeaux; **~ rouge** claret

border /bɔʀde/ [1] *vtr* **(a)** to line (**de** with)
(b) ‹plants› to border ‹lake›
(c) to tuck [sb] in
(d) to edge ‹garment› (**de** with)

bordereau, *pl* **~x** /bɔʀdəʀo/ *nm* form, slip

bordure /bɔʀdyʀ/ **1** *nf* **(a)** (of sports ground, carpet) border
(b) (of road, platform) edge
2 en bordure de *phr* **(a)** next to ‹park, canal, track›
(b) on the edge of ‹park›; on the side of ‹road›
(c) just outside ‹village›

boréal, **~e**, *mpl* **-aux** /bɔʀeal, o/ *adj* boreal

borgne /bɔʀɲ/ *adj* one-eyed

borne /bɔʀn/ **1** *nf* **(a)** **~ (kilométrique)** kilometre (GB) marker
(b) bollard (GB), post (US)
(c) (colloq) kilometre (GB)
(d) (for electricity) terminal
2 bornes *nf pl* leur ambition est sans **~s** their ambition knows no bounds
■ **~ téléphonique** emergency telephone; taxi stand telephone

borné, **~e** /bɔʀne/ *adj* narrow-minded

borner: se borner /bɔʀne/ [1] *v refl* (**+ v être**) **(a)** se **~ à faire** to content oneself with doing
(b) se **~ à faire** to be limited to doing

bosquet /bɔskɛ/ *nm* grove

bosse /bɔs/ *nf* **(a)** hump
(b) bump
(c) dent
IDIOMS **avoir la ~ de** (colloq) to have a flair for; **rouler sa ~** to knock about

bosseler /bɔsle/ [19] *vtr* to dent; (in metalwork) to emboss

bosser /bɔse/ [1] *vi* (colloq) to work

bossu, **~e** /bɔsy/ *adj* hunchbacked

bot /bo/ *adj m* **pied ~** club foot

botanique /bɔtanik/ **1** *adj* botanical
2 *nf* botany

botte /bɔt/ *nf* **(a)** boot
(b) (of flowers) bunch; (of hay) bale
■ **~s de caoutchouc** wellington boots

botter /bɔte/ [1] *vtr* **(a)** ça le botte (colloq)! he loves it!
(b) to kick

bottin® /bɔtɛ̃/ *nm* telephone directory

bottine /bɔtin/ *nf* ankle-boot

bouc /buk/ *nm* **(a)** billy goat
(b) goatee
■ **~ émissaire** scapegoat

boucan /bukɑ̃/ *nm* (colloq) din, racket (colloq)

bouche /buʃ/ *nf* mouth; **faire la fine ~ devant qch** to turn one's nose up at sth
■ **~ d'aération** air vent; **~ d'égout** manhole; **~ d'incendie** fire hydrant; **~ de métro** tube (GB) *or* subway (US) entrance

bouché, **~e**[1] /buʃe/ **1** *pp* ▶ BOUCHER[1]
2 *pp adj* **(a)** blocked
(b) ‹profession› oversubscribed
(c) (colloq) dim, (colloq) stupid
(d) cidre **~** bottled cider

bouche-à-bouche /buʃabuʃ/ *nm inv* mouth-to-mouth resuscitation

bouche-à-oreille /buʃaɔʀɛj/ *nm inv* le **~** word of mouth

bouchée[2] /buʃe/ *nf* mouthful; **pour une ~ de pain** for next to nothing; **mettre les ~s doubles** to double one's efforts

boucher[1] /buʃe/ [1] **1** *vtr* **(a)** to cork
(b) to block, to clog (up)
(c) to fill ‹crack›
2 se boucher *v refl* (**+ v être**) **(a)** se **~ le nez** to hold one's nose; se **~ les oreilles** to put one's fingers in one's ears
(b) to get blocked
IDIOMS en **~ un coin à qn** (colloq) to amaze sb

boucher[2], **-ère** /buʃe, ɛʀ/ *nm,f* butcher

boucherie /buʃʀi/ *nf* **(a)** butcher's shop
(b) butcher's trade
(c) slaughter

bouchon /buʃɔ̃/ *nm* **(a)** cork
(b) (screw)cap
(c) (of wax) plug
(d) traffic jam
(e) (in fishing) float

boucle /bukl/ *nf* **(a)** buckle; **~ d'oreille** earring
(b) curl
(c) loop
(d) (Comput) loop

bouclé, **~e** /bukle/ *adj* curly

boucler /bukle/ [1] *vtr* **(a)** to fasten ‹belt›
(b) (colloq) to lock ‹door›
(c) (colloq) to cordon off ‹district›
(d) (colloq) to complete ‹investigation›
(e) (colloq) to lock [sb] up
IDIOMS **la ~** (colloq) to shut up; **~ la boucle** to come full circle

bouclier /buklije/ *nm* shield

bouddhisme /budism/ *nm* Buddhism

bouder /bude/ [1] *vi* to sulk

bouderie /budʀi/ *nf* sulking

boudin /budɛ̃/ *nm* ≈ blood sausage

boudiné, **~e** /budine/ *adj* podgy

boudiner /budine/ [1] *vtr* être boudiné dans qch to be squeezed into sth

boue /bu/ *nf* (a) (gen, figurative) mud
(b) silt

bouée /bwe/ *nf* (a) rubber ring
(b) buoy
■ ~ de sauvetage *or* de secours lifebelt (GB), life preserver (US)

boueux, -euse /buø, øz/ *adj* muddy

bouffant, ~e /bufã, ãt/ *adj* (a) baggy
(b) ⟨sleeves⟩ puffed
(c) ⟨hairstyle⟩ bouffant

bouffe /buf/ *nf* (colloq) (a) eating
(b) food
(c) meal

bouffée /bufe/ *nf* (of tobacco, steam) puff; une ~ d'air frais a breath of fresh air
■ ~ de chaleur hot flush (GB), hot flash (US)

bouffer (colloq) /bufe/ [1] **1** *vtr* to eat
2 *vi* to eat; (greedily) to stuff oneself (colloq)

bouffi, ~e /bufi/ *adj* puffy

bouffon /bufɔ̃/ *nm* (a) clown
(b) jester; buffoon

bouffonnerie /bufɔnʀi/ *nf* (a) (actions) antics
(b) (for comic effect) buffoonery
(c) (intrinsic stupidity) ridiculousness
(d) (in theatre) farce

bougeoir /buʒwaʀ/ *nm* (a) candleholder
(b) candlestick

bougeotte /buʒɔt/ *nf* (colloq) avoir la ~ to be restless

bouger /buʒe/ [13] **1** *vtr* to move
2 *vi* (a) to move
(b) (colloq) ⟨sector, company⟩ to be on the move
(c) (colloq) ville qui bouge lively town
3 se bouger *v refl* (+ *v être*) (colloq) (a) to get a move on (colloq)
(b) to put some effort in

bougie /buʒi/ *nf* (a) candle
(b) (Tech) spark plug

bougonner /bugɔne/ [1] *vi* to grumble

bouillabaisse /bujabɛs/ *nf* fish soup

bouillant, ~e /bujã, ãt/ *adj* boiling (hot)

bouille /buj/ *nf* (colloq) face

bouilli, ~e /buji/ ▶ BOUILLIR

bouillie /buji/ *nf* (a) gruel; en ~ mushy; mettre qn/qch en ~ to reduce sb/sth to a pulp
(b) baby cereal

bouillir /bujiʀ/ [31] *vi* (a) to boil
(b) to be seething (de with)

bouilloire /bujwaʀ/ *nf* kettle

bouillon /bujɔ̃/ *nm* (a) broth
(b) (Culin) stock
(c) bouillir à gros ~s to boil fiercely

bouillonnant, ~e /bujɔnã, ãt/ *adj* ⟨water⟩ foaming; ⟨person⟩ lively

bouillonner /bujɔne/ [1] *vi* (a) to bubble
(b) ~ d'activité to be bustling with activity

bouillotte /bujɔt/ *nf* hot-water bottle

boulanger, -ère /bulãʒe, ɛʀ/ *nm,f* baker

boulangerie /bulãʒʀi/ *nf* bakery

boulangerie-pâtisserie, *pl* **boulangeries-pâtisseries** /bulãʒʀipɑtisʀi/ *nf* bakery (*selling cakes and pastries*)

boule /bul/ *nf* (gen) ball; (in bowling) bowl; mettre qch en ~ to roll sth up into a ball
■ ~ de neige snowball; ~ Quiès® earplug
IDIOMS il a perdu la ~ (colloq) he's gone mad; mettre qn en ~ (colloq) to make sb furious

bouleau, *pl* ~**x** /bulo/ *nm* birch

bouledogue /buldɔg/ *nm* bulldog

boulet /bulɛ/ *nm* (a) ~ (de canon) cannonball
(b) ball and chain
(c) (figurative) millstone

boulette /bulɛt/ *nf* (a) (of bread, paper) pellet
(b) ~ de viande meatball
(c) (colloq) blunder

boulevard /bulvaʀ/ *nm* boulevard
■ ~ périphérique ring road (GB), beltway (US)

bouleversant, ~e /bulvɛʀsã, ãt/ *adj* deeply moving

bouleversement /bulvɛʀsəmã/ *nm* upheaval

bouleverser /bulvɛʀse/ [1] *vtr* (a) to move [sb] deeply
(b) ⟨experience⟩ to shatter
(c) to turn ⟨sth⟩ upside down ⟨house, files⟩
(d) to disrupt ⟨schedule⟩
(e) to change [sth] dramatically ⟨lifestyle⟩

boulier /bulje/ *nm* abacus

boulimie /bulimi/ *nf* bulimia

boulon /bulɔ̃/ *nm* bolt

boulot, -otte /bulo, ɔt/ **1** *adj* tubby
2 *nm* (colloq) (a) work
(b) job

boulotter /bulɔte/ [1] *vtr, vi* (colloq) to eat

boum[1] /bum/ *nm* (a) bang
(b) (colloq) en plein ~ ⟨business⟩ booming; faire un ~ ⟨birth rates⟩ to soar

boum[2] /bum/ *nf* party

bouquet /bukɛ/ *nm* (a) ~ (de fleurs) bunch of flowers; bouquet
(b) (of firework display) final flourish; c'est le ~! (colloq) (figurative) that's the limit! (colloq)

bouquin /bukɛ̃/ *nm* (colloq) book

bouquiner /bukine/ [1] *vtr, vi* (colloq) to read

bourbier /buʀbje/ *nm* quagmire

bourde /buʀd/ *nf* blunder

bourdon /buʀdɔ̃/ *nm* bumblebee

bourdonnement /buʀdɔnmã/ *nm* (of insect) buzzing; (of engine) hum; (of plane) drone

bourdonner /buʀdɔne/ [1] *vi* to buzz; to hum

bourg /buʀ/ *nm* market town

bourgeois, ~e /buʀʒwa, az/ **1** *adj* bourgeois
2 *nm,f* (a) middle-class person
(b) (in Ancien Regime) bourgeois
(c) burgher

bourgeoisie /buRʒwazi/ *nf* (a) middle classes
(b) bourgeoisie

bourgeon /buRʒɔ̃/ *nm* bud; **en ~s** in bud

bourgeonner /buRʒɔne/ [1] *vi* to bud

bourrage /buRaʒ/ *nm* **~ de crâne** brainwashing

bourrasque /buRask/ *nf* (of wind) gust

bourratif, **-ive** /buRatif, iv/ *adj* very filling, stodgy

bourre /buR/ *nf* (colloq) **être à la ~** to be pushed for time

bourré, **~e** /buRe/ *adj* ⟨*train, museum*⟩ packed; ⟨*case, bag*⟩ bulging (**de** with); **~ de fric** (colloq) stinking rich (colloq)

bourreau, *pl* **~x** /buRo/ *nm* executioner

bourrelet /buRlɛ/ *nm* roll of fat

bourrer /buRe/ [1] *vtr* (a) to cram [sth] full; to fill ⟨*pipe*⟩
(b) (colloq) **~ qn de** to dose sb up with ⟨*medicine*⟩

bourricot /buRiko/ *nm* donkey

bourrique /buRik/ *nf* (a) donkey
(b) (colloq) pig-headed person

bourru, **~e** /buRy/ *adj* gruff

bourse /buRs/ *nf* (a) grant (GB), scholarship (US)
(b) purse

Bourse /buRs/ *nf* (a) stock exchange
(b) shares; **une société de ~** a broking (GB) *or* brokerage (US) firm

boursicoter /buRsikɔte/ [1] *vi* to dabble in stocks and shares

boursier, **-ière** /buRsje, ɛR/ ⓵ *adj* **le marché ~** share prices
⓶ *nm,f* grant holder (GB), scholarship student (US)

boursouflé, **~e** /buRsufle/ *adj*
(a) blistered
(b) puffy
(c) ⟨*body*⟩ bloated

bousculade /buskylad/ *nf* (a) jostling; (accidental) crush
(b) rush

bousculer /buskyle/ [1] ⓵ *vtr* (a) to push, to jostle ⟨*person*⟩
(b) to rush
⓶ **se bousculer** *v refl* (+ *v être*) to fall over each other (**pour faire** to do)

bouse /buz/ *nf* **une ~ (de vache)** a cowpat

bousiller /buzije/ [1] *vtr* (colloq) to wreck ⟨*engine*⟩; to smash up ⟨*car*⟩

boussole /busɔl/ *nf* compass

bout /bu/ *nm* (a) end; tip; (of shoe) toe; **au ~ du jardin** at the bottom of the garden; **aller jusqu'au ~** to go all the way; **aller (jusqu') au ~ de** to follow through ⟨*idea, demand*⟩; **elle est à ~** she can't take any more; **ne me pousse pas à ~** don't push me; **être à ~ d'arguments** to have run out of arguments; **venir à ~ de** to overcome ⟨*difficulty*⟩; to get through ⟨*task, meal*⟩; **au ~ du compte** in the end; **à ~ portant** at point-blank range
(b) (of bread, paper) piece; (of land) bit

■ **~ de chou** (colloq) sweet little thing (colloq); **~ d'essai** screen test
IDIOMS **tenir le bon ~** (colloq) to be on the right track; **ne pas être au ~ de ses peines** not to be out of the woods yet

boutade /butad/ *nf* witticism

boute-en-train /butɑ̃tRɛ̃/ *nmf inv* live wire (figurative)

bouteille /butɛj/ *nf* (gen) bottle; (of gas) cylinder
IDIOMS **prendre de la ~** (colloq) to be getting on (a bit)

boutique /butik/ *nf* shop (GB), store (US)

boutiquier, **-ière** /butikje, ɛR/ *nm,f* shopkeeper

bouton /butɔ̃/ *nm* (a) (on clothes) button
(b) knob; button
(c) (Med) spot (GB), pimple (US)
(d) (flower) bud
■ **~ de fièvre** cold sore; **~ de manchette** cuff link; **~ de porte** doorknob; **~ d'or** buttercup

boutonner /butɔne/ [1] *vtr*, **se boutonner** *v refl* (+ *v être*) to button up

boutonneux, **-euse** /butɔnø, øz/ *adj* spotty (GB), pimply (US)

boutonnière /butɔnjɛR/ *nf* buttonhole

bouture /butyR/ *nf* cutting

bovin, **~e** /bɔvɛ̃, in/ ⓵ *adj* bovine
⓶ *nm* bovine; **des ~s** cattle

box, *pl* **boxes** /bɔks/ *nm* (a) lock-up garage
(b) (for horse) stall
(c) (in bar) alcove
■ **~ des accusés** (Law) dock

boxe /bɔks/ *nf* (Sport) boxing; **~ française** savate

boxer /bɔkse/ [1] *vi* (Sport) to box

boxeur /bɔksœR/ *nm* (Sport) boxer

boyau, *pl* **~x** /bwajo/ *nm* (a) gut
(b) catgut
(c) (for sausage) casing
(d) tubeless tyre (GB) *or* tire (US)

boycotter /bɔjkɔte/ [1] *vtr* to boycott

BP *written abbr* ▶ **BOÎTE**

bracelet /bRaslɛ/ *nm* (a) bracelet; bangle
(b) wristband; **~ de montre** watchstrap

braconnier /bRakɔnje/ *nm* poacher

brader /bRade/ [1] *vtr* (a) to sell cheaply
(b) to sell off

braderie /bRadRi/ *nf* (a) street market
(b) discount store
(c) clearance sale

braguette /bRagɛt/ *nf* flies (GB), fly (US)

braille /bRaj/ *nm* Braille

brailler /bRaje/ [1] *vi* (colloq) (a) to yell
(b) ⟨*child, singer*⟩ to bawl

braire /bRɛR/ [58] *vi* to bray

braise /bRɛz/ *nf* live embers

brancard /bRɑ̃kaR/ *nm* stretcher

branchage /bRɑ̃ʃaʒ/ *nm* branches

branche /bRɑ̃ʃ/ *nf* (a) (of tree) branch
(b) **céleri en ~s** sticks of celery
(c) field, sector

····>

(d) (of family) branch
(e) (of candelabra) branch; (of spectacles) arm; (of star) point

branché, ~e /bʀɑ̃ʃe/ adj (colloq) trendy (colloq)

branchement /bʀɑ̃ʃmɑ̃/ nm **(a)** (electrical) connection
(b) (for water) branch pipe; (for electricity) lead (GB), cable (US)

brancher /bʀɑ̃ʃe/ [1] vtr **(a)** to plug in
(b) to connect (up) ⟨water, electricity⟩
(c) (colloq) ~ qn sur to get sb onto ⟨topic⟩
(d) (colloq) je vais au cinéma, ça te branche? I'm going to the cinema, are you interested?

branchie /bʀɑ̃ʃi/ nf (of fish) gill

brandir /bʀɑ̃diʀ/ [3] vtr to brandish

branlant, ~e /bʀɑ̃lɑ̃, ɑ̃t/ adj ⟨chair⟩ rickety; ⟨tooth⟩ loose; ⟨argument⟩ shaky

branle /bʀɑ̃l/ nm mettre qch en ~ to set [sth] in motion ⟨project, convoy⟩

branle-bas /bʀɑ̃lba/ nm inv commotion
■ ~ de combat (Mil) action stations

branler /bʀɑ̃le/ [1] vi ⟨wall⟩ to wobble; ⟨chair⟩ to be rickety; ⟨tooth⟩ to be loose

braquage /bʀakaʒ/ nm (colloq) robbery

braquer /bʀake/ [1] **1** vtr **(a)** to point ⟨gun, camera⟩ (sur, vers at); to turn or fix ⟨eyes⟩ (sur, vers on)
(b) ~ à gauche/droite to turn hard left/right
(c) (colloq) to point a gun at
(d) (colloq) to rob ⟨bank⟩
(e) (colloq) ~ qn contre qn/qch to turn sb against sb/sth
2 vi ⟨driver⟩ to turn the wheel full lock (GB) or all the way (US)
3 se braquer v refl (+ v être) to dig one's heels in

bras /bʀɑ/ nm inv **(a)** arm; ~ dessus ~ dessous arm in arm; porter qch à bout de ~ (figurative) to keep sth afloat; en ~ de chemise in one's shirtsleeves
(b) manpower, labour (GB)
(c) (of river) branch; ~ de mer sound
(d) (of armchair) arm
■ ~ droit right hand man; ~ de fer arm wrestling; (figurative) trial of strength
IDIOMS les ~ m'en tombent I'm absolutely speechless; avoir le ~ long to have a lot of influence

brasier /bʀazje/ nm inferno

bras-le-corps: à bras-le-corps /abʀalkɔʀ/ phr ⟨lift⟩ bodily

brassage /bʀasaʒ/ nm **(a)** (of beer) brewing
(b) (mixing) (of people) intermingling; (of ideas, cultures) cross-fertilization

brassard /bʀasaʀ/ nm armband

brasse /bʀas/ nf (Sport) breaststroke

brasser /bʀase/ [1] vtr **(a)** to toss around ⟨ideas⟩; to shuffle around ⟨papers⟩; to intermingle ⟨population⟩; il brasse des millions he handles big money
(b) to brew ⟨beer⟩

brasserie /bʀasʀi/ nf **(a)** brasserie
(b) brewery

brasseur, -euse /bʀasœʀ, øz/ nm,f brewer

brassière /bʀasjɛʀ/ nf **(a)** baby's top
(b) crop top

brave /bʀav/ adj **(a)** nice; un ~ homme a nice man
(b) brave; un homme ~ a brave man

braver /bʀave/ [1] vtr to defy ⟨person⟩; to brave ⟨storm⟩

bravo /bʀavo/ excl bravo!; well done!

bravoure /bʀavuʀ/ nf bravery

break /bʀɛk/ nm estate car (GB), station wagon (US)

brebis /bʀəbi/ nf inv ewe

brèche /bʀɛʃ/ nf **(a)** hole, gap
(b) (Mil) breach

bréchet /bʀeʃɛ/ nm wishbone

bredouille /bʀəduj/ adj empty-handed

bredouiller /bʀəduje/ [1] vtr, vi to mumble

bref, brève¹ /bʀɛf, bʀɛv/ **1** adj brief; short
2 adv (en) ~ in short

breloque /bʀəlɔk/ nf (on bracelet) charm

Brésil /bʀezil/ pr nm Brazil

Bretagne /bʀətaɲ/ pr nf Brittany

bretelle /bʀətɛl/ **1** nf **(a)** (gen) strap
(b) slip road (GB), ramp (US)
2 bretelles nf pl braces

breton, -onne /bʀətɔ̃, ɔn/ **1** adj Breton
2 nm (language) Breton

breuvage /bʀœvaʒ/ nm beverage

brève² /bʀɛv/ **1** adj f ▶ BREF 1
2 nf news flash

brevet /bʀəvɛ/ nm **(a)** ~ (d'invention) patent
(b) ~ de secourisme first aid certificate; ~ de pilote pilot's licence (GB)
■ ~ de technicien supérieur, BTS advanced vocational diploma

breveter /bʀəvte/ [20] vtr (faire) ~ to patent

bréviaire /bʀevjɛʀ/ nm breviary

bribes /bʀib/ nf pl (of conversation) snatches

bric: de bric et de broc /dəbʀiked(ə)bʀɔk/ phr ⟨furnished⟩ with bits and pieces

bric-à-brac /bʀikabʀak/ nm inv bric-à-brac

bricolage /bʀikɔlaʒ/ nm DIY (GB), do-it-yourself

bricole /bʀikɔl/ nf acheter une ~ to buy a little something; des ~s bits and pieces

bricoler /bʀikɔle/ [1] **1** vtr (colloq) **(a)** to tinker with
(b) to throw [sth] together
2 vi to do DIY (GB), to fix things (US)

bride /bʀid/ nf **(a)** bridle
(b) button loop
IDIOMS partir à ~ abattue to dash off; avoir la ~ sur le cou to have free rein

bridé, ~e /bʀide/ adj yeux ~s slanting eyes

b

brièvement /bʀijɛvmɑ̃/ adv briefly
brigade /bʀigad/ nf (a) (Mil) brigade
 (b) (in police) squad
brigadier /bʀigadje/ nm (a) ≈ corporal
 (b) fire chief
brigand /bʀigɑ̃/ nm brigand, bandit
brillamment /bʀijamɑ̃/ adv brilliantly
brillant, ∼e /bʀijɑ̃, ɑ̃t/ ① adj (a) bright;
 shiny; glistening
 (b) brilliant
 ② nm (cut) diamond, brilliant
briller /bʀije/ [1] vi (a) ⟨sun⟩ to shine;
 ⟨flame⟩ to burn brightly; ⟨gem⟩ to sparkle;
 ⟨nose⟩ to be shiny
 (b) ∼ de ⟨eyes⟩ to blaze with ⟨anger⟩
 (c) ⟨person⟩ to shine; **elle brille par son
 esprit** she's extremely witty
brimade /bʀimad/ nf bullying
brimer /bʀime/ [1] vtr (a) to bully
 (b) **se sentir brimé** to feel picked on
brin /bʀɛ̃/ nm (a) (of parsley) sprig; (of straw)
 wisp; (of grass) blade
 (b) **un ∼ de** a bit of
brindille /bʀɛ̃dij/ nf twig
bringue /bʀɛ̃g/ nf (colloq) (a) drinking
 party
 (b) rave-up (colloq)
 (c) (girl) **(grande) ∼** beanpole
brinquebaler /bʀɛ̃kbale/ [1] vi ⟨load⟩ to
 rattle about; ⟨vehicle⟩ to jolt along
brio /bʀijo/ nm brilliance; (Mus) brio
brioche /bʀijɔʃ/ nf (a) brioche, (sweet)
 bun
 (b) (colloq) paunch
brioché, ∼e /bʀijɔʃe/ adj (Culin) brioche
brique /bʀik/ nf (a) brick
 (b) (for milk, juice) carton
briquer /bʀike/ [1] vtr to polish [sth] up
briquet /bʀike/ nm (cigarette) lighter
brise /bʀiz/ nf breeze; **bonne ∼** fresh
 breeze
brise-glace /bʀizglas/ nm inv icebreaker
briser /bʀize/ [1] ① vtr (a) (gen) to break;
 to break down ⟨resistance⟩
 (b) to shatter ⟨dream⟩; to destroy ⟨career,
 person⟩
 (c) to shatter ⟨person⟩
 ② **se briser** v refl (+ v être) (a) to break
 (b) ⟨dream⟩ to be shattered
 (c) ⟨voice⟩ to break
brise-tout /bʀiztu/ nm inv (person)
 butterfingers
briseur, -euse /bʀizœʀ, øz/ nm,f wrecker
 ■ ∼ **de grève** strike breaker
brisure /bʀizyʀ/ nf (a) crack
 (b) fragment
britannique /bʀitanik/ adj British
Britannique /bʀitanik/ nmf **un/une ∼** a
 British man/woman; **les ∼s** the British
 (people)
broc /bʀo/ nm ewer
brocante /bʀokɑ̃t/ nf (a) bric-à-brac trade
 (b) flea market

broche /bʀoʃ/ nf (a) brooch
 (b) (for roasting) spit
 (c) (in surgery) pin
brocher /bʀoʃe/ [1] vtr to bind [sth] (with
 paper) ⟨book⟩; **livre broché** paperback
brochet /bʀoʃɛ/ nm (Zool) pike
brochette /bʀoʃɛt/ nf (a) skewer
 (b) kebab
brochure /bʀoʃyʀ/ nf (a) booklet
 (b) (travel) brochure
brocoli /bʀokoli/ nm broccoli
broder /bʀode/ [1] vtr, vi to embroider
broderie /bʀodʀi/ nf embroidery
bromure /bʀomyʀ/ nm bromide
bronche /bʀɔ̃ʃ/ nf **les ∼s** the bronchial
 tubes
broncher /bʀɔ̃ʃe/ [1] vi **sans ∼** without
 turning a hair
bronchite /bʀɔ̃ʃit/ nf bronchitis
bronzage /bʀɔ̃zaʒ/ nm (sun)tan
bronze /bʀɔ̃z/ nm bronze
bronzé, ∼e /bʀɔ̃ze/ adj ⟨person⟩
 (sun-)tanned
bronzer /bʀɔ̃ze/ [1] vi to get a tan, to go
 brown
brossage /bʀosaʒ/ nm (of hair, teeth)
 brushing
brosse /bʀos/ nf brush; **donner un coup de
 ∼ à qch** to give sth a brush; **avoir les
 cheveux (taillés) en ∼** to have a crew cut
brosser /bʀose/ [1] ① vtr (a) to brush; to
 scrub
 (b) to give a quick outline of
 ② **se brosser** v refl (+ v être) to brush
 oneself down; **se ∼ les dents** to brush one's
 teeth
brouette /bʀuɛt/ nf wheelbarrow
brouhaha /bʀuaa/ nm hubbub
brouillard /bʀujaʀ/ nm fog
brouille /bʀuj/ nf (a) quarrel
 (b) rift
brouiller /bʀuje/ [1] ① vtr (a) to make
 [sth] cloudy ⟨liquid⟩; to blur ⟨text, vision⟩;
 ∼ les cartes to confuse or cloud the issue
 (b) to jam ⟨signal⟩; to interfere with
 ⟨reception⟩
 ② **se brouiller** v refl (+ v être) (a) to fall
 out (**avec** with)
 (b) ⟨liquid⟩ to become cloudy; ⟨vision⟩ to
 become blurred; ⟨mind⟩ to become confused;
 avoir le teint brouillé to look ill
brouillon, -onne /bʀujɔ̃, ɔn/ ① adj
 (a) untidy
 (b) disorganized
 (c) muddled
 ② nm (a) rough draft
 (b) rough paper
broussaille /bʀusaj/ nf (a) undergrowth
 (b) scrub
 (c) bushes
brousse /bʀus/ nf bush; **en pleine ∼**
 (colloq) in the sticks (colloq)
brouter /bʀute/ [1] vtr to nibble; to graze

brouteur , **-euse** /bʀutœʀ øz/ nm,f
browser

broyer /bʀwaje/ [23] vtr (a) to grind
⟨wheat⟩
(b) to crush
IDIOMS ∼ du noir to brood

broyeur, **-euse** /bʀwajœʀ, øz/ nm
(machine) crusher, grinder

bru /bʀy/ nf daughter-in-law

brugnon /bʀyɲɔ̃/ nm nectarine

bruiner /bʀɥine/ [1] v impers to drizzle

bruissement /bʀɥismɑ̃/ nm (of leaves)
rustle; (of brook) babbling

bruit /bʀɥi/ nm (a) noise; ∼ étouffé thud;
un ∼ de ferraille a clang
(b) noise, din; ∼ infernal or d'enfer awful
racket; sans ∼ silently
(c) le film a fait beaucoup de ∼ the film
attracted a lot of attention
(d) ∼ (de couloir) rumour (GB)

bruitage /bʀɥitaʒ/ nm sound effects

bruiteur /bʀɥitœʀ/ nm sound effects
engineer

brûlant, **∼e** /bʀylɑ̃, ɑ̃t/ adj (a) ⟨tea⟩
boiling hot; ⟨sand, radiator, person⟩ burning
hot; ⟨sun⟩ blazing
(b) ⟨issue⟩ burning
(c) ⟨passion⟩ burning

brûlé, **∼e** /bʀyle/ **1** nm,f un grand ∼ a
third degree burns victim; service des
grands ∼s burns unit
2 nm ça sent le ∼ there's a smell of
burning

brûle-parfum(s) /bʀylpaʀfœ̃/ nm inv
incense burner

brûle-pourpoint: à brûle-pourpoint
/abʀylpuʀpwɛ̃/ phr point-blank

brûler /bʀyle/ [1] **1** vtr (a) to burn
⟨papers⟩; to set fire to ⟨house⟩
(b) to burn ⟨fuel⟩; to use ⟨electricity⟩
(c) ⟨acid⟩ to burn; ⟨water⟩ to scald; j'ai les
yeux qui me brûlent my eyes are stinging
(d) (colloq) ∼ un feu (rouge) to jump (colloq)
the lights
2 vi (a) ⟨wood⟩ to burn; ⟨forest, town⟩ to be
on fire
(b) ∼ (d'envie) de faire to be longing to do
3 se brûler v refl (+ v être) to burn
oneself

brûlure /bʀylyʀ/ nf (a) burn; ∼s d'estomac
heartburn
(b) burn mark

brume /bʀym/ nf mist; fog; haze

brumeux, **-euse** /bʀymø, øz/ adj (a) hazy;
misty
(b) ⟨idea⟩ hazy

brun, **∼e** /bʀœ̃, bʀyn/ **1** adj brown, dark;
dark-haired
2 nm,f dark-haired man/woman
3 nm brown

brunir /bʀyniʀ/ [3] vi (a) ⟨skin⟩ to tan
(b) (Culin) to brown

brushing /bʀœʃiŋ/ nm blow-dry

brusque /bʀysk/ adj (a) ⟨tone, person⟩
abrupt
(b) ⟨movement⟩ sudden; ⟨bend⟩ sharp

brusquement /bʀyskəmɑ̃/ adv
(a) abruptly
(b) suddenly; ⟨brake⟩ sharply

brusquer /bʀyske/ [1] vtr (a) to be brusque
with
(b) to rush

brut, **∼e¹** /bʀyt/ adj (a) ⟨material⟩ raw;
⟨oil⟩ crude; ⟨stone⟩ rough; ⟨sugar⟩ unrefined
(b) ⟨cider, champagne⟩ dry
(c) ⟨salary⟩ gross

brutal, **∼e**, mpl **-aux** /bʀytal, o/ adj
(a) ⟨blow⟩ violent; ⟨pain, death⟩ sudden
(b) ⟨tone⟩ brutal; ⟨gesture, temper⟩ violent
(c) stark

brutalement /bʀytalmɑ̃/ adv (a) ⟨repress⟩
brutally; ⟨close⟩ violently
(b) ⟨die, stop⟩ suddenly

brutaliser /bʀytalize/ [1] vtr to ill-treat

brutalité /bʀytalite/ nf (a) brutality
(b) suddenness

brute² /bʀyt/ **1** adj f ▶ BRUT
2 nf brute; comme une ∼ ⟨hit⟩ savagely

Bruxelles /bʀysɛl/ pr n Brussels

bruyant, **∼e** /bʀɥijɑ̃, ɑ̃t/ adj (a) noisy;
loud
(b) resounding

BTS /betees/ nm: abbr ▶ BREVET

bu, **∼e** /by/ ▶ BOIRE

buanderie /bɥɑ̃dʀi/ nf laundry room

buccal, **∼e**, mpl **-aux** /bykal, o/ adj oral

bûche /byʃ/ nf (a) log (of wood)
(b) (colloq) tumble, fall
(c) (Culin) ∼ de Noël yule log

bûcher¹ /byʃe/ [1] vi (colloq) to slog away
(colloq)

bûcher² /byʃe/ nm (a) le ∼ the stake
(b) (funeral) pyre

bûcheron /byʃʀɔ̃/ nm lumberjack

bûchette /byʃet/ nf (for fire) stick

bucolique /bykɔlik/ adj bucolic, pastoral

budget /bydʒɛ/ nm budget

budgétaire /bydʒetɛʀ/ adj ⟨deficit⟩ budget;
⟨year⟩ financial (GB), fiscal (US)

budgétiser /bydʒetize/ [1] vtr to include
[sth] in the budget

buée /bɥe/ nf (a) condensation
(b) steam

buffet /byfɛ/ nm (a) sideboard
(b) dresser
(c) (station) buffet
(d) (Culin) buffet

buffle /byfl/ nm buffalo

buis /bɥi/ nm (a) box tree
(b) boxwood

buisson /bɥisɔ̃/ nm (a) bush
(b) shrub

buissonnière /bɥisɔnjɛʀ/ adj f faire
l'école ∼ to play truant (GB), to play hooky
(US) (colloq)

bulbe /bylb/ nm (Bot) bulb

bulgare /bylgaʀ/ *adj, nm* Bulgarian
Bulgarie /bylgaʀi/ *pr nf* Bulgaria
bulldozer /byldozœʀ/ *nm* bulldozer
bulle /byl/ *nf* (a) bubble
  (b) speech bubble
bulletin /byltɛ̃/ *nm* (a) bulletin, report;
  ∼ **de santé** medical bulletin
  (b) certificate; ∼ **de naissance** birth
  certificate
  (c) form; ∼ **de salaire** payslip; ∼ **de
  participation** entry form
  (d) bulletin, official publication
  (e) ballot *or* voting paper
bulletin-réponse, *pl* **bulletins-
  réponse** /byltɛ̃ʀepɔ̃s/ *nm* reply coupon
bulot /bylo/ *nm* whelk
buraliste /byʀalist/ *nmf* (a) (for smokers'
  supplies) tobacconist; (for cigarettes and
  newspapers) newsagent (GB), newsdealer (US)
  (b) (counter staff) clerk
bureau, *pl* ∼**x** /byʀo/ *nm* (a) desk
  (b) study
  (c) office
  (d) board
  ■ ∼ **d'accueil** reception; ∼ **de poste** post
  office; ∼ **de tabac** tobacconist's; ∼ **de vote**
  polling station; **Bureau international du
  travail, BIT** International Labour Office, ILO
bureaucratie /byʀokʀasi/ *nf*
  bureaucracy
bureautique /byʀotik/ *nf* office
  automation
burin /byʀɛ̃/ *nm* chisel
buriné, ∼**e** /byʀine/ *adj* ⟨face⟩ craggy
burlesque /byʀlɛsk/ *adj* ludicrous;
  farcical

bus /bys/ *nm inv* bus
buse /byz/ *nf* (a) buzzard
  (b) (colloq) clot (GB) (colloq), clod (colloq)
busqué, ∼**e** /byske/ *adj* ⟨nose⟩ hooked
buste /byst/ *nm* (a) (in sculpture) bust
  (b) (Anat) chest
  (c) bust, breasts
bustier /bystje/ *nm* (a) long-line bra
  (b) bustier
but /by(t)/ *nm* (a) goal; aim, purpose; **aller
  droit au** ∼ to go straight to the point
  (b) (in football) goal
  (c) (in archery) target
  IDIOMS **déclarer de** ∼ **en blanc** to declare
  point-blank
buté, ∼**e** /byte/ *adj* stubborn, obstinate
buter /byte/ [1] *vi* ∼ **contre qch** to trip over
  sth; to bump into sth; ∼ **sur** *or* **contre** to
  come up against ⟨obstacle⟩
butin /bytɛ̃/ *nm* (from robbery) haul
butiner /bytine/ [1] *vi* to gather pollen
butte /byt/ *nf* mound
  IDIOMS **être en** ∼ **à** to come up against
  ⟨difficulties⟩; to be the butt of ⟨jokes⟩
buvable /byvabl/ *adj* (a) ⟨medicine⟩ to be
  taken orally
  (b) drinkable
buvard /byvaʀ/ *nm* (**papier**) ∼ blotting
  paper
buvette /byvɛt/ *nf* refreshment area
buveur, -euse /byvœʀ, øz/ *nm,f* drinker;
  c'est un gros ∼ he's a heavy drinker; **un** ∼
  de thé/bière a tea/beer drinker

Cc

c, C /se/ *nm inv* c, C; **c cédille** c cedilla
c' ▶ CE 2
ça /sa/ *pron* (a) that; this; **c'est pour** ∼ **qu'il
  est parti** that's why he left; **sans** ∼
  otherwise; ∼, **c'est bizarre** that's strange; **la
  rue a** ∼ **de bien qu'elle est calme** one good
  thing about the street is that it's quiet
  (b) it; that; ∼ **fait mal** it hurts; that hurts;
  ∼ **criait de tous les côtés** there was
  shouting everywhere
  IDIOMS ∼ **alors!** well I never! (colloq); ∼, **oui!**
  definitely!; **elle est bête et méchante avec** ∼
  she's stupid and what's more she's nasty; **et
  avec** ∼? anything else?; **rien que** ∼! (ironic)
  is that all!; **c'est** ∼! that's right!; ∼ **y est,** ∼
  recommence! here we go again!; ∼ **y est, j'ai
  fini!** that's it, I've finished!

CA *written abbr* ▶ CHIFFRE

caban /kabɑ̃/ *nm* sailor's jacket
cabane /kaban/ *nf* (a) hut
  (b) shed
  (c) (slang) prison
cabaret /kabaʀɛ/ *nm* cabaret
cabas /kaba/ *nm* shopping bag
cabillaud /kabijo/ *nm* cod
cabine /kabin/ *nf* cabin; cab; booth;
  cubicle
  ■ ∼ **d'essayage** fitting room; ∼ **de pilotage**
  cockpit; ∼ **téléphonique** phone box (GB),
  phone booth
cabinet /kabinɛ/ [1] *nm* (a) (gen) office;
  (of doctor, dentist) surgery (GB), office (US);
  (of judge) chambers
  (b) practice; ∼ **de médecins** medical
  practice; **ouvrir un** ∼ to set up in practice
  (c) agency

 ⋯⋯

(d) (Pol) cabinet; ~ **ministériel** minister's personal staff

[2] **cabinets** *nm pl* toilet

■ ~ **de toilette** bathroom

cabinet-conseil, *pl* **cabinets-conseil** /kabinɛkɔ̃sɛj/ *nm* firm of consultants

câble /kɑbl/ *nm* **(a)** cable; rope **(b)** cable television

câbler /kɑble/ [1] *vtr* **(a)** to install cable television in ⟨*house, town*⟩ **(b)** to cable ⟨*message*⟩

cabochard, **~e** /kabɔʃaʀ, aʀd/ *adj* (colloq) stubborn

caboche /kabɔʃ/ *nf* (colloq) head

cabosser /kabɔse/ [1] *vtr* to dent

cabot /kabo/ *nm* (colloq) dog, mutt (colloq)

cabotin, **~e** /kabɔtɛ̃, in/ *adj* **être** ~ to like playing to the gallery

cabrer: se cabrer /kabʀe/ [1] *v refl* (+ *v être*) **(a)** ⟨*horse*⟩ to rear (**devant** at) **(b)** ⟨*person*⟩ to jib

cabri /kabʀi/ *nm* (Zool) kid

cabriole /kabʀijɔl/ *nf* (of clown, child) caper

CAC® /kak/ *nm* (*abbr* = **Compagnie des agents de change**) indice ~ **40**, ~ **40** Paris Stock Exchange index

caca /kaka/ *nm* (baby talk) poo (GB) (colloq), poop (US) (colloq)

cacahuète /kakawɛt/ *nf* peanut

cacao /kakao/ *nm* cocoa

cacatoès /kakatɔɛs/ *nm* cockatoo

cachalot /kaʃalo/ *nm* sperm whale

cache¹ /kaʃ/ *nm* **se servir d'un** ~ **pour apprendre une liste de vocabulaire** to cover up the answers while learning a list of vocabulary

cache² /kaʃ/ *nf* ~ **d'armes** arms cache

caché, **~e** /kaʃe/ [1] *pp* ▶ **CACHER**

[2] *pp adj* ⟨*beauty, sense*⟩ hidden; ⟨*pain, desire*⟩ secret

cache-cache /kaʃkaʃ/ *nm inv* hide and seek (GB), hide-and-go-seek (US)

cache-col /kaʃkɔl/ *nm inv* scarf

cachemire /kaʃmiʀ/ *nm* cashmere

cache-nez /kaʃne/ *nm inv* scarf, muffler

cache-pot /kaʃpo/ *nm inv* flowerpot holder

cacher /kaʃe/ [1] [1] *vtr* to hide; ~ **son jeu** (figurative) to keep one's cards close to one's chest; ~ **qch à qn** to conceal sth from sb

[2] **se cacher** *v refl* (+ *v être*) **(a)** to hide; (temporarily) to go into hiding; **il ne s'en cache pas** he makes no secret of it **(b)** ⟨*sun*⟩ to disappear

cache-sexe /kaʃsɛks/ *nm inv* G-string

cachet /kaʃɛ/ *nm* **(a)** tablet **(b)** (for letter) stamp; seal; ~ **de la poste** postmark **(c)** (of actor) fee

cacheter /kaʃte/ [20] *vtr* to seal

cachette /kaʃɛt/ *nf* hiding place; **en** ~ on the sly

cachot /kaʃo/ *nm* **(a)** prison cell **(b)** dungeon

cachotterie /kaʃɔtʀi/ *nf* little secret

cachottier, **-ière** /kaʃɔtje, ɛʀ/ *adj* secretive

cachou /kaʃu/ *nm* cachou

cacophonie /kakɔfɔni/ *nf* cacophony

cactus /kaktys/ *nm inv* cactus

c-à-d (*written abbr* = **c'est-à-dire**) ie

cadastre /kadastʀ/ *nm* **(a)** land register **(b)** land registry

cadavérique /kadaveʀik/ *adj* ⟨*complexion*⟩ deathly pale

cadavre /kadavʀ/ *nm* corpse, body

caddie® /kadi/ *nm* shopping trolley

cadeau, *pl* **~x** /kado/ [1] *nm* present, gift; **faire un** ~ **à qn** to give sb a present; **il ne fait pas de ~x** (examiner, judge) he's very strict

[2] **(-)cadeau** (*combining form*) gift; **papier(-)~** wrapping paper

cadenas /kadna/ *nm* padlock

cadence /kadɑ̃s/ *nf* **(a)** rhythm **(b)** (of work) rate

cadet, **-ette** /kadɛ, ɛt/ [1] *adj* **(a)** younger **(b)** youngest

[2] *nm,f* **(a)** younger son/daughter, younger child **(b)** youngest child **(c)** younger brother/sister **(d)** (Sport) *athlete between the ages of 15 and 17*

IDIOMS **c'est le** ~ **de mes soucis** it's the least of my worries

cadrage /kadʀaʒ/ *nm* **(a)** framing **(b)** composition

cadran /kadʀɑ̃/ *nm* (of watch) face; (of meter) dial; ~ **solaire** sundial

cadre /kadʀ/ [1] *nm* **(a)** frame **(b)** setting; surroundings **(c)** **cela sort du** ~ **de mes fonctions** that's not part of my duties **(d)** framework **(e)** executive; ~ **supérieur** senior executive; **les ~s moyens** middle management **(f)** **faire partie des ~s** to be on the company's books **(g)** (of bicycle) frame **(h)** (on form) space, box

[2] **dans le cadre de** *phr* **(a)** on the occasion of **(b)** (of negotiations) within the framework of; (of campaign, plan) as part of

cadrer /kadʀe/ [1] [1] *vtr* to centre (GB) ⟨*picture*⟩

[2] *vi* to tally, to fit (**avec** with)

cadreur /kadʀœʀ/ *nm* cameraman

caduc, **caduque** /kadyk/ *adj* **(a)** obsolete **(b)** (Law) null and void **(c)** ⟨*leaf*⟩ deciduous

cætera ▶ ET CÆTERA

cafard /kafaʀ/ *nm* **(a)** (colloq) depression; **avoir le** ~ to be down in the dumps (colloq) **(b)** cockroach

cafardeux, -euse /kafaʀdø, øz/ *adj* glum; gloomy

café /kafe/ *nm* **(a)** coffee; ~ **en grains** coffee beans; ~ **soluble** instant coffee **(b)** café
■ ~ **crème** espresso with milk; ~ **au lait** coffee with milk; **peau** ~ **au lait** coffee-coloured (GB) skin

café-concert, *pl* **cafés-concerts** /kafekɔ̃sɛʀ/ *nm* café with live music

caféine /kafein/ *nf* caffeine

cafétéria /kafeteʀja/ *nf* cafeteria

cafetière /kaftjɛʀ/ *nf* coffee pot; coffee maker

cafouillage /kafujaʒ/ *nm* (colloq) bungling (colloq)

cafouiller /kafuje/ [1] *vi* (colloq) ⟨*person*⟩ to get flustered; ⟨*machine*⟩ to be on the blink (colloq); ⟨*organization*⟩ to get in a muddle (colloq)

cage /kaʒ/ *nf* **(a)** cage **(b)** (Sport) (colloq) goal
■ ~ **d'ascenseur** lift (GB) or elevator (US) shaft; ~ **d'escalier** stairwell; ~ **à lapins** rabbit hutch; ~ **thoracique** rib cage

cageot /kaʒo/ *nm* crate

cagette /kaʒɛt/ *nf* tray

cagibi /kaʒibi/ *nm* store cupboard

cagnotte /kaɲɔt/ *nf* **(a)** kitty **(b)** jackpot

cagoule /kagul/ *nf* balaclava; hood

cahier /kaje/ *nm* **(a)** notebook; (Sch) exercise book **(b)** (in printing) section
■ ~ **de brouillon** rough book; ~ **de textes** homework notebook

cahin-caha /kaɛ̃kaa/ *adv* (colloq) with difficulty

cahot /kao/ *nm* jolt

cahoter /kaɔte/ [1] *vi* ⟨*vehicle*⟩ to bounce along

cahoteux, ~euse /kaɔtø, øz/ *adj* ⟨*road*⟩ rough, bumpy

cahute /kayt/ *nf* hut, shack

caïd /kaid/ *nm* (in criminal underworld) boss; **jouer les** ~**s** to act tough

caillasse /kajas/ *nf* stones

caille /kaj/ *nf* (Zool) quail

cailler /kaje/ [1] **1** **se cailler** *v refl* (+ *v être*) **(a)** ⟨*milk*⟩ to curdle **(b)** (colloq) ⟨*person*⟩ to be freezing **2** *v impers* **ça caille** it's freezing

caillot /kajo/ *nm* clot

caillou, *pl* ~**x** /kaju/ *nm* **(a)** pebble; **gros** ~ stone **(b)** (colloq) nut (colloq); **ne plus avoir un poil sur le** ~ to be as bald as a coot (colloq)

caillouteux, -euse /kajutø, øz/ *adj* stony

caïman /kaimã/ *nm* cayman

Caire /kɛʀ/ *pr n* **le** ~ Cairo

caisse /kɛs/ *nf* **(a)** crate **(b)** (of car) shell, body **(c)** (slang) car

(d) (for money) till; cash register; cash box; **les** ~**s de l'Etat** the Treasury coffers; **voler la** ~ to steal the takings
(e) cash desk; (in supermarket) checkout (counter); (in bank) cashier's desk
(f) fund
■ ~ **d'épargne** ≈ savings bank; ~ **noire** slush fund; ~ **à outils** toolbox

caissette /kɛsɛt/ *nf* small box *or* case

caissier, -ière /kesje, ɛʀ/ *nm,f* cashier

cajoler /kaʒɔle/ [1] *vtr* to cuddle ⟨*child*⟩

cajoleur, -euse /kaʒɔlœʀ, øz/ *adj* affectionate

cajou /kaʒu/ *nm* **noix de** ~ cashew nut

cake /kɛk/ *nm* fruit cake

cal /kal/ *nm* callus

calamar /kalamaʀ/ *nm* squid

calamité /kalamite/ *nf* disaster, calamity

calandre /kalɑ̃dʀ/ *nf* (Aut) (radiator) grille (GB)

calcaire /kalkɛʀ/ **1** *adj* ⟨*water*⟩ hard; ⟨*soil*⟩ chalky; ⟨*rock*⟩ limestone
2 *nm* **(a)** limestone **(b)** fur (GB), sediment (US)

calciner /kalsine/ [1] *vtr* **(a)** to char; (in oven) to burn [sth] to a crisp **(b)** (in chemistry) to calcine

calcium /kalsjɔm/ *nm* calcium

calcul /kalkyl/ *nm* **(a)** calculation; **faire le** ~ **de qch** to calculate sth **(b)** arithmetic; ~ **mental** mental arithmetic **(c)** (scheming) calculation; **agir par** ~ to act out of self-interest **(d)** (Med) stone

calculateur, -trice¹ /kalkylatœʀ, tʀis/ *adj* calculating

calculatrice² /kalkylatʀis/ *nf* (pocket) calculator

calculer /kalkyle/ [1] **1** *vtr* **(a)** to calculate, to work out **(b)** to weigh up ⟨*advantages, chances*⟩; **tout bien calculé** all things considered **(c)** ~ **son coup** to plan one's move
2 *vi* to calculate

calculette /kalkylɛt/ *nf* pocket calculator

cale /kal/ *nf* **(a)** wedge; (for wheel) chock; (for raising vehicle) block **(b)** (Naut) (ship's) hold

calé, ~e /kale/ *adj* (colloq) bright; ~ **en qch** brilliant at sth

calebasse /kalbas/ *nf* calabash, gourd

calèche /kalɛʃ/ *nf* barouche, carriage

caleçon /kalsɔ̃/ *nm* **(a)** boxer shorts; ~ **long** long johns (colloq) **(b)** (for woman) leggings

calédonien, -ienne /kaledɔnjɛ̃, ɛn/ *adj* **(a)** New Caledonian **(b)** Caledonian

calembour /kalɑ̃buʀ/ *nm* pun, play on words

calendrier /kalɑ̃dʀije/ *nm* **(a)** calendar **(b)** schedule **(c)** dates

cale-pied, pl ~**s** /kalpje/ nm toe clip
calepin /kalpɛ̃/ nm notebook
caler /kale/ [1] **1** vtr **(a)** to wedge ‹wheel›; to steady ‹piece of furniture›; to support ‹row of books›; **bien calé dans mon fauteuil** ensconced in my armchair
(b) (colloq) **ça cale** it fills you up
2 vi ‹car› to stall
3 se caler v refl (+ v être) to settle (**dans** in)
calfeutrer /kalføtʀe/ [1] **1** vtr to stop up ‹crack›; to draughtproof ‹door›
2 se calfeutrer v refl (+ v être) to shut oneself away
calibre /kalibʀ/ nm **(a)** (of gun) bore, calibre (GB); (of pipe, cable) diameter; **arme de gros ~** large-bore weapon
(b) (of eggs, fruit) size, grade
(c) gauge
calibrer /kalibʀe/ [1] vtr **(a)** (Tech) to calibrate
(b) to grade, to size ‹eggs, fruit›
calice /kalis/ nm chalice
calife /kalif/ nm caliph
califourchon: **à califourchon** /akalifuʀʃɔ̃/ phr astride
câlin, ~**e**, in/ **1** adj affectionate
2 nm cuddle
câliner /kaline/ [1] vtr to cuddle
calleux, -**euse** /kalø, øz/ adj calloused
calligraphie /kaligʀafi/ nf calligraphy
calligraphier /kaligʀafje/ [2] vtr to write [sth] in a decorative hand
callosité /kalozite/ nf callus
calmant, ~**e** /kalmɑ̃, ɑ̃t/ **1** adj soothing
2 nm sedative
calmar /kalmaʀ/ nm squid
calme /kalm/ **1** adj **(a)** ‹sea, situation› calm; ‹night› still; ‹place, life› quiet
(b) ‹person› calm
2 nm **(a)** peace (and quiet)
(b) calm; (of crowd) calmness; (of night) stillness; **dans le ~** peacefully
(c) composure; **conserver son ~** to keep calm; **du ~!** calm down!; quiet!
calmement /kalməmɑ̃/ adv calmly
calmer /kalme/ [1] **1** vtr **(a)** to calm down ‹person›; to calm ‹stock market›; to defuse ‹situation›; to tone down ‹discussion›; **~ les esprits** to calm people down
(b) to ease ‹pain›; to take the edge off ‹hunger›; to quench ‹thirst›
2 se calmer v refl (+ v être) **(a)** ‹person, situation› to calm down; ‹agitation, storm› to die down; ‹debate› to quieten (GB) or quiet (US) down; ‹ardour› to cool
(b) ‹pain› to ease
calomnie /kalɔmni/ nf slander
calomnier /kalɔmnje/ [2] vtr to slander
calorie /kalɔʀi/ nf calorie
calorifère /kalɔʀifɛʀ/ adj heat-conveying
calorique /kalɔʀik/ adj calorie; **ration/valeur ~** calorie intake/content
calotte /kalɔt/ nf **(a)** skull cap

(b) (colloq) slap
(c) ~ **glaciaire** icecap
calque /kalk/ nm **(a)** tracing
(b) tracing paper
(c) replica
calquer /kalke/ [1] vtr **(a)** to copy ‹behaviour›
(b) to trace ‹pattern, design› (**sur** from)
calumet /kalymɛ/ nm ~ **de la paix** peace pipe
calvados /kalvados/ nm calvados (apple brandy distilled in Normandy)
calvaire /kalvɛʀ/ nm **(a)** ordeal
(b) (monument) wayside cross
(c) Calvary
calvitie /kalvisi/ nf baldness
camaïeu /kamajø/ nm monochrome
camarade /kamaʀad/ nmf **(a)** friend; ~ **d'atelier** workmate
(b) comrade
camaraderie /kamaʀadʀi/ nf comradeship
Cambodge /kãbɔdʒ/ pr nm Cambodia
cambouis /kãbwi/ nm dirty grease
cambré, ~**e** /kãbʀe/ adj ‹back› arched; ‹foot, shoe› with a high instep
cambrer /kãbʀe/ [1] **1** vtr to curve, to arch
2 se cambrer v refl (+ v être) to arch one's back
cambriolage /kãbʀijɔlaʒ/ nm burglary
cambrioler /kãbʀijɔle/ [1] vtr to burgle (GB), to burglarize (US)
cambrioleur, -**euse** /kãbʀijɔlœʀ, øz/ nm,f burglar
cambrousse /kãbʀus/ nf (colloq) **la ~ the** sticks (colloq), the country; **en pleine ~** in the middle of nowhere
cambrure /kãbʀyʀ/ nf curve; (of foot) arch
■ ~ **des pieds** instep; ~ **des reins** small of the back
camée /kame/ nm cameo
caméléon /kameleɔ̃/ nm chameleon
camelote /kamlɔt/ nf (colloq) junk (colloq)
camembert /kamãbɛʀ/ nm **(a)** (Culin) Camembert
(b) (colloq) pie chart
camer: **se camer** /kame/ [1] v refl (+ v être) (slang) to be on drugs
caméra /kameʀa/ nf (cine-)camera (GB), movie camera (US)
caméscope® /kameskɔp/ nm camcorder
camion /kamjɔ̃/ nm truck
camion-citerne, pl **camions-citernes** /kamjɔ̃sitɛʀn/ nm tanker
camionnette /kamjɔnɛt/ nf van
camionneur /kamjɔnœʀ/ nm truck driver
camisole /kamizɔl/ nf camisole; ~ **de force** straitjacket
camomille /kamɔmij/ nf camomile
camouflage /kamuflaʒ/ nm **(a)** (Mil) camouflage
(b) (figurative) concealing; disguising (**en** as)

camoufler /kamufle/ [1] *vtr* **(a)** (Mil) to camouflage
(b) to cover up ⟨*crime, mistake, truth*⟩; to conceal ⟨*intention, feelings*⟩
(c) to hide ⟨*money*⟩

camp /kã/ *nm* **(a)** (gen) camp
(b) (Sport, Pol) side
IDIOMS ficher (colloq) **le ~** to split (colloq), to leave

campagnard, ~e /kãpaɲaʀ, aʀd/ **1** *adj* country, rustic
2 *nm,f* country person

campagne /kãpaɲ/ *nf* **(a)** country; (open) countryside
(b) campaign; **faire ~** to campaign

campanule /kãpanyl/ *nf* bellflower

campement /kãpmã/ *nm* camp, encampment

camper /kãpe/ [1] **1** *vtr* to portray ⟨*character*⟩; to depict ⟨*landscape,scene*⟩
2 *vi* to camp
3 se camper *v refl* (+ *v être*) **se ~ devant qn/qch** to stand squarely in front of sb/sth

campeur, -euse /kãpœʀ, øz/ *nm,f* camper

camphre /kãfʀ/ *nm* camphor

camping /kãpiŋ/ *nm* **(a)** camping; **faire du ~ sauvage** to camp rough
(b) campsite (GB), campground (US)

camping-car, *pl* **~s** /kãpiŋkaʀ/ *nm* (controversial) camper

camping-gaz® /kãpiŋgaz/ *nm inv* (gas) camping stove

campus /kãpys/ *nm inv* campus

Canada /kanada/ *pr nm* Canada

Canadair® /kanadɛʀ/ *nm* water bomber

canadienne /kanadjɛn/ *nf* **(a)** sheepskin-lined jacket
(b) ridge tent

canal, *pl* **-aux** /kanal, o/ *nm* **(a)** canal
(b) channel
(c) (Anat) duct

canalisation /kanalizasjõ/ *nf* **(a)** pipe
(b) mains

canaliser /kanalize/ [1] *vtr* **(a)** to canalize ⟨*river*⟩
(b) (figurative) to channel

canapé /kanape/ *nm* **(a)** sofa; **~ convertible** sofa bed
(b) (Culin) canapé

canaque /kanak/ *adj* Kanak

canard /kanaʀ/ *nm* **(a)** duck; **~ laqué** Peking duck
(b) (colloq) rag (colloq), newspaper
(c) (Mus) wrong note
IDIOMS ça ne casse pas trois pattes à un ~ (colloq) it's nothing to write home about

canarder /kanaʀde/ [1] *vtr* (colloq) to snipe at

canari /kanaʀi/ *nm* canary

canasson /kanasõ/ *nm* (slang) nag (colloq), horse

cancan /kãkã/ *nm* **(a)** (colloq) gossip
(b) cancan

cancaner /kãkane/ [1] *vi* (colloq) to gossip

cancer /kãsɛʀ/ *nm* cancer

Cancer /kãsɛʀ/ *pr nm* Cancer

cancéreux, -euse /kãseʀø, øz/ *adj* ⟨*cell*⟩ cancerous; ⟨*person*⟩ with cancer

cancérigène /kãseʀiʒɛn/ *adj* carcinogenic

cancérologie /kãseʀɔlɔʒi/ *nf* cancer research; **service de ~** cancer ward

cancre /kãkʀ/ *nm* dunce

cancrelat /kãkʀəla/ *nm* cockroach

candeur /kãdœʀ/ *nf* ingenuousness

candi /kãdi/ *adj m* **sucre ~** sugar candy

candidat, ~e /kãdida, at/ *nm,f* (Pol) candidate; (for job) applicant; (in competition) contestant; **être ~ aux élections** to stand for election (GB), to run for office (US); **être ~ (à un poste)** to apply (for a post); **pour la vaisselle, il n'y a pas beaucoup de ~s!** (humorous) when it comes to doing the dishes, there aren't many takers

candidature /kãdidatyʀ/ *nf*
(a) candidature, candidacy; **retirer sa ~** to stand down (GB), to drop out (US)
(b) (for a post) application; **faire acte de ~** to apply

candide /kãdid/ *adj* ingenuous

cane /kan/ *nf* (female) duck

caneton /kantõ/ *nm* duckling

canette /kanɛt/ *nf* **(a) ~ (de bière)** (small) bottle of beer
(b) can; **~ de bière** can of beer
(c) (of sewing machine) spool

canevas /kanva/ *nm inv* **(a)** canvas
(b) tapestry work
(c) (figurative) framework

caniche /kaniʃ/ *nm* poodle

canicule /kanikyl/ *nf* **(a)** scorching heat
(b) heatwave

canif /kanif/ *nm* penknife

canin, ~e¹ /kanɛ̃, in/ *adj* canine

canine² /kanin/ *nf* canine (tooth)

caniveau, *pl* **~x** /kanivo/ *nm* gutter

cannabis /kanabis/ *nm* cannabis

canne /kan/ *nf* **(a)** (walking) stick
(b) (Bot) cane
■ **~ à pêche** fishing rod

canneberge /kanbɛʀʒ/ *nf* cranberry

cannelle /kanɛl/ *nf* cinnamon

cannette = CANETTE

cannibale /kanibal/ *adj*, *nmf* cannibal

canoë /kanɔe/ *nm* **(a)** canoe
(b) canoeing

canoë-kayak /kanɔekajak/ *nm* canoeing

canon /kanõ/ **1** *adj m inv* **droit ~** canon law
2 *nm* **(a)** (big) gun; cannon; **tirer un coup de ~** to fire a gun; **entendre des coups de ~** to hear cannon fire
(b) (of firearm) barrel
(c) (Mus) canon; **chanter en ~** to sing in a round
(d) (rule, principle) canon ⋯⟶

(e) (in religion) canon

cañon /kanjɔ̃, kanjɔn/ *nm* canyon

canonique /kanɔnik/ *adj* **droit ~** canon law; **d'âge ~** (humorous) of a venerable age

canoniser /kanɔnize/ [1] *vtr* to canonize

canot /kano/ *nm* (small) boat, dinghy; **~ pneumatique** rubber dinghy; **~ de sauvetage** (on ship) lifeboat; (on plane) life raft

canotier /kanɔtje/ *nm* boater

canson® /kɑ̃sɔ̃/ *nm* drawing paper

cantaloup /kɑ̃talu/ *nm* cantaloupe melon

cantate /kɑ̃tat/ *nf* cantata

cantatrice /kɑ̃tatris/ *nf* (opera) singer

cantine /kɑ̃tin/ *nf* **(a)** canteen (GB), cafeteria; **manger à la ~** (child) to have school dinners
(b) tin trunk

cantique /kɑ̃tik/ *nm* hymn, canticle

canton /kɑ̃tɔ̃/ *nm* canton

cantonade: à la cantonade /alakɑ̃tɔnad/ *phr* **parler à la ~** to speak to no-one in particular

cantonais, ~e /kɑ̃tɔnɛ, ɛz/ [1] *adj* Cantonese
[2] *nm* (language) Cantonese

cantonal, ~e, *mpl* **-aux** /kɑ̃tɔnal, o/ *adj* cantonal

cantonner /kɑ̃tɔne/ [1] *vtr* **~ qn dans un lieu** to confine sb to a place; **~ qn dans le rôle de** to reduce sb to the role of

cantonnier /kɑ̃tɔnje/ *nm* road-mender

cantonnière /kɑ̃tɔnjɛʀ/ *nf* pelmet

canular /kanylaʀ/ *nm* hoax

canule /kanyl/ *nf* cannula

canyon = CAÑON

caoutchouc /kautʃu/ *nm* **(a)** rubber
(b) rubber plant
(c) rubber band

caoutchouteux, -euse /kautʃutø, øz/ *adj* rubbery

cap /kap/ *nm* **(a)** (in geography) cape
(b) mark; **passer le ~ de la cinquantaine** to pass the fifty mark
(c) (direction) course; **maintenir le ~** to hold one's course; **mettre le ~ sur** to head for

Cap /kap/ *pr n* **le ~** Cape Town

CAP /seape/ *nm: abbr* ▶ CERTIFICAT

capable /kapabl/ *adj* capable (de faire of doing); **ils sont bien ~s de nous mentir** I wouldn't put it past them to lie to us

capacité /kapasite/ [1] *nf* **(a)** ability
(b) capacity
[2] **capacités** *nf pl* (talent) abilities

cape /kap/ *nf* cape; cloak
IDIOMS **rire sous ~** to laugh up one's sleeve

capeline /kaplin/ *nf* wide-brimmed hat

CAPES /kapɛs/ *nm* (*abbr* = **certificat d'aptitude professionnelle à l'enseignement secondaire**) *secondary school teaching qualification*

capharnaüm /kafaʀnaɔm/ *nm* shambles (colloq)

capillaire /kapilɛʀ/ [1] *adj* **(a)** capillary
(b) soins ~s hair care
[2] *nm* capillary

capitaine /kapitɛn/ *nm* **(a)** (Mil) (in army, navy) ≈ captain
(b) (Sport) captain

capitainerie /kapitɛnʀi/ *nf* port authority

capital, ~e¹, *mpl* **-aux** /kapital, o/
[1] *adj* **(a)** (importance) major; (role, question) key; **il est ~ de faire** it's essential to do
(b) (letter) capital
(c) peine ~e capital punishment
[2] *nm* **(a)** capital
(b) le ~ humain/industriel human/industrial resources
[3] **capitaux** *nm pl* capital, funds

capitale² /kapital/ *nf* **(a)** capital (city)
(b) capital (letter); **en ~s d'imprimerie** in block capitals

capitalisation /kapitalizasjɔ̃/ *nf* capitalization

capitaliser /kapitalize/ [1] *vtr* to capitalize

capitalisme /kapitalism/ *nm* capitalism

capitaliste /kapitalist/ *adj, nmf* capitalist

capitonner /kapitɔne/ [1] *vtr* to pad

capitulation /kapitylasjɔ̃/ *nf* capitulation (devant to); **~ sans conditions** unconditional surrender

capituler /kapityle/ [1] *vi* to capitulate

caporal, *pl* **-aux** /kapɔral, o/ *nm* (Mil) (in army) ≈ corporal

capot /kapo/ *nm* (Aut) bonnet (GB), hood (US)

capotage /kapɔtaʒ/ *nm* collapse

capote /kapɔt/ *nf* **(a)** great-coat
(b) (of car, pram) hood (GB), top
(c) (colloq) **~ (anglaise)** condom

capoter /kapɔte/ [1] *vi* **(a)** to collapse
(b) (car) to overturn

câpre /kɑpʀ/ *nf* caper

caprice /kapʀis/ *nm* **(a)** (of person) whim; **céder aux ~s de qn** to indulge sb's whims; **c'est un ~ de la nature** (of plant, animal) it's a freak of nature
(b) faire un ~ to throw a tantrum

capricieusement /kapʀisjøzmɑ̃/ *adv* capriciously; whimsically

capricieux, -ieuse /kapʀisjø, øz/ *adj* (person) capricious; (machine) temperamental; (weather) changeable; (destiny) fickle

capricorne /kapʀikɔrn/ *nm* capricorn beetle

Capricorne /kapʀikɔrn/ *pr nm* Capricorn

capsule /kapsyl/ *nf* **(a)** (of bottle) cap; top
(b) (Med) capsule
(c) ~ spatiale space capsule

capter /kapte/ [1] *vtr* **(a)** to get (channel, programme); to pick up (signal)
(b) to catch (attention)
(c) to soak up (light)

captif, -ive /kaptif, iv/ *adj, nm,f* captive

captivant, **~e** /kaptivã, ãt/ adj
enthralling; gripping; riveting; captivating

captiver /kaptive/ [1] vtr ⟨beauty⟩ to
captivate; ⟨music⟩ to enthrall; ⟨story, person⟩
to fascinate

captivité /kaptivite/ nf captivity

capture /kaptyR/ nf capture

capturer /kaptyRe/ [1] vtr to capture

capuche /kapyʃ/ nf hood; **à ~** with a
hood

capuchon /kapyʃɔ̃/ nm **(a)** (of garment)
hood
(b) (of pen) cap

capucine /kapysin/ nf nasturtium

caquet /kakɛ/ nm prattle; **rabattre le ~ à
qn** (colloq) to put sb in his/her place

caqueter /kakte/ [20] vi ⟨hen⟩ to cackle

car¹ /kaR/ conj because, for

car² /kaR/ nm bus; **~ de police** police van;
~ (de ramassage) scolaire school bus

carabine /kaRabin/ nf rifle

carabiné, **~e** /kaRabine/ adj (colloq)
⟨fever⟩ raging; ⟨cold⟩ stinking (colloq)

caracoler /kaRakɔle/ [1] vi **(a)** to be well
ahead
(b) ⟨horse⟩ to prance; ⟨rider⟩ to parade

caractère /kaRaktɛR/ nm **(a)** (written)
character; **~s d'imprimerie** block capitals;
en petits/gros ~s in small/large print
(b) nature, temperament; **avoir mauvais ~**
to be bad-tempered
(c) (personality) character; **il n'a aucun ~** he's
got no backbone
(d) (of house, place) character
(e) characteristic
(f) nature; **à ~ commercial** of a commercial
nature
IDIOMS **avoir un ~ de cochon** (colloq), **avoir
un sale ~** to have a vile temper

caractériel, **-ielle** /kaRakteRjɛl/ adj
⟨problems⟩ emotional; ⟨person⟩ disturbed

caractériser /kaRakteRize/ [1] **1** vtr to
characterize
2 se caractériser v refl (+ v être) to be
characterized

caractéristique /kaRakteRistik/ **1** adj
characteristic
2 nf characteristics

carafe /kaRaf/ nf carafe

caraïbe /kaRaib/ adj Caribbean

Caraïbes /kaRaib/ pr nf pl Caribbean
(islands)

carambolage /kaRãbɔlaʒ/ nm pile-up

caramboler /kaRãbɔle/ [1] vtr to collide
with

caramel /kaRamɛl/ nm **(a)** caramel
(b) toffee (GB), toffy (US); **~ mou** ≈ fudge

carapace /kaRapas/ nf shell, carapace

carat /kaRa/ nm carat; **or 18 ~s** 18-carat
gold

caravane /kaRavan/ nf **(a)** caravan (GB),
trailer (US)
(b) (convoy) caravan

caravelle /kaRavɛl/ nf (boat) caravel

carbone /kaRbɔn/ nm **(a)** carbon
(b) carbon paper
(c) sheet of carbon paper

carbonique /kaRbɔnik/ adj carbonic;
neige ~ dry ice

carbonisé, **~e** /kaRbɔnize/ adj burned-
out; charred; burned to a cinder

carboniser /kaRbɔnize/ [1] vtr **(a)** to
carbonize
(b) to reduce [sth] to ashes

carburant /kaRbyRã/ nm fuel

carburateur /kaRbyRatœR/ nm
carburettor (GB), carburetor (US)

carburer /kaRbyRe/ [1] vi **(a) il carbure au
vin rouge** he runs on red wine
(b) to work flat out

carcan /kaRkã/ nm **(a)** (device) iron collar
(b) ~ administratif administrative
constraints

carcasse /kaRkas/ nf carcass

carcéral, **~e**, mpl **-aux** /kaRseRal, o/
adj prison

cardan /kaRdã/ nm universal joint

cardiaque /kaRdjak/ adj **être ~** to have a
heart condition; **crise ~** heart attack

cardinal, **~e**, mpl **-aux** /kaRdinal, o/
1 adj cardinal
2 nm **(a)** cardinal
(b) cardinal number

cardiologie /kaRdjɔlɔʒi/ nf cardiology

cardiologue /kaRdjɔlɔg/ nmf cardiologist

carême /kaRɛm/ nm **le ~** Lent

carence /kaRãs/ nf **(a)** (Med) deficiency
(b) lack
(c) les ~s de la loi the shortcomings of the
law

carène /kaRɛn/ nf hull (below the
waterline)

caressant, **~e** /kaRɛsã, ãt/ adj
affectionate; soft

caresse /kaRɛs/ nf caress, stroke; **faire
une ~** or **des ~s à** to stroke

caresser /kaRese/ [1] vtr **(a)** to stroke, to
caress; **~ qn du regard** to look at sb lovingly
(b) to entertain ⟨hope, idea⟩; to cherish
⟨dream⟩
IDIOMS **~ qn dans le sens du poil** to stay on
the right side of sb

cargaison /kaRgɛzɔ̃/ nf **(a)** cargo
(b) (colloq) load

cargo /kaRgo/ nm (Naut) freighter, cargo
ship

caricatural, **~e**, mpl **-aux**
/kaRikatyRal, o/ adj **(a)** grotesque
(b) caricatural

caricature /kaRikatyR/ nf caricature;
c'est une ~ de procès it's a mockery of a
trial

caricaturer /kaRikatyRe/ [1] vtr to
caricature

caricaturiste /kaRikatyRist/ nmf
caricaturist

carie /kaʀi/ nf la ~ (dentaire) (tooth) decay; avoir une carie to have a hole in one's tooth

carié, **~e** /kaʀje/ adj decayed

carier: se carier /kaʀje/ [2] v refl (+ v être) ⟨tooth⟩ to decay

carillon /kaʀijɔ̃/ nm (a) (of church) (set of) bells; (tune) chimes
(b) (chiming) clock; (sound) chimes
(c) (door) chimes

carillonner /kaʀijɔne/ [1] vi (a) ⟨bells⟩ to ring out, to peal out
(b) (at door) to ring (loudly)

caritatif, -ive /kaʀitatif, iv/ adj charitable; une association caritative a charity

carlingue /kaʀlɛ̃g/ nf (of plane) cabin

carmin /kaʀmɛ̃/ nm, adj inv carmine

carnage /kaʀnaʒ/ nm carnage, massacre

carnassier, -ière /kaʀnasje, ɛʀ/ adj carnivorous

carnaval, pl **~s** /kaʀnaval/ nm carnival

carnet /kaʀnɛ/ nm (a) notebook
(b) (of tickets, vouchers, stamps) book
■ ~ de chèques chequebook (GB), checkbook (US); ~ de correspondance (Sch) mark book; ~ de santé health record

carnivore /kaʀnivɔʀ/ ❶ adj carnivorous
❷ nm carnivore

carotide /kaʀɔtid/ adj, nf carotid

carotte /kaʀɔt/ nf carrot
IDIOMS manier la ~ et le bâton to use stick-and-carrot tactics

caroube /kaʀub/ nf carob

carpe¹ /kaʀp/ nm (Anat) carpus

carpe² /kaʀp/ nf (fish) carp
IDIOMS il est resté muet comme une ~ he never said a word

carpette /kaʀpɛt/ nf (a) rug
(b) (colloq) doormat (colloq)

carré, ~e /kaʀe/ ❶ adj (a) ⟨shape⟩ square; il est ~ d'épaules he has broad shoulders
(b) ⟨metre, root⟩ square
❷ nm (a) square
(b) (of sky, ground) patch; (of chocolate) piece; avoir une coupe au ~ to have one's hair cut in a bob; ~ blanc 'suitable for adults only' sign on French TV
(c) (in mathematics) square
(d) ~ d'agneau rack of lamb

carreau, pl **~x** /kaʀo/ nm (a) (floor) tile; (wall) tile
(b) window-pane; faire les ~x to clean the windows
(c) (on paper) square; (on fabric) check
(d) (in cards) diamonds
IDIOMS rester sur le ~ (colloq) to be left high and dry (colloq); se tenir à ~ (colloq) to watch one's step

carrefour /kaʀfuʀ/ nm (a) junction; crossroads
(b) (figurative) crossroads

carrelage /kaʀlaʒ/ nm (a) tiled floor
(b) tiles

carreler /kaʀle/ [19] vtr to tile

carrelet /kaʀlɛ/ nm plaice

carrément /kaʀemɑ̃/ adv (a) la situation devient ~ inquiétante quite frankly the situation is becoming worrying; il vaut ~ mieux les jeter it would be better just to throw them out
(b) completely; dans un cas pareil, appelle ~ la police in such a case, don't hesitate to call the police
(c) ⟨ask, say⟩ straight out; ⟨express⟩ clearly
(d) allez-y ~! go straight ahead!

carrière /kaʀjɛʀ/ nf (a) career; faire ~ dans to make a career in
(b) quarry; ~ de sable sandpit

carriole /kaʀjɔl/ nf (a) cart
(b) (colloq) jalopy (colloq), car

carrossable /kaʀɔsabl/ adj suitable for motor vehicles

carrosse /kaʀɔs/ nm (horse-drawn) coach

carrosserie /kaʀɔsʀi/ nf (a) bodywork
(b) coachbuilding
(c) body repair work

carrossier /kaʀɔsje/ nm coachbuilder

carrousel /kaʀuzɛl/ nm merry-go-round, carousel

carrure /kaʀyʀ/ nf (a) shoulders
(b) calibre (GB)

cartable /kaʀtabl/ nm (a) schoolbag, satchel
(b) briefcase

carte /kaʀt/ nf (a) card; ~ à jouer playing card
(b) pass
(c) map; chart
(d) ~ génétique genetic map
(e) menu; repas à la ~ à la carte meal
■ ~ d'abonnement season ticket; ~ d'adhérent membership card; ~ bleue® credit card; ~ de crédit credit card; ~ grise logbook; ~ d'identité ID card; ~ orange® season ticket (in the Paris region); ~ postale postcard; ~ à puce smart card; ~ de réduction discount card; ~ de retrait (automatique) cashcard; ~ de séjour resident's permit; ~ vermeil® senior citizen's railcard; ~ des vins wine list; ~ de visite (social) visiting card; (professional) business card; ~ de vœux greetings card

cartel /kaʀtɛl/ nm (a) cartel
(b) coalition

carter /kaʀtɛʀ/ nm (of engine) crankcase; (of gearbox) casing

cartilage /kaʀtilaʒ/ nm (a) (Anat, Zool) cartilage
(b) (Culin) gristle

cartomancie /kaʀtɔmɑ̃si/ nf fortune-telling

cartomancien, -ienne /kaʀtɔmɑ̃sjɛ̃, ɛn/ nm,f fortune-teller

carton /kaʀtɔ̃/ nm (a) cardboard; en ~ ⟨folder⟩ cardboard; ⟨cups⟩ paper
(b) (cardboard) box
(c) card
■ ~ à dessin portfolio

IDIOMS faire un ~ (colloq) to do great (colloq)

cartonné, ~e /kaʀtɔne/ *adj* **couverture** ~**e** (of book) hard cover

cartonner (colloq) /kaʀtɔne/ [1] *vi* to score

carton-pâte /kaʀtɔpat/ *nm inv* pasteboard

cartouche /kaʀtuʃ/ *nf* **(a)** cartridge; (of gas) refill
(b) ~ **de cigarettes** carton of cigarettes

cas /kɑ/ **1** *nm inv* case; **auquel** ~ in which case; **au** ~ **où il viendrait** in case he comes; **prends ta voiture, au** ~ **où** take your car, just in case; **en** ~ **de besoin** if necessary; **en** ~ **de décès** in the event of death; **le** ~ **échéant** if need be; **dans le** ~ **contraire, vous devrez...** should the opposite occur, you will have to...; **dans le meilleur/pire des** ~ at best/worst; **en aucun** ~ under no circumstances; **c'est le** ~ **de le dire!** you can say that again!; **être dans le même** ~ **que qn** to be in the same position as sb; **n'aggrave pas ton** ~ don't make things worse for yourself; **un** ~ **rare** a rare occurrence; **c'est un** ~ **de renvoi** it's grounds for dismissal
2 en tout cas, en tous les cas *phr*
(a) in any case, at any rate
(b) at least
■ ~ **de conscience** moral dilemma; ~ **social** socially disadvantaged person
IDIOMS il a fait grand ~ **de son avancement** he made a big thing of his promotion

casanier, -ière /kazanje, ɛʀ/ *adj* ⟨person⟩ stay-at-home; ⟨existence⟩ unadventurous

casaque /kazak/ *nf* (of jockey) jersey, silk

cascade /kaskad/ *nf* **(a)** waterfall
(b) stunt

cascadeur, -euse /kaskadœʀ, øz/ *nm,f* stuntman/stuntwoman

case /kɑz/ *nf* **(a)** hut, cabin
(b) (in board games) square
(c) (on form) box
■ ~ **départ** (in board game) start; **retour à la** ~ **départ** (figurative) back to square one.
IDIOMS il lui manque une ~ (colloq) he's got a screw loose (colloq)

caser (colloq) /kɑze/ [1] **1** *vtr* **(a)** to put, to stick (colloq)
(b) to marry off
(c) to find a place *or* job for
2 se caser *v refl* (+ *v être*) to get married

caserne /kazɛʀn/ *nf* barracks
■ ~ **de sapeurs-pompiers** fire station

casher /kaʃɛʀ/ *adj inv* kosher

casier /kazje/ *nm* **(a)** (in gym) locker
(b) pigeonhole
(c) ~ **judiciaire** police record

casino /kazino/ *nm* casino

casque /kask/ *nm* **(a)** helmet; crash helmet; safety helmet
(b) headphones
(c) hairdryer

casqué, ~e /kaske/ *adj* helmeted

casquette /kaskɛt/ *nf* cap; **porter plusieurs** ~**s** (figurative) to wear several hats

cassant, ~e /kasɑ̃, ɑ̃t/ *adj* **(a)** brittle
(b) curt, abrupt

casse¹ /kɑs/ *nm* (slang) break-in, heist (US) (colloq)

casse² /kɑs/ *nf* **(a)** breakage
(b) breaker's yard, scrap yard; **mettre à la** ~ to scrap

cassé, ~e /kase/ *adj* ⟨voice⟩ hoarse

casse-cou /kasku/ *nmf inv* daredevil

casse-croûte /kaskʀut/ *nm inv* snack

casse-noisettes /kasnwazɛt/, **casse-noix** /kasnwa/ *nm inv* nutcrackers

casser /kase/ [1] **1** *vtr* to break ⟨object, bone⟩; to crack ⟨nut⟩; ~ **les prix** to slash prices; ~ **la figure** (colloq) **à qn** to beat sb up (colloq)
2 *vi* **(a)** to break
(b) (colloq) ⟨couple⟩ to split up
3 se casser *v refl* (+ *v être*) **(a)** to break
(b) **se** ~ **une** *or* **la jambe** to break one's leg; **se** ~ **la figure** (colloq) ⟨pedestrian⟩ to fall over (GB) *or* down; ⟨venture⟩ to fail; ⟨people⟩ to have a scrap (colloq); **il ne s'est pas cassé la tête** (colloq) he didn't exactly strain himself
(c) (colloq) to go away
IDIOMS ~ **les pieds** (colloq) **à qn** to annoy sb; ~ **la croûte** to eat; **ça te prendra trois heures, à tout** ~ (colloq) it'll take you three hours at the very most

casserole /kasʀɔl/ *nf* saucepan, pan
IDIOMS chanter comme une ~ (colloq) to sing atrociously

casse-tête /kastɛt/ *nm inv* **(a)** headache, problem
(b) puzzle

cassette /kasɛt/ *nf* **(a)** tape, cassette
(b) casket

casseur /kasœʀ/ *nm* **(a)** scrap dealer
(b) rioting demonstrator

cassis /kasis/ *nm inv* **(a)** blackcurrant
(b) (in road) dip

cassonade /kasɔnad/ *nf* soft brown sugar

cassoulet /kasulɛ/ *nm*: meat and bean stew

cassure /kasyʀ/ *nf* **(a)** break
(b) split

castagnettes /kastaɲɛt/ *nf pl* castanets

caste /kast/ *nf* **(a)** caste
(b) (derogatory) (social) class

castor /kastɔʀ/ *nm* beaver

castrer /kastʀe/ [1] *vtr* to castrate

cataclysme /kataklism/ *nm* cataclysm

catacombes /katakɔ̃b/ *nf pl* catacombs

catadioptre /katadjɔptʀ/ *nm* reflector

catalepsie /katalɛpsi/ *nf* catalepsy

catalogue /katalɔg/ *nm* catalogue (GB); **acheter sur** ~ to buy by mail order

cataloguer /katalɔge/ [1] *vtr* **(a)** to catalogue (GB) ⟨objects⟩
(b) to label ⟨people⟩

catalyse /kataliz/ *nf* catalysis

catalytique /katalitik/ *adj* catalytic

catamaran /katamaʀɑ̃/ nm catamaran

cataplasme /kataplasm/ nm poultice

catapulter /katapylte/ [1] vtr to catapult

cataracte /kataʀakt/ nf cataract

catastrophe /katastʀɔf/ nf disaster; **en ~** in a panic; **atterrissage en ~** crash landing

catastropher /katastʀɔfe/ [1] vtr to devastate

catastrophique /katastʀɔfik/ adj disastrous

catch /katʃ/ nm wrestling

catcheur, -euse /katʃœʀ, øz/ nm,f wrestler

catéchisme /kateʃism/ nm catechism

catégorie /kategɔʀi/ nf (a) category; **de première/deuxième ~** top-/low-grade
(b) (of staff) grade
(c) (in sociology) group
(d) (Sport) class

catégorique /kategɔʀik/ adj categorical

cathédrale /katedʀal/ nf cathedral

cathode /katɔd/ nf cathode

catholicisme /katɔlisism/ nm (Roman) Catholicism

catholique /katɔlik/ adj, nmf Catholic; **ce n'est pas très ~** (humorous) (colloq) it's a bit unorthodox

cauchemar /koʃmaʀ/ nm nightmare

causant, -e /kozɑ̃, ɑ̃t/ adj (colloq) talkative

cause /koz/ nf (a) cause; **pour la ~ de la liberté** in the cause of freedom
(b) reason; **pour ~ de maladie** because of illness; **avoir pour ~ qch** to be caused by sth; **à ~ de** because of
(c) case; **être en ~** ⟨system, fact⟩ to be at issue; ⟨person⟩ to be involved; **mettre hors de ~** (gen) to clear; **remettre en ~** to call [sth] into question ⟨policy, right⟩; to cast doubt on ⟨project, efficiency⟩; to undermine ⟨efforts⟩; **remise en ~** (of system) reappraisal; **avoir gain de ~** to win one's case
IDIOMS **en toute connaissance de ~** in full knowledge of the facts

causer /koze/ [1] **1** vtr (a) to cause; **~ des soucis** to give cause for concern
(b) (colloq) to talk about; **~ travail** to talk shop
2 causer de v+prep to talk about
3 vi to talk; to chat

causette /kozɛt/ nf (colloq) chat; **faire la ~** to have a little chat

caustique /kostik/ adj caustic

cautériser /koteʀize/ [1] vtr to cauterize

caution /kosjɔ̃/ nf (a) (when renting) deposit; (in finance) guarantee, security; (Law) bail
(b) support

cautionner /kosjone/ [1] vtr (a) to give one's support to
(b) to stand surety for

cavalcade /kavalkad/ nf (a) stampede, rush
(b) cavalcade

cavale /kaval/ nf (colloq) escape; **en ~** on the run

cavaler /kavale/ [1] vi (colloq) to rush about

cavalerie /kavalʀi/ nf cavalry

cavaleur, -euse /kavalœʀ, øz/ adj (colloq) **être ~** to be a womanizer/man-chaser

cavalier, -ière /kavalje, ɛʀ/ **1** adj cavalier
2 nm,f (a) (horse) rider; **être bon ~** to be a good rider
(b) (dancing) partner
3 nm (a) cavalryman
(b) (in chess) knight
IDIOMS **faire ~ seul** to go it alone

cave /kav/ nf cellar; **avoir une bonne ~** to have good wines

caveau, pl **~x** /kavo/ nm vault

caverne /kavɛʀn/ nf cavern

caviar /kavjaʀ/ nm caviar

cavité /kavite/ nf cavity

CCP /sesepe/ nm: abbr ▶ COMPTE

CD /sede/ nm (abbr = **compact disc**) CD

CD-I /sedei/ nm inv (abbr = **compact disc interactif**) CD-I

ce /sə/ **1** (**cet** /sɛt/ before vowel or mute h, **cette** /sɛt/, pl **ces** /se/) adj (a) this; that; **~ crayon(-ci)** this pencil; **~ livre(-là)** that book; **cette nuit** tonight; last night; **un de ces jours** one of these days
(b) (colloq) **cet entretien, ça s'est bien passé?** how did the interview go?
(c) **et pour ces dames?** what are the ladies having?
(d) **elle a eu cette chance que la corde a tenu** she was lucky in that the rope held
(e) **cette arrogance!** what arrogance!; **j'ai un de ces rhumes!** I've got an awful cold!
2 (**c'** before e) pron **qui est-~?** who's that?; who is it?; **~ faisant** in so doing; **c'est tout dire** that says it all; **fais ~ que tu veux** do what you like; **c'est ~ à quoi il a fait allusion** that's what he was alluding to; **il a fait faillite, ~ qui n'est pas surprenant** he's gone bankrupt, which is hardly surprising; **il tient à ~ que vous veniez** he's very keen that you should come; **~ que c'est grand!** it's so big!

CE /seə/ nm: abbr ▶ COURS

ceci /səsi/ pron this; **à ~ près que** except that; **cet hôtel a ~ de bien que... de bien que...** one good thing about this hotel is that...

cécité /sesite/ nf blindness

céder /sede/ [14] **1** vtr (a) to give up ⟨seat, share⟩; to yield ⟨right⟩; to make over ⟨property⟩; **~ le passage** to give way; **~ la place** (figurative) to give way
(b) to sell
2 céder à v+prep to give in to, to yield to
3 vi (a) to give in
(b) ⟨beam⟩ to give way; ⟨handle⟩ to break off; ⟨door⟩ to yield

cédille /sedij/ nf cedilla

cèdre /sɛdʀ/ nm cedar

CEE /seəə/ nf: abbr ▶ COMMUNAUTÉ

CEEA /seəəa/ *nf* (*abbr* = **Communauté européenne de l'énergie atomique**) EAEC
CEI /seəi/ *nf*: *abbr* ▶ COMMUNAUTÉ
ceinture /sɛ̃tyʀ/ *nf* **(a)** belt
(b) waistband
(c) girdle
(d) waist; **avoir de l'eau jusqu'à la ~** to be waist-deep in water
(e) (Sport) waist hold; **~ noire** black belt
(f) ring
■ **~ de sauvetage** lifebelt; **~ de sécurité** safety *or* seat belt
IDIOMS **faire ~** (colloq) to go without; **se serrer la ~** to tighten one's belt
ceinturer /sɛ̃tyʀe/ [1] *vtr* to encircle
ceinturon /sɛ̃tyʀɔ̃/ *nm* belt
cela /səla/ *pron*

■ **Note** *Cela* and *ça* are equivalent in many cases. See the entry *ça* for more information.
– *Cela* is used in formal contexts and in the expressions shown below.

(a) it; that; **quant à ~** as for that; **~ dit** having said that
(b) ~ va sans dire it *or* that goes without saying; **voyez-vous ~!** did you ever hear of such a thing!
célébration /selebʀasjɔ̃/ *nf* celebration
célèbre /selɛbʀ/ *adj* famous
célébrer /selebʀe/ [14] *vtr* **(a)** to celebrate ‹*event, mass*›; to perform ‹*rite*›
(b) to praise ‹*person*›
célébrité /selebʀite/ *nf* **(a)** fame
(b) celebrity
céleri /sɛlʀi/ *nm* **(a)** celery
(b) celeriac
céleri-rave, *pl* **céleris-raves** /selʀiʀav/ *nm* celeriac
céleste /selɛst/ *adj* celestial; heavenly; divine
célibat /seliba/ *nm* **(a)** single status
(b) celibacy
célibataire /selibatɛʀ/ **1** *adj* single
2 *nmf* bachelor/single woman
celle ▶ CELUI
celle-ci ▶ CELUI-CI
celle-là ▶ CELUI-LÀ
celles-ci ▶ CELUI-CI
celles-là ▶ CELUI-LÀ
cellier /selje/ *nm* cellar
cellophane® /selɔfan/ *nf* cellophane®
cellulaire /selylɛʀ/ *adj* cell; cellular
cellule /selyl/ *nf* **(a)** cell
(b) unit; **~ familiale** family unit
cellulite /selylit/ *nf* **(a)** cellulite
(b) cellulitis
celte /sɛlt/ *adj, nm* Celtic
Celte /sɛlt/ *nmf* Celt
celui /səlɥi/, **celle** /sɛl/, *mpl* **ceux** /sø/, *fpl* **celles** /sɛl/ *pron* the one; **le train du matin ou ~ du soir?** the morning train or the evening one?; **ceux, celles** those; the ones; **ceux d'entre vous qui veulent partir** those of you who want to leave; **ceux qu'il a vendus** the ones he sold; **faire ~ qui n'entend pas** to pretend not to hear
celui-ci /səlɥisi/, **celle-ci** /sɛlsi/, *mpl* **ceux-ci** /søsi/, *fpl* **celles-ci** /sɛlsi/ *pron* **(a)** this one; **ceux-ci, celles-ci** these
(b) je n'ai qu'une chose à dire et c'est celle-ci I have only one thing to say and it's this
(c) elle essaya la fenêtre mais celle-ci était coincée she tried the window but it was jammed; **il entra, suivi de son père et de son frère; ~ portait un paquet** he came in, followed by his father and his brother; the latter was carrying a parcel
celui-là /səlɥila/, **celle-là** /sɛlla/, *mpl* **ceux-là** /søla/, *fpl* **celles-là** /sɛlla/ *pron* **(a)** that one; **ceux-là, celles-là** those (ones)
(b) si je n'ai qu'un conseil à te donner, c'est ~ if I only have one piece of advice for you, it's this
(c) the former
(d) il fit une autre proposition, plus réaliste celle-là he made another proposal, a more realistic one this time
(e) (colloq) **il exagère, ~!** that guy's pushing it a bit! (colloq)
(f) (colloq) **elle est bien bonne, celle-là!** that's a good one!; **je ne m'attendais pas à celle-là** I didn't expect that!; **~ même** the very one
cendre /sɑ̃dʀ/ *nf* ash
cendré, ~e /sɑ̃dʀe/ *adj* **blond ~** ash blond
cendrier /sɑ̃dʀije/ *nm* ashtray
Cène /sɛn/ *nf* **la ~** the Last Supper
censé, ~e /sɑ̃se/ *adj* **être ~ faire** to be supposed to do
censeur /sɑ̃sœʀ/ *nm* (Sch) *school official in charge of discipline*
censure /sɑ̃syʀ/ *nf* **(a)** censorship
(b) board of censors
(c) censure
censurer /sɑ̃syʀe/ [1] *vtr* **(a)** to censor
(b) to ban
cent /sɑ̃/ **1** *adj* a hundred, one hundred
2 *nm* **(a)** hundred
(b) (euro-currency) cent
3 pour cent *phr* per cent
IDIOMS **faire les ~ pas** to pace up and down; **être aux ~ coups** (colloq) to be worried sick (colloq); **attendre ~ sept ans** (colloq) to wait for ages
centaine /sɑ̃tɛn/ *nf* **(a)** hundred
(b) about a hundred
centenaire /sɑ̃tnɛʀ/ **1** *adj* hundred-year-old, centenarian
2 *nmf* **c'est une ~** she's a hundred years old
3 *nm* centenary, centennial
centième /sɑ̃tjɛm/ *adj* hundredth
centilitre /sɑ̃tilitʀ/ *nm* centilitre (GB)
centime /sɑ̃tim/ *nm* centime
centimètre /sɑ̃timɛtʀ/ *nm* **(a)** centimetre (GB) ···›

(b) ne pas avancer d'un ∼ not to move an inch
(c) tape measure

central, ∼e¹, *mpl* **-aux** /sɑ̃tral, o/
1 *adj* **(a)** central; **court ∼** (in tennis) centre (GB) court; **ordinateur ∼** host computer
(b) main
2 *nm* **∼ (téléphonique)** (telephone) exchange

centrale² /sɑ̃tral/ *nf* **(a)** power station
(b) prison

centraliser /sɑ̃tralize/ [1] *vtr* to centralize

centralisme /sɑ̃tralism/ *nm* centralism

centre /sɑ̃tr/ *nm* centre (GB); **il se prend pour le ∼ du monde** he thinks the whole world revolves around him
■ **∼ aéré** children's outdoor activity centre; **∼ commercial** shopping centre (GB); **∼ de documentation et d'information, CDI** learning resources centre (GB); **∼ hospitalier** hospital complex; **∼ hospitalier universitaire, CHU ≈** teaching hospital

centrer /sɑ̃tre/ [1] *vtr* to centre (GB)

centre-ville, *pl* **centres-villes** /sɑ̃trəvil/ *nm* town centre (GB), city centre (GB)

centrifuge /sɑ̃trify3/ *adj* centrifugal

centrifugeuse /sɑ̃trify3øz/ *nf* **(a)** juice extractor
(b) centrifuge

centriste /sɑ̃trist/ *adj, nmf* centrist

centuple /sɑ̃typl/ *nm* **dix mille est le ∼ de cent** ten thousand is a hundred times one hundred; **au ∼** a hundred times over

cep /sɛp/ *nm* **∼ (de vigne)** vine stock

cépage /sepaʒ/ *nm* grape variety; **∼ cabernet** Cabernet grape

cèpe /sɛp/ *nm* cep

cependant /səpɑ̃dɑ̃/ **1** *conj* yet, however
2 cependant que *phr* whereas, while

céramique /seramik/ *nf* **(a)** ceramic
(b) ceramics

cerceau, *pl* **∼x** /sɛrso/ *nm* hoop

cercle /sɛrkl/ *nm* **(a)** circle; **en ∼** in a circle; **décrire des ∼s** ⟨*plane, bird*⟩ to circle (overhead); **le ∼ de famille** the family circle
(b) circle, society; club
(c) hoop

cercler /sɛrkle/ [1] *vtr* to hoop ⟨*barrel*⟩; **les noms cerclés en rouge** the names circled in red

cercueil /sɛrkœj/ *nm* coffin

céréale /sereal/ *nf* cereal, grain

céréalier, -ière /serealje, ɛr/ *adj* ⟨*production*⟩ cereal; ⟨*region*⟩ cereal-growing

cérébral, ∼e, *mpl* **-aux** /serebral, o/ *adj* **(a)** cerebral
(b) intellectual

cérémonial, *pl* **∼s** /seremɔnjal/ *nm* ceremonial

cérémonie /seremɔni/ **1** *nf* ceremony; **tenue** *or* **habit de ∼** ceremony dress

2 cérémonies *nf pl* ceremony; **faire des ∼s** to stand on ceremony; **sans ∼s** ⟨*dinner, invitation*⟩ informal; ⟨*receive*⟩ informally

cérémonieux, -ieuse /seremɔnjø, øz/ *adj* ceremonious; **d'un air ∼** ceremoniously

cerf /sɛr/ *nm* stag

cerfeuil /sɛrfœj/ *nm* chervil

cerf-volant, *pl* **cerfs-volants** /sɛrvolɑ̃/ *nm* **(a)** kite
(b) stag beetle

cerise /s(ə)riz/ *nf* cherry

cerisier /s(ə)rizje/ *nm* cherry (tree)

cerne /sɛrn/ *nm* ring

cerné, ∼e /sɛrne/ *adj* **avoir les yeux ∼s** to have rings under one's eyes

cerner /sɛrne/ [1] *vtr* **(a)** to surround
(b) to define ⟨*problem*⟩; to figure out ⟨*person*⟩; to determine ⟨*personality*⟩
(c) to outline ⟨*drawing*⟩

certain, ∼e /sɛrtɛ̃, ɛn/ **1** *adj* **(a)** **être ∼ de** to be certain *or* sure of
(b) ⟨*fact*⟩ certain, sure; ⟨*date, price, influence*⟩ definite; ⟨*rate*⟩ fixed
2 *det* **elle restera un ∼ temps** she'll stay for some time; **un ∼ nombre d'erreurs** a certain number of mistakes; **d'une ∼e manière** in a way; **il avait déjà un ∼ âge** he was already getting on in years
3 certains, certaines *det pl* some; **à ∼s moments** sometimes, at times
4 certains, certaines *pron pl* some people; **∼s d'entre eux** some of them

certainement /sɛrtɛnmɑ̃/ *adv* **(a)** most probably
(b) certainly; **mais ∼!** certainly!, of course!

certes /sɛrt/ *adv* **ce ne sera ∼ pas facile mais...** admittedly it won't be easy but...

certificat /sɛrtifika/ *nm* **(a)** certificate
(b) testimonial
■ **∼ d'aptitude professionnelle, CAP** *vocational training qualification*; **∼ de décès** death certificate; **∼ médical** medical certificate; **∼ de résidence** proof of residence; **∼ de scolarité** proof of attendance (*at school or university*); **∼ de travail** *document from a previous employer giving dates and nature of employment*

certifié, ∼e /sɛrtifje/ *adj* **professeur ∼** fully qualified teacher

certifier /sɛrtifje/ [2] *vtr* **(a)** to certify; **copie certifiée conforme** certified copy
(b) **elle m'a certifié que** she assured me that

certitude /sɛrtityd/ *nf* **(a)** certainty; **on sait avec ∼ que** we know for certain that
(b) **avoir la ∼ que** to be certain that

cérumen /serymɛn/ *nm* earwax

cerveau, *pl* **∼x** /sɛrvo/ *nm* **(a)** brain
(b) mind
(c) (person) brain (colloq); **exode** *or* **fuite des ∼x** brain drain; **c'est un ∼** he/she has an outstanding mind
(d) brains; nerve centre (GB)
IDIOMS avoir le ∼ dérangé to be deranged

cervelas /sɛrvəla/ *nm* saveloy

cervelet /sɛʀvəlɛ/ *nm* cerebellum

cervelle /sɛʀvɛl/ *nf* (a) brains; ～ **de veau** (Culin) calf's brains
(b) (colloq) **il n'a rien dans la** ～ he's brainless; ～ **d'oiseau** birdbrain (colloq)

cervical, ～**e**, *mpl* **-aux** /sɛʀvikal, o/ *adj* cervical

ces ▶ CE 1

CES /seəes/ *nm*: *abbr* ▶ COLLÈGE

césar /sezaʀ/ *nm* César (*film award*)

césarienne /sezaʀjɛn/ *nf* caesarian (section)

cessation /sesasjɔ̃/ *nf* suspension

cesse /sɛs/ *nf* **sans** ～ constantly

cesser /sese/ [1] **1** *vtr* to stop, to cease; to end; ～ **de faire** to stop doing; to give up doing
2 *vi* ⟨activity⟩ to cease; ⟨wind⟩ to drop; ⟨rain⟩ to stop; **faire** ～ to put an end *or* a stop to, to end

cessez-le-feu /seselfø/ *nm inv* ceasefire

cession /sesjɔ̃/ *nf* transfer

c'est-à-dire /setadiʀ/ *phr* (a) that is (to say)
(b) ～ **que** which means (that); '**le travail est trop dur**'—'～?' 'the work is too hard'— 'what do you mean?'

cet ▶ CE 1

CET /seate/ *nm*: *abbr* ▶ COLLÈGE

cette ▶ CE 1

ceux ▶ CELUI

ceux-ci ▶ CELUI-CI

ceux-là ▶ CELUI-LÀ

CFDT /seɛfdete/ *nf* (*abbr* = **Confédération française démocratique du travail**) CFDT (*French trade union*)

CGC /seʒese/ *nf* (*abbr* = **Confédération générale des cadres**) CGC (*French trade union*)

CGT /seʒete/ *nf* (*abbr* = **Confédération générale du travail**) CGT (*French trade union*)

chacal, *pl* ～**s** /ʃakal/ *nm* jackal

chacun, ～**e** /ʃakœ̃, yn/ *pron* (a) each (one); **ils ont** ～ **sa** *or* **leur chambre** they each have their own room
(b) everyone; ～ **pour soi** every man for himself

chagrin, ～**e** /ʃagʀɛ̃, in/ **1** *adj* despondent
2 *nm* grief; **faire du** ～ **à qn** to cause sb grief; **avoir du** ～ to be sad; **avoir un gros** ～ to be very upset; ～ **d'amour** unhappy love affair

chagriner /ʃagʀine/ [1] *vtr* (a) to pain, to grieve
(b) to worry

chahut /ʃay/ *nm* racket (colloq)

chahuter /ʃayte/ [1] **1** *vtr* to play up ⟨teacher⟩; to heckle ⟨speaker⟩
2 *vi* to mess around

chaîne /ʃɛn/ **1** *nf* (a) chain; **attacher qn**

avec des ～**s** to chain sb up; **des catastrophes en** ～ a series of disasters; **réaction en** ～ chain reaction
(b) assembly line; **produire (qch) à la** ～ to mass-produce (sth)
(c) network; ～ **de solidarité** support network
(d) ～ (**de télévision**) (television) channel
(e) ～ **hi-fi/stéréo** hi-fi/stereo system
2 **chaînes** *nf pl* snow chains
■ ～ **de fabrication** production line

chaînette /ʃɛnɛt/ *nf* chain

chaînon /ʃɛnɔ̃/ *nm* link; ～ **manquant** missing link

chair /ʃɛʀ/ **1** *adj inv* flesh-coloured (GB)
2 *nf* flesh; meat; **bien en** ～ plump
■ ～ **de poule** gooseflesh, goose pimples; **donner la** ～ **de poule à qn** ⟨cold⟩ to give sb gooseflesh; ⟨fear⟩ to make sb's flesh creep

chaire /ʃɛʀ/ *nf* (a) pulpit
(b) (at university) chair
(c) rostrum

chaise /ʃɛz/ *nf* chair
■ ～ **haute** high-chair; ～ **longue** deckchair; ～ **roulante** wheelchair
IDIOMS **être assis entre deux** ～**s** to be in an awkward position

châle /ʃal/ *nm* shawl

chalet /ʃalɛ/ *nm* chalet

chaleur /ʃalœʀ/ **1** *nf* (a) heat; warmth; **coup de** ～ heat stroke; ～ **animale** body heat
(b) (of person, welcome, colour) warmth
(c) (Zool) (**être**) **en** ～ (to be) on heat
2 **chaleurs** *nf pl* **les grandes** ～**s** the hot season

chaleureusement /ʃaləʀøzmɑ̃/ *adv* warmly; wholeheartedly

chaleureux, **-euse** /ʃaləʀø, øz/ *adj* ⟨person, greeting⟩ warm; ⟨audience⟩ enthusiastic

challenge /ʃalɑ̃ʒ/ *nm* (a) (Sport) tournament
(b) trophy

challenge(u)r /ʃalɑ̃ʒœʀ/ *nm* challenger

chaloupe /ʃalup/ *nf* (a) rowing boat (GB), rowboat (US)
(b) (motor) launch

chalumeau, *pl* ～**x** /ʃalymo/ *nm* blowtorch

chalut /ʃaly/ *nm* trawl

chalutier /ʃalytje/ *nm* (a) trawler
(b) trawlerman

chamailler: se chamailler /ʃamaje/ [1] *v refl* (+ *v être*) (colloq) to squabble

chamarré, ～**e** /ʃamaʀe/ *adj* (a) richly ornamented
(b) brightly coloured (GB)

chambard /ʃɑ̃baʀ/ *nm* (colloq) din, racket (colloq)

chambardement /ʃɑ̃baʀdəmɑ̃/ *nm* (colloq) (a) shake-up (colloq)
(b) mess

chambouler /ʃɑ̃bule/ [1] *vtr* (colloq) (a) to upset ⟨plans, routine⟩

(b) to turn [sth] upside down ⟨*house*⟩; to mess [sth] up ⟨*papers*⟩

chambranle /ʃɑ̃bʀɑ̃l/ *nm* frame

chambre /ʃɑ̃bʀ/ *nf* **(a)** bedroom; room; ~ pour une personne single room; ~ à deux lits twin room; faire ~ à part to sleep in separate rooms
(b) musique de ~ chamber music
(c) (in parliament) house
(d) (in administration) chamber
■ ~ à air inner tube; ~ d'amis guest room; ~ de commerce chamber of commerce; ~ à coucher bedroom; bedroom suite; '~s d'hôte' 'bed and breakfast'; ~ noire camera obscura; darkroom

chambrée /ʃɑ̃bʀe/ *nf* (Mil) soldiers occupying barrack room

chambrer /ʃɑ̃bʀe/ [1] *vtr* **(a)** to bring [sth] to room temperature
(b) (colloq) (mock) to tease

chameau, *pl* ~**x** /ʃamo/ *nm* (Zool) camel

chamelier /ʃaməlje/ *nm* camel driver

chamelle /ʃamɛl/ *nf* she-camel

chamois /ʃamwa/ *nm* (Zool) chamois

champ /ʃɑ̃/ ⒈ *nm* field; (figurative) field, domain; en pleins ~s in open country; avoir le ~ libre to have a free hand
⒉ à tout bout de champ *phr* (colloq) all the time
■ ~ de courses racetrack

champagne /ʃɑ̃paɲ/ *nm* champagne

champagnisé /ʃɑ̃paɲize/ *adj* vin ~ sparkling wine

champenois, ~**e** /ʃɑ̃pənwa, az/ *adj* **(a)** of the Champagne region
(b) méthode ~e champagne method

champêtre /ʃɑ̃pɛtʀ/ *adj* ⟨*scene*⟩ rural; bal ~ village dance; déjeuner ~ country picnic

champignon /ʃɑ̃piɲɔ̃/ *nm* **(a)** (Culin) mushroom; ~ vénéneux toadstool
(b) (Bot, Med) fungus
(c) (colloq) throttle, accelerator
■ ~ atomique mushroom cloud; ~ de Paris button mushroom (GB), champignon (US)

champion, -**ionne** /ʃɑ̃pjɔ̃, ɔn/ *nm,f* champion; le ~ en titre the titleholder

championnat /ʃɑ̃pjɔna/ *nm* championship

chance /ʃɑ̃s/ *nf* **(a)** (good) luck; coup de ~ stroke of luck; avoir de la ~ to be lucky; avoir la ~ de trouver une maison to be lucky enough to find a house; par ~ luckily, fortunately; tenter *or* courir sa ~ to try one's luck
(b) chance (de of); il y a de fortes ~s (pour) que there's every chance that; il a ses ~s he stands a good chance; mettre toutes les ~s de son côté to take no chances; 'il va pleuvoir?'—'il y a des ~s' 'is it going to rain?'—'probably'
(c) chance, opportunity

chancelant, ~**e** /ʃɑ̃slɑ̃, ɑ̃t/ *adj* **(a)** ⟨*gait*⟩ unsteady; ⟨*object*⟩ rickety, shaky; ⟨*person*⟩ staggering; d'un pas ~ unsteadily

(b) ⟨*courage, faith*⟩ wavering; ⟨*empire*⟩ tottering

chanceler /ʃɑ̃sle/ [19] *vi* **(a)** ⟨*person*⟩ to stagger; ⟨*object*⟩ to wobble
(b) ⟨*courage*⟩ to waver
(c) ⟨*empire*⟩ to totter; ⟨*health*⟩ to be precarious

chancelier /ʃɑ̃səlje/ *nm* chancellor

chancellerie /ʃɑ̃sɛlʀi/ *nf* Ministry of Justice

chanceux, -**euse** /ʃɑ̃sø, øz/ *adj* lucky

chandail /ʃɑ̃daj/ *nm* sweater, jumper (GB)

chandelier /ʃɑ̃dəlje/ *nm* candelabra (GB)

chandelle /ʃɑ̃dɛl/ *nf* **(a)** candle; un dîner aux ~s a candlelit dinner
(b) (Sport) shoulder stand
IDIOMS devoir une fière ~ à to be hugely indebted to; faire des économies de bouts de ~s to make cheeseparing economies

change /ʃɑ̃ʒ/ *nm* **(a)** exchange rate
(b) (foreign) exchange; perdre au ~ (figurative) to lose out

changeant, ~**e** /ʃɑ̃ʒɑ̃, ɑ̃t/ *adj* changeable

changement /ʃɑ̃ʒmɑ̃/ *nm* change; ~ en mieux/pire change for the better/worse

changer /ʃɑ̃ʒe/ [13] ⒈ *vtr* **(a)** to exchange ⟨*object*⟩; to change ⟨*secretary, job*⟩
(b) to change ⟨*money*⟩; to cash ⟨*traveller's cheque*⟩
(c) to change ⟨*purchased item*⟩
(d) ~ qch de place to move sth
(e) to change ⟨*situation, appearance*⟩; cette coiffure te change you look different with your hair like that; qu'est-ce que ça change? what difference does it make?; cela ne change rien au fait que that doesn't alter the fact that
(f) ~ qn/qch en to turn sb/sth into
(g) cela nous change de la pluie it makes a change from the rain; pour ne pas ~ as usual
(h) to change ⟨*baby*⟩
⒉ changer de *v+prep* to change; ~ d'avis to change one's mind; ~ de domicile to move house; ~ de trottoir to cross over to the other side of the road; nous avons changé de route au retour we came back by a different route
⒊ *vi* to change
⒋ se changer *v refl* (+ *v être*) **(a)** to get changed
(b) se ~ en to turn *or* change into

changeur, -**euse** /ʃɑ̃ʒœʀ, øz/ ⒈ *nm,f* money changer
⒉ *nm* change machine

chanoine /ʃanwan/ *nm* canon

chanson /ʃɑ̃sɔ̃/ *nf* **(a)** song; vedette de la ~ singing star
(b) c'est toujours la même ~ (colloq) it's always the same old story; je connais la ~ (colloq) I've heard it all before

chansonnier, -**ière** /ʃɑ̃sɔnje, ɛʀ/ *nm,f* cabaret artist

chant /ʃɑ̃/ *nm* **(a)** singing

(b) (of bird, whale) song; (of cock) crow(ing); (of cricket) chirp(ing); (of cicada) shrilling
(c) song
(d) ode; canto
■ ~ **de Noël** Christmas carol

chantage /ʃɑ̃taʒ/ *nm* blackmail

chantant, ~e /ʃɑ̃tɑ̃, ɑ̃t/ *adj* singsong

chanter /ʃɑ̃te/ [1] **1** *vtr* (a) to sing
(b) (colloq) **qu'est-ce qu'il nous chante?** what's he talking about?
2 chanter à *v+prep* (colloq) **ça te chante d'y aller?** do you fancy (colloq) going?
3 *vi* (a) to sing; ~ **juste/faux** to sing in tune/out of tune
(b) ⟨*bird*⟩ to sing; ⟨*cock*⟩ to crow
(c) **faire ~ qn** to blackmail sb

chanteur, -euse /ʃɑ̃tœʀ, øz/ *nm,f* singer

chantier /ʃɑ̃tje/ *nm* (a) building site; **en ~** ⟨*building*⟩ under construction; **notre maison sera en ~ tout l'hiver** the work on our house will go on all winter; **mettre en ~** to undertake ⟨*project*⟩
(b) builder's yard
(c) (colloq) mess

chantonner /ʃɑ̃tɔne/ [1] *vtr, vi* to hum

chantre /ʃɑ̃tʀ/ *nm* eulogist (**de** of); (poet) bard

chanvre /ʃɑ̃vʀ/ *nm* hemp

chaos /kao/ *nm inv* chaos

chaotique /kaɔtik/ *adj* chaotic

chaparder /ʃapaʀde/ [1] *vtr* (colloq) to pinch (colloq)

chape /ʃap/ *nf* ~ **de béton** concrete screed

chapeau, *pl* ~**x** /ʃapo/ **1** *nm* hat
2 *excl* (colloq) well done!
■ ~ **haut de forme** top hat; ~ **melon** bowler (hat) (GB), derby (hat) (US); ~ **de roue** (Aut) hubcap; **démarrer sur les ~x de roues** (colloq) ⟨*car, driver*⟩ to shoot off at top speed
IDIOMS **tirer son ~ à** to take one's hat off to

chapeauter /ʃapote/ [1] *vtr* (colloq) to head; **le ministère chapeaute notre équipe** our team works under the ministry

chapelet /ʃaplɛ/ *nm* (a) rosary
(b) (of onions, insults, islands) string

chapelier, -ière /ʃapəlje, ɛʀ/ *nm,f* hatter

chapelle /ʃapɛl/ *nf* (a) chapel
(b) clique, coterie

chapelure /ʃaplyʀ/ *nf* breadcrumbs

chaperon /ʃapʀɔ̃/ *nm* chaperon(e)

chapiteau, *pl* ~**x** /ʃapito/ *nm*
(a) marquee (GB), tent; (of circus) big top
(b) (of pillar) capital

chapitre /ʃapitʀ/ *nm* (a) (of book) chapter
(b) subject
IDIOMS **avoir voix au ~** to have a say in the matter

chapka /ʃapka/ *nf* fur hat

chaque /ʃak/ *det* each, every

char /ʃaʀ/ *nm* (a) (Mil) tank
(b) chariot
(c) (in carnival) float
■ ~ **d'assaut** (Mil) tank; ~ **à bœufs** oxcart; ~ **à voile** (Sport) sand yacht; ice yacht

charabia /ʃaʀabja/ *nm* (colloq) gobbledygook (colloq)

charade /ʃaʀad/ *nf* riddle

charbon /ʃaʀbɔ̃/ *nm* coal; ~ **de bois** charcoal
IDIOMS **être sur des ~s ardents** to be like a cat on a hot tin roof

charcuter /ʃaʀkyte/ [1] *vtr* (colloq) to hack [sb] about

charcuterie /ʃaʀkytʀi/ *nf* (a) cooked pork meats
(b) pork butcher's

charcutier, -ière /ʃaʀkytje, ɛʀ/ *nm,f* pork butcher

chardon /ʃaʀdɔ̃/ *nm* thistle

charentais, ~e[1] /ʃaʀɑ̃tɛ, ɛz/ *adj* from the Charente region

charentaise[2] /ʃaʀɑ̃tɛz/ *nf* carpet slipper

charge /ʃaʀʒ/ **1** *nf* (a) burden, load; (of vehicle) load; (of ship) cargo, freight; **prise en ~** (in taxi) minimum fare
(b) **avoir la ~ de qn/qch** to be responsible for sb/sth; **avoir trois enfants à ~** to have three children to support; **prendre en ~** ⟨*guardian*⟩ to take charge of ⟨*child*⟩; ⟨*social security system*⟩ to accept financial responsibility for ⟨*sick person*⟩; to take care of ⟨*fees*⟩
(c) ~ **de notaire** ≈ solicitor's office
(d) (legal) charge
(e) (Mil) charge
2 charges *nf pl* (a) expenses, costs
(b) (payable by tenant) ~**s** (**locatives**) service charges
■ ~**s patronales** employer's social security contributions.
IDIOMS **revenir à la ~** to try again

chargé, ~e /ʃaʀʒe/ **1** *pp* ▶ CHARGER
2 *pp adj* **être ~ de** to be heavy *or* laden (down) with; **un regard ~ de menaces** a threatening look; **être ~ de famille** to have dependents
3 *adj* ⟨*person, vehicle*⟩ loaded; ⟨*day*⟩ busy; **avoir un casier judiciaire ~** to have had several previous convictions
■ ~ **d'affaires** chargé d'affaires; ~ **de cours** part-time lecturer; ~ **de mission** representative

chargement /ʃaʀʒəmɑ̃/ *nm* (a) (goods) load; cargo
(b) (action) loading

charger /ʃaʀʒe/ [13] **1** *vtr* (a) to load
(b) to charge ⟨*battery*⟩
(c) ~ **qn de faire** to give sb the responsibility of doing; **c'est lui qui est chargé de l'enquête** he is in charge of the investigation
(d) to bring evidence against ⟨*accused*⟩
(e) ⟨*police*⟩ to charge at ⟨*crowd*⟩
2 se charger *v refl* (+ *v être*) **se ~ de** to take responsibility for; **je m'en charge** I'll see to it

chargeur /ʃaʀʒœʀ/ *nm* (a) (Mil) magazine
(b) (of camera) cartridge
(c) (Comput) loader

chariot /ʃaʀjo/ *nm* **(a)** trolley (GB), cart (US)
(b) truck
(c) waggon (GB)
(d) (of typewriter) carriage

charisme /kaʀism/ *nm* charisma

charitable /ʃaʀitabl/ *adj* charitable

charitablement /ʃaʀitabləmɑ̃/ *adv* charitably; kindly

charité /ʃaʀite/ *nf* **(a)** charity
(b) par (pure) ∼ out of the kindness of one's heart

charlatan /ʃaʀlatɑ̃/ *nm* **(a)** quack (colloq)
(b) con man
(c) (politician) fraud

charlot /ʃaʀlo/ *nm* (colloq) clown

charlotte /ʃaʀlɔt/ *nf* **(a)** (Culin) charlotte
(b) mobcap

charmant, ∼e /ʃaʀmɑ̃, ɑ̃t/ *adj* charming

charme /ʃaʀm/ **1** *nm* **(a)** charm; **faire du** ∼ **à qn** to make eyes at sb; **cela ne manque pas de** ∼ (lifestyle, novel) it's not without its charms; (proposition) it's not unattractive
(b) spell
2 charmes *nm pl* (euphemistic) physical attributes
IDIOMS **se porter comme un** ∼ to be as fit as a fiddle

charmer /ʃaʀme/ [1] *vtr* to charm

charmeur, -euse /ʃaʀmœʀ, øz/ **1** *adj* winning, engaging
2 *nm,f* charmer

charnel, -elle /ʃaʀnɛl/ *adj* carnal

charnier /ʃaʀnje/ *nm* mass grave

charnière /ʃaʀnjɛʀ/ *nf* **(a)** hinge
(b) (figurative) bridge; junction; **rôle(-)**∼ pivotal role

charnu, ∼e /ʃaʀny/ *adj* (lip) fleshy, thick

charogne /ʃaʀɔɲ/ *nf* rotting carcass

charpente /ʃaʀpɑ̃t/ *nf* (of roof) roof structure; (of building) framework; (of person) build

charpentier /ʃaʀpɑ̃tje/ *nm* carpenter

charpie /ʃaʀpi/ *nf* **réduire** *or* **mettre qch en** ∼ to tear sth to shreds

charretier /ʃaʀtje/ *nm* carter
IDIOMS **jurer comme un** ∼ to swear like a trooper

charrette /ʃaʀɛt/ *nf* cart; ∼ **à bras** handcart

charrier /ʃaʀje/ [2] **1** *vtr* **(a)** to carry, to haul
(b) (river) to carry (sth) along
(c) (colloq) to tease [sb] unmercifully
2 *vi* (colloq) to go too far

charrue /ʃaʀy/ *nf* plough (GB), plow (US).
IDIOMS **mettre la** ∼ **avant les bœufs** to put the cart before the horse

charte /ʃaʀt/ *nf* charter

charter /ʃaʀtɛʀ/ *adj inv* (plane, flight) charter

chasse /ʃas/ *nf* **(a)** hunting; shooting; ∼ **au trésor** treasure hunt; **la** ∼ **est ouverte** it's the open season
(b) ∼ **gardée** private hunting (ground); (figurative) preserve
(c) donner la ∼ **à, prendre en** ∼ to chase
■ ∼ **à courre** hunting; ∼ **d'eau** (toilet) flush; **tirer la** ∼ to pull the chain
IDIOMS **qui va à la** ∼ **perd sa place** (Proverb) leave your place and you lose it

chassé-croisé, *pl* **chassés-croisés** /ʃasekrwaze/ *nm* continual coming and going

chasse-neige /ʃasnɛʒ/ *nm inv* snowplough (GB), snowplow (US)

chasser /ʃase/ [1] **1** *vtr* **(a)** (animal) to hunt (prey)
(b) (hunter) to shoot (GB), to hunt
(c) (person) to chase away (animal, intruder); (rain) to drive away (tourists); to fire (domestic servant)
(d) to dispel (smoke, doubt)
2 *vi* to go hunting

chasseur, -euse /ʃasœʀ, øz/ **1** *nm,f* hunter
2 *nm* **(a)** (Mil) fighter (aircraft); fighter pilot
(b) (in hotel) bellboy
■ ∼ **alpin** soldier trained for mountainous terrain; ∼ **de têtes** head-hunter

châssis /ʃasi/ *nm inv* **(a)** (of window) frame
(b) (Aut) chassis

chaste /ʃast/ *adj* (gen) chaste; (person) celibate

chasteté /ʃastəte/ *nf* chastity

chat /ʃa/ *nm* cat; tomcat
■ ∼ **de gouttière** ordinary cat; alley cat; ∼ **perché** off-ground tag.
IDIOMS **donner sa langue au** ∼ to give in; **il n'y a pas un** ∼ the place is deserted; **avoir un** ∼ **dans la gorge** to have a frog in one's throat; **il ne faut pas réveiller le** ∼ **qui dort** (Proverb) let sleeping dogs lie; **s'entendre comme chien et** ∼ to fight like cat and dog

châtaigne /ʃatɛɲ/ *nf* (sweet) chestnut

châtaignier /ʃatɛɲe/ *nm* (sweet) chestnut (tree); **une table de** *or* **en** ∼ a chestnut table

châtain /ʃatɛ̃/ *adj m* (hair) brown

château, *pl* **∼x** /ʃato/ *nm* **(a)** castle
(b) palace
(c) mansion
■ ∼ **de cartes** house of cards; ∼ **d'eau** water tower; ∼ **fort** fortified castle
IDIOMS **mener la vie de** ∼ to live the life of Riley (GB), to live like a prince

châtelain, ∼e /ʃatlɛ̃, ɛn/ *nm,f* **(a)** lord/ lady of the manor
(b) owner of a manor

châtier /ʃatje/ [2] *vtr* to punish

chatière /ʃatjɛʀ/ *nf* catflap

châtiment /ʃatimɑ̃/ *nm* punishment

chatoiement /ʃatwamɑ̃/ *nm* shimmering

chaton /ʃatɔ̃/ *nm* **(a)** kitten
(b) catkin

chatouille /ʃatuj/ *nf* (colloq) tickle

chatouiller /ʃatuje/ [1] *vtr* to tickle
  IDIOMS ∼ les côtes à qn (euphemistic) to tan
  sb's hide
chatouilleux, -euse /ʃatujø, øz/ *adj*
  (a) ticklish
  (b) touchy (**sur** about)
chatoyant, ∼e /ʃatwajɑ̃, ɑ̃t/ *adj*
  shimmering; iridescent
chatoyer /ʃatwaje/ [23] *vi* to shimmer
châtrer /ʃɑtʀe/ [1] *vtr* to castrate
chatte /ʃat/ *nf* (female) cat
chaud, ∼e /ʃo, ʃod/ 1 *adj* (a) hot; warm
  (b) ⟨colour, voice⟩ warm
  (c) ils n'ont pas été très ∼s pour faire they
  were not very keen on doing
  (d) ⟨region⟩ turbulent; ⟨discussion⟩ heated;
  un des points ∼s du globe one of the flash
  points of the world
  (e) quartier ∼ (colloq) red light district
  2 *adv* il fait ∼ it's warm; it's hot; ça ne me
  fait ni ∼ ni froid it doesn't matter one way
  or the other to me
  3 *nm* heat; avoir ∼ to be warm; to be hot;
  nous avons eu ∼ (figurative) we had a narrow
  escape; se tenir ∼ to keep warm
  4 à chaud *phr* à ∼ ⟨analyse⟩ on the spot;
  ⟨reaction⟩ immediate
  ■ ∼ et froid (Med) chill
chaudement /ʃodmɑ̃/ *adv* (gen) warmly;
  ⟨recommend⟩ heartily
chaudière /ʃodjɛʀ/ *nf* boiler
chaudron /ʃodʀɔ̃/ *nm* cauldron
chaudronnerie /ʃodʀɔnʀi/ *nf*
  boilermaking industry; boilerworks
chaudronnier, -ière /ʃodʀɔnje, ɛʀ/
  nm,f boilermaker
chauffage /ʃofaʒ/ *nm* (a) heating
  (b) heater
chauffagiste /ʃofaʒist/ *nmf* heating
  engineer
chauffant, ∼e /ʃofɑ̃, ɑ̃t/ *adj* heating
chauffard /ʃofaʀ/ *nm* (colloq) reckless
  driver
chauffe /ʃof/ *nf* (Tech) fire chamber
chauffe-eau /ʃofo/ *nm inv* water-heater
chauffe-plat /ʃofpla/ *nm inv* dish
  warmer
chauffer /ʃofe/ [1] 1 *vtr* (a) to heat
  ⟨house⟩; to heat (up) ⟨object, meal⟩
  (b) ⟨sun⟩ to warm
  2 *vi* (a) ⟨food, oven⟩ to heat up; ⟨engine⟩ to
  warm up; to overheat
  (b) ⟨radiator⟩ to give out heat
  (c) (colloq) ça va ∼! there's going to be big
  trouble!
  3 se chauffer *v refl* (+ *v être*) (a) se ∼
  au soleil to bask in the sun
  (b) se ∼ au charbon to have coal-fired
  heating
chaufferie /ʃofʀi/ *nf* (a) boiler room
  (b) (in boat) stokehold
chauffeur /ʃofœʀ/ *nm* (a) driver
  (b) chauffeur

chauffeuse /ʃoføz/ *nf* low armless easy
  chair
chaume /ʃom/ *nm* (a) (in field) stubble
  (b) thatch
chaumière /ʃomjɛʀ/ *nf* (a) thatched
  cottage
  (b) faire jaser dans les ∼s to cause tongues
  to wag
chaussée /ʃose/ *nf* (a) roadway, highway;
  (in town) street
  (b) (road) surface
  (c) causeway
chausse-pied, *pl* ∼**s** /ʃospje/ *nm*
  shoehorn
chausser /ʃose/ [1] 1 *vtr* to put [sth] on
  ⟨shoes, spectacles⟩
  2 *vi* je chausse du 41 I take a (size) 41
  3 se chausser *v refl* (+ *v être*) (a) to put
  (one's) shoes on
  (b) to buy (one's) shoes
chaussette /ʃosɛt/ *nf* sock
  IDIOMS laisser tomber qn comme une vieille
  ∼ (colloq) to cast sb off like an old rag
chausseur /ʃosœʀ/ *nm* shoe shop
  manager; shoemaker
chausson /ʃosɔ̃/ *nm* (a) slipper
  (b) bootee
  (c) ballet shoe
  ■ ∼ aux pommes (Culin) apple turnover
chaussure /ʃosyʀ/ *nf* shoe; ∼ montante
  ankle boot
  IDIOMS trouver ∼ à son pied ⟨man, woman⟩
  to find the right person
chauve /ʃov/ *adj* bald
chauve-souris, *pl* **chauves-souris**
  /ʃovsuʀi/ *nf* (Zool) bat
chauvin, ∼e /ʃovɛ̃, in/ *adj* chauvinistic
chaux /ʃo/ *nf* lime
chavirer /ʃaviʀe/ [1] 1 *vtr* to overwhelm
  2 *vi* (a) ⟨boat⟩ to capsize
  (b) faire ∼ les cœurs to be a heartbreaker
  (c) ⟨objects⟩ to tip over
chef /ʃɛf/ *nm* (a) leader
  (b) superior, boss (colloq)
  (c) head; (of sales department) manager;
  architecte en ∼ chief architect
  (d) ∼ cuisinier *or* de cuisine chef
  (e) (colloq) ace; se débrouiller comme un ∼
  to manage splendidly
  (f) de mon/leur (propre) ∼ on my/their own
  initiative
  (g) au premier ∼ primarily, first and
  foremost
  ■ ∼ d'accusation (Law) count of indictment;
  ∼ d'atelier (shop) foreman; ∼ d'équipe
  foreman; (Sport) team captain; ∼ d'État head
  of state; ∼ de gare stationmaster
chef-d'œuvre, *pl* **chefs-d'œuvre**
  /ʃɛdœvʀ/ *nm* masterpiece
chef-lieu, *pl* **chefs-lieux** /ʃɛfljø/ *nm*
  administrative centre
chemin /ʃ(ə)mɛ̃/ *nm* (a) country road;
  lane; ∼ (de terre) dirt track; path
  (b) way; sur le ∼ du retour on the way
  back; reprendre le ∼ du bureau to go back to ⋯⋗

work; **on a fait un bout de ~ ensemble** we walked along together for a while; **~ faisant, en ~** on *or* along the way; **l'idée fait son ~** the idea is gaining ground; **prendre le ~ de la faillite** to be heading for bankruptcy; **s'arrêter en ~** to stop off on the way; (figurative) to stop

■ **~ de fer** railway, railroad (US); rail

cheminée /ʃ(ə)mine/ *nf* **(a)** chimney; chimney stack
(b) fireplace
(c) mantelpiece
(d) (of ship) funnel

cheminement /ʃ(ə)minmɑ̃/ *nm* **(a)** slow progression
(b) le ~ de sa pensée his/her train of thought

cheminer /ʃ(ə)mine/ [1] *vi* **(a)** to walk (along)
(b) ⟨idea⟩ to progress, to develop

cheminot /ʃ(ə)mino/ *nm* railway worker (GB), railroader (US)

chemise /ʃ(ə)miz/ *nf* **(a)** shirt
(b) folder
■ **~ de nuit** nightgown; (for man) nightshirt
IDIOMS **je m'en moque comme de ma première ~** (colloq) I don't give two hoots (GB) (colloq) *or* a hoot (US) (colloq); **changer d'avis comme de ~** (colloq) to change one's mind at the drop of a hat

chemiserie /ʃ(ə)mizri/ *nf* shirt-making trade; shirt factory; shirt shop

chemisier /ʃ(ə)mizje/ *nm* blouse

chenal, *pl* **-aux** /ʃənal, o/ *nm* channel, fairway

chenapan /ʃənapɑ̃/ *nm* scallywag (colloq), rascal

chêne /ʃɛn/ *nm* **(a)** oak (tree)
(b) oak

chenet /ʃənɛ/ *nm* firedog, andiron

chenil /ʃənil/ *nm* **(a)** (dog) kennel
(b) kennels

chenille /ʃənij/ *nf* (Aut, Zool) caterpillar

cheptel /ʃɛptɛl/ *nm* **~ (vif)** livestock

chèque /ʃɛk/ *nm* cheque (GB), check (US)
■ **~ en blanc** blank cheque (GB) *or* check (US); **~ en bois** (colloq) rubber cheque (GB) (colloq) *or* check (US); **~ sans provision** bad cheque (GB) *or* check (US); **~ de voyage** traveller's cheque (GB) *or* check (US)

chèque-cadeau, *pl* **chèques-cadeaux** /ʃɛkkado/ *nm* gift token

chèque-voyage, *pl* **chèques-voyage** /ʃɛkvwajaʒ/ *nm* traveller's cheque

chéquier /ʃekje/ *nm* chequebook (GB), checkbook (US)

cher, chère¹ /ʃɛʀ/ **1** *adj* **(a)** dear; beloved; **un être ~** a loved one
(b) (as term of address) dear
(c) expensive; **pas ~** cheap
2 *nm,f* **mon ~/ma chère** my dear
3 *adv* **(a)** a lot (of money); **coûter plus/moins ~** to cost more/less; **acheter ~** to buy at a high price

(b) (figurative) ⟨pay, cost⟩ dearly
IDIOMS **ne pas donner ~ de la peau de qn** (colloq) not to rate sb's chances highly

chercher /ʃɛʀʃe/ [1] **1** *vtr* **(a)** to look for ⟨person, object, trouble⟩; to try to find ⟨answer, ideas⟩; to try to remember ⟨name⟩; **~ fortune** to seek one's fortune; **~ qn du regard** to look about for sb
(b) ~ à faire to try to do
(c) aller ~ qn/qch to go and get sb/sth; to pick sb/sth up
(d) où est-il allé ~ cela? what made him think that?
(e) une maison dans ce quartier, ça va ~ dans les 800 000 francs a house in this area must fetch (GB) *or* get (US) about 800,000 francs
2 se chercher *v refl* (+ *v être*) **(a)** to try to find oneself
(b) se ~ des excuses to try to find excuses for oneself
(c) (colloq) to be out to get each other (colloq)

chercheur, -euse /ʃɛʀʃœʀ, øz/ *nm,f* researcher
■ **~ d'or** gold-digger

chère² /ʃɛʀ/ **1** *adj f* ▶ CHER
2 *nf* **faire bonne ~** to eat well

chèrement /ʃɛʀmɑ̃/ *adv* **~ acquise** gained at great cost

chéri, ~e /ʃeri/ **1** *pp* ▶ CHÉRIR
2 *pp adj* beloved
3 *nm,f* **(a)** darling
(b) (colloq) boyfriend/girlfriend

chérir /ʃeriʀ/ [3] *vtr* to cherish ⟨person⟩; to hold [sth] dear ⟨idea⟩

chérubin /ʃerybɛ̃/ *nm* cherub

chétif, -ive /ʃetif, iv/ *adj* ⟨child⟩ puny

cheval, *pl* **-aux** /ʃ(ə)val, o/ **1** *nm*
(a) horse; **monter à ~** to ride a horse; **remède de ~** strong medicine; **fièvre de ~** raging fever
(b) (Sport) horse-riding
(c) horsemeat
2 à cheval sur *phr* **(a)** astride
(b) spanning
(c) in between
(d) être à ~ sur qch to be a stickler for sth
■ **~ à bascule** rocking horse; **~ de bataille** hobbyhorse; **chevaux de bois** merry-go-round horses

chevaleresque /ʃ(ə)valʀɛsk/ *adj*
(a) ⟨literature⟩ courtly
(b) ⟨person⟩ chivalrous

chevalerie /ʃ(ə)valʀi/ *nf* chivalry

chevalet /ʃ(ə)valɛ/ *nm* easel

chevalier /ʃ(ə)valje/ *nm* knight

chevalière /ʃ(ə)valjɛʀ/ *nf* signet ring

cheval-vapeur, *pl* **chevaux-vapeur** /ʃ(ə)valvapœʀ, ʃ(ə)vovapœʀ/ *nm* horsepower

chevauchée /ʃ(ə)voʃe/ *nf* ride

chevaucher /ʃ(ə)voʃe/ [1] **1** *vtr* **(a)** to sit astride ⟨animal, chair⟩
(b) to overlap
2 se chevaucher *v refl* (+ *v être*) to overlap

chevelu, **~e** /ʃəvly/ adj long-haired

chevelure /ʃəvlyʀ/ nf hair

chevet /ʃəvɛ/ nm bedhead; **être au ~ de qn** to be at sb's bedside

cheveu, pl **~x** /ʃəvø/ [1] nm hair; **être à un ~ de** to be within a hair's breadth of; **ne tenir qu'à un ~** to hang by a thread [2] **cheveux** nm pl hair
IDIOMS **avoir un ~ sur la langue** to have a lisp; **venir comme un ~ sur la soupe** to come at an awkward moment; **se faire des ~x (blancs)** (colloq) to worry oneself to death; **couper les ~x en quatre** to split hairs; **être tiré par les ~x** to be far-fetched

cheville /ʃ(ə)vij/ nf (a) (Anat) ankle
(b) Rawlplug®; peg; dowel
IDIOMS **il n'arrive pas à la ~ de Paul** he can't hold a candle to Paul; **être en ~ avec qn** (colloq) to be in cahoots with sb (colloq)

chèvre¹ /ʃɛvʀ/ nm goat's cheese

chèvre² /ʃɛvʀ/ nf goat; nanny-goat
IDIOMS **devenir ~** (colloq) to go nuts (slang)

chevreau, pl **~x** /ʃəvʀo/ nm (Zool) kid

chèvrefeuille /ʃɛvʀəfœj/ nm honeysuckle

chevreuil /ʃəvʀœj/ nm (a) roe (deer); roebuck
(b) (Culin) venison

chevronné, **~e** /ʃəvʀɔne/ adj ⟨person⟩ experienced

chevrotant, **~e** /ʃəvʀɔtɑ̃, ɑ̃t/ adj ⟨voice⟩ quavering

chevroter /ʃəvʀɔte/ [1] vtr, vi to quaver

chevrotine /ʃəvʀɔtin/ nf buckshot

chez /ʃe/ prep (a) **~ qn** at sb's place; **rentre ~ toi** go home; **de ~ qn** ⟨telephone⟩ from sb's place; **fais comme ~ toi** make yourself at home
(b) (referring to shop, office) **aller ~ le boucher** to go to the butcher's; **être convoqué ~ le patron** to be called in before the boss
(c) (referring to a region) **~ nous** where I come from; where I live
(d) among; **~ l'animal** in animals
(e) **ce que j'aime ~ elle, c'est son humour** what I like about her is her sense of humour
(f) in; **~ Cocteau** in Cocteau

chic /ʃik/ [1] adj (a) smart (GB), chic
(b) (colloq) chic, fashionable
(c) (colloq) ⟨person⟩ nice
[2] nm chic; **avoir le ~ pour faire** to have a knack for doing; **avec ~** with style

chicane /ʃikan/ nf chicane; (on road, ski slope) double bend; **en ~** on alternate sides

chicaner /ʃikane/ [1] vi to squabble

chiche /ʃiʃ/ [1] adj (a) mean (GB), stingy
(b) **être ~ de faire** (colloq) to be quite capable of doing
[2] excl **'je vais le faire'—'~!'** (colloq) 'I'll do it'—'I dare you!'

chichement /ʃiʃmɑ̃/ adv ⟨live⟩ frugally; ⟨give⟩ stingily; ⟨pay⟩ poorly

chichi /ʃiʃi/ nm fuss

chicon /ʃikɔ̃/ nm chicory

chicorée /ʃikɔʀe/ nf (a) (plant) chicory; (salad vegetable) endive (GB), chicory (US)
(b) (Culin) (powder) chicory; (drink) chicory coffee

chien, chienne¹ /ʃjɛ̃, ʃjɛn/ [1] adj (colloq) **ne pas être ~** not to be too hard
[2] nm (a) dog
(b) (of rifle) hammer
[3] **de chien** phr (colloq) ⟨job, weather⟩ rotten; **ça me fait un mal de ~** it hurts like hell (colloq)
■ **~ d'aveugle** guide dog; **~ de berger** sheepdog; **~ de garde** guard dog; (figurative) watchdog; **~ de race** pedigree dog
IDIOMS **être couché en ~ de fusil** to be curled up; **ce n'est pas fait pour les ~s** (colloq) it's there to be used

chiendent /ʃjɛ̃dɑ̃/ nm couch grass; **brosse de ~** scrubbing brush

chienlit /ʃjɑ̃li/ nf havoc, chaos

chien-loup, pl **chiens-loups** /ʃjɛ̃lu/ nm Alsatian (GB), German shepherd

chienne² /ʃjɛn/ [1] adj f ▶ CHIEN
[2] nf (animal) bitch

chiffon /ʃifɔ̃/ nm (a) rag, (piece of) cloth; **parler ~s** to talk (about) clothes
(b) duster

chiffonné, **~e** /ʃifɔne/ adj (a) ⟨face⟩ tired-looking
(b) (colloq) ⟨person⟩ troubled, ruffled

chiffonner /ʃifɔne/ [1] [1] vtr (a) to crease, to crumple
(b) (colloq) to bother ⟨person⟩
[2] **se chiffonner** v refl (+ v être) to crease

chiffonnier /ʃifɔnje/ nm **se battre comme des ~s** to fight like cat and dog

chiffrable /ʃifʀabl/ adj calculable; **les pertes ne sont pas ~s** it's impossible to put a figure on the losses

chiffre /ʃifʀ/ nm (a) figure
(b) monogram
■ **~ d'affaires, CA** turnover (GB), sales (US); **~ arabe** Arabic numeral; **~ romain** Roman numeral; **~ de vente** sales (figures)

chiffrer /ʃifʀe/ [1] [1] vtr (a) to put a figure on ⟨cost, loss⟩; to cost ⟨job⟩; **~ à** to put the cost of ⟨sth⟩ at ⟨job⟩
(b) to encode ⟨message⟩
[2] vi (colloq) to add up; **ça chiffre vite** it soon adds up
[3] **se chiffrer** v refl (+ v être) **se ~ à** to amount to, to come to

chignole /ʃiɲɔl/ nf hand drill

chignon /ʃiɲɔ̃/ nm bun; chignon

Chili /ʃili/ pr nm Chile

chimère /ʃimɛʀ/ nf (a) wild dream, pipe dream
(b) (in mythology) Chimaera

chimérique /ʃimeʀik/ adj ⟨hope⟩ wild; ⟨person⟩ fanciful

chimie /ʃimi/ nf chemistry

chimiothérapie /ʃimjoteʀapi/ nf chemotherapy

chimique /ʃimik/ *adj* (a) chemical; ⟨fibre⟩ man-made
(b) ⟨food, taste⟩ synthetic

chimiste /ʃimist/ *nmf* chemist

chimpanzé /ʃɛ̃pɑ̃ze/ *nm* chimpanzee

chiné, **~e** /ʃine/ *adj* chiné

Chine /ʃin/ *pr nf* China

chiner /ʃine/ [1] *vi* (colloq) to bargain-hunt, to antique (US)

chinois, **~e** /ʃinwa, az/ ⟨1⟩ *adj* Chinese
⟨2⟩ *nm* (language) Chinese
IDIOMS **pour moi c'est du ~** it's double-Dutch (GB) *or* Greek to me

chiot /ʃjo/ *nm* puppy, pup

chiper /ʃipe/ [1] *vtr* (colloq) to pinch (colloq)

chipie /ʃipi/ *nf* (colloq) cow (colloq)

chipoter /ʃipɔte/ [1] *vi* (colloq) (a) to quibble (**sur** over)
(b) to pick at one's food

chipoteur, **-euse** /ʃipɔtœʀ, øz/ *adj* (colloq) (a) difficult
(b) fussy

chips /ʃips/ *nf inv* crisp (GB), potato chip (US)

chique /ʃik/ *nf* plug (of tobacco)
IDIOMS **couper la ~ à qn** to shut sb up (colloq)

chiqué /ʃike/ *nm* (colloq) (a) **c'est du ~** it's a put-on
(b) **faire du ~** to put on *or* give oneself airs

chiquenaude /ʃiknod/ *nf* flick

chiquer /ʃike/ [1] *vtr* **tabac à ~** chewing tobacco

chiromancie /kiʀɔmɑ̃si/ *nf* palmistry

chirurgical, **~e**, *mpl* **-aux** /ʃiʀyʀʒikal, o/ *adj* surgical

chirurgie /ʃiʀyʀʒi/ *nf* surgery

chirurgien /ʃiʀyʀʒjɛ̃/ *nm* surgeon

chlore /klɔʀ/ *nm* chlorine

chlorer /klɔʀe/ [1] *vtr* to chlorinate

chlorhydrique /klɔʀidʀik/ *adj* hydrochloric

chloroforme /klɔʀɔfɔʀm/ *nm* chloroform

chlorophylle /klɔʀɔfil/ *nf* chlorophyll

chlorure /klɔʀyʀ/ *nm* chloride

choc /ʃɔk/ ⟨1⟩ *adj inv* **'prix ~!'** 'huge reductions'
⟨2⟩ *nm* (a) impact, shock; collision; **sous le ~** under the impact
(b) (noise) crash, smash; thud; clang; chink
(c) (confrontation) (gen, Mil) clash; (Sport) encounter; **de ~** ⟨journalist⟩ ace (colloq)
(d) (emotional, physical) shock

chocolat /ʃɔkɔla/ *nm* chocolate; **~ noir** *or* **à croquer** plain (GB) *or* dark (US) chocolate

chœur /kœʀ/ *nm* (a) choir; (in opera, play) chorus; (figurative) chorus (**de** of); **en ~** ⟨say⟩ in unison; ⟨laugh⟩ all together
(b) (in church) chancel, choir

choir /ʃwaʀ/ [51] *vi* to fall; **laisser ~ qn** to drop sb

choisir /ʃwaziʀ/ [3] *vtr* to choose

choix /ʃwa/ *nm inv* (a) choice; **arrêter son ~ sur** to settle *or* decide on
(b) **de ~** ⟨item⟩ choice; ⟨candidate⟩ first-rate; **les places de ~** the best seats; **un morceau de ~** (of meat) a prime cut; **de second ~** of inferior quality

choléra /kɔleʀa/ *nm* cholera

cholestérol /kɔlesteʀɔl/ *nm* cholesterol

chômage /ʃomaʒ/ *nm* unemployment; **mettre qn au ~** to make sb redundant (GB), to lay sb off
■ **~ technique** layoffs

chômé, **~e** /ʃome/ *adj* **jour ~** day off; **fête ~e** national holiday

chômer /ʃome/ [1] *vi* (a) to be idle
(b) to be out of work

chômeur, **-euse** /ʃomœʀ, øz/ *nm,f* unemployed person

chope /ʃɔp/ *nf* beer mug, tankard

choquant, **~e** /ʃɔkɑ̃, ɑ̃t/ *adj* shocking

choquer /ʃɔke/ [1] *vtr* (a) to shock ⟨person⟩; to offend ⟨sight, sensibility⟩
(b) ⟨news⟩ to shake ⟨person⟩; ⟨accident⟩ to shake [sb] (up)

chorale /kɔʀal/ *nf* choir

chorégraphie /kɔʀegʀafi/ *nf* choreography

choriste /kɔʀist/ *nmf* chorister; member of the choir; member of the chorus

chorus /kɔʀys/ *nm inv* chorus; **faire ~ avec qn** (figurative) to join in with sb

chose /ʃoz/ *nf* (a) (object, abstract) thing; **de deux ~s l'une** it's got to be one thing or the other; **une ~ communément admise** a widely accepted fact; **en mettant les ~s au mieux** at best; **mettre les ~s au point** to clear things up; **avant toute ~** before anything else; above all else
(b) matter; **la ~ en question** the matter in hand
(c) **être un peu porté sur la ~** (colloq) to be keen on sex

chou, *pl* **~x** /ʃu/ *nm* (a) cabbage
(b) choux bun (GB), pastry shell (US)
(c) dear, darling
■ **~ de Bruxelles** Brussels sprout; **~ à la crème** cream puff; **~ rave** kohlrabi
IDIOMS **bête comme ~** really easy; **faire ~ blanc** (colloq) to draw a blank; **faire ses ~x gras de qch** (colloq) to use sth to one's advantage; **rentrer dans le ~ de qn** (colloq) to beat sb up; to give sb a piece of one's mind

choucas /ʃuka/ *nm* jackdaw

chouchou /ʃuʃu/ *nm* (colloq) (a) (teacher's) pet; (of adoring public) darling
(b) (for hair) scrunchie

chouchouter /ʃuʃute/ [1] *vtr* (colloq) to pamper

choucroute /ʃukʀut/ *nf* sauerkraut

chouette /ʃwɛt/ ⟨1⟩ *adj* (colloq) great (colloq), neat (US) (colloq)
⟨2⟩ *nf* (a) owl
(b) **vieille ~** old harridan

chou-fleur, pl **choux-fleurs** /ʃuflœʀ/ nm cauliflower

chourer /ʃuʀe/ [1] vtr (colloq) to pinch (colloq); **se faire ~ qch** to have sth pinched

choyer /ʃwaje/ [23] vtr to pamper

chrétien, -ienne /kʀetjɛ̃, ɛn/ adj, nm,f Christian

chrétienté /kʀetjẽte/ nf **la ~** Christendom

Christ /kʀist/ pr n **le ~** Christ

christianisme /kʀistjanism/ nm Christianity

chromatique /kʀɔmatik/ adj chromatic

chrome /kʀom/ nm chromium

chromosome /kʀɔmozom/ nm chromosome

chronique /kʀɔnik/ **1** adj chronic **2** nf (in newspaper) column, page

chroniqueur, -euse /kʀɔnikœʀ, øz/ nm,f columnist, editor

chronologie /kʀɔnɔlɔʒi/ nf chronology

chronologique /kʀɔnɔlɔʒik/ adj chronological

chronomètre /kʀɔnɔmɛtʀ/ nm stopwatch

chronométrer /kʀɔnɔmetʀe/ [14] vtr to time

chrysalide /kʀizalid/ nf chrysalis

chu ▶ CHOIR

CHU /seaʃy/ nm: abbr ▶ CENTRE

chuchotement /ʃyʃɔtmɑ̃/ nm whisper

chuchoter /ʃyʃɔte/ [1] vtr, vi to whisper

chuintant, -e /ʃɥɛ̃tɑ̃, ɑ̃t/ adj **bruit ~** hissing sound

chuinter /ʃɥɛ̃te/ [1] vi ⟨steam⟩ to hiss gently; ⟨tyre⟩ to swish

chum /tʃœm/ nm (colloq) friend; boyfriend

chut /ʃyt/ excl shh!, hush!

chute /ʃyt/ nf (a) (gen) fall; (of empire) collapse; (of hair) loss; (of pressure) drop (b) (of film) ending; (of story) punch line (c) (of cloth) offcut
■ **~ d'eau** waterfall; **la ~ des reins** the small of the back

Chypre /ʃipʀ/ pr nf Cyprus

ci /si/ **1** det **cette page-~** this page; **ces jours-~** (past) these last few days; (future) in the next few days; (present) at the moment **2** pron this; **~ et ça** this and that

ci-après /siapʀe/ adv below

cible /sibl/ nf target

cibler /sible/ [1] vtr to target

ciboulette /sibulɛt/ nf (Bot) chive; (Culin) chives

cicatrice /sikatʀis/ nf scar

cicatrisant, -e /sikatʀizɑ̃, ɑ̃t/ adj healing

cicatrisation /sikatʀizasjɔ̃/ nf healing

cicatriser /sikatʀize/ [1] vtr, **se cicatriser** v refl (+ v être) to heal

ci-contre /sikɔ̃tʀ/ adv opposite

ci-dessous /sidəsu/ adv below

ci-dessus /sidəsy/ adv above

cidre /sidʀ/ nm cider

cidrerie /sidʀəʀi/ nf cider-works

ciel /sjɛl/, pl **cieux** /sjø/ nm (a) sky; **carte du ~** star chart; **à ~ ouvert** ⟨pool⟩ open-air; ⟨sewer⟩ open (b) heaven; **c'est le ~ qui t'envoie** you're a godsend

cierge /sjɛʀʒ/ nm (church) candle

cieux ▶ CIEL

cigale /sigal/ nf cicada

cigare /sigaʀ/ nm cigar

cigarette /sigaʀɛt/ nf cigarette

ci-gît /siʒi/ phr here lies

cigogne /sigɔɲ/ nf stork

ci-inclus, ~e /siɛ̃kly, yz/ adj, adv enclosed

ci-joint, ~e /siʒwɛ̃, ɛ̃t/ adj, adv enclosed

cil /sil/ nm eyelash

ciller /sije/ [1] vi **~ (des yeux)** to blink; **sans ~** without batting an eyelid

cime /sim/ nf (tree)top

ciment /simɑ̃/ nm cement

cimenter /simɑ̃te/ [1] **1** vtr to cement **2 se cimenter** v refl (+ v être) ⟨friendship⟩ to grow stronger

cimenterie /simɑ̃tʀi/ nf cement works

cimetière /simtjɛʀ/ nm cemetery, graveyard

cinéaste /sineast/ nmf film director

ciné-club, pl **~s** /sineklœb/ nm film club

cinéma /sinema/ nm (a) **(salle de) ~** cinema (GB), movie theater (US) (b) cinema; film industry; **faire du ~** to be in films (c) (figurative) (colloq) **arrête ton ~** cut out the play-acting; stop making such a fuss (colloq)
■ **~ d'art et d'essai** cinema showing art films (GB), art house (US)

cinémathèque /sinematɛk/ nf film archive

cinématographique /sinematɔgʀafik/ adj film (GB), movie (US)

cinéphile /sinefil/ nmf cinema enthusiast

cinglant, -e /sɛ̃glɑ̃, ɑ̃t/ adj (a) ⟨wind⟩ biting; ⟨rain⟩ driving (b) ⟨remark, irony⟩ scathing

cinglé, ~e /sɛ̃gle/ adj (colloq) mad (colloq), crazy (colloq)

cingler /sɛ̃gle/ [1] vtr (a) ⟨rain, wind⟩ to sting ⟨face⟩ (b) (with whip) to lash

cinoche /sinɔʃ/ nm (colloq) (a) cinema, pictures (colloq) (b) cinema, movie theater (US)

cinq /sɛ̃k/ adj inv, pron, nm inv five

cinquantaine /sɛ̃kɑ̃tɛn/ nf about fifty

cinquante /sɛ̃kɑ̃t/ adj inv, pron, nm inv fifty

cinquantenaire /sɛ̃kɑ̃tnɛʀ/ nm fiftieth anniversary

cinquantième /sɛ̃kɑ̃tjɛm/ adj fiftieth

cinquième /sɛ̃kjɛm/ **1** adj fifth ⋯⟡

2 *nf* (a) (Sch) second year of secondary school, age 12–13
(b) (Aut) fifth (gear)

cintre /sɛ̃tʀ/ *nm* (a) (clothes) hanger
(b) (in architecture) curve

cintré, **~e** /sɛ̃tʀe/ *adj* ⟨coat⟩ waisted; ⟨shirt⟩ tailored

cirage /siʀaʒ/ *nm* (shoe) polish
IDIOMS être dans le **~** (colloq) to be half-conscious

circoncire /siʀkɔ̃siʀ/ [64] *vtr* to circumcise

circoncision /siʀkɔ̃sizjɔ̃/ *nf* male circumcision

circonférence /siʀkɔ̃feʀɑ̃s/ *nf* circumference

circonflexe /siʀkɔ̃flɛks/ *adj* accent **~** circumflex (accent)

circonscription /siʀkɔ̃skʀipsjɔ̃/ *nf* district

circonscrire /siʀkɔ̃skʀiʀ/ [67] *vtr* (a) to contain ⟨fire, epidemic⟩; to limit ⟨subject⟩
(b) to define

circonspection /siʀkɔ̃spɛksjɔ̃/ *nf* caution

circonstance /siʀkɔ̃stɑ̃s/ **1** *nf*
(a) circumstance
(b) situation; **en toute ~** in any event; **pour la ~** for the occasion
2 de circonstance *phr* ⟨poem⟩ for the occasion; **faire une tête de ~** to assume a suitable expression
■ **~s atténuantes** (Law) extenuating *or* mitigating circumstances

circuit /siʀkɥi/ *nm* (a) (Sport, Tech) circuit
(b) (in tourism) tour
(c) (figurative) **être mis hors ~** ⟨person⟩ to be put on the sidelines; **vivre en ~ fermé** to live in a closed world

circulaire /siʀkylɛʀ/ *adj, nf* circular

circulation /siʀkylasjɔ̃/ *nf* (a) traffic
(b) circulation; **la libre ~ des personnes** the free movement of people; **disparaître de la ~** to go out of circulation

circulatoire /siʀkylatwaʀ/ *adj* circulatory

circuler /siʀkyle/ [1] *vi* (a) ⟨train, bus⟩ to run
(b) ⟨person⟩ to get around; to move about; (by car) to travel
(c) ⟨banknotes, rumour, information⟩ to circulate; **faire ~** to circulate; to spread ⟨rumour⟩
(d) ⟨blood, air⟩ to circulate

cire /siʀ/ *nf* wax

ciré /siʀe/ *nm* oilskin

cirer /siʀe/ [1] *vtr* to polish ⟨shoes, floor⟩

cirque /siʀk/ *nm* (a) circus
(b) (figurative) (colloq) racket (colloq); **arrête ton ~!** stop your nonsense!

cirrhose /siʀoz/ *nf* cirrhosis

cisaille /sizaj/ *nf* pair of shears; **~s** shears

cisailler /sizaje/ [1] *vtr* (a) to shear; to cut
(b) to shear off

ciseau, *pl* **~x** /sizo/ **1** *nm* (a) (Tech) chisel
(b) (Sport) scissors jump; scissors hold
2 ciseaux *nm pl* scissors

ciseler /sizle/ [17] *vtr* to chisel

ciselure /sizlyʀ/ *nf* chasing

citadelle /sitadɛl/ *nf* citadel

citadin, **~e** /sitadɛ̃, in/ **1** *adj* city
2 *nm,f* city-dweller

citation /sitasjɔ̃/ *nf* quotation

cité /site/ *nf* (a) (gen) city; town
(b) housing estate
■ **~ universitaire** student halls of residence (GB), dormitories (US)

citer /site/ [1] *vtr* (a) to quote ⟨author, passage⟩
(b) to name ⟨title, book⟩; to cite ⟨person, example, fact⟩
(c) (Law) to summon ⟨witness⟩

citerne /sitɛʀn/ *nf* tank

citoyen, **-enne** /sitwajɛ̃, ɛn/ *nm,f* citizen

citoyenneté /sitwajɛnte/ *nf* citizenship

citrique /sitʀik/ *adj* citric

citron /sitʀɔ̃/ *nm* (a) lemon
(b) (colloq) head, nut (colloq)
■ **~ givré** lemon sorbet; **~ vert** lime

citronnade /sitʀɔnad/ *nf* lemon squash (GB), lemonade (US)

citronnelle /sitʀɔnɛl/ *nf* (Bot) citronella

citronnier /sitʀɔnje/ *nm* lemon tree

citrouille /sitʀuj/ *nf* pumpkin

civet /sivɛ/ *nm* ≈ stew

civière /sivjɛʀ/ *nf* stretcher

civil, **~e** /sivil/ **1** *adj* (gen) civilian; ⟨marriage⟩ civil; ⟨funeral⟩ non religious
2 *nm* civilian; **en ~** in civilian clothes; in plain clothes; **dans le ~** in civilian life

civilisation /sivilizasjɔ̃/ *nf* civilization

civiliser /sivilize/ [1] *vtr* to civilize

civique /sivik/ *adj* civic

claie /klɛ/ *nf* (a) wicker rack
(b) fence, hurdle

clair, **~e** /klɛʀ/ **1** *adj* (a) ⟨colour⟩ light; ⟨complexion⟩ fair
(b) ⟨room⟩ bright
(c) ⟨weather, water⟩ clear
(d) ⟨text⟩ clear; **passer le plus ~ de son temps** to spend most of one's time
2 *adv* ⟨speak⟩ clearly; **il faisait ~** it was already light; **voir ~** to see well
3 *nm* (a) light; **mettre ses idées au ~** to get one's ideas straight; **tirer une affaire au ~** to get to the bottom of things
(b) light colours (GB)
■ **~ de lune** moonlight
IDIOMS **c'est ~ comme de l'eau de roche** it's crystal clear

clairière /klɛʀjɛʀ/ *nf* clearing, glade

clairon /klɛʀɔ̃/ *nm* (a) bugle
(b) bugler

claironnant, **~e** /klɛʀɔnɑ̃, ɑ̃t/ *adj* strident

claironner /klɛʀɔne/ [1] *vtr* to shout [sth] from the rooftops

clairsemé, **~e** /klɛʀsəme/ *adj* ⟨houses⟩ scattered; ⟨hair⟩ thin; ⟨population⟩ sparse

clairvoyance /klɛʀvwajɑ̃s/ *nf* perceptiveness

clairvoyant, **~e** /klɛʀvwajɑ̃, ɑ̃t/ *adj* perceptive

clamer /klame/ [1] *vtr* to proclaim

clameur /klamœʀ/ *nf* roar

clan /klɑ̃/ *nm* clan

clandestin, **~e** /klɑ̃dɛstɛ̃, in/ *adj* ⟨organization⟩ underground; ⟨immigration⟩ illegal; **passager ~** stowaway

clandestinement /klɑ̃dɛstinmɑ̃/ *adv* illegally

clandestinité /klɑ̃dɛstinite/ *nf* secret *or* clandestine nature; **dans la ~** ⟨live⟩ in hiding; ⟨operate⟩ in secret

clap /klap/ *nm* clapperboard

clapet /klapɛ/ *nm* **(a)** valve
(b) (colloq) mouth, trap (colloq)

clapier /klapje/ *nm* rabbit hutch

clapoter /klapɔte/ [1] *vi* to lap

claquage /klakaʒ/ *nm* pulled *or* strained muscle

claque /klak/ *nf* **(a)** slap
(b) (colloq) slap in the face
(c) (in theatre) claque
IDIOMS **en avoir sa ~** (colloq) to be fed up

claqué, **~e** /klake/ *adj* (colloq) knackered (slang), done in (colloq)

claquement /klakmɑ̃/ *nm* (of door) bang; (of whip) crack; (of tongue) click; (of flag) flapping

claquemurer: se claquemurer /klakmyʀe/ [1] *v refl* (+ *v être*) to shut oneself away (**dans** in)

claquer /klake/ [1] **1** *vtr* **(a)** to slam ⟨door⟩
(b) (colloq) to exhaust ⟨person⟩
(c) (colloq) to blow (colloq) ⟨money⟩
2 *vi* ⟨door⟩ to bang; (closing) to slam shut; ⟨flag⟩ to flap; **elle claque des dents** her teeth are chattering
3 se claquer *v refl* (+ *v être*) **se ~ un muscle** to pull *or* strain a muscle

claquettes /klakɛt/ *nf pl* tap dancing

clarifier /klaʀifje/ [2] *vtr* to clarify

clarinette /klaʀinɛt/ *nf* clarinet

clarté /klaʀte/ *nf* **(a)** light
(b) (of water) clarity; (of complexion) fairness
(c) (of style) clarity

classe /klas/ *nf* **(a)** (Sch) (group) class, form (GB); (level) year, form (GB), grade (US); **après la ~** after school
(b) (Sch) classroom
(c) (in society, transport) class; **les ~s sociales** social classes
(d) **avoir de la ~** to have class
(e) (Mil) **faire ses ~s** to do one's basic training
■ **~ d'âge** age group; **~ verte** *educational schooltrip to the countryside*; **~s**

préparatoires (aux grandes écoles) *preparatory classes for entrance to Grandes Écoles*

classement /klasmɑ̃/ *nm*
(a) classification
(b) filing; **faire du ~ dans ses papiers** to sort one's papers out
(c) grading; **~ trimestriel** (Sch) termly position (in class)
(d) (Sport) ranking; **en tête du ~** in first place
(e) (of hotel) rating

classer /klase/ [1] **1** *vtr* **(a)** to classify
(b) to file (away) ⟨documents⟩
(c) (Law) to close ⟨case⟩
(d) to list ⟨old building⟩
(e) to class ⟨country, pupils⟩; to rank ⟨song, player⟩
(f) (colloq) to size [sb] up
2 se classer *v refl* (+ *v être*) to rank

classeur /klasœʀ/ *nm* **(a)** ring binder
(b) file

classicisme /klasisism/ *nm* **(a)** (in art) classicism
(b) (in clothes, tastes) traditionalism

classification /klasifikasjɔ̃/ *nf* classification

classifier /klasifje/ [2] *vtr* to classify

classique /klasik/ **1** *adj* **(a)** classical; **faire des études ~s** (Sch) to do classics
(b) classic; ⟨method⟩ classic, standard; ⟨consequence⟩ usual; **de coupe ~** of classic cut; **c'est ~!** (colloq) it's typical!; **c'est le coup ~!** (colloq) it's the same old story!
2 *nm* classic

clause /kloz/ *nf* clause

claustrophobie /klostʀɔfɔbi/ *nf* claustrophobia

clavecin /klavsɛ̃/ *nm* harpsichord

clavicule /klavikyl/ *nf* collarbone

clavier /klavje/ *nm* keyboard; **~ numérique** numeric keypad

claviste /klavist/ *nmf* **(a)** typesetter
(b) (Comput) keyboarder

clé /kle/ **1** *nf* **(a)** (of lock, tin) key; **sous ~** under lock and key; **fermer à ~** to lock; **prix ~s en main** ⟨car⟩ on the road price (GB), sticker price (US); **usine ~s en main** turnkey factory
(b) (solution) key (**de** to)
(c) spanner (GB), wrench
(d) (of flute) key; (of violin) peg; **~ de fa** bass clef
2 (-)clé (*combining form*) **poste/mot(-)~** key post/word
3 à la clé *phr* at stake; **avec, à la ~, une récompense** with a reward thrown in
■ **~ anglaise**, **~ à molette** adjustable spanner (GB) *or* wrench (US)

clef = CLÉ

clément, **~e** /klemɑ̃, ɑ̃t/ *adj* **(a)** ⟨judge⟩ lenient
(b) ⟨temperature, winter⟩ mild

clémentine /klemɑ̃tin/ *nf* clementine

cleptomanie /klɛptɔmani/ *nf* kleptomania

clerc /klɛʀ/ *nm* (Law) clerk

clergé /klɛʀʒe/ *nm* clergy

cliché /kliʃe/ *nm* (a) snapshot
(b) cliché

client, ~e /klijã, ãt/ *nm,f* (of shop) customer; (of solicitor) client; (of hotel) guest; (in taxi) fare
IDIOMS **c'est à la tête du ~** it depends whether they like the look of you

clientèle /klijãtɛl/ *nf* (of shop) customers; (of solicitor) clients; (of doctor) patients; **se faire une ~** to build up a clientele

cligner /kliɲe/ [1] *v+prep* **~ des yeux** to blink; **~ de l'œil** to wink

clignotant /kliɲɔtã/ *nm* (Aut) indicator (GB), blinker (US)

clignoter /kliɲɔte/ [1] *vi* ⟨*light*⟩ to flash; to flash on and off; ⟨*star*⟩ to twinkle

climat /klima/ *nm* climate

climatique /klimatik/ *adj* climatic

climatisation /klimatizasjɔ̃/ *nf* air-conditioning

climatiser /klimatize/ [1] *vtr* to air-condition

climatiseur /klimatizœʀ/ *nm* air-conditioner

clin /klɛ̃/ *nm* **~ d'œil** wink; (figurative) allusion; **en un ~ d'œil** in a flash

clinique /klinik/ **1** *adj* clinical
2 *nf* private hospital; **~ vétérinaire** veterinary clinic

clinquant, ~e /klɛ̃kã, ãt/ *adj* flashy (colloq)

clip /klip/ *nm* (a) pop video
(b) clip-on (earring)

clique /klik/ *nf* clique; **prendre ses ~s et ses claques** to pack up and go

cliquer /klike/ [1] *vi* (Comput) to click (**sur** on)

cliqueter /klikte/ [20] *vi* ⟨*keys*⟩ to jingle; ⟨*chain, machine*⟩ to rattle

clitoris /klitɔris/ *nm* clitoris

clivage /klivaʒ/ *nm* divide; **~ d'opinion** division of opinion

clochard, ~e /klɔʃaʀ, aʀd/ *nm,f* tramp

cloche /klɔʃ/ *nf* (a) bell
(b) (colloq) clod (colloq), idiot
(c) **à fromage** cover of cheese dish
IDIOMS **entendre plusieurs sons de ~** to hear several versions; **sonner les ~s à qn** to bawl sb out (colloq)

cloche-pied: à cloche-pied /aklɔʃpje/ *phr* **sauter à ~** to hop

clocher¹ /klɔʃe/ [1] *vi* (colloq) **il y a quelque chose qui cloche** there's something wrong

clocher² /klɔʃe/ *nm* steeple; church *or* bell tower; **querelle de ~** local quarrel

clochette /klɔʃɛt/ *nf* (little) bell

cloison /klwazɔ̃/ *nf* (a) partition
(b) screen; **~ extensible** folding room-divider

cloisonner /klwazɔne/ [1] *vtr* (a) to partition ⟨*room*⟩; to divide up ⟨*space*⟩
(b) to divide up ⟨*society*⟩; to compartmentalize ⟨*administration*⟩

cloître /klwatʀ/ *nm* cloister

cloîtrer /klwatʀe/ [1] **1** *vtr* to shut [sb] away
2 **se cloîtrer** *v refl* (+ *v être*) to shut oneself away

clone /klon/ *nm* clone

clope /klɔp/ *nm or f* (colloq) fag (GB) (colloq), ciggy (colloq), cigarette

clopin-clopant /klɔpɛ̃klɔpã/ *phr* (colloq) **aller ~** to hobble along

cloporte /klɔpɔʀt/ *nm* woodlouse

cloque /klɔk/ *nf* blister

clore /klɔʀ/ [79] **1** *vtr* (a) to close ⟨*debate*⟩
(b) to end, to conclude ⟨*programme*⟩
(c) to close ⟨*eyes*⟩
2 **se clore** *v refl* (+ *v être*) to end (**par** with)

clos, ~e /klo, oz/ **1** *pp* ▶ CLORE
2 *pp adj* ⟨*system*⟩ closed; ⟨*area*⟩ enclosed; **monde ~** self-contained world

clôture /klotyʀ/ *nf* (a) fence; wire fence; railings
(b) (of debate, session) close; (of subscription) closing; **discours de ~** closing speech

clôturer /klotyʀe/ [1] *vtr* (a) to fence in ⟨*land*⟩
(b) ⟨*person*⟩ to close ⟨*list*⟩; ⟨*speech*⟩ to end ⟨*debate*⟩

clou /klu/ **1** *nm* (a) nail; stud
(b) (of show) star attraction; (of evening) high point
(c) (Med) boil
2 **clous** *nm pl* (a) pedestrian crossing (GB), crosswalk (US)
(b) (colloq) **des ~s!** no way!
■ **~ de girofle** (Bot, Culin) clove
IDIOMS **enfoncer le ~** to drive the point home

clouer /klue/ [1] *vtr* to nail down ⟨*lid*⟩; to nail together ⟨*planks*⟩; **~ au sol** (figurative) to pin [sb] down; **être cloué au lit** to be confined to bed

clown /klun/ *nm* clown

clownerie /klunʀi/ *nf* clowning; **arrête tes ~s** stop clowning about

club /klœb/ *nm* (a) club
(b) **~ de vacances** holiday camp

CM /seɛm/ *nm: abbr* ▶ COURS

CNPF /seɛnpeɛf/ *nm* (*abbr* = **Conseil national du patronat français**) *national council of French employers*

CNRS /seɛnɛʀɛs/ *nm* (*abbr* = **Centre national de la recherche scientifique**) *national centre for scientific research*

coaguler /kɔagyle/ [1] *vi*, **se coaguler** *v refl* (+ *v être*) ⟨*blood*⟩ to coagulate

coalition /kɔalisjɔ̃/ *nf* coalition

coasser /kɔase/ [1] *vi* to croak

cobaye /kɔbaj/ *nm* guinea pig

cobra /kɔbʀa/ nm cobra

cocaïne /kɔkain/ nf cocaine

cocarde /kɔkaʀd/ nf **(a)** rosette; (on uniform) cockade
(b) (on vehicle) official badge

cocasse /kɔkas/ adj comical

coccinelle /kɔksinɛl/ nf ladybird, ladybug (US)

coccyx /kɔksis/ nm coccyx

coche /kɔʃ/ nm (stage)coach
IDIOMS **manquer le ~** to miss the boat

cocher[1] /kɔʃe/ [1] vtr to tick (GB), to check (US)

cocher[2] /kɔʃe/ nm coachman; cabman

cochère /kɔʃɛʀ/ adj f **porte ~** carriage entrance

cochon, -onne /kɔʃɔ̃, ɔn/ **1** adj (colloq)
(a) ⟨film⟩ dirty; ⟨person⟩ dirty-minded
(b) ⟨person⟩ messy, dirty
2 nm,f (colloq) (a) pig (colloq), slob (colloq); **de ~** ⟨job⟩ botched; ⟨weather⟩ lousy (colloq)
(b) sex maniac
3 nm **(a)** (Zool) pig, hog
(b) (Culin) pork
■ **~ d'Inde** Guinea pig; **~ de lait** sucking pig

cochonnaille /kɔʃɔnaj/ nf (colloq): products made from pork such as salami, bacon, pâté and ham

cochonnerie /kɔʃɔnʀi/ nf (colloq) **(a)** junk (colloq); **il ne mange que des ~s** he only eats junk food
(b) mess; **faire des ~s** to make a mess

cocker /kɔkɛʀ/ nm (cocker) spaniel

cocktail /kɔktɛl/ nm **(a)** cocktail
(b) (figurative) mixture
(c) cocktail party

coco /koko/ nm coconut

cocon /kɔkɔ̃/ nm cocoon

cocorico /kɔkɔʀiko/ nm cock-a-doodle-do

cocotier /kɔkɔtje/ nm coconut palm

cocotte /kɔkɔt/ nf **(a)** (colloq) (baby talk) hen
(b) (colloq) **ma ~** honey (colloq)
(c) (Culin) casserole (GB), pot

cocotte-minute®, pl **cocottes-minute** /kɔkɔtminyt/ nf pressure cooker

codage /kɔdaʒ/ nm coding, encoding

code /kɔd/ **1** nm code
2 **codes** nm pl (of vehicle) dipped (GB) or dimmed (US) (head)lights, low beam
■ **~ accès** password; **~ (à) barres** bar code; **~ confidentiel** personal identification number, PIN; **~ de la nationalité** regulations as to nationality; **~ postal** post code (GB), zip code (US); **~ de la route** (Aut) highway code (US), rules of the road (US); **passer son ~** (colloq) to take the written part of a driving test

coder /kɔde/ [1] vtr to code, to encode

codétenu, ~e /kɔdetny/ nm,f fellow prisoner

codifier /kɔdifje/ [2] vtr to codify ⟨laws⟩; to standardize ⟨language, custom⟩

codirecteur, -trice /kɔdiʀɛktœʀ, tʀis/ nm,f joint manager; joint director

coefficient /kɔefisjɑ̃/ nm **(a)** ratio
(b) margin
(c) weighting factor in an exam; **la chimie est au ~ 4** chemistry results are multiplied by 4
(d) (in arithmetic, physics) coefficient

coéquipier, -ière /koekipje, ɛʀ/ nm,f team mate

cœur /kœʀ/ **1** nm **(a)** heart; **il a le ~ malade** he has a heart condition; **serrer qn sur or contre son ~** to hold sb close; **écouter son ~** to go with one's feelings; **aller droit au ~ de qn** to touch sb deeply; **avoir un coup de ~ pour qch** to fall in love with sth; **ça me fait mal au ~ de voir** it sickens me to see; **problème de ~** emotional problem; **parler à ~ ouvert** to speak openly; **avoir bon ~** to be kind-hearted; **je n'ai plus le ~ à rien** I don't feel like doing anything any more
(b) (Culin) heart
(c) (figurative) (of fruit, rock) core; (of problem, debate) heart; **au ~ de** (of region, town) in the middle of; (of building, problem, system) at the heart of; **au ~ de l'hiver** in the dead of winter
(d) (person) **mon (petit) ~** sweetheart
(e) courage; **le ~ m'a manqué** my courage failed me; **redonner du ~ à qn** to give sb new heart
(f) (Games) (card) heart; (suit) hearts
2 **à cœur** phr **avoir à ~ de faire** to be intent on doing; **prendre qch à ~** to take sth seriously
3 **de bon cœur** phr willingly; **rire de bon ~** to laugh heartily
4 **par cœur** phr by heart; **connaître qn par ~** to know sb inside out
IDIOMS **avoir mal au ~** to feel sick (GB) or nauseous (US); **avoir du ~ au ventre** to be brave; **avoir le ~ sur la main** to be open-handed; **il ne le porte pas dans son ~** he's not his favourite (GB) person; **j'irai mais le ~ n'y est pas** I'll go but my heart isn't in it; **si le ~ t'en dit** if you feel like it; **avoir qch sur le ~** to be resentful about sth

coexister /koɛgziste/ [1] vi to coexist

coffre /kɔfʀ/ nm **(a)** chest; **~ à jouets** toy box
(b) (for valuables) safe; (individual) safety deposit box; **la salle des ~s** the strongroom
(c) (of car) boot (GB), trunk (US)
IDIOMS **avoir du ~** (colloq) to have a powerful voice

coffre-fort, pl **coffres-forts** /kɔfʀəfɔʀ/ nm safe

coffret /kɔfʀɛ/ nm **(a)** casket; **~ à bijoux** jewellery (GB) or jewelry (US) box
(b) (of records, cassettes, books) boxed set

cogérer /kɔʒeʀe/ [14] vtr to co-manage

cogestion /kɔʒɛstjɔ̃/ nf joint management

cogiter /kɔʒite/ [1] vi to cogitate, to think

cognac /kɔɲak/ nm cognac (brandy from the Cognac area)

cogner /kɔɲe/ [1] **1** *vtr* to knock
2 *vi* (a) ~ **contre** ⟨*shutter*⟩ to bang against; ⟨*branch*⟩ to knock against; ⟨*projectile*⟩ to hit; ~ **à la porte** to bang on the door
(b) (colloq) ⟨*boxer*⟩ to hit out
(c) ⟨*heart*⟩ to pound
3 se cogner *v refl* (*+ v être*) to bump into something; **se ~ le pied contre une pierre** to stub one's toe on a stone

cognitif, -ive /kɔgnitif, iv/ *adj* cognitive

cohabitation /kɔabitasjɔ̃/ *nf* (a) living with somebody
(b) *situation where the French President is in political opposition to the government*

cohabiter /kɔabite/ [1] *vi* ⟨*people*⟩ to live together; ⟨*things*⟩ to coexist

cohérence /kɔeRɑ̃s/ *nf* (a) coherence; consistency
(b) (in physics) cohesion

cohérent, ~e /kɔeRɑ̃, ɑ̃t/ *adj* coherent; consistent

cohéritier, -ière /kɔeRitje, ɛR/ *nm,f* joint heir

cohésion /kɔezjɔ̃/ *nf* cohesion

cohorte /kɔɔRt/ *nf* (colloq) crowd, group

cohue /kɔy/ *nf* crowd; **c'est la ~** it's a crush

coi, coite /kwa, kwat/ *adj* **se tenir ~** to remain quiet

coiffant, ~e /kwafɑ̃, ɑ̃t/ *adj* **gel ~** styling gel

coiffe /kwaf/ *nf* (gen) headgear; (of nun) wimple

coiffer /kwafe/ [1] **1** *vtr* (a) ~ **qn** to do sb's hair; to comb sb's hair
(b) **coiffé d'une casquette** wearing a cap
2 se coiffer *v refl* (*+ v être*) (a) to do *or* comb one's hair
(b) **se ~ de qch** to put sth on
IDIOMS ~ **qn au poteau** (colloq) *or* **sur le fil** (colloq) to beat sb by a whisker

coiffeur, -euse[1] /kwafœR, øz/ *nm,f* hairdresser

coiffeuse[2] /kwaføz/ *nf* dressing table

coiffure /kwafyR/ *nf* (a) hairstyle
(b) hairdressing
(c) headgear

coin /kwɛ̃/ **1** *nm* (a) corner; **à tous les ~s de rue** everywhere; **aux quatre ~s de la ville** all over the town; **aller au ~** (as punishment) to go and stand in the corner; **j'ai dû poser mon sac dans un ~** I must have put my bag down somewhere; **au ~ du feu** by the fire
(b) (of eye, mouth) corner; **un sourire en ~** a half-smile; **un regard en ~** a sidelong glance
(c) (of ground) plot; (of lawn) patch; **un ~ de paradis** an idyllic spot
(d) (in region) **un ~ de France** a part of France; **dans le ~** around here, in these parts; around there, in those parts; **le café du ~** the local café; **les gens du ~** the locals; **connaître les bons ~s pour manger** to know all the good places to eat
(e) (for photograph) corner; (for file) reinforcing corner

(f) (Tech) wedge
2 coin(-) (*combining form*) ~**-repas/-salon** dining/living area

coincé, ~e /kwɛ̃se/ **1** *pp* ▶ COINCER
2 *pp adj* (a) stuck; trapped; ~ **entre** ⟨*house*⟩ wedged between
(b) (colloq) **j'ai le dos ~, je suis ~** my back has gone (colloq)
(c) (figurative) (colloq) stuck (colloq)
(d) (colloq) ill at ease
(e) (colloq) uptight (colloq)

coincer /kwɛ̃se/ [12] **1** *vtr* (a) to wedge ⟨*object*⟩; to wedge [sth] open/shut ⟨*door*⟩; ⟨*snow*⟩ to trap ⟨*person*⟩
(b) to jam ⟨*drawer, zip*⟩
(c) (colloq) to catch ⟨*person*⟩; **se faire ~ par** to get caught by
(d) (colloq) to catch [sb] out ⟨*person*⟩
2 *vi* (a) ⟨*zip, drawer*⟩ to stick
(b) (colloq) **ça coince** there's a problem
3 se coincer *v refl* (*+ v être*) (a) ⟨*object*⟩ to get stuck *or* jammed
(b) **se ~ les doigts** to get one's fingers caught

coïncidence /kɔɛ̃sidɑ̃s/ *nf* coincidence

coïncider /kɔɛ̃side/ [1] *vi* to coincide

coing /kwɛ̃/ *nm* quince

coite ▶ COI

col /kɔl/ *nm* (a) collar
(b) (in mountains) pass
(c) (of bottle) neck
(d) (Anat) neck
■ ~ **blanc** white-collar worker

colère /kɔlɛR/ *nf* (a) anger; **être en ~** to be angry; **passer sa ~ sur qn** to take out *or* vent one's anger on sb; **sous le coup de la ~** in a fit of anger
(b) **faire** *or* **piquer** (colloq) **une ~** to have a fit; to throw a tantrum

coléreux, -euse /kɔleRø, øz/ *adj* ⟨*person*⟩ quick-tempered

colifichet /kɔlifiʃɛ/ *nm* trinket; knick-knack

colimaçon /kɔlimasɔ̃/ *nm* snail; **escalier en ~** spiral staircase

colin /kɔlɛ̃/ *nm* (fish) hake; coley

colin-maillard /kɔlɛ̃majaR/ *nm* **jouer à ~** to play blind man's buff

colique /kɔlik/ *nf* (a) diarrhoea
(b) stomach pain; (in babies) colic

colis /kɔli/ *nm* parcel
■ ~ **piégé** parcel bomb; ~ **postal** parcel sent by mail

colite /kɔlit/ *nf* colitis

collaborateur, -trice /kɔlabɔRatœR, tRis/ *nm,f* (a) colleague; assistant
(b) employee
(c) (journalist) contributor
(d) (derogatory) collaborator

collaboration /kɔlabɔRasjɔ̃/ *nf* (a) (to newspaper) contribution; (work on project) collaboration
(b) (in Second World War) collaboration

collaborer /kɔlabɔʀe/ [1] *vi* (a) ~ à to contribute to ‹newspaper›; to collaborate on ‹project›
(b) (as working partner) to collaborate

collage /kɔlaʒ/ *nm* collage; (in photography) montage

collant, ~e /kɔlã, ãt/ **1** *adj*
(a) ‹substance, object› sticky
(b) ‹dress› skintight
2 *nm* tights (GB), panty hose (US)

collation /kɔlasjɔ̃/ *nf* light meal

colle /kɔl/ *nf* (a) glue; (wallpaper) paste
(b) (colloq) (hard question) poser (colloq); test
(c) (colloq) (students' slang) detention

collecte /kɔlɛkt/ *nf* (a) collection; **faire une ~** to raise funds
(b) (prayer) collect

collecter /kɔlɛkte/ [1] *vtr* to collect

collecteur, -trice /kɔlɛktœʀ, tʀis/ *nm,f* collector
■ **~ de fonds** fundraiser; **~ d'impôts** tax collector

collectif, -ive /kɔlɛktif, iv/ **1** *adj* collective; ‹dismissals› mass; ‹heating› shared; ‹ticket› group
2 *nm* (a) collective
(b) action group

collection /kɔlɛksjɔ̃/ *nf* (a) collection; **~ de timbres** stamp collection
(b) (of books) series; (by same author) set

collectionner /kɔlɛksjɔne/ [1] *vtr* (a) to collect
(b) (figurative) **~ les erreurs** to make one mistake after another

collectionneur, -euse /kɔlɛksjɔnœʀ, øz/ *nm,f* collector

collectivement /kɔlɛktivmã/ *adv* (gen) collectively; ‹resign› en masse, as a body

collectivité /kɔlɛktivite/ *nf* (a) group
(b) community
■ **~ locale** local authority (GB), local government (US)

collège /kɔlɛʒ/ *nm* (a) secondary school (GB), junior high school (US) ‹up to age 16›
(b) college; **~ électoral** (Pol) electoral college
■ **~ d'enseignement secondaire, CES** secondary school (GB), junior high school (US); **~ d'enseignement technique, CET** *technical secondary school in France*

collégial, ~e, *mpl* **-iaux** /kɔleʒjal, o/ *adj* ‹church› collegial; ‹system› collegiate

collégien, -ienne /kɔleʒjɛ̃, ɛn/ *nm,f* schoolboy/schoolgirl

collègue /kɔlɛg/ *nmf* colleague

coller /kɔle/ [1] **1** *vtr* (a) to stick, to glue ‹wood, paper›; to paste up ‹poster›; to hang ‹wallpaper›; to stick [sth] on ‹label›; to stick down ‹envelope›
(b) **~ qch contre** *or* **à qch** to press sth against sth; **il la colla contre le parapet** he pushed her up against the parapet
(c) (colloq) to stick (colloq); **je leur ai collé la facture sous le nez** I stuck the bill (right) under their noses; **~ une amende/une gifle à qn** to fine/slap sb

(d) (colloq) (in exam) **se faire ~** to fail
(e) (colloq) to give [sb] detention ‹pupil›
2 *vi* (a) to stick
(b) (colloq) **~ avec** to be consistent *or* fit with
3 **se coller** *v refl* (+ *v être*) (a) **se ~ à** *or* **contre qn/qch** to press oneself against sb/sth
(b) (colloq) **dès qu'il rentre, il se colle devant son ordinateur** as soon as he comes in he's glued (colloq) to his computer

collerette /kɔlʀɛt/ *nf* (a) ruff
(b) ruffle

collet /kɔlɛ/ *nm* **être ~ monté** to be prim

collier /kɔlje/ *nm* (a) necklace; **~ de perles** string of pearls
(b) (of animal) collar
(c) beard
IDIOMS **donner un coup de ~** to get one's head down; to put one's back into it

collimateur /kɔlimatœʀ/ *nm* **avoir qn dans le ~** (colloq) to have it in for sb (colloq)

colline /kɔlin/ *nf* hill

collision /kɔlizjɔ̃/ *nf* collision

colloque /kɔl(l)ɔk/ *nm* conference, symposium

collyre /kɔliʀ/ *nm* eyedrops

colmater /kɔlmate/ [1] *vtr* to plug, to seal off ‹leak›; to seal ‹crack›

colombe /kɔlɔ̃b/ *nf* dove

colombier /kɔlɔ̃bje/ *nm* dovecote

colon /kɔlɔ̃/ *nm* colonist

côlon /kolɔ̃, kɔlɔ̃/ *nm* colon

colonel /kɔlɔnɛl/ *nm* (Mil) (in army) ≈ colonel; (in air force) ≈ group captain (GB), ≈ colonel (US)

colonial, ~e, *mpl* **-iaux** /kɔlɔnjal, o/ *adj, nm,f* colonial

colonialisme /kɔlɔnjalism/ *nm* colonialism

colonie /kɔlɔni/ *nf* (gen) colony; **~ (de vacances)** holiday camp (for children)

colonnade /kɔlɔnad/ *nf* colonnade

colonne /kɔlɔn/ *nf* column.
■ **~ vertébrale** (Anat) spinal column

colorant, ~e /kɔlɔʀã, ãt/ **1** *adj* colouring (GB)
2 *nm* (a) colouring (GB) agent
(b) dye
(c) (in chemistry) stain
(d) (Culin) colouring (GB)

coloration /kɔlɔʀasjɔ̃/ *nf* (a) colouring (GB); dyeing; staining; tinting
(b) colour (GB)

coloré, ~e /kɔlɔʀe/ *adj* (a) (gen) coloured (GB)
(b) ‹life, crowd› colourful (GB); ‹style› lively

colorer /kɔlɔʀe/ [1] *vtr* to colour (GB); to tint; to stain; to dye

colorier /kɔlɔʀje/ [2] *vtr* to colour in (GB), to color (US)

coloris /kɔlɔʀi/ *nm inv* colour (GB); shade

colossal, ~e, *mpl* **-aux** /kɔlɔsal, o/ *adj* colossal, huge

colosse /kɔlɔs/ *nm* giant

colporter /kɔlpɔʀte/ [1] *vtr* **(a)** to spread ⟨*news*⟩

(b) to peddle ⟨*goods*⟩

coltiner: se coltiner /kɔltine/ [1] *v refl* (+ *v être*) (colloq) **(a)** to lug (colloq) ⟨*heavy object*⟩

(b) to get stuck with (colloq) ⟨*chore, person*⟩

colza /kɔlza/ *nm* rape

coma /kɔma/ *nm* coma

comateux, -euse /kɔmatø, øz/ *adj* comatose

combat /kɔ̃ba/ *nm* **(a)** (Mil) fighting; ~s aériens air battles; **mettre hors de** ~ to disable

(b) (in politics) struggle; **livrer un** ~ to campaign

(c) (Sport) bout; **hors de** ~ out of action

■ ~ **de coqs** cock fight

combatif, -ive /kɔ̃batif, iv/ *adj*
(a) assertive
(b) aggressive

combativité /kɔ̃bativite/ *nf* fighting spirit

combattant, ~e /kɔ̃batɑ̃, ɑ̃t/ *nm,f* combatant

combattre /kɔ̃batʀ/ [61] *vtr, vi* to fight

combien¹ /kɔ̃bjɛ̃/ ① *adv* **(a)** ~ **mesure le salon?** how big is the lounge?; **j'aimerais savoir** ~ **il a payé son costume** I'd like to know how much he paid for that suit; ~ **êtes-vous?** how many of you are there?

(b) (to what extent) **je ne saurais te dire** ~ **il me manque** I can't tell you how much I miss him

② **combien de** *det* **(a)** how many, how much

(b) ~ **de temps faut-il?** how long does it take?

combien² /kɔ̃bjɛ̃/ *nmf inv* **(a)** **tu es le/la** ~? (in queue) how many people are before you?

(b) **le** ~ **sommes-nous?** what's the date today?

(c) (for measurements) **tu chausses du** ~? what size shoes do you take?

(d) **tu le vois tous les** ~? how often do you see him?

combinaison /kɔ̃binɛzɔ̃/ *nf* **(a)** combining; combination

(b) (of safe) combination
(c) (full-length) slip
(d) jumpsuit
(e) overalls (GB), coveralls (US)

■ ~ **de plongée** wetsuit

combine /kɔ̃bin/ *nf* (colloq) trick (colloq); scheme

combiné /kɔ̃bine/ *nm* handset, receiver

combiner /kɔ̃bine/ [1] *vtr* **(a)** to combine
(b) to work out ⟨*plan*⟩

comble /kɔ̃bl/ ① *adj* ⟨*room*⟩ packed

② *nm* **(a)** **le** ~ **de l'injustice/du mauvais goût** the height of injustice/of bad taste; **pour** ~ **de malchance j'ai...** to crown it all, I...; **c'est un** *or* **le** ~! (colloq) that's the limit!

(b) roof space; **de fond en** ~ from top to bottom; completely

③ **combles** *nm pl* attic

combler /kɔ̃ble/ [1] *vtr* **(a)** to fill (in) ⟨*ditch*⟩

(b) to fill in ⟨*gaps*⟩; to make up ⟨*deficit*⟩
(c) to fulfil (GB) ⟨*need, desire*⟩; **la vie m'a comblé** I've had a wonderful life; ~ **qn** to fill sb with joy

combustible /kɔ̃bystibl/ ① *adj* combustible

② *nm* fuel; ~ **nucléaire** nuclear fuel

combustion /kɔ̃bystjɔ̃/ *nf* combustion

comédie /kɔmedi/ *nf* **(a)** comedy
(b) play-acting; **jouer la** ~ to put on an act
(c) (colloq) scene; **faire une** ~ to make a scene

■ ~ **musicale** musical

comédien, -ienne /kɔmedjɛ̃, ɛn/ ① *adj* **il est (un peu)** ~ (figurative) he puts it on

② *nm,f* actor/actress

comestible /kɔmɛstibl/ ① *adj* edible

② **comestibles** *nm pl* food

comète /kɔmɛt/ *nf* comet

comique /kɔmik/ ① *adj* **(a)** comic
(b) funny

② *nmf* comic actor/actress; comedian

③ *nm* **(a)** clown
(b) comedy

comité /kɔmite/ *nm* **(a)** committee
(b) group

commandant /kɔmɑ̃dɑ̃/ *nm* (in army) ≈ major; (in air force) ≈ squadron leader (GB), ≈ major (US)

■ ~ **de bord** captain

commande /kɔmɑ̃d/ *nf* **(a)** order
(b) commission; **passer** ~ **de qch à qn** to commission sb to do sth
(c) (Tech) control; **levier de** ~ control lever; **être aux** *or* **tenir les** ~s to be at the controls; (figurative) to be in control
(d) (Comput) command

commandement /kɔmɑ̃dmɑ̃/ *nm* **(a)** (Mil) command

(b) (in religion) commandment

commander /kɔmɑ̃de/ [1] ① *vtr* **(a)** to order [sth] (**à qn** from sb)

(b) to commission ⟨*book, survey*⟩
(c) (Mil) to command ⟨*army*⟩; to order ⟨*attack*⟩
(d) ~ **qn** to order sb about
(e) **les circonstances commandent la prudence** the circumstances call for caution
(f) ⟨*machine*⟩ to control ⟨*mechanism*⟩

② **commander à** *v+prep* **(a)** ~ **à** to be in command of
(b) ~ **à** to order, to command

③ *vi* to give the orders, to be in charge

④ **se commander** *v refl* (+ *v être*) **ça ne se commande pas** it's not something you can control

commanditer /kɔmɑ̃dite/ [1] *vtr* **(a)** to finance ⟨*company*⟩

(b) to sponsor ⟨*project*⟩
(c) to be behind ⟨*crime*⟩

commando /kɔmɑ̃do/ *nm* commando

comme /kɔm/ **1** *adv* how

2 *conj* **(a)** as; **ici ~ en Italie** here as in Italy; **il est paresseux, ~ sa sœur d'ailleurs** he's lazy, just like his sister; **jolie ~ tout** really pretty

(b) (in comparisons) **il est grand ~ sa sœur** he's as tall as his sister; **c'est tout ~** (colloq) it comes to the same thing; **elle me traite ~ un enfant** she treats me like a child

(c) like; **un manteau ~ le tien** a coat like yours; **~ ça** like that; **puisque c'est ~ ça** if that's the way it is

(d) as if, as though; **~ pour faire** as if to do

(e) (colloq) **elle a eu ~ un évanouissement** she sort of fainted

(f) avare ~ il est, il ne te donnera rien he's so mean, he won't give you anything

(g) as; **travailler ~ jardinier** to work as a gardener

(h) as, since; **~ elle était seule** as *or* since she was alone

(i) as; **~ il traversait la rue** as he was crossing the road

IDIOMS ~ quoi! which just shows!; **~ ci ~ ça** (colloq) so-so (colloq)

commémoration /kɔmemɔrasjɔ̃/ *nf* commemoration

commémorer /kɔmemɔre/ [1] *vtr* to commemorate

commencement /kɔmɑ̃smɑ̃/ *nm* beginning

commencer /kɔmɑ̃se/ [12] **1** *vtr* **(a)** to start, to begin

(b) ~ à *or* **de faire** to start *or* begin to do; **ça commence à bien faire!** (colloq) it's getting to be a bit much!

2 *vi* to start, to begin; **pour ~** for a start; **vous êtes tous coupables à ~ par toi** you're all guilty starting with you

3 *v impers* **il commence à neiger** it's starting *or* beginning to snow

comment /kɔmɑ̃/ *adv* **(a)** how; **~ faire?** how can it be done?; **~ t'appelles-tu?** what's your name?; **~ ça se fait?** (colloq) how come? (colloq)

(b) ~? qu'est-ce que tu dis? pardon? what did you say?; **Paul ~?** Paul who?

(c) ~ est leur maison/fils? what's their house/son like?; **~ trouvez-vous ma robe?** what do you think of my dress?

(d) ~ cela? what do you mean?; **~ donc!** but of course!; **et ~** (donc)**!** (colloq) and how! (colloq); **'c'était bon?'—'et ~!'** (colloq) 'was it nice?'—'it certainly was!'

commentaire /kɔmmɑ̃tɛr/ *nm*
(a) comment
(b) commentary

commentateur, -trice /kɔmmɑ̃tatœr, tris/ *nm,f* commentator

commenter /kɔmmɑ̃te/ [1] *vtr* **(a)** to comment on ⟨*decision, event*⟩
(b) to give a commentary on ⟨*film, visit*⟩
(c) to commentate on ⟨*match*⟩

commérage /kɔmeraʒ/ *nm* gossip

commerçant, ~e /kɔmɛrsɑ̃, ɑ̃t/ **1** *adj*
⟨*street*⟩ shopping; ⟨*nation*⟩ trading

2 *nm,f* shopkeeper, storekeeper (US); retailer

commerce /kɔmɛrs/ *nm* **(a)** shop, store (US); **dans le ~** in the shops *or* stores (US)
(b) business
(c) trade; **faire le ~ de** to trade in; **faire ~ de** to sell; **faire du ~** to be in business

commercial, ~e, *mpl* **-iaux** /kɔmɛrsjal, o/ **1** *adj* **(a)** commercial; **carrière ~e** career in sales and marketing
(b) trade
2 *nm,f* sales and marketing person

commercialisation /kɔmɛrsjalizasjɔ̃/ *nf* marketing

commercialiser /kɔmɛrsjalize/ [1] *vtr* to market

commère /kɔmɛr/ *nf* gossip

commettre /kɔmɛtr/ [60] *vtr* to make ⟨*error*⟩; to commit ⟨*crime*⟩; to carry out ⟨*attack*⟩

commis /kɔmi/ *nm* **(a)** (in office) clerk
(b) shop assistant (GB), salesclerk (US)

commissaire /kɔmisɛr/ *nm* **(a) ~ (de police)** ≈ police superintendent
(b) commissioner
(c) (of sports event) steward; (of exhibition) organizer

commissaire-priseur, *pl* **commissaires-priseurs** /kɔmisɛrprizœr/ *nm* auctioneer

commissariat /kɔmisarja/ *nm* **~ (de police)** police station

commission /kɔmisjɔ̃/ **1** *nf*
(a) committee
(b) commission; **payé à la ~** paid on a commission basis
(c) errand
(d) faire la ~ à qn to give sb the message
2 commissions *nf pl* (colloq) shopping

commissionnaire /kɔmisjɔnɛr/ *nm* (Econ) agent, broker

commissure /kɔmisyr/ *nf* corner

commode /kɔmɔd/ **1** *adj* **(a)** (gen) convenient; ⟨*tool*⟩ handy
(b) easy
(c) ne pas être (très) ~ to be strict; to be difficult (to deal with)
2 *nf* chest of drawers

commodité /kɔmɔdite/ *nf* convenience

commotion /kɔmosjɔ̃/ *nf* **(a) ~ (cérébrale)** concussion (*of the brain*)
(b) (figurative) shock

commun, ~e[1] /kɔmœ̃, yn/ **1** *adj*
(a) common; ⟨*policy, property*⟩ joint; ⟨*friend*⟩ mutual; ⟨*room, memories, experience*⟩ shared; **d'un ~ accord** by mutual agreement; **après dix ans de vie ~e** after living together for ten years
(b) ⟨*person, tastes*⟩ common; ⟨*face*⟩ plain
(c) elle est d'une beauté peu ~e she's uncommonly beautiful
2 *nm* ordinary; **le ~ des mortels** ordinary mortals; **hors du ~** exceptional
3 en commun *phr* ⟨*work, write*⟩ jointly, ···▸

together; **avoir qch en ∼** to have sth in common; **nous mettons tout en ∼** we share everything

communal, **∼e**, *mpl* **-aux** /kɔmynal, o/ *adj* ‹*budget, resources*› local council (GB), local government (US); ‹*building*› local council (GB), community (US)

communautaire /kɔmynotɛʀ/ *adj*
(a) (referring to the EC) ‹*budget, law*› Community
(b) **la vie ∼** life in a community

communauté /kɔmynote/ *nf*
(a) community
(b) commune; **vivre en ∼** to live in a commune
■ **Communauté économique européenne, CEE** European Economic Community, EEC; **Communauté des États indépendants, CEI** Commonwealth of Independent States, CIS

commune² /kɔmyn/ **1** *nf* village; town **2 communes** *nf pl* **la Chambre des ∼s** the (House of) Commons

communément /kɔmynemã/ *adv* generally

communicatif, -ive /kɔmynikatif, iv/ *adj* (a) ‹*person*› talkative
(b) ‹*gaiety*› infectious

communication /kɔmynikasjɔ̃/ *nf*
(a) **∼** (téléphonique) (telephone) call; **mettre qn en ∼ avec qn** to put sb through to sb
(b) report; (at conference) paper
(c) **demander ∼ d'un dossier à qn** to ask sb for a file
(d) (between people) communication, contact
(e) (media) communications
(f) (by phone, radio) **moyens de ∼** communications

communier /kɔmynje/ [2] *vi* to receive Communion

communion /kɔmynjɔ̃/ *nf* (a) Communion
(b) (figurative) communion
■ **∼ (privée)** first communion

communiqué /kɔmynike/ *nm*
(a) communiqué, press release
(b) statement

communiquer /kɔmynike/ [1] **1** *vtr*
(a) to announce ‹*date, result*›; to give ‹*address*›
(b) ‹*person*› to pass on ‹*document*›; to convey ‹*idea*›
2 *vi* (a) to communicate
(b) ‹*rooms*› to be adjoining
3 se communiquer *v refl* (+ *v être*)
(a) ‹*people*› to pass [sth] on to each other
(b) ‹*fire, disease*› to spread

communisme /kɔmynism/ *nm* communism

commutateur /kɔmytatœʀ/ *nm* switch

commuter /kɔmyte/ [1] *vtr* to commute

compact, **∼e** /kɔpakt/ *adj* (a) ‹*fog, crowd*› dense; ‹*earth*› compact
(b) ‹*car*› compact

compagne /kɔ̃paɲ/ *nf* (a) (female) companion
(b) (female animal) mate

compagnie /kɔ̃paɲi/ *nf* (a) company; **en ∼ de** together with
(b) **salut la ∼!** hello everybody!
(c) (commercial) company
(d) theatre company
■ **∼ aérienne** airline; **∼ d'assurance** insurance company; **∼ pétrolière** oil company

compagnon /kɔ̃paɲɔ̃/ *nm* (a) companion
(b) partner
(c) mate
(d) journeyman
■ **∼ de route** fellow traveller (GB)

comparable /kɔ̃paʀabl/ *adj* comparable

comparaison /kɔ̃paʀɛzɔ̃/ *nf*
(a) comparison; **c'est sans ∼ le plus confortable** it's far and away the most comfortable
(b) simile
(c) **adjectif de ∼** comparative adjective

comparaître /kɔ̃paʀɛtʀ/ [73] *vi* (Law) to appear

comparatif, -ive /kɔ̃paʀatif, iv/ *adj* comparative

comparé, **∼e** /kɔ̃paʀe/ *adj* ‹*literature, law*› comparative

comparer /kɔ̃paʀe/ [1] **1** *vtr* to compare **2 se comparer** *v refl* (+ *v être*) (a) **se ∼ à qn/qch** to compare oneself with sb/sth
(b) to be comparable

comparse /kɔ̃paʀs/ *nmf* (a) (in theatre) extra
(b) sidekick (colloq)

compartiment /kɔ̃paʀtimã/ *nm* compartment

compartimenter /kɔ̃paʀtimãte/ [1] *vtr*
(a) **∼ un grenier** to divide up a loft with partitions
(b) (figurative) to compartmentalize ‹*administration*›

compas /kɔ̃pa/ *nm* compass

compassion /kɔ̃pasjɔ̃/ *nf* compassion

compatible /kɔ̃patibl/ *adj* compatible

compatir /kɔ̃patiʀ/ [3] *vi* to sympathize

compatissant, **∼e** /kɔ̃patisã, ãt/ *adj* compassionate

compatriote /kɔ̃patʀijɔt/ *nmf* fellow-countryman/-countrywoman, compatriot

compensation /kɔ̃pãsasjɔ̃/ *nf* compensation

compensé, **∼e** /kɔ̃pãse/ *adj* (a) **semelle ∼e** wedge heel
(b) (Med) compensated

compenser /kɔ̃pãse/ [1] *vtr* to compensate for; to make up for; to offset

compère /kɔ̃pɛʀ/ *nm* partner; accomplice

compétence /kɔ̃petãs/ *nf* (a) ability; competence, skill
(b) (Law) competence; **relever de la ∼ de qn** to fall within the competence of sb
(c) domain

compétent, **∼e** /kɔ̃petã, ãt/ *adj* competent

compétitif, -ive /kɔ̃petitif, iv/ *adj*
competitive

compétition /kɔ̃petisjɔ̃/ *nf* competition;
en ~ pour competing for; **faire de la ~** to
compete; **sport de ~** competitive sport

complaire: se complaire /kɔ̃plɛR/ [59]
v refl (+ v être) **se ~ à faire** to take pleasure
in doing

complaisance /kɔ̃plɛzɑ̃s/ *nf* **(a)** kindness
(b) (derogatory) soft attitude; **décrire la
situation sans ~** to give an objective
assessment of the situation
(c) (derogatory) complacency

complaisant, ~e /kɔ̃plɛzɑ̃, ɑ̃t/ *adj*
(a) obliging
(b) (derogatory) indulgent
(c) (derogatory) complacent, self-satisfied

complément /kɔ̃plemɑ̃/ *nm* **(a)** **~ de
salaire** extra payment
(b) (to funding, programme) supplement
(c) **~ de nom** possessive phrase; **~ d'objet
direct/indirect** direct/indirect object

complémentaire /kɔ̃plemɑ̃tɛR/ *adj*
(a) ⟨*training, information*⟩ further; ⟨*activity,
amount*⟩ supplementary
(b) complementary

complet, -ète /kɔ̃plɛ, ɛt/ [1] *adj* **(a)** (gen)
complete; ⟨*failure*⟩ total; ⟨*inquiry, range*⟩
full; ⟨*survey*⟩ comprehensive
(b) ⟨*train, hotel*⟩ full; **être (réuni) au (grand)
~** to be all present
[2] *nm* suit; **~ veston** two-/three-piece suit

complètement /kɔ̃plɛtmɑ̃/ *adv*
completely; ⟨*read*⟩ right through; **~ réveillé**
fully awake

compléter /kɔ̃plete/ [14] [1] *vtr* **(a)** to
complete ⟨*collection*⟩; to top up ⟨*sum*⟩
(b) ⟨*person*⟩ to complement ⟨*person*⟩
(c) to complete ⟨*sentence*⟩
[2] **se compléter** *v refl (+ v être)*
⟨*elements, people*⟩ to complement each other

complexe /kɔ̃plɛks/ [1] *adj* complex
[2] *nm* **(a)** (psychological) complex; **il n'a pas
de ~** he has no inhibitions
(b) (place) complex; **un ~ sportif** a sports
complex

complexer /kɔ̃plekse/ [1] *vtr* (colloq) to
give [sb] a complex

complexité /kɔ̃plɛksite/ *nf* complexity

complication /kɔ̃plikasjɔ̃/ *nf*
complication

complice /kɔ̃plis/ [1] *adj* **(a)** **être ~ de
qch** to be a party to sth
(b) ⟨*air*⟩ of complicity
[2] *nmf* accomplice

complicité /kɔ̃plisite/ *nf* **(a)** complicity
(b) bond

compliment /kɔ̃plimɑ̃/ [1] *nm*
compliment
[2] **compliments** *nm pl* (gen)
compliments; **(tous) mes ~s!**
congratulations!

complimenter /kɔ̃plimɑ̃te/ [1] *vtr* to
compliment

compliqué, ~e /kɔ̃plike/ *adj*
complicated; ⟨*mind*⟩ tortuous

compliquer /kɔ̃plike/ [1] [1] *vtr* to
complicate
[2] **se compliquer** *v refl (+ v être)* **(a)** to
become more complicated
(b) **se ~ la vie** *or* **l'existence** to make life
difficult for oneself

complot /kɔ̃plo/ *nm* plot

comploter /kɔ̃plɔte/ [1] *vtr, vi* to plot

comportement /kɔ̃pɔRtəmɑ̃/ *nm* **(a)** (gen)
behaviour (GB)
(b) (of sportsman, car) performance

comporter /kɔ̃pɔRte/ [1] [1] *vtr* **(a)** to
include
(b) to comprise, to consist of
(c) to entail, to involve
[2] **se comporter** *v refl (+ v être)* **(a)** to
behave, to act
(b) ⟨*sportsman, car*⟩ to perform

composant /kɔ̃pozɑ̃/ *nm* (Tech)
component

composante /kɔ̃pozɑ̃t/ *nf* element;
component

composé, ~e /kɔ̃poze/ [1] *adj* ⟨*salad*⟩
mixed
[2] *nm* (in chemistry) compound

composer /kɔ̃poze/ [1] [1] *vtr* ⟨*elements,
people*⟩ to make up
(b) ⟨*person*⟩ to put [sth] together
⟨*programme, menu*⟩; to select ⟨*team*⟩; to
make up ⟨*bouquet*⟩
(c) ⟨*artist*⟩ to compose ⟨*piece of music*⟩; to
paint ⟨*picture*⟩
(d) to dial ⟨*number*⟩
[2] **se composer** *v refl (+ v être)* **se ~ de**
to be made up of

compositeur, -trice /kɔ̃pozitœR, tRis/
nm,f **(a)** (Mus) composer
(b) typesetter

composition /kɔ̃pozisjɔ̃/ *nf*
(a) (of government, delegation) make-up; (of team)
line-up; (of product) ingredients; (of drug)
composition
(b) (of government) formation; (of team)
selection; (of list, menu) drawing up; **de ma ~**
of my invention
(c) (of piece of music, picture) composition;
(of letter) writing
(d) (Sch) end-of-term test
(e) typesetting
IDIOMS **être de bonne ~** to be good-natured

composter /kɔ̃pɔste/ [1] *vtr* to
(date)stamp; to punch ⟨*ticket*⟩

compote /kɔ̃pɔt/ *nf* (Culin) stewed fruit,
compote

compréhensible /kɔ̃pReɑ̃sibl/ *adj*
(a) understandable
(b) comprehensible

compréhensif, -ive /kɔ̃pReɑ̃sif, iv/ *adj*
understanding

compréhension /kɔ̃pReɑ̃sjɔ̃/ *nf*
understanding; comprehension

comprendre /kɔ̃pRɑ̃dR/ [52] [1] *vtr* **(a)** to
understand; **c'est à n'y rien ~** it's   ···⊹

completely baffling; **mal ~ to** misunderstand;
être compris comme une menace to be
interpreted as a threat; **se faire ~ to** make
oneself understood
(b) to consist of, to comprise
(c) to include
2 se comprendre *v refl* (+ *v être*)
(a) ⟨*people*⟩ to understand each other *or* one
another
(b) je me comprends I know what I'm trying
to say
(c) ⟨*attitude*⟩ to be understandable

compresse /kɔ̃pʀɛs/ *nf* compress

compresser /kɔ̃pʀese/ [1] *vtr* to compress

compression /kɔ̃pʀesjɔ̃/ *nf* **(a)** (Tech)
compression
(b) reduction
(c) cut; **~s budgétaires** budget cuts

comprimé /kɔ̃pʀime/ *nm* tablet

comprimer /kɔ̃pʀime/ [1] *vtr* **(a)** to
constrict; to squeeze ⟨*tube*⟩
(b) (Med) to compress
(c) (Tech) **air comprimé** compressed air

compris, ~e /kɔ̃pʀi, iz/ **1** *pp* ▶
COMPRENDRE
2 *pp adj* including; **service ~/non ~**
service included/not included
3 tout compris *phr* in total, all in (GB)
(colloq)
4 y compris *phr* including

compromettant, ~e /kɔ̃pʀɔmetɑ̃, ɑ̃t/
adj compromising

compromettre /kɔ̃pʀɔmɛtʀ/ [60] **1** *vtr*
(a) to endanger, to jeopardize
(b) to compromise ⟨*person*⟩; to damage
⟨*reputation*⟩
2 se compromettre *v refl* (+ *v être*) to
compromise oneself

compromis /kɔ̃pʀɔmi/ *nm* compromise

comptabiliser /kɔ̃tabilize/ [1] *vtr* to
count

comptabilité /kɔ̃tabilite/ *nf*
(a) accountancy
(b) bookkeeping; **faire sa ~ to** do one's
accounts
(c) accounts department

comptable /kɔ̃tabl/ **1** *adj* **(a)** ⟨*year*⟩
accounting; ⟨*department*⟩ accounts
(b) ⟨*noun*⟩ countable
2 *nmf* accountant; bookkeeper

comptant /kɔ̃tɑ̃/ *adv* cash

compte /kɔ̃t/ **1** *nm* **(a)** count; **faire le ~
de qch** to work out ⟨*expenditure*⟩; to count
(up) ⟨*objects*⟩; **comment fais-tu ton ~ pour
faire...?** how do you manage to
do...?; **tout ~ fait** all things considered; **en
fin de ~ at** the end of the day
(b) (of money) amount; (of objects, people)
number; **il n'y a pas le ~** that's not the right
amount; that's not the right number; **il a son
~** (colloq) he's done for (colloq); (drunk) he's
had a drop too much; **nous avons eu notre ~
d'ennuis** (figurative) we've had more than our
fair share of problems; **à ce ~~-là** in that case

(c) prendre qch en ~, tenir ~ de qch to take
sth into account
(d) être *or* **travailler à son ~** to be self-
employed; **pour le ~ de qn** on behalf of sb;
y trouver son ~ to get something out of it
(e) account; **~ en banque** bank account;
mettre qch sur le ~ de qn to charge sth to
sb's account; (figurative) to put sth down to sb
(f) rendre ~ de qch à qn to give an account
of sth to sb; **to account for sth to sb; devoir
rendre des ~s à qn** to be answerable to sb;
demander des ~s à qn to ask for an
explanation from sb
(g) se rendre ~ de to realize; to notice
(h) dire qch sur le ~ de qn to say sth about
sb
(i) (in boxing) count
2 à bon compte *phr* **s'en tirer à bon ~**
to get off lightly
■ **~ chèques** current account (GB), checking
account (US); **~ d'épargne** savings account;
~ épargne logement savings account (for
purchasing a property); **~ chèque postal,
CCP** post office account; **~ joint** joint
account; **~ à rebours** countdown

compte-gouttes /kɔ̃tgut/ *nm inv*
dropper; **au ~** (figurative) sparingly

compter /kɔ̃te/ [1] **1** *vtr* **(a)** to count; **on
compte deux millions de chômeurs** there is a
total of two million unemployed; **il a toujours
compté ses sous** he has always watched the
pennies; **sans ~** ⟨*give, spend*⟩ freely; **ses
jours sont comptés** his/her days are
numbered
(b) ~ une bouteille pour trois to allow a
bottle between three people
(c) (as fee, price) **~ qch à qn** to charge sb for
sth
(d) to count, to include; **sans ~ les soucis**
not to mention the worry
(e) to have; **notre club compte des gens
célèbres** our club has some well-known
people among its members
(f) ~ faire to intend to do
(g) il comptait que je lui prête de l'argent he
expected me to lend him some money
2 *vi* **(a)** to count; **~ au nombre de, ~ parmi**
to be counted among
(b) to matter; **c'est l'intention qui compte** it's
the thought that counts; **ça compte
beaucoup pour moi** it means a lot to me
(c) to count; **ça ne compte pas, il a triché** it
doesn't count, he cheated
(d) ~ avec to reckon with; to take [sb/sth]
into account; **~ sans** not to take [sb/sth]
into account
(e) ~ sur to count on ⟨*person, help*⟩; (for
support) to rely on ⟨*person, resource*⟩;
(in anticipation) to reckon on ⟨*sum, income*⟩
3 se compter *v refl* (+ *v être*) **leurs
victoires se comptent par douzaines** they
have had dozens of victories
4 à compter de *phr* as from
5 sans compter que *phr* and what is
more; especially as

compte(-)rendu, *pl* **comptes(-) rendus** /kɔ̃tRɑ̃dy/ *nm* (gen) report; (of book) review

compteur /kɔ̃tœR/ *nm* meter; clock. ■ ~ **kilométrique** ≈ milometer; ~ **de vitesse** speedometer

comptine /kɔ̃tin/ *nf* nursery rhyme

comptoir /kɔ̃twaR/ *nm* **(a)** (of café) bar **(b)** (of shop) counter

comte /kɔ̃t/ *nm* (title) count; earl

comtesse /kɔ̃tɛs/ *nf* countess

con, conne /kɔ̃, kɔn/ *nm,f* (vulgar) bloody idiot (GB) (slang), stupid jerk (colloq); **idée à la** ~ lousy idea (colloq)

concasser /kɔ̃kase/ [1] *vtr* (Culin, Tech) to crush

concave /kɔ̃kav/ *adj* concave

concéder /kɔ̃sede/ [14] *vtr* to concede

concentration /kɔ̃sɑ̃tRasjɔ̃/ *nf* concentration

concentré, ~e /kɔ̃sɑ̃tRe/ ① *pp* ▶ CONCENTRER
② *pp adj* **(a)** **un air** ~ **a** look of concentration
(b) concentrated; ⟨lait⟩ condensed
③ *nm* (Culin) ~ **de tomate** tomato purée (GB) or paste (US)

concentrer /kɔ̃sɑ̃tRe/ [1] ① *vtr* to concentrate
② **se concentrer** *v refl* (+ *v être*) to concentrate; ⟨attention⟩ to be concentrated

concept /kɔ̃sɛpt/ *nm* concept

conception /kɔ̃sɛpsjɔ̃/ *nf* **(a)** conception **(b)** design **(c)** idea

concernant /kɔ̃sɛRnɑ̃/ *prep* **(a)** concerning **(b)** as regards, with regard to

concerner /kɔ̃sɛRne/ [1] *vtr* **(a)** to concern **(b)** to affect

concert /kɔ̃sɛR/ ① *nm* (Mus) concert ② **de concert** *phr* **ils ont agi de** ~ they worked together

concertation /kɔ̃sɛRtasjɔ̃/ *nf* **(a)** consultation **(b)** cooperation

concerté, ~e /kɔ̃sɛRte/ *adj* concerted

concerter: se concerter /kɔ̃sɛRte/ [1] *v refl* (+ *v être*) to consult each other

concerto /kɔ̃sɛRto/ *nm* concerto

concession /kɔ̃sesjɔ̃/ *nf* **(a)** (compromise) concession; **film sans** ~**s** uncompromising film
(b) (awarding of right) concession (**de** of)
(c) (right, contract) (of mine, site) concession; (Aut) dealership

concessionnaire /kɔ̃sesjɔnɛR/ *nmf* (commercial) agent; (Aut) dealer

concevoir /kɔ̃s(ə)vwaR/ [5] ① *vtr* **(a)** to design ⟨product, system⟩
(b) to conceive ⟨child⟩
(c) to understand ⟨attitude⟩
(d) to see ⟨phenomenon, activity⟩
(e) (formal) to conceive ⟨hatred⟩
② **se concevoir** *v refl* (+ *v être*) **(a)** to be conceivable
(b) to be understandable

concierge /kɔ̃sjɛRʒ/ *nmf* caretaker (GB), superintendent (US)

concile /kɔ̃sil/ *nm* council

conciliabule /kɔ̃siljabyl/ *nm* consultation, confab (colloq)

conciliant, ~e /kɔ̃siljɑ̃, ɑ̃t/ *adj* conciliatory

conciliation /kɔ̃siljasjɔ̃/ *nf* conciliation

concilier /kɔ̃silje/ [2] *vtr* to reconcile

concis, ~e /kɔ̃si, iz/ *adj* concise

concision /kɔ̃sizjɔ̃/ *nf* conciseness

concitoyen, -enne /kɔ̃sitwajɛ̃, ɛn/ *nm,f* fellow-citizen

conclave /kɔ̃klav/ *nm* conclave

conclu, ~e /kɔ̃kly/ ▶ CONCLURE

concluant, ~e /kɔ̃klyɑ̃, ɑ̃t/ *adj* conclusive

conclure /kɔ̃klyR/ [78] *vtr* **(a)** to conclude (**que** that)
(b) to conclude ⟨deal, agreement⟩; **'marché conclu!'** 'it's a deal!'
(c) ⟨person⟩ to conclude ⟨speech⟩
(d) to bring [sth] to a close ⟨festival⟩

conclusion /kɔ̃klyzjɔ̃/ ① *nf*
(a) conclusion; **tirer les** ~**s d'une expérience** to learn from an experience; **ne tire pas de** ~**s hâtives** don't jump to conclusions
(b) (of deal, treaty) conclusion
(c) (of speech, session) close
② **conclusions** *nf pl* **(a)** (of analysis, autopsy) results; (of inquiry) findings
(b) (Law) (of expert) opinion; (of jury) verdict; (of plaintiff) pleadings

concocter /kɔ̃kɔkte/ [1] *vtr* (colloq) to concoct ⟨dish⟩; to devise ⟨programme⟩

concombre /kɔ̃kɔ̃bR/ *nm* cucumber

concordance /kɔ̃kɔRdɑ̃s/ *nf* concordance; compatibility
■ ~ **des temps** sequence of tenses

concorder /kɔ̃kɔRde/ [1] *vi* ⟨results, evidence⟩ to tally; ⟨estimates⟩ to agree

concourir /kɔ̃kuRiR/ [26] ① *vi* to compete
② **concourir à** *v+prep* ~ **à qch/à faire** ⟨factors⟩ to combine to bring about sth/to do; ⟨factor, person⟩ to help bring about sth/do

concours /kɔ̃kuR/ *nm inv* **(a)** (gen) competition; (agricultural) show; ~ **de beauté** beauty contest
(b) competitive examination; ~ **d'entrée** entrance examination
(c) help, assistance; support; cooperation
■ ~ **de circonstances** combination of circumstances

concret, -ète /kɔ̃kRɛ, ɛt/ *adj* **(a)** ⟨result⟩ concrete
(b) ⟨mind, person⟩ practical

concrètement /kɔ̃kRɛtmɑ̃/ *adv* **(a)** in concrete terms
(b) in practical terms

concrétisation /kɔ̃kretizasjɔ̃/ *nf* concrete expression; fulfilment (GB); achievement

concrétiser /kɔ̃kretize/ [1] **1** *vtr* to make ⟨sth⟩ a reality ⟨*plan, project*⟩
2 se concrétiser *v refl* (+ *v être*) ⟨*dream*⟩ to become a reality; ⟨*offer*⟩ to materialize

concubin, **~e** /kɔ̃kybɛ̃, in/ *nm,f* common law husband/wife

concubinage /kɔ̃kybinaʒ/ *nm* cohabitation

concurrence /kɔ̃kyʀɑ̃s/ *nf* competition; **prix défiant toute ~** unbeatable price; **jusqu'à ~ de** up to a limit of

concurrencer /kɔ̃kyʀɑ̃se/ [12] *vtr* to compete with

concurrent, **~e** /kɔ̃kyʀɑ̃, ɑ̃t/ **1** *adj* rival
2 *nm,f* (for a job) rival; (Sport) competitor; (in competitive examination) candidate

concurrentiel, **-ielle** /kɔ̃kyʀɑ̃sjɛl/ *adj* competitive

condamnable /kɔ̃danabl/ *adj* reprehensible

condamnation /kɔ̃danasjɔ̃/ *nf* (a) (Law) conviction; sentence
(b) condemnation

condamné, **~e** /kɔ̃dane/ **1** *adj*
(a) ⟨*person*⟩ terminally ill
(b) ⟨*door*⟩ sealed up
2 *nm,f* convicted prisoner

condamner /kɔ̃dane/ [1] *vtr* (a) (Law) to sentence; **~ qn à une amende** to fine sb; **~ qn pour vol** to convict sb of theft
(b) ⟨*law*⟩ to punish ⟨*thieving, smuggling*⟩
(c) ⟨*person, country*⟩ to condemn ⟨*act, decision*⟩
(d) **~ qn à faire** to compel sb to do
(e) to seal up ⟨*window*⟩; to shut up ⟨*room*⟩
(f) (figurative) to spell death for ⟨*society, industry*⟩
(g) **les médecins l'ont condamné** the doctors have given up hope of saving him

condensation /kɔ̃dɑ̃sasjɔ̃/ *nf* condensation

condensé /kɔ̃dɑ̃se/ *nm* summary; digest

condenser /kɔ̃dɑ̃se/ [1] *vtr*, **se condenser** *v refl* (+ *v être*) to condense

condescendance /kɔ̃desɑ̃dɑ̃s/ *nf* condescension

condescendant, **~e** /kɔ̃desɑ̃dɑ̃, ɑ̃t/ *adj* condescending

condiment /kɔ̃dimɑ̃/ *nm* (Culin) seasoning; condiment

condisciple /kɔ̃disipl/ *nmf* fellow student

condition /kɔ̃disjɔ̃/ **1** *nf* (a) condition; **à ~ d'avoir le temps** provided (that) one has the time; **sous ~** ⟨*freed*⟩ conditionally; **sans ~(s)** ⟨*acceptance*⟩ unconditional; ⟨*accept*⟩ unconditionally; **imposer ses ~s** to impose one's own terms; **~ préalable** precondition
(b) (Law) (of contract, treaty) term
(c) **la ~ ouvrière** (the conditions of) working-class life
(d) **~** (**sociale**) social status

2 conditions *nf pl* (a) conditions; **dans ces ~s** in these conditions; in that case
(b) terms

conditionnel, **-elle** /kɔ̃disjɔnɛl/ **1** *adj* conditional
2 *nm* conditional

conditionnement /kɔ̃disjɔnmɑ̃/ *nm*
(a) conditioning
(b) packaging
■ **~ sous vide** vacuum packing

conditionner /kɔ̃disjɔne/ [1] *vtr* (a) to condition
(b) to package

condoléances /kɔ̃dɔleɑ̃s/ *nf pl* condolences

condom /kɔ̃dɔm/ *nm* condom

condor /kɔ̃dɔʀ/ *nm* condor

conducteur, **-trice** /kɔ̃dyktœʀ, tʀis/
1 *adj* (a) conductive
(b) ⟨*principle*⟩ guiding
2 *nm,f* (of vehicle) driver
3 *nm* conductor

conduire /kɔ̃dɥiʀ/ [69] **1** *vtr* (a) to take ⟨*person*⟩; (in car) to drive
(b) ⟨*leader, studies*⟩ to lead; **la route qui conduit à Oxford** the road that goes to Oxford; **~ qn au désespoir** to drive sb to despair
(c) to drive ⟨*car, train*⟩; to ride ⟨*motorbike*⟩
(d) to conduct ⟨*research*⟩; to carry out ⟨*project*⟩; to run ⟨*business*⟩
(e) to conduct ⟨*electricity, heat*⟩
2 se conduire *v refl* (+ *v être*) to behave

conduit¹, **~e** /kɔ̃dɥi, ɥit/ ▶ CONDUIRE

conduit² /kɔ̃dɥi/ *nm* (a) conduit
(b) (Anat) canal
■ **~ de fumée** flue; **~ de ventilation** ventilation shaft

conduite /kɔ̃dɥit/ *nf* (a) behaviour (GB); (of pupil) conduct
(b) (of inquiry) conducting; (of building works) supervision; (of company) management
(c) (of vehicle) driving; (of motorbike) riding
(d) (Aut) **voiture avec ~ à gauche** left-hand drive car
(e) (exam) driving test
(f) pipe

cône /kon/ *nm* cone

confection /kɔ̃fɛksjɔ̃/ *nf* (a) clothing industry
(b) making

confectionner /kɔ̃fɛksjɔne/ [1] *vtr* (gen) to make; to prepare ⟨*meal*⟩

confédération /kɔ̃fedeʀasjɔ̃/ *nf* confederation.
■ **la Confédération helvétique** Switzerland

confédéré, **~e** /kɔ̃fedeʀe/ *adj* confederate

conférence /kɔ̃feʀɑ̃s/ *nf* (a) lecture
(b) conference
(c) debate
■ **~ au sommet** summit meeting

conférencier, **-ière** /kɔ̃feʀɑ̃sje, ɛʀ/ *nm,f* speaker; lecturer

conférer /kɔ̃feʀe/ [14] *vtr* to give; to confer

confesser /kɔ̃fese/ [1] **1** *vtr* **(a)** to confess ⟨*sin*⟩
(b) ~ qn to hear sb's confession
2 se confesser *v refl* (+ *v être*) **(a)** to go to confession
(b) se ~ à un ami to confide in a friend

confession /kɔ̃fesjɔ̃/ *nf* **(a)** confession
(b) faith

confessionnal, *pl* **-aux** /kɔ̃fesjɔnal, o/ *nm* confessional

confetti /kɔ̃feti/ *nm* confetti

confiance /kɔ̃fjɑ̃s/ *nf* **(a)** trust; de ~ ⟨*person*⟩ trustworthy; ⟨*mission*⟩ which requires trust; avoir ~ en qn, faire ~ à qn to trust sb; mettre qn en ~ to win sb's trust
(b) (in ability, self) confidence ~ en soi (self-)confidence

confiant, **~e** /kɔ̃fjɑ̃, ɑ̃t/ *adj* **(a)** confident
(b) (self-)confident
(c) trusting

confidence /kɔ̃fidɑ̃s/ *nf* secret, confidence; être dans la ~ to be in on the secret

confident, **~e** /kɔ̃fidɑ̃, ɑ̃t/ *nmf* confidant/confidante

confidentialité /kɔ̃fidɑ̃sjalite/ *nf* confidentiality

confidentiel, **-ielle** /kɔ̃fidɑ̃sjɛl/ *adj* confidential

confier /kɔ̃fje/ [2] **1** *vtr* **(a)** ~ qch à qn to entrust sb with sth ⟨*mission*⟩; to entrust sth to sb ⟨*money, letters*⟩
(b) ~ qch à qn to confide sth to sb ⟨*intentions*⟩
2 se confier *v refl* (+ *v être*) to confide

configuration /kɔ̃figyʀasjɔ̃/ *nf* **(a)** shape; la ~ des lieux the layout of the premises
(b) configuration
(c) set-up

confiné, **~e** /kɔ̃fine/ *adj* **(a)** ⟨*atmosphere*⟩ stuffy; ⟨*air*⟩ stale
(b) ⟨*space*⟩ confined, restricted

confiner /kɔ̃fine/ [1] **1** *vtr* to confine
2 confiner à *v+prep* to border on
3 se confiner *v refl* (+ *v être*) to shut oneself away *or* up

confins /kɔ̃fɛ̃/ *nm pl* boundaries

confirmation /kɔ̃fiʀmasjɔ̃/ *nf* confirmation

confirmer /kɔ̃fiʀme/ [1] **1** *vtr* to confirm ⟨*order, fact*⟩; to uphold ⟨*decision*⟩; to be evidence of ⟨*attitude, quality*⟩; to affirm ⟨*intention*⟩
2 se confirmer *v refl* (+ *v être*) ⟨*news*⟩ to be confirmed; ⟨*testimony*⟩ to be corroborated

confiserie /kɔ̃fizʀi/ *nf* **(a)** confectioner's (shop)
(b) confectionery

confisquer /kɔ̃fiske/ [1] *vtr* to confiscate, to seize

confit, **~e** /kɔ̃fi, it/ **1** *adj* ⟨*fruits*⟩ crystallized
2 *nm* confit; ~ de canard confit of duck

confiture /kɔ̃fityʀ/ *nf* (Culin) jam, preserve; marmalade
IDIOMS donner de la ~ aux cochons to cast pearls before swine

conflictuel, **-elle** /kɔ̃fliktɥɛl/ *adj* ⟨*subject*⟩ controversial; ⟨*relationship*⟩ confrontational

conflit /kɔ̃fli/ *nm* conflict
■ ~ de générations generation gap; ~ social industrial strife

confluence /kɔ̃flyɑ̃s/ *nf* confluence; (figurative) convergence

confluent /kɔ̃flyɑ̃/ *nm* confluence

confondre /kɔ̃fɔ̃dʀ/ [53] **1** *vtr* **(a)** to mix up, to confuse; tous secteurs confondus all sectors taken together
(b) to merge
(c) (formal) to stagger, to amaze
(d) to expose ⟨*traitor*⟩
2 se confondre *v refl* (+ *v être*)
(a) ⟨*shapes, colours*⟩ to merge; ⟨*events, facts*⟩ to become confused
(b) ⟨*interests, hopes*⟩ to coincide
(c) (formal) se ~ en excuses to apologize profusely

conforme /kɔ̃fɔʀm/ *adj* **(a)** être ~ à to comply with ⟨*regulations*⟩
(b) être ~ à l'original to conform to the original

conformément /kɔ̃fɔʀmemɑ̃/ *adv* ~ à in accordance with

conformer: se conformer /kɔ̃fɔʀme/ [1] *v refl* (+ *v être*) to comply with ⟨*regulations*⟩

conformisme /kɔ̃fɔʀmism/ *nm* conformity

conformiste /kɔ̃fɔʀmist/ *adj, nmf* conformist

conformité /kɔ̃fɔʀmite/ *nf* **(a)** ~ à la loi compliance with the law; en ~ avec ⟨*act*⟩ in accordance with
(b) similarity; vérifier la ~ de la traduction à l'original to check that the translation is faithful to the original
(c) (of tastes, points of view) correspondence

confort /kɔ̃fɔʀ/ *nm* comfort; maison tout ~ house with all mod cons (GB) (colloq) *or* modern conveniences

confortable /kɔ̃fɔʀtabl/ *adj* comfortable

confortablement /kɔ̃fɔʀtabləmɑ̃/ *adv* comfortably

conforter /kɔ̃fɔʀte/ [1] *vtr* to consolidate ⟨*position*⟩; to reinforce ⟨*situation*⟩

confrère /kɔ̃fʀɛʀ/ *nm* (at work) colleague; (in association) fellow member

confrérie /kɔ̃fʀeʀi/ *nf* brotherhood

confrontation /kɔ̃fʀɔ̃tasjɔ̃/ *nf* **(a)** (of ideas, witnesses) confrontation; (of texts) comparison
(b) (between people) debate; clash

confronter /kɔ̃fʀɔ̃te/ [1] *vtr* **(a)** to confront ⟨*witnesses*⟩
(b) to compare ⟨*texts*⟩

confus, **~e** /kɔ̃fy, yz/ *adj* **(a)** confused
(b) ⟨*feeling, fear*⟩ vague

(c) sorry; embarrassed

confusément /kɔ̃fyzemɑ̃/ *adv* ⟨explain⟩ confusedly; ⟨feel⟩ vaguely

confusion /kɔ̃fyzjɔ̃/ *nf* **(a)** confusion
(b) embarrassment
(c) mix-up

congé /kɔ̃ʒe/ *nm* **(a)** leave; **prendre quatre jours de** ~ to take four days off; **être en** ~ **de maladie** to be on sick leave
(b) notice; **donner (son)** ~ **à qn** to give sb notice
(c) prendre ~ **de qn** to take leave of sb

congédier /kɔ̃ʒedje/ [2] *vtr* to dismiss

congélateur /kɔ̃ʒelatœʀ/ *nm* freezer; (in refrigerator) freezer compartment

congelé, ~e /kɔ̃ʒle/ *adj* frozen; **produits** ~**s** frozen foods

congeler /kɔ̃ʒle/ [17] **1** *vtr* to freeze
2 se congeler *v refl* (+ *v être*) to freeze

congénital, ~e, mpl -aux /kɔ̃ʒenital, o/ *adj* congenital

congère /kɔ̃ʒɛʀ/ *nf* snowdrift

congestion /kɔ̃ʒɛstjɔ̃/ *nf* congestion
■ ~ **cérébrale** stroke

congestionner /kɔ̃ʒɛstjɔne/ [1] *vtr* **(a)** **il est tout congestionné** he's all flushed
(b) to congest ⟨street⟩

conglomérat /kɔ̃glɔmeʀa/ *nm*
(a) conglomerate
(b) (mixture) conglomeration

congrégation /kɔ̃gʀegasjɔ̃/ *nf* congregation; (humorous) assembly

congrès /kɔ̃gʀɛ/ *nm* conference; **le Congrès** (US) Congress

congressiste /kɔ̃gʀesist/ *nmf* (conference) delegate

conifère /kɔnifɛʀ/ *nm* conifer

conique /kɔnik/ *adj* cone-shaped

conjecture /kɔ̃ʒɛktyʀ/ *nf* conjecture; **vaines** ~**s** idle speculation

conjecturer /kɔ̃ʒɛktyʀe/ [1] *vtr* to speculate

conjoint, ~e /kɔ̃ʒwɛ̃, ɛ̃t/ **1** *adj* ⟨action⟩ joint; ⟨questions⟩ linked
2 *nm,f* spouse; **les** ~**s** the husband and wife

conjointement /kɔ̃ʒwɛ̃tmɑ̃/ *adv*
(a) jointly
(b) at the same time

conjonction /kɔ̃ʒɔ̃ksjɔ̃/ *nf* conjunction

conjonctivite /kɔ̃ʒɔ̃ktivit/ *nf* conjunctivitis

conjoncture /kɔ̃ʒɔ̃ktyʀ/ *nf* situation; circumstances

conjoncturel, -elle /kɔ̃ʒɔ̃ktyʀɛl/ *adj* ⟨situation⟩ economic

conjugaison /kɔ̃ʒygɛzɔ̃/ *nf* **(a)** (of verb) conjugation
(b) (figurative) combination

conjugal, ~e, mpl -aux /kɔ̃ʒygal, o/ *adj* ⟨love⟩ conjugal; ⟨life⟩ married

conjugalement /kɔ̃ʒygalmɑ̃/ *adv* ⟨live⟩ as man and wife

conjuguer /kɔ̃ʒyge/ [1] *vtr* **(a)** to conjugate ⟨verb⟩
(b) to combine ⟨efforts⟩

conjuration /kɔ̃ʒyʀasjɔ̃/ *nf* **(a)** conspiracy
(b) (of evil spirits) conjuration

conjurer /kɔ̃ʒyʀe/ [1] *vtr* **(a)** to avert ⟨crisis⟩; to ward off ⟨danger⟩
(b) je vous en conjure I beg you

connaissance /kɔnɛsɑ̃s/ *nf*
(a) knowledge; **prendre** ~ **d'un texte** to acquaint oneself with a text; **en** ~ **de cause** with full knowledge of the facts
(b) consciousness; **sans** ~ unconscious
(c) acquaintance; **faire (plus ample)** ~ **avec qn** to get to know sb (better); **en pays de** ~ among familiar faces; on familiar ground

connaisseur, -euse /kɔnɛsœʀ, øz/ *nm,f* connoisseur, expert

connaître /kɔnɛtʀ/ [73] **1** *vtr* **(a)** to know; **faire** ~ **à qn** to make [sth] known to sb ⟨decision⟩; to introduce sb to ⟨music⟩; **je l'ai connu en Chine** I met him in China; **tu connais la nouvelle?** have you heard the news?
(b) to experience ⟨hunger, failure⟩; to enjoy ⟨success⟩; to have ⟨difficulties⟩; ~ **une forte croissance** to show a rapid growth
2 se connaître *v refl* (+ *v être*) **(a)** to know oneself
(b) to know each other; **ils se sont connus à Rome** they met in Rome
(c) s'y ~ **en vin** to know all about wine
IDIOMS **on connaît la chanson** *or* **musique!** we've heard it all before!; ~ **qch comme sa poche** to know sth like the back of one's hand

conne (vulgar) ▶ **CON**

connecter /kɔnɛkte/ [1] *vtr* to connect

connexion /kɔnɛksjɔ̃/ *nf* connection

connivence /kɔnivɑ̃s/ *nf* connivance; **signe de** ~ sign of complicity

connotation /kɔnɔtasjɔ̃/ *nf* connotation

connu, ~e /kɔny/ ▶ **CONNAÎTRE**

conquérant, ~e /kɔ̃keʀɑ̃, ɑ̃t/ *nm,f* conqueror

conquérir /kɔ̃keʀiʀ/ [35] *vtr* to conquer; to capture ⟨market⟩; to win over ⟨audience⟩.
IDIOMS **se croire en pays** *or* **terrain conquis** to lord it over everyone

conquête /kɔ̃kɛt/ *nf* conquest

conquis, ~e ▶ **CONQUÉRIR**

consacré, ~e /kɔ̃sakʀe/ *adj* **formule** ~**e** time-honoured (GB) expression; **artiste** ~ recognized artist

consacrer /kɔ̃sakʀe/ [1] **1** *vtr* **(a)** to devote; **pouvez-vous me** ~ **un instant?** can you spare me a moment?
(b) to sanction
(c) to consecrate
2 se consacrer *v refl* (+ *v être*) **se** ~ **à** to devote oneself to

consanguin, ~e /kɔ̃sɑ̃gɛ̃, in/ *adj* ⟨marriage⟩ between blood relations

consciemment /kɔ̃sjamɑ̃/ *adv*
consciously

conscience /kɔ̃sjɑ̃s/ *nf* **(a)** conscience;
avoir bonne/mauvaise ∼ to have a clear/a
guilty conscience
(b) awareness; **prendre ∼ de** to become
aware of; **prise de ∼** realization; **perdre ∼** to
lose consciousness
■ **∼ professionnelle** conscientiousness

consciencieusement /kɔ̃sjɑ̃sjøzmɑ̃/
adv **(a)** conscientiously
(b) dutifully

consciencieux, -ieuse /kɔ̃sjɑ̃sjø, øz/
adj conscientious

conscient, ∼e /kɔ̃sjɑ̃, ɑ̃t/ *adj* **(a)** aware
(b) conscious

conscrit /kɔ̃skRi/ *nm* conscript (GB),
draftee (US)

consécration /kɔ̃sekRasjɔ̃/ *nf* **(a)** (of author)
recognition
(b) consecration

consécutif, -ive /kɔ̃sekytif, iv/ *adj*
consecutive; **∼ à** resulting from; following

consécutivement /kɔ̃sekytivmɑ̃/ *adv*
consecutively

conseil /kɔ̃sej/ *nm* **(a)** advice; **quelques
∼s de prudence** a few words of warning; **il
est de bon ∼** he always gives good advice;
∼s d'entretien cleaning *or* care instructions
(b) council
(c) consultant
■ **∼ d'administration** board of directors; **∼ de
classe** (Sch) staff meeting; **∼ de discipline**
disciplinary committee; **∼ général** *council of
a French department*

conseiller¹, -ère /kɔ̃seje, ɛR/ **1** *nm,f*
(a) adviser (GB)
(b) counsellor (GB)
2 *nm* councillor (GB)
■ **∼ commercial** commercial counsellor (GB);
∼ culturel cultural counsellor (GB); **∼ d'État**
member of the Council of State; **∼ général**
councillor for a French department;
∼ municipal town councillor (GB);
∼ d'orientation careers adviser

conseiller² /kɔ̃seje/ [1] *vtr* to recommend;
to advise; **∼ à qn de faire** to advise sb to do

consensus /kɔ̃sɛ̃sys/ *nm inv* consensus

consentant, ∼e /kɔ̃sɑ̃tɑ̃, ɑ̃t/ *adj* willing;
(Law) consenting

consentement /kɔ̃sɑ̃tmɑ̃/ *nm* consent

consentir /kɔ̃sɑ̃tiR/ [30] **1** *vtr* to grant; to
allow
2 consentir à *v+prep* **∼ à qch/à faire** to
agree to sth/to do

conséquence /kɔ̃sekɑ̃s/ *nf* consequence;
être lourd de ∼s to have serious
consequences; **sans ∼(s)** of no consequence;
ne pas tirer à ∼ to be of no consequence;
avoir pour ∼ le chômage to result in
unemployment; **agir en ∼** to act
accordingly; **avoir des qualifications et un
salaire en ∼** to have qualifications and a
corresponding salary

conséquent, ∼e /kɔ̃sekɑ̃, ɑ̃t/ **1** *adj*
(a) substantial
(b) consistent
2 par conséquent *phr* therefore, as a
result

conservateur, -trice /kɔ̃sɛRvatœR,
tRis/ **1** *adj* **(a)** conservative
(b) **produit ∼** preservative
2 *nm,f* **(a)** conservative
(b) (museum) curator

conservation /kɔ̃sɛRvasjɔ̃/ *nf*
conservation; preservation; **lait longue ∼**
long-life milk (GB)

conservatoire /kɔ̃sɛRvatwaR/ *nm*
academy; **∼ de musique** conservatoire

conserve /kɔ̃sɛRv/ **1** *nf* **(a)** **la ∼, les ∼s**
canned food; **boîte de ∼** can
(b) preserve
2 de conserve *phr* in concert

conserver /kɔ̃sɛRve/ [1] *vtr* **(a)** to keep; to
retain; **∼ l'anonymat** to remain anonymous
(b) (Culin) to preserve; (in vinegar) to pickle
(c) ⟨activity⟩ to keep [sb] young

conserverie /kɔ̃sɛRvəRi/ *nf* **(a)** cannery,
canning plant
(b) canning industry

considérable /kɔ̃sideRabl/ *adj*
considerable, significant; **l'enjeu est ∼** the
stakes are high

considération /kɔ̃sideRasjɔ̃/ *nf*
(a) consideration; **prendre qch en ∼** to
consider sth, to take sth into account; **en ∼
de** in view of; **sans ∼ de** irrespective of
(b) consideration, factor
(c) respect, esteem

considérer /kɔ̃sideRe/ [14] **1** *vtr* **(a)** to
consider, to take into account
(b) to consider, to regard; **∼ qn/qch comme
(étant)** to consider sb/sth to be, to regard sb/
sth as being; **être bien considéré** to be
highly regarded
2 se considérer *v refl* (+ *v être*) **se ∼
(comme)** **(a)** to consider oneself (to be)
(b) to regard one another as being

consignation /kɔ̃siɲasjɔ̃/ *nf* **(a)** deposit
(b) **en ∼** on consignment

consigne /kɔ̃siɲ/ *nf* **(a)** orders,
instructions; **passer la ∼ à qn** to pass the
word on to sb; **'∼s à suivre en cas
d'incendie'** 'fire regulations'
(b) left luggage office (GB), baggage
checkroom (US)
(c) (on bottle) deposit
■ **∼ automatique** left luggage lockers (GB),
baggage lockers (US)

consigné, ∼e /kɔ̃siɲe/ *adj* ⟨bottle⟩
returnable

consigner /kɔ̃siɲe/ [1] *vtr* **(a)** to record, to
write down
(b) to confine ⟨soldier⟩; to give [sb]
detention ⟨pupil⟩

consistance /kɔ̃sistɑ̃s/ *nf* **(a)** consistency;
avoir de la/manquer de ∼ to be quite thick/
to be too runny   ···⟶

(b) substance, weight; **sans** ∼ ⟨*person*⟩ spineless; ⟨*rumour*⟩ groundless

consistant, ∼e /kɔ̃sistɑ̃, ɑ̃t/ *adj* ⟨*meal, investment*⟩ substantial; ⟨*dish*⟩ nourishing

consister /kɔ̃siste/ [1] *vi* **(a)** ∼ **en** *or* **dans** to consist in; ∼ **à faire** to consist in doing **(b)** ∼ **en** to consist of, to be made up of; **en quoi consiste cette aide?** what form does this aid take?

consœur /kɔ̃sœʀ/ *nf* **(a)** female colleague **(b)** counterpart

consolant, ∼e /kɔ̃sɔlɑ̃, ɑ̃t/ *adj* comforting

consolation /kɔ̃sɔlasjɔ̃/ *nf* consolation

console /kɔ̃sɔl/ *nf* console; ∼ **de jeu vidéo** games console

consoler /kɔ̃sɔle/ [1] **1** *vtr* to console; **si ça peut te** ∼ if it is any comfort to you **2 se consoler** *v refl* (+ *v être*) to find consolation; **se** ∼ **de** to get over

consolidable /kɔ̃sɔlidabl/ *adj* **(a)** ⟨*debt*⟩ fundable **(b)** ⟨*structure*⟩ reinforceable

consolidation /kɔ̃sɔlidasjɔ̃/ *nf* **(a)** (of wall) strengthening; (of position) consolidation **(b)** (of debt) consolidation, funding; (of turnover, balance sheet) consolidation; (of currency) strengthening

consolider /kɔ̃sɔlide/ [1] **1** *vtr* to consolidate, to strengthen **2 se consolider** *v refl* (+ *v être*) **(a)** to grow stronger, to be strengthened **(b)** to consolidate

consommable /kɔ̃sɔmabl/ **1** *adj* edible; drinkable **2 consommables** *nm pl* (Econ, Comput) consumables

consommateur, -trice /kɔ̃sɔmatœʀ, tʀis/ *nm,f* **(a)** consumer **(b)** (in bar) customer

consommation /kɔ̃sɔmasjɔ̃/ *nf* **(a)** consumption; **faire une grande** ∼ **de** to use a lot of; **de** ∼ ⟨*goods, society*⟩ consumer **(b)** drink **(c)** consummation

consommé, ∼e /kɔ̃sɔme/ *nm* consommé

consommer /kɔ̃sɔme/ [1] *vtr* **(a)** to consume; to use **(b)** to eat ⟨*food*⟩; to drink ⟨*tea*⟩; to take ⟨*drugs*⟩

consonance /kɔ̃sɔnɑ̃s/ *nf* consonance; **mot aux** ∼**s étrangères** foreign-sounding word

consonne /kɔ̃sɔn/ *nf* consonant

conspirateur, -trice /kɔ̃spiʀatœʀ, tʀis/ *nm,f* conspirator

conspiration /kɔ̃spiʀasjɔ̃/ *nf* conspiracy

conspirer /kɔ̃spiʀe/ [1] **1** *vi* to conspire, to plot **2 conspirer à** *v+prep* to conspire to bring about; ∼ **à faire** to conspire to do

constamment /kɔ̃stamɑ̃/ *adv* constantly

constance /kɔ̃stɑ̃s/ *nf* **(a)** consistency; constancy

(b) steadfastness

constant, ∼e¹ /kɔ̃stɑ̃, ɑ̃t/ *adj* **(a)** constant; consistent **(b)** continuous; continual

constante² /kɔ̃stɑ̃t/ *nf* constant

constat /kɔ̃sta/ *nm* certified *or* official report
■ ∼ **(à l')amiable**: accident report drawn up by the parties involved; ∼ **d'échec** admission of failure

constatation /kɔ̃statasjɔ̃/ *nf* observation

constater /kɔ̃state/ [1] *vtr* **(a)** to notice, to note; ∼ **(par) soi-même** to see for oneself **(b)** to ascertain, to establish **(c)** to record

constellation /kɔ̃stɛlasjɔ̃/ *nf* constellation

constellé, ∼e /kɔ̃stɛlle/ *adj* ∼ **de** spangled with; riddled with; spotted with

consternant, ∼e /kɔ̃stɛʀnɑ̃, ɑ̃t/ *adj* **(a)** distressing **(b)** appalling

consternation /kɔ̃stɛʀnasjɔ̃/ *nf* consternation

consterner /kɔ̃stɛʀne/ [1] *vtr* to fill [sb] with consternation, to dismay

constipation /kɔ̃stipasjɔ̃/ *nf* constipation

constipé, ∼e /kɔ̃stipe/ *adj* constipated

constiper /kɔ̃stipe/ [1] *vtr* to make [sb] constipated

constitué, ∼e /kɔ̃stitɥe/ *adj* **(a) personne bien/mal** ∼**e** person of sound/unsound constitution **(b)** constituted

constituer /kɔ̃stitɥe/ [1] **1** *vtr* **(a)** to be, to constitute ⟨*crime, reason*⟩ **(b)** to form, to set up ⟨*team, commission*⟩ **(c)** to make up ⟨*whole*⟩ **(d)** (Law) to settle; ∼ **qn héritier** to appoint sb as heir **2 se constituer** *v refl* (+ *v être*) **(a)** to build up ⟨*network, reserve*⟩ **(b) se** ∼ **en** to form ⟨*party*⟩ **(c) se** ∼ **prisonnier** to give oneself up

constitutif, -ive /kɔ̃stitytif, iv/ *adj* **(a)** (basic) constituent **(b)** (Pol) founding; constitutional

constitution /kɔ̃stitysjɔ̃/ *nf* **(a)** (of company) setting up; (of capital) accumulation; (of application) preparing **(b)** constitution

constructeur, -trice /kɔ̃stʀyktœʀ, tʀis/ *nm,f* **(a)** (car) manufacturer **(b)** builder

constructif, -ive /kɔ̃stʀyktif, iv/ *adj* constructive

construction /kɔ̃stʀyksjɔ̃/ *nf* **(a)** construction; building; **en** ∼ under construction; **de** ∼ **japonaise** Japanese built **(b) la** ∼ the construction industry; ∼ **navale** shipbuilding

construire /kɔ̃stʀɥiʀ/ [69] **1** *vtr* to build; to construct

2 **se construire** *v refl* (+ *v être*) (a) ça s'est beaucoup construit par ici there's been a lot of building here
(b) se ~ avec le subjonctif to take the subjunctive

consul /kɔ̃syl/ *nm* consul

consulat /kɔ̃syla/ *nm* consulate

consultant, ~e /kɔ̃syltã, ãt/ *nm,f* consultant

consultation /kɔ̃syltasjɔ̃/ *nf*
(a) consultation; consulting; ~ électorale election
(b) surgery hours (GB), office hours (US)

consulter /kɔ̃sylte/ [1] **1** *vtr* to consult; ~ le peuple to hold a general election
2 *vi* ‹doctor› to see patients
3 **se consulter** *v refl* (+ *v être*) to consult together; se ~ du regard to exchange glances

consumer /kɔ̃syme/ [1] **1** *vtr* ‹fire› to consume
2 **se consumer** *v refl* (+ *v être*) to burn

contact /kɔ̃takt/ *nm* (a) contact; garder le ~ to keep in touch; entrer en ~ avec to get in touch with; elle est devenue plus sociable à ton ~ she's become more sociable through spending time with you
(b) mettre/couper le ~ to switch on/switch off the ignition

contacter /kɔ̃takte/ [1] *vtr* to contact, to get in touch with

contagieux, -ieuse /kɔ̃taʒjø, øz/ *adj*
(a) contagious
(b) ‹laughter› infectious

contagion /kɔ̃taʒjɔ̃/ *nf* contagion

contamination /kɔ̃taminasjɔ̃/ *nf* contamination

contaminer /kɔ̃tamine/ [1] *vtr* to contaminate; to infect

conte /kɔ̃t/ *nm* tale, story

contemplatif, -ive /kɔ̃tãplatif, iv/ *adj* contemplative

contemplation /kɔ̃tãplasjɔ̃/ *nf* contemplation

contempler /kɔ̃tãple/ [1] *vtr* to survey; to contemplate; to look at

contemporain, ~e /kɔ̃tãpɔʀɛ̃, ɛn/ *adj, nm,f* contemporary

contenance /kɔ̃t(ə)nɑ̃s/ *nf* (a) (of container) capacity
(b) bearing, attitude; perdre ~ to lose one's composure

contenant /kɔ̃t(ə)nã/ *nm* packaging

conteneur /kɔ̃t(ə)nœʀ/ *nm* container
■ ~ vert (for bottles) bottle bank

contenir /kɔ̃t(ə)niʀ/ [36] **1** *vtr* (a) to contain ‹substance, error›
(b) ‹container› to hold; ‹hall› to accommodate ‹spectators›
(c) to contain ‹crowd›
2 **se contenir** *v refl* (+ *v être*) to contain oneself

content, ~e /kɔ̃tã, ãt/ **1** *adj* happy, pleased, glad; ~ de soi pleased with oneself

2 *nm* avoir son ~ de to have had one's fill of

contentement /kɔ̃tãtmã/ *nm* contentment

contenter /kɔ̃tãte/ [1] **1** *vtr* to satisfy ‹customer, curiosity›; facile à ~ easy to please
2 **se contenter** *v refl* (+ *v être*) se ~ de qch to content oneself with sth

contentieux /kɔ̃tãsjø/ *nm* (a) bone of contention
(b) legal department
(c) litigation

contenu, ~e /kɔ̃t(ə)ny/ **1** *pp* ▶ CONTENIR
2 *pp adj* restrained; suppressed
3 *nm* contents; content

conter /kɔ̃te/ [1] *vtr* to tell, to recount

contestable /kɔ̃tɛstabl/ *adj* questionable

contestataire /kɔ̃tɛstatɛʀ/ **1** *adj* anti-authority
2 *nmf* protester

contestation /kɔ̃tɛstasjɔ̃/ *nf* (a) protest
(b) challenging; être sujet à ~, prêter à ~ to be questionable; sans ~ possible beyond dispute
(b) la ~ dissent

conteste: sans conteste /sãkɔ̃tɛst/ *phr* unquestionably

contesté, ~e /kɔ̃tɛste/ *adj* controversial

contester /kɔ̃tɛste/ [1] **1** *vtr* to question; to contest; to dispute; to challenge
2 *vi* (a) to raise objections
(b) to protest

contexte /kɔ̃tɛkst/ *nm* context

contigu, -uë /kɔ̃tigy/ *adj* ‹rooms› adjoining

continent, ~e /kɔ̃tinã, ãt/ **1** *adj* continent
2 *nm* (a) continent
(b) mainland

continental, ~e, mpl -aux /kɔ̃tinãtal, o/ *adj* (a) continental
(b) mainland

contingent /kɔ̃tɛ̃ʒã/ *nm* (a) contingent; (Mil) conscripts, draft (US)
(b) quota
(c) (Law, figurative) share

continu, ~e /kɔ̃tiny/ *adj* continuous

continuation /kɔ̃tinɥasjɔ̃/ *nf* continuation

continuel, -elle /kɔ̃tinɥɛl/ *adj* continual

continuer /kɔ̃tinɥe/ [1] **1** *vtr* to continue
2 *vi* to continue, to go on

continuité /kɔ̃tinɥite/ *nf* continuity

contondant, ~e /kɔ̃tɔ̃dã, ãt/ *adj* blunt

contorsion /kɔ̃tɔʀsjɔ̃/ *nf* contortion

contorsionner: se contorsionner /kɔ̃tɔʀsjone/ [1] *v refl* (+ *v être*) to tie oneself in knots

contorsionniste /kɔ̃tɔʀsjonist/ *nmf* contortionist

contour /kɔ̃tuʀ/ *nm* (a) outline, contour
(b) ~s (of road, river) twists and turns

contourner /kɔ̃tuʀne/ [1] *vtr* to go round; to by-pass ⟨town⟩; to get round ⟨problem⟩

contraceptif, -ive /kɔ̃tʀasɛptif, iv/
1 *adj* contraceptive
2 *nm* contraceptive

contraception /kɔ̃tʀasɛpsjɔ̃/ *nf* contraception

contractant, ~e /kɔ̃tʀaktɑ̃, ɑ̃t/ **1** *adj* contracting
2 *nm,f* contracting party

contracter /kɔ̃tʀakte/ [1] **1** *vtr* (a) to tense ⟨muscle⟩
(b) to incur ⟨debt⟩; to take out ⟨loan⟩
(c) to contract ⟨disease⟩
2 se contracter *v refl* (+ *v être*) ⟨muscle, word⟩ to contract; ⟨face, person⟩ to tense up

contraction /kɔ̃tʀaksjɔ̃/ *nf* (a) tenseness
(b) contraction

contractuel, -elle /kɔ̃tʀaktɥɛl/ **1** *adj* contractual; personnel ~ contract staff
2 *nm,f* (a) contract employee
(b) traffic warden (GB), meter reader (US)

contradiction /kɔ̃tʀadiksjɔ̃/ *nf* contradiction

contradictoire /kɔ̃tʀadiktwaʀ/ *adj* contradictory; ~ à in contradiction to

contraignant, ~e /kɔ̃tʀɛɲɑ̃, ɑ̃t/ *adj* restrictive

contraindre /kɔ̃tʀɛ̃dʀ/ [54] **1** *vtr* (a) ~ qn à faire to force sb to do
(b) to restrain, to curb
2 se contraindre *v refl* (+ *v être*) se ~ à to force oneself to

contraint, ~e¹ /kɔ̃tʀɛ̃, ɛ̃t/ *adj* (a) ~ et forcé (Law) under duress
(b) strained, forced

contrainte² /kɔ̃tʀɛ̃t/ *nf* (a) pressure; coercion
(b) constraint
(c) sans ~ without restraint, freely

contraire /kɔ̃tʀɛʀ/ **1** *adj* (a) opposite; contrary; ⟨interests⟩ conflicting; être ~ aux usages to be contrary to custom; dans le cas ~ (should it be) otherwise
(b) adverse
2 *nm* le ~ the opposite, the contrary; ne dites pas le ~ don't deny it; au ~! on the contrary!

contrairement /kɔ̃tʀɛʀmɑ̃/ *adv* ~ à ce qu'on pourrait penser contrary to what one might think; ~ à qn unlike sb

contrariant, ~e /kɔ̃tʀaʀjɑ̃, ɑ̃t/ *adj*
(a) ⟨person⟩ contrary
(b) ⟨event⟩ annoying

contrarier /kɔ̃tʀaʀje/ [2] *vtr* (a) to upset
(b) to annoy
(c) to frustrate, to thwart

contrariété /kɔ̃tʀaʀjete/ *nf* vexation

contraste /kɔ̃tʀast/ *nm* contrast

contrasté, ~e /kɔ̃tʀaste/ *adj*
(a) contrasting
(b) ⟨photo⟩ with good contrast
(c) ⟨results⟩ uneven

contraster /kɔ̃tʀaste/ [1] **1** *vtr* to contrast ⟨colours⟩; to give contrast to ⟨photo⟩
2 *vi* to contrast

contrat /kɔ̃tʀa/ *nm* contract
■ ~ emploi solidarité, CES part-time low-paid work for the long-term unemployed

contravention /kɔ̃tʀavɑ̃sjɔ̃/ *nf*
(a) parking ticket; speeding ticket; fine
(b) minor offence (GB)

contre¹ /kɔ̃tʀ/ **1** *prep* (a) against; 22% ~ 18% hier 22% as against 18% yesterday; allongés l'un ~ l'autre lying side by side
(b) versus
(c) (in exchange) for; échange-la ~ une bleue exchange it for a blue one
2 par contre *phr* on the other hand

contre² /kɔ̃tʀ/ **1** *nm* (a) le pour et le ~ the pros and cons
(b) (Sport) counter-attack
2 *pref* counter

contre-accusation, *pl* ~s /kɔ̃tʀakyzasjɔ̃/ *nf* counter-charge

contre-allée, *pl* ~s /kɔ̃tʀale/ *nf* service road; side path

contre-attaque, *pl* ~s /kɔ̃tʀatak/ *nf* counter-attack

contrebalancer /kɔ̃tʀəbalɑ̃se/ [12] *vtr*
(a) to counterbalance
(b) to offset

contrebande /kɔ̃tʀəbɑ̃d/ *nf* (a) smuggling
(b) smuggled goods, contraband

contrebandier, -ière /kɔ̃tʀəbɑ̃dje, ɛʀ/ *nm,f* smuggler

contrebas: en contrebas /ɑ̃kɔ̃tʀəba/ *phr* (down) below; en ~ de below

contrebasse /kɔ̃tʀəbas/ *nf* double bass

contrecarrer /kɔ̃tʀəkaʀe/ [1] *vtr* to thwart, to foil; to counteract

contrechamp /kɔ̃tʀəʃɑ̃/ *nm* reverse shot

contrecœur: à contrecœur /akɔ̃tʀəkœʀ/ *phr* reluctantly

contrecoup /kɔ̃tʀəku/ *nm* effects; after-effects; par ~ as a result

contre-courant, *pl* ~s /kɔ̃tʀəkuʀɑ̃/ *nm* counter-current; nager à ~ to swim against the current; aller à ~ de la mode to go against the fashion

contredire /kɔ̃tʀədiʀ/ [65] **1** *vtr* to contradict
2 se contredire *v refl* (+ *v être*) (a) to contradict oneself
(b) to contradict each other

contrée /kɔ̃tʀe/ *nf* (a) land
(b) region

contre-enquête, *pl* ~s /kɔ̃tʀɑ̃kɛt/ *nf* second enquiry (GB)

contre-espionnage, *pl* ~s /kɔ̃tʀɛspjɔnaʒ/ *nm* counter-intelligence

contre-expertise *pl* ~s /kɔ̃tʀɛkspɛʀtiz/ *nf* second opinion

contrefaçon /kɔ̃tʀəfasɔ̃/ *nf* (a) forging, counterfeiting
(b) forgery, counterfeit

contrefacteur /kɔ̃tʁəfaktœʁ/ *nm* (of notes, credit cards, paintings) forger; (of coins) counterfeiter; (of software, invention) pirate

contrefaire /kɔ̃tʁəfɛʁ/ [10] *vtr* **(a)** to forge, to counterfeit
(b) to imitate
(c) to disguise

contrefort /kɔ̃tʁəfɔʁ/ *nm* **(a)** foothills
(b) buttress
(c) (of shoe) back

contre-indiqué, **~e**, *mpl* **~s** /kɔ̃tʁɛ̃dike/ *adj* contra-indicated; inadvisable

contre-interrogatoire, *pl* **~s** /kɔ̃tʁɛ̃teʁɔgatwaʁ/ *nm* cross-examination

contre-jour, *pl* **~s** /kɔ̃tʁəʒuʁ/ *nm* backlighting; **à ~** against *or* into the light

contremaître, **-esse** /kɔ̃tʁəmɛtʁ, kɔ̃tʁəmɛtʁɛs/ *nm,f* foreman/forewoman

contrepartie /kɔ̃tʁəpaʁti/ *nf*
(a) equivalent
(b) compensation; **en ~** in compensation; in return; **mais la ~ est que le salaire est élevé** but this is offset by the high salary

contre-pied, *pl* **~s** /kɔ̃tʁəpje/ *nm* **prendre le ~ de ce que dit qn** to say the opposite of what sb says

contreplaqué /kɔ̃tʁəplake/ *nm* plywood

contrepoids /kɔ̃tʁəpwa/ *nm* counterweight

contrer /kɔ̃tʁe/ [1] *vtr* to counter; to block

contresens /kɔ̃tʁəsɑ̃s/ *nm*
(a) misinterpretation
(b) mistranslation
(c) **à ~** in the opposite direction; the wrong way; against the grain

contretemps /kɔ̃tʁətɑ̃/ *nm inv*
(a) setback, contretemps
(b) **à ~** (Mus) on the off-beat; out of time; (figurative) at the wrong moment

contre-valeur, *pl* **~s** /kɔ̃tʁəvalœʁ/ *nf* exchange value

contrevenir /kɔ̃tʁəvəniʁ/ [36] *v+prep* **~ à** to contravene

contribuable /kɔ̃tʁibɥabl/ *nmf* taxpayer

contribuer /kɔ̃tʁibɥe/ [1] *v+prep* **~ à** to contribute to; to pay one's share of; **cela y a beaucoup contribué** it was a major factor

contribution /kɔ̃tʁibysjɔ̃/ *nf*
(a) contribution; **mettre qn à ~** to call upon sb's services
(b) **~s** taxes; tax office

contrit, **~e** /kɔ̃tʁi, it/ *adj* contrite, apologetic

contrôle /kɔ̃tʁol/ *nm* **(a)** control
(b) check; **~ de police** police check; **~ des billets** ticket inspection
(c) (Sch) test; **~ de géographie** geography test
(d) check-up
(e) monitoring; **sous ~ médical** under medical supervision
■ **~ continu** (des connaissances) continuous assessment; **~ fiscal** tax investigation; **~ technique** (des véhicules) MOT (test)

contrôler /kɔ̃tʁole/ [1] **1** *vtr* **(a)** to control
(b) to monitor
(c) to check; to inspect; to test
2 se contrôler *v refl* (+ *v être*) to control oneself

contrôleur, **-euse** /kɔ̃tʁolœʁ, øz/ *nm,f* inspector; **~ aérien** air-traffic controller

contrordre /kɔ̃tʁɔʁdʁ/ *nm* **(a)** ordres et **~s** conflicting orders; **j'irai vendredi, sauf ~** I'll go on Friday, unless I hear to the contrary
(b) counter command

controverse /kɔ̃tʁovɛʁs/ *nf* controversy

controversé, **~e** /kɔ̃tʁovɛʁse/ *adj* controversial

contusion /kɔ̃tyzjɔ̃/ *nf* bruise

convaincant, **~e** /kɔ̃vɛ̃kɑ̃, ɑ̃t/ *adj*
(a) convincing
(b) persuasive

convaincre /kɔ̃vɛ̃kʁ/ [57] **1** *vtr* to convince; to persuade
2 se convaincre *v refl* (+ *v être*) to convince oneself

convaincu, **~e** /kɔ̃vɛ̃ky/ **1** *pp* ▶ CONVAINCRE
2 *pp adj* **(a)** convinced; **d'un ton ~** with conviction
(b) ⟨*supporter*⟩ staunch

convalescence /kɔ̃valesɑ̃s/ *nf* convalescence

convalescent, **~e** /kɔ̃valesɑ̃, ɑ̃t/ *adj*, *nm,f* convalescent

convenable /kɔ̃vnabl/ *adj* **(a)** suitable
(b) reasonable
(c) decent; proper; respectable

convenablement /kɔ̃vnabləmɑ̃/ *adv* properly; reasonably well; decently

convenance /kɔ̃vnɑ̃s/ *nf* **(a)** pour **~ personnelle** for personal reasons; **à votre ~** at your convenience
(b) **~s** (social) conventions

convenir /kɔ̃vniʁ/ [36] **1** *vtr* **(a)** to admit
(b) to agree
2 convenir à *v+prep* to suit; to be suitable for
3 convenir de *v+prep* **(a)** **~ de** to admit, to acknowledge
(b) **~ de** to agree on
4 *v impers* **(a)** **il convient de faire/que vous fassiez** one/you should do
(b) **ce qu'il est convenu d'appeler le réalisme** what is commonly called realism; **comme convenu** as agreed

convention /kɔ̃vɑ̃sjɔ̃/ *nf* **(a)** agreement
(b) convention; **de ~** conventional

conventionné, **~e** /kɔ̃vɑ̃sjɔne/ *adj* ⟨*doctor, costs*⟩ national health service; ⟨*clinic*⟩ registered; **médecin non ~** private doctor

conventionnel, **-elle** /kɔ̃vɑ̃sjɔnɛl/ *adj*
(a) conventional
(b) contractual

convenu, **~e** /kɔ̃v(ə)ny/ **1** *pp* ▶ CONVENIR

C

2 *pp adj* (a) ‹*date, terms*› agreed
(b) ‹*phrase*› conventional; ‹*smile*› polite

convergence /kɔ̃vɛrʒɑ̃s/ *nf* convergence

converger /kɔ̃vɛrʒe/ [13] *vi* to converge

conversation /kɔ̃vɛrsasjɔ̃/ *nf*
conversation; **avoir de la ~** to be a good
conversationalist; **dans la ~ courante** in
everyday speech

converser /kɔ̃vɛrse/ [1] *vi* to converse

conversion /kɔ̃vɛrsjɔ̃/ *nf* conversion

converti, ~e /kɔ̃vɛrti/ **1** *pp* ▶ CONVERTIR
2 *nm,f* convert

convertible /kɔ̃vɛrtibl/ *adj* (a) convertible
(b) **canapé ~** sofa-bed

convertir /kɔ̃vɛrtir/ [3] **1** *vtr* to convert
2 se convertir *v refl* (+ *v être*) to convert;
‹*company*› to change products

convertisseur /kɔ̃vɛrtisœr/ *nm*
converter

convexe /kɔ̃vɛks/ *adj* convex

conviction /kɔ̃viksjɔ̃/ *nf* conviction

convier /kɔ̃vje/ [2] *vtr* to invite ‹*person*›

convive /kɔ̃viv/ *nmf* guest

convivial, ~e, *mpl* **-iaux** /kɔ̃vivjal, o/
adj (a) convivial
(b) user-friendly

convivialité /kɔ̃vivjalite/ *nf*
(a) friendliness; conviviality
(b) user-friendliness

convocation /kɔ̃vɔkasjɔ̃/ *nf* (a) (of meeting)
convening; (of person) summoning; (Mil)
calling up
(b) notice to attend; (Law) summons; (Mil)
call-up papers; **~ aux examens** notification
of examination timetables

convoi /kɔ̃vwa/ *nm* (a) convoy; ‹~
exceptionnel’ (Aut) ‘wide *or* dangerous load’
(b) train

convoiter /kɔ̃vwate/ [1] *vtr* to covet

convoitise /kɔ̃vwatiz/ *nf* **la ~**
covetousness; **~ de** lust for

convoquer /kɔ̃vɔke/ [1] *vtr* to call, to
convene ‹*meeting*›; to send for ‹*pupil*›; to
summon ‹*witness*›; to call up ‹*soldier*›; **être
convoqué à un examen** to be asked to attend
an exam

convoyer /kɔ̃vwaje/ [23] *vtr* to escort

convoyeur, -euse /kɔ̃vwajœr/ *nm,f*
(a) prison escort
(b) courier; **~ de fonds** security guard

convulsif, -ive /kɔ̃vylsif, iv/ *adj*
(a) convulsive
(b) ‹*laughter*› nervous

convulsion /kɔ̃vylsjɔ̃/ *nf* convulsion

convulsionner /kɔ̃vylsjɔne/ [1] *vtr* to
convulse

coopératif, -ive /kɔɔperatif, iv/ **1** *adj*
cooperative
2 coopérative *nf* cooperative

coopération /kɔɔperasjɔ̃/ *nf*
(a) cooperation
(b) cultural/technical aid

coopérer /kɔɔpere/ [14] *vi* to cooperate

coordinateur, -trice /kɔɔrdinatœr,
tris/ **1** *adj* coordinating
2 *nm,f* coordinator

coordination /kɔɔrdinasjɔ̃/ *nf*
(a) coordination
(b) joint committee

coordonné, ~e /kɔɔrdɔne/ **1** *pp* ▶
COORDONNER
2 *pp adj* coordinated; coordinating
3 coordonnés *nm pl* (in fashion)
coordinates

coordonnées /kɔɔrdɔne/ *nf pl* (a) (on
graph, map) coordinates
(b) information
(c) address and telephone number

coordonner /kɔɔrdɔne/ [1] *vtr* to
coordinate

copain, copine /kɔpɛ̃, in/ **1** *adj* pally
(GB) (colloq), chummy (colloq)
2 *nm,f* (a) friend
(b) boyfriend/girlfriend

copeau, *pl* **~x** /kɔpo/ *nm* shaving

Copenhague /kɔpɛnag/ *pr n* Copenhagen

copie /kɔpi/ *nf* (a) copying; copy
(b) (Sch) paper

copier /kɔpje/ [2] *vtr* (a) to copy
(b) (Sch) **~ sur qn** to copy *or* crib from sb

copieur, -ieuse /kɔpjœr, øz/ **1** *nm,f*
(Sch) cheat
2 *nm* photocopier

copieusement /kɔpjøzmɑ̃/ *adv* heartily;
lavishly; copiously

copieux, -ieuse /kɔpjø, øz/ *adj* ‹*meal*›
hearty; ‹*portion*› generous; ‹*notes*› copious

copilote /kɔpilɔt/ *nmf* co-pilot; co-driver

copine ▶ COPAIN

coprésident, ~e /kɔprezidɑ̃, ɑ̃t/ *nm,f*
joint president; co-chair

coproduction /kɔprɔdyksjɔ̃/ *nf* coproduction

copropriété /kɔprɔprijete/ *nf* joint
ownership; co-ownership

coq /kɔk/ *nm* cockerel, rooster; cock; **au
chant du ~** at cockcrow; **le ~ du village**
(figurative) the local Casanova
■ **~ de bruyère** grouse
IDIOMS **être comme un ~ en pâte** to be in
clover; **sauter du ~ à l’âne** to hop from one
subject to another

coque /kɔk/ *nf* (a) (of boat) hull;
(of hydroplane) fuselage; (of car) body
(b) cockle
(c) (of nut) shell

coquelicot /kɔkliko/ *nm* poppy

coqueluche /kɔklyʃ/ *nf* (a) whooping-
cough
(b) (colloq) idol

coquet, -ette /kɔkɛ, ɛt/ *adj* (a) **être ~** to
be particular about one’s appearance
(b) pretty
(c) (colloq) ‹*sum*› tidy (colloq)

coquetier /kɔktje/ *nm* eggcup

coquetterie /kɔkɛtri/ *nf* interest in one’s
appearance; vanity; **par ~** out of vanity

coquillage /kɔkijaʒ/ *nm* **(a)** shellfish
(b) shell

coquille /kɔkij/ *nf* **(a)** shell
(b) scallop-shaped dish; ~ **de saumon**
salmon served in a shell
(c) misprint
(d) (Med) spinal jacket
■ ~ **Saint-Jacques** scallop; scallop shell

coquillette /kɔkijɛt/ *nf* small macaroni

coquin, ~e /kɔkɛ̃, in/ ① *adj*
(a) mischievous
(b) naughty, saucy
② *nm,f* rascal

cor /kɔr/ *nm* **(a)** (Mus) horn
(b) (Med) corn
IDIOMS **réclamer** *or* **demander qch à ~ et à
cri** to clamour (GB) for sth

corail, *pl* **-aux** /kɔraj, o/ *adj inv, nm*
coral

Coran /kɔrɑ̃/ *pr nm* **le ~** the Koran

corbeau, *pl* **~x** /kɔrbo/ *nm* **(a)** crow;
grand ~ raven
(b) (colloq) writer of a poison-pen letter

corbeille /kɔrbɛj/ *nf* **(a)** basket
(b) dress circle

corbillard /kɔrbijar/ *nm* hearse

corde /kɔrd/ *nf* **(a)** rope
(b) ~ **(à sauter)** skipping rope
(c) (of racket, instrument) string
■ ~ **à linge** clothes line; ~ **raide** tightrope;
~**s vocales** vocal chords
IDIOMS **mériter la ~** to deserve to be
hanged; **pleuvoir** *or* **tomber des ~s** to be
raining cats and dogs (colloq); **tirer sur la ~**
to push one's luck; **faire jouer la ~ sensible**
to tug at the heartstrings; **usé jusqu'à la ~**
threadbare

cordée /kɔrde/ *nf* roped party (of
climbers)

cordelière /kɔrdəljɛr/ *nf* cord

cordial, ~e, *mpl* **-iaux** /kɔrdjal, o/ *adj*
cordial; warm-hearted; warm

cordialement /kɔrdjalmɑ̃/ *adv* warmly;
~ **(vôtre** *or* **à vous)** yours sincerely

cordialité /kɔrdjalite/ *nf* warmth;
friendliness

cordillère /kɔrdijɛr/ *nf* cordillera

cordon /kɔrdɔ̃/ *nm* **(a)** cord; string; lace
(b) flex (GB), cord (US)
(c) cordon
(d) row
(e) ribbon
■ ~ **ombilical** umbilical cord

cordonnerie /kɔrdɔnri/ *nf*
(a) shoemaking
(b) shoe repairing
(c) cobbler's

cordonnier /kɔrdɔnje/ *nm* cobbler
IDIOMS **les ~s sont toujours les plus mal
chaussés** it's always the baker's children
who have no bread

Corée /kɔre/ *pr nf* Korea

coriace /kɔrjas/ *adj* tough

coriandre /kɔrjɑ̃dr/ *nf* coriander

Corinthe /kɔrɛ̃t/ *pr n* **raisins de ~**
currants

corne /kɔrn/ *nf* **(a)** horn; antler; **à ~s**
horned; **blesser d'un coup de ~** to gore
(b) (Mus) horn
(c) (colloq) **avoir de la ~ aux pieds** to have
calluses on one's feet
■ ~ **d'abondance** horn of plenty, cornucopia;
~ **de brume** foghorn

cornée /kɔrne/ *nf* cornea

corneille /kɔrnɛj/ *nf* crow

cornemuse /kɔrnəmyz/ *nf* bagpipes

corner /kɔrne/ [1] *vtr* to turn down the
corner of ⟨*page*⟩; **page cornée** dog-eared
page

cornet /kɔrne/ *nm* **(a)** (paper) cone
(b) (ice-cream) cone, cornet (GB)
■ ~ **à dés** dice cup; ~ **à pistons** cornet

corniche /kɔrniʃ/ *nf* **(a)** cornice
(b) moulding (GB), molding (US)
(c) ledge (of rock)
(d) cliff road

cornichon /kɔrniʃɔ̃/ *nm* gherkin

Cornouailles /kɔrnuaj/ *pr nf* Cornwall

corollaire /kɔrɔlɛr/ *nm* corollary

corolle /kɔrɔl/ *nf* **(a)** corolla
(b) **en ~** ⟨*skirt*⟩ flared

coron /kɔrɔ̃/ *nm* miners' terraced houses

corporatif, -ive /kɔrpɔratif, iv/ *adj*
corporate

corporation /kɔrpɔrasjɔ̃/ *nf* corporation

corporel, -elle /kɔrpɔrɛl/ *adj* ⟨*needs*⟩
bodily; ⟨*punishment*⟩ corporal

corps /kɔr/ *nm inv* body; ⟨*combat*⟩ ~ **à ~**
hand-to-hand combat; **se donner ~ et âme à**
to give oneself body and soul to; **faire ~
avec** ⟨*person*⟩ to stand solidly behind;
⟨*building*⟩ to be joined to; **prendre ~** to take
shape
■ ~ **enseignant** teaching profession; ~ **et
biens** (to sink) with all hands;
~ **expéditionnaire** expeditionary force;
~ **gras** fatty substance; ~ **médical** medical
profession
IDIOMS **tenir au ~** to be nourishing

corpulence /kɔrpylɑ̃s/ *nf* stoutness

corpulent, ~e /kɔrpylɑ̃, ɑ̃t/ *adj* stout,
corpulent

correct, ~e /kɔrɛkt/ *adj* **(a)** ⟨*calculation*⟩
correct; ⟨*copy*⟩ accurate
(b) ⟨*outfit*⟩ proper; ⟨*conduct*⟩ correct
(c) (colloq) ⟨*result, wine*⟩ reasonable, decent
(d) ⟨*person*⟩ polite; fair, correct

correctement /kɔrɛktəmɑ̃/ *adv*
(a) correctly
(b) properly
(c) decently, reasonably well

correcteur, -trice /kɔrɛktœr, tris/
① *adj* corrective
② *nm,f* **(a)** examiner (GB), grader (US)
(b) proofreader

correction /kɔrɛksjɔ̃/ *nf* **(a)** correcting;
proofreading; marking (GB), grading (US)
(b) correction ⋯⋅❩

(c) thrashing
(d) correctness; good manners

correctionnel, -elle[1] /kɔrɛksjɔnɛl/ *adj*
tribunal ∼ magistrate's court

correctionnelle[2] /kɔrɛksjɔnɛl/ *nf*
magistrate's court

corrélation /kɔrelasjɔ̃/ *nf* correlation; **être
en** ∼ **avec qn** to be related to sth

correspondance /kɔrɛspɔ̃dɑ̃s/ *nf*
(a) letters; mail; correspondence; **faire sa** ∼
to write some letters; **vendu par** ∼ available
by mail order
(b) correspondence
(c) connection; **trains/vols en** ∼ connecting
trains/flights

correspondant, ∼e /kɔrɛspɔ̃dɑ̃, ɑ̃t/
1 *adj* corresponding
2 *nm,f* correspondent; (Sch) pen pal

correspondre /kɔrɛspɔ̃dr/ [6]
1 correspondre à *v+prep* to correspond
to; to match; to suit ⟨*tastes*⟩
2 *vi* to correspond, to write
3 se correspondre *v refl* (+ *v être*) to
correspond

corrida /kɔrida/ *nf* bullfight

corridor /kɔridɔr/ *nm* corridor

corrigé /kɔriʒe/ *nm* (Sch) correct version

corriger /kɔriʒe/ [13] **1** *vtr* (a) to correct;
to proofread ⟨*manuscript*⟩; to mark (GB), to
grade (US) ⟨*exam papers*⟩; to redress
⟨*situation*⟩
(b) to adjust ⟨*position*⟩; to modify ⟨*theory*⟩;
∼ **le tir** (Mil) to alter one's aim; (figurative) to
adjust one's tactics
(c) to give [sb] a hiding (colloq); to spank
⟨*child*⟩
2 se corriger *v refl* (+ *v être*) (a) to
correct oneself
(b) **se** ∼ **d'un défaut** to cure oneself of a
fault

corroborer /kɔrɔbɔre/ [1] *vtr* to
corroborate

corroder /kɔrɔde/ [1] *vtr* to corrode

corrompre /kɔrɔ̃pr/ [53] *vtr* (a) to bribe
(b) to corrupt

corrompu, ∼e /kɔrɔ̃py/ **1** *pp* ▶
CORROMPRE
2 *pp adj* corrupt

corrosif, -ive /kɔrozif, iv/ *adj*
(a) ⟨*substance*⟩ corrosive
(b) ⟨*humour*⟩ caustic

corrosion /kɔrozjɔ̃/ *nf* corrosion

corruption /kɔrypsjɔ̃/ *nf* (a) corruption
(b) bribery

corsage /kɔrsaʒ/ *nm* (a) blouse
(b) bodice

corsaire /kɔrsɛr/ *nm* (a) corsair
(b) pedal pushers

corse /kɔrs/ *adj, nm* Corsican

corsé, ∼e /kɔrse/ *adj* ⟨*coffee*⟩ strong;
⟨*sauce, story*⟩ spicy; ⟨*problem*⟩ tough; ⟨*bill*⟩
steep

Corse /kɔrs/ *pr nf* Corsica

corser /kɔrse/ [1] **1** *vtr* (a) to make [sth]
more difficult; **pour** ∼ **l'affaire** (just) to
complicate matters
(b) to make [sth] spicier ⟨*sauce*⟩
2 se corser *v refl* (+ *v être*) to get more
complicated

corset /kɔrsɛ/ *nm* corset

corso /kɔrso/ *nm* ∼ **fleuri** procession of
floral floats

cortège /kɔrtɛʒ/ *nm* procession

corvée /kɔrve/ *nf* chore; (Mil) fatigue (duty)

cosmétique /kɔsmetik/ *adj, nm* cosmetic

cosmique /kɔsmik/ *adj* cosmic

cosmonaute /kɔsmonot/ *nmf* cosmonaut

cosmopolite /kɔsmɔpɔlit/ *adj*
cosmopolitan

cosse /kɔs/ *nf* (of pea) pod; (of grain) husk

cossu, ∼e /kɔsy/ *adj* ⟨*person*⟩ well-to-do;
⟨*interior*⟩ plush; ⟨*house*⟩ smart

costaud /kɔsto/ *adj* (colloq) strong, sturdy;
hefty (colloq)

costume /kɔstym/ *nm* (a) suit
(b) costume; **répétition en** ∼ dress rehearsal

costumer: se costumer /kɔstyme/ [1]
v refl (+ *v être*) **se** ∼ **en** to dress up as; **soirée
costumée** fancy-dress party

cotation /kɔtasjɔ̃/ *nf* quotation

cote /kɔt/ *nf* (a) (of stocks, commodities)
quotation; (stock exchange) list
(b) (of stamp) quoted value
(c) (at races) odds
(d) (of person, film) rating; **avoir la** ∼ **auprès
de** (colloq) to be popular with; to be well
thought of by
(e) (on plan) dimension
(f) (on map) spot height
■ ∼ **d'alerte** flood level; (figurative) danger level;
∼ **de popularité** popularity rating

coté, ∼e /kɔte/ **1** *pp* ▶ COTER
2 *pp adj* **être** ∼ to be well thought of

côte /kot/ **1** *nf* (a) coast
(b) hill; **dans une** ∼ on a hill
(c) rib
(d) chop; ∼ **de bœuf** rib roast
2 côte à côte *phr* side by side
■ **Côte d'Azur** French riviera

côté /kote/ **1** *nm* (a) side; **du** ∼ **droit/
gauche** on the righthand/lefthand side;
chambre ∼ **rue** room overlooking the street;
par certains ∼s in some respects; ∼ **santé**
healthwise; **de mon** ∼, **je pense que...** for
my part, I think that...; **d'un** ∼**... d'un autre**
∼**...** on the one hand... on the other hand...
(b) way, direction; **de tous** ∼s ⟨*come*⟩ from
all directions; ⟨*run*⟩ all over the place; **du** ∼
de Nice ⟨*live*⟩ near Nice; **aller du** ∼ **de Dijon**
to head for Dijon
2 à côté *phr* (a) nearby; **les gens d'à** ∼
the people next door; **à** ∼ **de** next to; **le
ballon est passé à** ∼ **(du but)** the ball went
wide (of the goal); **répondre à** ∼ (by mistake)
to miss the point; (on purpose) to sidestep the
question
(b) by comparison

(c) on the side; **elle est étudiante et travaille à ~** she's a student and works on the side
3 **de côté** phr **(a)** sideways
(b) aside; **mettre qch de ~** to put sth aside ⟨money, object⟩
4 **aux côtés de** phr **aux ~s de qn** ⟨to be⟩ at sb's side; ⟨to work⟩ alongside sb

coteau, pl **~x** /kɔto/ nm **(a)** hillside
(b) hill
(c) (sloping) vineyard

côtelette /kotlɛt/ nf (Culin) chop

coter /kɔte/ [1] vtr **(a)** to quote, to list ⟨shares⟩; to price ⟨car⟩
(b) to rate ⟨film⟩

côtier, -ière /kotje, ɛR/ adj coastal; inshore

cotisation /kɔtizasjɔ̃/ nf **(a)** contribution
(b) subscription

cotiser /kɔtize/ [1] 1 vi **(a)** to pay one's contributions
(b) to pay one's subscription (à to)
2 **se cotiser** v refl (+ v être) to club together (GB), to go in together

coton /kɔtɔ̃/ nm **(a)** cotton
(b) thread
(c) cotton wool (GB), cotton (US)
IDIOMS **filer un mauvais ~** to be in a bad way; **élever un enfant dans du ~** to give a child a very sheltered upbringing; **j'ai les jambes en ~** (after shock) my legs have turned to jelly

cotonnade /kɔtɔnad/ nf cotton fabric

cotonneux, -euse /kɔtɔnø, øz/ adj ⟨fog⟩ like cotton-wool; ⟨cloud⟩ fleecy

côtoyer /kotwaje/ [23] 1 vtr to walk alongside ⟨river⟩; to move in ⟨milieu⟩; to mix with ⟨people⟩; to be in close contact with ⟨death⟩
2 **se côtoyer** v refl (+ v être) ⟨people⟩ to mix

cotte /kɔt/ nf overalls
■ **~ de mailles** coat of mail

cou /ku/ nm neck; **être endetté jusqu'au ~** to be up to one's eyes in debt

couchage /kuʃaʒ/ nm bedding; **un studio avec ~ pour six** a studio that sleeps six

couchant /kuʃɑ̃/ 1 adj **au soleil ~** at sunset
2 nm **(a)** sunset
(b) west

couche /kuʃ/ nf **(a)** layer; (of paint) coat
(b) nappy (GB), diaper (US)
(c) class, sector

couché, ~e /kuʃe/ 1 pp ▶ COUCHER
2 pp adj ⟨grass⟩ flattened; ⟨writing⟩ sloping

couche-culotte, pl **couches-culottes** /kuʃkylɔt/ nf disposable nappy (GB) or diaper (US)

coucher /kuʃe/ [1] 1 nm bedtime
2 vtr **(a)** to put [sb] to bed; to lay out ⟨wounded person⟩
(b) to lay [sth] on its side; to lay [sth] down
(c) to flatten ⟨grass⟩
3 vi to sleep; **~ sous les ponts** to sleep rough (GB) or outdoors

4 **se coucher** v refl (+ v être) **(a)** to lie (down)
(b) to go to bed
(c) ⟨stem⟩ to bend; ⟨boat⟩ to list; **se ~ sur** ⟨cyclist⟩ to lean forward over ⟨handlebars⟩
(d) ⟨sun⟩ to set
■ **~ de soleil** sunset

couchette /kuʃɛt/ nf couchette, berth

couci-couça /kusikusa/ adv (colloq) so-so (colloq)

coucou /kuku/ 1 nm **(a)** cuckoo
(b) cowslip
(c) (colloq) (old) crate (colloq), plane
(d) cuckoo clock
2 excl (colloq) **(a)** cooee!
(b) peekaboo!

coude /kud/ nm **(a)** elbow; **travailler ~ à ~** to work shoulder to shoulder
(b) (in river, pipe) bend
IDIOMS **se serrer les ~s** to stick together

coudé, ~e¹ /kude/ adj bent at an angle

coudée² /kude/ nf **avoir les ~s franches** to have elbow room

cou-de-pied, pl **cous-de-pied** /kudpje/ nm instep

couder /kude/ [1] vtr to bend

coudre /kudR/ [76] vtr to sew; to sew [sth] on; to stitch [sth] on; to stitch (up)
IDIOMS **leur histoire est cousue de fil blanc** you can see through their story

couenne /kwan/ nf (bacon) rind

couette /kwɛt/ nf duvet

couffin /kufɛ̃/ nm Moses basket (GB), bassinet (US)

couiner /kwine/ [1] vi to squeak, to squeal

coulant, ~e /kulɑ̃, ɑ̃t/ adj ⟨camembert⟩ runny; ⟨person⟩ easy-going

coulée /kule/ nf (of lava) flow; (of paint) drip

couler /kule/ [1] 1 vtr **(a)** to cast ⟨metal, statue⟩; to pour ⟨concrete⟩
(b) to sink ⟨ship⟩
(c) (colloq) to put [sth] out of business; to bring [sb] down
2 vi **(a)** ⟨blood⟩ to flow; ⟨paint, cheese⟩ to run; **faire ~ qch** to run ⟨bath⟩
(b) ⟨tap, pen⟩ to leak; ⟨nose⟩ to run
(c) ⟨boat⟩ to sink; ⟨company⟩ to go under
3 **se couler** v refl (+ v être) **se ~ dans/entre** to slip into/between

couleur /kulœR/ nf **(a)** colour (GB); **de ~** ⟨person⟩ coloured (GB); **sans ~** colourless (GB); **plein de ~** colourful (GB)
(b) paint
(c) **les ~s** (washing) coloureds (GB); (flag) the colours (GB)
(d) (in cards) suit
(e) **sous ~ de faire** while pretending to do
IDIOMS **ne pas voir la ~ de qch** (colloq) never to get a sniff of sth (colloq); **il m'en a fait voir de toutes les ~s** (colloq) he put me through the mill

couleuvre /kulœvR/ nf grass snake
IDIOMS **avaler des ~s** (colloq) to believe anything one is told

coulissant, ∼**e** /kulisɑ̃, ɑ̃t/ adj sliding

coulisse /kulis/ nf (a) les ∼s, la ∼ the wings; en ∼ backstage; (figurative) behind the scenes
(b) runner

coulisser /kulise/ [1] vi to slide

couloir /kulwaʀ/ nm (a) corridor (GB), hallway; passage; bruits de ∼s rumours (GB)
(b) lane; ∼ aérien air (traffic) lane

coup /ku/ nm (a) knock; blow; ∼ à la porte knock at the door; à ∼s de bâton with a stick; donner un ∼ de qch à qn to hit sb with sth; donner un ∼ de poing à qn to punch sb; porter un ∼ (sévère) à (figurative) to deal [sb/sth] a (severe) blow; sa fierté en a pris un ∼ it was a blow to his/her pride; sous le ∼ de la colère in (a fit of) anger; être sous le ∼ d'une forte émotion to be in a highly emotional state
(b) (noise) knock; bang; thump, thud; au douzième ∼ de minuit on the last stroke of midnight; sur le ∼ de dix heures (colloq) around ten; ∼ de sifflet whistle blast
(c) un (petit) ∼ de chiffon a (quick) wipe; un ∼ de peinture a lick of paint
(d) (in tennis, golf, cricket) stroke; shot; (in chess) move; (with dice) throw; (in boxing) punch; tous les ∼s sont permis no holds barred
(e) ∼ de feu/fusil (gun)shot/(rifle) shot
(f) (colloq) job (colloq), racket (colloq); trick (colloq); monter un ∼ to plan a job (colloq); il a raté son ∼ (colloq) he blew it (colloq); être dans le ∼ to be in on it; to be up to date; qui a fait le ∼? who did it?
(g) time; du premier ∼ first time; à tous les ∼s every time; ce ∼-ci this time; du ∼ (colloq) as a result; après ∼ afterward(s); ∼ sur ∼ in succession; tout d'un ∼, tout à ∼ suddenly, all of a sudden; d'un ∼, d'un seul ∼ just like that; en un seul ∼ in one go (colloq); sur le ∼ at the time; instantly, on the spot; pleurer un bon ∼ to have a good cry
(h) à ∼s de subventions by means of subsidies
(i) (colloq) drink
■ ∼ bas blow below the belt; ∼s et blessures assault and battery; ∼ dur blow; ∼ franc free kick; ∼ monté put-up job

■ Note For translations of expressions such as coup d'envoi, coup de fil etc, look up the entries at envoi, fil etc.

IDIOMS tenir le ∼ ⟨shoes⟩ to last out; ⟨repair⟩ to hold; ⟨person⟩ to hold on; être aux cent ∼s (colloq) to be worried sick (colloq); faire les quatre cents ∼s (colloq) to be a real tearaway; attraper le ∼ pour faire (colloq) to get the knack of doing

coupable /kupabl/ **1** adj guilty; ⟨negligence⟩ culpable; ⟨indifference⟩ shameful
2 nmf culprit

coupant, ∼**e** /kupɑ̃, ɑ̃t/ adj sharp

coup-de-poing, pl **coups-de-poing** /kudpwɛ̃/ nm ∼ américain knuckle-duster (GB), brass knuckles (US)

coupe /kup/ nf (a) cutting; cutting out; cut

(b) haircut
(c) (Sport) cup; la ∼ du Monde the World Cup
(d) (fruit) bowl; (champagne) glass
(e) section; ∼ transversale cross section
■ ∼ en brosse crew cut
IDIOMS la ∼ est pleine enough is enough; être sous la ∼ de qn to be under sb's control

coupe-feu /kupfø/ nm inv firebreak

coupe-gorge /kupgɔʀʒ/ nm inv rough place; rough area

coupe-papier /kuppapje/ nm inv paper knife

couper /kupe/ [1] **1** vtr (a) to cut; to cut down; to chop; to cut out; to cut off; ∼ qch en tranches to slice sth
(b) ⟨road⟩ to cut across; ∼ la route à qn to cut in on sb
(c) to cut off ⟨road, supplies⟩; to spoil ⟨appetite⟩; to take the edge off ⟨hunger⟩; to turn off ⟨water⟩; ∼ le souffle à qn to take sb's breath away; ∼ la parole à qn to interrupt sb
(d) ∼ qn de qn/qch to cut sb off from sb/sth
(e) to dilute ⟨wine⟩
(f) (in cards) to cut ⟨pack⟩; to trump ⟨card⟩
2 vi attention ça coupe! be careful, it's sharp; ∼ à travers champs to cut across country
3 se couper v refl (+ v être) to cut oneself
IDIOMS c'est ton tour de faire à manger, tu n'y couperas pas it's your turn to cook, you won't get out of it

couperet /kupʀɛ/ nm cleaver; (of guillotine) blade; la nouvelle est tombée comme un ∼ the news came as a bolt from the blue

couperose /kupʀoz/ nf broken veins

coupe-vent /kupvɑ̃/ nm inv
(a) windcheater (GB), windbreaker (US)
(b) windbreak

couple /kupl/ nm (a) couple; pair
(b) relationship

couplet /kuplɛ/ nm (a) verse
(b) couplet

coupole /kupɔl/ nf cupola, dome

coupon /kupɔ̃/ nm (a) remnant
(b) ticket voucher
(c) multiuse ticket (in travel pass)

coupon-réponse, pl **coupons-réponses** /kupɔ̃ʀepɔ̃s/ nm reply coupon

coupure /kupyʀ/ nf (a) cut; ∼ d'électricité or de courant power cut
(b) break
(c) gap
(d) (bank)note (GB), bill (US)
■ ∼ de journal or de presse (newspaper) cutting

cour /kuʀ/ nf (a) courtyard; (school) playground; (farm) yard
(b) (of sovereign) court; (of celebrity) entourage
(c) courtship
(d) (Law) court
■ ∼ d'arrivée arrivals area; ∼ de départ departures area; ∼ martiale court-martial; ∼ de récréation playground

courage /kuʀaʒ/ *nm* **(a)** courage, bravery;
avoir du ~ to be brave
(b) energy; **je n'ai même pas le ~ de me
doucher** I don't even have the energy to
have a shower; **bon ~!** good luck!; **perdre ~**
to lose heart; **je n'ai pas eu le ~ de dire non**
I didn't have the heart to say no

courageusement /kuʀaʒøzmã/ *adv*
courageously, bravely

courageux, -euse /kuʀaʒø, øz/ *adj*
courageous, brave

couramment /kuʀamã/ *adv* **(a)** fluently
(b) ⟨*used*⟩ widely; **cela se fait ~** it's very
common

courant¹ /kuʀã/ *prep* **~ janvier** (some
time) in January

courant², ~e /kuʀã, ãt/ ⓵ *adj* **(a)** ⟨*word,
practice, mistake*⟩ common
(b) ⟨*language*⟩ everyday; ⟨*procedure*⟩ usual,
ordinary; ⟨*size*⟩ standard
(c) ⟨*month, price*⟩ current; **le 15 du mois ~**
the 15th of this month
⓶ *nm* **(a)** current; **il n'y a plus de ~** the
power has gone off
(b) trend; **un ~ politique** a political trend
(c) **dans le ~ de** in the course of
⓷ **au courant** *phr* **être au ~ de** to know
about ⟨*news*⟩; to be up to date on
⟨*technique*⟩; **mettre qn au ~** to put sb in the
picture; **tenir qn au ~** to keep sb posted
■ **~ d'air** draught (GB), draft (US)

courbatu, ~e /kuʀbaty/ *adj* stiff

courbature /kuʀbatyʀ/ *nf* ache; **avoir des
~s** to be stiff

courbaturé, ~e /kuʀbatyʀe/ *adj* stiff;
aching

courbe /kuʀb/ ⓵ *adj* curved
⓶ *nf* **(a)** curve
(b) bend
■ **~ de température** temperature chart

courber /kuʀbe/ [1] *vtr* to bend; **~ le dos**
(figurative) to bow down

courbette /kuʀbɛt/ *nf* (low) bow; **faire des
~s** (figurative) to bow and scrape

courbure /kuʀbyʀ/ *nf* curve

coureur, -euse /kuʀœʀ, øz/ *nm,f* runner;
~ automobile racing driver; **~ de jupons**
philanderer

courge /kuʀʒ/ *nf* gourd; (vegetable)
marrow

courgette /kuʀʒɛt/ *nf* courgette (GB),
zucchini (US)

courir /kuʀiʀ/ [26] ⓵ *vtr* **(a)** to compete in
⟨*trials*⟩
(b) **~ le monde** to roam the world
(c) **~ les cocktails** to do the round of the
cocktail parties; **~ les boutiques** to go
round the shops (GB) *or* stores (US)
(d) **~ un (grand) danger** to be in (great)
danger; **~ un (gros) risque** to run a (big)
risk; **faire ~ un risque à qn** to put sb at risk
(e) (colloq)**~ les filles** to chase after girls
⓶ *vi* **(a)** to run; to race; **~ après qn/qch** to
run after sb/sth; to chase after sb/sth; **les**

voleurs courent toujours the thieves are still
at large; **~ à la catastrophe** to be heading
for disaster
(b) ⟨*rumour*⟩ to go around
IDIOMS tu peux toujours ~! (colloq) you can
go whistle for it! (colloq); **laisser ~** (colloq) to
let things ride

couronne /kuʀɔn/ *nf* **(a)** crown
(b) **~ de fleurs** garland; wreath
(c) ring-shaped loaf
(d) (in Paris) **la petite/grande ~** the inner/
outer suburbs

couronnement /kuʀɔnmã/ *nm*
coronation

couronner /kuʀɔne/ [1] *vtr* to crown

courre /kuʀ/ *vtr* **chasse à ~** hunting

courriel /kuʀjɛl/ *nm* e-mail

courrier /kuʀje/ *nm* **(a)** mail, post (GB);
faire son ~ to write letters
(b) **~ des lecteurs** letters to the editor; **~ du
cœur** problem page; **~ électronique**
electronic mail

courroie /kuʀwa/ *nf* **(a)** strap
(b) (on machine) belt

cours /kuʀ/ *nm inv* **(a)** lesson, class; **avoir
~** to have a class; **faire ~** to teach
(b) course book, textbook
(c) school; **~ de théâtre** drama school
(d) price; exchange rate
(e) (of river) course
(f) (of tale, events) course; (of ideas) flow; **la vie
reprend son ~** life returns to normal;
donner libre ~ à to give free rein to
⟨*imagination*⟩; **au** *or* **dans le ~ de** in the
course of, during; **en ~** ⟨*month*⟩ current;
⟨*project*⟩ under way; ⟨*work*⟩ in progress; **en
~ de journée** in the course of the day
■ **~ d'eau** watercourse; **~ élémentaire
première année, CE1** *second year of primary
school, age 7–8*; **~ moyen première année,
CM1** *fourth year of primary school, age 9–10*;
~ particulier(s) private tuition (GB), private
tutoring (US); **~ préparatoire, CP** *first year of
primary school, age 6–7*

course /kuʀs/ *nf* **(a)** running; run; racing;
race; **faire la ~ avec qn** to race sb; **c'est la
course tous les matins pour me préparer** I'm
always in a rush in the morning to get
ready
(b) (in taxi) journey; **c'est 50 francs la ~** the
fare is 50 francs
(c) **faire une ~** to run an errand; **faire les
~s** to do the shopping
(d) (of star, planet) path; (of clouds) passage
■ **~ de haies** (in athletics) hurdles; (for horses)
steeplechase; **~ d'obstacles** obstacle race;
(figurative) obstacle course; **~ de vitesse**
(in athletics) sprint; (on motorbikes) speedway
race
IDIOMS ne plus être dans la ~ to be out of
touch; **être à bout de ~** to be worn out

coursier, -ière /kuʀsje, ɛʀ/ *nm,f*
messenger

court, ~e /kuʀ, kuʀt/ **1** *adj* (a) short; de **~e durée** short-lived; short-term; **avoir le souffle ~** to get out of breath easily
(b) ⟨*defeat, victory, majority*⟩ narrow
2 *adv* **couper ~ à qch** to put paid to sth; **s'arrêter ~** to stop short
3 *nm* **~ de tennis** tennis court
■ **~ métrage** short (film); **~e échelle: faire la ~e échelle à qn** to give sb a leg up (colloq)
IDIOMS **être à ~ de** to be short of ⟨*money*⟩; **prendre qn de ~** to catch sb unprepared

court-circuit, *pl* **~s** /kuʀsiʀkɥi/ *nm* shortcircuit

courtier, -ière /kuʀtje, ɛʀ/ *nm,f* broker

courtiser /kuʀtize/ [1] *vtr* to woo

courtois, ~e /kuʀtwa, az/ *adj* ⟨*person, tone*⟩ courteous; ⟨*genre, tradition*⟩ courtly

courtoisie /kuʀtwazi/ *nf* courtesy

couru, ~e /kuʀy/ **1** *pp* ▶ COURIR
2 *pp adj* ⟨*place*⟩ popular
IDIOMS **c'est ~ d'avance** (colloq) it's a foregone conclusion

cousin, ~e /kuzɛ̃, in/ *nm,f* cousin

coussin /kusɛ̃/ *nm* cushion

cousu, ~e /kuzy/ ▶ COUDRE

coût /ku/ *nm* cost; **~ de la vie** cost of living

coûtant /kutɑ̃/ *adj m* **prix ~** cost price

couteau, *pl* **~x** /kuto/ *nm* (a) knife; **donner un coup de ~ à qn** to stab sb
(b) razor shell (GB) *or* clam (US)
(c) knife edge
IDIOMS **être à ~x tirés avec qn** to be at daggers drawn with sb; **avoir le ~ sous la gorge** to have a pistol to one's head

coûter /kute/ [1] **1** *vtr* to cost
2 *vi* to cost; **~ cher** to be expensive; **ça m'a coûté de m'excuser** it was hard for me to apologize
3 *v impers* **il t'en coûtera d'avoir fait cela** you will pay for doing this; **coûte que coûte, quoi qu'il en coûte** at all costs
IDIOMS **~ les yeux de la tête** to cost an arm and a leg (colloq)

coûteux, -euse /kutø, øz/ *adj* costly

coutume /kutym/ *nf* custom; **avoir ~ de faire** to be in the habit of doing
IDIOMS **une fois n'est pas ~** it does no harm just this once

coutumier, -ière /kutymje, ɛʀ/ *adj* customary

couture /kutyʀ/ *nf* (a) sewing; dressmaking; **faire de la ~** to sew
(b) seam
IDIOMS **sous toutes les ~s** from every angle; **battre qn à plates ~s** to beat sb hollow

couturier /kutyʀje/ *nm* dress designer

couturière /kutyʀjɛʀ/ *nf* dressmaker

couvent /kuvɑ̃/ *nm* convent

couver /kuve/ [1] **1** *vtr* (a) to sit on ⟨*eggs*⟩; **la poule couve** the hen is brooding
(b) to overprotect; **~ qn/qch du regard** to look fondly at sb/sth; to gaze longingly at sb/sth
(c) to be coming down with ⟨*illness*⟩

2 *vi* ⟨*rebellion*⟩ to brew; ⟨*fire, anger*⟩ to smoulder (GB), to smolder (US)

couvercle /kuvɛʀkl/ *nm* (a) lid
(b) screwtop

couvert, ~e /kuvɛʀ, ɛʀt/ **1** *pp* ▶ COUVRIR
2 *pp adj* (a) covered (de in, with); **être ~ de diplômes** to have a lot of qualifications
(b) ⟨*pool*⟩ indoor; ⟨*market*⟩ covered
(c) ⟨*sky*⟩ overcast
3 *nm* (a) place setting; **mettre le ~** to lay the table; **un ~ en argent** a silver knife, fork and spoon
(b) cover charge
4 **à couvert** *phr* **se mettre à ~** to take cover
5 **sous le couvert de** *phr* under the pretence (GB) of; **sous ~ de la plaisanterie** under the guise of a joke

couverture /kuvɛʀtyʀ/ *nf* (a) blanket; (small) rug (GB), lap robe (US)
(b) (of book, magazine) cover
(c) (media) coverage
IDIOMS **tirer la ~ à soi** to turn a situation to one's own advantage

couveuse /kuvøz/ *nf* incubator

couvre-feu, *pl* **~x** /kuvʀəfø/ *nm* curfew

couvre-lit, *pl* **~s** /kuvʀəli/ *nm* bedspread

couvreur /kuvʀœʀ/ *nm* roofer

couvrir /kuvʀiʀ/ [32] **1** *vtr* (a) to cover ⟨*furniture, wall, fire, card*⟩; to roof ⟨*house*⟩; **~ qn de qch** (with blows, jewels, compliments) to shower sb with sth
(b) ⟨*sound*⟩ to drown out
(c) ⟨*transmitter, inspector*⟩ to cover ⟨*region*⟩
(d) to wrap [sb] up; to cover [sb] up
(e) to cover up for ⟨*mistake, person*⟩
(f) (with gun) to cover ⟨*soldier*⟩
(g) to cover ⟨*distance*⟩
(h) ⟨*book, journalist*⟩ to cover ⟨*story, event*⟩
(i) ⟨*sum*⟩ to cover ⟨*expenses*⟩
2 **se couvrir** *v refl* (+ *v être*) (a) to wrap up; to put on a hat
(b) ⟨*sky*⟩ to become overcast
(c) **se ~ de** to become covered with
(d) (against accusations) to cover oneself

CP /sepe/ *nm: abbr* ▶ COURS

crabe /kʀab/ *nm* crab

crachat /kʀaʃa/ *nm* spit

crachement /kʀaʃmɑ̃/ *nm* (a) spitting
(b) crackling

cracher /kʀaʃe/ [1] **1** *vtr* (a) to spit out; **c'est le portrait de sa mère tout craché** (colloq) she's the spitting image of her mother
(b) to belch (out) ⟨*flames, smoke*⟩
2 *vi* to spit; **je ne cracherais pas dessus** (colloq) I wouldn't turn up my nose at it

cracheur /kʀaʃœʀ/ *nm* **~ de feu** fire-eater

crachin /kʀaʃɛ̃/ *nm* drizzle

crachoir /kʀaʃwaʀ/ *nm* spittoon

crachoter /kʀaʃɔte/ [1] *vi* (a) to cough and splutter
(b) to crackle

crack /kʀak/ *nm* (a) (genius) ace
(b) (colloq) (drug) crack (colloq)

craie /kʀɛ/ *nf* chalk

craindre /kʀɛ̃dʀ/ [54] *vtr* **(a)** to fear, to be afraid of
(b) to be sensitive to ⟨*cold*⟩; to dislike ⟨*sun*⟩

craint, ~e¹ /kʀɛ̃, ɛ̃t/ ▶ CRAINDRE

crainte² /kʀɛ̃t/ *nf* fear; **avoir des ~s au sujet de qn** to be worried about sb; **n'ayez ~, soyez sans ~** have no fear

craintif, -ive /kʀɛ̃tif, iv/ *adj* timorous, timid

cramoisi, ~e /kʀamwazi/ *adj* crimson

crampe /kʀɑ̃p/ *nf* cramp

crampon /kʀɑ̃pɔ̃/ *nm* crampon; **chaussures à ~s** (for football) boots with studs (GB) *or* cleats (US); (for running) spiked shoes

cramponner: se cramponner /kʀɑ̃pɔne/ [1] *v refl* (+ *v être*) to hold on tightly

cran /kʀɑ̃/ ⟨1⟩ *nm* **(a)** notch; (in belt) hole; **monter d'un ~** to move up a notch
(b) nick
(c) (colloq) **avoir du ~** to have guts (colloq)
(d) (in hair) wave
⟨2⟩ **à cran** *phr* **être à ~** to be on edge
■ **~ d'arrêt** flick knife (GB), switchblade (US); **~ de sûreté** safety catch

crâne /kʀɑn/ *nm* **(a)** skull
(b) (colloq) head; **ne rien avoir dans le ~** to have no brains; **bourrer le ~ à qn** (colloq) to brainwash sb

crânement /kʀɑnmɑ̃/ *adv* gallantly; proudly

crânien, -ienne /kʀɑnjɛ̃, ɛn/ *adj* cranial; **boîte crânienne** cranium

crapaud /kʀapo/ *nm* toad

crapule /kʀapyl/ *nf* crook

crapuleux, -euse /kʀapylø, øz/ *adj* villainous

craqueler: se craqueler /kʀakle/ [19] *v refl* (+ *v être*) to crack

craquement /kʀakmɑ̃/ *nm* **(a)** creaking sound, creak
(b) cracking sound, crack

craquer /kʀake/ [1] ⟨1⟩ *vtr* **(a)** to split ⟨*trousers*⟩
(b) to strike ⟨*match*⟩
⟨2⟩ *vi* **(a)** ⟨*seam*⟩ to split; ⟨*branch*⟩ to crack
(b) ⟨*floor*⟩ to creak
(c) (colloq) ⟨*person*⟩ to crack up (colloq)

crasse /kʀas/ *nf* grime, filth

crasseux, -euse /kʀasø, øz/ *adj* filthy, grimy

cratère /kʀatɛʀ/ *nm* crater

cravache /kʀavaʃ/ *nf* whip

cravate /kʀavat/ *nf* tie

crawl /kʀol/ *nm* crawl

crayon /kʀɛjɔ̃/ *nm* pencil; **~ noir** lead pencil; **~ optique** light pen

créance /kʀeɑ̃s/ *nf* **(a)** debt (*owed by a debtor*)
(b) letter of credit

créancier, -ière /kʀeɑ̃sje, ɛʀ/ *nm,f* creditor

créateur, -trice /kʀeatœʀ, tʀis/ *nm,f* creator; designer

créatif, -ive /kʀeatif, iv/ *adj* creative

création /kʀeasjɔ̃/ *nf* **(a)** creation; **la ~ d'une entreprise** the setting up of a company; **la ~ d'un nouveau produit** the development of a new product; **tous les livres de la ~** all the books in the world
(b) (work of art) creation; (play) first production; (commercial) new product

créativité /kʀeativite/ *nf* creativity

créature /kʀeatyʀ/ *nf* creature

crèche /kʀɛʃ/ *nf* **(a)** crèche (GB), day-nursery
(b) (at Christmas) crib (GB), crèche (US)

crédibilité /kʀedibilite/ *nf* credibility

crédible /kʀedibl/ *adj* credible

crédit /kʀedi/ *nm* **(a)** funds; **les ~s de la recherche** research funding
(b) credit; **accorder un ~** to grant credit terms; **faire ~ à qn** to give sb credit; **porter une somme au ~ d'un compte** to credit sb's account with a sum of money; **mettre** *or* **porter qch au ~ de qn** (figurative) to give sb credit for sth

créditer /kʀedite/ [1] *vtr* to credit

créditeur, -trice /kʀeditœʀ, tʀis/ *adj* **être ~** to be in credit

credo /kʀedo/ *nm* creed

crédule /kʀedyl/ *adj* gullible, credulous

créer /kʀee/ [11] ⟨1⟩ *vtr* (gen) to create; to develop ⟨*new product*⟩; to set up ⟨*company*⟩
⟨2⟩ **se créer** *v refl* (+ *v être*) **se ~ des problèmes** to bring trouble on oneself

crémaillère /kʀemajɛʀ/ *nf* **pendre la ~** to have a house-warming (party)

crémation /kʀemasjɔ̃/ *nf* cremation

crématoire /kʀematwaʀ/ *nm* crematorium

crème¹ /kʀɛm/ *adj inv* cream

crème² /kʀɛm/ *nf* **(a)** cream
(b) cream dessert
(c) (colloq) **la ~ des linguistes** the very best linguists
■ **~ Chantilly** whipped cream; **~ glacée** dairy ice cream; **~ de marrons** chestnut spread; **~ renversée** caramel custard

crémerie /kʀɛmʀi/ *nf* cheese shop (GB) *or* store (US)

crémeux, -euse /kʀemø, øz/ *adj* creamy

créneau, *pl* **~x** /kʀeno/ *nm* **(a)** parallel parking
(b) (Econ) market
(c) gap, niche
(d) crenel; **les ~x** crenellations
■ **~ horaire** time slot; **~ publicitaire** advertising slot

créole /kʀeɔl/ *adj, nm* Creole

crêpe¹ /kʀɛp/ *nm* **(a)** crepe
(b) black veil

crêpe² /kʀɛp/ *nf* pancake, crêpe

crêper /kʀepe/ [1] *vtr* to backcomb (GB), to tease ⟨*hair*⟩

crépi /kʀepi/ nm rendering

crépitement /kʀepitmɑ̃/ nm crackling, crackle; sizzling

crépiter /kʀepite/ [1] vi ⟨fire⟩ to crackle; ⟨oil⟩ to sizzle; ⟨rain⟩ to patter

crépon /kʀepɔ̃/ nm crepe paper

crépu, ~e /kʀepy/ adj frizzy

crépuscule /kʀepyskyl/ nm twilight, dusk

crescendo /kʀeʃɛndo/ **1** adv aller ~ ⟨noise⟩ to intensify
2 nm crescendo

cresson /kʀesɔ̃, kʀəsɔ̃/ nm watercress

crête /kʀɛt/ nf (a) (of cock) comb; (of bird) crest
(b) (of mountain, wave) crest; (of roof) ridge

crétin, ~e /kʀetɛ̃, in/ nm,f moron (colloq)

creuser /kʀøze/ [1] **1** vtr (a) to dig a hole in ⟨ground⟩; to drill a hole in ⟨tooth⟩; to dig into ⟨rock⟩
(b) to dig ⟨hole, canal, grave⟩; to sink ⟨well⟩
(c) ⟨wrinkles⟩ to furrow ⟨face⟩; ~ les reins to arch one's back
(d) to deepen, to increase ⟨deficit, inequalities⟩
(e) to go into [sth] in depth ⟨question, subject⟩
2 se creuser v refl (+ v être) ⟨cheeks⟩ to become hollow; ⟨gap⟩ to widen
IDIOMS ça creuse (colloq) it really gives you an appetite; se ~ (la tête or la cervelle) (colloq) to rack one's brains

creux, -euse /kʀø, øz/ **1** adj (a) ⟨trunk, tooth, sound, cheeks⟩ hollow; ⟨stomach, speech⟩ empty; ⟨analysis⟩ shallow; un plat ~ a shallow dish; assiette creuse soup dish
(b) ⟨day, period⟩ slack, off-peak
2 adv sonner ~ to make a hollow sound
3 nm (a) hollow; le ~ des reins the small of the back; le ~ de l'aisselle the armpit; le ~ de la vague the trough of the wave; être au ~ de la vague (figurative) to be at rock bottom
(b) (colloq) avoir un petit ~ to have the munchies (colloq)

crevaison /kʀəvɛzɔ̃/ nf puncture

crevasse /kʀəvas/ nf (a) crevasse
(b) crack, fissure
(c) chapped skin

crève /kʀɛv/ nf (colloq) chill; attraper la ~ to catch a chill or one's death (of cold)

crever /kʀəve/ [16] **1** vtr to puncture, to burst; ~ les yeux de qn to poke sb's eyes out; ça crève les yeux it's blindingly obvious; ça crève le cœur it's heartbreaking
2 vi (a) to burst; to burst open
(b) to die; ~ de faim to be starving
(c) ~ d'envie to be eaten up with envy; ~ d'orgueil to be terribly full of oneself
3 se crever v refl (+ v être) il s'est crevé un œil he put his eye out
IDIOMS marche ou crève sink or swim

crevette /kʀəvɛt/ nf ~ grise shrimp; ~ rose prawn

cri /kʀi/ nm (a) cry; shout; scream; un ~ aigu a shriek; à grands ~s loudly; pousser les hauts ~s to protest loudly
(b) (of bird) call

criant, ~e /kʀijɑ̃, ɑ̃t/ adj clear, striking

criard, ~e /kʀijaʀ, aʀd/ adj ⟨voice⟩ shrill; ⟨colour⟩ garish

crible /kʀibl/ nm (for minerals) screen; (for sand) riddle; passer au ~ (figurative) to sift through

cribler /kʀible/ [1] vtr (a) ~ qn/qch de balles to riddle sb/sth with bullets
(b) ~ qn de reproches to heap reproaches on sb

cric /kʀik/ nm (for car) jack

criée /kʀije/ nf (vente à la) ~ auction

crier /kʀije/ [2] **1** vtr (a) to shout
(b) to proclaim; to protest ⟨innocence⟩
2 crier à v+prep on a crié au scandale quand... there was an outcry when...
3 vi (a) to shout; to cry; to scream
(b) ⟨animal⟩ to give a cry; ⟨monkey⟩ to chatter; ⟨gull⟩ to cry; ⟨pig⟩ to squeal

crieur, -ieuse /kʀijœʀ, øz/ nm,f ~ de journaux news vendor

crime /kʀim/ nm (a) crime
(b) murder; ~ crapuleux murder for money

criminalité /kʀiminalite/ nf crime

criminel, -elle /kʀiminɛl/ **1** adj criminal
2 nm,f (a) criminal
(b) murderer

crin /kʀɛ̃/ nm horsehair; à tout ~ (figurative) dyed-in-the-wool

crinière /kʀinjɛʀ/ nf mane

crique /kʀik/ nf cove

criquet /kʀikɛ/ nm locust

crise /kʀiz/ nf (a) crisis; ~ agricole crisis in the agricultural industry; la ~ the economic crisis, the slump
(b) shortage; ~ de l'emploi job shortage
(c) (Med) attack; ~ d'appendicite appendicitis; ~ de toux coughing fit
(d) fit; ~ de colère fit of rage; faire une ~ to have a tantrum; to have a fit (colloq)
■ ~ cardiaque heart attack; ~ de foie indigestion; ~ de nerfs hysterics

crisper /kʀispe/ [1] **1** vtr l'angoisse crispait son visage his/her face was tense with worry
2 se crisper v refl (+ v être) ⟨hands⟩ to clench; ⟨face, person⟩ to tense (up); ⟨smile⟩ to freeze

crisser /kʀise/ [1] vi ⟨shoes, chalk⟩ to squeak; ⟨snow⟩ to crunch; ⟨tyres, brakes⟩ to screech

cristal, pl -aux /kʀistal, o/ nm crystal

cristallin, ~e /kʀistalɛ̃, in/ **1** adj
(a) crystalline
(b) crystal clear
2 nm (of eye) (crystalline) lens

cristalliser /kʀistalize/ [1] vtr, vi, v refl (+ v être) to crystallize

critère /kʀitɛʀ/ nm (a) criterion; ~s de

gestion/de confort standards of management/comfort; **le ~ déterminant** the crucial factor

(b) specification; **remplir les ~s d'âge et de diplôme** to meet the requirements as far as age and qualifications are concerned

critiquable /kʀitikabl/ *adj* questionable

critique¹ /kʀitik/ **1** *adj* critical **2** *nmf* critic

critique² /kʀitik/ *nf* (a) criticism; **faire une ~ à qn** to criticize sb
(b) review; **faire la ~ d'un film** to review a film
(c) **la ~ littéraire** literary criticism

critiquer /kʀitike/ [1] *vtr* to criticize

croasser /kʀɔase/ [1] *vi* to caw

croc /kʀo/ *nm* fang

croche /kʀɔʃ/ *nf* quaver (GB), eighth note (US); **double ~** semiquaver (GB), sixteenth note (US)

croche-pied, *pl* **~s** /kʀɔʃpje/ *nm* (colloq) **faire un ~ à qn** to trip sb up

crochet /kʀɔʃɛ/ *nm* (a) hook
(b) picklock
(c) crochet hook; **faire du ~** to crochet
(d) square bracket
(e) **faire un ~** to make a detour
(f) (in boxing) hook
(g) fang
IDIOMS **vivre aux ~s de qn** (colloq) to sponge off sb (colloq)

crocheter /kʀɔʃte/ [18] *vtr* to pick ⟨*lock*⟩

crochu, **~e** /kʀɔʃy/ *adj* ⟨*nose*⟩ hooked; ⟨*hands*⟩ clawed

crocodile /kʀɔkɔdil/ *nm* crocodile

croire /kʀwaʀ/ [71] **1** *vtr* (a) to believe; **faire ~ à qn** to make sb believe
(b) to think; **je crois savoir que** I happen to know that; **il est malin, faut pas ~!** (colloq) he's clever, believe me!; **tu ne crois pas si bien dire** you don't know how right you are; **on croirait de la soie** it looks *or* feels like silk
(c) **si l'on en croit l'auteur, à en ~ l'auteur** if we are to believe the author; **crois-en mon expérience** take my word for it
2 croire à *v+prep* to believe ⟨*story*⟩; to believe in ⟨*ghosts*⟩
3 croire en *v+prep* to believe in
4 se croire *v refl* (+ *v être*) **il se croit beau** he thinks he's handsome

croisade /kʀwazad/ *nf* crusade

croisé, **~e¹** /kʀwaze/ **1** *pp* ▶ CROISER
2 *pp adj* (a) ⟨*legs*⟩ crossed; ⟨*arms*⟩ folded
(b) crossbred
(c) ⟨*agreements*⟩ reciprocal

croisée² /kʀwaze/ *nf* (a) junction; **à la ~ des chemins** at the crossroads
(b) window

croisement /kʀwazmɑ̃/ *nm*
(a) crossroads; crossing, junction
(b) (of threads, straps) crossing
(c) crossbreeding; hybrid, cross(breed)

croiser /kʀwaze/ [1] **1** *vtr* (a) to cross; **~ les bras** to fold one's arms

(b) **~ qn/qch** to pass sb/sth (coming the other way)
(c) to meet; **mon regard croisa le sien** our eyes met
(d) to cross(breed)
2 se croiser *v refl* (+ *v être*) ⟨*cars*⟩ to pass each other; ⟨*letters*⟩ to cross in the post (GB) *or* mail (US); ⟨*roads*⟩ to intersect; ⟨*lines*⟩ to cross

croisière /kʀwazjɛʀ/ *nf* cruise

croissance /kʀwasɑ̃s/ *nf* growth

croissant /kʀwasɑ̃/ *nm* (a) croissant
(b) crescent; **~ de lune** crescent moon

croître /kʀwatʀ/ [72] *vi* (a) to grow; **faire ~** to grow
(b) ⟨*noise*⟩ to get *or* grow louder

croix /kʀwa/ *nf* cross; **bras en ~** arms out on either side of the body
IDIOMS **ton argent, tu peux faire une ~ dessus** (colloq) you can kiss your money goodbye; **un jour à marquer d'une ~** a red-letter day

Croix-Rouge /kʀwaʀuʒ/ *nf* **la ~** the Red Cross

croquant, **~e** /kʀɔkɑ̃, ɑ̃t/ *adj* crunchy

croque-madame /kʀɔkmadam/ *nm inv*: toasted ham and cheese sandwich topped with a fried egg

croque-monsieur /kʀɔkməsjø/ *nm inv*: toasted ham and cheese sandwich

croque-mort, *pl* **~s** /kʀɔkmɔʀ/ *nm* (colloq) undertaker

croquer /kʀɔke/ [1] **1** *vtr* (a) to crunch
(b) to sketch; **belle à ~** as pretty as a picture
2 *vi* (a) to be crunchy
(b) **~ dans une pomme** to bite into an apple

croquette /kʀɔkɛt/ *nf* croquette

croquis /kʀɔki/ *nm* sketch

crosse /kʀɔs/ *nf* (a) (of rifle) butt
(b) (of cane) crook
(c) (Sport) stick

crotte /kʀɔt/ *nf* dropping; **c'est de la ~ de chien** it's dog mess

crotter /kʀɔte/ [1] *vtr* to muddy; **bottes crottées** muddy boots

crottin /kʀɔtɛ̃/ *nm* (a) dung
(b) (*small round*) goat's cheese

crouler /kʀule/ [1] *vi* (a) to collapse; to crumble
(b) **~ sous** to be weighed down by ⟨*parcels, debts, work*⟩; **~ sous le poids de** ⟨*table*⟩ to groan under the weight of ⟨*books*⟩

croupe /kʀup/ *nf* (of horse) croup

croupi, **~e** /kʀupi/ *adj* stagnant

croupier /kʀupje/ *nm* croupier

croupir /kʀupiʀ/ [3] *vi* (a) ⟨*water*⟩ to stagnate
(b) **~ en prison** to rot in jail

croustillant, **~e** /kʀustijɑ̃, ɑ̃t/ *adj*
(a) crispy; crunchy
(b) ⟨*story, details*⟩ spicy

croustiller /kʀustije/ [1] *vi* ⟨*bread*⟩ to be crusty; ⟨*chocolate*⟩ to be crunchy

croûte /kʀut/ nf (a) (of bread) crust; (of cheese) rind; **casser la ~** (colloq) to have a bite to eat
(b) (Culin) **pâté en ~** pâté en croute or in pastry
(c) (Med) scab
(d) (colloq) daub, bad painting

croûton /kʀutɔ̃/ nm (a) crust
(b) (Culin) crouton

croyance /kʀwajɑ̃s/ nf belief

croyant, ~e /kʀwajɑ̃, ɑ̃t/ adj **être ~** to be a believer

CRS /sɛɛʀɛs/ nm (abbr = **compagnie républicaine de sécurité**) **un ~** a member of the French riot police

cru¹, ~e¹ /kʀy/ ▶ CROIRE

cru², ~e² /kʀy/ [1] adj (a) raw; uncooked; ⟨milk⟩ unpasteurized; **se faire manger tout ~** (colloq) to be eaten alive (colloq)
(b) ⟨light, colour⟩ harsh
(c) ⟨language⟩ crude
[2] nm vineyard; vintage; vintage year; **du meilleur ~** ⟨collection⟩ vintage; **du ~** ⟨wine, author⟩ local

crû, crue³ /kʀy/ ▶CROÎTRE

cruauté /kʀyote/ nf cruelty

cruche /kʀyʃ/ nf jug (GB), pitcher (US)

crucial, ~e, mpl **-iaux** /kʀysjal, o/ adj crucial

crucifier /kʀysifje/ [2] vtr to crucify

crucifix /kʀysifi/ nm crucifix

crudité /kʀydite/ nf **~s** raw vegetables, crudités

crue⁴ /kʀy/ [1] adj f ▶ CRU² 1
[2] nf rise in water level; flood; **en ~** in spate

cruel, -elle /kʀyɛl/ adj cruel

cruellement /kʀyɛlmɑ̃/ adv (a) cruelly
(b) **manquer ~ de qch** to be desperately short of sth
(c) terribly; **la pénurie de carburant se fait ~ sentir** the fuel shortage is being sorely felt

crûment /kʀymɑ̃/ adv (a) bluntly
(b) crudely

crustacé /kʀystase/ nm shellfish

crypte /kʀipt(ə)/ nf crypt

crypté, ~e /kʀipte/ adj coded; encrypted

cube /kyb/ [1] adj cubic
[2] nm (a) cube
(b) building block

cubique /kybik/ adj (a) cubic
(b) cube-shaped

cucul /kyky/ adj (colloq) corny (colloq); silly

cueillette /kœjɛt/ nf (a) (of fruits, flowers) picking
(b) crop

cueilli, ~e /kœji/ ▶ CUEILLIR

cueillir /kœjiʀ/ [27] vtr (a) to pick ⟨fruit, flowers⟩
(b) (colloq) to arrest ⟨criminal⟩

cuiller, cuillère /kɥijɛʀ/ nf spoon; spoonful; **~ à café** teaspoon; coffee spoon
IDIOMS **il n'y va pas avec le dos de la ~**

(colloq) he doesn't do things by halves; **en deux coups de ~ à pot** in two shakes of a lamb's tail (colloq)

cuillerée /kɥij(ə)ʀe/ nf spoonful

cuir /kɥiʀ/ nm (a) leather
(b) rawhide; hide
■ **~ chevelu** scalp

cuirassé /kɥiʀase/ nm battleship

cuire /kɥiʀ/ [69] [1] vtr (a) to cook; to bake; to roast; **~ à la vapeur** to steam; **à ~** ⟨apple⟩ cooking
(b) to fire ⟨porcelain⟩
[2] vi (a) ⟨food⟩ to cook; to be cooking; **laissez ~ à petit feu** allow to simmer gently
(b) (colloq) **on cuit sur la plage** it's baking (hot) on the beach
(c) ⟨graze⟩ to sting; **ça me cuit** it stings

cuisant, ~e /kɥizɑ̃, ɑ̃t/ adj (a) ⟨defeat, regret⟩ bitter; ⟨remark⟩ stinging
(b) ⟨pain⟩ burning

cuisine /kɥizin/ nf (a) kitchen
(b) galley
(c) kitchen furniture
(d) cooking
(e) (colloq) intrigues

cuisiner /kɥizine/ [1] vtr, vi to cook

cuisinier, -ière¹ /kɥizinje, ɛʀ/ nm,f cook; chef

cuisinière² /kɥizinjɛʀ/ nf cooker

cuissarde /kɥisaʀd/ nf wader; thighboot

cuisse /kɥis/ nf thigh; **des ~s de grenouille** frogs' legs

cuisson /kɥisɔ̃/ nf (a) cooking; baking; roasting
(b) (of pottery) firing

cuistot /kɥisto/ nm (colloq) cook

cuit, ~e¹ /kɥi, kɥit/ pp ▶ CUIRE
IDIOMS **c'est ~** (colloq) we've had it (colloq); **c'est du tout ~** (colloq) it's a piece of cake (colloq); it's in the bag (colloq); **elle attend que ça (lui) tombe tout ~** (colloq) she expects things to fall straight into her lap

cuite² /kɥit/ nf **tenir une ~** to be plastered (colloq)

cuivre /kɥivʀ/ [1] nm (a) **~ (rouge)** copper
(b) **~ (jaune)** brass
[2] **cuivres** nm pl (a) copperware
(b) brass
(c) (Mus) **les ~s** the brass

cul /ky/ nm (a) (slang) bottom, arse (GB) (vulgar), ass (US) (slang)
(b) (of bottle) bottom; **~ sec!** (colloq) bottoms up! (colloq)

culasse /kylas/ nf (a) cylinder head
(b) breechblock

culbute /kylbyt/ nf somersault

culbuter /kylbyte/ [1] vi ⟨person⟩ to take a tumble; ⟨vehicle⟩ to overturn

cul-cul (colloq) = CUCUL

cul-de-jatte, pl **culs-de-jatte** /kydʒat/ nmf person who has had both legs amputated

cul-de-sac, pl **culs-de-sac** /kydsak/ nm (a) cul-de-sac

(b) dead end

culinaire /kylinɛʀ/ *adj* culinary

culminant, ∼e /kylminɑ̃, ɑ̃t/ *adj* point ∼ (of mountain) highest point *or* peak; (of career) peak; (of crisis) height; (of holiday) high point

culminer /kylmine/ [1] *vi* **(a)** ∼ **au-dessus de qch** to tower above sth
(b) ⟨*inflation, unemployment*⟩ to reach its peak

culot /kylo/ *nm* (colloq) cheek (colloq); **y aller au ∼** to bluff

culotte /kylɔt/ *nf* **(a)** pants (GB), panties (US)
(b) **en ∼(s) courte(s)** in short trousers (GB) *or* pants (US)

culotté, ∼e /kylɔte/ *adj* (colloq) cheeky

culpabilisation /kylpabilizasjɔ̃/ *nf* making guilty; feeling of guilt

culpabiliser /kylpabilize/ [1] **1** *vtr* to make [sb] feel guilty
2 *vi* to feel guilty

culpabilité /kylpabilite/ *nf* guilt

culte /kylt/ *nm* **(a)** cult
(b) religion

cultivateur, -trice /kyltivatœʀ, tʀis/ *nm,f* farmer

cultiver /kyltive/ [1] **1** *vtr* to grow; to cultivate
2 se cultiver *v refl* (+ *v être*) to improve one's mind

culture /kyltyʀ/ **1** *nf* **(a)** cultivation; **la ∼ du blé** wheat growing
(b) crop; **∼ d'hiver** winter crop
(c) (in biology) culture
(d) (of society) culture; **∼ de masse** mass culture
(e) knowledge; **∼ classique** classical education
(f) arts; **subventionner la ∼** to subsidize the arts
2 cultures *nf pl* cultivated land
■ **∼ physique** physical exercise

culturel, -elle /kyltyʀɛl/ *adj* cultural

culturisme /kyltyʀism/ *nm* body-building

cumin /kymɛ̃/ *nm* cumin

cumul /kymyl/ *nm* **(a)** **∼ de fonctions** holding of several posts concurrently
(b) (Law) **∼ des peines** ≈ sentences to be served consecutively

cumuler /kymyle/ [1] *vtr* **(a)** to hold [sth] concurrently ⟨*offices*⟩; to draw [sth] concurrently ⟨*salaries*⟩
(b) to accumulate ⟨*handicaps, degrees*⟩
(c) to combine ⟨*results*⟩; to add up ⟨*amounts*⟩

cumulus /kymylys/ *nm inv* cumulus

cupide /kypid/ *adj* grasping

cupidité /kypidite/ *nf* avarice, greed, cupidity

cure /kyʀ/ *nf* **faire une ∼** to go for a course of treatment in a spa

■ **∼ d'amaigrissement** slimming course (GB), reducing treatment (US); **∼ de sommeil** sleep therapy

curé /kyʀe/ *nm* (parish) priest

cure-dents /kyʀdɑ̃/ *nm inv* toothpick

curer /kyʀe/ [1] **1** *vtr* to clean out ⟨*pipe, pond*⟩
2 se curer *v refl* (+ *v être*) **se ∼ les ongles** to clean one's nails

curieusement /kyʀjøzmɑ̃/ *adv* **(a)** oddly, strangely
(b) oddly enough

curieux, -ieuse /kyʀjø, øz/ **1** *adj*
(a) inquisitive, curious
(b) strange
(c) **esprit ∼** person with an enquiring mind; **être ∼ d'apprendre** to be keen to learn
2 *nm,f* onlooker

curiosité /kyʀjozite/ *nf* curiosity

curriculum vitae /kyʀikylɔmvite/ *nm inv* curriculum vitae, résumé (US)

curry /kyʀi/ *nm* **(a)** curry powder
(b) curry

curseur /kyʀsœʀ/ *nm* cursor

cursus /kyʀsys/ *nm inv* course

cutané, ∼e /kytane/ *adj* ⟨*irritation*⟩ skin

cutter /kytœʀ/ *nm* Stanley knife®

cuve /kyv/ *nf* vat; tank

cuvée /kyve/ *nf* vatful; **la ∼ 1959** the 1959 vintage; **∼ du patron** house wine

cuvette /kyvɛt/ *nf* **(a)** bowl; **∼ des wc** lavatory bowl *or* pan
(b) (in land) basin

CV /seve/ *nm* **(a)** (*abbr* = **curriculum vitae**) CV (GB), résumé (US)
(b) (*written abbr* = **cheval-vapeur**) HP

cybercafé /sibɛʀkafe/ *nm* cybercafe

cyberjargon /sibɛʀʒaʀgɔ̃/ *nm* netspeak

cyclable /siklabl/ *adj* **piste ∼** cycle track

cycle /sikl/ *nm* **(a)** cycle; **∼ infernal** vicious cycle
(b) series
(c) (Sch) **premier ∼** *first two years of a university degree course leading to a diploma;* **deuxième ∼** *final two years of a university degree course;* **troisième ∼** postgraduate (GB) *or* graduate (US) studies
(d) (bi)cycle

cyclique /siklik/ *adj* cyclic

cyclisme /siklism/ *nm* cycling; cycle racing

cycliste /siklist/ **1** *adj* ⟨*club*⟩ cycling; ⟨*race*⟩ cycle; **coureur ∼** racing cyclist
2 *nmf* cyclist; **short de ∼** cycling shorts

cyclone /siklon/ *nm* **(a)** cyclone
(b) (in weather) depression

cygne /siɲ/ *nm* swan; **∼ mâle** cob; **∼ femelle** pen; **jeune ∼** cygnet

cylindre /silɛ̃dʀ/ *nm* **(a)** cylinder
(b) roller

cylindrée /silɛ̃dʀe/ *nf* capacity, size; **∼ de 1200 cm³** 1200 cc engine

cymbale /sɛ̃bal/ *nm* cymbal

cynique /sinik/ *adj* cynical
cynisme /sinism/ *nm* cynicism

cyprès /sipʀɛ/ *nm* cypress
cystite /sistit/ *nf* cystitis

Dd

d, D /de/ *nm inv* d, D
d' ▶ DE
DAB /deabe/ *nm*: (*abbr* = **distributeur automatique de billets**) automatic teller machine, ATM
dactylographie /daktilɔgʀafi/ *nf* typing
dada /dada/ *nm* (colloq) **(a)** (baby talk) horsie (colloq)
(b) hobby
(c) hobbyhorse
dadais /dadɛ/ *nm inv* (colloq) clumsy youth; **espèce de grand ∼!** you great oaf!
daigner /deɲe/ [1] *vtr* to deign (**faire** to do)
daim /dɛ̃/ *nm* **(a)** (fallow) deer
(b) venison
(c) buckskin
(d) suede
dallage /dalaʒ/ *nm* paving
dalle /dal/ *nf* **(a)** slab
(b) flagstone
(c) concrete foundation slab
IDIOMS **avoir la ∼** (colloq) to be ravenous; **que ∼** (slang) nothing at all, zilch (colloq)
daller /dale/ [1] *vtr* to pave
daltonien, -ienne /daltɔnjɛ̃, ɛn/ *adj* colour (GB)-blind
dam /dɑ(m)/ *nm* **au grand ∼ de** to the great displeasure of
dame /dam/ *nf* **(a)** lady
(b) (in cards, chess) queen; (in draughts) King
[2] dames *nf pl* draughts (GB), checkers (US)
damier /damje/ *nm* draughtboard (GB), checkerboard (US)
damnation /danasjɔ̃/ *nf* damnation
damner /dɑne/ [1] **[1]** *vtr* to damn
[2] se damner *v refl* (+ *v être*) to damn oneself; **se ∼ pour qch** (colloq) to sell one's soul for sth
dancing /dɑ̃siŋ/ *nm* dance hall
dandiner: se dandiner /dɑ̃dine/ [1] *v refl* (+ *v être*) ⟨duck⟩ to waddle
Danemark /danmaʀk/ *pr nm* Denmark
danger /dɑ̃ʒe/ *nm* danger
■ **∼ public** danger to the public; (figurative) menace
dangereusement /dɑ̃ʒʀøzmɑ̃/ *adv* dangerously
dangereux, -euse /dɑ̃ʒʀø, øz/ *adj* dangerous
danois, ∼e /danwa, az/ **[1]** *adj* Danish

[2] *nm* **(a)** (language) Danish
(b) (dog) Great Dane
dans /dɑ̃/ *prep* **(a)** in; **être ∼ la cuisine** to be in the kitchen; **être ∼ un avion/bateau** to be on a plane/boat
(b) into; **entrer ∼ une pièce** to go into a room; **monter ∼ un avion** to get on a plane
(c) **boire ∼ un verre** to drink out of a glass; **prendre qch ∼ un placard** to take sth out of a cupboard
(d) **∼ deux heures** in two hours; **fait ∼ les deux heures** done within two hours; **je t'appellerai ∼ la journée** I'll phone you during the day
(e) **∼ les 30 francs** about 30 francs
danse /dɑ̃s/ *nf* **(a)** dance
(b) dancing; **faire de la ∼** to take dancing classes
■ **∼ classique** classical ballet
danser /dɑ̃se/ [1] *vtr, vi* to dance
IDIOMS **ne pas savoir sur quel pied ∼** not to know what to do
danseur, -euse /dɑ̃sœʀ, øz/ *nm,f* dancer; **∼ étoile** principal dancer
dard /daʀ/ *nm* **(a)** (Zool) sting
(b) spear
dare-dare /daʀdaʀ/ *adv* (colloq) double quick
darne /daʀn/ *nf* (fish) steak
dartre /daʀtʀ/ *nf* scurf patch
date /dat/ *nf* **(a)** date; **∼ limite** deadline; **∼ limite de vente** sell-by date
(b) time; **depuis cette ∼** from that time; **un ami de longue ∼** a longstanding friend; **le dernier scandale en ∼** the latest scandal
dater /date/ [1] **[1]** *vtr* to date; **à ∼ du 31 juillet** as from 31 July
[2] *vi* **(a)** **∼ de** to date from
(b) to be dated
dation /dasjɔ̃/ *nf* **∼ (en paiement)** payment in kind
datte /dat/ *nf* (Bot, Culin) date
dattier /datje/ *nm* date palm
daube /dob/ *nf* **bœuf en ∼** beef casserole
dauphin /dofɛ̃/ *nm* **(a)** dolphin
(b) heir apparent
(c) dauphin
daurade /dɔʀad/ *nf* (sea) bream
davantage /davɑ̃taʒ/ *adv* **(a)** more
(b) longer; **rester ∼** to stay longer
DCA /desea/ *nf* (*abbr* = **défense contre les aéronefs**) antiaircraft defence (GB)

DDASS /das/ *nf* (*abbr* = **Direction départementale de l'action sanitaire et sociale**) regional social services department

de (**d'** *before vowel or mute h*) /də, d/

■ Note You will find translations for expressions such as *d'abord, de travers, pomme de terre, chemin de fer* etc, at the entries ABORD, TRAVERS, POMME and CHEMIN etc.

1 *prep* (a) from; **venir ~ Paris** to come from Paris; **il est ~ père italien** his father is Italian
(b) by; **un poème ~ Victor Hugo** a poem by Victor Hugo
(c) of; **les chapeaux ~ Paul** Paul's hats; **le 20 du mois** the 20th of the month; **deux heures d'attente** a two-hour wait; **deux heures ~ libres** two hours free
(d) than; **plus/moins ~ dix** more/less than ten
(e) in; **d'un ton monocorde** in a monotone
(f) with; **pousser qch du pied** to push sth aside with one's foot
(g) **travailler ~ nuit** to work at night; **ne rien faire ~ la journée** to do nothing all day
(h) **être content ~ faire** to be happy to do
2 *det* **de, de l', de la, du** some; any; **voulez-vous ~ la bière?** would you like some beer?; **je n'ai pas d'argent** I haven't got any money

dé /de/ *nm* (a) dice; **les ~s sont jetés** the die is cast
(b) **~ (à coudre)** thimble

DEA /deaa/ *nm* (*abbr* = **diplôme d'études approfondies**) postgraduate certificate (*prior to doctoral thesis*)

déambulateur /deãbylatœʀ/ *nm* zimmer® (frame)

déambuler /deãbyle/ [1] *vi* to wander (about)

débâcle /debɑkl/ *nf* (a) (Mil) rout
(b) (figurative) collapse

déballage /debalaʒ/ *nm* (colloq) jumble; outpouring

déballer /debale/ [1] *vtr* (a) to unpack
(b) to display

débandade /debãdad/ *nf* (a) stampede
(b) disarray

débarbouiller /debaʀbuje/ [1] **1** *vtr* to wash
2 **se débarbouiller** *v refl* (+ *v être*) to wash one's face

débarcadère /debaʀkadɛʀ/ *nm* landing stage, jetty

débardeur /debaʀdœʀ/ *nm* tank top

débarquement /debaʀkəmã/ *nm*
(a) (of goods) unloading
(b) (of passengers) disembarkation
(c) (Mil) landing

débarquer /debaʀke/ [1] **1** *vtr* to unload ⟨goods⟩
2 *vi* (a) to disembark
(b) (Mil) to land
(c) (colloq) to turn up (colloq) (**chez qn** at sb's place)

débarras /debaʀa/ *nm inv* (a) junk room
(b) **bon ~!** (colloq) good riddance!

débarrasser /debaʀase/ [1] **1** *vtr* (a) to clear (out)
(b) **~** ⟨qn⟩ **de** to free [sb] from ⟨complex⟩; **~ qn** (**de son manteau**) to take sb's coat
2 **se débarrasser** *v refl* (+ *v être*) **se ~ de** to get rid of; to dispose of
IDIOMS **~ le plancher** (colloq) to clear off (colloq)

débat /deba/ *nm* debate

débattre /debatʀ/ [61] **1** *vtr* to negotiate
2 **débattre de** *or* **sur** *v+prep* (a) **~ de** *or* **sur** to discuss
(b) **~ de** *or* **sur** to debate
3 **se débattre** *v refl* (+ *v être*) to struggle

débauche /deboʃ/ *nf* (a) debauchery
(b) profusion

débaucher /deboʃe/ [1] *vtr* (a) to corrupt
(b) to lay [sb] off
(c) (colloq) to tempt [sb] away

débile /debil/ **1** *adj* (colloq) daft (colloq)
2 *nmf* **~ mental** (Med) retarded person

débilité /debilite/ *nf* (a) debility
(b) (colloq) stupidity

débiner (colloq) /debine/ [1] **1** *vtr* to badmouth (colloq)
2 **se débiner** *v refl* (+ *v être*) to clear off (colloq); to make oneself scarce (colloq)

débit /debi/ *nm* (a) debit; **la somme est inscrite au ~** the sum has been debited
(b) (when speaking) delivery
(c) (of river) rate of flow
(d) (of liquid) flow; (of gas) output
■ **~ de boissons** bar

débiter /debite/ [1] *vtr* (a) to debit
(b) to reel [sth] off; **~ des bêtises** to talk a lot of nonsense
(c) to cut [sth] up

débiteur, -trice /debitœʀ, tʀis/ **1** *adj* **compte ~** debit account; **pays ~** debtor nation
2 *nm,f* debtor

déblayer /debleje/ [21] *vtr* (a) to clear away ⟨earth, snow⟩
(b) to clear ⟨place⟩

débloquer /debloke/ [1] **1** *vtr* (a) to unlock ⟨steering wheel⟩; to unjam ⟨mechanism⟩
(b) to unfreeze ⟨prices⟩; to end the deadlock in ⟨situation⟩
(c) to make [sth] available ⟨credit⟩
2 *vi* (colloq) to be off one's rocker (colloq)

déboires /debwaʀ/ *nm pl*
(a) disappointments
(b) trials, difficulties
(c) setbacks

déboiser /debwaze/ [1] *vtr* to deforest

déboîter /debwate/ [1] **1** *vtr* to disconnect ⟨tubes⟩
2 *vi* ⟨car⟩ to pull out
3 **se déboîter** *v refl* (+ *v être*) **se ~ le genou** to dislocate one's knee

débonnaire /debonɛʀ/ *adj* good-humoured (GB); kindly

débordant, ~**e** /debɔʀdɑ̃, ɑ̃t/ *adj*
(a) ⟨*imagination*⟩ overactive
(b) ~ **de** brimming with ⟨*energy*⟩; bursting with ⟨*health*⟩

débordé, ~**e** /debɔʀde/ **1** *pp* ▶ DÉBORDER
2 *pp adj* (a) overwhelmed
(b) overloaded

débordement /debɔʀdəmɑ̃/ *nm* (of protest) flood; (of enthusiasm) excess

déborder /debɔʀde/ [1] **1** *vtr* (a) ⟨*problem, feeling*⟩ to go beyond
(b) **se laisser** ~ to let oneself be overwhelmed
(c) (Mil, Sport) to outflank
2 **déborder de** *v+prep* to be brimming over with; to be bursting with
3 *vi* (a) ⟨*river*⟩ to overflow
(b) ⟨*liquid*⟩ to overflow; to boil over
(c) to jut out

débouché /debuʃe/ *nm* (a) market; ~**s à l'exportation** export outlets
(b) job opportunity

déboucher /debuʃe/ [1] **1** *vtr* (a) to unblock
(b) to open; to uncork
2 *vi* ~ **sur** ⟨*street*⟩ to open onto; ⟨*talks*⟩ to lead to
3 **se déboucher** *v refl* (+ *v être*) (a) to come unblocked
(b) ⟨*ears*⟩ to pop
(c) **se** ~ **les oreilles/le nez** to unblock one's ears/nose

débouler /debule/ [1] **1** *vtr* to charge down
2 *vi* (a) to tumble down
(b) (colloq) to turn up

déboulonner /debulɔne/ [1] *vtr* to unbolt

débourser /debuʀse/ [1] *vtr* to pay out

déboussoler /debusɔle/ [1] *vtr* (colloq) to confuse

debout /dəbu/ **1** *adj inv*, *adv* (a) standing; ⟨*object*⟩ upright; **se mettre** ~ to stand up; **je ne tiens plus** ~ I'm falling asleep on my feet
(b) **ton histoire tient** ~ (colloq) your story seems likely
(c) (out of bed) **être** ~ to be up
2 *excl* get up!

déboutonner /debutɔne/ [1] **1** *vtr* to unbutton
2 **se déboutonner** *v refl* (+ *v être*) to come undone

débraillé, ~**e** /debʀaje/ *adj* ⟨*person*⟩ dishevelled (GB); ⟨*clothes, style*⟩ sloppy

débrancher /debʀɑ̃ʃe/ [1] *vtr* to unplug ⟨*appliance*⟩; to disconnect ⟨*alarm system*⟩

débrayer /debʀeje/ [21] *vi* (Aut) to declutch

débridé, ~**e** /debʀide/ *adj* unbridled

débris /debʀi/ *nm inv* (a) fragment; **des** ~ **de verre** broken glass
(b) piece of wreckage

débrouillard, ~**e** /debʀujaʀ, aʀd/ *adj* resourceful

débrouiller /debʀuje/ [1] **1** *vtr* (a) to disentangle ⟨*threads*⟩
(b) to solve ⟨*riddle*⟩

2 **se débrouiller** *v refl* (+ *v être*) (a) to manage
(b) to get by; **il se débrouille bien en espagnol** he speaks good Spanish

débroussailler /debʀusaje/ [1] *vtr* to clear the undergrowth from; (figurative) to do the groundwork on

débusquer /debyske/ [1] *vtr* to flush [sb/sth] out

début /deby/ **1** *nm* beginning; start
2 **débuts** *nm pl* (a) debut
(b) early stages

débutant, ~**e** /debytɑ̃, ɑ̃t/ **1** *adj* ⟨*driver, skier*⟩ novice; ⟨*engineer*⟩ recently qualified
2 *nm,f* beginner

débuter /debyte/ [1] *vi* (a) ⟨*day, novel*⟩ to begin, to start; ⟨*person*⟩ to start off
(b) to start out (**comme** as)
(c) ⟨*performer*⟩ to make one's debut

deçà /dəsa/ **1** *adv* ~, **delà** here and there
2 **en deçà** *phr* (a) on this side
(b) below

décacheter /dekaʃte/ [20] *vtr* to unseal

décade /dekad/ *nf* (a) 10-day period
(b) (controversial) decade

décadence /dekadɑ̃s/ *nf* decadence; decline

décadent, ~**e** /dekadɑ̃, ɑ̃t/ *adj*
(a) decadent
(b) in decline

décaféiné, ~**e** /dekafeine/ *adj* decaffeinated

décalage /dekalaʒ/ *nm* (a) gap
(b) discrepancy
(c) interval, time-lag
(d) shift
■ ~ **horaire** time difference

décalcomanie /dekalkɔmani/ *nf* transfer

décaler /dekale/ [1] **1** *vtr* (a) to bring forward ⟨*date, departure time*⟩
(b) to put (GB) *or* move (US) back ⟨*date, departure time*⟩
(c) to move [sth] forward ⟨*object*⟩
(d) to move [sth] back ⟨*object*⟩
2 **se décaler** *v refl* (+ *v être*) **se** ~ **sur la droite** to move *or* shift to the right

décalquer /dekalke/ [1] *vtr* (a) to trace (**sur** from)
(b) to transfer (**sur** onto)

décamper /dekɑ̃pe/ [1] *vi* (colloq) to run off

décanter /dekɑ̃te/ [1] **1** *vtr* to allow [sth] to settle ⟨*liquid*⟩; to clarify ⟨*waste water*⟩
2 **se décanter** *v refl* (+ *v être*) (a) ⟨*liquid*⟩ to settle
(b) ⟨*situation, ideas*⟩ to become clearer

décapant, ~**e** /dekapɑ̃, ɑ̃t/ *adj*
(a) scouring
(b) (colloq) ⟨*humour*⟩ abrasive, caustic

décaper /dekape/ [1] *vtr* (a) to clean
(b) to strip ⟨*furniture*⟩; ~ **avec un abrasif** to scour
(c) (colloq) ⟨*alcohol, soap*⟩ to be harsh

décapitation /dekapitasjɔ̃/ *nf* decapitation; beheading

décapiter /dekapite/ [1] *vtr* to behead; to
decapitate

décapotable /dekapɔtabl/ *adj* **une
(voiture)** ~ a convertible

décapsuler /dekapsyle/ [1] *vtr* to take
the top off

décapsuleur /dekapsylœR/ *nm* bottle-
opener

décathlon /dekatlɔ̃/ *nm* decathlon

décéder /desede/ [14] *vi* (+ *v être*) to die

décelable /deslabl/ *adj* detectable

déceler /desle/ [17] *vtr* **(a)** to detect
(b) to reveal ⟨*anomaly, feeling*⟩
(c) to indicate ⟨*presence*⟩

décembre /desɑ̃bR/ *nm* December

décemment /desamɑ̃/ *adv* decently

décence /desɑ̃s/ *nf* decency

décennie /deseni/ *nf* decade

décent, ~e /desɑ̃, ɑ̃t/ *adj* **(a)** decent
(b) proper

décentraliser /desɑ̃tralize/ [1] *vtr* to
decentralize

décentrer /desɑ̃tre/ [1] *vtr* to move away
from the centre (GB)

déception /desɛpsjɔ̃/ *nf* disappointment

décerner /deseRne/ [1] *vtr* to award

décès /desɛ/ *nm inv* death

décevant, ~e /desəvɑ̃, ɑ̃t/ *adj*
disappointing

décevoir /desəvwaR/ [5] *vtr* **(a)** to
disappoint
(b) to fail to fulfil (GB) ⟨*hope*⟩

déchaîné, ~e /deʃene/ ①*pp* ▸
DÉCHAÎNER
②*pp adj* stirred up; ~ **contre** furious with

déchaîner /deʃene/ [1] ①*vtr* to rouse
⟨*feelings*⟩; to excite ⟨*people*⟩
②**se déchaîner** *v refl* (+ *v être*) **(a)** ⟨*sea*⟩
to rage; ⟨*feelings*⟩ to burst out
(b) to go wild

déchanter /deʃɑ̃te/ [1] *vi* to become
disenchanted

décharge /deʃaRʒ/ *nf* **(a)** ⟨of firearm⟩
discharge
(b) ~ **municipale** (municipal) dump
(c) ~ **électrique** electric shock
(d) (Law) acquittal

décharger /deʃaRʒe/ [13] ①*vtr* **(a)** to
unload ⟨*vessel, goods*⟩
(b) to unload ⟨*firearm*⟩
(c) to fire ⟨*gun*⟩
(d) ~ **qn de** to relieve sb of ⟨*task*⟩
(e) to discharge ⟨*battery*⟩
(f) to unburden ⟨*conscience*⟩
②**se décharger** *v refl* (+ *v être*) **(a)** se ~
de qch to off-load sth
(b) ⟨*battery*⟩ to run down

décharné, ~e /deʃaRne/ *adj* ⟨*body*⟩
emaciated; ⟨*finger*⟩ bony

déchausser: se déchausser /deʃose/
[1] *v refl* (+ *v être*) **(a)** to take off one's shoes
(b) ⟨*teeth*⟩ to work loose due to receding
gums

dèche /dɛʃ/ *nf* (colloq) **être dans la** ~ to be
broke (colloq)

déchéance /deʃeɑ̃s/ *nf* **(a)** decline
(b) degeneration

déchet /deʃɛ/ ① *nm* **(a)** scrap
(b) waste
(c) wreck
② **déchets** *nm pl* waste material, waste;
~**s industriels** industrial waste; ~ **nucléaires**
nuclear waste

déchetterie /deʃɛtRi/ *nf* waste reception
centre (GB)

déchiffrer /deʃifRe/ [1] *vtr* **(a)** to decipher
(b) (Mus) to sight-read

déchiqueté, ~e /deʃikte/ ① *pp* ▸
DÉCHIQUETER
② *pp adj* jagged, ragged

déchiqueter /deʃikte/ [20] *vtr* **(a)** to tear
[sth] to shreds
(b) ⟨*machine, animal*⟩ to tear to pieces

déchirant, ~e /deʃiRɑ̃, ɑ̃t/ *adj* **(a)** heart-
rending
(b) agonizing

déchirer /deʃiRe/ [1] ① *vtr* **(a)** to tear up
⟨*paper, material*⟩
(b) to tear ⟨*garment*⟩
(c) to split ⟨*group*⟩; **déchiré entre X et Y** torn
between X and Y
② **se déchirer** *v refl* (+ *v être*) **(a)** to tear
(b) se ~ **un muscle** to tear a muscle
(c) to tear each other apart

déchirure /deʃiRyR/ *nf* (gen, Med) tear

déchoir /deʃwaR/ [51] *vi* to demean
oneself; ~ **de son rang** to come down in the
world

déchu, ~e /deʃy/ *adj* ① *pp* ▸ DÉCHOIR
② *adj* ⟨*monarch*⟩ deposed; ⟨*angel*⟩ fallen

décibel /desibɛl/ *nm* decibel

décidé, ~e /deside/ ① *pp* ▸ DÉCIDER
② *pp adj* determined; resolute

décidément /desidemɑ̃/ *adv* really

décider /deside/ [1] ① *vtr* **(a)** to decide;
c'est décidé it's settled
(b) to persuade (**à faire** to do)
② **décider de** *v+prep* to decide on; to fix
③ **se décider** *v refl* (+ *v être*) **(a)** to make
up one's mind
(b) se ~ **pour** to decide on

décideur /desidœR/ *nm* decision-maker

décimal, ~e[1], *mpl* **-aux** /desimal, o/
adj decimal

décimale[2] /desimal/ *nf* decimal

décimer /desime/ [1] *vtr* to decimate

décisif, -ive /desizif, iv/ *adj* **(a)** decisive
(b) conclusive

décision /desizjɔ̃/ *nf* **(a)** decision
(b) decisiveness

déclamer /deklame/ [1] *vtr* to declaim

déclaration /deklaRasjɔ̃/ *nf* **(a)** statement;
declaration
(b) notification
(c) (Law) statement; ~ **de vol/perte** report of
theft/loss
■ ~ **d'impôts** (income-)tax return

déclaré, **~e** /deklare/ adj ⟨enemy⟩ avowed; ⟨hatred⟩ professed

déclarer /deklare/ [1] **1** vtr (a) to declare; **il a été déclaré coupable** he was found guilty
(b) to declare ⟨goods, revenue⟩; to report ⟨theft⟩; to register ⟨birth⟩; **non déclaré** undeclared; illegal
2 se déclarer v refl (+ v être) (a) ⟨fire, epidemic⟩ to break out; ⟨fever⟩ to start
(b) **se ~ pour/contre** to come out for/against

déclenchement /deklɑ̃ʃmɑ̃/ nm (of mechanism) release; (of illness) onset; (of reaction) start

déclencher /deklɑ̃ʃe/ [1] **1** vtr (a) to spark (off) ⟨protest⟩; to cause ⟨reaction, explosion⟩; to start ⟨avalanche⟩
(b) to launch ⟨offensive⟩; to start ⟨strike, debate⟩
(c) to set off ⟨mechanism⟩
2 se déclencher v refl (+ v être) (a) to go off; to be activated
(b) to break out; to begin

déclic /deklik/ nm (a) trigger
(b) (of camera) click

déclin /deklɛ̃/ nm decline

déclinaison /deklinɛzɔ̃/ nf declension

décliner /dekline/ [1] **1** vtr (a) to decline; to turn [sth] down
(b) **~ son identité** to give one's name
(c) to decline
2 vi ⟨light, talent⟩ to fade; ⟨health⟩ to deteriorate; ⟨enthusiasm⟩ to wane; ⟨sun⟩ to go down
3 se décliner v refl (+ v être) to decline

décocher /dekɔʃe/ [1] vtr to shoot ⟨arrow⟩

décoder /dekɔde/ [1] vtr to decode

décodeur /dekɔdœr/ nm decoder

décoiffer /dekwafe/ [1] vtr **~ qn** to ruffle sb's hair ·

décoincer /dekwɛ̃se/ [12] vtr to unjam ⟨mechanism, door⟩; to free ⟨key⟩

décollage /dekɔlaʒ/ nm take-off

décoller /dekɔle/ [1] **1** vtr to peel off ⟨sticker⟩
2 vi ⟨plane⟩ to take off
3 se décoller v refl (+ v être) to come off

décolleté, **~e** /dekɔlte/ **1** adj low-cut
2 nm low neckline

décolleuse /dekɔløz/ nf steam stripper

décolonisation /dekɔlɔnizasjɔ̃/ nf decolonization

décolorant, **~e** /dekɔlɔrɑ̃, ɑ̃t/ adj bleaching

décolorer /dekɔlɔre/ [1] vtr (a) to bleach
(b) to cause to fade

décombres /dekɔ̃br/ nm pl rubble

décommander /dekɔmɑ̃de/ [1] **1** vtr to call [sth] off
2 se décommander v refl (+ v être) to cry off (GB), to beg off

décomposer /dekɔ̃poze/ [1] **1** vtr (a) to break down ⟨argument, water⟩
(b) to distort ⟨features⟩

2 se décomposer v refl (+ v être) (a) to decompose
(b) to fall apart

décomposition /dekɔ̃pozisjɔ̃/ nf
(a) decomposition
(b) disintegration

décompte /dekɔ̃t/ nm (a) discount
(b) count; **faire le ~ de** to count [sth] up ⟨votes, points⟩

décompter /dekɔ̃te/ [1] vtr (a) to deduct (de from)
(b) to count ⟨votes, points⟩

déconcentrer /dekɔ̃sɑ̃tre/ [1] vtr to distract

déconcertant, **~e** /dekɔ̃sɛrtɑ̃, ɑ̃t/ adj disconcerting; **d'une facilité ~e** ridiculously easy

déconcerter /dekɔ̃sɛrte/ [1] vtr to disconcert

déconfit, **~e** /dekɔ̃fi, it/ adj crestfallen

déconfiture /dekɔ̃fityr/ nf (a) (of person) failure; (of party, team) defeat
(b) (of company) collapse

décongeler /dekɔ̃ʒle/ [17] vtr, vi to defrost

décongestionner /dekɔ̃ʒɛstjɔne/ [1]
1 vtr (a) to ease the pressure on ⟨university, services⟩; ⟨motorway⟩ to relieve congestion in ⟨street, town⟩
(b) to clear ⟨nose⟩
2 se décongestionner v refl (+ v être) to clear

déconnecter /dekɔnɛkte/ [1] vtr (a) to disconnect ⟨appliance⟩
(b) to dissociate

déconner /dekɔne/ [1] vi (slang) (a) to kid around (colloq); **faut pas ~!** come off it! (colloq)
(b) to mess around (colloq); to piss around (GB) (slang)
(c) to play up (colloq)

déconseiller /dekɔ̃seje/ [1] vtr to advise against

déconsidérer /dekɔ̃sidere/ [14] **1** vtr to discredit
2 se déconsidérer v refl (+ v être) **tu t'es déconsidéré** it was unworthy of you

décontenancer /dekɔ̃tnɑ̃se/ [12] vtr to disconcert

décontracté, **~e** /dekɔ̃trakte/ **1** pp ▶ DÉCONTRACTER
2 pp adj (a) relaxed
(b) casual
(c) laid-back (colloq)

décontracter /dekɔ̃trakte/ [1] vtr, **se décontracter** v refl (+ v être) to relax

décontraction /dekɔ̃traksjɔ̃/ nf
(a) relaxation
(b) ease
(c) casual attitude

déconvenue /dekɔ̃vəny/ nf disappointment

décor /dekɔr/ nm (a) decor
(b) setting; **j'ai besoin de changer de ~** I need a change of scene; **partir dans le ~** (colloq) to drive off the road

(c) (of film) set; **tourné en** ~ **naturel** shot on location

décorateur, -trice /dekɔratœr, tris/ nm,f **(a)** interior decorator
(b) set designer

décoratif, -ive /dekɔratif, iv/ adj
(a) ornamental
(b) decorative

décoration /dekɔrasjɔ̃/ nf **(a)** decorating
(b) (gen, Mil) decoration
(c) interior design

décorer /dekɔre/ [1] vtr to decorate

décortiquer /dekɔrtike/ [1] vtr to shell ⟨nut⟩; to peel ⟨prawn⟩

décote /dekɔt/ nf (Econ) drop

découcher /dekuʃe/ [1] vi to spend the night away from home

découdre /dekudr/ [76] **1** vtr to undo, to unpick (GB) ⟨hem, seam⟩
2 vi **en** ~ **to** have a fight (**avec** with)

découler /dekule/ [1] vi **(a)** to follow (**de** from)
(b) to result (**de** from)

découpage /dekupaʒ/ nm cut-out

découper /dekupe/ [1] vtr to cut up ⟨tart⟩; to carve ⟨roast⟩; to divide up ⟨land⟩

découragé, ~e /dekuraʒe/ adj ⟨person⟩ disheartened; ⟨expression⟩ despondent; ⟨tone⟩ dejected

décourageant, ~e /dekuraʒɑ̃, ɑ̃t/ adj disheartening

découragement /dekuraʒmɑ̃/ nm discouragement, despondency

décourager /dekuraʒe/ [13] vtr **(a)** to dishearten
(b) to discourage
(c) to deter

décousu, ~e /dekuzy/ **1** pp ▶ DÉCOUDRE
2 pp adj ⟨hem⟩ which has come undone
3 adj ⟨story⟩ rambling; ⟨conversation⟩ casual

découvert, ~e[1] /dekuvɛr, ɛrt/ **1** pp ▶ DÉCOUVRIR
2 pp adj **(a)** bare; **avoir la tête** ~**e** to be bare-headed
(b) ⟨truck⟩ open; ⟨car⟩ open-topped
3 nm overdraft; **être à** ~ to be overdrawn

découverte[2] /dekuvɛrt/ nf discovery

découvrir /dekuvrir/ [32] **1** vtr **(a)** to discover; **faire** ~ **qch à qn** to introduce sb to sth
(b) to show ⟨arm, back⟩
(c) to leave [sth] exposed ⟨border⟩
2 se découvrir v refl (+ v être) **(a)** to remove one's hat
(b) **elle s'est découvert un talent** she found she had a talent

décrasser /dekrase/ vtr [1] to get [sb/sth] clean

décrépit, ~e /dekrepi, it/ adj ⟨person⟩ decrepit; ⟨building⟩ dilapidated; ⟨wall⟩ crumbling

décrépitude /dekrepityd/ nf degeneration; decay; decrepitude

décret /dekrɛ/ nm decree

décréter /dekrete/ [14] vtr **(a)** to order
(b) to decree (**que** that)
(c) to declare (**que** that)

décrire /dekrir/ [67] vtr **(a)** to describe
(b) to follow

décrocher /dekrɔʃe/ [1] **1** vtr **(a)** to take down ⟨picture⟩
(b) to uncouple ⟨wagon⟩
(c) ~ **son téléphone** to pick up the receiver; to take the phone off the hook
(d) (colloq) to get ⟨contract⟩
2 vi to give up
IDIOMS ~ **le gros lot** to hit the jackpot

décroissant, ~e /dekrwasɑ̃, ɑ̃t/ adj fading; lessening; **par** or **en ordre** ~ in descending order

décroître /dekrwɑtr/ [72] vi ⟨level⟩ to fall; ⟨moon⟩ to wane; ⟨day⟩ to get shorter; ⟨light, noise⟩ to fade; ⟨inflation⟩ to go down

décrypter /dekripte/ [1] vtr **(a)** to decipher ⟨signs⟩
(b) to interpret ⟨statement⟩

déçu, ~e /desy/ ▶ DÉCEVOIR

déculpabiliser /dekylpabilize/ [1] vtr to free [sb] of guilt

décupler /dekyple/ [1] vtr, vi to increase tenfold

dédaigner /dedeɲe/ [1] vtr to despise

dédaigneux, -euse /dedɛɲø, øz/ adj disdainful, scornful; **être** ~ **du danger** to be unmindful of danger

dédain /dedɛ̃/ nm contempt, disdain

dédale /dedal/ nm **(a)** (of buildings) maze
(b) (of laws, formalities) labyrinth

dedans /dədɑ̃/ **1** adv inside
2 en dedans phr inside

dédicace /dedikas/ nf **(a)** dedication (**à qn** to sb)
(b) inscription

dédicacer /dedikase/ [12] vtr **(a)** to dedicate ⟨book⟩ (**à** to)
(b) to sign ⟨book, photo⟩

dédier /dedje/ [2] vtr **(a)** to dedicate ⟨novel⟩ (**à** to)
(b) to devote ⟨life⟩ (**à** to)

dédire: se dédire /dedir/ [65] v refl (+ v être) to back out

dédommagement /dedɔmaʒmɑ̃/ nm compensation

dédommager /dedɔmaʒe/ [13] vtr **(a)** to compensate
(b) ~ **qn de qch** to make it up to sb for sth

dédouaner /dedwane/ [1] vtr to clear through customs

dédoubler: se dédoubler /deduble/ [1] v refl (+ v être) ⟨nail⟩ to split; ⟨image⟩ to split in two; ⟨cable⟩ to come apart

dédramatiser /dedramatize/ [1] vi to play things down

déductible /dedyktibl/ adj deductible (**de** from); ~ **des impôts** tax-deductible

déduction /dedyksjɔ̃/ nf deduction

déduire /dedɥiʀ/ [69] **1** *vtr* **(a)** to deduce
(b) to infer
(c) to deduct
2 se déduire *v refl* (+ *v être*) **(a)** to be
inferred
(b) to be deduced
(c) to be deducted

déesse /dees/ *nf* goddess

défaillance /defajɑ̃s/ *nf* failure

défaillant, ~e /defajɑ̃, ɑ̃t/ *adj* **(a)** ⟨*motor,
system*⟩ faulty
(b) ⟨*organization*⟩ inefficient
(c) ⟨*health, memory*⟩ failing; ⟨*person*⟩
fainting

défaillir /defajiʀ/ [28] *vi* **(a)** to faint; **se
sentir ~** to feel faint
(b) ⟨*health, memory*⟩ to fail; **soutenir qn sans
~** to show unflinching support for sb

défaire /defɛʀ/ [10] **1** *vtr* to undo; to untie
2 se défaire *v refl* (+ *v être*) **(a)** to come
undone
(b) se ~ de to get rid of; to part with; to rid
oneself of
(c) ⟨*face*⟩ to fall; **avoir la mine défaite** to look
haggard

défaite /defɛt/ *nf* defeat

défaut /defo/ **1** *nm* **(a)** fault, failing;
prendre qn en ~ to catch sb out
(b) defect; flaw; **présenter des ~s** to be
faulty; **~ de fabrication** manufacturing fault;
~ de prononciation speech impediment
(c) shortage; **faire ~** ⟨*money, resources*⟩ to be
lacking
2 à défaut de *phr* **à ~ de** (**quoi**) failing
(which); **à ~ de pouvoir acheter, elle loue**
since she can't buy, she has to rent

défaveur /defavœʀ/ *nf* **il s'est trompé de
30 francs en ma ~** he overcharged me by 30
francs

défavorable /defavɔʀabl/ *adj* ⟨*situation*⟩
unfavourable (GB) (**à** to); ⟨*person*⟩ opposed
(**à** to)

défavorisé, ~e /defavɔʀize/ *adj*
(a) underprivileged
(b) disadvantaged

défavoriser /defavɔʀize/ [1] *vtr* **(a)** to
discriminate against
(b) to put [sb] at a disadvantage

défection /defɛksjɔ̃/ *nf* **(a)** defection
(b) non-appearance
(c) (of friends) desertion

défectueux, -euse /defɛktɥø, øz/ *adj*
⟨*material*⟩ faulty, defective; ⟨*reasoning*⟩
flawed

défendre /defɑ̃dʀ/ [6] **1** *vtr* **(a) ~ à qn de
faire** to forbid sb to do
(b) to defend ⟨*person, country, interests*⟩
(c) to fight for ⟨*right*⟩; to stand up for
⟨*friend, principle*⟩; **~ une cause** to champion
a cause
(d) (Law, Sport) to defend
2 se défendre *v refl* (+ *v être*) **(a)** to
defend oneself; to stand up for oneself
(b) to be tenable
(c) to protect oneself

(d) (colloq) to get by
(e) on ne peut se ~ de penser que... one
can't help thinking that...

défense /defɑ̃s/ *nf* **(a)** '**~ de fumer**' 'no
smoking'; **~ d'en parler devant lui** don't
mention it in front of him
(b) (Med, Mil, Sport) defence (GB)
(c) protection; **sans ~** helpless; unprotected;
la ~ de l'environnement the protection of the
environment; **prendre la ~ de** to stand up
for
(d) (Zool) tusk

défenseur /defɑ̃sœʀ/ *nm* defender

défensive /defɑ̃siv/ *nf* **sur la ~** on the
defensive

déférence /defeʀɑ̃s/ *nf* **marques de ~**
marks of respect

déferler /defɛʀle/ [1] *vi* **(a)** ⟨*wave*⟩ to break
(**sur** on)
(b) ⟨*violence*⟩ to erupt
(c) ~ sur ⟨*people*⟩ to pour into ⟨*country,
town*⟩

défi /defi/ *nm* **(a)** challenge; **mettre qn au ~
de faire** to challenge sb to do
(b) air de ~ defiant look

défiance /defjɑ̃s/ *nf* distrust, mistrust

défiant, ~e /defjɑ̃, ɑ̃t/ *adj* distrustful,
wary

déficience /defisjɑ̃s/ *nf* deficiency

déficit /defisit/ *nm* **(a)** deficit
(b) (Med) deficiency

déficitaire /defisitɛʀ/ *adj* showing a
deficit; showing a loss; showing a shortfall

défier /defje/ [2] *vtr* **(a)** to challenge ⟨*rival*⟩
(b) to defy ⟨*danger, death*⟩; **prix défiant toute
concurrence** unbeatable price

défigurer /defigyʀe/ [1] *vtr* to disfigure

défilé /defile/ *nm* **(a)** parade
(b) (protest) march
(c) (of visitors, candidates) stream
(d) gorge
■ **~ aérien** flypast (GB), flyover (US);
~ militaire march-past; **~ de mode** fashion
show

défiler /defile/ [1] **1** *vi* **(a)** to parade;
⟨*protesters*⟩ to march
(b) ⟨*people*⟩ to come and go
(c) ⟨*images, landscape*⟩ to unfold
(d) (Comput) to scroll
2 se défiler *v refl* (+ *v être*) (colloq) to
wriggle out of it

définir /definiʀ/ [3] *vtr* to define

définitif, -ive /definitif, iv/ **1** *adj*
⟨*accounts, report*⟩ final; ⟨*edition*⟩ definitive;
⟨*refusal*⟩ flat
2 en définitive *phr* at the end of the day

définition /definisjɔ̃/ *nf* definition

définitivement /definitivmɑ̃/ *adv* for
good

défiscalisé, ~e /defiskalize/ *adj* tax-
exempt

déflagration /deflagʀasjɔ̃/ *nf* detonation

défoncer /defɔ̃se/ [12] *vtr* to break down
⟨*door*⟩; to smash in ⟨*back of a car*⟩

déformation /defɔʀmasjɔ̃/ *nf*
(a) distortion
(b) deformity
(c) c'est de la ~ **professionnelle** it's a habit that comes from the job

déformé, **~e** /defɔʀme/ *adj* ⟨*face, image, truth*⟩ distorted; ⟨*object, mind*⟩ warped; **chaussée ~e** uneven (road) surface

déformer /defɔʀme/ [1] **1** *vtr* (a) to bend [sth] (out of shape)
(b) to distort
(c) **on a déformé mes propos** my words have been twisted
2 se déformer *v refl* (+ *v être*) to lose its shape

défoulement /defulmɑ̃/ *nm* letting off steam

défouler /defule/ [1] **1** *vtr* **ça me défoule** it helps me (to) unwind
2 se défouler *v refl* (+ *v être*) (a) to let off steam
(b) **se ~ sur qn** to take it out on sb

défraîchi, **~e** /defʀeʃi/ *adj* ⟨*garment, curtain*⟩ worn; ⟨*material, beauty*⟩ faded

défrayer /defʀeje/ [21] *vtr* (a) **~ la chronique** to be the talk of the town
(b) **~ qn** to pay *or* meet sb's expenses

défricher /defʀiʃe/ [1] *vtr* to clear, to reclaim

défriser /defʀize/ [1] *vtr* to straighten

défroisser /defʀwase/ [1] *vtr* to smooth out

défunt, **~e** /defœ̃, œ̃t/ **1** *adj* (a) former
(b) late
2 *nm,f* **le ~** the deceased

dégagé, **~e** /degaʒe/ *adj* (a) ⟨*road, sky*⟩ clear; ⟨*forehead*⟩ bare
(b) ⟨*look*⟩ casual

dégagement /degaʒmɑ̃/ *nm* (a) clearing
(b) (in football) clearance

dégager /degaʒe/ [13] **1** *vtr* (a) to free; **~ qn d'une responsabilité** to relieve sb of a responsibility; **~ des crédits** to make funds available
(b) to unblock ⟨*nose*⟩
(c) to clear ⟨*way*⟩; **'dégagez, s'il vous plaît'** 'move along please'; **dégage!** (colloq) get lost! (colloq)
(d) to find ⟨*idea, sense*⟩
(e) to emit ⟨*odour, gas*⟩; **~ de la chaleur** to give off heat
2 se dégager *v refl* (+ *v être*) (a) to free oneself/itself
(b) ⟨*weather, sky*⟩ to clear
(c) **se ~ de** to come out of
(d) to become clear

dégaine /degɛn/ *nf* (colloq) odd appearance

dégainer /degene/ [1] *vtr* to draw ⟨*gun*⟩

dégarnir: se dégarnir /degaʀniʀ/ [3] *v refl* (+ *v être*) to be going bald

dégât /dega/ *nm* damage

dégel /deʒɛl/ *nm* thaw

dégeler /deʒle/ [17] **1** *vtr* (a) to improve ⟨*relations*⟩

(b) to unfreeze ⟨*credit*⟩
2 *vi* to thaw (out)
3 se dégeler *v refl* (+ *v être*)
(a) ⟨*relations, situation*⟩ to thaw
(b) ⟨*audience*⟩ to warm up

dégénérer /deʒeneʀe/ [14] *vi* (a) ⟨*incident*⟩ to get out of hand; **~ en** to degenerate into
(b) ⟨*plant, species*⟩ to degenerate

dégingandé, **~e** /deʒɛ̃gɑ̃de/ *adj* lanky

dégivrer /deʒivʀe/ [1] *vtr* (a) to de-ice ⟨*windscreen*⟩
(b) to defrost ⟨*fridge*⟩

déglingué, **~e** /deglɛ̃ge/ *adj* (colloq) dilapidated

déglutir /deglytiʀ/ [3] *vtr, vi* to swallow

dégonflé, **~e** /degɔ̃fle/ **1** *adj* ⟨*balloon*⟩ deflated; ⟨*tyre*⟩ flat
2 *nm,f* (colloq) chicken (colloq), coward

dégonfler /degɔ̃fle/ [1] **1** *vtr* to deflate ⟨*tyre*⟩
2 *vi* ⟨*swelling, bump*⟩ to go down
3 se dégonfler *v refl* (+ *v être*) (a) to deflate; to go down
(b) (colloq) to chicken out (colloq)

dégot(t)er /degɔte/ [1] *vtr* (colloq) to find

dégouliner /deguline/ [1] *vi* (a) to trickle
(b) to drip (**de** with)

dégoupiller /degupije/ [1] *vtr* **~ une grenade** to pull the pin out of a grenade

dégourdi, **~e** /deguʀdi/ *adj* smart

dégourdir: se dégourdir /deguʀdiʀ/ [3] *v refl* (+ *v être*) **se ~ les jambes** to stretch one's legs

dégoût /degu/ *nm* disgust

dégoûtant, **~e** /degutɑ̃, ɑ̃t/ *adj* (a) filthy
(b) (colloq) disgusting; revolting

dégoûté, **~e** /degute/ *adj* disgusted; **faire le ~** to turn one's nose up

dégoûter /degute/ [1] *vtr* (a) to disgust
(b) to make [sb] feel sick
(c) **~ qn de qch/de faire** to put sb off sth/off doing

dégradant, **~e** /degʀadɑ̃, ɑ̃t/ *adj* degrading

dégradation /degʀadasjɔ̃/ *nf* (a) damage
(b) deterioration
(c) decline; **la ~ des conditions de vie** the deterioration in the standard of living; **la ~ du pouvoir d'achat** the erosion in purchasing power

dégradé, **~e** /degʀade/ **1** *adj* **tons ~s** shaded tones; **coupe ~e** layered cut
2 *nm* (in colours) gradation

dégrader /degʀade/ [1] **1** *vtr* (a) to damage
(b) (Mil) to cashier ⟨*officer*⟩
(c) to degrade ⟨*person*⟩
2 se dégrader *v refl* (+ *v être*) to deteriorate

dégrafer /degʀafe/ [1] **1** *vtr* to undo
2 se dégrafer *v refl* (+ *v être*) to come undone

dégraisser /degʀese/ [1] *vtr* to trim the fat off

degré /dəgʀe/ *nm* (a) degree; **par ~s**
gradually; **à un moindre ~** to a lesser extent;
susceptible au plus haut ~ extremely
touchy; **brûlures du premier ~** first-degree
burns; **~ de parenté** degree of kinship
(b) step; **enseignement du second ~**
secondary education; **c'est à prendre au
deuxième ~** it is not to be taken literally
(c) **titrer 40° d'alcool** ≈ to be 70% proof
■ **~ Celsius** degree Celsius; **~ Fahrenheit**
degree Fahrenheit

dégressif, -ive /degʀesif, iv/ *adj* ⟨*tax*⟩
graduated; **tarifs ~s** tapering charges

dégringolade /degʀɛ̃gɔlad/ *nf* (colloq)
(a) (gen) fall
(b) (Econ) collapse

dégringoler (colloq) /degʀɛ̃gɔle/ [1] **1** *vtr*
to race down ⟨*stairs, hill*⟩
2 *vi* (a) ⟨*person*⟩ to take a tumble; ⟨*books*⟩
to tumble down
(b) to drop sharply

dégriser /degʀize/ [1] *vtr* (a) to sober [sb]
up
(b) to bring [sb] to his/her senses

déguerpir /degɛʀpiʀ/ [3] *vi* to leave

déguisé, ~e /degize/ *adj* (a) in fancy
dress; in disguise
(b) ⟨*party*⟩ fancy-dress
(c) ⟨*attempt*⟩ concealed; ⟨*compliment*⟩
disguised

déguisement /degizmɑ̃/ *nm* costume

déguiser /degize/ [1] **1** *vtr* (a) to dress
[sb] up (en as)
(b) to disguise
2 **se déguiser** *v refl* (+ *v être*) (a) to dress
up
(b) to disguise oneself

dégustation /degystasjɔ̃/ *nf* tasting

déguster /degyste/ [1] *vtr* to savour (GB)
⟨*drink, victory*⟩; to enjoy ⟨*performance*⟩

déhanchement /deɑ̃ʃmɑ̃/ *nm* (a) swaying
hips
(b) lopsidedness

déhancher: se déhancher /deɑ̃ʃe/ [1]
v refl (+ *v être*) to wiggle one's hips

dehors /dəɔʀ/ **1** *adv* outside; **mettre qn ~**
to throw sb out; to fire sb; to expel sb
2 *excl* get out!
3 **en dehors de** *phr* (a) outside
(b) apart from

déjà /deʒa/ *adv* (a) already
(b) before, already; **je te l'ai ~ dit** I've told
you before
(c) (colloq) **il s'est excusé, c'est ~ quelque
chose** he apologized, that's something at
least; **elle est ~ assez riche!** she's rich
enough as it is; **c'est combien, ~?** how
much was it again?

déjà-vu /deʒavy/ *nm inv* déjà vu; **c'est du
~** (colloq) we've seen it all before

déjeuner¹ /deʒœne/ [1] *vi* to have lunch

déjeuner² /deʒœne/ *nm* lunch

déjouer /deʒwe/ [1] *vtr* to frustrate
⟨*precaution, manoeuvre*⟩; to foil ⟨*plan*⟩; to
evade ⟨*inspection*⟩

delà /dəla/ *adv* **deçà** *or* **de-ci, ~** here and
there

délabré, ~e /delabʀe/ *adj* ⟨*house,
equipment*⟩ dilapidated; ⟨*health*⟩ damaged

délabrement /delabʀəmɑ̃/ *nm*
dilapidation

délabrer /delabʀe/ [1] **1** *vtr* to ruin
2 **se délabrer** *v refl* (+ *v être*) ⟨*house*⟩ to
become run-down; ⟨*business, country*⟩ to go
to rack and ruin; ⟨*health*⟩ to deteriorate

délacer /delase/ [12] *vtr* to undo; to unlace

délai /delɛ/ *nm* (a) **dans un ~ de 24 heures**
within 24 hours; **respecter un ~** to meet a
deadline; **dans les meilleurs ~s** as soon as
possible
(b) extension; **demander un ~** to ask for
extra time
■ **~ de livraison** delivery *or* lead time

délaisser /delese/ [1] *vtr* (a) to abandon
⟨*activity*⟩
(b) to neglect ⟨*friends*⟩

délassement /delasmɑ̃/ *nm* relaxation

délasser /delase/ [1] *vtr, v refl* (+ *v être*) to
relax; **ça délasse** it's relaxing

délateur, -trice /delatœʀ, tʀis/ *nm,f*
informer

délation /delasjɔ̃/ *nf* informing

délavé, ~e /delave/ *adj* (a) ⟨*colour, sky*⟩
washed-out; ⟨*jeans*⟩ faded
(b) waterlogged

délayer /deleje/ [21] *vtr* to thin ⟨*paint*⟩; to
mix ⟨*flour*⟩

délectation /delɛktasjɔ̃/ *nf* delight

délecter: se délecter /delɛkte/ [1] *v refl*
(+ *v être*) **se ~ à faire/en faisant** to delight in
doing

délégation /delegasjɔ̃/ *nf* delegation

délégué, ~e /delege/ *nm,f* delegate
■ **~ syndical** union representative

déléguer /delege/ [14] *vtr* (a) to appoint
[sb] as a delegate
(b) to delegate ⟨*responsibility, power*⟩

délester /deleste/ [1] *vtr* (a) to get rid of
the ballast from
(b) to divert traffic away from

délibération /deliberasjɔ̃/ *nf* deliberation;
mettre qch en ~ to debate sth

délibéré, ~e /delibeʀe/ *adj* ⟨*act,
violation*⟩ deliberate; ⟨*choice, policy*⟩
conscious

délibérément /deliberemɑ̃/ *adv* ⟨*wound,
provoke*⟩ deliberately; ⟨*accept, choose*⟩
consciously

délibérer /delibeʀe/ [14] **1** **délibérer de**
or **sur** *v+prep* to discuss
2 *vi* to be in session

délicat, ~e /delika, at/ *adj* (a) ⟨*dish*⟩
subtle; ⟨*person*⟩ refined
(b) tactful
(c) thoughtful; **des procédés peu ~s**
unscrupulous means
(d) ⟨*balance, task*⟩ delicate; ⟨*business,
moment*⟩ sensitive; ⟨*mission*⟩ tricky
(e) ⟨*skin*⟩ delicate

délicatement /delikatmã/ *adv*
(a) delicately
(b) tactfully

délicatesse /delikatɛs/ *nf* (a) delicacy; **la**
~ **de ses traits** his/her fine features
(b) sensitivity
(c) delicacy, trickiness

délice /delis/ *nm* delight

délicieusement /delisjøzmã/ *adv*
(a) deliciously
(b) delightfully

délicieux, -ieuse /delisjø, øz/ *adj*
(a) delicious
(b) ⟨*feeling, music*⟩ delightful; ⟨*joy*⟩ exquisite

délié, ~e /delje/ *adj* (a) ⟨*waist*⟩ slender
(b) ⟨*movement*⟩ loose
(c) ⟨*mind*⟩ nimble

délier /delje/ [2] *vtr* to untie; ~ **qn de** to
release sb from ⟨*promise*⟩
IDIOMS ~ **la langue à qn** to loosen sb's
tongue

délimiter /delimite/ [1] *vtr* (a) to mark
the boundary of
(b) to form the boundary of
(c) to define ⟨*role*⟩; to define the scope of
⟨*subject*⟩

délinquance /delɛ̃kãs/ *nf* crime; **la** ~
juvénile juvenile delinquency

délinquant, ~e /delɛ̃kã, ãt/ ①️ *adj*
delinquent
②️ *nm,f* offender

déliquescence /delikesãs/ *nf* decline

délirant, ~e /delirã, ãt/ *adj* (a) ⟨*welcome*⟩
ecstatic
(b) (colloq) ⟨*scenario*⟩ crazy (colloq)

délire /delir/ *nm* (a) (Med) delirium
(b) (colloq) madness
(c) frenzy; **salle en** ~ ecstatic audience

délirer /delire/ [1] *vi* (a) (Med) to be
delirious
(b) (colloq) to be mad

délit /deli/ *nm* offence (GB).
■ ~ **de fuite** hit-and-run offence; ~ **d'initié**
insider dealing

délivrance /delivrãs/ *nf* relief

délivrer /delivre/ [1] *vtr* (a) to free, to
liberate; ~ **qn de** to relieve sb of
(b) to issue ⟨*passport*⟩

délocalisation /delɔkalizasjɔ̃/ *nf*
relocation

déloger /delɔʒe/ [13] *vtr* (a) to evict
⟨*tenant*⟩
(b) to flush out ⟨*rebels, game*⟩
(c) to remove ⟨*dust*⟩

déloyal, ~e, *mpl* **-aux** /delwajal, o/ *adj*
⟨*person*⟩ disloyal; ⟨*competition*⟩ unfair

deltaplane /deltaplan/ *nm* hang-glider

déluge /delyʒ/ *nm* downpour; ~ **de** flood
of ⟨*tears, complaints*⟩; **le Déluge** the Flood
IDIOMS **après moi le** ~ I don't care what
happens after I'm gone

déluré, ~e /delyre/ *adj* (a) smart,
resourceful
(b) forward

démagogie /demagɔʒi/ *nf* demaguery,
demagogy; **faire de la** ~ to try to gain
popularity

démagogique /demagɔʒik/ *adj*
demagogic

demain /dəmɛ̃/ *adv* tomorrow; **l'Europe de**
~ the Europe of the future
IDIOMS ~ **il fera jour** tomorrow is another
day; **ce n'est pas** ~ **la veille!** that's not going
to happen in a hurry!

démancher: se démancher /demãʃe/
[1] *v refl* (+ *v être*) ⟨*tool*⟩ to come off its
handle

demande /dəmãd/ *nf* (a) request,
application, claim (de for); ~ **de dommages**
et intérêts claim for damages; **faire une** ~ **de**
mutation to apply for a transfer
(b) (in economics) demand
(c) application form
■ ~ **d'emploi** job application; '~**s d'emploi'**
'situations wanted'; ~ **en mariage** marriage
proposal

demandé, ~e /dəmãde/ *adj* **très** ~
⟨*destination*⟩ very popular; ⟨*product*⟩ in
great demand

demander /dəmãde/ [1] ①️ *vtr* (a) to ask
for ⟨*advice, money, help*⟩; to apply for
⟨*nationality*⟩; to claim ⟨*damages*⟩; ~ **le**
divorce to sue for divorce; ~ **en mariage** to
propose to; **'on demande un plombier'**
'plumber wanted'; **fais ce qu'on te demande!**
do as you're told!; **je ne demande pas mieux**
there's nothing I would like better
(b) ~ **qch à qn** to ask sb sth; **il m'a demandé**
de tes nouvelles he asked after you
(c) to send for ⟨*priest*⟩; to dial ⟨*number*⟩; **le**
patron vous demande the boss wants to see
you
(d) to call for ⟨*reforms*⟩; to require ⟨*effort,*
qualification⟩; to need ⟨*attention*⟩
②️ **se demander** *v refl* (+ *v être*) to
wonder

demandeur¹, -euse /dəmãdœr, øz/
nm,f applicant.
■ ~ **d'asile** asylum-seeker; ~ **d'emploi** job-
seeker

demandeur², -eresse /dəmãdœr,
d(ə)rɛs/ *nm,f* (Law) plaintiff

démangeaison /demãʒɛzɔ̃/ *nf* itch

démanger /demãʒe/ [13] *vtr* **ça me**
démange it itches, it's itching; **l'envie de le**
gifler me démangeait I was itching to slap
him

démanteler /demãtle/ [17] *vtr* to
dismantle; to break up

démaquillage /demakijaʒ/ *nm* make-up
removal

démaquillant, ~e /demakijã, ãt/ ①️ *adj*
⟨*milk*⟩ cleansing
②️ *nm* make-up remover

démaquiller: se démaquiller
/demakije/ [1] *v refl* (+ *v être*) to remove
one's make-up

démarcation /demarkasjɔ̃/ *nf*
demarcation

démarchage /demaʀʃaʒ/ nm door-to-door selling; ~ **électoral** canvassing; ~ **téléphonique** cold calling

démarche /demaʀʃ/ nf **(a)** walk **(b)** step; **faire une** ~ **auprès de qn to** approach sb; **faire des** ~**s pour obtenir qch** to take steps to obtain sth **(c)** reasoning; ~ **de la pensée** thought process

démarcher /demaʀʃe/ [1] vtr **(a)** to sell door-to-door **(b)** to canvass

démarque /demaʀk/ nf (of goods) mark-down (de of)

démarquer /demaʀke/ [1] **1** vtr to mark down ⟨goods⟩ **2** se **démarquer** v refl (+ v être) **(a)** se ~ **de** to distance oneself from **(b)** (Sport) to get free of one's marker

démarrage /demaʀaʒ/ nm **(a)** starting up **(b)** spurt ■ ~ **en côte** hill start

démarrer /demaʀe/ [1] **1** vtr to start (up) **2** vi **(a)** ⟨vehicle⟩ to pull away; ⟨engine⟩ to start; ⟨driver⟩ to drive off; ⟨business⟩ to start up; ⟨campaign⟩ to get under way; ⟨person⟩ to start off **(b)** (Sport) to put on a spurt

démarreur /demaʀœʀ/ nm (in car) starter

démasquer /demaske/ [1] vtr to unmask ⟨person⟩; to uncover ⟨plot⟩

démazouter /demazute/ [1] vtr to clean the oil from ⟨beach⟩

démêlé /demele/ nm wrangle; **avoir des** ~**s avec la justice** to get into trouble with the law

démêler /demele/ [1] vtr **(a)** to disentangle; to untangle **(b)** to sort out ⟨situation⟩

démembrement /demɑ̃bʀəmɑ̃/ nm **(a)** break-up, dismemberment **(b)** (of estate) division

démembrer /demɑ̃bʀe/ [1] vtr to divide up, to dismember

déménagement /demenaʒmɑ̃/ nm **(a)** moving house; move **(b)** removal; **entreprise de** ~**s** removals firm (GB), moving company (US)

déménager /demenaʒe/ [13] **1** vtr **(a)** to move ⟨furniture⟩; to relocate ⟨offices⟩ **(b)** to clear ⟨room⟩ **2** vi **(a)** to move (house) **(b)** (colloq) to push off (colloq) **(c)** (colloq) to be off one's rocker (colloq)

déménageur /demenaʒœʀ/ nm removal (GB) or moving (US) man

démence /demɑ̃s/ nf **(a)** insanity **(b)** dementia

démener: se démener /dem(ə)ne/ [16] v refl (+ v être) **(a)** to thrash about **(b)** to put oneself out, to exert oneself

dément, ~**e** /demɑ̃, ɑ̃t/ adj **(a)** insane, mad **(b)** (colloq) terrific (colloq)

démenti /demɑ̃ti/ nm denial

démentiel, -ielle /demɑ̃sjɛl/ adj insane

démentir /demɑ̃tiʀ/ [30] vtr **(a)** to deny **(b)** ⟨person⟩ to refute ⟨statement⟩; ⟨fact⟩ to give the lie to ⟨statement⟩; to belie ⟨appearance⟩

démesure /deməzyʀ/ nf **(a)** (of ambition) excesses **(b)** excessive size

démesuré, ~**e** /deməzyʀe/ adj excessive, immoderate

démettre /demɛtʀ/ [60] **1** vtr **(a)** to dislocate ⟨joint⟩ **(b)** to dismiss ⟨employee⟩ **2** se **démettre** v refl (+ v être) se ~ **l'épaule** to dislocate one's shoulder

demeurant: au demeurant /odəmœʀɑ̃/ phr as it happens, for all that

demeure /dəmœʀ/ **1** nf **(a)** residence **(b)** **mettre qn en** ~ **de faire** to require sb to do **2** **à demeure** phr permanently; permanent IDIOMS **il n'y a pas péril en la** ~ there's no rush

demeuré, ~**e** /dəmœʀe/ adj retarded

demeurer /dəmœʀe/ [1] **1** vi **(a)** (+ v avoir) to reside, to live **(b)** (+ v être) to remain **2** v impers **il n'en demeure pas moins que** nonetheless, the fact remains that

demi, ~**e**[1] /d(ə)mi/ **1** **et demi, et demie** phr and a half; **il est trois heures et** ~**e** it's half past three **2** nm,f half **3** nm **(a)** glass of beer **(b)** (Sport) ~ **de mêlée/d'ouverture** scrum/stand-off half **4** **à demi** phr half; **à** ~ **éveillé** half awake **5** **demi-** (combining form) **(a)** half; **une** ~-**pomme** half an apple **(b)** partial; **une** ~-**victoire** a partial victory

demi-cercle, pl ~**s** /d(ə)misɛʀkl/ nm semicircle

demie[2] /d(ə)mi/ **1** adj ▶ DEMI 1,2 **2** nf **il est déjà la** ~ it's already half past

demi-écrémé, ~**e,** mpl ~**s** /d(ə)miekʀeme/ adj semi-skimmed

demi-finale, pl ~**s** /d(ə)mifinal/ nf semifinal

demi-fond, pl ~**s** /d(ə)mifɔ̃/ nm middle-distance running

demi-frère, pl ~**s** /d(ə)mifʀɛʀ/ nm half-brother; stepbrother

demi-gros /d(ə)migʀo/ nm inv wholesale direct to the public

demi-heure, pl ~**s** /d(ə)mijœʀ/ nf half an hour

demi-journée, pl ~**s** /d(ə)miʒuʀne/ nf half a day; **à la** ~ on a half-day basis

démilitariser /demilitaʀize/ [1] vtr to demilitarize

demi-litre, pl ~**s** /d(ə)militʀ/ nm half a litre (GB)

demi-mesure, pl ~**s** /d(ə)mim(ə)zyʀ/ nf
half-measure

demi-mot: à demi-mot /ad(ə)mimo/ phr
j'ai compris à ~ I didn't need to have it
spelt out

déminer /demine/ [1] vtr to clear [sth] of
mines

demi-pension /d(ə)mipɑ̃sjɔ̃/ nf half
board

demi-pensionnaire, pl ~**s**
/d(ə)mipɑ̃sjɔnɛʀ/ nmf (Sch) pupil who has
school lunches

démis, ~**e** /demi, iz/ 1 pp ▶ DÉMETTRE
2 pp adj dislocated

demi-sel /d(ə)misɛl/ adj ⟨butter⟩ slightly
salted

demi-sœur, pl ~**s** /d(ə)misœʀ/ nf half-
sister; stepsister

démission /demisjɔ̃/ nf **(a)** resignation
(de from)
(b) (figurative) failure to take responsibility

démissionner /demisjɔne/ [1] vi **(a)** to
resign (de from)
(b) to abdicate one's responsibilities

demi-tarif, pl ~**s** /d(ə)mitaʀif/ 1 adj
half-price
2 adv half-price
3 nm half-price ticket

demi-tour, pl ~**s** /d(ə)mituʀ/ nm half-
turn; **faire** ~ to turn back

démobiliser /demɔbilize/ [1] vtr **(a)** to
demobilize
(b) to demotivate

démocrate /demɔkʀat/ 1 adj democratic
2 nmf democrat

démocratie /demɔkʀasi/ nf democracy

démocratique /demɔkʀatik/ adj
democratic

démocratiser: se démocratiser
/demɔkʀatize/ [1] v refl (+ v être) **(a)** to
become more democratic
(b) to become more accessible

démodé, ~**e** /demɔde/ adj old-fashioned

démoder: se démoder /demɔde/ [1]
v refl (+ v être) to go out of fashion

démographie /demɔgʀafi/ nf
demography

démographique /demɔgʀafik/ adj
demographic

demoiselle /d(ə)mwazɛl/ nf **(a)** young
lady
(b) single woman
■ ~ **d'honneur** bridesmaid

démolir /demɔliʀ/ [3] vtr to demolish; to
wreck; to destroy

démolition /demɔlisjɔ̃/ nf demolition

démon /demɔ̃/ nm demon, devil
■ ~ **de midi** ≈ middle-age lust

démoniaque /demɔnjak/ adj demonic

démonstrateur, -trice /demɔ̃stʀatœʀ,
tʀis/ nm,f (for products) demonstrator

démonstratif, -ive /demɔ̃stʀatif, iv/ adj
demonstrative

démonstration /demɔ̃stʀasjɔ̃/ nf
(a) display; ~ **de courage** display of
courage; ~**s d'amitié** a show of friendship
(b) demonstration
(c) (of theory) demonstration, proof

démontable /demɔ̃tabl/ adj ⟨furniture⟩
that can be taken apart

démonté, ~**e** /demɔ̃te/ adj ⟨sea⟩ stormy

démonte-pneu, pl ~**s** /demɔ̃t(ə)pnø/
nm tyre-lever (GB), tire iron (US)

démonter /demɔ̃te/ [1] 1 vtr **(a)** to
dismantle, to take [sth] to pieces ⟨machine⟩;
to remove ⟨wheel⟩
(b) (colloq) to fluster; **ne pas se laisser** ~ to
remain unruffled
2 **se démonter** v refl (+ v être)
(a) ⟨furniture⟩ to come apart
(b) (colloq) ⟨person⟩ to become flustered

démontrer /demɔ̃tʀe/ [1] vtr to
demonstrate, to prove

démoralisant, ~**e** /demɔʀalizɑ̃, ɑ̃t/ adj
demoralizing

démoraliser /demɔʀalize/ [1] vtr to
demoralize

démordre /demɔʀdʀ/ [6] v+prep **il n'en
démord pas** he sticks by it, he's sticking to
it

démotiver /demɔtive/ vtr to demotivate

démouler /demule/ [1] vtr to turn [sth]
out of the tin (GB) or pan (US) ⟨cake⟩; to
remove [sth] from the mould (GB) or mold
(US) ⟨statue⟩

démultiplier /demyltiplije/ [2] vtr **(a)** to
reduce ⟨speed⟩
(b) to increase ⟨powers, capacity⟩

démuni, ~**e** /demyni/ adj destitute;
penniless; ~ **de** devoid of, without ⟨talent⟩

démunir /demyniʀ/ [3] 1 vtr to divest (de
of)
2 **se démunir** v refl (+ v être) **se** ~ **de
qch** to leave oneself without sth

démystifier /demistifje/ [2] vtr **(a)** ~ **qn**
to dispel sb's illusions
(b) to demystify

démythifier /demitifje/ [2] vtr to
demythologize

dénatalité /denatalite/ nf fall in the
birthrate

dénationaliser /denasjɔnalize/ [1] vtr to
denationalize

dénaturé, ~**e** /denatyʀe/ adj **(a)** ⟨alcohol⟩
denatured
(b) ⟨tastes⟩ warped; ⟨parents⟩ unnatural

dénaturer /denatyʀe/ [1] vtr **(a)** to
denature
(b) to distort ⟨facts⟩
(c) to spoil ⟨taste, sauce⟩

dénicher /denife/ [1] vtr **(a)** (colloq) to dig
out (colloq) ⟨object⟩; to track down ⟨person⟩;
to find ⟨right address⟩
(b) to flush out ⟨thief, animal⟩

dénier /denje/ [2] vtr to deny

deniers /dənje/ nm pl money; ~**s publics**
or **de l'État** public funds

d

dénigrement /denigrəmɑ̃/ *nm*
denigration

dénigrer /denigre/ [1] *vtr* to denigrate

dénivellation /denivɛlasjɔ̃/ *nf*
(a) difference in level
(b) gradient

dénombrable /denɔ̃brabl/ *adj* countable;
non ∼ uncountable

dénombrement /denɔ̃brəmɑ̃/ *nm* count

dénombrer /denɔ̃bre/ [1] *vtr* to count

dénomination /denɔminasjɔ̃/ *nf* name,
designation

dénommer /denɔme/ [1] *vtr* to name

dénoncer /denɔ̃se/ [12] **1** *vtr* to denounce
2 se dénoncer *v refl* (+ *v être*) to give
oneself up

dénonciation /denɔ̃sjasjɔ̃/ *nf*
denunciation

dénoter /denɔte/ [1] *vtr* denote

dénouement /denumɑ̃/ *nm*
(a) denouement
(b) outcome

dénouer /denwe/ [1] **1** *vtr* (a) to undo
⟨knot⟩
(b) to unravel ⟨intrigue⟩; to resolve ⟨crisis⟩
2 se dénouer *v refl* (+ *v être*) (a) ⟨laces⟩
to come undone
(b) ⟨crisis⟩ to resolve itself

dénoyauter /denwajote/ [1] *vtr* to stone
(GB), to pit (US)

denrée /dɑ̃re/ *nf* (a) foodstuff; ∼ de base
staple
(b) commodity

dense /dɑ̃s/ *adj* dense; concentrated; heavy

densité /dɑ̃site/ *nf* (a) density
(b) denseness

dent /dɑ̃/ *nf* (a) tooth; à pleines *or* belles
∼s with relish; ne rien avoir à se mettre
sous la ∼ to have nothing to eat
(b) (of comb) tooth; (of fork) prong; en ∼s de
scie ⟨blade⟩ serrated; ⟨results⟩ which go up
and down
(c) crag
■ ∼ de lait milk tooth
IDIOMS avoir une ∼ contre qn to bear sb a
grudge; avoir les ∼s longues to be ambitious

dentaire /dɑ̃tɛr/ *adj* dental

denté, ∼**e** /dɑ̃te/ *adj* (a) toothed
(b) dentate

dentelé, ∼**e** /dɑ̃t(ə)le/ *adj* ⟨coast⟩
indented; ⟨crest⟩ jagged; ⟨stamp⟩ perforated;
⟨leaf⟩ dentate

dentelle /dɑ̃tɛl/ *nf* lace
IDIOMS il ne fait pas dans la ∼ he's not one
to bother with niceties

dentelure /dɑ̃tlyr/ *nf* (of stamp)
perforation; (of crest) jagged outline; (of leaf)
serration

dentier /dɑ̃tje/ *nm* dentures

dentifrice /dɑ̃tifris/ *nm* toothpaste

dentiste /dɑ̃tist/ *nmf* dentist

dentition /dɑ̃tisjɔ̃/ *nf* dentition

dénuder /denyde/ [1] **1** *vtr* to strip

2 se dénuder *v refl* (+ *v être*) (a) to strip
(off)
(b) to become bare

dénué, ∼**e** /denye/ *adj* ∼ de lacking in;
∼ de sens senseless

dénuement /denymɑ̃/ *nm* destitution;
bareness

déodorant, ∼**e** /deɔdɔrɑ̃, ɑ̃t/ **1** *adj*
deodorant
2 *nm* deodorant

déontologie /deɔ̃tɔlɔʒi/ *nf* (professional)
ethics

dépannage /depanaʒ/ *nm* repair

dépanner /depane/ [1] *vtr* (a) to fix ⟨car,
machine⟩
(b) to tow away
(c) (colloq) to help [sb] out

dépanneur, **-euse¹** /depanœr, øz/ *nm,f*
engineer

dépanneuse² /depanøz/ *nf* breakdown
truck (GB), tow truck (US)

dépareillé, ∼**e** /depareje/ *adj* (a) odd;
articles ∼s oddments
(b) incomplete

déparer /depare/ [1] *vtr* to spoil, to mar

départ /depar/ *nm* (a) departure; ∼ des
grandes lignes main line departures;
téléphone avant ton ∼ phone before you
leave; être sur le ∼ to be about to leave
(b) resignation; le ∼ en retraite retirement
(c) (gen, Sport) start; donner le (signal du) ∼
aux coureurs to start the race; prendre un
nouveau ∼ (figurative) to make a fresh start;
au ∼ at first; at the outset; de ∼ initial;
⟨language⟩ source; ⟨salary⟩ starting

départager /departaʒe/ [13] *vtr* to decide
between ⟨competitors⟩

département /departəmɑ̃/ *nm*
department

départemental, ∼**e**, *mpl* **-aux**
/departəmɑ̃tal, o/ *adj* ⟨election⟩ local; ⟨road⟩
secondary

dépassé, ∼**e** /depɑse/ *adj* (a) outdated,
outmoded
(b) (colloq) overwhelmed

dépassement /depɑsmɑ̃/ *nm*
(a) overtaking
(b) overrun; ∼ d'horaire overrunning the
schedule; le ∼ de la dose prescrite exceeding
the stated dose
(c) ∼ de soi surpassing oneself
■ ∼ budgétaire cost overrun; ∼ de capacité
(Comput) overflow

dépasser /depɑse/ [1] **1** *vtr* (a) to
overtake (GB), to pass (US) ⟨car, pedestrian⟩;
to go past ⟨place⟩
(b) to exceed ⟨figure, dose, limit⟩; elle le
dépasse de cinq centimètres she's five
centimetres (GB) taller than him; il a
dépassé la cinquantaine he's over *or* past
fifty; ∼ la mesure *or* les bornes to go too far
(c) to be ahead of, to outstrip ⟨rival⟩; ça me
dépasse! it's beyond me!
2 *vi* to jut *or* stick out; ⟨underskirt⟩ to show

dépassionner /depasjɔne/ [1] *vtr* to defuse ⟨discussion⟩

dépatouiller: se dépatouiller /depatuje/ [1] *v refl* (+ *v être*) (colloq) to get by

dépaysé, **∼e** /depeize/ *adj* **il est complètement ∼** he's like a fish out of water; **il n'est pas ∼ ici** he feels at home here

dépaysement /depeizmã/ *nm* (a) change of scenery
(b) disorientation

dépayser /depeize/ [1] *vtr* (a) to provide [sb] with a pleasant change of scenery
(b) to disorient

dépecer /dep(ə)se/ [16] *vtr* to tear apart, to cut up

dépêche /depɛʃ/ *nf* dispatch

dépêcher /depeʃe/ [16] **1** *vtr* to dispatch (à to)
2 se dépêcher *v refl* (+ *v être*) to hurry up

dépeigné, **∼e** /depeɲe/ *adj* dishevelled (GB)

dépeindre /depɛ̃dʀ/ [55] *vtr* to depict

dépenaillé, **∼e** /depənaje/ *adj* ragged

dépénaliser /depenalize/ [1] *vtr* to decriminalize

dépendance /depãdãs/ *nf*
(a) dependence, dependency
(b) outbuilding
(c) dependent, dependent territory

dépendant, **∼e** /depãdã, ãt/ *adj* dependent (**de** on); **∼s l'un de l'autre** interdependent

dépendre /depãdʀ/ [6] *v+prep* (a) **∼ de** to depend on
(b) **∼ de** to be dependent on
(c) **∼ de** ⟨organization⟩ to come under the control of; ⟨employee⟩ to be responsible to
(d) **∼ de** ⟨environment⟩ to be the responsibility of
(e) **∼ de** ⟨territory⟩ to be a dependency of
(f) **∼ de** ⟨building, land⟩ to belong to

dépens /depã/ *nm pl* **aux ∼ de** at the expense of; **vivre aux ∼ des autres** to live off other people

dépense /depãs/ *nf* (a) spending, expenditure; **∼s publiques** public expenditure
(b) expense; **réduire ses ∼s** to cut down on expenses
(c) outlay; **une ∼ de 300 francs** an outlay of 300 francs
(d) consumption; **∼ d'énergie physique** expenditure of physical energy

dépenser /depãse/ [1] **1** *vtr* to spend ⟨money, time⟩; to use up ⟨energy, fuel⟩
2 se dépenser *v refl* (+ *v être*) to get (enough) exercise

dépensier, **-ière** /depãsje, ɛʀ/ *adj* extravagant

déperdition /depɛʀdisjɔ̃/ *nf* loss

dépérir /depeʀiʀ/ [3] *vi* ⟨person⟩ to waste away; ⟨plant⟩ to wilt; ⟨economy⟩ to be on the decline

dépêtrer: se dépêtrer /depɛtʀe/ [1] *v refl* (+ *v être*) **se ∼ de** to extricate oneself from

dépeuplement /depœpləmã/ *nm* depopulation

dépeupler /depœple/ [1] *vtr* to depopulate ⟨region⟩; to reduce the wildlife in ⟨forest⟩

déphasé, **∼e** /defaze/ *adj* (a) (colloq) out of step
(b) out of phase

dépiauter /depjote/ [1] *vtr* (colloq) to skin ⟨animal⟩

dépilation /depilasjɔ̃/ *nf* hair removal

dépilatoire /depilatwaʀ/ *adj* depilatory, hair-removing

dépistable /depistabl/ *adj* detectable

dépistage /depistaʒ/ *nm* screening (de for); **test de ∼ du sida** Aids test

dépister /depiste/ [1] *vtr* (a) to track down ⟨criminal, game⟩
(b) to detect ⟨illness⟩

dépit /depi/ **1** *nm* pique; **par ∼** out of pique
2 en dépit de *phr* in spite of; **en ∼ du bon sens** in a very illogical way

dépité, **∼e** /depite/ *adj* piqued (**de** at)

déplacé, **∼e** /deplase/ *adj* inappropriate; **c'est ∼** it's out of place; it's uncalled for

déplacement /deplasmã/ *nm* (a) trip; **ça vaut le ∼!** it's worth the trip!; **frais de ∼** travelling (GB) expenses
(b) moving; shifting; transfer (**vers** to)
(c) displacement
■ **∼ de vertèbre** slipped disc

déplacer /deplase/ [12] **1** *vtr* to move ⟨object, person⟩; to displace ⟨population⟩; to shift ⟨attention⟩; to change ⟨issue⟩
2 se déplacer *v refl* (+ *v être*) (a) to move; **se ∼ une vertèbre** to slip a disc
(b) to get about; to travel
(c) ⟨doctor⟩ to go out on call

déplaire /deplɛʀ/ [59] **1** *vi* **le spectacle a déplu** the show was not well received
2 déplaire à *v+prep* **cela m'a déplu** I didn't like it; **la situation n'est pas pour me ∼** the situation quite suits me
3 *v impers* **ne vous en déplaise** (ironic) whether you like it or not

déplaisant, **∼e** /deplɛzã, ãt/ *adj* unpleasant

déplâtrer /deplɑtʀe/ [1] *vtr* to remove the cast from ⟨limb⟩

dépliant /deplijã/ *nm* (a) leaflet
(b) fold-out page

déplier /deplije/ [2] *vtr* to unfold ⟨newspaper⟩; to open out ⟨map⟩

déploiement /deplwamã/ *nm* (a) display; array
(b) deployment

déplorable /deplɔʀabl/ *adj* (a) regrettable
(b) appalling, deplorable

déplorer /deplɔʀe/ [1] *vtr* to deplore

déployer /deplwaje/ [23] *vtr* **(a)** to display ⟨*talent, wealth*⟩; to expend ⟨*energy*⟩
(b) to deploy ⟨*troops*⟩
(c) to spread ⟨*wings*⟩; to unfurl ⟨*sail*⟩

déplumer: se déplumer /deplyme/ [1] *v refl* (+ *v être*) ⟨*bird*⟩ to lose its feathers

dépoli, **∼e** /depɔli/ *adj* **verre ∼** frosted glass

dépolitiser /depɔlitize/ [1] *vtr* to depoliticize

dépolluer /depɔlɥe/ [1] *vtr* to rid [sth] of pollution, to clean up

dépollution /depɔlysjɔ̃/ *nf* cleanup

dépopulation /depɔpylasjɔ̃/ *nf* depopulation

déportation /depɔʀtasjɔ̃/ *nf*
(a) internment in a concentration camp
(b) deportation

déporté, **∼e** /depɔʀte/ *nm,f* **(a)** prisoner interned in a concentration camp
(b) transported convict

déporter /depɔʀte/ [1] **1** *vtr* **(a)** to send [sth] to a concentration camp
(b) to deport
2 se déporter *v refl* (+ *v être*) to swerve

déposant, **∼e** /depozɑ̃, ɑ̃t/ *nm,f*
(a) depositor
(b) deponent

déposer /depoze/ [1] **1** *vtr* **(a)** to dump ⟨*rubbish*⟩; to lay ⟨*wreath*⟩; to drop off, to leave ⟨*parcel, passenger*⟩; to deposit ⟨*money*⟩; **∼ les armes** to lay down one's arms
(b) to register ⟨*trademark*⟩; to submit ⟨*file, offer*⟩; to lodge ⟨*complaint*⟩; **∼ son bilan** to file a bankruptcy petition
(c) ⟨*river*⟩ to deposit ⟨*alluvium*⟩
2 *vi* (Law) to make a statement, to testify
3 se déposer *v refl* (+ *v être*) ⟨*dust*⟩ to settle; ⟨*deposit*⟩ to collect

dépositaire /depozitɛʀ/ *nmf* **(a)** agent; **∼ agréé** authorized dealer
(b) trustee

déposition /depozisjɔ̃/ *nf* (Law) statement; deposition; evidence

déposséder /deposede/ [14] *vtr* to dispossess

dépôt /depo/ *nm* **(a)** warehouse; depot
(b) outlet; **l'épicerie fait ∼ de pain the** grocer's sells bread
(c) (of trademark) registration; (of bill) introduction
(d) date limite de ∼ des déclarations d'impôt deadline for income tax returns
(e) deposit
(f) police cells
■ **∼ de bilan** voluntary liquidation; **∼ d'ordures** (rubbish) tip *or* dump (GB), garbage dump (US)

dépotoir /depotwaʀ/ *nm* **(a)** dump
(b) (colloq) shambles (colloq)

dépôt-vente, *pl* **dépôts-ventes** /depovɑ̃t/ *nm* secondhand shop (GB) *or* store ⟨*where goods are sold on commission*⟩

dépouille /depuj/ *nf* **(a)** skin, hide
(b) body; **∼ mortelle** mortal remains

(c) **∼s** spoils

dépouillé, **∼e** /depuje/ *adj* **(a)** ⟨*style*⟩ spare
(b) ⟨*tree*⟩ bare

dépouillement /depujmɑ̃/ *nm* **(a)** (of votes) counting, count; (of mail) going through
(b) asceticism
(c) (of style) sobriety

dépouiller /depuje/ [1] *vtr* **(a)** to skin ⟨*animal*⟩
(b) to lay [sth] bare ⟨*region*⟩
(c) to rob ⟨*person*⟩
(d) to count ⟨*votes*⟩; to go through ⟨*mail*⟩

dépourvu, **∼e** /depuʀvy/ **1** *adj* **∼ de** devoid of ⟨*interest, charm*⟩; without ⟨*heating*⟩
2 *nm* **prendre qn au ∼** to take sb by surprise

dépoussiérer /depusjeʀe/ [14] *vtr* to dust; (figurative) to revamp

dépravation /depʀavasjɔ̃/ *nf* depravity

dépraver /depʀave/ [1] *vtr* to deprave

dépréciation /depʀesjasjɔ̃/ *nf* depreciation

déprécier /depʀesje/ [2] *vtr* **(a)** to depreciate
(b) to disparage, to depreciate

déprédateur -trice /depʀedatœʀ, tʀis/ *nm,f* vandal

déprédations /depʀedasjɔ̃/ *nf pl* damage

dépressif, -ive /depʀesif, iv/ *adj, nm,f* depressive

dépression /depʀesjɔ̃/ *nf* depression; **∼ nerveuse** nervous breakdown

dépressurisation /depʀesyʀizasjɔ̃/ *nf*
(a) depressurization
(b) loss of pressure

déprimant, **∼e** /depʀimɑ̃, ɑ̃t/ *adj* depressing

déprime /depʀim/ *nf* (colloq) depression

déprimer /depʀime/ [1] **1** *vtr* to depress
2 *vi* (colloq) to be depressed

déprogrammer /depʀɔgʀame/ [1] *vtr* to cancel

depuis /dəpɥi/ **1** *adv* since; **∼ je n'ai plus de nouvelles** since then I haven't had any news
2 *prep* **(a)** since; **∼ quand vis-tu là-bas?** how long have you been living there?; **∼ le début jusqu'à la fin** from start to finish
(b) for; **il pleut ∼ trois jours** it's been raining for three days; **∼ quand?** how long?; **∼ peu** recently; **∼ toujours** always
(c) from; **∼ ma fenêtre** from my window
3 depuis que *phr* since, ever since; **il pleut ∼ que nous sommes arrivés** it's been raining ever since we arrived

député /depyte/ *nm* **(a)** (in politics) deputy; (in GB) member of Parliament; **être ∼ au Parlement européen** to be a Euro-MP *ou* member of the European Parliament
(b) representative

député-maire, *pl* **députés-maires** /depytemɛʀ/ *nm* deputy and mayor

déqualifier /dekalifje/ [2] *vtr* to deskill

der /dɛʀ/ *nf* (colloq) last; **la ~ des ~s** the war to end all wars

déraciné, ~e /deʀasine/ *nm,f* uprooted person

déracinement /deʀasinmɑ̃/ *nm*
(a) uprooting
(b) rootlessness

déraciner /deʀasine/ [1] *vtr* (a) to uproot
(b) to eradicate ⟨prejudice⟩

déraillement /deʀajmɑ̃/ *nm* derailment

dérailler /deʀaje/ [1] *vi* (a) to be derailed; **faire ~ un train** to derail a train
(b) (colloq) to lose one's marbles (colloq); to talk through one's hat (colloq)

dérailleur /deʀajœʀ/ *nm* derailleur

déraisonnable /deʀɛzɔnabl/ *adj* unrealistic; senseless; unreasonable

déraisonner /deʀɛzɔne/ [1] *vi* to talk nonsense

dérangé, ~e /deʀɑ̃ʒe/ *adj* (a) upset
(b) (colloq) deranged

dérangeant, ~e /deʀɑ̃ʒɑ̃, ɑ̃t/ *adj* disturbing

dérangement /deʀɑ̃ʒmɑ̃/ *nm* (a) trouble, inconvenience
(b) ~ **intestinal** stomach upset
(c) **être en ~** ⟨lift, phone⟩ to be out of order

déranger /deʀɑ̃ʒe/ [13] **1** *vtr* to disturb ⟨person⟩; to upset ⟨routine, plans⟩; to affect ⟨mind⟩; **excusez-moi de vous ~** (I'm) sorry to bother you; **est-ce que la fumée vous dérange?** do you mind if I smoke?
2 se déranger *v refl* (+ *v être*) (a) to go out, to come out; **je me suis dérangé pour rien, c'était fermé** I wasted my time going there, it was shut
(b) to get up; to move
(c) to put oneself out

dérapage /deʀapaʒ/ *nm* (a) skid
(b) blunder
(c) loss of control

déraper /deʀape/ [1] *vi* (a) ⟨prices, discussion⟩ to get out of control
(b) ⟨knife⟩ to slip
(c) to skid
(d) ⟨skier⟩ to sideslip

dératisation /deʀatizasjɔ̃/ *nf* pest control (for rats)

déréglé, ~e /deʀegle/ *adj* ⟨mind⟩ unbalanced; ⟨life⟩ irregular; ⟨mechanism⟩ out, disturbed

dérèglement /deʀɛɡləmɑ̃/ *nm*
(a) (in machine) fault
(b) disorder

déréglementer /deʀeɡləmɑ̃te/ [1] *vtr* to deregulate

dérégler /deʀegle/ [14] *vtr* to affect ⟨weather, organ⟩; to upset ⟨process, mechanism⟩; **~ la radio** to lose the station on the radio; **~ le réveil** to set the alarm clock wrong

dérider /deʀide/ [1] **1** *vtr* to cheer [sb] up
2 se dérider *v refl* (+ *v être*) to start smiling

dérision /deʀizjɔ̃/ *nf* scorn, derision; **tourner qn/qch en ~** to ridicule sb/sth

dérisoire /deʀizwaʀ/ *adj* pathetic; trivial

dérivatif, -ive /deʀivatif, iv/ **1** *adj* derivative
2 *nm* (a) diversion (à from)
(b) (Med) derivative

dérivation /deʀivasjɔ̃/ *nf* diversion (GB), detour

dérive /deʀiv/ *nf* drift; **à la ~** adrift

dérivé, ~e /deʀive/ *nm* by-product

dériver /deʀive/ [1] **1 dériver de** *v+prep*
(a) **~ de** to stem from
(b) **~ de** to be derived from
2 *vi* to drift

dermatologie /dɛʀmatɔlɔʒi/ *nf* dermatology

derme /dɛʀm/ *nm* dermis

dernier, -ière¹ /dɛʀnje, ɛʀ/ **1** *adj*
(a) last; ⟨floor, shelf⟩ top; **je les veux jeudi ~ délai** I want them by Thursday at the latest
(b) latest; **les dernières nouvelles** the latest news; **ces ~ temps** recently
(c) **du ~ ridicule** utterly ridiculous; **c'était la dernière chose à faire** it was the worst possible thing to do
2 *nm, f* last; **arriver le ~** to arrive last; **c'est bien le ~ de mes soucis** that is the least of my worries; **être le ~ de la classe** to be bottom of the class; **le petit ~** the youngest child; **ce ~** the latter; **le ~ des ~s** the lowest of the low
3 en dernier *phr* last; **j'irai chez eux en ~** I'll go to them last
■ **~ cri** latest fashion; **dernières volontés** last requests

dernière² /dɛʀnjɛʀ/ *nf* (a) **la ~** the latest
(b) last performance

dernièrement /dɛʀnjɛʀmɑ̃/ *adv* recently

dernier-né, dernière-née, *mpl* **derniers-nés** /dɛʀnjene, dɛʀnjɛʀne/ *nm,f* (a) youngest (child)
(b) latest model

dérobade /deʀɔbad/ *nf* evasion

dérobé, ~e /deʀɔbe/ **1** *adj* ⟨door, stairs⟩ concealed
2 à la dérobée *phr* furtively

dérober /deʀɔbe/ [1] **1** *vtr* to steal
2 se dérober *v refl* (+ *v être*) (a) to be evasive
(b) to shirk responsibility
(c) **se ~ à** to shirk ⟨duty⟩
(d) ⟨ground, knees⟩ to give way

dérogation /deʀɔɡasjɔ̃/ *nf* (a) (special) dispensation
(b) infringement (à of)

dérogatoire /deʀɔɡatwaʀ/ *adj* special; **clause ~** derogation clause

déroger /deʀɔʒe/ [13] *v+prep* **~ à** to infringe ⟨law⟩; to depart from ⟨principles⟩; to ignore ⟨obligation⟩; to break with ⟨tradition⟩

dérouiller /deʀuje/ [1] (colloq) *vi* to get a hiding (colloq) *or* beating; to suffer

déroulement /deʀulmɑ̃/ *nm* (a) le ~ des événements the sequence of events; **veiller au bon** ~ **de** to make sure [sth] goes smoothly; ~ **de carrière** career development
(b) uncoiling, unwinding

dérouler /deʀule/ [1] **1** *vtr* to unroll ⟨*carpet*⟩; to uncoil ⟨*rope*⟩; to unwind ⟨*wire, film*⟩
2 se dérouler *v refl* (+ *v être*) (a) to take place
(b) ⟨*negotiations*⟩ to proceed; ⟨*story*⟩ to unfold

déroutant, **~e** /deʀutɑ̃, ɑ̃t/ *adj* puzzling

déroute /deʀut/ *nf* crushing defeat, rout; **mettre en** ~ to rout; **en** ~ in disarray

dérouter /deʀute/ [1] *vtr* (a) to puzzle
(b) to divert

derrière¹ /deʀjeʀ/ **1** *prep* behind; ~ **les apparences** beneath the surface; **il faut toujours être** ~ **son dos** you have to keep after him
2 *adv* behind; (of room) at the back; (in car) in the back

derrière² /deʀjeʀ/ *nm* (a) (of house, object) back; **de** ~ ⟨*bedroom*⟩ back
(b) (colloq) behind (colloq), backside (colloq)

des /de/ **1** *det* ▸ UN 1
2 *det* ▸ DE

dès /dɛ/ **1** *prep* from; ~ **(l'âge de) huit ans** from the age of eight; ~ **maintenant** straight away; **je vous téléphone** ~ **mon arrivée** I'll phone you as soon as I arrive; ~ **Versailles il y a des embouteillages** there are traffic jams from Versailles onwards
2 dès que *phr* as soon as
3 dès lors *phr* (a) from then on, from that time on, henceforth
(b) therefore, consequently
4 dès lors que *phr* (a) once, from the moment that
(b) since

désabusé, **~e** /dezabyze/ *adj* disillusioned; cynical

désaccord /dezakɔʀ/ *nm* disagreement; **être en** ~ to disagree (**avec** with; **sur** over)

désaccordé, **~e** /dezakɔʀde/ *adj* out-of-tune

désaccoutumer /dezakutyme/ **se désaccoutumer** *v refl* se ~ **de qch** to break one's dependence on sth

désactiver /dezaktive/ *vt* to deactivate

désaffecté, **~e** /dezafɛkte/ *adj* disused

désaffection /dezafɛksjɔ̃/ *nf* disaffection (**pour** with)

désagréable /dezagʀeabl/ *adj* unpleasant

désagrégation /dezagʀegasjɔ̃/ *nf* disintegration, break-up, collapse

désagréger: se désagréger /dezagʀeʒe/ [15] *v refl* (+ *v être*) to disintegrate, to break up

désagrément /dezagʀemɑ̃/ *nm* inconvenience

désaltérant, **~e** /dezalteʀɑ̃, ɑ̃t/ *adj* thirst-quenching

désaltérer /dezalteʀe/ [14] **1** *vtr* ~ **qn** to quench sb's thirst
2 se désaltérer *v refl* (+ *v être*) to quench one's thirst

désamorcer /dezamɔʀse/ [12] *vtr* to defuse ⟨*explosive, crisis*⟩; to drain ⟨*pump*⟩

désappointement /dezapwɛ̃tmɑ̃/ *nm* disappointment

désappointer /dezapwɛte/ [1] *vtr* to disappoint

désapprobateur, **-trice** /dezapʀɔbatœʀ, tʀis/ *adj* disapproving

désapprobation /dezapʀɔbasjɔ̃/ *nf* disapproval

désapprouver /dezapʀuve/ [1] *vtr* to disapprove of

désarçonner /dezaʀsɔne/ [1] *vtr* (a) to throw ⟨*rider*⟩
(b) to take [sb] aback

désargenté, **~e** /dezaʀʒɑ̃te/ *adj* (colloq) hard up (colloq), penniless

désarmant, **~e** /dezaʀmɑ̃, ɑ̃t/ *adj* disarming

désarmé, **~e** /dezaʀme/ **1** *pp* ▸ DÉSARMER
2 *pp adj* (a) disarmed
(b) ⟨*ship*⟩ laid up

désarmement /dezaʀməmɑ̃/ *nm*
(a) disarmament
(b) (of ship) laying up

désarmer /dezaʀme/ [1] **1** *vtr* (a) to disarm
(b) to lay up ⟨*ship*⟩
2 *vi* (a) to disarm
(b) ⟨*person*⟩ to give up the fight; ⟨*anger*⟩ to abate

désarroi /dezaʀwa/ *nm* distress; confusion

désarticulé, **~e** /dezaʀtikyle/ *adj* ⟨*chair*⟩ wrecked; ⟨*puppet*⟩ with broken joints

désastre /dezastʀ/ *nm* disaster

désastreux, **-euse** /dezastʀø, øz/ *adj* disastrous

désavantage /dezavɑ̃taʒ/ *nm*
(a) disadvantage
(b) drawback, disadvantage

désavantager /dezavɑ̃taʒe/ [13] *vtr* to put [sb/sth] at a disadvantage, to disadvantage

désavantageux, **-euse** /dezavɑ̃taʒø, øz/ *adj* unfavourable (GB), disadvantageous

désaveu /dezavø/ *nm* (a) denial
(b) rejection

désavouer /dezavwe/ [1] *vtr* (a) to deny
(b) to disown

désaxé, **~e** /dezakse/ **1** *pp* ▸ DÉSAXER
2 *pp adj* deranged
3 *nm,f* deranged person

désaxer /dezakse/ [1] *vtr* (a) to put [sth] out of true ⟨*wheel*⟩
(b) to unbalance ⟨*person*⟩

desceller /desele/ [1] **1** *vtr* to work [sth] free
2 se desceller *v refl* (+ *v être*) to work loose

descendance /desɑ̃dɑ̃s/ *nf* descendants

descendant, **~e** /desɑ̃dɑ̃, ɑ̃t/ *nm,f* descendant

descendre /desɑ̃dʀ/ [6] **1** *vtr* (+ *v avoir*)
(a) to take [sb/sth] down (à to), to bring [sb/ sth] down (de from)
(b) to lower ⟨*shelf, blind*⟩; to wind [sth] down ⟨*window* ⟩
(c) to go down, to come down ⟨*road, steps, river*⟩; **~ la rivière à la nage** to swim down the river
(d) (colloq) to bump off (colloq) ⟨*person*⟩; to shoot down ⟨*plane*⟩
(e) (colloq) to down ⟨*bottle*⟩
2 *vi* (+ *v être*) (a) to go down (à to), to come down (de from); ⟨*night*⟩ to fall; **tu es descendu à pied?** did you walk down?; **la route descend en pente douce** the road slopes down gently
(b) **~ de** to step off ⟨*step*⟩; to get off ⟨*train, bike, horse*⟩; to get out of ⟨*car*⟩
(c) ⟨*temperature, prices*⟩ to drop, to go down; ⟨*tide*⟩ to go out
(d) **~ dans le Midi** to go down to the South (of France)
(e) **~ dans un hôtel** to stay at a hotel
(f) **~ de** to be descended from

descente /desɑ̃t/ *nf* (a) descent; **la ~ a pris une heure** it took an hour to come down
(b) **à ma ~ du train** when I got off the train
(c) **~ de police** police raid; **la police a fait une ~ dans l'immeuble** the police raided the building
(d) (in skiing) downhill (event)
■ **~ de lit** (bedside) rug

descriptif, **-ive** /deskʀiptif, iv/ *adj* descriptive

description /deskʀipsjɔ̃/ *nf* description; **faire une ~ de qch** to describe sth

désembuer /dezɑ̃bɥe/ [1] *vtr* to demist (GB), to defog (US)

désemparé, **~e** /dezɑ̃paʀe/ **1** *pp* ▶
DÉSEMPARER
2 *pp adj* distraught, at a loss

désemparer /dezɑ̃paʀe/ [1] *vtr* to throw [sb] into confusion

désemplir /dezɑ̃pliʀ/ [3] *vi* **ne pas ~** to be always full

désenchanté, **~e** /dezɑ̃ʃɑ̃te/ *adj* disillusioned, disenchanted (de with)

désenchantement /dezɑ̃ʃɑ̃tmɑ̃/ *nm* disillusionment, disenchantment

désenclaver /dezɑ̃klave/ [1] *vtr* to open up ⟨*region*⟩

désendettement /dezɑ̃dɛtmɑ̃/ *nm* reduction of the debt

désenfler /dezɑ̃fle/ [1] *vi* to become less swollen, to go down

désengagement /dezɑ̃ɡaʒmɑ̃/ *nm*
(a) (Econ) disengagement
(b) withdrawal (de from)

désengager: **se désengager**
/dezɑ̃ɡaʒe/ [13] *v refl* (+ *v être*) to withdraw (de from)

désensibiliser /desɑ̃sibilize/ [1] *vtr* to desensitize

désenvoûter /dezɑ̃vute/ [1] *vtr* to break the spell on

désépaissir /dezepɛsiʀ/ [3] *vtr* (a) to thin ⟨*sauce*⟩
(b) to thin [sth] out ⟨*hair*⟩

déséquilibre /dezekilibʀ/ *nm*
(a) unsteadiness; **en ~** ⟨*table*⟩ unstable; ⟨*person*⟩ off balance
(b) imbalance
(c) derangement

déséquilibré, **~e** /dezekilibʀe/ **1** *pp* ▶
DÉSÉQUILIBRER
2 *pp adj* (Med) unbalanced
3 *nm,f* lunatic

déséquilibrer /dezekilibʀe/ [1] *vtr* (a) to make [sb] lose their balance; to make [sth] unstable
(b) to destabilize ⟨*country*⟩
(c) (Med) to unbalance

désert, **~e** /dezɛʀ, ɛʀt/ **1** *adj*
(a) uninhabited; **île ~e** desert island
(b) deserted
2 *nm* desert

déserter /dezɛʀte/ [1] *vtr, vi* to desert

déserteur /dezɛʀtœʀ/ *nm* deserter

désertion /dezɛʀsjɔ̃/ *nf* (a) desertion
(b) defection

désertique /dezɛʀtik/ *adj* (a) ⟨*climate, region*⟩ desert
(b) barren

désespérant, **~e** /dezɛspeʀɑ̃, ɑ̃t/ *adj* ⟨*person, situation*⟩ hopeless

désespéré, **~e** /dezɛspeʀe/ **1** *pp* ▶
DÉSESPÉRER
2 *pp adj* ⟨*person*⟩ in despair; ⟨*situation*⟩ hopeless; ⟨*attempt*⟩ desperate; **cri ~** cry of despair

désespérément /dezɛspeʀemɑ̃/ *adv* despairingly; desperately; hopelessly

désespérer /dezɛspeʀe/ [14] **1** *vtr* to drive [sb] to despair
2 désespérer de *v+prep* **~ de qn** to despair of sb; **il ne désespère pas de le sauver** he hasn't given up hope of saving him
3 *vi* to despair, to lose hope
4 se désespérer *v refl* (+ *v être*) to despair

désespoir /dezɛspwaʀ/ *nm* despair; **mettre** *or* **réduire qn au ~** to drive sb to despair

déshabillé /dezabije/ *nm* negligee

déshabiller /dezabije/ [1] **1** *vtr* to undress
2 se déshabiller *v refl* (+ *v être*) (a) to undress
(b) to take one's coat off

déshabituer /dezabitɥe/ [1] *vtr* **~ qn du tabac** to get sb out of the habit of smoking

désherbant /dezɛʀbɑ̃/ *nm* weedkiller

désherber /dezɛʀbe/ [1] *vtr* to weed

déshérité /dezeʀite/ **1** *pp* ▶ DÉSHÉRITER ⋯⟶

2 *pp adj* underprivileged; disadvantaged; deprived
3 *nm,f* les ~s the underprivileged

déshériter /dezeRite/ [1] *vtr* to disinherit

déshonorant, ~e /dezɔnɔRɑ̃, ɑ̃t/ *adj* dishonourable (GB), degrading

déshonorer /dezɔnɔRe/ [1] **1** *vtr* to bring disgrace on ⟨*family*⟩; to bring [sth] into disrepute ⟨*profession*⟩
2 se déshonorer *v refl* (+ *v être*) to disgrace oneself

déshumaniser /dezymanize/ [1] **1** *vtr* to dehumanize
2 se déshumaniser *v refl* (+ *v être*) to become dehumanized

déshydratation /dezidRatasjɔ̃/ *nf*
(a) dehydration
(b) drying

déshydrater /dezidRate/ [1] *vtr* to dehydrate

desiderata /dezideRata/ *nm pl* wishes

désignation /deziɲasjɔ̃/ *nf* designation

désigner /deziɲe/ [1] *vtr* (a) ⟨*word*⟩ to designate; ⟨*triangle*⟩ to represent
(b) to point out
(c) to choose; **être tout désigné pour** to be just right for

désillusion /dezil(l)yzjɔ̃/ *nf* disillusion

désincarcérer /dezɛ̃kaRseRe/ [14] *vtr* to free

désincarné, ~e /dezɛ̃kaRne/ *adj* disembodied

désinence /dezinɑ̃s/ *nf* ending

désinfectant, ~e /dezɛ̃fɛktɑ̃, ɑ̃t/ **1** *adj* disinfecting
2 *nm* disinfectant

désinfecter /dezɛ̃fɛkte/ [1] *vtr* to disinfect

désintégrer: se désintégrer /dezɛ̃tegRe/ [14] *v refl* (+ *v être*) to disintegrate

désintéressé, ~e /dezɛ̃teRese/ **1** *pp* ▶ DÉSINTÉRESSER
2 *pp adj* ⟨*person, act*⟩ selfless, unselfish; ⟨*advice*⟩ disinterested

désintéressement /dezɛ̃teRɛsmɑ̃/ *nm*
(a) disinterestedness; **agir avec ~** to act disinterestedly
(b) (Econ) paying off

désintéresser: se désintéresser /dezɛ̃teRese/ [1] *v refl* (+ *v être*) **se ~ de** to lose interest in

désintérêt /dezɛ̃teRɛ/ *nm* lack of interest

désintoxiquer /dezɛ̃tɔksike/ [1] *vtr* to detoxify; **se faire ~** to undergo detoxification

désinvolte /dezɛ̃vɔlt/ *adj* casual, offhand

désinvolture /dezɛ̃vɔltyR/ *nf* casual manner

désir /deziR/ *nm* wish, desire; **prendre ses ~s pour des réalités** to delude oneself

désirable /deziRabl/ *adj* desirable

désirer /deziRe/ [1] *vtr* to want; **effets non**

désirés unwanted effects; **que désirez-vous?** what would you like? **laisser à ~** to leave something to be desired

désistement /dezistəmɑ̃/ *nm* withdrawal

désister: se désister /deziste/ [1] *v refl* (+ *v être*) to stand down (GB), to withdraw

désobéir /dezɔbeiR/ [3] *v+prep* to disobey; **~ à qn** to disobey sb

désobéissance /dezɔbeisɑ̃s/ *nf* disobedience

désobéissant, ~e /dezɔbeisɑ̃, ɑ̃t/ *adj* disobedient

désobligeant, ~e /dezɔbliʒɑ̃, ɑ̃t/ *adj* discourteous

désobliger /dezɔbliʒe/ [13] *vtr* to offend

désodorisant /dezɔdɔRizɑ̃/ *nm* deodorant

désodoriser /dezɔdɔRize/ [1] *vtr* to freshen

désœuvré, ~e /dezœvRe/ *adj* at a loose end (GB) (colloq), at loose ends (US) (colloq)

désœuvrement /dezœvRəmɑ̃/ *nm* **par ~** for lack of anything better to do

désolation /dezɔlasjɔ̃/ *nf* (a) grief
(b) desolation

désolé, ~e /dezɔle/ **1** *pp* ▶ DÉSOLER
2 *pp adj* (a) sorry
(b) desolate

désoler /dezɔle/ [1] **1** *vtr* (a) to upset, to distress
(b) to depress; **tu me désoles!** I despair of you!
2 se désoler *v refl* (+ *v être*) to be upset

désopilant, ~e /dezɔpilɑ̃, ɑ̃t/ *adj* hilarious

désordonné, ~e /dezɔRdɔne/ *adj* ⟨*person*⟩ untidy; ⟨*meeting*⟩ disorderly; ⟨*movements*⟩ uncoordinated; ⟨*existence*⟩ wild

désordre /dezɔRdR/ **1** *adj inv* (colloq) **faire ~** to look untidy *or* messy
2 *nm* (a) untidiness; mess; **pièce en ~** untidy room; **il a tout mis en ~** he made such a mess
(b) chaos; **semer le ~** to cause chaos
(c) **dans le ~** in any order; **gagner dans le ~** (at races) to win with a combination forecast
(d) disorder; **~s mentaux** mental disorders

désorganisation /dezɔRganizasjɔ̃/ *nf* disruption; disorganization

désorganisé, ~e /dezɔRganize/ *adj* disorganized

désorienter /dezɔRjɑ̃te/ [1] *vtr* (a) to disorientate (GB)
(b) to confuse, to bewilder

désormais /dezɔRmɛ/ *adv* (a) from now on
(b) from then on

désosser /dezɔse/ [1] *vtr* (Culin) to bone

despote /dɛspɔt/ *nm* despot

despotique /dɛspɔtik/ *adj* despotic

desquelles ▶ LEQUEL

desquels ▶ LEQUEL

DESS /deəɛsɛs/ *nm* (*abbr* = **diplôme d'études supérieures spécialisées**) *postgraduate degree taken after a Master's*

dessaisir /desɛziʀ/ [3] **1** *vtr* **(a)** ~ qn de to relieve sb of ⟨responsibility⟩
(b) ~ qn de to divest sb of ⟨property⟩
2 se dessaisir *v refl* (+ *v être*) se ~ de to relinquish

dessaler /desale/ [1] *vtr* **(a)** to desalinate
(b) (Culin) to desalt

dessécher /deseʃe/ [14] **1** *vtr* to dry [sth] out; **arbre desséché** withered tree
2 se dessécher *v refl* (+ *v être*) ⟨hair⟩ to become dry; ⟨tree⟩ to wither; ⟨ground⟩ to dry out

dessein /desɛ̃/ *nm* design, intention; **à ~** deliberately

desserré, ~e /deseʀe/ *adj* loose

desserrement /deseʀmɑ̃/ *nm*
(a) loosening
(b) (Econ) relaxation; ~ **du crédit** relaxation of credit

desserrer /deseʀe/ [1] **1** *vtr* **(a)** to loosen; to release; to undo
(b) to relax ⟨grip, credit⟩
2 se desserrer *v refl* (+ *v être*) ⟨screw⟩ to work loose; ⟨knot⟩ to come undone
IDIOMS **il n'a pas desserré les dents** he never once opened his mouth

dessert /desɛʀ/ *nm* dessert

desserte /desɛʀt/ *nf* **(a)** (transport) service; **la ~ d'une ville par les transports en commun** public transport services to and from a city
(b) sideboard

desservir /desɛʀviʀ/ [30] *vtr* **(a)** ⟨train⟩ to serve ⟨town⟩
(b) to lead to ⟨room, floor⟩
(c) ⟨hospital⟩ to serve

dessin /desɛ̃/ *nm* **(a)** drawing; **tu veux que je te fasse un ~?** (colloq) do I have to spell it out for you?
(b) design
(c) pattern
(d) outline
■ ~ **animé** cartoon

dessinateur, -trice /desinatœʀ, tʀis/ *nm,f* **(a)** draughtsman (GB), draftsman (US)
(b) designer
■ ~ **de bande dessinée** (strip) cartoonist

dessiner /desine/ [1] **1** *vtr* **(a)** to draw
(b) to design ⟨material, decor⟩; to draw up ⟨plans⟩
2 *vi* to draw
3 se dessiner *v refl* (+ *v être*) **(a)** ⟨future⟩ to take shape
(b) se ~ **à l'horizon** to appear on the horizon; **il se dessinait nettement dans la lumière** he was clearly outlined in the light

dessoûler /desule/ [1] *vtr* to sober up

dessous¹ /dəsu/ **1** *adv* underneath
2 en dessous *phr* **(a)** underneath; **il habite juste en ~** he lives on the floor below
(b) **la taille en ~** the next size down

3 en dessous de *phr* below; **les enfants en ~ de 13 ans** children under 13

dessous² /dəsu/ **1** *nm inv* (of plate, tongue) underside; (of arm) inside (part); **le ~ du pied** the sole of the foot; **l'étagère de** *or* **du ~** the shelf below; the bottom shelf
2 *nm pl* **(a)** underwear
(b) inside story

dessous-de-plat /d(ə)sudpla/ *nm inv*
(a) table mat
(b) plate stand
(c) trivet

dessous-de-table /d(ə)sudtabl/ *nm inv* backhanders (colloq) (GB), bribes

dessus¹ /dəsy/ *adv* on top; **le prix est marqué ~** the price is on it; **passe ~** go over it; **compte ~** count on it; **'ton rapport est fini?'—'non, je travaille** *or* **suis ~'** 'is your report finished?'—'no, I'm working on it'

dessus² /dəsy/ *nm inv* (of shoe) upper; (of table, head) top; (of hand) back; **les voisins du ~** the people who live on the floor above
IDIOMS **reprendre le ~** to regain the upper hand; (after illness) to get back on one's feet

dessus-de-lit /d(ə)sydli/ *nm inv* bedspread

déstabiliser /destabilize/ [1] *vtr* to unsettle ⟨person⟩; to destabilize ⟨country⟩

destin /dɛstɛ̃/ *nm* **(a)** fate
(b) destiny

destinataire /dɛstinatɛʀ/ *nmf*
(a) addressee
(b) beneficiary
(c) payee

destination /dɛstinasjɔ̃/ **1** *nf* destination
2 à destination de *phr* ⟨train⟩ bound for

destinée /dɛstine/ *nf* destiny

destiner /dɛstine/ [1] **1** *vtr* **(a)** ~ **qch à qn** to design sth for sb; **être destiné à faire** to be designed *or* intended to do; to be destined to do
(b) **la lettre ne leur était pas destinée** the letter wasn't for them
2 se destiner *v refl* (+ *v être*) **elle se destine à une carrière de juriste** she's decided on a legal career

destituer /dɛstitɥe/ [1] *vtr* to discharge ⟨officer⟩; to depose ⟨monarch⟩

destitution /dɛstitysjɔ̃/ *nf* discharge; deposition

destructeur, -trice /dɛstʀyktœʀ, tʀis/ *adj* destructive

destruction /dɛstʀyksjɔ̃/ *nf* destruction

désuet, -ète /dezɥɛ, ɛt/ *adj* ⟨decor⟩ old-world; ⟨style⟩ old-fashioned; ⟨word⟩ obsolete

désunion /dezynjɔ̃/ *nf* **(a)** division
(b) discord

désunir /dezyniʀ/ [3] *vtr* to divide, to break up

détachant /detaʃɑ̃/ *nm* stain remover

détaché, ~e /detaʃe/ **1** *pp* ▶ DÉTACHER
2 *pp adj* **(a)** detached, unconcerned

(b) ⟨*teacher, diplomat*⟩ on secondment (GB), transferred

détachement /detaʃmɑ̃/ *nm*
(a) detachment (**de** from)
(b) (Mil) detachment
(c) secondment

détacher /detaʃe/ [1] **1** *vtr* (a) to untie; to unfasten; to undo
(b) to take down ⟨*poster*⟩
(c) ~ **les yeux** *or* **le regard de qch** to take one's eyes off sth
(d) to second (GB), to transfer
(e) to remove the stain(s) from
2 se détacher *v refl* (+ *v être*)
(a) ⟨*prisoner, animal*⟩ to break loose; ⟨*boat*⟩ to come untied
(b) to come undone
(c) ⟨*coupon*⟩ to come out; ⟨*wallpaper*⟩ to come away
(d) to grow away from ⟨*person*⟩
(e) ⟨*pattern*⟩ to stand out
(f) **se** ~ **de** to detach oneself from; to pull away from

détail /detaj/ *nm* (a) detail
(b) breakdown; **analyse de** ~ detailed analysis
(c) retail; **acheter (qch) au** ~ to buy (sth) retail

détailler /detaje/ [1] *vtr* (a) to detail; to itemize
(b) to scrutinize

détartrer /detaʀtʀe/ [1] *vtr* (a) to descale ⟨*kettle*⟩
(b) to scale ⟨*teeth*⟩

détaxe /detaks/ *nf* (a) tax removal
(b) tax refund
(c) export rebate

détecter /detɛkte/ [1] *vtr* to detect

détecteur /detɛktœʀ/ *nm* detector; ~ **de mines** mine detector

détection /detɛksjɔ̃/ *nf* detection

détective /detɛktiv/ *nm* detective

déteindre /detɛ̃dʀ/ [55] *vi* (a) ⟨*garment*⟩ to fade
(b) ⟨*colour*⟩ to run
(c) (figurative) to rub off

détendre /detɑ̃dʀ/ [6] **1** *vtr* (a) to release ⟨*spring*⟩
(b) to slacken ⟨*rope, spring*⟩
(c) to relax ⟨*muscle*⟩; to calm ⟨*atmosphere, mind*⟩
2 *vi* (a) to be relaxing
(b) to be entertaining
3 se détendre *v refl* (+ *v être*) (a) ⟨*rope, spring*⟩ to slacken
(b) ⟨*person, muscle*⟩ to relax

détendu, ~**e** /detɑ̃dy/ **1** *pp* ▶ DÉTENDRE
2 *pp adj* (a) relaxed
(b) slack

détenir /det(ə)niʀ/ [36] *vtr* (a) to keep ⟨*objects*⟩; to hold ⟨*power, record*⟩; to possess ⟨*arms*⟩; to have ⟨*secret, evidence*⟩
(b) to detain ⟨*suspect*⟩

détente /detɑ̃t/ *nf* (a) relaxation
(b) détente

(c) (on gun) trigger
IDIOMS être lent *or* **dur à la** ~ (colloq) to be slow on the uptake

détention /detɑ̃sjɔ̃/ *nf* (a) (of passport, drugs, record) holding; (of arms, secret) possession
(b) detention; ~ **préventive** custody

détenu, ~**e** /detəny/ *nm,f* prisoner

détergent /detɛʀʒɑ̃/ *nm* detergent

détériorer /deteʀjɔʀe/ [1] **1** *vtr* to damage
2 se détériorer *v refl* (+ *v être*) ⟨*situation, weather*⟩ to deteriorate; ⟨*foodstuff*⟩ to go bad

déterminant, ~**e** /detɛʀminɑ̃, ɑ̃t/ *adj* ⟨*role, factor*⟩ decisive

détermination /detɛʀminasjɔ̃/ *nf* determination

déterminé, ~**e** /detɛʀmine/ **1** *pp* ▶ DÉTERMINER
2 *pp adj* (a) determined
(b) given

déterminer /detɛʀmine/ [1] *vtr* (a) to determine ⟨*reason, responsibility*⟩
(b) to work out ⟨*policy, terms*⟩
(c) to determine ⟨*attitude, decision*⟩
(d) ~ **qn à faire** to make sb decide to do

déterrer /deteʀe/ [1] *vtr* to dig [sb/sth] up

détestable /detɛstabl/ *adj* ⟨*style, weather*⟩ appalling; ⟨*habits*⟩ revolting; ⟨*person*⟩ hateful

détester /detɛste/ [1] *vtr* (a) to detest, to loathe ⟨*person*⟩
(b) to hate

détonateur /detɔnatœʀ/ *nm* (a) detonator
(b) (figurative) catalyst

détonation /detɔnasjɔ̃/ *nf* detonation

détonner /detɔne/ [1] *vi* to be out of place

détordre /detɔʀdʀ/ [6] *vtr* to straighten ⟨*iron bar*⟩; to unwind ⟨*cable*⟩

détour /detuʀ/ *nm* (a) detour; **ça vaut le** ~ it's worth the trip
(b) roundabout means
(c) circumlocution; **il me l'a dit sans** ~**s** he told me straight
(d) (in road, river) bend

détourné, ~**e** /deturne/ **1** *pp* ▶ DÉTOURNER
2 *pp adj* ⟨*reference*⟩ oblique; ⟨*means*⟩ indirect

détournement /deturnəmɑ̃/ *nm*
(a) misappropriation
(b) hijacking
(c) (of traffic) diversion
■ ~ **de mineur** (Law) corruption of a minor

détourner /deturne/ [1] **1** *vtr* (a) to divert ⟨*attention*⟩
(b) ~ **les yeux** *or* **le regard** *or* **la tête** to look away
(c) to divert ⟨*traffic, river, flight*⟩; ~ **la conversation** to change the subject
(d) to hijack ⟨*plane, ship*⟩; to misappropriate ⟨*funds*⟩
2 se détourner *v refl* (+ *v être*) (a) **se** ~ **de** to turn away from ⟨*friend*⟩
(b) to look away

détracteur, -trice /detʀaktœʀ, tʀis/
nm,f detractor

détraqué, ~e /detʀake/ *nm,f* (colloq)
deranged person

détraquer /detʀake/ [1] **1** *vtr* **(a)** to bust
[sth] (colloq); to make [sth] go wrong
(b) (colloq) ⟨*medicine*⟩ to upset ⟨*stomach*⟩; to
damage ⟨*health*⟩
2 se détraquer *v refl* (+ *v être*)
⟨*mechanism*⟩ to break down; ⟨*weather*⟩ to
break

détremper /detʀɑ̃pe/ [1] *vtr* to saturate
⟨*ground*⟩; to soak ⟨*garment*⟩

détresse /detʀɛs/ *nf* distress

détriment: au détriment de
/odetʀimɑ̃də/ *phr* to the detriment of

détritus /detʀity(s)/ *nm pl* refuse, rubbish
(GB), garbage (US)

détroit /detʀwɑ/ *nm* straits

détromper /detʀɔ̃pe/ [1] **1** *vtr* to set [sb]
straight
2 se détromper *v refl* (+ *v être*)
détrompez-vous! don't you believe it!

détrôner /detʀone/ [1] *vtr* to dethrone

détruire /detʀɥiʀ/ [69] *vtr* to destroy

dette /dɛt/ *nf* debt; **avoir une ~ envers qn**
to be indebted to sb

DEUG /dœg/ *nm* (*abbr* = **diplôme
d'études universitaires générales**)
*university diploma taken after two years'
study*

deuil /dœj/ *nm* **(a)** bereavement
(b) mourning, grief
IDIOMS **faire son ~ de qch** (colloq) to kiss sth
goodbye (colloq)

deux /dø/ **1** *adj inv* **(a)** two; **~ fois** twice;
des ~ côtés de la rue on either side *or* both
sides of the street; **tous les ~ jours** every
other day; **à nous ~** I'm all yours; (to enemy)
it's just you and me now
(b) a few, a couple of
(c) second; **le deux mai** the second of May
(GB), May second (US)
2 *pron* **elles sont venues toutes les ~** they
both came
3 *nm inv* two
IDIOMS **faire ~ poids, ~ mesures** to have
double standards; **un tiens vaut mieux que ~
tu l'auras** (Proverb) a bird in the hand is
worth two in the bush; **en ~ temps, trois
mouvements** very quickly; **je n'ai fait ni une
ni ~** I didn't have a second's hesitation

deuxième /døzjɛm/ **1** *adj* second; **dans
un ~ temps nous étudierons…** secondly, we
will study…
2 *nmf* second
■ **~ classe** second class, standard class (GB)

deuxièmement /døzjɛmmɑ̃/ *adv*
secondly

deux-points /døpwɛ̃/ *nm inv* colon

deux-roues /døʀu/ *nm inv* two-wheeled
vehicle

dévaler /devale/ [1] *vtr* to hurtle down; to
tear down

dévaliser /devalize/ [1] *vtr* **(a)** to rob
⟨*person, bank, safe*⟩
(b) to clean out (colloq) ⟨*shop, larder*⟩

dévaloriser /devalɔʀize/ [1] **1** *vtr* **(a)** to
depreciate
(b) to belittle
2 se dévaloriser *v refl* (+ *v être*) **(a)** to
lose value; to lose prestige
(b) to put oneself down

dévaluation /devalɥasjɔ̃/ *nf* devaluation

dévaluer /devalɥe/ [1] *vtr* to devalue

devancer /dəvɑ̃se/ [12] *vtr* **(a)** to be ahead
of, to outstrip ⟨*competitor*⟩
(b) to anticipate ⟨*demand, desire*⟩; to
forestall ⟨*attack, criticisms*⟩

devant¹ /dəvɑ̃/ **1** *prep* **(a)** in front of;
tous les hommes sont égaux ~ la loi all
men are equal in the eyes of the law; **fuir ~
le danger** to run away from danger; **le bus
est passé ~ moi sans s'arrêter** the bus went
straight past me without stopping
(b) outside; **il attendait ~ la porte** he was
waiting outside the door; he was waiting by
the door
(c) ahead of; **la voiture ~ nous** the car
ahead *or* in front of us; **laisser passer
quelqu'un ~ (soi)** to let somebody go first;
avoir toute la vie ~ soi to have one's whole
life ahead of one
2 *adv* **(a)** 'où est la poste?'—'tu es juste ~'
'where's the post office?'—'you're right in
front of it'
(b) pars ~, je te rejoins go ahead, I'll catch
up with you
(c) (of hall, theatre) at the front; (in car) in the
front

devant² /dəvɑ̃/ *nm* front
IDIOMS **prendre les ~s** to take the initiative

devanture /dəvɑ̃tyʀ/ *nf* **(a)** (shop)front
(b) shop *or* store (US) window

dévastation /devastasjɔ̃/ *nf* devastation

dévaster /devaste/ [1] *vtr* **(a)** ⟨*army*⟩ to
lay waste to; ⟨*storm, fire*⟩ to destroy
(b) ⟨*burglar*⟩ to wreck

déveine /devɛn/ *nf* (colloq) rotten luck
(colloq), bad luck

développement /devlɔpmɑ̃/ *nm*
(a) development; **pays en voie de ~**
developing nation *or* country
(b) (in photography) developing

développer /devlɔpe/ [1] **1** *vtr* to
develop
2 se développer *v refl* (+ *v être*) ⟨*body,
ability*⟩ to develop; ⟨*plant, company, town*⟩ to
grow

devenir¹ /dəvniʀ/ [36] *vi* (+ *v être*) to
become; **et Paul, qu'est-ce qu'il devient?** and
what is Paul up to these days?

devenir² /dəvniʀ/ *nm* future

dévergonder: se dévergonder
/devɛʀgɔ̃de/ [1] *v refl* (+ *v être*) to be going to
the bad

déverser /devɛʀse/ [1] **1** *vtr* to pour
⟨*liquid*⟩; to drop ⟨*bombs*⟩; to dump ⟨*refuse,*   ····⟶

sand⟩; to discharge ⟨waste⟩; to disgorge
⟨crowd⟩; ~ **du pétrole** to dump oil; to spill oil
2 se déverser v refl (+ v être) ⟨river⟩ to
flow; ⟨sewer, crowd⟩ to pour

dévêtir /devetiʀ/ [33] **1** vtr to undress
2 se dévêtir v refl (+ v être) to get
undressed

déviation /devjasjɔ̃/ nf **(a)** diversion (GB),
detour (US)
(b) departure, deviation
(c) (of compass) deviation
(d) (of light) deflection

dévider /devide/ [1] vtr to unwind ⟨cable⟩

dévier /devje/ [2] **1** vtr to deflect ⟨ball,
trajectory⟩; to divert ⟨traffic⟩
2 vi **(a)** ⟨bullet, ball⟩ to deflect; ⟨vehicle⟩ to
veer off course
(b) ~ **de** to deviate from ⟨plan⟩
(c) ⟨tool⟩ to slip
(d) ⟨conversation⟩ to drift

devin /dəvɛ̃/ nm soothsayer, seer

deviner /dəvine/ [1] vtr **(a)** to guess
⟨secret⟩; to foresee, to tell ⟨future⟩
(b) to sense ⟨danger⟩
(c) to make out, to discern

devinette /dəvinɛt/ nf riddle

devis /d(ə)vi/ nm inv estimate, quote

dévisager /devizaʒe/ [13] vtr to stare at

devise /dəviz/ nf **(a)** currency
(b) (foreign) currency
(c) motto

deviser /dəvize/ [1] vi to converse

dévisser /devise/ [1] vtr to unscrew

dévoiler /devwale/ [1] vtr **(a)** to unveil
(b) to reveal; to uncover

devoir¹ /dəvwaʀ/ [44] **1** v aux **(a)** to have
to; **je dois aller au travail** I've got to or I must
go to work; **il a dû accepter** he had to accept;
il aurait dû partir he should have left
(b) **il a dû accepter** he must have accepted;
elle doit avoir 13 ans she must be about 13
years old
(c) **cela devait arriver** it was bound to
happen; **un incident qui devait avoir de
graves conséquences** an incident which was
to have serious consequences; **ils doivent
arriver vers 10 heures** they're due to arrive
around 10 o'clock
2 vtr to owe; **il me doit des excuses** he owes
me an apology
3 se devoir v refl (+ v être) **(a)** **je me dois
de le faire** it's my duty to do it
(b) **les époux se doivent fidélité** spouses owe
it to each other to be faithful
(c) **un homme de son rang se doit d'avoir un
chauffeur** a man of his standing has to have
a chauffeur
4 comme il se doit phr **(a)** **agir comme
il se doit** to behave in the correct way
(b) **comme il se doit, elle est en retard!** as
you might expect, she's late!

devoir² /dəvwaʀ/ nm **(a)** duty; **il est de
mon ~ de** it's my duty to
(b) test; homework

dévolu /devɔly/ nm **jeter son ~ sur** to set
one's heart on ⟨object⟩; to set one's cap at
⟨person⟩

dévorant, **~e** /devɔʀɑ̃, ɑ̃t/ adj ⟨hunger⟩
voracious; ⟨flames, passion⟩ all-consuming

dévorer /devɔʀe/ [1] vtr **(a)** to devour
⟨food, book⟩; ~ **qn de baisers** to smother sb
with kisses
(b) ⟨obsession⟩ to consume

dévot, **~e** /devo, ɔt/ adj devout

dévotion /devosjɔ̃/ nf **(a)** devoutness
(b) (religious) devotion (à to)
(b) passion (pour for)

dévoué, **~e** /devwe/ adj devoted (à to)

dévouement /devumɑ̃/ nm devotion

dévouer: se dévouer /devwe/ [1] v refl
(+ v être) **(a)** to devote or dedicate oneself
(b) to put oneself out

dévoyer /devwaje/ [23] **1** vtr to deprave
[sb], to lead [sb] astray
2 se dévoyer v refl (+ v être) to go astray

dextérité /dɛksteʀite/ nf dexterity, skill

dézipper /dezipe/ vt (Comput) to unzip

diabète /djabɛt/ nm diabetes

diabétique /djabetik/ adj, nmf diabetic

diable /djɑbl/ **1** nm **(a)** devil; **en ~**
diabolically; fiendishly; **un (petit) ~** a little
devil
(b) two-wheeled trolley (GB), hand truck (US)
2 excl my God!; **pourquoi ~** why on earth
IDIOMS habiter au ~ to live miles from
anywhere; **que le ~ t'emporte!** to hell with
you!; **ce n'est pas le ~!** it's not that difficult!;
avoir le ~ au corps to be like someone
possessed; **tirer le ~ par la queue** to live
from hand to mouth

diablement /djɑbləmɑ̃/ adv terrifically

diabolique /djabɔlik/ adj **(a)** diabolic;
⟨invention⟩ fiendish
(b) ⟨person⟩ demonic; ⟨scheme, smile⟩
devilish
(c) ⟨precision⟩ uncanny

diabolo /djabɔlo/ nm ~ **menthe** mint
cordial and lemonade (GB) or soda (US)

diadème /djadɛm/ nm **(a)** tiara
(b) diadem

diagnostic /djagnɔstik/ nm (gen, Med)
diagnosis

diagnostiquer /djagnɔstike/ [1] vtr to
diagnose

diagonal, **~e¹**, mpl **-aux** /djagɔnal, o/
adj diagonal

diagonale² /djagɔnal/ nf diagonal; **lire qch
en ~** to skim through sth

diagramme /djagʀam/ nm graph

dialecte /djalɛkt/ nm dialect

dialogue /djalɔg/ nm dialogue (GB)

dialoguer /djalɔge/ [1] vi to have talks

dialoguiste /djalɔgist/ nmf screenwriter

dialyse /djaliz/ nf dialysis

diamant /djamɑ̃/ nm diamond

diamantaire /djamɑ̃tɛʀ/ nm **(a)** diamond
cutter

(b) diamond merchant

diamétralement /djametRalmɑ̃/ *adv* diametrically

diamètre /djamɛtR/ *nm* diameter

diapason /djapazɔ̃/ *nm* (a) (note) diapason
(b) tuning fork
IDIOMS **se mettre au ~** to fall in step

diaphragme /djafRagm/ *nm* diaphragm

diapo /djapo/ *nf* (colloq) slide

diaporama /djaporama/ *nm* slide show

diapositive /djapozitiv/ *nf* slide, transparency

diarrhée /djaRe/ *nf* diarrhoea

dico /diko/ *nm* (colloq) dictionary

dictateur /diktatœR/ *nm* dictator

dictature /diktatyR/ *nf* dictatorship

dictée /dikte/ *nf* dictation

dicter /dikte/ [1] *vtr* (a) to dictate
(b) to motivate

diction /diksjɔ̃/ *nf* diction; elocution

dictionnaire /diksjɔnɛR/ *nm* dictionary

dicton /diktɔ̃/ *nm* saying

didacticiel /didaktisjɛl/ *nm* educational software program

didactique /didaktik/ *adj* (a) (work, tone) didactic
(b) (term, language) technical, specialist

dièse /djɛz/ *adj, nm* sharp; **do ~ C** sharp

diesel /djezɛl/ *nm* diesel

diète /djɛt/ *nf* (Med) light diet

diététicien, -ienne /djetetisjɛ̃, ɛn/ *nm,f* dietitian

diététique /djetetik/ [1] *adj* dietary; **produits ~s** health foods; **magasin ~** health-food shop
[2] *nf* dietetics

dieu, pl ~x /djø/ *nm* (a) god
(b) **sur le terrain c'est un ~** he's brilliant on the sports field
IDIOMS **nager comme un ~** to be a superb swimmer; **être dans le secret des ~x** to be privy to the secrets of those on high

Dieu /djø/ *nm* God
IDIOMS **se prendre pour ~ le père** to think one is God Almighty; **chaque jour que ~ fait** day in, day out; **il vaut mieux s'adresser à ~ qu'à ses saints** (Proverb) always go straight to the top

diffamation /difamasjɔ̃/ *nf* slander; (Law) libel

diffamatoire /difamatwaR/ *adj* (in writing) libellous; (verbally) slanderous; **écrit ~** libel

diffamer /difame/ [1] *vtr* (gen) to slander, to defame; (Law) to libel

différé, ~e /difeRe/ [1] *pp* ▶ DIFFÉRER
[2] *pp adj* (a) postponed
(b) (payment) deferred
(c) (programme) pre-recorded
[3] *nm* (of match, event) recording

différemment /difeRamɑ̃/ *adv* differently

différence /difeRɑ̃s/ *nf* difference; **à la ~ de** unlike; **le droit à la ~** the right to be different

différenciation /difeRɑ̃sjɑsjɔ̃/ *nf* differentiation

différencier /difeRɑ̃sje/ [2] [1] *vtr* (a) to differentiate; **rien ne les différencie** there's no way of telling them apart
(b) to make [sb/sth] different
[2] **se différencier** *v refl* (+ *v être*)
(a) (person, organization) to differentiate oneself
(b) to differ
(c) to become different

différend /difeRɑ̃/ *nm* disagreement

différent, ~e /difeRɑ̃, ɑ̃t/ *adj* different, various; **pour ~es raisons** for various reasons

différentiel, -ielle /difeRɑ̃sjɛl/ *adj* differential

différer /difeRe/ [14] [1] *vtr* to postpone (departure, meeting); to defer (payment)
[2] *vi* to differ

difficile /difisil/ *adj* (a) (gen) difficult; (victory) hard-won; **le plus ~ reste à faire** the worst is yet to come
(b) (person, personality) difficult
(c) fussy (sur about); **tu n'es pas ~!** you're easy to please!

difficilement /difisilmɑ̃/ *adv* with difficulty; **~ supportable** hard to bear

difficulté /difikylte/ *nf* difficulty

difforme /difɔRm/ *adj* (body, limb) deformed; (object) strangely shaped; (tree) twisted

difformité /difɔRmite/ *nf* deformity

diffus, ~e /dify, yz/ *adj* (light, heat) diffuse; (feeling) vague

diffuser /difyze/ [1] *vtr* (a) to broadcast
(b) to spread; **~ le signalement de qn** to send out a description of sb
(c) to distribute (article, book)
(d) to diffuse (light, heat)

diffusion /difyzjɔ̃/ *nf* (a) broadcasting; **la ~ du film** the showing of the film
(b) dissemination, diffusion
(c) (commercial) distribution
(d) (of newspaper) circulation

digérer /diʒeRe/ [14] *vtr* (a) to digest
(b) (colloq) to swallow (insult); to stomach (defeat)

digeste /diʒɛst/ *adj* easily digestible

digestif, -ive /diʒɛstif, iv/ [1] *adj* digestive
[2] *nm* liqueur (taken after dinner); brandy

digestion /diʒɛstjɔ̃/ *nf* digestion

digicode® /diʒikɔd/ *nm* digital (access) lock

digital, ~e, mpl -aux /diʒital, o/ *adj* digital

digne /diɲ/ *adj* (a) dignified
(b) worthy; **~ de confiance** *or* **de foi** trustworthy

dignement /diɲmɑ̃/ *adv* (a) with dignity
(b) fittingly

dignité /diɲite/ *nf* (a) dignity; **avoir sa ~** to have one's pride ⋯⋮

(b) (title) dignity

digression /digʀesjɔ̃/ nf digression

digue /dig/ nf **(a)** sea wall
(b) dyke (GB), dike (US)
(c) harbour (GB) wall

dilapider /dilapide/ [1] vtr to squander

dilatation /dilatasjɔ̃/ nf **(a)** (of gas) expansion
(b) (Med) dilation

dilater /dilate/ [1] vtr **(a)** to dilate ⟨pupil, cervix⟩; to distend ⟨stomach⟩
(b) to expand ⟨gas⟩

dilemme /dilɛm/ nm dilemma

dilettante /dilɛtɑ̃t/ nmf amateur

dilettantisme /dilɛtɑ̃tism/ nm amateurism; (pejorative) dilettantism

diligence /diliʒɑ̃s/ nf **(a)** stagecoach
(b) haste

diligent, ~**e** /diliʒɑ̃, ɑ̃t/ adj diligent

diluant /dilɥɑ̃/ nm thinner

diluer /dilɥe/ [1] vtr **(a)** to dilute
(b) to thin [sth] down

diluvien, -ienne /dilyvjɛ̃, ɛn/ adj pluies diluviennes torrential rain

dimanche /dimɑ̃ʃ/ nm Sunday.
IDIOMS ce n'est pas tous les jours ~ not every day is a holiday

dimension /dimɑ̃sjɔ̃/ nf **(a)** dimension
(b) size
(c) dimension, aspect
(d) (of problem) dimensions

diminué, ~**e** /diminɥe/ **1** pp ▶ DIMINUER
2 pp adj ⟨person⟩ weak

diminuer /diminɥe/ [1] **1** vtr **(a)** to reduce; to lower
(b) to dampen ⟨enthusiasm, courage⟩
(c) to belittle ⟨person, achievement⟩
(d) to weaken ⟨strength⟩; to sap ⟨strength⟩
2 vi **(a)** to come or go down; to be reduced; to fall; to decrease; les jours diminuent the days are getting shorter
(b) ⟨activity, violence⟩ to fall off; ⟨tension⟩ to decrease; ⟨noise, flames, rumours⟩ to die down; ⟨strength⟩ to diminish

diminutif /diminytif/ nm **(a)** diminutive
(b) pet name

diminution /diminysjɔ̃/ nf decrease; reduction; (in production, trade) fall-off

dinde /dɛ̃d/ nf turkey (hen)

dindon /dɛ̃dɔ̃/ nm turkey (cock)
IDIOMS être le ~ de la farce to be fooled or duped

dindonneau, pl ~**x** /dɛ̃dɔno/ nm turkey

dîner¹ /dine/ [1] vi to have dinner
IDIOMS qui dort dîne (Proverb) when you're asleep you don't feel hungry

dîner² /dine/ nm dinner

dînette /dinɛt/ nf doll's tea set

dingo /dɛ̃go/ adj inv (colloq) crazy (colloq)

dingue (colloq) /dɛ̃g/ **1** adj **(a)** ⟨person⟩ crazy (colloq)
(b) ⟨noise, success⟩ wild; ⟨price, speed⟩ ridiculous

2 nmf **(a)** nutcase (colloq)
(b) un ~ de musique a music freak (colloq)

dinosaure /dinozɔʀ/ nm dinosaur

diocèse /djɔsɛz/ nm diocese

dioxyde /dijɔksid/ nm dioxide

diphtongue /diftɔ̃g/ nf diphthong

diplomate /diplɔmat/ **1** adj diplomatic
2 nmf diplomat

diplomatie /diplɔmasi/ nf diplomacy

diplomatique /diplɔmatik/ adj diplomatic

diplôme /diplom/ nm **(a)** certificate, diploma; il n'a aucun ~ he hasn't got any qualifications
(b) (at university) degree; diploma
(c) (in army, police) staff exam

diplômé, ~**e** /diplome/ **1** adj une infirmière ~e a qualified nurse
2 nm,f graduate

dire¹ /diʀ/ [65] **1** vtr **(a)** to say ⟨words, prayer⟩; to read ⟨lesson⟩; to tell ⟨story, joke⟩; ~ qch entre ses dents to mutter sth
(b) to tell; c'est ce qu'on m'a dit so I've been told; faire ~ à qn que to let sb know that...; je me suis laissé ~ que... I heard that...; c'est pas pour ~, mais.. (colloq) I don't want to make a big deal of it, but (colloq)...; à qui le dites-vous! (colloq) don't I know it!; je ne vous le fais pas ~! (colloq) you don't need to tell me!; dis donc, où tu te crois? (colloq) hey! where do you think you are?
(c) to say ⟨que that⟩; on dit que... it is said that...; si l'on peut ~ if one might say so; autant ~ que... you might as well say that...; si j'ose ~ if I may say so; c'est (tout) ~! need I say more?; cela dit having said that; tu peux le ~! (colloq) you can say that again! (colloq); à vrai ~ actually; entre nous soit dit between you and me; soit dit en passant incidentally; c'est ~ si j'ai raison it just goes to show I'm right; c'est beaucoup ~ that's going a bit far; c'est vite dit that's easy for you to say; ce n'est pas dit I'm not that sure; comment ~? how shall I put it?; pour ainsi ~ so to speak; autrement dit in other words; comme dirait l'autre (colloq) as they say; il n'y a pas à ~, elle est belle (colloq) you have to admit, she's beautiful
(d) (law) to state; ⟨measuring device⟩ to show; vouloir ~ to mean
(e) ~ à qn de faire to tell sb to do
(f) to think; on dirait de l'estragon it looks or tastes like tarragon; ça ne me dit rien de faire I don't feel like doing; notre nouveau jardinier ne me dit rien (qui vaille) I don't think much of our new gardener
2 se dire v refl (+ v être) **(a)** to tell oneself; il faut (bien) se ~ que... one must realize that...
(b) to exchange ⟨insults⟩; se ~ adieu to say goodbye to each other
(c) to claim to be
(d) ça ne se dit pas you can't say that
3 se dire v impers il ne s'est rien dit d'intéressant à la réunion nothing of interest was said during the meeting

dire² /diʀ/ nm au ~ de, selon les ~s de according to

direct /diʀɛkt/ **1** adj **(a)** ⟨contact, descendant, tax⟩ direct; ⟨superior⟩ immediate
(b) ⟨route, access⟩ direct; **ce train est ~ pour Lille** this train is nonstop to Lille
(c) direct, frank
2 nm **(a)** live broadcasting; **en ~ de** live from
(b) (in boxing) jab; **~ du gauche** left jab
(c) express (train)

directement /diʀɛktəmɑ̃/ adv **(a)** ⟨travel, go⟩ straight
(b) directly

directeur, -trice /diʀɛktœʀ, tʀis/ **1** adj **principe ~** guiding principle; **idée directrice d'un ouvrage** central theme of a book
2 nm,f **(a)** headmaster/headmistress (GB), principal (US); (of private school) principal
(b) (of hotel, cinema) manager/manageress
(c) director; head
■ **~ de banque** bank manager; **~ général** managing director (GB), chief executive officer (US); **~ de prison** prison governor (GB), warden (US); **~ sportif** (team) manager

direction /diʀɛksjɔ̃/ nf **(a)** direction; **il a pris la ~ du nord** he headed north; **en ~ de** toward(s); **indiquer la ~ à qn** to tell sb the way; **prenez la ~ Nation** take the train going to 'Nation'
(b) (gen) management; supervision; (of newspaper) editorship; (of movement) leadership; **orchestre sous la ~ de** orchestra conducted by
(c) management; **la ~ et les ouvriers** management and workers
(d) manager's office; head office
(e) (Aut) steering

directive /diʀɛktiv/ nf directive

directrice ▶ DIRECTEUR

dirigeable /diʀiʒabl/ adj, nm dirigible

dirigeant, ~e /diʀiʒɑ̃, ɑ̃t/ **1** adj ⟨class⟩ ruling
2 nm leader

diriger /diʀiʒe/ [13] **1** vtr **(a)** to be in charge of ⟨people⟩; to run ⟨service, party⟩; to manage ⟨company⟩; to lead ⟨investigation⟩; to direct ⟨operation⟩
(b) to steer; to pilot; **il vous dirigera dans la ville** he'll guide you around the town
(c) to turn ⟨light, jet⟩ (sur on); to point ⟨gun, telescope⟩ (sur at)
(d) to dispatch ⟨goods⟩; to direct ⟨convoy⟩
(e) (Mus) to conduct
(f) to direct ⟨actors⟩; to manage ⟨theatre company⟩
2 se diriger v refl (+ v être) **se ~ vers** to make for; **avoir du mal à se ~ dans le noir** to have difficulty finding one's way in the dark

dirigisme /diʀiʒism/ nm planned economy

discale /diskal/ adj f hernie ~ slipped disc

discernement /disɛʀnəmɑ̃/ nm judgment

discerner /disɛʀne/ [1] vtr **(a)** to detect ⟨sign, smell, expression⟩; to make out ⟨shape, noise⟩
(b) to make out ⟨motives⟩; **~ le vrai du faux** to discriminate between truth and untruth

disciple /disipl/ nmf **(a)** follower
(b) disciple

disciplinaire /disiplinɛʀ/ adj disciplinary

discipline /disiplin/ nf **(a)** discipline
(b) discipline, specialism
(c) (Sch) subject
(d) sport

discipliner /disipline/ [1] vtr **(a)** to discipline
(b) to control ⟨troops⟩; to discipline ⟨thoughts, feelings⟩
(c) to keep [sth] under control ⟨hair⟩

disco /disko/ **1** adj inv disco
2 nm disco music

discontinu, ~e /diskɔ̃tiny/ adj ⟨movement⟩ intermittent; ⟨line⟩ broken

discordance /diskɔʀdɑ̃s/ nf **(a)** (of opinions) conflict
(b) (of colours) clash
(c) (of sounds) dissonance

discordant, ~e /diskɔʀdɑ̃, ɑ̃t/ adj **(a)** ⟨sound, instrument⟩ discordant; ⟨voice⟩ strident
(b) ⟨colours⟩ clashing
(c) ⟨opinions⟩ conflicting

discorde /diskɔʀd/ nf discord, dissension

discothèque /diskɔtɛk/ nf **(a)** music library
(b) record collection
(c) discotheque

discourir /diskuʀiʀ/ [26] vi **~ de** or **sur qch** to hold forth on sth

discours /diskuʀ/ nm inv **(a)** speech (sur on)
(b) talk; **assez de ~, des actes!** let's have less talk and more action!
(c) views; **il tient toujours le même ~** his views haven't changed
(d) (in linguistics) speech; discourse

discrédit /diskʀedi/ nm disrepute; **jeter le ~ sur** to discredit

discréditer /diskʀedite/ [1] vtr to discredit

discret, -ète /diskʀɛ, ɛt/ adj **(a)** ⟨person⟩ unassuming; ⟨colour⟩ sober; ⟨charm⟩ subtle; ⟨lighting⟩ subdued; ⟨smile, perfume⟩ discreet; ⟨place⟩ quiet
(b) discreet (sur about)
(c) not inquisitive

discrètement /diskʀɛtmɑ̃/ adv discreetly; soberly; quietly

discrétion /diskʀesjɔ̃/ **1** nf discretion; **dans la plus grande ~** in the greatest secrecy
2 à discrétion phr **il y avait à boire à ~** you could drink as much as you liked
3 à la discrétion de phr at the discretion of

discrimination /diskʀiminasjɔ̃/ *nf* discrimination

discriminatoire /diskʀiminatwaʀ/ *adj* discriminatory (**à l'encontre de** against)

discriminer /diskʀimine/ [1] *vtr* to discriminate between ⟨*things, people*⟩

disculper /diskylpe/ [1] **1** *vtr* to exculpate **2 se disculper** *v refl* (+ *v être*) to vindicate oneself (**auprès de qn** in the eyes of)

discussion /diskysjɔ̃/ *nf* (a) discussion; **relancer la** ~ to revive the debate
(b) argument

discutable /diskytabl/ *adj* debatable; questionable

discuté, ~e /diskyte/ **1** *pp* ▶ DISCUTER **2** *pp adj* controversial

discuter /diskyte/ [1] **1** *vtr* (a) to discuss, to debate
(b) to question
2 discuter de *v+prep* to discuss
3 *vi* (a) to talk (**avec qn** to sb)
(b) to argue
4 se discuter *v refl* (+ *v être*) **ça se discute, ça peut se** ~ that's debatable

diseur, -euse /dizœʀ, øz/ *nm,f* ~ **de bonne aventure** fortune-teller

disgrâce /disgʀas/ *nf* disgrace

disgracieux, -ieuse /disgʀasjø, øz/ *adj* ugly; unsightly

disjoindre /disʒwɛ̃dʀ/ [56] **1** *vtr* (a) to loosen
(b) to separate
2 se disjoindre *v refl* to come loose

disjoncter /disʒɔ̃kte/ [1] *vi* **ça a disjoncté** the trip switch has gone

disjoncteur /disʒɔ̃ktœʀ/ *nm* circuit breaker

dislocation /dislɔkasjɔ̃/ *nf*
(a) dismemberment
(b) ~ (**articulaire**) dislocation (of a joint)

disloquer /dislɔke/ [1] *vtr* (a) to dismember ⟨*empire, state*⟩
(b) to dislocate ⟨*shoulder, arm*⟩

disparaître /dispaʀɛtʀ/ [73] *vi* (a) to disappear; to vanish; **disparaissez!** out of my sight!; **des centaines de personnes disparaissent chaque année** hundreds of people go missing every year
(b) ⟨*pain, smell*⟩ to go; ⟨*stain*⟩ to come out; ⟨*fever*⟩ to subside; **faire** ~ to get rid of ⟨*pain, dandruff*⟩; to remove ⟨*stain*⟩
(c) (euphemistic) to die; to die out; to become extinct; **voir** ~ to witness the end of ⟨*civilization*⟩

disparate /dispaʀat/ *adj* ill-assorted; mixed

disparition /dispaʀisjɔ̃/ *nf*
(a) disappearance; (of species) extinction; **une espèce en voie de** ~ an endangered species
(b) (euphemistic) death

disparu, ~e /dispaʀy/ **1** *pp* ▶ DISPARAÎTRE

2 *pp adj* (a) missing; **porté** ~ (Mil) missing in action
(b) ⟨*civilization, traditions*⟩ lost; ⟨*species*⟩ extinct
(c) (euphemistic) dead
3 *nm,f* (a) missing person
(b) **les** ~**s** the dead

dispendieux, -ieuse /dispɑ̃djø, øz/ *adj* expensive, extravagant

dispense /dispɑ̃s/ *nf* (a) exemption (**de** from)
(b) certificate of exemption

dispenser /dispɑ̃se/ [1] **1** *vtr* (a) to give ⟨*lessons, advice*⟩
(b) ~ **qn de (faire) qch** to exempt sb from (doing) sth; to excuse sb from (doing) sth; **je vous dispense de commentaire** I don't need any comment from you
2 se dispenser *v refl* (+ *v être*) **se** ~ **de (faire) qch** to spare oneself (the trouble of doing) sth

disperser /dispɛʀse/ [1] **1** *vtr* to scatter ⟨*objects, family*⟩; to disperse ⟨*crowd, smoke*⟩; to break up ⟨*gathering, collection*⟩
2 se disperser *v refl* (+ *v être*) to disperse; to scatter; to break up

disponibilité /dispɔnibilite/ **1** *nf* availability
2 disponibilités *nf pl* available funds

disponible /dispɔnibl/ *adj* available

dispos, ~e /dispo, oz/ *adj* **frais et** ~ fresh as a daisy

disposé, ~e /dispoze/ **1** *pp* ▶ DISPOSER
2 *pp adj* (a) arranged; laid out
(b) ~ **à faire** willing to do
(c) **être bien** ~ to be in a good mood; **être bien** ~ **à l'égard de** *or* **envers qn** to be well-disposed toward(s) sb

disposer /dispoze/ [1] **1** *vtr* (a) to arrange; to position
(b) **les machines dont nous disposons** the machines we have at our disposal
2 se disposer *v refl* (+ *v être*) (a) **se** ~ **à faire** to be about to do
(b) **se** ~ **en cercle autour de qn** to form a circle around sb

dispositif /dispozitif/ *nm* (a) device; system
(b) operation; ~ **policier** police operation

disposition /dispozisjɔ̃/ **1** *nf*
(a) arrangement; layout; position
(b) disposal; **à la** ~ **du public** for public use
(c) measure, step
2 dispositions *nf pl* aptitude

disproportionné, ~e /dispʀɔpɔʀsjɔne/ *adj* ⟨*effort, demand*⟩ disproportionate; ⟨*head*⟩ out of proportion with one's body

dispute /dispyt/ *nf* argument

disputé, ~e /dispyte/ *adj* (a) ⟨*title, match*⟩ keenly contested
(b) ⟨*place, person*⟩ sought-after (**de** by)
(c) ⟨*issue, plan*⟩ controversial

disputer /dispyte/ [1] **1** *vtr* (a) to compete in ⟨*competition*⟩; to compete for ⟨*cup*⟩; to play ⟨*match*⟩; to run ⟨*race*⟩

(b) (colloq) to tell [sb] off

2 **se disputer** *v refl* (+ *v être)* **(a)** to argue **(sur** about; **pour** over); **nous nous sommes disputés** we had an argument **(b)** to fight over ⟨*inheritance, bone*⟩ **(c)** ⟨*tournament*⟩ to take place

disquaire /diskɛR/ *nmf* record dealer

disqualifier /diskalifje/ [2] **1** *vtr* to disqualify; **se faire ~** (**par**) to be disqualified (by) **2** **se disqualifier** *v refl* (+ *v être)* to discredit oneself **(en faisant** by doing)

disque /disk/ *nm* **(a)** record; **passer un ~** to play a record **(b)** (gen, Tech) disc; (Comput) disk **(c)** (Sport) discus ∎ **~ compact** compact disc; **~ dur** hard disk; **~ souple** flexi-disc; floppy disk; **~ de stationnement** parking disc

disquette /diskɛt/ *nf* diskette, floppy disk

dissection /disɛksjɔ̃/ *nf* dissection

dissemblable /disɑ̃blabl/ *adj* dissimilar, different

dissémination /diseminasjɔ̃/ *nf* spread; dispersal; scattering; dissemination

disséminer /disemine/ [1] **1** *vtr* to spread ⟨*germs, ideas*⟩; to disperse ⟨*pollen*⟩ **2** **se disséminer** *v refl* (+ *v être)* ⟨*people*⟩ to scatter; ⟨*germs, ideas*⟩ to spread

dissension /disɑ̃sjɔ̃/ *nf* disagreement **(au sein de** within)

disséquer /diseke/ [14] *vtr* to dissect

dissert /disɛR/ *nf* essay

dissertation /disɛRtasjɔ̃/ *nf* essay

disserter /disɛRte/ [1] *vi* to speak **(sur** on)

dissidence /disidɑ̃s/ *nf* **(a)** dissent; dissidence; rebellion **(b) la ~** the dissidents

dissident, ~e /disidɑ̃, ɑ̃t/ **1** *adj* dissident **2** *nm,f* **(a)** dissident **(b)** dissenter

dissimulation /disimylasjɔ̃/ *nf* concealment

dissimuler /disimyle/ [1] *vtr* to conceal **(qch à qn** sth from sb)

dissipation /disipasjɔ̃/ *nf* **(a)** (of misunderstanding) clearing up **(b)** (of fog, clouds) clearing **(c)** (of attention) wandering **(d)** restlessness

dissipé, ~e /disipe/ *adj* ⟨*pupil*⟩ badly-behaved; ⟨*life*⟩ dissipated

dissiper /disipe/ [1] **1** *vtr* **(a)** to dispel ⟨*doubt*⟩; to clear up ⟨*misunderstanding*⟩; to disperse ⟨*smoke*⟩ **(b)** to distract ⟨*person*⟩ **2** **se dissiper** *v refl* (+ *v être)* **(a)** ⟨*doubt*⟩ to vanish; ⟨*misunderstanding*⟩ to be cleared up; ⟨*mist*⟩ to clear **(b)** to behave badly

dissocier /disɔsje/ [2] *vtr* to separate **(de** from)

dissolu, ~e /disɔly/ *adj* ⟨*life*⟩ dissolute; ⟨*morals*⟩ loose

dissolution /disɔlysjɔ̃/ *nf* dissolution

dissolvant, ~e /disɔlvɑ̃, ɑ̃t/ **1** *adj* solvent **2** *nm* **(a)** nail varnish **(b)** solvent

dissonance /disɔnɑ̃s/ *nf* dissonance

dissonant, ~e /disɔnɑ̃, ɑ̃t/ *adj* ⟨*voice*⟩ dissonant; ⟨*colours*⟩ clashing

dissoudre /disudR/ [75] **1** *vtr* **(a)** to dissolve ⟨*assembly*⟩; to disband ⟨*movement*⟩ **(b)** to dissolve ⟨*substance*⟩ **2** **se dissoudre** *v refl* (+ *v être)* **(a)** ⟨*organization*⟩ to disband **(b)** ⟨*substance*⟩ to dissolve

dissous, -oute /disu, ut/ ▶ DISSOUDRE

dissuader /disɥade/ [1] *vtr* to dissuade; to put [sb] off; to deter

dissuasif, -ive /disɥazif, iv/ *adj* **(a)** dissuasive; deterrent **(b)** prohibitive

dissuasion /disɥazjɔ̃/ *nf* (Mil) deterrence

dissymétrie /disimetri/ *nf* asymmetry

distance /distɑ̃s/ *nf* **(a)** distance; **Paris est à quelle ~ de Londres?** how far is Paris from London?; **j'ai couru sur une ~ de deux kilomètres** I ran for two kilometres (GB); **être à faible ~ de** not to be far (away) from; **prendre ses ~s avec** to distance oneself from; **tenir** *or* **garder ses ~s** to stand aloof; **tenir la ~** ⟨*runner*⟩ to stay the course; **à ~** from a distance; **commande à ~** remote control **(b)** gap; **à une semaine de ~** one week apart

distancer /distɑ̃se/ [12] *vtr* to outdistance; to outrun; **se laisser ~** to get left behind

distancier: se distancier /distɑ̃sje/ [2] *v refl* (+ *v être)* to distance oneself **(de** from)

distant, ~e /distɑ̃, ɑ̃t/ *adj* **(a)** ⟨*place, noise*⟩ distant; **~s de trois kilomètres** three kilometres (GB) apart **(b)** ⟨*person*⟩ distant; ⟨*attitude*⟩ reserved; ⟨*relations*⟩ cool

distendre /distɑ̃dR/ **1** *vtr* **(a)** to distend ⟨*stomach*⟩; to stretch ⟨*skin*⟩, ⟨*cable*⟩ **(b)** to weaken ⟨*bond*⟩, ⟨*tie*⟩ **2** **se distendre** *v refl* (+ *v être)* **(a)** to slacken **(b)** to cool

distiller /distile/ [1] *vtr* to distil (GB)

distillerie /distilRi/ *nf* **(a)** distillery **(b)** distilling

distinct, ~e /distɛ̃, ɛ̃kt/ *adj* **(a)** distinct **(de** from) **(b)** ⟨*sound*⟩ distinct; ⟨*voice*⟩ clear **(c)** ⟨*firm*⟩ separate

distinctif, -ive /distɛ̃ktif, iv/ *adj* ⟨*mark*⟩ distinguishing; ⟨*feature*⟩ distinctive

distinction /distɛ̃ksjɔ̃/ *nf* **(a)** distinction; **sans ~** without discrimination; indiscriminately **(b)** honour (GB); **~ honorifique** award **(c)** refinement

d

distingué, **~e** /distẽge/ adj distinguished

distinguer /distẽge/ [1] **1** vtr **(a)** to distinguish between; **il est difficile de les ~** it's difficult to tell them apart
(b) to distinguish, to make out
(c) to discern
(d) to set [sb] apart; to make [sth] different
(e) to single [sb] out for an honour (GB)
2 se distinguer v refl (+ v être) **(a) se ~ de** to differ from; to set oneself apart from
(b) to distinguish oneself
(c) to be distinguishable
(d) to draw attention to oneself

distordre /distɔʀdʀ/ **1** vtr to contort; **distordu par** contorted with
2 se distordre v refl to become contorted

distorsion /distɔʀsjɔ̃/ nf distortion

distraction /distʀaksjɔ̃/ nf **(a)** leisure, entertainment; **les ~s sont rares ici** there's not much to do around here
(b) recreation
(c) absent-mindedness

distraire /distʀɛʀ/ [58] **1** vtr **(a)** to amuse; to entertain
(b) ~ qn de qch to take sb's mind off sth
(c) to distract (**de** from; **par** by)
2 se distraire v refl (+ v être) **(a)** to amuse oneself; to enjoy oneself
(b) j'ai besoin de me ~ I need to take my mind off things

distrait, **~e** /distʀɛ, ɛt/ adj ⟨person⟩ absent-minded; inattentive; ⟨air⟩ distracted; ⟨look⟩ vague

distraitement /distʀɛtmɑ̃/ adv absent-mindedly; **regarder ~ qch** to look vaguely at sth; **écouter ~** to listen with half an ear

distrayant, **~e** /distʀɛjɑ̃, ɑ̃t/ adj entertaining

distribuer /distʀibɥe/ [1] vtr **(a)** to distribute (**à** to); to allocate (**à** to); **~ les cartes** to deal; **~ le courrier** to deliver the mail
(b) to supply ⟨water, heat⟩

distributeur, **-trice** /distʀibytœʀ, tʀis/
1 nm,f distributor
2 nm **(a)** dispenser; vending machine; **~ de tickets** ticket machine; **~ de billets (de banque)** cash dispenser
(b) retailing group
■ **~ automatique de billets, DAB** automatic teller machine, ATM

distribution /distʀibysjɔ̃/ nf **(a)** (sector) retailing
(b) (in commerce) distribution
(c) (of water, electricity) supply
(d) (supplying) distribution, handing out; (of jobs, duties) allocation
(e) (geographically) distribution, layout
(f) (of actors) casting; cast
■ **~ d'actions gratuites** allocation of bonus shares; **~ automatique** automatic dispensing; **~ du courrier** postal delivery

dithyrambique /ditiʀɑ̃bik/ adj ⟨speech⟩, ⟨comments⟩ ecstatic; ⟨praise⟩ extravagant

diurétique /djyʀetik/ adj, nm diuretic

divagation /divagasjɔ̃/ nf ravings; rambling

divaguer /divage/ [1] vi **(a)** to rave; **la fièvre le fait ~** he's delirious with fever
(b) to ramble; to talk nonsense
(c) to stray

divan /divɑ̃/ nm divan; couch

divergence /divɛʀʒɑ̃s/ nf divergence; difference

divergent, **~e** /divɛʀʒɑ̃, ɑ̃t/ adj divergent

diverger /divɛʀʒe/ [13] vi to diverge (**de** from); to differ (**de** from)

divers, **~e** /divɛʀ, ɛʀs/ adj **(a)** various; **les gens les plus ~** all sorts of people
(b) miscellaneous

diversement /divɛʀsəmɑ̃/ adv variously, in different ways

diversification /divɛʀsifikasjɔ̃/ nf diversification; **une entreprise en voie de ~** a company in the process of diversifying; **une ~ de la clientèle** targeting a wider clientele

diversifier /divɛʀsifje/ [2] vtr to widen the range of; to diversify

diversion /divɛʀsjɔ̃/ nf (Mil) diversion

diversité /divɛʀsite/ nf diversity; variety

divertir /divɛʀtiʀ/ [3] **1** vtr to entertain; to amuse
2 se divertir v refl (+ v être) to amuse oneself; **pour se ~** for fun

divertissant, **~e** /divɛʀtisɑ̃, ɑ̃t/ adj amusing; entertaining; enjoyable

divertissement /divɛʀtismɑ̃/ nm entertainment; recreation

dividende /dividɑ̃d/ nm dividend

divin, **~e** /divɛ̃, in/ adj divine

divinité /divinite/ nf deity; divinity

diviser /divize/ [1] **1** vtr to divide
2 se diviser v refl (+ v être) **(a)** to become divided (**sur** over)
(b) to be divided
(c) to be divisible
(d) to divide; to fork

divisible /divizibl/ adj divisible

division /divizjɔ̃/ nf division

divisionnaire /divizjɔnɛʀ/ adj **commissaire ~** Chief Superintendent

divorce /divɔʀs/ nm divorce (**d'avec** from); **prononcer le ~ entre deux époux** to grant a divorce to a couple

divorcé, **~e** /divɔʀse/ nm,f divorcee

divorcer /divɔʀse/ [12] vi to get divorced

divulgation /divylgasjɔ̃/ nf disclosure

divulguer /divylge/ [1] vtr to disclose

dix /dis, but before consonant di, before vowel or mute h diz/ adj inv, pron, nm inv ten
IDIOMS **ne rien savoir faire de ses ~ doigts** to be useless; **un de perdu, ~ de retrouvés** (Proverb) there's plenty more fish in the sea

dix-huit /dizɥit/ adj inv, pron, nm inv eighteen

dix-huitième /dizɥitjɛm/ adj eighteenth

dixième /dizjɛm/ adj tenth

dix-neuf /diznœf/ *adj inv, pron, nm inv*
nineteen

dix-neuvième /diznœvjɛm/ *adj*
nineteenth

dix-sept /dis(s)ɛt/ *adj inv, pron, nm inv*
seventeen

dix-septième /dis(s)ɛtjɛm/ *adj*
seventeenth

dizaine /dizɛn/ *nf* (a) ten
(b) about ten; **des ～s de personnes** dozens
of people

do /do/ *nm inv* (Mus) (note) C; (in sol-fa) doh

docile /dɔsil/ *adj* ⟨animal, person⟩ docile

dock /dɔk/ *nm* (a) dock
(b) warehouse

docteur /dɔktœʀ/ *nm* doctor; **jouer au ～**
to play doctors and nurses

doctorat /dɔktɔʀa/ *nm* PhD, doctorate

doctrinaire /dɔktʀinɛʀ/ *adj* ⟨attitude⟩
doctrinaire; ⟨tone⟩ sententious

doctrine /dɔktʀin/ *nf* doctrine

document /dɔkymɑ̃/ *nm* (a) document;
～ sonore audio material; **avec ～s à l'appui**
with documentary evidence
(b) document, paper

documentaire /dɔkymɑ̃tɛʀ/ ⨯1⨯ *adj*
documentary; **à titre ～** for your information
⨯2⨯ *nm* documentary (**sur** on, about)

documentaliste /dɔkymɑ̃talist/ *nmf*
information officer; (school) librarian

documentation /dɔkymɑ̃tasjɔ̃/ *nf*
(a) material (**sur** on)
(b) research
(c) brochures
(d) **centre de ～** resource centre (GB)

documenter: se documenter
/dɔkymɑ̃te/ ⨯1⨯ *v refl* (+ *v être*) **se ～ sur qch**
to research sth

dodeliner /dɔdline/ ⨯1⨯ *vi* **il dodelinait de
la tête** his head was nodding

dodo /dodo/ *nm* (baby talk) **faire ～** to sleep

dodu, -e /dɔdy/ *adj* plump

dogmatique /dɔgmatik/ *adj* dogmatic

dogme /dɔgm/ *nm* dogma

dogue /dɔg/ *nm* mastiff

doigt /dwa/ *nm* finger; **petit ～** little finger
(GB), pinkie; **bout des ～s** fingertips; **du bout
des ～s** (figurative) reluctantly; **connaître une
ville sur le bout des ～s** to know a city like
the back of one's hand; **montrer du ～** to
point at; (figurative) to point the finger at
■ **～ de pied** toe
IDIOMS **se brûler les ～s** to get one's fingers
burned; **être à deux ～s de** to be a whisker
away from; **filer entre les ～s de qn** ⟨money,
thief⟩ to slip through sb's fingers; **se faire
taper sur les ～s** to get one's knuckles
rapped; **lever le ～** to put one's hand up

doigté /dwate/ *nm* (a) tact
(b) (of pianist) fingering

doléance /dɔleɑ̃s/ *nf* complaint

dollar /dɔlaʀ/ *nm* dollar

DOM /dɔm/ *nm inv* (*abbr* = **département
d'outre-mer**) *French overseas
(administrative) department*

domaine /dɔmɛn/ *nm* (a) estate
(b) field, domain
(c) territory

domanial, ～e, mpl -iaux /dɔmanjal, o/
adj state-owned

dôme /dom/ *nm* dome

domestique /dɔmɛstik/ ⨯1⨯ *adj* (a) ⟨staff,
animal⟩ domestic
(b) ⟨market⟩ domestic, home
⨯2⨯ *nmf* servant

domestiquer /dɔmɛstike/ [1] *vtr* to
domesticate ⟨animal⟩

domicile /dɔmisil/ ⨯1⨯ *nm* place of
residence; (of company) registered address
⨯2⨯ **à domicile** *phr* **travail à ～** working at
or from home; **'livraisons à ～'** 'home
deliveries'

domicilié, ～e /dɔmisilje/ *adj* (a) **être ～
à Arras** to live in Arras
(b) **j'habite à Paris, mais je suis ～e à
Rennes** I live in Paris, but my official
address is in Rennes

dominance /dɔminɑ̃s/ *nf* dominance

dominant, ～e[1] /dɔminɑ̃, ɑ̃t/ *adj*
(a) ⟨colour, gene⟩ dominant; ⟨wind, tendency⟩
prevailing; ⟨feature, idea⟩ main
(b) ⟨class⟩ ruling

dominante[2] /dɔminɑ̃t/ *nf* (a) dominant
feature
(b) (Univ) main subject, major

dominateur, -trice /dɔminatœʀ, tʀis/
adj domineering; overbearing; imperious

domination /dɔminasjɔ̃/ *nf* domination;
être sous la ～ de to be dominated by

dominer /dɔmine/ [1] ⨯1⨯ *vtr* (a) to
dominate; to tower above; **de là, on domine
toute la vallée** from there you get a view of
the whole valley
(b) to dominate ⟨match, sector⟩
(c) ⟨theme⟩ to dominate
(d) to master ⟨subject⟩; to overcome ⟨fear⟩;
～ la situation to be in control of the
situation
⨯2⨯ *vi* (a) to rule, to hold sway
(b) to be in the lead
(c) ⟨impression⟩ to prevail; ⟨taste⟩ to stand
out
⨯3⨯ **se dominer** *v refl* (+ *v être*) to control
oneself

dominical, ～e, mpl -aux /dɔminikal,
o/ *adj* ⟨walk, mass⟩ Sunday

domino /dɔmino/ *nm* domino

dommage /dɔmaʒ/ *nm* (a) **c'est ～** it's a
shame *or* pity
(b) damage
(c) (Law) tort
■ **～s corporels** personal injury; **～s et
intérêts** damages

dommageable /dɔmaʒabl/ *adj* harmful
(**pour** to)

dommages-intérêts /dɔmaʒɛtɛʀɛ/ *nm pl* damages; **10 000 francs de ~** 10,000 francs in damages

dompter /dɔ̃te/ [1] *vtr* to tame ⟨*wild animal*⟩; to bring [sb] to heel ⟨*unruly person*⟩; to subdue ⟨*insurgents*⟩; to overcome ⟨*passion*⟩

dompteur, -euse /dɔ̃tœʀ, øz/ *nm,f* tamer

DOM-TOM /dɔmtɔm/ *nm pl* (*abbr* = **départements et territoires d'outre-mer**) French overseas departments and territories

don /dɔ̃/ *nm* (a) donation; **faire ~ de** to give (à to); **~ de soi** self-sacrifice
(b) gift; **avoir le ~ de faire** to have a talent for doing
■ **~ du sang** blood donation

donation /dɔnasjɔ̃/ *nf* (a) donation
(b) (Law) gift

donc /dɔ̃k/ *conj* so, therefore; **j'étais ~ en train de lire, lorsque...** so I was reading, when...; **je disais ~ que...** as I was saying...; **entrez ~!** do come in!; **mais où est-il ~ passé?** where on earth has he gone?

donjon /dɔ̃ʒɔ̃/ *nm* (of castle) keep

donne /dɔn/ *nf* (in cards) deal

donné, ~e[1] /dɔne/ [1] *pp* ▶ DONNER
[2] *pp adj* (a) **il n'est pas ~ à tout le monde de faire** not everyone can do
(b) given; **à un moment ~** at one point; all of a sudden
(c) cheap
[3] **étant donné (que)** *phr* given (that)

donnée[2] /dɔne/ *nf* (a) fact, element
(b) data

donner /dɔne/ [1] [1] *vtr* (a) to give ⟨*present, headache, advice, dinner, lesson*⟩; **~ l'heure à qn** to tell sb the time; **je lui donne 40 ans** I'd say he/she was 40; **~ faim à qn** to make sb feel hungry; **elle donne sa fille à garder à mes parents** she has my parents look after her daughter; **j'ai donné ma voiture à réparer** I've taken my car in to be repaired; **les sondages le donnent en tête** the polls put him in the lead
(b) to show ⟨*film*⟩; to put on ⟨*play*⟩; to give ⟨*performance*⟩
(c) to produce, to yield ⟨*fruit, juice*⟩; to produce ⟨*results*⟩
(d) to show ⟨*signs*⟩
(e) (colloq) to inform on ⟨*accomplice*⟩
[2] *vi* (a) **le poirier va bien ~ cette année** the pear tree will yield a good crop this year
(b) **ne plus savoir où ~ de la tête** (figurative) not to know which way to turn
(c) **~ sur** ⟨*room, window*⟩ to overlook; ⟨*door*⟩ to give onto; **~ au nord** to face north; **la cuisine donne dans le salon** the kitchen leads into the living-room
(d) **~ dans** to tend toward(s)
(e) **~ de sa personne** to give of oneself
[3] **se donner** *v refl* (+ *v être*) (a) **se ~ à** to devote oneself to
(b) **se ~ le temps de faire** to give oneself time to do

(c) **se ~ pour but de faire** to make it one's aim to do
(d) **se ~ de grands airs** to put on airs
(e) **se ~ des coups** to exchange blows; **se ~ le mot** to pass the word on
IDIOMS **donnant donnant: je fais la cuisine, tu fais la vaisselle** fair's fair: I cook, you do the washing-up; **avec lui, c'est donnant donnant** he never does anything for nothing

donneur, -euse /dɔnœʀ, øz/ *nm,f* (Med) donor

dont /dɔ̃/ *rel pron* (a) whose, of which; **la jeune fille ~ on nous disait qu'elle avait 20 ans** the girl who they said was 20; **Sylvaine est quelqu'un ~ on se souvient** Sylvaine is somebody (that) you remember; **la maladie ~ il souffre** the illness which he's suffering from; **la façon ~ il a été traité** the way in which he has been treated
(b) **il y a eu plusieurs victimes ~ mon père** there were several victims, one of whom was my father; **des boîtes ~ la plupart sont vides** boxes, most of which are empty

dopage /dɔpaʒ/ *nm* (a) (of horses) doping
(b) illegal drug-taking

doper /dɔpe/ [1] *vtr* to dope

dorade /dɔʀad/ *nf* (sea) bream

doré, ~e /dɔʀe/ [1] *pp* ▶ DORER
[2] *pp adj* (a) ⟨*paint*⟩ gold; ⟨*frame*⟩ gilt; ⟨*dome*⟩ gilded; ⟨*hair*⟩ golden; ⟨*skin*⟩ tanned; ⟨*bread*⟩ golden brown; **~ à l'or fin** gilded
(b) ⟨*exile*⟩ luxurious; **jeunesse ~e** gilded youth
[3] *nm* gilt

dorénavant /dɔʀenavɑ̃/ *adv* from now on

dorer /dɔʀe/ [1] [1] *vtr* (a) to gild
(b) (Culin) to glaze
[2] *vi* (Culin) to brown
[3] **se dorer** *v refl* (+ *v être*) **se ~ au soleil** to sunbathe

dorloter /dɔʀlɔte/ [1] *vtr* to pamper

dormeur, -euse /dɔʀmœʀ, øz/ *nm,f* sleeper; **c'est un gros ~** he sleeps a lot

dormir /dɔʀmiʀ/ [30] *vi* (a) to sleep; **~ debout** (figurative) to be dead on one's feet; **ça m'empêche de ~** it keeps me awake; **il n'en dort plus** he's losing sleep over it
(b) ⟨*money*⟩ to lie idle
IDIOMS **ne ~ que d'un œil** to sleep with one eye open; **~ sur ses deux oreilles, ~ tranquille** to rest easy; **~ comme un loir** to sleep like a log; **~ à poings fermés** to be fast asleep

dorsal, ~e, *mpl* **-aux** /dɔʀsal, o/ *adj* ⟨*pain*⟩ back; ⟨*fin*⟩ dorsal

dortoir /dɔʀtwaʀ/ [1] *nm* dormitory
[2] **(-)dortoir** (*combining form*) **ville-~** dormitory town

dorure /dɔʀyʀ/ *nf* gilt

dos /do/ *nm inv* (a) back; **avoir le ~ rond** or **voûté** to stoop; **mal de ~** backache; **voir qn de ~** to see sb from behind; **robe décolletée dans le ~** dress with a low back; **il n'a rien sur le ~** (colloq) he's wearing hardly

anything; **tourner le ~ à** to have one's back
to; to turn one's back to; (figurative) to turn
one's back on
(b) (of book) spine; (of blade) blunt edge
IDIOMS **mettre qch sur le ~ de** (colloq) to
blame sth on; **il a bon ~ le réveil!** (colloq) it's
easy to blame it on the alarm-clock!
dosage /dozaʒ/ *nm* **(a)** amount;
measurement
(b) mix; mixing
(c) proportions
dos-d'âne /dodɑn/ *nm inv* hump
dose /doz/ *nf* **(a)** dose; **forcer la ~** (colloq) to
go a bit far (colloq)
(b) measure
doser /doze/ [1] *vtr* **(a)** to measure
(b) to use [sth] in a controlled way
dossard /dosar/ *nm* number (*worn by an
athlete*)
dossier /dosje/ *nm* **(a)** file, dossier;
~ médical medical records; **~ d'inscription**
(Sch) registration form; **sélection sur ~**
selection by written application
(b) (Law) file; case
(c) **le ~ brûlant de la pollution** the
controversial problem of pollution
(d) file, folder
(e) (of chair) back
dot /dɔt/ *nf* dowry
dotation /dɔtasjɔ̃/ *nf* allocation;
endowment
doter /dote/ [1] *vtr* **(a)** **~ qn de qch** to
allocate sth to sb
(b) **~ qn/qch de** to equip sb/sth with
(c) **~ qn/qch de** to endow sb/sth with
douane /dwan/ *nf* **(a)** customs
(b) (on goods) duty
douanier, -ière /dwanje, ɛr/ **1** *adj*
customs
2 *nm* customs officer
double /dubl/ **1** *adj* double; **l'avantage est
~** the advantage is twofold; **valise à ~ fond**
suitcase with a false bottom; **~ nationalité**
dual nationality; **avoir le don de ~ vue** to
have second sight; **en ~ exemplaire** in
duplicate
2 *adv* double
3 *nm* **(a)** double; **leur piscine fait le ~ de la
nôtre** their swimming-pool is twice as big as
ours
(b) copy; **un ~ des clés** a spare set of keys
(c) (in tennis) doubles
doublé, ~e /duble/ **1** *pp* ▶ DOUBLER
2 *pp adj* **(a)** ⟨coat⟩ lined
(b) ⟨film⟩ dubbed
doublement /dubləmɑ̃/ **1** *adv* in two
ways; **il est ~ coupable** he's guilty on two
counts
2 *nm* (of quantity) doubling
doubler /duble/ [1] **1** *vtr* **(a)** to double
(b) to line (**de** with)
(c) to dub ⟨film⟩; to stand in for ⟨actor⟩
(d) to overtake (GB), to pass (US); **'défense
de ~'** 'no overtaking' (GB), 'no passing' (US)
2 *vi* to double

3 se doubler *v refl* (+ *v être*) **se ~ de qch**
to be coupled with sth
doublure /dublyr/ *nf* **(a)** lining
(b) (for actor) double
douce ▶ DOUX
douceâtre /dusɑtr/ *adj* sickly sweet
doucement /dusmɑ̃/ *adv* **(a)** gently;
~ avec le vin! go easy on the wine!
(b) quietly
(c) slowly
doucereux, -euse /dusrø, øz/ *adj*
⟨person⟩ smooth; ⟨words⟩ sugary; ⟨smile⟩
unctuous
douceur /dusœr/ **1** *nf* **(a)** softness;
mildness; mellowness; smoothness;
gentleness; **~ de vivre** relaxed rhythm of
life; **avec ~** gently
(b) sweet (GB), candy (US)
2 **en douceur** *phr* **(a)** smoothly;
atterrissage en ~ smooth landing
(b) **shampooing qui lave en ~** mild
shampoo
douche /duʃ/ *nf* shower; **~ froide** cold
shower; (figurative) letdown (colloq)
■ **~ écossaise** alternating hot and cold
shower; (figurative) bucket of cold water
doucher /duʃe/ [1] **1** *vtr* **(a)** to give [sb] a
shower
(b) (colloq) to dampen ⟨enthusiasm⟩
2 se doucher *v refl* (+ *v être*) to take a
shower
doué, ~e /dwe/ *adj* **(a)** gifted, talented;
être ~ pour to have a gift for
(b) **~ de** endowed with, gifted with
douille /duj/ *nf* **(a)** cartridge (case)
(b) (light) socket
douillet, -ette /dujɛ, ɛt/ *adj*
(a) oversensitive to pain
(b) cosy (GB), cozy (US)
douleur /dulœr/ *nf* **(a)** pain; **médicament
contre la ~** painkiller
(b) grief
douloureuse ▶ DOULOUREUX
douloureusement /dulurøzmɑ̃/ *adv*
(a) grievously; terribly
(b) painfully
douloureux, -euse /dulurø, øz/ *adj*
(a) painful
(b) ⟨event⟩ distressing; ⟨question⟩ painful
doute /dut/ **1** *nm* doubt; **laisser qn dans le
~** to leave sb in a state of uncertainty;
mettre qch en ~ to call sth into question;
dans le ~, j'ai préféré ne rien dire not being
sure I didn't say anything; **il fait peu de ~
que** there's little doubt that; **nul ~ que**
there's no doubt that
2 sans doute *phr* probably; **sans aucun
~** without any doubt
douter /dute/ [1] **1** *vtr* **(a)** **~ que** to doubt
that *or* whether
(b) **~ de qch** to have doubts about sth; **elle
l'affirme mais j'en doute** she says it's true
but I have my doubts; **elle ne doute de rien!**
(colloq) (ironic) she's so sure of herself!
2 *vi* to doubt

3 **se douter** *v refl* (+ *v être*) **se ~ de** to suspect; **je m'en doutais!** I thought so!; **je me doute (bien) qu'il devait être furieux** I can (well) imagine that he was furious; **nous étions loin de nous ~ que** we didn't have the least idea that

douteux, -euse /dutø, øz/ *adj*
(a) uncertain
(b) ambiguous
(c) dubious
(d) ‹*deal, character*› shady

douve /duv/ *nf* moat

Douvres /duvʀ/ *n pr* Dover

doux, douce /du, dus/ *adj* ‹*light, voice, substance*› soft; ‹*cider*› sweet; ‹*cheese, shampoo, weather*› mild; ‹*person, slope*› gentle

IDIOMS **filer ~** (colloq) to keep a low profile; **se la couler douce** (colloq) to take it easy; **en douce** (colloq) on the sly

douzaine /duzɛn/ *nf* (a) dozen; **à la ~** by the dozen
(b) about twelve, a dozen or so

douze /duz/ *adj inv, pron, nm inv* twelve

douzième /duzjɛm/ *adj* twelfth

doyen, -enne /dwajɛ̃, ɛn/ *nm,f* (a) oldest person
(b) the (most) senior member
(c) dean

Dr (*written abbr* = **docteur**) Dr

draconien, -ienne /dʀakɔnjɛ̃, ɛn/ *adj* draconian; very strict

dragée /dʀaʒe/ *nf* (a) sugared almond
(b) sugar-coated pill

dragon /dʀagɔ̃/ *nm* (a) dragon
(b) (Mil) dragoon

draguer /dʀage/ [1] *vtr* (a) (colloq) to come on to (colloq)
(b) to dredge, to drag ‹*river, canal*›

dragueur, -euse /dʀagœʀ, øz/ *nm,f* (colloq) **c'est un drôle de ~** (colloq) he's a terrible flirt

drain /dʀɛ̃/ *nm* drain

drainage /dʀɛnaʒ/ *nm* (a) drainage
(b) (Med) draining (off)

drainer /dʀɛne/ [1] *vtr* to drain

dramatique /dʀamatik/ *adj* (a) tragic; **ce n'est pas ~** it's not the end of the world
(b) dramatic; **art ~** drama; **auteur ~** playwright

dramatiquement /dʀamatikmɑ̃/ *adv* tragically

dramatiser /dʀamatize/ [1] *vtr* to dramatize

dramaturge /dʀamatyʀʒ/ *nmf* playwright

drame /dʀam/ *nm* (a) tragedy; **tourner au ~** to take a tragic turn
(b) drama; play; **~ lyrique** opera

drap /dʀa/ *nm* (a) sheet
(b) woollen (GB) cloth
■ **~ de plage** beach towel

IDIOMS **se mettre dans de beaux ~s** to land oneself in a fine mess

drapeau, *pl* **~x** /dʀapo/ *nm* flag; **être sous les ~x** to be doing military service

drap-housse, *pl* **draps-housses** /dʀaus/ *nm* fitted sheet

dressage /dʀɛsaʒ/ *nm* (a) training; (of horse) breaking in
(b) dressage

dresser /dʀɛse/ [1] **1** *vtr* (a) to train ‹*animal*›; to break in ‹*horse*›; to teach [sb] how to behave ‹*person*›
(b) to put up ‹*scaffolding*›
(c) to prick up ‹*ears*›
(d) to lay out ‹*buffet*›
(e) to draw up ‹*list*›; **~ un procès-verbal à qn** to give sb a ticket
(f) **~ qn contre** to set sb against
2 **se dresser** *v refl* (+ *v être*) (a) to stand up
(b) **se ~ contre** to rebel against
(c) ‹*statue, obstacle*› to stand; to tower up

dresseur, -euse /dʀɛsœʀ, øz/ *nm,f* trainer

dribbler /dʀible/ [1] *vi* to dribble

drogue /dʀɔg/ *nf* drug; **la ~** drugs; **c'est devenu une ~** it has become an addiction

drogué, ~e /dʀɔge/ *nm,f* drug-addict

droguer /dʀɔge/ [1] **1** *vtr* (a) ‹*doctor*› to dope
(b) to dope ‹*animal, sportsman*›; to drug ‹*victim*›; to doctor ‹*drink*›
2 **se droguer** *v refl* (+ *v être*) (a) to dope oneself (à, de with)
(b) to take drugs

droguerie /dʀɔgʀi/ *nf* hardware shop (GB) or store (US)

droguiste /dʀɔgist/ *nmf* owner of a hardware shop

droit, ~e¹ /dʀwa, at/ **1** *adj* ‹*line, road, nose*› straight; ‹*writing*› upright; **se tenir ~** to stand up straight; to sit up strait; **s'écarter du ~ chemin** to stray from the strait and narrow
(b) right; **du côté ~** on the right-hand side
(c) ‹*person*› straight(forward)
(d) ‹*skirt*› straight
(e) ‹*angle*› right
2 *adv* straight; **continuez tout ~** carry straight on; **marcher ~** to toe the line
3 *nm* (a) right; **être dans son (bon) ~** to be within one's rights; **cela leur revient de ~** it's theirs by right; **avoir ~ à** to be entitled to; **il a eu ~ à une amende** (ironic) he got a fine; **avoir le ~ de faire** to be allowed to do; **to have the right to do; avoir le ~ de vie ou de mort sur qn** to have power of life and death over sb; **il s'imagine qu'il a tous ses ~s** he thinks he can do whatever he likes; **être en ~ de** to be entitled to
(b) **le ~** law; **faire son ~** to study law
(c) fee
(d) (in boxing) right
■ (**prisonnier de**) **~ commun** nonpolitical prisoner; **~ d'entrée** entrance fee; **~ de passage** right of way (GB), easement (US); **un ~ de regard sur** a say in; **~s d'auteur**

royalties; ∼s **de douane** customs duties; **les ∼s de l'homme** human rights; ∼s **de succession** inheritance tax

droite² /dʁwat/ *nf* (a) right; **la porte de ∼** the door on the right; **à ta ∼** on your right; **demander à ∼ et à gauche** to ask everywhere; to ask everybody
(b) **voter à ∼** to vote for the right; **de ∼** right-wing
(c) straight line

droitier, -ière /dʁwatje, ɛʁ/ *nm,f* right-hander

droiture /dʁwatyʁ/ *nf* honesty, uprightness

drôle /dʁol/ *adj* (a) funny, odd; **faire (tout) ∼ à qn** to give sb a funny feeling; **faire une ∼ de tête** to make a bit of a face
(b) funny, amusing
(c) (colloq) **un ∼ de courage** a lot of courage
IDIOMS **j'en ai entendu de ∼s** I heard some funny things; **en faire voir de ∼s à qn** to lead sb a merry dance

drôlement /dʁolmɑ̃/ *adv* (a) (colloq) really
(b) oddly

drôlerie /dʁolʁi/ *nf* **avec ∼** amusingly

dromadaire /dʁɔmadɛʁ/ *nm* dromedary

dru, ∼e /dʁy/ ① *adj* ⟨*hair*⟩ thick
② *adv* (a) ⟨*grow*⟩ thickly
(b) **la pluie tombait ∼** it was raining heavily

druide /dʁɥid/ *nm* druid

DS /deɛs/ *nf: Citroen car of the 1950s*

DST /deɛste/ *nf* (*abbr* = **Direction de la surveillance du territoire**) *French counterintelligence agency*

du /dy/ *det* ▶ DE

dû, due, *mpl* **dus** /dy/ ① *pp* ▶ DEVOIR¹
② *pp adj* (a) owed, owing, due (à to); **en bonne et due forme** in due form
(b) **∼ à** due to
③ *nm* **réclamer son ∼** to claim one's due

dualité /dɥalite/ *nf* duality

dubitatif, -ive /dybitatif, iv/ *adj* sceptical (GB), skeptical (US)

duc /dyk/ *nm* duke

duchesse /dyʃɛs/ *nf* duchess

duel /dɥɛl/ *nm* duel (à with); (figurative) battle

dulcinée /dylsine/ *nf* lady-love

dune /dyn/ *nf* dune

duo /dyo, dɥo/ *nm* (a) duet; **en ∼** as a duo
(b) double act (GB), duo (US)
(c) (colloq) pair

dupe /dyp/ ① *adj* **être ∼** to be taken in *or* fooled (**de** by)
② *nf* dupe; **un marché de ∼s** a fool's bargain

duper /dype/ [1] *vtr* to fool; **facile à ∼** gullible

duperie /dypʁi/ *nf* trickery

duplex /dyplɛks/ *nm inv* maisonette (GB), duplex apartment (US)

duplicata /dyplikata/ *nm inv* duplicate

duquel ▶ LEQUEL

dur, ∼e /dyʁ/ ① *adj* (a) ⟨*ground, toothbrush, bread*⟩ hard; ⟨*meat*⟩ tough; ⟨*brush, cardboard*⟩ stiff; ⟨*plastic*⟩ rigid
(b) ⟨*zip, handle, pedal*⟩ stiff; ⟨*steering*⟩ heavy
(c) ⟨*sound, light, colour*⟩ harsh
(d) ⟨*face, expression*⟩ severe
(e) ⟨*parents, boss*⟩ hard; harsh; ⟨*policy*⟩ hardline
(f) ⟨*living conditions*⟩ harsh
(g) ⟨*job, sport*⟩ hard; tough; ⟨*climate, necessity*⟩ harsh
(h) ⟨*exam*⟩ hard, difficult
(i) ⟨*water*⟩ hard
② *nm,f* (a) tough nut (colloq); **jouer les ∼s** to act tough
(b) hardliner
③ *adv* ⟨*work, hit*⟩ hard
④ *nm* **construction en ∼** permanent structure
⑤ **à la dure** *phr* **élevé à la ∼e** brought up the hard way
IDIOMS **∼ d'oreille** hard of hearing; **avoir la tête ∼e** to be stubborn; to be dense; **avoir la vie ∼e** ⟨*habit*⟩ to die hard; **mener la vie ∼e à qn** to give sb a hard time

durable /dyʁabl/ *adj* ⟨*impression*⟩ lasting; ⟨*interest*⟩ enduring; ⟨*material*⟩ durable

durablement /dyʁabləmɑ̃/ *adv* on a permanent basis

durant /dyʁɑ̃/ *prep* (a) for; **des heures ∼** for hours and hours
(b) during

durcir /dyʁsiʁ/ [3] ① *vtr* (a) to harden ⟨*ground, features, position*⟩
(b) to step up ⟨*strike action*⟩; **∼ sa politique en matière de** to take a harder line on
② *vi* ⟨*clay, artery*⟩ to harden; ⟨*cement, glue*⟩ to set; ⟨*bread*⟩ to go hard
③ **se durcir** *v refl* (+ *v être*) (a) to harden
(b) to become harsher; to intensify

durcissement /dyʁsismɑ̃/ *nm*
(a) hardening
(b) intensification

durée /dyʁe/ *nf* (a) (of reign, studies) length; (of contract) term; (of cassette) playing time; **séjour d'une ∼ de trois mois** three-month stay; **contrat à ∼ déterminée** fixed-term contract; **de courte ∼** ⟨*peace*⟩ short-lived; ⟨*absence*⟩ brief; ⟨*loan*⟩ short-term
(b) ∼ **(de vie)** life; **pile longue ∼** long-life battery

durement /dyʁmɑ̃/ *adv* (a) badly
(b) harshly
(c) ⟨*look*⟩ severely
(d) ⟨*hit*⟩ hard

durer /dyʁe/ [1] *vi* (a) to last
(b) to go on; **ça ne peut plus ∼** it can't go on any longer; **faire ∼** to prolong ⟨*meeting*⟩; **faire ∼ le plaisir** (ironic) to prolong the agony
(c) ⟨*festival*⟩ to run

dures /dyʁ/ *nf pl* **en faire voir de ∼ à ses parents** to give one's parents a hard time

dureté /dyʁte/ *nf* (a) (of material, face) hardness; (of meat) toughness; (of brush) stiffness ⋯⋯

(b) (of expression, tone, climate) harshness; (of look) severity; **avec ~** ⟨look⟩ severely; ⟨punish⟩ harshly

durillon /dyRijɔ̃/ nm callus

durite /dyRit/ nf radiator hose

DUT /deyte/ nm (abbr = **diplôme universitaire de technologie**) two-year diploma from a university institute of technology

duvet /dyvɛ/ nm **(a)** (of bird) down **(b)** sleeping bag

duveteux, -euse /dyvtø, øz/ adj downy

dynamique /dinamik/ **1** adj dynamic, lively
2 nf **(a)** dynamics

(b) process

dynamiser /dinamize/ [1] vtr to make [sb/sth] more dynamic; to revitalize

dynamisme /dinamism/ nm dynamism; **être plein de ~** to be very dynamic

dynamite /dinamit/ nf dynamite

dynamiter /dinamite/ [1] vtr to dynamite; (figurative) to destroy

dynastie /dinasti/ nf dynasty

dysenterie /disɑ̃tRi/ nf dysentery

dysfonctionnement /disfɔ̃ksjɔnmɑ̃/ nm **(a)** (Med) dysfunction **(b)** malfunctioning

dyslexie /dislɛksi/ nf dyslexia

Ee

e, E /ə/ nm inv e, E; **e dans l'o** o and e joined together

eau, pl **~x** /o/ **1** nf **(a)** water; **l'~ de source** spring water; **prendre l'~** ⟨shoe⟩ to let in water; **être en ~** to be dripping with sweat; **mettre à l'~** to launch ⟨ship⟩; **se jeter à l'~** to throw oneself into the water; (figurative) to take the plunge; **tomber à l'~** (figurative) to fall through; **nettoyer le sol à grande ~** to sluice the floor down

(b) rain

2 eaux nf pl **(a)** water; waters
(b) (Med) waters

■ **~ bénite** holy water; **~ de chaux** limewater; **~ douce** fresh water; **~ de Javel** ≈ (chloride) bleach; **~ de mer** seawater; **~ oxygénée** hydrogen peroxide; **~ plate** plain water; still mineral water; **~ de rose: à l'~ de rose** ⟨novel⟩ sentimental; **~x et forêts** forestry commission; **~x usées** waste water **IDIOMS mettre l'~ à la bouche de qn** to make sb's mouth water; **ou dans ces ~x-là** (colloq) or thereabouts; **vivre d'amour et d'~ fraîche** to live on love alone

EAU written abbr ▶ ÉMIRATS

eau-de-vie, pl **eaux-de-vie** /odvi/ nf brandy, eau de vie; **à l'~** in brandy

ébahir /ebaiR/ [3] **1** vtr to dumbfound
2 s'ébahir v refl (+ v être) to be dumbfounded

ébattre: s'ébattre /ebatR/ [61] v refl (+ v être) to frolic (about); to frisk about; to splash about

ébauche /eboʃ/ nf **(a)** (for sculpture) rough shape; (for picture) preliminary sketch; (of novel) preliminary draft; **être encore à l'état d'~** to be still at an early stage
(b) **l'~ d'un sourire** a hint of a smile

ébaucher /eboʃe/ [1] **1** vtr to sketch out ⟨picture, solution⟩; to draft ⟨novel, plan⟩; to rough-hew ⟨statue⟩; to begin ⟨conversation⟩
2 s'ébaucher v refl (+ v être) ⟨solution, novel⟩ to begin to take shape; ⟨friendship⟩ to begin to develop; ⟨talks⟩ to start

ébène /ebɛn/ nf ebony

ébéniste /ebenist/ nmf cabinetmaker

éberluer /ebɛRlɥe/ [1] vtr to dumbfound

éblouir /ebluiR/ [3] vtr to dazzle

éblouissement /ebluismɑ̃/ nm **(a)** dazzle **(b)** dizzy spell

éborgner /ebɔRɲe/ [1] vtr **~ qn** to blind sb in one eye; (humorous) to poke sb's eye out

éboueur /ebuœR/ nm dustman (GB), garbageman (US)

ébouillanter /ebujɑ̃te/ [1] vtr **(a)** to scald **(b)** to blanch ⟨vegetables⟩

éboulement /ebulmɑ̃/ nm (of wall, cliff) collapse; **~ (de rochers)** rockfall

éboulis /ebuli/ nm inv mass of fallen rocks; heap of fallen earth

ébouriffer /ebuRife/ [1] vtr to tousle; to ruffle

ébranler /ebRɑ̃le/ [1] vtr **(a)** to rattle ⟨windowpane⟩; to shake ⟨house⟩; to weaken ⟨building⟩
(b) to shake ⟨person, confidence⟩

ébrécher /ebReʃe/ [14] vtr to chip ⟨cup⟩

ébriété /ebRijete/ nf intoxication

ébrouer: s'ébrouer /ebRue/ [1] v refl (+ v être) **(a)** ⟨horse⟩ to snort
(b) ⟨person, dog⟩ to shake oneself/itself; ⟨bird⟩ to flap its wings

ébruiter /ebRɥite/ [1] **1** vtr to divulge
2 s'ébruiter v refl (+ v être) ⟨news⟩ to get out

ébullition /ebylisjɔ̃/ nf (Culin) boiling

IDIOMS être en ~ ⟨crowd⟩ to be in a fever of excitement; ⟨country, brain⟩ to be in a ferment

écaille /ekaj/ *nf* **(a)** (on fish, reptile) scale; (on oyster) shell
(b) tortoiseshell; **lunettes en ~** horn-rimmed glasses
(c) flake

écailler /ekaje/ [1] **1** *vtr* **(a)** (Culin) to scale ⟨fish⟩; to open ⟨oyster⟩
(b) ~ **qch** to chip [sth] off
2 **s'écailler** *v refl* (+ *v être*) to flake away

écarlate /ekaʀlat/ *adj* scarlet

écart /ekaʀ/ **1** *nm* **(a)** (between objects) distance, gap; (between dates) interval; (between ideas) gap
(b) (between versions, in prices) difference; ~ **des salaires** pay differential
(c) **faire un** ~ ⟨horse⟩ to shy; ⟨car⟩ to swerve
(d) lapse; ~s **de langage** bad language
2 **à l'écart** *phr* **être à l'**~ to be isolated; **se tenir à l'**~ to stand apart; to keep oneself to oneself; not to join in; **mettre qn à l'**~ to push sb aside; to ostracize sb; **entraîner qn à l'**~ to take sb aside
3 **à l'écart de** *phr* away from; **tenir qn à l'**~ **de** to keep sb away from ⟨place⟩; to keep sb out of ⟨activity, talks⟩

écarté, ~e /ekaʀte/ **1** *pp* ▶ ÉCARTER
2 *pp adj* **(a)** ⟨fingers⟩ spread; ⟨knees, legs⟩ apart; ⟨teeth⟩ widely spaced
(b) ⟨place⟩ isolated

écarteler /ekaʀtəle/ [17] *vtr* (kill) to quarter [sb]

écartement /ekaʀtəmɑ̃/ *nm* distance, space

écarter /ekaʀte/ [1] **1** *vtr* **(a)** to move [sth] further apart ⟨objects⟩; to open ⟨curtains⟩; to spread ⟨fingers, legs⟩
(b) to move [sth] aside ⟨chair⟩; to remove ⟨obstacle⟩; to push [sb] aside; to move [sb] on
(c) to dispel ⟨suspicion⟩; to eliminate ⟨risk, rival⟩
(d) to reject ⟨idea⟩; to rule out ⟨possibility⟩
2 **s'écarter** *v refl* (+ *v être*) **(a)** ⟨crowd, clouds⟩ to part; ⟨shutters⟩ to open
(b) to move away; **s'**~ **de** to move away from ⟨direction, standard⟩; to stray from ⟨path, subject⟩

ecchymose /ekimoz/ *nf* bruise

ecclésiastique /eklezjastik/ *nm* cleric

écervelé, ~e /esɛʀvəle/ *nm,f* featherbrain

échafaud /eʃafo/ *nm* **(a)** scaffold
(b) guillotine

échafaudage /eʃafodaʒ/ *nm* scaffolding

échafauder /eʃafode/ [1] *vtr* to put [sth] together ⟨plan⟩; to develop ⟨theory⟩

échalas /eʃala/ *nm inv* **(a)** cane, stake
(b) (colloq) beanpole (colloq)

échalote /eʃalot/ *nf* shallot

échancré, ~e /eʃɑ̃kʀe/ *adj* **(a)** ⟨dress⟩ low-cut; ⟨briefs⟩ high-cut; **trop ~** ⟨sleeve⟩ cut too wide

(b) ⟨blouse⟩ open-necked
(c) ⟨coast⟩ indented

échange /eʃɑ̃ʒ/ **1** *nm* **(a)** exchange; **elles ont fait l'**~ **de leurs manteaux** they've swapped coats
(b) trade; ~s **commerciaux** trade
(c) (cultural, linguistic) exchange
(d) (Sport) rally
2 **en échange** *phr* in exchange, in return
3 **en échange de** *phr* in exchange for, in return for
■ ~ **de bons procédés** quid pro quo

échanger /eʃɑ̃ʒe/ [13] *vtr* **(a)** to exchange; ~ **des insultes** to trade insults
(b) (Sport) ~ **des balles** to rally

échangeur /eʃɑ̃ʒœʀ/ *nm* interchange (GB), grade separation (US)

échantillon /eʃɑ̃tijɔ̃/ *nm* sample

échappatoire /eʃapatwaʀ/ *nf* way out (à of)

échappement /eʃapmɑ̃/ *nm* (Aut) **(tuyau d')**~ exhaust (pipe)

échapper /eʃape/ [1] **1** **échapper à** *v+prep* **(a)** ~ **à** to get away from; (cleverly) to elude
(b) ~ **à** to escape ⟨death, failure⟩; (to manage) to avoid ⟨accident⟩
(c) ~ **à** to escape from ⟨social background⟩; **je sens qu'il m'échappe** ⟨partner⟩ I feel he is drifting away from me; ⟨child⟩ I feel he's growing away from me
(d) ~ **à qn** or **des mains de qn** to slip out of sb's hands
(e) **un soupir m'a échappé** I let out a sigh
(f) **le titre m'échappe** the title escapes me
(g) ~ **à** to defy ⟨logic⟩; ~ **à la règle** to be an exception to the rule
2 **s'échapper** *v refl* (+ *v être*) **(a)** to run away; to fly away; to escape; to get away
(b) ⟨gas, smoke⟩ to escape
(c) to get away; **s'**~ **pour quelques jours** to get away for a few days
IDIOMS l'~ **belle** to have a narrow escape

écharde /eʃaʀd/ *nf* splinter

écharpe /eʃaʀp/ *nf* **(a)** scarf
(b) sash

échasse /eʃas/ *nf* stilt

échauder /eʃode/ [1] *vtr* to put [sb] off.
IDIOMS chat échaudé craint l'eau froide (Proverb) once bitten, twice shy

échauffement /eʃofmɑ̃/ *nm* (Sport) warm-up

échauffer /eʃofe/ [1] *vtr* **(a)** (Sport) to warm up
(b) to stir ⟨imagination⟩; to stir up ⟨person, debate⟩
(c) to start [sth] fermenting
IDIOMS ~ **les oreilles de qn** to vex sb

échéance /eʃeɑ̃s/ *nf* **(a)** (of debt) due date; (of share, policy) maturity date; (of loan) redemption date; **arriver à** ~ ⟨payment⟩ to fall due; ⟨investment, policy⟩ to mature
(b) expiry date

(c) à longue/brève ~ ⟨forecast⟩ long-/short-term; ⟨strengthen, change⟩ in the long/short term
(d) payment; repayment
(e) date; deadline

échéancier /eʃeɑ̃sje/ nm schedule of due dates; schedule of repayments

échéant: le cas échéant /ləkazeʃeɑ̃/ phr if need be, should the case arise

échec /eʃɛk/ **1** nm **(a)** failure; setback; **faire ~ à qn** to thwart sb
(b) (gen, Mil) defeat
(c) faire ~ au roi to put the king in check
2 échecs nm pl **les ~s** chess; chess set

échelle /eʃɛl/ nf **(a)** ladder; **~ coulissante** extending ladder (GB), extension ladder (US); **faire la courte ~ à qn** to give sb a leg up
(b) (of map, model) scale; **plan à l'~** scale plan; **à l'~ mondiale** on a worldwide scale; **~ des salaires** pay scale
(c) (colloq) (in stocking) ladder

échelon /eʃlɔ̃/ nm **(a)** (of ladder) rung
(b) grade; **sauter les ~s** to get accelerated promotion
(c) level

échelonner /eʃlɔne/ [1] **1** vtr **(a)** to space [sth] out ⟨objects⟩
(b) to spread ⟨payments, work⟩; to stagger ⟨holidays⟩
(c) to grade ⟨exercises⟩
2 s'échelonner v refl (+ v être) **(a)** to be positioned at intervals
(b) ⟨payments⟩ to be spread; ⟨departures⟩ to be staggered

écheveau, pl **~x** /eʃvo/ nm hank, skein

échevelé, ~e /eʃəvle/ adj **(a)** tousled
(b) ⟨rhythm⟩ frenzied; ⟨romanticism⟩ unbridled

échine /eʃin/ nf **(a)** (Anat) spine
(b) (Culin) ≈ spare rib
IDIOMS **courber l'~ devant** to submit to

échiquier /eʃikje/ nm **(a)** chessboard
(b) chequered (GB) or checkered (US) pattern

Échiquier /eʃikje/ pr nm **l'~** the Exchequer, the Treasury

écho /eko/ nm **(a)** echo; **faire ~ à qch, se faire l'~ de qch** to echo sth
(b) response; **nous n'avons eu aucun ~ des pourparlers** we have heard nothing about the talks

échographie /ekoɡʁafi/ nf (Med) scan

échoir /eʃwaʁ/ [51] vi (+ v être) ⟨rent⟩ to fall due; ⟨draft⟩ to be payable

échoppe /eʃɔp/ nf stall

échouer /eʃwe/ **1** vtr to beach ⟨boat⟩
2 échouer à v+prep to fail ⟨exam, test⟩
3 vi **(a)** ⟨person, attempt⟩ to fail
(b) to end up (dans in)
4 s'échouer v refl (+ v être) ⟨boat⟩ to run aground; ⟨whale⟩ to be beached

échu, ~e /eʃy/ **1** pp ▶ ÉCHOIR
2 adj expired; **payer à terme ~** to pay in arrears

éclabousser /eklabuse/ [1] vtr **(a)** to splash

(b) il a été éclaboussé par ces rumeurs the rumours (GB) have damaged his reputation

éclair /eklɛʁ/ **1** adj inv **rencontre ~** brief meeting; **attaque ~** lightning strike; **guerre ~** blitzkrieg
2 nm **(a)** flash of lightning; **passer comme un ~** to flash past
(b) (of explosion, diamonds) flash; (of eyes) glint
(c) (of lucidity, triumph) moment; **il a eu un ~ de génie** he had a brainwave (GB) or brainstorm (US)
(d) (Culin) éclair

éclairage /eklɛʁaʒ/ nm lighting; light; **~ au gaz** gaslight

éclairagiste /eklɛʁaʒist/ nm (in theatre, films) electrician

éclairant, ~e /eklɛʁɑ̃, ɑ̃t/ adj flare

éclaircie /eklɛʁsi/ nf sunny spell

éclaircir /eklɛʁsiʁ/ [3] **1** vtr **(a)** to lighten ⟨colour⟩; to lighten the colour (GB) of ⟨paint, hair⟩
(b) to shed light on [sth]
2 s'éclaircir v refl (+ v être) **(a)** ⟨weather⟩ to clear; **l'horizon s'éclaircit** (figurative) the outlook is getting brighter
(b) ⟨colour⟩ to fade; ⟨hair⟩ to get lighter
(c) ⟨situation, mystery⟩ to become clearer
(d) ⟨crowd, forest⟩ to thin out
(e) s'~ les cheveux to lighten one's hair; **s'~ la voix** or **la gorge** to clear one's throat

éclaircissement /eklɛʁsismɑ̃/ nm
(a) explanation
(b) clarification

éclairé, ~e /ekleʁe/ adj ⟨person, advice⟩ enlightened; ⟨art lover⟩ well-informed

éclairer /ekleʁe/ [1] **1** vtr **(a)** to light ⟨street, room⟩; ⟨sun⟩ to light up ⟨place, object⟩
(b) to give [sb] some light
(c) ⟨remark⟩ to throw light on ⟨text, situation⟩
(d) to enlighten [sb]
2 vi ⟨lamp, candle⟩ to give out light
3 s'éclairer v refl (+ v être) **(a)** ⟨screen, face⟩ to light up
(b) s'~ à l'électricité to have electric lighting

éclaireur /eklɛʁœʁ/ nm **(a)** scout (GB), Boy Scout (US)
(b) (Mil) scout

éclaireuse /eklɛʁøz/ nf guide (GB), Girl Guide (US)

éclat /ekla/ nm **(a)** splinter; **un ~ d'obus** a piece of shrapnel; **voler en ~s** to shatter
(b) (of light, star) brightness; (of spotlight) glare; (of snow) sparkle
(c) (of colour, material) brilliance; (of hair, plumage) shine; (of metal) lustre (GB)
(d) (of face, smile) radiance; (of eyes) sparkle; **sans ~** ⟨eyes⟩ dull; ⟨beauty⟩ lifeless
(e) splendour (GB); **manquer d'~** ⟨ceremony⟩ to lack sparkle
(f) scene, fuss; **faire un ~** to make a scene
■ **~ de colère** fit of anger; **~ de rire** roar of laughter; **des ~s de voix** raised voices
IDIOMS **rire aux ~s** to roar with laughter

éclatant, ~e /eklatã, ãt/ *adj* (a) ⟨*light*⟩ dazzling; ⟨*sun*⟩ blazing
(b) ⟨*colour, plumage*⟩ bright; **d'une blancheur ~e** sparkling white
(c) ⟨*beauty, smile*⟩ radiant; ⟨*victory*⟩ brilliant
(d) ⟨*proof*⟩ striking
(e) ⟨*laughter*⟩ ringing

éclaté, ~e /eklate/ *adj* (gen) fragmented; ⟨*family*⟩ divided

éclatement /eklatmã/ *nm* (a) bursting
(b) explosion
(c) break-up (**en** into)

éclater /eklate/ [1] *vi* (a) ⟨*tyre, bubble*⟩ to burst; ⟨*shell, firework*⟩ to explode; ⟨*bottle*⟩ to shatter; **faire ~** to burst ⟨*bubble*⟩; to detonate ⟨*bomb*⟩
(b) ⟨*pipe, boil*⟩ to burst
(c) ⟨*laughter, firing*⟩ to break out; ⟨*shot*⟩ to ring out
(d) ⟨*scandal, news*⟩ to break; ⟨*truth*⟩ to come out
(e) ⟨*war*⟩ to break out; ⟨*storm*⟩ to break
(f) **laisser ~ sa joie** to be wild with joy
(g) ⟨*coalition*⟩ to break up (**en** into); ⟨*party*⟩ to split
(h) to lose one's temper; **~ de rire** to burst out laughing

éclectique /eklɛktik/ *adj* eclectic

éclipse /eklips/ *nf* eclipse

éclipser /eklipse/ [1] **1** *vtr* (a) to eclipse
(b) to obscure
(c) to outshine
2 s'éclipser *v refl* (+ *v être*) (colloq) to slip away

éclopé, ~e /eklɔpe/ *adj* injured, lame

éclore /eklɔʀ/ [79] *vi* (a) ⟨*chick, egg*⟩ to hatch; ⟨*flower*⟩ to bloom; **faire ~ un œuf** to incubate an egg
(b) ⟨*idea*⟩ to dawn; ⟨*talent*⟩ to bloom

écluse /eklyz/ *nf* lock

écœurant, ~e /ekœʀã, ãt/ *adj* (a) ⟨*food, smell*⟩ sickly
(b) nauseating
(c) (humorous) sickening

écœurement /ekœʀmã/ *nm* nausea

écœurer /ekœʀe/ [1] *vtr* (a) to make [sb] feel sick
(b) (figurative) to sicken

éco-guerrier, -ière /ekɔgeʀje, ɛʀ/ *nm,f* eco-warrior

école /ekɔl/ *nf* (a) school
(b) education system
(c) (grande) ⟨ *higher education institution with competitive entrance examination*; **une ~ de commerce** a business school
(d) training (**de** in); **être à bonne ~** to be in good hands
(e) (of art) school; **faire ~** to gain a following
■ **~ élémentaire** primary school;
~ d'infirmières nursing college; **~ maternelle** nursery school; **~ normale** primary teacher training college; **~ primaire** primary school;
École nationale d'administration, ENA

Grande École for top civil servants; **École normale supérieure, ENS** *Grande École from which the educational élite is recruited*

écolier, -ière /ekɔlje, ɛʀ/ *nm,f* schoolboy/schoolgirl

écologie /ekɔlɔʒi/ *nf* ecology

écologique /ekɔlɔʒik/ *adj* ecological; ⟨*speech*⟩ on the environment; ⟨*interest*⟩ environmental; ⟨*product*⟩ environment-friendly

écologiste /ekɔlɔʒist/ **1** *adj*
(a) ⟨*candidate*⟩ Green
(b) ⟨*measure*⟩ ecological
2 *nmf* (a) environmentalist
(b) Green (candidate)
(c) ecologist

écomusée /ekomyze/ *nm* ≈ open air museum

éconduire /ekõdɥiʀ/ [69] *vtr* to turn [sb] away

économat /ekɔnɔma/ *nm* bursar's office

économe /ekɔnɔm/ **1** *adj* thrifty
2 *nm* (Culin) potato peeler

économie /ekɔnɔmi/ **1** *nf* (a) (of country) economy
(b) (discipline) economics
(c) (amount saved) saving; **faire l'~ de** to save the cost of ⟨*trip*⟩
(d) economy, thrift; **par ~** in order to save money; **s'exprimer avec une grande ~ de paroles** to express oneself succinctly
2 économies *nf pl* savings; **faire des ~s** to save up; to save money
■ **~ d'entreprise** managerial economics; **~ de marché** free market (economy)
IDIOMS **il n'y a pas de petites ~s** every little helps

économique /ekɔnɔmik/ *adj* (a) ⟨*policy, crisis*⟩ economic
(b) economical

économiser /ekɔnɔmize/ [1] *vtr* (a) to save (up) ⟨*money*⟩; **~ ses forces** to pace oneself
(b) to save ⟨*petrol, water, energy*⟩
(c) to economize

économiste /ekɔnɔmist/ *nmf* economist

écoper /ekɔpe/ [1] *vtr* to bail out

ecoproduit /ecɔpʀɔdɥi/ *nm* eco-product

écorce /ekɔʀs/ *nf* (of tree) bark; (of fruit) peel; (of chestnut) skin
■ **~ terrestre** earth's crust

écorché, ~e /ekɔʀʃe/ *adj* **~ (vif)** hypersensitive

écorcher /ekɔʀʃe/ [1] *vtr* (a) to skin ⟨*animal*⟩; to flay ⟨*person*⟩
(b) to graze ⟨*face, hand*⟩
(c) to mispronounce ⟨*word*⟩

écorchure /ekɔʀʃyʀ/ *nf* graze

écossais, ~e /ekɔsɛ, ɛz/ **1** *adj* Scottish; ⟨*whisky*⟩ Scotch; ⟨*language*⟩ Scots; ⟨*skirt*⟩ tartan
2 *nm* (a) (dialect) Scots
(b) (Scottish) Gaelic
(c) tartan (cloth)

Écossais, **~e** /ekɔsɛ, ɛz/ nm,f Scotsman/ Scotswoman, Scot

Écosse /ekɔs/ pr nf Scotland

écosser /ekɔse/ [1] vtr to shell

écot /eko/ nm share

écoulement /ekulmɑ̃/ nm **(a)** (of water, traffic) flow; (of time) passing
(b) (Med) discharge
(c) (of banknotes, drugs) circulation

écouler /ekule/ [1] **1** vtr **(a)** to sell ⟨product⟩; **les stocks sont écoulés** stocks are exhausted
(b) to fence ⟨stolen goods⟩; to pass ⟨banknote⟩
2 **s'écouler** v refl (+ v être) **(a)** ⟨time, life⟩ to pass
(b) ⟨river⟩ to flow
(c) ⟨oil, water⟩ to escape
(d) ⟨water⟩ to drain away
(e) ⟨product⟩ to move

écourter /ekurte/ [1] vtr to cut short ⟨stay⟩

écoute /ekut/ nf **(a)** **être à l'~ de** to be listening to ⟨programme⟩; to be (always) ready to listen to ⟨problems⟩
(b) audience; **heure de grande ~** peak listening time; peak viewing time
(c) **un centre d'~(s)** monitoring centre (GB); **je suis sur ~(s)** my phone is being tapped

écouter /ekute/ [1] **1** vtr **(a)** to listen to [sb/sth]; **~ qn chanter** to listen to sb singing; **~ aux portes** to eavesdrop
(b) **~ son cœur** to follow one's own inclination
2 **s'écouter** v refl (+ v être) **(a)** **s'~ parler** to like the sound of one's own voice
(b) to cosset oneself
(c) **si je m'écoutais** if it was up to me

écouteur /ekutœʀ/ nm **(a)** (on phone) earpiece
(b) earphones
(c) headphones

écoutille /ekutij/ nf (Naut) hatch

écrabouiller /ekʀabuje/ [1] vtr (colloq) to squash

écran /ekʀɑ̃/ nm **(a)** (gen) screen; **crever l'~** ⟨actor⟩ to have a great screen presence; **une vedette du petit ~** a TV star
(b) cinema (GB), movie theater (US)
(c) (on machine) display
(d) **crème ~ total** sun block
■ **~ antibruit** soundproofing; **~ de contrôle** monitor; **~ à cristaux liquides** liquid crystal display, LCD; **~ solaire** sunscreen; **~ tactile** touch screen; **~ de visualisation** VDU screen

écrasant, **~e** /ekʀazɑ̃, ɑ̃t/ adj **(a)** ⟨weight⟩ enormous
(b) ⟨heat⟩ sweltering; ⟨victory⟩ resounding; ⟨responsibility⟩ heavy

écraser /ekʀaze/ [1] **1** vtr **(a)** to crush ⟨finger, person⟩; to squash, to crush ⟨insect, hat, fruit, box⟩; ⟨driver⟩ to run over ⟨person, animal⟩; **se faire ~** to get run over
(b) to flatten ⟨vegetation⟩
(c) (Culin) to mash ⟨fruit⟩
(d) **~ sa cigarette** to stub out one's cigarette; **~ une larme** to wipe away a tear

(e) to press ⟨nose, face⟩ (**contre** against)
(f) to crush ⟨rebellion⟩; to thrash (colloq) ⟨opponent⟩
(g) to outshine
(h) to put [sb] down
(i) ⟨fatigue, heat⟩ to overcome
2 **s'écraser** v refl (+ v être) **(a)** ⟨car, train⟩ to crash; ⟨driver, motorcyclist⟩ to have a crash; ⟨insect⟩ to splatter (**contre** on)
(b) (colloq) to shut up (colloq)
(c) (colloq) to keep one's head down

écrémé, **~e** /ekʀeme/ adj skimmed

écrémer /ekʀeme/ [14] vtr **(a)** to skim ⟨milk⟩
(b) to cream off the best of ⟨candidates⟩

écrevisse /ekʀəvis/ nf crayfish (GB), crawfish (US)

écrier: s'écrier /ekʀije/ [2] v refl (+ v être) to exclaim

écrin /ekʀɛ̃/ nm (for jewellery) case

écrire /ekʀiʀ/ [67] **1** vtr **(a)** to write
(b) to spell
2 vi to write
3 **s'écrire** v refl (+ v être) **(a)** to be written
(b) to be spelled

écrit, **~e** /ekʀi, it/ **1** pp ▶ ÉCRIRE
2 pp adj written; **c'était ~** it was bound to happen
3 nm **(a)** work, piece of writing
(b) document; **par ~** in writing
(c) written examination
IDIOMS **les paroles s'envolent, les ~s restent** never put anything in writing; (as security) get it in writing

écriteau, pl **~x** /ekʀito/ nm sign

écritoire /ekʀitwaʀ/ nf writing case

écriture /ekʀityʀ/ **1** nf **(a)** handwriting
(b) (in printing) hand
(c) (text, activity) writing
(d) script; **~ phonétique** phonetic script
2 **écritures** nf pl accounts; **tenir les ~s** to do the books

Écriture /ekʀityʀ/ nf **les (saintes) ~s** the Scriptures; **l'~ sainte** Holy Writ

écrivain /ekʀivɛ̃/ nm writer

écrou /ekʀu/ nm (Tech) nut

écrouer /ekʀue/ [1] vtr (Law) to commit [sb] to prison

écroulé, **~e** /ekʀule/ adj overwhelmed; **~ de rire** (colloq) doubled up with laughter

écrouler: s'écrouler /ekʀule/ [1] v refl (+ v être) to collapse; to fade; to crumble

écru, **~e** /ekʀy/ adj **(a)** ⟨canvas⟩ unbleached; ⟨wool⟩ undyed; ⟨silk⟩ raw
(b) (colour) ecru

écu /eky/ nm **(a)** (in EU) ecu
(b) ≈ crown
(c) shield

ECU /eky/ nm: (abbr = **European currency unit**) ECU

écueil /ekœj/ nm **(a)** reef
(b) (figurative) pitfall

écuelle /ekɥɛl/ nf **(a)** bowl
(b) bowlful

écume /ekym/ *nf* **(a)** (on water) foam; (on beer) froth; (on metal) dross
(b) (at mouth) foam, froth
écumer /ekyme/ [1] ⃞1 *vtr* **(a)** to skim
(b) to scour, to search
⃞2 *vi* ⟨*sea*⟩ to foam; ⟨*wine*⟩ to froth
écumoire /ekymwaʀ/ *nf* skimming ladle
écureuil /ekyʀœj/ *nm* squirrel
écurie /ekyʀi/ *nf* **(a)** stable
(b) (Sport) stable
(c) (figurative) pigsty
écusson /ekysɔ̃/ *nm* **(a)** (Mil) flash (GB)
(b) (of school) crest, badge; (of club, movement) badge; (of car) insignia
(c) (in heraldry) coat of arms
écuyer, -ère /ekɥije, ɛʀ/ ⃞1 *nm,f*
(a) horseman/horsewoman
(b) riding instructor
(c) bareback rider
⃞2 *nm* **(a)** squire
(b) equerry
eczéma /egzema/ *nm* eczema
éden /edɛn/ *nm* paradise
Éden /edɛn/ *pr nm* Eden
édenté, ∼e /edɑ̃te/ *adj* **(a)** toothless
(b) gap-toothed
(c) ⟨*comb*⟩ broken
EDF /œdeɛf/ *nf* (*abbr* = **Électricité de France**) *French electricity board*
édicter /edikte/ [1] *vtr* to enact ⟨*law*⟩
édifiant, ∼e /edifjɑ̃, ɑ̃t/ *adj* **(a)** edifying
(b) enlightening
édifice /edifis/ *nm* **(a)** building
(b) structure
édifier /edifje/ [2] *vtr* **(a)** to build [sth]
(b) to build ⟨*empire*⟩
(c) to edify
(d) to enlighten
Édimbourg /edɛ̃buʀ/ *pr n* Edinburgh
édit /edi/ *nm* edict
éditer /edite/ [1] *vtr* **(a)** to publish ⟨*book, author*⟩; to release ⟨*record*⟩
(b) (Comput) to edit
éditeur, -trice /editœʀ, tʀis/ ⃞1 *nm,f* editor
⃞2 *nm* **(a)** publisher
(b) (Comput) editor
édition /edisjɔ̃/ ⃞1 *nf* **(a)** (of book) publication; (of record) release
(b) (book, print) edition; (record) release
(c) publishing; **société d'∼** publishing firm
(d) editing
(e) (paper) **∼ du soir** evening edition
⃞2 **éditions** *nf pl* **les ∼s de la Roulotte** la Roulotte (Publishing Company)
éditorial, ∼e, *mpl* **-iaux** /editɔʀjal, o/
⃞1 *adj* ⟨*policy, service*⟩ editorial
⃞2 *nm* editorial, leader
édredon /edʀədɔ̃/ *nm* eiderdown
éducateur, -trice /edykatœʀ, tʀis/
⃞1 *adj* educational
⃞2 *nm,f* youth worker
éducatif, -ive /edykatif, iv/ *adj* educational

éducation /edykasjɔ̃/ *nf* **(a)** education; **faire l'∼ de qn** to educate sb
(b) training
(c) manners
■ **Éducation nationale, EN** Ministry of Education; (system) state education
édulcorer /edylkɔʀe/ [1] *vtr* **(a)** to sweeten
(b) to tone down ⟨*letter, remark*⟩
éduquer /edyke/ [1] *vtr* to educate; to train
effacé, ∼e /efase/ *adj* retiring
effacement /efasmɑ̃/ *nm* **(a)** deletion; **touche d'∼** (Comput) delete key
(b) (of cassette) erasure
(c) self-effacement
effacer /efase/ [12] ⃞1 *vtr* **(a)** to rub out; to delete; to erase
(b) to wipe ⟨*tape*⟩; to clear ⟨*file*⟩; to clean ⟨*blackboard*⟩
(c) ⟨*rain*⟩ to erase ⟨*tracks*⟩; ⟨*snow*⟩ to cover (up) ⟨*tracks*⟩; ⟨*cream*⟩ to remove ⟨*wrinkles*⟩
(d) to blot out ⟨*memory*⟩; to remove ⟨*differences*⟩
(e) to write off ⟨*debt*⟩
⃞2 **s'effacer** *v refl* (+ *v être*) **(a)** ça s'efface you can rub it out
(b) ⟨*inscription, drawing, memory*⟩ to fade; ⟨*impression*⟩ to wear off; ⟨*fear*⟩ to disappear
(c) to step aside
(d) to stay in the background
effaceur /efasœʀ/ *nm* correction pen
effarant, ∼e /efaʀɑ̃, ɑ̃t/ *adj* astounding
effarer /efaʀe/ [1] *vtr* to alarm
effaroucher /efaʀuʃe/ [1] *vtr* **(a)** to frighten [sb/sth] away
(b) to alarm
effectif, -ive /efɛktif, iv/ ⃞1 *adj* real
⃞2 *nm* (of school) number of pupils; (of university) number of students; (of company) workforce; (of army) strength
effectivement /efɛktivmɑ̃/ *adv*
(a) indeed
(b) actually, really
effectuer /efɛktɥe/ [1] *vtr* to do ⟨*work, repairs*⟩; to make ⟨*payment, trip*⟩; to carry out ⟨*transaction*⟩; to conduct ⟨*survey*⟩; to serve ⟨*sentence*⟩
efféminé, ∼e /efemine/ *adj* effeminate
effervescence /efɛʀvesɑ̃s/ *nf*
(a) effervescence
(b) turmoil
effervescent, ∼e /efɛʀvesɑ̃, ɑ̃t/ *adj*
(a) effervescent
(b) (figurative) ⟨*crowd*⟩ seething; ⟨*personality*⟩ effervescent
effet /efɛ/ ⃞1 *nm* **(a)** effect; **prendre ∼** ⟨*measure, law*⟩ to take effect; **sous l'∼ de l'alcool** under the influence of alcohol; **couper tous ses ∼s à qn** to steal sb's thunder
(b) impression; **être du plus mauvais ∼** to be in the worst possible taste; **faire un drôle d'∼** to make one feel strange; **un ∼ de surprise** an element of surprise ····⋗

(c) à cet ∼ for that purpose

2 en effet *phr* indeed

3 effets *nm pl* things, clothes

∎ ∼ **de serre** greenhouse effect; ∼**s secondaires** (Med) side effects

efficace /efikas/ *adj* effective; efficient

efficacement /efikasmã/ *adv* efficiently; effectively

efficacité /efikasite/ *nf* (of action, remedy) effectiveness; (of person, device) efficiency

effigie /efiʒi/ *nf* **(a)** effigy; à l'∼ de ⟨medal, stamp⟩ with the head of

(b) logo

effilé, ∼**e** /efile/ *adj* ⟨almonds⟩ flaked

effiler /efile/ [1] **1** *vtr* **(a)** to sharpen

(b) to string ⟨green beans⟩

2 s'effiler *v refl* (+ *v être*) to fray

effilocher /efilɔʃe/ [1] **1** *vtr* to shred

2 s'effilocher *v refl* (+ *v être*) to fray

efflanqué, ∼**e** /eflãke/ *adj* emaciated

effleurer /eflœʀe/ [1] *vtr* to touch lightly, to brush (against); **l'idée ne m'a même pas effleuré** the idea didn't even cross my mind

effluent /eflyã/ *nm* effluent

effluve /eflyv/ *nm* **(a)** unpleasant smell

(b) fragrance

effondrement /efɔ̃dʀəmã/ *nm* **(a)** collapse

(b) subsidence

effondrer: s'effondrer /efɔ̃dʀe/ [1] *v refl* (+ *v être*) **(a)** ⟨roof, person⟩ to collapse; ⟨dream⟩ to crumble; ⟨hopes⟩ to fall

(b) être effondré par la nouvelle to be distraught at the news

efforcer: s'efforcer /efɔʀse/ [12] *v refl* (+ *v être*) to try hard (**de faire** to do)

effort /efɔʀ/ *nm* **(a)** effort; **fais un petit** ∼ **d'imagination!** use a bit of imagination!; **avec mon dos, je ne peux pas faire d'**∼ with this back of mine, I can't do anything strenuous

(b) (in physics) stress; strain

effraction /efʀaksjɔ̃/ *nf* breaking and entering

∎ ∼ **informatique** computer hacking

effrayant, ∼**e** /efʀɛjã, ãt/ *adj* ⟨sight, ugliness⟩ frightening; ⟨thinness, paleness⟩ dreadful

effrayer /efʀeje/ [21] *vtr* **(a)** to frighten; to alarm

(b) ⟨difficulty, price⟩ to put [sb] off

effréné, ∼**e** /efʀene/ *adj* ⟨rhythm, competition⟩ frenzied; ⟨ambition⟩ wild

effriter /efʀite/ [1] **1** *vtr* to crumble; to break up

2 s'effriter *v refl* (+ *v être*) to crumble (away)

effroi /efʀwa/ *nm* dread, terror

effronté, ∼**e** /efʀɔ̃te/ *adj* cheeky; shameless

effroyable /efʀwajabl/ *adj* dreadful

effroyablement /efʀwajabləmã/ *adv*

(a) horribly

(b) (colloq) terribly

effusion /efyzjɔ̃/ *nf* effusion

∎ ∼ **de sang** bloodshed

égal, ∼**e**, *mpl* **-aux** /egal, o/ **1** *adj*

(a) equal (**à** to); **à prix** ∼, **je préfère celui-là** if the price is the same, I'd rather have that one

(b) ⟨ground⟩ level; ⟨light⟩ even; ⟨colour⟩ uniform; ⟨weather⟩ settled; ⟨pulse, breathing⟩ steady; **d'un pas** ∼ at an even pace

(c) ça m'est ∼ I don't mind (either way); I don't care

2 *nmf* equal; **traiter d'**∼ **à** ∼ **avec qn** to deal with sb as an equal

IDIOMS **rester** ∼ **à soi-même** to be one's usual self; **combattre à armes** ∼**es** to be on an equal footing

égalable /egalabl/ *adj* **difficilement** ∼ unparalleled; incomparably superior

également /egalmã/ *adv* **(a)** also, too

(b) equally

égaler /egale/ [1] *vtr* **(a)** to equal ⟨record⟩; to be as good as ⟨person⟩; to be as high as ⟨price⟩

(b) **trois plus trois égalent six** three plus three equals six *or* is six

égalisation /egalizasjɔ̃/ *nf* **(a)** levelling (GB) out

(b) (Sport) **le penalty a permis l'**∼ the penalty evened (GB) *or* tied (US) the score

égaliser /egalize/ [1] **1** *vtr* **(a)** to level ⟨ground⟩

(b) to make [sth] the same size ⟨planks⟩

2 *vi* (Sport) to equalize (GB), to tie (US)

égalitaire /egalitɛʀ/ *adj*, *nmf* egalitarian

égalité /egalite/ *nf* **(a)** equality

(b) (Sport) **être à** ∼ to be level (GB), to be tied (US); ∼**! deuce!**

égard /egaʀ/ **1** *nm* **(a)** consideration; **sans** ∼ **pour** without regard for

(b) à l'∼ **de qn** toward(s) sb; **à cet** ∼ in this respect

2 égards *nm pl* **avec des** ∼**s** with respect; **être plein d'**∼**s envers qn** to be attentive to sb's every need

égaré, ∼**e** /egaʀe/ *adj* **(a)** stray

(b) ⟨look⟩ wild

égarement /egaʀmã/ *nm* **(a)** distraction, madness

(b) confusion

(c) erratic behaviour (GB)

égarer /egaʀe/ [1] **1** *vtr* **(a)** to lead [sb] astray

(b) to mislay

2 s'égarer *v refl* (+ *v être*) **(a)** to get lost

(b) (figurative) ⟨mind⟩ to wander; ⟨person⟩ to ramble

égayer /egeje/ [21] *vtr* to enliven; to lighten; to brighten; to cheer [sb] up

égérie /eʒeʀi/ *nf* muse

égide /eʒid/ *nf* aegis

églantine /eglãtin/ *nf* wild rose, dog-rose

églefin /egləfɛ̃/ *nm* haddock

église /egliz/ *nf* church

ego /ego/ *nm inv* ego

égocentrique /egosãtʀik/ *adj*, *nmf* egocentric

égoïsme /egɔism/ *nm* selfishness

égoïste /egɔist/ *adj* selfish

égorger /egɔʀʒe/ [13] *vtr* ~ qn to cut sb's throat

égosiller: s'égosiller /egozije/ [1] *v refl* (+ *v être*) **(a)** to shout oneself hoarse
(b) to sing at the top of one's voice
(c) to yell

égout /egu/ *nm* sewer

égoutter /egute/ [1] **1** *vtr* to drain
2 s'égoutter *v refl* (+ *v être*) ⟨*dishes, rice, vegetables*⟩ to drain; ⟨*washing*⟩ to drip dry

égouttoir /egutwaʀ/ *nm* draining rack (GB), (dish) drainer (US)

égratigner /egʀatiɲe/ [1] **1** *vtr* to scratch, to graze
2 s'égratigner *v refl* (+ *v être*) to scratch oneself; to graze oneself

égratignure /egʀatiɲyʀ/ *nf* scratch; graze

égrener /egʀəne/ [16] *vtr* **(a)** to shell ⟨*peas*⟩; to remove the seeds from ⟨*melon*⟩
(b) to chime out ⟨*notes*⟩; ~ son chapelet to tell one's beads

Égypte /eʒipt/ *pr nf* Egypt

égyptien, -ienne /eʒipsjɛ̃, ɛn/ **1** *adj* Egyptian
2 *nm* (language) Egyptian

éhonté, ~e /eɔ̃te/ *adj* ⟨*liar, lie*⟩ brazen

Éire /ɛʀ/ *pr n* Éire, Republic of Ireland

éjectable /eʒɛktabl/ *adj* siège ~ ejector seat (GB), ejection seat (US)

éjecter /eʒɛkte/ [1] *vtr* **(a)** (in accident) to throw [sb/sth] out
(b) (Tech) to eject

élaboration /elabɔʀasjɔ̃/ *nf* development; working out; drafting; putting together

élaboré, ~e /elabɔʀe/ *adj* sophisticated; elaborate

élaborer /elabɔʀe/ [1] *vtr* to work [sth] out; to draw [sth] up; to put [sth] together

élaguer /elage/ [1] *vtr* to prune

élan /elɑ̃/ *nm* **(a)** (Sport) run up; saut sans ~ standing jump
(b) momentum
(c) impetus
(d) enthusiasm; ~ patriotique patriotic fervour (GB)
(e) impulse; ~ de tendresse surge of tenderness
(f) (Zool) elk

élancé, ~e /elɑ̃se/ *adj* slender

élancement /elɑ̃smɑ̃/ *nm* throbbing pain

élancer: s'élancer /elɑ̃se/ [12] *v refl* (+ *v être*) **(a)** to dash forward
(b) s'~ vers le ciel ⟨*tree, spire*⟩ to soar up toward(s) the sky

élargi, ~e /elaʀʒi/ *adj* enlarged; expanded

élargir /elaʀʒiʀ/ [3] **1** *vtr* **(a)** to widen ⟨*road*⟩; to let out ⟨*garment*⟩
(b) to stretch ⟨*shoes, sweater*⟩
(c) to extend ⟨*contacts, law*⟩; to broaden ⟨*knowledge*⟩; to increase ⟨*majority*⟩

2 s'élargir *v refl* (+ *v être*) ⟨*group*⟩ to expand; ⟨*gap*⟩ to increase; ⟨*road*⟩ to widen; ⟨*person*⟩ to fill out; ⟨*garment*⟩ to stretch

élastique /elastik/ **1** *adj* **(a)** ⟨*waistband*⟩ elasticated (GB), elasticized (US)
(b) ⟨*gas, fibre*⟩ elastic
(c) ⟨*rule, timetable*⟩ flexible; ⟨*budget*⟩ elastic
2 *nm* **(a)** rubber band
(b) (in haberdashery) elastic
(c) (Sport) bungee cord
IDIOMS les lâcher avec un ~ (colloq) to be tight-fisted

élastomère /elastɔmɛʀ/ *nm* elastomer

électeur, -trice /elɛktœʀ, tʀis/ *nm,f* voter

élection /elɛksjɔ̃/ *nf* **(a)** election
(b) choice; mon pays d'~ my chosen country

électoral, ~e, mpl -aux /elɛktɔʀal, o/ *adj* electoral; election

électorat /elɛktɔʀa/ *nm* electorate, voters

électricien, -ienne /elɛktʀisjɛ̃, ɛn/ *nm,f* electrician

électricité /elɛktʀisite/ *nf* electricity

électrifier /elɛktʀifje/ [2] *vtr* to electrify ⟨*railtracks*⟩

électrique /elɛktʀik/ *adj* **(a)** electrical
(b) (figurative) ⟨*atmosphere*⟩ electric

électriser /elɛktʀize/ [1] *vtr* to electrify

électro(-) /elɛktʀo/ *pref* electro; ~cardiogramme electrocardiogram

électrochoc /elɛktʀoʃɔk/ *nm* ~s electroshock therapy, EST

électrocuter: s'électrocuter /elɛktʀokyte/ [1] *v refl* (+ *v être*) to be electrocuted

électrode /elɛktʀɔd/ *nf* electrode

électrogène /elɛktʀoʒɛn/ *adj* groupe ~ (electricity) generator

électromécanicien, -ienne /elɛktʀomekanisjɛ̃, ɛn/ *nm,f* electrical engineer

électroménager /elɛktʀomenaʒe/ **1** *adj m* appareil ~ household appliance
2 *nm* **(a)** domestic electrical appliances
(b) electrical goods industry

électron /elɛktʀɔ̃/ *nm* electron

électronicien, -ienne /elɛktʀonisjɛ̃, ɛn/ *nm,f* electronics engineer

électronique /elɛktʀonik/ **1** *adj* **(a)** ⟨*circuit*⟩ electronic
(b) ⟨*microscope*⟩ electron
2 *nf* electronics

électrophone /elɛktʀofɔn/ *nm* record player

élégamment /elegamɑ̃/ *adv* ⟨*dress*⟩ elegantly

élégance /elegɑ̃s/ *nf* elegance; avec ~ ⟨*dress*⟩ elegantly; ⟨*lose*⟩ gracefully; ⟨*behave*⟩ honourably (GB); ⟨*resolve problem*⟩ neatly

élégant, ~e /elegɑ̃, ɑ̃t/ *adj* elegant; ce n'est pas très ~ de ta part it's not very decent of you

élément /elemɑ̃/ **1** *nm* **(a)** (in structure, ensemble) element; (in device) component; ∼ **moteur** driving force
(b) factor, element; **l'∼-clé de** the key element in
(c) (of furniture) unit
(d) fact; **disposer de tous les ∼s** to have all the facts
(e) (person) **bon ∼** good pupil; good player
(f) (chemical) element
2 éléments *nm pl* elements

élémentaire /elemɑ̃tɛʀ/ *adj* **(a)** ⟨principle⟩ basic
(b) elementary

éléphant /elefɑ̃/ *nm* elephant

éléphanteau, *pl* **∼x** /elefɑ̃to/ *nm* (elephant) calf

élevage /elvaʒ/ *nm* **(a)** livestock farming; **faire de l'∼ de porcs** to breed pigs; **d'∼** ⟨oysters⟩ farmed; ⟨pheasant⟩ captive-bred
(b) farm; **un ∼ de visons** a mink farm
(c) stock (**de** of)

élévateur /elevatœʀ/ *nm* elevator

élévation /elevasjɔ̃/ *nf* **(a)** rise (**de** in)
(b) (to rank) elevation
(c) (in architecture) elevation

élevé, **∼e** /elve/ *adj* **(a)** ⟨level, price, rank⟩ high
(b) ⟨plateau⟩ high
(c) ⟨sentiment⟩ fine; ⟨principles⟩ high; ⟨ideal⟩ lofty; ⟨language⟩ elevated

élève /elɛv/ *nmf* (gen) student; (Sch) pupil; ∼ **officier** trainee officer

élever /elve/ [16] **1** *vtr* **(a)** to put up, to erect
(b) to raise ⟨temperature, level⟩
(c) to lift, to raise ⟨load⟩
(d) la poésie élève l'âme poetry is elevating *or* uplifting
(e) to raise ⟨objection⟩
(f) to bring [sb] up; **c'est mal élevé** it's bad manners (**de faire** to do)
(g) to rear ⟨cattle⟩; to keep ⟨bees⟩
2 s'élever *v refl* (+ *v être*) **(a)** ⟨rate⟩ to rise
(b) s'∼ à ⟨expenses⟩ to come to; ⟨death toll⟩ to stand at
(c) to rise (up); **s'∼ dans les airs** ⟨smoke⟩ to rise up into the air; ⟨bird⟩ to soar into the air
(d) ⟨voice, protests⟩ to be heard
(e) s'∼ contre qch to protest against sth
(f) ⟨statue⟩ to stand; **s'∼ au-dessus de qch** to rise above sth

éleveur, **-euse** /elvœʀ, øz/ *nm,f* breeder

elfe /ɛlf/ *nm* elf

élider /elide/ [1] *vtr* to elide

éligible /eliʒibl/ *adj* eligible for office

élimé, **∼e** /elime/ *adj* threadbare

élimer /elime/ [1] **1** *vtr* to wear [sth] thin
2 s'élimer *v refl* (+ *v être*) to wear thin

élimination /eliminasjɔ̃/ *nf* **(a)** (gen) elimination, defeat
(b) (of stain) removal ∼ **déchets** waste disposal

éliminatoire /eliminatwaʀ/ *adj* ⟨question, match⟩ qualifying; ⟨mark⟩ eliminatory

éliminer /elimine/ [1] *vtr* to eliminate

élire /eliʀ/ [66] *vtr* to elect **se faire ∼** to be elected; ∼ **domicile** to take up residence

élision /elizjɔ̃/ *nf* elision

élite /elit/ *nf* **l'∼** the elite; **d'∼** ⟨troops⟩ elite, crack; ⟨student⟩ high-flying; ⟨athlete⟩ top

élitisme /elitism/ *nm* elitism

élixir /eliksiʀ/ *nm* elixir

elle /ɛl/ *pron f* she; it; **∼s** they; **je les vois plus souvent qu'∼** I see them more often than she does; I see them more often than (I see) her; **le bol bleu est à ∼** the blue bowl is hers

ellébore /elebɔʀ/ *nm* hellebore

elle-même, *pl* **elles-mêmes** /ɛlmɛm/ *pron* herself; itself; **elles-mêmes** themselves; **'Mme Roc?'—'∼'** 'Mrs Roc?'—'speaking'

elles *pron* ▶ ELLE

ellipse /elips/ *nf* ellipsis

elliptique /eliptik/ *adj* **(a)** elliptical
(b) elliptic

élocution /elɔkysjɔ̃/ *nf* diction; **défaut d'∼** speech impediment

éloge /elɔʒ/ *nm* **(a)** praise; **être tout à l'∼ de qn** to do sb great credit
(b) eulogy; ∼ **funèbre** funeral oration

élogieux, **-ieuse** /elɔʒjø, øz/ *adj* full of praise; laudatory

éloigné, **∼e** /elwaɲe/ *adj* **(a)** distant; ∼ **tout** remote; **deux usines ∼es de cinq kilomètres** two factories five kilometres (GB) apart
(b) ⟨memories⟩ distant; ⟨event⟩ remote; ∼ **dans le temps** distant (in time)
(c) ⟨cousin⟩ distant

éloignement /elwaɲmɑ̃/ *nm* **(a)** distance
(b) remoteness

éloigner /elwaɲe/ [1] **1** *vtr* **(a)** to move [sb/sth] away
(b) ils font tout pour l'∼ de moi they are doing everything to drive us apart
2 s'éloigner *v refl* (+ *v être*) **(a)** to move away; **ne t'éloigne pas trop** don't go too far away
(b) s'∼ de to move away from ⟨party line⟩; to stray from ⟨subject⟩

élongation /elɔ̃gasjɔ̃/ *nf* (Med) pulled muscle

éloquence /elɔkɑ̃s/ *nf* eloquence

éloquent, **∼e** /elɔkɑ̃, ɑ̃t/ *adj* eloquent

élu, **∼e** /ely/ *nm,f* **(a)** elected representative
(b) beloved
(c) (in religion) **les ∼s** the Chosen Ones

élucider /elyside/ [1] *vtr* to solve ⟨crime, problem⟩; to clarify ⟨circumstances⟩

élucubrations /elykybʀasjɔ̃/ *nf pl* rantings

éluder /elyde/ [1] *vtr* to evade

Élysée /elize/ *pr nm* (**palais de**) l'∼ *the official residence of the French President*

émacier: s'émacier /emasje/ [2] *v refl* (+ *v être*) to become emaciated

e-mail /emaj/ *nm* e-mail

émail, *pl* **-aux** /emaj, o/ *nm* enamel

émaillé, ∼**e** /emaje/ *adj* ⟨*utensil*⟩ enamel; ⟨*metal*⟩ enamelled

émanation /emanasjɔ̃/ *nf* emanation; ∼**s de gaz** gas fumes

émancipation /emɑ̃sipasjɔ̃/ *nf* emancipation

émanciper /emɑ̃sipe/ [1] **1** *vtr* to emancipate ⟨*people*⟩; to liberate ⟨*country*⟩

2 s'émanciper *v refl* (+ *v être*) to become emancipated; **femme émancipée** liberated woman

émaner /emane/ [1] **1** *vi* ∼ **de** to emanate from; to come from

2 *v impers* **il émane d'elle un charme fou** she exudes charm

émaux ▸ ÉMAIL

emballage /ɑ̃balaʒ/ *nm* packaging; wrapping; packing.
■ ∼ **sous vide** vacuum packing

emballant, ∼**e** /ɑ̃balɑ̃, ɑ̃t/ *adj* (colloq) exciting

emballer /ɑ̃bale/ [1] **1** *vtr* (**a**) to pack, to wrap
(**b**) (colloq) **être emballé par** to be taken with

2 s'emballer *v refl* (+ *v être*) (**a**) ⟨*horse*⟩ to bolt
(**b**) (colloq) to get carried away
(**c**) to get all worked up (colloq)
(**d**) (colloq) ⟨*engine*⟩ to race
(**e**) ⟨*prices, inflation*⟩ to shoot up; ⟨*currency*⟩ to shoot up in value

embarcadère /ɑ̃baʀkadɛʀ/ *nm* pier; wharf

embarcation /ɑ̃baʀkasjɔ̃/ *nf* boat

embardée /ɑ̃baʀde/ *nf* (of car) swerve

embargo /ɑ̃baʀgo/ *nm* embargo

embarquement /ɑ̃baʀkəmɑ̃/ *nm* boarding

embarquer /ɑ̃baʀke/ [1] **1** *vtr* (**a**) to load ⟨*goods*⟩; to take [sb] on board
(**b**) (colloq) to take ⟨*object*⟩; ⟨*police*⟩ to pick up ⟨*criminal*⟩

2 *vi* (**a**) to board
(**b**) to sail (**pour** for)

3 s'embarquer *v refl* (+ *v être*) (**a**) to board
(**b**) (colloq) **s'∼ dans** to launch into ⟨*explanation*⟩

embarras /ɑ̃baʀa/ *nm inv*
(**a**) embarrassment
(**b**) awkward position; difficult situation
(**c**) **n'avoir que l'∼ du choix** to have too much to choose from

embarrassant, ∼**e** /ɑ̃baʀasɑ̃, ɑ̃t/ *adj*
(**a**) awkward; embarrassing
(**b**) cumbersome

embarrassé, ∼**e** /ɑ̃baʀase/ **1** *pp* ▸ EMBARRASSER

2 *pp adj* (**a**) embarrassed; **être bien ∼ pour répondre** to be at a loss for an answer
(**b**) ⟨*room*⟩ cluttered; ∼ **d'une grosse valise** weighed down with a large suitcase

embarrasser /ɑ̃baʀase/ [1] **1** *vtr* (**a**) to embarrass
(**b**) to clutter [sth] (up); **cette armoire m'embarrasse plutôt qu'autre chose** this wardrobe is more of a nuisance than anything else

2 s'embarrasser *v refl* (+ *v être*) **s'∼ de** to burden oneself with ⟨*baggage, person*⟩

embauche /ɑ̃boʃ/ *nf* appointment (GB), hiring (US); **salaire d'∼** starting salary

embaucher /ɑ̃boʃe/ [1] *vtr* (**a**) to take on (GB), to hire
(**b**) (colloq) to recruit

embaumer /ɑ̃bome/ [1] **1** *vtr* (**a**) ⟨*smell*⟩ to fill ⟨*place*⟩; ⟨*place*⟩ to smell of ⟨*wax*⟩
(**b**) to embalm

2 *vi* to be fragrant

embaumeur, **-euse** /ɑ̃bomœʀ, øz/ *nm,f* embalmer

embellir /ɑ̃beliʀ/ [3] **1** *vtr* (**a**) to improve [sth]; to make [sb] more attractive
(**b**) to embellish ⟨*story, truth*⟩

2 *vi* to become more attractive

embellissement /ɑ̃belismɑ̃/ *nm* (of house) improving; **travaux d'∼** improvements

emberlificoter /ɑ̃bɛʀlifikɔte/ [1] (colloq) **1** *vtr* (**a**) to entangle
(**b**) to take [sb] in (colloq)

2 s'emberlificoter *v refl* (+ *v être*) to get entangled; to get tangled up (**dans** in)

embêtant, ∼**e** /ɑ̃bɛtɑ̃, ɑ̃t/ *adj*
(**a**) annoying
(**b**) boring

embêtement /ɑ̃bɛtmɑ̃/ *nm* problem

embêter /ɑ̃bete/ [1] **1** *vtr* (**a**) to bother
(**b**) to pester; to annoy
(**c**) to bore

2 s'embêter *v refl* (+ *v être*) (**a**) to be bored
(**b**) **s'∼ à faire** to go to the bother of doing

emblée: d'emblée /dɑ̃ble/ *phr*
(**a**) straightaway
(**b**) at first sight

emblématique /ɑ̃blematik/ *adj* emblematic; symbolic

emblème /ɑ̃blɛm/ *nm* emblem

embobiner /ɑ̃bɔbine/ [1] *vtr* (colloq) to hoodwink

emboîter /ɑ̃bwate/ [1] **1** *vtr* to fit [sth] together; ∼ **qch dans** to fit sth into

2 s'emboîter *v refl* (+ *v être*) ⟨*part*⟩ to fit (**dans** into); ⟨*parts*⟩ to fit together
IDIOMS ∼ **le pas à qn** to fall in behind sb

embonpoint /ɑ̃bɔ̃pwɛ̃/ *nm* stoutness; **avoir de l'∼** to be stout

embouché, ∼**e** /ɑ̃buʃe/ *adj* **mal ∼** coarse; in a foul mood

embouchure /ɑ̃buʃyʀ/ *nf* (of river) mouth; (of instrument) mouthpiece; (of pipe) opening

e

embourber: **s'embourber** /ɑ̃buʀbe/ [1] *v refl* (+ *v être*) **(a)** to get stuck in the mud
(b) to get bogged down

embourgeoiser: **s'embourgeoiser** /ɑ̃buʀʒwaze/ [1] *v refl* (+ *v être*) ⟨*person*⟩ to become middle-class; ⟨*area*⟩ to become gentrified

embout /ɑ̃bu/ *nm* (of cigar, cane) tip; (of hosepipe) nozzle; (of pipe) mouthpiece

embouteillage /ɑ̃butɛjaʒ/ *nm* traffic jam

emboutir /ɑ̃butiʀ/ [3] *vtr* **(a)** to stamp, to press ⟨*part, metal*⟩
(b) (colloq) to crash into ⟨*vehicle*⟩

embranchement /ɑ̃bʀɑ̃ʃmɑ̃/ *nm*
(a) junction
(b) side road
(c) (on railways) branch line

embrasé, **~e** /ɑ̃bʀaze/ *adj* **(a)** burning
(b) glowing

embrasement /ɑ̃bʀazmɑ̃/ *nm* **(a)** blaze
(b) dazzling illumination
(c) unrest

embraser /ɑ̃bʀaze/ [1] **1** *vtr* **(a)** to set [sth] ablaze
(b) to set [sth] alight ⟨*country*⟩
2 **s'embraser** *v refl* (+ *v être*) **(a)** to catch fire
(b) ⟨*country*⟩ to erupt into violence
(c) ⟨*sky*⟩ to be set ablaze
(d) to burn with desire

embrasser /ɑ̃bʀase/ [1] **1** *vtr* **(a)** to kiss; **je t'embrasse** lots of love
(b) to embrace; to hug
(c) to take up ⟨*career, cause*⟩
2 **s'embrasser** *v refl* (+ *v être*) **(a)** to kiss (each other)
(b) to embrace; to hug
IDIOMS **~** qn comme du bon pain to hug sb warmly

embrasure /ɑ̃bʀazyʀ/ *nf* **~** de fenêtre window; **~** de porte doorway

embrayage /ɑ̃bʀɛjaʒ/ *nm* **(a)** clutch
(b) clutch pedal

embrayer /ɑ̃bʀeje/ [21] *vi* ⟨*driver*⟩ to engage the clutch; (Tech) to engage

embrigader /ɑ̃bʀigade/ [1] *vtr* **(a)** to recruit
(b) (Mil) to brigade

embrouillamini /ɑ̃bʀujamini/ *nm* (colloq) muddle

embrouille /ɑ̃bʀuj/ *nf* (colloq) shady goings-on (colloq)

embrouiller /ɑ̃bʀuje/ [1] **1** *vtr* to tangle ⟨*wires*⟩
(b) to confuse ⟨*matter, person*⟩
2 **s'embrouiller** *v refl* (+ *v être*) **(a)** to become tangled
(b) ⟨*ideas, person*⟩ to become confused

embroussaillé, **~e** /ɑ̃bʀusaje/ *adj* ⟨*path*⟩ overgrown; ⟨*hair*⟩ bushy

embrumé, **~e** /ɑ̃bʀyme/ *adj* **(a)** misty
(b) ⟨*mind*⟩ befuddled; ⟨*look*⟩ glazed

embruns /ɑ̃bʀœ̃/ *nm pl* spray

embryon /ɑ̃bʀijɔ̃/ *nm* embryo

embûche /ɑ̃byʃ/ *nf* **(a)** trap; **dresser des ~s** to set traps
(b) hazard; pitfall; **semé d'~s** hazardous; (figurative) fraught with pitfalls

embuer /ɑ̃bɥe/ [1] **1** *vtr* to mist up, to fog up
2 **s'embuer** *v refl* (+ *v être*) ⟨*window*⟩ to mist up, to fog up; ⟨*eyes*⟩ to mist over

embuscade /ɑ̃byskad/ *nf* ambush

embusquer: **s'embusquer** /ɑ̃byske/ [1] *v refl* (+ *v être*) to lie in ambush

éméché, **~e** /emeʃe/ *adj* (colloq) tipsy

émeraude /emʀod/ *nf* emerald

émergence /emɛʀʒɑ̃s/ *nf* emergence

émerger /emɛʀʒe/ [13] *vi* to emerge

émeri /emʀi/ *nm* emery

émérite /emeʀit/ *adj* **(a)** outstanding
(b) **professeur ~** emeritus professor

émerveiller /emɛʀveje/ [1] **1** *vtr* **~** qn to fill sb with wonder
2 **s'émerveiller** *v refl* (+ *v être*) **s'~** de or devant qch to marvel at sth

émetteur, -trice /emetœʀ, tʀis/ **1** *adj*
(a) ⟨*station*⟩ broadcasting
(b) ⟨*bank*⟩ issuing
2 *nm* **(a)** transmitter
(b) (of loan, card) issuer

émettre /emɛtʀ/ [60] *vtr* **(a)** to express ⟨*opinion, wish*⟩; to put forward ⟨*hypothesis*⟩
(b) to utter ⟨*cry*⟩; to produce ⟨*sound, heat*⟩
(c) to issue ⟨*document*⟩
(d) to broadcast ⟨*programme*⟩
(e) to send out ⟨*signal*⟩
(f) to emit ⟨*radiation*⟩

émeute /emøt/ *nf* riot

émietter /emjete/ [1] **1** *vtr* to crumble [sth]
2 **s'émietter** *v refl* (+ *v être*) to crumble

émigrant, **~e** /emigʀɑ̃, ɑ̃t/ *nm,f* emigrant

émigration /emigʀasjɔ̃/ *nf* emigration

émigré, **~e** /emigʀe/ *nm,f* emigrant; émigré

émigrer /emigʀe/ [1] *vi* **(a)** to emigrate
(b) ⟨*bird*⟩ to migrate

émincer /emɛ̃se/ [12] *vtr* to slice [sth] thinly

éminemment /eminamɑ̃/ *adv* eminently

éminence /eminɑ̃s/ *nf* **(a)** hillock
(b) (Anat) protuberance

Éminence /eminɑ̃s/ *nf* Eminence

éminent, **~e** /eminɑ̃, ɑ̃t/ *adj* distinguished, eminent

émirat /emiʀa/ *nm* emirate

Émirats /emiʀa/ *pr nm pl* **~ arabes unis**, **EAU** United Arab Emirates

émis, **~e** /emi, iz/ ▶ **ÉMETTRE**

émissaire /emisɛʀ/ *nm* emissary

émission /emisjɔ̃/ *nf* **(a)** programme (GB)
(b) (of document) issue
(c) (of waves, signals) emission

emmagasiner /ɑ̃magazine/ [1] *vtr* **(a)** to store

(b) to stockpile ⟨*goods*⟩; to store up ⟨*knowledge*⟩

emmanchure /ɑ̃mɑ̃ʃyʀ/ *nf* armhole

emmêler /ɑ̃mele/ [1] **1** *vtr* **(a)** to tangle **(b)** to confuse ⟨*matter*⟩
2 s'emmêler *v refl* (+ *v être*) to get tangled up in; **s'~ les pieds dans** to get one's feet caught in

emménagement /ɑ̃menaʒmɑ̃/ *nm* moving in

emménager /ɑ̃menaʒe/ [13] *vi* to move in

emmener /ɑ̃mne/ [16] *vtr* **(a)** to take ⟨*person*⟩ (**à, jusqu'à** to); **veux-tu que je t'emmène en voiture?** do you want a lift (GB) *or* a ride (US)?
(b) (colloq) (controversial) to take [sth] with one ⟨*object*⟩
(c) to take [sb] away

emmerder /ɑ̃mɛʀde/ [1] (slang) **1** *vtr* to annoy, to hassle (colloq); **~ le monde** to be a pain in the arse (GB) (colloq) *or* ass (US) (slang)
2 s'emmerder *v refl* (+ *v être*) **(a)** to be bored stiff (colloq)
(b) **s'~ à faire** to go to the trouble of doing; **tu t'emmerdes pas!** you're doing all right for yourself!; you've got a nerve!

emmitoufler /ɑ̃mitufle/ [1] **1** *vtr* to wrap [sb/sth] up warmly
2 s'emmitoufler *v refl* (+ *v être*) to wrap (oneself) up warmly

émoi /emwa/ *nm* agitation, turmoil

émoluments /emolymɑ̃/ *nm pl* remuneration

émonder /emɔ̃de/ [1] *vtr* to prune

émotif, -ive /emɔtif, iv/ *adj* emotional

émotion /emosjɔ̃/ *nf* emotion

émotivité /emɔtivite/ *nf* **enfant d'une grande ~** highly emotional child

émousser /emuse/ [1] **1** *vtr* **(a)** to blunt **(b)** to dull ⟨*curiosity, sensitivity*⟩
2 s'émousser *v refl* (+ *v être*) **(a)** to become blunt
(b) ⟨*curiosity*⟩ to become dulled

émoustiller /emustije/ [1] *vtr* **(a)** to exhilarate
(b) to titillate

émouvant, ~e /emuvɑ̃, ɑ̃t/ *adj* moving

émouvoir /emuvwaʀ/ [43] **1** *vtr* to move, to touch; **~ l'opinion** to cause a stir
2 s'émouvoir *v refl* (+ *v être*) **(a)** to be touched *or* moved
(b) **s'~ de** to become concerned about; to be bothered by

empailler /ɑ̃paje/ [1] *vtr* to stuff

empailleur, -euse /ɑ̃pajœʀ, øz/ *nm,f* taxidermist

empaler /ɑ̃pale/ [1] **1** *vtr* to impale
2 s'empaler *v refl* (+ *v être*) to become impaled

empaqueter /ɑ̃pakte/ [20] *vtr* to package; to wrap [sth] up

emparer: s'emparer /ɑ̃paʀe/ [1] *v refl* (+ *v être*) **(a)** **s'~ de** (gen) to get hold of, to seize; to take over ⟨*town*⟩; to seize ⟨*power*⟩
(b) **s'~ de** ⟨*feeling*⟩ to take hold of [sb]

empâter: s'empâter /ɑ̃pate/ [1] *v refl* (+ *v être*) to become puffy; to put on weight

empêchement /ɑ̃pɛʃmɑ̃/ *nm* unforeseen difficulty; **j'ai un ~** something's cropped up

empêcher /ɑ̃peʃe/ [1] **1** *vtr* to prevent, to stop; **~ qn de faire** to prevent sb (from) doing
2 s'empêcher *v refl* (+ *v être*) **je n'ai pas pu m'~ de rire** I couldn't help laughing
3 *v impers* **(il) n'empêche** all the same; **il n'empêche que** the fact remains that

empereur /ɑ̃pʀœʀ/ *nm* emperor

empesé, ~e /ɑ̃paze/ *adj* ⟨*collar*⟩ starched; ⟨*person, manner*⟩ starchy

empester /ɑ̃pɛste/ [16] **1** *vtr* to stink [sth] out (GB), to stink up (US)
2 *vi* to stink

empêtrer: s'empêtrer /ɑ̃petʀe/ [1] *v refl* (+ *v être*) **s'~ dans** to get entangled in ⟨*briars*⟩; to get tangled up in ⟨*lies*⟩

emphase /ɑ̃faz/ *nf* **(a)** grandiloquence **(b)** emphasis

emphatique /ɑ̃fatik/ *adj* **(a)** grandiloquent
(b) emphatic

empiècement /ɑ̃pjɛsmɑ̃/ *nm* (of garment) yoke

empiéter /ɑ̃pjete/ [14] *vi* to encroach

empiffrer: s'empiffrer /ɑ̃pifʀe/ [1] *v refl* (+ *v être*) (colloq) to stuff oneself

empiler /ɑ̃pile/ [1] **1** *vtr* to pile [sth] (up)
2 s'empiler *v refl* (+ *v être*) to pile up

empire /ɑ̃piʀ/ *nm* empire

Empire /ɑ̃piʀ/ *nm* **l'~** the Empire.
■ **l'~ d'Orient** the Byzantine Empire; **l'~ d'Occident** the Western Empire

empirer /ɑ̃piʀe/ [1] *vi* to get worse

empirique /ɑ̃piʀik/ *adj* empirical

empirisme /ɑ̃piʀism/ *nm* empiricism

emplacement /ɑ̃plasmɑ̃/ *nm* **(a)** site
(b) parking space

emplette /ɑ̃plɛt/ *nf* purchase

emplir /ɑ̃pliʀ/ [3] *vtr*, **s'emplir** *v refl* (+ *v être*) to fill (**de** with)

emploi /ɑ̃plwa/ *nm* **(a)** job
(b) employment
(c) use; **téléviseur couleur à vendre, cause double ~** colour (GB) TV for sale, surplus to requirements
(d) usage
■ **~ du temps** timetable
IDIOMS **avoir la tête de l'~** to look the part

employé, ~e /ɑ̃plwaje/ *nm,f* employee
■ **~ de banque** bank clerk; **~ municipal** local authority employee

employer /ɑ̃plwaje/ [23] **1** *vtr* to employ ⟨*person*⟩; to use ⟨*word, product*⟩
2 s'employer *v refl* (+ *v être*) **(a)** to be used
(b) **s'~ à faire** to apply oneself to doing

employeur, -euse /ɑ̃plwajœʀ, øz/ *nm,f*
employer

empocher /ɑ̃pɔʃe/ [1] *vtr* to pocket

empoigner /ɑ̃pwaɲe/ [1] *vtr* to grab ⟨hold of⟩

empoisonnant, ~e /ɑ̃pwazɔnɑ̃, ɑ̃t/ *adj* (colloq) annoying, irritating

empoisonné, ~e /ɑ̃pwazɔne/ **1** *pp* ▸ EMPOISONNER

2 *pp adj* ⟨foodstuff⟩ poisoned; ⟨atmosphere⟩ sour

empoisonnement /ɑ̃pwazɔnmɑ̃/ *nm*
(a) poisoning
(b) (colloq) trouble

empoisonner /ɑ̃pwazɔne/ [1] **1** *vtr* to poison; ~ **la vie de qn** to make sb's life a misery

2 **s'empoisonner** *v refl* (+ *v être*) to poison oneself; **il s'est empoisonné avec une huître pas fraîche** he got food poisoning from eating a bad oyster

empoisonneur, -euse /ɑ̃pwazɔnœʀ, øz/ *nm,f* (a) poisoner
(b) (colloq) nuisance

emportement /ɑ̃pɔʀtəmɑ̃/ *nm* fit of anger; **avec ~** angrily

emporter /ɑ̃pɔʀte/ [1] **1** *vtr* (a) to take ⟨object⟩; **pizzas à ~** takeaway pizzas (GB), pizzas to go (US)
(b) ⟨ambulance⟩ to take [sb] away; ⟨plane⟩ to carry [sb] away
(c) ⟨wind, river⟩ to sweep [sb/sth] away; ⟨shell, bullet⟩ to take [sth] off ⟨ear, leg⟩
(d) **une leucémie l'a emporté** he died of leukaemia
(e) to take ⟨position⟩
(f) **l'~** to win; to prevail; **l'~ sur qch** to overcome sth

2 **s'emporter** *v refl* (+ *v être*) to lose one's temper

empoté, ~e /ɑ̃pɔte/ *adj* (colloq) clumsy, awkward

empreindre: s'empreindre /ɑ̃pʀɛ̃dʀ/ [55] *v refl* (+ *v être*) to become marked (**de** with), to become imbued (**de** with)

empreinte /ɑ̃pʀɛ̃t/ *nf* (a) footprint; track
(b) stamp, mark
■ **~s digitales** fingerprints

empressement /ɑ̃pʀɛsmɑ̃/ *nm*
(a) eagerness; **avec ~** eagerly
(b) attentiveness

empresser: s'empresser /ɑ̃pʀese/ [1] *v refl* (+ *v être*) **s'~ de faire** to hasten to do; **s'~ autour** *or* **auprès de qn** to fuss over sb

emprise /ɑ̃pʀiz/ *nf* hold, influence

emprisonnement /ɑ̃pʀizɔnmɑ̃/ *nm*
imprisonment; **peine d'~** prison sentence

emprisonner /ɑ̃pʀizɔne/ [1] *vtr* (a) to imprison (**à, dans** in)
(b) to keep [sb] prisoner

emprunt /ɑ̃pʀœ̃/ *nm* (a) (money) loan; **faire un ~** to take out a loan
(b) borrowing; **d'~** ⟨car, name⟩ borrowed
(c) (object, book) loan; **c'est un ~ fait à un musée** it's on loan from a museum

(d) (of idea, word) borrowing

emprunté, ~e /ɑ̃pʀœ̃te/ *adj* awkward

emprunter /ɑ̃pʀœ̃te/ [1] *vtr* (a) to borrow
(b) to take ⟨road⟩

empuantir /ɑ̃pɥɑ̃tiʀ/ [3] *vtr* to stink out (GB), to stink up (US)

ému, ~e /emy/ **1** *pp* ▸ ÉMOUVOIR

2 *pp adj* moved; touched; nervous; **trop ~ pour parler** too overcome to speak

3 *adj* ⟨words⟩ full of emotion; ⟨memory⟩ fond

émulation /emylasjɔ̃/ *nf* competitiveness

émule /emyl/ *nm,f* imitator; **être l'~ de qn** to model oneself on sb

émulsifiant /emylsifjɑ̃/ *nm* emulsifier

émulsion /emylsjɔ̃/ *nf* emulsion

en /ɑ̃/ **1** *prep* (a) in; into; to; **vivre ~ ville** to live in town; **aller ~ Allemagne** to go to Germany; **~ hiver/1991** in winter/1991; **~ semaine** during the week; **voyager ~ train** to travel by train
(b) **il est toujours ~ manteau** he always wears a coat
(c) as; **je vous parle ~ ami** I'm speaking (to you) as a friend
(d) into; **traduire ~ anglais** to translate into English
(e) **c'est ~ or** it's (made of) gold; **le même ~ bleu/plus grand** the same in blue/only bigger; **~ hauteur, le mur fait trois mètres** the wall is three metres (GB) high
(f) (used with gerund) **je l'ai croisé ~ sortant** I met him as I was leaving; **prends un café ~ attendant** have a cup of coffee while you're waiting; **l'enfant se réveilla ~ hurlant** the child woke up screaming; **ouvrez cette caisse ~ soulevant le couvercle** open this box by lifting the lid; **tu aurais moins chaud ~ enlevant ta veste** you'd be cooler if you took your jacket off

2 *pron* (a) (indicating means) **il sortit son épée et l'~ transperça** he took out his sword and ran him/her through
(b) (indicating cause) **ça l'a tellement bouleversé qu'il ~ est tombé malade** it distressed him so much that he fell ill (GB) *or* became sick (US)
(c) (representing person) **ils aiment leurs enfants et ils ~ sont aimés** they love their children and they are loved by them
(d) (representing thing) **'veux-tu du vin?'—'oui, j'~ veux'** 'would you like some wine?'—'yes, I'd like some'; **il n'~ reste pas beaucoup** there isn't much (of it) left; there aren't many left; **j'~ suis fier** I'm proud of it
(e) (colloq) **tu ~ as un beau chapeau!** what a nice hat you've got!

ENA /ena/ *nf: abbr* ▸ ÉCOLE

énarque /enaʀk/ *nm,f* graduate of the ENA

encadré /ɑ̃kɑdʀe/ *nm* (in newspaper) box

encadrement /ɑ̃kɑdʀəmɑ̃/ *nm*
(a) supervision
(b) supervisory staff; managerial staff; (Mil) officers
(c) (of picture) frame

encadrer /ɑ̃kɑdʀe/ [1] *vtr* (a) to supervise ‹*staff*›; to train ‹*soldier*›
(b) to flank ‹*person*›; to frame ‹*face, window*›; ~ **de rouge** to outline [sth] in red
(c) to frame ‹*picture*›

encaisser /ɑ̃kese/ [1] *vtr* (a) to cash ‹*cheque, sum of money*›
(b) (colloq) to take ‹*blow, defeat*›; **je ne peux pas ~ ton frère** I can't stand your brother
IDIOMS ~ **le coup** (colloq) to take it all in one's stride

encart /ɑ̃kaʀ/ *nm* insert; ~ **publicitaire** promotional insert

en-cas /ɑ̃kɑ/ *nm inv* snack

encastrer /ɑ̃kastʀe/ [1] **1** *vtr* to build in ‹*oven, refrigerator*›; to fit ‹*sink, hotplate*›; **baignoire encastrée** sunken bath
2 s'encastrer *v refl* (+ *v être*) to fit (**dans** into)

encaustique /ɑ̃kostik/ *nf* wax polish

enceinte /ɑ̃sɛ̃t/ **1** *adj f* ‹*woman*› pregnant
2 *nf* (a) (**mur d'**)~ surrounding wall
(b) (of prison, palace) compound; (of church) interior

encens /ɑ̃sɑ̃/ *nm inv* incense

encenser /ɑ̃sɑ̃se/ [1] *vtr* to sing the praises of ‹*person*›; to acclaim ‹*work of art*›

encercler /ɑ̃sɛʀkle/ [1] *vtr* (a) to surround, to encircle
(b) (with pen) to circle

enchaînement /ɑ̃ʃɛnmɑ̃/ *nm* (a) (of events) chain
(b) sequence
(c) (in music, sport) transition

enchaîner /ɑ̃ʃɛne/ [1] **1** *vtr* to chain up ‹*person, animal*›; ~ **à** to chain to
2 *vi* to go on; ~ **avec une nouvelle chanson** to move on to a new song
3 s'enchaîner *v refl* (+ *v être*) ‹*shots, sequences in film*› to follow on

enchantement /ɑ̃ʃɑ̃tmɑ̃/ *nm* enchantment, spell; **comme par ~** as if by magic

enchanter /ɑ̃ʃɑ̃te/ [1] *vtr* (a) to delight; **ça ne m'enchante guère** it doesn't exactly thrill me; **enchanté (de faire votre connaissance)!** how do you do!
(b) **forêt enchantée** enchanted forest

enchanteur, -eresse /ɑ̃ʃɑ̃tœʀ, tʀɛs/
1 *adj* enchanting
2 *nm,f* (a) enchanter/enchantress
(b) (figurative) charmer

enchère /ɑ̃ʃɛʀ/ **1** *nf* bid
2 enchères *nf pl* **vente aux ~s** auction

enchérir /ɑ̃ʃeʀiʀ/ [3] *vi* to bid; ~ **sur qn** to bid more than sb; ~ **sur une offre** to make a higher bid

enchevêtrement /ɑ̃ʃ(ə)vɛtʀəmɑ̃/ *nm* (of threads) tangle; (of corridors, streets) labyrinth

enchevêtrer /ɑ̃ʃ(ə)vetʀe/ [1] **1** *vtr* (a) to tangle [sth] up ‹*threads*›
(b) **être enchevêtré** ‹*sentence, plot*› to be muddled; ‹*case*› to be complicated

2 s'enchevêtrer *v refl* (+ *v être*)
(a) ‹*branches, threads*› to get tangled
(b) ‹*phrases, ideas*› to become muddled

enclave /ɑ̃klav/ *nf* enclave

enclencher /ɑ̃klɑ̃ʃe/ [1] **1** *vtr* (a) to set [sth] in motion ‹*process*›
(b) to engage ‹*mechanism*›
2 s'enclencher *v refl* (+ *v être*)
(a) ‹*process*› to get under way
(b) ‹*mechanism*› to engage

enclin, ~e /ɑ̃klɛ̃, in/ *adj* inclined (**à** to)

enclos /ɑ̃klo/ *nm inv* (gen) enclosure; (for animals) pen

enclume /ɑ̃klym/ *nf* (Tech, Anat) anvil

encoche /ɑ̃kɔʃ/ *nf* notch

encoder /ɑ̃kɔde/ [1] *vtr* to encode

encodeur /ɑ̃kɔdœʀ/ *nm* (Comput) encoder

encolure /ɑ̃kɔlyʀ/ *nf* (a) (of garment) neckline
(b) collar size
(c) (of animal) neck

encombrant, ~e /ɑ̃kɔ̃bʀɑ̃, ɑ̃t/ *adj*
(a) bulky; cumbersome
(b) ‹*person, matter*› troublesome

encombre: sans encombre /sɑ̃zɑ̃kɔ̃bʀ/ *phr* without a hitch

encombré, ~e /ɑ̃kɔ̃bʀe/ *adj* ‹*road, sky*› congested (**de** with); ‹*room*› cluttered

encombrement /ɑ̃kɔ̃bʀəmɑ̃/ *nm*
(a) traffic congestion
(b) (of switchboard) jamming
(c) (of room) cluttering
(d) (of furniture) bulk

encombrer /ɑ̃kɔ̃bʀe/ [1] **1** *vtr* (a) ‹*object, people*› to clutter up ‹*room*›; to obstruct ‹*road, path*›
(b) to jam ‹*switchboard*›; to clutter up ‹*mind*›
2 s'encombrer *v refl* (+ *v être*) **s'~ de** to burden oneself with; **s'~ l'esprit** to clutter up one's mind (**de** with)

encontre: à l'encontre de /alɑ̃kɔ̃tʀədə/ *phr* (a) counter to
(b) against
(c) toward(s)

encorder: s'encorder /ɑ̃kɔʀde/ [1] *v refl* (+ *v être*) to rope up

encore /ɑ̃kɔʀ/ **1** *adv* (a) still; **il n'est ~ que midi** it's only midday; **tu en es ~ là?** haven't you got (GB) *or* gotten (US) beyond that by now?; **qu'il soit impoli passe ~, mais...** the fact that he's rude is one thing, but...
(b) **pas ~** not yet; **il n'est pas ~ rentré** he hasn't come home yet; he still hasn't come home; **cela ne s'est ~ jamais vu** it has never been seen before
(c) again; ~ **toi** you again!; ~**!** encore!, more!; ~ **une fois** once more, once again; **qu'est-ce que j'ai ~ fait?** what have I done now?
(d) more; **mange ~ un peu** have some more to eat; **c'est ~ mieux** it's even better

(e) ~ un gâteau? another cake?; **pendant ~ trois jours** for another three days; **qu'est-ce qu'il te faut ~?** what more do you need?

(f) ~ faut-il qu'elle accepte but she still has to accept; **si ~ il était généreux!** if he were at least generous!

(g) only, just; **il y a ~ trois mois** only three months ago

2 **et encore** *phr* if that; **c'est tout au plus mangeable, et ~!** it's only just edible, if that!

3 **encore que** *phr* even though

encourageant, ~e /ãkuraʒã, ãt/ *adj* encouraging

encouragement /ãkuraʒmã/ *nm* encouragement

encourager /ãkuraʒe/ [13] *vtr* **(a)** to encourage (**à faire** to do)
(b) to cheer [sb] on

encourir /ãkurir/ [26] *vtr* to incur

encrasser /ãkrase/ [1] *vtr* **(a)** to clog [sth] (up) ⟨*filter, artery*⟩; to make [sth] sooty ⟨*chimney*⟩
(b) to dirty; (Aut) to foul up ⟨*spark plugs*⟩

encre /ãkr/ *nf* ink
■ ~ **de Chine** Indian (GB) *or* India (US) ink; ~ **sympathique** invisible ink
IDIOMS **cela a fait couler beaucoup d'~** a lot of ink has been spilled over this; **se faire un sang d'~** to be worried sick

encrier /ãkrije/ *nm* inkwell; ink pot

encroûter: s'encroûter /ãkrute/ [1] *v refl* (colloq) to get in a rut

encyclopédie /ãsiklɔpedi/ *nf* encyclopedia

endetté, ~e /ãdete/ *adj* in debt

endettement /ãdɛtmã/ *nm* debt

endetter /ãdete/ [1] **1** *vtr* to put [sb] into debt
2 **s'endetter** *v refl* (+ *v être*) to get into debt

endiablé, ~e /ãdjable/ *adj* ⟨*rhythm*⟩ furious

endiguer /ãdige/ [1] *vtr* to confine ⟨*river*⟩; to contain ⟨*demonstrators*⟩; to curb ⟨*speculation*⟩

endimanché, ~e /ãdimãʃe/ *adj* in one's Sunday best

endive /ãdiv/ *nf* chicory (GB), endive (US)

endoctriner /ãdɔktrine/ [1] *vtr* to indoctrinate

endolori, ~e /ãdɔlɔri/ *adj* aching

endolorir /ãdɔlɔrir/ [3] *vtr* to make [sb/sth] ache

endommager /ãdɔmaʒe/ [13] *vtr* to damage

endormi, ~e /ãdɔrmi/ *adj* **(a)** ⟨*person, animal*⟩ sleeping, asleep
(b) ⟨*village, mind*⟩ sleepy

endormir /ãdɔrmir/ [30] **1** *vtr* **(a)** to send [sb] to sleep ⟨*child*⟩; ⟨*person, substance*⟩ to put [sb] to sleep ⟨*patient*⟩
(b) (from boredom) ⟨*person, lecture*⟩ to send [sb] to sleep ⟨*person*⟩
(c) to dupe ⟨*person, opinion, enemy*⟩

(d) to allay ⟨*suspicion*⟩; to numb ⟨*faculties*⟩
2 **s'endormir** *v refl* (+ *v être*) **(a)** to fall asleep
(b) to get to sleep
(c) (figurative) to sit back

endossable /ãdosabl/ *adj* ⟨*cheque*⟩ endorsable

endosser /ãdose/ [1] *vtr* **(a)** to take on ⟨*role, responsibility*⟩
(b) to endorse ⟨*cheque*⟩

endroit /ãdrwa/ **1** *nm* **(a)** place; **par ~s** in places; **à quel ~?** where?
(b) (of fabric) right side; **à l'~** (of object) the right way up; (of garment) the right way round (GB) *or* around (US)
2 **à l'endroit de** *phr* toward(s)

enduire /ãdɥir/ [69] **1** *vtr* to coat (**de** with)
2 **s'enduire** *v refl* (+ *v être*) **s'~ de** to put [sth] on

enduit /ãdɥi/ *nm* **(a)** coating
(b) filler

endurance /ãdyrãs/ *nf* **(a)** (of person) stamina; ~ **à** resistance to
(b) (of engine) endurance

endurant, ~e /ãdyrã, ãt/ *adj* ⟨*person, athlete*⟩ tough; ⟨*engine, vehicle*⟩ hard-wearing

endurcir /ãdyrsir/ [3] **1** *vtr* **(a)** ⟨*sport, hard work*⟩ to strengthen ⟨*body, character*⟩
(b) ⟨*ordeal*⟩ to harden ⟨*person*⟩
2 **s'endurcir** *v refl* (+ *v être*) **(a)** to become stronger
(b) to become hardened

endurer /ãdyre/ [1] *vtr* **(a)** to endure; **faire ~ qch à qn** to put sb through sth
(b) to put up with

énergétique /enɛrʒetik/ *adj* **(a)** ⟨*needs, resources*⟩ energy
(b) ⟨*food*⟩ high-calorie

énergie /enɛrʒi/ *nf* energy; **faire des économies d'~** to save energy; **trouver des ~s douces** to find safe energy sources; **avec l'~ du désespoir** driven on by despair; **avec ~** ⟨*work*⟩ energetically; ⟨*protest*⟩ strongly
■ ~ **éolienne** windpower; ~ **nucléaire** nuclear power *ou* energy; ~ **solaire** solar power

énergique /enɛrʒik/ *adj* **(a)** ⟨*person, gesture*⟩ energetic; ⟨*handshake*⟩ vigorous; ⟨*face, expression*⟩ resolute
(b) ⟨*action*⟩ tough; ⟨*protest*⟩ strong; ⟨*refusal*⟩ firm; ⟨*intervention*⟩ forceful

énergumène /enɛrgymɛn/ *nmf* oddball

énervant, ~e /enɛrvã, ãt/ *adj* irritating

énervé, ~e /enɛrve/ *adj* **(a)** irritated
(b) nervous; ⟨*child*⟩ overexcited

énervement /enɛrvəmã/ *nm* **(a)** irritation
(b) agitation; **elle pleura d'~** she was so on edge that she cried

énerver /enɛrve/ [1] **1** *vtr* **(a)** to put [sb] on edge
(b) ~ **qn** to get on sb's nerves, to irritate sb
2 **s'énerver** *v refl* (+ *v être*) to get worked up

enfance /ãfãs/ *nf* childhood; **la petite ~** early childhood

IDIOMS c'est l'∼ de l'art it's child's play

enfant /ɑ̃fɑ̃/ *nmf* child; infant; **être ∼ unique** to be an only child
■ ∼ **de chœur** altar boy; **ce n'est pas un ∼ de chœur** (figurative) he's no angel

enfanter /ɑ̃fɑ̃te/ [1] *vtr* to give birth to

enfantillage /ɑ̃fɑ̃tijaʒ/ *nm* childishness

enfantin, ∼e /ɑ̃fɑ̃tɛ̃, in/ *adj* (a) simple, easy
(b) **mode ∼e** children's fashion
(c) childish

enfer /ɑ̃fɛʀ/ *nm* Hell; (figurative) hell; **aller à un train d'∼** (colloq) to go hell for leather (colloq); **soirée d'∼** (colloq) hell of a party (colloq)

enfermer /ɑ̃fɛʀme/ [1] **1** *vtr* (a) to shut [sth] in ⟨*animal*⟩; to lock [sth] up ⟨*money, jewellery*⟩; to lock [sb] up ⟨*person*⟩; **elle est bonne à ∼** (colloq) she's stark raving mad (colloq)
(b) ∼ **qn dans un rôle** to confine sb to a role; ∼ **qn dans une situation** to trap sb in a situation
2 s'enfermer *v refl* (+ *v être*) (a) (gen) to lock oneself in; (accidentally) to get locked in; (in order to be alone) to shut oneself away; **ne reste pas enfermé toute la journée!** don't stay cooped up indoors all day!
(b) **s'∼ dans** to retreat into; **s'∼ dans le mutisme** to remain obstinately silent

enfiévré, ∼e /ɑ̃fjevʀe/ *adj* ⟨*imagination*⟩ fevered; ⟨*atmosphere*⟩ feverish; ⟨*speech*⟩ fiery

enfilade /ɑ̃filad/ *nf* (of traps) succession; (of houses, tables) row

enfiler /ɑ̃file/ [1] **1** *vtr* (a) to slip on
(b) to thread ⟨*piece of thread, needle*⟩
2 s'enfiler *v refl* (+ *v être*) (a) (colloq) to guzzle down
(b) **s'∼ dans** to take ⟨*street*⟩

enfin /ɑ̃fɛ̃/ *adv* finally; lastly; ∼ **et surtout** last but not least; ∼ **seuls!** alone at last!; **mais ∼, cessez de vous disputer!** for heaven's sake, stop arguing!; **il pleut tous les jours, ∼ presque** it rains every day, well almost

enflammé, ∼e /ɑ̃flame/ *adj* (a) burning, on fire
(b) ⟨*person, declaration*⟩ passionate; ⟨*speech*⟩ impassioned
(c) (Med) ⟨*throat, wound*⟩ inflamed
(d) ⟨*sky*⟩ ablaze

enflammer /ɑ̃flame/ [1] **1** *vtr* (a) to set fire to [sth]
(b) to inflame ⟨*public opinion, mind*⟩; to fire ⟨*imagination*⟩; to fuel ⟨*anger*⟩
2 s'enflammer *v refl* (+ *v être*) (a) ⟨*house, paper*⟩ to go up in flames; ⟨*wood*⟩ to catch fire
(b) ⟨*eyes*⟩ to blaze; ⟨*imagination*⟩ to be fired (de with; à la vue de by); ⟨*country*⟩ to explode; **s'∼ pour qn** to become passionate about sb; **s'∼ pour qch** to get carried away by sth

enfler /ɑ̃fle/ [1] **1** *vtr* to exaggerate ⟨*story, event*⟩

2 *vi* (a) ⟨*part of body*⟩ to swell (up); ⟨*river, sea*⟩ to swell
(b) ⟨*rumour, anger*⟩ to spread
3 s'enfler *v refl* (+ *v être*) ⟨*anger*⟩ to mount; ⟨*voice*⟩ to rise; ⟨*rumour*⟩ to grow

enfoncement /ɑ̃fɔ̃smɑ̃/ *nm* (a) recess; dip
(b) **l'∼ du pays dans la récession** the country's slide into recession

enfoncer /ɑ̃fɔ̃se/ [12] **1** *vtr* (a) to push in ⟨*cork, stake*⟩; ∼ **ses mains dans ses poches** to dig one's hands into one's pockets; ∼ **son doigt dans** to stick one's finger into; ∼ **un clou dans qch** to knock a nail into sth
(b) to break down ⟨*door*⟩; to break through ⟨*enemy lines*⟩; ∼ **des portes ouvertes** to state the obvious
(c) **ne m'enfonce pas davantage** don't rub it in
2 s'enfoncer *v refl* (+ *v être*) (a) **s'∼ dans la neige** to sink in the snow; **s'∼ dans l'erreur** to make error after error; **les piquets s'enfoncent facilement** the posts go in easily; **s'∼ une épine dans le doigt** to get a thorn in one's finger; **s'∼ dans la forêt** to go into the forest
(b) (colloq) to make things worse for oneself

enfouir /ɑ̃fwiʀ/ [3] **1** *vtr* (a) to bury
(b) ∼ **qch dans un sac** to shove sth into a bag
2 s'enfouir *v refl* (+ *v être*) **s'∼ sous les couvertures** to burrow under the blankets

enfourcher /ɑ̃fuʀʃe/ [1] *vtr* to mount ⟨*horse*⟩; to get on ⟨*motorbike*⟩

enfourner /ɑ̃fuʀne/ [1] *vtr* (a) to put [sth] in the oven
(b) (colloq) to stuff down ⟨*food*⟩

enfreindre /ɑ̃fʀɛ̃dʀ/ [55] *vtr* to infringe

enfuir: s'enfuir /ɑ̃fɥiʀ/ [9] *v refl* (+ *v être*)
(a) to run away; ⟨*bird*⟩ to fly away
(b) to escape

enfumer /ɑ̃fyme/ [1] *vtr* to fill [sth] with smoke; **tu nous enfumes avec tes cigares!** you're smoking us out with your cigars!

engagé, ∼e /ɑ̃ɡaʒe/ *nm,f* enlisted man/ woman

engageant, ∼e /ɑ̃ɡaʒɑ̃, ɑ̃t/ *adj* ⟨*person, manner*⟩ welcoming; ⟨*dish, place*⟩ inviting

engagement /ɑ̃ɡaʒmɑ̃/ *nm*
(a) commitment; **prendre l'∼ de faire** to undertake to do
(b) involvement
(c) (Mil) enlistment

engager /ɑ̃ɡaʒe/ [13] **1** *vtr* (a) to hire ⟨*staff*⟩; to enlist ⟨*soldier*⟩; to engage ⟨*artist*⟩
(b) to begin ⟨*process, reform policy*⟩; **nous avons engagé la conversation** we struck up a conversation
(c) to commit, to bind ⟨*person*⟩
(d) to stake ⟨*honour*⟩; ∼ **sa parole** to give one's word
(e) ∼ **qch dans** to put sth in
(f) to lay out ⟨*capital*⟩
(g) ∼ **qn à faire** to urge sb to do

(h) (Sport) ∼ **qn dans une compétition** to enter sb for a competition

(i) to pawn ⟨*valuables*⟩

2 **s'engager** *v refl* (+ *v être*) **(a)** to promise (**à faire** to do); **s'**∼ **vis-à-vis de qn** to make a commitment to sb

(b) **s'**∼ **dans un projet** to embark on a project

(c) to get involved

(d) **s'**∼ **sur une route** to go into a road

(e) ⟨*lawsuit*⟩ to begin

(f) **s'**∼ **dans l'armée** to join the army

engelure /ãʒlyʀ/ *nf* chilblain

engendrer /ãʒɑ̃dʀe/ [1] *vtr* **(a)** to engender

(b) ⟨*woman*⟩ to give birth to; ⟨*man*⟩ to father

engin /ãʒɛ̃/ *nm* **(a)** device

(b) vehicle

(c) piece of equipment

englober /ãglɔbe/ [1] *vtr* to include

engloutir /ãglutiʀ/ [3] *vtr* **(a)** ⟨*sea, storm, fog*⟩ to engulf, to swallow up

(b) (colloq) to gulp ⟨*sth*⟩ down

(c) ⟨*person*⟩ to squander ⟨*money*⟩

engoncé, ∼**e** /ãgõse/ *adj* **il était** ∼ **dans une veste trop étroite** he was squeezed into a tight jacket

engorger /ãgɔʀʒe/ [13] *vtr* **(a)** to block (up) ⟨*pipes, drains*⟩

(b) to clog up ⟨*roads*⟩

engouement /ãgumã/ *nm* (for thing, activity) passion; (for person) infatuation

engouer: s'engouer /ãgwe/ [1] *v refl* (+ *v être*) **s'**∼ **de** to develop a passion for

engouffrer: s'engouffrer /ãgufʀe/ [1] *v refl* (+ *v être*) (into a room) to rush; (into a taxi) to dive

engourdi, ∼**e** /ãguʀdi/ *adj* ⟨*limb, body*⟩ numb (**par, de** with); ⟨*person*⟩ drowsy; ⟨*town*⟩ sleepy; ⟨*mind*⟩ dull(ed)

engourdir: s'engourdir /ãguʀdiʀ/ [3] *v refl* (+ *v être*) ⟨*limb*⟩ to go numb; ⟨*mind*⟩ to grow dull

engourdissement /ãguʀdismã/ *nm* **(a)** (physical) numbness; (mental) drowsiness

(b) (of body) numbing; (of mind) dulling

engrais /ãgʀɛ/ *nm inv* manure; fertilizer

engraisser /ãgʀese/ [1] **1** *vtr* **(a)** to fatten ⟨*cattle*⟩

(b) to fertilize ⟨*soil*⟩

2 *vi* to get fat

3 **s'engraisser** *v refl* (+ *v être*) (colloq) **s'**∼ **(sur le dos de qn)** to grow fat (off sb's back) (colloq)

engranger /ãgʀãʒe/ [13] *vtr* to gather in ⟨*harvest*⟩; (figurative) to store; to store up

engrenage /ãgʀənaʒ/ *nm* **(a)** gears

(b) (figurative) (of violence) spiral

engueuler (slang) /ãgœle/ [1] **1** *vtr* to tell [sb] off; to give [sb] an earful (colloq)

2 **s'engueuler** *v refl* (+ *v être*) to have a row

enhardir: s'enhardir /ãaʀdiʀ/ [3] *v refl* (+ *v être*) to become bolder

énième /ɛnjɛm/ *adj* umpteenth

énigmatique /enigmatik/ *adj* enigmatic

énigme /enigm/ *nf* **(a)** enigma, mystery

(b) riddle; **parler par** ∼**s** to speak in riddles

enivrant, ∼**e** /ãnivʀã, ãt/ *adj* intoxicating

enivrement /ãnivʀəmã/ *nm* intoxication

enivrer /ãnivʀe/ [1] **1** *vtr* **(a)** to make [sb] drunk

(b) ∼ **qn** ⟨*success*⟩ to go to sb's head

2 **s'enivrer** *v refl* (+ *v être*) to get drunk

enjambée /ãʒãbe/ *nf* stride; **avancer/s'éloigner à grandes** ∼**s** to stride forward/off

enjamber /ãʒãbe/ [1] *vtr* to step over ⟨*obstacle*⟩

enjeu, *pl* ∼**x** /ãʒø/ *nm* (Games) stake; **analyser l'**∼ **des élections** to analyse (GB) what is at stake in the elections

enjoindre /ãʒwɛ̃dʀ/ [56] *vtr* ∼ **à qn de faire** to enjoin sb to do

enjôler /ãʒole/ [1] *vtr* to beguile

enjoliver /ãʒɔlive/ [1] *vtr* to embellish

enjoliveur /ãʒɔlivœʀ/ *nm* hubcap

enjoué, ∼**e** /ãʒwe/ *adj* ⟨*character*⟩ cheerful; ⟨*tone*⟩ light-hearted

enlacer /ãlase/ [12] **1** *vtr* to embrace; ⟨*snake*⟩ to wrap itself around ⟨*prey*⟩

2 **s'enlacer** *v refl* (+ *v être*) ⟨*people*⟩ to embrace; ⟨*body*⟩ to intertwine

enlaidir /ãlediʀ/ [3] *vtr* to spoil ⟨*landscape*⟩; to make [sb] look ugly ⟨*person*⟩

enlevé, ∼**e** /ãlve/ *adj* lively

enlèvement /ãlɛvmã/ *nm* kidnapping (GB), abduction

enlever /ãlve/ [16] **1** *vtr* **(a)** to take [sth] away, to remove ⟨*piece of furniture, book*⟩; to take [sth] down ⟨*curtains, pictures*⟩; to take [sth] off ⟨*garment*⟩; to move, to remove ⟨*vehicle*⟩

(b) to remove ⟨*stain, paint*⟩

(c) to take ⟨*person, object*⟩ away; ∼ **à qn l'envie de partir** to put sb off going

(d) to kidnap; to carry [sb] off

(e) to carry [sth] off ⟨*trophy*⟩; to capture ⟨*market*⟩

2 **s'enlever** *v refl* (+ *v être*) **(a)** ⟨*varnish*⟩ to come off; ⟨*stain*⟩ to come out

(b) ⟨*part, section*⟩ to be detachable

(c) (colloq) **enlève-toi de là** get off (colloq)

enlisement /ãlizmã/ *nm* sinking; (of negotiations) stalemate; (of movement) collapse

enliser /ãlize/ [1] **1** *vtr* to get [sth] stuck

2 **s'enliser** *v refl* (+ *v être*) **(a)** ⟨*boat, vehicle*⟩ to get stuck

(b) ⟨*inquiry, negotiations*⟩ to drag on

enluminure /ãlyminyʀ/ *nf* illumination

enneigé, ∼**e** /ãneʒe/ *adj* ⟨*summit*⟩ snowy; ⟨*road*⟩ covered in snow

enneigement /ãnɛʒmã/ *nm* **bulletin d'**∼ snow report

ennemi, ∼**e** /ɛnmi/ **1** *adj* **(a)** (Mil) enemy

(b) (gen) hostile

2 *nm,f* enemy

3 *nm* (Mil) enemy; **passer à l'**∼ to go over to the enemy

ennui /ɑ̃nɥi/ *nm* (a) boredom; **tromper l'~**
to escape from boredom; **quel ~!** what a
bore!
(b) problem; **avoir des ~s** to have problems;
j'ai des ~s avec la police I'm in trouble
with the police; **s'attirer des ~s** to get into
trouble

ennuyé, ~e /ɑ̃nɥije/ *adj* (a) bored
(b) embarrassed; **j'étais très ~ de laisser les
enfants seuls** I felt awful about leaving the
children on their own
(c) **j'aurais été très ~ si je n'avais pas eu la
clé** I would have been in real trouble if I
hadn't had the key

ennuyer /ɑ̃nɥije/ [22] **1** *vtr* (a) to bore
(b) to bother; **si ça ne vous ennuie pas trop**
if you don't mind
(c) to annoy
(d) to hassle (colloq)
2 s'ennuyer *v refl* (+ *v être*) (a) to be
bored; to get bored
(b) **s'~ de** to miss ⟨friend⟩

ennuyeux, -euse /ɑ̃nɥijø, øz/ *adj*
(a) boring
(b) tedious
(c) annoying
IDIOMS **être ~ comme la pluie** to be as dull
as ditchwater

énoncé /enɔ̃se/ *nm* (a) (of exam subject)
wording (**de** of); **l'~ d'une théorie** the
exposition of a theory
(b) (of fact) statement (**de** of)

énoncer /enɔ̃se/ [12] *vtr* to pronounce
⟨verdict⟩; to set out, to state ⟨facts⟩; to
expound ⟨theory⟩

enorgueillir: s'enorgueillir
/ɑ̃nɔʁɡœjiʁ/ [3] *v refl* (+ *v être*) to pride
oneself (**de** on)

énorme /enɔʁm/ *adj* (a) ⟨object, person⟩
huge, enormous
(b) ⟨success, effort⟩ tremendous; ⟨mistake⟩
terrible; ⟨lie⟩ outrageous

énormément /enɔʁmemɑ̃/ *adv* a
tremendous amount; a great deal; **~ de
temps** a tremendous amount of time; **ça m'a
~ plu** I liked it immensely

énormité /enɔʁmite/ *nf* (a) (of figure, size)
hugeness; (of lie) enormity
(b) outrageous remark

enquérir: s'enquérir /ɑ̃keʁiʁ/ [35] *v refl*
(+ *v être*) **s'~ de** to enquire about

enquête /ɑ̃kɛt/ *nf* (a) (Law) inquiry,
investigation; (into a death) inquest; **~ de
police** police investigation
(b) (by journalist) investigation
(c) (by sociologist) survey

enquêter /ɑ̃kete/ [1] *vi* ⟨policeman⟩ to
carry out an investigation; ⟨expert⟩ to hold
an inquiry

enquêteur, -trice /ɑ̃ketœʁ, tʁis/ *nm,f*
(a) investigating officer
(b) pollster
(c) interviewer

enquiquinant, ~e /ɑ̃kikinɑ̃, ɑ̃t/ *adj*
(colloq) annoying; boring

enquiquiner /ɑ̃kikine/ [1] (colloq) **1** *vtr*
~ qn to get on sb's nerves; to pester sb
2 s'enquiquiner *v refl* (+ *v être*) **s'~ à
faire** to go to the trouble of doing

enraciner: s'enraciner /ɑ̃ʁasine/ [1]
v refl (+ *v être*) (a) to take root
(b) (figurative) ⟨person⟩ to put down roots;
⟨custom, idea⟩ to take root

enragé, ~e /ɑ̃ʁaʒe/ *adj* (a) fanatical
(b) enraged
(c) (Med) rabid
IDIOMS **manger de la vache ~e** (colloq) to go
through hard times

enrageant, ~e /ɑ̃ʁaʒɑ̃, ɑ̃t/ *adj*
infuriating

enrager /ɑ̃ʁaʒe/ [13] *vi* to be furious; **faire
~ qn** to tease sb

enrayer /ɑ̃ʁeje/ [21] **1** *vtr* (a) to check
⟨epidemic, development⟩; to curb ⟨inflation⟩;
to stop [sth] escalating ⟨crisis⟩
(b) to jam ⟨mechanism, gun⟩
2 s'enrayer *v refl* (+ *v être*) to get
jammed

enregistrement /ɑ̃ʁəʒistʁəmɑ̃/ *nm*
(a) (of music) recording
(b) (of data) recording; (of order) taking down
(c) (of baggage) check-in

enregistrer /ɑ̃ʁəʒistʁe/ [1] *vtr* (a) to
record ⟨cassette, album⟩
(b) to note ⟨progress, failure⟩; to record
⟨rise, drop⟩
(c) to make a record of ⟨expenses⟩; to take
⟨order⟩; to record ⟨data⟩; to set ⟨record⟩
(d) to register ⟨birth, claim⟩
(e) to check in ⟨baggage⟩
(f) **c'est enregistré, j'enregistre** (colloq) I've
made a mental note of it

enrhumer: s'enrhumer /ɑ̃ʁyme/ [1] *v refl*
(+ *v être*) to catch a cold

enrichir /ɑ̃ʁiʃiʁ/ [3] **1** *vtr* (a) to make
[sb] rich ⟨person⟩; to bring wealth to
⟨country⟩
(b) to enrich, to enhance ⟨collection, book⟩
2 s'enrichir *v refl* (+ *v être*) (a) ⟨person⟩
to become or grow rich
(b) to be enriched

enrichissant, ~e /ɑ̃ʁiʃisɑ̃, ɑ̃t/ *adj*
⟨experience⟩ rewarding; ⟨relationship⟩
fulfilling

enrober /ɑ̃ʁɔbe/ [1] *vtr* (a) to coat
(b) (figurative) to wrap up ⟨news⟩

enrôlement /ɑ̃ʁolmɑ̃/ *nm* (in the army)
enlistment; (in political party) enrolment (GB)

enrôler /ɑ̃ʁole/ [1] **1** *vtr* to recruit
2 s'enrôler *v refl* (+ *v être*) to enlist

enrouer: s'enrouer /ɑ̃ʁwe/ [1] *v refl*
(+ *v être*) ⟨voice⟩ to go hoarse; ⟨person⟩ to
make oneself hoarse; **d'une voix enrouée**
hoarsely

enrouler /ɑ̃ʁule/ [1] **1** *vtr* (a) to wind
(b) to wrap
2 s'enrouler *v refl* (+ *v être*) (a) ⟨thread,
tape⟩ to wind
(b) ⟨person, animal⟩ to curl up

ENS /œɛnɛs/ *nf: abbr* ▶ ÉCOLE

ensabler: **s'ensabler** /ãsable/ [1] *v refl*
(+ *v être*) ⟨*vehicle*⟩ to get stuck in the sand;
⟨*boat*⟩ to get stranded (*on a sandbank*)

ensanglanter /ãsãglãte/ [1] *vtr* **(a)** to
cover [sth] with blood
(b) to bring bloodshed to ⟨*country*⟩

enseignant, **~e** /ãsɛɲã, ãt/ **1** *adj* **corps**
~ teaching profession
2 *nm,f* (Sch) teacher; (at university) lecturer

enseigne /ãsɛɲ/ *nf* **(a)** (shop) sign;
~ lumineuse neon sign
(b) (Mil, Naut) ensign
IDIOMS nous sommes logés à la même ~ we
are in the same boat

enseignement /ãsɛɲmã/ *nm*
(a) education; **l'~ supérieur** higher
education
(b) teaching; **méthodes d'~** teaching
methods
(c) lesson
■ **~ par correspondance** distance learning;
~ professionnel vocational training;
~ religieux religious instruction

enseigner /ãsɛɲe/ [1] *vtr* to teach

ensemble /ãsãbl/ **1** *adv* **(a)** together
(b) at the same time
2 *nm* **(a)** group; **un ~ de personnes** a group
of people; **une vue d'~** an overall view; **plan**
d'~ d'une ville general plan of a town; **dans**
l'~ by and large; **dans l'~ de** throughout;
dans son *or* **leur ~** as a whole
(b) (of luggage, measures) set
(c) unity, cohesion; **former un bel ~** to form
a harmonious whole
(d) (of gestures) coordination; (of sounds)
unison; **un mouvement d'~** a coordinated
movement
(e) (in mathematics) set
(f) (Mus) ensemble
(g) (of offices) complex; **~ hôtelier** hotel
complex; **~ industriel** industrial estate (GB)
or park (US)
(h) (set of clothes) outfit; suit

ensevelir /ãsəvəlir/ [3] *vtr* to bury

ensoleillé, **~e** /ãsɔleje/ *adj* sunny

ensommeillé, **~e** /ãsɔmeje/ *adj* sleepy

ensorcelé, **~e** /ãsɔrsəle/ *adj* enchanted

ensorceler /ãsɔrsəle/ [19] *vtr* **(a)** to cast
or to put a spell on
(b) to bewitch, to enchant

ensorceleur, **-euse** /ãsɔrsəlœr, øz/
nm,f charmer

ensuite /ãsɥit/ *adv* **(a)** then; after; next;
très bien, mais ~? fine, but then what?; **il ne**
me l'a dit qu'~ he only told me later
(b) secondly

ensuivre: **s'ensuivre** /ãsɥivr/ [19] *v refl*
(+ *v être*) to follow, to ensue

entacher /ãtaʃe/ [1] *vtr* to mar ⟨*relations*⟩

entaille /ãtaj/ *nf* **(a)** cut; gash
(b) notch

entailler /ãtaje/ [1] **1** *vtr* to cut into;
(deeply) to make a gash in
2 **s'entailler** *v refl* (+ *v être*) **s'~ le doigt**
to cut one's finger, to gash one's finger

entame /ãtam/ *nf* **(a)** (Culin) first slice
(b) (in cards) lead

entamer /ãtame/ [1] *vtr* **(a)** to start ⟨*day,*
activity⟩; to initiate ⟨*procedure*⟩; to open
⟨*negotiations*⟩
(b) to undermine ⟨*credibility*⟩
(c) to eat into ⟨*savings*⟩
(d) to cut into ⟨*loaf, roast*⟩; to open ⟨*bottle,*
jar⟩; to start eating ⟨*dessert*⟩
(e) to cut into ⟨*skin, wood*⟩
(f) to eat into ⟨*metal*⟩

entartrer /ãtartre/ [1] **1** *vtr* to fur up
(GB), to scale up
2 **s'entartrer** *v refl* (+ *v être*) to scale up;
⟨*teeth*⟩ to be covered in tartar

entassement /ãtasmã/ *nm* **(a)** piling up;
cramming together
(b) pile; heap

entasser /ãtase/ [1] **1** *vtr* **(a)** to pile
⟨*books, clothes*⟩
(b) to hoard ⟨*money, old things*⟩
(c) to pack, to cram ⟨*people, objects*⟩ (**dans**
into)
2 **s'entasser** *v refl* (+ *v être*) ⟨*objects*⟩ to
pile up; ⟨*people*⟩ to squeeze (**dans** into; **sur**
onto)

entendement /ãtãdmã/ *nm*
understanding; **cela dépasse l'~** it's beyond
belief

entendre /ãtãdr/ [6] **1** *vtr* **(a)** to hear
⟨*noise, word*⟩; **faire ~ un cri** to give a cry; **je**
n'en ai jamais entendu parler I've never
heard of it; **on n'entend plus parler de lui** his
name is not mentioned any more
(b) ⟨*judge*⟩ to hear ⟨*witness*⟩; **à t'~, tout va**
bien according to you, everything is fine; **elle**
ne veut rien ~ she won't listen
(c) to understand; **il agit comme il l'entend**
he does as he likes; **elle a laissé ~ que** she
intimated that; **ils ne l'entendent pas de cette**
oreille they don't see it that way
(d) to mean; **qu'entends-tu par là?** what do
you mean by that?
(e) **~ faire** to intend doing; **j'entends qu'on**
fasse ce que je dis I expect people to do
what I say
2 **s'entendre** *v refl* (+ *v être*) **(a)** to get on
or along
(b) to agree (**sur** on)
(c) ⟨*noise*⟩ to be heard
(d) to hear oneself; ⟨*two or more people*⟩ to
hear each other
(e) **phrase qui peut s'~ de plusieurs façons**
sentence which can be understood in several
ways

entendu, **~e** /ãtãdy/ **1** *pp* ▶ ENTENDRE
2 *pp adj* **(a)** **'tu viens demain?'—'~!'** 'will
you come tomorrow?'—'OK!' (colloq)
(b) **d'un air ~** with a knowing look
3 **bien entendu** *phr* of course

entente /ãtãt/ *nf* **(a)** harmony; **vivre en**
bonne ~ avec qn to be on good terms with
sb
(b) understanding
(c) arrangement

entériner /ãterine/ [1] *vtr* **(a)** to ratify

(b) to confirm

enterré, **~e** /ɑ̃teʀe/ *adj* buried; **mort et ~** dead and buried

enterrement /ɑ̃tɛʀmɑ̃/ *nm* (a) burial
(b) funeral; **faire une tête d'~** (colloq) to look gloomy

enterrer /ɑ̃teʀe/ [1] *vtr* to bury
IDIOMS **~ sa vie de garçon** to have a stag party

entêtant, **~e** /ɑ̃tetɑ̃, ɑ̃t/ *adj* ⟨aroma⟩ heady; ⟨music⟩ insistent

en-tête, *pl* **~s** /ɑ̃tɛt/ *nm* heading

entêtement /ɑ̃tɛtmɑ̃/ *nm* stubbornness

entêter: **s'entêter** /ɑ̃tete/ [1] *v refl* (+ *v être*) (a) to be stubborn
(b) to persist

enthousiasme /ɑ̃tuzjasm/ *nm* enthusiasm

enthousiasmer /ɑ̃tuzjasme/ [1] *vtr* to fill [sb] with enthusiasm

enthousiaste /ɑ̃tuzjast/ *adj* enthusiastic

enticher: **s'enticher** /ɑ̃tiʃe/ [1] *v refl* (+ *v être*) **s'~ de** to become infatuated with ⟨person⟩

entier, **-ière** /ɑ̃tje, ɛʀ/ **1** *adj* (a) whole; **manger un pain ~** to eat a whole loaf; **des heures entières** for hours on end; **lait ~** full-fat milk
(b) ⟨success, satisfaction⟩ complete; **avoir l'entière responsabilité de qch** to have full responsibility for sth
(c) ⟨object, reputation⟩ intact; **le mystère reste ~** the mystery remains unsolved
(d) **avoir un caractère ~** to be thoroughgoing
2 *nm* (in mathematics) integer

entièrement /ɑ̃tjɛʀmɑ̃/ *adv* entirely, completely; **~ équipé** fully equipped

entonner /ɑ̃tɔne/ [1] *vtr* to start singing ⟨song⟩

entonnoir /ɑ̃tɔnwaʀ/ *nm* (a) funnel
(b) crater

entorse /ɑ̃tɔʀs/ *nf* (a) (Med) sprain
(b) (figurative) infringement (à of); **faire une ~ au règlement** to bend the rules

entortiller /ɑ̃tɔʀtije/ [1] **1** *vtr* (a) to wind (autour de qch round (GB) sth)
(b) to tangle up
2 **s'entortiller** *v refl* (+ *v être*) ⟨thread, wool⟩ to get entangled (dans in)

entourage /ɑ̃tuʀaʒ/ *nm* (a) family circle
(b) circle (of friends); **on dit dans son ~ que** people close to him/her say that

entouré, **~e** /ɑ̃tuʀe/ **1** *pp* ▶ ENTOURER
2 *adj* (a) ⟨person⟩ popular
(b) **nos patients sont très ~s** our patients are well looked after

entourer /ɑ̃tuʀe/ [1] **1** *vtr* (a) to surround
(b) **~ qch de qch** to put sth around sth; **~ qch de mystère** to shroud sth in mystery
(c) to rally round (GB) or around (US) ⟨sick person⟩
2 **s'entourer** *v refl* (+ *v être*) **s'~ d'objets**

to surround oneself with things; **s'~ de précautions** to take every possible precaution

entracte /ɑ̃tʀakt/ *nm* intermission

entraider: **s'entraider** /ɑ̃tʀede/ [1] *v refl* (+ *v être*) to help each other *or* one another

entrailles /ɑ̃tʀɑj/ *nf pl* (of animal) innards

entrain /ɑ̃tʀɛ̃/ *nm* (a) (of person) spirit, go (GB) (colloq); **retrouver son ~** to cheer up
(b) (of party, discussion) liveliness; **sans ~** half-hearted

entraînant, **~e** /ɑ̃tʀenɑ̃, ɑ̃t/ *adj* lively

entraînement /ɑ̃tʀenmɑ̃/ *nm* (a) training, coaching
(b) practice (GB); **avoir de l'~** to be highly trained; **l'~ à la lecture** reading practice (GB)
(c) training session

entraîner /ɑ̃tʀene/ [1] **1** *vtr* (a) to lead to; **une panne a entraîné l'arrêt de la production** a breakdown brought production to a standstill
(b) ⟨river, current⟩ to carry [sb/sth] away ⟨swimmer, boat⟩; **il a entraîné qn/qch dans sa chute** he dragged sb/sth down with him
(c) to take, to lead ⟨person⟩; **~ qn à faire** ⟨person⟩ to make sb do; ⟨circumstances⟩ to lead sb to do
(d) (figurative) to carry [sb] away ⟨person, group⟩
(e) to train, to coach ⟨athlete, team⟩ (à for); to train ⟨horse, soldier⟩ (à for)
(f) ⟨engine, piston⟩ to drive ⟨machine, wheel, turbine⟩
2 **s'entraîner** *v refl* (+ *v être*) (a) ⟨player, soldiers⟩ to train
(b) to prepare oneself

entraîneur /ɑ̃tʀenœʀ/ *nm* (of athlete) coach

entrave /ɑ̃tʀav/ *nf* hindrance; (on freedom) restriction

entraver /ɑ̃tʀave/ [1] *vtr* to hinder, to impede

entre /ɑ̃tʀ/ *prep*

■ Note You will find translations for expressions such as *entre parenthèses*, *entre nous* etc, at the entries PARENTHÈSE, NOUS etc.

(a) between; **~ midi et deux** at lunchtime; **'doux ou très épicé?'—'~ les deux'** 'mild or very spicy?'—'in between'; **~ son travail et l'informatique, il n'a pas le temps de sortir** what with work and his computer he doesn't have time to go out
(b) among; **organiser une soirée ~ amis** to organize a party among friends; **chacune d'~ elles** each of them; **~ hommes** as one man to another; **~ nous** between you and me; **nous sommes ~ nous** there's just the two of us; we're among friends; **les enfants sont souvent cruels ~ eux** children are often cruel to each other

entrebâillement /ɑ̃tʀəbɑjmɑ̃/ *nm* (in door, shutter, window) gap (de in)

entrebâiller /ɑ̃tʀəbɑje/ [1] *vtr* to half-open

entrechoquer /ɑ̃tʀəʃɔke/ [1] **1** *vtr* to clatter ⟨*saucepans*⟩; to clink ⟨*glasses*⟩
2 s'entrechoquer *v refl* (+ *v être*)
(a) ⟨*glasses*⟩ to clink
(b) ⟨*ideas, interests*⟩ to clash

entrecôte /ɑ̃tʀəkot/ *nf* (a) entrecôte (steak)
(b) rib steak

entrecouper /ɑ̃tʀəkupe/ [1] **1** *vtr* to punctuate
2 s'entrecouper *v refl* (+ *v être*) to intersect

entrecroiser /ɑ̃tʀəkʀwaze/ [1] *vtr* to intertwine

entre-deux-guerres /ɑ̃tʀədøgɛʀ/ *nm or f inv* interwar period

entrée /ɑ̃tʀe/ *nf* (a) entrance (de to); se retrouver à l'~ du bureau to meet outside the office
(b) (on motorway) (entry) slip road (GB), on-ramp (US)
(c) (in house) hall; (in hotel) lobby; (door) entry
(d) l'~ dans la récession the beginning of the recession; d'~ (de jeu) from the very start
(e) l'~ d'un pays dans une organisation the entry of a country into an organization; '~ libre' 'admission free'; '~ interdite' 'no entry'
(f) ticket; deux ~s gratuites two free tickets
(g) (of person) entrance; réussir son ~ ⟨*actor*⟩ to enter on cue
(h) (Culin) starter
(i) (in bookkeeping) ~s receipts
■ ~ des artistes stage door; ~ en matière introduction

entrée-sortie, *pl* **entrées-sorties** /ɑ̃tʀesɔʀti/ *nf* (Comput) input-output

entrefaites: **sur ces entrefaites** /syʀsezɑ̃tʀəfɛt/ *phr* at that moment, just then

entrefilet /ɑ̃tʀəfilɛ/ *nm* brief article

entrejambes /ɑ̃tʀəʒɑ̃b/ *nm inv* crotch

entrelacer /ɑ̃tʀəlase/ [12] *vtr*, **s'entrelacer** *v refl* (+ *v être*) to intertwine, to interlace

entremêler: **s'entremêler** /ɑ̃tʀəmele/ [1] *v refl* (+ *v être*) (gen) to be mixed; ⟨*hair, branches*⟩ to get tangled

entremets /ɑ̃tʀəmɛ/ *nm* dessert

entremetteur, -euse /ɑ̃tʀəmɛtœʀ, øz/ *nm,f* (a) matchmaker
(b) go-between

entremise /ɑ̃tʀəmiz/ *nf* intervention; il l'a su par mon ~ he heard of it through me

entreposer /ɑ̃tʀəpoze/ [1] *vtr* to store

entrepôt /ɑ̃tʀəpo/ *nm* (a) warehouse
(b) stockroom

entreprenant, ~e /ɑ̃tʀəpʀənɑ̃, ɑ̃t/ *adj* enterprising

entreprendre /ɑ̃tʀəpʀɑ̃dʀ/ [52] *vtr* (a) to start, to undertake; ~ de faire to set about doing; to undertake to do
(b) ~ qn sur un sujet to engage sb in conversation about sth

entrepreneur, -euse /ɑ̃tʀəpʀənœʀ, øz/ *nm,f* (a) builder
(b) contractor
(c) owner-manager (*of a small firm*)

entreprise /ɑ̃tʀəpʀiz/ *nf* (a) firm, business; petites et moyennes ~s small and medium-sized businesses
(b) business, industry; la libre ~ free enterprise
(c) undertaking; venture
■ ~ unipersonnelle à responsabilité limitée, EURL company owned by a sole proprietor

entrer /ɑ̃tʀe/ [1] **1** *vtr* (+ *v avoir*) (a) to bring [sth] in; to take [sth] in
(b) (in computing) to enter
2 *vi* (+ *v être*) (a) to get in, to enter; to go in; to come in; fais-la ~ show her in; 'défense d'~' (on door) 'no entry'; (on gate) 'no trespassing'; je ne fais qu'~ et sortir I can only stay a minute
(b) to fit (in); je n'arrive pas à faire ~ la pièce dans la fente I can't get the coin into the slot
(c) ~ dans to enter ⟨*period, debate*⟩; to join ⟨*company, army, party*⟩; ~ à to enter ⟨*school, charts*⟩; to get into ⟨*university*⟩; ~ en to enter into ⟨*negotiations*⟩; ~ dans la vie de qn to come into sb's life; ~ dans la légende ⟨*person*⟩ to become a legend; ⟨*fact*⟩ to become legendary; cela n'entre pas dans mes attributions it's not part of my duties; ~ dans une colère noire to fly into a blind rage

entresol /ɑ̃tʀəsɔl/ *nm* mezzanine

entre-temps /ɑ̃tʀətɑ̃/ *adv* meanwhile

entretenir /ɑ̃tʀətniʀ/ [36] **1** *vtr* (a) to look after ⟨*garment, house*⟩; to maintain ⟨*road*⟩; ~ sa forme to keep in shape
(b) to support ⟨*family*⟩; to keep ⟨*mistress*⟩
(c) to keep [sth] going ⟨*conversation, fire*⟩; to keep [sth] alive ⟨*friendship*⟩
(d) ~ qn de qch to speak to sb about sth
2 s'entretenir *v refl* (+ *v être*) (a) s'~ de qch to discuss sth
(b) s'~ facilement ⟨*house, fabric*⟩ to be easy to look after

entretien /ɑ̃tʀətjɛ̃/ *nm* (a) (of house) upkeep; (of car, road) maintenance; (of plant, skin) care
(b) cleaning
(c) (gen) discussion; (for a job) interview; (in newspaper) interview

entre-tuer: **s'entre-tuer** /ɑ̃tʀətɥe/ [1] *v refl* (+ *v être*) to kill each other

entrevoir /ɑ̃tʀəvwaʀ/ [46] *vtr* (a) to catch a glimpse of; (indistinctly) to make out
(b) to glimpse ⟨*truth, solution*⟩
(c) to foresee ⟨*difficulty*⟩; laisser ~ qch ⟨*result, sign*⟩ to point to sth

entrevue /ɑ̃tʀəvy/ *nf* meeting; (Pol) talks

entrouvrir /ɑ̃tʀuvʀiʀ/ [32] **1** *vtr* to open [sth] a little
2 s'entrouvrir *v refl* (+ *v être*) (gen) ⟨*door, country*⟩ to half-open; ⟨*lips*⟩ to part

énumération /enymeʀasjɔ̃/ *nf* (a) listing
(b) catalogue (GB)

énumérer /enymeʀe/ [14] *vtr* to enumerate

envahir /ɑ̃vaiʀ/ [3] *vtr* **(a)** ⟨*troops, crowd*⟩ to invade; ⟨*animal*⟩ to overrun
(b) to flood ⟨*market*⟩

envahissant, ~e /ɑ̃vaisɑ̃, ɑ̃t/ *adj*
(a) intrusive
(b) pervasive; invasive

envahisseur /ɑ̃vaisœʀ/ *nm* invader

enveloppe /ɑ̃vlɔp/ *nf* **(a)** (for letter) envelope; **sous ~** in an envelope
(b) (for parcel) wrapping; (of grains) husk; (of peas, beans) pod
■ **~ budgétaire** budget

enveloppé, ~e /ɑ̃vlɔpe/ *adj* ⟨*person*⟩ plump

envelopper /ɑ̃vlɔpe/ [1] **1** *vtr* **(a)** ⟨*person*⟩ to wrap [sb/sth] (up); ⟨*sheet*⟩ to cover
(b) ⟨*fog, silence*⟩ to envelop; ⟨*mystery*⟩ to surround
2 s'envelopper *v refl* (+ *v être*) to wrap oneself (up)

envenimer /ɑ̃vnime/ [1] **1** *vtr* to inflame ⟨*debate*⟩; to aggravate ⟨*situation*⟩
2 s'envenimer *v refl* (+ *v être*) ⟨*dispute*⟩ to worsen; ⟨*situation*⟩ to turn ugly

envergure /ɑ̃vɛʀgyʀ/ *nf* **(a)** (of plane) wingspan
(b) (figurative) (of person) stature; (of project) scale; **un projet d'~** a substantial project; **sans ~** ⟨*project*⟩ limited; ⟨*person*⟩ of no account

envers¹ /ɑ̃vɛʀ/ *prep* toward(s), to.
IDIOMS **~ et contre tous/tout** in spite of everyone/everything

envers² /ɑ̃vɛʀ/ **1** *nm inv* (of sheet of paper) back; (of piece of cloth) wrong side; (of garment) inside; (of coin) reverse
2 à l'envers *phr* **(a)** the wrong way
(b) upside down
(c) inside out
(d) back to front
(e) the wrong way round (GB) *or* around (US); **mettre ses chaussures à l'~** to put one's shoes on the wrong feet
(f) **passer un film à l'~** to run a film backward(s)

envie /ɑ̃vi/ *nf* **(a)** (gen) urge (**de faire** to do); (for food) craving; **avoir ~ de qch** to feel like sth; **avoir ~ de dormir** to want to go to bed; **mourir d'~ de faire** to be dying to do (colloq); **donner (l')~ à qn de faire** to make sb want to do
(b) envy; **il te fait ~ ce jouet?** would you like that toy?
(c) birthmark

envier /ɑ̃vje/ [2] *vtr* to envy

envieux, -ieuse /ɑ̃vjø, øz/ **1** *adj* envious
2 *nm,f* **faire des ~** to make people jealous

environ /ɑ̃viʀɔ̃/ *adv* about

environnant, ~e /ɑ̃viʀɔnɑ̃, ɑ̃t/ *adj* surrounding

environnement /ɑ̃viʀɔnmɑ̃/ *nm* environment

environner /ɑ̃viʀɔne/ [1] *vtr* to surround

environs /ɑ̃viʀɔ̃/ *nm pl* **être des ~** to be from the area; **aux ~ de** (place) in the vicinity of; (time, moment) around; (amount) in the region of

envisageable /ɑ̃vizaʒabl/ *adj* possible

envisager /ɑ̃vizaʒe/ [13] *vtr* **(a)** to plan (**de faire** to do)
(b) to envisage ⟨*hypothesis, situation*⟩; to foresee ⟨*problem, possibility*⟩; **~ le pire** to imagine the worst
(c) to consider

envoi /ɑ̃vwa/ *nm* **(a)** **tous les ~s de colis sont suspendus** parcel post is suspended; **faire un ~ de** to send ⟨*flowers, books*⟩
(b) **demander l'~ (immédiat) de troupes** to ask for troops to be dispatched (immediately)
(c) **l'~ de la fusée** the rocket launch; **donner le coup d'~ de** to kick off ⟨*match*⟩; to open ⟨*festival*⟩
■ **~ recommandé** registered post (GB) *or* mail (US); **~ contre remboursement** cash on delivery

envol /ɑ̃vɔl/ *nm* (of bird) flight; (of plane) takeoff

envolée /ɑ̃vɔle/ *nf* **(a)** flight of fancy
(b) (in prices) surge (**de** in); (of political party) rise.

envoler: s'envoler /ɑ̃vɔle/ [1] *v refl* (+ *v être*) **(a)** ⟨*bird*⟩ to fly off; ⟨*plane, passenger*⟩ to take off; ⟨*paper, hat*⟩ to be blown away
(b) ⟨*prices*⟩ to soar
(c) to vanish
(d) (colloq) to do a runner (colloq)

envoûtement /ɑ̃vutmɑ̃/ *nm*
(a) bewitchment
(b) spell

envoûter /ɑ̃vute/ [1] *vtr* to bewitch

envoyé, ~e /ɑ̃vwaje/ **1** *adj* **ça c'est (bien) ~!** (colloq) well said!
2 *nm,f* envoy; **~ spécial** special correspondent

envoyer /ɑ̃vwaje/ [24] **1** *vtr* **(a)** to send; **~ qn étudier à Genève** to send sb off to study in Geneva
(b) to throw ⟨*pebble*⟩; to fire ⟨*missile*⟩; **~ qch dans l'œil de qn** to hit sb in the eye with sth; **~ le ballon dans les buts** to put the ball in the net
2 s'envoyer *v refl* (+ *v être*) to exchange; **s'~ des baisers** to blow each other kisses
IDIOMS **~ qn promener** (colloq) to send sb packing (colloq); **tout ~ promener** (colloq) to drop the lot (colloq); **il ne me l'a pas envoyé dire** (colloq) and he told me in no uncertain terms

enzyme /ɑ̃zim/ *nm or f* enzyme

éolien, -ienne¹ /eɔljɛ̃, ɛn/ *adj* ⟨*generator*⟩ wind

éolienne² /eɔljɛn/ *nf* (aeolian) windmill

épagneul /epaɲœl/ *nm* spaniel

e

épais, **épaisse** /epɛ, ɛs/ **1** adj (a) thick;
il n'est pas bien ~ ce petit! (colloq) he's a
skinny little fellow!
(b) ⟨mind⟩ dull
(c) ⟨night⟩ deep
2 adv a lot, much

épaisseur /epɛsœʀ/ nf (a) thickness;
couper qch dans (le sens de) l'~ to cut sth
sideways
(b) layer

épaissir /epesiʀ/ [3] **1** vtr (a) to thicken
(b) to deepen ⟨mystery⟩
2 vi (a) ⟨sauce⟩ to thicken; ⟨jelly⟩ to set
(b) to put on weight
3 **s'épaissir** v refl (+ v être) ⟨sauce, waist,
mist⟩ to thicken; ⟨mystery⟩ to deepen

épancher: s'épancher /epɑ̃ʃe/ [1] v refl
(+ v être) to open one's heart (auprès de to)

épanoui, **~e** /epanwi/ adj ⟨flower⟩ in full
bloom; ⟨smile⟩ beaming; ⟨person⟩ well-
adjusted

épanouir /epanwiʀ/ [3] **1** vtr (a) ⟨sun⟩ to
open (out) ⟨flower⟩; ⟨joy⟩ to light up ⟨face⟩
(b) (figurative) to make [sb/sth] blossom
2 **s'épanouir** v refl (+ v être) ⟨flower⟩ to
bloom; ⟨face⟩ to light up; ⟨person⟩ to blossom

épanouissant, **~e** /epanwisɑ̃, ɑ̃t/ adj
fulfilling

épanouissement /epanwismɑ̃/ nm
(a) (of flower) blooming
(b) (of person) development; (of talent)
flowering

épargnant, **~e** /epaʀɲɑ̃, ɑ̃t/ nm,f saver

épargne /epaʀɲ/ nf savings

épargner /epaʀɲe/ [1] **1** vtr (a) to save
⟨money⟩
(b) to spare; ~ qch à qn to spare sb sth
2 vi to save
3 **s'épargner** v refl (+ v être) to save
oneself

éparpiller /epaʀpije/ [1] vtr,
s'éparpiller v refl (+ v être) to scatter

épars, **~e** /epaʀ, aʀs/ adj scattered

épatant, **~e** /epatɑ̃, ɑ̃t/ adj (colloq)
marvellous (GB)

épate /epat/ nf (colloq) faire de l'~ to show
off

épaté, **~e** /epate/ adj (a) nez ~ pug nose,
flat nose
(b) (colloq) amazed (de by)

épater /epate/ [1] vtr (colloq) (a) to impress;
ça t'épate, hein? surprised, aren't you?
(b) to amaze

épaule /epol/ nf shoulder
IDIOMS changer son fusil d'~ to change
one's tactics; avoir la tête sur les ~s to have
one's head screwed on (colloq)

épauler /epole/ [1] **1** vtr (a) to help
(b) to take aim with ⟨rifle⟩
2 vi to take aim

épaulette /epolɛt/ nf (a) shoulder-pad
(b) (shoulder-)strap
(c) (Mil) epaulette

épave /epav/ nf (a) wreck

(b) (car) (gen) wreck; (after accident) write-off
(colloq)
(c) (person) wreck

épée /epe/ nf sword; c'est un coup d'~
dans l'eau it was a complete waste of effort

épeler /eple/ [19] vtr to spell ⟨word⟩

éperdu, **~e** /epɛʀdy/ adj ⟨need, desire⟩
overwhelming; ⟨glance⟩ desperate; ⟨love⟩
boundless

éperdument /epɛʀdymɑ̃/ adv ⟨in love⟩
madly; je me moque ~ de ce qu'il pense I
couldn't care less what he thinks

éperon /epʀɔ̃/ nm spur

épervier /epɛʀvje/ nm (Zool) sparrowhawk

éphémère /efemɛʀ/ adj ephemeral;
fleeting; short-lived

épi /epi/ nm (a) (of corn) ear; (of flower) spike;
~ de maïs corn cob
(b) (unmanageable) tuft of hair (GB), cow-
lick (US)

épice /epis/ nf spice

épicé, **~e** /epise/ adj spicy; hot

épicentre /episɑ̃tʀ/ nm epicentre (GB)

épicer /epise/ [12] vtr to spice; to add spice
to

épicerie /episʀi/ nf (a) grocer's (shop)
(GB), grocery (store) (US); ~ fine delicatessen
(b) grocery trade
(c) groceries

épicier, **-ière** /episje, ɛʀ/ nm,f grocer

épidémie /epidemi/ nf epidemic

épiderme /epidɛʀm/ nm skin

épidermique /epidɛʀmik/ adj skin;
⟨sensitivity⟩ extreme; réaction ~ gut reaction

épier /epje/ [2] vtr (a) to spy on ⟨person,
behaviour⟩
(b) to be on the lookout for

épilation /epilasjɔ̃/ nf removal of
unwanted hair

épilepsie /epilɛpsi/ nf crise d'~ epileptic
fit

épiler /epile/ [1] vtr to remove unwanted
hair from; to wax ⟨leg⟩; to pluck ⟨eyebrows⟩

épilogue /epilɔg/ nm epilogue (GB)

épiloguer /epilɔge/ [1] vi to go on and on
(sur about)

épinard /epinaʀ/ nm spinach
IDIOMS ça met du beurre dans les ~s (colloq)
it brings in a nice bit of extra money

épine /epin/ nf thorn; ~ dorsale spine
IDIOMS ôter à qn une ~ du pied to take a
weight off sb's shoulders

épineux, **-euse** /epinø, øz/ adj ⟨stem,
character⟩ prickly; ⟨problem⟩ tricky;
⟨question⟩ vexed

épingle /epɛ̃gl/ nf pin; ~ de or à nourrice,
~ de sûreté safety pin
IDIOMS monter qch en ~ to blow sth up out
of proportion; être tiré à quatre ~s (colloq) to
be immaculately dressed; tirer son ~ du jeu
to get out while the going is good

épinière /epinjɛʀ/ adj f moelle ~ spinal
cord

épique /epik/ *adj* epic; **c'était ~** (humorous) (colloq) it was quite something (colloq)

épisode /epizɔd/ *nm* episode; **roman à ~s** serialized novel

épisodique /epizɔdik/ *adj* sporadic

épistolaire /epistɔlɛʀ/ *adj* epistolary; **ils ont des relations ~s** they correspond

épitaphe /epitaf/ *nf* epitaph

épithète /epitɛt/ *nf* attributive adjective

éploré, ~e /eplɔʀe/ *adj* (a) grief-stricken
  (b) tearful

éplucher /eplyʃe/ [1] *vtr* to peel; (figurative) to go through [sth] with a fine-tooth comb

épluchure /eplyʃyʀ/ *nf* ~s peelings

éponge /epɔ̃ʒ/ *nf* (a) sponge
  (b) terry-towelling (GB)
  IDIOMS passer l'~ to forget the past

éponger /epɔ̃ʒe/ [13] *vtr* (a) to mop (up)
  (b) to absorb ⟨*deficit*⟩; to pay off ⟨*debts*⟩

épopée /epɔpe/ *nf* (a) epic
  (b) saga

époque /epɔk/ *nf* (a) time; **vivre avec son ~** to move with the times; **quelle ~!** what's the world coming to!; **à mon ~** in my day
  (b) (historical) era
  (c) en costume d'~ in period costume; **des meubles d'~** antique furniture

épouse /epuz/ *nf* wife, spouse

épouser /epuze/ [1] *vtr* (a) to marry ⟨*person*⟩
  (b) to adopt ⟨*cause, idea*⟩

épousseter /epuste/ [20] *vtr* to dust

époustoufler /epustufle/ [1] *vtr* (colloq) to amaze

épouvantable /epuvɑ̃tabl/ *adj* (a) (gen) dreadful
  (b) appalling

épouvantail /epuvɑ̃taj/ *nm* (a) scarecrow
  (b) (colloq) (ugly person) fright
  (c) spectre (GB)

épouvante /epuvɑ̃t/ *nf* (a) terror
  (b) horror

épouvanter /epuvɑ̃te/ [1] *vtr* (a) to terrify
  (b) to horrify

époux /epu/ ⓵ *nm inv* husband
  ⓶ *nm pl* **les ~** the (married) couple

éprendre: s'éprendre /epʀɑ̃dʀ/ [52] *v refl* (+ *v être*) **s'~ de qn** to become enamoured of sb

épreuve /epʀœv/ *nf* (a) ordeal
  (b) test; **mettre à rude ~** to put [sb] to a severe test ⟨*person*⟩; to be very hard on ⟨*car, shoes*⟩; to tax ⟨*patience, nerves*⟩; **à toute ~** unfailing; **l'~ du feu** ordeal by fire; **à l'~ du feu/des balles** fire-/bullet-proof
  (c) (part of an) examination; **~ écrite** written examination
  (d) (Sport) **~ d'athlétisme** athletics event
  (e) (photograph, print) proof

épris, ~e /epʀi, iz/ *adj* in love (**de** with)

éprouvant, ~e /epʀuvɑ̃, ɑ̃t/ *adj* gruelling (GB); trying

éprouver /epʀuve/ [1] *vtr* (a) to feel ⟨*regret, love*⟩; to have ⟨*sensation, difficulty*⟩; **~ de la jalousie** to be jealous
  (b) to test
  (c) ⟨*death, event*⟩ to distress ⟨*person*⟩; ⟨*storm*⟩ to hit ⟨*region*⟩

éprouvette /epʀuvɛt/ *nf* (a) test tube
  (b) sample

EPS /œpeɛs/ *nf* (*abbr* = **éducation physique et sportive**) PE

épuisant, ~e /epɥizɑ̃, ɑ̃t/ *adj* exhausting

épuisé, ~e /epɥize/ ⓵ *pp* ▶ ÉPUISER
  ⓶ *pp adj* (a) exhausted, worn out
  (b) ⟨*publication, livre*⟩ out of print; ⟨*item*⟩ out of stock

épuisement /epɥizmɑ̃/ *nm* (a) exhaustion
  (b) jusqu'à ~ des stocks while stocks last

épuiser /epɥize/ [1] ⓵ *vtr* (a) to exhaust, to wear [sb] out
  (b) to exhaust ⟨*subject, mine*⟩
  ⓶ **s'épuiser** *v refl* (+ *v être*) (a) to exhaust oneself
  (b) ⟨*stocks, provisions*⟩ to be running out

épuisette /epɥizɛt/ *nf* (a) landing net
  (b) shrimp net

épurateur /epyʀatœʀ/ *nm* purifier

épuration /epyʀasjɔ̃/ *nf* (a) (of gas, liquid) purification; (of sewage) treatment
  (b) purge

épurer /epyʀe/ [1] *vtr* (a) to purify ⟨*water, gas*⟩
  (b) to purge ⟨*party*⟩
  (c) to expurgate ⟨*text*⟩

équateur /ekwatœʀ/ *nm* equator

équation /ekwasjɔ̃/ *nf* equation

équerre /ekɛʀ/ *nf* (a) set square; **en** *or* **d'~** at right angles
  (b) flat angle bracket

équestre /ekɛstʀ/ *adj* equestrian; **centre ~** riding school

équilibre /ekilibʀ/ *nm* (a) balance; **être en ~ sur** ⟨*object*⟩ to be balanced on; ⟨*person*⟩ to balance on
  (b) equilibrium; **manquer d'~** to be unstable; **retrouver son ~** to get back to normal

équilibrer /ekilibʀe/ [1] *vtr* to balance

équilibriste /ekilibʀist/ *nmf* acrobat

équinoxe /ekinɔks/ *nm* equinox

équipage /ekipaʒ/ *nm* crew

équipe /ekip/ *nf* team; crew; shift; **travailler en ~** to work as a team; **~ de tournage** film crew; **l'~ de nuit** the night shift

équipé, ~e[1] /ekipe/ ⓵ *pp* ▶ ÉQUIPER
  ⓶ *pp adj* **bien/mal ~** well-/ill-equipped; **cuisine ~e** fitted kitchen

équipée[2] /ekipe/ *nf* escapade

équipement /ekipmɑ̃/ *nm* (a) equipment; kit
  (b) ~s facilities

équiper /ekipe/ [1] ⓵ *vtr* to equip ⟨*hospital, vehicle*⟩; to provide ⟨*town*⟩; to fit out ⟨*person*⟩ ⋯⋗

2 s'équiper *v refl* (+ *v être*) to equip oneself

équipier, -ière /ekipje, ɛʀ/ *nm,f* (a) team member
(b) crew member

équitable /ekitabl/ *adj* fair-minded; fair

équitablement /ekitabləmɑ̃/ *adv* equitably, fairly

équitation /ekitasjɔ̃/ *nf* (horse-)riding

équité /ekite/ *nf* equity

équivalence /ekivalɑ̃s/ *nf* (a) equivalence
(b) titre admis en ∼ recognized qualification

équivalent, ∼e /ekivalɑ̃, ɑ̃t/ *adj*
(a) equivalent
(b) identical

équivaloir /ekivalwaʀ/ [45] *v+prep* ∼ à to be equivalent to ⟨*quantity*⟩; to amount to ⟨*effect*⟩

équivoque /ekivɔk/ **1** *adj* (a) ambiguous
(b) ⟨*reputation*⟩ dubious; ⟨*behaviour*⟩ questionable
2 *nf* ambiguity; **sans** ∼ ⟨*reply*⟩ unequivocal; ⟨*condemn*⟩ unequivocally

érable /eʀabl/ *nm* maple (tree)

érafler /eʀafle/ [1] **1** *vtr* to scratch
2 s'érafler *v refl* (+ *v être*) to scratch oneself

érailler: s'érailler /eʀaje/ [1] *v refl* (+ *v être*) to become hoarse

ère /ɛʀ/ *nf* (a) era; en l'an 10 de notre ∼ in the year 10 AD
(b) age; à l'∼ atomique in the nuclear age

érection /eʀɛksjɔ̃/ *nf* erection

éreinter /eʀɛ̃te/ [1] *vtr* (colloq) to exhaust

ergot /ɛʀgo/ *nm* (a) (of cock) spur; (of dog) dewclaw
(b) ergot

ergoter /ɛʀgɔte/ [1] *vi* to split hairs

ériger /eʀiʒe/ [13] **1** *vtr* to erect ⟨*statue*⟩
2 s'ériger *v refl* (+ *v être*) s'∼ en to set oneself up as

ermite /ɛʀmit/ *nm* (a) hermit
(b) recluse

éroder /eʀode/ [1] *vtr* to erode

érosion /eʀozjɔ̃/ *nf* erosion

érotique /eʀɔtik/ *adj* erotic

érotisme /eʀɔtism/ *nm* eroticism

errance /ɛʀɑ̃s/ *nf* restless wandering

errant, ∼e /ɛʀɑ̃, ɑ̃t/ *adj* wandering; rootless; **chien** ∼ stray dog

errer /eʀe/ [1] *vi* ⟨*person, gaze*⟩ to wander; ⟨*animal*⟩ to roam

erreur /eʀœʀ/ *nf* (a) mistake; ∼ de jugement error of judgment; induire qn en ∼ to mislead sb; sauf ∼ de ma part if I'm not mistaken
(b) (Law) error

erroné, ∼e /eʀone/ *adj* incorrect, erroneous

ersatz /ɛʀzats/ *nm* ersatz

érudit, ∼e /eʀydi, it/ *nm,f* scholar

érudition /eʀydisjɔ̃/ *nf* erudition, scholarship

éruption /eʀypsjɔ̃/ *nf* eruption

es /ɛ/ ▶ ÊTRE¹

ès /ɛs/ *prep* licence ∼ lettres ≈ arts degree, B.A. (degree)

esbroufe /ɛzbʀuf/ *nf* (colloq) faire de l'∼ to swank (colloq), to show off

escabeau, *pl* ∼**x** /ɛskabo/ *nm* stepladder

escadrille /ɛskadʀij/ *nf* squadron

escadron /ɛskadʀɔ̃/ *nm* (Mil) company; ∼ de la mort death squad

escalade /ɛskalad/ *nf* (a) (Sport) climbing; ascent
(b) escalation

escalader /ɛskalade/ [1] *vtr* to scale ⟨*wall*⟩; to climb ⟨*mountain*⟩

escale /ɛskal/ *nf* (gen) stopover; (for ship) port of call; ∼ **technique** (for plane) refuelling (GB) stop; (for ship) overhaul

escalier /ɛskalje/ *nm* (a) staircase
(b) stairs
■ ∼ **mécanique** *or* **roulant** escalator; ∼ **de service** backstairs

escalope /ɛskalɔp/ *nf* escalope

escamotable /ɛskamɔtabl/ *adj* ⟨*landing gear*⟩ retractable; ⟨*ladder*⟩ foldaway

escamoter /ɛskamɔte/ [1] *vtr*
(a) ⟨*magician*⟩ to make [sth] disappear
(b) to evade ⟨*issue*⟩

escampette /ɛskɑ̃pɛt/ *nf* (colloq) prendre la poudre d'∼ to scarper (colloq), to skedaddle (colloq)

escapade /ɛskapad/ *nf* escapade

escargot /ɛskaʀgo/ *nm* snail

escarpé, ∼e /ɛskaʀpe/ *adj* (a) steep
(b) craggy

escarpement /ɛskaʀpəmɑ̃/ *nm* steep slope

escarpin /ɛskaʀpɛ̃/ *nm* court shoe (GB), pump (US)

escarre /ɛskaʀ/ *nf* bedsore

escient /esjɑ̃/ *nm* à bon ∼ wittingly; à mauvais ∼ ill-advisedly

esclaffer: s'esclaffer /ɛsklafe/ [1] *v refl* (+ *v être*) to guffaw

esclandre /ɛsklɑ̃dʀ/ *nm* scene

esclavage /ɛsklavaʒ/ *nm* slavery; (figurative) tyranny

esclave /ɛsklav/ *nm,f* slave

escompte /ɛskɔ̃t/ *nm* discount

escompter /ɛskɔ̃te/ [1] *vtr* to anticipate; ∼ **faire** to count on doing, to hope to do

escorte /ɛskɔʀt/ *nf* escort

escorter /ɛskɔʀte/ [1] *vtr* to escort

escrime /ɛskʀim/ *nf* fencing

escrimer: s'escrimer /ɛskʀime/ [1] *v refl* (+ *v être*) (colloq) s'∼ à faire to knock oneself out trying to do (colloq)

escroc /ɛskʀo/ *nm* swindler, crook

escroquer /ɛskʀɔke/ [1] *vtr* to swindle

escroquerie /ɛskʀɔkʀi/ *nf* (a) fraud, swindling; tentative d'∼ attempted fraud
(b) swindle

ésotérique /ezɔteʀik/ *adj* esoteric
espace /ɛspas/ *nm* (a) space
 (b) ~ **de loisirs** leisure complex
 (c) gap
 (d) **en l'~ de** in the space of; **l'~ d'un instant** for a moment
■ ~ **vert** open space; ~ **vital** living space
espacer /ɛspase/ [12] **1** *vtr* to space [sth] out
 2 s'espacer *v refl* (+ *v être*) to become less frequent
espadon /ɛspadɔ̃/ *nm* swordfish
espadrille /ɛspadʀij/ *nf* espadrille
Espagne /ɛspaɲ/ *pr nf* Spain
 IDIOMS **bâtir des châteaux en** ~ to build castles in the air
espagnol, ~e /ɛspaɲɔl/ **1** *adj* Spanish
 2 *nm* (language) Spanish
espalier /ɛspalje/ *nm* (a) espalier
 (b) fruit-wall
espèce /ɛspɛs/ **1** *nf* (a) species; **l'~ humaine** mankind
 (b) kind
 2 espèces *nf pl* **en** ~**s** in cash
espérance /ɛspeʀɑ̃s/ *nf* hope; ~ **de vie** life expectancy
espérer /ɛspeʀe/ [14] **1** *vtr* (a) ~ **qch** to hope for sth
 (b) to expect; **je n'en espérais pas tant** it's more than I expected
 2 *vi* to hope
espiègle /ɛspjɛgl/ *adj* mischievous
espion, -ionne /ɛspjɔ̃, ɔn/ *nm,f* spy
espionnage /ɛspjɔnaʒ/ *nm* espionage, spying
espionner /ɛspjɔne/ [1] *vtr* to spy on
esplanade /ɛsplanad/ *nf* esplanade
espoir /ɛspwaʀ/ *nm* hope; **reprendre** ~ to feel hopeful again; **avec** ~ hopefully
esprit /ɛspʀi/ *nm* (a) mind; **avoir l'~ mal placé** to have a dirty mind (colloq); **avoir un** ~ **de synthèse** to be good at synthesizing information; **avoir l'~ de contradiction** to be contrary; **dans mon** ~ **c'était facile** the way I saw it, it was easy; **cela ne t'est jamais venu à l'~?** didn't it ever occur to you?; **avoir l'~ ailleurs** to be miles away; **les choses de l'~** spiritual matters
 (b) wit; **faire de l'~** to try to be witty; ~ **d'à-propos** ready wit
 (c) **dans un** ~ **de vengeance** in a spirit of revenge; **ils ont l'~ de famille** they're a very close family
 (d) **l'un des plus grands** ~**s de son temps** one of the greatest minds of his/her time; **calmer les** ~**s** to calm people down; **les** ~**s sont échauffés** feelings are running high
 (e) spirit; **croire aux** ~**s** to believe in ghosts
■ ~ **de corps** solidarity; ~ **d'équipe** team spirit
 IDIOMS **perdre ses** ~**s** to faint; **les grands** ~**s se rencontrent** great minds think alike
esquimau, -aude, *mpl* ~**x** /ɛskimo, od/ **1** *adj* Eskimo; **chien** ~ husky
 2 *nm* (a) Eskimo

 (b) ®chocolate-covered ice lolly (GB), ice-cream bar (US)
esquinter /ɛskɛ̃te/ [1] *vtr* (colloq) to damage
esquisse /ɛskis/ *nf* (a) sketch
 (b) outline
esquisser /ɛskise/ [1] *vtr* to sketch ⟨*portrait*⟩; to outline ⟨*programme*⟩
esquiver /ɛskive/ [1] **1** *vtr* to dodge, to duck ⟨*blow*⟩; to sidestep ⟨*issue*⟩
 2 s'esquiver *v refl* (+ *v être*) to slip away
essai /esε/ **1** *nm* (a) (Tech, Med) trial; test; **être à l'~** to undergo trials; to be tested; ~ **sur route** road test
 (b) try, attempt; **un coup d'~** a try; **prendre qn à l'~** to give sb a try-out
 (c) essay
 (d) (in rugby) try
 2 essais *nm pl* (Aut) (Sport) qualifying round
essaim /esɛ̃/ *nm* swarm
essayage /esɛjaʒ/ *nm* fitting
essayer /eseje/ [21] **1** *vtr* (a) to try; ~ **sa force** to test one's strength
 (b) to test ⟨*weapon, product*⟩; to run trials on ⟨*car*⟩
 (c) to try on ⟨*clothes*⟩; to try ⟨*size, colour*⟩; to try out ⟨*car*⟩
 2 *vi* to try; ~ **à la poste** to try the post office; **j'essaierai que tout se passe bien** I'll try to make sure everything goes all right
 3 s'essayer *v refl* (+ *v être*) **s'~ à** to have a go at, to try one's hand at
essayiste /esɛjist/ *nmf* essayist
essence /esɑ̃s/ *nf* (a) petrol (GB), gasoline (US)
 (b) essential oil
 (c) tree species
■ ~ **à briquet** lighter fuel (GB), lighter fluid (US); ~ **ordinaire** ≈ 2-star petrol (GB), regular gasoline (US); ~ **sans plomb** unleaded (petrol) (GB), unleaded gasoline (US); ~ **super** ≈ 4-star petrol (GB), premium gasoline (US)
essentiel, -ielle /esɑ̃sjɛl/ **1** *adj* essential
 2 *nm* **c'est l'~** that's the main thing; **aller à l'~** to get to the heart of the matter; **l'~ des voix** the bulk of the vote; **pour l'~** mainly; **en voyage je n'emporte que l'~** when I travel I only take the bare essentials
essentiellement /esɑ̃sjɛlmɑ̃/ *adv*
 (a) mainly
 (b) essentially
esseulé, ~e /esœle/ *adj* forlorn
essieu, *pl* ~**x** /esjø/ *nm* axle
essor /esɔʀ/ *nm* (of technology, area) development; **être en plein** ~ to be booming
essorage /esɔʀaʒ/ *nm* wringing; spin-drying
essorer /esɔʀe/ [1] *vtr* (a) to wring
 (b) to spin-dry ⟨*washing*⟩; to spin ⟨*lettuce*⟩
essoufflement /esuflǝmɑ̃/ *nm* breathlessness; (figurative) loss of impetus

essouffler /esufle/ [1] **1** *vtr* to leave [sb]
breathless; **être essoufflé** to be out of breath
2 **s'essouffler** *v refl* (+ *v être*) **(a)** to get
breathless
(b) to run out of steam

essuie-glace, *pl* **~s** /esɥiglas/ *nm*
windscreen wiper (GB), windshield wiper
(US)

essuie-mains /esɥimɛ̃/ *nm inv* hand
towel

essuie-tout /esɥitu/ *nm inv* kitchen roll,
kitchen paper

essuyer /esɥije/ [22] **1** *vtr* **(a)** to dry
⟨*glass, hands*⟩; to wipe ⟨*table*⟩; **~ la vaisselle**
to dry up; **~ ses larmes** to wipe away one's
tears
(b) to suffer ⟨*defeat, losses*⟩; to meet with
⟨*failure*⟩
2 **s'essuyer** *v refl* (+ *v être*) to dry oneself;
s'~ les mains to dry one's hands

est¹ /ɛ/ ▶ ÊTRE¹

est² /ɛst/ **1** *adj inv* east; eastern
2 *nm* **(a)** east; **un vent d'~** an easterly wind
(b) **l'Est** the East; **de l'Est** eastern

estafette® /ɛstafɛt/ *nf* van

estampe /ɛstɑ̃p/ *nf* **(a)** engraving
(b) print

estamper /ɛstɑ̃pe/ [1] *vtr* (colloq) to rip [sb]
off (colloq)

esthète /ɛstɛt/ *nmf* aesthete

esthéticienne /ɛstetisjɛn/ *nf* beautician

esthétique /ɛstetik/ **1** *adj* aesthetic;
⟨*decor*⟩ aesthetically pleasing; ⟨*pose*⟩ graceful
2 *nf* aesthetics

estimable /ɛstimabl/ *adj* **(a)** worthy
(b) laudable
(c) **difficilement ~** hard to estimate

estimation /ɛstimasjɔ̃/ *nf* estimate;
valuation

estime /ɛstim/ *nf* respect

estimer /ɛstime/ [1] *vtr* **(a)** to feel;
~ nécessaire de faire to consider it
necessary to do
(b) to think highly of ⟨*friend, artist*⟩
(c) to value ⟨*painting*⟩; to assess ⟨*damage*⟩;
une vitesse estimée à 150 km/h an estimated
speed of 150 kph
(d) to reckon

estival, **~e**, *mpl* **-aux** /ɛstival, o/ *adj*
(a) summer
(b) summery

estivant, **~e** /ɛstivɑ̃, ɑ̃t/ *nm,f* summer
visitor

estomac /ɛstɔma/ *nm* stomach; **avoir l'~
bien accroché** to have a strong stomach.
IDIOMS **avoir l'~ dans les talons** (colloq) to be
famished

estomper /ɛstɔ̃pe/ [1] **1** *vtr* to blur
⟨*shape*⟩; to gloss over ⟨*details*⟩
2 **s'estomper** *v refl* (+ *v être*) ⟨*landscape*⟩
to become blurred; ⟨*hatred, memories*⟩ to
fade

estrade /ɛstrad/ *nf* platform

estragon /ɛstragɔ̃/ *nm* tarragon

estropié, **~e** /ɛstrɔpje/*nm,f* cripple

estropier /ɛstrɔpje/ [2] **1** *vtr* to maim
2 **s'estropier** *v refl* (+ *v être*) to maim
oneself

estuaire /ɛstɥɛr/ *nm* estuary

esturgeon /ɛstyrʒɔ̃/ *nm* sturgeon

et /e/ *conj* and; **~ voilà qu'il sort un couteau
de sa poche!** and next thing he whips a
knife out of his pocket!; **~ alors?** so what?

étable /etabl/ *nf* cowshed

établi, **~e** /etabli/ **1** *pp* ▶ ÉTABLIR
2 *pp adj* **(a)** ⟨*reputation, use*⟩ established
(b) ⟨*power, regime*⟩ ruling; ⟨*order*⟩
established
3 *nm* workbench

établir /etablir/ [3] **1** *vtr* **(a)** to set up
⟨*home*⟩
(b) to establish ⟨*rule, link, reputation,
innocence, fact*⟩; to introduce ⟨*tax, discipline*⟩;
to set ⟨*record, standard*⟩
(c) to draw up ⟨*list, plan, budget, file*⟩; to
make out ⟨*cheque, bill*⟩; to prepare ⟨*quote*⟩; to
make ⟨*diagnosis*⟩; to draw ⟨*parallel*⟩
2 **s'établir** *v refl* (+ *v être*) **(a)** ⟨*person*⟩ to
settle (**à, en** in); **s'~ à son compte** to set up
one's own business
(b) ⟨*links*⟩ to develop

établissement /etablismɑ̃/ *nm*
(a) organization; **~ bancaire** banking
institution
(b) (of relations, regime) establishment; (of tax,
sanctions) introduction
(c) premises
■ **~ commercial** commercial establishment;
~ de crédit finance company;
~ d'enseignement supérieur higher
education institution; **~ scolaire** school

étage /etaʒ/ *nm* **(a)** floor; **le premier ~** the
first floor (GB), the second floor (US); **à l'~**
upstairs
(b) (of tower) level; (of aquaduct, cake) tier

étagère /etaʒɛr/ *nf* shelf

étaient /etɛ/ ▶ ÊTRE¹

étain /etɛ̃/ *nm* **(a)** tin
(b) pewter

étais /etɛ/ ▶ ÊTRE¹

était /etɛ/ ▶ ÊTRE¹

étal /etal/ *nm* **(a)** (market) stall
(b) butcher's block

étalage /etalaʒ/ *nm* **(a)** window display
(b) display; **faire ~ de ses connaissances** to
flaunt one's knowledge

étalagiste /etalaʒist/ *nmf* window dresser

étalement /etalmɑ̃/ *nm* (of holidays)
staggering; (of payments) spreading

étaler /etale/ [1] **1** *vtr* **(a)** to spread out
⟨*sheet*⟩; to roll [sth] out ⟨*pastry*⟩
(b) to scatter
(c) to spread ⟨*butter, glue*⟩; to apply ⟨*paint,
ointment*⟩
(d) to spread ⟨*work, payments*⟩; to stagger
⟨*departures*⟩

(e) to flaunt ‹*wealth, knowledge*›; to display ‹*merchandise*›; **~ qch au grand jour** to bring sth out into the open

2 s'étaler *v refl* (+ *v être*) **(a)** ‹*butter, paint*› to spread

(b) ‹*person*› to sprawl, to spread out

(c) (colloq) **s'~ de tout son long** to fall flat on one's face; **s'étaler** *or* **se faire ~ à un examen** to fail an exam

étalon /etalɔ̃/ *nm* **(a)** stallion

(b) standard

étalon-or /etalɔ̃ɔʀ/ *nm inv* gold standard

étamine /etamin/ *nf* stamen

étanche /etɑ̃ʃ/ *adj* **~ (à l'eau)** waterproof; watertight; **~ (à l'air)** airtight

étanchéité /etɑ̃ʃeite/ *nf* waterproofness; watertightness; airtightness

étancher /etɑ̃ʃe/ [1] *vtr* to quench ‹*thirst*›

étang /etɑ̃/ *nm* pond

étant /etɑ̃/ ▶ DONNÉ 3, ÊTRE¹

étape /etap/ *nf* **(a)** stop

(b) (in journey) stage; (in race) leg

(c) (figurative) stage, step; **brûler les ~s** to go too far too fast

état /eta/ **1** *nm* **(a)** condition; **mettre qn hors d'~ de nuire** to put sb out of harm's way; **leur ~ de santé est excellent** they're in excellent health; **maintenir qch en ~ de marche** to keep sth in working order; **hors d'~ de marche** ‹*car*› off the road; ‹*machine*› out of order; **j'ai laissé les choses en l'~** I left everything as it was

(b) state; **être dans un drôle d'~** (colloq) to be in a hell of a state (colloq); **être dans un ~ second** to be in a trance; **ce n'est encore qu'à l'~ de projet** it's still only at the planning stage

(c) statement

2 faire ~ de *phr* **(a)** to cite ‹*document*›

(b) to mention ‹*conversation*›

(c) to state ‹*preferences*›

(d) to make a point of mentioning ‹*success*›

■ **~ d'âme** qualm; feeling; **~ civil** registry office (GB); civil status; **~ d'esprit** state of mind; **~ de fait** fact; **~ des lieux** inventory and report on state of repair; **~s de service** service record

IDIOMS **être/se mettre dans tous ses ~s** (colloq) to be in/to get into a state (colloq)

État /eta/ *nm* **(a)** state, State

(b) state, government

étatique /etatik/ *adj* state (GB), public (US)

état-major, *pl* **états-majors** /etamaʒɔʀ/ *nm* **(a)** (Mil) staff

(b) headquarters

États-Unis /etazyni/ *pr nm pl* **~ (d'Amérique)** United States (of America)

étau, *pl* **~x** /eto/ *nm* vice (GB), vise (US); (figurative) **l'~ se resserre** the net is tightening

étayer /eteje/ [21] *vtr* **(a)** to prop up

(b) (figurative) to support ‹*theory*›

été¹ /ete/ ▶ ÊTRE¹

été² /ete/ *nm* summer

éteindre /etɛ̃dʀ/ [55] **1** *vtr* **(a)** to put out ‹*fire, cigarette*›; to blow out ‹*candle*›

(b) to switch off ‹*light, TV, oven*›; to turn off ‹*gas*›

2 s'éteindre *v refl* (+ *v être*) **(a)** ‹*cigarette, fire, light*› to go out; ‹*radio*› to go off

(b) (euphemistic) to pass away *or* on

(c) ‹*desire, passion*› to fade

éteint, **~e** /etɛ̃, ɛ̃t/ **1** *pp* ▶ ÉTEINDRE

2 *pp adj* **(a)** ‹*gaze*› dull

(b) ‹*volcano*› extinct; ‹*star*› extinct, dead

étendard /etɑ̃daʀ/ *nm* standard, flag

étendre /etɑ̃dʀ/ [6] **1** *vtr* **(a)** to stretch ‹*arms, legs*›

(b) to spread (out) ‹*cloth*›; **~ le linge** to hang out the washing

(c) to extend ‹*embargo*›

2 s'étendre *v refl* (+ *v être*) **(a)** ‹*land, forest*› to stretch

(b) ‹*strike, epidemic*› to spread; ‹*town*› to expand, to grow

(c) ‹*law, measure*› **s'~ à** to apply to

(d) ‹*period, work*› to stretch, to last

(e) to lie down

(f) **s'~ sur** to dwell on

étendu, **~e¹** /etɑ̃dy/ **1** *pp* ▶ ÉTENDRE

2 *pp adj* ‹*city*› sprawling; ‹*region, plain*› vast; ‹*vocabulary, knowledge, damage*› extensive

étendue² /etɑ̃dy/ *nf* **(a)** expanse

(b) size

(c) scale, extent; range

éternel, -elle /etɛʀnɛl/ *adj* endless; eternal

éternellement /etɛʀnɛlmɑ̃/ *adv*

(a) forever

(b) permanently

(c) perpetually

(d) eternally

éterniser: s'éterniser /etɛʀnize/ [1] *v refl* (+ *v être*) to drag on; ‹*visitor*› to stay for ages (colloq)

éternité /etɛʀnite/ *nf* eternity

éternuement /etɛʀnymɑ̃/ *nm* sneeze

éternuer /etɛʀnɥe/ [1] *vi* to sneeze

êtes /ɛt/ ▶ ÊTRE¹

éther /etɛʀ/ *nm* ether

éthique /etik/ **1** *adj* ethical

2 *nf* **(a)** ethics

(b) code of ethics

ethnie /etni/ *nf* ethnic group

ethnique /ɛtnik/ *adj* ethnic

ethnologie /ɛtnɔlɔʒi/ *nf* ethnology

éthylique /etilik/ *adj, nmf* alcoholic

éthylisme /etilism/ *nm* alcoholism

étiez /etje/ ▶ ÊTRE¹

étincelant, **~e** /etɛ̃slɑ̃, ɑ̃t/ *adj* ‹*sun*› blazing; ‹*star*› twinkling; ‹*gemstone, glass*› sparkling; ‹*feathers, colour*› brilliant

étinceler /etɛ̃sle/ [19] *vi* to twinkle; to sparkle

étincelle /etɛ̃sɛl/ *nf* spark; **jeter des ~s** to glitter; **faire des ~s** to do brilliantly

étioler: s'étioler /etjɔle/ [1] *v refl* (+ *v être*)
to wilt

étions /etjɔ̃/ ▶ ÊTRE[1]

étiquetage /etiktaʒ/ *nm* labelling (GB)
■ ~ **génétique** gene tagging

étiqueter /etikte/ [20] *vtr* to label

étiquette /etikɛt/ *nf* (a) label
(b) tag; **porter une** ~ to be labelled (GB);
candidat sans ~ independent candidate
(c) etiquette

étirer /etire/ [1] **1** *vtr* to stretch
2 s'étirer *v refl* (+ *v être*) (a) ⟨person⟩ to
stretch
(b) ⟨procession, road⟩ to stretch out

étoffe /etɔf/ *nf* (a) fabric
(b) (figurative) substance; **avoir l'**~ **d'un grand
homme** to have the makings of a great man

étoffer /etɔfe/ [1] **1** *vtr* to expand
2 s'étoffer *v refl* (+ *v être*) to put on
weight

étoile /etwal/ *nf* star
■ ~ **filante** shooting star; ~ **de mer** starfish;
~ **polaire** Pole Star
IDIOMS **coucher** *or* **dormir à la belle** ~ to
sleep out in the open

étoilé, ~**e** /etwale/ *adj* (a) starry
(b) ⟨glass, windscreen⟩ crazed

étole /etɔl/ *nf* stole

étonnamment /etɔnamɑ̃/ *adv*
surprisingly

étonnant, ~**e** /etɔnɑ̃, ɑ̃t/ *adj*
(a) surprising
(b) amazing

étonnement /etɔnmɑ̃/ *nm* surprise

étonner /etɔne/ [1] **1** *vtr* to surprise
2 s'étonner *v refl* (+ *v être*) to be
surprised

étouffant, ~**e** /etufɑ̃, ɑ̃t/ *adj* (a) stifling
(b) oppressive

étouffé, ~**e** /etufe/ *adj* (a) ⟨sound, voice⟩
muffled
(b) ⟨sob⟩ choked; ⟨laughter⟩ suppressed

étouffement /etufmɑ̃/ *nm* asphyxiation

étouffer /etufe/ [1] **1** *vtr* (a) to suppress
⟨protest⟩
(b) to hush up ⟨scandal⟩
(c) to suffocate ⟨person⟩; to choke ⟨plant⟩; **la
générosité ne les étouffe pas** generosity is
not their middle name
(d) to smother ⟨fire⟩
(e) to stifle ⟨yawn⟩; to hold back ⟨sigh⟩
(f) to deaden ⟨noise⟩
2 *vi* to feel stifled; **on étouffe ici!** (colloq) it's
stifling in here!; **mourir étouffé** to die of
suffocation
3 s'étouffer *v refl* (+ *v être*) to choke

étourderie /eturdəri/ *nf* absent-
mindedness

étourdi, ~**e** /eturdi/ *adj* (a) absent-
minded
(b) unthinking

étourdir /eturdir/ [3] **1** *vtr* (a) to stun, to
daze
(b) ~ **qn** ⟨noise⟩ to make sb's head spin

2 s'étourdir *v refl* (+ *v être*) **s'**~ **de
paroles** to become intoxicated with words

étourdissant, ~**e** /eturdisɑ̃, ɑ̃t/ *adj*
⟨noise⟩ deafening; ⟨speed⟩ dizzying

étourdissement /eturdismɑ̃/ *nm* **avoir
un** ~ to feel dizzy

étrange /etrɑ̃ʒ/ **1** *adj* strange; **chose** ~
elle n'a pas répondu strangely enough she
didn't answer
2 *nm* (a) strangeness
(b) **l'**~ **the** bizarre

étrangement /etrɑ̃ʒmɑ̃/ *adv*
(a) curiously; **vous me rappelez** ~ **un ami**
it's strange but you remind me of a friend
(b) surprisingly

étranger, -ère /etrɑ̃ʒe, ɛr/ **1** *adj*
(a) foreign
(b) ~ **à** ⟨person⟩ not involved in ⟨case⟩;
outside ⟨group⟩; ⟨fact⟩ with no bearing on
⟨problem⟩; **se sentir** ~ to feel like an
outsider
(c) unfamiliar
2 *nm,f* (a) foreigner
(b) outsider
(c) stranger
3 *nm* **à l'**~ abroad

étrangeté /etrɑ̃ʒte/ *nf* strangeness

étranglé, ~**e** /etrɑ̃gle/ *adj* (a) ⟨voice⟩
choked; ⟨sound⟩ muffled
(b) ⟨street⟩ narrow

étranglement /etrɑ̃gləmɑ̃/ *nm*
(a) strangulation
(b) (of road, valley) narrow section

étrangler /etrɑ̃gle/ [1] **1** *vtr* (a) to
strangle
(b) to choke
2 s'étrangler *v refl* (+ *v être*) (a) to
strangle oneself
(b) to choke

étrangleur, -euse /etrɑ̃glœr, øz/ *nm,f*
strangler

être[1] /ɛtr/ [7] *vi* (+ *v avoir*)

■ **Note** You will find translations for fixed phrases
using *être* such as *être en train de, être sur le
point de, quoi qu'il en soit, étant donné* etc. at
the entries TRAIN, POINT, QUOI, DONNÉ etc.

(a) to be; **nous sommes pauvres** we are poor
(b) (as auxiliary verb) **elles sont tombées** they
have fallen; they fell; **elle s'était vengée** she
had taken her revenge
(c) (to go) **je n'ai jamais été en Chine** I've
never been to China
(d) (with *ce*) **est-ce leur voiture?** is it their
car?; **c'est grave?** is it serious?; **qui est-ce?**
who is he/she?; who is that?; who is it?; **est-
ce que tu parles russe?** do you speak
Russian?; **qu'est-ce que c'est?** what is it?; **ce
sont mes enfants** these are my children; they
are my children; **c'est cela** that's right; **c'est
à Pierre/lui de choisir** it's Pierre's/his turn to
choose; it's up to Pierre/to him to choose; **il
aurait pu s'excuser, ne serait-ce qu'en
envoyant un mot** he could have apologized if
only by sending a note
(e) (with *il*) **il est facile de critiquer** it is easy

to criticize; **il n'est pas jusqu'à l'Antarctique qui ne soit pollué** even the Antarctic is polluted; **il n'en est rien** this isn't at all the case

(f) (with *en*) **où en étais-je?** where was I?; **je ne sais plus où j'en suis** I'm lost; **'où en es-tu de tes recherches?'**—**'j'en suis à mi-chemin'** 'how far have you got in your research?'—'I'm halfway through'; **j'en suis à me demander si…** I'm beginning to wonder whether…; ~ **en uniforme** to be wearing a uniform

(g) (with *y*) **j'y suis** I'm with you, I get it (colloq); **je n'y suis pas** I don't get it (colloq); **nous partons, vous y êtes?** we're leaving, do you understand?; we're leaving, are you ready?

(h) (with *à* and *de*) **ce livre est à moi/à mon frère** this book is mine/my brother's; **à qui est ce chien?** whose dog is this?; **je suis à vous tout de suite** I'll be with you right away; **je suis à vous** I'm all yours; ~ **à ce qu'on fait** to have one's mind on what one is doing; **elle est d'un ridicule!** she's so ridiculous!

être² /ɛtʀ/ *nm* **(a)** ~ **humain** human being; **les** ~**s animés et inanimés** animate and inanimate things; **un** ~ **sans défense** a defenceless (GB) creature
(b) person; **un** ~ **cher** a loved one
(c) de tout son ~ with one's whole being; **blessé au plus profond de son** ~ hurt to the core

étreindre /etʀɛ̃dʀ/ [55] *vtr* to embrace, to hug ⟨*friend*⟩; to clasp ⟨*opponent*⟩

étreinte /etʀɛ̃t/ *nf* embrace; grip

étrenner /etʀene/ [1] *vtr* to use [sth] for the first time

étrennes /etʀɛn/ *nf pl* **(a)** gift
(b) money

étrier /etʀije/ *nm* stirrup
IDIOMS mettre à qn le pied à l'~ (figurative) to get sb started

étriper /etʀipe/ [1] *vtr* (figurative) (colloq) ~ **qn** to skin sb alive

étriqué, ~**e** /etʀike/ *adj* ⟨*jacket*⟩ skimpy; ⟨*life*⟩ restricted

étroit, ~**e** /etʀwa, at/ **1** *adj* **(a)** narrow; **avoir l'esprit** ~ to be narrow-minded
(b) ⟨*links*⟩ close; **en** ~ **e collaboration** closely
2 à l'étroit *phr* **nous sommes un peu à l'**~ we're a bit cramped; **je me sens un peu à l'**~ **dans cette jupe** this skirt feels a bit too tight

étroitement /etʀwatmã/ *adv* closely

étroitesse /etʀwatɛs/ *nf* narrowness

étude /etyd/ **1** *nf* **(a)** study
(b) survey
(c) (mise à l')~ consideration; **à l'**~ under consideration
(d) (of lawyer) office
(e) (Sch) study room (GB), study hall (US)
(f) study period

2 études *nf pl* studies; **faire des** ~**s** to be a student; **je n'ai pas fait d'**~**s (supérieures)** I didn't go to university *or* college
■ ~ **de marché** market research

étudiant, ~**e** /etydjɑ̃, ɑ̃t/ *nm,f* student

étudié, ~**e** /etydje/ *adj* **(a)** carefully prepared
(b) studied

étudier /etydje/ [2] **1** *vtr* to study; to examine ⟨*file, situation*⟩; to learn ⟨*lesson*⟩
2 *vi* **(a)** to be a student
(b) to be studying

étui /etɥi/ *nm* case; ~ **à revolver** holster

étuve /etyv/ *nf* **(a)** steam room; **le grenier est une** ~ (figurative) the attic is like an oven
(b) incubator

étymologie /etimɔlɔʒi/ *nf* etymology

eu, ~**e** /y/ ▶ AVOIR¹

eucalyptus /økaliptys/ *nm inv* eucalyptus

eucharistie /økaʀisti/ *nf* **(a)** Eucharist
(b) Sacrament

eûmes /ym/ ▶ AVOIR¹

eunuque /ønyk/ *nm* eunuch

euphémisme /øfemism/ *nm* euphemism

euphorie /øfɔʀi/ *nf* euphoria

euphorique /øfɔʀik/ *adj* euphoric

euphorisant, ~**e** /øfɔʀizɑ̃, ɑ̃t/ **1** *adj* stimulating; uplifting; euphoriant
2 *nm* (Med) stimulant

eurasien, -ienne /øʀazjɛ̃, ɛn/ *adj* Eurasian

Euratom /øʀatɔm/ *nf* (*abbr* = **European atomic energy commission**) Euratom

eurent /yʀ/ ▶ AVOIR¹

EURL /œyɛʀɛl/ *nf*: *abbr* ▶ ENTREPRISE

euro /øʀoøʀo/ *nm* (currency) euro

eurochèque /øʀoʃɛk/ *nm* Eurocheque

euroconnecteur /øʀokɔnɛktœʀ/ *nm* scart socket; scart plug

eurocrate /øʀokʀat/ *nmf* eurocrat

eurodéputé, -e /øʀodepyte/ *nm,f* Euro MP

euromarché /øʀomaʀʃe/ *nm* Euromarket

Europe /øʀɔp/ *pr nf* Europe; **l'**~ **communautaire** the European community

européaniser /øʀɔpeanize/ [1] **1** *vtr* to europeanize; ~ **un débat** to broaden a debate to a European level
2 s'européaniser *v refl* (+ *v être*) ⟨*country*⟩ to become europeanized; ⟨*economy*⟩ to become adapted to a European framework

européen, -éenne /øʀɔpeɛ̃, ɛn/ *adj* European

eurosceptique /øʀosɛptik/ *nmf* eurosceptic

Eurotunnel /øʀotynɛl/ *nm* Eurotunnel

eus /y/ ▶ AVOIR¹

eusse /ys/ ▶ AVOIR¹

eussent /ys/ ▶ AVOIR¹

eusses /ys/ ▶ AVOIR¹

eussiez /ysje/ ▶ AVOIR[1]

eussions /ysjɔ̃/ ▶ AVOIR[1]

eut /y/ ▶ AVOIR[1]

eût /yt/ ▶ AVOIR[1]

eûtes /yt/ ▶ AVOIR[1]

euthanasie /øtanazi/ *nf* euthanasia

eux /ø/ *pron* **(a)** they; **je sais que ce n'est pas ∼ qui ont fait ça** I know they weren't the ones who did it
(b) them; **les inviter, ∼, quelle idée!** invite THEM, what an idea!; **c'est à ∼** it's theirs

eux-mêmes /ømɛm/ *pron* themselves; **les experts ∼ reconnaissent que...** even the experts admit that...

évacuation /evakɥasjɔ̃/ *nf* **(a)** evacuation
(b) discharge; **il y a un problème d'∼ de l'eau** the water doesn't drain away

évacuer /evakɥe/ [1] *vtr* **(a)** to evacuate
(b) to drain off
(c) (figurative) to shrug off ⟨*problem*⟩

évader: **s'évader** /evade/ [1] *v refl*
(+ *v être*) **(a)** to escape; **faire ∼ qn** to help sb to escape
(b) (figurative) to get away ⟨de from⟩

évaluable /evalɥabl/ *adj* assessable

évaluation /evalɥasjɔ̃/ *nf* **(a)** (of collection, house) valuation; **faire l'∼ de** to value
(b) (of costs, damages) assessment; estimate, appraisal (US)
(c) (of staff) appraisal

évaluer /evalɥe/ [1] *vtr* **(a)** to estimate ⟨*size, length*⟩; to assess ⟨*risks, costs*⟩
(b) to value ⟨*inheritance*⟩
(c) to assess ⟨*employee, student*⟩

Évangile /evɑ̃ʒil/ *nm* Gospel

évanouir: **s'évanouir** /evanwiʀ/ [3] *v refl*
(+ *v être*) **(a)** to faint
(b) ⟨*feeling*⟩ to fade

évanouissement /evanwismɑ̃/ *nm*
(a) blackout, fainting fit
(b) fading

évaporation /evapɔʀasjɔ̃/ *nf* evaporation

évaporer: **s'évaporer** /evapɔʀe/ [1] *v refl*
(+ *v être*) **(a)** to evaporate
(b) (colloq) to vanish

évaser /evaze/ [1] **1** *vtr* to flare
2 **s'évaser** *v refl* (+ *v être*) ⟨*duct*⟩ to open out; ⟨*skirt*⟩ to be flared

évasif, -ive /evazif, iv/ *adj* evasive

évasion /evazjɔ̃/ *nf* escape

Ève /ɛv/ *pr nf* Eve; **en tenue d'∼** in her birthday suit
IDIOMS **elle ne le connaît ni d'∼ ni d'Adam** she doesn't know him from Adam

évêché /eveʃe/ *nm* **(a)** diocese
(b) bishop's palace

éveil /evɛj/ *nm* awakening

éveiller /eveje/ [1] **1** *vtr* **(a)** to arouse ⟨*curiosity, suspicions*⟩; to stimulate ⟨*intelligence*⟩; to awaken ⟨*conscience*⟩; **un enfant éveillé** a bright child
(b) to wake (up) ⟨*sleeper*⟩; **être éveillé** to be awake
2 **s'éveiller** *v refl* (+ *v être*) **(a)** to wake up

(b) ⟨*imagination*⟩ to start to develop

événement /evenmɑ̃/ *nm* event

événementiel, -ielle /evenmɑ̃sjɛl/ *adj* factual

éventail /evɑ̃taj/ *nm* **(a)** fan
(b) range

éventaire /evɑ̃tɛʀ/ *nm* stall

éventer: **s'éventer** /evɑ̃te/ [1] *v refl*
(+ *v être*) ⟨*perfume, coffee*⟩ to go off; ⟨*wine*⟩ to pass its best; ⟨*beer, lemonade*⟩ to go flat

éventrer /evɑ̃tʀe/ [1] *vtr* **(a)** ⟨*person*⟩ to disembowel; ⟨*bull*⟩ to gore
(b) to rip open

éventualité /evɑ̃tɥalite/ *nf* **(a)** eventuality
(b) possibility; **dans l'∼ de** in the event of

éventuel, -elle /evɑ̃tɥɛl/ *adj* possible

éventuellement /evɑ̃tɥɛlmɑ̃/ *adv*
(a) possibly
(b) if necessary

évêque /evɛk/ *nm* bishop ⟨de of⟩

évertuer: **s'évertuer** /evɛʀtɥe/ [1] *v refl*
(+ *v être*) to try one's best ⟨à faire to do⟩

éviction /eviksjɔ̃/ *nf* **(a)** ousting ⟨de from⟩
(b) (Law) eviction

évidemment /evidamɑ̃/ *adv* of course

évidence /evidɑ̃s/ **1** *nf* **(a)** obviousness
(b) obvious fact; **se rendre à l'∼** to face the facts; **de toute ∼, à l'∼** obviously
2 **en évidence** *phr* **laisser qch en ∼** to leave sth in an obvious place; **mettre en ∼** to highlight ⟨*feature*⟩

évident, ∼e /evidɑ̃, ɑ̃t/ *adj* obvious; **ce n'est pas ∼** (colloq) not necessarily; it's not so easy

évider /evide/ [1] *vtr* to hollow out; to scoop out

évier /evje/ *nm* sink

évincer /evɛ̃se/ [12] *vtr* to oust ⟨*rival*⟩

évitable /evitabl/ *adj* avoidable

éviter /evite/ [1] *vtr* **(a)** to avoid; **∼ à qn de faire** to save sb (from) doing
(b) to dodge ⟨*bullet, blow*⟩

évocation /evɔkasjɔ̃/ *nf* **(a)** evocation; reminiscence
(b) mention ⟨de of⟩

évolué, ∼e /evɔlɥe/ *adj* **(a)** civilized
(b) evolved

évoluer /evɔlɥe/ [1] *vi* **(a)** to evolve, to change
(b) to develop
(c) to glide

évolutif, -ive /evɔlytif, iv/ *adj* progressive

évolution /evɔlysjɔ̃/ *nf* **(a)** evolution
(b) development
(c) progress
(d) progression
(e) change; **en pleine ∼** undergoing rapid change

évolutionniste /evɔlysjɔnist/ *adj* evolutionary

évoquer /evɔke/ [1] *vtr* **(a)** to recall
(b) to mention, to bring up

(c) to bring back ⟨*memory*⟩; to be reminiscent of ⟨*childhood*⟩
(d) to evoke

ex /ɛks/ *nm* **(a)** (*written abbr* = **exemple**) eg
(b) (*written abbr* = **exemplaire**) copy

ex- /ɛks/ *pref* ~**champion** former champion

exacerber /ɛgzasɛrbe/ [1] *vtr* to exacerbate

exact, ~**e** /ɛgza(kt), akt/ *adj* **(a)** correct
(b) accurate
(c) exact
(d) punctual

exactement /ɛgzaktəmɑ̃/ *adv* exactly

exactitude /ɛgzaktityd/ *nf* **(a)** correctness
(b) accuracy
(c) exactness
(d) punctuality

ex æquo /ɛgzeko/ *adv* **ils sont premiers ~** they've tied for first place

exagération /ɛgzaʒerasjɔ̃/ *nf* exaggeration

exagéré, ~**e** /ɛgzaʒere/ *adj*
(a) exaggerated
(b) excessive; **d'une sensibilité ~e** oversensitive

exagérément /ɛgzaʒeremɑ̃/ *adv* excessively

exagérer /ɛgzaʒere/ [14] **1** *vtr* to exaggerate
2 *vi* to go too far

exaltant, ~**e** /ɛgzaltɑ̃, ɑ̃t/ *adj* thrilling; inspiring

exaltation /ɛgzaltasjɔ̃/ *nf* **(a)** elation
(b) stimulation
(c) glorification

exalté, ~**e** /ɛgzalte/ **1** *pp* ▶ EXALTER
2 *pp adj* impassioned

exalter /ɛgzalte/ [1] *vtr* **(a)** to glorify
(b) to heighten
(c) to elate, to thrill

examen /ɛgzamɛ̃/ *nm* **(a)** (Sch, Univ) examination, exam; **passer un ~** to take an exam; **~ de rattrapage** retake, resit (GB)
(b) (Med) examination
(c) examination; consideration; review; **être en cours d'~** to be under review; to be under consideration
(d) inspection
■ **~ blanc** mock (exam), practice exam; **~ de conscience** self-examination; **~ spécial d'entrée à l'université, ESEU** *university entrance exam for students not having the baccalaureate*

examinateur, **-trice** /ɛgzaminatœr, tris/ *nm,f* examiner

examiner /ɛgzamine/ [1] *vtr* **(a)** to examine; to review; **~ qch de près** to have a close look at sth
(b) (Med) to examine ⟨*patient, wound*⟩

exaspération /ɛgzasperasjɔ̃/ *nf*
(a) exasperation
(b) intensification

exaspérer /ɛgzaspere/ [14] *vtr* **(a)** to exasperate, to infuriate
(b) to exacerbate

exaucer /ɛgzose/ [12] *vtr* to grant

excavatrice /ɛkskavatris/ *nf* excavator

excédant, ~**e** /ɛksedɑ̃, ɑ̃t/ *adj* exasperating, infuriating

excédent /ɛksedɑ̃/ *nm* surplus; **~ de bagages** excess baggage

excédentaire /ɛksedɑ̃tɛr/ *adj* surplus

excéder /ɛksede/ [14] *vtr* **(a)** to exceed
(b) to infuriate

excellence /ɛksɛlɑ̃s/ *nf* excellence

Excellence /ɛksɛlɑ̃s/ *nf* **Son ~** His/Her Excellency

excellent, ~**e** /ɛksɛlɑ̃, ɑ̃t/ *adj* excellent

exceller /ɛksele/ [1] *vi* to excel

excentré, ~**e** /ɛksɑ̃tre/ *adj* **(a)** ⟨*area*⟩ outlying
(b) **être ~** ⟨*axis*⟩ to be off-centre (GB)

excentricité /ɛksɑ̃trisite/ *nf* eccentricity

excentrique /ɛksɑ̃trik/ *adj, nmf* eccentric

excepté, ~**e** /ɛksɛpte/ **1** *pp* ▶ EXCEPTER
2 *prep* except
3 **excepté que** *phr* except that

excepter /ɛksɛpte/ [1] *vtr* **si l'on excepte** except for, apart from

exception /ɛksɛpsjɔ̃/ *nf* exception; **faire ~** to be an exception; **à l'~ de, ~ faite de** except for; **sauf ~** with the occasional exception; **d'~** ⟨*person*⟩ exceptional; ⟨*law*⟩ emergency

exceptionnel, **-elle** /ɛksɛpsjɔnɛl/ *adj* (gen) exceptional; ⟨*price*⟩ bargain; ⟨*meeting*⟩ extraordinary

exceptionnellement /ɛksɛpsjɔnɛlmɑ̃/ *adv* exceptionally

excès /ɛksɛ/ *nm inv* excess; **commettre des ~** to go too far; **des ~ de langage** bad language; **tomber dans l'~ inverse** to go to the opposite extreme; **~ de confiance/zèle** overconfidence/overzealousness
■ **~ de vitesse** speeding

excessif, **-ive** /ɛksesif, iv/ *adj*
(a) excessive
(b) extreme; **il est ~** he is a man of extremes

excision /ɛksizjɔ̃/ *nf* **(a)** excision
(b) female circumcision

excitant, ~**e** /ɛksitɑ̃, ɑ̃t/ **1** *adj*
(a) ⟨*substance*⟩ stimulating
(b) exciting; thrilling
2 *nm* stimulant

excitation /ɛksitasjɔ̃/ *nf* **(a)** excitement
(b) arousal
(c) stimulation

excité, ~**e** /ɛksite/ **1** *adj* **(a)** ⟨*crowd*⟩ in a frenzy; ⟨*atmosphere*⟩ frenzied
(b) ⟨*person*⟩ thrilled, excited
(c) (sexually) aroused
2 *nm,f* **(a)** rowdy
(b) fanatic
(c) neurotic

···⟩

IDIOMS être ~ **comme une puce** (colloq) to be like a cat on a hot tin roof

exciter /ɛksite/ [1] **1** *vtr* (a) to arouse ⟨*anger*⟩; to kindle ⟨*desire*⟩
(b) to thrill
(c) to arouse
(d) to tease ⟨*animal*⟩; to get [sb] excited ⟨*child*⟩; ⟨*coffee*⟩ to get [sb] hyped up
(e) to stimulate ⟨*palate*⟩
2 s'exciter *v refl* (+ *v être*) to get excited

exclamatif, -ive /ɛksklamatif, iv/ *adj* exclamatory

exclamation /ɛksklamasjɔ̃/ *nf* exclamation

exclamer: s'exclamer /ɛksklame/ [1] *v refl* (+ *v être*) to exclaim

exclu, ~e /ɛkskly/ **1** *pp* ▶ EXCLURE
2 *pp adj* excluded; **c'est exclu!** it's out of the question!; **se sentir** ~ to feel left out

exclure /ɛksklyʀ/ [78] *vtr* (a) to exclude ⟨*person*⟩; to rule out ⟨*possibility*⟩
(b) to expel ⟨*member*⟩

exclusif, -ive /ɛksklyzif, iv/ *adj* exclusive; **concessionnaire** ~ sole agent

exclusion /ɛksklyzjɔ̃/ **1** *nf* (a) exclusion; ~ **sociale** social exclusion
(b) expulsion
(c) suspension
2 à l'exclusion de *phr* with the exception of

exclusivité /ɛksklyzivite/ *nf* exclusive rights; **en** ~ ⟨*publish*⟩ exclusively; ⟨*product*⟩ exclusive

excommunier /ɛkskɔmynje/ [2] *vtr* to excommunicate

excrément /ɛkskʀemɑ̃/ *nm* excrement

excrétion /ɛkskʀesjɔ̃/ *nf* excretion

excroissance /ɛkskʀwasɑ̃s/ *nf* (a) (Med) growth, excrescence
(b) (in botany) outgrowth

excursion /ɛkskyʀsjɔ̃/ *nf* excursion, trip

excuse /ɛkskyz/ *nf* (a) excuse
(b) apology

excuser /ɛkskyze/ [1] **1** *vtr* to forgive; to pardon; to excuse; **excusez-moi** I'm sorry; **vous êtes tout excusé** it's quite all right
2 s'excuser *v refl* (+ *v être*) to apologize

exécrable /ɛgzekʀabl/ *adj* loathsome; dreadful; detestable

exécrer /ɛgzekʀe/ [14] *vtr* to loathe

exécutant, ~e /ɛgzekytɑ̃, ɑ̃t/ *nm,f*
(a) performer
(b) **il dit n'avoir été qu'un** ~ he claims he was only obeying orders

exécuter /ɛgzekyte/ [1] **1** *vtr* (a) to carry out ⟨*task, mission*⟩; to do ⟨*exercise*⟩
(b) to carry out ⟨*orders, threat*⟩; to fulfil (GB) ⟨*contract*⟩; to enforce ⟨*law, ruling*⟩
(c) to execute ⟨*prisoner*⟩; to kill ⟨*victim*⟩
(d) (Mus) to perform
2 s'exécuter *v refl* (+ *v être*) to comply

exécutif, -ive /ɛgzekytif, ive/ *adj* executive

exécution /ɛgzekysjɔ̃/ *nf* (a) execution,

carrying out; enforcement; fulfilment (GB); **mettre à** ~ to carry out ⟨*threat*⟩; **travaux en cours d'**~ work in progress; **veiller à la bonne** ~ **d'une tâche** to see that a job is done well
(b) execution; ~ **capitale** capital punishment

exemplaire /ɛgzɑ̃plɛʀ/ **1** *adj*
(a) exemplary; **élève** ~ model pupil
(b) (Law) exemplary
2 *nm* (a) copy; print
(b) specimen

exemplarité /ɛgzɑ̃plaʀite/ *nf* deterrent nature (**de** of)

exemple /ɛgzɑ̃pl/ **1** *nm* (a) example; **sans** ~ unprecedented; **être l'**~ **de la gentillesse** to be a model of kindness; **donner qn en** ~ to hold sb up as an example
(b) warning (**pour** to)
2 par exemple *phr* for example; **ça par** ~! how amazing!; well, honestly!

exemplifier /ɛgzɑ̃plifje/ [2] *vtr* to exemplify

exempt, ~e /ɛgzɑ̃, ɑ̃t/ *adj* exempt; ~ **d'impôt** tax-free

exempter /ɛgzɑ̃te/ [1] *vtr* to exempt

exercer /ɛgzɛʀse/ [12] **1** *vtr* (a) to exercise ⟨*right*⟩; to exert ⟨*authority*⟩
(b) to exercise ⟨*profession*⟩; to practise (GB) ⟨*art*⟩
(c) to exercise ⟨*body*⟩
2 s'exercer *v refl* (+ *v être*) (a) ⟨*athlete*⟩ to train; ⟨*musician*⟩ to practise (GB)
(b) ⟨*influence, force*⟩ to be exerted

exercice /ɛgzɛʀsis/ *nm* exercise; **faire de l'**~ to get some exercise; **dans l'**~ **de ses fonctions** in the course of one's duty; while at work; **en** ~ ⟨*minister, president*⟩ incumbent; **entrer en** ~ to take up one's duties

exergue /ɛgzɛʀg/ *nm* (a) epigraph
(b) inscription

exhaler /ɛgzale/ [1] *vtr* to exhale

exhausser /ɛgzose/ [1] *vtr* to raise

exhaustif, -ive /ɛgzostif, iv/ *adj* exhaustive

exhiber /ɛgzibe/ [1] **1** *vtr* to flaunt ⟨*wealth*⟩; to show ⟨*animal*⟩; to expose ⟨*body*⟩
2 s'exhiber *v refl* (+ *v être*) (a) to expose oneself
(b) to flaunt oneself

exhibition /ɛgzibisjɔ̃/ *nf* (a) (of animals) show; exhibition
(b) (Sport) demonstration, display
(c) (of wealth) parade; (of emotion) display

exhibitionniste /ɛgzibisjɔnist/ *adj, nmf* exhibitionist

exhortation /ɛgzɔʀtasjɔ̃/ *nf* exhortation; ~ **au calme** call for calm

exhorter /ɛgzɔʀte/ [1] *vtr* to motivate; ~ **qn à faire** to urge *or* exhort sb to do

exhumer /ɛgzyme/ [1] *vtr* (a) to exhume
(b) to excavate

exigeant, ~e /ɛgziʒɑ̃, ɑ̃t/ *adj* demanding

exigence /ɛgziʒɑ̃s/ *nf* demand (**de qch** for sth)

exiger /ɛgziʒe/ [13] *vtr* (**a**) to demand ⟨*answer, reforms*⟩
(**b**) to require

exigibilité /ɛgziʒibilite/ *nf* (of tax, bill) payability; (of debt) repayability

exigible /ɛgziʒibl/ *adj* due

exigu, -uë /ɛgzigy/ *adj* ⟨*room*⟩ cramped; ⟨*entrance*⟩ narrow; ⟨*space*⟩ confined

exil /ɛgzil/ *nm* exile; **en** ∼ in exile

exilé, ∼e /ɛgzile/ *nm,f* exile

exiler /ɛgzile/ [1] **1** *vtr* to exile
2 s'exiler *v refl* (+ *v être*) to go into exile

existence /ɛgzistɑ̃s/ *nf* (**a**) existence
(**b**) (colloq) life

existentialisme /ɛgzistɑ̃sjalism/ *nm* existentialism

exister /ɛgziste/ [1] *vi* to exist; **si le paradis existe** if there is a heaven; **la maison existe encore** the house is still standing

exode /ɛgzɔd/ *nm* exodus; ∼ **rural** rural depopulation

exonération /ɛgzɔneʀasjɔ̃/ *nf* exemption

exonérer /ɛgzɔneʀe/ [14] *vtr* to exempt

exorbitant, ∼e /ɛgzɔʀbitɑ̃, ɑ̃t/ *adj* ⟨*price*⟩ exorbitant; ⟨*demands*⟩ outrageous

exorbité, ∼e /ɛgzɔʀbite/ *adj* bulging

exorciser /ɛgzɔʀsize/ [1] *vtr* to exorcize

exotique /ɛgzɔtik/ *adj* exotic

exotisme /ɛgzɔtism/ *nm* exoticism

expansif, -ive /ɛkspɑ̃sif, iv/ *adj* communicative, outgoing

expansion /ɛkspɑ̃sjɔ̃/ *nf* (**a**) growth; **en (pleine)** ∼ (rapidly) growing
(**b**) expansion

expansivité /ɛkspɑ̃sivite/ *nf* expansiveness

expatriation /ɛkspatʀijasjɔ̃/ *nf* expatriation

expatrié, ∼e /ɛkspatʀije/ *adj, nm,f* expatriate

expatrier /ɛkspatʀije/ [2] **1** *vtr* to deport
2 s'expatrier *v refl* (+ *v être*) to emigrate

expectative /ɛkspɛktativ/ *nf* **rester dans l'**∼ to wait and see

expédient /ɛkspedjɑ̃/ *nm* expedient; **vivre d'**∼**s** to live by one's wits

expédier /ɛkspedje/ [2] *vtr* (**a**) to send; to post (GB), to mail (US); to dispatch; ∼ **qch à qn** to send sb sth
(**b**) to get rid of ⟨*person*⟩; to polish off ⟨*work, meal*⟩; ∼ **un procès en une heure** to get a trial over within one hour

expéditeur, -trice /ɛkspeditœʀ, tʀis/ *nm,f* sender

expéditif, -ive /ɛkspeditif, iv/ *adj* ⟨*person*⟩ brisk; ⟨*method*⟩ cursory; **une justice expéditive** summary justice

expédition /ɛkspedisjɔ̃/ *nf* expedition

expéditionnaire /ɛkspedisjɔnɛʀ/ **1** *adj* expeditionary
2 *nmf* (**a**) forwarding agent

(**b**) copyist

expérience /ɛkspeʀjɑ̃s/ *nf* (**a**) experience; **avoir de l'**∼ to be experienced; **j'en ai fait l'**∼ **à mes dépens** I learned that lesson to my cost
(**b**) experiment

expérimental, ∼e, *mpl* **-aux** /ɛkspeʀimɑ̃tal, o/ *adj* experimental

expérimentation /ɛkspeʀimɑ̃tasjɔ̃/ *nf* experimentation
■ ∼ **animale** experiments on animals

expérimenté, ∼e /ɛkspeʀimɑ̃te/ *adj* experienced

expérimenter /ɛkspeʀimɑ̃te/ [1] *vtr* to test

expert /ɛkspɛʀ/ *nm* (**a**) expert (**en** on); **l'avis d'un** ∼ expert advice
(**b**) adjuster

expert-comptable, *pl* **experts-comptables** /ɛkspɛʀkɔ̃tabl/ *nm* ≈ chartered accountant (GB), certified public accountant (US)

expert-conseil, *pl* **experts-conseils** /ɛkspɛʀkɔ̃sɛj/ *nm* consultant

expertise /ɛkspɛʀtiz/ *nf* (**a**) valuation (GB), appraisal (US); assessment
(**b**) expertise

expertiser /ɛkspɛʀtize/ [1] *vtr* to value (GB), to appraise (US) ⟨*jewellery*⟩; to assess ⟨*damages*⟩

expier /ɛkspje/ [2] *vtr* to atone for, to expiate

expiration /ɛkspiʀasjɔ̃/ *nf* (**a**) exhalation
(**b**) expiry (GB), expiration (US)

expirer /ɛkspiʀe/ [1] **1** *vtr* to exhale
2 *vi* (**a**) ⟨*contract*⟩ to expire
(**b**) to breathe out

explicatif, -ive /ɛksplikatif, iv/ *adj* explanatory

explication /ɛksplikasjɔ̃/ *nf* explanation; **nous avons eu une bonne** ∼ we've talked things through

explicite /ɛksplisit/ *adj* ⟨*text, film*⟩ explicit; ⟨*answer*⟩ definite

explicitement /ɛksplisitmɑ̃/ *adv* ⟨*mention*⟩ explicitly; ⟨*condemn*⟩ unequivocally; ⟨*ask*⟩ specifically

expliciter /ɛksplisite/ [1] *vtr* to clarify

expliquer /ɛksplike/ [1] **1** *vtr* (**a**) to explain
(**b**) (Sch) to analyse (GB) ⟨*text*⟩
2 s'expliquer *v refl* (+ *v être*) **s'**∼ **qch** to understand sth; **tout finira par s'**∼ everything will become clear

exploit /ɛksplwa/ *nm* exploit, feat

exploitant, ∼e /ɛksplwatɑ̃, ɑ̃t/ *nm,f* ∼ **agricole** farmer

exploitation /ɛksplwatasjɔ̃/ *nf*
(**a**) exploitation
(**b**) ∼ **agricole** farm; ∼ **commerciale** business concern
(**c**) (of land, forest) exploitation; (of airline, shipping line) operation

e

exploiter /ɛksplwate/ [1] *vtr* **(a)** to exploit ⟨*person*⟩
(b) to work ⟨*mine*⟩; to mine ⟨*coal*⟩; to exploit ⟨*forest*⟩; to run ⟨*firm*⟩; to operate ⟨*airline*⟩
(c) to make the most of ⟨*gift, knowledge*⟩

explorateur, -trice /ɛksplɔratœr, tris/ *nm,f* explorer

exploration /ɛksplɔrasjɔ̃/ *nf* exploration

explorer /ɛksplɔre/ [1] *vtr* to explore

exploser /ɛksploze/ [1] *vi* to explode; to blow up; **faire ∼** to blow up; to explode; to cause [sth] to blow up

explosif, -ive /ɛksplozif, iv/ **1** *adj* explosive
2 *nm* explosive; **attentat à l'∼** bomb attack

explosion /ɛksplozjɔ̃/ *nf* **(a)** explosion
(b) outburst
(c) (in market) boom

export /ɛkspɔr/ *nm* export

exportateur, -trice /ɛkspɔrtatœr, tris/ *nm,f* exporter

exportation /ɛkspɔrtasjɔ̃/ *nf* export

exporter /ɛkspɔrte/ [1] *vtr* to export

exposé, ∼e /ɛkspoze/ **1** *pp* ▶ EXPOSER
2 *pp adj* **(a)** exposed; **maison ∼e au sud** south-facing house
(b) on show; on display
3 *nm* **(a)** **∼ de** account of; **faire un** *or* **l'∼ des faits** to give a statement of the facts
(b) (Sch) talk; **faire un ∼** to give a talk

exposer /ɛkspoze/ [1] **1** *vtr* **(a)** to exhibit ⟨*art*⟩; to display, to put [sth] on display ⟨*goods*⟩
(b) to state ⟨*facts*⟩; to outline ⟨*idea, plan*⟩; to explain ⟨*situation*⟩
(c) to risk ⟨*life, reputation*⟩
(d) to expose ⟨*skin, body*⟩; **ne reste pas exposé au soleil** stay out of the sun
2 **s'exposer** *v refl* (+ *v être*) **(a)** to put oneself at risk; **s'∼ à** to lay oneself open to ⟨*criticism*⟩
(b) **s'∼ au soleil** to go out in the sun

exposition /ɛkspozisjɔ̃/ *nf* **(a)** (of art) exhibition; (of animals, plants) show; (for trade) fair
(b) (in shop) display
(c) (of situation, facts) exposition
(d) (of house) aspect
(e) (to light, radiation) exposure

exprès¹ /ɛksprɛ/ *adv* **(a)** deliberately, on purpose; **comme par un fait ∼** as ill-luck would have it
(b) specially

exprès², -esse /ɛksprɛs/ **1** *adj* express
2 **exprès** *adj inv* **envoyer qch en** *or* **par ∼** to send sth special delivery *or* express

express /ɛksprɛs/ **1** *adj inv* express
2 *nm inv* **(a)** express (train)
(b) espresso

expressément /ɛksprɛsemã/ *adv* expressly

expressif, -ive /ɛksprɛsif, iv/ *adj* expressive

expression /ɛksprɛsjɔ̃/ *nf* expression; **réduire qch à sa plus simple ∼** (figurative) to reduce sth to a minimum
■ **∼ corporelle** self-expression through movement

expressivité /ɛksprɛsivite/ *nf* expressiveness

exprimable /ɛksprimabl/ *adj* **difficilement ∼** hard to express

exprimer /ɛksprime/ [1] **1** *vtr* to express
2 **s'exprimer** *v refl* (+ *v être*) **(a)** to express oneself; **si j'ose m'∼ ainsi** if I may put it that way
(b) to be expressed

expropriation /ɛksprɔprijasjɔ̃/ *nf* compulsory purchase; expropriation

exproprier /ɛksprɔprije/ [2] *vtr* **∼ qn** to put a compulsory purchase order on sb's property

expulser /ɛkspylse/ [1] *vtr* **(a)** to evict
(b) to deport
(c) to expel
(d) (Sport) to send [sb] off

expulsion /ɛkspylsjɔ̃/ *nf* **(a)** eviction
(b) deportation
(c) expulsion

expurger /ɛkspyrʒe/ [13] *vtr* to purge

exquis, ∼e /ɛkski, iz/ *adj* exquisite; delightful

exsangue /ɛgzɑ̃g/ *adj* bloodless

exsuder /ɛksyde/ [1] **1** *vtr* to exude
2 *vi* to ooze (**de** from)

extase /ɛkstaz/ *nf* ecstasy

extasier: s'extasier /ɛkstazje/ [2] *v refl* (+ *v être*) to go into ecstasy *or* raptures

extatique /ɛkstatik/ *adj* ecstatic

extensible /ɛkstɑ̃sibl/ *adj* **(a)** extensible
(b) extendable

extensif, -ive /ɛkstɑ̃sif, iv/ *adj*
(a) extensive
(b) extended

extension /ɛkstɑ̃sjɔ̃/ *nf* extension; **prendre de l'∼** ⟨*industry*⟩ to expand; ⟨*strike*⟩ to spread

exténuer /ɛkstenɥe/ [1] *vtr* to exhaust

extérieur, ∼e /ɛksterjœr/ **1** *adj*
(a) outside
(b) outer
(c) foreign
(d) outward
2 *nm* **(a)** outside; **à l'∼** outside, outdoors; **d'∼** outdoor
(b) exterior, appearance
(c) **en ∼** ⟨*filmed*⟩ on location

extérieurement /ɛksterjœrmã/ *adv*
(a) on the outside
(b) outwardly

extérioriser /ɛksterjɔrize/ [1] *vtr* to show

extermination /ɛkstɛrminasjɔ̃/ *nf* extermination

exterminer /ɛkstɛrmine/ [1] *vtr* to exterminate; to wipe out

externat /ɛkstɛrna/ *nm* **(a)** (Sch) day school

(b) préparer l'~ to prepare for medical school entrance exams; **faire son ~** to be a non-resident student doctor (in a hospital)

externe /ɛkstɛʀn/ **1** *adj* external; outside; exterior

2 *nmf* **(a)** (Sch) day pupil
(b) (Med) non-residential medical student (GB), extern (US)

extincteur /ɛkstɛ̃ktœʀ/ *nm* fire extinguisher

extinction /ɛkstɛ̃ksjɔ̃/ *nf* **(a)** (Med) **avoir une ~ de voix** to have lost one's voice
(b) extinction; **espèce en voie d'~** endangered species
(c) après l'~ de l'incendie after the fire was put out; **après l'~ des feux** after lights out

extirper /ɛkstiʀpe/ [1] *vtr* **(a)** to eradicate
(b) (colloq) to drag ‹person› **(de** out of, from)

extorquer /ɛkstɔʀke/ [1] *vtr* to extort

extorsion /ɛkstɔʀsjɔ̃/ *nf* extortion

extra /ɛkstʀa/ **1** *adj inv* **(a)** (colloq) great (colloq)
(b) ‹product› of superior quality
2 *nm inv* **(a)** extra; **se payer un petit ~** to have a little treat
(b) faire des ~ to do a few extra jobs
(c) extra worker

extracommunautaire, *pl* ~**s** /ɛkstʀakɔmynotɛʀ/ *adj* non-EEC

extraction /ɛkstʀaksjɔ̃/ *nf* **(a)** (of oil, gas) extraction; (of coal, diamonds) mining; (of marble, slate) quarrying
(b) (of bullet, tooth) extraction

extrader /ɛkstʀade/ [1] *vtr* to extradite

extraire /ɛkstʀɛʀ/ [58] *vtr* **(a)** to extract ‹mineral›; to mine ‹gold, coal›; to quarry ‹slate, marble›
(b) to extract; to pull out; to remove

extrait /ɛkstʀɛ/ *nm* **(a)** (from book, film) extract, excerpt; (from speech) extract
(b) essence, extract; **~ de viande** meat extract
■ **~ (d'acte) de naissance** birth certificate; **~ de casier judiciaire (de qn)** copy of (sb's) criminal record; **~ de compte** abstract of accounts

extra-long, -longue, *mpl* ~**s** /ɛkstʀalɔ̃, ɔ̃g/ *adj* ‹cigarette› king-size; ‹clothing› extra-long

extralucide /ɛkstʀalysid/ *adj* clairvoyant

extraordinaire /ɛkstʀaɔʀdinɛʀ/ *adj*
(a) extraordinary, amazing, remarkable; **c'est quand même ~!** it's incredible!
(b) ‹expenses, measures› extraordinary

extraordinairement /ɛkstʀaɔʀdinɛʀmɑ̃/ *adv* amazingly, extraordinarily

extrapoler /ɛkstʀapole/ [1] *vtr, vi* to extrapolate

extrascolaire /ɛkstʀaskɔlɛʀ/ *adj* extracurricular

extraterrestre /ɛkstʀatɛʀɛstʀ/ *nmf* extraterrestrial, alien

extra-utérin, ~**e**, *mpl* ~**s** /ɛkstʀayteʀɛ̃, in/ *adj* **grossesse** ~**e** ectopic pregnancy

extravagance /ɛkstʀavagɑ̃s/ *nf*
(a) eccentricity
(b) extravagance

extravagant, ~**e** /ɛkstʀavagɑ̃, ɑ̃t/ *adj*
(a) eccentric
(b) extravagant
(c) exorbitant

extraverti, ~**e** /ɛkstʀavɛʀti/ *adj, nm,f* extrovert

extrême /ɛkstʀɛm/ **1** *adj* **(a)** furthest; **dans l'~ nord/sud du pays** in the extreme North/South of the country
(b) extreme
(c) drastic
2 *nm* extreme; **c'est pousser la logique à l'~** that's taking logic to extremes; **à l'~ inverse** at the other extreme

extrêmement /ɛkstʀɛmmɑ̃/ *adv* extremely

Extrême-Orient /ɛkstʀɛmɔʀjɑ̃/ *pr nm* **l'~** the Far East

extrémiste /ɛkstʀemist/ *adj, nmf* extremist

extrémité /ɛkstʀemite/ *nf* **(a)** end; (of finger) tip; (of mast) top; (of town, field) edge; **aux deux ~s** at both ends
(b) extreme

exubérance /ɛgzybeʀɑ̃s/ *nf* exuberance

exubérant, ~**e** /ɛgzybeʀɑ̃, ɑ̃t/ *adj* exuberant

exultation /ɛgzyltasjɔ̃/ *nf* exultation

exulter /ɛgzylte/ [1] *vi* to be exultant (**de** with), to exult (**de faire** at doing)

exutoire /ɛgzytwaʀ/ *nm* outlet

e

Ff

f, F /ɛf/ *nm inv* (a) (letter f, F
(b) F3 2-bedroom flat (GB) *or* apartment
(c) (*written abbr* = **franc**) 50 F 50 F

fa /fa/ *nm inv* (Mus) (note) F; (in sol-fa) fa

fable /fɑbl/ *nf* (a) tale
(b) fable
(c) tall story

fabricant /fabʀikɑ̃/ *nm* manufacturer

fabrication /fabʀikasjɔ̃/ *nf* making;
manufacture; ~ **en série** mass production.
■ ~ **assistée par ordinateur, FAO** computer-
aided manufacturing, CAM

fabrique /fabʀik/ *nf* factory

fabriquer /fabʀike/ [1] *vtr* (a) to make; to
manufacture
(b) to invent ‹*alibi*›; **qu'est-ce que tu
fabriques?** (colloq) what are you up to?

fabulateur, -trice /fabylatœʀ, tʀis/ *nm,f*
compulsive liar

fabuler /fabyle/ [1] *vi* (a) to make things
up
(b) to confabulate

fabuleusement /fabyløzmɑ̃/ *adv*
fabulously

fabuleux, -euse /fabylø, øz/ *adj* ‹*beauty*›
fabulous; ‹*sum*› fantastic; ‹*creature*› mythical

fac /fak/ *nf* (colloq) (a) faculty
(b) university

façade /fasad/ *nf* (a) (of building) front;
~ **nord** north side
(b) façade

face /fas/ ① *nf* (a) face
(b) side; **le côté** ~ **d'une pièce** the heads side
of a coin
(c) **faire** ~ to face up to things; **se faire** ~ to
face each other; to be opposite one another;
faire ~ **à** to face ‹*place*›; (figurative) to face
‹*adversary, challenge*›; to cope with
‹*spending*›; to meet ‹*demand*›
② **de face** *phr* ‹*photo*› fullface; ‹*lighting*›
frontal
③ **en face** *phr* **il habite en** ~ he lives
opposite; **voir les choses en** ~ to see things
as they are; **l'équipe d'en** ~ the opposing
team
④ **en face de** *phr* (a) **en** ~ **de l'église**
opposite the church (GB), across from the
church
(b) compared with
⑤ **face à** *phr* (a) **mon lit est** ~ **à la fenêtre**
my bed faces the window
(b) ~ **à cette situation** in view of this
situation
IDIOMS se voiler la ~ not to face facts

face-à-face /fasafas/ *nm inv* (a) one-to-
one debate (GB), one-on-one debate (US)
(b) encounter

facétie /fasesi/ *nf* facetious remark;
practical joke

facétieux, -ieuse /fasesjø, øz/ *adj*
mischievous

facette /fasɛt/ *nf* facet

fâché, ~e /fɑʃe/ ① *pp* ▶ FÂCHER
② *pp adj* angry; **être** ~ **avec qn** to have
fallen out with sb

fâcher: se fâcher /fɑʃe/ [1] *v refl* (+ *v être*)
(a) to get angry
(b) to fall out

fâcheux, -euse /fɑʃø, øz/ *adj* ‹*influence*›
detrimental; ‹*delay*› unfortunate; ‹*news*›
distressing

facial, ~e, *mpl* **-iaux** /fasjal, o/ *adj*
facial

faciès /fasjɛs/ *nm inv* (a) facies
(b) face

facile /fasil/ ① *adj* (a) easy; **avoir la larme**
~ to be quick to cry
(b) easy-going
② *adv* (colloq) easily

facilement /fasilmɑ̃/ *adv* (a) easily
(b) (colloq) **j'ai mis** ~ **deux heures pour venir**
it took me a good two hours to get here

facilité /fasilite/ ① *nf* (a) (of work) easiness;
(of use, maintenance) ease
(b) fluency
② **facilités** *nf pl* (a) **donner toutes** ~**s**
pour faire to afford every opportunity to do
(b) ~**s (de paiement)** easy terms

faciliter /fasilite/ [1] *vtr* to make [sth]
easier

façon /fasɔ̃/ ① *nf* (a) way; **de toute** ~, **de
toutes les** ~**s** anyway; **de** ~ **à faire** in order
to do; in such a way as to do; **de** ~ **(à ce)
qu'elle fasse** so (that) she does; **elle nous a
joué un tour à sa** ~ she played a trick of her
own on us; ~ **de parler** so to speak
(b) **un peigne** ~ **ivoire** an imitation ivory
comb
(c) (of garment) making-up
② **façons** *nf pl* **en voilà des** ~**s!** what a
way to behave!; **sans** ~**s** ‹*meal*› informal;
‹*person*› unpretentious

façonner /fasɔne/ [1] *vtr* (a) to
manufacture; to make
(b) to hew ‹*wood*›; to fashion ‹*clay*›
(c) to shape, to mould (GB), to mold (US)

fac-similé, *pl* ~**s** /faksimile/ *nm*
facsimile

facteur, -trice /faktœʀ, tʀis/ ① *nm,f*
postman/postwoman
② *nm* factor

factice /faktis/ *adj* ‹*smile*› forced;
‹*jewellery*› imitation; ‹*flower, beauty*›
artificial

faction /faksjɔ̃/ *nf* **(a)** faction
(b) (Mil) guard duty

factrice ▸ FACTEUR 1

factuel, -elle /faktɥɛl/ *adj* factual

facturation /faktyʀasjɔ̃/ *nf* **(a)** invoicing
(b) invoicing department

facture /faktyʀ/ *nf* bill; invoice

facturer /faktyʀe/ [1] *vtr* to invoice
⟨goods⟩

facturette /faktyʀɛt/ *nf* credit card slip

facturier, -ière[1] /faktyʀje, ɛʀ/ **1** *nm,f*
invoice clerk
2 *nm* invoice book

facturière[2] /faktyʀjɛʀ/ *nf* invoicing
machine

facultatif, -ive /fakyltatif, iv/ *adj*
optional

faculté /fakylte/ *nf* **(a)** (mental) faculty;
ability
(b) option
(c) (at university) faculty
(d) (Law) right

fade /fad/ *adj* ⟨person, book⟩ dull; ⟨food,
taste⟩ tasteless; ⟨colour⟩ drab

fadeur /fadœʀ/ *nf* blandness; dreariness

fagot /fago/ *nm* bundle of firewood

fagoter /fagɔte/ [1] (colloq) **1** *vtr* to do [sb]
up (colloq)
2 se fagoter *v refl* to do oneself up
(colloq); (être) **mal fagoté** (to be) badly
dressed

faible /fɛbl/ **1** *adj* **(a)** (gen) weak; ⟨sight⟩
poor; ⟨constitution⟩ frail; **être ~ avec qn** to
be too soft on sb
(b) ⟨proportion, increase⟩ small; ⟨income,
speed⟩ low; ⟨means, impact⟩ limited; ⟨chance⟩
slim
(c) ⟨noise, glow⟩ faint; ⟨lighting⟩ dim; ⟨wind,
rain⟩ light
(d) ⟨result⟩ poor; ⟨argument⟩ feeble
(e) ⟨pupil, class⟩ slow; **~ d'esprit** feeble-
minded
(f) le mot est ~! that's putting it mildly!
2 *nmf* weak-willed person
3 *nm* weakness; **avoir un ~ pour qn** to
have a soft spot for sb

faiblement /fɛbləmɑ̃/ *adv* weakly;
⟨influence, increase⟩ slightly; ⟨lit⟩ dimly

faiblesse /fɛblɛs/ *nf* **(a)** weakness;
(of invalid) frailty
(b) inadequacy
(c) (of voice) faintness; (of lighting) dimness

faiblir /fɛbliʀ/ [3] *vi* **(a)** ⟨person, pulse⟩ to
get weaker; ⟨sight⟩ to be failing
(b) ⟨person, currency⟩ to weaken
(c) ⟨athlete⟩ to flag; ⟨plot⟩ to decline;
⟨interest⟩ to wane; ⟨speed⟩ to slacken
(d) ⟨storm⟩ to abate; ⟨noise⟩ to grow faint

faïence /fajɑ̃s/ *nf* earthenware
IDIOMS se regarder en chiens de ~ to look
daggers at each other

faille /faj/ *nf* **(a)** (in geology) fault
(b) flaw; **sans ~** unfailing
(c) rift

faillir /fajiʀ/ [28] *vi* **(a)** elle a failli le gifler
she almost *or* (very) nearly slapped him
(b) sans ~ unfailingly

faillite /fajit/ *nf* **(a)** bankruptcy
(b) failure

faim /fɛ̃/ *nf* hunger; **avoir ~** to be hungry;
mourir de ~ to die of starvation; (figurative) to
be starving; **je suis resté sur ma ~** I was
disappointed

fainéant, ~e /feneɑ̃, ɑ̃t/ *adj* lazy

fainéantise /feneɑ̃tiz/ *nf* laziness

faire /fɛʀ/ [10]

■ **Note** You will find translations for expressions
such as *faire peur, faire semblant* etc., at the
entries PEUR, SEMBLANT etc.

1 *vtr* **(a)** to make; **~ son lit/une faute** to
make one's bed/a mistake; **~ des jaloux** to
make people jealous; **deux et deux font
quatre** two and two is four
(b) to do; **~ de la recherche** to do research;
j'ai à ~ I have things to do; **que fait-il?** what
does he do?; what is he doing?; **que veux-tu
que j'y fasse?** what do you want me to do
about it?; **~ médecine/du violon** to do *or*
study medicine/to study *or* play the violin;
~ une école de commerce to go to business
school; **~ un numéro de téléphone/une lettre**
to dial a number/to write a letter; **~ du
tennis/de la couture** to play tennis/to sew;
~ un poulet to do *or* cook a chicken
(c) to do ⟨distance, journey⟩; to go round
⟨shops⟩; to go through ⟨region, museums⟩; **j'ai
fait tous les tiroirs mais je ne l'ai pas trouvé**
I went through all the drawers but I
couldn't find it
(d) (colloq) to have ⟨diabetes, complex⟩
(e) ~ le malade to pretend to be ill
(f) leur départ ne m'a rien fait their
departure didn't affect me at all; **ça y fait**
(colloq) it has an effect; **pour ce que ça fait!**
(colloq) for all the good it does!
(g) to say; **'bien sûr', fit-elle** 'of course,' she
said; **le canard fait 'coin-coin'** ducks go
'quack'
(h) ça m'a fait rire it made me laugh;
~ manger un bébé to feed a baby; **fais voir**
show me; **fais-leur prendre un rendez-vous**
get them to make an appointment;
~ traverser la rue à un vieillard to help an
old man across the road
(i) ~ réparer sa voiture to have *or* get one's
car repaired
(j) je n'en ai rien à ~ (colloq) I couldn't care
less; **ça ne fait rien!** it doesn't matter!;
qu'est-ce que ça peut bien te ~? (colloq)
what is it to you?; **il sait y ~** he's got the
knack; **il ne fait que pleuvoir** it never stops
raining; **je ne fais qu'obéir aux ordres** I'm
only obeying orders
2 *vi* **(a)** to do, to act; **fais comme tu veux** do
as you like
(b) to look; **~ jeune** to look young
(c) ça fait 15 ans que j'habite ici I've been
living here for 15 years; **ça fait 2 mètres de
long** it's 2 metres (GB) long ⋯⫶

(d) to go (to the toilet); **tu as fait?** have you been?

(e) (colloq) ~ **avec** to make do with; to put up with

3 **se faire** *v refl* (+ *v être*) **(a)** se ~ **un café** to make oneself a coffee; **se ~ comprendre** to make oneself understood

(b) to get, to become; **il se fait tard** it's getting late

(c) **s'en ~** to worry; **il ne s'en fait pas!** he's not the sort of person to worry about things!; (as criticism) he's got a nerve!

(d) **se ~ à** to get used to

(e) **ça se fait encore ici** it's still done here; **ça ne se fait pas** it's not the done thing

(f) ⟨*colour, style*⟩ to be in (fashion)

(g) **c'est ce qui se fait de mieux** it's the best there is

(h) **comment se fait-il que...?** how is it that...?, how come...?

faire-part /fɛʀpaʀ/ *nm inv* announcement

faire-valoir /fɛʀvalwaʀ/ *nm inv* **être le ~ de** ⟨*actor*⟩ to be a foil for

fais /fɛ/ ▶FAIRE

faisaient /fɛzɛ/ ▶ FAIRE

faisais /fɛzɛ/ ▶ FAIRE

faisait /fɛzɛ/ ▶ FAIRE

faisan /fəzɑ̃/ *nm* (cock) pheasant

faisane /fəzan/ *nf* (**poule**) ~ hen pheasant

faisant /fɛzɑ̃/ ▶ FAIRE

faisceau, *pl* ~**x** /fɛso/ *nm* **(a)** beam; ~ **lumineux** beam of light

(b) bundle

faisiez /fɛzje/ ▶ FAIRE

faisions /fɛzjɔ̃/ ▶ FAIRE

faisons /fɛzɔ̃/ ▶ FAIRE

fait, ~**e** /fɛ, fɛt/ **1** *pp* ▶ FAIRE

2 *pp adj* **(a)** done; **c'en est ~ de** that's the end of; **c'est bien ~ (pour toi)!** (colloq) it serves you right!

(b) ~ **de** *or* **en** made (up) of; **idée toute** ~**e** ready-made idea; **elle est bien** ~**e** she's got a great figure; **la vie est mal** ~**e** life is unfair

(c) ~ **pour qch/pour faire** meant for sth/to do

(d) ⟨*programme, device*⟩ designed

(e) (colloq) done for

(f) **un fromage bien** ~ a ripe cheese

3 *nm* **(a)** fact; **le** ~ **est là** *or* **les** ~**s sont là, il t'a trompé** the fact (of the matter) is that he cheated you; **les** ~**s et gestes de qn** sb's movements

(b) **de ce** ~ because of this *or* that; **être le** ~ **de qn** to be due to sb

(c) event

(d) **aller droit au** ~ to go straight to the point

4 **au fait** /ofɛt/ *phr* by the way

5 **de fait** *phr* **(a)** ⟨*situation*⟩ de facto

(b) ⟨*exist, result in*⟩ effectively

(c) indeed

6 **en fait** *phr* in fact, actually

7 **en fait de** *phr* as regards

■ ~ **divers** (short) news item; ~ **de société** fact of life

IDIOMS **être au** ~ **de** to be informed about; **prendre qn sur le** ~ to catch sb in the act

faîte /fɛt/ *nm* (of mountain) summit; (of house) rooftop; (of tree) top

faites /fɛt/ ▶ FAIRE

falaise /falɛz/ *nf* cliff

fallacieux, -ieuse /falasjø, øz/ *adj* ⟨*argument*⟩ fallacious; ⟨*pretext*⟩ false

falloir /falwaʀ/ [50] **1** *v impers* **(a)** **il faut qn/qch** we need sb/sth; sb/sth is needed; **il va** ~ **deux jours/du courage** it will take two days/courage; **il me/te/leur faut qch** I/you/ they need sth; **il me faut ce livre!** I've got to have that book!

(b) **il faut faire** we/you etc have (got) to do; we/you etc must do; we/you etc should do; **il ne faut pas la déranger** she mustn't be disturbed; **il fallait le faire** it had to be done; **faut le faire!** (colloq) (admiring) it takes a bit of doing!; (critical) would you believe it?; **comme il faut** ⟨*behave*⟩ properly

(c) **il faut que tu fasses** you have (got) to do, you must do; you should do

2 **s'en falloir** *v refl* (+ *v être*) **peu s'en faut** very nearly; **elle a perdu, mais il s'en est fallu de peu** she lost, but only just

IDIOMS **il faut ce qu'il faut!** there's no point in skimping!; **en moins de temps qu'il ne faut pour le dire** before you could say Jack Robinson

fallu /faly/ ▶ FALLOIR

falsification /falsifikasjɔ̃/ *nf*

(a) falsification

(b) forging

falsifier /falsifje/ [2] *vtr* **(a)** to falsify, to tamper with ⟨*document*⟩; to distort ⟨*facts*⟩

(b) to forge

famé, ~**e** /fame/ *adj* **un quartier mal** ~ a disreputable *or* seedy area

famélique /famelik/ *adj* emaciated, scrawny

fameux, -euse /famø, øz/ *adj* **(a)** much talked-about

(b) famous

(c) excellent

familial, ~**e,** *mpl* **-iaux** /familjal, o/ *adj*

(a) ⟨*meal, life, firm*⟩ family

(b) **voiture** ~**e** estate car (GB), station wagon (US)

familiariser /familjaʀize/ [1] *vtr* to familiarize

familiarité /familjaʀite/ *nf* familiarity

familier, -ière /familje, ɛʀ/ *adj* **(a)** ⟨*face, landscape*⟩ familiar

(b) ⟨*word*⟩ informal, colloquial

(c) ⟨*attitude*⟩ informal; ⟨*person, gesture*⟩ familiar

(d) **animal** ~ pet

familièrement /familjɛʀmɑ̃/ *adv*

(a) commonly

(b) informally

(c) with undue familiarity

famille /famij/ *nf* family; **c'est de** ~ it runs in the family

famine /famin/ *nf* famine

fanatique /fanatik/ 1 adj ‹believer›
fanatical; ‹admiration, love› ardent
2 nmf (a) fanatic
(b) (colloq) enthusiast, freak (colloq)

fanatisme /fanatism/ nm fanaticism

faner /fane/ [1] 1 vi (a) to wither
(b) to make hay
2 **se faner** v refl (+ v être) (a) ‹plant› to
wither, to wilt
(b) ‹beauty, colour› to fade

fanfare /fɑ̃faʀ/ nf brass band; **annoncer
qch en** ~ to trumpet sth

fanfaron, -onne /fɑ̃faʀɔ̃, ɔn/ nm,f
boaster, swaggerer; **faire le** ~ to boast

fanfaronner /fɑ̃faʀɔne/ [1] vi to boast

fanion /fanjɔ̃/ nm pennant

fantaisie /fɑ̃tezi/ nf (a) imaginativeness;
manquer de ~ ‹person› to be staid; ‹life› to
be dull
(b) whim, fancy
(c) **s'offrir une petite** ~ to spoil oneself; **un
bijou** ~ a piece of costume jewellery (GB) or
jewelry (US)

fantaisiste /fɑ̃tezist/ adj (a) ‹person›
unreliable; ‹figures› doubtful
(b) ‹idea› far-fetched

fantasme /fɑ̃tasm/ nm fantasy

fantasque /fɑ̃task/ adj ‹character›
unpredictable; ‹tale› fanciful

fantassin /fɑ̃tasɛ̃/ nm infantryman,
footsoldier

fantastique /fɑ̃tastik/ 1 adj fantastic
2 nm **le** ~ fantasy

fantoche /fɑ̃tɔʃ/ adj puppet

fantôme /fɑ̃tom/ 1 nm ghost
2 **(-)fantôme** (combining form) ‹train,
city› ghost; **image(-)**~ (on screen) ghost;
société(-)~ (Law) dummy company

FAO /ɛfao/ nf (Comput) (abbr = **fabrication
assistée par ordinateur**) CAM

faon /fɑ̃/ nm (Zool) fawn

faramineux, -euse /faʀaminø, øz/ adj
(colloq) colossal, staggering; incredible

farandole /faʀɑ̃dɔl/ nf (dance) farandole;
≈ conga

farce /faʀs/ nf (a) practical joke; **magasin
de** ~**s et attrapes** joke shop (GB), novelty
store (US)
(b) joke
(c) (in theatre) farce
(d) stuffing, forcemeat

farceur, -euse /faʀsœʀ, øz/ nm,f
practical joker

farcir /faʀsiʀ/ [3] vtr (Culin) to stuff

fard /faʀ/ nm make-up; **sans** ~ ‹beauty›
natural; ‹truth› simple
■ ~ **à joues** blusher; ~ **à paupières** eye-
shadow
IDIOMS piquer un ~ (colloq) to go as red as a
beetroot (GB), to turn as red as a beet (US)

fardeau, pl ~**x** /faʀdo/ nm burden

farder /faʀde/ [1] 1 vtr to disguise ‹truth›
2 **se farder** v refl (+ v être) ‹actor› to
make up; ‹woman› to use make-up

farfelu, ~**e** /faʀfəly/ adj (colloq) ‹idea›
harebrained (colloq); ‹person› scatter-brained
(colloq); ‹show› bizarre

farfouiller /faʀfuje/ [1] vi (colloq) to
rummage around or about (**dans** in)

farine /faʀin/ nf (a) flour
(b) baby cereal
■ ~ **d'avoine** oatmeal
IDIOMS se faire rouler dans la ~ (colloq) to be
had (colloq)

farineux, -euse /faʀinø, øz/ adj ‹food›
starchy; ‹potato› floury

farniente /faʀnjɛnte/ nm **le** ~ lazing
about, lazing around

farouche /faʀuʃ/ adj (a) ‹child, animal›
timid, shy; ‹adult› unsociable
(b) ‹look, warrior› fierce
(c) ‹enemy, hatred› bitter; ‹adversary› fierce;
‹supporter› staunch; ‹will› iron

farouchement /faʀuʃmɑ̃/ adv ‹opposed,
independent› fiercely; ‹refuse› doggedly

fascicule /fasikyl/ nm (a) booklet
(b) fascicule

fascinant, ~**e** /fasinɑ̃, ɑ̃t/ adj ‹person,
film› fascinating; ‹charm, music›
spellbinding

fascination /fasinasjɔ̃/ nf fascination

fasciner /fasine/ [1] vtr ‹speaker, music› to
hold [sb] spellbound; ‹sea, person› to
fascinate

fascisant, ~**e** /faʃizɑ̃, ɑ̃t/ adj fascistic

fascisme /faʃism/ nm fascism

fasse /fas/ ▶ FAIRE

fassent /fas/ ▶ FAIRE

fasses /fas/ ▶ FAIRE

fassiez /fasje/ ▶ FAIRE

fassions /fasjɔ̃/ ▶ FAIRE

faste /fast/ 1 adj auspicious
2 nm splendour (GB), pomp; **avec** ~ with
pomp

fastidieux, -ieuse /fastidjø, øz/ adj
tedious

fatal, ~**e** /fatal/ adj (a) inevitable
(b) fatal, disastrous
(c) ‹moment, day› fateful

fatalement /fatalmɑ̃/ adv inevitably

fatalisme /fatalism/ nm fatalism

fatalité /fatalite/ nf (a) **la** ~ fate
(b) mischance
(c) inevitability

fatidique /fatidik/ adj fateful

fatigant, ~**e** /fatigɑ̃, ɑ̃t/ adj (a) ‹sport,
journey› tiring; ‹climate› wearing
(b) ‹work› arduous
(c) ‹person› tiresome; ‹film, conversation›
tedious

fatigue /fatig/ nf (a) tiredness; **être mort
de** ~, **tomber de** ~ to be dead tired
(b) (Med) fatigue; ~ **visuelle** eyestrain

fatigué, ~**e** /fatige/ 1 pp ▶ FATIGUER
2 pp adj ‹voice› strained; ‹eyes, smile›
weary

fatiguer /fatige/ [1] **1** *vtr* **(a)** to make
[sb/sth] tired; to strain ⟨*eyes*⟩
(b) to tire [sb] out
(c) to wear [sb] out
(d) to wear out ⟨*engine*⟩
2 *vi* **(a)** (colloq) to get tired
(b) ⟨*engine, car*⟩ to be labouring (GB)
3 se fatiguer *v refl* (+ *v être*) **(a)** to get
tired
(b) to tire oneself out
(c) se ~ les yeux to strain one's eyes
(d) se ~ à faire to bother doing

fatras /fatʀa/ *nm inv* jumble

faubourg /fobuʀ/ *nm* working class area
(*on the outskirts*)

fauché, ~**e** /foʃe/ *adj* (colloq) broke (colloq),
penniless

faucher /foʃe/ [1] *vtr* **(a)** to mow; to scythe
(b) ⟨*car, bullet*⟩ to mow [sb] down
(c) (colloq) to steal

faucheuse /foʃøz/ *nf* mowing machine

faucille /fosij/ *nf* sickle

faucon /fokõ/ *nm* falcon, hawk (US)

faudra ▸ FALLOIR

faufiler /fofile/ [1] **1** *vtr* to baste
2 se faufiler *v refl* (+ *v être*) **(a)** se ~ à
l'extérieur to slip out
(b) se ~ dans ⟨*mistakes*⟩ to creep into ⟨*text*⟩
(c) ⟨*route*⟩ to snake in and out

faune /fon/ *nf* **(a)** wildlife, fauna; la ~
marine marine life
(b) (derogatory) set, crowd

faussaire /foseʀ/ *nmf* forger

fausse ▸ FAUX¹ 1

faussement /fosmã/ *adv* **(a)** falsely,
wrongly
(b) deceptively

fausser /fose/ [1] *vtr* to distort ⟨*result,
mechanism*⟩; to damage ⟨*lock*⟩; to buckle
⟨*blade*⟩
IDIOMS ~ compagnie à qn to give sb the slip

faut ▸ FALLOIR

faute /fot/ *nf* **(a)** mistake, error; il a fait un
(parcours) sans ~ he's never put a foot
wrong
(b) (gen) misdemeanour (GB); (Law) civil
wrong; être en ~ to be at fault; prendre qn
en ~ to catch sb out
(c) fault; c'est (de) ma ~ it's my fault; par la
~ de qn because of sb; rejeter la ~ sur qn to
lay the blame on sb
(d) ~ de temps through lack of time; ~ de
mieux for want of anything better; ~ de quoi
otherwise, failing which; sans ~ without fail
(e) (Sport) foul; (in tennis) fault

fauteuil /fotœj/ *nm* **(a)** chair, armchair
(b) (in theatre) seat

fauteur /fotœʀ/ *nm* ~ de troubles
troublemaker; ~ de guerre warmonger

fautif, -ive /fotif, iv/ **1** *adj* **(a)** at fault
(b) ⟨*memory*⟩ faulty; ⟨*reference*⟩ inaccurate
2 *nm,f* culprit

fauve /fov/ **1** *adj* tawny
2 *nm* **(a)** wild animal

(b) big cat
(c) (colour) fawn

fauvette /fovɛt/ *nf* warbler

faux¹, fausse /fo, fos/ **1** *adj* **(a)** ⟨*result,
number, idea*⟩ wrong; ⟨*impression, promise,
accusation*⟩ false
(b) ⟨*beard, tooth, eyelashes*⟩ false
(c) ⟨*wood, marble, diamonds*⟩ imitation, fake;
⟨*door, drawer*⟩ false
(d) ⟨*passport, money*⟩ forged
(e) ⟨*policeman, bishop*⟩ bogus; ⟨*candour,
humility*⟩ feigned
(f) ⟨*hope*⟩ false; ⟨*fear*⟩ groundless
(g) deceitful
2 *adv* ⟨*play, sing*⟩ out of tune
3 *nm inv* **(a)** le ~ falsehood
(b) fake; forgery
■ fausse couche (Med) miscarriage; fausse
facture bogus invoice; fausse fenêtre blind
window; fausse joie ill-founded joy; faire une
fausse joie à qn to raise sb's hopes in vain;
fausse monnaie forged *or* counterfeit
currency; fausse note jarring note; fausse
piste wrong track; ~ ami *foreign word which
looks deceptively like a word in one's own
language*; ~ en écriture(s) falsification of
accounts; ~ frais extras, incidental expenses;
~ jeton (colloq) two-faced person; ~ nom
assumed name; ~ pas slip; mistake; faux
pas; ~ pli crease; ~ témoignage perjury

faux² /fo/ *nf inv* scythe

faux-filet, *pl* ~**s** /fofilɛ/ *nm* sirloin

faux-monnayeur, *pl* ~**s** /fomɔnɛjœʀ/
nm forger, counterfeiter

faux-semblant, *pl* ~**s** /fosãblã/ *nm* les
~s pretence (GB)

faveur /favœʀ/ **1** *nf* favour (GB); régime *or*
traitement de ~ preferential treatment; des
mesures en ~ des handicapés measures to
help the disabled; intervenir en ~ de qn to
intervene on sb's behalf
2 à la faveur de *phr* thanks to; à la ~ de
la nuit under cover of darkness

favorable /favɔʀabl/ *adj* favourable (GB);
être ~ à qch to be in favour (GB) of sth

favori, -ite /favɔʀi, it/ **1** *adj, nm,f*
favourite (GB)
2 favoris *nm pl* sideburns

favoriser /favɔʀize/ [1] *vtr* **(a)** to favour
(GB); les milieux favorisés the privileged
classes
(b) to encourage, to promote

favorite ▸ FAVORI 1

favoritisme /favɔʀitism/ *nm* favouritism
(GB)

fax /faks/ *nm inv* **(a)** fax
(b) fax machine

fayot¹ /fajo/ *nm* (colloq) bean

fayot², -otte /fajo, ɔt/ *nm,f* (colloq) creep
(colloq), crawler (colloq)

FB (*written abbr* = **franc belge**) BFr

fébrile /febril/ *adj* **(a)** ⟨*emotion, gesture*⟩
feverish; ⟨*person*⟩ nervous
(b) (Med) feverish

fébrilité /febʀilite/ *nf* (a) agitation; **avec ~** agitatedly
(b) nervousness

fécal, ~e, *mpl* **-aux** /fekal, o/ *adj* faecal

fécond, ~e /fekɔ̃, ɔ̃d/ *adj* (a) fertile
(b) fruitful

fécondation /fekɔ̃dasjɔ̃/ *nf* (of female) impregnation; (of plant) pollination; (of egg) fertilization

féconder /fekɔ̃de/ [1] *vtr* to impregnate ⟨*female*⟩; to inseminate ⟨*animal*⟩; to pollinate ⟨*plant*⟩; to fertilize ⟨*egg, ovum*⟩

fécondité /fekɔ̃dite/ *nf* (a) fertility
(b) (of author) productivity

fécule /fekyl/ *nf* starch

féculent /fekylɑ̃/ *nm* starch; starchy food

fédéral, ~e, *mpl* **-aux** /fedeʀal, o/ *adj* federal

fédéralisme /fedeʀalism/ *nm* federalism

fédératif, -ive /fedeʀatif, iv/ *adj* federal

fédération /fedeʀasjɔ̃/ *nf* federation

fée /fe/ *nf* fairy; **~ du logis** perfect housewife
IDIOMS **avoir des doigts de ~** to have nimble fingers

féerie /fe(e)ʀi/ *nf* (a) **c'est une vraie ~** it's magical
(b) extravaganza

féerique /fe(e)ʀik/ *adj* ⟨*beauty*⟩ enchanting; ⟨*landscape, moment*⟩ enchanted

feignant, ~e /feɲɑ̃, ɑ̃t/ = FAINÉANT

feindre /fɛ̃dʀ/ [55] *vtr* to feign; **~ de faire/d'être** to pretend to do/to be

feinte /fɛ̃t/ *nf* (a) feint; **faire une ~** (in football, rugby) to dummy (GB), to fake (US)
(b) (colloq) trick, ruse

fêlé, ~e /fɛle/ *adj* (colloq) cracked (colloq)

fêler /fɛle/ [1] *vtr*, **se fêler** *v refl* (+ *v être*) to crack

félicitations /felisitasjɔ̃/ *nf pl* congratulations

féliciter /felisite/ [1] **1** *vtr* to congratulate
2 se féliciter *v refl* (+ *v être*) **se ~ de qch** to be very pleased about sth

félin, ~e /felɛ̃, in/ **1** *adj* (a) feline; **exposition ~e** cat show
(b) ⟨*grace*⟩ feline; ⟨*eyes*⟩ catlike
2 *nm* feline; **les ~s** felines, the cat family

fêlure /fɛlyʀ/ *nf* crack

femelle /fəmɛl/ **1** *adj* female; **éléphant ~** cow elephant; **moineau ~** hen sparrow
2 *nf* female; (in pair) mate

féminin, ~e /feminɛ̃, in/ **1** *adj* ⟨*sex, occupation*⟩ female; ⟨*magazine, record*⟩ women's; ⟨*team, club*⟩ ladies'; ⟨*appearance*⟩ feminine
2 *nm* feminine; **au ~** in the feminine

féminiser: se féminiser /feminize/ [1] *v refl* (+ *v être*) ⟨*profession*⟩ to become more open to women; to become predominantly female

féministe /feminist/ *adj, nmf* feminist

féminité /feminite/ *nf* femininity

femme /fam/ *nf* (a) woman
(b) wife
■ **~ d'affaires** businesswoman; **~ de chambre** chambermaid; **~ au foyer** housewife; **~ d'intérieur** homemaker; **~ de service** cleaner, cleaning lady; **~ de tête** assertive woman; ▶ BON, JEUNE
IDIOMS **souvent ~ varie** woman is fickle

fémur /femyʀ/ *nm* thighbone; **se casser le col du ~** to break one's hip

FEN /fɛn/ *nf* (*abbr* = **Fédération de l'éducation nationale**) FEN (*French teachers' union*)

fendiller: se fendiller /fɑ̃dije/ [1] *v refl* (+ *v être*) ⟨*lips*⟩ to chap; ⟨*earth*⟩ to craze over; ⟨*wood*⟩ to crack

fendre /fɑ̃dʀ/ [6] **1** *vtr* (a) to chop ⟨*wood*⟩; to slit ⟨*material*⟩
(b) to crack ⟨*wall, stone*⟩; to split ⟨*lip*⟩
(c) **~ le cœur à qn** to break sb's heart
(d) **~ l'air** to slice through the air; **~ la foule** to push one's way through the crowd
2 se fendre *v refl* (+ *v être*) (a) to crack
(b) (colloq) to cough up (colloq) ⟨*money*⟩; **tu ne t'es pas fendu!** that didn't break the bank!
IDIOMS **se ~ la pêche** (colloq) to split one's sides (colloq); **avoir la bouche fendue jusqu'aux oreilles** to be grinning from ear to ear

fenêtre /fənɛtʀ/ *nf* window
■ **~ à guillotine** sash window
IDIOMS **jeter l'argent par les ~s** to throw money away

fenouil /fənuj/ *nm* fennel

fente /fɑ̃t/ *nf* (a) slit; (for coin, card) slot; (of jacket) vent
(b) crack; (in wood) split; (in rock) crevice

féodal, ~e, *mpl* **-aux** /feɔdal, o/ *adj* feudal

fer /fɛʀ/ *nm* (a) iron; **de ~** ⟨*discipline, fist, will*⟩ iron
(b) (on shoe) steel tip
(c) branding iron
(d) **croiser le ~ avec** to cross swords with
■ **~ à cheval** horseshoe; **~ forgé** wrought iron; **~ à repasser** iron
IDIOMS **croire dur comme ~** to believe wholeheartedly; **tomber les quatre ~s en l'air** (colloq) to fall flat on one's back

fera /fəʀa/ ▶ FAIRE

ferai /fəʀɛ/ ▶ FAIRE

feraient /fəʀɛ/ ▶ FAIRE

ferais /fəʀɛ/ ▶ FAIRE

ferait /fəʀɛ/ ▶ FAIRE

feras /fəʀa/ ▶ FAIRE

fer-blanc, *pl* **fers-blancs** /fɛʀblɑ̃/ *nm* tinplate

ferez /fəʀe/ ▶ FAIRE

férié, ~e /feʀje/ *adj* **jour ~** public holiday (GB), holiday (US)

feriez /fəʀje/ ▶ FAIRE

ferions /fəʀjɔ̃/ ▶ FAIRE

ferme¹ /fɛʀm/ **1** *adj* (a) firm   ⋯⋗

(b) (Law) **peine de prison** ~ custodial sentence

2 *adv* ⟨*argue, campaign*⟩ vigorously; ⟨*believe*⟩ firmly; **tenir** ~ to stand one's ground

IDIOMS **attendre de pied** ~ to be ready and waiting

ferme² /fɛʀm/ *nf* farm, farmhouse

fermement /fɛʀməmɑ̃/ *adv* firmly

ferment /fɛʀmɑ̃/ *nm* ferment

fermenter /fɛʀmɑ̃te/ [1] *vi* to ferment

fermer /fɛʀme/ [1] **1** *vtr* **(a)** to close, to shut ⟨*door, book, eyes*⟩; to clench ⟨*fist*⟩; to draw ⟨*curtain*⟩; to turn off ⟨*tap, gas, radio*⟩; to do up ⟨*jacket*⟩; ~ **à clé** to lock (up)
(b) to close ⟨*shop, airport, road*⟩; (definitively) to close [sth] down
2 *vi* to close (down)
3 **se fermer** *v refl* (+ *v être*) **(a)** ⟨*door*⟩ to shut; ⟨*flower*⟩ to close up; ⟨*coat, bracelet*⟩ to fasten
(b) ⟨*person*⟩ to clam up; ⟨*face*⟩ to harden
IDIOMS ~ **les yeux sur** to turn a blind eye to

fermeté /fɛʀməte/ *nf* firmness

fermette /fɛʀmɛt/ *nf* farmhouse-style cottage

fermeture /fɛʀmətyʀ/ *nf* **(a)** (of business, account) closing; (definitive) closure, closing down
(b) (on handbag) clasp; (on garment) fastening
■ ~ **éclair®**, ~ **à glissière** zip (GB), zipper (US)

fermier, -ière /fɛʀmje, ɛʀ/ **1** *adj* free-range
2 *nm,f* farmer

fermoir /fɛʀmwaʀ/ *nm* (on necklace, bag) clasp

féroce /feʀɔs/ *adj* **(a)** fierce; ferocious
(b) ⟨*appetite*⟩ voracious

férocité /feʀɔsite/ *nf* **(a)** (of animal) ferociousness
(b) (of remark) savagery
(c) (of person) fierceness

ferons /fəʀɔ̃/ ▶ FAIRE

feront /fəʀɔ̃/ ▶ FAIRE

ferraille /feʀɑj/ *nf* **(a)** scrap metal
(b) scrapheap
(c) (colloq) small change

ferrailleur /feʀɑjœʀ/ *nm* scrap (metal) dealer

ferronnerie /feʀɔnʀi/ *nf* **(a)** ironworks
(b) wrought iron work
(c) iron work

ferroviaire /feʀɔvjɛʀ/ *adj* ⟨*transport, collision*⟩ rail; ⟨*station, tunnel*⟩ railway (GB), railroad (US)

fertile /fɛʀtil/ *adj* fertile; ⟨*year*⟩ productive

fertilisant /fɛʀtilizɑ̃/ *nm* fertilizer

fertilité /fɛʀtilite/ *nf* fertility

fervent, ~e /fɛʀvɑ̃, ɑ̃t/ *adj* ⟨*believer*⟩ fervent; ⟨*admirer*⟩ ardent

ferveur /fɛʀvœʀ/ *nf* (of prayer) fervour (GB); (of love) ardour (GB)

fesse /fɛs/ *nf* buttock

IDIOMS **coûter la peau des** ~**s** (colloq) to cost an arm and a leg (colloq)

fessée /fese/ *nf* smack on the bottom, spanking

festin /fɛstɛ̃/ *nm* feast

festival /fɛstival/ *nm* festival

festivités /fɛstivite/ *nf pl* festivities

festoyer /fɛstwaje/ [23] *vi* to feast

fêtard, ~e /fɛtaʀ, aʀd/ *nm,f* (colloq) reveller

fête /fɛt/ *nf* **(a)** public holiday (GB), holiday (US)
(b) (saint's) name-day; **ça va être ma** ~**!** (colloq) I'm going to cop it! (colloq)
(c) festival
(d) (day of) celebration
(e) party; **faire la** ~ to live it up (colloq)
(f) fête, fair, celebrations
■ ~ **foraine** funfair; ~ **du travail** May Day, Labour Day (GB)
IDIOMS **faire sa** ~ **à qn** (colloq) to give sb a working over (colloq)

fêter /fete/ [1] *vtr* to celebrate ⟨*event*⟩

fétiche /fetiʃ/ **1** *adj* lucky
2 *nm* **(a)** mascot
(b) fetish

fétide /fetid/ *adj* foul; foul-smelling

feu¹, ~e /fø/ *adj* late; ~ **la reine, la** ~**e reine** the late queen

feu², pl ~x /fø/ *nm* **(a)** fire; ▶ HUILE
(b) light; **sous le** ~ **des projecteurs** under the glare of the spotlights; (figurative) in the spotlight
(c) traffic light; **j'ai le** ~ **vert de mon patron** my boss has given me the go-ahead
(d) (on cooker) ring (GB), burner (US); **faire cuire à petit** ~ cook over a gentle heat
(e) **avez-vous du** ~**?** have you got a light?
(f) passion; **dans le** ~ **de la discussion** in the heat of the discussion
(g) ~**!** (Mil) fire!; **faire** ~ to fire; **coup de** ~ shot
(h) (Mil) action
■ ~ **d'artifice** fireworks display; firework; ~ **de cheminée** chimney fire; open fire; ~ **follet** will-o'-the-wisp; ~ **de joie** bonfire; ~ **de signalisation**, ~ **tricolore** traffic light; ~**x de croisement** dipped (GB) or dimmed (US) headlights; ~**x de détresse** warning lights; ~**x de route** headlights
IDIOMS **il n'y a pas le** ~**!** (colloq) there's no rush!; **ne pas faire long** ~ (colloq) not to last long; **il n'y a vu que du** ~ (colloq) he fell for it; **mourir à petit** ~ to die a slow death

feuillage /fœjaʒ/ *nm* foliage, leaves

feuille /fœj/ *nf* **(a)** (Bot) leaf
(b) (of paper, metal) sheet
■ ~ **de chou** (colloq) rag (colloq), newspaper; ~ **d'impôts** tax return; ~ **de maladie** *a form for reclaiming medical expenses from the social security office*; ~ **de paie** payslip (GB), pay stub (US)

feuillet /fœjɛ/ *nm* **(a)** (in book) leaf
(b) page

feuilleté, ~e /fœjte/ *adj* **pâte ~e** puff pastry

feuilleter /fœjte/ [20] *vtr* to leaf through [sth]

feuilleton /fœjtɔ̃/ *nm* serial; soap (opera)

feutre /føtʀ/ *nm* **(a)** felt
(b) felt-tip (pen)

feutré, ~e /føtʀe/ *adj* ‹*atmosphere*› hushed; ‹*sound*› muffled

fève /fɛv/ *nf* **(a)** broad bean
(b) lucky charm (*hidden in Twelfth Night cake*)

février /fevʀije/ *nm* February

FF (*written abbr* = **franc français**) FFr

fiabilité /fjabilite/ *nf* reliability

fiable /fjabl/ *adj* reliable

fiançailles /fjɑ̃saj/ *nf pl* engagement

fiancé, ~e /fjɑ̃se/ *nm,f* fiancé/fiancée

fiancer: se fiancer /fjɑ̃se/ [12] *v refl* (+ *v être*) to get engaged

fibre /fibʀ/ *nf* fibre (GB)

ficeler /fisle/ [19] *vtr* to tie up ‹*parcel*›

ficelle /fisɛl/ *nf* **(a)** string
(b) trick; **la ~ est un peu grosse** it's a bit obvious
(c) thin baguette
IDIOMS tirer sur la ~ to push one's luck

fiche /fiʃ/ *nf* **(a)** index card; slip
(b) form; **~ d'inscription** enrolment (GB) form
(c) plug; **prise à trois ~s** three-pin plug
■ **~ d'état civil** *record of personal details for administrative purposes*; **~ de paie** payslip (GB), pay stub (US)

ficher /fiʃe/ [1] **1** *vtr* **(a)** to put [sth] on a file; to open a file on [sb]; **être fiché (par la police)** to be on police files
(b) to drive ‹*stake, nail*›
(c) (colloq) to do; **qu'est-ce que tu fiches?** what the heck are you doing? (colloq); **n'en avoir rien à ~** not to give a damn (colloq)
(d) (colloq) **~ un coup à qn** (figurative) to be a real blow to sb; **~ la paix à qn** to leave sb alone
(e) (colloq) **~ qch quelque part** to chuck sth somewhere (colloq); **~ qn dehors** to kick sb out (colloq)
2 se ficher *v refl* (+ *v être*) **(a)** ‹*arrow, knife*› to stick
(b) (colloq) **se ~ de qn** to make fun of sb; **se ~ du monde** to have a hell of a nerve (colloq)
(c) (colloq) **se ~ de ce que qn fait** not to give a damn (about) what sb does (colloq)

fichier /fiʃje/ *nm* file; (in library) index

fichu (colloq) /fiʃy/ **1** *pp* ▶ FICHER 1 C, D, E, 2
2 *adj* **(a)** ‹*weather, job*› rotten (colloq); ‹*rain*› dreadful; ‹*car, TV*› damned (colloq)
(b) ‹*person, car*› done for (colloq); **s'il pleut c'est ~** if it rains that's the end of that
(c) **être bien ~** to be well designed; ‹*book*› to be well laid out; **je suis mal ~** I feel lousy (colloq)

(d) **être ~ de faire** to be quite capable of doing

fictif, -ive /fiktif, iv/ *adj* imaginary; false

fiction /fiksjɔ̃/ *nf* **(a)** fiction
(b) (on TV) drama

fidèle /fidɛl/ **1** *adj* **(a)** ‹*person, dog*› faithful; **être ~ au poste** to be always there
(b) loyal
(c) true (à to)
(d) ‹*translation*› faithful
2 *nmf* **(a)** loyal supporter
(b) **les ~s** the faithful

fidèlement /fidɛlmɑ̃/ *adv* **(a)** faithfully
(b) loyally

fidéliser /fidelize/ [1] *vtr* to secure the loyalty of ‹*clients*›

fidélité /fidelite/ *nf* **(a)** fidelity
(b) loyalty
(c) (of translation) accuracy

fiduciaire /fidysjɛʀ/ *adj* fiduciary; **société ~** trust company

fief /fjɛf/ *nm* **(a)** fief
(b) (figurative) territory; (of party) stronghold

fieffé, ~e /fjefe/ *adj* **~ menteur** incorrigible liar

fier¹, fière /fjɛʀ/ *adj* proud; **avoir fière allure** to cut a fine figure

fier²: se fier /fje/ [2] *v refl* (+ *v être*) **(a)** se **~ à** to trust ‹*person, promise*›
(b) **se ~ à** to rely on ‹*person, instrument*›; to trust to ‹*chance*›

fierté /fjɛʀte/ *nf* pride

fièvre /fjɛvʀ/ *nf* **(a)** (high) temperature; **avoir de la ~** to have a (high) temperature
(b) frenzy
(c) fervour (GB); **~ électorale** election fever
■ **~ de cheval** (colloq) raging fever

fiévreusement /fjevʀøzmɑ̃/ *adv* frantically; feverishly

fiévreux, -euse /fjevʀø, øz/ *adj* **(a)** (Med) feverish
(b) (agitated) frantic
(c) (passionate) feverish

figer /fiʒe/ [13] **1** *vtr* to congeal ‹*grease*›; to thicken ‹*sauce*›; to clot ‹*blood*›
2 se figer *v refl* (+ *v être*) **(a)** ‹*smile, person*› to freeze
(b) ‹*grease*› to congeal; ‹*blood*› to clot

fignoler /fiɲole/ [1] **1** *vtr* **(a)** to put the finishing touches to
(b) to take great pains over
2 *vi* to fiddle about

figue /fig/ *nf* fig; **~ de Barbarie** prickly pear

figuier /figje/ *nm* fig tree

figurant, ~e /figyʀɑ̃, ɑ̃t/ *nm,f* (in films) extra; (in theatre) bit player

figuratif, -ive /figyʀatif, iv/ *adj* figurative, representational; **artiste non ~** abstract artist

figuration /figyʀasjɔ̃/ *nf* **faire de la ~** (in films) to be an extra; (figurative) to have a token role

figure /figyʀ/ *nf* **(a)** face   ⋯▸

(b) faire ~ d'amateur to look like an amateur; **reprendre ~ humaine** to look half-human again

(c) (in history, politics) figure

(d) (in drawing) figure

IDIOMS prendre ~ to take shape; **faire bonne ~** to keep an air of composure; to make the right impression; to do well

figurer /figyʀe/ [1] **1** *vtr* to represent **2** *vi* ⟨*name, object*⟩ to appear **3 se figurer** *v refl* (+ *v être*) to imagine

figurine /figyʀin/ *nf* figurine

fil /fil/ **1** *nm* **(a)** thread; ▶ COUDRE

(b) yarn

(c) string; **~ de fer** wire

(d) wire; (on appliance) flex (GB), cord (US); (on phone) lead; **coup de ~** (colloq) (phone) call; **au bout du ~** (colloq) on the phone

(e) (of conversation, text) thread; **perdre le ~ des événements** to lose track of events

(f) (of razor) edge

2 au fil de *phr* in the course of; **au ~ des ans** over the years; **aller au ~ de l'eau** to go with the flow

■ **~ conducteur** (of heat) conductor; (of novel) thread; (of inquiry) lead; **~ directeur** guiding principle

IDIOMS ne tenir qu'à un ~ to hang by a thread

filament /filamɑ̃/ *nm* filament

filature /filatyʀ/ *nf* **(a)** textile mill

(b) spinning

(c) prendre qn en ~ to tail sb (colloq)

file /fil/ *nf* **(a) ~ (d'attente)** queue (GB), line (US)

(b) line; **~ indienne** single file

(c) lane; **se garer en double ~** to double-park

filer /file/ [1] **1** *vtr* **(a)** to spin ⟨*wool, cotton*⟩

(b) to spin ⟨*web, cocoon*⟩

(c) to ladder (GB), to get a run in ⟨*tights*⟩

(d) to tail [sb] (colloq)

(e) (colloq) to give [sth] (**à qn** to sb)

2 *vi* (colloq) **(a)** to go off, to leave

(b) to rush

(c) ⟨*time*⟩ to fly by; ⟨*prisoner*⟩ to get away; **~ entre les mains** to slip through one's fingers

filet /file/ *nm* **(a)** net; **~ à provisions** string bag; **coup de ~** (police) raid

(b) fillet

(c) (of water) trickle; (of smoke) wisp; **~ de citron** dash of lemon juice

filial, ~e¹, *mpl* **-iaux** /filjal, o/ *adj* filial

filiale² /filjal/ *nf* subsidiary

filiation /filjasjɔ̃/ *nf* filiation

filière /filjɛʀ/ *nf* **(a)** (Sch) course of study

(b) (Econ) field

(c) suivre la ~ habituelle to climb up the usual career ladder

(d) official channels

(e) ~ (clandestine) de la drogue drugs ring

filiforme /filifɔʀm/ *adj* spindly; threadlike

filigrane /filigʀan/ *nm* filigree

filin /filɛ̃/ *nm* rope

fille /fij/ *nf* **(a)** daughter

(b) girl; **~ mère** unmarried mother

fillette /fijɛt/ *nf* **(a)** little girl

(b) (colloq) half bottle

filleul /fijœl/ *nm* godson, godchild

filleule /fijœl/ *nf* goddaughter, godchild

film /film/ *nm* **(a)** film, movie (US)

(b) (thin) film

■ **~ d'animation** cartoon

filmer /filme/ [1] *vtr* to film

filmique /filmik/ *adj* film; cinematic

filon /filɔ̃/ *nm* vein, seam

filou /filu/ *nm* crook; cheat; rascal

fils /fis/ *nm inv* son; **Dupont ~** Dupont Junior

filtre /filtʀ/ *nm* filter

filtrer /filtʀe/ [1] **1** *vtr* **(a)** to filter

(b) to screen ⟨*visitors, calls*⟩

2 *vi* ⟨*information*⟩ to leak out; ⟨*idea, liquid*⟩ to filter through

fîmes /fim/ ▶ FAIRE

fin¹, fine /fɛ̃, fin/ **1** *adj* **(a)** ⟨*rain, sand, brush*⟩ fine; ⟨*slice, layer*⟩ thin

(b) ⟨*ankle, waist*⟩ slender; ⟨*features*⟩ fine; ⟨*dish*⟩ delicate

(c) ⟨*person*⟩ perceptive; ⟨*taste, humour*⟩ subtle; **vraiment c'est ~!** that's really clever!; **jouer au plus ~ avec qn** to try to outsmart sb; **avoir l'air ~** (colloq) to look a fool

(d) avoir l'ouïe ~e to have a keen sense of hearing

(e) au ~ fond de in the remotest part of ⟨*country*⟩; **le ~ mot de l'histoire** the truth of the matter

2 *adv* **(a) être ~ prêt** to be all set

(b) ⟨*write, grind*⟩ finely; ⟨*slice*⟩ thinly

3 *nm* **le ~ du ~** the ultimate

■ **~e mouche** sly customer (colloq); **~es herbes** mixed herbs

fin² /fɛ̃/ *nf* **(a)** end, ending; **à la ~ des années 70** in the late '70s; **tu vas te taire à la ~!** (colloq) for God's sake, be quiet!; **chômeur en ~ de droits** unemployed person no longer entitled to benefit

(b) end, death

(c) end, aim, purpose

■ **~ de série** oddment

final, ~e¹, *mpl* **-aux** /final, o/ *adj* final

finale² /final/ *nf* (Sport) final

finalement /finalmɑ̃/ *adv* **(a)** in the end, finally

(b) in fact, actually

finaliser /finalize/ [1] *vtr* to finalize; to complete

finalité /finalite/ *nf* **(a)** purpose, aim

(b) finality

finance /finɑ̃s/ **1** *nf* **(a) la ~** finance

(b) financiers

2 finances *nf pl* **les ~s** finances; **moyennant ~s** for a consideration

financement /finɑ̃smɑ̃/ *nm* financing

financer /finɑ̃se/ [12] *vtr* to finance

financier, -ière /finɑ̃sje, ɛʀ/ **1** *adj* financial

2 *nm* **(a)** financier
(b) small cake

finaud, -e /fino, od/ *nm,f* (Comput) hacker

finesse /finɛs/ *nf* **(a)** (of thread, writing) fineness; (of layer, paper) thinness
(b) (of dish) delicacy; (of face) fineness; (of waist) slenderness
(c) (of remark, person) perceptiveness; (of actor) sensitivity
(d) (of senses) keenness
(e) les ~s d'une langue the subtleties of a language

fini, ~e /fini/ **1** *pp* ▶ FINIR
2 *pp adj* être ~ to be over, to be finished
3 *nm* finish

finir /finiʀ/ [3] **1** *vtr* **(a)** to finish (off), to complete; to end ⟨day⟩
(b) to use up ⟨supplies⟩
2 *vi* to finish, to end; ⟨contract, lease⟩ to run out; le film finit bien the film has a happy ending; ça va mal ~! it'll end in tears!; ~ par faire to end up doing; ils finiront bien par céder they're bound to give in in the end; en ~ avec qn/qch to have done with sb/sth; finissons-en! let's get it over with!

finissant /finisɑ̃/ ▶ FINIR

finition /finisjɔ̃/ *nf* **(a)** finishing
(b) finish

finlandais, ~e /fɛ̃lɑ̃dɛ, ɛz/ *adj* Finnish
Finlandais, ~e /fɛ̃lɑ̃dɛ, ɛz/ *nm,f* Finn
Finlande /fɛ̃lɑ̃d/ *pr nf* Finland

finnois, ~e /finwa, az/ **1** *adj* Finnish
2 *nm* (language) Finnish

fioriture /fjɔʀityʀ/ *nf* embellishment

fioul /fjul/ *nm* fuel oil

firent /fiʀ/ ▶ FAIRE

firme /fiʀm/ *nf* firm

fis /fi/ ▶ FAIRE

fisc /fisk/ *nm* tax office

fiscal, ~e, *mpl* **-aux** /fiskal, o/ *adj* fiscal, tax

fiscaliser /fiskalize/ [1] *vtr* **(a)** to tax
(b) to fund [sth] by taxation

fiscalité /fiskalite/ *nf* **(a)** taxation
(b) tax system

fisse /fis/ ▶ FAIRE
fissent /fis/ ▶ FAIRE
fisses /fis/ ▶ FAIRE

fissible /fisibl/ *adj* fissionable, fissile
fissiez /fisje/ ▶ FAIRE

fission /fisjɔ̃/ *nf* fission; ~ nucléaire nuclear fission

fissionner /fisjɔne/ [1] *vtr, vi* to split

fissions /fisjɔ̃/ ▶ FAIRE

fissure /fisyʀ/ *nf* **(a)** crack
(b) (Anat) fissure

fissurer /fisyʀe/ [1] *vtr* to crack, to fissure

fit /fi/ ▶ FAIRE

fites /fit/ ▶ FAIRE

fixation /fiksasjɔ̃/ *nf* **(a)** fixing; fastening
(b) (on ski) binding
(c) fixation

fixe /fiks/ *adj* **(a)** fixed
(b) permanent

fixé, ~e /fikse/ **1** *pp* ▶ FIXER
2 *pp adj* tu es ~ maintenant! you've got the picture now! (colloq)
(b) nous ne sommes pas encore très ~s we haven't really decided yet

fixer /fikse/ [1] **1** *vtr* **(a)** to fix (à to)
(b) to set ⟨date, price⟩; to establish ⟨boundaries⟩; ~ son choix sur to decide on
(c) to fix ⟨colour, emulsion⟩
(d) to focus ⟨attention⟩; to stare at ⟨person⟩
2 se fixer *v refl* (+ *v être*) **(a)** ⟨part⟩ to be attached
(b) to set oneself ⟨goal, limit⟩

flacon /flakɔ̃/ *nm* **(a)** (small) bottle
(b) decanter
(c) (in laboratory) flask

flagada /flagada/ *adj inv* (colloq) weary

flageller /flaʒele/ [1] *vtr* to flog; (as religious punishment) to flagellate

flageoler /flaʒole/ [1] *vi* avoir les jambes qui flageolent to feel wobbly

flageolet /flaʒolɛ/ *nm* flageolet

flagrant, ~e /flagʀɑ̃, ɑ̃t/ *adj* ⟨difference⟩ obvious; ⟨injustice⟩ flagrant; ⟨lie⟩ blatant; prendre qn en ~ délit to catch sb red-handed

flair /flɛʀ/ *nm* **(a)** sense of smell, nose
(b) intuition

flairer /fleʀe/ [1] *vtr* **(a)** to sniff ⟨object⟩; le chien a flairé une piste the dog has picked up a scent
(b) ⟨animal⟩ to scent; ⟨person⟩ to smell
(c) to sense ⟨danger⟩

flamand, ~e /flamɑ̃, ɑ̃d/ **1** *adj* Flemish
2 *nm* (language) Flemish

flamant /flamɑ̃/ *nm* flamingo

flambant /flɑ̃bɑ̃/ *adv* ~ neuf brand new

flambeau, *pl* **~x** /flɑ̃bo/ *nm* torch

flambée /flɑ̃be/ *nf* **(a)** fire; faire une ~ to light a fire
(b) (of hatred) flare-up; (of prices) explosion

flamber /flɑ̃be/ [1] **1** *vtr* to flambé ⟨pancake⟩
2 *vi* to burn

flamboyant, ~e /flɑ̃bwajɑ̃, ɑ̃t/ *adj* ⟨fire, light⟩ blazing; ⟨colour⟩ flaming

flamme /flɑm/ *nf* **(a)** flame; en ~s on fire
(b) love, passion
IDIOMS descendre en ~s to shoot down; être tout feu tout ~ to be wildly enthusiastic

flan /flɑ̃/ *nm* (Culin) custard tart (GB) *or* flan (US)
IDIOMS en rester comme deux ronds de ~ (colloq) to be dumbfounded

flanc /flɑ̃/ *nm* (of person, mountain) side; (of animal) flank; être sur le ~ (colloq) to be exhausted

flancher /flɑ̃ʃe/ [1] *vi* (colloq) **(a)** to lose one's nerve
(b) to crack up
(c) ⟨heart, engine⟩ to give out

flanelle /flanɛl/ *nf* flannel

flâner /flɑne/ [1] *vi* to stroll; to loaf around (colloq)

flâneur, -euse /flɑnœʀ, øz/ *nm,f*
(a) stroller
(b) loafer (colloq), idler

flanquer /flɑ̃ke/ [1] **1** *vtr* (a) to flank; **il est toujours flanqué de son adjoint** his assistant never leaves his side
(b) (colloq) to give ⟨*blow, fine*⟩; ~ **qch par terre** to throw sth to the ground; to drop sth; to knock sth to the ground
2 se flanquer *v refl* (+ *v être*) (colloq) **se ~ dans** to run into

flapi, ~e /flapi/ *adj* (colloq) worn out

flaque /flak/ *nf* ~ **(d'eau)** puddle; ~ **d'huile** pool of oil

flash, *pl* ~**es** /flaʃ/ *nm* (a) (on camera) flash
(b) ~ **(d'information)** news headlines; ~ **publicitaire** advert (GB), commercial (US)

flasque¹ /flask/ *adj* ⟨*skin, flesh*⟩ flabby

flasque² /flask/ *nf* flask

flatter /flate/ [1] **1** *vtr* to flatter
2 se flatter *v refl* (+ *v être*) to pride oneself

flatterie /flatʀi/ *nf* flattery

flatteur, -euse /flatœʀ, øz/ *adj*
(a) ⟨*portrait*⟩ flattering
(b) ⟨*person, remarks*⟩ sycophantic

flatulence /flatylɑ̃s/ *nf* wind, flatulence

fléau, *pl* ~**x** /fleo/ *nm* (a) scourge
(b) (figurative) curse, plague
(c) (person) pest

flèche /flɛʃ/ *nf* (a) arrow; **partir en ~** to shoot off; **monter en ~** ⟨*prices*⟩ to soar
(b) barbed remark
(c) spire

flécher /fleʃe/ [14] *vtr* to signpost

fléchette /fleʃɛt/ *nf* (a) dart
(b) (game) darts

fléchir /fleʃiʀ/ [3] **1** *vtr* (a) to bend
(b) to sway ⟨*person, opinion*⟩; to weaken ⟨*will*⟩
2 *vi* (a) ⟨*knees*⟩ to bend; ⟨*legs*⟩ to give way
(b) ⟨*attention*⟩ to flag; ⟨*courage*⟩ to waver; ⟨*will*⟩ to weaken; ⟨*demand*⟩ to fall off

flegmatique /flɛgmatik/ *adj* phlegmatic

flegme /flɛgm/ *nm* phlegm, composure

flemmard, ~e /flemaʀ, aʀd/ *nm,f* (colloq) lazybones (colloq), lazy devil (colloq)

flemme /flɛm/ *nf* (colloq) laziness

flétan /fletɑ̃/ *nm* halibut

flétrir /fletʀiʀ/ [3] **1** *vtr* to blacken ⟨*reputation*⟩
2 se flétrir *v refl* (+ *v être*) ⟨*plant*⟩ to wither; ⟨*flower, beauty*⟩ to fade; ⟨*fruit*⟩ to shrivel

fleur /flœʀ/ *nf* (a) flower; **être en ~s** ⟨*garden*⟩ to be full of flowers; ⟨*plant, shrub*⟩ to be in bloom; ⟨*tree, lilac*⟩ to be in blossom; **à ~s** flowery
(b) **à ~ d'eau** just above the water
■ ~ **des champs** wild flower; ~ **de lys** fleur-de-lis
IDIOMS **être ~ bleue** to be romantic; **avoir**

une sensibilité à ~ de peau to be hypersensitive; **avoir les nerfs à ~ de peau** to be a bundle of nerves; **faire une ~ à qn** (colloq) to do sb a favour (GB)

fleuret /flœʀɛ/ *nm* (sword) foil

fleurette /flœʀɛt/ *nf* (Culin) **crème ~** whipping cream

fleuri, ~e /flœʀi/ **1** *pp* ▶ FLEURIR
2 *pp adj* (a) ⟨*garden*⟩ full of flowers; ⟨*tree*⟩ in blossom; in bloom
(b) ⟨*table*⟩ decorated with flowers
(c) ⟨*wallpaper*⟩ flowery

fleurir /flœʀiʀ/ [3] *vi* (a) ⟨*rose bush*⟩ to flower; ⟨*cherry tree*⟩ to blossom
(b) ⟨*new buildings*⟩ to spring up; ⟨*posters*⟩ to appear
(c) to thrive, to flourish

fleuriste /flœʀist/ *nmf* (a) florist
(b) flower shop

fleuve /flœv/ **1** *nm* river
2 (-)fleuve (*combining form*) interminable;
▶ ROMAN-FLEUVE

flexible /flɛksibl/ *adj* (a) ⟨*blade, tube*⟩ flexible; ⟨*body*⟩ supple
(b) ⟨*person, timetable*⟩ flexible

flexion /flɛksjɔ̃/ *nf* (of object) bending; (of arm, leg) flexing

flic /flik/ *nm* (colloq) cop (colloq), policeman

flipper /flipœʀ/ *nm* (Games) (a) pinball machine
(b) (device in machine) flipper
(c) (game) pinball

flirter /flœʀte/ [1] *vi* to flirt

flocon /flɔkɔ̃/ *nm* (of snow) flake; (of dust) speck; (of wool) bit; ~**s d'avoine** oat flakes (GB), oatmeal (US)

flop /flɔp/ *nm* (colloq) flop

flopée /flɔpe/ *nf* (colloq) **(toute) une ~ de gamins** masses of kids (colloq)

floraison /flɔʀɛzɔ̃/ *nf* flowering

floral, ~e, *mpl* **-aux** /flɔʀal, o/ *adj* floral

floralies /flɔʀali/ *nf pl* flower show

flore /flɔʀ/ *nf* flora

florilège /flɔʀilɛʒ/ *nm* anthology

florin /flɔʀɛ̃/ *nm* (Dutch currency) guilder

florissant, ~e /flɔʀisɑ̃, ɑ̃t/ *adj*
(a) ⟨*activity*⟩ thriving
(b) ⟨*complexion*⟩ ruddy

flot /flo/ **1** *nm* (a) (of letters, refugees) flood; (of visitors) stream
(b) **les ~s** the deep, the sea
2 à flot *phr* **couler à ~(s)** to flow

flottant, ~e /flɔtɑ̃, ɑ̃t/ *adj* ⟨*wood, line*⟩ floating; ⟨*clothes, hair*⟩ flowing

flotte /flɔt/ *nf* (a) fleet
(b) (colloq) rain
(c) (colloq) water

flottement /flɔtmɑ̃/ *nm* (a) wavering
(b) (of currency) floating

flotter /flɔte/ [1] **1** *vi* (a) to float; ~ **à la dérive** to drift

(b) ⟨*mist*⟩ to drift; ⟨*flag*⟩ to fly; ~ **au vent** to flutter in the wind; **elle flotte dans ses vêtements** her clothes are hanging off her
(c) ⟨*currency*⟩ to float
2 *v impers* (colloq) to rain

flotteur /flɔtœʀ/ *nm* float

flou, **~e** /flu/ **1** *adj* **(a)** ⟨*outline*⟩ blurred
(b) (figurative) vague, hazy
2 *nm* **(a)** fuzziness
(b) (figurative) vagueness
■ ~ **artistique** soft focus; (figurative) artistry

flouer /flue/ [1] *vtr* (colloq) to cheat; **se faire ~** to be had (colloq)

fluctuant, **~e** /flyktɥɑ̃, ɑ̃t/ *adj* ⟨*prices, opinions*⟩ fluctuating; ⟨*person*⟩ fickle

fluet, **-ette** /flyɛ, ɛt/ *adj* ⟨*body, person*⟩ slight; ⟨*voice*⟩ thin, reedy

fluide /flɥid/ **1** *adj* **(a)** ⟨*oil, paint*⟩ fluid
(b) ⟨*style*⟩ fluent; ⟨*traffic*⟩ moving freely
2 *nm* **(a)** (in physics) fluid
(b) (of clairvoyant) (psychic) powers

fluo /flyo/ *adj inv* (colloq) fluorescent

fluor /flyɔʀ/ *nm* fluorine

fluorescent, **~e** /flyɔʀɛsɑ̃, ɑ̃t/ *adj* fluorescent

flûte /flyt/ **1** *nf* **(a)** (Mus) flute; **petite ~** piccolo
(b) (champagne) flute
(c) French stick
2 *excl* (colloq) damn! (colloq), darn it! (colloq)
■ ~ **à bec** recorder; ~ **de Pan** panpipes

fluvial, **~e**, *mpl* **-iaux** /flyvjal, o/ *adj* fluvial, river

flux /fly/ *nm inv* **(a)** (gen, Econ) flow
(b) (in physics) flux
(c) **le ~ et le reflux** flood tide and ebb tide; (figurative) the ebb and flow
(d) influx

FMI /ɛfɛmi/ *nm: abbr* ▶ FONDS

foc /fɔk/ *nm* jib

focal, **~e**, *mpl* **-aux** /fɔkal, o/ *adj* focal

focaliser /fɔkalize/ [1] *vtr* to focus ⟨*rays*⟩; to focalize ⟨*electron beam*⟩

fœtus /fetys/ *nm inv* foetus

foi /fwa/ *nf* **(a)** faith; **avoir la ~** to be a believer
(b) **ma ~ oui** well yes; **en toute bonne ~ je crois que** in all sincerity, I believe that; **il est de mauvaise ~** he doesn't mean a word of it
(c) **sur la ~ de témoins** on the evidence of witnesses; **qui fait** *or* **faisant ~** ⟨*text, signature*⟩ authentic; **sous la ~ du serment** under oath
IDIOMS **sans ~ ni loi** fearing neither God nor man

foie /fwa/ *nm* liver; **crise de ~** indigestion

foin /fwɛ̃/ *nm* hay; **tas de ~** haystack; **la saison des ~s** the haymaking season

foire /fwaʀ/ *nf* **(a)** fair; ~ **du livre** book fair
(b) fun fair
(c) (colloq) bedlam; **faire la ~** (colloq) to live it up (colloq)

fois /fwa/ **1** *nf inv* time; **une ~** once; **deux** ~ **twice; quatre ~ trois font douze** four times three is twelve; **l'autre ~** last time; **une (bonne) ~ pour toutes** once and for all; **une ~ sur deux** half the time; **une ~ sur trois** every third time; **deux ~ sur cinq** two times out of five; **toutes les ~ que** every time (that); **deux ~ plus petit** half as big; **c'est dix ~ trop lourd!** it's far too heavy!; **régler en trois ~** to pay in three instalments (GB); **pour la énième ~** for the hundredth time; **(à) la première ~** the first time; **la première ~ que je vous ai parlé** when I first talked to you
2 **à la fois** *phr* deux à la ~ two at a time; **elle est à la ~ intelligente et travailleuse** she's both clever and hardworking
3 **des fois** *phr* (colloq) sometimes; **tu n'as pas vu mon chien, des ~?** you wouldn't have seen my dog, by any chance?
4 **des fois que** *phr* (colloq) in case
IDIOMS **il était une ~** once upon a time there was

foisonner /fwazɔne/ [1] *vi* to abound

fol ▶ FOU 1

folâtrer /fɔlɑtʀe/ [1] *vi* to romp about; to frisk

folichon, **-onne** /fɔliʃɔ̃, ɔn/ *adj* (colloq) **pas ~** far from brilliant

folie /fɔli/ *nf* **(a)** madness; **aimer qn/qch à la ~** to be mad (GB) *or* crazy about sb/sth
(b) act of folly; **elle a fait une ~ en acceptant** she was mad to accept
(c) extravagance
■ ~ **des grandeurs** delusions of grandeur

folk /fɔlk/ *nm* folk music

folklo /fɔlklo/ *adj* (colloq) eccentric, crazy (colloq)

folklore /fɔlklɔʀ/ *nm* **(a)** folklore
(b) (colloq) razzmatazz (colloq)

folklorique /fɔlklɔʀik/ *adj* **(a)** ⟨*music*⟩ folk; ⟨*costume*⟩ traditional
(b) (colloq) eccentric

folle ▶ FOU 1, 2

follement /fɔlmɑ̃/ *adv* **s'amuser ~** to have a terrific time

follet /fɔlɛ/ *adj m* **feu ~** will-o'-the-wisp

fomenter /fɔmɑ̃te/ [1] *vtr* to instigate

foncé, **~e** /fɔ̃se/ *adj* ⟨*colour*⟩ dark; ⟨*pink*⟩ deep

foncer /fɔ̃se/ [12] **1** *vtr* **(a)** to make [sth] darker *or* deeper ⟨*colour*⟩
(b) (Culin) to line
2 *vi* **(a)** (colloq) ⟨*person, vehicle*⟩ to tear along (colloq); **fonce!** get a move on! (colloq); go for it! (colloq); ~ **vers/dans** to rush toward(s)/into; ~ **sur qch/vers la sortie** to make a dash for sth/for the exit; ~ **sur qn** to charge at sb; ~ **à New York** to dash over to New York
(b) ⟨*colour*⟩ (gen) to darken; ⟨*pink, mauve*⟩ to deepen; ⟨*fabric*⟩ to go darker

fonceur, **-euse** /fɔ̃sœʀ, øz/ (colloq) **1** *adj* dynamic
2 *nm,f* go-getter (colloq)

foncier, -ière /fɔ̃sje, ɛʀ/ adj ‹income› from land; **impôt ~** property tax

foncièrement /fɔ̃sjɛʀmɑ̃/ adv fundamentally

fonction /fɔ̃ksjɔ̃/ nf **(a)** (in administration, company) post; duties; **dans l'exercice de leurs ~s** while carrying out their duties; **occuper la ~ de** to hold the position of; **voiture de ~** company car
(b) en ~ de according to
(c) function; **avoir pour ~ de faire** to be designed to do; **faire ~ de** to serve as
(d) profession; **~ enseignante** teaching profession
■ **~ publique** civil service

fonctionnaire /fɔ̃ksjɔnɛʀ/ nmf civil servant; (higher ranking) government official

fonctionnalité /fɔ̃ksjɔnalite/ nf functionality

fonctionnel, -elle /fɔ̃ksjɔnɛl/ adj functional

fonctionnement /fɔ̃ksjɔnmɑ̃/ nm
(a) (of institution) functioning
(b) (of machinery) working; **mauvais ~** malfunction; **en ~** in service

fonctionner /fɔ̃ksjɔne/ [1] vi to work; **~ à l'essence** to run on petrol (GB) or gas (US)

fond /fɔ̃/ **1** nm **(a)** (of vessel, lake, valley) bottom; (of cupboard, wardrobe) back; **~ de la mer** seabed; **~ de l'océan** ocean floor; **toucher le ~** (in water) to touch the bottom; (figurative) to hit rock bottom
(b) (of shop, yard) back; (of corridor, room) far end; **la chambre du ~** the back bedroom; **au ~ des bois** deep in the woods; **de ~ en comble** from top to bottom
(c) les problèmes de ~ the basic problems; **un débat de ~** an in-depth debate; **au ~ or dans le ~, le problème est simple** basically, the problem is simple
(d) (of text) content
(e) regarder qn au ~ des yeux (suspiciously) to give sb a searching look; **elle a un bon ~** she's very good at heart
(f) background; **~ musical** background music
(g) un ~ de porto a drop of port
(h) (Naut) **il y a 20 mètres de ~** the water is 20 metres (GB) deep
(i) (Sport) **épreuve de ~** long-distance event
2 à fond phr **(a) connaître qch à ~** to be an expert in sth; **être à ~ pour** (colloq) to support wholeheartedly; **respirer à ~** to breathe deeply; **mettre la radio à ~** to turn the radio right up
(b) (colloq) **rouler à ~** to drive at top speed
■ **~ d'artichaut** artichoke bottom; **~ de teint** foundation (GB), make-up base (US)

fondamental, ~e, mpl -aux /fɔ̃damãtal, o/ adj **(a)** basic, fundamental
(b) essential

fondamentalement /fɔ̃damãtalmã/ adv
(a) fundamentally
(b) radically

fondant, ~e /fɔ̃dã, ãt/ adj **(a)** ‹ice› melting
(b) ‹pear› which melts in the mouth

fondateur, -trice /fɔ̃datœʀ, tʀis/ nm,f founder; **groupe ~** founding group

fondation /fɔ̃dasjɔ̃/ **1** nf foundation
2 fondations nf pl foundations

fondé, ~e /fɔ̃de/ **1** pp ▶ FONDER
2 pp adj justifiable, well-founded, legitimate; **non ~, mal ~** ‹accusation› groundless
■ **~ de pouvoir** (of company) authorized representative; (of bank) senior banking executive

fondement /fɔ̃dmã/ nm foundation; **être sans or dénué de ~** to be unfounded

fonder /fɔ̃de/ [1] **1** vtr **(a)** to found
(b) to base
2 se fonder v refl (+ v être) **se ~ sur** ‹theory, method› to be based on; ‹person› to go on

fonderie /fɔ̃dʀi/ nf **(a)** foundry
(b) casting

fondre /fɔ̃dʀ/ [6] **1** vtr **(a)** to melt down ‹metal›; to smelt ‹mineral›
(b) to cast ‹statue›
2 vi **(a)** ‹snow, butter› to melt
(b) ‹sugar› to dissolve
(c) ‹savings› to melt away
(d) (emotionally) to soften; **~ en larmes** to dissolve into tears
3 se fondre v refl (+ v être) **se ~ dans** ‹person, figure› to blend in with

fonds /fɔ̃/ **1** nm inv **(a)** (in gallery, museum) collection
(b) fund
2 nm pl funds
■ **~ d'amortissement** sinking fund; **~ bloqués** frozen assets; **~ de commerce** business; **~ de placement** investment fund; **~ de prévoyance** provident fund; **~ propres** equity capital; **~ de roulement** working capital; **~ de solidarité** mutual aid fund; **Fonds monétaire international, FMI** International Monetary Fund, IMF

fondu, ~e¹ /fɔ̃dy/ **1** pp ▶ FONDRE
2 pp adj ‹butter› melted; ‹metal› molten

fondue² /fɔ̃dy/ nf (Culin) fondue; **~ savoyarde** cheese fondue; **~ bourguignonne** fondue bourguignonne (meat dipped in hot oil)

font /fɔ̃/ ▶ FAIRE

fontaine /fɔ̃tɛn/ nf **(a)** fountain
(b) spring

fonte /fɔ̃t/ nf **(a)** cast iron
(b) melting down, smelting
(c) thawing; **~ des neiges** thaw

fonts /fɔ̃/ nm pl **~ baptismaux** font

foot /fut/ nm (colloq) = FOOTBALL

football /futbol/ nm football (GB), soccer

footballeur, -euse /futbolœʀ, øz/ nm,f football or soccer player

footing /futiŋ/ nm jogging

forage /fɔʀaʒ/ nm drilling

forain, -aine /fɔʀɛ̃, ɛn/ **1** *adj* fairground
  2 *nm* stallkeeper; **les** ~**s** fairground people

forçat /fɔʀsa/ *nm* **(a)** convict
  (b) galley slave

force /fɔʀs/ **1** *nf* **(a)** strength; ~**s** strength;
avoir de la ~ to be strong; **c'est au-dessus
de mes** ~**s** it's too much for me; **de toutes
ses** ~**s** with all one's might; **ils sont de** ~
égale aux échecs they are evenly matched
at chess
  (b) force; **de** ~ by force; **faire manger de** ~
to force [sb] to eat; **entrer de** ~ **dans un lieu**
to force one's way into a place
  (c) ~ **de vente** sales force; ~**s** (Mil) forces;
d'importantes ~**s de police** large numbers of
police
  2 à force *phr* (colloq) **à** ~, **elle l'a cassé**
she ended up breaking it
  3 à force de *phr* **réussir à** ~ **de travail** to
succeed by dint of hard work; **il est aphone
à** ~ **de crier** he's been shouting so much
(that) he's lost his voice
  ■ ~ **de dissuasion** (Mil) deterrent force; ~ **de
frappe** nuclear weapons; ~**s de l'ordre**
forces of law and order

forcé, ~e /fɔʀse/ **1** *pp* ▶ FORCER
  2 *pp adj* **(a)** (gen) forced
  (b) ⟨*consequence*⟩ inevitable; **c'est** ~**!** (colloq)
there's no way around it! (colloq)

forcément /fɔʀsemɑ̃/ *adv* inevitably; **pas**
~ not necessarily

forcené, ~e /fɔʀsəne/ **1** *adj* ⟨*rhythm*⟩
furious; ⟨*activity*⟩ frenzied
  2 *nm,f* **(a)** maniac
  (b) crazed gunman

forcer /fɔʀse/ [12] **1** *vtr* **(a)** to force
  (b) to break through ⟨*fence, enclosure*⟩; ~ **la
porte de qn** to force one's way into sb's
house; ~ **le passage** to force one's way
through
  2 forcer sur *v+prep* to overdo ⟨*salt,
colour*⟩
  3 *vi* **(a)** to overdo it
  (b) serrez sans ~ do not tighten too much;
ne force pas! don't force it!
  4 se forcer *v refl* (+ *v être*) to force
oneself
  IDIOMS ~ **la main à qn** to force sb's hand

forcing /fɔʀsiŋ/ *nm* (colloq) **faire du** ~ to go
all out

forer /fɔʀe/ [1] *vtr* to drill

forestier, -ière /fɔʀɛstje, ɛʀ/ *adj* ⟨*area*⟩
forested; **chemin** ~ forest path; **exploitation
forestière** (place) forestry plantation

foret /fɔʀɛ/ *nm* drill

forêt /fɔʀɛ/ *nf* forest; ~ **tropicale** rain forest
  IDIOMS **c'est l'arbre qui cache la** ~ you can't
see the wood for the trees

forfait /fɔʀfɛ/ *nm* **(a)** fixed rate; **un** ~ **de 15
francs** a fixed price of 15 francs
  (b) package; ~ **avion-auto** fly-drive package
  (c) ~ **skieur** ski pass
  (d) (of player) withdrawal; **déclarer** ~ to give
up; (Sport) to withdraw

forfaitaire /fɔʀfetɛʀ/ *adj* **prix** ~ contract
or all-inclusive price; **indemnité** ~ basic
allowance

forge /fɔʀʒ/ *nf* **(a)** forge
  (b) ironworks

forgé, ~e /fɔʀʒe/ **1** *pp* ▶ FORGER
  2 *pp adj* ⟨*object, metal*⟩ wrought

forger /fɔʀʒe/ [13] *vtr* **(a)** to forge
  (b) to form ⟨*character*⟩

forgeron /fɔʀʒəʀɔ̃/ *nm* blacksmith
  IDIOMS **c'est en forgeant qu'on devient** ~
(Proverb) practice makes perfect

formaliser: se formaliser /fɔʀmalize/
[1] *v refl* (+ *v être*) to take offence (GB) (**de**
to)

formalité /fɔʀmalite/ *nf* formality; **les** ~**s
à accomplir pour obtenir un visa** the
necessary procedure to obtain a visa; **par
pure** ~ as a matter of form

format /fɔʀma/ *nm* format, size

formatage /fɔʀmataʒ/ *nm* (Comput)
formatting; **faire un** ~ to format

formateur, -trice /fɔʀmatœʀ, tʀis/ *adj*
formative

formation /fɔʀmasjɔ̃/ *nf* **(a)** education;
training; **avoir une** ~ **littéraire** to have an
arts background; **en** ~ undergoing training
  (b) training course
  (c) (of government, team) forming
  (d) group
  ■ ~ **continue**, ~ **permanente** adult continuing
education; ~ **professionnelle** professional
training

forme /fɔʀm/ **1** *nf* **(a)** shape; form; **en** ~
de in the shape of; **sous** ~ **de** in the form
of; **sans** ~ shapeless; **pour la** ~ as a matter
of form
  (b) (of payment) method
  (c) (physical condition) form; **en pleine** ~ in
great shape
  2 formes *nf pl* **(a)** (of person) figure
  (b) (of object, building) lines
  (c) faire qch dans les ~**s** to do sth in the
correct manner; **y mettre les** ~**s** to be
tactful

formé, ~e /fɔʀme/ **1** *pp* ▶ FORMER
  2 *pp adj* **(a)** made up; formed
  (b) educated; trained
  (c) ⟨*writing, sentence*⟩ formed

formel, -elle /fɔʀmɛl/ *adj* **(a)** ⟨*refusal,
denial, person*⟩ categorical; ⟨*order*⟩ strict;
être ~ **sur qch** ⟨*person*⟩ to be definite about
sth
  (b) c'est purement ~ it's just a formality

formellement /fɔʀmɛlmɑ̃/ *adv*
  (a) categorically; strictly
  (b) officially; ~ **identifié** clearly identified

former /fɔʀme/ [1] **1** *vtr* **(a)** to form
⟨*circle, rectangle*⟩
  (b) to form, to constitute
  (c) to train ⟨*staff*⟩; to educate ⟨*person,
tastes*⟩; to develop ⟨*intelligence*⟩
  (d) to form ⟨*abscess, film*⟩
  2 se former *v refl* (+ *v être*) **(a)** to form
  (b) to be formed

(c) to train, to be trained
(d) ⟨character, style⟩ to develop

formidable /fɔʀmidabl/ adj (a) ⟨force⟩ tremendous
(b) (colloq) great, marvellous (GB)
(c) (colloq) incredible

formol /fɔʀmɔl/ nm formalin

formulaire /fɔʀmylɛʀ/ nm form

formulation /fɔʀmylasjɔ̃/ nf formulation; wording; **la ~ de cette idée est difficile** it's not easy to express that idea

formule /fɔʀmyl/ nf (a) expression; **~ toute faite** set phrase
(b) (in travel, tourism) option; **~ à 75F** (in restaurant) set menu at 75F
(c) method
(d) concept
(e) (in science) formula
(f) (of car) **~ un** Formula One
(g) of magazine) format
■ **~ magique** magic words

formuler /fɔʀmyle/ [1] vtr (gen) to express; to put [sth] into words ⟨idea⟩

fort, ~e /fɔʀ, fɔʀt/ ❶ adj (a) strong; **armée ~e de 10 000 hommes** 10,000-strong army; **~ d'un chiffre d'affaires en hausse** boasting an increased turnover
(b) ⟨noise⟩ loud; ⟨light⟩ bright; ⟨heat, activity⟩ intense; ⟨temperature, fever, rate⟩ high; ⟨blow, jolt⟩ hard; ⟨rain⟩ heavy; ⟨spice⟩ hot; ⟨majority⟩ large; ⟨lack, shortage⟩ great; ⟨drop, increase⟩ sharp; **~e émigration** high level of emigration
(c) (at school subject) good
(d) ⟨person⟩ stout; ⟨hips⟩ broad; ⟨bust⟩ large; ⟨thighs⟩ big
(e) (colloq) **c'est un peu ~!** that's a bit much! (colloq)
❷ adv (a) extremely, very
(b) ⟨doubt⟩ very much; **avoir ~ à faire** (colloq) to have a lot to do
(c) ⟨hit⟩ hard; ⟨squeeze⟩ tight; ⟨breathe⟩ deeply; ⟨speak⟩ loudly; **y aller un peu ~** (colloq) to go a bit too far
(d) **il ne va pas très ~** he's not very well
❸ nm (a) fort
(b) strong person
❹ **au plus fort de** phr **au plus ~ de l'été** at the height of summer
■ **~e tête** rebel
IDIOMS **c'est plus ~ que moi/qu'elle** I/she just can't help it

fortement /fɔʀtəmã/ adv ⟨criticize⟩ strongly; ⟨rise⟩ sharply; ⟨industrialized⟩ highly; ⟨shaken⟩ deeply; ⟨damaged⟩ badly; ⟨displease, dislike⟩ greatly; ⟨armed⟩ heavily; **il est ~ question de...** it is highly likely that...

forteresse /fɔʀtəʀɛs/ nf stronghold

fortiche /fɔʀtiʃ/ adj (colloq) smart, clever (en at)

fortifiant /fɔʀtifjã/ nm (Med) tonic

fortification /fɔʀtifikasjɔ̃/ nf fortification

fortifier /fɔʀtifje/ [2] vtr (a) to strengthen ⟨nails, hair⟩

(b) ⟨meal⟩ to fortify; ⟨holiday, vitamins⟩ to do [sb] good
(c) to reinforce ⟨construction⟩

fortuit, ~e /fɔʀtɥi, it/ adj ⟨meeting⟩ accidental; ⟨incident, discovery⟩ fortuitous

fortune /fɔʀtyn/ nf (a) fortune
(b) **de ~** makeshift
IDIOMS **faire contre mauvaise ~ bon cœur** to put on a brave face

fortuné, ~e /fɔʀtyne/ adj wealthy

fosse /fos/ nf (a) pit
(b) grave
(c) sandpit
■ **~ commune** communal grave; **~ septique** septic tank

fossé /fose/ nm (a) (gen) ditch; (of castle) moat
(b) (figurative) gap; rift

fossette /fosɛt/ nf dimple

fossile /fosil/ adj, nm fossil

fossiliser /fosilize/ [1] vtr, **se fossiliser** v refl (+ v être) to fossilize

fossoyeur /foswajœʀ/ nm gravedigger

fou (**fol** before vowel or mute h), **folle** /fu, fɔl/ ❶ adj (a) (insane) mad; **devenir ~** to go mad; **un tueur ~** a crazed killer
(b) ⟨person, idea⟩ mad (GB), crazy; ⟨look⟩ wild; ⟨story⟩ crazy; **être ~ furieux** (colloq) to be raving mad; **être ~ à lier** (colloq) to be stark raving mad (colloq); **entre eux c'est l'amour ~** they're madly in love; **~ de qn** crazy about sb
(c) ⟨success⟩ huge; **un monde ~** a huge crowd; **avoir un mal ~ à faire** to find it incredibly difficult to do
(d) ⟨vehicle, horse⟩ runaway; ⟨lock of hair⟩ stray; **avoir le ~ rire** to have a fit of the giggles
❷ nm,f madman/madwoman; **envoyer qn chez les ~s** (colloq) to send sb to the nuthouse (colloq); **courir comme un ~** to run like mad; **c'est un ~ d'art contemporain** he's mad about contemporary art
❸ nm (a) fool, court jester
(b) (in chess) bishop
IDIOMS **faire les ~s** (colloq) to fool about; **plus on est de ~s plus on rit** (colloq) the more the merrier

foudre /fudʀ/ nf lightning; **coup de ~** love at first sight; **avoir le coup de ~ pour** to be really taken with

foudroyant, ~e /fudʀwajã, ãt/ adj ⟨attack⟩ lightning; ⟨look⟩ furious; ⟨death⟩ sudden

foudroyer /fudʀwaje/ [23] vtr (a) to strike ⟨tree⟩; **mort foudroyé** struck dead by lightning; **~ qn du regard** to look daggers at sb (colloq)
(b) ⟨bad news⟩ to devastate

fouet /fwɛ/ nm (a) whip; **dix coups de ~** ten lashes of the whip; **le grand air m'a donné un coup de ~** the fresh air invigorated me; **se heurter de plein ~** to collide head-on
(b) (Culin) whisk; **~ mécanique** hand whisk

fouetter /fwɛte/ [1] *vtr* (a) to whip, to flog ⟨*person*⟩; to whip ⟨*animal*⟩
(b) **la pluie leur fouettait le visage** the rain lashed their faces
IDIOMS **il n'y a pas de quoi ~ un chat** (colloq) it's no big deal (colloq); **avoir d'autres chats à ~** (colloq) to have other fish to fry

foufou, **fofolle** /fufu, fɔfɔl/ *adj* (colloq) scatterbrained

fougère /fuʒɛʀ/ *nf* (a) fern
(b) bracken

fougue /fug/ *nf* enthusiasm

fougueusement /fugøzmɑ̃/ *adv* enthusiastically

fougueux, **-euse** /fugø, øz/ *adj* spirited; enthusiastic

fouille /fuj/ *nf* (a) (of place, person, baggage) search
(b) excavation

fouillé, **~e** /fuje/ [1] *pp* ▶ FOUILLER
[2] *pp adj* ⟨*study, portrait, piece of work*⟩ detailed; ⟨*style*⟩ elaborate

fouiller /fuje/ [1] [1] *vtr* (a) to search; to frisk
(b) to dig ⟨*site*⟩
[2] *vi* **~ dans** (gen) to rummage through; to search ⟨*memory*⟩; to delve into ⟨*past*⟩

fouillis /fuji/ *nm inv* mess; jumble

fouine /fwin/ *nf* (Zool) stone marten

fouiner /fwine/ [1] *vi* (a) to forage about
(b) **~ dans** to rummage through ⟨*objects, papers*⟩; to poke one's nose into ⟨*life, past*⟩

foulard /fulaʀ/ *nm* scarf, headscarf

foule /ful/ *nf* crowd; mob; **il y avait ~ à la réunion** there were masses of people at the meeting; **venir en ~ à** to flock to
(b) mass

foulée /fule/ *nf* (of horse, athlete) stride; **courir dans la ~ de qn** (Sport) to tail sb; **dans la ~ il a...** while he was at it, he...

fouler /fule/ [1] [1] *vtr* to tread ⟨*grapes*⟩
[2] **se fouler** *v refl* (+ *v être*) (a) (Med) **se ~ le poignet** to sprain one's wrist
(b) (colloq) **tu ne t'es pas foulé** you didn't kill yourself (colloq)

foulure /fulyʀ/ *nf* sprain

four /fuʀ/ *nm* (a) oven; **cuire au ~** to roast, to bake
(b) furnace; kiln
■ **~ crématoire** crematory (furnace); **~ à micro-ondes** microwave oven

fourbu, **~e** /fuʀby/ *adj* exhausted

fourche /fuʀʃ/ *nf* fork; **faire une ~** to fork

fourcher /fuʀʃe/ [1] *vi* **ma langue a fourché** it was a slip of the tongue

fourchette /fuʀʃɛt/ *nf* (a) fork
(b) (of prices, temperature) range; (of income) bracket; **~ horaire** period

fourchu, **~e** /fuʀʃy/ *adj* ⟨*branch*⟩ forked; **cheveux ~s** split ends

fourgon /fuʀgɔ̃/ *nm* (a) van
(b) (of train) goods wagon (GB), freight car (US)
■ **~ à bestiaux** cattle truck

fourgonnette /fuʀgɔnɛt/ *nf* (small) van

fourguer (slang) /fuʀge/ [1] *vtr* to flog (colloq) (**à** to), to sell [sth] off (**à** to)

fourmi /fuʀmi/ *nf* (Zool) ant; **travail de ~** laborious task
IDIOMS **avoir des ~s dans les jambes** to have pins and needles in one's legs

fourmilier /fuʀmilje/ *nm* anteater

fourmilière /fuʀmiljɛʀ/ *nf* ant hill

fourmillement /fuʀmijmɑ̃/ *nm* (a) **un ~ de gens** a mass of people
(b) tingling sensation

fourmiller /fuʀmije/ [1] [1] **fourmiller de** *v+prep* to be chock-full of ⟨*mistakes*⟩; to be swarming with ⟨*visitors*⟩
[2] *vi* to abound

fournaise /fuʀnɛz/ *nf* blaze; **la ville est une ~ en été** the town is baking hot in summer

fourneau, *pl* **~x** /fuʀno/ *nm* (a) (Tech) furnace
(b) stove

fournée /fuʀne/ *nf* batch

fourni, **~e** /fuʀni/ [1] *pp* ▶ FOURNIR
[2] *pp adj* ⟨*hair*⟩ thick; ⟨*grass*⟩ lush

fournir /fuʀniʀ/ [3] [1] *vtr* to supply ⟨*document, equipment*⟩; to provide ⟨*energy*⟩; to contribute ⟨*effort*⟩; to produce ⟨*proof*⟩
[2] **se fournir** *v refl* (+ *v être*) **se ~ chez** or **auprès de** to get [sth] from

fournisseur, **-euse** /fuʀnisœʀ, øz/
[1] *adj* **pays ~** exporting country
[2] *nm* supplier; **~ de drogue** drug dealer
■ **~ d'accès** (Comput) service provider

fourniture /fuʀnityʀ/ *nf* (a) supply, provision
(b) **~s scolaires/de bureau** school/office stationery; **~s de laboratoire** laboratory equipment

fourrage /fuʀaʒ/ *nm* forage; **~ sec** fodder

fourré, **~e** /fuʀe/ [1] *pp* ▶ FOURRER
[2] *pp adj* (a) (Culin) filled
(b) fur-lined; lined
(c) (colloq) **toujours ~ au café** always hanging about at the café
[3] *nm* thicket

fourrer /fuʀe/ [1] [1] *vtr* (a) (colloq) to stick (colloq); **~ qch dans la tête de qn** to put sth into sb's head
(b) (Culin) to fill
(c) to line ⟨*garment*⟩
[2] **se fourrer** *v refl* (+ *v être*) (colloq) (a) **se ~ dans un coin** to get into a corner
(b) **se ~ une idée dans la tête** to get an idea into one's head

fourre-tout /fuʀtu/ *adj inv* **sac ~** holdall (GB), carryall (US)

fourreur /fuʀœʀ/ *nm* furrier

fourrière /fuʀjɛʀ/ *nf* pound; **mettre une voiture à la ~** to impound a car

fourrure /fuʀyʀ/ *nf* fur, coat

fourvoyer: se fourvoyer /fuʀvwaje/ [23] *v refl* (+ *v être*) to make a mistake

f

foutoir /futwaʀ/ nm (slang) shambles (colloq); complete chaos

foutre /futʀ/ [6] (slang) **1** vtr **(a)** n'en avoir rien à ~ not to give a damn (colloq)
(b) ~ qch quelque part to stick sth somewhere (colloq)
2 se foutre v refl (+ v être) **(a)** il ne s'est pas foutu de toi! he's been very generous!; se ~ du monde to have a bloody (GB) or hell of a (US) nerve (slang)
(b) not to give a damn (colloq)
IDIOMS ~ le camp to bugger off (GB) (colloq), to split (US) (colloq)

foutu, ~e /futy/ (slang) **1** pp ▶ FOUTRE
2 pp adj **(a)** (before n) bloody awful (GB) (slang), damned (US)
(b) être ~ ⟨person, garment⟩ to have had it (colloq)
(c) être mal ~ to be unattractive; to feel lousy (colloq)
(d) être ~ de faire to be totally capable of doing

foyer /fwaje/ nm **(a)** home; fonder un ~ to get married
(b) (family) household
(c) hostel
(d) club
(e) (for fire) hearth
(f) (of resistance) pocket; un ~ d'incendie a fire
(g) (of rebellion) seat; (of epidemic) source
(h) (in optics) focus; lunettes à double ~ bifocals
■ ~ fiscal household for tax purposes; ~ de placement foster home

fracas /fʀaka/ nm inv (of falling object) crash; (of waves) roar; (of town, battle) din

fracassant, ~e /fʀakasã, ãt/ adj ⟨noise⟩ deafening; ⟨news⟩ sensational; ⟨success⟩ stunning

fracasser /fʀakase/ [1] **1** vtr to smash
2 se fracasser v refl (+ v être) to crash

fraction /fʀaksjɔ̃/ nf **(a)** (in mathematics) fraction
(b) (of sum of money) part; (of company) section; en une ~ de seconde in a split second

fractionnement /fʀaksjɔnmã/ nm division; fragmentation

fractionner /fʀaksjone/ [1] vtr to divide up ⟨work, group⟩; to split ⟨party⟩

fracture /fʀaktyʀ/ nf fracture; ~ du poignet fractured wrist

fracturer /fʀaktyʀe/ [1] **1** vtr to break down ⟨door⟩; to break ⟨window⟩; to force ⟨safe⟩
2 se fracturer v refl (+ v être) se ~ la cheville to break one's ankle

fragile /fʀaʒil/ adj **(a)** fragile
(b) ⟨person⟩ frail; ⟨eye⟩ sensitive; ⟨heart⟩ weak

fragiliser /fʀaʒilize/ [1] vtr to weaken

fragilité /fʀaʒilite/ nf **(a)** fragility
(b) frailty

fragment /fʀagmã/ nm **(a)** (of cup, bone) fragment

(b) (of book, novel) passage

fragmentaire /fʀagmãtɛʀ/ adj patchy; sketchy; sporadic

fragmentation /fʀagmãtasjɔ̃/ nf
(a) division; splitting up
(b) fragmentation

fragmenter /fʀagmãte/ [1] vtr to break up ⟨substance⟩; to divide up ⟨work⟩

fraîche ▶ FRAIS 1, 5

fraîchement /fʀɛʃmã/ adv **(a)** freshly, newly
(b) coldly; elle a été ~ accueillie she was given a cool reception

fraîcheur /fʀɛʃœʀ/ nf **(a)** coolness; coldness; la ~ du soir the cold evening air
(b) freshness

frais, fraîche /fʀɛ, fʀɛʃ/ **1** adj **(a)** cool; cold; 'servir ~' 'serve chilled'
(b) ⟨news, snow⟩ fresh; ⟨paint⟩ wet
(c) ⟨complexion⟩ fresh
(d) ⟨troops⟩ fresh; de l'argent ~ more money
2 adv il fait ~ it's cool
3 nm prendre le ~ to get some fresh air; mettre au ~ to put in a cool place; to put to cool
4 nm pl **(a)** expenses; aux ~ de l'entreprise paid for by the company; rentrer dans ses ~ to cover one's expenses; faire les ~ de qch to bear the brunt of sth
(b) fees
(c) costs
5 à la fraîche phr in the cool of the morning; in the cool of the evening
■ ~ d'annulation cancellation fees; ~ de déplacement (of employee) travel expenses; (for repairman) call-out charge; ~ divers miscellaneous costs; ~ d'expédition (for parcel) postage and packing; ~ de fonctionnement running costs; ~ de garde childminding fees; ~ d'inscription (gen) registration fees; (for school) school fees (GB), tuition fees (US); (at university) tuition fees; ~ de port postage; ~ professionnels professional expenses; ~ de scolarité tuition fees, school fees (GB)

fraise /fʀɛz/ nf **(a)** strawberry; ~ des bois wild strawberry
(b) (tool, instrument) reamer; milling-cutter; (of dentist) drill
IDIOMS ramener sa ~ (colloq) to stick one's nose in (colloq)

fraiseur, -euse¹ /fʀɛzœʀ, øz/ nmf cutter

fraiseuse² /fʀɛzøz/ nf milling machine

fraisier /fʀɛzje/ nm **(a)** strawberry plant
(b) strawberry gateau

framboise /fʀãbwaz/ nf **(a)** raspberry
(b) raspberry liqueur

framboisier /fʀãbwazje/ nm raspberry cane; raspberry bush

franc, franche /fʀã, fʀãʃ/ **1** adj
(a) ⟨person⟩ frank, straight; ⟨reply⟩ straight; ⟨laughter, expression⟩ open, honest; jouer ~ jeu to play fair
(b) duty-free; ~ de port postage paid
2 nm (currency) franc; ~ lourd new franc

français, **~e** /fʀɑ̃sɛ, ɛz/ **1** *adj* French **2** *nm* (language) French

Français, **~e** /fʀɑ̃sɛ, ɛz/ *nm,f* Frenchman/Frenchwoman

France /fʀɑ̃s/ *pr nf* France

franche ▶ FRANC 1

franchement /fʀɑ̃ʃmɑ̃/ *adv* **(a)** frankly, candidly; **je lui ai demandé ~** I asked him straight out
(b) ⟨lean⟩ firmly; ⟨enter⟩ boldly
(c) really; **il m'a franchement agacé** he really annoyed me; **~!** (well) really!

franchir /fʀɑ̃ʃiʀ/ [3] *vtr* to cross ⟨line⟩; to get over ⟨fence⟩; to cover ⟨distance⟩

franchise /fʀɑ̃ʃiz/ *nf* **(a)** frankness, sincerity
(b) exemption
(c) (in insurance) excess (GB), deductible (US)
(d) (to sell goods) franchise
■ **~ de bagages** baggage allowance; **~ fiscale** tax exemption; **~ postale** 'postage paid'; **en ~ postale** post free

franchiser /fʀɑ̃ʃize/ [1] *vtr* to franchise

franchissement /fʀɑ̃ʃismɑ̃/ *nm* crossing; clearing; **~ de la ligne continue** crossing the white line

franciser /fʀɑ̃size/ [1] *vtr* to gallicize

franc-jeu /fʀɑ̃ʒø/ *nm* fair play

franc-maçon, **-onne**, *pl* **francs-maçons**, **franc-maçonnes** /fʀɑ̃masɔ̃, ɔn/ *nm,f* Freemason

franc-maçonnerie, *pl* **~s** /fʀɑ̃masɔnʀi/ *nf* **la ~** Freemasonry

franco /fʀɑ̃ko/ *adv* **(a)** **~ de port** postage paid, carriage paid
(b) (colloq) **y aller ~** to go right ahead

francophone /fʀɑ̃kɔfɔn/ **1** *adj* French-speaking; ⟨literature⟩ in the French language
2 *nmf* French speaker

francophonie /fʀɑ̃kɔfɔni/ *nf* French-speaking world

franc-parler /fʀɑ̃paʀle/ *nm* **avoir son ~** to speak one's mind

frange /fʀɑ̃ʒ/ *nf* **(a)** (on rug, curtain, garment) fringe
(b) (hair) fringe (GB), bangs (US)

frangin /fʀɑ̃ʒɛ̃/ *nm* (colloq) brother

frangine /fʀɑ̃ʒin/ *nf* (colloq) sister

franglais /fʀɑ̃glɛ/ *nm* Franglais

franquette: à la bonne franquette /alabɔnfʀɑ̃kɛt/ *phr* (colloq) **recevoir qn à la bonne ~** to have sb over for an informal meal

frappé, **~e** /fʀape/ **1** *pp* ▶ FRAPPER
2 *pp adj* ⟨cocktail⟩ frappé; ⟨coffee⟩ iced

frapper /fʀape/ [1] **1** *vtr* **(a)** (gen) to hit, to strike; **~ à coups de pied** to kick; **~ à coups de poing** to punch; **~ un grand coup** (gen) to hit hard; (on door) to knock
(b) to strike ⟨coin⟩
(c) ⟨unemployment, epidemic⟩ to hit ⟨region⟩; **les taxes qui frappent les produits français** duties imposed on French goods

(d) **ce qui m'a frappé c'est...** what struck me was...; **j'ai été frappé de voir que...** I was amazed to see that...
2 *vi* **(a)** to hit, to strike; **~ dans ses mains** to clap one's hands
(b) to knock; **on a frappé** there was a knock at the door
(c) ⟨criminals⟩ to strike

frasque /fʀask/ *nf* escapade

fraternel, **-elle** /fʀatɛʀnɛl/ *adj* fraternal, brotherly

fraternellement /fʀatɛʀnɛlmɑ̃/ *adv* in a brotherly fashion

fraternisation /fʀatɛʀnizasjɔ̃/ *nf* fraternizing

fraterniser /fʀatɛʀnize/ [1] *vi* to fraternize

fraternité /fʀatɛʀnite/ *nf* fraternity

fraude /fʀod/ *nf* (Law) fraud; **~ fiscale** tax fraud; **~ électorale** vote or election rigging; **en ~** ⟨enter⟩ illegally

frauder /fʀode/ [1] *vi* (on public transport) to travel without a ticket; (in cinema) to slip in without paying

fraudeur, **-euse** /fʀodœʀ, øz/ *nm,f* swindler; tax evader; cheat

frauduleux, **-euse** /fʀodylø, øz/ *adj* fraudulent

frayer /fʀeje/ [21] **1** *vtr* **~ un passage à qn à travers la foule** to clear a path for sb through the crowd; **~ le chemin** or **la voie à qch** (figurative) to pave the way for sth
2 **se frayer** *v refl* (+ *v être*) **se ~ un chemin dans** or **à travers** to make one's way through

frayeur /fʀɛjœʀ/ *nf* **(a)** fear
(b) fright

fredonner /fʀədɔne/ [1] *vtr* to hum

free-lance /fʀilɑ̃s/ *nmf* freelance, freelancer; **travailler en ~** to work freelance *or* as a freelancer

freezer /fʀizœʀ/ *nm* icebox

frégate /fʀegat/ *nf* (Naut) frigate

frein /fʀɛ̃/ *nm* brake; **donner un coup de ~** to slam on the brakes; **mettre un ~ à** to curb
IDIOMS **ronger son ~** to champ at the bit

freinage /fʀɛnaʒ/ *nm* braking

freiner /fʀɛne/ [1] **1** *vtr* **(a)** to slow down ⟨vehicle⟩
(b) to impede ⟨person⟩
(c) to curb ⟨inflation⟩
2 *vi* **(a)** to brake; **~ à fond** to slam on the brakes
(b) (in skiing) to slow down

frelaté, **~e** /fʀəlate/ *adj* ⟨alcohol⟩ adulterated; ⟨taste⟩ unnatural

frêle /fʀɛl/ *adj* frail

frelon /fʀəlɔ̃/ *nm* hornet

frémir /fʀemiʀ/ [3] *vi* **(a)** ⟨leaf⟩ to quiver; ⟨water⟩ to ripple
(b) (with emotion) ⟨lip⟩ to tremble; ⟨person⟩ to quiver; to shudder
(c) (Culin) to start to come to the boil

frémissant, ~e /fʀemisɑ̃, ɑ̃t/ *adj* faire
cuire dans l'eau ~e simmer gently in water

frémissement /fʀemismɑ̃/ *nm* **(a)** quiver,
tremor
(b) (of person, hand) quiver, shudder

frêne /fʀɛn/ *nm* ash (tree)

frénésie /fʀenezi/ *nf* frenzy

frénétique /fʀenetik/ *adj* frenzied;
frenetic

frénétiquement /fʀenetikmɑ̃/ *adv* ⟨*fight*⟩
frantically; ⟨*dance*⟩ frenziedly; ⟨*applaud*⟩
wildly

fréquemment /fʀekamɑ̃/ *adv* frequently

fréquence /fʀekɑ̃s/ *nf* frequency

fréquent, ~e /fʀekɑ̃, ɑ̃t/ *adj* **(a)** frequent
(b) common

fréquentable /fʀekɑ̃tabl/ *adj* respectable;
ce ne sont pas des gens ~s they are not the
sort of people one should associate with

fréquentation /fʀekɑ̃tasjɔ̃/ *nf*
(a) company; avoir de bonnes/mauvaises ~s
to keep good/bad company
(b) ~ des théâtres theatregoing (GB)

fréquenté, ~e /fʀekɑ̃te/ ⓵ *pp* ▸
FRÉQUENTER
⓶ *pp adj* popular, busy; lieu bien ~ place
that attracts the right sort of people

fréquenter /fʀekɑ̃te/ [1] ⓵ *vtr* **(a)** to
associate with ⟨*person*⟩; to move in ⟨*milieu*⟩
(b) to attend ⟨*school*⟩; to go to ⟨*restaurant*⟩
⓶ **se fréquenter** *v refl* (+ *v être*) ⟨*friends*⟩
to see one another

frère /fʀɛʀ/ *nm* brother

fresque /fʀɛsk/ *nf* **(a)** fresco
(b) panorama

fret /fʀɛt/ *nm* freight

frétiller /fʀetije/ [1] *vi* ⟨*fish*⟩ to wriggle;
~ de la queue ⟨*dog*⟩ to wag its tail

freudien, -ienne /fʀødjɛ̃, ɛn/ *adj, nm,f*
Freudian

friable /fʀijabl/ *adj* ⟨*rock, biscuit*⟩ crumbly

friand, ~e /fʀijɑ̃, ɑ̃d/ ⓵ *adj* être ~ de qch
to be very fond of sth
⓶ *nm* (Culin) puff; ~ au fromage cheese puff

friandise /fʀijɑ̃diz/ *nf* sweet (GB), candy
(US)

fric /fʀik/ *nm* (colloq) dough (colloq), money

friche /fʀiʃ/ *nf* waste land

friction /fʀiksjɔ̃/ *nf* **(a)** (Med) rub
(b) friction

frictionner /fʀiksjɔne/ [1] ⓵ *vtr* to give
[sb] a rub ⟨*person*⟩; to rub ⟨*head, feet*⟩
⓶ **se frictionner** *v refl* (+ *v être*) to rub
oneself down

frigidaire® /fʀiʒidɛʀ/ *nm* refrigerator

frigide /fʀiʒid/ *adj* frigid

frigo /fʀigo/ *nm* (colloq) fridge (colloq)

frigorifique /fʀigɔʀifik/ *adj* refrigerated

frileux, -euse /fʀilø, øz/ *adj* **(a)** sensitive
to the cold
(b) ⟨*attitude, policy*⟩ cautious

frimas /fʀima/ *nm pl* cold weather

frime /fʀim/ *nf* (colloq) pour la ~ for show;
c'est de la ~ it's all an act

frimer /fʀime/ [1] *vi* (colloq) to show off
(colloq)

frimousse /fʀimus/ *nf* (colloq) little face

fringale /fʀɛ̃gal/ *nf* (colloq) j'ai la ~ I'm
absolutely starving (colloq)

fringuer: se fringuer /fʀɛ̃ge/ [1] *v refl*
(+ *v être*) (colloq) to dress

friper /fʀipe/ [1] *vtr*, **se friper** *v refl*
(+ *v être*) to crease, to crumple

fripon, -onne /fʀipɔ̃, ɔn/ *nm,f* (colloq)
rascal

fripouille /fʀipuj/ *nf* (colloq) crook (colloq)

frire /fʀiʀ/ [64] *vtr, vi* to fry

frisé, ~e¹ /fʀize/ ⓵ *pp* ▸ FRISER
⓶ *pp adj* ⟨*hair*⟩ curly; ⟨*person*⟩ curly-haired

frisée² /fʀize/ *nf* curly endive

friser /fʀize/ [1] ⓵ *vtr* **(a)** to curl; se faire
~ to have one's hair curled
(b) to border on; cela frise les 10% it's
approaching 10%
⓶ *vi* to curl; ⟨*person*⟩ to have curly hair

frisson /fʀisɔ̃/ *nm* shiver, shudder; j'ai des
~s I keep shivering; grand ~ great thrill

frissonner /fʀisɔne/ [1] *vi* **(a)** (with cold) to
shiver; (with fear) to shudder
(b) ⟨*leaves*⟩ to tremble
(c) ⟨*water, milk*⟩ to simmer

frit /fʀi/ ▸ FRIRE

frite /fʀit/ *nf* (Culin) chip (GB), French fry
(US)

friterie /fʀitʀi/ *nf* chip shop (GB), French-
fries stall (US)

friteuse /fʀitøz/ *nf* chip pan (GB), deep fat
fryer (US)

friture /fʀityʀ/ *nf* **(a)** frying
(b) (for frying) fat; oil
(c) fried food
(d) (fish) petite ~ ≈ whitebait
(e) (on radio) crackling

frivole /fʀivɔl/ *adj* frivolous

froid, ~e /fʀwa, fʀwad/ ⓵ *adj* cold;
(figurative) cold, cool
⓶ *adv* il fait ~ it's cold
⓷ *nm* **(a)** cold; coup de ~ chill; prendre ~
to catch a cold
(b) coldness; ils sont en ~ avec moi
relations between them and me are strained;
jeter un ~ to cast a chill
⓸ **à froid** *phr* démarrage à ~ cold start
IDIOMS il fait un ~ de canard (colloq) it is
bitterly cold; donner ~ dans le dos to send a
shiver down the spine; ne pas avoir ~ aux
yeux to be fearless

froidement /fʀwadmɑ̃/ *adv* **(a)** coolly;
abattre ~ to shoot [sb] down in cold blood
(b) regarder les choses ~ to look at things
with a cool head

froideur /fʀwadœʀ/ *nf* (gen) coldness;
(of reception) coolness

froissement /fʀwasmɑ̃/ *nm* **(a)** (of paper,
fabric) crumpling; (noise) rustling
(b) (Med) strain

froisser /fʀwase/ [1] **1** *vtr* (a) to crease ⟨*fabric*⟩; to crumple ⟨*paper*⟩
(b) to offend ⟨*person*⟩
(c) (Med) to strain
2 se froisser *v refl* (+ *v être*) (a) to crease
(b) to be hurt *or* offended
(c) (Med) to strain

frôlement /fʀolmɑ̃/ *nm* (a) brushing
(b) rustling; fluttering

frôler /fʀole/ [1] **1** *vtr* (a) ⟨*person*⟩ to brush (against)
(b) ⟨*bullet, car*⟩ to miss narrowly; **il a frôlé la mort** he came close to dying
2 se frôler *v refl* (+ *v être*) ⟨*people*⟩ to brush against each other

fromage /fʀɔmaʒ/ *nm* cheese; **∼ maigre** low-fat cheese; **∼ de tête** brawn (GB), head cheese (US)

fromager /fʀɔmaʒe/ *nm* (a) cheesemaker
(b) cheese seller

fromagerie /fʀɔmaʒʀi/ *nf* cheese shop

froment /fʀɔmɑ̃/ *nm* wheat

froncement /fʀɔ̃smɑ̃/ *nm* **avoir un léger ∼ de sourcils** to frown slightly

froncer /fʀɔ̃se/ [12] *vtr* (a) to gather ⟨*pleats*⟩
(b) **∼ les sourcils** to frown

fronde /fʀɔ̃d/ *nf* (a) ⟨*weapon*⟩ sling
(b) ⟨*toy*⟩ catapult (GB), slingshot (US)
(c) revolt

frondeur, -euse /fʀɔ̃dœʀ, øz/ *adj* rebellious

front /fʀɔ̃/ **1** *nm* (a) forehead
(b) (Mil) front
(c) façade
2 de front *phr* **ils marchaient à quatre de ∼** they were walking four abreast; **mener plusieurs tâches de ∼** to have several jobs on the go
IDIOMS **avoir le ∼ de faire** to have the face *or* effrontery to do

frontal, ∼e, *mpl* **-aux** /fʀɔ̃tal, o/ *adj* ⟨*attack*⟩ frontal; ⟨*collision*⟩ head-on

frontalier, -ière /fʀɔ̃talje, ɛʀ/ **1** *adj* border; **travailleur ∼** person who works across the border
2 *nm,f* person living near the border

frontière /fʀɔ̃tjɛʀ/ *nf* (a) frontier, border; **∼ naturelle** natural boundary
(b) **∼s entre les disciplines** boundaries between disciplines

fronton /fʀɔ̃tɔ̃/ *nm* pediment

frottement /fʀɔtmɑ̃/ *nm* (a) rubbing
(b) friction

frotter /fʀɔte/ [1] **1** *vtr* (a) to rub
(b) to scrub
2 *vi* to rub
3 se frotter *v refl* (+ *v être*) (a) **se ∼ les yeux** to rub one's eyes
(b) to scrub oneself
(c) **se ∼ à** to take on ⟨*person*⟩
IDIOMS **qui s'y frotte s'y pique** if you go looking for trouble, you'll find it

frottis /fʀɔti/ *nm inv* (Med) smear

froussard, ∼e /fʀusaʀ, aʀd/ *nm,f* (colloq) chicken (colloq), coward

frousse /fʀus/ *nf* (colloq) fright

fructifier /fʀyktifje/ [2] *vi* ⟨*capital*⟩ to yield a profit; ⟨*business*⟩ to flourish

fructueux, -euse /fʀyktɥø, øz/ *adj*
(a) ⟨*relationship, meeting*⟩ fruitful; ⟨*attempt, career*⟩ successful
(b) (financially) profitable

frugal, ∼e, *mpl* **-aux** /fʀygal, o/ *adj* frugal

fruit /fʀɥi/ *nm* fruit
■ **∼ de la passion** passion fruit; **∼ sec** dried fruit; **∼s de mer** seafood

fruité, ∼e /fʀɥite/ *adj* ⟨*alcohol, aroma*⟩ fruity

fruitier, -ière /fʀɥitje, ɛʀ/ **1** *adj* fruit
2 *nm,f* fruiterer (GB), fruit seller (US)

fruste /fʀyst/ *adj* unsophisticated

frustrant, ∼e /fʀystʀɑ̃, ɑ̃t/ *adj* frustrating

frustré, ∼e /fʀystʀe/ *adj* frustrated

frustrer /fʀystʀe/ [1] *vtr* (a) **∼ qn** to thwart sb
(b) **∼ qn de qch** to deprive sb of sth; to cheat sb (out) of sth
(c) to frustrate

fuel /fjul/ *nm* = FIOUL

fugace /fygas/ *adj* fleeting; ⟨*symptom*⟩ elusive

fugitif, -ive /fyʒitif, iv/ **1** *adj*
(a) ⟨*prisoner*⟩ escaped
(b) fleeting, elusive
2 *nm,f* fugitive

fugue /fyg/ *nf* (a) **faire une ∼** to run away
(b) (Mus) fugue

fugueur, -euse /fygœʀ, øz/ *nm,f* runaway ⟨*child*⟩

fui, ∼e /fɥi/ ▶ FUIR

fuir /fɥiʀ/ [29] **1** *vtr* (a) to flee ⟨*country, oppression*⟩
(b) to avoid ⟨*discussion, person*⟩; to steer clear of ⟨*crowd*⟩; to stay out of ⟨*sun*⟩
2 *vi* (a) ⟨*person*⟩ to flee; ⟨*animal*⟩ to run away; **faire ∼** to scare [sb] off ⟨*person*⟩
(b) ⟨*tap, gas, pen*⟩ to leak
(c) **∼ devant ses responsabilités** not to face up to one's responsibilities

fuite /fɥit/ *nf* (a) (gen) flight; (of prisoner) escape; **prendre la ∼** to flee; to escape
(b) (of information) leak
(c) (of liquid, gas) leak

fulgurant, ∼e /fylgyʀɑ̃, ɑ̃t/ *adj* ⟨*attack*⟩ lightning; ⟨*progression*⟩ dazzling; ⟨*imagination*⟩ brilliant

fulminer /fylmine/ [1] *vi* to fulminate

fumé, ∼e[1] /fyme/ **1** *pp* ▶ FUMER
2 *pp adj* (a) (Culin) smoked
(b) ⟨*lenses*⟩ tinted; ⟨*glass*⟩ smoked

fumée[2] /fyme/ *nf* (a) smoke; **∼s** (from factory) fumes; **partir en ∼** (figurative) to go up in smoke
(b) steam

fumer /fyme/ [1] **1** *vtr* to smoke   ⋯⟩

2 *vi* **(a)** ⟨*person, chimney*⟩ to smoke
(b) ⟨*soup*⟩ to steam; ⟨*acid*⟩ to give off fumes
IDIOMS ~ comme un pompier *or* sapeur to smoke like a chimney

fûmes /fym/ ▸ ÊTRE¹

fumet /fymɛ/ *nm* (Culin) (of meat) aroma; (of wine) bouquet

fumeur, -euse¹ /fymœR, øz/ *nm,f* smoker; **zone non ~s** non-smoking area

fumeux, -euse² /fymø, øz/ *adj* ⟨*theory, ideas*⟩ woolly (GB), wooly (US)

fumier /fymje/ *nm* manure

fumigène /fymiʒɛn/ *adj* **grenade ~** smoke grenade

fumiste /fymist/ *nm,f* (colloq) **(a)** shirker
(b) phoney (colloq)

fumisterie /fymistəri/ *nf* **(a)** (colloq) joke; **c'est de la ~** it's a joke
(b) chimney engineering; stove fitting

fumoir /fymwaR/ *nm* smoking-room

funambule /fynãbyl/ *nmf* tightrope walker

funèbre /fynɛbR/ *adj* **(a)** cérémonie/service **~** funeral ceremony/service
(b) gloomy

funérailles /fyneRɑj/ *nf pl* funeral

funéraire /fyneRɛR/ *adj* ⟨*ceremony*⟩ funeral; ⟨*monument*⟩ funerary

funeste /fynɛst/ *adj* fatal; fateful

funiculaire /fynikylɛR/ *nm* funicular

fur: au fur et à mesure /ofyReaməzyR/ *phr* as one goes along; **le chemin se rétrécissait au ~ et à mesure qu'on avançait** the path grew progressively narrower as we went along

furent /fyR/ ▸ ÊTRE¹

furet /fyRɛ/ *nm* ferret

fureter /fyRte/ [18] *vi* to rummage

fureur /fyRœR/ *nf* **(a)** rage, fury
(b) frenzy; **avec ~** frenziedly; **ce sport fait ~ en ce moment** that sport is all the rage at the moment

furibond, -e /fyRibɔ̃, ɔ̃d/ *adj* furious

furie /fyRi/ *nf* rage, fury

furieusement /fyRjøzmã/ *adv*
(a) furiously, violently
(b) (colloq) **j'ai ~ envie de dormir** I'm dying to go to sleep

furieux, -ieuse /fyRjø, øz/ *adj* **(a)** furious, angry
(b) (colloq) ⟨*desire*⟩ terrible
(c) ⟨*battle*⟩ intense

furoncle /fyRɔ̃kl/ *nm* boil

furtif, -ive /fyRtif, iv/ *adj* **(a)** furtive; **marcher d'un pas ~** to creep along
(b) fleeting

furtivement /fyRtivmã/ *adv* furtively

fus /fy/ ▸ ÊTRE¹

fusain /fyzɛ̃/ *nm* charcoal crayon; charcoal drawing

fuseau, *pl* **~x** /fyzo/ *nm* **(a)** spindle; **en ~** tapering
(b) ski pants
(c) **~ horaire** time zone

fusée /fyze/ *nf* **(a)** rocket
(b) (Aut) stub axle

fuselage /fyzlaʒ/ *nm* fuselage

fuselé, ~e /fyzle/ *adj* tapering, spindle-shaped

fuser /fyze/ [1] *vi* to ring out; **les rires fusaient** laughter came from all sides

fusible /fyzibl/ *nm* fuse

fusil /fyzi/ *nm* **(a)** gun, shotgun; (Mil) rifle
(b) sharpening steel
(c) gas igniter

fusillade /fyzijad/ *nf* **(a)** gunfire
(b) shoot-out

fusiller /fyzije/ [1] *vtr* **(a)** to shoot
(b) (colloq) to wreck
IDIOMS **~ qn du regard** to look daggers at sb

fusil-mitrailleur, *pl* **fusils-mitrailleurs** /fyzimitRajœR/ *nm* light machine gun

fusion /fyzjɔ̃/ *nf* **(a)** (of metal, ice) melting; **roche en ~** molten rock
(b) (in biology, physics) fusion
(c) (of companies, parties) merger; (of systems, cultures) fusion; (of peoples) mixing

fusionner /fyzjone/ [1] *vtr, vi* to merge

fusse /fys/ ▸ ÊTRE¹

fussent /fys/ ▸ ÊTRE¹

fusses /fys/ ▸ ÊTRE¹

fussiez /fysje/ ▸ ÊTRE¹

fussions /fysjɔ̃/ ▸ ÊTRE¹

fut¹ /fy/ ▸ ÊTRE¹

fût¹ /fy/ ▸ ÊTRE¹

fût² /fy/ *nm* cask, barrel; drum

futaie /fytɛ/ *nf* forest of tall trees

futé, ~e /fyte/ **1** *adj* wily, crafty; **ce n'est pas très ~** that isn't *or* wasn't very clever
2 *nm,f* **(petit) ~** cunning little devil

fûtes /fyt/ ▸ ÊTRE¹

futile /fytil/ *adj* trivial; superficial

futilité /fytilite/ **1** *nf* superficiality
2 futilités *nf pl* **(a)** banalities
(b) trifles; trifling activities
(c) trivial details

futur, ~e /fytyR/ **1** *adj* future; **mon ~ mari** my husband-to-be
2 *nm* future

fuyant, ~e /fɥijã, ãt/ *adj* ⟨*look*⟩ shifty

fuyard, ~e /fɥijaR, aRd/ *nm,f* runaway

Gg

g, G /ʒe/ *nm inv* (a) (letter) g, G
(b) (*written abbr* = **gramme**) 250 g 250 g

gabarit /gabaʀi/ *nm* (a) (of vehicle) size
(b) (colloq) (of person) calibre (GB); (physical)
build

gabonais, **~e** /gabɔnɛ, ɛz/ *adj* Gabonese

gâcher /gɑʃe/ [1] *vtr* (a) to waste ⟨*food,
talent*⟩; to throw away ⟨*life*⟩
(b) to spoil ⟨*party*⟩

gâchette /gɑʃɛt/ *nf* (a) (of gun) tumbler
(b) (controversial) trigger
(c) (on lock) tumbler

gâchis /gɑʃi/ *nm inv* (a) waste
(b) mess

gadget /gadʒɛt/ *nm* gadget

gadin /gadɛ̃/ *nm* (colloq) **ramasser** *or*
prendre un ~ to fall flat on one's face

gadoue /gadu/ *nf* (colloq) mud

gaélique /gaelik/ *adj, nm* Gaelic

gaffe /gaf/ *nf* (colloq) (a) blunder; **faire une
~** to make a blunder
(b) **faire ~** to watch out

gag /gag/ *nm* (a) (in film, show) gag
(b) joke

gaga /gaga/ *adj inv* (colloq) (a) gaga (colloq)
(b) silly

gage /gaʒ/ **1** *nm* (a) security; **mettre qch
en ~** to pawn sth; **être le ~ de qch** to be a
guarantee of sth
(b) (Games) forfeit
(c) pledge
2 gages *nm pl* wages; **tueur à ~s** hired
killer

gager /gaʒe/ [13] *vtr* **~ que** to suppose that,
to wager that

gageure /gaʒyʀ/ *nf* challenge

gagnant, **~e** /gaɲɑ̃, ɑ̃t/ **1** *adj* winning
2 *nm,f* winner; winning horse; winning
ticket

gagne-pain /gaɲpɛ̃/ *nm inv* livelihood

gagne-petit /gaɲpəti/ *nmf inv* low-wage
earner

gagner /gaɲe/ [1] **1** *vtr* (a) to win; **~ d'une
longueur** to win by a length; **c'est gagné!**
we've done it!; **à tous les coups on gagne!**
every one a winner!
(b) to earn; **il gagne bien sa vie** he makes a
good living
(c) to gain ⟨*reputation, advantage, time*⟩;
~ de la vitesse to gather speed
(d) to save ⟨*time*⟩; **~ de la place en faisant**
to make more room by doing
(e) to win ⟨sb⟩ over
(f) to reach ⟨*place*⟩
(g) ⟨*blaze, disease*⟩ to spread to ⟨*place*⟩
(h) ⟨*fear*⟩ to overcome

(i) to beat ⟨sb⟩; **~ qn de vitesse** to outstrip
sb
2 *vi* (a) to win
(b) **le film gagne à être vu en version
originale** the film is best seen in the original
version
(c) to gain
(d) **y ~** to come off better; **y ~ en** to gain in
⟨*comfort*⟩
(e) ⟨*sea*⟩ to encroach

gagneur, **-euse** /gaɲœʀ, øz/ *nm,f* winner

gai, **~e** /gɛ/ *adj* (a) ⟨*person*⟩ happy; ⟨*smile,
expression*⟩ cheerful; ⟨*conversation*⟩ light-
hearted
(b) (ironic) **c'est ~** great!
(c) merry, tipsy

gaiement /gɛmɑ̃/ *adv* (a) cheerfully,
merrily; gaily
(b) (ironic) happily

gaieté /gete/ *nf* gaiety, cheerfulness

gaillard, **~e** /gajaʀ, aʀd/ *nm,f* strapping
lad/girl

gain /gɛ̃/ *nm* (a) earnings; **mes ~s au jeu**
my winnings
(b) (on stock exchange) gain
(c) saving; **c'est un ~ de temps
considérable** it saves a considerable amount
of time

gaine /gɛn/ *nf* (a) (for dagger) sheath
(b) girdle
(c) (Tech) sheathing; casing
(d) (Bot) sheath

gainer /gene/ [1] *vtr* to sheathe

gala /gala/ *nm* gala

galamment /galamɑ̃/ *adv* gallantly

galant, **~e** /galɑ̃, ɑ̃t/ *adj* (a) gallant,
gentlemanly
(b) romantic

galanterie /galɑ̃tʀi/ *nf* gallantry

galaxie /galaksi/ *nf* galaxy

galbe /galb/ *nm* curve

galbé, **~e** /galbe/ *adj* shapely

gale /gal/ *nf* (a) scabies
(b) (on dog, cat) mange; (on sheep) scab
(c) (Bot) scab

galère /galɛʀ/ *nf* (a) galley
(b) (colloq) hell
IDIOMS être dans la même ~ to be in the
same boat

galérer /galere/ [14] *vi* (colloq) to have a
hard time

galerie /galʀi/ *nf* (a) gallery
(b) tunnel
■ **~ marchande** shopping arcade; **~ de toit**
roof rack; **Galerie des Glaces** hall of mirrors ⋯❖

IDIOMS amuser la ~ (colloq) to play to the gallery; **pour épater la ~** (colloq) to impress the crowd

galet /galɛ/ nm **(a)** pebble
(b) (Tech) roller

galette /galɛt/ nf **(a)** round flat biscuit, cookie (US)
(b) pancake
■ **~ des Rois** Twelfth Night cake

Galles /gal/ pr nf pl **le pays de ~** Wales

gallois, ~e /galwɑ, az/ **1** adj Welsh
2 nm (language) Welsh

Gallois, ~e /galwɑ, az/ nm,f Welshman/ Welshwoman; **les ~** the Welsh

gallon /galɔ̃/ nm gallon

galoche /galɔʃ/ nf clog; **menton en ~** protruding chin

galon /galɔ̃/ nm **(a)** (for trimming) braid
(b) (Mil) stripe; **prendre du ~** to be promoted

galop /galo/ nm **(a)** gallop; **petit ~** canter; **grand ~** full gallop; **au ~!** (figurative) hurry up!
(b) (Mus) galop
IDIOMS chassez le naturel il revient au ~ (Proverb) what's bred in the bone will come out in the flesh

galopade /galɔpad/ nf **(a)** gallop
(b) (colloq) (figurative) stampede

galoper /galɔpe/ [1] vi **(a)** to gallop
(b) (colloq) ⟨child⟩ to charge (around)

galopin /galɔpɛ̃/ nm rascal

galvaniser /galvanize/ [1] vtr (lit, fig) to galvanize

gamba /gɑ̃ba, pl as/ nf large (Mediterranean) prawn

gambader /gɑ̃bade/ [1] vi to gambol

gamelle /gamɛl/ nf (of soldier) dixie (GB), mess kit; (of camper) billycan (GB), tin dish; (of worker) lunchbox; (for pet) dish
IDIOMS prendre une ~ (colloq) to fall flat on one's face (colloq); (figurative) to come a cropper

gamin, ~e /gamɛ̃, in/ **1** adj ⟨air, look⟩ youthful; ⟨attitude⟩ childish
2 nm,f kid (colloq); **~ des rues** street urchin

gaminerie /gaminʀi/ nf childish behaviour

gamme /gam/ nf **(a)** (Mus) scale
(b) range; **produit (de) bas de ~** low quality product; cheap product; **~ de produits** product range

gammée /game/ adj f **croix ~** swastika

ganglion /gɑ̃glijɔ̃/ nm ganglion

gangrène /gɑ̃gʀɛn/ nf **(a)** (Med) gangrene
(b) (figurative) canker

gangrener /gɑ̃gʀəne/ [16] **1** vtr to corrupt
2 se gangrener v refl (+ v être) **(a)** (Med) to become gangrenous
(b) (figurative) to become corrupt

gangster /gɑ̃gstɛʀ/ nm **(a)** gangster
(b) swindler

gant /gɑ̃/ nm glove
■ **~ de boxe** boxing glove; **~ de ménage** rubber glove; **~ de toilette** ≈ (face) flannel (GB), wash cloth (US)

IDIOMS son tailleur lui va comme un ~ her suit fits her like a glove; **mettre** or **prendre des ~s avec qn** to handle sb with kid gloves

garage /gaʀaʒ/ nm **(a)** garage
(b) garage, filling station
■ **~ à vélos** bicycle shed

garagiste /gaʀaʒist/ nmf **(a)** garage owner
(b) car mechanic

garant, ~e /gaʀɑ̃, ɑ̃t/ **1** adj **être** or **se porter ~ de qn/qch** to vouch for sb/sth
2 nm,f guarantor

garanti, ~e[1] /gaʀɑ̃ti/ **1** pp ▶ GARANTIR
2 adj **(a)** with a guarantee
(b) guaranteed

garantie[2] /gaʀɑ̃ti/ nf **(a)** (gen, Law) guarantee
(b) (in finance) security; guarantee
(c) (in insurance) cover; **montant des ~s** sum insured

garantir /gaʀɑ̃tiʀ/ [3] vtr **(a)** to guarantee; **~ qch à qn** to guarantee sb sth
(b) to safeguard ⟨security⟩
(c) to guarantee ⟨loan, product⟩

garçon /gaʀsɔ̃/ nm **(a)** boy
(b) young man; **un brave** or **gentil ~** a nice chap (GB) or guy (US)
(c) bachelor
(d) ~ (de café) waiter
■ **~ d'écurie** stableboy; **~ d'honneur** best man; **~ manqué** tomboy

garçonnet /gaʀsɔnɛ/ nm little boy

garçonnière /gaʀsɔnjɛʀ/ nf bachelor flat (GB) or apartment

garde[1] /gaʀd/ nm **(a)** guard
(b) (for invalid, patient) carer; (in prison) warder
■ **~ champêtre** ≈ local policeman (appointed by the municipality); **~ du corps** bodyguard; **~ forestier** forest warden; **Garde des Sceaux** French Minister of Justice

garde[2] /gaʀd/ nf **(a)** nurse
(b) (gen, Mil, Sport) guard; **la vieille ~** the old guard; **monter la ~** ⟨soldier⟩ to mount guard; **monter la ~ auprès de qn** to keep watch over sb; to stand guard over sb; **être de ~** ⟨doctor⟩ to be on call; ⟨soldier⟩ to be on guard duty
(c) **mettre qn en ~** to warn sb; **prendre ~** to watch out; to be careful
(d) (of sword) hilt
(e) (page de) **~** endpaper
■ **~ à vue** (Law) ≈ police custody

garde-à-vous /gaʀdavu/ nm inv **se mettre au ~** to stand to attention

garde-chasse, pl **gardes-chasses** /gaʀdəʃas/ nm game warden; gamekeeper

garde-côte, pl **~s** /gaʀdəkot/ nm coastguard ship

garde-fou, pl **~s** /gaʀdəfu/ nm **(a)** parapet
(b) safeguard

garde-malade, pl **gardes-malades** /gaʀdmalad/ nmf home nurse

garde-manger /gaʀdmɑ̃ʒe/ nm inv meat safe

garder /gaʀde/ [1] **1** *vtr* **(a)** to keep ⟨*object*⟩; to keep on ⟨*hat, sweater*⟩; to keep on ⟨*employee*⟩
(b) ⟨*soldier*⟩ to guard; ⟨*person*⟩ to look after
2 se garder *v refl* (+ *v être*) **(a) se ~ de faire** to be careful not to do
(b) ⟨*foodstuff*⟩ to keep

garderie /gaʀdəʀi/ *nf* **(a)** day nursery
(b) after-school child-minding facility

garde-robe, *pl* **~s** /gaʀdəʀɔb/ *nf* wardrobe

gardien, -ienne[1] /gaʀdjɛ̃, ɛn/ *nm,f*
(a) (in premises) security guard; (in apartment block) caretaker (GB), janitor (US); (in park) keeper; (in prison) warder; (in museum) attendant
(b) (Sport) keeper
■ **~ de but** goalkeeper; **~ de nuit** night watchman; **~ de la paix** police officer

gardiennage /gaʀdjɛnaʒ/ *nm* (of premises) security; (of apartment block) caretaking

gardienne[2] /gaʀdjɛn/ *nf* **(a)** ▶ GARDIEN
(b) ~ d'enfant childminder (GB), day-care lady (US)

gardon /gaʀdɔ̃/ *nm* roach
IDIOMS **être frais comme un ~** to be as fresh as a daisy

gare /gaʀ/ **1** *nf* (railway) station
2 *excl* **~ (à toi)!** (threat) careful!, watch it! (colloq)
■ **~ maritime** harbour (GB) station; **~ routière** coach station (GB), bus station (US)
IDIOMS **sans crier ~** without any warning

garenne /gaʀɛn/ *nf* (rabbit) warren

garer /gaʀe/ [1] **1** *vtr* to park
2 se garer *v refl* (+ *v être*) **(a)** to park
(b) ⟨*vehicle*⟩ to pull over

gargariser: se gargariser /gaʀgaʀize/ [1] *v refl* (+ *v être*) to gargle

gargarisme /gaʀgaʀism/ *nm* **(a)** gargling
(b) mouthwash

gargouille /gaʀguj/ *nf* **(a)** gargoyle
(b) waterspout

gargouiller /gaʀguje/ [1] *vi* ⟨*water, fountain*⟩ to gurgle; ⟨*stomach*⟩ to rumble

garnement /gaʀnəmɑ̃/ *nm* brat (colloq)

garni, ~e /gaʀni/ **1** *pp* ▶ GARNIR
2 *adj* **bien ~** ⟨*wallet*⟩ full; ⟨*fridge*⟩ well-stocked; ⟨*buffet*⟩ copious

garnir /gaʀniʀ/ [3] *vtr* **(a)** ⟨*objects*⟩ to fill ⟨*room*⟩; ⟨*person*⟩ to stock ⟨*shelves*⟩
(b) to stuff ⟨*cushion*⟩
(c) (Culin) to decorate ⟨*cake*⟩; to garnish ⟨*meat*⟩

garnison /gaʀnizɔ̃/ *nf* garrison

garniture /gaʀnityʀ/ *nf* **(a)** (Culin) side dish; (for dessert) decoration; (for meat, fish) garnish
(b) (on hat, garment) trimming
■ **~ de cheminée** mantelpiece ornaments

garrigue /gaʀig/ *nf* garrigue, scrubland (in southern France)

garrot /gaʀo/ *nm* **(a)** (Med) tourniquet

(b) (Zool) withers; **le cheval mesure 1,50 m au ~** ≈ the horse is 15 hands

gars /ga/ *nm inv* (colloq) **(a)** boy
(b) chap (GB) (colloq), guy (US) (colloq)

Gascogne /gaskɔɲ/ *pr nf* Gascony

Gascon, -onne /gaskɔ̃, ɔn/ *nm,f* Gascon
IDIOMS **faire une offre de ~** to raise false hopes

gas-oil /gazwal/ *nm* diesel (GB), fuel oil (US)

gaspillage /gaspijaʒ/ *nm* **(a)** wasting; waste
(b) squandering

gaspiller /gaspije/ [1] *vtr* **(a)** to waste ⟨*time, food*⟩
(b) to squander ⟨*resources, talent*⟩

gastronome /gastʀɔnɔm/ *nmf* gourmet, gastronome

gastronomie /gastʀɔnɔmi/ *nf* gastronomy

gastronomique /gastʀɔnɔmik/ *adj* (Culin) gourmet, gastronomic

gâteau, *pl* **~x** /gato/ *nm* cake; gâteau
■ **~ apéritif** cocktail biscuit; **~ de cire** honeycomb; **~ de riz** ≈ rice pudding; **~ sec** biscuit (GB), cookie (US)
IDIOMS **c'est du ~!** (colloq) it's a piece of cake! (colloq); **c'est pas du ~!** (colloq) it's no picnic!

gâter /gate/ [1] **1** *vtr* to spoil; to ruin ⟨*teeth*⟩
2 se gâter *v refl* (+ *v être*) **(a)** to go bad; to rot
(b) to take a turn for the worse

gâterie /gatʀi/ *nf* little treat

gâteux, -euse /gatø, øz/ *adj* **(a)** senile
(b) il est ~ avec sa fille (colloq) he's dotty about his daughter (colloq)

gauche[1] /goʃ/ *adj* **(a)** left
(b) ⟨*person, manner*⟩ awkward; ⟨*style*⟩ clumsy
IDIOMS **se lever du pied ~** (colloq) to get out of bed on the wrong side (GB), to get up on the wrong side of the bed (US)

gauche[2] /goʃ/ *nf* **(a)** left; **à ~** ⟨*drive*⟩ on the left; ⟨*go, look*⟩ to the left; ⟨*turn*⟩ left; **de ~** ⟨*page*⟩ left-hand
(b) Left; **de ~** left-wing
IDIOMS **passer l'arme à ~** (colloq) to kick the bucket (colloq); **jusqu'à la ~** (colloq) completely; **mettre de l'argent à ~** (colloq) to put money aside

gauchement /goʃmɑ̃/ *adv* awkwardly

gaucher, -ère /goʃe, ɛʀ/ *adj* left-handed

gaucherie /goʃʀi/ *nf* awkwardness

gauchiste /goʃist/ *adj, nmf* leftist

gaufre /gofʀ/ *nf* **(a)** waffle
(b) honeycomb

gaufrette /gofʀɛt/ *nf* wafer

gaufrier /gofʀije/ *nm* waffle iron

Gaule /gol/ *pr nf* Gaul

Gaulois, ~e /golwa, az/ *nm,f* Gaul

gaver /gave/ [1] **1** *vtr* to force-feed ⟨*geese*⟩ ⋯⟶

2 se gaver *v refl* (+ *v être*) **(a)** to stuff oneself
(b) se ~ de to devour ⟨*novels*⟩
gay /gɛ/ *adj inv, nm* gay, homosexual
gaz /gɑz/ **1** *nm inv* gas
2 *nm pl* **(a)** (Aut) air-fuel mixture; **rouler à pleins ~** (colloq) to go at full throttle
(b) (Med) wind
■ **~ d'échappement** exhaust fumes; **~ de ville** mains gas
IDIOMS **il y a de l'eau dans le ~** (colloq) there's trouble brewing
gaze /gɑz/ *nf* gauze
gazéifier /gazeifje/ [2] *vtr* to carbonate ⟨*drink*⟩
gazelle /gazɛl/ [1] *vtr* to gas
gazer /gaze/ [1] **1** *vtr* to gas
2 *vi* (colloq) **ça gaze** things are fine
gazette /gazɛt/ *nf* newspaper
gazeux, -euse /gazø, øz/ *adj* **(a)** ⟨*drink*⟩ fizzy
(b) gaseous
gazinière /gazinjɛʀ/ *nf* gas cooker (GB), gas stove
gazoduc /gazɔdyk/ *nm* gas pipeline
gazole /gazɔl/ *nm* diesel (oil) (GB), fuel oil (US)
gazon /gazɔ̃/ *nm* **(a)** grass, turf
(b) lawn
gazouiller /gazuje/ [1] *vi* to twitter; to babble
GDF /ʒedeɛf/ (*abbr* = **Gaz de France**) *French gas board*
géant, ~e /ʒeɑ̃, ɑ̃t/ **1** *adj* **(a)** huge
(b) giant
2 *nm,f* giant/giantess
geignement /ʒɛɲəmɑ̃/ *nm* moan, groan
geindre /ʒɛ̃dʀ/ [55] *vi* (in pain) to moan, to groan; to whimper; (complainingly) to whine
gel /ʒɛl/ *nm* **(a)** frost; **résistant au ~** frost-resistant
(b) ~ des prix/salaires price/wage freeze
(c) après le ~ du projet after the project had been put on ice
(d) gel
gélatine /ʒelatin/ *nf* gelatine (GB), gelatin (US)
gelé, ~e¹ /ʒəle/ **1** *pp* ▶ GELER
2 *adj* **(a)** ⟨*water, ground*⟩ frozen; ⟨*toe*⟩ frost-bitten; **j'ai les oreilles ~es** my ears are frozen
(b) ⟨*prices, negotiations*⟩ frozen
gelée² /ʒəle/ *nf* **(a)** (from fruit) jelly; (from meat, fish) gelatinous stock; **œuf en ~** egg in aspic
(b) gel
(c) frost
■ **~ blanche** hoarfrost
geler /ʒəle/ [17] **1** *vtr* **(a)** to freeze; to nip ⟨*plant*⟩
(b) to freeze ⟨*salaries*⟩; to suspend ⟨*plan*⟩
2 *vi* ⟨*water, ground, finger, foot*⟩ to freeze; ⟨*plant*⟩ to be frosted
3 *v impers* **il gèle** it's freezing

gélule /ʒelyl/ *nf* capsule
Gémeaux /ʒemo/ *pr nm pl* Gemini
gémir /ʒemiʀ/ [3] *vi* to moan; to whimper
gémissement /ʒemismɑ̃/ *nm* moan
gemme /ʒɛm/ *nf* **(a)** gem, gemstone
(b) resin
gênant, ~e /ʒɛnɑ̃, ɑ̃t/ *adj* **(a)** ⟨*box*⟩ cumbersome; ⟨*problem*⟩ annoying
(b) embarrassing
gencive /ʒɑ̃siv/ *nf* gum
gendarme /ʒɑ̃daʀm/ *nm* **(a)** (Mil) gendarme, French policeman
(b) dried sausage
■ **~ couché** road hump
gendarmerie /ʒɑ̃daʀm(ə)ʀi/ *nf*
(a) ≈ police station
(b) ~ (nationale) gendarmerie
gendre /ʒɑ̃dʀ/ *nm* son-in-law
gêne /ʒɛn/ *nf* **(a)** embarrassment
(b) discomfort
(c) inconvenience
(d) poverty
gêné, ~e /ʒɛne/ **1** *pp* ▶ GÊNER
2 *adj* **(a)** embarrassed
(b) short of money
gène /ʒɛn/ *nm* gene
généalogie /ʒenealɔʒi/ *nf* genealogy
généalogique /ʒenealɔʒik/ *adj* genealogical; **arbre ~** family tree
gêner /ʒene/ [1] **1** *vtr* **(a)** to disturb, to bother
(b) ⟨*smoke, noise*⟩ to bother
(c) to embarrass
(d) ⟨*belt*⟩ to restrict ⟨*breathing*⟩
(e) ⟨*person*⟩ to get in the way of ⟨*progress*⟩
2 se gêner *v refl* (+ *v être*) **(a)** to get in each other's way
(b) je vais me ~ (colloq) see if I don't; **ne vous gênez pas pour moi** don't mind me
général, ~e¹, mpl -aux /ʒeneʀal, o/
1 *adj* general; **de l'avis ~** in most people's opinion; **en ~, de façon ~e** generally, in general; **en règle ~e** as a rule
2 *nm* general
générale² /ʒeneʀal/ *nf* **(a)** dress rehearsal
(b) general's wife
généralement /ʒeneʀalmɑ̃/ *adv* generally
généralisation /ʒeneʀalizasjɔ̃/ *nf* widespread use; generalization; spread
généralisé, ~e /ʒeneʀalize/ *adj* ⟨*conflict*⟩ widespread; ⟨*process*⟩ general; ⟨*cancer*⟩ generalized
généraliser /ʒeneʀalize/ [1] **1** *vtr* to bring [sth] into general use
2 *vi* to generalize
3 se généraliser *v refl* (+ *v être*) ⟨*technique*⟩ to become standard; ⟨*tax*⟩ to become widely applicable; ⟨*strike, illness*⟩ to spread
généraliste /ʒeneʀalist/ *adj* non-specialized; **(médecin) ~** GP, general practitioner
généralité /ʒeneʀalite/ *nf* generality

générateur, -trice /ʒeneʀatœʀ, tʀis/
1 *adj* être ~ de to generate
2 *nm* generator

génération /ʒeneʀasjɔ̃/ *nf* generation

générer /ʒeneʀe/ [14] *utr* to generate

généreusement /ʒeneʀøzmɑ̃/ *adv*
generously; liberally

généreux, -euse /ʒeneʀø, øz/ *adj*
(a) ⟨person, nature⟩ generous; ⟨idea, gesture⟩
noble
(b) ⟨portion⟩ generous; **poitrine généreuse**
large bust

générique /ʒeneʀik/ 1 *adj* generic
2 *nm* credits; **le ~ de fin** closing credits

générosité /ʒeneʀozite/ *nf* generosity

genèse /ʒənɛz/ *nf* (a) (of plan) genesis;
(of state) birth
(b) **la Genèse** Genesis

genêt /ʒənɛ/ *nm* (Bot) broom

généticien, -ienne /ʒenetisjɛ̃, ɛn/ *nm,f*
geneticist

génétique /ʒenetik/ 1 *adj* genetic
2 *nf* genetics

génétiquement /ʒenetikmɑ̃/ *adv*
genetically; ~ **modifié** genetically modified

Genève /ʒənɛv/ *pr n* Geneva

genévrier /ʒənevʀije/ *nm* juniper

génial, ~e, mpl -iaux /ʒenjal, o/ *adj*
(a) brilliant
(b) (colloq) great (colloq)

génie /ʒeni/ *nm* (a) genius; **idée de ~**
brainwave
(b) spirit; genie
(c) engineering

genièvre /ʒənjɛvʀ/ *nm* Dutch gin

génisse /ʒenis/ *nf* heifer

génital, ~e, mpl -aux /ʒenital, o/ *adj*
genital

génocide /ʒenɔsid/ *nm* genocide

génoise /ʒenwaz/ *nf* ≈ sponge cake

genou, pl ~x /ʒ(ə)nu/ 1 *nm* knee; **sur les
~x de qn** on sb's lap
2 **à genoux** *phr* **se mettre à ~x** to kneel
down; to go down on one's knees
IDIOMS faire du ~ à qn (colloq) to play footsie
with sb (colloq); **mettre qn sur les ~x** (colloq)
to wear sb out

genouillère /ʒənujɛʀ/ *nf* (Sport) knee pad;
(Med) knee support

genre /ʒɑ̃ʀ/ *nm* (a) sort, kind, type; **un peu
dans le ~ de ta robe** a bit like your dress
(b) **pour se donner un ~** (in order) to make
oneself look different
(c) (in grammar) gender
(d) genre
(e) (Bot, Zool) genus
■ **le ~ humain** mankind

gens /ʒɑ̃/ *nm pl* (a) people
(b) servants; retinue
■ ~ **d'église** clergymen; ~ **de lettres** writers;
~ **de maison** servants; ~ **du voyage**
travelling (GB) people

gentil, -ille /ʒɑ̃ti, ij/ *adj* (a) kind, nice
(b) good; **sois ~** be a good boy

(c) **c'est bien ~ tout ça, mais...** that's all
very well, but...

gentilhomme, pl gentilshommes
/ʒɑ̃tijɔm, ʒɑ̃tizɔm/ *nm* gentleman;
~ **campagnard** country gentleman

gentillesse /ʒɑ̃tijɛs/ *nf* (a) kindness
(b) (ironic) **échanger des ~s** to exchange
insults

gentiment /ʒɑ̃timɑ̃/ *adv* (a) kindly
(b) quietly

géographie /ʒeɔgʀafi/ *nf* geography

geôlier, -ière /ʒolje, ɛʀ/ *nm,f* jailer

géologie /ʒeɔlɔʒi/ *nf* geology

géomètre /ʒeɔmɛtʀ/ *nm,f* land surveyor

géométrie /ʒeɔmetʀi/ *nf* geometry; **à ~
variable** ⟨doctrine⟩ flexible

géométrique /ʒeɔmetʀik/ *adj* geometric

Géorgie /ʒeɔʀʒi/ *pr nf* (a) (in US) Georgia
(b) (in Europe) Georgia

gérable /ʒeʀabl/ *adj* manageable; **situation
difficilement ~** a situation which is hard to
handle

gérance /ʒeʀɑ̃s/ *nf* management; **mettre
en ~** to appoint a manager for ⟨shop,
company⟩; to appoint a managing agent for
⟨property⟩

géranium /ʒeʀanjɔm/ *nm* geranium

gérant, ~e /ʒeʀɑ̃, ɑ̃t/ *nm,f* manager;
(of property) (managing) agent

gerbe /ʒɛʀb/ *nf* (a) bouquet; wreath
(b) (of water) spray
(c) (of wheat) sheaf

gercer /ʒɛʀse/ [12] *vi* to become chapped

gerçure /ʒɛʀsyʀ/ *nf* (in skin, lips) crack

gérer /ʒeʀe/ [14] *vtr* (a) to manage
⟨production, time⟩; to run ⟨business⟩
(b) to handle ⟨situation⟩

gériatrie /ʒeʀjatʀi/ *nf* geriatrics

germain, ~e /ʒɛʀmɛ̃, ɛn/ *adj* (a) ⟨cousin⟩
~ first cousin
(b) Germanic

germanique /ʒɛʀmanik/ *adj, nm*
Germanic

germanophone /ʒɛʀmanɔfɔn/ *nm,f*
German speaker

germe /ʒɛʀm/ *nm* (of embryo, seed) germ;
(of potato) sprout

germer /ʒɛʀme/ [1] *vi* (a) ⟨wheat⟩ to
germinate
(b) ⟨idea, suspicion⟩ to form

gérondif /ʒeʀɔ̃dif/ *nm* gerund, gerundive

gésier /ʒezje/ *nm* gizzard

gésir /ʒeziʀ/ [37] *vi* (formal) **ci-gît Luc Pichon**
here lies Luc Pichon

geste /ʒɛst/ *nm* (a) movement; gesture;
joindre le ~ à la parole to suit the action to
the word
(b) gesture, act

gesticuler /ʒɛstikyle/ [1] *vtr* (a) to
gesticulate
(b) to fidget

gestion /ʒɛstjɔ̃/ *nf* (a) management
(b) (of situation) handling　····⟫

(c) (of classroom) management

■ ~ **administrative** administration; ~ **des déchets** waste management; ~ **des stocks** stock (GB) *or* inventory (US) control; ~ **de portefeuille** portfolio management; ~ **de la production assistée par ordinateur** computer-aided production management

gestionnaire /ʒɛstjɔnɛʀ/ *nmf* administrator

■ ~ **de fichiers** (Comput) file-management system; ~ **de portefeuille** portfolio manager

gestuel, -elle[1] /ʒɛstɥɛl/ *adj* gestural

gestuelle[2] /ʒɛstɥɛl/ *nf* body language

geyser /ʒezɛʀ/ *nm* geyser

ghetto /geto/ *nm* ghetto

gibecière /ʒibsjɛʀ/ *nf* gamebag

gibier /ʒibje/ *nm* game; **gros** ~ big game; (figurative) big-time criminals

giboulée /ʒibule/ *nf* shower

giclée /ʒikle/ *nf* spurt; squirt

gicler /ʒikle/ [1] *vi* to spurt; to squirt

gifle /ʒifl/ *nf* slap in the face

gifler /ʒifle/ [1] *vtr* to slap [sb] across the face

gigantesque /ʒigɑ̃tɛsk/ *adj* huge, gigantic

gigaoctet /ʒigaɔktɛ/ *nm* gigabyte

GIGN /ʒeiʒeɛn/ *nm* (*abbr* = **Groupe d'intervention de la gendarmerie nationale**) *branch of the police specialized in cases of armed robbery, terrorism etc*

gigogne /ʒigɔɲ/ *adj* **tables** ~**s** nest of tables

gigot /ʒigo/ *nm* leg of lamb

gigoter /ʒigɔte/ [1] *vi* **(a)** to wriggle
(b) to fidget

gilet /ʒilɛ/ *nm* **(a)** cardigan
(b) waistcoat (GB), vest (US)

■ ~ **pare-balles** bulletproof vest; ~ **de sauvetage** lifejacket

gin /dʒin/ *nm* gin; ~ **tonic** gin and tonic

gingembre /ʒɛ̃ʒɑ̃bʀ/ *nm* ginger

girafe /ʒiʀaf/ *nf* (Zool) giraffe

giratoire /ʒiʀatwaʀ/ *adj* gyratory

■ **sens** ~ roundabout (GB), traffic circle (US)

girofle /ʒiʀɔfl/ *nm* **un clou de** ~ a clove

girolle /ʒiʀɔl/ *nf* chanterelle

girouette /ʒiʀwɛt/ *nf* windvane

gisement /ʒizmɑ̃/ *nm* (of oil, minerals) deposit

gît ▶ GÉSIR

gitan, -e /ʒitɑ̃, an/ *nm,f* Gypsy (GB)

gîte /ʒit/ *nm* **(a)** shelter
(b) (of hare) form

■ ~ **rural** self-catering cottage

givrant /ʒivʀɑ̃/ *adj m* **brouillard** ~ freezing fog

givre /ʒivʀ/ *nm* frost; ice

givré, -e /ʒivʀe/ *adj* **(a)** frosty; frost-covered; frozen
(b) (colloq) crazy
(c) (Culin) ⟨*glass*⟩ frosted

givrer /ʒivʀe/ [1] *vi*, **se givrer** *v refl* (+ *v être*) to frost over

glaçage /glasaʒ/ *nm* (Culin) (on dessert) icing

glace /glas/ *nf* **(a)** ice; **de** ~ ⟨*face*⟩ stony
(b) ice cream
(c) mirror
(d) sheet of glass; (of shop window) glass; (of car) window

IDIOMS rester de ~ to remain unmoved

glacé, -e /glase/ *adj* **(a)** ⟨*rain*⟩ ice-cold; ⟨*hands*⟩ frozen; **thé** ~ iced tea
(b) ⟨*cake*⟩ iced
(c) ⟨*atmosphere*⟩ frosty; ⟨*smile*⟩ chilly
(d) ⟨*paper*⟩ glossy

glacer /glase/ [12] **1** *vtr* **(a)** to freeze ⟨*body*⟩; to chill [sb] to the bone
(b) to intimidate; ~ **le sang de qn** to make sb's blood run cold
2 se glacer *v refl* (+ *v être*) to freeze

glaciaire /glasjɛʀ/ *adj* glacial

glacial, ~e, *mpl* ~**s** *or* **-iaux** /glasjal, o/ *adj* **(a)** icy
(b) ⟨*person, reception*⟩ frosty; ⟨*silence*⟩ stony; ⟨*look*⟩ icy

glacier /glasje/ *nm* **(a)** glacier
(b) ice-cream maker
(c) ice-cream parlour (GB)

glacière /glasjɛʀ/ *nf* coolbox (GB), ice chest (US)

glaçon /glasɔ̃/ *nm* ice cube

glaire /glɛʀ/ *nf* **(a)** mucus
(b) albumen

glaise /glɛz/ *nf* clay

glaive /glɛv/ *nm* double-edged sword

gland /glɑ̃/ *nm* **(a)** acorn
(b) (Anat) glans
(c) tassel

glande /glɑ̃d/ *nf* (Anat) gland

glaner /glane/ [1] *vtr* to glean

glapir /glapiʀ/ [3] *vi* **(a)** ⟨*pup*⟩ to yap; ⟨*fox*⟩ to bark
(b) ⟨*person*⟩ to shriek

glas /glɑ/ *nm inv* toll, knell

glauque /glok/ *adj* murky; ⟨*street*⟩ squalid

glissade /glisad/ *nf* slide; skid

glissant, ~e /glisɑ̃, ɑ̃t/ *adj* slippery

glissement /glismɑ̃/ *nm* **(a)** sliding
(b) (in sense) shift; (among voters) swing; (in prices) fall

glisser /glise/ [1] **1** *vtr* to slip ⟨*object*⟩ (**dans** into); to slip in ⟨*remark, criticism*⟩
2 *vi* **(a)** to be slippery
(b) to slip
(c) to slide; to glide
(d) ~ **sur** to have no effect on
3 se glisser *v refl* (+ *v être*) **se** ~ **dans** to slip into; to sneak into; to creep into

glissière /glisjɛʀ/ *nf* slide; **fermeture à** ~ zip (GB), zipper (US)

global, ~e, *mpl* **-aux** /glɔbal, o/ *adj* ⟨*sum*⟩ total; ⟨*result, cost*⟩ overall; ⟨*agreement, solution*⟩ global; ⟨*study*⟩ comprehensive

globalement /glɔbalmɑ̃/ *adv* on the whole

globe /glɔb/ *nm* (a) ~ (terrestre) earth, globe; **parcourir le ~** to globe-trot
(b) round glass lampshade; glass case
(c) (in architecture) dome
■ ~ **oculaire** eyeball

globule /glɔbyl/ *nm* globule; blood cell
■ ~ **blanc** white cell; ~ **rouge** red cell

gloire /glwaʀ/ *nf* (a) glory, fame
(b) credit; **faire qch pour la ~** to do sth (just) for the sake of it
(c) glory, praise
(d) **tirer ~ de** to pride oneself on
(e) celebrity; star

glorieux, -ieuse /glɔʀjø, øz/ *adj* glorious

glorifier /glɔʀifje/ [2] **1** *vtr* to glorify
2 se glorifier *v refl* (+ *v être*) to glory (de in), to boast (de about)

glose /gloz/ *nf* gloss; note

gloser /gloze/ [1] *vi* to ramble on (sur about)

glossaire /glɔsɛʀ/ *nm* glossary

glotte /glɔt/ *nf* glottis

gloussement /glusmɑ̃/ *nm* (of hen) clucking; (of person) chuckle

glousser /gluse/ [1] *vi* ⟨hen⟩ to cluck; ⟨person⟩ to chuckle

glouton, -onne /glutɔ̃, ɔn/ *adj* ⟨person⟩ gluttonous; ⟨appetite⟩ voracious

glu /gly/ *nf* (a) bird lime
(b) glue

gluant, ~e /glyɑ̃, ɑ̃t/ *adj* (a) sticky
(b) slimy

glucide /glysid/ *nm* carbohydrate

glycémie /glisemi/ *nf* **taux de ~** blood sugar level

glycérine /gliseʀin/ *nf* glycerin

gnognotte /nɔɲɔt/ *nf* (colloq) **c'est pas de la ~!** it's not your common or garden variety

gnome /gnom/ *nm* gnome

gnon /ɲɔ̃/ *nm* (colloq) dent; bruise; **prendre un ~** to get hit

go: **tout de go** /go/ *phr* ⟨say⟩ straight out

goal /gol/ *nm* (colloq) goalkeeper, goalie (colloq)

gobelet /gɔblɛ/ *nm* cup; tumbler; beaker; ~ **en carton** paper cup

gober /gɔbe/ [1] *vtr* (a) to suck ⟨egg⟩; to swallow [sth] whole
(b) (colloq) to fall for (colloq) ⟨story⟩

godasse /gɔdas/ *nf* (colloq) shoe

godet /gɔdɛ/ *nm* (a) goblet
(b) pot

goéland /gɔelɑ̃/ *nm* gull

goémon /gɔemɔ̃/ *nm* wrack

gogo: **à gogo** /gogo/ *phr* (colloq) galore; **vin à ~** wine galore

goguette: **en goguette** /ɑ̃gɔgɛt/ *phr* (colloq) **partir en ~** to go on a spree

goinfre /gwɛ̃fʀ/ *nmf* (colloq) greedy pig (colloq)

goinfrer: **se goinfrer** /gwɛ̃fʀe/ [1] *v refl* (+ *v être*) (colloq) to stuff oneself (colloq) (de with)

goître /gwatʀ/ *nm* goitre (GB)

golden /gɔldɛn/ *nf inv* Golden Delicious (apple)

golf /gɔlf/ *nm* (a) golf
(b) golf course

golfe /gɔlf/ *nm* gulf; bay

gomme /gɔm/ **1** *nf* (a) eraser, rubber (GB)
(b) (substance) gum
2 à la gomme *phr* (colloq) ⟨idea⟩ pathetic, useless; ⟨machine⟩ useless; ⟨plan⟩ hopeless
IDIOMS mettre (toute) la ~ (colloq) to step on it (colloq); to give it full throttle (colloq); to turn it up full blast

gommer /gɔme/ [1] *vtr* (a) to rub [sth] out
(b) to smooth out ⟨wrinkle⟩; to erase ⟨past, boundaries⟩; to iron out ⟨differences⟩

gond /gɔ̃/ *nm* hinge; **sortir de ses ~s** to come off its hinges; to fly off the handle (colloq)

gondole /gɔ̃dɔl/ *nf* (a) gondola
(b) sales shelf

gondoler: **se gondoler** /gɔ̃dɔle/ [1] *v refl* (+ *v être*) ⟨paper⟩ to crinkle; ⟨wood⟩ to warp

gonflable /gɔ̃flabl/ *adj* inflatable

gonflé, ~e /gɔ̃fle/ **1** *pp* ▶ GONFLER
2 *adj* (a) ⟨tyre, balloon⟩ inflated; ⟨cheeks⟩ puffed out
(b) swollen; bloated; puffy; **yeux ~s de sommeil** eyes puffy with sleep
(c) (colloq) **être ~** to have guts (colloq); (critical) to have a nerve (colloq)

gonfler /gɔ̃fle/ [1] **1** *vtr* (a) to blow up, to inflate ⟨balloon, tyre⟩; to fill ⟨lungs, sail⟩; to puff out ⟨cheeks⟩; **être gonflé à bloc** to be fully inflated; to be raring to go (colloq)
(b) to flex ⟨muscle⟩; to make [sth] bulge ⟨pocket, bag⟩; to saturate ⟨sponge⟩; to make [sth] swollen ⟨river⟩; to swell ⟨bud⟩
(c) **il est gonflé d'orgueil** he's full of his own importance
(d) to increase ⟨profits⟩; to push up ⟨prices⟩; to inflate ⟨statistics⟩
2 *vi* (gen) to swell (up); (Culin) to rise

gonfleur /gɔ̃flœʀ/ *nm* (air) pump

gong /gɔ̃g/ *nm* (a) gong
(b) (in boxing) bell

goret /gɔʀɛ/ *nm* (a) piglet
(b) (colloq) (child) little pig (colloq)

gorge /gɔʀʒ/ *nf* (a) throat; **avoir mal à la ~** to have a sore throat; **tenir qn à la ~** to have sb by the throat; (figurative) to have a stranglehold over sb; **avoir la ~ serrée** or **nouée** to have a lump in one's throat; to have one's heart in one's mouth; **à ~ déployée, à pleine ~** ⟨sing⟩ at the top of one's voice; ⟨laugh⟩ uproariously; **ta remarque m'est restée en travers de la ~** I found your comment hard to swallow
(b) bosom, breast
(c) gorge ····÷

IDIOMS faire des ~s chaudes de qn/qch to laugh sb/sth to scorn

gorgé, ~e¹ /gɔʀʒe/ *adj* ~ d'eau ⟨land⟩ waterlogged; ⟨sponge⟩ saturated with water; fruit ~ de soleil fruit bursting with sunshine

gorgée² /gɔʀʒe/ *nf* sip; gulp

gorger /gɔʀʒe/ [13] **se gorger** *v refl* (+ *v être*) se ~ de nourriture to gorge oneself

gorille /gɔʀij/ *nm* **(a)** gorilla
(b) (colloq) bodyguard

gosier /gozje/ *nm* throat, gullet

gosse /gɔs/ *nmf* (colloq) **(a)** kid (colloq); sale ~ brat (colloq)
(b) il est beau ~ he's a good-looking fellow

gothique /gɔtik/ *adj, nm* Gothic

gouache /gwaʃ/ *nf* gouache, poster paint

gouaille /gwaj/ *nf* cheek, cheekiness

goudron /gudʀɔ̃/ *nm* tar

goudronner /gudʀɔne/ [1] *vtr* to tarmac

gouffre /gufʀ/ *nm* chasm, abyss; le ~ de Padirac the caves of Padirac

goujat /guʒa/ *nm* boor

goujon /guʒɔ̃/ *nm* (Zool) gudgeon

goulée /gule/ *nf* (colloq) gulp

goulet /gulɛ/ *nm* **(a)** narrows
(b) gully
■ ~ d'étranglement bottleneck

goulot /gulo/ *nm* (of bottle) neck

goulu, ~e /guly/ *adj* greedy

goulûment /gulymɑ̃/ *adv* greedily

goupillon /gupijɔ̃/ *nm* **(a)** bottle brush
(b) holy water sprinkler

gourd, ~e¹ /guʀ, guʀd/ *adj* numb

gourde² /guʀd/ **1** *adj* (colloq) dumb (colloq), gormless (GB) (colloq)
2 *nf* **(a)** flask; gourd
(b) (colloq) dope (colloq)

gourdin /guʀdɛ̃/ *nm* bludgeon, cudgel

gourmand, ~e /guʀmɑ̃, ɑ̃d/ *adj* fond of good food; il est ~ (de sucreries) he has a sweet tooth

gourmandise /guʀmɑ̃diz/ **1** *nf* weakness for sweet things; weakness for good food
2 **gourmandises** *nf pl* sweets (GB), candies (US)

gourmet /guʀmɛ/ *nm* gourmet

gourmette /guʀmɛt/ *nf* chain bracelet

gourou /guʀu/ *nm* guru

gousse /gus/ *nf* pod; ~ d'ail clove of garlic

gousset /gusɛ/ *nm* **(a)** (pocket) fob
(b) gusset

goût /gu/ *nm* **(a)** (gen) taste; palate; donner du ~ à qch to give sth flavour (GB)
(b) de bon ~ in good taste; s'habiller sans ~ to have no dress sense; avoir le mauvais ~ de faire to be tactless enough to do
(c) liking; ne pas être du ~ de tout le monde not to be to everyone's liking; not to be everyone's cup of tea; chacun ses ~s each to his own; être au ~ du jour to be trendy; faire qch par ~ to do sth for pleasure

IDIOMS tous les ~s sont dans la nature (Proverb) it takes all sorts to make a world

goûter¹ /gute/ [1] **1** *vtr* **(a)** to taste, to try
(b) to enjoy ⟨peace, solitude⟩
2 goûter à *v+prep* **(a)** ~ à to try ⟨food, drink⟩
(b) ~ à to have a taste of ⟨freedom, power⟩

goûter² /gute/ *nm* **(a)** snack
(b) children's party

goutte /gut/ **1** *nf* **(a)** drop (de of); ~ de pluie raindrop; à grosses ~s ⟨rain⟩ heavily; ⟨perspire⟩ profusely
(b) (Med) gout
2 gouttes *nf pl* (Med) drops

IDIOMS se ressembler comme deux ~s d'eau to be as alike as two peas in a pod

goutte-à-goutte /gutagut/ *nm inv* (Med) drip

gouttelette /gutlɛt/ *nf* droplet

goutter /gute/ [1] *vi* to drip

gouttière /gutjɛʀ/ *nf* gutter; drainpipe

gouvernail /guvɛʀnaj/ *nm* **(a)** rudder
(b) helm

gouvernant, ~e¹ /guvɛʀnɑ̃, ɑ̃t/ **1** *adj* ruling
2 gouvernants *nm pl* les ~s the government

gouvernante² /guvɛʀnɑ̃t/ *nf* housekeeper

gouverne /guvɛʀn/ *nf* pour votre ~ for your information

gouvernement /guvɛʀnəmɑ̃/ *nm* government

gouvernemental, ~e, mpl -aux /guvɛʀnəmɑ̃tal, o/ *adj* government; governmental

gouverner /guvɛʀne/ [1] *vtr* **(a)** to govern, to rule
(b) ⟨money⟩ to rule
(c) to steer ⟨ship⟩

gouverneur /guvɛʀnœʀ/ *nm* governor

grabataire /gʀabatɛʀ/ *adj* bedridden

grabuge /gʀabyʒ/ *nm* (colloq) faire du ~ to raise hell (colloq)

grâce /gʀɑs/ **1** *nf* **(a)** (of person, gesture) grace; (of landscape) charm
(b) de bonne ~ with (a) good grace
(c) favour (GB); faire à qn la ~ d'accepter to do sb the honour (GB) of accepting
(d) mercy; ~ présidentielle presidential pardon; je vous fais ~ des détails I'll spare you the details
(e) ~ à Dieu! thank God!
2 grâce à *phr* thanks to

Grâce /gʀɑs/ *nf* Grace; votre ~ your Grace

gracier /gʀasje/ [2] *vtr* to pardon, to reprieve

gracieusement /gʀasjøzmɑ̃/ *adv* **(a)** free of charge
(b) gracefully

gracieux, -ieuse /gʀasjø, øz/ *adj*
(a) graceful
(b) gracious

grade /gʀad/ *nm* rank; monter en ~ to be promoted

gradé, ~e /gʀade/ *nm,f* noncommissioned officer

gradin /gʀadɛ̃/ *nm* (in hall) tier; (in arena) terrace

gradué, ~e /gʀadɥe/ *adj* **règle ~e** ruler

graduer /gʀadɥe/ [1] *vtr* **(a)** to increase ⟨*difficulty*⟩
(b) to graduate ⟨*instrument*⟩

graffiti /gʀafiti/ *nm pl* graffiti

graillon /gʀajɔ̃/ *nm* (colloq) **ça sent le ~** it smells of stale fat

grain /gʀɛ̃/ *nm* **(a)** grain; **nourri au ~** corn-fed (GB) *or* grain-fed
(b) grain; **~ de poivre** peppercorn; **~ de café** coffee bean; **~ de moutarde** mustard seed; **~ de raisin** grape
(c) speck
(d) le ~ the grain; **à gros ~** coarse grained
■ **~ de beauté** beauty spot, mole
IDIOMS **avoir un ~** (colloq) to be loony (colloq); **mettre son ~ de sel** (colloq) to put one's oar in (colloq)

graine /gʀɛn/ *nf* seed; birdseed; **monter en ~** ⟨*vegetable*⟩ to run to seed; ⟨*child*⟩ to shoot up
IDIOMS **prends-en de la ~** (colloq) let that be an example to you

graisse /gʀɛs/ *nf* **(a)** (gen) fat; (of seal, whale) blubber
(b) (Tech) grease

graisser /gʀɛse/ [1] *vtr* to grease ⟨*pan*⟩; to lubricate ⟨*mechanism*⟩

graisseux, -euse /gʀɛsø, øz/ *adj* (gen) greasy; (Med) fatty

grammaire /gʀamɛʀ/ *nf* grammar

grammatical, ~e, *mpl* **-aux** /gʀamatikal, o/ *adj* grammatical

gramme /gʀam/ *nm* gram

grand, ~e /gʀɑ̃, gʀɑ̃d/ **1** *adj* **(a)** ⟨*person, tree, tower*⟩ tall; ⟨*arm, stride, journey*⟩ long; ⟨*margin, angle*⟩ wide; ⟨*place, object, fire*⟩ big
(b) ⟨*crowd, family, fortune*⟩ large, big; **pas ~ monde** not many people; **il fait ~ jour** it's broad daylight; **laver à ~e eau** to wash [sth] in plenty of running water; to wash [sth] down
(c) ⟨*dreamer, collector, friend*⟩ great; ⟨*cheat, gambler*⟩ big; ⟨*drinker, smoker*⟩ heavy; **c'est un ~ timide** he's very shy
(d) ⟨*discovery, news, expedition*⟩ great; ⟨*date*⟩ important; ⟨*role*⟩ major; ⟨*problem, decision*⟩ big
(e) main
(f) ⟨*company, brand*⟩ leading; **les ~es industries** the big industries
(g) ⟨*painter, wine*⟩ great; ⟨*heart, spirit*⟩ noble
(h) ⟨*brother, sister*⟩ elder; ⟨*pupil*⟩ senior (GB), older; **assez ~ pour faire** old enough to do
(i) ⟨*height, length, value, distance*⟩ great; ⟨*size, quantity*⟩ large; ⟨*speed*⟩ high
(j) ⟨*kindness, friendship, danger, interest*⟩ great; ⟨*noise*⟩ loud; ⟨*cold*⟩ severe; ⟨*heat*⟩ intense; ⟨*wind*⟩ strong, high; ⟨*storm*⟩ big, violent; **à ma ~e surprise** much to my surprise

(k) ⟨*family, name*⟩ great; **la ~e bourgeoisie** the upper middle class
(l) ⟨*reception, plan*⟩ grand
(m) ⟨*word*⟩ big; ⟨*phrase*⟩ high-sounding; **faire de ~s gestes** to wave one's arms about; **et voilà, tout de suite les ~s mots** there you go, straight off the deep end
2 *nm,f* big boy/girl; (Sch) senior (GB) *or* older pupil
3 *adv* wide; **ouvrir tout ~ les bras** to throw one's arms open; **ouvrir ~ ses oreilles** to prick up one's ears; **voir ~** to think big
4 *nm* **les ~s de ce monde** the great and the good; the world's leaders
5 en grand *phr* ⟨*open*⟩ wide; **faire les choses en ~** to do things on the grand scale
■ **~s axes** main roads; ~ **banditisme** organized crime; **le ~ capital** big money; **~ duc** eagle owl; **~ écart** (Sport) splits; **le ~ écran** the big screen; **~ ensemble** high-density housing complex; **le ~ large** the high seas; **~ magasin** department store; **le ~ monde** high society; **le Grand Nord** the Far North; **Grand Pardon** Day of Atonement; **~ prêtre** high priest; **~ prix** grand prix; **le ~ public** the general public; **produit ~ public** consumer product; **la ~e banlieue** the outer suburbs; **la ~e cuisine** haute cuisine; **la Grande Guerre** the First World War; **la ~e muraille de Chine** the Great Wall of China; **~e personne** grown-up, adult; **~e puissance** superpower; **~e roue** big wheel (GB), Ferris wheel (US); **~e surface** supermarket; **~es eaux** fountains; **dès qu'on la gronde, ce sont les ~es eaux** the minute you tell her off, she turns on the waterworks; **~es lignes** main train routes; **~es marées** spring tides; **~es ondes** long wave; **les ~s blessés** the seriously injured; **~s fauves** big cats

grand-angle, *pl* **grands-angles** /gʀɑ̃tɑ̃gl, gʀɑ̃zɑ̃gl/ *adj* wide-angle; **un (objectif) ~** a wide-angle lens

grand-chose /gʀɑ̃ʃoz/ *pron* **pas ~** not much, not a lot; **il n'y a plus ~ à faire** there isn't much left to do

Grande-Bretagne /gʀɑ̃dbʀətaɲ/ *pr nf* Great Britain

grandement /gʀɑ̃dmɑ̃/ *adv* greatly; a great deal; extremely

grandeur /gʀɑ̃dœʀ/ *nf* **(a)** size; **~ nature** ⟨*reproduction*⟩ full-scale; ⟨*portrait*⟩ life-size
(b) scale
(c) greatness

Grand-Guignol /gʀɑ̃giɲɔl/ *nm* **c'est du ~** it's farcical

grandiloquence /gʀɑ̃dilɔkɑ̃s/ *nf* pomposity, grandiloquence

grandiloquent, ~e /gʀɑ̃dilɔkɑ̃, ɑ̃t/ *adj* pompous, grandiloquent

grandiose /gʀɑ̃djoz/ *adj* ⟨*site, decor*⟩ grandiose; ⟨*party*⟩ spectacular; ⟨*gesture*⟩ grand

grandir /gʀɑ̃diʀ/ [3] **1** *vtr* **(a)** to magnify
(b) to make [sb] look taller
(c) to exaggerate
2 *vi* **(a)** to grow; to grow up ···⟩

(b) ⟨company⟩ to expand; ⟨crowd, anxiety⟩ to grow

3 se grandir v refl (+ v être) to make oneself (look) taller

grandissant, ~e /gʀɑ̃disɑ̃, ɑ̃t/ adj growing

grand-mère, pl **grands-mères** /gʀɑ̃mɛʀ/ nf grandmother

grand-oncle, pl **grands-oncles** /gʀɑ̃tɔ̃kl, gʀɑ̃zɔ̃kl/ nm great-uncle

grand-peine /gʀɑ̃pɛn/ **1** nf avoir ~ à faire to have great difficulty doing **2 à grand-peine** phr à ~ with great difficulty

grand-père, pl **grands-pères** /gʀɑ̃pɛʀ/ nm grandfather

grand-route, pl **~s** /gʀɑ̃ʀut/ nf main road

grand-rue, pl **~s** /gʀɑ̃ʀy/ nf high street

grands-parents /gʀɑ̃paʀɑ̃/ nm pl grandparents

grand-tante, pl **grand(s)-tantes** /gʀɑ̃tɑ̃t/ nf great-aunt

grand-voile, pl **grand(s)-voiles** /gʀɑ̃vwal/ nf mainsail

grange /gʀɑ̃ʒ/ nf barn

granit(e) /gʀanit/ nm granite

granité, ~e /gʀanite/ adj grained

granulé /gʀanyle/ nm granule

graphie /gʀafi/ nf **(a)** written form **(b)** spelling

graphique /gʀafik/ **1** adj **(a)** ⟨work⟩ graphic **(b)** ⟨screen⟩ graphic; ⟨software⟩ graphics **2** nm graph

graphisme /gʀafism/ nm **(a)** style of drawing **(b)** handwriting **(c)** graphic design

graphologie /gʀafɔlɔʒi/ nf graphology

grappe /gʀap/ nf (of fruit) bunch; (of flowers) cluster

grappiller /gʀapije/ [1] vtr to pick up ⟨fruit⟩; to glean ⟨information⟩

grappin /gʀapɛ̃/ nm mettre le ~ sur qn (colloq) to get sb in one's clutches

gras, grasse /gʀɑ, gʀɑs/ **1** adj **(a)** ⟨substance⟩ fatty; ⟨fish⟩ oily; ⟨paper⟩ greasy **(b)** coarse, vulgar **(c)** (in printing) bold **(d)** loose, phlegmy **2** adv manger ~ to eat fatty foods **3** nm **(a)** (from meat) fat **(b)** grease **(c)** (of arm, calf) le ~ the fleshy part

grassement /gʀɑsmɑ̃/ adv ⟨pay⟩ handsomely; ⟨feed⟩ lavishly

grassouillet, -ette /gʀasujɛ, ɛt/ adj (colloq) chubby, plump

graticiel /gʀatisjɛl/ nm freeware

gratifiant, ~e /gʀatifjɑ̃, ɑ̃t/ adj gratifying

gratification /gʀatifikasjɔ̃/ nf **(a)** gratification **(b)** bonus

gratifier /gʀatifje/ [2] vtr ~ qn de qch to give sb sth; **se sentir gratifié** to feel gratified

gratin /gʀatɛ̃/ nm **(a)** gratin (breadcrumbs and cheese) **(b)** (colloq) le ~ the upper crust (colloq)

gratiné, ~e /gʀatine/ adj **(a)** (Culin) au gratin **(b)** (colloq) ⟨person⟩ weird; ⟨problem⟩ mind-bending (colloq)

gratiner /gʀatine/ [1] vtr (faire) ~ un plat to brown a dish

gratis /gʀatis/ **1** adj inv free **2** adv free (GB), for free

gratitude /gʀatityd/ nf gratitude; **avoir de la ~ pour qn** to be grateful to sb

gratte-ciel /gʀatsjɛl/ nm inv skyscraper

gratte-papier /gʀatpapje/ nm inv (colloq) pen pusher

gratter /gʀate/ [1] **1** vtr **(a)** to scratch; to scrape (off) **(b)** to make [sb] itch; **ça me gratte partout** I'm itching all over **2** vi ~ à la porte to scratch at the door **3 se gratter** v refl (+ v être) to scratch; **se ~ la tête** to scratch one's head

grattoir /gʀatwaʀ/ nm **(a)** (tool) scraper **(b)** (on matchbox) striking strip

gratuit, ~e /gʀatɥi, it/ adj **(a)** ⟨place, service⟩ free **(b)** ⟨violence⟩ gratuitous; ⟨accusation⟩ spurious; ⟨exercise⟩ pointless

gratuité /gʀatɥite/ nf la ~ de l'enseignement free education

gratuitement /gʀatɥitmɑ̃/ adv **(a)** free (GB), for free **(b)** ⟨work⟩ for nothing **(c)** gratuitously

gravats /gʀava/ nm pl rubble

grave /gʀav/ adj **(a)** ⟨problem, injury⟩ serious **(b)** ⟨expression⟩ grave, solemn **(c)** ⟨voice⟩ deep; ⟨note⟩ low; ⟨sound⟩ low-pitched

gravement /gʀavmɑ̃/ adv **(a)** gravely, solemnly **(b)** seriously

graver /gʀave/ [1] vtr to engrave

graveur, -euse /gʀavœʀ, øz/ nm,f engraver; ~ sur bois wood engraver

gravier /gʀavje/ nm du ~ gravel

gravillon /gʀavijɔ̃/ nm grit

gravir /gʀaviʀ/ [3] vtr to climb up

gravitation /gʀavitasjɔ̃/ nf gravitation; ~ universelle Newton's law of gravitation

gravité /gʀavite/ nf **(a)** seriousness **(b)** solemnity **(c)** (in physics) gravity

graviter /gʀavite/ [1] vi to orbit

gravure /gʀavyʀ/ nf **(a)** la ~ engraving **(b)** engraving **(c)** print, reproduction

gré /gʀe/ nm (a) contre le ∼ de qn against sb's will; de ∼ ou de force one way or another
(b) (formal) savoir ∼ à qn de qch to be grateful to sb for sth
(c) j'ai flâné au ∼ de mon humeur I strolled where the mood took me

grec, grecque /gʀɛk/ ① adj Greek; Grecian
② nm (language) Greek

Grec, Grecque /gʀɛk/ nm,f Greek

Grèce /gʀɛs/ pr nf Greece; ∼ antique Ancient Greece

grecque ▸ GREC

greffe /gʀɛf/ nf (a) (of organ) transplant; (of skin) graft
(b) (in agriculture) grafting; graft

greffer /gʀefe/ [1] ① vtr (a) to transplant ⟨organ⟩; to graft ⟨tissue⟩
(b) to graft ⟨tree⟩
② se greffer v refl (+ v être) se ∼ sur qch ⟨problem, event⟩ to come along on top of sth

greffier, -ière /gʀefje, ɛʀ/ nm,f clerk of the court (GB), court clerk (US)

grégaire /gʀegɛʀ/ adj gregarious

grège /gʀɛʒ/ adj, nm oatmeal

grêle /gʀɛl/ ① adj (a) skinny; spindly
(b) ⟨voice⟩ reedy; ⟨sound⟩ thin
② nf hail

grêlé, ∼e /gʀele/ adj pockmarked

grêler /gʀele/ [1] v impers il grêle it's hailing

grêlon /gʀelɔ̃/ nm hailstone

grelot /gʀəlo/ nm small bell

grelotter /gʀəlɔte/ [1] vi to shiver

grenade /gʀənad/ nf (a) grenade
(b) pomegranate

Grenade /gʀənad/ ① pr n Granada
② pr nf la ∼ Grenada

grenadine /gʀənadin/ nf grenadine

grenaille /gʀənaj/ nf (a) steel filings
(b) lead shot

grenat /gʀəna/ adj inv dark red

grenier /gʀənje/ nm attic, loft; ∼ à grain granary

grenouille /gʀənuj/ nf frog

grès /gʀɛ/ nm inv (a) sandstone
(b) (piece of) stoneware

grésillement /gʀezijmɑ̃/ nm (a) crackling
(b) sizzling

grésiller /gʀezije/ [1] vi (a) ⟨radio⟩ to crackle
(b) ⟨butter, oil⟩ to sizzle

grève /gʀɛv/ nf (a) strike; mouvement de ∼ industrial action
(b) shore
■ ∼ de la faim hunger strike; ∼ sur le tas sit-down strike; ∼ du zèle work-to-rule

grever /gʀəve/ [16] vtr to put a strain on ⟨budget⟩; l'entreprise est grevée de charges the company has crippling overheads

gréviste /gʀevist/ nmf striker

gribouillage /gʀibujaʒ/ nm (colloq) scribble

gribouiller /gʀibuje/ [1] vtr (colloq) to scribble

grief /gʀijɛf/ nm grievance

grièvement /gʀijɛvmɑ̃/ adv ⟨injured⟩ seriously; ⟨burned⟩ badly; ⟨affected⟩ severely

griffe /gʀif/ nf (a) claw; tomber entre les ∼s de qn to fall into sb's clutches
(b) (on garment) label
(c) signature stamp
(d) (in jewellery) claw

griffer /gʀife/ [1] ① vtr to scratch
② se griffer v refl (+ v être) to scratch oneself

griffonner /gʀifɔne/ [1] vtr (a) to scrawl
(b) to sketch

griffure /gʀifyʀ/ nf scratch

grignoter /gʀiɲɔte/ [1] ① vtr (a) to nibble
(b) to encroach on ⟨territory⟩; to conquer ⟨corner of market⟩
(c) to fritter away ⟨inheritance⟩
② vi (a) ⟨rodent⟩ to gnaw
(b) ⟨person⟩ to nibble

gri-gri, pl **gris-gris** /gʀigʀi/ nm lucky charm

gril /gʀil/ nm grill (GB), broiler (US)

grillage /gʀijaʒ/ nm wire netting; chicken wire; wire mesh

grille /gʀij/ nf (a) railings; (iron) gate; (of sink, sewer) drain; (of air vent) grille; (in oven, fridge) shelf; (in fireplace, stove) grate
(b) (of crossword) grid
(c) (on TV, radio) schedule, listings
(d) (for assessing results) model
(e) (in administration) scale

grillé, ∼e /gʀije/ ① pp ▸ GRILLER
② pp adj (a) ⟨meat⟩ grilled; ⟨bread⟩ toasted; ⟨almonds⟩ roasted
(b) crispy, well-browned
(c) burned out; l'ampoule est ∼e the bulb has blown
(d) (colloq) ⟨spy⟩ exposed

grille-pain /gʀijpɛ̃/ nm inv toaster

griller /gʀije/ [1] ① vtr to grill ⟨meat⟩; to toast ⟨bread⟩; to roast ⟨almonds⟩
(b) (colloq) to jump (colloq) ⟨light⟩; to ignore ⟨give way sign⟩
(c) (colloq) to give the game away about [sb]
(d) (colloq) ∼ un adversaire to manage to get ahead of one's opponent
② vi (a) to grill; faire ∼ to grill; to toast; to roast
(b) ⟨bulb⟩ to blow

grillon /gʀijɔ̃/ nm cricket

grimaçant, ∼e /gʀimasɑ̃, ɑ̃t/ adj grimacing

grimace /gʀimas/ nf grimace; funny face

grimacer /gʀimase/ [12] vi to grimace

grimer: se grimer /gʀime/ [1] v refl (+ v être) to make oneself up

grimpant, ∼e /gʀɛ̃pɑ̃, ɑ̃t/ adj climbing

grimper /gʀɛ̃pe/ [1] ① vtr to climb ⟨stairs⟩ ···⟩

2 vi (a) ~ **aux arbres** to climb (up) trees; **grimpe sur mon dos** get on my back
(b) (colloq) ⟨road⟩ to be steep
(c) (colloq) ⟨prices⟩ to climb

grimpeur, -euse /gʀɛ̃pœʀ, øz/ nm,f rock climber

grinçant, ~e /gʀɛ̃sɑ̃, ɑ̃t/ adj ⟨tone⟩ scathing; ⟨joke⟩ caustic; ⟨laugh⟩ nasty

grincement /gʀɛ̃smɑ̃/ nm creak(ing); squeak(ing); screech(ing)

grincer /gʀɛ̃se/ [12] vi ⟨door⟩ to creak; ⟨violin⟩ to screech; ⟨chalk⟩ to squeak; ~ **des dents** to grind one's teeth; (figurative) to gnash one's teeth

gringalet /gʀɛ̃galɛ/ nm runt

griotte /gʀijɔt/ nf morello cherry

grippe /gʀip/ nf flu; ~ **intestinale** gastric flu (GB), intestinal flu (US)
IDIOMS **prendre qn/qch en** ~ (colloq) to take a sudden dislike to sb/sth

gris, ~e /gʀi, iz/ **1** adj (a) grey (GB), gray (US)
(b) dreary; dull
(c) tipsy
2 nm inv grey (GB), gray (US)

grisaille /gʀizaj/ nf (a) dullness
(b) (of weather) greyness (GB), grayness (US)

grisant, ~e /gʀizɑ̃, ɑ̃t/ adj (a) ⟨speed⟩ exhilarating; ⟨success⟩ intoxicating
(b) ⟨perfume⟩ heady

grisâtre /gʀizɑtʀ/ adj ⟨colour, sky⟩ greyish (GB), grayish (US); ⟨morning⟩ dull

griser /gʀize/ [1] vtr ⟨speed⟩ to exhilarate; ⟨success⟩ to intoxicate; **se laisser** ~ **par le pouvoir** to let power go to one's head

griserie /gʀizʀi/ nf exhilaration (**de** of)

grisonnant, ~e /gʀizɔnɑ̃, ɑ̃t/ adj greying

grisonner /gʀizɔne/ [1] vi to go grey

grisou /gʀizu/ nm firedamp

grive /gʀiv/ nf thrush

grivois, ~e /gʀivwa, az/ adj bawdy; coarse

grivoiserie /gʀivwazʀi/ nf suggestive remark

grizzli, grizzly /gʀizli/ nm grizzly bear

grogne /gʀɔɲ/ nf (colloq) discontent

grognement /gʀɔɲəmɑ̃/ nm grunt; growl

grogner /gʀɔɲe/ [1] vi (a) to groan; (figurative) to grumble
(b) ⟨pig⟩ to grunt; ⟨dog⟩ to growl

grognon /gʀɔɲɔ̃/ adj grouchy (colloq)

groin /gʀwɛ̃/ nm snout

grommeler /gʀɔmle/ [19] vi to grumble

grondement /gʀɔ̃dmɑ̃/ nm (of torrent, machine) roar; (of crowd) angry murmur

gronder /gʀɔ̃de/ [1] **1** vtr to tell [sb] off
2 vi (a) ⟨thunder⟩ to rumble; ⟨machine, wind⟩ to roar
(b) ⟨rebellion⟩ to be brewing

groom /gʀum/ nm bellboy (GB), bellhop (US)

gros, grosse /gʀo, gʀos/ **1** adj (a) big, large

(b) thick
(c) fat
(d) ⟨customer, market⟩ big; ⟨damage⟩ considerable
(e) ⟨problem⟩ serious, big; ⟨flaw⟩ big, major
(f) ⟨cold⟩ bad; ⟨sobs⟩ loud; ⟨voice⟩ deep; ⟨rain⟩ heavy; ⟨smoker⟩ heavy
2 adv (a) ⟨write⟩ big
(b) ⟨bet, lose⟩ a lot of money; (figurative) a lot
3 nm inv (a) **le** ~ **de** the majority of ⟨spectators⟩; the bulk of ⟨work⟩; most of ⟨winter⟩
(b) wholesale trade
(c) **la pêche au** ~ game fishing
4 **en** ~ phr (a) roughly; **en** ~ **je suis d'accord avec toi** basically, I agree with you
(b) wholesale
(c) in big letters
■ ~ **bonnet** (colloq) big shot (colloq); ~ **lot** first prize; ~ **mot** swearword; ~ **œuvre** shell (of a building); ~ **plan** close-up; ~ **sel** cooking salt; ~ **titre** headline; **grosse caisse** bass drum; **grosse tête** (colloq) brain (colloq)
IDIOMS **en avoir** ~ **sur le cœur** or **la patate** (colloq) to be very upset; **c'est un peu** ~ **comme histoire!** that's a bit of a tall story!

groseille /gʀozɛj/ nf redcurrant; ~ **à maqureau** gooseberry

grosse ▶ GROS

grossesse /gʀosɛs/ nf pregnancy
■ ~ **nerveuse** phantom pregnancy (GB), false pregnancy

grosseur /gʀosœʀ/ nf (a) size
(b) (of thread) thickness
(c) (Med) lump

grossier, -ière /gʀosje, ɛʀ/ adj
(a) ⟨person, gesture⟩ rude; ⟨language⟩ bad
(b) ⟨laugh⟩ coarse
(c) ⟨imitation⟩ crude
(d) ⟨sketch, idea⟩ rough; ⟨work⟩ crude
(e) ⟨error⟩ glaring

grossièrement /gʀosjɛʀmɑ̃/ adv
(a) ⟨calculate⟩ roughly
(b) ⟨built⟩ crudely
(c) ⟨speak⟩ rudely

grossièreté /gʀosjɛʀte/ nf (a) rudeness
(b) dirty word
(c) coarseness

grossir /gʀosiʀ/ [3] **1** vtr (a) to enlarge ⟨image⟩
(b) to increase ⟨numbers⟩; to boost ⟨profits⟩
(c) to exaggerate ⟨incident⟩
(d) to make [sb] look fat
2 vi (a) to put on weight
(b) (gen) to grow; ⟨river⟩ to swell

grossissant, ~e /gʀosisɑ̃, ɑ̃t/ adj magnifying

grossiste /gʀosist/ nmf wholesaler

grosso modo /gʀosomodo/ adv roughly

grotesque /gʀotɛsk/ adj ridiculous

grotte /gʀot/ nf (a) cave
(b) grotto

grouiller /gʀuje/ [1] **1** vi to swarm about; to mill about

2 se grouiller *v refl* (+ *v être*) (colloq) to get a move on (colloq)

groupage /gʀupaʒ/ *nm* bulking; **envoi en ~** collective shipment

groupe /gʀup/ *nm* **(a)** (gen, Econ) group; **par ~s de deux** in pairs, in twos
(b) (of objects) group; cluster
■ **~ d'autodéfense** vigilante group; **~ électrogène** (electricity) generator; **~ de pression** pressure group; **~ sanguin** blood group; **~ scolaire** school; **~ des Sept**, G7 Group of Seven, G7 countries

groupement /gʀupmã/ *nm* **(a)** association, group
(b) grouping

grouper /gʀupe/ [1] **1** *vtr* to put together
2 se grouper *v refl* (+ *v être*) to gather (autour de around); to form a group; **se ~ par trois** to form groups of three; **restez groupés** keep together

groupuscule /gʀupyskyl/ *nm* small group

gruau, *pl* **~x** /gʀyo/ *nm* **(a)** gruel
(b) fine wheat flour

grue /gʀy/ *nf* (Tech, Zool) crane
IDIOMS **faire le pied de ~** (colloq) to hang around

grumeau, *pl* **~x** /gʀymo/ *nm* lump

gruyère /gʀyjɛʀ/ *nm* Gruyère, Swiss cheese

Guadeloupe /gwadlup/ *pr nf* **la ~** Guadeloupe

gué /ge/ *nm* ford; **passer un ruisseau à ~** to ford a stream

guenille /gənij/ *nf* rag; **en ~s** in rags

guenon /gənɔ̃/ *nf* female monkey

guépard /gepaʀ/ *nm* cheetah

guêpe /gɛp/ *nf* wasp

guêpier /gepje/ *nm* **(a)** wasps' nest
(b) tight corner; **dans quel ~ es-tu allé te fourrer?** (colloq) what kind of mess have you got (GB) *or* gotten (US) yourself into?

guêpière /gepjɛʀ/ *nf* basque, bodyshaper with suspenders (GB) *or* garters (US)

guère /gɛʀ/ *adv* hardly; **il n'avait ~ le choix** he didn't really have a choice

guéridon /geʀidɔ̃/ *nm* pedestal table

guérilla /geʀija/ *nf* **(a)** guerilla warfare
(b) guerillas

guérir /geʀiʀ/ [3] **1** *vtr* **(a)** to cure ‹person, disease›
(b) ~ qn de to cure sb of ‹habit›
2 *vi* to recover; to heal; to get better
3 se guérir *v refl* (+ *v être*) **se ~ de** to overcome ‹shyness›

guérison /geʀizɔ̃/ *nf* recovery; healing

guérite /geʀit/ *nf* **(a)** sentry box
(b) (on toll road) booth

guerre /gɛʀ/ *nf* war; warfare; **les pays en ~** the warring nations
■ **~ chimique** chemical war; chemical warfare; **~ éclair** blitzkrieg, lightning war; **~ mondiale** world war; **Première/Deuxième Guerre mondiale** World War I/II; **~ nucléaire** nuclear war; nuclear warfare; **~ de 14** 1914-18 war; **~ de Sécession** American Civil War; **~ d'usure** war of attrition; **~ des prix** price war
IDIOMS **à la ~ comme à la ~** in time of hardship you have to make the best of things; **c'est de bonne ~** it's only fair; **de ~ lasse, elle renonça** realizing that she was fighting a losing battle, she gave up

guerrier, -ière /geʀje, ɛʀ/ *nm,f* warrior

guet /gɛ/ *nm* **(a)** lookout; **faire le ~** to be on the lookout
(b) (Mil) watch

guet-apens, *pl* **guets-apens** /gɛtapã/ *nm* ambush; (figurative) trap

guêtre /gɛtʀ/ *nf* **(a)** (Sport) leggings
(b) gaiter

guetter /gete/ [1] *vtr* **(a)** to watch ‹prey, criminal, reaction›; to watch out for ‹sign›; to look out for ‹postman›
(b) to threaten

guetteur, -euse /getœʀ, øz/ *nm,f* lookout

gueule /gœl/ *nf* **(a)** (slang) face; **il a la ~ de l'emploi** he really looks the part
(b) (slang) mouth; **(ferme) ta ~!** shut your face (GB) *or* mouth! (colloq)
(c) (of animal) mouth
■ **~ de bois** (colloq) hangover
IDIOMS **faire la ~** (slang) to be sulking

gueuler (slang) /gœle/ [1] **1** *vtr* to yell; to bawl out
2 *vi* to yell, to bawl; to kick up a real fuss; **~ après qn** to have a go at sb (colloq)

gui /gi/ *nm* mistletoe

guichet /giʃɛ/ *nm* window; (in bank) counter; (in museum, station) ticket office; (in theatre, cinema) box office; **la pièce se jouera à ~s fermés** the play is sold out
■ **~ automatique** automatic teller machine

guichetier, -ière /giʃtje, ɛʀ/ *nm,f* ticket clerk

guide /gid/ *nm* guide

guider /gide/ [1] *vtr* **(a)** (gen) to guide
(b) to show [sb] the way

guidon /gidɔ̃/ *nm* handlebars

guigne /giɲ/ *nf* (colloq) bad luck

guignol /giɲɔl/ *nm* **(a)** puppet show, ≈ Punch and Judy show
(b) (derogatory) clown

guillemets /gijmɛ/ *nm pl* inverted commas (GB), quotation marks

guillotine /gijɔtin/ *nf* guillotine

guimauve /gimov/ *nf* **(a)** (Bot) (marsh) mallow
(b) (confectionery) marshmallow

guimbarde /gɛ̃baʀd/ *nf* Jew's harp

guindé, ~e /gɛ̃de/ *adj* formal

guingois: de guingois /dəgɛ̃gwa/ *phr* **être de ~** to be lopsided

guirlande /giʀlãd/ *nf* garland; tinsel
■ **~ électrique** set *or* string of fairy lights

guise /giz/ *nf* **(a)** **'à votre ~'** 'just as you like *or* please'

(b) en ~ de by way of
guitare /gitaʀ/ *nf* guitar
guitariste /gitaʀist/ *nmf* guitarist
gustatif, -ive /gystatif, iv/ *adj* ⟨organ⟩ taste
guttural, ~e, *mpl* **-aux** /gytyʀal, o/ *adj* guttural
Guyana /gɥijana/ *pr nf* Guyana;
République de ~ Republic of Guyana
Guyane /gɥijan/ *pr nf* ~ **(française)** (French) Guyana; ~ **hollandaise** Dutch Guiana

gym /ʒim/ *nf* (colloq) (Sch) physical education; (Sport) gymnastics
gymnase /ʒimnɑz/ *nm* gymnasium
gymnaste /ʒimnast/ *nmf* gymnast
gymnastique /ʒimnastik/ *nf* gymnastics; exercises
■ ~ **corrective** ≈ physiotherapy exercises
gynécologie /ʒinekɔlɔʒi/ *nf* gynaecology
gyrophare /ʒiʀɔfaʀ/ *nm* flashing light, emergency rotating light

H h

h, H /aʃ/ *nm inv* **(a)** (letter) h, H; **h muet** mute h
(b) (*written abbr* = **heure**) 9 h 10 9.10
ha /ˈa/ (*written abbr* = **hectare**) ha
habile /abil/ *adj* clever, skilful (GB)
habilement /abilmɑ̃/ *adv* skilfully (GB); cleverly
habileté /abilte/ *nf* skill; skilfulness (GB)
habillé, ~e /abije/ *adj* ⟨dress⟩ smart; ⟨dinner⟩ formal
habillement /abijmɑ̃/ *nm* clothing
habiliter /abilite/ [1] *vtr* to authorize
habiller /abije/ [1] **1** *vtr* **(a)** to dress; to dress [sb] up
(b) to clothe; to provide [sb] with clothing
(c) to make [sb's] clothes
(d) un rien l'habille she looks good in anything
2 s'habiller *v refl* (+ *v être*) **(a)** to get dressed; to dress up; **s'~ long/court** to wear long/short skirts
(b) **s'~ chez** to get one's clothes from
habilleur, -euse /abijœʀ, øz/ *nm,f* dresser
habit /abi/ *nm* **(a)** ~**s** clothes
(b) outfit, costume
(c) (of monk, nun) habit
■ ~ **de lumière** matador's costume; ~**s du dimanche** Sunday best
habitable /abitabl/ *adj* **(a)** habitable
(b) **surface** ~ living space
habitacle /abitakl/ *nm* **(a)** (aviat) cockpit; (of rocket) cabin
(b) (Aut) interior
(c) (Naut) binnacle
habitant, ~e /abitɑ̃, ɑ̃t/ *nm,f* inhabitant; resident; **loger chez l'~** to stay as a paying guest
habitat /abita/ *nm* **(a)** (Bot, Zool) habitat
(b) housing
habitation /abitasjɔ̃/ *nf* **(a)** house, dwelling; home

(b) living; **immeuble d'~** block of flats (GB), apartment building (US)
■ ~ **à loyer modéré, HLM** ≈ (block of) council flats (GB), low-rent apartment (building) (US)
habité, ~e /abite/ *adj* **(a)** inhabited
(b) ⟨rocket⟩ manned
habiter /abite/ [1] **1** *vtr* to live in
2 *vi* to live
habitude /abityd/ **1** *nf* **(a)** habit; **par ~** out of habit; **ils ont l'~ de se coucher tôt** they usually go to bed early; **avoir l'~ de** to be used to
(b) custom
2 d'habitude *phr* usually
habitué, ~e /abitɥe/ *nm,f* regular
habituel, -elle /abitɥɛl/ *adj* usual
habituellement /abitɥɛlmɑ̃/ *adv* usually
habituer /abitɥe/ [1] **1** *vtr* **(a)** ~ **qn à** to get sb used to
(b) to teach
2 s'habituer *v refl* (+ *v être*) **s'~ à** to get used to
hache /ˈaʃ/ *nf* axe (GB), ax (US)
IDIOMS enterrer la ~ de guerre to bury the hatchet
haché, ~e /ˈaʃe/ *adj* **(a)** ⟨meat⟩ minced
(b) ⟨speech⟩ disjointed
hache-légumes /ˈaʃlegym/ *nm inv* vegetable chopper
hacher /ˈaʃe/ [1] *vtr* to mince; to chop
hachette /ˈaʃɛt/ *nf* hatchet
hachis /ˈaʃi/ *nm inv* mince; ~ **de persil** chopped parsley
■ ~ **Parmentier** ≈ shepherd's pie
hachisch /ˈaʃiʃ/ *nm* hashish
hachoir /ˈaʃwaʀ/ *nm* **(a)** mincer
(b) chopper
hachurer /ˈaʃyʀe/ [1] *vtr* to hatch
haddock /ˈadɔk/ *nm* smoked haddock
hagard, ~e /ˈagaʀ, aʀd/ *adj* ⟨person⟩ dazed; ⟨eyes⟩ wild

haï, ~e /'ai/ ► HAÏR
haie /'ɛ/ nf **(a)** hedge
(b) (Sport) hurdle; fence; **course de ~s** hurdle race; steeple chase
(c) line, row; **faire une ~ d'honneur** to form a guard of honour (GB)
haillon /'ajɔ̃/ nm rag; **en ~s** in rags
haine /'ɛn/ nf hatred; **s'attirer la ~ de qn** to earn sb's hatred
haineux, -euse /'ɛnø, øz/ adj full of hatred
haïr /'aiʀ/ [25] vtr to hate
haïssable /'aisabl/ adj detestable, hateful
halage /'alaʒ/ nm **chemin de ~** towpath
hâle /'al/ nm (sun)tan
hâlé, ~e /'ale/ adj tanned
haleine /alɛn/ nf breath; breathing; **hors d'~** out of breath; **un travail de longue ~** a long-drawn-out job
haler /'ale/ [1] vtr to tow ⟨boat⟩; to haul in ⟨chain⟩
haleter /'alte/ [18] vi **(a)** to gasp for breath; to pant
(b) ⟨machine⟩ to puff; ⟨chest⟩ to heave
hall /'ol/ nm entrance hall (GB), lobby (US); **~ (de gare)** concourse
halle /'al/ nf covered market
hallucination /alysinasjɔ̃/ nf hallucination; **avoir des ~s** to hallucinate; to be seeing things
halluciné, ~e /alysine/ adj ⟨eyes⟩ wild
hallucinogène /alysinɔʒɛn/ adj hallucinogenic
halo /'alo/ nm halo; **entouré d'un ~ de mystère** shrouded in mystery
halogène /alɔʒɛn/ adj halogen
halte /'alt/ [1] nf **(a)** stop
(b) stopping place
[2] excl stop!; (Mil) halt!
halte-garderie, pl **haltes-garderies** /'altəgardəri/ nf ≈ playgroup
haltère /altɛr/ nm dumbbell; barbell; **faire des ~s** to do weightlifting
haltérophilie /alterɔfili/ nf weightlifting
hamac /'amak/ nm hammock
hameau, pl **~x** /'amo/ nm hamlet
hameçon /amsɔ̃/ nm hook; **mordre à l'~** to take the bait
hanche /'ɑ̃ʃ/ nf (of person) hip
handicap /'ɑ̃dikap/ nm handicap
handicapé, ~e /'ɑ̃dikape/ [1] adj
(a) disabled
(b) **être ~** to be at a disadvantage
[2] nm,f disabled person
handicaper /'ɑ̃dikape/ [1] vtr to handicap
hangar /'ɑ̃gaʀ/ nm shed; warehouse; hangar
hanneton /'antɔ̃/ nm cockchafer (GB), June bug (US)
hanter /'ɑ̃te/ [1] vtr to haunt
hantise /'ɑ̃tiz/ nf dread
happer /'ape/ [1] vtr to catch ⟨insect⟩;

happé par ⟨arm⟩ caught up in ⟨machine⟩; ⟨person⟩ hit by ⟨train⟩; (figurative) swallowed up by ⟨crowd⟩
haranguer /'aʀɑ̃ge/ [1] vtr to harangue
haras /'aʀa/ nm inv stud farm
harassement /'aʀasmɑ̃/ nm exhaustion
harasser /'aʀase/ [1] vtr to exhaust
harcèlement /'aʀsɛlmɑ̃/ nm harassment
harceler /'aʀsəle/ [17] vtr **(a)** to pester
(b) to harass
hardi, ~e /'aʀdi/ adj bold, daring
hardiesse /'aʀdjɛs/ nf **(a)** boldness
(b) brazenness
hareng /'aʀɑ̃/ nm herring
hargne /'aʀɲ/ nf aggression
hargneux, -euse /'aʀɲø, øz/ adj aggressive
haricot /'aʀiko/ nm (Bot) bean; **~ blanc** haricot bean; **~ vert** French bean
IDIOMS **c'est la fin des ~s** (colloq) we've had it (colloq)
harmonica /aʀmɔnika/ nm mouth organ, harmonica
harmonie /aʀmɔni/ nf harmony
harmonieux, -ieuse /aʀmɔnjø, øz/ adj harmonious; ⟨movements⟩ graceful
harmoniser /aʀmɔnize/ [1] [1] vtr **(a)** to coordinate ⟨colours⟩
(b) to harmonize; to make ⟨sth⟩ consistent; to bring into line
(c) (Mus) to harmonize
[2] **s'harmoniser** v refl (+ v être) **bien s'~** ⟨colours⟩ to go together well
harnachement /'aʀnaʃmɑ̃/ nm **(a)** (for horse) harness
(b) (colloq) (clothes) get-up (colloq)
harnacher /'aʀnaʃe/ [1] vtr **(a)** to harness ⟨horse⟩
(b) (colloq) to rig out (colloq) ⟨person⟩
harnais /'aʀnɛ/ nm inv harness
harpe /'aʀp/ nf harp
harpie /'aʀpi/ nf harpy
harpon /'aʀpɔ̃/ nm harpoon
harponner /'aʀpɔne/ [1] vtr to harpoon
hasard /'azaʀ/ nm chance; **par ~** by chance; **par un curieux ~** by a curious coincidence; **par un heureux ~** by a stroke of luck; **ce n'est pas un ~ si...** it's no accident that...; **le ~ a voulu que...** as luck would have it,...; **au ~** ⟨choose⟩ at random; ⟨walk⟩ aimlessly; ⟨answer⟩ off the top of one's head; **comme par ~,** il a oublié son argent (ironic) surprise, surprise, he's forgotten his money; **à tout ~** just in case, on the off chance; **les ~s de la vie** the fortunes of life
IDIOMS **le ~ fait bien les choses** fate is a great provider
hasarder /'azaʀde/ [1] [1] vtr **(a)** to venture ⟨advice⟩
(b) to risk ⟨life⟩
[2] **se hasarder** v refl (+ v être) to venture

hasardeux, -euse /'azaʀdø, øz/ *adj*
risky

hâte /'ɑt/ *nf* (a) haste; **à la ~** hastily
(b) **j'ai ~ de partir/qu'elle parte** I can't wait
to leave/for her to leave

hâter /'ɑte/ [1] **1** *vtr* to hasten; **~ le pas** to
quicken one's step
2 se hâter *v refl* (+ *v être*) to hurry, to
rush

hâtif, -ive /'ɑtif, iv/ *adj* (a) ⟨*judgment*⟩
hasty, hurried
(b) ⟨*plant*⟩ early

hâtivement /'ɑtivmɑ̃/ *adv* hurriedly,
hastily

hausse /'os/ *nf* increase, rise; **être en ~**
⟨*prices*⟩ to be rising; ⟨*goods*⟩ to be going up
in price; **en ~ de 10%** up 10%

haussement /'osmɑ̃/ *nm* **~ d'épaules**
shrug

hausser /'ose/ [1] **1** *vtr* to raise; **~ les
épaules** to shrug one's shoulders
2 se hausser *v refl* (+ *v être*) **se ~ sur la
pointe des pieds** to stand on tiptoe

haut, ~e[1] /'o, 'ot/ **1** *adj* (a) high; tall;
l'étagère la plus ~e the top shelf; **à ~e voix**
⟨*speak*⟩ loudly; ⟨*read*⟩ aloud, out loud; **à ~
risque** very risky; **au plus ~ point**
immensely
(b) ⟨*rank, society*⟩ high; ⟨*person, post*⟩ high-
ranking; **~e surveillance** close supervision
(c) (in geography) upper; **la ~e Égypte** Upper
Egypt
(d) **le ~ Moyen Âge** the early Middle Ages
2 *adv* (a) high; **un personnage ~ placé** a
high-ranking person; **plus ~ sur la page**
higher up on the page; **'voir plus ~'** see
above; **de ~** from above
(b) (in time) far back
(c) loud(ly); **dire qch tout ~** to say sth aloud;
n'avoir jamais un mot plus ~ que l'autre
never to raise one's voice
3 *nm* (a) top; **le ~ du corps** the top half of
the body; **l'étagère du ~** the top shelf; **les
pièces du ~** the upstairs rooms; **parler du ~
d'un balcon** to speak from a balcony
(b) **faire 50 mètres de ~** to be 50 metres (GB)
high
4 en haut *phr* upstairs; on an upper floor;
en ~ de at the top of
■ **~ en couleur** ⟨*character*⟩ colourful (GB);
~ fait heroic deed; **~ lieu de** centre (GB) of
or for; **en ~ lieu** in high places; **~e mer** open
sea; **~es sphères** high social circles
IDIOMS **voir les choses de ~** to have a
detached view of things; **tomber de ~** to be
dumbfounded; **connaître des ~s et des bas**
to have one's ups and downs; **~ les mains!**
hands up!; **gagner ~ la main** to win hands
down; **prendre qch de ~** to react indignantly

hautain, ~e[1] /'otɛ̃, ɛn/ *adj* haughty

hautbois /'obwa/ *nm inv* (a) oboe
(b) oboist

haut-de-forme, *pl* **hauts-de-
formes** /'odfɔʀm/ *nm* top hat

haute[2] /'ot/ **1** *adj f* ▶ HAUT 1

2 *nf* (colloq) **les gens de la ~** the upper crust

haute(-)fidélité, *pl* **hautes(-)
fidélités** /'otfidelite/ *nf* hi-fi, high fidelity

hauteur /'otœʀ/ **1** *nf* (a) height; **prendre
de la ~** ⟨*plane*⟩ to climb; **dans le sens de la
~** upright; **à ~ d'homme** at head height
(b) hill; **gagner les ~s** to reach high
ground
(c) haughtiness
(d) (of voice) pitch
2 à la hauteur de *phr* (a) **arriver à la ~
de** to come up to; to draw level with;
raccourcir une jupe à la ~ des genoux to
shorten a dress to the knee
(b) (figurative) **être à la ~** to measure up; **être
à la ~ de sa tâche** to be equal to one's job
IDIOMS **tomber de toute sa ~** to fall
headlong

haut-fond, *pl* **hauts-fonds** /'ofɔ̃/ *nm*
shallows

haut(-)fourneau, *pl* **hauts(-)
fourneaux** /'ofuʀno/ *nm* blast furnace

haut-le-cœur /'olkœʀ/ *nm inv* retching,
heaving; **avoir un ~** to retch

haut-parleur, *pl* **~s** /'opaʀlœʀ/ *nm*
loudspeaker

havane /'avan/ **1** *adj inv* tobacco-brown
2 *nm* (a) Havana tobacco
(b) Havana cigar

havre /'ɑvʀ/ *nm* haven

Haye /'ɛ/ *pr n* **la ~** the Hague

heaume /'om/ *nm* helmet

hebdomadaire /ɛbdomadɛʀ/ *adj, nm*
weekly

hébergement /ebɛʀʒəmɑ̃/ *nm*
(a) accommodation
(b) housing

héberger /ebɛʀʒe/ [13] *vtr* to put [sb]
up; to accommodate; to provide shelter
for

hébété, ~e /ebete/ *adj* ⟨*look*⟩ stupid

hébraïque /ebʀaik/ *adj* Hebrew

hébreu, *pl* **~x** /ebʀø/ **1** *adj m* Hebrew
2 *nm* (language) Hebrew
IDIOMS **pour moi, c'est de l'~** it's all Greek
to me

HEC /aʃəse/ *nf* (*abbr* = **Hautes études
commerciales**) *major business school*

hécatombe /ekatɔ̃b/ *nf* massacre,
slaughter

hectare /ɛktaʀ/ *nm* hectare

hecto /ɛkto/ **1** *nm* (*abbr* =
hectogramme) hectogram
2 hecto(-) (*combining form*) hecto

hein /'ɛ̃/ *excl* (colloq) what (colloq)?, sorry?; **ça
t'étonne, ~?** that's surprised you, hasn't it?

hélas /'elas/ *excl* alas; **~ non!** unfortunately
not!

héler /'ele/ [14] *vtr* to hail

hélice /elis/ *nf* (a) (screw) propeller
(b) helix

hélicoptère /elikɔptɛʀ/ *nm* helicopter

héliporté, **~e** /eliporte/ *adj* helicopter-borne

hellène /ellɛn/ *adj* Hellenic

helvétique /ɛlvetik/ *adj* Helvetic, Swiss; **la Confédération ~** Switzerland

helvétisme /ɛlvetism/ *nm* Swiss French expression

hématologie /ematɔlɔʒi/ *nf* haematology

hématome /ematom/ *nm* bruise

hémicycle /emisikl/ *nm* semicircular auditorium

hémisphère /emisfɛʀ/ *nm* hemisphere

hémoglobine /emɔglɔbin/ *nf* haemoglobin

hémophile /emɔfil/ **1** *adj* haemophilic
2 *nmf* haemophiliac

hémorragie /emɔʀaʒi/ *nf*
(a) haemorrhage, bleeding
(b) (of capital) outflow

hémorroïdes /emɔʀɔid/ *nf pl* piles, haemorrhoids

henné /ene/ *nm* henna

hennir /ˈeniʀ/ [3] *vi* to neigh, to whinny

hépatique /epatik/ **1** *adj* hepatic
2 *nmf* person with a liver complaint

hépatite /epatit/ *nf* hepatitis

héraldique /eʀaldik/ *adj* heraldic

herbacé, **~e** /ɛʀbase/ *adj* herbaceous

herbage /ɛʀbaʒ/ *nm* pasture

herbe /ɛʀb/ **1** *nf* (a) grass; **mauvaise ~** weed
(b) (Culin) herb
2 en herbe *phr* (a) ⟨wheat⟩ in the blade
(b) ⟨musician⟩ budding
IDIOMS **couper l'~ sous le pied de qn** to pull the rug from under sb's feet

herbeux, **-euse** /ɛʀbø, øz/ *adj* grassy

herbier /ɛʀbje/ *nm* herbarium

herbivore /ɛʀbivɔʀ/ **1** *adj* herbivorous
2 *nm* herbivore

herboriste /ɛʀbɔʀist/ *nmf* herbalist

herboristerie /ɛʀbɔʀistəʀi/ *nf* (a) herb trade
(b) herbalist's shop (GB) *or* store (US)

héréditaire /eʀeditɛʀ/ *adj* hereditary; (figurative) ⟨enemy⟩ traditional

hérédité /eʀedite/ *nf* (a) heredity
(b) (of title) hereditary nature

hérésie /eʀezi/ *nf* (a) heresy
(b) (humorous) sacrilege

hérétique /eʀetik/ **1** *adj* heretical
2 *nmf* heretic

hérissé, **~e** /ˈeʀise/ *adj* ⟨hair⟩ bristling, standing up on end; **~ de** spiked with ⟨nails⟩

hérisser /ˈeʀise/ [1] **1** *vtr* (a) ⟨bird⟩ to ruffle (up) ⟨feathers⟩
(b) **~ qch de** to spike sth with
(c) (colloq) **ça me hérisse** it makes my hackles rise
2 se hérisser *v refl* (+ *v être*) ⟨hair⟩ to stand on end

hérisson /ˈeʀisɔ̃/ *nm* hedgehog

héritage /eʀitaʒ/ *nm* (a) inheritance; **laisser qch en ~ to** bequeath sth; **recevoir qch en ~ to** inherit sth
(b) heritage

hériter /eʀite/ [1] **1** *vtr* to inherit
2 hériter de *v+prep* to inherit
3 *vi* to inherit; to come into an inheritance; **~ de qn** to receive an inheritance from sb

héritier, **-ière** /eʀitje, ɛʀ/ *nm,f* heir/heiress

hermétique /ɛʀmetik/ *adj* (a) hermetic; airtight; watertight
(b) ⟨milieu⟩ impenetrable; ⟨poetry, author⟩ abstruse; ⟨face⟩ inscrutable

hermétiquement /ɛʀmetikmɑ̃/ *adv*
(a) ⟨sealed⟩ hermetically
(b) ⟨speak⟩ abstrusely

hermine /ɛʀmin/ *nf* (a) stoat
(b) ermine

hernie /ˈɛʀni/ *nf* (a) hernia
(b) (in tyre) bulge

héroïne /eʀɔin/ *nf* (a) heroine
(b) heroin

héroïque /eʀɔik/ *adj* heroic; epic

héroïsme /eʀɔism/ *nm* heroism

héron /ˈeʀɔ̃/ *nm* heron

héros /ˈeʀo/ *nm inv* hero

herse /ˈɛʀs/ *nf* (a) harrow
(b) portcullis

hertzien, **-ienne** /ɛʀtzjɛ̃, ɛn/ *adj* ⟨wave⟩ Hertzian; ⟨station⟩ radio-relay

hésitant, **~e** /ezitɑ̃, ɑ̃t/ *adj* (a) hesitant
(b) ⟨start⟩ shaky

hésitation /ezitasjɔ̃/ *nf* (a) indecision, hesitancy
(b) hesitation

hésiter /ezite/ [1] *vi* to hesitate; **elle hésite encore** she's still undecided; **il n'y a pas à ~** it's got to be done; **j'hésite sur le chemin à prendre** I'm not sure which path to take; **~ à faire** to be hesitant to do

hétéroclite /eteʀɔklit/ *adj* ⟨population, work⟩ heterogeneous; ⟨objects⟩ miscellaneous

hétérogène /eteʀɔʒɛn/ *adj* mixed, heterogeneous

hétérosexuel, **-elle** /eteʀɔsɛksɥɛl/ *adj*, *nm,f* heterosexual

hêtre /ˈɛtʀ/ *nm* (a) beech (tree)
(b) beechwood

heure /œʀ/ *nf* (a) hour; **24 ~s sur 24** 24 hours a day; **dans l'~ qui a suivi** within the hour; **d'~ en ~** ⟨increase⟩ by the hour; **à trois ~s d'avion de Paris** three hours from Paris by plane; **à trois ~s de marche de Paris** a three-hour walk from Paris; **faire du 60 à l'~** (colloq) to do 60 km per hour; **payé à l'~** paid by the hour; **une petite ~** an hour at the most
(b) time; **quelle ~ est-il?** what time is it?; **il est 10 ~s** it's 10 (o'clock); **il est 10 ~s 20** it's 20 past 10; **il est 10 ~s moins 20** it's 20 to 10; **mettre sa montre à l'~** to set one's watch; ···⫶·

l'∼ **tourne** time is passing; ∼**s d'ouverture**
opening times; **être à l'**∼ to be on time; **à
une** ∼ **avancée (de la nuit)** late at night; **de
bonne** ∼ early; **c'est son** ∼ it's his/her
usual time; **à l'**∼ **où je te parle** as we speak;
de la première ∼ from the very beginning; **à
la première** ∼ at first light; **ta dernière** ∼ **est
arrivée** your time has come; **à l'**∼ **actuelle,
pour l'**∼ at the present time; **l'**∼ **du déjeuner**
lunchtime; **l'**∼ **est grave** the situation is
serious; **il est peintre à ses** ∼**s** he paints in
his spare time; **à la bonne** ∼**!** well done!
(c) era, age; **vivre à l'**∼ **des satellites** to live
in the satellite era
∎ ∼ **d'affluence** peak hour; ∼ **d'été** summer
time (GB), daylight saving(s) time; ∼ **H** (Mil,
figurative) zero hour; ∼ **d'hiver** winter time
(GB), standard time; ∼ **de pointe** rush hour;
∼**s supplémentaires** overtime

heureusement /œʀøzmɑ̃/ *adv*
fortunately

heureux, -euse /œʀø, øz/ *adj* (a) happy;
∼ **en ménage** happily married; **très** ∼ **de
faire votre connaissance** (very) pleased to
meet you
(b) ⟨*ending*⟩ happy; ⟨*proportions*⟩ pleasing;
⟨*choice*⟩ fortunate; ⟨*surprise*⟩ pleasant
(c) ⟨*winner*⟩ lucky; **'il a réussi!'—'encore** ∼**!'**
'he succeeded!'—'just as well!'
IDIOMS **attendre un** ∼ **événement** to be
expecting a baby

heurt /œʀ/ *nm* (a) collision
(b) (figurative) (between people) clash; **sans** ∼**s**
⟨*do*⟩ smoothly; ⟨*relationship*⟩ smooth

heurter /œʀte/ [1] **1** *vtr* (a) ⟨*object*⟩ to hit;
⟨*person*⟩ to collide with, to bump into
(b) (figurative) to go against ⟨*convention*⟩; to
hurt ⟨*feelings*⟩
2 *vi* ∼ **contre** to strike
3 se heurter *v refl* (+ *v être*) to collide;
(figurative) to clash; **se** ∼ **à** to bump into
⟨*table*⟩; to come up against ⟨*refusal, problem*⟩

hévéa /evea/ *nm* rubber tree

hexagonal, ∼e, mpl -aux /ɛgzagɔnal,
o/ *adj* (a) hexagonal
(b) (colloq) ⟨*policy*⟩ inward-looking

hexagone /ɛgzagon/ *nm* (a) hexagon
(b) (colloq) **l'Hexagone** France

hiberner /ibɛʀne/ [1] *vi* to hibernate

hibou, pl -x /ibu/ *nm* owl

hic /ik/ *nm* (colloq) snag; **voilà le** ∼ there's
the snag

hideux, -euse /idø, øz/ *adj* hideous

hier /jɛʀ/ *adv* yesterday; **ça ne date pas d'**∼
it's nothing new

hiérarchie /jeʀaʀʃi/ *nf* hierarchy

hiérarchique /jeʀaʀʃik/ *adj* hierarchical;
mon supérieur ∼ my immediate superior;
par la voie ∼ through the correct channels

hiérarchiser /jeʀaʀʃize/ [1] *vtr* to
organize [sth] into a hierarchy ⟨*structure*⟩

hiératique /jeʀatik/ *adj* hieratic

hiéroglyphe /jeʀɔglif/ *nm* hieroglyph; **les**
∼**s** hieroglyphics

hi-fi /ifi/ *adj inv, nf inv* hi-fi

hilarant, ∼e /ilaʀɑ̃, ɑ̃t/ *adj* hilarious; **gaz**
∼ laughing gas

hilare /ilaʀ/ *adj* **être** ∼ to be laughing

hilarité /ilaʀite/ *nf* mirth, hilarity

hindou, ∼e /ɛ̃du/ *adj, nm,f* Hindu

hindouisme /ɛ̃duism/ *nm* Hinduism

hippique /ipik/ *adj* equestrian; **concours**
∼ showjumping event (GB), horse show

hippocampe /ipɔkɑ̃p/ *nm* sea horse

hippodrome /ipɔdrom/ *nm* racecourse
(GB), racetrack (US)

hippopotame /ipɔpɔtam/ *nm*
hippopotamus

hirondelle /iʀɔ̃dɛl/ *nf* swallow

hirsute /ˈiʀsyt/ *adj* dishevelled (GB),
unkempt

hispanique /ispanik/ *adj, nmf* Hispanic

hispano-américain, ∼e, mpl ∼s
/ispanoameʀikɛ̃, ɛn/ *adj* Hispanic-American,
Spanish-American

hispanophone /ispanofɔn/ *nmf* Spanish
speaker

hisse /ˈis/ *excl* **oh** ∼**!** heave-ho!

hisser /ˈise/ [1] **1** *vtr* to hoist ⟨*flag*⟩
2 se hisser *v refl* (+ *v être*) to heave
oneself up

histoire /istwaʀ/ *nf* (a) history; **l'**∼ **jugera**
posterity will be the judge
(b) story; **tout ça, c'est des** ∼**s!** (colloq) that's
all fiction!; **une** ∼ **à dormir debout** a tall
story; **raconter des** ∼**s** to tell fibs
(c) matter, business; ∼ **d'amour** love affair;
∼ **de famille** family matter; **il m'est arrivé
une drôle d'**∼ a funny thing happened to me
(d) fuss; trouble; **elle fait toujours des** ∼**s**
she's always making a fuss; **ça va faire des**
∼**s** it will cause trouble; **c'est une femme à**
∼**s** she's a troublemaker; **une vie sans** ∼**s**
an uneventful life; **ça a été toute une** ∼ **pour
faire** it was a terrible job doing; **au travail, et
pas d'**∼**s!** (colloq) get on with it, no messing
about! (colloq)
(e) (colloq) ∼ **de rire** just for fun

historien, -ienne /istɔʀjɛ̃, ɛn/ *nm,f*
historian

historique /istɔʀik/ *adj* (a) historical
(b) historic
(c) **passé** ∼ past historic

hit-parade, pl ∼s /ˈitpaʀad/ *nm* charts

hiver /ivɛʀ/ *nm* winter

hivernage /ivɛʀnaʒ/ *nm* wintering

hivernal, ∼e, mpl -aux /ivɛʀnal, o/ *adj*
(a) winter
(b) wintry

hiverner /ivɛʀne/ [1] *vi* ⟨*animals*⟩ to winter

HLM /aʃɛlɛm/ *nm or f: abbr* ▶ HABITATION

hochement /ˈɔʃmɑ̃/ *nm* nod; shake of the
head

hocher /ˈɔʃe/ [1] *vtr* ∼ **la tête** to nod; to
shake one's head

hochet /ˈɔʃɛ/ *nm* rattle

hockey /ˈɔkɛ/ *nm* hockey

holà /ˈɔla/ *excl* hey (there)!

IDIOMS **mettre le ~ à qch** to put an end *or* a stop to sth

holding /'ɔldiŋ/ *nm or f* holding company

hold-up, *pl* ~ *or* ~**s** /'ɔldœp/ *nm* hold-up

hollandais, ~**e** /'ɔlɑ̃dɛ, ɛz/ **1** *adj* Dutch
2 *nm* (language) Dutch

Hollandais, ~**e** /'ɔlɑ̃dɛ, ɛz/ *nm,f* Dutchman/Dutchwoman; **les ~** the Dutch

Hollande /'ɔlɑ̃d/ *pr nf* Holland

holocauste /ɔlɔkost/ *nm* holocaust

homard /'ɔmaʀ/ *nm* lobster

homéopathie /ɔmeɔpati/ *nf* homeopathy

homéopathique /ɔmeɔpatik/ *adj* homeopathic; **à doses ~s** (figurative) in small doses

homicide /ɔmisid/ *nm* homicide; manslaughter; murder

hommage /ɔmaʒ/ *nm* homage, tribute; **présenter ses ~s** to pay one's respects

hommasse /ɔmas/ *adj* mannish

homme /ɔm/ *nm* man; **l'~** man; mankind; **un ~ à la mer!** man overboard!; **comme un seul ~** as one; **leur ~ de confiance** their right-hand man; **il n'est pas ~ à se venger** he's the not the type to want revenge
■ **~ d'affaires** businessman; **~ des cavernes** caveman; **~ d'esprit** wit; **~ d'État** statesman; **~ à femmes** womanizer; **~ au foyer** house-husband; **~ de main** hired hand; **~ de paille** front, straw man (US); **~ de terrain** man with practical experience; **~ à tout faire** handyman; **~ de troupe** private; **~s en blanc** surgeons
IDIOMS **un ~ averti en vaut deux** (Proverb) forewarned is forearmed

homme-grenouille, *pl* **hommes-grenouilles** /ɔmgʀənuj/ *nm* frogman

homme-orchestre, *pl* **hommes-orchestres** /ɔmɔʀkɛstʀ/ *nm* one-man band

homogène /ɔmɔʒɛn/ *adj* homogeneous

homogénéité /ɔmɔʒeneite/ *nf* homogeneity

homologue /ɔmɔlɔg/ **1** *adj* homologous
2 *nmf* counterpart, opposite number

homologuer /ɔmɔlɔge/ [1] *vtr* **(a)** to approve ‹*product*›
(b) (Sport) to recognize officially

homonyme /ɔmɔnim/ *nm* **(a)** homonym
(b) namesake

homosexualité /ɔmɔsɛksɥalite/ *nf* homosexuality

homosexuel, ~**elle** /ɔmɔsɛksɥɛl/ *adj, nm,f* homosexual

Hongrie /'ɔ̃gʀi/ *pr nf* Hungary

honnête /ɔnɛt/ *adj* **(a)** honest
(b) decent; respectable
(c) fair, reasonable

honnêtement /ɔnɛtmɑ̃/ *adv* **(a)** ‹*say, manage*› honestly; ‹*reply*› frankly; ‹*behave*› properly; ‹*judge*› fairly
(b) fairly, reasonably; **s'acquitter ~ d'une tâche** to do a decent job

honnêteté /ɔnɛte/ *nf* honesty

honneur /ɔnœʀ/ *nm* **(a)** honour (GB); **à toi l'~!** you do the honours (GB)!; **j'ai l'~ de vous informer que** I beg to inform you that; **j'ai l'~ de solliciter** I would respectfully request; **d'~** ‹*stairs*› main
(b) credit; **c'est tout à leur ~** it's all credit to them
(c) mettre qn à l'~ to honour (GB) sb; **être à l'** *or* **en ~** to be in favour (GB); **faire ~ à un repas** to do justice to a meal; **faire les ~s de la maison à qn** to show sb around the house; **avoir les ~s de la presse** to be mentioned in the press; **en quel ~?** (colloq) (ironic) any particular reason why?
IDIOMS **en tout bien tout ~** with no hidden motive

honnir /'ɔniʀ/ [3] *vtr* **honni soit qui mal y pense** evil unto him who evil thinks

honorabilité /ɔnɔʀabilite/ *nf* integrity

honorable /ɔnɔʀabl/ *adj* **(a)** honourable (GB)
(b) ‹*score*› creditable; ‹*salary*› decent

honorablement /ɔnɔʀabləmɑ̃/ *adv*
(a) honourably (GB)
(b) decently

honoraire /ɔnɔʀɛʀ/ **1** *adj* ‹*member*› honorary
2 **honoraires** *nm pl* fee, fees

honorer /ɔnɔʀe/ [1] *vtr* **(a)** to honour (GB) ‹*god, person, memory*›
(b) to honour (GB) ‹*promise, debt*›
(c) to be a credit to ‹*country, profession*›

honorifique /ɔnɔʀifik/ *adj* honorary

honoris causa /ɔnɔʀiskoza/ *phr* **être nommé docteur ~** to be awarded an honorary doctorate

honte /'ɔ̃t/ *nf* **(a)** shame; **avoir ~ de** to be ashamed of; **sans fausse ~** quite openly
(b) disgrace; **faire la ~ de** to be a disgrace to; **quelle ~!** what a disgrace!

honteusement /'ɔ̃tøzmɑ̃/ *adv*
(a) shamefully
(b) shamelessly

honteux, **-euse** /'ɔ̃tø, øz/ *adj*
(a) disgraceful
(b) ashamed

hôpital, *pl* **-aux** /ɔpital, o/ *nm* hospital
IDIOMS **c'est l'~ qui se moque de la charité** it's the pot calling the kettle black

hoquet /'ɔkɛ/ *nm* **avoir le ~** to have hiccups

hoqueter /'ɔkte/ [20] *vi* ‹*person*› to hiccup

horaire /ɔʀɛʀ/ **1** *adj* per hour, hourly; **tranche** *or* **plage ~** time-slot
2 *nm* timetable, schedule; **les ~s libres** *or* **à la carte** flexitime

horde /'ɔʀd/ *nf* horde

horizon /ɔʀizɔ̃/ *nm* horizon

horizontal, ~**e**[1], *mpl* **-aux** /ɔʀizɔ̃tal, o/ *adj* horizontal

horizontale[2] /ɔʀizɔ̃tal/ *nf* horizontal

horloge /ɔʀlɔʒ/ *nf* clock

horloger, -ère /ɔrlɔʒe, ɛr/ nm,f
watchmaker

horlogerie /ɔrlɔʒʀi/ nf (a) watchmaking
(b) watchmaker's (shop)

hormis /'ɔrmi/ prep (formal) save, except
(for)

hormonal, ~e, mpl **-aux** /ɔrmɔnal, o/
adj ⟨problem⟩ hormonal; ⟨treatment⟩
hormone

hormone /ɔrmɔn/ nf hormone

horodateur /ɔrɔdatœr/ nm parking ticket
machine

horoscope /ɔrɔskɔp/ nm horoscope

horreur /ɔrœr/ nf (a) horror; **quelle ~!**
how horrible!
(b) **dire des ~s de** or **sur qn** to say awful
things about sb
(c) loathing; **avoir ~ de qn/de faire** to loathe
sb/doing

horrible /ɔribl/ adj (a) horrible
(b) revolting
(c) hideous

horriblement /ɔribləmɑ̃/ adv ⟨damaged⟩
horribly; ⟨cold⟩ terribly

horrifier /ɔrifje/ [2] vtr to horrify

horripiler /ɔripile/ [1] vtr to exasperate

hors /'ɔr/

■ **Note** You will find translations for expressions
such as hors série, hors d'usage etc. at the
entries SÉRIE, USAGE etc.

1 prep outside; **longueur ~ tout** overall
length
2 hors de phr out of, outside; **~ d'ici!** get
out of here!
IDIOMS **être ~ de soi** to be beside oneself

hors-bord /'ɔrbɔr/ nm inv speedboat

hors-d'œuvre /'ɔrdœvr/ nm inv starter,
hors d'oeuvre

hors-jeu /'ɔrʒø/ nm inv (**pour**) **~** for
offside

hors-la-loi /'ɔrlalwa/ nm inv outlaw

hors-piste /'ɔrpist/ nm inv off-piste skiing

hortensia /ɔrtɑ̃sja/ nm hydrangea

horticulteur, -trice /ɔrtikyltœr, tris/
nm,f horticulturist

hospice /ɔspis/ nm home; **~ de vieillards**
old people's home

hospitalier, -ière /ɔspitalje, ɛr/ adj
(a) hospital; **centre ~** hospital
(b) hospitable

hospitalisation /ɔspitalizasjɔ̃/ nf
hospitalization; **~ à domicile** home (medical)
care

hospitaliser /ɔspitalize/ [1] vtr to
hospitalize

hospitalité /ɔspitalite/ nf hospitality

hostie /ɔsti/ nf Host

hostile /ɔstil/ adj hostile

hostilité /ɔstilite/ nf hostility

hôte /ot/ **1** nm (a) host
(b) occupant
2 nm,f guest

hôtel /otɛl/ nm hotel
■ **~ particulier** town house; **~ de passe** hotel
used by prostitutes; **~ des ventes** saleroom;
~ de ville ≈ town hall

hôtelier, -ière /otəlje, ɛr/ **1** adj
⟨industry⟩ hotel; ⟨school⟩ hotel management
2 nm,f hotelier

hôtellerie /otɛlʀi/ nf hotel business

hôtesse /otɛs/ nf (at home, at exhibition)
hostess; (in company) receptionist; (in boat)
stewardess
■ **~ d'accueil** receptionist; **~ de l'air** air
hostess

hotte /'ɔt/ nf (a) basket
(b) hood
■ **~ aspirante** extractor hood (GB), ventilator
(US); **la ~ du Père Noël** Santa Claus's sack

houblon /'ublɔ̃/ nm hop, hops

houille /'uj/ nf coal

houiller, -ère /'uje, ɛr/ adj ⟨industry⟩
coal; ⟨area⟩ coalmining

houle /'ul/ nf swell

houlette /'ulɛt/ nf (of shepherd) crook; **sous
la ~ de** (figurative) under the leadership of

houleux, -euse /'ulø, øz/ adj (a) ⟨sea⟩
rough
(b) ⟨meeting⟩ stormy

houppe /'up/ nf (a) (of hair) tuft; (of threads)
tassel
(b) powder puff

houppette /'upɛt/ nf powder puff

hourra /'uʀa/ nm cheer

houspiller /'uspije/ [1] vtr to scold

housse /'us/ nf cover, slipcover; dustcover;
garment bag

houx /'u/ nm inv holly

HT (written abbr = **hors taxes**) exclusive
of tax

hublot /'yblo/ nm (in plane) window; (in boat)
porthole

huche /'yʃ/ nf (a) chest
(b) **~ à pain** bread bin

huer /'ɥe/ [1] vtr to boo

huile /ɥil/ nf (a) oil
(b) oil painting
■ **~ de coude** (humorous) elbow grease;
~ solaire suntan oil
IDIOMS **tout/ça baigne dans l'~** (colloq)
everything/it is going smoothly; **jeter** or
verser de l'~ sur le feu to add fuel to the fire

huiler /ɥile/ [1] vtr to oil

huileux, -euse /ɥilø, øz/ adj oily

huis /'ɥi/ nm inv **à ~ clos** (Law) in camera;
(figurative) behind closed doors

huissier /ɥisje/ nm (a) **~ (de justice)**
bailiff
(b) porter; usher

huit /'ɥit, but before consonant 'ɥi/ **1** adj
inv eight; **mardi en ~** a week on Tuesday
2 pron eight
3 nm inv (a) eight
(b) a figure of eight

huitaine /'ɥitɛn/ nf (a) about a week; **sous ~** within a week
(b) about eight

huitième /'ɥitjɛm/ [1] adj eighth
[2] nf (Sch) fourth year of primary school, age 9–10

huître /ɥitʀ/ nf oyster

hululement /'ylylmɑ̃/ nm hooting

hululer /'ylyle/ [1] vi to hoot

humain, ~e /ymɛ̃, ɛn/ [1] adj (a) human; **pertes ~es** loss of life
(b) ⟨regime⟩ humane; ⟨person⟩ human, understanding
[2] nm human (being)

humainement /ymɛnmɑ̃/ adv
(a) humanly
(b) humanely

humaniser /ymanize/ [1] [1] vtr to humanize
[2] **s'humaniser** v refl (+ v être) to become more human

humanitaire /ymanitɛʀ/ adj humanitarian

humanité /ymanite/ nf humanity

humble /œbl/ adj humble

humblement /œblɑ̃mɑ̃/ adv humbly

humecter /ymɛkte/ [1] vtr to moisten

humer /'yme/ [1] vtr to sniff; to smell

humeur /ymœʀ/ nf (a) mood; **être de bonne/mauvaise ~** to be in a good/bad mood
(b) temperament; **être d'~ égale** to be even-tempered; **être d'~ inégale** to be moody; **elle est connue pour sa bonne ~** she's known for her good humour
(c) bad temper; **geste d'~** bad-tempered gesture; **avec ~** bad-temperedly

humide /ymid/ adj (a) damp
(b) ⟨climate⟩ humid; ⟨season⟩ rainy; **il fait froid et ~** it's cold and damp; **il fait une chaleur ~** it's muggy

humidifier /ymidifje/ [2] vtr to humidify

humidité /ymidite/ nf (a) dampness, damp
(b) humidity

humiliant, ~e /ymiljɑ̃, ɑ̃t/ adj humiliating

humiliation /ymiljasjɔ̃/ nf humiliation

humilier /ymilje/ [2] vtr to humiliate

humilité /ymilite/ nf (a) humility
(b) (of task) humble nature

humoriste /ymɔʀist/ nmf (a) humorist
(b) joker

humoristique /ymɔʀistik/ adj humorous; **dessin ~** cartoon

humour /ymuʀ/ nm humour (GB); **avoir de l'~** to have a sense of humour (GB); **faire de l'~** to make jokes

huppé, ~e /'ype/ adj (a) (colloq) ⟨person⟩ upper-crust
(b) ⟨bird⟩ crested

hurlement /'yʀləmɑ̃/ nm (of animal) howl, howling; (of person) yell, howl; (of siren) wail, wailing

hurler /'yʀle/ [1] [1] vtr to yell
[2] vi (a) to yell; (with pain, anger) to howl
(b) ⟨siren⟩ to wail; ⟨wind⟩ to roar; ⟨radio⟩ to blare
IDIOMS **~ avec les loups** to follow the crowd; **~ à la mort** to bay at the moon

hurluberlu, ~e /yʀlybɛʀly/ nm,f oddball (colloq)

hutte /'yt/ nf hut

hybride /ibʀid/ adj, nm hybrid

hydratant, ~e /idʀatɑ̃, ɑ̃t/ adj moisturizing

hydratation /idʀatasjɔ̃/ nf (a) hydration
(b) moisturizing

hydrate /idʀat/ nm **~ de carbone** carbohydrate

hydrater /idʀate/ [1] [1] vtr (a) to hydrate
(b) to moisturize ⟨skin⟩
[2] **s'hydrater** v refl (+ v être) **bien s'~** to take plenty of fluids

hydraulique /idʀolik/ adj hydraulic

hydravion /idʀavjɔ̃/ nm seaplane, hydroplane

hydro /idʀo/ pref hydro; **~électrique** hydroelectric

hydrocarbure /idʀɔkaʀbyʀ/ nm hydrocarbon

hydrocution /idʀɔkysjɔ̃/ nf immersion hypothermia

hydrofuge /idʀɔfyʒ/ adj water-repellent

hydrogène /idʀɔʒɛn/ nm hydrogen

hydroglisseur /idʀɔglisœʀ/ nm hydroplane

hydrophile /idʀɔfil/ adj absorbent

hydroxyde /idʀɔksid/ nm hydroxide

hyène /'jɛn/ nf hyena

hygiaphone® /iʒjafɔn/ nm grill (perforated communication panel)

hygiène /iʒjɛn/ nf hygiene; **bonne ~ alimentaire** healthy diet
■ **~ corporelle** personal hygiene

hygiénique /iʒjenik/ adj (a) hygienic
(b) ⟨lifestyle⟩ healthy

hymen /imɛn/ nm (a) hymen
(b) nuptial bond

hymne /imn/ nm hymn; **~ national** national anthem

hyperactif, -ive /ipɛʀaktif, iv/ adj hyperactive

hyperclassique /ipɛʀklasik/ adj ⟨reaction⟩ absolutely classic; **roman ~** great classic

hypermarché /ipɛʀmaʀʃe/ nm hypermarket (GB), large supermarket

hypermétrope /ipɛʀmetʀɔp/ adj longsighted

hypernerveux, -euse /ipɛʀnɛʀvø, øz/ adj highly strung

hypersensible /ipɛʀsɑ̃sibl/ adj hypersensitive

h

hypersophistiqué, **~e** /ipɛʀsɔfistike/ *adj* very sophisticated

hyperspécialisé, **~e** /ipɛʀspesjalize/ *adj* highly specialized

hypertension /ipɛʀtɑ̃sjɔ̃/ *nf* ~ (**artérielle**) high blood pressure

hypertexte /ipɛʀtɛkst/ *nm* hypertext

hypertoile /ipɛʀtwal/ *nf* World Wide Web

hypertrophie /ipɛʀtʀɔfi/ *nf* (a) (Med) enlargement
(b) (of town) overdevelopment

hypertrophier: s'hypertrophier /ipɛʀtʀɔfje/ [2] *v refl* (+ *v être*) (a) (Med) to hypertrophy
(b) (*town*) to become overdeveloped

hypnose /ipnoz/ *nf* hypnosis

hypnotique /ipnɔtik/ *adj, nm* hypnotic

hypnotiser /ipnɔtize/ [1] *vtr* to hypnotize; (figurative) to mesmerize

hypnotiseur, **-euse** /ipnɔtizœʀ, øz/ *nm,f* hypnotist

hypocalorique /ipɔkalɔʀik/ *adj* low-calorie

hypocondriaque /ipɔkɔ̃dʀijak/ *adj, nmf* hypochondriac

hypocrisie /ipɔkʀizi/ *nf* hypocrisy

hypocrite /ipɔkʀit/ **1** *adj* hypocritical
2 *nmf* hypocrite

hypodermique /ipɔdɛʀmik/ *adj* hypodermic

hypokhâgne /ipɔkaɲ/ *nf: first year preparatory class in humanities for entrance to École normale supérieure*

hypotension /ipɔtɑ̃sjɔ̃/ *nf* ~ (**artérielle**) low blood pressure

hypothécaire /ipɔtekɛʀ/ *adj* mortgage; **créancier/débiteur** ~ mortgagee/mortgager

hypothèque /ipɔtɛk/ *nf* mortgage

hypothéquer /ipɔteke/ [14] *vtr* to mortgage

hypothèse /ipɔtɛz/ *nf* hypothesis

hypothétique /ipɔtetik/ *adj* hypothetical

hystérie /isteʀi/ *nf* hysteria

hystérique /isteʀik/ *adj* hysterical

I i

i, I /i/ *nm inv* i, I
IDIOMS **mettre les points sur les i** to make things crystal clear

ibérique /iberik/ *adj* Iberian

iceberg /ajsbɛʀg, isbɛʀg/ *nm* iceberg

ici /isi/ *adv* (a) here; **c'est** ~ **que...** this is where...; **par** ~ this way; around here; **les gens d'**~ the locals; **je vois ça d'**~! I can just picture it!
(b) **jusqu'**~ until now; until then; **d'**~ **peu** shortly; **d'**~ **deux jours** two days from now; **d'**~ **là** by then; **il l'aime bien, mais d'**~ **à ce qu'il l'épouse...** he likes her, but as for marrying her...

ici-bas /isiba/ *adv* here below

icône /ikon/ *nf* icon

id. *written abbr* = IDEM

idéal, **~e** /ideal, o/ *mpl* **-aux** **1** *adj* ideal
2 *nm* ideal; **dans l'**~ ideally

idéalisme /idealism/ *nm* idealism

idée /ide/ *nf* idea; thought; **avoir de l'**~ to be inventive; **avoir une** ~ **derrière la tête** to have something in mind; **se faire des** ~s to imagine things; **avoir les** ~s **larges** to be broad-minded; **changer d'**~ to change one's mind; **avoir de la suite dans les** ~s to be single-minded; not to be easily deterred; **avoir dans l'**~ **de faire** to plan to do; **tu ne m'ôteras pas de l'**~ **que...** I still think that...; **ça ne m'est pas venu à l'**~ it never occurred to me
■ ~ **fixe** obsession; ~ **de génie** brainwave (colloq); ~ **noire** dark thought; ~ **reçue** received idea

idem /idɛm/ *adv* ditto

identification /idɑ̃tifikasjɔ̃/ *nf* identification

identifier /idɑ̃tifje/ [2] **1** *vtr* to identify
2 **s'identifier** *v refl* (+ *v être*) (a) to become identified
(b) to identify

identique /idɑ̃tik/ *adj* (a) identical
(b) unchanged

identité /idɑ̃tite/ *nf* (a) identity
(b) similarity

idéologie /ideɔlɔʒi/ *nf* ideology

idiomatique /idjɔmatik/ *adj* idiomatic

idiome /idjom/ *nm* idiom

idiot, **~e** /idjo, ɔt/ **1** *adj* stupid
2 *nm* idiot; **faire l'**~ to behave like an idiot

idiotie /idjɔsi/ *nf* (a) stupid thing
(b) stupidity

idolâtrer /idolatʀe/ [1] *vtr* to idolize

idole /idɔl/ *nf* idol

idylle /idil/ *nf* (a) love affair
(b) (in literature) idyll

idyllique /idilik/ *adj* idyllic

if /if/ *nm* (a) yew (tree)

(b) yew (wood)

IFOP /ifɔp/ *nm* (*abbr* = **Institut français d'opinion publique**) French institute for opinion polls

ignare /iɲaʀ/ *adj* ignorant

ignifuge /iɲifyʒ/ *adj* fireproofing

ignifuger /iɲifyʒe/ [13] *vtr* to fireproof

ignoble /iɲɔbl/ *adj* (a) ⟨*person, conduct*⟩ vile
(b) ⟨*place*⟩ squalid; ⟨*food*⟩ revolting

ignominie /iɲɔmini/ *nf* (a) ignominy
(b) dreadful thing

ignorance /iɲɔʀɑ̃s/ *nf* ignorance

ignorant, **~e** /iɲɔʀɑ̃, ɑ̃t/ *adj* ignorant

ignoré, **~e** /iɲɔʀe/ *adj* unknown; ignored

ignorer /iɲɔʀe/ [1] *vtr* (a) j'ignore comment/si I don't know how/whether; **~ tout de qch** to know nothing of *or* about sth; **~ l'existence de** to be unaware of the existence of
(b) to ignore ⟨*person*⟩

iguane /igwan/ *nm* iguana

il /il/ [1] *pron m* he; it; **~s** they
[2] *pron impers* it; **~ pleut** it's raining

île /il/ *nf* island
■ **l'~ de Beauté** Corsica

illégal, **~e**, *mpl* **-aux** /ilegal, o/ *adj* illegal

illégalité /ilegalite/ *nf* illegality; **être dans l'~** to be in breach of the law

illégitime /ileʒitim/ *adj* ⟨*child*⟩ illegitimate

illégitimité /ileʒitimite/ *nf* (of child) illegitimacy; (of love) illicitness

illettré, **~e** /iletʀe/ *adj*, *nm,f* illiterate

illicite /ilisit/ *adj* illicit; unlawful

illico /iliko/ *adv* (colloq) straightaway

illimité, **~e** /ilimite/ *adj* unlimited

illisible /ilizibl/ *adj* (a) illegible
(b) unreadable

illogique /ilɔʒik/ *adj* illogical

illumination /ilyminasjɔ̃/ [1] *nf*
(a) floodlighting
(b) flash of inspiration
[2] **illuminations** *nf pl* (in town) illuminations

illuminé, **~e** /ilymine/ [1] *adj*
(a) ⟨*monument*⟩ floodlit
(b) ⟨*face*⟩ radiant
[2] *nm,f* (a) visionary
(b) crank

illuminer /ilymine/ [1] *vtr* (a) to illuminate; to floodlight
(b) ⟨*smile*⟩ to light up ⟨*face*⟩
[2] **s'illuminer** *v refl* (+ *v être*) to light up

illusion /ilyzjɔ̃/ *nf* illusion; **se faire des ~s** to delude oneself; **il ne fait pas ~** he doesn't fool anyone

illusionner: s'illusionner /ilyzjɔne/ *v refl* (+ *v être*) to delude oneself (**sur qch/qn** about sth/sb)

illusionniste /ilyzjɔnist/ *nmf* conjurer

illusoire /ilyzwaʀ/ *adj* illusory

illustrateur, **-trice** /ilystʀatœʀ, tʀis/ *nm,f* illustrator

illustration /ilystʀasjɔ̃/ *nf* illustration

illustre /ilystʀ/ *adj* illustrious

illustré /ilystʀe/ *nm* comic

illustrer /ilystʀe/ [1] [1] *vtr* to illustrate
[2] **s'illustrer** *v refl* (+ *v être*) to distinguish oneself

îlot /ilo/ *nm* (a) islet
(b) **~s de végétation** isolated patches of vegetation

ils ▸ IL 1

image /imaʒ/ *nf* (a) picture
(b) (on film) frame
(c) reflection, image
(d) **à l'~ de ses prédécesseurs...** just like his/her predecessors...
(e) image; **les ~s d'un poème** the imagery of a poem
■ **~ d'Épinal** *simplistic print of traditional French life*; (figurative) clichéd image; **~ de marque** brand image; corporate image; (public) image

imagé, **~e** /imaʒe/ *adj* ⟨*style*⟩ colourful (GB)

imagerie /imaʒʀi/ *nf* (a) imagery
(b) print trade
(c) imaging

imaginable /imaʒinabl/ *adj* conceivable, imaginable

imaginaire /imaʒinɛʀ/ *adj* imaginary

imaginatif, **-ive** /imaʒinatif, iv/ *adj* imaginative

imagination /imaʒinasjɔ̃/ *nf* imagination

imaginer /imaʒine/ [1] [1] *vtr* (a) to imagine, to picture
(b) to suppose
(c) to devise, to think up
[2] **s'imaginer** *v refl* (+ *v être*) (a) to imagine, to picture
(b) to picture oneself; **s'~ à 60 ans** to picture oneself at 60
(c) to think

imbattable /ɛ̃batabl/ *adj* unbeatable

imbécile /ɛ̃besil/ [1] *adj* idiotic
[2] *nmf* fool; **faire l'~** to play the fool

imberbe /ɛ̃bɛʀb/ *adj* beardless

imbiber /ɛ̃bibe/ [1] [1] *vtr* to soak
[2] **s'imbiber** *v refl* (+ *v être*) **s'~ de** to become soaked with

imbriquer: s'imbriquer /ɛ̃bʀike/ [1] *v refl* (+ *v être*) (a) ⟨*slates*⟩ to overlap
(b) ⟨*issues*⟩ to be interlinked; ⟨*parts*⟩ to interlock

imbu, **~e** /ɛ̃by/ *adj* full; **~ de sa personne** full of oneself

imbuvable /ɛ̃byvabl/ *adj* (a) undrinkable
(b) (colloq) unbearable

imitateur, **-trice** /imitatœʀ, tʀis/ *nm,f*
(a) impressionist
(b) (of painting) imitator

imitation /imitasjɔ̃/ *nf* imitation; (of person) impression

i

imiter /imite/ [1] *vtr* **(a)** to imitate; to forge ‹*signature*›
(b) to do an impression of [sb]
(c) il part, je vais l'~ he's leaving and I'm going to do the same

immaculé, ~**e** /imakyle/ *adj* immaculate

immangeable /ɛ̃mɑ̃ʒabl/ *adj* inedible

immanquablement /ɛ̃mɑ̃kabləmɑ̃/ *adv* inevitably

immatriculation /imatrikylasjɔ̃/ *nf* registration; numéro d'~ registration (GB) or license (US) number

immatriculer /imatrikyle/ [1] *vtr* to register; to register (GB) or license (US) ‹*car*›

immédiat, ~**e** /imedja, at/ ① *adj* immediate
② *nm* dans l'~ for the time being

immédiatement /imedjatmɑ̃/ *adv* immediately

immense /imɑ̃s/ *adj* (gen) huge; ‹*pain, regret*› immense; ‹*joy, courage*› great

immensité /imɑ̃site/ *nf* (of place) immensity; (of knowledge) breadth

immerger /imɛrʒe/ [13] *vtr* to immerse ‹*object*›; to bury [sth] at sea

immersion /imɛrsjɔ̃/ *nf* **(a)** (of body, object) immersion; (of corpse) burial at sea
(b) flooding

immettable /ɛ̃metabl/ *adj* (colloq) unwearable

immeuble /imœbl/ *nm* **(a)** building
(b) real asset

immigrant, ~**e** /imigrɑ̃, ɑ̃t/ *adj*, *nm,f* immigrant

immigration /imigrasjɔ̃/ *nf* immigration

immigré, ~**e** /imigre/ *adj*, *nm,f* immigrant

immigrer /imigre/ [1] *vi* to immigrate

imminent, ~**e** /iminɑ̃, ɑ̃t/ *adj* imminent

immiscer: s'immiscer /imise/ [12] *v refl* (+ *v être*) to interfere

immobile /imɔbil/ *adj* (gen) motionless; ‹*vehicle*› stationary; ‹*stare*› fixed

immobilier /imɔbilje/ *nm* l'~ property (GB), real estate (US)

immobiliser /imɔbilize/ [1] ① *vtr* **(a)** to bring [sth] to a standstill ‹*vehicle*›; to stop ‹*machine*›
(b) to immobilize ‹*person*›
(c) to tie up ‹*capital*›
② **s'immobiliser** *v refl* (+ *v être*) to come to a halt; to stop

immobilisme /imɔbilism/ *nm* opposition to change

immobilité /imɔbilite/ *nf* **(a)** immobility
(b) stillness

immodéré, ~**e** /imɔdere/ *adj*
(a) excessive
(b) immoderate

immoler /imɔle/ [1] *vtr* to sacrifice (à to)

immonde /imɔ̃d/ *adj* **(a)** filthy
(b) revolting

immondices /imɔ̃dis/ *nf pl* refuse (GB), trash (US)

immoral, ~**e**, *mpl* **-aux** /imɔral, o/ *adj* immoral

immortaliser /imɔrtalize/ [1] *vtr* to immortalize

immortel, **-elle**[1] /imɔrtɛl/ *adj* immortal

immortelle[2] /imɔrtɛl/ *nf* everlasting (flower)

immuable /imɥabl/ *adj* **(a)** immutable
(b) unchanging
(c) perpetual

immuniser /imynize/ [1] *vtr* to immunize

immunitaire /imynitɛr/ *adj* (Med) immune

immunité /imynite/ *nf* immunity

impact /ɛ̃pakt/ *nm* impact; mark

impair, ~**e** /ɛ̃pɛr/ ① *adj* ‹*number*› odd; ‹*day, year*› odd-numbered
② *nm* indiscretion, faux pas

imparable /ɛ̃parabl/ *adj* **(a)** unstoppable
(b) unanswerable
(c) irrefutable

impardonnable /ɛ̃pardɔnabl/ *adj* unforgivable

imparfait, ~**e** /ɛ̃parfɛ, ɛt/ ① *adj* imperfect
② *nm* l'~ the imperfect (tense)

impartial, ~**e**, *mpl* **-iaux** /ɛ̃parsjal, o/ *adj* impartial

impartir /ɛ̃partir/ [3] *vtr* to give; dans les temps impartis within the given time

impasse /ɛ̃pas/ *nf* **(a)** dead end
(b) deadlock

impassible /ɛ̃pasibl/ *adj* impassive

impatience /ɛ̃pasjɑ̃s/ *nf* impatience

impatient, ~**e** /ɛ̃pasjɑ̃, ɑ̃t/ *adj* impatient

impatienter /ɛ̃pasjɑ̃te/ [1] ① *vtr* to irritate
② **s'impatienter** *v refl* (+ *v être*) to get impatient

impayable /ɛ̃pɛjabl/ *adj* (colloq) priceless

impayé, ~**e** /ɛ̃pɛje/ *adj* unpaid

impeccable /ɛ̃pɛkabl/ *adj* perfect; impeccable; spotless

impénétrable /ɛ̃penetrabl/ *adj*
(a) impenetrable
(b) inscrutable

impénitent, ~**e** /ɛ̃penitɑ̃, ɑ̃t/ *adj* ‹*drinker*› inveterate; ‹*bachelor*› confirmed

impensable /ɛ̃pɑ̃sabl/ *adj* unthinkable

imper /ɛ̃pɛr/ *nm* (colloq) raincoat, mac (GB) (colloq)

impératif, **-ive** /ɛ̃peratif, iv/ ① *adj* imperative
② *nm* **(a)** (of situation) imperative; (for quality) necessity
(b) (in grammar) imperative

impératrice /ɛ̃peratris/ *nf* empress

imperceptible /ɛ̃pɛrsɛptibl/ *adj* imperceptible

imperfection /ɛ̃pɛrfɛksjɔ̃/ *nf* imperfection

impérial, ∼**e**[1], *mpl* **-iaux** /ɛ̃peʀjal, o/ *adj* imperial

impériale[2] /ɛ̃peʀjal/ *nf* **autobus à** ∼ double-decker bus

impérialisme /ɛ̃peʀjalism/ *nm* imperialism

impérieux, **-ieuse** /ɛ̃peʀjø, øz/ *adj*
(a) imperious
(b) pressing

impérissable /ɛ̃peʀisabl/ *adj* imperishable

imperméable /ɛ̃pɛʀmeabl/ **[1]** *adj*
(a) ⟨material⟩ waterproof; ⟨ground⟩ impermeable
(b) impervious
[2] *nm* raincoat

impertinence /ɛ̃pɛʀtinãs/ *nf*
(a) impertinence
(b) impertinent remark

impertinent, ∼**e** /ɛ̃pɛʀtinã, ãt/ *adj* impertinent

imperturbable /ɛ̃pɛʀtyʀbabl/ *adj* imperturbable; unruffled

imperturbablement /ɛ̃pɛʀtyʀbabləmã/ *adv* ⟨continue, listen⟩ unperturbed

impétueux, **-euse** /ɛ̃petɥø, øz/ *adj* (gen) impetuous; ⟨torrent⟩ raging

impie /ɛ̃pi/ *adj* impious

impitoyable /ɛ̃pitwajabl/ *adj* merciless, pitiless; relentless; ruthless

implacable /ɛ̃plakabl/ *adj* implacable; tough; harsh

implacablement /ɛ̃plakabləmã/ *adv* relentlessly; ruthlessly

implantation /ɛ̃plãtasjõ/ *nf* establishment; setting up; installation; settlement

implanté, ∼**e** /ɛ̃plãte/ *adj* (a) ⟨factory, party⟩ established; ⟨population⟩ settled
(b) ⟨roots⟩ established; **dents mal** ∼**es** crooked teeth

implanter /ɛ̃plãte/ **[1]** **[1]** *vtr* (a) to establish ⟨factory⟩; to build ⟨supermarket⟩; to open ⟨agency⟩; to introduce ⟨product, fashion⟩; to instil (GB) ⟨ideas⟩
(b) (Med) to implant
[2] **s'implanter** *v refl* (+ *v être*) ⟨company, product⟩ to establish itself; ⟨factory⟩ to be built; ⟨person⟩ to settle; ⟨party⟩ to gain a following

implication /ɛ̃plikasjõ/ *nf* (a) involvement
(b) implication
(c) commitment

implicite /ɛ̃plisit/ *adj* implicit

implicitement /ɛ̃plisitmã/ *adv* implicitly; (Comput) by default

impliquer /ɛ̃plike/ **[1]** *vtr* (a) to implicate
(b) to involve ⟨staff⟩
(c) to involve (**de faire** doing)
(d) to mean

implorer /ɛ̃plɔʀe/ **[1]** *vtr* (a) to beseech, to implore
(b) to beg for

imploser /ɛ̃ploze/ **[1]** *vi* to implode

impoli, ∼**e** /ɛ̃pɔli/ *adj* rude, impolite

impolitesse /ɛ̃pɔlites/ *nf* rudeness

impondérable /ɛ̃põdeʀabl/ *nm* imponderable

impopulaire /ɛ̃pɔpylɛʀ/ *adj* unpopular

importance /ɛ̃pɔʀtãs/ *nf* (a) importance; **quelle** ∼? what does it matter?
(b) size; (of damage) extent; **prendre de l'**∼ to increase in size
(c) **prendre de l'**∼ ⟨person⟩ to become more important

important, ∼**e** /ɛ̃pɔʀtã, ãt/ **[1]** *adj*
(a) important
(b) significant; considerable; sizeable; large; lengthy
(c) **prendre un air** ∼ to adopt a self-important manner
[2] *nm,f* **jouer les** ∼**s** to act important (colloq)

importateur, **-trice** /ɛ̃pɔʀtatœʀ, tʀis/
[1] *adj* importing
[2] *nm,f* importer

importation /ɛ̃pɔʀtasjõ/ *nf* (a) importation
(b) import

importer /ɛ̃pɔʀte/ **[1]** **[1]** *vtr* to import
[2] *v impers* **peu importe** or **qu'importe que...** it doesn't matter or what does it matter if...; **n'importe quel enfant** any child; **n'importe qui** anybody, anyone; **n'importe lequel** any; **n'importe où** anywhere; **prends n'importe quoi** take anything; **elle dit n'importe quoi** she talks nonsense

importun, ∼**e** /ɛ̃pɔʀtœ̃, yn/ **[1]** *adj*
(a) troublesome; tiresome; **visiteur** ∼ unwelcome visitor
(b) ⟨visit⟩ ill-timed; ⟨remark⟩ ill-chosen
[2] *nm,f* unwelcome visitor; tiresome individual

importuner /ɛ̃pɔʀtyne/ **[1]** *vtr* (a) to bother
(b) to disturb

imposable /ɛ̃pozabl/ *adj* ⟨person⟩ liable to tax; ⟨income⟩ taxable

imposant, ∼**e** /ɛ̃pozã, ãt/ *adj* imposing

imposer /ɛ̃poze/ **[1]** **[1]** *vtr* (a) ⟨person⟩ to impose ⟨sanctions, deadline⟩; to lay down ⟨rule⟩; **elle nous a imposé le silence** she made us be quiet
(b) to impose ⟨idea, opinion⟩; to set ⟨fashion⟩
(c) to command ⟨respect⟩
(d) to tax
[2] **en imposer** *v+prep* **elle en impose à ses élèves** she inspires respect in her pupils
[3] **s'imposer** *v refl* (+ *v être*) (a) ⟨choice, solution⟩ to be obvious; ⟨change⟩ to be called for; **une visite au Louvre s'impose** a visit to the Louvre is a must
(b) to impose ⟨sth⟩ on oneself; **s'**∼ **de travailler le soir** to make it a rule to work in the evening
(c) to impose (**à qn** on sb)
(d) **s'**∼ **comme leader** to establish oneself/itself as the leader; **s'**∼ **sur un marché** to establish itself in a market
(e) ⟨person⟩ to make one's presence felt; ⟨will⟩ to impose itself

imposition /ɛ̃pozisjɔ̃/ *nf* taxation
impossibilité /ɛ̃posibilite/ *nf*
impossibility; **être dans l'~ de faire** to be
unable to do
impossible /ɛ̃posibl/ **1** *adj* impossible
2 *nm* **l'~** the impossible; **faire** *or* **tenter l'~**
to do everything one can
imposteur /ɛ̃postœʀ/ *nm* impostor
imposture /ɛ̃postyʀ/ *nf* **(a)** deception
(b) fraud
impôt /ɛ̃po/ *nm* tax; **après ~** after tax
■ **~ sur le revenu** income tax
impotent, ~e /ɛ̃potã, ãt/ **1** *adj* infirm
2 *nm,f* person with impaired mobility
impraticable /ɛ̃pratikabl/ *adj* impassable
imprécis, ~e /ɛ̃presi, iz/ *adj* ⟨*outline,
memory*⟩ vague; ⟨*concept*⟩ hazy; ⟨*aim*⟩
inaccurate; ⟨*results*⟩ imprecise; ⟨*person*⟩
vague
imprécision /ɛ̃presizjɔ̃/ *nf* imprecision;
vagueness; inaccuracy
imprégner /ɛ̃preɲe/ [14] **1** *vtr* to
impregnate
2 **s'imprégner** *v refl* (+ *v être*) **s'~ de** to
become soaked with ⟨*water*⟩; to immerse
oneself in ⟨*language*⟩
imprenable /ɛ̃prənabl/ *adj* **avec vue ~**
with unobstructed view guaranteed
imprésario /ɛ̃presarjo/ *nm* agent,
impresario
impression /ɛ̃presjɔ̃/ *nf* **(a)** impression;
faire bonne ~ to make a good impression;
j'ai l'~ d'être surveillé I feel I am being
watched
(b) printing; **faute d'~** misprint
(c) pattern
impressionnant, ~e /ɛ̃presjɔnã, ãt/
adj **(a)** impressive
(b) disturbing
impressionner /ɛ̃presjɔne/ [1] *vtr* **(a)** to
impress
(b) ⟨*image*⟩ to disturb
(c) to act on ⟨*retina*⟩
impressionnisme /ɛ̃presjɔnism/ *nm*
Impressionism
impressionniste /ɛ̃presjɔnist/ *nmf*
Impressionist
imprévisible /ɛ̃previzibl/ *adj*
unpredictable
imprévu, ~e /ɛ̃prevy/ **1** *adj*
(a) unforeseen
(b) unexpected
2 *nm* **(a)** hitch
(b) **l'~** the unexpected; **plein d'~** ⟨*person,
film*⟩ quirky; ⟨*trip*⟩ with a few surprises
(c) unforeseen expense
imprimante /ɛ̃primãt/ *nf* printer
■ **~ à jet d'encre** ink-jet printer; **~ (à) laser**
laser printer; **~ à marguerite** daisywheel
printer; **~ matricielle** dot matrix printer
imprimé, ~e /ɛ̃prime/ **1** *pp* ▶ IMPRIMER
2 *pp adj* printed (**de** with)
3 *nm* **(a)** form
(b) printed matter

(c) print; **un ~ à fleurs** a floral print
imprimer /ɛ̃prime/ [1] *vtr* **(a)** to print
⟨*text*⟩
(b) to put ⟨*stamp, seal*⟩
(c) to leave an imprint of [sth]
imprimerie /ɛ̃primʀi/ *nf* **(a)** printing;
atelier d'~ printing shop
(b) printing works
(c) printers, print workers
imprimeur /ɛ̃primœʀ/ *nm* printer
improbable /ɛ̃prɔbabl/ *adj* unlikely
improductif, -ive /ɛ̃prɔdyktif, iv/ *adj*
unproductive; **capitaux ~s** idle capital
impromptu, ~e /ɛ̃prɔ̃pty/ **1** *adj*
impromptu
2 *adv* impromptu
impropre /ɛ̃prɔpr/ *adj* ⟨*term, usage*⟩
incorrect; **~ à** unfit for ⟨*human
consumption*⟩
improvisation /ɛ̃prɔvizasjɔ̃/ *nf*
improvisation
improvisé, ~e /ɛ̃prɔvize/ *adj* ⟨*speech*⟩
improvised; ⟨*meal*⟩ impromptu; ⟨*means*⟩
makeshift; ⟨*solution*⟩ ad hoc; ⟨*cook*⟩ stand-in
improviser /ɛ̃prɔvize/ [1] **1** *vtr* to
improvise ⟨*meal, speech*⟩; to concoct ⟨*excuse,
alibi*⟩
2 *vi* to improvise
3 **s'improviser** *v refl* (+ *v être*) **(a)** **s'~
cuisinier** to act as a cook
(b) **un camp pour réfugiés ne s'improvise
pas** you can't create a refugee camp just like
that
improviste: à l'improviste /alɛ̃prɔvist/
phr unexpectedly
imprudemment /ɛ̃prydamã/ *adv* ⟨*speak*⟩
carelessly; ⟨*act*⟩ unwisely
imprudence /ɛ̃prydãs/ *nf* **(a)** carelessness
(b) **commettre une ~** to do something foolish
imprudent, ~e /ɛ̃prydã, ãt/ *adj* ⟨*person,
words*⟩ careless; ⟨*action*⟩ rash
impudence /ɛ̃pydãs/ *nf* impudence
impudent, ~e /ɛ̃pydã, ãt/ *adj* impudent
impudeur /ɛ̃pydœʀ/ *nf* immodesty;
shamelessness
impuissance /ɛ̃pɥisãs/ *nf* (gen, Med)
impotence; **~ à faire** inability to do
impuissant, ~e /ɛ̃pɥisã, ãt/ *adj*
(a) powerless, helpless
(b) (Med) impotent
impulsif, -ive /ɛ̃pylsif, iv/ *adj* impulsive
impulsion /ɛ̃pylsjɔ̃/ *nf* **(a)** (gen) impulse;
(Tech) pulse
(b) (figurative) impetus
impunément /ɛ̃pynemã/ *adv* with
impunity; **on ne joue pas ~ avec sa santé**
you don't play fast and loose with your
health and get away with it
impuni, ~e /ɛ̃pyni/ *adj* unpunished
impunité /ɛ̃pynite/ *nf* impunity
impur, ~e /ɛ̃pyr/ *adj* **(a)** ⟨*thoughts*⟩
impure
(b) ⟨*air*⟩ dirty; ⟨*blood*⟩ tainted
(c) ⟨*ore*⟩ impure

impureté /ɛ̃pyʀte/ *nf* impurity
imputable /ɛ̃pytabl/ *adj* **(a)** attributable
(à to)
(b) chargeable (**sur** to)
imputer /ɛ̃pyte/ [1] *vtr* to attribute, to
impute
inabordable /inabɔʀdabl/ *adj* **(a)** ⟨*coast*⟩
inaccessible
(b) ⟨*prices*⟩ prohibitive
inacceptable /inaksɛptabl/ *adj*
unacceptable
inaccessible /inaksesibl/ *adj*
(a) inaccessible
(b) ⟨*person*⟩ unapproachable
inaccoutumé /inakutyme/ *adj* unusual
inachevé, ～e /inaʃve/ *adj* unfinished
inactif, -ive /inaktif, iv/ ⟨1⟩ *adj* idle;
⟨*person*⟩ inactive; ⟨*population*⟩ non-working
⟨2⟩ *nm,f* non-worker; **les ～s** the non-
working population
inactivité /inaktivite/ *nf* inactivity
inadaptation /inadaptasjɔ̃/ *nf* **(a)** (of law,
equipment) inappropriateness (**à** for)
(b) (emotional, social) maladjustment (**à** to)
inadapté, ～e /inadapte/ *adj* **(a)** ⟨*child*⟩
maladjusted
(b) ⟨*means*⟩ inappropriate; ⟨*tool*⟩ unsuitable;
⟨*law*⟩ ill-adapted
inadéquat, ～e /inadekwa, at/ *adj*
inadequate; unsuitable
inadmissible /inadmisibl/ *adj*
(a) intolerable
(b) unacceptable
inadvertance: par inadvertance
/paʀinadvɛʀtɑ̃s/ *phr* inadvertently
inaltérable /inalteʀabl/ *adj*
(a) ⟨*substance*⟩ unalterable, non-corroding;
⟨*colour*⟩ fade-resistant
(b) ⟨*character*⟩ constant; ⟨*principle*⟩
immutable; ⟨*hope*⟩ steadfast
inaltéré, ～e /inalteʀe/ *adj* ⟨*substance*⟩
unaltered; ⟨*sky, air*⟩ pure
inamovible /inamɔvibl/ *adj* irremovable
inanimé, ～e /inanime/ *adj* ⟨*matter*⟩
inanimate; ⟨*person*⟩ unconscious; lifeless
inanition /inanisjɔ̃/ *nf* starvation
inaperçu, ～e /inapɛʀsy/ *adj* **passer ～** to
go unnoticed
inapte /inapt/ *adj* unfit
inaptitude /inaptityd/ *nf* unfitness
inarticulé, ～e /inaʀtikyle/ *adj*
inarticulate
inassouvi, ～e /inasuvi/ *adj* ⟨*appetite*⟩
insatiable; ⟨*person, desire*⟩ unsatisfied
inattaquable /inatakabl/ *adj* **(a)** (Mil)
unassailable
(b) irreproachable
(c) irrefutable
inattendu, ～e /inatɑ̃dy/ *adj* unexpected
inattentif, -ive /inatɑ̃tif, iv/ *adj*
(a) inattentive; distracted
(b) heedless

inattention /inatɑ̃sjɔ̃/ *nf* inattention;
faute d'～ careless mistake
inaudible /inodibl/ *adj* inaudible
inaugural, ～e, mpl -aux /inogyʀal, o/
adj **(a)** ⟨*ceremony*⟩ inauguration
(b) ⟨*flight*⟩ maiden
inauguration /inogyʀasjɔ̃/ *nf* (of building)
inauguration; (of exhibition) opening
inaugurer /inogyʀe/ [1] *vtr* **(a)** to unveil
⟨*statue, plaque*⟩; to open ⟨*motorway, school*⟩
(b) to open ⟨*conference*⟩
(c) to mark the start of ⟨*period*⟩
inavouable /inavwabl/ *adj* shameful
inavoué, ～e /inavwe/ *adj* ⟨*crime, vice*⟩
unconfessed; ⟨*aim*⟩ undisclosed; ⟨*fear*⟩
hidden
incalculable /ɛ̃kalkylabl/ *adj*
(a) innumerable
(b) incalculable
incandescent, ～e /ɛ̃kɑ̃dɛsɑ̃, ɑ̃t/ *adj*
incandescent; white-hot; glowing
incapable /ɛ̃kapabl/ *adj* **(a)** ～ **de faire**
incapable of doing; unable to do
(b) incompetent
incapacité /ɛ̃kapasite/ *nf* **(a)** inability;
être dans l'～ de faire to be unable to do
(b) incompetence
(c) disability
(d) (Law) incapacity
incarcération /ɛ̃kaʀseʀasjɔ̃/ *nf*
imprisonment
incarcérer /ɛ̃kaʀseʀe/ [14] *vtr* to imprison
incarnation /ɛ̃kaʀnasjɔ̃/ *nf* incarnation
incarné, ～e /ɛ̃kaʀne/ *adj* **(a)** **c'est la
bêtise ～e** he/she is stupidity itself
(b) ⟨*nail*⟩ ingrowing
incarner /ɛ̃kaʀne/ [1] ⟨1⟩ *vtr* **(a)** to embody
(b) to play, to portray
⟨2⟩ **s'incarner** *v refl* (+ *v être*) to become
incarnate
incartade /ɛ̃kaʀtad/ *nf* **(a)** misdemeanour
(GB)
(b) (in riding) shy; **faire une ～** to shy
incassable /ɛ̃kasabl/ *adj* unbreakable
incendiaire /ɛ̃sɑ̃djɛʀ/ ⟨1⟩ *adj* **(a)** ⟨*bomb*⟩
incendiary
(b) ⟨*statement*⟩ inflammatory
⟨2⟩ *nmf* arsonist
incendie /ɛ̃sɑ̃di/ *nm* fire; ～ **criminel** arson
incendier /ɛ̃sɑ̃dje/ [2] *vtr* **(a)** to burn
(down), to torch
(b) (colloq) to haul [sb] over the coals
incertain, ～e /ɛ̃sɛʀtɛ̃, ɛn/ *adj* ⟨*person,
date, result*⟩ uncertain; ⟨*effect*⟩ unknown;
⟨*colour*⟩ indeterminate; ⟨*smile*⟩ vague;
⟨*weather*⟩ unsettled; ⟨*step*⟩ hesitant
incertitude /ɛ̃sɛʀtityd/ *nf* uncertainty
incessamment /ɛ̃sesamɑ̃/ *adv* very
shortly
incessant, ～e /ɛ̃sesɑ̃, ɑ̃t/ *adj* ⟨*noise,
rain*⟩ incessant; ⟨*activity*⟩ unceasing
inceste /ɛ̃sɛst/ *nm* incest

incestueux, -euse /ɛ̃sɛstɥø, øz/ adj incestuous

inchangé, ~e /ɛ̃ʃɑ̃ʒe/ adj unchanged

incidemment /ɛ̃sidamɑ̃/ adv (a) in passing
(b) by chance

incidence /ɛ̃sidɑ̃s/ nf (a) impact
(b) incidence

incident, ~e /ɛ̃sidɑ̃, ɑ̃t/ nm incident; ~ de parcours hitch; l'~ est clos the matter is closed

incinérateur /ɛ̃sineratœʀ/ nm
(a) incinerator
(b) crematorium (GB), crematory (US)

incinération /ɛ̃sinerasjɔ̃/ nf
(a) incineration
(b) cremation

incinérer /ɛ̃sineʀe/ [14] vtr (a) to burn; to incinerate
(b) to cremate

inciser /ɛ̃size/ [1] vtr to make an incision in

incisif, -ive[1] /ɛ̃sizif, iv/ adj ⟨criticism⟩ incisive; ⟨portrait⟩ telling; ⟨look⟩ piercing

incision /ɛ̃sizjɔ̃/ nf incision

incisive[2] /ɛ̃siziv/ [1] adj f ▸ INCISIF
[2] nf incisor

incitation /ɛ̃sitasjɔ̃/ nf (a) incentive
(b) (Law) incitement

inciter /ɛ̃site/ [1] vtr ⟨person, situation⟩ to encourage; ⟨event, decision⟩ to prompt; ~ qn à la prudence to make sb cautious

inclassable /ɛ̃klasabl/ adj unclassifiable

inclinable /ɛ̃klinabl/ adj adjustable

inclinaison /ɛ̃klinɛzɔ̃/ nf (of hill) incline; (of wall, seat) angle; (of roof) slope; (of boat) list

inclination /ɛ̃klinasjɔ̃/ nf inclination

incliné, ~e /ɛ̃kline/ adj (a) ⟨ground⟩ sloping; ⟨roof⟩ steep
(b) ⟨wall⟩ leaning

incliner /ɛ̃kline/ [1] [1] vtr to tilt ⟨sunshade⟩; to tip up ⟨bottle⟩; ~ le buste to lean forward
[2] **s'incliner** v refl (+ v être) (a) to lean forward; (politely) to bow
(b) s'~ devant qch to bow to sth, to accept sth
(c) to give in (colloq)
(d) s'~ devant le courage de qn to admire sb's courage

inclure /ɛ̃klyʀ/ [78] vtr (a) to include
(b) to enclose

inclus, ~e /ɛ̃kly, yz/ [1] pp ▸ INCLURE
[2] pp adj (a) jusqu'à jeudi ~ up to and including Thursday (GB), through Thursday (US)
(b) enclosed

inclusion /ɛ̃klyzjɔ̃/ nf inclusion

inclusivement /ɛ̃klyzivmɑ̃/ adv jusqu'au 4 mai ~ till 4 May inclusive

incognito /ɛ̃kɔɲito/ [1] adv incognito
[2] nm garder l'~ to remain incognito

incohérence /ɛ̃kɔeʀɑ̃s/ nf (a) incoherence
(b) discrepancy

incohérent, ~e /ɛ̃kɔeʀɑ̃, ɑ̃t/ adj ⟨talk, behaviour⟩ incoherent; ⟨attitude⟩ illogical

incollable /ɛ̃kɔlabl/ adj (a) (colloq) elle est ~ en latin you can't catch her out in Latin
(b) riz ~ easy-cook rice

incolore /ɛ̃kɔlɔʀ/ adj colourless (GB); ⟨glass⟩ clear

incomber /ɛ̃kɔ̃be/ [1] v+prep ~ à ⟨task⟩ to fall to; ⟨responsibility⟩ to lie with

incommode /ɛ̃kɔmɔd/ adj
(a) inconvenient; awkward
(b) uncomfortable

incommodé, ~e /ɛ̃kɔmɔde/ [1] pp ▸ INCOMMODER
[2] pp adj unwell, indisposed

incommoder /ɛ̃kɔmɔde/ [1] vtr to bother

incomparable /ɛ̃kɔ̃paʀabl/ adj incomparable

incompatible /ɛ̃kɔ̃patibl/ adj incompatible

incompétence /ɛ̃kɔ̃petɑ̃s/ nf (gen) incompetence; (Law) incompetency

incompétent, ~e /ɛ̃kɔ̃petɑ̃, ɑ̃t/ adj incompetent

incomplet, -ète /ɛ̃kɔ̃plɛ, ɛt/ adj incomplete

incompréhensible /ɛ̃kɔ̃pʀeɑ̃sibl/ adj incomprehensible

incompréhension /ɛ̃kɔ̃pʀeɑ̃sjɔ̃/ nf
(a) incomprehension
(b) lack of understanding

incompressible /ɛ̃kɔ̃pʀɛsibl/ adj
(a) incompressible
(b) ⟨costs⟩ fixed

incompris, ~e /ɛ̃kɔ̃pʀi, iz/ nm,f misunderstood person

inconcevable /ɛ̃kɔ̃svabl/ adj inconceivable

inconditionnel, -elle /ɛ̃kɔ̃disjɔnɛl/
[1] adj unconditional
[2] nm,f devoted admirer; fan

inconfortable /ɛ̃kɔ̃fɔʀtabl/ adj
(a) uncomfortable
(b) awkward

incongru, ~e /ɛ̃kɔ̃gʀy/ adj ⟨behaviour⟩ unseemly; ⟨remark⟩ incongruous

incongruité /ɛ̃kɔ̃gʀɥite/ nf incongruity

inconnu, ~e /ɛ̃kɔny/ [1] adj unknown; ⟨territories⟩ unexplored
[2] nm,f (a) unknown (person)
(b) stranger

inconsciemment /ɛ̃kɔ̃sjamɑ̃/ adv
(a) subconsciously
(b) unintentionally, unconsciously

inconscience /ɛ̃kɔ̃sjɑ̃s/ nf
(a) recklessness
(b) (Med) unconsciousness

inconscient, ~e /ɛ̃kɔ̃sjɑ̃, ɑ̃t/ [1] adj
(a) unthinking; foolhardy
(b) (Med) unconscious
(c) ⟨act, gesture⟩ unconscious, automatic
[2] nm,f c'est un ~ he's irresponsible
[3] nm l'~ the unconscious

inconséquent, **~e** /ɛ̃kɔ̃sekɑ̃, ɑ̃t/ *adj*
⟨*person, behaviour*⟩ inconsistent

inconsidéré, **~e** /ɛ̃kɔ̃sideʀe/ *adj*
(a) ⟨*remark, act*⟩ ill-considered
(b) ⟨*consumption*⟩ excessive

inconsidérément /ɛ̃kɔ̃sideʀemɑ̃/ *adv*
⟨*drink*⟩ to excess; ⟨*spend*⟩ wildly

inconsistant, **~e** /ɛ̃kɔ̃sistɑ̃, ɑ̃t/ *adj*
⟨*argument, plot*⟩ flimsy; ⟨*programme*⟩
lacking in substance; ⟨*person*⟩ characterless

inconstant, **~e** /ɛ̃kɔ̃stɑ̃, ɑ̃t/ *adj* fickle

incontestable /ɛ̃kɔ̃tɛstabl/ *adj*
unquestionable, indisputable

incontesté, **~e** /ɛ̃kɔ̃tɛste/ *adj* ⟨*victory*⟩
undisputed; ⟨*fact*⟩ uncontested

incontinent, **~e** /ɛ̃kɔ̃tinɑ̃, ɑ̃t/ *adj*
incontinent

incontournable /ɛ̃kɔ̃tuʀnabl/ *adj* ⟨*facts*⟩
that cannot be ignored

incontrôlable /ɛ̃kɔ̃tʀolabl/ *adj*
(a) unverifiable
(b) uncontrollable

inconvenance /ɛ̃kɔ̃vnɑ̃s/ *nf* impropriety

inconvenant, **~e** /ɛ̃kɔ̃vnɑ̃, ɑ̃t/ *adj*
unsuitable; improper, unseemly

inconvénient /ɛ̃kɔ̃venjɑ̃/ *nm* drawback,
disadvantage; **si vous n'y voyez pas d'~** if
you have no objection

incorporer /ɛ̃kɔʀpɔʀe/ [1] *vtr* (a) (Culin) to
blend
(b) to incorporate

incorrect, **~e** /ɛ̃kɔʀɛkt/ *adj* (a) incorrect;
faulty; inaccurate
(b) ⟨*behaviour*⟩ improper; ⟨*term*⟩ unsuitable;
⟨*person*⟩ impolite
(c) unfair

incorrection /ɛ̃kɔʀɛksjɔ̃/ *nf* (of style,
language) incorrectness; (of behaviour)
impropriety

incorrigible /ɛ̃kɔʀiʒibl/ *adj* incorrigible

incrédule /ɛ̃kʀedyl/ *adj* incredulous

incrédulité /ɛ̃kʀedylite/ *nf* incredulity

incriminer /ɛ̃kʀimine/ [1] *vtr* ⟨*person*⟩ to
accuse; ⟨*evidence*⟩ to incriminate; **l'article
incriminé** the offending article

incroyable /ɛ̃kʀwajabl/ *adj* incredible,
unbelievable; **~ mais vrai** strange but true

incrustation /ɛ̃kʀystasjɔ̃/ *nf* (a) inlaying
(b) inlay
(c) encrustation

incruster /ɛ̃kʀyste/ [1] **1** *vtr* (a) to inlay
(b) **incrusté de diamants** encrusted with
diamonds
2 s'incruster *v refl* (+ *v être*) ⟨*pebble,
shell*⟩ to become embedded

incubation /ɛ̃kybasjɔ̃/ *nf* incubation

incuber /ɛ̃kybe/ [1] *vtr* to incubate, to
hatch

inculpation /ɛ̃kylpasjɔ̃/ *nf* (Law) charge

inculpé, **~e** /ɛ̃kylpe/ *nm,f* **l'~** ≈ the
accused

inculper /ɛ̃kylpe/ [1] *vtr* (Law) to charge

inculquer /ɛ̃kylke/ [1] *vtr* to inculcate

inculte /ɛ̃kylt/ *adj* uncultivated

incurable /ɛ̃kyʀabl/ *adj*, *nmf* incurable

incursion /ɛ̃kyʀsjɔ̃/ *nf* incursion, foray

incurver /ɛ̃kyʀve/ [1] *vtr*, **s'incurver**
v refl (+ *v être*) to curve, to bend

Inde /ɛ̃d/ *pr nf* India

indécence /ɛ̃desɑ̃s/ *nf* (gen) indecency;
(of remark) impropriety

indécent, **~e** /ɛ̃desɑ̃, ɑ̃t/ *adj* indecent;
⟨*luxury*⟩ obscene

indéchiffrable /ɛ̃deʃifʀabl/ *adj*
(a) indecipherable
(b) ⟨*mystery*⟩ incomprehensible

indécis, **~e** /ɛ̃desi, iz/ **1** *adj* (a) **il est
encore ~** he hasn't decided yet
(b) indecisive
2 *nm,f* (a) indecisive person
(b) (in opinion poll) 'don't know'; (in election)
floating voter

indécision /ɛ̃desizjɔ̃/ *nf* (a) indecision,
uncertainty
(b) indecisiveness

indécrottable /ɛ̃dekʀɔtabl/ *adj* (colloq)
hopeless (colloq)

indéfini, **~e** /ɛ̃defini/ *adj* (a) ⟨*number*⟩
indeterminate
(b) ⟨*sadness*⟩ undefined; ⟨*duration*⟩
indefinite
(c) (in grammar) indefinite

indéfiniment /ɛ̃definimɑ̃/ *adv*
indefinitely

indéfinissable /ɛ̃definisabl/ *adj*
undefinable

indélébile /ɛ̃delebil/ *adj* indelible

indélicatesse /ɛ̃delikatɛs/ *nf*
(a) indelicacy, tactlessness
(b) dishonesty
(c) act of dishonesty

indemne /ɛ̃dɛmn/ *adj* unscathed,
unharmed

indemnisation /ɛ̃dɛmnizasjɔ̃/ *nf*
(a) indemnification
(b) indemnity, compensation

indemniser /ɛ̃dɛmnize/ [1] *vtr* to
indemnify

indemnité /ɛ̃dɛmnite/ *nf* (a) (Law)
indemnity, compensation
(b) allowance
■ **~ de chômage** unemployment benefit;
~ journalière sick pay; **~ de licenciement**
severance pay

indéniable /ɛ̃denjabl/ *adj* undeniable

indentation /ɛ̃dɑ̃tasjɔ̃/ *nf* indentation

indépendamment /ɛ̃depɑ̃damɑ̃/ **1** *adv*
independently
2 indépendamment de *phr*
(a) regardless of
(b) in addition to

indépendance /ɛ̃depɑ̃dɑ̃s/ *nf*
independence

indépendant, **~e** /ɛ̃depɑ̃dɑ̃, ɑ̃t/ **1** *adj*
(a) independent
(b) ⟨*room*⟩ separate; **maison ~e** detached
house ····⟩

2 *nm,f* freelance, self-employed person

indépendantiste /ɛ̃depɑ̃dɑ̃tist/ **1** *adj*
⟨*organization*⟩ (pro-)independence
2 *nmf* **(a)** freedom fighter
(b) member of an independence movement

indescriptible /ɛ̃dɛskʀiptibl/ *adj*
indescribable

indésirable /ɛ̃deziʀabl/ *adj* ⟨*person*⟩
undesirable; **effets ~s** (Med) adverse
reactions

indéterminé, ~e /ɛ̃detɛʀmine/ *adj*
⟨*form, quantity*⟩ indeterminate; ⟨*reason*⟩
unspecified

index /ɛ̃dɛks/ *nm inv* **(a)** index; **mettre qn/
qch à l'~** to blacklist sb/sth
(b) forefinger

indexer /ɛ̃dɛkse/ [1] *vtr* **(a)** to index-link;
~ qch sur qch to index sth to sth
(b) to index

indicateur, -trice /ɛ̃dikatœʀ, tʀis/
1 *adj* **panneau** *or* **poteau ~** signpost
2 *nm* **(a)** informer
(b) indicator
(c) gauge, indicator

indicatif, -ive /ɛ̃dikatif, iv/ **1** *adj*
indicative
2 *nm* **(a)** (in grammar) indicative
(b) **~** (**téléphonique**) dialling (GB) code
(c) theme tune

indication /ɛ̃dikasjɔ̃/ *nf* **(a)** indication
(b) information; **sauf ~ contraire** unless
otherwise indicated
(c) (for use) instruction
(d) indication, clue

indice /ɛ̃dis/ *nm* **(a)** sign, indication
(b) (in inquiry) clue
(c) (Econ) index; **~ du coût de la vie** cost of
living index
(d) **l'~ d'écoute** audience ratings

indicible /ɛ̃disibl/ *adj* inexpressible

indien, -ienne /ɛ̃djɛ̃, ɛn/ *adj* **(a)** Indian
(b) (North American) Indian

indifféremment /ɛ̃difeʀamɑ̃/ *adv*
(a) equally
(b) **servir ~ de salon ou de bureau** to be
used either as a living room or a study

indifférence /ɛ̃difeʀɑ̃s/ *nf* indifference

indifférent, ~e /ɛ̃difeʀɑ̃, ɑ̃t/ *adj*
(a) indifferent
(b) irrelevant

indifférer /ɛ̃difeʀe/ [14] *vtr* to leave [sb]
indifferent

indigence /ɛ̃diʒɑ̃s/ *nf* destitution, extreme
poverty

indigène /ɛ̃diʒɛn/ **1** *adj* **(a)** ⟨*fauna, flora*⟩
indigenous
(b) ⟨*population, custom*⟩ local; native
2 *nmf* local; native

indigeste /ɛ̃diʒɛst/ *adj* indigestible

indigestion /ɛ̃diʒɛstjɔ̃/ *nf* **(a)** indigestion
(b) **avoir une ~ de qch** to be fed up with sth
(colloq)

indignation /ɛ̃diɲasjɔ̃/ *nf* indignation

indigne /ɛ̃diɲ/ *adj* **(a)** ⟨*conduct*⟩
disgraceful; ⟨*mother, son*⟩ bad
(b) **~ de qn** unworthy of sb

indigné, ~e /ɛ̃diɲe/ *adj* indignant

indigner /ɛ̃diɲe/ [1] **1** *vtr* to make [sb]
indignant, to outrage [sb]
2 s'indigner *v refl* (+ *v être*) to be
indignant

indignité /ɛ̃diɲite/ *nf* **(a)** despicableness
(b) despicable act, disgraceful act

indigo /ɛ̃digo/ *adj inv, nm* indigo

indiqué, ~e /ɛ̃dike/ **1** *pp* ► INDIQUER
2 *pp adj* **(a)** ⟨*treatment*⟩ recommended
(b) **à l'heure ~e** at the specified time; **le
village est très mal ~** the village is very
badly signposted

indiquer /ɛ̃dike/ [1] *vtr* **(a)** ⟨*person*⟩ to
point out, to point to; ⟨*signpost*⟩ to show the
way to; **pouvez-vous m'~ la banque la plus
proche?** can you tell me where the nearest
bank is?
(b) to indicate (**que** that)
(c) **je peux t'~ un bon médecin** I can give
you the name of a good doctor
(d) to give; **l'heure indiquée sur le
programme est fausse** the time given on the
programme (GB) is wrong
(e) ⟨*meter, map*⟩ to show; **le restaurant n'est
pas indiqué** there are no signs to the
restaurant

indirect, ~e /ɛ̃diʀɛkt/ *adj* indirect

indiscipline /ɛ̃disiplin/ *nf* lack of
discipline

indiscipliné, ~e /ɛ̃disipline/ *adj*
undisciplined, unruly

indiscret, -ète /ɛ̃diskʀɛ, ɛt/ *adj*
(a) ⟨*person*⟩ inquisitive; **à l'abri des regards
~s** away from prying eyes
(b) ⟨*person, question*⟩ indiscreet; **il est ~** he
can't keep a secret

indiscrétion /ɛ̃diskʀesjɔ̃/ *nf*
(a) inquisitiveness; **sans ~, combien
gagnez-vous?** if you don't mind my asking,
how much do you earn?
(b) lack of discretion
(c) indiscreet remark

indiscutable /ɛ̃diskytabl/ *adj*
indisputable, unquestionable

indispensable /ɛ̃dispɑ̃sabl/ **1** *adj*
essential; **être ~ à qn** to be indispensable to
sb
2 *nm* **l'~** the essentials

indisposé, ~e /ɛ̃dispoze/ *adj* unwell,
indisposed

indisposer /ɛ̃dispoze/ [1] *vtr* **(a)** to annoy
(b) to upset [sb], to make [sb] feel ill

indisposition /ɛ̃dispozisjɔ̃/ *nf*
indisposition

indissociable /ɛ̃disɔsjabl/ *adj*
inseparable

indistinct, ~e /ɛ̃distɛ̃, ɛkt/ *adj* indistinct

individu /ɛ̃dividy/ *nm* **(a)** individual
(b) human being, person

(c) un sinistre ∼ a sinister individual or character; un ∼ armé an armed man
(d) (in scientific study) subject

individualiser /ɛ̃dividɥalize/ [1] **1** vtr
(a) to tailor [sth] to individual needs
(b) to individualize
2 s'individualiser v refl (+ v être) to become more individual

individualiste /ɛ̃dividɥalist/ adj individualistic

individuel, -elle /ɛ̃dividɥɛl/ adj (gen) individual; ⟨responsibility⟩ personal; ⟨room⟩ single; **maison individuelle** (detached) house

indivisible /ɛ̃divizibl/ adj indivisible

Indochine /ɛ̃dɔʃin/ pr nf Indochina

indo-européen, -éenne /ɛ̃doøʁɔpeɛ̃, ɛn/ mpl ∼s Indo-European

indolence /ɛ̃dɔlɑ̃s/ nf laziness, indolence

indolent, ∼e /ɛ̃dɔlɑ̃, ɑ̃t/ adj lazy, indolent

indolore /ɛ̃dɔlɔʀ/ adj painless

indomptable /ɛ̃dɔ̃tabl/ adj ⟨person, courage⟩ indomitable; ⟨anger, passion, person⟩ uncontrollable; ⟨animal⟩ untamable; **avec une énergie ∼** with tireless energy

Indonésie /ɛ̃dɔnezi/ pr nf Indonesia

indu, ∼e /ɛ̃dy/ adj ⟨hour⟩ ungodly (colloq), unearthly; ⟨remark, reaction⟩ inappropriate

indubitable /ɛ̃dybitabl/ adj indubitable

indubitablement /ɛ̃dybitabləmɑ̃/ adv undoubtedly

induction /ɛ̃dyksjɔ̃/ nf induction

induire /ɛ̃dɥiʀ/ [69] vtr (a) ⟨event, measures⟩ to lead to, to bring about
(b) to infer, to conclude
(c) to induce; **∼ qn en erreur** to mislead sb
(d) to induce ⟨current⟩

indulgence /ɛ̃dylʒɑ̃s/ nf (a) (of parent, audience) indulgence
(b) (of jury) leniency

indulgent, ∼e /ɛ̃dylʒɑ̃, ɑ̃t/ adj (a) ⟨parent, audience⟩ indulgent
(b) ⟨jury⟩ lenient

industrialisation /ɛ̃dystʀializasjɔ̃/ nf industrialization

industrialiser /ɛ̃dystʀialize/ [1] **1** vtr to industrialize
2 s'industrialiser v refl (+ v être) to become industrialized

industrie /ɛ̃dystʀi/ nf (a) industry; **l'∼ hôtelière** the hotel trade
(b) industrial concern

industriel, -ielle /ɛ̃dystʀijɛl/ **1** adj industrial; **pain ∼** factory-baked bread
2 nm,f industrialist, manufacturer

inébranlable /inebʀɑ̃labl/ adj
(a) unshakeable, unwavering
(b) immovable

inédit, ∼e /inedi, it/ adj ⟨book⟩ (previously) unpublished; ⟨situation⟩ (totally) new

ineffable /inefabl/ adj ineffable, unutterable

inefficace /inefikas/ adj (a) ineffective

(b) inefficient

inefficacité /inefikasite/ nf
(a) ineffectiveness, inefficacy
(b) inefficiency

inégal, ∼e, mpl -aux /inegal, o/ adj unequal; uneven; irregular; ⟨mood⟩ changeable, erratic

inégalable /inegalabl/ adj incomparable

inégalé, ∼e /inegale/ adj unequalled (GB), unrivalled (GB)

inégalement /inegalmɑ̃/ adv
(a) unequally
(b) unevenly

inégalité /inegalite/ nf (a) disparity
(b) inequality
(c) (of mood) changeability; (of surface) unevenness

inéluctable /inelyktabl/ adj, nm inevitable

inénarrable /inenaʀabl/ adj hilarious

inepte /inɛpt/ adj ⟨person⟩ inept; ⟨judgment⟩ inane; ⟨remark⟩ idiotic

ineptie /inɛpsi/ nf (a) inanity
(b) idiotic remark
(c) (action) stupid thing

inépuisable /inepɥizabl/ adj inexhaustible

inerte /inɛʀt/ adj (a) inert
(b) apathetic

inertie /inɛʀsi/ nf (a) inertia
(b) apathy, inertia

inespéré, ∼e /inɛspeʀe/ adj ⟨victory⟩ unhoped for; **c'est une occasion ∼e de faire** this is a heaven-sent opportunity to do

inestimable /inɛstimabl/ adj ⟨value⟩ inestimable; ⟨help⟩ invaluable

inévitable /inevitabl/ adj inevitable; unavoidable

inexact, ∼e /inɛgza, akt/ adj inaccurate

inexactitude /inɛgzaktityd/ nf
(a) inaccuracy
(b) unpunctuality

inexcusable /inɛkskyzabl/ adj inexcusable

inexistant, ∼e /inɛgzistɑ̃, ɑ̃t/ adj ⟨means, help⟩ nonexistent

inexpérience /inɛkspeʀjɑ̃s/ nf inexperience

inexpérimenté, ∼e /inɛkspeʀimɑ̃te/ adj inexperienced

inexplicable /inɛksplikabl/ adj inexplicable

inexpressif, -ive /inɛkspʀesif, iv/ adj inexpressive

inexprimable /inɛkspʀimabl/ adj inexpressible

in extremis /inɛkstʀemis/ phr at the last minute

infaillible /ɛ̃fajibl/ adj infallible

infaisable /ɛ̃fəzabl/ adj unfeasible, impossible

infamant, ∼e /ɛ̃famɑ̃, ɑ̃t/ adj
(a) ⟨remark⟩ defamatory

···▷

(b) ⟨act⟩ infamous

infâme /ɛ̃fɑm/ adj **(a)** ⟨food, smell⟩ revolting

(b) ⟨person⟩ despicable; ⟨crime⟩ odious

infamie /ɛ̃fami/ nf **(a)** infamy

(b) infamous act

(c) slanderous remark

infanterie /ɛ̃fɑ̃tʀi/ nf infantry

infantile /ɛ̃fɑ̃til/ adj **(a)** ⟨illness⟩ childhood; ⟨mortality⟩ infant; ⟨psychology⟩ child

(b) ⟨person, behaviour⟩ infantile, childish

infantilisme /ɛ̃fɑ̃tilism/ nm childishness

infarctus /ɛ̃faʀktys/ nm inv heart attack

infatigable /ɛ̃fatigabl/ adj tireless

infatué, ～e /ɛ̃fatɥe/ adj **être ～ de sa personne** to be full of oneself

infect, ～e /ɛ̃fɛkt/ adj foul; revolting

infecter /ɛ̃fɛkte/ [1] **1** vtr **(a)** (Med) to infect

(b) (figurative) to poison

2 **s'infecter** v refl (+ v être) to become infected, to go septic

infectieux, -ieuse /ɛ̃fɛksjø, øz/ adj infectious

infection /ɛ̃fɛksjɔ̃/ nf **(a)** (Med) infection

(b) (figurative) **c'est une ～!** it stinks to high heaven! (colloq)

inférieur, ～e /ɛ̃feʀjœʀ/ **1** adj **(a)** lower; ⟨size⟩ smaller; ⟨length⟩ shorter; **～ à la moyenne** below average; **être en nombre ～** to be fewer in number

(b) inferior

(c) (in mathematics) **si a est ～ à b** if a is less than b

2 nm,f inferior

infériorité /ɛ̃feʀjɔʀite/ nf inferiority

infernal, ～e, mpl **-aux** /ɛ̃fɛʀnal, o/ adj **(a)** ⟨noise, heat⟩ infernal; **cycle ～** unstoppable chain of events

(b) ⟨situation⟩ diabolical; **ce gosse est ～** (colloq) that child is a monster

infertile /ɛ̃fɛʀtil/ adj barren, infertile

infester /ɛ̃fɛste/ [1] vtr to infest, to overrun; **infesté de puces** flea-ridden

infidèle /ɛ̃fidɛl/ **1** adj unfaithful; disloyal

2 nmf infidel

infidélité /ɛ̃fidelite/ nf **(a)** infidelity; **faire des ～s à** to be unfaithful to

(b) disloyalty

infiltration /ɛ̃filtʀasjɔ̃/ nf **(a)** **～s d'eau** water seepage

(b) (of spies) infiltration

(c) (Med) injection

infiltrer /ɛ̃filtʀe/ [1] **1** vtr to infiltrate

2 **s'infiltrer** v refl (+ v être) **(a)** ⟨liquid⟩ to seep; ⟨light, cold⟩ to filter in

(b) ⟨person⟩ **s'～ dans** to infiltrate ⟨group, place⟩

infime /ɛ̃fim/ adj tiny, minute

infini, ～e /ɛ̃fini/ **1** adj infinite

2 nm **l'～** infinity

infiniment /ɛ̃finimɑ̃/ adv immensely; **～ plus** infinitely more

infinité /ɛ̃finite/ nf **l'～** infinity; **une ～ de** an endless number of

infinitif /ɛ̃finitif/ nm infinitive

infirme /ɛ̃fiʀm/ **1** adj (gen) disabled; (because of age) infirm

2 nmf disabled person; **les ～s** the disabled

infirmer /ɛ̃fiʀme/ [1] vtr (gen, Law) to invalidate

infirmerie /ɛ̃fiʀməʀi/ nf (gen) infirmary; sick room; sick bay

infirmier /ɛ̃fiʀmje/ nm male nurse

infirmière /ɛ̃fiʀmjɛʀ/ nf nurse

infirmité /ɛ̃fiʀmite/ nf (gen) disability; (through old age) infirmity

inflammable /ɛ̃flamabl/ adj flammable

inflammation /ɛ̃flamasjɔ̃/ nf (Med) inflammation

inflammatoire /ɛ̃flamatwaʀ/ adj (Med) inflammatory

inflation /ɛ̃flasjɔ̃/ nf inflation

infléchir /ɛ̃fleʃiʀ/ [3] vtr, **s'infléchir** v refl (+ v être) to soften; to deflect

inflexible /ɛ̃flɛksibl/ adj inflexible

infliger /ɛ̃fliʒe/ [13] vtr to impose ⟨fine⟩

influençable /ɛ̃flyɑ̃sabl/ adj impressionable

influence /ɛ̃flyɑ̃s/ nf influence

influencer /ɛ̃flyɑ̃se/ [12] vtr to influence ⟨person⟩; to affect ⟨situation⟩

influent, ～e /ɛ̃flyɑ̃, ɑ̃t/ adj influential

influer /ɛ̃flye/ [1] v+prep **～ sur** to have an influence on

informateur, -trice /ɛ̃fɔʀmatœʀ, tʀis/ nm,f **(a)** (gen) informant

(b) (police) informer

informaticien, -ienne /ɛ̃fɔʀmatisjɛ̃, ɛn/ nm,f computer scientist

information /ɛ̃fɔʀmasjɔ̃/ nf **(a)** information; **une ～** a piece of information

(b) (in newspaper, on television) **une ～** a piece of news; **écouter les ～s** to listen to the news; **contrôler l'～** to control the media

(c) (Comput) data, information

informatique /ɛ̃fɔʀmatik/ **1** adj computer

2 nf computer science, computing

informatisation /ɛ̃fɔʀmatizasjɔ̃/ nf computerization

informatiser /ɛ̃fɔʀmatize/ [1] **1** vtr to computerize

2 **s'informatiser** v refl (+ v être) to become computerized

informe /ɛ̃fɔʀm/ adj shapeless

informer /ɛ̃fɔʀme/ [1] **1** vtr to inform

2 **s'informer** v refl (+ v être) **(a)** to keep oneself informed

(b) **s'～ de qch** to enquire about sth

(c) **s'～ sur qn** to make enquiries about sb

infortune /ɛ̃fɔʀtyn/ nf misfortune

infortuné, ～e /ɛ̃fɔʀtyne/ **1** adj ill-fated

2 nm,f unfortunate

infra /ɛ̃fʀa/ adv below; **voir ～** see below

infraction /ɛ̃fʀaksjɔ̃/ nf offence (GB); **être en ~** to be in breach of the law

infranchissable /ɛ̃fʀɑ̃ʃisabl/ adj ⟨obstacle⟩ insurmountable; ⟨border⟩ impassable

infrarouge /ɛ̃fʀaʀuʒ/ adj, nm infrared; **missile guidé par ~** heat-seeking missile

infrastructure /ɛ̃fʀastʀyktyʀ/ nf
(a) facilities
(b) (Econ) infrastructure

infructueux, -euse /ɛ̃fʀyktɥø, øz/ adj fruitless

infuser /ɛ̃fyze/ [1] vi ⟨tea⟩ to brew, to infuse

infusion /ɛ̃fyzjɔ̃/ nf (a) herbal tea
(b) infusion

ingénier: **s'ingénier** /ɛ̃ʒenje/ [2] v refl (+ v être) to do one's utmost (à faire to do)

ingénierie /ɛ̃ʒeniʀi/ nf engineering

ingénieur /ɛ̃ʒenjœʀ/ nm engineer

ingénieur-conseil, pl **ingénieurs-conseils** /ɛ̃ʒenjœʀkɔ̃sɛj/ nm consulting engineer

ingénieux, -ieuse /ɛ̃ʒenjø, øz/ adj ingenious

ingéniosité /ɛ̃ʒenjozite/ nf ingenuity

ingénu, ~e /ɛ̃ʒeny/ adj ingenuous

ingénuité /ɛ̃ʒenɥite/ nf ingenuousness; **en toute ~** in all innocence

ingérence /ɛ̃ʒeʀɑ̃s/ nf interference (dans in)

ingérer /ɛ̃ʒeʀe/ [14] [1] vtr to ingest
[2] **s'ingérer** v refl (+ v être) to interfere

ingestion /ɛ̃ʒɛstjɔ̃/ nf ingestion

ingrat, ~e /ɛ̃gʀa, at/ adj (a) ungrateful
(b) ⟨face, landscape⟩ unattractive
(c) ⟨task, role⟩ thankless; ⟨land, soil⟩ unproductive

ingratitude /ɛ̃gʀatityd/ nf ingratitude

ingrédient /ɛ̃gʀedjɑ̃/ nm ingredient

ingurgiter /ɛ̃gyʀʒite/ [1] vtr to gulp down

inhabitable /inabitabl/ adj uninhabitable

inhabité, ~e /inabite/ adj uninhabited

inhabituel, -elle /inabitɥɛl/ adj unusual

inhalation /inalasjɔ̃/ nf inhalation

inhaler /inale/ [1] vtr to inhale

inhérent, ~e /ineʀɑ̃, ɑ̃t/ adj inherent

inhibition /inibisjɔ̃/ nf inhibition

inhumain, ~e /inymɛ̃, ɛn/ adj inhuman

inhumation /inymasjɔ̃/ nf (a) burial
(b) funeral

inhumer /inyme/ [1] vtr to bury

inimaginable /inimaʒinabl/ adj
(a) unimaginable
(b) unthinkable

inimitable /inimitabl/ adj inimitable

ininflammable /inɛ̃flamabl/ adj nonflammable

inintéressant, ~e /inɛ̃teʀesɑ̃, ɑ̃t/ adj uninteresting

ininterrompu, ~e /inɛ̃teʀɔ̃py/ adj
(a) ⟨process⟩ uninterrupted; ⟨drop⟩ continuous; ⟨traffic⟩ endless
(b) ⟨procession⟩ unbroken

initial, ~e¹, mpl **-iaux** /inisjal, o/ adj initial

initiale² /inisjal/ nf initial

initiateur, -trice /inisjatœʀ, tʀis/ nm,f
(a) originator; instigator
(b) instructor

initiation /inisjasjɔ̃/ nf (a) introduction
(b) initiation

initiative /inisjativ/ nf initiative; **avoir l'esprit d'~** to have initiative

initié, ~e /inisje/ [1] adj (Comput) **~ à l'informatique** computer literate
[2] nm,f (a) initiate
(b) insider trader
(c) (Comput) **~ à l'informatique** computer-literate person

initier /inisje/ [2] [1] vtr (a) to introduce
(b) to initiate
[2] **s'initier** v refl (+ v être) **s'~ à qch** to learn sth

injecter /ɛ̃ʒɛkte/ [2] vtr to inject

injection /ɛ̃ʒɛksjɔ̃/ nf injection

injonction /ɛ̃ʒɔ̃ksjɔ̃/ nf injunction, command

injure /ɛ̃ʒyʀ/ nf insult, abuse

injurier /ɛ̃ʒyʀje/ [1] vtr to insult, to swear at

injurieux, -ieuse /ɛ̃ʒyʀjø, øz/ adj ⟨remark⟩ abusive; ⟨attitude⟩ insulting

injuste /ɛ̃ʒyst/ adj unfair

injustement /ɛ̃ʒystəmɑ̃/ adv unjustly; unfairly

injustice /ɛ̃ʒystis/ nf injustice; unfairness; **réparer une ~** to right a wrong

injustifié, ~e /ɛ̃ʒystifje/ adj unjustified

inlassable /ɛ̃lasabl/ adj ⟨person⟩ tireless; ⟨curiosity⟩ insatiable; ⟨efforts⟩ unremitting

inlassablement /ɛ̃lasabləmɑ̃/ adv tirelessly

inné, ~e /inne/ adj innate

innocemment /inɔsamɑ̃/ adv innocently; **pas ~** disingenuously

innocence /inɔsɑ̃s/ nf innocence

innocent, ~e /inɔsɑ̃, ɑ̃t/ adj innocent

innocenter /inɔsɑ̃te/ [1] vtr to prove [sb] innocent

innombrable /innɔ̃bʀabl/ adj
(a) countless
(b) ⟨crowd⟩ vast

innommable /innɔmabl/ adj unspeakable

innovateur, -trice /inɔvatœʀ, tʀis/ nm,f innovator

innover /inɔve/ [1] vi to innovate

inoculer /inɔkyle/ [1] vtr to inoculate

inodore /inɔdɔʀ/ adj ⟨substance⟩ odourless (GB)

inoffensif, -ive /inɔfɑ̃sif, iv/ adj harmless

inondation /inɔ̃dasjɔ̃/ nf (a) flood ┈┄➔

(b) flooding

inonder /inɔ̃de/ [1] *vtr* to flood

inopérant, **~e** /inɔperɑ̃, ɑ̃t/ *adj* ineffective

inopiné, **~e** /inɔpine/ *adj* unexpected

inopportun, **~e** /inɔpɔrtœ̃, yn/ *adj*
(a) inappropriate
(b) ill-timed

inoubliable /inublijabl/ *adj* unforgettable

inouï, **~e** /inwi/ *adj* ⟨*event*⟩ unprecedented; ⟨*success*⟩ incredible; **c'est ~** that's unheard of

inox /inɔks/ *nm inv* stainless steel

inoxydable /inɔksidabl/ *adj* ⟨*metal*⟩ non-oxidizing; **acier ~** stainless steel

inqualifiable /ɛ̃kalifjabl/ *adj* unspeakable

inquiet, **-iète** /ɛ̃kjɛ, ɛt/ *adj* (a) anxious
(b) worried

inquiétant, **~e** /ɛ̃kjetɑ̃, ɑ̃t/ *adj*
(a) worrying
(b) frightening

inquiéter /ɛ̃kjete/ [14] **1** *vtr* (a) to worry
(b) **les douaniers ne l'ont pas inquiété** the customs officers didn't bother him
2 s'inquiéter *v refl* (+ *v être*) (a) to worry
(b) **s'~ de qch** to enquire about sth

inquiétude /ɛ̃kjetyd/ *nf* (a) anxiety, concern
(b) worry; **il n'y a pas d'~ à avoir** there's nothing to worry about

inquisiteur, **-trice** /ɛ̃kizitœr, tris/
1 *adj* inquisitive
2 *nm,f* inquisitor

inquisition /ɛ̃kizisjɔ̃/ *nf* inquisition

insaisissable /ɛ̃sezisabl/ *adj* ⟨*person, character*⟩ elusive; ⟨*nuance*⟩ imperceptible

insalubre /ɛ̃salybr/ *adj* insanitary

insanité /ɛ̃sanite/ *nf* (a) rubbish, nonsense
(b) insanity

insatiable /ɛ̃sasjabl/ *adj* insatiable

insatisfaction /ɛ̃satisfaksjɔ̃/ *nf* dissatisfaction

insatisfait, **~e** /ɛ̃satisfɛ, ɛt/ *adj* dissatisfied (**de** with); unsatisfied

inscription /ɛ̃skripsjɔ̃/ *nf* (a) (in school) enrolment (GB); (at university) registration
(b) **l'~ au club coûte 200 francs** the membership fee for the club is 200 francs; **~ électorale** registration as a voter
(c) inscription; graffiti

inscrire /ɛ̃skrir/ [67] **1** *vtr* (a) to enrol (GB) ⟨*pupil*⟩; to register ⟨*student*⟩
(b) to write down ⟨*name, date*⟩
2 s'inscrire *v refl* (+ *v être*) (a) to enrol (GB); to register; **s'~ au chômage** to register as unemployed; **s'~ à un parti** to join a party
(b) **s'~ dans le cadre de** to be in line with
(c) **s'~ en faux contre qch** to dispute the validity of sth

inscrit, **~e** /ɛ̃skri, it/ **1** *pp* ▶ **INSCRIRE**
2 *nm,f* registered student; registered voter

insecte /ɛ̃sɛkt/ *nm* insect

insecticide /ɛ̃sɛktisid/ *nm* insecticide

insécurité /ɛ̃sekyrite/ *nf* insecurity

INSEE *nm* (*abbr* **Institut National de la Statistique et des Études Économiques**) French national institute of statistics and economic studies

insémination /ɛ̃seminasjɔ̃/ *nf* insemination; **~ artificielle** artificial insemination

insensé, **~e** /ɛ̃sɑ̃se/ *adj* (a) insane
(b) (*colloq*) ⟨*crowd, traffic jam*⟩ phenomenal

insensibiliser /ɛ̃sɑ̃sibilize/ [1] *vtr* (Med) to anaesthetize

insensibilité /ɛ̃sɑ̃sibilite/ *nf* insensitivity

insensible /ɛ̃sɑ̃sibl/ *adj* (a) impervious
(b) insensitive

insensiblement /ɛ̃sɑ̃sibləmɑ̃/ *adv* imperceptibly

inséparable /ɛ̃separabl/ *adj* inseparable

insérer /ɛ̃sere/ [14] **1** *vtr* to insert
2 s'insérer *v refl* (+ *v être*) (gen) to be inserted

insertion /ɛ̃sɛrsjɔ̃/ *nf* (a) insertion
(b) integration

insidieux, **-ieuse** /ɛ̃sidjø, øz/ *adj* insidious

insigne /ɛ̃siɲ/ **1** *adj* ⟨*honour, favour*⟩ great
2 *nm* badge

insignifiant, **~e** /ɛ̃siɲifjɑ̃, ɑ̃t/ *adj* insignificant

insinuation /ɛ̃sinɥasjɔ̃/ *nf* insinuation

insinuer /ɛ̃sinɥe/ [1] **1** *vtr* to insinuate
2 s'insinuer *v refl* (+ *v être*) **s'~ dans** ⟨*person*⟩ to worm one's way into; ⟨*liquid*⟩ to seep into

insipide /ɛ̃sipid/ *adj* insipid

insistance /ɛ̃sistɑ̃s/ *nf* insistence

insistant, **~e** /ɛ̃sistɑ̃, ɑ̃t/ *adj* insistent

insister /ɛ̃siste/ [1] *vi* (a) to insist; **'ça ne répond pas'—'insiste'** 'there's no reply!'—'keep trying'
(b) **~ sur** to stress ⟨*danger, need*⟩; to put the emphasis on ⟨*spelling*⟩
(c) **~ sur** to pay particular attention to ⟨*stain*⟩

insolation /ɛ̃sɔlasjɔ̃/ *nf* sunstroke

insolence /ɛ̃sɔlɑ̃s/ *nf* (a) insolence
(b) insolent remark

insolent, **~e** /ɛ̃sɔlɑ̃, ɑ̃t/ *adj* (a) ⟨*child, tone*⟩ insolent
(b) ⟨*rival, winner*⟩ arrogant

insolite /ɛ̃sɔlit/ *adj, nm* unusual

insoluble /ɛ̃sɔlybl/ *adj* insoluble

insolvable /ɛ̃sɔlvabl/ *adj* insolvent

insomniaque /ɛ̃sɔmnjak/ *adj, nmf* insomniac

insomnie /ɛ̃sɔmni/ *nf* insomnia

insondable /ɛ̃sɔ̃dabl/ *adj* unfathomable

insonorisation /ɛ̃sɔnɔrizasjɔ̃/ *nf* soundproofing

insonoriser /ɛ̃sɔnɔrize/ [1] *vtr* to soundproof

insouciance /ɛ̃susjɑ̃s/ *nf* carefreeness

insouciant, ~e /ɛsusjɑ̃, ɑ̃t/ adj carefree

insoumission /ɛ̃sumisjɔ̃/ nf
(a) insubordination
(b) (Mil) draft-dodging

insoupçonné, ~e /ɛ̃supsɔne/ adj
unsuspected

insoutenable /ɛ̃sutnabl/ adj (a) ‹pain›
unbearable
(b) ‹opinion› untenable

inspecter /ɛ̃spɛkte/ [1] vtr to inspect

inspecteur, -trice /ɛ̃spɛktœr, tris/ nm,f
inspector
■ ~ de police ≈ detective constable (GB);
~ du travail health and safety inspector

inspection /ɛ̃spɛksjɔ̃/ nf (a) inspection
(b) inspectorate

inspiration /ɛ̃spirasjɔ̃/ nf inspiration

inspirer /ɛ̃spire/ [1] **1** vtr (a) to inspire
‹person›; être bien/mal inspiré de faire to be
well-/ill-advised to do; un roman inspiré des
vieux contes populaires a novel based on old
folk tales
(b) to appeal to; ça ne m'inspire pas that
doesn't appeal to me
(c) ~ la méfiance à qn to inspire distrust in
sb
2 vi to breathe in, to inhale
3 s'inspirer v refl (+ v être) s'~ de to
draw one's inspiration from

instabilité /ɛ̃stabilite/ nf (gen) instability

instable /ɛ̃stabl/ adj (gen) unstable;
‹weather› unsettled

installateur, -trice /ɛ̃stalatœr, tris/
nm,f fitter

installation /ɛ̃stalasjɔ̃/ **1** nf
(a) installation, putting in
(b) system; ~ électrique (electric) wiring
(c) move; depuis mon ~ à Paris since I
moved to Paris
2 installations nf pl facilities

installé, ~e /ɛ̃stale/ **1** pp ▶ INSTALLER
2 pp adj ‹person› living (à in); ‹company›
based; être bien ~ dans un fauteuil to be
ensconced in an armchair; ils sont bien ~s
dans leur nouvelle maison they're very snug
in their new home; c'est un homme ~
(figurative) he's very nicely set up

installer /ɛ̃stale/ [1] **1** vtr (a) to install, to
put in ‹central heating, sink›; to put up
‹shelves›; to connect ‹gas›
(b) to put ‹guest› (dans in); ~ qn dans un
fauteuil to sit sb in an armchair; ~ qn à un
poste to appoint sb to a post
2 s'installer v refl (+ v être) (a) ‹recession›
to set in; ‹illness› to take hold; le doute
commence à s'~ dans leur esprit they're
beginning to have doubts
(b) s'~ à son compte to set up one's own
business
(c) to settle; partir s'~ à l'étranger to go and
live abroad; je viendrai te voir quand tu
seras installé I'll come and see you when
you're settled in; s'~ au soleil to sit in the

sun; s'~ à son bureau to settle down at
one's desk; installe-toi, j'arrive! make
yourself at home, I'm coming!

instamment /ɛ̃stamɑ̃/ adv insistently

instance /ɛ̃stɑ̃s/ nf (a) authority; les ~s
d'un parti politique the leaders of a political
party
(b) être en ~ de divorce to be engaged in
divorce proceedings

instant, ~e /ɛ̃stɑ̃, ɑ̃t/ nm moment,
instant; à tout or chaque ~ all the time; par
~s at times; pour l'~ for the moment; il
devrait arriver d'un ~ à l'autre he should
arrive any minute now; à l'~ même où just
when

instantané, ~e /ɛ̃stɑ̃tane/ **1** adj
instantaneous; ‹drink, soup› instant
2 nm snapshot

instar: à l'instar de /alɛstardə/ phr
following the example of

instaurer /ɛ̃stɔre/ [1] vtr to establish
‹regime, dialogue›; to impose ‹curfew›

instigateur, -trice /ɛ̃stigatœr, tris/
nm,f (a) instigator
(b) originator

instigation /ɛ̃stigasjɔ̃/ nf à l'~ de qn at
sb's instigation

instiller /ɛ̃stile/ [1] vtr to instil (GB)

instinct /ɛ̃stɛ̃/ nm instinct; d'~
instinctively

instinctif, -ive /ɛ̃stɛ̃ktif, iv/ adj
instinctive

instituer /ɛ̃stitɥe/ [1] vtr to institute

institut /ɛ̃stity/ nm (a) institute
(b) ~ de beauté beauty salon or parlour
(GB)
■ Institut universitaire de formation des
maîtres, IUFM primary teacher training
college; Institut universitaire de technologie,
IUT university institute of technology

instituteur, -trice /ɛ̃stitytœr, tris/ nm,f
(primary school) teacher

institution /ɛ̃stitysjɔ̃/ nf (a) institution
(b) private school

institutrice ▶ INSTITUTEUR

instructeur /ɛ̃stryktœr/ nm (gen, Mil)
instructor

instructif, -ive /ɛ̃stryktif, iv/ adj (gen)
instructive; ‹experience› enlightening

instruction /ɛ̃stryksjɔ̃/ **1** nf (a) (gen)
education; (Mil) training
(b) (Law) preparation of a case for trial
2 instructions nf pl instructions
■ ~ civique civics; ~ religieuse religious
instruction

instruire /ɛ̃strɥir/ [69] **1** vtr (a) to teach
‹child›; to train ‹soldiers›
(b) (Law) ~ une affaire to prepare a case for
trial
2 s'instruire v refl (+ v être) to learn

instruit, ~e /ɛ̃strɥi, it/ adj educated

instrument /ɛ̃strymɑ̃/ nm (gen, Mus)
instrument; ~ à cordes/à percussion/à vent ···⊹

string/percussion/wind instrument; **jouer d'un ~** to play an instrument; **être l'~ de qn** to be sb's tool

■ **~s de bord** controls

insu: **à l'insu de** /alɛ̃syd/ *phr* **à l'~ de qn** without sb knowing

insubordination /ɛ̃sybɔrdinasjɔ̃/ *nf* insubordination

insubordonné, ~e /ɛ̃sybɔrdɔne/ *adj* rebellious; insubordinate

insuffisamment /ɛ̃syfizamɑ̃/ *adv* insufficiently; inadequately

insuffisance /ɛ̃syfizɑ̃s/ *nf*
(a) insufficiency, shortage
(b) poor standard; **l'~ de la production** the shortfall in production
(c) (Med) insufficiency

insuffisant, ~e /ɛ̃syfizɑ̃, ɑ̃t/ *adj*
(a) insufficient
(b) inadequate

insuffler /ɛ̃syfle/ [1] *vtr* to instil (GB); **~ la vie à qn** to breathe life into sb

insulaire /ɛ̃sylɛr/ *adj* ⟨population⟩ island; ⟨mentality⟩ insular

insultant, ~e /ɛ̃syltɑ̃, ɑ̃t/ *adj* insulting

insulte /ɛ̃sylt/ *nf* insult

insulter /ɛ̃sylte/ [1] *vtr* to insult; to shout abuse at; ⟨attitude⟩ to be an insult to

insupportable /ɛ̃sypɔrtabl/ *adj* unbearable

insurgé, ~e /ɛ̃syrʒe/ *nm,f* insurgent, rebel

insurger: **s'insurger** /ɛ̃syrʒe/ [13] *v refl* (+ *v être*) (a) to rise up
(b) to protest

insurmontable /ɛ̃syrmɔ̃tabl/ *adj* insurmountable; insuperable; unconquerable

insurrection /ɛ̃syrɛksjɔ̃/ *nf* insurrection

intact, ~e /ɛ̃takt/ *adj* intact

intarissable /ɛ̃tarisabl/ *adj* ⟨imagination⟩ inexhaustible; ⟨source⟩ never-ending

intégral, ~e, *mpl* -aux /ɛ̃tegral, o/ *adj*
(a) ⟨payment⟩ full, in full
(b) ⟨tan⟩ all-over
(c) ⟨text⟩ unabridged; **version ~e** uncut version

intégralement /ɛ̃tegralmɑ̃/ *adv* ⟨pay⟩ in full

intégralité /ɛ̃tegralite/ *nf* **l'~ de leur salaire** their entire salary

intégrante /ɛ̃tegrɑ̃t/ *adj f* **faire partie ~ de qch** to be an integral part of sth

intégration /ɛ̃tegrasjɔ̃/ *nf* integration

intègre /ɛ̃tegr/ *adj* ⟨person, life⟩ honest

intégrer /ɛ̃tegre/ [14] **1** *vtr* (a) to insert
(b) to integrate ⟨population⟩
(c) (colloq) **il vient d'~ Harvard** he has just got into Harvard
2 **s'intégrer** *v refl* (+ *v être*)
(a) ⟨population⟩ to integrate
(b) ⟨building⟩ to fit in

intégrisme /ɛ̃tegrism/ *nm* fundamentalism

intégrité /ɛ̃tegrite/ *nf* integrity

intellect /ɛ̃telɛkt/ *nm* intellect

intellectuel, -elle /ɛ̃telɛktɥɛl/ **1** *adj* ⟨work⟩ intellectual; ⟨effort⟩ mental
2 *nm,f* intellectual

intelligence /ɛ̃teliʒɑ̃s/ *nf* (a) intelligence
(b) **agir d'~ avec qn** to act in agreement with sb

intelligent, ~e /ɛ̃teliʒɑ̃, ɑ̃t/ *adj* intelligent; clever

intelligible /ɛ̃teliʒibl/ *adj* intelligible

intempéries /ɛ̃tɑ̃peri/ *nf pl* bad weather

intempestif, -ive /ɛ̃tɑ̃pɛstif, iv/ *adj* untimely; ⟨curiosity, zeal⟩ misplaced

intemporel, -elle /ɛ̃tɑ̃pɔrɛl/ *adj* timeless

intenable /ɛ̃t(ə)nabl/ *adj* (a) ⟨situation⟩ unbearable
(b) ⟨child⟩ difficult

intendance /ɛ̃tɑ̃dɑ̃s/ *nf* (Sch) administration

intendant, ~e /ɛ̃tɑ̃dɑ̃, ɑ̃t/ **1** *nm,f* (Sch) bursar
2 *nm* (Mil) quartermaster; paymaster

intense /ɛ̃tɑ̃s/ *adj* (gen) intense; ⟨red, green⟩ vivid; ⟨traffic⟩ heavy

intensif, -ive /ɛ̃tɑ̃sif, iv/ *adj* intensive

intensification /ɛ̃tɑ̃sifikasjɔ̃/ *nf* intensification

intensifier /ɛ̃tɑ̃sifje/ [2] *vtr*, **s'intensifier** *v refl* (+ *v être*) to intensify

intensité /ɛ̃tɑ̃site/ *nf* intensity

intensivement /ɛ̃tɑ̃sivmɑ̃/ *adv* intensively

intenter /ɛ̃tɑ̃te/ [1] *vtr* **~ un procès à qn** to sue sb

intention /ɛ̃tɑ̃sjɔ̃/ *nf* intention; **c'est l'~ qui compte** it's the thought that counts; **à l'~ de qn** ⟨remark⟩ aimed at sb

intentionné, ~e /ɛ̃tɑ̃sjɔne/ *adj* **bien/mal ~** well-/ill-intentioned

intentionnel, -elle /ɛ̃tɑ̃sjɔnɛl/ *adj* intentional

interaction /ɛ̃tɛraksjɔ̃/ *nf* interaction

interbancaire /ɛ̃tɛrbɑ̃kɛr/ *adj* interbank

intercalaire /ɛ̃tɛrkalɛr/ **1** *adj* **feuille** or **feuillet ~** insert
2 *nm* divider

intercaler /ɛ̃tɛrkale/ [1] *vtr* to insert

intercéder /ɛ̃tɛrsede/ [14] *vi* to intercede

intercepter /ɛ̃tɛrsɛpte/ [1] *vtr* to intercept

interchangeable /ɛ̃tɛrʃɑ̃ʒabl/ *adj* interchangeable

interclasse /ɛ̃tɛrklas/ *nm* break (between classes)

interdiction /ɛ̃tɛrdiksjɔ̃/ *nf* (a) banning; '**~ de dépasser'** 'no overtaking' (GB), 'no passing' (US)
(b) ban; **lever une ~** to lift a ban

■ **~ de séjour** prohibition on residence

interdire /ɛ̃tɛrdir/ [65] *vtr* to ban; **~ à qn de faire, ~ que qn fasse** to forbid sb to do

interdisciplinaire /ɛ̃tɛrdisiplinɛr/ *adj* (Sch) cross-curricular; (Univ) interdisciplinary

interdit, **~e** /ɛ̃tɛʀdi, it/ ⟦1⟧ *pp* ▶
INTERDIRE
⟦2⟧ *pp adj* prohibited, forbidden; **entrée ~e**
no entry *or* admittance; **film ~ aux moins de
13 ans** film unsuitable for children under 13
⟦3⟧ *adj* dumbfounded
⟦4⟧ *nm* proscription; taboo

intéressant, **~e** /ɛ̃teʀesɑ̃, ɑ̃t/ ⟦1⟧ *adj*
(a) interesting
(b) ⟨*prices, conditions*⟩ attractive; **il est plus
~ de payer au comptant qu'à crédit** it's
better to pay in cash rather than by credit
⟦2⟧ *nm,f* **faire l'~** *or* **son ~** to show off

intéressé, **~e** /ɛ̃teʀese/ ⟦1⟧ *pp* ▶
INTÉRESSER
⟦2⟧ *pp adj* **(a)** interested
(b) attentive
(c) **les parties ~es** those concerned; **les
personnes ~es aux bénéfices** people with a
share in the profits
(d) ⟨*person*⟩ self-interested; ⟨*action*⟩
motivated by self-interest; **ses conseils
étaient ~s** he/she had a selfish motive for
giving that advice
⟦3⟧ *nm,f* person concerned

intéressement /ɛ̃teʀesmɑ̃/ *nm* share in
the profits

intéresser /ɛ̃teʀese/ [1] ⟦1⟧ *vtr* **(a)** to
interest; **ça ne m'intéresse pas** I'm not
interested
(b) ⟨*problem, decision*⟩ to concern
(c) **~ les salariés aux bénéfices** to offer a
profit-sharing scheme to employees
⟦2⟧ **s'intéresser** *v refl* (+ *v être*) **s'~ à** (gen)
to be interested in; to take an interest in

intérêt /ɛ̃teʀɛ/ *nm* **(a)** interest; **recherche
digne d'~** worthwhile research; **l'~
supérieur de la nation** the higher good of the
country; **je ne vois pas l'~ de cette réforme**
I can't see the point of this reform; **par ~**
⟨*act*⟩ out of self-interest; ⟨*marry*⟩ for money
(b) (financial) interest

interférence /ɛ̃tɛʀfeʀɑ̃s/ *nf* interference

interférer /ɛ̃tɛʀfeʀe/ [14] *vi* to interfere

intérieur, **~e** /ɛ̃teʀjœʀ/ ⟦1⟧ *adj*
(a) internal, interior; ⟨*sea*⟩ inland; ⟨*pocket*⟩
inside; **le côté ~** the inside
(b) domestic; **sur le plan ~** on the domestic
front
(c) ⟨*regulations*⟩ internal
⟦2⟧ *nm* (of box, newspaper) inside; (of car, house)
interior; **à l'~** inside; indoors; **à l'~ des
terres** inland; **d'~** ⟨*game*⟩ indoor; **être fier de
son ~** to be proud of one's home

intérim /ɛ̃teʀim/ *nm* **(a)** interim (period);
président par ~ acting president; **assurer
l'~ de** to stand in for
(b) temporary work; **travailler en ~** to temp
(colloq)

intérimaire /ɛ̃teʀimɛʀ/ *adj* ⟨*committee*⟩
interim; ⟨*minister*⟩ acting; ⟨*job, staff*⟩
temporary

intérioriser /ɛ̃teʀjɔʀize/ [1] *vtr* to
internalize

interjection /ɛ̃tɛʀʒɛksjɔ̃/ *nf* interjection

interligne /ɛ̃tɛʀliɲ/ *nm* line space

interlocuteur, **-trice** /ɛ̃tɛʀlɔkytœʀ,
tʀis/ *nm,f* **(a)** **mon ~** the person I am/was
talking to
(b) (in negotiations) representative
(c) **Louis est notre seul ~** Louis is our only
contact

interloquer /ɛ̃tɛʀlɔke/ [1] *vtr* to take [sb]
aback

interlude /ɛ̃tɛʀlyd/ *nm* interlude

intermède /ɛ̃tɛʀmɛd/ *nm* interlude

intermédiaire /ɛ̃tɛʀmedjɛʀ/ ⟦1⟧ *adj* ⟨*rate,
stage*⟩ intermediate
⟦2⟧ *nmf* (in negotiations) go-between; (in industry)
middleman
⟦3⟧ *phr* **par l'~ de** through

interminable /ɛ̃tɛʀminabl/ *adj*
(a) interminable, never-ending
(b) endless

intermittence /ɛ̃tɛʀmitɑ̃s/ *nf* **par ~**
⟨*rain*⟩ on and off; ⟨*work*⟩ intermittently

intermittent, **~e** /ɛ̃tɛʀmitɑ̃, ɑ̃t/ *adj*
⟨*rain, fever*⟩ intermittent; ⟨*noise, efforts*⟩
sporadic

internat /ɛ̃tɛʀna/ *nm* boarding school

international, **~e**, *mpl* **-aux**
/ɛ̃tɛʀnasjɔnal, o/ *adj* international

interne /ɛ̃tɛʀn/ ⟦1⟧ *adj* (gen) internal;
⟨*training*⟩ in-house; ⟨*ear*⟩ inner
⟦2⟧ *nmf* **(a)** (Sch) boarder
(b) **~ (en médecine)** houseman (GB), intern
(US)

internement /ɛ̃tɛʀnəmɑ̃/ *nm* (Med)
committal (to a psychiatric institution)

interner /ɛ̃tɛʀne/ [1] *vtr* to commit ⟨*mental
patient*⟩

Internet /ɛ̃tɛʀnɛt/ *nm* Internet; **naviguer
sur (l')~** to surf the Internet

interpellation /ɛ̃tɛʀpelasjɔ̃/ *nf* **procéder
à des ~s** to take people in for questioning

interpeller /ɛ̃tɛʀpele/ [1] *vtr* **(a)** to call
out to; to shout at
(b) to question; (in police station) to take [sb]
in for questioning

interphone® /ɛ̃tɛʀfɔn/ *nm* **(a)** intercom
(b) entry phone

interposer: s'interposer /ɛ̃tɛʀpoze/ [1]
v refl (+ *v être*) to intervene; **par personne
interposée** through an intermediary

interprétariat /ɛ̃tɛʀpʀetaʀja/ *nm*
interpreting

interprétation /ɛ̃tɛʀpʀetasjɔ̃/ *nf* **(a)** (gen,
Mus) interpretation
(b) (profession) interpreting

interprète /ɛ̃tɛʀpʀɛt/ *nmf* **(a)** interpreter
(b) performer
(c) spokesperson

interpréter /ɛ̃tɛʀpʀete/ [14] *vtr* **(a)** to play
⟨*role, sonata*⟩; to sing ⟨*song*⟩
(b) to interpret

interpréteur /ɛ̃tɛʀpʀetœʀ/ *nm* (Comput)
interpreter

interrogateur, **-trice** /ɛ̃tɛʀɔgatœʀ,
tʀis/ *adj* enquiring; **d'un air ~** enquiringly

interrogatif, -ive /ɛ̃tɛʀɔgatif, iv/ *adj* interrogative

interrogation /ɛ̃tɛʀɔgasjɔ̃/ *nf* **(a)** (of witness) questioning
(b) (in grammar) question
(c) (Sch) test; ∼ **orale** oral test

interrogatoire /ɛ̃tɛʀɔgatwaʀ/ *nm* (gen) interrogation; (by police) questioning

interroger /ɛ̃tɛʀɔʒe/ [13] **1** *vtr* **(a)** (gen) to question; to ask; (figurative) to examine ‹conscience›; **être interrogé comme témoin** (Law) to be called as a witness
(b) ∼ **son répondeur** to check one's calls
(c) (Sch) to test
2 s'interroger *v refl* (+ *v être*) **s'**∼ **sur** to wonder about

interrompre /ɛ̃tɛʀɔ̃pʀ/ [53] **1** *vtr* **(a)** to interrupt; to break off ‹dialogue›; ‹person› to cease ‹activity›; ∼ **son repas pour faire** to stop eating to do
(b) to put an end to ‹holiday›; to stop ‹treatment›; to terminate ‹pregnancy›
2 s'interrompre *v refl* (+ *v être*)
(a) ‹person, conversation› to break off
(b) ‹rain› to stop

interrupteur /ɛ̃tɛʀyptœʀ/ *nm* switch

interruption /ɛ̃tɛʀypsjɔ̃/ *nf* **(a)** break; **sans** ∼ continuously
(b) ending; **l'**∼ **du dialogue entre** the breaking off of the dialogue (GB) between

intersection /ɛ̃tɛʀsɛksjɔ̃/ *nf* intersection

interstice /ɛ̃tɛʀstis/ *nm* (in floor) crack; (in shutters, blinds) chink

intervalle /ɛ̃tɛʀval/ *nm* **(a)** space; **à** ∼**s réguliers** at regular intervals
(b) interval; **dans l'**∼ meanwhile, in the meantime

intervenir /ɛ̃tɛʀvəniʀ/ [36] *vi* **(a)** ‹changes› to take place; ‹agreement› to be reached
(b) ‹speaker› to speak
(c) (in emergency) ‹police› to intervene
(d) ∼ **auprès de qn pour qn** to intercede with sb on sb's behalf

intervention /ɛ̃tɛʀvɑ̃sjɔ̃/ *nf*
(a) intervention
(b) speech; lecture
(c) (Med) ∼ **(chirurgicale)** operation

intervertir /ɛ̃tɛʀvɛʀtiʀ/ [3] *vtr* to invert

interviewer /ɛ̃tɛʀvjuve/ [1] *vtr* to interview

intestin /ɛ̃tɛstɛ̃/ *nm* bowel, intestine

intestinal, ∼e, *mpl* **-aux** /ɛ̃tɛstinal, o/ *adj* intestinal

intime /ɛ̃tim/ **1** *adj* **(a)** ‹life, diary› private; ‹friend, relationship› intimate; ‹hygiene› personal
(b) ‹gathering› intimate; ‹conversation› private; ‹dinner› quiet
(c) ‹room› cosy (GB), cozy (US)
(d) ‹knowledge› intimate
2 *nmf* close friend

intimement /ɛ̃timmɑ̃/ *adv* intimately; **je suis** ∼ **convaincu que...** I'm absolutely convinced that...

intimidation /ɛ̃timidasjɔ̃/ *nf* intimidation; **d'**∼ ‹measures, remarks› intimidatory

intimider /ɛ̃timide/ [1] *vtr* to intimidate

intimité /ɛ̃timite/ *nf* **(a)** intimacy
(b) privacy; **dans la plus stricte** ∼ in the strictest privacy
(c) private life
(d) (of house, setting) cosiness

intitulé /ɛ̃tityle/ *nm* title, heading

intituler /ɛ̃tityle/ [1] **1** *vtr* to call
2 s'intituler *v refl* (+ *v être*) to be called, to be entitled

intolérable /ɛ̃tɔleʀabl/ *adj* intolerable; deeply shocking

intolérance /ɛ̃tɔleʀɑ̃s/ *nf* intolerance

intolérant, ∼e /ɛ̃tɔleʀɑ̃, ɑ̃t/ *adj* intolerant

intonation /ɛ̃tɔnasjɔ̃/ *nf* intonation

intoxication /ɛ̃tɔksikasjɔ̃/ *nf* **(a)** (Med) poisoning
(b) (figurative) disinformation

intoxiquer /ɛ̃tɔksike/ [1] **1** *vtr* to poison
2 s'intoxiquer *v refl* (+ *v être*) to poison oneself

intraitable /ɛ̃tʀɛtabl/ *adj* inflexible

intra-muros /ɛ̃tʀamyʀos/ *adj inv* **Paris** ∼ Paris itself

intransigeance /ɛ̃tʀɑ̃ziʒɑ̃s/ *nf* intransigence

intransigeant, ∼e /ɛ̃tʀɑ̃ziʒɑ̃, ɑ̃t/ *adj* ‹attitude› uncompromising; ‹person› intransigent

intraveineuse /ɛ̃tʀavɛnøz/ *nf* intravenous injection

intrépide /ɛ̃tʀepid/ *adj* intrepid, bold

intrépidité /ɛ̃tʀepidite/ *nf* boldness

intrigant, ∼e /ɛ̃tʀigɑ̃, ɑ̃t/ *nm,f* schemer

intrigue /ɛ̃tʀig/ *nf* **(a)** intrigue
(b) plot; **une** ∼ **policière** a detective story

intriguer /ɛ̃tʀige/ [1] *vtr* to intrigue

intrinsèque /ɛ̃tʀɛ̃sɛk/ *adj* intrinsic

introduction /ɛ̃tʀɔdyksjɔ̃/ *nf* **(a)** (gen) introduction
(b) (of key, probe) insertion

introduire /ɛ̃tʀɔdɥiʀ/ [69] **1** *vtr* **(a)** to insert ‹object›
(b) to usher [sb] in ‹visitor›; (surreptitiously) to smuggle [sb] in
(c) to introduce ‹person›
(d) to introduce ‹product, idea›
2 s'introduire *v refl* (+ *v être*) **s'**∼ **dans** to get into

introduit, ∼e /ɛ̃tʀɔdɥi, it/ ▶ INTRODUIRE

introspection /ɛ̃tʀɔspɛksjɔ̃/ *nf* introspection

introverti, ∼e /ɛ̃tʀɔvɛʀti/ *nm,f* introvert

intrus, ∼e /ɛ̃tʀy, yz/ *nm,f* intruder

intrusion /ɛ̃tʀyzjɔ̃/ *nf* **(a)** (gen) intrusion
(b) interference

intuitif, ∼ive /ɛ̃tɥitif, iv/ *adj* intuitive

intuition /ɛ̃tɥisjɔ̃/ *nf* intuition

inusable /inyzabl/ *adj* hardwearing

inusité, ∼e /inyzite/ *adj* uncommon

inutile /inytil/ *adj* useless; pointless; needless; **(il est) ~ de faire** there's no point in doing; **~ de dire que** needless to say; **sans risques ~s** without unnecessary risks

inutilement /inytilmɑ̃/ *adv* unnecessarily; needlessly; in vain

inutilisable /inytilizabl/ *adj* unusable

inutilité /inytilite/ *nf* (of expense, action) pointlessness

invalide /ɛ̃valid/ [1] *adj* disabled
[2] *nmf* disabled person

invalidité /ɛ̃validite/ *nf* (Med) disability

invariable /ɛ̃vaʀjabl/ *adj* invariable

invasion /ɛ̃vazjɔ̃/ *nf* invasion

invendable /ɛ̃vɑ̃dabl/ *adj* unsaleable

invendu, **~e** /ɛ̃vɑ̃dy/ *adj* unsold

inventaire /ɛ̃vɑ̃tɛʀ/ *nm* **(a)** stocktaking (GB), inventory (US)
(b) stocklist (GB), inventory (US)
(c) (of wardrobe, suitcase) list of contents

inventer /ɛ̃vɑ̃te/ [1] [1] *vtr* to invent; to devise; **je n'invente rien** I'm not making it up
[2] **s'inventer** *v refl* (+ *v être*) **ça ne s'invente pas** that has to be true
IDIOMS **il n'a pas inventé la poudre** (colloq) he is not very bright

inventeur, **-trice** /ɛ̃vɑ̃tœʀ, tʀis/ *nm,f* inventor

inventif, **-ive** /ɛ̃vɑ̃tif, iv/ *adj* **(a)** inventive
(b) resourceful

invention /ɛ̃vɑ̃sjɔ̃/ *nf* **(a)** invention
(b) fabrication; **c'est de l'~ pure** it's a complete fabrication

inventorier /ɛ̃vɑ̃tɔʀje/ [2] *vtr* to make out an inventory of

inverse /ɛ̃vɛʀs/ [1] *adj* (gen) opposite; **dans l'ordre ~** (referring to list) in reverse order
[2] *nm* (gen) **l'~** the opposite; **à l'~** conversely; **à l'~ de ce qu'il croyait** contrary to what he thought

inversement /ɛ̃vɛʀsəmɑ̃/ *adv* (gen) conversely

inverser /ɛ̃vɛʀse/ [1] *vtr* **(a)** to invert ⟨*position*⟩; to reverse ⟨*roles*⟩; **image inversée** mirror image
(b) to reverse ⟨*electric current*⟩

inversion /ɛ̃vɛʀsjɔ̃/ *nf* inversion; reversal

invertébré, **~e** /ɛ̃vɛʀtebʀe/ *adj* invertebrate

invertir /ɛ̃vɛʀtiʀ/ [3] *vtr* to reverse; to switch [sth] round ⟨*words*⟩

investigation /ɛ̃vɛstigasjɔ̃/ *nf* investigation; **d'~** investigative

investir /ɛ̃vɛstiʀ/ [3] [1] *vtr* **(a)** to invest ⟨*capital*⟩
(b) to invest ⟨*person, ambassador*⟩
(c) ⟨*police*⟩ to go into; ⟨*tourists, demonstrators*⟩ to take over
(d) ⟨*army*⟩ to besiege
[2] **s'investir** *v refl* (+ *v être*) **s'~ dans** to put a lot of oneself into; to invest emotionally in

investissement /ɛ̃vɛstismɑ̃/ *nm* (gen) investment; (Mil) investing

investisseur /ɛ̃vɛstisœʀ/ *nm* investor

investiture /ɛ̃vɛstityʀ/ *nf* investiture

invétéré, **~e** /ɛ̃veteʀe/ *adj* ⟨*drinker, thief*⟩ inveterate; ⟨*liar*⟩ compulsive

invincible /ɛ̃vɛ̃sibl/ *adj* ⟨*people*⟩ invincible

inviolable /ɛ̃vjɔlabl/ *adj* (gen) inviolable; ⟨*door, safe*⟩ impregnable

invisible /ɛ̃vizibl/ *adj* **(a)** invisible; **la route était ~ depuis la maison** the road could not be seen from the house
(b) ⟨*danger*⟩ unseen

invitation /ɛ̃vitasjɔ̃/ *nf* invitation

invité, **~e** /ɛ̃vite/ *nm,f* guest

inviter /ɛ̃vite/ [1] *vtr* to invite; **ceci invite à penser que...** this suggests that...

invivable /ɛ̃vivabl/ *adj* unbearable

invocation /ɛ̃vɔkasjɔ̃/ *nf* invocation

involontaire /ɛ̃vɔlɔ̃tɛʀ/ *adj* ⟨*reaction*⟩ involuntary; ⟨*mistake*⟩ unintentional

invoquer /ɛ̃vɔke/ [1] *vtr* to invoke

invraisemblable /ɛ̃vʀɛsɑ̃blabl/ *adj*
(a) ⟨*story*⟩ unlikely; ⟨*explanation*⟩ implausible
(b) (colloq) fantastic, incredible

invraisemblance /ɛ̃vʀɛsɑ̃blɑ̃s/ *nf*
(a) unlikelihood
(b) improbability

invulnérable /ɛ̃vylneʀabl/ *adj* invulnerable

iode /jɔd/ *nm* iodine

iota /jɔta/ *nm inv* iota
IDIOMS **ne pas changer d'un ~** not to change one iota; **ne pas bouger d'un ~** not to move an inch

ira /iʀa/ ▶ ALLER[1]

irai /iʀe/ ▶ ALLER[1]

iraient /iʀe/ ▶ ALLER[1]

irais /iʀe/ ▶ ALLER[1]

irait /iʀe/ ▶ ALLER[1]

iras /iʀa/ ▶ ALLER[1]

irascible /iʀasibl/ *adj* ⟨*person*⟩ quick-tempered

irez /iʀe/ ▶ ALLER[1]

iriez /iʀje/ ▶ ALLER[1]

irions /iʀjɔ̃/ ▶ ALLER[1]

iris /iʀis/ *nm inv* **(a)** (flower) iris
(b) (of eye) iris

irisé, **~e** /iʀize/ *adj* iridescent

irlandais, **~e** /iʀlɑ̃dɛ, ɛz/ [1] *adj* Irish
[2] *nm* (language) Irish

Irlandais, **~e** /iʀlɑ̃dɛ, ɛz/ *nm,f* Irishman/Irishwoman

Irlande /iʀlɑ̃d/ *pr nf* Ireland; **la République d'~** the Republic of Ireland; **l'~ du Nord** Northern Ireland

ironie /iʀɔni/ *nf* irony; **faire de l'~** to be ironic

ironique /iʀɔnik/ *adj* ironic

ironiser /iʀɔnize/ [1] *vi* to be ironic (**sur** about)

irons /iʀɔ̃/ ▶ ALLER¹

iront /iʀɔ̃/ ▶ ALLER¹

irradier /iʀadje/ [2] **1** vtr to irradiate
2 vi to radiate

irrattrapable /iʀatʀapabl/ adj
irretrievable

irréalisable /iʀealizabl/ adj ⟨dream⟩
impossible; ⟨plan⟩ unworkable

irrécupérable /iʀekypeʀabl/ adj
(a) irrecoverable
(b) damaged beyond repair
(c) ⟨delinquent⟩ beyond help

irréductible /iʀedyktibl/ nmf diehard

irréel, -elle /iʀeɛl/ adj unreal

irréfléchi, ~e /iʀefleʃi/ adj ill-considered

irréfutable /iʀefytabl/ adj irrefutable

irrégularité /iʀegylaʀite/ nf irregularity

irrégulier, -ière /iʀegylje, ɛʀ/ adj
(a) irregular; uneven
(b) ⟨procedure⟩ irregular; **immigré en
situation irrégulière** illegal immigrant
(c) ⟨athlete⟩ whose performance is uneven

irrégulièrement /iʀegyljɛʀmɑ̃/ adv
(a) illegally
(b) irregularly; unevenly; erratically

irrémédiable /iʀ(ʀ)emedjabl/ adj
irreparable

irremplaçable /iʀɑ̃plasabl/ adj
irreplaceable

irréparable /iʀepaʀabl/ **1** adj ⟨car⟩
beyond repair; ⟨damage, crime⟩ irreparable
2 nm **commettre l'~** to go beyond the point
of no return

irrépressible /iʀepʀesibl/ adj ⟨gen⟩
irrepressible; ⟨tears⟩ uncontrollable

irréprochable /iʀepʀɔʃabl/ adj ⟨life,
employee⟩ beyond reproach; ⟨work⟩ perfect

irrésistible /iʀezistibl/ adj irresistible;
⟨person, joke⟩ hilarious

irrésolu, ~e /iʀezɔly/ adj ⟨person⟩
indecisive; ⟨problem, mystery⟩ unsolved

irrespirable /iʀespiʀabl/ adj ⟨air⟩
unbreathable; ⟨atmosphere⟩ stifling

irresponsable /iʀespɔ̃sabl/ adj
irresponsible

irrévérencieux, -ieuse /iʀeveʀɑ̃sjø,
øz/ adj irreverent

irréversible /iʀevɛʀsibl/ adj irreversible

irrévocable /iʀevɔkabl/ adj irrevocable

irrigation /iʀigasjɔ̃/ nf **(a)** (of land)
irrigation
(b) (Med) supply of blood

irriguer /iʀige/ [1] vtr to irrigate

irritation /iʀitasjɔ̃/ nf ⟨gen, Med⟩ irritation

irriter /iʀite/ [1] **1** vtr **(a)** to irritate, to
annoy
(b) (Med) to irritate

2 s'irriter v refl (+ v être) **(a)** to get angry
(b) (Med) to become irritated

irruption /iʀypsjɔ̃/ nf **faire ~ dans** to burst
into ⟨room⟩

islam /islam/ nm **l'~** Islam

islamique /islamik/ adj Islamic

islamisme /islamism/ nm Islam

Islande /islɑ̃d/ pr nf Iceland

isolant, ~e /izɔlɑ̃, ɑ̃t/ adj insulating

isolation /izɔlasjɔ̃/ nf insulation

isolement /izɔlmɑ̃/ nm **(a)** (of village)
remoteness; (of house) isolated location
(b) (of patient, politician) isolation; (of prisoner)
solitary confinement

isoler /izɔle/ [1] **1** vtr **(a)** to isolate ⟨sick
person, dissident⟩; to put [sb] in solitary
confinement ⟨prisoner⟩
(b) to isolate ⟨gene, substance⟩
(c) to soundproof; to insulate
(d) to insulate ⟨wire⟩
2 s'isoler v refl (+ v être) to isolate oneself

isoloir /izɔlwaʀ/ nm voting or polling (GB)
booth

isotherme /izotɛʀm/ adj refrigerated;
boîte ~ ice box; **sac ~** cool bag

issu, ~e¹ /isy/ adj **être ~ de** to come
from; to result from

issue² /isy/ nf **(a)** exit; **'sans ~'** 'no exit'
(b) solution; **situation sans ~** situation with
no solution
(c) outcome; **à l'~ de** at the end of; **à l'~ de
trois jours de pourparlers** at the close of
three days of talks
■ **~ de secours** emergency exit

Italie /itali/ pr nf Italy

italien, -ienne /italjɛ̃, ɛn/ **1** adj Italian
2 nm (language) Italian

italique /italik/ nm italics

itinéraire /itineʀeʀ/ nm **(a)** ⟨gen⟩ route;
(detailed) itinerary
(b) (figurative) career
■ **~ bis** alternative route; **~ de délestage**
relief route

itinérant, ~e /itineʀɑ̃, ɑ̃t/ adj
⟨exhibition⟩ touring; ⟨life⟩ peripatetic;
⟨circus⟩ travelling

IUFM /iyefɛm/ nm: abbr ▶ INSTITUT

IUT /iyte/ nm: abbr ▶ INSTITUT

ivoire /ivwaʀ/ adj inv, nm ivory

ivoirien, -ienne /ivwaʀjɛ̃, ɛn/ adj of the
Ivory Coast

ivre /ivʀ/ adj **(a)** drunk, intoxicated
(b) **~ de rage** wild with rage

ivresse /ivʀes/ nf **(a)** intoxication
(b) exhilaration

ivrogne /ivʀɔɲ/ nmf drunkard

Jj

j, **J** /ʒi/ *nm inv* j, J; **le jour J** D-day

j' ▸ JE

jabot /ʒabo/ *nm* **(a)** (of bird) crop
(b) (of shirt) jabot

jacasser /ʒakase/ [1] *vi* to chatter

jachère /ʒaʃɛʀ/ *nf* **(terre en)** ∼ fallow land

jacinthe /ʒasɛ̃t/ *nf* hyacinth

jackpot /(d)ʒakpɔt/ *nm* **(a)** jackpot
(b) slot machine

jacquet /ʒakɛ/ *nm* backgammon

jacter /ʒakte/ [1] *vi* (slang) to jaw (colloq), to talk

jade /ʒad/ *nm* jade

jadis /ʒadis/ *adv* formerly, in the past

jaguar /ʒagwaʀ/ *nm* jaguar

jaillir /ʒajiʀ/ [3] *vi* ‹liquid› to gush out; ‹tears› to flow; ‹flame› to shoot up; ‹truth› to emerge

jais /ʒɛ/ *nm inv* **(a)** jet
(b) **(noir) de** ∼ jet-black

jalon /ʒalɔ̃/ *nm* **(a)** marker
(b) (figurative) **poser les** ∼**s de** to prepare the ground for

jalonner /ʒalɔne/ [1] *vtr* **(a)** ‹trees› to line ‹road›; ‹incidents› to punctuate ‹career›
(b) to mark out ‹road›

jalousement /ʒaluzmɑ̃/ *adv* jealously; enviously

jalouser /ʒaluze/ [1] *vtr* to be jealous of

jalousie /ʒaluzi/ *nf* **(a)** jealousy
(b) slatted blind

jaloux, -ouse /ʒalu, uz/ **1** *adj* jealous
2 *nm,f* jealous man/woman

jamais /ʒamɛ/ *adv* **(a)** never; **rien n'est** ∼ **certain** nothing is ever certain; **sait-on** ∼? you never know; ∼ **de la vie!** never!
(b) ever; **plus belle que** ∼ prettier than ever; **si** ∼ if
(c) **à tout** ∼ forever
(d) **ne...** ∼ **que** only; **il ne fait** ∼ **que son devoir** he is only doing his duty

jambe /ʒɑ̃b/ *nf* leg; **avoir de bonnes** ∼**s** to have strong legs; **courir à toutes** ∼**s** to run as fast as one's legs can carry one; **j'ai les** ∼**s comme du coton** (colloq) I feel weak at the knees; **traîner la** ∼ (colloq) to trudge along
IDIOMS cela me fait une belle ∼ (colloq) a fat lot of good that does me (colloq); **il ne tient plus sur ses** ∼**s** he can hardly stand up; **prendre ses** ∼**s à son cou** to take to one's heels; **tenir la** ∼ **à qn** to keep talking to sb; **par-dessus** *or* **par-dessous la** ∼ in a slipshod manner

jambon /ʒɑ̃bɔ̃/ *nm* ham

■ ∼ **blanc** *or* **de Paris** cooked ham; ∼ **de pays** cured ham

jambonneau, *pl* ∼**x** /ʒɑ̃bɔno/ *nm* knuckle of ham

jante /ʒɑ̃t/ *nf* **(a)** rim
(b) wheel

janvier /ʒɑ̃vje/ *nm* January

Japon /ʒapɔ̃/ *pr nm* Japan

japonais, ∼e /ʒapɔnɛ, ɛz/ **1** *adj* Japanese
2 *nm* (language) Japanese

jappement /ʒapmɑ̃/ *nm* yapping

japper /ʒape/ [1] *vi* to yap

jaquette /ʒakɛt/ *nf* **(a)** morning coat
(b) dust jacket
(c) (on tooth) crown

jardin /ʒaʀdɛ̃/ *nm* garden (GB), yard (US); **chaise de** ∼ garden chair (GB), patio chair (US)

■ ∼ **d'acclimatation** = ∼ ZOOLOGIQUE; ∼ **d'agrément** ornamental garden; ∼ **d'enfants** kindergarten; ∼ **potager** vegetable garden; ∼ **public** park; ∼ **zoologique** zoo

jardinage /ʒaʀdinaʒ/ *nm* gardening

jardiner /ʒaʀdine/ [1] *vi* to do some gardening

jardinier, -ière¹ /ʒaʀdinje, ɛʀ/ **1** *adj* garden
2 *nm,f* gardener

jardinière² /ʒaʀdinjɛʀ/ *nf* jardinière

jargon /ʒaʀgɔ̃/ *nm* **(a)** jargon; ∼ **administratif** officialese
(b) gibberish

jarre /ʒaʀ/ *nf* (earthenware) jar

jarret /ʒaʀɛ/ *nm* **(a)** (of human) ham, hollow of the knee
(b) (of animal) hock
(c) (Culin) ∼ **de veau** knuckle of veal

jarretelle /ʒaʀtɛl/ *nf* suspender (GB), garter (US)

jars /ʒaʀ/ *nm inv* gander

jaser /ʒaze/ [1] *vi* to gossip

jasmin /ʒasmɛ̃/ *nm* jasmine

jatte /ʒat/ *nf* bowl, basin

jauge /ʒoʒ/ *nf* gauge; ∼ **d'huile** dipstick

jaunâtre /ʒonɑtʀ/ *adj* yellowish

jaune /ʒon/ **1** *adj* yellow; ∼ **d'or** golden yellow; ∼ **paille** straw-coloured (GB); ∼ **poussin** bright yellow; **teint** ∼ sallow complexion
2 *nm* **(a)** yellow
(b) ∼ **(d'œuf)** (egg) yolk
(c) blackleg (GB), scab
IDIOMS rire ∼ (colloq) to give a forced laugh

jaunir /ʒoniʀ/ [3] **1** *vtr* to turn [sth] yellow, to make [sth] go yellow **2** *vi* to go yellow

jaunisse /ʒonis/ *nf* jaundice; **il va en faire une ∼!** (colloq) that'll put his nose out of joint!

java /ʒava/ *nf* (a) popular dance (b) (colloq) rave-up (colloq)

Javel /ʒavɛl/ *nf* (**eau de**) ∼ ≈ bleach

javelliser /ʒavelize/[1] *vtr* to chlorinate

javelot /ʒavlo/ *nm* javelin

J.-C. (*written abbr* = **Jésus-Christ**) **avant ∼** BC; **après ∼** AD

je (**j'** *before vowel or mute h*) /ʒ(ə)/ *pron* I

jean /dʒin/ *nm* (a) (pair of) jeans (b) denim

jeannette /ʒanɛt/ *nf* ≈ Brownie

je-ne-sais-quoi /ʒənsɛkwa/ *nm inv* **avoir un ∼** to have a certain something

jérémiades /ʒeʀemjad/ *nf pl* moaning

jerrican /ʒeʀikan/ *nm* jerrycan

jersey /ʒɛʀzɛ/ *nm* (a) jersey (b) stocking stitch

jésuite /ʒezɥit/ *adj, nm* Jesuit

Jésus /ʒezy/ *pr n* Jesus

jet¹ /ʒɛ/ *nm* (a) throwing; throw (b) jet; spurt; burst; **passer au ∼** to hose down; **premier ∼** (figurative) first sketch; **d'un seul ∼** (write) in one go ∎ **∼ d'eau** fountain; hosepipe

jet² /dʒɛt/ *nm* jet (plane)

jetable /ʒətabl/ *adj* disposable

jetée /ʒəte/ *nf* pier; jetty

jeter /ʒəte/ [20] **1** *vtr* (a) to throw; to hurl; to throw away *or* out; **∼ qch à qn** to throw sth to sb ⟨*ball*⟩; to throw sth at sb ⟨*stone*⟩; **∼ qn dehors** to throw sb out; **∼ quelques idées sur le papier** (figurative) to jot down a few ideas; **bon à ∼** fit for the bin (GB) *or* the garbage (US) (b) to give ⟨*cry, light*⟩; to cast ⟨*glance, shadow*⟩ (c) to create ⟨*confusion, terror*⟩; **∼ l'émoi dans la ville** to throw the town into turmoil **2** **se jeter** *v refl* (+ *v être*) (a) **se ∼ du haut d'un pont** to throw oneself off a bridge; **se ∼ sur** ⟨*opponent*⟩ to pounce on ⟨*prey, newspaper*⟩; **se ∼ au cou de qn** to fling oneself around sb's neck; **se ∼ à l'eau** to jump into the water; (figurative) to take the plunge; (aller) **se ∼ contre un arbre** to crash into a tree (b) ⟨*river*⟩ to flow

jeton /ʒ(ə)tɔ̃/ *nm* (for machine) token; (in board games) counter; (at casino) chip

jeu, *pl* **∼x** /ʒø/ *nm* (a) **le ∼** play; **un ∼** a game; **faire un ∼** to play a game; **par ∼** for fun; **entrer en ∼** to come into the picture; **se prendre** *or* **se piquer au ∼** to get hooked; **mettre en ∼** to bring [sth] into play; to stake; **hors ∼** offside; **ils ont beau ∼ de me critiquer** it's easy for them to criticize me (b) **le ∼** gambling; **ton avenir est en ∼** your future is at stake

(c) (in cards) hand; **cacher bien son ∼** (figurative) to keep it quiet (d) (of cards) deck; **∼ d'échecs** chess set (e) (of actor) acting; (of musician) playing; (of sportsman) game (f) (of keys, spanners) set ∎ **∼ d'argent** game played for money; **∼ de construction** construction set; **∼ électronique** computer game; **le ∼ de massacre** ≈ coconut shy (GB); **∼ de mots** pun; **∼ de l'oie** ≈ snakes and ladders (GB); **∼ de société** board game; party game; **∼ télévisé** (TV) game show; **∼x Olympiques, JO** Olympic Games IDIOM'S **jouer le ∼** to play the game; **c'est pas de** *or* **du ∼!** (colloq) that's not fair!; **faire le ∼ de qn** to play into sb's hands

jeu-concours, *pl* **jeux-concours** /ʒøkɔ̃kuʀ/ *nm* competition

jeudi /ʒødi/ *nm* Thursday IDIOMS **ça aura lieu la semaine des quatre ∼s!** (colloq) it won't happen, not in a month of Sundays!

jeun: à jeun /aʒœ̃/ *phr* (a) on an empty stomach (b) (colloq) sober

jeune /ʒœn/ **1** *adj* (a) (gen) young; ⟨*industry*⟩ new; ⟨*face, hairstyle*⟩ youthful; **nos ∼s années** our youth; **de massacre** ≈ coconut **∼ âge** youth; **le ∼ marié** the groom; **la ∼ mariée** the bride (b) younger; **mon ∼ frère** my younger brother **2** *nmf* young person; **les ∼s** young people **3** *adv* **s'habiller ∼** to wear young styles; **faire ∼** to look young ∎ **∼ femme** young woman; **∼ fille** girl; **∼ homme** young man; **∼ loup** up-and-coming executive; **∼ premier** romantic lead

jeûne /ʒøn/ *nm* (a) fasting; fast (b) period of fasting

jeûner /ʒøne/ [1] *vi* to fast

jeunesse /ʒœnɛs/ *nf* (a) youth; **une seconde ∼** a new lease of life; **une erreur de ∼** a youthful indiscretion (b) young people IDIOMS **il faut que ∼ se passe** youth will have its fling; **les voyages forment la ∼** travel broadens the mind

jf *written abbr* = **JEUNE FEMME** *or* **FILLE**; ▶ **JEUNE**

jh *written abbr* = **JEUNE HOMME**; ▶ **JEUNE**

JO /ʒio/ *nm pl: abbr* ▶ **JEU**

joaillerie /ʒɔajʀi/ *nf* (a) jeweller's shop (GB), jewelry store (US) (b) jewellery (GB), jewelry (US)

joaillier, -ière /ʒɔalje, ɛʀ/ *nm,f* jeweller (GB), jeweler (US)

Joconde /ʒɔkɔ̃d/ *n pr* **la ∼** the Mona Lisa

joggeur, -euse /dʒɔgœʀ, øz/ *nm,f* jogger

joie /ʒwa/ *nf* joy; **au comble de la ∼** overjoyed; **se faire une ∼ de faire** to look forward to doing; to be delighted to do IDIOMS **s'en donner à cœur ∼** to enjoy oneself to the full; (figurative) to have a field day

joignable /ʒwaɲabl/ *adj* il n'est pas ~ en ce moment he's not available at the moment

joindre /ʒwɛ̃dʀ/ [56] **1** *vtr* (a) to get hold of ⟨person⟩
(b) to enclose ⟨cheque⟩; to attach ⟨card⟩
(c) to link ⟨points⟩; to put [sth] together ⟨planks, feet⟩; ~ l'intelligence à la simplicité to be intelligent without being pretentious
2 se joindre *v refl* (+ *v être*) (a) se ~ à to join ⟨person, group⟩; to join in ⟨conversation⟩
(b) ⟨lips⟩ to meet; ⟨hands⟩ to join
IDIOMS ~ les deux bouts (colloq) to make ends meet

joint¹, ~e /ʒwɛ̃, ɛ̃t/ ▶ JOINDRE

joint² /ʒwɛ̃/ *nm* (in wood) joint; (on pipes) seal

jointure /ʒwɛ̃tyʀ/ *nf* joint

jojo (colloq) /ʒoʒo/ **1** *adj inv* il n'est pas ~ ton chapeau your hat isn't very nice; ce n'est pas ~ ce qu'ils lui ont fait what they did to him/her wasn't very nice
2 *nm* un affreux ~ a horrible brat (colloq); a weirdo (colloq)

joli, ~e /ʒɔli/ **1** *adj* (gen) nice; ⟨face⟩ pretty; ⟨sum⟩ tidy; faire ~ to look nice
2 *nm* c'est du ~! (ironic) very nice!
■ ~ cœur smooth talker; faire le ~ cœur to play Romeo
IDIOMS être ~ à croquer *or* comme un cœur to be as pretty as a picture

joliment /ʒɔlimɑ̃/ *adv* (a) prettily, nicely
(b) (colloq) ⟨happy, well⟩ really; ⟨handle⟩ nicely

jonc /ʒɔ̃/ *nm* rush

joncher /ʒɔ̃ʃe/ [1] *vtr* ⟨papers, leaves⟩ to be strewn over ⟨ground⟩

jonction /ʒɔ̃ksjɔ̃/ *nf* (a) junction
(b) link-up

jongler /ʒɔ̃gle/ [1] *vi* to juggle

jonque /ʒɔ̃k/ *nf* junk

jonquille /ʒɔ̃kij/ *nf* daffodil

jouable /ʒwabl/ *adj* (a) feasible; le pari est ~ the gamble might pay off
(b) ⟨piece of music⟩ playable; une pièce qui n'est pas ~ a play that's impossible to stage

joue /ʒu/ *nf* (a) cheek
(b) (Mil) en ~! aim!; mettre qn en ~ to take aim at sb

jouer /ʒwe/ [1] **1** *vtr* (a) ⟨children, musician⟩ to play
(b) to back ⟨horse⟩; to stake ⟨money⟩; to risk ⟨reputation, life⟩; c'est joué d'avance it's a foregone conclusion; tout n'est pas encore joué the game isn't over yet; ~ le tout pour le tout to go for broke (colloq)
(c) qu'est-ce qu'on joue au théâtre/cinéma? what's on at the theatre/cinema?
(d) ~ les imbéciles to play dumb
2 jouer à *v+prep* to play ⟨tennis, game⟩; to play with ⟨doll⟩; ~ à qui perd gagne to play 'loser takes all'; ~ à la marchande to play shops
3 jouer de *v+prep* (a) ~ de to play ⟨instrument⟩
(b) ~ de to use ⟨influence⟩

4 *vi* (a) to play; arrête de ~ avec ta bague! stop fiddling with your ring!; à toi de ~! your turn!; (figurative) the ball's in your court!; bien joué! well played!; (figurative) well done!
(b) to gamble; ~ avec to gamble with ⟨life, health⟩; ~ aux courses to bet on the horses; ~ sur to bank on ⟨credulity⟩
(c) to act; il joue bien he's a good actor
(d) ⟨argument, clause⟩ to apply; ⟨age⟩ to matter; faire ~ ses relations to make use of one's connections
5 se jouer *v refl* (+ *v être*) (a) ⟨future, peace⟩ to be at stake; ⟨drama⟩ to be played out
(b) se ~ de to make light work of ⟨obstacle⟩

jouet /ʒwɛ/ *nm* (a) toy
(b) plaything

joueur, -euse /ʒwœʀ, øz/ **1** *adj*
(a) playful
(b) être ~/joueuse to be a gambling man/woman
2 *nm,f* (a) player; être beau/mauvais ~ to be a good/bad loser
(b) gambler

joufflu, ~e /ʒufly/ *adj* ⟨person⟩ chubby-cheeked; ⟨face⟩ chubby

joug /ʒu/ *nm* yoke

jouir /ʒwiʀ/ [3] *v+prep* ~ de to enjoy; to enjoy the use of ⟨property⟩; ⟨place⟩ to have ⟨view, climate⟩

jouissance /ʒwisɑ̃s/ *nf* (a) (Law) use
(b) pleasure

joujou, *pl* ~x /ʒuʒu/ *nm* (baby talk) toy

jour /ʒuʀ/ *nm* (a) day; quel ~ sommes-nous? what day is it today?; un ~ ou l'autre some day; ~ pour ~ to the day; à ce ~ to date; à ~ up to date; mettre à ~ to bring up to date ⟨work⟩; to revise ⟨edition⟩; mise à ~ updating; de nos ~s nowadays; d'un ~ à l'autre ⟨expected⟩ any day now; ⟨change⟩ from one day to the next; du ~ au lendemain overnight; d'un ~ ⟨fashion⟩ passing; ⟨queen⟩ for a day; vivre au ~ le ~ to live one day at a time; le ~ se lève it's getting light; au lever du ~ at daybreak; le petit ~ the early morning; de ~ ⟨work⟩ days; ⟨travel⟩ in the daytime
(b) daylight; light; en plein ~ in broad daylight; se faire ~ ⟨truth⟩ to come to light; éclairer qch d'un ~ nouveau to shed new light on sth; je t'ai vu sous ton vrai ~ I saw you in your true colours (GB)
(c) (figurative) donner le ~ à qn to bring sb into the world; voir le ~ ⟨person⟩ to come into the world; ⟨work of art⟩ to see the light of day; mes ~s sont comptés my days are numbered; des ~s difficiles hard times; les beaux ~s reviennent spring will soon be here
(d) (in wall) gap; ~s openwork ⟨embroidery⟩
■ ~ de l'An New Year's Day; ~ férié bank holiday (GB), legal holiday (US); ~ de fermeture closing day; ~ ouvrable working day

journal, *pl* -aux /ʒuʀnal, o/ *nm*
(a) newspaper
(b) magazine
(c) news (bulletin)

·····➤

(d) journal

■ ~ **de bord** logbook; ~ **intime** diary; **Journal officiel** *government publication listing new acts, laws etc*

journalier, -ière /ʒuʀnalje, ɛʀ/ *adj* daily

journalisme /ʒuʀnalism/ *nm* journalism

journaliste /ʒuʀnalist/ *nmf* journalist

journalistique /ʒuʀnalistik/ *adj* journalistic

journée /ʒuʀne/ *nf* day; ~ **de repos** day off; **dans la** ~ during the day; **la** ~ **d'hier/de mardi** yesterday/Tuesday; **faire des** ~**s de huit heures** to work an eight-hour day

joute /ʒut/ *nf* **(a)** (figurative) jousting, battle; ~ **oratoire** *or* **verbale** sparring match
(b) joust

jouvence /ʒuvɑ̃s/ *nf* **fontaine de** ~ Fountain of Youth

jouxter /ʒukste/ [1] *vtr* to adjoin

jovial, ~e, *mpl* ~**s** *or* **-iaux** /ʒɔvjal, o/ *adj* jovial

jovialité /ʒɔvjalite/ *nf* joviality

joyau, *pl* ~**x** /ʒwajo/ *nm* jewel, gem

joyeusement /ʒwajøzmɑ̃/ *adv* merrily, cheerfully

joyeux, -euse /ʒwajø, øz/ *adj* merry, cheerful

jubilation /ʒybilasjɔ̃/ *nf* joy, jubilation

jubilé /ʒybile/ *nm* jubilee

jubiler /ʒybile/ [1] *vi* to be jubilant

jucher /ʒyʃe/ [1] *vtr*, **se jucher** *v refl* (+ *v être*) to perch

judaïsme /ʒydaism/ *nm* Judaism

judas /ʒyda/ *nm inv* peephole

judiciaire /ʒydisjɛʀ/ *adj* judicial

judicieux, -ieuse /ʒydisjø, øz/ *adj* judicious, sensible

judo /ʒydo/ *nm* judo

juge /ʒyʒ/ *nm* judge; **être à la fois** ~ **et partie** to be judge and jury

■ ~ **d'instruction** examining magistrate; ~ **de touche** linesman

jugé: au jugé /oʒyʒe/ *phr* ⟨*value*⟩ by guesswork; ⟨*shoot*⟩ blind

jugement /ʒyʒmɑ̃/ *nm* judgment; **passer en** ~ ⟨*case*⟩ to come to court

jugeote /ʒyʒɔt/ *nf* (colloq) common sense

juger /ʒyʒe/ [13] **1** *vtr* **(a)** to judge ⟨*person, competition*⟩; **mal** ~ **qn** to misjudge sb
(b) to consider; ~ **utile de faire** to consider it useful to do
(c) (Law) to try ⟨*case*⟩; to judge ⟨*case*⟩; **le tribunal jugera** the court will decide
2 juger de *v+prep* to assess; **j'en jugerai par moi-même** I'll judge for myself; **à en** ~ **par** judging by

juguler /ʒygyle/ [1] *vtr* to stamp out ⟨*epidemic, uprising*⟩; to curb ⟨*inflation*⟩

juif, juive /ʒɥif, ʒɥiv/ **1** *adj* Jewish
2 *nm,f* Jew

juillet /ʒɥijɛ/ *nm* July; **le 14** ~ Bastille Day

juin /ʒɥɛ̃/ *nm* June

juive ▶ JUIF

jumeau, -elle¹, *mpl* ~**x** /ʒymo, ɛl/ *adj, nm,f* twin

jumelage /ʒymlaʒ/ *nm* twinning

jumeler /ʒymle/ [19] *vtr* to twin

jumelle² /ʒymɛl/ *nf*, **jumelles** *nf pl* binoculars; ~**s de théâtre** opera glasses

jument /ʒymɑ̃/ *nf* mare

jungle /ʒœ̃gl/ *nf* jungle

junte /ʒœ̃t/ *nf* junta

jupe /ʒyp/ *nf* skirt
IDIOMS **il est toujours dans les** ~**s de sa mère** he's tied to his mother's apron strings

jupe-culotte, *pl* **jupes-culottes** /ʒypkylɔt/ *nf* culottes, divided skirt

jupette /ʒypɛt/ *nf* short skirt

jupon /ʒypɔ̃/ *nm* petticoat
IDIOMS **courir le** ~ to womanize

juré, ~e /ʒyʀe/ **1** *pp* ▶ JURER
2 *pp adj* **(a)** on oath; sworn-in
(b) ⟨*enemy*⟩ sworn
3 *nm* juror; **les** ~**s** the members of the jury

jurer /ʒyʀe/ [1] **1** *vtr* to swear; **on leur a fait** ~ **le secret** they were sworn to secrecy; ~ **de tuer qn** to vow to kill sb; **ah mais je te jure!** (colloq) honestly! (colloq)
2 jurer de *v+prep* to swear to
3 *vi* **(a)** to swear
(b) ⟨*colours*⟩ to clash
(c) **ne** ~ **que par** to swear by
4 se jurer *v refl* (+ *v être*) **(a)** to swear [sth] to one another
(b) to vow
IDIOMS **il ne faut** ~ **de rien** (Proverb) never say never

juridiction /ʒyʀidiksjɔ̃/ *nf* **(a)** jurisdiction
(b) courts

juridique /ʒyʀidik/ *adj* legal; **vide** ~ gap in the law

jurisprudence /ʒyʀispʀydɑ̃s/ *nf* case law

juriste /ʒyʀist/ *nmf* **(a)** jurist
(b) lawyer

juron /ʒyʀɔ̃/ *nm* swearword

jury /ʒyʀi/ *nm* **(a)** jury
(b) panel of judges
(c) board of examiners

jus /ʒy/ *nm inv* **(a)** juice
(b) (from meat) juices; gravy
(c) electricity; **prendre le** ~ to get a shock

jusque (jusqu' before vowel) /ʒysk/
1 *prep* **(a)** **aller jusqu'à Paris** to go as far as Paris; to go all the way to Paris; **courir jusqu'au bout du jardin** to run right down to the bottom of the garden (GB) *or* the end of the yard (US); **suivre qn** ~ **dans sa chambre** to follow sb right into his/her room; **la nouvelle est arrivée jusqu'à nous** the news has reached us; **jusqu'où comptez-vous aller?** how far do you intend to go?
(b) **jusqu'à, jusqu'en** until, till; **jusqu'à présent, jusqu'ici** (up) until now
(c) **monter jusqu'à 20°** to go up to 20°
(d) to the point of; **aller jusqu'à faire** to go so far as to do

(e) even; **des détritus ∼ sous la table** rubbish everywhere, even under the table
②jusqu'à ce que *phr* until
jusque-là /ʒyskəla/ *adv* **(a)** until then, up to then
(b) up to here; up to there
IDIOMS en avoir ∼ de qn/qch (colloq) to have had it up to here with sb/sth (colloq); **s'en mettre ∼** (colloq) to stuff one's face (colloq)
justaucorps /ʒystokɔʀ/ *nm inv* leotard
juste /ʒyst/ **①** *adj* **(a)** ⟨*person*⟩ just, fair
(b) ⟨*cause*⟩ just; ⟨*anger*⟩ righteous; ⟨*word, answer*⟩ right, correct
(c) ⟨*balance, watch*⟩ accurate; **∼ milieu** happy medium; **à ∼ titre** with good reason; **dire des choses ∼s** to make some valid points; **apprécier qn à sa ∼ valeur** to get a fair picture of sb
(d) (Mus) ⟨*piano, voice*⟩ in tune; ⟨*note*⟩ true
(e) c'est un peu ∼ (in width, time) it's a bit tight; (in quantity) it's barely enough
② *adv* **(a)** ⟨*sing*⟩ in tune; ⟨*guess*⟩ right; **elle a vu ∼** she was right; **viser ∼** to aim straight
(b) just; **∼ à temps** just in time
(c) (tout) ∼ only just; **j'arrive ∼** I've only just arrived; **c'est tout ∼ s'il sait lire** he can hardly read
③ au juste *phr* exactly
④ *nm* righteous man; **les ∼s** the righteous
justement /ʒystəmɑ̃/ *adv* **(a)** precisely
(b) just
(c) correctly
(d) justifiably
justesse /ʒystɛs/ **①** *nf* **(a)** correctness; **avec ∼** correctly
(b) accuracy; **avec ∼** accurately

②de justesse *phr* ⟨*succeed*⟩ only just
justice /ʒystis/ *nf* **(a)** justice; **rendre la ∼** to dispense justice; **il faut leur rendre cette ∼ qu'ils sont…** one has to acknowledge that they are…; **ce n'est que ∼** it is only fair; **se faire ∼** to take the law into one's own hands; to take one's own life
(b) la ∼ the law; the legal system; the courts; **action en ∼** legal action
justicier, -ière /ʒystisje, ɛʀ/ *nm,f* righter of wrongs
justificatif, -ive /ʒystifikatif, iv/ *nm* documentary evidence; **∼ de domicile** proof of domicile; **∼ de frais** receipt
justification /ʒystifikasjɔ̃/ *nf*
(a) justification
(b) explanation; documentary evidence
justifié, ∼e /ʒystifje/ **①** *pp* ▶ JUSTIFIER
② *pp adj* **(a)** justified; **non ∼** unjustified
justifier /ʒystifje/ **②** **①** *vtr* to justify ⟨*method, absence*⟩; to vindicate ⟨*guilty party*⟩; to explain ⟨*ignorance*⟩; **les faits ont justifié nos craintes** events proved our fears to have been justified; **tu essaies toujours de la ∼** you are always making excuses for her
②justifier de *v+prep* to give proof of
③se justifier *v refl* (+ *v être*) **(a)** to make excuses; (in court) to clear oneself
(b) ⟨*decision*⟩ to be justified (by)
jute /ʒyt/ *nm* jute; (toile de) ∼ hessian
juteux, -euse /ʒytø, øz/ *adj* ⟨*fruit*⟩ juicy
juvénile /ʒyvenil/ *adj* youthful; juvenile
juxtaposer /ʒykstapoze/ [1] *vtr* to juxtapose
juxtaposition /ʒykstapozisjɔ̃/ *nf* juxtaposition

k

Kk

k, K /ka/ *nm inv* k, K
kafkaïen, -ïenne /kafkajɛ̃, ɛn/ *adj* Kafkaesque
kakatoès /kakatɔɛs/ *nm inv* cockatoo
kaki /kaki/ **①** *adj inv* khaki
② *nm* **(a)** persimmon
(b) khaki
kaléidoscope /kaleidɔskɔp/ *nm* kaleidoscope
kanak = CANAQUE
kangourou /kɑ̃guʀu/ **①** *adj inv* **poche ∼** front pocket; **slip ∼** pouch-front briefs
② *nm* **(a)** kangaroo
(b) ®baby carrier
karaté /kaʀate/ *nm* karate
karité /kaʀite/ *nm* shea; **beurre de ∼** shea butter
kart /kaʀt/ *nm* go-kart

karting /kaʀtiŋ/ *nm* go-karting; **faire du ∼** to go karting
kasher /kaʃeʀ/ *adj inv* kosher
kayak /kajak/ *nm* kayak; **faire du ∼** to go kayaking
képi /kepi/ *nm* kepi
kératine /keʀatin/ *nf* keratin
kermesse /kɛʀmɛs/ *nf* fete
kérosène /keʀɔzɛn/ *nm* kerosene
kF (*written abbr* = KILOFRANC)
kg (*written abbr* = **kilogramme**) kg
kibboutz, *pl* **-tzim** /kibuts, kibutsim/ *nm* kibbutz
kick /kik/ *nm* kick-start
kidnapper /kidnape/ [1] *vtr* to kidnap; **se faire ∼** to be kidnapped

kidnappeur, -euse /kidnapœʀ, øz/ *nm,f* kidnapper

kif-kif /kifkif/ *adj inv* (colloq) **c'est ~ (bourricot)** it's all the same

kilo[1] /kilo/ *pref* kilo

kilo[2] /kilo/ *nm* (*abbr* = **kilogramme**) kilo; **prendre des ~s** to put on weight

kilofranc /kilofʀɑ̃/ *nm* 1,000 French francs

kilogramme /kilogʀam/ *nm* kilogram

kilométrage /kilometʀaʒ/ *nm* ≈ mileage

kilomètre /kilomɛtʀ/ *nm* kilometre (GB)

kilomètre-heure *pl* **kilomètres-heure** /kilometʀœʀ/ *nm* kilometre (GB) per hour

kilométrique /kilometʀik/ *adj* ⟨*distance*⟩ in kilometres (GB); ⟨*price*⟩ per kilometre (GB)

kilo-octet /kiloɔktɛ/ *nm* kilobyte

kilotonne /kilotɔn/ *nf* kiloton

kilowattheure /kilowatœʀ/ *nm* kilowatt-hour

kimono /kimono/ *nm* (a) kimono
(b) judo suit

kinésithérapeute /kineziteʀapøt/ *nmf* physiotherapist (GB), physical therapist (US)

kinésithérapie /kineziteʀapi/ *nf* physiotherapy (GB), physical therapy (US)

kiosque /kjɔsk/ *nm* kiosk
■ **~ à musique** bandstand

kiwi /kiwi/ *nm* kiwi

klaxon® /klaksɔn/ *nm* (car) horn

klaxonner /klaksɔne/ [1] *vi* to sound one's horn (GB), to honk the horn

kleptomane /klɛptɔman/ *adj*, *nmf* kleptomaniac

knock-out /nɔkaut/ [1] *adj inv* knocked out
[2] *nm* knockout

Ko (*written abbr* = **kilo-octet**) KB

KO /kao/ [1] *adj inv* (*abbr* = **knocked out**)
(a) KO'd (colloq); **mettre qn ~** to KO sb (colloq)
(b) (colloq) exhausted
[2] *nm* (*abbr* = **knockout**) KO (colloq)

koala /kɔala/ *nm* koala (bear)

kopeck /kɔpɛk/ *nm* kopeck; **ça ne vaut pas un ~** it's not worth a penny

krach /kʀak/ *nm* (on stock exchange) crash

kraft /kʀaft/ *nm* (**papier**) **~** brown paper

kurde /kyʀd/ *adj*, *nm* Kurdish

Kurde /kyʀd/ *nmf* Kurd

kW (*written abbr* = **kilowatt**) kW

K-way® /kawe/ *nm* windcheater (GB), windbreaker (US)

kyrielle /kiʀjɛl/ *nf* **une ~ de** a string of

kyste /kist/ *nm* cyst

Ll

l, L /ɛl/ *nm inv* (a) (letter) l, L
(b) (*written abbr* = **litre**) 20 l | 20 l

l' ▶ LE

la[1] *det, pron* ▶ LE

la[2] /la/ *nm* (Mus) (note) A; (in sol-fa) lah; **donner le ~** to give an A; (figurative) to set the tone

là /la/ *adv* (a) there; here; **viens ~** come here; **~ où je travaille** where I work; **pas par ici, par ~** not this way, that way; **de ~ au village** from there to the village
(b) then; **d'ici ~** between now and then; by then; **et ~, le téléphone a sonné** and then the phone rang; **en ce temps-~** in those days; **ce jour-~** that day
(c) **s'il en est (arrivé) ~, c'est que...** if he's got to that point, it's because...; **alors ~ tu exagères!** now you're going too far!; **que vas-tu chercher ~?** what are you thinking of?; **il a fallu en passer par ~** there was no alternative; **qu'entendez-vous par ~?** what do you mean by that?; **si tu vas par ~** if you are saying that; **de ~** hence; from that

là-bas /labɑ/ *adv* over there

labeur /labœʀ/ *nm* hard work

labo /labo/ *nm* (colloq) lab (colloq)

laboratoire /labɔʀatwaʀ/ *nm* laboratory
■ **~ d'analyses médicales** medical laboratory; **~ de langues** language laboratory; **~ pharmaceutique** pharmaceutical company

laborieusement /labɔʀjøzmɑ̃/ *adv* laboriously

laborieux, -ieuse /labɔʀjø, øz/ *adj*
(a) ⟨*work, process*⟩ arduous; ⟨*style*⟩ laboured (GB)
(b) **les classes laborieuses** the working classes

labour /labuʀ/ *nm* ploughing; **cheval de ~** plough horse

labourer /labuʀe/ [1] *vtr* to plough (GB), to plow (US)

labyrinthe /labiʀɛ̃t/ *nm* maze; labyrinth

lac /lak/ *nm* (a) lake
(b) reservoir

lacer /lase/ [12] *vtr* to lace up ⟨*shoes, corset*⟩

lacérer /laseʀe/ [14] *vtr* to lacerate; to slash

lacet /lasɛ/ *nm* (a) lace; **chaussures à ~s** lace-up shoes; **nouer ses ~s** to do up one's laces
(b) (in road) **une route en ~s** a twisting road

lâche /lɑʃ/ [1] *adj* **(a)** ⟨*person, crime*⟩ cowardly
(b) ⟨*belt*⟩ loose
(c) ⟨*regulation*⟩ lax
[2] *nmf* coward

lâchement /lɑʃmã/ *adv* **ils se sont ~ enfuis** they fled like cowards; **il a été ~ assassiné** he was foully murdered

lâcher[1] /lɑʃe/ [1] [1] *vtr* **(a)** to drop ⟨*object*⟩; to let go of ⟨*rope*⟩; **lâche-moi** let go of me; (figurative) (colloq) give me a break (colloq); **~ prise** to lose one's grip
(b) to reveal ⟨*information*⟩; to let out ⟨*scream*⟩
(c) to let ⟨sb/sth⟩ go ⟨*person, animal*⟩
(d) to drop ⟨*friend, activity*⟩; **la peur ne la lâche plus depuis** she's been living in constant terror ever since
[2] *vi* ⟨*rope*⟩ to give way; ⟨*brakes*⟩ to fail; **ses nerfs ont lâché** he/she went to pieces

lâcher[2] /lɑʃe/ *nm* (of balloons, birds) release

lâcheté /lɑʃte/ *nf* **(a)** cowardice; **par ~** out of cowardice
(b) cowardly act

laconique /lakɔnik/ *adj* laconic; terse

lacrymal, ~e, *mpl* **-aux** /lakʀimal, o/ *adj* lachrymal

lacrymogène /lakʀimɔʒɛn/ *adj* ⟨*grenade, bomb*⟩ teargas; **gaz ~** teargas

lacté, ~e /lakte/ *adj* **(a)** ⟨*product*⟩ milk
(b) ⟨*liquid*⟩ milky; **la voie ~e** the Milky Way

lacune /lakyn/ *nf* (in knowledge, law) gap

là-dedans /lad(ə)dã/ *adv* in here; in there; **et moi ~ qu'est-ce que je fais?** (colloq) and where do I come in?

là-dessous /lad(ə)su/ *adv* under here; under there; **il y a qch de louche ~** (colloq) there's something fishy about all this (colloq)

là-dessus /lad(ə)sy/ *adv* **(a)** on here; on there
(b) **qu'as-tu à dire ~?** what have you got to say about it?
(c) **~ il a raccroché** with that he hung up

ladite ▶ LEDIT

lagon /lagõ/ *nm* lagoon

lagune /lagyn/ *nf* lagoon

là-haut /lao/ *adv* **(a)** up here; up there; **tout ~** (all the) way up there
(b) upstairs
(c) in heaven

laïc /laik/ *nm* layman

laïcité /laisite/ *nf* secularism; secularity

laid, ~e /lɛ, lɛd/ *adj* **(a)** ugly
(b) disgusting

laideur /lɛdœʀ/ *nf* ugliness

lainage /lɛnaʒ/ *nm* **(a)** woollen (GB) material
(b) woollen (GB) garment

laine /lɛn/ *nf* wool; **de or en ~** woollen (GB), wool
■ **~ peignée** worsted; **~ de verre** glass wool; **~ vierge** new wool (GB), virgin wool

laïque /laik/ [1] *adj* ⟨*school*⟩ nondenominational (GB), public (US); ⟨*state, mind*⟩ secular
[2] *nmf* layman/laywoman; **les ~s** lay people

laisse /lɛs/ *nf* (for dog) lead (GB), leash (US)

laissé-pour-compte, laissée-pour-compte, *mpl* **laissés-pour-compte** /lesepuʀkõt/ *nm,f* **les laissés-pour-compte** (gen) the forgotten people; **les laissés-pour-compte de la révolution technologique** the casualties of the technological revolution

laisser /lese/ [1] [1] *vtr* to leave; **~ la liberté à qn** to let sb go free; **je te laisse** I must go; **~ le choix à qn** to give sb the choice; **laisse ce jouet à ton frère** let your brother have the toy; **laisse-le, ça lui passera** ignore him, he'll get over it; **cela me laisse sceptique** I'm sceptical (GB) *or* skeptical (US)
[2] *v aux* **~ qn/qch faire** to let sb/sth do; **laisse-moi faire** let me do it; leave it to me; **laisse faire!** so what!
[3] **se laisser** *v refl* (+ *v être*) **se ~ bercer par les vagues** to be lulled by the waves; **il se laisse insulter** he puts up with insults; **elle n'est pas du genre à se ~ faire** she won't be pushed around; **il ne veut pas se ~ faire** he won't let you touch him; **se ~ aller** to let oneself go

laisser-aller /leseale/ *nm inv*
(a) scruffiness
(b) sloppiness

laissez-passer /lesepase/ *nm inv* pass

lait /lɛ/ *nm* milk
■ **~ de chaux** whitewash; **~ concentré non sucré** evaporated milk; **~ demi-écrémé** low-fat milk; **~ écrémé** skimmed milk (GB), skim *or* nonfat milk (US); **~ maternel** breastmilk; **~ de poule** eggnog

laitage /lɛtaʒ/ *nm* dairy product

laitance /lɛtãs/ *nf* (Culin, Zool) soft roe

laiterie /lɛtʀi/ *nf* **(a)** dairy
(b) dairy industry

laiteux, -euse /lɛtø, øz/ *adj* ⟨*liquid, white*⟩ milky; ⟨*complexion*⟩ creamy

laitier, -ière /lɛtje, ɛʀ/ [1] *adj* ⟨*industry, product*⟩ dairy; ⟨*production, cow*⟩ milk
[2] *nm,f* milkman/milkwoman

laiton /lɛtõ/ *nm* brass

laitue /lɛty/ *nf* lettuce

laïus /lajys/ *nm inv* (colloq) speech

lama /lama/ *nm* **(a)** (animal) llama
(b) (religious leader) lama

lambda /lãbda/ *adj inv* (colloq) average

lambeau, *pl* **~x** /lãbo/ *nm* (of cloth) rag; (of paper, hide) strip; (of flesh) bit

lambris /lãbʀi/ *nm inv* panelling (GB); marble walls; (on ceiling) mouldings (GB), moldings (US)

lambrisser /lãbʀise/ [1] *vtr* to panel

lame /lam/ *nf* **(a)** (of knife, saw) blade
(b) knife
(c) sword; **une fine ~** an expert swordsman ·····>

(d) (of metal, wood) strip; (on blind) slat
■ ~ **de fond** ground swell; (figurative) upheaval;
~ **de rasoir** razor blade

lamé /lame/ *nm* lamé; **en** ~ lamé

lamelle /lamɛl/ *nf* **(a)** (of wood, metal) small strip
(b) (Culin) sliver; **découper en fines** ~s to slice thinly
(c) (Bot) (of mushroom) gill

lamentable /lamɑ̃tabl/ *adj* pathetic, awful

lamentablement /lamɑ̃tabləmɑ̃/ *adv*
⟨*fail*⟩ miserably; ⟨*cry*⟩ piteously

lamentation /lamɑ̃tasjɔ̃/ *nf* wailing

lamenter: se lamenter /lamɑ̃te/ [1] *v refl*
(+ *v être*) to moan; **se** ~ **sur son propre sort**
to feel sorry for oneself

lampadaire /lɑ̃padɛʀ/ *nm* **(a)** standard
(GB) *or* floor (US) lamp
(b) streetlight

lampe /lɑ̃p/ *nf* **(a)** lamp, light
(b) (light) bulb
■ ~ **à bronzer** sun lamp; ~ **de chevet** bedside
light; ~ **électrique** torch (GB), flashlight (US);
~ **de poche** pocket torch (GB), flashlight
(US); ~ **témoin** indicator light; ~ **tempête**
hurricane lamp

lampée /lɑ̃pe/ *nf* (colloq) gulp

lampion /lɑ̃pjɔ̃/ *nm* paper lantern

lance /lɑ̃s/ *nf* (gen) spear; (in jousting) lance
■ ~ **d'incendie** fire hose nozzle

lancée /lɑ̃se/ *nf* **sur ma** ~ while I was at it;
continuer sur sa ~ to continue to forge
ahead

lancement /lɑ̃smɑ̃/ *nm* **(a)** (of ship,
company) launching; (of process) setting up
(b) (of product, book) launch; (of loan) floating;
(of actor) promotion
(c) (of missile) launching; launch

lance-pierres /lɑ̃spjɛʀ/ *nm inv* catapult
IDIOMS **payer qn avec un** ~ (colloq) to pay sb
peanuts (colloq)

lancer[1] /lɑ̃se/ [12] **1** *vtr* **(a)** to throw ⟨*ball,
pebble, javelin*⟩; ~ **le poids** to put the shot
(b) to launch ⟨*rocket, ship*⟩; to fire ⟨*arrow*⟩;
to drop ⟨*bomb*⟩; to start up ⟨*engine*⟩
(c) to throw out ⟨*smoke, flames*⟩; to give
⟨*look*⟩; to put about ⟨*rumour*⟩; to issue
⟨*ultimatum*⟩; to send out ⟨*invitation*⟩
(d) to hurl ⟨*insult*⟩; to make ⟨*accusation*⟩;
lança-t-il he said
2 *vi* (colloq) to throb; **mon doigt me lance** my
finger is throbbing
3 se lancer *v refl* (+ *v être*) **(a) se** ~ **dans
des dépenses** to get involved in expense; **se**
~ **dans les affaires** to go into business
(b) se ~ **dans le vide** to jump
(c) to throw [sth] to each other ⟨*ball*⟩; to
exchange ⟨*insults*⟩

lancer[2] /lɑ̃se/ *nm* **(a)** (Sport) ~ **du disque**
discus event; ~ **du poids** shot put (event)
(b) le ~, **la pêche au** ~ rod and reel fishing

lance-roquettes /lɑ̃sʀɔkɛt/ *nm inv*
rocket launcher

lancinant, ~**e** /lɑ̃sinɑ̃, ɑ̃t/ *adj* ⟨*pain*⟩
shooting; ⟨*music, rhythm*⟩ insistent

landau /lɑ̃do/ *nm* pram (GB), baby carriage
(US)

lande /lɑ̃d/ *nf* moor

langage /lɑ̃gaʒ/ *nm* language
■ ~ **administratif** official jargon; ~ **des
sourds-muets** sign language

lange /lɑ̃ʒ/ *nm* **(a)** swaddling clothes
(b) nappy (GB), diaper (US)

langer /lɑ̃ʒe/ [13] *vtr* **(a)** to wrap [sb] in
swaddling clothes ⟨*baby*⟩
(b) to put a nappy (GB) *or* diaper (US) on
⟨*baby*⟩

langoureux, -euse /lɑ̃guʀø, øz/ *adj*
languorous

langouste /lɑ̃gust/ *nf* spiny lobster

langoustine /lɑ̃gustin/ *nf* langoustine

langue /lɑ̃g/ *nf* **(a)** tongue; **tirer la** ~ to
stick out one's tongue; (for doctor) to put out
one's tongue; (figurative) to be dying of thirst;
to struggle financially
(b) language; speech
(c) mauvaise ~ malicious gossip
(d) ~ **de terre** spit of land
■ ~ **de bois** political cant; ~ **maternelle**
mother tongue; ~ **verte** slang
IDIOMS **avoir la** ~ **bien pendue** (colloq) to be
very talkative; **avoir qch sur le bout de la** ~
to have sth on the tip of one's tongue

languette /lɑ̃gɛt/ *nf* (on shoe) tongue; (on
satchel, bag) strap; (of ham) long narrow strip

langueur /lɑ̃gœʀ/ *nf* languor

languir /lɑ̃giʀ/ [3] **1** *vi* **(a)** ⟨*conversation*⟩
to languish; ⟨*economy*⟩ to be sluggish
(b) je languis de vous revoir I'm longing to
see you; **faire** ~ **qn** to keep sb in suspense
2 se languir *v refl* (+ *v être*) to pine

languissant, ~**e** /lɑ̃gisɑ̃, ɑ̃t/ *adj*
⟨*economy*⟩ sluggish; ⟨*conversation*⟩ desultory

lanière /lanjɛʀ/ *nf* (gen) strap; (of whip) lash

lanterne /lɑ̃tɛʀn/ *nf* **(a)** lantern
(b) (Aut) sidelight (GB), parking light (US)
IDIOMS **éclairer la** ~ **de qn** to enlighten sb

laper /lape/ [1] *vtr* to lap (up) ⟨*soup, milk*⟩

lapider /lapide/ [1] *vtr* **(a)** to stone [sb] to
death
(b) to throw stones at

lapin /lapɛ̃/ *nm* **(a)** rabbit; ~ **de garenne**
wild rabbit; **coup du** ~ rabbit punch;
(in accident) whiplash injury; **cage** *or* **cabane à**
~s rabbit hutch; (figurative) (colloq) tower
block
(b) rabbit(skin)
IDIOMS **poser un** ~ **à qn** (colloq) to stand sb
up; **se faire tirer comme des** ~s (colloq) to be
picked off like flies; **c'est un chaud** ~ (colloq)
he's a randy devil

lapine /lapin/ *nf* doe rabbit

laps /laps/ *nm inv* ~ **de temps** period of
time

lapsus /lapsys/ *nm inv* slip

laquais /lakɛ/ *nm inv* lackey

laque /lak/ *nf* **(a)** hairspray
(b) lacquer; gloss paint (GB), enamel (US)

laqué, ~**e** /lake/ *adj* ⟨*paint*⟩ gloss

laquelle ▶ LEQUEL

laquer /lake/ [1] *vtr* to lacquer; to paint [sth] in gloss (GB) *or* enamel (US)

larbin /laʀbɛ̃/ *nm* (derogatory) (colloq) servant

lard /laʀ/ *nm* ≈ fat streaky bacon

larder /laʀde/ [1] *vtr* (Culin) to lard; ~ qn de coups de couteau (figurative) to stab sb repeatedly

lardon /laʀdɔ̃/ *nm* (Culin) bacon cube

large /laʀʒ/ **1** *adj* **(a)** ⟨shoulders, hips⟩ broad; ⟨avenue, bed⟩ wide; ⟨coat⟩ loose-fitting; ⟨trousers⟩ loose; ⟨skirt⟩ full; ⟨jumper⟩ big; ⟨smile⟩ broad; ⟨curve⟩ long; ~ de trois mètres three metres (GB) wide
(b) ⟨advance, profit⟩ substantial; ⟨choice, public⟩ wide; ⟨majority⟩ large; au sens ~ in a broad sense
(c) ⟨person⟩ generous
(d) ⟨life⟩ comfortable
(e) avoir les idées ~s, être ~ d'esprit to be broad-minded
2 *adv* **(a)** ⟨plan⟩ on a generous scale; ⟨calculate, measure⟩ on the generous side
(b) s'habiller ~ to wear loose-fitting clothes
3 *nm* **(a)** faire quatre mètres de ~ to be four metres (GB) wide
(b) open sea; au ~ offshore
IDIOMS ne pas en mener ~ (colloq) to be worried sick (colloq)

largement /laʀʒəmɑ̃/ *adv* **(a)** widely
(b) largely, to a large extent; être ~ responsable de qch to be largely responsible for sth
(c) arriver ~ en tête to be a clear winner; ~ en dessous de la limite well under the limit
(d) tu as ~ le temps you've got plenty of time
(e) easily; une chaîne en or vaudrait ~ le double a gold chain would easily be worth twice as much
(f) ⟨contribute⟩ generously

largesse /laʀʒɛs/ *nf* generous gift

largeur /laʀʒœʀ/ *nf* **(a)** width, breadth; dans le sens de la ~ widthwise
(b) ~ d'esprit broad-mindedness

largué, ~e /laʀge/ *adj* (colloq) **(a)** lost, out of one's depth
(b) out of touch

larguer /laʀge/ [1] *vtr* **(a)** (Mil) to drop ⟨bomb, missile⟩; to drop ⟨parachutist⟩; to release ⟨satellite⟩
(b) to unfurl ⟨sail⟩; ~ les amarres to cast off; (figurative) to set off
(c) (colloq) to give up ⟨studies⟩; to chuck (colloq) ⟨boyfriend, girlfriend⟩

larme /laʀm/ *nf* **(a)** tear; elle a ri aux ~s she laughed till she cried; avoir la ~ à l'œil to be a bit weepy
(b) (colloq) drop

larmoyant, ~e /laʀmwajɑ̃, ɑ̃t/ *adj*
(a) ⟨eyes⟩ full of tears
(b) ⟨voice⟩ whining; ⟨speech⟩ maudlin

larmoyer /laʀmwaje/ [23] *vi* **(a)** ⟨eyes⟩ to water

(b) ⟨person⟩ to whine

larron /laʀɔ̃/ *nm* **(a)** (humorous) scoundrel
(b) thief
IDIOMS s'entendre comme ~s en foire to be as thick as thieves

larvaire /laʀvɛʀ/ *adj* ⟨state⟩ embryonic

larve /laʀv/ *nf* **(a)** (Zool) larva
(b) (person) wimp (colloq)

larvé, ~e /laʀve/ *adj* latent

laryngite /laʀɛ̃ʒit/ *nf* laryngitis

larynx /laʀɛ̃ks/ *nm inv* larynx

las, lasse /lɑ, lɑs/ *adj* weary

lasagnes /lazaɲ/ *nf pl* lasagna

lascar /laskaʀ/ *nm* (colloq) fellow

lascif, -ive /lasif, iv/ *adj* ⟨person, look⟩ lascivious; ⟨temperament⟩ lustful

laser /lazɛʀ/ *nm* laser

lassant, ~e /lasɑ̃, ɑ̃t/ *adj* **(a)** ⟨speech⟩ tedious; ⟨reproaches⟩ tiresome
(b) tiring

lasser /lase/ [1] **1** *vtr* **(a)** to bore ⟨person, audience⟩
(b) to weary ⟨person, audience⟩
2 se lasser *v refl* (+ *v être*) ⟨person⟩ to grow tired; sans se ~ without tiring; patiently

lassitude /lasityd/ *nf* weariness

lasso /laso/ *nm* lasso; prendre au ~ to lasso

latence /latɑ̃s/ *nf* latency

latent, ~e /latɑ̃, ɑ̃t/ *adj* ⟨danger, illness⟩ latent; ⟨anxiety, jealousy⟩ underlying

latéral, ~e, mpl -aux /lateʀal, o/ *adj* ⟨door, exit⟩ side; ⟨tunnel, aisle⟩ lateral

latéralement /lateʀalmɑ̃/ *adv* sideways

latin, ~e /latɛ̃, in/ **1** *adj* **(a)** ⟨texts⟩ Latin
(b) ⟨temperament⟩ Latin; ⟨culture⟩ Mediterranean
(c) langues ~es Romance languages
2 *nm* (language) Latin
IDIOMS c'est à y perdre son ~ you can't make head or tail of it

latino-américain, ~e, mpl ~s /latinoameʀikɛ̃, ɛn/ *adj* Latin-American

latitude /latityd/ *nf* latitude
IDIOMS avoir toute ~ de faire to be entirely free to do

latte /lat/ *nf* **(a)** lath; (of floor) board
(b) (of bed base) slat

laudatif, -ive /lodatif, iv/ *adj* laudatory

lauréat, ~e /loʀea, at/ *nm,f*
(a) (of competition) winner
(b) (in exam) successful candidate

laurier /loʀje/ **1** *nm* **(a)** (Bot) laurel; ~ commun bay (tree)
(b) (Culin) feuille de ~ bay leaf
2 lauriers *nm pl* laurels; s'endormir sur ses ~s to rest on one's laurels

laurier-rose, pl lauriers-roses /loʀjeʀoz/ *nm* oleander

lavable /lavabl/ *adj* washable

lavabo /lavabo/ *nm* washbasin, washbowl

lavage /lavaʒ/ *nm* **(a)** washing; cleaning ⋯⋯

(b) (washing machine cycle) wash ■ ~ **de cerveau** brainwashing; **faire un ~ d'estomac à qn** to pump sb's stomach (out)

lavande /lavɑ̃d/ *adj inv, nf* lavender

lave /lav/ *nf* lava; **coulée de ~** lava flow

lave-glace, *pl* ~**s** /lavglas/ *nm* windscreen (GB) *or* windshield (US) washer

lave-linge /lavlɛ̃ʒ/ *nm inv* washing machine

lavement /lavmɑ̃/ *nm* (Med) enema

laver /lave/ [1] **1** *vtr* **(a)** to wash ⟨clothes, child, car⟩; ~ **son linge** to do one's washing; ~ **la vaisselle** to do the dishes; ~ **qch à grande eau** to wash sth down
(b) to clean ⟨wound⟩
(c) to clear; ~ **qn d'une accusation** to clear sb of an accusation
2 **se laver** *v refl* (+ *v être*) **(a)** to wash; **se ~ les mains** to wash one's hands; **se ~ les dents** to brush one's teeth
(b) to be washable
(c) **se ~ d'un affront** to take revenge for an insult
IDIOMS **je m'en lave les mains** I'm washing my hands of it

laverie /lavʀi/ *nf* ~ **(automatique)** launderette, laundromat® (US)

lave-vaisselle /lavvɛsɛl/ *nm inv* dishwasher

lavis /lavi/ *nm inv* wash drawing

lavoir /lavwaʀ/ *nm* wash house

laxatif /laksatif/ *nm* laxative

laxisme /laksism/ *nm* laxity

laxiste /laksist/ *adj* lax

layette /lɛjɛt/ *nf* baby clothes, layette

le, la[1] (**l'** before vowel or mute h), *pl* **les** /lə, la, l, lɛ/ **1** *det* **(a)** the; **la table de la cuisine** the kitchen table; **les Dupont** at the Duponts; **elle aime les chevaux** she likes horses; **arriver sur** *or* **vers les 11 heures** to arrive at about 11 o'clock
(b) elle s'est cogné ~ bras she banged her arm
(c) a, an; **50 francs ~ kilo** 50 francs a kilo
(d) (oh) la jolie robe! what a pretty dress!
2 *pron* him; her; it; them; **je ne les comprends pas** I don't understand them
3 *pron neutre* **je ~ savais** I knew; I knew it; **je ~ croyais aussi, mais...** I thought so too, but...; **espérons-~!** let's hope so!

lé /le/ *nm* (of cloth, wallpaper) width

LEA /ɛlaa/ *nf pl* (abbr = **langues étrangères appliquées**) *university language course with emphasis on business and management*

leadership /lidœʀʃip/ *nm* **(a)** leading role
(b) supremacy

lèche-bottes (colloq) /lɛʃbɔt/ **1** *nmf inv* crawler (GB) (colloq), bootlicker (colloq)
2 *nm* crawling (GB) (colloq), bootlicking (colloq)

lécher /leʃe/ [1] **1** *vtr* **(a)** to lick ⟨spoon, plate⟩
(b) ⟨flames⟩ to lick; ⟨sea⟩ to lap against

2 **se lécher** *v refl* (+ *v être*) **se ~ les doigts** to lick one's fingers

lèche-vitrines /lɛʃvitʀin/ *nm inv* window-shopping

leçon /ləsɔ̃/ *nf* lesson; ~ **particulière** private lesson; **cela lui servira de ~** that'll teach him a lesson

lecteur, -trice /lɛktœʀ, tʀis/ **1** *nm,f*
(a) reader
(b) teaching assistant
2 *nm* **(a)** (Comput) reader; ~ **optique** optical scanner *or* reader; ~ **de disquettes** disk drive
(b) player; ~ **laser** CD player

lecture /lɛktyʀ/ *nf* **(a)** (of book, newspaper) reading; **faire la ~ à qn** to read to sb
(b) reading, interpretation
(c) reading material; **tu as pris de la ~?** have you brought something to read?
(d) (of music, X-ray, disk) reading
(e) (of cassette, CD) play; playing

ledit, ladite, *pl* **lesdits, lesdites** /lədi, ladit, ledi, ledit/ *adj* the aforementioned

légal, ~e, *mpl* **-aux** /legal, o/ *adj* legal; lawful

légalement /legalmɑ̃/ *adv* legally; lawfully

légaliser /legalize/ [1] *vtr* to legalize

légalité /legalite/ *nf* **(a)** legality
(b) lawfulness

légataire /legatɛʀ/ *nmf* legatee

légendaire /leʒɑ̃dɛʀ/ *adj* legendary

légende /leʒɑ̃d/ *nf* **(a)** legend
(b) (accompanying picture) caption; (on map) key
(c) tall story

léger, -ère /leʒe, ɛʀ/ **1** *adj* **(a)** light; **se sentir plus ~** (figurative) to have a great weight off one's mind
(b) ⟨Culin⟩ ⟨meal⟩ light
(c) ⟨person⟩ nimble; ⟨step⟩ light
(d) ⟨laugh⟩ gentle; ⟨blow, knock⟩ soft; ⟨error, delay⟩ slight; ⟨taste, hope⟩ faint; ⟨wind, rain⟩ light; ⟨cloud⟩ thin; ⟨injury⟩ minor
(e) ⟨tea, drink⟩ weak; ⟨perfume, wine⟩ light; ⟨tobacco⟩ mild (GB), light (US)
(f) ⟨action⟩ ill-considered; ⟨remark⟩ thoughtless; ⟨argument, proof⟩ weak
(g) (colloq) **c'est un peu ~** it's a bit skimpy
(h) ⟨woman, way of life⟩ loose; ⟨husband, mood⟩ fickle
(i) (Mil) light
2 *adv* ⟨travel⟩ light; **cuisiner/manger ~** to cook/to eat light meals
3 **à la légère** *phr* (gen) without thinking; ⟨accuse⟩ rashly; **prendre qch à la légère** not to take sth seriously

légèrement /leʒɛʀmɑ̃/ *adv* **(a)** ⟨move⟩ gently; ⟨perfume⟩ lightly; ⟨tremble, injured⟩ slightly
(b) ⟨Culin⟩ ⟨eat⟩ lightly
(c) ⟨walk, run⟩ lightly, nimbly
(d) ⟨act, speak⟩ without thinking

légèreté /leʒɛʀte/ *nf* **(a)** lightness; nimbleness

(b) thoughtlessness; fickleness; **la ∼ de ses mœurs** his/her loose morals

légiférer /leʒifeʀe/ [14] *vi* to legislate

légion /leʒjɔ̃/ *nf* **(a)** (Mil) legion
 (b) army
 ■ **la Légion (étrangère)** the Foreign Legion

légionnaire /leʒjɔnɛʀ/ *nm* (Roman) legionary; (in Foreign Legion) legionnaire

législateur, -trice /leʒislatœʀ, tʀis/ *nm,f* legislator, law-maker

législatif, -ive /leʒislatif, iv/ *adj* legislative; **élections législatives** ≈ general election

législation /leʒislasjɔ̃/ *nf* legislation

législature /leʒislatyʀ/ *nf* **(a)** term of office
 (b) legislature

légiste /leʒist/ *nm* jurist

légitime /leʒitim/ *adj* **(a)** ⟨child, right⟩ legitimate; ⟨union, heir⟩ lawful
 (b) ⟨action⟩ legitimate; ⟨anger⟩ justifiable
 (c) ⟨reward⟩ just
 ■ **∼ défense** self-defence (GB)

légitimité /leʒitimite/ *nf* **(a)** legitimacy
 (b) (of an act) lawfulness

legs /lɛg/ *nm inv* (Law, gen) legacy; (of personal belongings) bequest

léguer /lege/ [14] *vtr* **(a)** (in one's will) to leave
 (b) to hand down ⟨traditions⟩; to pass on ⟨flaw⟩

légume /legym/ *nm* vegetable; **∼s secs** pulses

leitmotiv /lajtmɔtiv/ *nm* leitmotiv

Léman /lemɑ̃/ *n pr* **le lac ∼** Lake Geneva

lendemain /lɑ̃dəmɛ̃/ **1** *nm* **(a) le ∼, la journée du ∼** the following day; **dès le ∼** the (very) next day; **le ∼ de l'accident** the day after the accident; **du jour au ∼** overnight
 (b) au ∼ de (in the period) after; **au ∼ de la guerre** just after the war
 (c) le ∼ tomorrow, the future; **sans ∼** ⟨happiness, success⟩ short-lived
 2 **lendemains** *nm pl* **(a)** outcome; consequences
 (b) future; **des ∼s difficiles** difficult days ahead

lénifiant, ∼e /lenifjɑ̃, ɑ̃t/ *adj* soothing

lent, ∼e[1] /lɑ̃, ɑ̃t/ *adj* slow; ⟨film, vehicle⟩ slow-moving; ⟨poison⟩ slow-acting

lente[2] /lɑ̃t/ *nf* (Zool) nit

lentement /lɑ̃t(ə)mɑ̃/ *adv* slowly

lenteur /lɑ̃tœʀ/ *nf* slowness; **avec ∼** slowly

lentille /lɑ̃tij/ *nf* **(a)** (Bot, Culin) lentil
 (b) lens; **∼s de contact** contact lenses

léopard /leɔpaʀ/ *nm* **(a)** leopard
 (b) leopardskin

lèpre /lɛpʀ/ *nf* leprosy

lépreux, -euse /lepʀø, øz/ *nm,f* leper

lequel /ləkɛl/, **laquelle** /lakɛl/, lesquels *mpl*, **lesquelles** *fpl* /lekɛl/, (with à) **auquel, auxquels** *mpl*,

auxquelles *fpl* /okɛl/, (with de) **duquel** /dykɛl/, **desquels** *mpl*, **desquelles** *fpl* /dekɛl/ **1** **lequel, laquelle, lesquels, lesquelles** *adj* who; which; **il m'a présenté son cousin, ∼ cousin vit en Grèce** he introduced me to his cousin, who lives in Greece; **auquel cas** in which case
 2 *rel pron* who; which; **les gens contre lesquels ils luttaient** the people (who) they were fighting against
 3 *pron* which; **lesquels sont les plus compétents?** which are the most competent?

les ▶ LE

lesbienne /lɛsbjɛn/ *nf* lesbian

lesdites ▶ LEDIT

lesdits ▶ LEDIT

lèse-majesté /lɛzmaʒɛste/ *nf inv* lese-majesty

léser /leze/ [14] *vtr* to wrong ⟨person⟩; to prejudice ⟨interests⟩

lésiner /lezine/ [1] *vi* **ne pas ∼ sur** to be liberal with ⟨ingredients, money, compliments⟩

lésion /lezjɔ̃/ *nf* (Med) lesion

lesquels, lesquelles ▶ LEQUEL

lessive /lesiv/ *nf* **(a)** washing powder; washing liquid
 (b) washing

lessiver /lesive/ [1] *vtr* **(a)** to wash
 (b) (colloq) **être lessivé** to be washed out (colloq)

lessiveuse /lesivøz/ *nf* boiler, copper (GB)

lest /lɛst/ *nm* **(a)** ballast; **jeter** *or* **lâcher du ∼** to jettison ballast
 (b) (on fishing net) weight

leste /lɛst/ *adj* **(a)** ⟨person, animal⟩ agile, nimble
 (b) ⟨joke, remark⟩ risqué

lestement /lɛstəmɑ̃/ *adv* nimbly

lester /lɛste/ [1] *vtr* **(a)** to ballast
 (b) (colloq) to stuff sth

létal, ∼e, *mpl* **-aux** /letal, o/ *adj* lethal

léthargie /letaʀʒi/ *nf* lethargy

léthargique /letaʀʒik/ *adj* **(a)** ⟨person⟩ lethargic; ⟨industry⟩ sluggish
 (b) (Med) lethargic

lettre /lɛtʀ/ **1** *nf* **(a)** (of alphabet) letter; **∼ majuscule** *or* **capitale** capital letter; **∼ d'imprimerie** block letter; **en toutes ∼s** in full; **c'est écrit en toutes ∼s dans le rapport** it's down in black and white in the report; **les Romains furent des urbanistes avant la ∼** the Romans were city planners before the concept was invented; **à la ∼, au pied de la ∼** to the letter; **il prend tout ce qu'on lui dit à la ∼** he takes everything you say literally
 (b) (message) letter; **∼ de rupture** letter ending a relationship
 2 **lettres** *nf pl* **(a)** (university subject) French; (more general) arts (GB), humanities (US)
 (b) letters; **femme de ∼s** woman of letters; **avoir des ∼s** to be well read
 ■ **∼ explicative** covering letter; **∼ de** ····⟩

recommandation letter of recommendation; ~ **recommandée** registered letter; ~**s classiques** French and Latin; ~**s modernes** French language and literature
IDIOMS passer comme une ~ à la poste (colloq) ⟨reform⟩ to go through smoothly; ⟨excuse⟩ to be accepted without any questions

lettré, ~**e** /letʀe/ nm,f man/woman of letters

leu: à la queue leu leu /alakølølø/ phr in single file

leucémie /løsemi/ nf leukaemia

leur /lœʀ/ **1** pron them; il ~ a écrit he wrote to them; il ~ a fallu faire they had to do
2 det (pl **leurs**) their; un de ~s amis a friend of theirs; pendant ~ absence while they were away
3 le leur, la leur, les leurs pron theirs; c'est le ~ it's theirs; il est des ~s he's one of them; ils m'ont demandé d'être des ~s they asked me to come along; ils vivent loin des ~s they live far away from their families

leurre /lœʀ/ nm (a) illusion
(b) (in fishing, hunting) lure
(c) (Mil) decoy

leurrer /lœʀe/ [1] **1** vtr to delude
2 se leurrer v refl (+ v être) to delude oneself

levain /ləvɛ̃/ nm (fermenting agent) starter; (for bread) leaven (GB), sourdough (US)

levant /ləvɑ̃/ **1** adj m soleil ~ rising sun
2 nm east; au ~ in the east; du ~ au couchant from east to west

levé, ~**e**[1] /ləve/ **1** pp ▶ LEVER[1]
2 pp adj (a) voter à main ~e to vote by a show of hands
(b) up; elle est toujours la première ~e she's always the first up

levée[2] /ləve/ nf (a) (of embargo, sentence, martial law) lifting; (of diplomatic immunity) removal; (of secrecy, taboo) ending; (of session) close
(b) (of mail) collection
(c) (embankment) levee
■ ~ de boucliers outcry

lever[1] /ləve/ [16] **1** vtr (a) to raise; ~ la main or le doigt (for permission to speak) to put up one's hand; ~ la main sur qn to raise a hand to sb; ~ les bras au ciel to throw up one's hands; lève les pieds quand tu marches! don't drag your feet!; ~ les yeux or la tête to look up
(b) to lift ⟨object⟩; to raise ⟨barrier⟩; ~ son verre to raise one's glass
(c) (out of bed) to get [sb] up ⟨child, sick person⟩
(d) to lift ⟨embargo, restriction⟩; to raise ⟨siege⟩; to end ⟨taboo, secret⟩; to remove ⟨obstacle⟩; to close ⟨session⟩
(e) to levy ⟨tax⟩
(f) to flush out ⟨game, partridges⟩
2 vi (a) (Culin) ⟨dough⟩ to rise

(b) ⟨seedlings, corn⟩ to come up
3 se lever v refl (+ v être) (a) to get up
(b) to stand up; se ~ de table to leave the table
(c) ⟨person, people⟩ to rise up
(d) ⟨sun⟩ to rise; le jour se lève it's getting light
(e) ⟨wind⟩ to rise
(f) ⟨fog, mist⟩ to clear; ⟨weather⟩ to clear up

lever[2] /ləve/ nm (a) être là au ~ des enfants to be there when the children get up
(b) au ~ du jour at daybreak

lève-tard /lɛvtaʀ/ nmf inv late riser

lève-tôt /lɛvto/ nmf inv early riser

levier /ləvje/ nm lever; soulever qch avec un ~ to lever sth up.
■ ~ de changement de vitesse (Aut) gear lever (GB), gear stick (US); ~ de commande control stick

lévitation /levitasjɔ̃/ nf levitation

lèvre /lɛvʀ/ nf lip; avoir le sourire aux ~s to be smiling; du bout des ~s ⟨eat⟩ half-heartedly; ⟨reply⟩ grudgingly
IDIOMS être suspendu aux ~s de qn to hang on sb's every word

lévrier /levʀije/ nm greyhound

levure /ləvyʀ/ nf yeast; ~ chimique baking powder

lexical, ~**e**, mpl **-aux** /lɛksikal, o/ adj lexical

lexique /lɛksik/ nm (a) glossary; (bilingual) vocabulary (book)
(b) lexicon, lexis

lézard /lezaʀ/ nm (a) lizard
(b) lizardskin

lézarde /lezaʀd/ nf crack

lézarder /lezaʀde/ [1] **1** vtr to crack
2 vi (colloq) ~ au soleil to bask in the sun
3 se lézarder v refl (+ v être) to crack

liaison /ljɛzɔ̃/ nf (a) link; la ~ Calais–Douvres the Calais–Dover line
(b) ~ radio radio contact; ~ satellite satellite link
(c) assurer la ~ entre différents services to liaise between different services
(d) (love) affair
(e) (between words) liaison

liane /ljan/ nf creeper, liana

liant, ~**e** /ljɑ̃, ɑ̃t/ adj sociable

liasse /ljas/ nf (of banknotes) wad; (of letters, papers, documents) bundle

Liban /libɑ̃/ pr nm Lebanon

libellé /libɛle/ nm wording

libeller /libɛle/ [1] vtr (a) to draw up ⟨contract⟩
(b) to word ⟨article⟩
(c) to make out ⟨cheque⟩

libellule /libɛllyl/ nf dragonfly

libéral, ~**e**, mpl **-aux** /libeʀal, o/ adj
(a) liberal
(b) (in politics) Liberal
(c) free-market

libéralisation /liberalizasjɔ̃/ *nf*
liberalization; ~ **des mœurs** relaxation of
moral standards

libéraliser /liberalize/ [1] **1** *vtr* to
liberalize
2 se libéraliser *v refl* (+ *v être*) ⟨*country,
attitudes*⟩ to become more liberal

libéralisme /liberalism/ *nm* liberalism

libéralité /liberalite/ *nf* liberality

libérateur, -trice /liberatœr, tris/
1 *adj* liberating
2 *nm,f* (de pays, ville, personne) liberator

libération /liberasjɔ̃/ *nf* (a) (of prisoner,
hostage) release
(b) (of country, population) liberation; ~ **des
femmes** women's liberation
(c) relief
(d) (of prices) deregulation

Libération /liberasjɔ̃/ *nf* (of 1944) **la** ~ the
Liberation

libéré, ~e /libere/ **1** *pp* ▶ LIBÉRER
2 *pp adj* (a) ⟨*man, woman*⟩ liberated
(b) ⟨*country, area, town*⟩ free
(c) ⟨*post, premises*⟩ vacant

libérer /libere/ [14] **1** *vtr* (a) to liberate
⟨*country, town*⟩; to free ⟨*companion, hostage*⟩
(b) to release ⟨*prisoner, hostage*⟩; to free
⟨*slave, animal*⟩
(c) to allow [sb] to go ⟨*employee*⟩
(d) to liberate ⟨*person, imagination*⟩; (of post,
duties) to relieve ⟨*minister*⟩; ~ **qn de
l'emprise de qn** to get sb away from sb's
influence
(e) to release ⟨*emotion*⟩; to give free rein to
⟨*imagination*⟩
(f) to relieve ⟨*mind, person*⟩; ~ **sa
conscience** to unburden oneself
(g) to vacate ⟨*apartment, office*⟩; ~ **la
chambre avant midi** (in hotel) to check out
before noon
(h) to free ⟨*arm, hand*⟩; to release ⟨*spring,
catch*⟩
(i) to liberalize ⟨*economy, trade*⟩; to
deregulate ⟨*prices*⟩; ~ **les loyers** to lift rent
controls
(j) to release ⟨*gas, energy*⟩
2 se libérer *v refl* (+ *v être*) (a) to free
oneself/itself; **se** ~ **d'une dette** to pay a debt
(b) **j'essaierai de me** ~ **mercredi** I'll try and
be free on Wednesday

libertaire /libɛrtɛr/ *adj, nmf* libertarian

liberté /libɛrte/ *nf* (a) (gen) freedom; **être
en** ~ to be free; **élever des animaux en** ~ to
raise animals in a natural habitat; **espèce
vivant en** ~ species in the wild; **l'assassin
est toujours en** ~ the killer is still at large;
prendre la ~ **de faire** to take the liberty of
doing; ~ **de pensée** freedom of thought
(b) (Law) **mettre qn en** ~ **conditionnelle** to
release sb on parole; **mise en** ~ **surveillée**
release on probation

libertin, ~e /libɛrtɛ̃, in/ *adj, nm,f*
libertine

libido /libido/ *nf* libido

libraire /librɛr/ *nmf* bookseller

librairie /librɛri/ *nf* (a) bookshop (GB),
bookstore
(b) bookselling business

librairie-papeterie, *pl* **librairies-
papeteries** /librɛripapetri/ *nf*
stationer's and bookshop

libre /libr/ *adj* (a) ⟨*person, country*⟩ free;
~ **à elle de partir** it's up to her whether she
goes or not; **être** ~ **de ses actes** to do as one
wishes
(b) ⟨*person*⟩ free and easy; ⟨*manner*⟩ free;
⟨*opinion*⟩ candid; ⟨*morality*⟩ easygoing
(c) ⟨*hand, thumb*⟩ free; ⟨*road, way*⟩ clear
(d) ⟨*person, room*⟩ available; ⟨*seat*⟩ free
(e) ⟨*WC*⟩ vacant; **la ligne n'est pas** ~ (on
telephone) the number is engaged (GB) *or*
busy (US)
■ ~ **arbitre** free will; ~ **circulation** freedom of
movement
IDIOMS **être** ~ **comme l'air** to be as free as a
bird

libre-échange /librɛʃɑ̃ʒ/ *nm* free trade

librement /librəmɑ̃/ *adv* freely

libre-service, *pl* **libres-services**
/librəsɛrvis/ **1** *adj inv* self-service
2 *nm* (a) **le** ~ self-service
(b) self-service shop (GB) *or* store (US); self-
service restaurant
■ ~ **bancaire** automatic teller

lice /lis/ *nf* **être en** ~ to have entered the
lists

licence /lisɑ̃s/ *nf* (a) (bachelor's) degree;
~ **en droit** law degree
(b) (Law) licence (GB); **produit sous** ~
licensed product

licencié, ~e /lisɑ̃sje/ **1** *pp* ▶ LICENCIER
2 *pp adj* ⟨*student*⟩ graduate
3 *nm,f* (a) graduate (GB), college graduate
(US)
(b) ~ **(économique)** redundant employee
(GB), laid-off worker

licenciement /lisɑ̃simɑ̃/ *nm* dismissal;
~ **(économique)** redundancy (GB), lay-off;
~ **abusif** unfair dismissal; ~ **collectif** mass
redundancy; ~ **sec** compulsory redundancy
(*without compensation*)

licencier /lisɑ̃sje/ [2] *vtr* (a) to make [sb]
redundant (GB), to lay [sb] off
(b) to dismiss (GB), to let [sb] go

licencieux, -ieuse /lisɑ̃sjø, øz/ *adj*
licentious

lichen /likɛn/ *nm* lichen

licite /lisit/ *adj* lawful

licorne /likɔrn/ *nf* unicorn

lie /li/ *nf* (a) dregs, lees
(b) (figurative) dregs

lie-de-vin /lidvɛ̃/ *adj inv* wine-coloured
(GB)

liège /ljɛʒ/ *nm* cork; **bouchon en** ~ cork

liégeois, ~e /ljeʒwa, az/ *adj* of Liège;
café ~ *iced coffee topped with whipped cream*

lien /ljɛ̃/ *nm* (a) strap; string
(b) connection, link (**entre** between) ····▷

(c) (gen) link, tie (**avec** with); (emotional) tie, bond; **~s économiques** economic links; **~s de parenté** family ties

lier /lje/ [1] **①** *vtr* **(a)** to tie (sb/sth) up; **il avait les mains liées** his hands were tied **(b)** to bind; **ils sont très liés** they are very close **(c)** to link ‹*ideas, events*› **(d)** **~ amitié avec qn** to strike up a friendship with sb **(e)** (Mus) to slur ‹*notes*› **②** **se lier** *v refl* (+ *v être*) to make friends

lierre /ljɛʀ/ *nm* ivy

liesse /ljɛs/ *nf* jubilation; **en ~** jubilant

lieu /ljø/ **①** *nm* **(a)** (*pl* **~x**) place; **~ de passage** thoroughfare; **en tous ~x** everywhere; **en ~ et place de qn** ‹*sign, act*› on behalf of sb; **en dernier ~** lastly; **avoir ~** to take place; **tenir ~ de** to serve as ‹*bedroom, study*›; **il y a ~ de s'inquiéter** there is cause for anxiety; **s'il y a ~** if necessary; **donner ~ à** to cause ‹*scandal*› **(b)** (*pl* **~s**) coley **②** **au lieu de** *phr* instead of **③** **lieux** *nm pl* **(a)** **sur les ~x** at *or* on the scene; on the spot; **repérer les ~x** to have a scout around **(b)** premises; **visiter les ~x** to visit the premises ■ **~ commun** platitude; **~ public** public place

lieue /ljø/ *nf* league; **~ marine** marine league **IDIOMS j'étais à cent** *or* **mille ~s d'imaginer** I never for a moment imagined

lieutenant /ljøtnɑ̃/ *nm* **(a)** (Mil) (in army) ≈ lieutenant (GB), ≈ first lieutenant (US); (in air force) ≈ flying officer (GB), ≈ first lieutenant (US) **(b)** (on boat) first officer

lièvre /ljɛvʀ/ *nm* (Zool) hare **IDIOMS courir plusieurs ~s à la fois** to try to do too many things at once

lifting /liftiŋ/ *nm* face-lift

ligament /ligamɑ̃/ *nm* ligament

ligaturer /ligatyʀe/ [1] *vtr* (Med) to tie

lignage /liɲaʒ/ *nm* lineage

ligne /liɲ/ *nf* **(a)** (gen) line; **lire les ~s de la main de qn** to read sb's palm; **~ droite** straight line; (driving) straight piece of road; **la dernière ~ droite avant l'arrivée** the home straight; **je vous écris ces quelques ~s pour vous dire...** this is just a quick note to tell you...; **à la ~!** new paragraph! **(b)** (in public transport) service; route; (of train, underground) line; **~ de chemin de fer** railway line; **~s intérieures** domestic flights **(c)** cable; **~ aérienne** overhead cable **(d)** (telephone) line **(e)** figure; **garder la ~** to stay slim **(f)** (of body) contours; (of face) shape; (of hills) outline; **la ~ aérodynamique d'une voiture** the aerodynamic lines of a car **(g)** (of clothes, furniture, style) look **(h)** outline; **raconter un événement dans ses grandes ~s** to give an outline of events **(i)** fishing line; **pêche à la ~** angling

(j) line; row; **les ~s ennemies** (Mil) the 'enemy lines **(k)** (Comput) **en ~** on line ■ **~ de conduite** line of conduct; **se donner comme ~ de conduite de faire** to make it a rule to do; **~ de démarcation** (Mil) demarcation line; **~ de mire** line of sight; **~ de tir** line of fire **IDIOMS être en première ~** to be in the front line; (figurative) to be in the firing line; **entrer en ~ de compte** to be taken into account

lignée /liɲe/ *nf* **(a)** descendants; lineage; **de haute ~** of noble descent **(b)** tradition

lignite /liɲit/ *nm* brown coal, lignite

ligoter /ligɔte/ [1] *vtr* to truss ‹*person*› up

ligue /lig/ *nf* league

liguer: se liguer /lige/ [1] *v refl* (+ *v être*) ‹*people*› to join forces

lilas /lila/ *adj inv, nm* lilac

lilliputien, -ienne /lilipysjɛ̃, ɛn/ *adj, nm,f* Lilliputian

limace /limas/ *nf* (Zool) slug

limaçon /limasɔ̃/ *nm* snail

limaille /limaj/ *nf* filings

limande /limɑ̃d/ *nf* (Zool) dab

limande-sole, *pl* **limandes-soles** /limɑ̃dsɔl/ *nf* (Zool) lemon sole

lime /lim/ *nf* **(a)** (Tech) file; **~ à ongles** nail file **(b)** (Bot) lime **(c)** (Zool) lima

limer /lime/ [1] **①** *vtr* **(a)** to file ‹*nail, metal*›; to file down ‹*key*› **(b)** to file through ‹*bars of cage*› **②** **se limer** *v refl* (+ *v être*) **se ~ les ongles** to file one's nails

limier /limje/ *nm* **(a)** bloodhound **(b)** (colloq) sleuth

limitatif, -ive /limitatif, iv/ *adj* limiting, restrictive

limitation /limitasjɔ̃/ *nf* (of power, liberty) limitation, restriction; (of prices, interest rates) control; **~ de vitesse** speed limit

limite /limit/ **①** *nf* **(a)** border **(b)** (of estate, piece of land) boundary; (of sea, forest, village) edge **(c)** limit; **connaître ses ~s** to know one's (own) limitations; **vraiment, il dépasse les ~s!** he's really going too far!; **à la ~, je préférerais qu'il refuse** I'd almost prefer it if he refused **(d)** **à la ~ de** on the verge of; **activités à la ~ de la légalité** activities bordering on the illegal **(e)** **dans une certaine ~** up to a point, to a certain extent; **dans la ~ de, dans les ~s de** within the limits of **②** **(-)limite** (*combining form*) **date(-)~** deadline; **date(-)~ de vente** sell-by date; **vitesse(-)~** maximum speed ■ **~ d'âge** age limit

limiter /limite/ [1] **①** *vtr* to limit, to

restrict ⟨*power, duration, number*⟩; **cela limite nos possibilités** that rather limits our scope

2 se limiter *v refl* (+ *v être*) **(a) se ~ à deux verres de bière par jour** to limit oneself to two glasses of beer a day; **je me limiterai à quelques observations** I'll confine myself to a few observations
(b) se ~ à to be limited to; **la vie ne se limite pas au travail** there's more to life than work

limitrophe /limitʀɔf/ *adj* ⟨*country, region*⟩ adjacent; ⟨*city*⟩ border

limoger /limɔʒe/ [13] *vtr* to dismiss

limon /limɔ̃/ *nm* **(a)** silt
(b) (on horse-drawn carriage) shaft

limonade /limɔnad/ *nf* lemonade (GB), lemon soda (US)

limousine /limuzin/ *nf* (Aut) limousine

limpide /lɛ̃pid/ *adj* **(a)** clear, limpid
(b) (figurative) ⟨*explanation, style*⟩ clear, lucid

limpidité /lɛ̃pidite/ *nf* clarity

lin /lɛ̃/ *nm* **(a)** flax
(b) linen

linceul /lɛ̃sœl/ *nm* shroud

linéaire /lineɛʀ/ *adj* linear

linge /lɛ̃ʒ/ *nm* **(a)** linen; **~ sale** dirty linen
(b) washing; **corde** *or* **fil à ~** clothes line
(c) ~ (de corps) underwear
(d) cloth
■ **~ de maison** household linen; **~ de toilette** bathroom linen

lingère /lɛ̃ʒɛʀ/ *nf* laundry woman

lingerie /lɛ̃ʒʀi/ *nf* **(a)** linen room
(b) lingerie

lingot /lɛ̃go/ *nm* ingot

linguiste /lɛ̃gɥist/ *nmf* linguist

linguistique /lɛ̃gɥistik/ **1** *adj* linguistic
2 *nf* linguistics

linotte /linɔt/ *nf* linnet

linteau, *pl* **~x** /lɛ̃to/ *nm* lintel

lion /ljɔ̃/ *nm* lion; **~ de mer** sealion
IDIOMS **avoir mangé du ~** (colloq) to be full of beans (GB) (colloq), to be full of pep (US) (colloq)

Lion /ljɔ̃/ *pr nm* Leo

lionceau, *pl* **~x** /ljɔ̃so/ *nm* lion cub

lionne /ljɔn/ *nf* lioness

lipide /lipid/ *nm* lipid

liquéfier /likefje/ [2] *vtr*, **se liquéfier** *v refl* (+ *v être*) to liquefy

liquette /likɛt/ *nf* (colloq) shirt

liqueur /likœʀ/ *nf* liqueur

liquidation /likidasjɔ̃/ *nf* **(a)** (Law) (of property) liquidation; (of debts) settlement
(b) clearance; **~ totale (du stock)** total clearance

liquide /likid/ **1** *adj* **(a)** liquid; **miel ~** clear honey
(b) argent ~ cash
2 *nm* **(a)** liquid
(b) cash

■ **~ correcteur** correction fluid, white-out (fluid) (US); **~ de frein** brake fluid

liquider /likide/ [1] *vtr* **(a)** to settle ⟨*accounts*⟩; to liquidate ⟨*company, business*⟩
(b) to clear ⟨*goods, stock*⟩
(c) (colloq) to liquidate (colloq) ⟨*enemy, witness*⟩
(d) (colloq) to demolish ⟨*meal*⟩; to empty ⟨*glass*⟩

liquidité /likidite/ *nf* **des ~s** liquid assets

lire¹ /liʀ/ [66] *vtr* to read; **~ qch en diagonale** to skim through sth; **~ sur les lèvres de qn** to lip-read what sb is saying; **~ dans les pensées de qn** to read sb's mind

lire² /liʀ/ *nf* lira

lis /lis/ *nm inv* lily

liseré /lizʀe/ *nm*, **liséré** /lizeʀe/ *nm* (on dress) edging; piping

liseron /lizʀɔ̃/ *nm* bindweed, convolvulus

liseuse /lizøz/ *nf* **(a)** bed jacket
(b) small reading lamp

lisible /lizibl/ *adj* **(a)** legible
(b) readable

lisière /lizjɛʀ/ *nf* **(a)** (of wood, field) edge; (of village) outskirts
(b) (on piece of fabric) selvage

lisse /lis/ *adj* ⟨*skin, surface*⟩ smooth; ⟨*tyre*⟩ worn

lisser /lise/ [1] *vtr* to smooth ⟨*hair, garment*⟩; to stroke ⟨*beard*⟩

liste /list/ *nf* (gen) list; (at election) list (of candidates) (GB), ticket (US)
■ **~ d'attente** waiting list; **~ électorale** electoral roll; **~ de mariage** wedding list
IDIOMS **être sur ~ rouge** to be ex-directory (GB), to have an unlisted number (US)

lister /liste/ [1] *vtr* to list

lit /li/ *nm* **(a)** bed; **~ à une place** *or* **d'une personne** single bed; **~ à deux places** *or* **de deux personnes** double bed; **aller** *or* **se mettre au ~** to go to bed; **garder le ~** to stay in bed; **tirer qn du ~** to drag sb out of bed; **au ~!** bedtime!; **~ métallique** iron bedstead; **le ~ n'était pas défait** the bed had not been slept in
(b) (Law) marriage
(c) (of river) bed; **la rivière est sortie de son ~** the river has overflowed its banks
■ **~ de camp** camp bed (GB), cot (US); **~ pliant** folding bed; **~s superposés** bunk beds

litanie /litani/ *nf* litany

literie /litʀi/ *nf* bedding

lithographie /litɔgʀafi/ *nf* **(a)** lithography
(b) lithograph

litière /litjɛʀ/ *nf* **(a)** (for cattle) litter; (for horses) bedding; (for cats) cat litter
(b) (mode of transport) litter

litige /litiʒ/ *nm* dispute; **point de ~** bone of contention; point at issue; **les parties en ~** the litigants

litigieux, -ieuse /litiʒjø, øz/ *adj* ⟨*case, point, argument*⟩ contentious

litre /litʀ/ *nm* **(a)** (measure) litre (GB)
(b) litre (GB) bottle

L

littéraire /liteRER/ **1** *adj* ⟨*work, criticism*⟩
literary; **études ~s** arts studies
2 *nm,f* (a) literary person
(b) arts *or* liberal arts (US) student

littéral, **~e**, *mpl* **-aux** /literal, o/ *adj*
literal

littéralement /literalmɑ̃/ *adv* literally;
verbatim

littérature /literatyR/ *nf* literature

littoral, **~e**, *mpl* **-aux** /litɔral, o/ **1** *adj*
coastal
2 *nm* coast

liturgie /lityRʒi/ *nf* liturgy

livide /livid/ *adj* deathly pale

living /liviŋ/ *nm* living-room

livraison /livRɛzõ/ *nf* delivery; **'~s à
domicile'** 'we deliver'; **il est venu prendre ~
de la commande** he came to pick up the
order

livre¹ /livR/ *nm* book; **c'est mon ~ de
chevet** it's my bedside book; (figurative) it's my
bible
■ **~ blanc** blue book; **~ de bord** logbook;
~ d'or visitors' book; **~ de poche®**
paperback; **~ scolaire** schoolbook

livre² /livR/ *nf* (a) pound; **~ sterling** pound
sterling; **~ irlandaise** Irish pound, punt
(b) (unit of weight) half a kilo; (in UK) pound

livrée /livre/ *nf* livery

livrer /livre/ [1] **1** *vtr* (a) to deliver
⟨*goods*⟩; **~ qn** to deliver sb's order
(b) to hand [sb] over ⟨*criminal*⟩; to betray
⟨*accomplice, secret*⟩
(c) **être livré à soi-même** to be left to one's
own devices
(d) **il nous livre un peu de lui-même** he
reveals something of himself
2 **se livrer** *v refl* (+ *v être*) (a) **se ~ à un
trafic de drogue** to engage in drug trafficking
(b) **se ~ à** ⟨*criminal*⟩ to give oneself up to
(c) **se ~ à un ami** to confide in a friend

livret /livRɛ/ *nm* (a) booklet
(b) libretto
■ **~ de caisse d'épargne** ≈ savings book (GB),
bankbook (*for a savings account*) (US); **~ de
famille** family record book (*of births,
marriages and deaths*)

livreur, **-euse** /livRœR, øz/ *nm,f* delivery
man/woman

lobe /lɔb/ *nm* lobe; **~ de l'oreille** ear lobe

local, **~e**, *pl* **-aux** /lɔkal, o/ **1** *adj*
⟨*newspaper, authorities*⟩ local; ⟨*pain,
showers*⟩ localized
2 *nm* (a) place; **les scouts ont besoin d'un
~** the scouts need a place to meet
(b) **~ commercial** commercial premises; **les
locaux du journal** the newspaper offices

localement /lɔkalmɑ̃/ *adv* on a local
level; **appliquer la crème ~** apply the cream
locally

localisation /lɔkalizasjõ/ *nf* (a) location
(b) **la ~ d'un incendie** localizing a fire

localiser /lɔkalize/ [1] *vtr* (a) to locate
⟨*person, noise*⟩

(b) to confine, to localize ⟨*fire*⟩

localité /lɔkalite/ *nf* locality

locataire /lɔkatɛR/ *nmf* tenant

locatif, **-ive** /lɔkatif, iv/ *adj* rental

location /lɔkasjõ/ *nf* (a) (by owner) renting
out; (by tenant) renting; **agence de ~** rental
agency
(b) rented accommodation
(c) rent
(d) (of equipment) hire; **~ de voitures** car hire,
car rental; **contrat de ~** rental agreement;
~ de vidéos video rental
(e) (of theatre seats) reservation, booking (GB)

location-vente, *pl* **locations-
ventes** /lɔkasjõvɑ̃t/ *nf* 100% mortgage
scheme

locomotion /lɔkɔmɔsjõ/ *nf* locomotion

locomotive /lɔkɔmɔtiv/ *nf* engine,
locomotive; **~ à vapeur** steam engine

locuteur, **-trice** /lɔkytœR, tRis/ *nm,f*
speaker

locution /lɔkysjõ/ *nf* phrase; idiom

logarithme /lɔgaRitm/ *nm* logarithm, log

loge /lɔʒ/ *nf* (a) (caretaker's dwelling) lodge
(b) (of actor) dressing room; (in theatre) box
(c) (in freemasonry) Lodge
(d) loggia

logé, **~e** /lɔʒe/ **1** *pp* ▶ LOGER
2 *pp adj* housed; **être ~, nourri, blanchi** to
have bed, board and one's laundry done

logement /lɔʒmɑ̃/ *nm* (a) accommodation;
~ individuel flat (GB), apartment (US); house
(b) housing; **la crise du ~** the housing crisis

loger /lɔʒe/ [13] **1** *vtr* (a) to house ⟨*student*⟩
(b) to put [sb] up ⟨*friend*⟩; to provide
accommodation for ⟨*refugees*⟩
(c) ⟨*hotel*⟩ to have accommodation for
(d) to put; **je n'ai pas pu ~ tous mes
meubles dans le salon** I couldn't fit all my
furniture in the living room
(e) **~ une balle dans la tête de qn** to shoot sb
in the head
2 *vi* (a) to live
(b) to stay; **~ à l'hôtel** to stay at a hotel
3 **se loger** *v refl* (+ *v être*) (a) to find
accommodation; **se nourrir et se ~** to pay for
food and accommodation
(b) **se ~ dans qch** to get stuck in sth; ⟨*dust*⟩
to collect in sth; **la balle est venue se ~ dans
le genou** the bullet lodged in his/her knee

logeur, **-euse** /lɔʒœR, øz/ *nm,f* lodger

loggia /lɔdʒja/ *nf* loggia

logiciel /lɔʒisjɛl/ *nm* (a) software; **~ de
base** system(s) software
(b) program
(c) (Comput) **~ de navigation** browser

logique /lɔʒik/ **1** *adj* (a) logical; **il n'est
pas ~ avec lui-même** he is not consistent
(b) (colloq) reasonable; **ce serait ~ qu'ils
soient en colère** one could understand why
they would be angry
2 *nf* logic; **manquer de ~** to be illogical;
c'est dans la ~ des choses it's in the nature
of things; **en toute ~** logically

logiquement /lɔʒikmɑ̃/ *adv* logically

logis /lɔʒi/ *nm inv* home, dwelling

logistique /lɔʒistik/ *nf* logistics

logo /lɔgo/ *nm* logo

loi /lwa/ *nf* **(a)** law; **voter une ~** to pass a law
(b) la ~ the law; **enfreindre la ~** to break the law; **tomber sous le coup de la ~** to be *or* constitute an offence (GB); **faire la ~** (figurative) to lay down the law
(c) rule; law; **la ~ du milieu** the law of the underworld; **c'est la ~ des séries** things always happen in a row
■ **~ d'amnistie** *act granting amnesty to some offenders*; **~ communautaire** community law; **~ informatique et libertés** data protection act; **~ de la jungle** law of the jungle

loin /lwɛ̃/ **1** *adv* **(a)** a long way, far (away); **c'est ~** it's a long way; **c'est trop ~** it's too far; **il habite plus ~** he lives further *or* farther away; **du plus ~ qu'il m'aperçut** as soon as he saw me; **voir plus ~** (in text) see below
(b) (in time) **tout cela est bien ~** that was all a long time ago; **aussi ~ que je me souvienne** as far back as I can remember; **l'été n'est plus très ~ maintenant** summer isn't far off now
(c) (figurative) **de là à dire qu'il est incompétent il n'y a pas ~** that comes close to saying he's incompetent; **il n'est pas bête, ~ s'en faut!** he's not stupid, far from it!; **ça va beaucoup plus ~** it goes much further
2 loin de *phr* **(a)** (in space) far from; **est-ce encore ~ d'ici?** is it much further *or* farther from here?
(b) (in time) far from; **cela ne fait pas ~ de quatre ans que je suis ici** I've been here for almost four years now
(c) (figurative) far from, a long way from; **~ de moi cette idée!** nothing could be further from my mind!; **avec l'imprimante, il faut compter pas ~ de 50 000 francs** if you include the printer, you're talking about 50,000 francs or thereabouts
3 de loin *phr* from a distance; **je ne vois pas très bien de ~** I can't see very well at a distance; **c'est de ~ ton meilleur roman** it's by far your best novel
4 au loin *phr* **au ~** in the distance
5 de loin en loin *phr* **(a)** **on pouvait voir des maisons de ~ en ~** you could see houses scattered here and there
(b) every now and then
IDIOMS **~ des yeux, ~ du cœur** (Proverb) out of sight, out of mind

lointain, ~e /lwɛ̃tɛ̃, ɛn/ **1** *adj*
(a) ⟨*country, past*⟩ distant
(b) ⟨*link*⟩ remote
(c) ⟨*person*⟩ distant
2 *nm* background; **dans le ~** ⟨*see, hear*⟩ in the distance

loir /lwaʀ/ *nm* (edible) dormouse

loisir /lwaziʀ/ *nm* **(a)** spare time; **(tout) à ~** at (great) leisure

(b) avoir tout ~ de faire to have plenty of time to do
(c) leisure activity

lombaire /lɔ̃bɛʀ/ *nf* lumbar vertebra

londonien, -ienne /lɔ̃dɔnjɛ̃, ɛn/ *adj* (of) London

Londres /lɔ̃dʀ/ *pr n* London

long, longue /lɔ̃, lɔ̃g/ **1** *adj* long; **plus/ trop ~ de deux mètres** two metres (GB) longer/too long; **être ~** (à faire) ⟨*person*⟩ to be slow (to do); **être en longue maladie** to be on extended sick leave; **il guérira, mais ce sera ~** he will get better, but it's going to take a long time; **être ~ à la détente** (colloq) to be slow on the uptake (colloq)
2 *adv* **(a) en dire ~/trop ~/plus ~** to say a lot/too much/more (**sur qn/qch** about sb/sth)
(b) s'habiller ~ to wear longer skirts
3 *nm* **(a) un câble de six mètres de ~** a cable six metres (GB) long, a six-metre (GB) long cable; **en ~** lengthwise; **en ~ et en large** ⟨*tell*⟩ in great detail; **marcher de ~ en large** to pace up and down; **en ~, en large et en travers** (colloq) ⟨*tell*⟩ at great length; **le ~ du mur** along the wall; up *or* down the wall; **tomber de tout son ~** to fall flat (on one's face)
4 à la longue *phr* in the end, eventually
■ **~ métrage** feature-length film

long-courrier, pl ~s /lɔ̃kuʀje/ *nm*
(a) ocean-going ship
(b) long-haul aircraft

longer /lɔ̃ʒe/ [13] *vtr* **(a)** ⟨*person, train*⟩ to go along ⟨*forest, coast*⟩; to follow ⟨*river*⟩
(b) ⟨*garden, road*⟩ to run alongside ⟨*lake, field*⟩

longévité /lɔ̃ʒevite/ *nf* longevity

longiligne /lɔ̃ʒiliɲ/ *adj* lanky, rangy

longitude /lɔ̃ʒityd/ *nf* longitude

longitudinal, ~e, *mpl* -aux /lɔ̃ʒitydinal, o/ *adj* longitudinal, lengthwise

longtemps /lɔ̃tɑ̃/ *adv* ⟨*wait, sleep*⟩ (for) a long time; **il t'a fallu ~?** did it take you long?; **~ avant/après** long before/after; **je peux te garder plus ~?** can I keep it a bit longer?; **il n'y a pas ~ qu'il travaille ici** he hasn't worked here long; **il y a** *or* **ça fait ~ qu'il n'a pas téléphoné** he hasn't phoned for ages (colloq); **il est mort depuis ~** he died a long time ago; **il n'y a pas si ~ c'était encore possible** it was still possible until quite recently

longue ▶ LONG 1, 4

longuement /lɔ̃gmɑ̃/ *adv* ⟨*hesitate, talk*⟩ for a long time; ⟨*explain, interview*⟩ at length

longueur /lɔ̃gœʀ/ **1** *nf* **(a)** (in space, time) length; **la maison est tout en ~** the house is long and narrow; **traîner en ~** ⟨*film, book*⟩ to go on forever
(b) (in race, swimming) length; **avoir une ~ d'avance sur qn** (Sport) to be one length ahead of sb; (figurative) to be ahead of sb; **le saut en ~** the long *or* broad (US) jump
(d) length

2 longueurs *nf pl* (in film, book, speech) overlong passages

3 à longueur de *phr* à ~ **de journée** all day long; à ~ **d'année** all year round; à ~ **d'émissions** programme (GB) after programme (GB)

■ ~ **d'onde** wavelength

longue-vue, *pl* **longues-vues** /lɔ̃gvy/ *nf* telescope

look /luk/ *nm* (colloq) look; image

looping /lupiŋ/ *nm* loop

lopin /lɔpɛ̃/ *nm* ~ **(de terre)** patch of land

loquace /lɔkas/ *adj* talkative, loquacious

loque /lɔk/ **1** *nf* ~ **(humaine)** (human) wreck

2 loques *nf pl* rags

loquet /lɔkɛ/ *nm* latch

lorgner /lɔʀɲe/ [1] *vtr* (colloq) to give [sb] the eye ⟨*person*⟩ (colloq); to cast longing glances at ⟨*jewel, cake*⟩; to have one's eye on ⟨*inheritance, job*⟩

lorgnette /lɔʀɲɛt/ *nf* **(a)** opera-glasses

(b) spy-glass

lorgnon /lɔʀɲɔ̃/ *nm* **(a)** lorgnette

(b) pince-nez

lors: lors de /lɔʀ/ *phr* **(a)** during

(b) at the time of

lorsque (lorsqu' *before vowel or mute h*) /lɔʀsk(ə)/ *conj* when

losange /lɔzɑ̃ʒ/ *nm* (shape) lozenge; **en** ~ diamond-shaped

lot /lo/ *nm* **(a)** (of inheritance) share; (of land) plot

(b) (in lottery) prize; **gagner le gros** ~ to hit the jackpot

(c) (of objects for sale) batch; (at auction) lot

(d) (of person) **être au-dessus du** ~ to be above the average

(e) fate, lot

loterie /lɔtʀi/ *nf* raffle; (in fair) tombola (GB), raffle (US); (large scale) lottery

loti, ~e /lɔti/ *adj* **bien/mal** ~ well/badly off

lotion /lɔsjɔ̃/ *nf* lotion

lotir /lɔtiʀ/ [3] *vtr* **terrain(s) à** ~ plots for sale

lotissement /lɔtismɑ̃/ *nm* housing estate (GB), subdivision (US)

loto /lɔto/ *nm* lotto; **le** ~ **national** national lottery

lotte /lɔt/ *nf* monkfish; (freshwater) burbot

lotus /lɔtys/ *nm inv* lotus

louable /luabl/ *adj* commendable, praiseworthy

louage /luaʒ/ *nm* **voiture de** ~ rented car (GB), rental car (US)

louange /luɑ̃ʒ/ *nf* praise

loubard /lubaʀ/ *nm* (colloq) hooligan, delinquent youth

louche /luʃ/ **1** *adj* ⟨*person, past, affair*⟩ shady; ⟨*place*⟩ seedy

2 *nf* ladle; ladleful

loucher /luʃe/ [1] *vi* to have a squint

louer /lue/ [1] *vtr* **(a)** ⟨*owner, landlord*⟩ to

let (GB), to rent out ⟨*house*⟩; to hire out ⟨*premises*⟩; to rent out ⟨*equipment*⟩; **'à** ~**'** 'for rent', 'to let' (GB)

(b) ⟨*tenant*⟩ to rent ⟨*house*⟩; to hire ⟨*room*⟩; to rent ⟨*equipment, film*⟩

(c) to hire ⟨*staff*⟩

(d) to praise; **Dieu soit loué** thank God

loufoque /lufɔk/ *adj* (colloq) crazy (colloq)

louis /lwi/ *nm inv* ~ **d'or** (gold) louis

loukoum /lukum/ *nm* Turkish delight

loulou /lulu/ *nm* **(a)** spitz

(b) (colloq) hooligan, delinquent youth

(c) (colloq) pet (GB) (colloq), honey (US)

loup /lu/ *nm* **(a)** wolf; **le grand méchant** ~ the big bad wolf; **à pas de** ~ stealthily

(b) ~ **(de mer)** (sea) bass

(c) domino, mask

■ **(vieux)** ~ **de mer** old salt, old tar

IDIOMS **avoir une faim de** ~ to be ravenous; **être connu comme le** ~ **blanc** to be known to everybody; **hurler avec les** ~**s** to follow the herd *or* crowd; **se jeter dans la gueule du** ~ to stick one's head in the lion's mouth; **les** ~**s ne se mangent pas entre eux** (Proverb) (there is) honour (GB) among thieves; **quand on parle du** ~ **(on en voit la queue)** (Proverb) speak of the devil; **l'homme est un** ~ **pour l'homme** (Proverb) dog eat dog

loupe /lup/ *nf* magnifying glass

louper (colloq) /lupe/ [1] **1** *vtr* **(a)** to miss ⟨*train, opportunity, visitor*⟩; **il n'en loupe pas une** he's always opening his big mouth

(b) to flunk (colloq) ⟨*exam*⟩; to screw up (colloq) ⟨*sauce, piece of work*⟩

2 *vi* **j'avais dit que ça se casserait, ça n'a pas loupé** I said it would break, and sure enough it did; **tu vas tout faire** ~ you'll mess everything up

loup-garou, *pl* **loups-garous** /lugaʀu/ *nm* werewolf

loupiote /lupjɔt/ *nf* (colloq) small lamp

lourd, ~e /luʀ, luʀd/ **1** *adj* **(a)** ⟨*person, object, metal*⟩ heavy

(b) ⟨*stomach, head, steps*⟩ heavy; ⟨*gesture*⟩ clumsy

(c) ⟨*meal, food*⟩ heavy; ⟨*wine*⟩ heady; ~ **à digérer** heavy on the stomach

(d) ⟨*equipment, weapons*⟩ heavy

(e) ⟨*fine, taxation*⟩ heavy

(f) ⟨*defeat, responsibility*⟩ heavy; ⟨*mistake*⟩ serious

(g) ⟨*administration, structure*⟩ unwieldy; ⟨*staff numbers*⟩ large

(h) ⟨*person, animal*⟩ ungainly; ⟨*body, object, architecture*⟩ heavy; ⟨*building*⟩ cumbersome, ponderous

(i) ⟨*joke*⟩ flat; ⟨*style*⟩ clumsy

(j) ⟨*atmosphere, silence*⟩ heavy; ⟨*heat*⟩ sultry

(k) **être** ~ **de dangers** to be fraught with danger

2 *adv* **(a)** **peser** ~ to weigh a lot; (figurative) to carry a lot of weight

(b) (of weather) **il fait** ~ it's close

(c) (colloq) **pas** ~ not a lot, not much; **dix personnes, ça ne fait pas** ~ ten people, that's not a lot

IDIOMS **avoir la main** ～**e** to be heavy-handed; **avoir la main** ～**e avec le sel/le parfum** to overdo the salt/the perfume

lourdement /luʀdəmɑ̃/ *adv* (a) heavily; **se tromper** ～ to be gravely mistaken
(b) **marcher** ～ to walk clumsily; **insister** ～ **sur** to keep going on about

lourdeur /luʀdœʀ/ *nf* (a) (of organization) complexity
(b) heaviness
(c) (of style) clumsiness; (in a text) clumsy expression
(d) weight
(e) (of person) oafishness; (of joke) poorness; (of architecture) ungainliness
(f) (of weather) closeness

loutre /lutʀ/ *nf* (a) otter
(b) otterskin

louve /luv/ *nf* she-wolf

louveteau, *pl* ～**x** /luvto/ *nm* (Zool) wolf cub

louvoyer /luvwaje/ [23] *vi* (a) ⟨ship⟩ to tack
(b) (figurative) to manoeuvre (GB), to maneuver (US)

lover: se lover /lɔve/ [1] *v refl* (+ *v être*) ⟨snake⟩ to coil itself up; ⟨person⟩ to curl up

loyal, ～**e**, *mpl* **-aux** /lwajal, o/ *adj*
(a) ⟨friend⟩ true; ⟨servant⟩ loyal, faithful
(b) ⟨procedure, conduct⟩ honest; ⟨competition, game⟩ fair

loyalisme /lwajalism/ *nm* loyalty

loyaliste /lwajalist/ *adj, nmf* loyalist

loyauté /lwajote/ *nf* (a) loyalty
(b) honesty

loyer /lwaje/ *nm* rent

lu, ～**e** /ly/ ▶ LIRE¹

lubie /lybi/ *nf* whim

lubricité /lybʀisite/ *nf* lechery; lewdness

lubrifiant /lybʀifjɑ̃/ *nm* lubricant

lubrifier /lybʀifje/ [2] *vtr* to lubricate

lubrique /lybʀik/ *adj* ⟨person⟩ lecherous; ⟨look, dance⟩ lewd

lucarne /lykaʀn/ *nf* (small) window; (in roof) skylight

lucide /lysid/ *adj* clear-sighted; lucid

lucidité /lysidite/ *nf* lucidity; clear-headedness; clarity; **juger en toute** ～ to judge without any illusions

luciole /lysjɔl/ *nf* firefly

lucratif, **-ive** /lykʀatif, iv/ *adj* lucrative

ludique /lydik/ *adj* ⟨activity⟩ play

ludothèque /lydɔtɛk/ *nf* toy library

luette /lyɛt/ *nf* uvula

lueur /lyœʀ/ *nf* (faint) light; **les** ～**s de la ville** the city lights; **à la** ～ **d'une bougie** by candlelight; **à la** ～ **des événements d'hier** in the light of yesterday's events; **les dernières** ～**s du soleil couchant** the dying glow of the sunset

luge /lyʒ/ *nf* (a) toboggan (GB), sled (US)
(b) (Sport) luge

lugubre /lygybʀ/ *adj* gloomy; mournful

lui¹ /lɥi/ *pron* ① *pron m* (a) he; **elle lit,** ～ **regarde la télévision** she's reading, he's watching TV; ～ **seul a le droit de parler** he alone has the right to talk
(b) him; **à cause de** ～ because of him; **je les vois plus souvent que** ～ I see them more often than he does; I see them more often than I see him; **c'est à** ～ it's his, it belongs to him; it's his turn; **c'est à** ～ **de choisir** it's up to him to choose
② *pron m/f* it; **le parti lance un appel, apportez-**～ **votre soutien** the party is launching an appeal—give it your support; **l'Espagne a signé, le Portugal,** ～**, n'a pas encore donné son accord** Spain has signed while Portugal hasn't yet agreed
③ *pron f* her; **je** ～ **ai annoncé la nouvelle** I told her the news

lui² /lɥi/ ▶ LUIRE

lui-même /lɥimɛm/ *pron* (a) (referring to person) himself; **'M. Greiner?'—'**～**'** (on phone) 'Mr Greiner?'—'speaking'
(b) (referring to object, concept) itself

luire /lɥiʀ/ [69] *vi* to shine; to glow; **leur regard luisait de colère** their eyes blazed with anger

luisant, ～**e** /lɥizɑ̃, ɑ̃t/ *adj* shining; glistening

lumbago /lœbago/ *nm* back pain

lumière /lymjɛʀ/ ① *nf* (a) light; ～ **naturelle/électrique** natural/electric light; **la** ～ **du jour** daylight; **il y a une** ～ **très particulière dans cette région** there's a very special quality to the light in this region; **les** ～**s de la ville** the city lights; **à la** ～ **d'une chandelle** by candlelight; **à la** ～ **des récents événements** in the light of recent events
(b) (person) **ce n'est pas une** ～ he'll never set the world on fire
② **lumières** *nf pl* (a) (of vehicle) lights
(b) (colloq) **j'ai besoin de vos** ～**s** I need to pick your brains

Lumières /lymjɛʀ/ *nf pl* **le siècle des** ～ the Age of Enlightenment

luminaire /lyminɛʀ/ *nm* light (fitting)

lumineux, **-euse** /lyminø, øz/ *adj*
(a) luminous; **panneau** ～ electronic display (board); **enseigne lumineuse** neon sign; **rayon** ～ ray of light
(b) **idée lumineuse** brilliant idea
(c) ⟨smile, gaze⟩ radiant

luminosité /lyminozite/ *nf* brightness, luminosity

lump /lœmp/ *nm* **œufs de** ～ lumpfish roe

lunaire /lynɛʀ/ *adj* lunar

lunatique /lynatik/ *nmf* moody person

lunch /lœʃ/ *nm* buffet (lunch); buffet (supper)

lundi /lœdi/ *nm* Monday

lune /lyn/ *nf* moon; **pleine** ～ full moon.
■ ～ **de miel** honeymoon; ～ **rousse** ≈ April moon
IDIOMS **être dans la** ～ (colloq) to have one's head in the clouds; **avoir l'air de tomber de la** ～ to look blank; **demander la** ～ (colloq) to ⋯▸

cry for the moon; **promettre la** ~ (colloq) to promise the earth; **décrocher la** ~ to do the impossible

luné, ~**e** /lyne/ adj (colloq) **mal** ~ grumpy

lunette /lynɛt/ **1** nf lavatory seat
2 lunettes nf pl **(a)** glasses
(b) (protective) goggles; ~**s de natation** swimming goggles
■ ~ **arrière** (Aut) rear window; ~**s noires** dark glasses; ~**s de soleil** sunglasses

lunule /lynyl/ nf (on nail) half-moon

lurette /lyRɛt/ nf (colloq) **il y a** or **cela fait belle** ~ **que je ne l'ai pas vue** it's been ages since I last saw her (colloq)

luron /lyRɔ̃/ nm fellow

lustre /lystR/ **1** nm **(a)** (gen) (decorative) ceiling light; (made of glass) chandelier
(b) sheen
(c) (of place, institution) prestigious image; **donner un nouveau** ~ **à** to give fresh appeal to
2 lustres nm pl (colloq) **depuis des** ~**s** for ages (colloq)

lustré, ~**e** /lystRe/ adj **(a)** glossy; (through wear) shiny
(b) ⟨fabric⟩ glazed

lustrer /lystRe/ [1] vtr to polish ⟨shoes, mirror⟩

luth /lyt/ nm **(a)** (Mus) lute
(b) (Zool) leatherback

luthier /lytje/ nm stringed instrument maker

lutin /lytɛ̃/ nm goblin

lutte /lyt/ nf **(a)** conflict; struggle; fight; ~ **d'influence** power struggle; **la** ~ **contre le cancer** the fight against cancer
(b) (Sport) wrestling
■ ~ **armée** armed conflict; ~ **de classes** class war; ~ **d'intérêts** clash of interests

lutter /lyte/ [1] vi to struggle; to fight; ~ **contre qn** to fight against sb; ~ **contre** to fight ⟨crime, unemployment, illness⟩; to fight against ⟨violence⟩; to contend with ⟨noise, bad weather⟩; **Louis luttait contre le sommeil** Louis was struggling to stay awake

lutteur, **-euse** /lytœR, øz/ nm,f (gen) fighter; (Sport) wrestler

luxation /lyksasjɔ̃/ nf dislocation

luxe /lyks/ nm luxury; **s'offrir le** ~ **de faire** to afford the luxury of doing; (figurative) to give oneself the satisfaction of doing; **je l'ai nettoyé et ce n'était pas du** ~ (colloq) I gave it a much needed clean; **avoir des goûts de** ~ to have expensive tastes

Luxembourg /lyksɑ̃buR/ pr nm Luxembourg

Luxembourgeois, ~**e** /lyksɑ̃buRʒwa, az/ nm,f **(a)** native of Luxembourg
(b) inhabitant of Luxembourg

luxer: se luxer /lykse/ [1] v refl (+ v être) **se** ~ **l'épaule** to dislocate one's shoulder

luxueux, **-euse** /lyksɥø, øz/ adj luxurious

luxure /lyksyR/ nf lust

luxuriant, ~**e** /lyksyRjɑ̃, ɑ̃t/ adj luxuriant

luzerne /lyzɛRn/ nf alfalfa, lucerne (GB)

lycée /lise/ nm secondary school (preparing students aged 15–18 for the baccalaureate)

lycéen, **-éenne** /liseɛ̃, ɛn/ nm,f secondary school student

lymphatique /lɛ̃fatik/ adj **(a)** lethargic
(b) lymphatic

lyncher /lɛ̃ʃe/ [1] vtr to lynch

lynx /lɛ̃ks/ nm inv lynx
IDIOMS **avoir un œil** or **des yeux de** ~ to have very keen eyesight

lyonnais, ~**e**[1] /ljɔnɛ, ɛz/ adj of Lyons

lyonnaise[2] /ljɔnɛz/ nf **(a)** (Culin) **à la** ~ à la lyonnaise
(b) regional game of boules

lyophiliser /ljofilize/ [1] vtr to freeze-dry

lyre /liR/ nf lyre

lyrique /liRik/ adj **(a)** (Mus) ⟨song, composer⟩ operatic; ⟨singer, season⟩ opera
(b) ⟨poetry, poet⟩ lyric; ⟨content, tone⟩ lyrical

lyrisme /liRism/ nm lyricism

lys /lis/ nm inv lily

M m

m, **M** /ɛm/ *nm inv* **(a)** (letter) m, M
 (b) (*written abbr* = **mètre**) 30 m 30 m
m' ▶ ME
M. (*written abbr* = **Monsieur**) Mr
ma ▶ MON
macabre /makabʀ/ *adj* macabre
macadam /makadam/ *nm* tarmac®
macaque /makak/ *nm* macaque
macaron /makaʀɔ̃/ *nm* **(a)** macaroon
 (b) lapel badge; sticker
macédoine /masedwan/ *nf* mixed diced
 vegetables
macérer /maseʀe/ [14] *vi* ⟨*plant, fruit*⟩ to
 soak, to steep; ⟨*meat*⟩ to marinate
mâche /maʃ/ *nf* corn salad, lamb's lettuce
mâcher /maʃe/ [1] *vtr* to chew
 IDIOMS ~ **la besogne** *or* **le travail à qn** to
 break the back of the work for sb; **il ne**
 mâche pas ses mots he doesn't mince his
 words
machette /maʃɛt/ *nf* machete
machiavélique /makjavelik/ *adj*
 Machiavellian
machin /maʃɛ̃/ *nm* (colloq) **(a)** thing,
 thingummy (colloq), whatsit (colloq)
 (b) old fogey
Machin, ~**e** /maʃɛ̃, in/ *nm,f* (colloq)
 what's-his-name (colloq)/what's-her-name
 (colloq)
machinal, ~**e**, *mpl* **-aux** /maʃinal, o/
 adj ⟨*gesture, reaction*⟩ mechanical
machination /maʃinasjɔ̃/ *nf* plot
machine /maʃin/ *nf* **(a)** machine; **taper à**
 la ~ to type; **coudre à la** ~ to machine-sew;
 faire deux ~**s (de linge)** (colloq) to do two
 loads of washing
 (b) (Naut) engine; **faire** ~ **arrière** to go astern;
 (figurative) to back-pedal
 ■ ~ **à calculer** calculating machine; ~ **à**
 coudre sewing machine; ~ **à écrire**
 typewriter; ~ **à laver** washing machine; ~ **à**
 laver la vaisselle dishwasher; ~ **à sous** slot
 machine, one-armed bandit
machinerie /maʃinʀi/ *nf* **(a)** machinery
 (b) machine room; (Naut) engine room
machiste /ma(t)ʃist/ *adj*, *nm* male
 chauvinist
mâchoire /maʃwaʀ/ *nf* jaw
mâchouiller /maʃuje/ [1] *vtr* (colloq) to
 chew (on)
maçon /masɔ̃/ *nm* bricklayer; builder;
 mason
maçonnerie /masɔnʀi/ *nf* building;
 bricklaying; masonry work
maculer /makyle/ [1] *vtr* to smudge; ~ **qch**
 de sang to spatter sth with blood

madame, *pl* **mesdames** /madam,
 medam/ *nf* **(a)** (addressing a woman whose name
 you do not know) **Madame** (in letter) Dear
 Madam; **bonsoir** ~**!** good evening!;
 mesdames et messieurs bonsoir good
 evening ladies and gentlemen
 (b) (addressing a woman whose name you know, for
 example Bon) Mrs, Ms; (in a letter) **Madame**
 Dear Ms Bon; **bonjour**, ~ good morning,
 Mrs Bon
 (c) (polite form of address) madam; '~ **a**
 sonné?' 'you rang, Madam?'
Madeleine /madlɛn/ *pr n* **pleurer comme**
 une ~ to cry one's eyes out
mademoiselle, *pl*
 mesdemoiselles /madmwazɛl,
 medmwazɛl/ *nf* **(a)** (addressing a woman whose
 name you do not know) **Mademoiselle** (in letter)
 Dear Madam; **bonjour**, ~**!** good morning!;
 mesdames, mesdemoiselles, messieurs
 ladies and gentlemen
 (b) (addressing a woman whose name you know, for
 example Bon) Miss, Ms; (in a letter)
 Mademoiselle Dear Miss Bon; **bonjour**, ~
 good morning, Miss Bon
 (c) (polite form of address) madam; '~ **a**
 sonné?' 'you rang, Madam?'
madone /madɔn/ *nf* madonna
madrier /madʀije/ *nm* beam
maestria /maɛstʀija/ *nf* brilliance,
 panache
maf(f)ia /mafja/ *nf* mafia; **la Mafia** the
 Mafia
maf(f)ieux, **-ieuse** /mafjø, øz/ *adj*
 mafia
magasin /magazɛ̃/ *nm* **(a)** shop, store;
 grand ~ department store; **faire les** ~**s** to go
 shopping
 (b) **avoir en** ~ to have in stock
magasinier, **-ière** /magazinje, ɛʀ/ *nm,f*
 (a) stock controller
 (b) warehouse keeper
magazine /magazin/ *nm* magazine
mage /maʒ/ *nm* magus; **les rois** ~**s** the
 (Three) Wise Men
maghrébin, ~**e** /magʀebɛ̃, in/ *adj* North
 African, Maghrebi
magicien, **-ienne** /maʒisjɛ̃, ɛn/ *nm,f*
 (a) magician/enchantress
 (b) conjuror
 (c) (figurative) wizard
magie /maʒi/ *nf* **(a)** magic
 (b) conjuring
magique /maʒik/ *adj* **(a)** magic; **formule**
 ~ magic words
 (b) (figurative) magical

m

magistère /maʒistɛʀ/ *nm: high-level University degree*

magistral, ~e, *mpl* **-aux** /maʒistʀal, o/ *adj* **(a)** brilliant; **réussir un coup ~** to bring off a masterstroke
(b) magisterial

magistrat /maʒistʀa/ *nm* magistrate

magistrature /maʒistʀatyʀ/ *nf*
(a) magistracy
(b) public office

magma /magma/ *nm* **(a)** magma
(b) (figurative) jumble

magnanime /maɲanim/ *adj* magnanimous

magnat /maɲa/ *nm* magnate, tycoon

magner: **se magner** /maɲe/ [1] *v refl* (+ *v être*) (slang) to get a move on (colloq)

magnésie /maɲezi/ *nf* magnesia

magnétique /maɲetik/ *adj* magnetic

magnétiser /maɲetize/ [1] *vtr* **(a)** to magnetize
(b) to hypnotize, to mesmerize

magnétiseur, -euse /maɲetizœʀ, øz/ *nm,f* healer

magnétisme /maɲetism/ *nm* magnetism

magnéto(phone) /maɲeto(fɔn)/ *nm* tape recorder

magnétoscope /maɲetoskɔp/ *nm* VCR, video recorder

magnificence /maɲifisɑ̃s/ *nf* magnificence, splendour (GB)

magnifier /maɲifje/ [1] *vtr* **(a)** to idealize ‹*memory*›, ‹*feeling*›
(b) to glorify ‹*heroism*›, ‹*act*›

magnifique /maɲifik/ *adj* gorgeous, magnificent

magot /mago/ *nm* (colloq) pile (of money) (colloq)

magouille /maguj/ *nf* (colloq) **(a)** wangling (colloq), fiddling (colloq)
(b) trick; **~s politiques** political skulduggery; **~s électorales** election rigging

magret /magʀɛ/ *nm* **~ de canard** duck breast

Mahomet /maɔme/ *pr n* Mohammed

mai /mɛ/ *nm* May; **le premier ~** May Day

maigre /mɛgʀ/ **1** *adj* **(a)** ‹*person*› thin
(b) ‹*meat*› lean; ‹*cheese*› low-fat
(c) ‹*day*› without meat; **faire** *or* **manger ~** to abstain from meat
(d) ‹*talents, savings*› meagre (GB); ‹*applause*› scant
(e) ‹*lawn, hair*› sparse
2 *nmf* thin man/woman; **c'est une fausse ~** she looks thinner than she is

maigrement /mɛgʀəmɑ̃/ *adv* ‹*paid*› poorly

maigreur /mɛgʀœʀ/ *nf* **(a)** thinness
(b) meagreness (GB)

maigrichon, -onne /mɛgʀiʃɔ̃, ɔn/ *adj* skinny

maigrir /mɛgʀiʀ/ [3] *vi* to lose weight

mail /maj/ *nm* **(a)** mall

(b) (game) pall-mall
(c) e-mail (message)

mailer /majle/ *vt* to e-mail

mailing /meliŋ/ *nm* (controversial) **(a)** direct mail advertising
(b) mail shot
(c) mailing pack

maille /maj/ *nf* **(a)** stitch; **une ~ qui file** (in tights) a ladder
(b) mesh; **passer à travers les ~s** to slip through the net
(c) (in fence) link
IDIOMS **avoir ~ à partir avec qn** to have a brush with sb

maillet /majɛ/ *nm* mallet

maillon /majɔ̃/ *nm* (in chain) link

maillot /majo/ *nm* **(a)** ~ **(de corps)** vest (GB), undershirt (US)
(b) (of footballer) shirt; (of cyclist) jersey
(c) swimsuit
■ **~ de bain** swimsuit; **le ~ jaune** the leader in the Tour de France

main /mɛ̃/ *nf* **(a)** hand; **se donner** *or* **se tenir la ~** to hold hands; **saluer qn de la ~** to wave at sb; **haut les ~s!** hands up!; **demander la ~ de qn** to ask for sb's hand in marriage; **avoir qch bien en ~(s)** to hold sth firmly; (figurative) to have sth well in hand; **si tu lèves la ~ sur elle** if you lay a finger on her; **à la ~** ‹*sew*› by hand; ‹*adjust*› manually; **fait ~** handmade; **vol à ~ armée** armed robbery; **donner un coup de ~ à qn** to give sb a hand
(b) **une ~ secourable** a helping hand; **une ~ criminelle** someone with criminal intentions
(c) **avoir qch sous la ~** to have sth to hand; **cela m'est tombé sous la ~** I just happened to come across it; **mettre la ~ sur qch** to get one's hands on sth; **je n'arrive pas à mettre la ~ dessus** I can't lay my hands on it; **je l'ai eu entre les ~s mais** I did have it but; **être entre les ~s de qn** ‹*power*› to be in sb's hands; **prendre qn/qch en ~s** to take sb/sth in hand; **à ne pas mettre entre toutes les ~s** ‹*book*› not for general reading; **tomber entre les ~s de qn** to fall into sb's hands; **les ~s vides** empty-handed; **je le lui ai remis en ~s propres** I gave it to him/her in person; **de la ~ à la ~** ‹*sell*› privately; ‹*be paid*› cash (in hand)
(d) **écrit de la ~ du président** written by the president himself; **de ma plus belle ~** in my best handwriting
(e) **avoir le coup de ~** to have the knack; **se faire la ~** to practise (GB)
(f) (in cards) hand; deal
(g) **à ~ droite/gauche** on the right/left
■ **~ courante** handrail
IDIOMS **j'en mettrais ma ~ au feu** *or* **à couper** I'd swear to it; **d'une ~ de fer** with an iron rod; **il n'y est pas allé de ~ morte!** (colloq) he didn't pull his punches!; **avoir la ~ leste** to be always ready with a slap; **faire ~ basse sur** to help oneself to ‹*goods*›; to take

over ⟨*market, country*⟩; **en venir aux ~s** to come to blows; **avoir la ~ heureuse** to be lucky

mainate /mɛnat/ *nm* mynah bird

main-d'œuvre, *pl* **mains-d'œuvre** /mɛ̃dœvʀ/ *nf* labour (GB)

main-forte /mɛ̃fɔʀt/ *nf inv* **prêter ~ à qn** to come to sb's aid

mainmise /mɛ̃miz/ *nf* seizure

maint, **~e** /mɛ̃, mɛ̃t/ *det* many, many a; **à ~es reprises** many times

maintenance /mɛ̃tnɑ̃s/ *nf* maintenance

maintenant /mɛ̃t(ə)nɑ̃/ *adv* now; nowadays; **commence dès ~** start straightaway

maintenir /mɛ̃t(ə)niʀ/ [36] **1** *vtr* **(a)** to keep; to maintain; to keep up; **~ qch debout** to keep sth upright
(b) to support ⟨*wall, ankle*⟩
(c) to stand by ⟨*decision*⟩; **~ que** to maintain that; **~ sa candidature** ⟨*politician*⟩ not to withdraw one's candidacy
2 **se maintenir** *v refl* (+ *v être*) ⟨*trend*⟩ to persist; ⟨*price*⟩ to remain stable; ⟨*weather*⟩ to remain fair; ⟨*political system*⟩ to remain in force; ⟨*currency*⟩ to hold steady

maintien /mɛ̃tjɛ̃/ *nm* **(a)** maintaining; **assurer le ~ de l'ordre** to maintain order
(b) support
(c) deportment

maire /mɛʀ/ *nm* mayor
■ **~ adjoint** deputy mayor

mairie /mɛʀi/ *nf* **(a)** town council (GB) *or* hall (US); **être élu à la ~ de** to be elected mayor of
(b) town hall

mais /mɛ/ *conj* but; **incroyable ~ vrai** strange but true; **il est bête, ~ bête!** (colloq) he's so incredibly stupid!; **~, vous pleurez!** good heavens, you're crying!; **~ j'y pense** now that I come to think of it

maïs /mais/ *nm inv* **(a)** maize (GB), corn (US)
(b) sweetcorn; **épi de ~** corn on the cob

maison /mɛzɔ̃/ **1** *adj inv* ⟨*product*⟩ home-made
2 *nf* **(a)** house
(b) home
(c) family, household; **gens de ~** domestic staff
(d) firm; **avoir 15 ans de ~** to have been with the firm for 15 years
■ **~ d'arrêt** prison; **~ bourgeoise** *imposing town house*; **~ de campagne** house in the country; **~ close** brothel; **~ de correction** institution for young offenders; **~ de la culture** ≈ community arts centre (GB); **~ des jeunes et de la culture, MJC** ≈ youth club; **~ de maître** manor; **~ mère** headquarters; main branch; **~ de passe** brothel; **~ de retraite** old people's *or* retirement home; **~ de santé** nursing home; **la Maison Blanche** the White House
IDIOMS **c'est gros comme une ~** (colloq) it sticks out a mile

maisonnée /mɛzɔne/ *nf* household; family

maître, **-esse¹** /mɛtʀ, ɛs/ **1** *adj* **(a)** **être ~ de soi** to have self-control; **être ~ chez soi** to be master in one's own house; **être ~ de son véhicule** to be in control of one's vehicle
(b) main; key; major
2 *nm,f* **(a)** teacher
(b) (of house) master/mistress
(c) (of animal) owner
3 *nm* **(a)** ruler; **être (le) seul ~ à bord** to be in sole command; **être son propre ~** to be one's own master/mistress; **régner en ~ absolu** to reign supreme
(b) master; **être passé ~ dans l'art de qch/de faire** to be a past master of sth/at doing; **en ~** masterfully
(c) (*also* **Me**) Maître (*form of address given to members of the legal profession*)
■ **~ d'hôtel** maître d'hôtel (GB), maître d' (US); **~ à penser** mentor; **maîtresse femme** strong-minded woman
IDIOMS **trouver son ~** to meet one's match

maître-assistant, **~e**, *mpl* **maîtres-assistants** /mɛtʀasistɑ̃, ɑ̃t/ *nm,f* ≈ senior lecturer (GB), senior instructor (US)

maître-chanteur, *pl* **maîtres-chanteurs** /mɛtʀəʃɑ̃tœʀ/ *nm* blackmailer

maître-nageur, *pl* **maîtres-nageurs** /mɛtʀanaʒœʀ/ *nm* **(a)** swimming instructor
(b) pool attendant

maîtresse² /mɛtʀɛs/ **1** *adj f* ▶ MAÎTRE 1
2 *nf* **(a)** ▶ MAÎTRE 2
(b) mistress

maîtrise /mɛtʀiz/ *nf* **(a)** mastery
(b) perfect command
(c) **~ (de soi)** self-control
(d) master's degree

maîtriser /mɛtʀize/ [1] **1** *vtr* **(a)** to control ⟨*feelings*⟩; to bring [sth] under control ⟨*fire*⟩; to overcome ⟨*opponent*⟩
(b) to master ⟨*language*⟩
2 **se maîtriser** *v refl* (+ *v être*) to have self-control

maïzena® /maizena/ *nf* cornflour

majesté /maʒɛste/ *nf* majesty

majestueux, **-euse** /maʒɛstɥø, øz/ *adj* majestic; stately

majeur, **~e** /maʒœʀ/ **1** *adj* **(a)** **être ~** to be over 18 *or* of age
(b) main, major; **en ~e partie** for the most part
(c) (Mus) major
2 *nm* middle finger

majoration /maʒɔʀasjɔ̃/ *nf* increase

majordome /maʒɔʀdɔm/ *nm* butler

majorer /maʒɔʀe/ [1] *vtr* to increase

majoritaire /maʒɔʀitɛʀ/ *adj* majority

majoritairement /maʒɔʀitɛʀmɑ̃/ *adv*
(a) by a majority (vote) ⸱⸱⸱⸢

(b) province ~ **catholique** predominantly Catholic province

majorité /maʒɔʀite/ *nf* **(a)** majority; **ils sont en** ~ they are in the majority; **ce sont, en** ~, **des enfants** they are, for the most part, children
(b) la ~ the government, the party in power

majuscule /maʒyskyl/ ① *adj* capital
② *nf* capital (letter)

mal, *mpl* **maux** /mal, mo/ ① *adj inv*
(a) wrong; **qu'a-t-elle fait de** ~? what has she done wrong?
(b) bad; **ce ne serait pas** ~ **de déménager** it wouldn't be a bad idea to move out
(c) (colloq) **il n'est pas mal** ⟨*film*⟩ it's not bad; ⟨*man*⟩ he's not bad(-looking)
② *nm* **(a)** trouble, difficulty; **avoir du** ~ **à faire** to find it difficult to do; **se donner du** ~ to go to a lot of trouble; **ne te donne pas ce** ~**!** don't bother!
(b) pain; **faire** ~ to hurt, to be painful; **se faire** ~ to hurt oneself; **j'ai** ~ it hurts; **avoir** ~ **partout** to ache all over; **elle avait très** ~ she was in pain; **avoir** ~ **à la tête** to have a headache; **avoir** ~ **à la gorge** to have a sore throat; **j'ai** ~ **au genou** my knee hurts; **j'ai** ~ **au cœur** I feel sick (GB) *or* nauseous
(c) illness, disease
(d) être en ~ **de** to be short of ⟨*inspiration*⟩; to be lacking in ⟨*affection*⟩
(e) harm; **faire du** ~ **à** to harm, to hurt; **une douche ne te ferait pas de** ~ (humorous) a shower wouldn't do you any harm
(f) le ~ evil; **qu'elle parte, est-ce vraiment un** ~? is it really a bad thing that she is leaving?; **sans penser à** ~ without meaning any harm; **dire du** ~ **de qn/qch** to speak ill of sb/sth
③ *adv* **(a)** badly; not properly; **elle travaille** ~ her work isn't good; **je t'entends** ~ I can't hear you very well
(b) with difficulty; **on voit** ~ **comment** it's difficult to see how
(c) ⟨*diagnosed, addressed*⟩ wrongly; **j'avais** ~ **compris** I had misunderstood; ~ **informé** ill-informed
(d) se trouver ~ to faint; **être** ~ ⟨*assis or couché or installé*⟩ not to be comfortable; **être au plus** ~ to be critically ill
④ **pas mal** *phr* **(a)** ⟨*travel, read*⟩ quite a lot
(b) il ne s'en est pas ~ **tiré** (in exam) he coped quite well; (in dangerous situation) he got off lightly
■ ~ **de l'air** airsickness; ~ **de mer** seasickness; ~ **du pays** homesickness; ~ **du siècle** world-weariness; ~ **des transports** travel sickness

malade /malad/ ① *adj* ⟨*person*⟩ ill, sick; ⟨*animal*⟩ sick; ⟨*organ, plant*⟩ diseased; **tomber** ~ to fall ill *or* sick, to get sick (US); **être** ~ **en voiture/en avion** to get carsick/airsick; **j'en suis** ~ (figurative) (colloq) it makes me sick; ~ **d'inquiétude** worried sick
② *nmf* **(a)** sick man/woman
(b) patient

■ ~ **imaginaire** hypochondriac; ~ **mental** mentally ill person

maladie /maladi/ *nf* illness, disease; **il va en faire une** ~ (colloq) (figurative) he'll have a fit (colloq)
■ ~ **sexuellement transmissible, MST** sexually transmitted disease, STD; ~ **du sommeil** sleeping sickness

maladif, -ive /maladif, iv/ *adj* ⟨*child*⟩ sickly; ⟨*jealousy*⟩ pathological

maladresse /maladʀɛs/ *nf* **(a)** clumsiness, awkwardness
(b) tactlessness
(c) blunder

maladroit, ~**e** /maladʀwa, wat/ ① *adj*
(a) clumsy
(b) tactless
② *nm,f* **(a)** clumsy person
(b) tactless person

maladroitement /maladʀwatmɑ̃/ *adv*
(a) clumsily, awkwardly
(b) tactlessly; ineptly

malaise /malɛz/ *nm* **(a)** dizzy turn; **avoir un** ~ to feel faint
(b) (figurative) uneasiness; unrest
■ ~ **cardiaque** mild heart attack

malaxer /malakse/ [1] *vtr* **(a)** to cream ⟨*butter*⟩; to knead ⟨*dough*⟩
(b) to mix ⟨*cement*⟩

malchance /malʃɑ̃s/ *nf* bad luck, misfortune; **par** ~ as ill luck would have it

malchanceux, -euse /malʃɑ̃sø, øz/ *adj* unlucky

maldonne /maldɔn/ *nf* misunderstanding

mâle /mɑl/ ① *adj* **(a)** male; ⟨*elephant*⟩ bull; ⟨*antelope, rabbit*⟩ buck; ⟨*sparrow*⟩ cock; **cygne** ~ cob; **canard** ~ drake
(b) manly
② *nm* **(a)** male
(b) (humorous) he-man (colloq)

malédiction /malediksjɔ̃/ *nf* curse

maléfice /malefis/ *nm* evil spell

maléfique /malefik/ *adj* evil

malencontreusement
/malɑ̃kɔ̃tʀøzmɑ̃/ *adv* inopportunely; unfortunately

malencontreux, -euse /malɑ̃kɔ̃tʀø, øz/ *adj* unfortunate

malentendant, ~**e** /malɑ̃tɑ̃dɑ̃, ɑ̃t/ *nm,f* **les** ~**s** the hearing-impaired

malentendu /malɑ̃tɑ̃dy/ *nm* misunderstanding

malfaçon /malfasɔ̃/ *nf* defect

malfaisant, ~**e** /malfəzɑ̃, ɑ̃t/ *adj* evil; harmful

malfaiteur /malfɛtœʀ/ *nm* criminal

malformation /malfɔʀmasjɔ̃/ *nf* malformation

malgache /malgaʃ/ *adj, nm* Malagasy

malgré /malgʀe/ *prep* in spite of, despite; ~ **cela,** ~ **tout** nevertheless; ~ **moi** against my wishes; reluctantly

malhabile /malabil/ *adj* clumsy

malheur /malœʀ/ *nm* (a) le ~ misfortune, adversity; **faire le ~ de qn** to bring sb nothing but unhappiness
(b) misfortune; accident; **un grand ~** a tragedy; **un ~ est si vite arrivé!** accidents can so easily happen!
(c) misfortune; **ceux qui ont le ~ de faire** those who are unfortunate enough to do; **j'ai eu le ~ de le leur dire** I made the mistake of telling them; **par ~** as bad luck would have it; **si par ~ la guerre éclatait** if, God forbid, war should break out; **porter ~** to be bad luck
IDIOMS **faire un ~** (colloq) to be a sensation; to go wild; **à quelque chose ~ est bon** (Proverb) every cloud has a silver lining

malheureusement /malœʀøzmɑ̃/ *adv* unfortunately

malheureux, -euse /malœʀø, øz/ **1** *adj*
(a) ⟨*person, life*⟩ unhappy, miserable; ⟨*victim, choice, word*⟩ unfortunate; **c'est ~ que** it's a pity *or* shame that
(b) (colloq) ⟨*sum*⟩ paltry, pathetic
2 *nm,f* (a) poor wretch; **le ~!** poor man!
(b) poor person; **les ~** the poor
IDIOMS **être ~ comme les pierres** to be as miserable as sin

malhonnête /malɔnɛt/ *adj* dishonest

malhonnêteté /malɔnɛtte/ *nf* dishonesty

malice /malis/ *nf* (a) mischief
(b) malice; **être sans ~** to be harmless

malicieux, -ieuse /malisjø, øz/ *adj* mischievous

malin, maligne /malɛ̃, maliɲ/ **1** *adj*
(a) clever; **j'ai eu l'air ~!** (ironic) I looked like a total fool!
(b) malicious
(c) (Med) malignant
2 *nm,f* **c'est un ~** he's a crafty one
IDIOMS **à ~, ~ et demi** (Proverb) there's always someone who will outwit you

malingre /malɛ̃gʀ/ *adj* ⟨*person, tree*⟩ sickly

malintentionné, ~e /malɛ̃tɑ̃sjɔne/ *adj* malicious

malle /mal/ *nf* trunk

malléabilité /maleabilite/ *nf* malleability

mallette /malɛt/ *nf* briefcase

malmener /malməne/ [16] *vtr* (a) to manhandle
(b) to give [sb] a rough ride

malnutrition /malnytʀisjɔ̃/ *nf* malnutrition

malodorant, ~e /malɔdɔʀɑ̃, ɑ̃t/ *adj* foul-smelling

malotru, ~e /malɔtʀy/ *nm,f* boor

Malouines /malwin/ *pr nf pl* **les (îles) ~** the Falklands

malpoli, ~e /malpɔli/ *adj* rude

malpropre /malpʀɔpʀ/ **1** *adj* dirty
2 *nm,f* **se faire renvoyer comme un ~** to be chucked out (colloq)

malsain, ~e /malsɛ̃, ɛn/ *adj* unhealthy

Malte /malt/ *pr nf* Malta

malthusianisme /maltyzjanism/ *nm* Malthusianism

maltraiter /maltʀɛte/ [1] *vtr* to mistreat

malus /malys/ *nm inv* loaded premium

malveillance /malvɛjɑ̃s/ *nf* malice

malveillant, ~e /malvɛjɑ̃, ɑ̃t/ *adj* malicious

malvenu, ~e /malvəny/ *adj* out of place

malversation /malvɛʀsasjɔ̃/ *nf*
(a) malpractice
(b) embezzlement

malvoyant, ~e /malvwajɑ̃, ɑ̃t/ *nmf* partially sighted person

maman /mamɑ̃/ *nf* mum (GB) (colloq), mom (US) (colloq)

mamelle /mamɛl/ *nf* udder; teat

mamelon /mamlɔ̃/ *nm* (a) nipple
(b) hillock

mamie /mami/ *nf* (colloq) granny (colloq), grandma (colloq)

mammifère /mamifɛʀ/ *nm* mammal

mammouth /mamut/ *nm* mammoth

mamy = MAMIE

manager[1], **manageur** /manaʒœʀ/ *nm* manager

manager[2] /manaʒe/ [13] *vtr* to manage

manche[1] /mɑ̃ʃ/ *nm* (a) (of tool) handle; (of violin) neck
(b) (colloq) clumsy idiot
■ ~ **à balai** broomhandle; broomstick; joystick

manche[2] /mɑ̃ʃ/ *nf* (a) sleeve; **sans ~s** sleeveless
(b) (Sport) round; (in cards) hand; (in bridge) game; (in tennis) set
IDIOMS **avoir qn dans la ~** to have sb in one's pocket; **c'est une autre paire de ~s** (colloq) it's a different ball game (colloq)

Manche /mɑ̃ʃ/ *pr nf* **la ~** the (English) Channel

manchette /mɑ̃ʃɛt/ *nf* (a) (double) cuff
(b) oversleeve
(c) headline

manchot, -otte /mɑ̃ʃo, ɔt/ **1** *adj* one-armed; one-handed; **il est ~** he's only got one arm; **ne pas être ~** (colloq) to be pretty good with one's hands (colloq)
2 *nm* penguin

mandarine /mɑ̃daʀin/ *nf* mandarin orange

mandat /mɑ̃da/ *nm* (a) ~ (**postal**) money order
(b) term of office; **exercer son ~** to be in office
(c) mandate
■ ~ **d'arrêt** (arrest) warrant; ~ **d'expulsion** expulsion order; eviction order; ~ **de perquisition** search warrant

mandataire /mɑ̃datɛʀ/ *nmf*
(a) representative, agent
(b) proxy

mandater /mɑ̃date/ [1] *vtr* to appoint [sb] as one's representative; to give a mandate to

mandat-lettre, *pl* **mandats-lettres** /mɑ̃dalɛtʀ/ *nm* postal order

mandibule /mɑ̃dibyl/ *nf* mandible

mandoline /mɑ̃dɔlin/ *nf* mandolin

manège /manɛʒ/ *nm* (a) merry-go-round (b) riding school (c) (little) trick, (little) game; **j'ai bien observé ton ∼** I know what you are up to

manette /manɛt/ *nf* (a) lever; joystick (b) (figurative) ∼s controls

mangeable /mɑ̃ʒabl/ *adj* edible

mangeoire /mɑ̃ʒwaʀ/ *nf* manger; trough; feeding tray

manger¹ /mɑ̃ʒe/ [13] **1** *vtr* (a) to eat; **il n'y a rien à ∼ dans la maison** there's no food in the house (b) to use up ⟨savings⟩; to go through ⟨inheritance⟩; to take up ⟨time⟩ (c) ⟨rust, acid⟩ to eat away (d) ∼ **ses mots** to mumble **2** *vi* to eat; ∼ **au restaurant** to eat out; ∼ **à sa faim** to eat one's fill; **donner à ∼ à qn** to feed sb; **to give sb something to eat; faire à ∼** to cook; **inviter qn à ∼** to invite sb for a meal; ∼ **chinois** to have a Chinese meal; **on mange mal ici** the food is not good here **3 se manger** *v refl* (+ *v être*) **ça se mange?** can you eat it?; **le gaspacho se mange froid** gazpacho is served cold

manger² /mɑ̃ʒe/ *nm* food

mangeur, -euse /mɑ̃ʒœʀ, øz/ *nm,f* **bon/gros ∼** good/big eater ■ **mangeuse d'hommes** man-eater

mangouste /mɑ̃gust/ *nf* (a) mongoose (b) mangosteen

mangue /mɑ̃g/ *nf* mango

maniable /manjabl/ *adj* ⟨object, car⟩ easy to handle; ⟨book⟩ manageable in size

maniaque /manjak/ **1** *adj* particular, fussy **2** *nmf* (a) fusspot (GB), fussbudget (US) (b) fanatic; **c'est un ∼ de l'ordre** he's obsessive about tidiness (c) maniac (d) (Med) manic

maniaquerie /manjakʀi/ *nf* fussiness

manichéen, -éenne /manikeɛ̃, ɛn/ *adj* Manichean; dualistic

manie /mani/ *nf* (a) habit; **c'est une vraie ∼** it's an absolute obsession (b) quirk, idiosyncrasy (c) (Med) mania

maniement /manimɑ̃/ *nm* handling; (of machine) operation; (of language) command ■ ∼ **d'armes** arms drill

manier /manje/ [2] **1** *vtr* to handle **2 se manier** *v refl* (+ *v être*) **se ∼ aisément** ⟨tool⟩ to be easy to handle; ⟨car⟩ to handle well IDIOMS ∼ **la fourchette avec entrain** (colloq) (humorous) to have a hearty appetite

maniéré, ∼e /manjeʀe/ *adj* affected

manière /manjɛʀ/ *nf* (a) way; **d'une certaine ∼** in a way; **leur ∼ de vivre/penser** their way of life/thinking; **de toutes les ∼s possibles** in every possible way; **de telle ∼ que** in such a way that; **de ∼ à faire** so as to do; **de ∼ à ce que** so that; **à ma ∼** my (own) way; **de quelle ∼?** how?; **de toute ∼, de toutes ∼s** anyway, in any case; **la ∼ forte** strong-arm tactics, force (b) style; **à la ∼ de qn/qch** in the style of sb/sth (c) manners; **faire des ∼s** to stand on ceremony

manifestant, ∼e /manifɛstɑ̃, ɑ̃t/ *nm,f* demonstrator

manifestation /manifɛstasjɔ̃/ *nf* (a) demonstration (b) event; ∼**s sportives** sporting events (c) (of phenomenon) appearance (d) (of feeling) expression, manifestation ■ ∼ **silencieuse** vigil; ∼ **de soutien** rally

manifeste /manifɛst/ **1** *adj* obvious, manifest **2** *nm* manifesto

manifester /manifɛste/ [1] **1** *vtr* to show ⟨courage⟩; to express ⟨desire, fears⟩; ∼ **sa présence** to make one's presence known **2** *vi* to demonstrate; **appeler à ∼ le 5 juin** to call a demonstration for 5 June **3 se manifester** *v refl* (+ *v être*) (a) ⟨symptom⟩ to manifest itself; ⟨phenomenon⟩ to appear; ⟨worry⟩ to show itself (b) ⟨witness⟩ to come forward; ⟨person⟩ to appear; to get in touch

manigance /manigɑ̃s/ *nf* little scheme

manigancer /manigɑ̃se/ [12] *vtr* ∼ **quelque chose** to be up to something; ∼ **un mauvais coup** to hatch up a scheme

manipulateur, -trice /manipylatœʀ, tʀis/ *nm,f* (a) technician (b) (pejorative) manipulator

manipulation /manipylasjɔ̃/ *nf* (a) (of object) handling (b) manipulation (c) (Sch) experiment

manipuler /manipyle/ [1] *vtr* (a) to handle ⟨object⟩; to use ⟨words⟩ (b) to manipulate ⟨person⟩

manitou /manitu/ *nm* (colloq) big noise (colloq); **un grand ∼ de la finance** a big noise in the financial world

manivelle /manivɛl/ *nf* handle IDIOMS **donner le premier tour de ∼** to start filming

manne /man/ *nf* godsend

mannequin /mankɛ̃/ *nm* (a) (fashion) model (b) dummy

manœuvre¹ /manœvʀ/ *nm* unskilled worker

manœuvre² /manœvʀ/ *nf* manoeuvre (GB), maneuver (US); **champ de ∼** military training area; **fausse ∼** mistake

manœuvrer /manœvʀe/ [1] **1** *vtr* (a) to manoeuvre (GB), to maneuver (US) ⟨vehicle⟩ (b) to operate ⟨machine⟩

(c) to manipulate ⟨*person*⟩
[2] *vi* to manoeuvre (GB), to maneuver (US)

manoir /manwaʀ/ *nm* manor (house)

manomètre /manɔmɛtʀ/ *nm* pressure
gauge

manquant, ~e /mãkã, ãt/ *adj* missing

manque /mãk/ [1] *nm* **(a)** ~ **de** lack of;
shortage of; ~ **de chance, il est tombé
malade** just his luck, he fell ill
(b) gap; **en ~ d'affection** in need of
affection; **être en ~** ⟨*drug addict*⟩ to be
suffering from withdrawal symptoms
[2] **à la manque** *phr* (colloq) **une idée à la
~** a useless idea

manqué, ~e /mãke/ [1] *pp* ▶ MANQUER
[2] *pp adj* ⟨*attempt*⟩ failed; ⟨*opportunity*⟩
missed

manquer /mãke/ [1] [1] *vtr* **(a)** to miss; **un
film à ne pas ~** a film not to be missed; **tu
l'as manquée de cinq minutes** you missed
her/it by five minutes
(b) ~ **son coup** (colloq) to fail
(c) (colloq) **la prochaine fois je ne le
manquerai pas** next time I won't let him get
away with it
[2] **manquer à** *v+prep* **(a)** ~ **à qn** to be
missed by sb; **ma tante me manque** I miss
my aunt
(b) ~ **à sa parole** to break one's word
[3] **manquer de** *v+prep* **(a)** ~ **de** to lack;
on ne manque de rien we don't want for
anything; **elle ne manque pas de charme**
she's not without charm; **on manque d'air ici**
it's stuffy in here
(b) **je ne manquerai pas de vous le faire
savoir** I'll be sure to let you know; **et
évidemment, ça n'a pas manqué!** (colloq) and
sure enough that's what happened!
(c) **il a manqué (de) casser un carreau** he
almost broke a windowpane
[4] *vi* **(a)** **les vivres vinrent à ~** the supplies
ran out; **le courage leur manqua** their
courage failed them; **ce n'est pas l'envie qui
m'en manque** it's not that I don't want to
(b) ⟨*person*⟩ to be absent; to be missing
[5] *v impers* **il lui manque un doigt** he's got a
finger missing; **il nous manque deux joueurs
pour former une équipe** we're two players
short of a team; **il ne manquerait plus que
ça!** (colloq) that would be the last straw!
[6] **se manquer** *v refl* (+ *v être*) to miss
each other

mansarde /mãsaʀd/ *nf* attic room

mansardé, ~e /mãsaʀde/ *adj* ⟨*room*⟩
attic

mansuétude /mãsɥetyd/ *nf* indulgence

manteau, pl ~x /mãto/ *nm* coat
■ ~ **de cheminée** mantelpiece
IDIOMS **sous le ~** illicitly

manucure /manykyʀ/ [1] *nmf* manicurist
[2] *nf* manicure

manuel, -elle /manɥel/ [1] *adj* manual
[2] *nm* manual; (Sch) textbook
■ ~ **de conversation** phrase book

manuellement /manɥelmã/ *adv*
manually

manufacture /manyfaktyʀ/ *nf* **(a)** factory
(b) manufacture

manufacturer /manyfaktyʀe/ [1] *vtr* to
manufacture

manu militari /manymilitaʀi/ *adv*
forcibly

manuscrit, ~e /manyskʀi, it/ [1] *adj*
handwritten
[2] *nm* manuscript

manutention /manytãsjɔ̃/ *nf* handling

manutentionnaire /manytãsjɔnɛʀ/ *nm*
warehouseman

mappemonde /mapmɔ̃d/ *nf* **(a)** map of
the world (in two hemispheres)
(b) globe

maquereau, pl ~x /makʀo/ *nm*
mackerel

maquette /makɛt/ *nf* scale model

maquillage /makijaʒ/ *nm* **(a)** making-up
(b) make-up

maquiller /makije/ [1] [1] *vtr* **(a)** to make
[sb] up
(b) to doctor ⟨*truth*⟩; ~ **un crime en accident**
to disguise a crime as an accident
[2] **se maquiller** *v refl* (+ *v être*) **(a)** to put
make-up on
(b) to wear make-up

maquilleur, -euse /makijœʀ, øz/ *nm,f*
make-up artist

maquis /maki/ *nm inv* maquis; **prendre le
~** to go underground

maquisard, ~e /makizaʀ, aʀd/ *nm,f*
member of the Resistance

marabout /maʀabu/ *nm* **(a)** marabou
(b) marabout

maraîchage /maʀɛʃaʒ/ *nm* market
gardening (GB), truck farming (US)

maraîcher, -ère /maʀɛʃe, ɛʀ/ [1] *adj*
produits ~s market garden produce (GB),
truck (US)
[2] *nm,f* market gardener (GB), truck farmer
(US)

marais /maʀɛ/ *nm inv* marsh; swamp
■ ~ **salant** saltern

marasme /maʀasm/ *nm* stagnation

marathon /maʀatɔ̃/ *nm* marathon

marathonien, -ienne /maʀatɔnjɛ̃, ɛn/
nm,f marathon runner

marâtre /maʀɑtʀ/ *nf* cruel mother

maraude /maʀod/ *nf* pilfering; **en ~**
⟨*person*⟩ on the prowl

marauder /maʀode/ [1] *vi* **(a)** to pilfer
(b) to prowl around

maraudeur, -euse /maʀodœʀ, øz/ *nm,f*
petty thief

marbre /maʀbʀ/ *nm* **(a)** marble
(b) marble top
(c) marble statue
IDIOMS **rester de ~** to remain stony-faced; **la
nouvelle les laissa de ~** they were
completely unmoved by the news

m

marbrer /maʀbʀe/ [1] *vtr* to marble

marbrerie /maʀbʀəʀi/ *nf* marble industry; marble masonry

marbrier, -ière¹ /maʀbʀije, ɛʀ/ *nm* marble mason

marbrière² /maʀbʀijɛʀ/ *nf* marble quarry

marbrure /maʀbʀyʀ/ *nf* marbling

marc /maʀ/ *nm* marc.
■ ∼ **de café** coffee grounds

marcassin /maʀkasɛ̃/ *nm* young wild boar

marchand, ∼e /maʀʃɑ̃, ɑ̃d/ **1** *adj* ⟨quality⟩ marketable; ⟨sector⟩ trade; ⟨value⟩ market
2 *nm,f* shopkeeper; stallholder; ∼ **d'armes/de bestiaux** arms/cattle dealer; ∼ **de charbon/vins** coal/wine merchant
■ ∼ **ambulant** hawker; ∼ **de couleurs** ironmonger (GB), hardware merchant; ∼ **de glaces** ice cream vendor; ∼ **en gros** wholesaler; ∼ **de journaux** newsagent; news vendor; ∼ **des quatre saisons** costermonger (GB), fruit and vegetable merchant; ∼ **de sable** sandman; ∼ **de tapis** carpet salesman

marchandage /maʀʃɑ̃daʒ/ *nm* haggling

marchander /maʀʃɑ̃de/ [1] *vtr* **(a)** to haggle over
(b) (figurative) ∼ **sa peine** not to put oneself out

marchandise /maʀʃɑ̃diz/ *nf* goods, merchandise; **tromper qn sur la ∼** to swindle sb

marche /maʀʃ/ *nf* **(a)** walking; walk; pace, step; **faire de la ∼** to go walking; **à 10 minutes de ∼** 10 minutes' walk away
(b) march; **fermer la ∼** to bring up the rear; **ouvrir la ∼** to be at the head of the march
(c) (of vehicle) progress; (of events) course; (of time) march; **bus en ∼** moving bus; **dans le sens contraire de la ∼** facing backward(s)
(d) (of mechanism) operation; (of organization) running; **en état de ∼** in working order; **mettre en ∼** to start (up) ⟨machine⟩; to switch on ⟨TV⟩
(e) step; **les ∼s** the stairs
■ ∼ **arrière** reverse; **faire ∼ arrière** to reverse; (figurative) to backpedal; ∼ **avant** forward; ∼ **à suivre** procedure
IDIOMS **prendre le train en ∼** to join halfway through; to climb onto the bandwagon

marché /maʀʃe/ *nm* **(a)** market; **faire son ∼** to do one's shopping at the market
(b) deal; **conclure un ∼ avec qn** to strike a deal with sb; ∼ **conclu!** it's a deal!; **bon/meilleur ∼** cheap/cheaper; **par-dessus le ∼** (colloq) to top it all
■ ∼ **de l'emploi** job market; ∼ **libre** free market; ∼ **noir** black market; ∼ **aux puces** flea market; ∼ **du travail** labour (GB) market; **Marché commun** Common Market

marchepied /maʀʃəpje/ *nm* **(a)** step
(b) steps

marcher /maʀʃe/ [1] *vi* **(a)** to walk; ⟨demonstrators⟩ to march
(b) to tread; **se laisser ∼ sur les pieds** (figurative) to let oneself be walked over
(c) ⟨mechanism, system⟩ to work; **ma radio marche mal** my radio doesn't work properly; **faire ∼ qch** to get sth to work; ∼ **au gaz** to run on gas; **les bus ne marchent pas le soir** the buses don't run in the evenings
(d) (colloq) ⟨bien⟩/∼ **mal** ⟨work, relationship⟩ to go well/not to go well; ⟨film, student⟩ to do well/not to do well; ⟨actor⟩ to go down well/not to go down well
(e) (colloq) **c'est trop risqué, je ne marche pas** it's too risky, count me out; **ça marche!** it's a deal!
(f) (colloq) to fall for it
(g) **faire ∼ qn** to pull sb's leg; **faire ∼ son monde** (colloq) to be good at giving orders
IDIOMS **il ne marche pas, il court!** (colloq) he's as gullible as they come

marcheur, -euse /maʀʃœʀ, øz/ *nm,f* walker

mardi /maʀdi/ *nm* Tuesday

mare /maʀ/ *nf* **(a)** pond
(b) ∼ **de** pool of ⟨blood⟩

marécage /maʀekaʒ/ *nm* marsh, swamp

marécageux, -euse /maʀekaʒø, øz/ *adj* ⟨ground⟩ marshy, swampy; ⟨plant⟩ marsh

maréchal, *pl* **-aux** /maʀeʃal, o/ *nm* ≈ field marshal (GB), general of the army (US)

maréchal-ferrant, *pl* **maréchaux-ferrants** /maʀeʃalfɛʀɑ̃, maʀeʃofɛʀɑ̃/ *nm* farrier

marée /maʀe/ *nf* tide; **la ∼ monte/descend** the tide is coming in/is going out; **à ∼ haute/basse** at high/low tide
■ ∼ **noire** oil slick
IDIOMS **contre vents et ∼s** come hell or high water; against all odds

marelle /maʀɛl/ *nf* hopscotch

marémoteur, -trice /maʀemɔtœʀ, tʀis/ *adj* tidal; **usine marémotrice** tidal power station

mareyeur, -euse /maʀejœʀ, øz/ *nm,f* fish wholesaler

margarine /maʀgaʀin/ *nf* margarine

marge /maʀʒ/ **1** *nf* **(a)** margin
(b) leeway; **on a 10 minutes de ∼** we've got 10 minutes to spare
(c) scope; **tu devrais me laisser plus de ∼ de décision** you should allow me more scope for making decisions
(d) profit margin; mark-up
2 **en marge de** *phr* **vivre en ∼ de la loi** to live outside the law; **se sentir en ∼** to feel like an outsider
■ ∼ **bénéficiaire** profit margin; ∼ **commerciale** gross profit; ∼ **d'erreur** margin of error; ∼ **de sécurité** safety margin

marginal, ∼e, *mpl* **-aux** /maʀʒinal, o/ **1** *adj* **(a)** marginal
(b) ⟨artist⟩ fringe
(c) on the margins of society
2 *nm,f* dropout; **les marginaux** the fringe elements of society

marginaliser /maʀʒinalize/ [1] *vtr* to marginalize

marguerite /maʀgəʀit/ *nf* daisy

mari /maʀi/ *nm* husband

mariage /maʀjaʒ/ *nm* (a) marriage; né d'un premier ~ from a previous marriage; ~ de raison marriage of convenience; faire un riche ~ to marry into money
(b) wedding
(c) (figurative) (of colours) marriage; (of companies) merger; (of parties) alliance; (of techniques) fusion
■ ~ blanc marriage in name only; ~ civil civil wedding; ~ religieux church wedding

Marianne /maʀjan/ *pr n* Marianne (*female figure personifying the French Republic*)

marié, ~e /maʀje/ **1** *pp* ▶ MARIER
2 *pp adj* married
3 *nm,f* le (jeune) ~ the (bride)groom; la (jeune) ~e the bride; les ~s the newlyweds

marier /maʀje/ [2] **1** *vtr* to marry
2 se marier *v refl* (+ *v être*) (a) to get married
(b) (colours) to blend

marijuana /maʀiʀwana/ *nf* marijuana

marin, ~e[1] /maʀɛ̃, in/ **1** *adj* (a) (life) marine; (salt) sea; (drilling) offshore
(b) pull ~ seaman's jersey; costume ~ sailor suit
2 *nm* sailor
■ ~ d'eau douce fair-weather sailor; ~ pêcheur fisherman
IDIOMS avoir le pied ~ not to get seasick

marine[2] /maʀin/ **1** *adj inv* navy (blue)
2 *nm* marine

marine[3] /maʀin/ *nf* navy; de ~ nautical

mariner /maʀine/ [1] *vtr, vi* to marinate

marinière /maʀinjɛʀ/ *nf* smock

marionnette /maʀjɔnɛt/ *nf* (a) puppet
(b) ~s puppet show
■ ~ à fils marionette

marionnettiste /maʀjɔnetist/ *nmf* puppeteer

maritalement /maʀitalmɑ̃/ *adv* (live) as man and wife

maritime /maʀitim/ *adj* (climate, commerce) maritime; (area) coastal; (company) shipping

marivaudage /maʀivodaʒ/ *nm* (a) gallant banter
(b) refined affectation (*in the style of Marivaux*)

marjolaine /maʀʒɔlɛn/ *nf* marjoram

marmaille (colloq) /maʀmaj/ *nf* rabble of kids (colloq)

marmelade /maʀməlad/ *nf* stewed fruit

marmite /maʀmit/ *nf* (a) (cooking-)pot
(b) potful
IDIOMS faire bouillir la ~ (colloq) to bring home the bacon

marmiton /maʀmitɔ̃/ *nm* chef's assistant

marmonner /maʀmɔne/ [1] *vtr* to mumble, to mutter

marmot /maʀmo/ *nm* (colloq) kid (colloq), brat (colloq)

marmotte /maʀmɔt/ *nf* (a) marmot
(b) (figurative) sleepyhead (colloq)

maroquinerie /maʀɔkinʀi/ *nf* (a) leather shop
(b) leather industry; leather trade; (articles de) ~ leather goods

marotte /maʀɔt/ *nf* (a) pet subject, hobby horse; pet *or* favourite (GB) hobby
(b) puppet

marquant, ~e /maʀkɑ̃, ɑ̃t/ *adj* (fact) memorable; (memory) lasting

marque /maʀk/ *nf* (a) brand, make; de ~ (product) branded; (guest) distinguished; (person) eminent
(b) mark; sign; ~ de doigts fingermarks; on voit encore les ~s (de coups) you can still see the bruises; ~ du pluriel plural marker; laisser sa ~ to make one's mark
(c) (Sport) score; à vos ~s, prêts, partez! on your marks, get set, go!
■ ~ déposée registered trademark; ~ de fabrication manufacturer's brand name; ~ de fabrique trademark

marqué, ~e /maʀke/ **1** *pp* ▶ MARQUER
2 *pp adj* (a) il a le corps ~ de traces de coups he's bruised all over; elle est restée ~e par la guerre the war left its mark on her; visage ~ worn face
(b) (difference) marked

marquer /maʀke/ [1] **1** *vtr* (a) to mark (goods); to brand (cattle)
(b) to mark, to signal (beginning, end)
(c) to mark (body, object)
(d) (figurative) (event, work) to leave its mark on (person); c'est quelqu'un qui m'a beaucoup marqué he/she was a strong influence on me
(e) to write [sth] down (information); to mark (price); qu'est-ce qu'il y a de marqué? what does it say?
(f) to show; ~ la mesure (Mus) to beat time; il faut ~ le coup let's celebrate
(g) ~ un temps (d'arrêt) to pause
(h) (Sport) to score (goal); to mark (opponent)
2 *vi* (a) to leave a mark
(b) (Sport) to score

marqueur /maʀkœʀ/ *nm* marker pen

marquis, ~e /maʀki, iz/ *nm,f* marquis/ marchioness

marraine /maʀɛn/ *nf* (a) godmother
(b) sponsor
■ ~ de guerre *soldier's wartime female penfriend*

marrant, ~e /maʀɑ̃, ɑ̃t/ *adj* (colloq) funny

marre /maʀ/ *adv* (colloq) en avoir ~ to be fed up (colloq)

marrer: se marrer /maʀe/ [1] *v refl* (+ *v être*) (colloq) (a) to have a great time
(b) to have a good laugh

marron, -onne /maʀɔ̃, ɔn/ **1** *adj* crooked

2 *adj inv* brown; ~ **clair/foncé** light/dark brown
3 *nm* (a) chestnut
(b) brown
■ ~ **glacé** marron glacé; ~**s chauds** roast chestnuts

marronnier /maʀɔnje/ *nm* chestnut (tree)

mars /maʀs/ *nm inv* March
IDIOMS **arriver comme** ~ **en carême** to come as sure as night follows day

Marseillaise /maʀsɛjɛz/ *nf* Marseillaise (*French national anthem*)

marsouin /maʀswɛ̃/ *nm* porpoise

marteau, *pl* ~**x** /maʀto/ *nm* hammer; (*of judge*) gavel; (*on door*) knocker

marteler /maʀtəle/ [17] *vtr* (a) to hammer, to pound
(b) to rap out ⟨*words*⟩

martial, ~**e**, *mpl* **-iaux** /maʀsjal, o/ *adj* ⟨*art, law*⟩ martial; ⟨*music, step*⟩ military

martinet /maʀtinɛ/ *nm* (a) (Zool) swift
(b) whip

martingale /maʀtɛ̃gal/ *nf* (a) (*on jacket*) half belt
(b) (*for horse*) martingale

martre /maʀtʀ/ *nf* (a) marten
(b) sable

martyr, ~**e**[1] /maʀtiʀ/ **1** *adj* martyred; **enfant** ~ battered child
2 *nm,f* martyr

martyre[2] /maʀtiʀ/ *nm* (a) martyrdom
(b) agony; **souffrir le** ~ to suffer agony

martyriser /maʀtiʀize/ [1] *vtr* (a) to torment ⟨*victim, animal*⟩; to batter ⟨*child*⟩
(b) to martyr

marxisme /maʀksism/ *nm* Marxism

mas /mɑ/ *nm inv* farmhouse (*in Provence*)

mascarade /maskaʀad/ *nf* (a) farce; ~ **de justice** travesty of justice
(b) masked ball

mascotte /maskɔt/ *nf* mascot

masculin, ~**e** /maskylɛ̃, in/ **1** *adj* ⟨*population, sex, part*⟩ male; ⟨*sport*⟩ man's; ⟨*magazine, team*⟩ men's; ⟨*face, noun*⟩ masculine
2 *nm* masculine

masochisme /mazɔʃism/ *nm* masochism

masochiste /mazɔʃist/ *nmf* masochist

masque /mask/ *nm* (a) mask
(b) face-pack
(c) expression
■ ~ **à gaz** gas mask; ~ **de plongée** diving mask; ~ **de soudeur** face shield
IDIOMS **jeter le** ~ to show one's true colours (GB)

masqué, ~**e** /maske/ *adj* (a) ⟨*bandit*⟩ masked
(b) (figurative) concealed

masquer /maske/ [1] **1** *vtr* (a) to conceal ⟨*defect*⟩; to mask ⟨*problem*⟩
(b) to block ⟨*opening, light*⟩
2 se masquer *v refl* (+ *v être*) to hide [sth] from oneself ⟨*truth*⟩

massacrante /masakʀɑ̃t/ *adj f* **être d'humeur** ~ to be in a foul mood

massacre /masakʀ/ *nm* massacre, slaughter

massacrer /masakʀe/ [1] *vtr* (a) to massacre, to slaughter
(b) (figurative) (colloq) to slaughter (colloq) ⟨*opponent*⟩; to massacre ⟨*piece of music*⟩; to botch ⟨*job*⟩; to criticize ⟨*play, actor*⟩

massage /masaʒ/ *nm* massage

masse /mas/ *nf* (a) mass; ~ **rocheuse** rocky mass; **une** ~ **humaine** a mass of humanity
(b) **une** ~ **de** a lot of; **des** ~**s de** (colloq) masses of; **départs en** ~ mass exodus
(c) **la** ~, **les** ~**s** the masses; **culture de** ~ mass culture
■ ~ **d'armes** mace; ~ **monétaire** money supply; ~ **salariale** (total) wage bill
IDIOMS (**se laisser**) **tomber comme une** ~ to collapse; **dormir comme une** ~ to sleep like a log (colloq)

massepain /maspɛ̃/ *nm* marzipan cake

masser /mase/ [1] **1** *vtr* to massage
2 se masser *v refl* (+ *v être*) (a) to mass
(b) **se** ~ **les jambes** to massage one's legs

masseur, -euse /masœʀ, øz/ *nm,f* masseur/masseuse

massicot /masiko/ *nm* (*for paper*) guillotine

massif, -ive /masif, iv/ **1** *adj*
(a) ⟨*features*⟩ heavy; ⟨*silhouette*⟩ massive
(b) ⟨*dose*⟩ massive; ⟨*redundancies*⟩ mass
(c) ⟨*gold, oak*⟩ solid
2 *nm* (a) massif
(b) (*flower*) bed

massivement /masivmɑ̃/ *adv* ⟨*demonstrate*⟩ in great numbers; ⟨*inject*⟩ in massive doses; ⟨*approve*⟩ overwhelmingly

mass media /masmedja/ *nm pl* mass media

massue /masy/ *nf* (gen, Sport) club, bludgeon

mastic /mastik/ **1** *adj inv* putty-coloured (GB)
2 *nm* (*for windows*) putty; (*for holes*) filler

mastiquer /mastike/ [1] *vtr* to chew

mastoc /mastɔk/ *adj inv* (colloq) huge

mastodonte /mastɔdɔ̃t/ *nm* (a) mastodon
(b) (figurative) (*person*) colossus, hulk (colloq); (*animal*) monster

masturber /mastyʀbe/ [1] *vtr*, **se masturber** *v refl* (+ *v être*) to masturbate

m'as-tu-vu /matyvy/ *nmf inv* (colloq) show-off

mat, ~**e** /mat/ **1** *adj* (a) ⟨*paint*⟩ matt (GB), matte (US)
(b) ⟨*complexion*⟩ olive
(c) ⟨*sound*⟩ dull
2 *nm* (**échec et**) ~**!** checkmate!

mât /mɑ/ *nm* (a) mast
(b) pole; climbing pole; ~ **de drapeau** flagpole

matador /matadɔʀ/ *nm* matador

match /matʃ/ nm match; (in team sports) match (GB), game (US); **~ nul** draw (GB), tie (US); **faire ~ nul** to draw (GB), to tie (US)
■ **~ de classement** league match

matelas /matla/ nm inv mattress; **~ pneumatique** air bed

matelassé, ~e /matlase/ adj ⟨material⟩ quilted; ⟨door⟩ padded

matelot /matlo/ nm **(a)** sailor
(b) ≈ ordinary seaman (GB), ≈ seaman apprentice (US)

mater /mate/ [1] vtr to bring [sb/sth] into line ⟨rebels⟩; to take [sb/sth] in hand ⟨child, horse⟩

matérialiser /materjalize/ [1] **1** vtr
(a) to realize ⟨dream⟩; to make [sth] happen ⟨plan⟩
(b) to mark; 'chaussée non matérialisée sur 3 km' 'no road markings for 3 km'
2 se matérialiser v refl (+ v être) to materialize

matérialisme /materjalism/ nm materialism

matérialiste /materjalist/ adj materialistic

matériau, pl ~x /materjo/ nm material; **~x de construction** building materials

matériel, -ielle /materjɛl/ **1** adj ⟨cause, conditions⟩ material; ⟨means⟩ practical
2 nm **(a)** equipment; **~ agricole** farm machinery
(b) material
■ **~ informatique** hardware

matériellement /materjɛlmɑ̃/ adv
(a) **c'est ~ possible** it can be done
(b) financially

maternel, -elle¹ /matɛrnɛl/ adj
(a) ⟨instinct⟩ maternal; ⟨love⟩ motherly
(b) ⟨aunt⟩ maternal; **du côté ~** on the mother's side

maternelle² /matɛrnɛl/ nf nursery school

maternellement /matɛrnɛlmɑ̃/ adv in a motherly way

materner /matɛrne/ [1] vtr **(a)** to mother
(b) to mollycoddle

maternité /matɛrnite/ nf **(a)** motherhood
(b) pregnancy; **de ~ leave** maternity
(c) maternity hospital

mathématicien, -ienne /matematisjɛ̃, ɛn/ nm,f mathematician

mathématiquement /matematikmɑ̃/ adv **(a)** mathematically
(b) logically

mathématiques /matematik/ nf pl mathematics

matheux, -euse /matø, øz/ nm,f (colloq) mathematician

maths /mat/ nf pl (colloq) maths (GB) (colloq), math (US) (colloq)

matière /matjɛr/ nf **(a)** material; **fournir la ~ d'un roman** to provide the material for a novel
(b) matter; **en ~ d'emploi** as far as employment is concerned; **~ à réflexion** food for thought
(c) (Sch) subject
■ **~s fécales** faeces; **~s grasses** fat; **~ grise** grey (GB) or gray (US) matter; **~ première** raw material

Matignon /matiɲɔ̃/ pr n: offices of the French Prime Minister

matin /matɛ̃/ nm morning; **de bon ~** early in the morning
IDIOMS **être du ~** to be a morning person

matinal, ~e, mpl -aux /matinal, o/ adj ⟨walk⟩ morning; ⟨hour⟩ early; **être ~** to be an early riser, to be up early

mâtiné, ~e /matine/ adj **un anglais ~ de français** a mixture of English and French

matinée /matine/ nf **(a)** morning
(b) matinée
IDIOMS **faire la grasse ~** to sleep in

matines /matin/ nf pl matins

matraquage /matrakaʒ/ nm
(a) bludgeoning
(b) (figurative) **~ publicitaire** hype (colloq)

matraque /matrak/ nf club; truncheon (GB), billy (US); **c'est le coup de ~** (figurative) (colloq) it costs a fortune

matraquer /matrake/ [1] vtr **(a)** to club
(b) ⟨media⟩ to bombard ⟨public⟩

matriarcal, ~e, mpl -aux /matrijarkal, o/ adj matriarchal

matrice /matris/ nf **(a)** matrix
(b) (Tech) die

matricule /matrikyl/ nm reference number; (Mil) service number

matrimonial, ~e, mpl -iaux /matrimɔnjal, o/ adj marriage, matrimonial

matrone /matrɔn/ nf matronly woman

maturation /matyrasjɔ̃/ nf ripening; maturing

maturité /matyrite/ nf maturity

maudire /modir/ [80] vtr to curse

maudit, ~e /modi, it/ **1** pp ▶ MAUDIRE
2 adj (colloq) blasted (colloq)
3 nm,f damned soul; **les ~s** the damned

maugréer /mogree/ [11] vi to grumble (**contre** about)

maure /mɔr/ adj Moorish

maussade /mosad/ adj ⟨mood⟩ sullen; ⟨weather⟩ dull; ⟨landscape⟩ bleak

mauvais, ~e /mɔvɛ, ɛz/ **1** adj **(a)** bad, poor; ⟨lawyer, doctor⟩ incompetent; ⟨wage⟩ low; **du ~ tabac** cheap tobacco
(b) ⟨address⟩ wrong
(c) ⟨day, moment⟩ bad; ⟨method⟩ wrong
(d) bad; ⟨surprise⟩ nasty; ⟨taste, smell⟩ unpleasant; **par ~ temps** in bad weather; **ça a un ~ goût** it tastes horrible
(e) ⟨cold, wound⟩ nasty; ⟨sea⟩ rough
(f) ⟨person, smile⟩ nasty; ⟨intentions, thoughts⟩ evil; **préparer un ~ coup** to be up to mischief
2 adv **sentir ~** to smell; **sentir très ~** to stink; **il fait ~** the weather is bad   ⋯⋯⟶

3 *nm* il n'y a pas que du ~ dans le projet the project isn't all bad

■ ~ **esprit** scoffing person; scoffing attitude; ~ **garçon** tough guy; ~ **traitements** ill-treatment; ~e **herbe** weed; ~es **rencontres** bad company

IDIOMS l'avoir ~e (colloq) to be furious

mauve¹ /mov/ *adj*, *nm* mauve

mauve² /mov/ *nf* mallow

mauviette /movjɛt/ *nf* wimp (colloq)

maux ▶ MAL

maxi- /maksi/ *pref* ~**jupe** maxi-skirt; ~-**bouteille** one-and-a-half litre (GB) bottle

maxillaire /maksilɛʀ/ *nm* jawbone

maxima ▶ MAXIMUM

maximal, ~**e**, *mpl* **-aux** /maksimal, o/ *adj* maximum

maxime /maksim/ *nf* maxim

maximum, *pl* ~**s** *or* **maxima** /maksimɔm, maksima/ **1** *adj* maximum
2 *nm* (a) maximum; **10 francs au grand ~** 10 francs at the very most; **au ~** ⟨work⟩ to the maximum; ⟨reduce⟩ as much as possible; **obtenir le ~ d'avantages** to get as many advantages as possible; **faire le ~** to do one's utmost
(b) (Law) maximum sentence

mayonnaise /majɔnɛz/ *nf* mayonnaise

mazagran /mazagʀɑ̃/ *nm*: *thick china goblet for coffee*

mazout /mazut/ *nm* (fuel) oil

me (**m'** *before vowel or mute h*) /m(ə)/ *pron*
(a) me; **tu ne m'as pas fait mal** you didn't hurt me
(b) myself; **je ~ lave (les mains)** I wash (my hands)

Me *written abbr* = MAÎTRE 3 C

méandre /meɑ̃dʀ/ *nm* meander; **les ~s de l'administration** the maze of officialdom; **les ~s de ta pensée** the rambling development of your ideas

mec /mɛk/ *nm* (colloq) guy (colloq); **mon ~** my man (colloq)

mécanicien, **-ienne** /mekanisjɛ̃, ɛn/
1 *adj* mechanical
2 *nm,f* mechanic
3 *nm* (of train) engine driver (GB), (locomotive) engineer (US); (of plane) flight engineer; (of boat) engineer

mécanique /mekanik/ **1** *adj* mechanical; ⟨toy⟩ clockwork; ⟨razor⟩ hand
2 *nf* (a) mechanics; **une merveille de ~** a marvel of engineering
(b) (colloq) machine

mécaniquement /mekanikmɑ̃/ *adv* mechanically; **fabriqué ~** machine-made

mécaniser /mekanize/ [1] *vtr*, **se mécaniser** *v refl* (+ *v être*) to mechanize

mécanisme /mekanism/ *nm* mechanism

mécano /mekano/ *nm* (colloq) mechanic

mécénat /mesena/ *nm* patronage

mécène /mesɛn/ *nm* patron of the arts

méchamment /meʃamɑ̃/ *adv*
(a) spitefully, maliciously; viciously; **traiter qn ~** to treat sb badly
(b) (colloq) ⟨damage⟩ badly; ⟨good⟩ terribly

méchanceté /meʃɑ̃ste/ *nf* (a) nastiness; **par pure ~** out of pure spite
(b) maliciousness, viciousness
(c) malicious act; malicious remark

méchant, ~**e** /meʃɑ̃, ɑ̃t/ **1** *adj*
(a) ⟨person⟩ nasty, malicious; ⟨animal⟩ vicious; ⟨flu, business⟩ nasty, bad
(b) (colloq) fantastic (colloq), terrific (colloq)
2 *nm,f* (a) villain, baddie (colloq)
(b) naughty boy/girl

mèche /mɛʃ/ *nf* (a) (of hair) lock
(b) (in hair) streak
(c) (of candle) wick
(d) (Med) packing
(e) (of explosive) fuse
(f) (drill) bit

IDIOMS **être de ~ avec qn** (colloq) to be in cahoots with sb (colloq); **vendre la ~** to let the cat out of the bag

méchoui /meʃwi/ *nm* North African style barbecue; spit-roast lamb

méconnaissable /mekɔnɛsabl/ *adj* unrecognizable

méconnaissance /mekɔnɛsɑ̃s/ *nf*
(a) ignorance
(b) misreading

méconnaître /mekɔnɛtʀ/ [73] *vtr* to misread; to be mistaken about

méconnu, ~**e** /mekɔny/ *adj* ⟨artist, work⟩ neglected; ⟨value⟩ unrecognized

mécontent, ~**e** /mekɔ̃tɑ̃, ɑ̃t/ *adj* dissatisfied; ⟨voter⟩ discontented; **pas ~** rather pleased

mécontentement /mekɔ̃tɑ̃tmɑ̃/ *nm*
(a) dissatisfaction
(b) discontent
(c) annoyance

mécontenter /mekɔ̃tɑ̃te/ [1] *vtr* to annoy; to anger

Mecque /mɛk/ *pr n* **la ~** Mecca

médaille /medaj/ *nf* (a) medal; ~ **d'or** gold medal
(b) coin
(c) medallion

médaillon /medajɔ̃/ *nm* (a) locket
(b) (in art, architecture) medallion

médecin /mɛdsɛ̃/ *nm* doctor; ~ **traitant** general practitioner, GP (GB)

■ ~ **de garde** duty doctor, doctor on duty; ~ **légiste** forensic surgeon

médecine /mɛdsin/ *nf* medicine

■ ~ **scolaire** ≈ school health service; ~ **du travail** ≈ occupational medicine; ~**s douces** *or* **parallèles** alternative medicine

média /medja/ **1** *nm* medium
2 médias *nm pl* **les ~s** the media

médiateur, **-trice** /medjatœʀ, tʀis/
1 *adj* mediatory
2 *nm* mediator; ombudsman

médiathèque /medjatɛk/ *nf* multimedia library

médiation /medjasjɔ̃/ *nf* mediation

médiatique /medjatik/ *adj* ⟨exploitation⟩ by the media; ⟨success⟩ media

médiatisation /medjatizasjɔ̃/ *nf* media coverage

médiatiser /medjatize/ [1] *vtr* to give [sth] publicity in the media

médical, ∼**e**, *mpl* **-aux** /medikal, o/ *adj* medical

médicament /medikamɑ̃/ *nm* medicine, drug

médication /medikasjɔ̃/ *nf* medication

médicinal, ∼**e**, *mpl* **-aux** /medisinal, o/ *adj* medicinal

médico-légal, ∼**e**, *mpl* **-aux** /medikolegal, o/ *adj* forensic; **certificat** ∼ autopsy report

médico-pédagogique, *pl* ∼**s** /medikopedagɔʒik/ *adj* **institut** ∼ special school

médiéval, ∼**e**, *mpl* **-aux** /medjeval, o/ *adj* medieval

médiocre /medjɔkʀ/ *adj* mediocre; ⟨pupil, intelligence⟩ below average; ⟨soil, light, return, food⟩ poor; ⟨interest, success⟩ limited; ⟨income⟩ meagre (GB)

médiocrement /medjɔkʀəmɑ̃/ *adv* rather badly

médiocrité /medjɔkʀite/ *nf* (a) mediocrity (b) meagreness (GB)

médire /mediʀ/ [65] *v+prep* ∼ **de** to speak ill of

médisance /medizɑ̃s/ *nf* malicious gossip

médisant, ∼**e** /medizɑ̃, ɑ̃t/ *adj* malicious

médit /medi/ ▶ MÉDIRE

méditation /meditasjɔ̃/ *nf* meditation

méditer /medite/ [1] ① *vtr* to mull over; **longuement médité** ⟨plan⟩ carefully considered
② *vi* to meditate; ∼ **sur** to meditate on ⟨existence⟩; to ponder on *or* over ⟨problem⟩

Méditerranée /mediteʀane/ *pr nf* **la** (**mer**) ∼ the Mediterranean (Sea)

méditerranéen, **-éenne** /mediteʀaneɛ̃, ɛn/ *adj* Mediterranean

médium /medjɔm/ *nm* medium

méduse /medyz/ *nf* jellyfish

méduser /medyze/ [1] *vtr* to dumbfound

meeting /mitiŋ/ *nm* meeting

méfait /mefɛ/ ① *nm* misdemeanour (GB); crime
② **méfaits** *nm pl* detrimental effect

méfiance /mefjɑ̃s/ *nf* mistrust, suspicion; ∼ **de qn envers qn/qch** sb's wariness of sb/sth

méfiant, ∼**e** /mefjɑ̃, ɑ̃t/ *adj* suspicious; **elle est d'un naturel** ∼ she's always very wary

méfier: **se méfier** /mefje/ [2] *v refl* (+ *v être*) (a) **se** ∼ **de qn/qch** not to trust sb/sth; **sans se** ∼ quite trustingly

(b) **se** ∼ **de qch** to be wary of sth; **méfie-toi!** be careful!; watch it!

méga /mega/ *pref* mega; ∼**hertz** megahertz

mégalomane /megalɔman/ *adj*, *nmf* megalomaniac

mégaoctet /megaɔktɛ/ *nm* megabyte

mégarde: **par mégarde** /paʀmegaʀd/ *phr* inadvertently

mégère /meʒɛʀ/ *nf* shrew

mégot /mego/ *nm* cigarette butt

meilleur, ∼**e**¹ /mɛjœʀ/ ① *adj* (a) better (**que** than)
(b) best; **au** ∼ **prix** ⟨buy⟩ at the lowest price; ⟨sell⟩ at the highest price
② *nm,f* **le** ∼, **la** ∼**e** the best one
③ *adv* better; **il fait** ∼ **qu'hier** the weather is better than it was yesterday
④ *nm* **le** ∼ the best bit; **pour le** ∼ **et pour le pire** for better or for worse

meilleure² /mɛjœʀ/ *nf* **ça c'est la** ∼! that's the best one yet!

mélancolie /melɑ̃kɔli/ *nf* (gen) melancholy; (Med) melancholia

mélancolique /melɑ̃kɔlik/ ① *adj* melancholy
② *nmf* melancholic

mélancoliquement /melɑ̃kɔlikmɑ̃/ *adv* melancholically, in a melancholy fashion

mélange /melɑ̃ʒ/ *nm* (of teas, tobaccos) blend; (of products, ideas) combination; (of colours) mixture; **c'est un** ∼ (**coton et synthétique**) it's a mix (of cotton and synthetic fibres (GB))

mélanger /melɑ̃ʒe/ [13] ① *vtr* (a) to blend ⟨teas, oils, tobaccos⟩; to mix ⟨colours, shades⟩
(b) to put together ⟨styles, people, objects⟩
(c) to mix up; ∼ **les cartes** to shuffle (the cards)
② **se mélanger** *v refl* (+ *v être*) (a) ⟨teas, oils, tobaccos⟩ to blend; ⟨colours, shades⟩ to mix, to blend together
(b) ⟨ideas⟩ to get muddled

mélangeur /melɑ̃ʒœʀ/ *nm* mixer

mélasse /melas/ *nf* black treacle (GB), molasses

mêlée /mele/ *nf* (a) mêlée; ∼ **générale** free-for-all
(b) (Sport) scrum
(c) (figurative) fray

mêler /mele/ [1] ① *vtr* (a) to mix ⟨products, colours⟩; to blend ⟨ingredients, cultures⟩; to combine ⟨influences⟩
(b) **être mêlé à un scandale** to be involved in a scandal
② **se mêler** *v refl* (+ *v être*) (a) ⟨cultures, religions⟩ to mix; ⟨smells, voices⟩ to mingle
(b) **se** ∼ **à** to mingle with ⟨crowd⟩; to mix with ⟨people⟩; to join in ⟨conversation⟩
(c) **se** ∼ **de** to meddle in; **mêle-toi de tes affaires** (colloq) mind your own business

méli-mélo, *pl* **mélis-mélos** /melimelo/ *nm* jumble, mess

mélo /melo/ *adj* (colloq) slushy (colloq), schmaltzy (colloq)

m

mélodie /melɔdi/ *nf* (a) melody, tune
(b) melodiousness

mélodrame /melɔdʀam/ *nm* melodrama

mélomane /melɔman/ *nmf* music lover

melon /məlɔ̃/ *nm* (a) melon
(b) bowler (hat) (GB), derby (hat) (US)

membrane /mɑ̃bʀan/ *nf* (Anat) membrane

membre /mɑ̃bʀ/ *nm* (a) member; **les pays
~s** the member countries
(b) limb; **~ postérieur** hind limb

mémé /meme/ *nf* (colloq) gran (colloq),
granny (colloq)

même /mɛm/ **1** *adj* (a) same
(b) **c'est l'intelligence ~** he's/she's
intelligence itself
(c) **le jour ~ où** the very same day that;
c'est cela ~ that's it exactly
2 *adv* (a) even; **je ne m'en souviens ~
plus** I can't even remember now
(b) very; **c'est ici ~ que je l'ai rencontré**
I met him at this very place
3 de même *phr* **agir** *or* **faire de ~** to do
the same; **il en va de ~ pour** the same is
true of
4 de même que *phr* **le prix du café, de
~ que celui du tabac, a augmenté de 10%** the
price of coffee, as well as that of tobacco, has
risen by 10%
5 même si *phr* even if
6 *pron* **le ~, la ~, les ~s** the same; **ce sac
est le ~ que celui de Pierre** this bag is the
same as Pierre's

mémento /memɛ̃to/ *nm* guide

mémo /memo/ *nm* (colloq) note

Mémo-Appel /memoapɛl/ *nm* reminder
call service

mémoire¹ /memwaʀ/ **1** *nm* (a) memo
(b) dissertation
2 mémoires *nm pl* memoirs

mémoire² /memwaʀ/ *nf* (a) memory; **si
j'ai bonne ~** if I remember rightly; **ne pas
avoir de ~** to have a bad memory; **de ~
d'homme** in living memory; **en ~ de** to the
memory of, in memory of; **pour ~** for the
record; for reference
(b) (Comput) memory; storage; **mettre des
données en ~** to input data
■ **~ centrale** main storage *or* memory;
~ morte read-only memory, ROM; **~ vive**
random access memory, RAM

Mémophone /memofɔn/ *nm* public
voicemail service

mémorable /memɔʀabl/ *adj* memorable

mémorial, **~e**, *mpl* **-iaux** /memɔʀjal, o/
nm memorial

mémoriser /memɔʀize/ [1] *vtr* to
memorize

menaçant, **~e** /mənasɑ̃, ɑ̃t/ *adj*
menacing

menace /mənas/ *nf* threat; **sous la ~**
under duress; **sous la ~ d'une arme** at
gunpoint

menacer /mənase/ [12] *vtr* (a) to threaten
‹*person*›

(b) to pose a threat to; **être menacé** ‹*stability,
economy*› to be in jeopardy; ‹*life*› to be in
danger; ‹*population*› to be at risk

ménage /menaʒ/ *nm* (a) household; **se
mettre en ~ avec qn** to set up home with sb;
scènes de ~ domestic rows; **monter son ~**
to buy the household goods
(b) housework; **faire le ~** to do the cleaning;
faire des ~ to do domestic cleaning work
IDIOMS **faire bon ~** to be compatible

ménagement /menaʒmɑ̃/ *nm* **avec ~s**
gently; **sans ~s** ‹*say*› bluntly; ‹*push*›
roughly

ménager¹ /menaʒe/ [13] **1** *vtr* (a) to
handle [sb] carefully; to deal carefully with
[sb]; to be gentle with [sb]; to be careful with
[sth]; **~ la susceptibilité de qn** to humour
(GB) sb
(b) to be careful with ‹*clothes, savings*›; **il ne
ménage pas sa peine** he spares no effort
2 se ménager *v refl* (+ *v être*) to take it
easy

ménager², **-ère¹** /menaʒe, ɛʀ/ *adj* ‹*jobs*›
domestic; ‹*equipment*› household; **appareils
~s** domestic appliances; **travaux ~s**
housework

ménagère² /menaʒɛʀ/ *nf* (a) housewife
(b) canteen of cutlery

ménagerie /menaʒʀi/ *nf* menagerie

mendiant, **~e** /mɑ̃djɑ̃, ɑ̃t/ *nm,f* beggar

mendicité /mɑ̃disite/ *nf* begging

mendier /mɑ̃dje/ [2] **1** *vtr* to beg for
2 *vi* to beg

mener /məne/ [16] **1** *vtr* (a) **~ qn quelque
part** to take sb somewhere; to drive sb
somewhere
(b) to lead ‹*people, country*›; to run
‹*company*›; **il ne se laisse pas ~ par sa
grande sœur** he won't be bossed about by his
sister (colloq)
(c) **~ au village** ‹*road*› to go *or* lead to the
village
(d) **~ à** to lead to; **cette histoire peut te ~
loin** it could be a very nasty business; **~ à
bien** to complete [sth] successfully; to bring
[sth] to a successful conclusion; to handle
[sth] successfully
(e) to carry out ‹*study, reform*›; to run
‹*campaign*›; **~ une enquête** to hold an
investigation; **~ sa vie comme on l'entend** to
live as one pleases
2 *vi* (Sport) to be in the lead
IDIOMS **~ la danse** *or* **le jeu** to call the tune

ménestrel /menɛstʀɛl/ *nm* minstrel

meneur, **-euse** /mənœʀ, øz/ *nm,f* leader

menhir /meniʀ/ *nm* menhir

méninge /menɛ̃ʒ/ **1** *nf* (Anat) meninx
2 méninges *nf pl* (colloq) brains (colloq)

méningite /menɛ̃ʒit/ *nf* meningitis

ménisque /menisk/ *nm* meniscus

ménopause /menɔpoz/ *nf* menopause

menotte /mənɔt/ **1** *nf* tiny hand
2 menottes *nf pl* handcuffs

mensonge /mɑ̃sɔ̃ʒ/ *nm* (a) lie

(b) le ~ lying

mensonger, -ère /mãsɔ̃ʒe, ɛʀ/ *adj*
⟨*accusations*⟩ false; ⟨*advertising*⟩ misleading

mensualité /mãsyalite/ *nf* monthly
instalment (GB)

mensuel, -elle /mãsyɛl/ **1** *adj* monthly
2 *nm* monthly magazine

mensuellement /mãsyɛlmã/ *adv* once a
month, monthly

mensurations /mãsyʀasjɔ̃/ *nf pl*
measurements

mental, ~e, *mpl* **-aux** /mãtal, o/ *adj*
mental; **handicapé** ~ mentally handicapped
person

mentalité /mãtalite/ *nf* mentality

menteur, -euse /mãtœʀ, øz/ **1** *adj*
⟨*person*⟩ untruthful; ⟨*statement*⟩ full of lies
2 *nm,f* liar

menthe /mãt/ *nf* **(a)** mint; ~ **poivrée**
peppermint; ~ **verte** spearmint
(b) mint tea
(c) ~ (à l'eau) mint cordial

menthol /mãtɔl/ *nm* menthol

mentholé, ~e /mãtɔle/ *adj* mentholated;
menthol

mention /mãsjɔ̃/ *nf* **(a)** mention; **faire** ~
de qch to mention sth
(b) (Sch) ~ **passable** *pass with 50 to 60%*;
~ **très bien** *pass with 80% upward(s)*
(c) note; **rayer la** ~ **inutile** *or* **les** ~**s inutiles**
delete as appropriate

mentionner /mãsjɔne/ [1] *vtr* to mention

mentir /mãtiʀ/ [30] *vi* **(a)** to lie, to tell
lies
(b) ⟨*figures*⟩ to be misleading
2 se mentir *v refl* (+ *v être*) **(a)** to fool
oneself
(b) to lie to one another

menton /mãtɔ̃/ *nm* chin

menu, ~e /məny/ **1** *adj* **(a)** ⟨*person*⟩
slight; ⟨*foot, piece*⟩ tiny; ⟨*writing*⟩ small
(b) ⟨*jobs*⟩ small; ⟨*details*⟩ minute; ~ **fretin**
small fry
2 *adv* ⟨*write*⟩ small; ⟨*chop*⟩ finely
3 *nm* menu
4 par le menu *phr* in (great) detail
■ ~ **fretin** small fry; ~**e monnaie** small
change

menuiserie /mənɥizʀi/ *nf* woodwork

menuisier /mənɥizje/ *nm* joiner (GB),
finish carpenter

méprendre: se méprendre /mepʀɑ̃dʀ/
[52] *v refl* (+ *v être*) to be mistaken

mépris /mepʀi/ *nm inv* contempt; **au** ~ **de**
la loi regardless of the law

méprisable /mepʀizabl/ *adj* contemptible

méprisant, ~e /mepʀizɑ̃, ɑ̃t/ *adj*
⟨*gesture*⟩ contemptuous; ⟨*person*⟩ disdainful

méprise /mepʀiz/ *nf* mistake

mépriser /mepʀize/ [1] *vtr* to despise
⟨*person, wealth*⟩; to scorn ⟨*danger, offer*⟩

mer /mɛʀ/ *nf* **(a)** sea; **une** ~ **d'huile** a glassy
sea; **en pleine** ~ out at sea; **la** ~ **monte** the
tide is coming in

(b) seaside
IDIOMS ce n'est pas la ~ **à boire** it's not all
that difficult

mercantile /mɛʀkãtil/ *adj* mercenary

mercenaire /mɛʀsənɛʀ/ *adj, nmf*
mercenary

mercerie /mɛʀsəʀi/ *nf* haberdasher's shop
(GB), notions store (US)

merci¹ /mɛʀsi/ *nm, excl* thank you

merci² /mɛʀsi/ *nf* mercy; **on est toujours à**
la ~ **d'un accident** there's always the risk of
an accident

mercredi /mɛʀkʀədi/ *nm* Wednesday

mercure /mɛʀkyʀ/ *nm* mercury

mercurochrome® /mɛʀkyʀokʀom/ *nm*
Mercurochrome®, antiseptic

merde /mɛʀd/ *nf, excl* (vulgar) shit (slang)

mère /mɛʀ/ **1** *nf* **(a)** mother
(b) ~ **supérieure** Mother Superior
2 (-)mère (*combining form*) **cellule/maison**
~ parent cell/company
■ ~ **célibataire** single mother; ~ **de famille**
mother; housewife; ~ **porteuse** surrogate
mother; ~ **poule** mother hen

merguez /mɛʀgɛz/ *nf inv* spicy sausage

méridien /meʀidjɛ̃/ *nm* meridian

méridional, ~e, *mpl* **-aux** /meʀidjɔnal,
o/ **1** *adj* southern
2 *nm,f* Southerner

meringue /məʀɛ̃g/ *nf* meringue

mérite /meʀit/ *nm* merit; credit; **au** ~
according to merit; **vanter les** ~**s de** to sing
the praises of

mériter /meʀite/ [1] **1** *vtr* to deserve;
~ **réflexion** to be worth considering
2 se mériter *v refl* (+ *v être*) **ça se mérite**
it's something that has to be earned

merlan /mɛʀlã/ *nm* whiting

merle /mɛʀl/ *nm* blackbird

mérou /meʀu/ *nm* grouper

merveille /mɛʀvɛj/ **1** *nf* marvel, wonder
2 à merveille *phr* wonderfully

merveilleux, -euse /mɛʀvɛjø, øz/ *adj*
marvellous (GB), wonderful

mes ▸ MON

mésaventure /mezavɑ̃tyʀ/ *nf*
misadventure

mesdames ▸ MADAME

mesdemoiselles ▸ MADEMOISELLE

mésentente /mezãtãt/ *nf* dissension;
disagreement

mésestimer /mezɛstime/ [1] *vtr* to
underrate; to underestimate

mesquin, ~e /mɛskɛ̃, in/ *adj* **(a)** petty-
minded; petty
(b) ⟨*person*⟩ mean (GB), cheap (US) (colloq)

mesquinerie /mɛskinʀi/ *nf* **(a)** meanness
(b) stinginess
(c) mean trick; mean remark

message /mesaʒ/ *nm* message;
~ **publicitaire** commercial

messager, -ère /mesaʒe, ɛʀ/ *nm,f*
(a) messenger

(b) envoy

messagerie /mesaʒʀi/ *nf* **(a)** freight forwarding
■ ~ **électronique** electronic mail service, e-mail; ~ **vocale** voice messaging

messe /mɛs/ *nf* mass; ~**s basses** (colloq) whispering

messie /mesi/ *nm* messiah

messieurs ▶ MONSIEUR

mesure /məzyʀ/ *nf* **(a)** measure; **prendre des ~s** to take measures; to take steps
(b) measurement; **c'est du sur ~** it's made to measure; **tu as un emploi du ~** the job is tailor-made for you; **c'est une adversaire à ta ~** she is a match for you
(c) unité de ~ unit of measurement; **instrument de ~** measuring device; **deux ~s de lait pour une ~ d'eau** two parts milk to one of water
(d) moderation; **dépasser la ~** to go too far
(e) (Mus) bar; **battre la ~** to beat time
(f) **être en ~ de rembourser** to be in a position to reimburse; **dans la ~ du possible** as far as possible; **dans la ~ où** insofar as

mesurer /məzyʀe/ [1] 1 *vtr* **(a)** to measure; ~ **le tour de cou de qn** to take sb's neck measurement
(b) to measure ⟨*productivity, gap*⟩; to assess ⟨*difficulties, risks, effects*⟩; to consider ⟨*consequences*⟩; ~ **ses paroles** to weigh one's words
2 *vi* ~ **20 mètres carrés** to be 20 metres (GB) square; **elle mesure 1,60 m** she's 1.60 m tall
3 **se mesurer** *v refl* (+ *v être*) **(a) se ~ en mètres** to be measured in metres (GB)
(b) se ~ à *or* **avec qn** to pit one's strength against sb

métal, *pl* **-aux** /metal, o/ *nm* metal; **pièce de** *or* **en ~** metal coin; ~ **jaune** gold

métallique /metalik/ *adj* **(a)** metal; **c'est ~** it's made of metal
(b) metallic

métallisé, ~**e** /metalize/ *adj* ⟨*green, blue*⟩ metallic

métallurgie /metalyʀʒi/ *nf*
(a) metalworking industry
(b) metallurgy

métallurgique /metalyʀʒik/ *adj* metallurgical

métamorphose /metamɔʀfoz/ *nf* metamorphosis

métamorphoser /metamɔʀfoze/ [1]
1 *vtr* to transform [sb/sth] completely
2 **se métamorphoser** *v refl* (+ *v être*) **se ~ en** to metamorphose into

métaphore /metafɔʀ/ *nf* metaphor

métayage /metejaʒ/ *nm* tenant farming, sharecropping

métayer, -ère /meteje, ɛʀ/ *nm,f* tenant farmer (GB), sharecropper (US)

météo /meteo/ *nf* weather forecast

météore /meteɔʀ/ *nm* meteor

météorite /meteɔʀit/ *nm or nf* meteorite

météorologie /meteɔʀɔlɔʒi/ *nf* meteorology

météorologique /meteɔʀɔlɔʒik/ *adj* meteorological; **conditions ~s** weather conditions

météorologiste /meteɔʀɔlɔʒist/,
météorologue /meteɔʀɔlɔg/ *nmf* meteorologist

métèque /metɛk/ *nm* (offensive) foreigner, dago (offensive)

méthane /metan/ *nm* methane

méthode /metɔd/ *nf* **(a)** method
(b) (for languages) course book (GB), textbook (US)
(c) way; **j'ai ma ~ pour le convaincre** I've got a way of convincing him

méthodique /metɔdik/ *adj* methodical

méthodiquement /metɔdikmɑ̃/ *adv* methodically; **procédons ~** let's take things step by step

méticuleux, -euse /metikylø, øz/ *adj* meticulous; painstaking

métier /metje/ *nm* **(a)** job; profession; trade; craft; **avoir 20 ans de ~** to have 20 years' experience; **c'est le ~ qui rentre!** you learn by your mistakes!
(b) ~ **à tisser** weaving loom

métis, -isse /metis/ *nm,f* person of mixed race

métissage /metisaʒ/ *nm* (of people) miscegenation; (of plants, animals) crossing

métrage /metʀaʒ/ *nm* **(a)** (of material) length
(b) long ~ feature(-length) film

mètre /mɛtʀ/ *nm* **(a)** metre (GB); **le 60 ~s** the 60 metres (GB); **piquer un cent ~s** (colloq) to break into a run
(b) rule (GB), yardstick (US); ~ **ruban** *or* **de couturière** tape measure

métrique /metʀik/ *adj* metric

métro /metʀo/ *nm* underground (GB), subway (US).
IDIOMS ~, **boulot, dodo** (colloq) the daily grind

métronome /metʀɔnɔm/ *nm* metronome

métropole /metʀɔpɔl/ *nf* **(a)** metropolis
(b) major city
(c) Metropolitan France

métropolitain, ~e /metʀɔpɔlitɛ̃, ɛn/ *adj*
(a) ⟨*network*⟩ underground (GB), subway (US)
(b) from Metropolitan France

métropolite /metʀɔpɔlit/ *nm* metropolitan

mets /mɛ/ *nm inv* dish, delicacy

mettable /metabl/ *adj* wearable

metteur /metœʀ/ *nm* ~ **en scène** director

mettre /mɛtʀ/ [60] 1 *vtr* **(a)** to put; to put in ⟨*heating, shower*⟩; to put up ⟨*curtains, shelves*⟩; **je mets les enfants à la crèche** I send the children to a creche; **mets ton écharpe** put your scarf on; ~ **le linge à sécher** to put the washing out to dry; **faire ~ le téléphone** to have a telephone put in
(b) to wear
(c) ~ **qn en colère** to make sb angry

(d) to put on ⟨radio, TV, heating⟩; **mets moins fort!** turn it down!; **∼ le réveil** to set the alarm
(e) to put up ⟨sign⟩; **qu'est-ce que je dois ∼?** what shall I put?; **je t'ai mis un mot** I've left you a note; **∼ en musique** to set to music; **∼ en anglais** to put into English
(f) y ∼ du sien to put oneself into it; **combien pouvez-vous ∼?** how much can you afford?; how much can you put in?; **elle a mis une heure** it took her an hour (**pour faire** to do)
(g) (Sch) **je vous ai mis trois sur vingt** I've given you three out of twenty
(h) (colloq) **mettons qu'il vienne, qu'est-ce que vous ferez?** supposing he comes, what will you do?
2 vi **∼ bas** ⟨animal⟩ to give birth; to calve
3 se mettre v refl (+ v être) **(a) se ∼ devant la fenêtre** to stand in front of the window; **se ∼ au lit** to go to bed; **se ∼ debout** to stand up; **où est-ce que ça se met?** where does this go?
(b) to spill [sth] on oneself
(c) je ne sais pas quoi me ∼ I don't know what to put on
(d) se ∼ à l'anglais to take up English; **il va se ∼ à pleuvoir** it's going to start raining
(e) je préfère me ∼ bien avec lui I prefer to get on the right side of him; **se ∼ à l'aise** to make oneself comfortable

meuble /mœbl/ **1** adj ⟨soil⟩ loose
2 nm **un ∼** a piece of furniture
IDIOMS **sauver les ∼s** to salvage something

meublé /mœble/ nm furnished apartment

meubler /mœble/ [1] vtr to furnish; **la plante meuble bien la pièce** the plant makes the room look more cosy (GB) or cozy (US)

meugler /møgle/ [1] vi to moo

meule /møl/ nf **(a)** millstone
(b) grindstone
(c) ∼ de foin haystack

meunier, -ière /mønje, ɛʀ/ nm,f miller

meurtre /mœʀtʀ/ nm murder

meurtrier, -ière /mœʀtʀije, ɛʀ/ **1** adj ⟨fighting, repression⟩ bloody; ⟨explosion, accident⟩ fatal; ⟨epidemic⟩ deadly; ⟨arm⟩ lethal
2 nm,f murderer

meurtrir /mœʀtʀiʀ/ [3] vtr **(a)** to hurt
(b) to bruise
(c) to wound ⟨self-esteem⟩

meute /møt/ nf pack of hounds

mexicain, ∼e /mɛksikɛ̃, ɛn/ adj Mexican

Mexico /mɛksiko/ pr n Mexico City

Mexique /mɛksik/ pr nm Mexico

mezzanine /medzanin/ nf mezzanine

MF /ɛmɛf/ nf (abbr = **modulation de fréquence**) frequency modulation, FM

mi /mi/ nm inv (Mus) (note) E; (in sol-fa) mi, me

mi- /mi/ pref **à la ∼-mai/saison** in mid-May/-season; **∼-chinois, ∼-français** half Chinese, half French

miam-miam /mjammjam/ excl (colloq) yum-yum! (colloq)

miauler /mjole/ [1] vi to miaow (GB), to meow

mi-bas /miba/ nm inv knee sock, long sock

miche /miʃ/ nf round loaf

mi-chemin: à mi-chemin /amiʃmɛ̃/ phr halfway; (figurative) halfway through

mi-clos, ∼e /miklo, oz/ adj half-closed

micmac /mikmak/ nm (colloq) shady goings-on (colloq)

mi-côte: à mi-côte /amikot/ phr halfway up; halfway down

mi-course: à mi-course /amikuʀs/ phr halfway through the race; (figurative) halfway through

micro¹ /mikʀo/ pref micro

micro² /mikʀo/ nm microphone, mike (colloq); **∼ caché** bug

microbe /mikʀɔb/ nm germ, microbe

microclimat /mikʀoklima/ nm microclimate

microcosme /mikʀɔkɔsm/ nm microcosm

micro-cravate, pl **micros-cravates** /mikʀokʀavat/ nm lapel-microphone

micro-édition /mikʀoedisjɔ̃/ nf desktop publishing

microfilm /mikʀɔfilm/ nm microfilm

micro-informatique /mikʀoɛ̃fɔʀmatik/ nf microcomputing

micro-ondes /mikʀoɔ̃d/ nm inv microwave (colloq)

micro-ordinateur, pl **∼s** /mikʀoɔʀdinatœʀ/ nm microcomputer

microphone /mikʀofɔn/ nm microphone

microprocesseur /mikʀopʀɔsesœʀ/ nm microprocessor

microscope /mikʀɔskɔp/ nm microscope

microscopique /mikʀɔskɔpik/ adj microscopic; (figurative) tiny

microsillon /mikʀɔsijɔ̃/ nm (disque) ∼ microgroove record

mi-cuisse: à mi-cuisse /amikɥis/ phr above one's knees

midi /midi/ nm **(a)** twelve o'clock, midday, noon; **je fais mes courses entre ∼ et deux** (colloq) I go shopping in my lunch hour
(b) lunchtime
(c) le Midi the South of France

midinette /midinɛt/ nf bimbo (colloq)

mi-distance: à mi-distance /amidistɑ̃s/ phr halfway

mie /mi/ nf bread without the crusts

miel /mjɛl/ nm honey
IDIOMS **être tout sucre tout ∼** to be as nice as pie (colloq)

mielleux, -euse /mjɛlø, øz/ adj ⟨tone⟩ unctuous, honeyed; ⟨person⟩ fawning

mien, mienne /mjɛ̃, mjɛn/ **1** det **ces idées, je les ai faites miennes** I adopted these ideas

2 **le mien, la mienne, les miens, les miennes** *pron* mine

miette /mjɛt/ *nf* crumb; **réduire en ∼s** to smash [sth] to bits ⟨*vase*⟩; to shatter ⟨*hopes*⟩; **elle n'en perd pas une ∼** (colloq) she's taking it all in

mieux /mjø/ **1** *adj inv* better; **le ∼, la ∼, les ∼** the best; the nicest; the most attractive; **ce qu'il y a de ∼** the best
2 *adv* (a) better; **je ne peux pas te dire ∼** that's all I can tell you; **qui dit ∼?** any other offers?; any advance on that bid?; **de ∼ en ∼** better and better; **on la critiquait à qui ∼ ∼** each person criticized her more harshly than the last
(b) **le ∼, la ∼, les ∼** the best; (of two) the better
3 *nm inv* **le ∼ est de refuser** the best thing is to refuse; **il y a un/du ∼** there is an/some improvement; **je ne demande pas ∼ que de rester ici** I'm perfectly happy staying here; **fais pour le ∼, fais au ∼** do whatever is best; **tout va pour le ∼** everything's fine; **elle est au ∼ avec sa voisine** she is on very good terms with her neighbour (GB)

mièvre /mjɛvʀ/ *adj* vapid; soppy

mièvrerie /mjɛvʀəʀi/ *nf* vapidity; soppiness

mi-figue /mifig/ *adj inv* **∼ mi-raisin** ⟨*smile*⟩ half-hearted; ⟨*compliment*⟩ ambiguous

mignon, -onne /miɲɔ̃, ɔn/ *adj* (a) cute
(b) sweet, kind

migraine /migʀɛn/ *nf* splitting headache

migration /migʀasjɔ̃/ *nf* migration

migratoire /migʀatwaʀ/ *adj* migratory

migrer /migʀe/ [1] *vi* to migrate

mi-hauteur: **à mi-hauteur** /amiotœʀ/ *phr* halfway up; halfway down

mi-jambe: **à mi-jambe** /amiʒɑ̃b/ *phr* (up) to one's knees

mijaurée /miʒɔʀe/ *nf* **ne fais pas ta ∼** don't put on such airs

mijoter /miʒɔte/ [1] **1** *vtr* (Culin) to prepare
2 *vi* (Culin) to simmer

mijoteuse® /miʒɔtøz/ *nf* slow cooker

mikado /mikado/ *nm* spillikins

mil /mil/ *adj* = MILLE 1

milice /milis/ *nf* militia; **∼ de quartier** local vigilante group

Milice /milis/ *nf* **la ∼** the Milice (*French wartime paramilitary organization which collaborated with the Germans against the Resistance*)

milicien, -ienne /milisjɛ̃, ɛn/ *nm,f*
(a) militiaman/militiawoman
(b) member of the Milice

milieu, *pl* **∼x** /miljø/ **1** *nm* (a) middle; **au beau** *or* **en plein ∼** right in the middle; **au ∼ de la nuit** halfway through the night
(b) middle ground
(c) environment; **en ∼ rural** in the country
(d) background, milieu; **le ∼** the underworld
2 **au milieu de** *phr* (a) among; **être au ∼ de ses amis** to be with one's friends

(b) surrounded by; **au ∼ du désastre** in the midst of disaster

militaire /militɛʀ/ **1** *adj* military; army
2 *nm* serviceman

militairement /militɛʀmɑ̃/ *adv* (a) by military means; **zone occupée ∼** military occupied zone
(b) with military efficiency; along military lines

militant, ∼e /militɑ̃, ɑ̃t/ **1** *adj* militant
2 *nm,f* (of organization) active member, activist; (for cause) campaigner

militantisme /militɑ̃tism/ *nm* political activism

militariste /militaʀist/ *adj* militaristic

militer /milite/ [1] *vi* (a) to campaign
(b) to be a political activist

mille /mil/ **1** *adj inv* a thousand, one thousand; **deux/trois ∼** two/three thousand
2 *nm inv* (a) a thousand, one thousand
(b) bull's eye; **taper dans le ∼** to hit the bull's-eye; (figurative) to hit the nail on the head
3 *nm* (a) **∼** (**marin** *or* **nautique**) (nautical) mile
(b) (air) mile
4 **pour mille** *phr* per thousand
IDIOMS **je vous le donne en ∼** you'll never guess (in a million years)

millénaire /milenɛʀ/ **1** *adj* (a) **un arbre ∼** a one-thousand-year-old tree
(b) ⟨*tradition*⟩ age-old
2 *nm* (a) **pendant des ∼s** for thousands of years
(b) millennium, millenary

mille-pattes /milpat/ *nm inv* centipede, millipede

millésime /milezim/ *nm* vintage, year

milli /mili/ *pref* milli; **∼mètre** millimetre (GB)

milliard /miljaʀ/ *nm* billion

milliardaire /miljaʀdɛʀ/ *nmf* multimillionaire, billionaire

millième /miljɛm/ *adj* thousandth

millier /milje/ *nm* (a) thousand
(b) **un ∼** about a thousand

million /miljɔ̃/ *nm* million

millionième /miljɔnjɛm/ *adj* millionth

millionnaire /miljɔnɛʀ/ **1** *adj* **être ∼** ⟨*firm*⟩ to be worth millions; ⟨*person*⟩ to be a millionaire
2 *nmf* millionaire

mime /mim/ *nm* mime

mimer /mime/ [1] *vtr* (a) to mime
(b) to mimic

mimétisme /mimetism/ *nm* (a) (Zool) mimicry
(b) **par ∼** through unconscious imitation

mimique /mimik/ *nf* funny face

minable /minabl/ *adj* (colloq) (a) ⟨*salary, person*⟩ pathetic
(b) ⟨*place*⟩ crummy (colloq); ⟨*existence*⟩ miserable

minage /minaʒ/ *nm* mining

minaret /minaʀɛ/ *nm* minaret

minauder /minode/ [1] *vi* (a) to mince about
(b) to simper

mince /mɛ̃s/ *adj* (a) slim, slender; ⟨face, slice⟩ thin
(b) ⟨consolation⟩ small; ⟨chance⟩ slim

minceur /mɛ̃sœʀ/ *nf* slimness; slenderness; thinness

mincir /mɛ̃siʀ/ [3] *vi* to lose weight

mine /min/ *nf* (a) expression; faire ∼ d'accepter to pretend to accept; elle nous a dit, ∼ de rien, que (colloq) she told us, casually, that; il est doué, ∼ de rien (colloq) it may not be obvious, but he's very clever
(b) avoir bonne ∼ ⟨person⟩ to look well
(c) (in pencil) lead
(d) mine; ∼ d'or gold mine
(e) (Mil) mine
IDIOMS ne pas payer de ∼ (colloq) not to look anything special (colloq)

miner /mine/ [1] *vtr* (a) to sap ⟨morale, energy⟩; to undermine ⟨health⟩
(b) (Mil) to mine

minerai /minʀɛ/ *nm* ore; ∼ de fer iron ore

minéral, ∼**e**, *mpl* **-aux** /mineʀal, o/
[1] *adj* ⟨water⟩ mineral; ⟨chemistry⟩ inorganic
[2] *nm* mineral

minéralogique /mineʀalɔʒik/ *adj* plaque ∼ number plate (GB), license plate (US)

minerve /minɛʀv/ *nf* (Med) surgical collar (GB), neck brace (US)

minet /minɛ/ *nm* (a) pussycat
(b) (colloq) pretty boy (colloq)

minette /minɛt/ *nf* (a) pussycat
(b) (colloq) cool chick (colloq)

mineur, ∼**e** /minœʀ/ [1] *adj* (a) (Law) under 18
(b) ⟨detail⟩ minor
(c) (Mus) en ré ∼ in D minor
[2] *nm,f* (Law) person under 18
[3] *nm* miner; ∼ de fond pit worker

mini- /mini/ *pref* mini

miniature /minjatyʀ/ *adj, nf* miniature

miniaturisation /minjatyʀizasjɔ̃/ *nf* miniaturization

minibus /minibys/ *nm inv* minibus

minicassette® /minikasɛt/ *nf* minicassette®

minier, -ière /minje, ɛʀ/ *adj* mining

mini-informatique /miniɛ̃fɔʀmatik/ *nf* minicomputing

mini-jupe, *pl* ∼**s** /miniʒyp/ *nf* mini-skirt

minimal, ∼**e**, *mpl* **-aux** /minimal, o/ *adj* minimal, minimum

minimalisme /minimalism/ *nm* minimalism

minime /minim/ [1] *adj* negligible
[2] *nmf* (Sport) junior (7 to 13 years old)

minimiser /minimize/ [1] *vtr* to minimize

minimum, *pl* ∼**s** or **minima** /minimɔm, minima/ [1] *adj* minimum

[2] *nm* (a) minimum; un ∼ de bon sens a certain amount of common sense; il faut au ∼ deux heures pour faire le trajet the journey takes at least two hours
(b) (Law) minimum sentence
■ ∼ vital subsistence level

mini-ordinateur, *pl* ∼**s** /miniɔʀdinatœʀ/ *nm* minicomputer

minipilule /minipilyl/ *nf* low-dose combined pill

ministère /ministɛʀ/ *nm* ministry; (in UK, US) department

ministériel, -ielle /ministeʀjɛl/ *adj* ministerial, cabinet

ministre /ministʀ/ *nm* (a) minister; (in UK) Secretary of State; (in US) Secretary
(b) (of religion) minister

Minitel® /minitɛl/ *nm* Minitel (*terminal linking phone users to a database*)

minitéler /minitele/ [14] *vtr* to contact via Minitel

minitéliste /minitɛlist/ *n* Minitel user

minivague /minivag/ *nf* soft perm

minois /minwa/ *nm inv* fresh young face

minoration /minɔʀasjɔ̃/ *nf*
(a) undervaluation; underestimation
(b) reduction; ∼ des prix cut in prices

minorer /minɔʀe/ [1] *vtr* (a) to reduce (de by)
(b) to undervalue; to underestimate

minoritaire /minɔʀitɛʀ/ *adj* minority

minorité /minɔʀite/ *nf* (a) minority; être mis en ∼ to be defeated
(b) (age) minority
■ ∼ de blocage blocking minority

minoterie /minɔtʀi/ *nf* (a) flour mill
(b) flour-milling

minou /minu/ *nm* pussycat

minuit /minɥi/ *nm* midnight

minuscule /minyskyl/ [1] *adj* ⟨person, thing⟩ tiny; ⟨quantity⟩ tiny, minute
[2] *nf* small letter; (in printing) lower-case letter

minutage /minytaʒ/ *nm* (precise) timing

minute /minyt/ *nf* minute; la ∼ de vérité the moment of truth

minuter /minyte/ [1] *vtr* (a) to time
(b) to work out the timing of

minuterie /minytʀi/ *nf* (a) time-switch
(b) automatic lighting

minuteur /minytœʀ/ *nm* timer

minutie /minysi/ *nf* meticulousness

minutieusement /minysjøzmã/ *adv* with meticulous care; in great detail

minutieux, -ieuse /minysjø, øz/ *adj* meticulous; ⟨description⟩ detailed

mioche /mjɔʃ/ *nmf* (colloq) kid (colloq)

mirabelle /miʀabɛl/ *nf* (a) mirabelle (*small yellow plum*)
(b) plum brandy

miracle /miʀakl/ [1] *adj inv* un médicament ∼ a wonder drug; une méthode ∼ a magic formula ⋯❖

m

2 *nm* **(a)** miracle; **faire un ∼** to work a miracle; (figurative) to work miracles; **comme par ∼** as if by magic
(b) miracle play

miraculeux, -euse /miʀakylø, øz/ *adj* miraculous; ⟨*product, remedy*⟩ which works wonders

mirador /miʀadɔʀ/ *nm* watchtower

mirage /miʀaʒ/ *nm* mirage

mi-raisin /miʀɛzɛ̃/ *adj inv* ▶ MI-FIGUE

miraud, ∼e /miʀo, od/ *adj* (colloq) shortsighted

mirobolant, ∼e /miʀɔbɔlɑ̃, ɑ̃t/ *adj* (colloq) fabulous (colloq)

miroir /miʀwaʀ/ *nm* mirror

miroitement /miʀwatmɑ̃/ *nm* sparkling; shimmering

miroiter /miʀwate/ [1] *vi* to shimmer; **faire ∼ qch à qn** to hold out the prospect of sth to sb

mis, ∼e[1] /mi, miz/ ▶ METTRE

misanthrope /mizɑ̃tʀɔp/ **1** *adj* misanthropic
2 *nmf* misanthropist, misanthrope

mise[2] /miz/ *nf* **une ∼ de cinq francs** a five-franc bet
■ **∼ de fonds** investment; **∼ en plis** set
IDIOMS **être de ∼** ⟨*conduct*⟩ to be proper

miser /mize/ [1] **1** *vtr* to bet
2 *vi* **(a) ∼ sur** to bet on, to place a bet on
(b) ∼ sur qn to place all one's hopes in sb

misérabilisme /mizeʀabilism/ *nm*
(a) sordid realism
(b) tendency to dwell on the dark side

misérable /mizeʀabl/ **1** *adj* **(a)** ⟨*person*⟩ destitute, poor; ⟨*life*⟩ poor
(b) ⟨*salary*⟩ meagre (GB)
2 *nmf* **(a)** pauper
(b) scoundrel

misère /mizeʀ/ *nf* **(a)** destitution; **réduire qn à la ∼** to reduce sb to poverty
(b) misery, wretchedness
(c) trouble, woe; **on a tous nos petites ∼s** we all have our troubles
(d) être payé une ∼ to be paid a pittance

miséreux, -euse /mizeʀø, øz/ *nm,f* destitute person; **les ∼** the destitute

miséricorde /mizeʀikɔʀd/ *nf, excl* mercy

misogyne /mizɔʒin/ *adj* misogynous

misogynie /mizɔʒini/ *nf* misogyny

missel /misɛl/ *nm* missal

missile /misil/ *nm* missile

mission /misjɔ̃/ *nf* mission

missionnaire /misjɔnɛʀ/ *adj, nmf* missionary

missive /misiv/ *nf* missive

mistral /mistʀal/ *nm* mistral

mitaine /mitɛn/ *nf* fingerless mitten

mite /mit/ *nf* (clothes) moth

mi-temps[1] /mitɑ̃/ *nm inv* part-time job

mi-temps[2] /mitɑ̃/ *nf inv* (Sport) half-time

miteux, -euse /mitø, øz/ *adj* seedy; shabby

mitigé, ∼e /mitiʒe/ *adj* ⟨*reception*⟩ lukewarm; ⟨*success*⟩ qualified

mitonner /mitɔne/ [1] *vtr* to cook [sth] lovingly

mitoyen, -enne /mitwajɛ̃, ɛn/ *adj* ⟨*hedge*⟩ dividing; **mur ∼** party wall

mitraille /mitʀaj/ *nf* hail of bullets

mitrailler /mitʀaje/ [1] *vtr* **(a)** to machine-gun
(b) ∼ qn de questions to fire questions at sb
(c) (colloq) to take photo after photo of [sb/sth]

mitraillette /mitʀajɛt/ *nf* submachine gun

mitrailleuse /mitʀajøz/ *nf* machine gun

mi-voix: à mi-voix /amivwa/ *phr* in a low voice

mixage /miksaʒ/ *nm* sound mixing

mixer[1] /mikse/ [1] *vtr* to mix

mixer[2] /miksɛʀ/ = MIXEUR

mixeur /miksœʀ/ *nm* **(a)** mixer
(b) blender

mixité /miksite/ *nf* (gen) mixing of sexes; (Sch) coeducation

mixte /mikst/ *adj* **(a)** ⟨*school*⟩ coeducational; ⟨*class*⟩ mixed
(b) ⟨*couple, marriage*⟩ mixed; ⟨*economy*⟩ mixed; **société ∼** joint venture

mixture /mikstyʀ/ *nf* **(a)** concoction
(b) (in pharmacy) mixture
(c) mishmash (colloq)

MJC /ɛmʒise/ *nf* (abbr = **maison des jeunes et de la culture**) ≈ youth club

MLF /ɛmɛlɛf/ *nm* (abbr = **mouvement de libération des femmes**) ≈ Women's Lib

Mlle (*written abbr* = **Mademoiselle**) Ms, Miss

mm (*written abbr* = **millimètre**) mm

MM. (*written abbr* = **Messieurs**) Messrs

Mme (*written abbr* = **Madame**) Ms, Mrs

mnémotechnique /mnemɔtɛknik/ *adj* mnemonic

Mo (*written abbr* = **mégaoctet**) Mb, MB

mobile /mɔbil/ **1** *adj* (gen) mobile; ⟨*leaf*⟩ loose
2 *nm* **(a)** motive
(b) mobile

mobilier, -ière /mɔbilje, ɛʀ/ **1** *adj* **biens ∼s** movable property
2 *nm* furniture

mobilisation /mɔbilizasjɔ̃/ *nf* mobilization

mobiliser /mɔbilize/ [1] **1** *vtr* to mobilize ⟨*soldier*⟩; to call up ⟨*civilian*⟩
2 se mobiliser *v refl* (+ *v être*) to rally

mobilité /mɔbilite/ *nf* mobility

mobylette® /mɔbilɛt/ *nf* moped

mocassin /mɔkasɛ̃/ *nm* moccasin, loafer

moche /mɔʃ/ *adj* (colloq) **(a)** ⟨*person*⟩ ugly; ⟨*garment*⟩ ghastly
(b) ⟨*incident*⟩ dreadful
(c) ⟨*act*⟩ nasty

modalité /mɔdalite/ **1** *nf* modality
2 modalités *nf pl* terms; practical details

mode¹ /mɔd/ *nm* (a) way, mode; ~ **de paiement** method of payment
(b) (in grammar) mood
■ ~ **d'emploi** instructions for use

mode² /mɔd/ *nf* (a) fashion; **lancer une** ~ to start a fashion; **à la** ~ ⟨*garment, club*⟩ fashionable; ⟨*singer*⟩ popular
(b) fashion industry

modèle /mɔdɛl/ **1** *adj* (gen) model; ⟨*conduct*⟩ perfect, exemplary
2 *nm* (a) (gen) model; **prendre** ~ **sur qn** to do as sb does/did; ~ **à suivre** somebody to look up to; **la tente grand** ~ large-size tent; **le** ~ **au-dessus** the next size up; ~ **de signature** specimen signature
(b) pattern; ~ **déposé** registered pattern
■ ~ **réduit** scale model

modeler /mɔdle/ [17] *vtr* to model ⟨*clay*⟩; to mould (GB) or mold (US) ⟨*character*⟩

modélisme /mɔdelism/ *nm* modelling

modération /mɔderasjɔ̃/ *nf*
(a) moderation
(b) (in price, tax) reduction

modéré, ~e /mɔdere/ *adj* ⟨*party, speed, words*⟩ moderate; ⟨*price*⟩ reasonable; ⟨*temperament*⟩ even; ⟨*enthusiasm*⟩ mild

modérément /mɔderemɑ̃/ *adv*
(a) relatively
(b) slightly

modérer /mɔdere/ [14] *vtr* to curb ⟨*expenses*⟩; to moderate ⟨*language*⟩; to reduce ⟨*speed*⟩

moderne /mɔdɛrn/ *adj* modern

moderniser /mɔdɛrnize/ [1] *vtr* to modernize; to update

modernité /mɔdɛrnite/ *nf* modernity

modeste /mɔdɛst/ *adj* ⟨*sum, apartment, person*⟩ modest; ⟨*cost*⟩ moderate; ⟨*background*⟩ humble

modestement /mɔdɛstəmɑ̃/ *adv* modestly

modestie /mɔdɛsti/ *nf* modesty

modification /mɔdifikasjɔ̃/ *nf* modification

modifier /mɔdifje/ [2] *vtr* to change; to alter, to modify

modique /mɔdik/ *adj* ⟨*sum, resources*⟩ modest

modiste /mɔdist/ *nf* milliner

modulation /mɔdylasjɔ̃/ *nf* modulation
■ ~ **de fréquence, MF** frequency modulation, FM

module /mɔdyl/ *nm* (gen, Sch) module

moduler /mɔdyle/ [1] *vtr* (a) to modulate
(b) to adjust ⟨*price*⟩; to adapt ⟨*policy*⟩

moelle /mwal/ *nf* marrow
■ ~ **épinière** spinal cord

moelleux, -euse /mwalø, øz/ *adj*
(a) ⟨*carpet*⟩ thick; ⟨*bed*⟩ soft
(b) ⟨*wine*⟩ mellow

mœurs /mœr(s)/ *nf pl* (a) customs; habits; lifestyle; **l'évolution des** ~ the change in attitudes
(b) morals; **des** ~ **dissolues** loose morals; **la police des** ~, **les Mœurs** (colloq) the vice squad
(c) (of animals) behaviour
IDIOMS **autres temps, autres** ~ other days, other ways

mohair /mɔɛr/ *nm* mohair

moi¹ /mwa/ *pron* (a) I, me; **c'est** ~ it's me
(b) me; **pour** ~ for me; **des amis à** ~ friends of mine; **c'est à** ~ it's mine; it's my turn

moi² /mwa/ *nm* **le** ~ the self

moignon /mwaɲɔ̃/ *nm* stump

moi-même /mwamɛm/ *pron* myself

moindre /mwɛ̃dr/ *adj* (a) lesser; **à** ~ **prix** more cheaply
(b) **le** ~ the least; **je n'en ai pas la** ~ **idée** I haven't got the slightest idea

moine /mwan/ *nm* monk
IDIOMS **l'habit ne fait pas le** ~ (Proverb) you can't judge a book by its cover

moineau, *pl* ~**x** /mwano/ *nm* sparrow

moins¹ /mwɛ̃/ **1** *prep* (a) minus
(b) **il est huit heures** ~ **dix** it's ten (minutes) to eight; **il était** ~ **une** (colloq) it was a close shave (colloq)
2 *adv* (comparative) less; (superlative) **le** ~ the least; **le** ~ **difficile** the less difficult; the least difficult; **de** ~ **en** ~ less and less; ~ **je sors,** ~ **j'ai envie de sortir** the less I go out, the less I feel like going out; **il n'en est pas** ~ **vrai que** it's nonetheless true that; **il ressemble à son frère en** ~ **gros** he looks like his brother, only thinner; **à tout le** ~, **pour le** ~ to say the least; **il y avait deux fourchettes en** ~ **dans la boîte** there were two forks missing from the box
3 **moins de** *quantif* ~ **de livres** fewer books; ~ **de sucre** less sugar; **les** ~ **de 20 ans** people under 20
4 **à moins de** *phr* unless
5 **à moins que** *phr* unless
6 **au moins** *phr* at least
7 **du moins** *phr* at least

moins² /mwɛ̃/ *nm inv* minus
■ ~ **que rien** good-for-nothing, nobody

moiré, ~e /mware/ *adj* moiré; watered

mois /mwa/ *nm inv* month

moisi /mwazi/ *nm* mould (GB), mold (US)

moisir /mwazir/ [3] *vi* ⟨*foodstuff*⟩ to go mouldy (GB) or moldy (US); ⟨*object, plant*⟩ to become mildewed

moisissure /mwazisyr/ *nf* (a) mould (GB), mold (US)
(b) mildew

moisson /mwasɔ̃/ *nf* harvest

moissonner /mwasɔne/ [1] *vtr* to harvest

moissonneuse /mwasɔnøz/ *nf* reaper

moite /mwat/ *adj* ⟨*heat*⟩ muggy; ⟨*skin*⟩ sweaty

moiteur /mwatœr/ *nf* (of air) mugginess; (of skin) sweatiness

moitié /mwatje/ *nf* half; **à** ~ **vide** half empty

moitié-moitié /mwatjemwatje/ adv half-and-half

moka /mɔka/ nm (a) mocha
(b) mocha cake

molaire /mɔlɛʀ/ nf molar

molécule /mɔlekyl/ nf molecule

moleskine /mɔlɛskin/ nf (a) imitation leather
(b) moleskin

molester /mɔlɛste/ [1] vtr to manhandle

molette /mɔlɛt/ nf (of spanner) adjusting knob

mollasson, -onne /mɔlasɔ̃, ɔn/ adj (colloq) sluggish

molle ▶ MOU 1

mollement /mɔlmɑ̃/ adv (a) idly
(b) ⟨work⟩ without much enthusiasm; ⟨protest⟩ half-heartedly

mollet /mɔlɛ/ [1] adj m œuf ~ soft-boiled egg
[2] nm (Anat) calf

molleton /mɔltɔ̃/ nm (a) flannel; flannelette
(b) (table) felt
(c) (ironing board) cover

molletonner /mɔltɔne/ [1] vtr to line with fleece

mollir /mɔliʀ/ [3] vi (a) ⟨courage⟩ to fail; ⟨resistance⟩ to grow weaker; ⟨person⟩ to soften
(b) ⟨knees⟩ to give way; ⟨arm⟩ to go weak

mollusque /mɔlysk/ nm mollusc (GB), mollusk (US)

molosse /mɔlɔs/ nm huge dog

môme /mom/ nmf (colloq) kid (colloq); brat (colloq)

moment /mɔmɑ̃/ nm moment; le ~ venu when the time comes/came; il devrait arriver d'un ~ à l'autre he should arrive any minute now; à un ~ donné at some point; at a given moment; à ce ~-là at that time; just then; in that case; au ~ où at the time (when); au ~ où il quittait son domicile as he was leaving his home; jusqu'au ~ où until; du ~ que as long as, provided; il arrive toujours au bon or mauvais ~! he certainly picks his moment to call!; un ~! just a moment!; ça va prendre un ~ it will take a while; au bout d'un ~ after a while; par ~s at times; les ~s forts du film the film's highlights; dans ses meilleurs ~s, il fait penser à Orson Welles at his best, he reminds one of Orson Welles; à mes ~s perdus in my spare time

momentané, ~e /mɔmɑ̃tane/ adj momentary

momentanément /mɔmɑ̃tanemɑ̃/ adv for a moment, momentarily

momie /mɔmi/ nf mummy

mon, ma, pl mes /mɔ̃, ma, mɛ/ det my; j'ai ~ idée I have my own ideas about that

monacal, ~e, mpl -aux /mɔnakal, o/ adj monastic

monarchie /mɔnaʀʃi/ nf monarchy

monarchiste /mɔnaʀʃist/ adj, nmf monarchist

monarque /mɔnaʀk/ nm monarch

monastère /mɔnastɛʀ/ nm monastery

monceau, pl ~x /mɔ̃so/ nm (of rubbish) pile

mondain, ~e /mɔ̃dɛ̃, ɛn/ [1] adj ⟨life, ball⟩ society; ⟨conversation⟩ polite
[2] nm,f socialite

monde /mɔ̃d/ nm (a) world; pas le moins du ~ not in the least; aller or voyager de par le ~ to travel the world; c'est le bout du ~! it's in the back of beyond!; ce n'est pas le bout du ~! it's not such a big deal!; à la face du ~ for all the world to see; en ce bas ~ here below; elle n'est plus de ce ~ she's no longer with us; je n'étais pas encore au ~ I wasn't yet born; le ~ médical the medical world; le ~ animal the animal kingdom; un ~ nous sépare we are worlds apart
(b) people; tout le ~ everybody; tout mon petit ~ my family and friends
(c) society; le beau or grand ~ high society
IDIOMS se faire un ~ de qch to get all worked up about sth; depuis que le ~ est ~ since the beginning of time; c'est un ~! (colloq) that's a bit much!

mondial, ~e, mpl -iaux /mɔ̃djal, o/ adj world; ⟨success⟩ worldwide; seconde guerre ~e Second World War

mondialement /mɔ̃djalmɑ̃/ adv être ~ connu to be world famous

mondialisation /mɔ̃djalizasjɔ̃/ nf globalization

mondialiser /mɔ̃djalize/ [1] vtr to globalize; to cause [sth] to spread worldwide

mondialisme /mɔ̃djalism/ nm internationalism

mondovision /mɔ̃dɔvizjɔ̃/ nf satellite broadcasting

monétaire /mɔnetɛʀ/ adj ⟨system, stability⟩ monetary; ⟨market⟩ money

monétariste /mɔnetaʀist/ adj, nmf monetarist

monétique /mɔnetik/ nf electronic banking

monétiser /mɔnetize/ [1] vtr to monetize

Mongolie /mɔ̃gɔli/ pr nf Mongolia

mongolien, -ienne /mɔ̃gɔljɛ̃, ɛn/ (controversial) nm,f Down's syndrome child

moniteur, -trice /mɔnitœʀ, tʀis/ [1] nm,f
(a) (Aut, Sport) instructor
(b) (in holiday camp) group leader (GB), counselor (US)
[2] nm (a) (TV) monitor
(b) (Comput) monitor system

monitorat /mɔnitɔʀa/ nm tutoring; tutorial system

monnaie /mɔnɛ/ nf (a) currency; fausse ~ forged or counterfeit currency
(b) change; faire de la ~ to get some change
(c) coin; battre ~ to mint or strike coins; l'hôtel de la Monnaie, la Monnaie the Mint
(d) (Econ) money

■ ~ **d'échange** trading currency; bargaining chip; ~ **de papier** paper money
IDIOMS rendre à qn la ~ **de sa pièce** to pay sb back in his/her own coin; **c'est** ~ **courante** it's commonplace

monnayable /mɔnɛjabl/ *adj* **(a)** (in finance) convertible
(b) ⟨*skill*⟩, ⟨*qualification*⟩ marketable

monnayer /mɔnɛje/ [21] *vtr* **(a)** to convert [sth] into cash
(b) to capitalize on ⟨*talent, experience*⟩; ~ **qch contre qch** to exchange sth for sth

mono¹ /mono/ *pref* mono; ~**chrome** monochrome; ~**lingue** monolingual

mono² /mono/ *nf* (in hi-fi) mono

monocellulaire /mɔnosɛlylɛʀ/ *adj*
famille ~ nuclear family

monocle /mɔnɔkl/ *nm* monocle

monocorde /mɔnɔkɔʀd/ *adj* ⟨*voice, speech*⟩ monotonous; ⟨*instrument*⟩ single-string

monogame /mɔnogam/ *adj* monogamous

monogamie /mɔnogami/ *nf* monogamy

monoï /mɔnɔj/ *nm inv* coconut oil (*used in cosmetics*)

monologue /mɔnɔlɔg/ *nm* monologue (GB)
■ ~ **intérieur** stream of consciousness

mononucléose /mɔnonykleoz/ *nf*
mononucleosis; ~ **infectieuse** glandular fever

monoparental, ~e, mpl -aux
/mɔnopaʀɑ̃tal, o/ *adj* **famille** ~**e** single-parent family

monopole /mɔnɔpɔl/ *nm* monopoly

monopoliser /mɔnɔpɔlize/ [1] *vtr* to monopolize

monoprocesseur /mɔnopʀɔsɛsœʀ/ *nm* single-chip computer

monoski /mɔnɔski/ *nm* **(a)** monoski
(b) monoskiing

monothéiste /mɔnoteist/ *adj* monotheistic

monotone /mɔnɔtɔn/ *adj* monotonous

monotonie /mɔnɔtɔni/ *nf* monotony

monoxyde /mɔnɔksid/ *nm* monoxide

Monseigneur, *pl* **Messeigneurs**
/mɔ̃sɛɲœʀ, mesɛɲœʀ/ *nm* Your Highness; Your Eminence; ~ **le duc de Parme** His Grace, the duke of Parma

monsieur, *pl* **messieurs** /məsjø, mesjø/ *nm* **(a)** (addressing a man whose name you do not know) **Monsieur** (in a letter) Dear Sir; **bonjour** ~**!** good morning!
(b) (addressing a man whose name you know, for instance Hallé) **Monsieur** (in a letter) Dear Mr Hallé; **bonjour** ~**!** good morning, Mr Hallé
(c) (polite form of address) **'Monsieur a sonné?'** 'you rang, sir?'
(d) man; **le double messieurs** the men's doubles; **c'était un (grand)** ~**!** he was a (true) gentleman!
■ ~ **Tout le Monde** the man in the street

monstre /mɔ̃stʀ/ ⒈ *adj* (colloq) ⟨*task, success, publicity*⟩ huge; ⟨*nerve*⟩ colossal
⒉ *nm* **(a)** monster
(b) freak (of nature)
■ ~ **marin** sea monster

monstrueux, -euse /mɔ̃stʀyø, øz/ *adj*
(a) ⟨*crime, cruelty*⟩ monstrous
(b) hideous; **d'une laideur monstrueuse** hideously ugly
(c) ⟨*error*⟩ colossal

monstruosité /mɔ̃stʀyozite/ *nf*
(a) (of conduct) monstrousness
(b) atrocity
(c) monstrosity; **dire des** ~**s** to say preposterous things

mont /mɔ̃/ *nm* mountain
■ **le** ~ **Blanc** Mont Blanc

montage /mɔ̃taʒ/ *nm* **(a)** set-up
(b) (of machine) assembly; (of tent) putting up; **chaîne de** ~ assembly line
(c) (of film) editing; **salle de** ~ cutting room
(d) (of gem) setting
■ ~ **photo** photomontage; ~ **sonore** sound montage

montagnard, ~e /mɔ̃taɲaʀ, aʀd/ ⒈ *adj* ⟨*people, plant*⟩ mountain; ⟨*custom*⟩ highland
⒉ *nm,f* mountain dweller

montagne /mɔ̃taɲ/ *nf* **(a)** mountain
(b) la ~ the mountains; **de** ~ ⟨*road, animal*⟩ mountain; **il neige en haute** ~ it's snowing on the upper slopes
■ ~**s russes** big dipper, roller coaster
IDIOMS se faire une ~ **de qch** to get really worked up about sth

montagneux, -euse /mɔ̃taɲø, øz/ *adj*
mountainous

montant, ~e /mɔ̃tɑ̃, ɑ̃t/ ⒈ *adj* **(a)** ⟨*cabin, group*⟩ going up
(b) ⟨*road*⟩ uphill
(c) ⟨*neck*⟩ high; ⟨*socks*⟩ long; **chaussures** ~**es** ankle boots
⒉ *nm* **(a)** sum; **le** ~ **des pertes** the total losses; **d'un** ~ **de** ⟨*deficit, savings*⟩ amounting to; ⟨*cheque*⟩ to the amount of; ⟨*goods*⟩ for a total of
(b) (of door, window) upright, jamb; transom; (of scaffolding) pole; (of ladder) upright

mont-de-piété, *pl* **monts-de-piété**
/mɔ̃dpjete/ *nm* pawnshop, pawnbroker's

monte-charge /mɔ̃tʃaʀʒ/ *nm inv* goods lift (GB) *or* elevator (US)

montée /mɔ̃te/ *nf* **(a)** (up slope) climb; (of mountain) ascent
(b) (of plane) climb
(c) rising; rise; **la** ~ **des eaux** the rise in the water level; **une brusque** ~ **d'adrénaline** a rush of adrenaline
(d) (in prices) rise; (in danger) increase
(e) hill; **une légère** ~ a slight slope

monter /mɔ̃te/ [1] ⒈ *vtr* (+ *v avoir*) **(a)** to take [sb/sth] up; to take [sb/sth] upstairs; to bring [sb/sth] up; to bring [sb/sth] upstairs; **impossible de** ~ **le piano par l'escalier** it's impossible to get the piano up the stairs
(b) to put [sth] up; to raise ⟨*shelf*⟩

⋯⋖

(c) to go up [sth]; to come up [sth]; ∼ **la colline à bicyclette** to cycle up the hill
(d) to turn up ⟨*volume, gas*⟩
(e) ∼ **les blancs en neige** beat *or* whisk the eggwhites until stiff
(f) ∼ **qn contre qn** to set sb against sb
(g) to ride ⟨*horse*⟩
(h) (Zool) to mount
(i) to assemble ⟨*appliance, unit*⟩; to put up ⟨*tent, scaffolding*⟩; ∼ **un film** to edit a film
(j) to hatch ⟨*plot*⟩; to set up ⟨*company*⟩; to stage ⟨*play*⟩; **monté de toutes pièces** ⟨*story*⟩ fabricated from beginning to end
2 *vi* (+ *v être*) **(a)** to go up; to go upstairs; to come up; to come upstairs; ⟨*plane*⟩ to climb; ⟨*bird*⟩ to fly up; ⟨*sun, mist*⟩ to rise; **tu es monté à pied?** did you walk up?; did you come up on foot?; ∼ **sur** to get onto ⟨*footpath*⟩; to climb onto ⟨*stool*⟩; ∼ **à l'échelle** to climb (up) the ladder; **faites-les** ∼ send them up
(b) ∼ **dans une voiture/dans un train** to get in a car/on a train; ∼ **sur** to get on ⟨*bike, horse*⟩
(c) ⟨*road*⟩ to go uphill, to climb; ⟨*ground*⟩ to rise; ∼ **jusqu'à** ⟨*path, wall*⟩ to go up to; ∼ **en lacets** to wind its way up
(d) ⟨*garment, water*⟩ to come up (**jusqu'à** to)
(e) ⟨*temperature, price*⟩ to rise, to go up; ⟨*tide*⟩ to come in
(f) ∼ **à** *or* **sur Paris** to go up to Paris
(g) ∼ **(à cheval)** to ride
(h) (Mil) ∼ **à l'assaut** *or* **l'attaque** to mount an attack
(i) ⟨*employee*⟩ to rise, to move up; ⟨*artist*⟩ to rise
(j) ⟨*anger, emotion*⟩ to mount; ⟨*tears*⟩ to well up; **le ton monta** the discussion became heated
(k) ∼ **à la tête de qn** to go to sb's head
(l) (Aut, Tech) ∼ **à 250 km/h** to go up to 250 km/h
IDIOMS **se** ∼ **la tête** (colloq) to get worked up (colloq)

monteur, -euse /mɔ̃tœʀ, øz/ *nm,f*
(a) fitter
(b) (in film-making) editor
(c) paste-up artist

montgolfière /mɔ̃ɡɔlfjɛʀ/ *nf* hot-air balloon

monticule /mɔ̃tikyl/ *nm* **(a)** hillock
(b) mound

montrable /mɔ̃tʀabl/ *adj* ⟨*person*⟩ presentable; ⟨*images*⟩ suitable for viewing

montre /mɔ̃tʀ/ *nf* watch; **trois heures** ∼ **en main** three hours exactly

Montréal /mɔ̃ʀeal/ *pr n* Montreal

montrer /mɔ̃tʀe/ [1] **1** *vtr* **(a)** to show; ∼ **qch à qn** to show sb sth
(b) to show ⟨*feelings, knowledge*⟩
(c) ⟨*person*⟩ to point out ⟨*track, place, object*⟩; ⟨*survey, table*⟩ to show ⟨*trend, results*⟩; ∼ **qn du doigt** to point at sb; to point the finger at sb

2 se montrer *v refl* (+ *v être*) **(a)** to show oneself to be; to prove (to be); **il faut se** ∼ **optimiste** we must try to be optimistic
(b) ⟨*person*⟩ to show oneself; ⟨*sun*⟩ to come out
IDIOMS ∼ **les dents** to bare one's teeth; ∼ **le bout de son nez** to show one's face; to peep through

monture /mɔ̃tyʀ/ *nf* **(a)** (for rider) mount
(b) (of glasses) frames; (of ring) setting

monument /mɔnymɑ̃/ *nm* **(a)** monument
(b) (historic) building; **visiter les** ∼**s de Paris** to see the sights of Paris
(c) **un des** ∼**s de la littérature européenne** a masterpiece of European literature
■ ∼ **historique** ancient monument; ∼ **aux morts** war memorial

monumental, ∼e, *mpl* **-aux** /mɔnymɑ̃tal, o/ *adj* monumental

moquer: se moquer /mɔke/ [1] *v refl* (+ *v être*) **(a)** **se** ∼ **de** to make fun of
(b) **se** ∼ to not care about
(c) **se** ∼ **du monde** to take people for fools

moquerie /mɔkʀi/ *nf* **(a)** mocking remark
(b) mockery

moquette /mɔkɛt/ *nf* wall-to-wall carpet

moqueur, -euse /mɔkœʀ, øz/ *adj* mocking

moral, ∼e¹, *mpl* **-aux** /mɔʀal, o/ **1** *adj*
(a) moral; **n'avoir aucun sens** ∼ to have no sense of right and wrong
(b) ⟨*torture*⟩ mental; ⟨*support*⟩ moral
(c) ⟨*person*⟩ moral; ⟨*conduct*⟩ ethical
2 *nm* **(a)** morale; **avoir le** ∼ to be in good spirits; **avoir le** ∼ **à zéro** (colloq) to feel very down; **remonter le** ∼ **de qn** to raise sb's spirits
(b) mind; **au** ∼ **comme au physique** mentally and physically

morale² /mɔʀal/ *nf* **(a)** morality; **leur** ∼ their moral code
(b) moral; **faire la** ∼ **à qn** to give sb a lecture
(c) **la** ∼ moral philosophy, ethics

moralement /mɔʀalmɑ̃/ *adv* **(a)** morally, ethically
(b) psychologically

moralisant, ∼e /mɔʀalizɑ̃, ɑ̃t/ *adj* moralizing

moralisateur, -trice /mɔʀalizatœʀ, tʀis/ *adj* moralizing, moralistic

moraliser /mɔʀalize/ [1] *vtr* to clean up; to reform

moraliste /mɔʀalist/ *nmf* moralist

moralité /mɔʀalite/ *nf* **(a)** morals
(b) (of action) morality
(c) moral; ∼**, ne faites confiance à personne** the moral is: don't trust anybody

morbide /mɔʀbid/ *adj* morbid

morbidité /mɔʀbidite/ *nf* morbidity

morceau, *pl* ∼**x** /mɔʀso/ *nm* **(a)** piece, bit; ∼ **de sucre** sugar lump; **manger un** ∼ (colloq) to have a snack
(b) (of meat) cut; **bas** ∼ cheap cut
(c) (Mus) piece; ∼ **de piano** piano piece
(d) (from book) extract

IDIOMS recoller les ~x to patch things up

morceler /mɔrsale/ [19] *vtr* to divide [sth] up

mordant, ~e /mɔrdɑ̃, ɑ̃t/ [1] *adj*
(a) caustic, scathing
(b) ⟨cold⟩ biting
[2] *nm* (a) sarcasm
(b) (colloq) (of person, team) zip (colloq)

mordiller /mɔrdije/ [1] *vtr* to nibble at

mordoré, ~e /mɔrdɔre/ *adj* golden brown

mordre /mɔrdr/ [6] [1] *vtr* to bite
[2] **mordre à** *v+prep* ~ **à l'appât** *or* **l'hameçon** to take the bait
[3] *vi* (a) ~ **dans une pomme** to bite into an apple
(b) ~ **sur** to go over ⟨white line⟩; to encroach on ⟨territory⟩
(c) (colloq) to fall for it (colloq)
[4] **se mordre** *v refl* (+ *v être*) **se ~ la langue** to bite one's tongue
IDIOMS je m'en suis mordu les doigts I could have kicked myself

mordu, ~e /mɔrdy/ [1] *adj* (colloq) (a) être ~ **de qch** to be mad about sth (colloq)
(b) smitten
[2] *nm,f* (colloq) fan; les ~s du ski skiing fans

morfondre: se morfondre /mɔrfɔ̃dr/ [6] *v refl* (+ *v être*) (a) se ~ **à attendre** *or* **en attendant** to wait dejectedly
(b) to pine

morgue /mɔrg/ *nf* (a) morgue; (hospital) mortuary
(b) arrogance

moribond, ~e /mɔribɔ̃, ɔ̃d/ [1] *adj* ⟨person, civilization⟩ moribund
[2] *nm,f* dying man/woman

morille /mɔrij/ *nf* morel (mushroom)

morne /mɔrn/ *adj* (a) gloomy; ⟨face⟩ glum
(b) ⟨landscape, life⟩ dreary

morose /mɔroz/ *adj* morose; gloomy

morosité /mɔrozite/ *nf* gloom

morphine /mɔrfin/ *nf* morphine

morphologie /mɔrfɔlɔʒi/ *nf* morphology

morpion /mɔrpjɔ̃/ *nm* noughts and crosses (GB), tick-tack-toe (US)

mors /mɔr/ *nm inv* bit; **prendre le ~ aux dents** to take the bit between its/one's teeth

morse /mɔrs/ *nm* (a) walrus
(b) (code) ~ Morse code

morsure /mɔrsyr/ *nf* (a) bite; ~ **de chien** dogbite
(b) la ~ **du froid** the biting cold

mort¹ /mɔr/ *nf* death; **mourir de sa belle ~** to die peacefully in old age; **il n'y a pas eu ~ d'homme** there were no fatalities; **trouver la ~** to die; **mise à ~** (of condemned) killing; (of bull) dispatch; **à ~** ⟨fight⟩ to the death; ⟨war⟩ ruthless; ⟨brake, squeeze⟩ like mad (colloq)
■ ~ **cérébrale** brain death
IDIOMS la ~ **dans l'âme** with a heavy heart

mort², ~e /mɔr, mɔrt/ [1] *pp* ▶ MOURIR
[2] *pp adj* (a) dead

(b) je suis ~ **de froid** I'm freezing to death; je suis ~ (colloq) I'm dead tired
(c) ⟨district⟩ dead; ⟨season⟩ slack
(d) ⟨civilization⟩ dead; ⟨city⟩ lost
[3] *nm,f* dead person, dead man/woman
[4] *nm* (a) fatality; **il y a eu 12 ~s** there were 12 dead
(b) body; **faire le ~** to play dead; to lie low
IDIOMS ne pas y aller de main ~e (colloq) not to pull any punches

mortalité /mɔrtalite/ *nf* mortality

mort-aux-rats /mɔrora/ *nf inv* rat poison

mortel, -elle /mɔrtɛl/ [1] *adj* (a) ⟨blow, illness⟩ fatal; ⟨poison⟩ lethal; ⟨venom⟩ deadly
(b) ⟨cold⟩ deathly
(c) ⟨enemy⟩ mortal
(d) ⟨person, meeting⟩ deadly boring
(e) ⟨being⟩ mortal
[2] *nm,f* mortal

mortellement /mɔrtɛlmɑ̃/ *adv*
(a) ⟨injured⟩ fatally
(b) ⟨boring⟩ deadly

mortier /mɔrtje/ *nm* mortar

mort-né, ~e, *mpl* ~s /mɔrne/ *adj*
(a) stillborn
(b) ⟨plan⟩ abortive

mortuaire /mɔrtɥɛr/ *adj* cérémonie ~ funeral ceremony; veillée ~ wake

morue /mɔry/ *nf* cod

morve /mɔrv/ *nf* nasal mucus, snot (slang)

mosaïque /mozaik/ *nf* mosaic

Moscou /mɔsku/ *pr n* Moscow

mosquée /mɔske/ *nf* mosque

mot /mo/ *nm* (a) word; **à ~s couverts** in veiled terms; **au bas ~** at least; **il est bête et le ~ est faible!** he's stupid and that's putting it mildly!; **dire un ~ à qn** to have a word with sb; **il ne dit jamais un ~ plus haut que l'autre** he never raises his voice; **avoir son ~ à dire** to be entitled to one's say
(b) note; **je t'ai laissé un ~** I left you a note
■ ~ **d'esprit** witticism; ~ **d'ordre** watchword; ~ **d'ordre de grève** strike call; ~ **de passe** password; ~s **croisés** crossword; ~s **doux** sweet nothings
IDIOMS ne pas avoir peur des ~s to call a spade a spade; **manger ses ~s** to mumble; **se donner le ~** to pass the word around

motard, ~e /mɔtar, ard/ [1] *nm,f* (colloq) biker (colloq)
[2] *nm* police motorcyclist

mot-clé, *pl* mots-clés /mokle/ *nm* key word

moteur, -trice /mɔtœr, tris/ [1] *adj*
(a) ⟨force, principle⟩ driving; **la voiture a quatre roues motrices** the car has four-wheel drive
(b) (Med) **troubles ~s** motor problems
[2] *nm* (a) motor
(b) engine
(c) être le ~ **de qch** to be the driving force behind sth

motif /mɔtif/ *nm* (a) grounds; **des ~s d'espérer** grounds for hope ⋯▸

(b) reason

(c) motive

(d) pattern; **à ~ floral** with a floral pattern

motion /mɔsjɔ̃/ *nf* motion

motivant, **~e** /mɔtivã, ãt/ *adj* ‹*salary*› attractive; ‹*work*› rewarding

motivation /mɔtivasjɔ̃/ *nf* **(a)** motivation **(b)** motive; **~s profondes** deeper motives

motivé, **~e** /mɔtive/ *adj* **(a)** motivated **(b)** ‹*complaint*› justifiable

motiver /mɔtive/ [1] *vtr* **(a)** to motivate **(b)** to lead to ‹*decision, action*›; **motivé par** caused by

moto /mɔto/ *nf* **(a)** (motor)bike **(b)** motorcycling

motocyclette /motosiklɛt/ *nf* motorcycle

motocyclisme /motosiklism/ *nm* motorcycle racing

motocycliste /motosiklist/ **1** *adj* motorcycle

2 *nmf* motorcyclist

motoneige /motonɛʒ/ *nf* snowmobile

motoriser /mɔtɔrize/ [1] *vtr* to motorize; **être motorisé** (colloq) to have transport (GB) *or* transportation (US)

motrice ▶ MOTEUR 1

motte /mɔt/ *nf* ~ **(de terre)** clod (of earth); **~ de gazon** sod, piece of turf; **~ (de beurre)** slab of butter

motus /mɔtys/ *excl* (colloq) ~ **(et bouche cousue)**! keep it under your hat!

mou (mol before vowel or mute *h*), **molle** /mu, mɔl/ **1** *adj* **(a)** ‹*substance, cushion*› soft; ‹*blow*› dull

(b) ‹*stomach*› flabby

(c) ‹*person*› listless; ‹*growth*› sluggish

(d) ‹*parent*› soft

(e) ‹*speech*› feeble

2 *nm* **(a)** wimp (colloq)

(b) (in butchery) lights (GB), lungs (US)

(c) (in rope) slack; **donner du ~ à qn** (colloq) to give sb a bit of leeway

mouchard, **~e** /muʃaR, aRd/ **1** *nmf* (colloq) **(a)** grass (GB) (colloq), informer

(b) sneak (colloq)

2 *nm* **(a)** tachograph

(b) spyhole

moucharder /muʃaRde/ [1] *vtr* (colloq) **(a)** ~ **qn** to inform on sb; to squeal (colloq) on sb

(b) to sneak (colloq)

mouche /muʃ/ *nf* **(a)** fly

(b) patch, beauty spot

(c) bull's eye; **faire ~** to hit the bull's eye; (figurative) to be right on target

(d) (Sport) (on foil) button

■ **~ verte** greenbottle; **~ du vinaigre** fruit fly

IDIOMS **quelle ~ les a piqués?** (colloq) what's got (GB) *or* gotten (US) into them?; **prendre la ~** to fly off the handle

moucher /muʃe/ [1] **1** *vtr* ~ **qn** to blow sb's nose; (figurative) (colloq) to put sb in their place

2 se moucher *v refl* (+ *v être*) to blow one's nose

IDIOMS **il ne se mouche pas du pied** *or* **du coude** (colloq) he's full of airs and graces

moucheron /muʃRɔ̃/ *nm* midge

moucheté, **~e** /muʃte/ *adj* **(a)** ‹*material*› flecked; ‹*plumage, fish*› speckled; ‹*coat*› spotted; ‹*horse*› dappled

(b) (Sport) ‹*foil*› buttoned

mouchoir /muʃwaR/ *nm* handkerchief; tissue

moudre /mudR/ [77] *vtr* to grind

moue /mu/ *nf* pout; **faire la ~ to** pout; (doubtfully) to pull a face

mouette /mwɛt/ *nf* (sea)gull

moufle /mufl/ *nf* mitten

mouiller /muje/ [1] **1** *vtr* **(a)** to wet; to get [sth] wet

(b) to drop ‹*anchor*›; to lay ‹*mine*›

2 *vi* to anchor, to drop anchor

3 se mouiller *v refl* (+ *v être*) to get wet

mouillette /mujɛt/ *nf* (colloq) soldier (colloq), finger of bread (*eaten with a boiled egg*)

moulage /mulaʒ/ *nm* **(a)** casting; **faire un ~ de qch** to take a cast of sth

(b) (of grain) milling

moulant, **~e** /mulã, ãt/ *adj* tight-fitting

moule[1] /mul/ *nm* **(a)** mould (GB), mold (US)

(b) tin, pan (US); **~ à gaufre** waffle iron

moule[2] /mul/ *nf* mussel

mouler /mule/ [1] *vtr* **(a)** to mould (GB), to mold (US) ‹*substance*›; to cast ‹*bronze*›; to mint ‹*medal*›

(b) to take a cast of

(c) ‹*garment*› to hug

moulin /mulɛ̃/ *nm* mill

■ **~ à paroles** (colloq) chatterbox; **~ à vent** windmill

IDIOMS **apporter de l'eau au ~ de qn** to fuel sb's arguments; **on ne peut être à la fois au four et au ~** one can't be in two places at once; **on y entre comme dans un ~** (colloq) one can just slip in

mouliner /muline/ [1] *vtr* to grind, to mill

moulinet /mulinɛ/ *nm* **faire des ~s avec les bras** to wave one's arms about

moulu, **~e** /muly/ **1** *pp* ▶ MOUDRE

2 *pp adj* ‹*coffee, pepper*› ground

3 *adj* (colloq) ~ **(de fatigue)** worn out

moumoute /mumut/ *nf* (colloq) **(a)** toupee

(b) sheepskin jacket

mourant, **~e** /muRã, ãt/ *adj* ‹*person, animal*› dying; ‹*light*› fading; ‹*voice*› faint

mourir /muRiR/ [34] *vi* (+ *v être*) to die; **~ de froid** to die of exposure; to die of cold; **je meurs de soif/de froid** I'm dying of thirst/freezing to death; **c'était à ~ (de rire)!** it was hilarious!; **~ debout** to be active to the end

IDIOMS **partir c'est ~ un peu** to say goodbye is to die a little; **je ne veux pas ~ idiot** (colloq) I want to know

mouroir /muRwaR/ *nm* (derogatory) old people's home, twilight home

mousquetaire /muskətɛʀ/ *nm*
musketeer

mousqueton /muskətɔ̃/ *nm* snap clasp

moussant, ~e /musɑ̃, ɑ̃t/ *adj* ⟨gel⟩
foaming

mousse¹ /mus/ *nm* ship's apprentice

mousse² /mus/ *nf* **(a)** moss
(b) foam; (from soap) lather; (on milk) froth; (on
beer) head
(c) ~ au chocolat chocolate mousse
(d) foam rubber
■ ~ carbonique fire foam; ~ à raser shaving
foam

mousseline /muslin/ *nf* **(a)** muslin
(b) chiffon

mousser /muse/ [1] *vi* to foam; to lather
IDIOMS se faire ~ (colloq) to blow one's own
trumpet

mousseux, -euse /musø, øz/ *adj*
(a) ⟨wine⟩ sparkling; ⟨beer⟩ fizzy
(b) ⟨lace⟩ frothy

mousson /musɔ̃/ *nf* monsoon

moustache /mustaʃ/ [1] *nf* moustache
(GB), mustache (US)
[2] **moustaches** *nf pl* (Zool) whiskers

moustachu, ~e /mustaʃy/ *adj* ⟨person⟩
with a moustache (GB) *or* mustache (US)

moustiquaire /mustikɛʀ/ *nf* mosquito
net

moustique /mustik/ *nm* mosquito

moutarde /mutaʀd/ *adj inv, nf* mustard
IDIOMS la ~ me monte au nez! (colloq) I'm
beginning to see red!

mouton /mutɔ̃/ [1] *nm* **(a)** sheep
(b) mutton
(c) sheepskin
(d) (derogatory) sheep
[2] **moutons** *nm pl* **(a)** small fleecy clouds
(b) whitecaps
(c) fluff
■ ~ à cinq pattes rare bird
IDIOMS revenons à nos ~s (colloq) let's get
back to the point

mouture /mutyʀ/ *nf* **(a)** (of coffee) grind
(b) première/nouvelle ~ first/new version

mouvant, ~e /muvɑ̃, ɑ̃t/ *adj* **(a)** ⟨ground⟩
unstable
(b) ⟨group⟩ shifting
(c) ⟨opinion⟩ changing

mouvement /muvmɑ̃/ *nm* **(a)** (gen)
movement; faire un ~ to move; ~ perpétuel
perpetual motion; accélérer le ~ to speed up
(b) bustle; suivre le ~ (figurative) to follow the
crowd
(c) impulse, reaction; un ~ de colère a
surge of anger
(d) le ~ étudiant the student protest
movement; ~ de grève strike, industrial
action
(e) le ~ des idées the evolution of ideas; un
milieu en ~ a changing environment
(f) (Econ) le ~ du marché market
fluctuations; ~ de hausse upward trend

mouvementé, ~e /muvmɑ̃te/ *adj*
(a) ⟨life, week, trip⟩ eventful, hectic

(b) ⟨terrain⟩ rough

mouvoir: se mouvoir /muvwaʀ/ [43]
v refl (+ *v être*) to move

moyen, -enne¹ /mwajɛ̃, ɛn/ [1] *adj*
(a) medium; medium-sized
(b) ⟨income⟩ middle; ⟨level⟩ intermediate
(c) average, mean; le Français ~ the
average Frenchman
[2] *nm* **(a)** means, way (de faire of doing);
employer les grands ~s to resort to drastic
measures; (il n'y a) pas ~ de lui faire
comprendre qu'il a tort it's impossible to
make him realize he's wrong
(b) (of expression, production) means;
(of investigation, payment) method
[3] **au moyen de** *phr* by means of
[4] **par le moyen de** *phr* by means of
[5] **moyens** *nm pl* **(a)** means; faute de ~s
through lack of money; avoir de petits ~s
not to be very well off
(b) resources; donner à qn les ~s de faire to
give sb the means to do
(c) ability; perdre ses ~s to go to pieces
■ ~ de locomotion *or* transport means of
transport (GB) *or* transportation (US); Moyen
Âge Middle Ages

moyenâgeux, -euse /mwajɛnaʒø, øz/
adj **(a)** medieval
(b) antiquated

moyen-courrier, *pl* ~**s** /mwajɛ̃kuʀje/
nm medium-haul airliner

moyennant /mwajɛnɑ̃/ *prep* ~ finances
for a fee; ~ quoi in view of which; in return
for which

moyenne² /mwajɛn/ [1] *adj f* ▶ MOYEN
[2] *nf* **(a)** average; la ~ d'âge the average
age; en ~ on average
(b) half marks (GB), 50%
(c) (Aut) average speed

moyennement /mwajɛnmɑ̃/ *adv*
⟨intelligent, wealthy⟩ moderately; ⟨like⟩ to a
certain extent

Moyen-Orient /mwajɛnɔʀjɑ̃/ *pr nm*
Middle East

moyeu, *pl* ~**x** /mwajø/ *nm* hub

MST /ɛmɛste/ *nf: abbr* ▶ MALADIE

mû, mue¹ /my/ ▶ MOUVOIR

mucoviscidose /mykovisidoz/ *nf* cystic
fibrosis

mucus /mykys/ *nm inv* mucus

mue² /my/ *nf* **(a)** (of insect) metamorphosis;
(of reptile) sloughing of the skin; (of bird,
mammal) moulting (GB), molting (US); (of stag)
casting
(b) (of snake, insect) slough, sloughed skin
(c) breaking (GB) *or* changing (US) of voice

muer /mɥe/ [1] [1] *vi* **(a)** ⟨insect⟩ to
metamorphose; ⟨snake⟩ to slough its skin;
⟨bird, mammal⟩ to moult (GB), to molt (US)
(b) sa voix mue, il mue his voice is breaking
(GB) *or* changing (US)
[2] **se muer** *v refl* (+ *v être*) **(a)** to be
transformed
(b) to transform oneself

m

muet, -ette /mɥɛ, ɛt/ **1** *adj* **(a)** dumb; speechless
(b) ⟨*witness*⟩ silent
(c) ⟨*vowel, consonant*⟩ mute
(d) ⟨*film*⟩ silent; ⟨*role*⟩ non-speaking
2 *nm,f* mute

mufle /myfl/ **1** *adj* boorish, loutish
2 *nm* **(a)** (Zool) muffle; muzzle
(b) boor, lout

muflerie /myfləʀi/ *nf* boorishness

mugir /myʒiʀ/ [3] *vi* **(a)** to low; to bellow
(b) ⟨*wind*⟩ to howl; ⟨*siren*⟩ to wail; ⟨*torrent*⟩ to roar

mugissement /myʒismɑ̃/ *nm* **(a)** (of cow) lowing; (of bull, ox) bellowing
(b) (of wind) howling; (of waves) roar

muguet /mygɛ/ *nm* lily of the valley

mulâtre /mylɑtʀ/ *adj* mulatto

mule /myl/ *nf* **(a)** female mule
(b) (slipper) mule

mulet /mylɛ/ *nm* (male) mule

mulot /mylo/ *nm* fieldmouse

multi /mylti/ *pref* multi; ∼**colore** multicoloured (GB); ∼**media** multimedia; ∼**programmation** multiple programming

multicarte /myltikaʀt/ *adj inv* représentant ∼ representative for several firms

multifonction /myltifɔ̃ksjɔ̃/ *adj inv* multipurpose; (Comput) multifunction

multipare /myltipaʀ/ *adj* multiparous

multiple /myltipl/ **1** *adj* **(a)** ⟨*reasons, occasions*⟩ numerous, many; ⟨*births*⟩ multiple; à choix ∼ multiple-choice
(b) ⟨*causes, facets*⟩ many, various
(c) (in science) multiple
2 *nm* multiple

multipliable /myltiplijabl/ *adj* multiplicable

multiplication /myltiplikasjɔ̃/ *nf* **(a)** ∼ de increase in the number of
(b) (in mathematics, science) multiplication

multiplicité /myltiplisite/ *nf* multiplicity

multiplier /myltiplije/ [2] **1** *vtr* **(a)** to multiply
(b) to increase ⟨*risks, fortune*⟩; to increase the number of ⟨*trains, accidents*⟩
2 se multiplier *v refl* (+ *v être*)
(a) ⟨*branches, villas*⟩ to grow in number; ⟨*incidents*⟩ to be on the increase; ⟨*difficulties*⟩ to increase
(b) ⟨*animals, germs*⟩ to multiply

multipropriété /myltipʀɔpʀijete/ *nf* time-sharing

multirisque /myltiʀisk/ *adj* assurance ∼ comprehensive insurance

multisalle /myltisal/ *adj inv* cinéma ∼ cinema complex, multiplex

multitude /myltityd/ *nf* **(a)** une ∼ de a mass of ⟨*tourists, objects*⟩; a lot of ⟨*reasons, ideas*⟩
(b) multitude, throng

municipal, ∼e, *mpl* **-aux** /mynisipal, o/ *adj* ⟨*council*⟩ local, town; city; ⟨*park, pool*⟩ municipal; arrêté ∼ bylaw

municipales /mynisipal/ *nf pl* local elections

municipalité /mynisipalite/ *nf*
(a) municipality
(b) town council; city council

munir /myniʀ/ [3] **1** *vtr* to provide; ∼ un bâtiment d'un escalier de secours to put a fire escape on a building; muni de fitted with
2 se munir *v refl* (+ *v être*) se ∼ de to bring; to take

munitions /mynisjɔ̃/ *nf pl* ammunition

muqueuse /mykøz/ *nf* mucous membrane

mur /myʀ/ **1** *nm* wall; faire les pieds au ∼ to do a handstand against the wall; (figurative) to tie oneself up in knots
2 murs *nm pl* (of business) premises; (of palace, embassy) confines; être dans ses ∼s to own one's own house
■ ∼ porteur *or* porteur load-bearing wall; ∼ du son sound barrier; Mur des lamentations Wailing Wall
IDIOMS faire le ∼ to go over the wall; mettre qn au pied du ∼ to call sb's bluff; être au pied du ∼ to be up against the wall

mûr, ∼e[1] /myʀ/ *adj* **(a)** ripe
(b) mature; l'âge ∼ middle age; après ∼e réflexion after careful consideration
(c) ready; il est ∼ pour des aveux he's ready to confess
(d) ⟨*situation*⟩ at a decisive stage
IDIOMS en voir des vertes et des pas ∼es (colloq) to go through a lot

muraille /myʀɑj/ *nf* great wall

mural, ∼e, *mpl* **-aux** /myʀal, o/ *adj* ⟨*covering, map*⟩ wall; ⟨*plant*⟩ climbing

mûre[2] /myʀ/ **1** *adj f* ▶ MÛR
2 *nf* blackberry

mûrement /myʀmɑ̃/ *adv* ∼ réfléchi carefully thought through

murer /myʀe/ [1] *vtr* to build a wall around [sth]; to brick [sth] up; to block [sth] off

muret /myʀɛ/ *nm* low wall

mûrier /myʀje/ *nm* mulberry tree

mûrir /myʀiʀ/ [3] **1** *vtr* **(a)** to ripen ⟨*fruit*⟩
(b) to mature ⟨*person*⟩; to develop ⟨*plan*⟩
2 *vi* **(a)** ⟨*fruit*⟩ to ripen
(b) ⟨*person, talent*⟩ to mature; ⟨*plan, idea*⟩ to evolve; ⟨*passion*⟩ to develop
(c) ⟨*abscess*⟩ to come to a head

murmure /myʀmyʀ/ *nm* **(a)** murmur
(b) ∼s mutterings
(c) (of wind) whisper

murmurer /myʀmyʀe/ [1] **1** *vtr* **(a)** to murmur
(b) to say; on murmure qu'il est riche he is rumoured (GB) to be rich
2 *vi* **(a)** ⟨*person*⟩ to murmur; ⟨*wind*⟩ to whisper

musaraigne /myzaʀɛɲ/ *nf* (Zool) shrew

musc /mysk/ *nm* musk

muscade /myskad/ *nf* nutmeg

muscle /myskl/ *nm* muscle

musclé, ~e /myskle/ *adj* **(a)** muscular
(b) ⟨*music, speech*⟩ powerful; ⟨*reaction*⟩
strong; ⟨*intervention*⟩ tough
(c) (Econ) competitive

muscler /myskle/ [1] *vtr* **(a)** ~ **les bras**
to develop the arm muscles
(b) to strengthen
2 se muscler *v refl* (+ *v être*) to develop
one's muscles

musculaire /myskylɛR/ *adj* muscle;
muscular

musculation /myskylasjɔ̃/ *nf* **(exercices
de)** ~ (gen) bodybuilding; (Med) exercises to
strengthen the muscles; **salle de** ~ weights
room

musculature /myskylatyR/ *nf*
musculature

muse /myz/ *nf* **(a)** Muse
(b) (figurative) muse

museau, *pl* ~**x** /myzo/ *nm* **(a)** muzzle;
snout; nose
(b) (colloq) face

musée /myze/ *nm* museum; art gallery
(GB), art museum (US); **une ville** ~ a city of
great historical and artistic importance

museler /myzəle/ [19] *vtr* to muzzle

muselière /myzəljɛR/ *nf* muzzle

musette¹ /myzɛt/ *nm* accordion music

musette² /myzɛt/ *nf* **(a)** haversack
(b) lunchbag

muséum /myzeɔm/ *nm* ~ **(d'histoire
naturelle)** natural history museum

musical, ~e, *mpl* **-aux** /myzikal, o/ *adj*
⟨*event*⟩ musical; ⟨*critic*⟩ music; ⟨*choice*⟩ of
music

music-hall, *pl* ~**s** *nm* /mysikol/ music
hall

musicien, -ienne /myzisjɛ̃, ɛn/ **1** *adj*
musical
2 *nm,f* musician

musique /myzik/ *nf* music; **travailler en** ~
to work with music in the background;
mettre en ~ to set [sth] to music; **faire de la**
~ to play an instrument; **une** ~ **de film** a
film score
IDIOMS connaître la ~ (colloq) to know the
score (colloq); **je ne peux pas aller plus vite
que la** ~ (colloq) I can't go any faster than
I'm already going; **être réglé comme du
papier à** ~ (colloq) ⟨*person*⟩ to be as regular
as clockwork; ⟨*conference, project*⟩ to go very
smoothly

musulman, ~e /myzylmɑ̃, an/ *adj*, *nm,f*
Muslim

mutabilité /mytabilite/ *nf* mutability

mutant, ~e /mytɑ̃, ɑ̃t/ *adj*, *nm,f* mutant

mutation /mytasjɔ̃/ *nf* **(a)** transfer
(b) transformation; **en pleine** ~ undergoing
radical transformation
(c) mutation

muter /myte/ [1] *vtr* to transfer ⟨*official*⟩

mutilation /mytilasjɔ̃/ *nf* mutilation

mutilé, ~e /mytile/ *nm,f* disabled person;
~ **de guerre** disabled war veteran

mutiler /mytile/ [1] *vtr* to mutilate

mutin, ~e /mytɛ̃, in/ **1** *adj* mischievous
2 *nm* mutineer; rioter

mutiner: se mutiner /mytine/ [1] *v refl*
(+ *v être*) to mutiny; to riot

mutinerie /mytinRi/ *nf* mutiny; riot

mutisme /mytism/ *nm* silence

mutuel, -elle¹ /mytɥɛl/ *adj* mutual

mutuelle² /mytɥɛl/ *nf* mutual insurance
company

mutuellement /mytɥɛlmɑ̃/ *adv*
mutually; **s'aider** ~ to help each other

myope /mjɔp/ *adj* short-sighted

myopie /mjɔpi/ *nf* short-sightedness

myosotis /mjɔzɔtis/ *nm inv* forget-me-not

myriade /miRjad/ *nf* myriad (**de** of)

myrrhe /miR/ *nf* myrrh

myrtille /miRtij/ *nf* bilberry, blueberry

mystère /mistɛR/ *nm* **(a)** mystery
(b) secrecy
(c) rite

mystérieusement /misteRjøzmɑ̃/ *adv*
mysteriously

mystérieux, -ieuse /misteRjø, øz/ *adj*
mysterious

mysticisme /mistisism/ *nm* mysticism

mystification /mistifikasjɔ̃/ *nf* **(a)** hoax
(b) myth

mystique /mistik/ **1** *adj* mystical
2 *nf* **(a)** mysticism
(b) mystique
(c) blind belief

mythe /mit/ *nm* myth

mythique /mitik/ *adj* mythical

mythologie /mitɔlɔʒi/ *nf* mythology

mythologique /mitɔlɔʒik/ *adj*
mythological

mythomane /mitɔman/ *adj*, *nm,f*
mythomaniac

m

Nn

n, N /ɛn/ **1** *nm inv* **(a)** (letter) n, N
(b) n° (*written abbr* = **numéro**) no
2 **N** *nf* (*abbr* = **nationale**) la N7 the N7

n' ▶ NE

nabot, ~e /nabo, ɔt/ *nm,f* (offensive) dwarf

nacelle /nasɛl/ *nf* **(a)** (of hot-air balloon) gondola
(b) carrycot (GB), carrier (US)
(c) (of worker) cradle

nacre /nakʀ/ *nf* mother-of-pearl

nacré, ~e /nakʀe/ *adj* pearly

nage /naʒ/ *nf* **(a)** swimming; **200 mètres quatre ~s** 200 metres (GB) medley; **traverser à la ~** to swim across
(b) être en ~ to be in a sweat
■ **~ indienne** sidestroke; **~ libre** freestyle

nageoire /naʒwaʀ/ *nf* **(a)** (of fish) fin
(b) (of seal) flipper

nager /naʒe/ [13] **1** *vtr* to swim
2 *vi* **(a)** to swim
(b) (figurative) **~ dans le bonheur** to bask in contentment; **elle nage dans sa robe** her dress is far too big for her
(c) (colloq) to be absolutely lost
IDIOMS **~ entre deux eaux** to run with the hare and hunt with the hounds

nageur, -euse /naʒœʀ, øz/ *nm,f* swimmer

naguère /nagɛʀ/ *adv* **(a)** quite recently
(b) formerly

naïf, naïve /naif, iv/ *adj* naïve

nain, ~e /nɛ̃, nɛn/ **1** *adj* ⟨tree⟩ dwarf; ⟨dog⟩ miniature
2 *nm,f* dwarf

naissance /nɛsɑ̃s/ *nf* **(a)** (gen) birth; (of rumour) start; **de ~** ⟨Italian, French⟩ by birth; ⟨deaf⟩ from birth; **à ma ~** when I was born
(b) à la ~ du cou at the base of the neck

naissant, ~e /nɛsɑ̃, ɑ̃t/ *adj* new

naître /nɛtʀ/ [74] *vi* (+ *v être*) **(a)** to be born; **elle est née le 5 juin** she was born on 5 June; **le bébé doit ~ à la fin du mois** the baby is due at the end of the month; **l'enfant à ~** the unborn baby *or* child; **je l'ai vu ~** (figurative) I have known him since he was a baby
(b) (figurative) ⟨idea⟩ to be born; ⟨company⟩ to come into existence; ⟨love⟩ to spring up; ⟨day⟩ to break; **faire ~** to give rise to ⟨hope⟩; **voir ~** to see the birth of ⟨newspaper, century⟩

naïve ▶ NAÏF

naïvement /naivmɑ̃/ *adv* naively; artlessly

naïveté /naivte/ *nf* naivety

nanisme /nanism/ *nm* dwarfism

nantir /nɑ̃tiʀ/ [3] *vtr* **~ qn de** to provide sb with; to award [sth] to sb

nantis /nɑ̃ti/ *nm pl* **les ~** the well-off

naphtaline /naftalin/ *nf* mothballs

nappe /nap/ *nf* **(a)** tablecloth
(b) (of oil, gas) layer; (of water, fire) sheet; (of fog) blanket

napper /nape/ [1] *vtr* (Culin) to coat; to glaze

napperon /napʀɔ̃/ *nm* mat

narcisse /naʀsis/ *nm* (flower) narcissus

narcissisme /naʀsisism/ *nm* narcissism

narco(-) /naʀko/ *pref* drug; **~-dollars/-trafiquant** drug money/trafficker

narcotique /naʀkɔtik/ *adj, nm* narcotic

narguer /naʀge/ [1] *vtr* to taunt ⟨person⟩

narine /naʀin/ *nf* nostril

narquois, ~e /naʀkwa, az/ *adj* mocking

narrateur, -trice /naʀatœʀ, tʀis/ *nm,f* narrator

narratif, -ive /naʀatif, iv/ *adj* narrative

narration /naʀasjɔ̃/ *nf* narration

narrer /naʀe/ [1] *vtr* to relate

nasal, ~e, mpl -aux /nazal, o/ *adj* nasal; **hémorragie ~e** heavy nosebleed

naseau, pl ~x /nazo/ *nm* nostril

nasillard, ~e /nazijaʀ, aʀd/ *adj* ⟨voice⟩ nasal; ⟨instrument⟩ tinny

nasillement /nazijmɑ̃/ *nm* nasal twang

nasiller /nazije/ [1] *vi* **(a)** to speak with a nasal voice
(b) ⟨duck⟩ to quack

nasse /nas/ *nf* **(a)** keepnet
(b) (figurative) net

natal, ~e, mpl ~s /natal/ *adj* native

nataliste /natalist/ *adj* ⟨policy⟩ pro-birth

natalité /natalite/ *nf* **(taux de) ~** birthrate

natation /natasjɔ̃/ *nf* swimming

natif, -ive /natif, iv/ *adj* **~ de** native of

nation /nasjɔ̃/ *nf* nation
■ **les Nations unies** the United Nations

national, ~e¹, mpl -aux /nasjɔnal, o/ *adj* national

nationale² /nasjɔnal/ *nf* ≈ A road (GB), highway (US)

nationalisation /nasjɔnalizasjɔ̃/ *nf* nationalization

nationaliser /nasjɔnalize/ [1] *vtr* to nationalize

nationalisme /nasjɔnalism/ *nm* nationalism

nationalité /nasjɔnalite/ *nf* nationality

nativité /nativite/ *nf* nativity

natte /nat/ *nf* **(a)** plait, braid (US)
(b) mat

natter /nate/ [1] *vtr* to plait

naturalisation /natyʀalizasjɔ̃/ *nf*
naturalization

naturalisé, ~e /natyʀalize/ *adj*
naturalized

naturaliser /natyʀalize/ [1] *vtr* to
naturalize ⟨foreigner, species⟩; to assimilate
⟨word, custom⟩

naturalisme /natyʀalism/ *nm* naturalism

nature /natyʀ/ **1** *adj inv* (a) ⟨yoghurt⟩
plain; ⟨tea⟩ black
(b) (colloq) ⟨person⟩ natural
2 *nf* (a) nature; **protection de la ~**
protection of the environment; **en pleine ~**
in the heart of the countryside; **lâcher qn
dans la ~** to leave sb in the middle of
nowhere; (figurative) to let sb loose
(b) **de ~ à faire** likely to do; **des offres de
toute ~** offers of all kinds
(c) **peindre d'après ~** to paint from life;
plus vrai que ~ larger than life
(d) **en ~** ⟨pay⟩ in kind
■ **~ humaine** human nature; **~ morte** still
life; ▸ PETIT

naturel, -elle /natyʀɛl/ **1** *adj* natural
2 *nm* (a) nature, disposition; **être d'un ~
craintif** to be timid by nature
(b) **il manque de ~** he's not very natural
(c) **au ~** ⟨rice⟩ plain; ⟨tuna⟩ in brine

naturisme /natyʀism/ *nm* nudism

naturiste /natyʀist/ *nmf* naturist (GB),
nudist

naufrage /nofʀaʒ/ *nm* shipwreck, sinking;
faire ~ ⟨ship⟩ to be wrecked; ⟨sailor⟩ to be
shipwrecked; ⟨company⟩ to collapse

naufragé, ~e /nofʀaʒe/ **1** *adj*
shipwrecked
2 *nm,f* survivor (of a shipwreck); castaway

nauséabond, ~e /nozeabɔ̃, ɔ̃d/ *adj*
sickening, nauseating

nausée /noze/ *nf* nausea

nautique /notik/ *adj* ⟨science⟩ nautical;
⟨sports⟩ water

nautisme /notism/ *nm* water sports

naval, ~e, *mpl* **~s** /naval/ *adj*
(a) ⟨industry⟩ shipbuilding
(b) (Mil) naval

navet /navɛ/ *nm* (a) turnip
(b) rubbishy film (GB), turkey (US) (colloq)

navette /navɛt/ *nf* shuttle; shuttle service;
faire la ~ (to work) to commute
■ **~ spatiale** space shuttle

navigable /navigabl/ *adj* navigable

navigant, ~e /navigã, ãt/ *adj* **personnel
~** (on plane) flight personnel; (Naut) seagoing
personnel; **mécanicien ~** flight engineer

navigateur, -trice /navigatœʀ, tʀis/
nm,f (a) a navigator
(b) sailor
(c) (Comput) browser

navigation /navigasjɔ̃/ *nf* navigation
■ **~ de plaisance** boating; yachting

naviguer /navige/ [1] *vi* (a) ⟨ship, sailor⟩
to sail; ⟨pilot, plane⟩ to fly; **en état de ~**
⟨ship⟩ seaworthy

(b) to navigate
(c) (Comput) to browse; **~ sur l'Internet** to
surf the Internet

navire /naviʀ/ **1** *nm* ship
2 navire- (combining form) **~-école/-usine**
training/factory ship; **~-s-citernes** tankers
■ **~ amiral** flagship; **~ de guerre** warship

navrant, ~e /navʀã, ãt/ *adj*
(a) depressing
(b) distressing

navré, ~e /navʀe/ *adj* **je suis vraiment ~**
I am terribly sorry; **avoir l'air ~** to look sad

nazi, ~e /nazi/ *adj, nm,f* Nazi

nazisme /nazism/ *nm* Nazism

ne /nə/ (**n'** before vowel or mute h) *adv*

■ **Note** In cases where *ne* is used with *pas,
jamais, guère, rien, plus, aucun, personne* etc,
one should consult the corresponding entry.
– *ne* + verb + *que* is treated in the entry below.

je n'ai que 100 francs I've only got 100
francs; **il n'y a que lui pour être aussi
désagréable** only he can be so unpleasant;
tu n'es qu'un raté you're nothing but a loser
(colloq); **je n'ai que faire de tes conseils** you
can keep your advice

né, ~e /ne/ **1** *pp* ▸ NAÎTRE
2 *pp adj* **bien ~** highborn; **Madame Masson
~e Roux** Mrs Masson née Roux
3 **(-)né** (combining form) **musicien(-)/
écrivain(-)~** born musician/writer

néanmoins /neãmwɛ̃/ *adv* nevertheless

néant /neã/ *nm* (a) **le ~** nothingness;
réduire à ~ to destroy ⟨argument, hopes⟩
(b) **'revenus: ~'** 'income: nil'

nébuleux, -euse /nebylø, øz/ *adj*
(a) ⟨sky⟩ cloudy
(b) ⟨idea⟩ vague, nebulous

nécessaire /neseseʀ/ **1** *adj* necessary
(à for); **plus qu'il n'est ~** more than is
necessary; **les voix ~s pour renverser le
gouvernement** the votes needed in order to
overthrow the government
2 *nm* (a) **faire le ~** to do what is necessary
(b) essentials; **le strict ~** the bare essentials
■ **~ de couture** sewing kit; **~ à ongles**
manicure set; **~ de toilette** toiletries

nécessairement /neseseʀmã/ *adv*
necessarily; **passe-t-on ~ par Oslo?** do you
have to go via Oslo?

nécessité /nesesite/ *nf* (a) necessity;
~ urgente urgent need; **~ de qch/de faire/
d'être** need for sth/to do/to be; **de première
~** vital; **par ~** out of necessity; **être dans la
~ de faire** to have no choice but to do
(b) need; **être dans la ~** to be in need
IDIOMS **~ fait loi** (Proverb) necessity knows
no law

nécessiter /nesesite/ [1] *vtr* to require

nécessiteux, -euse /nesesitø, øz/ *nm,f*
needy person; **les ~** the needy

nec plus ultra /nɛkplyzyltʀa/ *nm inv* **le
~ the last word** (de in)

nécrologie /nekʀɔlɔʒi/ *nf* deaths column

nécrologique /nekʀɔlɔʒik/ *adj* obituary

n

nectar /nɛktaʀ/ nm nectar

néerlandais, ~e /neeʀlɑ̃dɛ, ɛz/ **1** adj Dutch

2 nm (language) Dutch

Néerlandais, ~e /neeʀlɑ̃dɛ, ɛz/ nm,f Dutchman/Dutchwoman; les ~ the Dutch

nef /nɛf/ nf nave; ~ latérale side aisle

néfaste /nefast/ adj harmful

négatif, -ive¹ /negatif, iv/ **1** adj negative

2 nm negative

négation /negasjɔ̃/ nf (a) negation

(b) (in grammar) negative

négative² /negativ/ **1** adj f ▶ NÉGATIF 1

2 nf répondre par la ~ to reply in the negative

négativement /negativmɑ̃/ adv negatively

négligé, ~e /neɡliʒe/ **1** adj ⟨person⟩ sloppy; ⟨house⟩ neglected; ⟨injury⟩ untreated

2 nm negligée

négligeable /neɡliʒabl/ adj ⟨amount⟩ negligible; ⟨person⟩ insignificant

négligemment /neɡliʒamɑ̃/ adv

(a) nonchalantly

(b) carelessly

négligence /neɡliʒɑ̃s/ nf (a) negligence

(b) oversight

négligent, ~e /neɡliʒɑ̃, ɑ̃t/ adj ⟨employee⟩ negligent, careless; ⟨glance⟩ casual

négliger /neɡliʒe/ [13] **1** vtr (gen) to neglect; to leave untreated ⟨cold⟩; to ignore ⟨rule⟩; une offre qui n'est pas à ~ an offer that's worth considering; ~ de faire to fail to do

2 se négliger v refl (+ v être) (a) not to take care over one's appearance

(b) not to look after oneself

négoce /negɔs/ nm trade (avec with)

négociable /negɔsjabl/ adj negotiable

négociant, ~e /negɔsjɑ̃, ɑ̃t/ nm,f merchant; wholesaler

négociateur, -trice /negɔsjatœʀ, tʀis/ nm,f negotiator

négociation /negɔsjasjɔ̃/ nf negotiation

négocier /negɔsje/ [2] vtr, vi to negotiate

nègre /nɛɡʀ/ nm (a) (offensive) Negro

(b) ghostwriter

négresse /negʀɛs/ nf (offensive) Negress

négritude /negʀityd/ nf black identity, negritude

négroïde /negʀɔid/ adj Negroid

neige /nɛʒ/ nf snow; ~ fondue slush; sleet; aller à la ~ to go skiing; blancs battus en ~ stiffly beaten eggwhites

IDIOMS être blanc comme ~ to be completely innocent

neiger /neʒe/ [13] v impers to snow

nénuphar /nenyfaʀ/ nm waterlily

néo /neo/ pref neo

néologisme /neɔlɔʒism/ nm neologism

néon /neɔ̃/ nm (a) neon

(b) neon light

néo-zélandais, ~e /neozelɑ̃dɛ, ɛz/ adj New Zealand

Néo-Zélandais, ~e /neozelɑ̃dɛ, ɛz/ nm,f New Zealander

népotisme /nepɔtism/ nm nepotism

nerf /nɛʀ/ (a) nerve; être malade des ~s to suffer from nerves

(b) spirit, go (colloq); redonner du ~ à qn to put new heart into sb

IDIOMS jouer avec les ~s de qn to be deliberately annoying; ses ~s ont lâché he/ she went to pieces; avoir les ~s à fleur de peau to have frayed nerves; avoir les ~s en pelote (colloq) or en boule (colloq) or à vif to be really wound up; être sur les ~s, avoir ses ~s (colloq) to be on edge; taper (colloq) or porter sur les ~s de qn to get on sb's nerves; être à bout de ~s to be at the end of one's tether or rope (US); passer ses ~s sur (colloq) qn/qch to take it out on sb/sth; l'argent est le ~ de la guerre money is the sinews of war

nerveusement /nɛʀvøzmɑ̃/ adv (a) ⟨wait⟩ nervously

(b) être épuisé ~ to be suffering from nervous exhaustion

nerveux, -euse /nɛʀvø, øz/ **1** adj

(a) ⟨person⟩ tense

(b) ⟨engine⟩ responsive; ⟨horse⟩ vigorous

(c) (Anat) ⟨cell⟩ nerve; ⟨system⟩ nervous

2 nm,f nervous person

nervosité /nɛʀvozite/ nf (a) nervousness

(b) excitability

(c) (of engine) responsiveness

nervure /nɛʀvyʀ/ nf (of leaf) nervure

n'est-ce pas /nɛspa/ adv c'est joli, ~? it's pretty, isn't it?; ~ qu'il est gentil? isn't he nice?

net, nette /nɛt/ **1** adj (a) ⟨price, weight⟩ net

(b) ⟨change⟩ marked; ⟨tendency⟩ distinct

(c) ⟨victory, memory⟩ clear; ⟨situation⟩ clearcut; ⟨handwriting⟩ neat; ⟨break⟩ clean; en avoir le cœur ~ to be clear in one's mind about it

(d) ⟨house, hands⟩ clean; (figurative) ⟨conscience⟩ clear; faire place nette to clear everything away

2 adv ⟨stop⟩ dead; ⟨kill⟩ outright; ⟨refuse⟩ flatly; la corde a cassé ~ the rope snapped

Net /nɛt/ nm le ~ the Net

netiquette /netikɛt/ nf netiquette

nettement /nɛtmɑ̃/ adv (a) ⟨increase, deteriorate⟩ markedly; ⟨dominate⟩ clearly; ⟨prefer⟩ definitely

(b) ⟨see, say⟩ clearly; ⟨refuse⟩ flatly; ⟨remember⟩ distinctly

netteté /nɛtte/ nf (a) (of image, features) sharpness; (of result, statement) definite nature

(b) (of place) cleanness; (of work) neatness

nettoyage /netwajaʒ/ nm (a) clean(up); ~ de printemps spring-cleaning

(b) cleaning; (of skin) cleansing; ~ à sec dry-cleaning

(c) opération de ~ (colloq) (by army, police) mopping-up operation

nettoyant /nɛtwajɑ̃/ nm cleaning agent

nettoyer /netwaje/ [23] vtr **(a)** (gen) to clean; to clean up ⟨garden⟩; to clean out ⟨river⟩; to clean off ⟨stain⟩
(b) (figurative) ⟨police⟩ to clean up ⟨town⟩

neuf¹ /nœf/ adj inv, pron, nm inv nine

neuf², **neuve** /nœf, nœv/ **1** adj new; tout ~ brand new; 'état ~' 'as new' **2** nm inv new; quoi de ~? what's new?; habillé de ~ dressed in new clothes; faire du ~ avec du vieux to revamp things
IDIOMS faire peau neuve to undergo a transformation

neurasthénie /nørasteni/ nf depression

neurasthénique /nørastenik/ nmf depressive

neuro /nøro/ pref neuro

neurone /nørɔn/ nm neurone

neutralisation /nøtralizasjɔ̃/ nf neutralization

neutraliser /nøtralize/ [1] vtr to neutralize

neutralité /nøtralite/ nf neutrality

neutre /nøtr/ adj neutral; neuter

neutron /nøtrɔ̃/ nm neutron

neuvième /nœvjɛm/ **1** adj ninth **2** nf (Sch) third year of primary school, age 8–9

neveu, pl ~**x** /n(ə)vø/ nm nephew

névralgie /nevralʒi/ nf neuralgia

névralgique /nevralʒik/ adj **(a)** neuralgic **(b)** point ~ key point

névrose /nevroz/ nf neurosis

névrosé, ~**e** /nevroze/ adj, nm,f neurotic

New York /njujɔrk/ pr n **(a)** New York City **(b)** l'État de ~ New York (State)

nez /ne/ nm nose; ~ en trompette turned-up nose; ça sent le parfum à plein ~ (colloq) there's a strong smell of perfume; je n'ai pas mis le ~ dehors (colloq) I didn't set foot outside; mettre le ~ à la fenêtre (colloq) to show one's face at the window; lever le ~ to look up; tu as le ~ dessus (colloq) it's staring you in the face; avoir du ~, avoir le ~ fin (figurative) to be shrewd
IDIOMS mener qn par le bout du ~ (colloq) to have sb under one's thumb; avoir qn dans le ~ (colloq) to have it in for sb; avoir un coup or verre dans le ~ (colloq) to have had one too many (colloq); au ~ (et à la barbe) de qn right under sb's nose; filer or passer sous le ~ de qn to slip through sb's fingers; se casser le ~ (colloq) to fail

NF /ɛnɛf/ adj, nf (abbr = **norme française**) French manufacturing standard

ni /ni/ conj nor, or; elle ne veut ~ ne peut changer she doesn't want to change, nor can she; elle ne veut pas le voir ~ lui parler she doesn't want to see him or talk to him; ~... ~ neither... nor; ~ l'un ~ l'autre neither of them; il ne m'a dit ~ oui ~ non he didn't say yes or no

IDIOMS ~ vu ~ connu (colloq) on the sly (colloq); c'est ~ fait ~ à faire (colloq) it's a botched job (colloq); il n'a fait ~ une ~ deux (colloq) he didn't have a second's hesitation

niais, ~**e** /njɛ, njɛz/ adj stupid

niaiserie /njɛzri/ nf **(a)** stupidity **(b)** stupid or inane remark

nicaraguayen, -**enne** /nikaragwajɛ̃, ɛn/ adj Nicaraguan

niche /niʃ/ nf **(a)** kennel, doghouse (US) **(b)** recess; (for statue) niche **(c)** (colloq) trick

nichée /niʃe/ nf (of birds) brood; (of mice) litter

nicher /niʃe/ [1] **1** vi **(a)** ⟨bird⟩ to nest **(b)** (colloq) ⟨person⟩ to live **2** se nicher v refl (+ v être) **(a)** ⟨bird⟩ to nest **(b)** ⟨person, cottage⟩ to nestle

nickel /nikɛl/ **1** adj (colloq) spotless **2** nm nickel

nicotine /nikɔtin/ nf nicotine

nid /ni/ nm nest
■ ~ d'aigle eyrie; ~ d'ange snuggle suit; ~ à poussière dust trap; ~ de résistance pocket of resistance

nid-d'abeilles, pl **nids-d'abeilles** /nidabɛj/ nm honeycomb weave

nid-de-poule, pl **nids-de-poule** /nidpul/ nm pothole

nièce /njɛs/ nf niece

nième /ɛnjɛm/ = ÉNIÈME

nier /nje/ [2] vtr to deny ⟨fact, existence⟩

nigaud, ~**e** /nigo, od/ adj silly

nigérian, ~**e** /niʒerjɑ̃, an/ adj Nigerian

nigérien, -**ienne** /niʒerjɛ̃, ɛn/ adj of Niger

nihiliste /niilist/ adj, nmf nihilist

nîmois, ~**e** /nimwa, az/ adj of Nîmes

nipper: se nipper /nipe/ [1] v refl (+ v être) (colloq) to get rigged out in one's Sunday best (colloq)

nippes /nip/ nf pl (colloq) rags (colloq), old clothes

nippon, -**onne** /nipɔ̃, ɔn/ adj Japanese

niveau, pl ~**x** /nivo/ nm (gen) level; (of knowledge, education) standard; au ~ du sol at ground level; être de ~ to be level; arrivé au ~ du bus, il... when he drew level with the bus he...; bâtiment sur deux ~**x** two-storey (GB) or two-story (US) building; '~ bac + 3' baccalaureate or equivalent plus 3 years' higher education; de haut ~ ⟨athlete⟩ top; ⟨candidate⟩ high-calibre (GB); au plus haut ~ ⟨discussion⟩ top-level
■ ~ de langue register; ~ social social status; ~ sonore sound level; ~ de vie standard of living

nivelage /nivlaʒ/ nm standardization

niveler /nivle/ [19] vtr **(a)** to level ⟨ground⟩ **(b)** to bring ⟨sth⟩ to the same level ⟨salaries⟩; ~ par le bas/haut to level down/up

n

nobiliaire /nɔbiljɛʀ/ *adj* nobiliary

noble /nɔbl/ **1** *adj* (gen) noble; ⟨*family*⟩ aristocratic; ⟨*person*⟩ of noble birth
2 *nmf* nobleman/noblewoman

noblement /nɔbləmɑ̃/ *adv* (a) nobly
(b) handsomely

noblesse /nɔblɛs/ *nf* nobility; **la petite ~** the gentry

noce /nɔs/ *nf* (a) (colloq) party; **faire la ~** (figurative) (colloq) to live it up (colloq), to party (colloq)
(b) wedding party
(c) **~s** wedding

noceur, -euse /nɔsœʀ, øz/ *nmf* (colloq) party animal (colloq)

nocif, -ive /nɔsif, iv/ *adj* noxious, harmful

noctambule /nɔktɑ̃byl/ *nmf* night owl

nocturne[1] /nɔktyʀn/ *adj* ⟨*attack*⟩ night; ⟨*animal*⟩ nocturnal; **la vie ~** nightlife

nocturne[2] /nɔktyʀn/ *nf* (a) (in sport) evening fixture
(b) (of shop) late-night opening

Noël /nɔɛl/ *nm* Christmas; '**Joyeux ~**' 'Merry Christmas'; **de ~** ⟨*tree, gift*⟩ Christmas

nœud /nø/ *nm* (a) (gen) knot; **faire un ~ de cravate** to tie a tie
(b) (of matter) crux; (of play) core
■ **~ coulant** slipknot; **~ papillon** bow tie; **~ de vipères** nest of vipers

noir, ~e[1] /nwaʀ/ **1** *adj* (a) (gen) black; ⟨*eyes*⟩ dark; ⟨*person, race*⟩ black; **être ~ de coups** to be black and blue; **être ~ de monde** to be swarming with people
(b) ⟨*street*⟩ dark; **il fait ~** it's dark
(c) ⟨*year*⟩ bad, bleak; ⟨*poverty*⟩ dire; ⟨*idea*⟩ gloomy, dark
(d) ⟨*look*⟩ black; ⟨*plot, design*⟩ evil, dark; **se mettre dans une colère ~e** to fly into a towering rage
2 *nm* (a) (colour) black
(b) **avoir du ~ sur le visage** to have a black mark on one's face
(c) darkness
(d) **au ~** ⟨*sell*⟩ on the black market; **travailler au ~** to work without declaring one's earnings; to moonlight (colloq)
(e) (colloq) **un (petit) ~** an espresso
IDIOMS **voir tout en ~** to look on the black side (of things)

Noir, ~e /nwaʀ/ *nmf* black man/woman

noirâtre /nwaʀɑtʀ/ *adj* blackish

noiraud, ~e /nwaʀo, od/ *adj* swarthy

noirceur /nwaʀsœʀ/ *nf* (gen) blackness; (of hair, night) darkness

noircir /nwaʀsiʀ/ [3] **1** *vtr* (a) ⟨*coal*⟩ to make [sth] dirty; ⟨*smoke*⟩ to blacken
(b) (figurative) **~ du papier** to scribble away; **~ la situation** to paint a black picture of the situation
2 *vi* ⟨*banana*⟩ to go black; ⟨*wall*⟩ to get dirty; ⟨*metal*⟩ to tarnish; ⟨*person*⟩ to get brown
3 **se noircir** *v refl* (+ *v être*) ⟨*sky*⟩ to darken; **se ~ le visage** to blacken one's face

noire /nwaʀ/ **1** *adj f* ▸ NOIR 1
2 *nf* (Mus) crotchet (GB), quarter note (US)

noise /nwaz/ *nf* **chercher ~** *or* **des ~s à qn** to pick a quarrel with sb

noisetier /nwaztje/ *nm* hazel (tree)

noisette /nwazɛt/ *nf* (a) hazelnut
(b) **~ de beurre** small knob of butter

noix /nwa/ *nf inv* (a) walnut (GB), English walnut (US)
(b) **~ de beurre** knob of butter
■ **~ de cajou** cashew nut; **~ de coco** coconut; **~ (de) muscade** nutmeg

nom /nɔ̃/ **1** *nm* (a) name; **petit ~** first name; **~ et prénom** full name; **donner un ~ à** to name; **sans ~** unspeakable; **George Sand, de son vrai ~ Aurore Dupin** George Sand, whose real name was Aurore Dupin; **parler en son propre ~** to speak for oneself
(b) noun
2 **au nom de** *phr* (a) in the name of
(b) on behalf of
■ **~ de baptême** Christian name; **~ d'emprunt** pseudonym; **~ de famille** surname; **~ de jeune fille** maiden name
IDIOMS **traiter qn de tous les ~s** (colloq) to call sb all the names under the sun; **appeler les choses par leur ~** to call a spade a spade

nomade /nɔmad/ *nmf* nomad

nombre /nɔ̃bʀ/ *nm* number; **un ~ à deux chiffres** a two-digit number; **un certain ~ de** some; **être en ~ inférieur** ⟨*players*⟩ to be fewer in number; ⟨*group*⟩ to be smaller; **ils étaient au ~ de 30** there were 30 of them; **écrasé sous le ~** (of people) overcome by sheer weight of numbers; (of letters) overwhelmed by the sheer volume; **bon ~ de** a good many; **~ de fois** many times

nombreux, -euse /nɔ̃bʀø, øz/ *adj* ⟨*population, collection*⟩ large; ⟨*people, objects*⟩ numerous, many; **ils étaient peu ~** there weren't many of them; **ils ont répondu à l'appel** a great many people responded to the appeal; **les touristes deviennent trop ~** the number of tourists is becoming excessive

nombril /nɔ̃bʀil/ *nm* navel; **elle se prend pour le ~ du monde** (colloq) she thinks she's God's gift to mankind

nombrilisme /nɔ̃bʀilism/ *nm* (colloq) navel-gazing (colloq)

nombriliste *adj* (colloq) egocentric

nomenclature /nɔmɑ̃klatyʀ/ *nf* nomenclature; (in dictionary) word list

nominal, ~e, *mpl* -aux /nɔminal, o/ *adj* (gen) nominal; ⟨*list*⟩ of names

nominatif, -ive /nɔminatif, iv/ **1** *adj* ⟨*list*⟩ of names; ⟨*invitation*⟩ personal; ⟨*share*⟩ registered
2 *nm* nominative

nomination /nɔminasjɔ̃/ *nf*
(a) appointment
(b) letter of appointment
(c) (controversial) nomination

nominativement /nɔminativmɑ̃/ *adv* by name

nominer /nɔmine/ [1] *vtr* to nominate

nommément /nɔmemɑ̃/ *adv* specifically, by name

nommer /nɔme/ [1] **1** *vtr* **(a)** to appoint; **être nommé à Paris** to be posted to Paris **(b)** to name ‹*person*›; to call ‹*thing*›; **pour ne ~ personne** to mention no names **2 se nommer** *v refl* (+ *v être*) **(a)** to be called **(b)** to give one's name

non /nɔ̃/ **1** *adv* **(a)** no; **'tu y vas?'—'~'** 'are you going?'—'no, I'm not'; **ah, ça ~!** definitely not!; **faire ~ de la tête** to shake one's head; **je pense que ~** I don't think so; **je te dis que ~** no, I tell you; **il paraît que ~** apparently not; **tu trouves ça drôle? moi ~** do you think that's funny? I don't; **~ sans raison** not without reason; **~ moins difficile** just as difficult; **qu'il soit d'accord ou ~** whether he agrees or not; **tu viens, oui ou ~?** are you coming or not?; **sois un peu plus poli, ~ mais!** (colloq) be a bit more polite, for heaven's sake! **(b)** non; **~ alcoolisé** nonalcoholic; **~ négligeable** considerable **2** *nm inv* **(a)** no **(b)** 'no' vote **3 non plus** *phr* **je ne suis pas d'accord ~ plus** I don't agree either; **il n'a pas aimé le film, moi ~ plus** he didn't like the film and neither did I **4 non(-)** (/nɔn/ *before vowel or mute h*) (*combining form*) **~-fumeur** nonsmoker; **~-syndiqué** non union member

nonagénaire /nɔnaʒenɛʁ/ *adj* **être ~** to be in one's nineties

non-aligné, ~e, *mpl* **~s** /nɔnaliɲe/ *nm,f* nonaligned country

nonante /nɔnɑ̃t/ *adj inv*, *pron* ninety

non-assistance /nɔnasistɑ̃s/ *nf* **~ à personne en danger** failure to render assistance

nonchalance /nɔ̃ʃalɑ̃s/ *nf* nonchalance

nonchalant, ~e /nɔ̃ʃalɑ̃, ɑ̃t/ *adj* nonchalant

non-dit /nɔ̃di/ *nm inv* **le ~** what is left unsaid

non-figuratif, -ive, *mpl* **~s** /nɔ̃figyʁatif, iv/ *adj* abstract

non-fonctionnement /nɔ̃fɔ̃ksjɔnmɑ̃/ *nm* failure to operate

non-initié, ~e, *mpl* **~s** /nɔninisje/ *nm,f* layman, lay person

non-inscrit, ~e, *mpl* **~s** /nɔnɛ̃skʁi, it/ *nm,f* independent

non-lieu, *pl* **~x** /nɔ̃ljø/ *nm* (Law) dismissal (of a charge); **il y a eu ~** the case was dismissed

nonne /nɔn/ *nf* nun

nonnette /nɔnɛt/ *nf* small iced gingerbread

non-recevoir /nɔ̃ʁəsəvwaʁ/ *nm* **fin de ~** flat refusal

non-reconduction, *pl* **~s** /nɔ̃ʁəkɔ̃dyksjɔ̃/ *nf* (of contract) nonrenewal

non-respect /nɔ̃ʁɛspɛ/ *nm* **~ de** failure to comply with ‹*clause*›; failure to respect ‹*person*›

non-sens /nɔ̃sɑ̃s/ *nm inv* nonsense

non-spécialiste, *pl* **~s** /nɔ̃spesjalist/ *nmf* layman

non-violent, ~e, *mpl* **~s** /nɔ̃vjɔlɑ̃, ɑ̃t/ *nm,f* advocate of nonviolence

non-voyant, ~e, *mpl* **~s** /nɔ̃vwajɑ̃, ɑ̃t/ *nm,f* visually handicapped person

nord /nɔʁ/ **1** *adj inv* north; northern **2** *nm* **(a)** north; **le vent du ~** the north wind; **le ~ de l'Europe** northern Europe **(b) le Nord** the North; **la Corée du Nord** North Korea IDIOMS **il ne perd pas le ~!** (colloq) he's got his head screwed on! (colloq)

nord-africain, ~e, *mpl* **~s** /nɔʁafʁikɛ̃, ɛn/ *adj* North African

nord-américain, ~e, *mpl* **~s** /nɔʁameʁikɛ̃, ɛn/ *adj* North American

nord-est /nɔʁ(d)ɛst/ **1** *adj inv* northeast; northeastern **2** *nm* northeast

nordique /nɔʁdik/ *adj* Nordic

nord-ouest /nɔʁ(d)wɛst/ **1** *adj inv* northwest; northwestern **2** *nm* northwest

Nord-Sud /nɔʁsyd/ *adj inv* North-South

normal, ~e[1], *mpl* **-aux** /nɔʁmal, o/ *adj* normal; **il est ~ que** it is natural that; **il n'est pas ~ que** it is not right that

normale[2] /nɔʁmal/ *nf* **(a)** average **(b)** norm; **retour à la ~** return to normal

normalement /nɔʁmalmɑ̃/ *adv* normally

normalisation /nɔʁmalizasjɔ̃/ *nf* **(a)** normalization **(b)** standardization

normaliser /nɔʁmalize/ [1] *vtr* **(a)** to normalize ‹*relations*› **(b)** to standardize ‹*sizes*›

normalité /nɔʁmalite/ *nf* normality

normand, ~e /nɔʁmɑ̃, ɑ̃d/ **1** *adj* **(a)** ‹*conquest*› Norman **(b)** ‹*coast*› Normandy; ‹*team*› from Normandy **2** *nm* Norman (French)

Normand, ~e /nɔʁmɑ̃, ɑ̃d/ *nm,f* Norman IDIOMS **une réponse de ~** a noncommittal reply

normatif, -ive /nɔʁmatif, iv/ *adj* normative

norme /nɔʁm/ *nf* (gen) norm; (Tech) standard

Norvège /nɔʁvɛʒ/ *pr nf* Norway

norvégien, -ienne /nɔʁveʒjɛ̃, ɛn/ **1** *adj* Norwegian **2** *nm* (language) Norwegian

nos ▶ NOTRE

nostalgie /nɔstalʒi/ *nf* nostalgia

nostalgique /nɔstalʒik/ *adj* nostalgic

notable /nɔtabl/ **1** *adj* ‹*fact*› notable; ‹*progress*› significant ····⫶

2 *nm* notable

notaire /nɔtɛʀ/ *nm* notary public

notamment /nɔtamɑ̃/ *adv* (a) notably
(b) in particular

notation /nɔtasjɔ̃/ *nf* (a) notation
(b) (of pupil) marking (GB), grading (US);
(of staff) grading

note /nɔt/ *nf* (a) bill (GB), check (US); **faire
la ～ de qn** to write out sb's bill (GB) *or*
check (US)
(b) (Mus) note; (figurative) note, touch; **forcer la
～** to overdo it
(c) mark (GB), grade (US); **～ éliminatoire** fail
mark (GB) *or* grade (US)
(d) (written) note; **prendre qch en ～** to make a
note of sth; **prendre (bonne) ～ de qch**
(figurative) to take (due) note of sth
■ **～ de frais** expense account; **～ d'honoraires**
bill; **～ de service** memorandum

noter /nɔte/ [1] *vtr* (a) to write down ⟨idea,
address⟩
(b) to notice ⟨change⟩; **notez (bien) que je
n'ai rien à lui reprocher** mind you I haven't
got anything particular against him; **il faut
quand même ～** it has to be said
(c) to mark (GB), to grade (US) ⟨exercise⟩; to
give a mark (GB) *or* grade (US) to ⟨pupil⟩; to
grade ⟨employee⟩

notice /nɔtis/ *nf* (a) note
(b) instructions

notifier /nɔtifje/ [2] *vtr* **～ qch à qn** (gen) to
notify sb of sth; (Law) to give sb notice of sth

notion /nɔsjɔ̃/ *nf* (a) notion; **perdre la ～ de**
to lose all sense of
(b) **～s** basic knowledge

notoire /nɔtwaʀ/ *adj* ⟨fact, position⟩ well-
known; ⟨swindler, stupidity⟩ notorious

notoirement /nɔtwaʀmɑ̃/ *adv* manifestly;
notoriously

notoriété /nɔtɔʀjete/ *nf* (a) fame; (of product)
reputation; **il est de ～ (publique) que** it's
common knowledge that
(b) (person) celebrity

notre, *pl* **nos** /nɔtʀ, no/ *det* our; **à nos
âges** at our age; **c'était ～ avis à tous** we all
felt the same; **nos enfants à nous** (colloq) our
children

nôtre, *pl* **nos** /nɔtʀ/ 1 *det* **nous avons fait ～s ces
idées** we've adopted these ideas
2 **le nôtre, la nôtre, les nôtres** *pron*
ours; **soyez des ～s!** won't you join us?; **les
～s** our own people; (team, group) our side

nouer /nwe/ [1] 1 *vtr* (a) (gen) to tie; to
knot ⟨tie⟩; to tie up ⟨parcel⟩; **avoir la gorge
nouée** to have a lump in one's throat
(b) to establish ⟨relations⟩; to engage in
⟨dialogue⟩
2 **se nouer** *v refl* (+ *v être*) (a) ⟨plot⟩ to
take shape
(b) ⟨diplomatic relations⟩ to be established;
⟨dialogue, friendship⟩ to begin

nougat /nuga/ *nm* nougat

nouilles /nuj/ *nf pl* noodles, pasta

nounou /nunu/ *nf* (colloq) nanny (GB), nurse

nounours /nunuʀs/ *nm inv* (colloq) teddy
bear

nourrice /nuʀis/ *nf* (a) childminder (GB),
babysitter (US)
(b) wet nurse

nourrir /nuʀiʀ/ [3] 1 *vtr* (a) to feed
⟨person, animal⟩; to nourish ⟨skin, leather⟩;
bien nourri well-fed; **～ au sein/au biberon** to
breast-/to bottle-feed; **mon travail ne me
nourrit pas** I don't make enough to live on
(b) (figurative) to harbour (GB) ⟨hopes⟩; to feed
⟨fire⟩; to fuel ⟨passion⟩
2 **se nourrir** *v refl* (+ *v être*) ⟨animal⟩ to
feed; ⟨person⟩ to eat; **se ～ de** to live on
⟨vegetables⟩; to feed on ⟨illusions⟩

nourrissant, **～e** /nuʀisɑ̃, ɑ̃t/ *adj*
nourishing

nourrisson /nuʀisɔ̃/ *nm* infant

nourriture /nuʀityʀ/ *nf* (a) food
(b) diet

nous /nu/ *pron* (a) (subject) we; (object) us;
～ sommes en avance we're early; **donne-～
l'adresse** give us the address; **entre ～, il
n'est pas très intelligent** between you and
me, he isn't very intelligent; **une maison à ～**
a house of our own; **pensons à ～** let's think
of ourselves
(b) (with reflexive verb) **～ ～ soignons** we look
after ourselves; **～ ～ aimons** we love each
other

nous-même, *pl* **nous-mêmes**
/numɛm/ *pron* ourselves

nouveau (**nouvel** *before vowel or mute
h*), **nouvelle**[1], *mpl* **～x** /nuvo, nuvɛl/
1 *adj* (gen) new; ⟨attempt, attack⟩ fresh; **tout
～** brand-new; **se faire faire un ～ costume** to
have a new suit made; to have another suit
made; **une nouvelle fois** once again; **les ～x
élus** the newly-elected members; **les ～x
mariés** the newlyweds
2 *nm,f* (in school) new boy/girl; (in company)
new employee; (in army) new recruit
3 *nm* **téléphone-moi s'il y a du ～** give me a
call if there is anything new to report; **j'ai du
～ pour toi** I've got some news for you
4 **à nouveau, de nouveau** *phr* (once)
again

nouveau-né, **～e**, *mpl* **～s** /nuvone/
nm,f newborn baby

nouveauté /nuvote/ *nf* (a) novelty; **ce
n'est pas une ～!** that's nothing new!
(b) (gen) new thing; (book) new publication;
(record) new release; (car, machine) new model

nouvel ▸ NOUVEAU 1

nouvelle[2] /nuvɛl/ 1 *adj f* ▸ NOUVEAU 1
2 *nf* (a) ▸ NOUVEAU 2
(b) news; **une ～** a piece of news; **tu connais
la ～?** have you heard the news?; **recevoir
des ～s de qn** to hear from sb; (through
somebody else) to hear news of sb; **il m'a
demandé de tes ～s** he asked after you; **aux
dernières ～s, il se porte bien** (colloq) the last
I heard he was doing fine; **il aura de mes ～s!**

(colloq) he'll be hearing from me!; **goûte ce petit vin, tu m'en diras des ~s** (colloq) have a taste of this wine, it's really good!
(c) short story

nouvellement /nuvɛlmɑ̃/ *adv* recently

Nouvelle-Zélande /nuvɛlzelɑ̃d/ *pr nf* New Zealand

nouvelliste /nuvelist/ *nmf* short-story writer

novateur, -trice /nɔvatœʀ, tʀis/ **1** *adj* innovative
2 *nm,f* innovator, pioneer

novembre /nɔvɑ̃bʀ/ *nm* November

novice /nɔvis/ **1** *adj* inexperienced, green
2 *nmf* novice

noyade /nwajad/ *nf* drowning

noyau, *pl* **~x** /nwajo/ *nm* (a) stone (GB), pit (US)
(b) small group; **~x de résistance** pockets of resistance
(c) nucleus

noyauter /nwajote/ [1] *vtr* to infiltrate

noyé, ~e /nwaje/ *nm,f* drowned person

noyer[1] /nwaje/ [23] **1** *vtr* (gen) to drown; to flood ⟨village, engine⟩; **~ qn sous un flot de paroles** to talk sb's head off (colloq)
2 se noyer *v refl* (+ *v être*) to drown; ⟨suicide⟩ to drown oneself; **mourir noyé** to drown
IDIOMS **se ~ dans un verre d'eau** to make a mountain out of a molehill

noyer[2] /nwaje/ *nm* walnut (tree)

nu, ~e /ny/ **1** *adj* ⟨person⟩ naked; ⟨wall, tree, coastline⟩ bare; ⟨truth⟩ plain; **pieds ~s** barefoot; **torse ~** stripped to the waist
2 *nm* (in art) nude
3 à nu *phr* **être à ~** to be exposed; **mettre son cœur à ~** to open one's heart

nuage /nɥaʒ/ *nm* cloud; **sans ~s** ⟨sky⟩ cloudless; ⟨happiness⟩ unclouded; **~ de lait** dash of milk
IDIOMS **descendre de son ~** to come back to earth

nuageux, -euse /nɥaʒø, øz/ *adj* ⟨sky⟩ cloudy

nuance /nɥɑ̃s/ *nf* (a) (of colour) shade
(b) (of meaning) nuance; **sans ~** ⟨commentary⟩ clearcut; ⟨personality⟩ straightforward
(c) slight difference; **à cette ~ près que** with the small reservation that
(d) (Mus) nuance

nuancer /nɥɑ̃se/ [12] *vtr* (a) to qualify ⟨opinion⟩; to modify ⟨view of situation⟩; **peu nuancé** unsubtle
(b) to moderate ⟨remarks, statements⟩

nucléaire /nykleɛʀ/ **1** *adj* nuclear
2 *nm* **le ~** nuclear energy; nuclear technology

nudité /nydite/ *nf* (a) nakedness, nudity
(b) (of place, wall) bareness

nuée /nye/ *nf* (of insects) swarm; (of people) horde

nues /ny/ *nf pl* **tomber des ~** (colloq) to be flabbergasted (colloq); **porter qn aux ~** to praise sb to the skies

nui /nɥi/ ▸ NUIRE

nuire /nɥiʀ/ [69] **1 nuire à** *v+prep* to harm ⟨person⟩; to be harmful to ⟨health, interests, reputation⟩; to damage ⟨crops⟩
2 se nuire *v refl* (+ *v être*) (a) to do each other a lot of harm
(b) to do oneself a lot of harm

nuisance /nɥizɑ̃s/ *nf* nuisance

nuisible /nɥizibl/ *adj* ⟨substance, waste⟩ dangerous; ⟨influence⟩ harmful; **insecte ~** (insect) pest; **~ à** detrimental to

nuit /nɥi/ *nf* night; **cette ~** last night; tonight; **voyager de ~** to travel by night; **avant la ~** before dark; **à la tombée de la ~** at nightfall; **il fait ~** it's dark; **il faisait ~ noire** it was pitch dark; **ça se perd dans la ~ des temps** it is lost in the mists of time
■ **~ blanche** sleepless night; **~ bleue** *night of terrorist bomb attacks*
IDIOMS **c'est le jour et la ~** they're as different as chalk and cheese; **attends demain pour donner ta réponse: la ~ porte conseil** wait till tomorrow to give your answer: sleep on it first

nuitée /nɥite/ *nf* (in a hotel) overnight stay

nul, nulle /nyl/ **1** *adj* (a) (colloq) ⟨person⟩ hopeless; ⟨piece of work⟩ worthless; ⟨film⟩ trashy (colloq)
(b) (Law) ⟨contract⟩ void; ⟨will⟩ invalid; ⟨elections⟩ null and void; ⟨vote⟩ spoiled
(c) (Sport) **match ~** tie, draw (GB); nil-all draw
(d) ⟨difference⟩ nil
(e) **~ homme/pays** no man/country; **~ autre que vous** no-one else but you
2 *nm,f* (colloq) idiot (colloq); **c'est un ~** he's a dead loss (colloq)
3 *pron* no-one
4 nulle part *phr* nowhere

nullement /nylmɑ̃/ *adv* not at all

nullité /nylite/ *nf* (a) (Law) nullity; **frapper de ~** to render void
(b) (of argument) invalidity; (of book, film) (colloq) worthlessness
(c) (colloq) (person) idiot (colloq)

numéraire /nymeʀɛʀ/ *nm* cash

numéral, ~e, *mpl* **-aux** /nymeʀal, o/ **1** *adj* numeral
2 *nm* numeral

numération /nymeʀasjɔ̃/ *nf* (Math) numeration
■ **~ globulaire** blood count

numérique /nymeʀik/ *adj* (gen) numerical; ⟨display⟩ digital; **clavier ~** keypad

numéro /nymeʀo/ *nm* (a) number; **~ de téléphone** telephone number
(b) (magazine) issue; **suite au prochain ~** to be continued
(c) (in show) act
(d) (colloq) **quel ~!** what a character!

■ ~ **d'abonné** customer's number; ~ **d'appel gratuit** freefone number (GB), toll-free number (US); ~ **vert** = ~ D'APPEL GRATUIT IDIOMS **tirer le bon** ~ to be lucky

numérotation /nymeʀɔtasjɔ̃/ *nf* numbering

numéroter /nymeʀɔte/ [1] *vtr* to number

numerus clausus /nymeʀyskloːzys/ *nm inv* quota

nunuche /nynyʃ/ *adj* (colloq) bird-brained (colloq), silly

nu-pied, *pl* ~**s** /nypje/ *nm* sandal

nuptial, ~**e**, *mpl* **-iaux** /nypsjal, o/ *adj* ⟨*mass*⟩ nuptial; ⟨*room*⟩ bridal; **cérémonie** ~**e** wedding

nuque /nyk/ *nf* nape (of the neck)

nurse /nœʀs/ *nf* nanny (GB), nurse

nutritif, **-ive** /nytʀitif, iv/ *adj* ⟨*skin cream*⟩ nourishing; ⟨*value*⟩ nutritive

nutrition /nytʀisjɔ̃/ *nf* nutrition

nymphe /nɛ̃f/ *nf* nymph

nymphéa /nɛ̃fea/ *nm* waterlily

nymphomane /nɛ̃fɔman/ *adj*, *nf* nymphomaniac

Oo

o, **O** /o/ *nm inv* o, O

oasis /ɔazis/ *nf inv* oasis

obéir /ɔbeiʀ/ [3] *v+prep* (a) to obey; ~ **à** to obey ⟨*order*⟩
(b) ⟨*brakes, vehicle*⟩ to respond

obéissance /ɔbeisɑ̃s/ *nf* obedience

obéissant, ~**e** /ɔbeisɑ̃, ɑ̃t/ *adj* obedient

obélisque /ɔbelisk/ *nm* obelisk

obèse /ɔbɛz/ *adj* obese

objecter /ɔbʒɛkte/ [1] *vtr* to object

objectif, **-ive** /ɔbʒɛktif, iv/ 1 *adj* objective
2 *nm* (a) objective
(b) lens
(c) target

objection /ɔbʒɛksjɔ̃/ *nf* objection

objectivité /ɔbʒɛktivite/ *nf* objectivity

objet /ɔbʒɛ/ 1 *nm* (a) object; ~ **fragile** fragile item; ~**s personnels** personal possessions
(b) (of debate, research) subject; (of hatred, desire) object; **faire l'**~ **de** to be the subject of ⟨*inquiry, research*⟩; to be subjected to ⟨*surveillance*⟩; to be the object of ⟨*desire, hatred*⟩
(c) purpose, object; '~**: réponse à votre lettre du...**' 're: your letter of...'
(d) (Law) ~ **d'un litige** matter at issue
2 **-objet** (*combining form*) as an object; **femme**-~ woman as an object

■ ~**s trouvés** lost property; ~ **volant non identifié, ovni** unidentified flying object, UFO

obligataire /ɔbligatɛʀ/ (Fin) *adj* ⟨*market, issue*⟩ bond; **emprunt** ~ bond issue

obligation /ɔbligasjɔ̃/ *nf* (a) obligation, responsibility; duty
(b) necessity; **se voir** *or* **se trouver dans l'**~ **de faire** to be forced to do
(c) (Econ) bond
(d) (Law) obligation

■ ~**s militaires, OM** military service

obligatoire /ɔbligatwaʀ/ *adj*
(a) compulsory
(b) (colloq) inevitable

obligatoirement /ɔbligatwaʀmɑ̃/ *adv* inevitably, necessarily

obligé, ~**e** /ɔblige/ 1 *pp* ▶ OBLIGER
2 *pp adj* (a) (constrained) **se voir** ~ **de faire** to be forced to do
(b) (indebted) **être** ~ **à qn de** to be obliged *or* grateful to sb for
(c) (necessary) essential; **un passage** ~ (**pour**) (figurative) a prerequisite (for)
3 *nm,f* (a) **être l'**~ **de qn** to be obliged *or* indebted to sb
(b) (in law) obligor

obligeamment /ɔbliʒamɑ̃/ *adv* obligingly

obligeance /ɔbliʒɑ̃s/ *nf* **avoir l'**~ **de** to be kind enough to

obligeant, ~**e** /ɔbliʒɑ̃, ɑ̃t/ *adj* obliging; kind

obliger /ɔbliʒe/ [13] 1 *vtr* (a) ~ **qn à faire** to force sb to do; ⟨*rules*⟩ to make it compulsory for sb to; ⟨*duty*⟩ to compel sb to; **je suis obligé de partir** I have to go
(b) ~ **qn** to oblige sb
2 **s'obliger** *v refl* (+ *v être*) **s'**~ **à faire** to force oneself to do

oblique /ɔblik/ *adj* slanting; sidelong; oblique

obliquement /ɔblikmɑ̃/ *adv* at an angle; diagonally

oblitération /ɔbliteʀasjɔ̃/ *nf* (of stamp) cancelling (GB); (**cachet d'**)~ postmark

oblitérer /ɔbliteʀe/ [14] *vtr* to cancel, to obliterate ⟨*stamp*⟩

oblong, **-ongue** /ɔblɔ̃, ɔ̃g/ *adj* oblong

obnubiler /ɔbnybile/ [1] *vtr* to obsess

obscène /ɔpsɛn/ *adj* obscene

obscur, ~**e** /ɔpskyʀ/ *adj* (a) dark
(b) obscure
(c) lowly
(d) vague

obscurcir ⋯◆ occurrence

obscurcir /ɔpskyʀsiʀ/ [3] **1** *vtr* (a) to make [sth] dark *‹place›*
(b) to obscure *‹view›*
2 s'obscurcir *v refl* (+ *v être*) (a) *‹sky, place›* to darken
(b) *‹situation›* to become confused

obscurément /ɔpskyʀemɑ̃/ *adv* (a) *‹feel›* vaguely
(b) *‹live›* in obscurity

obscurité /ɔpskyʀite/ *nf* darkness

obsédant, **~e** /ɔpsedɑ̃, ɑ̃t/ *adj* *‹memory, dream, music›* haunting; *‹rhythm›* insistent

obsédé, **~e** /ɔpsede/ *nm,f* ~ (**sexuel**) sex maniac

obséder /ɔpsede/ [14] *vtr* *‹memory, dream›* to haunt; *‹idea, problem›* to obsess

obsèques /ɔpsɛk/ *nf pl* funeral

obséquieux, **-ieuse** /ɔpsekjø, øz/ *adj* obsequious

observateur, **-trice** /ɔpsɛʀvatœʀ, tʀis/
1 *adj* observant
2 *nm,f* observer

observation /ɔpsɛʀvasjɔ̃/ *nf*
(a) observation
(b) observation, remark; comment
(c) reproach

observatoire /ɔpsɛʀvatwaʀ/ *nm*
(a) observatory
(b) look-out post

observer /ɔpsɛʀve/ [1] **1** *vtr* (a) to watch, to observe
(b) to notice, to observe *‹phenomenon, reaction›*
(c) to observe *‹rules, treaty›*; to keep to *‹diet›*; to maintain *‹strategy›*; ~ **le silence** to keep quiet
2 s'observer *v refl* (+ *v être*) (a) to watch each other
(b) to keep a check on oneself

obsession /ɔpsesjɔ̃/ *nf* obsession

obsolète /ɔpsɔlɛt/ *adj* obsolete

obstacle /ɔpstakl/ *nm* (a) obstacle
(b) (in horseriding) fence

obstétricien, **-ienne** /ɔpstetʀisjɛ̃, ɛn/ *nm,f* obstetrician

obstétrique /ɔpstetʀik/ *nf* obstetrics

obstination /ɔpstinasjɔ̃/ *nf* obstinacy

obstiné, **~e** /ɔpstine/ **1** *pp* ▶ OBSTINER
2 *pp adj* (a) stubborn
(b) dogged

obstinément /ɔpstinemɑ̃/ *adv* obstinately

obstiner: **s'obstiner** /ɔpstine/ [1] *v refl* (+ *v être*) to persist

obstruction /ɔpstʀyksjɔ̃/ *nf* obstruction

obstruer /ɔpstʀye/ [1] **1** *vtr* to obstruct
2 s'obstruer *v refl* (+ *v être*) to get blocked

obtempérer /ɔptɑ̃peʀe/ [14] *v+prep* to comply; ~ **à** to comply with *‹order›*

obtenir /ɔptəniʀ/ [36] *vtr* to get, to obtain

obtention /ɔptɑ̃sjɔ̃/ *nf* getting, obtaining

obturation /ɔptyʀasjɔ̃/ *nf* (a) blocking (up)
(b) **vitesse d'~** shutter speed

obturer /ɔptyʀe/ [1] *vtr* to block up

obtus, **~e** /ɔpty, yz/ *adj* obtuse

obus /ɔby/ *nm inv* shell

occasion /ɔkazjɔ̃/ *nf* (a) occasion; **à l'~** some time; **à** *or* **en plusieurs ~s** on several occasions; **les grandes ~s** special occasions
(b) opportunity, chance; **être l'~ de qch** to give rise to sth
(c) second-hand buy
(d) bargain

occasionnel, **-elle** /ɔkazjɔnɛl/ *adj* occasional

occasionner /ɔkazjɔne/ [1] *vtr* to cause

occident /ɔksidɑ̃/ *nm* (a) west
(b) **l'Occident** the West

occidental, **~e**, *mpl* **-aux** /ɔksidɑ̃tal, o/ *adj* western

Occidental, **~e**, *mpl* **-aux** /ɔksidɑ̃tal, o/ *nm,f* Westerner

occitan /ɔksitɑ̃/ *nm* langue d'oc

occulte /ɔkylt/ *adj* (a) occult
(b) secret

occulter /ɔkylte/ [1] *vtr* (a) to eclipse
(b) to obscure *‹issue›*; to conceal *‹truth›*

occultisme /ɔkyltism/ *nm* occultism

occupant, **~e** /ɔkypɑ̃, ɑ̃t/ **1** *adj* occupying
2 *nm,f* (of house) occupier; (of vehicle) occupant

occupation /ɔkypasjɔ̃/ *nf* (a) (pastime) occupation
(b) occupation, job
(c) occupancy
(d) (of country, factory) occupation

occupé, **~e** /ɔkype/ **1** *pp* ▶ OCCUPER
2 *pp adj* (a) *‹person, life›* busy
(b) *‹seat›* taken; *‹phone›* engaged (GB); busy; *‹toilet›* engaged
(c) (Mil) *‹country›* occupied

occuper /ɔkype/ [1] **1** *vtr* (a) to live in, to occupy *‹flat, house›*; to be in *‹shower, cell›*; to sit in *‹seat›*
(b) to take up *‹space, time›*
(c) to occupy *‹person, mind›*; **ça m'occupe!** it keeps me busy!; **le sujet qui nous occupe** the matter which we are dealing with
(d) to have *‹employment›*; to hold *‹job, office›*
(e) *‹strikers, army›* to occupy *‹place›*; ~ **les locaux** to stage a sit-in
2 s'occuper *v refl* (+ *v être*) (a) to keep oneself busy *or* occupied
(b) **s'~ de** to see to, to take care of *‹dinner, tickets›*; to be dealing with *‹file, matter›*; to take care of *‹child, animal, plant›*; to attend to *‹customer›*; to be in charge of *‹finance, library›*; **occupe-toi de tes affaires** (colloq) *or* **de ce qui te regarde!** (colloq) mind your own business! (colloq)

occurrence /ɔkyʀɑ̃s/ *nf* (a) case, instance; **en l'~** in this case
(b) occurrence

O

OCDE /osedeə/ *nf* (*abbr* = **Organisation de coopération et de développement économiques**) OECD

océan /oseã/ *nm* ocean

océanique /oseanik/ *adj* oceanic

océanographe /oseanɔgraf/ *nmf* oceanographer

ocre /ɔkʀ/ *adj inv, nm* ochre (GB)

octante /ɔktãt/ *adj inv, pron* (in Belgian, Canadian, Swiss, French) eighty

octave /ɔktav/ *nf* octave

octet /ɔktɛt/ *nm* (a) (Comput) byte
(b) (in physics) octet

octobre /ɔktɔbʀ/ *nm* October

octogénaire /ɔktɔʒenɛʀ/ *nmf* octogenarian

octogonal, ~**e**, *mpl* **-aux** /ɔktɔgɔnal, o/ *adj* octagonal

octroi /ɔktʀwa/ *nm* (a) granting
(b) octroi

octroyer /ɔktʀwaje/ [23] *vtr* ~ **à qn** to grant sb *(pardon, favour)*; to allocate sb sth *(budget)*

oculaire /ɔkylɛʀ/ *adj* **troubles** ~**s** eye trouble; **témoin** ~ eyewitness

oculiste /ɔkylist/ *nmf* oculist, ophthalmologist

ode /ɔd/ *nf* ode

odeur /ɔdœʀ/ *nf* smell

odieux, -ieuse /ɔdjø, øz/ *adj* horrible

odorant, ~**e** /ɔdɔʀã, ãt/ *adj* which has a smell

odorat /ɔdɔʀa/ *nm* sense of smell

OECE /ɔəseə/ *nf* (*abbr* = **Organisation européenne de coopération économique**) OEEC

œdème /edɛm/ *nm* (Med) oedema

œdipe /edip/ *nm* Oedipus complex

œil, *pl* **yeux** /œj, jø/ *nm* eye; **ouvrir l'**~ to keep one's eyes open; **fermer les yeux sur qch** to turn a blind eye to sth; **acheter qch les yeux fermés** to buy sth with complete confidence; **avoir l'**~ **à tout** to be vigilant; **jeter un** ~ **à** *or* **sur qch** to have a quick look at sth; **aux yeux de tous** openly; **jeter un coup d'**~ **à qch** to glance at sth; **avoir le coup d'**~ to have a good eye; **regarder qch d'un** ~ **neuf** to see sth in a new light; **voir qch d'un mauvais** ~ to take a dim view of sth; **à mes yeux** in my opinion
■ ~ **de verre** glass eye
IDIOMS mon ~**!** (colloq) my eye! (colloq), my foot! (colloq); **à l'**~ (colloq) for nothing, for free (colloq); **faire les gros yeux à qn** to glare at sb; **dévorer qn/qch des yeux** to gaze longingly at sb/sth; **faire les yeux doux à qn** to make eyes at sb; **tourner de l'**~ (colloq) to faint; **cela me sort par les yeux** (colloq) I've had it up to here (colloq); **avoir bon pied bon** ~ to be as fit as a fiddle; **sauter aux yeux** to be obvious

œillade /œjad/ *nf* (a) wink
(b) glance

œillère /œjɛʀ/ *nf* blinker

œillet /œjɛ/ *nm* (a) carnation
(b) (in shoe, tarpaulin) eyelet; (in belt) hole; (made of metal) grommet

œilleton /œjtɔ̃/ *nm* (in door) peephole

œnologie /enɔlɔʒi/ *nf* oenology

œsophage /ezɔfaʒ/ *nm* oesophagus

œstrogène /ɛstʀɔʒɛn/ *nm* oestrogen

œuf /œf, *pl* ø/ *nm* egg; ~**s de cabillaud** cod's roe
■ ~ **à la coque** boiled egg; ~ **dur** hard-boiled egg; ~ **sur le plat** fried egg; ~**s brouillés** scrambled eggs

œuvre /œvʀ/ *nf* (a) (artistic, literary) work; ~**s complètes** complete works
(b) **être à l'**~ to be at work; **voir qn à l'**~ to see sb in action; **mettre en** ~ to implement *(reform)*; to display *(ingenuity)*; **tout mettre en** ~ **pour faire** to make every effort to do
■ ~ **d'art** work of art; ~ **de bienfaisance** *or* **de charité** charity

off /ɔf/ *adj inv* (colloq) **voix** ~ voice-over

offensant, ~**e** /ɔfãsã, ãt/ *adj* offensive (**pour à**)

offense /ɔfãs/ *nf* insult

offenser /ɔfãse/ [1] **1** *vtr* to offend
2 s'offenser *v refl* (+ *v être*) to take offence (GB)

offensif, -ive¹ /ɔfãsif, iv/ *adj* (Mil) offensive

offensive² /ɔfãsiv/ *nf* (Mil, figurative) offensive

offert, -e /ɔfɛʀ, ɛʀt/ ▶ OFFRIR

office /ɔfis/ **1** *nm* (a) **faire** ~ **de table** to serve as a table
(b) ~ **religieux** service
(c) butlery
2 d'office *phr* **d'**~ without consultation; **nos propositions ont été rejetées d'**~ our proposals were dismissed out of hand; **commis d'**~ *(lawyer)* appointed by the court
■ ~ **du tourisme** tourist information office

officiel, -ielle /ɔfisjɛl/ **1** *adj* official; **être en visite officielle** to be on a state visit
2 *nm* official

officier¹ /ɔfisje/ [2] *vi* to officiate

officier² /ɔfisje/ *nm* officer

officieusement /ɔfisjøzmã/ *adv* unofficially

officieux, -ieuse /ɔfisjø, øz/ *adj* unofficial

officine /ɔfisin/ *nf* dispensary; pharmacy

offrande /ɔfʀãd/ *nf* offering

offrant /ɔfʀã/ **1** *pres p* ▶ OFFRIR
2 *nm* **vendre qch au plus** ~ to sell sth to the highest bidder

offre /ɔfʀ/ *nf* (a) offer; **répondre à une** ~ **d'emploi** to reply to a job advertisement
(b) (Econ) supply
■ ~ **d'achat** bid; ~ **publique d'achat**, OPA takeover bid

offrir /ɔfʀiʀ/ [4] **1** *vtr* (a) ~ **qch à qn** to give sth to sb
(b) to buy (**à qn** for sb)

(c) to offer ⟨*choice*⟩; to offer ⟨*resignation*⟩; to present ⟨*problems*⟩
2 s'offrir *v refl* (+ *v être*) **(a) s'~** to buy oneself ⟨*flowers*⟩; **ils ne peuvent pas s'~ le théâtre** they can't afford to go to the theatre (GB); **s'~ un jour de vacances** to give oneself a day off
(b) ⟨*solution*⟩ to present itself; **s'~ en spectacle** to make an exhibition of oneself
offusquer /ɔfyske/ [1] **1** *vtr* to offend
2 s'offusquer *v refl* (+ *v être*) to be offended

ogive /ɔʒiv/ *nf* rib

ogre /ɔgʀ/ *nm* ogre

oh /o/ *excl* oh!; **~ hisse!** heave-ho!

oie /wa/ *nf* goose; **~ blanche** naïve young girl

oignon /ɔɲɔ̃/ *nm* **(a)** onion
(b) (of flower) bulb
IDIOMS **occupe-toi de tes ~s** (colloq) mind your own business (colloq)

oiseau, *pl* **~x** /wazo/ *nm* bird; **un (drôle d')~** an oddball (colloq)
IDIOMS **trouver l'~ rare** (colloq) to find the one person in a million

oiseau-mouche, *pl* **oiseaux-mouches** /wazomuʃ/ *nm* hummingbird

oiseleur /wazlœʀ/ *nm* bird-catcher

oisellerie /wazɛlʀi/ *nf* bird shop

oisif, -ive /wazif, iv/ **1** *adj* idle
2 *nm,f* idler; **les ~s** the idle rich

oisillon /wazijɔ̃/ *nm* fledgling

oisiveté /wazivte/ *nf* idleness
IDIOMS **l'~ est mère de tous les vices** (Proverb) the devil makes work for idle hands

olé: **olé olé** /ɔleɔle/ *phr* (colloq) ⟨*joke*⟩ naughty

oléagineux, -euse /ɔleaʒinø, øz/ **1** *adj* oleaginous
2 *nm inv* oleaginous plant

oléiculture /ɔleikyltyʀ/ *nf* olive-growing

oléoduc /ɔleɔdyk/ *nm* (oil) pipeline

olfactif, -ive /ɔlfaktif, iv/ *adj* olfactory

oligo-élément, *pl* **~s** /ɔligoelemɑ̃/ *nm* trace element

olivâtre /ɔlivɑtʀ/ *adj* olive-greenish; sallow

olive /ɔliv/ *nf* olive

oliveraie /ɔlivʀɛ/ *nf* olive grove

olivier /ɔlivje/ *nm* **(a)** olive tree
(b) olive wood

olympiade /ɔlɛ̃pjad/ **1** *nf* Olympiad
2 olympiades *nf pl* Olympics

olympique /ɔlɛ̃pik/ *adj* Olympic

ombilic /ɔ̃bilik/ *nm* umbilicus, navel

ombrage /ɔ̃bʀaʒ/ *nm* shade
IDIOMS **porter ~ à qn** to offend sb; **prendre ~ de qch** to take umbrage at sth

ombrager /ɔ̃bʀaʒe/ [13] *vtr* to shade

ombrageux, -euse /ɔ̃bʀaʒø, øz/ *adj* tetchy

ombre /ɔ̃bʀ/ *nf* **(a)** shade; **tu leur fais de l'~** you're (standing) in their light; (figurative) you put them in the shade; **rester dans l'~ de qn** to be in sb's shadow
(b) shadow
(c) darkness
(d) laisser certains détails dans l'~ to be deliberately vague about certain details
(e) hint; **une ~ de tristesse passa dans son regard** a look of sadness crossed his/her face
■ **~ chinoise** shadow puppet; **~ à paupières** eye shadow
IDIOMS **jeter une ~ au tableau** to spoil the picture

ombrelle /ɔ̃bʀɛl/ *nf* parasol, sunshade

omelette /ɔmlɛt/ *nf* omelette

omettre /ɔmɛtʀ/ [60] *vtr* to leave out, to omit

omission /ɔmisjɔ̃/ *nf* omission

omnibus /ɔmnibys/ *nm inv* slow *or* local train

omniprésent, ~e /ɔmnipʀezɑ̃, ɑ̃t/ *adj* omnipresent

omnisports /ɔmnispɔʀ/ *adj inv* **salle ~** sports hall; **club ~** (multi-)sports club

omnivore /ɔmnivɔʀ/ *nmf* omnivore

omoplate /ɔmɔplat/ *nf* shoulder blade

OMS /ɔɛmɛs/ *nf* (*abbr* = **Organisation mondiale de la santé**) WHO

on /ɔ̃/ *pron* **(a) ~ a refait la route** the road was resurfaced; **~ a prétendu que** it was claimed that; **il pleut des cordes, comme ~ dit** it's raining cats and dogs, as they say
(b) we; **mon copain et moi, ~ va en Afrique** my boyfriend and I are going to Africa
(c) you; **alors, ~ se promène?** so you're taking a stroll then?
(d) ~ fait ce qu'~ peut! one does what one can!; **toi, ~ ne t'a rien demandé** nobody asked you for your opinion; **~ ne m'a pas demandé mon avis** they didn't ask me for my opinion

once /ɔ̃s/ *nf* ounce

oncle /ɔ̃kl/ *nm* uncle

onctueux, -euse /ɔ̃ktɥø, øz/ *adj*
(a) smooth, creamy
(b) unctuous

onde /ɔ̃d/ *nf* wave; **grandes ~s** long wave; **sur les ~s** on the air

ondée /ɔ̃de/ *nf* shower

on-dit /ɔ̃di/ *nm inv* **les ~** hearsay

ondoyant, ~e /ɔ̃dwajɑ̃, ɑ̃t/ *adj* rippling; lithe; swaying

ondoyer /ɔ̃dwaje/ [23] *vi* to undulate; to sway

ondulant, ~e /ɔ̃dylɑ̃, ɑ̃t/ *adj* swaying; undulating

ondulation /ɔ̃dylasjɔ̃/ *nf* **(a)** undulation; swaying
(b) curves; wave

ondulé, ~e /ɔ̃dyle/ *adj* ⟨*hair, shape*⟩ wavy; ⟨*cardboard*⟩ corrugated

onéreux, -euse /ɔneʀø, øz/ *adj* expensive

O

ONG /ɔɛnʒe/ nf (abbr = **organisation non gouvernementale**) NGO

ongle /ɔ̃gl/ nm nail
IDIOMS jusqu'au bout des ~s through and through

onglet /ɔ̃glɛ/ nm (a) tab; avec ~s with thumb-index
(b) (Culin) prime cut of beef

onirique /ɔniʀik/ adj dream-like

onomatopée /ɔnɔmatɔpe/ nf onomatopoeia

ont /ɔ̃/ ▸ AVOIR¹

ONU /ɔny, oɛny/ nf (abbr = **Organisation des Nations unies**) UN, UNO

onyx /ɔniks/ nm inv onyx

onze /ɔ̃z/ adj inv, pron, nm inv eleven

onzième /ɔ̃zjɛm/ **1** adj eleventh
2 nf (Sch) first year of primary school, age 6–7

OPA /opea/ nf (abbr = **offre publique d'achat**) takeover bid

opaque /ɔpak/ adj (a) opaque
(b) (figurative) ⟨text⟩ opaque; ⟨night⟩ dark; ⟨wood, fog⟩ impenetrable

OPEP /ɔpɛp/ nf (abbr = **Organisation des pays producteurs de pétrole**) OPEC

opéra /ɔpeʀa/ nm (a) opera
(b) opera house

opérateur, -trice /ɔpeʀatœʀ, tʀis/ nm,f operator; ~ de saisie keyboarder

opération /ɔpeʀasjɔ̃/ nf (a) ~ (chirurgicale) operation, surgery
(b) calculation
(c) (Tech) operation
(d) process
(e) transaction

opératoire /ɔpeʀatwaʀ/ adj (a) ⟨technique⟩ surgical; ⟨risk⟩ in operating
(b) operative

opercule /ɔpɛʀkyl/ nm (a) (Bot, Zool) operculum
(b) lid

opéré, ~e /ɔpeʀe/ nm,f person who has had an operation

opérer /ɔpeʀe/ [14] **1** vtr (a) to operate on; ~ qn de l'appendicite to remove sb's appendix; se faire ~ to have an operation, to have surgery
(b) to bring about ⟨change⟩
2 vi (a) (Med) to operate
(b) ⟨cure, charm⟩ to work
(c) to proceed
(d) ⟨thief⟩ to operate

opérette /ɔpeʀɛt/ nf operetta, light opera

ophtalmologiste /ɔftalmɔlɔʒist/ nmf ophthalmologist

opiner /ɔpine/ [1] vi ~ du bonnet or de la tête to nod in agreement

opiniâtre /ɔpinjɑtʀ/ adj ⟨resistance⟩ dogged; ⟨work⟩ relentless; ⟨person⟩ tenacious

opinion /ɔpinjɔ̃/ nf (a) opinion; mon ~ est faite my mind is made up
(b) l'~ (publique) public opinion

opium /ɔpjɔm/ nm opium

opportun, ~e /ɔpɔʀtœ̃, yn/ adj appropriate

opportuniste /ɔpɔʀtynist/ nmf opportunist

opportunité /ɔpɔʀtynite/ nf
(a) appropriateness
(b) opportunity

opposant, ~e /ɔpozɑ̃, ɑ̃t/ nm,f opponent

opposé, ~e /ɔpoze/ **1** adj (a) ⟨direction⟩ opposite
(b) ⟨opinion⟩ opposite; ⟨parties, sides⟩ opposing; ⟨interests⟩ conflicting
(c) opposed
2 à l'opposé phr (a) à l'~ de mes frères in contrast to my brothers
(b) il est parti à l'~ he went off in the opposite direction

opposer /ɔpoze/ [1] **1** vtr (a) to put up ⟨resistance, argument⟩
(b) ~ à to match or pit [sb] against ⟨person, team⟩
(c) ⟨problem⟩ to divide ⟨people⟩
(d) to compare
2 s'opposer v refl (+ v être) (a) s'~ à qch to be opposed to sth
(b) s'~ à to stand in the way of ⟨change⟩
(c) to contrast
(d) ⟨ideas, opinions⟩ to conflict; ⟨people⟩ to disagree
(e) ⟨teams⟩ to confront each other

opposition /ɔpozisjɔ̃/ nf (a) opposition; par ~ à in contrast with or to
(b) faire ~ à un chèque to stop a cheque (GB) or check (US)

oppressant, ~e /ɔpʀɛsɑ̃, ɑ̃t/ adj oppressive

oppresser /ɔpʀɛse/ [1] vtr to oppress; se sentir oppressé to feel breathless

oppression /ɔpʀɛsjɔ̃/ nf oppression

opprimer /ɔpʀime/ [1] vtr to oppress ⟨people⟩

opter /ɔpte/ [1] vi to opt

opticien, -ienne /ɔptisjɛ̃, ɛn/ nm,f optician

optimal, ~e, mpl **-aux** /ɔptimal, o/ adj optimum

optimiser /ɔptimize/ [1] vtr to optimize

optimisme /ɔptimism/ nm optimism

optimiste /ɔptimist/ adj optimistic

option /ɔpsjɔ̃/ nf option; en ~ optional

optique /ɔptik/ **1** adj (a) (Anat) optic
(b) optical
2 nf (a) optics
(b) perspective

opulence /ɔpylɑ̃s/ nf opulence

or¹ /ɔʀ/ conj and yet; ~, ce jour-là, il... now, on that particular day, he...

or² /ɔʀ/ **1** adj inv gold; ⟨hair⟩ golden
2 nm (a) gold; en ~ gold; ⟨husband⟩ marvellous (GB); ⟨opportunity⟩ golden
(b) gilding

oracle /ɔʀakl/ nm oracle

orage /ɔʀaʒ/ nm storm

orageux, -euse /ɔRaʒø, øz/ *adj* stormy

oraison /ɔRɛzɔ̃/ *nf* prayer; ~ **funèbre** funeral oration

oral, ~e, *mpl* **-aux** /ɔRal, o/ ⬚1 *adj*
(a) oral
(b) (Med) **par voie ~e** orally
⬚2 *nm* (Sch) oral (examination)

oralement /ɔRalmɑ̃/ *adv* (a) (Med) orally
(b) verbally

orange¹ /ɔRɑ̃ʒ/ *adj inv* orange; ⟨light⟩ amber (GB), yellow (US)

orange² /ɔRɑ̃ʒ/ *nf* orange

orangeade /ɔRɑ̃ʒad/ *nf* orangeade

oranger /ɔRɑ̃ʒe/ *nm* orange tree

orangerie /ɔRɑ̃ʒRi/ *nf* orangery

orateur, -trice /ɔRatœR, tRis/ *nm,f*
(a) speaker
(b) orator

orbite /ɔRbit/ *nf* (a) orbit
(b) eye-socket

orchestral, ~e, *mpl* **-aux** /ɔRkɛstRal, o/ *adj* orchestral

orchestration /ɔRkɛstRasjɔ̃/ *nf* orchestration

orchestre /ɔRkɛstR/ *nm* (a) orchestra
(b) band
(c) orchestra stalls (GB), orchestra (US)

orchestrer /ɔRkɛstRe/ [1] *vtr* to orchestrate

orchidée /ɔRkide/ *nf* orchid

ordinaire /ɔRdinɛR/ ⬚1 *adj* (a) ordinary; ⟨quality⟩ standard; ⟨reader, tourist⟩ average; **journée peu ~** unusual day
(b) **très ~** ⟨meal, wine⟩ very average; ⟨person⟩ very ordinary
⬚2 *nm* **sortir de l'~** to be out of the ordinary
⬚3 **à l'ordinaire, d'ordinaire** *phr* usually

ordinal, ~e, *mpl* **-aux** /ɔRdinal, o/ *adj* ordinal

ordinateur /ɔRdinatœR/ *nm* computer

ordination /ɔRdinasjɔ̃/ *nf* ordination

ordonnance /ɔRdɔnɑ̃s/ *nf* prescription

ordonner /ɔRdɔne/ [1] *vtr* (a) to order
(b) to put [sth] in order
(c) to ordain

ordre /ɔRdR/ *nm* (a) (command) order; **j'ai des ~s** I'm acting under orders; **à vos ~s!** (Mil) yes, sir!; **jusqu'à nouvel ~** until further notice
(b) (sequence) order; **par ~ alphabétique** in alphabetical order
(c) tidiness, orderliness
(d) (orderly state) order; **rappeler qn à l'~** to reprimand sb; **tout est rentré dans l'~** everything is back to normal; **rétablir l'~** (public) to restore law and order
(e) nature; **c'est dans l'~ des choses** it's in the nature of things; **de l'~ de 30%** in the order of 30% (GB), on the order of 30% (US); **de premier ~** first-rate
(f) (in religion) order; **entrer dans les ~s** to take (holy) orders

(g) **libellez le chèque à l'~ de X** make the cheque (GB) *or* check (US) payable to X
■ **~ du jour** agenda

ordure /ɔRdyR/ ⬚1 *nf* filth
⬚2 **ordures** *nf pl* refuse (GB), garbage (US)

ordurier, -ière /ɔRdyRje, ɛR/ *adj* filthy

orée /ɔRe/ *nf* (a) edge
(b) (figurative) start

oreille /ɔRɛj/ *nf* (a) ear; **n'écouter que d'une ~** to half-listen; **ouvre-bien les ~s!** listen carefully
(b) hearing; **avoir l'~ fine** to have keen hearing
(c) **à l'abri des ~s indiscrètes** where no-one can hear
IDIOMS tirer les ~s à qn to tell sb off

oreiller /ɔRɛje/ *nm* pillow

oreillons /ɔRɛjɔ̃/ *nm pl* mumps

ores: d'ores et déjà /dɔRzedeʒa/ *phr* already

orfèvre /ɔRfɛvR/ *nmf* goldsmith; **être ~ en la matière** to be an expert in the field

orfèvrerie /ɔRfɛvRəRi/ *nf* (a) goldsmith's art
(b) goldsmith's and silversmith's

organe /ɔRgan/ *nm* organ

organigramme /ɔRganigRam/ *nm* organization chart

organique /ɔRganik/ *adj* organic

organisation /ɔRganizasjɔ̃/ *nf* organization

organiser /ɔRganize/ [1] ⬚1 *vtr* to organize
⬚2 **s'organiser** *v refl* (+ *v être*)
(a) ⟨opposition⟩ to get organized
(b) to organize oneself
(c) ⟨fight, help⟩ to be organized

organisme /ɔRganism/ *nm* (a) body
(b) organism
(c) organization, body

orgasme /ɔRgasm/ *nm* orgasm

orge /ɔRʒ/ *nf* barley

orgie /ɔRʒi/ *nf* orgy

orgue /ɔRg/ (Mus) organ

orgueil /ɔRgœj/ *nm* pride

orgueilleux, -euse /ɔRgœjø, øz/ *adj* overproud

orient /ɔRjɑ̃/ *nm* (a) east
(b) **l'Orient** the East

oriental, ~e, *mpl* **-aux** /ɔRjɑ̃tal, o/ *adj* eastern; oriental

Oriental, ~e, *mpl* **-aux** /ɔRjɑ̃tal, o/ *nm,f* Asian; **les Orientaux** Asians

orientation /ɔRjɑ̃tasjɔ̃/ *nf* (a) (of house) aspect; (of aerial) angle
(b) (of inquiry) direction
(c) (Sch) **changer d'~** to change courses

orienter /ɔRjɑ̃te/ [1] ⬚1 *vtr* (a) to adjust ⟨aerial, lamp⟩
(b) **~ la conversation sur** to bring the conversation around to
(c) to direct ⟨person⟩
(d) (Sch) to give [sb] career advice ⋯⟶

O

2 **s'orienter** *v refl* (+ *v être*) **(a)** to get *or* find one's bearings
(b) s'~ vers ⟨*person*⟩ to turn toward(s); s'~ vers les carrières scientifiques to go in for a career in science

orifice /ɔʀifis/ *nm* **(a)** orifice
(b) (of pipe) mouth; (of tube) neck

originaire /ɔʀiʒinɛʀ/ *adj* ⟨*plant, animal*⟩ native; famille ~ d'Asie Asian family

original, ~e, *mpl* **-aux** /ɔʀiʒinal, o/
1 *adj* **(a)** original
(b) eccentric
2 *nm* original

originalité /ɔʀiʒinalite/ *nf* originality

origine /ɔʀiʒin/ *nf* origin; être d'~ modeste to come from a modest background; dès l'~ right from the start; à l'~ originally

originel, -elle /ɔʀiʒinɛl/ *adj* original

orme /ɔʀm/ *nm* **(a)** elm (tree)
(b) elm (wood)

ornement /ɔʀnəmã/ *nm* **(a)** ornament
(b) decorative detail

orner /ɔʀne/ [1] *vtr* to decorate

ornière /ɔʀnjɛʀ/ *nf* rut

ornithologie /ɔʀnitɔlɔʒi/ *nf* ornithology

ornithorynque /ɔʀnitɔʀɛ̃k/ *nm* (duck-billed) platypus, duckbill (US)

orphelin, ~e /ɔʀfəlɛ̃, in/ *nm,f* orphan

orphelinat /ɔʀfəlina/ *nm* orphanage

orque /ɔʀk/ *nm or f* killer whale

orteil /ɔʀtɛj/ *nm* toe; gros ~ big toe

orthodoxe /ɔʀtɔdɔks/ *adj, nmf* Orthodox

orthographe /ɔʀtɔgʀaf/ *nf* spelling

orthographier /ɔʀtɔgʀafje/ [2] *vtr* to spell

orthopédie /ɔʀtɔpedi/ *nf* orthopedics

orthophoniste /ɔʀtɔfɔnist/ *nmf* speech therapist

ortie /ɔʀti/ *nf* (stinging) nettle

orvet /ɔʀvɛ/ *nm* slowworm, blindworm

os /ɔs, *pl* o/ *nm inv* bone; en chair et en ~ in the flesh
IDIOMS il y a un ~ (colloq) there's a hitch; tomber sur un ~ (colloq) to come across a snag; être trempé jusqu'aux ~ (colloq) to be soaked to the skin (colloq)

osciller /ɔsile/ [1] *vi* **(a)** ⟨*pendulum*⟩ to swing; ⟨*boat*⟩ to rock; ⟨*head*⟩ to roll from side to side
(b) ⟨*currency*⟩ to fluctuate
(c) to vacillate

osé, ~e /oze/ *adj* **(a)** risqué
(b) ⟨*behaviour*⟩ daring; ⟨*words*⟩ outspoken

oseille /ozɛj/ *nf* **(a)** sorrel
(b) (colloq) dough (colloq), money

oser /oze/ [1] *vtr* to dare; si j'ose dire if I may say so

osier /ozje/ *nm* **(a)** (tree) osier
(b) wicker, osier

osmose /ɔsmoz/ *nf* osmosis

ossature /ɔsatyʀ/ *nf* skeleton; ~ du visage bone structure

ossements /ɔsmã/ *nm pl* remains

osseux, -euse /ɔsø, øz/ *adj* **(a)** bony
(b) ⟨*disease*⟩ bone

ostentatoire /ɔstãtatwaʀ/ *adj* ostentatious

ostéopathe /ɔsteɔpat/ *nmf* osteopath

ostracisme /ɔstʀasism/ *nm* ostracism

ostréiculture /ɔstʀeikyltyʀ/ *nf* oyster farming

otage /ɔtaʒ/ *nm* hostage

OTAN /ɔtã/ *nf* (abbr = **Organisation du traité de l'Atlantique Nord**) NATO

otarie /ɔtaʀi/ *nf* eared seal, otary

ôter /ote/ [1] **1** *vtr* **(a)** to take off ⟨*clothes, glasses*⟩; to remove ⟨*bones, stain*⟩
(b) ~ qch à qn to take sth away from sb
(c) (in mathematics) 4 ôté de 9, il reste 5 9 minus *or* take away 4 leaves 5
2 **s'ôter** *v refl* (+ *v être*) s'~ qch de l'esprit to get sth out of one's mind *or* head

otite /ɔtit/ *nf* inflammation of the ear

oto-rhino-laryngologiste, *pl* **~s** /otoʀinolaʀɛ̃gɔlɔʒist/ *nmf* ENT specialist

ou /u/ *conj* or; ~ (bien)... ~ (bien)... either... or...

où /u/ **1** *adv* where; je l'ai perdu je ne sais ~ I've lost it somewhere or other; par ~ êtes-vous passés pour venir? which way did you come?; ~ en êtes-vous? where have you got to?; ~ allons-nous? what are things coming to!
2 *rel pron* **(a)** where; le quartier ~ nous habitons the area we live in; d'~ s'élevait de la fumée out of which smoke was rising; ~ qu'ils aillent wherever they may go
(b) la misère ~ elle se trouvait the poverty in which she was living; au train *or* à l'allure ~ vont les choses (at) the rate things are going; le travail s'est accumulé, d'~ ce retard there is a backlog of work, hence the delay
(c) when; le matin ~ je l'ai rencontré the morning I met him

ouate /wat/ *nf* **(a)** cotton wool (GB), cotton (US)
(b) wadding

oubli /ubli/ *nm* **(a)** l'~ de qch forgetting sth; (of duty) neglect of sth
(b) omission
(c) oblivion; tomber dans l'~ to be completely forgotten

oublier /ublije/ [2] **1** *vtr* **(a)** to forget ⟨*name, date, fact*⟩; to forget about ⟨*worries, incident*⟩; se faire ~ to keep a low profile
(b) to leave out ⟨*person, detail*⟩
(c) to neglect ⟨*duty, friend*⟩
2 **s'oublier** *v refl* (+ *v être*) **(a)** to be forgotten
(b) to leave oneself out

oubliettes /ublijɛt/ *nf pl* oubliette

oued /wɛd/ *nm* wadi

ouest /wɛst/ **1** *adj inv* west; western
2 *nm* **(a)** west
(b) l'Ouest the West

ouf /uf/ **1** *nm* faire ~ to breathe a sigh of relief

2 *excl* phew!

oui /wi/ **1** *adv* yes; **alors c'est ～?** so the answer is yes?; **découvrir si ～ ou non** to discover whether or not; **dire ～ à qch** to welcome sth; to agree to sth; **faire ～ de la tête** to nod; **lui, prudent? un lâche, ～!** him, cautious? a coward, more like! (colloq); **je crois que ～** I think so
2 *nm inv* (a) yes
(b) 'yes' vote; **le ～ l'a emporté** the ayes have it
IDIOMS **pour un ～ (ou) pour un non** ⟨*get angry*⟩ for the slightest thing; ⟨*change one's mind*⟩ at the drop of a hat

ouï, ～e /wi/ ▶ OUÏR

ouï-dire /widiʀ/ *nm inv* **par ～** by hearsay

ouïe /wi/ *nf* (a) hearing; **être tout ～** to be all ears
(b) (of fish) gill

ouïr /wiʀ/ [38] *vtr* to hear; **j'ai ouï dire que** word has reached me that

ouistiti /wistiti/ *nm* marmoset

ouragan /uʀagɑ̃/ *nm* hurricane

ourler /uʀle/ [1] *vtr* to hem

ourlet /uʀlɛ/ *nm* hem

ours /uʀs/ *nm inv* (a) bear
(b) **il est un peu ～** he's a bit surly
■ **～ blanc** polar bear; **～ en peluche** teddy bear; **～ polaire** = **～ BLANC**
IDIOMS **vendre la peau de l'～ avant de l'avoir tué** (Proverb) to count one's chickens before they're hatched

ourse /uʀs/ *nf* she-bear

oursin /uʀsɛ̃/ *nm* (sea) urchin

ourson /uʀsɔ̃/ *nm* bear cub

outil /uti/ *nm* tool; **～ de travail** work tool

outrage /utʀaʒ/ *nm* insult
■ **～ à agent** *verbal assault of a policeman*

outrager /utʀaʒe/ [13] *vtr* to offend

outrance /utʀɑ̃s/ *nf* **à ～** excessively

outrancier, -ière /utʀɑ̃sje, ɛʀ/ *adj* extreme

outre /utʀ/ **1** *prep* in addition to
2 *adv* **passer ～** to pay no heed
3 **outre mesure** *phr* unduly
4 **en outre** *phr* in addition

outre-Atlantique /utʀatlɑ̃tik/ *adv* across the Atlantic; **d'～** American

outre-Manche /utʀəmɑ̃ʃ/ *adv* across the Channel; **d'～** British

outremer /utʀəmɛʀ/ *adj inv, nm* ultramarine

outre-mer /utʀəmɛʀ/ *adv* overseas

outrer /utʀe/ [1] *vtr* (a) to outrage
(b) to exaggerate

outre-tombe /utʀətɔ̃b/ *adv* **une voix d'～** a voice from beyond the grave

ouvert, ～e /uvɛʀ, ɛʀt/ **1** *pp* ▶ OUVRIR
2 *pp adj* (a) open; **grand ～** wide open; **être ～ aux idées nouvelles** to be open to new ideas
(b) ⟨*gas*⟩ on; ⟨*tap*⟩ running
(c) ⟨*question*⟩ open-ended

ouvertement /uvɛʀtəmɑ̃/ *adv* openly; blatantly

ouverture /uvɛʀtyʀ/ *nf* (a) opening; **heures d'～** opening hours
(b) openness; **～ d'esprit** open-mindedness; **～ à l'Ouest** opening-up to the West
(c) (Mus) overture

ouvrable /uvʀabl/ *adj* ⟨*day*⟩ working; ⟨*hours*⟩ business

ouvrage /uvʀaʒ/ *nm* (a) work
(b) book, work
(c) piece of work; **～ de broderie** piece of embroidery
IDIOMS **avoir du cœur à l'～** to work with a will

ouvragé, ～e /uvʀaʒe/ *adj* finely wrought

ouvrant, ～e /uvʀɑ̃, ɑ̃t/ *adj* **toit ～** sunroof

ouvré, ～e /uvʀe/ *adj* **jour ～** working day

ouvre-boîtes /uvʀəbwat/ *nm inv* can-opener

ouvreur, -euse /uvʀœʀ, øz/ *nm,f* usher/usherette

ouvrier, -ière /uvʀije, ɛʀ/ **1** *adj* of the workers; **classe ouvrière** working class
2 *nm,f* worker; workman

ouvrir /uvʀiʀ/ [32] **1** *vtr* (gen) to open; to undo ⟨*collar, shirt, zip*⟩; to initiate ⟨*dialogue*⟩; to open up ⟨*possibilities, market*⟩; **ne pas ～ la bouche** not to say a word; **～ les bras à qn** to welcome sb with open arms; **～ l'esprit à qn** to open sb's mind
2 *vi* (a) to open the door; **ouvre-moi!** let me in!
(b) to open
(c) to be opened
3 **s'ouvrir** *v refl* (+ *v être*) (gen) to open; ⟨*shirt, dress*⟩ to come undone; ⟨*dialogue, process*⟩ to be initiated; ⟨*country, economy*⟩ to open up; ⟨*ground, scar*⟩ to open up; ⟨*person*⟩ to cut open ⟨*head*⟩; **s'～ les veines** to slash one's wrists; **s'～ à qn** to open one's heart to sb

ovaire /ɔvɛʀ/ *nm* ovary

ovale /ɔval/ *adj, nm* oval

ovation /ɔvasjɔ̃/ *nf* (a) ovation
(b) accolade

ovationner /ɔvasjɔne/ [1] *vtr* to greet [sb] sth] with wild applause

ovni /ɔvni/ *nm* (*abbr* = **objet volant non identifié**) unidentified flying object, UFO

ovulation /ɔvylasjɔ̃/ *nf* ovulation

ovule /ɔvyl/ *nm* (a) (Anat) ovum
(b) (Bot) ovule

oxyde /ɔksid/ *nm* oxide; **～ de carbone** carbon monoxide

oxyder /ɔkside/ [1] *vtr*, **s'oxyder** *v refl* (+ *v être*) to oxidize

oxygène /ɔksiʒɛn/ *nm* (a) oxygen
(b) air

oxygéner /ɔksiʒene/ [14] **1** *vtr* to oxygenate

⋯⋗

2 s'oxygéner *v refl* (+ *v être*) ⟨person⟩ to get some fresh air

ozone /ozon/ *nf* ozone; **la couche d'~** the ozone layer

Pp

p, P /pe/ *nm inv* p, P

PAC *nf* (*abbr* **politique agricole commune**) CAP

pacha /paʃa/ *nm* pasha

pachyderme /paʃidɛʀm/ *nm* (Zool) pachyderm; **de ~** (figurative) heavy

pacifier /pasifje/ [1] *vtr* to establish peace in

pacifique /pasifik/ **1** *adj* peaceful
2 *nmf* peace-loving person

Pacifique /pasifik/ *pr nm* **le ~** the Pacific

pacifiste /pasifist/ *adj, nmf* pacifist

pacotille /pakɔtij/ *nf* **de la ~** cheap rubbish

pacte /pakt/ *nm* pact

PAF /paf/ **1** *nm: abbr* ▶ PAYSAGE
2 *nf: abbr* ▶ POLICE

pagaie /pagɛ/ *nf* (Naut) paddle

pagaille (colloq) /pagaj/ **1** *nf* mess; **semer la ~** to cause chaos
2 en pagaille *phr* in a mess

paganisme /paganism/ *nm* paganism

pagayer /pageje/ [21] *vi* to paddle

page¹ /paʒ/ *nf* page (boy)

page² /paʒ/ *nf* page; **en première ~** on the front page; **tourner la ~** (figurative) to turn over a new leaf
■ **~ d'accueil** (Comput) home page; **~ de publicité** commercial break
IDIOMS **être à la ~** to be up to date

pagination /paʒinasjɔ̃/ *nf* pagination

paginer /paʒine/ [1] *vtr* to paginate

pagne /paɲ/ *nm* **(a)** loincloth
(b) grass skirt

pagode /pagɔd/ *nf* pagoda

paie /pɛ/ *nf* pay; **bulletin** *or* **fiche de ~** payslip
IDIOMS **ça fait une ~ que je ne l'ai pas vu** (colloq) it's ages since I saw him (colloq)

paiement /pɛmɑ̃/ *nm* payment

païen, -ïenne /pajɛ̃, ɛn/ *adj, nm,f* pagan

paillard, ~e /pajaʀ, aʀd/ *adj* bawdy

paillasse /pajas/ *nf* **(a)** straw mattress
(b) lab bench
(c) draining board

paillasson /pajasɔ̃/ *nm* doormat

paille /paj/ **1** *adj inv* **jaune ~** straw yellow
2 *nf* straw; **~ de fer** steel wool
IDIOMS **être sur la ~** (colloq) to be penniless; **tirer à la courte ~** to draw lots

paillette /pajɛt/ *nf* **(a)** sequin, spangle (US); **robe à ~s** sequined *or* spangled (US) dress
(b) glitter
(c) savon en ~s soap flakes

pain /pɛ̃/ *nm* **(a)** bread; **des miettes de ~** breadcrumbs
(b) loaf; **un petit ~** a (bread) roll
(c) ~ de viande meat loaf
(d) (of soap) bar
■ **~ blanc** white bread; **~ de campagne** farmhouse bread; **~ complet** wholemeal bread; **~ d'épices** gingerbread; **~ grillé** toast; **~ au lait** milk roll; **~ de mie** sandwich loaf; **~ de seigle** rye bread; **~ de son** bran loaf
IDIOMS **se vendre comme des petits ~s** to sell like hot cakes; **ça ne mange pas de ~** (colloq) it doesn't cost anything; **je ne mange pas de ce ~-là** (colloq) I won't have anything to do with it

pair, ~e¹ /pɛʀ/ **1** *adj* ⟨number⟩ even
2 *nm* **(a)** peer; **c'est une cuisinière hors ~** she's an excellent cook
(b) aller *or* **marcher de ~ avec qch** to go hand in hand with sth
3 au pair *phr* **travailler au ~** to work as an au pair

paire² /pɛʀ/ *nf* pair; **donner une ~ de gifles à qn** to box sb's ears
IDIOMS **les deux font la ~!** they're two of a kind!

paisible /pɛzibl/ *adj* peaceful, quiet, calm

paisiblement /pɛzibləmɑ̃/ *adv* peacefully

paître /pɛtʀ/ [74] *vi* to graze
IDIOMS **envoyer ~ qn** (colloq) to send sb packing (colloq)

paix /pɛ/ *nf inv* peace; **avoir la ~** to get some peace; **laisser qn en ~** to leave sb alone; **la ~!** (colloq) be quiet!

pakistanais, ~e /pakistanɛ, ɛz/ *adj* Pakistani

palabrer /palabʀe/ [1] *vi* to discuss endlessly

palace /palas/ *nm* luxury hotel

palais /palɛ/ *nm inv* **(a)** palate
(b) palace
(c) (Law) **~ (de justice)** law courts
■ **~ des sports** sports centre (GB)

palan /palɑ̃/ *nm* hoist

pale /pal/ *nf* (of propeller, oar) blade

pâle /pal/ *adj* pale; **vert ~** pale green
IDIOMS **faire ~ figure à côté de** to pale into insignificance beside

palefrenier, -ière /palfʀənje, ɛʀ/ *nm,f*
groom

paléolithique /paleɔlitik/ *adj, nm*
Paleolithic

paléontologie /paleɔtɔlɔʒi/ *nf*
paleontology

palet /palɛ/ *nm* **(a)** (in ice hockey) puck
(b) quoit

paletot /palto/ *nm* jacket
IDIOMS tomber sur le ~ de qn (colloq) to lay
into sb (colloq)

palette /palɛt/ *nf* **(a)** palette
(b) range; une ~ d'activités a range of
activities
(c) (of pork, mutton) ≈ shoulder

pâleur /pɑlœʀ/ *nf* paleness; pallor

palier /palje/ *nm* **(a)** landing; mon voisin
de ~ my neighbour (GB) on the same floor
(b) level; plateau
(c) (in diving) ~ (de décompression)
(decompression) stage

palière /paljɛʀ/ *adj f* porte ~ entry door

pâlir /pɑliʀ/ [3] *vi* **(a)** to fade
(b) to grow pale

palissade /palisad/ *nf* fence

palliatif /paljatif/ *nm* palliative

pallier /palje/ [2] *vtr* to compensate for

palmarès /palmaʀɛs/ *nm inv* **(a)** honours
(GB) list; list of (award) winners
(b) record of achievements
(c) hit parade
(d) bestsellers list

palme /palm/ *nf* **(a)** palm leaf
(b) palm (tree)
(c) (for diver) flipper
(d) (Mil) ≈ bar
(e) prize

palmé, ~e /palme/ *adj* **(a)** ⟨feet⟩ webbed
(b) ⟨leaf⟩ palmate

palmier /palmje/ *nm* palm (tree)

palombe /palɔb/ *nf* wood pigeon

palourde /paluʀd/ *nf* clam

palpable /palpabl/ *adj* palpable; tangible

palper /palpe/ [1] *vtr* **(a)** (Med) to palpate
(b) to feel

palpitant, ~e /palpitã, ãt/ *adj* thrilling

palpitation /palpitasjɔ̃/ *nf* **(a)** (Med)
palpitation
(b) twitching

palpiter /palpite/ [1] *vi* ⟨heart⟩ to beat; to
flutter; ⟨vein⟩ to pulse

paludisme /palydism/ *nm* malaria

pâmer: se pâmer /pɑme/ [1] *v refl*
(+ *v être*) se ~ devant qch to swoon over sth

pamphlet /pɑ̃flɛ/ *nm* satirical tract

pamphlétaire /pɑ̃fletɛʀ/ *nmf*
pamphleteer

pamplemousse /pɑ̃pləmus/ *nm*
grapefruit

pan /pɑ̃/ **1** *nm* **(a)** (of cliff, house) section;
(of life) part
(b) (of tower) side; ~s d'un manteau coat-tails

2 *excl* (also onomatopoeic) bang!; thump!;
whack!

pan- /pɑ̃, pan/ *pref* Pan; ~-russe Pan-
Russian; ~-européen Pan-European

panacée /panase/ *nf* panacea

panache /panaʃ/ *nm* **(a)** panache
(b) plume

panaché, ~e /panaʃe/ **1** *adj* ⟨bouquet,
salad⟩ mixed; ⟨tulip, ivy⟩ variegated
2 *nm* shandy (GB), shandygaff (US)

panacher /panaʃe/ [1] *vtr* to mix

panama /panama/ *nm* panama (hat)

panaris /panaʀi/ *nm inv* whitlow

pancarte /pɑ̃kaʀt/ *nf* **(a)** notice (GB), sign
(US)
(b) placard (GB), sign (US)

pancréas /pɑ̃kʀeas/ *nm inv* pancreas

panda /pɑ̃da/ *nm* panda

paner /pane/ [1] *vtr* to coat with
breadcrumbs

panier /panje/ *nm* **(a)** basket
(b) (in dishwasher) rack
(c) (Sport) basket
■ ~ à linge linen basket; ~ à salade salad
shaker; Black Maria (GB), paddy wagon (US)
IDIOMS être un ~ percé (colloq) to spend
money like water; ils sont tous à mettre
dans le même ~ (colloq) they are all about
the same; le dessus du ~ (colloq) the pick of
the bunch; mettre au ~ to throw [sth] out; to
get rid of [sth]

panique /panik/ *nf* panic; semer *or* jeter la
~ to spread panic; être pris de ~ to be
panic-stricken

paniquer /panike/ [1] *vi* (colloq) to panic

panne /pan/ *nf* (of vehicle, machine)
breakdown; (of engine) failure; ~ de courant
power failure; tomber en ~ sèche *or*
d'essence to run out of petrol (GB) *or* gas
(US); être en ~ de (colloq) to be out of
⟨coffee⟩; to have run out of ⟨ideas⟩

panneau, *pl* ~x /pano/ *nm* **(a)** sign;
board
(b) notice board
(c) panel
■ ~ indicateur signpost; ~ publicitaire
hoarding (GB), billboard; ~ de signalisation
routière road sign; ~ solaire solar panel
IDIOMS tomber dans le ~ (colloq) to fall for it
(colloq)

panonceau, *pl* ~x /panõso/ *nm* sign;
board

panoplie /panɔpli/ *nf* **(a)** outfit
(b) display of weapons

panorama /panɔʀama/ *nm* **(a)** panorama
(b) (of art, culture) survey

panoramique /panɔʀamik/ *adj* **(a)** ⟨view,
visit⟩ panoramic
(b) ⟨windscreen⟩ wrap-around
(c) ⟨screen⟩ wide

panse /pɑ̃s/ *nf* **(a)** (of cow) paunch
(b) (colloq) belly (colloq)
(c) (of jug) belly

pansement /pɑ̃smɑ̃/ nm dressing;
~ **(adhésif)** plaster (GB), Band-Aid®

panser /pɑ̃se/ [1] vtr to dress ⟨wound⟩; to put a dressing on ⟨arm, leg⟩

pantalon /pɑ̃talɔ̃/ nm trousers (GB), pants (US); ~ **de pyjama** pyjama (GB) or pajama (US) bottoms

panthère /pɑ̃tɛʀ/ nf panther

pantin /pɑ̃tɛ̃/ nm puppet

pantois, ~e /pɑ̃twa, az/ adj flabbergasted

pantomime /pɑ̃tɔmim/ nf **(a)** mime
(b) mime show

pantouflard, ~e /pɑ̃tuflaʀ, aʀd/ adj (colloq) **qu'est-ce que tu es ~!** what a stay-at-home you are!

pantoufle /pɑ̃tufl/ nf slipper

panure /panyʀ/ nf breadcrumbs

PAO /peao/ nf **(a)** abbr ▶ PRODUCTION
(b) abbr ▶ PUBLICATION

paon /pɑ̃/ nm peacock

paonne /pan/ nf peahen

papa /papa/ nm dad (colloq), daddy (colloq); father; **fils** or **fille à ~** spoiled little rich kid (colloq)

pape /pap/ nm **(a)** pope
(b) (figurative) high priest

paperasse /papʀas/ nf (colloq) **(a)** bumph (GB) (colloq), documents
(b) paperwork

papeterie /papɛtʀi/ nf **(a)** stationer's (shop), stationery shop (GB) or store (US)
(b) stationery
(c) (colloq) papermaking industry
(d) paper mill

papi /papi/ nm (colloq) granddad (colloq), grandpa (colloq)

papier /papje/ nm **(a)** paper
(b) ~s **(d'identité)** (identity) papers or documents
(c) (colloq) (newspaper) article, piece (colloq)
■ ~ **alu** (colloq), ~ **(d')aluminium** aluminium (GB) or aluminum (US) foil, kitchen foil; ~ **brouillon** rough paper (GB), scrap paper; ~ **cadeau** gift wrap; ~ **d'emballage** wrapping paper; ~ **hygiénique** toilet paper; ~ **journal** newsprint; ~ **à lettres** writing paper; ~ **peint** wallpaper; ~ **de verre** sandpaper; ~s **gras** litter
IDIOMS **être dans les petits ~s de qn** (colloq) to be in sb's good books; ▶ MUSIQUE

papier-calque, pl **papiers-calque** /papjekalk/ nm tracing paper

papillon /papijɔ̃/ nm **(a)** butterfly; ~ **de nuit** moth
(b) (brasse) ~ butterfly (stroke)

papillonner /papijɔne/ [1] vi **(a)** to flit about
(b) to flirt incessantly

papillote /papijɔt/ nf **(a)** (Culin) foil parcel
(b) (for hair) curlpaper

papoter /papɔte/ [1] vi (colloq) to chatter

paprika /papʀika/ nm paprika

papy = PAPI

Pâque /pɑk/ nf **la ~ juive** Passover

paquebot /pakbo/ nm liner

pâquerette /pakʀɛt/ nf daisy
IDIOMS **être au ras des ~s** (colloq) to be very basic

Pâques /pɑk/ nm, nf pl Easter

paquet /pakɛ/ nm **(a)** packet (GB), package (US); (of cigarettes, coffee) packet (GB), pack (US)
(b) parcel
(c) (of clothes) bundle
(d) (colloq) masses
(e) (colloq) packet (GB) (colloq), bundle (US) (colloq)
■ ~ **de muscles** (colloq) muscleman
IDIOMS **mettre le ~** (colloq) to pull out all the stops

paquet-cadeau, pl **paquets-cadeaux** /pakɛkado/ nm gift-wrapped present

par /paʀ/ **1** prep **(a)** **elle est arrivée ~ la droite** she came from the right; **le peintre a terminé** or **fini ~ la cuisine** the painter did the kitchen last
(b) ~ **le passé** in the past; ~ **une belle journée d'été** on a beautiful summer's day; **ils sortent même ~ moins 40°** they go outdoors even when it's minus 40°
(c) per; ~ **jour/an** a day/year; ~ **personne** per person
(d) by; **payer ~ carte de crédit** to pay by credit card; **être pris ~ son travail** to be taken up with one's work; **deux ~ deux** ⟨work⟩ in twos; ⟨walk⟩ two by two
(e) in; ~ **étapes** in stages; ~ **endroits** in places
(f) **l'accident est arrivé ~ sa faute** it was his/her fault that the accident happened; ~ **jalousie** out of jealousy
(g) through; **tu peux me faire passer le livre ~ ta sœur** you can get the book to me via your sister; **entre ~ le garage** come in through the garage
2 de par phr (formal) **(a)** **voyager de ~ le monde** to travel all over the world
(b) **de ~ leurs origines** by virtue of their origins

parabole /paʀabɔl/ nf **(a)** parable
(b) parabola

parachever /paʀaʃve/ [16] vtr **(a)** to complete
(b) to put the finishing touches to

parachutage /paʀaʃytaʒ/ nm airdrop

parachute /paʀaʃyt/ nm parachute

parachuter /paʀaʃyte/ [1] vtr to parachute

parachutisme /paʀaʃytism/ nm parachuting

parachutiste /paʀaʃytist/ nmf
(a) parachutist
(b) paratrooper

parade /paʀad/ nf **(a)** (Mil) parade
(b) (in fencing) parry
(c) (by animal) display

parader /paʀade/ [1] vi to strut about

paradis /paradi/ nm inv **(a)** heaven
(b) paradise
■ ~ **terrestre** Garden of Eden
IDIOMS tu ne l'emporteras pas au ~ (colloq)
you'll live to regret it

paradisiaque /paradizjak/ adj heavenly

paradoxal, ~**e**, mpl **-aux** /paradɔksal,
o/ adj paradoxical

paradoxe /paradɔks/ nm paradox

paraffine /parafin/ nf **(a)** paraffin (GB),
kerosene (US)
(b) paraffin wax

parages /paraʒ/ nm pl neighbourhood
(GB); **elle est dans les** ~ she is around
somewhere

paragraphe /paragraf/ nm paragraph

paraître /paretr/ [73] **1** vi **(a)** to come
out, to be published; **'à** ~**'** 'forthcoming
titles'
(b) to appear, to seem, to look
(c) to appear; to show; **elle ne laisse rien** ~
de ses sentiments she doesn't let her
feelings show at all; ~ **en public** to appear
in public; ~ **à son avantage** to look one's
best
2 v impers **il paraît qu'il a menti** apparently
he lied; **oui, il paraît** so I hear

parallèle¹ /paralɛl/ **1** adj **(a)** parallel
(b) ‹market› unofficial; ‹medicine›
alternative
2 nm parallel

parallèle² /paralɛl/ nf parallel line

parallèlement /paralɛlmã/ adv **(a)** ~ **à**
parallel to
(b) at the same time

paralyser /paralize/ [1] vtr **(a)** (Med) to
paralyse (GB)
(b) to paralyse (GB) [sth]; to bring [sth] to a
halt

paralysie /paralizi/ nf paralysis

paralytique /paralitik/ adj, nmf paralytic

paramédical, ~**e**, mpl **-aux**
/paramedikal, o/ adj paramedical

paramètre /parametr/ nm parameter

paranoïaque /paranɔjak/ adj, nmf
paranoiac

paranormal, ~**e**, mpl **-aux**
/paranɔrmal, o/ adj paranormal

parapente /parapãt/ nm **(a)** paraglider
(b) paragliding

paraphe /paraf/ nm **(a)** initials
(b) signature

paraphrase /parafraz/ nf paraphrase

paraplégique /parapleʒik/ adj, nmf
paraplegic

parapluie /paraplɥi/ nm umbrella

parascolaire /paraskɔlɛr/ adj
extracurricular

parasitaire /parazitɛr/ adj parasitic(al)

parasite /parazit/ **1** adj ‹organism›
parasitic(al); ‹idea› intrusive
2 nm **(a)** parasite
(b) (on TV, radio) ~**s** interference

parasol /parasɔl/ nm beach umbrella; sun
umbrella

paratonnerre /paratɔnɛr/ nm lightning
rod

paravent /paravã/ nm screen

parc /park/ nm **(a)** park
(b) playpen
(c) (for animals) pen
(d) (of facilities) (total) number; (of capital goods)
stock; ~ **automobile** fleet of cars; (nationwide)
number of cars (on the road); ~ **immobilier**
housing stock
■ ~ **d'attractions** amusement or theme park;
~ **de loisirs** theme park; ~ **national** national
park; ~ **naturel** nature park

parce: parce que /pars(ə)k(ə)/ phr
because

parcelle /parsɛl/ nf **(a)** plot (of land)
(b) une ~ **de bonheur** a bit of happiness

parchemin /parʃəmɛ̃/ nm parchment

par-ci /parsi/ adv ~ **par-là** here and there

parcimonie /parsimɔni/ nf parsimony

parcmètre /parkmɛtr/ nm parking meter

parcourir /parkurir/ [26] vtr **(a)** to travel
all over ‹country›; ~ **la ville** to go all over
town
(b) to cover ‹distance›
(c) to glance through ‹letter›; to scan
‹horizon›

parcours /parkur/ nm inv **(a)** (of bus,
traveller) route; (of river) course; ~ **fléché**
waymarked trail
(b) (Sport) course; ~ **de golf** round of golf
(c) career; **son** ~ (of artist) the development
of his/her art; **incident de** ~ hitch

par-delà /pardəla/ prep beyond

par-derrière /pardɛrjɛr/ adv **(a)** passer
~ to go round (GB) or to the back; **ils m'ont
attaqué** ~ they attacked me from behind
(b) **critiquer qn** ~ to criticize sb behind his/
her back

par-dessous /pardəsu/ prep, adv
underneath

pardessus /pardəsy/ nm inv overcoat

par-dessus /pardəsy/ **1** adv **(a)** **pose
ton sac dans un coin et mets ton manteau** ~
put your bag in a corner and put your coat
on top of it
(b) **le mur n'est pas haut, passe** ~ the wall
isn't high, climb over it
2 prep **(a)** **saute** ~ **le ruisseau** jump over
the stream
(b) **ce que j'aime** ~ **tout** what I like best of
all

par-devant /pardəvã/ adv **(a)** passer ~
to come round by the front
(b) **il te fait des sourires** ~ **mais dit du mal
de toi dans ton dos** he's all smiles to your
face but says nasty things about you behind
your back

pardon /pardɔ̃/ nm **(a)** forgiveness;
pardon; **je te demande** ~ I'm sorry
(b) ~**!** sorry!; ~ **madame/monsieur, je
cherche...** excuse me please, I'm looking
for...

p

pardonnable /paʀdɔnabl/ *adj* forgivable;
ils ne sont pas ~s it's unforgivable of them

pardonner /paʀdɔne/ [1] **1** *vtr* to forgive;
pardonnez-moi, mais... excuse me, but...
2 *vi* **ne pas ~** ⟨*illness, error*⟩ to be fatal

pare-balles /paʀbal/ *adj inv* bulletproof

pare-brise /paʀbʀiz/ *nm inv* windscreen
(GB), windshield (US)

pare-chocs /paʀʃɔk/ *nm inv* bumper

pareil, -eille /paʀɛj/ **1** *adj* (a) similar;
c'est toujours ~ avec toi it's always the
same with you; **à nul autre ~** without equal
(b) such; **je n'ai jamais dit une chose pareille**
I never said any such thing
2 *nm,f* equal; **d'un dynamisme sans ~**
incredibly dynamic; **pour moi c'est du ~ au
même** (colloq) it makes no difference to me
3 *adv* (colloq) **faire ~** to do the same

parent, ~e /paʀɑ̃, ɑ̃t/ **1** *adj* ⟨*languages*⟩
similar; **~ avec** ⟨*person*⟩ related to
2 *nm,f* (a) relative, relation
(b) (Zool) parent
3 *nm* (a) parent
(b) **~s** forebears
■ **~ pauvre** poor relation

parental, ~e, *mpl* **-aux** /paʀɑ̃tal, o/ *adj*
parental

parenté /paʀɑ̃te/ *nf* (a) (between people)
blood relationship
(b) (between stories) connection

parenthèse /paʀɑ̃tɛz/ *nf* (a) bracket;
ouvrir une ~ (figurative) to digress; **entre ~s**
(figurative) incidentally
(b) interlude

parer /paʀe/ [1] **1** *vtr* (a) to ward off
(b) to protect
(c) to adorn
(d) **~ qn/qch de qch** to attribute sth to sb/
sth
2 parer à *v+prep* **~ à toute éventualité** to
be prepared for all contingencies; **~ au plus
pressé** to deal with the most urgent matters
first

pare-soleil /paʀsɔlɛj/ *nm inv* visor

paresse /paʀɛs/ *nf* laziness

paresser /paʀɛse/ [1] *vi* to laze (around)

paresseux, -euse /paʀɛsø, øz/ **1** *adj*
lazy
2 *nm,f* lazy person
3 *nm* (Zool) sloth

parfaire /paʀfɛʀ/ [10] *vtr* to complete
⟨*education, works*⟩; to perfect ⟨*technique*⟩

parfait, ~e /paʀfɛ, ɛt/ **1** *adj* (a) perfect
(b) ⟨*likeness*⟩ exact; ⟨*discretion*⟩ absolute
(c) ⟨*tourist*⟩ archetypal; ⟨*example*⟩ classic
2 *nm* (in grammar) perfect

parfaitement /paʀfɛtmɑ̃/ *adv* ⟨*happy,
capable*⟩ perfectly; ⟨*tolerate, accept*⟩ fully

parfois /paʀfwa/ *adv* sometimes

parfum /paʀfœ̃/ *nm* (a) perfume
(b) (of flower, fruit) scent; (of bath salts)
fragrance; (of wine) bouquet; (of coffee) aroma
(c) flavour (GB)

IDIOMS mettre qn au ~ (colloq) to put sb in
the picture

parfumé, ~e /paʀfyme/ **1** *pp* ▶
PARFUMER
2 *pp adj* (a) ⟨*flower*⟩ sweet-scented; ⟨*fruit,
air*⟩ fragrant
(b) ⟨*handkerchief*⟩ scented
(c) **glace ~e au café** coffee-flavoured (GB) ice
cream

parfumer /paʀfyme/ [1] **1** *vtr* (a) **les
fleurs parfument la pièce** the room is
fragrant with flowers
(b) to put scent on ⟨*handkerchief*⟩; to put
scent in ⟨*bath*⟩
(c) to flavour (GB)
2 se parfumer *v refl* (+ *v être*) (a) to
wear perfume
(b) to put perfume on

parfumerie /paʀfymʀi/ *nf* perfumery

pari /paʀi/ *nm* (a) bet
(b) betting
(c) gamble

parier /paʀje/ [2] *vtr* to bet; **il y a fort** or
gros à ~ que it's a safe bet that; **je l'aurais
parié!** I knew it!

Paris /paʀi/ *pr n* Paris

parisien, -ienne /paʀizjɛ̃, ɛn/ *adj*
Parisian, Paris

parité /paʀite/ *nf* parity; **à ~** at parity

parjure /paʀʒyʀ/ *nm* perjury

parking /paʀkiŋ/ *nm* car park (GB),
parking lot (US)

par-là /paʀla/ *adv* **par-ci ~** here and there

parlant, ~e /paʀlɑ̃, ɑ̃t/ *adj* (a) ⟨*gesture*⟩
eloquent; ⟨*evidence, figure*⟩ which speaks for
itself
(b) **le cinéma ~** the talkies (colloq); **un film ~**
a talking picture

Parlement /paʀləmɑ̃/ *nm* Parliament

parlementaire /paʀləmɑ̃tɛʀ/ **1** *adj*
parliamentary
2 *nmf* (a) Member of Parliament
(b) negotiator

parlementer /paʀləmɑ̃te/ [1] *vi* to
negotiate

parler /paʀle/ [1] **1** *vtr* (a) to speak;
~ (l')italien to speak Italian
(b) **~ affaires/politique** to talk (about)
business/politics
2 parler à *v+prep* **~ à qn** to talk or speak
to sb
3 parler de *v+prep* (a) **~ de qn/qch** to
talk about sb/sth; to mention sb/sth; **~ de
tout et de rien, ~ de choses et d'autres** to
talk about this and that; **les journaux en ont
parlé** it was in the papers; **faire ~ de soi** to
get oneself talked about; to make the news;
qui parle de vous expulser? who said
anything about throwing you out?; **ta
promesse, parlons-en!** some promise!; **n'en
parlons plus!** let's drop it; that's the end of
it; **on m'a beaucoup parlé de vous** I've heard
a lot about you
(b) **~ de** ⟨*book, film*⟩ to be about
4 *vi* to talk, to speak; **parle plus fort** speak

up, speak louder; ~ **en connaissance de
cause** to know what one is talking about;
une prime? tu parles! (colloq) you
must be joking! (colloq); **il s'écoute** ~ he
loves the sound of his own voice

5 se parler *v refl* (+ *v être*) **(a)** to talk *or*
speak (to each other)
(b) to be on speaking terms
(c) ⟨*language, dialect*⟩ to be spoken
IDIOMS **trouver à qui** ~ to meet one's match

parloir /paʀlwaʀ/ *nm* (in school) visitors'
room; (in prison) visiting room; (in convent)
parlour (GB)

parme /paʀm/ *adj inv, nm* mauve

Parmentier /paʀmɑ̃tje/ *pr n* **hachis** ~
cottage pie, shepherd's pie

parmi /paʀmi/ *prep* **(a)** among, amongst
(b) demain il sera ~ **nous** he'll be with us
tomorrow
(c) choisir ~ **huit destinations** to choose
from eight destinations

parodie /paʀɔdi/ *nf* **(a)** parody
(b) mockery

parodier /paʀɔdje/ [2] *vtr* to parody

paroi /paʀwa/ *nf* **(a)** (of tunnel) side; (of cave)
wall; (of tube, pipe) inner surface
(b) (of house) wall
(c) ~ **rocheuse** rock face
(d) (Anat) wall

paroisse /paʀwas/ *nf* parish

paroissial, ~**e,** *mpl* **-iaux** /paʀwasjal,
o/ *adj* parish

parole /paʀɔl/ *nf* **(a)** speech; **avoir la** ~
facile to have the gift of the gab (colloq)
(b) laisser la ~ **à qn** to let sb speak; **temps
de** ~ speaking time
(c) word; ~**s en l'air** empty words; **une** ~
blessante a hurtful remark
(d) (*promise*) word; **donner sa** ~ to give one's
word; ~ **d'honneur!** cross my heart!,
I promise!; **ma** ~**!** (upon) my word!
(e) words; **c'est** ~ **d'évangile** it's gospel
truth; ~**s** words, lyrics; **film sans** ~**s** silent
film

parolier, -ière /paʀɔlje, ɛʀ/ *nm,f* **(a)** lyric
writer
(b) librettist

paroxysme /paʀɔksism/ *nm* (of pleasure)
paroxysm; (of battle) climax; (of ridiculousness)
height

parpaing /paʀpɛ̃/ *nm* breeze-block, cinder
block

parquer /paʀke/ [1] *vtr* **(a)** to pen ⟨*cattle*⟩
(b) to coop up ⟨*people*⟩
(c) to park ⟨*car*⟩

parquet /paʀkɛ/ *nm* **(a)** parquet (floor)
(b) (Law) **le** ~ ≈ the prosecution

parrain /paʀɛ̃/ *nm* **(a)** godfather
(b) (of candidate) sponsor; (of organization)
patron

parrainer /paʀene/ [1] *vtr* **(a)** to be patron
of ⟨*organization*⟩
(b) to sponsor ⟨*programme, race*⟩

parricide /paʀisid/ *nm* parricide

parsemer /paʀsəme/ [16] *vtr* **une pelouse
parsemée de fleurs** a lawn dotted with
flowers

part /paʀ/ **1** *nf* **(a)** (of cake) slice; (of meat,
rice) helping; (of market, legacy) share; **avoir sa**
~ **de misères** to have one's (fair) share of
misfortunes
(b) proportion; **une grande** ~ **de** a high
proportion *or* large part of; **pour une bonne**
~ to a large *or* great extent; **à** ~ **entière**
⟨*member*⟩ full; ⟨*science*⟩ in its own right
(c) share; **faire sa** ~ **de travail** to do one's
share of the work; **prendre** ~ **à** to take part
in; **il m'a fait** ~ **de ses projets** he told me
about his plans
(d) de toute(s) ~**(s)** from all sides; **de** ~ **et
d'autre** on both sides, on either side; **de** ~
en ~ ⟨*pierce*⟩ right *or* straight through
(e) pour ma/notre ~ for my/our part; **d'une**
~**...**, **d'autre** ~**...** on (the) one hand... on the
other hand...; **prendre qch en mauvaise** ~ to
take sth badly
2 à part *phr* **(a)** ⟨*file*⟩ separately; **mettre
qch à** ~ to put sth to one side; **prendre qn à**
~ to take sb aside; **une salle à** ~ a separate
room; **blague à** ~ joking aside
(b) être un peu à ~ ⟨*person*⟩ to be out of the
ordinary; **un cas à** ~ a special case
(c) apart from; **à** ~ **ça** apart from that
3 de la part de *phr* **(a) de la** ~ **de**
⟨*write, act*⟩ on behalf of
(b) de la ~ **de qn** from sb; **donne-leur le
bonjour de ma** ~ say hello to them for me;
de leur ~**, rien ne m'étonne** nothing they do
surprises me
IDIOMS **faire la** ~ **des choses** to put things
in perspective

partage /paʀtaʒ/ *nm* **(a)** dividing, sharing;
recevoir qch en ~ to be left sth (in a will)
(b) distribution
(c) sharing, division; **régner sans** ~ to reign
absolutely; **une victoire sans** ~ a total
victory
(d) division, partition

partagé, ~**e** /paʀtaʒe/ **1** *pp* ▶ PARTAGER
2 *pp adj* **(a)** ⟨*opinion, unions*⟩ divided
(b) ⟨*reactions, feelings*⟩ mixed
(c) être ~ to be torn
(d) ⟨*grief*⟩ shared; **les torts sont** ~**s** they are
both to blame
(e) ⟨*affection*⟩ mutual

partager /paʀtaʒe/ [13] **1** *vtr* **(a)** to share;
faire ~ **qch à qn** to let sb share in sth; **il sait
nous faire** ~ **ses émotions** he knows how to
get his feelings across
(b) to divide ⟨*country, room*⟩
(c) to divide [sth] (up), to split ⟨*inheritance,
work*⟩
2 se partager *v refl* (+ *v être*) **(a)** to
share ⟨*money, work, responsibility*⟩
(b) to be divided, to be split
(c) ⟨*costs, responsibility*⟩ to be shared; ⟨*cake*⟩
to be cut (up)

partance /paʀtɑ̃s/ *nf* **en** ~ about to take
off; about to sail; about to leave; **être en** ~
pour *or* **vers** to be bound for

p

partenaire /paʀtənɛʀ/ nmf partner; qui
était le ~ d'Arletty? who played opposite
Arletty?
■ ~s sociaux ≈ unions and management

partenariat /paʀtənaʀja/ nm partnership

parterre /paʀtɛʀ/ nm (a) (in garden) bed
(b) stalls (GB), orchestra (US)

parti, ~e¹ /paʀti/ ① adj (colloq) être ~ to
be tight (colloq)
② nm (a) group; party; les ~s de
l'opposition the opposition parties
(b) option; prendre ~ to commit oneself;
prendre le ~ de qn to side with sb
(c) bon ~ suitable match
■ ~ pris bias
IDIOMS prendre son ~ de qch to come to
terms with sth; tirer ~ de to take advantage
of [sth]; to turn [sth] to good account

partial, ~e, mpl **-iaux** /paʀsjal, o/ adj
biased (GB)

partialité /paʀsjalite/ nf bias

participant, ~e /paʀtisipɑ̃, ɑ̃t/ nm,f
participant

participation /paʀtisipasjɔ̃/ nf
(a) participation; involvement
(b) contribution; ~ aux frais (financial)
contribution

participe /paʀtisip/ nm participle; ~ passé
past participle

participer /paʀtisipe/ [1] v+prep (a) ~ à
to participate in, to take part in; to be
involved in
(b) ~ à to contribute to

particularisme /paʀtikylaʀism/ nm
distinctive identity

particularité /paʀtikylaʀite/ nf (a) special
feature
(b) (of disease, situation) particular nature

particule /paʀtikyl/ nf particle; nom à ~
aristocratic name

particulier, -ière /paʀtikylje, ɛʀ/ ① adj
(a) particular
(b) ⟨rights, privileges, role⟩ special; ⟨example,
objective⟩ specific
(c) ⟨car, secretary⟩ private
(d) ⟨case, situation⟩ unusual; ⟨talent, effort⟩
special; ⟨habits⟩ odd; ⟨accent, style⟩
distinctive, unusual; c'est quelqu'un de très
~ he's/she's somebody out of the ordinary;
he's/she's weird
② en particulier phr (a) in private
(b) individually
(c) in particular, particularly
③ nm (simple) ~ private individual

particulièrement /paʀtikyljɛʀmɑ̃/ adv
(a) particularly, exceptionally
(b) in particular

partie² /paʀti/ ① adj f ▶ PARTI 1
② nf (a) part; (of amount, salary) proportion,
part; la majeure ~ des gens most people; en
~ partly, in part; faire ~ des premiers to be
among the first; cela fait ~ de leurs
avantages that's one of their advantages
(b) line (of work); il est de la ~ it's in his
line of work)

(c) game; faire une ~ to have a game;
gagner la ~ to win the game; (figurative) to
win the day; j'espère que tu seras de la ~ I
hope you can come; ce n'est que ~ remise
maybe next time
(d) (in contract, negotiations) party; les ~s en
présence the parties involved; être ~
prenante dans to be actively involved in
(e) (Mus) part
■ ~ civile plaintiff; ~ de pêche fishing trip;
~ de plaisir fun
IDIOMS avoir affaire à forte ~ to have a
tough opponent; prendre qn à ~ to take sb to
task

partiel, -ielle /paʀsjɛl/ adj ⟨payment⟩
part; ⟨destruction, agreement⟩ partial

partir /paʀtiʀ/ [30] ① vi (+ v être) (a) to
leave, to go; ~ à pied to leave on foot; ~ en
courant to run off; ~ sans laisser d'adresse
to disappear without trace; ~ loin/à Paris to
go far away/to Paris; ~ en week-end to go
away for the weekend; ~ à la pêche to go
fishing; ~ en tournée to set off on tour (GB)
or on a tour; ~ en retraite to retire
(b) ⟨vehicle, train⟩ to leave; ⟨plane⟩ to take
off; ⟨motor⟩ to start; les coureurs sont partis
the runners are off; à vos marques, prêts,
partez! on your marks, get set, go!
(c) ⟨bullet⟩ to be fired; ⟨cork⟩ to shoot out;
⟨capsule⟩ to shoot off; ⟨retort⟩ to slip out; le
coup de feu est parti the gun went off; il était
tellement énervé que la gifle est partie toute
seule he was so angry that he slapped him/
her before he could stop himself
(d) ⟨path, road⟩ to start; ~ favori to start
favourite (GB); ~ battu d'avance to be
doomed from the start; ~ de rien to start
from nothing; c'est parti! go!; et voilà, c'est
parti, il pleut! (colloq) here we go, it's raining!;
être bien parti to have got (GB) or gotten (US)
off to a good start; être bien parti pour
gagner to seem all set to win; c'est mal parti
(colloq) things don't look too good
(e) ~ de to start from ⟨idea⟩; ~ du principe
que to work on the assumption that; ~ d'une
bonne intention to be well-meant
(f) ⟨stain⟩ to come out; ⟨smell⟩ to go;
⟨enamel, button⟩ to come off
(g) ⟨parcel, application⟩ to be sent (off)
(h) quand il est parti on ne l'arrête plus
(colloq) once he starts or gets going there's no
stopping him
② à partir de phr from; à ~ de 16 heures/
de 2 000 francs from 4 o'clock onwards/2,000
francs; à ~ du moment où as soon as; as
long as; fabriqué à ~ d'un alliage made from
an alloy

partisan, ~e /paʀtizɑ̃, an/ ① adj
(a) partisan
(b) ~ de qch/de faire in favour (GB) of sth/of
doing; être ~ du moindre effort (colloq) to be
lazy
② nm,f (gen) supporter, partisan; (Mil)
partisan

partition /paʀtisjɔ̃/ nf (Mus) score

partout /paʀtu/ adv (a) everywhere; avoir

mal ~ to ache all over; **un peu ~ dans le monde** more or less all over the world; **~ où je vais** wherever I go
(b) (Sport) **trois (points** *or* **buts) ~** three all
IDIOMS fourrer son nez ~ (colloq) to stick one's nose into everything (colloq)

parure /paʀyʀ/ *nf* **(a)** finery
(b) set of jewels

parution /paʀysjɔ̃/ *nf* publication

parvenir /paʀvəniʀ/ [36] *v+prep* (+ *v être*)
(a) ~ **à** to reach ⟨*place, person*⟩; **faire ~ qch à qn** to send sth to sb; to get sth to sb
(b) ~ **à** to reach ⟨*agreement*⟩; to achieve ⟨*balance*⟩
(c) ~ **à faire** to manage to do

parvenu, ~e /paʀvəny/ *nm,f* upstart

parvis /paʀvi/ *nm inv* (of church) square

pas¹ /pa/ *adv* **(a)** **je ne prends ~ de sucre** I don't take sugar; **ils n'ont ~ le téléphone** they haven't got a phone; **je ne pense ~** I don't think so; **elle a aimé le film, mais lui ~** she liked the film but he didn't
(b) (in expressions, exclamations) ~ **du tout** not at all; ~ **le moins du monde** not in the least; ~ **tant que ça,** ~ **plus que ça** not all that much; ~ **d'histoires!** I don't want any arguments *or* fuss!; ~ **de chance!** hard luck!; ~ **possible!** I can't believe it!; ~ **vrai?** (colloq) isn't that so?

pas² /pa/ *nm inv* **(a)** step; **marcher à ~ feutrés** to walk softly; **faire ses premiers ~** to take one's first steps; **faire le premier ~** to make the first move; **suivre qn ~ à ~** to follow sb everywhere; **de là à dire qu'il s'en fiche** (colloq), **il n'y a qu'un ~** there's only a fine line between that and saying he doesn't care; **j'habite à deux ~ (d'ici)** I live very near here; **l'hiver arrive à grands ~** winter is fast approaching; **apprendre les ~ du tango** to learn how to tango
(b) pace; **marcher d'un bon ~** to walk at a brisk pace; **marcher au ~** to march; (on horseback) to walk; **'roulez au ~'** 'dead slow' (GB), '(very) slow' (US); **mettre qn au ~** to bring sb to heel; **partir au ~ de course** to rush off; **j'y vais de ce ~** I'm on my way now
(c) footstep
(d) footprint; **revenir sur ses ~** to retrace one's steps
IDIOMS se tirer d'un mauvais ~ to get out of a tight corner; **sauter le ~** to take the plunge; **prendre le ~ sur qch** to overtake sth

pascal, ~e, *mpl* **~s** *or* **-aux** /paskal, o/ *adj* ⟨*weekend*⟩ Easter; ⟨*candle, lamb*⟩ paschal

pas-de-porte /padpɔʀt/ *nm inv* key money

passable /pasabl/ *adj* **(a)** ⟨*film*⟩ fairly good; ⟨*results*⟩ reasonable
(b) (Sch) fair

passablement /pasabləmɑ̃/ *adv* ⟨*drunk, annoyed*⟩ rather; ⟨*drink, worry*⟩ quite a lot

passade /pasad/ *nf* fad

passage /pasaʒ/ *nm* **(a)** traffic; **interdire le ~ des camions dans la ville** to ban lorries from (driving through) the town
(b) stay; **ton ~ dans la ville a été bref** your stay in the town was brief
(c) **attendre le ~ du boulanger** to wait for the baker's van to come; **je peux te prendre au ~** I can pick you up on the way; **des hôtes de ~** short-stay guests; **so servir au ~** to help oneself; (figurative) to take a cut (of the profits); to pocket some of the profits
(d) '~ **interdit, voie privée**' 'no entry, private road'; **pour céder le ~ à l'ambulance** in order to let the ambulance go past
(e) **chaque ~ de votre chanson à la radio** every time your song is played on the radio
(f) way, path; **prévoir le ~ de câbles** to plan the route of cables
(g) ~ **(de qch) à qch** transition (from sth) to sth
(h) alley; passageway
(i) (in novel) passage; (in film) sequence
■ ~ **à l'acte** acting out; ~ **à niveau** level crossing (GB), grade crossing (US); ~ **pour piétons** pedestrian crossing; ~ **à tabac** beating; ~ **à vide** bad patch; unproductive period

passager, -ère /pasaʒe, ɛʀ/ **1** *adj* ⟨*situation, crisis*⟩ temporary; ⟨*feeling*⟩ passing; ⟨*shower*⟩ brief; ⟨*unease*⟩ slight, short-lived
2 *nm,f* passenger; ~ **clandestin** stowaway

passant, ~e /pasɑ̃, ɑ̃t/ **1** *adj* ⟨*street*⟩ busy
2 *nm,f* passer-by
3 *nm* (on belt, watchstrap) loop

passation /pasasjɔ̃/ *nf* ~ **des pouvoirs** transfer of power

passe¹ /pas/ *nm* (colloq) **(a)** master key
(b) pass

passe² /pas/ *nf* **(a)** (Sport) pass
(b) **être dans une ~ difficile** to be going through a difficult patch; **être en ~ de faire** to be (well) on the way to doing

passé, ~e /pase/ **1** *pp* ▸ PASSER
2 *pp adj* **(a)** ⟨*years, experiences*⟩ past; ~ **de mode** dated
(b) **l'année passée** last year
(c) ⟨*colour, material*⟩ faded
3 *nm* **(a)** past
(b) past (tense)
4 *prep* after; ~ **8 heures il s'endort dans son fauteuil** come eight o'clock he goes to sleep in his armchair
■ ~ **antérieur** past anterior; ~ **composé** present perfect; ~ **simple** past historic

passéisme /paseism/ *nm* attachment to the past

passe-montagne, *pl* **~s** /pasmɔ̃taɲ/ *nm* balaclava

passe-partout /paspaʀtu/ *adj inv* ⟨*expression*⟩ catch-all; ⟨*garment*⟩ for all occasions

passe-passe /paspas/ *nm inv* **tour de ~** conjuring trick; (figurative) sleight of hand

passeport /paspɔʀ/ *nm* passport

passer /pase/ [1] **1** *vtr* **(a)** to cross ⟨*river, border*⟩; to go through ⟨*door, customs*⟩; to get over ⟨*hedge, obstacle*⟩; **il m'a fait ~ la frontière** he got me across the border; **~ qch à la douane** to get sth through customs
(b) to go past, to pass; **quand vous aurez passé le feu, tournez à droite** turn right after the lights; **le malade ne passera pas la nuit** the patient won't last the night
(c) **~ le doigt sur la table** to run one's finger over the table-top; **~ la tête à la fenêtre** to stick one's head out of the window
(d) to pass ⟨*object*⟩; to pass [sth] on ⟨*instructions, disease*⟩; **~ sa colère sur ses collègues** to take one's anger out on one's colleagues
(e) to lend; to give
(f) (on phone) **tu peux me ~ Chris?** can you put Chris on?; **je vous le passe** I'm putting you through
(g) to take, to sit ⟨*examination*⟩; to have ⟨*interview*⟩; **faire ~ un test à qn** to give sb a test
(h) to spend ⟨*time*⟩; **dépêche-toi, on ne va pas y ~ la nuit!** (colloq) hurry up, or we'll be here all night!
(i) **elle leur passe tout** she lets them get away with murder
(j) to skip ⟨*page, paragraph*⟩; **je vous passe les détails** I'll spare you the details
(k) **~ l'aspirateur** to vacuum
(l) to filter ⟨*coffee*⟩; to strain ⟨*fruit juice, sauce*⟩; to purée ⟨*vegetables*⟩
(m) to slip [sth] on ⟨*garment, ring*⟩; to slip into ⟨*dress*⟩
(n) to play ⟨*record, cassette*⟩; to show ⟨*film, slides*⟩; to place ⟨*ad*⟩
(o) to enter into ⟨*agreement*⟩; to place ⟨*order*⟩
(p) (Aut) **~ la troisième** to go into third gear
(q) (Games) **~ son tour** to pass
2 *vi* (+ *v être*) **(a)** to go past *or* by, to pass; **~ sur un pont** to go over a bridge; **le facteur n'est pas encore passé** the postman hasn't been yet; **~ à côté de** ⟨*person*⟩ to pass; ⟨*road*⟩ to run alongside; **~ à pied/à bicyclette** to walk/cycle past
(b) **je ne fais que ~** I've just popped in (GB) *or* dropped by for a minute; **~ dans la matinée** ⟨*plumber*⟩ to come by in the morning; **~ prendre qn/qch** to pick sb/sth up
(c) to go; **passons au salon** let's go into the lounge; **les contrebandiers sont passés en Espagne** the smugglers have crossed into Spain
(d) to get through; **tu ne passeras pas, c'est trop étroit** you'll never get through, it's too narrow; **il m'a fait signe de ~** he waved me on; **vas-y, ça passe!** go on, there's plenty of room!; **~ par-dessus bord** to fall overboard; **il est passé par la fenêtre** he fell out of the window; he got in through the window
(e) **~ par** to go through; **~ par le standard** to go through the switchboard; **je ne sais jamais ce qui se passe par la tête** I never know what's going on in your head
(f) (colloq) **il accuse le patron, ses collègues,** **bref, tout le monde y passe** he's accusing the boss, his colleagues—basically, everyone in sight; **que ça te plaise ou non, il va falloir y ~** whether you like it or not, there's no alternative; **on ne peut pas faire autrement que d'en ~ par là** there is no other way around it
(g) **~ sur** to pass over ⟨*question, mistake*⟩; **~ à côté d'une question** to miss the point; **laisser ~ une occasion** to miss an opportunity
(h) **soit dit en ~** incidentally
(i) ⟨*comments, speech*⟩ to go down well; ⟨*law, measure, candidate*⟩ to get through; ⟨*attitude, doctrine*⟩ to be accepted; **j'ai mangé quelque chose qui n'est pas passé** I ate something which didn't agree with me; **que je sois critiqué, passe encore, mais calomnié, non!** criticism is one thing, but I draw the line at slander; **~ au premier tour** to be elected in the first round; **~ dans la classe supérieure** to move up to the year above; **(ça) passe pour cette fois** (colloq) I'll let it go this time
(j) **~ à l'ennemi** to go over to the enemy; **~ de main en main** to be passed around; **~ constamment d'un sujet à l'autre** to flit from one subject to another; **~ à un taux supérieur** to go up to a higher rate
(k) **~ pour un imbécile** to look a fool; **~ pour un génie** to pass as a genius; **il passe pour l'inventeur de l'ordinateur** he's supposed to have invented computers; **il se fait ~ pour mon frère** he passes himself off as my brother
(l) ⟨*pain, crisis*⟩ to pass; **quand l'orage sera** *or* **aura passé** when the storm is over; **ça passera** ⟨*bad mood*⟩ it'll pass; ⟨*hurt*⟩ you'll get over it; **~ de mode** to go out of fashion; **faire ~ à qn l'envie de faire** to cure sb of the desire to do; **ce médicament fait ~ les maux d'estomac** this medicine relieves stomach ache
(m) ⟨*performer, group*⟩ (on stage) to be appearing; (on TV, radio) to be on; ⟨*show, film*⟩ to be on; ⟨*music*⟩ to be playing
(n) ⟨*avant/après*⟩ to come before/after; **il fait ~ sa famille avant ses amis** he puts his family before his friends
(o) (colloq) **où étais-tu passé?** where did you get to?; **où est passé mon livre?** where has my book got to?
(p) ⟨*time*⟩ to pass, to go by; **je ne vois pas le temps ~** I don't know where the time goes
(q) to turn to; **~ à l'étape suivante** to move on to the next stage; **nous allons ~ au vote** let's vote now
(r) **~ de père en fils** to be handed down from father to son; **l'expression est passée dans la langue** the expression has become part of the language
(s) to be promoted to; **elle est passée maître dans l'art de mentir** she's an accomplished liar
(t) ⟨*money, amount*⟩ to go on *or* into; ⟨*product, material*⟩ to go into
(u) (colloq) **y ~** to die
(v) ⟨*colour, material*⟩ to fade
(w) ⟨*coffee*⟩ to filter

(x) ~ **en marche arrière** to go into reverse; **la troisième passe mal** third gear is a bit stiff

(y) (in bridge, poker) to pass

3 se passer *v refl* (+ *v être*) **(a)** to happen; **tout s'est passé très vite** it all happened very fast; **tout se passe comme si le yen avait été dévalué** it's as if the yen had been devalued

(b) to take place; **la scène se passe au Viêt Nam** the scene is set in Vietnam

(c) ‹*examination, negotiations*› to go; **ça ne se passera pas comme ça!** I won't leave it at that!

(d) ‹*period*› to go by, to pass; **deux ans se sont passés depuis** that was two years ago

(e) se ~ **de** to do without ‹*object, activity, person*›; to go without ‹*meal, sleep*›; **se** ~ **de commentaires** to speak for itself

(f) se ~ **la langue sur les lèvres** to run one's tongue over one's lips; **se** ~ **la main sur le front** to put a hand to one's forehead

(g) ils se sont passé des documents they exchanged some documents

IDIOMS **qu'est-ce qu'elle nous a passé!** (colloq) she really went for us! (colloq)

passerelle /pasʀɛl/ *nf* **(a)** footbridge
(b) link
(c) (to boat) gangway; (to plane) steps

passe-temps /pastɑ̃/ *nm inv* pastime, hobby

passeur, -euse /pasœʀ, øz/ *nm,f*
(a) ferryman/ferrywoman
(b) smuggler; (for drugs) courier

passible /pasibl/ *adj* (Law) ~ **de** ‹*crime*› punishable by; ‹*person*› liable to

passif, -ive /pasif, iv/ **1** *adj* passive
2 *nm* **(a)** passive (voice)
(b) debit; **mettre qch au** ~ **de qn** to count sth amongst sb's failures

passion /pasjɔ̃/ *nf* passion

passionnant, ~e /pasjɔnɑ̃, ɑ̃t/ *adj* exciting, fascinating, riveting

passionné, ~e /pasjɔne/ **1** *adj* ‹*love*› passionate; ‹*debate, argument*› impassioned; **être** ~ **de** *or* **pour qch** to have a passion for sth
2 *nm,f* enthusiast

passionnel, -elle /pasjɔnɛl/ *adj* ‹*debate*› passionate; ‹*crime*› of passion

passionner /pasjɔne/ [1] **1** *vtr* **(a)** to fascinate; **la botanique le passionne** he has a passion for botany
(b) to inflame ‹*debate*›
2 se passionner *v refl* (+ *v être*) to have a passion (**pour** for)

passivité /pasivite/ *nf* passivity

passoire /paswaʀ/ *nf* **(a)** colander
(b) strainer

pastel /pastɛl/ **1** *adj inv* ‹*shade*› pastel
2 *nm* pastel

pastèque /pastɛk/ *nf* watermelon

pasteur /pastœʀ/ *nm* **(a)** minister, pastor
(b) priest
(c) shepherd

pasteuriser /pastœʀize/ [1] *vtr* to pasteurize

pastiche /pastiʃ/ *nm* pastiche

pastille /pastij/ *nf* **(a)** pastille, lozenge; ~ **contre la toux** cough drop
(b) ~ **de menthe** peppermint
(c) spot
(d) (of cloth, rubber) patch; (of plastic) disc

pastoral, ~e¹, *mpl* -aux /pastɔʀal, o/ *adj* pastoral

pastorale² /pastɔʀal/ *nf* (Mus) pastoral

patachon /pataʃɔ̃/ *nm* (colloq) **mener une vie de** ~ to live in the fast lane

patata /patata/ *excl* (colloq) ▶ PATATI

patate /patat/ *nf* (colloq) **(a)** spud (colloq); ~ **douce** sweet potato
(b) blockhead (colloq), idiot

patati /patati/ *excl* (colloq) ~, **patata** and so on and so forth

pataud, ~e /pato, od/ *adj* clumsy

patauger /patoʒe/ [13] *vi* **(a)** to splash about; to paddle
(b) to flounder

pâte /pɑt/ **1** *nf* **(a)** pastry; dough; batter
(b) paste
2 pâtes *nf pl* ~**s (alimentaires)** pasta
■ ~ **d'amandes** marzipan; ~**s de fruit(s)** fruit jellies; ~ **à modeler** Plasticine®; ~ **à tartiner** spread

IDIOMS **mettre la main à la** ~ to pitch in

pâté /pɑte/ *nm* **(a)** pâté
(b) pie; ~ **en croûte** ≈ pie
(c) ~ **de maisons** block (of houses)
(d) (ink)blot
(e) sandcastle

pâtée /pɑte/ *nf* dog food; cat food; swill

patelin /patlɛ̃/ *nm* (colloq) small village

patente /patɑ̃t/ *nf: licence* (GB) *to exercise a trade or profession*

patère /pateʀ/ *nf* peg, hook

paternalisme /patɛʀnalism/ *nm* paternalism

paternaliste /patɛʀnalist/ *adj* paternalistic

paternel, -elle /patɛʀnɛl/ *adj* **(a)** paternal
(b) fatherly

paternité /patɛʀnite/ *nf* **(a)** fatherhood; (Law) paternity
(b) authorship

pâteux, -euse /pɑtø, øz/ *adj*
(a) ‹*substance*› doughy; ‹*gruel*› mushy
(b) ‹*voice*› thick

pathétique /patetik/ *adj* moving

pathologique /patɔlɔʒik/ *adj* pathological

patiemment /pasjamɑ̃/ *adv* patiently

patience /pasjɑ̃s/ *nf* patience
IDIOMS **prendre son mal en** ~ to resign oneself to one's fate

patient, ~e /pasjɑ̃, ɑ̃t/ *adj, nm,f* patient

patienter /pasjɑ̃te/ [1] *vi* to wait

patin /patɛ̃/ *nm* **(a)** skate ····⦂

(b) (Tech) (on helicopter) skid; (on sledge) runner
■ ~ **à glace** ice skate; ice-skating; ~ **à roulettes** roller skate; roller-skating

patinage /patinaʒ/ nm skating

patine /patin/ nf patina; finish, sheen

patiner /patine/ [1] **1** vtr to apply a finish to
2 vi **(a)** to skate
(b) (Aut) ⟨wheel⟩ to spin; ⟨clutch⟩ to slip; **faire ~ l'embrayage** to slip the clutch
3 se patiner v refl (+ v être) to acquire a patina

patineur, -euse /patinœr, øz/ nm,f skater

patinoire /patinwar/ nf ice rink

pâtir /pɑtir/ [3] vi ~ **de** to suffer as a result of

pâtisserie /pɑtisri/ nf **(a)** cake shop, pâtisserie
(b) pastry, cake

pâtissier, -ière /pɑtisje, ɛr/ nm,f confectioner, pastry cook

patois /patwa/ nm inv patois, dialect

patraque /patrak/ adj (colloq) **être ~** to be under the weather (colloq)

patriarche /patrijarʃ/ nm patriarch

patrie /patri/ nf homeland, country

patrimoine /patrimwan/ nm **(a)** (of person, family) patrimony; (of firm) capital
(b) heritage
■ ~ **génétique** gene pool

patriote /patrijot/ **1** adj patriotic
2 nmf patriot; **en ~** patriotically

patriotisme /patrijotism/ nm patriotism

patron, -onne /patrɔ̃, ɔn/ **1** nm,f boss (colloq)
2 nm (sewing) pattern
■ ~ **de pêche** skipper, master

patronal, ~e, mpl -aux /patronal, o/ adj ⟨organization⟩ employers'

patronat /patrona/ nm employers

patronne ▶ PATRON 1

patronner /patrone/ [1] vtr to sponsor

patronyme /patronim/ nm patronymic

patrouille /patruj/ nf patrol

patrouiller /patruje/ [1] vi to be on patrol

patte /pat/ nf **(a)** leg; paw; foot; **donner la ~** to give its paw; **retomber sur ses ~s** to fall on its feet
(b) (colloq) leg, foot; **tu es toujours dans mes ~s** you are always getting under my feet; **marcher à quatre ~s** to walk on all fours; to crawl; **traîner la ~** to limp
(c) (colloq) hand; **bas les ~s!** (colloq) keep your hands to yourself!; hands off! (colloq)
(d) (on shelving unit) lug; (on garment) flap
(e) sideburn
■ ~**s d'éléphant** flares; ~ **folle** (colloq) gammy leg (GB), game leg (US); ~**s de mouche** spidery scrawl
IDIOMS **faire ~ de velours** ⟨cat⟩ to draw in its claws; ⟨person⟩ to switch on the charm;

montrer ~ blanche to prove one is acceptable; **se tirer dans les ~s** to pull dirty tricks on each other

patte-d'oie ou pl **pattes-d'oie** /patdwa/ nf **(a)** crow's-foot
(b) junction

pâturage /pɑtyraʒ/ nm pasture

pâture /pɑtyr/ nf **(a)** feed; **être jeté en ~** (figurative) to be thrown to the lions
(b) pasture

paume /pom/ nf palm (of the hand)

paumé, ~e /pome/ adj (colloq) **(a)** ⟨person⟩ mixed up (GB), out of it (US) (colloq)
(b) ⟨place⟩ godforsaken

paumer (colloq) /pome/ [1] **1** vtr, vi to lose
2 se paumer v refl (+ v être) to get lost

paupière /popjɛr/ nf eyelid

paupiette /popjɛt/ nf ~ **de veau** stuffed escalope of veal

pause /poz/ nf **(a)** break; **faire une ~** to take a break
(b) (in process) pause
(c) (Mus) rest

pauvre /povr/ **1** adj **(a)** poor
(b) sparse; ~ **en sucre** low in sugar; lacking sugar
(c) **un ~ type** (colloq) a poor guy (colloq); a dead loss (colloq)
2 nmf (colloq) **le/la ~!** poor man/woman!; poor thing!
3 nm **un ~** a poor man; ~ **d'esprit** half-wit

pauvrement /povrəmɑ̃/ adv poorly

pauvresse /povrɛs/ nf poor wretch, pauper

pauvreté /povrəte/ nf **(a)** poverty
(b) shabbiness

pavage /pavaʒ/ nm paving

pavaner: se pavaner /pavane/ [1] v refl (+ v être) to strut (about)

pavé /pave/ nm cobblestone; **se retrouver sur le ~** to find oneself out on the street
IDIOMS **lancer un ~ dans la mare** to set the cat among the pigeons; **tenir le haut du ~** to head the field

paver /pave/ [1] vtr to lay [sth] with cobblestones

pavillon /pavijɔ̃/ nm **(a)** (detached) house
(b) (for exhibition) pavilion; (of hospital) wing
(c) (of ear) auricle
(d) (of loudspeaker) horn
(e) (Naut) flag

pavillonnaire /pavijonɛr/ adj **zone ~** residential area; **banlieue ~** suburb consisting of houses (as opposed to high-rise buildings)

pavoiser /pavwaze/ [1] vi (colloq) to crow

pavot /pavo/ nm poppy

payable /pɛjabl/ adj payable; ~ **à la commande** cash with order

payant, ~e /pɛjɑ̃, ɑ̃t/ adj **(a)** ⟨person⟩ paying
(b) ⟨show⟩ not free
(c) (colloq) lucrative, profitable

paye /pɛj/ = PAIE

payement /pɛjmɑ̃/ = PAIEMENT

payer /peje/ [21] **1** vtr **(a)** to pay; to pay for; **il est payé pour le savoir!** he knows that to his cost!; **faire ~ qch à qn** to charge sb for sth; **~ qch à qn** (colloq) to buy sb sth
(b) to pay for ⟨mistake, carelessness⟩
2 vi **(a)** ⟨efforts, sacrifice⟩ to pay off; ⟨profession, activity⟩ to pay
(b) (colloq) to be funny
3 se payer v refl (+ v être) **(a)** ⟨service, goods⟩ to have to be paid for
(b) (colloq) to treat oneself to ⟨holiday⟩; to get ⟨cold, bad mark⟩; to get landed with ⟨job⟩; **se ~ un arbre** to crash into a tree
IDIOMS **se ~ du bon temps** (colloq) to have a good time; **se ~ la tête de qn** (colloq) to take the mickey out of sb (GB) (colloq), to razz sb (US) (colloq)

pays /pei/ nm **(a)** country
(b) la Bourgogne est le ~ du bon vin Burgundy is the home of good wine; **gens du ~** local people
IDIOMS **voir du ~** to do some travelling (GB)

paysage /peizaʒ/ nm landscape, scenery
■ **~ audiovisuel français, PAF** French radio and TV scene

paysager, -ère /peizaʒe, ɛR/ adj
(a) environmental
(b) ⟨garden⟩ landscaped

paysagiste /peizaʒist/ nmf (**jardinier**) **~** landscape gardener

paysan, -anne /peizɑ̃, an/ **1** adj ⟨life⟩ rural; ⟨ways⟩ peasant; ⟨soup, bread⟩ country
2 nm,f **(a)** ≈ small farmer
(b) (derogatory) peasant

paysannerie /peizanRi/ nf small farmers; peasantry

Pays-Bas /peibɑ/ pr nm pl **les ~** The Netherlands

PC /pese/ nm **(a)** (Pol) (abbr = **parti communiste**) CP, Communist Party
(b) (abbr = **personal computer**) PC

PCF /peseɛf/ nm (abbr = **parti communiste français**) French Communist Party

PCV /peseve/ nm (abbr = **paiement contre vérification**) reverse charge call (GB), collect call (US)

PDG /pedeʒe/ nm (abbr = **président-directeur général**) chief executive officer

péage /peaʒ/ nm **(a)** toll
(b) tollbooth

peau, pl **~x** /po/ nf **(a)** skin; **n'avoir que la ~ sur les os** to be all skin and bone
(b) leather; **gants de ~** leather gloves
(c) peel
(d) (colloq) life; **risquer sa ~** to risk one's life; **faire la ~ à qn** to kill sb; **vouloir la ~ de qn** to want sb dead
IDIOMS **être bien dans sa ~** (colloq) to feel good about oneself; **avoir qn dans la ~** (colloq) to be crazy about sb (colloq); **prendre une balle dans la ~** (colloq) to be shot

peaufiner /pofine/ [1] vtr to put the finishing touches to ⟨work, text⟩

Peau-Rouge, pl **Peaux-Rouges** /poRuʒ/ nmf Red Indian

péché /peʃe/ nm sin; **ce serait un ~ de rater ça** (colloq) it would be a crime to miss that; **le chocolat, c'est mon ~ mignon** I've got a weakness for chocolate

pêche /pɛʃ/ nf **(a)** peach
(b) fishing; **aller à la ~** to go fishing
(c) (colloq) clout (colloq)
(d) (colloq) **avoir la ~** to be feeling great
■ **~ à la ligne** angling

pécher /peʃe/ [14] vi to sin; **~ par excès de confiance** to be overconfident; **le roman pèche sur un point** the novel has one shortcoming

pêcher¹ /pɛʃe/ [1] **1** vtr to go fishing for
2 vi to fish; **~ à la mouche** to fly-fish; **~ à la ligne** to angle

pêcher² /pɛʃe/ nm peach tree

pécheresse /peʃRɛs/ nf sinner

pêcherie /pɛʃRi/ nf **(a)** fish factory
(b) fishing ground

pécheur /peʃœR/ nm sinner

pêcheur /pɛʃœR/ nm fisherman

pectoral, pl **-aux** /pɛktɔRal, o/ nm pectoral muscle

pécule /pekyl/ nm savings, nest egg (colloq)

pécuniaire /pekynjɛR/ adj financial

pédagogie /pedagɔʒi/ nf **(a)** education, pedagogy
(b) teaching skills
(c) teaching method

pédagogique /pedagɔʒik/ adj ⟨activity⟩ educational; ⟨system⟩ education; ⟨method⟩ teaching

pédagogue /pedagɔg/ nmf educationalist

pédale /pedal/ nf pedal
IDIOMS **perdre les ~s** (colloq) to lose one's grip

pédaler /pedale/ [1] vi to pedal

pédalier /pedalje/ nm (of bicycle) chain transmission; (of piano) pedals

pédalo® /pedalo/ nm pedalo (GB), pedal boat

pédant, ~e /pedɑ̃, ɑ̃t/ adj pedantic

pédérastie /pedeRasti/ nf **(a)** pederasty
(b) homosexuality

pédestre /pedɛstR/ adj **randonnée ~** ramble

pédiatre /pedjatR/ nmf paediatrician

pédiatrie /pedjatRi/ nf paediatrics

pédicure /pedikyR/ nmf chiropodist (GB), podiatrist (US)

pedigree /pedigRe/ nm pedigree

pédologue /pedɔlɔg/ nmf pedologist

pédophilie /pedɔfili/ nf paedophilia

pègre /pɛgR/ nf underworld

peigne /pɛɲ/ nm comb

peigner /peɲe/ [1] **1** vtr to comb ⟨hair, wool⟩ ⋯⟶

2 **se peigner** *v refl* (+ *v être*) to comb one's hair

peignoir /pɛɲwaʀ/ *nm* dressing gown (GB), robe (US); **~ de bain** bathrobe

peinard, ~e /penaʀ, aʀd/ *adj* (colloq) ⟨*job*⟩ cushy (colloq); ⟨*place*⟩ snug

peindre /pɛ̃dʀ/ [55] **1** *vtr* (a) to paint
(b) to depict
2 *vi* to paint

peine /pɛn/ **1** *nf* (a) sorrow, grief; **avoir de la ~** to feel sad; **faire de la ~ à qn** ⟨*person*⟩ to hurt sb; ⟨*event, remark*⟩ to upset sb
(b) effort, trouble; **c'est ~ perdue** it's a waste of effort; **il n'est pas au bout de ses ~s** his troubles are far from over; he's still got a long way to go; **ce n'est pas la ~ de crier** there's no need to shout; **pour ta ~** for your trouble
(c) difficulty; **sans ~** easily; **avec ~** with difficulty
(d) (Law) penalty, sentence; **~ de prison** prison sentence; **'défense de fumer sous ~ d'amende'** 'no smoking, offenders will be fined'
2 **à peine** *phr* hardly; **il était à ~ arrivé qu'il pensait déjà à repartir** no sooner had he arrived than he was thinking of leaving again
■ **~ capitale** capital punishment; **~ de cœur** heartache; **~ de mort** death penalty

peiner /pene/ [1] **1** *vtr* to sadden, to upset
2 *vi* ⟨*person*⟩ to struggle; ⟨*car*⟩ to labour (GB)

peint, ~e /pɛ̃, ɛ̃t/ ▶ PEINDRE

peintre /pɛ̃tʀ/ *nm* painter

peinture /pɛ̃tyʀ/ *nf* (a) paint
(b) paintwork
(c) painting; **je ne peux pas le voir en ~** (colloq) I can't stand the sight of him
(d) portrayal

peinturlurer /pɛ̃tyʀlyʀe/ [1] *vtr* to daub

péjoratif, -ive /peʒɔʀatif, iv/ *adj* pejorative

Pékin /pekɛ̃/ *pr n* Beijing, Peking

PEL /peɛl/ *nm*: *abbr* ▶ PLAN

pelage /pəlaʒ/ *nm* coat, fur

pelé, ~e /pəle/ *adj* ⟨*animal*⟩ mangy; ⟨*hill*⟩ bare

pêle-mêle /pɛlmɛl/ *adv* higgledy-piggledy

peler /pəle/ [17] **1** *vtr* to peel
2 *vi* (a) ⟨*skin, nose*⟩ to peel
(b) (colloq) **~ (de froid)** to freeze

pèlerin /pɛlʀɛ̃/ *nm* pilgrim

pèlerinage /pɛlʀinaʒ/ *nm* pilgrimage

pélican /pelikɑ̃/ *nm* pelican

pelisse /pəlis/ *nf* fur-trimmed coat, pelisse

pelle /pɛl/ *nf* shovel; spade; **à la ~** (colloq) by the dozen.
■ **~ à tarte** cake slice

pelleteuse /pɛltøz/ *nf* mechanical digger

pellicule /pelikyl/ **1** *nf* film
2 **pellicules** *nf pl* dandruff

pelote /p(ə)lɔt/ *nf* (of wool) ball

peloton /p(ə)lɔtɔ̃/ *nm* (a) platoon; **~ d'exécution** firing squad
(b) (in cycling) pack; **dans le ~ de tête** in the leading pack

pelotonner: se pelotonner /p(ə)lɔtɔne/ [1] *v refl* (+ *v être*) (a) to snuggle up
(b) to huddle up

pelouse /p(ə)luz/ *nf* lawn; **'~ interdite'** 'keep off the grass'

peluche /p(ə)lyʃ/ *nf* (a) plush; **jouet en ~** cuddly toy (GB), stuffed animal (US)
(b) fluff

pelucher /p(ə)lyʃe/ [1] *vi* to become fluffy

pelure /p(ə)lyʀ/ *nf* (of vegetable, fruit) peel; (of onion) skin

pelvis /pɛlvis/ *nm inv* pelvis

pénal, ~e, *mpl* **-aux** /penal, o/ *adj* criminal

pénaliser /penalize/ [1] *vtr* to penalize

pénalité /penalite/ *nf* penalty

penaud, ~e /pəno, od/ *adj* sheepish

penchant /pɑ̃ʃɑ̃/ *nm* (a) fondness
(b) weakness
(c) tendency

penché, ~e /pɑ̃ʃe/ **1** *pp* ▶ PENCHER
2 *pp adj* ⟨*tree*⟩ leaning; ⟨*writing*⟩ slanting

pencher /pɑ̃ʃe/ [1] **1** *vtr* to tilt; to tip [sth] up; **~ la tête en avant** to bend one's head forward(s)
2 *vi* (a) ⟨*tower, tree*⟩ to lean; ⟨*boat*⟩ to list; ⟨*picture*⟩ to slant
(b) **~ pour** to incline toward(s) ⟨*theory*⟩; to be in favour (GB) of ⟨*solution*⟩
3 **se pencher** *v refl* (+ *v être*) (a) to lean
(b) to bend down
(c) **se ~ sur** to look into ⟨*problem*⟩

pendable /pɑ̃dabl/ *adj* **jouer un tour ~ à qn** to play a rotten trick on sb

pendaison /pɑ̃dɛzɔ̃/ *nf* hanging

pendant /pɑ̃dɑ̃/ **1** *prep* for; **je t'ai attendu ~ des heures** I waited for you for hours; **~ combien de temps avez-vous vécu à Versailles?** how long did you live in Versailles?; **il a été malade ~ tout le trajet** he was sick throughout the journey; **~ ce temps(-là)** meanwhile
2 **pendant que** *phr* while

pendeloque /pɑ̃dlɔk/ *nf* pendant, drop (on earring)

pendentif /pɑ̃dɑ̃tif/ *nm* pendant

penderie /pɑ̃dʀi/ *nf* (a) wardrobe
(b) walk-in cupboard (GB) *or* closet

pendouiller /pɑ̃duje/ [1] *vi* (colloq) to dangle down

pendre /pɑ̃dʀ/ [6] **1** *vtr* (a) to hang ⟨*person*⟩
(b) to hang ⟨*picture, curtains*⟩; to hang up ⟨*clothes*⟩
2 *vi* (a) ⟨*object, clothes*⟩ to hang; ⟨*arms, legs*⟩ to dangle
(b) ⟨*strips, lock of hair*⟩ to hang down; ⟨*cheek, breasts*⟩ to sag
3 **se pendre** *v refl* (+ *v être*) (a) to hang oneself

(b) se ~ à to hang from ⟨*branch*⟩; **se ~ au cou de qn** to throw one's arms around sb's neck
IDIOMS ça te pend au nez (colloq) you've got it coming to you

pendu, ~e /pɑ̃dy/ **1** *pp* ▶ PENDRE
2 *pp adj* **(a)** ⟨*person*⟩ hanged
(b) ⟨*object*⟩ hung, hanging; **être ~ aux lèvres de qn** to hang on sb's every word; **être toujours ~ au téléphone** to spend all one's time on the telephone
3 *nm,f* hanged man/woman

pendulaire /pɑ̃dylɛʀ/ *adj* pendular

pendule¹ /pɑ̃dyl/ *nm* pendulum

pendule² /pɑ̃dyl/ *nf* clock
IDIOMS remettre les ~s à l'heure to set the record straight

pénétrant, ~e /penetʀɑ̃, ɑ̃t/ *adj* ⟨*wind*⟩ penetrating; ⟨*cold*⟩ piercing; ⟨*comment*⟩ shrewd; ⟨*mind, look*⟩ penetrating

pénétration /penetʀasjɔ̃/ *nf* penetration

pénétré, ~e /penetʀe/ **1** *pp* ▶ PÉNÉTRER
2 *pp adj* earnest, intense; **être ~ de** to be imbued with ⟨*feeling*⟩

pénétrer /penetʀe/ [14] **1** *vtr* **(a)** ⟨*rain*⟩ to soak *or* seep into ⟨*ground*⟩; ⟨*sun*⟩ to penetrate ⟨*foliage*⟩
(b) to fathom ⟨*secret, thoughts*⟩
(c) to penetrate
(d) ⟨*idea, fashion*⟩ to reach ⟨*group*⟩
2 *vi* **~ dans** to enter, to get into; to penetrate; **faire ~ la pommade en massant doucement** rub the ointment into your skin

pénible /penibl/ *adj* ⟨*effort*⟩ painful; ⟨*work*⟩ hard; ⟨*journey*⟩ difficult; ⟨*person*⟩ tiresome

péniblement /peniblǝmɑ̃/ *adv* ⟨*walk*⟩ with difficulty; ⟨*reach*⟩ barely

péniche /peniʃ/ *nf* barge

pénicilline /penisilin/ *nf* penicillin

péninsulaire /penɛ̃sylɛʀ/ *adj* peninsular

péninsule /penɛ̃syl/ *nf* peninsula

pénis /penis/ *nm inv* penis

pénitence /penitɑ̃s/ *nf* **(a)** penance
(b) punishment

pénitencier /penitɑ̃sje/ *nm* prison

pénitentiaire /penitɑ̃sjɛʀ/ *adj* ⟨*institution*⟩ penal; ⟨*regime*⟩ prison

pénombre /penɔ̃bʀ/ *nf* half-light

pensable /pɑ̃sabl/ *adj* thinkable; **ce n'est pas ~** it's unthinkable

pense-bête, *pl* **pense-bêtes** /pɑ̃sbɛt/ *nm* reminder

pensée /pɑ̃se/ *nf* **(a)** thought; **être perdu dans ses ~s** to be lost in thought
(b) mind; **nous serons avec vous par la ~** we'll be with you in spirit
(c) thinking
(d) (Bot) pansy

penser /pɑ̃se/ [1] **1** *vtr* **(a)** to think; **~ du bien de qn** to think well of sb; **je n'en pense rien** I have no opinion about it; **c'est bien ce que je pensais!** I thought as much!; **tu penses vraiment ce que tu dis?** do you

really mean what you're saying?; **tout porte à ~ que** there's every indication that; **vous pensez si j'étais content!** you can imagine how pleased I was!; **'il s'est excusé?'— 'penses-tu!'** 'did he apologize?'—'you must be joking!'
(b) ça me fait ~ qu'il faut que je leur écrive that reminds me that I must write to them
(c) ~ faire to be thinking of doing, to intend to do
(d) to think [sth] up ⟨*plan, device*⟩
2 penser à *v+prep* **(a) ~ à** to think of, to think about; **ne pensez plus à rien** empty your mind; **sans ~ à mal** without meaning any harm; **tu n'y penses pas!** you can't be serious!; **n'y pensons plus!** let's forget about it!
(b) ~ à to remember; **il me fait ~ à mon père** he reminds me of my father
(c) ~ à faire to be thinking of doing
3 *vi* to think; **je lui ai dit ma façon de ~!** I gave him/her a piece of my mind!; **~ tout haut** to think out loud

penseur /pɑ̃sœʀ/ *nm* thinker

pensif, -ive /pɑ̃sif, iv/ *adj* pensive, thoughtful

pension /pɑ̃sjɔ̃/ *nf* **(a)** pension
(b) boarding house
(c) boarding school
■ **~ alimentaire** alimony; **~ complète** full board; **~ de famille** family hotel

pensionnaire /pɑ̃sjɔnɛʀ/ *nmf* **(a)** (in hotel) resident
(b) (in prison) inmate
(c) (Sch) boarder

pensionnat /pɑ̃sjɔna/ *nm* boarding school

pensionné, ~e /pɑ̃sjɔne/ *nm,f* pensioner

pensivement /pɑ̃sivmɑ̃/ *adv* pensively

pentagone /pɛ̃tagɔn/ *nm* pentagon

pente /pɑ̃t/ *nf* slope; **toit en ~** sloping roof
IDIOMS être sur la mauvaise ~ ⟨*person*⟩ to be going astray; ⟨*company*⟩ to be going downhill; **remonter la ~** to get back on one's feet

Pentecôte /pɑ̃tkot/ *nf* Pentecost; **à la ~** at Whitsun

pénurie /penyʀi/ *nf* shortage

pépé /pepe/ *nm* (colloq) **(a)** grandpa (colloq)
(b) old man

pépère /pepɛʀ/ *adj* (colloq) ⟨*life*⟩ cushy (colloq); ⟨*place*⟩ nice

pépin /pepɛ̃/ *nm* **(a)** pip; **sans ~s** seedless
(b) (colloq) slight problem
(c) (colloq) umbrella

pépinière /pepinjɛʀ/ *nf* (for trees, plants) nursery

pépite /pepit/ *nf* nugget

péquenaud, ~e /pɛkno, od/ *nm,f* (colloq) country bumpkin (colloq)

perçant, ~e /pɛʀsɑ̃, ɑ̃t/ *adj* **(a)** ⟨*cry, voice*⟩ shrill; ⟨*gaze*⟩ piercing
(b) ⟨*vision*⟩ sharp

percée /pɛʀse/ *nf* **(a)** opening ····⊹

p

(b) breakthrough

perce-neige /pɛʁsənɛʒ/ *nm inv or nf inv* snowdrop

perce-oreille, *pl* ~**s** /pɛʁsɔʁɛj/ *nm* earwig

percepteur /pɛʁsɛptœʁ/ *nm* tax inspector

perceptible /pɛʁsɛptibl/ *adj* (a) ⟨sound⟩ perceptible
(b) ⟨tax⟩ payable

perception /pɛʁsɛpsjɔ̃/ *nf* (a) tax office
(b) perception

percer /pɛʁse/ [12] **1** *vtr* (a) to pierce ⟨body, surface⟩; to burst ⟨abscess, eardrum⟩
(b) to make ⟨door⟩; to bore ⟨tunnel⟩; to build ⟨road⟩; ~ un trou dans to make a hole in
(c) to pierce ⟨silence, air⟩; to break through ⟨clouds⟩
(d) to penetrate ⟨secret⟩; ~ qn à jour to see through sb
(e) ~ ses dents to be teething
2 *vi* (a) ⟨sun⟩ to break through; ⟨plant⟩ to come up; ⟨tooth⟩ to come through
(b) (Mil, Sport) to break through
(c) ⟨actor⟩ to become known

perceuse /pɛʁsøz/ *nf* drill

percevable /pɛʁsəvabl/ *adj* ⟨tax⟩ payable

percevoir /pɛʁsəvwaʁ/ [5] *vtr* (a) to collect ⟨tax⟩; to receive ⟨rent⟩
(b) to perceive ⟨change⟩; to feel ⟨vibration⟩; être perçu comme to be seen as

perche /pɛʁʃ/ *nf* (a) (gen) pole; (of ski tow) T-bar; (for microphone) boom
(b) (colloq) (grande) ~ beanpole (colloq)
(c) (Zool) perch
IDIOMS tendre la ~ à qn to throw sb a line

perché, ~**e** /pɛʁʃe/ *pp adj* perched; voix haut ~e high-pitched voice; ma valise est ~e en haut de l'armoire my suitcase is on top of the wardrobe

percher /pɛʁʃe/ [1] **1** *vtr* ~ qch sur une étagère to stick sth up on a shelf
2 *vi* to perch; to roost
3 se percher *v refl* (+ *v être*) to perch

perchoir /pɛʁʃwaʁ/ *nm* (a) perch
(b) (Pol) (colloq) Speaker's Chair

perclus, ~**e** /pɛʁkly, yz/ *adj* crippled

percolateur /pɛʁkɔlatœʁ/ *nm* (espresso) coffee machine

percussions /pɛʁkysjɔ̃/ *nf pl* les ~ percussion instruments; percussion section; drums

percutant, ~**e** /pɛʁkytɑ̃, ɑ̃t/ *adj* ⟨criticism⟩ hard-hitting; ⟨slogan⟩ punchy (colloq)

percuter /pɛʁkyte/ [1] **1** *vtr* ⟨car, driver⟩ to hit
2 *vi* ~ contre ⟨vehicle⟩ to crash into; ⟨shell⟩ to explode against
3 se percuter *v refl* (+ *v être*) to collide

perdant, ~**e** /pɛʁdɑ̃, ɑ̃t/ **1** *adj* losing; être ~ to have lost out
2 *nm,f* loser

perdition /pɛʁdisjɔ̃/ *nf* (a) lieu de ~ den of iniquity

(b) en ~ ⟨ship⟩ in distress

perdre /pɛʁdʁ/ [6] **1** *vtr* (a) to lose; ~ de vue to lose sight of; leurs actions ont perdu 9% their shares have dropped 9%
(b) to shed ⟨leaves, flowers⟩
(c) to miss ⟨chance⟩
(d) to waste ⟨day, years⟩; perdre son temps to waste one's time
(e) je perds mes chaussures my shoes are too big; je perds mon pantalon my trousers are falling down
(f) to bring [sb] down; cet homme te perdra that man will be your undoing
2 *vi* to lose; j'y perds I lose out
3 se perdre *v refl* (+ *v être*) (a) to get lost; se ~ dans ses pensées to be lost in thought
(b) ⟨tradition⟩ to die out
IDIOMS ~ la raison *or* l'esprit to go out of one's mind

perdrix /pɛʁdʁi/ *nf inv* partridge

perdu, ~**e** /pɛʁdy/ **1** *pp* ▶ PERDRE
2 *pp adj* (a) lost; chien ~ stray dog; balle ~e stray bullet; c'est ~ d'avance it's hopeless
(b) ⟨day, opportunity⟩ wasted; c'est du temps ~ it's a waste of time
(c) ⟨harvest⟩ ruined; il est ~ there's no hope for him
(d) ⟨person⟩ lost
3 *adj* remote, isolated
IDIOMS se lancer à corps ~ dans to throw oneself headlong into; ce n'est pas ~ pour tout le monde somebody will do all right out of it

père /pɛʁ/ *nm* father; Dupont ~ Dupont senior; le ~ Dupont (colloq) old Dupont (colloq)
■ le ~ Noël Santa Claus

péremption /peʁɑ̃psjɔ̃/ *nf* date de ~ use-by date

péremptoire /peʁɑ̃ptwaʁ/ *adj* peremptory

perfection /pɛʁfɛksjɔ̃/ *nf* perfection

perfectionnement /pɛʁfɛksjɔnmɑ̃/ *nm* improvement

perfectionner /pɛʁfɛksjɔne/ [1] **1** *vtr* to perfect ⟨technique⟩; to refine ⟨art⟩
2 se perfectionner *v refl* (+ *v être*) to improve

perfectionniste /pɛʁfɛksjɔnist/ *adj, nmf* perfectionist

perfide /pɛʁfid/ *adj* perfidious, treacherous

perfidie /pɛʁfidi/ *nf* perfidy, treachery

perforation /pɛʁfɔʁasjɔ̃/ *nf* perforation

perforer /pɛʁfɔʁe/ [1] *vtr* (a) to pierce; to perforate
(b) to punch; carte perforée punch card

performance /pɛʁfɔʁmɑ̃s/ *nf* (a) result, performance
(b) achievement

performant, ~**e** /pɛʁfɔʁmɑ̃, ɑ̃t/ *adj* ⟨car, equipment⟩ high-performance; ⟨person, techniques⟩ efficient; ⟨company⟩ competitive

perfusion /pɛʁfyzjɔ̃/ *nm* (Med) drip (GB), IV (US)

péricliter /peʁiklite/ [1] *vi* to be going downhill

péridurale /peʀidyʀal/ nf epidural

péril /peʀil/ nm peril, danger; **à ses risques et ~s** at his/her own risk; **il n'y a pas ~ en la demeure** what's the hurry?

périlleux, -euse /peʀijø, øz/ adj perilous

périmé, ~e /peʀime/ adj (a) out-of-date; **son passeport est ~** his/her passport has expired
(b) ⟨idea, custom⟩ outdated

périmètre /peʀimɛtʀ/ nm (a) perimeter
(b) area

périnée /peʀine/ nm perineum

période /peʀjɔd/ nf period; era

périodique /peʀjɔdik/ **1** adj (a) ⟨fever⟩ recurring
(b) **serviette ~** sanitary towel (GB), sanitary napkin (US)
2 nm periodical

péripétie /peʀipesi/ nf (a) incident
(b) event
(c) adventure
(d) **les ~s d'une intrigue** the twists and turns of a plot

périphérie /peʀifeʀi/ nf periphery

périphérique /peʀifeʀik/ **1** adj (gen) peripheral; ⟨area⟩ outlying; **radio ~** broadcasting station situated outside the territory to which it transmits
2 nm ring road (GB), beltway (US)

périphrase /peʀifʀɑz/ nf circumlocution

périple /peʀipl/ nm journey; voyage

périr /peʀiʀ/ [3] vi to die, to perish

périscolaire /peʀiskɔlɛʀ/ adj extracurricular

périscope /peʀiskɔp/ nm periscope

périssable /peʀisabl/ adj perishable

Péritel® /peʀitɛl/ nf **prise ~** scart socket; scart plug

perle /pɛʀl/ nf (a) pearl; **~ fine** real pearl
(b) (figurative) gem; **~ rare** real treasure
(c) (colloq) howler (colloq)

perler /pɛʀle/ [1] vi ⟨drop, tear⟩ to appear

permanence /pɛʀmanɑ̃s/ **1** nf
(a) permanence
(b) persistence
(c) **~ téléphonique** manned line; **assurer or tenir une ~** to be on duty; to hold a surgery (GB), to have office hours (US)
(d) permanently manned office
(e) (Sch) (private) study room (GB), study hall (US)
2 **en permanence** phr (a) permanently
(b) constantly

permanent, ~e¹ /pɛʀmanɑ̃, ɑ̃t/ adj
(a) ⟨staff, exhibition⟩ permanent; ⟨committee⟩ standing
(b) ⟨tension, danger⟩ constant; ⟨show⟩ continuous

permanente² /pɛʀmanɑ̃t/ nf perm

perméable /pɛʀmeabl/ adj permeable

permettre /pɛʀmɛtʀ/ [60] **1** vtr (a) **~ à qn de faire** to allow sb to do, to give sb permission to do; **(vous) permettez! j'étais là**

avant! excuse me! I was here first!; **il est menteur comme c'est pas permis** (colloq) he's an incredible liar
(b) **~ à qn de faire** to allow or enable sb to do, to give sb the opportunity to do; **leurs moyens ne le leur permettent pas** they can't afford it; **autant qu'il est permis d'en juger** as far as one can tell
2 **se permettre** v refl (+ v être) (a) **je peux me ~ ce genre de plaisanterie avec lui** I can get away with telling him that kind of joke; **se ~ de faire** to take the liberty of doing
(b) **je ne peux pas me ~ d'acheter une nouvelle voiture** I can't afford to buy a new car

permis, ~e /pɛʀmi, iz/ **1** pp ▸ PERMETTRE
2 pp adj permitted
3 nm inv permit, licence (GB)
■ **~ de conduire** driver's licence (GB); driving test; **~ de séjour** residence permit; **~ de travail** work permit

permission /pɛʀmisjɔ̃/ nf (a) permission
(b) (Mil) leave; **partir en ~** to go on leave

permutable /pɛʀmytabl/ adj interchangeable

permuter /pɛʀmyte/ [1] vtr to switch [sth] around ⟨letters, labels⟩

pernicieux, -ieuse /pɛʀnisjø, øz/ adj pernicious

Pérou /peʀu/ pr nm Peru
IDIOMS **ce n'est pas le ~** it's not a fortune

perpendiculaire /pɛʀpɑ̃dikylɛʀ/ adj, nf perpendicular

perpète /pɛʀpɛt/ nf (colloq) **être condamné à ~** (prisoners' slang) to get life (colloq); **habiter à ~** to live miles away

perpétrer /pɛʀpetʀe/ [14] vtr to perpetrate

perpétuel, -elle /pɛʀpetɥɛl/ adj perpetual

perpétuellement /pɛʀpetɥɛlmɑ̃/ adv constantly, perpetually

perpétuer /pɛʀpetɥe/ [1] vtr to perpetuate

perpétuité /pɛʀpetɥite/ nf perpetuity; **à ~** (Law) ⟨imprisonment⟩ life

perplexe /pɛʀplɛks/ adj perplexed, baffled

perplexité /pɛʀplɛksite/ nf perplexity

perquisition /pɛʀkizisjɔ̃/ nf search

perquisitionner /pɛʀkizisjɔne/ [1] vtr to search ⟨house⟩

perron /peʀɔ̃/ nm flight of steps

perroquet /peʀɔkɛ/ nm parrot

perruche /peʀyʃ/ nf budgerigar (GB), parakeet (US)

perruque /peʀyk/ nf wig

persan, ~e /pɛʀsɑ̃, an/ adj Persian

perse /pɛʀs/ adj Persian

persécuter /pɛʀsekyte/ [1] vtr to persecute

persécution /pɛʀsekysjɔ̃/ nf persecution

persévérance /pɛʀseveʀɑ̃s/ nf perseverance

p

persévérer /pɛʀseveʀe/ [14] vi (a) to
persevere
(b) to persist
persienne /pɛʀsjɛn/ nf (louvred (GB))
shutter
persiflage /pɛʀsiflaʒ/ nm mockery
persifleur, -euse /pɛʀsiflœʀ, øz/ adj
⟨tone, comment⟩ mocking
persil /pɛʀsi(l)/ nm parsley
persistance /pɛʀsistɑ̃s/ nf persistence
persistant, ~e /pɛʀsistɑ̃, ɑ̃t/ adj ⟨heat,
problem⟩ continuing; ⟨smell, snow⟩ lingering;
⟨cough, symptom⟩ persistent
persister /pɛʀsiste/ [1] vi ⟨symptom, pain⟩
to persist; ⟨inflation⟩ to continue; je persiste
à croire que I still think that
personnage /pɛʀsɔnaʒ/ nm (a) character
(b) figure; un ~ public a public figure
personnaliser /pɛʀsɔnalize/ [1] vtr to
add a personal touch to
personnalité /pɛʀsɔnalite/ nf
(a) personality
(b) important person
personne¹ /pɛʀsɔn/ pron anyone,
anybody; no-one, nobody; ~ n'est parfait
nobody's perfect
personne² /pɛʀsɔn/ nf person; dix ~s ten
people; les ~s âgées the elderly; bien fait de
sa ~ good-looking; le respect de la ~ respect
for the individual; il s'en occupe en ~ he's
dealing with it personally; c'est la cupidité
en ~ he/she is greed personified
■ ~ à charge dependant; ~ civile or morale
artificial person, legal entity
personnel, -elle /pɛʀsɔnɛl/ [1] adj
(a) ⟨friend, effects⟩ personal; ⟨papers⟩ private
(b) individual
(c) selfish
(d) ⟨pronoun⟩ personal
[2] nm staff; workforce; employees, personnel
personnellement /pɛʀsɔnɛlmɑ̃/ adv
personally
personnifier /pɛʀsɔnifje/ [2] vtr to
personify
perspective /pɛʀspɛktiv/ nf (a) (in art)
perspective
(b) view
(c) perspective, angle
(d) prospect
perspicace /pɛʀspikas/ adj perceptive
perspicacité /pɛʀspikasite/ nf insight,
perspicacity
persuader /pɛʀsɥade/ [1] vtr to persuade
persuasif, -ive /pɛʀsɥazif, iv/ adj
persuasive
persuasion /pɛʀsɥazjɔ̃/ nf persuasion
perte /pɛʀt/ nf (a) loss; à ~ de vue as far as
the eye can see
(b) waste
(c) ruin; courir or aller à sa ~ to be heading
for a fall
pertinemment /pɛʀtinamɑ̃/ adv
(a) perfectly well
(b) pertinently

pertinence /pɛʀtinɑ̃s/ nf pertinence
pertinent, ~e /pɛʀtinɑ̃, ɑ̃t/ adj pertinent
perturbant, ~e /pɛʀtyʀbɑ̃, ɑ̃t/ adj
disturbing
perturbation /pɛʀtyʀbasjɔ̃/ nf
(a) disruption
(b) disturbance
(c) upheaval
perturber /pɛʀtyʀbe/ [1] vtr to disrupt
⟨traffic, market, meeting⟩; to interfere with
⟨development⟩; to disturb ⟨sleep⟩
pervenche /pɛʀvɑ̃ʃ/ nf (a) periwinkle
(b) (colloq) (female) traffic warden (GB),
meter maid (US) (colloq)
pervers, ~e /pɛʀvɛʀ, ɛʀs/ [1] adj
(a) wicked
(b) perverted
(c) ⟨effect⟩ pernicious
[2] nm,f pervert
perversion /pɛʀvɛʀsjɔ̃/ nf perversion
perversité /pɛʀvɛʀsite/ nf perversity
pervertir /pɛʀvɛʀtiʀ/ [3] vtr to corrupt
pesant, ~e /pəzɑ̃, ɑ̃t/ adj (a) heavy
(b) cumbersome
(c) ⟨atmosphere, silence⟩ oppressive
IDIOMS valoir son ~ d'or to be worth its
weight in gold
pesanteur /pəzɑ̃tœʀ/ nf (a) (of style)
heaviness; (of bureaucracy) inertia
(b) gravity
pèse-personne, pl ~s /pɛzpɛʀsɔn/ nm
bathroom scales
peser /pəze/ [16] [1] vtr (a) to weigh
(b) to weigh up; ~ ses mots to choose one's
words carefully; tout bien pesé all things
considered
[2] vi (a) to weigh; je pèse 70 kg I weigh 70
kg; ~ lourd to weigh a lot
(b) to carry weight; ~ dans/sur une décision
to have a decisive influence in/on a decision
(c) ~ sur ⟨suspicion⟩ to hang over ⟨person⟩
(d) ⟨tax, debts⟩ to weigh [sb/sth] down
⟨person, country⟩
(e) ⟨person, decision⟩ to influence (greatly)
⟨policy⟩
peseta /pezeta/ nf peseta
pessimisme /pesimism/ nm pessimism
pessimiste /pesimist/ [1] adj pessimistic
[2] nmf pessimist
peste /pɛst/ nf (a) plague
(b) (colloq) pest (colloq)
IDIOMS je me méfie de lui comme de la ~
(colloq) I don't trust him an inch
pester /pɛste/ [1] vi ~ contre qn/qch to
curse sb/sth
pesticide /pɛstisid/ nm pesticide
pet /pɛ/ nm (colloq) fart (colloq)
pétale /petal/ nm petal
pétanque /petɑ̃k/ nf petanque
pétarader /petaʀade/ [1] vi to backfire
pétard /petaʀ/ nm banger (GB), firecracker
(US); être en ~ (colloq) to be hopping mad
(GB) (colloq), to be real mad (US) (colloq)
péter /pete/ [14] vi (a) (slang) to fart (colloq)

(b) (colloq) ⟨*balloon*⟩ to burst; ⟨*situation*⟩ to blow up; ⟨*thread*⟩ to snap

pétillant, ∼e /petijɑ̃, ɑ̃t/ *adj* sparkling

pétiller /petije/ [1] *vi* ⟨*drink*⟩ to fizz; ⟨*firewood*⟩ to crackle; ⟨*eyes*⟩ to sparkle

petit, ∼e /p(ə)ti, it/ **1** *adj* **(a)** small, little; short; **une toute ∼e pièce** a tiny room; **se faire tout ∼** (figurative) to try to make oneself inconspicuous

(b) ⟨*walk, distance*⟩ short

(c) young, little; **c'est notre ∼ dernier** he's our youngest

(d) ⟨*eater*⟩ light; ⟨*wage*⟩ low; ⟨*cry, worry*⟩ little; ⟨*hope*⟩ slight; ⟨*detail, defect*⟩ minor; ⟨*job*⟩ modest

(e) **une ∼e trentaine de personnes** under thirty people

2 *adv* **tailler ∼** to be small-fitting; **∼ à ∼** little by little

■ **∼ ami** boyfriend; **∼ bois** kindling; **∼ coin** (colloq) (euphemistic) loo (GB) (colloq), bathroom (US); **∼ déjeuner** breakfast; **∼ noir** (colloq) coffee; **∼ nom** (colloq) first name; **∼ pois** (garden) pea, petit pois; **∼ pot** jar of baby food; **∼ rat (de l'Opéra)** pupil at Paris Opéra's ballet school; **∼ salé** streaky salted pork; **∼e amie** girlfriend; **∼e annonce** classified advertisement; **∼e nature** weakling; **∼e reine** cycling; **∼e voiture** toy car; **∼s chevaux** ≈ ludo

petit-beurre, *pl* **petits-beurre** /p(ə)tibœʀ/ *nm* petit beurre biscuit

petit-cousin, petite-cousine, *mpl* **petits-cousins** /p(ə)tikuzɛ̃, p(ə)titkuzin/ *nm,f* second cousin

petite-fille, *pl* **petites-filles** /p(ə)titfij/ *nf* granddaughter

petitesse /p(ə)tites/ *nf* **(a)** pettiness **(b)** small size

petit-fils, *pl* **petits-fils** /p(ə)tifis/ *nm* grandson

pétition /petisjɔ̃/ *nf* petition

petit-lait /p(ə)tilɛ/ *nm* **ça se boit comme du ∼!** (colloq) it slips down nicely!

petit-nègre /p(ə)tinɛgʀ/ *nm inv* (colloq) pidgin French

petits-enfants /p(ə)tizɑ̃fɑ̃/ *nm pl* grandchildren

pétrifiant, ∼e /petʀifjɑ̃, ɑ̃t/ *adj* petrifying

pétrifier /petʀifje/ [2] *vtr* **(a)** to petrify **(b)** (figurative) to transfix

pétrin /petʀɛ̃/ *nm* dough trough

IDIOMS **être dans le ∼** to be in a fix (colloq)

pétrir /petʀiʀ/ [3] *vtr* **(a)** to knead ⟨*dough*⟩ **(b)** to mould (GB), to mold (US) ⟨*personality*⟩

pétrole /petʀɔl/ *nm* oil, petroleum

pétrolette /petʀɔlɛt/ *nf* (colloq) moped

pétrolier, -ière /petʀɔlje, ɛʀ/ **1** *adj* oil **2** *nm* oil tanker

pétulant, ∼e /petylɑ̃, ɑ̃t/ *adj* exuberant

peu /pø/

■ Note See the entries *avant, depuis, d'ici* and *sous* for the use of *peu* with these words.

1 *adv* **(a)** not much; **il parle ∼** he doesn't talk much; **elle gagne très ∼** she earns very little; **deux semaines c'est trop ∼** two weeks isn't long enough; **si ∼ que ce soit** however little; **très ∼ pour moi!** (colloq) thanks, but no thanks!

(b) not very; **assez ∼ connu** little-known; **elle n'est pas ∼ fière** she's more than a little proud

2 *pron* few, not many

3 **de peu** *phr* only just

4 **peu de** *quantif* **∼ de mots** few words; **∼ de temps** little time

5 *nm* **le ∼ de** the little ⟨*trust, freedom*⟩; the few ⟨*books, friends*⟩; the lack of ⟨*interest*⟩

6 **un peu** *phr* **(a)** a little, a bit; **reste encore un ∼** stay a little longer; **parle un ∼ plus fort** speak a little louder; **un ∼ plus de** a few more ⟨*books*⟩; a little more ⟨*time*⟩; **un ∼ beaucoup** more than a bit

(b) just; **répète un ∼ pour voir!** (colloq) you just try saying that again!; **pour un ∼ ils se seraient battus** they very nearly had a fight

7 **peu à peu** *phr* gradually, little by little

8 **pour peu que** *phr* if; **pour ∼ qu'il ait bu, il va nous raconter sa vie** one drink, and he'll tell us his life story

peuplade /pœplad/ *nf* small tribe

peuple /pœpl/ *nm* people

peuplement /pœpləmɑ̃/ *nm* population

peupler /pœple/ [1] **1** *vtr* **(a)** to populate ⟨*country*⟩; to stock ⟨*forest, pond*⟩

(b) ⟨*animals, plants*⟩ to colonize ⟨*region*⟩; ⟨*students*⟩ to fill ⟨*street*⟩

2 **se peupler** *v refl* (+ *v être*) to fill up

peuplier /pøplije/ *nm* poplar

peur /pœʀ/ *nf* fear; fright; scare; **être mort or vert** (colloq) **de ∼** to be scared to death; **une ∼ panique s'empara de lui** he was panic-stricken; **avoir ∼** to be afraid; **j'en ai bien ∼** I'm afraid so; **faire ∼ à qn** to frighten sb; **maigre à faire ∼** terribly thin

peureusement /pœʀøzmɑ̃/ *adv* fearfully

peureux, -euse /pœʀø, øz/ *adj* fearful

peut-être /pøtɛtʀ/ *adv* perhaps, maybe

phalange /falɑ̃ʒ/ *nf* phalanx

phallocrate /falɔkʀat/ *nm* male chauvinist

phalloïde /falɔid/ *adj* **amanite ∼** death cap

phallus /falys/ *nm inv* phallus

pharaon /faʀaɔ̃/ *nm* pharaoh

phare /faʀ/ *nm* **(a)** headlight **(b)** lighthouse

pharmacie /faʀmasi/ *nf* **(a)** chemist's (shop) (GB), drugstore (US), pharmacy **(b)** medicine cabinet **(c)** (science) pharmacy

pharmacien, -ienne /faʀmasjɛ̃, ɛn/ *nm,f* (dispensing) chemist (GB), pharmacist

pharyngite /faʀɛ̃ʒit/ *nf* pharyngitis

p

pharynx /faʀɛ̃ks/ nm inv pharynx
phase /faz/ nf (a) stage
  (b) phase
phénoménal, ~e, mpl -aux
/fenɔmenal, o/ adj phenomenal
phénomène /fenɔmɛn/ nm
  (a) phenomenon
  (b) (colloq) **c'est un ~** he/she's quite a
character
philanthropie /filɑ̃tʀɔpi/ nf philanthropy
philatélie /filateli/ nf stamp collecting
philatéliste /filatelist/ nmf philatelist
philosophe /filɔzɔf/ nmf philosopher
philosophie /filɔzɔfi/ nf philosophy
philosophique /filɔzɔfik/ adj
philosophical
phobie /fɔbi/ nf phobia
phonétique /fɔnetik/ **1** adj phonetic
  2 nf phonetics
phonographe /fɔnɔgʀaf/ nm gramophone
(GB), phonograph (US)
phoque /fɔk/ nm (a) seal
  (b) sealskin
phosphate /fɔsfat/ nm phosphate
phosphore /fɔsfɔʀ/ nm phosphorus
phosphorescent, ~e /fɔsfɔʀesɑ̃, ɑ̃t/
adj phosphorescent
photo /fɔto/ nf (a) photography
  (b) photo
  ■ ~ **d'identité** passport photo
photocomposition /fɔtokɔ̃pozisjɔ̃/ nf
filmsetting (GB), photocomposition (US)
photocopie /fɔtokɔpi/ nf photocopy
photocopier /fɔtokɔpje/ [2] vtr to
photocopy
photocopieur /fɔtokɔpjœʀ/ nm
photocopier
photocopieuse /fɔtokɔpjøz/ nf
photocopier
photogénique /fɔtoʒenik/ adj photogenic
photographe /fɔtogʀaf/ nmf
photographer
photographie /fɔtogʀafi/ nf
  (a) photography
  (b) photograph, picture
photographier /fɔtogʀafje/ [2] vtr to
photograph, to take a photo of
photographique /fɔtogʀafik/ adj
photographic
photomaton® /fɔtomatɔ̃/ nm photo booth
photosynthèse /fɔtosɛ̃tez/ nf
photosynthesis
photothèque /fɔtotɛk/ nf picture library
phrase /fʀɑz/ nf (a) sentence
  (b) phrase; **avoir une ~ malheureuse** to say
the wrong thing; **~ toute faite** stock phrase
  (c) (Mus) phrase
phréatique /fʀeatik/ adj **nappe ~** ground
water
physicien, **-ienne** /fizisjɛ̃, ɛn/ nm,f
physicist
physiologie /fizjɔlɔʒi/ nf physiology

physiologique /fizjɔlɔʒik/ adj
physiological
physionomie /fizjɔnɔmi/ nf (a) face
  (b) (figurative) (of country) face; (of area)
appearance, look
physiothérapie /fizjɔteʀapi/ nf
physiotherapy (GB), physical therapy (US)
physique¹ /fizik/ **1** adj physical
  2 nm (a) physical appearance
  (b) physique; **avoir un ~ séduisant** to look
attractive
  IDIOMS **avoir le ~ de l'emploi** to look the
part
physique² /fizik/ nf physics
piaf /pjaf/ nm (colloq) little bird
piaffer /pjafe/ [1] vi (a) ⟨horse⟩ to paw the
ground
  (b) ⟨person⟩ to be impatient; **~ d'impatience**
to be champing at the bit
piailler /pjaje/ [1] vi ⟨bird⟩ to chirp
pianiste /pjanist/ nmf pianist
piano /pjano/ **1** nm piano; **jouer qch au ~**
to play sth on the piano
  2 adv (Mus) piano
  ■ ~ **à queue** grand piano
pianoter /pjanɔte/ [1] vi to tinkle on the
piano
PIB /peibe/ nm: abbr ▶ PRODUIT
pic /pik/ **1** nm (a) peak
  (b) pick
  (c) woodpecker
  2 **à pic** phr ⟨cliff⟩ sheer; ⟨ravine⟩ very
steep
  IDIOMS **tomber à ~** to come just at the right
time
pichenette /piʃnɛt/ nf flick
pichet /piʃɛ/ nm jug (GB), pitcher
pick-up /pikœp/ nm inv (colloq) record
player
picorer /pikɔʀe/ [1] vi ⟨bird⟩ to peck about
picotement /pikɔtmɑ̃/ nm tingling;
tickling
picoter /pikɔte/ [1] **1** vtr to sting ⟨eyes,
nose, skin⟩; to tickle ⟨throat⟩
  2 vi ⟨throat⟩ to tickle; ⟨eyes⟩ to sting
pie /pi/ nf (a) magpie
  (b) (colloq) chatterbox (colloq)
pièce /pjɛs/ **1** nf (a) room
  (b) coin; **~ de monnaie** coin
  (c) play; **~ de théâtre** play
  (d) bit, piece; **en ~s** in bits; **mettre qn/qch
en ~s** to pull sb/sth to pieces
  (e) part; **~ de rechange** spare part
  (f) patch
  (g) document; **juger sur ~s** to judge on the
actual evidence; **c'est inventé de toutes ~s**
(figurative) it's a complete fabrication
  (h) piece, item; (in chess set, puzzle) piece; **~ de
collection** collector's item; **on n'est pas aux
~s** (colloq) we're not in a sweat-shop
  2 **-pièces** (combining form) (a) **un trois-
~s cuisine** a three-roomed apartment with
kitchen
  (b) **un deux-~s** a two-piece swimsuit

■ ~ **à conviction** exhibit; ~ **détachée** spare part; **en ~s détachées** in kit form; dismantled; ~ **d'identité** identity papers; ~ **maîtresse** showpiece; key element; ~ **montée** layer cake

piécette /pjesɛt/ *nf* small coin

pied /pje/ *nm* **(a)** foot; **être ~s nus** to be barefoot(ed); **sauter à ~s joints** to jump with one's feet together; (figurative) to jump in with both feet; **coup de ~** kick; **à ~** on foot; **promenade à ~** walk; **taper du ~** to stamp one's foot; to tap one's foot; **de la tête aux ~s** from head to foot; **portrait en ~** full-length portrait; **avoir conscience de là où on met les ~s** (colloq) to know what one is letting oneself in for; **sur un ~ d'égalité** on an equal footing
(b) (of hill, stairs) foot, bottom; (of glass) stem; (of lamp) base; (of camera) stand
(c) (of celery, lettuce) head; ~ **de vigne** vine
(d) (measurement) foot
■ ~ **à coulisse** calliper rule
IDIOMS **être sur ~** ⟨*person*⟩ to be up and about; ⟨*business*⟩ to be up and running; **mettre sur ~** to set up; **j'ai ~** I can touch the bottom; **perdre ~** to go out of one's depth; to lose ground; **être à ~ d'œuvre** to be ready to get down to work; **elle joue au tennis comme un ~** (colloq) she's hopeless at tennis; **faire un ~ de nez à qn** to thumb one's nose at sb; **faire du ~ à qn** to play footsy with sb (colloq); **faire des ~s et des mains pour obtenir** (colloq) to work really hard at getting; **ça lui fera les ~s** (colloq) that will teach him a lesson; **c'est le ~** (colloq) that's terrific (colloq); **mettre à ~** to suspend; **lever le ~** (colloq) to slow down

pied-à-terre /pjetatɛR/ *nm inv* pied-à-terre

pied-bot, *pl* **pieds-bots** /pjebo/ *nm* person with a club foot

piédestal, *pl* **-aux** /pjedɛstal, o/ *nm* pedestal

pied-noir, *pl* **pieds-noirs** /pjenwaR/ *nmf* (colloq): French colonial born in Algeria

piège /pjɛʒ/ *nm* **(a)** trap; **il s'est laissé prendre au ~** he walked into the trap
(b) pitfall

piéger /pjeʒe/ [15] *vtr* **(a)** to trap ⟨*animal, criminal*⟩
(b) to trick, to trap ⟨*person*⟩
(c) to booby-trap ⟨*letter, parcel, car*⟩

piercing /piRsiŋ/ *nm* **le ~** body piercing; **elle a un ~ au nombril** she has a pierced navel

pierre /pjɛR/ *nf* stone; rock; **poser la première ~** to lay the foundation stone
IDIOMS **jeter la ~ à qn** to accuse sb; **faire d'une ~ deux coups** to kill two birds with one stone

pierreries /pjɛRRi/ *nf pl* gems

pierreux, -euse /pjɛRø, øz/ *adj* stony

piété /pjete/ *nf* piety; **de ~** devotional

piétiner /pjetine/ [1] **1** *vtr* **(a)** to trample [sth] underfoot

(b) to trample on
2 *vi* **(a)** ~ **d'impatience** to hop up and down with impatience
(b) to shuffle along; to trudge along
(c) to make no headway

piéton, -onne /pjetɔ̃, ɔn/ **1** *adj* pedestrianized
2 *nm,f* pedestrian

piétonnier, -ière /pjetɔnje, ɛR/ *adj* pedestrianized

piètre /pjɛtR/ *adj* ⟨*actor, writer*⟩ very mediocre; ⟨*health, results*⟩ very poor; **c'est une ~ consolation** that's small comfort

pieu, *pl* **~x¹** /pjø/ *nm* stake

pieuvre /pjœvR/ *nf* octopus

pieux², pieuse /pjø, øz/ *adj* **(a)** pious, religious
(b) ⟨*affection, silence*⟩ reverent
■ ~ **mensonge** white lie

pif /pif/ *nm* (colloq) **(a)** nose, conk (GB) (colloq), schnozzle (US) (colloq)
(b) intuition; **j'ai eu du ~** I had a hunch (colloq); **au ~** ⟨*measure*⟩ roughly; ⟨*decide*⟩ just like that

pige /piʒ/ *nf* **travailler à la ~, faire des ~s** to do freelance work

pigeon /piʒɔ̃/ *nm* **(a)** pigeon
(b) (colloq) sucker (colloq)
■ ~ **voyageur** carrier pigeon

pigeonnier /piʒɔnje/ *nm* pigeon house; pigeon loft; dovecote

piger /piʒe/ [13] *vtr* (colloq) to understand

pigiste /piʒist/ *nmf* freelance

pigment /pigmɑ̃/ *nm* pigment

pigmenter /pigmɑ̃te/ [1] *vtr* to alter the pigmentation of

pignon /piɲɔ̃/ *nm* **(a)** gable
(b) gearwheel
(c) pine kernel
IDIOMS **avoir ~ sur rue** to be well-established

pilaf /pilaf/ *nm* pilau; **riz ~** pilau rice

pile¹ /pil/ *adv* (colloq) **(a)** **s'arrêter ~** to stop dead
(b) exactly; **à 10 heures et demie ~** at ten-thirty sharp; ~ **à l'heure** right on time; **tu tombes ~** you're just the person I wanted to see

pile² /pil/ *nf* **(a)** pile; stack
(b) ~ **(électrique)** battery; **à ~s** battery-operated
(c) pier
(d) (of coin) **le côté ~** the reverse side; **jouer à ~ ou face** to play heads or tails
■ ~ **bouton** button battery; ~ **solaire** solar cell

piler /pile/ [1] **1** *vtr* to grind; to crush
2 *vi* (colloq) ⟨*car*⟩ to pull up short; ⟨*driver*⟩ to slam on the brakes

pileux, -euse /pilø, øz/ *adj* **système ~** hair

pilier /pilje/ *nm* **(a)** pillar
(b) (figurative) mainstay
(c) (in rugby) prop forward

p

pillage /pijaʒ/ nm pillage, plundering; looting

pillard, ~e /pijaʀ, aʀd/ nm,f looter; pillager

piller /pije/ [1] vtr to pillage ⟨town⟩; to loot ⟨shop⟩; to plunder ⟨temple⟩

pilleur, -euse /pijœʀ, øz/ nm,f looter; plunderer

pilon /pilɔ̃/ nm (a) pestle
(b) (of poultry) drumstick

pilonnage /pilɔnaʒ/ nm (Mil) bombardment

pilotage /pilɔtaʒ/ nm piloting

pilote /pilɔt/ ⟦1⟧ nm pilot
⟦2⟧ (-)pilote (combining form) projet(-)~ pilot project; hôpital(-)~ experimental hospital
■ ~ **automobile** racing driver

piloter /pilɔte/ [1] vtr to pilot ⟨plane, ship⟩; to drive ⟨car⟩

pilotis /pilɔti/ nm inv stilts

pilule /pilyl/ nf pill
IDIOMS **avaler la** ~ (colloq) to grin and bear it; **faire passer la** ~ (colloq) to sweeten the pill

pimbêche /pɛ̃bɛʃ/ nf stuck-up madam (colloq)

piment /pimɑ̃/ nm (a) hot pepper
(b) spice
■ ~ **rouge** hot red pepper, chilli; ~ **vert** green chilli pepper

pimpant, ~e /pɛ̃pɑ̃, ɑ̃t/ adj spruce, smart

pin /pɛ̃/ nm pine (tree); **pomme de** ~ pine cone

pinailler /pinɑje/ [1] vi (slang) to split hairs

pince /pɛ̃s/ nf (a) (pair of) pliers; (pair of) tongs
(b) (in garment) dart; **un pantalon à** ~**s** pleat front trousers (GB) or pants (US)
(c) (of crab) pincer, claw
■ ~ **à cheveux** hair grip; ~ **coupante** wire cutters; ~ **à dessin** bulldog clip; ~ **à épiler** tweezers; ~ **à linge** clothes peg; ~ **à sucre** sugar tongs; ~ **à vélo** bicycle clip

pincé, ~e¹ /pɛ̃se/ adj ⟨smile⟩ tight-lipped; **prendre un air** ~ to become stiff or starchy

pinceau, pl ~**x** /pɛ̃so/ nm (paint) brush

pincée² /pɛ̃se/ ⟦1⟧ adj f ▶ PINCÉ
⟦2⟧ nf (of pepper, salt) pinch

pincement /pɛ̃smɑ̃/ nm pinch; **avoir un** ~ **de cœur** to feel a twinge of sadness

pince-monseigneur, pl **pinces-monseigneur** /pɛ̃smɔ̃sɛɲœʀ/ nf jemmy, slim jim

pince-nez /pɛ̃sne/ nm inv pince-nez

pincer /pɛ̃se/ [12] ⟦1⟧ vtr (a) ⟨person⟩ to pinch; ⟨crab⟩ to nip
(b) (colloq) to nab (colloq), to catch ⟨thief⟩
(c) ~ **les lèvres** to purse one's lips
(d) to pluck ⟨string⟩
(e) ⟨wind, cold⟩ to sting ⟨face⟩
⟦2⟧ **se pincer** v refl (+ v être) to pinch oneself; **se** ~ **le nez** to hold one's nose; **elle s'est pincée en refermant le tiroir** she caught her fingers closing the drawer

IDIOMS **en** ~ **pour qn** (colloq) to be stuck on sb (colloq)

pince-sans-rire /pɛ̃ssɑ̃ʀiʀ/ nmf inv **c'est un** ~ he has a deadpan sense of humour (GB)

pincettes /pɛ̃sɛt/ nf pl **il n'est pas à prendre avec des** ~ (colloq) he's like a bear with a sore head (colloq)

pinède /pinɛd/ nf pine forest

pingouin /pɛ̃gwɛ̃/ nm (a) auk
(b) penguin

ping-pong®, pl ~**s** /piŋpɔ̃ŋ/ nm table tennis, ping-pong®

pingre /pɛ̃gʀ/ adj stingy, niggardly

pingrerie /pɛ̃gʀəʀi/ nf stinginess

pin-pon /pɛ̃pɔ̃/ nm: sound of a two-tone siren

pin's /pins/ nm inv lapel badge

pintade /pɛ̃tad/ nf guinea fowl

pintadeau, pl ~**x** /pɛ̃tado/ nm young guinea fowl

pinte /pɛ̃t/ nf (a) pint (GB) (= 0,57 litre)
(b) ≈ quart (US) (= 0,94 litre)
(c) pot, tankard

pinter: se pinter /pɛ̃te/ [1] v refl (+ v être) (colloq) to get plastered (colloq) or drunk

pin-up /pinœp/ nf inv (colloq) glamour (GB) girl

pioche /pjɔʃ/ nf (a) mattock; pickaxe (GB), pickax (US)
(b) (Games) stack

piocher /pjɔʃe/ [1] vtr (a) to dig [sth] over ⟨soil⟩
(b) (Games) to take [sth] from the stack ⟨card⟩

piolet /pjɔlɛ/ nm ice axe (GB), ice pick (US)

pion, pionne /pjɔ̃, pjɔn/ ⟦1⟧ nm,f (colloq) (Sch) student paid to supervise pupils
⟦2⟧ nm (a) (in games) counter; (in chess) pawn; (in draughts) draught (GB), checker (US)
(b) (figurative) pawn

pionnier, -ière /pjɔnje, ɛʀ/ adj, nm,f pioneer

pipe /pip/ nf pipe
IDIOMS **casser sa** ~ (colloq) to kick the bucket (colloq)

pipeau, pl ~**x** /pipo/ nm (reed-)pipe
IDIOMS **c'est du** ~ (colloq) it's no great shakes (colloq); **c'est pas du** ~ (colloq) it's for real (colloq)

pipelette /piplɛt/ nf (colloq) gossip(monger)

piper /pipe/ [1] vtr (a) (colloq) **ne pas** ~ (mot) not to say a word
(b) to load ⟨dice⟩

pipi /pipi/ nm (colloq) pee (colloq); wee-wee (colloq)

piquant, ~e /pikɑ̃, ɑ̃t/ ⟦1⟧ adj (a) ⟨stem, thistle⟩ prickly; ⟨nail⟩ sharp
(b) ⟨mustard, sauce⟩ hot; ⟨cheese⟩ sharp
⟦2⟧ nm (a) (of stem, thistle) prickle; (of hedgehog, cactus) spine; (of barbed wire) spike, barb
(b) (of story) spiciness; (of situation) piquancy

pique¹ /pik/ nm (Games) spades

pique² /pik/ *nf* (a) cutting remark
(b) pike; (of picador) lance

piqué, **~e** /pike/ *adj* ⟨*wood*⟩ worm-eaten;
⟨*linen, mirror, fruit*⟩ spotted; ⟨*paper*⟩ foxed

pique-assiette /pikasjɛt/ *nmf inv* (colloq)
sponger (colloq)

pique-nique, *pl* **~s** /piknik/ *nm* picnic

piquer /pike/ [1] **1** *vtr* (a) to sting; to bite;
to prick
(b) (colloq) to give [sb] an injection; **faire ~
un animal** to have an animal put down
(c) ⟨*mildew, rust*⟩ to spot ⟨*linen, mirror*⟩; to
fox ⟨*paper, book*⟩
(d) **ses yeux la piquaient** her eyes were
stinging; **ça me pique partout** I'm itchy all
over
(e) (colloq) to pinch (GB) (colloq), to steal
⟨*book, idea*⟩; to borrow ⟨*pencil, pullover*⟩
(f) to catch; **ils se sont fait ~ à tricher
pendant l'examen** they got caught cheating
in the exam
(g) **~ qn au vif** to cut sb to the quick
(h) to arouse ⟨*curiosity*⟩
(i) (colloq) **~ un fou rire** to have a fit of the
giggles; **~ une crise de nerfs** to throw a fit
(colloq); **~ un cent mètres** to break into a run
(j) **~ une tête** to dive
2 *vi* (a) ⟨*beard*⟩ to be bristly; ⟨*wool*⟩ to be
scratchy; ⟨*throat, eyes*⟩ to sting
(b) ⟨*bird*⟩ to swoop down; ⟨*plane*⟩ to dive;
~ du nez ⟨*person*⟩ to nod off; ⟨*plane*⟩ to go
into a nosedive
(c) (colloq) **arrête de ~ dans le plat** stop
picking (things out of the dish)
3 **se piquer** *v refl* (+ *v être*) (a) to prick
oneself; **se ~ aux orties** to get stung by
nettles
(b) to inject oneself
(c) **se ~ de pouvoir réussir seul** to claim
that one can manage on one's own
IDIOMS **quelle mouche t'a piqué?** (colloq)
what's eating you? (colloq); **son article n'était
pas piqué des hannetons** (colloq) his/her
article didn't pull any punches

piquet /pikɛ/ *nm* (a) stake
(b) peg
(c) (in skiing) gate pole
(d) (of sunshade) pole
(e) picket; **~ de grève** (strike) picket, picket
line

piquette /pikɛt/ *nf* (colloq) plonk (GB)
(colloq), cheap wine

piqûre /pikyʀ/ *nf* (a) injection, shot
(b) (of thorn, pin) prick; (of nettle, bee) sting;
(of mosquito) bite
(c) stitch; stitching

pirate /piʀat/ *nm* pirate
■ **~ de l'air** hijacker, skyjacker

pirater /piʀate/ [1] *vtr* to pirate

piraterie /piʀatʀi/ *nf* piracy
■ **~ aérienne** hijacking, skyjacking;
~ informatique computer hacking

pire /piʀ/ **1** *adj* (a) worse (**que** than)
(b) worst; **les ~s mensonges** the most
wicked lies

2 *nm* **le ~** the worst; **au ~** at the very
worst

pirogue /piʀɔg/ *nf* dugout canoe

pirouette /piʀwɛt/ *nf* pirouette; **s'en tirer
par une ~** to dodge the question skilfully
(GB)

pis /pi/ **1** *adj inv* worse
2 *adv* worse; **tant ~** too bad
3 *nm inv* (of cow) udder

pis-aller /pizale/ *nm inv* makeshift
solution

pisciculteur, **-trice** /pisikyltœʀ, tʀis/
nm,f fish farmer

pisciculture /pisikyltyʀ/ *nf* fish farming

piscine /pisin/ *nf* swimming pool

pisse /pis/ *nf* (slang) piss (slang)

pissenlit /pisɑ̃li/ *nm* dandelion
IDIOMS **manger les ~s par la racine** (slang) to
be pushing up the daisies (colloq)

pisser (slang) /pise/ [1] **1** *vtr* **~ le sang**
⟨*person, nose, injury*⟩ to pour with blood
2 *vi* to pee (colloq), to piss (slang)
IDIOMS **il pleut comme vache qui pisse** it's
pissing down (slang); **laisse ~!** forget it!

pissotière /pisɔtjɛʀ/ *nf* (colloq) street
urinal

pistache /pistaʃ/ *nf* pistachio

piste /pist/ *nf* (a) trail; **être sur une fausse
~** to be on the wrong track
(b) (in police investigation) lead
(c) (in stadium) track; (in horseracing)
racecourse (GB), racetrack (US); (in motor
racing) racetrack; (in circus) ring; (in skiing)
slope; (in cross-country skiing) trail; **~ de danse**
dance floor; **entrer en ~** (at circus) to come
into the ring; (figurative) to enter the fray
(d) track, path; (in desert) trail
(e) (in airport) runway
(f) (on record, cassette) track
■ **~ cyclable** cycle lane; cycle path

pister /piste/ [1] *vtr* to trail, to track

pistil /pistil/ *nm* pistil

pistolet /pistɔlɛ/ *nm* (a) pistol, gun; **tirer
au ~** to fire a pistol
(b) (Tech) gun; **~ à peinture** spray gun

pistolet-mitrailleur, *pl* **pistolets-
mitrailleurs** /pistɔlɛmitʀajœʀ/ *nm*
submachine gun

piston /pistɔ̃/ *nm* (a) (Tech) piston
(b) (colloq) contacts; **avoir du ~** to have
connections in the right places

pistonner /pistɔne/ [1] *vtr* (colloq) to pull
strings for

pitance /pitɑ̃s/ *nf* fare

piteusement /pitøzmɑ̃/ *adv* pitifully,
pathetically

piteux, **-euse** /pitø, øz/ *adj* (a) ⟨*results*⟩
poor, pitiful
(b) ⟨*air*⟩ crestfallen

pitié /pitje/ *nf* pity; mercy; **prendre qn en ~**
to take pity on sb; **il fait ~** he's a pitiful
sight; **par ~, tais-toi!** for pity's sake, be
quiet!

piton /pitɔ̃/ *nm* (a) hook

(b) (in climbing) piton
(c) (of mountain) peak
pitoyable /pitwajabl/ *adv* **(a)** pitiful
(b) pathetic
pitoyablement /pitwajabləmɑ̃/ *adv*
(a) pitifully
(b) ⟨fail⟩ miserably; ⟨sing⟩ pathetically
pitre /pitʀ/ *nm* clown, buffoon
pitrerie /pitʀəʀi/ *nf* clowning
pittoresque /pitɔʀɛsk/ *adj* picturesque;
colourful (GB)
pivert /pivɛʀ/ *nm* green woodpecker
pivoine /pivwan/ *nf* peony
pivot /pivo/ *nm* **(a)** (Tech) pivot
(b) (of economy, strategy, group) linchpin; (of plot)
kingpin
(c) (Sport) (player) pivot, post
(d) (of tooth) post and core
pivotant, ~e /pivotɑ̃, ɑ̃t/ *adj* ⟨chair⟩
swivel; ⟨sign⟩ pivoting; ⟨door⟩ revolving
pivoter /pivɔte/ [1] *vi* ⟨person, animal,
panel⟩ to pivot; ⟨door⟩ to revolve; ⟨chair⟩ to
swivel
PJ /peʒi/ *nf* **(a)** (*abbr* = **police judiciaire**)
detective division of the French police force
(b) (*abbr* = **pièce(s) jointe(s)**) enc
PL (*written abbr* = **poids lourd**) HGV (GB),
heavy truck (US)
placard /plakaʀ/ *nm* **(a)** cupboard; **mettre
au ~** (figurative) to put [sth] on ice ⟨plan⟩; to
shunt [sb] aside ⟨person⟩
(b) poster, bill
placarder /plakaʀde/ [1] *vtr* **(a)** to post, to
stick
(b) to cover [sth] with posters
place /plas/ *nf* **(a)** room, space
(b) (in theatre, cinema, bus) seat; **payer sa ~**
(in cinema, theatre) to pay for one's ticket; (on
train) to pay one's fare
(c) place; **remettre qch à sa ~** to put sth
back in its place; **être en bonne ~ pour
gagner** to be well-placed *or* in a good
position to win; **la ~ d'un mot dans une
phrase** the position of a word in a sentence;
sur ~ to/on the scene; on the spot; **il faut
savoir rester à sa ~** you must know your
place; **tenir une grande ~ dans la vie de qn**
to play a large part in sb's life
(d) **à la ~ de** instead of, in place of; (**si
j'étais) à ta ~** if I were in your position
(e) **en ~** ⟨system, structure⟩ in place; ⟨troops⟩
in position; ⟨leader, party, regime⟩ ruling; **ne
plus tenir en ~** to be restless; **mettre en ~** to
put [sth] in place ⟨programme⟩; to put [sth]
in position ⟨team⟩; to establish, to set up
⟨network, institution⟩
(f) (in town) square; **la ~ du village** the
village square
(g) (Econ) market; **~ financière** financial
market
(h) job; **perdre sa ~** to lose one's job
(i) **être dans la ~** to be on the inside; **avoir
un pied dans la ~** to have a foot in the door
placé, ~e /plase/ [1] *pp* ▶ PLACER
[2] *pp adj* **(a)** (located) **être ~** ⟨object, tap,

window⟩ to be; ⟨chair, table, statue⟩ to be
placed; ⟨person⟩ (gen) to be; (at the theatre,
cinema) to be sitting; **être bien/mal ~**
⟨building, shop⟩ to be well/badly situated;
⟨person⟩ (at table, at a function) to have a good/
bad place
(b) (in a hierarchy) **être bien ~ sur une liste** to
have a good position on the list; **il est bien ~
pour le poste** he's a likely candidate for the
job; **avoir des amis haut ~s** to have friends
in high places
(c) **être bien/mal ~ pour faire** (to succeed) to
be well/badly placed to do; (to know, judge) to
be in a (good)/in no position to do
placebo /plasebo/ *nm* placebo
placement /plasmɑ̃/ *nm* **(a)** investment
(b) **assurer le ~ des diplômés** to ensure that
graduates find employment
(c) (of child) fostering
placenta /plasɛ̃ta/ *nm* placenta
placer /plase/ [12] [1] *vtr* **(a)** to put, to place
⟨object⟩; to seat ⟨person⟩; **~ sa confiance en
qn** to put one's trust in sb; **~ ses espoirs en
qn** to pin one's hopes on sb; **mal placé**
⟨pride⟩ misplaced
(b) to place, to find a job for ⟨person⟩
(c) to invest ⟨money⟩
(d) to slip in ⟨remark, anecdote⟩; **je n'arrive
pas à en ~ une avec elle!** (colloq) I can't get a
word in edgeways (GB) *or* edgewise (US) with
her!
(e) to place [sb] in care ⟨child⟩
[2] **se placer** *v refl* (+ *v être*) **(a)** **se ~ près
de** to sit next to
(b) **se ~ premier** to come first
placeur, -euse /plasœʀ, øz/ *nm,f* usher/
usherette
placide /plasid/ *adj* placid, calm
placier, -ière /plasje, ɛʀ/ *nm,f* **(a)** sales
representative
(b) market superintendent
plafond /plafɔ̃/ *nm* **(a)** ceiling; (of tent,
vehicle, tunnel) roof
(b) ceiling, limit
plafonnement /plafɔnmɑ̃/ *nm* **(a)** setting
a ceiling on ⟨pay⟩; setting a limit on
⟨spending⟩
(b) (on pay) ceiling (**de** on); (on spending)
limitation (**de** of)
plafonnier /plafɔnje/ *nm* (gen) flush-fitting
ceiling light; (in car) interior light
plage /plaʒ/ *nf* beach
■ **~ arrière** rear window shelf; **~ horaire** time
slot
plagiaire /plaʒjɛʀ/ *nmf* plagiarist
plagiat /plaʒja/ *nm* plagiarism
plagier /plaʒje/ [2] *vtr* to plagiarize
plaid /plɛd/ *nm* tartan rug (GB), plaid
blanket (US)
plaidant, ~e /plɛdɑ̃, ɑ̃t/ *adj* litigant
plaider /plede/ [1] [1] *vtr* to plead ⟨case⟩
[2] *vi* **(a)** to plead
(b) **~ en faveur de qn** ⟨circumstances⟩ to
speak in favour (GB) of sb
plaidoirie /plɛdwaʀi/ *nf* plea

plaidoyer /plɛdwaje/ *nm* **(a)** speech for the defence (GB)
(b) plea

plaie /plɛ/ *nf* **(a)** wound; sore; cut
(b) ⟨colloq⟩ cet enfant, quelle ∼! ⟨colloq⟩ that child is such a pain! ⟨colloq⟩

plaignant, ∼**e** /plɛɲɑ̃, ɑ̃t/ *nm,f* plaintiff

plaindre /plɛ̃dʀ/ [54] **1** *vtr* to pity
2 se plaindre *v refl* (+ *v être*) **(a)** to complain
(b) ⟨*injured person*⟩ to moan

plaine /plɛn/ *nf* plain

plain-pied: **de plain-pied** /dəplɛ̃pje/ *phr* une maison de ∼ a single-storey (GB) *or* single-story (US) house

plainte /plɛ̃t/ *nf* **(a)** (gen, Law) complaint
(b) moan, groan

plaintif, -**ive** /plɛ̃tif, iv/ *adj* plaintive

plaintivement /plɛ̃tivmɑ̃/ *adv* plaintively, dolefully

plaire /plɛʀ/ [59] **1 plaire à** *v+prep*
(a) elle plaît aux hommes men find her attractive; elle m'a plu tout de suite I liked her straight away
(b) mon travail me plaît I like my job; un modèle qui plaît beaucoup a very popular model
2 se plaire *v refl* (+ *v être*) **(a)** ⟨*people, couple*⟩ to like each other
(b) ils se plaisent ici they like it here
(c) il se plaît à dire qu'il est issu du peuple he likes to say that he's a son of the people
3 *v impers* s'il te plaît, s'il vous plaît please

plaisamment /plɛzamɑ̃/ *adv*
(a) agreeably
(b) amusingly

plaisance /plɛzɑ̃s/ *nf* la navigation de ∼ boating; bateau de ∼ pleasure boat

plaisancier, -**ière** /plɛzɑ̃sje, ɛʀ/ *nm,f* amateur sailor

plaisant, ∼**e** /plɛzɑ̃, ɑ̃t/ *adj* **(a)** pleasant
(b) amusing, funny

plaisanter /plɛzɑ̃te/ [1] *vi* to joke

plaisanterie /plɛzɑ̃tʀi/ *nf* joke

plaisir /plɛziʀ/ *nm* pleasure; prendre un malin ∼ à faire to take a wicked delight in doing; faire ∼ à qn to please sb; faites-moi le ∼ de vous taire! would you please shut up! ⟨colloq⟩; faire durer le ∼ to make the pleasure last; (ironic) to prolong the agony

plan /plɑ̃/ *nm* **(a)** (of town, underground) map; (in building) plan, map
(b) (for building) plan; tirer des ∼s to draw up plans
(c) (of machine) blueprint
(d) (of essay, book) outline, framework
(e) (in cinematography) shot; premier ∼ foreground
(f) level; au premier ∼ de l'actualité at the forefront of the news; sur le ∼ politique from a political point of view
(g) plan; c'est le bon ∼ ⟨colloq⟩ it's a good idea
■ ∼ d'eau artificial lake; ∼ d'épargne

savings plan; ∼ d'épargne-logement, PEL savings scheme entitling depositor to a cheap mortgage.
IDIOMS laisser qn en ∼ ⟨colloq⟩ to leave sb in the lurch; laisser qch en ∼ ⟨colloq⟩ to leave sth unfinished

planche /plɑ̃ʃ/ *nf* **(a)** (gen) plank; (for kneading dough) board; faire la ∼ to float on one's back
(b) plate
■ ∼ à roulettes (Sport) skateboard; ∼ de salut lifeline; ∼ à voile windsurfing board
IDIOMS monter sur les ∼s to go on the stage; avoir du pain sur la ∼ ⟨colloq⟩ to have one's work cut out

plancher[1] /plɑ̃ʃe/ [1] *vi* (students' slang) to work

plancher[2] /plɑ̃ʃe/ *nm* **(a)** floor
(b) (Econ) floor; atteindre un ∼ to bottom out

planchiste /plɑ̃ʃist/ *nmf* windsurfer

plancton /plɑ̃ktɔ̃/ *nm* plankton

plané /plane/ *adj m* vol ∼ glide; faire un vol ∼ (figurative) to go flying

planer /plane/ [1] *vi* **(a)** ⟨*plane, bird*⟩ to glide
(b) laisser ∼ le doute to allow uncertainty to persist
(c) ⟨colloq⟩ to have one's head in the clouds

planétaire /planetɛʀ/ *adj* planetary; (figurative) global

planète /planɛt/ *nf* planet

planeur /planœʀ/ *nm* **(a)** glider
(b) gliding

planifier /planifje/ [2] *vtr* to plan

planning /planiŋ/ *nm* (controversial) ⟨colloq⟩ schedule
■ ∼ familial family planning service

planque /plɑ̃k/ *nf* ⟨colloq⟩ (for person) hideout

planquer ⟨colloq⟩ /plɑ̃ke/ [1] **1** *vtr* to hide ⟨*person*⟩; to hide [sth] away ⟨*object*⟩
2 se planquer *v refl* (+ *v être*) to hide

plan-séquence, *pl* **plans-séquences** /plɑ̃sekɑ̃s/ *nm* sequence shot

plant /plɑ̃/ *nm* young plant

plantaire /plɑ̃tɛʀ/ *adj* (Anat) plantar; voûte ∼ arch of the foot

plantation /plɑ̃tasjɔ̃/ *nf* **(a)** plantation
(b) (of flowers) bed; (of vegetables) patch

plante /plɑ̃t/ *nf* **(a)** plant; ∼ verte houseplant; ∼ grasse succulent
(b) ∼ (des pieds) sole (of the foot)

planter /plɑ̃te/ [1] **1** *vtr* **(a)** to plant ⟨*flowers, shrub*⟩
(b) to drive in ⟨*stake*⟩; to knock in ⟨*nail*⟩; ∼ un couteau dans to stick a knife into
(c) to pitch ⟨*tent*⟩; ∼ le décor to set the scene
(d) ∼ (là) to drop ⟨*tool*⟩; to abandon ⟨*car*⟩
2 se planter *v refl* (+ *v être*) **(a)** ⟨colloq⟩ aller se ∼ devant qch to go and stand in front of sth
(b) ⟨colloq⟩ to crash

····≫

(c) (colloq) to get it wrong; **il s'est planté en histoire** he made a mess of the history exam

plantureux, **-euse** /plɑ̃tyʀø, øz/ adj ‹bosom› ample; ‹woman› buxom

plaque /plak/ nf (of ice) patch; (on skin) blotch; (of glass) plate; (of marble) slab; (on door of surgery) brass plate; (of policeman) badge
■ ~ **d'égout** manhole cover;
~ **d'immatriculation** number plate (GB), license plate (US)
IDIOMS **être à côté de la** ~ (colloq) to be completely mistaken

plaqué, **~e** /plake/ adj ~ **or** gold-plated

plaquer /plake/ [1] ① vtr **(a)** ~ **qn contre qch** to pin sb against sth
(b) (colloq) to leave ‹job, spouse›
② **se plaquer** v refl (+ v être) **se** ~ **contre un mur** to flatten oneself against a wall

plaquette /plakɛt/ nf **(a)** (of butter) packet
(b) (of pills) ≈ blister strip
■ ~ **de frein** brake shoe

plastic /plastik/ nm plastic explosive

plasticage /plastikaʒ/ nm bomb attack (de on)

plastifier /plastifje/ [2] vtr to coat [sth] with plastic

plastique[1] /plastik/ nm plastic

plastique[2] /plastik/ nf (of object, statue) formal beauty; (of person) physique

plastiquer /plastike/ [1] vtr to carry out a bomb attack on

plastron /plastʀɔ̃/ nm shirt front

plat, **~e** /pla, plat/ ① adj **(a)** flat
(b) ‹boat› flat-bottomed; ‹watch, lighter› slimline; ‹hair› limp
(c) ‹style, description› lifeless
② nm **(a)** dish
(b) course
③ **à plat** phr **(a)** **poser qch à** ~ to lay sth down flat; **à** ~ **ventre** flat on one's stomach; **tomber à** ~ ‹joke› to fall flat
(b) ‹tyre› flat; ‹battery› flat (GB), dead
(c) (colloq) **être à** ~ ‹person› to be run down
■ ~ **de résistance** main course
IDIOMS **mettre les pieds dans le** ~ (colloq) to put one's foot in it; **faire tout un** ~ **de qch** (colloq) to make a big deal about sth

platane /platan/ nm plane tree

plateau, pl **~x** /plato/ nm **(a)** tray
(b) ~ **de tournage** film set
(c) (in geography) plateau
(d) (of weighing scales) pan

plate-bande, pl **plates-bandes** /platbɑ̃d/ nf border, flower bed

platée /plate/ nf (colloq) plateful (de of)

plate-forme, pl **plates-formes** /platfɔʀm/ nf platform; ~ **pétrolière** oil rig

platine[1] /platin/ adj inv, nm platinum

platine[2] /platin/ nf (record player) turntable

platitude /platityd/ nf platitude

platonique /platɔnik/ adj platonic

plâtre /plɑtʀ/ nm **(a)** plaster
(b) (Med) plaster cast

plâtrer /plɑtʀe/ [1] vtr **(a)** to plaster ‹wall›
(b) (Med) ~ **le bras de qn** to put sb's arm in plaster

plâtreux, **-euse** /plɑtʀø, øz/ adj chalky

plâtrier, **-ière** /plɑtʀije, ɛʀ/ nm,f plasterer

plausible /plozibl/ adj plausible

playback /plɛbak/ nm inv miming, lip syncing; **chanter en** ~ to lip-sync (a song)

plébiscite /plebisit/ nm plebiscite

plébisciter /plebisite/ [1] vtr **(a)** to elect [sb] with a huge majority
(b) to vote overwhelmingly in favour (GB) of

pléiade /plejad/ nf galaxy, pleiad

plein, **~e** /plɛ̃, plɛn/ ① adj **(a)** full
(b) **un** ~ **panier** a basketful; **prendre à** ~**es mains** to pick up a handful of ‹earth, sand, coins›
(c) ‹brick, wall› solid; ‹cheeks, face› plump; ‹shape› rounded
(d) ‹power, effect› full; ‹satisfaction, confidence› complete
(e) ‹day, month› whole, full; ‹moon› full
(f) **en** ~**e poitrine/réunion/forêt** (right) in the middle of the chest/meeting/forest; **en** ~ **jour** in broad daylight; **en** ~ **été** at the height of summer
(g) (Zool) ~**e** ‹animal› pregnant; ‹cow› in calf
(h) (colloq) sloshed (colloq), drunk
(i) **veste** ~**e peau** jacket made out of full skins
② adv **(a)** **avoir des billes** ~ **les poches** to have one's pockets full of marbles; **il a des idées** ~ **la tête** he's full of ideas
(b) **être orienté** ~ **sud** to face due south
③ nm **faire le** ~ **de** to fill up with ‹water, petrol›; **le** ~ **s'il vous plaît** fill it up please
④ **plein de** (colloq) quantif ~ **de** lots of, loads (colloq) of
⑤ **à plein** phr fully
⑥ **tout plein** phr (colloq) really
IDIOMS **en avoir** ~ **le dos** (colloq) to be fed up

plein-air /plɛnɛʀ/ nm inv (Sch) (outdoor) games

pleinement /plɛnmɑ̃/ adv fully

plein-emploi /plɛnɑ̃plwa/ nm inv full employment

plein-temps, pl **pleins-temps** /plɛ̃tɑ̃/ nm full-time job

plénier, **-ière** /plenje, ɛʀ/ adj plenary

pléonasme /pleonasm/ nm pleonasm

pleurer /plœʀe/ [1] ① vtr to mourn ‹friend›
② vi **(a)** to cry, to weep
(b) ‹eyes› to water
(c) ~ **sur qn/qch** to shed tears over sb/sth; **arrête de** ~ **sur ton sort!** stop feeling sorry for yourself!
(d) (colloq) ‹person› to whine
IDIOMS **elle n'a plus que ses yeux pour** ~ all she can do is cry

pleureur /plœʀœʀ/ adj m **saule** ~ weeping willow

pleureuse /plœʀøz/ nf (hired) mourner

pleurnicher /plœRniʃe/ [1] *vi* (colloq) to snivel

pleurnicheur, **-euse** /plœRniʃœR, øz/ *nm,f* (colloq) sniveller

pleurs /plœR/ *nm pl* tears; **en** ~ in tears

pleuvoir /pløvwaR/ [39] ① *v impers* to rain; **il pleut** it's raining; **il pleut à torrents** it's pouring with rain
② *vi* ⟨*blows, bombs*⟩ to rain down

pli /pli/ *nm* (a) (gen) fold; (in trousers) crease; (in skirt) pleat
(b) (Games) trick
(c) letter; **sous** ~ **cacheté** in a sealed envelope
IDIOMS **ça ne fait pas un** ~ (colloq) there's no doubt about it; **c'est un** ~ **à prendre** it's something you've got to get used to

pliage /plijaʒ/ *nm* folding

pliant, ~**e** /plijɑ̃, ɑ̃t/ ① *adj* folding
② *nm* folding stool, campstool

plier /plije/ [2] ① *vtr* (a) to fold; to fold up
(b) to bend ⟨*stem, arm*⟩
(c) to submit
② *vi* (a) ⟨*tree, branch, joint*⟩ to bend; ⟨*plank, floor*⟩ to sag
(b) to give in
③ **se plier** *v refl* (+ *v être*) (a) to fold
(b) **se** ~ **à** to submit to
IDIOMS **être plié (en deux** *or* **quatre)** (colloq) to be doubled up with laughter

plinthe /plɛ̃t/ *nf* skirting board (GB), baseboard (US)

plisser /plise/ [1] ① *vtr* (a) to pleat ⟨*cloth*⟩
(b) to crease ⟨*garment*⟩
(c) ~ **le front** to knit one's brows; ~ **les yeux** to screw up one's eyes
② *vi* ⟨*stocking*⟩ to wrinkle; ⟨*skirt*⟩ to be creased

pliure /plijyR/ *nf* fold; **la** ~ **du genou** the back of the knee

plomb /plɔ̃/ *nm* (a) lead; **sans** ~ ⟨*petrol*⟩ unleaded; **soleil de** ~ burning sun; **ciel de** ~ leaden sky
(b) (in hunting) **un** ~ a lead pellet; **du** ~ lead shot
(c) fuse
IDIOMS **avoir du** ~ **dans l'aile** (colloq) to be in a bad way (colloq); **cela va leur mettre du** ~ **dans la cervelle** (colloq) that will knock some sense into them

plombage /plɔ̃baʒ/ *nm* (in dentistry) filling

plomber /plɔ̃be/ [1] *vtr* to fill ⟨*tooth*⟩

plombier /plɔ̃bje/ *nm* plumber

plonge /plɔ̃ʒ/ *nf* (colloq) washing up, dishwashing (US)

plongée /plɔ̃ʒe/ *nf* (a) (skin) diving
(b) scuba diving
(c) snorkelling (GB); ~ **sous-marine** deep-sea diving; **faire de la** ~ to go diving

plongeoir /plɔ̃ʒwaR/ *nm* (a) diving-board
(b) springboard

plongeon /plɔ̃ʒɔ̃/ *nm* (a) dive
(b) fall

plonger /plɔ̃ʒe/ [13] ① *vtr* to plunge

② *vi* (a) to dive
(b) ⟨*bird*⟩ to swoop down
③ **se plonger** *v refl* (+ *v être*) (a) to plunge
(b) to bury oneself

plongeur, **-euse** /plɔ̃ʒœR, øz/ *nm,f*
(a) diver
(b) dishwasher

plot /plo/ *nm* (a) (electrical) contact
(b) (of wood) block

plouc /pluk/ *nm* (colloq) country bumpkin (colloq)

plouf /pluf/ ① *nm inv* splash; **faire un** ~ to go splash
② *excl* splash!

ployer /plwaje/ [23] *vi* ⟨*branch, person*⟩ to bend; ~ **sous un fardeau** to be weighed down by a burden

plu /ply/ ▶ PLAIRE; PLEUVOIR

pluie /plɥi/ *nf* (a) rain; **sous une** ~ **battante** in driving rain
(b) (of missiles, insults) hail; (of sparks, compliments) shower
■ ~**s acides** acid rain
IDIOMS **il n'est pas né de la dernière** ~ (colloq) he wasn't born yesterday (colloq); **faire la** ~ **et le beau temps** to call the shots (colloq)

plume /plym/ *nf* (a) (Zool) feather
(b) (pen) nib; **écrire au fil de la** ~ to write as the thoughts come into one's head
IDIOMS **voler dans les** ~**s de qn** (colloq) to fly at sb

plumeau, *pl* ~**x** /plymo/ *nm* (a) feather duster
(b) tuft

plumer /plyme/ [1] *vtr* to pluck ⟨*bird*⟩

plumier /plymje/ *nm* pencil box

plupart: la plupart /laplypaR/ *nf inv* **la** ~ **des gens** most people; **la** ~ **du temps** most of the time, mostly

pluridisciplinaire /plyRidisiplinɛR/ *adj* multidisciplinary

pluriel, **-elle** /plyRjɛl/ ① *adj* plural
② *nm* plural

plus[1] /ply, plys, plyz/ ① *prep* plus
② *adv* (a) (comparative) more; (superlative) **le** ~ the most; **il travaille** ~ **(que moi)** he works more (than I do); ~ **j'y pense, moins je comprends** the more I think about it, the less I understand; ~ **ça va** as time goes on; **qui** ~ **est** furthermore; **de** ~ **en** ~ more and more; ~ **petit** smaller; **le** ~ **petit** the smallest; **trois heures** ~ **tôt** three hours earlier; **deux fois** ~ **cher** twice as expensive; **il est on ne peut** ~ **désagréable** he's as unpleasant as can be; **il est** ~ **ou moins artiste** he's an artist of sorts; **il a été** ~ **ou moins poli** he wasn't particularly polite
(b) (in negative constructions) **elle ne fume** ~ she doesn't smoke any more; **il n'y a** ~ **d'œufs** there are no more eggs; ~ **jamais ça!** never again!; ~ **que trois jours avant Noël!** only three days to go until Christmas!
③ **plus de** *quantif* **deux fois** ~ **de livres**

que twice as many books as; **il a gagné le ~
d'argent** he won the most money; **les gens de
~ de 60 ans** people over 60
4 **au plus** *phr* at the most
5 **de plus** *phr* (a) furthermore, what's
more
(b) **donnez-moi deux pommes de ~** give me
two more apples; **une fois de ~** once more
6 **en plus** *phr* **en ~ (de cela)** on top of
that; **les taxes en ~** plus tax

plus² /plys/ *nm inv* (a) **le signe ~** the plus
sign
(b) (colloq) plus (colloq)

plusieurs /plyzjœʀ/ **1** *adj* several; **une ou
~ personnes** one or more people
2 *pron* **~ ont déjà signé** several people
have already signed

plus-value, *pl* **~s** /plyvaly/ *nf*
(a) (of property) increase in value; (sales profit)
capital gain
(b) surcharge
(c) (Econ) surplus value

plutôt /plyto/ *adv* rather; instead; **passe ~
le matin** call round (GB) *or* come by (US) in
the morning preferably; **~ mourir!** I'd rather
die!; **demande ~ à Corinne** ask Corinne
instead; **dis ~ que tu n'as pas envie de le
faire** why don't you just say that you don't
want to do it?; **la nouvelle a été ~ bien
accueillie** the news went down rather well

pluvieux, -ieuse /plyvjø, øz/ *adj* wet,
rainy

PME /peɛmə/ *nf pl* (*abbr* = **petites et
moyennes entreprises**) small and
medium-sized enterprises, SMEs

PMI /peɛmi/ *nf pl* (*abbr* = **petites et
moyennes industries**) small and
medium-sized industries

PMU /peɛmy/ *nm* (*abbr* = **Pari mutuel
urbain**) *French state-controlled betting
system*

PNB /peɛnbe/ *nm* (*abbr* = **produit
national brut**) gross national product,
GNP

pneu /pnø/ *nm* tyre (GB), tire (US)

pneumatique /pnømatik/ *adj* inflatable

pneumonie /pnømɔni/ *nf* pneumonia

poche¹ /pɔʃ/ *nm* (livre de) **~** paperback

poche² /pɔʃ/ *nf* (a) (in garment, bag) pocket;
en ~ in one's pocket; **il avait 1 000 francs en
~** he had 1,000 francs on him; **s'en mettre
plein** *or* **se remplir les ~s** (colloq) to line one's
pockets; **faire les ~s de qn** to pick sb's
pocket
(b) **~ de gaz/d'air** gas/air pocket
(c) **avoir des ~s sous les yeux** to have bags
under one's eyes
(d) (Zool) (of kangaroo) pouch
■ **~ revolver** hip pocket
IDIOMS **c'est dans la ~** (colloq) it's in the bag
(colloq); **en être de sa ~** (colloq) to be out of
pocket; **ne pas avoir les yeux dans sa ~**
(colloq) not to miss a thing (colloq); **connaître
un endroit comme sa ~** (colloq) to know a
place like the back of one's hand

pocher /pɔʃe/ [1] *vtr* (Culin) to poach

pochette /pɔʃɛt/ *nf* (a) (for pencils) case; (for
credit cards) wallet; (for make-up, glasses) pouch;
(for document) folder; (for record) sleeve
(b) (of matches) book
(c) clutch bag

pochoir /pɔʃwaʀ/ *nm* stencil

podium /pɔdjɔm/ *nm* podium

poêle¹ /pwal/ *nm* (a) stove
(b) (on coffin) pall

poêle² /pwal/ *nf* frying pan

poème /pɔɛm/ *nm* poem; **c'est tout un ~**
(colloq) it's quite something

poésie /pɔezi/ *nf* (a) poetry
(b) poem

poète /pɔɛt/ *nm* (a) poet
(b) dreamer

poétique /pɔetik/ *adj* poetic

poids /pwɑ/ *nm inv* (a) weight; **peser son
~** to be very heavy; **adversaire de ~**
opponent to be reckoned with
(b) burden; **être un ~ pour qn** to be a
burden on sb; **avoir un ~ sur la conscience**
to have a guilty conscience
(c) influence
(d) **des ~ en laiton** brass weights
(e) (in athletics) shot; **lancer le ~** to put the
shot
■ **~ et haltères** weightlifting; **~ lourd** (Sport)
heavyweight; heavy truck
IDIOMS **avoir** *or* **faire deux ~ deux mesures**
to have double standards

poignant, ~e /pwaɲɑ̃, ɑ̃t/ *adj* (a) poignant
(b) heart-rending, harrowing

poignard /pwaɲaʀ/ *nm* dagger; **coup de ~**
stab

poignarder /pwaɲaʀde/ [1] *vtr* to stab

poigne /pwaɲ/ *nf* **avoir de la ~** to have a
strong grip; **homme à ~** strong man

poignée /pwaɲe/ *nf* (a) handful
(b) (of door, drawer, bag) handle; (of sword) hilt
■ **~ de main** handshake

poignet /pwaɲɛ/ *nm* (a) wrist
(b) (of shirt) cuff

poil /pwal/ *nm* (a) (on body, animal) hair; **à ~**
(slang) stark naked; **caresser dans le sens du
~** to stroke [sth] the way the fur lies; to
butter [sb] up (colloq); **ça marche au ~** (colloq)
it works like a dream
(b) (colloq) (of irony) touch; (of commonsense)
shred; **à un ~ près** by a whisker
(c) (of cloth) nap; (of brush) bristle
■ **~ à gratter** itching powder
IDIOMS **être de bon/mauvais ~** (colloq) to be
in a good/bad mood; **hérisser le ~ de qn**
(colloq) to put sb's back up (colloq); **avoir un ~
dans la main** (colloq) to be bone idle

poilu, ~e /pwaly/ *adj* hairy

poinçon /pwɛ̃sɔ̃/ *nm* (a) (tool) punch
(b) (on gold) die, stamp; hallmark

poinçonner /pwɛ̃sɔne/ [1] *vtr* (a) to
punch, to clip
(b) to hallmark

poinçonneur, -euse /pwɛ̃sɔnœʀ, øz/ *nm,f* ticket-puncher

poindre /pwɛ̃dʀ/ [56] *vi* ⟨*day*⟩ to break

poing /pwɛ̃/ *nm* fist; **coup de ~** punch; **montrer le ~** to shake one's fist; **être pieds et ~s liés** (figurative) to have one's hands tied
IDIOMS dormir à ~s fermés to sleep like a log

point /pwɛ̃/ **1** *nm* (a) point; **un ~ de rencontre** a meeting point; **~ de vente** (sales) outlet
(b) (at sea) position; **faire le ~** to take bearings; (figurative) to take stock of the situation
(c) **être sur le ~ de faire** to be just about to do; **au ~ où j'en suis, ça n'a pas d'importance!** I'm past caring!
(d) **il m'agace au plus haut ~** he annoys me intensely; **je ne le pensais pas bête à ce ~** I didn't think he was that stupid; **à tel ~ que** to such an extent that; **douloureux au ~ que** so painful that
(e) (on agenda) item, point; **un ~ de détail** a minor point; **en tout ~, en tous ~s** in every respect *or* way
(f) dot; **un ~ de colle** a spot of glue; **un ~ de rouille** a speck of rust; **~ d'intersection** point of intersection
(g) (Games, Sport) point; **compter les ~s** to keep (the) score
(h) (Sch) mark (GB), point (US); **être un bon ~ pour** to be a plus point for
(i) full stop (GB), period (US); **mettre un ~ final à qch** (figurative) to put a stop to sth; **tu vas te coucher un ~ c'est tout!** (colloq) you're going to bed and that's final!
(j) (Med) pain; **avoir un ~ à la poitrine** to have a pain in one's chest
(k) (in sewing, knitting) stitch
2 **à point** *phr* (a) **à ~ nommé** just at the right moment
(b) **à ~** ⟨*meat*⟩ medium rare
3 **au point** *phr* **être au ~** ⟨*system, machine*⟩ to be well designed; ⟨*show*⟩ to be well put together; **mettre au ~** to perfect ⟨*system, method*⟩; to develop ⟨*vaccine, machine*⟩; **faire la mise au ~** (in photography) to focus; **faire une mise au ~** (figurative) to set the record straight
■ **~ argent** cash point; **~ chaud** trouble *or* hot spot; **~ de côté** (pain) stitch; **~ de départ** starting point; **nous revoilà à notre ~ de départ** (figurative) we're back to square one; **~ d'eau** water tap (GB) *or* faucet (US); **~ d'exclamation** exclamation mark; **~ faible** weak point; **~ fort** strong point; **~ d'interrogation** question mark; **~ de mire** (Mil) target; (figurative) focal point; **~ mort** neutral; **être au ~ mort** (in car) to be in neutral; ⟨*business, trade*⟩ to be at a standstill; ⟨*situation*⟩ problem; **~ noir** (Med) blackhead; (of situation) problem; **~ de repère** landmark; point of reference; **~ de suture** (Med) stitch; **~ de vue** point of view; viewpoint; **du ~ de vue du sens** as far as meaning is concerned; **~s de suspension** suspension points
IDIOMS être mal en ~ to be in a bad way

pointage /pwɛ̃taʒ/ *nm* (a) (on list) ticking off (GB), checking off (US)
(b) (of employee) clocking in

pointe /pwɛ̃t/ **1** *nf* (a) (of knife) point; (of shoe) toe; (of hair) end; (of railing) spike; (of spear) tip; **en ~** pointed
(b) **de ~** ⟨*technology*⟩ advanced, state-of-the-art; ⟨*sector, industry*⟩ high-tech; **à la ~ du progrès** state-of-the-art
(c) high; **une vitesse de ~ de 200 km/h** a maximum *or* top speed of 200 km/h; **heure de ~** rush hour; **aux heures de ~** at peak time
(d) (of garlic) touch; (of accent) hint
(e) blocked shoe
2 **pointes** *nf pl* **faire des ~s** to dance on points
■ **~ du pied** tiptoe

pointer /pwɛ̃te/ [1] **1** *vtr* (a) to tick off (GB), to check off (US) ⟨*names, figures*⟩; to check ⟨*list*⟩
(b) to point ⟨*weapon*⟩; **~ le doigt vers** to point at; **~ son nez** (colloq) to show one's face
2 *vi* (a) ⟨*employee*⟩ to clock in; **~ à l'agence pour l'emploi** to sign on at the unemployment office
(b) ⟨*sun, plant*⟩ to come up; ⟨*day*⟩ to break
3 **se pointer** *v refl* (+ *v être*) (colloq) to turn up

pointillé, ~e /pwɛ̃tije/ **1** *adj* dotted
2 *nm* dotted line

pointilleux, -euse /pwɛ̃tijø, øz/ *adj* ⟨*person*⟩ fussy, pernickety

pointu, ~e /pwɛ̃ty/ *adj* (a) (gen) pointed; ⟨*scissors*⟩ with a sharp point
(b) ⟨*check*⟩ close, thorough
(c) ⟨*question, approach*⟩ precise

pointure /pwɛ̃tyʀ/ *nf* (of glove, shoe) size

point-virgule, *pl* **points-virgules** /pwɛ̃viʀgyl/ *nm* semicolon

poire /pwaʀ/ *nf* (a) pear
(b) (colloq) sucker (colloq)
IDIOMS couper la ~ en deux to split the difference; **garder une ~ pour la soif** to save something for a rainy day

poireau, *pl* **~x** /pwaʀo/ *nm* leek

poirier /pwaʀje/ *nm* (a) pear (tree)
(b) **faire le ~** to do a headstand

pois /pwa/ *nm inv* (a) (Bot, Culin) pea; **petit ~** (garden) pea
(b) dot; **à ~** polka dot, spotted
■ **~ cassé** split pea; **~ chiche** chickpea

poison /pwazɔ̃/ *nm* poison

poisse /pwas/ *nf* (colloq) (a) rotten luck (colloq)
(b) drag (colloq)

poisseux, -euse /pwasø, øz/ *adj* ⟨*hands, table*⟩ sticky; ⟨*atmosphere*⟩ muggy; ⟨*restaurant*⟩ greasy

poisson /pwasɔ̃/ *nm* fish; **les ~s d'eau douce/de mer** freshwater/saltwater fish
■ **~ rouge** goldfish
IDIOMS être comme un ~ dans l'eau to be in one's element

poissonnerie /pwasɔnʀi/ *nf* fishmonger's (shop) (GB), fish shop (US)

poissonnier, -ière /pwasɔnje, ɛʀ/ *nm,f* fishmonger (GB), fish vendor (US)

Poissons /pwasɔ̃/ *pr nm pl* Pisces

poitrail /pwatʀaj/ *nm* breast

poitrine /pwatʀin/ *nf* (a) chest; **tour de ~** chest size
(b) breasts; **tour de ~** bust size
■ **~ fumée** ≈ smoked streaky bacon

poivre /pwavʀ/ *nm* pepper

poivré, ~e /pwavʀe/ *adj* ‹sauce› peppery

poivrer /pwavʀe/ [1] *vtr* to add pepper to

poivron /pwavʀɔ̃/ *nm* sweet pepper, capsicum

poivrot, ~e /pwavʀo, ɔt/ *nm,f* ‹colloq› drunk

poker /pɔkɛʀ/ *nm* poker; **coup de ~** gamble

polaire /pɔlɛʀ/ *adj* polar; arctic

polar /pɔlaʀ/ *nm* ‹colloq› detective novel

polariser /pɔlaʀize/ [1] *vtr*, **se polariser** *v refl* (+ *v être*) (a) to polarize
(b) to focus

pôle /pol/ *nm* (a) pole
(b) centre (GB)

polémique /pɔlemik/ *nf* debate

poli, ~e /pɔli/ ① *pp* ▶ POLIR
② *pp adj* ‹metal, style› polished
③ *adj* polite
④ *nm* shine

police /pɔlis/ *nf* (a) police; police force
(b) security service
(c) **faire la ~** to keep order
(d) (in insurance) policy
■ **~ judiciaire, PJ** detective division of the French police force; **~ de l'air et des frontières, PAF** border police; **~ des mœurs** *or* **mondaine** vice squad; **~ secours** ≈ emergency services

policier, -ière /pɔlisje, ɛʀ/ ① *adj* (gen) police; ‹novel› detective
② *nm* policeman; **femme ~** policewoman

poliment /pɔlimɑ̃/ *adv* politely

polir /pɔliʀ/ [3] *vtr* to polish ‹stone, metal›

polisson, -onne /pɔlisɔ̃, ɔn/ *nm,f* naughty child

politesse /pɔlitɛs/ *nf* politeness; **rendre la ~ à qn** to return the compliment

politicien, -ienne /pɔlitisjɛ̃, ɛn/ *nm,f* politician

politique¹ /pɔlitik/ *adj* (gen) political; ‹behaviour, act› calculating

politique² /pɔlitik/ *nf* (a) politics; **faire de la ~** ‹militant› to be involved in politics
(b) policy; **notre ~ des prix** our pricing policy
IDIOMS **pratiquer la ~ de l'autruche** to stick one's head in the sand; **pratiquer la ~ du pire** to envisage the worst-case scenario

politiser /pɔlitize/ [1] *vtr* to politicize

pollen /pɔl(l)ɛn/ *nm* pollen

polluant, ~e /pɔl(l)ɥɑ̃, ɑ̃t/ ① *adj* polluting

② *nm* pollutant

polluer /pɔl(l)ɥe/ [1] *vtr* to pollute

pollution /pɔl(l)ysjɔ̃/ *nf* pollution

polo /pɔlo/ *nm* (a) polo shirt
(b) (Sport) polo

polochon /pɔlɔʃɔ̃/ *nm* ‹colloq› bolster; **bataille de ~s** pillow fight

Pologne /pɔlɔɲ/ *pr nf* Poland

polonais, ~e /pɔlɔnɛ, ɛz/ ① *adj* Polish
② *nm* (language) Polish

Polonais, ~e *nm,f* Pole

poltronnerie /pɔltʀɔnʀi/ *nf* cowardice

polycopier /pɔlikɔpje/ [2] *vtr* to duplicate

polyculture /pɔlikyltyʀ/ *nf* mixed farming

polygame /pɔligam/ *adj* polygamous

polyglotte /pɔliglɔt/ *adj, nm,f* polyglot

Polytechnique /pɔlitɛknik/ *nf*: **Grande École de Science and Technology**

polyvalence /pɔlivalɑ̃s/ *nf* (a) versatility
(b) (of employee) flexibility

polyvalent, ~e /pɔlivalɑ̃, ɑ̃t/ *adj* ‹equipment› multipurpose; ‹employee› who does several jobs

pommade /pɔmad/ *nf* (Med) ointment
IDIOMS **passer de la ~ à qn** ‹colloq› to butter sb up ‹colloq›

pomme /pɔm/ *nf* (a) apple
(b) (of watering can) rose; (of shower) showerhead; (of walking stick) pommel, knob
(c) ‹colloq› mug (GB) ‹colloq›, sucker ‹colloq›; **ça va encore être pour ma ~** I'm in for it again ‹colloq›
■ **~ d'Adam** Adam's apple; **~ de pin** pine cone; **~ de terre** potato; **~s frites** chips (GB), (French) fries
IDIOMS **tomber dans les ~s** ‹colloq› to faint

pommeau, *pl* ~x /pɔmo/ *nm* knob; pommel

pommette /pɔmɛt/ *nf* cheekbone

pommier /pɔmje/ *nm* apple tree

pompe /pɔ̃p/ *nf* (a) pump
(b) (slang) shoe
(c) pomp
(d) (Sport) ‹colloq› press-up (GB), push-up
■ **~ à essence** petrol pump (GB), gas pump (US); **~s funèbres** undertaker's (GB), funeral director's
IDIOMS **avoir un coup de ~** ‹colloq› to be knackered (GB) (slang) *or* pooped ‹colloq›

pomper /pɔ̃pe/ [1] *vtr* (a) to pump ‹liquid, air›
(b) (students' slang) to copy
IDIOMS **~ l'air à qn** ‹colloq› to get on sb's nerves

pompette /pɔ̃pɛt/ *adj* ‹colloq› tipsy ‹colloq›, drunk

pompeux, -euse /pɔ̃pø, øz/ *adj* pompous

pompier, -ière /pɔ̃pje, ɛʀ/ ① *adj* pompous
② *nm* fireman, firefighter; **appeler les ~s** to call the fire brigade (GB) *or* department (US)

pompiste /pɔ̃pist/ *nmf* petrol (GB) *or* gas (US) pump attendant

pompon /pɔ̃pɔ̃/ *nm* (on hat) pompom, bobble; (on slipper) pompom
IDIOMS **décrocher le ~** (colloq) to win first prize

pomponner: se pomponner /pɔ̃pɔne/ [1] *v refl* (+ *v être*) to get dolled up

ponce /pɔ̃s/ *nf* **pierre ~** pumice stone

poncer /pɔ̃se/ [12] *vtr* (a) (Tech) to sand
(b) to pumice

ponceuse /pɔ̃søz/ *nf* sander

ponction /pɔ̃ksjɔ̃/ *nf* (a) (Med) puncture
(b) levy

ponctualité /pɔ̃ktɥalite/ *nf* punctuality

ponctuation /pɔ̃ktɥasjɔ̃/ *nf* punctuation

ponctuel, -elle /pɔ̃ktɥɛl/ *adj* (a) ⟨person⟩ punctual
(b) ⟨action⟩ limited; ⟨problem⟩ isolated

ponctuer /pɔ̃ktɥe/ [1] *vtr* to punctuate

pondéré, ~e /pɔ̃dere/ *adj* (a) ⟨person⟩ levelheaded
(b) ⟨factor⟩ weighted

pondre /pɔ̃dʀ/ [6] *vtr* (a) to lay ⟨egg⟩
(b) (colloq) to churn out (colloq) ⟨poetry, articles⟩

poney /pɔnɛ/ *nm* pony

pont /pɔ̃/ ⓵ *nm* (a) bridge
(b) link, tie; **couper les ~s** to break off all contact
(c) extended weekend (*including days between a public holiday and a weekend*)
(d) deck
⓶ **ponts** *nm pl* **~s (et chaussées)** highways department
■ **~ aérien** airlift; **~ à péage** toll bridge
IDIOMS **coucher sous les ~s** to sleep rough, to be a tramp; **il coulera beaucoup d'eau sous les ~s avant que…** it will be a long time before…; **faire un ~ d'or à qn** to offer sb a large sum to accept a job

pontife /pɔ̃tif/ *nm* (a) pontiff; **le souverain ~** the pope
(b) (colloq) pundit (colloq)

pontificat /pɔ̃tifika/ *nm* pontificate

pontifier /pɔ̃tifje/ [2] *vi* to pontificate

pont-levis, *pl* **ponts-levis** /pɔ̃ləvi/ *nm* drawbridge

ponton /pɔ̃tɔ̃/ *nm* (a) landing stage
(b) pontoon

pope /pɔp/ *nm* pope, orthodox priest

popote /pɔpɔt/ *nf* (colloq) cooking

populace /pɔpylas/ *nf* **la ~** the masses

populaire /pɔpylɛʀ/ *adj* (a) ⟨suburb⟩ working-class; ⟨art, novel⟩ popular; ⟨edition⟩ cheap; ⟨restaurant⟩ basic; **classe ~** working class
(b) ⟨tradition⟩ folk; **culture ~** folklore
(c) popular
(d) ⟨revolt⟩ popular; ⟨will⟩ of the people
(e) ⟨expression, term⟩ vulgar
(f) **République ~** People's Republic

popularité /pɔpylarite/ *nf* popularity

population /pɔpylasjɔ̃/ *nf* population

populeux, -euse /pɔpylø, øz/ *adj* densely populated, populous

porc /pɔʀ/ *nm* (a) pig, hog (US)
(b) pork
(c) pigskin

porcelaine /pɔʀsəlɛn/ *nf* porcelain, china

porcelet /pɔʀsəlɛ/ *nm* piglet

porc-épic, *pl* **~s** /pɔʀkepik/ *nm* porcupine

porche /pɔʀʃ/ *nm* porch

porcherie /pɔʀʃəri/ *nf* pigsty

porcin, ~e /pɔʀsɛ̃, in/ *adj* porcine

pore /pɔʀ/ *nm* pore

poreux, -euse /pɔʀø, øz/ *adj* porous

porno /pɔʀno/ *adj*, *nm* (colloq) porn (colloq)

pornographique /pɔʀnɔgʀafik/ *adj* pornographic

port /pɔʀ/ *nm* (a) harbour (GB); port
(b) haven
(c) wearing; carrying
(d) bearing
(e) (transport) carriage; postage
■ **~ d'attache** port of registry; home base; **~ de pêche** fishing harbour (GB); fishing port; **~ de plaisance** marina
IDIOMS **arriver à bon ~** to arrive safe and sound

portable /pɔʀtabl/ ⓵ *adj* portable; **ordinateur ~** laptop computer
⓶ *nm* mobile (phone)

portail /pɔʀtaj/ *nm* (of park) gate; (of church) great door

portant, ~e /pɔʀtɑ̃, ɑ̃t/ *adj* (a) ⟨wall⟩ load-bearing
(b) **bien ~** in good health
IDIOMS **à bout ~** at point-blank range

portatif, -ive /pɔʀtatif, iv/ *adj* portable

porte /pɔʀt/ *nf* (a) door; gate; **devant la ~ de l'hôpital** outside the hospital; **aux ~s du désert** at the edge of the desert; **ouvrir sa ~ à qn** to let sb in; **c'est la ~ ouverte à la criminalité** it's an open invitation to crime; **mettre à la ~** to expel; to fire; **ce n'est pas la ~ à côté** (colloq) it's quite far
(b) gateway; **la victoire leur ouvre la ~ de la finale** the victory clears the way to the final for them
(c) (in airport) gate
(d) (car) door
■ **~ battante** swing door; **~ d'écluse** lock gate; **~ d'entrée** front door; main entrance; **~ de service** service entrance; **~ de sortie** escape route
IDIOMS **prendre la ~** to leave; **entrer par la petite/grande ~** to start at the bottom/top

porté, ~e[1] /pɔʀte/ *adj* **être ~ sur qch** to be keen on sth

porte-à-faux /pɔʀtafo/ *nm inv* **être en ~** ⟨wall⟩ to be out of plumb; ⟨construction⟩ to be cantilevered; ⟨person⟩ to be in an awkward position

porte-à-porte /pɔʀtapɔʀt/ *nm inv*
(a) door-to-door selling
(b) door-to-door canvassing

P

porte-avions /pɔʀtavjɔ̃/ *nm inv* aircraft
carrier

porte-bagages /pɔʀt(ə)bagaʒ/ *nm inv*
carrier; luggage rack; roof rack

porte-bébé /pɔʀt(ə)bebe/ *nm inv* baby
carrier

porte-bonheur /pɔʀt(ə)bɔnœʀ/ *nm inv*
lucky charm

porte-clés, **porte-clefs** /pɔʀt(ə)kle/
nm inv key ring

porte-documents /pɔʀt(ə)dɔkymã/ *nm
inv* briefcase, attaché case

portée² /pɔʀte/ **1** *adj f* ▸ PORTÉ
2 *nf* (a) range; être à ~ de main *or* à la ~
de la main to be within reach; to be to hand
(b) c'est à la ~ de n'importe qui anybody
can do it; anybody can understand it; se
mettre à la ~ de qn to come down to sb's
level
(c) impact
(d) (of kittens) litter
(e) (Mus) staff, stave (GB)

porte-fenêtre, *pl* **portes-fenêtres**
/pɔʀt(ə)fənɛtʀ/ *nf* French window

portefeuille /pɔʀt(ə)fœj/ **1** *adj* jupe ~
wrap-over skirt
2 *nm* (a) wallet, billfold (US)
(b) portfolio

porte-jarretelles /pɔʀt(ə)ʒaʀtɛl/ *nm inv*
suspender belt (GB), garter belt (US)

portemanteau, *pl* **~x** /pɔʀt(ə)mãto/ *nm*
(a) coat rack
(b) coat stand
(c) coat hanger

portemine /pɔʀt(ə)min/ *nm* propelling
(GB) *or* mechanical (US) pencil

porte-monnaie /pɔʀt(ə)mɔnɛ/ *nm inv*
purse (GB), coin purse (US)

porte-parapluies /pɔʀt(ə)paʀaplɥi/ *nm
inv* umbrella stand

porte-parole /pɔʀt(ə)paʀɔl/ *nm inv*
spokesperson, spokesman/spokeswoman

porte-plume /pɔʀt(ə)plym/ *nm inv*
penholder

porter /pɔʀte/ [1] **1** *vtr* (a) to carry
(b) ~ qch quelque part to take sth
somewhere; ~ qch à qn to take sb sth
(c) (wall, chair) to carry, to bear (weight)
(d) to wear (dress, contact lenses); to have
(moustache)
(e) to have (initials, date, name); to bear
(seal); il porte bien son nom the name suits
him
(f) to bear (flowers)
(g) ~ qch à to bring sth up to, to put sth up
to (rate, number); ~ la température de l'eau
à 80°C to heat the water to 80°C
(h) ~ son regard vers to look at; si tu portes
la main sur elle if you lay a finger on her;
~ un jugement sur qch to pass judgment on
sth
(i) ~ qch sur un registre to enter sth on a
register; se faire ~ malade to report sick;
~ plainte to lodge a complaint

(j) tout nous porte à croire que everything
leads us to believe that
(k) ~ bonheur *or* chance to be lucky
2 **porter sur** *v+prep* (debate) to be about;
(measure) to concern; (ban) to apply to
3 *vi* une voix qui porte a voice that carries;
le coup a porté the blow hit home
4 **se porter** *v refl* (+ *v être*) (a) se ~ bien/
mal (person) to be well/ill; (business) to be
going well/badly
(b) se ~ sur (suspicion) to fall on; (infection)
to spread to

porte-savon /pɔʀt(ə)savɔ̃/ *nm inv*
soapdish

porte-serviettes /pɔʀt(ə)sɛʀvjɛt/ *nm inv*
towel rail

porteur, -euse /pɔʀtœʀ, øz/ **1** *adj*
(a) être ~ d'un virus to carry a virus
(b) mur ~ load-bearing wall
(c) (market, sector) expanding
(d) (current, wave, frequency) carrier
2 *nm,f* holder, bearer
3 *nm* (a) porter; messenger
(b) (of cheque) bearer; ~ d'actions
shareholder
■ ~ sain (Med) symptom-free carrier

porte-voix /pɔʀt(ə)vwɑ/ *nm inv*
megaphone

portier /pɔʀtje/ *nm* porter

portière /pɔʀtjɛʀ/ *nf* (of car) door

portillon /pɔʀtijɔ̃/ *nm* gate

portion /pɔʀsjɔ̃/ *nf* (a) (Culin) portion;
helping
(b) part, portion; (of road) stretch
IDIOMS réduire qn à la ~ congrue to give sb
the strict minimum

portique /pɔʀtik/ *nm* (a) portico
(b) (in gym) frame
(c) swing frame

porto /pɔʀto/ *nm* port

portoricain, **~e** /pɔʀtɔʀikɛ̃, ɛn/ *adj*
Puerto Rican

portrait /pɔʀtʀɛ/ *nm* (a) portrait
(b) description, picture
(c) tu es tout le ~ de ton père you're the
spitting image of your father
(d) (colloq) face; se faire tirer le ~ to have
one's photo taken

portrait-robot, *pl* **portraits-robots**
/pɔʀtʀɛʀɔbo/ *nm* photofit®, identikit®

portuaire /pɔʀtɥɛʀ/ *adj* port

portugais, **~e** /pɔʀtygɛ, ɛz/ **1** *adj*
Portuguese
2 *nm* (language) Portuguese

Portugal /pɔʀtygal/ *pr nm* Portugal

pose /poz/ *nf* (a) (of window) putting in;
(of cupboard) fitting; (of carpet) laying
(b) pose; prendre une ~ to strike a pose
(c) (in photography) exposure

posé, **~e** /poze/ *adj* (air, person)
composed; (gesture, voice) controlled

posément /pozemã/ *adv* calmly, carefully

poser /poze/ [1] **1** *vtr* (a) to put down
(book, glass)

(b) to put in ‹window›; to install ‹radiator›; to fit ‹lock›; to lay ‹tiling, cable›; to plant ‹bomb›; to put up ‹wallpaper, curtains›
(c) to assert ‹theory›; ~ **sa candidature à un poste** to apply for a job; ~ **une addition** to write a sum down
(d) to ask ‹question›; to set ‹riddle›; **ça ne pose aucun problème** that's no problem at all
(e) (Mus) to place ‹voice›
2 vi **(a)** to pose
(b) to put on airs
3 se poser v refl (+ v être) **(a)** ‹bird, insect› to settle
(b) ‹plane› to land
(c) ‹eyes› to fall
(d) se ~ en to claim to be; to present oneself as
(e) se ~ des questions to ask oneself questions
(f) ‹problem, case› to arise; **la question ne se pose pas** there's no question of it; it goes without saying

poseur, -euse /pozœʀ, øz/ nm,f poser (colloq)
■ ~ de bombes bomber; ~ de moquette carpet fitter

positif, -ive /pozitif, iv/ adj **(a)** ‹reply› affirmative
(b) ‹interview› constructive; ‹outcome› positive
(c) ‹reaction› favourable (GB)
(d) ‹person, attitude› positive
(e) ‹number› positive

position /pozisjɔ̃/ nf **(a)** position; **en ~ horizontale** horizontally; **placer qn dans une ~ difficile** to put sb in a difficult or an awkward position
(b) (in ranking) place, position
(c) position, stance; **prendre ~ sur un problème** to take a stand on an issue; **camper sur ses ~s** to stand one's ground
(d) (bank) balance

positivement /pozitivmɑ̃/ adv ‹answer› positively; ‹react, judge› favourably (GB)

posologie /pozɔlɔʒi/ nf dosage

possédant, ~e /posedɑ̃, ɑ̃t/ nm,f **les ~s** the rich, the wealthy

possédé, ~e /posede/ nm,f **les ~s** the possessed

posséder /posede/ [14] vtr **(a)** to own, to possess ‹property, army›; to hold ‹responsibility›
(b) to have ‹skill, quality›
(c) to speak [sth] fluently; to have a thorough knowledge of [sth]
(d) ‹anger, pain› to overwhelm
(e) (colloq) **il nous a bien possédés** he really had us there (colloq)

possesseur /posesœʀ/ nm (of property) owner; (of diploma) holder; (of passport) bearer

possessif, -ive /posesif, iv/ adj possessive

possession /posesjɔ̃/ nf possession

possibilité /posibilite/ **1** nf
(a) possibility
(b) opportunity; ~ **d'embauche** job opportunity
2 **possibilités** nf pl **(a)** (of person) abilities; (of device) potential uses
(b) resources

possible /posibl/ **1** adj **(a)** possible; **dès que ~** as soon as possible; **tout le courage ~** the utmost courage; **tous les cas ~s et imaginables** every conceivable case; **le plus cher ~** ‹sell› at the highest possible price; **autant que ~** as much as possible; **il n'y a pas d'erreur ~, c'est lui** it's him, without a shadow of a doubt; **tout est ~** anything is possible; **pas ~!** (colloq) I don't believe it!; you're joking!; ʻtu vas acheter une voiture?'—ʻ~' ʻare you going to buy a car?'—ʻmaybe'
(b) (colloq) **il a une chance pas ~** he's incredibly lucky
2 nm **faire (tout) son ~** to do one's best

post(-) /post/ pref post(-)

postal, ~e, mpl **-aux** /postal, o/ adj ‹van› post office (GB), mail (US); ‹services› postal

poste¹ /post/ nm **(a)** position, job; post; ~s **vacants** or **à pourvoir** vacancies
(b) (Sport) position
(c) post; ~ **(de travail)** work station; **il est toujours fidèle au ~** you can always rely on him
(d) ~ **de police** police station
(e) ~ **de radio** radio set
(f) (tele)phone; extension
(g) shift
(h) (in accountancy) item
■ ~ **d'aiguillage** signal box; ~ **de douane** customs post; ~ **de pilotage** flight deck; ~ **de secours** first-aid station

poste² /post/ nf post office; **envoyer par la ~** to send [sth] by post (GB), to mail (US)
■ ~ **aérienne** airmail; ~ **restante** poste restante (GB), general delivery (US)

poster¹ /poste/ [1] **1** vtr **(a)** to post (GB), to mail (US)
(b) to post ‹guard›; to put [sb] in place ‹spy›
2 se poster v refl (+ v être) **se ~ devant** to station oneself in front of

poster² /postɛʀ/ nm poster

postérieur, ~e /posterjœʀ/ adj **(a)** ‹date› later; ‹event› subsequent; **un écrivain ~ à Flaubert** a writer who came after Flaubert
(b) ‹part, section› posterior; ‹legs› hind

postérité /posterite/ nf posterity; **passer à la ~** ‹person› to go down in history; ‹work› to become part of the cultural heritage

posthume /postym/ adj posthumous

postiche /postiʃ/ **1** adj ‹beard› false
2 nm **(a)** hairpiece; toupee; wig
(b) false moustache (GB) or mustache (US)
(c) false beard

postier, -ière /postje, ɛʀ/ nm,f postal worker

postillon /pɔstijɔ̃/ *nm* (colloq) drop of saliva

postillonner /pɔstijɔne/ [1] *vi* (colloq) to spit (saliva)

post-scriptum /pɔstskʁiptɔm/ *nm inv* postscript

postsynchroniser /pɔstsɛ̃kʁɔnize/ [1] *vtr* to dub, to add the soundtrack to

postulant, **~e** /pɔstylɑ̃, ɑ̃t/ *nm,f* candidate

postulat /pɔstyla/ *nm* premise; postulate

postuler /pɔstyle/ [1] *vi* to apply

posture /pɔstyʁ/ *nf* (a) posture
(b) position

pot /po/ *nm* (a) container; jar; carton, tub; (earthenware) pot; jug; un ~ de peinture a tin of paint
(b) (chamber) pot
(c) (colloq) drink
(d) (colloq) do (GB) (colloq), drinks party
(e) (colloq) avoir du ~ to be lucky
■ ~ catalytique catalytic converter; ~ d'échappement (Aut) silencer (GB), muffler (US); exhaust
IDIOMS payer les ~s cassés to pick up the pieces; tourner autour du ~ (colloq) to beat about the bush

potable /pɔtabl/ *adj* (a) eau ~ drinking water
(b) (colloq) decent

potage /pɔtaʒ/ *nm* soup

potager /pɔtaʒe/ *nm* kitchen garden

pot-au-feu /pɔtofø/ *nm inv* (a) boiled beef (*with vegetables*)
(b) boiling beef

pot-de-vin, *pl* **pots-de-vin** /podvɛ̃/ *nm* bribe, backhander (GB) (colloq)

pote /pɔt/ *nm* (colloq) mate (GB) (colloq), pal (US) (colloq)

poteau, *pl* **~x** /pɔto/ *nm* post; goalpost
■ ~ électrique electricity pole (*supplying domestic power lines*)

potelé, **~e** /pɔtle/ *adj* chubby

potence /pɔtɑ̃s/ *nf* gallows

potentiel, **-ielle** /pɔtɑ̃sjɛl/ **1** *adj* potential
2 *nm* potential

poterie /pɔtʁi/ *nf* (a) pottery
(b) piece of pottery

potiche /pɔtiʃ/ *nf* vase

potier, **-ière** /pɔtje, ɛʁ/ *nm,f* potter

potin /pɔtɛ̃/ *nm* (colloq) (a) gossip
(b) din (colloq)

potion /posjɔ̃/ *nf* potion

potiron /pɔtiʁɔ̃/ *nm* pumpkin (GB), winter squash (US)

pot-pourri, *pl* **pots-pourris** /popuʁi/ *nm* (a) (Mus) medley
(b) potpourri

pou, *pl* **~x** /pu/ *nm* louse
IDIOMS chercher des ~x (colloq) to nitpick (colloq); être laid comme un ~ (colloq) to be as ugly as sin

poubelle /pubɛl/ *nf* bin (GB), trash can (US); dustbin (GB), garbage can (US)

pouce /pus/ *nm* (a) thumb
(b) big toe
(c) inch; ne pas bouger d'un ~ not to budge an inch
IDIOMS se tourner *or* rouler les ~s (colloq) to twiddle one's thumbs; manger sur le ~ to have a quick bite to eat; donner un coup de ~ à qn to help sb get started

poudre /pudʁ/ *nf* (gen) powder; ~ (à canon) gunpowder; ~ à récurer scouring powder
IDIOMS mettre le feu aux ~s to bring things to a head; jeter de la ~ aux yeux to try to impress

poudrer /pudʁe/ [1] *vtr* to powder

poudreux, **-euse** /pudʁø, øz/ *adj* powdery

poudrier /pudʁije/ *nm* powder compact

poudrière /pudʁijɛʁ/ *nf* (a) powder magazine
(b) (figurative) time bomb

pouf /puf/ *nm* (a) pouffe
(b) faire ~ to fall with a soft thud

pouffer /pufe/ [1] *vi* ~ (de rire) to burst out laughing

pouilleux, **-euse** /pujø, øz/ *adj* (a) (colloq) seedy
(b) flea-ridden

poulailler /pulaje/ *nm* (a) henhouse; hen run
(b) hens
(c) (colloq) (in theatre) le ~ the Gods (GB), the gallery

poulain /pulɛ̃/ *nm* (a) colt; foal
(b) protégé

poularde /pulaʁd/ *nf* fattened chicken

poule /pul/ *nf* (a) hen
(b) boiling fowl
(c) (colloq) ma ~ my pet (colloq), honey (US) (colloq)
■ ~ d'eau moorhen; ~ faisane hen pheasant; ~ mouillée wimp (colloq); ~ naine bantam; ~ au pot boiled chicken
IDIOMS quand les ~s auront des dents (colloq) pigs might fly; tuer la ~ aux œufs d'or to kill the goose that lays the golden egg

poulet /pulɛ/ *nm* chicken
■ ~ d'élevage ≈ battery chicken; ~ fermier ≈ free-range chicken

pouliche /puliʃ/ *nf* filly

poulie /puli/ *nf* pulley

poulpe /pulp/ *nm* octopus

pouls /pu/ *nm inv* pulse

poumon /pumɔ̃/ *nm* lung; ~ d'acier *or* artificiel iron lung; à pleins ~s (*shout*) at the top of one's voice; (*breathe*) deeply

poupe /pup/ *nf* stern; avoir le vent en ~ to have the wind in one's sails

poupée /pupe/ *nf* doll

poupon /pupɔ̃/ *nm* (a) tiny baby
(b) baby doll

pouponner /pupɔne/ [1] *vi* (colloq) to play the doting father/mother

pour¹ /puʀ/ *prep* **(a)** (in order) to; ∼ **faire** to do; in order to do; **pour ne pas faire** so as not to do; **c'était** ∼ **rire** *or* **plaisanter** it was a joke; ∼ **que** so that; ∼ **ainsi dire** so to speak **(b)** for; **le train** ∼ **Paris** the train for Paris *or* to Paris; **ce sera prêt** ∼ **vendredi?** will it be ready by Friday?; ∼ **toujours** forever; **le bébé c'est** ∼ **quand?** when is the baby due?; **se battre** ∼ **une femme** to fight over a woman; **c'est fait** *or* **étudié** ∼**!** (colloq) that's what it's for; **je suis** ∼ (colloq) I'm in favour (GB) **(c)** about; as regards; **se renseigner** ∼ to find out about; ∼ **l'argent** as regards the money, as for the money; ∼ **moi, il a tort** as far as I am concerned, he's wrong **(d)** **elle a** ∼ **ambition d'être pilote** her ambition is to be a pilot **(e)** **elle avait** ∼ **elle de savoir écouter** she had the merit of being a good listener **(f)** ∼ **autant que je sache** as far as I know; ∼ **être intelligente, ça elle l'est!** she really is intelligent! **(g)** **j'ai mis** ∼ **200 francs d'essence** I've put in 200 francs' worth of petrol (GB) *or* gas (US); **merci** ∼ **tout** thank you for everything; **je n'y suis** ∼ **rien** I had nothing to do with it; **je n'en ai pas** ∼ **longtemps** it won't take long **(h)** **dix** ∼ **cent** ten per cent; **une cuillère de vinaigre** ∼ **quatre d'huile** one spoonful of vinegar to four of oil; ∼ **une large part** to a large extent

pour² /puʀ/ *nm* **le** ∼ **et le contre** the pros and the cons

pourboire /puʀbwaʀ/ *nm* tip

pourcentage /puʀsɑ̃taʒ/ *nm* **(a)** percentage **(b)** commission **(c)** cut (colloq)

pourchasser /puʀʃase/ [1] *vtr* **(a)** to hunt ⟨*animal, criminal*⟩ **(b)** to pursue ⟨*person*⟩

pourparlers /puʀpaʀle/ *nm pl* talks; **être en** ∼ ⟨*people*⟩ to be engaged in talks

pourpre /puʀpʀ/ *adj, nm* crimson

pourquoi /puʀkwa/ **1** *adv, conj* why; ∼ **donc?** but why?; ∼ **pas** *or* **non?** why not?; ∼ **pas un week-end à Paris?** what *or* how about a weekend in Paris?; **va donc savoir** ∼**!** God knows why! **2** *nm inv* **le** ∼ **et le comment** the why and the wherefore

pourri, ∼e /puʀi/ **1** *pp* ▶ POURRIR **2** *pp adj* **(a)** (gen) rotten; ⟨*vegetation*⟩ rotting **(b)** (colloq) ⟨*weather, car*⟩ rotten (colloq); ⟨*person*⟩ crooked (colloq) **3** *nm* rotten part; **ça sent le** ∼ it smells rotten

pourrir /puʀiʀ/ [3] **1** *vtr* **(a)** to rot ⟨*wood*⟩ **(b)** to spoil ⟨*person*⟩ **(c)** (colloq) to spoil [sb] rotten (colloq) **2** *vi* **(a)** ⟨*food*⟩ to go bad **(b)** ⟨*wood*⟩ to rot **(c)** ⟨*person*⟩ to rot; ⟨*situation*⟩ to deteriorate

pourriture /puʀityʀ/ *nf* **(a)** rot, decay **(b)** corruption, rottenness

poursuite /puʀsɥit/ *nf* **(a)** pursuit; **être à la** ∼ **de** to be in pursuit of **(b)** chase **(c)** continuation **(d)** ∼ ⟨*judiciaire*⟩ (judicial) proceedings

poursuivre /puʀsɥivʀ/ [62] **1** *vtr* **(a)** to chase **(b)** ⟨*person*⟩ to hound; ⟨*nightmare*⟩ to haunt; ∼ **qn de ses assiduités** to force one's attentions on sb **(c)** to seek (after) ⟨*honours, truth*⟩; to pursue ⟨*goal*⟩ **(d)** to continue ⟨*journey, studies*⟩; to pursue ⟨*talks*⟩ **(e)** (Law) ∼ **qn** (**en justice** *or* **devant les tribunaux**) to sue sb **2** *vi* to continue; ∼ **sur un sujet** to continue talking on a subject **3 se poursuivre** *v refl* (+ *v être*) ⟨*talks, conflict, journey*⟩ to continue

pourtant /puʀtɑ̃/ *adv* though; **et** ∼ and yet; **techniquement** ∼, **le film est parfait** technically, however, the film is perfect

pourtour /puʀtuʀ/ *nm* **(a)** perimeter; circumference **(b)** surrounding area

pourvoir /puʀvwaʀ/ [40] **1** *vtr* **(a)** to fill ⟨*post*⟩ **(b)** ∼ **qn de** to endow sb with **2 pourvoir à** *v+prep* to provide for **3 se pourvoir** *v refl* (+ *v être*) **se** ∼ **de** to provide oneself with ⟨*currency*⟩; to equip oneself with ⟨*boots*⟩

pourvoyeur, -euse /puʀvwajœʀ, øz/ *nm,f* ∼ **de** source of ⟨*jobs, funding*⟩

pourvu, ∼e /puʀvy/ **1** *pp* ▶ POURVOIR **2 pourvu que** *phr* **(a)** provided (that), as long as **(b)** let's hope; ∼ **que ça dure!** let's hope it lasts!

pousse /pus/ *nf* **(a)** (Bot) shoot **(b)** growth

poussé, ∼e¹ /puse/ **1** *pp* ▶ POUSSER **2** *pp adj* ⟨*inquiry*⟩ thorough; ⟨*studies*⟩ advanced

poussée² /puse/ *nf* **(a)** (of water, crowd) pressure; (of wind) force **(b)** thrust **(c)** (Med) attack; ∼ **de fièvre** sudden high temperature **(d)** (in price) (sharp) rise; (in racism, violence) upsurge

pousser /puse/ [1] **1** *vtr* **(a)** to push ⟨*wheelbarrow, person*⟩; to move *or* shift [sth] (out of the way), to push [sth] aside; ∼ **une porte** to push a door to; to push a door open; ∼ **qn du coude** to give sb a dig *or* to nudge sb with one's elbow **(b)** ∼ **qn à faire** to encourage sb to do; to urge sb to do; ⟨*hunger, despair*⟩ to drive sb to do; ∼ **à la consommation** to encourage people to buy more; to encourage people to drink more

⋯⟶

(c) to push ‹*pupil*›; to keep [sb] at it
‹*employee*›; to drive [sth] hard ‹*car*›
(d) to push ‹*product, protégé*›
(e) to pursue ‹*studies, research*›; c'est ~ un
peu loin la plaisanterie that's taking the joke
a bit far
(f) to let out ‹*cry*›; to heave ‹*sigh*›
2 vi **(a)** ‹*child*› to grow; ‹*plant*› to grow; to
sprout; ‹*tooth*› to come through; ‹*buildings*›
to spring up; je fais ~ des légumes I grow
vegetables; se laisser ~ les cheveux to grow
one's hair
(b) ~ plus loin to go on further
(c) (colloq) to overdo it, to go too far
3 se pousser v refl (+ v être) to move
over
IDIOMS à la va comme je te pousse (colloq)
any old how

poussette /pusɛt/ nf pushchair (GB),
stroller (US)

poussière /pusjɛʀ/ nf **(a)** dust; tomber en
~ to crumble away; to fall to bits
(b) speck of dust
IDIOMS 10 francs/20 ans et des ~s (colloq)
just over 10 francs/20 years

poussiéreux, -euse /pusjeʀø, øz/ adj
(a) dusty
(b) outdated, fossilized

poussin /pusɛ̃/ nm chick

poussoir /puswaʀ/ nm (push) button

poutre /putʀ/ nf **(a)** beam
(b) girder

pouvoir¹ /puvwaʀ/ [49] **1** v aux **(a)** to be
able to; peux-tu soulever cette boîte? can you
lift this box?; dès que je pourrai as soon as I
can; je n'en peux plus I've had it (colloq); I'm
full (colloq); tout peut arriver anything could
happen; il ne peut pas ne pas gagner he's
bound to win; on peut toujours espérer
there's no harm in wishing; qu'est-ce que
cela peut (bien) te faire? (colloq) what
business is it of yours?
(b) to be allowed to; est-ce que je peux me
servir de ta voiture? can I use your car?; on
peut dire que it can be said that; on peut ne
pas faire l'accord the agreement is optional
(c) pouvez-vous/pourriez-vous me tenir la
porte s'il vous plaît? can you/could you hold
the door (open) for me please?
(d) puisse cette nouvelle année exaucer vos
vœux les plus chers may the new year bring
you everything you could wish for; s'il croit
que je vais payer il peut toujours attendre if
he thinks I'm going to pay he's got another
think coming; ce qu'il peut être grand! how
tall he is!
2 vtr que puis-je pour vous? what can I do
for you?; je fais ce que je peux I'm doing my
best
3 v impers il peut faire très froid en janvier
it can get very cold in January; ce qu'il a pu
pleuvoir! you wouldn't believe how much it
rained!
4 il se peut v impers il se peut que les

prix augmentent en juin prices may or might
rise in June; cela se pourrait qu'il soit fâché
he might be angry
5 on ne peut plus phr il est on ne peut
plus timide he is as shy as can be
6 on ne peut mieux phr ils s'entendent
on ne peut mieux they get on extremely well
IDIOMS autant que faire se peut as far as
possible

pouvoir² /puvwaʀ/ nm **(a)** (gen) power;
~ d'achat purchasing power; avoir le ~ de
faire to be able to do, to have the power to
do; je n'ai pas le ~ de décider it's not up to
me to decide
(b) (Pol) power; avoir tous ~s to have or
exercise full powers; le ~ en place the
government in power
■ le ~ judiciaire the judiciary; ~ législatif
legislative power; ~s publics authorities

pragmatisme /pʀagmatism/ nm
pragmatism

praire /pʀɛʀ/ nf clam

prairie /pʀeʀi/ nf meadow

praline /pʀalin/ nf sugared (GB) or sugar-
coated (US) almond

praliné, ~e /pʀaline/ **1** adj praline
2 nm praline

praticable /pʀatikabl/ adj ‹*road*› passable

praticien, -ienne /pʀatisjɛ̃, ɛn/ nm,f
(a) general practitioner, GP
(b) practitioner

pratiquant, ~e /pʀatikɑ̃, ɑ̃t/ adj
practising (GB); être très ~ to be very devout

pratique /pʀatik/ **1** adj practical; ‹*device*›
handy; ‹*place, route*› convenient
2 nf **(a)** ~ des arts martiaux est très
répandue many people practise (GB) martial
arts; cela nécessite de longues heures de ~
it takes hours of practice; avoir une bonne ~
de l'anglais to have a good working
knowledge of English
(b) practical experience
(c) practice; mettre qch en ~ to put sth into
practice
(d) les ~s religieuses religious practices

pratiquement /pʀatikmɑ̃/ adv **(a)** in
practice
(b) practically, virtually; ~ jamais hardly
ever

pratiquer /pʀatike/ [1] **1** vtr **(a)** to play
‹*tennis*›; to do ‹*yoga*›; to take part in
‹*activity*›; to practise (GB) ‹*language*›; il est
croyant mais ne pratique pas he believes in
God but doesn't practise (GB) his religion
(b) to use ‹*method, blackmail*›; to pursue
‹*policy*›; to charge ‹*rate of interest*›
(c) to carry out ‹*examination, graft*›
2 se pratiquer v refl (+ v être) ‹*sport*› to
be played; ‹*technique, policy, strategy*› to be
used; ‹*price, tariff*› to be charged

pré /pʀe/ nm meadow

pré- /pʀe/ pref pre(-); ~-accord preliminary
agreement

préalable /pʀealabl/ **1** adj ‹*notice*› prior;
‹*study*› preliminary

2 *nm* precondition; preliminary
3 au préalable *phr* first, beforehand
préalablement /pʀealabləmɑ̃/ *adv*
beforehand
préambule /pʀeɑ̃byl/ *nm* **(a)** preamble
(b) forewarning
préau, *pl* ∼**x** /pʀeo/ *nm* (of school) covered
playground; (of prison) exercise yard
préavis /pʀeavi/ *nm inv* notice
précaire /pʀekɛʀ/ *adj* ⟨*existence*⟩
precarious; ⟨*job*⟩ insecure; ⟨*construction*⟩
flimsy
précariser /pʀekaʀize/ [1] *vtr* ∼ **l'emploi**
to casualize labour (GB)
précarité /pʀekaʀite/ *nf* precariousness;
la ∼ **de l'emploi** job insecurity
précaution /pʀekosjɔ̃/ *nf* precaution;
caution; **par** ∼ as a precaution
précédemment /pʀesedamɑ̃/ *adv*
previously
précédent, ∼**e** /pʀesedɑ̃, ɑ̃t/ **1** *adj*
previous
2 *nm,f* **le** ∼, **la** ∼**e** the previous one
3 *nm* precedent; **sans** ∼ unprecedented
précéder /pʀesede/ [14] *vtr* **(a)** ⟨*person*⟩ to
go in front of, to precede; ⟨*vehicle*⟩ to be in
front of
(b) il m'avait précédé de cinq minutes he'd
got there five minutes ahead of me
(c) ⟨*paragraph, crisis*⟩ to precede; **la**
semaine qui a précédé votre départ the week
before you left
précepte /pʀesɛpt/ *nm* precept
précepteur, **-trice** /pʀesɛptœʀ, tʀis/
nm,f (private) tutor
prêcher /pʀeʃe/ [1] **1** *vtr* **(a)** to preach
(b) to advocate
2 *vi* to preach
IDIOMS ∼ **le faux pour savoir le vrai** to tell a
lie in order to get at the truth
précieusement /pʀesjøzmɑ̃/ *adv*
carefully
précieux, **-ieuse** /pʀesjø, øz/ *adj*
(a) ⟨*stone, book*⟩ precious; ⟨*piece of*
furniture⟩ valuable
(b) ⟨*information*⟩ very useful; ⟨*collaborator*⟩
valued
(c) ⟨*friendship, right*⟩ precious; ⟨*friend*⟩ very
dear
(d) ⟨*style, language*⟩ precious
précipice /pʀesipis/ *nm* precipice
précipitamment /pʀesipitamɑ̃/ *adv*
hurriedly
précipitation /pʀesipitasjɔ̃/ **1** *nf* haste
2 précipitations *nf pl* rainfall,
precipitation
précipité, ∼**e** /pʀesipite/ *adj* **(a)** rapid
(b) hasty, precipitate
précipiter /pʀesipite/ [1] **1** *vtr* **(a)** ∼ **qn**
dans le vide (from roof) to push sb off; (out of
window) to push sb out
(b) to hasten ⟨*departure, decision*⟩; to
precipitate ⟨*event*⟩; ∼ **les choses** to rush
things

2 se précipiter *v refl* (+ *v être*) **(a) il**
s'est précipité dans le vide he jumped off
(b) to rush; **se** ∼ **au secours de qn** to rush
to sb's aid; **se** ∼ **sur** to rush at ⟨*person*⟩; to
rush for ⟨*object*⟩
(c) to rush
(d) ⟨*action*⟩ to move faster
précis, ∼**e** /pʀesi, iz/ **1** *adj*
(a) ⟨*programme, criterion*⟩ specific; ⟨*idea,*
date⟩ definite; ⟨*moment*⟩ particular
(b) ⟨*person, gesture*⟩ precise; ⟨*figure, data*⟩
accurate; ⟨*place*⟩ exact
2 *nm inv* handbook
précisément /pʀesizemɑ̃/ *adv* precisely
préciser /pʀesize/ [1] **1** *vtr* **(a)** to add;
faut-il le *or* **est-il besoin de** ∼ needless to
say
(b) to state; ∼ **ses intentions** to state one's
intentions
(c) to specify; **pouvez-vous** ∼**?** could you be
more specific?
(d) to clarify ⟨*ideas*⟩
2 se préciser *v refl* (+ *v être*) **(a)** ⟨*danger,*
future⟩ to become clearer; ⟨*plan, trip*⟩ to
take shape
(b) ⟨*shape, reality*⟩ to become clear
précision /pʀesizjɔ̃/ *nf* **(a)** precision
(b) accuracy; **localiser avec** ∼ to pinpoint;
instrument de ∼ precision instrument
(c) detail
précité, ∼**e** /pʀesite/ *adj* aforementioned
précoce /pʀekɔs/ *adj* **(a)** precocious
(b) ⟨*season*⟩ early
(c) ⟨*senility*⟩ premature
précompte /pʀekɔ̃t/ *nm* deduction; ∼ **de**
l'impôt deduction of tax at source
préconçu, ∼**e** /pʀekɔ̃sy/ *adj*
preconceived
préconiser /pʀekɔnize/ [1] *vtr* to
recommend
précuit, ∼**e** /pʀekɥi, it/ *adj* precooked
précurseur, ∼**e** /pʀekyʀsœʀ/ **1** *adj m*
precursory; **signes** ∼**s de l'orage** signs that
herald a storm
2 *nm* pioneer; ∼ **de** precursor of
prédateur /pʀedatœʀ/ *nm* **(a)** predator
(b) hunter-gatherer
prédécesseur /pʀedesesœʀ/ *nm*
predecessor
prédestiner /pʀedɛstine/ [1] *vtr* to
predestine
prédicateur, **-trice** /pʀedikatœʀ, tʀis/
nm,f preacher
prédiction /pʀediksjɔ̃/ *nf* prediction
prédilection /pʀedilɛksjɔ̃/ *nf*
predilection, liking; **de** ∼ favourite (GB)
prédire /pʀediʀ/ [65] *vtr* to predict
prédisposer /pʀedispoze/ [1] *vtr* to
predispose
prédominant, ∼**e** /pʀedɔminɑ̃, ɑ̃t/ *adj*
predominant
prédominer /pʀedɔmine/ [1] *vi* to
predominate

p

préétablir /pʀeetabliʀ/ [3] *vtr* to pre-establish

préexister /pʀeɛgziste/ [1] *vi* to pre-exist

préfabriqué /pʀefabʀike/ *nm*
(a) prefabricated material
(b) prefab (colloq)

préface /pʀefas/ *nf* preface

préfacer /pʀefase/ [12] *vtr* to write a *or* the preface to

préfectoral, ~e, mpl -aux /pʀefɛktɔʀal, o/ *adj* ⟨*level, authorization*⟩ prefectoral; ⟨*administration, building*⟩ prefectural

préfecture /pʀefɛktyʀ/ *nf* (a) prefecture
(b) *main city of a French department*
■ ~ **de police** police headquarters (*in some large French cities*)

préférable /pʀefeʀabl/ *adj* preferable

préféré, ~e /pʀefeʀe/ *adj, nm,f* favourite (GB)

préférence /pʀefeʀɑ̃s/ *nf* preference; **achète cette marque de ~** if you can, buy this brand

préférentiel, -ielle /pʀefeʀɑ̃sjɛl/ *adj* preferential

préférer /pʀefeʀe/ [14] *vtr* to prefer; **j'aurais préféré ne jamais l'apprendre** I wish I'd never found out

préfet /pʀefɛ/ *nm* prefect

préfigurer /pʀefigyʀe/ [1] *vtr* to prefigure

préfixe /pʀefiks/ *nm* prefix

préhistoire /pʀeistwaʀ/ *nf* prehistory

préjudice /pʀeʒydis/ *nm* harm, damage; **~ moral** moral wrong; **porter ~ à qn** to harm sb; **au ~ de qn** to the detriment of sb

préjugé /pʀeʒyʒe/ *nm* prejudice; **~(s) en faveur de qn** bias in favour (GB) of sb

préjuger /pʀeʒyʒe/ [13] *vtr*, **préjuger de** *v+prep* to prejudge

prélasser: se prélasser /pʀelase/ [1] *v refl* (+ *v être*) to lounge

prélat /pʀela/ *nm* prelate

prélavage /pʀelavaʒ/ *nm* prewash

prêle /pʀɛl/ *nf* (Bot) horsetail

prélèvement /pʀelɛvmɑ̃/ *nm*
(a) sampling; sample; **faire un ~ de sang** to take a blood sample
(b) **faire un ~ bancaire de 100 francs** to make a debit of 100 francs
■ ~ **automatique** direct debit; ~ **à la source** deduction at source

prélever /pʀelve/ [16] *vtr* (a) to take a sample of ⟨*blood, water*⟩; to remove ⟨*organ*⟩
(b) to debit
(c) to deduct ⟨*tax*⟩
(d) to take ⟨*percentage*⟩

préliminaire /pʀeliminɛʀ/ **1** *adj* preliminary
2 préliminaires *nm pl* preliminaries

prélude /pʀelyd/ *nm* prelude

préluder /pʀelyde/ [1] *v+prep* ~ **à** to be a prelude to

prématuré, ~e /pʀematyʀe/ **1** *adj* premature

2 *nm,f* premature baby

préméditation /pʀemeditasjɔ̃/ *nf* premeditation

préméditer /pʀemedite/ [1] *vtr* to premeditate

premier, -ière¹ /pʀəmje, ɛʀ/ **1** *adj*
(a) first; ⟨dans⟩ **les ~s temps** at first
(b) ⟨*artist, power*⟩ leading; ⟨*student*⟩ top; **être ~** to be top; to be first; **c'est le ~ prix** it's the cheapest
(c) ⟨*impression*⟩ first, initial
(d) ⟨*quality*⟩ prime; ⟨*objective*⟩ primary
2 *nm,f* first; **je préfère le ~** I prefer the first one; **arriver le ~** to come first; **être le ~ de la classe** to be top of the class
3 *nm* (a) first floor (GB), second floor (US)
(b) first; **le ~ de l'an** New Year's Day
(c) first arrondissement
4 en premier *phr* first
■ ~ **âge** ⟨*clothes*⟩ for babies up to six months; ~ **de cordée** (Sport) leader; ~ **ministre** prime minister; **le ~ venu** just anybody; the first person to come along; **~s secours** first aid

première² /pʀəmjɛʀ/ **1** ▶ **PREMIER 1, 2**
2 *nf* (a) first; ~ **mondiale** world first
(b) première
(c) (Sch) sixth year of secondary school, *age 16-17*
(d) (Aut) first (gear)
(e) (colloq) first class
3 de première *phr* (colloq) first-rate

premièrement /pʀəmjɛʀmɑ̃/ *adv*
(a) firstly, first
(b) for a start, for one thing

prémisse /pʀemis/ *nf* premise, premiss (GB)

prémolaire /pʀemɔlɛʀ/ *nf* premolar

prémonition /pʀemɔnisjɔ̃/ *nf* premonition

prémonitoire /pʀemɔnitwaʀ/ *adj* premonitory

prémunir /pʀemyniʀ/ [3] **1** *vtr* to protect
2 se prémunir *v refl* (+ *v être*) to protect oneself

prenant, ~e /pʀənɑ̃, ɑ̃t/ *adj* ⟨*film*⟩ fascinating; ⟨*voice*⟩ captivating; ⟨*work*⟩ absorbing

prendre /pʀɑ̃dʀ/ [52]

■ Note *Prendre* is very often translated by *to take* but see the entry below for a wide variety of usages.
– For translations of certain fixed phrases such as *prendre froid, prendre soin de, prendre parti* etc, refer to the entries FROID, SOIN, PARTI.

1 *vtr* (a) to take; ~ **un vase dans le placard** to take a vase out of the cupboard; **prenez donc une chaise** take a seat; ~ **un congé** to take time off; ~ **le train/l'avion** to take the train/plane; **on m'a pris tous mes bijoux** I had all my jewellery (GB) *or* jewelry (US) stolen; **la guerre leur a pris deux fils** they lost two sons in the war; ~ **les mensurations de qn** to take sb's measurements; ~ **les choses comme elles sont** to take things as they

come; **ne le prends pas mal** don't take it the wrong way; **je vous ai pris pour quelqu'un d'autre** I thought you were someone else
(b) ~ **un accent** to pick up an accent; to put on an accent
(c) to bring; **n'oublie pas de ~ des bottes** don't forget to bring a pair of boots
(d) to get ⟨food, petrol⟩; ~ **de l'argent au distributeur** to get some money out of the cash dispenser
(e) to have ⟨drink, meal⟩; to take ⟨medicine⟩; **aller ~ une bière** to go for a beer
(f) to choose ⟨topic, question⟩
(g) to charge; **il prend 15% au passage** (colloq) he takes a cut of 15%
(h) to take up ⟨space, time⟩
(i) to take [sb] on; to engage [sb]
(j) to pick [sb/sth] up; ~ **les enfants à l'école** to collect the children from school
(k) to catch; **elle s'est fait ~ en train de voler** she got caught stealing
(l) (colloq) **qu'est-ce qui te prend?** what's the matter with you?; **ça te/leur prend souvent?** are you/they often like this?
(m) to involve ⟨spectator, reader⟩; **être pris par un livre/film** to get involved in a book/film
(n) to get ⟨slap, sunburn⟩; to catch ⟨cold⟩
(o) **il est très gentil quand on sait le ~** he's very nice when you know how to handle him
(p) to take [sth] down ⟨address⟩
(q) **où a-t-il pris qu'ils allaient divorcer?** where did he get the idea they were going to get divorced?
(r) to take over ⟨management, power⟩; to assume ⟨control⟩; **je prends ça sur moi** I'll see to it; **elle a pris sur elle de leur parler** she took it upon herself to talk to them
(s) to put on ⟨weight⟩; to gain ⟨lead⟩
(t) to take on ⟨lease⟩; to take ⟨job⟩
(u) to take on ⟨rival⟩
(v) to take, to seize ⟨town⟩; to capture ⟨ship, tank⟩; to take ⟨chesspiece, card⟩
2 vi **(a)** ~ **à gauche/vers le nord** to go left/north
(b) ⟨wood⟩ to catch; ⟨fire⟩ to break out
(c) ⟨jelly, glue⟩ to set; ⟨mayonnaise⟩ to thicken
(d) ⟨strike, innovation⟩ to be a success; ⟨idea, fashion⟩ to catch on; ⟨dye, cutting⟩ to take
(e) ~ **sur son temps libre pour traduire un roman** to translate a novel in one's spare time
(f) ~ **sur soi** to take a hold on oneself, to get a grip on oneself
(g) (colloq) **ça ne prend pas!** it won't work!
(h) (colloq) **c'est toujours moi qui prends!** I'm always the one who gets it in the neck!
(colloq) **il en a pris pour 20 ans** he got 20 years
3 **se prendre** v refl (+ v être) **(a)** **en Chine le thé se prend sans sucre** in China they don't put sugar in their tea
(b) **les mauvaises habitudes se prennent vite** bad habits are easily picked up

(c) **se ~ par la taille** to hold each other around the waist
(d) **se ~ les doigts dans la porte** to catch one's fingers in the door
(e) (colloq) **il s'est pris une gifle** he got a slap in the face
(f) **se ~ à faire** to find oneself doing; **se ~ de sympathie pour qn** to take to sb
(g) **pour qui est-ce que tu te prends?** who do you think you are?
(h) **s'en ~ à** to attack ⟨person, press⟩; to take it out on [sb]; to go for [sb]
(i) **savoir s'y ~ avec** to have a way with ⟨children⟩
(j) **il faut s'y ~ à l'avance pour avoir des places** you have to book ahead to get seats; **tu t'y es pris trop tard** you left it too late; **il s'y est pris à plusieurs fois** he tried several times; **elle s'y prend mal** she goes about it the wrong way
IDIOMS **c'est à ~ ou à laisser** take it or leave it

preneur, -euse /prənœr, øz/ nm,f **il n'y a pas ~** there are no takers; **trouver ~** to attract a buyer; to find a buyer

prénom /prenɔ̃/ nm first name, forename

prénommer /prenɔme/ [1] **1** vtr to name, to call
2 **se prénommer** v refl (+ v être) to be called

prénuptial, ~e, pl **-iaux** /prenypsjal, o/ adj prenuptial; prior to marriage

préoccupant, ~e /preɔkypɑ̃, ɑ̃t/ adj worrying

préoccupation /preɔkypasjɔ̃/ nf worry

préoccuper /preɔkype/ [1] **1** vtr **(a)** to worry; **avoir l'air préoccupé** to look worried
(b) to preoccupy
(c) to concern
2 **se préoccuper** v refl (+ v être) **se ~ de** to be concerned about ⟨situation⟩; to think about ⟨future⟩

préparateur, -trice /preparatœr, tris/ nm,f ~ **en pharmacie** pharmacist's assistant

préparatifs /preparatif/ nm pl preparations

préparation /preparasjɔ̃/ nf
(a) preparation
(b) training

préparatoire /preparatwar/ adj preliminary

préparer /prepare/ [1] **1** vtr **(a)** (gen) to prepare; to make ⟨meal⟩; to get [sth] ready ⟨clothes, file⟩; to plan ⟨holidays, future⟩; to draw up ⟨plan⟩; to hatch ⟨plot⟩; **il est en train de ~ le dîner** he's getting dinner ready; **des plats préparés** ready-to-eat meals
(b) ~ **qn à qch** to prepare sb for sth; to coach sb for sth ⟨race, examination⟩; **essaie de la ~ avant de lui annoncer la nouvelle** try and break the news to her gently
2 **se préparer** v refl (+ v être) **(a)** to get ready
(b) to prepare
(c) ⟨storm, trouble⟩ to be brewing; ⟨changes⟩ ⋯⊹

to be in the offing; **un coup d'État se prépare dans le pays** a coup d'état is imminent in the country
(d) se ~ une tasse de thé to make or fix (US) oneself a cup of tea

prépondérance /pʀepɔ̃deʀɑ̃s/ *nf* predominance

prépondérant, ~e /pʀepɔ̃deʀɑ̃, ɑ̃t/ *adj* predominant

préposé, ~e /pʀepoze/ *nm,f* **(a)** official; **~ des douanes** customs official; **~ au vestiaire** cloakroom attendant
(b) postman/postwoman

préposition /pʀepozisjɔ̃/ *nf* preposition

prépuce /pʀepys/ *nm* foreskin

préretraite /pʀeʀətʀɛt/ *nf* early retirement

prérogative /pʀeʀɔgativ/ *nf* prerogative; **~ de qn/qch sur** primacy of sb/sth over

près /pʀɛ/ **1** *adv* **(a)** close; **ce n'est pas tout ~** it's quite a way; **se raser de ~** to have a close shave
(b) ça pèse 10 kg, à quelques grammes ~ it weighs 10 kg, give or take a few grams; à ceci *or* cela ~ que except that; il m'a remboursé au centime ~ he paid me back to the very last penny; gagner à deux voix ~ to win by two votes; à une exception ~ with only one exception
2 près de *phr* **(a)** near; être ~ du but to be close to achieving one's goal; j'aimerais être ~ de toi I'd like to be with you
(b) near, nearly; je ne suis pas ~ de recommencer I'm not about to do that again; le problème n'est pas ~ d'être résolu the problem is nowhere near solved
(c) close; ils sont très ~ l'un de l'autre they are very close
(d) nearly, almost; cela coûte ~ de 1 000 francs it costs nearly 1,000 francs
3 de près *phr* closely; se suivre de ~ ⟨*competitors*⟩ to be close together; ⟨*siblings*⟩ to be close in age
4 à peu près *phr* ~ vide practically empty; ~ 200 francs about 200 francs; à peu ~ de la même façon in much the same way

présage /pʀezaʒ/ *nm* **(a)** omen
(b) harbinger
(c) prediction

présager /pʀezaʒe/ [13] *vtr* ⟨*event*⟩ to presage; ⟨*person*⟩ to predict; laisser ~ to suggest

presbyte /pʀɛsbit/ *adj* longsighted (GB), farsighted (US)

presbytère /pʀɛsbitɛʀ/ *nm* presbytery

presbytie /pʀɛsbisi/ *nf* longsightedness (GB), farsightedness (US)

préscolaire /pʀeskɔlɛʀ/ *adj* preschool

prescription /pʀɛskʀipsjɔ̃/ *nf* prescription; 'se conformer aux ~s du médecin' 'to be taken in accordance with doctor's instructions'

prescrire /pʀɛskʀiʀ/ [67] *vtr* **(a)** (Med) to prescribe
(b) to stipulate

présélection /pʀeselɛksjɔ̃/ *nf*
(a) shortlisting
(b) (Tech) presetting

présélectionner /pʀeselɛksjɔne/ [1] *vtr*
(a) to shortlist
(b) to preselect; to preset

présence /pʀezɑ̃s/ *nf* (gen) presence; (at work) attendance; il fait de la ~, c'est tout he's present and not much else; les forces en ~ dans le conflit the forces involved in the conflict; il a besoin d'une ~ he needs company; avoir beaucoup de ~ (sur scène) to have great stage presence
■ ~ d'esprit presence of mind

présent, ~e[1] /pʀezɑ̃, ɑ̃t/ **1** *adj*
(a) present; M. Maquanne, ici ~ Mr Maquanne, who is here with us; avoir qch à l'esprit to have [sth] in mind ⟨*advice*⟩; to have [sth] fresh in one's mind ⟨*memory*⟩
(b) actively involved; un chanteur très ~ sur scène a singer with a strong stage presence
2 *nm,f* la liste des ~s the list of those present
3 *nm* **(a)** le ~ the present
(b) (in grammar) present (tense)
(c) gift, present
4 à présent *phr* at present; now

présentable /pʀezɑ̃tabl/ *adj* presentable

présentateur, -trice /pʀezɑ̃tatœʀ, tʀis/ *nm,f* presenter; newsreader (GB), newscaster (US)

présentation /pʀezɑ̃tasjɔ̃/ *nf*
(a) introduction; faire les ~s to make the introductions
(b) appearance
(c) (of dish, letter) presentation; (of products) display
(d) show, showing; ~ de mode fashion show
(e) (of programme) presentation
(f) (of card, ticket) production; (of cheque) presentation
(g) presentation, exposé

présente[2] /pʀezɑ̃t/ **1** *adj f* ▶ PRÉSENT 1
2 *nf* **(a)** par la ~ hereby
(b) ▶ PRÉSENT 2

présenter /pʀezɑ̃te/ [1] **1** *vtr* **(a)** to introduce; to present
(b) to show ⟨*ticket, card, menu*⟩
(c) to present ⟨*programme, show, collection*⟩; to display ⟨*goods*⟩
(d) to present ⟨*receipt, bill*⟩; to submit ⟨*estimate, report*⟩; to introduce ⟨*proposal, bill*⟩; ~ une liste pour les élections to put forward a list (of candidates) for the elections
(e) to present ⟨*situation, budget, theory*⟩; to set out ⟨*objections, point of view*⟩; ~ qn comme (étant) un monstre to portray sb as a monster
(f) to offer ⟨*condolences*⟩; ~ des excuses to apologize
(g) to involve ⟨*risk, difficulty*⟩; to show ⟨*differences*⟩; to offer ⟨*advantage*⟩; to have ⟨*aspect, feature*⟩
2 *vi* ~ bien to have a smart appearance
3 se présenter *v refl* (+ *v être*) **(a)** il faut

se ~ à la réception you must go to
reception; **présentez-vous à 10 heures** come
at 10 o'clock
(b) to introduce oneself
(c) se ~ à to take ⟨*examination*⟩; to stand
for ⟨*election*⟩
(d) ⟨*opportunity*⟩ to arise; ⟨*solution*⟩ to
emerge
(e) se ~ en, se ~ sous forme de ⟨*product*⟩
to come in the form of
(f) l'affaire se présente bien things are
looking good

présentoir /pʀezɑ̃twaʀ/ *nm* **(a)** display
stand *or* unit
(b) display shelf

préservatif /pʀezɛʀvatif/ *nm* condom

préservation /pʀezɛʀvasjɔ̃/ *nf*
protection; preservation

préserver /pʀezɛʀve/ [1] *vtr* **(a)** to
preserve
(b) to protect

présidence /pʀezidɑ̃s/ *nf* **(a)** presidency;
chairmanship
(b) presidential palace

président /pʀezidɑ̃/ *nm* president;
chairman
■ ~ de la République President of the
Republic

président-directeur, *pl*
présidents-directeurs
/pʀezidɑ̃diʀɛktœʀ/ *nm* ~ général chairman
and managing director (GB), chief executive
officer

présidente /pʀezidɑ̃t/ *nf* **(a)** president;
chairwoman, chairperson; chairman
(b) First Lady

présidentiel, -ielle /pʀezidɑ̃sjɛl/ *adj*
presidential

présidentielles /pʀezidɑ̃sjɛl/ *nf pl*
presidential election

présider /pʀezide/ [1] *vtr* **(a)** to chair
(b) to be the president of; to be the
chairman/chairwoman of; to preside over

présomption /pʀezɔ̃psjɔ̃/ *nf* **(a)** (Law)
presumption
(b) assumption
(c) plein de ~ presumptuous

présomptueux, -euse /pʀezɔ̃ptɥø, øz/
adj arrogant; presumptuous

presque /pʀɛsk/ *adv* almost, nearly; il y a
trois ans ~ jour pour jour it's nearly three
years to the day; c'était le bonheur ou ~ it
was as close to happiness as one can get; il
ne reste ~ rien there's hardly anything left

presqu'île /pʀɛskil/ *nf* peninsula

pressant, ~e /pʀesɑ̃, ɑ̃t/ *adj* ⟨*need*⟩
pressing; ⟨*appeal*⟩ urgent; ⟨*salesman*⟩
insistent

presse /pʀɛs/ *nf* **(a)** press; newspapers;
avoir bonne ~ to be well thought of
(b) (gen) press; (printing) press; mettre sous
~ to send [sth] to press; 'sous ~' 'in
preparation'

pressé, ~e /pʀese/ *adj* **(a)** ⟨*person*⟩ in a
hurry; ⟨*steps*⟩ hurried

(b) ~ de faire keen to do
(c) ⟨*business*⟩ urgent; parer au plus ~ to do
the most urgent thing(s) first

presse-ail /pʀesaj/ *nm inv* garlic press

presse-citron /pʀesitʀɔ̃/ *nm inv* lemon
squeezer

pressentiment /pʀesɑ̃timɑ̃/ *nm*
premonition

pressentir /pʀesɑ̃tiʀ/ [30] *vtr* to have a
premonition about

presse-papiers /pʀɛspapje/ *nm inv*
paperweight

presser /pʀese/ [1] **1** *vtr* **(a)** ~ qn de faire
to urge sb to do
(b) to press ⟨*debtor*⟩; to harry ⟨*enemy*⟩
(c) ⟨*hunger, necessity*⟩ to drive [sb] on
(d) to increase ⟨*rhythm*⟩; ~ le pas *or*
mouvement to hurry
(e) to press ⟨*button*⟩
(f) to squeeze ⟨*hand, object*⟩
(g) to squeeze ⟨*orange, sponge*⟩; to press
⟨*grapes*⟩
(h) to press ⟨*record*⟩
2 *vi* ⟨*matter*⟩ to be pressing; ⟨*work*⟩ to be
urgent; le temps presse time is running out
3 se presser *v refl* (+ *v être*) **(a)** se ~
autour de qn/qch to press around sb/sth
(b) to hurry up
(c) to flock

pressing /pʀesiŋ/ *nm* dry-cleaner's

pression /pʀesjɔ̃/ *nf* **(a)** (gen) pressure;
~ artérielle blood pressure; sous ~ under
pressure; pressurized; faire ~ sur to press
on ⟨*surface*⟩; to put pressure on ⟨*person*⟩
(b) snap (fastener)

pressoir /pʀeswaʀ/ *nm* **(a)** pressing shed
(b) press; ~ à pommes cider press

pressurer /pʀesyʀe/ [1] *vtr* **(a)** to press
⟨*fruit, seeds*⟩
(b) (colloq) (exploiter) to milk (colloq)

pressuriser /pʀesyʀize/ [1] *vtr* to
pressurize

prestance /pʀɛstɑ̃s/ *nf* avoir de la ~ to
have great presence

prestataire /pʀɛstatɛʀ/ *nm* **(a)** ~ de
service (service) contractor, service
provider
(b) recipient ⟨*of a state benefit*⟩

prestation /pʀɛstasjɔ̃/ *nf* **(a)** benefit
(b) provision; ~ de service (provision of a)
service
(c) service
(d) performance; ~ télévisée televised
appearance

prestidigitation /pʀɛstidiʒitasjɔ̃/ *nf*
conjuring

prestige /pʀɛstiʒ/ *nm* prestige; le ~ de
l'uniforme the glamour (GB) of a uniform

prestigieux, -ieuse /pʀɛstiʒjø, øz/ *adj*
prestigious

présumer /pʀezyme/ [1] **1** *vtr* to
presume; le présumé terroriste the alleged
terrorist
2 présumer de *v+prep* (trop) ~ de ses
forces to overestimate one's strength

p

présupposer /pʀesypoze/ [1] *vtr* to presuppose

prêt, ∼e /pʀɛ, pʀɛt/ **1** *adj* ready; **être fin ∼** to be all set; **il est ∼ à tout** he will stop at nothing
2 *nm* **(a) le service de ∼ de la bibliothèque** the library loans service
(b) loan
■ **∼ immobilier** property loan; **∼ personnalisé** personal loan

prêt-à-porter /pʀɛtapɔʀte/ *nm* ready-to-wear

prétendant, ∼e /pʀetɑ̃dɑ̃, ɑ̃t/ **1** *nm,f*
(a) candidate
(b) pretender
2 *nm* suitor

prétendre /pʀetɑ̃dʀ/ [6] **1** *vtr* to claim; **à ce qu'il prétend** according to him; **on le prétend très spirituel** he is said to be very witty
2 prétendre à *v+prep* to claim ‹*damages*›; to aspire to ‹*job*›
3 se prétendre *v refl* (+ *v être*) **il se prétend artiste** he makes out *or* claims he is an artist

prétendu, ∼e /pʀetɑ̃dy/ *adj* ‹*culprit*› alleged; ‹*doctor*› would-be

prétendument /pʀetɑ̃dymɑ̃/ *adv* supposedly

prête-nom, *pl* **∼s** /pʀɛtnɔ̃/ *nm* frontman, man of straw; **société ∼** dummy (US) company

prétentieux, -ieuse /pʀetɑ̃sjø, øz/
1 *adj* pretentious
2 *nm,f* pretentious person

prétention /pʀetɑ̃sjɔ̃/ **1** *nf*
(a) pretentiousness; **être sans ∼** to be unpretentious
(b) avoir la ∼ de faire to claim to do
2 prétentions *nf pl* **quelles sont vos ∼s?** what salary are you asking for?

prêter /pʀete/ [1] **1** *vtr* **(a)** to lend ‹*money, object*›; **∼ sur gages** to loan against security
(b) ∼ attention à to pay attention to; **∼ la main à qn** to lend sb a hand; **∼ l'oreille** to listen; **∼ serment** to take an oath
(c) ∼ à qn to attribute [sth] to sb
2 prêter à *v+prep* to give rise to ‹*confusion*›; **son attitude prête à rire** his/her attitude is ridiculous; **tout prête à croire** *or* **penser que** all the indications would suggest that
3 se prêter *v refl* (+ *v être*) **(a) se ∼ à** to take part in
(b) roman qui se prête à une adaptation cinématographique novel which lends itself to a film adaptation

prétérit /pʀeteʀit/ *nm* preterite

prêteur, -euse /pʀetœʀ, øz/ **1** *adj* **il n'est pas ∼** he's very possessive about his belongings
2 *nm,f* **∼ sur gages** pawnbroker

prétexte /pʀetɛkst/ *nm* excuse, pretext;

donner qch comme ∼, prendre ∼ de qch to use sth as an excuse; **sous aucun ∼** on no account

prétexter /pʀetɛkste/ [1] **1** *vtr* to use [sth] as an excuse, to plead
2 prétexter de *v+prep* **∼ de qch pour faire** to use sth as an excuse for doing

prêtre /pʀɛtʀ/ *nm* priest

prêtresse /pʀɛtʀɛs/ *nf* priestess

preuve /pʀœv/ *nf* **(a)** proof; **une ∼** a piece of evidence; **apporter la ∼ de/que** to offer proof of/that; **la ∼ est faite de/que** now there is proof of/that; **∼ en main** with concrete proof; **faire ses ∼s** to prove oneself
(b) demonstration; **faire ∼ de** to show; **∼ de bonne volonté** gesture of goodwill

prévaloir /pʀevalwaʀ/ [45] **1** *vi* to prevail
2 se prévaloir *v refl* (+ *v être*) **se ∼ de son ancienneté** to claim seniority

prévenance /pʀevnɑ̃s/ *nf* consideration

prévenant, ∼e /pʀevnɑ̃, ɑ̃t/ *adj* considerate

prévenir /pʀevniʀ/ [36] *vtr* **(a)** to tell
(b) to call ‹*doctor, police*›
(c) to warn
(d) to prevent ‹*disaster*›
(e) to anticipate ‹*wishes*›
IDIOMS **mieux vaut ∼ que guérir** (Proverb) prevention is better than cure

préventif, -ive /pʀevɑ̃tif, iv/ *adj* preventive

prévention /pʀevɑ̃sjɔ̃/ *nf* prevention; **faire de la ∼** to take preventive action

prévenu, ∼e /pʀevny/ *nm,f* (Law) defendant

prévisible /pʀevizibl/ *adj* predictable

prévision /pʀevizjɔ̃/ *nf* **(a)** forecasting; **en ∼ de** in anticipation of
(b) prediction; forecast; **∼s météorologiques** weather forecast

prévisionnel, -elle /pʀevizjɔnɛl/ *adj* projected

prévisionniste /pʀevizjɔnist/ *nmf* forecaster

prévoir /pʀevwaʀ/ [42] *vtr* **(a)** to predict ‹*change*›; to foresee ‹*event, victory*›; to anticipate ‹*reaction*›; to forecast ‹*result, weather*›; **c'était à ∼!** that was predictable!
(b) to plan ‹*meeting, journey, building*›; to set the date for ‹*return, move*›; (Law) to make provision for ‹*case, eventuality*›; **ce n'était pas prévu!** that wasn't meant to happen!; **remplissez le formulaire prévu à cet effet** fill in the appropriate form; **tout a été prévu** all the arrangements have been made
(c) to make sure one takes ‹*coat, umbrella*›
(d) to expect ‹*visitor, shortage, strike*›
(e) to allow ‹*sum of money, time*›

prévoyance /pʀevwajɑ̃s/ *nf* foresight

prévoyant, ∼e /pʀevwajɑ̃, ɑ̃t/ *adj* far-sighted

prévu, ∼e /pʀevy/ ▶ PRÉVOIR

prier /pʀije/ [2] **1** *vtr* **(a) ∼ qn de faire** to ask sb to do; **je vous prie d'excuser mon**

retard I'm so sorry I'm late; **je vous prie de vous taire** will you kindly be quiet; **elle ne s'est pas fait ∼** she didn't have to be asked twice
(b) to pray to ⟨*god*⟩; **∼ que** to pray that
2 *vi* to pray

prière /pRijɛR/ *nf* (a) prayer; **faire sa ∼** to say one's prayers
(b) request; plea, entreaty; **∼ de ne pas fumer** no smoking please

prieuré /pRijœRe/ *nm* (a) priory
(b) priory church

primaire /pRimɛR/ **1** *adj* (a) primary
(b) ⟨*person*⟩ limited; ⟨*reasoning*⟩ simplistic
2 *nm* (a) (Sch) **le ∼** primary education
(b) (Econ) **le ∼** the primary sector
(c) **le ∼** the palaeozoic era

primate /pRimat/ *nm* primate

primauté /pRimote/ *nf* primacy

prime /pRim/ **1** *adj* (a) **de ∼ abord** at first, initially
(b) **A ∼** A prime
2 *nf* (a) bonus; free gift
(b) allowance
(c) subsidy
(d) (in insurance) premium
■ **∼ d'ancienneté** seniority bonus; **∼ de risque** danger money

primer /pRime/ [1] **1** *vtr* (a) to take precedence over, to prevail over
(b) to award a prize to
2 **primer sur** *v+prep* (controversial) ▶ PRIMER 1A
3 *vi* **pour moi, c'est la qualité qui prime** what counts for me is quality

primeur /pRimœR/ **1** *nf* **avoir la ∼ de l'information** to be the first to hear sth
2 **primeurs** *nf pl* early fruit and vegetables

primevère /pRimvɛR/ *nf* primrose

primitif, -ive /pRimitif, iv/ *adj* (gen) primitive; ⟨*budget*⟩ initial; ⟨*project, state*⟩ original

primordial, ∼e, mpl -iaux /pRimɔRdjal, o/ *adj* essential, vital

prince /pRɛ̃s/ *nm* prince
IDIOMS **être bon ∼** to be magnanimous

princesse /pRɛ̃sɛs/ *nf* princess
IDIOMS **aux frais de la ∼** (colloq) at the company's expense; at sb's expense

princier, -ière /pRɛ̃sje, ɛR/ *adj* ⟨*title, tastes, sum*⟩ princely; ⟨*luxury*⟩ dazzling

principal, ∼e, mpl -aux /pRɛ̃sipal, o/ **1** *adj* (a) ⟨*factor*⟩ main; ⟨*task*⟩ principal
(b) ⟨*country, role*⟩ leading
(c) ⟨*inspector*⟩ chief
2 *nm* (a) **le ∼** the main thing
(b) (Sch) principal

principalement /pRɛ̃sipalmɑ̃/ *adv* mainly

principauté /pRɛ̃sipote/ *nf* principality

principe /pRɛ̃sip/ **1** *nm* (a) principle; **par ∼** on principle
(b) assumption

(c) (concept) principle; **quel est le ∼ de la machine à vapeur?** how does a steam engine work?
2 **en principe** *phr* (a) as a rule
(b) in theory

printanier, -ière /pRɛ̃tanje, ɛR/ *adj* ⟨*sun*⟩ spring; ⟨*weather*⟩ spring-like

printemps /pRɛ̃tɑ̃/ *nm inv* (a) spring
(b) (colloq) **mes 60 ∼** my 60 summers

prion /pRijɔ̃/ *nm* prion

priori ▶ A PRIORI

prioritaire /pRijɔRitɛR/ *adj* ⟨*file, project*⟩ priority; **être ∼** to have priority

priorité /pRijɔRite/ *nf* priority; **avoir la ∼** to have right (GB) *or* the right (US) of way

pris, ∼s[1] /pRi, pRiz/ **1** *pp* ▶ PRENDRE
2 *pp adj* (a) busy; **j'ai les mains ∼es** I've got my hands full; **les places sont toutes ∼es** all the seats are taken
(b) ⟨*nose*⟩ stuffed up; ⟨*lungs*⟩ congested
(c) **∼ de** overcome with; **∼ de panique** panic-stricken

prise[2] /pRiz/ *nf* (a) storming; **la ∼ de la Bastille** the storming of the Bastille
(b) catching; **une belle ∼** a fine catch
(c) (in judo, wrestling) hold
(d) **n'offrir aucune ∼** to have no handholds; to have no footholds; **avoir ∼ sur qn** to have a hold over sb; **donner ∼ à** to lay oneself open to
(e) socket (GB), outlet (US); plug; jack; **∼ multiple** (multiplug) adaptor; trailing socket
■ **∼ de bec** (colloq) row, argument; **∼ en charge** (of expenses) payment; **∼ de conscience** realization; **∼ de contact** initial contact; **∼ de courant** socket (GB), outlet (US); **∼ d'eau** water supply point; **∼ de sang** blood test; **∼ de vue** shooting; shot
IDIOMS **être aux ∼s avec des difficultés** to be grappling with difficulties

priser /pRize/ [1] *vtr* (a) to hold [sth] in esteem
(b) **∼ (du tabac)** to take snuff

prisme /pRism/ *nm* prism

prison /pRizɔ̃/ *nf* prison; **condamné à trois ans de ∼** sentenced to three years' imprisonment

prisonnier, -ière /pRizɔnje, ɛR/ **1** *adj* **il est ∼** he is a prisoner
2 *nm,f* prisoner

privatif, -ive /pRivatif, iv/ *adj* private

privation /pRivasjɔ̃/ *nf* (a) (of rights) deprivation
(b) want; **s'imposer des ∼s** to make sacrifices

privatisation /pRivatizasjɔ̃/ *nf* privatization

privatiser /pRivatize/ [1] *vtr* to privatize

privé, ∼e /pRive/ **1** *pp* ▶ PRIVER
2 *pp adj* **∼ de** deprived of; **tu seras ∼ de dessert!** you'll go without dessert!
3 *adj* (gen) private; ⟨*interview*⟩ unofficial
4 *nm* (a) (Econ) private sector
(b) (Sch) **le ∼** private schools ····⟩

(c) en ~ in private

priver /pʀive/ [1] **1** *vtr* ~ qn/qch de to deprive sb/sth of; ~ qn de sorties to forbid sb to go out
2 se priver *v refl* (+ *v être*) pourquoi se ~? why deprive ourselves?; **se** ~ **de** qch/de faire to go or do without sth/doing

privilège /pʀivilɛʒ/ *nm* privilege

privilégié, ~e /pʀivileʒje/ **1** *pp* ▶ PRIVILÉGIER
2 *pp adj* **(a)** privileged
(b) fortunate
(c) ⟨*moment, links*⟩ special; ⟨*treatment*⟩ preferential

privilégier /pʀivileʒje/ [2] *vtr* **(a)** to favour (GB)
(b) to give priority to

prix /pʀi/ *nm inv* **(a)** price; **à** or **au** ~ **coûtant** at cost price; **acheter** qch **à** ~ **d'or** to pay a small fortune for sth; **il faut être prêt à y mettre le** ~ you have to be prepared to pay for it; **mettre** qch **à** ~ **à 50 francs** to start the bidding for sth at 50 francs
(b) (figurative) price; **à tout** ~ at all costs; **attacher beaucoup de** ~ **à** to value [sth] highly ⟨*friendship*⟩
(c) prize

pro(-) /pʀo/ *pref* pro(-)

probabilité /pʀobabilite/ *nf* **(a)** probability, likelihood
(b) les ~s probability theory

probable /pʀobabl/ *adj* probable, likely

probablement /pʀobabləmɑ̃/ *adv* probably

probant, ~e /pʀobɑ̃, ɑ̃t/ *adj* ⟨*argument, demonstration*⟩ convincing; ⟨*force, proof*⟩ conclusive

probatoire /pʀobatwaʀ/ *adj* examen ~ assessment test; épreuve ~ aptitude test

probité /pʀobite/ *nf* integrity, probity

problématique /pʀoblematik/ *adj* ⟨*situation*⟩ problematic; ⟨*outcome*⟩ uncertain

problème /pʀoblɛm/ *nm* problem

procédé /pʀosede/ *nm* **(a)** process
(b) practice (GB); **échange de bons** ~s exchange of courtesies

procéder /pʀosede/ [14] **1** *v+prep* to carry out ⟨*check, survey*⟩; to undertake ⟨*reform*⟩; ~ **à un tirage au sort/un vote** to hold a draw/a vote
2 procéder de *v+prep* to be a product of
3 *vi* to go about things; ~ **par élimination** to use a process of elimination

procédure /pʀosedyʀ/ *nf* **(a)** proceedings
(b) procedure

procès /pʀosɛ/ *nm inv* **(a)** trial
(b) lawsuit, case; **intenter un** ~ **à** qn to sue sb
(c) indictment; **faire le** ~ **de** qn/qch to put sb/sth in the dock
IDIOMS sans autre forme de ~ without further ado

processeur /pʀosesœʀ/ *nm* processor

procession /pʀosesjɔ̃/ *nf* procession

processus /pʀosesys/ *nm inv* **(a)** process
(b) (Med) evolution

procès-verbal, *pl* **-aux** /pʀosɛvɛʀbal, o/ *nm* **(a)** (of meeting) minutes
(b) statement of offence (GB)

prochain, ~e /pʀoʃɛ̃, ɛn/ **1** *adj* **(a)** next; **en juin** ~ next June; **à la** ~**e!** (colloq) see you! (colloq)
(b) ⟨*meeting*⟩ coming, forthcoming; ⟨*departure, war*⟩ imminent; **un jour** ~ one day soon
2 *nm* fellow man; **aime ton** ~ love thy neighbour (GB)

prochainement /pʀoʃɛnmɑ̃/ *adv* soon

proche /pʀoʃ/ **1** *adj* **(a)** nearby; ~ **de** close to, near
(b) ⟨*departure*⟩ imminent; **la victoire est** ~ victory is at hand; **la fin est** ~ the end is (drawing) near
(c) ⟨*event*⟩ recent; ⟨*memory*⟩ real, vivid
(d) similar; ~ **de** ⟨*figure, language*⟩ close to; ⟨*attitude*⟩ verging on
(e) ⟨*people*⟩ close; (on form) (**plus**) ~ **parent** next of kin
2 *nm* **(a)** close relative
(b) close friend

Proche-Orient /pʀoʃoʀjɑ̃/ *pr nm* le ~ the Near East

proclamation /pʀoklamasjɔ̃/ *nf* proclamation

proclamer /pʀoklame/ [1] *vtr* **(a)** to proclaim
(b) to declare

procréer /pʀokʀee/ [11] *vi* to procreate

procuration /pʀokyʀasjɔ̃/ *nf* **(a)** power of attorney
(b) proxy; proxy form

procurer /pʀokyʀe/ [1] **1** *vtr* to bring; to give
2 se procurer *v refl* (+ *v être*) **(a)** to obtain
(b) to buy

procureur /pʀokyʀœʀ/ *nm* prosecutor

prodige /pʀodiʒ/ *nm* **(a)** prodigy
(b) feat; **faire des** ~s to work wonders; ~ **technique** technical miracle

prodigieux, -ieuse /pʀodiʒjø, øz/ *adj* ⟨*quantity*⟩ prodigious; ⟨*person*⟩ wonderful

prodigue /pʀodig/ *adj* **(a)** extravagant
(b) être ~ **de** to be lavish with

prodiguer /pʀodige/ [1] *vtr* **(a)** to give lots of ⟨*advice*⟩
(b) to give ⟨*treatment, first aid*⟩

producteur, -trice /pʀodyktœʀ, tʀis/ **1** *adj* **pays** ~ **de pétrole** oil-producing country
2 *nm,f* producer

productif, -ive /pʀodyktif, iv/ *adj* ⟨*work*⟩ productive; ⟨*investment*⟩ profitable

production /pʀodyksjɔ̃/ *nf* **(a)** (gen) production; (of energy) generation
(b) (gen) products, goods
■ ~ **assisteé par ordinateur, PAO** computer aided manufacturing, **CAM**

productivité /pʀɔdyktivite/ *nf* productivity

produire /pʀɔdɥiʀ/ [69] **1** *vtr* (a) (gen) to produce; **cette usine produit peu** this factory has a low output; **un artiste/écrivain qui produit beaucoup** a prolific artist/writer
(b) to bring in ⟨*money, wealth*⟩; to yield ⟨*interest*⟩
(c) to produce, to have ⟨*effect, result*⟩; to create, to make ⟨*impression*⟩; to cause ⟨*sensation, emotion*⟩
2 se produire *v refl* (+ *v être*) (a) ⟨*event*⟩ to occur, to happen
(b) ⟨*singer*⟩ to perform

produit /pʀɔdɥi/ *nm* (a) product; **des ~s** goods, products; **~s alimentaires** foodstuffs; **~s agricoles** agricultural produce
(b) income; yield, return; profit; **vivre du ~ de sa terre** to live off the land; **le ~ de la vente** the proceeds of the sale
(c) (of research) result; (of activity) product
■ **~ chimique** chemical; **~ d'entretien** cleaning product, household product; **~ intérieur brut, PIB** gross domestic product, GDP; **~ national brut, PNB** gross national product, GNP

proéminent, ~e /pʀɔeminã, ãt/ *adj* prominent

profanateur, -trice /pʀɔfanatœʀ, tʀis/ *nm,f* profaner

profanation /pʀɔfanasjɔ̃/ *nf* desecration; defilement; debasement

profane /pʀɔfan/ **1** *adj* secular
2 *nmf* (a) layman/laywoman
(b) nonbeliever
3 *nm* **le ~ et le sacré** the sacred and the profane

profaner /pʀɔfane/ [1] *vtr* to desecrate ⟨*temple*⟩; to defile ⟨*memory*⟩; to debase ⟨*institution*⟩

proférer /pʀɔfeʀe/ [14] *vtr* to hurl ⟨*insults*⟩; to make ⟨*threats*⟩; to utter ⟨*words*⟩

professer /pʀɔfese/ [1] *vtr* to profess

professeur /pʀɔfesœʀ/ *nm* (in school) teacher; (in higher education) lecturer (GB), professor (US); (holding university chair) professor; **~ des écoles** primary school teacher

profession /pʀɔfesjɔ̃/ *nf* (a) occupation; profession; **exercer la ~ d'infirmière** to be a nurse by profession; **être sans ~** to have no occupation
(b) declaration, profession
■ **~ libérale** profession

professionnalisme /pʀɔfesjɔnalism/ *nm* professionalism

professionnel, -elle /pʀɔfesjɔnɛl/
1 *adj* (a) ⟨*qualifications*⟩ professional; ⟨*life, environment*⟩ working; ⟨*disease*⟩ occupational; ⟨*training*⟩ vocational
(b) ⟨*player*⟩ professional
2 *nm,f* professional; **le salon est réservé aux ~s** the fair is restricted to people in the trade

professionnellement /pʀɔfesjɔnɛlmã/ *adv* professionally

professoral, ~e, *mpl* **-aux** /pʀɔfesɔʀal, o/ *adj* professorial

profil /pʀɔfil/ *nm* profile; **être de ~** to be in profile; **se mettre de ~** to turn sideways

profiler /pʀɔfile/ [1] **1** *vtr* **la tour profile sa silhouette dans le ciel** the tower is silhouetted *or* outlined against the sky
2 se profiler *v refl* (+ *v être*) ⟨*shape*⟩ to stand out; ⟨*problem*⟩ to emerge; ⟨*events*⟩ to approach

profit /pʀɔfi/ *nm* (a) benefit, advantage; **au ~ des handicapés** in aid of the handicapped; **mettre à ~** to make the most of ⟨*free time, course*⟩; to turn [sth] to good account ⟨*situation*⟩; to make good use of ⟨*idea*⟩
(b) profit; **être une source de ~ pour** to be a source of wealth for

profitable /pʀɔfitabl/ *adj* (a) beneficial
(b) profitable

profiter /pʀɔfite/ [1] **1 profiter à** *v+prep* **~ à qn** to benefit sb
2 profiter de *v+prep* to use ⟨*advantage*⟩; to make the most of ⟨*holiday, situation*⟩; to take advantage of ⟨*visit, weakness, person*⟩
3 *vi* (colloq) ⟨*person*⟩ to grow; ⟨*plant*⟩ to thrive

profiteur, -euse /pʀɔfitœʀ, øz/ *nm,f* profiteer

profond, ~e /pʀɔfɔ̃, ɔ̃d/ **1** *adj* (a) deep; **peu ~** shallow
(b) ⟨*boredom*⟩ acute; ⟨*sigh*⟩ heavy; ⟨*feeling, sleep, colour*⟩ deep
(c) ⟨*change, ignorance*⟩ profound
(d) ⟨*mind, remark*⟩ profound; ⟨*gaze*⟩ penetrating
(e) **la France ~e** provincial France; **l'Amérique ~e** small-town America
2 *adv* deeply, deep down

profondément /pʀɔfɔ̃demã/ *adv* (a) ⟨*dig*⟩ deep
(b) deeply; greatly; profoundly; **détester ~** to loathe

profondeur /pʀɔfɔ̃dœʀ/ *nf* (a) depth; **avoir une ~ de 3 mètres** to be 3 metres (GB) deep
(b) (of feeling) depth; (of remark, work) profundity; **en ~** ⟨*analysis*⟩ in-depth; ⟨*work*⟩ thorough

profusion /pʀɔfyzjɔ̃/ *nf* profusion; abundance

progéniture /pʀɔʒenityʀ/ *nf* progeny

progiciel /pʀɔʒisjɛl/ *nm* software package

programmateur, -trice /pʀɔgʀamatœʀ, tʀis/ **1** *nm,f* programme (GB) planner
2 *nm* timer

programmation /pʀɔgʀamasjɔ̃/ *nf* programming

programme /pʀɔgʀam/ *nm*
(a) programme (GB)
(b) (of action) plan; (of work) programme (GB); **c'est tout un ~!** (humorous) that'll take some doing! ⋯⋗

(c) (Sch) syllabus
(d) (Comput) program

programmer /pRɔgRame/ [1] *vtr* **(a)** to schedule ‹*broadcast*›; to plan ‹*work*›
(b) (Comput) to program

programmeur, -euse /pRɔgRamœR, øz/ *nm,f* (computer) programmer

progrès /pRɔgRɛ/ *nm inv* **(a)** progress; les ~ de la médecine advances in medicine; être en ~ ‹*person*› to be making progress; ‹*results*› to be improving
(b) increase; être en ~ de 10% to be up by 10%
(c) (of illness) progression

progresser /pRɔgRese/ [1] *vi* **(a)** to rise; to increase; ~ de 3% ‹*rate*› to rise by 3%; ‹*party*› to gain 3%
(b) ‹*politician*› to make gains; ‹*illness*› to spread; ‹*crime*› to be on the increase
(c) ‹*pupil, inquiry, country*› to make progress; ‹*relations*› to improve; ‹*technology*› to progress
(d) ‹*climber*› to make progress; ‹*army*› to advance

progressif, -ive /pRɔgResif, iv/ *adj* progressive

progression /pRɔgRɛsjɔ̃/ *nf* **(a)** progress; advance; spread; increase
(b) (in mathematics, music) progression

progressiste /pRɔgResist/ *adj* progressive

prohibé, ~e /pRɔibe/ *adj* ‹*goods, substance, weapon*› prohibited; ‹*trade, action*› illegal; port d'arme ~ illegal possession of a firearm

prohiber /pRɔibe/ [1] *vtr* to prohibit

prohibitif, -ive /pRɔibitif, iv/ *adj*
(a) ‹*price*› prohibitive
(b) ‹*law*› prohibition

prohibition /pRɔibisjɔ̃/ *nf* prohibition

proie /pRwɑ/ *nf* prey; être en ~ à l'angoisse to be racked by anxiety; pays en ~ à la guerre civile country in the grip of civil war

projecteur /pRɔʒɛktœR/ *nm*
(a) searchlight; floodlight; être sous les ~s to be in the spotlight
(b) projector

projectile /pRɔʒɛktil/ *nm* missile; projectile

projection /pRɔʒɛksjɔ̃/ *nf* **(a)** l'éruption commença par une ~ de cendres the eruption began with a discharge of ashes
(b) le cuisinier a reçu des ~s d'huile bouillante the cook got spattered with scalding oil
(c) projection; showing; salle de ~ screening room

projectionniste /pRɔʒɛksjɔnist/ *nmf* projectionist

projet /pRɔʒɛ/ *nm* **(a)** plan; en ~, à l'état de ~ at the planning stage
(b) project
(c) (rough) draft
(d) (in architecture) execution plan
∎ ~ de loi (government) bill

projeter /pRɔʒte/ [20] *vtr* **(a)** to throw; le 'choc l'a projeté par terre the shock sent him hurtling to the ground
(b) to cast ‹*shadow*›
(c) to show ‹*film*›
(d) to plan (de faire to do)

prolétaire /pRɔletɛR/ *adj, nmf* proletarian

prolétariat /pRɔletaRja/ *nm* proletariat

proliférer /pRɔlifeRe/ [14] *vi* to proliferate

prolifique /pRɔlifik/ *adj* prolific

prolixe /pRɔliks/ *adj* verbose, prolix

prologue /pRɔlɔg/ *nm* prologue

prolongation /pRɔlɔ̃gasjɔ̃/ *nf* continuation; extension; (Sport) extra time

prolongé, ~e /pRɔlɔ̃ʒe/ *adj* ‹*effort*› sustained; ‹*stay*› extended; ‹*exhibition*› prolonged

prolongement /pRɔlɔ̃ʒmɑ̃/ *nm* **(a)** (of road, stay) extension
(b) la rue Berthollet se trouve dans le ~ de la rue de la Glacière Rue de la Glacière becomes Rue Berthollet

prolonger /pRɔlɔ̃ʒe/ [13] **1** *vtr* to extend ‹*stay*›; to prolong ‹*meeting, life*›
2 se prolonger *v refl* (+ *v être*) **(a)** to persist; to go on
(b) ‹*street*› se ~ jusqu'à to go as far as

promenade /pRɔmnad/ *nf* **(a)** walk; ride; drive
(b) walkway; promenade

promener /pRɔmne/ [16] **1** *vtr* **(a)** to take [sb] out ‹*person*›; to take [sth] out for a walk ‹*animal*›; ça te promènera (colloq) it'll get you out
(b) to carry ‹*object*›
(c) to show [sb] around
2 se promener *v refl* (+ *v être*) to go for a walk/drive/ride

promeneur, -euse /pRɔmnœR, øz/ *nm,f* walker

promesse /pRɔmɛs/ *nf* **(a)** promise; avoir la ~ de qn to have sb's word; tenir ses ~s to keep one's promises
(b) ~ de vente agreement to sell
∎ ~ en l'air *or* de Gascon *or* d'ivrogne empty *or* idle promise

prometteur, -euse /pRɔmɛtœR, øz/ *adj* promising

promettre /pRɔmɛtR/ [60] **1** *vtr* **(a)** ~ qch à qn to promise sb sth; je te promets qu'il le regrettera he'll regret it, I guarantee you
(b) une soirée qui promet bien des surprises an evening that holds a few surprises in store
2 *vi* ‹*pupil*› **(a)** to show promise; un film qui promet a film which sounds interesting
(b) (colloq) cet enfant promet! that child is going to be a handful!; ça promet! that promises to be fun!
3 se promettre *v refl* (+ *v être*) **(a)** to promise oneself
(b) se ~ de faire to resolve to do

promiscuité /pRɔmiskɥite/ *nf* lack of privacy

promontoire /pRɔmɔ̃twaR/ *nm*
promontory

promoteur, -trice /pRɔmɔtœR, tRis/
nm,f ~ **(immobilier)** property developer

promotion /pRɔmɔsjɔ̃/ *nf* **(a)** promotion
(b) (special) offer; **en** ~ on (special) offer

promotionnel, -elle /pRɔmɔsjɔnɛl/ *adj*
promotional

promouvoir /pRɔmuvwaR/ [43] *vtr* to
promote

prompt, ~e /pRɔ̃, pRɔ̃t/ *adj* ⟨*reaction*⟩
prompt; ⟨*gesture, glance*⟩ swift; ⟨*return*⟩
sudden

promulguer /pRɔmylge/ [1] *vtr* to
promulgate

prôner /pRone/ [1] *vtr* to advocate

pronom /pRɔnɔ̃/ *nm* pronoun

pronominal, ~e, *mpl* **-aux**
/pRɔnɔminal, o/ *adj* pronominal

prononcé, ~e /pRɔnɔ̃se/ *adj* ⟨*accent,
taste*⟩ strong; ⟨*wrinkles*⟩ deep; **avoir un goût
~ pour** to be particularly fond of

prononcer /pRɔnɔ̃se/ [12] **1** *vtr* **(a)** to
pronounce ⟨*word*⟩
(b) to mention ⟨*name*⟩; to say ⟨*phrase*⟩
(c) to deliver ⟨*speech*⟩
(d) to pronounce ⟨*death penalty*⟩; ~ **le
divorce** to grant a divorce
2 se prononcer *v refl* (+ *v être*) **(a)** to be
pronounced
(b) se ~ contre/en faveur de qch to declare
oneself against/in favour (GB) of sth; **se ~
sur qch** to give one's opinion on sth

prononciation /pRɔnɔ̃sjasjɔ̃/ *nf*
pronunciation

pronostic /pRɔnɔstik/ *nm* **(a)** forecast
(b) prediction
(c) (medical) prognosis

pronostiquer /pRɔnɔstike/ [1] *vtr* (in sport)
to forecast ⟨*result*⟩; to herald ⟨*defeat, victory*⟩

propagande /pRɔpagɑ̃d/ *nf* propaganda

propagateur, -trice /pRɔpagatœR, tRis/
nm,f proponent

propagation /pRɔpagasjɔ̃/ *nf* spread;
propagation

propager /pRɔpaʒe/ [13] **1** *vtr* to spread
⟨*rumour, disease*⟩; to propagate ⟨*species,
sound*⟩
2 se propager *v refl* (+ *v être*) to spread;
to propagate

propane /pRɔpan/ *nm* propane

propension /pRɔpɑ̃sjɔ̃/ *nf* propensity

prophète /pRɔfɛt/ *nm* prophet

prophétie /pRɔfesi/ *nf* prophecy

prophétiser /pRɔfetize/ [1] *vtr* to
prophesy

propice /pRɔpis/ *adj* favourable (GB);
trouver le moment ~ to find the right
moment

proportion /pRɔpɔRsjɔ̃/ *nf* proportion; **en
~, ils sont mieux payés** they are
proportionately better paid; **être sans ~
avec** to be out of (all) proportion to; **toutes
~s gardées** relatively speaking

proportionnel, -elle¹ /pRɔpɔRsjɔnɛl/
adj proportional

proportionnelle² /pRɔpɔRsjɔnɛl/ *nf*
proportional representation

proportionner /pRɔpɔRsjɔne/ [1] *vtr* ~
qch à qch to make sth proportional to sth;
proportionné à proportional to

propos /pRɔpo/ **1** *nm inv* **(a) à ~, je...** by
the way, I...; **à ~ de** about; **à ~ de qui?**
about who?; **à ce ~, je voudrais...** in this
connection, I would like...
(b) à ~ at the right moment; **mal à ~** at
(just) the wrong moment
2 *nm pl* comments; '~ **recueillis par J.
Brun'** 'interview by J. Brun'

proposer /pRɔpoze/ [1] **1** *vtr* **(a)** to
suggest
(b) to offer ⟨*drink, dish*⟩
(c) to put forward ⟨*solution*⟩; to propose
⟨*strategy*⟩
2 se proposer *v refl* (+ *v être*) **(a) se ~
pour faire** to offer to do
(b) se ~ de faire to intend to do

proposition /pRɔpozisjɔ̃/ *nf* **(a)** suggestion
(b) proposal
(c) clause
■ ~ **de loi** ≈ bill

propre /pRɔpR/ **1** *adj* **(a)** clean; **nous voilà
~s!** (figurative) we're in a fine mess now!
(b) tidy, neat
(c) ⟨*person, life*⟩ decent; **des affaires pas très
~s** unsavoury (GB) business
(d) own; **ma ~ voiture** my own car; **ce sont
tes ~s paroles** you said so yourself; those
were your very words
(e) of one's own; **chaque pays a des lois qui
lui sont ~s** each country has its own
particular laws
(f) ⟨*baby*⟩ toilet-trained; ⟨*animal*⟩
housetrained (GB), housebroken (US)
2 propre à *phr* **(a)** ~ **à** peculiar to
(b) ~ **à faire** likely to do; liable to do
(c) ~ **à** appropriate for; **produit déclaré ~ à
la consommation** product fit for
consumption
3 *nm* **(a) mettre qch au ~** to make a fair
copy of sth
(b) c'est du ~! (ironic) that's very nice!
**(c) le ~ de cette nouvelle technologie est de
faire** what is peculiar to this new technology
is that it does; ~ **à rien** good-for-nothing

proprement /pRɔpRəmɑ̃/ *adv* **(a)** purely;
à ~ parler strictly speaking
(b) absolutely
(c) really
(d) literally; **l'air est devenu ~ irrespirable**
the air has become literally unbreathable
(e) specifically
(f) well and truly; **le professeur l'a ~ remis
à sa place** he was well and truly put in his
place by the teacher
(g) neatly
(h) ⟨*earn living*⟩ honestly; ⟨*live*⟩ decently

propreté /pRɔpRəte/ *nf* **(a)** cleanliness;
d'une ~ douteuse not very clean
(b) honesty

p

propriétaire /prɔprijetɛr/ nmf (a) owner;
un petit ∼ a small-scale property owner; ils
sont ∼s de leur maison they own their own
house; faire le tour du ∼ to look round (GB)
or around the house
(b) landlord/landlady

propriété /prɔprijete/ nf (a) ownership
(b) property; ∼ privée private property
(c) (of substance) property
(d) (of term) aptness
■ ∼ artistique et littéraire copyright

propulser /prɔpylse/ [1] vtr to propel

propulseur /prɔpylsœr/ ① adj m
propellent
② nm engine; ∼ (de fusée) (rocket) engine
■ ∼ à hélice propeller

propulsion /prɔpylsjɔ̃/ nf propulsion; à ∼
nucléaire nuclear-powered

prorata /prɔrata/ nm inv proportion

proroger /prɔrɔʒe/ [13] vtr (a) to defer
⟨date⟩; to renew ⟨passport⟩
(b) to adjourn ⟨meeting⟩

prosaïque /prɔzaik/ adj prosaic

proscription /prɔskripsjɔ̃/ nf
(a) proscription
(b) banishment; frapper qn de ∼ to banish
sb

proscrire /prɔskrir/ [67] vtr to ban; to
banish

proscrit, ∼e /prɔskri, it/ nm,f outcast

prose /proz/ nf (a) prose; poème en ∼
prose poem
(b) (humorous) distinctive prose

prosélytisme /prɔzelitism/ nm
proselytizing

prospecter /prɔspɛkte/ [1] vtr (a) to
canvass
(b) to prospect

prospecteur, -trice /prɔspɛktœr, tris/
nm,f (a) canvasser
(b) prospector

prospectif, -ive /prɔspɛktif, iv/ adj long-
term

prospection /prɔspɛksjɔ̃/ nf
(a) canvassing
(b) prospecting

prospectus /prɔspɛktys/ nm inv leaflet

prospère /prɔspɛr/ adj thriving;
prosperous

prospérer /prɔspere/ [14] vi to thrive; to
prosper

prospérité /prɔsperite/ nf prosperity

prostate /prɔstat/ nf prostate (gland)

prosternation /prɔstɛrnasjɔ̃/ nf
(a) prostration
(b) (figurative) self-abasement

prosternement /prɔstɛrnəmɑ̃/ nm
(a) prostrate position
(b) prostration

prosterner: se prosterner /prɔstɛrne/
[1] v refl (+ v être) (a) to prostrate oneself
(b) (figurative) to grovel

prostitué /prɔstitɥe/ nm (male) prostitute

prostituée /prɔstitɥe/ nf prostitute

prostituer: se prostituer /prɔstitɥe/ [1]
v refl (+ v être) to prostitute oneself

prostitution /prɔstitysjɔ̃/ nf prostitution

prostration /prɔstrasjɔ̃/ nf prostration

protagoniste /prɔtagɔnist/ nmf
protagonist

protecteur, -trice /prɔtɛktœr, tris/
① adj (a) protective
(b) patronizing
② nm,f protector

protection /prɔtɛksjɔ̃/ nf (a) protection;
être sous haute ∼ to be under tight security;
de ∼ ⟨screen, measures⟩ protective; ⟨zone,
system⟩ protection
(b) protective device
■ ∼ sociale social welfare system

protectionnisme /prɔtɛksjɔnism/ nm
protectionism

protectionniste /prɔtɛksjɔnist/ adj, nmf
protectionist

protégé, ∼e /prɔteʒe/ nm,f protégé

protéger /prɔteʒe/ [15] ① vtr to protect
② se protéger v refl (+ v être) to protect
oneself

protège-slip, pl ∼s /prɔtɛʒslip/ nm
panty-liner

protège-tibia, pl ∼s /prɔtɛʒtibja/ nm
shinpad

protéine /prɔtein/ nf protein

protestant, ∼e /prɔtɛstɑ̃, ɑ̃t/ adj, nm,f
Protestant

protestantisme /prɔtɛstɑ̃tism/ nm
Protestantism

protestataire /prɔtɛstatɛr/ nmf protester

protestation /prɔtɛstasjɔ̃/ nf protest

protester /prɔtɛste/ [1] ① protester de
v+prep ∼ de son innocence to protest one's
innocence
② vi to protest

prothèse /prɔtɛz/ nf prosthesis; artificial
limb; dentures; ∼ auditive hearing aid

prothésiste /prɔtezist/ nmf prosthetist

protocolaire /prɔtɔkɔlɛr/ adj formal;
official; question ∼ question of protocol

protocole /prɔtɔkɔl/ nm (a) formalities;
protocol
(b) ∼ d'accord draft agreement

prototype /prɔtɔtip/ nm prototype

protubérance /prɔtyberɑ̃s/ nf
protuberance

protubérant, ∼e /prɔtyberɑ̃, ɑ̃t/ adj
protruding

prou /pru/ adv peu ou ∼ more or less

proue /pru/ nf prow, bow(s)

prouesse /prues/ nf feat; (ironic) exploit

prouver /pruve/ [1] ① vtr (a) to prove
(b) to show
(c) to demonstrate
② se prouver v refl (+ v être) (a) to prove
to oneself
(b) ils se sont prouvé qu'ils s'aimaient they
proved their love for each other

IDIOMS n'avoir plus rien à ~ to have proved oneself

provenance /pʀɔvnɑ̃s/ *nf* origin; **en ~ de** from

provençal, ~e, *mpl* **-aux** /pʀɔvɑ̃sal, o/ *adj* Provençal; **à la ~e** (Culin) (à la) provençale

provenir /pʀɔvniʀ/ [36] *vi* (a) to come (**de** from); **provenant de** from
(b) to stem (**de** from)

proverbe /pʀɔvɛʀb/ *nm* proverb

proverbial, ~e, *mpl* **-iaux** /pʀɔvɛʀbjal, o/ *adj* proverbial

providence /pʀɔvidɑ̃s/ ⒈ *nf* (a) salvation
(b) providence
⒉ **(-)providence** (*combining form*) État(-) ~ welfare state

providentiel, -ielle /pʀɔvidɑ̃sjɛl/ *adj* providential

province /pʀɔvɛ̃s/ *nf* (a) province
(b) **la ~** the provinces; **ville de ~** provincial town

provincial, ~e, *mpl* **-iaux** /pʀɔvɛ̃sjal, o/ *adj, nm,f* provincial

proviseur /pʀɔvizœʀ/ *nm* headteacher (GB) *or* principal (US) (*of a lycée*)

provision /pʀɔvizjɔ̃/ ⒈ *nf* (a) stock; supply
(b) deposit; credit (balance)
⒉ **provisions** *nf pl* food shopping

provisoire /pʀɔvizwaʀ/ *adj* provisional; temporary

provisoirement /pʀɔvizwaʀmɑ̃/ *adv* provisionally

provocant, ~e /pʀɔvɔkɑ̃, ɑ̃t/ *adj* provocative

provocateur, -trice /pʀɔvɔkatœʀ, tʀis/ *nm,f* agitator

provocation /pʀɔvɔkasjɔ̃/ *nf* provocation

provoquer /pʀɔvɔke/ [1] *vtr* (a) to cause ‹*accident*›; to provoke ‹*reaction, anger*›; **~ l'accouchement** to induce labour (GB)
(b) to provoke; **~ qn en duel** to challenge sb to a duel
(c) (sexually) to arouse

proxénète /pʀɔksenɛt/ *nm* procurer, pimp

proxénétisme /pʀɔksenetism/ *nm* procuring

proximité /pʀɔksimite/ *nf* (a) nearness, proximity; **à ~** nearby; **à ~ de** near
(b) imminence; **à cause de la ~ de Noël** because it is/was so close to Christmas

prude /pʀyd/ *adj* prudish

prudemment /pʀydamɑ̃/ *adv* (a) carefully
(b) cautiously

prudence /pʀydɑ̃s/ *nf* caution; **avec ~** cautiously; with caution; **par ~** as a precaution; **redoubler de ~** to be doubly careful

prudent, ~e /pʀydɑ̃, ɑ̃t/ *adj* (a) careful; **ce n'est pas ~ de faire** it isn't safe to do
(b) cautious
(c) wise

prud'homme /pʀydɔm/ *nm* Conseil des **~s** ≈ industrial tribunal (GB), labor relations board (US)

prune /pʀyn/ *nf* (a) plum
(b) plum brandy
IDIOMS **pour des ~s** (colloq) for nothing

pruneau, *pl* **~x** /pʀyno/ *nm* prune

prunelle /pʀynɛl/ *nf* (a) sloe; ≈ sloe gin
(b) (of eye) pupil

prunier /pʀynje/ *nm* plum tree

Prusse /pʀys/ *pr nf* Prussia

PS /pɛɛs/ *nm* (*abbr* = **post-scriptum**) PS

psalmodier /psalmɔdje/ [2] *vi* to chant psalms

psaume /psom/ *nm* psalm

pseudo- /psødo/ *pref* pseudo; **~-équilibre** so-called balance; **~-savant** self-styled scientist

pseudonyme /psødɔnim/ *nm* pseudonym

psy /psi/ *nmf* (colloq) shrink (colloq), therapist

psychanalyse /psikanaliz/ *nf* psychoanalysis

psychanalyser /psikanalize/ [1] *vtr* to psychoanalyse (GB)

psyché /psiʃe/ *nf* (a) cheval glass
(b) psyche

psychiatrie /psikjatʀi/ *nf* psychiatry

psychiatrique /psikjatʀik/ *adj* psychiatric

psychique /psiʃik/ *adj* mental

psychisme /psiʃism/ *nm* psyche

psychologie /psikɔlɔʒi/ *nf* (a) psychology
(b) (psychological) insight

psychologique /psikɔlɔʒik/ *adj* psychological

psychologue /psikɔlɔg/ ⒈ *adj* **être ~** to understand people very well
⒉ *nmf* psychologist

psychopathe /psikɔpat/ *nmf* psychopath

psychose /psikoz/ *nf* (a) psychosis
(b) **~ de la guerre** obsessive fear of war

psychosomatique /psikosɔmatik/ *adj* psychosomatic

psychothérapeute /psikoteʀapøt/ *nmf* psychotherapist

psychothérapie /psikoteʀapi/ *nf* psychotherapy

PTT /petete/ *nf pl* (*abbr* = **Administration des postes et télécommunications et de la télédiffusion**) *former French postal and telecommunications service*

pu /py/ ▶ POUVOIR[1]

puant, ~e /pɥɑ̃, ɑ̃t/ *adj* (a) stinking; smelly
(b) (colloq) **un type ~** an incredibly arrogant guy (colloq)

puanteur /pɥɑ̃tœʀ/ *nf* stench

pub /pyb/ *nf* (colloq): *abbr* ▶ PUBLICITÉ

pubère /pybɛʀ/ *adj* pubescent

puberté /pybɛʀte/ *nf* puberty

pubis /pybis/ *nm inv* pubes; pubis

p

public, -ique /pyblik/ **1** *adj* public; ⟨*education*⟩ state (GB), public (US); ⟨*company*⟩ state-owned; **la dette publique** the national debt
2 *nm* (a) public; **'interdit au ~'** 'no admittance'; **'avis au ~'** 'public notice'
(b) audience; spectators; **tous ~s** for all ages
(c) readership
(d) **avoir un ~** to have a following
(e) **le ~** the public sector

publication /pyblikasjɔ̃/ *nf* publication
■ **~ assistée par ordinateur, PAO** desktop publishing, DTP

publicitaire /pyblisitɛʀ/ **1** *adj* ⟨*campaign*⟩ advertising; ⟨*gift*⟩ promotional
2 *nmf* **il/elle est ~** he/she's in advertising
3 *nm* advertising agency

publicité /pyblisite/ *nf* (a) advertising; **faire de la ~ pour** to advertise
(b) (*also* **pub** (colloq)) advertisement, advert (GB), ad (colloq)
(c) publicity; **faire une mauvaise ~ à qn/qch** to give sb/sth a bad press
■ **~ comparative** knocking copy (colloq); **~ mensongère** misleading advertising

publier /pyblije/ [2] *vtr* to publish

publiquement /pyblikmɑ̃/ *adv* publicly

puce /pys/ *nf* (a) flea
(b) (silicon) chip; **~ à mémoire** memory chip
IDIOMS **ça m'a mis la ~ à l'oreille** that set me thinking; **secouer les ~ à qn** (colloq) to bawl sb out (colloq)

puceau, *pl* **~x** /pyso/ *adj m* (colloq) **il est encore ~** he's still a virgin

pucelle /pysɛl/ *adj f* (colloq) **être ~** to be a virgin

puceron /pysʀɔ̃/ *nm* aphid

pudeur /pydœʀ/ *nf* (a) sense of modesty; **sans ~** shamelessly
(b) decency; sense of propriety

pudibond, ~e /pydibɔ̃, ɔ̃d/ *adj* prudish

pudique /pydik/ *adj* (a) modest
(b) discreet

pudiquement /pydikmɑ̃/ *adv* (a) modestly
(b) discreetly

puer /pɥe/ [1] **1** *vtr* to stink of
2 *vi* to stink; **il puait des pieds** his feet stank

puéricultrice /pɥerikyltʀis/ *nf* pediatric nurse

puériculture /pɥerikyltyʀ/ *nf* childcare

puéril, ~e /pɥeril/ *adj* childish; puerile

puis /pɥi/ *adv* (a) then; **des poires et ~ des pêches** pears and peaches; **et ~ quoi encore!** (colloq) what next?
(b) **il va être en colère? et ~ (après)?** (colloq) so what if he's angry!

puisard /pɥizaʀ/ *nm* soakaway (GB), sink hole (US)

puiser /pɥize/ [1] *vtr* **~ qch dans qch** to draw sth from sth

puisque (**puisqu'** *before vowel or mute h*) /pɥisk(ə)/ *conj* since; **~ c'est comme ça, je m'en vais** if that's how it is, I'm off

puissance /pɥisɑ̃s/ *nf* (a) power; **la ~ militaire** military strength *or* might
(b) (country) power; **une grande ~** a superpower
(c) (of light) intensity; (of sound) volume
(d) (in algebra) power; **dix ~ trois** ten to the power (of) three

puissant, ~e /pɥisɑ̃, ɑ̃t/ **1** *adj* powerful; strong
2 puissants *nm pl* **les ~s** the powerful

puits /pɥi/ *nm* (a) well; **~ de pétrole** oil well
(b) shaft
■ **~ de science** fount of knowledge

pull /pyl/ *nm* (colloq) sweater

pull-over, *pl* **~s** /pylɔvɛʀ/ *nm* sweater

pullulement /pylylmɑ̃/ *nm*
(a) proliferation
(b) multitude

pulluler /pylyle/ [1] *vi* (a) to proliferate
(b) **les touristes pullulent dans la région** the area is swarming with tourists

pulmonaire /pylmɔnɛʀ/ *adj* ⟨*disease*⟩ lung; ⟨*artery*⟩ pulmonary

pulpe /pylp/ *nf* (of fruit) pulp; (of potato) flesh

pulpeux, -euse /pylpø, øz/ *adj* ⟨*body, lips*⟩ luscious; ⟨*fruit*⟩ fleshy

pulsation /pylsasjɔ̃/ *nf* beat; **~s cardiaques** heartbeat; heartbeats

pulsion /pylsjɔ̃/ *nf* impulse, urge

pulvérisation /pylveʀizasjɔ̃/ *nf* (a) (liquid) spraying
(b) (of solid) pulverization (GB)

pulvériser /pylveʀize/ [1] *vtr* (a) to spray
(b) to pulverize
(c) to shatter (colloq) ⟨*record*⟩

puma /pyma/ *nm* puma

punaise /pynez/ *nf* (a) drawing pin (GB), thumbtack (US)
(b) (Zool) bug

punaiser /pyneze/ [1] *vtr* (colloq) to pin *ou* tack (US) [sth] up

punch¹ /pɔ̃ʃ/ *nm* (drink) punch

punch² /pœnʃ/ *nm* (a) punch
(b) energy; **avoir du ~** ⟨*slogan*⟩ to be punchy (colloq); ⟨*person*⟩ to have drive

punching-ball, *pl* **~s** /pœnʃiŋbol/ *nm* punchball (GB), punching bag (US)

punir /pyniʀ/ [3] *vtr* to punish

punitif, -ive /pynitif, iv/ *adj* punitive

punition /pynisjɔ̃/ *nf* (a) punishment
(b) **il n'a pas fait sa ~** he hasn't done the task he was given as punishment

pupille¹ /pypij/ *nmf* ward; **~ de l'État** child in care; **~ de la Nation** war orphan

pupille² /pypij/ *nf* (of eye) pupil

pupitre /pypitʀ/ *nm* (a) control panel; console
(b) music stand; music rest
(c) desk
(d) lectern

pupitreur, -euse /pypitʀœʀ, øz/ *nm,f* computer operator

pur, ∼e /pyʀ/ **1** adj **(a)** (gen) pure;
⟨diamond⟩ flawless; ⟨voice, sky⟩ clear
(b) ⟨truth⟩ pure; ⟨coincidence, madness⟩
sheer; **en ∼e perte** to no avail; **c'est de la
paresse ∼e et simple** it's laziness, pure and
simple; **∼ et dur** hardline
(c) ⟨tradition⟩ true; **un ∼ produit de** a
typical product of; **à l'état ∼** ⟨genius⟩ sheer
2 nm,f virtuous person

purée /pyʀe/ nf purée; **∼ (de pommes de
terre)** mashed potatoes
■ **∼ de pois** pea souper (GB), fog

purement /pyʀmɑ̃/ adv purely

pureté /pyʀte/ nf purity

purgatif, -ive /pyʀgatif, iv/ adj purgative

purgatoire /pyʀgatwaʀ/ nm **le ∼**
purgatory

purge /pyʀʒ/ nf **(a)** purgative
(b) purge

purger /pyʀʒe/ [13] vtr **(a)** (Med) to purge
(b) to bleed ⟨radiator⟩; to drain ⟨pipe⟩; to
purify ⟨metal⟩
(c) (Law) to serve ⟨sentence⟩

purificateur /pyʀifikatœʀ/ nm
∼ d'atmosphère or **d'air** air purifier

purification /pyʀifikasjɔ̃/ nf purification

purifier /pyʀifje/ [2] vtr to purify; to
cleanse

purin /pyʀɛ̃/ nm slurry

puriste /pyʀist/ nmf purist

puritain, ∼e /pyʀitɛ̃, ɛn/ **1** adj
puritanical; Puritan
2 nm,f puritan; Puritan

pur-sang /pyʀsɑ̃/ nm inv thoroughbred

pus /py/ nm inv pus

pustule /pystyl/ nf pustule

putois /pytwa/ nm inv **(a)** polecat
(b) skunk (fur)

putréfaction /pytʀefaksjɔ̃/ nf
putrefaction; **en état de ∼** decomposing

putsch /putʃ/ nm putsch

puzzle /pœzl, pyzl/ nm jigsaw puzzle

PV /peve/ nm (colloq) (abbr = **procès-
verbal**) fine; parking ticket; speeding ticket

PVC /pevese/ nm (abbr = **chlorure de
polyvinyle**) PVC

pygmée /pigme/ nmf pygmy

pyjama /piʒama/ nm (pair of) pyjamas
(GB), (pair of) pajamas (US)

pylône /pilon/ nm pylon; (for radio, TV
transmitter) mast; (of bridge) tower

pyramide /piʀamid/ nf pyramid

pyrénéen, -éenne /piʀeneɛ̃, ɛn/ adj
Pyrenean

pyrex® /piʀɛks/ nm inv Pyrex®

pyrogravure /piʀogʀavyʀ/ nf pokerwork

pyromane /piʀɔman/ nmf pyromaniac;
(Law) arsonist

python /pitɔ̃/ nm python

Qq

q, Q /ky/ nm inv q, Q

qcm /kyseɛm/ nm (abbr = **questionnaire
à choix multiple**) multiple-choice
questionnaire, mcq

QG /kyʒe/ nm: abbr ▶ QUARTIER

QI /kyi/ nm: abbr ▶ QUOTIENT

qu' ▶ QUE

quadragénaire /kwadʀaʒenɛʀ/ nmf
forty-year-old

quadrature /kwadʀatyʀ/ nf quadrature;
c'est la ∼ du cercle it's like squaring the
circle

quadriennal, ∼e, mpl **-aux**
/kwadʀijɛnal, o/ adj **(a)** ⟨plan⟩ four-year
(b) quadrennial

quadrillage /kadʀijaʒ/ nm cross-ruling

quadrillé, ∼e /kadʀije/ adj ⟨paper⟩
squared

quadriller /kadʀije/ [1] vtr **(a)** ⟨police⟩ to
spread one's net over
(b) to cross-rule ⟨paper⟩

quadrimoteur /k(w)adʀimɔtœʀ/ nm
four-engined plane

quadrupède /k(w)adʀypɛd/ adj, nm
quadruped

quadruple /k(w)adʀypl/ nm **le ∼ de cette
quantité** four times this amount

quadruplé, ∼e /k(w)adʀyple/ nm,f
quadruplet, quad

quai /ke/ nm **(a)** quay; **le navire est à ∼** the
ship has docked
(b) (of river) bank
(c) (station) platform
■ **∼ d'embarquement** loading dock; **Quai des
Orfèvres** criminal investigation department
of the French police force; **Quai d'Orsay**
French Foreign Office

qualificatif, -ive /kalifikatif, iv/ **1** adj
qualifying
2 nm **(a)** (in grammar) qualifier
(b) term, word

qualification /kalifikasjɔ̃/ nf
(a) qualification
(b) skills; **sans ∼** unskilled

qualifié, ∼e /kalifje/ adj ⟨staff, labour⟩
skilled; qualified

qualifier /kalifje/ [2] **1** vtr **(a)** to describe ⋯⟶

(b) to qualify
2 se qualifier *v refl* (+ *v être*) (Sport) to qualify

qualitatif, -ive /kalitatif, iv/ *adj* qualitative

qualité /kalite/ *nf* **(a)** quality; **de première ~** of the highest quality; **avoir beaucoup de ~s** to have many qualities
(b) en (sa) ~ de représentant in his/her capacity as a representative; **nom, prénom et ~** surname, first name and occupation

quand /kɑ̃, kɑ̃t/ **1** *conj* **(a)** when; **~ il arrivera, vous lui annoncerez la nouvelle** when he gets here, you can tell him the news; **~ je pense que ma fille va avoir dix ans!** to think that my daughter's almost ten!; **~ je vous le disais!** I told you so!
(b) whenever; **~ il pleut plus de trois jours la cave est inondée** whenever it rains for more than three days, the cellar floods
(c) even if; **~ (bien même) la terre s'écroulerait, il continuerait à dormir** he'd sleep through an earthquake
2 *adv* when; **de ~ date votre dernière réunion?** when was your last meeting?; **depuis ~ habitez-vous ici?** how long have you been living here?; **à ~ la semaine de 30 heures?** (colloq) when will we get a 30-hour working week?
3 quand même *phr* still; **ils ne veulent pas de moi, mais j'irai ~ même!** they don't want me, but I'm still going!; **~ même, tu exagères!** (colloq) come on, that's going too far!

quant: **quant à** /kɑ̃ta/ *phr* **(a)** as for; **la France, ~ à elle,... as for France, it...
(b) about, concerning

quantifier /kɑ̃tifje/ **[2]** *vtr* to quantify

quantitatif, -ive /kɑ̃titatif, iv/ *adj* quantitative

quantité /kɑ̃tite/ *nf* **(a)** quantity, amount
(b) des ~s de scores of ⟨*people*⟩; a lot of ⟨*things*⟩; **du pain/vin en ~** plenty of bread/wine

quarantaine /kaʁɑ̃tɛn/ *nf* **(a)** about forty
(b) être en ~ to be in quarantine; to be ostracized

quarante /kaʁɑ̃t/ *adj inv, pron, nm inv* forty

quarante-cinq /kaʁɑ̃tsɛ̃k/ *adj inv, pron, nm inv* forty-five
■ **~ tours** single

quarantième /kaʁɑ̃tjɛm/ *adj* fortieth

quart /kaʁ/ *nm* **(a)** quarter; **un ~ d'heure** a quarter of an hour; **les trois ~s du temps** (colloq) most of the time
(b) a quarter-litre (GB) bottle; a quarter-litre (GB) pitcher
(c) (Naut) **être de ~** to be on watch
■ **~ de cercle** quadrant; **~ de tour** 90° turn; **faire qch au ~ de tour** (colloq) to do sth immediately

quartier /kaʁtje/ *nm* **(a)** area, district; **de ~** ⟨*cinema, grocer*⟩ local

(b) quarter; **un ~ de pommes** a slice of apple; **un ~ d'orange** an orange segment
(c) (of moon) quarter
(d) (Mil) **~s** quarters; **avoir ~ libre** to be off duty; to have time off
■ **~ général, QG** headquarters, HQ
IDIOMS **ne pas faire de ~** to show no mercy

quart-monde /kaʁmɔ̃d/ *nm inv* underclass

quartz /kwaʁts/ *nm* quartz

quasi /kazi/ **1** *adv* almost
2 quasi- (*combining form*) **~-indifférence** virtual indifference; **la ~-totalité de** almost all of; **à la ~-unanimité** almost unanimously

quasiment /kazimɑ̃/ *adv* (colloq) practically

quaternaire /kwatɛʁnɛʁ/ *adj, nm* Quaternary

quatorze /katɔʁz/ *adj inv, pron, nm inv* fourteen
IDIOMS **chercher midi à ~ heures** (colloq) to complicate matters

quatorzième /katɔʁzjɛm/ *adj* fourteenth

quatrain /katʁɛ̃/ *nm* quatrain

quatre /katʁ/ *adj inv, pron, nm inv* four
IDIOMS **faire les ~ volontés de qn** to give in to sb's every whim; **être tiré à ~ épingles** to be dressed up to the nines (colloq); **ne pas y aller par ~ chemins** not to beat about the bush; **je vais leur parler entre ~ yeux** I'm going to talk to them face to face; **monter un escalier ~ à ~** to go up the stairs four at a time; **être entre ~ planches** (colloq) to be six feet under

quatre-heures /katʁœʁ/ *nm inv* afternoon snack (*for children*)

quatre-quarts /kat(ʁə)kaʁ/ *nm inv* pound cake

quatre-vingt(s) /katʁəvɛ̃/ *adj, pron, nm* eighty

quatre-vingt-dix /katʁəvɛ̃dis/ *adj inv, pron, nm inv* ninety

quatre-vingt-dixième /katʁəvɛ̃dizjɛm/ *adj* ninetieth

quatre-vingtième /katʁəvɛ̃tjɛm/ *adj* eightieth

quatrième /katʁijɛm/ **1** *adj* fourth
2 *nf* **(a)** (Sch) *third year of secondary school, age 13–14*
(b) (Aut) fourth (gear)
■ **le ~ âge** very old people
IDIOMS **en ~ vitesse** (colloq) in double quick time (colloq)

quatuor /kwatɥɔʁ/ *nm* quartet

que (qu' *before vowel or mute h*) /kə/
1 *conj* **(a)** that; **je pense qu'il a raison** I think he's right; **je veux ~ tu m'accompagnes** I want you to come with me
(b) so (that); **approche, ~ je te regarde** come closer so I can look at you
(c) whether; **~ cela vous plaise ou non** whether you like it or not
(d) si vous venez et ~ vous ayez le temps if you come and (if you) have the time

(e) il n'était pas sitôt parti qu'elle appela la police no sooner had he left than she called the police

(f) ~ tout le monde sorte! everyone must leave!; **~ ceux qui n'ont pas compris le disent** let anyone who hasn't understood say so; **qu'il crève!** (slang) let him rot! (colloq)

(g) than; as; **plus gros ~ moi** fatter than me; **aussi grand ~ mon frère** as tall as my brother

② *pron* what; **~ dire?** what can you say?; **je ne sais pas ce qu'il a dit** I don't know what he said; **qu'est-ce que c'est que ça?** what's that?

③ *rel pron* that; who(m); which; **je n'aime pas la voiture ~ tu as achetée** I don't like the car (that) you've bought

④ *adv* **c'est joli** it's so pretty; **~ de monde** what a lot of people

Québec /kebɛk/ **①** *pr nm* **le ~** Quebec
② *pr n* Quebec

québécois, ~e /kebekwa, az/ *adj* of Quebec

Québécois, ~e /kebekwa, az/ *nm,f* Quebecois, Quebecker

quel, quelle /kɛl/ **①** *det* who; what; which; **je me demande quelle est la meilleure solution** I wonder what the best solution is; **de ces deux médicaments, ~ est le plus efficace?** which of these two medicines is more effective?

② *adj* **(a)** what; which; **quelle heure est-il?** what time is it?; **dans ~ tiroir l'as-tu mis?** which drawer did you put it in?; **~ âge as-tu?** how old are you?

(b) what; how; **quelle coïncidence!** what a coincidence!

(c) quelle que soit la route que l'on prenne whatever *or* whichever road we take; **~ que soit le vainqueur** whoever the winner may be

quelconque /kɛlkɔ̃k/ **①** *adj* ⟨person⟩ ordinary; ordinary-looking; ⟨novel, actor⟩ poor; ⟨restaurant⟩ second-rate; ⟨place⟩ characterless

② *adj* any; **si pour une raison ~** if for some reason or other; **si le livre avait un intérêt ~** if the book was in any way interesting

quelle ▸ QUEL

quelque /kɛlk/ **①** *quantif* some; a few; any; **depuis ~ temps** for some time; **je voudrais ajouter ~s mots** I'd like to add a few words; **ça dure trois heures et ~s** it lasts over three hours; **si pour ~ raison que ce soit** if for whatever reason

② *adv* **(a) les ~ deux mille spectateurs** the two thousand odd spectators

(b) however; **~ admirable que soit son attitude** however admirable his/her attitude may be

③ quelque chose *pron* something; anything; **il y a ~ chose qui ne va pas** something's wrong; **si ~ chose leur arrive** if anything should happen to them; **il a ~**

chose de son grand-père he's got a look of his grandfather about him; **ça me dit ~ chose** it rings a bell

④ quelque part *phr* somewhere; anywhere

⑤ quelque peu *phr* somewhat

quelquefois /kɛlkəfwa/ *adv* sometimes

quelques-uns, quelques-unes /kɛlkəzœ̃, yn/ *pron* some, a few

quelqu'un /kɛlkœ̃/ *pron* someone, somebody; anyone, anybody; **~ d'autre** someone else; **c'est ~ de compétent** he/she is competent

quémander /kemɑ̃de/ [1] *vtr* to beg

qu'en-dira-t-on /kɑ̃diratɔ̃/ *nm inv* gossip

quenelle /kənɛl/ *nf*: dumpling made of flour and egg, flavoured with meat or fish

quenotte /kənɔt/ *nf* (colloq) toothy-peg (colloq), tooth

quenouille /kənuj/ *nf* distaff

querelle /kəʀɛl/ *nf* **(a)** quarrel; **chercher ~ à qn** to pick a quarrel with sb

(b) dispute

quereller: se quereller /kəʀele/ [1] *v refl* (+ *v être*) to quarrel

question /kɛstjɔ̃/ *nf* **(a)** question; **je ne me suis jamais posé la ~** I've never really thought about it; **pose-leur la ~** ask them

(b) matter, question; issue; **~ d'habitude!** it's a matter of habit; **en ~** in question; at issue; **(re)mettre en ~** to reappraise; to reassess; **se remettre en ~** to take a new look at oneself; **la ~ n'est pas là** that's not the point; **il est ~ d'elle dans l'article** she's mentioned in the article; **il n'est pas ~ que tu partes** you can't possibly leave; **pas ~!** no way! (colloq)

(c) (colloq) **~ santé, ça va** where health is concerned, things are OK

questionnaire /kɛstjɔnɛʀ/ *nm* questionnaire

questionner /kɛstjɔne/ [1] *vtr* to question

quête /kɛt/ *nf* **(a)** collection; **faire la ~** to take the collection; to pass the hat round; to collect for charity

(b) search; **la ~ du Graal** the quest for the Holy Grail

quêter /kete/ [1] *vi* to take the collection; **~ pour une œuvre** to collect for a charity

quetsche /kwɛtʃ/ *nf* (sweet purple) plum

queue /kø/ *nf* **(a)** tail

(b) (of flower) stem; (of apple) stalk (GB), stem (US)

(c) (of pot) handle

(d) (Sport) cue

(e) (of procession) tail(-end); (of train) rear, back; **ils arrivent en ~ (de peloton) des grandes entreprises** they come at the bottom of the league table of companies

(f) faire la ~ to stand in a queue (GB), to stand in line (US)

IDIOMS une histoire sans ~ ni tête (colloq) a cock and bull story; **la ~ basse** with one's tail between one's legs; **il n'y en avait pas la** ⋯⟶

q

~ **d'un(e)** (colloq) there were none to be seen; **faire une ~ de poisson à qn** to cut in front of sb; **finir en ~ de poisson** to fizzle out

queue-de-cheval, *pl* **queues-de-cheval** /kødʃøval/ *nf* ponytail

queue-de-pie, *pl* **queues-de-pie** /kødpi/ *nf* (colloq) tails, tailcoat

queux /kø/ *nm inv* **maître ~ chef**

qui /ki/ **1** *pron* who; whom; **~ veut-elle voir?** who does she want to speak to?

2 *rel pron* (a) who; that; which; **est-ce vous ~ venez d'appeler?** was it you who called just now?; **ce ~ me plaît chez lui** what I like about him

(b) **~ que vous soyez** whoever you are; **je n'ai jamais frappé ~ que ce soit** I've never hit anybody

quiche /kiʃ/ *nf* quiche, flan

quiconque /kikɔ̃k/ **1** *rel pron* whoever, anyone who

2 *pron* anyone, anybody

quiétude /kjetyd/ *nf* tranquillity

quignon /kiɲɔ̃/ *nm* crusty end (of a loaf)

quille /kij/ *nf* (a) skittle

(b) (Naut) keel

IDIOMS **être reçu comme un chien dans un jeu de ~s** (colloq) to be given a very unfriendly welcome

quincaillerie /kɛ̃kajʀi/ *nf* (a) hardware shop (GB) *or* store (US)

(b) hardware

(c) hardware business

quinconce /kɛ̃kɔ̃s/ *nm* **en ~** in staggered rows

quinquagénaire /kɛ̃kaʒenɛʀ/ *nmf* fifty-year-old

quinquennal, **~e**, *mpl* **-aux** /kɛ̃kenal, o/ *adj* ⟨plan⟩ five-year

(b) five-yearly

quintal, *pl* **-aux** /kɛ̃tal, o/ *nm* quintal

quinte /kɛ̃t/ *nf* (a) (Mus) fifth

(b) **une ~ (de toux)** a coughing fit

quintette /kɛ̃tɛt/ *nm* quintet

quintuple /kɛ̃typl/ *nm* **le ~ de cette quantité** five times the amount

quintuplé, **~e** /kɛ̃typle/ *nm,f* quintuplet, quin (GB), quint (US)

quinzaine /kɛ̃zɛn/ *nf* (a) fortnight (GB), two weeks; **sous ~** within 2 weeks

(b) about fifteen

quinze /kɛ̃z/ *adj inv, pron, nm inv* fifteen

quinzième /kɛ̃zjɛm/ *adj* fifteenth

quiproquo /kipʀɔko/ *nm* misunderstanding

quittance /kitɑ̃s/ *nf* (a) receipt

(b) bill

quitte /kit/ **1** *adj* (a) **nous sommes ~s, je suis ~ avec lui** we're quits

(b) **en être ~ pour la peur/un rhume** to get off with a fright/a cold

2 **quitte à** *phr* **~ à aller à Londres, autant que ce soit pour quelques jours** if you're going to London anyway, you might as well go for a few days

■ **~ ou double** double or quits

quitter /kite/ [1] **1** *vtr* (a) to leave ⟨place, person, road⟩

(b) to leave ⟨job, organization⟩; **~ la scène** to give up acting; **il ne l'a pas quittée des yeux de tout le repas** he didn't take his eyes off her throughout the meal; **ne quittez pas** hold the line

(c) ⟨company⟩ to move from ⟨street⟩; to move out of ⟨building⟩

(d) **un grand homme nous a quittés** a great man has passed away

(e) to take off ⟨garment, hat⟩

2 **se quitter** *v refl* (+ *v être*) to part; **ils ne se quittent plus** they're inseparable now

qui-vive /kiviv/ *nm inv* **être sur le ~** to be on the alert

quoi /kwa/ **1** *pron* (a) what; **à ~ penses-tu?** what are you thinking about?; **à ~ bon recommencer?** what's the point of starting again?

(b) **~ qu'elle puisse en dire** whatever she may say; **~ qu'il en soit** be that as it may

2 *rel pron* **il n'y a rien sur ~ vous puissiez fonder vos accusations** there's nothing on which to base your accusations; **à ~ il a répondu** to which he replied; **après ~ ils sont partis** after which they left; **(il n'y a) pas de ~!** my pleasure; **il n'y a pas de ~ se fâcher** there's no reason to get angry; **il n'a (même) pas de ~ s'acheter un livre** he hasn't (even) got enough money to buy a book

quoique (**quoiqu'** *before vowel or mute* h) /kwak(ə)/ *conj* although, though; **nous sommes mieux ici qu'à Paris, ~** we're better off here than in Paris, but then (again)

quota /kɔta/ *nm* quota (**sur on**)

quote-part, *pl* **quotes-parts** /kɔtpaʀ/ *nf* share

quotidien, **-ienne** /kɔtidjɛ̃, ɛn/ **1** *adj*

(a) daily

(b) everyday

2 *nm* (a) daily ⟨paper⟩

(b) everyday life

quotidiennement /kɔtidjɛnmɑ̃/ *adv* every day, daily

quotient /kɔsjɑ̃/ *nm* quotient

■ **~ intellectuel, QI** intelligence quotient, IQ

Rr

r, R /ɛʁ/ *nm inv* r, R

rab /ʁab/ *nm* (colloq) **(a)** extra; **faire du ~** to do extra hours
(b) demander du ~ to ask for seconds

rabâcher /ʁabɑʃe/ [1] **1** *vtr* to keep repeating
2 *vi* to keep harping on

rabais /ʁabɛ/ *nm inv* discount

rabaisser /ʁabese/ [1] **1** *vtr* to belittle
2 se rabaisser *v refl* (+ *v être*) to demean oneself

rabat /ʁaba/ *nm* (of bag, table, pocket) flap

rabat-joie /ʁabaʒwa/ *adj inv* **être ~** to be a killjoy

rabattre /ʁabatʁ/ [61] **1** *vtr* **(a)** ⟨*person*⟩ to shut ⟨*lid*⟩; to put *or* fold up ⟨*foldaway seat, tray*⟩
(b) to turn [sth] down ⟨*collar, sheet*⟩
(c) ⟨*player*⟩ to smash ⟨*ball*⟩
(d) ~ le gibier to beat the undergrowth for game
2 se rabattre *v refl* (+ *v être*) **(a)** ⟨*lid*⟩ to shut; ⟨*leaf of table*⟩ to fold up
(b) ⟨*driver, vehicle*⟩ to pull back in
(c) se ~ sur to make do with

rabbin /ʁabɛ̃/ *nm* rabbi; **grand ~** chief rabbi

râblé, ~e /ʁɑble/ *adj* **(a)** ⟨*animal*⟩ sturdy
(b) ⟨*person*⟩ stocky

rabot /ʁabo/ *nm* (tool) plane

raboter /ʁabɔte/ [1] *vtr* to plane

rabougri, ~e /ʁabugʁi/ *adj* ⟨*tree*⟩ stunted

rabrouer /ʁabʁue/ [1] *vtr* to snub

racaille /ʁakɑj/ *nf* scum

raccommoder /ʁakɔmɔde/ [1] *vtr* **(a)** to darn ⟨*socks*⟩
(b) (colloq) to reconcile ⟨*people*⟩

raccompagner /ʁakɔ̃paɲe/ [1] *vtr* **~ qn chez lui** to walk/to drive sb (back) home

raccord /ʁakɔʁ/ *nm* **(a)** (in wallpaper) join
(b) (in painting) touch-up
(c) (in film) link shot

raccordement /ʁakɔʁdəmɑ̃/ *nm* link road

raccorder /ʁakɔʁde/ [1] *vtr* to connect

raccourci /ʁakuʁsi/ *nm* (road) shortcut

raccourcir /ʁakuʁsiʁ/ [3] **1** *vtr* **(a)** (gen) to shorten
(b) to cut ⟨*text, speech*⟩
2 *vi* ⟨*days*⟩ to get shorter, to draw in
IDIOMS **tomber sur qn à bras raccourcis** (colloq) to lay into sb

raccrocher /ʁakʁɔʃe/ [1] **1** *vtr* to hang [sth] back up
2 *vi* to hang up

3 se raccrocher *v refl* (+ *v être*) **se ~ à** to grab hold of ⟨*rail*⟩; (figurative) to cling to ⟨*person, excuse*⟩

race /ʁas/ *nf* **(a)** race
(b) (Zool) breed; **chien de ~** pedigree (dog)

racheter /ʁaʃte/ [18] **1** *vtr* **(a)** to buy [sth] back
(b) to buy some more ⟨*wine*⟩
(c) to buy new ⟨*sheets*⟩
(d) to buy out ⟨*company, factory*⟩; **je rachète votre voiture 5 000 francs** I'll buy your car off you for 5,000 francs
(e) to redeem ⟨*sinner*⟩
2 se racheter *v refl* (+ *v être*) to redeem oneself

rachitique /ʁaʃitik/ *adj* ⟨*animal, plant, person*⟩ scrawny

rachitisme /ʁaʃitism/ *nm* rickets

racial, ~e, *mpl* **-iaux** /ʁasjal, o/ *adj* racial; **émeutes ~es** race riots

racine /ʁasin/ *nf* root

racisme /ʁasism/ *nm* racism

raciste /ʁasist/ *adj, nmf* racist

racket /ʁakɛt/ *nm* extortion racket; racketeering

raclée /ʁɑkle/ *nf* (colloq) hiding (colloq)

racler /ʁɑkle/ [1] **1** *vtr* **(a)** to scrape [sth] clean ⟨*plate*⟩
(b) to scrape off ⟨*rust*⟩
(c) to scrape against
2 se racler *v refl* (+ *v être*) **se ~ la gorge** to clear one's throat

raclette /ʁɑklɛt/ *nf* **(a)** raclette (*Swiss cheese dish*)
(b) scraper

racolage /ʁakɔlaʒ/ *nm* touting (de for); soliciting (de for)

racoler /ʁakɔle/ [1] *vtr* ⟨*prostitute*⟩ to solicit

racontar /ʁakɔ̃taʁ/ *nm* (colloq) **des ~s** idle gossip

raconter /ʁakɔ̃te/ [1] *vtr* to tell ⟨*story*⟩; to describe ⟨*incident*⟩; **~ qch à qn** to tell sb sth; **qu'est-ce que tu racontes?** what are you talking about?

racornir /ʁakɔʁniʁ/ [3] *vtr,* **se racornir** *v refl* (+ *v être*) **(a)** to harden
(b) to shrivel (up)

radar /ʁadaʁ/ *nm* radar

rade /ʁad/ *nf* harbour (GB); **rester en ~** (colloq) ⟨*person*⟩ to be left stranded

radeau, *pl* **~x** /ʁado/ *nm* raft

radiateur /ʁadjatœʁ/ *nm* radiator; **~ électrique** electric heater

radiation /ʁadjasjɔ̃/ *nf* radiation

r

radical, ~**e**, *mpl* **-aux** /ʁadikal, o/ *adj*,
nm,f radical

radicalement /ʁadikalmɑ̃/ *adv* radically;
completely

radier /ʁadje/ [2] *vtr* ~ **un médecin** to
strike off a doctor (GB), to take away a
doctor's license (US); ~ **un avocat** to disbar a
lawyer

radieux, -ieuse /ʁadjø, øz/ *adj* **(a)** ⟨*sun*⟩
dazzling
(b) ⟨*weather*⟩ glorious
(c) ⟨*face, smile*⟩ radiant; ⟨*person*⟩ radiant
with joy

radin, ~**e** /ʁadɛ̃, in/ *adj* (colloq) stingy
(colloq)

radinerie /ʁadinʁi/ *nf* (colloq) stinginess
(colloq)

radio¹ /ʁadjo/ ⓵ *adj inv* ⟨*contact, signal*⟩
radio
⓶ *nm* radio operator

radio² /ʁadjo/ *nf* **(a)** radio
(b) X-ray

radioactivité /ʁadjoaktivite/ *nf*
radioactivity

radiocassette /ʁadjokasɛt/ *nm* radio
cassette player

radiodiffuser /ʁadjodifyze/ [1] *vtr* to
broadcast

radiographie /ʁadjoɡʁafi/ *nf*
(a) radiography
(b) X-ray (photograph)

radiologue /ʁadjoloɡ/ *nmf* radiologist

radiophonique /ʁadjofɔnik/ *adj* radio

radio-réveil, *pl* **radios-réveils**
/ʁadjoʁevɛj/ *nm* clock radio

radioscopie /ʁadjoskɔpi/ *nf* fluoroscopy

radiothérapie /ʁadjoteʁapi/ *nf*
radiotherapy

radis /ʁadi/ *nm inv* radish; **je n'ai plus un**
~ (colloq) I haven't got a penny

radoter /ʁadɔte/ [1] *vi* **(a)** to talk nonsense
(b) to repeat oneself

radoucir: se radoucir /ʁadusiʁ/ [3] *v refl*
(+ *v être*) ⟨*person*⟩ to soften up; ⟨*weather*⟩ to
turn milder

radoucissement /ʁadusismɑ̃/ *nm* **la**
météo annonce un ~ the forecast is for
milder weather

rafale /ʁafal/ *nf* **(a)** (of wind, rain) gust;
(of snow) flurry
(b) (of gunfire) burst

raffermir /ʁafɛʁmiʁ/ [3] *vtr* **(a)** to tone
⟨*skin*⟩; to tone up ⟨*muscles*⟩
(b) to strengthen ⟨*position*⟩; to steady
⟨*market*⟩

raffinage /ʁafinaʒ/ *nm* refining

raffiné, ~**e** /ʁafine/ *adj* refined; ⟨*food*⟩
sophisticated

raffinement /ʁafinmɑ̃/ *nm* **(a)** refinement
(b) elegance

raffiner /ʁafine/ [1] *vtr* to refine

raffinerie /ʁafinʁi/ *nf* refinery; ~ **de**
pétrole oil refinery

raffoler /ʁafɔle/ [1] *v+prep* ~ **de** to be
crazy about (colloq)

raffut /ʁafy/ *nm* (colloq) **(a)** racket (colloq)
(b) stink (colloq), row

rafiot /ʁafjo/ *nm* (colloq) boat, (old) tub
(colloq)

rafistoler /ʁafistɔle/ [1] *vtr* (colloq) to patch
up

rafle /ʁafl/ *nf* **(a)** raid
(b) roundup

rafler /ʁafle/ [1] *vtr* (colloq) **(a)** to make off
with, to swipe (colloq)
(b) to walk off with ⟨*medal, reward*⟩

rafraîchir /ʁafʁeʃiʁ/ [3] ⓵ *vtr* ⟨*rain*⟩ to
cool ⟨*atmosphere*⟩; **le thé glacé te rafraîchira**
the iced tea will cool you down
⓶ **se rafraîchir** *v refl* (+ *v être*) ⟨*weather*⟩
to get cooler; ⟨*person*⟩ to refresh oneself
IDIOMS ~ **la mémoire de qn** (colloq) to refresh
sb's memory

rafraîchissant, ~**e** /ʁafʁeʃisɑ̃, ɑ̃t/ *adj*
refreshing

rafraîchissement /ʁafʁeʃismɑ̃/ *nm*
refreshment

ragaillardir /ʁaɡajaʁdiʁ/ [3] *vtr* to cheer
[sb] up

rage /ʁaʒ/ *nf* **(a)** rabies
(b) rage; **être fou de** ~ to be in a mad rage;
faire ~ ⟨*disease*⟩ to be rife; ⟨*epidemic, fire*⟩ to
rage
■ ~ **de dents** raging toothache

rageant, ~**e** /ʁaʒɑ̃, ɑ̃t/ *adj* (colloq)
infuriating

rageusement /ʁaʒøzmɑ̃/ *adv* furiously;
angrily

ragot /ʁaɡo/ *nm* (colloq) malicious gossip

ragoût /ʁaɡu/ *nm* stew, ragout

rai /ʁɛ/ *nm* ~ **de lumière** ray of light

raï /ʁaj/ *nm*: *music from the Maghreb with*
Western influences

raid /ʁɛd/ *nm* **(a)** (Mil) raid
(b) (Sport) trek

raide /ʁɛd/ *adj* **(a)** (gen) stiff; ⟨*hair*⟩ straight;
⟨*rope*⟩ taut
(b) steep
(c) (colloq) **je trouve ça un peu** ~ that's a bit
steep
IDIOMS **être** ~ **comme un piquet** to be stiff as
a ramrod; **tomber** ~ to be flabbergasted

raideur /ʁɛdœʁ/ *nf* **(a)** stiffness
(b) steepness

raidir /ʁɛdiʁ/ [3] ⓵ *vtr* to tense ⟨*arm, body*⟩
⓶ **se raidir** *v refl* (+ *v être*) ⟨*body*⟩ to tense
up; **se** ~ **contre la douleur** to brace oneself
against pain

raie /ʁɛ/ *nf* **(a)** (in hair) parting (GB), part
(US)
(b) scratch
(c) (Zool) skate

rail /ʁaj/ *nm* rail, track
■ ~ **de sécurité** crash barrier

raillerie /ʁajʁi/ *nf* mockery

rainette /ʁɛnɛt/ *nf* tree frog

rainure /ʁenyʁ/ *nf* groove

raisin ···⋮· ramollir ····⋮

raisin /rɛzɛ̃/ *nm* grapes; **~s secs** raisins
raison /rɛzɔ̃/ *nf* **(a)** reason; **~ d'agir** reason
for action; **en ~ d'une panne** owing to a
breakdown; **à plus forte ~** even more so,
especially; **avec ~** justifiably; **comme de ~**
as one might expect
(b) avoir ~ to be right; **donner ~ à qn** to
agree with sb
(c) reason; **se rendre à la ~** to see reason;
ramener qn à la ~ to bring sb to his/her
senses; **se faire une ~ de qch** to resign
oneself to sth; **plus que de ~** more than is
sensible; **avoir ~ de qn/qch** to get the better
of sb/sth; **à ~ de** at the rate of
raisonnable /rɛzɔnabl/ *adj* reasonable;
moderate; sensible
raisonné, ~e /rɛzɔne/ **1** *pp* ▶
RAISONNER
2 *pp adj* **(a)** ⟨*attitude*⟩ cautious; ⟨*decision*⟩
carefully thought out
(b) ⟨*enthusiasm*⟩ measured
raisonnement /rɛzɔnmɑ̃/ *nm* reasoning;
selon le même ~ by the same token; **il tient
le ~ suivant** his argument is as follows; **je
ne tiens pas le même ~** I look at it
differently
raisonner /rɛzɔne/ [1] **1** *vtr* to reason
with
2 *vi* to think
3 se raisonner *v refl* (+ *v être*) ⟨*person*⟩
to be more sensible, to pull oneself together
rajeunir /raʒœniʀ/ [3] **1** *vtr* **(a)** to make
[sb] look/feel younger
(b) ~ qn to make sb out to be younger
(c) to bring *or* inject new blood into
2 *vi* to look/to feel younger
rajeunissement /raʒœnismɑ̃/ *nm*
**(a) nous avons enregistré un ~ de la
population** we see that the population is
getting younger
(b) modernization
(c) updating
(d) rejuvenation
rajouter /raʒute/ [1] *vtr* to add; **en ~**
(colloq) to exaggerate
rajuster /raʒyste/ [1] *vtr* to straighten
⟨*clothing*⟩
râle /rɑl/ *nm* **(a)** rale
(b) groan
(c) death rattle
ralenti, ~e /ralɑ̃ti/ **1** *pp* ▶ RALENTIR
2 *pp adj* ⟨*gesture, rhythm, growth*⟩ slower
3 *nm* slow motion
ralentir /ralɑ̃tiʀ/ [3] *vtr, vi,* **se ralentir**
v refl (+ *v être*) to slow down
ralentissement /ralɑ̃tismɑ̃/ *nm*
(a) slowing down
(b) tailback
ralentisseur /ralɑ̃tisœʀ/ *nm* speed ramp
râler /rɑle/ [1] *vi* **(a)** (colloq) to moan (colloq);
ça me fait ~ it annoys me
(b) to groan
râleur, -euse /rɑlœʀ, øz/ *nm,f* (colloq)
moaner (colloq)
ralliement /ralimɑ̃/ *nm* rallying

rallier /ralje/ [2] **1** *vtr* **~ qn à sa cause** to
win sb over
2 se rallier *v refl* (+ *v être*) **se ~ à** to
rally to ⟨*republicans*⟩; to come round to
⟨*opinion*⟩
rallonge /ralɔ̃ʒ/ *nf* **(a)** extension cord,
extension lead (GB)
(b) (of table) leaf
rallonger /ralɔ̃ʒe/ [13] **1** *vtr* to extend; to
lengthen
2 *vi* **les jours rallongent** the days are
drawing out
rallye /rali/ *nm* (car) rally
ramadan /ramadɑ̃/ *nm* Ramadan; **faire le
~** to keep Ramadan
ramage /ramaʒ/ **1** *nm* (of bird) song
2 ramages *nm pl* foliage pattern
ramassage /ramasaʒ/ *nm* **car de ~** (for
employees) works *or* company bus; (for pupils)
school bus
ramassé, ~e /ramase/ **1** *pp* ▶
RAMASSER
2 *pp adj* **(a)** stocky, squat
(b) être ~ sur soi-même to be hunched up
ramasser /ramase/ [1] **1** *vtr* to collect; to
pick up; to dig up ⟨*potatoes*⟩; **se faire ~ dans
une rafle** (colloq) to get picked up in a
(police) raid
2 se ramasser *v refl* (+ *v être*) **(a)** to
huddle up
(b) (colloq) to come a cropper (colloq); **se faire
~ à un examen** to fail an exam
ramassis /ramasi/ *nm inv* (derogatory)
(of people) bunch; (of ideas, objects) jumble
rambarde /rɑ̃baʀd/ *nf* guardrail
rame /ram/ *nf* **(a)** oar
(b) (of paper) ream
(c) une ~ de métro a metro train
rameau, *pl* **~x** /ramo/ *nm* (Bot) branch
ramener /ramne/ [16] **1** *vtr*
(a) ~ l'inflation à 5% to reduce inflation to 5
per cent
(b) to restore ⟨*order*⟩; **~ qn à la réalité** to
bring sb back to reality; **~ qn à la vie** to
bring sb round; **~ toujours tout à soi** always
to relate everything to oneself
(c) to take [sb/sth] back
(d) to bring back; to return
2 se ramener *v refl* (+ *v être*) **se ~ à** to
come down to, to boil down to
ramequin /ramkɛ̃/ *nm* ramekin
ramer /rame/ [1] *vi* to row
rameur, -euse /ramœʀ, øz/ *nm,f* rower
rameuter /ramøte/ [1] *vtr* to round up
ramification /ramifikasjɔ̃/ *nf* **(a)** network
(b) ramification
ramifier: se ramifier /ramifje/ [2] *v refl*
(+ *v être*) ⟨*stem, nerve*⟩ to branch; ⟨*branch*⟩
to divide
ramollir /ramɔliʀ/ [3] **1** *vtr* to soften
2 se ramollir *v refl* (+ *v être*) **(a)** to
become soft
(b) (colloq) ⟨*person*⟩ to get soft

r

ramollissement /Ramɔlismɑ̃/ *nm*
softening

ramoner /Ramɔne/ [1] *vtr* to sweep
⟨*chimney*⟩

ramoneur /Ramɔnœʀ/ *nm* chimney sweep

rampant, ~e /Rɑ̃pɑ̃, ɑ̃t/ *adj* (a) ⟨*animal*⟩
crawling; ⟨*plant*⟩ creeping
(b) ⟨*inflation*⟩ creeping

rampe /Rɑ̃p/ *nf* (a) banister; hand-rail
(b) (in theatre) **la ~** the footlights
■ **~ d'accès** (for motorway) sliproad (GB),
entrance ramp (US); (of building) ramp

ramper /Rɑ̃pe/ [1] *vi* (a) to crawl
(b) to creep

ramure /RamyR/ *nf* (a) (of tree) branches
(b) antlers

rancard /Rɑ̃kaR/ *nm* (slang) (a) ⟨*rendezvous*⟩
date
(b) (information) tip

rancart /Rɑ̃kaR/ *nm* (colloq) **mettre au ~** to
shunt [sb] aside

rance /Rɑ̃s/ *adj* rancid

rancœur /Rɑ̃kœʀ/ *nf* resentment

rançon /Rɑ̃sɔ̃/ *nf* (a) ransom
(b) **la ~ de la gloire** the price of fame

rancune /Rɑ̃kyn/ *nf* (a) resentment
(b) grudge; **sans ~!** no hard feelings

rancunier, -ière /Rɑ̃kynje, ɛR/ *adj* **être ~**
to be a person who holds grudges

randonnée /Rɑ̃dɔne/ *nf* hiking

randonneur, -euse /Rɑ̃dɔnœʀ, øz/ *nm,f*
hiker, rambler

rang /Rɑ̃/ *nm* (a) row; (in necklace) strand; **se
mettre en ~s** ⟨*children*⟩ to get into (a) line
(b) (Mil, figurative) rank; **sortir du ~** to rise or
come up through the ranks; **serrer les ~s** to
close ranks
(c) (in a hierarchy) rank; **être au 5ᵉ ~
mondial des exportateurs** to be the 5th largest
exporter in the world; **acteur de second ~**
second-rate actor; **des personnes de son ~**
people of one's own station

rangé, ~e[1] /Rɑ̃ʒe/ **1** *pp* ▶ RANGER[1]
2 *pp adj* ⟨*life*⟩ orderly; ⟨*person*⟩ well-
behaved

rangée[2] /Rɑ̃ʒe/ *nf* row

rangement /Rɑ̃ʒmɑ̃/ *nm* (a) **c'est un
maniaque du ~** he's obsessively tidy
(b) storage space

ranger[1] /Rɑ̃ʒe/ [13] **1** *vtr* (a) to put away;
où ranges-tu tes verres? where do you keep
the glasses?
(b) to arrange, to put into order; **~ un
animal dans les mammifères** to class an
animal as a mammal
(c) to tidy
2 **se ranger** *v refl* (+ *v être*) (a) to line up
(b) ⟨*vehicle, driver*⟩ to pull over
(c) **se ~ à l'avis de qn** to go along with sb
(d) to settle down

ranger[2] /Rɑ̃dʒɛR/ *nm* (a) ranger
(b) heavy-duty boot

ranimer /Ranime/ [1] *vtr* (a) to revive
⟨*person*⟩

(b) to rekindle ⟨*fire, hope*⟩; to stir up
⟨*quarrel*⟩

rapace /Rapas/ **1** *adj* ⟨*person*⟩ rapacious
2 *nm* bird of prey

rapacité /Rapasite/ *nf* (a) (of an animal)
ferocity
(b) (of trader) greed

rapatrié, ~e /Rapatrije/ *nm,f* repatriate
(**de** from)

rapatrier /Rapatrije/ [2] *vtr* to repatriate

râpe /Rɑp/ *nf* (Culin) grater

râper /Rɑpe/ [1] *vtr* to grate ⟨*cheese, carrot*⟩;
c'est râpé (figurative) (colloq) it's off (colloq)

rapetisser /Rap(ə)tise/ [1] *vi* to shrink

râpeux, -euse /Rɑpø, øz/ *adj* rough

raphia /Rafja/ *nm* raffia

rapide /Rapid/ **1** *adj* quick, rapid; fast
2 *nm* (a) rapids; **descendre un ~** to shoot
the rapids
(b) (train) express

rapidement /Rapidmɑ̃/ *adv* quickly; fast

rapidité /Rapidite/ *nf* speed

rapiécer /Rapjese/ [14] *vtr* to patch

rappel /Rapɛl/ *nm* (a) reminder; **~ à l'ordre**
call to order
(b) (lettre de) **~** reminder
(c) back pay
(d) (of ambassador) recall; (of actors) curtain
call
(e) (Med) booster

rappeler /Raple/ [19] **1** *vtr* (a) **~ qch à qn**
to remind sb of sth; **rappelons-le** let's not
forget; **~ qn à l'ordre** to call sb to order
(b) to call [sb] back
(c) (on phone) to call or ring [sb] back
2 **se rappeler** *v refl* (+ *v être*) to
remember

rappliquer /Raplike/ [1] *vi* (colloq) (a) to
turn up (colloq)
(b) to come back

rapport /RapɔR/ **1** *nm* (a) connection, link;
être sans ~ avec, n'avoir aucun ~ avec to
have nothing to do with
(b) **~s** relations; **avoir or entretenir de bons
~s avec qn** to be on good terms with sb
(c) **être en ~ avec qn** to be in touch with sb
(d) **sous tous les ~s** in every respect
(e) report
(f) return, yield; **immeuble de ~** block of
flats (GB) or apartment block (US) that is
rented out
(g) ratio; **bon ~ qualité prix** good value for
money
2 **par rapport à** *phr* (a) compared with;
par ~ au dollar against the dollar
(b) **le nombre de voitures par ~ au nombre
d'habitants** the number of cars per head of
the population
(c) with regard to, toward(s); **l'attitude de la
population par ~ à l'immigration** people's
attitudes to immigration
■ **~ de force** power struggle; **~s sexuels**
sexual relations

rapporter /RapɔRte/ [1] **1** *vtr* (a) to bring
back; to take back

(b) to bring in ⟨*income*⟩; **~ 10%** to yield *or* return 10%

(c) to report; **on m'a rapporté que** I was told that

2 *vi* **(a)** to bring in money

(b) (colloq) to tell tales

3 **se rapporter** *v refl* (+ *v être*) **se ~ à** to relate to, to bear a relation to

rapproché, **~e** /ʀapʀɔʃe/ **1** *pp* ▶ RAPPROCHER

2 *pp adj* close together

rapprochement /ʀapʀɔʃmɑ̃/ *nm*

(a) rapprochement

(b) connection

rapprocher /ʀapʀɔʃe/ [1] **1** *vtr* **(a)** to move [sth] closer

(b) to bring [sth] forward(s) ⟨*date*⟩

(c) to bring [sb] (closer) together ⟨*people*⟩

(d) to compare

2 **se rapprocher** *v refl* (+ *v être*) to get closer, to get nearer; **leurs peintures se rapprochent des fresques antiques** their paintings are similar to classical frescoes

rapt /ʀapt/ *nm* kidnapping (GB), abduction

raquette /ʀakɛt/ *nf* **(a)** (for tennis) racket; (for table-tennis) bat (GB), paddle (US)

(b) snowshoe

rare /ʀɑʀ/ *adj* **(a)** (not common) (gen) rare; ⟨*job*⟩ unusual; ⟨*intelligence*⟩ exceptional; **il est ~ qu'il vienne en train** it's unusual for him to come by train

(b) (not numerous) few, rare; ⟨*visits*⟩ infrequent; (not abundant) (gen) scarce; ⟨*hair*⟩ thin; ⟨*vegetation*⟩ sparse; **se faire ~** ⟨*product*⟩ to become scarce; **vous vous faites ~ ces temps-ci** you are not around much these days

raréfier /ʀaʀefje/ [2] **1** *vtr* **(a)** to rarefy ⟨*air, gas*⟩

(b) to make [sth] rare

2 **se raréfier** *v refl* (+ *v être*) ⟨*air*⟩ to become thinner; ⟨*gas*⟩ to rarefy; ⟨*food, money*⟩ to become scarce; ⟨*species*⟩ to become rare

rarement /ʀaʀmɑ̃/ *adv* rarely, seldom

rareté /ʀaʀte/ *nf* shortage, scarcity; rarity

rarissime /ʀaʀisim/ *adj* extremely rare

ras, **~e** /ʀɑ, ʀɑz/ **1** *adj* ⟨*hair*⟩ close-cropped; ⟨*fur*⟩ short; **à poil ~** ⟨*animal*⟩ short-haired; ⟨*carpet*⟩ short-piled; **en ~e campagne** in (the) open country; **une cuillère à café ~e** a level teaspoonful; **à ~ bord** to the brim

2 *adv* short; **couper (à) ~** to cut [sth] very short ⟨*hair, lawn*⟩

3 **au ras de** *phr* **au ~ du sol** at ground level

IDIOMS **faire table ~e de** to make a clean sweep of

RAS /ɛʀɑɛs/ (*abbr* = **rien à signaler**) nothing to report

rasade /ʀazad/ *nf* **(a)** glassful

(b) swig (colloq)

rasage /ʀazaʒ/ *nm* **(a)** (action) shaving

(b) (result) shave

ras-de-cou /ʀadku/ *nm inv* **(a)** crew-neck sweater

(b) choker

rase-mottes /ʀazmɔt/ *nm inv* **faire du ~, voler en ~** to fly low

raser /ʀaze/ [1] **1** *vtr* **(a)** to shave; to shave off; **~ de près** to give [sb] a close shave

(b) to demolish; to raze [sth] to the ground

(c) ⟨*bullet*⟩ to graze; ⟨*plane, bird*⟩ to skim

2 **se raser** *v refl* (+ *v être*) to shave

IDIOMS **~ les murs** to hug the walls

ras-le-bol /ʀalbɔl/ *nm inv* (colloq) discontent

rasoir /ʀazwaʀ/ **1** *adj inv* (colloq) boring

2 *nm* **~ mécanique** razor; **~ électrique** electric shaver

rassasier /ʀasazje/ [2] **1** *vtr* ⟨*food*⟩ to fill [sb] up

2 **se rassasier** *v refl* (+ *v être*) to eat one's fill

rassemblement /ʀasɑ̃bləmɑ̃/ *nm*

(a) rally

(b) gathering

(c) meeting

rassembler /ʀasɑ̃ble/ [1] **1** *vtr* to gather [sb/sth] together ⟨*people*⟩; to round up ⟨*sheep, herd*⟩; to unite ⟨*citizens, nation*⟩; to gather ⟨*information, proof*⟩; **~ ses forces** to summon up one's strength

2 **se rassembler** *v refl* (+ *v être*) **(a)** to gather

(b) to assemble

rasseoir: **se rasseoir** /ʀaswaʀ/ [41] *v refl* (+ *v être*) to sit down (again)

rasséréner /ʀaseʀene/ [14] *vtr* to calm [sb] down ⟨*person*⟩

rassis, **~e** /ʀasi, iz/ *adj* ⟨*bread*⟩ stale

rassurant, **~e** /ʀasyʀɑ̃, ɑ̃t/ *adj* reassuring

rassurer /ʀasyʀe/ [1] **1** *vtr* to reassure

2 **se rassurer** *v refl* (+ *v être*) to reassure oneself; **rassure-toi** don't worry; **je suis rassuré** I'm relieved

rat /ʀa/ *nm* **(a)** rat

(b) skinflint, cheapskate (colloq)

ratatiner: **se ratatiner** /ʀatatine/ [1] *vpr* **(a)** ⟨*fruit*⟩ to shrivel

(b) ⟨*face, person*⟩ to become wizened

ratatouille /ʀatatuj/ *nf* ratatouille

rate /ʀat/ *nf* **(a)** (Zool) female rat

(b) (Anat) spleen

raté, **~e** /ʀate/ **1** *pp* ▶ RATER

2 *pp adj* **(a)** ⟨*actor, painter*⟩ failed; **une vie ~e** a wasted life

(b) ⟨*opportunity*⟩ missed

3 *nm,f* (person) failure

4 **ratés** *nm pl* (in negotiations, system) hiccups

râteau, *pl* **~x** /ʀato/ *nm* rake

râtelier /ʀatəlje/ *nm* hayrack

IDIOMS **manger à tous les ~s** to run with the hare and hunt with the hounds

r

rater /ʀate/ [1] **1** *vtr* **(a)** to fail ⟨*exam*⟩; to spoil ⟨*sauce*⟩; **elle a raté son coup** (colloq) she has failed
(b) to miss ⟨*train, target*⟩
2 *vi* ⟨*plan*⟩ to fail; **il dit toujours des bêtises, ça ne rate jamais** (colloq) he can always be relied upon to say something stupid

ratifier /ʀatifje/ [2] *vtr* **(a)** to ratify ⟨*treaty, contract*⟩
(b) to confirm ⟨*plan, proposal*⟩

ration /ʀasjɔ̃/ *nf* **(a)** ration
(b) share

rationaliser /ʀasjɔnalize/ [1] *vtr* to rationalize

rationnel, -elle /ʀasjɔnɛl/ *adj* rational

rationnement /ʀasjɔnmɑ̃/ *nm* rationing

rationner /ʀasjɔne/ [1] **1** *vtr* to ration ⟨*petrol*⟩; to impose rationing on ⟨*population*⟩
2 se rationner *v refl* (+ *v être*) to cut down

ratisser /ʀatise/ [1] *vtr* **(a)** to rake over; to rake up
(b) to comb ⟨*area*⟩

raton /ʀatɔ̃/ *nm* young rat
■ ~ **laveur** racoon

rattachement /ʀataʃmɑ̃/ *nm* **(a)** (of country) unification
(b) (of person) **demander son** ~ **à** to ask to be posted to

rattacher /ʀataʃe/ [1] *vtr* **(a)** to attach ⟨*region*⟩; to post ⟨*employee*⟩
(b) to retie; to fasten [sth] again
(c) **plus rien ne la rattache à Lyon** she no longer has any ties with Lyons

rattrapage /ʀatʀapaʒ/ *nm* **(a)** (Econ) adjustment
(b) catching up; **cours de** ~ remedial lesson

rattraper /ʀatʀape/ [1] **1** *vtr* **(a)** to catch up with ⟨*competitor*⟩
(b) to catch ⟨*fugitive*⟩
(c) to make up for ⟨*lost time, deficit*⟩; to make up ⟨*points, distance*⟩; ~ **son retard** to catch up
(d) to put right ⟨*error*⟩; to smooth over ⟨*blunder*⟩; to save ⟨*situation*⟩
(e) to catch ⟨*object*⟩
2 se rattraper *v refl* (+ *v être*) **(a)** to redeem oneself
(b) to make up for it
(c) (Sch) to catch up
(d) to make up one's losses
(e) **se** ~ **de justesse** to stop oneself just in time; **se** ~ **à une branche** to save oneself by catching hold of a branch

rature /ʀatyʀ/ *nf* crossing-out; deletion

raturer /ʀatyʀe/ [1] *vtr* to cross out

rauque /ʀok/ *adj* **(a)** husky
(b) hoarse

ravage /ʀavaʒ/ *nm* **les** ~**s de la guerre** the ravages of war; **faire des** ~**s** to wreak havoc; ⟨*epidemic*⟩ to take a terrible toll; **tu vas faire des** ~**s avec ta mini-jupe** (humorous) you'll knock them dead in that mini-skirt

ravagé, ~e /ʀavaʒe/ *adj* (colloq) crazy

ravager /ʀavaʒe/ [13] *vtr* **(a)** ⟨*fire, war*⟩ to devastate, to ravage
(b) ⟨*disease*⟩ to ravage ⟨*face*⟩; ⟨*grief*⟩ to tear [sb] apart

ravalement /ʀavalmɑ̃/ *nm* **(a)** cleaning
(b) refacing
(c) (figurative) facelift

ravaler /ʀavale/ [1] *vtr* **(a)** to clean; to reface; to renovate ⟨*building*⟩
(b) to revamp ⟨*image*⟩
(c) to suppress ⟨*anger*⟩; ~ **ses larmes** to hold back one's tears

ravier /ʀavje/ *nm* small dish (*for hors-d'œuvre*)

ravigoter /ʀavigɔte/ [1] *vtr* (colloq) ⟨*fresh air*⟩ to invigorate; ⟨*drink*⟩ to perk [sb] up

ravin /ʀavɛ̃/ *nm* ravine

ravir /ʀaviʀ/ [3] *vtr* **(a)** to delight; **ça te va à** ~ it really suits you
(b) to steal

raviser: se raviser /ʀavize/ [1] *v refl* (+ *v être*) to change one's mind

ravissant, ~e /ʀavisɑ̃, ɑ̃t/ *adj* beautiful

ravisseur, -euse /ʀavisœʀ, øz/ *nm,f* kidnapper (GB), abductor

ravitaillement /ʀavitajmɑ̃/ *nm* supplies

ravitailler /ʀavitaje/ [1] **1** *vtr* **(a)** to provide [sb] with fresh supplies ⟨*town*⟩
(b) to refuel
2 se ravitailler *v refl* (+ *v être*) to obtain fresh supplies

raviver /ʀavive/ [1] *vtr* to rekindle; to revive

rayé, ~e /ʀeje/ **1** *pp* ▶ RAYER
2 *pp adj* **(a)** ⟨*fabric*⟩ striped
(b) ⟨*record*⟩ scratched

rayer /ʀeje/ [21] *vtr* **(a)** to cross [sth] out; '~ **la mention inutile**' 'delete whichever does not apply'
(b) **la ville a été rayée de la carte** the town was wiped off the map
(c) to scratch

rayon /ʀejɔ̃/ *nm* **(a)** radius; **dans un** ~ **de 10 km** within a 10 km radius; ~ **d'action** range; (figurative) sphere of activity
(b) ray; beam; **les** ~**s X** X-rays; **être soigné aux** ~**s** to undergo radiation treatment
(c) (of wheel) spoke
(d) shelf; ~ **de bibliothèque** (book)shelf
(e) (in big store) department; (in small shop) section; **tous nos modèles sont en** ~ all our styles are on display
(f) (colloq) **c'est mon** ~ that's my department (colloq); **il en connaît un** ~ **à ce sujet** he knows a lot about it

rayonnage /ʀejɔnaʒ/ *nm* shelves

rayonnant, ~e /ʀejɔnɑ̃, ɑ̃t/ *adj* radiant

rayonne /ʀejɔn/ *nf* rayon

rayonnement /ʀejɔnmɑ̃/ *nm* **(a)** radiation
(b) radiance
(c) (of country) influence

rayonner /ʀejɔne/ [1] *vi* **(a)** ⟨*light, heat*⟩ to radiate
(b) ⟨*star*⟩ to shine

(c) ⟨person⟩ to glow
(d) ⟨city⟩ to exert its influence
(e) ⟨soldiers⟩ to patrol; ⟨tourists⟩ to tour around
(f) ⟨streets⟩ to radiate

rayure /ʀɛjyʀ/ nf **(a)** stripe
(b) scratch

raz-de-marée /ʀɑdmaʀe/ nm inv tidal wave

razzia /ʀazja/ nf raid

ré /ʀe/ nm inv (note) D; (in sol-fa) re

réabonner /ʀeabɔne/ [1] vtr ~ qn to renew sb's subscription (à to)

réaccoutumer /ʀeakutyme/ [1] vtr ~ qn à qch to get sb used to sth again

réacheminer /ʀeaʃ(ə)mine/ vt to redirect

réacteur /ʀeaktœʀ/ nm **(a)** ~ (nucléaire) (nuclear) reactor
(b) jet engine

réaction /ʀeaksjɔ̃/ nf **(a)** reaction; response
(b) avion à ~ jet aircraft

réactionnaire /ʀeaksjɔnɛʀ/ adj, nmf reactionary

réactualiser /ʀeaktyalize/ [1] vtr (gen) to update; to relaunch ⟨debate⟩

réadapter: se **réadapter** /ʀeadapte/ [1] v refl to readjust (à qch to sth)

réaffirmer /ʀeafiʀme/ [1] vtr to reaffirm, to reassert

réagir /ʀeaʒiʀ/ [3] vi to react; to respond

réalisable /ʀealizabl/ adj feasible; workable

réalisateur, -trice /ʀealizatœʀ, tʀis/ nm,f director

réalisation /ʀealizasjɔ̃/ nf **(a)** (of dream) fulfilment (GB)
(b) (of study) carrying out
(c) achievement
(d) (of film) production

réaliser /ʀealize/ [1] **1** vtr **(a)** to fulfil (GB) ⟨ambition⟩; to achieve ⟨ideal, feat⟩
(b) to make ⟨model⟩; to carry out ⟨survey, study⟩
(c) to direct ⟨film⟩
(d) to realize
2 se **réaliser** v refl (+ v être) **(a)** ⟨dream⟩ to come true; ⟨predictions⟩ to be fulfilled
(b) se ~ (dans qch) to find fulfilment (GB) (in sth)

réalisme /ʀealism/ nm realism

réaliste /ʀealist/ adj (gen) realistic; (in art) realist

réalité /ʀealite/ nf la ~ reality; en ~ in reality; tenir compte des ~s to take the facts into consideration

réanimation /ʀeanimasjɔ̃/ nf **(a)** (service de) ~ intensive care (unit)
(b) resuscitation

réapparaître /ʀeapaʀɛtʀ/ [73] vi ⟨sun⟩ to come out again; ⟨illness⟩ to recur

réapprovisionner /ʀeapʀɔvizjɔne/ [1] vtr to restock ⟨shop⟩

réarmer /ʀeaʀme/ [1] vtr **(a)** to rearm

(b) to reload ⟨gun⟩

réassortir /ʀeasɔʀtiʀ/ [3] vtr to replenish

rébarbatif, -ive /ʀebaʀbatif, iv/ adj off-putting; forbidding

rebâtir /ʀ(ə)batiʀ/ [3] vtr to rebuild

rebattre /ʀ(ə)batʀ/ [61] vtr ~ les oreilles de qn avec une histoire to go on (and on) about something

rebattu, ~e /ʀ(ə)baty/ **1** pp ▸ REBATTRE
2 pp adj ⟨joke, story⟩ hackneyed

rebelle /ʀəbɛl/ **1** adj **(a)** rebel
(b) rebellious
(c) ⟨curl, lock of hair⟩ stray; ⟨stain⟩ stubborn
2 nmf rebel

rebeller: se **rebeller** /ʀəbɛle/ [1] v refl (+ v être) to rebel

rébellion /ʀebɛljɔ̃/ nf rebellion

rebiffer: se **rebiffer** /ʀ(ə)bife/ [1] vpr (colloq) to rebel

rebiquer /ʀ(ə)bike/ [1] vi (colloq) to stick up

reboiser /ʀ(ə)bwaze/ [1] vtr to reafforest

rebond /ʀ(ə)bɔ̃/ nm **(a)** bounce
(b) recovery

rebondi, ~e /ʀ(ə)bɔ̃di/ adj **(a)** ⟨shape⟩ round, rounded; ⟨cheek⟩ chubby; ⟨stomach⟩ fat; ⟨buttocks⟩ rounded
(b) (figurative) ⟨wallet⟩ bulging

rebondir /ʀ(ə)bɔ̃diʀ/ [3] vi **(a)** to bounce
(b) to start up again; to take a new turn

rebondissement /ʀ(ə)bɔ̃dismɑ̃/ nm (of controversy) sudden revival; (in trial) new development

rebord /ʀ(ə)bɔʀ/ nm **(a)** ledge; ~ de fenêtre windowsill
(b) rim
(c) edge

rebours: à **rebours** /aʀ(ə)buʀ/ phr ⟨count, walk⟩ backward(s)

rebouteux, -euse /ʀ(ə)butø, øz/ nm,f (colloq) bonesetter

rebrousse-poil: à **rebrousse-poil** /aʀ(ə)bʀuspwal/ phr the wrong way

rebrousser /ʀ(ə)bʀuse/ [1] vtr ~ chemin to turn back

rébus /ʀebys/ nm inv rebus

rebut /ʀ(ə)by/ nm rubbish; mettre qch au ~ to throw sth on the scrapheap

rebuter /ʀ(ə)byte/ [1] vtr **(a)** to disgust; to repel
(b) to put [sb] off

récalcitrant, ~e /ʀekalsitʀɑ̃, ɑ̃t/ adj recalcitrant

recaler /ʀ(ə)kale/ [1] vtr (colloq) to fail ⟨candidate⟩

récapitulatif /ʀekapitylatif/ nm summary of the main points

récapituler /ʀekapityle/ [1] vtr to sum up

receler /ʀəs(ə)le, ʀsəle/ [17] vtr **(a)** ~ des marchandises to possess stolen goods
(b) to contain

receleur, -euse /ʀ(ə)s(ə)lœʀ, ʀsəlœʀ, øz/ nm,f possessor of stolen goods

r

récemment /ʀesamã/ *adv* recently

recensement /ʀ(ə)sãsmã/ *nm* (a) census
(b) inventory

recenser /ʀ(ə)sãse/ [1] *vtr* (a) to take a census of ⟨*population*⟩
(b) to list ⟨*objects*⟩

récent, **~e** /ʀesã, ãt/ *adj* recent; ⟨*house*⟩ new

recentrer /ʀəsãtʀe/ [1] *vtr*, **se recentrer** *v refl* (+ *v être*) to refocus

récépissé /ʀesepise/ *nm* receipt

réceptacle /ʀesɛptakl/ *nm* container; **~ à verre** bottle bank

récepteur /ʀesɛptœʀ/ *nm* receiver

réceptif, -ive /ʀesɛptif, iv/ *adj* receptive

réception /ʀesɛpsjõ/ *nf* (a) reception
(b) welcome
(c) **s'occuper de la ~ des marchandises** to take delivery of the goods

réceptionner /ʀesɛpsjɔne/ [1] *vtr* (a) to take delivery of ⟨*goods*⟩
(b) to catch ⟨*ball*⟩

réceptionniste /ʀesɛpsjɔnist/ *nmf* receptionist

récession /ʀesesjõ/ *nf* recession

recette /ʀ(ə)sɛt/ *nf* (a) **~ (de cuisine)** recipe
(b) formula, recipe
(c) takings; **faire ~** to bring in money; (figurative) to be a success; **les ~s et (les) dépenses** receipts and expenses

receveur, -euse /ʀəs(ə)vœʀ, øz/ *nm,f* (on bus) conductor
■ **~ des postes** postmaster

recevoir /ʀəsvwaʀ, ʀ(ə)səvwaʀ/ [5] *vtr*
(a) to receive, to get; **il a reçu une tuile sur la tête** he got hit on the head by a tile; **je n'ai d'ordre à ~ de personne** I don't take orders from anyone
(b) to welcome ⟨*guests*⟩; **être bien reçu** to be well received; to get a good reception; **ils reçoivent beaucoup** they do a lot of entertaining; **Laval reçoit Caen** (Sport) Laval is playing host to Caen
(c) to see ⟨*patients*⟩
(d) to receive ⟨*radio signal*⟩
(e) (Sch) to pass ⟨*candidate*⟩; **être reçu à un examen** to pass an exam

rechange: **de rechange** /dəʀ(ə)ʃãʒ/ *phr* ⟨*part*⟩ spare; ⟨*solution*⟩ alternative

réchapper /ʀeʃape/ [1] *v+prep* **~ de** to come through ⟨*illness, accident*⟩

recharge /ʀ(ə)ʃaʀʒ/ *nf* refill; reload

rechargeable /ʀ(ə)ʃaʀʒabl/ *adj* ⟨*lighter, pen*⟩ refillable; ⟨*battery, appliance*⟩ rechargeable

recharger /ʀ(ə)ʃaʀʒe/ [13] *vtr* to reload; to refill; to recharge ⟨*battery*⟩

réchaud /ʀeʃo/ *nm* stove; **~ électrique** electric ring (GB), hotplate

réchauffé, ~e /ʀeʃofe/ [1] *pp* ▶
RÉCHAUFFER
[2] *pp adj* ⟨*joke, story*⟩ hackneyed

[3] *nm* **c'est du ~** there's nothing new about it

réchauffement /ʀeʃofmã/ *nm* warming (up); **le ~ de la planète** global warming

réchauffer /ʀeʃofe/ [1] [1] *vtr* (a) (Culin) to reheat, to heat [sth] up
(b) to warm up ⟨*person, hands, room*⟩
[2] **se réchauffer** *v refl* (+ *v être*) to warm up

rêche /ʀɛʃ/ *adj* ⟨*hands, fabric*⟩ rough

recherche /ʀ(ə)ʃɛʀʃ/ *nf* (a) research
(b) search; **être à la ~ de** to be looking for
(c) **~ de** pursuit of ⟨*happiness*⟩
(d) **sans ~** without affectation
■ **~ d'emploi** job-hunting

recherché, ~e /ʀ(ə)ʃɛʀʃe/ [1] *pp* ▶
RECHERCHER
[2] *pp adj* (a) sought-after
(b) in demand
(c) ⟨*dress*⟩ meticulous; ⟨*style*⟩ original
(d) ⟨*aim*⟩ intended

rechercher /ʀ(ə)ʃɛʀʃe/ [1] *vtr* (a) to look for; **il est recherché par la police** he's wanted by the police; **'recherchons vendeuse qualifiée'** 'qualified sales assistant (GB) or clerk (US) required'
(b) to seek ⟨*security*⟩; to fish for ⟨*compliments*⟩

rechigner /ʀ(ə)ʃiɲe/ [1] [1] *v+prep* **~ à faire** to balk at doing
[2] *vi* to grumble

rechute /ʀəʃyt/ *nf* relapse

rechuter /ʀ(ə)ʃyte/ [1] *vi* (a) (Med) to have a relapse
(b) (Econ) ⟨*price, currency*⟩ to fall again

récidive /ʀesidiv/ *nf* (a) (Law) second offence (GB)
(b) (figurative) repetition
(c) (Med) recurrence

récidiver /ʀesidive/ [1] *vi* (Law) to reoffend

récidiviste /ʀesidivist/ *nmf* second offender, recidivist; habitual offender

récif /ʀesif/ *nm* reef

récipient /ʀesipjã/ *nm* container

réciprocité /ʀesipʀɔsite/ *nf* reciprocity

réciproque /ʀesipʀɔk/ [1] *adj* reciprocal
[2] *nf* reverse; **la ~ est vraie** the reverse is true

réciproquement /ʀesipʀɔkmã/ *adv* **et ~** and vice versa

récit /ʀesi/ *nm* (a) story
(b) narrative

récital /ʀesital/ *nm* recital

récitation /ʀesitasjõ/ *nf* **apprendre une ~** to learn a text (off) by heart

réciter /ʀesite/ [1] *vtr* to recite

réclamation /ʀeklamasjõ/ *nf*
(a) complaint
(b) claim; **sur ~** on request

réclame /ʀeklam/ *nf* (a) publicity
(b) advertisement
(c) **'en ~'** 'on offer' (GB), 'on sale'

réclamer /ʀeklame/ [1] [1] *vtr* to ask for ⟨*person, thing, money*⟩; to call for ⟨*reform,* inquiry>; to claim ⟨compensation⟩; **travail qui réclame de l'attention** work that requires attention

[2] **se réclamer** v refl (+ v être) **se ~ de** ⟨person, group⟩ to claim to be representative of

reclasser /Rəklase/ [1] vtr (a) to reclassify ⟨documents⟩
(b) to redeploy

reclus, **~e** /Rəkly, yz/ adj reclusive; **vivre ~** to live as a recluse

réclusion /Reklyzjɔ̃/ nf (a) (Law) imprisonment
(b) reclusion

recoin /Rəkwɛ̃/ nm corner; (figurative) recess

récolte /Rekɔlt/ nf harvest; crop

récolter /Rekɔlte/ [1] vtr (a) to harvest ⟨corn⟩; to dig up ⟨potatoes⟩
(b) ⟨bee⟩ to collect ⟨pollen⟩; ⟨person⟩ to win ⟨points⟩; to collect ⟨information⟩

recommandable /Rəkɔmɑ̃dabl/ adj **un individu peu ~** a disreputable individual

recommandation /Rəkɔmɑ̃dasjɔ̃/ nf recommendation

recommandé, **~e** /Rəkɔmɑ̃de/ [1] pp ▶
RECOMMANDER
[2] pp adj ⟨letter⟩ registered

recommander /Rəkɔmɑ̃de/ [1] [1] vtr
(a) to advise
(b) to recommend
[2] **se recommander** v refl (+ v être) **se ~ de qn** to give sb's name as a reference

recommencement /Rəkɔmɑ̃smɑ̃/ nm **l'histoire est un éternel ~** history is constantly repeating itself

recommencer /Rəkɔmɑ̃se/ [12] vtr (a) to start [sth] again
(b) to do [sth] again

récompense /Rekɔ̃pɑ̃s/ nf (a) reward
(b) award

récompenser /Rekɔ̃pɑ̃se/ [1] vtr to reward

réconciliation /Rekɔ̃siljasjɔ̃/ nf reconciliation

réconcilier /Rekɔ̃silje/ [2] [1] vtr **~ Pierre avec Paul** to bring Pierre and Paul back together; **~ morale et politique** to reconcile morality with politics
[2] **se réconcilier** v refl (+ v être) ⟨friends⟩ to make up; ⟨nations⟩ to be reconciled

reconduction /Rəkɔ̃dyksjɔ̃/ nf renewal

reconduire /Rəkɔ̃dɥiR/ [69] vtr (a) to see [sb] out; **~ qn chez lui** to take sb home
(b) to extend ⟨strike, ceasefire⟩; to renew ⟨mandate⟩

réconfort /Rekɔ̃fɔR/ nm comfort

réconfortant, **~e** /Rekɔ̃fɔRtɑ̃, ɑ̃t/ adj
(a) comforting
(b) cheering
(c) fortifying

réconforter /Rekɔ̃fɔRte/ [1] vtr (a) to comfort; to console
(b) **~ qn** to cheer sb up

(c) to fortify

reconnaissance /R(ə)kɔnɛsɑ̃s/ nf
(a) gratitude; **en ~ de** in appreciation of
(b) recognition
(c) (of wrongs) admission, admitting; (of qualities) recognition, recognizing
(d) (Mil) reconnaissance

reconnaissant, **~e** /R(ə)kɔnɛsɑ̃, ɑ̃t/ adj grateful

reconnaître /R(ə)kɔnɛtR/ [73] [1] vtr (a) to recognize ⟨person⟩
(b) to identify; **je reconnais bien là leur générosité** it's just like them to be so generous
(c) to admit ⟨facts, errors⟩
(d) to recognize ⟨trade union, regime⟩; **~ un enfant** to recognize a child legally
(e) to acknowledge
[2] **se reconnaître** v refl (+ v être) **se ~ à qch** to be recognizable by sth

reconnu, **~e** /R(ə)kɔny/ [1] pp ▶
RECONNAÎTRE
[2] pp adj ⟨fact⟩ recognized

reconquérir /R(ə)kɔ̃keRiR/ [35] vtr to reconquer, to recover ⟨territory⟩; (figurative) to regain ⟨esteem⟩; to win back ⟨person, right⟩

reconstituer /R(ə)kɔ̃stitɥe/ [1] vtr to re-form ⟨association⟩; to reconstruct ⟨crime⟩; to recreate ⟨era, decor⟩; to piece [sth] together again ⟨broken object⟩; to build up again ⟨reserves⟩

reconstitution /R(ə)kɔ̃stitysjɔ̃/ nf (of crime, event) reconstruction

reconstruire /R(ə)kɔ̃stRɥiR/ [69] vtr (a) to reconstruct
(b) to rebuild

reconversion /R(ə)kɔ̃vɛRsjɔ̃/ nf (of worker) redeployment; (of region) redevelopment; (of economy) restructuring; (of factory) conversion

reconvertir /R(ə)kɔ̃vɛRtiR/ [3] [1] vtr to redeploy ⟨staff⟩; to convert ⟨factory⟩; to adapt ⟨equipment⟩
[2] **se reconvertir** v refl (+ v être) ⟨staff⟩ to switch to a new type of employment; ⟨company⟩ to switch to a new type of production

recopier /R(ə)kɔpje/ [2] vtr (a) to copy out
(b) to write up ⟨notes⟩

record /R(ə)kɔR/ [1] adj inv record
[2] nm (Sport, figurative) record

recoudre /R(ə)kudR/ [76] vtr (a) to sew [sth] back on ⟨button⟩
(b) (Med) to stitch up ⟨wound⟩

recoupement /R(ə)kupmɑ̃/ nm cross-check

recouper /R(ə)kupe/ [1] [1] vtr to cut [sth] again ⟨hair, hedge⟩; to recut ⟨garment⟩
[2] **se recouper** v refl (+ v être)
(a) ⟨versions⟩ to tally; ⟨results⟩ to add up
(b) ⟨lines⟩ to intersect

recourbé, **~e** /R(ə)kuRbe/ adj (gen) curved; ⟨nose, beak⟩ hooked

recourir /R(ə)kuRiR/ [26] v+prep **~ à** to use ⟨remedy⟩; to resort to ⟨strategy⟩

recours /ʀ(ə)kuʀ/ *nm inv* (a) recourse; resort; **sans autre ~ que** with no other way out but; **avoir ~ à** to have recourse to ⟨*remedy*⟩; to resort to ⟨*strategy*⟩; to go to ⟨*expert*⟩
(b) (Law) appeal

recouvrement /ʀ(ə)kuvʀəmɑ̃/ *nm* (of tax, contributions) collection; (of sum, debt) recovery

recouvrer /ʀ(ə)kuvʀe/ [1] *vtr* to recover; to collect ⟨*tax*⟩

recouvrir /ʀ(ə)kuvʀiʀ/ [32] *vtr* (a) to cover
(b) to re-cover
(c) to hide, to conceal

recracher /ʀ(ə)kʀaʃe/ [1] *vtr* to spit out

récréation /ʀekʀeasjɔ̃/ *nf* (a) playtime (GB), break (GB), recess (US)
(b) recreation

recréer /ʀ(ə)kʀee/ [11] *vtr* to recreate

récrier: se récrier /ʀekʀije/ [2] *v refl* (+ *v être*) to exclaim

récrimination /ʀekʀiminasjɔ̃/ *nf* recrimination

récriminer /ʀekʀimine/ [1] *vi* to rail

recroqueviller: se recroqueviller /ʀ(ə)kʀɔkvije/ [1] *v refl* (+ *v être*) (a) ⟨*person*⟩ to huddle up
(b) ⟨*leaf, petal*⟩ to shrivel up

recrudescence /ʀ(ə)kʀydesɑ̃s/ *nf* (of violence, interest) fresh upsurge; (of bombing, demands) new wave; (of fire) renewed outbreak

recrudescent, ~e /ʀ(ə)kʀydesɑ̃, ɑ̃t/ *adj* **être ~** to be on the increase

recrue /ʀəkʀy/ *nf* recruit

recrutement /ʀ(ə)kʀytmɑ̃/ *nm* recruitment

recruter /ʀ(ə)kʀyte/ [1] *vtr* to recruit

rectangle /ʀɛktɑ̃gl/ *nm* rectangle

rectangulaire /ʀɛktɑ̃gylɛʀ/ *adj* rectangular

recteur /ʀɛktœʀ/ *nm* (Sch, Univ) chief education officer

rectificatif, -ive /ʀɛktifikatif, iv/ *nm*
(a) (in newspaper) correction
(b) (to law) amendment

rectification /ʀɛktifikasjɔ̃/ *nf* correction; rectification; adjustment

rectifier /ʀɛktifje/ [2] *vtr* to correct, to rectify; to adjust

rectiligne /ʀɛktiliɲ/ *adj* straight

recto /ʀɛkto/ *nm* front; **~ verso** on both sides

rectorat /ʀɛktɔʀa/ *nm* ≈ local education authority (GB), ≈ board of education (US)

rectum /ʀɛktɔm/ *nm* rectum

reçu, ~e /ʀ(ə)sy/ **1** *pp* ▶ RECEVOIR
2 *pp adj* ⟨*candidate*⟩ successful
3 *nm* receipt

recueil /ʀ(ə)kœj/ *nm* collection; anthology

recueillement /ʀəkœjmɑ̃/ *nm*
(a) contemplation
(b) reverence

recueilli, ~e /ʀəkœji/ **1** *pp* ▶ RECUEILLIR

2 *pp adj* ⟨*air*⟩ rapt; ⟨*person*⟩ rapt in prayer; ⟨*crowd, silence*⟩ reverential

recueillir /ʀəkœjiʀ/ [27] **1** *vtr* (a) to collect ⟨*donations, anecdotes*⟩; to gather ⟨*evidence, testimonies*⟩
(b) to get ⟨*votes, news*⟩; to gain ⟨*consensus*⟩; to win ⟨*praise*⟩
(c) to collect ⟨*water, resin*⟩; to gather ⟨*honey*⟩
(d) to take in ⟨*orphan*⟩
(e) to record ⟨*impressions, opinions*⟩
2 se recueillir *v refl* (+ *v être*) to engage in private prayer

recul /ʀ(ə)kyl/ *nm* (a) detachment; **avec le ~** with hindsight, in retrospect; **prendre du ~** to stand back
(b) (in production) drop, fall; (of doctrine) decline
(c) (of army) pulling back; (of tide, floodwaters) recession; **avoir un mouvement de ~** to recoil; **feu de ~** reversing light

reculé, ~e /ʀəkyle/ *adj* remote

reculer /ʀ(ə)kyle/ [1] **1** *vtr* (a) to move back ⟨*object*⟩
(b) (in car) to reverse (GB), to back up
(c) to put off ⟨*event, decision*⟩; to put back ⟨*date*⟩
2 *vi* (a) ⟨*person*⟩ to move back; to stand back; ⟨*driver, car*⟩ to reverse
(b) ⟨*army*⟩ to pull *or* draw back
(c) ⟨*forest*⟩ to be gradually disappearing; ⟨*river*⟩ to go down; ⟨*sea*⟩ to recede
(d) ⟨*currency, exports*⟩ to fall; ⟨*doctrine*⟩ to decline; **faire ~ le chômage** to reduce unemployment
(e) to back down; **ne ~ devant rien** to stop at nothing
3 se reculer *v refl* (+ *v être*) (gen) to move back; to stand back

reculons: à reculons /aʀ(ə)kylɔ̃/ *phr* **aller à ~** to go backward(s)

récupérable /ʀekypeʀabl/ *adj*
(a) ⟨*material*⟩ reusable
(b) ⟨*object*⟩ which can be made good again
(c) ⟨*delinquent*⟩ who can be rehabilitated

récupération /ʀekypeʀasjɔ̃/ *nf*
(a) salvage; recycling
(b) recovery
(c) appropriation

récupérer /ʀekypeʀe/ [14] **1** *vtr* (a) to get back ⟨*money, strength*⟩
(b) to retrieve
(c) to salvage ⟨*scrap iron*⟩; to reclaim ⟨*rags*⟩
(d) to save ⟨*boxes*⟩
(e) to make up ⟨*days*⟩
(f) to appropriate ⟨*ideas*⟩
2 *vi* to recover

récurer /ʀekyʀe/ [1] *vtr* to scour; to scrub

récurrent, ~e /ʀekyʀɑ̃, ɑ̃t/ *adj* recurrent

récuser /ʀekyze/ [1] **1** *vtr* to challenge ⟨*jury*⟩
2 se récuser *v refl* (+ *v être*) ⟨*judge*⟩ to decline to act in a case

recyclable /ʀ(ə)siklabl/ *adj* recyclable

recyclage /ʀ(ə)siklaʒ/ *nm* (a) recycling
(b) retraining

recycler /R(ə)sikle/ [1] **1** *vtr* **(a)** to recycle ⟨*material*⟩

(b) ~ le personnel to retrain the staff

2 se recycler *v refl* (+ *v être*) **(a)** to retrain

(b) to change jobs

rédacteur, -trice /Redaktœr, tris/ *nm,f*
(a) author, writer
(b) editor

rédaction /Redaksjɔ̃/ *nf* **(a)** writing
(b) editing
(c) editorial offices
(d) editorial staff
(e) (Sch) essay (GB), theme (US)

reddition /Redisjɔ̃/ *nf* surrender

rédemption /Redãpsjɔ̃/ *nf* redemption

redescendre /RədɛsãdR/ [6] **1** *vtr* (gen) to take [sb/sth] back down; ⟨*person*⟩ to go/ come back down ⟨*stairs*⟩

2 *vi* (+ *v être*) to go (back) down; to go down again

redevable /Rədvabl, R(ə)dəvabl/ *adj* être ~ de qch à qn to owe sth to sb; être ~ de l'impôt to be liable for tax

redevance /Rədvãs, R(ə)dəvãs/ *nf* **(a)** (gen) charge; (for television) licence (GB) *or* license (US) fee; (for telephone) rental charge
(b) royalty

rédhibitoire /RedibitwaR/ *adj* ⟨*cost*⟩ prohibitive; ⟨*obstacle*⟩ insurmountable

rediffuser /R(ə)difyze/ [1] *vtr* to repeat, to rerun ⟨*programme*⟩

rédiger /Rediʒe/ [13] *vtr* to write ⟨*article*⟩; to write up ⟨*notes*⟩; to draft ⟨*contract*⟩

redingote /R(ə)dɛ̃gɔt/ *nf* (for man) frock coat; (for woman) fitted coat

redire /RədiR/ [65] *vtr* to repeat; **trouver quelque chose à ~ à qch** to find fault with sth

redite /R(ə)dit/ *nf* (needless) repetition

redondance /R(ə)dɔ̃dãs/ *nf* redundancy

redondant, ~e /R(ə)dɔ̃dã, ãt/ *adj*
(a) superfluous
(b) redundant

redonner /R(ə)dɔne/ [1] *vtr* ~ qch à qn to give sb sth again

redorer /R(ə)dɔRe/ [1] *vtr* to regild; ~ son blason ⟨*person*⟩ to restore one's image

redoublant, ~e /R(ə)dublã, ãt/ *nm,f* student repeating a year

redoublement /R(ə)dubləmã/ *nm* intensification

redoubler /R(ə)duble/ [1] **1** *vtr* (Sch) ~ une classe to repeat a year

2 redoubler de *v+prep* ~ de prudence to be twice as careful; la tempête a redoublé de violence the storm has become even fiercer

3 *vi* **(a)** to repeat a year
(b) to intensify

redoutable /R(ə)dutabl/ *adj* ⟨*weapon, exam*⟩ formidable; ⟨*disease*⟩ dreadful

redouter /R(ə)dute/ [1] *vtr* to fear

redressement /RədRɛsmã/ *nm* maison de ~ reformatory

redresser /R(ə)dRese/ [1] **1** *vtr* **(a)** to straighten (up); to put [sth] up again; ~ la tête to lift one's head up

(b) to put [sth] back on its feet ⟨*economy*⟩; to turn [sth] around ⟨*company*⟩; to aid the recovery of ⟨*currency*⟩

(c) to straighten up ⟨*glider, steering wheel*⟩; ~ la barre to right the helm; (figurative) to put things back on an even keel

(d) to rectify ⟨*error*⟩

2 se redresser *v refl* (+ *v être*) **(a)** to stand up; to sit up; to stand up straight; to sit up straight

(b) ⟨*economy, plant*⟩ to recover; ⟨*country*⟩ to get back on its feet

redresseur /RədRɛsœR/ *nm* ~ de torts righter of wrongs

réductible /Redyktibl/ *adj* ⟨*costs*⟩ which can be reduced *or* cut

réduction /Redyksjɔ̃/ *nf* **(a)** discount, reduction; ~ étudiants concession for students

(b) cutting, reducing
(c) reduction, cut; ~s d'effectifs staff cuts
(d) (of statue) small replica

réduire /RedɥiR/ [68] **1** *vtr* **(a)** to reduce; to cut ⟨*tax*⟩; to cut down on ⟨*staff, spending*⟩

(b) to reduce ⟨*photograph*⟩; to scale down ⟨*drawing*⟩; to cut ⟨*text*⟩

(c) ~ qch en poudre to crush sth to powder; être réduit en cendres ⟨*city*⟩ to be reduced to ashes; ⟨*dreams*⟩ to turn to ashes

(d) ~ à to reduce to; voilà à quoi j'en suis réduit! this is what I've been reduced to!

(e) to reduce ⟨*sauce*⟩

2 *vi* ⟨*sauce*⟩ to reduce; ⟨*spinach*⟩ to shrink

3 se réduire *v refl* (+ *v être*) **(a)** ⟨*costs*⟩ to be reduced; ⟨*imports*⟩ to be cut

(b) cela se réduit à bien peu de chose it doesn't amount to very much

réduit, ~e /Redɥi, it/ **1** *pp* ▶ RÉDUIRE

2 *pp adj* **(a)** ⟨*rate, speed*⟩ reduced, lower; ⟨*time*⟩ shorter; ⟨*activity*⟩ reduced; ⟨*group*⟩ smaller; visibilité ~e restricted visibility

(b) ⟨*means, choice*⟩ limited; ⟨*group*⟩ small
(c) ⟨*size*⟩ small

3 *nm* cubbyhole

rééditer /Reedite/ [1] *vtr* to reprint ⟨*book*⟩

rééducation /Reedykasjɔ̃/ *nf*
(a) physiotherapy; ~ de la parole speech therapy
(b) rehabilitation

rééduquer /Reedyke/ [1] *vtr* to restore normal functioning to ⟨*limb*⟩; to rehabilitate

réel, réelle /Reɛl/ **1** *adj* (gen) real; ⟨*fact*⟩ true

2 *nm* le ~ the real

réellement /Reɛlmã/ *adv* really

réembaucher /Reãboʃe/ [1] *vtr* to take [sb] on again

réemployer /Reãplwaje/ [23] *vtr* to reinvest ⟨*funds*⟩; to re-employ ⟨*staff*⟩

rééquilibrer /ReekilibRe/ [1] *vtr* **(a)** (Aut) to balance ⟨*wheels*⟩
(b) to balance ⟨*budget*⟩

r

réévaluer /ʀeevalɥe/ [1] *vtr* (a) to revalue ⟨*currency*⟩; to revise ⟨*tax*⟩
(b) to reappraise

réexpédier /ʀeɛkspedje/ [2] *vtr* (a) to forward, to redirect
(b) to send [sth] back

réf (*written abbr* = **référence**) ref

refaire /ʀəfɛʀ/ [10] **1** *vtr* (a) to do [sth] again ⟨*exercise*⟩; to make [sth] again ⟨*journey, mistake*⟩; ∼ **le même chemin** to go back the same way; ∼ **un numéro de téléphone** to redial a number
(b) **je vais** ∼ **de la soupe** I'll make some more soup
(c) **vouloir** ∼ **le monde** to want to change the world; **se faire** ∼ **le nez** to have one's nose re-modelled (GB); ∼ **sa vie** to start all over again
(d) to redo ⟨*roof*⟩; to redecorate ⟨*room*⟩; to resurface ⟨*road*⟩
2 se refaire *v refl* (+ *v être*) (a) **se** ∼ **une santé** to recuperate; **se** ∼ **une beauté** to redo one's make-up
(b) **se** ∼ **à** to get used to [sth] again
(c) **on ne se refait pas** a person can't change

réfection /ʀefɛksjɔ̃/ *nf* repairing

réfectoire /ʀefɛktwaʀ/ *nm* refectory; (Mil) mess

référence /ʀefeʀɑ̃s/ **1** *nf* (a) reference; **en** *or* **par** ∼ **à** in reference to; **faire** ∼ **à** to refer to; **lui? ce n'est pas une** ∼**!** who, him? well, he's not much of an example!
(b) reference number
2 références *nf pl* references

référendum /ʀefeʀɛ̃dɔm/ *nm* referendum

référer /ʀefeʀe/ [14] **1 référer à** *v+prep* **en** ∼ **à** to consult
2 se référer *v refl* (+ *v être*) (a) **se** ∼ **à** to refer to
(b) **se** ∼ **à** to consult

refermer /ʀ(ə)fɛʀme/ [1] **1** *vtr* (a) to close
(b) to close [sth] again
2 se refermer *v refl* (+ *v être*) ⟨*door*⟩ to close; ⟨*wound*⟩ to close up

réfléchi, ∼**e** /ʀefleʃi/ *adj* (a) ⟨*person*⟩ reflective, thoughtful
(b) ⟨*decision*⟩ considered; ⟨*action*⟩ well-considered; **c'est tout** ∼ my mind is made up
(c) ⟨*image*⟩ reflected
(d) ⟨*verb*⟩ reflexive

réfléchir /ʀefleʃiʀ/ [3] **1** *vtr* to reflect ⟨*heat*⟩
2 réfléchir à *v+prep* to think about
3 *vi* to think; **mais réfléchis donc un peu!** use your brain!
4 se réfléchir *v refl* (+ *v être*) to be reflected

réflecteur /ʀeflɛktœʀ/ *nm* reflector

reflet /ʀ(ə)flɛ/ *nm* (a) reflection
(b) glint; shimmer; sheen; **cheveux châtains aux** ∼**s roux** brown hair with auburn highlights

refléter /ʀ(ə)flete/ [14] **1** *vtr* to reflect; **son visage reflétait son émotion** his/her emotion showed in his/her face

2 se refléter *v refl* (+ *v être*) to be reflected

réflexe /ʀeflɛks/ **1** *adj* reflex
2 *nm* (a) reflex
(b) reaction; **manquer de** ∼ to be slow to react; **par** ∼ automatically
∎ ∼ **conditionné** conditioned reflex

réflexion /ʀeflɛksjɔ̃/ *nf* (a) thought, reflection
(b) thinking, reflection; ∼ **faite** *or* **à la** ∼, **je n'irai pas** on second thoughts, I won't go; **donner matière à** ∼ to be food for thought
(c) remark, comment; **s'attirer des** ∼**s** to attract criticism
(d) study; **document de** ∼ discussion paper
(e) (of image) reflection

refluer /ʀ(ə)flɥe/ [1] *vi* ⟨*liquid*⟩ to flow back

reflux /ʀ(ə)fly/ *nm inv* ebb tide

refonte /ʀ(ə)fɔ̃t/ *nf* (a) overhaul
(b) (of contract) rewriting

reforestation /ʀ(ə)fɔʀɛstasjɔ̃/ *nf* reafforestation

réformateur, **-trice** /ʀefɔʀmatœʀ, tʀis/ *nm,f* reformer

réforme /ʀefɔʀm/ *nf* (a) reform
(b) (Mil) discharge
(c) **la Réforme** the Reformation

réformé, ∼**e** /ʀefɔʀme/ *nm,f* Calvinist

reformer /ʀ(ə)fɔʀme/ [1] *vtr* to re-form

réformer /ʀefɔʀme/ [1] *vtr* (a) to reform
(b) (Mil) to declare [sb] unfit for service ⟨*conscript*⟩; to discharge ⟨*soldier*⟩

refoulé, ∼**e** /ʀ(ə)fule/ *nm,f* repressed *or* inhibited person

refoulement /ʀ(ə)fulmɑ̃/ *nm* (a) (of impulse) repression
(b) pushing back; turning back; driving back; forcing back

refouler /ʀ(ə)fule/ [1] *vtr* (a) to suppress ⟨*memory*⟩; to repress ⟨*tendency*⟩; to hold back ⟨*tears*⟩
(b) to force [sth] back ⟨*liquid*⟩; to push back ⟨*enemy*⟩; to turn back ⟨*immigrant*⟩

réfractaire /ʀefʀaktɛʀ/ *adj* (a) ∼ **à** resistant to ⟨*influence*⟩; impervious to ⟨*music*⟩
(b) refractory

réfracter /ʀefʀakte/ [1] *vtr* to refract

réfraction /ʀefʀaksjɔ̃/ *nf* refraction

refrain /ʀ(ə)fʀɛ̃/ *nm* (a) chorus
(b) (old) refrain

refréner /ʀ(ə)fʀene/, **réfréner** /ʀefʀene/ [14] *vtr* to curb

réfrigérant, ∼**e** /ʀefʀiʒeʀɑ̃, ɑ̃t/ *adj* cooling

réfrigérateur /ʀefʀiʒeʀatœʀ/ *nm* refrigerator

réfrigérer /ʀefʀiʒeʀe/ [14] *vtr* to refrigerate ⟨*food*⟩; to cool ⟨*place*⟩

refroidir /ʀəfʀwadiʀ/ [3] **1** *vtr* (a) to cool down; to cool
(b) ∼ **qn** to dampen sb's spirits
2 *vi* (a) to cool down
(b) to get cold

3 **se refroidir** *v refl* (+ *v être*) ⟨*weather*⟩ to get colder; ⟨*joint*⟩ to stiffen up; ⟨*person*⟩ to get cold

refroidissement /ʀəfʀwadismã/ *nm*
(a) drop in temperature
(b) cooling
(c) (Med) chill

refuge /ʀ(ə)fyʒ/ *nm* (a) refuge
(b) (mountain) refuge
(c) (for animals) sanctuary
(d) traffic island

réfugié, ~e /ʀefyʒje/ *nm,f* refugee

réfugier: se réfugier /ʀefyʒje/ [2] *v refl* (+ *v être*) to take refuge

refus /ʀ(ə)fy/ *nm inv* refusal; **ce n'est pas de ~** (colloq) I wouldn't say no (colloq)
■ **~ de priorité** failure to give way

refuser /ʀ(ə)fyze/ [1] **1** *vtr* (a) (gen) to refuse; to turn down ⟨*offer*⟩; **~ de faire** to refuse to do
(b) to reject ⟨*budget, manuscript, racism*⟩; to refuse to accept ⟨*fact*⟩; to turn away ⟨*spectator*⟩
2 **se refuser** *v refl* (+ *v être*) (a) **ça ne se refuse pas** it's too good to pass up (colloq); I wouldn't say no (colloq)
(b) to deny oneself ⟨*pleasure*⟩; **on ne se refuse rien!** (colloq) you're certainly not stinting yourself!
(c) **se ~ à** to refuse to accept ⟨*evidence*⟩; to refuse to adopt ⟨*solution*⟩

réfuter /ʀefyte/ [1] *vtr* to refute

regagner /ʀ(ə)gaɲe/ [1] *vtr* (a) to get back to ⟨*place*⟩
(b) to regain ⟨*esteem*⟩

regain /ʀ(ə)gɛ̃/ *nm* **~ de** rise in ⟨*inflation*⟩; revival of ⟨*interest*⟩; resurgence of ⟨*violence*⟩

régal /ʀegal/ *nm* (a) culinary delight; **c'est un ~!** it's delicious!
(b) (figurative) delight; **un ~ pour les yeux** a feast for the eyes

régalade /ʀegalad/ *nf* **boire à la ~** to drink without letting one's lips touch the bottle

régaler: se régaler /ʀegale/ [1] *v refl* (+ *v être*) (a) **je me régale** it's delicious; **les enfants se sont régalés avec ton dessert** the children really enjoyed your dessert
(b) (figurative) **se ~ avec** to enjoy [sth] thoroughly ⟨*film*⟩; **se ~ de** to love ⟨*anecdote*⟩

regard /ʀ(ə)gaʀ/ **1** *nm* (a) look; **porter son ~ sur qch** to look at sth; **détourner le ~** to look away; **j'ai croisé son ~** our eyes met; **à l'abri des ~s indiscrets** far from prying eyes
(b) expression; **son ~ triste** his/her sad expression; **sous le ~ amusé de qn** under the amused eye of sb; **jeter un ~ noir à qn** to give sb a black look
(c) **le ~ des autres** other people's opinion; **porter un ~ nouveau sur qch** to take a fresh look at sth
2 **au regard de** *phr* (formal) **au ~ de la loi** in the eyes of the law
3 **en regard** *phr* **avec une carte en ~** with a map on the opposite page

regardant, ~e /ʀəgaʀdã, ãt/ *adj* **ne pas être très ~** not to be very particular *or* fussy

regarder /ʀ(ə)gaʀde/ [1] **1** *vtr* (a) to look at ⟨*person, scene, landscape*⟩; **~ qch méchamment/fixement/longuement** to glare/stare/gaze at sth; **~ qn en face** to look sb in the face; **~ la réalité** *or* **les choses en face** to face facts; **~ qn de haut** to look down one's nose at sb
(b) to watch ⟨*film, TV*⟩; **regarde bien comment je fais** watch what I do carefully
(c) to look at ⟨*watch, map*⟩; to have a look at ⟨*tyres, oil*⟩; **~ qch dans** to look sth up in ⟨*dictionary*⟩; **~ si** to have a look and see if
(d) to look at ⟨*situation*⟩; **~ pourquoi/si/qui** to see why/if/who
(e) (colloq) to concern ⟨*person*⟩; **ça ne vous regarde pas** it's none of your business
(f) **elle ne regarde que ses intérêts** she thinks only of her own interests
2 **regarder à** *v+prep* to think about; **ne pas ~ à la dépense** to spare no expense; **à y ~ de plus près** on closer examination
3 *vi* to look; **~ en l'air/par terre** to look up/down; **regarde où tu mets les pieds** watch where you put your feet
4 **se regarder** *v refl* (+ *v être*) (a) to look at oneself
(b) to look at one another

régate /ʀegat/ *nf* regatta

régence /ʀeʒɑ̃s/ *nf* (a) regency
(b) **la Régence** the Regency

régénérer /ʀeʒeneʀe/ [14] **1** *vtr* (a) to regenerate
(b) to reactivate
2 **se régénérer** *v refl* (+ *v être*) (a) ⟨*cells*⟩ to regenerate
(b) (figurative) to regain one's strength

régent, ~e /ʀeʒã, ãt/ *nm,f* regent

régenter /ʀeʒɑ̃te/ [1] *vtr* (a) to rule
(b) to regulate

régie /ʀeʒi/ *nf* (a) state control; local government control
(b) **~ d'État** state-owned company
(c) stage management; production department
(d) central control room

regimber /ʀ(ə)ʒɛ̃be/ [1] *vi* (a) ⟨*person*⟩ to balk (**contre** at)
(b) ⟨*horse*⟩ to jib

régime /ʀeʒim/ *nm* (a) diet; **être au ~** to be on a diet
(b) (Pol) system (of government); government; regime
(c) (in administration) system, regime; **~ de faveur** preferential treatment
(d) (Law) **~ matrimonial** marriage settlement
(e) (of engine) (running) speed; **tourner à plein ~** ⟨*engine*⟩ to run at top speed; ⟨*factory*⟩ to work at full capacity
(f) (of bananas) bunch

régiment /ʀeʒimã/ *nm* regiment

région /ʀeʒjɔ̃/ *nf* region; area

r

régional, ~**e**, *mpl* **-aux** /Reʒjɔnal, o/ *adj*
regional

régionalisme /Reʒjɔnalism/ *nm*
regionalism

régir /ReʒiR/ [3] *vtr* to govern

régisseur /ReʒisœR/ *nm* (a) (of estate)
steward, manager
(b) stage manager

registre /R(ə)ʒistR/ *nm* (a) register; **les ~s
de la police** police records
(b) (of novel) style
(c) (of language, voice) register; **cet acteur a un
~ limité** this actor has a limited range

réglable /Reglabl/ *adj* (a) adjustable
(b) payable

réglage /Reglaʒ/ *nm* regulating; setting;
adjustment

réglé, ~**e** /Regle/ *adj* (a) ruled, lined
(b) ⟨*life*⟩ well-ordered
(c) **l'affaire est ~e** the matter is settled

règle /Regl/ **1** *nf* (a) ruler
(b) rule; **~s de sécurité** safety regulations;
respecter les ~s du jeu to play by the rules;
dans les ~s de l'art by the rule book; **en ~
générale** as a rule
2 règles *nf pl* period
3 en règle *phr* ⟨*request*⟩ formal; ⟨*papers,
accounts*⟩ in order; **subir un interrogatoire en
~** to be given a grilling; **pour passer la
frontière, il faut être en ~** to cross the
border, your papers must be in order

règlement /Regləmɑ̃/ *nm* (a) regulations,
rules
(b) payment
(c) settlement
■ **~ de comptes** settling of scores

réglementaire /Regləmɑ̃tɛR/ *adj*
⟨*uniform*⟩ regulation; ⟨*format*⟩ prescribed;
⟨*procedure*⟩ statutory

réglementation /Regləmɑ̃tasjɔ̃/ *nf*
(a) rules, regulations
(b) control

réglementer /Regləmɑ̃te/ [1] *vtr* to
regulate

régler /Regle/ [14] *vtr* (a) to settle ⟨*debt*⟩; to
pay ⟨*bill*⟩; to pay for ⟨*purchase, work*⟩; **avoir
des comptes à ~ avec qn** (figurative) to have a
score to settle with sb; **son compte à qn**
(colloq) to sort sb out
(b) to settle, to sort out ⟨*problem*⟩
(c) to settle ⟨*details, terms*⟩
(d) to adjust ⟨*height*⟩; to regulate ⟨*speed*⟩; to
tune ⟨*engine*⟩; to set ⟨*pressure*⟩
(e) **~ sa conduite sur celle de qn** to model
one's behaviour (GB) on sb's
(f) to rule (lines on) ⟨*paper*⟩

réglisse /Reglis/ *nf* liquorice (GB), licorice
(US)

régnant, ~**e** /Reɲɑ̃, ɑ̃t/ *adj* ⟨*dynasty*⟩
reigning; ⟨*ideology*⟩ prevailing

règne /Rɛɲ/ *nm* (a) reign; rule
(b) (figurative) reign
(c) (in biology) kingdom

régner /Reɲe/ [14] *vi* (a) ⟨*sovereign*⟩ to
reign, to rule

(b) ⟨*boss*⟩ to be in control; **~ en maître sur**
to reign supreme over
(c) ⟨*confusion, fear*⟩ to reign; ⟨*smell*⟩ to
prevail; **la confiance règne!** (ironic) there's
trust for you!; **faire ~** to give rise to
⟨*insecurity*⟩; to impose ⟨*order*⟩

regonfler /R(ə)gɔ̃fle/ [1] *vtr* (a) to reinflate
⟨*tyre*⟩; to blow [sth] up again ⟨*balloon*⟩
(b) (colloq) to increase ⟨*staff*⟩; to boost ⟨*sales,
profits*⟩

regorger /R(ə)gɔRʒe/ [13] *vi* **~ de** ⟨*shop*⟩ to
be packed with; ⟨*region*⟩ to have an
abundance of

régresser /Regrese/ [1] *vi* (a) ⟨*waters*⟩ to
recede; ⟨*unemployment*⟩ to go down
(b) ⟨*industry*⟩ to be in decline
(c) ⟨*epidemic*⟩ to die out

régressif, **-ive** /Regresif, iv/ *adj*
regressive

régression /Regresjɔ̃/ *nf* (a) decline
(b) regression

regret /RəgRɛ/ *nm* regret; **j'apprends avec
~ que** I'm sorry to hear that; **j'ai le ~ de
vous annoncer** I regret to inform you

regrettable /RəgRɛtabl/ *adj* regrettable

regretter /RəgRɛte/ [1] *vtr* (a) to be sorry
about, to regret ⟨*situation, action*⟩; **je regrette
de ne pas pouvoir t'aider** I'm sorry I can't
help you
(b) to regret ⟨*decision*⟩; **~ d'avoir fait** to
regret doing; **je ne regrette rien** I have no
regrets
(c) to miss ⟨*person, place*⟩; **notre regretté
collègue** (formal) our late colleague

regroupement /R(ə)gRupmɑ̃/ *nm*
(a) grouping; pooling; bringing together
(b) merger
(c) getting [sb/sth] back together; rounding
up

regrouper /R(ə)gRupe/ [1] **1** *vtr* (a) to
group [sth] together; to bring [sth] together;
to pool ⟨*interests*⟩; **~ deux chapitres en un
seul** to merge two chapters into one
(b) to reassemble ⟨*pupils*⟩; to round up
⟨*animals*⟩
2 se regrouper *v refl* (+ *v être*)
(a) ⟨*companies*⟩ to group together;
⟨*malcontents*⟩ to gather
(b) ⟨*runners*⟩ to bunch together again

régularisation /RegylaRizasjɔ̃/ *nf*
(a) (of situation) sorting out, regularization
(b) (of watercourse) regulation

régulariser /RegylaRize/ [1] *vtr* (a) to sort
out, to regularize ⟨*position, situation*⟩
(b) to regulate ⟨*flow*⟩; to stabilize ⟨*price,
market*⟩

régularité /RegylaRite/ *nf* (a) regularity
(b) (of rhythm, production, progress) steadiness;
(of features) regularity; (of writing) neatness;
(of surface) evenness; (of quantity) consistency
(c) legality

régulateur, **-trice** /RegylatœR, tRis/
1 *adj* regulating
2 *nm* regulator

régulation /ʀegylasjɔ̃/ *nf* regulation, control

régulier, -ière /ʀegylje, ɛʀ/ *adj* (a) (gen) regular; ⟨*flow, rise, effort*⟩ steady; ⟨*quality*⟩ consistent; ⟨*thickness*⟩ even; ⟨*writing*⟩ neat; ⟨*life*⟩ (well-)ordered; **vol** ∼ scheduled flight
(b) ⟨*person*⟩ honest; ⟨*papers, ballot*⟩ in order; ⟨*government*⟩ legitimate
(c) ⟨*verb*⟩ regular

régulièrement /ʀegyljɛʀmɑ̃/ *adv*
(a) regularly
(b) steadily
(c) evenly
(d) normally

régurgiter /ʀegyʀʒite/ [1] *vtr* to regurgitate

réhabiliter /ʀeabilite/ [1] **1** *vtr* (a) to rehabilitate
(b) to renovate
2 se réhabiliter *v refl* (+ *v être*) to redeem oneself

réhabituer /ʀeabitɥe/ [1] *vtr* to reaccustom (qn à qch sb to sth; qn à faire sb to doing)

rehausser /ʀəose/ [1] *vtr* (a) to raise
(b) to enhance ⟨*prestige*⟩
(c) to set off ⟨*pattern*⟩

réimplanter /ʀeɛ̃plɑ̃te/ [1] *vtr* to re-establish ⟨*factory, industry*⟩

réimprimer /ʀeɛ̃pʀime/ [1] *vtr* to reprint

rein /ʀɛ̃/ (Anat) **1** *nm* kidney; ∼ **artificiel** kidney machine
2 reins *nm pl* **les** ∼**s** the small of the back; **une serviette autour des** ∼**s** a towel around one's waist

réincarner: se réincarner /ʀeɛ̃kaʀne/ [1] *v refl* (+ *v être*) to be reincarnated

reine /ʀɛn/ *nf* (a) queen
(b) (figurative) **être la** ∼ **des imbéciles** (colloq) to be a prize idiot

reine-claude, *pl* **reines-claudes** /ʀɛnklod/ *nf* greengage

reinette /ʀɛnɛt/ *nf* rennet apple

réinscrire: se réinscrire /ʀeɛ̃skʀiʀ/ [67] *v refl* (+ *v être*) to re-enrol

réinsérer /ʀeɛ̃seʀe/ [14] *vtr* (a) to reintegrate
(b) to reinsert

réinstaller /ʀeɛ̃stale/ [1] **1** *vtr* to put [sth] back
2 se réinstaller *v refl* (+ *v être*) **se** ∼ **dans un fauteuil** to settle (oneself) back into an armchair

réintégrer /ʀeɛ̃tegʀe/ [14] *vtr* (a) to return to ⟨*place, group, system*⟩
(b) ∼ **qn** (**dans ses fonctions**) to reinstate sb

réitérer /ʀeiteʀe/ [14] *vtr* to repeat

rejaillir /ʀ(ə)ʒajiʀ/ [3] *vi* (a) ⟨*liquid*⟩ to splash back; to spurt back
(b) ∼ **sur qn** ⟨*success*⟩ to reflect on sb; ⟨*scandal*⟩ to affect sb adversely

rejaillissement /ʀ(ə)ʒajismɑ̃/ *nm* (of scandal) adverse effect; (of success) reflection

rejet /ʀ(ə)ʒɛ/ *nm* (a) (gen) rejection; (of complaint) dismissal; (of motion) defeat; (of request) denial
(b) (of waste) discharge; disposal; ∼**s** waste

rejeter /ʀaʒte, ʀʒəte/ [20] **1** *vtr* (a) to reject ⟨*advice, candidacy, outsider*⟩; to turn down ⟨*offer*⟩; to deny ⟨*request*⟩; to set aside ⟨*decision*⟩
(b) ∼ **qch sur qn** to shift sth onto sb ⟨*blame*⟩
(c) ⟨*factory*⟩ to discharge ⟨*waste*⟩; to eject ⟨*smoke*⟩
(d) ⟨*person, company*⟩ to dispose of ⟨*waste*⟩; ⟨*sea*⟩ to wash up ⟨*body, debris*⟩
(e) ∼ **[qch] en arrière** to throw back ⟨*head, hair*⟩
2 se rejeter *v refl* (+ *v être*) **se** ∼ **la faute** to blame each other

rejeton /ʀəʒ(ə)tɔ̃, ʀʒətɔ̃/ *nm* (a) offshoot
(b) (colloq) offspring

rejoindre /ʀ(ə)ʒwɛ̃dʀ/ [56] **1** *vtr* (a) to meet up with
(b) to catch up with
(c) to join; to rejoin
(d) to get to; to get back to, to return to
(e) ∼ **qn sur qch** to concur with sb on sth
2 se rejoindre *v refl* (+ *v être*) ⟨*people*⟩ to meet up; ⟨*roads*⟩ to meet

rejouer /ʀ(ə)ʒwe/ [1] *vtr* (gen) to play [sth] again; to replay ⟨*match, point*⟩

réjoui, ∼e /ʀeʒwi/ *adj* cheerful

réjouir /ʀeʒwiʀ/ [3] **1** *vtr* (a) to delight ⟨*person*⟩; to gladden ⟨*heart*⟩
(b) to amuse
2 se réjouir *v refl* (+ *v être*) to rejoice; **se** ∼ **de qch** to be delighted at ⟨*news*⟩; to be delighted with ⟨*success*⟩

réjouissance /ʀeʒwisɑ̃s/ **1** *nf* rejoicing
2 réjouissances *nf pl* celebrations; **quel est le programme des** ∼**s?** (colloq) what delights are in store for us?

réjouissant, ∼e /ʀeʒwisɑ̃, ɑ̃t/ *adj*
(a) heartening, delightful
(b) amusing

relâche /ʀ(ə)lɑʃ/ *nf* (a) (of theatre, cinema) closure; **faire** ∼ to be closed
(b) break, rest; **sans** ∼ relentlessly

relâchement /ʀ(ə)lɑʃmɑ̃/ *nm*
(a) (of discipline, effort) slackening; (of morals) loosening
(b) (of muscle) slackening

relâcher /ʀ(ə)lɑʃe/ [1] **1** *vtr* (a) to loosen ⟨*hold*⟩
(b) to release ⟨*captive*⟩
(c) to relax ⟨*discipline*⟩; ∼ **son attention** to let one's attention wander; ∼ **ses efforts** to let up
2 se relâcher *v refl* (+ *v être*) (a) ⟨*hold, tie*⟩ to loosen; ⟨*muscle*⟩ to relax
(b) ⟨*effort*⟩ to slacken; ⟨*zeal*⟩ to flag; ⟨*pupil*⟩ to grow slack

r

relais /ʀ(ə)lɛ/ nm inv **(a)** intermediary;
prendre le ~ (de qn/qch) to take over (from
sb/sth)
(b) (Sport) relay
(c) restaurant; hotel
(d) (Tech) relay; ~ hertzien radio relay
station

relance /ʀ(ə)lɑ̃s/ nf (of industry, idea) revival;
(of economy) reflation; (in inflation) rise; **mesures
de** ~ reflationary measures

relancer /ʀ(ə)lɑ̃se/ [12] vtr **(a)** to throw
[sth] again ⟨ball⟩; to throw [sth] back (again)
⟨ball⟩
(b) to restart ⟨engine⟩; to relaunch
⟨company⟩; to revive ⟨idea⟩; to reopen
⟨debate⟩; to boost ⟨investment⟩; to reflate
⟨economy⟩
(c) ⟨creditor⟩ to chase [sb] up; ⟨person⟩ to
pester

relater /ʀ(ə)late/ [1] vtr (formal) to recount

relatif, -ive¹ /ʀ(ə)latif, iv/ **1** adj relative;
le risque est très ~ there is relatively little
risk
2 nm relative (pronoun)

relation /ʀ(ə)lasjɔ̃/ **1** nf **(a)** connection
(b) acquaintance; ~s d'affaires business
acquaintances
(c) relationship; avoir de bonnes ~s avec qn
to have a good relationship with sb; entrer
en ~ avec qn to get in touch with sb
2 relations nf pl relations
■ ~s extérieures foreign affairs; ~s publiques
public relations

relative² /ʀ(ə)lativ/ **1** adj f ▶ RELATIF 1
2 nf relative (clause)

relativement /ʀ(ə)lativmɑ̃/ **1** adv
relatively
2 relativement à phr in relation to

relativiser /ʀ(ə)lativize/ [1] vtr to put [sth]
into perspective

relativité /ʀ(ə)lativite/ nf relativity

relax /ʀəlaks/ adj inv (colloq) ⟨person⟩ laid-
back (colloq); ⟨clothes⟩ casual; ⟨party⟩
informal

relaxant, ~e /ʀəlaksɑ̃, ɑ̃t/ adj relaxing

relaxation /ʀəlaksasjɔ̃/ nf relaxation

relaxer /ʀəlakse/ [1] **1** vtr **(a)** to discharge
⟨defendant⟩
(b) to relax ⟨muscle, person⟩
2 se relaxer v refl (+ v être) to relax

relayer /ʀ(ə)leje/ [21] **1** vtr **(a)** to take
over from, to relieve
(b) to relay ⟨broadcast⟩
2 se relayer v refl (+ v être) **(a)** to take
turns
(b) to take over from each other

reléguer /ʀ(ə)lege/ [14] vtr (gen) to relegate;
to consign ⟨object⟩; ~ qn/qch au second plan
to push sb/sth into the background

relent /ʀ(ə)lɑ̃/ nm **(a)** lingering odour (GB)
(b) (figurative) whiff

relevé, ~e /ʀəlve, ʀləve/ **1** adj spicy
2 nm **(a)** noting down; faire le ~ de to list
⟨mistakes⟩; to make a note of ⟨expenses⟩; to
read ⟨meter⟩

(b) ~ bancaire bank statement

relève /ʀ(ə)lɛv/ nf **(a)** la ~ s'effectue à 20
heures the changeover takes place at 8 pm;
la ~ de la garde the changing of the guard;
prendre la ~ to take over
(b) relief; relief team

relever /ʀəlve, ʀləve/ [16] **1** vtr **(a)** to pick
up ⟨person, stool⟩; to put [sth] back up
(again)
(b) to raise ⟨lever⟩
(c) ~ la tête to raise one's head; to look up;
(figurative) to refuse to accept defeat
(d) to turn up ⟨collar⟩; to lift ⟨skirt⟩; to wind
up ⟨car window⟩; to raise ⟨sail, blind⟩; ~ ses
cheveux to put one's hair up
(e) to note, to notice; to point out; ~ la
moindre inexactitude to seize on the slightest
inaccuracy
(f) to take down ⟨date, name⟩; to take
⟨prints⟩; ~ le compteur to read the meter
(g) to take in ⟨exam papers⟩
(h) to react to ⟨remark⟩; to lift ⟨skirt⟩; ~ le défi/un pari to
take up the challenge/a bet
(i) to rebuild ⟨wall⟩; to put [sth] back on its
feet ⟨country, economy⟩
(j) to raise ⟨standard, price⟩; to increase
⟨productivity⟩
(k) to relieve ⟨team⟩; ~ la garde to change
the guard
(l) to spice up ⟨dish, story⟩
(m) ~ qn de ses fonctions to relieve sb of
their duties
2 relever de v+prep **(a)** ~ de
⟨department⟩ to come under ⟨Ministry⟩; cela
ne relève pas de mes fonctions that's not
part of my duties
(b) cela relève de la gageure this comes close
to being impossible
3 se relever v refl (+ v être) **(a)** to pick
oneself up; to get up again
(b) se ~ automatiquement to be raised
automatically
(c) ⟨blind⟩ to be raised
(d) se ~ de to recover from

relief /ʀəljɛf/ nm **(a)** relief; (on medal, coin)
raised pattern; en ~ ⟨globe of the world⟩ in
relief; ⟨letters⟩ raised; cinéma en ~ three-
dimensional cinema; mettre qch en ~ to
accentuate sth; un ~ accidenté a hilly
landscape
(b) depth; l'effet de ~ the effect of depth

relier /ʀəlje/ [2] vtr **(a)** to link; to link up;
to link together; to join up; to connect
(b) to bind ⟨book⟩; relié cuir leather-bound

religieuse¹ /ʀəliʒjøz/ **1** adj f ▶
RELIGIEUX 1
2 nf **(a)** nun
(b) (Culin) religieuse

religieusement /ʀəliʒjøzmɑ̃/ adv
(a) religiously
(b) ⟨listen⟩ with rapt attention
(c) ⟨get married⟩ in church

religieux, -ieuse² /ʀəliʒjø, øz/ **1** adj
(a) religious; ⟨school, wedding⟩ church;
⟨music⟩ sacred
(b) (figurative) ⟨silence⟩ reverent

2 *nm* monk

religion /ʀ(ə)liʒjɔ̃/ *nf* **(a)** religion
(b) faith
(c) entrer en ~ to enter the Church

reliquaire /ʀ(ə)likɛʀ/ *nm* reliquary

reliquat /ʀ(ə)lika/ *nm* (of sum) remainder;
(of account) balance

relique /ʀ(ə)lik/ *nf* relic

relire /ʀ(ə)liʀ/ [66] *vtr* to reread; to read
[sth] over

reliure /ʀəljyʀ/ *nf* **(a)** binding
(b) bookbinding

reloger /ʀ(ə)lɔʒe/ [13] *vtr* to rehouse

reluire /ʀ(ə)lɥiʀ/ [69] *vi* to shine; to glisten
IDIOMS il sait passer la brosse à ~ he's a
real flatterer

reluisant, ~**e** /ʀ(ə)lɥizɑ̃, ɑ̃t/ *adj* shiny;
glistening; **peu** ~ (figurative) far from brilliant

remâcher /ʀ(ə)mɑʃe/ [1] *vtr* **(a)** to chew
[sth] again
(b) (colloq) to ruminate over ⟨problem, past⟩

remaniement /ʀ(ə)manimɑ̃/ *nm*
modification; revision; reorganization

remanier /ʀ(ə)manje/ [2] *vtr* to modify; to
redraft; to reorganize; to reshuffle

remarier: se remarier /ʀ(ə)maʀje/ [2]
v refl (+ *v être*) to remarry

remarquable /ʀ(ə)maʀkabl/ *adj*
(a) remarkable
(b) striking
(c) noteworthy

remarquablement /ʀ(ə)maʀkabləmɑ̃/
adv remarkably

remarque /ʀ(ə)maʀk/ *nf* **(a)** remark; **faire
des** ~**s** to comment
(b) (written) comment
(c) critical remark, criticism

remarqué, ~**e** /ʀ(ə)maʀke/ *adj*
⟨initiative⟩ noteworthy; ⟨increase⟩ noticeable

remarquer /ʀ(ə)maʀke/ [1] **1** *vtr* **(a)** to
point out
(b) to observe
(c) to notice; **remarque, ce n'est pas très
important** mind you, it's not very important;
se faire ~ to draw attention to oneself
(d) ~ **un visage dans la foule** to spot a face
in the crowd
2 se remarquer *v refl* (+ *v être*) **(a)** to
attract attention
(b) to show

remballer /ʀɑ̃bale/ [1] *vtr* to pack [sth] up
again

rembarrer /ʀɑ̃baʀe/ [1] *vtr* (colloq) to send
[sb] packing (colloq)

remblai /ʀɑ̃blɛ/ *nm* **(a)** embankment; **route
en** ~ raised road
(b) filling in; banking up
(c) (terre de) ~ (for railway, road) ballast; (for
ditch) fill; (for excavation) backfill

rembobiner /ʀɑ̃bɔbine/ [1] *vtr* to rewind

rembourrer /ʀɑ̃buʀe/ [1] *vtr* to stuff
⟨chair⟩; to pad ⟨shoulders⟩

remboursable /ʀɑ̃buʀsabl/ *adj* ⟨loan,
debt⟩ repayable; ⟨ticket, medicine, treatment⟩
refundable

remboursement /ʀɑ̃buʀsəmɑ̃/ *nm*
(a) repayment
(b) refund
(c) reimbursement

rembourser /ʀɑ̃buʀse/ [1] *vtr* **(a)** to pay
off, to repay ⟨loan, debt⟩
(b) to give a refund to ⟨customer⟩; to refund
the price of ⟨item⟩
(c) to reimburse ⟨expenses, employee⟩; ~ **un
ami** to pay a friend back

rembrunir: se rembrunir /ʀɑ̃bʀyniʀ/ [3]
v refl (+ *v être*) ⟨face⟩ to darken, to cloud
over

remède /ʀ(ə)mɛd/ *nm* medicine; remedy,
cure
■ ~ **de bonne femme** folk remedy; ~ **de
cheval** strong medicine
IDIOMS aux grands maux les grands ~**s**
desperate times call for desperate measures

remédier /ʀ(ə)medje/ [2] *v+prep* ~ **à** to
remedy

remembrement /ʀ(ə)mɑ̃bʀəmɑ̃/ *nm*
regrouping of lands

remémorer: se remémorer
/ʀ(ə)memɔʀe/ [1] *v refl* (+ *v être*) to recall, to
recollect

remerciement /ʀ(ə)mɛʀsimɑ̃/ *nm*
thanks; **je n'ai pas eu un seul** ~ I didn't get
a word of thanks; **lettre de** ~ thank-you
letter

remercier /ʀ(ə)mɛʀsje/ [2] *vtr* **(a)** to
thank; **je vous remercie** thank you
(b) (ironic) to dismiss

remettre /ʀ(ə)mɛtʀ/ [60] **1** *vtr* **(a)** ~ **qch
dans/sur** to put sth back in/on; ~ **qch en
mémoire à qn** to remind sb of sth
(b) ~ **à qn** to hand [sth] over to sb ⟨keys⟩; to
hand [sth] in to sb ⟨letter⟩; to present [sth]
to sb ⟨reward⟩
(c) ~ **qch droit** *or* **d'aplomb** to put sth
straight again
(d) to postpone ⟨visit⟩
(e) to put [sth] on again ⟨heating⟩; to play
[sth] again ⟨record⟩
(f) ~ **une vis** to put a new screw in
(g) to add some more ⟨salt⟩; to add another
⟨nail⟩
(h) to put [sth] back on ⟨coat⟩
(i) (Med) to put [sth] back in place ⟨joint⟩
(j) ⟨medicine⟩ to make [sb] feel better
(k) ~ **qn/le visage de qn** to remember sb/
sb's face
(l) (colloq) ~ **ça** to start again; **on s'est bien
amusé, quand est-ce qu'on remet ça?** that
was fun, when are we going to do it again?
2 se remettre *v refl* (+ *v être*) **(a) se** ~ **à
un endroit** to go *or* get back to a place
(b) se ~ **au travail** to go back to work; **se** ~
au dessin to start drawing again
(c) se ~ **en jean** to wear jeans again
(d) se ~ **de** to recover from ⟨illness⟩; to get
over ⟨shock⟩ ····⟶

r

(e) s'en ~ à qn to leave it to sb; s'en ~ à la décision de qn to accept sb's decision
(f) se ~ avec qn to get back together with sb

réminiscence /ʀeminisɑ̃s/ *nf*
(a) reminiscence
(b) recollection

remise /ʀ(ə)miz/ *nf* **(a)** attendre la ~ des clés to wait for the keys to be handed over; ~ des prix prizegiving; ~ des médailles medals ceremony
(b) discount
(c) une ~ de peine a remission
(d) ~ de fonds remittance of funds
(e) shed

remiser /ʀ(ə)mize/ [1] *vtr* to put [sth] away (dans in)

rémission /ʀemisjɔ̃/ *nf* remission; sans ~ ⟨punish⟩ mercilessly; ⟨rain⟩ without stopping

remmener /ʀɑ̃mne/ [16] *vtr* to take [sb] back

remodeler /ʀəmɔdle/ [17] *vtr* to restructure; to reshape; to replan

remontant /ʀ(ə)mɔ̃tɑ̃/ *nm* pick-me-up (colloq), tonic

remontée /ʀ(ə)mɔ̃te/ *nf* **(a)** climb up; la ~ de la Saône en péniche going up the Saône by barge
(b) (in price) rise; (in violence) increase
■ ~ mécanique (Sport) ski lift

remonte-pente, *pl* ~s /ʀ(ə)mɔ̃tpɑ̃t/ *nm* ski-tow

remonter /ʀəmɔ̃te/ [1] **1** *vtr* (+ *v avoir*)
(a) ~ qch to take sth back up/upstairs; to bring sth back up/upstairs
(b) to put [sth] back up; ~ un seau d'un puits to pull a bucket up from a well
(c) to raise ⟨shelf, blind⟩; to wind [sth] back up ⟨car window⟩; to roll up ⟨sleeves⟩; to turn up ⟨collar⟩; to pull up ⟨socks⟩
(d) to go/to come back up; to climb back up; to drive back up
(e) to sail up ⟨river⟩; to go up ⟨road⟩; ~ une filière *or* piste to follow a trail
(f) ~ qn *or* le moral de qn to cheer sb up
(g) to put [sth] back together again; to put [sth] back ⟨wheel⟩
(h) to wind [sth] up; être remonté à bloc (colloq) to be full of energy
(i) to revive ⟨play, show⟩
2 *vi* (+ *v être*) **(a)** ⟨person⟩ to go/to come back up; ⟨tide⟩ to come in again; ⟨price, temperature⟩ to rise again; ~ sur to step back onto ⟨pavement⟩; to climb back onto ⟨wall⟩; ~ à la surface ⟨diver⟩ to surface; ⟨oil, object⟩ to rise to the surface; ~ dans les sondages to move up in the opinion polls
(b) ~ dans le temps to go back in time; ~ à ⟨historian⟩ to go back to; ⟨event⟩ to date back to; faire ~ to trace (back) ⟨origins⟩
(c) ⟨skirt⟩ to ride up
(d) les odeurs d'égout remontent dans la maison the smell from the drains reaches our house

3 se remonter *v refl* (+ *v être*) se ~ le moral to cheer oneself up; to cheer each other up

remontoir /ʀ(ə)mɔ̃twaʀ/ *nm* winder

remontrance /ʀəmɔ̃tʀɑ̃s/ *nf* reprimand

remontrer /ʀəmɔ̃tʀe/ [1] *vi* en ~ à qn to teach sb a thing or two

remords /ʀəmɔʀ/ *nm inv* remorse

remorquage /ʀəmɔʀkaʒ/ *nm* towing

remorque /ʀəmɔʀk/ *nf* **(a)** towrope; prendre en ~ to tow ⟨car⟩
(b) trailer

remorquer /ʀəmɔʀke/ [1] *vtr* to tow ⟨vehicle⟩

remorqueur /ʀəmɔʀkœʀ/ *nm* tug

remous /ʀ(ə)mu/ *nm inv* **(a)** eddy
(b) backwash; wash
(c) (of ideas) turmoil; (in crowd) stir

rempailler /ʀɑ̃paje/ [1] *vtr* to reseat ⟨chair⟩

rempart /ʀɑ̃paʀ/ *nm* **(a)** rampart; battlements; les ~s de la ville the city walls
(b) defence (GB)

remplaçable /ʀɑ̃plasabl/ *adj* replaceable

remplaçant, ~e /ʀɑ̃plasɑ̃, ɑ̃t/ *nm,f*
(a) (gen) substitute; (at school) supply (GB) *or* substitute (US) teacher; (actor) stand-in
(b) successor

remplacement /ʀɑ̃plasmɑ̃/ *nm* replacement; faire des ~s ⟨teacher⟩ to do supply (GB) *or* substitute (US) teaching; ⟨temp⟩ to do temporary work; produit de ~ substitute

remplacer /ʀɑ̃plase/ [12] *vtr* **(a)** to stand in for, to cover for ⟨colleague⟩
(b) to replace; on peut ~ le vinaigre par du jus de citron you can use lemon juice instead of vinegar

remplir /ʀɑ̃pliʀ/ [3] *vtr* **(a)** to fill (up) ⟨container⟩; to fill in ⟨form⟩; ~ qch à moitié to half fill sth; ~ qn de joie to fill sb with joy; une vie bien remplie a full life
(b) to carry out ⟨role, mission⟩; to fulfil (GB) ⟨duty, role⟩

remplissage /ʀɑ̃plisaʒ/ *nm* **(a)** filling
(b) (derogatory) faire du ~ to pad out one's work

remplumer: se remplumer /ʀɑ̃plyme/ [1] *v refl* (colloq) (financially) to get back on one's feet; (physically) to put some weight back on

rempocher /ʀɑ̃pɔʃe/ [1] *vtr* to put [sth] back in one's pocket

remporter /ʀɑ̃pɔʀte/ [1] *vtr* to win ⟨seat, title, victory⟩; ~ un vif succès to be a great success

rempoter /ʀɑ̃pɔte/ [1] *vtr* to repot

remuant, ~e /ʀəmɥɑ̃, ɑ̃t/ *adj* **(a)** rowdy
(b) boisterous; energetic

remue-ménage /ʀ(ə)mymenaʒ/ *nm inv*
(a) commotion
(b) bustle

remuer /ʀ(ə)mɥe/ [1] **1** *vtr* **(a)** to move ⟨*hand, head*⟩; to wiggle ⟨*toe, hips*⟩; to wag ⟨*tail*⟩
(b) to shake ⟨*object*⟩
(c) to move ⟨*object*⟩
(d) to stir ⟨*soup*⟩; to toss ⟨*salad*⟩
(e) to turn over ⟨*earth*⟩; to poke ⟨*ashes*⟩
(f) (figurative) to rake up ⟨*past*⟩; to stir up ⟨*memories*⟩
(g) to upset ⟨*person*⟩
2 *vi* ⟨*person*⟩ to move; ⟨*leaves*⟩ to flutter; ⟨*boat*⟩ to bob up and down
3 se remuer *v refl* (+ *v être*) (colloq) **(a)** to get a move on (colloq)
(b) se ~ pour obtenir to make an effort to get

rémunérateur, -trice /ʀemyneʀatœʀ, tʀis/ *adj* lucrative

rémunération /ʀemyneʀasjɔ̃/ *nf* pay; payment

rémunérer /ʀemyneʀe/ [14] *vtr* to pay ⟨*person*⟩; to pay for ⟨*work*⟩

renâcler /ʀ(ə)nɑkle/ [1] *vi* **(a)** ⟨*person*⟩ to show reluctance
(b) ⟨*animal*⟩ to snort

renaissance /ʀ(ə)nɛsɑ̃s/ *nf* rebirth; revival

Renaissance /ʀ(ə)nɛsɑ̃s/ *nf* Renaissance

renaître /ʀ(ə)nɛtʀ/ [74] *vi* (+ *v être*) **(a)** to come back to life
(b) ⟨*hope, desire*⟩ to return; faire ~ l'espoir to bring new hope

rénal, ~e, *mpl* **-aux** /ʀenal, o/ *adj* ⟨*artery*⟩ renal; ⟨*infection*⟩ kidney

renard /ʀ(ə)naʀ/ *nm* **(a)** fox
(b) wily old fox

renarde /ʀ(ə)naʀd/ *nf* vixen

renardeau, *pl* **~x** /ʀ(ə)naʀdo/ *nm* fox cub

renchérir /ʀɑ̃ʃeʀiʀ/ [3] *vi* **(a)** to add; ~ sur ce que dit qn to add something to what sb says
(b) to go one step further
(c) to raise the bidding

rencontre /ʀɑ̃kɔ̃tʀ/ *nf* **(a)** meeting; encounter; faire la ~ de qn to meet sb
(b) (Sport) match (GB), game (US); ~ d'athlétisme athletics meeting (GB), track meet (US)
■ ~ au sommet summit meeting

rencontrer /ʀɑ̃kɔ̃tʀe/ [1] **1** *vtr* **(a)** to meet ⟨*person*⟩; ~ qn sur son chemin to come across sb
(b) to encounter, to meet with ⟨*problem, opposition*⟩
(c) to come across ⟨*object, word*⟩
(d) to meet ⟨*player, team*⟩
2 se rencontrer *v refl* (+ *v être*) **(a)** to meet
(b) ⟨*quality, object, person*⟩ to be found

rendant /ʀɑ̃dɑ̃/ ▶ RENDRE

rendement /ʀɑ̃dmɑ̃/ *nm* **(a)** (from land, investment) yield; (of machine, worker) output
(b) (of factory) productivity; (of machine, worker) efficiency

(c) (of sportsman, pupil) performance

rendez-vous /ʀɑ̃devu/ *nm inv* **(a)** appointment; date; sur ~ by appointment; j'ai ~ avec un ami I'm meeting a friend; le soleil n'était pas au ~ the sun didn't shine
(b) meeting
(c) gathering; meeting place

rendormir: se rendormir /ʀɑ̃dɔʀmiʀ/ [30] *v refl* (+ *v être*) to go back to sleep

rendre /ʀɑ̃dʀ/ [6] **1** *vtr* **(a)** (gen) to give back, to return; to repay, to pay back ⟨*loan*⟩; to return ⟨*greeting, invitation, goods*⟩; ~ la pareille à qn to pay sb back; il la déteste mais elle le lui rend bien he hates her and she feels the same about him
(b) ~ la santé/vue à qn to restore sb's health/sight
(c) ~ qch possible to make sth possible; ~ qn fou to drive sb mad
(d) to hand in ⟨*homework*⟩
(e) ⟨*land*⟩ to yield ⟨*crop, quantity*⟩
(f) to convey ⟨*atmosphere, nuance*⟩; ça ne rendra rien en couleurs it won't come out in colour (GB)
(g) (colloq) to bring up ⟨*food, bile*⟩
(h) to pronounce ⟨*sentence*⟩; to return ⟨*verdict*⟩
(i) les tomates rendent de l'eau (à la cuisson) tomatoes give out water during cooking
2 *vi* **(a)** ⟨*land*⟩ to be productive; ⟨*plant*⟩ to produce a good crop
(b) (colloq) to throw up (colloq)
3 se rendre *v refl* (+ *v être*) **(a)** se ~ à Rome/en ville to go to Rome/to town
(b) se ~ indispensable/malade to make oneself indispensable/ill
(c) to give oneself up; to surrender
(d) se ~ à qch to bow to ⟨*argument*⟩
IDIOMS ~ l'âme *or* l'esprit to pass away

rendu, -e ▶ /ʀɑ̃dy/ RENDRE

rêne /ʀɛn/ *nf* rein

renfermé, ~e /ʀɑ̃fɛʀme/ **1** *pp* ▶ RENFERMER
2 *pp adj* ⟨*person*⟩ withdrawn; ⟨*feeling*⟩ hidden
3 *nm* odeur de ~ musty smell

renfermer /ʀɑ̃fɛʀme/ [1] **1** *vtr* to contain
2 se renfermer *v refl* (+ *v être*) to become withdrawn

renflé, ~e /ʀɑ̃fle/ *adj* ⟨*vase*⟩ rounded; ⟨*dome*⟩ bulbous; ⟨*stomach*⟩ bulging

renflement /ʀɑ̃fləmɑ̃/ *nm* bulge

renflouer /ʀɑ̃flue/ [1] *vtr* **(a)** to raise ⟨*ship*⟩
(b) to bail out ⟨*person, company*⟩

renfoncement /ʀɑ̃fɔ̃smɑ̃/ *nm* recess; ~ de porte doorway

renforcer /ʀɑ̃fɔʀse/ [12] **1** *vtr* to reinforce; to strengthen
2 se renforcer *v refl* (+ *v être*) ⟨*power*⟩ to increase; ⟨*control*⟩ to become tighter; ⟨*team, numbers*⟩ to grow; ⟨*sector*⟩ to grow stronger

renfort /ʀɑ̃fɔʀ/ *nm* **(a)** (Mil) reinforcement ⋯⟶

(b) support; **annoncé à grand ~ de publicité** well-publicized

(c) (Sport) substitute

renfrogné, **~e** /Rɑ̃fRɔɲe/ *adj* sullen

renfrogner: **se renfrogner** /Rɑ̃fRɔɲe/ [1] *v refl* (+ *v être*) to become sullen

rengaine /Rɑ̃gɛn/ *nf* **c'est toujours la même ~** (figurative) it's the same old thing every time

rengainer /Rɑ̃gene/ [1] *vtr* to sheathe ⟨*sword*⟩; to put [sth] back in its holster ⟨*pistol*⟩

rengorger: **se rengorger** /Rɑ̃gɔRʒe/ [13] *v refl* (+ *v être*) ⟨*bird*⟩ to puff out its breast; ⟨*person*⟩ to swell with conceit

reniement /Rə(ə)nimɑ̃/ *nm* disavowal

renier /Rənje/ [2] **1** *vtr* to renounce ⟨*religion, opinion*⟩; to disown ⟨*child, work, friend*⟩

2 se renier *v refl* (+ *v être*) to go back on what one has said *or* promised

reniflement /R(ə)nifləmɑ̃/ *nm* (a) sniffing

(b) sniff

renifler /R(ə)nifle/ [1] *vtr, vi* to sniff

renne /Rɛn/ *nm* reindeer

renom /Rənɔ̃/ *nm* (a) fame

(b) reputation

renommé, **~e¹** /Rənɔme/ *adj* famous

renommée² /Rənɔme/ *nf* (a) reputation

(b) fame

renoncement /R(ə)nɔ̃smɑ̃/ *nm* renunciation

renoncer /R(ə)nɔ̃se/ [12] *v+prep* to give up; **~ à** to give up; to abandon; to renounce; **~ à faire** to abandon the idea of doing

renonciation /R(ə)nɔ̃sjasjɔ̃/ *nf* giving up

renouer /Rənwe/ [1] **1** *vtr* (a) to retie ⟨*laces*⟩

(b) to pick up the thread of ⟨*conversation*⟩

2 ~ avec *v+prep* to get back in touch with ⟨*person*⟩; to revive ⟨*tradition*⟩; to go back to ⟨*past*⟩

renouveau, *pl* **~x** /Rənuvo/ *nm* revival

renouveler /Rənuvle/ [19] **1** *vtr* (a) (gen) to renew; to repeat ⟨*suggestion, experience*⟩; to replace ⟨*equipment, team*⟩; to change ⟨*water*⟩

(b) to revitalize ⟨*genre, style*⟩

2 se renouveler *v refl* (+ *v être*) (a) **une pièce où l'air ne se renouvelle pas** a room which isn't aired

(b) ⟨*artist*⟩ to try out new ideas

(c) ⟨*experience*⟩ to be repeated

renouvellement /Rənuvɛlmɑ̃/ *nm*

(a) renewal

(b) replacement

(c) revitalization

rénovateur, **-trice** /Renɔvatœr, tRis/ *nm,f* reformer

rénovation /Renɔvasjɔ̃/ *nf* renovation

rénover /Renɔve/ [1] *vtr* (a) to renovate ⟨*area, house*⟩; to restore ⟨*furniture*⟩

(b) to reform ⟨*institution, policy*⟩; to revamp ⟨*project*⟩

renseignement /Rɑ̃sɛɲmɑ̃/ **1** *nm*

(a) information; **est-ce que je peux vous demander un ~?** can I ask you something?; **~s pris** upon investigation; **'pour tous ~s, s'adresser à...'** 'all enquiries to...'

(b) (Mil) intelligence

2 renseignements *nm pl* (a) information

(b) directory enquiries (GB) *or* assistance (US)

renseigner /Rɑ̃sene/ [1] **1** *vtr* **~ qn** to give information to sb

2 se renseigner *v refl* (+ *v être*) to find out, to enquire; to make enquiries

rentabilisation /Rɑ̃tabilizasjɔ̃/ *nf* **la ~ de l'entreprise est notre premier objectif** our primary aim is to make the company profitable

rentabiliser /Rɑ̃tabilize/ [1] *vtr* to secure a return on ⟨*investment*⟩; to make a profit on ⟨*product*⟩; to make [sth] profitable ⟨*business*⟩

rentabilité /Rɑ̃tabilite/ *nf* (a) profitability

(b) return

rentable /Rɑ̃tabl/ *adj* profitable

rente /Rɑ̃t/ *nf* (a) private income

(b) annuity; **~ viagère** life annuity

(c) government stock

rentrée /Rɑ̃tRe/ *nf* (a) (general) return to work (*after the slack period of the summer break in France*); **~ (des classes** *or* **scolaire)** start of the (new) school year; **mon livre sera publié à la ~** my book will be published in the autumn (GB) *or* fall (US)

(b) return (to work)

(c) comeback; **~ politique** political comeback

(d) receipts; **~ (d'argent)** income; takings

■ **~ parlementaire** reassembly of Parliament

rentrer /Rɑ̃tRe/ [1] **1** *vtr* (a) to bring [sth] in; to take [sth] in

(b) to raise ⟨*landing gear*⟩; to draw in ⟨*claws*⟩; **rentrez le ventre!** hold your stomach in!

(c) to tuck ⟨*shirt*⟩ (**dans** into)

2 *vi* (+ *v être*) (a) to go in; to get in; to fit; **~ dans un arbre** (colloq) to hit a tree

(b) **~ dans** to go back into; to come back into

(c) **~ (chez soi)** to get (*or* go *or* come) back (home); to return (home)

(d) **~ dans ses frais** to recoup one's money

(e) ⟨*money*⟩ to come in

(f) **faire ~ qch dans la tête de qn** to get sth into sb's head

IDIOMS **il m'est rentré dedans** (slang) he bumped *or* ran into me; he crashed into me

renversant, **~e** /Rɑ̃vɛRsɑ̃, ɑ̃t/ *adj* astounding, astonishing

renverse /Rɑ̃vɛRs/ *nf* **tomber à la ~** to fall flat on one's back

renversement /Rɑ̃vɛRsəmɑ̃/ *nm*

(a) reversal

(b) overthrow; removal from office

renverser /Rɑ̃vɛRse/ [1] **1** *vtr* (a) to knock over; to knock down

(b) to spill

(c) to turn [sth] upside down

(d) to reverse
(e) to overthrow; to vote [sb/sth] out of office
2 **se renverser** *v refl* (+ *v être*) ⟨boat⟩ to capsize; ⟨bottle⟩ to fall over; ⟨liquid⟩ to spill

renvoi /ʀɑ̃vwa/ *nm* **(a)** expulsion; dismissal
(b) return; ~ **d'un colis** return of a parcel
(c) postponement
(d) cross-reference
(e) belch, burp (colloq)

renvoyer /ʀɑ̃vwaje/ [24] *vtr* **(a)** to throw [sth] back ⟨ball⟩; to reflect ⟨light, heat⟩; to echo ⟨sound⟩
(b) to return ⟨mail⟩
(c) to send [sb] back; ~ **qn chez lui** to send sb home
(d) to expel; to dismiss
(e) to postpone ⟨debate⟩; to adjourn ⟨case⟩
(f) ~ **à** to refer to

réorganisation /ʀeɔʀganizasjɔ̃/ *nf* reorganization

réorienter /ʀeɔʀjɑ̃te/ [1] *vtr* to reorientate ⟨pupil⟩, ⟨student⟩ (vers toward(s)); to reshape ⟨policy⟩

réouverture /ʀeuvɛʀtyʀ/ *nf* reopening

repaire /ʀ(ə)pɛʀ/ *nm* den; hideout

répandre /ʀepɑ̃dʀ/ [6] **1** *vtr* **(a)** to spread ⟨substance⟩; to pour ⟨liquid⟩; to spill ⟨liquid⟩
(b) to scatter ⟨seeds, rubbish⟩
(c) to spread ⟨news, religion⟩; to give off ⟨heat, smoke, smell⟩
2 **se répandre** *v refl* (+ *v être*) to spread

répandu, ~**e** /ʀepɑ̃dy/ *adj* widespread

réparable /ʀepaʀabl/ *adj* **(a)** ⟨object⟩ repairable
(b) ⟨mistake⟩ which can be put right

reparaître /ʀ(ə)paʀɛtʀ/ [73] *vi* **(a)** = RÉAPPARAÎTRE
(b) ⟨magazine⟩ to be back in print

réparateur, -trice /ʀepaʀatœʀ, tʀis/
1 *adj* refreshing
2 *nm,f* engineer (GB), fixer (US)

réparation /ʀepaʀasjɔ̃/ *nf* **(a)** repairing, mending; repair
(b) compensation
(c) redress

réparer /ʀepaʀe/ [1] *vtr* **(a)** to repair, to mend, to fix
(b) to put [sth] right ⟨error⟩; to make up for ⟨oversight⟩
(c) to compensate for ⟨damage⟩

reparler /ʀ(ə)paʀle/ [1] *vtr* **(a)** ~ **de** to discuss [sth] again (à qn, avec qn with sb)
(b) ~ **à qn** to be back on speaking terms with sb

repartie /ʀepaʀti/ *nf* rejoinder; **elle a de la** ~ she always has a ready reply

repartir /ʀ(ə)paʀtiʀ/ [30] *vi* (+ *v être*) **(a)** to leave (again); to go back
(b) ⟨person⟩ to set off again; ⟨machine⟩ to start again; ⟨sector⟩ to pick up again
(c) ~ **à zéro** to start again from scratch

répartir /ʀepaʀtiʀ/ [3] **1** *vtr* **(a)** to share [sth] out; to split ⟨profits, expenses⟩; to distribute ⟨weight⟩

(b) to spread ⟨payments⟩
2 **se répartir** *v refl* (+ *v être*) **(a)** to share out, to split
(b) ⟨work, votes⟩ to be split; **se** ~ **en** ⟨people, objects⟩ to divide (up) into

répartition /ʀepaʀtisjɔ̃/ *nf* **(a)** sharing out; dividing up
(b) distribution

repas /ʀ(ə)pɑ/ *nm inv* meal

repassage /ʀ(ə)pasaʒ/ *nm* ironing

repasser /ʀ(ə)pase/ [1] **1** *vtr* **(a)** to iron
(b) to cross [sth] again ⟨river, border⟩
(c) to take [sth] again ⟨exam⟩
(d) to pass [sth] again ⟨tool, salt⟩; **je te repasse Jean** (on phone) I'll put you back on to Jean
(e) (colloq) ~ **qch à qn** to give sb sth ⟨cold⟩
2 *vi* (+ *v être*) **(a)** to go past again; **si tu repasses à Lyon, viens me voir** if you're ever back in Lyons, come and see me
(b) ⟨film⟩ to be showing again
(c) **quand elle fait la vaisselle, je dois** ~ **derrière elle** I always have to do the dishes again after she's done them

repêchage /ʀ(ə)pɛʃaʒ/ *nm* **(a)** recovery (from water)
(b) épreuve de ~ resit (GB), retest (US)

repêcher /ʀ(ə)peʃe/ [1] *vtr* to recover; to fish out

repeindre /ʀ(ə)pɛ̃dʀ/ [55] *vtr* to repaint

repenser /ʀ(ə)pɑ̃se/ [1] **1** *vtr* to rethink
2 **repenser à** *v+prep* to think back to ⟨childhood⟩; to think again about ⟨anecdote⟩

repenti, ~**e** /ʀ(ə)pɑ̃ti/ *adj* repentant

repentir[1]: **se repentir** /ʀ(ə)pɑ̃tiʀ/ [30] *v refl* (+ *v être*) **(a)** to regret
(b) to repent

repentir[2] /ʀ(ə)pɑ̃tiʀ/ *nm* repentance

repérable /ʀ(ə)peʀabl/ *adj* that can be spotted

repérage /ʀ(ə)peʀaʒ/ *nm* (Mil) location (**de** of)

répercussion /ʀepɛʀkysjɔ̃/ *nf* repercussion

répercuter /ʀepɛʀkyte/ [1] **1** *vtr* **(a)** to pass [sth] on ⟨increase⟩
(b) to send back ⟨sound⟩
2 **se répercuter** *v refl* (+ *v être*) ⟨sound⟩ to echo; ⟨increase⟩ to be reflected (**sur** in)

repère /ʀ(ə)pɛʀ/ *nm* **(a)** marker; (reference) mark
(b) (event) landmark; (date) reference point

repérer /ʀ(ə)peʀe/ [14] **1** *vtr* **(a)** (colloq) to spot; ~ **les lieux** to check out a place
(b) to locate ⟨target⟩
2 **se repérer** *v refl* (+ *v être*) to get one's bearings

répertoire /ʀepɛʀtwaʀ/ *nm* **(a)** notebook with thumb index
(b) ~ **téléphonique** telephone book
(c) repertoire

répertorier /ʀepɛʀtɔʀje/ [2] *vtr* **(a)** to list; to index
(b) to identify

r

répéter /Repete/ [14] **1** *vtr* **(a)** to repeat; ~ qch à qn to say sth to sb again; **je te répète que tu as tort** I'm telling you, you're wrong **(b)** to rehearse ⟨*play*⟩; to rehearse for ⟨*concert*⟩

2 se répéter *v refl* (+ *v être*) **(a)** to repeat oneself
(b) **j'ai beau me ~ que** no matter how often I tell myself that
(c) ⟨*incident*⟩ to be repeated

répétitif, -ive /Repetitif, iv/ *adj* repetitive

répétition /Repetisjɔ̃/ *nf* **(a)** repetition
(b) rehearsal; **~ générale** dress rehearsal

repeupler /R(ə)pœple/ [1] *vtr* **(a)** to repopulate
(b) to restock
(c) to reforest

repiquer /R(ə)pike/ [1] *vtr* to transplant ⟨*rice*⟩; to prick out ⟨*seedlings*⟩

répit /Repi/ *nm* respite

replacer /R(ə)plase/ [12] *vtr* ~ qch dans son contexte to set sth back in context

replanter /R(ə)plɑ̃te/ [1] *vtr* **(a)** to transplant
(b) to replant

replâtrer /R(ə)plɑtRe/ [1] *vtr* **(a)** to replaster
(b) to patch up ⟨*group*⟩

replet, -ète /Rəplɛ, ɛt/ *adj* plump, chubby

repli /R(ə)pli/ *nm* **(a)** double fold
(b) fold
(c) (Mil) withdrawal
(d) ~ sur soi(-même) withdrawal

replier /R(ə)plije/ [2] **1** *vtr* **(a)** to fold up ⟨*map*⟩
(b) to fold [sth] back ⟨*sheet*⟩
(c) to fold up ⟨*deckchair, fan*⟩; to close ⟨*umbrella, penknife*⟩
(d) **elle replia ses jambes** she tucked her legs under her; **~ ses ailes** ⟨*bird*⟩ to fold its wings

2 se replier *v refl* (+ *v être*) **(a)** ⟨*blade*⟩ to fold up
(b) ⟨*army*⟩ to withdraw
(c) **se ~ sur soi-même** ⟨*person*⟩ to become withdrawn

réplique /Replik/ *nf* **(a)** retort, rejoinder; **il a la ~ facile** he's always ready with an answer
(b) line; **donner la ~ à qn** to play opposite sb
(c) replica; **elle est la ~ de sa mère** she is the image of her mother

répliquer /Replike/ [1] **1** *vtr* to retort
2 répliquer à *v+prep* to argue with ⟨*person*⟩; to respond to ⟨*criticism*⟩
3 *vi* **(a)** to answer back
(b) to retaliate, to respond

répondant, ~e /Repɔ̃dɑ̃, ɑ̃t/ *nm,f* referee; (Law) surety, guarantor

répondeur /Repɔ̃dœR/ *nm* ~ **(téléphonique)** (telephone) answering machine

répondre /Repɔ̃dR/ [6] **1** *vtr* to answer, to reply; **il m'a été répondu que** I was told that; **qu'as-tu à ~?** what's your answer?

2 répondre à *v+prep* **(a)** ~ **à** to reply to, to answer ⟨*person, question, letter*⟩; to answer ⟨*phone*⟩
(b) ~ **à** to talk back to
(c) ~ **à** to answer, to meet ⟨*needs*⟩; to fulfil (GB) ⟨*wishes*⟩; to fit ⟨*description*⟩; to come up to ⟨*expectations*⟩
(d) ~ **à** to respond to ⟨*appeal, criticism*⟩; to return ⟨*greeting*⟩; **à un sourire** to smile back; **les freins ne répondent plus** the brakes have failed

3 répondre de *v+prep* ~ **de qn** to vouch for sb; ~ **de ses actes** to answer for one's actions

réponse /Repɔ̃s/ *nf* **(a)** answer, reply
(b) response

report /RəpɔR/ *nm* **(a)** adjournment; postponement; deferment
(b) transfer

reportage /R(ə)pɔRtaʒ/ *nm* **(a)** report
(b) reporting

reporter¹ /R(ə)pɔRte/ [1] **1** *vtr* **(a)** to put back ⟨*date*⟩; to postpone ⟨*event*⟩; to defer ⟨*judgment*⟩
(b) to carry forward ⟨*result*⟩; to copy out ⟨*name*⟩
(c) to take [sth] back ⟨*goods*⟩
(d) to transfer ⟨*affection*⟩; ~ **son agressivité sur qn** to take one's aggression out on sb
2 se reporter *v refl* (+ *v être*) **se ~ à** to refer to; to think back to

reporter² /RəpɔRtɛR/ *nm* reporter

repos /Rəpo/ *nm inv* rest; **mon jour de ~** my day off

reposant, ~e /Rəpozɑ̃, ɑ̃t/ *adj* peaceful, restful; soothing; relaxing

repose-pieds /R(ə)pozpje/ *nm inv* footrest

reposer /Rəpoze/ [1] **1** *vtr* **(a)** to rest; **avoir le visage reposé** to look rested; **lire qch à tête reposée** to read sth at one's leisure
(b) to put [sth] down ⟨*phone*⟩; to put [sth] down again
(c) to ask [sth] again ⟨*question*⟩
2 *vi* **(a)** to rest; **'ici repose le Dr Grunard'** 'here lies Dr Grunard'; **laisser ~ la terre** to rest the land; **'laisser ~ la pâte'** 'let the dough stand'
(b) ~ **sur** to be based on; **la poutre repose sur...** the beam is supported by...
3 se reposer *v refl* (+ *v être*) **(a)** to have a rest, to rest
(b) **se ~ sur qn** to rely on sb

repose-tête /Rəpoztɛt/ *nm inv* head rest

repoussant, ~e /Rəpusɑ̃, ɑ̃t/ *adj* hideous

repousser /R(ə)puse/ [1] **1** *vtr* **(a)** to push [sth] to ⟨*door*⟩; to push back ⟨*object*⟩
(b) to push away ⟨*objects*⟩; to push back ⟨*lock of hair*⟩
(c) to push *or* drive back ⟨*crowd, animal*⟩; (Mil) to repel ⟨*attack*⟩
(d) to dismiss ⟨*objection*⟩; to decline ⟨*help*⟩; to turn down ⟨*request*⟩
(e) to revolt
(f) to postpone ⟨*event*⟩; to move [sth] back ⟨*date*⟩

2 *vi* to grow again; to grow back

répréhensible /ʀepʀeɑ̃sibl/ *adj* reprehensible

reprendre /ʀ(ə)pʀɑ̃dʀ/ [52] **1** *vtr* **(a)** ~ du **pain/vin** to have some more bread/wine; **j'en ai repris deux fois** I had three helpings
(b) to pick [sth] up again ⟨*object, tool*⟩; to take [sth] back ⟨*present*⟩; to collect ⟨*person, car*⟩
(c) to take [sb] on again ⟨*employee*⟩; ⟨*shop*⟩ to take [sth] back ⟨*item*⟩; **si on me reprend ma vieille voiture** if I can trade in my old car
(d) to resume ⟨*walk, story*⟩; to take up [sth] again ⟨*studies*⟩; to revive ⟨*play, tradition*⟩; ~ **le travail** to go back to work; **tu reprends le train à quelle heure?** what time is your train back?; ~ **une histoire au début** to go back to the beginning of a story
(e) to take over ⟨*business, shop*⟩
(f) **on ne me reprendra plus à lui rendre service!** you won't catch me doing him/her any favours again!
(g) ~ **confiance** to regain one's confidence
(h) to alter ⟨*clothes*⟩; ~ **le travail de qn** to correct sb's work
(i) to take up ⟨*idea, thesis, policy*⟩
(j) to repeat ⟨*argument*⟩; to take up ⟨*slogan, news*⟩
(k) to correct ⟨*pupil*⟩
(l) **mon mal de dents m'a repris** my toothache has come back
2 *vi* **(a)** ⟨*business*⟩ to pick up again; ⟨*plant*⟩ to recover
(b) to start again
(c) **'c'est étrange,' reprit-il** 'it's strange,' he continued
3 **se reprendre** *v refl* (+ *v être*) **(a)** to correct oneself
(b) to pull oneself together
(c) **s'y ~ à trois fois pour faire** to make three attempts to do *or* at doing

représailles /ʀ(ə)pʀezaj/ *nf pl* reprisals; retaliation

représentant, **~e** /ʀ(ə)pʀezɑ̃tɑ̃, ɑ̃t/ *nm,f*
(a) representative
(b) ~ **(de commerce)** sales representative

représentatif, -ive /ʀəpʀezɑ̃tatif, iv/ *adj* representative

représentation /ʀəpʀezɑ̃tasjɔ̃/ *nf*
(a) representation
(b) performance
(c) commercial travelling (GB); ~ **exclusive** sole agency

représenter /ʀəpʀezɑ̃te/ [1] **1** *vtr*
(a) (in painting) to depict; to portray
(b) to represent; to mean; **les enfants représentent les deux tiers de la population** children make up two thirds of the population
(c) to represent ⟨*person, company*⟩
(d) to perform ⟨*play*⟩
2 **se représenter** *v refl* (+ *v être*) **(a)** to imagine ⟨*scene*⟩
(b) ⟨*opportunity*⟩ to arise again
(c) **se ~ à un examen** to retake an examination

répressif, -ive /ʀepʀesif, iv/ *adj* repressive

répression /ʀepʀesjɔ̃/ *nf* suppression

réprimande /ʀepʀimɑ̃d/ *nf* reprimand

réprimander /ʀepʀimɑ̃de/ [1] *vtr* to reprimand

réprimer /ʀepʀime/ [1] *vtr* to suppress; to repress ⟨*desire*⟩

repris /ʀ(ə)pʀi/ *nm inv* ~ **de justice** ex-convict

reprise /ʀəpʀiz/ *nf* **(a)** (of work, negotiations) resumption; (of play, film) rerun; **à plusieurs** *or* **maintes ~s** on several occasions, repeatedly
(b) (of demand, production) increase; (of business) revival; (of economy) upturn
(c) (of goods) return, taking back; trade-in; (of company) takeover
(d) key money
(e) (Aut) acceleration
(f) mend; darn
(g) (in boxing) round; (in football) start of second half

repriser /ʀəpʀize/ [1] *vtr* to mend; to darn

réprobation /ʀepʀɔbasjɔ̃/ *nf* disapproval

reproche /ʀ(ə)pʀɔʃ/ *nm* reproach; **j'ai un ou deux ~s à vous faire** I've one or two criticisms to make; **sans ~** beyond reproach

reprocher /ʀəpʀɔʃe/ [1] **1** *vtr* **(a)** ~ **qch à qn** to criticize *or* reproach sb for sth; **on ne peut rien lui ~** he's/she's beyond reproach; **elle me reproche de ne jamais lui écrire** she complains that I never write to her
(b) **les faits qui lui sont reprochés** the charges against him/her
2 **se reprocher** *v refl* (+ *v être*) **se ~ qch** to blame *or* reproach oneself for sth

reproducteur, -trice /ʀəpʀɔdyktœʀ, tʀis/ *adj* **(a)** reproductive
(b) ⟨*animal*⟩ breeding

reproduction /ʀ(ə)pʀɔdyksjɔ̃/ *nf*
(a) reproduction
(b) reproduction, copy; **droit de ~** copyright

reproduire /ʀ(ə)pʀɔdɥiʀ/ [69] **1** *vtr* (gen) to reproduce; to recreate ⟨*conditions*⟩
2 **se reproduire** *v refl* (+ *v être*) **(a)** ⟨*man, plants*⟩ to reproduce
(b) ⟨*situation*⟩ to recur

réprouver /ʀepʀuve/ [1] *vtr* to condemn

reptile /ʀɛptil/ *nm* reptile

repu, ~e /ʀəpy/ *adj* full

républicain, ~e /ʀepyblikɛ̃, ɛn/ *adj*, *nm,f* republican

république /ʀepyblik/ *nf* republic; **on est en ~** it's a free country

répudier /ʀepydje/ [2] *vtr* **(a)** to repudiate ⟨*spouse*⟩
(b) to renounce ⟨*right, faith*⟩

répugnance /ʀepyɲɑ̃s/ *nf* **(a)** revulsion
(b) reluctance; **avec ~** reluctantly

répugnant, ~e /ʀepyɲɑ̃, ɑ̃t/ *adj*
(a) revolting
(b) disgusting

r

⋯❖

(c) loathsome

répugner /Repyɲe/ [1] *v+prep* **(a)** ~ à ⟨*food*⟩ to disgust ⟨*person*⟩
(b) ~ à ⟨*person*⟩ to be averse to ⟨*work*⟩; ~ à faire to be reluctant to do

répulsion /Repylsjɔ̃/ *nf* repulsion

réputation /Repytasjɔ̃/ *nf* reputation; **se faire une** ~ to make a name for oneself

réputé, ~**e** /Repyte/ *adj* **(a)** ⟨*company*⟩ reputable; ⟨*writer*⟩ of repute; ⟨*product*⟩ well-known; ~ **pour qch** renowned for sth; **l'avocat le plus** ~ **de Paris** the best lawyer in Paris
(b) ~ **cher** reputed to be expensive

requérir /RəkeRiR/ [35] *vtr* **(a)** to request
(b) to require

requête /Rəkɛt/ *nf* **(a)** request
(b) (Law) petition

requiem /Rekwijɛm/ *nm inv* requiem

requin /R(ə)kɛ̃/ *nm* (Zool, figurative) shark

requis, ~**e** /Rəki, iz/ [1] *pp* ▶ **REQUÉRIR**
[2] *pp adj* ⟨*patience*⟩ necessary; ⟨*age*⟩ required

réquisition /Rekizisjɔ̃/ *nf* requisitioning

réquisitionner /Rekizisjɔne/ [1] *vtr* **(a)** to requisition
(b) to commandeer ⟨*premises*⟩; to conscript ⟨*workers*⟩

réquisitoire /Rekizitwaʀ/ *nm* closing speech for the prosecution

RER /ɛʀəɛʀ/ *nm* (abbr = **réseau express régional**) *rapid-transit rail system in the Paris region*

rescapé, ~**e** /Reskape/ **[1]** *adj* surviving
[2] *nm,f* survivor

rescousse: à la rescousse /alaʀɛskus/ *phr* **aller à la** ~ **de qn** to go to sb's rescue

réseau, *pl* ~**x** /Rezo/ *nm* network

réservation /Rezɛrvasjɔ̃/ *nf* reservation, booking (GB)

réserve /Rezɛrv/ *nf* **(a)** reservation; **sous** ~ **de changement** subject to alteration; '**sous** (**toute**) ~' (in a programme) 'to be confirmed'
(b) stock; **des** ~**s de sucre** a stock of sugar; ~(**s**) **d'argent** money in reserve
(c) (Econ) ~**s de charbon** coal reserves; ~**s d'eau** water supply
(d) (of person, manner) reserve
(e) stockroom
(f) (in museum) storeroom
(g) ~ **naturelle** nature reserve
(h) ~ **indienne** Indian reservation
(i) (Mil) **officier de** ~ reserve officer

réservé, ~**e** /Rezɛrve/ **[1]** *pp* ▶ **RÉSERVER**
[2] *pp adj* **(a)** ⟨*fishing*⟩ private
(b) ~ **à la clientèle** for patrons only; **voie** ~**e aux autobus** bus lane; '**tous droits** ~**s**' 'all rights reserved'
(c) ⟨*person*⟩ reserved

réserver /Rezɛrve/ [1] **[1]** *vtr* **(a)** to reserve, to book ⟨*seat, ticket*⟩
(b) to put aside ⟨*goods*⟩
(c) to set aside ⟨*money, time*⟩
(d) ~ **un bon accueil à qn** to give sb a warm

welcome; **sans savoir ce que l'avenir nous réserve** without knowing what the future has in store for us
(e) ~ **son jugement** to reserve judgment
[2] se réserver *v refl* (+ *v être*) **se** ~ **les meilleurs morceaux** to save the best bits for oneself; **se** ~ **le droit de faire** to reserve the right to do; **il se réserve pour la candidature à la présidence** he's saving himself for the presidential race

réserviste /Rezɛrvist/ *nmf* reservist

réservoir /Rezɛrvwaʀ/ *nm* **(a)** tank
(b) reservoir

résidant, ~**e** /Rezidɑ̃, ɑ̃t/ *adj* resident

résidence /Rezidɑ̃s/ *nf* **(a)** residence
(b) place of residence; **assigné à** ~ under house arrest
■ ~ **principale/secondaire** main/second home; ~ **universitaire** (university) hall of residence (GB), residence hall (US)

résident, ~**e** /Rezidɑ̃, ɑ̃t/ *nm,f* resident

résidentiel, -**ielle** /Rezidɑ̃sjɛl/ *adj* residential

résider /Rezide/ [1] *vi* **(a)** to live
(b) ~ **dans qch** to lie in sth

résidu /Rezidy/ *nm* **(a)** residue
(b) remnant
(c) waste

résignation /Rezɪɲasjɔ̃/ *nf* resignation (à to)

résigner: se résigner /Reziɲe/ [1] *v refl* (+ *v être*) to resign oneself

résiliation /Reziljasjɔ̃/ *nf* (of contract) termination

résilier /Rezilje/ [2] *vtr* to terminate ⟨*contract*⟩

résine /Rezin/ *nf* resin

résineux /Rezinø/ *nm* conifer

résistance /Rezistɑ̃s/ *nf* **(a)** resistance; **manquer de** ~ ⟨*person*⟩ to lack stamina
(b) (in electricity) (gen) resistance; (of household appliance) element

résistant, ~**e** /Rezistɑ̃, ɑ̃t/ **[1]** *adj*
(a) ⟨*person*⟩ tough, resilient; ⟨*plant*⟩ hardy
(b) ⟨*metal*⟩ resistant; ⟨*fabric, garment*⟩ hard-wearing
[2] *nm,f* Resistance fighter

résister /Reziste/ [1] *v+prep* (gen) to resist; ~ **à** to resist ⟨*offer*⟩; to stand ⟨*strain*⟩; to withstand ⟨*pressure*⟩; to get through ⟨*ordeal*⟩; **le mur n'a pas résisté** the wall collapsed; ~ **à l'épreuve du temps** to stand the test of time; **il ne supporte pas qu'on lui résiste** he doesn't like it when people stand up to him

résolu, ~**e** /Rezɔly/ **[1]** *pp* ▶ **RÉSOUDRE**
[2] *pp adj* resolute, determined

résolument /Rezɔlymɑ̃/ *adv* resolutely

résolution /Rezɔlysjɔ̃/ *nf* **(a)** (gen, Pol) resolution
(b) resolve
(c) solution

résonance /Rezɔnɑ̃s/ *nf* (gen) resonance

résonner /Rezɔne/ [1] *vi* **(a)** ⟨step, laughter⟩ to ring out; ⟨alarm⟩ to resound; ⟨cymbals⟩ to clash
(b) ⟨room⟩ to echo; ∼ **de** to resound with

résorber /Rezɔrbe/ [1] **1** *vtr* to absorb ⟨deficit, surplus⟩; to reduce ⟨inflation⟩
2 se résorber *v refl* (+ *v être*) **(a)** ⟨deficit⟩ to be reduced
(b) (Med) to be resorbed

résorption /Rezɔrpsjɔ̃/ *nf* (of unemployment, inflation) reduction (**de** of)

résoudre /Rezudʀ/ [75] **1** *vtr* to solve ⟨equation, problem⟩; to resolve ⟨crisis⟩
2 se résoudre *v refl* (+ *v être*) **se ∼ à faire** to resolve *or* make up one's mind to do; **être résolu à faire** to be determined to do

respect /Respɛ/ *nm* (gen) respect; **manquer de ∼ à qn** to be disrespectful to sb; **le ∼ de soi** self-respect
IDIOMS sauf votre ∼ with all due respect; **tenir qn en ∼** to keep sb at bay

respectabilité /Respɛktabilite/ *nf* respectability

respectable /Respɛktabl/ *adj* respectable

respecter /Respɛkte/ [1] **1** *vtr* (gen) to respect; to treat [sth] with respect; to honour (GB) ⟨commitment⟩; **faire ∼ l'ordre/la loi** to enforce order/the law
2 se respecter *v refl* (+ *v être*) to respect oneself; **tout homme qui se respecte** any self-respecting man

respectif, -ive /Respɛktif, iv/ *adj* respective

respectueux, -euse /Respɛktɥø, øz/ *adj* respectful; **∼ de la loi** law-abiding; **salutations respectueuses** yours faithfully

respirable /Respirabl/ *adj* **(a)** breathable
(b) ⟨atmosphere⟩, ⟨mood⟩ bearable

respiration /Respirasjɔ̃/ *nf* **(a)** breathing; **avoir une ∼ difficile** to have breathing difficulties
(b) breath; **retenir sa ∼** to hold one's breath

respiratoire /Respiratwar/ *adj* respiratory

respirer /Respire/ [1] **1** *vtr* **(a)** to breathe in ⟨air, dust⟩
(b) to smell ⟨perfume⟩
(c) ⟨person, place⟩ to exude
2 *vi* **(a)** to breathe
(b) (figurative) to catch one's breath; **laisse-moi ∼** let me get my breath back

resplendir /Resplɑ̃dir/ [3] *vi* **(a)** ⟨light⟩ to shine brightly; ⟨snow⟩ to sparkle
(b) **∼ de santé** to be glowing with health

resplendissant, ∼e /Resplɑ̃disɑ̃, ɑ̃t/ *adj* **(a)** ⟨light⟩ brilliant
(b) ⟨beauty⟩ radiant

responsabiliser /Respɔ̃sabilize/ [1] *vtr* to give [sb] a sense of responsibility

responsabilité /Respɔ̃sabilite/ *nf* (gen) responsibility; (Law) liability; **avoir la ∼ de** to be responsible for; **engageant la ∼ de la société** for which the company is liable
■ **∼ civile** (in insurance) personal liability

responsable /Respɔ̃sabl/ **1** *adj*
(a) ⟨person, error⟩ responsible
(b) accountable; (Law) liable
(c) **être ∼ de qn/qch** to be in charge of sb/sth
(d) ⟨person, attitude, act⟩ responsible
2 *nmf* **(a)** (gen) person in charge; (of shop, project) manager; (of party) leader; (of department) head
(b) **les ∼s de la catastrophe** the people responsible for the catastrophe
(c) **le grand ∼ c'est le tabac** smoking is the main cause

resquiller /Reskije/ [1] *vi* (colloq) (on train) not to pay the fare; (at show) to sneak in (colloq)

resquilleur, -euse /Reskijœr, øz/ *nm,f* (colloq) fare dodger

ressac /Rəsak/ *nm* backwash

ressaisir: se ressaisir /R(ə)sezir/ [3] *v refl* (+ *v être*) to pull oneself together

ressasser /R(ə)sase/ [1] *vtr* to brood over ⟨failure⟩; to dwell on ⟨misfortunes⟩

ressemblance /R(ə)sɑ̃blɑ̃s/ *nf*
(a) resemblance, likeness
(b) (between things) similarity

ressemblant, ∼e /R(ə)sɑ̃blɑ̃, ɑ̃t/ *adj* **un portrait ∼** a portrait which is a good likeness

ressembler /R(ə)sɑ̃ble/ [1]
1 ressembler à *v+prep* to look like, to resemble; to be like
2 se ressembler *v refl* (+ *v être*) **(a)** to look alike
(b) to be alike

ressemeler /R(ə)səmle/ [19] *vtr* to resole

ressentiment /R(ə)sɑ̃timɑ̃/ *nm* resentment

ressentir /R(ə)sɑ̃tir/ [30] **1** *vtr* to feel
2 se ressentir *v refl* (+ *v être*) **se ∼ de** to feel the effects of; to suffer from

resserrer /R(ə)sere/ [1] **1** *vtr* **(a)** to tighten ⟨knot, screw, grip⟩
(b) **resserrez les rangs!** close up a bit!
(c) to tighten up on ⟨discipline, supervision⟩
2 se resserrer *v refl* (+ *v être*) **(a)** ⟨road⟩ to narrow
(b) ⟨friendship⟩ to become stronger
(c) ⟨link, knot, grip⟩ to tighten
(d) ⟨gap⟩ to close
(e) ⟨group of people⟩ to draw closer together
(f) ⟨discipline⟩ to become stricter

resservir /R(ə)servir/ [30] **1** *vtr* **(a)** to serve [sth] (up) again
(b) to give [sb] another helping
2 se resservir *v refl* (+ *v être*) to take another helping

ressort /R(ə)sɔr/ *nm* **(a)** (Tech) spring
(b) **avoir du ∼** to have resilience
(c) **être du ∼ de qn** to be within sb's province; (Law) to fall within the jurisdiction of ⟨court⟩; **en premier ∼** in the first resort

ressortir /R(ə)sɔrtir/ [30] **1** *vtr* **(a)** to take [sth] out again ⋯⟶

(b) to bring [sth] out again; to dig out (colloq) ⟨affair, scandal⟩

2 vi (+ v être) **(a)** ⟨person⟩ to go out again
(b) ⟨bullet⟩ to come out
(c) to stand out; **voici ce qui ressort de l'étude** the results of the study are as follows; **faire** ~ to bring to light ⟨contradiction⟩; ⟨make-up⟩ to accentuate ⟨eyes⟩
(d) ⟨film, record⟩ to be re-released
3 v impers (+ v être) **il ressort que** it emerges that

ressortissant, ~e /R(ə)sɔrtisɑ̃, ɑ̃t/ nm,f national

ressouder /R(ə)sude/ [1] vtr to solder [sth] again

ressource /R(ə)suRs/ nf **(a)** resource; **les ~s énergétiques** energy resources
(b) option; **en dernière** ~ as a last resort
(c) avoir de la ~ (colloq) to be resourceful
(d) ~s means; être sans ~s to have no means of support

ressourcer: se ressourcer /R(ə)suRse/ [12] v refl (+ v être) to recharge one's batteries

ressusciter /Resysite/ [1] **1** vtr **(a)** to revive ⟨tradition⟩; to resurrect ⟨past⟩
(b) to raise [sb] from the dead; (figurative) to bring [sb] back to life
2 vi ⟨dead person⟩ to rise from the dead

restant, ~e /Restɑ̃, ɑ̃t/ **1** adj remaining
2 nm **(a) le** ~ the remainder; the rest
(b) un ~ **de poulet** some left-over chicken

restaurant /Restɔrɑ̃/ nm restaurant
■ ~ **universitaire, RU** university canteen (GB), cafeteria

restaurateur, -trice /Restɔratœr, tris/ nm,f **(a)** restaurant owner
(b) restorer

restauration /Restɔrasjɔ̃/ nf **(a)** catering; ~ **rapide** fast-food industry
(b) restoration

restaurer /Restɔre/ [1] **1** vtr **(a)** to feed
(b) to restore
2 se restaurer v refl (+ v être) to have something to eat

reste /Rest/ **1** nm **le** ~ the rest; the remainder; **un** ~ **de tissu** some left-over material; **au** ~, **du** ~ besides
2 restes nm pl **(a)** remains
(b) leftovers
IDIOMS sans demander son ~ without further ado; **être en** ~ **avec qn** to feel indebted to sb; **pour ne pas être en** ~ so as not to be outdone

rester /Reste/ [1] (+ v être) **1** vi **(a)** to stay, to remain; **que ça reste entre nous!** this is strictly between you and me!
(b) to remain; **restez assis!** remain seated!; don't get up!; ~ **sans manger** to go without food; ~ **paralysé** to be left paralysed; ~ **les bras croisés** (figurative) to stand idly by
(c) to be left, to remain
(d) ⟨memory, work of art⟩ to live on

(e) ~ **sur une bonne impression** to be left with a good impression
(f) en ~ **à** to go no further than; **je compte bien ne pas en** ~ **là** I won't let the matter rest there; **restons-en là pour le moment** let's leave it at that for now
2 v impers **il reste une minute** there is one minute left; **il ne me reste plus que lui** he's all I've got left; **il reste que, il n'en reste pas moins que** the fact remains that

restituer /Restitɥe/ [1] vtr **(a)** to restore
(b) to reconstruct ⟨text⟩; to reproduce ⟨sound⟩

restitution /Restitysjɔ̃/ nf **(a)** return; restoration
(b) reproduction

restreindre /RestRɛ̃dR/ [55] **1** vtr to curb, to cut back on; to limit; to restrict
2 se restreindre v refl (+ v être)
(a) ⟨possibilities⟩ to become restricted; ⟨influence⟩ to wane
(b) se ~ **(dans ses dépenses)** to cut back (on one's expenses)

restreint, ~e /RestRɛ̃, ɛ̃t/ adj ⟨public, vocabulary⟩ limited; ⟨team⟩ small

restrictif, -ive /Restriktif, iv/ adj restrictive

restriction /Restriksjɔ̃/ nf **(a)** restriction; ~**s salariales** wage restraints; **sans** ~ freely
(b) sans ~ ⟨approve⟩ without reservations; ⟨support⟩ unreservedly

restructurer /Rəstryktyre/ [1] vtr to restructure; to redevelop ⟨area⟩

résultat /Rezylta/ nm (gen) result; (of research) results, findings; (of negotiations, inquiry) result, outcome; **sans** ~ without success

résulter /Rezylte/ [1] **1 résulter de** v+prep to be the result of, to result from
2 v impers **il résulte de ce que vous venez de dire que** it follows from what you have just said that; **il en résulte que** as a result

résumé /Rezyme/ nm summary, résumé; **en** ~ to sum up; **faire un** ~ **de qch (à qn)** to give (sb) a rundown of or on sth

résumer /Rezyme/ [1] **1** vtr **(a)** to summarize ⟨text⟩
(b) to sum up ⟨news⟩
2 se résumer v refl (+ v être) **(a)** to sum up
(b) se ~ **à** to come down to

résurgence /RezyRʒɑ̃s/ nf resurgence; revival

resurgir /R(ə)syRʒiR/ [3] vi to reappear

résurrection /RezyRɛksjɔ̃/ nf
(a) resurrection
(b) revival
(c) rebirth

rétablir /Retablir/ [3] **1** vtr **(a)** to restore; ~ **la circulation** to get the traffic moving again
(b) to re-establish ⟨truth, facts⟩
(c) ~ **qn dans ses fonctions** to reinstate sb in his/her job

2 **se rétablir** *v refl* (+ *v être*) **(a)** to recover
(b) ⟨*calm*⟩ to return; ⟨*situation*⟩ to return to normal

rétablissement /ʀetablismã/ *nm*
(a) restoration
(b) re-establishment
(c) recovery

rétamer (colloq) /ʀetame/ [1] **1** *vtr* (tire) to wear [sb] out; (beat) to hammer (colloq)
2 **se rétamer** *v refl* (+ *v être*) (colloq) to fall, to come a cropper (colloq)

retape /ʀ(ə)tap/ *nf* (slang) **faire de la ~ pour qch** to beat the drum for sth

retaper /ʀ(ə)tape/ [1] *vtr* (colloq) **(a)** to do up ⟨*house*⟩
(b) to put [sb] on his/her feet again

retard /ʀ(ə)taʀ/ *nm* **(a)** lateness
(b) delay; **avoir du ~** to be late; **nous sommes en ~ sur l'emploi du temps** we're behind schedule; **prendre du ~** to fall *or* get behind; **avoir du courrier en ~** to have a backlog of mail; **sans ~** without delay
(c) backwardness; **il a deux ans de ~** (Sch) he's two years behind at school

retardataire /ʀ(ə)taʀdatɛʀ/ *nmf* latecomer

retardé, ~e /ʀətaʀde/ *adj* ⟨*person*⟩ backward

retardement: à retardement /aʀ(ə)taʀdəmã/ *phr* ⟨*mechanism, device*⟩ delayed-action; **bombe à ~** time-bomb; ⟨*act, get angry*⟩ after the event

retarder /ʀ(ə)taʀde/ [1] **1** *vtr* **(a)** to make [sb] late; **être retardé** ⟨*train*⟩ to be delayed
(b) to hold [sb] up
(c) to put off, to postpone ⟨*departure, operation*⟩
(d) to put back ⟨*clock*⟩
2 *vi* ⟨*clock*⟩ to be slow

retenir /ʀət(ə)niʀ, ʀtəniʀ/ [36] **1** *vtr* **(a)** to keep ⟨*person*⟩; **~ qn prisonnier** to hold sb captive; **~ qn à dîner** to ask sb to stay for dinner
(b) to hold [sb] up, to detain ⟨*person*⟩
(c) to hold ⟨*object, attention*⟩; to hold back ⟨*hair, dog, crowd*⟩; to stop ⟨*person*⟩; **~ sa langue** to hold one's tongue; **~ qn par la manche** to catch hold of sb's sleeve; **votre réclamation a retenu toute notre attention** your complaint is receiving our full attention
(d) to hold back ⟨*tears*⟩; to hold ⟨*breath*⟩; to stifle ⟨*scream, yawn*⟩; to contain, to suppress ⟨*anger*⟩
(e) to retain ⟨*heat, water, odour*⟩
(f) to reserve, to book ⟨*table, room*⟩; to set ⟨*date*⟩
(g) to deduct ⟨*sum*⟩
(h) to remember; **toi, je te retiens!** (colloq) I won't forget this!
(i) to accept ⟨*argument, plan*⟩; (Law) to uphold ⟨*charge*⟩
(j) (in mathematics) **je pose 5 et je retiens 2** I put down 5 and carry 2

2 **se retenir** *v refl* (+ *v être*) **(a)** to stop oneself; **se ~ à qch** to hang on to sth
(b) **se ~ de pleurer** to hold back the tears
(c) (colloq) to control oneself

rétention /ʀetãsjɔ̃/ *nf* **(a)** (Med) retention
(b) withholding

retentir /ʀ(ə)tãtiʀ/ [3] *vi* to ring out; to resound

retentissant, ~e /ʀ(ə)tãtisã, ãt/ *adj*
(a) ⟨*failure*⟩ resounding; ⟨*trial, film*⟩ sensational
(b) ⟨*cry, noise*⟩ ringing; resounding

retentissement /ʀ(ə)tãtismã/ *nm* (gen) effect; (of book, artist) impact

retenue /ʀət(ə)ny/ *nf* **(a)** restraint; **perdre toute ~** to lose one's inhibitions; **boire sans ~** to drink to excess
(b) deduction
(c) (Sch) detention
(d) **tu as oublié la ~ des dizaines** you forgot to carry over from the tens column

réticence /ʀetisãs/ *nf* **(a)** reluctance
(b) **ses ~s en ce qui concerne le passé** his/her reticence about the past

réticent, ~e /ʀetisã, ãt/ *adj* **(a)** hesitant
(b) reluctant

rétif, -ive /ʀetif, iv/ *adj* restive; rebellious

rétine /ʀetin/ *nf* retina

retiré, ~e /ʀətiʀe/ *adj* **(a)** ⟨*life*⟩ secluded
(b) ⟨*place*⟩ remote

retirer /ʀətiʀe/ [1] **1** *vtr* **(a)** to take off ⟨*garment, piece of jewellery*⟩
(b) to take out, to remove; **~ ses troupes d'un pays** to withdraw one's troops from a country
(c) to withdraw ⟨*foot, hand*⟩; **retire ta main** move your hand away
(d) to withdraw ⟨*permission, privilege*⟩; to take away ⟨*right, property*⟩; **~ un produit de la vente** to recall a product; **~ une pièce de l'affiche** to close a play
(e) to withdraw ⟨*complaint, offer, support*⟩; **je retire ce que j'ai dit** I take back what I said
(f) to collect, to pick up ⟨*ticket, luggage*⟩; to withdraw ⟨*money*⟩
(g) to get, to derive ⟨*profits*⟩; **il en retire 10 000 francs par an** he gets 10,000 francs a year out of it
2 **se retirer** *v refl* (+ *v être*) **(a)** to withdraw, to leave; **un homme retiré de la politique** a man retired from political life
(b) **la mer se retire** the tide is going out

retombées /ʀətɔ̃be/ *nf pl*
(a) **~ radioactives** radioactive fallout
(b) effects, consequences
(c) (of invention) spin-offs

retomber /ʀətɔ̃be/ [1] *vi* (+ *v être*) **(a)** to fall again; **~ en enfance** to regress to childhood
(b) ⟨*person, cat, projectile*⟩ to land; ⟨*ball, curtain*⟩ to come down; ⟨*fog*⟩ to set in again; **ça va te ~ sur le nez** (figurative) (colloq) it'll come down on your head
(c) ⟨*anger*⟩ to subside; ⟨*interest*⟩ to wane

r

⋯▸

(d) ⟨currency, temperature⟩ to fall
(e) ~ **sur qn** ⟨responsibility⟩ to fall on sb; **faire** ~ **la responsabilité sur qn** to pass the buck to sb (colloq)

retordre /ʀ(ə)tɔʀdʀ/ [6] vtr **donner du fil à** ~ **à qn** to give sb a hard time

rétorquer /ʀetɔʀke/ [1] vtr to retort

retors, **~e** /ʀətɔʀ, ɔʀs/ adj ⟨person⟩ crafty; ⟨argument⟩ devious

rétorsion /ʀetɔʀsjɔ̃/ nf retaliation

retouche /ʀ(ə)tuʃ/ nf alteration; ⟨of photograph, picture⟩ retouching

retoucher /ʀ(ə)tuʃe/ [1] vtr to make alterations to; to touch up

retour /ʀ(ə)tuʀ/ nm return; **(billet de)** ~ return ticket (GB), round trip (ticket) (US); **au** ~ on the way back; **être de** ~ **(à la maison)** to be back (home); **on attend le** ~ **au calme** people are waiting for things to calm down; **il connaît maintenant le succès et c'est un juste** ~ **des choses** he's successful now, and deservedly so; **elle s'engage, en** ~, **à payer la facture** she undertakes for her part to pay the bill; **'sans** ~ **ni consigne'** 'no deposit or return'; **par** ~ **du courrier** by return of post (GB), by the next mail (US)
■ ~ **d'âge** change of life; **~ en arrière** flashback; ~ **de bâton** (colloq) backlash
IDIOMS être sur le ~ (colloq) to be over the hill (colloq)

retournement /ʀ(ə)tuʀnəmɑ̃/ nm reversal; **un** ~ **de l'opinion publique** a turn around in public opinion

retourner /ʀ(ə)tuʀne/ [1] **1** vtr (+ v avoir)
(a) to turn [sth] over; to turn ⟨mattress⟩
(b) to turn [sth] inside out
(c) to turn over ⟨earth⟩; to toss ⟨salad⟩
(d) to return ⟨compliment, criticism⟩; ~ **la situation** to reverse the situation
(e) to turn [sth] upside down ⟨room⟩; ⟨news, film⟩ to shake ⟨person⟩
(f) to send [sth] back, to return
2 vi (+ v être) to go back, to return
3 se retourner v refl (+ v être) **(a)** to turn around
(b) to turn over; **il n'a pas arrêté de se** ~ **(dans son lit)** he kept tossing and turning
(c) (colloq) to get organized
(d) se ~ **contre qn** ⟨person⟩ to turn against sb; ⟨arguments⟩ to backfire on sb
(e) elle s'est retourné le doigt she bent back her finger
(f) s'en ~ **(chez soi)** to go back (home)
4 v impers **j'aime savoir de quoi il retourne** I like to know what's going on
IDIOMS ~ **qn comme une crêpe** (colloq) to make sb change their mind completely

retracer /ʀətʀase/ [12] vtr **(a)** to redraw ⟨line⟩
(b) to recount ⟨event⟩

rétractable /ʀetʀaktabl/ adj retractable

rétracter /ʀetʀakte/ [1] vtr, **se rétracter** v refl (+ v être) to retract

retrait /ʀ(ə)tʀɛ/ **1** nm (gen) withdrawal; ⟨of suitcase, packet⟩ collection; ~ **du permis (de conduire)** disqualification from driving
2 en retrait phr **maison en** ~ **de** ⟨road⟩ set back from ⟨road⟩; **se tenir en** ~ to stand back; **rester en** ~ to stay in the background

retraite /ʀ(ə)tʀɛt/ nf **(a)** retirement; **prendre sa** ~ to retire
(b) pension
(c) (Mil) retreat
(d) (place) retreat; ⟨of bandits⟩ hiding place
■ ~ **par capitalisation** loanback pension; ~ **complémentaire** private pension

retraité, **~e** /ʀətʀete/ nm,f retired person

retraiter /ʀətʀete/ [1] vtr to reprocess ⟨plutonium⟩

retranché, **~e** /ʀ(ə)tʀɑ̃ʃe/ adj entrenched

retranchement /ʀ(ə)tʀɑ̃ʃmɑ̃/ nm entrenchment; **pousser qn dans ses derniers** ~**s** to drive sb into a corner

retrancher /ʀ(ə)tʀɑ̃ʃe/ [1] **1** vtr **(a)** to cut out ⟨word⟩
(b) to subtract ⟨amount⟩; to deduct ⟨costs⟩
2 se retrancher v refl (+ v être) (Mil, gen) to take up position; to entrench oneself

retransmettre /ʀətʀɑ̃smɛtʀ/ [60] vtr **(a)** to broadcast; **retransmis par satellite** relayed by satellite
(b) to retransmit

retransmission /ʀətʀɑ̃smisjɔ̃/ nf
(a) broadcast
(b) relay
(c) retransmission

rétrécir /ʀetʀesiʀ/ [3] vi, **se rétrécir** v refl (+ v être) **(a)** to narrow
(b) to shrink

rétrécissement /ʀetʀesismɑ̃/ nm
(a) shrinkage
(b) narrowing
(c) contraction

rétribuer /ʀetʀibɥe/ [1] vtr to remunerate

rétribution /ʀetʀibysjɔ̃/ nf remuneration

rétro /ʀetʀo/ nm **(a)** nostalgic style
(b) retro fashions

rétroactif, **-ive** /ʀetʀoaktif, iv/ adj (Law, gen) retroactive

rétrograde /ʀetʀogʀad/ adj ⟨person⟩ reactionary; ⟨policy, measure⟩ retrograde

rétrograder /ʀetʀogʀade/ [1] **1** vtr **(a)** to demote
(b) (Sport) to relegate
2 vi (Aut) to change down (GB), to downshift (US)

rétrospectif, **-ive**[1] /ʀetʀɔspɛktif, iv/ adj retrospective

rétrospective[2] /ʀetʀɔspɛktiv/ nf (gen) retrospective; ⟨of films⟩ festival

rétrospectivement /ʀetʀɔspɛktivmɑ̃/ adv in retrospect; looking back

retroussé, **~e** /ʀətʀuse/ adj ⟨nose⟩ turned up; ⟨lip⟩ curling

retrousser /ʀ(ə)tʀuse/ [1] vtr to hitch up (GB), to hike up (US) ⟨skirt⟩; to roll up ⟨sleeves⟩

retrouvailles /ʀətʀuvaj/ *nf pl* (a) reunion
(b) reconciliation

retrouver /ʀətʀuve/ [1] **1** *vtr* (a) to find ‹*lost object*›
(b) to find [sth] again ‹*work, object*›
(c) to regain ‹*strength, health*›
(d) to remember ‹*name, tune*›
(e) to be back in ‹*place*›
(f) to recognize ‹*person, style*›; **je retrouve sa mère en elle** I can see her mother in her
(g) to join, to meet ‹*person*›
2 se retrouver *v refl* (+ *v être*) (a) to meet (again); **on s'est retrouvé en famille** the family got together; **comme on se retrouve!** fancy seeing you here!
(b) **se ∼ enceinte** to find oneself pregnant; **se ∼ sans argent** to be left penniless
(c) **se** *or* **s'y ∼ dans** to find one's way around in ‹*place, mess*›; to follow, to understand ‹*explanation*›; **il y a trop de changements, on ne s'y retrouve plus** there are too many changes, we don't know if we're coming or going
(d) (colloq) **s'y ∼** to break even; (making profit) to do well
(e) ‹*quality*› to be found; ‹*problem*› to occur
(f) **se ∼ dans qn/qch** to see *or* recognize oneself in sb/sth

rétroviseur /ʀetʀovizœʀ/ *nm* (a) rear-view mirror
(b) wing mirror (GB), outside rear-view mirror (US)

réunification /ʀeynifikasjɔ̃/ *nf* reunification

réunifier /ʀeynifje/ [2] **1** *vtr* to reunify
2 se réunifier *v refl* (+ *v être*) to be reunified

réunion /ʀeynjɔ̃/ *nf* (a) meeting; **être en ∼** ‹*person*› to be at a meeting
(b) gathering
(c) reunion
(d) (of different talents) combination; (of poems) collection
(e) union

réunir /ʀeyniʀ/ [3] **1** *vtr* (a) ‹*conference*› to bring together ‹*participants*›; ‹*organizer*› to get [sb] together ‹*participants*›
(b) to call [sb] together ‹*delegates*›; to convene ‹*assembly*›
(c) to have [sb] round (GB) *or* over ‹*friends*›
(d) to join ‹*edges*›
(e) to unite ‹*provinces*›
(f) **∼ les conditions nécessaires** to fulfil (GB) all the necessary conditions
(g) to raise ‹*funds*›
(h) to assemble ‹*elements, evidence*›; to gather [sth] together ‹*documents*›
(i) ‹*road, canal*› to connect
2 se réunir *v refl* (+ *v être*) to meet; to get together

réussir /ʀeysiʀ/ [3] **1** *vtr* to achieve ‹*unification*›; to carry out [sth] successfully ‹*operation*›; to make a success of ‹*life*›
2 réussir à *v+prep* (a) **∼ à faire** to succeed in doing; **∼ à un examen** to pass an exam

(b) **∼ à qn** ‹*life, method*› to turn out well for sb; ‹*rest*› to do sb good
3 *vi* (a) to succeed
(b) ‹*attempt*› to be successful
(c) ‹*person*› to do well

réussite /ʀeysit/ *nf* (gen) success

revaloir /ʀ(ə)valwaʀ/ [45] *vtr* **je te revaudrai ça** (vengefully) I'll get even with you for that; (in gratitude) I'll return the favour (GB)

revalorisation /ʀ(ə)valɔʀizasjɔ̃/ *nf*
(a) (increase) **une ∼ des salaires de 3%** a 3% wage increase
(b) (renewed esteem) **la ∼ des enseignants** the enhanced prestige of teachers

revaloriser /ʀ(ə)valɔʀize/ [1] *vtr* (a) to increase ‹*salary*›; to revalue ‹*currency*›
(b) to reassert the value of ‹*traditions*›
(c) to renovate ‹*area*›

revanche /ʀ(ə)vɑ̃ʃ/ **1** *nf* (a) revenge
(b) (Sport) return match (GB) *or* game (US)
2 en revanche *phr* on the other hand

rêvasser /ʀɛvase/ [1] *vi* to daydream

rêve /ʀɛv/ *nm* (a) dreaming
(b) dream; **fais de beaux ∼s!** sweet dreams!
(c) **une maison de ∼** a dream house
(c) **c'est le ∼** this is just perfect

rêvé, ∼e /ʀeve/ *adj* ideal, perfect

revêche /ʀavɛʃ/ *adj* ‹*manner, tone*› sour; ‹*person*› crabby

réveil /ʀevɛj/ *nm* (a) waking (up)
(b) (after anaesthetic) **j'ai eu des nausées au ∼** I felt nauseous when I regained consciousness
(c) (of movement) resurgence; (of pain) return; (of volcano) return to activity
(d) (Mil) reveille
(e) alarm clock

réveille-matin /ʀevɛjmatɛ̃/ *nm inv* alarm clock

réveiller /ʀeveje/ [1] **1** *vtr* (a) to wake [sb] up, to wake
(b) to revive ‹*person*›; to awaken ‹*feeling*›; to arouse ‹*curiosity*›; to stir up ‹*memory*›
2 se réveiller *v refl* (+ *v être*) (a) to wake up; to awaken
(b) to regain consciousness
(c) ‹*volcano*› to become active again
(d) ‹*pain, appetite*› to come back; ‹*memory*› to be reawakened

réveillon /ʀevɛjɔ̃/ *nm* **∼ du Nouvel An** New Year's Eve party

réveillonner /ʀevɛjɔne/ [1] *vi* to celebrate Christmas Eve; to see the New Year in

révélateur, -trice /ʀevelatœʀ, tʀis/
1 *adj* ‹*detail, fact*› revealing, telling
2 *nm* (in photography) developer

révélation /ʀevelasjɔ̃/ *nf* revelation

révéler /ʀevele/ [14] **1** *vtr* (a) to reveal; to give away ‹*secret*›
(b) to show
(c) to discover ‹*artist*›
(d) (in photography) to develop
2 se révéler *v refl* (+ *v être*) **se ∼ faux** to turn out to be wrong

r

revenant, **~e** /Rəv(ə)nã, ãt/ *nm,f* ghost

revendeur, **-euse** /R(ə)vãdœR, øz/ *nm,f*
(a) stockist
(b) **un ~ de drogue** a drug dealer
(c) seller (of stolen goods)

revendicatif, **-ive** /R(ə)vãdikatif, iv/ *adj*
protest; **journée revendicative** day of protest

revendication /R(ə)vãdikasjõ/ *nf*
(of workers) demand; (of country) claim

revendiquer /R(ə)vãdike/ [1] *vtr* (a) to
demand ‹pay rise›; to claim ‹territory›
(b) to claim responsibility for ‹attack›
(c) to proclaim ‹origins›

revendre /R(ə)vãdR/ [6] *vtr* (a) to sell [sth]
retail, to retail
(b) to resell ‹car, house›; to sell on ‹stolen
object›; **avoir de l'énergie à ~** to have energy
to spare

revenir /Rəvnir, Rvənir/ [36] (+ *v être*) **1** *vi*
(a) to come back; to come again
(b) ‹person, animal, vehicle› to come back, to
return; **~ de loin** (figurative) to have had a
close shave; **mon chèque m'est revenu** my
cheque (GB) *or* check (US) was returned
(c) **~ à** to return to, to come back to
‹method, story›
(d) ‹appetite, memory› to come back; ‹sun› to
come out again; ‹season› to return; ‹idea,
theme› to recur; **~ à la mémoire** *or* **l'esprit de
qn** to come back to sb; **ça me revient!** now I
remember!
(e) **~ à 100 francs** to come to 100 francs; **ça
revient cher** it works out expensive
(f) **~ sur** to go back over ‹question, past›; to
go back on ‹decision, promise›; to retract
‹confession›
(g) **~ de** to get over ‹illness, surprise›; to
lose ‹illusion›; **la vie à la campagne, j'en suis
revenu** as for life in the country, I've seen it
for what it is; **je n'en reviens pas des
progrès que tu as faits** (colloq) I'm amazed at
the progress you've made
(h) **~ aux oreilles de qn** ‹remark› to reach
sb's ears
(i) **~ à qn** ‹property› to go to sb; ‹honour› to
fall to sb; **ça leur revient de droit** it's theirs
by right; **la décision revient au rédacteur** it is
the editor's decision
(j) (Culin) **faire ~** to brown
2 *v impers* **c'est à vous qu'il revient de
trancher** it is for you to decide
IDIOMS **il a une tête qui ne me revient pas**
I don't like the look of him

revenu /Rəv(ə)ny, Rvəny/ *nm* income;
(of state) revenue
■ **~ minimum d'insertion**, **RMI** *minimum
benefit paid to those with no other source of
income*

rêver /Reve/ [1] **1** *vtr* (a) to dream
(b) to dream of ‹success, revenge›
2 *vi* to dream

réverbération /ReveRbeRasjõ/ *nf* (a) glare
(b) reflection
(c) reverberation

réverbère /ReveRbeR/ *nm* street lamp *or*
light

réverbérer /ReveRbere/ [14] **1** *vtr* to
reflect
2 se réverbérer *v refl* (+ *v être*) ‹light,
heat› to be reflected; ‹sound› to reverberate

révérence /ReveRãs/ *nf* (a) curtsey; bow
(b) reverence
IDIOMS **tirer sa ~** (colloq) to take one's leave

révérencieux, **-ieuse** /ReveRãsjø, øz/
adj deferential (envers to); **attitude peu
révérencieuse** irreverent attitude

révérend, **~e** /ReveRã, ãd/ *nm,f*
(a) Father/Mother Superior
(b) reverend

révérer /ReveRe/ [14] *vtr* to revere

rêverie /RevRi/ *nf* (a) daydreaming
(b) daydream

revers /R(ə)veR/ *nm inv* (a) (of hand) back;
(of cloth) wrong side; (of coin) reverse; **le ~ de
la médaille** (figurative) the downside (colloq)
(b) (on jacket) lapel; (of trousers) turn-up (GB),
cuff (US)
(c) (in tennis) backhand (stroke)
(d) setback

réversibilité /ReveRsibilite/ *nf*
reversibility; (in law) reversion

réversible /ReveRsibl/ *adj* (gen) reversible

revêtement /R(ə)vɛtmã/ *nm* (a) (of road)
surface
(b) coating; covering

revêtir /R(ə)vetiR/ [33] **1** *vtr* (a) to assume
‹gravity, solemnity›; to have ‹disadvantage›;
to take on ‹significance›; **~ la forme de** to
take the form of
(b) to put on ‹garment›
(c) **~ qch de** to cover sth with ‹carpet, tiles›
2 se revêtir *v refl* (+ *v être*) **se ~ de** to
put on ‹cloak›; to become covered with
‹snow›

rêveur, **-euse** /RevœR, øz/ **1** *adj* dreamy
2 *nm,f* dreamer

revient /R(ə)vjɛ̃/ *nm* **prix de ~** cost price

revigorer /R(ə)vigoRe/ [1] *vtr* to revive

revirement /R(ə)viRmã/ *nm* turnaround

réviser /Revize/ [1] *vtr* (a) to revise
‹position, prices›; to review ‹constitution›
(b) to overhaul ‹car, boiler›; to revise
‹manuscript›
(c) (Sch) to revise (GB), to review (US)

révision /Revizjõ/ *nm* (a) revision; review
(b) (of car) service; (of manuscript) revision;
(of accounts) audit
(c) (Sch) revision (GB), review (US)

revitaliser /R(ə)vitalize/ [1] *vtr* to
revitalize

revivifier /R(ə)vivifje/ [2] *vtr* to revive; to
revivify

revivre /R(ə)vivR/ [63] **1** *vtr* (a) to go over,
to relive ‹event, past›; **faire ~ qch à qn** to
bring back memories of sth to sb
(b) to live through [sth] again ‹war›
2 *vi* (a) to come alive again
(b) to be able to breathe again
(c) **faire ~** to revive ‹tradition›

révocation /ʀevɔkasjɔ̃/ nf (of will) revocation; (of person) dismissal

revoici /ʀ(ə)vwasi/ prep (colloq) ∼ **Marianne!** here's Marianne again!

revoilà /ʀ(ə)vwala/ = REVOICI

revoir¹ /ʀ(ə)vwaʀ/ [46] vtr **(a)** to see [sb/sth] again
(b) to go over ⟨exercise, lesson⟩; to review ⟨method⟩; to check through ⟨accounts⟩

revoir²: au revoir /ɔʀ(ə)vwaʀ/ phr goodbye

révoltant, ∼e /ʀevɔltɑ̃, ɑ̃t/ adj appalling

révolte /ʀevɔlt/ nf **(a)** revolt
(b) rebellion

révolté, ∼e /ʀevɔlte/ adj **(a)** (insubordinate) rebellious
(b) (shocked) appalled

révolter /ʀevɔlte/ [1] **1** vtr to appal (GB)
2 se révolter v refl (+ v être) **(a)** to rebel
(b) to be appalled

révolu, ∼e /ʀevɔly/ adj **(a) ce temps est ∼** those days are over or past
(b) avoir 12 ans ∼s to be over 12 years of age

révolution /ʀevɔlysjɔ̃/ nf **(a)** revolution
(b) turmoil
(c) (of planet) revolution

révolutionnaire /ʀevɔlysjɔnɛʀ/ adj, nmf revolutionary

révolutionner /ʀevɔlysjɔne/ [1] vtr to revolutionize

revolver /ʀevɔlvɛʀ/ nm **(a)** revolver
(b) handgun; **coup de ∼** gunshot

révoquer /ʀevɔke/ [1] vtr **(a)** to revoke ⟨will⟩
(b) to dismiss ⟨person⟩

revue /ʀ(ə)vy/ nf **(a)** (gen) magazine; (academic) journal
(b) (Mil) parade; **passer en ∼** to review ⟨troops⟩; to inspect ⟨equipment⟩
(c) revue
(d) examination; **passer qch en ∼** to go over sth
■ **∼ de presse** review of the papers

révulser /ʀevylse/ [1] **1** vtr to appal (GB)
2 se révulser v refl (+ v être) ⟨eyes⟩ to roll (upward(s)); ⟨face⟩ to contort

révulsion /ʀevylsjɔ̃/ nf (Med, gen) revulsion

rez-de-chaussée /ʀɛdʃose/ nm inv ground floor (GB), first floor (US)

RF (written abbr = **République française**) French Republic

rhabiller: se rhabiller /ʀabije/ [1] v refl (+ v être) to get dressed again
IDIOMS il peut aller se ∼! (slang) he can go back where he came from!

rhapsodie /ʀapsɔdi/ nf rhapsody

rhésus /ʀezys/ nm inv **(a) facteur ∼** rhesus factor
(b) rhesus monkey

rhétorique /ʀetɔʀik/ **1** adj rhetorical
2 nf rhetoric

Rhin /ʀɛ̃/ pr nm **le ∼ the** Rhine

rhinocéros /ʀinɔseʀɔs/ nm inv rhinoceros

rhubarbe /ʀybaʀb/ nf rhubarb

rhum /ʀɔm/ nm rum

rhumatisme /ʀymatism/ nm rheumatism

rhume /ʀym/ nm cold; **∼ des foins** hay fever

ri /ʀi/ ▶ RIRE¹

ribambelle /ʀibɑ̃bɛl/ nf (colloq) (of children) flock; (of friends) host; (of names) whole string

Ricain, ∼e (colloq) /ʀikɛ̃, ɛn/ (offensive or humorous) nm,f Yank (colloq)

ricaner /ʀikane/ [1] vi **(a)** to snigger
(b) to giggle

riche /ʀiʃ/ **1** adj (gen) rich; ⟨person⟩ rich, wealthy; ⟨library⟩ well-stocked; ⟨decor⟩ elaborate; **une ∼ idée** an excellent idea
2 nmf rich man/woman; **les ∼s** the rich

richement /ʀiʃmɑ̃/ adv richly, lavishly ⟨furnished, decorated⟩

richesse /ʀiʃɛs/ **1** nf **(a)** wealth; **c'est toute notre ∼** it's all we have
(b) (of jewellery) magnificence; (of garment) richness
(c) (of foodstuff) richness
(d) (of fauna, vocabulary) richness; (of documentation) wealth
2 richesses nf pl wealth; **∼s naturelles** natural resources

richissime /ʀiʃisim/ adj (colloq) fabulously rich

ricin /ʀisɛ̃/ nm **huile de ∼** castor oil

ricocher /ʀikɔʃe/ [1] vi ⟨bullet⟩ to ricochet (**sur off**); (off an obstacle) to rebound (**sur off**)

ricochet /ʀikɔʃɛ/ nm (of bullet) ricochet; (of stone) bounce; **faire des ∼s** to skim stones

rictus /ʀiktys/ nm inv (fixed) grin, rictus

ride /ʀid/ nf (on face, fruit) wrinkle; (on lake) ripple

rideau, pl ∼x /ʀido/ nm **(a)** curtain
(b) (of shop) roller shutter
(c) (of flames) wall
■ **∼ de fumée** blanket of smoke

rider /ʀide/ [1] **1** vtr **(a)** to wrinkle ⟨face, skin⟩
(b) to ripple ⟨surface, lake⟩
2 se rider v refl (+ v être) **(a)** ⟨skin⟩ to wrinkle
(b) ⟨lake⟩ to ripple

ridicule /ʀidikyl/ **1** adj **(a)** ridiculous
(b) ⟨wage⟩ ridiculously low, pathetic
2 nm **(a)** ridicule
(b) (of situation) absurdity

ridiculiser /ʀidikylize/ [1] **1** vtr to ridicule; to wipe the floor with ⟨competitor⟩
2 se ridiculiser v refl (+ v être) ⟨person⟩ to make a fool of oneself

ridule /ʀidyl/ nf fine wrinkle

rien¹ /ʀjɛ̃/ **1** pron **(a)** nothing; **il n'y a plus ∼** there's nothing left; **∼ n'y fait!** nothing's any good!; **∼ d'autre** nothing else; **'pourquoi?'—'pour ∼'** 'why?'—'no reason'; **'merci'—'de ∼'** 'thank you'—'you're welcome' or 'not at all'; **en moins de ∼** in ····❖

no time at all!; **ça ou ∼, c'est pareil** it makes no odds; **c'est trois fois ∼** (colloq) it's next to nothing

(b) ∼ que la bouteille pèse deux kilos the bottle alone weighs two kilos; **elle voudrait un bureau ∼ qu'à elle** (colloq) she would like an office all to herself; **∼ que ça?** (colloq) is that all?; **ils habitent un château, ∼ que ça!** (ironic) they live in a castle, no less! *or* if you please!

(c) anything; **sans que j'en sache ∼** without my knowing anything about it

(d) (Sport, gen) nil; (in tennis) love

2 de rien (du tout) *phr* **un petit bleu de ∼ (du tout)** a tiny bruise

3 en rien *phr* at all, in any way

IDIOMS **∼ à faire!** it's no good *or* use!; **ce n'est pas ∼!** (exploit) it's quite something!; (task) it's no joke!; (sum of money) it's not exactly peanuts! (colloq)

rien² /ʀjɛ̃/ **1** *nm* **un ∼ le fâche** the slightest thing annoys him; **se disputer pour un ∼ to** quarrel over nothing; **les petits ∼s qui rendent la vie agréable** the little things which make life pleasant; **un/une ∼ du tout** a worthless person

2 un rien *phr* (colloq) a (tiny) bit

rieur, rieuse /ʀijœʀ, øz/ *adj* ⟨person, tone⟩ cheerful; ⟨face, eyes⟩ laughing

rigide /ʀiʒid/ *adj* **(a)** rigid
(b) stiff

rigidité /ʀiʒidite/ *nf* rigidity

rigolade /ʀiɡɔlad/ *nf* (colloq) **(a) quelle ∼!** what a laugh! (colloq)
(b) joke
(c) réparer ça, c'est de la ∼! repairing this is a piece of cake (colloq)

rigole /ʀiɡɔl/ *nf* **(a)** channel
(b) rivulet

rigoler /ʀiɡɔle/ [1] *vi* (colloq) **(a)** to laugh
(b) to have fun
(c) to joke, to kid (colloq)

rigolo, -ote /ʀiɡɔlo, ɔt/ (colloq) **1** *adj*
(a) funny
(b) odd
2 *nm,f* **(a)** joker
(b) c'est un petit ∼ he's quite a little comedian

rigoriste /ʀiɡɔʀist/ *adj* ⟨attitude⟩ unbending, rigoristic; ⟨morals⟩ strict

rigoureusement /ʀiɡuʀøzmɑ̃/ *adv* completely; carefully

rigoureux, -euse /ʀiɡuʀø, øz/ *adj*
(a) ⟨discipline, person⟩ strict
(b) ⟨climate, working conditions⟩ harsh, severe
(c) ⟨research, demonstration⟩ meticulous; ⟨analysis⟩ rigorous

rigueur /ʀiɡœʀ/ **1** *nf* **(a)** strictness
(b) harshness
(c) rigour (GB)
(d) (Econ) austerity
2 de rigueur *phr* obligatory

3 à la rigueur *phr* à la ∼ **je peux te prêter 100 francs** at a pinch (GB) *or* in a pinch (US) I can lend you 100 francs
IDIOMS **tenir ∼ à qn de qch** to bear sb a grudge for sth

rillettes /ʀijɛt/ *nf pl* ≈ potted meat

rime /ʀim/ *nf* rhyme

rimer /ʀime/ [1] *vi* **(a)** to rhyme
(b) cela ne rime à rien it makes no sense

rimmel® /ʀimɛl/ *nm* mascara

rinçage /ʀɛ̃saʒ/ *nm* **(a)** rinsing
(b) rinse

rince-doigts /ʀɛ̃sdwa/ *nm inv* **(a)** finger bowl
(b) finger wipe

rincer /ʀɛ̃se/ [12] **1** *vtr* **(a)** to rinse
(b) to rinse [sth] out
2 se rincer *v refl* (+ *v être*) **se ∼ les mains/les cheveux** to rinse one's hands/hair

ring /ʀiŋ/ *nm* (boxing) ring

ringard, ∼e /ʀɛ̃ɡaʀ, aʀd/ *adj* (colloq) out of date

riper /ʀipe/ [1] *vi* ⟨foot⟩ to slip; ⟨bicycle⟩ to skid

riposte /ʀipɔst/ *nf* **(a)** reply, riposte
(b) response
(c) (Sport) (in fencing) riposte; (in boxing) counter

riposter /ʀipɔste/ [1] **1** *vtr* to retort
2 *vi* **(a)** to retort; **∼ à qn/qch par** to counter sb/sth with
(b) to respond
(c) (Mil) to return fire, to shoot back
(d) (in sport) to riposte

ripou, pl ∼x /ʀipu/ *adj* (slang) crooked (colloq), bent

riquiqui /ʀikiki/ *adj inv* (colloq) ⟨room, car⟩ poky (colloq); ⟨portion⟩ measly (colloq)

rire¹ /ʀiʀ/ [68] **1** *vi* **(a)** to laugh; **tu nous feras toujours ∼!** you're a real scream! (colloq)
(b) to have fun; **il faut bien ∼ un peu** you need a bit of fun now and again; **fini de ∼** the fun's over; **c'était pour ∼** it was a joke; **sans ∼** (colloq) seriously; **laisse-moi ∼** (colloq), **ne me fais pas ∼** (colloq) don't make me laugh
(c) ∼ de qn/qch to laugh at sb/sth
2 se rire *v refl* (+ *v être*) **se ∼ de qn** (formal) to laugh at sb; **se ∼ des difficultés** (formal) to make light of difficulties
IDIOMS **rira bien qui rira le dernier** (Proverb) he who laughs last laughs longest; **être mort de ∼** (colloq) to be doubled up (with laughter)

rire² /ʀiʀ/ *nm* laughter; **un ∼** a laugh; **il a eu un petit ∼** he chuckled
∎ **∼s préenregistrés** canned laughter

ris /ʀi/ *nm inv* **(a)** (Culin) **∼ (de veau)** calf's sweetbread
(b) (Naut) reef

risée /ʀize/ *nf* **être la ∼ de** to be the laughing stock of

risette /ʀizɛt/ *nf* (colloq) smile

risible /ʀizibl/ *adj* ridiculous, laughable

risque /ʀisk/ *nm* risk; c'est sans ∼ it's safe; à ∼s 〈*group, loan*〉 high-risk
■ les ∼s du métier occupational hazards

risqué, -e /ʀiske/ *adj* (a) risky; 〈*investment*〉 high-risk
(b) 〈*joke*〉 risqué; 〈*hypothesis*〉 daring

risquer /ʀiske/ [1] **1** *vtr* (a) to face 〈*accusation, condemnation*〉
(b) to risk 〈*death, criticism*〉; vas-y, tu ne risques rien go ahead, you're safe; (figurative) go ahead, you've got nothing to lose; ∼ gros to take a major risk
(c) to risk 〈*life, reputation, job*〉
(d) to venture 〈*look, question*〉; to attempt 〈*operation*〉; ∼ un œil to venture a glance; ∼ le coup (colloq) to risk it
2 risquer de *v+prep* (a) tu risques de te brûler you might burn yourself
(b) il ne veut pas ∼ de perdre son travail he doesn't want to risk losing his job
3 se risquer *v refl* (+ *v être*) (a) to venture; je ne m'y risquerais pas I wouldn't risk it
(b) se ∼ à dire to dare to say
4 *v impers* il risque de pleuvoir it might rain; il risque d'y avoir du monde there may well be a lot of people there
IDIOMS ∼ le tout pour le tout to stake *or* risk one's all

risque-tout /ʀiskətu/ *adj inv* daredevil

rissoler /ʀisɔle/ [1] *vtr, vi* (Culin) to brown

ristourne /ʀistuʀn/ *nf* discount, rebate

rite /ʀit/ *nm* rite

rituel, -elle /ʀitɥɛl/ *adj, nm* ritual

rivage /ʀivaʒ/ *nm* shore

rival, ∼e, *mpl* **-aux** /ʀival, o/ *adj, nm,f* rival

rivaliser /ʀivalize/ [1] *vi* to compete with; ∼ avec qch to rival sth

rivalité /ʀivalite/ *nf* rivalry

rive /ʀiv/ *nf* (a) (of river) bank
(b) (of sea, lake) shore

river /ʀive/ [1] *vtr* to clinch 〈*nail, rivet*〉; être rivé à (figurative) to be tied to 〈*one's work*〉; avoir les yeux rivés sur to have one's eyes riveted on

riverain, ∼e /ʀivʀɛ̃, ɛn/ *nm,f* (of street) resident; (beside river) riverside resident

rivet /ʀivɛ/ *nm* rivet

rivière /ʀivjɛʀ/ *nf* river
■ ∼ de diamants diamond necklace

rixe /ʀiks/ *nf* brawl

riz /ʀi/ *nm* rice

rizière /ʀizjɛʀ/ *nf* paddy field

RMI /ɛʀɛmi/ *nm* (*abbr* = **revenu minimum d'insertion**) *minimum benefit paid to those with no other source of income*

RN /ɛʀɛn/ *nf* (*abbr* = **route nationale**) ≈ A road (GB), highway (US)

robe /ʀɔb/ *nf* (a) (gen) dress
(b) (of lawyer) gown
(c) (of horse) coat; (of wine) colour (GB)
■ ∼ de chambre dressing gown, robe (US)

robinet /ʀɔbinɛ/ *nm* (for water) tap (GB), faucet (US); (for gas) tap (GB), valve (US)

robot /ʀɔbo/ *nm* robot; ∼ ménager food processor

robotique /ʀɔbɔtik/ *nf* robotics

robotisation /ʀɔbɔtizasjɔ̃/ *nf* automation

robotiser /ʀɔbɔtize/ [1] *vtr* to automate

robuste /ʀɔbyst/ *adj* robust, sturdy; 〈*appetite*〉 healthy; 〈*faith*〉 strong

robustesse /ʀɔbystɛs/ *nf* (a) robustness, sturdiness
(b) soundness

roc /ʀɔk/ *nm* rock

rocade /ʀɔkad/ *nf* bypass; ring road

rocaille /ʀɔkaj/ *nf* (a) loose stones
(b) rock garden

rocailleux, -euse /ʀɔkajø, øz/ *adj*
(a) 〈*terrain*〉 rocky, stony
(b) 〈*voice*〉 harsh, grating

rocambolesque /ʀɔkɑ̃bɔlɛsk/ *adj* fantastic, incredible

roche /ʀɔʃ/ *nf* rock

rocher /ʀɔʃe/ *nm* rock

rocheux, -euse /ʀɔʃø, øz/ *adj* rocky

rock /ʀɔk/ *nm* (a) rock (music)
(b) jive

rockeur, -euse /ʀɔkœʀ, øz/ *nm,f* (a) rock musician
(b) rock fan

rococo /ʀɔkoko/ *adj inv* 〈*art, style*〉 rococo

rodage /ʀɔdaʒ/ *nm* (of vehicle, engine) running in (GB), breaking in (US)

rodéo /ʀɔdeo/ *nm* rodeo

roder /ʀɔde/ [1] *vtr* (a) to run in (GB), to break in (US) 〈*engine*〉
(b) to polish up 〈*show*〉; être (bien) rodé 〈*department*〉 to be running smoothly

rôder /ʀode/ [1] *vi* to prowl; ∼ autour de qn to hang around sb

rôdeur, -euse /ʀodœʀ, øz/ *nm,f* prowler

rogne /ʀɔɲ/ *nf* (colloq) se mettre en ∼ to get mad (colloq)

rogner /ʀɔɲe/ [1] *vtr* (a) to trim 〈*angle*〉; to clip 〈*nails*〉
(b) ∼ sur to cut down on 〈*budget*〉

rognon /ʀɔɲɔ̃/ *nm* (Culin) kidney

roi /ʀwa/ *nm* king
■ les ∼s mages the (three) wise men
IDIOMS tirer les Rois to eat Twelfth Night cake

roitelet /ʀwatlɛ/ *nm* (a) wren
(b) kinglet

rôle /ʀol/ *nm* (a) (for actor) part, role; premier ∼ lead, leading role
(b) (gen) role; (of heart, part of body) function, role; à tour de ∼ in turn
IDIOMS avoir le beau ∼ (colloq) to have the easy job

romain, ∼e[1] /ʀɔmɛ̃, ɛn/ *adj* (a) Roman
(b) l'Église ∼e the Roman Catholic Church
(c) caractères ∼s roman typeface

romaine[2] /ʀɔmɛn/ *nf* cos lettuce

r

roman, **~e** /ʀɔmɑ̃, an/ **1** adj **(a)** ⟨church, style⟩ Romanesque; (in England) Norman
(b) ⟨language⟩ Romance
2 nm **(a)** novel; **~ courtois** courtly romance
(b) (style) **le ~** the Romanesque
■ **~ policier** detective story

romance /ʀɔmɑ̃s/ nf **(a)** love song
(b) romance

romancer /ʀɔmɑ̃se/ [12] vtr **(a)** to romanticize
(b) to fictionalize

romanche /ʀɔmɑ̃ʃ/ nm, adj Romans(c)h

romancier, **-ière** /ʀɔmɑ̃sje, ɛʀ/ nm,f novelist

romand, **~e** /ʀɔmɑ̃, ɑ̃d/ adj ⟨Swiss person⟩ French-speaking

romanesque /ʀɔmanɛsk/ **1** adj
(a) ⟨person⟩ romantic
(b) ⟨narrative, story⟩ fictional
2 nm **(a)** **le ~** fiction
(b) **le ~ d'une situation** the fantastical aspect of a situation

roman-feuilleton, pl **romans-feuilletons** /ʀɔmɑ̃fœjtɔ̃/ nm serial

roman-fleuve, pl **romans-fleuves** /ʀɔmɑ̃flœv/ nm roman-fleuve, saga

roman-photo, pl **romans-photos** /ʀɔmɑ̃foto/ nm photo-story

romantique /ʀɔmɑ̃tik/ adj, nmf romantic

romantisme /ʀɔmɑ̃tism/ nm romanticism

romarin /ʀɔmaʀɛ̃/ nm rosemary

rombière /ʀɔ̃bjɛʀ/ nf (slang) **une ~** an old bag (colloq)

rompre /ʀɔ̃pʀ/ [53] **1** vtr (gen) to break, to break off ⟨relationship⟩; to upset ⟨equilibrium⟩; to disrupt ⟨harmony⟩; to end ⟨isolation⟩
2 vi **~ avec** to break with ⟨habit, tradition⟩; to make a break from ⟨past⟩; to break away from ⟨background⟩; to break up with ⟨fiancé⟩
3 **se rompre** v refl (+ v être) to break

rompu, **~e** /ʀɔ̃py/ **1** pp ▶ ROMPRE
2 pp adj **~ (de fatigue)** worn-out

romsteck /ʀɔmstɛk/ nm rump steak

ronce /ʀɔ̃s/ nf bramble

ronchon, **-onne** /ʀɔ̃ʃɔ̃, ɔn/ adj (colloq) grumpy (colloq)

ronchonner /ʀɔ̃ʃɔne/ [1] vi (colloq) to grumble

rond, **~e¹** /ʀɔ̃, ʀɔ̃d/ **1** adj **(a)** ⟨object, hole⟩ round
(b) ⟨writing⟩ rounded; ⟨face⟩ round; ⟨person⟩ plump
(c) ⟨number⟩ round
(d) (colloq) drunk
2 nm circle; **faire des ~s dans l'eau** to make ripples in the water
■ **~ de serviette** napkin ring
IDIOMS **ouvrir des yeux ~s** to be wide-eyed with astonishment

ronde² /ʀɔ̃d/ **1** adj f ▶ ROND 1
2 nf **(a)** round dance; **entrer dans la ~** to join the dance
(b) (of policeman) patrol; (of soldiers) watch

(c) (Mus) semibreve (GB), whole note (US)
3 **à la ronde** phr around

rondelle /ʀɔ̃dɛl/ nf **(a)** slice
(b) (Tech) washer

rondement /ʀɔ̃dmɑ̃/ adv promptly

rondeur /ʀɔ̃dœʀ/ nf **(a)** roundness
(b) curve

rondin /ʀɔ̃dɛ̃/ nm log

rondouillard, **~e** /ʀɔ̃dujaʀ, aʀd/ adj (colloq) tubby (colloq)

rond-point, pl **ronds-points** /ʀɔ̃pwɛ̃/ nm roundabout (GB), traffic circle (US)

ronflant, **~e** /ʀɔ̃flɑ̃, ɑ̃t/ adj **(a)** ⟨stove⟩ roaring
(b) ⟨style⟩ high-flown

ronflement /ʀɔ̃fləmɑ̃/ nm **(a)** snore
(b) (of engine) purr

ronfler /ʀɔ̃fle/ [1] vi **(a)** ⟨sleeper⟩ to snore; ⟨engine⟩ to purr
(b) (colloq) to be fast asleep

ronger /ʀɔ̃ʒe/ [13] **1** vtr **(a)** ⟨mouse, dog⟩ to gnaw; ⟨worms⟩ to eat into; ⟨caterpillar⟩ to eat away
(b) ⟨acid, rust⟩ to erode
(c) ⟨disease⟩ to wear down
2 **se ronger** v refl (+ v être) **se ~ les ongles** to bite one's nails
IDIOMS **se ~ les sangs** (colloq) to worry oneself sick

rongeur /ʀɔ̃ʒœʀ/ nm rodent

ronronnement /ʀɔ̃ʀɔnmɑ̃/ nm (of cat, engine) purring

ronronner /ʀɔ̃ʀɔne/ [1] vi to purr

roquet /ʀɔkɛ/ nm **(a)** yappy little dog
(b) (colloq) bad-tempered little runt (colloq)

roquette /ʀɔkɛt/ nf rocket

rosace /ʀozas/ nf **(a)** rosette
(b) rose window
(c) (decorative motif) rose

rosaire /ʀozɛʀ/ nm rosary

rosâtre /ʀozɑtʀ/ adj pinkish

rosbif /ʀɔsbif/ nm joint of beef (GB), roast of beef (US); (meal) roast beef

rose¹ /ʀoz/ adj (gen) pink; ⟨cheeks⟩ rosy
IDIOMS **la vie n'est pas ~** life isn't a bed of roses

rose² /ʀoz/ nf (Bot) rose
■ **~ des sables** gypsum flower; **~ trémière** hollyhock
IDIOMS **envoyer qn sur les ~s** (colloq) to send sb packing (colloq); **découvrir le pot aux ~s** (colloq) to find out what is going on

rosé /ʀoze/ nm rosé

roseau, pl **~x** /ʀozo/ nm (Bot) reed

rosée /ʀoze/ nf dew

roseraie /ʀozʀɛ/ nf rose garden

rosier /ʀozje/ nm (Bot) rosebush, rose

rosir /ʀoziʀ/ [3] vi ⟨sky⟩ to turn pink; ⟨face⟩ to go pink

rosse /ʀɔs/ **1** adj (colloq) nasty, mean
2 nf **(a)** nag (colloq)
(b) meanie (colloq), nasty person

rosser /ʀɔse/ [1] *vtr* (colloq) to give *‹person›* a good thrashing; to beat *‹animal›*

rosserie /ʀɔsʀi/ *nf* **(a)** nasty remark; mean trick
(b) meanness; nastiness

rossignol /ʀɔsiɲɔl/ *nm* nightingale

rot /ʀo/ *nm* (colloq) burp (colloq); **faire un ~ to burp** (colloq)

rotation /ʀɔtasjɔ̃/ *nf* **(a)** (movement) rotation
(b) (Mil) turnaround
(c) (of crops, staff, shift) rotation

roter /ʀɔte/ [1] *vtr* (colloq) to burp (colloq), to belch

rôti /ʀoti/ *nm* **(a)** joint
(b) roast

rotin /ʀɔtɛ̃/ *nm* rattan

rôtir /ʀotiʀ/ [3] *vtr* to roast *‹meat›*; to toast, to grill *‹bread›*

rôtisseur, -euse /ʀotisœʀ, øz/ *nm,f* seller of roast meat

rôtissoire /ʀotiswaʀ/ *nf* rotisserie, roasting spit

rotonde /ʀɔtɔ̃d/ *nf* (building) rotunda

rotondité /ʀɔtɔ̃dite/ *nf* roundness

rotule /ʀɔtyl/ *nf* (Anat) kneecap
IDIOMS **être sur les ~s** (colloq) to be on one's last legs

roturier, -ière /ʀɔtyʀje, ɛʀ/ *nm,f* commoner

rouage /ʀwaʒ/ *nm* **(a)** (of machine) (cog)wheel; **les ~s** the parts *or* works
(b) (of administration) machinery; **les ~s bureaucratiques** the wheels of bureaucracy

roublard, ~e /ʀublaʀ, aʀd/ *adj* (colloq) crafty, cunning

roublardise /ʀublaʀdiz/ *nf* (colloq) craftiness, cunning

rouble /ʀubl/ *nm* rouble

roucouler /ʀukule/ [1] *vi* **(a)** *‹bird›* to coo
(b) *‹lovers›* to bill and coo

roue /ʀu/ *nf* wheel; **~ dentée** cogwheel
■ **~ motrice** driving wheel; **~ de secours** spare wheel *or* tyre (GB), spare tire (US)
IDIOMS **être la cinquième ~ du carrosse** to feel unwanted; **pousser qn à la ~** to be behind sb; **faire la ~** *‹peacock›* to spread its tail, to display; *‹person›* to strut around; (in gymnastics) to do a cartwheel

rouer /ʀwe/ [1] *vtr* **~ qn de coups** to beat sb up

rouerie /ʀuʀi/ *nf* **(a)** cunning
(b) cunning trick

rouet /ʀwɛ/ *nm* spinning wheel

rouge /ʀuʒ/ **1** *adj* **(a)** (gen) red; *‹person, face›* flushed
(b) *‹beard, hair, fur›* ginger
(c) red-hot
2 *nmf* (communist) Red
3 *nm* **(a)** red; **le ~ lui monta au visage** he/she went red in the face
(b) ~ à joues blusher, rouge; **~ à lèvres** lipstick

(c) le feu est au ~ the (traffic) lights are red; **passer au ~** to jump the lights (GB) *or* a red light
(d) (colloq) red (wine); **gros ~** (colloq) cheap red wine; **un coup de ~** (colloq) a glass of red wine
IDIOMS **être ~ comme une tomate** *or* **une écrevisse** (from embarrassment) to be as red as a beetroot (GB) *or* a beet (US); (from running) to be red in the face

rougeâtre /ʀuʒatʀ/ *adj* reddish

rougeaud, ~e /ʀuʒo, od/ *adj ‹person›* ruddy-faced; *‹face, complexion›* ruddy

rouge-gorge, *pl* **rouges-gorges** /ʀuʒgɔʀʒ/ *nm* robin (redbreast)

rougeoiement /ʀuʒwamɑ̃/ *nm* red glow

rougeole /ʀuʒɔl/ *nf* measles

rougeoyer /ʀuʒwaje/ [23] *vi ‹sun›* to glow fiery red; *‹fire›* to glow red

rouget /ʀuʒɛ/ *nm* red mullet, goatfish (US)

rougeur /ʀuʒœʀ/ *nf* **(a)** redness
(b) redness; flushing
(c) red blotch

rougir /ʀuʒiʀ/ [3] **1** *vtr* to redden
2 *vi* **(a)** to blush; to flush; to go red; **ne ~ de rien** to have no shame
(b) *‹fruit, sky›* to turn red
(c) *‹metal›* to become red hot

rougissant, ~e /ʀuʒisɑ̃, ɑ̃t/ *adj ‹person›* blushing; *‹sky›* reddening

rouille /ʀuj/ **1** *adj inv* red-brown
2 *nf* rust

rouiller /ʀuje/ [1] **1** *vtr* to rust
2 *vi* to rust, to go rusty
3 se rouiller *v refl* (+ *v être*) to get rusty

roulade /ʀulad/ *nf* (Sport) roll

roulant, ~e /ʀulɑ̃, ɑ̃t/ *adj* **table ~e** trolley; **personnel ~** train crew

roulé /ʀule/ *nm* (Culin) roll

rouleau, *pl* **~x** /ʀulo/ *nm* **(a)** roll
(b) breaker, roller
(c) (Tech) roller
(d) roller, curler
■ **~ compresseur** steamroller; **~ à pâtisserie** rolling pin

roulement /ʀulmɑ̃/ *nm* **(a)** (of thunder) rumble; (of drum) roll
(b) (of capital) circulation
(c) rotation; **travailler par ~** to work (in) shifts
(d) (Tech) **~ à billes** ball bearing

rouler /ʀule/ [1] **1** *vtr* **(a)** to roll *‹barrel, tyre›*; to wheel *‹cart›*
(b) to roll up *‹carpet, sleeve, paper›*; to roll *‹cigarette›*
(c) ~ les épaules to roll one's shoulders
(d) (colloq) **~ qn** to cheat sb
2 *vi* **(a)** *‹ball, person›* to roll
(b) *‹vehicle›* to go; **~ à gauche** to drive on the left; **les bus ne roulent pas le dimanche** the buses don't run on Sundays
3 se rouler *v refl* (+ *v être*) **se ~ dans** to roll in *‹grass, mud›*

roulette /ʀulɛt/ *nf* **(a)** caster

(b) roulette

(c) (dentist's) drill

IDIOMS **marcher comme sur des** ∼**s** (colloq) to go smoothly or like a dream

roulis /Ruli/ nm (of boat) rolling; (of car, train) swaying

roulotte /Rulɔt/ nf (horse-drawn) caravan (GB), trailer (US)

Roumanie /Rumani/ pr nf Romania

roupie /Rupi/ nf rupee

roupiller /Rupije/ [1] vtr (colloq) to sleep

roupillon /Rupijɔ̃/ nm (colloq) snooze (colloq), nap

rouquin, ∼**e** /Rukɛ̃, in/ nm,f (colloq) redhead

rouspéter /Ruspete/ [14] vi (colloq) to grumble

rousse /Rus/ adj f ▶ ROUX

rousseur /Rusœr/ nf (of hair, foliage) redness; (of shade) russet colour (GB)

roussi /Rusi/ nm ça sent le ∼ there's a smell of burning; (figurative) there's trouble brewing

roussir /Rusir/ [3] **1** vtr to turn [sth] brown

2 vi **(a)** to go brown

(b) (Culin) faire ∼ to brown

routage /Rutaʒ/ nm sorting and mailing

routard, ∼**e** /Rutar, ard/ nm,f (colloq) backpacker

route /Rut/ nf **(a)** road, highway (US); **tenir la** ∼ ⟨car⟩ to hold the road; (figurative) (colloq) ⟨argument⟩ to hold water; ⟨equipment⟩ to be well-made

(b) road; **il y a six heures de** ∼ it's a six-hour drive; **faire de la** ∼ (colloq) to do a lot of mileage

(c) route; ∼**s maritimes** sea routes

(d) way; **la** ∼ **sera longue** it will be a long journey; **j'ai changé d'avis en cours de** ∼ I changed my mind along the way; **être en** ∼ ⟨person⟩ to be on one's way; ⟨dish⟩ to be cooking; **être en** ∼ **pour** to be en route to; **faire fausse** ∼ to go off course; (figurative) to be mistaken; **se mettre en** ∼ to set off; **en** ∼! let's go!; **mettre en** ∼ to start ⟨machine, car⟩; to get [sth] going ⟨project⟩

■ ∼ **départementale** secondary road; ∼ **nationale** trunk road (GB), ≈ A road (GB), national highway (US)

routier, -ière /Rutje, ɛr/ **1** adj road

2 nm **(a)** lorry driver (GB), truck driver

(b) transport café (GB), truck stop (US)

routine /Rutin/ nf routine

routinier, -ière /Rutinje, ɛr/ adj ⟨person⟩ set in one's ways; ⟨work, life⟩ routine

rouvrir: se rouvrir /Ruvrir/ [32] v refl (+ v être) ⟨door⟩ to open (again); ⟨wound⟩ to open up (again)

roux, rousse /Ru, Rus/ **1** adj ⟨leaves⟩ russet; ⟨hair⟩ red; ⟨person⟩ red-haired; ⟨fur⟩ ginger

2 nm,f red-haired person, redhead

royal, ∼**e**, mpl **-aux** /Rwajal, o/ adj

(a) royal

(b) ⟨present⟩ fit for a king; ⟨tip, salary⟩ princely

(c) ⟨indifference⟩ supreme; ⟨peace⟩ blissful

royalement /Rwajalmɑ̃/ adv **(a)** royally; **être payé** ∼ to be paid handsomely

(b) (colloq) **il se moque** ∼ **de son travail** he really couldn't care less about his work

royaliste /Rwajalist/ adj, nmf royalist.

IDIOMS **être plus** ∼ **que le roi** to be more Catholic than the pope

royaume /Rwajom/ nm kingdom

Royaume-Uni /Rwajomyni/ pr nm le ∼ the United Kingdom

royauté /Rwajote/ nf **(a)** kingship

(b) monarchy

RSVP (written abbr = **répondez s'il vous plaît**) RSVP

ruade /Ryad/ nf **(a)** (by horse) buck

(b) (by person, party) attack

ruban /Rybɑ̃/ nm ribbon; ∼ **adhésif** adhesive tape, sticky tape (GB)

rubéole /Rybeɔl/ nf German measles

rubis /Rybi/ nm inv **(a)** ruby

(b) ruby (red)

rubrique /Rybrik/ nf **(a)** (of newspaper) section; ∼ **mondaine** social column

(b) category

ruche /Ryʃ/ nf **(a)** beehive

(b) hive of activity

rude /Ryd/ adj **(a)** ⟨job, day⟩ hard, tough; ⟨winter⟩ harsh; ⟨ordeal⟩ severe

(b) ⟨material, beard⟩ rough

(c) ⟨features⟩ coarse

(d) **c'est un** ∼ **gaillard** he's a strapping fellow

(e) ⟨opponent⟩ tough

rudement /Rydmɑ̃/ adv **(a)** roughly

(b) (colloq) really

rudesse /Rydɛs/ nf **(a)** harshness, severity

(b) coarseness

rudimentaire /Rydimɑ̃tɛr/ adj **(a)** basic

(b) (Anat) rudimentary

rudiments /Rydimɑ̃/ nm pl **avoir quelques** ∼ **de** to have a rudimentary knowledge of

rudoyer /Rydwaje/ [23] vtr to bully

rue /Ry/ nf street

IDIOMS **ça ne court pas les** ∼**s** (colloq) it's pretty thin on the ground; **descendre dans la** ∼ to take to the street

ruée /Rɥe/ nf rush; ∼ **vers l'or** gold rush

ruelle /Rɥel/ nf alleyway, back street

ruer /Rɥe/ [1] **1** vi ⟨horse⟩ to kick

2 se ruer v refl (+ v être) to rush

IDIOMS ∼ **dans les brancards** to rebel

rugby /Rygbi/ nm rugby; ∼ **à treize** rugby league; ∼ **à quinze** rugby union

rugbyman, pl **rugbymen** /Rygbiman, mɛn/ nm rugby player

rugir /Ryʒir/ [3] **1** vtr to bellow (out), to growl

2 vi ⟨animal, engine⟩ to roar; ⟨wind⟩ to howl

rugissement /ʀyʒismɑ̃/ *nm* (of animal, person) roar; (of wind) howling

rugosité /ʀygozite/ *nf* roughness

rugueux, -euse /ʀygø, øz/ *adj* rough

ruine /ʀɥin/ *nf* (a) (of building, person, reputation, company) ruin; (of civilization) collapse; (of hope) death; **en ~(s)** ruined; **ce n'est pas la ~** (colloq) it's not that expensive
(b) ruin
(c) wreck

ruiner /ʀɥine/ [1] **1** *vtr* (a) to ruin ⟨*person, economy*⟩; **~ qn** to be a drain on sb's resources
(b) to destroy ⟨*health, happiness*⟩
(c) to ruin ⟨*life*⟩; to shatter ⟨*hopes*⟩
2 se ruiner *v refl* (+ *v être*) to be ruined, to lose everything; to ruin oneself

ruineux -euse /ʀɥinø, øz/ *adj* very expensive

ruisseau, *pl* **~x** /ʀɥiso/ *nm* (a) stream, brook
(b) **~ de larmes** stream of tears

ruisseler /ʀɥisle/ [19] *vi* (a) ⟨*water*⟩ to stream; ⟨*grease*⟩ to drip
(b) to be streaming; **~ de sueur** to be dripping with sweat

ruissellement /ʀɥisɛlmɑ̃/ *nm* (of rain) streaming; (of grease) dripping

rumeur /ʀymœʀ/ *nf* (a) rumour (GB)
(b) (of voices, wind) murmur

ruminant /ʀyminɑ̃/ *nm* ruminant

ruminer /ʀymine/ [1] **1** *vtr* (a) to ruminate
(b) to brood on ⟨*misery*⟩; to chew over (colloq) ⟨*idea, plan*⟩
2 *vi* (a) to ruminate
(b) ⟨*person*⟩ to brood

rumsteck /ʀɔmstɛk/ *nm* rump steak

rupestre /ʀypɛstʀ/ *adj* (a) ⟨*plants*⟩ rock
(b) ⟨*paintings*⟩ cave, rock

rupture /ʀyptyʀ/ *nf* (a) (of relations) breaking-off
(b) breakdown
(c) break-up; **lettre de ~** letter ending a relationship
(d) (of dam, dyke) breaking; (of pipe) fracture

rural, ~e, *mpl* **-aux** /ʀyʀal, o/ *adj* ⟨*exodus, environment*⟩ rural; ⟨*road, life*⟩ country

ruse /ʀyz/ *nf* (a) trick, ruse; **~ de guerre** (humorous) cunning stratagem
(b) cunning, craftiness

rusé, ~e /ʀyze/ *adj* cunning, crafty

ruser /ʀyze/ [1] *vi* (a) to be crafty
(b) **~ avec** to trick ⟨*enemy, police*⟩

rush, *pl* **rushes** /ʀœʃ/ **1** *nm* (in race) final burst
2 rushes *nm pl* (of film) rushes

russe /ʀys/ *adj, nm* Russian

Russie /ʀysi/ *pr nf* Russia

rustaud, ~e /ʀysto, od/ *adj* rustic

rusticité /ʀystisite/ *nf* rustic character

rustine® /ʀystin/ *nf* (puncture-repair) patch

rustique /ʀystik/ *adj* rustic, country

rustre /ʀystʀ/ **1** *adj* uncouth
2 *nm* lout

rut /ʀyt/ *nm* rutting season

rutilant, ~e /ʀytilɑ̃, ɑ̃t/ *adj* sparkling; gleaming

Ruanda /ʀwɑ̃da/ *pr nm* Rwanda

rythme /ʀitm/ *nm* (a) rhythm; **marquer le ~** to beat time
(b) (of growth) rate; (of life) pace
■ **~ cardiaque** heart rate

rythmer /ʀitme/ [1] *vtr* (a) to give rhythm to
(b) to regulate ⟨*life, work*⟩

rythmique /ʀitmik/ *adj* rhythmic

Ss

s, S /ɛs/ *nm inv* s, S

s' (a) ▶ SE
(b) ▶ SI¹ 2

sa ▶ SON¹

sabbat /saba/ *nm* (a) Sabbath
(b) witches' Sabbath

sabbatique /sabatik/ *adj* (Univ) sabbatical

sable /sɑbl/ *nm* sand; **~s mouvants** quicksands

sablé, ~e /sable/ **1** *adj* **pâte ~e** shortcrust pastry
2 *nm* shortbread biscuit (GB) *or* cookie (US)

sabler /sable/ [1] *vtr* to grit ⟨*roadway*⟩

IDIOMS **~ le champagne** to crack open some champagne

sablier /sablije/ *nm* hourglass; egg timer

sablonneux, -euse /sablɔnø, øz/ *adj* sandy

sabot /sabo/ *nm* (a) clog
(b) (Zool) hoof

sabotage /sabotaʒ/ *nm* sabotage

saboter /sabɔte/ [1] *vtr* to sabotage

saboteur, -euse /sabɔtœʀ, øz/ *nm,f* (of equipment) saboteur

sabre /sɑbʀ/ *nm* (a) sword
(b) sabre (GB)

sabrer /sɑbʀe/ [1] *vtr* (colloq) to cut chunks out of ⟨*article*⟩

sac /sak/ *nm* (a) (gen) bag
(b) sack
(c) bag(ful), sack(ful)
(d) **mettre à ~** to sack ⟨*city, region*⟩; to ransack ⟨*shop, house*⟩
■ **~ de couchage** sleeping bag; **~ à dos** rucksack, backpack; **~ à main** handbag, purse (US); **~ postal** mail sack; **~ à provisions** shopping bag, carry-all (US)
IDIOMS **l'affaire est dans le ~** (colloq) it's in the bag (colloq); **avoir plus d'un tour dans son ~** to have more than one trick up one's sleeve; **vider son ~** (colloq) to get it off one's chest; **se faire prendre la main dans le ~** to be caught red-handed; **mettre dans le même ~** (colloq) to lump together

saccade /sakad/ *nf* jerk

saccadé, ~e /sakade/ *adj* ⟨*movement*⟩ jerky; ⟨*rhythm*⟩ staccato; ⟨*voice*⟩ clipped

saccager /sakaʒe/ [13] *vtr* (a) to wreck, to devastate ⟨*region*⟩; to vandalize ⟨*building*⟩
(b) to sack

saccharine /sakaʀin/ *nf* saccharin

SACEM /sasɛm/ *nf* (*abbr* = **Société des auteurs, compositeurs et éditeurs de musique**) *association of composers and music publishers to protect copyright and royalties*

sacerdoce /sasɛʀdɔs/ *nm* priesthood

sachet /saʃɛ/ *nm* (of powder) packet; (of herbs, spices) sachet; **~ de thé** tea bag

sacoche /sakɔʃ/ *nf* (a) bag
(b) (on bicycle) pannier (GB), saddlebag (US)

sacquer /sake/ [1] *vtr* (colloq) (a) to sack (colloq), to fire (colloq)
(b) ⟨*teacher*⟩ to mark [sb] strictly
(c) **je ne peux pas le ~** I can't stand the sight of him

sacre /sakʀ/ *nm* (of king) coronation; (of bishop) consecration

sacré, ~e /sakʀe/ *adj* (a) ⟨*art, object, place*⟩ sacred; ⟨*cause*⟩ holy
(b) ⟨*rule, right*⟩ sacred
(c) (colloq) **être un ~ menteur** to be a hell of a liar (colloq)
(d) (colloq) **~ Paul, va!** Paul, you old devil!
IDIOMS **avoir le feu ~** to be full of zeal

sacrement /sakʀəmɑ̃/ *nm* sacrament; **les derniers ~s** the last rites

sacrément /sakʀemɑ̃/ *adv* (colloq) incredibly (colloq)

sacrer /sakʀe/ [1] *vtr* to crown ⟨*king*⟩; to consecrate ⟨*bishop*⟩

sacrifice /sakʀifis/ *nm* sacrifice

sacrifier /sakʀifje/ [1] ① *vtr* to sacrifice
② **sacrifier à** *v+prep* to conform to ⟨*fashion*⟩
③ **se sacrifier** *v refl* (+ *v être*) (a) to sacrifice oneself
(b) (colloq) to make sacrifices

sacrilège /sakʀilɛʒ/ *nm* sacrilege

sacristie /sakʀisti/ *nf* (of catholic church) sacristy; (of protestant church) vestry

sacro-saint, ~e, *mpl* **~s** /sakʀosɛ̃, ɛ̃t/ *adj* sacrosanct

sadique /sadik/ ① *adj* sadistic
② *nmf* sadist

sadisme /sadism/ *nm* sadism

sadomasochisme /sadomazɔʃism/ *nm* sadomasochism

safari /safaʀi/ *nm* safari

safran /safʀɑ̃/ *adj inv, nm* saffron

saga /saga/ *nf* saga

sagacité /sagasite/ *nf* sagacity, shrewdness

sage /saʒ/ ① *adj* (a) wise, sensible
(b) good, well-behaved
(c) ⟨*tastes, fashion*⟩ sober
② *nm* (a) wise man, sage
(b) expert

sage-femme, *pl* **sages-femmes** /saʒfam/ *nf* midwife

sagement /saʒmɑ̃/ *adv* (a) wisely
(b) ⟨*sit, listen*⟩ quietly
(c) ⟨*dress*⟩ soberly

sagesse /saʒɛs/ *nf* (a) wisdom, common sense; (of advice) soundness; **la voix de la ~** the voice of reason
(b) good behaviour (GB)

Sagittaire /saʒitɛʀ/ *pr nm* Sagittarius

Sahara /saaʀa/ *pr nm* Sahara

saignant, ~e /sɛɲɑ̃, ɑ̃t/ *adj* (a) ⟨*meat*⟩ rare
(b) (figurative) (colloq) ⟨*criticism*⟩ savage

saignée /sɛɲe/ *nf* (a) (Med) bloodletting, bleeding
(b) (in budget) hole
(c) (in tree) cut

saignement /sɛɲ(ə)mɑ̃/ *nm* bleeding

saigner /sɛɲe/ [1] ① *vtr* (a) (Med) to bleed
(b) to kill ⟨*animal*⟩ (by slitting its throat); **~ un cochon** to stick a pig
② *vi* to bleed; **~ du nez** to have a nosebleed
IDIOMS **~ qn à blanc** to bleed sb dry; **se ~ (aux quatre veines) pour qn** to make big sacrifices for sb

saillant, ~e /sajɑ̃, ɑ̃t/ *adj* (a) ⟨*jaw*⟩ prominent; ⟨*muscle, eyes*⟩ bulging; ⟨*angle*⟩ salient
(b) ⟨*fact, episode*⟩ salient

saillie /saji/ *nf* (a) projection; **le balcon est en ~** the balcony juts out
(b) (Zool) covering

saillir /sajiʀ/ [28] *vi* (a) to jut out
(b) ⟨*ribs, muscles*⟩ to bulge

sain, ~e /sɛ̃, sɛn/ *adj* (gen) healthy, sound; ⟨*wound*⟩ clean; **~ d'esprit** sane; **~ de corps et d'esprit** sound in body and mind; **~ et sauf** ⟨*return*⟩ safe and sound

saindoux /sɛ̃du/ *nm inv* lard

sainement /sɛnmɑ̃/ *adv* (a) ⟨*live*⟩ healthily
(b) ⟨*reason*⟩ soundly

saint, ~e /sɛ̃, sɛ̃t/ ① *adj* (a) holy; **vendredi ~** Good Friday

(b) ~ **Paul** Saint Paul
2 *nm,f* saint
■ ~**e nitouche** goody-goody (colloq); **la Sainte Vierge** the Virgin Mary

Saint-Barthélémy /sɛ̃baʀtelemi/ *nf* **la ~** the St Bartholomew's Day massacre

saint-bernard /sɛ̃bɛʀnaʀ/ *nm inv* St Bernard

Saint-Esprit /sɛ̃tɛspʀi/ *pr nm* Holy Spirit

sainteté /sɛ̃te/ *nf* saintliness

saint-glinglin: **à la saint-glinglin** /alasɛ̃glɛ̃glɛ̃/ *phr* (colloq) probably never; **rester/attendre jusqu'à la ~** to stay/to wait till the cows come home (colloq)

saint-honoré /sɛ̃tɔnɔʀe/ *nm inv*: cream-filled tart topped with choux and caramel

Saint-Jacques /sɛ̃ʒak/ *pr n* **coquille ~** scallop

Saint-Jean /sɛ̃ʒɑ̃/ *nf* **la ~** Midsummer Day

Saint-Sylvestre /sɛ̃silvɛstʀ/ *nf* **la ~** New Year's Eve

saisie /sezi/ *nf* **(a)** (gen, Law) seizure
(b) keyboarding; ~ **de données** data capture

saisir /seziʀ/ **[3]** **1** *vtr* **(a)** to grab; to seize; ~ **au vol** to catch ⟨*ball*⟩; **'affaire à ~'** 'amazing bargain'
(b) to understand
(c) to catch ⟨*name, bits of conversation*⟩
(d) ⟨*emotion, cold*⟩ to grip ⟨*person*⟩
(e) to strike, to impress ⟨*person*⟩
(f) (Law) to seize ⟨*property*⟩; ~ **la justice d'une affaire** to refer a matter to a court
(g) (Comput) to capture ⟨*data*⟩; to key ⟨*text*⟩
2 **se saisir** *v refl* (+ *v être*) **se ~ de** to catch *or* grab hold of ⟨*object*⟩

saisissant, ~e /sezisɑ̃, ɑ̃t/ *adj* **(a)** ⟨*cold*⟩ piercing
(b) ⟨*effect, resemblance*⟩ striking

saison /sɛzɔ̃/ *nf* (gen) season; **en cette ~** at this time of year; **en toute ~** all (the) year round; **la haute/morte ~** the high/slack season; **prix hors ~** off-season prices

saisonnier, -ière /sɛzɔnje, ɛʀ/ **1** *adj* seasonal
2 *nm,f* (worker) seasonal worker

salace /salas/ *adj* salacious

salade /salad/ *nf* **(a)** lettuce
(b) salad
(c) (colloq) muddle; **raconter des ~s** to spin yarns (colloq)

saladier /saladje/ *nm* salad bowl

salaire /salɛʀ/ *nm* salary; wages

salaison /salɛzɔ̃/ *nf* salt meat

salamandre /salamɑ̃dʀ/ *nf* salamander

salant /salɑ̃/ *adj m* **marais ~** saltern

salarial, ~e, *mpl* **-iaux** /salaʀjal, o/ *adj*
(a) ⟨*policy, rise*⟩ wage
(b) **cotisation ~e** employee's contribution

salarié, ~e /salaʀje/ **1** *adj* ⟨*worker*⟩ wage-earning; ⟨*job*⟩ salaried
2 *nm,f* **(a)** wage earner
(b) salaried employee

salaud /salo/ *nm* (offensive) (slang) bastard (slang)

sale /sal/ **1** *adj* **(a)** (*after n*) dirty
(b) (*before n*) (colloq) ⟨*person*⟩ horrible; ⟨*animal, illness, habit*⟩ nasty; ⟨*weather*⟩ foul, horrible; ⟨*work, place*⟩ rotten; ~ **menteur!** you dirty liar!; **il a une ~ tête** he looks dreadful; **faire une ~ tête** to look annoyed; **un ~ coup** a very nasty blow; **un ~ caractère** a foul temper
2 *nm* **mettre qch au ~** to put sth in the wash

salé, ~e /sale/ *adj* **(a)** salt, salty
(b) salted; ⟨*snack*⟩ savoury (GB)
(c) (colloq) ⟨*bill*⟩ steep

salement /salmɑ̃/ *adv* **(a)** **manger ~** to be a messy eater
(b) (colloq) badly, seriously

saler /sale/ **[1]** *vtr* **(a)** to salt ⟨*food*⟩; ~ **et poivrer** to add salt and pepper
(b) to grit (GB), to salt (US) ⟨*road*⟩

saleté /salte/ *nf* **(a)** dirtiness; dirt; filth; **ramasser les ~s** to pick up the rubbish (GB) *or* trash (US); **faire des ~s** to make a mess
(b) (colloq) **c'est de la ~** (gadget, goods) it's rubbish; **c'est une vraie ~ ce virus!** it's a rotten bug!

salière /saljɛʀ/ *nf* saltcellar, saltshaker (US)

salir /saliʀ/ **[3]** **1** *vtr* **(a)** to dirty; to soil
(b) to sully ⟨*reputation*⟩
2 *vi* ⟨*industry, coal*⟩ to pollute
3 **se salir** *v refl* (+ *v être*) to get dirty, to dirty oneself

salissant, ~e /salisɑ̃, ɑ̃t/ *adj* **(a)** ⟨*colour*⟩ which shows the dirt
(b) ⟨*work*⟩ dirty

salive /saliv/ *nf* saliva

saliver /salive/ **[1]** *vi* to salivate; ~ **devant qch** to drool over sth

salle /sal/ *nf* **(a)** (gen) room; hall; (in restaurant) (dining) room; (in hospital) ward; (in theatre) auditorium; **faire ~ comble** ⟨*show*⟩ to be packed; **en ~** ⟨*sport*⟩ indoor
(b) audience
■ ~ **d'attente** waiting room; ~ **de bains** bathroom; ~ **de cinéma** cinema (GB), movie theater (US); ~ **de classe** classroom; ~ **de concert** concert hall; ~ **d'eau** shower room; ~ **d'embarquement** departure lounge; ~ **des fêtes** village hall; community centre (GB); ~ **de garde** (in hospital) staff room; ~ **de gymnastique** gymnasium; ~ **de jeu(x)** (in casino) gaming room; (for children) playroom; ~ **à manger** dining room; dining-room suite; ~ **de séjour** living room; ~ **des ventes** auction room

salon /salɔ̃/ *nm* **(a)** (gen) lounge; drawing room
(b) sitting-room suite; ~ **de jardin** garden furniture
(c) (trade) show; fair; exhibition; ~ **du livre** book fair
(d) (of intellectuals) salon
(e) (Comput) chatroom

S

■ ~ **de beauté** beauty salon; ~ **de coiffure** hairdressing salon; ~ **d'essayage** fitting room; ~ **de thé** tearoom

salopette /salɔpɛt/ *nf* overalls

salpêtre /salpɛtʀ/ *nm* saltpetre (GB)

salsifis /salsifi/ *nm inv* salsify

saltimbanque /saltɛ̃bɑ̃k/ *nmf* **(a)** street acrobat
(b) entertainer

salubre /salybʀ/ *adj* ‹lodgings› salubrious

salubrité /salybʀite/ *nf* (of air, climate) healthiness; (of dwelling) salubrity
■ ~ **publique** public health

saluer /salɥe/ [1] *vtr* **(a)** to greet ‹person›; ~ **qn de la tête** to nod to sb
(b) to say goodbye to ‹person›
(c) (Mil) to salute
(d) to welcome ‹decision, news›
(e) to pay tribute to ‹memory›

salut /saly/ *nm* **(a)** greeting; ~! hello!, hi!; bye!; ~ **de la tête** nod
(b) salute
(c) salvation

salutaire /salytɛʀ/ *adj* ‹experience› salutary; ‹effect› beneficial; ‹air› healthy

salutation /salytasjɔ̃/ *nf* greeting

salvateur, -trice /salvatœʀ, tʀis/ *adj* saving

salve /salv/ *nf* **(a)** salvo; **tirer une** ~ **d'honneur** to fire a salute
(b) ~ **d'applaudissements** burst of applause

samedi /samdi/ *nm* Saturday

SAMU /samy/ *nm* (abbr = **Service d'assistance médicale d'urgence**) ≈ mobile accident unit (GB), emergency medical service, EMS (US)

sanatorium /sanatɔʀjɔm/ *nm* sanatorium (GB), sanitarium (US)

sanctifier /sɑ̃ktifje/ [1] *vtr* to sanctify

sanction /sɑ̃ksjɔ̃/ *nf* (Law) penalty, sanction; disciplinary measure; (Sch) punishment

sanctionner /sɑ̃ksjɔne/ [1] *vtr* **(a)** to punish
(b) to give official recognition to ‹training›

sanctuaire /sɑ̃ktɥɛʀ/ *nm* **(a)** shrine
(b) sanctuary

sandale /sɑ̃dal/ *nf* sandal

sandwich, *pl* ~**s** *or* ~**es** /sɑ̃dwitʃ/ *nm* sandwich; **(pris) en** ~ sandwiched

sang /sɑ̃/ *nm* **(a)** blood; **être en** ~ to be covered with blood; **se terminer dans le** ~ to end in bloodshed
(b) de ~ ‹brother, ties› blood; **être du même** ~ to be kin
IDIOMS **il a ça dans le** ~ it's in his blood; **mettre qch à feu et à** ~ to put sth to fire and sword; **mon** ~ **n'a fait qu'un tour** my heart missed a beat; I saw red; **se faire du mauvais** ~ (colloq) to worry; **bon** ~! for God's sake! (colloq)

sang-froid /sɑ̃fʀwa/ *nm inv* composure; **garde ton** ~! keep calm!; **de** ~ in cold blood

sanglant, ~e /sɑ̃glɑ̃, ɑ̃t/ *adj* bloody

sangle /sɑ̃gl/ *nf* **(a)** (gen) strap
(b) (of saddle) girth
(c) (of seat, bed) webbing

sangler /sɑ̃gle/ [1] *vtr* to girth ‹horse›

sanglier /sɑ̃glije/ *nm* wild boar

sanglot /sɑ̃glo/ *nm* sob

sangloter /sɑ̃glɔte/ [1] *vi* to sob

sangsue /sɑ̃sy/ *nf* leech

sanguin, ~e¹ /sɑ̃gɛ̃, in/ *adj* blood

sanguinaire /sɑ̃ginɛʀ/ *adj* ‹crime› bloody; ‹person› bloodthirsty

sanguine² /sɑ̃gin/ ⓵ *adj f* ▶ SANGUIN
⓶ *nf* **(a)** blood orange
(b) red chalk drawing

sanguinolent, ~e /sɑ̃ginɔlɑ̃, ɑ̃t/ *adj* blood-stained

sanisette® /sanizɛt/ *nf* automatic public toilet

sanitaire /sanitɛʀ/ ⓵ *adj* ‹regulations› health; ‹conditions› sanitary
⓶ **sanitaires** *nm pl* **les** ~**s** (in house) the bathroom; (in campsite) the toilet block

sans /sɑ̃/ ⓵ *adv* without
⓶ *prep* **(a)** without; **un couple** ~ **enfant** a childless couple; ~ **cela** otherwise
(b) il est resté trois mois ~ **téléphoner** he didn't call for three months; **il est poli,** ~ **plus** he's polite, but that's as far as it goes
(c) on sera dix ~ **les enfants** there'll be ten of us not counting the children; **3 500 francs** ~ **l'hôtel** 3,500 francs not including accommodation
⓷ **sans que** *phr* without; **pars** ~ **qu'on te voie** leave without anyone seeing you
■ ~ **domicile fixe, SDF** of no fixed abode, NFA

sans-abri /sɑ̃zabʀi/ *nmf inv* **un** ~ a homeless person; **les** ~ the homeless

sans-emploi /sɑ̃zɑ̃plwa/ *nmf inv* unemployed person

sans-faute /sɑ̃fot/ *nm inv* faultless performance

sans-gêne /sɑ̃ʒɛn/ *adj inv* bad-mannered

santal /sɑ̃tal/ *nm* sandalwood

santé /sɑ̃te/ *nf* health; **avoir la** ~ to enjoy good health; **se refaire une** ~ to build up one's strength; **avoir une petite** ~ to be frail; **à votre** ~! cheers!; **à la** ~ **de Janet!** here's to Janet!

santon /sɑ̃tɔ̃/ *nm* Christmas crib figure

saoul, ~e = SOÛL

saper /sape/ [1] ⓵ *vtr* to undermine
⓶ **se saper** *v refl* (+ *v être*) (colloq) to dress

sapeur /sapœʀ/ *nm* sapper
IDIOMS **fumer comme un** ~ to smoke like a chimney

sapeur-pompier, *pl* **sapeurs-pompiers** /sapœʀpɔ̃pje/ *nm* fireman

saphir /safiʀ/ *nm* **(a)** sapphire
(b) (on record player) stylus

sapin /sapɛ̃/ *nm* **(a)** fir tree; ~ **de Noël** Christmas tree
(b) deal

saquer /sake/ [1] *vtr* (colloq) = SACQUER

sarbacane /saʀbakan/ *nf* blowpipe

sarcasme /saʀkasm/ *nm* **(a)** sarcasm
(b) sarcastic remark

sarcastique /saʀkastik/ *adj* sarcastic

sarcophage /saʀkɔfaʒ/ *nm* sarcophagus

sardine /saʀdin/ *nf* **(a)** (Zool) sardine
(b) (colloq) tent peg

sarment /saʀmɑ̃/ *nm* vine shoot

sarrasin /saʀazɛ̃/ *nm* buckwheat

sarrau /saʀo/ *nm* smock

sas /sɑs/ *nm inv* **(a)** airlock
(b) (on canal) lock
(c) (in bank) security double door system

satanique /satanik/ *adj* ⟨*smile, ruse*⟩
fiendish
(b) ⟨*cult*⟩ Satanic

satellite /satɛlit/ *nm* satellite

satiété /sasjete/ **1** *nf* satiation, satiety
2 **à satiété** *phr* **(a)** manger à ~ to eat
one's fill
(b) ⟨*say, repeat*⟩ ad nauseam

satin /satɛ̃/ *nm* satin

satiné, ~**e** /satine/ *adj* ⟨*fabric, cloth*⟩
satiny; ⟨*paint*⟩ satin-finish

satire /satiʀ/ *nf* satire

satirique /satiʀik/ *adj* satirical

satisfaction /satisfaksjɔ̃/ *nf* satisfaction;
la ~ de nos besoins the fulfilment (GB) of
our needs

satisfaire /satisfɛʀ/ **[10]** **1** *vtr* (gen) to
satisfy; to fulfil (GB) ⟨*aspiration,
requirement*⟩
2 **satisfaire à** *v+prep* to fulfil (GB)
⟨*obligation*⟩; to meet ⟨*norm, standard*⟩
3 **se satisfaire** *v refl* (+ *v être*) **se ~ de**
to be satisfied with ⟨*explanation*⟩; to be
content with ⟨*low salary*⟩

satisfaisant, ~**e** /satisfəzɑ̃, ɑ̃t/ *adj*
(a) satisfactory
(b) satisfying

satisfait, ~**e** /satisfɛ, ɛt/ *adj* ⟨*customer,
need, smile*⟩ satisfied; ⟨*desire*⟩ gratified;
⟨*person*⟩ happy

saturation /satyʀasjɔ̃/ *nf* (of market)
saturation; (in trains, hotels) overcrowding;
(of network) overloading; **arriver à ~** ⟨*market,
network*⟩ to reach saturation point; ⟨*person*⟩
to have had as much as one can take

saturé, ~**e** /satyʀe/ *adj* ⟨*market*⟩
saturated; ⟨*profession*⟩ overcrowded

saturer /satyʀe/ **[1]** *vtr* to saturate

satyre /satiʀ/ *nm* **(a)** satyr
(b) lecher

sauce /sos/ *nf* (Culin) sauce; **(r)allonger la ~**
(figurative) (colloq) to spin things out
IDIOMS **mettre qch à toutes les ~s** to adapt
sth to any purpose

saucière /sosjɛʀ/ *nf* sauceboat

saucisse /sosis/ *nf* sausage; **chair à ~**
sausage meat
■ **~ de Francfort** frankfurter

saucisson /sosisɔ̃/ *nm* (slicing) sausage;
~ à l'ail garlic sausage; **~ sec** ≈ salami

sauf¹ /sof/ **1** *prep* **(a)** except, but
(b) **~ contrordre** failing an order to the
contrary; **~ avis contraire** unless otherwise
stated; **~ erreur de ma part** if I'm not
mistaken
2 **sauf si** *phr* unless
3 **sauf que** *phr* except that

sauf², **sauve** /sof, sov/ *adj* **(a)** safe;
laisser la vie sauve à qn to spare sb's life
(b) ⟨*honour, reputation*⟩ intact

sauf-conduit, *pl* ~**s** /sofkɔ̃dɥi/ *nm* safe-
conduct

sauge /soʒ/ *nf* sage

saugrenu, ~**e** /sogʀəny/ *adj* crazy, potty
(GB) (colloq)

saule /sol/ *nm* willow

saumâtre /somɑtʀ/ *adj* ⟨*water*⟩ brackish;
⟨*taste*⟩ bitter and salty

saumon /somɔ̃/ *nm* salmon

saumure /somyʀ/ *nf* brine

sauna /sona/ *nm* sauna

saupoudrer /sopudʀe/ **[1]** *vtr* **(a)** to
sprinkle
(b) (figurative) to give [sth] sparingly

saur /sɔʀ/ *adj m* **hareng ~** kippered
herring

saut /so/ *nm* **(a)** jump; **faire un petit ~** to
skip; **au ~ du lit** first thing in the morning
(b) (Sport) **le ~** jumping
(c) (colloq) **faire un ~ chez qn** to pop in and
see sb
■ **~ à la corde** skipping; **~ à l'élastique**
bungee jumping; **~ en hauteur** high jump;
~ à la perche pole vault; **~ périlleux** mid-air
somersault

saute /sot/ *nf* **~ de température** sudden
change in temperature; **~ d'humeur** mood
swing

sauté, ~**e** /sote/ **1** *adj* (Culin) sautéed
2 *nm* (Culin) **~ d'agneau** sautéed lamb

saute-mouton /sotmutɔ̃/ *nm inv*
leapfrog

sauter /sote/ **[1]** **1** *vtr* **(a)** to jump
⟨*distance, height*⟩; to jump over ⟨*stream*⟩
(b) to skip ⟨*meal, paragraph*⟩; to leave out
⟨*details*⟩; (Sch) **~ une classe** to skip a year
(c) to miss ⟨*word, turn*⟩
2 *vi* **(a)** to jump; **~ à pieds joints** to jump
with one's feet together; **~ à la corde** to
skip; **faire ~ un enfant sur ses genoux** to
dandle a child on one's knee; **~ sur qn** to
pounce on sb; **~ à la gorge de qn** to go for
sb's throat; **~ au cou de qn** to greet sb with
a kiss
(b) **~ dans un taxi** to jump *or* hop into a
taxi
(c) **~ d'un sujet à l'autre** to skip from one
subject to another
(d) (colloq) **faire ~ une réunion** to cancel a
meeting; **faire ~ une contravention** to get
out of paying a parking ticket
(e) ⟨*bicycle chain, fan belt*⟩ to come off
(f) **faire ~ une serrure** to force a lock; **faire
~ les boutons** to burst one's buttons ⋯⋖

S

(g) ⟨bridge, building⟩ to be blown up, to go up; **faire ~ les plombs** to blow the fuses
(h) (Culin) **faire ~** to sauté ⟨onions⟩
IDIOMS **~ aux yeux** to be blindingly obvious; **et que ça saute!** (colloq) make it snappy! (colloq); **~ au plafond** (colloq) to jump for joy; to hit the roof (colloq); to be staggered

sauterelle /sotʀɛl/ *nf* grasshopper

sauterie /sotʀi/ *nf* party

sautillant, ~e /sotijɑ̃, ɑ̃t/ *adj* ⟨rhythm, gait⟩ bouncy; ⟨bird⟩ hopping

sautiller /sotije/ [1] *vi* **(a)** ⟨bird⟩ to hop
(b) ⟨child⟩ to skip along; to jump up and down

sauvage /sovaʒ/ **1** *adj* **(a)** ⟨animal, plant⟩ wild; ⟨tribe⟩ primitive
(b) ⟨behaviour⟩ savage, wild; ⟨struggle⟩ fierce
(c) unsociable
(d) illegal
2 *nmf* **(a)** savage
(b) unsociable person, loner

sauvagement /sovaʒmɑ̃/ *adv* savagely

sauvageon, -onne /sovaʒɔ̃, ɔn/ *nm,f* wild child

sauvagerie /sovaʒʀi/ *nf* savagery

sauve ▶ SAUF²

sauvegarde /sovɡaʀd/ *nf* (of heritage, peace, values) maintenance; (of rights) protection

sauvegarder /sovɡaʀde/ [1] *vtr* **(a)** to safeguard
(b) (Comput) to save; to back [sth] up ⟨file⟩

sauve-qui-peut /sovkipø/ *nm inv* stampede

sauver /sove/ [1] **1** *vtr* **(a)** (gen) to save; **~ la vie à qn** to save sb's life; **elle est sauvée** ⟨ill person⟩ she has pulled through (colloq)
(b) to salvage ⟨goods⟩
(c) ce qui le sauve à mes yeux, c'est sa générosité his redeeming feature for me is his generosity
2 se sauver *v refl* (+ *v être*) **(a)** to escape; to run away; (from danger) to run
(b) (colloq) **il faut que je me sauve** I've got to rush off now
IDIOMS **~ la situation** to save the day; **sauve qui peut!** run for your life!

sauvetage /sovtaʒ/ *nm* rescue; **cours de ~** life-saving training

sauveteur /sovtœʀ/ *nm* rescuer

sauvette: à la sauvette /alasovɛt/ *phr*
(a) ⟨prepare, sign⟩ in a rush
(b) ⟨film, record⟩ on the sly

sauveur /sovœʀ/ *nm* saviour (GB)

savamment /savamɑ̃/ *adv* **(a)** learnedly, eruditely
(b) skilfully (GB)

savane /savan/ *nf* savannah

savant, ~e /savɑ̃, ɑ̃t/ **1** *adj* **(a)** ⟨person⟩ learned, erudite
(b) ⟨study⟩ scholarly; ⟨calculation⟩ complicated
(c) ⟨manoeuvre⟩ clever; ⟨direction⟩ skilful (GB)
(d) ⟨animal⟩ performing

2 *nm,f* scholar
3 *nm* scientist

savate /savat/ *nf* (colloq) **(a)** old slipper
(b) old shoe

saveur /savœʀ/ *nf* flavour (GB); **sans ~** tasteless

savoir¹ /savwaʀ/ [47] **1** *vtr* **(a)** to know ⟨truth, answer⟩; **vous n'êtes pas sans ~ que** you are no doubt aware that; **va** *or* **allez ~!** who knows!; **est-ce que je sais, moi!** how should I know!; **pour autant que je sache** as far as I know; **comment l'as-tu su?** how did you find out?; **je l'ai su par elle** she told me about it; **ne ~ que faire pour...** to be at a loss as to how to...; **sachant que** knowing that; given that; **qui vous savez** you-know-who; **je ne sais qui** somebody or other; **tu en sais des choses!** you really know a thing or two!
(b) ~ faire to know how to do; **je sais conduire** I can drive; **~ écouter** to be a good listener; **elle sait y faire avec les hommes** she knows how to handle men
2 se savoir *v refl* (+ *v être*) **ça se saurait** people would know about it
3 à savoir *phr* that is to say
IDIOMS **ne pas ~ où donner de la tête** not to know whether one is coming or going

savoir² /savwaʀ/ *nm* **(a)** learning
(b) knowledge
(c) body of knowledge

savoir-faire /savwaʀfɛʀ/ *nm inv* know-how

savoir-vivre /savwaʀvivʀ/ *nm inv* manners

savon /savɔ̃/ *nm* **(a)** soap; **~ de Marseille** household soap
(b) (bar of) soap
IDIOMS **passer un ~ à qn** (colloq) to give sb a telling-off

savonner /savɔne/ [1] *vtr* to soap

savonnette /savɔnɛt/ *nf* small cake of soap

savourer /savuʀe/ [1] *vtr* to savour (GB)

savoureux, -euse /savuʀø, øz/ *adj* ⟨dish⟩ tasty; ⟨anecdote⟩ juicy

saxophone /saksɔfɔn/ *nm* saxophone

saxophoniste /saksɔfɔnist/ *nmf* saxophonist

scabreux, -euse /skabʀø, øz/ *adj* obscene

scalp /skalp/ *nm* **(a)** scalp
(b) scalping

scalpel /skalpɛl/ *nm* scalpel

scalper /skalpe/ [1] *vtr* to scalp

scandale /skɑ̃dal/ *nm* scandal; **faire (un** *or* **du) ~** (gen) to cause a scandal; ⟨person⟩ to cause a fuss; **la presse à ~** the gutter press; **c'est un ~!** it's scandalous!

scandaleux, -euse /skɑ̃dalø, øz/ *adj* scandalous, outrageous

scandaliser /skɑ̃dalize/ [1] **1** *vtr* to outrage
2 se scandaliser *v refl* (+ *v être*) to be shocked

scander /skɑ̃de/ [1] *vtr* **(a)** to scan
(b) to chant ⟨*slogan, name*⟩
scandinave /skɑ̃dinav/ *adj* Scandinavian
scanneur /skanœʀ/ *nm* scanner
scaphandre /skafɑ̃dʀ/ *nm* **(a)** deep-sea
diving suit
(b) spacesuit
scaphandrier /skafɑ̃dʀije/ *nm* deep-sea
diver
scarabée /skaʀabe/ *nm* **(a)** beetle
(b) scarab
scarlatine /skaʀlatin/ *nf* scarlet fever
scatologie /skatɔlɔʒi/ *nf* scatology
sceau, *pl* ∼**x** /so/ *nm* **(a)** seal; **sous le** ∼
du secret in strictest secrecy
(b) stamp, hallmark
scélérat, ∼**e** /seleʀa, at/ *nm,f* villain
scellé /sele/ *nm* seal; **apposer les** ∼**s** to
affix seals
sceller /sele/ [1] *vtr* **(a)** to seal
(b) to fix [sth] securely ⟨*shelf, bar*⟩
scénario /senaʀjo/ *nm* **(a)** screenplay,
script
(b) scenario; ∼ **catastrophe** nightmare
scenario
scénariste /senaʀist/ *nmf* scriptwriter
scène /sɛn/ *nf* **(a)** (in theatre) stage; **entrer
en** ∼ to come on
(b) scene; **la** ∼ **se passe à Paris** the scene is
set in Paris
(c) **quitter la** ∼ to give up the stage; **mettre
en** ∼ to stage ⟨*play*⟩; to direct ⟨*film*⟩
(d) scene; **occuper le devant de la** ∼
(figurative) to be in the news
(e) **faire une** ∼ to throw a fit (colloq)
(f) scene; ∼**s de panique** scenes of panic
■ ∼ **de ménage** domestic dispute
scepticisme /sɛptisism/ *nm* scepticism
(GB), skepticism (US)
sceptique /sɛptik/ **1** *adj* sceptical (GB),
skeptical (US); **laisser qn** ∼ to leave sb
unconvinced
2 *nmf* sceptic (GB), skeptic (US)
sceptre /sɛptʀ/ *nm* sceptre (GB)
schéma /ʃema/ *nm* **(a)** diagram
(b) outline
(c) pattern
schématique /ʃematik/ *adj* **(a)** ⟨*vision,
argument*⟩ simplistic
(b) schematic
schématiser /ʃematize/ [1] *vtr* to
simplify
schizophrénie /skizɔfʀeni/ *nf*
schizophrenia
sciatique /sjatik/ **1** *adj* **nerf** ∼ sciatic
nerve
2 *nf* **avoir une** ∼ to have sciatica
scie /si/ *nf* saw; ∼ **sauteuse** jigsaw
sciemment /sjamɑ̃/ *adv* knowingly
science /sjɑ̃s/ *nf* **(a)** science
(b) knowledge
■ ∼**s naturelles** ≈ biology (*sg*); ∼**s occultes**
black arts; **Sciences Po** (colloq) *Institute of
Political Science*

science-fiction /sjɑ̃sfiksjɔ̃/ *nf* science
fiction
scientifique /sjɑ̃tifik/ **1** *adj* scientific
2 *nmf* scientist
scier /sje/ [2] *vtr* **(a)** to saw
(b) (colloq) to stun
scierie /siʀi/ *nf* sawmill
scinder /sɛ̃de/ [1] **1** *vtr* to split ⟨*group*⟩
2 **se scinder** *v refl* (+ *v être*) to split up
scintillant, ∼**e** /sɛ̃tijɑ̃, ɑ̃t/ *adj* twinkling
scintiller /sɛ̃tije/ [1] *vi* ⟨*diamond*⟩ to
sparkle; ⟨*star*⟩ to twinkle; ⟨*water*⟩ to glisten
scission /sisjɔ̃/ *nf* **(a)** split, schism
(b) fission
sciure /sjyʀ/ *nf* ∼ **(de bois)** sawdust
sclérose /skleʀoz/ *nf* **(a)** (Med) sclerosis
(b) fossilization, ossification
■ ∼ **en plaques** multiple sclerosis, MS
scléroser /skleʀoze/ [1] **1** *vtr* (Med) to
sclerose
2 **se scléroser** *v refl* (+ *v être*)
(a) ⟨*institution, person*⟩ to become fossilized
(b) (Med) ⟨*tissue*⟩ to become hardened
scolaire /skɔlɛʀ/ *adj* ⟨*holidays, book*⟩
school; ⟨*reform, publication*⟩ educational;
⟨*failure*⟩ academic; **établissement** ∼ school
scolarisation /skɔlaʀizasjɔ̃/ *nf* schooling
scolariser /skɔlaʀize/ [1] *vtr* to send [sb]
to school
scolarité /skɔlaʀite/ *nf* **(a)** schooling;
durant ma ∼ when I was at school; **la** ∼
obligatoire compulsory education
(b) (in university) registrar's office
scoliose /skɔljoz/ *nf* scoliosis
scooter /skutœʀ/ *nm* (motor) scooter
score /skɔʀ/ *nm* **(a)** (Sch, Sport) score; ∼ **nul**
draw (GB), tie (US)
(b) results
scorie /skɔʀi/ *nf* **(a)** scoria
(b) slag
scorpion /skɔʀpjɔ̃/ *nm* (Zool) scorpion
Scorpion /skɔʀpjɔ̃/ *pr nm* Scorpio
scotch, *pl* ∼**es** /skɔtʃ/ *nm* **(a)** Scotch
(whisky)
(b) ®Sellotape® (GB), Scotch® tape (US)
scotcher /skɔtʃe/ [1] *vtr* to Sellotape®
(GB), to Scotch-tape® (US)
scout, ∼**e** /skut/ **1** *adj* scout
2 *nm,f* boy scout/girl scout
scribe /skʀib/ *nm* scribe
scribouillard, ∼**e** /skʀibujaʀ, aʀd/ *nm,f*
(colloq) pen pusher (GB) (colloq), pencil pusher
(US)
script /skʀipt/ *nm* **(a)** **écrire en** ∼ to print
(b) script
scripte /skʀipt/ *nmf* continuity man/girl
scrupule /skʀypyl/ *nm* scruple
scrupuleusement /skʀypyløzmɑ̃/ *adv*
scrupulously
scrupuleux, **-euse** /skʀypylø, øz/ *adj*
scrupulous; **peu** ∼ unscrupulous
scrutateur, **-trice** /skʀytatœʀ, tʀis/ *adj*
searching

S

scruter /skʀyte/ [1] *vtr* to scan ‹horizon›; to scrutinize ‹object›; to examine ‹ground, person›

scrutin /skʀytɛ̃/ *nm* (a) ballot; **dépouiller le ~** to count the votes
(b) polls; **jour du ~** polling day; **mode de ~** electoral system
■ **~ majoritaire** election by majority vote

sculpter /skylte/ [1] *vtr* to sculpt, to carve

sculpteur /skyltœʀ/ *nm* sculptor

sculptural, ~e, *mpl* **-aux** /skyltyʀal, o/ *adj* ‹art› sculptural; ‹shape, beauty› statuesque

sculpture /skyltyʀ/ *nf* sculpture; **la ~ sur bois** woodcarving

SDF /ɛsdeɛf/ ▶ SANS

se (**s'** *before vowel or mute h*) /sə, s/ *pron*
(a) oneself; himself; herself; itself; **il ~ regarde** he's looking at himself
(b) each other; **ils ~ regardaient** they were looking at each other
(c) **~ ronger les ongles** to bite one's nails; **il ~ lave les pieds** he's washing his feet
(d) **elle ~ comporte honorablement** she behaves honourably (GB); **l'écart ~ creuse** the gap is widening
(e) **les exemples ~ comptent sur les doigts de la main** the examples can be counted on the fingers of ones hand
(f) **comment ~ fait-il que...?** how come...?, how is it that...?

séance /seɑ̃s/ *nf* (a) (of court, parliament) session; (of committee) meeting; **~ tenante** immediately
(b) (in cinema) show
■ **~ de spiritisme** séance

seau, *pl* **~x** /so/ *nm* bucket, pail

sébile /sebil/ *nf* begging bowl

sec, sèche /sɛk, sɛʃ/ **1** *adj* (a) ‹weather, hair› dry; ‹fruit› dried
(b) ‹wine, cider› dry; **boire son gin ~** to like one's gin straight
(c) ‹person, statement› terse; ‹letter› curt
(d) ‹noise› sharp
2 *nm* **être à ~** ‹river› to have dried up; (figurative) ‹person› to have no money
3 *adv* (a) **se briser ~** to snap
(b) (colloq) ‹rain, drink› a lot
IDIOMS **aussi ~** (colloq) immediately

sécateur /sekatœʀ/ *nm* clippers

sécession /sesesjɔ̃/ *nf* secession

sèche /sɛʃ/ *adj f* ▶ SEC 1

sèche-cheveux /sɛʃʃəvø/ *nm inv* hairdrier (GB), blow-dryer

sèche-linge /sɛʃlɛ̃ʒ/ *nm inv* tumble-drier (GB), tumble-dryer

sèchement /sɛʃmɑ̃/ *adv* drily, coldly

sécher /seʃe/ [1] **1** *vtr* (a) (gen) to dry
(b) (colloq) to skip ‹class›
2 *vi* ‹hair, clothes› to dry; ‹mud› to dry up; **fleur séchée** dried flower; **mettre des vêtements à ~** to hang clothes up to dry

sécheresse /seʃʀɛs/ *nf* (a) drought
(b) dryness

(c) curt manner

séchoir /seʃwaʀ/ *nm* (a) clothes airer, clothes horse
(b) tumble-drier (GB), tumble-dryer

second, ~e¹ /səgɔ̃, ɔ̃d/ **1** *adj*
(a) (in sequence, series) second; **chapitre ~** chapter two; **en ~ lieu** secondly; **dans un ~ temps...** subsequently...; **c'est à prendre au ~ degré** it is not to be taken literally
(b) (in hierarchy) second; **de ~ ordre** second-rate; **politicien de ~ plan** minor politician; **jouer un ~ rôle** (in theatre) to play a supporting role; **jouer les ~s rôles** (figurative) to play second fiddle
2 *nm,f* second one
3 *nm* (a) second-in-command
(b) second floor (GB), third floor (US)
4 **en second** *phr* ‹arrive, leave› second

secondaire /səgɔ̃dɛʀ/ **1** *adj* (a) secondary
(b) minor
(c) (Sch) **école ~** secondary school (GB), high school (US)
(d) **effets ~s** side effects
2 *nm* (Sch) secondary school (GB) or high school (US) education

seconde² /səgɔ̃d/ **1** *adj f* ▶ SECOND 1
2 *nf* (a) ▶ SECOND 2
(b) second; **en une fraction de ~** in a split second
(c) (Sch) *fifth year of secondary school, age 15–16*
(d) **billet de ~** second-class ticket
(e) (Aut) second (gear)

seconder /səgɔ̃de/ [1] *vtr* ‹person› to assist

secouer /səkwe/ [1] **1** *vtr* (a) to shake ‹bottle, branch, person›; to shake out ‹rug, umbrella›; **~ la tête** to shake one's head; **être un peu secoué** (in car, plane) to have rather a bumpy ride
(b) to shake off ‹dust, snow, yoke›
(c) ‹crisis› to shake ‹person, country›
(d) (colloq) to get [sb] going (colloq)
2 **se secouer** *v refl* (+ *v être*) (a) to give oneself a shake
(b) (colloq) to pull oneself together
(c) (colloq) to wake up, to get moving (colloq)

secourable /səkuʀabl/ *adj* ‹person› helpful

secourir /səkuʀiʀ/ [26] *vtr* (a) to help
(b) to rescue
(c) to give first aid to

secourisme /səkuʀism/ *nm* first aid

secouriste /səkuʀist/ *nmf* first-aid worker

secours /səkuʀ/ **1** *nm inv* help; **au ~!** help!; **appeler** *or* **crier au ~** to shout for help; **porter ~ à qn** to help sb; **le ~ en mer** sea rescue operations; **de ~** ‹wheel› spare; ‹exit› emergency; ‹kit› first-aid; ‹team› rescue; ‹battery› back-up
2 *nm pl* (a) rescuers; reinforcements
(b) relief supplies; supplies; **premiers ~** first aid

secousse /səkus/ *nf* jolt; **~ (sismique)** (earth) tremor

S

secret, **-ète** /səkʀɛ, ɛt/ ﹎1 *adj* **(a)** secret
(b) ⟨person⟩ secretive
﹎2 *nm* **(a)** secret; **ne pas avoir de ∼s pour
qn** to have no secrets from sb; **il n'en fait
pas un ∼** he makes no secret of it
(b) secrecy; **mettre qn dans le ∼** to let sb in
on the secret; **en ∼** in secret; **encore une de
ces gaffes dont il a le ∼** another of those
blunders that only he knows how to make
(c) solitary confinement
■ ∼ **bancaire** bank confidentiality; ∼ **de
fabrication** industrial secret; ∼ **de
Polichinelle** open secret; ∼ **professionnel**
professional confidentiality

secrétaire /s(ə)kʀetɛʀ/ ﹎1 *nmf* secretary
﹎2 *nm* (piece of furniture) secretaire (GB),
secretary (US)
■ ∼ **de direction** personal assistant; ∼ **d'État**
(in France) minister; (in Great Britain, America)
Secretary of State; ∼ **de rédaction** sub-editor
(GB), copy-editor

secrétariat /s(ə)kʀetaʀja/ *nm*
(a) secretarial work
(b) secretariat

secrète ▸ SECRET 1

secrètement /səkʀɛtmɑ̃/ *adv* secretly

sécréter /sekʀete/ [14] *vtr* **(a)** to secrete
⟨sap, bile⟩
(b) to exude ⟨liquid⟩

sécrétion /sekʀesjɔ̃/ *nf* secretion

sectaire /sɛktɛʀ/ *adj, nmf* sectarian

secte /sɛkt/ *nf* sect; faction

secteur /sɛktœʀ/ *nm* **(a)** (Econ) sector;
∼ **tertiaire** service sector; ∼ **d'activité** sector
(b) area, territory; (Mil) sector
(c) (electrical) **le ∼** the mains; **appareil
fonctionnant sur ∼** mains-operated
appliance; **panne de ∼** power failure

section /sɛksjɔ̃/ *nf* **(a)** section; (of party,
trade union) branch; (of book) part
(b) (Sch) stream (GB), track (US)
■ ∼ **d'autobus** fare stage

sectionner /sɛksjɔne/ [1] *vtr* **(a)** to sever
(b) to divide up ⟨organization⟩

sectoriel, **-ielle** /sɛktɔʀjɛl/ *adj* sectoral

sectorisation /sɛktɔʀizasjɔ̃/ *nf* division

sectoriser /sɛktɔʀize/ [1] *vtr* to divide
[sth] into sectors

Sécu /seky/ *nf* National Health Service

séculaire /sekylɛʀ/ *adj* **(a)** ⟨tradition⟩
ancient
(b) ⟨house, tree⟩ hundred-year-old

séculier, **-ière** /sekylje, ɛʀ/ *adj* secular

secundo /sagɔ̃do/ *adv* secondly

sécuriser /sekyʀize/ [1] *vtr* **(a)** to
reassure
(b) to make [sb] feel secure

sécurité /sekyʀite/ *nf* **(a)** security; ∼ **de
l'emploi** job security; **de ∼** ⟨system⟩ security;
⟨reasons⟩ of security
(b) safety; **se sentir en ∼** to feel secure *or*
safe
■ ∼ **routière** road safety; ∼ **sociale** French
national health and pensions organization

sédatif /sedatif/ *nm* sedative

sédentaire /sedɑ̃tɛʀ/ *adj* sedentary

sédentariser /sedɑ̃taʀize/ [1] *vtr* to settle

sédentarité /sedɑ̃taʀite/ *nf* (of population)
settled way of life; (of job) sedentary nature

sédiment /sedimɑ̃/ *nm* sediment

sédimentation /sedimɑ̃tasjɔ̃/ *nf*
sedimentation

séducteur, **-trice** /sedyktœʀ, tʀis/
﹎1 *adj* seductive, attractive
﹎2 *nm,f* **(a)** charmer
(b) seducer/seductress

séduction /sedyksjɔ̃/ *nf* **(a)** charm
(b) seduction; **pouvoir de ∼** (of person) power
of seduction; (of money) lure; (of words)
seductive power

séduire /seduiʀ/ [1] *vtr* **(a)** ⟨person⟩ to
captivate; **il aime ∼** he likes to charm
people
(b) to appeal to ⟨person⟩
(c) ⟨person⟩ to win over
(d) to seduce

séduisant, **∼e** /seduizɑ̃, ɑ̃t/ *adj* ⟨person⟩
attractive; ⟨idea⟩ appealing

segment /sɛgmɑ̃/ *nm* segment

segmenter /sɛgmɑ̃te/ [1] *vtr*, **se
segmenter** *v refl* (+ *v être*) to segment

ségrégation /segʀegasjɔ̃/ *nf* segregation

seiche /sɛʃ/ *nf* cuttlefish

seigle /sɛgl/ *nm* rye; **pain de ∼** rye bread

seigneur /sɛɲœʀ/ *nm* lord; **être grand ∼**
to be full of largesse
■ ∼ **de la guerre** warlord
IDIOMS **à tout ∼ tout honneur** (Proverb) credit
where credit is due

Seigneur /sɛɲœʀ/ *nm* Lord; ∼**!** Good
Lord!

seigneurial, **∼e**, *mpl* **-iaux** /sɛɲœʀjal,
o/ *adj* ⟨home⟩ stately; ⟨manner⟩ lordly

sein /sɛ̃/ *nm* **(a)** (Anat) breast; **les ∼s nus**
topless; **nourrir (son enfant) au ∼** to breast-
feed (one's baby)
(b) **au ∼ de** within

séisme /seism/ *nm* earthquake, seism

seize /sɛz/ *adj inv, pron, nm inv* sixteen

seizième /sɛzjɛm/ *adj* sixteenth

séjour /seʒuʀ/ *nm* **(a)** stay; ∼**s à l'étranger**
(on CV) time spent abroad
(b) (**salle de**) ∼ living room
(c) **un ∼ champêtre** a rural retreat
■ ∼ **linguistique** language study vacation

séjourner /seʒuʀne/ [1] *vi* **(a)** ⟨person⟩ to
stay
(b) ⟨liquid⟩ to remain; ⟨snow⟩ to lie

sel /sɛl/ *nm* **(a)** salt; **gros ∼** coarse salt
(b) (figurative) **la situation ne manque pas de
∼** the situation has a certain piquancy
■ ∼**s de bain** bath salts

sélect, **∼e** /selɛkt/ *adj* (colloq) ⟨club, bar⟩
exclusive; ⟨clientele⟩ select

sélecteur, **-trice** /selɛktœʀ, tʀis/ ﹎1 *adj*
selective
﹎2 *nm* **(a)** (Comput) selector ···⫶

S

(b) (Aut) gear lever, gearshift

sélectif, -ive /selɛktif, iv/ *adj* selective

sélection /selɛksjɔ̃/ *nf* (gen) selection; (for a job) selection process; ~ **à l'entrée** selective entry

sélectionner /selɛksjɔne/ [1] *vtr* to select

self-service, *pl* ~**s** /sɛlfsɛʀvis/ *nm* self-service restaurant

selle /sɛl/ ① *nf* saddle; **remis en** ~ ⟨*player, regime*⟩ firmly (re)established
② **selles** *nf pl* (Med) stools

seller /sele/ [1] *vtr* to saddle

sellette /selɛt/ *nf* **être sur la** ~ to be in the hot seat

selon /səlɔ̃/ *prep* **(a)** according to; ~ **moi, il va pleuvoir** in my opinion, it's going to rain; ~ **les termes du président** in the President's words; **l'idée** ~ **laquelle** the idea that
(b) depending on ⟨*time, circumstances*⟩; **la situation varie** ~ **les régions** the situation varies from region to region; **c'est** ~ (colloq) it all depends

semailles /səmaj/ *nf pl* **(a)** sowing season
(b) seeds
(c) faire les ~ to sow

semaine /s(ə)mɛn/ *nf* **(a)** week
(b) week's wages
IDIOMS vivre à la petite ~ to live from day to day

sémantique /semɑ̃tik/ ① *adj* semantic
② *nf* semantics

semblable /sɑ̃blabl/ ① *adj* **(a)** similar
(b) identical
② *nmf* fellow creature; **eux et leurs** ~**s** they and their kind

semblant /sɑ̃blɑ̃/ *nm* **un** ~ **de légalité** a semblance of legality; **faire** ~ **d'être triste** to pretend to be sad

sembler /sɑ̃ble/ [1] ① *vi* to seem
② *v impers* **il semble bon de faire** it seems appropriate to do; **le problème est réglé à ce qu'il me semble** the problem has been solved, or so it seems to me; **faites comme bon vous semble** do whatever you think best; **elle a, semble-t-il, refusé** apparently, she refused

semelle /s(ə)mɛl/ *nf* sole
■ ~ **compensée** wedge heel; ~ **intérieure** insole
IDIOMS être dur comme de la ~ (colloq) to be as tough as old boots (GB) (colloq) *or* leather (US)

semence /s(ə)mɑ̃s/ *nf* seed

semer /s(ə)me/ [16] *vtr* **(a)** to sow ⟨*seeds*⟩
(b) to sow ⟨*discord, doubt*⟩; to spread ⟨*confusion, panic*⟩
(c) to scatter ⟨*objects*⟩; **semé de difficultés** plagued with difficulties; **ciel semé d'étoiles** star-spangled sky; **on récolte ce qu'on a semé** as you sow so shall you reap
(d) (colloq) to drop ⟨*purse, keys*⟩
(e) (colloq) to shake off ⟨*pursuer*⟩

semestre /s(ə)mɛstʀ/ *nm* (Sch) semester

semestriel, -ielle /səmɛstʀijɛl/ *adj*
(a) twice-yearly; half-yearly
(b) (at university) ⟨*exam*⟩ end-of-semester (GB), final (US); ⟨*class*⟩ one-semester

semeur, -euse /səmœʀ, øz/ *nm,f* sower;
~ **de troubles** troublemaker

semi /səmi/ *pref* ~**-automatic**
semiautomatic; ~**-liberté** relative freedom; ~**-remorque** articulated lorry (GB), tractor-trailer (US)

semi-échec, *pl* ~**s** /səmieʃɛk/ *nm* partial failure

sémillant, ~e /semijɑ̃, ɑ̃t/ *adj* spirited

séminaire /seminɛʀ/ *nm* **(a)** seminar
(b) seminary

séminariste /seminaʀist/ *nm* seminarist

sémiologie /semjɔlɔʒi/ *nf* semiology

sémiotique /semjɔtik/ ① *adj* semiotic
② *nf* semiotics

semis /s(ə)mi/ *nm inv* **(a)** sowing
(b) seedling
(c) seedbed

semonce /səmɔ̃s/ *nf* reprimand; **coup de** ~ warning shot

semoule /səmul/ *nf* semolina; **sucre** ~ caster sugar

sempiternel, -elle /sɑ̃pitɛʀnɛl/ *adj* perpetual

sénat /sena/ *nm* senate

sénateur /senatœʀ/ *nm* senator

sénile /senil/ *adj* senile

sénilité /senilite/ *nf* senility

sens /sɑ̃s/ ① *nm inv* **(a)** direction, way;
dans le ~ **de la largeur** widthways, across;
être dans le bon ~ to be the right way up;
retourner un problème dans tous les ~ to consider a problem from every angle; **courir dans tous les** ~ to run all over the place;
~ **dessus dessous** /sɑ̃d(ə)sydəsu/ upside down; (figurative) very upset; **aller dans le bon** ~ ⟨*reforms*⟩ to be a step in the right direction; **le** ~ **de l'histoire** the tide of history; **nous travaillons dans ce** ~ that's what we are working toward(s)
(b) meaning; **le** ~ **figuré d'un mot** the figurative sense of a word; **employer un mot au** ~ **propre** to use a word literally; **cela n'a pas de** ~ it doesn't make sense; it's absurd
(c) sense; **retrouver l'usage de ses** ~ to regain consciousness; **avoir le** ~ **pratique** to be practical; **ne pas avoir le** ~ **du ridicule** not to realize when one looks silly; **avoir le** ~ **des affaires** to have a flair for business;
n'avoir aucun ~ **des réalités** to live in a dream world
② *nm pl* senses; **plaisirs des** ~ sensual pleasures
■ ~ **giratoire** roundabout (GB), traffic circle (US); ~ **interdit** no-entry sign; one-way street;
~ **obligatoire** one-way sign; ~ **unique** one-way sign; one-way street

sensation /sɑ̃sasjɔ̃/ *nf* feeling, sensation;
aimer les ~**s fortes** to like one's thrills; **la décision a fait** ~ the decision caused a sensation; **un journal à** ~ a tabloid

sensationnel, -elle /sɑ̃sasjɔnɛl/ *adj*
(a) (colloq) fantastic (colloq)
(b) sensational, astonishing

sensé, ~e /sɑ̃se/ *adj* sensible

sensément /sɑ̃semɑ̃/ *adv* sensibly

sensibilisation /sɑ̃sibilizasjɔ̃/ *nf*
(a) **campagne de ~** awareness campaign
(b) (Med) sensitizing

sensibiliser /sɑ̃sibilize/ [1] *vtr* (a) **~ le
public à un problème** to increase public
awareness of an issue
(b) (Med) to sensitize

sensibilité /sɑ̃sibilite/ *nf* (a) sensibility
(b) (in photography) sensitivity

sensible /sɑ̃sibl/ *adj* (a) (gen) sensitive;
être ~ aux compliments to like
compliments; **je suis ~ au fait que** I am
aware that; **un être ~** a sentient being; **je
suis très ~ au froid** I really feel the cold
(b) ⟨skin⟩ sensitive; (because of injury) tender;
⟨limb⟩ sore; **j'ai la gorge ~** I often get a sore
throat
(c) ⟨rise, difference⟩ appreciable; ⟨effort⟩ real;
la différence est à peine ~ the difference is
hardly noticeable

sensiblement /sɑ̃sibləmɑ̃/ *adv*
(a) ⟨reduce, increase⟩ appreciably,
noticeably; ⟨different⟩ perceptibly
(b) ⟨alike⟩ roughly

sensiblerie /sɑ̃sibləri/ *nf* sentimentality

sensitif, -ive /sɑ̃sitif, iv/ *adj* sensory

sensoriel, -ielle /sɑ̃sɔrjɛl/ *adj* sensory;
organe ~ sense organ

sensualité /sɑ̃sɥalite/ *nf* sensuality

sensuel, -elle /sɑ̃sɥɛl/ *adj* sensual

sentence /sɑ̃tɑ̃s/ *nf* (a) sentence
(b) maxim

sentencieux, -ieuse /sɑ̃tɑ̃sjø, øz/ *adj*
sententious

senteur /sɑ̃tœr/ *nf* scent

senti, ~e /sɑ̃ti/ *adj* **bien ~** ⟨words⟩ well-
chosen; ⟨answer⟩ blunt; ⟨speech⟩ forthright

sentier /sɑ̃tje/ *nm* path, track; **hors des
~s battus** off the beaten track

sentiment /sɑ̃timɑ̃/ *nm* feeling; **il est
incapable de ~** he's incapable of emotion;
faire du ~ to sentimentalize; **prendre qn par
les ~s** to appeal to sb's better nature; **les
beaux** *or* **bons ~s** fine sentiments; **être
animé de mauvais ~s** to have bad
intentions; **~s affectueux** *or* **amicaux** best
wishes

sentimental, ~e, mpl -aux /sɑ̃timɑ̃tal,
o/ *adj* sentimental; romantic; **vie ~e** lovelife

sentinelle /sɑ̃tinɛl/ *nf* sentry

sentir /sɑ̃tir/ [30] **1** *vtr* (a) to smell
(b) to feel; **je ne sens rien** I can't feel
anything; **je ne sens plus mes pieds** my feet
are numb
(c) to be conscious of ⟨importance⟩; to feel
⟨beauty, force⟩; to appreciate ⟨difficulties⟩; to
sense ⟨danger, disapproval⟩; **je sens qu'il est**

sincère I feel that he's sincere; **je te sens
inquiet** I can tell you're worried; **se faire ~**
⟨need⟩ to be felt
2 *vi* (a) to smell; **ça sent l'ail** it smells of
garlic
(b) **le poisson commence à ~** the fish is
beginning to smell
(c) to smack of; **ciel nuageux qui sent
l'orage** cloudy sky that heralds a storm
3 se sentir *v refl* (+ *v être*) (a) to feel; **se
~ mieux** to feel better
(b) ⟨effect⟩ to be felt
IDIOMS je ne peux pas le ~ I can't stand
him

seoir /swar/ [41] **1 seoir à** *vtr* ⟨dress⟩ to
suit
2 *v impers* **il sied de faire** it is appropriate
to do

sépale /sepal/ *nm* sepal

séparable /separabl/ *adj* separable

séparation /separasjɔ̃/ *nf* (a) (gen, Law)
separation
(b) (between gardens) boundary; (figurative)
boundary, dividing line
■ **~ de biens** (Law) matrimonial division of
property; **~ de corps** (Law) judicial
separation

séparatisme /separatism/ *nm*
separatism

séparé, ~e /separe/ *adj* (a) **vivre ~** to
live apart
(b) separate

séparément /separemɑ̃/ *adv* separately

séparer /separe/ [1] **1** *vtr* (a) (gen) to
separate; to pull [sb] apart ⟨fighters⟩; **c'est
un malentendu qui les a séparés** they parted
because of a misunderstanding
(b) to distinguish between ⟨concepts, areas⟩
(c) to divide; **tout les sépare** they are worlds
apart
2 se séparer *v refl* (+ *v être*) (a) ⟨guests⟩
to part; ⟨partners, lovers⟩ to split up
(b) **se ~ de** to leave ⟨friend, group⟩; to split
up with; (Law) to separate from ⟨husband,
wife⟩
(c) **se ~ de** to let [sb] go ⟨employee⟩; to part
with ⟨personal possession⟩
(d) to divide; **la route se sépare (en deux)**
the road forks

sépia /sepja/ *adj inv* sepia

sept /sɛt/ *adj inv, pron, nm inv* seven
■ **les ~ Familles** (Games) Happy Families
**IDIOMS tourne ~ fois ta langue dans ta
bouche avant de parler** think before you
speak

septante /sɛptɑ̃t/ *adj inv, pron* seventy

septembre /sɛptɑ̃br/ *nm* September

septennat /sɛptena/ *nm* seven-year term
(of office)

septentrional, ~e, mpl -aux
/sɛptɑ̃trijonal, o/ *adj* northern

septicémie /sɛptisemi/ *nf* blood-
poisoning

septième /sɛtjɛm/ **1** *adj* seventh   ···⟶

2 *nf* (Sch) *fifth year of primary school, age 10–11*

■ le ~ **art** cinematography

septuagénaire /sɛptɥaʒenɛʀ/ *adj* être ~ to be in one's seventies

septuor /sɛptɥɔʀ/ *nm* septet

sépulture /sepyltyʀ/ *nf* **(a)** grave
 (b) burial

séquelle /sekɛl/ *nf* **(a)** after-effect
 (b) repercussion
 (c) consequence

séquence /sekɑ̃s/ *nf* sequence

séquestrer /sekɛstʀe/ [1] *vtr* (gen) to hold ⟨*hostage*⟩; (Law) to confine [sb] illegally

sera /səʀa/ ▶ ÊTRE¹

serai /səʀɛ/ ▶ ÊTRE¹

seraient /səʀɛ/ ▶ ÊTRE¹

sérail /seʀaj/ *nm* **(a)** seraglio
 (b) innermost circle

serais /səʀɛ/ ▶ ÊTRE¹

serait /səʀɛ/ ▶ ÊTRE¹

seras /səʀa/ ▶ ÊTRE¹

serein, **~e** /səʀɛ̃, ɛn/ *adj* ⟨*sky*⟩ clear; ⟨*person, face*⟩ serene; ⟨*criticism*⟩ objective

sereinement /səʀɛnmɑ̃/ *adv* ⟨*look*⟩ serenely; ⟨*speak*⟩ calmly; ⟨*judge*⟩ dispassionately

sérénade /seʀenad/ *nf* **(a)** serenade
 (b) (colloq) racket (colloq), din

sérénité /seʀenite/ *nf* **(a)** (of face, mind) serenity; (of person) equanimity
 (b) (of judge, verdict) impartiality
 (c) (of sky, weather) calmness

serez /səʀe/ ▶ ÊTRE¹

serf, **serve** /sɛʀ, sɛʀv/ *nm,f* serf

sergent /sɛʀʒɑ̃/ *nm* (Mil) (in army) ≈ sergeant

série /seʀi/ *nf* **(a)** series; **catastrophes en ~** a series of catastrophes
 (b) **numéro de ~** serial number; **~ limitée** limited edition; **modèle de ~** (gen) mass-produced model; (car) production model; **numéro hors ~** special issue
 (c) set, collection
 (d) (on television) series
 (e) (Sport) division

■ **~ noire** series of disasters

sérieusement /seʀjøzmɑ̃/ *adv* seriously; considerably

sérieux, **-ieuse** /seʀjø, øz/ **1** *adj*
 (a) serious; **être ~ dans son travail** to be serious about one's work; **avoir des lectures sérieuses** to read serious books
 (b) ⟨*situation, threat*⟩ serious; ⟨*clue, lead*⟩ important; ⟨*offer*⟩ genuine; **'pas ~ s'abstenir'** 'genuine enquiries only'
 (c) reliable
 (d) responsible; **cela ne fait pas très ~** that doesn't make a very good impression
 (e) ⟨*effort, need*⟩ real; ⟨*progress*⟩ considerable; ⟨*handicap*⟩ serious
 2 *nm* seriousness; **garder son ~** to keep a straight face; **perdre son ~** to start to laugh; **se prendre au ~** to take oneself seriously

seriez /səʀje/ ▶ ÊTRE¹

sérigraphie /seʀigʀafi/ *nf* **(a)** silkscreen printing
 (b) silkscreen print

serin /səʀɛ̃/ *nm* (Zool) canary

seriner /səʀine/ [1] *vtr* (colloq) **~ qch à qn** to drum sth into sb

seringue /səʀɛ̃g/ *nf* syringe

serions /səʀjɔ̃/ ▶ ÊTRE¹

serment /sɛʀmɑ̃/ *nm* **(a)** oath; **prêter ~** to take the oath
 (b) vow

■ **un ~ d'ivrogne** an empty promise

sermon /sɛʀmɔ̃/ *nm* **(a)** sermon
 (b) lecture

sermonner /sɛʀmɔne/ [1] *vtr* to lecture, to give [sb] a talking-to

séronégatif, **-ive** /seʀonegatif, iv/ *adj* HIV negative

serons /səʀɔ̃/ ▶ ÊTRE¹

seront /səʀɔ̃/ ▶ ÊTRE¹

séropositif, **-ive** /seʀopozitif, iv/ *adj*
 (a) (gen) seropositive
 (b) HIV positive

séropositivité /seʀopozitivite/ *nf* (HIV antibody) seropositivity

serpe /sɛʀp/ *nf* billhook

serpent /sɛʀpɑ̃/ *nm* (Zool) snake; **~ à sonnette** rattlesnake

serpenter /sɛʀpɑ̃te/ [1] *vi* ⟨*road, river*⟩ to wind

serpentin /sɛʀpɑ̃tɛ̃/ *nm* streamer

serpillière /sɛʀpijɛʀ/ *nf* floorcloth

serre /sɛʀ/ *nf* **(a)** greenhouse
 (b) talon, claw

serré, **~e** /seʀe/ **1** *adj* **(a)** ⟨*screw, nut*⟩ tight; ⟨*skirt, trousers*⟩ tight; **trop serré** too tight
 (b) ⟨*grass*⟩ thick; ⟨*writing*⟩ cramped
 (c) ⟨*deadlines, budget*⟩ tight; ⟨*bend*⟩ sharp; ⟨*control*⟩ strict; ⟨*struggle*⟩ hard; ⟨*debate*⟩ heated; ⟨*match*⟩ close
 (d) ⟨*coffee*⟩ very strong
 2 *adv* ⟨*write*⟩ in a cramped hand; ⟨*knit*⟩ tightly; **il va falloir jouer ~ si...** we can't take any chances if...

serre-livres /sɛʀlivʀ/ *nm inv* book end

serrement /sɛʀmɑ̃/ *nm* **(a)** **~ de main** handshake
 (b) **avoir** *or* **ressentir un ~ de cœur** to feel a pang

serrer /seʀe/ [1] **1** *vtr* **(a)** to grip ⟨*steering wheel, rope*⟩; **~ qn/qch dans ses bras** to hug sb/sth; **~ la main de qn** to shake hands with sb; **~ les poings** to clench one's fists; **ça me serre le cœur de voir ça** it wrings my heart to see that
 (b) to tighten ⟨*knot, screw*⟩; to turn [sth] off tightly ⟨*tap*⟩; **sans ~** ⟨*attach, screw*⟩ loosely
 (c) ⟨*shoes, clothes*⟩ to be too tight
 (d) **~ à droite** to get *or* stay in the right-hand lane; **~ qn de près** to be hot on sb's tail

(e) to push [sth] closer together ⟨*objects, tables*⟩; to squeeze ⟨*person*⟩; **être serrés** to be packed together
(f) to cut ⟨*expenses, prices*⟩
2 se serrer *v refl* (+ *v être*) **(a)** to squeeze up; **ils se sont serrés les uns contre les autres** they huddled together
(b) se ~ dans une jupe to squeeze oneself into a skirt; **nous nous sommes serré la main** we shook hands
(c) avoir la gorge qui se serre to have a lump in one's throat

serrure /sɛRyR/ *nf* lock; **trou de ~** keyhole

serrurerie /sɛRyRRi/ *nf* locksmith's

serrurier /sɛRyRje/ *nm* locksmith

sertir /sɛRtiR/ [3] *vtr* to set ⟨*stone*⟩

sérum /seRɔm/ *nm* serum; **~ de vérité** truth drug

servage /sɛRvaʒ/ *nm* serfdom

servante /sɛRvɑ̃t/ *nf* maidservant

serve ▶ SERF

serveur, -euse /sɛRvœR, øz/ *nm,f* waiter/waitress

servi, ~e /sɛRvi/ **1** *pp* ▶ SERVIR
2 *pp adj* **(a)** 'prends de la viande'—'merci je suis déjà ~' 'have some meat'—'I already have some, thank you'
(b) (colloq) **nous voulions du soleil, nous sommes ~s** we wanted some sunshine and we've certainly got it

serviable /sɛRvjabl/ *adj* obliging, helpful

service /sɛRvis/ **1** *nm* **(a)** favour (GB); **rendre un ~ à qn** to do sb a favour (GB)
(b) (in transport) service; **~ de bus** bus service
(c) être en ~ ⟨*lift*⟩ to be in working order; ⟨*motorway*⟩ to be open; ⟨*bus*⟩ to be running
(d) rendre ~ à qn ⟨*machine*⟩ to be a help to sb; ⟨*shop*⟩ to be convenient (for sb)
(e) service; **être au ~ de son pays** to serve one's country; **travailler au ~ de la paix** to work for peace; **'à votre ~!'** 'don't mention it!', 'not at all!'; **avoir 20 ans de ~ dans une entreprise** to have been with a firm 20 years; **être de** or **en ~** to be on duty; **état de ~(s)** record of service; **pharmacie de ~** duty chemist
(f) (at table) service; **faire le ~** to serve; to act as waiter
(g) (domestic) service; **entrer au ~ de qn** to go to work for sb; **prendre qn à son ~** to take sb on; **escalier de ~** back stairs
(h) department; **~ du personnel** personnel department; **~ des urgences** casualty department (GB), emergency room (US); **les ~s de sécurité** the security services; **chef de ~** (in administration) section head; (in hospital) senior consultant
(i) (Mil) **~** (**militaire**) military or national service
(j) set; **un ~ à thé** a tea set; **~ de table** dinner service
(k) (in church) service
(l) (Sport) service, serve; **être au ~** to serve

2 services *nm pl* services; **se passer des ~s de qn** to dispense with sb's services
■ ~ après-vente after-sales service; **~ d'ordre** stewards; **~ de presse** press office; press and publicity department; **~ public** public service

serviette /sɛRvjɛt/ *nf* **(a) ~** (**de toilette**) towel; **~** (**de table**) (table) napkin
(b) briefcase
■ ~ de bain bath towel; **~ hygiénique** sanitary towel (GB), sanitary napkin (US)

serviette-éponge, *pl* **serviettes-éponges** /sɛRvjɛtepɔ̃ʒ/ *nf* terry towel

servile /sɛRvil/ *adj* servile; slavish

servilement /sɛRvilmɑ̃/ *adv* ⟨*obey, imitate*⟩ slavishly; ⟨*flatter*⟩ obsequiously

servilité /sɛRvilite/ *nf* servility

servir /sɛRviR/ [30] **1** *vtr* **(a)** to serve; **qu'est-ce que je vous sers (à boire)?** what would you like to drink?; **tu es mal servi** you haven't got much; **'Madame est servie'** 'dinner is served, Madam'; **au moment de ~** before serving
(b) ⟨*situation*⟩ to help ⟨*person, cause*⟩; to serve ⟨*interests*⟩; ⟨*person*⟩ to further ⟨*ambition*⟩
(c) to deal ⟨*cards*⟩
2 servir à *v+prep* **(a) ~ à qn** to be used by sb; **~ à qch** to be used for sth; **les exercices m'ont servi à comprendre la règle** the exercises helped me to understand the rule
(b) to come in useful; **cela ne sert à rien de faire** there's no point in doing
3 servir de *v+prep* **~ d'intermédiaire à qn** to act as an intermediary for sb; **~ d'arme** to be used as a weapon
4 *vi* **(a)** (Mil) **~ dans** to serve in
(b) (Sport) to serve
(c) il a servi dix ans chez nous he was in our service for ten years
(d) ⟨*object*⟩ to be used
5 se servir *v refl* (+ *v être*) **(a)** (at table) to help oneself; **se ~ un verre de vin** to pour oneself a glass of wine
(b) (in shop) to serve oneself
(c) se ~ de qn/qch to use sb/sth; **se ~ d'une situation** to make use of a situation
(d) (Culin) to be served

serviteur /sɛRvitœR/ *nm* servant

servitude /sɛRvityd/ *nf* **(a)** servitude
(b) (figurative) constraint

ses ▶ SON¹

sésame /sezam/ *nm* sesame

session /sesjɔ̃/ *nf* **(a)** session
(b) examination session; **~ de rattrapage** retakes
(c) course

set /sɛt/ *nm* (Sport) set
■ ~ de table place mat

seuil /sœj/ *nm* **~** (**de la porte**) doorstep; doorway, threshold

seul, ~e /sœl/ **1** *adj* **(a)** alone, on one's own; **vous êtes ~ dans la vie?** are you ⸱⸱⸱⸦

single?; **elle veut vous parler ~ à ~ or ~e à ~(e)** she wants to speak to you in private; **parler tout ~** to talk to oneself
(b) by oneself, on one's own; **il a mangé un poulet à lui tout ~** he ate a whole chicken all by himself; **ça va tout ~** it's really easy; things are running smoothly
(c) only; **la ~e et unique personne** the one and only person; **pas un ~ client** not a single customer; **l'espion et l'ambassadeur sont une ~e et même personne** the spy and the ambassador are one and the same person; **d'une ~e pièce** in one piece; **à la ~e idée de faire** at the very idea of doing; **ils ont parlé d'une ~e voix** they were unanimous; **elle ~e pourrait vous le dire** only she could tell you
(d) lonely; **c'est un homme ~** he's a lonely man
2 *nm,f* **le ~, la ~e** the only one; **les ~s, les ~es** the only ones; **ils sont les ~s à croire que** they're alone in thinking that

seulement /sœlmɑ̃/ *adv* **(a)** only; **nous étions ~ deux** there were only the two of us; **'nous étions dix'—'~?'** 'there were ten of us'—'is that all?'; **elle revient ~ demain** she's not coming back until tomorrow
(b) **c'est possible, ~ je veux y réfléchir** it's possible, only *or* but I'd like to think about it
(c) **si ~** if only

sève /sɛv/ *nf* **(a)** sap
(b) (figurative) vigour (GB)

sévère /sevɛʀ/ *adj* ‹*look, tone, punishment*› severe; ‹*person, upbringing*› strict; ‹*selection*› rigorous; ‹*judgment*› harsh; ‹*losses*› heavy

sévèrement /sevɛʀmɑ̃/ *adv* severely; harshly; strictly

sévérité /severite/ *nf* **(a)** strictness, harshness
(b) sternness, severity

sévices /sevis/ *nm pl* physical abuse

sévir /seviʀ/ [3] *vi* **(a)** to clamp down
(b) ‹*storm, war*› to rage; ‹*poverty*› to be rife
(c) (figurative) ‹*doctrine*› to hold sway; ‹*phenomenon*› to be rife

sevrage /səvʀaʒ/ *nm* weaning

sevrer /səvʀe/ [16] *vtr* to wean

sexagénaire /sɛksaʒenɛʀ/ *nmf* sixty-year 1-old

sexe /sɛks/ *nm* **(a)** sex; **indépendamment du ~, de l'ethnie, de l'âge** irrespective of gender, race or age; **un bébé de ~ féminin** a female baby
(b) genitals

sexiste /sɛksist/ *adj, nmf* sexist

sexologue /sɛksɔlɔg/ *nmf* sex therapist

sextuor /sɛkstɥɔʀ/ *nm* sextet

sextuplé, ~e /sɛkstyple/ *nm,f* sextuplet

sexualité /sɛksɥalite/ *nf* sexuality

sexué, ~e /sɛksɥe/ *adj* sexed; sexual

sexuel, -elle /sɛksɥɛl/ *adj* (gen) sexual; ‹*education, gland*› sex

seyant, ~e /sejɑ̃, ɑ̃t/ *adj* becoming

SF /ɛsɛf/ *nf* (abbr = **science-fiction**) sci-fi

SFP /ɛsɛfpe/ *nf* (abbr = **Société française de production et de création audiovisuelles**) *TV and video production company*

shaker /ʃekœʀ/ *nm* cocktail shaker

shampooing /ʃɑ̃pwɛ̃/ *nm* shampoo

shampouiner /ʃɑ̃pwine/ [1] *vtr* to shampoo

shampouineur, -euse /ʃɑ̃pwinœʀ, øz/ *nm,f*: trainee hairdresser (who washes hair)

shérif /ʃeʀif/ *nm* sheriff

shetland /ʃetlɑ̃d/ *nm* **(a)** Shetland wool
(b) Shetland pony

shoot /ʃut/ *nm* **(a)** (Sport) shot
(b) (colloq) (of drug) fix (colloq)

shooter /ʃute/ [1] **1** *vi* to shoot
2 se shooter *v refl* (+ *v être*) (colloq) to shoot up (colloq)

short /ʃɔʀt/ *nm* shorts

si¹ /si/ **1** *adv* **(a)** yes; **'tu ne le veux pas?'— '~!'** 'don't you want it?'—'yes I do!'; **il n'ira pas, moi ~** he won't go, but I will
(b) so; **c'est un homme ~ agréable** he's such a pleasant man; **~ bien que** so; so much so that; **rien n'est ~ beau qu'un coucher de soleil** there's nothing so beautiful as a sunset; **est-elle ~ bête qu'on le dit?** is she as stupid as people say (she is)?
2 *conj* (**s'** before **il** or **ils**) **(a)** if; **~ j'étais riche** if I were rich; **~ j'avais su!** if only I'd known!; **vous pensez ~ j'étais content** you can imagine how happy I was!; **~ ce n'est (pas) toi, qui est-ce?** if it wasn't you, who was it?; **il n'a rien pris avec lui ~ ce n'est un livre** he didn't take anything with him apart from a book; **à quoi servent ces réunions ~ ce n'est à nous faire perdre notre temps?** what purpose do these meetings serve other than to waste our time?; **~ tant est qu'une telle distinction ait un sens** if such a distinction makes any sense
(b) **~ tu venais avec moi?** how about coming with me?
(c) whereas

si² /si/ *nm inv* (note) B; (in sol-fa) ti

siamois, ~e /sjamwa, az/ **1** *adj* **(a)** ‹*cat*› Siamese
(b) **des frères ~** male Siamese twins
2 *nm inv* **(a)** (language) Siamese
(b) Siamese cat

sibylle /sibil/ *nf* sibyl

SICAV /sikav/ *nf* (abbr = **société d'investissement à capital variable**) unit trust, mutual fund

sida /sida/ *nm* (abbr = **syndrome immunodéficitaire acquis**) Aids

side-car, *pl* **~s** /sidkaʀ/ *nm* **(a)** sidecar
(b) motorcycle combination

sidéral, ~e, *mpl* **-aux** /sideral, o/ *adj* sidereal

sidérer /sideʀe/ [14] *vtr* (colloq) to stagger (colloq)

sidérurgie /sideʀyʀʒi/ *nf* steel industry

sidérurgique /sideʀyʀʒik/ *adj* steel

siècle /sjɛkl/ nm (a) century; **au Vᵉ ~ après J.-C.** in the 5th century AD; **d'ici la fin du ~** by the turn of the century; **il y a des ~s** (colloq) **que je ne suis venu ici** I haven't been here for ages
(b) age; **le ~ de Louis XIV** the age of Louis XIV

sied ▶ SEOIR

siège /sjɛʒ/ nm (a) seat
(b) **~ (social)** (of company) head office; (of organization) headquarters
(c) (of MP) seat
(d) (Mil) siege
(e) (Anat) seat

siéger /sjeʒe/ [15] vi (a) to sit
(b) to be in session
(c) to have its headquarters

sien, sienne /sjɛ̃, sjɛn/ **[1]** det **cette maison est sienne à présent** the house is now his/hers
[2] le sien, la sienne, les siens, les siennes pron his/hers; **être de retour parmi les ~s** to be back with one's family; to be back among one's own friends; **faire des siennes** ⟨person⟩ to be up to mischief; ⟨computer⟩ to act up

sieste /sjɛst/ nf nap, siesta

sifflant, ~e /siflɑ̃, ɑ̃t/ adj (a) hissing; wheezing
(b) sibilant

sifflement /sifləmɑ̃/ nm (of person, train) whistle; (of kettle, wind) whistling; (of bird, insect) chirping; (of snake) hissing

siffler /sifle/ [1] **[1]** vtr (a) to whistle ⟨tune⟩; to whistle for ⟨dog⟩; to whistle at ⟨person⟩
(b) ⟨referee⟩ to blow one's whistle for ⟨foul⟩
(c) to hiss, to boo
[2] vi (a) (gen) to whistle; ⟨projectile⟩ to whistle through the air; ⟨bird⟩ to chirp; ⟨snake⟩ to hiss
(b) to blow one's whistle

sifflet /siflɛ/ nm (a) whistle; **coup de ~** whistle
(b) (of train) whistle; (of kettle) whistling
(c) hiss, boo
IDIOMS **couper le ~ à qn** (colloq) to shut sb up (colloq)

sifflotement /siflɔtmɑ̃/ nm whistling

siffloter /siflɔte/ [1] vi to whistle away to oneself

sigle /sigl/ nm acronym

signal, pl **-aux** /siɲal, o/ nm signal
■ **~ d'alarme** alarm signal; **~ sonore** (on answerphone) tone

signalement /siɲalmɑ̃/ nm description

signaler /siɲale/ [1] **[1]** vtr (a) **~ qch à qn** to point sth out to sb; to inform sb of sth
(b) **~ à qn que** to remind sb that
(c) to indicate ⟨roadworks, danger⟩
(d) to report ⟨fact⟩
[2] se signaler v refl (+ v être) **se ~ par qch** to distinguish oneself by sth

signalétique /siɲaletik/ adj descriptive; **fiche ~** specification sheet

signalisation /siɲalizasjɔ̃/ nf
(a) signalling (GB)
(b) signals
■ **~ routière** roadsigns and markings

signaliser /siɲalize/ [1] vtr to signpost ⟨road⟩; to mark out and light ⟨runway⟩

signataire /siɲatɛʀ/ nmf signatory

signature /siɲatyʀ/ nf (a) signature
(b) signing

signe /siɲ/ nm sign; **~ astral** star sign; **~ précurseur** omen; **~ distinctif** or **particulier** distinguishing feature; **c'était un ~ du destin** it was fate; **~s de ponctuation** punctuation marks; **faire ~ à qn** to wave to sb; (figurative) to get in touch with sb; **d'un ~ de la main/tête, elle m'a montré la cuisine** she pointed to/nodded her head in the direction of the kitchen; **faire ~ que oui** to indicate agreement
IDIOMS **il n'a pas donné ~ de vie depuis six mois** there's been no sign of him for six months

signer /siɲe/ [1] **[1]** vtr to sign; **il signe son troisième roman** he's written his third novel
[2] se signer v refl (+ v être) to cross oneself

signet /siɲɛ/ nm (Comput) bookmark; **créer un ~ sur** to bookmark ⟨site⟩

signifiant, ~e /siɲifjɑ̃, ɑ̃t/ adj significant

significatif, -ive /siɲifikatif, iv/ adj significant

signification /siɲifikasjɔ̃/ nf (a) meaning
(b) importance

signifié /siɲifje/ nm signified

signifier /siɲifje/ [1] vtr (a) to mean
(b) **~ qch à qn** to inform sb of sth

silence /silɑ̃s/ nm (a) silence; **'un peu de ~ s'il vous plaît'** 'quiet please'; **passer qch sous ~** to say nothing about sth
(b) (Mus) rest

silencieusement /silɑ̃sjøzmɑ̃/ adv silently

silencieux, -ieuse /silɑ̃sjø, øz/ **[1]** adj silent; quiet
[2] nm (a) (on gun) silencer
(b) (on exhaust) silencer (GB), muffler (US)

silex /silɛks/ nm inv flint; **en** or **de ~** flint

silhouette /silwɛt/ nf (a) silhouette; outline
(b) figure; shape

silice /silis/ nf silica

silicium /silisjɔm/ nm silicon

silicone /silikɔn/ nf silicone

sillage /sijaʒ/ nm (a) (of ship) wake; (of plane) vapour (GB) trail; slipstream
(b) (of person) wake

sillon /sijɔ̃/ nm (a) furrow
(b) line
(c) fissure
(d) groove

sillonner /sijɔne/ [1] vtr (a) ⟨roads⟩ to criss-cross; ⟨police⟩ to patrol; **~ la France en voiture** to drive all over France
(b) to furrow

silo /silo/ *nm* silo

simagrée /simagʀe/ *nf* play-acting

simiesque /simjɛsk/ *adj* ape-like

similaire /similɛʀ/ *adj* similar

similarité /similaʀite/ *nf* similarity

similicuir /similikɥiʀ/ *nm* imitation leather

similitude /similityd/ *nf* similarity

simple /sɛ̃pl/ **1** *adj* (a) (gen) simple; **c'est (bien) ~, il ne fait plus rien** he simply doesn't do anything any more
(b) ⟨*decor*⟩ plain; ⟨*person, air*⟩ unaffected
(c) ⟨*origins*⟩ modest
(d) ⟨*worker*⟩ ordinary; **c'est un ~ avertissement** it's just a warning; **le ~ fait de poser la question** the mere fact of asking the question; **par ~ curiosité** out of pure curiosity; **sur ~ présentation du passeport** on presentation of one's passport
(e) ⟨*ice-cream cone, knot*⟩ single
2 *nm* (a) **le prix varie du ~ au double** the price can turn out to be twice as high
(b) (Sport) **~ dames/messieurs** ladies'/men's singles
■ **~ d'esprit** simple-minded

simplement /sɛ̃pləmã/ *adv* (a) simply, merely, just; **vas-y, ~ fais attention** you can go, only be careful
(b) ⟨*dress, live*⟩ simply
(c) easily

simplet, -ette /sɛ̃plɛ, ɛt/ *adj* simple

simplicité /sɛ̃plisite/ *nf* (a) simplicity; **c'est d'une ~ enfantine** it's so easy a child could do it
(b) (of person) unpretentiousness; (of thing) simplicity; **avec ~** simply

simplification /sɛ̃plifikasjɔ̃/ *nf* simplification

simplifier /sɛ̃plifje/ [2] **1** *vtr* to simplify
2 se simplifier *v refl* (+ *v être*) **se ~ la vie** to make life easier for oneself

simpliste /sɛ̃plist/ *adj* simplistic

simulacre /simylakʀ/ *nm* (a) pretence (GB); **~ de procès** mock trial
(b) sham; **~ de justice** travesty of justice

simulateur, -trice /simylatœʀ, tʀis/
1 *nm,f* (a) shammer, faker
(b) malingerer
2 *nm* (Tech) simulator

simulation /simylasjɔ̃/ *nf* (a) simulation
(b) malingering

simuler /simyle/ [1] *vtr* to feign; to simulate

simultané, ~e /simyltane/ *adj* simultaneous

sincère /sɛ̃sɛʀ/ *adj* (gen) sincere; ⟨*friend*⟩ true; ⟨*emotion, offer*⟩ genuine; ⟨*opinion*⟩ honest

sincèrement /sɛ̃sɛʀmã/ *adv* (a) ⟨*think*⟩ really; ⟨*regret, thank, speak*⟩ sincerely
(b) frankly

sincérité /sɛ̃seʀite/ *nf* sincerity; honesty; genuineness

sinécure /sinekyʀ/ *nf* sinecure

sine qua non /sinekwanɔn/ *phr* **condition ~** sine qua non

singe /sɛ̃ʒ/ *nm* (a) monkey; ape; **les grands ~s** the apes
(b) mimic; **faire le ~** to clown around

singer /sɛ̃ʒe/ [13] *vtr* to ape; to feign

singeries /sɛ̃ʒʀi/ *nf pl* antics; **faire des ~** to monkey around; to pull funny faces

singulariser: se singulariser
/sɛ̃gylaʀize/ [1] *v refl* (+ *v être*) to draw attention to oneself

singularité /sɛ̃gylaʀite/ *nf* (a) peculiarity, singularity
(b) uniqueness

singulier, -ière /sɛ̃gylje, ɛʀ/ **1** *adj*
(a) peculiar, unusual
(b) **combat ~** single combat
2 *nm* (a) singular
(b) singularity

singulièrement /sɛ̃gyljɛʀmã/ *adv*
(a) oddly
(b) radically

sinistre /sinistʀ/ **1** *adj* sinister; ⟨*place, future*⟩ bleak; ⟨*evening*⟩ dreary
2 *nm* disaster; accident; blaze

sinistré, ~e /sinistʀe/ **1** *adj* stricken; **région ~e** disaster area
2 *nm,f* disaster victim

sinon /sinɔ̃/ **1** *conj* (a) otherwise, or else
(b) except, apart from
(c) not to say; **c'est devenu difficile ~ impossible** it has become difficult if not impossible
2 sinon que *phr* except that, other than that

sinueux, -euse /sinɥø, øz/ *adj* sinuous; winding; tortuous

sinus /sinys/ *nm inv* sinus

sinusite /sinyzit/ *nf* sinusitis

siphon /sifɔ̃/ *nm* (a) (gen) siphon
(b) U-bend

siphonné, ~e /sifɔne/ *adj* (colloq) nuts (colloq), crazy (colloq)

sire /siʀ/ *nm* Sire

sirène /siʀɛn/ *nf* (a) (gen) siren; (of boat) foghorn
(b) mermaid, siren
■ **~ d'alarme** fire alarm

sirop /siʀo/ *nm* (a) syrup (GB), sirup (US); cordial
(b) (medicine) syrup (GB), sirup (US), mixture; **~ pectoral** cough mixture

siroter /siʀɔte/ [1] *vtr* (colloq) to sip

sirupeux, -euse /siʀypø, øz/ *adj* syrupy (GB), sirupy (US)

sis, ~e /si, siz/ *adj* located

sismique /sismik/ *adj* seismic

sismographie /sismɔgʀafi/ *nf* seismography

site /sit/ *nm* (a) area; **~ touristique** place of interest; **~ archéologique** archaeological site
(b) site
■ **~ de bavardage** (Comput) chatroom; **~ vierge** green-field site; **~ Web** Web site

sitôt /sito/ **1** *adv* ~ **rentrés** as soon as we/they get back; as soon as we/they got back; **je n'y retournerai pas de** ~ I won't go back there in a hurry (colloq)

2 *conj* ~ **que** as soon as

IDIOMS ~ **dit,** ~ **fait** no sooner said than done

situation /situasjɔ̃/ *nf* **(a)** situation

(b) job, position

(c) location

■ ~ **de famille** marital status

situer /situe/ [1] **1** *vtr* **(a)** (in space and time) to place; **l'hôtel est bien situé** the hotel is in a good location

(b) ~ **une histoire en 2001/à Palerme** to set a story in 2001/in Palermo

2 **se situer** *v refl* (+ *v être*) **(a)** **se** ~ **à Paris en 1900** to be set in Paris in 1900

(b) **politiquement, je me situe plutôt à gauche** politically, I'm more to the left

six /sis, *but before consonant* si, *and before vowel or mute h* siz/ *adj inv, pron, nm inv* six

sixième /sizjɛm/ **1** *adj* sixth

2 *nf* (Sch) *first year of secondary school, age 11–12*

skaï® /skaj/ *nm* imitation leather

skate-board, *pl* ~**s** /skɛtbɔrd/ *nm*

(a) skateboard

(b) skateboarding

sketch, *pl* ~**es** /skɛtʃ/ *nm* sketch

ski /ski/ *nm* **(a)** ski

(b) **le** ~ skiing

■ ~ **de fond** cross-country skiing; ~ **nautique** water skiing; ~ **de piste** downhill skiing

skier /skje/ [2] *vi* to ski

skieur, -ieuse /skjœr, øz/ *nm,f* skier

slalom /slalɔm/ *nm* slalom

slalomer /slalɔme/ [1] *vi* **(a)** (Sport) to slalom

(b) (figurative) to zigzag

slave /slav/ *adj* Slavonic

Slave /slav/ *nmf* Slav

slip /slip/ *nm* **(a)** underpants

(b) slipway

slogan /slɔgɑ̃/ *nm* slogan

slow /slo/ *nm* slow dance

smala /smala/ *nf* (colloq) tribe (colloq)

SME /ɛsɛmø/ *nm: abbr* ▶ **SYSTÈME**

SMIC /smik/ *nm* (*abbr* = **salaire minimum interprofessionel de croissance**) guaranteed minimum wage

smoking /smɔkiŋ/ *nm* dinner jacket (GB), tuxedo

SNCF /ɛsɛnseɛf/ *nf* (*abbr* = **Société nationale des chemins de fer français**) French national railway company

snob /snɔb/ **1** *adj* (*person*) stuck-up (colloq); (*restaurant*) posh

2 *nmf* snob; **c'est un** ~ he's a snob

snober /snɔbe/ [1] *vtr* to snub

snobisme /snɔbism/ *nm* snobbery

sobre /sɔbr/ *adj* **(a)** (*person*) abstemious; sober; temperate; (*life*) simple

(b) (*style*) plain, sober

sobrement /sɔbrəmɑ̃/ *adv* soberly; in moderation; (*live*) frugally

sobriété /sɔbrijete/ *nf* sobriety, temperance; restraint; moderation

sobriquet /sɔbrikɛ/ *nm* nickname

soc /sɔk/ *nm* ploughshare (GB), plowshare (US)

sociabilité /sɔsjabilite/ *nf* sociability

sociable /sɔsjabl/ *adj* **(a)** sociable

(b) social

social, ~e, *mpl* **-iaux** /sɔsjal, o/ **1** *adj*

(a) social; **le milieu** ~ **de qn** sb's social background

(b) **conflit** ~ industrial dispute

2 *nm* **le** ~ social issues

socialement /sɔsjalmɑ̃/ *adv* socially; **être** ~ **pris en charge** to be in the care of the social services

socialiser /sɔsjalize/ [1] *vtr* **(a)** to socialize

(b) to collectivize

socialisme /sɔsjalism/ *nm* socialism

socialiste /sɔsjalist/ *adj, nmf* socialist

sociétaire /sɔsjetɛr/ *nmf* member

société /sɔsjete/ *nf* **(a)** society; **la haute** ~ high society

(b) company; ~ **de nettoyage** cleaning company

(c) (formal) **rechercher la** ~ **de qn** to seek sb's company

socioculturel, -elle /sɔsjokyltyrɛl/ *adj* sociocultural; **centre** ~ recreation centre (GB)

socio-démocrate, *pl* ~**s** /sɔsjodemɔkrat/ **1** *adj* social democratic

2 *nmf* social democrat

socio-éducatif, -ive, *mpl* ~**s** /sɔsjoedykatif, iv/ *adj* socioeducational

sociologie /sɔsjɔlɔʒi/ *nf* sociology

sociologue /sɔsjɔlɔg/ *nmf* sociologist

socioprofessionnel, -elle /sɔsjoprɔfɛsjɔnɛl/ *adj* social and occupational

socle /sɔkl/ *nm* pedestal, plinth; base; stand

socque /sɔk/ *nm* clog

socquette /sɔkɛt/ *nf* ankle sock, anklet (US)

soda /sɔda/ *nm* fizzy drink (GB), soda (US)

sodium /sɔdjɔm/ *nm* sodium

sodomiser /sɔdɔmize/ [1] *vtr* to sodomize, to bugger

sœur /sœr/ *nf* sister; ~ **jumelle** twin sister

sofa /sɔfa/ *nm* sofa

soi /swa/ *pron* **(a)** autour de ~ around one; **laisser la porte se refermer derrière** ~ to let the door shut behind one; **trouver en** ~ **les ressources nécessaires** to find the necessary inner resources; **garder qch pour** ~ to keep sth to oneself

····⟩

(b) la logique n'est pas un objectif en ~ logic is not an end in itself; **cela va de ~** it goes without saying

soi-disant /swadizɑ̃/ ① *adj inv* **(a)** self-styled

(b) (controversial) so-called

② *adv* supposedly; **elle a ~ la migraine** she has a migraine, or so she says

soie /swɑ/ *nf* **(a)** silk

(b) bristle

soient /swa/ ▶ ÊTRE¹

soierie /swari/ *nf* **(a)** silk

(b) silk industry

soif /swaf/ *nf* **(a)** thirst; **avoir ~** to be thirsty

(b) ~ de thirst for; hunger for; lust for; **avoir ~ d'affection** to crave affection

soignant, **~e** /swaɲɑ̃, ɑ̃t/ *adj* medical; **médecin ~** doctor, GP

soigné, **~e** /swaɲe/ ① *pp* ▶ SOIGNER

② *pp adj* **(a)** ⟨*nails*⟩ well-manicured; ⟨*hair, clothes*⟩ immaculate

(b) ⟨*publication*⟩ carefully produced; ⟨*work*⟩ meticulous; **peu ~** ⟨*work*⟩ careless

soigner /swaɲe/ [1] ① *vtr* **(a)** ⟨*doctor*⟩ to treat

(b) to look after ⟨*person, customer*⟩

(c) to take care over ⟨*appearance*⟩; to look after ⟨*hands*⟩

② **se soigner** *v refl* (+ *v être*) **(a)** to treat oneself; to look after oneself

(b) ⟨*illness*⟩ to be treatable

(c) to take care over one's appearance

soigneusement /swaɲøzmɑ̃/ *adv* carefully; meticulously; neatly

soigneux, **-euse** /swaɲø, øz/ *adj*

(a) ⟨*work*⟩ conscientious; ⟨*examination*⟩ careful

(b) ⟨*person*⟩ neat, tidy

soi-même /swamɛm/ *pron* oneself

soin /swɛ̃/ ① *nm* **(a)** care; **prendre ~ de qch** to take care of sth; **prendre ~ de qn/sa santé** to look after sb/one's health; **prendre ~ de sa petite personne** to coddle oneself; **laisser à qn le ~ de faire** to leave it to sb to do

(b) product; **~ antipelliculaire** dandruff treatment

② **soins** *nm pl* **(a)** (Med) treatment; care; **recevoir des ~s** to receive treatment; **~s dentaires** dental care; **les premiers ~s à donner aux brûlés** first-aid treatment for burns; **~s à domicile** homecare

(b) care; **~s corporels** *or* **du corps** body care

(c) 'aux bons ~s de' 'care of', 'c/o'

IDIOMS **être aux petits ~s pour qn** to attend to sb's every need

soir /swar/ *nm* evening; night; **le ~ du 3, le 3 au ~** on the evening of the 3rd; **il sort tous les samedis ~** he goes out every Saturday night; **6 heures du ~** 6 pm; **à ce ~!** see you tonight!

soirée /sware/ *nf* **(a)** evening; **dans** *or* **pendant la ~, en ~** in the evening

(b) party; **aller dans une ~** to go to a party

(c) evening performance *or* show

sois /swa/ ▶ ÊTRE¹

soit¹ /swa/ ① ▶ ÊTRE¹

② *conj* **(a)** ~, ~ either, or; ~ **du fromage,** ~ **un gâteau** either cheese, or a cake

(b) that is, ie; **toutes mes économies,** ~ **200 francs** all my savings, ie *or* that is, 200 francs

(c) (in mathematics) ~ **un triangle ABC** let ABC be a triangle

soit² /swat/ *adv* very well; **je me suis trompé,** ~**, mais là n'est pas la question** all right, so I was wrong, but that's not the point

soixantaine /swasɑ̃tɛn/ *nf* **(a)** about sixty

(b) avoir la ~ to be about sixty

soixante /swasɑ̃t/ *adj inv, pron, nm inv* sixty

soixante-dix /swasɑ̃tdis/ *adj inv, pron, nm inv* seventy

soixante-dixième /swasɑ̃tdizjɛm/ *adj* seventieth

soixantième /swasɑ̃tjɛm/ *adj* sixtieth

soja /sɔʒa/ *nm* soya bean (GB), soybean (US); **sauce de ~** soy sauce

sol /sɔl/ *nm* **(a)** ground; floor

(b) soil

(c) (Mus) (note) G; (in sol-fa) soh

solaire /sɔlɛr/ *adj* ⟨*energy*⟩ solar; ⟨*engine*⟩ solar-powered; ⟨*cream*⟩ sun

soldat /sɔlda/ *nm* soldier, serviceman

solde¹ /sɔld/ ① *nm* balance; **faire le ~ d'un compte** to settle an account

② **en solde** *phr* **acheter une veste en ~** to buy a jacket in a sale

③ **soldes** *nm pl* sales; sale

solde² /sɔld/ *nf* (Mil) pay; **avoir qn à sa ~** (figurative) to have sb in one's pay

solder /sɔlde/ [1] ① *vtr* **(a)** to sell off ⟨*merchandise*⟩

(b) to settle the balance of ⟨*account*⟩

② **se solder** *v refl* (+ *v être*) **se ~ par qch** to end in sth

solderie /sɔldəri/ *nf* discount shop

sole /sɔl/ *nf* (Zool) sole

soleil /sɔlɛj/ *nm* sun; ~ **de minuit** midnight sun; **en plein** ~ ⟨*sit*⟩ in (the) hot sun; ⟨*leave something*⟩ in direct sunlight; **quand il y a du** ~ when it's sunny; **attraper un coup** *or* **des coups de** ~ to get sunburned

solennel, **-elle** /sɔlanɛl/ *adj* (gen) solemn; ⟨*appeal, declaration*⟩ formal

solennité /sɔlanite/ *nf* solemnity

solfège /sɔlfɛʒ/ *nm* **(a)** music theory; ~ **chanté** sol-fa

(b) music theory book

solidaire /sɔlidɛr/ *adj* **(a)** ⟨*team, group*⟩ united

(b) (Tech) ⟨*parts*⟩ interdependent

solidariser: se solidariser /sɔlidarize/ [1] *v refl* (+ *v être*) **se ~ avec qn/qch** to stand by sb/sth

solidarité /sɔlidarite/ *nf* solidarity

solide /sɔlid/ ① *adj* **(a)** ⟨*food, matter*⟩ solid

(b) ⟨*house, friendship*⟩ solid; ⟨*shoes, bag*⟩ sturdy; ⟨*link, fastening, blade*⟩ strong; ⟨*position, base*⟩ firm
(c) ⟨*person, constitution, heart*⟩ strong; **avoir la tête ∼** (figurative) to have one's head screwed on (right)
(d) ⟨*business, experience, reasons*⟩ sound; ⟨*guarantees*⟩ firm
2 *nm* **(a)** solid; **manger du ∼** to eat solids
(b) ce qu'il te dit, c'est du ∼ what he says is sound
(c) les meubles anciens, c'est du ∼ antique furniture is solidly built

solidement /sɔlidmɑ̃/ *adv* ⟨*attach, establish*⟩ firmly; ⟨*barricaded*⟩ securely; **un rapport ∼ documenté** a well-documented report

solidifier /sɔlidifje/ [2] *vtr*, **se solidifier** *v refl* (+ *v être*) to solidify

solidité /sɔlidite/ *nf* **(a)** (of construction) solidity; (of machine) strength; (of link) firmness; (of clothes) hard-wearing quality; **d'une grande ∼** well-built; sturdy; strong; hard-wearing
(b) (of argument) soundness

soliloque /sɔlilɔk/ *nm* soliloquy

soliste /sɔlist/ *nmf* soloist

solitaire /sɔlitɛʀ/ **1** *adj* **(a)** ⟨*person, life*⟩ solitary; ⟨*old age, childhood*⟩ lonely; **navigateur ∼** single-handed yachtsman
(b) ⟨*house*⟩ isolated
2 *nmf* solitary person, loner; **en ∼** ⟨*live*⟩ alone; ⟨*sail*⟩ single-handed
3 *nm* **(a)** (diamond) solitaire
(b) rogue boar
(c) (Games) solitaire

solitude /sɔlityd/ *nf* **(a)** solitude
(b) loneliness

solliciter /sɔlisite/ [1] *vtr* **(a)** (formal) to seek ⟨*interview, post, advice*⟩
(b) to approach ⟨*person, organization*⟩; to canvass ⟨*customer, voter*⟩; **être très sollicité** to be assailed by requests; to be very much in demand

sollicitude /sɔlisityd/ *nf* concern, solicitude

solstice /sɔlstis/ *nm* solstice

soluble /sɔlybl/ *adj* soluble

solution /sɔlysjɔ̃/ *nf* **(a)** solution, solving; resolution
(b) solution; **une ∼ de facilité** an easy way out
(c) (in chemistry) solution

solutionner /sɔlysjɔne/ [1] *vtr* to solve

solvabilité /sɔlvabilite/ *nf* **(a)** solvency
(b) creditworthiness

solvable /sɔlvabl/ *adj* solvent; creditworthy

solvant /sɔlvɑ̃/ *nm* solvent

somatiser /sɔmatize/ [1] *vtr* to have a psychosomatic reaction to

sombre /sɔ̃bʀ/ *adj* **(a)** dark; **il fait ∼** it's dark
(b) ⟨*thought, future*⟩ dark, black; ⟨*conclusion*⟩ depressing; ⟨*air, person*⟩ solemn

(c) (*before n*) (colloq) ⟨*idiot*⟩ absolute; ⟨*affair*⟩ murky

sombrer /sɔ̃bʀe/ [1] *vi* **(a)** ⟨*ship*⟩ to sink
(b) ∼ dans ⟨*person*⟩ to sink into ⟨*despair, alcoholism*⟩

sommaire /sɔmmɛʀ/ **1** *adj* ⟨*explanation*⟩ cursory; ⟨*description*⟩ rough; ⟨*installation, meal*⟩ rough and ready; ⟨*execution*⟩ summary
2 *nm* **(a)** contents; **au ∼ de notre numéro de juillet** featured in our July issue
(b) (colloq) **au ∼ : un débat sur le chômage** a debate on unemployment is on the programme (GB)

sommairement /sɔmmɛʀmɑ̃/ *adv* summarily

sommation /sɔmmasjɔ̃/ *nf* (from police) warning; (from guard) challenge

somme[1] /sɔm/ *nm* nap, snooze (colloq)

somme[2] /sɔm/ *nf* **(a)** sum, amount
(b) sum total; **la ∼ de nos connaissances** the sum total of our knowledge; **il a fourni une grosse ∼ de travail** he did a great deal of work; **en ∼, ∼ toute** all in all

sommeil /sɔmɛj/ *nm* sleep; **avoir le ∼ agité** to sleep fitfully; **avoir le ∼ léger** to be a light sleeper

sommeiller /sɔmeje/ [1] *vi* **(a)** to doze
(b) to lie dormant

sommelier, -ière /sɔməlje, ɛʀ/ *nm,f* wine waiter, sommelier

sommer /sɔmme/ [1] *vtr* **∼ qn de faire** to command sb to do

sommes /sɔm/ ▶ ÊTRE[1]

sommet /sɔmɛ/ *nm* **(a)** (of mountain) peak; summit
(b) (gen) top; (of wave) crest; (of curve, career) peak
(c) (of glory, stupidity) height; **atteindre des ∼s** ⟨*prices, sales*⟩ to peak
(d) summit; **conférence au ∼** summit meeting
(e) (of triangle, angle) apex; (of cone) vertex

sommier /sɔmje/ *nm* (bed) base

somnambule /sɔmnɑ̃byl/ **1** *adj* **être ∼** to sleepwalk
2 *nmf* sleepwalker

somnifère /sɔmnifɛʀ/ **1** *adj* soporific
2 *nm* **(a)** soporific
(b) sleeping pill

somnolence /sɔmnɔlɑ̃s/ *nf* drowsiness

somnolent, ∼e /sɔmnɔlɑ̃, ɑ̃t/ *adj*
(a) drowsy
(b) ⟨*town*⟩ sleepy; ⟨*industry, country*⟩ lethargic

somnoler /sɔmnɔle/ [1] *vi* **(a)** to drowse
(b) ⟨*town*⟩ to be sleepy; ⟨*industry, country*⟩ to be lethargic

somptueux, -euse /sɔ̃ptɥø, øz/ *adj* sumptuous

somptuosité /sɔ̃ptɥozite/ *nf* sumptuousness

son[1], **sa**, *pl* **ses** /sɔ̃, sa, sɛ/ *det* his/her/ its; **ses enfants** his/her children; **ses pattes** ⋯✧

S

its paws; **elle a ∼ lundi** she's off on Monday;
she gets Mondays off; **∼ étourdie de sœur**
(colloq) his/her absent-minded sister

son² /sɔ̃/ *nm* **(a)** sound; **ingénieur du ∼**
engineer
(b) volume; **baisser le ∼** to turn the volume
down
(c) bran; **pain au ∼** bran loaf
■ **∼ et lumière** son et lumière

sonar /sɔnaʀ/ *nm* sonar

sonate /sɔnat/ *nf* sonata

sondage /sɔ̃daʒ/ *nm* **(a)** poll; survey
(b) (Med) catheterization; probe
(c) (Naut) sounding

sonde /sɔ̃d/ *nf* **(a)** (Med) catheter; probe
(b) sounding lead; sounding line
(c) drill
(d) taster

sonder /sɔ̃de/ [1] *vtr* **(a)** to poll; to survey;
to sound out
(b) to probe
(c) (Med) to catheterize; to probe
(d) (Naut) to sound

songe /sɔ̃ʒ/ *nm* dream

songer /sɔ̃ʒe/ [13] *v+prep* **∼ à** qch/**à faire** to
think of sth/of doing; **tu n'y songes pas!** you
can't be serious!

songeur, -euse /sɔ̃ʒœʀ, øz/ *adj* pensive

sonnant, -e /sɔnɑ̃, ɑ̃t/ *adj* **à trois heures**
∼es on the stroke of three

sonné, -e /sɔne/ [1] *pp* ▶ SONNER
[2] *pp adj* **(a)** groggy; shattered
(b) **elle a quarante ans bien ∼s** (colloq) she's
well into her forties

sonner /sɔne/ [1] [1] *vtr* **(a)** to ring ‹*bell*›
(b) ‹*clock*› to strike ‹*hour*›; ‹*person*› to sound
‹*retreat, alarm*›; to ring out ‹*vespers*›
(c) to ring for; **on ne t'a pas sonné!** (colloq)
did anyone ask you?
(d) (colloq) ‹*blow*› to make [sb] dizzy; ‹*news*›
to stagger
[2] **sonner de** *v+prep* to sound ‹*horn*›; to
play ‹*bagpipes*›
[3] *vi* **(a)** ‹*bell, phone*› to ring; ‹*hour*› to
strike; ‹*alarm clock*› to go off; ‹*alarm,*
trumpet› to sound; **leur dernière heure a**
sonné their last hour has come
(b) ‹*word, expression*› to sound

sonnerie /sɔnʀi/ *nf* **(a)** ringing; chimes;
système qui déclenche une ∼ system that
sets off an alarm
(b) (of horn) sounding

sonnet /sɔnɛ/ *nm* sonnet

sonnette /sɔnɛt/ *nf* bell; doorbell; **tirer la**
∼ d'alarme to pull the emergency cord;
(figurative) to sound the alarm

sonore /sɔnɔʀ/ *adj* **(a)** ‹*laugh, kiss, slap*›
resounding
(b) resonant; echoing; hollow-sounding
(c) ‹*vibrations*› sound; **le volume ∼ est tel**
que... the noise level is so high that...; **effets**
∼s sound effects; **un document ∼** a
recording
(d) ‹*consonant*› voiced

sonorisation /sɔnɔʀizasjɔ̃/ *nf* public
address system, PA system

sonorité /sɔnɔʀite/ *nf* **(a)** (of instrument,
voice) tone; **les ∼s de l'italien** the sound of
Italian
(b) (of hi-fi) sound quality
(c) resonance

sont /sɔ̃/ ▶ ÊTRE¹

sophistication /sɔfistikasjɔ̃/ *nf*
sophistication

sophistiqué, ∼e /sɔfistike/ *adj*
(a) sophisticated
(b) artificial, mannered

sophrologie /sɔfʀɔlɔʒi/ *nf* relaxation
therapy

soporifique /sɔpɔʀifik/ *adj, nm* soporific

soprano /sɔpʀano/ *nmf* soprano

sorbet /sɔʀbɛ/ *nm* sorbet

sorcellerie /sɔʀsɛlʀi/ *nf* witchcraft;
sorcery

sorcier /sɔʀsje/ [1] *adj m* (colloq) **ce n'est**
(pourtant) pas ∼! (but) it's dead easy! (colloq)
[2] *nm* **(a)** wizard; sorcerer
(b) witch doctor

sorcière /sɔʀsjɛʀ/ *nf* witch; sorceress

sordide /sɔʀdid/ *adj* squalid; sordid

sornettes /sɔʀnɛt/ *nf pl* tall stories

sort /sɔʀ/ *nm* **(a)** lot; **être satisfait de son ∼**
to be satisfied with one's lot
(b) fate; **le ∼ est contre moi** I'm ill-fated;
tirer qch au ∼ to draw lots for sth
(c) curse, spell; **jeter un ∼ à qn** to put a
curse on sb; **le ∼ en est jeté** the die is cast

sortable /sɔʀtabl/ *adj* **mon mari n'est pas**
∼ I can't take my husband anywhere

sorte /sɔʀt/ [1] *nf* sort, kind
[2] **de la sorte** *phr* in this way
[3] **de sorte que** *phr* **(a)** so that
(b) **la toile est peinte de ∼ que** the canvas is
painted in such a way that
(c) **de ∼ que je n'ai pas pu venir** with the
result that I couldn't come
[4] **en quelque sorte** *phr* in a way
[5] **en sorte de** *phr* **fais en ∼ d'être à**
l'heure try to be on time
[6] **en sorte que** *phr* **fais en ∼ que tout**
soit en ordre make sure everything is tidy

sortie /sɔʀti/ *nf* **(a)** exit; **je t'attendrai à la ∼**
I'll wait for you outside (the building); **à la**
∼ de la ville on the outskirts of the town; on
the edge of the town
(b) **à ma ∼ du tribunal** when I left the court;
se retrouver à la ∼ de l'école to meet after
school; **à la ∼ de l'hiver** at the end of winter
(c) **faire une ∼ fracassante** to make a
dramatic exit; **la ∼ de la récession/crise** the
end of the recession/crisis
(d) outing; **faire une ∼ avec l'école** to go on
a school outing; **ce soir, c'est mon soir de ∼**
tonight is my night out; **priver qn de ∼** to
keep sb in, ground sb (colloq)
(e) (of new product) launching; (of film) release;
(of book) publication; (of fashion collection)
showing

(f) (Tech) output; **faire une ∼ sur imprimante** to print

■ **∼ des artistes** stage-door; **∼ d'autoroute** exit; **∼ de bain** bathrobe

sortilège /sɔʀtilɛʒ/ *nm* spell

sortir¹ /sɔʀtiʀ/ [30] **1** *vtr* **(a)** to take [sb/ sth] out ⟨*person, dog*⟩

(b) to get [sb/sth] out; **∼ les mains de ses poches** to take one's hands out of one's pockets; **∼ la poubelle** to put the bin out; **∼ sa langue** to stick one's tongue out

(c) (colloq) to chuck (colloq) [sb] out ⟨*person*⟩; to send [sb] out ⟨*pupil*⟩

(d) **∼ qn de** to get sb out of ⟨*situation*⟩

(e) to bring out ⟨*book*⟩; to release ⟨*film*⟩; to show ⟨*collection*⟩

(f) to turn out ⟨*book, record, film, product*⟩

(g) to bring [sth] out ⟨*newspaper*⟩

(h) (colloq) to come out with (colloq) ⟨*remarks*⟩; **∼ une blague** to crack a joke

2 *vi* (+ *v être*) **(a)** to go out; to come out; **∼ déjeuner** to go out for lunch; **être sorti** to be out; **∼ en courant** to run out; **faire ∼ qn** to get sb outside; **laisser ∼ qn** to allow sb out

(b) to go out; **∼ avec qn** to go out with sb; **inviter qn à sortir** to ask sb out

(c) **∼ de** to leave; **∼ de chez qn** to leave sb's house; **sortez d'ici!** get out of here!; **∼ de son lit** to get out of bed; **∼ tout chaud du four** to be hot from the oven; **∼ de chez le médecin** to come out of the doctor's

(d) **∼ d'un rêve** to wake up from a dream; **∼ de la récession** to pull out of the recession; **∼ de l'hiver** to reach the end of winter

(e) **∼ à peine de l'enfance** to be just emerging from childhood; **∼ d'une guerre** to emerge from a war

(f) ⟨*water, smoke, cork*⟩ to come out; **faire ∼** to squeeze [sth] out ⟨*juice*⟩; to eject ⟨*cassette*⟩

(g) ⟨*bud, insect*⟩ to come out; ⟨*tooth*⟩ to come through

(h) to stick out

(i) ⟨*film, book, new model*⟩ to come out; **∼ tous les jours/tous les mois** ⟨*paper*⟩ to be published daily/monthly

(j) **∼ de** ⟨*person, product*⟩ to come from; **∼ de Berkeley** to have graduated from Berkeley; **d'où sors-tu à cette heure?** (colloq) where have you been?

(k) **∼ du sujet** ⟨*remark*⟩ to be beside the point; **cela sort de mes fonctions** that's not within my authority

(l) ⟨*number*⟩ to come up

(m) (Comput) to exit

3 **se sortir** *v refl* (+ *v être*) **(a)** **se ∼ de la pauvreté** to escape from poverty; **s'en ∼** to get out of it; to get over it; **s'en ∼ vivant** to escape with one's life

(b) **s'en ∼** to pull through; to cope; to manage; **s'en ∼ à peine** to scrape a living

sortir² /sɔʀtiʀ/ *nm* **au ∼ de** at the end of

SOS /ɛsoɛs/ *nm* **(a)** SOS

(b) emergency service; **∼ médecins** emergency medical service

(c) helpline; **∼ enfants battus** child abuse helpline

sosie /sozi/ *nm* double; **c'est ton ∼!** he/ she's the spitting image of you!

sot, sotte /so, sɔt/ **1** *adj* silly **2** *nm,f* silly thing; **petit ∼!** you silly thing!

sottement /sɔtmɑ̃/ *adv* foolishly, stupidly

sottise /sɔtiz/ *nf* **(a)** silliness, foolishness **(b)** silly remark; **dire des ∼s** to talk rubbish **(c)** **faire des ∼s** ⟨*children*⟩ to be naughty

sou /su/ *nm* **(a)** (colloq) penny (GB), cent (US); **il est près de ses ∼s** he's a penny-pincher; **c'est une affaire de gros ∼s** there's big money involved

(b) (colloq) **il n'a pas un ∼ de bon sens** he hasn't got a scrap of common sense

(c) (former unit of French currency) sou

soubassement /subasmɑ̃/ *nm* **(a)** (of building, pillar) base **(b)** bedrock

soubresaut /subʀəso/ *nm* start; jolt

soubrette /subʀɛt/ *nf* maid

souche /suʃ/ *nf* **(a)** (tree) stump; (vine) stock **(b)** stock; **de ∼ paysanne** of peasant stock **(c)** (of chequebook) stub
IDIOMS dormir comme une ∼ to sleep like a log

souci /susi/ *nm* **(a)** **se faire du ∼** to worry **(b)** problem; **j'ai d'autres ∼s (en tête)** I've got other things to worry about **(c)** (formal) **avoir le ∼ de qch** to care about sth; **avoir le ∼ de faire** to be anxious to do; **dans le seul ∼ de faire plaisir** with the sole intention of pleasing **(d)** marigold

soucier: se soucier /susje/ [2] *v refl* (+ *v être*) to care (de about); **sans se ∼ de qch/faire** without concerning oneself with sth/doing

soucieux, -ieuse /susjø, øz/ *adj* worried

soucoupe /sukup/ *nf* saucer
■ **∼ volante** flying saucer

soudain, ∼e /sudɛ̃, ɛn/ **1** *adj* sudden **2** *adv* suddenly, all of a sudden

soudainement /sudɛnmɑ̃/ *adv* suddenly

soude /sud/ *nf* **∼ caustique** caustic soda

souder /sude/ [1] **1** *vtr* **(a)** to weld **(b)** to join ⟨*edges*⟩; to bind [sb] together ⟨*people*⟩
2 se souder *v refl* (+ *v être*) ⟨*vertebrae*⟩ to fuse; ⟨*bone*⟩ to knit together

soudoyer /sudwaje/ [23] *vtr* to bribe

soudure /sudyʀ/ *nf* weld, join; welding

soufflant, ∼e /suflɑ̃, ɑ̃t/ *adj* **(a)** machine **∼e** blowing apparatus **(b)** (colloq) stunning

souffle /sufl/ *nm* **(a)** breath; **couper le ∼ à qn** to wind sb; (figurative) to take sb's breath away; **(en) avoir le ∼ coupé** to be winded; (figurative) to be speechless; **être à bout de ∼** ⟨*person*⟩ to be out of breath; ⟨*country, economy*⟩ to be running out of steam; **donner** ⋯⋗

un second or nouveau ∼ à qn/qch to put new life into sb/sth; avoir du ∼ ⟨saxophonist⟩ to have good lungs; ⟨singer⟩ to have a powerful voice; ⟨sportsman⟩ to be fit; (figurative) ⟨person⟩ to have staying power
(b) breathing
(c) breeze; pas un ∼ d'air not a breath of air
(d) spirit; ∼ révolutionnaire revolutionary spirit
(e) inspiration
(f) (from fan, explosion) blast
(g) (Med) ∼ au cœur heart murmur

soufflé, ∼e /sufle/ **1** adj (colloq) flabbergasted
2 nm (Culin) soufflé

souffler /sufle/ [1] **1** vtr (a) to blow out ⟨candle⟩
(b) to blow ⟨air, smoke, dust⟩
(c) to whisper ⟨words⟩; ∼ qch à l'oreille de qn to whisper sth in sb's ear; ∼ la réplique à un acteur to prompt an actor
(d) to suggest ⟨idea⟩
(e) to blow ⟨glass⟩; to blast ⟨metal⟩
(f) ⟨explosion⟩ to blow out ⟨window⟩; to blow up ⟨building⟩
(g) (colloq) to flabbergast
2 vi (a) ⟨wind⟩ to blow; le vent souffle fort there's a strong wind
(b) ⟨person⟩ to get one's breath back; ⟨horse⟩ to get its wind back
(c) to puff; suant et soufflant huffing and puffing
(d) ⟨person, animal⟩ to blow; ∼ dans une trompette to blow into a trumpet
(e) to tell sb the answer; on ne souffle pas! no prompting!
IDIOMS ∼ comme un bœuf or un phoque or une locomotive to puff and pant

soufflerie /sufləri/ nf (a) blower; blower house
(b) glassblower; glassblowing company

soufflet /suflɛ/ nm (a) bellows
(b) gusset

souffleur, -euse /suflœr, øz/ nm,f
(a) prompter
(b) ∼ (de verre) glassblower

souffrance /sufrɑ̃s/ nf suffering

souffrant, ∼e /sufrɑ̃, ɑ̃t/ adj unwell

souffre-douleur /sufrədulœr/ nm inv punch-bag (GB), punching-bag (US)

souffrir /sufrir/ [4] **1** vtr (a) ∼ tout de qn to put up with anything from sb; il ne souffre pas la critique he can't take criticism
(b) cette affaire ne peut ∼ aucun retard this matter brooks no delay
2 vi (a) ⟨person⟩ to suffer; ∼ de to suffer from; ma cheville me fait ∼ my ankle hurts; est-ce qu'il souffre? is he in pain?; faire ∼ ⟨person⟩ to make [sb] suffer; ⟨situation⟩ to upset; ∼ du racisme to be a victim of racism
(b) ⟨crops, economy⟩ to be badly affected; ⟨country, city⟩ to suffer

soufre /sufr/ nm sulphur (GB)

souhait /swɛ/ nm wish
IDIOMS à vos ∼s! bless you!

souhaitable /swɛtabl/ adj desirable

souhaiter /swete/ [1] vtr (a) to hope for
(b) ∼ qch à qn to wish sb sth; ∼ la bienvenue à qn to welcome sb; je vous souhaite d'obtenir très bientôt votre diplôme I hope you get your degree very soon
(c) il souhaite se rendre là-bas en voiture he would like to go by car

souiller /suje/ [1] vtr (a) to soil, to make [sth] dirty; être souillé de to be stained with
(b) to defile ⟨place, person⟩; to sully ⟨memory⟩

souillon /sujɔ̃/ nf slattern

souillure /sujyr/ nf stain

souk /suk/ nm (a) souk
(b) (colloq) mess; racket (colloq)

soûl, ∼e /su, sul/ **1** adj drunk
2 tout son soûl phr ⟨drink, eat⟩ one's fill

soulagement /sulaʒmɑ̃/ nm relief

soulager /sulaʒe/ [13] vtr (gen) to relieve; to ease ⟨conscience⟩; le comprimé m'a soulagé the tablet made me feel better; tu m'as soulagé d'un grand poids you've taken a great weight off my shoulders

soûlant, ∼e /sulɑ̃, ɑ̃t/ adj (colloq) elle est ∼e! she makes my head spin!

soûler /sule/ [1] **1** vtr (a) ⟨person⟩ to get [sb] drunk; ⟨alcohol⟩ to make [sb] drunk
(b) ⟨perfume⟩ to intoxicate
(c) (colloq) tu me soûles avec tes histoires you're making my head spin!
2 se soûler v refl (+ v être) to get drunk

soulèvement /sulɛvmɑ̃/ nm uprising

soulever /sulve/ [16] **1** vtr (a) to lift ⟨object⟩; to raise ⟨dust⟩; ∼ qn/qch de terre to pick sb/sth up
(b) to arouse ⟨enthusiasm, anger⟩; to stir up ⟨crowd⟩; to raise ⟨problems⟩
2 se soulever v refl (+ v être) (a) to raise oneself up
(b) to rise up
IDIOMS ça me soulève le cœur it turns my stomach; it makes me sick

soulier /sulje/ nm shoe
IDIOMS être dans ses petits ∼s to feel uncomfortable

souligner /suliɲe/ [1] vtr (a) to underline ⟨word⟩; to outline ⟨eyes⟩
(b) to emphasize

soumettre /sumɛtr/ [60] **1** vtr (a) to bring [sb/sth] to heel ⟨person, group, region⟩; to subdue ⟨rebels⟩
(b) ∼ qn/qch à to subject sb/sth to
(c) to submit
(d) ∼ un produit à une température élevée to subject a product to a high temperature
2 se soumettre v refl (+ v être) (a) to submit
(b) se ∼ à to accept ⟨rule⟩

soumis, ∼e /sumi, iz/ **1** pp ▶ soumettre
2 adj submissive

soumission /sumisjɔ̃/ nf submission

soupape /supap/ nf valve

soupçon /supsɔ̃/ nm (a) suspicion

(b) (colloq) (of milk, wine) drop; (of salt) pinch; (of flavour) hint

soupçonner /supsɔne/ [1] *vtr* to suspect

soupçonneux, -euse /supsɔnø, øz/ *adj* suspicious, mistrustful

soupe /sup/ *nf* **(a)** soup; à la ∼! (colloq) (humorous) grub's up! (colloq)
(b) (colloq) slush
■ ∼ **populaire** soup kitchen
IDIOMS **être** ∼ **au lait** (colloq) to be quick-tempered; **cracher dans la** ∼ (colloq) to look a gift horse in the mouth

soupente /supɑ̃t/ *nf* **(a)** loft, garret
(b) cupboard under the stairs

souper¹ /supe/ [1] *vi* to have late dinner

souper² /supe/ *nm* late dinner, supper

soupeser /supəze/ [16] *vtr* **(a)** to feel the weight of
(b) to weigh up ⟨arguments⟩

soupière /supjɛʀ/ *nf* soup tureen

soupir /supiʀ/ *nm* sigh

soupirail, *pl* **-aux** /supiʀaj, o/ *nm* cellar window

soupirer /supiʀe/ [1] *vi* to sigh

souple /supl/ *adj* **(a)** ⟨body⟩ supple; ⟨stalk⟩ flexible; ⟨hair⟩ soft
(b) ⟨step, style⟩ flowing; ⟨shape⟩ smooth
(c) ⟨rule⟩ flexible

souplesse /suplɛs/ *nf* **(a)** (of stalk) flexibility; (of hair) softness; (of body) suppleness
(b) (of step) litheness; (of gesture) grace; (of car) smoothness; (of style) fluidity
(c) (of rule) flexibility

source /suʀs/ *nf* **(a)** spring
(b) source; **prendre sa** ∼ **dans** *or* **à** ⟨river⟩ to rise in *or* at; **citer ses** ∼s to give one's sources
IDIOMS **ça coule de** ∼ it's obvious; **retour aux** ∼s return to basics

sourcil /suʀsi/ *nm* eyebrow

sourciller /suʀsije/ [1] *vi* to raise one's eyebrows; **sans** ∼ without batting an eyelid

sourd, ∼e /suʀ, suʀd/ **1** *adj* **(a)** deaf; ∼ **à** deaf to ⟨pleas⟩
(b) ⟨noise⟩ dull; ⟨voice⟩ muffled
(c) ⟨pain⟩ dull
(d) ⟨consonant⟩ voiceless, surd
2 *nm,f* deaf person; **les** ∼s the deaf
IDIOMS **faire la** ∼e **oreille** to turn a deaf ear; **comme un** ∼ ⟨shout⟩ at the top of one's voice; **comme un** ∼ like one possessed; **ce n'est pas tombé dans l'oreille d'un** ∼ it didn't go unheard

sourdine /suʀdin/ *nf* (Mus) mute; (on piano) soft pedal; **écouter la radio en** ∼ to have the radio on quietly

sourd-muet, sourde-muette, *pl* **sourds-muets, sourdes-muettes** /suʀmɥɛ, suʀdmɥɛt/ **1** *adj* deaf and dumb
2 *nm,f* deaf-mute

souriant, ∼e /suʀjɑ̃, ɑ̃t/ *adj* smiling

souriceau, *pl* ∼**x** /suʀiso/ *nm* young mouse

souricière /suʀisjɛʀ/ *nf* **(a)** mousetrap
(b) trap

sourire¹ /suʀiʀ/ [68] *vi* **(a)** to smile; ∼ **jusqu'aux oreilles** to grin from ear to ear
(b) ∼ **à qn** ⟨fate, fortune⟩ to smile on sb

sourire² /suʀiʀ/ *nm* smile; **le** ∼ **aux lèvres** with a smile on one's face

souris /suʀi/ *nf inv* mouse

sournois, ∼e /suʀnwa, az/ *adj* ⟨person, look⟩ sly; ⟨behaviour⟩ underhand; ⟨pain⟩ insidious

sous /su/ *prep* **(a)** under, underneath; **un journal** ∼ **le bras** a newspaper under one's arm; ∼ **la pluie** in the rain
(b) under; ∼ **le numéro 4757** under number 4757
(c) during; ∼ **la présidence de Mitterrand** during Mitterrand's presidency
(d) within; ∼ **peu** before long
(e) ∼ **traitement** undergoing treatment; ∼ **antibiotiques** on antibiotics

sous-alimenté, ∼e, *mpl* ∼**s** /suzalimɑ̃te/ *adj* undernourished

sous-bois /subwa/ *nm inv* undergrowth

sous-catégorie, *pl* ∼**s** /sukategɔʀi/ *nf* subcategory

sous-chef, *pl* ∼**s** /suʃɛf/ *nm* second-in-command

souscripteur, -trice /suskʀiptœʀ, tʀis/ *nm,f* subscriber (de to)

souscription /suskʀipsjɔ̃/ *nf*
(a) subscription
(b) ∼ **d'un contrat d'assurances** taking out an insurance policy

souscrire /suskʀiʀ/ [67] **1** *vtr* to take out ⟨insurance⟩; to sign ⟨contract⟩; to subscribe ⟨sum of money⟩
2 **souscrire à** *v+prep* to subscribe to

souscrit, ∼e /suskʀi, it/ **1** *pp* ▶ SOUSCRIRE
2 *pp adj* **(a)** subscribed
(b) subscript

sous-cutané, ∼e, *mpl* ∼**s** /sukytane/ *adj* subcutaneous

sous-développé, ∼e, *mpl* ∼**s** /sudevlɔpe/ *adj* underdeveloped

sous-directeur, -trice, *mpl* ∼**s** /sudiʀɛktœʀ, tʀis/ *nm,f* assistant manager

sous-direction, *pl* ∼**s** /sudiʀɛksjɔ̃/ *nf* division; ∼ **des affaires économiques et financières** economic and financial affairs division

sous-effectif, *pl* ∼**s** /suzefɛktif/ *nm* understaffing; **ils sont en** ∼ they're understaffed

sous-employer /suzɑ̃plwaje/ [23] *vtr* to underemploy

sous-entendre /suzɑ̃tɑ̃dʀ/ [6] *vtr* to imply

sous-entendu, ∼e, *mpl* ∼**s** /suzɑ̃tɑ̃dy/
1 *pp* ▶ SOUS-ENTENDRE
2 *pp adj* understood

3 *nm* innuendo

sous-équipé, ∼**e**, *mpl* ∼**s** /suzekipe/
adj underequipped

sous-estimer /suzestime/ [1] *vtr* to
underestimate

sous-évaluer /suzevalɥe/ [1] *vtr* to
underestimate; to undervalue

sous-fifre, *pl* ∼**s** /sufifʀ/ *nm* (colloq)
underling

sous-jacent, ∼**e**, *mpl* ∼**s** /suʒasɑ̃, ɑ̃t/
adj (a) ⟨idea, problem, tension⟩ underlying
(b) subjacent

sous-lieutenant, *pl* ∼**s** /suljøtnɑ̃/ *nm*
(in the army) ≈ second lieutenant; (in the air
force) ≈ pilot officer

sous-louer /sulwe/ [1] *vtr* to sublet; to
sublease

sous-main /sumɛ̃/ **1** *nm inv* desk blotter
2 en sous-main *phr* secretly

sous-marin, ∼**e**, *mpl* ∼**s** /sumaʀɛ̃, in/
1 *adj* submarine, underwater; deep-sea
2 *nm* (a) submarine
(b) (colloq) spy

sous-marque, *pl* ∼**s** /sumaʀk/ *nf* sub-
brand

sous-officier, *pl* ∼**s** /suzɔfisje/ *nm*
noncommissioned officer

sous-ordre, *pl* ∼**s** /suzɔʀdʀ/ *nm*
suborder

sous-payer /supeje/ [21] *vtr* to underpay

sous-préfecture, *pl* ∼**s** /supʀefɛktyʀ/
nf: administrative subdivision of a
department in France

sous-produit, *pl* ∼**s** /supʀɔdɥi/ *nm*
(a) by-product
(b) second-rate product

sous-prolétariat, *pl* ∼**s** /supʀɔletaʀja/
nm underclass

sous-pull, *pl* ∼**s** /supyl/ *nm* thin polo-
neck jumper

soussigné, ∼**e** /susiɲe/ *adj*, *nm,f*
undersigned

sous-sol, *pl* ∼**s** /susɔl/ *nm* (a) basement
(b) subsoil

sous-tasse, *pl* ∼**s** /sutas/ *nf* saucer

sous-titrage, *pl* ∼**s** /sutitʀaʒ/ *nm*
subtitling

sous-titre, *pl* ∼**s** /sutitʀ/ *nm* subtitle

sous-titrer /sutitʀe/ [1] *vtr* to subtitle

soustraction /sustʀaksjɔ̃/ *nf* subtraction

soustraire /sustʀɛʀ/ [58] **1** *vtr* (a) to
subtract
(b) to steal
(c) to take away ⟨person⟩; ∼ **qn/qch à la vue
de qn** to hide sb/sth from sb
(d) to shield ⟨person⟩; ∼ **qn à la mort** to save
sb's life
2 se soustraire *v refl* (+ *v être*) (a) se ∼
à to escape from
(b) se ∼ **à la justice** to escape justice

sous-traitance, *pl* ∼**s** /sutʀɛtɑ̃s/ *nf*
subcontracting; **travail donné en** ∼ work
contracted out

sous-verre /suvɛʀ/ *nm inv* (a) clip-frame
(b) coaster

sous-vêtement, *pl* ∼**s** /suvɛtmɑ̃/ *nm*
underwear

soutane /sutan/ *nf* cassock

soute /sut/ *nf* hold; ∼ **à bagages** baggage
hold

soutenable /sutnabl/ *adj* (a) bearable;
pas ∼ unbearable
(b) tenable

soutenance /sutnɑ̃s/ *nf* viva (voce) (GB),
orals (US)

soutènement /sutɛnmɑ̃/ *nm* retaining
structure; (in mine) props

souteneur /sutnœʀ/ *nm* pimp (colloq),
procurer

soutenir /sutniʀ/ [36] **1** *vtr* (a) (gen) to
support ⟨person, team, currency⟩; ∼ **à bout
de bras** to keep [sb/sth] afloat ⟨person,
project⟩; ∼ **qn contre qn** to side with sb
against sb; ∼ **le moral de qn** to keep sb's
spirits up
(b) to maintain ⟨contrary⟩; to defend
⟨paradox⟩; to uphold ⟨opinion⟩
(c) to keep [sb] going
(d) to keep [sth] going ⟨conversation⟩; to
keep up ⟨effort, pace⟩
(e) to withstand ⟨shock, attack, stares⟩; to
bear ⟨comparison⟩
(f) ∼ **sa thèse** to have one's viva (voce) (GB)
or defense (US)
2 se soutenir *v refl* (+ *v être*) to support
each other

soutenu, ∼**e** /sutny/ **1** *pp* ▶ SOUTENIR
2 *pp adj* ⟨effort, activity⟩ sustained;
⟨attention⟩ close; ⟨rhythm⟩ steady
3 *adj* (a) ⟨market⟩ firm; ⟨colour⟩ deep;
⟨language⟩ formal
(b) (Mus) ⟨note⟩ sustained

souterrain, ∼**e** /suteʀɛ̃, ɛn/ **1** *adj*
(a) underground
(b) **économie** ∼**e** black economy
2 *nm* underground passage, tunnel

soutien /sutjɛ̃/ *nm* support

soutien-gorge, *pl* **soutiens-gorge**
/sutjɛ̃gɔʀʒ/ *nm* bra

soutirer /sutiʀe/ [1] *vtr* ∼ **qch à qn** to
squeeze sth out of sb ⟨money⟩; to extract sth
from sb ⟨confession⟩

souvenance /suvnɑ̃s/ *nf* **à ma** ∼ as far as
I recall; **avoir** ∼ **de qch** to remember sth

souvenir¹: se souvenir /suvniʀ/ [36]
v refl (+ *v être*) **se** ∼ **de qn/qch** to remember
sb/sth

souvenir² /suvniʀ/ *nm* (a) memory; **garder
un bon** ∼ **de qch** to have happy memories of
sth; **ne pas avoir** ∼ **de** to have no
recollection of
(b) memory; **s'effacer du** ∼ **de qn** to fade
from sb's memory
(c) souvenir; memento; **en** ∼ as a souvenir;
as a memento; as a keepsake; **boutique de**
∼**s** souvenir shop (GB) or store (US)
(d) **mon bon** ∼ **à** remember me to

souvent /suvɑ̃/ *adv* often

s

souverain, **∼e** /suvʀɛ̃, ɛn/ **1** *adj*
(a) ⟨state⟩ sovereign; ⟨authority⟩ supreme
(b) ⟨happiness, scorn⟩ supreme
(c) ⟨remedy⟩ sovereign; ⟨advice, virtue⟩
sterling
(d) ⟨person⟩ haughty
2 *nm,f* sovereign, monarch

souverainement /suvʀɛnmɑ̃/ *adv* votre
attitude me déplaît ∼ I dislike your attitude
intensely

souveraineté /suvʀɛnte/ *nf* sovereignty

soviet /sɔvjɛt/ *nm* soviet; **Soviet suprême**
Supreme Soviet

soviétique /sɔvjetik/ *adj* Soviet

soyeux, **-euse** /swajø, øz/ *adj* silky

soyez /swaje/ ▶ ÊTRE¹

soyons /swajɔ̃/ ▶ ÊTRE¹

SPA /ɛspea/ *nf* (*abbr* = **Société
protectrice des animaux**) society for
the prevention of cruelty to animals

spacieux, **-ieuse** /spasjø, øz/ *adj*
spacious

spaghetti /spageti/ *nm inv* des ∼
spaghetti

sparadrap /spaʀadʀa/ *nm* (a) surgical *or*
adhesive tape
(b) (sticking) plaster (GB), Band-aid®

spartiate /spaʀsjat/ *adj*, *nmf* Spartan

spasme /spasm/ *nm* spasm

spasmophilie /spasmɔfili/ *nf*
spasmophilia

spatial, **∼e**, *mpl* **-iaux** /spasjal, o/ *adj*
(a) spatial
(b) space; **vaisseau** ∼ spaceship

spatule /spatyl/ *nf* (a) spatula
(b) filling-knife

speaker, **speakerine** /spikœʀ,
spikʀin/ *nm,f* announcer

spécial, **∼e**, *mpl* **-iaux** /spesjal, o/ *adj*
(a) special
(b) odd

spécialement /spesjalmɑ̃/ *adv*
(a) specially
(b) especially; **pas** ∼ not especially

spécialiser: se spécialiser
/spesjalize/ [1] *v refl* (+ *v être*) to specialize

spécialiste /spesjalist/ *nmf* specialist

spécialité /spesjalite/ *nf* speciality (GB),
specialty (US)

spécificité /spesifisite/ *nf* (a) specificity
(b) characteristic
(c) uniqueness

spécifier /spesifje/ [2] *vtr* to specify

spécifique /spesifik/ *adj* specific

spécimen /spesimɛn/ *nm* (a) specimen
(b) (free) sample
(c) (colloq) odd specimen (colloq)

spectacle /spɛktakl/ *nm* (a) sight; **se
donner** *or* **s'offrir en** ∼ to make an
exhibition of oneself
(b) show; ∼ **de danse** dance show; '∼s'
'entertainment'; **film à grand** ∼ spectacular
(c) show business

spectaculaire /spɛktakylɛʀ/ *adj*
spectacular

spectateur, **-trice** /spɛktatœʀ, tʀis/
nm,f (a) member of the audience
(b) spectator

spectre /spɛktʀ/ *nm* (a) ghost
(b) spectre (GB)
(c) ∼ **lumineux** spectrum of light

spéculateur, **-trice** /spekylatœʀ, tʀis/
nm,f speculator

spéculatif, **-ive** /spekylatif, iv/ *adj*
speculative

spéculation /spekylasjɔ̃/ *nf* (a) (Econ)
speculation; ∼ **sur** speculation in
(b) (gen) speculation (**sur** on, about)

spéculer /spekyle/ [1] *vi* to speculate; ∼ **à
la hausse/baisse** to bull/bear

spéléologie /speleɔlɔʒi/ *nf* (a) caving,
potholing (GB), spelunking (US)
(b) speleology

spermatozoïde /spɛʀmatozoid/ *nm* des
∼s spermatozoa

sperme /spɛʀm/ *nm* sperm

sphère /sfɛʀ/ *nf* sphere

sphérique /sfeʀik/ *adj* spherical

sphincter /sfɛ̃ktɛʀ/ *nm* sphincter

sphinx /sfɛ̃ks/ *nm inv* (a) Sphinx
(b) hawkmoth

spirale /spiʀal/ *nf* spiral

spiritisme /spiʀitism/ *nm* spiritualism

spiritualité /spiʀitɥalite/ *nf* spirituality

spirituel, **-elle** /spiʀitɥɛl/ *adj*
(a) spiritual
(b) witty

spiritueux, **-euse** /spiʀitɥø, øz/ *nm inv*
spirit

splendeur /splɑ̃dœʀ/ *nf* (of scenery, site)
splendour (GB); (of era, reign) glory

splendide /splɑ̃did/ *adj* splendid;
stunning

spolier /spɔlje/ [2] *vtr* to despoil (**de** of)

spongieux, **-ieuse** /spɔ̃ʒjø, øz/ *adj*
spongy

sponsoriser /spɔ̃sɔʀize/ [1] *vtr* to sponsor

spontané, **∼e** /spɔ̃tane/ *adj* spontaneous

spontanéité /spɔ̃taneite/ *nf* spontaneity

sporadique /spɔʀadik/ *adj* sporadic

spore /spɔʀ/ *nf* spore

sport /spɔʀ/ *nm* sport; sports; **aller aux** ∼s
d'hiver to go on a winter sports holiday (GB)
or vacation (US)

sportif, **-ive** /spɔʀtif, iv/ **1** *adj* (a) ⟨event⟩
sports; **je ne suis pas** ∼ I'm not the sporty
type
(b) ⟨appearance⟩ athletic, sporty (colloq)
2 *nm,f* sportsman/sportswoman; **c'est un** ∼
he's athletic

spot /spɔt/ *nm* (a) spotlight
(b) ∼ (**publicitaire**) commercial

squale /skwal/ *nm* shark

square /skwaʀ/ *nm* small public garden

squash /skwaʃ/ *nm* squash

S

squatter¹ /skwate/ [1] *vtr* to squat in

squatter² /skwatœʀ/ *nm* squatter

squelette /skəlɛt/ *nm* **(a)** skeleton
(b) (colloq) bag of bones (colloq)
(c) framework

squelettique /skəletik/ *adj* ⟨person, legs⟩
scrawny; ⟨tree⟩ skeletal; ⟨report⟩ sketchy

stabiliser /stabilize/ [1] **1** *vtr* to stabilize;
to consolidate
2 se stabiliser *v refl* (+ *v être*)
⟨unemployment⟩ to stabilize; ⟨person⟩ to
become stable

stabilité /stabilite/ *nf* stability

stable /stabl/ *adj* stable

stade /stad/ *nm* **(a)** (Sport) stadium
(b) stage; **à ce ~** at this stage

stage /staʒ/ *nm* **(a)** professional training
(b) work experience; **~ pratique** period of
work experience
(c) course; **suivre un ~ de formation** to go on
a training course

stagiaire /staʒjɛʀ/ *nmf* **(a)** trainee
(b) student teacher

stagnation /stagnasjɔ̃/ *nf* stagnation

stagner /stagne/ [1] *vi* to stagnate

stalactite /stalaktit/ *nf* stalactite

stalagmite /stalagmit/ *nf* stalagmite

stalle /stal/ *nf* stall

stand /stɑ̃d/ *nm* stand; stall
■ **~ de tir** shooting range; shooting gallery

standard /stɑ̃daʀ/ **1** *adj inv* standard
2 *nm* switchboard

standardisation /stɑ̃daʀdizasjɔ̃/ *nf*
standardization

standardiste /stɑ̃daʀdist/ *nmf*
switchboard operator

standing /stɑ̃diŋ/ *nm* **(a)** de **~**
⟨apartment⟩ luxury
(b) standard of living

star /staʀ/ *nf* star

starter /staʀtɛʀ/ *nm* (Aut) choke

station /stasjɔ̃/ *nf* **(a)** station; taxi-rank
(GB), taxi stand; **c'est à deux ~s d'ici** it's two
stops from here
(b) **~ (de radio)** (radio) station
(c) **~ balnéaire** seaside resort; **~ thermale**
spa
(d) **~ debout** *or* **verticale** upright posture *or*
position
(f) stop, pause

stationnaire /stasjɔnɛʀ/ *adj* **(a)** stationary
(b) stable

stationnement /stasjɔnmɑ̃/ *nm* parking

stationner /stasjɔne/ [1] *vi* to park

station-service, *pl* **stations-
service** /stasjɔ̃sɛʀvis/ *nf* service *or* filling
station

statique /statik/ *adj* static

statistique /statistik/ *nf* **(a)** statistics
(b) statistic

statue /staty/ *nf* statue

statuer /statɥe/ [1] *vi* to give a ruling

statuette /statɥɛt/ *nf* statuette

statu quo /statykwo/ *nm inv* status quo

stature /statyʀ/ *nf* **(a)** stature
(b) height

statut /staty/ *nm* **(a)** statute
(b) status

statutaire /statytɛʀ/ *adj* statutory

steak /stɛk/ *nm* steak; **un ~ haché** a
hamburger

sténodactylo /stenodaktilo/ **1** *nmf*
shorthand typist (GB), stenographer (US)
2 *nf* shorthand typing (GB), stenography
(US)

sténographier /stenɔgʀafje/ [2] *vtr* to
take [sth] down in shorthand

sténotypiste /stenɔtipist/ *nmf*
stenotypist

steppe /stɛp/ *nf* steppe

stéréo /steʀeo/ *adj inv*, *nf* stereo

stéréophonique /steʀeɔfɔnik/ *adj*
stereophonic

stéréotype /steʀeɔtip/ *nm* **(a)** stereotype
(b) cliché

stérile /steʀil/ *adj* (gen) sterile; ⟨land⟩
barren; ⟨discussion⟩ fruitless

stérilet /steʀilɛ/ *nm* coil, IUD

stériliser /steʀilize/ [1] *vtr* to sterilize

stérilité /steʀilite/ *nf* **(a)** sterility;
barrenness
(b) fruitlessness

sterling /stɛʀliŋ/ *adj inv* sterling; **livre ~**
pound sterling

sternum /stɛʀnɔm/ *nm* breastbone,
sternum

stéthoscope /stetɔskɔp/ *nm* stethoscope

stigmate /stigmat/ *nm* **(a)** scar
(b) mark

stimulant, ~e /stimylɑ̃, ɑ̃t/ *adj*
invigorating; bracing; stimulating

stimulation /stimylasjɔ̃/ *nf* stimulation

stimuler /stimyle/ [1] **1** *vtr* **(a)** to
stimulate ⟨organ, function⟩
(b) to spur [sb] on
2 *vi* **(a)** to be bracing
(b) (colloq) to act as a spur

stimulus, *pl* **stimuli** /stimylys, stimyli/
nm stimulus

stipuler /stipyle/ [1] *vtr* to stipulate

stock /stɔk/ *nm* stock; **avoir qch en ~** to
have sth in stock

stockage /stɔkaʒ/ *nm* **(a)** stocking;
stockpiling
(b) (Comput) storage

stocker /stɔke/ [1] *vtr* **(a)** to stock
(b) to stockpile
(c) to store ⟨data⟩

stoïque /stɔik/ *adj* stoical

stop /stɔp/ *nm* **(a)** stop sign
(b) (colloq) hitch-hiking (colloq); **prendre qn en
~** to give sb a lift (GB) *or* ride (US)

stopper /stɔpe/ [1] **1** *vtr* **(a)** to stop; to
halt ⟨development⟩
(b) to mend
2 *vi* to stop

store /stɔʀ/ *nm* **(a)** blind
(b) awning
strabisme /stʀabism/ *nm* squint
strapontin /stʀapɔ̃tɛ̃/ *nm* foldaway seat
stratagème /stʀataʒɛm/ *nm* stratagem
strate /stʀat/ *nf* stratum
stratégie /stʀateʒi/ *nf* strategy
stratégique /stʀateʒik/ *adj* strategic
stratifié, **~e** /stʀatifje/ *adj* **(a)** stratified
(b) laminated
stratosphère /stʀatɔsfɛʀ/ *nf*
stratosphere
stress /stʀɛs/ *nm inv* stress
stressant, **~e** /stʀɛsɑ̃, ɑ̃t/ *adj* stressful
stresser /stʀese/ [1] *vtr* to put [sb] on
edge; to put [sb] under stress
strict, **~e** /stʀikt/ *adj* **(a)** (gen) strict; **au
sens ~** in the strict sense of the word
(b) ⟨hairstyle, outfit⟩ severe
strident, **~e** /stʀidɑ̃, ɑ̃t/ *adj* ⟨noise⟩
piercing; ⟨voice⟩ strident
strie /stʀi/ *nf* **(a)** streak
(b) groove
(c) (in geology) **des ~s** striation
strip-tease /stʀiptiz/ *nm* striptease
strophe /stʀɔf/ *nf* stanza, verse
structure /stʀyktyʀ/ *nf* **(a)** structure
(b) organization; **~ d'accueil** shelter, refuge
structurer /stʀyktyʀe/ [1] *vtr* to structure
stuc /styk/ *nm* stucco
studieux, **-ieuse** /stydjø, øz/ *adj* ⟨pupil⟩
studious; ⟨holiday⟩ study
studio /stydjo/ *nm* **(a)** studio flat (GB),
studio apartment (US)
(b) studio
stupéfaction /stypefaksjɔ̃/ *nf*
stupefaction
stupéfait, **~e** /stypefɛ, ɛt/ *adj* astounded
stupéfiant, **~e** /stypefjɑ̃, ɑ̃t/ 1 *adj*
stunning
2 *nm* drug, narcotic
stupéfier /stypefje/ [2] *vtr* to astound
stupeur /stypœʀ/ *nf* **(a)** astonishment
(b) (Med) stupor
stupide /stypid/ *adj* stupid
stupidité /stypidite/ *nf* stupidity
style /stil/ *nm* **(a)** style; **~ de vie** lifestyle;
c'est bien ton ~ de faire it's just like you to
do
(b) **meubles de ~** (reproduction) period
furniture
(c) speech form; **~ indirect** indirect *or*
reported speech
stylé, **~e** /stile/ *adj* well-trained
styliser /stilize/ [1] *vtr* to stylize
styliste /stilist/ *nmf* fashion designer
stylo /stilo/ *nm* (fountain) pen; **~ bille** ballpoint pen; **~ feutre** felt-tip pen
su¹, **~e** /sy/ ▶ SAVOIR
su² /sy/ *nm* **au vu et au ~ de tous** openly
suaire /sɥɛʀ/ *nm* shroud
suant, **~e** /sɥɑ̃, ɑ̃t/ *adj* **(a)** sweaty

(b) (colloq) deadly dull
suave /sɥav/ *adj* ⟨perfume, music, smile⟩
sweet; ⟨voice⟩ mellifluous; ⟨person, manner⟩
suave
subalterne /sybaltɛʀn/ *nmf* subordinate;
(Mil) low-ranking officer, subaltern
subconscient /sybkɔ̃sjɑ̃/ *nm*
subconscious
subdiviser /sybdivize/ [1] *vtr* to subdivide
subir /sybiʀ/ [3] *vtr* **(a)** to be subjected to
⟨violence, pressure⟩; to suffer ⟨defeat,
damage⟩
(b) to take ⟨examination⟩; to have
⟨operation, test⟩; **~ l'influence de qn** to be
under sb's influence
(c) to put up with
(d) to undergo
subit, **~e** /sybi, it/ *adj* sudden
subitement /sybitmɑ̃/ *adv* suddenly
subjectif, **-ive** /sybʒɛktif, iv/ *adj*
subjective
subjectivité /sybʒɛktivite/ *nf*
subjectivity
subjonctif /sybʒɔ̃ktif/ *nm* subjunctive
subjuguer /sybʒyge/ [1] *vtr* **(a)** to
captivate, to enthral (GB)
(b) to subjugate
sublime /syblim/ *adj* sublime
sublimer /syblime/ [1] *vtr*, *vi* to sublimate
submerger /sybmɛʀʒe/ [13] *vtr* **(a)** to
submerge
(b) to flood ⟨market, switchboard⟩
(c) ⟨crowd, emotion⟩ to overwhelm
(d) **~ qn de travail** to inundate sb with
work
subodorer /sybɔdɔʀe/ [1] *vtr* to detect
subordination /sybɔʀdinasjɔ̃/ *nf*
subordination
subordonné, **~e¹** /sybɔʀdɔne/ *nm,f*
subordinate
subordonnée² /sybɔʀdɔne/ *nf*
subordinate clause; **~ relative** relative
clause
subordonner /sybɔʀdɔne/ [1] *vtr* **(a)** **être
subordonné à qn** to be subordinate to sb
(b) **être subordonné à qch** to be subject to
sth
suborner /sybɔʀne/ [1] *vtr* to bribe
⟨witness⟩
subreptice /sybʀɛptis/ *adj* surreptitious
subside /sybsid/ *nm* **(a)** grant
(b) allowance
subsidiaire /sybzidjɛʀ/ *adj* subsidiary;
question ~ tiebreaker
subsistance /sybzistɑ̃s/ *nf* subsistence;
(moyens de) ~ means of support
subsister /sybziste/ [1] *vi* **(a)** to remain
(b) ⟨custom⟩ to survive
(c) **ça leur suffit à peine pour ~** it's barely
enough for them to live on
substance /sypstɑ̃s/ *nf* substance
substantif /sypstɑ̃tif/ *nm* noun,
substantive

S

substituer /sypstitɥe/ [1] **1** vtr to substitute
2 se substituer v refl (+ v être) se ~ à to take the place of

substitut /sypstity/ nm substitute

substitution /sypstitysjɔ̃/ nf substitution; produit de ~ du sucre sugar substitute

subterfuge /sypterfyʒ/ nm ploy, subterfuge

subtil, **~e** /syptil/ adj subtle; skilful (GB)

subtiliser /syptilize/ [1] vtr ~ qch à qn to steal sth from sb

subtilité /syptilite/ nf subtlety

subvenir /sybvənir/ [36] v+prep ~ à to meet ‹expenses, needs›; ~ aux besoins de sa famille to provide for one's family

subvention /sybvɑ̃sjɔ̃/ nf (a) grant
(b) subsidy

subventionner /sybvɑ̃sjɔne/ [1] vtr to subsidize

subversif, -ive /sybversif, iv/ adj subversive

subversion /sybversjɔ̃/ nf subversion

suc /syk/ nm (of fruit) juice; (of plant) sap; ~s digestifs or gastriques gastric juices

succédané /syksedane/ nm substitute, ersatz

succéder /syksede/ [14] **1 succéder à** v+prep (a) ~ à to succeed ‹person›
(b) ~ à to follow
2 se succéder v refl (+ v être) to succeed or follow one another

succès /syksɛ/ nm inv success; avoir du ~, être un ~ to be a success; ‹record› to be a hit; à ~ ‹actor, film› successful

successeur /syksesœr/ nm successor

successif, -ive /syksesif, iv/ adj successive

succession /syksesjɔ̃/ nf (a) series, succession
(b) (Law) succession; prendre la ~ de to succeed
(c) inheritance, estate

succinct, ~e /syksɛ̃, ɛ̃t/ adj ‹essay› succinct; ‹speech› brief; ‹meal› frugal

succomber /sykɔ̃be/ [1] vi (a) to die
(b) to give way, to yield; ~ sous le poids to collapse under the weight
(c) ~ à to succumb to ‹charm, despair›; to give in to ‹temptation›

succulent, ~e /sykylɑ̃, ɑ̃t/ adj delicious

succursale /sykyrsal/ nf branch, outlet

sucer /syse/ [12] vtr to suck

sucette /sysɛt/ nf lollipop, lolly (colloq)

suçoter /sysɔte/ [1] vtr to suck

sucre /sykr/ nm (a) sugar
(b) sugar lump
■ ~ cristallisé granulated sugar; ~ glace icing sugar (GB), powdered sugar (US); ~ en poudre caster sugar (GB), superfine sugar (US); ~ roux brown sugar
IDIOMS casser du ~ sur le dos de qn to run sb down, to badmouth sb (colloq)

sucré, ~e /sykre/ adj sweet; sweetened

sucrer /sykre/ [1] vtr to put sugar in; to sweeten

sucrerie /sykrəri/ nf (a) sugar refinery
(b) ~s sweets (GB)

sucrier /sykrije/ nm sugar bowl

sud /syd/ **1** adj inv south; southern
2 nm (a) south; exposé au ~ south-facing
(b) le Sud the South

sudation /sydasjɔ̃/ nf sweating

sud-est /sydɛst/ **1** adj inv southeast; southeastern
2 nm southeast; le Sud-Est asiatique South East Asia

sudiste /sydist/ adj, nmf Confederate

sud-ouest /sydwɛst/ **1** adj inv southwest; southwestern
2 nm southwest

Suède /sɥɛd/ pr nf Sweden

suédois, ~e /sɥedwa, az/ **1** adj Swedish
2 nm (language) Swedish

Suédois, ~e /sɥedwa, az/ nm,f Swede

suer /sɥe/ [1] **1** vtr to sweat; ~ sang et eau to sweat blood and tears
2 vi to sweat; faire ~ qn (colloq) to bore sb stiff (colloq)

sueur /sɥœr/ nf sweat; j'en avais des ~s froides I was in a cold sweat about it

suffi /syfi/ ▶ SUFFIRE

suffire /syfir/ [64] **1** vi to be enough; un rien suffit à le mettre en colère it only takes the slightest thing to make him lose his temper
2 se suffire v refl (+ v être) se ~ (à soi-même) to be self-sufficient
3 v impers il suffit de me téléphoner all you have to do is phone me; il suffit d'une lampe pour éclairer la pièce one lamp is enough to light the room; il suffit que je sorte sans parapluie pour qu'il pleuve! every time I go out without my umbrella, it's guaranteed to rain; ça suffit (comme ça)! that's enough!

suffisamment /syfizamɑ̃/ adv enough

suffisance /syfizɑ̃s/ nf self-importance

suffisant, ~e /syfizɑ̃, ɑ̃t/ adj (a) sufficient
(b) self-important

suffixe /syfiks/ nm suffix

suffocant, ~e /syfɔkɑ̃, ɑ̃t/ adj
(a) suffocating
(b) staggering

suffocation /syfɔkasjɔ̃/ nf suffocation; choking

suffoquer /syfɔke/ [1] **1** vtr to suffocate
2 vi (a) to suffocate
(b) to choke

suffrage /syfraʒ/ nm suffrage; ~s exprimés recorded votes

suggérer /sygʒere/ [14] vtr to suggest

suggestif, -ive /sygʒestif, iv/ adj ‹music› evocative; ‹pose› suggestive; ‹dress› provocative

suggestion /sygʒestjɔ̃/ nf suggestion

suicidaire /sɥisidɛr/ adj suicidal

suicide /sɥisid/ *nm* suicide

suicider: **se suicider** /sɥiside/ [1] *v refl*
(+ *v être*) to commit suicide

suie /sɥi/ *nf* soot

suinter /sɥɛ̃te/ [1] *vi* (a) ⟨*liquid*⟩ to seep; to
ooze
(b) ⟨*walls*⟩ to sweat; ⟨*wound*⟩ to weep

suis /sɥi/ ▶ ÊTRE¹

suisse /sɥis/ **1** *adj* Swiss
2 *nm* (a) Swiss Guard
(b) verger

Suisse /sɥis/ *pr nf* Switzerland

suite /sɥit/ **1** *nf* (a) rest; **la ~ des**
événements what happens next
(b) (of story) continuation; (of series) next
instalment (GB); (of meal) next course
(c) sequel
(d) result; **les ~s** (of action) the
consequences; (of incident) the repercussions;
(of illness) the after-effects
(e) **donner ~ à** to follow up ⟨*complaint*⟩; to
deal with ⟨*order*⟩; **rester sans ~** ⟨*plan*⟩ to be
dropped
(f) **faire ~ à** to follow upon ⟨*incident*⟩;
prendre la ~ de qn to take over from sb
(g) **avoir de la ~ dans les idées** to be single-
minded
(h) (of incidents) series; (of successes) run
(i) (hotel) suite
(j) (of monarch) suite
(k) (Mus) suite
2 de suite *phr* in succession, in a row; **et**
ainsi de ~ and so on
3 par la suite *phr* (a) afterward(s)
(b) later
4 par suite de *phr* due to
5 à la suite de *phr* (a) following
(b) behind

suivant¹ /sɥivɑ̃/ *prep* (a) in accordance
with ⟨*tradition*⟩; **~ leur habitude** as they
usually do
(b) depending on
(c) according to

suivant², **~e** /sɥivɑ̃, ɑ̃t/ **1** *adj*
(a) following
(b) next
2 *nm,f* **le ~** the following one; the next one
3 le suivant, la suivante *phr* as
follows

suivi, **~e** /sɥivi/ **1** *pp* ▶ SUIVRE
2 *pp adj* (a) ⟨*work*⟩ steady; ⟨*effort*⟩
sustained; ⟨*correspondence*⟩ regular
(b) ⟨*policy*⟩ coherent
3 *nm* (a) monitoring
(b) follow-up; **~ des malades** follow-up care
for patients

suivre /sɥivʀ/ [62] **1** *vtr* (a) to follow
⟨*person, car*⟩; **suivez le guide!** this way,
please!
(b) to follow, to come after ⟨*period,*
incident⟩; **'à ~'** 'to be continued'
(c) to follow ⟨*route, coast*⟩; ⟨*road*⟩ to run
alongside ⟨*railway line*⟩; **~ le droit chemin**
to keep to the straight and narrow
(d) to follow ⟨*example*⟩; to obey ⟨*impulse*⟩

(e) to follow ⟨*lesson, match*⟩; to follow the
progress of ⟨*pupil, patient*⟩; **~ l'actualité** to
keep up with the news
(f) to do ⟨*course*⟩
(g) to follow ⟨*explanation, logic*⟩; **je vous**
suis I'm with you
(h) to keep pace with [sb/sth]
2 *vi* **faire ~ son courrier** to have one's mail
forwarded; **faire ~** please forward
3 se suivre *v refl* (+ *v être*) (a) ⟨*numbers,*
pages⟩ to be in order; ⟨*cards*⟩ to be
consecutive
(b) to happen one after the other
4 *v impers* **comme suit** as follows

sujet, **-ette** /syʒɛ, ɛt/ **1** *adj* **être ~ à** to
be prone to ⟨*migraine*⟩
2 *nm* (a) subject; **un ~ d'actualité** a topical
issue; **c'est à quel ~?** what is it about?; **au**
~ de about
(b) (Sch) question; **~ libre** topic of one's own
choice; **hors ~** off the subject
(c) cause; **c'est un ~ d'étonnement** it is
amazing
(d) **c'est un brillant ~** he's a brilliant
student
(e) (of kingdom) subject

sulfate /sylfat/ *nm* sulphate (GB)

sulfureux, **-euse** /sylfyʀø, øz/ *adj*
⟨*vapour*⟩ sulphurous (GB); ⟨*bath*⟩ sulphur
(GB)

sultan /syltɑ̃/ *nm* sultan

sultane /syltan/ *nf* sultana

summum /sɔm(m)ɔm/ *nm* height

sumo /sumo, symo/ *nm inv* sumo wrestling

super¹ /sypɛʀ/ *pref* super

super² /sypɛʀ/ **1** *adj inv* (colloq) great
(colloq)
2 *nm* four-star (petrol) (GB), super

superbe /sypɛʀb/ *adj* superb, magnificent

superbement /sypɛʀbəmɑ̃/ *adv*
(a) superbly
(b) haughtily

supercarburant /sypɛʀkaʀbyʀɑ̃/ *nm*
four-star petrol, super

supercherie /sypɛʀʃəʀi/ *nf* (a) deception
(b) hoax

supérette /sypeʀɛt/ *nf* minimarket

superficie /sypɛʀfisi/ *nf* area

superficiel, **-ielle** /sypɛʀfisjɛl/ *adj* (gen)
superficial; ⟨*layer*⟩ surface

superflu, **~e** /sypɛʀfly/ *adj*
(a) superfluous
(b) unnecessary

supérieur, **~e** /sypeʀjœʀ/ **1** *adj*
(a) ⟨*jaw, lip, floor*⟩ upper
(b) ⟨*ranks, classes*⟩ upper
(c) higher (à than); ⟨*size*⟩ bigger (à than);
⟨*length*⟩ longer (à than)
(d) ⟨*work, quality*⟩ superior (à to)
(e) ⟨*air, tone*⟩ superior
2 *nm,f* (a) superior; **~ hiérarchique**
immediate superior
(b) (in monastery, convent) Superior
3 *nm* higher education

S

supérieurement /sypeʀjœʀmɑ̃/ *adv*
exceptionally

supériorité /sypeʀjɔʀite/ *nf* superiority

superlatif, -ive /sypɛʀlatif, iv/ **1** *adj*
superlative
2 *nm* superlative

supermarché /sypɛʀmaʀʃe/ *nm*
supermarket

superposer /sypɛʀpoze/ [1] *vtr* (a) to
stack [sth] (up); **lits superposés** bunk beds
(b) to superimpose ⟨*drawings*⟩

superposition /sypɛʀpozisjɔ̃/ *nf*
superposition

superproduction /sypɛʀpʀɔdyksjɔ̃/ *nf*
blockbuster (colloq)

superpuissance /sypɛʀpɥisɑ̃s/ *nf*
superpower

superstitieux, -ieuse /sypɛʀstisjø, øz/
adj superstitious

superstition /sypɛʀstisjɔ̃/ *nf* superstition

superviser /sypɛʀvize/ [1] *vtr* to supervise

supplanter /syplɑ̃te/ [1] *vtr* to supplant

suppléant, ~e /sypleɑ̃, ɑ̃t/ *nm,f*
replacement; (for judge) deputy; (for teacher)
supply (GB) *or* substitute (US) teacher; (for
doctor) locum

suppléer /syplee/ [11] *v+prep* **~ à** to make
up for, to compensate for

supplément /syplemɑ̃/ *nm* (a) extra
charge; supplement; **le vin est en ~** the wine
is extra
(b) **~ d'informations** additional information
(c) (newspaper) supplement

supplémentaire /syplemɑ̃tɛʀ/ *adj*
additional, extra; **train ~** relief train

suppliant, ~e /syplijɑ̃, ɑ̃t/ *adj* ⟨*voice*⟩
pleading; ⟨*look*⟩ imploring

supplice /syplis/ *nm* torture

supplicier /syplisje/ [2] *vtr* (a) to torture
(b) to execute

supplier /syplije/ [2] *vtr* to beg, to beseech

support /sypɔʀ/ *nm* (a) support; **servir de
~ à qch** to serve as a support for sth
(b) (for ornaments) stand
(c) back-up; **~ audiovisuel** audio-visual aid

supportable /sypɔʀtabl/ *adj* bearable

supporter¹ /sypɔʀte/ [1] **1** *vtr* (a) to
support, to bear the weight of ⟨*structure*⟩
(b) to bear ⟨*costs*⟩
(c) to put up with ⟨*misery, behaviour,
person*⟩; to bear ⟨*suffering*⟩; ⟨*plant*⟩ to
withstand ⟨*cold*⟩; **elle ne supporte pas
d'attendre** she can't stand waiting
2 se supporter *v refl* (+ *v être*) **ils ne
peuvent plus se ~** they can't stand each
other any more

supporter² /sypɔʀtœʀ/ *nmf* supporter

supposer /sypoze/ [1] *vtr* (a) to suppose
(b) to assume
(c) to presuppose

supposition /sypozisjɔ̃/ *nf* supposition

suppositoire /sypozitwaʀ/ *nm*
suppository

suppôt /sypo/ *nm* **~ de Satan** fiend

suppression /sypʀesjɔ̃/ *nf* removal;
abolition; withdrawal; suppression;
elimination; breaking, ending; deletion; **~s
d'emplois** job cuts

supprimer /sypʀime/ [1] *vtr* (a) to cut
⟨*job*⟩; to stop ⟨*aid, vibration*⟩; to abolish ⟨*tax,
law*⟩; to remove ⟨*effect, obstacle*⟩; to do away
with ⟨*class*⟩; to withdraw ⟨*licence*⟩; to break
⟨*monopoly*⟩; to suppress ⟨*evidence*⟩; to cut out
⟨*sugar, salt*⟩; to delete ⟨*word*⟩; **~ un train** to
cancel a train
(b) to eliminate ⟨*person*⟩

suppurer /sypyʀe/ [1] *vi* to suppurate

supputer /sypyte/ [1] *vtr* to calculate, to
work out

supranational, ~e, *mpl* **-aux**
/sypʀanasjɔnal, o/ *adj* supranational

suprématie /sypʀemasi/ *nf* supremacy

suprême /sypʀɛm/ *adj* supreme

sur¹ /syʀ/ *prep* (a) on; **~ la table** on the
table; **prends un verre ~ la table** take a glass
from the table; **appliquer la lotion ~ vos
cheveux** apply the lotion to your hair; **la clé
est ~ la porte** the key is in the door; **écrire
~ du papier** to write on paper; **elle est ~ la
photo** she's in the photograph
(b) over; **un pont ~ la rivière** a bridge across
or over the river
(c) **une table d'un mètre ~ deux** a table that
measures one metre (GB) by two; **~ 150
hectares** over an area of 150 hectares
(d) **se diriger ~ Valence** to head for Valence
(e) ⟨*debate, essay, thesis*⟩ on; ⟨*poem*⟩ about
(f) **être ~ une affaire** to be involved in a
business deal
(g) **une personne ~ dix** one person out of *or*
in ten; **un mardi ~ deux** every other Tuesday
(h) **faire proposition ~ proposition** to make
one offer after another
(i) **ils se sont quittés ~ ces mots** with these
words, they parted; **~ le moment** at the time;
~ ce, je vous laisse with that, I must leave
you

sur², ~e /syʀ/ *adj* (slightly) sour

sûr, ~e /syʀ/ **1** *adj* (a) ⟨*information,
service, person*⟩ reliable; ⟨*opinion, investment*⟩
sound; **d'une main ~e** with a steady hand
(b) safe
(c) certain; **c'est ~ et certain** it's definite; **à
coup ~** definitely
(d) sure; **j'en suis ~ et certain** I'm positive; **il
est ~ de lui** he's self-confident; **j'en étais ~!** I
knew it!
2 *adv* **bien ~ (que oui)** of course
IDIOMS **être ~ de son coup** (colloq) to be
confident of success

surabondance /syʀabɔ̃dɑ̃s/ *nf*
overabundance

surabonder /syʀabɔ̃de/ [1] *vi* to abound

surajouter: se surajouter /syʀaʒute/
[1] *v refl* to be added on (à to)

suranné, ~e /syʀane/ *adj* ⟨*ideas*⟩
outmoded; ⟨*style*⟩ outdated

S

surcharge /syʀʃaʀʒ/ *nf* excess load, overload; **une ~ de travail** extra work

surchargé, ~e /syʀʃaʀʒe/ *adj* ⟨day⟩ overloaded; ⟨class⟩ overcrowded

surcharger /syʀʃaʀʒe/ [13] *vtr* to overload; **~ qn de travail** to overburden sb with work

surchauffer /syʀʃofe/ [1] *vtr* to overheat

surclasser /syʀklase/ [1] *vtr* to outclass

surconsommation /syʀkõsɔmasjõ/ *nf* (Econ) overconsumption; **~ de médicaments** excessive drug consumption

surcroît /syʀkʀwa/ *nm* increase; **un ~ de travail** extra work; **de ~** moreover

surdité /syʀdite/ *nf* deafness

surdoué, ~e /syʀdwe/ *adj* (exceptionally) gifted

sureau, *pl* **~x** /syʀo/ *nm* elder (tree)

sureffectif /syʀefɛktif/ *nm* excess staff

surélever /syʀelve/ [16] *vtr* to raise the height of ⟨house, road⟩

sûrement /syʀmɑ̃/ *adv* (a) most probably
(b) **~ pas** certainly not
(c) safely

surenchère /syʀɑ̃ʃɛʀ/ *nf* (a) higher bid
(b) **faire de la ~** to try to go one better

surenchérir /syʀɑ̃ʃeʀiʀ/ [3] *vi* (a) to make a higher bid
(b) to add; to chime in

surendetté, ~e /syʀɑ̃dete/ *adj* deeply in debt; overextended

surendettement /syʀɑ̃dɛtmɑ̃/ *nm* excessive debt

surestimer /syʀɛstime/ [1] **1** *vtr* to overvalue ⟨property⟩; to overrate ⟨qualities⟩
2 se surestimer *v refl* (+ *v être*) to rate oneself too highly

sûreté /syʀte/ *nf* (a) (of place, person) safety; (of country) security
(b) (of judgment) soundness; (of gesture) steadiness
(c) (on gun) safety catch; (on door) safety lock

surévaluer /syʀevalɥe/ [1] *vtr* to overvalue ⟨currency⟩; to overestimate ⟨cost⟩

surexciter /syʀɛksite/ [1] *vtr* to overexcite

surf /sœʀf/ *nm* surfing

surface /syʀfas/ *nf* (a) surface; **de ~** ⟨installations⟩ above ground; ⟨friendliness⟩ superficial; **faire ~** to surface
(b) surface area; **en ~** in area

surfait, ~e /syʀfɛ, ɛt/ *adj* overrated

surfer /sœʀfe/ [1] *vi* (a) to go surfing
(b) (Comput) **~ sur l'Internet** to surf the Internet

surfiler /syʀfile/ [1] *vtr* to oversew

surgelé, ~e /syʀʒəle/ *adj* deep-frozen; **les produits ~s** frozen food

surgeler /syʀʒəle/ [17] *vtr* to deep-freeze

surgénérateur /syʀʒeneʀatœʀ/ *nm* fast-breeder reactor

surgir /syʀʒiʀ/ [3] *vi* ⟨person⟩ to appear suddenly; ⟨difficulty⟩ to crop up; **faire ~ la vérité** to bring the truth to light

surhomme /syʀɔm/ *nm* superman

surhumain, ~e /syʀymɛ̃, ɛn/ *adj* superhuman

surimpression /syʀɛ̃pʀesjõ/ *nf* double exposure; **en ~** superimposed

surinformation /syʀɛ̃fɔʀmasjõ/ *nf* surfeit of information

sur-le-champ /syʀləʃɑ̃/ *adv* right away

surlendemain /syʀlɑ̃d(ə)mɛ̃/ *nm* **le ~** two days later

surligner /syʀliɲe/ [1] *vtr* to highlight

surligneur /syʀliɲœʀ/ *nm* highlighter (pen)

surmenage /syʀmənaʒ/ *nm* overwork

surmener /syʀmene/ [16] **1** *vtr* to overwork
2 se surmener *v refl* (+ *v être*) to push oneself too hard

surmontable /syʀmõtabl/ *adj* surmountable

surmonter /syʀmõte/ [1] *vtr* to overcome

surmultiplié, ~e /syʀmyltiplije/ *adj* **vitesse ~e** overdrive

surnager /syʀnaʒe/ [13] *vi* to float

surnaturel, -elle /syʀnatyʀɛl/ *adj*
(a) supernatural
(b) eerie

surnom /syʀnõ/ *nm* nickname

surnombre /syʀnõbʀ/ *nm* **en ~** ⟨objects⟩ surplus; ⟨staff⟩ excess; ⟨passenger⟩ extra

surnommer /syʀnɔme/ [1] *vtr* to nickname

surnuméraire /syʀnymeʀɛʀ/ *adj*, *nmf* supernumerary

surpasser /syʀpase/ [1] **1** *vtr* to surpass
2 se surpasser *v refl* (+ *v être*) to surpass oneself, to excel oneself

surpeuplé, ~e /syʀpœple/ *adj*
(a) overpopulated
(b) overcrowded

surplace /syʀplas/ *nm inv* **faire du ~** (in traffic jam) to be stuck; (in work, inquiry) to be getting nowhere; (in cycling) to do a track stand

surplomb /syʀplõ/ *nm* **en ~** overhanging

surplomber /syʀplõbe/ [1] *vtr* to overhang

surplus /syʀply/ *nm inv* (of goods) surplus

surpopulation /syʀpɔpylasjõ/ *nf* overpopulation

surprenant, ~e /syʀpʀənɑ̃, ɑ̃t/ *adj* surprising; amazing

surprendre /syʀpʀɑ̃dʀ/ [52] **1** *vtr* (a) to surprise
(b) to take (sb) by surprise; **se laisser ~ par la pluie** to get caught in the rain
(c) to catch ⟨thief⟩
(d) to overhear ⟨conversation⟩; to intercept ⟨smile⟩

····◈

2 vi ⟨behaviour⟩ to be surprising; ⟨show⟩ to surprise; ⟨person⟩ to surprise people

surprise /syʀpʀiz/ nf surprise; **créer la ∼** to cause a stir; **il m'a fait la ∼ de venir me voir** he came to see me as a surprise; **avoir la bonne ∼ d'apprendre que** to be pleasantly surprised to hear that; **voyage sans ∼** uneventful trip; **gagner sans ∼** to win as expected

surproduction /syʀpʀɔdyksjɔ̃/ nf overproduction

surqualifié, ∼e /syʀkalifje/ adj overqualified

surréalisme /suʀ(ʀ)ealism/ nm surrealism

surréaliste /suʀ(ʀ)ealist/ **1** adj
(a) surrealist
(b) ⟨landscape, vision⟩ surreal
2 nmf surrealist

surrégénérateur /syʀʀeʒeneʀatœʀ/ nm fast-breeder reactor

sursaut /syʀso/ nm (a) start; **en ∼** with a start
(b) (of energy, enthusiasm) sudden burst; (of pride, indignation) flash; **dans un dernier ∼** in a final spurt of effort

sursauter /syʀsote/ [1] vi to jump, to start

sursis /syʀsi/ nm inv (a) respite
(b) (Law) suspended sentence
(c) (Mil) deferment of military service

surtaxe /syʀtaks/ nf surcharge

surtaxer /syʀtakse/ [1] vtr to surcharge

surtout /syʀtu/ adv above all; **∼ quand/ que** especially when/as; **∼ pas!** certainly not!

surveillance /syʀvɛjɑ̃s/ nf (a) watch; (police) surveillance; **déjouer la ∼ de qn** to escape detection by sb
(b) supervision; **sous ∼ médicale** under medical supervision

surveillant, ∼e /syʀvɛjɑ̃, ɑ̃t/ nm,f
(a) (Sch) supervisor
(b) **∼ de prison** prison warder (GB) or guard
(c) store detective

surveiller /syʀveje/ [1] **1** vtr (a) (gen) to watch; to keep watch on ⟨building⟩
(b) to supervise ⟨work, pupils⟩; to monitor ⟨progress⟩
(c) **∼ sa santé** to take care of one's health
2 se surveiller v refl (+ v être) to watch oneself

survenir /syʀvəniʀ/ [36] vi (+ v être) ⟨death, storm⟩ to occur; ⟨difficulty, conflict⟩ to arise

survêtement /syʀvɛtmɑ̃/ nm tracksuit

survie /syʀvi/ nf survival

survivant, ∼e /syʀvivɑ̃, ɑ̃t/ nm,f survivor

survivre /syʀvivʀ/ [63] **1** survivre à v+prep ⟨person⟩ to survive ⟨event, injuries⟩; to outlive ⟨person⟩; ⟨work, influence⟩ to outlast ⟨person⟩
2 vi to survive

survol /syʀvɔl/ nm (a) flying over

(b) synopsis

survoler /syʀvɔle/ [1] vtr (a) to fly over ⟨place⟩
(b) to do a quick review of ⟨problem⟩

survolté, ∼e /syʀvɔlte/ adj (colloq) overexcited

sus: **en sus** /ɑ̃sys/ phr **être en ∼** to be extra; **en ∼ de** on top of; in addition to

susceptibilité /sysɛptibilite/ nf touchiness

susceptible /sysɛptibl/ adj (a) touchy
(b) **∼ de faire** likely to do

susciter /sysite/ [1] vtr (a) to spark off ⟨reaction, debate⟩; to create ⟨problem⟩
(b) to arouse ⟨enthusiasm, interest⟩; to give rise to ⟨fear⟩

susmentionné, ∼e adj aforementioned

suspect, ∼e /syspɛ, ɛkt/ **1** adj suspicious; ⟨information, logic⟩ dubious; ⟨foodstuff, honesty⟩ suspect; ⟨person⟩ suspicious-looking
2 nm,f suspect

suspecter /syspɛkte/ [1] vtr to suspect

suspendre /syspɑ̃dʀ/ [6] **1** vtr (a) to hang up; **être suspendu aux lèvres de qn** to be hanging on sb's every word
(b) to suspend ⟨programme, payment⟩; to end ⟨strike⟩; to adjourn ⟨session, inquiry⟩
(c) to suspend ⟨official, athlete⟩
2 se suspendre v refl (+ v être) to hang; **se ∼ à une corde** to hang from a rope

suspens: **en suspens** /ɑ̃syspɑ̃/ phr
(a) **laisser qch en ∼** to leave sth unresolved ⟨question⟩; to leave sth unfinished ⟨work⟩
(b) **tenir qn en ∼** to keep sb in suspense

suspense /syspɛns/ nm suspense; **film or roman à ∼** thriller

suspension /syspɑ̃sjɔ̃/ nf (a) (gen, Tech) suspension
(b) (of aid, work) suspension; (of session, trial) adjournment
(c) **en ∼** ⟨particles⟩ in suspension
(d) pendant, ceiling light

suspicieux, -ieuse /syspisjø, øz/ adj suspicious

suspicion /syspisjɔ̃/ nf suspicion

sustenter: **se sustenter** /systɑ̃te/ [1] v refl (+ v être) to have a little snack

susurrer /sysyʀe/ [1] vtr, vi to whisper

suture /sytyʀ/ nf suture; **point de ∼** stitch

suzerain, ∼e /syzʀɛ̃, ɛn/ nm,f suzerain

svelte /svɛlt/ adj slender

sveltesse /svɛltɛs/ nf slenderness

SVP (written abbr = **s'il vous plaît**) please

syllabe /sil(l)ab/ nf syllable

sylviculture /silvikyltyʀ/ nf forestry

symbiose /sɛ̃bjoz/ nf symbiosis

symbole /sɛ̃bɔl/ nm (a) symbol
(b) creed

symbolique /sɛ̃bɔlik/ adj (a) symbolic
(b) ⟨gesture⟩ token; ⟨price⟩ nominal

symboliser /sɛ̃bɔlize/ [1] vtr to symbolize

symétrie /simetʀi/ *nf* symmetry

symétrique /simetʀik/ *adj* (a) ‹design, face› symmetrical
(b) ‹relation› symmetric

sympa /sɛ̃pa/ *adj inv* (colloq) nice

sympathie /sɛ̃pati/ *nf* (a) avoir de la ∼ pour qn to like sb
(b) sympathy; croyez à toute ma ∼ you have my deepest sympathy

sympathique /sɛ̃patik/ *adj* nice; pleasant

sympathisant, ∼e /sɛ̃patizɑ̃, ɑ̃t/ *nm,f* sympathizer

sympathiser /sɛ̃patize/ [1] *vi* to get on well

symphonie /sɛ̃fɔni/ *nf* symphony

symphonique /sɛ̃fɔnik/ *adj* symphonic

symptomatique /sɛ̃ptɔmatik/ *adj* symptomatic

symptôme /sɛ̃ptom/ *nm* symptom

synagogue /sinagɔg/ *nf* synagogue

synchronique /sɛ̃kʀɔnik/ *adj* synchronic

synchronisation /sɛ̃kʀɔnizasjɔ̃/ *nf* synchronization

synchroniser /sɛ̃kʀɔnize/ [1] *vtr* to synchronize

syncope /sɛ̃kɔp/ *nf* (a) fainting fit; tomber en ∼ to faint
(b) (Mus) syncopation

syndic /sɛ̃dik/ *nm* property manager

syndical, ∼e, *mpl* -aux /sɛ̃dikal, o/ *adj* (trade) union

syndicalisme /sɛ̃dikalism/ *nm* (a) trade unionism
(b) union activities

syndicaliste /sɛ̃dikalist/ *nmf* union activist

syndicat /sɛ̃dika/ *nm* (a) trade union
(b) (employers') association
■ ∼ d'initiative tourist information office

syndiqué, ∼e /sɛ̃dike/ *adj* être ∼ to be a union member

syndrome /sɛ̃dʀom/ *nm* syndrome
■ ∼ immunodéficitaire acquis acquired immunodeficiency syndrome

synergie /sinɛʀʒi/ *nf* synergy (entre between)

synonyme /sinɔnim/ [1] *adj* synonymous
[2] *nm* synonym; dictionnaire de ∼s ≈ thesaurus

syntaxe /sɛ̃taks/ *nf* syntax

synthèse /sɛ̃tɛz/ *nf* (a) synthesis
(b) produit de ∼ synthetic product
(c) images de ∼ computer-generated images

synthétique /sɛ̃tetik/ *adj* (a) synthetic
(b) ‹vision› global

synthétiseur /sɛ̃tetizœʀ/ *nm* synthesizer

syphilis /sifilis/ *nf inv* syphilis

systématique /sistematik/ *adj* systematic

système /sistɛm/ *nm* (a) system; ∼ de canaux canal system *or* network
(b) ∼ pileux hair
■ le ∼ D (colloq) resourcefulness; ∼ monétaire européen, SME European Monetary System, EMS
IDIOMS taper sur le ∼ de qn (colloq) to get on sb's nerves

Tt

t, T /te/ *nm inv* t, T; en (forme de) T T-shaped

t' ▶ TE

ta ▶ TON¹

tabac /taba/ *nm* (a) tobacco
(b) tobacconist's (GB), smoke shop (US)
(c) (colloq) big hit
■ ∼ blond Virginia tobacco; ∼ brun dark tobacco; ∼ à priser snuff
IDIOMS passer qn à ∼ (colloq) to beat sb up

tabagie /tabaʒi/ *nf* c'est une vraie ∼ ici! it's really smoky in here!

tabagisme /tabaʒism/ *nm* tobacco addiction

tabernacle /tabɛʀnakl/ *nm* tabernacle

table /tabl/ *nf* (a) table; mettre *or* dresser la ∼ to set *or* lay the table; nous étions toujours à ∼ quand... we were still eating when...; passer *or* se mettre à ∼ to sit down at the table; (figurative) (colloq) to spill the beans (colloq)
(b) ∼ des négociations negotiating table
(c) ∼ de logarithmes log table
■ ∼ basse coffee table; ∼ de chevet bedside table (GB), night stand (US); ∼ d'écoute wiretapping set; être mis sur ∼ d'écoute to have one's phone tapped; ∼ des matières (table of) contents; ∼ de mixage mixing desk; ∼ de nuit = ∼ de chevet; ∼ ronde round table
IDIOMS mettre les pieds sous la ∼ to let others wait on you

tableau, *pl* ∼x /tablo/ *nm* (a) picture; painting
(b) (description) picture; en plus, il était ivre, tu vois un peu le ∼! (colloq) on top of that he was drunk, you can just imagine!
(c) table, chart

····⟶

(d) (Sch) blackboard

(e) (displaying information) (gen) board; (for trains) indicator board; ~ **horaire** timetable

(f) (in play) short scene

■ ~ **d'affichage** notice board; ~ **de bord** (in car) dashboard; (on plane, train) instrument panel; ~ **de chasse** (in hunting) total number of kills; (figurative) list of conquests

IDIOMS **jouer sur les deux ~x** to hedge one's bets

tablée /table/ *nf* table; **une grande ~** a large party

tabler /table/ [1] *vi* ~ **sur** to bank on (colloq)

tablette /tablet/ *nf* **(a)** (of chocolate) bar; (of chewing-gum) stick

(b) shelf

tablier /tablije/ *nm* **(a)** apron

(b) roadway

IDIOMS **rendre son ~** to give in (GB) or give (US) one's notice

tabloïd /tablɔid/ *adj, nm* tabloid

tabou /tabu/ ⟦1⟧ *adj* **(a)** taboo

(b) sacred

⟦2⟧ *nm* taboo

tabouret /taburɛ/ *nm* stool

tac /tak/ *nm* **répondre du ~ au ~** to answer as quick as a flash

tache /taʃ/ *nf* **(a)** stain; ~ **d'humidité** damp patch

(b) (figurative) stain, blot; **sans ~** (reputation) spotless

(c) (on fruit) mark; (on skin) blotch, mark

(d) (of colour) spot; patch

■ ~**s de rousseur** freckles

IDIOMS **faire ~ d'huile** to spread like wildfire

tâche /taʃ/ *nf* task, job; **tu ne me facilites pas la ~!** you're not making my job any easier!; **les ~s ménagères** household chores

tacher /taʃe/ [1] ⟦1⟧ *vtr* **(a)** (substance) to stain; (person) to get a stain on (garment)

(b) to tarnish, to stain (reputation)

⟦2⟧ *vi* to stain; **ça ne tache pas** it doesn't stain

tâcher /taʃe/ [1] *v+prep* ~ **de faire** to try to do

tacheté /taʃte/ *adj* (fur) speckled

tacite /tasit/ *adj* tacit

taciturne /tasityʀn/ *adj* taciturn

tact /takt/ *nm* tact; **avec ~** tactfully

tactile /taktil/ *adj* (sense) tactile

tactique /taktik/ ⟦1⟧ *adj* (gen, Mil) tactical

⟦2⟧ *nf* tactic; **la ~** tactics

taie /tɛ/ *nf* ~ **(d'oreiller)** pillowcase; ~ **(de traversin)** bolstercase

taillader /tajade/ [1] *vtr* to slash

taille /taj/ *nf* **(a)** waist, waistline

(b) size; **de grande/petite ~** large/small; **de ~** (problem, ambition) considerable; (event, question) very important; **être de ~ à faire** to be up to or capable of doing

(c) (of garment) size; '~ **unique**' 'one size'; **essaie la ~ au-dessus** try the next size up

(d) height; **être de grande/petite ~** to be tall/ short

(e) (of tree, shrub) pruning; (of hedge) clipping, trimming; (of diamond, glass) cutting

taillé, ~e /taje/ ⟦1⟧ *pp* ▶ TAILLER

⟦2⟧ *pp adj* **(a)** ~ **en athlète** built like an athlete

(b) **être ~ pour faire** to be cut out to do

(c) **cristal ~** cut glass

taille-crayons /tajkʀɛjɔ̃/ *nm inv* pencil sharpener

tailler /taje/ [1] ⟦1⟧ *vtr* **(a)** to cut (glass, marble); to sharpen (pencil); to prune (tree, shrub); to trim (hair, beard)

(b) to cut (steak); to carve (sculpture); to cut out (garment); **taillé sur mesure** (garment) custom-made; (figurative) (role) tailor-made

⟦2⟧ *vi* ~ **grand/petit** (garment) to be cut on the large/small side

⟦3⟧ **se tailler** *v refl* (+ *v être*) **(a)** to carve out [sth] for oneself (career, empire); to make [sth] for oneself (reputation)

(b) (slang) to beat it (colloq)

tailleur /tajœʀ/ *nm* **(a)** (woman's) suit

(b) tailor; **s'asseoir en ~** to sit down cross-legged

■ ~ **de pierre** stone-cutter

taillis /taji/ *nm inv* **(a)** undergrowth

(b) coppice

tain /tɛ̃/ *nm* **miroir sans ~** two-way mirror

taire /tɛʀ/ [59] ⟦1⟧ *vtr* **(a)** not to reveal (name, secret); to hush up (truth)

(b) to keep [sth] to oneself (sadness, resentment)

⟦2⟧ **se taire** *v refl* (+ *v être*) **(a)** (person) to be silent

(b) (person) to stop talking; (bird, journalist) to fall silent; **faire ~** to make [sb] be quiet (pupils); to silence (opponent, media); to put a stop to (rumours); **tais-toi!** be quiet!

(c) (noise) to stop; (orchestra) to fall silent

talc /talk/ *nm* talc, talcum powder

talent /talɑ̃/ *nm* talent; **de ~** talented

talentueux, -euse /talɑ̃tɥø, øz/ *adj* talented

talisman /talismɑ̃/ *nm* talisman

talkie-walkie, *pl* **talkies-walkies** /tokiwoki/ *nm* walkie-talkie

taloche /talɔʃ/ *nf* (colloq) clout (colloq)

talon /talɔ̃/ *nm* **(a)** (of foot, shoe) heel

(b) (of cheque, ticket) stub

(c) (in cards) pile

■ ~ **aiguille** stiletto heel

IDIOMS **être sur les ~s de qn** to be hard or hot on sb's heels

talonner /talɔne/ [1] *vtr* **(a)** ~ **qn** to be hot on sb's heels

(b) (person) to badger (person); (hunger, anxiety) to torment (person)

talonnette /talɔnɛt/ *nf* lift (in a shoe)

talus /taly/ *nm inv* **(a)** embankment

(b) bank, slope

tamanoir /tamanwaʀ/ *nm* anteater

tambouille /tɑ̃buj/ *nf* (colloq) grub (colloq)

tambour /tɑ̃buʀ/ *nm* drum; **mener qch ~ battant** to deal with sth briskly

tambourin /tɑ̃buRɛ̃/ nm tambourine

tambouriner /tɑ̃buRine/ [1] vi ~ **à la porte de qn** to hammer on sb's door

tamis /tami/ nm inv sieve

Tamise /tamiz/ pr nf **la** ~ the Thames

tamiser /tamize/ [1] vtr to sieve, to sift ⟨sand, flour⟩; to filter ⟨light, colours⟩

tampon /tɑ̃pɔ̃/ nm **(a)** (in office) stamp; ~ **(encreur)** (ink) pad
(b) (for sponging) (gen) pad; (Med) swab; ~ **à récurer** scouring pad
(c) ~ **hygiénique** tampon

tamponner /tɑ̃pɔne/ [1] vtr **(a)** to swab ⟨wound, cut⟩; to mop ⟨forehead⟩
(b) to stamp ⟨document⟩
(c) to crash into ⟨vehicle⟩

tamponneuse /tɑ̃pɔnøz/ adj f **auto** ~ bumper car, dodgem

tam-tam, pl ~**s** /tamtam/ nm tomtom

tanche /tɑ̃ʃ/ nf tench

tandem /tɑ̃dɛm/ nm **(a)** tandem
(b) (figurative) duo

tandis: **tandis que** /tɑ̃di(s)k(ə)/ phr while

tangent, ~**e**[1] /tɑ̃ʒɑ̃, ɑ̃t/ adj **(a)** tangent, tangential
(b) (colloq) **elle a été reçue, mais c'était** ~ she got through, but only by the skin of her teeth (colloq)

tangente[2] /tɑ̃ʒɑ̃t/ nf tangent

tangible /tɑ̃ʒibl/ adj tangible

tanguer /tɑ̃ge/ [1] vi ⟨ship, plane⟩ to pitch

tanière /tanjɛR/ nf **(a)** den
(b) lair

tank /tɑ̃k/ nm tank

tanner /tane/ [1] vtr **(a)** to tan ⟨leather, hides⟩
(b) ⟨sun⟩ to make [sth] leathery ⟨face, skin⟩

tannerie /tanRi/ nf **(a)** tannery
(b) tanning

tant /tɑ̃/ **1** adv **(a)** (so) much; **il a** ~ **insisté que** he was so insistent that; **vous m'en direz** ~**!** (colloq) you don't say!; **le moment** ~ **attendu** the long-awaited moment
(b) **n'aimer rien** ~ **que…** to like nothing so much as…; ~ **bien que mal** ⟨repair, lead⟩ after a fashion; ⟨manage⟩ more or less; **essayer** ~ **bien que mal de s'adapter** to be struggling to adapt
(c) ~ **que** as long as; **je ne partirai pas** ~ **qu'il ne m'aura pas accordé un rendez-vous** I won't leave until he's given me an appointment; **traite-moi de menteur** ~ **que tu y es!** (colloq) go ahead and call me a liar!
(d) (replacing number) **gagner** ~ **par mois** to earn so much a month
2 tant de quantif **Loulou, Pivachon et** ~ **d'autres** Loulou, Pivachon and so many others; ~ **de travail** so much work
3 (in phrases) ~ **pis** too bad; ~ **mieux** so much the better; ~ **mieux pour toi** good for you; ~ **et plus** a great deal; a great many; ~ **et si bien que** so much so that; **s'il avait un** ~ **soit peu de bon sens** if he had the

slightest bit of common sense; ~ **qu'à faire, autant repeindre toute la pièce** we may as well repaint the whole room while we're at it; **en** ~ **que** as; **en** ~ **que tel** as such; **si** ~ **est qu'il puisse y aller** that is if he can go at all; **je ne l'aime pas** ~ **que ça** I don't like him/her all that much

tante /tɑ̃t/ nf aunt

tantôt /tɑ̃to/ adv sometimes

taon /tɑ̃/ nm horsefly

tapage /tapaʒ/ nm **(a)** din, racket (colloq)
(b) furore (GB), furor (US)
(c) hype; ~ **médiatique** media hype
■ ~ **nocturne** disturbance of the peace at night

tapageur, -euse /tapaʒœR, øz/ adj
(a) ⟨person⟩ rowdy
(b) ⟨luxury⟩ showy; ⟨campaign⟩ hyped-up

tapant, ~**e** /tapɑ̃, ɑ̃t/ adj **à trois heures** ~**es** at three o'clock sharp or on the dot

tape /tap/ nf pat; slap

tape-à-l'œil /tapalœj/ adj inv (colloq) ⟨colour⟩ loud; ⟨jewellery, decor⟩ garish

taper /tape/ [1] **1** vtr **(a)** to hit ⟨person, dog⟩
(b) to type ⟨letter⟩
2 taper sur v+prep to hit; ~ **sur l'épaule de qn** to tap sb on the shoulder
3 vi **(a)** ~ **des mains** to clap one's hands; ~ **à la porte** to knock at the door; **le soleil tape aujourd'hui** (colloq) the sun is beating down today
(b) ~ **(à la machine)** to type
4 se taper v refl (+ v être) **(a)** (colloq) **se** ~ **dessus** to knock each other about
(b) **c'est à se** ~ **la tête contre les murs** (figurative) it's enough to drive you up the wall
(c) (colloq) to get stuck with (colloq) ⟨chore, person⟩
IDIOMS **elle m'a tapé dans l'œil** (colloq) I thought she was striking

tapette /tapet/ nf **(a)** carpet beater
(b) fly swatter
(c) mousetrap

tapeur, -euse /tapœR, øz/ nm,f (colloq) scrounger (colloq)

tapioca /tapjɔka/ nm tapioca

tapir[1]: **se tapir** /tapiR/ [3] v refl (+ v être) **(a)** ⟨person, animal⟩ to hide
(b) to crouch

tapir[2] /tapiR/ nm (Zool) tapir

tapis /tapi/ nm inv rug; carpet; mat; **mettre qch sur le** ~ (figurative) to bring sth up; **mettre** or **envoyer qn au** ~ to throw sb
■ ~ **de bain(s)** bathmat; ~ **roulant** moving walkway; (for luggage) carousel; (in factory, supermarket) conveyor belt

tapisser /tapise/ [1] vtr **(a)** to wallpaper; to decorate ⟨room⟩; to cover ⟨armchair⟩
(b) ⟨snow⟩ to carpet ⟨ground⟩; ⟨residue⟩ to line ⟨bottom of container⟩

tapisserie /tapisRi/ nf **(a)** tapestry
(b) wallpaper
(c) tapestry work   ···⫸

t

IDIOMS faire ~ to be a wallflower

tapissier, -ière /tapisje, ɛʀ/ nm,f
(a) upholsterer
(b) tapestry-maker

tapoter /tapɔte/ [1] vtr to tap ⟨table, object⟩; to pat ⟨cheeks, back⟩

taquin, ~e /takɛ̃, in/ adj ⟨person⟩ teasing

taquiner /takine/ [1] vtr ⟨person⟩ to tease

tarabiscoté, ~e /taʀabiskɔte/ adj ⟨design⟩ over-ornate; ⟨reasoning⟩ convoluted

tarama /taʀama/ nm taramasalata

taratata /taʀatata/ excl (colloq) nonsense!, rubbish! (colloq)

tard /taʀ/ **1** adv late; plus ~ later; bien plus ~ much later (on); au plus ~ at the latest; pas plus ~ qu'hier only yesterday
2 sur le tard phr ⟨marry⟩ late in life

tarder /taʀde/ [1] **1** vi (a) ~ à faire to take a long time doing; to put off or delay doing
(b) ⟨reaction⟩ to be a long time coming; les enfants ne vont pas ~ the children won't be long
2 v impers il me tarde de la revoir I'm longing to see her again

tardif, -ive /taʀdif, iv/ adj late; belated

tardivement /taʀdivmɑ̃/ adv ⟨arrive⟩ late; ⟨react⟩ rather belatedly

tare /taʀ/ nf (a) tare
(b) defect

taré, ~e /taʀe/ adj (colloq) crazy (colloq)

targette /taʀʒɛt/ nf bolt

targuer: se targuer /taʀge/ [1] v refl (+ v être) to claim, to boast

tarif /taʀif/ nm (a) (gen) rate; (on bus, train) fare; (for consultation) fee; payer plein ~ to pay full price; to pay full fare; ~ de nuit night-time rate
(b) price list
■ ~ douanier customs tariff

tarification /taʀifikasjɔ̃/ nf price setting; tariff

tarir /taʀiʀ/ [23] **1** vtr to dry up ⟨source, well⟩; to sap ⟨strength⟩
2 vi ne pas ~ d'éloges sur qn/qch to be full of praise for sb/sth
3 se tarir v refl (+ v être) to dry up

tarot /taʀo/ nm tarot (card game)

tartare /taʀtaʀ/ adj (a) Tartar
(b) (Culin) sauce ~ tartare sauce

tarte /taʀt/ nf (a) (Culin) tart
(b) (slang) wallop (colloq)
IDIOMS c'est pas de la ~ (colloq) it's no picnic (colloq)

tartelette /taʀtəlɛt/ nf (small) tart

tartine /taʀtin/ nf (a) slice of bread and butter
(b) (colloq) il en a écrit une ~ he wrote reams about it

tartiner /taʀtine/ [1] vtr to spread

tartre /taʀtʀ/ nm (in kettle) scale; (on teeth) tartar

tartufe /taʀtyf/ nm hypocrite

tas /tɑ/ **1** nm inv (a) heap, pile; en ~ ⟨put, place⟩ in a heap or pile; ~ de ferraille scrap heap; (figurative) (colloq) wreck
(b) (colloq) un ~, des ~ loads (colloq)
2 dans le tas phr (colloq) tirer dans le ~ to fire into the crowd
3 sur le tas phr apprendre sur le ~ to learn on the job; grève sur le ~ sit-down strike

tasse /tɑs/ nf cup; ~ à thé teacup
IDIOMS boire la ~ (colloq) to swallow a mouthful of water (when swimming)

tassement /tɑsmɑ̃/ nm contraction; ~ de vertèbres compression of the vertebrae

tasser /tɑse/ [1] **1** vtr to press down ⟨earth⟩; to pack down ⟨hay⟩; to pack ⟨clothes, people⟩ (dans into); il a la cinquantaine bien tassée (colloq) he's well over fifty
2 se tasser v refl (+ v être) (a) (with age) to shrink
(b) (in train, car) ⟨people⟩ to squash up
(c) (colloq) ⟨rumour, conflict⟩ to die down

tata /tata/ nf (colloq) auntie

tâter /tɑte/ [1] **1** vtr to feel; ~ le sol du pied to test the ground
2 se tâter v refl (+ v être) (colloq) je me tâte I'm thinking about it
IDIOMS ~ le terrain to put out feelers

tatillon, -onne /tatijɔ̃, ɔn/ adj nit-picking

tâtonnement /tɑtɔnmɑ̃/ nm ~s dans l'obscurité groping around in the dark; les ~s des chercheurs tentative research; après dix années de ~s after ten years of trial and error

tâtonner /tɑtɔne/ [1] vi to grope about or around

tâtons: à tâtons /atɑtɔ̃/ phr avancer à ~ to feel one's way along

tatouage /tatwaʒ/ nm tattoo

tatouer /tatwe/ [1] vtr to tattoo

tatoueur, -euse /tatwœʀ, øz/ nm,f tattooist

taudis /todi/ nm inv (a) hovel
(b) pigsty

taule /tol/ nf (slang) prison

taupe /top/ nf (a) (Zool) mole
(b) moleskin

taupinière /topinjɛʀ/ nf (a) molehill
(b) (mole) tunnels

taureau, pl ~x /tɔʀo/ nm (Zool) bull
IDIOMS prendre le ~ par les cornes to take the bull by the horns

Taureau /tɔʀo/ pr nm Taurus

tauromachie /tɔʀomaʃi/ nf bullfighting

taux /to/ nm inv (a) (gen) rate; ~ de chômage unemployment rate
(b) (Med) (of alcohol, albumen, sugar) level; (of bacteria, sperm) count

taxation /taksasjɔ̃/ nf (a) taxation
(b) assessment

taxe /taks/ nf tax; boutique hors ~s duty-free shop (GB) or store (US); 1 000 francs toutes ~s comprises 1,000 francs inclusive of tax

■ ∼ **de douane** customs duty; ∼ **foncière** property tax; ∼ **d'habitation** ≈ council tax (*paid by residents to cover local services*); ∼ **à la valeur ajoutée** value added tax

taxer /takse/ [1] *vtr* (a) (Econ) to tax
(b) ∼ **qn de laxisme** to accuse sb of being lax

taxi /taksi/ *nm* taxi, cab (US)

taxidermiste /taksidɛrmist/ *nmf* taxidermist

Tchad /tʃad/ *pr nm* Chad

tchador /tʃadɔr/ *nm* chador

tchao /tʃao/ *excl* (colloq) bye! (colloq), see you! (colloq)

tchèque /tʃɛk/ ① *adj* Czech; **République** ∼ Czech Republic
② *nm* (Ling) Czech

tchin(-tchin) /tʃin(tʃin)/ *excl* (colloq) cheers!

TD /tede/ *nm pl* (colloq) (*abbr* = **travaux dirigés**) (Sch) practical

te (**t'** *before vowel or mute h*) /t(ə)/ *pron*
(a) (direct or indirect object) you
(b) (reflexive pronoun) yourself; **va** ∼ **laver les mains** go and wash your hands

té /te/ *nm* T-square; **en** ∼ T-shaped

technicien, -ienne /tɛknisjɛ̃, ɛn/ *nm,f*
(a) technician
(b) technical expert
(c) engineer
■ ∼ **de surface** cleaner

technique¹ /tɛknik/ ① *adj* technical
② *nm* technical subjects

technique² /tɛknik/ *nf* (a) technique
(b) technology

technocrate /tɛknɔkrat/ *nmf* technocrat

technologie /tɛknɔlɔʒi/ *nf* technology

teck /tɛk/ *nm* teak; **en** ∼ teak

teckel /tekɛl/ *nm* dachshund

tee-shirt, *pl* ∼**s** /tiʃœrt/ *nm* T-shirt

teigne /tɛɲ/ *nf* (a) (Med) ringworm
(b) moth
(c) (colloq) **être méchant comme une** ∼ to be a nasty (GB) *or* real (US) piece of work (colloq)

teigneux, -euse /tɛɲø, øz/ *adj* (colloq) cantankerous

teindre /tɛ̃dr/ [73] ① *vtr* to dye; to stain
② **se teindre** *v refl* (+ *v être*) to dye one's hair

teint, ∼e¹ /tɛ̃, tɛ̃t/ ① *pp* ▶ TEINDRE
② *pp adj* dyed; stained
③ *nm* complexion; **avoir le** ∼ **rose** *or* **frais** to have a healthy glow to one's cheeks

teinte² /tɛ̃t/ *nf* (a) shade
(b) colour (GB)

teinter /tɛ̃te/ [1] ① *vtr* (a) to tint; to stain; to dye
(b) ∼ **qch de** to tinge sth with
② **se teinter** *v refl* (+ *v être*) **se** ∼ **de** to become tinged with

teinture /tɛ̃tyr/ *nf* dye; (for wood) stain

teinturerie /tɛ̃tyrri/ *nf* (dry-)cleaner's

teinturier, -ière /tɛ̃tyrje, ɛr/ *nm,f*
(a) dry-cleaner
(b) dyer

tel, telle /tɛl/ *adj* (a) such; **une telle conduite** such behaviour (GB)
(b) like; ∼ **père,** ∼ **fils** like father like son
(c) **telle est la vérité** that is the truth; **comme** ∼**, en tant que** ∼ as such; **ses affaires étaient restées telles quelles** his/her things were left as they were
(d) **avec un** ∼ **enthousiasme** with such enthusiasm; **de telle sorte** *or* **façon** *or* **manière que** in such a way that; so that
(e) **admettons qu'il arrive** ∼ **jour, à telle heure** suppose that he arrives on such and such a day, at such and such a time

télé /tele/ *adj inv, nf* (colloq) TV

télé-achat /teleaʃa/ *nm* teleshopping

téléchargeable /teleʃarʒabl/ *adj* (Comput) downloadable; uploadable

téléchargement /teleʃarʒmã/ *nm* (Comput) download; upload

télécharger /teleʃarʒe/ *vt* (Comput) to download; upload

télécommande /telekɔmãd/ *nf* remote control

télécommander /telekɔmãde/ [1] *vtr*
(a) to operate [sth] by remote control; **voiture télécommandée** remote-controlled car
(b) (figurative) to mastermind

télécommunication /telekɔmynikasjɔ̃/ *nf* telecommunications

téléconférence /telekɔ̃ferãs/ *nf*
(a) conference call
(b) teleconference

télécopie /telekɔpi/ *nf* fax

télécopier /telekɔpje/ [2] *vtr* to fax

télécopieur /telekɔpjœr/ *nm* fax machine, fax

télédiffuser /teledifyze/ [1] *vtr* to broadcast

télé-enseignement, *pl* ∼**s** /teleãsɛɲəmã/ *nm* distance learning

téléfilm /telefilm/ *nm* TV film, TV movie

télégramme /telegram/ *nm* telegram

télégraphier /telegrafje/ [1] *vtr* to telegraph

télégraphique /telegrafik/ *adj* ⟨pole, message⟩ telegraph; ⟨style⟩ telegraphic

téléguidage /telegidaʒ/ *nm* radio control

téléguider /telegide/ [1] *vtr* (a) to control [sth] by radio
(b) (figurative) to mastermind

télématique /telematik/ ① *adj* ⟨service, network⟩ viewdata (GB), videotex®
② *nf* telematics

téléobjectif /teleɔbʒɛktif/ *nm* telephoto lens

télépathie /telepati/ *nf* telepathy

téléphérique /teleferik/ *nm* cable car

téléphone /telefɔn/ *nm* phone ⋯

■ ~ **arabe** (colloq) grapevine, bush telegraph; ~ **portable** mobile phone; ~ **portatif** pocket car phone; **le ~ rouge** the hotline

téléphoner /telefɔne/ [1] *vi* to phone; to make a phone call; ~ **à qn** to phone sb

téléphonique /telefɔnik/ *adj* (tele)phone

télescope /teleskɔp/ *nm* telescope

télescoper /teleskɔpe/ [1] **1** *vtr* ⟨*truck, juggernaut*⟩ to crush ⟨*car*⟩

2 se télescoper *v refl* (+ *v être*) **(a)** ⟨*vehicles*⟩ to collide **(b)** ⟨*notions, tendencies*⟩ to overlap

télescopique /teleskɔpik/ *adj* telescopic

téléscripteur /teleskʀiptœʀ/ *nm* teleprinter, teletypewriter

télésiège /telesjɛʒ/ *nm* chair lift

téléski /teleski/ *nm* ski tow

téléspectateur, -trice /telespɛktatœʀ, tʀis/ *nm,f* viewer

télésurveillance /telesyʀvejɑ̃s/ *nf* electronic surveillance

télétransmission /teletʀɑ̃smisjɔ̃/ *nf* transmission

télétravail /teletʀavaj/ *nm* teleworking

télévente /televɑ̃t/ *nf* telesales

télévisé, ~e /televize/ *adj* television; televised

téléviseur /televizœʀ/ *nm* television (set)

télévision /televizjɔ̃/ *nf* television, TV

télex /telɛks/ *nm inv* telex; **par ~** by telex

télexer /telɛkse/ [1] *vtr* to telex

tellement /tɛlmɑ̃/ **1** *adv* (modifying an adjective or adverb) so; (modifying a verb or comparative) so much; **pas ~** not much; **il n'aime pas ~ lire** he doesn't like reading much; **j'ai de la peine à suivre ~ c'est compliqué** it's so complicated that I find it hard to follow

2 tellement de *quantif* (colloq) **il y a ~ de choses à voir** there's so much to see; **il a eu ~ de chance** he was so lucky; **il y en a ~ qui aimeraient le faire** so many people would like to do it

téméraire /temeʀɛʀ/ *adj* ⟨*person, plan*⟩ reckless; ⟨*judgment*⟩ rash; **courageux mais pas ~** brave but not foolhardy

témérité /temeʀite/ *nf* recklessness; rashness; **avoir la ~ de faire** to have the temerity to do

témoignage /temwaɲaʒ/ *nm* **(a)** story **(b)** account; **~s recueillis auprès de** accounts given by **(c)** evidence; testimony; **des ~s contradictoires/qui concordent** conflicting/ corroborating evidence **(d)** ~ **d'amitié** (gift) token of friendship; **les ~s de sympathie** expressions of sympathy

témoigner /temwaɲe/ [1] **1** *vtr* **(a)** (Law) to testify **(b)** ~ **de l'affection** to show affection **2 témoigner de** *v+prep* **(a)** ~ **de** to show **(b)** ~ **du courage de qn** to vouch for sb's courage **3** *vi* **(a)** (Law) to give evidence

(b) '**il était toujours poli**', **témoignent les voisins** neighbours (GB) say he was always polite

témoin /temwɛ̃/ *nm* **(a)** (gen, Law) witness; ~ **oculaire** eyewitness **(b)** (at duel) second **(c)** (Tech) indicator *or* warning light

tempe /tɑ̃p/ *nf* temple

tempérament /tɑ̃peʀamɑ̃/ *nm* disposition; **avoir du ~** to have a strong character

tempérance /tɑ̃peʀɑ̃s/ *nf* temperance

température /tɑ̃peʀatyʀ/ *nf* temperature

tempéré, ~e /tɑ̃peʀe/ *adj* temperate

tempérer /tɑ̃peʀe/ [14] *vtr* to temper; to moderate ⟨*argument*⟩

tempête /tɑ̃pɛt/ *nf* **(a)** gale; storm **(b)** uproar; **déclencher une ~ de protestations** to trigger a wave of protest

tempêter /tɑ̃pɛte/ [1] *vi* to rage

temple /tɑ̃pl/ *nm* **(a)** (gen) temple; (protestant) church **(b)** (figurative) temple

tempo /tɛmpo/ *nm* (Mus) tempo

temporaire /tɑ̃pɔʀɛʀ/ *adj* temporary

temporel, -elle /tɑ̃pɔʀɛl/ *adj* (gen) temporal

temporisateur, -trice /tɑ̃pɔʀizatœʀ, tʀis/ **1** *adj* temporizing **2** *nm,f* temporizer

temporiser /tɑ̃pɔʀize/ [1] *vi* to stall

temps /tɑ̃/ *nm inv* **(a)** weather; **un beau ~** fine weather; **le ~ est à la pluie** it looks like rain; **quel ~ fait-il?** what's the weather like?; **par tous les ~** in all weathers **(b)** time; **le ~ arrangera les choses** time will take care of everything; **peu de ~ avant** shortly before; **en peu de ~** in a short time; **dans peu de ~** shortly; **dans quelque ~** before long; **pendant ce ~(-là)** meanwhile; **qu'as-tu fait tout ce ~(-là)?** what have you been doing all this time?; **en un rien de ~** in no time at all; **les trois quarts du ~** most of the time; **le ~ de ranger mes affaires et j'arrive** just let me put my things away and I'll be with you; **on a (tout) le ~** we've got (plenty of) time; **avoir dix** *or* **cent fois le ~** to have all the time in the world; **laisser à qn le ~ de faire** to give sb time to do; **mettre** *or* **prendre du ~** to take time; **beaucoup de ~** a long time; **tu y as mis le ~!**, **tu en as mis du ~!** you (certainly) took your time!; **le ~ passe vite** time flies; **faire passer le ~** to while away the time; **avoir du ~ à perdre** to have time on one's hands; **c'est du ~ perdu**, **c'est une perte de ~** it's a waste of time; **le ~ presse!** time is short!; **j'ai trouvé le ~ long** (the) time seemed to drag; **finir dans les ~** to finish in time; **à ~** ⟨*leave, finish*⟩ in time; **juste à ~** just in time; **de ~ en ~**, **de ~ à autre** from time to time; **il était ~!** (impatiently) (and) about time too!; (with relief) just in the nick of time!; **en ~ utile** in time; **en ~ voulu** in due course; at the right time; **ne durer qu'un ~** to be short-lived

(c) au *or* du ~ des Grecs in the time of the
Greeks; au *or* du ~ où in the days when; le
bon vieux ~ the good old days; ces derniers
~ recently; ces ~-ci lately; de mon ~ in my
day; dans le ~ in those days; en ~ normal
usually; en d'autres ~ at any other time
(d) stage; en deux ~ in two stages; dans un
premier ~ first; dans un deuxième ~
subsequently; dans un dernier ~ finally
(e) (of verb) tense
(f) avoir un travail à ~ partiel/plein to have
a part-/full-time job
(g) (Sport) time; il a réalisé le meilleur ~ he
got the best time; améliorer son ~ d'une
seconde to knock a second off one's time
(h) (of engine) stroke
(i) (Mus) time; mesure à deux ~ two-four
time
■ ~ d'antenne airtime; ~ fort (Mus) forte;
(figurative) high point; ~ mort slack period;
~ universel Greenwich Mean Time, GMT
IDIOMS au ~ pour moi! my mistake!; par les
~ qui courent with things as they are; se
payer du bon ~ (colloq) to have a whale of a
time (colloq)

tenable /tənabl/ *adj* (a) bearable; la
situation n'est pas ~ the situation is
unbearable
(b) (defendable) tenable
(c) les élèves ne sont pas ~s aujourd'hui
the pupils are being impossible today

tenace /tənas/ *adj* (a) ⟨stain, headache⟩
stubborn; ⟨perfume⟩ long-lasting; ⟨fog, cough,
memory⟩ persistent
(b) ⟨person⟩ tenacious; persistent; ⟨will⟩
tenacious

ténacité /tenasite/ *nf* tenacity;
persistence

tenaille /tənɑj/ *nf* pincers

tenailler /tənɑje/ [1] *vtr* il était tenaillé par
le remords he was racked with remorse

tenancier, -ière /tənɑ̃sje, ɛR/ *nm,f*
(of café) landlord/landlady; (of hotel, casino)
manager/manageress

tenant, ~e /tənɑ̃, ɑ̃t/ ①① *nm,f* (Sport) ~ du
titre titleholder
② *nm* d'un seul ~ all in one piece
IDIOMS les ~s et les aboutissants de qch
the ins and outs of sth

tendance /tɑ̃dɑ̃s/ *nf* (a) tendency
(b) (in politics) tendency; toutes ~s politiques
confondues across party lines
(c) trend

tendancieux, -ieuse /tɑ̃dɑ̃sjø, øz/ *adj*
biased (GB), tendentious

tendeur /tɑ̃dœR/ *nm* (a) (of tent) guy rope
(b) (for roof rack) elastic strap

tendon /tɑ̃dɔ̃/ *nm* tendon

tendre¹ /tɑ̃dR/ [6] ①① *vtr* (a) to tighten
⟨rope, cable⟩; to stretch ⟨elastic, skin⟩; to
extend ⟨spring⟩; ~ le bras to reach out;
~ les bras à qn to greet sb with open arms;
~ la main to reach out; to hold out one's
hand; ~ la main à qn to hold one's hand out
to sb; (figurative) to lend sb a helping hand

(b) to spread ⟨cloth, sheet⟩
(c) to set ⟨trap⟩; to put up ⟨clothes line⟩
(d) ~ qch à qn to hold sth out to sb
② **tendre à** *v+prep* ~ à faire to tend to do
③ *vi* (a) ~ vers to strive for
(b) ~ vers to approach ⟨value⟩; to tend to
⟨zero⟩
④ **se tendre** *v refl* (+ *v être*) (a) to tighten
(b) to become strained

tendre² /tɑ̃dR/ ①① *adj* (a) ⟨wood, fibre⟩ soft;
⟨skin, vegetables⟩ tender
(b) ⟨shoot, grass⟩ new; ~ enfance earliest
childhood
(c) ⟨pink, green⟩ soft
(d) ⟨person⟩ loving; ⟨love, smile, words⟩
tender; ⟨temperament⟩ gentle; ne pas être ~
avec qn/qch to be hard on sb/sth
(e) ⟨husband, wife⟩ dear
② *nmf* soft-hearted person

tendrement /tɑ̃dRəmɑ̃/ *adv* tenderly

tendresse /tɑ̃dRɛs/ *nf* (a) tenderness
(b) affection

tendu, ~e /tɑ̃dy/ ①① *pp* ▶ TENDRE¹
② *pp adj* ⟨rope⟩ tight
③ *adj* ⟨person, meeting⟩ tense

ténèbres /tenɛbR/ *nf pl* les ~ darkness

ténébreux, -euse /tenebRø, øz/ *adj*
(a) dark
(b) obscure

teneur /tənœR/ *nf* (a) (of solid) content;
(of gas, liquid) level
(b) (of report) import

ténia /tenja/ *nm* tapeworm

tenir /təniR/ [36] ①① *vtr* (a) to hold; ~ qn
par la main to hold sb's hand; tiens! (giving sth
to sb) here you are!; tiens, regarde! hey,
look!; si je le tenais! if I could get my hands
on him!
(b) to keep [sb] under control; il nous tient
he's got a hold on us
(c) (Mil) to hold ⟨hill, bridge, city⟩
(d) to hold ⟨captive, animal⟩; je te tiens! I've
caught you!
(e) to have ⟨information⟩
(f) to hold ⟨job⟩; to run ⟨shop, house,
business⟩; to be in charge of ⟨switchboard,
reception⟩
(g) to keep; '~ hors de portée des enfants'
'keep out of reach of children'
(h) ~ sa tête droite to hold one's head
upright; ~ les yeux baissés to keep one's
eyes lowered
(i) to hold down ⟨load, cargo⟩; to hold up
⟨trousers, socks⟩
(j) to keep to ⟨itinerary⟩
(k) ~ la mer ⟨ship⟩ to be seaworthy; ~ le
coup to hold out; ~ le choc ⟨person⟩ to
stand the strain
(l) ⟨object⟩ to take up ⟨room⟩; ⟨person⟩ to
hold ⟨role, position⟩
(m) ~ qn/qch pour responsable to hold sb/
sth responsible; ~ qn pour mort to give sb
up for dead
② **tenir à** *v+prep* (a) ~ à to be fond of, to
like; ~ à la vie to value one's life

t

(b) j'y tiens I insist; **~ à ce que qn fasse** to insist that sb should do

3 tenir de *v+prep* **~ de qn** to take after sb
4 *vi* **(a)** ⟨*rope, shelf, dam*⟩ to hold; ⟨*stamp, glue*⟩ to stick; ⟨*bandage, structure*⟩ to stay in place; ⟨*hairstyle*⟩ to stay tidy
(b) ~ ⟨*bon*⟩ (gen) to hang on; (Mil) to hold out
(c) la neige tient the snow is settling; **les fleurs n'ont pas tenu** the flowers didn't last long
(d) ⟨*theory*⟩ to hold good; ⟨*alibi*⟩ to stand up
(e) ⟨*people, objects*⟩ to fit; **~ à six dans une voiture** to fit six into a car; **mon article tient en trois pages** my article takes up only three pages
5 se tenir *v refl* (+ *v être*) **(a) se ~ la tête à deux mains** to hold one's head in one's hands
(b) se ~ par le bras to be arm in arm; **se ~ par la main** to hold hands
(c) se ~ à qch to hold onto sth; **tiens-toi** *or* **tenez-vous bien** (figurative) (colloq) prepare yourself for a shock
(d) se ~ accroupi to be squatting; **se ~ au milieu** to be standing in the middle; **se ~ prêt** to be ready
(e) to behave; **se ~ bien/mal** to behave well/badly
(f) se ~ bien/mal to have (a) good posture/(a) bad posture; **tiens-toi droit!** stand up straight!
(g) ⟨*demonstration, exhibition*⟩ to be held
(h) ⟨*argument, book*⟩ to hold together; **ça se tient** it makes sense
(i) tenez-vous le pour dit! (colloq) I don't want to have to tell you again!
(j) s'en ~ à to keep to; **s'en ~ aux ordres** to stick to orders; **ne pas savoir à quoi s'en ~** not to know what to make of it
6 *v impers* **il ne tient qu'à toi de partir** it's up to you to decide whether to leave; **qu'à cela ne tienne!** never mind!

tennis /tenis/ **1** *nm inv* tennis; **~ de table** table tennis
2 *nm inv or nf inv* tennis shoe

tennisman, *pl* **tennismen** /tenisman, mɛn/ *nm* (male) tennis player

ténor /tenɔʀ/ *nm* tenor

tension /tɑ̃sjɔ̃/ *nf* **(a)** (of cable, muscle) tension
(b) (Med) **~** ⟨*artérielle*⟩ blood pressure; **être sous ~** to be under stress
(c) (in electricity) tension; **basse ~** low voltage; **sous ~** ⟨*wire*⟩ live; ⟨*machine*⟩ switched on
(d) (between people) tension

tentacule /tɑ̃takyl/ *nm* tentacle

tentateur, -trice /tɑ̃tatœʀ, tʀis/ *nm,f* tempter/temptress

tentation /tɑ̃tasjɔ̃/ *nf* temptation

tentative /tɑ̃tativ/ *nf* attempt; **~ de meurtre** (gen) murder attempt; (Law) attempted murder

tente /tɑ̃t/ *nf* tent

tenter /tɑ̃te/ [1] *vtr* **(a)** to attempt; **~ sa chance** to try one's luck; **~ le tout pour le tout** to risk one's all

(b) to tempt; **cela ne la tente guère** that doesn't appeal to her very much; **laisse-toi ~!** be a devil!; **~ le diable** to court disaster

tenture /tɑ̃tyʀ/ *nf* **(a)** curtain; **~s** draperies
(b) fabric wall covering

tenu, ~e[1] /təny/ **1** *pp* ▶ TENIR
2 *pp adj* **(a) bien/mal ~** ⟨*child*⟩ well/badly cared for; ⟨*house*⟩ well/badly kept
(b) ~ de faire required to do; **~ à** bound by

tenue[2] /təny/ *nf* **(a) ~** ⟨*vestimentaire*⟩ dress, clothes; **être en ~ légère** to be scantily dressed; **en ~** (Mil) uniformed
(b) avoir de la ~ to have good manners; **un peu de ~!** mind your manners!
(c) posture

ter /tɛʀ/ *adv* **(a)** (in address) ter; **15 ~ rue du Rocher** 15 ter rue du Rocher
(b) three times

térébenthine /teʀebɑ̃tin/ *nf* turpentine

tergal® /tɛʀgal/ *nm* Terylene®

tergiversation /tɛʀʒivɛʀsasjɔ̃/ *nf* equivocation

tergiverser /tɛʀʒivɛʀse/ [1] *vi* **(a)** to dither
(b) to shilly-shally

terme /tɛʀm/ **1** *nm* **(a)** term, word
(b) end; **mettre un ~ à qch** to put an end to sth; **toucher à son ~** to come to an end; **arriver à ~** ⟨*period, contract*⟩ to expire; **accoucher avant ~** to give birth prematurely
(c) passé ce ~ vous paierez des intérêts after this date, you will pay interest; **à moyen ~** ⟨*loan*⟩ medium-term
(d) trouver un moyen ~ to find a compromise
2 termes *nm pl* terms; **~s de l'échange** terms of trade; **en bons ~s** on good terms

terminaison /tɛʀminɛzɔ̃/ *nf* ending

terminal, ~e[1], *mpl* **-aux** /tɛʀminal, o/
1 *adj* ⟨*year*⟩ final; **phase ~e** (of operation) concluding phase; (of illness) terminal phase
2 *nm* terminal

terminale[2] /tɛʀminal/ *nf* (Sch) final year (*of secondary school*)

terminer /tɛʀmine/ [1] **1** *vtr* to finish; to end
2 *vi* to finish; **en ~ avec** to be through with; **pour ~** in conclusion
3 se terminer *v refl* (+ *v être*) **(a)** to end; **être terminé** to be over
(b) se ~ par ⟨*word, number, object*⟩ to end in

terminologie /tɛʀminɔlɔʒi/ *nf* terminology

terminus /tɛʀminys/ *nm inv* (of train) end of the line; (of bus) terminus

termite /tɛʀmit/ *nm* termite

ternaire /tɛʀnɛʀ/ *adj* (in maths, physics) ternary; (Mus) compound

terne /tɛʀn/ *adj* ⟨*hair, life*⟩ dull; ⟨*colour*⟩ drab; ⟨*eyes, expression*⟩ lifeless

ternir /tɛʀniʀ/ [3] **1** *vtr* **(a)** to tarnish ⟨*metal*⟩; to fade ⟨*fabric*⟩
(b) to tarnish ⟨*image, reputation*⟩

2 se ternir *v refl* (+ *v être*) to tarnish

terrain /tɛʀɛ̃/ *nm* **(a)** (gen) ground; (Mil) field
(b) plot of land
(c) land
(d) (for football, rugby, cricket) pitch, field; ground; (for volley-ball, handball, tennis) court; (in golf) course
(e) (figurative) **nous ne vous suivrons pas sur ce ~** we won't go along with you there; **un ~ d'entente** common ground; **travailler sur le ~** to do fieldwork; **~ favorable** (Med) predisposing factors; (in sociology) favourable (GB) environment; **déblayer le ~** to clear the ground; **préparer le ~** to pave the way; **tâter le ~** to put out feelers
■ **~ d'atterrissage** landing strip; **~ d'aviation** airfield; **~ de camping** campsite; **~ de jeu(x)** playground; **~ de sport(s)** sports ground; **~ vague** wasteland

terrasse /tɛʀas/ *nf* **(a)** terrace; **s'installer à la ~ d'un café** to sit at a table outside a café
(b) flat roof
(c) large balcony

terrassement /tɛʀasmã/ *nm* excavation; **faire des travaux de ~** to carry out excavation work

terrasser /tɛʀase/ [1] *vtr* (illness) to strike down; **terrassé par** (by heat, grief) prostrated by

terrassier /tɛʀasje/ *nm* building labourer

terre /tɛʀ/ **1** *nf* **(a)** ground; **sous ~** underground
(b) earth; soil; **sortir de ~** (plant) to come up
(c) land; **le retour à la ~** the movement back to the land; **aller à ~** to go ashore; **s'enfoncer à l'intérieur des ~s** to go deep inland
(d) earth; **il croit que la ~ entière est contre lui** he thinks the whole world is against him; **redescends sur ~!** come back to earth!
(e) **de la ~ (glaise)** clay; **un pot en ~** an earthenware pot
(f) (in electricity) earth (GB), ground (US)
2 terre à terre *phr* (question) basic; (conversation, person) pedestrian
3 par terre *phr* on the ground; on the floor; **c'est à se rouler par ~** (colloq) it's hilarious; **ça a fichu tous nos projets par ~** (colloq) it messed up all our plans (colloq)
■ **~ d'asile** country of refuge; **~ battue** trodden earth; **sur ~ battue** on a clay court
IDIOMS **avoir les pieds sur ~** (colloq) to have one's feet firmly planted on the ground

Terre /tɛʀ/ *nf* Earth; **sur la ~** on Earth

terreau, *pl* **~x** /tɛʀo/ *nm* compost; **~ de feuilles** leaf mould (GB), leaf mold (US)

terre-plein, *pl* **terres-pleins** /tɛʀplɛ̃/ *nm* (of road) central reservation (GB), median strip (US)

terrer: se terrer /tɛʀe/ [1] *v refl* (+ *v être*)
(a) (rabbit) to disappear into its burrow; (fox) to go to earth
(b) (fugitive) to hide

terrestre /tɛʀɛstʀ/ *adj* **(a)** (surface, diameter) of the Earth
(b) (animals) land
(c) (war, transport) land; **la vie/le paradis ~** life/heaven on earth

terreur /tɛʀœʀ/ *nf* terror; **c'est ma grande ~** it's my greatest fear

terrible /tɛʀibl/ *adj* **(a)** (gen) terrible; (thirst, desire) tremendous; **il est ~, il ne veut jamais avoir tort** (colloq) it's terrible the way he never wants to admit that he's wrong
(b) (colloq) terrific (colloq)

terriblement /tɛʀibləmã/ *adv* terribly; **il a ~ grandi** he's grown an awful lot

terrien, -ienne /tɛʀjɛ̃, ɛn/ *adj* **propriétaire ~** landowner

terrier /tɛʀje/ *nm* **(a)** (gen) hole; **un ~ de renard** a fox's earth
(b) (Zool) terrier

terrifiant, ~e /tɛʀifjã, ãt/ *adj* terrifying

terrifier /tɛʀifje/ [2] *vtr* to terrify

terrine /tɛʀin/ *nf* (gen) terrine; (round) earthenware bowl

territoire /tɛʀitwaʀ/ *nm* territory.
■ **~ d'outre-mer, TOM** French overseas (administrative) territory

territorial, ~e, *mpl* **-iaux** /tɛʀitɔʀjal, o/ *adj* **(a)** (waters, integrity) territorial
(b) (administration) divisional; regional

terroir /tɛʀwaʀ/ *nm* land; **vin du ~** local wine

terroriser /tɛʀɔʀize/ [1] *vtr* **(a)** to terrorize
(b) to terrify

terrorisme /tɛʀɔʀism/ *nm* terrorism

terroriste /tɛʀɔʀist/ *adj, nmf* terrorist

tertiaire /tɛʀsjɛʀ/ *adj* **(a)** (Econ) (sector, industry) service
(b) (in geology) Tertiary

tertio /tɛʀsjo/ *adv* thirdly

tes ▶ TON¹

tesson /tɛsɔ̃/ *nm* shard, fragment

test /tɛst/ *nm* test; **~ (de dépistage) du sida** Aids test; **faire passer des ~s à qn** (gen) to give sb tests; (Med) to carry out tests on sb

testament /tɛstamã/ *nm* (Law) will; (figurative) legacy

testamentaire /tɛstamãtɛʀ/ *adj* of a will

tester /tɛste/ [1] *vtr* to test

testicule /tɛstikyl/ *nm* testicle

tétanos /tetanos/ *nm inv* tetanus

têtard /tetaʀ/ *nm* (Zool) tadpole

tête /tɛt/ *nf* **(a)** head; **en pleine ~** (right) in the head; **~ baissée** (rush) headlong; **la ~ en bas** (hang) upside down; **se laver la ~** to wash one's hair; **au-dessus de nos ~s** overhead; **être tombé sur la ~** (figurative) (colloq) to have gone off one's rocker (colloq); **ma ~ est mise à prix** there's a price on my head; **vouloir la ~ de qn** to want sb's head; to be after sb's head; **risquer sa ~** to risk one's neck (colloq); **des ~s vont tomber** (figurative) heads will roll ⋯⟶

(b) face; **une bonne/sale ~** a nice/nasty face; **tu en fais une ~!** what a face!; **quelle ~ va-t-il faire?** how's he going to react?; **il (me) fait la ~** he's sulking; **il a une ~ à tricher** he looks like a cheat; **tu as une ~ à faire peur, aujourd'hui!** you look dreadful today!

(c) **de ~** ‹*quote, recite*› from memory; ‹*calculate*› in one's head; **tu n'as pas de ~!** you have a mind like a sieve!; **avoir qch en ~** to have sth in mind; **où avais-je la ~?** whatever was I thinking of?; **ça (ne) va pas, la ~?** (colloq) are you out of your mind or what?; **mets-lui ça dans la ~** drum it into him/her; **passer par la ~ de qn** ‹*idea*› to cross sb's mind; **monter la ~ à Pierre contre Paul** to turn Pierre against Paul; **j'ai la ~ qui tourne** my head's spinning; **monter à la ~ de qn** ‹*alcohol, success*› to go to sb's head; **il a encore toute sa ~** (à lui) he's still got all his faculties; **n'en faire qu'à sa ~** to go one's own way; **tenir ~ à qn** to stand up to sb

(d) (person) **avoir ses ~s** to have one's favourites (GB); **un dîner en ~ à ~** an intimate dinner for two; **par ~** (gen) a head, each; (in statistics) per capita

(e) (measurement) head; **avoir une ~ d'avance sur qn** to be a short length in front of sb

(f) **il a été nommé à la ~ du groupe** he was appointed head of the group; **prendre la ~ des opérations** to take charge of operations; **être à la ~ d'une immense fortune** to be the possessor of a huge fortune

(g) top; **être en ~** ‹of list, category› to be at the top; (in election, race, survey) to be in the lead; **en ~ de phrase** at the beginning of a sentence

(h) (of train) front; (of convoy) head; (of tree, mast) top; (of screw, nail) head; **en ~ de file** first in line

(i) (Sport) (in football) **faire une ~** to head the ball

(j) (Mil) (of missile) warhead

(k) **~ de lecture** (in tape recorder, video recorder) head

■ **~ en l'air** scatterbrain; **~ brûlée** daredevil; **~ à claques** (colloq) pain (colloq); **~ de linotte** = EN L'AIR; **~ de mort** skull; death's head; skull and crossbones; **~ de mule** (colloq) mule; **être une vraie ~ de mule** (colloq) to be as stubborn as a mule; **~ de Turc** (colloq) whipping boy

IDIOMS **j'en mettrais ma ~ à couper** I'd swear to it; **en avoir par-dessus la ~** (colloq) to be fed up to the back teeth (colloq); **ça me prend la ~** (colloq) it's a real drag (colloq)

tête-à-queue /tɛtakø/ *nm inv* **faire un ~** to slew round *or* around

tête-à-tête /tɛtatɛt/ *nm inv* (a) tête-à-tête (b) private meeting

tête-bêche /tɛtbɛʃ/ *adv* (a) top-to-tail (b) head-to-tail

tétée /tete/ *nf* (a) feeding (b) feed

téter /tete/ [14] **1** *vtr* to suck at ‹breast›; to feed from ‹bottle›; to suck ‹milk› **2** *vi* to suckle; **donner à ~ à** to feed ‹baby›

tétine /tetin/ *nf* (a) teat (GB), nipple (US) (b) dummy (GB), pacifier (US) (c) (of animal) teat

têtu, **~e** /tety/ *adj* stubborn

texte /tɛkst/ *nm* (a) text; '**~ intégral**' 'unabridged' (b) (Law) **~ de loi** bill; law

textile /tɛkstil/ **1** *adj* textile **2** *nm* (a) textile industry (b) **~s synthétiques** synthetic fibres (GB)

texto /tɛksto/ (colloq) = TEXTUELLEMENT

textuellement /tɛkstɥɛlmɑ̃/ *adv* ‹recount› word for word

texture /tɛkstyʀ/ *nf* (a) (of fabric, material) texture (b) (of novel) structure

TGV /teʒeve/ *nm* (*abbr* = **train à grande vitesse**) TGV, high-speed train

thé /te/ *nm* (a) tea (b) tea party

théâtral, **~e**, *mpl* **-aux** /teatʀal, o/ *adj* (a) ‹performance› stage; ‹season, company› theatre (GB); ‹production, technique› theatrical; **l'œuvre ~e de Racine** the plays of Racine (b) ‹gesture› histrionic; ‹tone› melodramatic

théâtre /teatʀ/ *nm* theatre (GB); **le ~ antique** Greek classical drama; **de ~** ‹actor, director, ticket› theatre (GB); ‹decor, costume› stage; **coup de ~** coup de théâtre; (figurative) dramatic turn of events; **faire du ~** (as profession) to be an actor; (at school) to do drama; **être le ~ d'affrontements** (figurative) to be the scene of fighting

■ **~ de Boulevard** farce

théière /tejɛʀ/ *nf* teapot

théine /tein/ *nf* theine

thématique /tematik/ **1** *adj* thematic **2** *nf* themes

thème /tɛm/ *nm* (a) topic, subject; (of film) theme (b) (translation) prose (c) (Mus) theme

■ **~ astral** birth chart

théologie /teɔlɔʒi/ *nf* theology

théorème /teɔʀɛm/ *nm* theorem

théoricien, **-ienne** /teɔʀisjɛ̃, ɛn/ *nm,f* theoretician

théorie /teɔʀi/ *nf* theory; **en ~** in theory

théorique /teɔʀik/ *adj* theoretical

thérapeute /teʀapøt/ *nmf* therapist

thérapeutique /teʀapøtik/ *adj* ‹effect› therapeutic; **choix ~** choice of treatment

thérapie /teʀapi/ *nf* (a) (Med) treatment (b) (in psychology) therapy

thermal, **~e**, *mpl* **-aux** /tɛʀmal, o/ *adj* ‹spring› thermal; **station ~e** spa

thermalisme /tɛʀmalism/ *nm* (a) balneology (b) hydrotherapy industry

thermes /tɛʀm/ *nm pl* (a) (Roman) thermae (b) thermal baths

thermique /tɛʀmik/ *adj* thermal

thermo /tɛRmo/ *pref* thermo; **∼nucléaire** thermonuclear

thermomètre /tɛRmɔmɛtR/ *nm* thermometer

thermostat /tɛRmɔsta/ *nm* thermostat

thèse /tɛz/ *nf* **(a)** (for doctorate) thesis (GB), dissertation (US)
(b) thesis, argument
(c) avancer la ∼ de l'accident to put forward the theory that it was an accident

thon /tɔ̃/ *nm* tuna

thonier *nm* tuna boat

thoracique /tɔRasik/ *adj* **cage ∼** ribcage

thorax /tɔRaks/ *nm inv* thorax

thym /tɛ̃/ *nm* thyme

thyroïde /tiRɔid/ *adj, nf* thyroid

tibia /tibja/ *nm* shinbone, tibia

tic /tik/ *nm* **(a)** tic; **être plein de ∼s** to be constantly twitching
(b) ∼ de langage verbal tic

ticket /tikɛ/ *nm* (for train, platform) ticket; **∼ de caisse** till receipt (GB), sales slip (US); **∼ modérateur** *patient's contribution towards the cost of medical treatment*

ticket-restaurant®, *pl* **tickets-restaurant** /tikɛRɛstɔRɑ̃/ *nm* luncheon voucher, meal ticket

tic-tac /tiktak/ *nm inv* **faire ∼** to tick

tiède /tjɛd/ *adj* **(a)** lukewarm; warm; mild
(b) (figurative) lukewarm

tièdement /tjɛdmɑ̃/ *adv* half-heartedly

tiédeur /tjedœR/ *nf* **(a)** (of season) mildness; (of air, room) warmth
(b) (figurative) half-heartedness

tiédir /tjediR/ [3] *vi* **(a) faire ∼** to warm *or* heat (up); **laisser ∼** to allow [sth] to cool
(b) ⟨feelings⟩ to cool; ⟨enthusiasm⟩ to wane

tien, tienne /tjɛ̃, tjɛn/ **le tien, la tienne, les tiens, les tiennes** *pron* yours; **un métier comme le ∼** a job like yours; **à la tienne!** cheers!; (ironic) good luck to you!

tiens ▸ TENIR

tierce¹ /tjɛRs/ *adj f* ▸ TIERS 1

tiercé /tjɛRse/ *nm* (Games) **jouer au ∼** to bet on the horses

tiers, tierce² /tjɛR, tjɛRs/ **1** *adj* third; **un pays ∼** (gen) another country; a non-member country; **une tierce personne** a third party
2 *nm inv* **(a)** third; **le ∼/les deux ∼ du travail** one third/two thirds of the work
(b) (person) outsider; (Law) third party
■ **le Tiers État** the Third Estate

tiers-monde /tjɛRmɔ̃d/ *nm* Third World

tiers-mondisme /tjɛRmɔ̃dism/ *nm* support for the Third World

tiers-mondiste /tjɛRmɔ̃dist/ **1** *adj* in support of the Third World
2 *nmf* supporter of the Third World

tige /tiʒ/ *nf* (of plant) (gen) stem, stalk

tigre /tigR/ *nm* (Zool) tiger

tigré, ∼e /tigRe/ *adj* **(a)** striped

(b) spotted

tigresse /tigRɛs/ *nf* (Zool, figurative) tigress

tilleul /tijœl/ *nm* **(a)** limetree
(b) limewood
(c) lime-blossom tea

tilt /tilt/ *nm* (colloq) **ça a fait ∼ (dans mon esprit)** (colloq) the penny dropped (colloq)

timbale /tɛ̃bal/ *nf* **(a)** (metal) tumbler
(b) (Mus) kettledrum; **∼s** timpani
(c) (Culin) timbale

timbre /tɛ̃bR/ *nm* **(a)** stamp
(b) postmark
(c) (of voice) tone, timbre
(d) (Med) patch

timbre-poste, *pl* **timbres-poste** /tɛ̃bRəpɔst/ *nm* postage stamp

timbrer /tɛ̃bRe/ [1] *vtr* to stamp

timide /timid/ *adj* ⟨person⟩ shy, timid; ⟨criticism⟩ timid; ⟨success⟩ limited

timidement /timidmɑ̃/ *adv* shyly; timidly; (without conviction) half-heartedly

timidité /timidite/ *nf* shyness

timoré, ∼e /timɔRe/ *adj* timorous

tintamarre /tɛ̃tamaR/ *nm* din; **faire du ∼** to make a din

tintement /tɛ̃tmɑ̃/ *nm* chiming; tinkling

tinter /tɛ̃te/ [1] *vi* ⟨bells⟩ to chime; ⟨doorbell⟩ to ring; ⟨small bell⟩ to tinkle; ⟨glass, coins⟩ to clink; ⟨keys⟩ to jingle; (Mus) ⟨triangle⟩ to ring

tintinnabuler /tɛ̃tinabyle/ [1] *vi* to tinkle

tipi /tipi/ *nm* te(e)pee

tique /tik/ *nf* (Zool) tick

tiquer /tike/ [1] *vi* (colloq) to wince; **sans ∼** without batting an eyelid (GB) *or* eyelash (US)

tir /tiR/ *nm* **(a)** (Mil) fire; **déclencher le ∼** to open fire
(b) (Sport) shooting
(c) ∼ de grenades grenade firing
(d) (in games, sports) (with ball) shot
(e) shooting

tirade /tiRad/ *nf* **(a)** declamation
(b) tirade

tirage /tiRaʒ/ *nm* **(a) ∼ (au sort)** draw; **désigner par ∼ (au sort)** to draw ⟨name, winner⟩
(b) impression
(c) edition; **∼ limité** limited edition
(d) (of book) run; (of newspaper) circulation

tiraillement /tiRajmɑ̃/ *nm* **(a)** pulling, tugging
(b) nagging pain; **∼s d'estomac** hunger pangs
(c) friction

tirailler /tiRaje/ [1] *vtr* to tug (at), to pull (at) ⟨rope, sleeve⟩; **être tiraillé entre son travail et sa famille** to be torn between one's work and one's family

tire-au-flanc /tiRoflɑ̃/ *nm inv* (colloq) shirker, skiver (colloq)

tire-bouchon, *pl* **∼s** /tiRbuʃɔ̃/ *nm* corkscrew; **en ∼** ⟨tail⟩ curly

tire-d'aile: **à tire-d'aile** /atiʀdɛl/ *phr* in a flurry of wings; (figurative) hurriedly

tirelire /tiʀliʀ/ *nf* piggy bank

tirer /tiʀe/ [1] **1** *vtr* **(a)** to pull ‹vehicle›; to pull up ‹chair, armchair›; to pull away ‹rug› **(b)** to pull ‹hair›; to pull on ‹rope›; to tug at ‹sleeve›; ~ **qn par le bras** to pull sb's arm **(c)** ~ **ses cheveux en arrière** to pull back one's hair; **avoir les traits tirés** to look drawn **(d)** to draw ‹bolt, curtain›; to pull down ‹blind›; to close ‹door, shutter› **(e)** to fire off ‹bullet, grenade›; to fire ‹missile›; to shoot ‹arrow› **(f)** (Sport) ~ **un penalty** to take a penalty **(g)** ~ **(au sort)** to draw ‹card, name, winner›; to draw for ‹partner› **(h)** (in astrology) ~ **les cartes à qn** to tell the cards for sb **(i)** to draw ‹wine›; to withdraw ‹money›; ~ **qch de sa poche** to pull sth out of one's pocket **(j)** ~ **le pays de la récession** to get the country out of recession; **tire-moi de là!** get me out of this! **(k)** ~ **[qch] de qn** to get [sth] from sb ‹information, confession›; ~ **[qch] de qch** to draw [sth] from sth ‹strength, resources›; to derive [sth] from sth ‹pride, satisfaction›; to make [sth] out of sth ‹money› **(l)** ~ **de qch** to base [sth] on sth ‹story, film›; to get [sth] from sth ‹name› **(m)** to print ‹book, negative›; to run off ‹proofs, copies› **(n)** to draw ‹line› **(o)** (colloq) **plus qu'une semaine à** ~ only one more week to go **(p)** ~ **un chèque** to draw a cheque (GB) *or* check (US)

2 *vi* **(a)** to pull; ~ **sur qch** to pull on sth; to tug at sth **(b)** (with firearm) to shoot; to fire **(c)** (in football) to shoot; (in handball, basketball) to take a shot **(d)** ~ **(au sort)** to draw lots **(e)** **la cheminée tire bien** the chimney draws well **(f)** ~ **à mille exemplaires** ‹periodical› to have a circulation of one thousand **(g)** ~ **sur le jaune/l'orangé** ‹colour› to be yellowish/orangy

3 **se tirer** *v refl* (+ *v être*) **(a)** **se** ~ **de** to come through ‹situation, difficulties› **(b)** **se** ~ **une balle** to shoot oneself; **se** ~ **dessus** to shoot at one another **(c)** (colloq) **s'en** ~ to cope; (from accident) to escape; (from illness) to pull through; **s'en** ~ **à bon prix** to get off lightly

tiret /tiʀɛ/ *nm* dash

tirette /tiʀɛt/ *nf* pull tab; cord

tireur, -euse /tiʀœʀ, øz/ *nm,f* **(a)** (Mil, Sport) marksman/markswoman **(b)** gunman

tiroir /tiʀwaʀ/ *nm* (in piece of furniture) drawer; **à** ~**s** (figurative) ‹novel, play› episodic **IDIOMS racler les fonds de** ~ to scrape some money together

tiroir-caisse, *pl* **tiroirs-caisses** /tiʀwaʀkɛs/ *nm* cash register

tisane /tizan/ *nf* herbal tea, tisane

tison /tizɔ̃/ *nm* (fire) brand

tisonnier /tizɔnje/ *nm* poker

tissage /tisaʒ/ *nm* **(a)** weaving **(b)** weave

tisser /tise/ [1] *vtr* **(a)** ‹person, machine› to weave **(b)** ‹spider› to spin ‹web›

tisserand, -e /tisʀɑ̃, ɑ̃d/ *nm,f* weaver

tissu /tisy/ *nm* **(a)** material, fabric **(b)** (Anat) ~ **osseux** bone tissue **(c)** (of intrigue) web; (of lies) pack; (of insults) string; ~ **social** social fabric

titan /titɑ̃/ *nm* titan; **de** ~ titanic

titane /titan/ *nm* titanium

titiller /titije/ [1] *vtr* to titillate

titre /titʀ/ *nm* **(a)** (of book, film, chapter) title; (in newspaper) headline; **avoir pour** ~ to be entitled; **les** ~**s de l'actualité** the headlines **(b)** (rank) title; ~ **mondial** world title; ~ **nobiliaire** *or* **de noblesse** title; **le** ~ **d'ingénieur** the status of qualified engineer; **en** ~ ‹professor, director› titular; ‹supplier› appointed; ‹mistress, rival› official; ~**s universitaires** university qualifications **(c)** **à juste** ~ quite rightly; **à** ~ **d'exemple** as an example; **à** ~ **définitif** on a permanent basis; **à** ~ **privé** in a private capacity; **à** ~ **gracieux** free; **à** ~ **indicatif** as a rough guide; **à quel** ~ **a-t-il été invité?** why was he invited? **(d)** (Law) deed; ~ **de propriété** title deed **(e)** (on stock exchange) security **(f)** (Econ) item; ~ **budgétaire** budgetary item **(g)** (of solution) titre (GB); (of wines, spirits) strength; (of precious metal) fineness ■ ~ **de gloire** claim to fame; ~ **de transport** ticket

titré, ~e /titʀe/ *adj* titled; **être** ~ to be titled

tituber /titybe/ [1] *vi* to stagger

titulaire /titylɛʀ/ **1** *adj* (gen) permanent; ‹lecturer› tenured **2** *nmf* **(a)** (gen) permanent staff member; tenured lecturer (GB) *or* professor (US) **(b)** holder; **être** ~ **de** to hold ‹degree, post›; to have ‹bank account›

titularisation /titylaʀizasjɔ̃/ *nf* confirmation in a post; (Univ) granting of tenure

titulariser /titylaʀize/ [1] *vtr* to give permanent status to ‹staff›; to grant tenure to ‹professor›

toast /tost/ *nm* toast

toboggan /tɔbɔɡɑ̃/ *nm* **(a)** slide **(b)** ® flyover (GB), overpass (US) **(c)** (Tech) (for rubble) chute

toc /tɔk/ **1** *nm* (colloq) **c'est du** ~ it's fake **2** *excl* ~**!** ~**!** knock! knock!

tocsin /tɔksɛ̃/ *nm* alarm (bell), tocsin

toge /tɔʒ/ *nf* **(a)** (of academic) gown; (of judge) robe

(b) toga

toi /twa/ *pron* **(a)** you; ~, ne dis rien don't say anything; **elle est plus âgée que** ~ she's older than you; **à** ~ (in game) your turn; **c'est à** ~ it's yours; **c'est à** ~ **de choisir** it's your turn to choose; it's up to you to choose **(b)** yourself; **reprends-**~ pull yourself together

toile /twal/ *nf* **(a)** cloth; ~ **de lin** linen (cloth); **de la grosse** ~ canvas **(b)** (in art) canvas; painting; ~ **de maître** master painting **(c)** (Naut) canvas
■ ~ **d'araignée** spider's web; cobweb; ~ **cirée** oilcloth; ~ **de jute** hessian; ~ **de tente** canvas; tent

toilettage /twalɛtaʒ/ *nm* (of animal) grooming

toilette /twalɛt/ ① *nf* **(a)** faire sa ~ ⟨*person*⟩ to have a wash; ⟨*animal*⟩ to wash itself; **faire la** ~ **d'un mort** to lay out a corpse **(b)** outfit; **en grande** ~ all dressed up ② **toilettes** *nf pl* toilet (GB), bathroom (US)

toiletter /twalete/ [1] *vtr* to groom ⟨*dog*⟩

toi-même /twamɛm/ *pron* yourself

toise /twaz/ *nf* height gauge

toiser /twaze/ [1] *vtr* to look [sb] up and down

toit /twa/ *nm* roof
■ **le** ~ **du Monde** the roof of the world; ~ **ouvrant** sunroof
IDIOMS **crier qch sur (tous) les** ~**s** to shout sth from the rooftops

toiture /twatyR/ *nf* **(a)** roof **(b)** roofing

tôle /tol/ *nf* **(a)** sheet metal **(b)** metal sheet *or* plate **(c)** (slang) = TAULE

tolérable /tɔlerabl/ *adj* bearable; tolerable

tolérance /tɔlerɑ̃s/ *nf* **(a)** tolerance; indulgence **(b)** ce n'est pas un droit, c'est une ~ it isn't legal but it is tolerated **(c)** (of medicine, noise) tolerance

tolérant, ~**e** /tɔlerɑ̃, ɑ̃t/ *adj* tolerant

tolérer /tɔlere/ [14] *vtr* to tolerate

tôlerie /tolRi/ *nf* sheet-metal working; sheet-metal trade; sheet-metal works

tollé /tɔle/ *nm* outcry, hue and cry

TOM /tɔm/ *nm: abbr* ▶ TERRITOIRE

tomate /tɔmat/ *nf* **(a)** tomato **(b)** tomato plant **(c)** *pastis with a dash of grenadine*

tombal, ~**e**, *mpl* **-aux** /tɔbal, o/ *adj* inscription ~**e** gravestone inscription

tombant, ~**e** /tɔbɑ̃, ɑ̃t/ *adj* ⟨*shoulders*⟩ sloping; ⟨*moustache, eyelids*⟩ drooping; ⟨*ears*⟩ floppy

tombe /tɔb/ *nf* **(a)** grave **(b)** gravestone

tombeau, *pl* ~**x** /tɔbo/ *nm* **(a)** tomb; **mettre qn au** ~ to lay sb in their grave

(b) c'est un ~ ⟨*person*⟩ he/she will keep quiet

tombée /tɔbe/ *nf* **à la** ~ **du jour** at close of day; **la** ~ **de la nuit** nightfall

tomber¹ /tɔbe/ [1] *vi* (+ *v être*) **(a)** (gen) to fall; ⟨*person, chair*⟩ to fall over; ⟨*tree, wall*⟩ to fall down; (from height) ⟨*person, vase*⟩ to fall off; ⟨*hair, teeth*⟩ to fall out; ⟨*plaster, covering*⟩ to come off; ⟨*rain, snow, theatre curtain*⟩ to fall; ⟨*fog*⟩ to come down; **du lit/de ma poche** to fall out of bed/out of my pocket; **le vent a fait** ~ **une tuile du toit** the wind blew a tile off the roof; **se laisser** ~ **dans un fauteuil** to flop into an armchair; **laisser** ~ **un gâteau sur le tapis** to drop a cake on the carpet **(b)** ⟨*rain, snow, theatre curtain*⟩ to fall; ⟨*fog*⟩ to come down; **qu'est-ce que ça tombe!** (colloq) it's pouring down!; **la foudre est tombée sur un arbre** the lightning struck a tree **(c)** ⟨*price, temperature*⟩ to fall; ⟨*anger*⟩ to subside; ⟨*fever*⟩ to come down; ⟨*wind*⟩ to drop; ⟨*day*⟩ to draw to a close; ⟨*conversation*⟩ to die down; **faire** ~ to bring down ⟨*price, temperature*⟩; to dampen ⟨*enthusiasm*⟩; **je tombe de sommeil** I can't keep my eyes open **(d)** ⟨*dictator, regime, city*⟩ to fall; ⟨*obstacle*⟩ to vanish; **faire** ~ to bring down ⟨*regime, dictator*⟩; (figurative) to break down ⟨*barriers*⟩ **(e)** ⟨*belly*⟩ to sag; ⟨*shoulders*⟩ to slope **(f)** ⟨*lock of hair*⟩ to fall; ~ **bien/mal** ⟨*garment, curtain*⟩ to hang well/badly **(g)** ~ **dans un piège** (figurative) to fall into a trap; ~ **sous le coup d'une loi** to fall within the provisions of a law; ~ **aux mains** *or* **entre les mains de qn** ⟨*document, power*⟩ to fall into sb's hand; ~ **malade/amoureux** to fall ill/in love **(h)** ⟨*decision, verdict*⟩ to be announced; ⟨*news*⟩ to break; ⟨*reply*⟩ to be given **(i)** ~ **sur** to come across ⟨*stranger, object*⟩; to run into ⟨*friend*⟩; ~ **sur la bonne page** to hit on the right page; **si tu prends cette rue, tu tomberas sur la place** if you follow that street, you'll come to the square **(j)** **c'est tombé juste au bon moment** it came just at the right time; **tu ne pouvais pas mieux** ~! you couldn't have come at a better time!; you couldn't have done better!; **tu tombes mal, j'allais partir** you're unlucky, I was just about to leave; **il faut toujours que ça tombe sur moi!** (colloq) (decision, choice) why does it always have to be me?; (misfortune) why does it always have to happen to me? **(k)** ⟨*birthday*⟩ to fall on ⟨*day*⟩ **(l)** **laisser** ~ to give up ⟨*job, activity*⟩; to drop ⟨*plan, habit*⟩; **laisse** ~! forget it!; **laisser** ~ **qn** to drop sb; to let sb down **(m)** ~ **sur qn** ⟨*soldiers, thugs*⟩ to fall on sb; ⟨*raiders, police*⟩ to descend on sb

tomber² /tɔbe/ *nm* hang; **ce velours a un beau** ~ this velvet hangs well

tombeur /tɔbœR/ *nm* (colloq) lady-killer

tombola /tɔbɔla/ *nf* tombola (GB), lottery

tome¹ /tɔm/ *nm* **(a)** volume **(b)** part, book

tome² /tɔm/ *nf* = TOMME

tomme /tɔm/ *nf* tomme *or* tome (cheese)

tommette /tɔmɛt/ *nf* hexagonal floor tile

ton¹, ta, *pl* **tes** /tɔ̃, ta, te/ *det* your; **un de tes amis** a friend of yours

ton² /tɔ̃/ *nm* (a) pitch; tone; **~ grave/aigu** low/high pitch; **d'un ~ dédaigneux** scornfully; **baisser le ~** to lower one's voice; (figurative) to moderate one's tone; **eh bien, si tu le prends sur ce ~** well, if you're going to take it like that
(b) (in linguistics) tone; **langue à ~s** tone language
(c) **donner le ~** to set the tone; to set the fashion; **de bon ~** in good taste
(d) (Mus) pitch; key; tone; (instrument) pitch pipe
(e) (of colour) shade; **~ sur ~** in matching tones

tonalité /tɔnalite/ *nf* (a) (Mus) key; tonality
(b) (of vowel) tone
(c) (of voice) tone
(d) (of colours) tonality
(e) dialling tone (GB), dial tone (US)

tondeuse /tɔ̃dœz/ *nf* (a) (for sheep) shears
(b) (for cutting hair) clippers
(c) **~ (à gazon)** lawnmower

tondre /tɔ̃dR/ [6] *vtr* to shear ⟨*sheep*⟩; to clip ⟨*dog*⟩; to mow ⟨*lawn*⟩; **~ qn** to shave sb's head

tongs /tɔ̃g/ *nf pl* flip-flops, thongs (US)

tonicité /tɔnisite/ *nf* (a) bracing effect
(b) tone

tonifiant, ~e /tɔnifjɑ̃, ɑ̃t/ *adj* (a) ⟨*climate, air*⟩ bracing
(b) ⟨*exercise, lotion*⟩ toning

tonifier /tɔnifje/ [2] *vtr* to tone up

tonique¹ /tɔnik/ *adj* (a) ⟨*drink*⟩ tonic; (figurative) ⟨*air*⟩ bracing; ⟨*book*⟩ stimulating
(b) **lotion ~** toning lotion
(c) ⟨*accent*⟩ tonic

tonique² /tɔnik/ *nf* (Mus) tonic

tonitruant, ~e /tɔnitRyɑ̃, ɑ̃t/ *adj* booming

tonitruer /tɔnitRye/ [1] *vi* to thunder

tonnage /tɔnaʒ/ *nm* tonnage

tonnant, ~e /tɔnɑ̃, ɑ̃t/ *adj* booming; thunderous

tonne /tɔn/ *nf* (1,000 kg) tonne, metric ton; **des ~s de choses à faire** (colloq) loads of things to do (colloq)

tonneau, *pl* **~x** /tɔno/ *nm* (a) barrel
(b) (of car) somersault
(c) (of plane) barrel roll
(d) (Naut) ton
IDIOMS **du même ~** (colloq) of the same kind

tonnelle /tɔnɛl/ *nf* arbour (GB)

tonner /tɔne/ [1] *vi, v impers* to thunder

tonnerre /tɔnɛR/ *nm* (a) thunder; **un coup de ~** a clap of thunder; (figurative) a thunderbolt
(b) (of cannons, artillery) thundering; **un ~ d'applaudissements** thunderous applause

(c) (colloq) **ça marche du ~** it's going fantastically well

tonsure /tɔ̃syR/ *nf* (of monk) tonsure

tonte /tɔ̃t/ *nf* (a) **~ (des moutons)** shearing
(b) fleece

tonton /tɔ̃tɔ̃/ *nm* (colloq) uncle; **~ Pierre** Uncle Pierre

tonus /tɔnys/ *nm inv* (a) (of person) energy, dynamism
(b) (of muscle) tone, tonus

top /tɔp/ *nm* pip, beep; **donner le ~ de départ** to give the starting signal

topaze /tɔpaz/ *nf* topaz

toper /tɔpe/ [1] *vi* **topons là!** let's shake on it!

topo /tɔpo/ *nm* (colloq) short talk; short piece; **c'est toujours le même ~** it's always the same old story (colloq)

topographie /tɔpɔgRafi/ *nf* topography

toquade /tɔkad/ *nf* (colloq) (a) (for thing) passion
(b) (on person) crush (colloq)

toque /tɔk/ *nf* (a) (of woman) toque; (of chef) chef's hat; (of judge) hat; **~ en fourrure** fur cap
(b) (of jockey) cap

toqué, ~e /tɔke/ *adj* (colloq) crazy (colloq)

torche /tɔRʃ/ *nf* torch
■ **~ électrique** torch (GB), flashlight

torcher /tɔRʃe/ [1] *vtr* (colloq) (a) to wipe
(b) to dash off ⟨*article, report*⟩; to cobble [sth] together

torchis /tɔRʃi/ *nm inv* cob (for walls)

torchon /tɔRʃɔ̃/ *nm* (a) (gen) cloth; **~ (de cuisine)** tea towel (GB), dish towel (US)
(b) (newspaper) (derogatory) rag (colloq)
(c) (colloq) messy piece of work
IDIOMS **le ~ brûle** (colloq) it's war

tordant, ~e /tɔRdɑ̃, ɑ̃t/ *adj* (colloq) hilarious

tordre /tɔRdR/ [6] **1** *vtr* (a) to twist ⟨*arm, wrist*⟩; to wring ⟨*neck*⟩
(b) to bend ⟨*nail, bar, bumper*⟩
(c) to wring out ⟨*washing*⟩
2 se tordre *v refl* (+ *v être*) (a) ⟨*person*⟩ se **~ la cheville** to twist one's ankle; **se ~ de douleur** to writhe in pain
(b) ⟨*bumper*⟩ to bend

tordu, ~e /tɔRdy/ *adj* (a) ⟨*nose, legs*⟩ crooked; ⟨*branches, trunk, iron bar*⟩ twisted
(b) (figurative) ⟨*idea*⟩ weird, strange; ⟨*logic, reasoning*⟩ twisted

tornade /tɔRnad/ *nf* tornado

torpeur /tɔRpœR/ *nf* torpor

torpille /tɔRpij/ *nf* torpedo

torpiller /tɔRpije/ [1] *vtr* to torpedo

torréfier /tɔRefje/ [2] *vtr* to roast

torrent /tɔRɑ̃/ *nm* torrent; **pleuvoir à ~s** to rain very heavily

torrentiel, -ielle /tɔRɑ̃sjɛl/ *adj* torrential

torride /tɔRid/ *adj* torrid; ⟨*sun*⟩ scorching

tors, torse¹ /tɔR, tɔRs/ *adj* (gen) twisted

torsade /tɔRsad/ *nf* (a) twist, coil

(b) cable stitch
(c) (in architecture) cable moulding (GB), cable molding (US)

torsader /tɔʀsade/ [1] *vtr* to twist; **une colonne torsadée** a cable column

torse² /tɔʀs/ *nm* **(a)** (gen) chest; **se mettre ~ nu** to strip to the waist
(b) (Anat) torso

torsion /tɔʀsjɔ̃/ *nf* **(a)** twisting
(b) torsion

tort /tɔʀ/ 1 *nm* **(a)** **avoir ~** to be wrong; **j'aurais bien ~ de m'inquiéter!** it would be silly of me to worry!; **être en ~** to be in the wrong; **donner ~ à qn** ⟨referee, judge⟩ to blame sb; ⟨facts⟩ to prove sb wrong
(b) fault; **les ~s sont partagés** there are faults on both sides; **avoir des ~s envers qn** to have wronged sb
(c) mistake; **j'ai eu le ~ de le croire** I made the mistake of believing him
(d) **faire du ~ à qn/qch** to harm sb/sth
2 **à tort** *phr* ⟨accuse⟩ wrongly; **à ~ et à travers** ⟨spend⟩ wildly; **parler à ~ et à travers** to talk a lot of nonsense

torticolis /tɔʀtikɔli/ *nm inv* stiff neck

tortillard /tɔʀtijaʀ/ *nm* (colloq) small local train

tortiller /tɔʀtije/ [1] 1 *vtr* to twist ⟨fibres, strands⟩; to twiddle ⟨handkerchief⟩
2 **se tortiller** *v refl* (+ *v être*) to wriggle

tortionnaire /tɔʀsjɔnɛʀ/ *nmf* torturer

tortue /tɔʀty/ *nf* **(a)** (sea) turtle
(b) tortoise, turtle (US)
(c) (butterfly) tortoiseshell

tortueux, -euse /tɔʀtɥø, øz/ *adj*
(a) ⟨road, staircase⟩ winding
(b) (figurative) ⟨behaviour⟩ devious; ⟨mind, reasoning⟩ tortuous

torture /tɔʀtyʀ/ *nf* torture

torturer /tɔʀtyʀe/ [1] 1 *vtr* **(a)** to torture ⟨person⟩
(b) ⟨thought, feeling⟩ to torment
(c) to distort ⟨text⟩; **style torturé** tortured style
2 **se torturer** *v refl* (+ *v être*) to torment oneself; **se ~ l'esprit** to rack one's brains

torve /tɔʀv/ *adj* ⟨look⟩ menacing, baleful

tôt /to/ *adv* **(a)** ⟨start⟩ early; **~ le matin** early in the morning
(b) soon, early; **le plus ~ serait le mieux** the sooner the better; **~ ou tard** sooner or later; **on ne m'y reprendra pas de si ~** I won't do that again in a hurry.

total, ~e, *mpl* **-aux** /tɔtal, o/ 1 *adj* complete, total
2 *nm* total
3 **au total** *phr* **au ~ cela fait 350 francs** altogether that comes to 350 francs

totalement /tɔtalmã/ *adv* totally, completely

totaliser /tɔtalize/ [1] *vtr* **(a)** to total ⟨profits⟩
(b) to have a total of ⟨points, votes⟩

totalitaire /tɔtalitɛʀ/ *adj* **(a)** ⟨regime, state⟩ totalitarian

(b) ⟨doctrine⟩ all-embracing

totalitarisme /tɔtalitaʀism/ *nm* totalitarianism

totalité /tɔtalite/ *nf* **la ~ du personnel** all the staff; **la ~ des dépenses** the total expenditure; **nous vous rembourserons en ~** we will refund you in full

totem /tɔtɛm/ *nm* **(a)** totem
(b) totem pole

toubib /tubib/ *nm* (colloq) doctor, quack (colloq)

toucan /tukã/ *nm* toucan

touchant, ~e /tuʃã, ãt/ *adj* moving; touching

touche /tuʃ/ *nf* **(a)** (gen) button; (on keyboard) key; (on stringed instrument) fret
(b) (of paintbrush) stroke; (of paint) dash; (of artist) touch
(c) (Sport) sideline, touchline; **mettre qn sur la ~** (figurative) to push sb aside
(d) (in fencing) hit
(e) (in fishing) bite

touche-à-tout /tuʃatu/ *adj inv* **être ~** to be into everything; to be a jack of all trades

toucher¹ /tuʃe/ [1] 1 *vtr* **(a)** **~ (de la main)** ⟨object, surface, person⟩; **~ du bois** (superstitiously) to touch wood; **~ le front de qn** to feel sb's forehead
(b) to be touching ⟨wall, ceiling, bottom of sth⟩; **~ le sol** to land
(c) to hit ⟨opponent, car, kerb⟩
(d) to touch, to move ⟨person⟩; **ça me touche beaucoup** I am very touched
(e) ⟨event, crisis⟩ to affect ⟨person, country⟩; ⟨storm⟩ to hit ⟨region, city⟩
(f) ⟨country, house⟩ to be next to
(g) ⟨person⟩ to get ⟨money⟩; to cash ⟨cheque⟩
2 **toucher à** *v*+*prep* **(a)** **~ à** to touch ⟨object⟩; **~ à tout** to be into everything; (figurative) to be a jack of all trades; **avec son air de ne pas y ~, c'est un malin** (colloq) he looks as if butter wouldn't melt in his mouth, but he's a sly one
(b) **~ à** to concern ⟨activity, issue⟩
(c) **~ à** to infringe on ⟨right, freedom⟩
(d) **~ à** to get on to ⟨problem⟩
3 **se toucher** *v refl* (+ *v être*) ⟨houses, gardens⟩ to be next to each other

toucher² /tuʃe/ *nm* **(a)** **le ~** touch, the sense of touch
(b) (of pianist) touch

touche-touche: à touche-touche /atuʃtuʃ/ *phr* (colloq) **être à ~** ⟨cars⟩ to be bumper to bumper; ⟨people⟩ to be on top of each other (colloq)

touffe /tuf/ *nf* (of hair, grass) tuft

touffu, ~e /tufy/ *adj* ⟨eyebrows, beard⟩ bushy; ⟨vegetation⟩ dense; ⟨bush⟩ thick; **au poil ~** with thick fur
(b) ⟨text⟩ dense

touiller /tuje/ [1] *vtr* (colloq) to stir ⟨sauce⟩

toujours /tuʒuʀ/ *adv* **(a)** always; **comme ~** as always; **de ~** ⟨friend⟩ very old; ⟨friendship⟩ long-standing; **~ plus vite** faster and faster ⋯⋗

(b) still; **il n'est ~ pas levé?** is he still not up?

(c) anyway; **on peut ~ essayer** we can always try; **c'est ~ ça de pris** *or* **de gagné** that's something at least; **~ est-il que** the fact remains that

toupet /tupɛ/ *nm* **(a)** (colloq) cheek (colloq), nerve (colloq)

(b) (of hair) tuft; quiff (GB), forelock (US)

toupie /tupi/ *nf* top; **faire tourner une ~** to spin a top

tour¹ /tuʀ/ *nm* **(a)** (gen) turn; (around axis) revolution; **donner un ~ de clé** to turn the key; **faire un ~ de manège** to have a go on the merry-go-round; **faire un ~ sur soi-même** ⟨*dancer*⟩ to spin around; ⟨*planet*⟩ to rotate; **fermer qch à double ~** to double-lock sth; **à ~ de bras** (colloq) ⟨*invest, buy up*⟩ left, right and centre (GB) (colloq)

(b) **faire le ~ de qch** (gen) to go around sth; to drive around sth; **la nouvelle a vite fait le ~ du village** the news spread rapidly through the village

(c) (of pond) edges; (of pipe, tree trunk) circumference; (of head, hips) measurement; (standard measurement) size

(d) walk, stroll; (on bicycle) ride; (in car) drive, spin; **je suis allé faire un ~ à Paris** I went to Paris

(e) look; **faire le ~ d'un problème** to have a look at a problem; **faire le ~ de ses relations** to go through one's acquaintances; **ce roman, on en a vite fait le ~** (colloq) there's not much to this novel

(f) (gen) turn; (in competition) round; **à qui le ~?** whose turn is it?; **chacun son ~** each one in his turn; **il perd plus souvent qu'à son ~** he loses more often than he would like; he loses more often than he should; **~ à ~** by turns; in turn

(g) **~ de scrutin** ballot, round of voting

(h) trick; **jouer un ~ à qn** to play a trick on sb; **ça te jouera des ~s** it's going to get you into trouble one of these days

(i) trick; **~ de cartes** card trick; **~ d'adresse** feat of skill

(j) (in situation) turn; **donner un ~ nouveau à qch** to give a new twist to sth

(k) (Tech) lathe

■ **~ de chant** song recital; **~ de garde** turn of duty; **~ de potier** potter's wheel; **~ de rein(s)** back strain

tour² /tuʀ/ *nf* **(a)** tower

(b) tower block (GB), high rise (US)

(c) (in chess) rook, castle

(d) siege-tower

tourbe /tuʀb/ *nf* peat

tourbière /tuʀbjɛʀ/ *nf* peat bog

tourbillon /tuʀbijɔ̃/ *nm* **(a)** whirlwind; whirlpool; **~ de poussière** whirl of dust

(b) (of memories) swirl; (of reforms) whirlwind

tourbillonner /tuʀbijɔne/ [1] *vi* ⟨*snow, leaves*⟩ to swirl, to whirl; ⟨*dancers*⟩ to twirl

tourelle /tuʀɛl/ *nf* (of building, tank) turret; (of submarine) conning tower

tourisme /tuʀism/ *nm* tourism

■ **~ vert** countryside holidays

touriste /tuʀist/ *nmf* tourist

touristique /tuʀistik/ *adj* ⟨*brochure, menu, season*⟩ tourist; ⟨*influx*⟩ of tourists; ⟨*town, area*⟩ which attracts tourists

tourment /tuʀmɑ̃/ *nm* torment

tourmente /tuʀmɑ̃t/ *nf* **(a)** storm

(b) turmoil

tourmenté, ~e /tuʀmɑ̃te/ *adj* **(a)** ⟨*person, face*⟩ tormented; ⟨*soul*⟩ tortured

(b) ⟨*era, life*⟩ turbulent

(c) ⟨*landscape*⟩ rugged

tourmenter /tuʀmɑ̃te/ [1] **1** *vtr* **(a)** to worry

(b) to torment

(c) ⟨*creditors*⟩ to harass

2 se tourmenter *v refl* (+ *v être*) to worry

tournage /tuʀnaʒ/ *nm* **(a)** shooting, filming

(b) film set

tournant, ~e /tuʀnɑ̃, ɑ̃t/ **1** *adj* **(a)** ⟨*seat*⟩ swivel; ⟨*sprinkler*⟩ rotating; ⟨*door*⟩ revolving

(b) ⟨*presidency*⟩ rotating; ⟨*strike*⟩ staggered

2 *nm* **(a)** (in road) bend

(b) turning point

(c) turn; **au ~ du siècle** at the turn of the century

(d) change of direction

tourné, ~e¹ /tuʀne/ *adj* **(a)** **~ vers** ⟨*eyes, look, person*⟩ turned toward(s); ⟨*activity, policy*⟩ oriented toward(s); **~ vers le passé/l'avenir** backward-/forward-looking; **porte ~e vers la mer** gate facing the sea

(b) bien ~ ⟨*compliment, letter*⟩ nicely phrased

(c) ⟨*milk*⟩ off

tourne-disque, *pl* **~s** /tuʀnədisk/ *nm* record player

tournée² /tuʀne/ *nf* **(a)** (of postman) round

(b) (of team, singer) tour

(c) (colloq) (of drinks) round

tournemain: en un tournemain /ɑ̃nɛ̃tuʀnəmɛ̃/ *phr* in no time

tourner /tuʀne/ [1] **1** *vtr* **(a)** to turn; **~ la tête vers** to turn to look at; **~ les yeux vers** to look at

(b) to shoot ⟨*film*⟩

(c) to get around ⟨*difficulty, law*⟩

(d) to phrase ⟨*letter, criticism*⟩

(e) **~ qn/qch en dérision** to deride sb/sth

(f) **~ et retourner qch dans son esprit** to mull sth over

(g) to stir ⟨*sauce*⟩; to toss ⟨*salad*⟩

2 *vi* **(a)** (gen) to turn; ⟨*planet*⟩ to rotate; ⟨*rotating door*⟩ to revolve; ⟨*dancer*⟩ to spin; **faire ~ qn** to turn; to spin; **faire ~ les tables** (in spiritualism) to do table-turning

(b) **~ autour de** (gen) to turn around; ⟨*planet*⟩ to revolve around; ⟨*plane*⟩ to circle

(c) **~ (en rond)** ⟨*person*⟩ to go round and round; ⟨*driver*⟩ to drive round and round; **~ en rond** (figurative) ⟨*discussion*⟩ to go round in circles

(d) ~ **autour de** ⟨*sum of money*⟩ to be (somewhere) in the region of

(e) ⟨*engine, factory*⟩ to run; ~ **rond** ⟨*engine*⟩ to run smoothly; ⟨*business*⟩ to be doing well; **faire** ~ to run ⟨*business, company*⟩; **mon frère ne tourne pas rond depuis quelque temps** (colloq) my brother has been acting strangely for some time

(f) **les choses ont bien/mal tourné pour lui** things turned out well/badly for him

(g) ⟨*director*⟩ to shoot; ~ **(dans un film)** ⟨*actor*⟩ to make a film (GB) *or* movie (US)

(h) ⟨*milk, meat*⟩ to go off

(i) ~ **autour de qn** to hang around sb

3̲ se tourner *v refl* (+ *v être*) **(a) se** ~ **vers qn/qch** to turn to sb/sth

(b) se ~ **vers qn/qch** to turn toward(s) sb/sth

(c) to turn around

tournesol /turnəsɔl/ *nm* sunflower

tournevis /turnəvis/ *nm inv* screwdriver

tourniquet /turnikɛ/ *nm* **(a)** turnstile
(b) revolving stand
(c) sprinkler

tournoi /turnwa/ *nm* tournament

tournoyer /turnwaje/ [23] *vi* **(a)** ⟨*leaves, papers*⟩ to swirl around; ⟨*vultures*⟩ to wheel; ⟨*flies*⟩ to fly around in circles
(b) ⟨*dancers*⟩ to whirl; **faire** ~ to twirl ⟨*stick, skirt*⟩

tournure /turnyr/ *nf* **(a)** turn; **prendre** ~ ⟨*plan*⟩ to take shape
(b) ~ **(de phrase)** turn of phrase
■ ~ **d'esprit** frame of mind

tourte /turt/ *nf* pie; ~ **à la viande** meat pie

tourteau, *pl* ~**x** /turto/ *nm* (Culin, Zool) crab

tourtereau, *pl* ~**x** /turtəro/ **1̲** *nm* (Zool) young turtle dove
2̲ tourtereaux *nm pl* (humorous) lovebirds

tourterelle /turtərɛl/ *nf* turtle dove

tous ▶ TOUT

Toussaint /tusɛ̃/ *nf* **la** ~ All Saints' Day

tousser /tuse/ [1] *vi* ⟨*person*⟩ to cough

toussotement /tusɔtmã/ *nm* cough; splutter

toussoter /tusɔte/ [1] *vi* ⟨*person*⟩ to have a slight cough; ⟨*engine*⟩ to splutter

tout /tu/, ~**e** /tut/, *mpl* **tous** /tu *adj*, tus *pron*/, *fpl* **toutes** /tut/

■ **Note** You will find translations for expressions such as *à tout hasard, tout compte fait, tout neuf* etc, at the entries HASARD, COMPTE, NEUF etc.

1̲ *pron* **(a) tout** everything; all; anything; ~ **est prétexte à querelle(s)** any pretext will do to start a quarrel; ~ **n'est pas perdu** all is not lost; **en** ~ in all; in every respect; **en** ~ **et pour** ~ all told; ~ **bien compté** *or* **pesé** *or* **considéré** all in all

(b) tous /tus/, **toutes** all; all of them/us/you; **tous ensemble** all together; **est-ce que ça conviendra à tous?** will it suit everybody?

2̲ *adj* **(a)** bois ~ **ton lait** drink all your milk; ~ **le reste** everything else; ~ **le monde** everybody; **manger** ~ **un pain** to eat a whole loaf; **il a plu** ~**e la journée** it rained all day (long)

(b) c'est ~ **un travail** it's quite a job

(c) all; everything; anything; ~ **ce qui compte** all that matters; ~ **ce qu'il dit n'est pas vrai** not all of what he says is true; **être** ~ **ce qu'il y a de plus serviable** to be most obliging

(d) any; **à** ~ **moment** at any time; constantly; ~ **autre que lui/toi aurait abandonné** anybody else would have given up

(e) **en** ~**e franchise** in all honesty; **il aurait** ~ **intérêt à placer cet argent** it would be in his best interests to invest this money

(f) **il a souri pour** ~**e réponse** his only reply was a smile

(g) **tous**, **toutes** all, every; **j'ai** ~**es les raisons de me plaindre** I have every reason to complain; **nous irons tous les deux** we'll both go; **je les prends tous les trois** I'm taking all three

(h) **tous/toutes les** every; **tous les deux jours** every other day; **tous les combien?** how often?

3̲ *adv* **(a)** very, quite; all; **être** ~ **étonné** to be very surprised; ~ **seul** all by oneself; ~ **en haut** right at the top; **la colline est** ~ **en fleurs** the hill is a mass of flowers; **veste** ~ **cuir** all leather jacket

(b) ~ **prêt** ready-made

(c) while; although; **il lisait** ~ **en marchant** he was reading as he walked; **elle le défendait** ~ **en le sachant coupable** she defended him although she knew he was guilty

(d) ~ **malin/roi qu'il est, il…** he may be clever/a king, but he…

4̲ **du tout** *phr* **(pas) du** ~ not at all

5̲ *nm* (*pl* ~**s**) whole; **le** ~ the (whole) lot; the main thing; **former un** ~ to make up *or* form a whole

6̲ **Tout-** (*combining form*) **le Tout-Paris/-Londres** the Paris/London smart set

■ ~ **à coup** suddenly; ~ **d'un coup** suddenly; all at once; ~ **à fait** quite, absolutely; ~ **à l'heure** in a moment; a little while ago, just now; **à** ~ **à l'heure!** see you later!; ~ **de même** all the same, even so; ~ **de même!** really!; ~ **de suite** at once

IDIOMS **être** ~ **yeux** ~ **oreilles** to be very attentive

tout-à-l'égout /tutalegu/ *nm inv* main drainage, main sewer

toutefois /tutfwa/ *adv* however

toute-puissance /tutpɥisãs/ *nf* omnipotence; supremacy

toutou /tutu/ *nm* (colloq) doggie (colloq), dog

tout-petit, *pl* ~**s** /tup(ə)ti/ *nm* **(a)** baby
(b) toddler

Tout-Puissant /tupɥisã/ *nm* **le** ~ the Almighty, God Almighty

tout-venant /tuv(ə)nã/ *nm inv* all and sundry

toux /tu/ *nf inv* cough
toxicité /tɔksisite/ *nf* toxicity
toxicodépendance /tɔksikodepɑ̃dɑ̃s/ *nf* drug dependency
toxicologie /tɔksikɔlɔʒi/ *nf* toxicology
toxicomane /tɔksikɔman/ *nmf* drug addict
toxicomanie /tɔksikɔmani/ *nf* drug addiction
toxine /tɔksin/ *nf* toxin
toxique /tɔksik/ *adj* toxic, poisonous
TP /tepe/ *nm pl: abbr* ▶ TRAVAIL
trac /tʀak/ *nm* (colloq) (of actor) stage fright; (before exam, conference) nerves; **avoir le ~** (gen) to feel nervous; ⟨*actor, performer*⟩ to have stage fright
traçage /tʀasaʒ/ *nm* **(a)** marking out; laying-out
(b) (Comput) tracing
tracas /tʀaka/ *nm inv* **(a)** trouble
(b) problems; **~ quotidiens** everyday problems
(c) worries; **se faire du ~ pour qn/qch** to worry about sb/sth
tracasser /tʀakase/ [1] ① *vtr* to bother ⟨*person*⟩
② **se tracasser** *v refl* (+ *v être*) to worry
tracasserie /tʀakasʀi/ *nf* **(a)** hassle (colloq)
(b) harassment
trace /tʀas/ *nf* **(a)** trail; **suivre qn à la ~** to track sb; (figurative) to follow sb's trail
(b) **~s** tracks; **~s d'ours/de ski** bear's/ski tracks; **~s de pas** footprints; **sur les ~s de Van Gogh** in the footsteps of Van Gogh
(c) (of burn) mark; (of wound) scar; (of paint) mark; (of blood, dampness) trace; **~s de doigts** fingermarks; **~s de coups** bruises
(d) (of activity) sign; (of presence) trace; **des ~s d'effraction** signs of a break-in
tracé /tʀase/ *nm* **(a)** (of town) layout; (of road) plan
(b) (of road, railway) route; (of river) course; (of border, coast) line
(c) (on graph, in sketch) line
tracer /tʀase/ [12] *vtr* **(a)** to draw ⟨*line, map, portrait*⟩; (on graph) to plot ⟨*curve*⟩; to write ⟨*word, letters*⟩
(b) **à 15 ans son avenir était déjà tout tracé** at 15, his/her future was already mapped out
(c) **~ le chemin à qn** (figurative) to show sb the way
trachée /tʀaʃe/ *nf* windpipe
trachée-artère, *pl* **trachées-artères** /tʀaʃeaʀtɛʀ/ *nf* windpipe, trachea
trachéite /tʀakeit/ *nf* tracheitis
tract /tʀakt/ *nm* pamphlet, tract
tractation /tʀaktasjɔ̃/ *nf* negotiation
tracter /tʀakte/ [1] *vtr* ⟨*vehicle*⟩ to tow ⟨*trailer*⟩; ⟨*cable*⟩ to pull up ⟨*cable car*⟩
tracteur /tʀaktœʀ/ *nm* tractor
traction /tʀaksjɔ̃/ *nf* **(a)** traction; **à ~ mécanique** mechanically drawn
(b) (Tech) tension

■ **~ arrière** (Aut) rear-wheel drive; **~ avant** (Aut) front-wheel drive
tradition /tʀadisjɔ̃/ *nf* **(a)** tradition
(b) legend; **la ~ veut que...** legend has it that...
traditionaliste /tʀadisjɔnalist/ *adj, nmf* traditionalist
traditionnel, **-elle** /tʀadisjɔnɛl/ *adj* traditional
traducteur, **-trice** /tʀadyktœʀ, tʀis/ *nm,f* translator
traduction /tʀadyksjɔ̃/ *nf* translation; **faire des ~s** to do translation work
traduire /tʀadɥiʀ/ [69] ① *vtr* **(a)** to translate
(b) ⟨*word, artist, book*⟩ to convey; ⟨*rebellion, violence*⟩ to be the expression of; ⟨*price rise*⟩ to be the result of
(c) (Law) **~ qn en justice** to bring sb to justice
② **se traduire** *v refl* (+ *v être*) **(a)** ⟨*joy, fear*⟩ to show
(b) ⟨*crisis, instability*⟩ to result; **se ~ par un échec** to result in failure
traduisible /tʀadɥizibl/ *adj* translatable
trafic /tʀafik/ *nm* **(a)** traffic; **~ d'armes** arms dealing; **~ de drogue** drug trafficking
(b) **~ (routier)** (road) traffic; **~ aérien** air traffic
trafiquant, **~e** /tʀafikɑ̃, ɑ̃t/ *nm,f* trafficker, dealer; **~ de drogue** drugs dealer
trafiquer /tʀafike/ [1] *vtr* **(a)** to fiddle with ⟨*car, meter*⟩
(b) (colloq) **je me demande ce qu'il trafique** I wonder what he's up to
tragédie /tʀaʒedi/ *nf* tragedy
tragédien, **-ienne** /tʀaʒedjɛ̃, ɛn/ *nm,f* tragic actor
tragique /tʀaʒik/ ① *adj* tragic
② *nm* tragedy
trahir /tʀaiʀ/ [3] ① *vtr* **(a)** to betray; to break ⟨*promise*⟩
(b) ⟨*writing, words*⟩ to betray ⟨*thoughts*⟩
(c) ⟨*translator, words*⟩ to misrepresent
(d) ⟨*strength, legs*⟩ to fail ⟨*person*⟩
② **se trahir** *v refl* (+ *v être*) to give oneself away, to betray oneself
trahison /tʀaizɔ̃/ *nf* **(a)** treachery; **~ de qn/qch** betrayal of sb/sth
(b) treason
train /tʀɛ̃/ ① *nm* **(a)** train; **par le** *or* **en ~** ⟨*travel*⟩ by train
(b) (convoy) train; **~ de péniches** train of barges
(c) series (**de** of)
(d) pace; **aller bon ~** to walk briskly; **aller bon ~** ⟨*rumours*⟩ to be flying around; ⟨*sales*⟩ to be going well; ⟨*conversation*⟩ to flow easily; **au ~ où vont les choses** (at) the rate things are going; **à fond de ~** (colloq) at top speed
(e) (Zool) **~ de derrière** hindquarters; **~ de devant** forequarter
② **en train** *phr* **(a)** **être en ~** to be full of energy

(b) mettre en ~ to get [sth] started ‹*process*›
(c) être en ~ de faire to be (busy) doing; **j'étais en ~ de dormir** I was sleeping
■ **~ d'atterrissage** undercarriage; **~ électrique** (toy) train set; **~ de vie** lifestyle

traînant, ~e /tʁɛnɑ̃, ɑ̃t/ *adj* shuffling; **voix ~e** drawl

traînard, ~e /tʁɛnaʁ, aʁd/ *nm,f* (colloq) slowcoach, slowpoke; straggler

traînasser (colloq) /tʁɛnase/ [1] *vi* **(a)** to loaf about (colloq)
(b) to take ages

traîne /tʁɛn/ *nf* **(a)** (of dress) train
(b) seine (net)
IDIOMS être à la ~ to lag behind

traîneau, *pl* **~x** /tʁɛno/ *nm* **(a)** sleigh
(b) (of vacuum cleaner) cylinder

traînée /tʁɛne/ *nf* **(a)** streak; **~ de sang** streak of blood
(b) trail

traîner /tʁɛne/ [1] **1** *vtr* **(a)** to drag [sb/ sth] (along) ‹*person, suitcase*›; to drag [sth] across the floor ‹*chair*›
(b) (colloq) to lug [sth] around (colloq) ‹*object*›; to drag [sth] around ‹*object*›
(c) ~ qn chez le médecin to drag sb off to the doctor's
(d) il traîne un rhume depuis deux semaines for two weeks now he's had a cold that he can't shake off; **~ les pieds** to drag one's feet
2 *vi* **(a) ~ dans les rues** to hang around on the streets; **j'ai traîné au lit** I slept in
(b) to take forever; **ne traîne pas, on doit terminer à 4 heures** get a move on (colloq), we've got to finish at four
(c) to dawdle
(d) ‹*building work, illness*› to drag on
(e) ~ par terre ‹*skirt*› to trail on the ground; ‹*curtains*› to trail on the floor
(f) ~ derrière qch to be trailing behind sth
(g) ‹*clothes, toys*› to be lying about or around; **laisser ~ qch** to leave sth lying about or around ‹*chequebook*›
3 **se traîner** *v refl* (+ *v être*) **(a)** ‹*injured person*› **se ~ par terre** to drag oneself along the ground
(b) se ~ jusqu'à la cuisine to drag oneself through to the kitchen
(c) ‹*train*› to crawl along; ‹*negotiations*› to drag on
IDIOMS ~ la jambe or **la patte** (colloq) to limp; **~ ses guêtres** (colloq) or **ses bottes** (colloq) to knock around (colloq)

train(-)train /tʁɛ̃tʁɛ̃/ *nm inv* (derogatory) (colloq) daily routine

traire /tʁɛʁ/ [58] *vtr* to milk ‹*cow, goat*›

trait¹, ~e /tʁɛ, ɛt/ ▶ TRAIRE

trait² /tʁɛ/ **1** *nm* **(a)** line; stroke; **souligner un mot d'un ~ rouge** to underline a word in red; **~ pour** ‹*replica*› line for line; ‹*reproduce*› line by line
(b) (of style, book) feature; (of person) trait; **~ caractéristique** characteristic; **~ de caractère** trait, characteristic

(c) ~ d'humour or **d'esprit** witticism; **~ de génie** stroke of genius
(d) avoir ~ à to relate to
(e) d'un (seul) ~ (gen) at one go
(f) de ~ ‹*animal*› draught (GB) or draft (US)
2 **traits** *nm pl* features
■ **~ d'union** hyphen; (figurative) link
IDIOMS tirer un ~ sur qch to put sth firmly behind one

traitant /tʁɛtɑ̃/ *adj m* **médecin ~** doctor, GP

traite /tʁɛt/ **1** *nf* **(a)** (Econ) draft, bill
(b) la ~ des Blanches the white slave trade
(c) milking; **la ~ des vaches** milking cows
2 **d'une traite** *phr* **d'une (seule) ~** ‹*recite*› in one breath; ‹*drink*› in one go

traité /tʁɛte/ *nm* **(a)** (Law) treaty; **~ commercial** trade agreement
(b) treatise

traitement /tʁɛtmɑ̃/ *nm* **(a)** (Med) treatment
(b) salary
(c) handling; **il faut accélérer le ~ des demandes** applications must be dealt with more quickly
(d) (of data) processing
(e) (Tech) (of water, waste) processing; (of wood) treatment
■ **~ de faveur** preferential treatment; **~ de texte** word-processing (package)

traiter /tʁɛte/ [1] **1** *vtr* **(a)** to treat ‹*person, animal, object*›
(b) (Med) to treat ‹*sick person, infection*›
(c) to deal with ‹*question, problem*›
(d) to treat ‹*wood, textile*›; to process ‹*waste*›
(e) to process ‹*data*›
(f) ~ qn de qch to call sb sth
2 **traiter de** *v+prep* to deal with
3 *vi* to negotiate, to do (GB) or make a deal
4 **se traiter** *v refl* (+ *v être*) **ils se sont traités de tous les noms** they called each other all sorts of names

traiteur /tʁɛtœʁ/ *nm* caterer

traître, traîtresse /tʁɛtʁ, tʁɛtʁɛs/ *nm,f* traitor; **en ~** by surprise

traîtrise /tʁɛtʁiz/ *nf* **(a)** act of treachery
(b) (of person) treachery

trajectoire /tʁaʒɛktwaʁ/ *nf* **(a)** (of bullet, missile) trajectory
(b) (of planet, satellite) path
(c) career

trajet /tʁaʒɛ/ *nm* **(a)** journey, trip; (by sea) crossing
(b) route

trame /tʁam/ *nf* **(a)** (of fabric) weft
(b) (of story) framework

tramer: se tramer /tʁame/ [1] *v refl* (+ *v être*) ‹*plot*› to be hatched

trampoline /tʁɑ̃pɔlin/ *nm* trampoline

tramway /tʁamwɛ/ *nm* **(a)** tram (GB), streetcar (US)
(b) tramway (GB), streetcar line (US)

tranchant, ~e /tʁɑ̃ʃɑ̃, ɑ̃t/ **1** *adj*
(a) sharp
(b) ‹*person*› forthright; ‹*tone*› curt

2 *nm* (of blade) sharp edge, cutting edge

tranche /tʀɑ̃ʃ/ *nf* **(a)** (of bread, meat, cheese) slice; (of lard, bacon) rasher
(b) (of operation) phase; (in timetable) period, time slot
(c) (of book, coin) edge
■ ~ **d'âge** age bracket

tranché, ~**e**[1] /tʀɑ̃ʃe/ **1** *pp* ▶ TRANCHER
2 *pp adj* ⟨salmon⟩ pre-sliced
3 *adj* **(a)** ⟨opinion, position, reply⟩ cut-and-dried; ⟨inequalities⟩ marked
(b) ⟨colours⟩ bold

tranchée[2] /tʀɑ̃ʃe/ *nf* **(a)** (Mil) trench
(b) (of road) cutting

trancher /tʀɑ̃ʃe/ [1] **1** *vtr* to slice, to cut ⟨bread, meat⟩; to cut through ⟨rope⟩; to cut [sth] off ⟨head⟩; to slit ⟨throat⟩
2 *vi* **(a)** ⟨colour, outline⟩ to stand out
(b) to come to a decision

tranquille /tʀɑ̃kil/ *adj* **(a)** quiet; calm; peaceful; **tiens-toi** ~**!** keep still!; be quiet!; **il s'est tenu** ~ **pendant quelques mois** he behaved himself for a few months
(b) **être** ~ to be *or* feel easy in one's mind; **sa mère n'est pas** ~ **quand il sort** his mother worries when he goes out
(c) **avoir la conscience** ~ to have a clear conscience

tranquillement /tʀɑ̃kilmɑ̃/ *adv* **(a)** **elle dort** ~ she's sleeping peacefully; **j'aimerais pouvoir travailler** ~ I wish I could work in peace
(b) quietly
(c) **nous avons marché** ~ we walked along at a leisurely pace
(d) **nous étions** ~ **en train de discuter** we were chatting away happily

tranquillisant, ~**e** /tʀɑ̃kilizɑ̃, ɑ̃t/ **1** *adj* reassuring, comforting
2 *nm* tranquillizer (GB)

tranquilliser /tʀɑ̃kilize/ [1] *vtr* to reassure

tranquillité /tʀɑ̃kilite/ *nf* **(a)** calmness; calm
(b) ~ **(d'esprit)** peace of mind

transaction /tʀɑ̃zaksjɔ̃/ *nf* transaction

transalpin, ~**e** /tʀɑ̃zalpɛ̃, in/ *adj*
(a) transalpine
(b) Italian

transat[1] /tʀɑ̃zat/ *nm* (colloq) **(a)** deckchair
(b) baby chair

transat[2] /tʀɑ̃zat/ *nf* (Sport) transatlantic race

transatlantique /tʀɑ̃zatlɑ̃tik/ *adj* transatlantic

transborder /tʀɑ̃sbɔʀde/ [1] *vtr* to transship ⟨goods⟩; to transfer ⟨passengers⟩

transbordeur /tʀɑ̃sbɔʀdœʀ/ *nm*
(a) transporter bridge
(b) traverser
(c) ferry

transcendant, ~**e** /tʀɑ̃sɑ̃dɑ̃, ɑ̃t/ *adj*
(a) (in philosophy) transcendent
(b) (colloq) wonderful

transcender /tʀɑ̃sɑ̃de/ [1] *vtr* to transcend

transcription /tʀɑ̃skʀipsjɔ̃/ *nf* transcription

transcrire /tʀɑ̃skʀiʀ/ [67] *vtr* to transcribe

transe /tʀɑ̃s/ *nf* trance

transférer /tʀɑ̃sfeʀe/ [14] *vtr* **(a)** (gen) to transfer; to relocate ⟨offices⟩
(b) (Law) to transfer, to convey ⟨property⟩

transfert /tʀɑ̃sfɛʀ/ *nm* **(a)** (of person, data, money, property) transfer; (of offices) relocation
(b) (psychological) transference

transfigurer /tʀɑ̃sfigyʀe/ [1] *vtr* to transform

transformable /tʀɑ̃sfɔʀmabl/ *adj* convertible

transformateur /tʀɑ̃sfɔʀmatœʀ/ *nm* transformer

transformation /tʀɑ̃sfɔʀmasjɔ̃/ *nf* transformation; (of mineral, energy) conversion

transformer /tʀɑ̃sfɔʀme/ [1] **1** *vtr* **(a)** to alter ⟨garment, façade⟩; to change ⟨person, landscape⟩
(b) ~ **qn/qch en** (gen) to turn sb/sth into; to transform sb/sth into; ~ **un garage en bureau** to convert a garage into an office
2 se transformer *v refl* (+ *v être*)
(a) ⟨person⟩ to transform oneself; to be transformed
(b) **se** ~ **en** ⟨embryo, larva, bud⟩ to turn into

transfrontalier, -ière /tʀɑ̃sfʀɔ̃talje, ɛʀ/ *adj* cross-border

transfuge /tʀɑ̃sfyʒ/ **1** *nmf* defector
2 *nm* (Mil) deserter

transfusé, ~**e** /tʀɑ̃sfyze/ **1** *pp* ▶ TRANSFUSER
2 *pp adj* ⟨blood⟩ transfused; ⟨person⟩ who has been given a blood transfusion

transfuser /tʀɑ̃sfyze/ [1] *vtr* to give a blood transfusion to

transfusion /tʀɑ̃sfyzjɔ̃/ *nf* transfusion

transgresser /tʀɑ̃sgʀese/ [1] *vtr* to break ⟨law, rule, taboo⟩; to defy ⟨ban⟩

transhumance /tʀɑ̃zymɑ̃s/ *nf* transhumance, seasonal migration of livestock to summer pastures

transi, ~**e** /tʀɑ̃zi/ **1** *pp* ▶ TRANSIR
2 *pp adj* chilled; ~ **de peur** paralysed (GB) with fear; **un amoureux** ~ a bashful lover

transiger /tʀɑ̃ziʒe/ [13] *vi* to compromise

transir /tʀɑ̃ziʀ/ [3] *vtr* to chill; to paralyse

transistor /tʀɑ̃zistɔʀ/ *nm* transistor

transit /tʀɑ̃zit/ *nm* transit; **en** ~ in transit

transitaire /tʀɑ̃zitɛʀ/ **1** *adj* transit; **pays** ~ transit point
2 *nmf* forwarding agent

transiter /tʀɑ̃zite/ [1] *vi* ~ **par** ⟨goods, passengers⟩ to pass through, to go via

transitif, -ive /tʀɑ̃zitif, iv/ *adj* transitive

transition /tʀɑ̃zisjɔ̃/ *nf* transition

transitoire /tʀɑ̃zitwaʀ/ *adj* transitional

translucide /tʀɑ̃slysid/ *adj* translucent

transmanche /tʀɑ̃smɑ̃ʃ/ adj inv cross-Channel

transmetteur /tʀɑ̃smɛtœʀ/ nm transmitter

transmettre /tʀɑ̃smɛtʀ/ [60] **1** vtr (a) to pass [sth] on, to convey ⟨information, order, news⟩; to pass [sth] on ⟨story, knowledge⟩; to pass [sth] down ⟨culture, fortune⟩; **transmets-leur mes félicitations** give them my congratulations
(b) to transmit ⟨image, signal, data⟩
(c) to broadcast ⟨news, programme⟩
(d) to hand [sth] on ⟨property, land⟩; to hand over ⟨power⟩
(e) (Med) to transmit ⟨virus, illness⟩
2 se transmettre v refl (+ v être) (a) to pass [sth] on to each other ⟨message, data⟩
(b) ⟨signals, data⟩ to be transmitted
(c) ⟨tradition, culture⟩ to be handed down; ⟨story⟩ to be passed on
(d) ⟨virus, illness⟩ to be transmitted

transmissible /tʀɑ̃smisibl/ adj transmissible, transmittable

transmission /tʀɑ̃smisjɔ̃/ nf
(a) transmission, passing on; **la ~ des connaissances** the communication of knowledge
(b) (of data, signals) transmission
(c) (of programme) broadcasting
(d) (of tradition, secret, culture) handing down; (of fortune, property) transfer
(e) (Aut, Med) transmission
■ **~ de pensées** thought transference

transparaître /tʀɑ̃spaʀɛtʀ/ [73] vi to show through; **laisser ~** ⟨face, words⟩ to betray; ⟨person⟩ to let [sth] show ⟨emotions⟩

transparence /tʀɑ̃spaʀɑ̃s/ nf (a) (of glass, fabric) transparency; (of water) clearness; **on voyait ses jambes en ~** (à travers sa jupe) you could see her legs through her skirt
(b) (of skin) translucency; (of colour) limpidity
(c) (of person) transparency; (of policy) openness

transparent, ~e /tʀɑ̃spaʀɑ̃, ɑ̃t/ **1** adj
(a) transparent; ⟨water⟩ clear
(b) ⟨complexion⟩ translucent
(c) ⟨person⟩ transparent
2 nm (for overhead projector) transparency

transpercer /tʀɑ̃spɛʀse/ [12] vtr
(a) ⟨sword, arrow⟩ to pierce ⟨body⟩; ⟨bullet⟩ to go through
(b) ⟨rain⟩ to go through
(c) ⟨pain⟩ to shoot through

transpiration /tʀɑ̃spiʀasjɔ̃/ nf
(a) sweating, perspiration
(b) sweat
(c) (Bot) transpiration

transpirer /tʀɑ̃spiʀe/ [1] vi (a) to sweat, to perspire
(b) ⟨secret⟩ to leak out

transplantation /tʀɑ̃splɑ̃tasjɔ̃/ nf
(a) transplant; **~ d'organes** organ transplants
(b) transplantation

transplanter /tʀɑ̃splɑ̃te/ [1] vtr to transplant

transport /tʀɑ̃spɔʀ/ **1** nm transport, transportation (US)
2 transports nm pl **~s en commun** public transport or transportation (US)

transportable /tʀɑ̃spɔʀtabl/ adj transportable; **il n'est pas ~** (injured person) he cannot be moved

transporter /tʀɑ̃spɔʀte/ [1] vtr (a) to carry ⟨person, object⟩; to transport ⟨passengers, goods⟩; **être transporté à l'hôpital** to be taken to hospital
(b) to carry ⟨pollen, virus, disease⟩
(c) **être transporté dans un monde féerique** to be transported to a magical world

transporteur /tʀɑ̃spɔʀtœʀ/ nm carrier; **~ aérien** air carrier; **~ routier** road haulier (GB), road haulage contractor (GB), trucking company (US)

transposer /tʀɑ̃spoze/ [1] vtr to transpose

transsexuel, -elle /tʀɑ̃sɛksɥɛl/ adj, nm,f transsexual

transsibérien, -ienne /tʀɑ̃ssibeʀjɛ̃, ɛn/ **1** adj trans-Siberian
2 nm **le Transsibérien** the Trans-Siberian Railway

transvaser /tʀɑ̃svaze/ [1] vtr to decant ⟨liquid⟩

transversal, ~e, mpl **-aux** /tʀɑ̃svɛʀsal, o/ adj transverse; **rue ~e** side street

trapèze /tʀapɛz/ nm (a) (Sport) trapeze
(b) (in geometry) trapezium (GB), trapezoid (US)

trapéziste /tʀapezist/ nmf trapeze artist

trappe /tʀap/ nf (gen) trap door

trappeur /tʀapœʀ/ nm trapper

trapu, ~e /tʀapy/ adj ⟨man, outline⟩ stocky

traquenard /tʀaknaʀ/ nm trap

traquer /tʀake/ [1] vtr (gen) to track down; ⟨photographer⟩ to hound ⟨film star⟩

traumatisant, ~e /tʀomatizɑ̃, ɑ̃t/ adj traumatic

traumatiser /tʀomatize/ [1] vtr to traumatize

traumatisme /tʀomatism/ nm (a) (Med) traumatism
(b) (psychological) trauma

travail, pl **-aux** /tʀavaj, o/ **1** nm (a) (gen) work; job; **se mettre au ~** to get down to work; **avoir du ~** to have work to do; **les gros travaux** the heavy work; (félicitations) **c'est du beau ~!** you've done a great job on that!; **qu'est-ce que c'est que ce ~?** what do you call this?; **ne me téléphone pas à mon ~** don't call me at work; **chercher du/un ~** to look for work/a job; **être sans ~** to be out of work; **le ~ temporaire** temporary work; **le ~ de nuit** nightwork
(b) (Econ) labour (GB); **entrer dans le monde du ~** to enter the world of work
(c) **le ~ musculaire** muscular effort ⋯⟫

(d) le ~ de working with or in ⟨*metal, wood, stone*⟩

(e) workmanship; un ~ superbe a superb piece of workmanship

(f) (of water, erosion) action

(g) (of wine) fermentation; (of wood) warping

(h) (of woman in childbirth) labour (GB)

2 travaux *nm pl* **(a)** (gen) work; (on road) roadworks (GB), roadwork (US); **faire faire des travaux dans sa maison** to have work done in one's house

(b) (of researcher) work

(c) (of commission) deliberations

(d) les **travaux agricoles** agricultural work; **travaux de couture** needlework

■ ~ **à la chaîne** assembly-line work; ~ **à domicile** working at or from home; ~ **au noir** (gen) *work for which no earnings are declared*; (holding two jobs) moonlighting; **travaux manuels** handicrafts; **travaux pratiques, TP** practical work; lab work; **travaux publics, TP** civil engineering

travaillé, ~e /tʀavaje/ **1** *pp* ▸
TRAVAILLER

2 *pp adj* ⟨*jewel*⟩ finely-worked; ⟨*carving*⟩ elaborate; ⟨*gold, silver*⟩ wrought; ⟨*style*⟩ polished

travailler /tʀavaje/ [1] **1** *vtr* **(a)** to work on ⟨*style, school subject, voice, muscles*⟩; to practise (GB) ⟨*sport, instrument*⟩

(b) to work ⟨*wood, metal*⟩; (Culin) to knead ⟨*dough*⟩; to cultivate ⟨*land*⟩

(c) ~ **qn** ⟨*idea, affair*⟩ to be on sb's mind; ⟨*jealousy, pain*⟩ to plague sb; **un doute me travaillait** I had a nagging doubt

2 travailler à *v+prep* to work on ⟨*project, essay*⟩; to work toward(s) ⟨*objective*⟩

3 *vi* **(a)** ⟨*person, machine, muscles*⟩ to work; **faire** ~ **son cerveau** to apply one's mind; ~ **en équipes** to work shifts

(b) ⟨*shop, hotel, shopkeeper*⟩ to do business; ~ **à perte** ⟨*company, business*⟩ to run at a loss

(c) nous voulons la paix et c'est dans ce sens que nous travaillons we want peace and we are working toward(s) it

(d) ⟨*athlete*⟩ to train; ⟨*musician*⟩ to practise (GB)

(e) ⟨*wood*⟩ to warp

travailleur, -euse /tʀavajœʀ, øz/ **1** *adj*
(a) ⟨*pupil*⟩ hardworking

(b) ⟨*classes*⟩ working

2 *nm,f* worker

travailliste /tʀavajist/ **1** *adj* Labour
2 *nmf* Labour MP

travée /tʀave/ *nf* **(a)** row

(b) (Tech) span

travelling /tʀavliŋ/ *nm* (in cinema) tracking; tracking shot

travers /tʀavɛʀ/ **1** *nm inv* **(a)** foible, quirk

(b) (Naut) beam

(c) (Culin) ~ **de porc** sparerib

2 à travers *phr* **(a)** ⟨*see, look*⟩ through

(b) ⟨*walk*⟩ across; **voyager à** ~ **le monde** to travel all over the world

(c) **voyager à** ~ **le temps** to travel through time

(d) through; **à** ~ **ces informations** through this information

3 au travers *phr* through; **passer au** ~ **de** (figurative) to escape ⟨*inspection*⟩

4 de travers *phr* **(a)** askew; **ta veste est boutonnée de** ~ your jacket is buttoned up wrongly; **il a le nez de** ~ he has a twisted nose; **j'ai avalé de** ~ it went down the wrong way; **regarder qn de** ~ to give sb filthy looks

(b) wrong; **comprendre de** ~ to misunderstand

5 en travers *phr* across; **un bus était en** ~ **de la route** a bus was stuck across the road; **se mettre en** ~ **de la route** ⟨*people*⟩ to stand in the middle of the road; **rester en** ~ **de la gorge de qn** (colloq) to be hard to swallow

traverse /tʀavɛʀs/ *nf* (on railway line) sleeper (GB), tie (US)

traversée /tʀavɛʀse/ *nf* **(a)** crossing; **la** ~ **du désert** crossing the desert; (figurative) (of company) a difficult period

(b) (of city) **évitez la** ~ **de Paris** avoid going through Paris

traverser /tʀavɛʀse/ [1] *vtr* **(a)** to cross ⟨*road, bridge, border, town, room*⟩; to go through ⟨*town, forest, tunnel*⟩; to make one's way through ⟨*group, crowd*⟩; **il traversa le jardin en courant** he ran across the garden (GB) or yard (US)

(b) ⟨*river*⟩ to run through ⟨*region*⟩; ⟨*road*⟩ to go through ⟨*region*⟩; ⟨*bridge, river*⟩ to cross ⟨*railway line, town*⟩

(c) ⟨*rain*⟩ to soak through ⟨*clothes*⟩; **la balle lui a traversé le bras** the bullet went right through his/her arm

(d) to go through ⟨*crisis*⟩; to live through ⟨*war*⟩

(e) ~ **l'esprit de qn** to cross sb's mind

traversin /tʀavɛʀsɛ̃/ *nm* bolster

travesti, ~e /tʀavɛsti/ **1** *pp* ▸ TRAVESTIR

2 *pp adj* in disguise; **rôle** ~ role played by a member of the opposite sex

3 *nm* **(a)** transvestite

(b) (actor) actor playing a female role; (in cabaret) drag artist (colloq)

travestir /tʀavɛstiʀ/ [3] **1** *vtr* **(a)** to dress [sb] up ⟨*person*⟩

(b) to distort ⟨*truth*⟩

2 se travestir *v refl* (+ *v être*) **(a)** to dress up

(b) to cross-dress

trébucher /tʀebyʃe/ [1] *vi* to stumble

trèfle /tʀɛfl/ *nm* **(a)** clover

(b) (Games) (card) club; (suit) clubs

(c) shamrock

tréfonds /tʀefɔ̃/ *nm inv* **le** ~ **de** the very depths of

treillage /tʀɛjaʒ/ *nm* **(a)** trellis

(b) lattice fence

treille /tʀɛj/ *nf* **(a)** (vine) arbour (GB)

(b) climbing vine

treillis /tʀɛji/ *nm inv* **(a)** (Mil) fatigues

(b) canvas

(c) trellis; ~ **métallique** wire grille

treize /tʀɛz/ adj inv, pron, nm inv thirteen

treizième /tʀɛzjɛm/ adj thirteenth

tréma /tʀema/ nm diaeresis; **i ~ i** diaeresis

tremblant, ~e /tʀɑ̃blɑ̃, ɑ̃t/ adj
(a) ⟨person, hands⟩ shaking
(b) ⟨voice⟩ trembling
(c) ⟨image, light⟩ flickering; ⟨sound⟩ tremulous

tremble /tʀɑ̃bl/ nm aspen

tremblement /tʀɑ̃bləmɑ̃/ nm (a) (of person, hands) shaking, trembling; (of lips) trembling
(b) (of voice) trembling
(c) (of leaves) quivering
■ ~ **de terre** earthquake

trembler /tʀɑ̃ble/ [1] vi (a) ⟨person, legs⟩ to shake, to tremble
(b) ⟨voice⟩ to tremble; ⟨sound, note⟩ to waver
(c) ⟨building, floor⟩ to shake
(d) (be afraid) to tremble; ~ **pour qn** to fear for sb
(e) ⟨light, image⟩ to flicker
(f) ⟨leaves⟩ to quiver

trembloter /tʀɑ̃blɔte/ [1] vi (a) ⟨person, hands⟩ to tremble slightly
(b) ⟨voice⟩ to tremble

trémolo /tʀemolo/ nm (a) (of voice) quaver
(b) (of instrument) tremolo

trémousser: se trémousser
/tʀemuse/ [1] v refl (+ v être) (a) to fidget
(b) to wiggle around

trempe /tʀɑ̃p/ nf **avoir la ~ d'un dirigeant** to have the makings of a leader

trempé, ~e /tʀɑ̃pe/ **1** pp ▶ TREMPER
2 pp adj (a) ⟨person, garments⟩ soaked (through); ⟨grass⟩ sodden
(b) (Tech) ⟨steel⟩ tempered; ⟨glass⟩ toughened

tremper /tʀɑ̃pe/ [1] **1** vtr (a) ⟨rain, person⟩ to soak ⟨person, garment⟩
(b) to dip; **j'ai juste trempé mes lèvres** I just had a sip
(c) to soak ⟨hands⟩
(d) (Tech) to temper
2 vi (a) ⟨clothes, vegetables⟩ to soak; **faire ~ qch** to soak sth
(b) (colloq) ~ **dans qch** to be mixed up in sth

tremplin /tʀɑ̃plɛ̃/ nm (a) springboard
(b) ski jump; water-ski jump

trentaine /tʀɑ̃tɛn/ nf (a) about thirty
(b) **avoir la ~** to be about thirty

trente /tʀɑ̃t/ adj inv, pron, nm inv thirty

trente-et-un /tʀɑ̃teœ̃/ nm **être sur son ~** (colloq) to be dressed up to the nines

trentenaire /tʀɑ̃tənɛʀ/ adj ⟨person⟩ in his/her thirties; ⟨tree, building⟩ around thirty years old

trente-six /tʀɑ̃tsis/ adj inv, pron, nm inv thirty-six
IDIOMS voir ~ chandelles (colloq) to see stars

trente-trois /tʀɑ̃tʀwa/ adj inv, pron, nm inv thirty-three
■ ~ **tours** LP

trentième /tʀɑ̃tjɛm/ adj thirtieth

trépas /tʀepɑ/ nm demise

trépidant, ~e /tʀepidɑ̃, ɑ̃t/ adj ⟨rhythm, speed⟩ pulsating; ⟨life⟩ hectic; ⟨story⟩ exciting

trépied /tʀepje/ nm (gen) tripod

trépigner /tʀepiɲe/ [1] vi (with anger, impatience) to stamp one's feet

très /tʀɛ/ adv very; ~ **connu** very well-known; **être ~ amoureux** to be very much in love; ~ **en avance** very early; ~ **volontiers** gladly; **'tu vas bien?'—'non, pas ~'** 'are you well?'—'no, not terribly'; **elle a ~ envie de partir** she's dying to leave (colloq)

trésor /tʀezɔʀ/ nm (a) treasure
(b) **déployer des ~s d'inventivité** to show infinite inventiveness
(c) (person) **mon ~** precious

trésorerie /tʀezɔʀʀi/ nf (a) funds; cash
(b) (of company) accounts
(c) government finance

trésorier, -ière /tʀezɔʀje, ɛʀ/ nm,f treasurer

tressaillement /tʀɛsajmɑ̃/ nm (a) (from surprise, fear) start; (of hope, pleasure) quiver; (from pain) wince
(b) (of person, muscle, animal) twitch; (of machine, ground) vibration

tressaillir /tʀɛsajiʀ/ [28] vi (a) (with surprise) to start; (with pleasure) to quiver
(b) ⟨person, muscle⟩ to twitch

tresse /tʀɛs/ nf (a) plait
(b) (of thread) braid

tresser /tʀɛse/ [1] vtr to plait ⟨hair, threads⟩; to weave ⟨straw, string⟩

tréteau, pl ~**x** /tʀeto/ nm trestle

treuil /tʀœj/ nm winch

trêve /tʀɛv/ nf (a) (Mil) truce
(b) respite; ~ **de plaisanteries!** that's enough joking!

tri /tʀi/ nm sorting; sorting out; **centre de ~** (postal) sorting office; **faire le ~ de** to sort ⟨mail⟩; to sort out ⟨documents, clothes⟩; **faire un ~ parmi des choses** to select among things

triage /tʀijaʒ/ nm **gare de ~** marshalling (GB) yard

triangle /tʀijɑ̃gl/ nm triangle
■ ~ **des Bermudes** Bermuda Triangle

triangulaire /tʀijɑ̃gylɛʀ/ adj
(a) triangular
(b) ⟨agreement, partnership⟩ three-way

triathlon /tʀiatlɔ̃/ nm triathlon

tribal, ~e, mpl **-aux** /tʀibal, o/ adj tribal

tribord /tʀibɔʀ/ nm starboard

tribu /tʀiby/ nf tribe

tribulations /tʀibylasjɔ̃/ nf pl tribulations

tribun /tʀibœ̃/ nm (a) tribune
(b) great orator

tribunal, pl **-aux** /tʀibynal, o/ nm (Law) court; **traîner qn devant les tribunaux** to take sb to court

t

tribune /tribyn/ *nf* (a) (in stadium) stand; (in court) gallery
(b) (of speaker) platform, rostrum
(c) (in newspaper) comments column

tribut /triby/ *nm* tribute

tributaire /tribytεr/ *adj* **être ~ de** ⟨*country, person*⟩ to depend on

tricentenaire /trisɑ̃tnεr/ *adj* three-hundred-year-old

triche /triʃ/ *nf* (colloq) **c'est de la ~** that's cheating

tricher /triʃe/ [1] *vi* to cheat; **~ sur son âge** to lie about one's age

tricherie /triʃri/ *nf* cheating

tricheur, -euse /triʃœr, øz/ *nm,f* cheat

tricolore /trikɔlɔr/ *adj* (a) three-coloured (GB); **feux ~s** traffic lights
(b) (colloq) French; **l'équipe ~** the French team

tricot /triko/ *nm* (a) knitting; **faire du ~** to knit
(b) knitwear; **en ~** knitted

tricoter /trikɔte/ [1] *vtr* to knit; **tricoté (à la) main** handknitted

tricycle /trisikl/ *nm* tricycle

trident /tridɑ̃/ *nm* trident

tridimensionnel, -elle /tridimɑ̃sjɔnεl/ *adj* three-dimensional

triennal, ~e, mpl -aux /trijenal, o/ *adj*
(a) ⟨*mandate*⟩ three-year
(b) ⟨*vote*⟩ three-yearly

trier /trije/ [2] *vtr* (a) to sort ⟨*mail*⟩
(b) to sort [sth] out ⟨*information*⟩; to select ⟨*clients*⟩
IDIOMS ~ sur le volet to handpick

trifouiller /trifuje/ [1] *vi* (colloq) **~ dans** to rummage through; to tinker with

trilingue /trilε̃g/ *adj* trilingual

trilogie /trilɔʒi/ *nf* trilogy

trimbal(l)er /trε̃bale/ [1] *vtr* (colloq) to lug [sth] around; to drag [sb] around

trimer /trime/ [1] *vi* (colloq) to slave away

trimestre /trimεstr/ *nm* (a) (period) quarter; (Sch) term
(b) quarterly income; quarterly payment

trimestriel, -ielle /trimεstrijεl/ *adj* (gen) quarterly; ⟨*exam*⟩ end-of-term

trimoteur /trimɔtœr/ *nm* three-engined plane

tringle /trε̃gl/ *nf* (a) (gen) rail
(b) (Tech) rod

trinité /trinite/ *nf* trinity

trinquer /trε̃ke/ [1] *vi* to clink glasses; **~ à qch** to drink to sth

trio /tri(j)o/ *nm* trio

triomphal, ~e, mpl -aux /trijɔ̃fal, o/ *adj* triumphant

triomphalisme /trijɔ̃falism/ *nm* triumphalism

triomphant, ~e /trijɔ̃fɑ̃, ɑ̃t/ *adj* triumphant

triomphateur, -trice /trijɔ̃fatœr, tris/ *adj* triumphant

triomphe /trijɔ̃f/ *nm* triumph; **faire un ~ à qn** to give sb a triumphal reception

triompher /trijɔ̃fe/ [1] **1 triompher de** *v+prep* to triumph over ⟨*enemy*⟩; to overcome ⟨*resistance*⟩
2 *vi* (a) ⟨*fighter*⟩ to triumph; ⟨*truth*⟩ to prevail
(b) to be triumphant

tripartisme /tripartism/ *nm* tripartite *or* three-party system

tripatouiller /tripatuje/ [1] *vtr* (colloq) to fiddle with (colloq) ⟨*object*⟩; to paw (colloq) ⟨*person*⟩

triperie /tripri/ *nf* (a) tripe shop
(b) tripe trade

tripes /trip/ *nf pl* (a) (Culin) tripe
(b) (colloq) guts, innards

triplace /triplas/ *adj* three-seater

triple /tripl/ **1** *adj* triple; **l'avantage est ~** the advantages are threefold; **en ~ exemplaire** in triplicate; **~ idiot!** (colloq) prize idiot! (colloq)
2 *nm* **coûter le ~** to cost three times as much

triplé, ~e /triple/ *nm,f* triplet

triplement /triplemɑ̃/ *adv* (a) in three respects
(b) trebly

tripler /triple/ [1] **1** *vtr* to treble ⟨*quantity, price*⟩
2 *vi* to treble (**de in**)

triporteur /tripɔrtœr/ *nm* delivery tricycle

tripot /tripo/ *nm* (a) gambling joint (colloq)
(b) dive (colloq)

tripotée /tripote/ *nf* (colloq) (a) (good) hiding (colloq)
(b) **une ~ de** hordes of

tripoter /tripote/ [1] *vtr* (colloq) to fiddle with ⟨*object*⟩

trique /trik/ *nf* cudgel; **battre à coups de ~** to cudgel
IDIOMS être maigre *or* **sec comme un coup de ~** to be as thin as a rake

trisaïeul, ~e /trizajœl/ *nm,f* great-great-grandfather/grandmother

trisannuel, -elle /trizanɥεl/ *adj* triennial

trisomie /trizɔmi/ *nf* trisomy; **~ 21** Down's Syndrome

trisomique /trizɔmik/ *adj* **enfant ~** Down's Syndrome child

triste /trist/ *adj* (a) (gen) sad; ⟨*town, existence*⟩ dreary; ⟨*weather, day*⟩ gloomy; ⟨*colour*⟩ drab
(b) ⟨*end, business, reputation*⟩ dreadful; ⟨*show, state*⟩ sorry; ⟨*character*⟩ unsavoury (GB); **c'est la ~ vérité** unfortunately, that's the truth of the matter; **faire la ~ expérience de qch** to learn about sth to one's cost

tristement /tristəmɑ̃/ *adv* sadly

tristesse /tristεs/ *nf* (gen) sadness; (of place, evening) dreariness; (of weather, day) gloominess

triton /tʀitɔ̃/ *nm* (Zool) **(a)** (mollusc) triton
(b) newt

triturer /tʀityʀe/ [1] *vtr* to fiddle with
⟨button⟩; to knead ⟨dough⟩
  IDIOMS se ∼ **la cervelle** (colloq) *or* **les
méninges** (colloq) to rack one's brains (colloq)

trivial, ∼**e**, *mpl* **-iaux** /tʀivjal, o/ *adj*
(a) coarse
(b) ordinary, everyday; ⟨style⟩ mundane

trivialité /tʀivjalite/ *nf* **(a)** coarseness
(b) triteness, triviality
(c) platitude

troc /tʀɔk/ *nm* barter; **faire du** ∼ to barter

troène /tʀɔɛn/ *nm* privet

troglodyte /tʀɔɡlɔdit/ *nm* cave-dweller

trogne /tʀɔɲ/ *nf* (colloq) mug (colloq), face

trognon /tʀɔɲɔ̃/ *nm* (of apple) core

trois /tʀwɑ/ *adj inv, pron, nm inv* three
  IDIOMS **être haut comme** ∼ **pommes** to be
kneehigh to a grasshopper; **jamais deux
sans** ∼ bad luck comes in threes

trois-huit /tʀwaɥit/ *nm pl* system of three
eight-hour shifts

troisième /tʀwazjɛm/ **1** *adj* third
2 *nf* **(a)** (Sch) *fourth year of secondary
school, age 14–15*
(b) (Aut) third (gear)
  ■ **le** ∼ **âge** the elderly

troisièmement /tʀwazjɛmmɑ̃/ *adv*
thirdly

trois-mâts /tʀwamɑ/ *nm inv* three-master

trois-quarts /tʀwakaʀ/ **1** *nm inv*
(a) three-quarter length coat
(b) (rugby player) three-quarter
2 **de trois-quarts** *phr* ⟨portrait⟩ three-
quarter length

trombe /tʀɔ̃b/ *nf* **(a)** (caused by whirlwind)
waterspout; **partir en** ∼ to go hurtling off
(b) ∼**s d'eau** masses of water; torrential
rain

trombone /tʀɔ̃bɔn/ *nm* **(a)** trombone
(b) trombonist
(c) paperclip

trompe /tʀɔ̃p/ *nf* **(a)** (Zool) (of elephant)
trunk; (of insect) proboscis
(b) (Mus) horn

trompe-la-mort /tʀɔ̃plamɔʀ/ *nmf inv*
daredevil

trompe-l'œil /tʀɔ̃plœj/ *nm inv* **(a)** (painting)
trompe l'œil
(b) (figurative) smokescreen

tromper /tʀɔ̃pe/ [1] **1** *vtr* **(a)** (gen) to
deceive; to be unfaithful to ⟨husband, wife⟩;
∼ **les électeurs** to mislead the voters
(b) ∼ **la vigilance de qn** to slip past sb's
guard
(c) **pour** ∼ **l'attente** to while away the time
2 **se tromper** *v refl* (+ *v être*) **(a)** to be
mistaken; **se** ∼ **sur qn** to be wrong about sb;
il ne faut pas s'y ∼, **qu'on ne s'y trompe pas**
make no mistake about it
(b) to make a mistake; **se** ∼ **de bus** to take
the wrong bus

tromperie /tʀɔ̃pʀi/ *nf* deceit

trompette¹ /tʀɔ̃pɛt/ *nm* (in army) bugler

trompette² /tʀɔ̃pɛt/ *nf* trumpet

trompettiste /tʀɔ̃petist/ *nmf* trumpet
(player)

trompeur, **-euse** /tʀɔ̃pœʀ, øz/ *adj*
⟨promise⟩ misleading; ⟨appearance⟩
deceptive

tronc /tʀɔ̃/ *nm* **(a)** (of tree, body) trunk;
(of column) shaft
(b) collection box
  ■ ∼ **commun** (of species) common origin;
(of disciplines) (common) core curriculum

tronche /tʀɔ̃ʃ/ *nf* (slang) mug (colloq), face

tronçon /tʀɔ̃sɔ̃/ *nm* section

tronçonneuse /tʀɔ̃sɔnøz/ *nf* chain saw

trône /tʀon/ *nm* throne

trôner /tʀone/ [1] *vi* **le professeur trônait au
milieu de ses étudiants** the professor was
holding court among his students; ∼ **sur**
⟨photograph⟩ to have pride of place on

tronquer /tʀɔ̃ke/ [1] *vtr* to truncate

trop /tʀo/ **1** *adv* too; too much; **beaucoup**
or **bien** ∼ **lourd** far *or* much too heavy; **j'ai**
∼ **mangé** I've had too much to eat; **j'ai** ∼
dormi I've slept too long; **nous sommes** ∼
peu nombreux there are too few of us; **12
francs c'est** ∼ **peu** 12 francs is too little; **ce
serait** ∼ **beau!** one should be so lucky!; **c'est**
∼ **bête!** how stupid!; ∼ **enthousiaste**
overenthusiastic; ∼ **c'est** ∼**!** enough is
enough!; **c'était** ∼ **drôle** it was so funny
2 **trop de** *quantif* ∼ **de pression/meubles**
too much pressure/furniture; ∼ **de livres/
monde** too many books/people
3 **de trop**, **en trop** *phr* **il y a une assiette
en** ∼ there's one plate too many; **il y a 12
francs de** ∼ there's 12 francs too much; **ta
remarque était de** ∼ your remark was
uncalled for; **se sentir de** ∼ to feel one is in
the way

trophée /tʀɔfe/ *nm* trophy

tropical, ∼**e**, *mpl* **-aux** /tʀɔpikal, o/ *adj*
tropical

tropique /tʀɔpik/ *nm* tropic

trop-perçu, *pl* ∼**s** /tʀɔpɛʀsy/ *nm*
(a) excess payment
(b) overpayment of tax; **remboursement d'un**
∼ tax refund

trop-plein, *pl* ∼**s** /tʀɔplɛ̃/ *nm* **(a)** (of energy)
excess
(b) (Tech) (from bath) overflow

troquer /tʀɔke/ [1] *vtr* (gen) ∼ **qch contre
qch** to swap sth for sth; to barter sth for sth

troquet /tʀɔkɛ/ *nm* (colloq) bar

trot /tʀo/ *nm* trot

trotte /tʀɔt/ *nf* (colloq) **ça fait une** ∼ it's a
fair walk

trotter /tʀɔte/ [1] *vi* **(a)** ⟨horse, rider⟩ to
trot
(b) ⟨person, mouse⟩ to scurry (about)
(c) (figurative) ∼ **dans la tête** ⟨thought⟩ to go
through one's mind; ⟨music⟩ to go through
one's head

trotteur /tʀɔtœʀ/ *nm* **(a)** trotter

    ····⟩

(b) *shoe with a low, broad heel*

trotteuse /tʀɔtøz/ *nf* (on watch) second hand

trottiner /tʀɔtine/ [1] *vi* (a) ⟨*horse*⟩ to jog
(b) ⟨*person, mouse*⟩ to scurry along

trottinette /tʀɔtinɛt/ *nf* scooter

trottoir /tʀɔtwaʀ/ *nm* pavement (GB), sidewalk (US); **le bord du ~** the kerb (GB) *or* curb (US)

trou /tʀu/ *nm* (a) hole
(b) (in timetable) (gen) gap; (in budget) deficit; (in savings) hole
(c) (colloq) **~ (perdu)** dump (colloq)
■ **~ d'aération** airhole; **~ d'air** air pocket; **~ de mémoire** memory lapse; **~ normand** *glass of spirits between courses to aid digestion*; **~ de serrure** keyhole

troublant, ~e /tʀublɑ̃, ɑ̃t/ *adj*
(a) disturbing; disconcerting
(b) (sexually) unsettling

trouble /tʀubl/ **1** *adj* (a) ⟨*liquid*⟩ cloudy; ⟨*glasses*⟩ smudgy
(b) ⟨*picture, outline*⟩ blurred
(c) ⟨*feeling*⟩ confused; ⟨*business, milieu*⟩ shady
2 *adv* **je vois ~** my eyes are blurred
3 *nm* (a) unrest; **~s ethniques** ethnic unrest
(b) trouble; **jeter le ~** to stir up trouble
(c) confusion; embarrassment
(d) emotion; **ressentir un ~** to feel a thrill of emotion
(e) (Med) **~s** disorders

trouble-fête /tʀubləfɛt/ *nmf inv* spoilsport

troubler /tʀuble/ [1] **1** *vtr* (a) to make [sth] cloudy ⟨*liquid*⟩; to blur ⟨*sight, picture*⟩
(b) to disturb ⟨*sleep, person*⟩; to disrupt ⟨*plans*⟩; **en ces temps troublés** in these troubled times
(c) to disconcert ⟨*person*⟩
2 **se troubler** *v refl* (+ *v être*) (a) ⟨*person*⟩ to become flustered
(b) ⟨*liquid*⟩ to become cloudy; **ma vue se troubla** my eyes became blurred

trouée /tʀue/ *nf* (a) gap
(b) (Mil) breach

trouer /tʀue/ [1] *vtr* to make a hole (*or* holes) in; to wear a hole (*or* holes) in; **semelle trouée** sole with a hole (*or* holes) in it

troufion /tʀufjɔ̃/ *nm* (slang) soldier

trouillard, ~e /tʀujaʀ, aʀd/ (slang) **1** *adj* cowardly
2 *nm,f* chicken (colloq), coward

trouille /tʀuj/ *nf* (slang) **avoir la ~** to be scared

troupe /tʀup/ *nf* (a) (Mil) troops
(b) (of actors) company; (on tour) troupe
(c) (of deer) herd; (of birds) flock; (of tourists) troop; (of children) troupe

troupeau, *pl* **~x** /tʀupo/ *nm* (of buffalo, cattle) herd; (of sheep) flock; (of geese) gaggle

trousse /tʀus/ *nf* (a) (little) case
(b) kit

■ **~ d'écolier** pencil case; **~ de médecin** doctor's bag; **~ de secours** first-aid kit; **~ de toilette** toilet bag
IDIOMS **être aux ~s de qn** to be hot on sb's heels

trousseau, *pl* **~x** /tʀuso/ *nm* (a) (of keys) bunch
(b) (of bride) trousseau; (of baby) clothes

trouvaille /tʀuvaj/ *nf* (a) (object) find
(b) bright idea, brainwave

trouvé, ~e /tʀuve/ **1** *pp* ▸ TROUVER
2 *pp adj* **réplique bien ~e** neat riposte; **tout ~** ⟨*solution*⟩ ready-made; ⟨*culprit*⟩ obvious

trouver /tʀuve/ [1] **1** *vtr* (a) (gen) to find; **~ qch par hasard** to come across sth; **~ un intérêt à qch** to find sth interesting; **~ à redire** to find fault; **~ le moyen de faire** to manage to do; **j'ai trouvé!** I've got it!; **tu as trouvé ça tout seul?** (ironic) did you work that out all by yourself?; **si tu continues tu vas me ~!** (colloq) don't push your luck! (colloq); **~ du plaisir à faire** to get pleasure out of doing; **aller ~ qn** to go and see sb
(b) **je trouve ça drôle** I think it's funny; **j'ai trouvé bon de vous prévenir** I thought it right to warn you; **je me demande ce qu'elle te trouve!** I wonder what she sees in you!; **je te trouve bien calme, qu'est-ce que tu as?** you're very quiet, what's the matter?
2 **se trouver** *v refl* (+ *v être*) (a) to be; **se ~ à Rome** to be in Rome; **se ~ dans l'impossibilité de faire** to be unable to do
(b) to feel; **j'ai failli me ~ mal** I nearly passed out
(c) **il se ~ beau** he thinks he's good-looking
(d) to find ⟨*excuse*⟩
3 *v impers* **il se trouve qu'elle ne leur avait rien dit** as it happened, she hadn't told them anything; **si ça se trouve ça te plaira** (colloq) you might like it

truand /tʀɥɑ̃/ *nm* (a) gangster
(b) crook

trublion /tʀyblijɔ̃/ *nm* troublemaker

truc /tʀyk/ *nm* (a) (colloq) knack; trick; **avoir un ~ pour gagner de l'argent** to know a good way of making money; **un ~ du métier** a trick of the trade
(b) thing; **il y a un tas de ~s à faire dans la maison** there are loads of things to do in the house (colloq); **il y a un ~ qui ne va pas** there's something wrong
(c) (colloq) thingummy (colloq), whatsit (colloq)
(d) (person) what's-his-name/what's-her-name, thingy (colloq)

trucage /tʀykaʒ/ *nm* (in cinema) special effect

truchement /tʀyʃmɑ̃/ *nm* **par le ~ de qch** through sth; **par le ~ de qn** through the intervention of sb

truculent, ~e /tʀykylɑ̃, ɑ̃t/ *adj* earthy

truelle /tʀyɛl/ *nf* trowel

truffe /tʀyf/ *nf* (a) (Culin) truffle
(b) (of dog) nose

truffer /tʀyfe/ [1] *vtr* **ta lettre est truffée de fautes** your letter is riddled with mistakes

truie /tʀɥi/ nf sow

truite /tʀɥit/ nf trout

truquage = TRUCAGE

truquer /tʀyke/ [1] vtr **(a)** to fiddle (colloq) ⟨accounts⟩
(b) to mark ⟨cards⟩
(c) to fix ⟨elections, match⟩

trust /tʀœst/ nm trust

tsar /tsaʀ/ nm tsar

tsé-tsé /tsetse/ nf inv (mouche) ~ tsetse (fly)

tsigane = TZIGANE

TTC (abbr = **toutes taxes comprises**) inclusive of tax

tu /ty/ pron you
IDIOMS être à ~ et à toi avec qn to be on familiar terms with sb

tuant, ~**e** /tɥɑ̃, ɑ̃t/ adj (colloq) exhausting

tuba /tyba/ nm **(a)** (Mus) tuba
(b) (of swimmer) snorkel

tube /tyb/ ⟨1⟩ nm **(a)** tube; pipe
(b) (colloq) (song) hit
⟨2⟩ **à pleins tubes** phr (colloq) mettre le son à pleins ~s to turn the sound right up (colloq)
■ ~ **cathodique** cathode ray tube; ~ **digestif** digestive tract; ~ **à essai** test tube

tubercule /tybɛʀkyl/ nm **(a)** (Bot) tuber
(b) (Anat) tuberosity

tuberculeux, -**euse** /tybɛʀkylø, øz/ adj tubercular; être ~ to have TB

tuberculose /tybɛʀkyloz/ nf tuberculosis, TB

tubulaire /tybylɛʀ/ adj tubular

TUC /tyk/ nm pl (abbr = **travaux d'utilité collective**) paid community service (for the young unemployed)

tué /tɥe/ nm person killed; sept ~s, cinq blessés seven people killed, five injured

tuer /tɥe/ [1] ⟨1⟩ vtr **(a)** (gen) to kill
(b) (colloq) to wear [sb] out
⟨2⟩ **se tuer** v refl (+ v être) **(a)** (accidentally) to be killed
(b) to kill oneself
(c) se ~ **au travail** to work oneself to death

tuerie /tɥʀi/ nf killings

tue-tête: **à tue-tête** /atytɛt/ phr at the top of one's voice

tueur, -**euse** /tɥœʀ, øz/ nm,f **(a)** killer
(b) slaughterman/slaughterwoman
■ ~ **à gages** hired or professional killer

tuile /tɥil/ nf **(a)** tile
(b) (colloq) blow; quelle ~! what a blow!
(c) (Culin) thin almond biscuit

tulipe /tylip/ nf tulip

tuméfier /tymefje/ [2] vtr to make [sth] swell up

tumeur /tymœʀ/ nf tumour (GB)

tumulte /tymylt/ nm **(a)** uproar
(b) turmoil

tumultueux, -**euse** /tymyltɥø, øz/ adj turbulent; tempestuous; stormy

tungstène /tœ̃gstɛn/ nm tungsten

tunique /tynik/ nf tunic

tunisien, -**ienne** /tynizjɛ̃, ɛn/ adj Tunisian

tunnel /tynɛl/ nm tunnel; le ~ **sous la Manche** the Channel Tunnel
IDIOMS voir le bout du ~ to see light at the end of the tunnel

turban /tyʀbɑ̃/ nm turban

turbin /tyʀbɛ̃/ nm (slang) daily grind (colloq), work

turbine /tyʀbin/ nf turbine

turboréacteur /tyʀboʀeaktœʀ/ nm turbojet (engine)

turbot /tyʀbo/ nm turbot

turbulence /tyʀbylɑ̃s/ nf **(a)** turbulence
(b) unruliness
(c) unrest

turbulent, ~**e** /tyʀbylɑ̃, ɑ̃t/ adj ⟨child⟩ unruly; ⟨class⟩ rowdy; ⟨teenager⟩ rebellious; être ~ **en classe** to be disruptive in class

turc, **turque** /tyʀk/ ⟨1⟩ adj Turkish
⟨2⟩ nm (language) Turkish

Turc, **Turque** /tyʀk/ nm,f Turk

turfiste /tœʀfist/ nmf racegoer, punter (colloq)

turlupiner /tyʀlypine/ [1] vtr (colloq) to bother

turpitude /tyʀpityd/ nf **(a)** turpitude, depravity
(b) base act; low remark

turque ▶ TURC 1

Turquie /tyʀki/ pr nf Turkey

turquoise /tyʀkwaz/ adj inv, nf turquoise

tutelle /tytɛl/ nf guardianship

tuteur, -**trice** /tytœʀ, tʀis/ ⟨1⟩ nm,f
(a) (Law) guardian
(b) tutor
⟨2⟩ nm (Bot) stake

tutoiement /tytwamɑ̃/ nm using the 'tu' form

tutoyer /tytwaje/ [23] vtr to address [sb] using the 'tu' form

tutu /tyty/ nm tutu

tuyau, pl ~**x** /tɥijo/ nm **(a)** (Tech) pipe
(b) (colloq) tip (colloq)
■ ~ **d'arrosage** hose; ~ **d'échappement** exhaust

tuyauterie /tɥijotʀi/ nf (Tech) piping

TVA /tevea/ nf (abbr = **taxe à la valeur ajoutée**) VAT

tympan /tɛ̃pɑ̃/ nm eardrum

type /tip/ ⟨1⟩ nm **(a)** type, kind; plusieurs accidents de ce ~ several accidents of this kind
(b) (classic) example; elle est le ~ même de la femme d'affaires she's the classic example of a business woman
(c) (physical) type
(d) (colloq) guy (colloq); sale ~! swine! (colloq); brave ~ nice chap (colloq)
⟨2⟩ (-)**type** (combining form) typical, classic

typer /tipe/ [1] vtr to portray [sb] as a type; to play [sb] as a type

t

typhoïde /tifɔid/ *adj, nf* typhoid
typhon /tifɔ̃/ *nm* typhoon
typique /tipik/ *adj* typical
typiquement /tipikmɑ̃/ *adv* typically; une famille ∼ américaine a typically American family
typographie /tipɔgRafi/ *nf* typography

typographique /tipɔgRafik/ *adj* typographical
tyran /tiRɑ̃/ *nm* tyrant
tyrannie /tiRani/ *nf* tyranny
tyrannique /tiRanik/ *adj* tyrannical
tyranniser /tiRanize/ [1] *vtr* to tyrannize
tzigane /dzigan, tsigɑ̃/ **1** *adj, nmf* gypsy **2** *nm* (language) Romany

U u

u, U /y/ *nm inv* u, U; en (forme de) U U-shaped
ubac /ybak/ *nm* north-facing side
ubiquité /ybikɥite/ *nf* ubiquity; je n'ai pas le don d'∼! I can't be everywhere at once!
ubuesque /ybyɛsk/ *adj* grotesque
ulcère /ylsɛR/ *nm* ulcer
ulcérer /ylseRe/ [14] *vtr* **(a)** to sicken, to revolt
(b) (Med) to ulcerate
ulcéreux, -euse /ylseRø, øz/ *adj* ⟨wound⟩ ulcerated
ULM /yɛlɛm/ *nm inv* (*abbr* = **ultraléger motorisé**) microlight; microlighting; faire de l'∼ to go microlighting
ultérieur, ∼e /ylteRjœR/ *adj* subsequent; une date ∼e a later date
ultérieurement /ylteRjœRmɑ̃/ *adv*
(a) subsequently
(b) later
ultimatum /yltimatɔm/ *nm* ultimatum
ultime /yltim/ *adj* **(a)** final
(b) ultimate
ultra /yltRa/ *adj, nmf* extremist
ultraconfidentiel, -ielle /yltRakɔ̃fidɑ̃sjɛl/ *adj* top secret
ultrafin, ∼e /yltRafɛ̃, in/ *adj* ⟨slice⟩ wafer-thin; ⟨stocking⟩ sheer; ⟨fibre⟩ ultra-fine
ultraléger, -ère /yltRaleʒe, ɛR/ *adj* ⟨material, cigarette⟩ ultra light; ⟨clothing, fabric, equipment⟩ very light
ultramoderne /yltRamɔdɛRn/ *adj* (gen) ultramodern; ⟨system, technology⟩ state-of-the-art
ultrarapide /yltRaRapid/ *adj* high-speed
ultrasecret, -ète /yltRasəkRɛ, ɛt/ *adj* top secret
ultrasensible /yltRasɑ̃sibl/ *adj* ⟨person⟩ hypersensitive; ⟨film⟩ ultrasensitive; ⟨issue⟩ highly sensitive
ultrason /yltRasɔ̃/ *nm* ultrasound
ultraviolet, -ette /yltRavjɔlɛ, ɛt/ **1** *adj* ultraviolet
2 *nm* ultraviolet ray; **séance d'∼s** session on a sunbed

ululer /ylyle/ [1] *vi* to hoot
un, une¹ /œ̃(n), yn/ **1** *det* (*pl* **des**) **(a)** a, an; one; **un homme** a man; **une femme** a woman; **avec ∼ sang-froid remarquable** with remarkable self-control; **il n'y avait pas ∼ arbre** there wasn't a single tree; **∼ accident est vite arrivé** accidents soon happen
(b) **il y avait des roses et des lis** there were roses and lilies; **il y a des gens qui trichent** there are some people who cheat
(c) **il fait ∼ froid** *or* **∼ de ces froids!** it's so cold!; **elle m'a donné une de ces gifles!** she gave me such a slap!; **il y a ∼ monde aujourd'hui!** there are so many people today!
2 *pron* (*pl* **uns, unes**) one; **(l')∼** de *or* **d'entre nous** one of us; **les ∼s pensent que...** some think that...
3 *adj* one, a, an; **trente et une personnes** thirty-one people; **∼ jour sur deux** every other day
4 *nm,f* one; **∼ par personne** one each; **les deux villes n'en font plus qu'une** the two cities have merged into one; **∼ à** *or* **par ∼** one by one
5 *nm* one; **page ∼** page one
IDIOMS fière comme pas une extremely proud; **∼ menteur comme pas ∼** he's the biggest liar; **∼ pour tous et tous pour ∼** all for one and one for all; ▶ DIX

unanime /ynanim/ *adj* unanimous
unanimement /ynanimmɑ̃/ *adv*
(a) ⟨adopted, elected⟩ unanimously
(b) (figurative) ⟨admired⟩ universally
unanimité /ynanimite/ *nf* unanimity; à l'∼ ⟨elected⟩ unanimously; à l'∼ moins deux voix with only two votes against; faire l'∼ to have unanimous support *or* backing
une² /yn/ **1** *det, pron, adj* ▶ UN 1, 2, 3, 4
2 *nf* la ∼ the front page; être à la ∼ to be in the headlines
uni, ∼e /yni/ **1** *pp* ▶ UNIR
2 *pp adj* **(a)** ⟨family⟩ close-knit; ⟨couple⟩ close; ⟨people, rebels⟩ united
(b) ⟨fabric, colour⟩ plain
(c) ⟨surface⟩ smooth, even
unicité /ynisite/ *nf* uniqueness

unidirectionnel, -elle /ynidirɛksjɔnɛl/ *adj* ⟨*transmitter*⟩ unidirectional; ⟨*receiver*⟩ one-way

unième /ynjɛm/ *adj* first; **vingt et ~** twenty-first

unification /ynifikasjɔ̃/ *nf* unification

unifier /ynifje/ [2] **1** *vtr* (a) to unify ⟨*country, market*⟩
(b) to standardize ⟨*procedure, system*⟩
2 s'unifier *v refl* (+ *v être*) ⟨*countries, groups*⟩ to unite

uniforme /ynifɔrm/ **1** *adj* (gen) uniform; ⟨*buildings, streets, existence*⟩ monotonous; ⟨*regulation*⟩ across-the-board
2 *nm* uniform; **en ~** uniformed

uniformément /ynifɔrmemã/ *adv* uniformly

uniformiser /ynifɔrmize/ [1] *vtr* to standardize ⟨*rate*⟩; to make [sth] uniform ⟨*colour*⟩

uniformité /ynifɔrmite/ *nf* (of tastes) uniformity; (of life, buildings) monotony

unijambiste /yniʒãbist/ **1** *adj* **être ~** to have only one leg
2 *nmf* one-legged person

unilatéral, ~e, *mpl* **-aux** /ynilateral, o/ *adj* unilateral; ⟨*parking*⟩ on one side only

unilingue /ynilɛ̃g/ *adj* unilingual, monolingual

uninominal, ~e, *mpl* **-aux** /yninominal, o/ *adj* (Pol) ⟨*ballot*⟩ for a single candidate

union /ynjɔ̃/ *nf* (a) union
(b) association; **~ de consommateurs** consumers' association
(c) marriage
■ **~ libre** cohabitation; **~ sportive, US sports** club; **Union européenne** European Union
IDIOMS **l'~ fait la force** (Proverb) united we stand, divided we fall

unique /ynik/ *adj* (a) only; **il est l'~ témoin** he's the only witness; **être fille** *or* **fils ~** to be an only child
(b) single; **parti ~** single party; **système à parti ~** one-party system; **'prix ~'** 'all at one price'
(c) unique; **une occasion ~** a unique opportunity; **~ en son genre** ⟨*person, object*⟩ one of a kind; ⟨*event*⟩ one-off (GB), one-shot (US)
(d) (colloq) **ce type est ~!** that guy's priceless! (colloq)

uniquement /ynikmã/ *adv* (gen) only; **en vente ~ par correspondance** available by mail order only; **c'était ~ pour te taquiner** it was only to tease you; **il pense ~ à s'amuser** all he thinks about is having fun; **~ dans un but commercial** purely for commercial ends

unir /ynir/ [3] **1** *vtr* (a) to unite ⟨*people, country*⟩; **des hommes unis par les mêmes idées** men brought together by the same ideas
(b) to combine ⟨*qualities, resources*⟩
(c) to join [sb] in matrimony

2 s'unir *v refl* (+ *v être*) (a) to unite
(b) to marry

unisexe /ynisɛks/ *adj* unisex

unisson /ynisɔ̃/ *nm* unison; **à l'~** (Mus) in unison; (figurative) in accord

unitaire /ynitɛr/ *adj* ⟨*cost*⟩ unit

unité /ynite/ *nf* (a) unity; **film qui manque d'~** film lacking in cohesion; **il y a ~ de vues entre eux** they share the same viewpoint
(b) unit; **~ monétaire** unit of currency; **20 francs l'~** 20 francs each; **vendre qch à l'~** to sell sth singly
■ **~ centrale (de traitement)** (Comput) central processing unit, CPU; **~ de disque** (Comput) disk drive

univers /yniver/ *nm inv* (a) universe
(b) whole world
(c) world; **l'~ de Kafka** Kafka's world

universaliser /yniversalize/ [1] *vtr* to universalize

universalité /yniversalite/ *nf* universality

universel, -elle /yniversɛl/ *adj* ⟨*language, theme*⟩ universal; ⟨*history*⟩ world; ⟨*remedy*⟩ all-purpose

universitaire /yniversitɛr/ **1** *adj* ⟨*town*⟩ university; ⟨*work*⟩ academic
2 *nmf* academic

université /yniversite/ *nf* university (GB), college (US)
■ **~ d'été** summer school

uns *pron* ▶ UN 2

Untel, Unetelle /œ̃tɛl, yntɛl/ *nm,f* **Monsieur ~** Mr so-and-so; **Madame Unetelle** Mrs so-and-so

urbain, ~e /yrbɛ̃, ɛn/ *adj* (a) urban; **vie ~e** city life
(b) (formal) urbane

urbanisation /yrbanizasjɔ̃/ *nf* urbanization

urbaniser /yrbanize/ [1] *vtr* to urbanize ⟨*region*⟩; **zone urbanisée** built-up area

urbanisme /yrbanism/ *nm* town planning (GB), city planning (US)

urbaniste /yrbanist/ *nmf* town planner (GB), city planner (US)

urée /yre/ *nf* urea

urètre /yrɛtr/ *nm* urethra

urgence /yrʒãs/ *nf* (a) urgency; **il y a ~** it's urgent, it's a matter of urgency; **d'~** ⟨*act*⟩ immediately; ⟨*summon*⟩ urgently; ⟨*measures, treatment*⟩ emergency; **de toute** *or* **d'extrême ~** as a matter of great urgency; **transporter qn d'~ à l'hôpital** to rush sb to hospital; **en ~** as a matter of urgency
(b) (Med) **une ~** an emergency; **le service des ~s, les ~s** the casualty department

urgent, ~e /yrʒã, ãt/ *adj* urgent

urinaire /yrinɛr/ *adj* urinary; **appareil ~** urinary tract

urinal, *pl* **-aux** /yrinal, o/ *nm* urinal

urine /yrin/ *nf* urine

uriner /yrine/ [1] *vi* to urinate

u

urinoir /yʀinwaʀ/ *nm* urinal

urne /yʀn/ *nf* **(a)** ~ ⟨électorale⟩ ballot box; **se rendre aux ~s** to go to the polls **(b)** urn

urologie /yʀɔlɔʒi/ *nf* urology

urologue /yʀɔlɔg/ *nmf* urologist

URSS /yeʀeses, yʀs/ *pr nf* (*abbr* = **Union des Républiques socialistes soviétiques**) USSR

urticaire /yʀtikɛʀ/ *nf* hives

uruguayen, -enne /yʀygwejɛ̃, ɛn/ *adj* Uruguayan

us /ys/ *nm pl* **les ~ et coutumes** the ways and customs

US /yɛs/ *nf* (*abbr* = **union sportive**) sports club

USA /yɛsa/ *nm pl* (*abbr* = **United States of America**) USA

usage /yzaʒ/ *nm* **(a)** use; **à l'~, par l'~** with use; **en ~** in use; **faire ~ de** to use ⟨*product*⟩; to exercise ⟨*authority*⟩; **faire bon/mauvais ~ de qch** to put sth to good/bad use; **faire de l'~** ⟨*garment*⟩ to last; **à ~ privé** for private use; **à ~s multiples** ⟨*appliance*⟩ multipurpose; **il a perdu l'~ d'un œil/l'~ de la parole** he's lost the use of one eye/the power of speech; **hors d'~** ⟨*garment*⟩ unwearable; ⟨*machine*⟩ out of order **(b)** (in a language) usage; **en ~** in usage **(c)** custom; **l'~ est de faire** the custom is to do; **it's usual practice to do; entrer dans l'~** ⟨*word*⟩ to come into common use; ⟨*behaviour*⟩ to become common practice; ⟨*politeness*⟩ customary; ⟨*precautions*⟩ usual
■ **~ de faux** (Law) use of false documents; **faux et ~ de faux** forgery and use of false documents

usagé, ~e /yzaʒe/ *adj* **(a)** ⟨*garment*⟩ well-worn; ⟨*tyre*⟩ worn **(b)** ⟨*syringe*⟩ used

usager /yzaʒe/ *nm* (of service) user; (of language) speaker; **~ de la route** road-user

usant, ~e /yzɑ̃, ɑ̃t/ *adj* exhausting, wearing

usé, ~e /yze/ **1** *pp* ▶ **USER**
2 *pp adj* ⟨*object*⟩ worn; ⟨*person*⟩ worn-down; ⟨*heart, eyes*⟩ worn-out; ⟨*joke*⟩ hackneyed; **~ jusqu'à la corde** ⟨*carpet*⟩ threadbare; ⟨*tyre*⟩ worn down to the tread; (figurative) ⟨*joke*⟩ hackneyed

user /yze/ **1** *vtr* to wear out ⟨*shoes*⟩; to wear down ⟨*person*⟩; **les piles sont usées** the batteries have run down *or* out; **~ ses vêtements jusqu'à la corde** to wear one's clothes out; **~ sa santé** to ruin one's health
2 **user de** *v+prep* (gen) to use; to exercise ⟨*right*⟩; to take ⟨*precautions*⟩; **~ de diplomatie** to be diplomatic
3 **s'user** *v refl* (+ *v être*) **(a)** ⟨*shoes*⟩ to wear out

(b) ⟨*person*⟩ **s'~ à la tâche** *or* **au travail** to wear oneself out with overwork; **s'~ la santé** to ruin one's health

usinage /yzinaʒ/ *nm* **(a)** (with a machine tool) machining **(b)** (industrial production) manufacture

usine /yzin/ *nf* factory, plant
■ **~ de traitement** recycling plant; **~ métallurgique** ironworks; **~ sidérurgique** steelworks

usiner /yzine/ [1] *vtr* **(a)** to machine **(b)** to manufacture

usité, ~e /yzite/ *adj* commonly used

ustensile /ystɑ̃sil/ *nm* utensil

usuel, -elle /yzɥɛl/ *adj* ⟨*object*⟩ everyday; ⟨*word*⟩ common

usufruit /yzyfʀɥi/ *nm* (Law) usufruct

usufruitier, -ière /yzyfʀɥitje, ɛʀ/ *nm,f* tenant for life

usure /yzyʀ/ *nf* **(a)** (of clothes) wear and tear; (of tyre, machine) wear; **résister à l'~** to wear well **(b)** (of energy, enemy) wearing down **(c)** **~ du temps** wearing effect of time **(d)** usury

usurier, -ière /yzyʀje, ɛʀ/ *nm,f* usurer

usurpateur, -trice /yzyʀpatœʀ, tʀis/ *nm,f* usurper

usurpation /yzyʀpasjɔ̃/ *nf* usurpation

usurper /yzyʀpe/ [1] *vtr* to usurp

ut /yt/ *nm* (Mus) C

utérus /yteʀys/ *nm inv* womb

utile /ytil/ **1** *adj* (gen) useful; **être ~** ⟨*person, book*⟩ to be helpful; ⟨*umbrella*⟩ to come in handy; **il est ~ de signaler** it's worth pointing out; **il n'a pas jugé ~ de me prévenir** he didn't think it necessary to let me know; **en quoi puis-je vous être ~?** how can I help you?
2 *nm* **joindre l'~ à l'agréable** to mix business with pleasure

utilement /ytilmɑ̃/ *adv* ⟨*intervene*⟩ effectively; ⟨*occupy oneself*⟩ usefully

utilisable /ytilizabl/ *adj* usable

utilisateur, -trice /ytilizatœʀ, tʀis/ *nm,f* user

utilisation /ytilizasjɔ̃/ *nf* use

utiliser /ytilize/ [1] *vtr* (gen) to use; to make use of ⟨*resources*⟩

utilitaire /ytilitɛʀ/ *adj* ⟨*role*⟩ practical; ⟨*object*⟩ functional, utilitarian; ⟨*vehicle*⟩ commercial

utilité /ytilite/ *nf* **(a)** usefulness; **d'une grande ~** ⟨*book, machine*⟩ very useful; ⟨*person*⟩ very helpful; **d'aucune ~** of no use **(b)** use; **je n'en ai pas l'~** I have no use for it

utopie /ytɔpi/ *nf* **(a)** Utopia **(b)** wishful thinking

utopique /ytɔpik/ *adj* utopian

UV /yve/ *nm pl* (*abbr* = **ultraviolets**) ultraviolet rays; **séance d'~** session on a sunbed

uvule /yvyl/ *nf* uvula

Vv

v, V /ve/ *nm inv* v, V; **en (forme de) V** V-shaped; **pull en V** V-necked sweater

va /va/ ▶ ALLER¹

vacance /vakɑ̃s/ **1** *nf* vacancy
  2 vacances *nf pl* holiday (GB), vacation (US); **être en ~s** to be on holiday (GB) *or* vacation (US)
  ■ **~s scolaires** (Sch) school holidays (GB) *or* vacation (US)

vacancier, -ière /vakɑ̃sje, ɛʀ/ *nm,f* holidaymaker (GB), vacationer (US)

vacant, ~e /vakɑ̃, ɑ̃t/ *adj* vacant

vacarme /vakaʀm/ *nm* din, racket (colloq)

vacataire /vakatɛʀ/ *nmf* **(a)** temporary employee
  (b) supply teacher (GB), substitute teacher (US)

vaccin /vaksɛ̃/ *nm* (Med) vaccine

vaccination /vaksinasjɔ̃/ *nf* vaccination

vacciner /vaksine/ [1] *vtr* **(a)** to vaccinate
  (b) (humorous) **je suis vacciné!** (colloq) I've learned my lesson!

vache /vaʃ/ **1** *adj* (colloq) mean, nasty
  2 *nf* **(a)** cow
  (b) cowhide
  ■ **~ à eau** water bottle; **~ à lait** (figurative) money-spinner (colloq); **années de ~s maigres** lean years
  IDIOMS **parler français comme une ~ espagnole** (colloq) to speak very bad French

vachement /vaʃmɑ̃/ *adv* (colloq) really

vacherie /vaʃʀi/ *nf* (colloq) **(a)** meanness
  (b) bitchy remark (colloq)
  (c) dirty trick
  (d) c'est une vraie ~ ce virus this virus is a damned nuisance (colloq)

vachette /vaʃɛt/ *nf* **(a)** young cow
  (b) calfskin

vacillant, ~e /vasijɑ̃, ɑ̃t/ *adj* **(a)** ⟨*legs*⟩ unsteady; ⟨*person*⟩ unsteady on one's legs; ⟨*light, flame*⟩ flickering
  (b) ⟨*power, majority*⟩ shaky

vaciller /vasije/ [1] *vi* **(a)** ⟨*person*⟩ to be unsteady on one's legs; ⟨*legs*⟩ to be unsteady
  (b) ⟨*person, object*⟩ to sway; ⟨*light, flame*⟩ to flicker
  (c) ⟨*health*⟩ to fail; ⟨*majority*⟩ to weaken

vadrouille /vadʀuj/ *nf* (colloq) stroll; **être en ~** to be wandering about

vadrouiller /vadʀuje/ [1] *vi* (colloq) to wander around

va-et-vient /vaevjɛ̃/ *nm inv* **(a)** comings and goings; **faire le ~** to go to and fro; to go back and forth
  (b) two-way switch

vagabond, ~e /vagabɔ̃, ɔ̃d/ **1** *adj* ⟨*dog*⟩ stray; ⟨*mood*⟩ ever-changing
  2 *nm,f* vagrant

vagabondage /vagabɔ̃daʒ/ *nm*
  (a) wandering
  (b) (Law) vagrancy

vagabonder /vagabɔ̃de/ [1] *vi* to wander

vagin /vaʒɛ̃/ *nm* vagina

vagissement /vaʒismɑ̃/ *nm* wail

vague¹ /vag/ **1** *adj* vague; **ce sont de ~s parents** they're distant relatives
  2 *nm* **(a) il regardait dans le ~** he was staring into space
  (b) avoir du ~ à l'âme to feel melancholic

vague² /vag/ *nf* wave; **faire des ~s** ⟨*wind*⟩ to make ripples; (figurative) ⟨*scandal*⟩ to cause a stir
  ■ **~ de chaleur** heatwave; **~ de froid** cold spell
  IDIOMS **être au creux de la ~** to be at a low ebb

vaguement /vagmɑ̃/ *adv* vaguely

vaillamment /vajamɑ̃/ *adv* courageously, valiantly

vaillance /vajɑ̃s/ *nf* courage; **avec ~** courageously

vaillant, ~e /vajɑ̃, ɑ̃t/ *adj* **(a)** courageous
  (b) strong

vain, ~e /vɛ̃, vɛn/ **1** *adj* **(a)** futile; **mes efforts ont été ~s** my efforts were in vain
  (b) ⟨*promises*⟩ empty; ⟨*hopes*⟩ vain
  (c) ⟨*person*⟩ vain
  2 en vain *phr* in vain

vaincre /vɛ̃kʀ/ [57] **1** *vtr* **(a)** to defeat ⟨*opponent*⟩
  (b) to overcome ⟨*prejudices, complex*⟩; to beat ⟨*unemployment, illness*⟩
  2 *vi* to win

vaincu, ~e /vɛ̃ky/ ▶ VAINCRE

vainement /vɛnmɑ̃/ *adv* in vain

vainqueur /vɛ̃kœʀ/ **1** *adj m* victorious
  2 *nm* victor; winner; prizewinner; conqueror

vais /vɛ/ ▶ ALLER¹

vaisseau, *pl* **~x** /vɛso/ *nm* **(a)** (Anat, Bot) vessel
  (b) (Naut) vessel; warship
  ■ **~ spatial** spaceship

vaisselier /vɛsəlje/ *nm* dresser

vaisselle /vɛsɛl/ *nf* **(a)** crockery, dishes
  (b) dishes; **faire la ~** to do the dishes

val, *pl* **~s** or **vaux** /val, vo/ *nm* valley
  IDIOMS **être toujours par monts et par vaux** to be always on the move

valable /valabl/ *adj* **(a)** ⟨*explanation*⟩ valid; ⟨*solution*⟩ viable
  (b) ⟨*document*⟩ valid
  (c) (colloq) ⟨*work, project*⟩ worthwhile

valdinguer /valdɛ̃ge/ [1] *vi* (colloq) to go flying (colloq)

valet /valɛ/ *nm* **(a)** manservant **(b)** (in cards) jack
■ ～ **de chambre** valet; ～ **de ferme** farm hand; ～ **de nuit** rack, valet (US)

valeur /valœr/ *nf* **(a)** value; **prendre de la** ～ to go up in value; **les objets de** ～ valuables
(b) (of person, artist) worth; (of work) value, merit; (of method, discovery) value; **attacher de la** ～ **à qch** to value sth; **mettre qch en** ～ to emphasize ⟨*fact, talent*⟩; to set off ⟨*eyes, painting*⟩; **se mettre en** ～ to make the best of oneself; to show oneself to best advantage
(c) validity
(d) value; **nous n'avons pas les mêmes** ～**s** we don't share the same values
(e) (on stock exchange) security; ～**s** securities, stock, stocks and shares
■ ～ **sûre** gilt-edged security (GB), blue chip; (figurative) safe bet; ～**s mobilières** securities

valeureux, -euse /valørø, øz/ *adj* valorous

validation /validasjɔ̃/ *nf* **(a)** validation **(b)** stamping

valide /valid/ *adj* **(a)** valid **(b)** able-bodied; fit

valider /valide/ [1] *vtr* to stamp ⟨*ticket*⟩; **faire** ～ to have [sth] recognized ⟨*diploma*⟩

validité /validite/ *nf* validity

valise /valiz/ *nf* suitcase; **faire ses** ～**s** to pack
IDIOMS **avoir des** ～**s sous les yeux** (colloq) to have bags under one's eyes

vallée /vale/ *nf* valley

vallon /valɔ̃/ *nm* dale, small valley

vallonné, ～e /valɔne/ *adj* ⟨*landscape*⟩ undulating; ⟨*country*⟩ hilly

valoir /valwar/ [45] **1** *vtr* ～ **qch à qn** to earn sb sth ⟨*praise, criticism*⟩; to win sb sth ⟨*friendship*⟩; to bring sb sth ⟨*problems*⟩
2 *vi* **(a)** ～ **une fortune/cher** to be worth a fortune/a lot; **ça vaut combien?** how much is it worth?; ～ **de l'or** (figurative) to be very valuable
(b) **que vaut ce film/vin?** what's that film/ wine like?; **il ne vaut pas mieux que son frère** he's no better than his brother; **ne rien** ～ to be rubbish; to be useless; to be worthless; **la chaleur ne me vaut rien** the heat doesn't suit me; **ça ne me dit rien qui vaille** I don't like the sound of it
(c) to be as good as; **ton travail vaut bien/ largement le leur** your work is just as good/ every bit as good as theirs; **rien ne vaut la soie** nothing beats silk
(d) to be worth; **le musée vaut le détour** the museum is worth a detour; **ça vaut la peine** *or* **le coup** (colloq) it's worth it
(e) ⟨*rule, criticism*⟩ to apply
(f) **faire** ～ to put [sth] to work ⟨*money*⟩; to point out ⟨*necessity*⟩; to emphasize ⟨*quality*⟩; to assert ⟨*right*⟩; **faire** ～ **que** to point out that; **se faire** ～ to push oneself forward

3 se valoir *v refl* (+ *v être*) to be the same
4 *v impers* **il vaut mieux faire, mieux vaut faire** it's better to do; **il vaut mieux que tu y ailles** you'd better go

valorisation /valɔrizasjɔ̃/ *nf* **(a)** (of product) promotion
(b) (of region, resources) development

valoriser /valɔrize/ [1] *vtr* **(a)** to promote ⟨*product*⟩; to make [sth] attractive ⟨*profession, course*⟩
(b) to develop ⟨*region, resources*⟩

valse /vals/ *nf* waltz

valse-hésitation, *pl* **valses- hésitations** /valsezitasjɔ̃/ *nf* shilly- shallying (colloq)

valser /valse/ [1] *vi* to waltz

valseur, -euse /valsœr, øz/ *nm,f* waltzer

valu, ～e /valy/ ▶ VALOIR

valve /valv/ *nf* valve

vamp /vãp/ *nf* (colloq) vamp

vampire /vãpir/ *nm* **(a)** vampire
(b) (figurative) bloodsucker
(c) (Zool) vampire bat

vampiriser /vãpirize/ [1] *vtr* (figurative) to cannibalize

van /vã/ *nm* **(a)** horsebox (GB), horse-car (US)
(b) van

vandale /vãdal/ *nmf* vandal

vandalisme /vãdalism/ *nm* vandalism

vanille /vanij/ *nf* vanilla; **une gousse de** ～ a vanilla pod

vanité /vanite/ *nf* **(a)** vanity; **tirer** ～ **de qch** to pride oneself on sth
(b) (of efforts) futility; (of promise) emptiness; (of undertaking) uselessness

vaniteux, -euse /vanitø, øz/ *adj* vain

vanne /van/ *nf* **(a)** gate; sluice gate; floodgate
(b) (colloq) dig (colloq)
IDIOMS **fermer les** ～**s** (colloq) to cut funding

vanner /vane/ [1] *vtr* (colloq) to tire [sb] out

vannerie /vanri/ *nf* basket-making; **objets en** ～ wickerwork

vantardise /vãtardiz/ *nf* **(a)** boastfulness
(b) boast

vanter /vãte/ [1] **1** *vtr* to praise, to extol
2 se vanter *v refl* **(a)** to boast
(b) **se** ～ **de faire** to pride oneself on doing

va-nu-pieds /vanypje/ *nmf inv* tramp, bum (US) (colloq)

vapeur /vapœr/ **1** *nf* steam; **bateau à** ～ steamboat; **renverser la** ～ (figurative) to backpedal; **faire cuire qch à la** ～ to steam sth
2 vapeurs *nf pl* fumes

vaporeux, -euse /vapɔrø, øz/ *adj* diaphanous

vaporisateur /vapɔrizatœr/ *nm* spray

vaporisation /vapɔrizasjɔ̃/ *nf* spraying

vaporiser /vapɔrize/ [1] *vtr* to spray

vaquer /vake/ [1] *v+prep* ～ **à ses occupations** to attend to one's business

varappe /varap/ *nf* rock-climbing

V

varappeur, -euse /varapœʀ, øz/ *nm,f*
rock climber

varech /vaʀɛk/ *nm* kelp

vareuse /vaʀøz/ *nf* (a) jersey
(b) (Mil) uniform jacket

variable /vaʀjabl/ **1** *adj* (a) variable
(b) ⟨*weather*⟩ changeable; ⟨*mood*⟩
unpredictable
2 *nf* variable

variante /vaʀjɑ̃t/ *nf* variant

variation /vaʀjasjɔ̃/ *nf* variation;
connaître de fortes ~s to fluctuate
considerably

varice /vaʀis/ *nf* varicose vein

varicelle /vaʀisɛl/ *nf* chicken pox

varié, ~e /vaʀje/ *adj* (a) varied
(b) various

varier /vaʀje/ [2] **1** *vtr* to vary; **pour ~ les
plaisirs** just for a (pleasant) change
2 *vi* to vary; **l'inflation varie de 4% à 6%**
inflation fluctuates between 4% and 6%

variété /vaʀjete/ **1** *nf* (a) variety; **une
grande ~ d'articles** a wide range of items
(b) (Bot) variety
(c) sort
2 variétés *nf pl* **spectacle de ~s** variety
show; **les ~s françaises** French popular
music

variole /vaʀjɔl/ *nf* smallpox

Varsovie /vaʀsɔvi/ *pr n* Warsaw

vas /va/ ▶ ALLER¹

vase¹ /vɑz/ *nm* vase
**IDIOMS c'est la goutte d'eau qui fait
déborder le ~** it's the last straw

vase² /vɑz/ *nf* silt, sludge

vasectomie /vazɛktɔmi/ *nf* vasectomy

vaseux, -euse /vazø, øz/ *adj* (a) muddy
(b) (colloq) **je me sens plutôt ~** I'm not really
with it (colloq)
(c) (colloq) ⟨*speech, explanation*⟩ woolly

vasistas /vazistas/ *nm inv* louvre (GB)
window

vasque /vask/ *nf* (a) (of fountain) basin
(b) bowl

vassal, ~e, *mpl* **-aux** /vasal, o/ *nm,f*
vassal

vaste /vast/ *adj* (a) ⟨*estate, sector*⟩ vast;
⟨*market*⟩ huge
(b) ⟨*audience, choice*⟩ large
(c) ⟨*fraud*⟩ massive; ⟨*campaign*⟩ extensive;
⟨*movement, attack*⟩ large-scale; ⟨*work*⟩ wide-
ranging

va-t-en-guerre /vatɑ̃gɛʀ/ *nm inv*
warmonger

va-tout /vatu/ *nm inv* **jouer/tenter son ~**
to stake/to risk everything

vaudeville /vodvil/ *nm* light comedy;
tourner au ~ to turn into a farce

vaudou /vodu/ *adj inv, nm* voodoo

vaurien, -ienne /voʀjɛ̃, ɛn/ *nm,f*
(a) rascal
(b) lout, yobbo (GB) (colloq), hoodlum (colloq)

vautour /votuʀ/ *nm* vulture

vautrer: se vautrer /votʀe/ [1] *v refl*
(+ *v être*) (a) **se ~ sur** to sprawl on
(b) **se ~ dans un fauteuil** to loll in an
armchair

va-vite: à la va-vite /alavavit/ *phr* in a
rush

veau, *pl* **~x** /vo/ *nm* (a) calf
(b) (Culin) veal
(c) calfskin

vecteur /vɛktœʀ/ *nm* (a) vector
(b) (figurative) vehicle
(c) (of disease) carrier

vécu, ~e /veky/ **1** *pp* ▶ VIVRE
2 *pp adj* ⟨*drama, story*⟩ real-life
3 *nm* personal experiences

vedette /vədɛt/ *nf* (a) star; **avoir la ~** to
have top billing
(b) (Naut) launch

végétal, ~e, *mpl* **-aux** /veʒetal, o/
1 *adj* vegetable
2 *nm* vegetable

végétalien, -ienne /veʒetaljɛ̃, ɛn/ *adj,
nm,f* vegan

végétarien, -ienne /veʒetaʀjɛ̃, ɛn/ *adj,
nm,f* vegetarian

végétatif, -ive /veʒetatif, iv/ *adj*
vegetative

végétation /veʒetasjɔ̃/ **1** *nf* vegetation
2 végétations *nf pl* (Med) adenoids

végéter /veʒete/ [14] *vi* ⟨*person*⟩ to
vegetate; ⟨*project*⟩ to stagnate

véhémence /veemɑ̃s/ *nf* vehemence

véhicule /veikyl/ *nm* vehicle
■ **~ utilitaire** commercial vehicle

véhiculer /veikyle/ [1] *vtr* to carry
⟨*people, goods, substance*⟩; **~ une image** to
promote an image

veille /vɛj/ *nf* (a) **la ~** the day before; **la ~
au soir** the night before; **à la ~ de** on the
eve of
(b) **être en état de ~** to be awake
(c) vigil

veillée /veje/ *nf* (a) evening; **à la ~** in the
evening
(b) vigil; **~ funèbre** wake

veiller /veje/ [1] **1** *vtr* to watch over ⟨*ill
person*⟩; to keep watch over ⟨*dead person*⟩
2 veiller à *v+prep* to look after ⟨*health*⟩;
~ à ce que to see to it that, to make sure
that
3 veiller sur *v+prep* to watch over ⟨*child*⟩
4 *vi* (a) to stay up
(b) to be on watch
(c) to be watchful
IDIOMS ~ au grain to be on one's guard

veilleur /vɛjœʀ/ *nm,f* **~ de nuit** night
watchman

veilleuse /vɛjøz/ *nf* (a) night light
(b) pilot light
(c) side light (GB), parking light (US)

veinard, ~e /venaʀ, aʀd/ *nm,f* (colloq)
lucky devil (colloq)

veine /vɛn/ *nf* (a) vein
(b) (in wood) grain ⋯⟶

(c) (of coal) seam
(d) inspiration; **dans la même** ∼ in the same
vein; **en** ∼ **de générosité** in a generous mood
(e) (colloq) luck; **il a de la** ∼ he's lucky

veiné, **∼e** /vene/ *adj* ‹skin, hand, marble›
veined; ‹wood› grained

veinure /venyʀ/ *nf* (in wood) grain; (in marble)
veining

vêler /vɛle/ [1] *vi* ‹cow› to calve

velléité /vɛlleite/ *nf* **(a)** vague desire
(b) vague attempt

vélo /velo/ *nm* (colloq) bike; **faire du** ∼ to
cycle
■ ∼ **d'appartement** exercise bike; ∼ **tout
terrain**, VTT mountain bike

vélo-cross /velokʀɔs/ *nm inv* **(a)** cyclo-
cross
(b) cyclo-cross bike

vélomoteur /velomɔtœʀ/ *nm* moped

velours /vəluʀ/ *nm inv* **(a)** velvet
(b) corduroy
IDIOMS **une main de fer dans un gant de** ∼
an iron fist in a velvet glove; **faire patte de** ∼
to switch on the charm

velouté, **∼e** /vəlute/ **1** *adj* ‹skin, voice›
velvety; ‹wine› smooth
2 *nm* **(a)** (Culin) ∼ **de champignons** cream of
mushroom soup
(b) softness; smoothness

velu, **∼e** /vəly/ *adj* **(a)** hairy
(b) (Bot) villous

vénal, **∼e**, *mpl* **-aux** /venal, o/ *adj*
‹person› venal; ‹behaviour› mercenary

vendable /vɑ̃dabl/ *adj* saleable (GB)

vendange /vɑ̃dɑ̃ʒ/ *nf* grape harvest

vendanger /vɑ̃dɑ̃ʒe/ [13] **1** *vtr* to harvest
‹grapes›; to pick the grapes from ‹vine›
2 *vi* to harvest the grapes

vendeur, **-euse** /vɑ̃dœʀ, øz/ *nm,f* **(a)** shop
assistant
(b) salesman/saleswoman
■ ∼ **ambulant** pedlar (GB), peddler (US); ∼ **de
journaux** news vendor

vendre /vɑ̃dʀ/ [6] **1** *vtr* **(a)** to sell; ∼ **à
crédit** to sell on credit; ∼ **en gros** to
wholesale; ∼ **au détail** to retail; **'à** ∼**'** 'for
sale'
(b) to betray ‹person›; to sell ‹secrets›
2 se vendre *v refl* (+ *v être*) **(a)** to be sold
(b) se ∼ **bien** to sell well
(c) to sell oneself; **se** ∼ **à l'ennemi** to sell out
to the enemy

vendredi /vɑ̃dʀədi/ *nm* Friday; ∼ **saint**
Good Friday

vendu, **∼e** /vɑ̃dy/ **1** *pp* ▶ VENDRE
2 *pp adj* bribed
3 *nm,f* traitor

vénéneux, **-euse** /venenø, øz/ *adj*
poisonous

vénérable /venerabl/ *adj* ‹person›
venerable; ‹tree, object› ancient

vénération /venerasjɔ̃/ *nf* veneration

vénérer /venere/ [14] *vtr* to venerate; to
revere

vénérien, **-ienne** /venerjɛ̃, ɛn/ *adj*
venereal

vengeance /vɑ̃ʒɑ̃s/ *nf* revenge

venger /vɑ̃ʒe/ [13] **1** *vtr* to avenge
2 se venger *v refl* (+ *v être*) to get one's
revenge; **se** ∼ **sur qn/qch** to take it out on
sb/sth

vengeur, **vengeresse** /vɑ̃ʒœʀ, vɑ̃ʒʀɛs/
adj vengeful; avenging; vindictive

véniel, **-ielle** /venjɛl/ *adj* ‹sin› venial

venimeux, **-euse** /vənimø, øz/ *adj*
venomous

venin /vənɛ̃/ *nm* venom

venir /vəniʀ/ [36] **1** *v aux* **(a)** venir de faire
to have just done; **elle vient de partir** she's
just left; **'vient de paraître'** (of book) 'new!'
(b) ∼ **aggraver la situation** to make the
situation worse
(c) le ballon est venu rouler sous mes pieds
the ball rolled up to my feet
(d) s'il venait à pleuvoir if it should rain
2 *vi* (+ *v être*) **(a)** to come; ∼ **de** to come
from; ∼ **après/avant** to come after/before;
allez, viens! come on!; **viens voir** come and
see; **j'en viens** I've just been there; **je viens
de sa part** he/she sent me to see you; **faire** ∼
qn to send for sb; to get sb to come; **faire** ∼
le médecin to call the doctor; **ça ne m'est
jamais venu à l'idée** it never crossed my
mind; **dans les jours à** ∼ in the next few
days
(b) en ∼ **à** to come to; **en** ∼ **aux mains** to
come to blows

vent /vɑ̃/ *nm* **(a)** wind; ∼ **d'est** east wind;
∼ **du large** seaward wind; **grand** ∼ gale,
strong wind; **il fait** *or* **il y a du** ∼ it's windy;
en plein ∼ exposed to the wind; in the open;
passer en coup de ∼ (figurative) to rush
through; **faire du** ∼ (with fan) to create a
breeze; ∼ **favorable**, **bon** ∼ favourable (GB)
wind; **avoir le** ∼ **en poupe** to sail *or* run
before the wind; (figurative) to have the wind
in one's sails; **coup de** ∼ fresh gale
(b) un ∼ **de liberté** a wind of freedom; **un** ∼
de folie a wave of madness
(c) (euphemistic) wind
IDIOMS **c'est du** ∼**!** it's just hot air!; **du** ∼**!**
(colloq) get lost! (colloq); **quel bon** ∼ **vous
amène?** to what do I owe the pleasure of
your visit?; **être dans le** ∼ to be trendy;
avoir ∼ **de qch** to get wind of sth; **contre** ∼**s
et marées** come hell or high water; against
all odds

vente /vɑ̃t/ *nf* sale; **en** ∼ **libre** (gen) freely
available; ‹medicines› available over the
counter; **mettre qch en** ∼ to put [sth] up for
sale
■ ∼ **par correspondance** mail order selling;
∼ **au détail** retailing; ∼ **aux enchères**
auction (sale); ∼ **en gros** wholesaling

ventilateur /vɑ̃tilatœʀ/ *nm* fan; ventilator

ventilation /vɑ̃tilasjɔ̃/ *nf* ventilation
(system)

ventiler /vɑ̃tile/ [1] *vtr* **(a)** to ventilate
(b) to break down ‹expenses, profits›

(c) to assign ‹staff›; to allocate ‹tasks, equipment›

ventouse /vɑ̃tuz/ nf (a) suction pad (GB), suction cup (US); faire ~ to stick
(b) plunger
(c) (Med) cupping glass

ventral, ~e, mpl **-aux** /vɑ̃tral, o/ adj ventral; parachute ~ lap-pack parachute

ventre /vɑ̃tr/ nm (a) stomach; avoir mal au ~ to have stomach ache; ça me donne mal au ~ de voir ça (figurative) (colloq) it makes me sick to see that sort of thing
(b) (of animal) (under)belly
(c) ne rien avoir dans le ~ (colloq) to have no guts (colloq); avoir la peur au ~ to feel sick with fear
(d) (of pot, boat, plane) belly
IDIOMS courir ~ à terre to run flat out

ventricule /vɑ̃trikyl/ nm ventricle

ventriloque /vɑ̃trilɔk/ nmf ventriloquist

ventripotent, ~e /vɑ̃tripɔtɑ̃, ɑ̃t/ adj (colloq) portly, fat-bellied

ventru, ~e /vɑ̃try/ adj ‹man› paunchy, pot-bellied; ‹pot, piece of furniture› rounded; ‹wall› bulging

venu, ~e¹ /vəny/ [1] pp ▶ VENIR
[2] pp adj bien ~ apt; mal ~ badly timed; il serait mal ~ de le leur dire it wouldn't be a good idea to tell them
[3] nm,f nouveau ~ newcomer

venue² /vəny/ nf visit; ~ au monde birth

vêpres /vepr/ nf pl vespers

ver /ver/ nm worm; woodworm; maggot
■ ~ à soie silkworm; ~ solitaire tapeworm; ~ de terre earthworm
IDIOMS tirer les ~s du nez à qn (colloq) to worm information out of sb

véracité /verasite/ nf truthfulness

véranda /verɑ̃da/ nf veranda

verbal, ~e, mpl **-aux** /verbal, o/ adj verbal; verb

verbaliser /verbalize/ [1] vi to record an offence (GB)

verbe /verb/ nm (a) verb
(b) language; avoir le ~ haut to be arrogant in one's speech

verdâtre /verdɑtr/ adj greenish

verdeur /verdœr/ nf sprightliness

verdict /verdikt/ nm verdict

verdir /verdir/ [3] vi (a) (gen) to turn green; ‹copper› to tarnish
(b) to turn pale

verdoyant, ~e /verdwajɑ̃, ɑ̃t/ adj green

verdure /verdyr/ nf (a) greenery
(b) green vegetables

véreux, **-euse** /verø, øz/ adj (a) ‹fruit› worm-eaten
(b) ‹politician, lawyer› bent (colloq), crooked

verge /verʒ/ nf (a) penis
(b) switch, birch

vergé /verʒe/ nm laid paper

verger /verʒe/ nm orchard

vergeture /verʒətyr/ nf stretch mark

verglacé, ~e /verglase/ adj icy

verglas /vergla/ nm inv black ice

vergogne: **sans vergogne** /sɑ̃vergɔɲ/ phr shamelessly

véridique /veridik/ adj true

vérifiable /verifjabl/ adj être facilement ~ to be easy to check or verify

vérification /verifikasjɔ̃/ nf (on equipment, identity) check; (of alibi, fact) verification

vérifier /verifje/ [2] [1] vtr to check; to verify
[2] se vérifier v refl (+ v être) ‹hypothesis, theory› to be borne out

véritable /veritabl/ adj real; true; genuine

véritablement /veritabləmɑ̃/ adv really

vérité /verite/ nf (a) truth; l'épreuve de ~ the acid test; à la ~ to tell the truth
(b) énoncer des ~s premières to state the obvious
(c) sincerity

verlan /verlɑ̃/ nm: French slang formed by inverting the syllables

vermeil, **-eille** /vermej/ [1] adj (a) bright red
(b) ‹wine› ruby
[2] nm vermeil

vermicelle /vermisel/ nm du ~, des ~s vermicelli

vermifuge /vermifyʒ/ nm wormer

vermillon /vermijɔ̃/ adj inv bright red

vermine /vermin/ nf (a) vermin
(b) (figurative) scum

vermoulu, ~e /vermuly/ adj worm-eaten

verni, ~e /verni/ [1] pp ▶ VERNIR
[2] pp adj varnished; patent-leather; glazed
[3] adj (colloq) lucky; il n'est pas ~ he's unlucky

vernir /vernir/ [3] [1] vtr to varnish; to glaze
[2] se vernir v refl (+ v être) se ~ les ongles to paint one's nails

vernis /verni/ nm inv (a) varnish; glaze
(b) (figurative) veneer; si on gratte le ~, on voit que... if you scratch the surface, you'll see that...
■ ~ à ongles nail varnish (GB) or polish

vernissage /vernisaʒ/ nm (a) (of art exhibition) preview, private view
(b) varnishing; glazing

vernissé, ~e /vernise/ adj (a) glazed
(b) glossy

verre /ver/ nm (a) glass; de or en ~ glass; un ~ à eau/vin a water/wine glass; ~s et couverts glassware and cutlery; lever son ~ à la santé de qn to raise one's glass to sb
(b) glass, glassful; un ~ d'eau/de vin a glass of water/wine
(c) drink
(d) lens; ~ grossissant magnifying glass
■ ~ de contact contact lens; ~ à pied stemmed glass

verrerie /verri/ nf (a) glassmaking
(b) glassworks, glass factory

verrière /vɛRjɛR/ *nf* **(a)** glass roof
(b) glass wall

verroterie /vɛRɔtRi/ *nf* glass jewellery (GB)
or jewelry (US)

verrou /vɛRu/ *nm* bolt
IDIOMS **être sous les ∼s** to be behind bars

verrouillage /vɛRujaʒ/ *nm* bolting;
locking; locking mechanism
■ ∼ **central** or **centralisé (des portes)** central
locking

verrouiller /vɛRuje/ [1] *vtr* to bolt
⟨*window, door*⟩; to lock ⟨*car door, gun*⟩

verrue /vɛRy/ *nf* wart; ∼ **plantaire** verruca

vers¹ /vɛR/ *prep*
■ Note When *vers* is part of an expression such
as *se tourner vers, tendre vers* etc, you will find
the translation at the entries TOURNER, TENDRE¹
3 etc.
– See below for other uses of *vers*.

(a) toward(s); **se déplacer de la gauche ∼ la
droite** to move from left to right
(b) near, around; about; toward(s); ∼ **cinq
heures** at about five o'clock; ∼ **le soir**
toward(s) evening

vers² /vɛR/ *nm inv* line (of verse)

versant /vɛRsɑ̃/ *nm* side

versatile /vɛRsatil/ *adj* unpredictable,
volatile

verse: **à verse** /avɛRs/ *phr* **il pleut à ∼** it's
pouring down

Verseau /vɛRso/ *pr nm* Aquarius

versement /vɛRsəmɑ̃/ *nm* **(a)** payment;
∼ **comptant** cash payment
(b) instalment (GB)
(c) deposit; **faire un ∼ sur son compte** to pay
money into one's account

verser /vɛRse/ [1] **1** *vtr* **(a)** to pour
(b) to pay ⟨*sum, pension*⟩
(c) to shed ⟨*tear, blood*⟩
(d) ∼ **une pièce à un dossier** to add a
document to a file
2 *vi* **(a)** to overturn
(b) to lapse
(c) ⟨*jug*⟩ to pour

verset /vɛRsɛ/ *nm* (in Bible, Koran) verse

verseur, -euse /vɛRsœR, øz/ *adj* pouring;
flacon ∼ bottle with a pouring spout

versifier /vɛRsifje/ [2] *vtr* to put [sth] into
verse

version /vɛRsjɔ̃/ *nf* **(a)** translation (*into
one's own language*)
(b) version
■ ∼ **originale, vo** (of film) original version

verso /vɛRso/ *nm* back; **voir au ∼** see
over(leaf)

vert, ∼e /vɛR, vɛRt/ **1** *adj* **(a)** green; **être
∼ de peur** to be white with fear
(b) ⟨*fruit*⟩ green, unripe; ⟨*wine*⟩ immature
(c) sprightly
(d) (*before n*) ⟨*reprimand*⟩ sharp, stiff
2 *nm* green
3 verts *nm pl* **les ∼s** the Greens

IDIOMS **avoir la main ∼e** to have green
fingers (GB) *or* a green thumb (US)

vert-de-gris /vɛRdəgRi/ **1** *adj inv* blue-
green
2 *nm inv* verdigris

vertébral, ∼e, *mpl* **-aux** /vɛRtebRal, o/
adj vertebral

vertébré /vɛRtebRe/ *nm* vertebrate

vertèbre /vɛRtɛbR/ *nf* vertebra

vertement /vɛRtəmɑ̃/ *adv* sharply

vertical, ∼e¹, *mpl* **-aux** /vɛRtikal, o/ *adj*
vertical; upright

verticale² /vɛRtikal/ *nf* vertical

verticalement /vɛRtikalmɑ̃/ *adv*
(a) vertically
(b) (in crossword) down

vertige /vɛRtiʒ/ *nm* **(a)** dizziness; vertigo;
avoir le ∼ to suffer from vertigo; to feel
dizzy
(b) avoir des ∼s to have dizzy or giddy
spells

vertigineux, -euse /vɛRtiʒinø, øz/ *adj*
dizzy, giddy; breathtaking; staggering

vertu /vɛRty/ **1** *nf* **(a)** virtue; **de petite ∼** of
easy virtue
(b) (of plant, remedy) property
2 en vertu de *phr* by virtue of ⟨*law*⟩; in
accordance with ⟨*agreement*⟩

vertueux, -euse /vɛRtɥø, øz/ *adj*
virtuous

verve /vɛRv/ *nf* eloquence

verveine /vɛRvɛn/ *nf* verbena (tea)

vésicule /vezikyl/ *nf* vesicle; ∼ **biliaire** gall
bladder

vespéral, ∼e, *mpl* **-aux** /vɛsperal, o/
adj evening

vessie /vesi/ *nf* bladder
IDIOMS **prendre des ∼s pour des lanternes**
(colloq) to think the moon is made of green
cheese

veste /vɛst/ *nf* jacket; ∼ **de survêtement**
tracksuit top
IDIOMS **retourner sa ∼** (colloq) to change
sides

vestiaire /vɛstjɛR/ *nm* (in gym) changing
room (GB), locker room; (in theatre)
cloakroom; **laisser sa fierté au ∼** to forget
one's pride

vestibule /vɛstibyl/ *nm* hall; foyer (GB),
lobby

vestige /vɛstiʒ/ *nm* **(a)** relic; **des ∼s
archéologiques** archaeological remains
(b) vestige

vestimentaire /vɛstimɑ̃tɛR/ *adj* **tenue ∼**
way of dressing; **mode ∼** fashion

veston /vɛstɔ̃/ *nm* (man's) jacket

vêtement /vɛtmɑ̃/ *nm* piece of clothing;
des ∼s clothes; '∼s pour hommes'
'menswear'; ∼**s de sport** sportswear

vétéran /veterɑ̃/ *nm* veteran

vétérinaire /veteRinɛR/ **1** *adj* veterinary
2 *nmf* veterinary surgeon (GB), veterinarian
(US)

v

vétille /vetij/ *nf* trifle

vêtir /vɛtiʀ/ [33] **1** *vtr* to dress ⟨person, doll⟩

2 se vêtir *v refl* (+ *v être*) to dress (oneself)

veto /veto/ *nm* veto; **mettre** *or* **opposer son** ∼ **à qch** to veto sth

vêtu, ∼e /vety/ ▶ VÊTIR

vétuste /vetyst/ *adj* (a) dilapidated
(b) outdated

vétusté /vetyste/ *nf* dilapidation (**de** of), run-down state (**de** of); outdated state (**de** of)

veuf, veuve /vœf, vœv/ **1** *adj* widowed
2 *nm,f* widower/widow

veule /vøl/ *adj* weak, spineless

veuvage /vœvaʒ/ *nm* widowhood

veuve *adj, nf* ▶ VEUF

vexant, ∼e /vɛksɑ̃, ɑ̃t/ *adj* (a) hurtful
(b) tiresome, vexing

vexation /vɛksasjɔ̃/ *nf* humiliation

vexer /vɛkse/ [1] **1** *vtr* (a) to offend
(b) to annoy
2 se vexer *v refl* (+ *v être*) to take offence (GB)

via /vja/ *prep* via; through

viabilité /vjabilite/ *nf* (a) viability
(b) (of road) suitability for vehicles

viable /vjabl/ *adj* (a) viable
(b) ⟨project⟩ feasible; ⟨situation⟩ bearable, tolerable

viaduc /vjadyk/ *nm* viaduct

viager /vjaʒe/ *nm* life annuity

viande /vjɑ̃d/ *nf* meat; ∼ **de bœuf/mouton** beef/mutton
■ ∼ **des Grisons** dried beef

vibrant, ∼e /vibʀɑ̃, ɑ̃t/ *adj* (a) vibrating
(b) ⟨voice⟩ resonant; ⟨speech⟩ vibrant; ⟨praise⟩ glowing; ⟨plea⟩ impassioned; ⟨crowd⟩ excited

vibration /vibʀasjɔ̃/ *nf* vibration; **traitement par ∼s** vibromassage

vibrer /vibʀe/ [1] *vi* (a) to vibrate
(b) ⟨voice⟩ to quiver; ⟨heart⟩ to thrill

vibromasseur /vibʀomasœʀ/ *nm* vibrator

vicaire /vikɛʀ/ *nm* curate

vice /vis/ *nm* (a) vice; **vivre dans le** ∼ to lead a dissolute life
(b) vice; **mon** ∼, **c'est le tabac** my vice is smoking
(c) fault, defect; ∼ **de fabrication** manufacturing defect

vice-président, ∼e, *mpl* ∼**s** /visprezidɑ̃, ɑ̃t/ *nm,f* (of state) vice-president; (of committee, company) vice-chair(man), vice-president (US)

vice-roi, *pl* ∼**s** /visʀwa/ *nm* viceroy

vice(-)versa /visvɛʀsa/ *adv* vice versa

vichy /viʃi/ *nm* (a) gingham
(b) vichy water

vicier /visje/ [2] *vtr* to pollute ⟨air⟩; to contaminate ⟨blood⟩

vicieux, -ieuse /visjø, øz/ *adj*
(a) lecherous; **il faut être** ∼ **pour aimer ça** you've got to be perverted to like that
(b) ⟨person⟩ sly; ⟨attack⟩ well-disguised; ⟨question⟩ trick; ⟨argument⟩ deceitful
(c) **un cercle** ∼ a vicious circle

vicinal, ∼e, *mpl* **-aux** /visinal, o/ *adj* **chemin** ∼ byroad

vicomte /vikɔ̃t/ *nm* viscount

vicomtesse /vikɔ̃tɛs/ *nf* viscountess

victime /viktim/ *nf* (a) victim, casualty; **être** ∼ **d'un infarctus** to suffer a heart attack
(b) sacrificial victim

victoire /viktwaʀ/ *nf* (gen) victory; (Sport) win

victorien, -ienne /viktɔʀjɛ̃, ɛn/ *adj* Victorian

victorieux, -ieuse /viktɔʀjø, øz/ *adj* ⟨army⟩ victorious; ⟨athlete⟩ winning; ⟨smile⟩ of victory

victuailles /viktɥaj/ *nf pl* provisions, victuals

vidange /vidɑ̃ʒ/ *nf* (a) emptying
(b) oil change; **huile de** ∼ waste oil
(c) (of washing machine) waste pipe

vidanger /vidɑ̃ʒe/ [13] **1** *vtr* (a) to empty, to drain ⟨tank, ditch⟩
(b) to drain off ⟨liquid⟩
2 *vi* ⟨washing machine⟩ to empty

vide /vid/ **1** *adj* (a) empty; ⟨tape, page⟩ blank; ⟨flat⟩ vacant; **tu l'as loué** ∼ **ou meublé?** are you renting it unfurnished or furnished?
(b) ⟨mind, day⟩ empty; ⟨look⟩ vacant
2 *nm* (a) space; **sauter** *or* **se jeter dans le** ∼ to jump; (figurative) to leap into the unknown; **parler dans le** ∼ to talk to oneself; to talk at random
(b) vacuum; void; **emballé sous** ∼ vacuum-packed; **faire le** ∼ **autour de soi** to drive everybody away; **j'ai besoin de faire le** ∼ **dans ma tête** I need to forget about everything
(c) emptiness; **le** ∼ **de l'existence** the emptiness of life
(d) gap; **combler un** *or* **le** ∼ to fill in a gap; (figurative) to fill a gap
3 à vide *phr* (a) empty
(b) with no result

vidéaste /videast/ *nmf* video director

vidéo /video/ **1** *adj inv* video
2 *nf* video; **tourner un film en** ∼ to make a video

vidéocassette /videokasɛt/ *nf* videotape

vidéoclip /videoklip/ *nm* (music) video

vidéoclub /videoklœb/ *nm* video store

vidéoconférence /videokɔ̃feʀɑ̃s/ *nf*
(a) videoconference
(b) videoconferencing

vidéodisque /videodisk/ *nm* videodisc

vide-ordures /vidɔʀdyʀ/ *nm inv* rubbish (GB) *or* garbage (US) chute

vidéothèque /videotɛk/ *nf* (a) video library ⋯⋗

(b) video collection

vide-poches /vidpɔʃ/ *nm inv* tidy

vider /vide/ [1] **1** *vtr* (a) to empty; to drain ⟨tank, pond⟩

(b) to empty [sth] (out) ⟨water, rubbish⟩

(c) (colloq) to throw [sb] out (colloq)

(d) (Culin) to gut ⟨fish⟩; to draw ⟨game⟩

(e) (colloq) to wear [sb] out; to drain

2 se vider *v refl* (+ *v être*) to empty; **en été, Paris se vide de ses habitants** in the summer all Parisians leave town

videur, -euse /vidœʀ, øz/ *nm,f* (colloq) bouncer

vie /vi/ *nf* (gen) life; **être en ~** to be alive; **il y a laissé sa ~** that was how he lost his life; **donner la ~ à qn** to bring sb into the world; **la ~ est chère** the cost of living is high; **mode de ~** lifestyle; **notre ~ de couple** our relationship; **donner de la ~ à une fête** to liven up a party; **sans ~** lifeless

■ **~ active** working life

IDIOMS **c'est la belle ~!** this is the life!; **avoir la ~ dure** ⟨prejudices⟩ to be ingrained; **mener la ~ dure à qn** to make life hard for sb; **faire la ~** (colloq) to have a wild time; to live it up (colloq); **à la ~, à la mort!** till death us do part!

vieil ▶ VIEUX

vieillard, ~e /vjɛjaʀ, aʀd/ *nm,f* old man/woman; **les ~s** old people

vieille ▶ VIEUX

vieillesse /vjɛjɛs/ *nf* (of person) old age; (of building, tree) great age

vieilli, ~e /vjɛji/ **1** *pp* ▶ VIEILLIR

2 *pp adj* (a) old-looking

(b) ⟨equipment⟩ outdated; ⟨expression⟩ dated

(c) **vin ~ en fût** wine matured in the cask

vieillir /vjɛjiʀ/ [3] **1** *vtr* (a) ⟨hairstyle⟩ to make [sb] look older

(b) ⟨illness⟩ to age ⟨person⟩

2 *vi* (a) to get older; **je vieillis** I'm getting old; **j'ai vieilli** I'm older; **notre population vieillit** we have an ageing population

(b) ⟨body, building⟩ to show signs of age; ⟨person⟩ to age; **il vieillit mal** he's losing his looks

(c) ⟨wine⟩ to mature

(d) ⟨work⟩ to become outdated

3 se vieillir *v refl* (+ *v être*) (a) to make oneself look older

(b) to make oneself out to be older

vieillissant, ~e /vjɛjisɑ̃, ɑ̃t/ *adj* ageing

vieillissement /vjɛjismɑ̃/ *nm* ageing

vieillot, -otte /vjɛjo, ɔt/ *adj* quaint; old-fashioned

viennois, ~e /vjenwa, az/ *adj* (a) (in Austria) Viennese; (in France) of Vienne

(b) (Culin) ⟨chocolate, coffee⟩ Viennese

viennoiserie /vjenwazʀi/ *nf* Viennese pastry

vierge /vjɛʀʒ/ **1** *adj* (a) virgin

(b) blank; unused; clean

(c) ⟨wool⟩ new; ⟨olive oil⟩ virgin

2 *nf* virgin

Vierge /vjɛʀʒ/ **1** *nf* (a) **la (Sainte) ~** the (Blessed) Virgin

(b) madonna

2 *pr nf* Virgo

Viêt Nam /vjɛtnam/ *pr nm* Vietnam

vietnamien, -ienne /vjɛtnamjɛ̃, ɛn/

1 *adj* Vietnamese

2 *nm* (language) Vietnamese

vieux (**vieil** before vowel or mute h), **vieille**, *mpl* **vieux** /vjø, vjɛj/ **1** *adj* old; **être ~ avant l'âge** to be old before one's time; **une institution vieille de 100 ans** a 100-year-old institution; **il est très vieille France** he's a gentleman of the old school

2 *nm,f* (a) old person; **un petit ~** a little old man; **les ~** old people; **mes ~** (colloq) my parents

(b) (colloq) **mon pauvre ~** you poor old thing **3** *adv* **vivre ~** to live to a ripe old age; **il s'habille ~** he dresses like an old man

4 *nm* **prendre un coup de ~** to age; **faire du neuf avec du ~** to revamp things

■ **vieille fille** old maid; **~ beau** ageing Romeo; **~ garçon** old bachelor; **~ jeu** old-fashioned; **~ rose** dusty pink

IDIOMS **~ comme le monde**, **~ comme Hérode** as old as the hills

vif, vive¹ /vif, viv/ **1** *adj* (a) ⟨colour, light⟩ bright

(b) ⟨person⟩ lively, vivacious; ⟨imagination⟩ vivid

(c) ⟨protests⟩ heated; ⟨opposition⟩ fierce; **sa réaction a été un peu vive** he/she reacted rather strongly

(d) ⟨contrast⟩ sharp; ⟨interest, desire⟩ keen; ⟨pain⟩ acute; ⟨success⟩ notable

(e) ⟨pace, movement⟩ brisk; **à vive allure** ⟨drive⟩ at high speed; **avoir l'esprit ~** to be very quick

(f) ⟨cold, wind⟩ biting; ⟨edge⟩ sharp; **air ~** fresh air; **cuire à feu ~** to cook over a high heat

(g) **de vive voix** in person

2 *nm* **à ~** ⟨flesh⟩ bared; ⟨knee⟩ raw; ⟨wire⟩ exposed; **avoir les nerfs à ~** to be on edge; **la plaie est à ~** it's an open wound; **piquer qn au ~** to cut sb to the quick

vigie /viʒi/ *nf* (Naut) (a) lookout

(b) crow's nest

vigilance /viʒilɑ̃s/ *nf* vigilance; **échapper à la ~ de qn** to escape sb's attention

vigilant, ~e /viʒilɑ̃, ɑ̃t/ *adj* ⟨person⟩ vigilant; ⟨eye⟩ watchful

vigile /viʒil/ *nm* (a) night watchman

(b) security guard

vigne /viɲ/ *nf* (a) vine

(b) vineyard

■ **~ vierge** Virginia creeper

vigneron, -onne /viɲ(ə)ʀɔ̃, ɔn/ *nm,f* winegrower

vignette /viɲɛt/ *nf* (a) *detachable label on medicines for reimbursement by social security*

(b) tax disc (GB)

(c) label

(d) vignette

vignoble /viɲɔbl/ *nm* vineyard

vigoureux, -euse /viguʀø, øz/ *adj*
(a) ⟨*person, handshake*⟩ vigorous; ⟨*athlete,
body*⟩ strong; ⟨*plant*⟩ sturdy
(b) ⟨*resistance, style*⟩ vigorous

vigueur /vigœʀ/ **1** *nf* **(a)** vigour (GB)
(b) strength
2 **en vigueur** *phr* ⟨*law, system*⟩ in force;
⟨*regime, conditions*⟩ current; **entrer en ~ to**
come into force

VIH /veiɑʃ/ *nm* (*abbr* = **virus
immunodéficitaire humain**) HIV

viking /vikiŋ/ *adj* Viking

vil, ~e /vil/ *adj* ⟨*person*⟩ base; ⟨*deed*⟩ vile,
base

vilain, ~e /vilɛ̃, ɛn/ **1** *adj* **(a)** ugly
(b) (colloq) ⟨*germ, creature*⟩ nasty; ⟨*child*⟩
naughty
(c) ⟨*fault*⟩ bad; ⟨*word*⟩ dirty
2 *nm,f* naughty boy/girl

vilenie /vileni/ *nf* **(a)** baseness (de of)
(b) vile *or* base act

villa /villa/ *nf* **(a)** ≈ detached house
(b) villa

village /vilaʒ/ *nm* village

villageois, ~e /vilaʒwa, az/ *nm,f*
villager

ville /vil/ *nf* **(a)** town; city; **la vieille ~** the
old town; **aller en ~** to go into town
(b) town *or* city council
■ **~ d'eau(x)** spa town; **~ franche** free city;
~ nouvelle new town

ville-dortoir, *pl* **villes-dortoirs**
/vildɔʀtwaʀ/ *nf* dormitory town (GB)

villégiature /vileʒjatyʀ/ *nf* holiday (GB),
vacation (US)

vin /vɛ̃/ *nm* wine; **~ blanc/rouge** white/red
wine; **~ de pays** *or* **de terroir** *quality wine
produced in a specific region*; **couper son ~**
to add water to one's wine
■ **~ d'appellation d'origine contrôlée**
appellation contrôlée wine (*with a guarantee
of origin*); **~ cuit** *wine which has undergone
heating during maturation*; **~ d'honneur**
reception
IDIOMS **avoir le ~ gai/triste** to get happy/
maudlin after one has had a few drinks;
mettre de l'eau dans son ~ to mellow;
quand le ~ est tiré, il faut le boire (Proverb)
once you have started something, you have
to see it through

vinaigre /vinɛgʀ/ *nm* vinegar
IDIOMS **tourner au ~** to turn sour

vinaigrette /vinɛgʀɛt/ *nf* French dressing

vinasse /vinas/ *nf* plonk (GB)
(colloq), cheap wine

vindicatif, -ive /vɛ̃dikatif, iv/ *adj*
vindictive

vingt /vɛ̃, vɛ̃t/ **1** *adj inv* twenty
2 *pron* twenty; (Sch) **j'ai eu ~ sur ~** ≈ I
got full marks (GB) *or* full credit (US)
3 *nm inv* twenty

vingtaine /vɛ̃tɛn/ *nf* about twenty

vingtième /vɛ̃tjɛm/ *adj* twentieth

vinicole /vinikɔl/ *adj* ⟨*sector, region*⟩ wine-
producing; ⟨*cellar, trade*⟩ wine

vinyle /vinil/ *nm* vinyl

viol /vjɔl/ *nm* **(a)** rape
(b) (of law, temple) violation

violacé, ~e /vjɔlase/ *adj* purplish

violation /vjɔlasjɔ̃/ *nf* **(a)** (of law, territory)
violation
(b) (of agreement, confidentiality) breach
■ **~ de domicile** forcible entry (*into a
person's home*)

violemment /vjɔlamã/ *adv* violently

violence /vjɔlãs/ *nf* **(a)** violence; **~ verbale**
verbal abuse; **par la ~** through violence;
with violence; **se faire ~** to force oneself
(b) act of violence; **~s à l'enfant** child abuse

violent, ~e /vjɔlã, ãt/ *adj* violent;
⟨*colour*⟩ harsh

violenter /vjɔlãte/ [1] *vtr* to assault
sexually

violer /vjɔle/ [1] *vtr* **(a)** to rape; **se faire ~**
to be raped
(b) to desecrate ⟨*tomb*⟩; **~ l'intimité de qn** to
invade sb's privacy
(c) to infringe ⟨*law*⟩

violet, -ette[1] /vjɔlɛ, ɛt/ **1** *adj* purple
2 *nm* purple

violette[2] /vjɔlɛt/ *nf* violet

violeur /vjɔlœʀ/ *nm* rapist

violon /vjɔlɔ̃/ *nm* violin
■ **~ d'Ingres** hobby
IDIOMS **accorder ses ~s** to agree on which
line to take

violoncelle /vjɔlɔ̃sɛl/ *nm* cello

violoncelliste /vjɔlɔ̃sɛlist/ *nmf* cellist

violoniste /vjɔlɔnist/ *nmf* violinist

vipère /vipɛʀ/ *nf* viper; **avoir une langue
de ~** to have a wicked tongue

virage /viʀaʒ/ *nm* **(a)** bend
(b) change of direction
(c) (in skiing) turn

virago /viʀago/ *nf* virago

viral, ~e, *mpl* **-aux** /viʀal, o/ *adj* viral

virement /viʀmã/ *nm* transfer; **faire un ~**
to make a transfer.
■ **~ automatique** standing order

virer /viʀe/ [1] **1** *vtr* **(a)** to transfer
⟨*money*⟩
(b) (colloq) to fire ⟨*employee*⟩; **se faire ~** to
get fired
2 **virer à** *v+prep* **~ au rouge** to turn red
3 *vi* **(a)** ⟨*vehicle*⟩ to turn; **~ de bord**
(figurative) to do a U-turn, to do a flip-flop (US)
(b) to change colour (GB); ⟨*colour*⟩ to change

virevolter /viʀvɔlte/ [1] *vi* to twirl

virginité /viʀʒinite/ *nf* virginity

virgule /viʀgyl/ *nf* **(a)** comma; **à la ~ près**
down to the last comma
(b) (decimal) point

viril, ~e /viʀil/ *adj* manly, virile;
masculine

virilité /viʀilite/ *nf* virility

V

virtualité /viʀtɥalite/ nf (a) virtuality
(b) potentiality
virtuel, -elle /viʀtɥɛl/ adj (a) potential
(b) (in science) virtual
virtuellement /viʀtɥɛlmɑ̃/ adv
(a) virtually
(b) potentially
virtuose /viʀtɥoz/ ⚊1⚊ adj virtuoso
⚊2⚊ nmf (a) (Mus) virtuoso
(b) master
virtuosité /viʀtɥozite/ nf (a) (Mus)
virtuosity
(b) brilliance
virulence /viʀylɑ̃s/ nf virulence
virulent, ~e /viʀylɑ̃, ɑ̃t/ adj virulent
virus /viʀys/ nm inv (a) (Med, Comput) virus
(b) bug (colloq), craze
vis /vis/ nf inv screw
IDIOMS serrer la ~ à qn to tighten the
screws on sb
visa /viza/ nm visa
■ ~ de censure (censor's) certificate
visage /vizaʒ/ nm face; à ~ découvert
openly
vis-à-vis /vizavi/ ⚊1⚊ nm inv (a) maison
sans ~ house with an open outlook
(b) assis en ~ sitting opposite each other
(c) (Sport) opponent
(d) meeting, encounter
⚊2⚊ vis-à-vis de phr (a) ~ de qch in
relation to sth; ~ de qn toward(s) sb
(b) beside
viscéral, ~e, mpl -aux /viseʀal, o/ adj
(a) réaction ~e gut reaction
(b) visceral
viscéralement /viseʀalmɑ̃/ adv
violently, virulently
viscère /visɛʀ/ nm (a) internal organ
(b) les ~s viscera
viscosité /viskozite/ nf viscosity
visée /vize/ nf (a) aim
(b) design
(c) sighting; aiming
viser /vize/ [1] ⚊1⚊ vtr (a) to aim at (target);
to aim for (heart, middle)
(b) to aim for (job, results); to aim at
(market)
(c) (law, campaign) to be aimed at; (remark,
allusion) to be meant for
⚊2⚊ viser à v+prep ~ à qch/à faire to aim at
sth/to do
⚊3⚊ vi to aim; ~ (trop) haut (figurative) to set
one's sights (too) high
viseur /vizœʀ/ nm (a) viewfinder
(b) (of gun) sight
visibilité /vizibilite/ nf visibility
visible /vizibl/ adj (a) visible
(b) obvious
visiblement /vizibləmɑ̃/ adv visibly
visière /vizjɛʀ/ nf (a) (of cap) peak
(b) eyeshade
vision /vizjɔ̃/ nf (a) eyesight, vision
(b) view; ~ globale global view
(c) sight

(d) avoir des ~s to see things, to have
visions
visionnaire /vizjɔnɛʀ/ adj, nmf visionary
visionner /vizjone/ [1] vtr to view (film,
slides)
visionneuse /vizjɔnøz/ nf viewer
visite /vizit/ nf visit; call; rendre ~ à qn to
pay sb a call; avoir de la ~ to have visitors
■ ~ de contrôle (Med) follow-up visit;
~ médicale medical (examination)
visiter /vizite/ [1] vtr (a) to visit (museum,
town)
(b) to view (apartment)
(c) to visit (patient)
visiteur, -euse /vizitœʀ, øz/ nm,f visitor
vison /vizɔ̃/ nm (a) mink
(b) mink (coat)
visqueux, -euse /viskø, øz/ adj
(a) viscous, viscid
(b) sticky, gooey (colloq)
visser /vise/ [1] vtr (a) to screw [sth] on
(b) être vissé sur sa chaise to be glued to
one's chair
visualisation /vizɥalizasjɔ̃/ nf
visualization; (Comput) display
visualiser /vizɥalize/ [1] vtr to visualize
visuel, -elle /vizɥɛl/ adj visual
vital, ~e, mpl -aux /vital, o/ adj vital
vitalité /vitalite/ nf vitality; energy
vitamine /vitamin/ nf vitamin
vitaminé, ~e /vitamine/ adj with added
vitamins
vite /vit/ adv (a) quickly; ~! quick!; ça ira
~ it'll soon be over; it won't take long; on a
pris un verre ~ fait (colloq) we had a quick
drink
(b) j'ai parlé trop ~ I spoke too hastily; I
spoke too soon; c'est ~ dit! that's easy to
say!
vitesse /vitɛs/ nf (a) speed; partir à toute
~ to rush away; à deux ~s (system) two-tier;
faire de la ~ to drive fast; prendre qn de ~
to outstrip sb; en ~ quickly; in a rush
(b) gear
IDIOMS à la ~ grand V, en quatrième ~ at
top speed
viticole /vitikɔl/ adj wine; wine-producing
viticulteur, -trice /vitikyltœʀ, tʀis/ nm,f
wine-grower
viticulture /vitikyltyʀ/ nf wine-growing
vitrage /vitʀaʒ/ nm windows; double ~
double glazing
vitrail, pl -aux /vitʀaj, o/ nm stained glass
window
vitre /vitʀ/ nf (a) windowpane
(b) pane of glass
(c) (of car, train) window
vitrerie /vitʀəʀi/ (a) glazier's
(b) glasswork
vitrier /vitʀije/ nm glazier
vitrifier /vitʀifje/ [2] vtr (a) to varnish
(floor)
(b) (Tech) to vitrify

vitrine /vitʀin/ nf **(a)** (shop or store) window; **faire les ~s** to go window-shopping **(b)** display cabinet (GB), curio cabinet (US) **(c)** (show)case

vitriol /vitʀijɔl/ nm vitriol

vitupérer /vitypeʀe/ [14] vi to rail

vivable /vivabl/ adj bearable; **ce n'est pas ~ ici** it is impossible to live here

vivace /vivas/ adj enduring

vivacité /vivasite/ nf **(a)** (of person) vivacity; (of feeling) intensity **(b)** (of intelligence) keenness; (of reaction, movement) swiftness; **avec ~** ⟨move, react⟩ swiftly **(c)** (of memory, colour, impression) vividness; (in eyes) spark; (of light) brightness

vivant, ~e /vivɑ̃, ɑ̃t/ **1** adj **(a)** living; **il est ~** he is alive; **un homard ~** a live lobster **(b)** ⟨person, style⟩ lively; ⟨description⟩ vivid **(c)** **être encore ~** ⟨custom⟩ to be still alive **2** nm **(a)** living being; **les ~s** the living **(b)** **du ~ de mon père** while my father was alive

vive² /viv/ **1** adj f ▶ VIF 1 **2** nf weever

vivement /vivmɑ̃/ adv ⟨encourage, react⟩ strongly; ⟨contrast, speak⟩ sharply; ⟨move, feel, regret⟩ deeply; ⟨rise⟩ swiftly

vivier /vivje/ nm **(a)** fishpond **(b)** fish-tank

vivifiant, ~e /vivifjɑ̃, ɑ̃t/ adj **(a)** invigorating **(b)** stimulating

vivifier /vivifje/ [2] vtr to invigorate

vivisection /viviseksjɔ̃/ nf vivisection

vivoter /vivɔte/ [1] vi to struggle along

vivre /vivʀ/ [63] **1** vtr to live through ⟨era⟩; to go through ⟨difficult times⟩; to experience ⟨love⟩ **(b)** to cope with ⟨divorce, failure, change⟩ **2** vi **(a)** to live; **~ vieux** to live to a great age; **vive la révolution!** long live the revolution!; **~ à la campagne** to live in the country; **être facile à ~** to be easy to live with; to be easy to get on with; **~ avec son temps** to move with the times; **se laisser ~** to take things easy; **apprendre à ~ à qn** (colloq) to teach sb some manners (colloq); **~ aux dépens de qn** to live off sb **(b)** ⟨fashion⟩ to last; **avoir vécu** ⟨person⟩ to have seen a great deal of life; (humorous) ⟨object⟩ to have had its day **(c)** ⟨town⟩ to be full of life IDIOMS **qui vivra verra** what will be will be

vivres /vivʀ/ nm pl **(a)** food, supplies **(b)** **couper les ~ à qn** to cut off sb's allowance

vizir /viziʀ/ nm vizier; **le Grand ~** the Grand Vizier

vo /veo/ nf: abbr ▶ VERSION

vocable /vɔkabl/ nm term

vocabulaire /vɔkabylɛʀ/ nm vocabulary

vocal, ~e, mpl -aux /vɔkal, o/ adj vocal

vocalement /vɔkalmɑ̃/ adv vocally

vocalise /vɔkaliz/ nf singing exercise

vocation /vɔkasjɔ̃/ nf **(a)** vocation, calling **(b)** purpose; **région à ~ agricole** farming area

vociférer /vɔsifeʀe/ [14] vtr, vi to shout

vodka /vɔdka/ nf vodka

vœu, pl ~x /vø/ nm **(a)** wish; **faire un ~** to make a wish **(b)** New Year's greetings; **adresser ses ~x à qn** to wish sb a happy New Year **(c)** vow; **~x de pauvreté** vows of poverty

vogue /vɔg/ nf fashion, vogue

voguer /vɔge/ [1] vi ⟨ship⟩ to sail IDIOMS **et vogue la galère!** come what may!

voici /vwasi/ **1** prep here is, this is; here are, these are; **~ mes clés** here are my keys; **~ un mois** a month ago; **~ bientôt deux mois qu'elle travaille chez nous** she's been working with us for nearly two months **2** **voici que** phr all of a sudden

voie /vwa/ nf **(a)** way; **montrer la ~ à qn** to show sb the way; **ouvrir la ~ à** to pave the way for; **être sur la bonne ~** ⟨person⟩ to be on the right track; **les travaux sont en bonne ~** the work is progressing; **par ~ de conséquence** consequently; **espèce en ~ de disparition** endangered species **(b)** channels; **par des ~ détournées** by roundabout means **(c)** lane; **route à trois ~s** three-lane road **(d)** (of railway) track; **le train entre en gare ~ 2** the train is arriving at platform 2 **(e)** **par ~ buccale** or **orale** orally ■ **~ aérienne** air route; **~ ferrée** railway track (GB), railroad track (US); **~ de garage** siding; **mettre qn sur une ~ de garage** (figurative) to shunt sb onto the sidelines; **Voie lactée** Milky Way; **~ privée** private road; **~ publique** public highway; **~ rapide** expressway; **~ sans issue** dead end; no through road; **~s respiratoires** respiratory tract

voilà /vwala/ **1** prep here is, this is; here are, these are; **voici mon fils et ~ ma fille** this is my son and this is my daughter; **me ~!** I'm coming!; here I am!; **le ~ qui se remet à rire!** there he goes again laughing!; **~ tout** that's all; **~ un mois** a month ago **2** **en voilà** phr **tu veux des fraises? en ~** you'd like some strawberries? here you are **3** **voilà que** phr (colloq) **et ~ qu'une voiture arrive** and the next thing you know, a car pulls up **4** excl **~! j'arrive!** (I'm) coming!; **(et) ~! il remet ça!** there he goes again! IDIOMS **il a de l'argent, en veux-tu en ~!** he has as much money as he could wish for!

voilage /vwalaʒ/ nm net curtain (GB), sheer curtain (US)

voile¹ /vwal/ nm **(a)** veil; **lever le ~ sur qch** to bring sth out in the open **(b)** voile

■ ~ **islamique** yashmak; ~ **du palais** soft palate, velum

voile² /vwal/ nf (Naut) **(a)** sail; **faire** ~ **vers** to sail toward(s)
(b) sailing

voilé, ~e /vwale/ adj **(a)** ⟨person, object⟩ veiled
(b) ⟨sun, sky⟩ hazy; ⟨eyes⟩ misty; ⟨voice⟩ with a catch in it; ⟨photo⟩ fogged
(c) ⟨threat, criticism⟩ veiled
(d) ⟨wheel⟩ buckled

voiler /vwale/ [1] **1** vtr **(a)** to veil ⟨landscape, sun⟩; ⟨person, fact⟩ to conceal ⟨event, fact⟩
(b) to buckle ⟨wheel⟩
(c) to mist ⟨eyes⟩
(d) to cover ⟨face, nudity⟩; to veil ⟨statue⟩
2 se voiler v refl (+ v être) **(a)** ⟨sky⟩ to cloud over; ⟨sun⟩ to become hazy; ⟨eyes⟩ to become misty
(b) ⟨person⟩ to wear a veil
IDIOMS **se ~ la face** to look the other way

voilette /vwalɛt/ nf veil

voilier /vwalje/ nm **(a)** sailing boat (GB), sailboat (US)
(b) yacht, sailing ship

voilure /vwalyʀ/ nf sails; **une ~ de 500m²** 500m² of sail

voir /vwaʀ/ [46] **1** vtr **(a)** to see; **faire ~ qch à qn** to show sb sth; **laisser ~ qch** to show sth; **~ si/pourquoi** to find out or to see if/why; **on l'a vue entrer** she was seen going in; **je le vois** or **verrais bien enseignant** I can just see him as a teacher; **aller ~ qn** to go to see sb; **le film est à ~** the film is worth seeing; **~ du pays** to see the world; **on voit bien qu'elle n'a jamais travaillé!** you can tell she's never worked!; **on n'a jamais vu ça!** it's unheard of!
(b) **avoir quelque chose à ~ avec** to have something to do with
2 voir à v+prep to see to; **voyez à ce que tout soit prêt** see to it that everything is ready
3 vi **(a)** ~, **y ~** to be able to see; ~ **double** to see double
(b) ~ **clair dans qch** to have a clear understanding of sth; **il faut ~** we'll have to see
4 se voir v refl (+ v être) **(a)** to see oneself
(b) ⟨stain⟩ to show; **la tour se voit de loin** the tower can be seen from far away; **ça ne s'est jamais vu!** it's unheard of!
(c) **se ~ obligé** or **dans l'obligation de faire** to find oneself forced to do
(d) to see each other; **ils ne peuvent pas se ~ (en peinture** (colloq)) they can't stand each other
IDIOMS **ne pas ~ plus loin que le bout de son nez** to see no further than the end of one's nose; **j'en ai vu d'autres** I've seen worse; **en faire ~ à qn** to give sb a hard time

voire /vwaʀ/ adv or even, not to say

voirie /vwaʀi/ nf road, rail and waterways network

voisin, ~e /vwazɛ̃, in/ **1** adj **(a)** ⟨house,

town⟩ neighbouring (GB); ⟨lake, forest⟩ nearby; ⟨room⟩ next; **les régions ~es de la Manche** the regions bordering the English Channel
(b) ⟨date, result⟩ close (**de** to)
(c) ⟨feelings, ideas⟩ similar; ⟨species⟩ (closely) related
2 nm,f neighbour (GB); **ma ~e de palier** the woman across the landing; **mon ~ de table** the man next to me at table

voisinage /vwazinaʒ/ nm
(a) neighbourhood (GB); **entretenir des rapports de bon ~** to maintain neighbourly (GB) relations
(b) proximity; **vivre dans le ~ d'une usine** to live close to a factory

voiture /vwatyʀ/ nf **(a)** car, automobile (US)
(b) carriage (GB), car (US); **en ~!** all aboard!
■ ~ **à bras** hand-drawn cart; ~ **de tourisme** saloon (car) (GB), sedan (US)

voiture-balai, pl **voitures-balais** /vwatyʀbalɛ/ nf support vehicle

voiture-lit, pl **voitures-lits** /vwatyʀli/ nf sleeper, sleeping car

voix /vwa/ nf inv **(a)** (gen) voice; **élever la ~** to raise one's voice; **à ~ haute** out loud; **rester sans ~** to remain speechless; **à portée de ~** within earshot; **faire entendre sa ~** (figurative) to make oneself heard
(b) vote
(c) **à la ~ active/passive** in the active/passive voice

vol /vɔl/ **1** nm **(a)** (of bird, plane) flight; **prendre son ~** to fly off; **à ~ d'oiseau** as the crow flies; **il y a trois heures de ~** it's a three-hour flight; **de ~** ⟨conditions⟩ flying; ⟨plan⟩ flight
(b) **un ~ de** a flock of ⟨birds⟩; a cloud of ⟨insects⟩; **de haut ~** (figurative) ⟨diplomat⟩ high-flying; ⟨burglar⟩ big-time
(c) theft, robbery
2 au vol phr **attraper une balle au ~** to catch a ball in mid-air; **saisir des bribes de conversation au ~** to catch snatches of conversation
■ ~ **à l'arraché** bag snatching; ~ **avec effraction** burglary; ~ **à l'étalage** shoplifting; ~ **à la tire** pickpocketing

volage /vɔlaʒ/ adj fickle

volaille /vɔlaj/ nf **(a)** poultry
(b) fowl

volant, ~e /vɔlã, ãt/ **1** adj flying
2 nm **(a)** steering wheel; **être au ~** to be at the wheel; **un brusque coup de ~** a sharp turn of the wheel; **un as du ~** an ace driver; **la sécurité au ~** safe driving
(b) flounce; **à ~s** flounced
(c) shuttlecock

volatil, ~e¹ /vɔlatil/ adj volatile

volatile² /vɔlatil/ nm **(a)** fowl
(b) bird

volatiliser: se volatiliser /vɔlatilize/ [1] v refl (+ v être) **(a)** to volatilize
(b) (humorous) to vanish into thin air

volcan /vɔlkɑ̃/ nm volcano

volcanique /vɔlkanik/ adj (a) ⟨region⟩
volcanic

(b) ⟨temperament⟩ explosive

volée /vɔle/ **1** nf (a) (of birds) flock, flight

(b) (of blows, stones) volley; **donner une ∼ à
qn** to give sb a good thrashing

(c) flight (of stairs)

(d) (Sport) volley

2 à toute volée phr **les cloches
sonnaient à toute ∼** the bells were pealing
out

voler /vɔle/ [1] **1** vtr (a) ∼ **qch à qn** to
steal sth from sb; **tu ne l'as pas volé!**
(figurative) it serves you right!

(b) ∼ **qn** to rob sb; ∼ **le client** to rip the
customer off (colloq)

2 vi (a) to fly; ∼ **au secours de qn** to rush
to sb's aid

(b) ∼ **en éclats** ⟨window⟩ to shatter

volet /vɔlɛ/ nm (a) shutter

(b) (of leaflet, brochure) (folding) section;
(of plan) part, component

voleter /vɔlte/ [20] vi to flutter

voleur, -euse /vɔlœR, øz/ **1** adj **être ∼**
⟨cat⟩ to be a thief; ⟨shopkeeper⟩ to be
dishonest

2 nm,f thief; swindler

IDIOMS **se sauver comme un ∼** to slip away
like a thief in the night

volière /vɔljɛR/ nf aviary

volley(-ball) /vɔlɛ(bol)/ nm volleyball

volontaire /vɔlɔ̃tɛR/ **1** adj (a) ⟨work⟩
voluntary; ⟨omission⟩ deliberate

(b) ⟨person, air⟩ determined; ⟨child⟩ self-
willed

2 nmf volunteer; **se porter ∼** to volunteer

volonté /vɔlɔ̃te/ **1** nf (a) will; **bonne ∼**
goodwill; **aller contre la ∼ de qn** to go
against sb's wishes; **manifester la ∼ de faire**
to show one's willingness to do

(b) willpower; **avoir une ∼ de fer** to have an
iron will

2 à volonté phr (a) **'vin/pain à ∼'**
'unlimited wine/bread'

(b) ⟨modifiable⟩ as required

volontiers /vɔlɔ̃tje/ adv (a) gladly; **j'irais
∼ à Paris** I'd love to go to Paris; **'tu me le
prêtes?'—'∼'** 'will you lend it to me?'—
'certainly'

(b) ⟨admit⟩ readily

volt /vɔlt/ nm volt

voltage /vɔltaʒ/ nm voltage

volte-face /vɔlt(ə)fas/ nf inv (a) **faire ∼** to
turn around

(b) (figurative) volte-face, U-turn

voltige /vɔltiʒ/ nf (haute) ∼ acrobatics

voltiger /vɔltiʒe/ [13] vi (a) to flutter

(b) to go flying

volubilité /vɔlybilite/ nf volubility

volume /vɔlym/ nm (gen) volume; **donner
du ∼ à ses cheveux** to give one's hair body;
∼ **sonore** sound level

volumineux, -euse /vɔlyminø, øz/ adj
voluminous, bulky

volupté /vɔlypte/ nf voluptuousness

voluptueux, -euse /vɔlyptɥø, øz/ adj
voluptuous

volute /vɔlyt/ nf (on pillar, column) volute;
(of violin) scroll; (of smoke) curl

vomi /vɔmi/ nm (colloq) vomit

vomir /vɔmiR/ [3] **1** vtr to bring up ⟨meal⟩;
to vomit ⟨bile⟩

2 vi ⟨person⟩ to be sick

vomissement /vɔmismɑ̃/ nm vomiting

vont /vɔ̃/ ▸ ALLER[1]

vorace /vɔRas/ adj voracious

voracité /vɔRasite/ nf voracity,
voraciousness

vos ▸ VOTRE

votant, ∼e /vɔtɑ̃, ɑ̃t/ nm,f voter

vote /vɔt/ nm (a) voting; (of law) passing

(b) vote

voter /vɔte/ [1] **1** vtr to vote ⟨budget⟩; to
pass ⟨parliamentary bill⟩; to vote for
⟨amnesty⟩

2 vi to vote; ∼ **blanc** to cast a blank vote

votre, pl **vos** /vɔtR, vo/ det your; **c'est
pour ∼ bien** it's for your own good; **à ∼
arrivée** when you arrive; when you arrived

vôtre /votR/ **1** det **mes biens sont ∼s** all I
have is yours; **'amicalement ∼'** 'best wishes'

2 le vôtre, la vôtre, les vôtres pron
yours; **à la ∼!** (colloq) cheers!

vouer /vwe/ [1] **1** vtr (a) ∼ **une
reconnaissance éternelle à qn** to be eternally
grateful to sb; ∼ **un véritable culte à qn** to
worship sb

(b) to doom; **film voué à l'échec** film doomed
to failure

(c) ∼ **sa vie à qch** to devote one's life to sth

2 se vouer v refl (+ v être) (a) **se ∼ à qch**
to devote oneself to sth

(b) **ils se vouent une haine féroce** they hate
each other intensely

vouloir[1] /vulwaR/ [48] **1** vtr (a) (gen) to
want; **qu'est-ce qu'ils nous veulent encore?**
(colloq) what do they want now?; **il en veut
15 000 francs** he wants 15,000 francs for it;
comme le veut la loi as the law demands;
que veux-tu boire? what do you want to
drink?; what would you like to drink?; **je
voudrais un kilo de poires** I'd like a kilo of
pears; **je comprends très bien que tu ne
veuilles pas répondre** I can quite understand
that you may not wish to reply; **sans le ∼**
⟨knock over, reveal⟩ by accident; ⟨annoy⟩
without meaning to; **que tu le veuilles ou
non** whether you like it or not; **elle fait ce
qu'elle veut de son mari** she twists her
husband around her little finger; **je ne vous
veux aucun mal** I don't wish you any harm;
tu ne voudrais pas me faire croire que you're
not trying to tell me that; **tu voudrais que je
leur fasse confiance?** do you expect me to
trust them?; **comment veux-tu que je le
sache?** how should I know?; **j'aurais voulu**

V

t'y voir! (colloq) I'd like to have seen you in the same position!; **tu l'auras voulu!** it'll be all your own fault!

(b) voulez-vous fermer la fenêtre? would you mind closing the window?; **voudriez-vous avoir l'obligeance de faire** (formal) would you be so kind as to do; **veuillez patienter** (on phone) please hold the line; **si vous voulez bien me suivre** if you'd like to follow me; **veux-tu te taire!** will you be quiet!; **ils ont bien voulu nous prêter leur voiture** they were kind enough to lend us their car; **je veux bien te croire** I'm quite prepared to believe you; **je veux bien qu'il soit malade mais** I know he's ill, but; **'ce n'est pas cher'—'si on veut!'** 'it's not expensive'—'or so you say!'

(c) ~ dire to mean; **qu'est-ce que ça veut dire?** what does that mean?; what's all this about?

(d) comme le veut la tradition as tradition has it

2 en vouloir v+prep **(a) en ~ à qn** to bear a grudge against sb; **je leur en veux de m'avoir trompé** I hold it against them for not being honest with me; **ne m'en veux pas** please forgive me

(b) en ~ à qch to be after sth

3 se vouloir v refl (+ v être) **(a)** ⟨person⟩ to like to think of oneself as; ⟨book, method⟩ to be meant to be

(b) s'en ~ to be cross with oneself; **s'en ~ de** to regret; **je m'en serais voulu de ne pas vous avoir prévenu** I would never have forgiven myself if I hadn't warned you

IDIOMS **~ c'est pouvoir** (Proverb) where there's a will there's a way

vouloir² /vulwaʀ/ nm will

voulu, ~e /vuly/ **1** pp ▶ VOULOIR¹

2 pp adj **(a)** required; **on n'obtient jamais les renseignements ~s** you never get the information you want; **en temps ~** in time; **au moment ~** at the right time

(b) ⟨omission⟩ deliberate; ⟨meeting⟩ planned

vous /vu/ pron **(a)** you; **je sais que ce n'est pas ~** I know it wasn't you; **c'est ~ qui avez gagné** you have won; **~ aussi, ~ avez l'air malade** you don't look very well either; **ce sont des amis à ~?** are they friends of yours?; **c'est à ~** it's yours, it belongs to you; it's your turn

(b) yourself; yourselves; **allez ~ laver les mains** go and wash your hands; **pensez à ~ deux** think of yourselves

vous-même, pl **vous-mêmes** /vumɛm/ pron **(a)** yourself; **vous me l'avez dit ~** you told me yourself

(b) allez-y ~s go yourselves; **vous verrez par ~s** you'll see for yourselves

voûte /vut/ nf (gen) vault; (of porch) archway; (of tunnel) roof; (figurative) (of leaves, branches) arch

■ **la ~ céleste** the sky; the heavens; **~ du palais** roof of the mouth; **~ plantaire** arch of the foot

voûté, ~e /vute/ adj **(a)** ⟨cellar⟩ vaulted

(b) ⟨back⟩ bent; **il est ~** he has a stoop

voûter /vute/ [1] **1** vtr **(a)** (in architecture) to vault ⟨room⟩

(b) to give [sb] a stoop

2 se voûter v refl (+ v être) ⟨person⟩ to develop a stoop; ⟨back⟩ to become bent

vouvoiement /vuvwamã/ nm using the 'vous' or polite form

vouvoyer /vuvwaje/ [23] vtr to address [sb] using the 'vous' form

voyage /vwajaʒ/ nm trip; journey; **partir en ~** to go on a trip; **le ~ aller** the outward journey; **aimer les ~s** to love travelling (GB)

■ **~ d'affaires** business trip; **être en ~ d'affaires** to be on a business trip; **~ d'études** study trip; **~ de noces** honeymoon; **~ organisé** package tour

voyager /vwajaʒe/ [13] vi to travel

voyageur, -euse /vwajaʒœʀ, øz/ nm,f **(a)** passenger; **'réservé aux ~s munis de billets'** 'ticketholders only'

(b) traveller (GB)

■ **~ de commerce** travelling (GB) salesman

voyagiste /vwajaʒist/ nmf tour operator

voyance /vwajãs/ nf clairvoyance

voyant, ~e /vwajã, ãt/ **1** adj ⟨colour⟩ loud

2 nm,f **(a)** clairvoyant

(b) sighted person

3 nm light; **~ d'huile** (Aut) oil warning light

voyelle /vwajɛl/ nf vowel

voyeur, -euse /vwajœʀ, øz/ nm,f voyeur

voyeurisme /vwajœʀism/ nm voyeurism

voyou /vwaju/ nm lout

vrac: en vrac /ãvʀak/ phr **(a)** loose, unpackaged

(b) in bulk

(c) jeter ses idées en ~ sur le papier to jot down one's ideas as they come

vrai, ~e /vʀɛ/ **1** adj true; real, genuine; **il n'y a rien de ~ dans ses déclarations** there's no truth in his statements; **la ~e raison de mon départ** the real reason for my leaving; **des ~s jumeaux** identical twins; **plus ~ que nature** ⟨picture, scene⟩ larger than life

2 nm truth; **il y a du ~ dans ce que tu dis** there's some truth in what you say; **être dans le ~** to be in the right; **pour de ~** for real; **à ~ dire, à dire ~** to tell the truth

3 adv to look real; **son discours sonne ~** his speech has the ring of truth

vraiment /vʀɛmã/ adv really

vraisemblable /vʀɛsãblabl/ adj ⟨excuse⟩ convincing; ⟨scenario⟩ plausible; ⟨hypothesis⟩ likely; **il est ~ que** it is likely that

vraisemblablement /vʀɛsãblabləmã/ adv probably

vraisemblance /vʀɛsãblãs/ nf (of hypothesis) likelihood; (of situation, explanation) plausibility

vrille /vʀij/ nf **(a)** spiral; (of airplane) tailspin; **descendre en ~** ⟨airplane⟩ to go into a spiral dive

(b) (Bot) tendril

(c) (Tech) gimlet

vrombir ⋯⋗ wishbone ⋯⋯

vrombir /vʀɔ̃biʀ/ [3] *vi* ⟨*engine*⟩ to roar; **faire ~ un moteur** to rev up an engine

VRP /veɛʀpe/ *nm* (*abbr* = **voyageur représentant placier**) representative, rep (colloq)

VTT /vetete/ ▶ **VÉLO**

vu, ~e¹ /vy/ [1] *pp* ▶ **VOIR**
  [2] *pp adj* (a) **être bien/mal ~** ⟨*person*⟩ to be/not to be well thought of; **c'est bien ~ de faire cela** it's good form to do that; **ce serait plutôt mal ~** it wouldn't go down well
  (b) **bien ~!** good point!; **c'est tout ~** my mind is made up
  (c) **~?** got it? (colloq)
  [3] *prep* in view of
  [4] **vu que** *phr* in view of the fact that

vue² /vy/ *nf* (a) sight; **avoir une bonne ~** to have good eyesight; **don de double ~** gift of second sight; **perdre qn de ~** (figurative) to lose touch with sb; **à ~** ⟨*shoot*⟩ on sight; ⟨*fly plane*⟩ without instruments; ⟨*payable*⟩ on demand
  (b) view; **à ma ~, il s'enfuit** he took to his heels when he saw me; **avoir ~ sur le lac** to look out onto the lake
  (c) (opinion) view; **~s** views; **~ optimiste des choses** optimistic view of things
  (d) **avoir des ~s sur qn/qch** to have designs on sb/sth
  (e) **en ~** in sight; ⟨*person*⟩ prominent; **mettre une photo bien en ~** to display a photo prominently; **c'est quelqu'un de très en ~** he's/she's very much in the public eye; **j'ai un terrain en ~** I have a plot of land in mind; I've got my eye on a piece of land; **en ~ de faire** with a view to doing
  ■ **~ d'ensemble** overall view
  IDIOMS à ~ d'œil *or* **de nez** (colloq) at a rough guess; **vouloir en mettre plein la ~ à qn** to try to dazzle sb

vulcanologue /vylkanɔlɔg/ *nmf* volcanologist

vulgaire /vylgɛʀ/ *adj* (a) vulgar, coarse
  (b) common, ordinary; **c'est un ~ employé** he's just a lowly employee

vulgairement /vylgɛʀmɑ̃/ *adv* (a) ⟨*speak*⟩ coarsely
  (b) commonly

vulgarisation /vylgaʀizasjɔ̃/ *nf* popularization; **revue de ~ scientifique** scientific review for the general public

vulgariser /vylgaʀize/ [1] [1] *vtr* to popularize; to bring [sth] into general use
  [2] **se vulgariser** *v refl* (+ *v être*) ⟨*technology*⟩ to become generally accessible; ⟨*expression*⟩ to come into general use

vulgarité /vylgaʀite/ *nf* vulgarity, coarseness

vulnérable /vylneʀabl/ *adj* vulnerable

vulve /vylv/ *nf* vulva

W w

w, W /dubləve/ *nm inv* (a) (letter) w, W
  (b) **W** (*written abbr* = **watt**) 60 W 60 W

wagon /vagɔ̃/ *nm* (a) wagon (GB), car (US); (for passengers) carriage (GB), car (US)
  (b) wagonload (GB), carload (US)
  ■ **~ à bestiaux** cattle truck (GB), cattle car (US); **~ de marchandises** goods wagon (GB), freight car (US)

wagon-bar, *pl* **wagons-bars** /vagɔ̃baʀ/ *nm* buffet car

wagon-citerne, *pl* **wagons-citernes** /vagɔ̃sitɛʀn/ *nm* tanker

wagon-lit, *pl* **wagons-lits** /vagɔ̃li/ *nm* sleeper, sleeping car (US)

wagonnet /vagɔnɛ/ *nm* trolley (GB), cart (US)

wagon-restaurant, *pl* **wagons-restaurants** /vagɔ̃ʀɛstɔʀɑ̃/ *nm* restaurant car (GB), dining car (US)

wallon, -onne /walɔ̃, ɔn/ [1] *adj* Walloon
  [2] *nm* (language) Walloon

Wallonie /walɔni/ *pr nf* Walloon area of Belgium

waters /watɛʀ/ *nm pl* (colloq) toilets

watt-heure, *pl* **watts-heures** /watœʀ/ *nm* watt-hour

WC /(dublə)vese/ *nm pl* toilet; **aller aux ~** to go to the toilet

winchester /winʃɛstɛʀ/ *nf* Winchester® rifle

wishbone /wiʃbon/ *nm* (Naut, Sport) wishbone boom

Xx

x, **X** /iks/ *nm inv* (letter) x, X; **il y a x temps que c'est fini** it's been over for ages; **porter plainte contre X** (Law) to take an action against person or persons unknown; **film classé X** X-rated movie

xénophobe /gzenɔfɔb/ **1** *adj* xenophobic **2** *nmf* xenophobe

xénophobie /gzenɔfɔbi/ *nf* xenophobia

xérès /kseʀɛs/ *nm inv* sherry

xylographe /ksilɔgraf/ *nm* xylographer

xylophène® /ksilɔfɛn/ *nm* wood preservative

Yy

y¹, **Y** /igʀɛk/ *nm inv* (letter) y, Y

y² /i/ *pron* **(a)** it; **tu t'∼ attendais?** were you expecting it?; **il n'∼ connaît rien** he knows nothing about it; **j'∼ pense parfois** I sometimes think about it; **elle n'∼ peut rien** there's nothing she can do about it; **j'∼ viens** I'm coming to that; **rien n'∼ fait** it's no use; **je n'∼ comprends rien** I don't understand a thing; **tu ∼ as gagné** you got the best deal; **plus difficile qu'il n'∼ paraît** harder than it seems

(b) there; **j'∼ ai mangé une fois** I ate there once; **n'∼ va pas** don't go

(c) **il ∼ a** there is/are; **du vin? il n'∼ en a plus** wine? there's none left; **il n'∼ a qu'à téléphoner** just phone

IDIOMS **∼ mettre du sien** to work at it

ya(c)k /'jak/ *nm* yak

yaourt /'jauʀ(t)/ *nm* yoghurt

yaourtière /'jauʀtjɛʀ/ *nf* yoghurt-maker

yéménite /'jemenit/ *adj* Yemeni

yen /'jɛn/ *nm* yen

yéti /'jeti/ *nm* yeti

yeux *nm pl* ▶ ŒIL

yoga /'jɔga/ *nm* yoga

yole /'jɔl/ *nf* skiff

yougoslave /'jugoslav/ *adj* Yugoslavian

youpi /'jupi/ *excl* (colloq) yippee!

youyou /'juju/ *nm* **(a)** ululation
(b) dinghy

Zz

z, **Z** /zɛd/ *nm inv* z, Z

zaïrois, **∼e** /zaiʀwa, az/ *adj* Zairean

zambien, **-ienne** /zɑ̃bjɛ̃, ɛn/ *adj* Zambian

zapper /zape/ [1] *vi* to flick through the TV channels

zébré, **∼e** /zebʀe/ *adj* ‹fabric› zebra-striped; **∼ de** streaked with

zèbre /zɛbʀ/ *nm* **(a)** zebra
(b) (figurative) (colloq) bloke (GB) (colloq), guy (colloq)

zébrure /zebʀyʀ/ *nf* stripe

zébu /zeby/ *nm* zebu

zélé, **∼e** /zele/ *adj* enthusiastic, zealous

zèle /zɛl/ *nm* zeal, enthusiasm; **faire du ∼** *or* **de l'excès de ∼** to be overzealous

zénith /zenit/ *nm* zenith; **à son ∼** ‹career› at its height

zéphyr /zefiʀ/ *nm* zephyr

zéro /zeʀo/ **1** *adj* **∼ heure** midnight, twenty-four hundred (hours); **il sera exactement ∼ heure vingt minutes dix secondes** the time will be twelve twenty and ten seconds; **j'ai eu ∼ faute dans ma dictée** I didn't make a single mistake in my dictation; **niveau/croissance ∼** zero level/ growth
2 *nm* **(a)** zero, nought (GB); **avoir un ∼ en latin** to get zero *or* nought in Latin; **remettre**

un compteur à ~ to reset a counter to zero; **avoir le moral à ~** (figurative) to be down in the dumps (colloq); **c'est beau à regarder mais question goût c'est ~** (colloq) it's nice to look at, but no marks for flavour (GB)
(b) (in sport) (gen) nil; (in tennis) love; **trois (buts) à ~** three nil
■ **~ de conduite** (Sch) bad mark for behaviour (GB)
IDIOMS partir de ~ to start from scratch; **tout reprendre à ~** to start all over again

zeste /zɛst/ *nm* **un ~ de citron** the zest of a lemon

zézayer /zezeje/ [21] *vi* to lisp

zibeline /ziblin/ *nf* sable

zieuter /zjøte/ [1] *vtr* (colloq) to get a load of (colloq), to take a look at

zigoto /zigoto/ *nm* (colloq) guy (colloq); **faire le ~** to clown around

zigue /zig/ *nm* (colloq) guy (colloq)

zigzag /zigzag/ *nm* zigzag; **route en ~** winding road; **faire des ~s** to zigzag (**parmi** through); **partir en ~** to zigzag off

zinc /zɛ̃g/ *nm* **(a)** zinc; **toiture de** *or* **en ~** tin roofing
(b) (colloq) counter, bar

zingueur /zɛ̃gœʀ/ *nm* roofer

zinzin (colloq) /zɛ̃zɛ̃/ **1** *adj inv* cracked (colloq)
2 *nm* thingamajig (colloq)

zip /zip/ *nm* zip (GB), zipper (US)

zippé, ~e /zipe/ *adj* zip-up

zipper /zipe/ *vt* (Comput) to zip

zizanie /zizani/ *nf* ill-feeling, discord

zizi /zizi/ *nm* (colloq) willy (GB) (colloq), penis

zodiac® /zodjak/ *nm* inflatable dinghy

zodiaque /zodjak/ *nm* zodiac

zona /zona/ *nm* shingles

zonage /zonaʒ/ *nm* zoning

zonard, ~e /zonaʀ, aʀd/ *nm,f* (colloq) dropout (colloq)

zone /zon/ *nf* **(a)** zone, area; **~ interdite** off-limits area; (on signpost) no entry
(b) **la ~** (colloq) the slum belt; **de seconde ~** second-rate
■ **~ d'activités** business park; **~ artisanale** small industrial estate (GB) *or* park; **~ bleue** restricted parking zone; **~ industrielle** industrial estate (GB) *or* park

zoner /zone/ [1] *vi* (colloq) to hang about (colloq)

zoo /zo/ *nm* zoo

zoologie /zɔɔlɔʒi/ *nf* zoology

zoom /zum/ *nm* **(a)** zoom lens
(b) zoom

zouave /zwav/ *nm* **(a)** (colloq) clown, comedian; **faire le ~** to clown around (colloq)
(b) (soldier) zouave

zoulou, ~e /zulu/ *adj* Zulu

zozo /zozo/ *nm* (colloq) ninny (GB) (colloq), jerk (colloq)

zozoter /zɔzɔte/ [1] *vi* to lisp

zut /zyt/ *excl* (colloq) damn! (colloq)

Z

473

Calendar
Culture
Letters

Calendar of French traditions, festivals, and holidays

Calendar

January

[1]	8	15	22	29
2	9	16	23	30
3	10	17	24	31
4	11	18	25	
5	12	19	26	
[6]	13	20	27	
7	14	21	28	

February

1	8	15	22
[2]	9	16	23
3	10	17	24
4	11	18	25
5	12	19	26
6	13	20	27
7	[14]	21	28

March

1	8	15	22	29
2	9	16	23	30
3	10	17	24	31
4	11	18	25	
5	12	19	26	
6	13	20	27	
7	14	21	28	

April

[1]	8	15	22	29
2	9	16	23	30
3	10	17	24	
4	11	18	25	
5	12	19	26	
6	13	20	27	
7	14	21	28	

May

[1]	[8]	15	22	29
2	9	16	23	30
3	10	17	24	31
4	11	18	25	
5	12	19	26	
6	13	20	27	
7	14	21	28	

June

1	8	15	22	29
2	9	16	23	30
3	10	17	[24]	
4	11	18	25	
5	12	19	26	
6	13	20	27	
7	14	21	28	

July

1	8	15	22	29
2	9	16	23	30
3	10	17	24	31
4	11	18	25	
5	12	19	26	
6	13	20	27	
7	[14]	21	28	

August

1	8	[15]	22	29
2	9	16	23	30
3	10	17	24	31
4	11	18	25	
5	12	19	26	
6	13	20	27	
7	14	21	28	

September

1	8	15	22	29
2	9	16	23	30
3	10	17	24	
4	11	18	25	
5	12	19	26	
6	13	20	27	
7	14	21	28	

October

1	8	15	22	29
2	9	16	23	30
3	10	17	24	31
4	11	18	25	
5	12	19	26	
6	13	20	27	
7	14	21	28	

November

[1]	8	15	22	29
2	9	16	23	30
3	10	17	24	
4	[11]	18	25	
5	12	19	26	
6	13	20	27	
7	14	21	28	

December

1	[8]	15	22	29
2	9	16	23	30
3	10	17	[24]	[31]
4	11	18	[25]	
5	12	19	[26]	
6	13	20	27	
7	14	21	28	

• •

1 January
le jour de l'an (New Year's Day) is a public holiday and a day of family celebration, with a large lunch, traditionally featuring seafood of various kinds.

6 January
la Fête des Rois (Epiphany or Twelfth night). Around this time, most families have a *galette des Rois*, a rich pastry cake filled with *frangipane* (almond paste). The cake contains a *fève*, literally a bean, as this is what was originally used. Nowadays the *fève* takes the form of a tiny plastic or ceramic figure. The person who gets the *fève* in their portion puts on the cardboard crown which comes with the cake.

2 February
la Chandeleur (Candlemas) is celebrated in the church but it is not a public holiday. However, it is traditional to eat *crêpes* (pancakes) on this day.

14 February
la Saint Valentin (St Valentine's Day). As in many other countries, people celebrate a romantic relationship with gifts of flowers or chocolates.

1 April
le premier avril (April Fool's Day). The French also take advantage of this occasion to play tricks on one another, calling out *poisson d'avril!* (literally 'April fish').

1 May
La Fête du Travail (International Labour Day) is a public holiday.

8 May
le 8 mai or **la Fête de la Victoire** is a public holiday commemorating Victory in Europe on 8 May 1945.

24 June
la Saint-Jean (Midsummer's Day). In many areas, bonfires (*les feux de la Saint-Jean*) are lit on Midsummer's Night. People are supposed to jump over these, re-enacting a pagan custom intended to ward off the cold of winter.

14 July
la Fête Nationale or le 14 juillet is usually called Bastille Day in English and is a public holiday in France. It commemorates the taking of the Bastille prison in Paris and the liberation of its prisoners by the people of Paris in 1789, one of the first events of the Revolution. All over France there are parades on the day of the 14th and firework displays and *bals* (local dances) either on the night of the 13th or or of the 14th.

15 August
l'Assomption (Feast of the Assumption) is a public holiday. Many people in France are either setting off on holiday around the 15th or else returning home, so this is traditionally a very busy time on the roads.

1 November
la Toussaint (All Saints' Day) is a public holiday and the day when people remember their dead relatives and friends, although properly speaking it is All Souls' Day the following day that is set aside for this in the church. People take flowers to the cemetery, particularly chrysanthemums, as these are in bloom at this time. Because of this association, it is best to avoid taking chrysanthemums as a gift for someone. Schoolchildren have a two-week holiday around this time.

11 November
le 11 novembre is a public holiday to commemorate the Armistice of 1918 and a day of remembrance for those who died in the two world wars and in subsequent conflicts. All towns and villages hold parades in which war veterans accompany local officials and a brass band to lay wreaths on the war memorial. In Paris, the President lays a wreath on the tomb of the unknown soldier beneath the *Arc de Triomphe* on the *Champs-Élysées*.

8 December
la fête de l'Immaculée Conception (Feast of the Immaculate Conception). In the city of Lyons, this is celebrated as

Calendar

la Fête de la Lumière (Festival of Light) said to commemorate the Virgin's intervention to prevent the plague reaching Lyons in the Middle Ages. People put rows of candles in coloured glass jars on the outsides of their windowsills, so that all the buildings in the centre of the city are illuminated.

24 December
la veille de Noël (Christmas Eve) is the time when most people exchange presents. Many people go to *la messe de minuit* (midnight mass).

25 December
Noël (Christmas) is a public holiday and a day of eating and drinking. Lunch will often start with a variety of seafood, oysters being particularly popular. Turkey is often eaten as a main course, sometimes with chestnut stuffing. A variety of cheeses will be followed by *la bûche de Noël*, a rich chocolate cake in the form of a snow-covered log. French people do not usually send Christmas cards, the custom being to send wishes for the coming year to more distant friends and relatives during the month of January.

26 December
There is no particular name for the day after Christmas Day and it is not a public holiday.

31 December
la Saint-Sylvestre (New Year's Eve). Many people have parties to celebrate *le réveillon du Nouvel An* (New Year's Eve Party). Once again, food plays a major part and, as at Christmas, this is a time to splash out on luxury foods such as *foie gras*. There will often be dancing and the New Year will be welcomed in with champagne.

Movable feasts

Mardi gras
Shrove Tuesday, the last day of carnival before the beginning of Lent on Ash Wednesday. Traditionally, *crêpes* (pancakes) are eaten for supper. In many areas of France, sugared fritters called *bugnes* in and around Lyons and *oreillettes* farther south, are eaten between *la fête des Rois* and *mardi gras*.

le Vendredi saint
Good Friday is celebrated in the church, but is not a public holiday.

Pâques
Easter Sunday, *le dimanche de Pâques*, is for many people the occasion for a big family lunch. Easter hunts are organised for children, with chocolate eggs, rabbits, hens, or fish traditionally hidden in the family garden. *Le lundi de Pâques* (Easter Monday) is a public holiday.

l'Ascension, the Thursday forty days after Easter, is a public holiday in France.

la Pentecôte (Whitsun) on the seventh Sunday after Easter represents for many people the first long weekend of the summer, as *le lundi de la Pentecôte* (Whit Monday) is a public holiday. Many families go to stay with friends or relatives in the country.

la Fête des mères (Mother's Day) is the Sunday after *Pentecôte*. This is another occasion for a big family meal, with presents for the mother. **La fête des pères** (Father's Day) is celebrated in similar fashion two weeks later.

A–Z of French Life and Culture

Académie française

A learned body whose main role nowadays is to monitor new developments in the French language and to make decisions as to what is acceptable and what is not, although these decisions are not always taken entirely seriously by the public at large. Its 40 members are elected for life on the basis of their contribution to scholarship or literature.

agrégation

A qualification awarded by **CONCOURS** for entry to the limited number of highest level teaching posts in secondary and higher education.

Alliance Française

A private organization which aims to spread awareness of French language and culture. It has centres in cities throughout the world, providing classes and a variety of cultural activities.

année scolaire

The French school year starts with the **RENTRÉE** *des classes* in early September and ends in early July. There is a week's holiday in late October/early November around *la Toussaint* (All Saints' Day, 1 November), two weeks around Christmas and New Year, two weeks in February, and two weeks in April. Many families go on skiing holidays during the February break.

ANPE - Agence nationale pour l'emploi

The national agency which assists jobseekers. The unemployed must register with *ANPE* to claim benefit and receive training.

Antenne 2 ▶ FRANCE 2

arrondissement

The three largest cities in France - Paris, Lyons, and Marseilles - are divided into numbered administrative areas called *arrondissements*. Each has its own mayor and council, and the number of the *arrondissement* is usually part of the postcode. The system makes for a convenient way for people to talk about which part of the city they live in e.g. '*le neuvième arrondissement*' or simply '*le neuvième*'.
An *arrondissement* is also a sub-division of a **DÉPARTEMENT**.

ARTE

A television channel, run jointly by France and Germany, which provides a high standard of cultural programmes.

Culture

Culture

Assemblée Nationale

The lower house of the French parliament, also called the **Chambre des députés**. There are 577 **DÉPUTÉS**, elected for a five-year term, often after two rounds of voting as at least 50% of the vote must be obtained.

Astérix

A hugely popular comic-book character invented by cartoonists Goscinny and Uderzo. *Astérix* is a tiny but invincible village leader in the ancient province of Gaul whose fictional adventures with his fellow-villagers often involve fighting and outwitting the occupying Romans and make for gentle mockery of cultures outside Gaul. The *Astérix* books have been translated into 40 languages.

autoroute

France has an extensive motorway system, which is largely financed by tolls calculated according to the distance travelled and the vehicle type. Tickets are obtained and tolls paid at *péages* (tollgates). There is a speed limit for standard vehicles of 130 km/h (approx. 80 mph) and 110 km/h (approx. 70 mph) in wet weather.

baccalauréat

The *baccalauréat*, generally known informally as the *Bac*, is the examination sat in the final year of the **LYCÉE** (*la terminale*), so usually at age 17 or 18. Students sit exams in a fairly broad range of subjects in a particular category: the *Bac S* places emphasis on the sciences, for example, whilst the *Bac L* has a literary bias. Some categories cater for students specializing in more directly job-based subjects such as agriculture. The final result is given as a single overall mark or grade out of 20, although the scores for individual subjects are also given. It is common to use the *Bac* as a point of reference in job adverts, so that *Bac + 4* would mean a person who had completed 4 years of full-time study after the *Bac*, with appropriate diplomas to show for it.

bachelier

The holder of the **BACCALAURÉAT**, entitled to enrol for university courses.

bande dessinée (BD)

Comic books of all sorts and for a wide variety of age and interest groups are immensely popular in France and form an important part of French culture. Cartoon characters such as *Astérix, Lucky Luke*, and *Tintin* are household names and older comic books are often collectors' items.

Basque

The Basque country extends on both sides of the Pyrenees with about one quarter of a million Basques living in France and ten times that number in Spain. The French Basque region (*le Pays basque français*) does not have

• •

any autonomous status nor is Basque recognized as an official language. It is, however, taught in some schools, and there are an estimated 40,000 Basque speakers in France.

BCBG
The letters *BCBG* stand for *bon chic bon genre,* although the full form is hardly ever used. *BCBG* is used to sum up a person, style of dress, lifestyle etc. as reflecting conventional upper middle-class or *bourgeois* values and tastes. In most cases, this is not intended as a compliment.

beur
A second-generation North African from the **MAGHREB** living in France.

boules
A type of bowls, also called **pétanque**, played all over France, using metal *boules* and a jack known as a *cochonnet.* Special areas (*terrains de boules*) are set aside for the game in towns and villages, although one of the obvious attractions of the game is that it can be played virtually anywhere, so a family lunch in the summer will often end in a game of *boules* (*une partie de boules*). There are some regional variations, notably in the size and form of the playing area and the size of the bowls.

brasserie
The original meaning of *brasserie* is 'brewery', and although the word is still used in this sense, it has come also to mean a type of bar-restaurant, usually serving simple, traditional French food at reasonable prices. Most *brasseries* offer a fixed-price menu, especially at lunchtime.

Breton
The ancient Celtic language of Brittany (*Bretagne*). It is related to Welsh, Irish, Scottish Gaelic, and Cornish. Recent decades have seen a revival of interest in the language going hand in hand with the assertion of a regional cultural identity and a movement for independence from France. Breton is fairly widely spoken and is taught in secondary schools in the region, although it is not recognized as an official language in France.

Brevet d'études professionnelles (BEP)
A vocational qualification awarded at the end of a two-year, practically-based course in a **LYCÉE** specializing in providing teaching directly related to the workplace.

Brevet de technicien (BT)
A vocational qualification awarded at the end of a three-year course in a special section of a **LYCÉE**. There is considerable competition for entry to courses, and the standards required result in a high dropout rate.

Brevet de technicien supérieur (BTS)
A vocational qualification awarded at the end of a two-year course after

Culture

• •

the **BACCALAURÉAT** in a specific professional field.

Brevet des collèges

A general educational qualification taken in a range of subjects by
students aged around 15 in the final year of **COLLÈGE**.

bureau de tabac

Tobacconists are either individual shops or else are to be found in a *bar-
tabac* or *café-tabac*. They are also often combined with a newsagents
(*marchand de journaux*). As well as being licensed to sell tobacco and
cigarettes, they have a state licence to sell stamps, **LOTO** tickets, the
VIGNETTE (road tax disc for motor vehicles), and certain other official
documents.

Canal Plus (Canal+)

A privately-owned French television channel broadcasting mainly feature
films. Viewers pay a subscription and access the channel using a decoder.

canton

A *canton* is an administrative unit of French local government which
contains several **COMMUNES**. It elects a member of the **CONSEIL
GÉNÉRAL**.

CAPES - certificat d'aptitude au professorat de l'enseignement du second degré

The qualification normally required in order to teach in a secondary
school. Qualification is by means of a competitive examination
(**CONCOURS**) usually at the end of a two-year course in a specialist
teacher-training institute (*IUFM: Institut universitaire pour la formation
des maîtres*).

Carte bleue

A credit card issued by French banks as part of the international Visa
network.

Carte grise

The registration document for a motor vehicle. It is an offence not to carry
it when driving the vehicle, and police checks are frequent. Vehicle
registration numbers depend on the **DÉPARTEMENT** in which the owner
lives and have to be changed if the owner moves to a different one.

Carte nationale d'identité

Although not obligatory, most French citizens possess a *carte nationale
d'identité* (national identity card), obtained from their local **MAIRIE**,
PRÉFECTURE, or *commissariat de police* (police station), as proof of
identity is often required, for example when paying by cheque. It is also
accepted as a travel document by all EC countries.

Catalan

The language spoken by 25 per cent of people in Spain and by some people in the Perpignan area of southwest France. It is taught in schools in the area but is not recognized as an official language in France.

CDI - Centre de documentation et d'information

A resource and information centre providing library and IT facilities in a school or college. The term has largely replaced *bibliothèque* (library) in this context.

CE - cycle élémentaire

Also called *cours élémentaire*, this is the programme for the two years of primary school for children aged 7 to 9 (*CE1* and *CE2*).

Césars

Prizes awarded annually for achievements in the film industry, so the French equivalent of the Oscars.

CFDT

A large and influential trade union which is close to the **PARTI SOCIALISTE**, but which has a much wider membership.

CGT

A large and influential trade union which has a tradition of association with the **PARTI COMMUNISTE**, but which has a much wider membership.

Chambre des députés ▶ ASSEMBLÉE NATIONALE

champignons

The French use the word *champignons* (mushrooms) to refer to any of the types of mushroom-like fungi that are to be found in the countryside, whether edible or not. Cultivated button mushrooms are called *champignons de Paris*. Hunting for edible *champignons* is almost a national leisure activity, and many varieties are highly prized. Advice on whether a *champignon* is edible or not can usually be obtained in a **PHARMACIE**.

Champs-Élysées

The world-famous avenue in central Paris, known for its luxury shops, hotels, and clubs. At one end is the *Arc de Triomphe*, the scene of the remembrance ceremony each year for the Armistice of 1918 and under which is the tomb of an unknown soldier, killed in World War I.

charcuterie

A shop or supermarket counter selling a wide variety of pork products. As well as cuts of pork, *charcutiers* usually sell chicken both raw and ready-cooked, and there will be various types of raw and cooked ham, a variety of pâtés, often homemade in small shops, and a selection of *saucissons*. Most *charcuteries* also offer a variey of salads, various types of savoury pastries, and a number of dishes, different every day, which can

Culture

• •

be reheated at home or on the premises. Some *charcuteries* also offer a catering service, in which case the shop will probably call itself a *charcutier-traiteur*. The word *charcuterie* is also used to mean pork products such as ham and *saucisson*.

chasse
La chasse (hunting) is a widely practised sport in France. Legislation as to the rights of hunters to hunt over privately-owned land varies according to the region and the amount of land concerned. During the hunting season, hunting is permitted on Thursdays, Saturdays, and Sundays. It is advisable not to stray from public footpaths when walking in the countryside on these days. The hunters (*les chasseurs*) are a powerful political lobby and are represented in the **ASSEMBLÉE NATIONALE**.

CHU - centre hospitalier universitaire
A teaching hospital attached to the medical faculty of a university.

Cinquième
La Cinquième is an educational television channel which broadcasts on the **ARTE** channel during the day.

Cinquième république
This is the present régime in France. The constitution was established in 1958 according to principles put forward by Charles de Gaulle

classe de neige
A period, generally a week, which a school class, usually of under-twelves, spends in a mountain area. Ski tuition is integrated with normal school work.

classe préparatoire
An intensive two-year course, provided by some prestigious **LYCÉES**, which prepares students for the competitive examinations (**CONCOURS**) by means of which students are selected for the **GRANDES ÉCOLES**.

classes
In French schools, after **CM**, classes go in reverse order, starting at age 11-12 in *sixième* and progressing through *cinquième, quatrième, troisième, seconde, première*, and ending in *terminale* at age 17 or 18, the year in which the **BACCALAURÉAT** is taken. Education in France is compulsory up to the end of *seconde*.

CM - Cycle moyen
Also called *Cours moyen* this is the programme for the two years of primary school for children aged 9 to 11 (*CM1* and *CM2*).

cohabitation
A period of power sharing between opposing political parties which can occur since the presidential mandate lasts for seven years, but legislative elections are five-yearly.

. . . .

collège
A state school for pupils between the ages of 11 and 15, between the
ÉCOLE PRIMAIRE and the **LYCÉE**. The organisation of the school and
the curriculum followed are laid down at national level.

colonie de vacances
A holiday village or summer camp for children. Originally set up as a
means of giving poorer city children a means of getting out into the
countryside, these are still largely state-subsidized. The informal word for
them is *colo*.

commune
The *commune* is the smallest administrative unit of French local
government. Each has its own **MAIRE** (mayor) and **CONSEIL**
MUNICIPAL and with other *communes* forms a **CANTON**.

concours
Entry into many areas of the public services, including the teaching
profession, as well as the most prestigious institutes of higher education,
depends on succeeding in a competitive examination or *concours*.
The number of candidates admitted depends on the number of posts or
places available in a given year.

conduite accompagnée (CA)
A learner driver who has passed the theory part of the driving test (*code de
la route*) in a state-approved driving school is allowed to practise driving a
vehicle accompanied by a qualified driver over the age of 28. Such drivers
are not allowed to drive on **AUTOROUTES** and are required to have a
white sticker with a red 'A' displayed on the rear of their vehicle.

conseil de classe
A committee representing each class in a **COLLÈGE** or **LYCÉE** consisting
of the class teachers, two elected parent members, and two elected class
members. It is chaired by the head teacher. The *conseil de classe* meets
regularly to discuss the progress of the class and any problems that have
arisen.

conseil général
The body of representatives elected every six years to implement public
policy in each **DÉPARTEMENT**.

conseil municipal
The *conseil municipal* is the local council elected for a 6-year term by the
inhabitants of a **COMMUNE**. The *conseil municipal* then elects the
MAIRE (mayor). It is responsible for the management of local public
services and amenities.

Culture

. . . .

conseil régional

Each member of a *conseil régional* is elected for a term of six years to represent a **DÉPARTEMENT**. The *conseillers régionaux* then appoint a president and an executive team.

CP - Cycle préparatoire

Also called *Cours préparatoire*, this is the first year of primary school, starting a child's formal education off at the statutory age of 6. Most children will have already attended an **ÉCOLE MATERNELLE**.

CRS - compagnies républicaines de sécurité

Special police units trained in public order techniques and riot control. They also police the **AUTOROUTES** and support mountain rescue and lifeguard work.

département

An administrative unit of government in France. Each *département* has a number and this appears as the first two digits in postcodes for addresses within the *département* and as the two-digit number at the end of registration numbers on motor vehicles.

député

An elected member of the **ASSEMBLÉE NATIONALE**.

DEUG - diplôme d'études universitaires générales

A qualification awarded after two years of university education in non-scientific subject areas. Students are required to pass this in order to go on to study for the **LICENCE**, and the **DEUG** is also accepted as a qualification for entry into professional life.

DEUST - Diplôme d'études universitaires de sciences et techniques

The equivalent of the **DEUG** in science and technology.

DOM - Département d'outre-mer

An overseas **DÉPARTEMENT** which also has the status of a region. At present there are four of these: Guadeloupe, Guyane, Martinique, and Réunion.

droguerie

As a shop or supermarket section, there seems little connection between the name, which might be literally translated as 'drugstore', and the merchandise displayed. However, *drogue* can also mean the raw ingredients of dyes, and *droguistes* were originally dye merchants. Nowadays you will find not only dyes but household products and cleaning utensils, candles, and a variey of other useful household items.

. . . .

DUT - diplôme universitaire de technologie
A qualification awarded after two years of higher education in an **IUT**. Courses are vocationally based and include a compulsory period of work experience.

école libre
Private sector school education, provided predominantly by the Catholic church.

école maternelle
A school providing free nursery education from age 3 to 6. Many children start at 2 and virtually all children attend between the ages of 4 and 6, which is the statutory school starting age and the time at which children move into the **ÉCOLE PRIMAIRE**

école primaire
A primary school for children between the ages of 6, the statutory minimum age for starting school, and 11.

école secondaire
Secondary education in France consists of two phases: **COLLÈGE** (11–15 years) and **LYCEE** (15/16–17/18 years).

EDF-GDF - Électricité de France-Gaz de France
The state-owned utility combining electricity generation and distribution of gas and electricity.

Élysée ▶ PALAIS DE L'ÉLYSÉE

Emmaüs
A charitable organization founded in 1954 by the Abbé Pierre, a Catholic priest and well-known public figure. The organisation, which has wide public support, aims to help underprivileged people. It has centres throughout France, run by volunteers who collect and sell secondhand furniture, clothes, and bric-à-brac.

Europe 1
A popular commercial French-language radio station, which broadcasts news, popular music, sport, and light entertainment from the Saarland in Germany.

Événement du jeudi - l'Événement du jeudi
A popular weekly news magazine.

Express - l'Express
A weekly news magazine offering in-depth coverage of political and cultural matters.

Culture

· ·

faculté

La faculté - and more usually and informally *la fac* - is the way that students refer to their university, particularly the location itself, so that *aller à la fac* would be the equivalent of 'to go into college'.

Figaro - le Figaro

A right-wing national daily newspaper with a wide circulation.

France 2

This is the main publicly-owned television channel and aims to provide a wide range of quality programmes.

France 3

A state-owned television channel which is regionally based and is required to promote regional diversity and to cover a wide range of beliefs and opinions.

France Culture

A 24-hour **RADIO FRANCE** radio station featuring serious talk programmes on a wide variety of cultural and social topics.

France Info

A 24-hour radio news station run by **RADIO FRANCE**.

France Inter

A **RADIO FRANCE** radio station broadcasting mainly light entertainment, including a considerable proportion of studio comedy shows, but also offering good news coverage.

France Musiques

A 24-hour **RADIO FRANCE** radio station. Its main focus is classical music but it also provides considerable coverage of jazz and world music.

France Télécom

The state-owned telephone company. It no longers holds a monopoly.

Front National

An extreme right-wing political party, founded in 1972 by Jean-Marie Le Pen.

Gendarmerie nationale

A section of the military which provides police services outside the major towns.

gîte rural

A farmhouse or other building in the country which has been turned into a holiday cottage. Houses displaying the official *gîte de France* sign must conform to certain standards.

grande école

A prestigious higher education establishment admitting students on the results of a **CONCOURS**. They have different areas of specialization and competition for entry is fierce, as they are widely believed to offer the highest level of education available and thus a guarantee of subsequent career success.

HLM - habitation à loyer modéré

Public housing, usually apartments, for which the rent is considerably lower than the average for private-sector housing. Tenants have the right to buy their homes, provided they undertake not to sell them within 5 years.

hôtel de ville ▶ MAIRIE

Humanité - l'Humanité

The communist national daily newspaper.

Internet

A wealth of useful information on French culture, society, and current affairs can be obtained on the Internet. All the main French newspapers have websites (e.g. http://www.lemonde.fr), as do the television channels (e.g. http://www.france3.fr and http://www.tf1.fr). The *Louvre* museum has an interesting site at http://web.culture.fr/louvre.

immatriculation ▶ PLAQUE D'IMMATRICULATION

IUT - Institut universitaire de technologie

An institute of technology attached to a university, which provides vocationally-based courses leading to the **DUT**.

Libération

A left-wing national daily newspaper published in Paris. A separate edition is published for Lyons.

licence

A university degree awarded after a year's study following the **DEUG**.

Loto

The French national lottery. People play the Loto using special machines which can be found in **BUREAUX DE TABAC** throughout France.

Luxembourg ▶ PALAIS DU LUXEMBOURG

lycée

A school providing the last three years of secondary education after **COLLÈGE**. The first year is *seconde* at the age of 15/16, going through *première*, and ending with *terminale* at age 17/18. As well as those which provide a conventional academic education, there are a number of different types of *lycée* offering a more vocationally-based education.

M6

A popular, privately-owned, commercial television channel.

magasins

Opening and closing times of shops (*les magasins*) vary according to the type of shop and the location. Department stores (*les grands magasins*) are generally open all day from 9 a.m. to 7 p.m. In larger towns, most other shops, with the exception of small food shops, are also open all day. Privately-owned food shops such as butchers and fishmongers generally open at 8 a.m. and do not close in the evening until 7 or 7.30. Most, however, are closed between midday and 2 or 3 p.m. In small towns, all the shops, with the exception of bakers, generally close for 2 or 3 hours in the middle of the day. In both small and large towns, it is always possible to find all types of food shops open on Sunday mornings until midday. In smaller towns, however, many of the shops are closed on Mondays.

Maghreb

The region of Islamic North Africa which covers the former French colony of Algeria and the former French protectorates of Morocco and Tunisia.

maire

The chief officer of a **COMMUNE** elected by the **CONSEIL MUNICIPAL**. He or she represents state authority locally, officiates at marriages, and supervises local elections.

mairie

The *mairie* (town hall) is the administrative headquarters of the **CONSEIL MUNICIPAL**. In larger towns the *mairie* is often called the **HÔTEL DE VILLE**.

marchés

All towns in France have a weekly market with stalls selling a variety of produce, and some areas in big cities have a market every day. Many stalls are held by local people selling their own produce. Despite supermarkets, many people do much of their food shopping *au marché*.

Marianne

The symbolic female figure often used to represent the French Republic. There are statues of her in public places all over France, and she also appears on the standard French stamp. She is always depicted wearing the Phrygian bonnet, a pointed cap which became one of the symbols of liberty as represented by the 1789 Revolution.

Marseillaise

The French national anthem, so called because it was the marching song of a group of republican volunteers from Marseilles a few years after the 1789 Revolution.

. . . .

Matignon

The *Hôtel Matignon* in the rue de Varenne in Paris is the official residence and office of the prime minister. *Hôtel* is used here in the sense of a large private town house, which would have been its original use in the eighteenth century.

Médecins du monde

A charitable organization which provides medical and humanitarian aid in areas stricken by war, famine, or natural disaster.

Médecins sans frontières

A charitable organisation which sends medical teams anywhere in the world where they are needed to cope with the effects on people of war and disaster.

Minitel

A computer terminal available in a variety of models to the subscribers of **FRANCE TÉLÉCOM**. It gives users access to the *Télétel* network, which has a huge variety of services, payable at different rates, including the telephone directory. It can now be accessed via the Internet.

MJC - Maison des jeunes et de la culture

A community youth centre offering a wide variety of services and activities.

Monde - le Monde

A national daily newspaper. Its political stance is left of centre, and it is entirely owned by its staff. It provides full coverage of national and international news and is known for its in-depth analysis of current issues. It is unusual in publishing virtually no photographs of current events.

Nouvel Observateur - le Nouvel Observateur

A left-wing weekly magazine providing in-depth articles on current political issues and good coverage of culture and the arts.

Occitan

The old language of the southern half of France. It is still spoken in a number of different dialects by an estimated four million people, and recent years have seen an immense revival of interest in promoting its survival. It can now be learned in many schools in the south, although it has no status as an official language in France.

Palais Bourbon

A large eighteenth-century residence on the left bank of the Seine which is now the seat of the **ASSEMBLÉE NATIONALE**.

Palais de l'Élysée

The official residence and office of the French President, situated just off the **CHAMPS-ÉLYSÉES** in Paris.

Culture

Culture

. . . .

Palais des Congrès

A huge conference centre. Several large cities have one of these, notably Paris and Lyons. As well as supplying luxury conference facilities, they have a large amount of exhibition space, and auditoriums where concerts and performances are held.

Palais du Luxembourg

A seventeenth century palace in the *jardin du Luxembourg* in Paris. It is now the seat of the **SÉNAT**.

paysan

Since *paysan* can be used in French to mean both 'small farmer' and, more offensively, 'peasant', small farmers are generally referred to as *agriculteurs*. However, many small farmers take pride in their identity as *paysans*, particularly in the more remote areas of the country, where small farms are still the usual form of cultivation. The difficulty of making a living with a limited amount of land has, however, led to many such farms being abandoned or amalgamated into larger units and a general movement of the traditional rural population towards the towns.

Parti communiste français (PCF)

The French Communist Party still has a significant following, but support for it has been decreasing steadily in recent years.

Parti socialiste (PS)

The main political party of the left.

permis de conduire

A driving licence can be issued to a person over the age of 18 who has passed both parts of the driving test. The first part is the theory test (*code de la route*) and consists of forty questions based on the highway code. This can be sat from the age of 16 onwards and gives the right to **CONDUITE ACCOMPAGNÉE**. The practical driving test has to be taken within two years of the theory test. It is compulsory to carry your driving licence with you when you are driving a vehicle.

pétanque ▶ BOULES

pharmacie

Pharmacies in France generally sell only medicines and closely related products such as toiletries and some brands of make-up and perfume. The products of the major perfume houses are to be found in *parfumeries*. Pharmacists traditionally play an active paramedical role, and people will often consult a pharmacist rather than a doctor in the case of minor ailments or accidents such as snake bites. Pharmacies are easily spotted by the green cross, which is lit up when the pharmacy is open. A *pharmacie de garde* (duty chemist) can dispense medicines outside normal opening hours as part of a local rota.

plaque d'immatriculation
A vehicle's registration plate. The last two figures indicate the number of the **DÉPARTEMENT** in which the owner lives. If you move into another *département*, you are obliged by law to change your registration plate accordingly.

PMU - pari mutuel urbain
The *PMU* sign is to be seen outside many **BUREAUX DE TABAC**. It indicates a state-regulated horse-race betting outlet. The most popular form of betting is the *tiercé*, in which punters have to predict the first three places in a given race.

Point - le Point
A centre-right weekly news magazine offering in-depth coverage of politics and economics.

police
There are three principal police forces: the *police municipale* who are responsible for routine local policing such as traffic offences, who are locally organized and are not armed, the *police nationale* who are nationally organized and generally armed, and the **GENDARMERIE NATIONALE** which is a branch of the military.

Poste - La Poste
The state monopoly postal service. Postboxes in France are yellow.

préfet
The most senior offical responsible for representing the state within the **DÉPARTEMENT**.

préfecture
The administrative headquarters of a **DÉPARTEMENT**.

Premier ministre
The chief minister of the government, appointed by the **PRÉSIDENT DE LA RÉPUBLIQUE** and responsible for the overall management of government affairs.

Président de la République
The president is the head of state and is elected for a term of 7 years. Under the constitution of the **CINQUIÈME RÉPUBLIQUE** the president plays a strong executive role in the governing of the country.

Prix Fémina
A literary prize awarded in November each year by a jury of women.

Prix Goncourt
A literary prize awarded each November for a novel published in that year. The event attracts considerable media coverage and speculation.

Culture

Prix Médicis

A literary prize awarded in November each year for an innovative novel or book of short stories.

Quai d'Orsay

The *ministère des Affaires étrangères* (ministry of Foreign Affairs) is situated here, so *Quai d'Orsay* is often used by journalists to mean the ministry.

Radio France

The state-owned radio broadcasting company.

région

The largest administrative unit in France, consisting of a number of **DÉPARTEMENTS**. Each has its own **CONSEIL RÉGIONAL** (regional council) which has responsibilities in education and economic planning.

rentrée

The week at the beginning of September when the new school year starts and around which much of French administrative life revolves. The preceding weeks see intensive advertising of associated merchandise, from books and stationery to clothes and sports equipment. Many stores and supermarkets have have a range of special purchases at bargain prices.

La rentrée littéraire marks the start of the literary year and *la rentrée parlementaire* signals the reassembly of parliament after the recess.

repas

Traditionally the midday meal was the big meal of the day, and for people who live in country areas this is still largely the case. Even in big cities many people continue to eat a big meal in the middle of the day, either in a family restaurant near their place of work or by buying a freshly cooked hot dish from a **CHARCUTERIE**. However, people living and working in the larger cities are tending more and more to have a snack lunch and to eat their main meal in the evening. In either case, the main meal virtually always consists of a number of courses, typically a starter such as *pâté, saucisson*, or salad, then meat or fish with a vegetable dish, followed by cheese and dessert. Cheese is virtually always eaten, as one might expect in a country that boasts a huge variety of different cheeses, and is always served before the dessert. In town and country alike, Sunday is the day for a big family meal in the middle of the day, and the **PÂTISSERIES** are usually crowded on Sunday mornings as people queue up to buy a large tart or cake for their hosts or guests.

. . . .

restaurants

France is rightly famed for the quality of its restaurants, from the small family-run business to the grand establishments. It is always possible to find restaurants and **BRASSERIES** offering fixed-price menus, which are generally good value for money. A basket of bread is usually included in the price of the meal, and most restaurants will have several inexpensive house wines, available in *pichets* (jugs) of ¼, ½, and 1 litre. Service is included in the bill, although many people do leave a tip if the meal and the service have been good.

restaurants du coeur

A charitable organization, widely publicized by virtue of having been set up by a much loved humourist called Coluche, who died in a motorcycle accident in 1986. It serves meals to the poor and homeless, particularly in the winter.

route départementale

These are signalled on French road maps as 'D' followed by a number and are marked in yellow. They are roads maintained by the **DÉPARTEMENT** and are secondary roads, not intended to be used for fast travel from place to place. Many of them have stretches marked in green on maps to highlight areas or views of particular beauty.

route nationale

A *route nationale* forms part of the state-maintained road network, outside the **AUTOROUTES** but providing fast roads for travel between towns and cities. They are signalled by 'N' followed by the road number and are marked in red on French road maps.

RPR - Rassemblement pour la République

The largest political party on the right, founded by Jacques Chirac in 1976.

SAMU - service d'aide médicale d'urgence

A 24 hour service coordinated by each **DÉPARTMENT** to provide mobile medical services and staff, ambulances, and helicopters to accident scenes and emergencies.

Sénat

The upper house of parliament which meets in the **PALAIS DU LUXEMBOURG**. It consists of 321 elected *sénateurs*. It votes laws and the state budget.

SNCF - Société nationale des chemins de fer français

The state-owned railway company, which also has access to private finance.

tabac ▶ BUREAU DE TABAC

• •

télécarte

A phone card for use in telephone kiosks, widely available from **FRANCE TÉLÉCOM**, *bureaux de poste, tabacs* and *marchands de journaux*.

TF1 - Télévision française 1

Originally a state-controlled television channel, now privately-owned, *TF1* has an obligation to ensure that 50% of its programmes are of French origin.

TGV - train à grande vitesse

The new-generation high-speed electric train. It runs on special tracks and can reach speeds of up to 300 km/h.

Tintin

A comic-book character invented by the Belgian cartoonist Hergé in 1929. *Tintin's* adventures with the irrepressible *Capitaine Haddock* are still bestsellers and have been translated into more than 40 languages.

TOM - territoire d'outre-mer

An overseas territory, constitutionally part of the French Republic and whose citizens have French nationality.

Tour de France

Probably the most famous cycle race in the world, the *Tour de France* takes place over a different route each year but always ends around July 14 on the **CHAMPS ÉLYSÉES**. The overall winner after each section of the race is entitled to wear *le maillot jaune* (yellow jersey).

UDF - Union pour la démocratie française

A political grouping, allowing various centre-right parties to work together at times of elections.

verlan

A type of slang in which syllables are reversed so that for example *l'envers = verlan, pourri = ripou*.

Verts - Les Verts

A left-wing political party committed to the protection of the environment.

vignette

The disc which by law must be displayed on the windscreen of a motor vehicle to certify that the road tax has been paid. This must be renewed every November, and is obtainable from a **BUREAU DE TABAC** on payment of the tax. Older vehicles pay a lower rate.

Letter-writing in French

Holiday postcard

■ *Beginnings (informal):* Cher *is used for a man,* Chère *for a woman. A letter to two males or to a male and female begins with* Chers. *For two female correspondents:* Chères Madeleine et Hélène. *For friends and relatives:* Chers amis, Chers cousins, *etc. For a family:* Chers tous.

■ *Address: On an envelope Mr, Mrs and Miss can be abbreviated to M., Mme, Mlle, although the full forms are considered preferable in more formal letters. There is no direct equivalent for Ms. If you do not know a woman's marital status use* Madame (Mme).

Road names such as rue, avenue, place *are not generally given capital letters.*

The name of the town comes after the postcode and on the same line.

14.7.2000

Cher Alexandre,

Grosses bises d'Edimbourg! Cela fait trois jours que nous sommes ici et nous n'avons pas encore vu la pluie! Espérons que ça va durer. La vieille ville est très belle et du château on a une vue splendide jusqu'à l'estuaire. Et en Normandie, comment ça va?

A bientôt pour des retrouvailles parisiennes.

Marie et Dominique

M. A. Pilnard

38 rue Glacière

75013 Paris

Letters

■ *Endings (informal):*
Bien amicalement,
Amitiés; A bientôt =
see you soon.

• •

Christmas and New Year wishes (informal)

- *On most personal letters French speakers do not put their address at the top of the letter. The date is given preceded by* le. *For the first day of the month* le 1er *is used. Generally, the name of the town in which the letter is written is placed before the date.*

① *The tradition of Christmas cards is much less widespread in France than in Great Britain. While Christmas greetings may be sent, it is more customary to send best wishes for the New Year in January.*

② *In the year 2000/2001 etc.* = en l'an 2000/2001 *etc., but* bonne année 2000/2001 *etc.*

Letters

le 18 décembre 1999①

Chers Steve et Michelle,

Nous vous souhaitons un Joyeux Noël① et une très bonne année 2000 ②! En espérant que ce nouveau millénaire vous apportera tout ce que vous désirez et que nous trouverons une occasion pour nous revoir!

Bises à vous deux,

Gérard

New Year wishes (formal)

le 5 janvier 2000

Je vous ① présente mes meilleurs vœux pour l'année 2000. Que cette année vous apporte, à vous et à votre famille, bonheur et prospérité.

Pierre Carlier

① *Note the use of the formal form* vous.

. . . .

Invitation (informal)

Invitations to parties are usually by word of mouth, but for more formal events such as weddings, invitations are sent out.

① *Note the use of the informal form* tu *betweeen good friends.*

Paris, le 28/04/00

Cher Denis,

Que fais-tu ① cet été? Pascal et moi avons décidé d'inviter tous les copains d'Orléans à nous rejoindre dans notre maison de Dordogne pour le weekend du 14 juillet. Il y aura fête au village avec bal populaire et feu d'artifice. Le petit vin du pays n'est pas mal non plus!

Nous comptons sur toi pour venir trinquer avec nous,

Bises,

Martine

Letters

■ *Endings (informal):* Bises *(= lots of love) is very informal and is appropriate for very good friends and family. Alternatives for close friends and family include* Bien à toi, Bons baisers *or affectionately* Je t'embrasse. *If the letter is addressed to more than one person use* Bien à vous *or* Je vous embrasse.

. . . .

Invitation (formal)

Christine et Félix Prévost
81 rue Esquemoise
59000 Lille

Lille, le 28 avril 2000

Chers amis,

Nous avons l'immense plaisir de vous annoncer le mariage de notre fils Victor et de mademoiselle Stéphanie Heusdens.

La cérémonie aura lieu à l'Hôtel de Ville à 15 heures le samedi 5 juin. Vous recevrez bientôt un faire-part et une invitation à dîner mais nous tenions à vous prévenir suffisamment tôt pour que vous puissiez arranger votre voyage. Nous espérons qu'il vous sera possible de vous joindre à nous.

Amicalement, ①

Christine et Félix

■ *In a more formal letter, especially where a reply is generally required, the sender's address is written on the left-hand side of the page. An alternative is in the centre of the page, particularly on printed stationery.*

① *Endings: Alternatives could be* Amitiés, Bien amicalement.

Accepting an invitation

Emilie Joly
2 rue de la Pompe
75016 Paris

le 16 mars 2000

Chère Madame Dubois,

Je vous ① remercie de bien vouloir me recevoir pour les deux premières semaines de juillet. Je serai très heureuse de vous revoir ainsi que Natalie, bien entendu. Nous avons passé un si bon séjour linguistique à Manchester l'été dernier que nous avions très envie de nous retrouver. Mes parents ne pouvant m'envoyer en Angleterre cette année, c'est avec un immense plaisir que j'accepte votre invitation.

Je vous prie de bien vouloir accepter, Madame, l'expression de mes sentiments les meilleurs,

Emilie

Letters

- In a more formal social letter where the correspondent is known personally by name it can be used in the opening greeting.

- The title of the person receiving the letter must be repeated in the closing formula. These formulas are more elaborate than in English, with a number of possible variations. Some of these are shown in the following letters in this section.

① Since the letter is from a young person to the mother of a friend, she uses the formal vous form and writes to her as Madame Dubois. Madame Dubois would address Emilie using tu.

. . . .

Replying to a job advertisement

- Address: The sender's address may be written or printed in the middle of the page or on the left-hand side. The address of the person receiving the letter is on the right-hand side or beneath the sender's address if it is in the central position. Where the name or job title of the person is known it is used in their address.

- Beginnings (formal): the standard opening for a business letter when the recipient is not personally known to you is Monsieur, Madame, Mademoiselle or Messieurs in the case of general correspondence to a company.

  If the person holds a very important position this can be used, e.g. Monsieur le Maire, Madame le Consul.

Alexander Smith
5, Winchester Drive
Stoke Gifford
Bristol BS34 8DP

Bristol, le 4 février 2000

Madame la Directrice
MEDIAPHOT
6 rue de la Victoire
62107 Calais

Madame,

L'annonce parue en page 13 dans 'Courrier Photo' concernant un poste de tireur m'a vivement intéressé. Je suis actuellement photographe indépendant mais je serais heureux de travailler à nouveau au sein d'une équipe d'entreprise. Je pense posséder l'expérience et les qualités requises pour vous donner toute satisfaction dans ce poste, comme vous pourrez le constater au vu de mon CV. Je suis de nationalité britannique mais je me débrouille bien en français. Je souhaite travailler à Calais car je vais prochainement me marier avec une Calaisienne.

Je me tiens à votre disposition pour un entretien éventuel, et vous prie d'agréer, Madame, l'expression de mes sentiments distingués.

A. Smith

P.J. ① : un CV avec photo ②

- Endings (formal): the form of address used in the opening should be inserted into the closing formula e.g. Madame, Monsieur le Maire, etc

  ① P.J. (pièce(s) jointe(s)) = enclosures (encl).

  ② In France prospective employers generally request a handwritten letter (lettre manuscrite) and a photograph to accompany an application or curriculum vitae.

. . . .

Curriculum Vitae

David Baker
67 Whiteley Avenue
St George
Bristol
BS5 6TW
Grande-Bretagne

Téléphone +44 (0)117 945 3421; Fax +44 (0)117 945 7225

e-mail dbaker@hotmail.com

Nationalité britannique

Né ① le 30.06.1979 à Londres

FORMATION ET DIPLOMES

1995: 'O Levels' dans sept matières (équivalent à un niveau de fin de Seconde)
John Radcliffe School, Croydon

1997: 'A Levels' en Mathématiques, Informatique, Allemand et Français
(équivalent au Baccalauréat)

EXPERIENCE PROFESSIONELLE

1998: Stage de quatre mois à Sempo-Informatik, Francfort au département
médias

1999: Contrat de formation de six mois à MEDIALAB, Paris (conception
d'images de synthèse)

DIVERS

Très bonne connaissance de l'outil informatique

Allemand et français courants

Permis de conduire

① *The feminine form* née *is used for a woman.*

■ *Where appropriate a heading* 'Situation de famille' *could give relevant personal details e.g.*
marié/-e, deux/trois enfants etc.; divorcé/-e, deux enfants; célibataire.

Letters

. . . .

Seeking a job as an au pair

Sally Paledra
5 Avon Crescent
Kenilworth
Warwickshire
CV8 2PQ

le 3 mars 2000

Madame,

Vos coordonnées m'ont été communiquées par l'agence 'Au Pair International', qui m'a demandé de vous écrire directement. Je suis en effet à la recherche d'un emploi au pair pour une période de neuf à dix mois à partir de septembre prochain.

J'aime beaucoup les enfants et ils apprécient également ma compagnie. J'ai une grande expérience du baby-sitting. J'ai aussi fait un stage d'un mois dans une crèche privée ①.

Je suis enthousiaste, discrète et je sais prendre des initiatives. J'ai étudié le français au lycée pendant cinq ans et je connais un peu la France pour y avoir passé des vacances à plusieurs reprises. J'ai aussi mon permis de conduire.

Dans l'espoir d'une réponse positive de votre part, je vous prie d'agréer, Madame, l'expression de mes salutations respectueuses.

S. Paledra

P.J. : un CV avec photo

---

① *Or be more specific, e.g.* pour des enfants de 3 mois à 3 ans.

■ *To supply references:* Vous trouverez également ci-joint les adresses de personnes pouvant fournir une lettre de recommandation *or* pouvant me recommander.

. . . .

Enquiry to a tourist office

M. et Mme Baude
13 La Faverolle
45000 Orléans

Syndicat d'initiative
de St Gervais
74170 Saint-Gervais-les-Bains

Orléans, le 24 mars 2000

Monsieur,

Nous vous serions reconnaissants de bien vouloir nous faire parvenir
toute la documentation dont vous disposez sur les villas de location à
proximité de la station thermale. Nous désirons également recevoir des
informations sur les activités de loisirs durant l'été.
Vous trouverez ci-joint une enveloppe timbrée ① pour la réponse.

Dans l'attente de votre réponse, je vous prie d'agréer, Monsieur,
l'expression de nos salutations distinguées.

J. Baude

Letters

① enveloppe timbrée = *stamped addressed envelope.*

■ Note that, unlike in English, a reference or the purpose of a business letter is placed, where
required, above the opening greeting. e.g. Objet: commande 99/08/21 *or* Réf: 000/23.

Letter-writing in French

....

Booking a hotel room

Miss Sylvia Daley
The Willows
49 North Terrace
Kings Barton
Nottinghamshire
NG8 4LQ
England

Hôtel Beauséjour
Chemin des Mimosas
06100 Grasse

le 8 avril 2000

Madame,

J'ai bien reçu le dépliant de votre hôtel et je vous en remercie.

Je souhaite réserver une chambre calme avec salle de bains, en pension complète ① pour la période du 7 au 18 juin. Pour les arrhes, je vous prie de m'informer de leur montant et des modalités de paiement possibles depuis la Grande-Bretagne.

En vous remerciant d'avance, je vous prie de croire, Madame, en mes sentiments les meilleurs.

S. Daley

① *Or* une chambre avec douche en demi-pension *or* avec petit déjeuner. *The term en suite does not exist for bathroom facilities in French.*

Letters

. . . .

Booking a campsite

Frances Good
22 Daniel Avenue
Caldwood
Leeds LS8 7RR
tel. 0113 2998767

Camping 'Les Embruns'
18 allée des Capucins
22116 Moëlan-sur-Mer

le 25 avril 2000

Monsieur,

Nous souhaitons réserver dans votre camping, pour la période du 2 au 15 juillet, deux emplacements de tente côte à côte ① et, si possible, pas trop loin de la plage ② . Il s'agit de deux tentes de deux personnes. Nous aurons également deux motos de 1000cc chacune.

Dès que nous aurons confirmation de votre part, nous vous adresserons le montant de la réservation.

Pouvez-vous nous indiquer à cet effet, les possibilités de paiement depuis l'étranger.

Veuillez croire, Monsieur, en l'expression de nos sentiments les meilleurs.

F. Good

① Or if you have a caravan un emplacement de caravane.

② Other requirements might be ombragé (shady), or abrité (sheltered).

Letters

. . . .

Cancelling a reservation

> *Mrs J. Warrington*
> *Downlands*
> *Steyning*
> *West Sussex*
> *BN44 6LZ*
>
> *Hôtel des Voyageurs*
> *9 cours Gambetta*
> *91949 Les Ulis*
>
> *le 15 février 2000*
>
> *Monsieur,*
>
> *Je suis au regret de devoir annuler la réservation de chambre pour deux personnes pour la nuit du 24 au 25 mars, que j'avais effectuée par téléphone le 18 janvier dernier.* ①
>
> *Je vous remercie de votre compréhension et vous prie d'agréer, Monsieur, l'expression de mes sentiments distingués.*
>
> *J. Warrington*

① *If reasons for the cancellation are specified these could include:* pour raisons de santé/de famille, en raison d'un décès dans la famille, *etc.*

Letters

Sending an e-mail

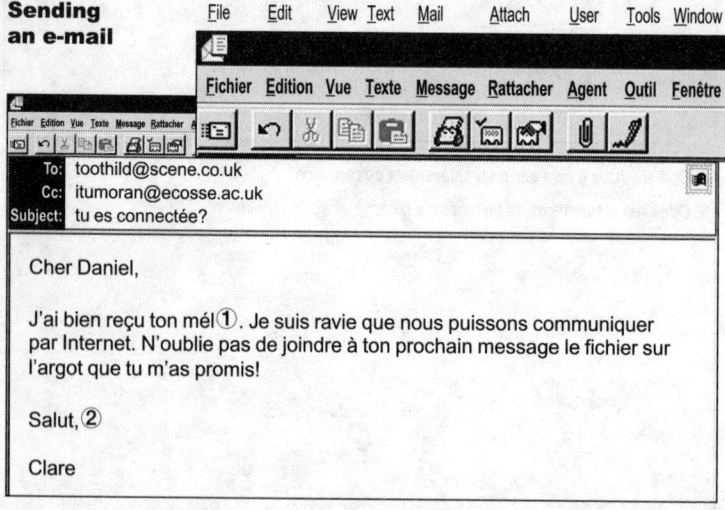

File   Edit   View Text   Mail   Attach   User   Tools Window

Fichier Edition Vue Texte Message Rattacher Agent Outil Fenêtre

To: toothild@scene.co.uk
Cc: itumoran@ecosse.ac.uk
Subject: tu es connectée?

Cher Daniel,

J'ai bien reçu ton mél①. Je suis ravie que nous puissons communiquer par Internet. N'oublie pas de joindre à ton prochain message le fichier sur l'argot que tu m'as promis!

Salut, ②

Clare

① *Note that* mél *is an abbreviated form of* message électronique. *To send an attachment =* joindre un fichier.

② *Endings (informal): An alternative could be* A bientôt *or simply* Bises *to a close friend in an informal context.*

a¹, A n (a) (letter) a, A m
(b) A (Mus) la m

a², an det un/une

■ Note The determiner or indefinite article *a* or *an* is translated by *un* + *masculine noun* and by *une* + *feminine noun*: *a tree* = un arbre; *a chair* = une chaise. There are, however, some cases where the article is not translated:
– with professions and trades: *her mother is a teacher* = sa mère est professeur;
– with other nouns used in apposition: *he's a widower* = il est veuf;
– with *what a*: *what a pretty house* = quelle jolie maison.
– When expressing prices in relation to weight, the definite article *le/la* is used in French: *ten francs a kilo* = dix francs le kilo. In other expressions where *a/an* means *per* the French translation is *par*: *twice a day* = deux fois par jour; but: *50 kilometres an hour* = 50 kilomètres/heure.

aback adv to be taken ~ être déconcerté/-e

abandon vtr abandonner ⟨person, hope⟩; renoncer à ⟨activity, attempt⟩

abbey n abbaye f

abbreviate vtr abréger (to en)

abbreviation n abréviation f

abdomen n abdomen m

abduct vtr enlever

abide vi to ~ by respecter ⟨rule, decision⟩

ability n (a) (capability) capacité f; to the best of one's ~ de son mieux
(b) (talent) talent m

able adj

■ Note *to be able to* meaning *can* is usually translated by the verb *pouvoir*. *I was not able to help him* = je ne pouvais pas l'aider.
– When *to be able to* implies the acquiring of a skill, *savoir* is used: *he's nine and he's still not able to read* = il a neuf ans et il ne sait toujours pas lire.

(a) to be ~ to do pouvoir faire; she was ~ to play the piano at the age of four elle savait jouer du piano à quatre ans
(b) ⟨lawyer, teacher⟩ compétent/-e; ⟨child⟩ doué/-e

able-bodied adj robuste, fort/-e

abnormal adj anormal/-e

abnormality n anomalie f

aboard ① adv à bord
② prep à bord de ⟨plane⟩; dans ⟨train⟩; ~ ship à bord

abolish vtr abolir ⟨law, right⟩; supprimer ⟨service, allowance⟩

abolition n (of law, right) abolition f; (of service) suppression f

abominable adj abominable

aborigine n aborigène mf

abort vtr faire avorter ⟨foetus⟩; interrompre ⟨plan⟩; abandonner ⟨computer program⟩

abortion n avortement m; to have an ~ se faire avorter

abortive adj ⟨attempt, project⟩ avorté/-e; ⟨coup, raid⟩ manqué/-e

about ① adj to be ~ to do être sur le point de faire
② adv (a) environ, à peu près; ~ an hour environ une heure; it's ~ the same c'est à peu près pareil; at ~ 6 pm vers 18 h; it's just ~ ready c'est presque prêt
(b) there was no-one ~ il n'y avait personne; there is a lot of flu ~ il y a beaucoup de grippes en ce moment; he's somewhere ~ il est dans les parages
③ prep (a) (concerning) a book ~ France un livre sur la France; what's it ~? (of book, film) ça parle de quoi?; may I ask what it's ~? pourriez-vous me dire de quoi il s'agit?; it's ~ my son au sujet de mon fils
(b) there's something odd ~ him il a quelque chose de bizarre; what I like ~ her is her honesty ce que j'aime chez elle c'est sa franchise
(c) (around) to wander ~ the streets errer dans les rues
(d) how *or* what ~ some tea? et si on prenait un thé?; how ~ going into town? et si on allait en ville?
(e) what ~ the legal costs? et les frais de justice?; what ~ you? et toi?
IDIOMS it's ~ time (that) somebody made an effort il serait temps que quelqu'un fasse un effort; ~ time too! ce n'est pas trop tôt! (colloq)

about-face n volte-face f inv

above ① prep au-dessus de; ~ the painting au-dessus du tableau; ~ it au-dessus; children ~ the age of 12 les enfants âgés de plus de 12 ans; ~ all else par-dessus tout; to hear sth ~ the shouting entendre qch au milieu des cris
② adj the ~ items les articles susmentionnés *or* figurant ci-dessus
③ adv (a) au-dessus; a desk with a shelf ~ un bureau avec une étagère au-dessus; the apartment ~ l'appartement du dessus
(b) (in text) see ~ voir ci-dessus
(c) (more) plus; children of 12 and ~ les enfants âgés de 12 ans et plus
④ above all phr surtout

above-mentioned adj susmentionné/-e

abrasive adj ⟨person, manner⟩ mordant/-e

a

abreast *adv* to walk three ~ marcher à trois de front; **to keep ~ of** se tenir au courant de

abroad *adv* à l'étranger; **from ~** de l'étranger

abrupt *adj* brusque

ABS *n* (*abbr* = **anti-lock braking system**) ABS; **~ brakes** freins *mpl* ABS

abscess *n* abcès *m*

abseiling *n* (GB) descente *f* en rappel

absence *n* absence *f*

absent *adj* absent/-e (**from** de)

absentee *n* absent/-e *m/f*

absent-minded *adj* distrait/-e

absolute *adj* absolu/-e

absolutely *adv* absolument

absorb *vtr* absorber; **~ed in one's work** plongé/-e dans son travail

absorbent *adj* absorbant/-e

abstain *vi* s'abstenir (**from** de)

abstract *adj* abstrait/-e

absurd *adj* absurde, ridicule

abundant *adj* abondant/-e

abuse ⒈ *n* (a) (maltreatment) mauvais traitement *m*; (sexual) sévices *mpl* (sexuels) (b) (of alcohol, power) abus *m*; **drug ~** usage *m* des stupéfiants (c) (insults) injures *fpl* ⒉ *vtr* (a) (hurt) maltraiter; (sexually) abuser de ⟨*woman*⟩; exercer des sévices sexuels sur ⟨*child*⟩ (b) abuser de ⟨*position, power, trust*⟩ (c) (insult) injurier

abusive *adj* ⟨*person*⟩ grossier/-ière; ⟨*words*⟩ injurieux/-ieuse

abyss *n* abîme *m*

academic ⒈ *n* universitaire *mf* ⒉ *adj* (a) ⟨*career, book*⟩ universitaire; ⟨*year*⟩ académique (b) (theoretical) théorique

academy *n* (school) école *f*; (learned society) académie *f*

accelerate *vi* accélérer

accelerator *n* accélérateur *m*

accent *n* accent *m*

accentuate *vtr* souligner

accept *vtr* (gen) accepter; (tolerate) admettre

acceptable *adj* acceptable

acceptance *n* acceptation *f*

access ⒈ *n* accès *m*; **to have ~ to** avoir accès à ⟨*information, funds, place*⟩ ⒉ *vtr* accéder à ⟨*database, information*⟩

accessible *adj* accessible (**to** à)

accessory *n* accessoire *m*; (on car) extra *m*

accident *n* accident *m*; **car/road ~** accident de voiture/de la route; **by ~** accidentellement; (by chance) par hasard

accidental *adj* (a) ⟨*death*⟩ accidentel/-elle (b) ⟨*mistake*⟩ fortuit/-e

accidentally *adv* (a) (by accident) accidentellement (b) (by chance) par hasard

accident-prone *adj* sujet/-ette aux accidents

accommodate *vtr* (a) (put up) loger (b) (hold, provide space for) contenir (c) (adapt to) s'adapter à ⟨*change, view*⟩ (d) (satisfy) satisfaire ⟨*need*⟩

accommodating *adj* accommodant/-e (**to** envers)

accommodation *n* (*also* **~s** (US)) logement *m*

accommodation officer *n* responsable *mf* de l'hébergement

accompany *vtr* accompagner

accomplice *n* complice *mf*

accomplish *vtr* accomplir ⟨*task, mission*⟩; réaliser ⟨*objective*⟩

accomplishment *n* réussite *f*

accord *n* accord *m*; **of my own ~** de moi-même

accordance: in accordance with *phr* ⟨*act*⟩ conformément à ⟨*rules, instructions*⟩; ⟨*be*⟩ conforme à ⟨*law, agreement*⟩

according: according to *phr* (a) ⟨*act*⟩ selon ⟨*law, principles*⟩; **~ to plan** comme prévu (b) d'après ⟨*newspaper, person*⟩

accordingly *adv* en conséquence

accordion *n* accordéon *m*

accost *vtr* (approach) aborder; (sexually) accoster

account ⒈ *n* (a) (in bank, post office, shop) compte *m* (**at, with** à); **in my ~** sur mon compte (b) **to take sth into ~, to take ~ of sth** tenir compte de qch (c) (description) compte-rendu *m* (d) **on ~ of** à cause de; **on no ~** sous aucun prétexte; **on my ~** à cause de moi ⒉ **accounts** *n pl* (a) (records) comptabilité *f*, comptes *mpl* (b) (department) (service *m*) comptabilité *f* ■ **account for** (a) (explain) expliquer ⟨*fact, behaviour*⟩; justifier ⟨*expense*⟩ (b) (represent) représenter ⟨*proportion, percentage*⟩

accountable *adj* responsable (**to** devant; **for** de)

accountancy *n* comptabilité *f*

accountant *n* comptable *mf*

account holder *n* titulaire *mf*

account number *n* numéro *m* de compte

accumulate ⒈ *vtr* accumuler ⒉ *vi* s'accumuler

accuracy *n* (of figures, watch) justesse *f*; (of map, aim) précision *f*; (of forecast) exactitude *f*

accurate *adj* ⟨*figures, watch, information*⟩ juste; ⟨*report, map, forecast*⟩ exact/-e

accurately *adv* ⟨*calculate*⟩ exactement; ⟨*report*⟩ avec exactitude; ⟨*assess*⟩ précisément

accusation *n* accusation *f*

accuse *vtr* accuser (**of** de)

accused n the ~ l'accusé/-e m/f

accuser n accusateur/-trice m/f

accustomed adj (a) to be ~ to sth/to doing avoir l'habitude de qch/de faire (b) (usual) habituel/-elle

ace n as m

ache ⓵ n douleur f (in à)
⓶ vi ⟨person⟩ avoir mal; my back ~s j'ai mal au dos

achieve vtr atteindre ⟨aim⟩; atteindre à ⟨perfection⟩; obtenir ⟨result⟩; réaliser ⟨ambition⟩

achievement n réussite f

aching adj ⟨body, limbs⟩ douloureux/-euse

acid n, adj acide (m)

acid rain n pluies fpl acides

acknowledge vtr admettre ⟨fact⟩; reconnaître ⟨error, problem, authority⟩; accuser réception de ⟨letter⟩

acknowledgement ⓵ n (a) (of error, guilt) aveu m
(b) (confirmation of receipt) accusé m de réception
⓶ **acknowledgements** n pl (in book) remerciements mpl

acne n acné f

acorn n gland m

acoustic adj acoustique

acoustic guitar n guitare f sèche

acoustics n pl the ~ are good l'acoustique f est bonne

acquaintance n connaissance f (with de)

acquainted adj to be ~ se connaître; to get or become ~ with sb faire la connaissance de qn; to get or become ~ with sth découvrir qch

acquiesce vi accepter; to ~ in sth donner son accord tacite à qch

acquire vtr acquérir ⟨expertise⟩; obtenir ⟨information⟩; faire l'acquisition de ⟨possessions⟩; acheter ⟨company⟩

acquit vtr (Law) acquitter; to be ~ted être disculpé/-e (of de)

acre n acre f, ≈ demi-hectare m

acrobat n acrobate mf

acrobatics n pl acrobaties fpl

across ⓵ prep (a) a journey ~ the desert un voyage à travers le désert; the bridge ~ the river le pont qui traverse la rivière; to go or travel ~ sth traverser qch; she leaned ~ the table elle s'est penchée au-dessus de la table
(b) (on the other side of) de l'autre côté de; ~ the street (from me) de l'autre côté de la rue
⓶ adv to help sb ~ aider qn à traverser; to go ~ to sb aller vers qn; to look ~ at sb regarder dans la direction de qn
⓷ **across from** phr en face de

acrylic n acrylique m

act ⓵ n (a) acte m; an ~ of kindness un acte de bonté
(b) (Law) loi f; Act of Parliament loi votée par le Parlement

(c) (in show) numéro m
(d) to put on an ~ jouer la comédie
⓶ vtr jouer ⟨part, role⟩
⓷ vi (a) (take action) agir
(b) (behave) agir, se comporter
(c) ⟨actor⟩ jouer, faire du théâtre
(d) (pretend) jouer la comédie, faire semblant
(e) (take effect) ⟨drug⟩ agir
(f) to ~ as ⟨person, object⟩ servir de
■ **act out** jouer ⟨role, part⟩; réaliser ⟨fantasy⟩

acting ⓵ n (performance) jeu m, interprétation f; (occupation) métier m d'acteur; I've done some ~ j'ai fait du théâtre
⓶ adj ⟨director, manager⟩ intérimaire

action n (a) (gen) action f; (steps) mesures fpl; to take ~ agir, prendre des mesures (against contre); to put a plan into ~ mettre un projet à exécution ~s speak louder than words mieux vaut agir que parler
(b) (fighting) action f, combat m; killed in ~ tué/-e au combat
(c) (in filming) action f; ~! moteur!

action film n film m d'action

action group n groupe m de pression

action-packed adj ⟨film⟩ plein/-e d'action; ⟨holiday⟩ bien rempli/-e

action replay n (GB) répétition f d'une séquence

activate vtr faire démarrer ⟨system⟩; actionner ⟨switch⟩; déclencher ⟨alarm⟩

active adj ⟨person, life⟩ actif/-ive; ⟨volcano⟩ en activité

activist n activiste mf

activity n activité f

activity holiday n (GB) ≈ vacances fpl sportives

actor n acteur m, comédien m

actress n actrice f, comédienne f

actual adj ⟨circumstances⟩ réel/réelle; ⟨words⟩ exact/-e; in ~ fact en fait; the ~ problem le problème lui-même

actually adv (a) (in fact) en fait; their profits have ~ risen en fait, leurs bénéfices ont augmenté; ~, I don't feel like it à vrai dire je n'en ai pas envie
(b) (really) vraiment; yes, it ~ happened! mais oui, c'est vraiment arrivé!

acupuncture n acupuncture f

acute adj (a) ⟨anxiety, pain⟩ vif/vive; ⟨boredom⟩ profond/-e
(b) ⟨illness⟩ aigu/aiguë
(c) ⟨mind⟩ pénétrant/-e
(d) ⟨accent, angle⟩ aigu/aiguë

ad n (abbr = **advertisement**) (a) (small) ~ (petite) annonce f (for pour)
(b) (on radio, TV) pub f (colloq) (for pour)

AD (abbr = **Anno Domini**) ap J.-C.

adamant adj catégorique (about sur); he is ~ that il maintient que

adapt ⓵ vtr adapter (to à; for pour; from de)
⓶ vi ⟨person⟩ s'adapter (to à)

a

adaptable adj souple

adapter, adaptor n adaptateur m

add vtr **(a)** ajouter, rajouter (onto, to à) **(b)** (also ∼ **together**) additionner ⟨numbers⟩; **to** ∼ **sth to** ajouter qch à ⟨figure, total⟩
■ **add up:** ¶ ∼ **up** ⟨facts, figures⟩ s'accorder; **to** ∼ **up to** s'élever à ⟨total⟩; ¶ ∼ **up [sth]** additionner ⟨cost, numbers⟩

adder n (snake) vipère f

addict n **(a)** (drug-user) toxicomane mf **(b)** (of TV, coffee) accro mf (colloq) (of de)

addicted adj **to be** ∼ (to alcohol, drugs) avoir une dépendance (to à); (to TV, coffee) être accro (colloq) (to de)

addiction n dépendance f (to à)

addictive adj ⟨drug, substance⟩ qui crée une dépendance; **to be** ∼ ⟨chocolate, power⟩ être comme une drogue

addition ⊡ n **(a)** (to list, house) ajout m **(b)** (in mathematics) addition f ⊡ **in addition** phr en plus

additional adj supplémentaire

additive n additif m

add-on adj supplémentaire

address ⊡ n adresse f; **to change (one's)** ∼ changer d'adresse ⊡ vtr **(a)** mettre l'adresse sur ⟨parcel, letter⟩; **to** ∼ **sth to sb** adresser qch à qn **(b)** (speak to) s'adresser à ⟨group⟩ **(c)** (aim) adresser ⟨remark, complaint⟩ (to à)

address book n carnet m d'adresses

adenoids n pl végétations fpl (adénoïdes)

adept adj expert/-e (at en)

adequate adj **(a)** (sufficient) suffisant/-e **(b)** (satisfactory) satisfaisant/-e

adhere vi adhérer (to à)

adhesive ⊡ n colle f, adhésif m ⊡ adj collant/-e; ∼ **tape** papier m collant, Scotch® m

adjacent adj contigu/contiguë; ∼ **to sth** attenant à qch

adjective n adjectif m

adjourn vtr ajourner ⟨trial⟩ (for pour; until à)

adjudicate vtr juger ⟨contest⟩; examiner ⟨case, claim⟩

adjust ⊡ vtr régler ⟨component, level, position, speed⟩; ajuster ⟨price, rate⟩; rajuster ⟨clothing⟩; modifier ⟨figures⟩ ⊡ vi ⟨person⟩ s'adapter (to à)

adjustable adj réglable

adjustment n **(a)** (of rates) rajustement m (of de); (of controls, machine) réglage m (of de) **(b)** (mental) adaptation f (to à) **(c)** (modification) modification f; **to make** ∼**s to** apporter des modifications à ⟨system, machine⟩

ad-lib vtr, vi improviser

administer vtr (also **administrate**) gérer ⟨company, affairs, estate⟩; gouverner ⟨territory⟩

administration n (gen) administration f; (paperwork) travail m administratif

administrative adj administratif/-ive

administrator n administrateur/-trice m/f

admirable adj admirable

admiral n amiral m

admiration n admiration f (for pour)

admire vtr admirer

admirer n admirateur/-trice m/f

admission n **(a)** (entry) entrée f, admission f (to dans); 'no ∼' 'entrée interdite' **(b)** (fee) (droit m d')entrée f **(c)** (confession) aveu m; **an** ∼ **of guilt** un aveu de culpabilité

admissions office n (Univ) service m d'inscriptions

admit vtr **(a)** reconnaître, admettre ⟨mistake, fact⟩; **to** ∼ **that...** reconnaître que...; **to** ∼ **to** reconnaître, admettre ⟨mistake, fact⟩ **(b)** (confess) reconnaître ⟨guilt⟩; **to** ∼ **to sth/doing** avouer qch/avoir fait **(c)** (let in) laisser entrer ⟨person⟩ (into dans); **to be** ∼**ted to hospital** être hospitalisé/-e

admittance n accès m, entrée f; 'no ∼' 'accès interdit au public'

admittedly adv il est vrai, il faut en convenir

adolescent ⊡ n adolescent/-e m/f ⊡ adj **(a)** (gen) adolescent/-e; ⟨crisis, rebellion⟩ d'adolescent; ⟨problem⟩ des adolescents **(b)** (childish) puéril/-e

adopt vtr adopter

adopted adj ⟨child⟩ adopté/-e; ⟨son, daughter⟩ adoptif/-ive

adoption n adoption f

adorable adj adorable

adore vtr adorer (doing faire)

adoring adj ⟨husband⟩ épris/-e; ⟨fan⟩ passionné/-e

adrenalin(e) n adrénaline f

Adriatic (Sea) pr n **the** ∼ la mer f Adriatique, l'Adriatique f

adrift adj, adv ⟨person, boat⟩ à la dérive; **to come** ∼ se détacher (of, from de)

adult ⊡ n adulte mf ⊡ adj (gen) adulte; ⟨life⟩ d'adulte; ⟨film, magazine⟩ pour adultes

adultery n adultère m (with avec)

adulthood n âge m adulte

advance ⊡ n **(a)** (forward movement) avance f; (progress) progrès m **(b)** (sum of money) avance f, acompte m (on sur) **(c) to make** ∼**s to sb** (gen) faire des démarches auprès de qn; (sexually) faire des avances à qn ⊡ vtr **(a)** avancer ⟨sum of money⟩ **(b)** faire avancer ⟨career, research⟩; servir ⟨cause, interests⟩

3 *vi* (a) (move forward) ⟨*person*⟩ avancer, s'avancer (**on, towards** vers); (Mil) ⟨*army*⟩ avancer (**on** sur)
(b) (progress) progresser, faire des progrès
4 **in advance** *phr* à l'avance

advanced *adj* ⟨*course, class*⟩ supérieur/-e; ⟨*student, stage*⟩ avancé/-e; ⟨*equipment, technology*⟩ de pointe, perfectionné/-e

advance warning *n* préavis *m*

advantage *n* (a) avantage *m*; **it is to our ~ to do** il est dans notre intérêt de faire
(b) (asset) atout *m*
(c) **to take ~ of** utiliser, profiter de ⟨*situation, offer, service*⟩; exploiter ⟨*person*⟩

advantageous *adj* avantageux/-euse

advent *n* (gen) apparition *f* (**of** de); **Advent** (prior to Christmas) l'Avent *m*

adventure *n* aventure *f*

adventure holiday *n* vacances *fpl* 'aventure'

adventurous *adj* aventureux/-euse

adverb *n* adverbe *m*

adverse *adj* ⟨*reaction, conditions, publicity*⟩ défavorable; ⟨*effect, consequences*⟩ négatif/-ive

advert *n* (GB) (colloq) (in paper) annonce *f*; (small ad) petite annonce *f*; (on TV, radio) pub *f* (colloq), spot *m* publicitaire

advertise **1** *vtr* faire de la publicité pour ⟨*product, event, service*⟩; mettre *or* passer une annonce pour ⟨*car, house, job*⟩
2 *vi* (a) (for publicity) faire de la publicité
(b) (in small ads) passer une annonce

advertisement *n* (a) (for product, event) publicité *f* (**for** pour); **a good/bad ~ for** une bonne/mauvaise publicité pour
(b) (to sell house, get job) annonce *f*; (in small ads) petite annonce *f*

advertising *n* publicité *f*

advertising agency *n* agence *f* de publicité

advertising campaign *n* campagne *f* publicitaire

advice *n* conseils *mpl* (**on** sur; **about** à propos de); **a piece of ~** un conseil; **it was good ~** c'était un bon conseil

advisable *adj* **it is ~ to do** il est recommandé de faire

advise *vtr* (a) conseiller, donner des conseils à (**about** sur); **to ~ sb to do** conseiller à qn de faire; **to ~ sb against doing** déconseiller à qn de faire
(b) recommander ⟨*rest, course of action*⟩
(c) (inform) **to ~ sb (of)** aviser qn (de)

adviser, **advisor** *n* conseiller/-ère *m/f* (**to** auprès de)

advisory service *n* service *m* d'aide et de conseil

Aegean (Sea) *pr n* **the ~** la mer Égée

aerial **1** *n* antenne *f*
2 *adj* aérien/-ienne

aerobics *n* aérobic *m*

aeroplane *n* (GB) avion *m*

aerosol *n* bombe *f* aérosol

aesthetic, **esthetic** (US) *adj* esthétique

affair *n* (a) affaire *f*; **state of ~s** situation *f*
(b) (relationship) liaison *f* (**with** avec)

affect *vtr* (a) (have effect on) avoir une incidence sur ⟨*price*⟩; affecter, avoir des conséquences pour ⟨*career, environment*⟩; affecter, toucher ⟨*region, population*⟩; influer sur ⟨*decision, outcome*⟩
(b) (emotionally) émouvoir
(c) (Med) atteindre ⟨*person*⟩; affecter ⟨*health, heart*⟩

affection *n* affection *f* (**for sb** pour qn)

affectionate *adj* affectueux/-euse

affinity *n* (a) (attraction) attirance *f* (**with, for** pour)
(b) (resemblance) ressemblance *f*

affinity card *n* carte *f* de fidélité

affluence *n* richesse *f*

afford *vtr* (a) (financially) **to be able to ~ sth** avoir les moyens d'acheter qch; **if I can ~ it** si j'ai les moyens; **I can't ~ to pay the rent** je n'ai pas les moyens de payer le loyer
(b) (spare) **to be able to ~** disposer de ⟨*time*⟩
(c) (risk) **to be able to ~** se permettre qch/de faire; **he can't ~ to wait** il ne peut pas se permettre d'attendre

affordable *adj* ⟨*price*⟩ abordable

afield *adv* **far ~** loin; **further ~** plus loin

afloat *adj, adv* **to stay ~** ⟨*person, object*⟩ rester à la surface (de l'eau); ⟨*boat*⟩ rester à flot

afraid *adj* (a) (scared) **to be ~** avoir peur (**of** de; **to do, of doing** de faire)
(b) (anxious) **she was ~ (that) there would be an accident** elle craignait un accident; **I'm ~ it might rain** je crains qu'il (ne) pleuve
(c) **I'm ~ I can't come** je suis désolé mais je ne peux pas venir; **I'm ~ so/not** je crains que oui/non

afresh *adv* à nouveau

Africa *pr n* Afrique *f*; **to ~** en Afrique

African **1** *n* Africain/-e *m/f*
2 *adj* africain/-e; ⟨*elephant*⟩ d'Afrique

African-American *n* Afro-américain/-e *m/f*

Afro-Caribbean *adj* antillais/-e

after **1** *adv* après; **soon** *or* **not long ~** peu après; **the year ~** l'année suivante *or* d'après; **the day ~** le lendemain
2 *prep* (a) après; **shortly ~ the strike** peu après la grève; **~ that** après (cela); **the day ~ tomorrow** après-demain; **to tidy up ~ sb** ranger derrière qn; **to ask ~ sb** demander des nouvelles de qn; **~ you!** après vous!
(b) **that's the house they're ~** c'est la maison qu'ils veulent acheter; **the police are ~ him** il est recherché par la police
(c) **year ~ year** tous les ans; **it was one disaster ~ another** on a eu catastrophe sur catastrophe
(d) **we called her Kate ~ my mother** nous l'avons appelée Kate comme ma mère ···>

(e) (US) **it's twenty ~ eleven** il est onze heures vingt

3 *conj* **(a)** (in the past) après avoir *or* être (+ *pp*), après que (+ *indicative*): **~ he had consulted Bill, he left** après avoir consulté Bill, il est parti; **~ he had changed she brought him to the office** après qu'il se fut changé, elle le conduisit au bureau; **~ we married/he left** après notre mariage/son départ

(b) (in the future) quand, une fois que

(c) why did he do that ~ we'd warned him? pourquoi a-t-il fait ça alors que nous l'avions prévenu?

4 after all *phr* après tout

after-effect *n* (Med) contrecoup *m*; (figurative) répercussion *f*

aftermath *n* conséquences *fpl*; **in the ~ of** à la suite de ⟨*war, scandal, election*⟩

afternoon *n* après-midi *m or f inv*; **in the ~** (dans) l'après-midi; **on Friday ~(s)** le vendredi après-midi; **good ~!** bonjour!

after-sales service *n* service *m* après-vente

after-shave *n* après-rasage *m*

aftershock *n* secousse *f* secondaire

after-sun *adj* après-soleil *inv*

aftertaste *n* arrière-goût *m*

afterthought *n* pensée *f* après coup

afterwards, afterward (US) *adv* **(a)** (after) après; **straight ~** tout de suite après

(b) (later) plus tard

again *adv* encore;

■ **Note** When used with a verb, *again* is often translated by adding the prefix *re* to the verb in French: *to start again* = recommencer; *to marry again* = se remarier; *I'd like to read that book again* = j'aimerais relire ce livre; *she never saw them again* = elle ne les a jamais revus. You can check *re*+ verbs by consulting the French side of the dictionary.

– For other uses of *again*, see below.

sing it ~! chante-le encore!; **once ~** encore une fois; **yet ~ he refused** il a encore refusé; **when you are well ~** quand tu seras rétabli; **I'll never go there ~** je n'y retournerai jamais; **~ and ~** à plusieurs reprises

against *prep* contre; **~ the wall** contre le mur; **I'm ~ it** je suis contre; **to be ~ doing** être contre l'idée de faire; **the pound fell ~ the dollar** la livre a baissé par rapport au dollar; **~ a background of** sur un fond de; **~ the light** à contre-jour

age **1** *n* **(a)** âge *m*; **to come of ~** atteindre la majorité; **to be under ~** (Law) être mineur/-e

(b) (era) ère *f*, époque *f* (of de); **the video ~** l'ère de la vidéo; **in this day and ~** à notre époque

(c) (colloq) **it's ~s since I've played golf** ça fait une éternité que je n'ai pas joué au golf; **I've been waiting for ~s** j'attends depuis des heures

2 *vtr, vi* vieillir

aged *adj* **(a)** **~ between 20 and 25** âgé/-e de 20 à 25 ans; **a boy ~ 12** un garçon de 12 ans

(b) (old) âgé/-e

age group *n* tranche *f* d'âge

ageism *n* discrimination *f* en raison de l'âge

agency *n* agence *f*

agenda *n* ordre *m* du jour

agent *n* agent *m* (**for sb** de qn)

aggravate *vtr* (make worse) aggraver; (annoy) exaspérer

aggression *n* (gen) agression *f*; (of person) agressivité *f*

aggressive *adj* agressif/-ive

aggro *n* (colloq) (violence) violence *f*; (hostility) hostilité *f*

agile *adj* agile

agitate *vi* faire campagne (**for** pour)

agitated *adj* agité/-e, inquiet/-iète

AGM *n* (*abbr* = **annual general meeting**) assemblée *f* générale annuelle

agnostic *n, adj* agnostique (*mf*)

ago *adv* **three weeks ~** il y a trois semaines; **long ~** il y a longtemps; **how long ~?** il y a combien de temps?; **not long ~** il y a peu de temps

agonize *vi* se tourmenter (**over, about** à propos de)

agonizing *adj* ⟨*pain, death*⟩ atroce; ⟨*choice*⟩ déchirant/-e

agony *n* (physical) douleur *f* atroce; (mental) angoisse *f*

agony aunt *n* journaliste *mf* responsable du courrier du cœur

agony column *n* courrier *m* du cœur

agree **1** *vtr* **(a)** (concur) être d'accord (**that** sur le fait que)

(b) (admit) convenir (**that** que)

(c) (consent) **to ~ to do** accepter de faire; **she ~d to speak to me** elle a accepté de me parler

(d) (settle on, arrange) se mettre d'accord sur ⟨*date, price*⟩; **to ~ to do** convenir de faire

2 *vi* **(a)** (hold same opinion) être d'accord (**with** avec; **about, on** sur; **about doing** pour faire); **I ~!** 'je suis bien d'accord!'

(b) (reach mutual understanding) se mettre d'accord (**about, on** sur)

(c) (consent) accepter; **to ~ to** consentir à ⟨*suggestion, terms*⟩

(d) (hold with, approve) **to ~ with** approuver ⟨*belief, idea, practice*⟩

(e) (tally) ⟨*stories, statements, figures*⟩ concorder (**with** avec)

(f) (suit) **to ~ with sb** ⟨*climate*⟩ être bon/bonne pour qn; ⟨*food*⟩ réussir à qn

(g) (in grammar) s'accorder (**with** avec; **in** en)

3 agreed *pp adj* convenu/-e; **is that ~d?** c'est entendu?

agreeable *adj* agréable

agreement *n* **(a)** accord *m* (**to do** pour faire); **to reach an ~** parvenir à un accord

(b) (undertaking) engagement *m*

(c) (contract) contrat *m*

(d) (in grammar) accord m

agricultural adj agricole

agriculture n agriculture f

aground adv to run ~ s'échouer

ahead ▢1 adv (a) ⟨run⟩ en avant; **to send sb on ~** envoyer qn en éclaireur; **to send one's luggage on ~** faire envoyer ses bagages; **a few kilometres ~** à quelques kilomètres
(b) (in time) **in the months ~** pendant les mois à venir
(c) (in leading position) **to be ~ in the polls** être en tête des sondages; **to be 30 points ~** avoir 30 points d'avance
▢2 **ahead of** phr (a) (in front of) devant ⟨person, vehicle⟩; **to be three metres ~ of sb** avoir trois mètres d'avance sur qn
(b) **to be ~ of sb** (in polls, ratings) avoir un avantage sur qn; **to be ~ of the others** ⟨pupil⟩ être plus avancé/-e que les autres

aid ▢1 n aide f (from de; to, for à); **in ~ of** au profit de ⟨charity⟩
▢2 adj ⟨organization⟩ d'entraide
▢3 vtr aider ⟨person⟩ (to do à faire); faciliter ⟨digestion, recovery⟩

aid agency n organisation f humanitaire

aide n aide mf, assistant/-e m/f

Aids n (abbr = **Acquired Immune Deficiency Syndrome**) sida m

Aids sufferer n sidéen/-éenne m/f

aid worker n employé/-e m/f d'une organisation humanitaire

aim ▢1 n (a) (purpose) but m
(b) (with weapon) **to take ~ at sb/sth** viser qn/qch
▢2 vtr (a) **to be ~ed at sb** ⟨campaign, product, remark⟩ viser qn
(b) braquer ⟨gun, camera⟩ (at sur); lancer ⟨ball, stone⟩ (at sur)
▢3 vi **to ~ for sth, to ~ at sth** viser qch; **to ~ at doing, to ~ to do** avoir l'intention de faire

air ▢1 n (a) (purpose) air m; **in the open ~** en plein air, au grand air; **to let the ~ out of sth** dégonfler qch; **he threw the ball up into the ~** il a jeté le ballon en l'air
(b) **to travel by ~** voyager par avion
(c) (on radio, TV) **to be/go on the ~** être/ passer à l'antenne
▢2 vtr (a) aérer ⟨garment, room, bed⟩
(b) exprimer ⟨opinion, view⟩; **to ~ one's grievances** exposer ses griefs
IDIOMS **to put on ~s** se donner de grands airs; **to vanish into thin ~** se volatiliser

air ambulance n avion m sanitaire

airbag n airbag m

air bed n (GB) matelas m pneumatique

air-conditioned adj climatisé/-e

air-conditioning n climatisation f, air m conditionné

aircraft n avion m, aéronef m

aircrew n équipage m d'un avion

airfare n tarif m d'avion

airfield n aérodrome m, terrain m d'aviation

air force n armée f de l'air, forces fpl aériennes

air-freshener n désodorisant m d'atmosphère

air gun n fusil m à air comprimé

airhead n (colloq) évaporé/-e m/f

air hostess n hôtesse f de l'air

airline n compagnie f aérienne

airmail n poste f aérienne; **by ~** par avion

airplane n (US) avion m

airport n aéroport m

air raid n attaque f aérienne, raid m (aérien)

airstrike n frappe f aérienne

air terminal n (at airport) aérogare f; (in town) terminal m

airtight adj étanche à l'air

air-traffic controller n contrôleur/-euse m/f aérien/-ienne, aiguilleur m du ciel

air travel n voyages mpl aériens

airwaves n pl ondes fpl

airy adj (a) ⟨room⟩ clair/-e et spacieux/-ieuse
(b) ⟨manner⟩ désinvolte, insouciant/-e

aisle n (a) (in church) (side passage) bas-côté m; (centre passage) allée f centrale
(b) (in train, plane) couloir m; (in cinema, shop) allée f

ajar adj, adv entrouvert/-e, entrebaillé/-e

alarm ▢1 n (a) (warning) alarme f; **smoke ~** détecteur m de fumée
(b) (fear) frayeur f; (concern) inquiétude f
▢2 vtr inquiéter ⟨person⟩

alarm clock n réveille-matin m, réveil m

alarmed adj effrayé/-e

album n album m

alcohol n alcool m; **~-free** sans alcool; **~ content** teneur f en alcool

alcoholic ▢1 n alcoolique mf
▢2 adj ⟨drink⟩ alcoolisé/-e; ⟨stupor⟩ alcoolique

alcoholism n alcoolisme m

alcopop n soda m alcoolisé

alcove n renfoncement m

ale n bière f

alert ▢1 n alerte f
▢2 adj (a) (lively) ⟨child⟩ éveillé/-e; ⟨adult⟩ alerte
(b) (attentive) vigilant/-e
▢3 vtr (a) alerter ⟨authorities⟩
(b) **to ~ sb to** mettre qn en garde contre ⟨danger⟩; attirer l'attention de qn sur ⟨fact, situation⟩

A-levels n pl (GB) (Sch) ≈ baccalauréat m

algebra n algèbre f

Algeria pr n Algérie f

alibi n (a) (Law) alibi m
(b) (excuse) excuse f

alien n (a) (gen, Law) étranger/-ère m/f (to à) ····❖

(b) (from space) extraterrestre *mf*

alienate *vtr* éloigner ⟨*supporters, colleagues*⟩

alight ① *adj* to set sth ∼ mettre le feu à qch
② *vi* ⟨*passenger*⟩ descendre (**from** de)

alike ① *adj* (identical) pareil/-eille; (similar) semblable; **to look** ∼ se ressembler
② *adv* ⟨*dress, think*⟩ de la même façon

alimony *n* pension *f* alimentaire

alive *adj* **(a)** vivant/-e, en vie; **to be burnt** ∼ être brûlé/-e vif/vive
(b) to come ∼ ⟨*party, place*⟩ s'animer; ⟨*history*⟩ prendre vie
(c) to be ∼ ⟨*tradition*⟩ être vivant/-e; ⟨*interest*⟩ être vif/vive
(d) ∼ **with** grouillant/-e de ⟨*insects*⟩

alkaline *adj* alcalin/-e

all

■ **Note** When *all* is used as a pronoun, it is generally translated by *tout*.
– When *all* is followed by a *that* clause, *all that* is translated by *tout ce que*: *after all* (*that*) *we've done* = après tout ce que nous avons fait.
– When referring to a specified group of people or objects, the translation of *all* reflects the number and gender of the people or objects referred to; *tous* is used for a group of people or objects of masculine or mixed or unspecified gender and *toutes* for a group of feminine gender: *we were all delighted* = nous étions tous ravis; '*where are the cups?*'—'*they're all in the kitchen*' = 'où sont les tasses?'—'elles sont toutes dans la cuisine'. ► 1
– In French, determiners agree in gender and number with the noun that follows: *all the time* = tout le temps; *all the family* = toute la famille; *all men* = tous les hommes; *all the books* = tous les livres; *all women* = toutes les femmes; *all the chairs* = toutes les chaises. ► 2
– As an adverb meaning *completely*, *all* is generally translated by *tout*: *he was all alone* = il était tout seul; *the girls were all excited* = les filles étaient tout excitées.
– However, when the adjective that follows is in the feminine and begins with a consonant the translation is *toute/toutes*: *she was all alone* = elle était toute seule; *the girls were all alone* = les filles étaient toutes seules. ► 3A
– For more examples and particular usages see the entry below.

① *pron* tout; **that's** ∼ **I want** c'est tout ce que je veux; **I spent it** ∼, **I spent** ∼ **of it** j'ai tout dépensé; ∼ **of our things** toutes nos affaires
② *det* tout/toute (+ *sg*); tous/toutes (+ *pl*); ∼ **those who came** (men, mixed group) tous ceux qui sont venus; (women) toutes celles qui sont venues; ∼ **his life** toute sa vie; ∼ **the time** tout le temps
③ *adv* **(a)** tout; **she's** ∼ **wet** elle est toute mouillée; ∼ **in white** tout en blanc; ∼ **along the canal** tout le long du canal; **to be** ∼ **for sth** être tout à fait pour qch; **tell me** ∼ **about it!** raconte-moi tout!
(b) (Sport) (they are) **six** ∼ (il y a) six partout

④ **all along** *phr* ⟨*know*⟩ depuis le début, toujours
⑤ **all the** *phr* ∼ **the more difficult** d'autant plus difficile; ∼ **the better!** tant mieux!
⑥ **all too** *phr* ⟨*easy, often*⟩ bien trop
⑦ **at all** *phr* **not at** ∼! (acknowledging thanks) de rien!; (answering query) pas du tout!; **it is not at** ∼ **certain** ce n'est pas du tout certain; **nothing at** ∼ rien du tout
⑧ **of all** *phr* **the easiest of** ∼ le plus facile; **first of** ∼ pour commencer

all clear *n* **to give sb the** ∼ donner le feu vert à qn (**to do** pour faire); ⟨*doctor*⟩ déclarer qn guéri/-e

allegation *n* allégation *f*

allege *vtr* **to** ∼ **that** (claim) prétendre que (+ *conditional*); (publicly) déclarer que (+ *conditional*); **it was** ∼**d that** il a été dit que

allegedly *adv* prétendument

allegiance *n* allégeance *f*

allergic *adj* allergique (**to** à)

allergist *n* allergologue *mf*

allergy *n* allergie *f* (**to** à)

alleviate *vtr* soulager ⟨*boredom, pain*⟩; réduire ⟨*overcrowding, stress*⟩

alley *n* (walkway) allée *f*; (for vehicles) ruelle *f*

alliance *n* alliance *f*

allied *adj* ⟨*group*⟩ allié/-e

all-important *adj* essentiel/-ielle

all-inclusive *adj* ⟨*fee, price*⟩ tout compris

all-in-one *adj* ⟨*garment*⟩ d'une seule pièce

all-night *adj* ⟨*party, meeting*⟩ qui dure toute la nuit; ⟨*service*⟩ ouvert/-e toute la nuit; ⟨*radio station*⟩ qui émet 24 heures sur 24

allocate *vtr* affecter ⟨*funds*⟩ (**for, to** à); accorder ⟨*time*⟩ (**to** à); assigner ⟨*tasks*⟩ (**to** à)

allot *vtr* attribuer ⟨*money*⟩ (**to** à); **in the** ∼**ted time** dans le temps imparti

allotment *n* (GB) parcelle *f* de terre

all-out *adj* ⟨*strike*⟩ total/-e; ⟨*attack*⟩ en règle; ⟨*effort*⟩ acharné/-e

all over ① *adj* fini/-e; **when it's** ∼ quand tout sera fini
② *adv* (everywhere) partout; **to be trembling** ∼ trembler de partout
③ *prep* partout dans ⟨*room, town*⟩; ∼ **China** partout en Chine

allow *vtr* **(a)** (authorize) permettre à, autoriser ⟨*person, organization*⟩ (**to do** à faire); **it isn't** ∼**ed** c'est interdit; **she isn't** ∼**ed to go out** elle n'a pas le droit de sortir
(b) (let) laisser; **he** ∼**ed the situation to get worse** il a laissé la situation s'aggraver
(c) (enable) **to** ∼ **sb/sth to do** permettre à qn/qch de faire; **it would** ∼ **the company to expand** cela permettrait à la société de s'agrandir
(d) (allocate) prévoir; **to** ∼ **two days for the job** prévoir deux jours pour faire le travail
(e) ⟨*referee*⟩ accorder ⟨*goal*⟩; ⟨*insurer*⟩ agréer ⟨*claim*⟩
(f) (condone) tolérer ⟨*rudeness, swearing*⟩
■ **allow for** tenir compte de

allowance n (a) (gen) allocation f; (from employer) indemnité f
(b) (tax) ~ abattement m fiscal
(c) (spending money) (for child) argent m de poche; (for student) argent m (pour vivre); (from trust, guardian) rente f
(d) your baggage ~ **is 40 kg** vous avez droit à 40 kg de bagages
(e) to make ~**(s) for sth** tenir compte de qch; **to make** ~**(s) for sb** essayer de comprendre qn

alloy wheel n jante f en alliage léger

all right, alright ① adj ⟨film, garment, place⟩ pas mal (colloq); **is my hair** ~? ça va mes cheveux?; **are you** ~? ça va?; **I'm** ~ **thanks** ça va merci; **is it** ~ **if…?** est-ce que ça va si…?
② adv (a) (giving agreement) d'accord
(b) ⟨work⟩ comme il faut; ⟨see, hear⟩ bien

all-round adj ⟨athlete⟩ complet/-ète; ⟨improvement⟩ général/-e

all-rounder n **to be a good** ~ être bon/ bonne en tout

all-time adj ⟨record⟩ absolu/-e; **the** ~ **greats** (people) les grands mpl; ~ **high record** m absolu

all told adv en tout

allusion n allusion f (**to** à)

ally ① n allié/-e m/f
② v refl **to** ~ **oneself with** s'allier avec

almond n (a) (nut) amande f
(b) (also ~ **tree**) amandier m

almost adv (a) (practically) presque; **we're** ~ **there** nous sommes presque arrivés; **it's** ~ **dark** il fait presque nuit
(b) he ~ **died/forgot** il a failli mourir/ oublier

alone ① adj seul/-e; **all** ~ tout seul/toute seule; **to leave sb** ~ laisser qn seul/-e; (in peace) laisser qn tranquille; **leave that bike** ~! ne touche pas à ce vélo!
② adv (a) ⟨work, live, travel⟩ seul/-e
(b) for this reason ~ rien que pour cette raison
IDIOMS to go it ~ (colloq) faire cavalier seul

along

■ Note When along is used as a preposition meaning all along it can usually be translated by le long de: there were trees along the road = il y avait des arbres le long de la route. For particular usages see the entry below.
– along is often used after verbs of movement. If the addition of along does not change the meaning of the verb, along will not be translated: as he walked along = tout en marchant.

① adv **to push sth** ~ pousser qch; **to be running** ~ courir; **I'll be** ~ **in a second** j'arrive tout de suite
② prep (a) (all along) le long de; **there were chairs** ~ **the wall** il y avait des chaises contre le mur
(b) to walk ~ **the beach** marcher sur la plage; **to look** ~ **the shelves** chercher dans les rayons; **halfway** ~ **the path** à mi-chemin

③ **along with** phr (accompanied by) accompagné/-e de; (at same time as) en même temps que

alongside ① prep (a) (all along) le long de
(b) to draw up ~ **sb** ⟨vehicle⟩ s'arrêter à la hauteur de qn
② adv à côté

aloud adv ⟨read⟩ à haute voix; ⟨think⟩ tout haut

alphabet n alphabet m

alphabetically adv par ordre alphabétique

alpine adj (also **Alpine**) alpin/-e

Alps pr n pl **the** ~ les Alpes fpl

already adv déjà; **it's 10 o'clock** ~ il est déjà 10 heures; **he's** ~ **left** il est déjà parti

alright = ALL RIGHT

Alsatian n (GB) (dog) berger m allemand

also adv aussi

alter ① vtr (a) changer ⟨person⟩; (radically) transformer ⟨person⟩; changer ⟨opinion, rule, timetable⟩; modifier ⟨amount, document⟩; affecter ⟨value, climate⟩
(b) retoucher ⟨dress, shirt⟩
② vi changer

alteration ① n modification f (**to, in** de)
② **alterations** n pl (building work) travaux mpl

alternate ① adj (a) (successive) ⟨chapters, layers⟩ en alternance
(b) (every other) **on** ~ **days** un jour sur deux
(c) (US) (other) autre
② vtr **to** ~ **sth and** or **with sth** alterner qch et qch
③ vi ⟨people⟩ se relayer; ⟨colours, patterns, seasons⟩ alterner (**with** avec)

alternately adv alternativement

alternative ① n (from two) alternative f, autre possibilité f; (from several) possibilité f; **to have no** ~ ne pas avoir le choix
② adj (a) ⟨date, flight, plan⟩ autre; ⟨accommodation, product⟩ de remplacement; ⟨solution⟩ de rechange
(b) (unconventional) alternatif/-ive

alternatively adv sinon; ~, **you can book by phone** vous avez aussi la possibilité de réserver par téléphone

alternative medicine n médecines fpl parallèles or douces

although conj bien que (+ subjunctive); ~ **he is shy** bien qu'il soit timide

altitude n altitude f

alto n (voice) (of female) contralto m; (of male) haute-contre f

altogether adv (a) (completely) complètement; **not** ~ **true** pas complètement vrai
(b) (in total) en tout; **how much is that** ~? ça fait combien en tout?

aluminium foil n papier m aluminium

always adv toujours; **he's** ~ **complaining** il n'arrête pas de se plaindre

Alzheimer's disease n maladie f d'Alzheimer

am adv (abbr = **ante meridiem**) **three ~** trois heures (du matin)

amalgamate ① vtr (merge) fusionner ‹companies, schools› **(with** avec; **into** en) ② vi ‹company, union› fusionner **(with** avec)

amateur ① n amateur m ② adj ‹sportsperson, musician› amateur; ‹sport› en amateur

amaze vtr surprendre; (stronger) stupéfier

amazed adj stupéfait/-e; **I'm ~ (that)** ça m'étonne que (+ subjunctive)

amazement n stupéfaction f

amazing adj extraordinaire

Amazon pr n Amazone m

ambassador n ambassadeur m

amber n (a) (resin, colour) ambre m (b) (GB) (traffic signal) orange m

ambiguous adj ambigu/ambiguë

ambition n ambition f **(to do** de faire)

ambitious adj ambitieux/-ieuse

ambulance n ambulance f; **~ crew** équipe f d'ambulanciers/-ières

ambush ① n embuscade f ② vtr tendre une embuscade à

amenable adj **~ to** ‹person› sensible à ‹reason, advice›

amend vtr amender ‹law›; modifier ‹document›

amendment n (to law) amendement m **(to** à); (to contract) modification f **(to** à)

amends n pl **to make ~** se racheter; **to make ~ for** réparer ‹damage›; **to make ~ to sb** (financially) dédommager qn

amenities n pl (of hotel) équipements mpl; (of house, sports club) installations fpl

America pr n Amérique f

American ① n (a) (person) Américain/-e m/f (b) (also **~ English**) américain m ② adj américain/-e; ‹embassy› des États-Unis

American Indian n Indien/-ienne m/f d'Amerique du Nord

amiable adj aimable **(to** avec)

amicable adj (friendly) amical/-e; **an ~ settlement** un arrangement à l'amiable

amiss ① adj **there is something ~** il y a quelque chose qui ne va pas ② adv **to take sth ~** prendre qch de travers

ammunition n munitions fpl

amnesty n amnistie f

among, amongst prep (a) (amidst) parmi; **~ the crowd** parmi la foule; **to be ~ friends** être entre amis (b) (one of) **~ the world's poorest countries** un des pays les plus pauvres du monde; **she was ~ those who survived** elle faisait partie des survivants; **to be ~ the first** être dans les premiers (c) (between) entre

amount n (of goods, food) quantité f; (of people, objects) nombre m; (of money) somme f; **a large ~ of** beaucoup de; **the full ~** le montant total

■ **amount to** (a) s'élever à ‹total› (b) (be equivalent to) revenir à ‹confession, betrayal›; **it ~s to the same thing** cela revient au même

amp n (a) (abbr = **ampere**) ampère m (b) (colloq) (abbr = **amplifier**) ampli m (colloq)

amphetamine n amphétamine f

ample adj (a) ‹provisions, resources› largement suffisant/-e **(for** pour); **there's ~ room** il y a largement la place (b) ‹proportions, bust› généreux/-euse

amplifier n amplificateur m

amputate vtr amputer; **to ~ sb's leg** amputer qn de la jambe

amuse ① vtr (a) (cause laughter) amuser; **to be ~d at** or **by** s'amuser de (b) (entertain) ‹game, story› distraire (c) (occupy) ‹activity, hobby› occuper ② v refl **to ~ oneself** (a) (entertain) se distraire (b) (occupy) s'occuper

amusement n (a) (mirth) amusement m **(at** face à) (b) (diversion) distraction f

amusement arcade n (GB) salle f de jeux électroniques

amusement park n parc m d'attractions

amusing adj amusant/-e

an ▶ A²

anachronism n anachronisme m

anaemic adj (Med) anémique

anaesthetic (GB), **anesthetic** (US) n, adj anesthésique (m)

anaesthetize (GB), **anesthetize** (US) vtr anesthésier

analogy n analogie f

analyse (GB), **analyze** (US) vtr analyser

analysis n analyse f

analytic(al) adj analytique

anarchist n, adj anarchiste (mf)

anarchy n anarchie f

anatomy n anatomie f

ancestor n ancêtre mf

anchor n ancre f; **to drop ~** jeter l'ancre

anchovy n anchois m

ancient adj (dating from BC) antique; (very old) ancien/-ienne; **~ Greek** grec ancien; **~ Greece** la Grèce antique; **~ monument** monument m historique

and conj et; **cups ~ plates** des tasses et des assiettes; **he stood up ~ went out** il s'est levé et il est sorti; **come ~ see** viens voir; **two hundred ~ sixty-two** deux cent soixante-deux; **faster ~ faster** de plus en plus vite

Andorra pr n Andorre f

angel n ange m

anger **1** n colère f (at devant; **towards** contre)
2 vtr mettre [qn] en colère ⟨person⟩

angle **1** n angle m
2 vi (a) (fish) pêcher (à la ligne)
(b) (colloq) **to ~ for sth** chercher à obtenir qch

Anglo-French adj anglo-français/-e, franco-britannique

angrily adv ⟨react, speak⟩ avec colère

angry adj ⟨person, expression⟩ furieux/-ieuse; ⟨scene, words⟩ de colère; **to be ~ (at or with sb)** être en colère (contre qn); **to get ~** se fâcher; **to make sb ~** mettre qn en colère

animal **1** n animal m, bête f
2 adj animal/-e

animal activist n militant/-e m/f pour les droits des animaux

animal experiment n expérience f sur les animaux

animal rights n pl droits mpl des animaux

animal testing n expérimentation f animale

animated adj animé/-e

animator n (cartoonist) animateur/-trice m/f

ankle n cheville f

ankle chain n chaîne f de cheville

ankle sock n socquette f

annex **1** n (also **annexe** (GB)) annexe f
2 vtr annexer ⟨territory, land, country⟩ (**to** à)

annihilate vtr anéantir

anniversary n anniversaire m (**of** de)

annotate vtr annoter

announce vtr annoncer (**that** que)

announcement n (a) (spoken) annonce f
(b) (written) avis m; (of birth, death) faire-part m inv

announcer n (on TV) speaker/-erine m/f; **radio ~** présentateur/-trice m/f de radio

annoy vtr ⟨person⟩ (by behaviour) agacer; (by opposing wishes) contrarier; ⟨noise⟩ gêner

annoyance n agacement m (**at** devant), contrariété f (**at** à cause de)

annoyed adj contrarié/-e (**at, by** par); (stronger) agacé/-e, fâché/-e (**at, by** par); **~ with sb** fâché/-e contre qn

annoying adj agaçant/-e (**to do** de faire)

annual **1** n (a) (book) album m (annuel)
(b) (plant) plante f annuelle
2 adj annuel/-elle

annually adv ⟨earn, produce⟩ par an; ⟨do, inspect⟩ tous les ans

anomaly n anomalie f

anonymous adj anonyme

anorak n anorak m

anorexia (nervosa) n anorexie f mentale

another

■ Note *Another* is translated by *un autre* or *une autre* according to the gender of the noun it

refers to: *another book* = un autre livre; *another chair* = une autre chaise.
– Note that *en* is always used with *un/une autre* in French to represent a noun that is understood: *that cake was delicious, can I have another (one)?* = ce gâteau était délicieux, est-ce que je peux en prendre un autre? For more examples and particular usages, see the entry below.

1 det (a) (an additional) un/-e autre, encore un/-e; **would you like ~ drink?** est-ce que tu veux un autre verre?; **I've broken ~ plate** j'ai encore cassé une assiette; **that will cost you ~ £5** cela vous coûtera 5 livres sterling de plus; **in ~ five weeks** dans cinq semaines
(b) (a different) un/-e autre; **~ time** une autre fois; **he has ~ job now** il a un nouveau travail maintenant
2 pron un/-e autre; **she had ~** elle en a pris un/-e autre; **one after ~** l'un/l'une après l'autre; **in one way or ~** d'une façon ou d'une autre

answer **1** n (gen) réponse f (**to** à); (to problem, puzzle) solution f (**to** à); **there's no ~** (to door) il n'y a personne; (on phone) ça ne répond pas; **the right/wrong ~** la bonne/ mauvaise réponse
2 vtr répondre à; **to ~ the door** aller or venir ouvrir la porte; **to ~ the phone** répondre au téléphone
3 vi (a) répondre; **to ~ to** répondre or correspondre à ⟨description⟩
(b) (be accountable) **to ~ to sb** être responsable devant qn

■ **answer back** répondre
■ **answer for** répondre de ⟨action, person⟩; **they have a lot to ~ for!** ils ont beaucoup de comptes à rendre!

answerable adj responsable (**to sb** devant qn; **for sth** de qch)

answering machine, **answerphone** n répondeur m (téléphonique)

ant n fourmi f

antagonize vtr (annoy) contrarier; (stronger) éveiller l'hostilité de

Antarctic **1** pr n **the ~** l'Antarctique m
2 adj antarctique

antelope n antilope f

antenatal adj prénatal/-e

antenatal class n (GB) cours m de préparation à l'accouchement

antenna n antenne f

anthropology n anthropologie f

anti **1** prep contre
2 **anti(-)** pref anti(-)

antibacterial adj antibactérien/-ienne

antibiotic n antibiotique m; **on ~s** sous antibiotiques

anticipate vtr (a) (foresee) prévoir, s'attendre à ⟨problem, delay⟩; **as ~d** comme prévu
(b) (guess in advance) anticiper ⟨needs, result⟩ ⋯⋗

a

(c) (pre-empt) devancer ⟨*person, act*⟩

anticipation n (a) (excitement) excitation f; (pleasure in advance) plaisir m anticipé
(b) (expectation) prévision f (of de)

anticlimax n déception f

anticlockwise adj, adv (GB) dans le sens inverse des aiguilles d'une montre

antidepressant n antidépresseur m

antidote n antidote m (to, for contre, à)

antihistamine n antihistaminique m

antique ① n (object) objet m ancien or d'époque; (furniture) meuble m ancien or d'époque
② adj ancien/-ienne

antique shop n magasin m d'antiquités

anti-Semitism n antisémitisme m

antiseptic n, adj antiseptique (m)

antisocial adj (a) ~ **behaviour** comportement m incorrect; (criminal behaviour) comportement m délinquant
(b) (reclusive) sauvage

anti-theft adj ⟨*lock, device*⟩ antivol inv

anti-virus software n logiciel m antivirus

antlers n pl bois mpl de cerf

anxiety n (a) (worry) grandes inquiétudes fpl (about à propos de; for pour); to be in a state of ~ être angoissé/-e
(b) (eagerness) désir m ardent (to do de faire)
(c) (in psychology) anxiété f

anxiety attack n crise f d'angoisse

anxious adj (a) (worried) très inquiet/-iète (about à propos de; for pour); to be ~ about doing s'inquiéter de faire
(b) ⟨*moment, time*⟩ angoissant/-e
(c) (eager) très désireux/-euse (to do de faire)

anxiously adv (a) (worriedly) avec inquiétude
(b) (eagerly) avec impatience

any

■ Note When *any* is used as a determiner in questions and conditional sentences it is translated by *du, de l', de la* or *des* according to the gender and number of the noun that follows: *is there any soap?* = y a-t-il du savon?; *is there any flour?* = y a-t-il de la farine?; *are there any questions?* = est-ce qu'il y a des questions?
– In negative sentences *any* is translated by *de* or *d'* (before a vowel or mute 'h'): *we don't have any money* = nous n'avons pas d'argent.
– When *any* is used as a pronoun in negative sentences and in questions it is translated by *en*: *we don't have any* = nous n'en avons pas; *have you got any?* = est-ce que vous en avez?
– For more examples and other uses see the entry below.

① det (a) (in questions, conditional sentences) du/ de l'/de la/des; is there ~ **tea**? est-ce qu'il y a du thé?; if you have ~ **money** si vous avez de l'argent
(b) (with negative) de, d'; I don't need ~ **advice** je n'ai pas besoin de conseils
(c) (no matter which) n'importe quel/quelle,

tout; ~ **pen will do** n'importe quel stylo fera l'affaire; you can have ~ **cup you like** vous pouvez prendre n'importe quelle tasse; I'm ready to help in ~ **way I can** je suis prêt à faire tout ce que je peux pour aider; come round and see me ~ **time** passe me voir quand tu veux
② pron, quantif (a) (in questions, conditional sentences) have you got ~? est-ce que vous en avez?; there is hardly ~ **left** il n'en reste presque pas; she doesn't like ~ **of them** (people) elle n'aime aucun d'entre eux/elles; (things) elle n'en aime aucun/-e
(c) (no matter which) n'importe lequel/laquelle; 'which colour would you like?'—'~' 'quelle couleur veux-tu?'—'n'importe laquelle'; ~ **of those pens** n'importe lequel de ces stylos; ~ **of them could do it** n'importe qui d'entre eux/elles pourrait le faire
③ adv have you got ~ **more of these?** est-ce que vous en avez d'autres?; do you want ~ **more wine?** voulez-vous encore du vin?; he doesn't live here ~ **more** il n'habite plus ici

anybody pron (also **anyone**) (a) (in questions, conditional sentences) quelqu'un; is there ~ **in the house?** est-ce qu'il y a quelqu'un dans la maison?; if ~ **asks, tell them I've gone out** si quelqu'un me cherche, dis que je suis sorti
(b) (with negative) personne; there wasn't ~ **in the house** il n'y avait personne dans la maison; I didn't have ~ **to talk to** il n'y avait personne avec qui j'aurais pu parler
(c) (no matter who) n'importe qui; ~ **could do it** n'importe qui pourrait le faire; ~ **who wants to, can go** tous ceux qui le veulent, peuvent y aller; ~ **can make a mistake** ça arrive à tout le monde de faire une erreur; ~ **would think you were deaf** c'est à croire que tu es sourd

anyhow adv (a) = ANYWAY A
(b) (carelessly) n'importe comment

anyone = ANYBODY

anything pron (a) (in questions, conditional sentences) quelque chose; is there ~ **to be done?** peut-on faire quelque chose?
(b) (with negative) rien; she didn't say ~ elle n'a rien dit; he didn't have ~ **to do** il n'avait rien à faire; don't believe ~ **he says** ne crois pas un mot de ce qu'il dit
(c) (no matter what) tout; ~ **is possible** tout est possible; she'll eat ~ elle mange tout; he was ~ **but happy** il n'était pas du tout heureux

anytime adv (also **any time**) n'importe quand; ~ **after 2 pm** n'importe quand à partir de 14 heures; ~ **you like** quand tu veux; he could arrive ~ **now** il pourrait arriver d'un moment à l'autre

anyway adv (a) (in any case) (also **anyhow**) de toute façon
(b) (all the same) quand même; I don't really like hats, but I'll try it on ~ je n'aime pas

vraiment les chapeaux, mais je vais quand même l'essayer; **thanks** ∼ merci quand même

(c) (at any rate) en tout cas; **we can't go out, not yet** ∼ nous ne pouvons pas sortir, pas pour l'instant en tout cas

(d) (well) '∼, **we arrived at the station...**' 'bref, nous sommes arrivés à la gare...'

anywhere adv **(a)** (in questions, conditional sentences) quelque part; **we're going to Spain, if** ∼ si on va quelque part, ce sera en Espagne

(b) (with negative) nulle part; **you can't go** ∼ tu ne peux aller nulle part; **there isn't** ∼ **to sit** il n'y a pas de place pour s'asseoir; **you won't get** ∼ **if you don't pass your exams** tu n'arriveras à rien si tu ne réussis pas tes examens; **crying isn't going to get you** ∼ ça ne t'avancera à rien de pleurer

(c) (no matter where) n'importe où; ∼ **you like** où tu veux; ∼ **in England** partout en Angleterre

apart ① adj, adv **(a)** (trees planted 10 metres ∼ des arbres plantés à 10 mètres d'intervalle

(b) (separated) séparé/-e; **we hate being** ∼ nous détestons être séparés; **they need to be kept** ∼ il faut les garder séparés

(c) (to one side) **he stood** ∼ **(from the group)** il se tenait à l'écart (du groupe)

② **apart from** phr **(a)** (separate from) à l'écart de; **it stands** ∼ **from the other houses** elle est à l'écart des autres maisons; **he lives** ∼ **from his wife** il vit séparé de sa femme

(b) (leaving aside) en dehors de, à part; ∼ **from being illegal, it's also dangerous** (mis) à part que c'est illégal, c'est aussi dangereux

apartheid n apartheid m

apartment n appartement m

apartment block n immeuble m

apartment house n (US) résidence f

apathetic adj (by nature) amorphe; (from illness, depression) apathique

apex n sommet m

APEX n (abbr = **Advance Purchase Excursion**) APEX m

apologetic adj ⟨gesture, letter⟩ d'excuse; **to be** ∼ **(about)** s'excuser (de)

apologize vi s'excuser **(to sb** auprès de qn; **for sth** de qch; **for doing** d'avoir fait)

apology n excuses fpl **(for sth** pour qch; **for doing** pour avoir fait); **to make an** ∼ s'excuser

apostrophe n apostrophe f

appal (GB), **appall** (US) vtr (shock) scandaliser; (horrify, dismay) horrifier

appalling adj **(a)** ⟨crime, conditions⟩ épouvantable

(b) ⟨manners, joke, taste⟩ exécrable; ⟨noise, weather⟩ épouvantable

apparatus n (gen) appareil m; (in gym) agrès mpl

apparent adj **(a)** (seeming) ⟨contradiction, willingness⟩ apparent/-e

(b) (clear) évident/-e; **for no** ∼ **reason** sans raison apparente

apparently adv apparemment

appeal ① n **(a)** (gen, Law) appel m **(for** à; **on behalf of** en faveur de)

(b) (attraction) charme m; (interest) intérêt m

② vi **(a)** (Law) faire appel **(against** de)

(b) (Sport) **to** ∼ **to** demander l'arbitrage de ⟨referee⟩; **to** ∼ **against** contester ⟨decision⟩

(c) **to** ∼ **for** lancer un appel à ⟨order, tolerance⟩; faire appel à ⟨witnesses⟩; **to** ∼ **for help** demander de l'aide

(d) (attract) **to** ∼ **to sb** ⟨idea⟩ tenter qn; ⟨person⟩ plaire à qn; ⟨place⟩ attirer qn

appeal fund n fonds m d'aide

appealing adj **(a)** (attractive) ⟨child⟩ attachant/-e; ⟨idea⟩ séduisant/-e; ⟨modesty⟩ charmant/-e

(b) ⟨look⟩ suppliant/-e

appear vi **(a)** (become visible) apparaître

(b) (turn up) arriver

(c) (seem) **to** ∼ **to be/to do** ⟨person⟩ avoir l'air d'être/de faire; **to** ∼ **depressed** avoir l'air déprimé; **it** ∼**s that** il semble que

(d) ⟨book, article, name⟩ paraître

(e) **to** ∼ **on stage** paraître en scène; **to** ∼ **on TV** passer à la télévision

(f) (Law) **to** ∼ **in court** comparaître devant le tribunal

appearance n **(a)** (arrival) (of person, vehicle) arrivée f; (of development, invention) apparition f; **to put in an** ∼ faire une apparition

(b) (on TV, in play, film) passage m

(c) (look) (of person) apparence f; (of district, object) aspect m; **to judge** or **go by** ∼**s** se fier aux apparences

appendicitis n appendicite f

appendix n appendice m; **to have one's** ∼ **removed** se faire opérer de l'appendicite

appetite n appétit m

appetite suppressant n anorexigène m

appetizer n (biscuit, olive etc) amuse-gueule m inv; (starter) hors-d'œuvre m

appetizing adj appétissant/-e

applaud vtr, vi applaudir

applause n applaudissements mpl; **there was a burst of** ∼ les applaudissements ont éclaté

apple n pomme f

applecore n trognon m de pomme

applet n (Comput) applet m, applette f

apple tree n pommier m

appliance n appareil m; **household** ∼ appareil électroménager

applicant n (for job, membership) candidat/-e m/f **(for** à); (for passport, benefit, loan) demandeur/-euse m/f **(for** de); (for citizenship) postulant/-e m/f **(for** à)

application n **(a)** (for job) candidature f **(for** à); (for membership, passport, loan) demande f **(for** de)

(b) (of ointment) application f **(to** à)

(c) (of law, penalty, rule) application f

application form n (gen) formulaire m de demande; (for job) formulaire m de candidature; (for membership) demande f d'inscription

apply ⓵ vtr (gen) appliquer; exercer ⟨pressure⟩ (to sur)
⓶ vi (a) to ~ (for) faire une demande (de) ⟨passport, loan, visa, permit⟩; poser sa candidature à ⟨job⟩; to ~ to faire une demande d'inscription à ⟨college⟩
(b) (be valid) ⟨definition, term⟩ s'appliquer (to à); ⟨ban, rule, penalty⟩ être en vigueur
⓷ v refl to ~ oneself s'appliquer

appoint vtr nommer ⟨person⟩ (to sth à qch; to do pour faire; as comme); fixer ⟨date, place⟩

appointment n (a) (meeting) rendez-vous m (at chez; with avec; to do pour faire); business ~ rendez-vous m d'affaires; to make an ~ prendre rendez-vous
(b) (to post) nomination f

appraisal n évaluation f

appreciate ⓵ vtr (a) apprécier ⟨help, effort⟩; être sensible à ⟨favour⟩; être reconnaissant/-e de ⟨kindness, sympathy⟩; I'd ~ it if you could reply soon je vous serais reconnaissant de répondre sans tarder
(b) (realize) se rendre (bien) compte de, être conscient/-e de
(c) (enjoy) apprécier ⟨music, art, food⟩
⓶ vi ⟨object⟩ prendre de la valeur; ⟨value⟩ monter

appreciation n (a) (gratitude) remerciement m (for pour)
(b) (enjoyment) appréciation f (of de)
(c) (increase) hausse f (of, in de)

appreciative adj (a) (grateful) reconnaissant/-e (of de)
(b) (admiring) admiratif/-ive

apprehensive adj inquiet/-iète; to be ~ about sth/doing appréhender qch/de faire

apprentice n apprenti/-e m/f (to de)

apprenticeship n apprentissage m

approach ⓵ n (a) (route of access) voie f d'accès
(b) (arrival) approche f
(c) (to problem) approche f
(d) to make ~es to sb faire des démarches auprès de qn
⓶ vtr (a) (draw near to) s'approcher de ⟨person, place⟩; (verge on) approcher de
(b) (deal with) aborder ⟨problem, subject⟩
(c) to ~ sb (about sth) s'adresser à qn (au sujet de qch); (more formally) faire des démarches auprès de qn (pour qch)
⓷ vi ⟨person, car⟩ (s')approcher; ⟨event, season⟩ approcher

approachable adj abordable, d'un abord facile

appropriate ⓵ adj (a) ⟨behaviour, choice, place⟩ approprié/-e (for pour); ⟨dress, gift⟩ qui convient (after n) (for à); ⟨punishment⟩ juste (for à); ⟨name⟩ bien choisi/-e
(b) (relevant) ⟨authority⟩ compétent/-e

⓶ vtr s'approprier ⟨property, document⟩; affecter ⟨funds, land⟩ (for à)

appropriately adv (a) ⟨behave, speak⟩ avec à-propos; ⟨dress⟩ convenablement
(b) ⟨designed, chosen, sited⟩ judicieusement

approval n approbation f (of de; to do pour faire); on ~ à l'essai

approve ⓵ vtr approuver ⟨product, plan⟩; accepter ⟨person⟩
⓶ vi to ~ of sb/sth apprécier qn/qch; he doesn't ~ of drinking il est contre l'alcool

approving adj approbateur/-trice

approximate adj approximatif/-ive

approximately adv (a) (about) environ; at ~ four o'clock vers quatre heures
(b) ⟨equal, correct⟩ à peu près

apricot n (fruit) abricot m

April n avril m

April Fools' Day n le premier avril

apron n tablier m

apt adj ⟨choice, description⟩ heureux/-euse; ⟨title, style⟩ approprié/-e (to, for à)

aptitude n aptitude f

aquarium n aquarium m

Aquarius n Verseau m

aquarobics n aquagym f

aquatic adj (gen) aquatique; ⟨sport⟩ nautique

aqueduct n aqueduc m

Arab ⓵ n (person) Arabe mf
⓶ adj arabe

Arabic ⓵ n (language) arabe m
⓶ adj arabe; ⟨lesson, teacher⟩ d'arabe

Arab-Israeli adj israélo-arabe

arbitrary adj arbitraire

arbitration n arbitrage m; to go to ~ ≈ aller aux prud'hommes

arcade n arcade f; shopping ~ galerie f marchande

arch ⓵ n arche f
⓶ vtr arquer; to ~ one's back ⟨person⟩ cambrer le dos; ⟨cat⟩ faire le dos rond
⓷ arch(-) pref par excellence; ~-enemy ennemi/-e m/f juré/-e; ~-rival grand rival

archaeologist (GB), **archeologist** (US) n archéologue mf

archaeology (GB), **archeology** (US) n archéologie f

archery n tir m à l'arc

architect n architecte mf

architecture n architecture f

archive n archive f

Arctic ⓵ pr n the ~ l'Arctique m
⓶ adj arctique

ardent adj ⟨defence, opposition, lover⟩ passionné/-e; ⟨supporter⟩ fervent/-e

area n (a) (region) région f; (of city) zone f; (district) quartier m; in the London ~ dans la région de Londres; residential ~ zone f résidentielle

(b) (in building) **dining** ~ coin *m* salle-à-manger; **no-smoking** ~ zone *f* non-fumeurs; **waiting** ~ salle *f* d'attente
(c) (of knowledge) domaine *m*; (of business) secteur *m*
(d) (in geometry) aire *f*, (of land) superficie *f*

area code *n* indicatif *m* de zone

arena *n* arène *f*

Argentina *pr n* Argentine *f*

argue ⃞1 *vtr* (debate) discuter (de), débattre (de); **to ~ that** (maintain) soutenir que
⃞2 *vi* **(a)** (quarrel) se disputer (**with** avec; **about, over** sur, pour)
(b) (debate) discuter (**about** de)
(c) (put one's case) argumenter (**for** en faveur de; **against** contre)

argument *n* **(a)** (quarrel) dispute *f* (**about** à propos de); **to have an** ~ se disputer
(b) (discussion) débat *m*, discussion *f* (**about** à propos de)
(c) (case) argument *m* (**for** en faveur de; **against** contre)

argumentative *adj* ergoteur/-euse

Aries *n* Bélier *m*

arise *vi* **(a)** ⟨problem⟩ survenir; ⟨question⟩ se poser; **if the need ~s** si le besoin se fait sentir
(b) (be the result of) résulter (**from** de)

aristocrat *n* aristocrate *mf*

arithmetic *n* arithmétique *f*

arm ⃞1 *n* bras *m*; (of chair) accoudoir *m*; ~ **in** ~ bras dessus bras dessous; **to have sth over/under one's** ~ avoir qch sur/sous le bras; **to fold one's** ~**s** croiser les bras
⃞2 **arms** *n pl* (weapons) armes *fpl*
⃞3 *vtr* (Mil) armer
IDIOMS **to keep sb at** ~**'s length** tenir qn à distance

armaments *n pl* armements *mpl*

armband *n* (for swimmer) bracelet *m* de natation; (for mourner) crêpe *m* de deuil

armchair *n* fauteuil *m*

armed *adj* armé/-e (**with** de); ⟨raid, robbery⟩ à main armée

armed forces, armed services *n pl* forces *fpl* armées

armour (GB), **armor** (US) *n* armure *f*

armoured (GB), **armored** (US) *adj* blindé/-e

armour-plated (GB), **armor-plated** (US) *adj* ⟨vehicle⟩ blindé/-e; ⟨ship⟩ cuirassé/-e

armpit *n* aisselle *f*

arms control *n* contrôle *m* des armements

arms race *n* course *f* aux armements

arms treaty *n* traité *m* sur le contrôle des armements

army ⃞1 *n* armée *f*; **to join the** ~ s'engager
⃞2 *adj* militaire

aroma *n* arôme *m*

aromatherapy *n* aromathérapie *f*

around ⃞1 *adv* **(a)** (approximately) environ, à peu près; **at** ~ **3 pm** vers 15 heures

(b) (in the vicinity) **to be (somewhere)** ~ être dans les parages; **are they** ~? est-ce qu'ils sont là?
(c) (in circulation) **CDs have been** ~ **for years** ça fait des années que les CD existent; **one of the most gifted musicians** ~ un des musiciens les plus doués du moment
(d) all ~ tout autour; **the only garage for miles** ~ le seul garage à des kilomètres à la ronde; **to ask sb (to come)** ~ dire à qn de passer
⃞2 *prep* **(a)** autour de ⟨fire, table⟩; **the villages** ~ **Dublin** les villages des environs de Dublin; **clothes scattered** ~ **the room** des vêtements éparpillés partout dans la pièce; **(all)** ~ **the world** partout dans le monde; **to walk** ~ **the town** se promener dans la ville; **the people** ~ **here** les gens d'ici
(b) (at) vers; ~ **midnight** vers minuit

arouse *vtr* éveiller ⟨interest, suspicion⟩; exciter ⟨anger, jealousy⟩; **to be ~d** ⟨person⟩ être excité/-e

arrange ⃞1 *vtr* **(a)** disposer ⟨chairs, ornaments⟩; arranger ⟨room, hair, clothes⟩; arranger, disposer ⟨flowers⟩
(b) (organize) organiser ⟨party, meeting, holiday⟩; fixer ⟨date, appointment⟩; **to ~ to do** s'arranger pour faire
(c) convenir de ⟨loan⟩
⃞2 *vi* **to ~ for sth** prendre des dispositions pour qch; **to ~ for sb to do** prendre des dispositions pour que qn fasse

arrangement *n* **(a)** (of objects, chairs) disposition *f*; (of flowers) composition *f*
(b) (agreement) entente *f*, accord *m*; **to come to an** ~ s'arranger
(c) (preparations) ~s préparatifs *mpl*; **to make** ~**s to do** s'arranger pour faire

array *n* gamme *f*

arrears *n pl* arriéré *m*; **I am in** ~ **with my payments** j'ai du retard dans mes paiements

arrest ⃞1 *n* arrestation *f*; **to be under** ~ être en état d'arrestation
⃞2 *vtr* arrêter

arrival *n* arrivée *f*; **on sb's** ~ à l'arrivée de qn

arrival(s) lounge *n* salon *m* d'arrivée

arrivals board *n* tableau *m* d'arrivée

arrival time *n* heure *f* d'arrivée

arrive *vi* **(a)** arriver (**at** à; **from** de)
(b) **to ~ at** parvenir à ⟨decision, solution⟩

arrogant *adj* arrogant/-e

arrow *n* flèche *f*

arson *n* incendie *m* criminel

arsonist *n* pyromane *mf*

art *n* art *m*; **I'm bad at** ~ je suis mauvais en dessin

artefact *n* objet *m* (fabriqué)

artery *n* artère *f*

art exhibition *n* (paintings) exposition *f* de tableaux; (sculpture) exposition *f* de sculpture

art gallery *n* (museum) musée *m* d'art; (commercial) galerie *f* d'art

arthritis *n* arthrite *f*

a

artichoke n artichaut m

article n article m (**about, on** sur)

artificial adj artificiel/-ielle

artificial limb n prothèse f, membre m artificiel

artificial respiration n respiration f artificielle

artillery n artillerie f

artisan n artisan m

artist n artiste mf

artistic adj ⟨talent⟩ artistique; ⟨temperament, person⟩ artiste

arts n pl (a) (culture) **the** ~ les arts mpl (b) (Univ) lettres fpl (c) ~ **and crafts** artisanat m

art school n école f des beaux-arts

arts student n étudiant/-e m/f en lettres

art student n étudiant/-e m/f des beaux-arts

as ▢1 conj (a) (comme; ~ **you know** comme vous le savez; ~ **usual** comme d'habitude; **do** ~ **I say** fais ce que je te dis; **leave it** ~ **it is** laisse-le tel quel; ~ **she was coming down the stairs** comme elle descendait l'escalier; ~ **she grew older** au fur et à mesure qu'elle vieillissait; ~ **a child, he...** (quand il était) enfant, il...
(b) (because, since) comme, puisque; ~ **you were out, I left a note** comme or puisque tu étais sorti, j'ai laissé un petit mot
(c) (although) strange ~ **it may seem** aussi curieux que cela puisse paraître; **try** ~ **he might, he could not forget it** il avait beau essayer, il ne pouvait pas oublier
(d) **the same...**~ le/la même...que; **I've got a jacket the same** ~ **yours** j'ai la même veste que toi
(e) **so** ~ **to do** pour faire, afin de faire
▢2 prep comme, en; **dressed** ~ **a sailor** habillé/-e en marin; **he works** ~ **a pilot** il travaille comme pilote; **a job** ~ **a teacher** un poste d'enseignant/-e; **to treat sb** ~ **an equal** traiter qn en égal
▢3 adv (in comparisons) **he is** ~ **intelligent** ~ **you** il est aussi intelligent que toi; ~ **fast** ~ **you can** aussi vite que possible; **he's twice** ~ **strong** ~ **me** il est deux fois plus fort que moi; **I have** ~ **much** or ~ **many** ~ **she has** j'en ai autant qu'elle; ~ **much** ~ **possible** autant que possible; ~ **little** ~ **possible** le moins possible; ~ **soon** ~ **possible** dès que possible; **he has a house in Nice** ~ **well** ~ **an apartment in Paris** il a une maison à Nice ainsi qu'un appartement à Paris
▢4 **as for** phr quant à, pour ce qui est de
▢5 **as from, as of** phr à partir de
▢6 **as if** phr comme (si); **it looks** ~ **if we've lost it** on dirait que nous avons perdu
▢7 **as long as** phr du moment que (+ indicative), pourvu que (+ subjunctive)
▢8 **as such** phr en tant que tel

asbestos n amiante m

ascend vtr gravir ⟨steps, hill⟩

ascent n ascension f

ascertain vtr établir (**that** que)

ash n (a) cendre f
(b) (also ~ **tree**) frêne m

ashamed adj honteux/-euse; **to be** ~ avoir honte (**of** de; **to do** de faire; **that** que (+ subjunctive))

ashen adj ⟨complexion⟩ terreux/-euse

ashore adv **to go** ~ débarquer; **washed** ~ rejeté/-e sur le rivage

ashtray n cendrier m

Asia pr n Asie f

Asian ▢1 n (from Far East) Asiatique mf; (in UK) personne f originaire du sous-continent indien
▢2 adj asiatique

aside ▢1 n **to say sth in an** ~ dire qch en aparté
▢2 adv **to stand** ~ s'écarter; **to put sth** ~ (save) mettre qch de côté; (in shop) réserver qch; **to take sb** ~ prendre qn à part
▢3 **aside from** phr à part

ask ▢1 vtr (a) demander; **to** ~ **a question** poser une question; **to** ~ **sb sth** demander qch à qn; **to** ~ **sb to do** demander à qn de faire
(b) (invite) inviter ⟨person⟩ (**to** à); **to** ~ **sb to dinner** inviter qn à dîner
▢2 vi (a) (request) demander
(b) (make enquiries) se renseigner; **to** ~ **about sb** s'informer au sujet de qn
▢3 v refl **to** ~ **oneself** se demander
■ **ask after** demander des nouvelles de ⟨person⟩
■ **ask for:** ¶ ~ **for** [sth] demander ⟨drink, money, help⟩; ¶ ~ **for** [sb] demander à voir; (on phone) demander à parler à

askance adv **to look** ~ **at sb/sth** considérer qn/qch avec méfiance

askew adj, adv de travers

asking price n prix m demandé

asleep adj **to be** ~ dormir; **to fall** ~ s'endormir; **to be sound** or **fast** ~ dormir à poings fermés

asparagus n asperge f

aspect n (a) aspect m
(b) (of house) orientation f

asphalt n bitume m

aspic n aspic m

aspiration n aspiration f (**to** à)

aspire vi aspirer (**to** à; **to do** à faire)

aspirin n aspirine® f

ass n (a) (donkey) âne m
(b) (colloq) (fool) idiot/-e m/f

assassin n assassin m

assassinate vtr assassiner

assassination n assassinat m

assault ▢1 n (a) (Law) agression f (**on** sur)
(b) (Mil) assaut m (**on** de)
▢2 vtr (a) (Law) agresser; **to be indecently** ~**ed** être victime d'une agression sexuelle
(b) (Mil) assaillir

assemble ▢1 vtr (a) (gather) rassembler
(b) (construct) assembler; **easy to** ~ facile à monter

2 *vi* ⟨*passengers, marchers*⟩ se rassembler; ⟨*parliament, team, family*⟩ se réunir

assembly *n* (a) (gen) assemblée *f*
(b) (Sch) rassemblement *m*
(c) (of components, machines) assemblage *m*

assembly line *n* chaîne *f* de montage

assent **1** *n* assentiment *m* (**to** à)
2 *vi* donner son assentiment (**to** à)

assert *vtr* (a) (state) affirmer (**that** que); **to ~ oneself** s'affirmer
(b) revendiquer ⟨*right, claim*⟩

assertion *n* déclaration *f* (**that** selon laquelle)

assertive *adj* assuré/-e

assess *vtr* (a) évaluer ⟨*person, problem*⟩; estimer ⟨*damage, value*⟩
(b) fixer ⟨*tax*⟩
(c) (Sch) contrôler ⟨*pupil*⟩

assessment *n* (a) (evaluation) appréciation *f* (**of** de); (of damage, value) estimation *f* (**of** de)
(b) (for tax) imposition *f*
(c) (Sch) contrôle *m*

asset *n* atout *m*; **~s** (private) avoir *m*; (of company) actif *m*

assign *vtr* (a) assigner ⟨*resources*⟩ (**to** à)
(b) **to ~ a task to sb** confier une tâche à qn
(c) (attribute) attribuer (**to** à)
(d) (appoint) nommer (**to** à)

assignment *n* (a) (specific duty) mission *f*
(b) (academic) devoir *m*

assimilate **1** *vtr* assimiler
2 *vi* s'assimiler (**into** dans)

assist **1** *vtr* (a) (help) aider; (in organization) assister (**to do, in doing** à faire)
(b) (facilitate) faciliter ⟨*development, process*⟩
2 *vi* aider (**in doing** à faire); **to ~ in** prendre part à ⟨*operation, rescue*⟩

assistance *n* aide *f* (**to** à); (more formal) assistance *f* (**to** à)

assistant **1** *n* (a) (helper) assistant/-e *m/f*; (in hierarchy) adjoint/-e *m/f*
(b) (*also* **shop ~**) vendeur/-euse *m/f*
(c) (GB) (**foreign language**) **~** (in school) assistant/-e *m/f*; (in university) lecteur/-trice *m/f*
2 *adj* ⟨*editor, manager*⟩ adjoint/-e

associate **1** *n* associé/-e *m/f*
2 *vtr* (a) associer ⟨*idea, memory*⟩ (**with** à)
(b) **to be ~d with** ⟨*person*⟩ faire partie de ⟨*movement, group*⟩; être mêlé/-e à ⟨*shady deal*⟩
3 *vi* **to ~ with sb** fréquenter qn

association *n* association *f*

assorted *adj* ⟨*objects, colours*⟩ varié/-e; ⟨*foodstuffs*⟩ assorti/-e

assortment *n* (of objects, colours) assortiment *m* (**of** de); (of people) mélange *m* (**of** de)

assume *vtr* (a) (suppose) supposer (**that** que)
(b) prendre ⟨*control, identity, office*⟩; assumer ⟨*responsibility*⟩; affecter ⟨*expression, indifference*⟩; **under an ~d name** sous un nom d'emprunt

assumption *n* supposition *f*

assurance *n* assurance *f*

assure *vtr* assurer; **to ~ sb that** assurer à qn que

asterisk *n* astérisque *m*

asthma *n* asthme *m*

asthmatic *n, adj* asthmatique (*mf*)

astonish *vtr* surprendre, étonner

astonished *adj* étonné/-e (**by, at** par; **to do** de faire)

astonishing *adj* étonnant/-e

astonishment *n* étonnement *m*

astound *vtr* stupéfier

astounding *adj* incroyable

astray *adv* (a) **to go ~** (go missing) se perdre
(b) **to lead sb ~** (confuse) induire qn en erreur; (corrupt) détourner qn du droit chemin

astride **1** *adv* à califourchon
2 *prep* à califourchon sur

astrologer, astrologist *n* astrologue *mf*

astrology *n* astrologie *f*

astronaut *n* astronaute *mf*

astronomer *n* astronome *mf*

astronomic, astronomical *adj* astronomique

astronomy *n* astronomie *f*

astute *adj* astucieux/-ieuse

asylum *n* asile *m*; **lunatic ~** asile de fous

asylum-seeker *n* demandeur/-euse *m/f* d'asile

at *prep*

■ Note *at* is often translated by *à*: *at the airport* = à l'aéroport; *at midnight* = à minuit; *at the age of 50* = à l'âge de 50 ans.
– Remember that *à* + *le* always becomes *au* and *à* + *les* always becomes *aux* (*au bureau, aux bureaux*).
– When *at* means *at the house, shop,* etc *of*, it is translated by *chez*: *at Amanda's* = chez Amanda; *at the hairdresser's* = chez le coiffeur.
– For examples and other usages, see the entry below.
– *At* is used with many verbs, adjectives and nouns (*look at, good at, at last*) etc. For translations consult the appropriate verb, adjective or noun entry.

(a) à; **~ school** à l'école; **~ 4 o'clock** à quatre heures; **~ Easter** à Pâques; **~ night** la nuit; **~ the moment** en ce moment
(b) chez; **~ my house** chez moi; **~ home** à la maison, chez soi

atheist *n, adj* athée (*mf*)

Athens *pr n* Athènes

athlete *n* athlète *mf*

athlete's foot *n* mycose *f*

athletic *adj* athlétique

athletics *n* (GB) athlétisme *m*; (US) sports *mpl*

Atlantic **1** *pr n* **the ~** l'Atlantique *m* ····⟶

a

2 *adj* ‹coast› atlantique

atlas *n* atlas *m*

ATM *n* (*abbr* = **automated teller machine**) guichet *m* automatique

atmosphere *n* (a) (air) atmosphère *f*
(b) (mood) ambiance *f*; (bad) atmosphère *f*

atom *n* atome *m*

atom bomb *n* bombe *f* atomique

atomic *adj* atomique, nucléaire

atrocious *adj* atroce

atrocity *n* atrocité *f*

attach *vtr* attacher (**to** à)

attaché *n* attaché/-e *m/f*

attaché case *n* attaché-case *m*

attached *adj* (a) (fond) **to be ~ to** être attaché/-e à
(b) ‹document› ci-joint/-e

attachment *n* (a) (affection) attachement *m*
(b) (device) accessoire *m*
(c) (in e-mail) pièce-jointe *f*

attack **1** *n* (a) (gen) attaque *f* (**on** contre); (criminal) agression *f* (**against, on** contre); (terrorist) attentat *m*
(b) (of illness) crise *f* (**of** de)
2 *vtr* (a) (gen) attaquer; (criminally) agresser ‹victim›
(b) s'attaquer à ‹task, problem›

attacker *n* (gen) agresseur *m*; (Mil, Sport) attaquant/-e *m/f*

attempt **1** *n* (a) tentative *f* (**to do** de faire); **to make an ~ to do** *or* **at doing** tenter de faire
(b) **to make an ~ on sb's life** attenter à la vie de qn
2 *vtr* tenter (**to do** de faire); **~ed murder** tentative de meurtre

attend **1** *vtr* assister à ‹ceremony, meeting›; aller à ‹church, school›; suivre ‹class, course›
2 *vi* être présent/-e
■ **attend to** s'occuper de ‹person, problem›

attendance *n* présence *f* (**at** à)

attendant *n* (in cloakroom, museum, car park) gardien/-ienne *m/f*; (at petrol station) pompiste *mf*; (at pool) surveillant/-e *m/f*

attention *n* (a) attention *f*; **to draw ~ to sth** attirer l'attention sur qch
(b) (Mil) **to stand to** *or* **at ~** être au garde-à-vous; **~!** garde-à-vous!

attention deficit disorder *n* troubles *mpl* chroniques de l'attention

attentive *adj* (alert) attentif/-ive; (solicitous) attentionné/-e (**to** à)

attic *n* grenier *m*; **the toys are in the ~** les jouets sont au grenier

attic room *n* mansarde *f*

attitude *n* attitude *f* (**to, towards** (GB) à l'égard de)

attorney *n* (US) avocat *m*

attract *vtr* attirer

attraction *n* (a) (favourable feature) attrait *m* (**of** de; **for** pour)
(b) (entertainment, sight) attraction *f*

(c) (sexual) attirance *f* (**to** pour)

attractive *adj* ‹person, offer› séduisant/-e; ‹child› charmant/-e; ‹place› attrayant/-e

attribute **1** *n* attribut *m*
2 *vtr* attribuer (**to** à)

aubergine *n* (GB) aubergine *f*

auburn *adj* auburn *inv*

auction **1** *n* enchères *fpl*
2 *vtr* (*also* **~ off**) vendre [qch] aux enchères

auctioneer *n* commissaire-priseur *m*

auction house *n* société *f* de commissaires-priseurs

audacity *n* audace *f*

audible *adj* audible

audience *n* (in cinema, concert, theatre) public *m*, salle *f*; (of radio programme) auditeurs *mpl*; (of TV programme) téléspectateurs *mpl*

audience ratings *n pl* indice *m* d'écoute

audio *adj* audio *inv*

audiobook *n* livre-cassette *m*

audiovisual, AV *adj* audiovisuel/-elle

audit **1** *n* audit *m*
2 *vtr* auditer, vérifier

audition **1** *n* audition *f* (**for** pour)
2 *vtr, vi* auditionner (**for** pour)

auditor *n* (a) commissaire *m* aux comptes
(b) (US) (student) auditeur/-trice *m/f*

auditorium *n* salle *f*

augur *vi* **to ~ well** être de bon augure

August *n* août *m*

aunt *n* tante *f*

au pair *n* (jeune) fille *f* au pair

aura *n* (of place) atmosphère *f*; (of person) aura *f*

aural *adj* (a) (gen) auditif/-ive
(b) (Sch) ‹comprehension, test› oral/-e

auspicious *adj* prometteur/-euse

austere *adj* austère

austerity *n* austérité *f*

Australia *pr n* Australie *f*

Australian **1** *n* Australien/-ienne *m/f*
2 *adj* australien/-ienne; ‹embassy› d'Australie

Austria *pr n* Autriche *f*

Austrian **1** *n* Autrichien/-ienne *m/f*
2 *adj* autrichien/-ienne; ‹embassy› d'Autriche

authentic *adj* authentique

author *n* auteur *m*

authoritarian *adj* autoritaire

authoritative *adj* (a) (forceful) autoritaire
(b) (reliable) ‹work› qui fait autorité; ‹source› bien informé/-e

authority *n* (a) autorité *f*; **the authorities** les autorités
(b) (permission) autorisation *f*

authorization *n* autorisation *f*

authorize *vtr* autoriser (**to do** à faire)

autism *n* autisme *m*

autobiographical *adj* autobiographique

autobiography *n* autobiographie *f*
Autocue® *n* prompteur *m*
autograph ① *n* autographe *m*
  ② *vtr* dédicacer
automatic ① *n* (a) (washing machine)
machine *f* à laver automatique
  (b) (car) voiture *f* (à changement de vitesse)
automatique
  (c) (gun) automatique *m*
  ② *adj* automatique
automatically *adv* automatiquement
automatic pilot *n* (device) pilote *m*
automatique
automation *n* automatisation *f*
automobile *n* automobile *f*
autonomy *n* autonomie *f*
autopsy *n* autopsie *f*
autumn *n* automne *m*; **in ~** en automne
auxiliary *n, adj* auxiliaire (*mf*)
availability *n* (of option, service) existence *f*;
  subject to ~ (of holidays, rooms, theatre seats)
dans la limite des places disponibles
available *adj* disponible (**for** pour; **to** à)
avalanche *n* avalanche *f*
avarice *n* cupidité *f*
avenge *vtr* venger
avenue *n* (a) (street, road) avenue *f*
  (b) (path, driveway) allée *f*
average ① *n* moyenne *f* (**of** de); **on (the)
~** en moyenne; **above/below (the) ~**
au-dessus de/au-dessous de la moyenne
  ② *adj* moyen/-enne
  ③ *vtr* faire en moyenne
averse *adj* opposé/-e (**to** à); **to be ~ to
doing** répugner à faire
aversion *n* aversion *f* (**to** pour)
avert *vtr* éviter; **to ~ one's eyes from sth**
détourner les yeux de qch
aviary *n* volière *f*
aviation *n* aviation *f*
avid *adj* ⟨collector, reader⟩ passionné/-e; **to
be ~ for sth** être avide de qch
avocado *n* (also **~ pear**) avocat *m*
avoid *vtr* (gen) éviter; esquiver ⟨issue,
question⟩; **to ~ doing** éviter de faire
await *vtr* attendre
awake ① *adj* (not yet asleep) éveillé/-e; (after
sleeping) réveillé/-e; **wide ~** bien réveillé/-e;
the noise kept me ~ le bruit m'a empêché
de dormir
  ② *vtr* réveiller ⟨person⟩
  ③ *vi* ⟨person⟩ se réveiller
award ① *n* (prize) prix *m* (**for** de)
  ② *vtr* décerner ⟨prize⟩; attribuer ⟨grant⟩;
accorder ⟨points, penalty⟩

award ceremony *n* cérémonie *f* de
remise de prix
award-winning *adj* ⟨book, film⟩
primé/-e; ⟨writer⟩ lauréat/-e
aware *adj* (conscious) conscient/-e (**of** de);
(informed) au courant (**of** de)
awareness *n* conscience *f* (**of** de; **that**
que)
away

■ **Note** *away* often appears after a verb in
English to show that an action is continuous or
intense. If *away* does not change the basic
meaning of the verb it is translated:
he was snoring away = il ronflait.

① *adj* (Sport) ⟨goal, match, win⟩ à
l'extérieur; **the ~ team** les visiteurs *mpl*
② *adv* (a) **to be ~** être absent/-e (**from** de);
to be ~ on business être en voyage
d'affaires; **to be ~ from home** ne pas être
chez soi, être absent/-e de chez soi; **she's ~
in Paris** elle est à Paris; **to crawl ~** partir en
rampant; **3 km ~** à 3 km; **London is two
hours ~** Londres est à deux heures d'ici; **my
birthday is two months ~** mon anniversaire
est dans deux mois
  (b) (Sport) ⟨play⟩ à l'extérieur
awe *n* crainte *f* mêlée d'admiration; **to
listen in ~** écouter impressionné/-e; **to be in
~ of sb** avoir peur de qn
awe-inspiring *adj* impressionnant/-e
awful *adj* (a) affreux/-euse, atroce; (in
quality) exécrable
  (b) **I feel ~** (ill) je ne me sens pas bien du
tout; (guilty) je culpabilise
  (c) (colloq) **an ~ lot (of)** énormément (de)
awfully *adv* extrêmement
awkward *adj* (a) ⟨tool⟩ peu commode;
⟨shape, design⟩ difficile
  (b) (clumsy) ⟨person, gesture⟩ maladroit/-e
  (c) ⟨issue, choice⟩ difficile; **at an ~ time** au
mauvais moment
  (d) (embarrassing) ⟨question⟩ embarrassant/-e;
⟨situation⟩ délicat/-e; ⟨silence⟩ gêné/-e
  (e) (uncooperative) ⟨person⟩ difficile (**about** à
propos de)
awning *n* (on shop) banne *f*, auvent *m*; (on
tent, house) auvent *m*; (on market stall) bâche *f*
awry ① *adj* de travers *inv*
  ② *adv* **to go ~** mal tourner
axe, ax (US) ① *n* hache *f*
  ② *vtr* virer (colloq) ⟨employee⟩; supprimer
⟨jobs⟩; abandonner ⟨plan⟩
axis *n* axe *m*
axle *n* essieu *m*

Bb

b, B *n* **(a)** (letter) b, B *m*
(b) B (Mus) si *m*

BA *n* (*abbr* = **Bachelor of Arts**) (degree)
diplôme *m* universitaire de lettres

babe *n* (colloq) super nana *f* (colloq)

baby ⊞ *n* bébé *m*
② *adj* ‹*clothes, food*› pour bébés; ‹*brother,
sister*› petit/-e (*before n*); ~ **seal** bébé phoque

babysit *vi* faire du babysitting

babysitter *n* baby-sitter *mf*

babysitting *n* baby-sitting *m*

baccalaureate *n* European/International
Baccalaureate baccalauréat *m* européen/
international

bachelor *n* célibataire *m*

Bachelor of Arts *n* (person) licencié/-e
m/f ès lettres

back ⊞ *n* **(a)** (of person, animal) dos *m*; **to
turn one's ~ on sb/sth** tourner le dos à
qn/qch; **behind sb's ~** dans le dos de qn
(b) (of page, cheque, hand, envelope, coat) dos *m*;
(of vehicle, plane, building, head) arrière *m*; (of
chair, sofa) dossier *m*; (of cupboard, drawer, fridge,
bus) fond *m*; **the ones at the ~ couldn't see**
ceux qui étaient derrière ne pouvaient pas
voir; **the steps at the ~ of the building**
l'escalier à l'arrière de l'immeuble; **at the ~
of the drawer** au fond du tiroir; **at the ~ of
the plane/bus** à l'arrière de l'avion/au fond
du bus; **in the ~ (of the car)** à l'arrière
(c) (Sport) arrière *m*; **left ~** arrière gauche
② *adj* ‹*paw, wheel*› arrière; ‹*bedroom*› du
fond; ‹*page*› dernier/-ière (*before n*); ‹*garden,
gate*› de derrière
③ *adv* **(a) to be ~** être de retour; **I'll be ~ in
five minutes** je reviens dans cinq minutes; **to
come ~** rentrer (**from** de); **to come ~ home**
rentrer chez soi
(b) to give/put sth ~ rendre/remettre qch; **to
phone ~** rappeler; **I'll write ~ (to him)** je lui
répondrai
(c) ‹*look, jump, lean*› en arrière
(d) ~ in 1964/April en 1964/avril
(e) to travel to London and ~ faire un
aller-retour à Londres
④ *vtr* **(a)** (support) soutenir ‹*candidate, bill*›;
apporter son soutien à ‹*project*›; justifier
‹*claim*› (**with** à l'aide de); financer ‹*venture*›
(b) to ~ the car into the garage rentrer la
voiture au garage en marche arrière
(c) (bet on) parier sur ‹*favourite, winner*›
⑤ **back and forth** *phr* **to go** *or* **travel ~
and forth** (commute) ‹*person, bus*› faire la
navette (**between** entre); **to go** *or* **walk ~ and
forth** faire des allées et venues (**between**
entre); **to sway ~ and forth** se balancer

■ **back away** reculer; **to ~ away from**
s'éloigner de ‹*person*›; chercher à éviter
‹*confrontation*›
■ **back down** céder
■ **back out**: ¶ ~ **out (a)** ‹*car, driver*› sortir
en marche arrière
(b) ‹*person*› se désister; **to ~ out of** annuler
‹*deal*›
¶ ~ **[sth] out: to ~ the car out of the garage**
faire sortir la voiture du garage en marche
arrière
■ **back up** confirmer ‹*claims, theory*›;
soutenir ‹*person*›; (Comput) sauvegarder

backache *n* **to have ~** avoir mal au dos

backbencher *n* (GB Pol) député *m* (sans
portefeuille ministériel)

backbone *n* colonne *f* vertébrale

back cover *n* dos *m*

backdate *vtr* antidater ‹*cheque, letter*›

back door *n* (of car) portière *f* arrière; (of
building) porte *f* de derrière

backdrop *n* toile *f* de fond

backer *n* **(a)** (supporter) allié/-e *m/f*
(b) (of project) commanditaire *m*; (of business)
bailleur *m* de fonds

backfire *vi* **(a)** ‹*scheme*› avoir l'effet
inverse; **to ~ on sb** se retourner contre qn
(b) ‹*car*› pétarader

backgammon *n* jaquet *m*

background ⊞ *n* **(a)** (of person) (social)
milieu *m*; (family) origines *fpl*; (professional)
formation *f*
(b) (of events, situation) contexte *m*; **against a ~
of violence** dans un climat de violence; **to
remain in the ~** rester au second plan;
voices in the ~ des voix en bruit de fond
(c) (of painting, photo, scene) arrière-plan *m*; **in
the ~** à l'arrière-plan
② *adj* **(a)** ‹*information*› sur les origines de
la situation; ~ **reading** lectures *fpl*
complémentaires
(b) ‹*music, lighting*› d'ambiance; ‹*noise*› de
fond

backhand *n* (Sport) revers *m*

backhander *n* (colloq) (bribe) pot-de-vin *m*

backing *n* **(a)** (support) soutien *m*
(b) (reverse layer) revêtement *m* intérieur

backing singer *n* chanteur/-euse *m/f*
d'accompagnement

backing vocals *n pl* chœurs *mpl*

backlash *n* réaction *f* violente (**against**
contre)

backlog *n* retard *m*; **I've got a huge ~ (of
work)** j'ai plein de travail en retard

back number *n* ancien numéro *m*

backpack ⊞ *n* sac *m* à dos

2 *vi* **to go ∼ing** partir en voyage avec son sac à dos

backpacker *n* routard/-e *m/f*

back pay *n* rappel *m* de salaire

back-pedal *vi* (figurative) faire marche arrière

back rest *n* dossier *m*

back seat *n* siège *m* arrière; **to take a ∼** (figurative) s'effacer

backside *n* (colloq) derrière *m* (colloq)

backstage *adv* dans les coulisses

backstreet **1** *n* petite rue *f*
2 *adj* ⟨*loanshark, abortionist*⟩ clandestin/-e

backstroke *n* dos *m* crawlé

back to back *adv* **to stand ∼** ⟨*two people*⟩ se mettre dos à dos

back to front *adj, adv* à l'envers

backtrack *vi* rebrousser chemin; (figurative) faire marche arrière

backup **1** *n* (gen) soutien *m*; (Mil) renforts *mpl*; (Comput) sauvegarde *f*
2 *adj* ⟨*copy, disk, file*⟩ de sauvegarde

backward **1** *adj* **(a)** ⟨*look, step*⟩ en arrière
(b) ⟨*nation*⟩ arriéré/-e
(c) ⟨*person*⟩ arriéré/-e
2 *adv* (*also* **backwards**) **(a)** ⟨*walk*⟩ à reculons; ⟨*lean, step, fall*⟩ en arrière; **to move ∼** reculer; **to walk ∼ and forward** faire des allées et venues
(b) ⟨*count*⟩ à rebours; ⟨*play*⟩ à l'envers

backwards = BACKWARD 2

backwater *n* village *m* tranquille, trou *m* (colloq)

backyard *n* **(a)** (GB) (courtyard) arrière-cour *f*
(b) (US) (back garden) jardin *m* de derrière

bacon *n* bacon *m*, ≈ lard *m*; **∼ and egg(s)** des œufs au bacon

bacteria *n pl* bactéries *fpl*

bad **1** *n* **the good and the ∼** le bon et le mauvais; **there is good and ∼ in everyone** il y a du bon et du mauvais dans chacun
2 *adj* **(a)** (gen) mauvais/-e (*before n*); ⟨*joke*⟩ stupide; ⟨*language*⟩ grossier/-ière; **to be ∼ at** ⟨*subject*⟩; **not ∼** (colloq) pas mal (colloq); **too ∼ !** (sympathetic) pas de chance!; (hard luck) tant pis!; **it will look ∼** cela fera mauvais effet; **to feel ∼** avoir mauvaise conscience (**about** à propos de)
(b) (serious) ⟨*accident, injury, mistake*⟩ grave; **a ∼ cold** un gros rhume
(c) **it's ∼ for you** *or* **your health** c'est mauvais pour la santé
(d) **to have a ∼ back** souffrir du dos; **to have a ∼ chest** être malade des poumons; **to be in a ∼ way** (colloq) aller très mal
(e) ⟨*fruit*⟩ pourri/-e; **to go ∼** pourrir

badge *n* (gen) badge *m*; (official) insigne *m*

badly *adv* **(a)** ⟨*begin, behave, sleep*⟩ mal; ⟨*made, worded*⟩ mal; **to go ∼** ⟨*exam, interview*⟩ mal se passer; **to do ∼** ⟨*candidate, company*⟩ obtenir de mauvais résultats; **to take sth ∼** mal prendre qch

(b) ⟨*suffer*⟩ beaucoup; ⟨*affect*⟩ sérieusement; ⟨*hurt, damaged*⟩ gravement
(c) **to want/need sth ∼** avoir très envie de/ grand besoin de qch

badly behaved *adj* désobéissant/-e

badly off *adj* pauvre

bad-mannered *adj* ⟨*person*⟩ mal élevé/-e

badminton *n* badminton *m*

bad-tempered *adj* (temporarily) irrité/-e; (habitually) irritable

baffle *vtr* rendre [qn] perplexe, confondre

baffled *adj* perplexe (**by** devant)

bag **1** *n* sac *m* (**of** de)
2 **bags** *n pl* bagages *mpl*; **to pack one's ∼s** faire ses bagages; (figurative) faire ses valises
IDIOMS to have ∼s under one's eyes avoir des valises sous les yeux (colloq)

baggage *n* bagages *mpl*

baggage allowance *n* franchise *f* de bagages

baggage reclaim *n* réception *f* des bagages

baggy *adj* large, ample

bagpipes *n* cornemuse *f*

bail *n* caution *f*; **to be (out) on ∼** être libéré/-e sous caution

■ **bail out**: ¶ **∼ out** (of plane) sauter; ¶ **∼ [sb] out** (gen) tirer [qn] d'affaire ⟨*person*⟩; (Law) payer la caution pour ⟨*person*⟩

bailiff *n* huissier *m*

bait *n* appât *m*

bake **1** *vtr* faire cuire [qch] au four ⟨*dish, vegetable*⟩; faire ⟨*bread, cake*⟩
2 *vi* **(a)** (make bread) faire du pain; (make cakes) faire de la pâtisserie
(b) (cook) ⟨*food*⟩ cuire

baked beans *n pl* haricots *mpl* blancs à la sauce tomate

baked potato *n* pomme *f* de terre en robe des champs (au four)

baker *n* boulanger/-ère *m/f*

bakery *n* boulangerie *f*

balance **1** *n* **(a)** équilibre *m* (**between** entre); **to lose one's ∼** perdre l'équilibre; **the right ∼** le juste milieu
(b) (scales) balance *f*; **to hang in the ∼** être en jeu
(c) (of account) solde *m*; **to pay the ∼** verser le surplus
2 *vtr* **(a)** mettre [qch] en équilibre ⟨*ball, plate*⟩ (**on** sur)
(b) (compensate for) (*also* **∼ out**) compenser, équilibrer
(c) (counterbalance) contrebalancer ⟨*weights*⟩
(d) (adjust) équilibrer ⟨*diet, budget*⟩; **to ∼ the books** dresser le bilan
3 *vi* **(a)** ⟨*person*⟩ se tenir en équilibre (**on** sur); ⟨*object*⟩ tenir en équilibre (**on** sur)
(b) (*also* **∼ out**) s'équilibrer
(c) ⟨*books, figures*⟩ être en équilibre
4 **balanced** *pp adj* ⟨*person, view, diet*⟩ équilibré/-e; ⟨*article, report*⟩ objectif/-ive

balance of payments n balance f des paiements

balance of power n équilibre m des forces

balance of trade n balance f du commerce extérieur

balance sheet n bilan m

balcony n (a) (in house, hotel) balcon m (b) (in theatre) deuxième balcon m

bald adj (a) ⟨man, head⟩ chauve (b) ⟨tyre⟩ lisse

Balkan ① **Balkans** pr n pl the ~s les Balkans mpl ② adj balkanique

ball ① n (a) (gen) balle f; (in football, rugby) ballon m; (in billiards) bille f (b) (of dough, clay) boule f (of de); (of wool, string) pelote f (of de) (c) (dance) bal m ② **balls** n pl (slang) (a) (testicles) couilles fpl (slang) (b) (rubbish) conneries fpl (slang)

ballet n ballet m

ball gown n robe f de bal

balloon n (a) ballon m (b) (also **hot air** ~) montgolfière f

ballot ① n (a) scrutin m (b) (also ~ **paper**) bulletin m de vote ② vtr consulter [qn] (par vote) (on sur)

ballot box n urne f (électorale)

ballpark figure n (colloq) chiffre m approximatif

ballpoint (pen) n stylo m (à) bille

ballroom n salle f de danse

ballroom dancing n danse f de salon

Baltic adj the ~ Sea la mer f Baltique

ban ① n interdiction f (on de) ② vtr (gen) interdire; suspendre ⟨athlete⟩; to ~ sb from doing interdire à qn de faire

banal adj banal/-e

banana n banane f

band n (a) (of people) groupe m (of de); (of musicians) (rock) groupe (de rock); (municipal) fanfare f; **jazz** ~ orchestre m de jazz (b) (strip) bande f (c) (GB) (of age, income tax) tranche f (d) (around arm) brassard m; (hair) ~ bandeau m

■ **band together** se réunir (to do pour faire)

bandage ① n bandage m ② vtr bander ⟨head, limb, wound⟩

bandit n bandit m

bandwagon n IDIOMS to jump or climb on the ~ prendre le train en marche

bang ① n (a) (of explosion) détonation f, boum m; (of door, window) claquement m (b) (knock) coup m ② adv (colloq) ~ in the middle en plein centre ③ vtr (a) taper sur ⟨drum, saucepan⟩; to ~ sth down on the table poser bruyamment

qch sur la table; to ~ one's head se cogner la tête (on contre); to ~ one's fist on the table taper du poing sur la table (b) (slam) claquer ⟨door, window⟩ ④ vi ⟨door, shutter⟩ claquer IDIOMS ~ goes (colloq) my holiday/my promotion je peux dire adieu à mes vacances/mon avancement

■ **bang into**: ¶ ~ into [sb/sth] heurter

bangle n bracelet m

banish vtr bannir (from de)

banister, bannister (GB) n rampe f (d'escalier)

bank ① n (a) banque f (b) (of river, lake) rive f; (of major river) bord m; (of canal) berge f (c) (mound) talus m; (of snow) congère f; (of flowers) massif m; (of fog, mist) banc m ② vi to ~ with the National avoir un compte (bancaire) à la Nationale

■ **bank on** compter sur ⟨person⟩ (to do pour faire); to ~ on doing escompter faire

bank account n compte m bancaire

bank card n carte f bancaire

bank charges n pl frais mpl bancaires

bank clerk n employé/-e m/f de banque

banker n banquier/-ière m/f

banker's draft n traite f bancaire

banker's order n virement m bancaire

bank holiday n (GB) jour m férié; (US) jour m de fermeture des banques

banking n (a) (business) opérations fpl bancaires (b) (profession) la banque

banking hours n pl heures fpl d'ouverture des banques

bank manager n directeur/-trice m/f d'agence bancaire

banknote n billet m de banque

bank robber n cambrioleur/-euse m/f de banque

bank robbery n cambriolage m de banque

bankroll vtr (colloq) financer

bankrupt adj ⟨person⟩ ruiné/-e; ⟨economy⟩ en faillite; to go ~ faire faillite

bankruptcy n faillite f

bank statement n relevé m de compte

banner n banderole f

baptism n baptême m

baptize vtr baptiser

bar ① n (a) (of metal, wood) barre f; (on cage, window) barreau m (b) (pub) bar m; (counter) comptoir m (c) ~ of soap savonnette f; ~ of chocolate tablette f de chocolat (d) (Law) (profession) the ~ le barreau (e) (Sport) barre f (f) (Mus) mesure f ② prep sauf; all ~ one tous sauf un seul/une seule ③ vtr (a) barrer ⟨way, path⟩; to ~ sb's way barrer le passage à qn

(b) (ban) exclure ⟨person⟩ (**from** sth de qch); **to ~ sb from** doing interdire à qn de faire

barbaric adj barbare

barbecue n barbecue m

barbed wire, **barbwire** (US) n (fil m de fer) barbelé m

barber n coiffeur m (pour hommes)

Barcelona pr n Barcelone

bar chart n histogramme m

bar code n code m à barres

bare ① adj (gen) nu/-e; ⟨cupboard, room⟩ vide; **with one's ~ hands** à mains nues; **the ~ minimum** le strict nécessaire
② vtr **to ~ one's teeth** montrer les dents

bareback adv ⟨ride⟩ à cru

barefoot ① adj **to be ~** être nu-pieds
② adv ⟨run, walk⟩ pieds nus

barely adv à peine

bargain ① n **(a)** (deal) marché m (**between** entre)
(b) (good buy) affaire f
② vi **(a)** (for deal) négocier (**with** avec)
(b) (over price) marchander (**with** avec)
■ **bargain for**, **bargain on** s'attendre à

bargaining ① n négociations fpl
② adj ⟨position, power⟩ de négociation

barge ① n péniche f; (for freight) chaland m
② vi **to ~ past sb** passer devant qn en le bousculant
■ **barge in** (enter noisily) faire irruption; (interrupt) interrompre brutalement

bark ① n **(a)** (of tree) écorce f
(b) (of dog) aboiement m
② vi aboyer (**at sb/sth** après qn/qch)

barley n orge f

barmaid n serveuse f de bar

barman n barman m

barn n (for crops) grange f; (for cattle) étable f

baron n baron m

barracks n caserne f

barrage n (gen) barrage m; (Mil) tir m de barrage

barrel n **(a)** (for beer, wine) tonneau m, fût m; (for oil) baril m
(b) (of gun) canon m

barricade n barricade f

barrier n barrière f

barrier cream n crème f protectrice

barring prep à moins de

barrister n (GB) avocat/-e m/f

barter vi (exchange) faire du troc; (haggle) marchander

base ① n (gen, Mil) base f; (of tree, lamp) pied m
② adj ignoble
③ vtr fonder (**on** sur); **the film is ~d on a true story** le film est tiré d'une histoire vraie; **to be ~d in Paris** ⟨person, company⟩ être basé/-e à Paris

baseball n base-ball m

basement n sous-sol m; **in the ~** au sous-sol

bash ① n (colloq) **(a)** (blow) coup m
(b) (attempt) tentative f; **to have a ~ at** sth, **to give** sth **a ~** s'essayer à qch
(c) (party) grande fête f
② vtr cogner ⟨person⟩; rentrer dans ⟨tree, wall, kerb⟩
■ **bash into**: **~ into** [sth] rentrer dans

bashful adj timide

basic adj **(a)** (gen) essentiel/-ielle; ⟨problem, principle⟩ fondamental/-e
(b) (elementary) ⟨knowledge, skill⟩ élémentaire; ⟨wage, training⟩ de base

basically adv fondamentalement

basics n pl essentiel m; **to get down to ~** aborder l'essentiel

basil n basilic m

basin n **(a)** (bowl) bol m
(b) (in bathroom) lavabo m; (portable) cuvette f

basis n base f (**for**, **of** de); **on a regular/ temporary ~** régulièrement/à titre provisoire

basket n panier m

basketball n (game) basket(-ball) m; (ball) ballon m de basket

bass n basse f

bass drum n grosse caisse f

bass guitar n basse f

bastard n **(a)** (illegitimate child) bâtard/-e m/f
(b) (slang) salaud m (slang)

baste vtr (Culin) arroser

bastion n bastion m

bat ① n **(a)** (in cricket, baseball) batte f; (in table tennis) raquette f
(b) (Zool) chauve-souris f
② vi (be batsman) être le batteur; (handle a bat) manier la batte

batch n (of loaves) fournée f; (of goods) lot m

bated adj **with ~ breath** en retenant son souffle

bath ① n bain m; (GB) (tub) baignoire f; **to have a ~** prendre un bain
② **baths** n pl **(a)** (for swimming) piscine f
(b) (in spa) thermes mpl
③ vtr (GB) baigner

bathe ① vtr laver ⟨wound⟩ (**in** dans; **with** à)
② vi **(a)** (swim) se baigner
(b) (US) (take bath) prendre un bain
(c) **to be ~d in** ruisseler de ⟨sweat⟩; être inondé/-e de ⟨light⟩

bather n baigneur/-euse m/f

bathing n baignade f

bathing cap n bonnet m de bain

bathing costume n costume m de bain

bath mat n tapis m de bain

bathrobe n sortie f de bain

bathroom n **(a)** salle f de bains
(b) (US) (lavatory) toilettes fpl

bathroom cabinet n armoire f de toilette

bathroom scales n pl pèse-personne m

bath towel n serviette f de bain

bathtub n baignoire f

baton n (GB) (policeman's) matraque f; (traffic policeman's) bâton m; (Mus) baguette f; (in relay race) témoin m

batsman n batteur m

batter ⓵ n pâte f
⓶ vtr battre

battered adj (a) ⟨kettle, hat⟩ cabossé/-e; ⟨suitcase⟩ très abîmé/-e
(b) ⟨wife⟩ battu/-e

battery n pile f; (in car) batterie f

battery charger n chargeur m de batteries

battery farming n élevage m en batterie

battery powered adj à piles

battle ⓵ n bataille f; (figurative) lutte f
⓶ vi combattre (**with sb** contre qn);
to ~ for sth/to do lutter pour qch/pour faire

battlefield n champ m de bataille

battleship n cuirassé m

bawdy adj ⟨song⟩ grivois/-e; ⟨person⟩ paillard/-e

bawl vi (weep) brailler; (shout) hurler

bay ⓵ n (a) (on coast) baie f
(b) (Bot) (also **~ tree**) laurier(-sauce) m
(c) **loading/parking ~** aire f de chargement/stationnement
⓶ vi ⟨dog⟩ aboyer (**at** contre, après)
IDIOMS **to hold sb/sth at ~** tenir qn/qch à distance

bay leaf n feuille f de laurier

bayonet n baïonnette f

BC (abbr = **Before Christ**) av. J.-C.

be

■ Note for translations of *there is, there are, here is* and *here are*, see the entries THERE and HERE

⓵ vi (a) être; **she is French** elle est française; **we are late** nous sommes en retard; **he is a doctor/widower** il est médecin/veuf; **it is Monday** c'est lundi; **it's me!** c'est moi!; **~ good!** sois sage!
(b) (physical and mental states) avoir; **I am cold/hot** j'ai froid/chaud; **are you hungry/thirsty?** as-tu faim/soif?; **his hands were cold** il avait froid aux mains
(c) (weather) faire; **it is cold/windy** il fait froid/du vent; **it is 40°** il fait 40°
(d) (health) aller; **how are you?** (polite) comment allez-vous?; (more informally) comment vas-tu?; (very informally) ça va?; **how is your son?** comment va votre fils?; ▶ WELL[1], FINE, BETTER
(e) (visit) **I've never been to Sweden** je ne suis jamais allé en Suède; **have you ever been to Africa?** tu es déjà allé en Afrique?; **has the postman been?** est-ce que le facteur est passé?
(f) (age) avoir; **how old are you?** quel âge as-tu?; **I am 23** j'ai 23 ans
(g) (in mathematics) faire; **2 plus 2 is 4** 2 et 2 font 4
(h) (cost) coûter; **how much is it?** combien ça coûte?
(i) (phrases) **so ~ it** d'accord; **if I were you** à ta place

⓶ v aux (a) (in passives) être; **the doors have been repainted** les portes ont été repeintes, on a repeint les portes; **it is said that...** on dit que...
(b) (in continuous tenses) **we are going to London tomorrow** nous allons à Londres demain; **it is raining** il pleut; **he is reading** il lit, il est en train de lire; ▶ FOR , SINCE
(c) (with infinitive) devoir; **you are to do it at once** tu dois le faire tout de suite; **they are to ~ married** ils vont se marier; **it was to ~ expected** il fallait s'y attendre; **it was nowhere to ~ found** il était introuvable
(d) (in tag questions) **it's a lovely house, isn't it?** c'est une très belle maison, n'est-ce pas?; **they're not in the garden, are they?** ils ne sont pas dans le jardin, par hasard?; **today is Tuesday, isn't it?** c'est bien mardi aujourd'hui?
(e) (in short answers) **'you are not going out'—'yes I am!'** 'tu ne sors pas'—'si!'; **'are you English?'—'yes, I am'** 'vous êtes anglais?'—'oui', 'oui, je suis anglais'

beach n plage f

beach ball n ballon m de plage

beach buggy n buggy m

beacon n (a) (on runway) balise f
(b) (lighthouse) phare m
(c) (also **radio ~**) radiobalise f

bead n (a) perle f; (string of) **~s** collier m
(b) (of sweat, dew) goutte f

beak n bec m

beam ⓵ n (a) (of light, torch) rayon m; (of car lights, lighthouse) faisceau m
(b) (wooden) poutre f
⓶ vtr transmettre ⟨signal⟩
⓷ vi rayonner

bean n haricot m

beansprout n germe m de soja

bear ⓵ n ours m
⓶ vtr (a) (carry) porter; **to ~ a resemblance to** ressembler à; **to ~ no relation to** n'avoir aucun rapport avec; **to ~ sth in mind** tenir compte de qch
(b) (endure) supporter; **I can't ~ to watch** je ne veux pas voir ça
(c) (stand up to) résister à ⟨scrutiny, inspection⟩
(d) (yield) donner ⟨fruit, crop⟩; ⟨investment⟩ rapporter ⟨interest⟩
⓷ vi (a) **to ~ left/right** ⟨person⟩ prendre à gauche/à droite
(b) **to bring pressure to ~ on sb** exercer une pression sur qn
■ **bear out** confirmer ⟨claim, story⟩; appuyer ⟨person⟩
■ **bear up** ⟨person⟩ tenir le coup; ⟨structure⟩ résister
■ **bear with**: **~ with [sb]** être indulgent/-e avec; **~ with me for a minute** pardonnez-moi un instant

bearable adj supportable

beard n barbe f

bearded adj barbu/-e

bearer *n* (of news, gift, letter) porteur/-euse *m/f*; (of passport) titulaire *mf*

bearing *n* (a) (of person) allure *f*
(b) **to have no/little ~ on sth** n'avoir aucun rapport/avoir peu de rapport avec qch
(c) **to take a compass ~** faire un relevé au compas

bearings *n pl* **to get one's ~** se repérer

beast *n* (a) (animal) bête *f*
(b) (colloq) (person) brute *f*

beat ① *n* (a) (of drum, heart) battement *m*
(b) (rhythm) rythme *m*
(c) (of policeman) ronde *f*
② *vtr* (a) battre; **to ~ sb with a stick** donner des coups de bâton à qn; **to ~ sb at tennis** battre qn au tennis; **to ~ time** (Mus) battre la mesure; **she beat me to it** elle a été plus rapide que moi
(b) **it ~s walking** c'est mieux que marcher; **you can't ~ Italian shoes** rien ne vaut les chaussures italiennes
③ *vi* ⟨waves, rain⟩ battre (**against** contre); ⟨person⟩ cogner (**at**, **on** à); ⟨heart, drum, wings⟩ battre
■ **beat back** repousser ⟨group, flames⟩
■ **beat down** ⟨rain⟩ tomber à verse (**on** sur); ⟨sun⟩ taper (**on** sur)
■ **beat off** repousser ⟨attacker⟩
■ **beat up** tabasser (colloq) ⟨person⟩

beating *n* (a) (punishment) raclée *f* (colloq), correction *f*
(b) (of drum, heart, wings) battement *m*

beautician *n* esthéticien/-ienne *m/f*

beautiful *adj* beau/belle (*before n*); ⟨weather, shot⟩ superbe; **a ~ place** un bel endroit.

■ **Note** the irregular form *bel* of the adjective *beau, belle* is used before masculine nouns beginning with a vowel or a mute 'h'.

beautifully *adv* (a) ⟨play, write⟩ admirablement
(b) ⟨furnished⟩ magnifiquement; **~ dressed** habillé/-e avec beaucoup de goût

beauty *n* beauté *f*

beauty parlour (GB), **beauty parlor** (US) *n* salon *m* de beauté

beauty queen *n* reine *f* de beauté

beauty salon *n* salon *m* de beauté

beauty spot *n* (a) (on skin) grain *m* de beauté; (fake) mouche *f*
(b) (place) beau site *m* or coin *m*

beaver *n* castor *m*

because ① *conj* parce que
② **because of** *phr* à cause de

beckon ① *vtr* faire signe à; **to ~ sb in** faire signe à qn d'entrer
② *vi* faire signe (**to sb to do** à qn de faire)

become ① *vi* devenir; **to ~ ill** tomber malade
② *v impers* **what has ~ of your brother?** qu'est-ce que ton frère est devenu?

becoming *adj* ⟨behaviour⟩ convenable; ⟨garment, haircut⟩ seyant/-e

bed *n* (a) lit *m*; **to go to ~** aller au lit
(b) (of flowers) parterre *m*
(c) (of sea) fond *m*; (of river) lit *m*

bed and breakfast, B and B *n* chambre *f* avec petit déjeuner, ≈ chambre *f* d'hôte

bedclothes *n pl* couvertures *fpl*

bedraggled *adj* dépenaillé/-e

bedridden *adj* alité/-e, cloué/-e au lit

bedroom *n* chambre *f* (à coucher)

bedside *n* chevet *m*

bedsit, bedsitter *n* (GB) chambre *f* meublée

bedspread *n* dessus *m* de lit

bedtime *n* **it's ~** c'est l'heure d'aller se coucher

bee *n* abeille *f*

beech *n* hêtre *m*

beef *n* bœuf *m*; **roast ~** rôti *m* de bœuf

beefburger *n* hamburger *m*

beehive *n* ruche *f*

beeline *n*
IDIOMS **to make a ~ for** se diriger tout droit vers

beep ① *n* (of electronic device) bip *m*; (of car) coup *m* de klaxon®
② *vi* ⟨device⟩ faire bip *or* bip-bip; ⟨car⟩ klaxonner

beer *n* bière *f*

bee sting *n* piqûre *f* d'abeille

beet *n* betterave *f*

beetle *n* scarabée *m*

beetroot *n* (GB) betterave *f*

before ① *prep* (a) avant; **the day ~ yesterday** avant-hier; **the day ~ the exam** la veille de l'examen
(b) (in front of) devant
(c) (US) (in telling time) **ten ~ six** six heures moins dix
② *adj* précédent/-e, d'avant; **the day ~** la veille; **the week ~** la semaine précédente (a) (beforehand)
③ *adv* (a) (beforehand) avant; **long ~** bien avant; (previously) auparavant
two months ~ deux mois auparavant
(b) (already) déjà; **have you been to India ~?** est-ce que tu es déjà allé en Inde?; **I've never seen him ~ in my life** c'est la première fois que je le vois; **you never told me ~** tu ne m'as jamais dit ça
④ *conj* avant de (+ *infinitive*), avant que (+ *subj*); **~ I go**, I would like to say that avant de partir, je voudrais dire que; **~ he goes**, I must remind him that avant qu'il parte, il faut que je lui rappelle que

beforehand *adv* (ahead of time) à l'avance; (earlier) auparavant, avant

befriend *vtr* (look after) prendre [qn] sous son aile; (make friends with) se lier d'amitié avec

beg ① *vtr* demander (**from** à); **to ~ sb for sth** demander qch à qn; **I ~ your pardon** je vous demande pardon

2 *vi* ‹person› mendier (**from** à); ‹dog› faire le beau; **to ~ for help** demander de l'aide

beggar *n* mendiant/-e *m/f*

begin **1** *vtr* commencer ‹journey, meeting, meal, game› (**with** par, avec); provoquer ‹debate, dispute›; lancer ‹campaign, trend›; déclencher ‹war›; **to ~ doing** commencer à faire

2 *vi* commencer; **to ~ with sth** commencer par qch; **to ~ again** recommencer

3 **to begin with** *phr* (at first) au début, au départ; (firstly) d'abord, premièrement

beginner *n* débutant/-e *m/f*

beginning *n* début *m*, commencement *m*; **in** *or* **at the ~** au départ, au début; **to go back to the ~** reprendre au début

beginnings *n pl* (of person, business) débuts *mpl*; (of movement) origines *fpl*

behalf: on ~ of (GB), **in ~ of** (US) *phr* ‹act, speak› au nom de, pour; ‹phone, write› de la part de; ‹negotiate› pour le compte de

behave **1** *vi* se comporter, se conduire (**towards** envers)

2 *v refl* **to ~ oneself** bien se comporter; **~ yourself!** tiens-toi bien!

behaviour (GB), **behavior** (US) *n* (gen) comportement *m* (**towards** envers); (Sch) conduite *f*; **to be on one's best ~** bien se tenir

behead *vtr* décapiter

behind **1** *n* (colloq) derrière *m* (colloq)

2 *adj* **to be ~** avoir du retard dans ‹work›; **to be too far ~** avoir trop de retard

3 *adv* ‹follow on› derrière; ‹look, glance› en arrière; **the car ~** la voiture de derrière

4 *prep* (a) derrière; **~ my back** derrière le dos; (figurative) derrière mon dos; **~ the scenes** en coulisses

(b) (supporting) **to be (solidly) ~ sb** soutenir qn (à fond)

beige *n, adj* beige (*m*)

Beijing *pr n* Pékin, Bei-jing

being *n* (a) (human) ~ être *m* (humain)

(b) **to come into ~** prendre naissance

Beirut *pr n* Beyrouth

Belarus *pr n* Bélarus *f*

belch **1** *n* renvoi *m*, rot *m*

2 *vtr* (also ~ **out**) vomir, cracher ‹smoke, fire›

3 *vi* avoir un renvoi

belfry *n* beffroi *m*, clocher *m*

Belgian **1** *n* Belge *mf*

2 *adj* belge; ‹embassy› de Belgique

Belgium *pr n* Belgique *f*

belie *vtr* démentir

belief *n* (a) (opinion) conviction *f* (**about** sur, à propos de)

(b) (confidence) confiance *f*, foi *f* (**in** dans)

(c) (religious faith) foi *f*

believable *adj* crédible

believe **1** *vtr* croire; **I don't ~ you!** ce n'est pas vrai!

2 *vi* **to ~ in** croire à ‹promises, ghosts›; croire en ‹God›

believer *n* (in God) croyant/-e *m/f*; (in progress, liberty) adepte *mf* (**in** de)

belittle *vtr* rabaisser

bell *n* (in church) cloche *f*; (handbell) clochette *f*; (on toy, cat) grelot *m*; (on bicycle) sonnette *f*; **door ~** sonnette *f*

IDIOMS **that name rings a ~** ce nom me dit quelque chose

belligerent **1** *n* belligérant *m*

2 *adj* ‹person› agressif/-ive; ‹country› belligérant/-e

bellow *vi* ‹bull› mugir (**with** de); ‹person› hurler

bellows *n pl* soufflet *m*

belly *n* ventre *m*

bellyache *n* (colloq) mal *m* au ventre

bellybutton *n* (colloq) nombril *m*

belong *vi* **to ~ to** ‹property› appartenir à ‹person›; ‹person› faire partie de ‹club, society, set›; **where do these books ~?** où vont ces livres?

belongings *n pl* affaires *fpl*; **personal ~** effets *mpl* personnels

beloved *n, adj* bien-aimé/-e (*m/f*)

below **1** *prep* au-dessous de; **~ freezing** au-dessous de zéro; **~ the surface** sous la surface

2 *adv* **the apartment ~** l'appartement du dessous; **the people (in the street) ~** les gens en bas (dans la rue); **the village ~** le village en contrebas; **100 metres ~** 100 mètres plus bas; **see ~** (on page) voir ci-dessous

belt **1** *n* (gen) ceinture *f*

(b) (Tech) courroie *f*

2 *vtr* (colloq) (hit) flanquer une beigne à (colloq) ‹person›

IDIOMS **to tighten one's ~** se serrer la ceinture; **that was below the ~** c'était un coup bas

▪ **belt out: ~ out** [sth], **~** [sth] **out** chanter [qch] à pleins poumons ‹song›

▪ **belt up** (a) (colloq) (shut up) la fermer (colloq), se taire

(b) (Aut) attacher sa ceinture de sécurité

bemused *adj* perplexe

bench *n* (a) (gen) banc *m*; (workbench) établi *m*

(b) (Law) (also **Bench**) (judges collectively) magistrature *f* (assise); (judges hearing a case) Cour *f*

benchmark **1** *n* (a) (gen) point *m* de référence

(b) (Comput) test *m* de performance

2 *vtr* évaluer les performances de ‹computer system›

bend **1** *n* (in road) tournant *m*, virage *m*; (in river) courbe *f*

2 *vtr* plier ‹arm, leg›; pencher ‹head›; tordre ‹pipe, nail, wire›

3 *vi* (a) ‹road, path› tourner; ‹branch› ployer

(b) ‹person› se pencher; **to ~ forward** se pencher en avant

▪ **bend down**, **bend over** se pencher

beneath ⓵ *prep* (a) sous; ～ **the calm exterior** sous des apparences calmes
(b) **it is ～ you to do** c'est indigne de toi de faire
⓶ *adv* en dessous; **the apartment ～** l'appartement en dessous

benefactor *n* bienfaiteur *m*

beneficial *adj* ⟨*effect, influence*⟩ bénéfique; ⟨*change*⟩ salutaire

beneficiary *n* bénéficiaire *mf*

benefit ⓵ *n* (a) (advantage) avantage *m* **(from** de)
(b) (financial aid) allocation *f*; **to be on ～(s)** (GB) toucher les allocations
⓶ *adj* ⟨*concert, match*⟩ de bienfaisance
⓷ *vtr* profiter à ⟨*person*⟩; être avantageux/-euse pour ⟨*group, nation*⟩
⓸ *vi* profiter; **to ～ from** tirer profit de; **to ～ from doing** gagner à faire
IDIOMS **to give sb the ～ of the doubt** accorder à qn le bénéfice du doute

benevolent *adj* bienveillant/-e

benign *adj* (a) ⟨*person, smile*⟩ bienveillant/-e
(b) (Med) bénin/-igne

bent *adj* (a) ⟨*nail, wire, stick*⟩ tordu/-e; ⟨*person*⟩ (stooped) courbé/-e
(b) **to be ～ on doing** vouloir à tout prix faire

bereaved *adj* endeuillé/-e, en deuil

bereavement *n* deuil *m*

berry *n* baie *f*

berserk *adj* **to go ～** être pris/-e de folie furieuse

berth ⓵ *n* (a) (bunk) couchette *f*
(b) (at dock) mouillage *m*
⓶ *vtr* faire mouiller ⟨*ship*⟩
⓷ *vi* ⟨*ship*⟩ venir à quai
IDIOMS **to give sb/sth a wide ～** (colloq) éviter qn/qch

beset *adj* **a country ～ by strikes** un pays en proie aux grèves

beside *prep* (a) (next to) à côté de; **～ the sea** au bord de la mer
(b) (in comparison with) par rapport à
IDIOMS **to be ～ oneself (with anger)** être hors de soi; **to be ～ oneself (with joy)** être fou/folle de joie

besides ⓵ *adv* (a) (moreover) d'ailleurs
(b) (in addition) en plus, aussi
⓶ *prep* en plus de

besiege *vtr* (Mil) assiéger; (figurative) assaillir

besotted *adj* follement épris/-e (**with** de)

best ⓵ *n* **the ～** le meilleur/la meilleure *m/f*; **the ～ of friends** les meilleurs amis/ meilleures amies du monde; **at ～** au mieux; **to make the ～ of sth** s'accommoder de qch; **to do one's ～ to do** faire de son mieux *or* faire (tout) son possible pour faire; **all the ～!** (good luck) bonne chance!; (cheers) à ta santé!
⓶ *adj* meilleur/-e; **the ～ book I've ever read** le meilleur livre que j'aie jamais lu; **my ～ dress** ma plus belle robe

⓷ *adv* le mieux; **～ of all** mieux que tout

best friend *n* meilleur ami/meilleure amie *m/f*

best man *n* témoin *m*

bestow *vtr* accorder ⟨*honour*⟩ (**on** à); conférer ⟨*title*⟩ (**on** à)

bestseller *n* bestseller *m*

best-selling *adj* ⟨*product*⟩ le/la plus vendu/-e; **the ～ novelist of 1999** le romancier qui s'est vendu le plus en 1999

bet ⓵ *n* pari *m*; (in casino) mise *f*
⓶ *vtr* parier (**on** sur)
⓷ *vi* parier (**on** sur); (in casino) miser

betray *vtr* trahir

betrayal *n* trahison *f*

better

■ Note When *better* is used as an adjective, it is translated by *meilleur* or *mieux* depending on the context (see 2 below, and note that *meilleur* is the comparative form of *bon*, *mieux* the comparative form of *bien*).

⓵ *n* **the ～ of the two** le meilleur/la meilleure *or* le/la mieux des deux; **so much the ～** tant mieux
⓶ *adj* meilleur/-e; mieux; **this wine is ～** ce vin est meilleur; **to get ～** ⟨*situation, weather*⟩ s'améliorer; ⟨*ill person*⟩ aller mieux; **things are getting ～** ça va mieux; **to be ～** ⟨*patient, cold*⟩ aller mieux; **to be a ～ swimmer than sb** nager mieux que qn; **to be ～ at** être meilleur/-e en ⟨*subject, sport*⟩; **it's ～ than nothing** c'est mieux que rien; **the bigger/sooner the ～** le plus grand/vite possible; **the less said about that the ～** mieux vaut ne pas parler de ça
⓷ *adv* mieux; **you had ～ do, you'd ～ do** (advising) tu ferais mieux de faire; (warning) tu as intérêt à faire; **we'd ～ leave** on ferait mieux de partir
⓸ *vtr* améliorer
IDIOMS **for ～ (or) for worse** advienne que pourra; (in wedding vow) pour le meilleur et pour le pire; **to get the ～ of** triompher de ⟨*opponent*⟩; **his curiosity got the ～ of him** sa curiosité a pris le dessus; **to go one ～** faire encore mieux (**than** que); **to think ～ of it** changer d'avis

better off *adj* (a) (more wealthy) plus riche (**than** que)
(b) (in better situation) mieux

betting *n* paris *mpl*

betting shop *n* (GB) bureau *m* de PMU

between ⓵ *prep* (a) entre; **～ you and me, ～ ourselves** entre nous; **～ now and next year** d'ici l'année prochaine
(b) **they drank the whole bottle ～ (the two of)** them ils ont bu toute la bouteille à eux deux
⓶ *adv* (also **in ～**) (in space) au milieu, entre les deux; (in time) entre-temps; **the two main roads and the streets (in) ～** les deux rues principales et les petites rues situées entre elles; **neither red nor orange, but somewhere in ～** ni rouge ni orange mais entre les deux

beverage n boisson f, breuvage m

beware ① excl prenez garde!, attention!
② vi se méfier (**of** de); ~ **of**... attention à...

bewildered adj ⟨person⟩ déconcerté/-e (**at**, **by** par); ⟨look⟩ perplexe

bewildering adj déconcertant/-e

bewitch vtr ensorceler

beyond ① prep (a) (in space and time) au-delà de
(b) ~ **one's means** au-dessus de ses moyens; ~ **all hope** au-delà de toute espérance; ~ **one's control** hors de son contrôle; **he is** ~ **help** on ne peut rien faire pour lui; **it's** ~ **me** ça me dépasse
(c) (other than) en dehors de, à part
② adv au-delà
③ conj à part (+ infinitive)
IDIOMS **to be in the back of** ~ être au bout du monde

bias ① n (a) (prejudice) parti m pris
(b) (tendency) tendance f
② vtr **to** ~ **sb against/in favour of** prévenir qn contre/en faveur de

biased, biassed adj ⟨person⟩ partial/-e; ⟨report⟩ manquant d'objectivité; **to be** ~ ⟨person⟩ avoir des partis pris; **to be** ~ **against** avoir un préjugé défavorable envers

bib n (baby's) bavoir m; (of apron, dungarees) bavette f

Bible n Bible f

biblical adj biblique

bibliography n bibliographie f

bicarbonate of soda n bicarbonate m de soude

bicentenary, bicentennial n bicentenaire m

biceps n biceps m

bicker vi se chamailler (**about** au sujet de)

bickering n chamailleries fpl

bicycle ① n bicyclette f, vélo m; **on a/by** ~ à bicyclette
② adj ⟨pump⟩ à bicyclette; ⟨bell, lamp⟩ de bicyclette; ⟨race⟩ cycliste

bicycle clip n pince f à vélo

bicycle lane n piste f cyclable

bid ① n (a) (at auction) enchère f (**for** sur; **to** de)
(b) (for contract) soumission f
(c) (attempt) tentative f (**to do** pour faire)
② vtr (a) offrir ⟨money⟩ (**for** pour)
(b) (say) **to** ~ **sb good morning** dire bonjour à qn
③ vi (at auction) enchérir (**for** sur); (for contract) soumissionner (**for** pour)

bidder n (at auction) enchérisseur/-euse m/f; **to go to the highest** ~ être adjugé/-e au plus offrant/-e

bidding n (at auction) enchères fpl

bide vi
IDIOMS **to** ~ **one's time** attendre le bon moment

bidet n bidet m

bifocals n pl verres mpl à double foyer

big adj (gen) grand/-e (before n); (bulky, fat) gros/grosse (before n); ⟨meal⟩ copieux/-ieuse; **to get** ~**(ger)** (taller) grandir; (fatter) grossir; **a** ~ **book** (thick) un gros livre; (large-format) un grand livre; **his** ~ **brother** son grand frère, son frère aîné; **a** ~ **mistake** une grave erreur; **to be in** ~ **trouble** être dans le pétrin (colloq); **to have** ~ **ideas, to think** ~ voir grand

bigamy n bigamie f

big business n (a) les grandes entreprises fpl
(b) **to be** ~ rapporter gros

big dipper n (GB) (at fair) montagnes fpl russes

big game n gros gibier m

bigheaded adj (colloq) prétentieux/-ieuse

bigmouth n (colloq) **he's such a** ~ ! il ne sait pas tenir sa langue!

big name n (in music, art) grand nom m; (in film, sport) star f; **to be a** ~ être connu/-e (**in** dans le monde de)

bigoted adj intolérant/-e, sectaire

bigotry n intolérance f, sectarisme m

big screen n grand écran m

big shot n (colloq) gros bonnet m (colloq)

big toe n gros orteil m

big top n (tent) grand chapiteau m

bike n (cycle) vélo m; (motorbike) moto f

biker n (colloq) motard m (colloq)

bikini n bikini® m

bilingual adj bilingue

bill ① n (a) (in restaurant) addition f; (for services, electricity) facture f; (from hotel, doctor, dentist) note f
(b) (Pol) projet m de loi
(c) (poster) affiche f
(d) (US) **dollar** ~ billet m d'un dollar
(e) (beak) bec m
② vtr **to** ~ **sb for sth** facturer qch à qn
IDIOMS **to fit** or **fill the** ~ faire l'affaire

billboard n panneau m d'affichage

billet vtr cantonner (**on, with** chez)

billiards n billard m

billion n (a thousand million) milliard m; (GB) (a million million) billion m

billionaire n milliardaire mf

billow vi ⟨clouds, smoke⟩ s'élever en tourbillons
■ **billow out** ⟨skirt, sail⟩ se gonfler; ⟨steam⟩ s'élever

billy goat n bouc m

bimbo n (colloq) ravissante idiote f (derogatory)

bin n (GB) (for rubbish) poubelle f

bind vtr (a) (tie up) attacher (**to** à)
(b) **to be bound by** être tenu/-e par ⟨law, oath⟩
(c) (also ~ **together**) unir ⟨people, community⟩
(d) relier ⟨book⟩

binder n (for papers, lecture notes) classeur m

binding ① n reliure f

2 adj ‹agreement, contract› qui engage
binge n (colloq) to go on a ∼ faire la noce
bingo n bingo m
bin liner n (GB) sac m poubelle
binoculars n pl jumelles fpl
biochemist n biochimiste mf
biochemistry n biochimie f
biodegradable adj biodégradable
biodiversity n diversité f biologique
bioengineering n génie m biologique
biographical adj biographique
biography n biographie f
biological adj biologique
biological clock n horloge f biologique
biological warfare n guerre f
  biologique
biologist n biologiste mf
biology n biologie f
biopsy n biopsie f
biotechnology n biotechnologie f
birch n bouleau m
bird n (a) (Zool) oiseau m
  (b) (GB) (colloq) (girl) nana f (colloq)
  IDIOMS to kill two ∼s with one stone faire
  d'une pierre deux coups
bird of prey n oiseau m de proie
bird's eye view n vue f d'ensemble
birdsong n chant m des oiseaux
bird-watching n to go ∼ observer les
  oiseaux
biro® n (GB) stylo-bille m, bic® m
birth n naissance f (of de)
birth certificate n certificat m de
  naissance
birth control n (in society) contrôle m des
  naissances; (by couple) contraception f
birthday n anniversaire m; Happy
  Birthday! Bon or Joyeux Anniversaire!
birthday party n (for child) goûter m
  d'anniversaire; (for adult) soirée f
  d'anniversaire
birthing pool n piscine f d'accouchement
birthmark n tache f de naissance
birth mother n mère f biologique
birthplace n lieu m de naissance
birthrate n taux m de natalité
birth sign n signe m du zodiaque
biscuit n (a) (GB) biscuit m, petit gâteau m
  (b) (US) pain m au lait
bisexual n, adj bisexuel/-elle (m/f)
bishop n (a) évêque m
  (b) (in chess) fou m
bit **1** n (a) (gen) morceau m (of de); (of paper,
  string, land) bout m (of de); (of book, film)
  passage m
  (b) (colloq) a ∼ (of) un peu (de); a little ∼ un
  petit peu
  (c) (of horse) mors m
  2 a bit phr (colloq) un peu; a ∼ early un
  peu trop tôt; she isn't a ∼ like me elle ne me
  ressemble pas du tout

IDIOMS ∼ by ∼ petit à petit; ∼s and pieces
  (fragments) morceaux mpl; (belongings) affaires
  fpl
bitch n (a) (dog) chienne f
  (b) (colloq derogatory) garce f (colloq)
bite **1** n (a) morsure f; (from insect) piqûre f
  (b) (mouthful) bouchée f; to have a ∼ to eat
  manger un morceau
  2 vtr ‹animal, person› mordre; ‹insect›
  piquer; to ∼ one's nails se ronger les ongles
  3 vi ‹fish› mordre
  ■ **bite off**: ∼ off [sth], ∼ [sth] off arracher
  [qch] d'un coup de dent
biting adj (a) ‹wind› cinglant/-e
  (b) ‹comment› mordant/-e
bitter adj (gen) amer/-ère; ‹wind› glacial/-e;
  ‹disappointment, truth› cruel/-elle
  IDIOMS to the ∼ end jusqu'au bout
bitterly adv ‹complain, speak› amèrement;
  ‹regret› profondément; it's ∼ cold il fait un
  froid terrible
bitterness n amertume f
bizarre adj bizarre
black **1** n (a) (colour) noir m
  (b) (also **Black**) (person) Noir/-e m/f
  (c) to be in the ∼ être créditeur/-trice
  2 adj (a) (gen) noir/-e; ‹night› obscur/-e;
  ‹tea› nature; to turn ∼ noircir
  (b) (also **Black**) ‹community, culture›
  noir/-e
  ■ **black out** ‹person› s'évanouir
black and white **1** n noir et blanc m
  2 adj ‹TV, camera film› noir et blanc inv;
  ‹movie, photography› (en) noir et blanc inv
blackberry n mûre f
blackbird n merle m
blackboard n tableau m (noir); on the ∼
  au tableau
black box n boîte f noire
blackcurrant n cassis m
blacken vtr noircir
black eye n œil m poché
blackhead n point m noir
black ice n verglas m
blacklist **1** n liste f noire
  2 vtr mettre [qn] à l'index
blackmail **1** n chantage m
  2 vtr faire chanter ‹victim›
blackmailer n maître-chanteur m
black market n on the ∼ au marché
  noir
blackout n (a) (power cut) panne f de
  courant; (in wartime) black-out m
  (b) (faint) étourdissement m
Black Sea pr n mer f Noire
black sheep n brebis f galeuse
blacksmith n forgeron m
black tie n (on invitation) '∼' tenue f de
  soirée'
bladder n vessie f
blade n (of knife, sword, axe) lame f; (of fan,
  propeller, oar) pale f; (of grass) brin m
blame **1** n responsabilité f (for de)   ⋯⋫

2 *vtr* I ~ you c'est ta faute; **to ~ sb for sth** reprocher qch à qn; **to ~ sth on sb** tenir qn responsable de qch; **to be to ~ for sth** être responsable de qch

3 *v refl* **to ~ oneself for sth** se sentir responsable de qch

blameless *adj* irréprochable

blancmange *n* blanc-manger *m*

bland *adj* ⟨*food, flavour*⟩ fade; ⟨*person*⟩ terne

blank **1** *n* **(a)** (empty space) blanc *m*; **my mind's a ~** j'ai la tête vide
(b) (cartridge) cartouche *f* à blanc
2 *adj* **(a)** ⟨*paper, page*⟩ blanc/blanche; ⟨*screen*⟩ vide; ⟨*cassette*⟩ vierge
(b) ⟨*expression*⟩ ébahi/-e; **my mind went ~** j'ai eu un trou de mémoire
■ **blank out**: **~** [sth] **out**, **~ out** [sth] rayer [qch] de sa mémoire

blank cheque (GB), **blank check** (US) *n* chèque *m* en blanc; (figurative) carte *f* blanche

blanket *n* **(a)** couverture *f*
(b) (of snow) couche *f*; (of cloud, fog) nappe *f*

blare *v* ■ **blare out**: **¶ ~ out** ⟨*music, radio*⟩ jouer à plein volume; **¶ ~ out** [sth] déverser ⟨*music*⟩

blasphemous *adj* ⟨*person*⟩ blasphémateur/-trice; ⟨*statement*⟩ blasphématoire

blasphemy *n* blasphème *m*

blast **1** *n* **(a)** (explosion) explosion *f*
(b) (of air) souffle *m*
(c) **at full ~** ⟨*play music*⟩ à plein volume
2 *vtr* (blow up) faire sauter; **to ~ a hole in the wall** percer un mur à l'explosif
■ **blast off** ⟨*rocket*⟩ décoller

blast-off *n* lancement *m*

blatant *adj* ⟨*lie, disregard*⟩ éhonté/-e; ⟨*abuse*⟩ flagrant/-e

blatantly *adv* ouvertement; **to be ~ obvious** sauter aux yeux

blaze **1** *n* (fire) incendie *m*; (in hearth) feu *m*, flambée *f*; **in a ~ of publicity** sous les feux des médias
2 *vtr* **to ~ a trail** faire œuvre de pionnier
3 *vi* (also **~ away**) **(a)** ⟨*fire, house*⟩ brûler
(b) ⟨*lights*⟩ briller

blazer *n* blazer *m*

blazing *adj* (violent) ⟨*argument*⟩ violent/-e; ⟨*fire*⟩ ronflant/-e; ⟨*building, car*⟩ embrasé/-e

bleach **1** *n* **(a)** (disinfectant) eau *f* de javel
(b) (for hair) décolorant *m*
2 *vtr* décolorer ⟨*hair*⟩; blanchir ⟨*linen*⟩

bleak *adj* ⟨*landscape*⟩ désolé/-e; ⟨*weather*⟩ maussade; ⟨*outlook, future*⟩ sombre

bleary *adj* ⟨*eyes*⟩ bouffi/-e; **to be ~-eyed** avoir les yeux bouffis

bleat *vi* ⟨*sheep, goat*⟩ bêler

bleed **1** *vtr* **to ~ sb dry** saigner qn à blanc
2 *vi* saigner; **my finger's ~ing** j'ai le doigt qui saigne

bleep **1** *n* (signal) bip *m*, bip-bip *m*
2 *vtr* **to ~ sb** appeler qn (au bip), biper qn

bleeper *n* (GB) bip *m*

blemish *n* (gen) imperfection *f*; (on fruit) tache *f*; (pimple) bouton *m*

blend **1** *n* mélange *m* (of de)
2 *vtr* mélanger ⟨*ingredients, colours, styles*⟩
3 *vi* **to ~ (together)** ⟨*colours, tastes, styles*⟩ se fondre; **to ~ with** ⟨*colours, tastes, sounds*⟩ se marier à; ⟨*smells*⟩ se mêler à
■ **blend in**: **¶ ~ in** s'harmoniser (**with** avec); **¶ ~** [sth] **in** incorporer ⟨*ingredient*⟩

blender *n* mixeur *m*, mixer *m*

bless *vtr* bénir; **~ you!** (after sneeze) à vos souhaits!; **to be ~ed with** jouir de ⟨*health, beauty*⟩

blessing *n* **(a)** bénédiction *f*
(b) (good thing) bienfait *m*; **a ~ in disguise** un bienfait caché

blight *n* (on society) plaie *f* (on de); **urban ~** délabrement *m* urbain

blind **1** *n* **(a)** **the ~** les aveugles *mpl*
(b) (on window) store *m*
2 *adj* ⟨*person*⟩ aveugle; **to go ~** perdre la vue; **~ in one eye** borgne
3 *vtr* **(a)** ⟨*injury, accident*⟩ rendre aveugle
(b) ⟨*sun, light*⟩ éblouir
(c) ⟨*pride, love*⟩ aveugler
IDIOMS **to turn a ~ eye** fermer les yeux (**to** sur)

blind alley *n* voie *f* sans issue

blind date *n* rendez-vous *m* avec un/-e inconnu/-e

blindfold **1** *n* bandeau *m*
2 *adj* (also **~ed**) aux yeux bandés
3 *adv* les yeux bandés
4 *vtr* bander les yeux à ⟨*person*⟩

blinding *adj* ⟨*light*⟩ aveuglant/-e; ⟨*headache*⟩ atroce

blindly *adv* ⟨*obey, follow*⟩ aveuglément

blindness *n* cécité *f*; (figurative) aveuglement *m*

blind spot *n* **(a)** (in eye) point *m* aveugle
(b) (in car, on hill) angle *m* mort

blink *vi* ⟨*person*⟩ cligner des yeux; ⟨*light*⟩ clignoter

blinker *n* **(a)** (Aut) clignotant *m*
(b) **~s** œillères *fpl*

blinkered *adj* ⟨*attitude, approach*⟩ borné/-e

blip *n* (on screen) spot *m*; (on graph) accident *m* (d'une courbe)

bliss *n* bonheur *m* parfait

blissfully *adv* **~ happy** au comble du bonheur; **~ ignorant** dans la plus parfaite ignorance

blister **1** *n* (on skin) ampoule *f*
2 *vi* ⟨*skin, paint*⟩ cloquer

blister pack *n* blister *m*, habillage *m* transparent

blithely *adv* (nonchalantly) avec insouciance; (cheerfully) allègrement

blitz **1** *n* bombardement *m* aérien
2 *vtr* bombarder

blizzard *n* tempête *f* de neige; (in Arctic regions) blizzard *m*

bloated adj ⟨face, body⟩ bouffi/-e; ⟨stomach⟩ ballonné/-e

blob n (a) (drop) grosse goutte f
(b) (shape) forme f floue

block **1** n (a) (slab) bloc m
(b) ~ of flats immeuble m (d'habitation); **office** ~ immeuble de bureaux
(c) (of houses) pâté m de maisons
(d) (for butcher, executioner) billot m
2 vtr bloquer ⟨exit, road, ball⟩; boucher ⟨drain, hole, artery, view⟩; **to have a ~ed nose** avoir le nez bouché
■ **block out**: ~ out [sth], ~ [sth] out (a) (hide) boucher ⟨view⟩; cacher ⟨light, sun⟩
(b) (suppress) refouler ⟨memory, problem⟩

blockade **1** n blocus m
2 vtr bloquer, faire le blocus de ⟨port⟩

blockage n obstruction f

blockbook vtr louer [qch] en groupe ⟨seats⟩

blockbuster n (colloq) (a) (book) livre m à succès, bestseller m
(b) (film) superproduction f

block capitals, **block letters** n pl **in** ~ (on form) en caractères mpl or capitales fpl d'imprimerie

bloke n (colloq) type m (colloq), mec m (colloq)

blonde **1** n blonde f
2 adj blond/-e

blood n sang m
IDIOMS **in cold** ~ de sang-froid

blood bank n banque f du sang

bloodcurdling adj à vous figer le sang dans les veines

blood donor n donneur/-euse m/f de sang

blood group n groupe m sanguin

blood pressure n tension f artérielle; **high** ~ hypertension f

blood relation n parent/-e m/f par le sang

bloodshed n effusion f de sang

bloodshot adj injecté/-e de sang

blood sport n sport m sanguinaire

bloodstained adj taché/-e de sang

bloodstream n sang m

blood test n analyse f de sang

bloodthirsty adj sanguinaire

blood type n groupe m sanguin

bloody **1** adj (a) ⟨hand, body⟩ ensanglanté/-e; ⟨battle⟩ sanglant/-e
(b) (GB) (colloq) sacré/-e (before n); ~ **fool!** espèce d'idiot!
2 adv (GB) (slang) sacrément (colloq)

bloom **1** n (flower) fleur f; **in** ~ en fleur
2 vi (a) (be in flower) être fleuri/-e; (come into flower) fleurir
(b) **to be ~ing with health** être resplendissant/-e de santé

blossom **1** n (flower) fleur f; (flowers) fleurs fpl
2 vi fleurir; (figurative) s'épanouir

blot **1** n (gen) tache f; (of ink) pâté m; (figurative) ombre f

2 vtr (a) (dry) sécher [qch] au buvard ⟨ink⟩
(b) (stain) tacher
■ **blot out** effacer ⟨memories⟩; masquer ⟨view⟩

blotch n (on skin) plaque f rouge; (of ink, colour) tache f

blotchy adj ⟨complexion⟩ marbré/-e

blotting paper n papier m buvard

blouse n chemisier m

blow **1** n coup m
2 vtr (a) **the wind blew the door shut** un coup de vent a fermé la porte; **to be blown off course** ⟨ship⟩ être dévié/-e par le vent
(b) ⟨person⟩ faire ⟨bubble, smoke ring⟩; souffler ⟨glass⟩; **to** ~ **one's nose** se moucher; **to** ~ **one's whistle** donner un coup de sifflet
(c) ⟨explosion⟩ faire ⟨hole⟩ (in dans); **to be blown to pieces** or **bits by** être réduit/-e en poussière par
(d) faire sauter ⟨fuse⟩; griller ⟨light bulb⟩
3 vi (a) ⟨wind⟩ souffler; ⟨person⟩ souffler (into dans; on sur)
(b) **to** ~ **in the wind** ⟨flag, clothes⟩ voler au vent
(c) ⟨fuse⟩ sauter; ⟨bulb⟩ griller; ⟨tyre⟩ éclater
■ **blow away**: ¶ ~ **away** s'envoler; ¶ ~ [sth] **away**, ~ **away** [sth] ⟨wind⟩ emporter ⟨object⟩
■ **blow down** ⟨wind⟩ faire tomber ⟨tree⟩
■ **blow off**: ¶ ~ **off** ⟨hat⟩ s'envoler; ¶ ~ [sth] **off** ⟨wind⟩ emporter ⟨hat⟩; ⟨explosion⟩ emporter ⟨roof⟩
■ **blow out** souffler ⟨candle⟩; éteindre ⟨flames⟩
■ **blow over** ⟨storm⟩ s'apaiser; ⟨affair⟩ être oublié/-e
■ **blow up**: ¶ ~ **up** ⟨building⟩ sauter; ⟨bomb⟩ exploser
¶ ~ [sb/sth] **up** (a) faire sauter ⟨building, person⟩; faire exploser ⟨bomb⟩
(b) gonfler ⟨tyre⟩
(c) agrandir ⟨photograph⟩

blow-dry **1** n brushing m
2 vtr **to** ~ **sb's hair** faire un brushing à qn

blowout n (a) (electrical) court-circuit m
(b) (of tyre) crevaison f
(c) (colloq) (meal) gueuleton m (colloq)

blowtorch n lampe f à souder

blubber n graisse f de baleine

bludgeon vtr **to** ~ **sb to death** tuer qn à coups de matraque

blue **1** n bleu m
2 adj (a) bleu/-e
(b) (colloq) ⟨movie⟩ porno (colloq); ⟨joke⟩ cochon/-onne (colloq)
IDIOMS **to appear/happen out of the** ~ apparaître/se passer à l'improviste

bluebell n jacinthe f des bois

blueberry n (US) myrtille f

blue cheese n (fromage m) bleu m

blue chip adj ⟨company, share⟩ de premier ordre

blue collar worker n ouvrier m, col m bleu

blue jeans n pl jean m

blueprint n bleu m; (figurative) projet m (**for** pour; **for doing** pour faire)

blues n pl (a) (Mus) **the** ~ le blues m
(b) (colloq) **to have the** ~ avoir le cafard (colloq)

bluff vtr, vi bluffer (colloq)
IDIOMS **to call sb's** ~ prendre qn au mot

blunder ① n bourde f
② vi (a) (make mistake) faire une bourde
(b) (move clumsily) **to** ~ **into sth** se cogner à qch

blunt ① adj (a) ⟨knife, scissors⟩ émoussé/-e; ⟨pencil⟩ mal taillé/-e; ⟨instrument⟩ contondant/-e
(b) ⟨person, manner⟩ abrupt/-e; ⟨criticism⟩ direct/-e
② vtr émousser ⟨knife⟩

bluntly adv franchement

blur ① n image f floue
② vtr brouiller

blurb n (on book cover) texte m de présentation; (derogatory) baratin m

blurred adj indistinct/-e; ⟨image, idea⟩ flou/-e; ⟨memory⟩ confus/-e; **to have** ~ **vision** avoir des troubles de la vue

blurt v ■ **blurt out** laisser échapper ⟨truth, secret⟩

blush vi rougir (**at** devant; **with** de)

blusher n fard m à joues

blustery adj ~ **wind** bourrasque f

blu-tak® n patafix® m

BO n (colloq) (abbr = **body odour**) odeur f corporelle; **he's got** ~ il sent mauvais

boar n (also **wild** ~) sanglier m

board ① n (a) (plank) planche f; **bare** ~s plancher nu
(b) (committee) conseil m; ~ **of directors** conseil d'administration
(c) (for chess, draughts) tableau m
(d) (in classroom) tableau m (noir)
(e) (notice board) panneau m d'affichage; (to advertise) panneau m
(f) (Comput) plaquette f
(g) (accommodation) **full** ~ pension f complète; **half** ~ demi-pension f; ~ **and lodging** le gîte et le couvert
② vtr monter à bord de ⟨plane, ship⟩; monter dans ⟨bus, train⟩; ⟨pirates⟩ aborder ⟨vessel⟩
③ **on board** phr à bord
IDIOMS **above** ~ légal/-e; **across the** ~ à tous les niveaux
■ **board up** boucher [qch] avec des planches ⟨window⟩; barricader [qch] avec des planches ⟨house⟩

boarder n (a) (lodger) pensionnaire m
(b) (school pupil) interne mf

board game n jeu m de société (à damier)

boarding n embarquement m

boarding card n carte f d'embarquement

boarding school n école f privée avec internat

board meeting n réunion f du conseil d'administration

boardroom n salle f du conseil

boast ① n vantardise f
② vtr s'enorgueillir de
③ vi se vanter (**about** de)

boastful adj vantard/-e

boat n (gen) bateau m; (sailing) voilier m; (rowing) barque f; (liner) paquebot m
IDIOMS **to be in the same** ~ (colloq) être tous/toutes dans la même galère

boater n (hat) canotier m

boathouse n abri m à bateaux

boating ① n navigation f de plaisance
② adj ⟨accident, enthusiast⟩ de bateau; ⟨trip⟩ en bateau

boatyard n chantier m de construction de bateaux

bob ① n (haircut) coupe f au carré
② vi (also ~ **up and down**) ⟨boat, float⟩ danser

bobsled, bobsleigh n bobsleigh m

bode vi **to** ~ **well/ill** être de bon/mauvais augure

bodily adj ⟨function⟩ physiologique; ⟨fluid⟩ organique

body n (a) (of person, animal) corps m
(b) (corpse) corps m, cadavre m
(c) (of car) carrosserie f
(d) (of water) étendue f
(e) (organization) organisme m
(f) (of wine) corps m; (of hair) volume m

bodybuilder n culturiste mf

body-building n culturisme m

bodyguard n garde m du corps

body language n langage m corporel

body piercing n piercing m

body warmer n gilet m matelassé

bodywork n carrosserie f

bog n (a) (marshy ground) marais m
(b) (also **peat** ~) tourbière f
IDIOMS **to get** ~**ged down in sth** s'enliser dans qch

boggle vi **the mind** ~**s!** c'est époustouflant!

bog-standard adj (colloq) ordinaire

bogus adj ⟨doctor, document⟩ faux/fausse (before n); ⟨claim⟩ bidon inv; ⟨company⟩ factice

bohemian adj ⟨lifestyle⟩ de bohème; ⟨person⟩ bohème

boil ① n (a) **to bring sth to the** ~ porter qch à ébullition
(b) (on skin) furoncle m
② vtr faire bouillir; **to** ~ **an egg** faire cuire un œuf
③ vi bouillir; **the kettle is** ~**ing** l'eau bout (dans la bouilloire); **to make sb's blood** ~ faire sortir qn de ses gonds
■ **boil down to** (figurative) se ramener à
■ **boil over** déborder

boiled egg n œuf m à la coque

boiled potatoes n pl pommes fpl de terre à l'anglaise

boiler n chaudière f

boiler suit n (GB) bleu m de travail

boiling adj ⟨liquid⟩ bouillant/-e; **it's ~ !**
(colloq) il fait une chaleur infernale!

boiling point n point m d'ébullition;
⟨figurative⟩ point m limite

boisterous adj ⟨adult, game⟩ bruyant/-e;
⟨child⟩ turbulent/-e

bold adj (a) (daring) ⟨person⟩ intrépide;
⟨attempt, plan⟩ audacieux/-ieuse
(b) (cheeky) ⟨person⟩ effronté/-e
(c) ⟨colour⟩ vif/vive; ⟨design⟩ voyant/-e; **~
print** caractères mpl gras

bollard n balise f

bolster [1] n traversin m
[2] vtr (also ~ **up**) soutenir

bolt [1] n (a) (lock) verrou m
(b) ~ **of lightning** coup m de foudre
[2] vtr (a) (lock) verrouiller
(b) (also ~ **down**) engloutir ⟨food⟩
[3] vi ⟨horse⟩ s'emballer; ⟨person⟩ détaler
(colloq)
[4] **bolt upright** phr droit/-e comme un i
IDIOMS a ~ **out of the blue** un coup de
tonnerre

bomb [1] n bombe f
[2] vtr bombarder ⟨town, house⟩

bombard vtr bombarder (**with** de)

bomb blast n explosion f

bomb disposal unit n équipe f de
déminage m

bomber n (a) (plane) bombardier m
(b) (terrorist) poseur/-euse mf de bombes

bomber jacket n blouson m d'aviateur

bombing n bombardement m; (by terrorists)
attentat m à la bombe

bomb scare n alerte f à la bombe

bombshell n obus m; (figurative) bombe f

bombsite n zone f touchée par une
explosion

Bomb Squad n brigade f antiterroriste

bona fide adj ⟨attempt⟩ sincère; ⟨member⟩
vrai/-e (before n); ⟨contract⟩ de bonne foi

bond [1] n (a) (link) liens mpl (**of** de;
between entre)
(b) (in finance) obligation f; **savings ~** bon m
d'épargne
[2] vtr (stick) faire adhérer
[3] vi ⟨person⟩ s'attacher (**with** à)

bone [1] n os m; (of fish) arête f
[2] vtr désosser ⟨joint, chicken⟩; enlever les
arêtes de ⟨fish⟩
IDIOMS ~ **of contention** sujet m de dispute;
to have a ~ to pick with sb avoir un compte
à régler avec qn

bone china n porcelaine f tendre or à l'os

bone dry adj complètement sec/sèche

bone idle adj flemmard/-e

bone-marrow transplant n greffe f
de moelle osseuse

bonfire n (of rubbish) feu m de jardin; (for
celebration) feu m de joie

Bonfire Night n (GB) la soirée du 5
novembre (fêtée avec feux de joie et feux
d'artifice)

bonnet n (a) (hat) bonnet m
(b) (GB) (Aut) capot m

bonus n (a) (payment) prime f
(b) (advantage) avantage m

bony adj ⟨person, body⟩ anguleux/-euse;
⟨finger, arm⟩ osseux/-euse

boo [1] n huée f
[2] excl (to give sb a fright) hou!; (to jeer) hou!
hou!
[3] vtr huer ⟨actor, speaker⟩
[4] vi pousser des huées

booby trap [1] n (a) mécanisme m piégé
(b) (practical joke) traquenard m
[2] vtr piéger

booing n huées fpl

book [1] n (a) livre m (**about** sur; **of** de);
history ~ livre d'histoire
(b) (exercise book) cahier m
(c) (of cheques, tickets, stamps) carnet m; ~ **of
matches** pochette f d'allumettes
[2] **books** n pl (accounts) livres mpl de
comptes
[3] vtr (a) réserver ⟨table, room, taxi, ticket⟩;
faire les réservations pour ⟨holiday⟩; **to be
fully ~ed** être complet/-ète
(b) ⟨policeman⟩ dresser un procès-verbal or
un P.V. (colloq) à ⟨motorist, offender⟩; (US)
(arrest) arrêter ⟨suspect⟩
(c) ⟨referee⟩ donner un carton jaune à
⟨player⟩
[4] vi réserver
IDIOMS **to be in sb's good ~s** être dans les
petits papiers de qn (colloq); **to be in sb's bad
~s** ne pas avoir la cote avec qn

bookcase n bibliothèque f

book club n club m du livre

booking n (GB) réservation f

booking form n bon m de réservation

booking office n (GB) bureau m de
location

bookkeeping n comptabilité f

booklet n brochure f

booklist n liste f de livres

bookmaker n bookmaker m

bookmark n [1] n (for page) marque-pages
m, signet m; (Comput) signet m
[2] vtr créer un signet sur ⟨website⟩

bookseller n libraire mf

bookshelf n (single) étagère f; (in bookcase)
rayon m

bookshop, book store (US) n
librairie f

book token n (GB) chèque-livre m

bookworm n mordu/-e mf (colloq) de la
lecture

boom [1] n (a) (of cannon, thunder)
grondement m; (of drum) boum m; (of
explosion) détonation f; ~**!** badaboum!
(b) (Econ) boom m; (in prices, sales) explosion f
(**in** de)
[2] vi (a) ⟨cannon, thunder⟩ gronder; ⟨voice⟩
retenir ⋯⟶

(b) ⟨*economy*⟩ prospérer; ⟨*exports, sales*⟩ monter en flèche; **business is** ∼ing les affaires vont bien

boon *n* **(a)** (asset) aide *f* précieuse (**to** à)
(b) (stroke of luck) aubaine *f* (**for** pour)

boost **1** *n* **to give sb/sth a** ∼ encourager qn/stimuler qch
2 *vtr* stimuler ⟨*economy, sales*⟩; encourager ⟨*investment*⟩; augmenter ⟨*profit*⟩; **to** ∼ **sb's confidence** redonner confiance à qn; **to** ∼ **morale** remonter le moral

booster *n* (Med) vaccin *m* de rappel

boot *n* **(a)** botte *f*; (of climber, hiker) chaussure *f*; (for workman, soldier) brodequin *m*; **football** ∼ (GB) chaussure *f* de football
(b) (GB) (of car) coffre *m*

■ **boot up** (Comput) ∼ **[sth] up,** ∼ **up [sth]** amorcer ⟨*computer*⟩

booth *n* (in language lab) cabine *f*; (at fair) baraque *f*; **polling** ∼ isoloir *m*; **telephone** ∼ cabine *f* (téléphonique)

bootlace *n* lacet *m* (de chaussure)

booze *n* (colloq) bibine *f* (colloq); (wine only) pinard *m* (colloq)

border **1** *n* **(a)** (frontier) frontière *f*; **to cross the** ∼ passer la frontière
(b) (edge) bord *m*
(c) (flower bed) plate-bande *f*
2 *vtr* **(a)** ⟨*road, land*⟩ longer ⟨*lake, forest*⟩; ⟨*country*⟩ border ⟨*ocean*⟩; avoir une frontière commune avec ⟨*country*⟩
(b) (surround) border
3 *adj* frontalier/-ière

■ **border on:** ∼ **on [sth] (a)** ⟨*country*⟩ être limitrophe de; ⟨*garden, land*⟩ toucher
(b) (verge on) friser ⟨*rudeness, madness*⟩

border dispute *n* différend *m* frontalier

borderline *n* frontière *f*, limite *f* (**between** entre); **a** ∼ **case** un cas limite

bore **1** *n* **(a)** (person) raseur/-euse *m/f* (colloq)
(b) (situation) **what a** ∼! quelle barbe!
(c) (of gun) calibre *m*
2 *vtr* **(a)** ennuyer ⟨*person*⟩
(b) (drill) percer ⟨*hole*⟩; creuser ⟨*well, tunnel*⟩

bored *adj* ⟨*expression*⟩ ennuyé/-e; **to be** *or* **get** ∼ s'ennuyer (**with** de)
IDIOMS **to be** ∼ **stiff** *or* ∼ **to tears** s'ennuyer à mourir

boredom *n* ennui *m*

boring *adj* ennuyeux/-euse

born *adj* né/-e; **to be** ∼ naître; **she was** ∼ **in May** elle est née en mai

borough *n* arrondissement *m* urbain

borrow *vtr* emprunter (**from** à)

borrower *n* emprunteur/-euse *m/f*

borrowing *n* emprunt *m*

Bosnia *pr n* Bosnie *f*

Bosnian *adj* bosniaque, bosnien/-ienne; ∼ **Serb/Muslim** Serbe/Musulman de Bosnie

bosom *n* poitrine *f*; **in the** ∼ **of one's family** au sein de sa famille; ∼ **friend** ami/-e *m/f* intime

boss *n* (colloq) patron/-onne *m/f*, chef *m*

■ **boss about** (colloq), **boss around** (colloq) mener [qn] par le bout du nez ⟨*person*⟩

bossy *adj* (colloq) autoritaire

botanic(al) *adj* botanique; ∼ **gardens** jardin *m* botanique

botany *n* botanique *f*

botch *vtr* (colloq) bâcler

both **1** *det* ∼ **sides of the road** les deux côtés de la rue; ∼ **children came** les enfants sont venus tous les deux; ∼ **her parents** ses deux parents
2 *conj* ∼ **here and abroad** ici comme à l'étranger
3 *pron, quantif* (of things) les deux; (of people) tous les deux; **let's take** ∼ **of them** prenons les deux; ∼ **of you are wrong** vous avez tort tous les deux

bother **1** *n* **(a)** (inconvenience) ennui *m*, embêtement *m* (colloq); **without any** ∼ sans aucune difficulté
(b) (GB) (colloq) (trouble) ennuis *mpl*; **to be in a spot of** ∼ avoir des ennuis
2 *vtr* **(a)** (worry) tracasser; **don't let it** ∼ **you** ne te tracasse pas avec ça
(b) (disturb) déranger; **I'm sorry to** ∼ **you** je suis désolé de vous déranger
3 *vi* **(a)** (take trouble) **please don't** ∼ s'il te plaît, ne te dérange pas; **don't** ∼ **doing** ce n'est pas la peine de faire
(b) (worry) **it's not worth** ∼ing **about** ça ne vaut pas la peine qu'on s'en occupe

bottle **1** *n* (gen) bouteille *f*; (for perfume, medicine) flacon *m*; (for baby) biberon *m*
2 *vtr* **(a)** embouteiller ⟨*milk, wine*⟩
(b) (GB) mettre ⟨qch⟩ en conserve ⟨*fruit*⟩
3 **bottled** *pp adj* ⟨*beer, gas*⟩ en bouteille; ∼**d water** eau *f* minérale

■ **bottle up** étouffer ⟨*anger, grief*⟩

bottle bank *n* réceptacle *m* à verre

bottle feed *vtr* nourrir [qn] au biberon

bottleneck *n* **(a)** (traffic jam) embouteillage *m*
(b) (narrow part of road) rétrécissement *m* de la chaussée

bottle-opener *n* décapsuleur *m*

bottle top *n* capsule *f* (de bouteille)

bottom **1** *n* **(a)** (of hill, steps, wall) pied *m*; (of page, list) bas *m*; (of bag, bottle, hole, river, sea, garden) fond *m*; (of boat) carène *f*; (of vase, box) dessous *m*; (of league) dernière place *f*; **at the** ∼ **of the pile** sous le tas; **to be** ∼ **of the class** être dernier/-ière de la classe
(b) (colloq) (buttocks) derrière *m* (colloq)
2 *adj* ⟨*layer, shelf*⟩ du bas; ⟨*sheet*⟩ de dessous; ⟨*bunk*⟩ inférieur/-e; ⟨*division, half*⟩ dernier/-ière (*before n*)
3 (colloq) **bottoms** *n pl* pyjama ∼**s** pantalon *m* de pyjama; **bikini** ∼**s** bas *m* de maillot de bain
IDIOMS **to get to the** ∼ **of a matter** découvrir le fin fond d'une affaire

bottom line *n* (decisive factor) **the** ∼ **is that** la vérité c'est que; **that's the** ∼ ça c'est le vrai problème

boulder *n* rocher *m*

b

bounce **1** *n* **(a)** (of ball) rebond *m*
(b) (of mattress, material) élasticité *f*; (of hair)
souplesse *f*
2 *vtr* faire rebondir ‹*ball*›
3 *vi* **(a)** ‹*ball, object*› rebondir (**off** sur; **over**
au dessus de); **to ~ up and down on sth**
‹*person*› sauter sur qch
(b) (colloq) ‹*cheque*› être sans provision
■ **bounce back** (after illness) se remettre; (in
career) faire un retour en force

bouncer *n* (colloq) videur *m*

bound **1** **bounds** *n pl* limites *fpl*; **to be**
out of ~s être interdit/-e d'accès
2 *adj* **(a)** **to be ~ to do sth** aller sûrement
faire qch; **it was ~ to happen** cela devait
arriver
(b) (obliged) (by promise, rules, terms) tenu/-e (**by**
par; **to do** de faire)
(c) **~ for** ‹*person, bus, train*› en route pour;
‹*aeroplane*› à destination de
3 *vi* bondir; **to ~ into the room** entrer dans
la pièce en coup de vent

boundary *n* (gen) limite *f* (**between** entre);
(of sports field) limites *fpl* du terrain

bouquet *n* bouquet *m*

bourgeois *adj* bourgeois/-e

bout *n* **(a)** (of fever, malaria) accès *m*; (of
insomnia) crise *f*; **drinking ~** soûlerie *f*
(b) (in boxing) combat *m*
(c) (period of activity) période *f*

boutique *n* boutique *f*

bow¹ *n* **(a)** (weapon) arc *m*
(b) (for violin) archet *m*
(c) (knot) nœud *m*

bow² **1** *n* **(a)** (movement) salut *m*; **to take a**
~ saluer
(b) (of ship) avant *m*, proue *f*
2 *vtr* baisser ‹*head*›; courber ‹*branch*›;
incliner ‹*tree*›
3 *vi* **(a)** saluer; **to ~ to sb** saluer qn
(b) **to ~ to pressure** céder à la pression

bowel *n* intestin *m*; **the ~s of the earth** les
entrailles *fpl* de la terre

bowl **1** *n* (for food) bol *m*; (for salad) saladier
m; (for soup) assiette *f* creuse; (for washing)
cuvette *f*; (of lavatory) cuvette *f*
2 *vtr* lancer ‹*ball*›
3 *vi* **(a)** lancer; **to ~ to sb** lancer la balle à
qn
(b) (US) (go bowling) aller au bowling
■ **bowl over (a)** (knock down) renverser
‹*person*›
(b) **to be ~ed over** (by news) être stupéfait/-e;
(by beauty, generosity) être bouleversé/-e

bowlegged *adj* ‹*person*› aux jambes
arquées

bowler *n* **(a)** (in cricket) lanceur *m*
(b) (*also* **~ hat**) chapeau *m* melon

bowling *n* (*also* **tenpin ~**) bowling *m*

bowling alley *n* bowling *m*

bowling green *n* terrain *m* de boules
(sur gazon)

bowls *n* jeu *m* de boules (sur gazon)

bow tie *n* nœud-papillon *m*

box **1** *n* **(a)** (cardboard) boîte *f*; (crate) caisse
f; **~ of matches** boîte d'allumettes
(b) (on page, form) case *f*
(c) (in theatre) loge *f*; (in stadium) tribune *f*
(d) (*also* **PO Box**) boîte *f* postale
2 *vtr* **(a)** (pack) mettre ‹qch› en caisse
(b) **to ~ sb's ears** gifler qn
3 *vi* (Sport) boxer

boxer *n* **(a)** (fighter) boxeur *m*
(b) (dog) boxer *m*

boxer shorts *n pl* caleçon *m* (court)

boxing *n* boxe *f*

Boxing Day *n* (GB) lendemain *m* de Noël

box number *n* numéro *m* de boîte postale

box office *n* guichet *m*

boy *n* garçon *m*

boy band *n* boys band *m*

boycott **1** *n* boycottage *m* (**against, of, on**
de)
2 *vtr* boycotter

boyfriend *n* (petit) copain *m* or ami *m*

bra *n* soutien-gorge *m*

brace **1** *n* **(a)** (for teeth) appareil *m*
dentaire
(b) (for broken limb) attelle *f*
2 **braces** *n pl* (GB) bretelles *fpl*
3 *vtr* ‹*person*› arc-bouter ‹*body, back*›
(**against** contre)
4 *v refl* **to ~ oneself** (physically) s'arc-bouter;
(mentally) se préparer (**for** à; **to do** à faire)

bracelet *n* bracelet *m*

bracing *adj* vivifiant/-e, tonifiant/-e

bracken *n* fougère *f*

bracket **1** *n* **(a)** (round) parenthèse *f*;
(square) crochet *m*; **in ~s** entre parenthèses
or crochets
(b) (for shelf) équerre *f*; (for lamp) applique *f*
(c) (category) **age ~** tranche *f* d'âge
2 *vtr* **(a)** (put in brackets) (round) mettre ‹qch›
entre parenthèses; (square) mettre ‹qch› entre
crochets
(b) (*also* **~ together**) mettre ‹qn› dans le
même groupe ‹*people*›

brag *vi* se vanter (**to** auprès de; **about** de)

braid *n* **(a)** (of hair) tresse *f*, natte *f*
(b) (trimming) galon *m*

brain *n* cerveau *m*; **~s** cervelle *f*

brainchild *n* grande idée *f*

brain damage *n* lésions *fpl* cérébrales

brain dead *adj* dans un coma dépassé

brain drain *n* fuite *f* des cerveaux

brain surgery *n* neurochirurgie *f*

brain teaser *n* (colloq) casse-tête *m inv*

brainwash *vtr* faire subir un lavage de
cerveau à

brainwashing *n* (of prisoners) lavage *m* de
cerveau; (of public) bourrage *m* (colloq) de
crâne

brainwave *n* idée *f* géniale, illumination *f*

brainy *adj* (colloq) doué/-e

braise *vtr* braiser

brake **1** *n* frein *m*
2 *vi* freiner

brake pad n plaquette f de frein
bramble n (a) ronce f
(b) (GB) (berry) mûre f
bran n son m
branch n (a) (of tree) branche f; (of road, railway) embranchement m
(b) (of shop) succursale f; (of bank) agence f; (of company) filiale f
■ **branch off** bifurquer
■ **branch out** se diversifier
brand ⊞ n marque f
⊠ vtr (a) marquer (au fer) ⟨animal⟩
(b) to ~ sb as sth désigner qn comme qch
branded adj ⟨goods⟩ de marque inv
brandish vtr brandir
brand leader n leader m du marché
brand name n marque f déposée
brand-new adj tout neuf/toute neuve
brandy n eau-de-vie f; (cognac) cognac m
brash adj ⟨person, manner⟩ bravache
brass n (a) (metal) laiton m, cuivre m jaune
(b) (Mus) (also ~ **section**) cuivres mpl
brass band n fanfare f
brat n (colloq) marmot m (colloq), môme mf (colloq)
bravado n bravade f
brave ⊞ n (Indian) brave m
⊠ adj (gen) courageux/-euse; ⟨smile⟩ brave; to put on a ~ face faire bonne contenance
⊞ vtr braver
bravely adv courageusement
bravery n courage m, bravoure f
brawl ⊞ n bagarre f
⊠ vi se bagarrer (with avec)
bray vi ⟨donkey⟩ braire; ⟨person⟩ brailler
brazen adj éhonté/-e
■ **brazen out**: ~ it out payer d'audace
Brazil pr n Brésil m
breach ⊞ n (a) (of rule) infraction f (of à); (of discipline, duty) manquement m (of à); (of copyright) violation f; to be in ~ of enfreindre ⟨law⟩; violer ⟨agreement⟩
(b) (gap) brèche f
⊠ vtr faire une brèche dans ⟨defence⟩
breach of contract n rupture f de contrat
breach of the peace n atteinte f à l'ordre public
bread n pain m
bread and butter n tartine f de pain beurré; (figurative) gagne-pain m
breadbin n (GB) boîte f or huche f à pain
breadboard n planche f à pain
breadcrumbs n pl miettes fpl de pain; (Culin) chapelure f
breadline n to be on the ~ être au seuil de l'indigence
bread roll n petit pain m
breadth n largeur f; (figurative) (of experience, knowledge) étendue f
breadwinner n soutien m de famille

break ⊞ n (a) (gap) (in wall) brèche f; (in row, line) espace m; (in circuit) rupture f
(b) (pause) (gen) pause f; (at school) récréation f; to take a ~ faire une pause; the Christmas ~ les vacances de Noël; to have a ~ from work arrêter de travailler; a ~ with the past une rupture avec le passé
(c) (also **commercial** ~) page f de publicité
(d) a lucky ~ un coup de veine (colloq)
⊠ vtr (a) (gen) casser; briser ⟨seal⟩; rompre ⟨silence, monotony, spell⟩; to ~ one's leg se casser la jambe
(b) enfreindre ⟨law⟩; to ~ one's promise manquer à sa promesse
(c) dépasser ⟨speed limit⟩; battre ⟨record⟩
(d) ⟨branches⟩ freiner ⟨fall⟩; ⟨hay⟩ amortir ⟨fall⟩
(e) débourrer ⟨horse⟩
(f) (in tennis) to ~ sb's serve faire le break
(g) to ~ the news to sb apprendre la nouvelle à qn
⊞ vi (a) (gen) se casser; ⟨arm, bone, leg⟩ se fracturer; ⟨bag⟩ se déchirer; to ~ in two se casser en deux
(b) ⟨waves⟩ se briser
(c) ⟨good weather⟩ se gâter; ⟨heatwave⟩ cesser
(d) ⟨storm, scandal, story⟩ éclater
(e) to ~ with sb rompre les relations avec qn; to ~ with tradition rompre avec la tradition
(f) ⟨boy's voice⟩ muer
■ **break away** (a) se détacher (from de)
(b) (escape) échapper
■ **break down**: ¶ ~ down (a) ⟨car, machine⟩ tomber en panne
(b) ⟨person⟩ s'effondrer, craquer (colloq); to ~ down in tears fondre en larmes
¶ ~ [sth] down (a) enfoncer ⟨door⟩; (figurative) faire tomber ⟨barriers⟩; vaincre ⟨resistance⟩
(b) (analyse) ventiler ⟨cost, statistics⟩; décomposer ⟨data, findings⟩ (into par)
■ **break even** rentrer dans ses frais
■ **break free** s'échapper
■ **break in**: ¶ ~ in (a) ⟨thief⟩ entrer (par effraction); ⟨police⟩ entrer de force
(b) (interrupt) interrompre
¶ ~ [sth] in débourrer ⟨horse⟩; assouplir ⟨shoe⟩
■ **break into** (a) entrer dans [qch] (par effraction) ⟨building⟩; forcer ⟨safe⟩
(b) entamer ⟨new packet, savings⟩
(c) to ~ into song/into a run se mettre à chanter/courir
■ **break off**: ¶ ~ off (a) ⟨end⟩ se casser; ⟨handle, piece⟩ se détacher
(b) ⟨speaker⟩ s'interrompre
~ [sth] off (a) casser ⟨branch, piece⟩
(b) rompre ⟨engagement⟩; interrompre ⟨conversation⟩
■ **break out** (a) ⟨epidemic, fire⟩ se déclarer; ⟨fight, riot, storm⟩ éclater; to ~ out in a rash avoir une éruption de boutons
(b) ⟨prisoner⟩ s'échapper (of de)
■ **break up**: ¶ ~ up (a) ⟨couple⟩ se séparer

(b) ⟨crowd, cloud⟩ se disperser; ⟨meeting⟩ se terminer
(c) (GB Sch) **schools** ~ **up on Friday** les cours finissent vendredi
¶ ~ **[sth] up** démanteler ⟨drugs ring⟩; séparer ⟨couple⟩; désunir ⟨family⟩; briser ⟨marriage⟩; mettre fin à ⟨demonstration⟩
breakaway n ⟨faction, group, state⟩ séparatiste
breakdown n **(a)** (of vehicle, machine) panne f
(b) (of communications, negotiations) rupture f; (of discipline, order) effondrement m
(c) to have a (nervous) ~ faire une dépression (nerveuse)
(d) (of figures, statistics) ventilation f
breakfast n petit déjeuner m
breakfast television n télévision f à l'heure du petit déjeuner
break-in n cambriolage m
breaking point n (figurative) **to be at** ~ être à bout
breakneck adj ⟨pace, speed⟩ fou/folle, insensé/-e
breakthrough n (gen) percée f; (in negotiations, investigation) progrès m
break-up n (of alliance, relationship) rupture f; (of political party, family, group) éclatement m; (of marriage) échec m
breakwater n brise-lames m inv
breast n **(a)** (woman's) sein m; (chest) poitrine f
(b) (Culin) (of poultry) blanc m, filet m
breast-feed vtr, vi allaiter
breast stroke n brasse f
breath n **(a)** souffle m; **out of** ~ à bout de souffle; **to hold one's** ~ retenir sa respiration; (figurative) retenir son souffle
(b) (from mouth) haleine f; (visible) respiration f; **to have bad** ~ avoir (une) mauvaise haleine
IDIOMS to take sb's ~ **away** couper le souffle à qn
breathalyse (GB), **breathalyze** (US) vtr faire subir un alcootest à ⟨driver⟩
Breathalyzer® n alcootest m
breathe ① vtr **(a)** respirer ⟨oxygen⟩
(b) souffler ⟨germs⟩ **(on** sur)
(c) don't ~ **a word!** pas un mot!
② vi **(a)** ⟨person, animal⟩ respirer; **to** ~ **heavily** souffler fort, haleter
(b) ⟨wine⟩ s'aérer
■ **breathe in**: ¶ ~ **in** inspirer; ¶ ~ **[sth] in** inhaler
■ **breathe out**: ¶ ~ **out** expirer; ¶ ~ **out,** ~ **[sth] out** exhaler
breather n pause f; **take a** ~ faire une pause
breathing n respiration f
breathing space n **(a)** (respite) répit m
(b) (postponement) délai m
breathless adj ⟨runner⟩ hors d'haleine; ⟨asthmatic⟩ haletant/-e

breathtaking adj ⟨feat, skill⟩ stupéfiant/-e; ⟨scenery⟩ à vous couper le souffle
breath test ① n alcootest m
② vtr faire subir un alcootest à ⟨driver⟩
breed ① n race f
② vtr élever ⟨animals⟩; (figurative) engendrer
③ vi se reproduire
④ **bred** pp adj **ill-/well-**~ mal/bien élevé/-e
breeder n (of animals) éleveur m
breeding n **(a)** (of animals) reproduction f
(b) (good manners) bonnes manières fpl
breeding ground n (figurative) foyer m **(for** de)
breeze ① n brise f
② vi **to** ~ **in/out** entrer/sortir d'un air dégagé; **to** ~ **through an exam** réussir un examen sans difficulté
brevity n brièveté f
brew ① vtr brasser ⟨beer⟩; préparer ⟨tea⟩; **freshly** ~**ed coffee** du café fraîchement passé
② vi **(a)** ⟨beer⟩ fermenter; ⟨tea⟩ infuser
(b) ⟨storm, crisis⟩ se préparer
brewer n brasseur m
brewery n brasserie f
bribe ① n pot-de-vin m
② vtr soudoyer ⟨police⟩; suborner ⟨witness⟩; acheter ⟨servant, voter⟩
bribery n corruption f
brick n brique f
bricklayer n maçon m
bridal adj ⟨gown⟩ de mariée; ⟨car⟩ des mariés; ⟨suite⟩ nuptial/-e
bride n (jeune) mariée f; **the** ~ **and groom** les (jeunes) mariés mpl
bridegroom n jeune marié m
bridesmaid n demoiselle f d'honneur
bridge ① n **(a)** pont m (over sur; across au-dessus de); (figurative) (link) rapprochement m
(b) (on ship) passerelle f
(c) (of nose) arête f; (of spectacles) arcade f
(d) (on guitar, violin) chevalet m
(e) (for teeth) bridge m
(f) (game) bridge m
② vtr **(a) to** ~ **a gap in [sth]** combler un vide dans ⟨conversation⟩; combler un trou dans ⟨budget⟩
(b) (span) enjamber ⟨two eras⟩
bridle ① n bride f
② vtr brider
③ vi se cabrer (at contre; with sous l'effet de)
bridle path n piste f cavalière
brief ① n **(a)** (GB) (remit) attributions fpl; (role) tâche f
(b) (Law) dossier m
② **briefs** n pl slip m
③ adj bref/brève; **in** ~ en bref
④ vtr (inform) informer (on de); (instruct) donner des instructions à (on sur)
briefcase n serviette f; (without handle) porte-documents m inv

b

briefing n briefing m (on sur)

briefly adv (a) (gen) brièvement; ⟨look, pause⟩ un bref instant
(b) (in short) en bref

brigade n brigade f

bright adj (a) ⟨colour⟩ vif/vive; ⟨garment⟩ aux couleurs vives; ⟨sunshine⟩ éclatant/-e; ⟨room, day⟩ clair/-e; ⟨star, eye, metal⟩ brillant/-e
(b) (clever) intelligent/-e; **a ∼ idea** une idée lumineuse
(c) **to look on the ∼ side** voir le bon côté des choses

brighten v ■ **brighten up**: ¶ ∼ **up (a)** ⟨person⟩ s'égayer (at à); ⟨face⟩ s'éclairer (at à)
(b) ⟨weather⟩ s'éclaircir; ¶ ∼ **[sth] up** égayer ⟨room, decor⟩

brightly adv (a) ⟨dressed⟩ de couleurs vives
(b) ⟨shine, burn⟩ d'un vif éclat

brightness n (a) (of colour, light, smile) éclat m
(b) (of room) clarté f

bright spark n (GB) (colloq) petit/-e futé/-e m/f (colloq)

brilliance n éclat m

brilliant adj (a) ⟨student, career, success⟩ brillant/-e
(b) (bright) éclatant/-e
(c) (GB) (colloq) (fantastic) super (colloq), génial/-e (colloq); **to be ∼ at sth** être doué/-e en qch

brilliantly adv (a) (very well) brillamment
(b) (very brightly) ⟨shine⟩ avec éclat

brim n bord m

brine n (a) (sea water) eau f de mer
(b) (for pickling) saumure f

bring vtr (a) apporter ⟨present, object, message⟩; amener ⟨person, animal, car⟩; **to ∼ sth with one** apporter qch; **to ∼ sb/sth into the room** faire entrer qn/qch dans la pièce
(b) apporter ⟨happiness, rain, change, hope⟩; **to ∼ a smile to sb's face** faire sourire qn
■ **bring about** provoquer ⟨change, disaster⟩; entraîner ⟨success, defeat⟩
■ **bring along** apporter ⟨object⟩; amener, venir avec ⟨friend, partner⟩
■ **bring back (a)** rapporter ⟨souvenir⟩ (from de); **to ∼ back memories** ranimer des souvenirs
(b) rétablir ⟨custom⟩; restaurer ⟨monarchy⟩
■ **bring down (a)** renverser ⟨government⟩
(b) réduire ⟨inflation, expenditure⟩; faire baisser ⟨price, temperature⟩
(c) (shoot down) abattre
■ **bring forward** avancer ⟨date⟩
■ **bring in** rapporter ⟨money, interest⟩; introduire ⟨legislation, measure⟩; rentrer ⟨harvest⟩; faire appel à ⟨expert, army⟩
■ **bring off** réussir ⟨feat⟩; conclure ⟨deal⟩
■ **bring on (a)** provoquer ⟨attack, migraine⟩
(b) faire entrer ⟨substitute player⟩
■ **bring out (a)** sortir ⟨edition, new model⟩
(b) (highlight) faire ressortir ⟨flavour, meaning⟩

■ **bring round (a)** (revive) faire revenir [qn] à soi
(b) (convince) convaincre
■ **bring up (a)** aborder, parler de ⟨subject⟩
(b) vomir, rendre ⟨food⟩
(c) élever ⟨child⟩; **well brought up** bien élevé/-e

brink n bord m

brisk adj (a) (efficient) ⟨manner, tone⟩ vif/vive; ⟨person⟩ efficace
(b) (energetic) ⟨trot⟩ rapide; **at a ∼ pace** à vive allure
(c) ⟨business, trade⟩ florissant/-e; **business was ∼** les affaires marchaient bien
(d) ⟨air⟩ vivifiant/-e; ⟨wind⟩ vif/vive

bristle ⟦1⟧ n (gen) poil m; (on pig) soie f
⟦2⟧ vi (a) ⟨hairs⟩ se dresser
(b) ⟨person⟩ se hérisser (at à; with de)

Britain pr n (also **Great ∼**) Grande-Bretagne f

British ⟦1⟧ n pl **the ∼** les Britanniques mpl
⟦2⟧ adj britannique; **the ∼ embassy** l'ambassade f de Grande-Bretagne

British Isles pr n pl **the ∼** îles fpl Britanniques

Briton n Britannique mf

Brittany pr n Bretagne f

brittle adj ⟨twig⟩ cassant/-e; ⟨nails, hair⟩ fragile

broach vtr aborder ⟨subject⟩

broad adj (a) (wide) large; **to have ∼ shoulders** être large d'épaules
(b) ⟨meaning⟩ large; ⟨outline⟩ général/-e
(c) ⟨accent⟩ fort/-e (before n); **in ∼ daylight** en plein jour

broad-based adj ⟨approach, campaign⟩ global/-e; ⟨education⟩ généralisé/-e

broad bean n fève f

broadcast ⟦1⟧ n émission f
⟦2⟧ vtr diffuser ⟨programme⟩ (to à)
⟦3⟧ vi ⟨station, channel⟩ émettre (on sur)

broadcaster n animateur/-trice m/f

broadcasting n (field) communication f audiovisuelle; (action) diffusion f; **to work in ∼** travailler dans l'audiovisuel

broaden ⟦1⟧ vtr étendre ⟨appeal, scope⟩; élargir ⟨horizons, knowledge⟩; **travel ∼s the mind** les voyages ouvrent l'esprit
⟦2⟧ vi s'élargir

broadminded adj ⟨person⟩ large d'esprit; ⟨attitude⟩ libéral/-e

broadsheet n journal m de grand format

brocade n brocart m

broccoli n (Bot) brocoli m; (Culin) brocolis mpl

brochure n (booklet) brochure f; (leaflet) dépliant m; (for hotel) prospectus m

broil vtr (US) faire griller ⟨meat⟩

broke adj (colloq) ⟨person⟩ fauché/-e (colloq)

broken adj (a) (gen) cassé/-e; ⟨glass, window, line⟩ brisé/-e; ⟨radio, machine⟩ détraqué/-e
(b) ⟨man, woman⟩ brisé/-e
(c) ⟨French⟩ mauvais/-e (before n)

b

broken-down adj ⟨machine⟩ en panne

broken-hearted adj to be ∼ avoir le cœur brisé

broken home n famille f désunie

broken marriage n foyer m désuni

broker n courtier m; **insurance** ∼ courtier m d'assurance; **real-estate** ∼ (US) agent m immobilier

brolly n (GB) (colloq) parapluie m

bronchitis n bronchite f

bronze n bronze m

brooch n broche f

brood ⓵ n (of birds) couvée f; (of mammals) nichée f

⓶ vi **(a)** (ponder) broyer du noir; **to** ∼ **about** ressasser, ruminer ⟨problem⟩

(b) ⟨bird⟩ couver

brook n ruisseau m

broom n balai m

broth n bouillon m

brothel n maison f close

brother n frère m

brother-in-law n beau-frère m

brotherly adj fraternel/-elle

brow n **(a)** (forehead) front m; (eyebrow) sourcil m

(b) (of hill) sommet m

brown ⓵ n (of object) marron m; (of hair, skin, eyes) brun m

⓶ adj **(a)** ⟨shoes, leaves, paint, eyes⟩ marron inv; ⟨hair⟩ châtain inv; **light/dark** ∼ marron clair/foncé

(b) (tanned) bronzé/-e; **to go** ∼ bronzer

⓷ vtr faire roussir ⟨sauce⟩; faire dorer ⟨meat, onions⟩

⓸ vi ⟨meat, potatoes⟩ dorer

brown bread n pain m complet

brown envelope n enveloppe f kraft

Brownie n jeannette f

brown paper n papier m kraft

brown rice n riz m complet

brown sugar n sucre m brun, cassonade f

browse vi **(a)** (in shop) regarder

(b) (graze) brouter

■ **browse through** feuilleter ⟨book⟩

browser n navigateur m

bruise ⓵ n (on skin) bleu m, ecchymose f (on sur); (on fruit) tache f (on sur)

⓶ vtr meurtrir ⟨person⟩; taler, abîmer ⟨fruit⟩; **to** ∼ **one's arm** se faire un bleu sur le bras

brunette n brune f

brunt n **to bear the** ∼ **of** être le plus touché/la plus touchée par ⟨disaster⟩; subir tout le poids de ⟨anger⟩

brush ⓵ n **(a)** (for hair, clothes, shoes) brosse f; (small, for sweeping up) balayette f; (broom) balai m; (for paint) pinceau m

(b) **to have a** ∼ **with death** frôler la mort; **to have a** ∼ **with the law** avoir des démêlés avec la justice

⓶ vtr brosser ⟨carpet, clothes⟩; **to** ∼ **one's hair/teeth** se brosser les cheveux/les dents

⓷ vi **to** ∼ **against** frôler; **to** ∼ **past sb** frôler qn en passant

■ **brush aside** repousser ⟨criticism, person⟩

■ **brush up (on)** se remettre à ⟨subject⟩

brushwood n (firewood) brindilles fpl; (brush) broussailles fpl

brusque adj brusque (**with** avec)

Brussels pr n Bruxelles

Brussels sprout n chou m de Bruxelles

brutal adj brutal/-e

brutality n brutalité f (**of** de)

brute ⓵ n **(a)** (man) brute f

(b) (animal) bête f

⓶ adj ⟨strength⟩ simple (before n); **by** ∼ **force** par la force

BSc n (GB) (Univ) (abbr = **Bachelor of Science**) diplôme m universitaire en sciences

BSE n (abbr = **Bovine Spongiform Encephalopathy**) ESB f, encéphalopathie f spongiforme bovine

bubble ⓵ n bulle f (**in** dans); **to blow** ∼**s** faire des bulles

⓶ vi ⟨fizzy drink⟩ pétiller; ⟨boiling liquid⟩ bouillonner; **to** ∼ **(over) with** déborder de ⟨enthusiasm, ideas⟩

bubble bath n bain m moussant

bubblewrap n bulle-pack® m

buck ⓵ n **(a)** (US) (colloq) dollar m

(b) (male animal) mâle m

⓶ vi ⟨horse⟩ ruer

IDIOMS **to pass the** ∼ refiler (colloq) la responsabilité à quelqu'un d'autre

bucket n seau m (**of** de)

buckle ⓵ n boucle f

⓶ vtr **(a)** attacher, boucler ⟨belt, shoe⟩

(b) (damage) gondoler

⓷ vi **(a)** ⟨metal, surface⟩ se gondoler; ⟨wheel⟩ se voiler

(b) ⟨belt, shoe⟩ s'attacher, se boucler

(c) ⟨knees, legs⟩ céder

bud ⓵ n (of leaf) bourgeon m; (of flower) bouton m

⓶ vi **(a)** (develop leaf buds) bourgeonner; (develop flower buds) boutonner

(b) ⟨flower, breast⟩ pointer

Buddha pr n Bouddha m

Buddhism n bouddhisme m

Buddhist n, adj bouddhiste (mf)

budding adj ⟨athlete, champion⟩ en herbe; ⟨talent, career, romance⟩ naissant/-e

buddy n (colloq) copain m, pote m (colloq)

budge ⓵ vtr **(a)** (move) bouger

(b) (persuade) faire changer d'avis à

⓶ vi **(a)** (move) bouger (**from, off** de)

(b) (give way) changer d'avis (**on** sur)

■ **budge over** (colloq), **budge up** (colloq) se pousser

budgerigar n perruche f

budget ⓵ n budget m (**for** pour)

⓶ vi **to** ∼ **for** budgétiser ses dépenses en fonction de ⟨increase, needs⟩

buff n (a) (colloq) (enthusiast) mordu/-e m/f
(b) (colour) chamois m

buffalo n (GB) buffle m; (US) bison m

buffer n tampon m

buffet¹ n buffet m

buffet² vtr ‹wind› ballotter ‹ship›; battre
‹coast›

buffoon n bouffon/-onne m/f

bug ⟨1⟩ n (a) (colloq) (insect) (gen) bestiole f;
(bedbug) punaise f
(b) (colloq) (also **stomach** ∼) ennuis mpl
gastriques
(c) (germ) microbe m
(d) (fault) (gen) défaut m; (Comput) bogue f or
m, bug m
(e) (hidden microphone) micro m caché
⟨2⟩ vtr (a) poser des micros dans ‹room,
building›; **the room is ∼ged** il y a un micro
(caché) dans la pièce
(b) (colloq) (annoy) embêter ‹person›

buggy n (a) (GB) (pushchair) poussette f
(b) (US) (pram) landau m
(c) (carriage) boghei m

bugle n clairon m

build ⟨1⟩ n (of person) carrure f
⟨2⟩ vtr (gen) construire; édifier ‹church,
monument›; bâtir ‹career, future›; fonder
‹empire›; créer ‹software, interface›; **to be
well built** ‹person› être bien bâti/-e
⟨3⟩ vi construire; **to ∼ on** tirer parti de
‹popularity, success›
■ **build up**: ¶ ∼ up ‹gas, deposits›
s'accumuler; ‹traffic› s'intensifier; ‹business,
trade› se développer; ‹tension, excitement›
monter; ¶ ∼ [sth] up accumuler ‹wealth›;
établir ‹trust›; constituer ‹collection›; créer
‹business›; établir ‹picture, profile›; se faire
‹reputation›; affermir ‹muscles›; **to ∼ oneself
up, to ∼ up one's strength** prendre des
forces

builder n (contractor) entrepreneur m en
bâtiment; (worker) ouvrier/-ière m/f du
bâtiment

building n (gen) bâtiment m; (with offices,
apartments) immeuble m; (palace, church) édifice
m

building contractor n entrepreneur m
en bâtiment

building site n chantier m (de
construction)

building society n (GB) société f
d'investissement et de crédit immobilier

build-up n (a) (in traffic, pressure)
intensification f (of de); (in weapons, stocks)
accumulation f (of de); (in tension)
accroissement m (of de)
(b) (publicity) **the ∼ to sth** les préparatifs de
qch

built-in adj ‹wardrobe› encastré/-e;
(figurative) intégré/-e

built-up adj ‹region› urbanisé/-e; ∼ **area**
agglomération f

bulb n (a) (electric) ampoule f (électrique)
(b) (of plant) bulbe m

Bulgaria pr n Bulgarie f

Bulgarian ⟨1⟩ n (a) (person) Bulgare mf
(b) (language) bulgare m
⟨2⟩ adj bulgare

bulge ⟨1⟩ n (in clothing, carpet) bosse f; (in pipe,
tube) renflement m; (in tyre) hernie f; (in wall)
bombement m; (in cheek) gonflement m
⟨2⟩ vi ‹bag, pocket, cheeks› être gonflé/-e;
‹wallet› être bourré/-e; ‹surface› se
boursoufler; ‹stomach› ballonner; **his eyes
were bulging** les yeux lui sortaient de la tête

bulimia (nervosa) n boulimie f

bulimic n, adj boulimique (mf)

bulk n (a) (of package, correspondence) volume
m; (of building, vehicle) masse f; **the ∼ of** la
majeure partie de
(b) **in ∼** ‹buy, sell› en gros; ‹transport› en
vrac

bulk-buying n achat m en gros

bulky adj ‹person› corpulent/-e; ‹package›
volumineux/-euse; ‹book› épais/-aisse

bull n (ox) taureau m; (elephant, whale) mâle m

bull bar n pare-buffle(s) m

bulldog n bouledogue m

bulldozer n bulldozer m, bouteur m

bullet n balle f

bulletin n bulletin m; **news ∼** bulletin
d'informations

bulletin board n (gen) tableau m
d'affichage; (Comput) messagerie f
électronique

bulletproof adj ‹glass, vehicle, door›
blindé/-e

bulletproof vest n gilet m pare-balles
inv

bullfight n corrida f

bullfighter n torero m

bullfighting n (gen) corridas fpl; (art)
tauromachie f

bullion n lingots mpl

bullock n bœuf m

bullring n arène f

bull's-eye n mille m

bully ⟨1⟩ n (child) petite brute f; (adult) tyran
m
⟨2⟩ vtr intimider; (stronger) tyranniser

bum n (colloq) (a) (GB) (buttocks) derrière m
(colloq)
(b) (US) (vagrant) clochard m

bumbag n (sacoche f) banane f

bumblebee n bourdon m

bumf, bumph n (GB) (colloq) paperasserie f
(colloq)

bump ⟨1⟩ n (a) (lump) (on body) bosse f (on à);
(on road) bosse f (on, in sur)
(b) (jolt) secousse f
(c) (sound) bruit m sourd
⟨2⟩ vtr cogner (against, on contre); **to ∼ one's
head** se cogner la tête
■ **bump into** rentrer dans ‹person, object›;
(meet) tomber sur (colloq) ‹person›

bumper ⟨1⟩ n pare-chocs m inv

b

2 *adj* ‹crop, sales, year› record (*after n*); ‹edition› exceptionnel/-elle

bumper car *n* auto *f* tamponneuse

bumpkin *n* (colloq) (*also* **country** ~) péquenaud/-e *m/f* (colloq)

bumpy *adj* ‹road› accidenté/-e; ‹wall› irrégulier/-ière; ‹landing› agité/-e

bun *n* (a) (cake) petit pain *m* sucré
(b) (hairstyle) chignon *m*

bunch *n* (of flowers) bouquet *m*; (of vegetables) botte *f*; (of grapes) grappe *f*; (of bananas) régime *m*; (of keys) trousseau *m*; (of people) groupe *m*

bundle **1** *n* (of clothes) ballot *m*; (of papers, notes) liasse *f*; (of books) paquet *m*; (of straw) botte *f*, ~ **of sticks** fagot *m* de bois; ~ **of nerves** boule *f* de nerfs
2 *vtr* **to** ~ **sb/sth into** fourrer (colloq) qn/qch dans

bundled software *n* ensemble *m* de logiciels complémentaires (*livré avec un ordinateur*)

bungalow *n* pavillon *m* (sans étage)

bungee jumping *n* saut *m* à l'élastique

bungle *vtr* rater (colloq) ‹attempt, burglary›

bunion *n* oignon *m*

bunk *n* (a) (on ship, train) couchette *f*
(b) (*also* ~ **bed**) lits *mpl* superposés
■ **bunk off** (colloq): **to** ~ **off school** sécher l'école

bunker *n* (a) (Mil) bunker *m*
(b) (in golf) bunker *m*
(c) (for coal) soute *f*

bunny *n* (a) (*also* ~ **rabbit**) (Jeannot) lapin *m*
(b) (*also* ~ **girl**) hôtesse *f*

bunting *n* guirlandes *fpl*

buoy **1** *n* (gen) bouée *f*; (for marking) balise *f* (flottante)
2 *vtr* (*also* ~ **up**) (a) revigorer ‹person, morale›
(b) stimuler ‹prices, economy›
(c) (keep afloat) maintenir à flot

buoyant *adj* (a) ‹object› qui flotte
(b) ‹person› vif/vive; ‹mood, spirits› enjoué/-e; ‹step› allègre
(c) ‹market, prices› ferme; ‹economy› en expansion

burden **1** *n* fardeau *m* (**to sb** pour qn)
2 *vtr* (a) (*also* ~ **down**) encombrer (**with** de)
(b) (figurative) (with work, taxes) accabler (**with** de); **I don't want to** ~ **you with my problems** je ne veux pas vous ennuyer avec mes problèmes

bureau *n* (a) (office) bureau *m*
(b) (US) (government department) service *m*
(c) (GB) (desk) secrétaire *m*
(d) (US) (chest of drawers) commode *f*

bureaucracy *n* bureaucratie *f*

bureaucrat *n* bureaucrate *mf*

bureaucratic *adj* bureaucratique

burgeoning *adj* ‹talent, love, industry, crime› croissant/-e; ‹population, industries› en plein essor

burger *n* hamburger *m*

burger bar *n* fast-food *m*

burglar *n* cambrioleur/-euse *m/f*

burglar alarm *n* sonnerie *f* d'alarme

burglary *n* (gen) cambriolage *m*; (Law) vol *m* avec effraction

burgle *vtr* cambrioler

burgundy **1** **Burgundy** *pr n* Bourgogne *f*
2 *n* (a) (*also* **Burgundy**) (wine) bourgogne *m*
(b) (colour) (couleur *f*) bordeaux *m*

burial *n* enterrement *m*

burly *adj* ‹person› solidement charpenté/-e

Burma *pr n* Birmanie *f*

burn **1** *n* brûlure *f*
2 *vtr* (gen) brûler; laisser brûler ‹food›
3 *vi* brûler
■ **burn down**: ¶ ~ **down** ‹house› être détruit/-e par le feu; ¶ ~ **[sth] down** réduire [qch] en cendres ‹house›
■ **burn up** brûler ‹calories›; dépenser ‹energy›

burner *n* (on cooker) brûleur *m*
IDIOMS **to put sth on the back** ~ mettre qch en veilleuse

burning **1** *n* **there's a smell of** ~ ça sent le brûlé
2 *adj* (a) (on fire) en flammes, en feu; (alight) ‹candle, lamp, fire› allumé/-e
(b) ‹desire› brûlant/-e; ‹passion› ardent/-e

burnt-out *adj* ‹building, car› calciné/-e; ‹person› usé/-e (par le travail)

burp (colloq) **1** *n* rot *m* (colloq), renvoi *m*
2 *vi* ‹person› roter (colloq); ‹baby› faire son rot (colloq)

burrow **1** *n* terrier *m*
2 *vi* ‹animal› creuser un terrier; **to** ~ **into/under sth** creuser dans/sous qch

bursary *n* (GB) (grant) bourse *f* (d'études)

burst **1** *n* (of flame) jaillissement *m*; (of gunfire) rafale *f*; (of activity, enthusiasm) accès *m*; **a** ~ **of laughter** un éclat de rire; **a** ~ **of applause** un tonnerre d'applaudissements
2 *vtr* (gen) crever; rompre ‹blood vessel›; **to** ~ **its banks** ‹river› déborder
3 *vi* (gen) crever; rompre; ‹pipe› éclater; ‹dam› rompre; **to be** ~**ing with health/pride** déborder de santé/fierté
■ **burst into** (a) faire irruption dans ‹room›
(b) **to** ~ **into flames** s'enflammer; **to** ~ **into tears** fondre en larmes
■ **burst out**: **to** ~ **out laughing** éclater de rire; **to** ~ **out crying** fondre en larmes
■ **burst through** rompre ‹barricade›; **to** ~ **through the door** entrer violemment

bury *vtr* enterrer

bus *n* autobus *m*, bus *m*; (long-distance) autocar *m*, car *m*; **by** ~ **en** (auto)bus, par le bus; **on the** ~ dans le bus

bus conductor *n* receveur *m* d'autobus

bus driver n conducteur/-trice m/f
d'autobus

bush n (a) buisson m
(b) (bushland) **the ~** la brousse f
IDIOMS **don't beat about the ~** cessez de
tourner autour du pot

bushfire n feu m de brousse

bushy adj ⟨hair, tail⟩ touffu/-e; ⟨beard⟩
épais/-aisse; ⟨eyebrows⟩ broussailleux/-euse

business ① n (a) (commerce) affaires fpl; **to
go into ~** se lancer dans les affaires; **she's
gone to Brussels on ~** elle est allée à
Bruxelles en voyage d'affaires; **to mix ~ with
pleasure** joindre l'utile à l'agréable; **he's in
the insurance ~** il travaille dans les
assurances
(b) (company, firm) affaire f, entreprise f; (shop)
commerce m, boutique f; **small ~es** les
petites entreprises
(c) **let's get down to ~** passons aux choses
sérieuses; **to go about one's ~** vaquer à ses
occupations
(d) (concern) **that's her ~** ça la regarde; **it's
none of your ~!** ça ne te regarde pas!; **mind
your own ~!** (colloq) occupe-toi de tes affaires!
(colloq)
② adj ⟨address, letter, transaction⟩
commercial/-e; ⟨meeting⟩ d'affaires
IDIOMS **she means ~!** elle ne plaisante pas!;
to work like nobody's ~ (colloq) travailler
d'arrache-pied

business associate n associé/-e m/f

business card n carte f de visite

business class n (on plane) classe f
affaires

business hours n pl (in office) heures fpl
de bureau; (of shop) heures fpl d'ouverture

businesslike adj sérieux/-ieuse

businessman n homme m d'affaires

business park n parc m d'affaires or
d'activités

business plan n projet m commercial

business school n école f de commerce

business studies n pl études fpl de
commerce

business trip n voyage m d'affaires

businesswoman n femme f d'affaires

busker n (GB) musicien/-ienne m/f
ambulant/-e

bus lane n couloir m d'autobus

bus pass n carte f de bus

bus shelter n abribus® m

bus station n gare f routière

bus stop n arrêt m de bus

bust ① n (a) (breasts) poitrine f
(b) (statue) buste m
② adj (colloq) (a) (broken) fichu/-e (colloq)
(b) (bankrupt) **to go ~** faire faillite

bustle ① n (activity) affairement m (of de);
hustle and ~ grande animation f
② vi ⟨person, crowd⟩ s'affairer; **to ~ in/out**
entrer/sortir d'un air affairé

bustling adj ⟨street, shop, town⟩ animé/-e

busy ① adj (a) ⟨person⟩ occupé/-e (**with**
avec; **doing** à faire)
(b) ⟨shop⟩ où il y a beaucoup de monde;
⟨junction, airport⟩ où le trafic est intense;
⟨road⟩ très fréquenté/-e; ⟨street, town⟩
animé/-e; ⟨day, week⟩ chargé/-e
(c) (engaged) ⟨line⟩ occupé/-e
② v refl **to ~ oneself doing** s'occuper à faire

busybody n (colloq) **he's a real ~** il se mêle
de tout

but ① conj mais
② prep sauf; **anybody ~ him** n'importe qui
sauf lui; **nobody ~ me knows how to do it** il
n'y a que moi qui sache le faire; **he's
nothing ~ a coward** ce n'est qu'un lâche; **the
last ~ one** l'avant-dernier
③ adv **one can't help ~ admire her** on ne
peut pas s'empêcher de l'admirer
④ **but for** phr **~ for you, I would have died**
sans toi je serais mort; **he would have gone
~ for me** si je n'avais pas été là il serait
parti

butane n butane m

butcher ① n boucher m; **~'s (shop)**
boucherie f
② vtr abattre ⟨animal⟩; massacrer ⟨people⟩

butchery n (a) (trade) boucherie f
(b) (slaughter) massacre m

butler n maître m d'hôtel, majordome m

butt ① n (a) (of rifle) crosse f; (of cigarette)
mégot m (colloq)
(b) (US) (colloq) (buttocks) derrière m (colloq)
(c) **to be the ~ of sb's jokes** être la cible des
blagues de qn
② vtr ⟨person⟩ donner un coup de tête à;
⟨animal⟩ donner un coup de corne à
∎ **butt in** interrompre

butter ① n beurre m
② vtr beurrer ⟨bread⟩
∎ **butter up** (colloq): **~ [sb] up, ~ up [sb]**
passer de la pommade à (colloq)

buttercup n bouton d'or m

butterfingers n empoté/-e m/f

butterfly n papillon m
IDIOMS **to have butterflies (in one's stomach)**
avoir le trac (colloq)

butterfly stroke n brasse f papillon

buttock n fesse f

button ① n (a) (on coat, switch) bouton m
(b) (US) (badge) badge m
(c) (Comput) bouton m
② vi ⟨dress⟩ se boutonner
∎ **button up** boutonner ⟨garment⟩

buttonhole ① n (a) (on garment)
boutonnière f
(b) (GB) (flower) (fleur f de) boutonnière f
② vtr (colloq) accrocher (colloq) ⟨person⟩

buttress n (a) contrefort m; (figurative)
soutien m
(b) (also **flying ~**) arc-boutant m

buxom adj ⟨woman⟩ à la poitrine
généreuse

buy ① n **a good ~** une bonne affaire
② vtr acheter (**from sb** à qn); **to ~ sth from
the supermarket/from the baker's** acheter qch

au supermarché/chez le boulanger; **to ∼ sb sth** acheter qch à qn; **to ∼ some time** gagner du temps

■ **buy off** acheter ⟨*person, witness*⟩

■ **buy out** racheter la part de ⟨*co-owner*⟩

■ **buy up** acheter systématiquement ⟨*shares, property*⟩

buyer *n* acheteur/-euse *m/f*

buyout *n* rachat *m* d'entreprise

buzz ①︎ *n* **(a)** (of insect) bourdonnement *m*
(b) (colloq) (phone call) **to give sb a ∼** passer un coup de fil à qn
(c) (colloq) (thrill) **it gives me a ∼** (from alcohol) ça me fait planer (colloq); **to get a ∼ out of doing** prendre son pied (colloq) en faisant
②︎ *vtr* **to ∼ sb** appeler qn au bip, biper qn
③︎ *vi* ⟨*bee, fly*⟩ bourdonner; ⟨*buzzer*⟩ sonner

buzzard *n* buse *f*

buzzer *n* (gen) sonnerie *f*; (on pocket) bip *m*

buzzword *n* (colloq) mot *m* à la mode

by ①︎ *prep* **(a)** (with passive verbs) par; **he was bitten ∼ a snake** il a été mordu par un serpent
(b) (with present participle) en; **∼ working extra hours** en faisant des heures supplémentaires; **to learn French ∼ listening to the radio** apprendre le français en écoutant la radio; **to begin ∼ doing** commencer par faire
(c) (by means of) par; **to pay ∼ cheque** payer par chèque; **∼ mistake/accident** par erreur/accident; **to travel to Rome ∼ Venice** aller à Rome en passant par Venise; **to travel ∼ bus/train** voyager en bus/train; **∼ bicycle** à bicyclette, en vélo; ⟨*read*⟩ **∼ candlelight** ⟨*dine*⟩ aux chandelles; ⟨*read*⟩ à la bougie
(d) (from) à; **I could tell ∼ the look on her face that** rien qu'à la regarder je savais que
(e) (near) à côté de, près de; **∼ the window** à côté de la fenêtre; **∼ the sea** au bord de la mer
(f) (showing authorship) de; **a film ∼ Claude Chabrol** un film de Claude Chabrol; **who is it ∼?** c'est de qui?
(g) (in time expressions) avant; **∼ midnight** avant minuit; **∼ this time next week** d'ici la

semaine prochaine; **∼ the time she had got downstairs he was gone** le temps qu'elle descende, il était parti; **he should be here ∼ now** il devrait être déjà là
(h) (according to) selon; **to play ∼ the rules** jouer selon les règles; **∼ my watch** à ma montre
(i) (showing amount) de; **prices have risen ∼ 20%** les prix ont augmenté de 20%; **he's taller than me ∼ two centimetres** il fait deux centimètres de plus que moi
(j) (in measurements) sur; **20 metres ∼ 10 metres** 20 mètres sur 10
(k) (showing rate, quantity) à; **paid ∼ the hour** payé à l'heure
(l) **little ∼ little** peu à peu; **day ∼ day** jour après jour; **one ∼ one** un par un, une par une; **∼ oneself** tout seul/toute seule; **to go** *or* **pass ∼ sb/sth** passer devant qn/qch
(m) (in compass directions) quart; **south ∼ south-west** sud quart sud-ouest
②︎ *adv* **(a)** (past) **to go ∼** passer; **the people walking ∼** les gens qui passent/passaient, les passants; **as time goes ∼** avec le temps
(b) (near) près; **he lives close ∼** il habite tout près
(c) (aside) **to put money ∼** mettre de l'argent de côté

bye *excl* (colloq) (*also* **∼-bye**) au revoir!

by(e)-election *n* (GB) élection *f* partielle

bygone *adj* ⟨*days, years, scene*⟩ d'antan; **a ∼ era** une époque révolue
IDIOMS **to let ∼s be ∼s** enterrer le passé

by(e)law *n* arrêté *m* municipal

bypass ①︎ *n* **(a)** (road) rocade *f*
(b) (pipe, channel) by-pass *m inv*
(c) (in electricity) dérivation *f*
(d) (Med) (*also* **∼ operation**) pontage *m*
②︎ *vtr* contourner ⟨*town, city*⟩

by-product *n* dérivé *m*; (figurative) effet *m* secondaire

bystander *n* spectateur/-trice *m/f*

byte *n* (Comput) octet *m*

byword *n* **to be a ∼ for** être synonyme de

Cc

c, C *n* **(a)** (letter) c, C *m*
(b) C (Mus) do *m*

cab *n* **(a)** (taxi) taxi *m*
(b) (for driver) cabine *f*

cabbage *n* chou *m*

cab-driver *n* chauffeur *m* de taxi

cabin *n* **(a)** (hut) cabane *f*; (in holiday camp) chalet *m*
(b) (in boat, plane) cabine *f*

cabin crew *n* personnel *m* de bord

cabinet *n* **(a)** (cupboard) petit placard *m*; **display ∼** vitrine *f*; **cocktail ∼** meuble *m* bar
(b) (GB) (Pol) cabinet *m*

cabinet minister *n* (GB) ministre *m*

cable ①︎ *n* câble *m*
②︎ *adj* ⟨*channel, network*⟩ câblé/-e

cable car *n* téléphérique *m*

cable TV *n* télévision *f* par câble

cab-rank, **cab stand** *n* station *f* de taxis

cackle *vi* ⟨hen⟩ caqueter; ⟨person⟩ (talk) caqueter; (laugh) ricaner

CAD *n* (*abbr* = **computer-aided design**) CAO *f*

CADCAM *n* (*abbr* = **computer-aided design and computer-aided manufacture**) CFAO *f*

caddy *n* caddie *m*

cadet *n* (Mil) élève *mf* officier

cadge *vtr* (colloq) to ∼ sth off *or* from sb taper (colloq) qch à qn ⟨cigarette, money⟩; to ∼ a meal/a lift se faire inviter/emmener en voiture

Caesarean, **Caesarian** *n* (also ∼ **section**) césarienne *f*

café *n* (a) ≈ snack-bar *m*; **pavement** ∼, **sidewalk** ∼ café *m*
(b) (US) bistro *m*

cafeteria *n* (gen) cafétéria *f*; (Sch) cantine *f*; (Univ) restaurant *m* universitaire

caffein(e) *n* caféine *f*; ∼**-free** décaféiné/-e

cage ⨯1⨯ *n* cage *f*
⨯2⨯ *vtr* mettre [qch] en cage ⟨animal⟩; **a** ∼**d animal** un animal en cage

cagoule *n* (GB) K-way® *m*

cahoots *n pl* (colloq) to be in ∼ être de mèche (colloq) (**with** avec)

Cairo *pr n* Le Caire

cajole *vtr* cajoler

cake *n* (a) (Culin) gâteau *m*; (sponge) génoise *f*
(b) (of soap, wax) pain *m*
IDIOMS it's a piece of ∼ (colloq) c'est du gâteau (colloq)

cake shop *n* ≈ pâtisserie *f*

calcium *n* calcium *m*

calculate *vtr* (a) calculer ⟨cost, distance, price⟩
(b) évaluer ⟨effect, probability⟩
(c) to be ∼d to do avoir été conçu/-e pour faire

calculated *adj* ⟨crime⟩ prémédité/-e; ⟨attempt, insult⟩ délibéré/-e; ⟨risk⟩ calculé/-e

calculating *adj* ⟨manner, person⟩ calculateur/-trice

calculation *n* calcul *m*

calculator *n* calculatrice *f*, calculette *f*

calendar *n* calendrier *m*

calf *n* (a) (Zool) veau *m*
(b) (also ∼**skin**) vachette *f*
(c) (Anat) mollet *m*

calibre (GB), **caliber** (US) *n* calibre *m*

California *pr n* Californie *f*

call ⨯1⨯ *n* (a) (also **phone** ∼) appel *m* (téléphonique) (**from** de); to make a ∼ appeler, téléphoner
(b) (cry) (human) appel *m* (**for** à); (animal) cri *m*
(c) (summons) appel *m*
(d) (visit) visite *f*
(e) (demand) demande *f* (**for** de)

(f) (need) there's no ∼ for sth il n'y a pas de raison pour qch
(g) (Sport) décision *f*
(h) to be on ∼ ⟨doctor⟩ être de garde; ⟨engineer⟩ être de service
⨯2⨯ *vtr* (a) (gen) appeler; what is he ∼ed? comment s'appelle-t-il?; the boss ∼ed me into his office le chef m'a fait venir dans son bureau
(b) (waken) réveiller ⟨person⟩; convoquer ⟨meeting⟩; fixer ⟨election⟩
(c) (waken) réveiller ⟨person⟩
(d) (describe as) to ∼ sb stupid traiter qn d'imbécile; I wouldn't ∼ it spacious je ne dirais pas que c'est spacieux
⨯3⨯ *vi* (a) (gen) appeler; who's ∼ing? qui est à l'appareil?
(b) (visit) passer; to ∼ at passer chez ⟨person, shop⟩; passer à ⟨bank, library⟩; ⟨train⟩ s'arrêter à ⟨town, station⟩

■ **call back**: ¶ ∼ back (on phone) rappeler; ¶ ∼ [sb] back rappeler ⟨person⟩

■ **call for**: ∼ for [sth] (a) (shout) appeler ⟨ambulance, doctor⟩; to ∼ for help appeler à l'aide
(b) (demand) réclamer
(c) (require) exiger ⟨treatment, skill⟩; nécessiter ⟨change⟩

■ **call in**: ¶ ∼ in (visit) passer; ¶ ∼ [sb] in faire entrer ⟨client, patient⟩; faire appel à ⟨expert⟩

■ **call off** abandonner ⟨investigation⟩; annuler ⟨deal, wedding⟩; rompre ⟨engagement⟩

■ **call on** (a) (visit) rendre visite à ⟨relative, friend⟩; visiter ⟨patient, client⟩
(b) to ∼ on sb to do demander à qn de faire

■ **call out**: ¶ ∼ out appeler; (louder) crier ¶ ∼ [sb] out (a) appeler ⟨doctor, troops⟩
(b) ⟨union⟩ lancer un ordre de grève à ⟨members⟩
∼ [sth] out appeler ⟨name, number⟩

■ **call up**: ¶ ∼ up appeler
¶ ∼ [sb/sth] up (a) (on phone) appeler
(b) (Mil) appeler [qn] sous les drapeaux ⟨soldier⟩

call box *n* (GB) cabine *f* téléphonique; (US) poste *m* téléphonique

call centre *n* centre *m* d'appels

caller *n* (a) (on phone) personne *f* qui appelle
(b) (visitor) visiteur/-euse *m/f*

callous *adj* inhumain/-e

call-out charge *n* frais *mpl* de déplacement

calm ⨯1⨯ *n* calme *m*; (in adversity) sang-froid *m*
⨯2⨯ *adj* calme; keep ∼! du calme!
⨯3⨯ *vtr* calmer

■ **calm down**: ¶ ∼ down se calmer ¶ ∼ [sb/sth] down calmer

calmly *adv* ⟨act, speak⟩ calmement; ⟨sleep, smoke⟩ tranquillement

Calor gas® *n* (GB) butane *m*

calorie *n* calorie *f*

camcorder *n* caméscope® *m*

camel *n* chameau *m*

camera n (a) (for photos) appareil m photo
(b) (for movies) caméra f

camera crew n équipe f de télévision

cameraman n cadreur m, cameraman m

camisole n caraco m

camouflage 1 n camouflage m
2 vtr camoufler (**with** avec)

camp 1 n camp m
2 vi camper; **to go ~ing** faire du camping

campaign 1 n campagne f
2 vi faire campagne (**for** pour; **against** contre)

campaigner n militant/-e m/f (**for** pour; **against** contre); (Pol) candidat/-e m/f en campagne (électorale)

camp bed n lit m de camp

camper n (a) (person) campeur/-euse m/f
(b) (also ~ **van**) camping-car m

campfire n feu m de camp

camping n camping m; **to go ~** faire du camping

campsite n terrain m de camping, camping m

campus n campus m

can¹ modal aux (a) (be able to) pouvoir; ~ **you come?** est-ce que tu peux venir?, peux-tu venir?; **we will do all we ~** nous ferons tout ce que nous pouvons or tout notre possible
(b) (know how to) savoir; **she ~ swim** elle sait nager; **I can't drive** je ne sais pas conduire; **he ~ speak French** il parle français
(c) (permission, requests, offers, suggestions) pouvoir; ~ **we park here?** est-ce que nous pouvons nous garer ici?; **you can't turn right** vous ne pouvez pas or vous n'avez pas le droit de tourner à droite; ~ **you do me a favour?** peux-tu or est-ce que tu peux me rendre un service?
(d) (with verbs of perception) ~ **they see us?** est-ce qu'ils nous voient?; **I can't feel a thing** je ne sens rien; **she can't understand English** elle ne comprend pas l'anglais
(e) (in expressions) **you can't be hungry!** tu ne peux pas avoir faim!; **you can't be serious!** tu veux rire!; **this can't be right** il doit y avoir une erreur; ~ **you believe it!** tu te rends compte?; **what ~ she want from me?** qu'est-ce qu'elle peut bien me vouloir?

can² 1 n (of food) boîte f; (of drink) cannette f; (aerosol) bombe f; (for petrol) bidon m; (of paint) pot m
2 vtr mettre [qch] en conserve

Canada pr n Canada m

Canadian 1 n Canadien/-ienne m/f
2 adj canadien/-ienne; ⟨embassy⟩ du Canada

canal n canal m

canal boat, **canal barge** n péniche f

Canaries pr n pl (also **Canary Islands**)
the ~ les Canaries fpl

cancel vtr (gen) annuler; mettre une opposition à ⟨cheque⟩

cancellation n annulation f

cancer n cancer m; **to have ~** avoir un cancer; **lung ~** cancer du poumon

Cancer n Cancer m

cancer patient n cancéreux/-euse m/f

cancer research n cancérologie f

candid adj franc/franche

candidate n candidat/-e m/f

candle n bougie f; (in church) cierge m

candlelight n lueur f de bougie

candlelit dinner n dîner m aux chandelles

candlestick n bougeoir m; (ornate) chandelier m

candy n (US) (sweets) bonbons mpl; (sweet) bonbon m

candyfloss n (GB) barbe f à papa

cane n (a) (material) rotin m; ~ **furniture** meubles en rotin
(b) (of sugar, bamboo) canne f
(c) (for walking) canne f; (for plant) tuteur m; (GB) (for punishment) badine f

canine n canine f

canister n boîte f métallique; **a tear gas ~** une bombe lacrymogène

cannabis n cannabis m

canned adj (a) ⟨food⟩ en boîte
(b) (colloq) ⟨laughter⟩ enregistré/-e

cannibal n cannibale mf

cannon n canon m

canoe 1 n (gen) canoë m; (dugout) pirogue f; (Sport) canoë-kayac m
2 vi faire du canoë

canoeing n **to go ~** faire du canoë-kayac

can-opener n ouvre-boîtes m inv

cantankerous adj acariâtre

canteen n (a) (GB) (dining room) cantine f
(b) (Mil) (flask) bidon m; (mess tin) gamelle f
(c) **a ~ of cutlery** une ménagère

canter vi ⟨rider⟩ faire un petit galop; ⟨horse⟩ galoper

canvas n toile f

canvass vtr (a) **to ~ voters** faire du démarchage électoral auprès des électeurs
(b) **to ~ opinion on sth** sonder l'opinion au sujet de qch
(c) (for business) prospecter ⟨area⟩

canvasser n agent m électoral

canyon n cañon m

canyoning n canyoning m

cap 1 n (a) casquette f; **baseball ~** casquette de baseball
(b) (of pen) capuchon m; (of bottle) capsule f
(c) (for tooth) couronne f
2 vtr (a) (limit) imposer une limite budgétaire à ⟨local authority⟩; plafonner ⟨budget⟩
(b) (cover) couronner (**with** de)
IDIOMS **to ~ it all** pour couronner le tout

capability n (a) (capacity) capacité f (**to do** de faire)
(b) (aptitude) aptitude f; **outside my capabilities** au-delà de mes compétences

capable adj (a) (competent) compétent/-e ⋯⟶

(b) (able) capable (**of** de)

capacity n **(a)** (of box, bottle) contenance f; (of building) capacité f d'accueil; **full to ~** comble

(b) (of factory) capacité f de production

(c) (role) **in my ~ as a doctor** en ma qualité de médecin

(d) (ability) **to have a ~ for** avoir des facilités pour ⟨learning, mathematics⟩; **a ~ for doing** une aptitude à faire

cape n **(a)** (cloak) cape f

(b) (on coast) cap m

caper n **(a)** (Culin) câpre f

(b) (colloq) (scheme) combine f

(c) (colloq) (antic) pitrerie f

Cape Town pr n Le Cap

capital ⟨1⟩ n **(a)** (letter) majuscule f

(b) (also ~ **city**) capitale f

(c) (money) capital m

⟨2⟩ adj **(a)** ⟨letter⟩ majuscule; ~ **A** A majuscule

(b) (Law) ⟨offence⟩ capital/-e

capital expenditure n dépenses fpl d'investissement

capital investment n dépenses fpl d'investissement

capitalism n capitalisme m

capitalist n, adj capitaliste (mf)

capitalize vi **to ~ on** tirer parti de ⟨situation, advantage⟩

capital punishment n peine f capitale

capitulate vi capituler (**to** devant)

Capricorn n Capricorne m

capsize vi chavirer

captain ⟨1⟩ n capitaine m

⟨2⟩ vtr être le capitaine de ⟨team⟩; commander ⟨ship, platoon⟩

caption n légende f

captivate vtr captiver, fasciner

captive n captif/-ive m/f

captivity n captivité f

captor n (of person) geôlier/-ière m/f

capture ⟨1⟩ n (of person, animal) capture f; (of stronghold) prise f

⟨2⟩ vtr **(a)** capturer ⟨person, animal⟩; prendre ⟨stronghold⟩

(b) saisir ⟨likeness⟩; rendre ⟨feeling⟩

car ⟨1⟩ n **(a)** (Aut) voiture f

(b) (on train) wagon m; **restaurant ~** wagon-restaurant m

⟨2⟩ adj ⟨industry, insurance⟩ automobile; ⟨journey, chase⟩ en voiture; ⟨accident⟩ de voiture

caramel n caramel m

carat n carat m; **18 ~ gold** or 18 carats

caravan ⟨1⟩ n caravane f; (horse-drawn) roulotte f

⟨2⟩ vi **to go ~ning** (GB) faire du caravanage

caravan site n camping m pour caravanes

carbohydrate n hydrate m de carbone

car bomb n bombe f dissimulée dans une voiture

carbon n carbone m

carbon copy n copie f carbone; (figurative) réplique f exacte

carbon dioxide n dioxyde m de carbone

carbon monoxide n monoxyde m de carbone

car boot sale n (GB) brocante f ⟨d'objets apportés dans le coffre de sa voiture⟩

carburettor (GB), **carburetor** (US) n carburateur m

card n carte f

IDIOMS to play one's ~s right bien jouer son jeu (colloq)

cardboard n carton m

cardboard box n (boîte f en) carton m

cardboard city n: zone urbaine où les sans-abri logent dans des cartons

card game n partie f de cartes

cardiac adj cardiaque

cardiac arrest n arrêt m du cœur

cardigan n cardigan m

card key n carte f magnétique

cardphone n téléphone m à carte

card trick n tour m de cartes

care ⟨1⟩ n **(a)** (attention) attention f, soin m; **to take ~ to do** prendre soin de faire; **'take ~!'** (be careful) 'fais attention!'; (goodbye) 'à bientôt!'; **'handle with ~'** 'fragile'

(b) (looking after) (of person, animal) soins mpl; (of car, plant, clothes) entretien m (of de); **to take ~ of** (deal with) s'occuper de ⟨child, client, garden, details⟩; (be careful with) prendre soin de ⟨machine, car⟩; (keep in good condition) entretenir ⟨car, teeth⟩; (look after) garder ⟨shop, watch⟩; **to take ~ of oneself** (look after oneself) prendre soin de soi; (cope) se débrouiller tout seul/toute seule; (defend oneself) se défendre

(c) (Med) soins mpl

(d) (GB) **to be in ~** ⟨child⟩ être (placé/-e) en garde

(e) (worry) souci m

⟨2⟩ vi **(a)** (be concerned) **to ~ about** s'intéresser à ⟨art, environment⟩; se soucier du bien-être de ⟨pupils, the elderly⟩; **I don't ~!** ça m'est égal!; **she couldn't ~ less about...** elle se moque or se fiche (colloq) complètement de...; **I'm past caring** je m'en moque

(b) (love) **to ~ about sb** aimer qn

■ **care for: ¶ ~ for [sth]** (a) (like) aimer; **would you ~ for a drink?** voulez-vous boire quelque chose?

(b) (maintain) entretenir ⟨car, garden⟩; prendre soin de ⟨skin, plant⟩

¶ ~ for [sb/sth] s'occuper de ⟨child, animal⟩; soigner ⟨patient⟩

care assistant n aide-soignant/-e m/f

career n carrière f

career break n interruption f de carrière

careers adviser, careers officer n conseiller/-ère m/f d'orientation

careers office n service m d'orientation professionnelle

carefree *adj* insouciant/-e

careful *adj* ⟨person, driving⟩ prudent/-e; ⟨planning, preparation⟩ minutieux/-ieuse; ⟨research, examination⟩ méticuleux/-euse; **to be ~ to do** *or* **about doing** prendre soin de faire; **to be ~ with sth** faire attention à qch; **be ~!** (fais) attention!

carefully *adv* ⟨walk, open, handle⟩ prudemment; ⟨write⟩ soigneusement; ⟨listen, read, look⟩ attentivement

careless *adj* ⟨person⟩ négligent/-e, imprudent/-e; ⟨work⟩ bâclé/-e; ⟨writing⟩ négligé/-e; ⟨driving⟩ négligent/-e; **~ mistake** faute d'étourderie; **it was ~ of me to do** ça a été de la négligence de ma part de faire

carelessness *n* négligence *f*

carer *n* (relative) *personne ayant un parent handicapé ou malade à charge*; (professional) aide *f* familiale

caress *vtr* caresser

caretaker *n* concierge *mf*

care worker *n* assistant/-e *m/f* social/-e

car ferry *n* ferry *m*

cargo *n* chargement *m*

cargo ship *n* cargo *m*

car hire *n* location *f* de voitures

car hire company *n* société *f* de location de voitures

Caribbean *pr n* **the ~ (sea)** la mer des Antilles *or* des Caraïbes

caricature *n* caricature *f*

caring *adj* (a) (loving) ⟨parent⟩ affectueux/-euse
(b) (compassionate) ⟨person, attitude⟩ compréhensif/-ive; ⟨society⟩ humain/-e

carjacking *n* vol *m* de voiture (avec agression du conducteur)

carnage *n* carnage *m*

carnation *n* œillet *m*

carnival *n* (a) carnaval *m*
(b) (US) (funfair) fête *f* foraine

carol *n* chant *m* de Noël

carousel *n* (a) (merry-go-round) manège *m*
(b) (for luggage, slides) carrousel *m*

car park *n* (GB) parc *m* de stationnement

carpenter *n* menuisier *m*

carpentry *n* menuiserie *f*

carpet *n* (fitted) moquette *f*; (loose) tapis *m*

carpet sweeper *n* balai *m* mécanique

car phone *n* téléphone *m* de voiture

car radio *n* autoradio *m*

carriage *n* (a) (ceremonial) carrosse *m*
(b) (of train) wagon *m*, voiture *f*
(c) (of goods) transport *m*; **~ paid** port *m* payé
(d) (of typewriter) chariot *m*

carriageway *n* chaussée *f*

carrier *n* (a) (transport company) transporteur *m*; (airline) compagnie *f* aérienne
(b) (of disease) porteur/-euse *m/f*
(c) (GB) (*also* **~ bag**) sac *m* (en plastique)

carrot *n* carotte *f*

carry ⚠1⚠ *vtr* (a) ⟨person⟩ porter; **to ~ sth in/out** apporter/emporter qch
(b) ⟨vehicle, pipe, vein⟩ transporter; ⟨tide, current⟩ emporter
(c) comporter ⟨warning⟩
(d) comporter ⟨risk, responsibility⟩; être passible de ⟨penalty⟩
(e) ⟨bridge, road⟩ supporter ⟨load, traffic⟩
(f) faire voter ⟨bill⟩; **the motion was carried by 20 votes to 13** la motion l'a emporté par 20 votes contre 13
(g) (Med) être porteur/-euse de ⟨disease, virus⟩
(h) (in mathematics) retenir
(i) (hold) porter ⟨head⟩
⚠2⚠ *vi* ⟨sound, voice⟩ porter
IDIOMS **to get carried away** (colloq) s'emballer (colloq), se laisser emporter
■ **carry forward** reporter ⟨balance, total⟩
■ **carry off** (gen) emporter; remporter ⟨prize⟩; **to ~ it off** (colloq) réussir, y arriver
■ **carry on**: ¶ **~ on** (a) (continue) continuer (doing à faire)
(b) (colloq) (behave) se conduire
¶ **~ on [sth]** maintenir ⟨tradition⟩; poursuivre ⟨activity, discussion⟩
■ **carry out** réaliser ⟨study⟩; effectuer ⟨experiment, reform, attack, repairs⟩; exécuter ⟨plan, orders⟩; mener ⟨investigation, campaign⟩; accomplir ⟨mission⟩; remplir ⟨duties⟩; mettre [qch] à exécution ⟨threat⟩; tenir ⟨promise⟩

carryall *n* (US) fourre-tout *m inv*

carrycot *n* (GB) porte-bébé *m*

carry-on *n* (colloq) cirque *m* (colloq)

carryout *n* repas *m* à emporter

car seat *n* siège-auto *m*

carsick *adj* **to be ~** avoir le mal de la route

cart ⚠1⚠ *n* charrette *f*
⚠2⚠ *vtr* (colloq) (*also* **~ around**, **~ about**) (colloq) trimballer (colloq) ⟨bags⟩

cartel *n* cartel *m*; **drug ~** cartel *m* de la drogue

car theft *n* vol *m* de voitures

carton *n* (of juice, milk) carton *m*, brique *f*; (of yoghurt, cream) pot *m*; (of cigarettes) cartouche *f*; (US) (for house removals) carton *m*

cartoon *n* (a) (film) dessin *m* animé
(b) (drawing) dessin *m* humoristique; (comic strip) bande *f* dessinée

cartridge *n* (for pen, gun, video) cartouche *f*; (for camera) chargeur *m*

cartwheel *n* **to do a ~** faire la roue

carve ⚠1⚠ *vtr* (a) tailler, sculpter ⟨wood, stone, figure⟩ (out of dans)
(b) graver ⟨letters, name⟩ (onto sur)
(c) découper ⟨meat⟩
⚠2⚠ *vi* découper
■ **carve out** (a) se faire ⟨niche, name⟩; se tailler ⟨reputation, market⟩
(b) creuser ⟨gorge, channel⟩
■ **carve up**: **~ up [sth]**, **~ [sth] up** partager ⟨proceeds⟩; morceler ⟨estate, territory⟩

carving *n* sculpture *f*

carving knife n couteau m à découper
car wash n lavage m automatique
case¹ ⓵ n (a) (gen) cas m; **in that** ~ en ce cas, dans ce cas-là; **in 7 out of 10** ~s 7 fois sur 10, dans 7 cas sur 10; **a** ~ **in point** un cas d'espèce, un exemple typique
(b) (Law) affaire f; procès m; **the** ~ **for the Crown** (GB), **the** ~ **for the State** (US) l'accusation f; **the** ~ **for the defence** la défense
(c) (argument) arguments mpl
⓶ **in any case** phr (a) (besides, anyway) de toute façon
(b) (at any rate) en tout cas
⓷ **in case** phr au cas où (+ conditional); **just in** ~ au cas où
⓸ **in case of** phr en cas de ⟨fire, accident⟩
case² n (a) (suitcase) valise f; (crate, chest) caisse f
(b) (display cabinet) vitrine f
(c) (for spectacles, binoculars, weapon) étui m; (for camera, watch) boîtier m
CASE n (abbr = **computer-aided software engineering**) CPAO f
case study n étude f de cas
cash ⓵ n (a) (notes and coin) espèces fpl, argent m liquide; **to pay in** ~ payer en espèces; **I haven't got any** ~ **on me** je n'ai pas d'argent liquide
(b) (money in general) argent m
(c) (payment) comptant m; **discount for** ~ remise f pour paiement comptant
⓶ vtr encaisser ⟨cheque⟩
■ **cash in**: ¶ **to** ~ **in on** tirer profit de, profiter de; ¶ ~ ⟨sth⟩ **in** se faire rembourser, réaliser ⟨bond, policy⟩; (US) encaisser ⟨check⟩
cash-and-carry n libre-service m de vente en gros
cash card n carte f de retrait
cash desk n caisse f
cash dispenser n (also **cashpoint**) distributeur m automatique de billets de banque, billetterie f
cashew nut n cajou m
cash flow n marge f brute d'auto-financement, MBA f
cashier n caissier/-ière m/f
cashless adj ⟨society⟩ sans argent liquide
cashmere n (lainage m en) cachemire m
cash on delivery, **COD** n envoi m contre remboursement
cashpoint = CASH DISPENSER
cash register n caisse f enregistreuse
casino n casino m
cask n fût m, tonneau m
casserole n (a) (container) daubière f, cocotte f
(b) (GB) (food) ragoût m cuit au four
cassette n cassette f
cassette deck n platine f à cassettes
cassette player n lecteur m de cassettes
cast ⓵ n (a) (list of actors) distribution f; (actors) acteurs mpl

(b) (Med) (also **plaster** ~) plâtre m
(c) (mould) moule m
⓶ vtr (a) jeter, lancer ⟨stone, fishing line⟩; projeter ⟨shadow⟩; **to** ~ **doubt on** émettre des doutes sur; **to** ~ **light on** éclairer; **to** ~ **a spell on** jeter un sort à
(b) jeter ⟨glance⟩ (at sur)
(c) distribuer les rôles de ⟨play, film⟩; **she was cast as Blanche** elle a joué Blanche
(d) couler ⟨plaster, metal⟩
(e) **to** ~ **one's vote** voter
castaway n naufragé/-e m/f
caste n caste f
caster sugar n (GB) sucre m en poudre
casting n distribution f
casting vote n voix f prépondérante
cast iron n fonte f; **a** ~ **alibi** un alibi en béton (colloq)
castle n (a) château m
(b) (in chess) tour f
cast-offs n pl vêtements mpl dont on n'a plus besoin, vieux vêtements
castrate vtr castrer
casual adj (a) (informal) ⟨clothes, person⟩ décontracté/-e
(b) ⟨acquaintance, relationship⟩ de passage; ~ **sex** relations fpl sexuelles non suivies
(c) ⟨attitude, gesture, remark⟩ désinvolte
(d) ⟨glance⟩ superficiel/-ielle
(e) ⟨work⟩ (temporary) temporaire; (occasional) occasionnel/-elle
casualize vtr **to** ~ **labour** précariser l'emploi
casually adv (a) ⟨enquire, remark⟩ d'un air détaché
(b) ⟨dressed⟩ simplement
casualty ⓵ n (a) (person) victime f
(b) (hospital ward) urgences fpl; **in** ~ aux urgences
⓶ **casualties** n pl (soldiers) pertes fpl; (civilians) victimes fpl
casual wear n vêtements mpl sport
cat n (domestic) chat m; (female) chatte f; **the big** ~s les grands félins mpl
IDIOMS **to let the** ~ **out of the bag** vendre la mèche; **to rain** ~s **and dogs** pleuvoir des cordes
catalogue, **catalog** (US) n catalogue m
catalyst n catalyseur m
catalytic converter n pot m catalytique
catapult n (hand-held) lance-pierres m inv
catarrh n catarrhe m
catastrophe n catastrophe f
catch ⓵ n (a) (on purse, door) fermeture f
(b) (drawback) piège m
(c) (act of catching) prise f; **to play** ~ jouer à la balle
(d) (in fishing) pêche f; (one fish) prise f
⓶ vtr (a) ⟨person⟩ attraper ⟨ball, fish, person⟩; **to** ~ **hold of sth** attraper qch; **to** ~ **sb's attention** or **eye** attirer l'attention de qn; **to** ~ **sight of sb/sth** apercevoir qn/qch
(b) (take by surprise) prendre, attraper; **to** ~ **sb**

doing surprendre qn en train de faire; **we got caught in the rain** nous avons été surpris par la pluie
(c) (grasp) prendre ⟨*bus, plane*⟩
(d) (grasp) prendre ⟨*hand, arm*⟩; agripper ⟨*branch, rope*⟩; captiver, éveiller ⟨*interest*⟩
(e) (hear) saisir (colloq), comprendre
(f) **to ∼ one's fingers in** se prendre les doigts dans ⟨*drawer, door*⟩; **to get one's shirt caught on** accrocher sa chemise à ⟨*nail*⟩; **to get caught in** se prendre dans ⟨*barbed wire, thorns*⟩
(g) attraper ⟨*cold, disease, flu*⟩
(h) **to ∼ fire** prendre feu, s'enflammer
3 *vi* **(a) to ∼ on** ⟨*shirt*⟩ s'accrocher à ⟨*nail*⟩; ⟨*wheel*⟩ frotter contre ⟨*frame*⟩
(b) ⟨*wood, fire*⟩ prendre
■ **catch on (a)** (become popular) devenir populaire (**with** auprès de)
(b) (understand) comprendre, saisir
■ **catch out (a)** (take by surprise) prendre [qn] de court; (doing something wrong) prendre [qn] sur le fait
(b) (trick) attraper, jouer un tour à
■ **catch up**: ¶ ∼ **up** (in race) regagner du terrain; (in work) rattraper son retard; **to ∼ up on** rattraper ⟨*work, sleep*⟩; se remettre au courant de ⟨*news*⟩; ¶ ∼ **[sb/sth] up** rattraper
catch-22 situation *n* situation *f* inextricable
catching *adj* contagieux/-ieuse
catchphrase *n* formule *f* favorite, rengaine *f*
catchy *adj* ⟨*tune*⟩ entraînant/-e; ⟨*slogan*⟩ accrocheur/-euse
categorical *adj* catégorique
categorize *vtr* classer (**by** d'après)
category *n* catégorie *f*
cater *vi* **(a)** ⟨*caterer*⟩ organiser des réceptions
(b) to ∼ for (GB) **or to** (US) accueillir ⟨*children, guests*⟩; pourvoir à ⟨*needs*⟩; ⟨*programme*⟩ s'adresser à ⟨*audience*⟩
caterer *n* traiteur *m*
catering *n* (provision) approvisionnement *m*; (trade, industry, career) restauration *f*
caterpillar *n* chenille *f*
cathedral *n* cathédrale *f*
Catholic *n, adj* catholique (*mf*)
Catholicism *n* catholicisme *m*
catnap *vi* faire un somme, sommeiller
Catseye® *n* (GB) plot *m* rétroréfléchissant
cattle *n* bétail *m*
catwalk *n* podium *m*; ∼ **show** défilé *m* de mode
cauliflower *n* chou-fleur *m*
cause **1** *n* cause *f* (**of** de); **there is ∼ for concern** il y a des raisons de s'inquiéter; **to have ∼ to do** avoir des raisons de faire; **with good ∼** à juste titre
2 *vtr* causer, occasionner ⟨*damage, grief, problem*⟩; provoquer ⟨*chaos, disease, controversy*⟩; entraîner ⟨*suffering*⟩; amener

⟨*confusion*⟩; **to ∼ sb problems** causer des problèmes à qn; **to ∼ trouble** créer des problèmes
caustic *adj* caustique
caution **1** *n* **(a)** (care) prudence *f*
(b) (wariness) circonspection *f*
(c) (warning) avertissement *m*
2 *vtr* **(a)** (warn) avertir (**that** que)
(b) (Sport) donner un avertissement à ⟨*player*⟩
IDIOMS to throw *or* **cast ∼ to the wind(s)** oublier toute prudence
cautionary *adj* ⟨*look, gesture*⟩ d'avertissement; **a ∼ tale** un conte moral
cautious *adj* **(a)** (careful) prudent/-e
(b) (wary) ⟨*person, reception, response*⟩ réservé/-e; ⟨*optimism*⟩ prudent/-e
cave *n* grotte *f*
■ **cave in (a)** ⟨*tunnel, roof*⟩ s'effondrer
(b) ⟨*person*⟩ céder
caveman *n* homme *m* des cavernes
caviar(e) *n* caviar *m*
caving *n* spéléologie *f*; **to go ∼** faire de la spéléologie
cavity *n* cavité *f*
cavort *vi* faire des cabrioles
caw *vi* croasser
cc *n* (*abbr* = **cubic centimetre**) cm³
CCTV *n* (*abbr* = **closed-circuit television**) télévision *f* en circuit fermé
CD *n* (*abbr* = **compact disc**) CD *m*
CD player, **CD system** *n* platine *f* laser
CD-ROM *n* CD-ROM *m*, disque *m* optique compact
cease *vtr, vi* cesser
cease-fire *n* cessez-le-feu *m inv*
cedar *n* cèdre *m*
cede *vtr, vi* céder (**to** à)
cedilla *n* cédille *f*
ceiling *n* plafond *m*
celebrate **1** *vtr* fêter; (more formally) célébrer
2 *vi* faire la fête
celebrated *adj* célèbre (**for** pour)
celebration *n* **(a)** (celebrating) célébration *f*
(b) (party) fête *f*
(c) (public festivities) ∼**s** cérémonies *fpl*
celebrity **1** *n* célébrité *f*
2 *adj* ⟨*guest*⟩ célèbre; ⟨*panel*⟩ de célébrités
celery *n* céleri *m*
celibate *adj* (chaste) chaste
cell *n* cellule *f*
cellar *n* cave *f*
cello *n* violoncelle *m*
cellphone, **cellular phone** *n* radiotéléphone *m*
cellulite *n* cellulite *f*
Celsius *adj* Celsius *inv*
Celt *n* Celte *mf*
Celtic *adj* celtique, celte
cement *n* ciment *m*

cement mixer n bétonnière f

cemetery n cimetière m

censor **1** n censeur mf
2 vtr censurer

censorship n censure f (of de)

censure **1** n censure f
2 vtr critiquer

census n recensement m

cent n cent m

centenary n centenaire m

center (US) = CENTRE

centigrade adj in degrees ~ en degrés Celsius

centimetre (GB), **centimeter** (US) n centimètre m

central adj (a) central/-e; ~ **London** le centre de Londres
(b) (in the town centre) situé/-e en centre-ville
(c) (key) principal/-e

Central America pr n Amérique f centrale

central heating n chauffage m central

centralize vtr centraliser

central locking n verrouillage m central or centralisé

central reservation n (GB) (Aut) terre-plein m central

centre (GB), **center** (US) **1** n centre m; in the ~ au centre; town ~, city ~ centre-ville m; the ~ of attention le centre de l'attention; the ~ of power le siège du pouvoir; shopping/sports ~ centre m commercial/sportif
2 vtr, vi centrer
■ **centre around**, **centre on** ⟨activities, person⟩ se concentrer sur; ⟨people, industry⟩ se situer autour de ⟨town⟩; ⟨life, thoughts⟩ être centré/-e sur ⟨person, work⟩

centre-forward n (Sport) avant-centre m

centre ground n centre m; to occupy the ~ être au centre

centre-half n (Sport) demi-centre m

centrepiece (GB), **centerpiece** (US) n (of table) décoration f centrale; (of exhibition) clou m

centre-stage to take/occupy ~ devenir/ être le point de mire

century n siècle m; in the 20th ~ au XXᵉ siècle; at the turn of the ~ au début du siècle

ceramic adj en céramique

ceramics n céramiques fpl

cereal n céréale f; breakfast ~ céréales pour le petit déjeuner

cerebral palsy n paralysie f motrice centrale

ceremony n cérémonie f; to stand on ~ faire des cérémonies

cert n (colloq) it's a (dead) ~! (colloq) ça ne fait pas un pli! (colloq)

certain adj (a) (sure) certain/-e, sûr/-e (about, of de); I'm ~ (of it) j'en suis certain

or sûr; absolutely ~ sûr et certain; I'm ~ that I checked je suis sûr d'avoir vérifié; I'm ~ that he refused je suis sûr qu'il a refusé
(b) (specific) ⟨amount, number, conditions⟩ certain/-e (before n); ~ **people** certains mpl; to a ~ **extent** dans une certaine mesure

certainly adv certainement

certainty n certitude f

certificate n (gen) certificat m; (of birth, death, marriage) acte m; **18-~ film** film interdit aux moins de 18 ans

certified adj certifié/-e

certified mail n (US) to send by ~ envoyer en recommandé

certified public accountant n (US) expert-comptable m

certify vtr (a) (confirm) certifier
(b) (authenticate) authentifier

cervical cancer n cancer m du col de l'utérus

cervical smear n frottis m vaginal

CFC n (abbr = **chlorofluorocarbon**) CFC m

chafe vi frotter (on, against sur)

chain **1** n (a) (metal links) chaîne f
(b) (on lavatory) chasse f (d'eau)
(c) (on door) chaîne f de sûreté
(d) (of shops, hotels) chaîne f (of de)
(e) (of events) série f; (of ideas) enchaînement m
2 vtr enchaîner ⟨person, animal⟩; to ~ a bicycle to sth attacher une bicyclette à qch avec une chaîne

chain reaction n réaction f en chaîne

chain saw n tronçonneuse f

chain-smoke vi fumer comme un sapeur (colloq), fumer sans arrêt

chain-smoker n gros fumeur/grosse fumeuse m/f

chain store n (single shop) magasin m faisant partie d'une chaîne; (retail group) magasin m à succursales multiples

chair **1** n (a) chaise f; (armchair) fauteuil m
(b) (chairperson) président/-e m/f
(c) (Univ) chaire f (of, in de)
2 vtr présider ⟨meeting⟩

chair lift n télésiège m

chairman n président/-e m/f; **Mr Chairman** monsieur le Président; **Madam Chairman** madame la Présidente

chairperson n président/-e m/f

chalet n (mountain) chalet m; (in holiday camp) bungalow m

chalk n craie f

challenge **1** n (a) défi m; to take up a ~ relever un défi
(b) (challenging task) challenge m; to rise to the ~ relever le challenge
2 vtr (a) défier ⟨person⟩ (to à; to do de faire)
(b) débattre ⟨ideas⟩; contester ⟨statement, authority⟩

challenger n challenger m (for de)

challenging adj (a) ⟨work⟩ stimulant/-e
(b) ⟨look⟩ provocateur/-trice

chamber ☐ n chambre f
☐ **chambers** n pl (Law) cabinet m; (GB Pol) **the upper/lower** ~ la Chambre des lords/des communes

chambermaid n femme f de chambre

chamber music n musique f de chambre

Chamber of Commerce n chambre f de commerce et d'industrie

chameleon n caméléon m

champagne n, adj champagne (m) inv

champion n champion/-ionne m/f

championship n championnat m

chance ☐ n (a) (opportunity) occasion f; **to have** or **get the** ~ **to do** avoir l'occasion de faire; **you've missed your** ~ tu as laissé passer l'occasion
(b) (likelihood) chance f; **there is a** ~ **that she'll get a job in Paris** il y a des chances qu'elle trouve un travail à Paris; **she has a good** ~ elle a de bonnes chances
(c) (luck) hasard m; **by** ~ par hasard
(d) (risk) risque m; **to take a** ~ prendre un risque
(e) (possibility) chance f; **not to stand a** ~ n'avoir aucune chance; **by any** ~ par hasard
☐ vtr **to** ~ **doing** courir le risque de faire; **to** ~ **it** tenter sa chance
IDIOMS **no** ~! (colloq) pas question! (colloq)

chancellor n chancelier m; (Univ) président m

Chancellor of the Exchequer n (GB) Chancelier m de l'Échiquier

chandelier n lustre m

change ☐ n (a) (gen) changement m; (adjustment) modification f; **the** ~ **in the schedule** la modification du programme; ~ **of plan** changement de programme; **a** ~ **of clothes** des vêtements de rechange; **a** ~ **for the better** un changement en mieux; **that makes a nice** ~ ça change agréablement; **she needs a** ~ elle a besoin de se changer les idées; **to need a** ~ **of air** avoir besoin de changer d'air; **for a** ~ pour changer
(b) (cash) monnaie f; **small** ~ petite monnaie; **she gave me 10 francs** ~ elle m'a rendu 10 francs; **have you got** ~ **for 50 francs?** pouvez-vous me changer un billet de 50 francs?
☐ vtr (a) (alter) changer; (in part) modifier; **to** ~ **sb/sth into** transformer qn/qch en; **to** ~ **one's mind** changer d'avis; **to** ~ **one's mind about doing** abandonner l'idée de faire; **to** ~ **colour** changer de couleur
(b) (change de) ⟨clothes, name, car, job, TV channel⟩; (in shop) échanger ⟨item⟩ (**for** pour); **to** ~ **places** (seats) changer de place (**with** avec)
(c) changer ⟨battery, tyre⟩; **to** ~ **a bed** changer les draps
(d) changer ⟨cheque, currency⟩ (**into, for** en)

☐ vi (a) ⟨situation, person⟩ changer; ⟨wind⟩ tourner; **the lights** ~**d from red to orange** les feux sont passés du rouge à l'orange
(b) (into different clothes) se changer; **to** ~ **into** passer ⟨garment⟩; **to** ~ **out of** ôter, enlever ⟨garment⟩
(c) (from bus, train) changer
☐ **changed** pp adj ⟨man, woman⟩ autre (before n)
■ **change round** déplacer ⟨large objects⟩; changer [qn/qch] de place ⟨workers, objects, words⟩

changeable adj ⟨condition, weather⟩ changeant/-e; ⟨price⟩ variable

changeover n passage m (**to** à)

changing adj ⟨colours, environment⟩ changeant/-e; ⟨attitude, world⟩ en évolution

changing room n (at sports centre) vestiaire m; (US) (in shop) cabine f d'essayage

channel ☐ n (a) (TV station) chaîne f; (radio band) canal m
(b) (groove) rainure f
(c) (in sea, river) chenal m
(d) **through the proper** ~**s** par la voie normale; **to go through official** ~**s** passer par la voie officielle
☐ vtr canaliser (**to, into** dans)

Channel pr n **the (English)** ~ la Manche

channel ferry n ferry m trans-Manche

channel-hop vi zapper (colloq)

Channel Islands pr n pl îles fpl Anglo-Normandes

Channel Tunnel pr n tunnel m sous la Manche

chant ☐ n (a) (of crowd) chant m scandé
(b) (of devotees) mélopée f
☐ vi ⟨crowd⟩ scander des slogans; ⟨choir, monks⟩ psalmodier

chaos n (gen) pagaille f (colloq); (economic, cosmic) chaos m; **in a state of** ~ ⟨house⟩ sens dessus dessous; ⟨country⟩ en plein chaos

chaotic adj désordonné/-e

chap ☐ n (GB) (colloq) type m (colloq)
☐ vtr gercer; ~**ped lips** lèvres gercées

chapel n chapelle f

chaperone ☐ n chaperon m
☐ vtr chaperonner

chaplain n aumônier m

chapter n chapitre m; **in** ~ **3** au chapitre 3

character n (a) (gen) caractère m
(b) (in book, play, film) personnage m (**from** de)
(c) **a real** ~ un sacré numéro (colloq); **a local** ~ une figure locale

characteristic ☐ n (gen) caractéristique f; (of person) trait m de caractère
☐ adj caractéristique (**of** de)

characterize vtr (a) (depict) dépeindre (**as** comme)
(b) (typify) caractériser; **to be** ~**d by** se caractériser par

character reference n références fpl

charade n comédie f

charades n pl (game) charades fpl

charcoal ☐ n (a) (fuel) charbon m de bois ⋯⟐

(b) (for drawing) fusain *m*
2 *adj* (*also* ~ **grey**) (gris) anthracite *inv*
charge **1** *n* **(a)** (fee) frais *mpl*; additional *or* extra ~ supplément *m*; **to reverse the** ~**s** (on phone) appeler en PCV
(b) (accusation) accusation *f* (**of** de); (Law) inculpation *f*; **murder** ~ inculpation d'assassinat; **to press** ~**s against sth** engager des poursuites contre qch
(c) (attack) charge *f* (**against** contre)
(d) to be in ~ (gen) être responsable (**of** de); (Mil) commander; **the person in** ~ le/la responsable; **to take** ~ prendre les choses en main
(e) (child) enfant *mf* dont on s'occupe; (pupil) élève *mf*; (patient) malade *mf*
(f) (explosive, electrical) charge *f*
2 *vtr* **(a)** prélever ⟨*commission*⟩; percevoir ⟨*interest*⟩ (**on** sur); **to** ~ **sb for sth** faire payer qch à qn; **how much do you** ~? vous prenez combien?; **I** ~ **£20 an hour** je prends 20 livres sterling de l'heure
(b) to ~ **sth to** mettre qch sur ⟨*account*⟩
(c) ⟨*police*⟩ inculper ⟨*suspect*⟩ (**with** de)
(d) (rush at) charger ⟨*enemy*⟩; ⟨*bull*⟩ foncer sur ⟨*person*⟩
(e) charger ⟨*battery*⟩
3 *vi* **to** ~ **into/out of** se précipiter dans/de ⟨*room*⟩
charge account *n* (US) compte-client *m*
charge card *n* (credit card) carte *f* de crédit; (store card) carte *f* d'achat
char-grilled *adj* ⟨*steak*⟩ grillé/-e au charbon de bois
charisma *n* charisme *m*
charismatic *adj* charismatique
charitable *adj* ⟨*person, act, explanation*⟩ charitable (**to** envers); ⟨*organization*⟩ caritatif/-ive
charity *n* **(a)** (virtue) charité *f*
(b) (organization) organisation *f* caritative; **to give to/collect money for** ~ donner à/ collecter des fonds pour des œuvres de bienfaisance
charity shop *n* magasin *m* d'articles d'occasion (*vendus au profit d'une œuvre de bienfaisance*)
charity work *n* travail *m* bénévole (*au profit d'une œuvre de bienfaisance*)
charm *n* **(a)** charme *m*
(b) lucky ~ porte-bonheur *m inv*
charming *adj* ⟨*person, place*⟩ charmant/-e; ⟨*child, animal*⟩ adorable
charred *adj* carbonisé/-e
chart **1** *n* **(a)** (graph) graphique *m*
(b) (table) tableau *m*
(c) (map) carte *f*
(d) the ~**s** le hit-parade
2 *vtr* **(a)** (on map) tracer ⟨*route*⟩
(b) enregistrer ⟨*progress*⟩
charter **1** *n* charte *f*
2 *vtr* affréter ⟨*plane*⟩
chartered accountant, CA *n* (GB) ≈ expert-comptable *m*
charter flight *n* (GB) vol *m* charter

chase **1** *n* poursuite *f* (**after** de)
2 *vtr* **(a)** pourchasser ⟨*person, animal*⟩; **to** ~ **sb/sth up** *or* **down the street** courir après qn/qch dans la rue
(b) (*also* ~ **after**) courir après ⟨*woman, man, success*⟩
■ **chase away, chase off** chasser ⟨*person, animal*⟩
chassis *n* châssis *m*
chastity *n* chasteté *f*
chat **1** *n* conversation *f*; **to have a** ~ bavarder (**with** avec; **about** sur)
2 *vi* bavarder (**with, to** avec)
■ **chat up** (GB) (colloq) draguer (colloq)
chatline *n* réseau *m* téléphonique; (sexual) ≈ téléphone *m* rose
chatroom *n* site *m* de bavardage, salon *m* virtuel
chat show *n* (GB) talk-show *m*
chatter **1** *n* (of person) bavardage *m*; (of birds) gazouillis *m*
2 *vi* ⟨*person*⟩ bavarder; ⟨*birds*⟩ gazouiller; **her teeth were** ~**ing** elle claquait des dents
chatterbox *n* moulin *m* à paroles (colloq)
chatty *adj* ⟨*person*⟩ ouvert/-e; ⟨*letter*⟩ vivant/-e
chauffeur **1** *n* chauffeur *m*; **a** ~-**driven car** une voiture avec chauffeur
2 *vtr* conduire
chauvinist *n, adj* **(a)** (gen) chauvin/-e (*m/f*)
(b) (*also* **male** ~) macho (*m*) (colloq)
cheap *adj* **(a)** bon marché *inv*; **to be** ~ être bon marché, ne pas coûter cher *inv*; ~**er** moins cher/-ère
(b) (shoddy) de mauvaise qualité
(c) ⟨*joke*⟩ facile; ⟨*trick*⟩ sale (*before n*)
cheapen *vtr* rabaisser
cheaply *adv* ⟨*produce, sell*⟩ à bas prix; **to eat** ~ manger pour pas cher
cheap rate *adj, adv* à tarif réduit
cheat **1** *n* tricheur/-euse *m/f*
2 *vtr* tromper; **to feel** ~**ed** se sentir lésé/-e; **to** ~ **sb (out) of** dépouiller qn de
3 *vi* tricher (**in** à); **to** ~ **at cards** tricher aux cartes; **to** ~ **on sb** tromper qn
Chechnya *pr n* Tchétchénie *f*
check **1** *n* **(a)** (for quality, security) contrôle *m* (**on** sur)
(b) (medical) examen *m*
(c) (restraint) frein *m* (**on** à)
(d) (in chess) ~! échec au roi!; **in** ~ en échec
(e) (*also* ~ **fabric**) tissu *m* à carreaux; (*also* ~ **pattern**) carreaux *mpl*
(f) (US) (cheque) chèque *m*
(g) (US) (bill) addition *f*
(h) (US) (receipt) ticket *m*
(i) (US) (tick) croix *f*
2 *adj* ⟨*shirt, skirt*⟩ à carreaux
3 *vtr* **(a)** (gen) vérifier; contrôler ⟨*ticket, area, work*⟩; prendre ⟨*temperature*⟩; examiner ⟨*watch, map, pocket*⟩
(b) (curb) contrôler ⟨*prices, inflation*⟩; freiner ⟨*growth*⟩; maîtriser ⟨*emotions*⟩

4 *vi* **(a)** vérifier; **to ~ with sb** demander à qn; **to ~ for** dépister ⟨*problems*⟩; chercher ⟨*leaks, flaws*⟩
(b) to ~ into arriver à ⟨*hotel*⟩
■ **check in**: ¶ ~ **in** (at airport) enregistrer; (at hotel) arriver (**at** à); ¶ ~ **[sb/sth] in** enregistrer ⟨*baggage, passengers*⟩
■ **check off** cocher ⟨*items*⟩
■ **check out**: ¶ ~ **out** (leave) partir; **to ~ out of** quitter ⟨*hotel*⟩; ¶ ~ **[sth] out** vérifier ⟨*information*⟩; examiner ⟨*package, building*⟩; se renseigner sur ⟨*club, scheme*⟩
■ **check up on** faire une enquête sur ⟨*person*⟩; vérifier ⟨*story, details*⟩

checkbook *n* (US) carnet *m* de chèques, chéquier *m*
checkered (US) = CHEQUERED
checkers (US) = CHEQUERS
check-in *n* enregistrement *m*
checking account *n* (US) compte *m* courant
checklist *n* liste *f* de contrôle
checkmate *n* échec *m* et mat
checkout *n* caisse *f*
checkout assistant *n* caissier/-ière *m/f*
checkpoint *n* poste *m* de contrôle
checkroom *n* (US) (cloakroom) vestiaire *m*; (for baggage) consigne *f*
checkup *n* **(a)** (at doctor's) examen *m* médical, bilan *m* de santé; **to have a ~** passer *or* se faire faire un examen médical
(b) (at dentist's) visite *f* de routine
cheek *n* **(a)** (of face) joue *f*; **~ to ~** joue contre joue
(b) culot *m* (colloq); **what a ~!** quel culot!
cheekbone *n* pommette *f*
cheeky *adj* ⟨*person*⟩ effronté/-e, insolent/-e; ⟨*question*⟩ impoli/-e; ⟨*grin*⟩ espiègle, coquin/-e
cheer **1** *n* acclamation *f*; **to get a ~** être acclamé/-e
2 cheers *excl* **(a)** (toast) à la vôtre! (colloq); (to close friend) à la tienne! (colloq)
(b) (GB) (colloq) (thanks) merci!
(c) (GB) (colloq) (goodbye) salut!
3 *vtr, vi* applaudir
■ **cheer up**: ¶ ~ **up** reprendre courage; **~ up!** courage!; ¶ ~ **[sb] up** remonter le moral à ⟨*person*⟩; ¶ ~ **[sth] up** égayer ⟨*room*⟩
cheerful *adj* ⟨*person, mood, music*⟩ joyeux/-euse; ⟨*tone*⟩ enjoué/-e; ⟨*colour*⟩ gai/-e
cheerleader *n* majorette *f*
cheese *n* fromage *m*; **~ sandwich** sandwich *m* au fromage
cheeseboard *n* (object) plateau *m* à fromage; (selection) plateau *m* de fromages
cheetah *n* guépard *m*
chef *n* chef *m* cuisinier
chemical **1** *n* produit *m* chimique
2 *adj* chimique
chemist *n* **(a)** (GB) pharmacien/-ienne *m/f*; **~'s (shop)** pharmacie *f*
(b) (scientist) chimiste *mf*

chemistry *n* chimie *f*
chemotherapy *n* chimiothérapie *f*
cheque (GB), **check** (US) *n* chèque *m*; **to make out** *or* **write a ~ for £20** faire un chèque de 20 livres sterling
chequebook (GB), **checkbook** (US) *n* chéquier *m*, carnet *m* de chèques
cheque card *n* (GB) carte *f* de garantie bancaire
chequered (GB), **checkered** (US) *adj*
(a) ⟨*cloth*⟩ à damiers
(b) ⟨*career, history*⟩ en dents de scie
chequers (GB), **checkers** (US) *n* jeu *m* de dames
cherish *vtr* caresser ⟨*hope*⟩; chérir ⟨*memory, person*⟩
cherry **1** *n* **(a)** (fruit) cerise *f*
(b) (*also* **~ tree**) cerisier *m*
2 *adj* (*also* **~-red**) rouge cerise *inv*
chess *n* échecs *mpl*; **a game of ~** une partie d'échecs
chessboard *n* échiquier *m*
chess set *n* jeu *m* d'échecs
chest *n* **(a)** (of person) poitrine *f*; **~ measurement** tour *m* de poitrine
(b) (furniture) coffre *m*; **~ of drawers** commode *f*
(c) (crate) caisse *f*
IDIOMS **to get something off one's ~** (colloq) vider son sac (colloq)
chestnut **1** *n* **(a)** (nut) marron *m*, châtaigne *f*
(b) (*also* **~ tree**) (horse) marronnier *m* (d'Inde); (sweet) châtaignier *m*
2 *adj* ⟨*hair*⟩ châtain *inv*; **a ~ horse** un (cheval) alezan
chew *vtr* mâcher ⟨*food, gum*⟩; mordiller ⟨*pencil*⟩; ronger ⟨*bone*⟩
chewing gum *n* chewing-gum *m*
chewy *adj* difficile à mâcher
chick *n* (fledgling) oisillon *m*; (of fowl) poussin *m*
chicken *n* **(a)** (fowl) poulet *m*, poule *f*
(b) (meat) poulet *m*
(c) (colloq) (coward) poule *f* mouillée
■ **chicken out** (colloq) se dégonfler (colloq)
chicken pox *n* varicelle *f*
chicken wire *n* grillage *m* (à mailles fines)
chickpea *n* pois *m* chiche
chicory *n* **(a)** (vegetable) endive *f*
(b) (in coffee) chicorée *f*
chief **1** *n* chef *m*
2 *adj* **(a)** ⟨*reason*⟩ principal/-e
(b) ⟨*editor*⟩ en chef
chief executive *n* directeur *m* général
chiefly *adv* notamment, surtout
chief of police *n* ≈ préfet *m* de police
Chief of Staff *n* (Mil) chef *m* d'état-major; (of White House) secrétaire *m* général
chiffon *n* mousseline *f*
chilblain *n* engelure *f*

child *n* enfant *mf*; **when I was a** ~ quand j'étais enfant

child abuse *n* mauvais traitements *mpl* infligés à un enfant; (sexual) sévices *mpl* sexuels exercés sur l'enfant

childbirth *n* accouchement *m*

childcare *n* (nurseries etc) structures *fpl* d'accueil pour les enfants d'âge préscolaire; (bringing up children) éducation *f* des enfants

childcare facilities *n pl* crèche *f*

childhood [1] *n* enfance *f*; **in (his) early** ~ dans sa prime enfance
[2] *adj* (friend, memory) d'enfance; (illness) infantile

childish *adj* puéril/-e

childless *adj* sans enfants

childlike *adj* enfantin/-e

childminder *n* (GB) nourrice *f*

children's home *n* maison *f* d'enfants

Chile *pr n* Chili *m*

chill [1] *n* (a) (coldness) fraîcheur *f*; **there is a** ~ **in the air** le fond de l'air est frais; **to send a** ~ **down sb's spine** donner des frissons à qn
(b) (illness) coup *m* de froid
[2] *adj* (a) (wind) frais/fraîche
(b) (reminder, words) brutal/-e
[3] *vtr* (a) mettre [qch] à refroidir (dessert, soup); rafraîchir (wine)
(b) (make cold) faire frissonner (person); **to** ~ **sb's** *or* **the blood** glacer le sang à qn
[4] *vi* (dessert) refroidir; (wine) rafraîchir
■ **chill out** (colloq) décompresser (colloq); ~ **out!** laisse faire!

chilli, chili *n* (a) (also ~ **pepper**) piment *m* rouge
(b) (also ~ **powder**) chili *m*
(c) (also ~ **con carne**) chili *m* con carne

chilly *adj* froid; **it's** ~ il fait froid

chime *n* carillon *m*

chimney *n* cheminée *f*

chimpanzee *n* chimpanzé *m*

chin *n* menton *m*

china [1] *n* porcelaine *f*
[2] *adj* (cup, plate) en porcelaine

China *pr n* Chine *f*

Chinese [1] *n* (a) (person) Chinois/-oise *m/f*
(b) (language) chinois *m*
[2] *adj* chinois/-oise; (embassy) de Chine

chink *n* (a) (in wall) fente *f*; (in curtain) entrebâillement *m*
(b) (sound) tintement *m*

chip [1] *n* (a) (fragment) fragment *m* (of de); (of wood) copeau *m*; (of glass) éclat *m*
(b) (in wood, china) ébréchure *f*
(c) (microchip) puce *f* (électronique)
[2] **chips** *n pl* (a) (GB) (fried potatoes) frites *fpl*
(b) (US) (crisps) chips *fpl*
[3] *vtr* ébrécher (glass, plate); écailler (paint); **to** ~ **a tooth** se casser une dent
IDIOMS **to have a** ~ **on one's shoulder** être amer/-ère

■ **chip in** (GB) (colloq) (financially) donner un peu d'argent

chipboard *n* aggloméré *m*

chip shop *n* marchand *m* de frites

chiropodist *n* pédicure *mf*

chiropractor *n* chiropraticien/-ienne *m/f*, chiropracteur *m*

chirp *vi* (bird) pépier

chisel [1] *n* ciseau *m*
[2] *vtr* ciseler

chitchat *n* (colloq) bavardage *m*

chivalry *n* (a) chevalerie *f*
(b) (courtesy) galanterie *f*

chive *n* ciboulette *f*

chlorine *n* chlore *m*

choc-ice *n* (GB) esquimau *m*

chock-a-block *adj* plein à craquer

chocolate [1] *n* chocolat *m*
[2] *adj* (sweets) en chocolat; (biscuit, cake, ice cream) au chocolat

choice *n* choix *m* (between, of entre); **to make a** ~ faire un choix, choisir; **to be spoilt for** ~ avoir l'embarras du choix; **out of** *or* **from** ~ par choix

choir *n* (of church, school) chorale *f*; (professional) chœur *m*

choirboy *n* petit chanteur *m*, jeune choriste *m*

choke [1] *n* (Aut) starter *m*
[2] *vtr* (a) (throttle) étrangler (person)
(b) (fumes, smoke) étouffer
[3] *vi* s'étouffer
■ **choke back** étouffer (cough, sob); **to** ~ **back one's tears** retenir ses larmes

cholera *n* choléra *m*

cholesterol *n* cholestérol *m*

choose [1] *vtr* (a) (select) choisir (from parmi)
(b) (decide) décider (to do de faire)
[2] *vi* (a) (select) choisir (between entre)
(b) (prefer) **to** ~ **to do** préférer faire

choosy *adj* difficile (about en ce qui concerne)

chop [1] *n* (Culin) côtelette *f*; **pork** ~ côtelette *f* de porc
[2] *vtr* (a) (also ~ **up**) couper (wood); couper, émincer (vegetable, meat); hacher (parsley, onion); **to** ~ **sth finely** hacher qch
(b) réduire (service, deficit)
IDIOMS **to** ~ **and change** (person) changer d'avis comme de chemise
■ **chop down** abattre (tree)
■ **chop off** couper (branch, end); trancher (head, hand, finger)

chopping board *n* planche *f* à découper

chopping knife *n* couteau *m* de cuisine

choppy *adj* (sea, water) agité/-e

chopstick *n* baguette *f* (chinoise)

chord *n* accord *m*

chore *n* tâche *f*; **to do the** ~**s** faire le ménage

choreograph *vtr* chorégraphier

chorus *n* (a) (singers) chœur *m*

(b) (piece of music) chœur m

(c) (refrain) refrain m

Christ pr n le Christ, Jésus-Christ

christen vtr baptiser

christening n baptême m

Christian [1] n chrétien/-ienne m/f

[2] adj chrétien/-ienne; ⟨attitude⟩ charitable

Christianity n christianisme m

Christian name n nom m de baptême

Christmas n ∼ (day) (jour m de) Noël; at ∼ à Noël; **Merry** ∼!, **Happy** ∼! Joyeux Noël!

Christmas card n carte f de Noël

Christmas eve n veille f de Noël

Christmas tree n sapin m de Noël

chrome n chrome m

chronic adj **(a)** ⟨illness⟩ chronique

(b) ⟨liar⟩ invétéré/-e; ⟨problem, shortage⟩ chronique

chronicle n chronique f

chronological adj chronologique

chubby adj ⟨child, finger⟩ potelé/-e; ⟨cheek⟩ rebondi/-e; ⟨face⟩ joufflu/-e; ⟨adult⟩ rondelet/-ette

chuck vtr (colloq) **(a)** (also ∼ **away**) balancer (colloq), jeter

(b) larguer (colloq) ⟨boyfriend, girlfriend⟩

chuckle vi glousser; **to** ∼ **at sth** rire de qch

chuffed adj (GB) (colloq) vachement (colloq) content/-e (**about, at, with** de)

chum n (colloq) copain/copine m/f (colloq), pote m (colloq)

chunk n **(a)** (of meat, fruit) morceau m; (of wood) tronçon m; (of bread) quignon m; **pineapple** ∼s ananas m en morceaux

(b) (of population, text, day) partie f (**of** de)

church [1] n **(a)** (Catholic, Anglican) église f; (Protestant) temple m

[2] adj ⟨bell, choir, steeple⟩ d'église; ⟨fête⟩ paroissial/-e; ⟨wedding⟩ religieux/-ieuse

churchgoer n pratiquant/-e m/f

church hall n salle f paroissiale

churchyard n cimetière m

churn [1] n **(a)** (for butter) baratte f

(b) (GB) (for milk) bidon m

[2] vtr **to** ∼ **butter** baratter

■ **churn out** pondre [qch] en série ⟨novels⟩; produire [qch] en série ⟨goods⟩

■ **churn up** faire des remous dans ⟨water⟩

chute n **(a)** (slide) toboggan m

(b) (for rubbish) vide-ordures m inv

(c) (for toboggan) piste f de toboggan

cicada n cigale f

cider n cidre m

cigar n cigare m

cigarette [1] n cigarette f

[2] adj ⟨ash, smoke⟩ de cigarette; ⟨case, paper⟩ à cigarettes

cigarette lighter n (portable) briquet m; (in car) allume-cigares m inv

cinder n (glowing) braise f; (ash) cendre f

Cinderella pr n Cendrillon

cinecamera n caméra f (d'amateur)

cine film n pellicule f cinématographique

cinema n cinéma m

cinemagoer n (regular) cinéphile mf, amateur m de cinéma; (spectator) spectateur/-trice m/f

cinnamon n cannelle f

circle [1] n **(a)** (gen) cercle m; **to go round in** ∼s tourner en rond; **to have** ∼s **under one's eyes** avoir les yeux cernés

(b) (in theatre) balcon m; **in the** ∼ au balcon

[2] vtr **(a)** ⟨plane⟩ tourner autour de ⟨airport⟩; ⟨person, animal, vehicle⟩ faire le tour de ⟨building⟩; tourner autour de ⟨person, animal⟩

(b) (surround) encercler

[3] vi tourner en rond (**around** autour de)

circuit n **(a)** (gen) circuit m

(b) (lap) tour m

circuit breaker n disjoncteur m

circular [1] n (newsletter) circulaire f; (advertisement) prospectus m

[2] adj ⟨object⟩ rond/-e; ⟨argument⟩ circulaire

circulate [1] vtr faire circuler

[2] vi **(a)** (gen) circuler

(b) (at party) **let's** ∼ on va aller faire connaissance

circulation n **(a)** (gen) circulation f

(b) (of newspaper) tirage m

circulation figures n pl chiffres mpl de tirage

circumcision n (of boy) circoncision f; (of girl) excision f

circumference n circonférence f

circumflex n accent m circonflexe

circumstances n pl **(a)** circonstances fpl; **in** or **under the** ∼ dans ces circonstances; **under no** ∼ en aucun cas

(b) (financial position) situation f

circumstantial adj ⟨evidence⟩ indirect/-e

circus n cirque m

CIS pr n (abbr = **Commonwealth of Independent States**) CEI f

cistern n (of lavatory) réservoir m de chasse d'eau; (in loft or underground) citerne f

citizen n **(a)** (of state) citoyen/-enne m/f; (when abroad) ressortissant/-e m/f

(b) (of town) habitant/-e m/f

citizenship n nationalité f

citrus fruit n agrume m

city n (grande) ville f; **the City** (GB) la City

city centre (GB), **city center** (US) n centre-ville m

civic adj ⟨administration, official⟩ municipal/-e; ⟨pride, responsibility⟩ civique

civic centre (GB), **civic center** (US) n centre m municipal (culturel et administratif)

civil adj **(a)** ⟨case, court, offence⟩ civil/-e

(b) (polite) courtois/-e

civil engineering n génie m civil

civilian n civil/-e m/f

civilization n civilisation f
civilized adj civilisé/-e
civil law n droit m civil
civil liberty n libertés fpl individuelles
civil rights n pl droits mpl civils
civil servant n fonctionnaire mf
civil service n fonction f publique
civil war n guerre f civile
claim ⓵ n (a) (demand) revendication f
(b) (in insurance) (against a person) réclamation f; (for fire, theft) demande f d'indemnisation
(c) (for welfare benefit) demande f d'allocation
(d) (assertion) affirmation f
⓶ vtr (a) (maintain) prétendre
(b) revendiquer ⟨money, property, responsibility, right⟩
(c) faire une demande de ⟨benefit⟩; faire une demande de remboursement de ⟨expenses⟩
⓷ vi (a) to ∼ for damages faire une demande pour dommages et intérêts
(b) (apply for benefit) faire une demande d'allocation
claimant n (a) (for benefit, compensation) demandeur/-euse m/f (to à)
(b) (to title, estate) prétendant/-e m/f (to à)
claim form n déclaration f de sinistre
clairvoyant n voyant/-e m/f, extralucide mf
clam n palourde f
■ **clam up** ne plus piper mot (on sb à qn)
clammy adj moite
clamour (GB), **clamor** (US) ⓵ n (shouting) clameur f
⓶ vi (a) (demand) to ∼ for sth réclamer qch; to ∼ for sb to do réclamer à qn de faire
(b) (rush, fight) se bousculer (for pour avoir; to do pour faire)
clamp ⓵ n (a) (on bench) valet m
(b) (also **wheel**∼) sabot m de Denver
⓶ vtr (a) cramponner ⟨two parts⟩; (at bench) fixer ⟨qch⟩ à l'aide d'un valet (onto à)
(b) serrer ⟨jaw, teeth⟩
(c) (also **wheel**∼) mettre un sabot de Denver à ⟨car⟩
■ **clamp down:** ¶ ∼ down on faire de la répression contre ⟨crime⟩; mettre un frein à ⟨extravagance⟩
clampdown n mesures fpl de répression (on sb contre qn; on sth de qch)
clan n clan m
clandestine adj clandestin/-e
clang ⓵ n fracas m, bruit m métallique
⓶ vi (gate) claquer avec un son métallique; ⟨bell⟩ retentir
clap ⓵ n to give sb a ∼ applaudir qn; a ∼ of thunder un coup de tonnerre
⓶ vtr to ∼ one's hands battre or taper des mains, frapper dans ses mains
⓷ vi applaudir
clapping n applaudissements mpl
claret n (a) (wine) bordeaux m (rouge)
(b) (colour) bordeaux m
clarification n éclaircissement m, clarification f

clarify vtr éclaircir, clarifier
clarinet n clarinette f
clarity n clarté f
clash ⓵ n (a) (confrontation) affrontement m
(b) (of cultures, interests, personalities) conflit m
(c) a ∼ of cymbals un coup de cymbales
⓶ vtr entrechoquer ⟨bin lids⟩; frapper ⟨cymbals⟩
⓷ vi (a) (fight, disagree) s'affronter; to ∼ with sb (fight) se heurter à qn; (disagree) se quereller avec qn (on, over au sujet de)
(b) (be in conflict) ⟨interests, beliefs⟩ être incompatibles
(c) (coincide) ⟨meetings⟩ avoir lieu en même temps (with que)
(d) ⟨colours⟩ jurer
clasp n (on bracelet, bag, purse) fermoir m; (on belt) boucle f
class ⓵ n (gen) classe f; (lesson) cours m (in de); to be in a ∼ of one's own être hors catégorie; to travel first/second ∼ voyager en première/deuxième classe; first/second ∼ degree ≈ licence f avec mention très bien/bien
⓶ vtr classer
class conscious adj soucieux/-ieuse des distinctions sociales
classic n, adj classique (m)
classical adj classique
classics n lettres fpl classiques
classification n (a) (category) classification f, catégorie f
(b) (categorization) classement m
classified ⓵ n (also ∼ ad) petite annonce f
⓶ adj (secret) confidentiel/-ielle
classify vtr (a) (file) classer
(b) (declare secret) classer [qch] confidentiel/-ielle
classmate n camarade mf de classe
classroom n salle f de classe
class system n système m de classes
classy adj (colloq) ⟨person, dress⟩ qui a de la classe; ⟨car, hotel⟩ de luxe; ⟨actor, performance⟩ de grande classe
clatter ⓵ n cliquetis m; (loud) fracas m
⓶ vi ⟨typewriter⟩ cliqueter; ⟨dishes⟩ s'entrechoquer
clause n (a) (in grammar) proposition f
(b) (in contract, treaty) clause f; (in will, act of Parliament) disposition f
claustrophobia n claustrophobie f
claw n (a) (gen) griffe f; (of bird of prey) serre f; (of crab, lobster) pince f
(b) (on hammer) arrache-clou m, pied-de-biche m
clay n argile f
clean ⓵ adj (a) (gen) propre; ⟨air, water⟩ pur/-e; my hands are ∼ j'ai les mains propres; ∼ and tidy d'une propreté irréprochable; a ∼ sheet of paper une feuille blanche
(b) ⟨joke⟩ anodin/-e

C

(c) ⟨reputation⟩ sans tache; ⟨record, licence⟩ vierge

(d) (Sport) ⟨tackle⟩ sans faute; ⟨hit⟩ précis/-e

(e) (neat) ⟨lines, profile⟩ pur/-e

2 vtr nettoyer; **to ∼ one's teeth** se brosser les dents

■ **clean out** nettoyer [qch] à fond ⟨cupboard, room⟩

■ **clean up**: ¶ ∼ **up (a)** tout nettoyer
(b) (wash oneself) se débarbouiller
¶ ∼ [sth] **up** nettoyer

clean-cut adj ⟨image, person⟩ soigné/-e

cleaner n (a) (woman) femme f de ménage; (man) agent m de nettoyage
(b) (detergent) produit m de nettoyage
(c) (shop) **cleaner's** pressing m

cleaning n (domestic) ménage m; (commercial) nettoyage m, entretien m

cleaning product n produit m d'entretien

cleanliness n propreté f

cleanse vtr nettoyer ⟨skin, wound⟩

cleanser n (a) (for face) démaquillant m
(b) (household) produit m d'entretien

clean-shaven adj **he's ∼** il n'a ni barbe ni moustache

clear **1** adj (a) (transparent) ⟨glass, liquid⟩ transparent/-e; ⟨blue⟩ limpide; ⟨lens, varnish⟩ incolore; ⟨honey⟩ liquide; ∼ **soup** consommé m
(b) (distinct) ⟨image, outline⟩ net/nette; ⟨sound, voice⟩ clair/-e
(c) (comprehensible) ⟨description, instruction⟩ clair/-e; **to make sth ∼ to sb** faire comprendre qch à qn; **is that ∼?** est-ce que c'est clair?
(d) (obvious) ⟨need, sign⟩ évident/-e; ⟨advantage⟩ net/nette (before n); ⟨majority⟩ large (before n); **it is ∼ that** il est clair que
(e) (not confused) ⟨idea, memory⟩ clair/-e; ⟨plan⟩ précis/-e; **to keep a ∼ head** garder les idées claires
(f) (empty) ⟨view⟩ dégagé/-e; ⟨table⟩ débarrassé/-e; ⟨space⟩ libre
(g) ⟨conscience⟩ tranquille
(h) ⟨skin⟩ net/nette; ⟨sky⟩ sans nuage; ⟨day, night⟩ clair/-e; **on a ∼ day** par temps clair/-e

2 adv **to jump ∼ of sth** éviter qch en sautant sur le côté; **to pull sb ∼ of** extraire qn de ⟨wreckage⟩; **to stay** or **steer ∼ of** éviter ⟨town centre, troublemakers⟩

3 vtr (a) enlever ⟨rubbish, papers, mines⟩; dégager ⟨snow⟩ (**from, off** de)
(b) déboucher ⟨drains⟩; débarrasser ⟨table, room⟩; vider ⟨desk⟩; évacuer ⟨area, building⟩; effacer ⟨screen⟩; défricher ⟨land⟩; **to ∼ one's throat** se racler la gorge; **to ∼ a path through sth** se frayer un chemin à travers qch
(c) dissiper ⟨fog, smoke⟩; disperser ⟨crowd⟩
(d) s'acquitter de ⟨debt⟩
(e) ⟨bank⟩ compenser ⟨cheque⟩
(f) innocenter ⟨accused⟩ (**of** de); **to ∼ one's name** blanchir son nom
(g) approuver ⟨request⟩; **to ∼ sth with sb** obtenir l'accord de qn pour qch

(h) franchir ⟨hurdle, wall⟩
(i) **to ∼ customs** passer à la douane

4 vi (a) ⟨liquid, sky⟩ s'éclaircir
(b) ⟨smoke, fog, cloud⟩ se dissiper
(c) ⟨air⟩ se purifier
(d) ⟨rash⟩ disparaître
(e) ⟨cheque⟩ être compensé/-e

■ **clear away**: ¶ ∼ **away** débarrasser; ¶ ∼ [sth] **away** balayer ⟨leaves⟩; enlever ⟨rubbish⟩; ranger ⟨papers, toys⟩

■ **clear up**: ¶ ∼ **up (a)** (tidy up) faire du rangement
(b) ⟨weather⟩ s'éclaircir; ⟨infection⟩ disparaître
¶ ∼ [sth] **up (a)** ranger ⟨mess, room, toys⟩; ramasser ⟨litter⟩
(b) résoudre ⟨problem⟩; dissiper ⟨misunderstanding⟩

clearance n (a) (of rubbish) enlèvement m; **land ∼** défrichement m du terrain
(b) (permission) autorisation f
(c) (also ∼ **sale**) liquidation f

clear-cut adj ⟨plan, division⟩ précis/-e; ⟨difference⟩ net/nette (before n); ⟨problem, rule⟩ clair/-e

clear-headed adj lucide

clearing n (glade) clairière f

clearly adv (a) ⟨speak, hear, think, write⟩ clairement; ⟨see⟩ bien; ⟨visible⟩ bien; ⟨labelled⟩ clairement
(b) (obviously) manifestement

clear-out n (colloq) **to have a ∼** faire du rangement

cleavage n décolleté m

cleaver n fendoir m

clef n clef f; **in the treble ∼** en clef de fa

cleft adj ⟨chin⟩ marqué/-e d'un sillon; ⟨palate⟩ fendu/-e

clench vtr serrer

clergy n clergé m

clergyman n ecclésiastique m

clerical adj (a) (of clergy) clérical/-e
(b) ⟨staff⟩ de bureau; ∼ **work** travail m de bureau

clerk n (a) (in office, bank) employé/-e m/f
(b) (GB) (to lawyer) ≈ clerc m; (in court) greffier/-ière m/f
(c) (US) (in hotel) réceptionniste mf; (in shop) vendeur/-euse m/f

clever adj (a) (intelligent) intelligent/-e
(b) (ingenious) ⟨solution, gadget, person⟩ astucieux/-ieuse, futé/-e
(c) (skilful) habile, adroit/-e

cliché n cliché m, lieu m commun

clichéd adj ⟨expression⟩ rebattu/-e; ⟨idea, technique⟩ éculé/-e; ⟨art, music⟩ bourré/-e (colloq) de clichés

click **1** n (a) (of machine, lock) déclic m
(b) (of fingers, heels, tongue) claquement m
(c) (Comput) clic m

2 vtr **to ∼ one's fingers** faire claquer ses doigts; **to ∼ one's heels** claquer des talons ····⟶

3 vi ⟨camera, lock⟩ faire un déclic; ⟨door⟩ faire un petit bruit sec; **to ~ on** cliquer sur ⟨icon⟩

client n client/-e m/f

clientele n clientèle f

cliff n (by sea) falaise f; (inland) escarpement m

climate n climat m

climax n (of war, conflict) paroxysme m; (of plot, speech, play) point m culminant; (of career) apogée m

climb **1** n (up hill) escalade f; (up tower) montée f; (up mountain) ascension f
2 vtr grimper ⟨hill⟩; faire l'ascension de ⟨mountain⟩; escalader ⟨lamppost, wall⟩; grimper à ⟨ladder, tree⟩; monter ⟨staircase⟩
3 vi **(a)** ⟨person⟩ grimper; **to ~ down** descendre ⟨rock face⟩; **to ~ over** enjamber ⟨stile⟩; passer par-dessus ⟨fence, wall⟩; escalader ⟨debris, rocks⟩; **to ~ up** grimper à ⟨ladder, tree⟩; monter ⟨steps⟩
(b) ⟨aircraft⟩ monter
(c) ⟨road⟩ monter
(d) (increase) monter
■ **climb down** revenir sur sa décision

climber n grimpeur/-euse m/f, alpiniste mf

climbing n escalade f

clinch vtr **(a) to ~ a deal** conclure une affaire
(b) décider de ⟨argument⟩

cling vi **(a) to ~ (on) to sb/sth** se cramponner à qn/qch; **to ~ together** se cramponner l'un à l'autre
(b) ⟨clothes⟩ coller (**to** à)
(c) ⟨smell⟩ résister

clingfilm n (GB) scellofrais® m

clinic n centre m médical

clinical adj **(a)** ⟨medicine⟩ clinique; ⟨approach⟩ objectif/-ive
(b) (unfeeling) froid/-e

clink **1** vtr faire tinter ⟨glass, keys⟩; **to ~ glasses with** trinquer avec
2 vi ⟨glass, keys⟩ tinter

clip **1** n **(a)** (on earring) clip m; (for hair) barrette f
(b) (from film) extrait m
2 vtr **(a)** tailler ⟨hedge⟩; couper ⟨nails, moustache⟩; tondre ⟨dog, sheep⟩
(b) accrocher ⟨microphone⟩ (**to** à); fixer ⟨brooch⟩ (**to** à)
IDIOMS **to ~ sb's wings** rogner les ailes à qn

clipart n clip-art m

clipboard n (gen) porte-bloc m inv à pince; (Comput) presse-papiers m inv

clip frame n sous-verre m inv

clip-ons n pl clips mpl

clippers n pl (for nails) coupe-ongles m inv; (for hair, hedge) tondeuse f

clipping n (from paper) coupure f de presse

cloak **1** n cape f
2 vtr **(a)** ~**ed in** enveloppé/-e dans ⟨darkness⟩; enveloppé/-e de ⟨secrecy⟩
(b) (disguise) masquer

cloakroom n **(a)** (for coats) vestiaire m

(b) (GB) (lavatory) toilettes fpl

clock n (large) horloge f; (small) pendule f; (Sport) chronomètre m; **to put the ~s forward/back one hour** avancer/reculer les pendules d'une heure; **to work around the ~** travailler 24 heures sur 24
■ **clock off** (GB) pointer (à la sortie)
■ **clock on** (GB) pointer

clock radio n radio-réveil m

clock tower n beffroi m

clockwise adj, adv dans le sens des aiguilles d'une montre

clockwork adj ⟨toy⟩ mécanique
IDIOMS **to go like ~** aller comme sur des roulettes

clog n sabot m

cloister n cloître m

clone **1** n clone m
2 vtr cloner

cloning n clonage m

close¹ **1** adj **(a)** (near) proche, voisin/-e (**to** de)
(b) ⟨relative, friend⟩ proche; ⟨resemblance⟩ frappant/-e
(c) ⟨contest, result⟩ serré/-e
(d) ⟨scrutiny⟩ minutieux/-ieuse; ⟨supervision⟩ étroit/-e; **to pay ~ attention to sth** faire une attention toute particulière à qch; **to keep a ~ watch or eye on sb/sth** surveiller étroitement qn/qch
(e) ⟨print, formation⟩ serré/-e
(f) ⟨weather⟩ lourd/-e; **it's ~** il fait lourd
2 adv **to live quite ~ (by)** habiter tout près; **to move sth ~r** approcher qch; **to follow ~ behind** suivre de près; **to hold sb ~** serrer qn; **~ together** serrés les uns contre les autres; **Christmas is ~** Noël approche
3 **close by** phr près de ⟨wall, bridge⟩; **the ambulance is ~ by** l'ambulance n'est pas loin
4 **close to** phr **(a)** (near) près de
(b) (on point of) au bord de ⟨tears, hysteria⟩; **to be ~ to doing** être sur le point de faire
(c) (almost) près de; **to come ~ to doing** faillir faire
IDIOMS **it was a ~ call** (colloq) or **shave** (colloq) or **thing** je l'ai/tu l'as etc échappé belle

close² **1** n fin f
2 vtr **(a)** fermer ⟨door, book⟩
(b) fermer ⟨border, port⟩; barrer ⟨road⟩; interdire l'accès à ⟨area⟩
(c) mettre fin à ⟨meeting⟩; fermer ⟨account⟩
(d) to ~ the gap réduire l'écart
(e) conclure ⟨deal⟩
3 vi **(a)** ⟨airport, polls, shop⟩ fermer; ⟨door, container, eyes, mouth⟩ se fermer
(b) (cease to operate) fermer définitivement
(c) ⟨meeting, play⟩ prendre fin; **to ~ with** se terminer par ⟨song⟩
(d) ⟨currency, index⟩ clôturer (**at** à)
(e) ⟨gap⟩ se réduire
4 **closed** pp adj fermé/-e; **behind ~d doors** à huis clos

■ **close down:** ¶ ~ **down** fermer définitivement; ¶ ~ **[sth] down** fermer [qch] définitivement

■ **close up:** ¶ ~ **up (a)** ⟨*flower, wound*⟩ se refermer; ⟨*group*⟩ se serrer
(b) ⟨*shopkeeper*⟩ fermer
¶ ~ **[sth] up (a)** fermer ⟨*shop*⟩
(b) boucher ⟨*hole*⟩

closed-circuit television, CCTV n télévision f en circuit fermé

close-fitting adj ⟨*garment*⟩ ajusté/-e, près du corps

close-knit adj ⟨*family, group*⟩ très uni/-e

closely adv ⟨*follow, watch*⟩ de près; ⟨*resemble*⟩ beaucoup; **to be ~ related** ⟨*people*⟩ être proches parents

close-run adj très serré/-e

closet ① n (US) ⟨*cupboard*⟩ placard m; (for clothes) penderie f
② adj ⟨*alcoholic, fascist*⟩ inavoué/-e

close-up ① n gros plan m; **in ~** en gros plan
② **close up** adv **(from)** ~ de près

closing ① n fermeture f
② adj ⟨*minutes, words*⟩ dernier/-ière (*before n*); ⟨*scene, stage*⟩ final/-e; ⟨*speech*⟩ de clôture

closing date n date f limite **(for** de)

closing-down sale, closing-out sale (US) n liquidation f

closing time n heure f de fermeture

closure n fermeture f

clot ① n caillot m
② vtr, vi coaguler, cailler

cloth n **(a)** (fabric) tissu m
(b) (for polishing, dusting) chiffon m; (for floor) serpillière f; (for drying dishes) torchon m; (for table) nappe f

clothes n pl vêtements mpl; **to put on/take off one's ~** s'habiller/se déshabiller

clothes brush n brosse f à habits

clotheshanger n cintre m

clothes line n corde f à linge

clothes peg n pince f à linge

clothes shop n magasin m de vêtements

clothing n vêtements mpl; **an item** *or* **article of ~** un vêtement

cloud ① n nuage m; **to cast a ~ over sth** jeter une ombre sur qch
② vtr **(a)** ⟨*steam, breath*⟩ embuer ⟨*mirror*⟩; ⟨*tears*⟩ brouiller ⟨*vision*⟩
(b) obscurcir ⟨*judgment*⟩; brouiller ⟨*memory*⟩; **to ~ the issue** brouiller les cartes
IDIOMS to be living in ~-cuckoo-land croire au père Noël

■ **cloud over** ⟨*sky*⟩ se couvrir (de nuages); ⟨*face*⟩ s'assombrir

cloudy adj **(a)** ⟨*weather*⟩ couvert/-e
(b) ⟨*liquid*⟩ trouble

clout n **(a)** (blow) claque f, coup m
(b) (influence) influence f **(with** auprès de, sur)

clove n **(a)** (spice) clou m de girofle
(b) (of garlic) gousse f

clover n trèfle m

clown n clown m

■ **clown around** (GB) faire le clown *or* le pitre

club n **(a)** (association) club m
(b) (colloq) (nightclub) boîte f de nuit
(c) (in cards) trèfle m
(d) (for golf) club m
(e) (weapon) massue f

■ **club together** cotiser

club car n (US) wagon-bar m de première classe

club class n classe f club *or* affaires

cluck vi ⟨*hen*⟩ glousser

clue n indication f **(to, as to** quant à); (in police investigation) indice m **(to** quant à); (in crossword) définition f; **I haven't (got) a ~** (colloq) je n'ai aucune idée

clued-up adj (colloq) calé/-e (colloq) **(about** sur)

clueless adj (colloq) nul/nulle (colloq) **(about** en)

clump n (of flowers, grass) touffe f; (of trees) massif m; (of earth) motte f

clumsiness n (carelessness) maladresse f; (awkwardness) gaucherie f; (of system) côté m peu pratique

clumsy adj ⟨*person, attempt*⟩ maladroit/-e; ⟨*object*⟩ grossier/-ière; ⟨*animal*⟩ pataud/-e; ⟨*tool*⟩ peu maniable; ⟨*style*⟩ lourd/-e

cluster ① n **(a)** (of flowers, berries) grappe f; (of people, islands, trees) groupe m; (of houses) ensemble m; (of diamonds) entourage m; (of stars) amas m
② vi ⟨*people*⟩ se rassembler **(around** autour de)

clutch ① n (Aut) embrayage m
② vtr tenir fermement

■ **clutch at** tenter d'attraper ⟨*branch, rail, person*⟩; saisir ⟨*arm*⟩

clutch bag n pochette f

clutches n pl **to fall into the ~ of** tomber sous les griffes *or* la patte (colloq) de

clutter ① n désordre m
② vtr (also ~ **up**) encombrer

c/o prep (abbr = **care of**) chez

Co n (abbr = **company**) Cie

coach ① n **(a)** (bus) (auto)car m
(b) (GB) (of train) wagon m
(c) (Sport) entraîneur/-euse m/f
(d) (for drama, voice) répétiteur/-trice m/f
(e) (horse-drawn) carrosse m
② vtr **(a)** (Sport) entraîner ⟨*team*⟩
(b) (teach) **to ~ sb** donner des leçons particulières à qn **(in** en)

coach station n gare f routière

coach trip n excursion f en autocar

coal n charbon m
IDIOMS to haul sb over the ~s (colloq) passer un savon à qn (colloq)

coalfield n bassin m houiller

coal fire n cheminée f (*où brûle un feu de charbon*)

coalition n coalition f

coalmine n mine f de charbon

coalminer n mineur m

coarse adj (a) ⟨texture⟩ grossier/-ière; ⟨skin⟩ épais/-aisse; ⟨sand, salt⟩ gros/grosse (before n)
(b) ⟨manners⟩ grossier/-ière; ⟨language, joke⟩ cru/-e

coast ① n côte f; off the ~ près de la côte ② vi ⟨car, bicycle⟩ descendre en roue libre

coastal adj côtier/-ière

coaster n (mat) dessous-de-verre m inv

coastguard n (a) (person) garde-côte m
(b) (organization) gendarmerie f maritime

coastline n littoral m

coat ① n (a) (garment) manteau m
(b) (of dog, cat) pelage m; (of horse, leopard) robe f
(c) (layer) couche f
② vtr to ~ sth with enduire qch de ⟨paint, adhesive⟩; couvrir qch de ⟨dust, oil⟩; enrober qch de ⟨breadcrumbs, chocolate, sauce⟩

coat hanger n cintre m

coat of arms n blason m, armoiries fpl

coat rack n portemanteau m

coax vtr cajoler; to ~ sb into doing persuader qn (gentiment) de faire

cobbler n cordonnier m

cobblestones n pl pavés mpl

cobweb n toile f d'araignée

cocaine n cocaïne f

cock ① n (a) (rooster) coq m
(b) (male bird) (oiseau m) mâle m
② vtr (a) to ~ an eyebrow hausser les sourcils; to ~ a leg ⟨dog⟩ lever la patte; to ~ an ear dresser l'oreille
(b) (tilt) pencher
(c) (Mil) armer ⟨gun⟩

cock-and-bull story n histoire f abracadabrante or à dormir debout

cockatoo n cacatoès m

cockerel n jeune coq m

cockle n coque f

cockpit n cockpit m, poste m de pilotage

cockroach n cafard m

cocktail n cocktail m

cocktail bar n bar m

cocky adj impudent/-e

cocoa n cacao m; (drink) chocolat m

coconut n noix f de coco

cocoon n cocon m

cod n morue f

COD n (abbr = **cash on delivery**) envoi m contre remboursement

code ① n (a) (gen) code m
(b) (also **dialling** ~) indicatif m
② vtr coder

codeine n codéine f

code name n nom m de code

codeword n (password) mot m de passe

coeducational adj mixte

coerce vtr exercer des pressions sur; to ~ sb into doing contraindre qn à faire

coexist vi coexister (with avec)

coffee ① n café m; a black/white ~ un café (noir)/au lait
② adj ⟨dessert⟩ au café; ⟨cup, filter, spoon⟩ à café

coffee break n pause(-)café f

coffee pot n cafetière f

coffee table n table f basse

coffin n cercueil m

cog n (tooth) dent f d'engrenage; (wheel) pignon m

cohabit vi cohabiter (with avec)

coherent adj cohérent/-e

coil ① n (a) (of rope, barbed wire) rouleau m; (of electric wire) bobine f; (of hair) boucle f; (of snake) anneau m
(b) (contraceptive) stérilet m
② vtr (also ~ up) enrouler ⟨hair, rope, wire⟩
③ vi s'enrouler (round autour de)

coin ① n pièce f (de monnaie); a pound ~ une pièce d'une livre
② vtr forger ⟨term⟩

coin box n (pay phone) cabine f (téléphonique) à pièces

coincide vi coïncider (with avec)

coincidence n coïncidence f, hasard m; it is a ~ that c'est par coïncidence que; by ~ par hasard

coincidental adj fortuit/-e

coin operated adj qui marche avec des pièces

coke n (a) (fuel) coke m
(b) (colloq) (cocaine) coke f (colloq)

Coke® n coca m

colander n passoire f

cold ① n (a) (chilliness) froid m; to feel the ~ être sensible au froid, être frileux/-euse
(b) (Med) rhume m; to have a ~ être enrhumé/-e, avoir un rhume
② adj (a) (chilly) froid; to be or feel ~ ⟨person⟩ avoir froid; the room was ~ il faisait froid dans la pièce; it's or the weather's ~ il fait froid; to go ~ ⟨food, water⟩ se refroidir
(b) ⟨manner⟩ froid/-e; to be ~ to or towards sb être froid/-e avec qn
IDIOMS in ~ blood de sang-froid; to be out ~ être sans connaissance

cold-blooded adj ⟨animal⟩ à sang froid; ⟨killer⟩ sans pitié

cold calling n démarchage m par téléphone

coldness n froideur f

cold shoulder n to give sb the ~ snober qn, battre froid à qn

cold sore n bouton m de fièvre

cold sweat n to bring sb out in a ~ donner des sueurs froides à qn

cold turkey n (colloq) (treatment) sevrage m; (reaction) réaction f de manque; to be ~ être en manque

Cold War n guerre f froide

coleslaw n salade f à base de chou cru

colic n coliques fpl

collaborate vi collaborer (**on, in** à; **with** avec)

collaboration n collaboration f

collaborator n collaborateur/-trice m/f

collapse ① n (a) (of regime, economy) effondrement m (**of, in** de)
(b) (of deal, talks) échec m
(c) (of company) faillite f (**of** de)
(d) (of person) (physical) écroulement m; (mental) effondrement m
(e) (of building, bridge) effondrement m; (of tunnel, wall) écroulement m
(f) (Med) (of lung) collapsus m
② vi (a) ⟨regime, economy⟩ s'effondrer; ⟨deal, talks⟩ échouer
(b) ⟨company⟩ faire faillite
(c) ⟨person⟩ s'écrouler
(d) ⟨building, bridge⟩ s'effondrer; ⟨tunnel, wall⟩ s'écrouler; ⟨chair⟩ s'affaisser (**under** sous)
(e) (Med) ⟨lung⟩ se dégonfler
(f) (fold) ⟨bike, pushchair⟩ se plier

collapsible adj pliant/-e

collar n (a) (on garment) col m
(b) (for animal) collier m
IDIOMS **to get hot under the** ～ se mettre en rogne (colloq)

collarbone n clavicule f

collar size n encolure f

collate vtr collationner

colleague n collègue mf

collect ① adv (US) **to call sb** ～ appeler qn en PCV
② vtr (a) ramasser ⟨wood, litter, rubbish⟩; rassembler ⟨information⟩; recueillir ⟨signatures⟩
(b) (as hobby) collectionner, faire collection de ⟨stamps, coins⟩
(c) ⟨objects⟩ prendre, ramasser ⟨dust⟩
(d) percevoir ⟨rent⟩; encaisser ⟨fares, money⟩; recouvrer ⟨debt⟩; toucher ⟨pension⟩; percevoir ⟨tax, fine⟩
(e) faire la levée de ⟨mail, post⟩
(f) (pick up) aller chercher ⟨person⟩; récupérer ⟨keys, book⟩
③ vi (a) ⟨dust, leaves⟩ s'accumuler; ⟨people⟩ se rassembler
(b) **to** ～ **for charity** faire la quête pour des bonnes œuvres
④ **collected** pp adj (a) ⟨person⟩ calme
(b) (assembled) **the** ～**ed works of Dickens** les œuvres complètes de Dickens

collection n (a) (of coins, records) collection f; (anthology) recueil m; **art** ～ collection f (de tableaux)
(b) (money) collecte f (**for** pour); (in church) quête f
(c) (of mail) levée f

collective adj collectif/-ive

collective ownership n copropriété f

collector n (a) (of coins, stamps) collectionneur/-euse m/f
(b) (of taxes) percepteur m; (of rent, debts) encaisseur m

collector's item n pièce f de collection

college n établissement m d'enseignement supérieur; (school, part of university) collège m; (US Univ) faculté f; **to go to** ～, **to be at** or **in** (US) ～ faire des études supérieures

college of further education, CFE n (GB) école ouverte aux adultes et aux jeunes pour terminer un cycle d'études secondaires

collide vi ⟨vehicle, plane⟩ entrer en collision (**with** avec)

collie n (dog) colley m

colliery n houillère f

collision n collision f

colloquial adj familier/-ière

colon n (a) (Anat) côlon m
(b) (punctuation) deux points mpl

colonel n colonel m

colonialist n, adj colonialiste (mf)

colonization n colonisation f

colonize vtr coloniser

colonizer n colon m

colony n colonie f

colour (GB), **color** (US) ① n (a) couleur f; **what** ～ **is it?** de quelle couleur est-il/elle?; **to put** ～ **into sb's cheeks** redonner des couleurs à qn
(b) (dye) (for food) colorant m; (for hair) teinture f
② vtr (a) (with paints, crayons) colorier; (with food dye) colorer
(b) (prejudice) fausser ⟨judgment⟩
③ vi ⟨person⟩ rougir
IDIOMS **to be off** ～ ne pas être en forme; **to show one's true** ～**s** se montrer sous son vrai jour

colour blind adj daltonien/-ienne

coloured (GB), **colored** (US) adj ⟨pen, paper, bead⟩ de couleur; ⟨picture⟩ en couleur; ⟨light, glass⟩ coloré/-e

colour film n (for camera) pellicule f couleur

colourful (GB), **colorful** (US) adj (a) ⟨dress, shirt⟩ aux couleurs vives
(b) ⟨story, life⟩ haut en couleur; ⟨character⟩ pittoresque

colouring (GB), **coloring** (US) n (a) (of animal) couleurs fpl; (of person) teint m
(b) (for food) colorant m

colour scheme n couleurs fpl, coloris m

colour supplement n supplément m illustré

colour television n télévision f (en) couleur

colt n poulain m

column n (a) (pillar) colonne f
(b) (on page, list) colonne f
(c) (newspaper article) rubrique f; **sports** ～ rubrique sportive

columnist n journaliste mf

coma n coma m; **in a** ～ dans le coma

comatose adj (Med) comateux/-euse; (figurative) abruti/-e

comb ① n peigne m   ····⫶

2 *vtr* **to ∼ sb's hair** peigner qn; **to ∼ one's hair** se peigner

combat **1** *n* combat *m*
2 *vtr* lutter contre, combattre

combat jacket *n* veste *f* de treillis

combination *n* combinaison *f*

combine **1** *n* groupe *m*
2 *vtr* (a) combiner ⟨*activities, colours, items*⟩ (with avec); associer ⟨*ideas, aims*⟩ (with à); **to ∼ forces** (merge) s'allier; (cooperate) collaborer
(b) (Culin) mélanger (with avec)
3 *vi* (a) ⟨*activities, colours, elements*⟩ se combiner
(b) ⟨*people, groups*⟩ s'associer; ⟨*firms*⟩ fusionner

combined *adj* (a) (joint) **∼ operation** collaboration *f*; **a ∼ effort** une collaboration
(b) (total) ⟨*salary, age*⟩ total/-e
(c) ⟨*effects*⟩ combiné/-e

combine harvester *n* moissonneuse-batteuse *f*

come *vi* (a) ⟨*person, day*⟩ venir; ⟨*bus, news, winter, war*⟩ arriver; ⟨*dustman, postman*⟩ passer; **to ∼ down** descendre ⟨*stairs, street*⟩; **to ∼ up** monter ⟨*stairs, street*⟩; **to ∼ into** entrer dans ⟨*house, room*⟩; **when the time ∼s** lorsque le moment sera venu; **(I'm) coming!** j'arrive!; **to ∼ to sb for** venir demander [qch] à qn ⟨*money, advice*⟩; **don't ∼ any closer** ne vous approchez pas (plus); **to ∼ as a shock/surprise** être un choc/une surprise
(b) (reach) **to ∼ up/down to** ⟨*water*⟩ venir jusqu'à; ⟨*dress, curtain*⟩ arriver à
(c) (happen) **how ∼?** comment ça se fait?; **to take things as they ∼** prendre les choses comme elles viennent; **∼ what may** advienne que pourra
(d) (begin) **to ∼ to do** finir par faire
(e) **to ∼ from** ⟨*person*⟩ être originaire de, venir de ⟨*city, country*⟩; ⟨*word, legend*⟩ venir de ⟨*language, country*⟩; ⟨*stamps, painting*⟩ provenir de ⟨*place*⟩; ⟨*smell, sound*⟩ venir de ⟨*place*⟩
(f) (in order) **to ∼ after** suivre, venir après; **to ∼ before** (in time, list, queue) précéder; (in importance) passer avant; **to ∼ first/last** (in race) arriver premier/dernier
(g) **when it ∼s to sth/to doing** lorsqu'il s'agit de qch/de faire
(h) **to ∼ true** se réaliser; **to ∼ undone** se défaire

■ **come across**: ¶ **∼ across** ⟨*meaning, message*⟩ passer; ⟨*feelings*⟩ transparaître; **∼ across as** donner l'impression d'être ⟨*liar, expert*⟩; paraître ⟨*honest*⟩; ¶ **∼ across [sth]** tomber sur ⟨*article*⟩
■ **come along** (a) ⟨*bus, person*⟩ arriver; ⟨*opportunity*⟩ se présenter
(b) (hurry up) **∼ along!** dépêche-toi!
(c) (attend) venir (**to** à)
(d) (progress) ⟨*pupil*⟩ faire des progrès; ⟨*book, work, project*⟩ avancer; ⟨*painting, tennis*⟩ progresser
■ **come apart** (a) (accidentally) ⟨*book, box*⟩ se déchirer; ⟨*toy, camera*⟩ se casser

(b) (intentionally) ⟨*components*⟩ se séparer; ⟨*machine*⟩ se démonter
■ **come around** (US) = COME ROUND
■ **come away** partir
■ **come back** (a) (return) revenir (**from** de; **to** à); (to one's house) rentrer
(b) ⟨*law, system*⟩ être rétabli/-e; ⟨*trend*⟩ revenir à la mode
■ **come down** (a) ⟨*person, lift, blind*⟩ descendre; ⟨*curtain*⟩ tomber
(b) ⟨*price, inflation, temperature*⟩ baisser; ⟨*cost*⟩ diminuer
(c) ⟨*snow, rain*⟩ tomber
(d) ⟨*ceiling, wall*⟩ s'écrouler; ⟨*hem*⟩ se défaire
(e) **to ∼ down with** attraper ⟨*flu*⟩
■ **come forward** (a) (step forward) s'avancer
(b) (volunteer) se présenter
■ **come in** (a) (enter) entrer (**through** par)
(b) ⟨*tide*⟩ monter
(c) **to ∼ in useful** être utile
(d) **to ∼ in for criticism** ⟨*person*⟩ être critiqué/-e; ⟨*plan*⟩ faire l'objet de nombreuses critiques
■ **come into** (a) hériter de ⟨*money*⟩; entrer en possession de ⟨*inheritance*⟩
(b) **luck doesn't ∼ into it** ce n'est pas une question de hasard
■ **come off** (a) ⟨*button, handle*⟩ se détacher; ⟨*lid*⟩ s'enlever; ⟨*paint*⟩ s'écailler
(b) ⟨*ink*⟩ s'effacer; ⟨*stain*⟩ partir
(c) ⟨*plan, trick*⟩ réussir
■ **come on** (a) **∼ on!** allez!
(b) ⟨*person, patient*⟩ faire des progrès; ⟨*bridge, novel*⟩ avancer; ⟨*plant*⟩ pousser
(c) ⟨*light*⟩ s'allumer; ⟨*heating, fan*⟩ se mettre en route
(d) ⟨*actor*⟩ entrer en scène
■ **come out** (a) ⟨*person, animal, vehicle*⟩ sortir (**of** de); ⟨*star*⟩ apparaître; ⟨*sun, moon*⟩ se montrer
(b) (strike) faire la grève; **to ∼ out on strike** faire la grève
(c) ⟨*contact lens, tooth*⟩ tomber; ⟨*contents*⟩ sortir; ⟨*cork*⟩ s'enlever
(d) ⟨*water, smoke*⟩ sortir (**through** par)
(e) ⟨*stain*⟩ s'en aller, partir
(f) ⟨*magazine, novel*⟩ paraître; ⟨*album, film, product*⟩ sortir
(g) ⟨*details, facts*⟩ être révélé/-e; ⟨*results*⟩ être connu/-e
(h) ⟨*photo, photocopy*⟩ être réussi/-e
(i) **to ∼ out with** sortir ⟨*excuse*⟩; raconter ⟨*nonsense*⟩; **to ∼ straight out with it** le dire franchement
(j) ⟨*homosexual*⟩ déclarer publiquement son homosexualité
■ **come over**: ¶ **∼ over** venir (**to do** faire); ¶ **what's ∼ over you?** qu'est-ce qui te prend?
■ **come round** (GB), **come around** (US)
(a) (regain consciousness) reprendre connaissance
(b) (visit) venir
(c) (change mind) changer d'avis
■ **come through**: ¶ **∼ through** (a) (survive) s'en tirer

(b) ⟨*heat, ink*⟩ traverser; ⟨*light*⟩ passer
¶ ∼ **through** [sth] se tirer de ⟨*crisis*⟩;
survivre à ⟨*operation, ordeal*⟩
■ **come to:** ¶ ∼ **to** reprendre connaissance;
¶ ∼ **to** [sth] ⟨*shopping*⟩ revenir à; ⟨*bill, total*⟩
s'élever à; **that** ∼**s to £40** cela fait 40 livres
sterling; **it may not** ∼ **to that** nous n'en
arriverons peut-être pas là
■ **come under (a) to** ∼ **under threat** être
menacé/-e
(b) (be classified under) être classé/-e dans le
rayon ⟨*reference, history*⟩
■ **come up (a)** ⟨*problem, issue*⟩ être
soulevé/-e; ⟨*name*⟩ être mentionné/-e
(b) ⟨*opportunity*⟩ se présenter; **something
urgent has** ∼ **up** j'ai quelque chose d'urgent
à faire
(c) ⟨*sun, moon*⟩ sortir; ⟨*daffodils*⟩ sortir
(d) (in law) ⟨*case*⟩ passer au tribunal
(e) to ∼ **up against** se heurter à ⟨*problem*⟩
(f) to ∼ **up with** trouver ⟨*answer, idea*⟩
comeback *n* come-back *m*; **to make a** ∼
⟨*person*⟩ faire un come-back; ⟨*trend*⟩ revenir
à la mode
comedian *n* (male) comique *m*
comedienne *n* actrice *f* comique
comedy *n* comédie *f*
comet *n* comète *f*
comeuppance *n* (colloq) **to get one's** ∼
avoir ce qu'on mérite
comfort ⓵ *n* **(a)** confort *m*; **to live in** ∼
vivre dans l'aisance; **home** ∼**s** le confort du
foyer
(b) (consolation) réconfort *m*, consolation *f*
⓶ *vtr* consoler; (stronger) réconforter
comfortable *adj* **(a)** ⟨*chair, clothes,
journey*⟩ confortable; ⟨*temperature*⟩ agréable
(b) ⟨*person*⟩ à l'aise
comfortably *adv* **(a)** (gen) confortablement;
(easily) facilement, aisément; **to be** ∼ **off** être
à l'aise
comforting *adj* réconfortant/-e
comic ⓵ *n* **(a)** = COMEDIAN
(b) (magazine) bande *f* dessinée
⓶ *adj* comique
comical *adj* cocasse, comique
comic strip *n* bande *f* dessinée
coming ⓵ *n* arrivée *f*; ∼**s and goings**
allées et venues *fpl*
⓶ *adj* ⟨*election, event*⟩ prochain/-e (*before n*);
⟨*months, weeks*⟩ à venir
comma *n* virgule *f*
command ⓵ *n* **(a)** (order) ordre *m*
(b) (military control) commandement *m*; **to be
in** ∼ commander
(c) (of language) maîtrise *f*; **to be in** ∼ **of the
situation** avoir la situation en main
(d) (Comput) commande *f*
⓶ *vtr* **(a)** ordonner à ⟨*person*⟩ **(to do** de
faire)
(b) inspirer ⟨*affection, respect*⟩
(c) (Mil) commander ⟨*regiment*⟩
commander *n* (gen) chef *m*; (Mil)
commandant *m*

commanding *adj* ⟨*manner, voice*⟩
impérieux/-ieuse; ⟨*presence*⟩ imposant/-e
commanding officer, CO *n*
commandant *m*
commando *n* commando *m*
commemorate *vtr* commémorer
commence *vtr, vi* commencer
commend *vtr* louer (**on** pour)
comment ⓵ *n* **(a)** (public) commentaire *m*
(**on** sur); (in conversation) remarque *f* (**on** sur);
(written) annotation *f*
(b) to be a ∼ **on** en dire long sur
⓶ *vi* faire des commentaires (**on** sur)
commentary *n* commentaire *m* (**on** de)
commentator *n* (sports)
commentateur/-trice *m/f*; (current affairs)
journaliste *mf*
commerce *n* commerce *m*
commercial ⓵ *n* annonce *f* publicitaire
⓶ *adj* commercial/-e
commercial break *n* publicité *f*
commercial traveller *n* voyageur *m*
de commerce
commiserate *vi* compatir (**with** avec;
about, over à propos de)
commission ⓵ *n* **(a)** (fee) commission *f*
(b) (order) commande *f* (**for** de)
(c) (committee) commission *f* (**on** sur)
⓶ *vtr* **(a)** commander ⟨*work*⟩ (**from** à); **to** ∼
sb to do charger qn de faire
(b) (Mil) **to be** ∼**ed (as) an officer** être
nommé/-e officier
commissioner *n* **(a)** (gen) membre *m*
d'une commission
(b) (GB) (in police) ≈ préfet *m* de police
(c) (in the EC) membre *m* de la Commission
européenne
commit *vtr* **(a)** commettre ⟨*crime, error,
sin*⟩; **to** ∼ **suicide** se suicider
(b) to ∼ **oneself** s'engager (**to** à)
(c) consacrer ⟨*money, time*⟩ (**to** à)
commitment *n* **(a)** (obligation) engagement
m (**to do** à faire)
(b) (sense of duty) attachement *m* (**to** à)
committed *adj* **(a)** (devoted) ⟨*parent,
teacher*⟩ dévoué/-e; ⟨*Christian, Socialist*⟩
fervent/-e; **to be** ∼ **to/to doing** se consacrer
à/à faire
(b) (with commitments) pris/-e
committee *n* comité *m*; (to investigate,
report) commission *f*
commodity *n* article *m*; (food) denrée *f*
common ⓵ *n* terrain *m* communal
⓶ **Commons** *n pl* (GB) (Pol) **the Commons**
les Communes *fpl*
⓷ *adj* **(a)** (frequent) courant/-e, fréquent/-e; **in**
∼ **use** d'un usage courant
(b) (shared) commun/-e (**to** à); **in** ∼ en
commun; **it is** ∼ **knowledge** c'est de
notoriété publique
(c) the ∼ **people** le peuple; **a** ∼ **criminal** un
criminel ordinaire
(d) (low-class) commun/-e; **it looks/sounds** ∼
ça fait commun

common-law husband n concubin m
common-law marriage n concubinage m
common-law wife n concubine f
commonly adv communément
Common Market n Marché m commun
commonplace adj (common) commun/-e; (trite) banal/-e
common room n salle f de détente
common sense n bon sens m, sens m commun
Commonwealth n the ～ le Commonwealth
Commonwealth of Independent States pr n Communauté f des États indépendants
commotion n (a) (noise) vacarme m, brouhaha m
(b) (disturbance) émoi m, agitation f
communal adj ‹property, area, showers› commun/-e; ‹garden› collectif/-ive; ‹life› communautaire
commune n communauté f
communicate ① vtr communiquer ‹ideas, feelings› (to à); transmettre ‹information› (to à)
② vi communiquer
communication n communication f
communication cord n (GB) sonnette f d'alarme
communications n pl (GB) communications fpl, liaison f
communications company n société f de communications
communication studies n pl études fpl en communication
communion n communion f
communism n communisme m
communist n, adj communiste (mf)
community n communauté f
community care n soins mpl en dehors du milieu hospitalier
community centre (GB), **community center** (US) n maison f de quartier
community service n travail m d'intérêt public
commute vi to ～ between Oxford and London faire le trajet entre Oxford et Londres tous les jours
commuter n navetteur/-euse m/f, migrant/-e m/f journalier/-ière
compact ① n poudrier m
② adj compact/-e
compact disc n disque m compact
companion n compagnon/compagne m/f
companionship n compagnie f
company n (a) (firm) société f; airline ～ compagnie f aérienne
(b) theatre ～ troupe f de théâtre, compagnie f théâtrale
(c) (Mil) compagnie f

(d) (companionship) compagnie f; to keep sb ～ tenir compagnie à qn
(e) (visitors) visiteurs mpl
company car n voiture f de fonction
company director n directeur/-trice m/f général/-e
company pension scheme n régime m de retraite de l'enterprise
company secretary n secrétaire mf général/-e
comparable adj comparable (to, with à)
comparative adj (a) (in grammar) comparatif/-ive
(b) (relative) relatif/-ive; in ～ terms en termes relatifs
(c) ‹study› comparatif/-ive
comparatively adv relativement
compare ① vtr comparer (with, to avec, à)
② vi être comparable (with à)
③ **compared with** prep phr ～d with sb/sth par rapport à qn/qch
④ v refl to ～ oneself with or to se comparer à
comparison n comparaison f; in or by ～ with par rapport à
compartment n compartiment m
compass n boussole f; (also **ship's ～**) compas m; the points of the ～ les points mpl cardinaux
compasses n pl (a pair of) ～ un compas
compassion n compassion f (for pour)
compassionate adj compatissant/-e; on ～ grounds pour raisons fpl personnelles
compatible adj compatible (with avec)
compel vtr contraindre (to do à faire), obliger (to do de faire)
compelling adj ‹reason, argument› convaincant/-e; ‹speaker› fascinant/-e
compensate ① vtr dédommager, indemniser
② vi to ～ for compenser
compensation n (a) (gen) compensation f (for de)
(b) (financial) indemnisation f
compete ① vi (a) (gen) rivaliser; to ～ against or with rivaliser avec (for pour obtenir)
(b) (commercially) ‹companies› se faire concurrence; to ～ with faire concurrence à (for pour obtenir)
(c) (in sport) être en compétition (against, with avec); to ～ in participer à ‹Olympics, race›
② **competing** pres p adj rival/-e
competence n (a) (ability) compétence f
(b) (skill) compétences fpl
competent adj compétent/-e, capable
competition n (a) (gen) concurrence f
(b) (contest) concours m; (race) compétition f
(c) (competitors) concurrence f
competitive adj (a) ‹person› qui a l'esprit de compétition; ‹environment› compétitif/-ive
(b) ‹price, product› compétitif/-ive
(c) ‹sport› de compétition

competitor n concurrent/-e m/f

compilation n (a) (collection) compilation f
(b) (act of compiling) (of reference book) rédaction f; (of dossier) constitution f

compile vtr (a) dresser ⟨list, catalogue⟩; établir ⟨report⟩
(b) (Comput) compiler

complacent adj suffisant/-e; **to be ~ about** être trop confiant/-e de ⟨success, future⟩

complain vi se plaindre (**to** à; **about** de; **of** de); (officially) se plaindre (**to** auprès de)

complaint n plainte f; (official) réclamation f; **there have been ~s about the noise** on s'est plaint du bruit; **to have grounds** or **cause for ~** avoir lieu de se plaindre

complement ⟨1⟩ n complément m
⟨2⟩ vtr compléter

complementary adj complémentaire (**to** de)

complementary medicine n médecine f parallèle

complete ⟨1⟩ adj (a) complet/-ète
(b) (finished) achevé/-e
⟨2⟩ vtr (a) (finish) terminer ⟨building, course, exercise⟩; achever ⟨task, journey⟩
(b) compléter ⟨collection, phrase⟩
(c) remplir ⟨form⟩

completely adv complètement

completion n achèvement m

complex ⟨1⟩ n complexe m; **sports ~** complexe sportif; **he's got a ~ about his weight** son poids le complexe
⟨2⟩ adj complexe

complexion n teint m

complexity n complexité f

compliance n conformité (**with** à)

compliant adj conciliant/-e

complicate vtr compliquer

complicated adj compliqué/-e

complication n (a) (problem) inconvénient m, problème m
(b) (Med) complication f

compliment ⟨1⟩ n compliment m; **to pay sb a ~** faire un compliment à qn
⟨2⟩ vtr complimenter, faire des compliments à

complimentary adj (a) ⟨remark⟩ flatteur/-euse
(b) (free) gratuit/-e

compliments n pl compliments mpl (**to** à)

comply vi **to ~ with** se conformer à ⟨orders⟩; respecter, observer ⟨rules⟩

component n (gen) composante f; (in car, machine) pièce f; (electrical) composant m

compose vtr (a) (gen) composer; **~d of** composé/-e de
(b) **to ~ oneself** se ressaisir

composed adj calme

composer n compositeur/-trice m/f

composition n (a) (gen) composition f
(b) (essay) rédaction f (**about, on** sur)

compost n compost m

composure n calme m

compound ⟨1⟩ n (a) (enclosure) enceinte f
(b) (in chemistry) composé m (**of** de)
(c) (word) mot m composé
⟨2⟩ adj (a) (gen) composé/-e
(b) (Med) ⟨fracture⟩ multiple

comprehend vtr comprendre

comprehensible adj compréhensible, intelligible

comprehension n compréhension f

comprehensive ⟨1⟩ n (GB Sch) (also **~ school**) école f (publique) secondaire
⟨2⟩ adj ⟨report, list⟩ complet/-ète, détaillé/-e; ⟨knowledge⟩ étendu/-e; **~ insurance policy** assurance f tous risques

compress ⟨1⟩ n compresse f
⟨2⟩ vtr comprimer

comprise vtr comprendre; **to be ~d of** être composé/-e de

compromise ⟨1⟩ n compromis m
⟨2⟩ vtr compromettre
⟨3⟩ vi transiger, arriver à un compromis; **to ~ on sth** trouver un compromis sur qch

compromising adj compromettant/-e

compulsive adj (a) (inveterate) invétéré/-e; (psychologically) compulsif/-ive
(b) (fascinating) fascinant/-e

compulsory adj obligatoire

computer n ordinateur m

computer-aided design, CAD n conception f assistée par ordinateur, CAO f

computer-aided learning, CAL n enseignement m assisté par ordinateur

computer crime n piratage m informatique

computer dating n organisation f de rencontres (en utilisant un ordinateur)

computer game n jeu m informatique

computer graphics n infographie f

computer hacker n pirate m informatique

computerize vtr mettre [qch] sur ordinateur ⟨accounts⟩; informatiser ⟨list⟩

computer literate adj **to be ~** avoir des notions d'informatique

computer program n programme m informatique

computer programmer n programmeur/-euse m/f

computer science n informatique f

computer scientist n informaticien/-ienne m/f

computing n informatique f

comrade n camarade mf

comradeship n camaraderie f

con (colloq) ⟨1⟩ n escroquerie f, arnaque f (slang)
⟨2⟩ vtr tromper, rouler (colloq), arnaquer (slang)

conceal vtr dissimuler (**from** à)

concede ⟨1⟩ vtr concéder
⟨2⟩ vi céder

conceit n suffisance f

conceited adj ‹person› vaniteux/-euse; ‹remark› suffisant/-e

conceive vtr, vi concevoir

concentrate **1** vtr concentrer ‹effort›; employer ‹resources›; centrer ‹attention›
2 vi (a) ‹person› se concentrer (on sur); to ~ on doing s'appliquer à faire
(b) to ~ on ‹film, journalist› s'intéresser surtout à

concentration n concentration f (on sur); to lose one's ~ se déconcentrer

concentration camp n camp m de concentration

concept n concept m

conception n conception f

concern **1** n (a) (worry) inquiétude f (about à propos de); to cause ~ être inquiétant/-e
(b) (preoccupation) préoccupation f; environmental ~s des préoccupations écologiques
(c) (company) entreprise f; a going ~ une affaire rentable
2 vtr (a) (worry) inquiéter
(b) (affect, interest) concerner, intéresser; to whom it may ~ à qui de droit; (in letter) Monsieur; as far as the pay is ~ed en ce qui concerne le salaire
(c) (be about) ‹book, programme› traiter de; ‹fax, letter› concerner

concerned adj (a) (anxious) inquiet/-ète (about à propos de); to be ~ for sb se faire du souci pour qn
(b) (involved) concerné/-e; all (those) ~ toutes les personnes concernées

concerning prep concernant

concert n concert m

concerted adj ‹action, campaign› concerté/-e; to make a ~ effort to do faire un sérieux effort pour faire

concert hall n salle f de concert

concertina **1** n concertina m
2 vi se plier en accordéon

concerto n concerto m

concession n (a) (compromise) concession f (on sur; to à)
(b) (discount) réduction f; '~s' 'tarif réduit'

conciliatory adj ‹gesture, terms› conciliant/-e; ‹measures› conciliatoire

concise adj concis/-e

conclude **1** vtr conclure
2 vi ‹story, event› se terminer (with par, sur); ‹speaker› conclure (with par)

concluding adj final/-e

conclusion n (a) (end) fin f
(b) (opinion, resolution) conclusion f

conclusive adj concluant/-e

concoct vtr concocter

concrete **1** n béton m
2 adj (a) ‹block› de béton; ‹base› en béton
(b) (real) concret/-ète

concuss vtr to be ~ed être commotionné/-e

concussion n commotion f cérébrale

condemn **1** vtr (a) (gen) condamner
(b) déclarer [qch] inhabitable ‹building›
2 condemned pp adj ‹cell› des condamnés à mort; ~ed man/woman condamné/-e m/f à mort

condensation n (on walls) condensation f; (on windows) buée f

condense **1** vtr condenser
2 vi se condenser

condensed milk n lait m concentré sucré

condescend vtr to ~ to do condescendre à faire

condescending adj condescendant/-e

condition n (a) (gen) condition f; on ~ that you come à condition que tu viennes
(b) (state) état m, condition f; to be in good/ bad ~ ‹house, car› être en bon/mauvais état
(c) (disease) maladie f

conditional adj conditionnel/-elle

conditioner n après-shampooing m, démêlant m

condolences n pl condoléances fpl

condom n préservatif m

condominium n (US) (also ~ unit) appartement m (dans une copropriété)

condone vtr tolérer

conducive adj ~ to favorable à

conduct **1** n conduite f (towards envers)
2 vtr (a) mener ‹business, campaign›
(b) mener ‹experiment, inquiry›; célébrer ‹ceremony›
(c) (Mus) diriger ‹orchestra›
(d) conduire ‹electricity, heat›

conductor n (a) (Mus) chef m d'orchestre
(b) (on bus) receveur m; (on train) chef m de train

conductress n receveuse f

cone n (a) (shape) cône m
(b) (also **ice-cream ~**) cornet m
(c) (for traffic) balise f

confectioner n (of sweets) confiseur/-euse m/f; (of cakes) pâtissier-confiseur m; ~'s (shop) pâtisserie-confiserie f

confectionery n (sweets) confiserie f; (cakes) pâtisserie f

confer **1** vtr conférer (on à)
2 vi conférer (about de; with avec)

conference n (academic, business) conférence f; (political) congrès m; peace ~ conférence pour la paix

confess **1** vtr (a) avouer (that que)
(b) confesser ‹sins›
2 vi avouer; to ~ to a crime avouer (avoir commis) un crime

confession n (a) (gen, Law) aveu m (of de)
(b) (in religion) confession f; to go to ~ se confesser

confetti n confettis mpl

confide vi to ~ in se confier à ‹person›

confidence *n* (a) (faith) confiance *f* (**in** en); **to have (every) ∼ in sb/sth** avoir (pleine) confiance en qn/qch
(b) (in politics) **vote of ∼** vote *m* de confiance; **motion of no ∼** motion *f* de censure
(c) (self-assurance) assurance *f*, confiance *f* en soi
(d) **to tell sb sth in ∼** dire qch à qn confidentiellement

confidence trick *n* escroquerie *f*

confident *adj* (a) (sure) sûr/-e, confiant/-e
(b) (self-assured) assuré/-e, sûr/-e de soi

confidential *adj* confidentiel/-ielle

confine *vtr* (a) confiner ⟨*person*⟩ (**in, to** dans); enfermer ⟨*animal*⟩ (**in** dans)
(b) (limit) limiter (**to** à)

confined *adj* (gen) confiné/-e; ⟨*space*⟩ restreint/-e

confinement *n* (in prison) détention *f*

confirm *vtr* confirmer; **to ∼ receipt of sth** accuser réception de qch

confirmation *n* confirmation *f*

confirmed *adj* ⟨*smoker, liar*⟩ invétéré/-e; ⟨*bachelor, sinner*⟩ endurci/-e

confiscate *vtr* confisquer (**from** à)

conflict ① *n* conflit *m*
② *vi* être en contradiction (**with** avec)

conflicting *adj* contradictoire

conform ① *vtr* conformer (**to** à)
② *vi* ⟨*person*⟩ se conformer (**with, to** à)

conformist *n, adj* conformiste (*mf*)

confront *vtr* affronter ⟨*danger, enemy*⟩; faire face à ⟨*problem*⟩

confrontation *n* affrontement *m*

confrontational *adj* provocateur/-trice

confuse *vtr* (a) (bewilder) troubler ⟨*person*⟩
(b) (mistake) confondre (**with** avec)
(c) (complicate) compliquer ⟨*argument*⟩; **to ∼ the issue** compliquer les choses

confused *adj* ⟨*person*⟩ troublé/-e; ⟨*account, thoughts, mind*⟩ confus/-e; **to get ∼** s'embrouiller

confusing *adj* déroutant/-e, peu clair/-e

confusion *n* confusion *f*

congeal *vi* ⟨*fat*⟩ se figer; ⟨*blood*⟩ se coaguler

congenial *adj* agréable

congenital *adj* congénital/-e

congested *adj* (a) ⟨*road*⟩ embouteillé/-e; ⟨*district*⟩ surpeuplé/-e
(b) ⟨*lungs*⟩ congestionné/-e

congestion *n* (a) traffic **∼** embouteillages *mpl*
(b) (of lungs) congestion *f*

conglomerate *n* conglomérat *m*

congratulate *vtr* féliciter (**on** de)

congratulations *n pl* félicitations *fpl*; **∼ on the birth of your new baby** félicitations à l'occasion de la naissance de votre bébé

congregate *vi* se rassembler

congregation *n* assemblée *f* des fidèles

congress *n* congrès *m* (**on** sur)

Congress *n* (US) Congrès *m*

congressman *n* (US) membre *m* du Congrès

conifer *n* conifère *m*

conjugal *adj* conjugal/-e

conjugate ① *vtr* conjuguer
② *vi* ⟨*verb*⟩ se conjuguer

conjunctivitis *n* conjonctivite *f*

conjure *vi* faire des tours de prestidigitation
■ **conjure up** évoquer ⟨*image*⟩

conjurer *n* prestidigitateur/-trice *m/f*

con man *n* arnaqueur *m* (slang), escroc *m*

connect *vtr* (a) raccorder ⟨*end, hose*⟩ (**to** à); accrocher ⟨*coach*⟩ (**to** à)
(b) ⟨*road, railway*⟩ relier ⟨*place, road*⟩ (**to, with** à)
(c) brancher ⟨*appliance*⟩ (**to** à)
(d) raccorder ⟨*phone, subscriber*⟩

connected *adj* (a) ⟨*idea, event*⟩ lié/-e (**to, with** à); **everything ∼ with music** tout ce qui se rapporte à la musique
(b) (in family) apparenté/-e (**to** à)

connecting *adj* (a) ⟨*flight*⟩ de correspondance
(b) ⟨*room*⟩ attenant/-e

connection *n* (a) (link) (between events) rapport *m*; (of person) lien *m* (**between** entre; **with** avec); **in ∼ with** au sujet de, à propos de
(b) (contact) relation *f*; **to have useful ∼s** avoir des relations
(c) (to mains) branchement *m*
(d) (to telephone network) raccordement *m*; (to number) mise *f* en communication (**to** avec); **bad ∼** mauvaise communication *f*
(e) (in travel) correspondance *f*
(f) (Comput) connexion *f*; **Internet ∼** connexion Internet

connive *vi* **to ∼ at** contribuer délibérément à; **to ∼ (with sb) to do** être de connivence *or* de mèche (colloq) (avec qn) pour faire

connoisseur *n* connaisseur/-euse *m/f*

connotation *n* connotation *f* (**of** de)

conquer *vtr* conquérir ⟨*territory, people*⟩; vaincre ⟨*enemy, unemployment*⟩

conqueror *n* conquérant/-e *m/f*

conquest *n* conquête *f*

conscience *n* conscience *f*; **they have no ∼** ils n'ont aucun sens moral; **to have a guilty ∼** avoir mauvaise conscience; **to have a clear ∼** avoir la conscience tranquille

conscientious *adj* consciencieux/-ieuse

conscientious objector, CO *n* objecteur *m* de conscience

conscious *adj* (a) (aware) conscient/-e (**of** de; **that** du fait que)
(b) (deliberate) ⟨*decision*⟩ réfléchi/-e; ⟨*effort*⟩ conscient/-e; ⟨*effort*⟩ consciencieux/-ieuse
(c) (awake) réveillé/-e

consciousness *n* **to lose/regain ∼** perdre/reprendre connaissance

conscript *n* appelé *m*

conscription n (system) conscription f

consecrate vtr consacrer

consecutive adj consécutif/-ive

consensus n consensus m (among au sein de; about quant à; on sur)

consent ① n consentement m; age of ~ âge m légal; by common or mutual ~ d'un commun accord
② vi consentir (to à); to ~ to sb doing consentir à ce que qn fasse

consequence n (a) conséquence f; as a ~ of du fait de ⟨change, process⟩; à la suite de ⟨event⟩
(b) (importance) importance f

consequently adv par conséquent

conservation n (a) (of nature) protection f (of de); energy ~ maîtrise f de l'énergie
(b) (of heritage) conservation f

conservation area n zone f protégée

conservationist n défenseur m des ressources naturelles

conservative ① n conservateur/-trice m/f
② adj (a) ⟨party⟩ conservateur/-trice
(b) ⟨taste, style⟩ classique

Conservative Party n (GB) parti m conservateur

conservatory n (a) (for plants) jardin m d'hiver
(b) (academy) conservatoire m

conserve ① n confiture f
② vtr (a) protéger ⟨forest⟩; sauvegarder ⟨wildlife⟩; conserver ⟨remains, ruins⟩
(b) économiser ⟨resources⟩; ménager ⟨energy⟩

consider vtr (a) (give thought to) considérer ⟨options, facts⟩; examiner ⟨evidence, problem⟩; étudier ⟨offer⟩
(b) (take into account) prendre [qch] en considération ⟨risk, cost⟩; songer à ⟨person⟩; faire attention à ⟨person's feelings⟩
(c) (envisage) to ~ doing envisager de faire; to ~ sb/sth as sth penser à qn/qch comme qch
(d) (regard) to ~ that considérer or estimer que; to ~ oneself (to be) a genius se considérer comme un génie

considerable adj considérable

considerate adj ⟨person⟩ attentionné/-e; ⟨behaviour⟩ courtois/-e; to be ~ towards sb avoir des égards pour qn

consideration n (a) considération f (for envers); to give sth careful ~ réfléchir longuement à qch; to take sth into ~ prendre qch en considération; out of ~ par considération
(b) (fee) for a ~ moyennant finance

considering prep, conj étant donné, compte tenu de

consign vtr expédier ⟨goods⟩ (to à)

consignment n (sending) expédition f; (goods) lot m, livraison f

consist vi to ~ of se composer de; to ~ in résider dans; to ~ in doing consister à faire

consistency n (a) (texture) consistance f
(b) (of view, policy) cohérence f

consistent adj (a) ⟨growth, level, quality⟩ régulier/-ière
(b) ⟨attempts, demands⟩ répété/-e
(c) ⟨argument⟩ cohérent/-e; ~ with en accord avec ⟨account, belief⟩

consistently adv (invariably) systématiquement; (repeatedly) à maintes reprises

consolation n consolation f (to pour)

console ① n (a) (control panel) console f
(b) (for hi-fi) meuble m hi-fi; (for video) meuble m vidéo
② vtr consoler (for, on de; with avec)

consolidate vtr (a) consolider ⟨position⟩
(b) réunir ⟨resources⟩; fusionner ⟨companies⟩

consonant n consonne f

consortium n consortium m

conspicuous adj ⟨feature, sign⟩ visible; ⟨garment⟩ voyant/-e; to be ~ se remarquer

conspiracy n conspiration f

conspirator n conspirateur/-trice m/f

conspire vi conspirer; to ~ to do ⟨people⟩ conspirer en vue de faire; ⟨events⟩ conspirer à faire

constable n (GB) agent m de police

constant adj ⟨problem, reminder, threat⟩ permanent/-e; ⟨care, temperature⟩ constant/-e; ⟨disputes, questions⟩ incessant/-e; ⟨attempts⟩ répété/-e; ⟨companion⟩ éternel/-elle

constantly adv constamment

constellation n constellation f

constipated adj constipé/-e

constipation n constipation f

constituency n (district) circonscription f électorale; (voters) électeurs mpl

constituent n (a) (Pol) électeur/-trice m/f
(b) (of character) trait m; (of event, work of art) élément m

constitute vtr constituer

constitution n constitution f

constitutional adj constitutionnel/-elle

constraint n contrainte f

constrict vtr comprimer ⟨flow, blood vessel⟩; gêner ⟨breathing, movement⟩

construct vtr construire (of avec; in en)

construction n construction f

construction site n chantier m

construction worker n ouvrier/-ière m/f du bâtiment

constructive adj constructif/-ive

consul n consul m

consulate n consulat m

consult ① vtr consulter (about sur)
② vi s'entretenir (about sur; with avec)

consultancy n (also ~ firm) cabinet-conseil m

consultant n (a) (expert) consultant/-e m/f, conseiller/-ère m/f (on, in en)
(b) (GB) (doctor) spécialiste mf

consultation *n* (for advice) consultation *f* (about sur); (for discussion) entretien *m* (about sur); after ~ with après avoir consulté

consumables *n pl* consommables *mpl*

consume *vtr* (a) (use up) consommer ⟨fuel, food, drink⟩
(b) to be ~d by or with être dévoré/-e par ⟨envy⟩; brûler de ⟨desire⟩; être rongé/-e par ⟨guilt⟩

consumer *n* consommateur/-trice *m/f*; (of electricity, gas) abonné/-e *m/f*

consumer advice *n* conseils *mpl* au consommateurs

consumer goods *n pl* biens *mpl* de consommation

consumer protection *n* défense *f* du consommateur

consumer society *n* société *f* de consommation

consummate *vtr* consommer ⟨marriage⟩

consumption *n* consommation *f*

contact [1] *n* (a) (gen) contact *m* (between entre; with avec); to be in/make ~ être en/se mettre en contact
(b) (acquaintance) connaissance *f*; (professional) contact *m*
[2] *vtr* contacter, se mettre en rapport avec

contact lens *n* lentille *f* or verre *m* de contact

contagious *adj* contagieux/-ieuse

contain *vtr* (a) contenir ⟨amount, ingredients⟩; contenir, comporter ⟨information, mistakes⟩
(b) (curb) maîtriser ⟨blaze⟩; enrayer ⟨epidemic⟩; limiter ⟨costs, problem⟩; retenir ⟨flood⟩

container *n* (for food, liquids) récipient *m*; (for plants) bac *m*; (for waste, for transporting) conteneur *m*

contaminate *vtr* contaminer

contamination *n* contamination *f*

contemplate *vtr* (a) (consider) envisager (doing de faire)
(b) (look at) contempler

contemporary [1] *n* contemporain/-e *m/f*
[2] *adj* (present-day) contemporain/-e; (up-to-date) moderne; (of same period) de l'époque

contempt *n* mépris *m* (for de); to hold sb/ sth in ~ mépriser qn/qch; ~ of court (Law) outrage *m* à magistrat

contemptible *adj* méprisable

contemptuous *adj* méprisant/-e

contend [1] *vtr* soutenir (that que)
[2] *vi* (a) (deal with) to ~ with affronter
(b) (compete) to ~ with sb for sth disputer qch à qn

contender *n* (a) (in competition) concurrent/-e *m/f*
(b) (for post) candidat/-e *m/f* (for à)

content [1] *n* (a) (quantity) teneur *f*
(b) (of book, essay) fond *m*
[2] *adj* satisfait/-e (with de)

contented *adj* ⟨person⟩ content/-e (with de); ⟨feeling⟩ de bien-être

contention *n* (a) (opinion) assertion *f*
(b) (dispute) dispute *f*

contentment *n* contentement *m*

contents *n pl* (gen) contenu *m*; (of house, for insurance) biens *mpl* mobiliers; list or table of ~ table *f* des matières

contest [1] *n* (a) (competition) concours *m*
(b) (struggle) lutte *f*
[2] *vtr* (a) contester ⟨decision, will⟩
(b) (compete for) disputer ⟨match⟩

contestant *n* (in competition, game) concurrent/-e *m/f*; (in fight) adversaire *mf*; (for job, in election) candidat/-e *m/f*

context *n* contexte *m*

continent *n* (a) continent *m*
(b) the Continent (GB) l'Europe *f* continentale

continental *adj* (a) continental/-e
(b) (GB) ⟨holiday⟩ en Europe continentale

continental breakfast *n* petit déjeuner *m* (avec café, pain, beurre et confiture)

continental quilt *n* (GB) couette *f*

contingency *n* imprévu *m*

contingency fund *n* fonds *m* de secours

contingency plan *n* plan *m* de réserve

continual *adj* continuel/-elle

continually *adv* continuellement

continuation *n* (a) (gen) continuation *f*
(b) (of story) suite *f*; (of route) prolongement *m*

continue [1] *vtr* continuer
[2] *vi* ⟨person⟩ continuer (doing, to do à or de faire); ⟨noise, debate, strike⟩ se poursuivre; to ~ with continuer, poursuivre ⟨task, treatment⟩

continuity *n* continuité *f*

continuous *adj* (a) ⟨growth, decline, noise⟩ continu/-e; ⟨care⟩ constant/-e; ⟨line⟩ ininterrompu/-e; ~ assessment (GB) contrôle *m* continu
(b) ⟨tense⟩ progressif/-ive

continuously *adv* (without a break) sans interruption; (repeatedly) continuellement

contort *vtr* tordre

contortion *n* contorsion *f*

contour *n* (a) (outline) contour *m*
(b) (also ~ line) courbe *f* hypsométrique or de niveau

contraband *n* contrebande *f*

contraception *n* contraception *f*

contraceptive [1] *n* contraceptif *m*
[2] *adj* contraceptif/-ive

contract [1] *n* contrat *m*
[2] *vtr* (a) (gen) contracter
(b) to be ~ed to do être tenu/-e par contrat de faire
[3] *vi* (a) to ~ to do s'engager par contrat à faire
(b) ⟨muscle, wood⟩ se contracter

contraction *n* contraction *f*

contract killer n tueur/-euse m/f à gages
contractor n (a) (business) entrepreneur/-euse m/f
(b) (worker) contractuel/-elle m/f
contradict vtr, vi contredire
contradiction n contradiction f
contradictory adj contradictoire (to à)
contraflow n (GB) circulation f à sens alterné
contraindication n contre-indication f
contrary ① n contraire m; **in** ~ **is** (bien) au contraire; **unless you hear anything to the** ~ sauf contrordre
② adj (a) ⟨idea, view⟩ contraire
(b) ⟨person⟩ contrariant/-e
③ **contrary to** phr contrairement à
contrast ① n contraste m; **in** ~ **to sth, by** ~ **with sth** par contraste avec qch; **in** ~ **to sb** à la différence de qn; **by** or **in** ~ par contre
② vtr **to** ~ **X with Y** faire ressortir le contraste (qui existe) entre X et Y
③ vi contraster (**with** avec)
contrasting adj ⟨examples⟩ opposé/-e; ⟨colour⟩ contrasté/-e; ⟨views⟩ très différent/-e
contribute ① vtr (a) verser ⟨sum⟩ (**to** à); **to** ~ **£5m** contribuer pour 5 millions de livres sterling
(b) (to gift, charity) donner (**to** à; **towards** pour)
(c) apporter ⟨ideas⟩ (**to** à); écrire ⟨article⟩ (**to** pour)
② vi (a) **to** ~ **to** or **towards** contribuer à ⟨change, decline⟩
(b) (to community life, research) participer (**to** à); (to programme, magazine) collaborer (**to** à)
(c) **to** ~ **to** cotiser à ⟨pension fund⟩
(d) (to charity) donner (de l'argent) (**to** à)
contribution n (a) (to tax, pension, profits, cost) contribution f (**towards** à)
(b) (to charity, campaign) don m; **to make a** ~ faire un don (**to** à)
(c) **sb's** ~ **to** le rôle que qn a joué dans ⟨success, undertaking⟩; ce que qn a apporté à ⟨science, sport⟩
(d) (to programme) participation f; (to magazine) article m
contributor n (to charity) donateur/-trice m/f, (in discussion) participant/-e m/f, (to magazine, book) collaborateur/-trice m/f
con trick n (colloq) escroquerie f, duperie f
contrive vtr (arrange) organiser; **to** ~ **to do** parvenir à faire
contrived adj (a) ⟨incident, meeting⟩ non fortuit/-e
(b) ⟨plot⟩ tiré/-e par les cheveux; ⟨style, effect⟩ étudié/-e
control ① n (a) (gen) contrôle m (**of** de); (of operation, project) direction f (**of** de); (of life, emotion, self) maîtrise f (**of, over** de); **to be in** ~ **of** contrôler ⟨territory⟩; diriger ⟨operation, organization⟩; maîtriser ⟨problem⟩; avoir le contrôle de ⟨ball, vehicle⟩ **to be in** ~ (**of oneself**) se maîtriser; **to bring** or **keep** [sth] **under** ~ maîtriser; **to lose** ~ (**of sth**) perdre le contrôle (de qch)

(b) (on vehicle, equipment) commande f; (on TV) bouton m de réglage; **to be at the** ~**s** être aux commandes
② vtr (a) dominer ⟨organization, situation⟩; contrôler ⟨territory⟩; diriger ⟨traffic, project⟩; être majoritaire dans ⟨company⟩
(b) maîtriser ⟨person, animal, inflation, fire⟩; endiguer ⟨epidemic⟩; dominer ⟨emotion⟩; retenir ⟨laughter⟩; **to** ~ **oneself** se contrôler
(c) commander ⟨machine⟩; manœuvrer ⟨boat, vehicle⟩; piloter ⟨plane⟩; contrôler ⟨ball⟩
(d) régler ⟨speed, temperature⟩; contrôler ⟨immigration, prices⟩
control panel n (on plane) tableau m de bord; (on machine) tableau m de contrôle; (on TV) (panneau m de) commandes fpl
control room n poste m de commande; (TV) (salle f de) régie f
control tower n tour f de contrôle
controversial adj (gen) controversé/-e; (open to criticism) qui prête à controverse
controversy n controverse f
conundrum n énigme f
convalesce vi se remettre
convene vtr organiser ⟨meeting⟩; convoquer ⟨group⟩
convenience n avantage m (**of doing** de faire); (of device, food, shop) commodité f; **for (the sake of)** ~ pour raisons de commodité; **at your** ~ quand cela vous conviendra
convenience foods n pl plats mpl (tout) préparés
convenient adj (a) ⟨place, time⟩ pratique; **to be** ~ **for sb** convenir à qn
(b) (useful, practical) pratique, commode
(c) ⟨shops⟩ situé/-e tout près; ⟨chair⟩ à portée de main
convent n couvent m
convention n (a) (gen) convention f
(b) (social norms) convenances fpl, conventions fpl
conventional adj (gen) conventionnel/-elle; ⟨person⟩ conformiste; ⟨medicine⟩ traditionnel/-elle
converge vi converger
conversant adj **to be** ~ **with** être versé/-e dans
conversation n conversation f
converse vi converser (**with** avec; **in** en)
conversion n (of currency, measurement) conversion f (**from** de; **into** en); (of building) aménagement m (**to, into** en); (to new beliefs) conversion f (**from** de; **to** à); (in rugby) transformation f
conversion rate n taux m de change
convert ① n converti/-e m/f (**to** à)
② vtr (a) (change into sth else) transformer; (modify) adapter
(b) convertir ⟨currency, measurement⟩ (**from** de; **to, into** en)
(c) aménager ⟨building, loft⟩ (**to, into** en)
(d) (to new beliefs) convertir (**to** à; **from** de)
(e) (in rugby) transformer ⟨try⟩

3 vi (a) ⟨sofa, device⟩ être convertible (**into** en)

(b) ⟨person⟩ se convertir (**to** à; **from** de)

convertible n décapotable f

convex adj convexe

convey vtr (a) ⟨person⟩ transmettre ⟨information⟩ (**to** à); exprimer ⟨condolences, feeling, idea⟩ (**to** à)

(b) ⟨words, images⟩ traduire ⟨mood, impression⟩

(c) ⟨vehicle⟩ transporter; ⟨pipes⟩ amener

conveyancing n rédaction f des actes de propriété

conveyor belt n (in factory) transporteur m à bande or à courroie; (for luggage) tapis m roulant

convict **1** n (imprisoned criminal) détenu/-e m/f; (deported criminal) bagnard m
2 vtr reconnaître or déclarer [qn] coupable (**of** de; **of doing** d'avoir fait)

conviction n (a) (Law) condamnation f (**for** pour)

(b) (belief) conviction f (**that** que)

convince vtr convaincre ⟨person⟩ (**to do** de faire)

convincing adj ⟨account, evidence⟩ convaincant/-e; ⟨victory, lead⟩ indiscutable

convoy n convoi m

convulsion n convulsion f

coo vi roucouler

cook **1** n cuisinier/-ière m/f
2 vtr faire cuire ⟨vegetables, pasta, eggs⟩; préparer ⟨meal⟩ (**for** pour)
3 vi ⟨person⟩ cuisiner, faire la cuisine; ⟨vegetable, meat, meal⟩ cuire

cook-chill foods n pl plats mpl préparés, plats mpl cuisinés

cooker n (GB) cuisinière f

cookery book n (GB) livre de cuisine

cookie n (a) (biscuit) gateau m sec, biscuit m

(b) (Comput) cookie m

cooking n cuisine f

cooking apple n pomme f à cuire

cooking chocolate n chocolat m pâtissier

cool **1** n (a) (coldness) fraîcheur f

(b) (colloq) (calm) sang-froid m; **to keep one's ~** (not get angry) ne pas s'énerver; (stay calm) garder son sang-froid; **to lose one's ~** (get angry) s'énerver; (panic) perdre son sang-froid
2 adj (a) ⟨day, drink, water, weather⟩ frais/fraîche; ⟨dress⟩ léger/-ère; ⟨colour⟩ froid/-e

(b) (calm) calme

(c) (unfriendly) froid/-e

(d) (casual) décontracté/-e, cool inv (colloq)

(e) (colloq) (trendy) branché/-e (colloq)
3 vtr (a) refroidir ⟨soup⟩; rafraîchir ⟨wine, room⟩

(b) calmer ⟨anger, ardour⟩
4 vi (a) (get colder) refroidir

(b) ⟨enthusiasm⟩ faiblir; ⟨friendship⟩ se dégrader

■ **cool down** ⟨engine, water⟩ refroidir; ⟨person, situation⟩ se calmer

cool bag n sac m isotherme

cool box n (GB) glacière f

cooling-off period n (in industrial relations) délai m de conciliation; (in contract) délai m de réflexion

coop n poulailler m

■ **coop up**: ¶ ~ [sb/sth] up enfermer, cloîtrer

cooperate vi coopérer (**with** avec; **in** à; **in doing** pour faire)

cooperation n coopération f (**on** à)

cooperative **1** n (a) (organization) coopérative f

(b) (US) (apartment house) immeuble m en copropriété
2 adj coopératif/-ive

coordinate **1** n (on map, graph) coordonnée f
2 vtr coordonner (**with** avec)

coordinates n pl (clothes) ensemble m

coordination n coordination f

coordinator n coordinateur/-trice m/f

cope vi s'en sortir (colloq), se débrouiller; **to ~ with** s'occuper de ⟨person, work⟩; faire face à ⟨demand, disaster, problem⟩; supporter ⟨death, depression, difficult person⟩

Copenhagen pr n Copenhague

copious adj (a) (plentiful) ⟨supply⟩ abondant/-e

(b) (generous) ⟨quantity, serving⟩ copieux/-ieuse

cop-out n (colloq) (excuse) excuse f bidon (colloq)

copper n (a) (metal) cuivre m

(b) (GB) (colloq) (coin) petite monnaie f

(c) (GB) (colloq) (policeman) flic m (colloq)

(d) (colour) couleur f cuivre

copy **1** n (a) (gen) copie f

(b) (of book, newspaper, report) exemplaire m
2 vtr copier (**from** sur)
3 vi copier

■ **copy down, copy out** recopier ⟨quote, address⟩

copyright n copyright m, droit m d'auteur

coral n corail m

cord **1** n cordon m
2 **cords** n pl (colloq) (also **corduroys**) pantalon m en velours (côtelé)

cordial **1** n (a) (fruit drink) sirop m de fruits

(b) (US) (liqueur) liqueur m
2 adj cordial/-e (**to, with** avec)

cordless adj ⟨telephone, kettle⟩ sans fil

cordon n cordon m

■ **cordon off** boucler ⟨street, area⟩; contenir ⟨crowd⟩

corduroy n velours m côtelé

core n (a) (of apple) trognon m

(b) (of problem) cœur m

(c) **rotten to the ~** pourri/-e jusqu'à l'os; **English to the ~** anglais/-e jusqu'au bout des ongles

···⊹

(d) (of nuclear reactor) cœur m
(e) (small group) noyau m; **hard** ~ noyau dur
core curriculum n tronc m commun
Corfu pr n Corfou f
cork n **(a)** (substance) liège m
(b) (object) bouchon m
corkscrew n tire-bouchon m
corn n **(a)** (GB) (wheat) blé m
(b) (US) (maize) maïs m
(c) (on foot) cor m
cornea n cornée f
corner ⃞1 n **(a)** (gen) coin m; **the house on
the** ~ la maison qui fait l'angle; **at the** ~ **of
the street** au coin de la rue; **to go round the**
~ tourner au coin de la rue; **just around the**
~ (nearby) tout près; (around the bend) juste
après le coin; **out of the** ~ **of one's eye** du
coin de l'œil
(b) (bend) virage m
(c) (in boxing) coin m (de repos); (in football,
hockey) corner m
⃞2 vtr **(a)** acculer ⟨animal, enemy⟩; coincer
(colloq) ⟨person⟩
(b) accaparer ⟨market⟩
IDIOMS **in a tight** ~ dans une impasse; **to cut**
~**s** (financially) faire des économies
corner shop n petite épicerie f
cornerstone n pierre f angulaire
cornflour n farine f de maïs
cornflower n bleuet m, barbeau m
corn on the cob n maïs m en épi
Cornwall pr n (comté m de) Cornouailles f
corny adj (colloq) ⟨joke⟩ (old) éculé/-e; (feeble)
faiblard/-e (colloq); ⟨film, story⟩ à la guimauve
coronary n infarctus m
coronation n couronnement m
coroner n coroner m
corporal n (gen) caporal m; (in artillery)
brigadier m
corporal punishment n châtiment m
corporel
corporate adj **(a)** ⟨accounts, funds⟩
appartenant/-e à une société; ⟨clients,
employees⟩ une société (or de sociétés)
(b) ⟨action⟩ commun/-e; ⟨decision⟩
collectif/-ive
**corporate identity, corporate
image** n image f de marque (d'une société)
corporate raider n raider m
(organisateur d'OPA)
corporation n (grande) société f
corps n corps m
corpse n cadavre m
correct ⃞1 adj **(a)** ⟨amount, answer,
decision⟩ correct/-e; ⟨figure, time⟩ exact/-e
(b) ⟨behaviour⟩ correct/-e, convenable
⃞2 vtr corriger
correcting fluid n liquide m correcteur
correction n correction f
correspond vi **(a)** (match) concorder,
correspondre (**with** à)
(b) (be equivalent) être équivalent/-e (**to** à)

(c) (exchange letters) correspondre (**with** avec;
about au sujet de)
correspondence n correspondance f
correspondence course n cours m
par correspondance
correspondent n **(a)** (journalist)
journaliste mf; (abroad) correspondant/-e m/f
(b) (letter writer) correspondant/-e m/f
corresponding adj (matching)
correspondant/-e; (similar) équivalent/-e
corridor n **(a)** couloir m
(b) (of land) corridor m
corroborate vtr corroborer
corrode ⃞1 vtr corroder
⃞2 vi se corroder
corrosion n corrosion f
corrugated adj ondulé/-e
corrugated iron n tôle f ondulée
corrupt ⃞1 adj corrompu/-e
⃞2 vtr corrompre
corruption n corruption f
Corsica pr n Corse f
cosh n (GB) matraque f
cosmetic ⃞1 n produit m de beauté
⃞2 adj (figurative) superficiel/-ielle
cosmetic surgery n chirurgie f
esthétique
cosmonaut n cosmonaute mf
cosmopolitan n, adj cosmopolite (mf)
cost ⃞1 n **(a)** (price) coût m, prix m (**of** de);
(expense incurred) frais mpl; **at** ~ au prix
coûtant
(b) (figurative) prix m; **at all** ~**s** à tout prix; **he
knows to his** ~ **that** il a appris à ses dépens
que
⃞2 vtr **(a)** coûter; **how much does it** ~?
combien ça coûte?; **the TV will** ~ **£100 to
repair** la réparation de la télé coûtera 100
livres sterling
(b) (estimate price of) calculer le prix de
revient de ⟨product⟩; calculer le coût de
⟨project, work⟩
co-star ⃞1 n co-vedette f
⃞2 vtr **a film** ~**ring X and Y** un film avec X
et Y
cost-cutting n réduction f des frais
cost-effective adj rentable
costly adv coûteux/-euse
cost of living n coût m de la vie
cost price n (for producer) prix m de
revient; (for consumer) prix m coûtant
costume n **(a)** (clothes) costume m
(b) (GB) (also **swimming** ~) maillot m de
bain
costume jewellery (GB), **costume
jewelry** (US) n bijoux mpl fantaisie
cosy (GB), **cozy** (US) adj (comfortable)
douillet/-ette; (intimate) intime; **it's** ~ **here** on
est bien ici
cot n **(a)** (GB) (for baby) lit m de bébé
(b) (US) (bed) lit m de camp
cot death n (GB) mort f subite du
nourrisson

cottage n maisonnette f; (thatched) chaumière f

cottage cheese n fromage m blanc à gros grains

cotton n (a) (plant, material) coton m (b) (thread) fil m de coton

cotton bud n Coton-Tige® m

cotton wool n ouate f (de coton)

couch n (a) (sofa) canapé m (b) (doctor's) lit m; (psychoanalyst's) divan m

couch potato n (colloq) pantouflard/-e m/f (colloq) (qui passe son temps devant la télé)

cough ① n toux f; **to have a ~** tousser ② vi tousser

cough mixture n (sirop m) antitussif m

could modal aux (a) (be able to) pouvoir; **I couldn't move** je ne pouvais pas bouger; **she couldn't come yesterday** elle n'a pas pu venir hier
(b) (know how to) savoir; **he couldn't swim** il ne savait pas nager; **she ~ speak four languages** elle parlait quatre langues
(c) (permission, requests, suggestions) pouvoir; **we ~ only go out at weekends** nous ne pouvions sortir or nous n'avions le droit de sortir que le week-end; **~ I speak to Annie?** est-ce que je pourrais parler à Annie?; **~ you help me?** pourrais-tu m'aider?
(d) (with verbs of perception) **I couldn't see a thing** je n'y voyais rien; **they couldn't understand me** ils ne me comprenaient pas; **we ~ hear them laughing** on les entendait rire
(e) **you ~ have died** tu aurais pu mourir; **they ~ have warned us** ils auraient pu nous prévenir; **I ~ be wrong** je me trompe peut-être; **if only I ~ start again** si seulement je pouvais tout recommencer

council n conseil m; **the town ~** le conseil municipal; **the Council of Europe** le Conseil de l'Europe

council estate n lotissement m de logements sociaux

council house n habitation f à loyer modéré

council housing n logements mpl sociaux

councillor, councilor (US) n conseiller/-ère m/f

council tax n (GB) ≈ impôts mpl locaux

counsel ① n (lawyer) avocat/-e m/f ② vtr conseiller (person) (about, on sur)

counselling (GB), **counseling** (US) n (advice) assistance f; (psychological) aide f psychosociale; **debt ~** assistance aux personnes endettées; **bereavement ~** aide psychosociale aux personnes endeuillées

counsellor, counselor (US) n conseiller/-ère m/f

count ① n (a) (numerical record) décompte m; (at election) dépouillement m; **at the last ~** au dernier décompte; **to keep (a) ~ of** tenir

compte de; **to lose ~** ne plus savoir où on en est dans ses calculs; **to be out for the ~** (colloq) être KO (colloq)
(b) (level) taux m; **cholesterol ~** taux de cholestérol
(c) (figure) chiffre m
(d) (Law) chef m d'accusation; **on three ~s** pour trois chefs d'accusation
(e) (nobleman) comte m
② vtr (a) compter (points, people, objects); énumérer (reasons, causes); **~ing the children** en comptant les enfants; **not ~ing my sister** sans compter ma sœur
(b) (consider) **to ~ sb as sth** considérer qn comme qch
③ vi compter; **it's the thought that ~s** c'est l'intention qui compte

■ **count against** jouer contre (person)

■ **count on** compter sur (person, event); **don't ~ on it!** ne comptez pas dessus!

■ **count up** calculer (cost, hours); compter (money, boxes)

countdown n compte m à rebours (**to** avant)

counter ① n (a) (in shop, snack bar) comptoir m; (in bank, post office) guichet m; (in pub, bar) bar m
(b) (in game) jeton m
② vtr répondre à (threat); neutraliser (effet); parer (blow); enrayer (inflation) ③ vi riposter (**with sth** par qch) ④ **counter to** phr (gen) contrairement à; (be, go, run) à l'encontre de

counteract vtr contrebalancer (influence); contrecarrer (negative effects)

counter-attack n contre-attaque f (**against** sur)

counter-clockwise adj, adv (US) dans le sens inverse des aiguilles d'une montre

counterfeit ① adj (signature, note) contrefait/-e; **~ money** fausse monnaie f ② vtr contrefaire

counterfoil n talon m, souche f

counterpart n (of person) homologue mf; (of company, institution) équivalent m

counter-productive adj contre-productif/-ive

countersign vtr contresigner

countess n comtesse f

countless adj **~ letters** un nombre incalculable de lettres; **on ~ occasions** je ne sais combien de fois

country n (a) pays m; **developing/third world ~** pays en voie de développement/du tiers monde; **~ of birth** pays natal
(b) (countryside) campagne f; **in the ~** à la campagne; **open ~** rase campagne; **across ~** à travers la campagne

country club n club m de loisirs

country dancing n danse f folklorique

country house n manoir m

country music n country music f

countryside n campagne f

county n comté m

county council n (GB) ≈ conseil m
régional

coup n (a) (also ∼ **d'état**) coup m d'État
(b) **to pull off a** ∼ réussir un beau coup

couple n (a) couple m
(b) **a** ∼ (**of**) (two) deux; (a few) deux ou trois;
a ∼ **of times** deux ou trois fois

coupon n (a) (voucher) bon m; **petrol** ∼ (GB)
bon d'essence
(b) (in ad) coupon m; **reply** ∼ coupon-réponse
m

courage n courage m

courageous adj courageux/-euse

courgette n courgette f

courier n (a) (also **travel** ∼)
accompagnateur/-trice m/f
(b) (for parcels, documents) coursier m; (for
drugs) transporteur m

course ☐ n (a) (gen) cours m (**of** de); **in the**
∼ **of** au cours de; **in the** ∼ **of time** avec le
temps; **in due** ∼ en temps utile; ∼ **of action**
moyen m d'action, parti m
(b) (route) cours m; (of boat, plane) cap m; **to be
on** ∼ ⟨boat, plane⟩ tenir le cap; **to go off** ∼
⟨ship⟩ dévier de son cap; **to change** ∼ (gen)
changer de direction; ⟨boat, plane⟩ changer de
cap
(c) (classes) cours m (**in** en; **of** de)
(d) (Med) **a** ∼ **of treatment** un traitement
(e) (Sport) (in golf) terrain m de golf m; (in
racing) champ m de courses
(f) (part of meal) plat m; **the main** ∼ le plat
principal; **five-**∼ **meal** repas m de cinq plats
② **of course** phr bien sûr, évidemment

course book n méthode f

coursework n devoirs mpl (de contrôle
continu)

court ☐ n (a) (Law) cour f, tribunal m; **to
go to** ∼ aller devant les tribunaux (**over**
pour); **to take sb to** ∼ poursuivre qn en
justice
(b) (for tennis, squash) court m; (for basketball)
terrain m
(c) (of sovereign) cour f
(d) (courtyard) cour f
② vtr courtiser ⟨woman, voters⟩

court case n procès m, affaire f

courteous adj courtois/-e (**to** envers)

courtesy n courtoisie f

courthouse n (Law) palais m de justice

court-martial vtr faire passer [qn] en
cour martiale

courtroom n salle f d'audience

courtyard n cour f

cousin n cousin/-e m/f

cove n (bay) avise f

cover ☐ n (a) (lid) couvercle m; (for duvet,
typewriter, cushion, furniture) housse f; (of record)
pochette f; (blanket) couverture f
(b) (shelter) abri m; **to take** ∼ se mettre à
l'abri; **under** ∼ à l'abri
(c) (for teacher, doctor) remplacement m
(d) (insurance) assurance f (**for** pour; **against**
contre)

② vtr (a) (gen) couvrir (**with** avec); recouvrir
⟨cushion, sofa, surface, person, cake⟩ (**with** de)
(b) (deal with) ⟨article, speaker⟩ traiter;
⟨journalist⟩ couvrir
(c) (insure) assurer, couvrir (**for, against**
contre; **for doing** pour faire)
■ **cover for** remplacer ⟨employee⟩
■ **cover up**: ¶ **to** ∼ **up for** couvrir ⟨friend⟩;
¶ ∼ [sth] **up** recouvrir ⟨object⟩; dissimuler
⟨mistake, truth⟩; étouffer ⟨scandal⟩

coverage n (gen) couverture f; **newspaper**
∼ couverture par les journaux; **live** ∼
reportage m en direct

cover charge n prix m de couvert

covering n (a) (for wall, floor) revêtement m
(b) (layer of snow, moss) couche f

covering letter n lettre f
d'accompagnement

cover note n (from insurance company)
attestation f d'assurance

covert adj ⟨operation⟩ secret/-ète; ⟨glance⟩
furtif/-ive; ⟨threat⟩ voilé/-e

cover-up n opération f de camouflage

cover version n version f

covetous adj cupide

cow n vache f

coward n lâche mf

cowardice n lâcheté f

cowardly adj lâche

cowboy n (a) (US) cowboy m
(b) (incompetent worker) fumiste m

cower vi se recroqueviller

cox ☐ n barreur m
② vtr, vi barrer

coy adj (a) ⟨smile, look⟩ de fausse modestie
(b) (reticent) réservé/-e (**about** à propos de)

cozy (US) = cosy

crab n crabe m

crack ☐ n (a) (in rock) fissure f; (in varnish,
ground) craquelure f; (in wall, cup, bone) fêlure f
(b) (in door) entrebâillement m; (in curtains)
fente f
(c) (also ∼ **cocaine**) crack m
(d) (noise) craquement m
(e) (colloq) (attempt) essai m, tentative f; **to
have a** ∼ **at doing** essayer de faire
② adj ⟨player⟩ de première; ⟨troops, shot⟩
d'élite
③ vtr (a) fêler ⟨bone, wall, cup⟩
(b) casser ⟨nut, egg⟩; **to** ∼ **a safe** fracturer
un coffre-fort; **to** ∼ **sth open** ouvrir qch; **to**
∼ **one's head open** se fendre le crâne
(c) déchiffrer ⟨code⟩
(d) faire claquer ⟨whip⟩; faire craquer
⟨knuckles, joints⟩
④ vi (a) ⟨bone, cup, wall, ice⟩ se fêler;
⟨varnish⟩ se craqueler; ⟨skin⟩ se crevasser;
⟨ground⟩ se fendre
(b) ⟨person⟩ craquer (colloq)
(c) ⟨knuckles, twig⟩ craquer; ⟨whip⟩ claquer
(d) ⟨voice⟩ se casser
■ **crack down** prendre des mesures
énergiques, sévir (**on** contre)

crackdown *n* mesure *f* sévère (**on** contre); **the** ~ **on drugs** l'action *f* antidrogue

cracker *n* (**a**) (biscuit) cracker *m*, biscuit *m* salé
(**b**) (for Christmas) diablotin *m*

crackle ⒈ *n* crépitement *m*
⒉ *vi* ⟨*fire, radio*⟩ crépiter; ⟨*hot fat*⟩ grésiller

cradle ⒈ *n* berceau *m*
⒉ *vtr* bercer ⟨*baby*⟩; tenir [qch] délicatement ⟨*object*⟩

craft *n* (**a**) (skill) métier *m*
(**b**) (craftwork) artisanat *m*; **arts and** ~**s** artisanat ⟨d'art⟩
(**c**) (boat) embarcation *f*

craftsman *n* artisan *m*

crafty *adj* astucieux/-ieuse

crag *n* rocher *m* escarpé

cram ⒈ *vtr* **to** ~ **sth into** enfoncer *or* fourrer (colloq) qch dans ⟨*bag, car*⟩; ~**med full** plein à craquer
⒉ *vi* ⟨*student*⟩ bachoter (**for** pour)

cramp ⒈ *n* crampe *f*
⒉ *vtr* gêner

cramped *adj* ⟨*house, office*⟩ exigu/-uë

cranberry *n* canneberge *f*

crane *n* grue *f*

crank *n* (**a**) (colloq) (freak) fanatique *mf*, fana *mf* (colloq)
(**b**) (handle) manivelle *f*

crash ⒈ *n* (**a**) (noise) fracas *m*
(**b**) (accident) accident *m*; **car** ~ accident de voiture; **train** ~ catastrophe *f* ferroviaire
(**c**) (of stock market) krach *m*
⒉ *vtr* **to** ~ **one's car** avoir un accident de voiture
⒊ *vi* (**a**) ⟨*car, plane*⟩ s'écraser; ⟨*vehicles, planes*⟩ se rentrer dedans, se percuter; **to** ~ **into sth** rentrer dans *or* percuter qch
(**b**) ⟨*share prices*⟩ s'effondrer
■ **crash out** (colloq) (go to sleep) pioncer (slang); (collapse) s'écrouler (colloq)

crash course *n* cours *m* intensif

crash diet *n* régime *m* d'amaigrissement intensif

crash helmet *n* casque *m*

crash landing *n* atterrissage *m* en catastrophe

crass *adj* grossier/-ière; ~ **ignorance** ignorance *f* crasse

crate *n* (for bottles, china) caisse *f*; (for fruit, vegetables) cageot *m*

crater *n* (of volcano) cratère *m*; (caused by explosion) entonnoir *m*

cravat *n* foulard *m* (pour homme)

crave *vtr* ⟨*also* ~ **for**⟩ avoir un besoin maladif de ⟨*drug*⟩; avoir soif de ⟨*affection*⟩; avoir envie de ⟨*food*⟩

crawl ⒈ *n* (**a**) (in swimming) crawl *m*
(**b**) **at a** ~ au pas; **to go at a** ~ ⟨*vehicle*⟩ rouler au pas
⒉ *vi* (**a**) ⟨*insect, snake, person*⟩ ramper
(**b**) ⟨*baby*⟩ marcher à quatre pattes
(**c**) ⟨*vehicle*⟩ rouler au pas
(**d**) ⟨*time*⟩ se traîner

(**e**) **to be** ~**ing with** fourmiller de ⟨*insects, tourists*⟩
(**f**) (colloq) (flatter) faire du lèche-bottes (colloq) (**to** à)

crayfish *n* (**a**) (freshwater) écrevisse *f*
(**b**) (spiny lobster) langouste *f*

crayon *n* (wax) craie *f* grasse; (pencil) crayon *m* de couleur

craze *n* vogue *f*; **to be the latest** ~ faire fureur

crazy *adj* (colloq) (gen) fou/folle; ⟨*idea*⟩ insensé/-e; ~ **about** fou/folle de ⟨*person*⟩; passionné/-e de ⟨*activity*⟩

crazy golf *n* (GB) mini-golf *m*

creak *vi* ⟨*hinge*⟩ grincer; ⟨*floorboard*⟩ craquer

cream ⒈ *n* crème *f*; **strawberries and** ~ fraises à la crème
⒉ *adj* (**a**) (couleur) crème *inv*
(**b**) ⟨*cake, bun*⟩ à la crème
■ **cream off**: ~ **off** [sth], ~ [sth] **off** prélever ⟨*best pupils*⟩; ramasser ⟨*profits*⟩

cream cheese *n* fromage *m* à tartiner

cream soda *n* soda *m* parfumé à la vanille

crease ⒈ *n* (intentional) pli *m*; (accidental) faux pli *m*
⒉ *vtr* froisser ⟨*paper, cloth*⟩
⒊ *vi* ⟨*cloth*⟩ se froisser

create *vtr* (gen) créer; provoquer ⟨*interest*⟩; poser ⟨*problem*⟩; faire ⟨*good impression*⟩

creation *n* création *f*

creative *adj* (**a**) ⟨*person*⟩ créatif/-ive
(**b**) ⟨*process, imagination*⟩ créateur/-trice

creator *n* créateur/-trice *m/f* (**of** de)

creature *n* (**a**) (living being) créature *f*
(**b**) (animal) animal *m*

crèche *n* (GB) (nursery) crèche *f*; (in shopping centre) halte-garderie *f*; **workplace** ~ crèche *f* d'entreprise

credentials *n pl* (**a**) (reputation) qualifications *fpl*
(**b**) (reference) pièce *f* d'identité

credibility *n* crédibilité *f*

credible *adj* crédible

credit ⒈ *n* (**a**) (merit) mérite *m* (**for** de); **to get/take the** ~ se voir attribuer/s'attribuer le mérite (**for** de); **to be a** ~ **to sb/sth** faire honneur à qn/qch
(**b**) (in business) crédit *m*; **to buy sth on** ~ acheter qch à crédit; **to be in** ~ être créditeur/-trice
⒉ *vtr* (**a**) **to** ~ **sb with** attribuer à qn ⟨*achievement*⟩
(**b**) créditer ⟨*account*⟩ (**with** de)

credit card *n* carte *f* de crédit

credit facilities *n pl* facilités *fpl* de crédit

credit note *n* avoir *m*

creditor *n* créancier/-ière *m/f*

credits *n pl* générique *m*

creditworthy *adj* solvable

credulous *adj* crédule, naïf/naïve

creed n (religious persuasion) croyance f; (opinions) principes mpl, credo m

creek n (a) (GB) crique f
(b) (US) (stream) ruisseau m

creep vi (a) to ~ in/out ⟨person⟩ entrer/sortir à pas de loup; to ~ under sth se glisser sous qch; to ~ along ⟨vehicle⟩ avancer lentement; ⟨insect, cat⟩ ramper
(b) ⟨plant⟩ grimper

creeper n (in jungle) liane f; (climbing plant) plante f grimpante

creepy adj (colloq) qui donne la chair de poule

creepy-crawly n (colloq) bestiole f (colloq)

cremate vtr incinérer

cremation n (a) (ceremony) crémation f
(b) (practice) incinération f

crematorium n (GB) crématorium m

crepe, **crêpe** n crêpe m

crescent n croissant m

crescent moon n croissant m de (la) lune

cress n cresson m

crest n (a) (ridge) crête f
(b) (coat of arms) armoiries fpl

Crete pr n Crète f

Creutzfeldt-Jacob disease, **CJD** n maladie f de Creutzfeldt-Jacob

crevice n fissure f

crew n (a) (on ship, plane) équipage m
(b) (on film, radio) équipe f

crewcut n coupe f (de cheveux) en brosse

crew neck sweater n pull m ras du cou

crib ① n (cot) lit m d'enfant
② vi copier (from sur)

crick n a ~ in one's neck un torticolis

cricket n (a) (insect) grillon m
(b) (game) cricket m

cricketer n joueur m de cricket

crime n (a) (minor) délit m; (serious) crime m (against contre)
(b) (phenomenon) criminalité f

criminal n, adj criminel/-elle (m/f)

criminal record n casier m judiciaire; to have a/no ~ avoir un casier judiciaire chargé/vierge

crimson ① n cramoisi m
② adj pourpre

cringe vi (a) (in fear) avoir un mouvement de recul
(b) (with embarrassment) avoir envie de rentrer sous terre

cripple ① n impotent/-e m/f
② vtr (a) estropier; ~d for life infirme à vie
(b) paralyser ⟨country, industry⟩

crisis n crise f (in dans; over à cause de)

crisp adj ⟨biscuit⟩ croustillant/-e; ⟨fruit⟩ croquant/-e; ⟨garment⟩ frais/fraîche; ⟨banknote, snow⟩ craquant/-e; ⟨air⟩ vif/vive; ⟨manner⟩ brusque

crispbread n pain m grillé suédois

crisps n pl (also **potato** ~) chips fpl

crisscross ① adj ⟨pattern⟩ en croisillons
② vi s'entrecroiser

criterion n critère m (for de)

critic n (a) (reviewer) critique m
(b) (opponent) détracteur/-trice m/f

critical adj ⟨point, condition, remark⟩ critique; ⟨stage⟩ crucial/-e; ⟨moment⟩ décisif/-ive; to be ~ of sb/sth critiquer qn/qch

critically adv (a) ⟨examine⟩ d'un œil critique
(b) ⟨ill⟩ très gravement

criticism n critique f

criticize vtr, vi critiquer

croak vi ⟨frog⟩ coasser

Croatia pr n Croatie f

crochet vtr faire [qch] au crochet; a ~(ed) sweater un pull au crochet

crockery n vaisselle f

crocodile n crocodile m

croissant n croissant m

crony n (petit/-e) copain/copine m/f

crook n (a) (person) escroc m
(b) (shepherd's) houlette f
(c) (of arm) creux m
IDIOMS by hook or by ~ coûte que coûte

crooked adj (a) ⟨line⟩ brisé/-e; ⟨picture, teeth, beam⟩ de travers
(b) (colloq) (dishonest) malhonnête

crop n (a) (produce) culture f; (harvest) récolte f
(b) (whip) cravache f

■ **crop up** ⟨matter, problem⟩ surgir; ⟨name⟩ être mentionné/-e; ⟨opportunity⟩ se présenter

cross ① n (a) croix f; to put a ~ against cocher ⟨name, item⟩
(b) (hybrid) croisement m
② adj (angry) fâché/-e (with contre); to get ~ se fâcher
③ vtr (a) (gen) traverser; franchir ⟨border, line⟩; it ~ed his mind that il lui est venu à l'esprit or l'idée que; to ~ one's legs croiser les jambes
(b) (intersect) couper
(c) barrer ⟨cheque⟩
④ vi se croiser

■ **cross off**, **cross out** barrer, rayer ⟨name, item⟩

cross-border adj trans-frontalier/-ière

cross-Channel adj trans-Manche

cross-check vtr, vi revérifier

cross-country n (a) (running) cross m
(b) (skiing) ski m de fond

cross cultural adj inter-culturel/-elle

cross-examine vtr (gen) interroger; (Law) faire subir un contre-interrogatoire à

cross-eyed adj ⟨person⟩ atteint/-e de strabisme; to be ~ loucher, avoir un strabisme

crossfire n feux mpl croisés; to get caught in the ~ être pris/-e entre deux feux

crossing n (a) (journey) traversée f

(b) (on road) passage *m* clouté; (level crossing) passage *m* à niveau

cross-legged *adv* ⟨*sit*⟩ en tailleur

cross-purposes *n pl* **we are at ∼** il y a un malentendu; (disagreement) nous sommes en désaccord

cross-reference *n* renvoi *m* (**to** à)

crossroads *n* carrefour *m*

cross-section *n* échantillon *m* (**of** de)

crossword *n* (also ∼ **puzzle**) mots *mpl* croisés

crotch *n* **(a)** (of body) entrecuisse *m*
(b) (in trousers) entrejambe *m*

crotchet *n* (GB) noire *f*

crouch *vi* (also ∼ **down**) ⟨*person*⟩ s'accroupir; (to spring) ⟨*animal*⟩ se ramasser

crow **1** *n* corbeau *m*
2 *vi* **(a)** (exult) exulter
(b) ⟨*cock*⟩ chanter
IDIOMS **as the ∼ flies** à vol d'oiseau

crowbar *n* pince-monseigneur *f*

crowd **1** *n* foule *f*; (watching sport, play) spectateurs *mpl*
2 *vtr* **(a)** entasser ⟨*people, furniture*⟩ (**into** dans)
(b) encombrer ⟨*room, house*⟩ (**with** de)
3 *vi* **to ∼ into** s'entasser dans ⟨*room, lift, vehicle*⟩

crowded *adj* **(a)** ⟨*place*⟩ plein/-e de monde; (jam-packed) bondé/-e; **to be ∼ with** être plein/-e de
(b) ⟨*schedule*⟩ chargé/-e

crowd-puller *n* (event) grosse attraction *f*

crown **1** *n* **(a)** (of monarch) couronne *f*
(b) (of hill) crête *f*; (of head) crâne *m*
(c) (on tooth) couronne *f*
2 *vtr* couronner

Crown court *n* (GB) ≈ cour *f* d'assises

crown jewels *n pl* joyaux *mpl* de la Couronne

crown prince *n* prince *m* héritier

crow's nest *n* nid *m* de pie

crucial *adj* crucial/-e

crucifix *n* crucifix *m*

crude *adj* **(a)** ⟨*method*⟩ rudimentaire; ⟨*estimate*⟩ approximatif/-ive
(b) ⟨*joke*⟩ grossier/-ière; ⟨*person*⟩ vulgaire
(c) (unprocessed) brut/-e; ∼ **oil** pétrole *m* brut

cruel *adj* cruel/-elle

cruelty *n* cruauté *f* (**to** envers)

cruise **1** *n* croisière *f*; **to go on a ∼** faire une croisière
2 *vtr* ⟨*driver, taxi*⟩ parcourir ⟨*street, city*⟩
3 *vi* ⟨*ship*⟩ croiser; ⟨*plane*⟩ voler

cruise missile *n* missile *m* de croisière

cruiser *n* **(a)** (cabin cruiser) petit bateau *m* de croisière
(b) (Mil) croiseur *m*

crumb *n* miette *f*

crumble **1** *vtr* émietter ⟨*bread*⟩
2 *vi* **(a)** ⟨*rock*⟩ s'effriter; ⟨*building*⟩ se délabrer

(b) ⟨*relationship, economy*⟩ se désagréger; ⟨*opposition*⟩ s'effondrer

crummy *adj* (colloq) **(a)** (substandard) minable (colloq)
(b) (unwell) **to feel ∼** se sentir patraque (colloq)

crumple *vtr* froisser ⟨*paper*⟩; **to ∼ sth into a ball** rouler qch en boule

crunch *vtr* croquer ⟨*apple, biscuit*⟩
IDIOMS **when** *or* **if it comes to the ∼** au moment crucial

crunchy *adj* croquant/-e

crusade *n* croisade *f*

crush **1** *n* bousculade *f*
2 *vtr* **(a)** écraser ⟨*can, fruit, person, vehicle*⟩ (**against** contre); broyer ⟨*arm, leg*⟩; piler ⟨*ice*⟩
(b) écraser ⟨*enemy, uprising*⟩; étouffer ⟨*protest*⟩
(c) chiffonner ⟨*garment, fabric*⟩

crushing *adj* ⟨*defeat, weight*⟩ écrasant/-e; ⟨*blow*⟩ percutant/-e; **a ∼ setback** un revers cuisant

crust *n* (gen) croûte *f*; **the earth's ∼** l'écorce *f* terrestre

crutch *n* béquille *f*

crux *n* **the ∼ of the matter** le point crucial

cry **1** *n* cri *m*
2 *vi* pleurer (**about** à cause de); **to ∼ with laughter** rire aux larmes
■ **cry out** **(a)** (with pain, grief) pousser un cri *or* des cris
(b) (call) crier, s'écrier
■ **cry off** (GB) (cancel) se décommander

cryogenics *n* cryogénie *f*

crypt *n* crypte *f*

cryptic *adj* ⟨*remark*⟩ énigmatique; ⟨*crossword*⟩ crypté/-e

crystal *n* cristal *m*

crystal ball *n* boule *f* de cristal

crystal clear *adj* **(a)** ⟨*water*⟩ cristallin/-e be a
(b) (obvious) clair/-e comme de l'eau de roche

CS gas *n* gaz *m* lacrymogène

cub *n* (Zool) petit *m*

Cuba *pr n* Cuba *f*

cubby-hole *n* (colloq) cagibi *m* (colloq)

cube **1** *n* (gen) cube *m*; **ice ∼** glaçon *m*
2 *vtr* couper ⟨qch⟩ en cubes ⟨*meat*⟩

cubic *adj* **(a)** cubique
(b) ⟨*metre, centimetre*⟩ cube

cubicle *n* (in changing room) cabine *f*; (in public toilets) cabinet *m*

cuckoo *n* coucou *m*

cucumber *n* concombre *m*

cuddle **1** *n* câlin *m*; **to give sb a ∼** faire un câlin à qn
2 *vtr* câliner

cuddly toy *n* (GB) peluche *f*

cue *n* **(a)** (line) réplique *f*; (action) signal *m*
(b) (Sport) queue *f* de billard

cuff *n* **(a)** poignet *m*
(b) (US) (on trousers) revers *m* ⋯⟩

IDIOMS off the ~ au pied levé

cuff link n bouton m de manchette

cul-de-sac n impasse f, cul-de-sac m

culinary adj culinaire

cull ① n massacre m
② vtr massacrer ⟨seals, whales⟩

culminate vtr aboutir (in à)

culottes n pl jupe-culotte f

culprit n coupable mf

cult ① n culte m; (contemporary religion) secte f
② adj a ~ film un film-culte; to be a ~
figure faire l'objet d'un culte

cultivate vtr cultiver

cultural adj culturel/-elle

cultural attaché n attaché-e m/f
culturel/-elle

culture n culture f

cultured adj cultivé-e; ⟨pearl⟩ de culture

culture shock n choc m culturel

culture vulture n (colloq) fana mf de
culture (colloq)

cumbersome adj encombrant/-e

cumulative adj cumulatif/-ive

cunning ① n (a) (of person) ruse f; (nastier)
fourberie f
② adj (a) ⟨person⟩ rusé-e; (nastier) fourbe
(b) ⟨trick⟩ habile; ⟨device⟩ astucieux/-ieuse

cup ① n (a) tasse f
(b) (trophy) coupe f
② vtr to ~ sth in one's hands prendre qch
dans le creux de ses mains

cupboard n placard m

curable adj guérissable

curate n vicaire m

curator n conservateur/-trice m/f

curb ① n (a) restriction f (on à)
(b) (US) (sidewalk) bord m du trottoir
② vtr refréner ⟨desires⟩; limiter ⟨powers⟩;
juguler ⟨spending⟩; restreindre
⟨consumption⟩

curdle vi ⟨milk⟩ se cailler; ⟨sauce⟩ tourner

cure ① n remède m (for à)
② vtr (a) (gen) guérir (of de)
(b) (Culin) (dry) sécher; (salt) saler; (smoke)
fumer

cure-all n panacée f (for contre)

curfew n couvre-feu m; ten o'clock ~
couvre-feu à partir de dix heures

curio n curiosité f, objet m rare

curiosity n curiosité f (about sur, au sujet
de); out of ~ par curiosité

curious adj curieux/-ieuse

curiously adv ⟨silent, detached⟩
étrangement; ~ enough chose assez curieuse

curl ① n boucle f
② vtr friser ⟨hair⟩
③ vi (a) ⟨hair⟩ friser
(b) (also ~ up) ⟨paper⟩ (se) gondoler; ⟨edges,
leaf⟩ se racornir
■ curl up ⟨person⟩ se pelotonner; ⟨cat⟩ se
mettre en rond; to ~ up in bed se blottir
dans son lit

curler n bigoudi m

curly adj ⟨hair⟩ (tight curls) frisé-e; (loose
curls) bouclé-e; ⟨tail, eyelashes⟩ recourbé-e

currant n raisin m de Corinthe

currency n monnaie f, devise f

current ① n courant m
② adj ⟨leader, situation, policy⟩ actuel/-elle;
⟨year, research⟩ en cours

current account n (GB) compte m
courant

current affairs n actualité f

currently adv actuellement, en ce moment

curriculum n programme m; in the ~ au
programme

curriculum vitae n curriculum vitae m

curry ① n curry m; chicken ~ curry de
poulet
② vtr to ~ favour chercher à se faire bien
voir (with sb de qn)

curse ① n (a) (scourge) fléau m
(b) (swearword) juron m
(c) (spell) malédiction f
② vtr maudire
③ vi jurer (at après)

cursor n curseur m

curt adj sec/sèche

curtail vtr (restrict) mettre une entrave à; (cut
back) réduire

curtain n rideau m

curtsey ① n révérence f
② vi faire la révérence (to à)

curve ① n courbe f
② vi ⟨line, wall⟩ s'incurver; ⟨road, railway⟩
faire une courbe

cushion ① n coussin m
② vtr amortir

cushy adj (colloq) peinard-e (colloq)

custard n (GB) (creamy) ≈ crème f anglaise

custodial sentence n peine f de prison

custodian n (of collection) gardien/-ienne
m/f; (in museum) conservateur/-trice m/f

custody n (a) (detention) détention f; to take
sb into ~ arrêter qn
(b) (of child) garde f

custom n (a) coutume f, usage m
(b) (customers) clientèle f

customary adj habituel/-elle; (more formal)
coutumier/-ière

customer n client/-e m/f

customer services n service m
clientèle

customize vtr fabriquer [qch] sur
commande ⟨car⟩

custom-made adj ⟨clothes⟩ fait-e sur
mesure

customs n douane f; to go through ~
passer à la douane

customs duties n pl droits mpl de
douane

customs hall n douane f

customs officer, **customs official**
n douanier/-ière m/f

cut $\boxed{1}$ *n* **(a)** (incision) entaille *f*; (in surgery) incision *f*
(b) (wound) coupure *f*
(c) (hairstyle) coupe *f*
(d) (colloq) (share) part *f*
(e) (reduction) réduction *f* (in de); job ~s suppression *f* d'emplois; **a ~ in salary** une baisse de salaire
$\boxed{2}$ *vtr* **(a)** (gen) couper; **to ~ oneself** se couper; **to ~ one's finger** se couper le doigt; **to have one's hair cut** se faire couper les cheveux
(b) tailler ⟨gem, suit, marble⟩; ⟨locksmith⟩ faire ⟨key⟩
(c) (edit) couper ⟨article, film⟩; supprimer ⟨scene⟩
(d) (reduce) réduire ⟨cost, inflation, list⟩ (by de); baisser ⟨price⟩
(e) to ~ a tooth percer une dent
(f) (record) faire, graver ⟨album⟩
(g) (Comput) couper ⟨text⟩
$\boxed{3}$ *vi* **(a)** (with knife, scissors) couper; **to ~ into** entamer ⟨cake⟩; couper ⟨fabric, paper⟩; inciser ⟨flesh⟩
(b) to ~ down a sidestreet couper par une petite rue
IDIOMS to ~ sb dead ignorer complètement qn
■ **cut back**: ¶ ~ **back** faire des économies
¶ ~ **[sth] back (a)** (reduce) réduire (**to** à)
(b) (prune) tailler
■ **cut down**: ¶ ~ **down** réduire sa consommation; **to ~ down on smoking** fumer moins; ¶ ~ **[sth] down (a)** (chop down) abattre
(b) (reduce) réduire
■ **cut off (a)** couper ⟨hair, piece, corner⟩; enlever ⟨excess, crusts⟩; amputer ⟨limb⟩
(b) (disconnect) couper ⟨mains service⟩
(c) to ~ off sb's allowance couper les vivres à qn
(d) to ~ sb off (on phone) couper qn; (interrupt) interrompre qn
(e) to feel ~ off se sentir isolé/-e
■ **cut out**: ¶ ~ **out** ⟨engine, fan⟩ s'arrêter
¶ ~ **[sth] out (a)** découper ⟨article, picture⟩ (**from** dans)
(b) (colloq) ~ **it out!** ça suffit!
■ **cut short** abréger ⟨holiday, discussion⟩
■ **cut up** couper
cut and paste *n* couper-coller *m*
cutback *n* réduction *f*; ~**s in** réductions dans le budget de ⟨defence, health⟩; **government** ~**s** réductions budgétaires du gouvernement

cute *adj* (colloq) **(a)** mignon/-onne
(b) (US) (clever) malin/-igne
cutlery *n* couverts *mpl*
cutlet *n* côtelette *f*
cut-off $\boxed{1}$ *n* (upper limit) limite *f*
$\boxed{2}$ **cut-offs** *n pl* jean *m* coupé
cut-price (GB), **cut-rate** (US) *adj* à prix réduit
cut-throat *adj* ⟨competition⟩ acharné/-e; **a ~ business** un milieu très dur
cutting $\boxed{1}$ *n* **(a)** (from newspaper) coupure *f* (**from** de)
(b) (in film-making) montage *m*
$\boxed{2}$ *adj* ⟨tone⟩ cassant/-e; ⟨remark⟩ désobligeant/-e
cutting edge *n* **to be at the ~ of** être à l'avant-garde de
CV, cv *n* (*abbr* = **curriculum vitae**) cv, CV *m*
cyanide *n* cyanure *m*
cybercafe *n* cybercafé *m*
cyberculture *n* cyberculture *f*
cyberspace *n* cyberespace *m*
cycle $\boxed{1}$ *n* **(a)** cycle *m*
(b) (bicycle) vélo *m*
$\boxed{2}$ *vi* faire du vélo
cycle lane *n* piste *f* cyclable
cycle race *n* course *f* cycliste
cycling *n* cyclisme *m*
cycling shorts *n pl* cuissard *m*
cyclist *n* (gen) cycliste *mf*; (Sport) coureur/-euse *m/f* cycliste
cyclone *n* cyclone *m*
cygnet *n* jeune cygne *m*
cylinder *n* **(a)** (in engine) cylindre *m*
(b) (of gas) bouteille *f*
(c) (GB) (*also* **hot water ~**) ballon *m* d'eau chaude
cynic *n* cynique *mf*
cynical *adj* cynique
cynicism *n* cynisme *m*
Cyprus *pr n* Chypre *f*
cyst *n* kyste *m*
Czech $\boxed{1}$ *n* **(a)** (person) Tchèque *mf*
(b) (language) tchèque *m*
$\boxed{2}$ *adj* tchèque
Czech Republic *pr n* République *f* tchèque

Dd

d, D *n* (a) (letter) d, D *m*
(b) **D** (Mus) ré *m*

dab ① *n* (of paint) touche *f*; (of butter) petit morceau *m*
② *vtr* tamponner ⟨*stain*⟩ (with de); **to ~ one's eyes** se tamponner les yeux

dabble *v* ■ **dabble in** faire [qch] en amateur ⟨*painting, politics*⟩

dachshund *n* teckel *m*

dad, Dad *n* (colloq) papa *m* (colloq) ; père *m*

daddy, Daddy *n* (colloq) papa *m* (colloq)

daffodil *n* jonquille *f*

daft *adj* (colloq) bête

dagger *n* poignard *m*
IDIOMS **to look ~s at sb** fusiller qn du regard

daily ① *n* (newspaper) quotidien *m*
② *adj* ⟨*visit, routine*⟩ quotidien/-ienne;
on a ~ basis tous les jours
(b) ⟨*wage, rate*⟩ journalier/-ière
③ *adv* quotidiennement; **twice ~** deux fois par jour

dainty *adj* ⟨*porcelain, handkerchief*⟩ délicat/-e; ⟨*shoe, hand, foot*⟩ mignon/-onne

dairy ① *n* (a) (on farm) laiterie *f*; (shop) crémerie *f*
(b) (company) société *f* laitière
② *adj* ⟨*butter*⟩ fermier/-ière; ⟨*cow, farm, product, cream*⟩ laitier/-ière

daisy *n* (common) pâquerette *f*; (garden) marguerite *f*
IDIOMS **to be as fresh as a ~** être frais/fraîche comme un gardon

dam *n* barrage *m*

damage ① *n* (a) (gen) dégâts *mpl* (to causés à)
(b) (Med) **brain ~** lésions *fpl* cérébrales
(c) (figurative) **to do ~ to** porter atteinte à; **the ~ is done** le mal est fait
② *vtr* (a) endommager ⟨*building*⟩; nuire à ⟨*environment, health*⟩; **to ~ one's eyesight** s'abîmer les yeux
(b) porter atteinte à ⟨*reputation*⟩

damages *n pl* (Law) dommages-intérêts *mpl*

damaging *adj* (to reputation, person) préjudiciable; ⟨*effect*⟩ préjudiciable; (to health, environment) nuisible (to pour)

damn (colloq) ① *n* **not to give a ~ about sb/sth** se ficher (colloq) éperdument de qn/qch
② *adj* (also **damned**) ⟨*key, car*⟩ fichu/-e (colloq) (before *n*)
③ *excl*! merde! (colloq), zut! (colloq)

damp ① *n* humidité *f*
② *adj* ⟨*clothes, house*⟩ humide; ⟨*skin*⟩ moite

dampen *vtr* (a) humecter ⟨*cloth*⟩

(b) refroidir ⟨*enthusiasm*⟩

damson *n* prune *f* (de Damas)

dance ① *n* (gen) danse *f*; (social occasion) soirée *f* dansante
② *vi* (a) ⟨*person*⟩ danser (with avec)
(b) ⟨*eyes*⟩ briller (with de)
■ **dance about, dance up and down** sautiller sur place

dancer *n* danseur/-euse *m/f*

dancing *n* danse *f*

dandruff *n* pellicules *fpl*

danger *n* danger *m* (of de; to pour); **to be in ~** être en danger; **to be in ~ of doing** risquer de faire

danger list *n* **on the ~** dans un état critique

dangerous *adj* dangereux/-euse (**for** pour; **to do** de faire)
IDIOMS **to be on ~ ground** avancer en terrain miné

dangerously *adv* (gen) dangereusement; ⟨*ill*⟩ gravement; **to live ~** prendre des risques

danger signal *n* signal *m* de danger

dangle ① *vtr* balancer ⟨*puppet, keys*⟩; laisser pendre ⟨*legs*⟩
② *vi* ⟨*puppet, keys*⟩ se balancer (from à); ⟨*earrings*⟩ pendiller; ⟨*legs*⟩ pendre

Danish ① *n* (language) danois *m*
② *adj* (gen) danois/-e; ⟨*embassy*⟩ du Danemark

dare ① *n* défi *m*
② *modal aux* oser; **to ~ (to) do** oser faire; **I ~ say** c'est bien possible
③ *vtr* **to ~ sb to do** défier qn de faire; **I ~ you!** chiche que tu ne le fais pas! (colloq)

daredevil *n, adj* casse-cou (*mf*) *inv*

daring *adj* (a) (courageous, novel) audacieux/-ieuse
(b) ⟨*suggestion, dress*⟩ osé/-e

dark ① *n* **in the ~** dans le noir *or* l'obscurité; **before ~** avant la (tombée de la) nuit; **after ~** après la tombée de la nuit
② *adj* (a) ⟨*room, alley, day, sky*⟩ sombre; **it is getting ~** il commence à faire noir *or* nuit; **it's ~** il fait noir *or* nuit
(b) ⟨*colour, suit*⟩ sombre; **a ~ blue dress** une robe bleu foncé
(c) ⟨*hair, complexion*⟩ brun/-e
(d) ⟨*secret, thought*⟩ noir/-e (before *n*)
IDIOMS **to be in the ~** être dans le noir; **to leave sb in the ~** laisser qn dans l'ignorance; **to keep sb in the ~ about sth** cacher qch à qn

darken ① *vtr* (a) obscurcir ⟨*sky, landscape*⟩; assombrir ⟨*house*⟩
(b) foncer ⟨*colour*⟩

d

2 *vi* **(a)** ‹*sky, room*› s'obscurcir
(b) (in colour) foncer; ‹*skin*› brunir

dark glasses *n pl* lunettes *fpl* noires

darkness *n* obscurité *f*; **in ~** dans l'obscurité

darkroom *n* chambre *f* noire

dark-skinned *adj* basané/-e

darling *n* **(a)** (my) **~** (to loved one) chéri/-e *m/f*; (to child) mon chou (colloq); (to acquaintance) mon cher/ma chère *m/f*
(b) (kind, lovable person) amour *m*, ange *m*

darn *vtr* repriser

dart *n* fléchette *f*; **to play ~s** jouer aux fléchettes

dartboard *n* cible *f*

dash **1** *n* **(a)** (rush) course *f* folle; **it was a mad ~** on a dû se presser
(b) (small amount) (of liquid) goutte *f*; (of powder) pincée *f*; (of colour) touche *f*
(c) (punctuation) tiret *m*
2 *vtr* **(a)** **to ~ sb/sth against** projeter qn/qch contre ‹*rocks*›
(b) anéantir ‹*hopes*›
3 *vi* se précipiter (into dans); **to ~ out of** sortir en courant de ‹*shop, room*›
■ **dash off**: ¶ **~ off** se sauver; ¶ **~ [sth] off** écrire [qch] en vitesse

dashboard *n* tableau *m* de bord

data *n pl* données *fpl*

database *n* base *f* de données

data entry *n* introduction *f* de données

data processing *n* (procedure) traitement *m* des données; (career) informatique *f*; (department) service *m* informatique

data protection *n* protection *f* de l'information

data security *n* sécurité *f* des données

data storage device *n* périphérique *m* de stockage

date **1** *n* **(a)** date *f*; **~ of birth** date de naissance; **what's the ~ today?** on est le combien aujourd'hui?; **at a later ~, at some future ~** plus tard
(b) (on coin) millésime *m*
(c) (meeting) rendez-vous *m*; **to have a lunch ~** être pris/-e à déjeuner
(d) who's your ~ for tonight? avec qui sors-tu ce soir?
(e) (fruit) datte *f*
2 *vtr* **(a)** (gen) dater
(b) sortir avec ‹*person*›
3 *vi* **to ~ from** or **back to** ‹*building*› dater de; ‹*problem, friendship*› remonter à
4 **to date** *phr* à ce jour, jusqu'ici

dated *adj* ‹*clothes, style*› démodé/-e; ‹*idea, custom*› dépassé/-e; ‹*language*› vieilli/-e; **the film seems ~ now** le film a mal vieilli

date rape *n* viol *m* (*au cours d'une sortie en tête à tête*)

dating agency *n* club *m* de rencontres

daughter *n* fille *f*

daughter-in-law *n* belle-fille *f*, bru *f*

daunting *adj* ‹*task, prospect*› décourageant/-e; ‹*person*› intimidant/-e

dawdle *vi* flâner, traînasser (colloq)

dawn **1** *n* aube *f*; **at ~** à l'aube; **at the crack of ~** à l'aube
2 *vi* **(a)** ‹*day*› se lever
(b) **it ~ed on me that** je me suis rendu compte que; **it suddenly ~ed on her why** elle a soudain compris pourquoi

dawn raid *n* descente *f* de police très tôt le matin

day *n* **(a)** jour *m*; **what ~ is it today?** quel jour sommes-nous aujourd'hui? **every ~** tous les jours; **every other ~** tous les deux jours; **from ~ to ~** ‹*live*› au jour le jour; ‹*change*› d'un jour à l'autre; **the ~ when** or **that** le jour où; **the ~ after** le lendemain; **the ~ before** la veille; **the ~ before yesterday** avant-hier; **the ~ after tomorrow** après-demain
(b) (with emphasis on duration) journée *f*; **all ~** toute la journée; **during the ~** pendant la journée
(c) (age, period) époque *f*; **in those ~s** à cette époque; **these ~s** ces temps-ci
IDIOMS **those were the ~s** c'était le bon temps; **that'll be the ~!** je voudrais voir ça!; **to call it a ~** s'arrêter là; **to save the ~** sauver la situation

daybreak *n* aube *f*

day-care *n* (for children) service *m* de garderie

daydream **1** *n* rêves *mpl*
2 *vi* rêvasser

daylight *n* **(a)** (light) jour *m*, lumière *f* du jour; **it was still ~** il faisait encore jour
(b) (dawn) lever *m* du jour, point *m* du jour

daylight robbery *n* (colloq) **it's ~!** c'est de l'arnaque! (colloq)

day nursery *n* garderie *f*

day release *n* formation *f* permanente

day return *n* (GB) aller-retour *m* valable une journée

daytime *n* journée *f*

day-to-day *adj* quotidien/-ienne

day-trip *n* excursion *f* pour la journée

daze *n* **in a ~** (from news) ahuri/-e; (from blow) étourdi/-e; (from drugs) hébété/-e

dazed *adj* (by news) ahuri/-e; (by blow) étourdi/-e

dazzle *vtr* éblouir; **to ~ sb with** éblouir qn par ‹*beauty, knowledge*›

dazzling *adj* éblouissant/-e

D-day *n* **(a)** (important day) jour *m* J
(b) (Mil) le 6 juin 1944 (*jour du débarquement des Alliés en Normandie*)

dead **1** *n* **(a)** **the ~** les morts *mpl*
(b) **at ~ of night** en pleine nuit; **in the ~ of winter** en plein hiver
2 *adj* mort/-e; **the ~ man/woman** le mort/la morte; **a ~ body** un cadavre; **to drop (down) ~** tomber raide mort/-e; **the phone went ~** la ligne a été coupée
3 *adv* (GB) ‹*certain, straight*› absolument; ⸱⸱⸱▸

~ **on time** pile (colloq) à l'heure; ~ **easy** (colloq) simple comme bonjour (colloq); **they were ~ lucky!** (colloq) ils ont eu du pot! (colloq); ~ **tired** (colloq) crevé/-e (colloq), claqué/-e (colloq); **to be ~ set on doing** être tout à fait décidé/-e à faire; **to stop ~** s'arrêter net

deaden *vtr* calmer ⟨*pain*⟩; amortir ⟨*blow*⟩; assourdir ⟨*sound*⟩

dead end 1 *n* impasse *f*
2 **dead-end** *adj* ⟨*job*⟩ sans perspectives

dead heat *n* (in athletics) arrivée *f* ex-aequo; (in horseracing) dead-heat *m inv*

deadline *n* date *f* or heure *f* limite, délai *m*; **to meet a ~** respecter un délai

deadlock *n* impasse *f*; **to reach (a) ~** aboutir à une impasse

dead loss *n* (colloq) **to be a ~** être nul/ nulle (colloq)

deadly 1 *adj* **(a)** ⟨*poison, enemy*⟩ mortel/-elle
(b) in ~ earnest avec le plus grand sérieux
2 *adv* ⟨*dull, boring*⟩ terriblement

deadpan *adj* ⟨*humour*⟩ pince-sans-rire *inv*

deaf 1 *n* **the ~** les sourds *mpl*, les malentendants *mpl*
2 *adj* **(a)** sourd/-e; **to go ~** devenir sourd/-e
(b) to turn a ~ ear to faire la sourde oreille à, rester sourd/-e à

deaf aid *n* (GB) prothèse *f* auditive

deafening *adj* assourdissant/-e

deaf without speech *adj* sourd-muet/ sourde-muette

deal 1 *n* **(a)** (agreement) accord *m*; (in business) affaire *f*; (with friend) marché *m*; **it's a ~!** marché conclu!
(b) a great *or* **good ~** beaucoup (of de)
2 *vtr* **(a)** porter ⟨*blow*⟩ (**to** à)
(b) distribuer ⟨*cards*⟩; donner ⟨*hand*⟩
3 *vi* **to ~ in** être dans le commerce de ⟨*commodity, shares*⟩
■ **deal with (a)** s'occuper de ⟨*problem, request*⟩
(b) traiter de ⟨*topic*⟩

dealer *n* **(a)** (in business) marchand/-e *m/f*; (large-scale) négociant/-e *m/f*
(b) (on stock exchange) opérateur/-trice *m/f*
(c) (in drugs) revendeur/-euse *m/f* de drogue, dealer *m* (colloq)
(d) (in cards) donneur/-euse *m/f*

dealing 1 *n* **(a)** (trading) vente *f*; **foreign exchange ~** opérations *fpl* de change; **share ~** transactions *fpl* boursières
(b) (trafficking) trafic *m*; **drug ~** le trafic de drogue
2 **dealings** *n pl* relations *fpl* (**with** avec)

dear 1 *n* **(my) ~** mon chéri/ma chérie *m/f*; (more formal) mon cher/ma chère *m/f*
2 *adj* **(a)** (gen) cher/chère; **he's my ~est friend** c'est mon meilleur ami; **to hold sb/sth ~** être attaché/-e à qn/qch, chérir qn/qch
(b) (in letter) cher/chère; **Dear Sir/Madam** Monsieur, Madame; **Dear Sirs** Messieurs;

~ **on time** pile (colloq) à l'heure; ~ **easy**

Dear Mr Jones Cher Monsieur; Dear Mr and Mrs Jones Cher Monsieur, Chère Madame; Dear Anne and Paul Chers Anne et Paul
3 *excl* **oh ~!** (dismay, surprise) oh mon Dieu!; (less serious) aïe!, oh là là!

death *n* mort *f*; (more formally) décès *m*; **to drink/to work oneself to ~** se tuer en buvant/au travail
IDIOMS **to be at ~'s door** être à l'article de la mort; **to frighten sb to ~** faire une peur bleue à qn (colloq); **to be bored to ~** (colloq) s'ennuyer à mourir; **I'm sick to ~ of this!** (colloq) j'en ai par-dessus la tête!

death camp *n* camp *m* de la mort

death penalty *n* peine *f* de mort

death row *n* quartier *m* des condamnés à mort

death sentence *n* condamnation *f* à mort

death threat *n* menaces *fpl* de mort

death toll *n* nombre *m* de morts

death trap *n* **to be a ~** être très dangereux/-euse

debar *vtr* **to ~red from doing** ne pas avoir le droit de faire

debatable *adj* discutable

debate *n* débat *m* (**on, about** sur); (informal discussion) discussion *f* (**about** à propos de); **to hold a ~ on** débattre de ⟨*issue*⟩

debauchery *n* débauche *f*

debit 1 *n* débit *m*
2 *vtr* débiter ⟨*account*⟩ (**with** de)

debit card *n* carte *f* bancaire (*sans paiement différé*)

debrief *vtr* interroger; **to be ~ed** ⟨*diplomat, agent*⟩ rendre compte (oralement) d'une mission; ⟨*defector, freed hostage*⟩ être interrogé/-e

debris *n* (of plane) débris *mpl*; (of building) décombres *mpl*; (rubbish) déchets *mpl*

debt *n* dette *f* (**to** envers); **to get into ~** s'endetter

debt collector *n* agent *m* de recouvrement

debtor *n* débiteur/-trice *m/f*

debug *vtr* déboguer ⟨*software*⟩

debut *n* débuts *mpl*

decade *n* décennie *f*

decadent *adj* décadent/-e

decaffeinated *adj* décaféiné/-e

decanter *n* (for wine, port) carafe *f* (à décanter); (for whisky) flacon *m* à whisky

decathlon *n* décathlon *m*

decay 1 *n* **(a)** (of vegetation, body) pourriture *f*; (of building) délabrement *m*
(b) tooth ~ carie *f* dentaire
(c) (of society) décadence *f*
2 *vi* ⟨*timber, vegetation*⟩ pourrir; ⟨*tooth*⟩ se carier; ⟨*building*⟩ se détériorer

deceased 1 *n* **the ~** le défunt/la défunte *m/f*
2 *adj* décédé/-e, défunt/-e

deceit *n* malhonnêteté *f*

deceitful adj malhonnête

deceive 1 vtr (a) tromper, duper ⟨friend⟩; to be ∼d être dupe
(b) tromper ⟨spouse, lover⟩
2 v refl to ∼ oneself se faire des illusions

December n décembre m

decency n (a) ⟨good manners⟩ politesse f
(b) ⟨propriety⟩ convenances fpl

decent adj (a) ⟨family, man, woman⟩ comme il faut, bien inv ⟨colloq⟩; **it's ∼ of him** c'est très gentil à lui
(b) ⟨adequate⟩ convenable
(c) ⟨good⟩ ⟨camera, education, result⟩ bon/ bonne ⟨before n⟩; ⟨profit⟩ appréciable; **to make a ∼ living** bien gagner sa vie
(d) ⟨behaviour, clothes, language⟩ décent/-e, correct/-e

decentralize vtr décentraliser

deception n duplicité f

deceptive adj trompeur/-euse

decide 1 vtr (a) **to ∼ to do** décider de faire; ⟨after much hesitation⟩ se décider à faire
(b) ⟨settle⟩ régler ⟨matter⟩; décider de ⟨fate, outcome⟩
2 vi décider; **to ∼ against** écarter ⟨plan, idea⟩; **to ∼ between** choisir, faire un choix entre ⟨applicants, books⟩
■ **decide on** (a) se décider pour ⟨hat, wallpaper⟩; fixer ⟨date⟩
(b) décider de ⟨course of action, size, budget⟩

deciduous adj ⟨tree⟩ à feuilles caduques

decimal adj ⟨system, currency⟩ décimal/-e; **∼ point** virgule f

decipher vtr déchiffrer

decision n décision f; **to make** or **take a ∼** prendre une décision

decision-maker n décideur/-euse m/f

decision-making n **to be good/bad at ∼** savoir/ne pas savoir prendre des décisions

decisive adj (a) ⟨manner, tone⟩ ferme
(b) ⟨battle, factor⟩ décisif/-ive; ⟨argument⟩ concluant/-e

deck n (a) ⟨on ship⟩ pont m; **on ∼** sur le pont; **below ∼(s)** sur le pont inférieur
(b) ⟨US⟩ ⟨terrace⟩ terrasse f
(c) **∼ of cards** jeu m de cartes
IDIOMS to clear the ∼s déblayer le terrain

deckchair n chaise f longue, transat m

declaration n déclaration f

declare vtr (a) déclarer ⟨that que⟩; annoncer ⟨intention, support⟩
(b) déclarer ⟨war⟩ ⟨on à⟩; proclamer ⟨independence⟩
(c) déclarer ⟨income⟩

decline 1 n (a) ⟨waning⟩ déclin m ⟨of de⟩; **to be in ∼** être sur le déclin
(b) ⟨drop⟩ baisse f ⟨in, of de⟩; **to be on the** or **in ∼** être en baisse
2 vi (a) ⟨drop⟩ ⟨demand, quality⟩ baisser ⟨by de⟩; ⟨support⟩ être en baisse
(b) ⟨wane⟩ être sur le déclin
(c) ⟨refuse⟩ refuser

decode vtr décoder ⟨code, message, signal⟩

decompose vi se décomposer

decompress vtr décomprimer, décompresser

decor n décoration f, ⟨in theatre⟩ décor m

decorate 1 vtr (a) décorer ⟨cake, tree⟩ ⟨with de, avec⟩
(b) **to ∼ a room** ⟨paint⟩ peindre une pièce; ⟨paper⟩ tapisser une pièce
2 vi faire des travaux de décoration

decoration n décoration f

decorative adj décoratif/-ive

decorator n peintre m, décorateur/-trice m/f

decoy 1 n leurre m
2 vtr attirer [qn] dans un piège

decrease 1 n diminution f ⟨in de⟩; ⟨in price⟩ baisse f ⟨in de⟩
2 vi ⟨population⟩ diminuer; ⟨price, popularity, rate⟩ baisser, diminuer

decreasing adj décroissant/-e

decree n (a) ⟨order⟩ décret m
(b) ⟨judgment⟩ jugement m, arrêt m

decrepit adj ⟨building⟩ délabré/-e; ⟨horse, old person⟩ décrépit/-e

decriminalize vtr décriminaliser, légaliser

dedicate vtr dédier ⟨book⟩ ⟨to à⟩; consacrer ⟨life⟩ ⟨to à⟩

dedicated adj ⟨teacher, mother, fan⟩ dévoué/-e; ⟨worker⟩ zélé/-e

dedication n (a) ⟨devotion⟩ dévouement m ⟨to à⟩; **∼ to duty** dévouement
(b) ⟨in a book, on music programme⟩ dédicace f

deduce vtr déduire ⟨that que⟩

deduct vtr prélever ⟨subscription, tax⟩ ⟨from sur⟩; déduire ⟨sum⟩ ⟨from de⟩

deduction n (a) ⟨from wages⟩ retenue f ⟨from sur⟩; ⟨of tax⟩ prélèvement m
(b) ⟨conclusion⟩ déduction f, conclusion f

deed n (a) ⟨action⟩ action f; **to do one's good ∼ for the day** faire sa bonne action or sa BA ⟨colloq⟩
(b) ⟨for property⟩ acte m de propriété

deep 1 adj (a) ⟨gen⟩ profond/-e; ⟨snow⟩ épais/épaisse; **a ∼-pile carpet** une moquette de haute laine; **how ∼ is the lake?** quelle est la profondeur du lac?; **the lake is 13 m ∼** le lac fait 13 m de profondeur
(b) ⟨dark⟩ ⟨colour⟩ intense; ⟨tan⟩ prononcé/-e; **∼ blue eyes** des yeux d'un bleu profond
(c) **to be ∼ in thought** être plongé/-e dans ses pensées; **to be ∼ in conversation** être en grande conversation
2 adv (a) ⟨dig, bury, cut⟩ profondément
(b) **∼ down** or **inside she was frightened** dans son for intérieur elle avait peur

deepen 1 vtr (a) creuser ⟨channel⟩
(b) approfondir ⟨knowledge, understanding⟩
2 vi (a) ⟨concern, love⟩ augmenter; ⟨knowledge⟩ s'approfondir; ⟨crisis⟩ s'aggraver; ⟨mystery⟩ s'épaissir; ⟨silence⟩ se faire plus profond
(b) ⟨voice⟩ devenir plus grave
(c) ⟨colour⟩ foncer

⋯⃗

3 **deepening** pres p adj ⟨mystery, need, rift⟩ croissant/-e; ⟨crisis⟩ de plus en plus grave; ⟨confusion⟩ de plus en plus grand/-e
deep-(fat-)fryer n friteuse f
deep-freeze n congélateur m
deep-fry vtr faire frire
deeply adv profondément
deep-rooted adj ⟨anxiety, prejudice⟩ profondément enraciné/-e
deep-sea adj ⟨diver, diving⟩ sous-marin/-e; ⟨fisherman, fishing⟩ hauturier/-ière
deer n (red) cerf m; (roe) chevreuil m; (fallow) daim m; (doe) biche f
de-escalate vtr faire baisser ⟨tension, violence⟩; désamorcer ⟨crisis⟩
deface vtr abîmer ⟨wall⟩; couvrir [qch] d'inscriptions, dégrader ⟨monument⟩
default **1** vi ne pas régler ses échéances
2 by default phr par défaut; **to win by ∼** gagner par forfait
defeat **1** n défaite f; **to admit ∼** ⟨team, troops⟩ concéder la défaite; ⟨person⟩ avouer son échec
2 vtr (a) vaincre ⟨enemy⟩; battre ⟨team, opposition, candidate⟩; **the government was ∼ed** le gouvernement a été mis en échec
(b) rejeter ⟨bill, proposal⟩
(c) **it ∼s me** ça me dépasse
defeatist n, adj défaitiste (mf)
defect **1** n (flaw) défaut m; (minor) imperfection f; **a speech ∼** un défaut d'élocution
2 vi faire défection; **to ∼ to the West** passer à l'Ouest
defective adj défectueux/-euse
defector n transfuge mf (from de)
defence (GB), **defense** (US) n (gen, Law, Sport) défense f; **in her ∼** à sa décharge
defenceless (GB), **defenseless** (US) adj ⟨person, animal⟩ sans défense; ⟨town, country⟩ sans défenses
defend vtr défendre ⟨fort, freedom, interests, title⟩; justifier ⟨behaviour, decision⟩
defendant n accusé/-e m/f
defender n défenseur m
defensive adj ⟨reaction, behaviour⟩ de défense; **to be (very) ∼** être sur la défensive
defer **1** vtr reporter ⟨meeting, decision⟩ (until à); remettre [qch] à plus tard ⟨departure⟩; différer ⟨payment⟩
2 vi **to ∼ to sb** s'incliner devant qn
deference n déférence f; **in ∼ to** par déférence pour
defiance n attitude f de défi
defiant adj ⟨person⟩ rebelle; ⟨behaviour⟩ provocant/-e
deficiency n (a) (shortage) insuffisance f (of, in de); (of vitamins) carence f (of en)
(b) (weakness) faiblesse f
deficient adj déficient/-e (in en)
deficit n déficit m
define vtr définir
definite adj ⟨plan, amount⟩ précis/-e;

⟨feeling, improvement, increase⟩ net/nette; ⟨decision, agreement⟩ ferme; **a ∼ answer** une réponse claire et nette; **nothing is ∼ yet** rien n'est encore sûr; **to be ∼ (sure)** être certain/-e (about de); (unyielding) être formel/-elle (about sur)
definitely adv sans aucun doute; **he ∼ said he wasn't coming** il a bien dit qu'il ne viendrait pas
definition n définition f
definitive adj définitif/-ive
deflate vtr dégonfler
deflationary adj déflationniste
deflect vtr (a) défléchir, dévier ⟨missile⟩
(b) détourner ⟨blame, criticism, attention⟩
deformed adj déformé/-e; (from birth) difforme
defraud vtr escroquer ⟨client, employer⟩; frauder ⟨tax office⟩
defrost **1** vtr décongeler ⟨food⟩; dégivrer ⟨refrigerator⟩
2 vi ⟨refrigerator⟩ dégivrer; ⟨food⟩ décongeler
deft adj adroit/-e de ses mains, habile
defunct adj défunt/-e
defuse vtr désamorcer
defy vtr (a) défier ⟨authority, person⟩
(b) **to ∼ sb to do** mettre qn au défi de faire
(c) défier ⟨description⟩; résister à ⟨efforts⟩
degenerate **1** adj dégénéré/-e
2 vi dégénérer
degrade vtr humilier ⟨person⟩
degrading adj ⟨conditions, film⟩ dégradant/-e; ⟨job⟩ avilissant/-e; ⟨treatment⟩ humiliant/-e
degree n (a) (measurement) degré m
(b) (from university) diplôme m universitaire; **first** or **bachelor's ∼** ≈ licence f
(c) **to such a ∼ that** à tel point que; **to a ∼, to some ∼** dans une certaine mesure; **by ∼s** petit à petit
(d) (US) **first ∼ murder** homicide m volontaire avec préméditation
degree ceremony n (GB Univ) cérémonie f de remise des diplômes
degree course n (GB Univ) programme m d'études universitaires
dehydrated adj déshydraté/-e; ⟨milk⟩ en poudre; **to become ∼** se déshydrater
de-icer n dégivrant m
deign vtr **to ∼ to do** condescendre à faire, daigner faire
deity n divinité f
dejected adj découragé/-e
delay **1** n (gen) retard m (of de; to, on sur); **a few minutes' ∼** un délai de quelques minutes; **without (further) ∼** sans (plus) tarder
2 vtr (a) différer ⟨decision, publication⟩; **to ∼ doing** attendre pour faire
(b) retarder ⟨train, arrival, post⟩
delayed adj **to be ∼** être retardé/-e
delegate **1** n délégué/-e m/f

2 *vtr* déléguer ⟨*responsibility, task*⟩ (**to** à)

delegation *n* délégation *f*

delete *vtr* supprimer (**from** de); (with pen) barrer; (on computer) effacer

delete key *n* touche *f* effacement

deliberate *adj* (a) (intentional) délibéré/-e; **it was ~** il/elle l'a fait etc exprès
(b) (measured) ⟨*movement*⟩ mesuré/-e

deliberately *adv* ⟨*do, say*⟩ exprès; ⟨*sarcastic, provocative*⟩ délibérément

delicacy *n* (a) (of object, situation) délicatesse *f*; (of mechanism) sensibilité *f*
(b) (food) (savoury) mets *m* raffiné; (sweet) friandise *f*

delicate *adj* (gen) délicat/-e; ⟨*features*⟩ fin/-e

delicatessen *n* (a) (shop) épicerie *f* fine
(b) (US) (eating-place) restaurant-traiteur *m*

delicious *adj* délicieux/-ieuse

delight **1** *n* joie *f*, plaisir *m*; **to take ~ in sth/in doing** prendre plaisir à qch/à faire
2 *vtr* ravir ⟨*person*⟩ (**with** par)

delighted *adj* ravi/-e (**at, by, with** de; **to do** de faire); **~ to meet you** enchanté

delightful *adj* charmant/-e

delinquency *n* délinquance *f*

delinquent *n, adj* délinquant/-e ⟨*m/f*⟩

delirious *adj* **to be ~** délirer

deliver **1** *vtr* (a) livrer ⟨*goods, groceries*⟩ (**to** à); distribuer ⟨*mail*⟩ (**to** à); remettre ⟨*note*⟩ (**to** à)
(b) mettre au monde ⟨*baby*⟩; délivrer ⟨*baby animal*⟩
(c) faire ⟨*speech*⟩; donner ⟨*ultimatum*⟩; rendre ⟨*verdict*⟩
2 *vi* ⟨*tradesman*⟩ livrer; ⟨*postman*⟩ distribuer le courrier

delivery *n* (a) (of goods, milk) livraison *f*; (of mail) distribution *f*; **on ~** à la livraison
(b) (of baby) accouchement *m*

delude *vtr* tromper; **to ~ oneself** se faire des illusions

deluge *n* déluge *m*

delusion *n* illusion *f*

demand **1** *n* (a) (gen) demande *f* (**for** de); **on ~** (gen) à la demande; ⟨*payable*⟩ à vue; **to be in ~** être très demandé/-e
(b) (pressure) exigence *f*
2 *vtr* (a) (request) demander ⟨*reform*⟩; (forcefully) exiger ⟨*ransom*⟩; réclamer ⟨*inquiry*⟩
(b) (require) demander ⟨*skill, time, patience*⟩ (**of sb** de qn); (more imperatively) exiger

demanding *adj* (a) ⟨*person*⟩ exigeant/-e
(b) ⟨*work, course*⟩ ardu/-e; ⟨*schedule*⟩ chargé/-e

demean *v refl* **to ~ oneself** s'abaisser

demeaning *adj* humiliant/-e

demented *adj* fou/folle

dementia *n* démence *f*

demerara (sugar) *n* sucre *m* roux cristallisé

demilitarize *vtr* démilitariser

demister *n* (GB) dispositif *m* antibuée

demo *n* (colloq) (a) (protest) manif *f* (colloq)
(b) (sample version) démo *f* (colloq), version *f* de démonstration

demobilize *vtr* démobiliser

democracy *n* démocratie *f*

democrat *n* démocrate *mf*

democratic *adj* démocratique

demolish *vtr* démolir

demolition *n* démolition *f*

demon *n* démon *m*

demonstrate **1** *vtr* (a) démontrer ⟨*theory, truth*⟩
(b) manifester ⟨*concern, support*⟩; montrer ⟨*skill*⟩
(c) faire la démonstration de ⟨*machine, product*⟩; **to ~ how to do** montrer comment faire
2 *vi* manifester (**for** en faveur de; **against** contre)

demonstration *n* (a) (march) manifestation *f* (**against** contre; **for** en faveur de)
(b) (of machine, theory) démonstration *f*

demonstrative *adj* démonstratif/-ive

demonstrator *n* manifestant/-e *m/f*

demoralize *vtr* démoraliser

demote *vtr* rétrograder

den *n* (a) (of lion) antre *m*; (of fox) tanière *f*
(b) (room) tanière *f*

denial *n* (of accusation, rumour) démenti *m*; (of guilt, rights, freedom) négation *f*

denim **1** *n* jean *m*; **~s** jean *m*
2 *adj* ⟨*jacket, skirt*⟩ en jean; **~ jeans** jean *m*

Denmark *pr n* Danemark *m*

denomination *n* (a) (name) dénomination *f*
(b) (faith) confession *f*
(c) (value) valeur *f*

denounce *vtr* (a) (inform on, criticize) dénoncer
(b) (accuse) accuser

dense *adj* dense

density *n* densité *f*

dent **1** *n* (in metal) bosse *f*
2 *vtr* cabosser ⟨*car*⟩

dental *adj* dentaire

dental floss *n* fil *m* dentaire

dental surgeon *n* chirurgien-dentiste *m*

dental surgery *n* (GB) (premises) cabinet *m* dentaire

dentist *n* dentiste *mf*

dentistry *n* médecine *f* dentaire

dentures *n pl* dentier *m*

deny *vtr* (a) démentir ⟨*rumour*⟩; nier ⟨*accusation*⟩; **to ~ doing** *or* **having done** nier avoir fait
(b) **to ~ sb sth** refuser qch à qn

deodorant *n* (personal) déodorant *m*; (for room) déodorisant *m*

depart *vi* (a) partir (**from** de; **for** pour)
(b) (deviate) **to ~ from** s'éloigner de

department n (a) (of company) service m
(b) (governmental) ministère m; (administrative)
service m; **social services** ~ services sociaux
(c) (in store) rayon m; **toy** ~ rayon jouets
(d) (in hospital) service m
(e) (in university) département m
(f) (in school) section f

departmental adj ⟨head, meeting⟩ de
service

department store n grand magasin m

departure n (of person, train) départ m; (from
truth, regulation) entorse f (**from** à); (from policy,
tradition) rupture f (**from** par rapport à)

departure gate n porte f de départ

departures board n tableau m des
départs

departure time n heure f de départ

depend vi **to** ~ **on** dépendre de, compter
sur (**for** pour); **to** ~ **on sb/sth to do** compter
sur qn/qch pour faire; **that** ~**s** cela dépend;
~**ing on the season** suivant la saison

dependable adj ⟨person⟩ digne de
confiance; ⟨machine⟩ fiable

dependant n personne f à charge

dependence, dependance (US) n (a)
(reliance) dépendance f (**on** vis-à-vis de)
(b) (addiction) dépendance f (**on** à)

dependent adj ⟨relative⟩ à charge; **to be**
~ (**up)on** (gen) dépendre de; (financially) vivre
à la charge de

depict vtr (visually) représenter; (in writing)
dépeindre (**as** comme)

depiction n peinture f, représentation f

deplete vtr réduire

deplorable adj déplorable

deplore vtr déplorer

deploy vtr déployer

depopulation n dépeuplement m

deport vtr expulser (**to** vers)

deportation n expulsion f

depose vtr déposer

deposit ⓵ n (a) (to bank account) dépôt m;
on ~ en dépôt
(b) (on house, hire purchase goods) versement m
initial (**on** sur); (on holiday, goods) acompte m,
arrhes fpl (**on** sur)
(c) (against damage, breakages) caution f
(d) (on bottle) consigne f
(e) (of silt, mud) dépôt m; (of coal, mineral)
gisement m
⓶ vtr déposer ⟨money⟩; **to** ~ **sth with sb**
confier qch à qn

deposit account n (GB) compte m de
dépôt

depot n (a) (gen) dépôt m
(b) (US) (station) (bus) gare f routière; (rail)
gare f ferroviaire

depress vtr (a) déprimer ⟨person⟩
(b) appuyer sur ⟨button⟩
(c) faire baisser ⟨prices⟩; affaiblir ⟨trading⟩

depressed adj (a) ⟨person⟩ déprimé/-e
(b) ⟨region, industry⟩ en déclin

depressing adj déprimant/-e

depression n dépression f; **to suffer from**
~ être dépressif/-ive

deprivation n (poverty) privations fpl

deprive vtr priver (**of** de)

deprived adj ⟨area, family⟩ démuni/-e;
⟨childhood⟩ malheureux/-euse

depth ⓵ n (a) (of hole, water) profondeur f;
(of layer) épaisseur f; **to be out of one's** ~ (in
water) ne plus avoir pied; (in situation) être
complètement perdu/-e
(b) (of colour, emotion) intensité f; (of crisis)
gravité f
(c) (of knowledge) étendue f; (of analysis, novel)
profondeur f; **to examine sth in** ~ examiner
qch en détail
⓶ **depths** n pl (of sea) profondeurs fpl; **in
the** ~**s of winter** au plus profond de l'hiver;
to be in the ~**s of despair** toucher le fond du
désespoir

deputize vi **to** ~ **for sb** remplacer qn

deputy ⓵ n (a) (aide) adjoint/-e m/f;
(replacement) remplaçant/-e m/f
(b) (politician) député m
⓶ adj adjoint/-e

deputy chairman n vice-président m

deputy president n vice-président m

derail vtr faire dérailler

deranged adj dérangé/-e

deregulate vtr libérer ⟨prices⟩; déréguler
⟨market⟩

derelict adj ⟨building⟩ délabré/-e

derision n moqueries fpl

derive vtr tirer ⟨benefit, income⟩ (**from** de)

derogatory adj désobligeant/-e (**about**
envers); ⟨term⟩ péjoratif/-ive

descend ⓵ vtr descendre ⟨steps, slope,
path⟩
⓶ vi (a) ⟨person, plane⟩ descendre (**from** de)
(b) ⟨rain, darkness, mist⟩ tomber (**on, over**
sur)
(c) **to** ~ **on sb** débarquer chez qn (colloq)
(d) **to be** ~**ed from** descendre de

descendant n descendant/-e m/f (**of** de)

descent n (a) descente f (**on, upon** sur)
(b) (extraction) descendance f

describe vtr décrire

description n description f (**of** de); (for
police) signalement m (**of** de)

descriptive adj descriptif/-ive

desecrate vtr profaner ⟨altar, shrine⟩

desert ⓵ n désert m
⓶ vtr abandonner ⟨person⟩ (**for** pour);
déserter ⟨cause⟩; abandonner ⟨post⟩
⓷ vi ⟨soldier⟩ déserter
IDIOMS **to get one's just** ~**s** avoir ce qu'on
mérite

desert boot n bottine f en croûte de cuir,
clarks® f inv

deserted adj désert/-e

deserter n déserteur m (**from** de)

desert island n île f déserte

deserve vtr mériter (**to do** de faire)

deserving *adj* ⟨*winner*⟩ méritant/-e; ⟨*cause*⟩ louable

design ⒈ *n* (a) (development) (of object, appliance) conception *f*; (of building, room) agencement *m*; (of clothing) création *f*
(b) (drawing, plan) plan *m* (for de)
(c) (art of designing) design *m*; (fashion) stylisme *m*
(d) (pattern) motif *m*; **a leaf** ~ un motif de feuilles
(e) (subject of study) arts *mpl* appliqués
⒉ *vtr* (a) ⟨*building, appliance*⟩; **to be** ~**ed for sth/to do** être conçu/-e pour qch/pour faire
(b) ⟨*designer*⟩ créer ⟨*costume, garment*⟩; dessiner ⟨*building, appliance*⟩

designate *vtr* **to** ~ **sb (as) sth** désigner qn (comme) qch; **to** ~ **sth (as) sth** classer qch (comme) qch; **to** ~ **sth for** destiner qch à

designer ⒈ *n* (gen) concepteur/-trice *m/f*; (of furniture, in fashion) créateur/-trice *m/f*; (of sets) décorateur/-trice *m/f*; **costume** ~ costumier/-ière *m/f*
⒉ *adj* ~ **clothes,** ~ **labels** vêtements *mpl* griffés; ~ **label** griffe *f*

design fault *n* faute *f* de conception

desirable *adj* (a) ⟨*outcome, solution*⟩ souhaitable; ⟨*area, position*⟩ convoité/-e; ⟨*job, gift*⟩ séduisant/-e
(b) (sexually) désirable

desire ⒈ *n* désir *m* (for de); **to have no** ~ **to do** n'avoir aucune envie de faire
⒉ *vtr* désirer; **it leaves a lot to be** ~**d** cela laisse beaucoup à désirer

desk *n* (a) bureau *m*; **writing** ~ secrétaire *m*
(b) (in classroom) (pupil's) table *f*; (teacher's) bureau *m*
(c) **reception** ~ réception *f*; **information** ~ bureau *m* de renseignements; **cash** ~ caisse *f*

desktop *n* (*also* ~ **computer**) ordinateur *m* de bureau

desktop publishing, DTP *n* micro-édition *f*, PAO *f*

desolate *adj* désolé/-e

despair ⒈ *n* désespoir *m*; **in** *or* **out of** ~ de désespoir
⒉ *vi* désespérer (**of** de; **of doing** de faire)

desperate *adj* ⟨*person, plea, situation*⟩ désespéré/-e; ⟨*criminal*⟩ prêt/-e à tout; **to be** ~ **for** avoir désespérément besoin de ⟨*affection, help*⟩; attendre désespérément ⟨*news*⟩

desperately *adv* (a) ⟨*plead, look, fight*⟩ désespérément; **to need sth** ~ avoir très besoin de qch
(b) ⟨*poor*⟩ terriblement; ⟨*ill*⟩ très gravement

desperation *n* désespoir *m*

despicable *adj* méprisable

despise *vtr* mépriser

despite *prep* malgré

despondent *adj* abattu/-e, découragé/-e

despot *n* despote *m*

dessert *n* dessert *m*

dessertspoon *n* cuillère *f* à dessert

dessert wine *n* vin *m* doux

destabilize *vtr* déstabiliser

destination *n* destination *f*

destined *adj* (a) destiné/-e (**for, to** à; **to do** à faire)
(b) (bound for) ~ **for Paris** à destination de Paris

destiny *n* destin *m*, destinée *f*

destitute *adj* sans ressources

destroy *vtr* (a) détruire ⟨*building, evidence*⟩; briser ⟨*career, person*⟩
(b) (kill) abattre ⟨*animal*⟩; détruire, anéantir ⟨*population, enemy*⟩

destruction *n* destruction *f*

destructive *adj* destructeur/-trice

detach *vtr* détacher (**from** de)

detachable *adj* ⟨*coupon, section, strap*⟩ détachable; ⟨*lever, collar*⟩ amovible

detached *adj* détaché/-e

detached house *n* maison *f* (individuelle)

detachment *n* détachement *m*

detail ⒈ *n* détail *m*; **in** (**more**) ~ (plus) en détail; **to go into** ~**s** entrer dans les détails; **to have an eye for** ~ prêter attention aux détails
⒉ *vtr* exposer [qch] en détail ⟨*plans*⟩; énumérer ⟨*items*⟩

detain *vtr* (a) (delay) retenir
(b) (keep in custody) placer [qn] en détention

detainee *n* détenu/-e *m/f*

detect *vtr* déceler ⟨*error, traces*⟩; détecter ⟨*crime, leak, sound*⟩; sentir ⟨*mood*⟩

detectable *adj* discernable

detection *n* (of disease, error) détection *f*; **crime** ~ la lutte contre la criminalité; **to escape** ~ ⟨*criminal*⟩ ne pas être découvert/-e; ⟨*error*⟩ ne pas être décelé/-e

detective *n* ≈ inspecteur/-trice *m/f* (de police); **private** ~ détective *m*

detective story *n* roman *m* policier

detector *n* détecteur *m*

detention *n* (a) (confinement) détention *f*
(b) (in school) retenue *f*, colle *f* (colloq)

detention centre *n* centre *m* de détention pour mineurs

deter *vtr* dissuader (**from doing** de faire)

detergent *n* détergent *m*

deteriorate *vi* se détériorer

determination *n* détermination *f*

determine *vtr* déterminer; **to** ~ **how** établir comment

determined *adj* ⟨*person*⟩ fermement décidé/-e (**to do** à faire); ⟨*air*⟩ résolu/-e

deterrent *n* (gen) moyen *m* de dissuasion; (Mil) force *f* de dissuasion

detest *vtr* détester (**doing** faire)

detonate *vtr* faire exploser ⟨*bomb*⟩

detour *n* détour *m*

detox (colloq) **1** *n* to be in ∼ être en cure de désintoxication
2 *adj* ⟨centre, treatment⟩ de désintoxication
detract *vi* to ∼ **from** porter atteinte à ⟨success, value⟩; nuire à ⟨image⟩; diminuer ⟨pleasure⟩
detriment *n* to the ∼ **of** au détriment de
detrimental *adj* nuisible (**to** à)
deuce *n* (in tennis) ∼! égalité!
devaluation *n* (of currency) dévaluation *f*
devastated *adj* ⟨land, region⟩ ravagé/-e; ⟨person⟩ anéanti/-e
devastation *n* dévastation *f*
develop **1** *vtr* (a) attraper ⟨illness⟩; prendre ⟨habit⟩; présenter ⟨symptom⟩
(b) élaborer ⟨plan⟩; mettre au point ⟨technique⟩; développer ⟨argument⟩
(c) développer ⟨mind, business, market⟩
(d) mettre en valeur ⟨land, site⟩; aménager ⟨city centre⟩
(e) (in photography) développer
2 *vi* (a) (evolve) ⟨child, society, country, plot⟩ se développer; ⟨skills⟩ s'améliorer; **to** ∼ **into** devenir
(b) (come into being) ⟨friendship, difficulty⟩ naître; ⟨crack⟩ se former; ⟨illness⟩ se déclarer
(c) (progress, advance) ⟨friendship⟩ se développer; ⟨difficulty, illness⟩ s'aggraver; ⟨crack, fault⟩ s'accentuer; ⟨game, story⟩ se dérouler
(d) (in size) ⟨town, business⟩ se développer
developer *n* (also **property** ∼) promoteur *m* (immobilier)
developing country *n* pays *m* en voie de développement
development *n* (a) (gen) développement *m*
(b) (of product) mise *f* au point; (of housing, industry) création *f*
(c) (of land) mise *f* en valeur; (of site, city centre) aménagement *m*
(d) (innovation) progrès *m*; **major** ∼**s** des découvertes *fpl* majeures (**in** dans le domaine de)
(e) (event) changement *m*; **recent** ∼**s in Europe** les derniers événements en Europe
deviate *vi* (a) (from norm) s'écarter (**from** de)
(b) (from course) dévier (**from** de)
device *n* (a) (household) appareil *m*
(b) (Tech) dispositif *m*
(c) (also **explosive** ∼, **incendiary** ∼) engin *m* explosif
(d) (means) moyen *m* (**for doing, to do** de or pour faire)
IDIOMS **to be left to one's own** ∼**s** être laissé/-e à soi-même
devil *n* (a) (also **Devil**) **the** ∼ le Diable
(b) (evil spirit) démon *m*
IDIOMS **speak of the** ∼! quand on parle du loup (on en voit la queue)! (colloq)
devil's advocate *n* avocat *m* du diable
devious *adj* retors/-e
devise *vtr* concevoir ⟨scheme, course⟩; inventer ⟨product, machine⟩
devoid *adj* ∼ **of** dépourvu/-e de

devolution *n* (a) (of powers) transfert *m* (**from** de; **to** à)
(b) (policy) régionalisation *f*
devote *vtr* consacrer (**to** à; **to doing** à faire); **to** ∼ **oneself** se consacrer (**to** à)
devoted *adj* ⟨person, animal⟩ dévoué/-e (**to** à); ⟨fan⟩ fervent/-e
devotion *n* (to person, work) dévouement *m* (**to** à); (to cause) attachement *m* (**to** à); (to God) dévotion *f* (**to** à)
devour *vtr* dévorer
devout *adj* ⟨Catholic, prayer⟩ fervent/-e; ⟨person⟩ pieux/pieuse
dew *n* rosée *f*
diabetes *n* diabète *m*
diabetic *n, adj* diabétique (*mf*)
diagnose *vtr* diagnostiquer
diagnosis *n* diagnostic *m*
diagonal **1** *n* diagonale *f*
2 *adj* diagonal/-e
diagonally *adv* en diagonale
diagram *n* schéma *m*; (in mathematics) figure *f*
dial **1** *n* cadran *m*
2 *vtr* faire, composer ⟨number⟩; appeler ⟨person⟩; **to** ∼ **999** (for police, ambulance) ≈ appeler police secours; (for fire brigade) ≈ appeler les pompiers
dialect *n* dialecte *m*
dialling code *n* (GB) indicatif *m*
dialling tone (GB), **dial tone** (US) *n* tonalité *f*
dialogue *n* dialogue *m*
dialogue box *n* boîte *f* de dialogue
dialysis *n* dialyse *f*
diameter *n* diamètre *m*
diamond *n* (a) (gem) diamant *m*
(b) (shape) losange *m*
(c) (in cards) carreau *m*
diaper *n* (US) couche *f* (de bébé)
diaphragm *n* diaphragme *m*
diarrhoea (GB), **diarrhea** (US) *n* diarrhée *f*
diary *n* (a) (for appointments) agenda *m*; **to put sth in one's** ∼ noter qch dans son agenda
(b) (journal) journal *m* intime
dice **1** *n* (object) dé *m*; (game) dés *mpl*
2 *vtr* couper [qch] en cubes ⟨vegetable, meat⟩
dictate **1** *vtr* (a) dicter ⟨letter⟩
(b) imposer ⟨terms⟩ (**to** à); déterminer ⟨outcome⟩
2 *vi* (a) **to** ∼ **to one's secretary** dicter une lettre (or un texte) à sa secrétaire
(b) **to** ∼ **to sb** imposer sa volonté à qn
dictation *n* dictée *f*
dictator *n* dictateur *m*
dictatorship *n* dictature *f*
dictionary *n* dictionnaire *m*
die *vi* mourir (**of, from** de); **to be dying** être

mourant/-e, se mourir; **to be dying to do**
mourir d'envie de faire; **to be dying for**
avoir une envie folle de

■ **die down** ⟨*emotion, row*⟩ s'apaiser;
⟨*fighting*⟩ s'achever; ⟨*storm*⟩ se calmer;
⟨*laughter*⟩ diminuer; ⟨*applause*⟩ se calmer

■ **die out** ⟨*species*⟩ disparaître

diesel *n* (a) (*also* ~ **fuel**, ~ **oil**) gazole *m*
(b) (*also* ~ **car**) diesel *m*

diesel engine *n* (moteur *m*) diesel *m*

diet *n* (a) (normal food) alimentation *f* (**of** à
base de)
(b) (slimming food) régime *m*; **to go on a** ~ se
mettre au régime

dietician *n* diététicien/-ienne *m/f*

differ *vi* (a) (be different) différer (**from** de; **in**
par)
(b) (disagree) différer (d'opinion) (**on** sur;
from sb de qn)

difference *n* (a) (be different) différence *f* (**in**, **of** de); **to**
tell the ~ **between** faire la différence entre;
it won't make any ~ ça ne changera rien; **it**
makes no ~ **to me** cela m'est égal
(b) (disagreement) différend *m* (**over** à propos
de; **with** avec); **a** ~ **of opinion** une
divergence d'opinion

different *adj* différent/-e (**from**, **to** (GB),
than (US) de)

differentiate ① *vtr* différencier (**from**
de)
② *vi* (a) (tell the difference) faire la différence
(**between** entre)
(b) (show the difference) faire la distinction
(**between** entre)

differently *adv* (in another way) autrement
(**from** que); (in different ways) différemment
(**from** de)

difficult *adj* difficile; **to find it** ~ **to do**
avoir du mal à faire; **to be** ~ **to get on with**
être difficile à vivre

difficulty *n* difficulté *f*; **to have** ~ (**in**)
doing avoir du mal à faire

diffident *adj* ⟨*person*⟩ qui manque
d'assurance; ⟨*smile, gesture*⟩ timide

dig ① *n* (a) (with elbow) coup *m* de coude (**in**
dans)
(b) (colloq) (jibe) **to take a** ~ **at sb** lancer une
pique (colloq) à qn
(c) (in archaeology) fouilles *fpl*; **to go on a** ~
aller faire des fouilles
② **digs** *n pl* (GB) chambre *f* (meublée)
③ *vtr* (a) creuser ⟨*hole, tunnel, grave*⟩ (**in**
dans)
(b) bêcher ⟨*garden*⟩; fouiller ⟨*site*⟩
(c) extraire ⟨*coal*⟩ (**out of** de)
④ *vi* ⟨*miner*⟩ creuser; ⟨*archaeologist*⟩
fouiller; ⟨*gardener*⟩ bêcher

■ **dig up** (a) déterrer ⟨*body, treasure,*
scandal⟩; arracher ⟨*roots, weeds*⟩; excaver
⟨*road*⟩
(b) bêcher ⟨*garden*⟩

digest *vtr* digérer ⟨*food*⟩; assimiler ⟨*facts*⟩

digestion *n* digestion *f*

digit *n* (a) (number) chiffre *m*
(b) (finger) doigt *m*; (toe) orteil *m*

digital *adj* ⟨*display, recording*⟩ numérique;
⟨*watch*⟩ à affichage numérique; ⟨*camera,*
TV⟩ numérique

dignified *adj* ⟨*person*⟩ digne; ⟨*manner*⟩
empreint/-e de dignité

dignity *n* dignité *f*

digress *vi* faire une digression; **to** ~ **from**
s'écarter de

dilapidated *adj* délabré/-e

dilate ① *vtr* dilater
② *vi* se dilater

dilemma *n* dilemme *m* (**about** à propos
de); **to be in a** ~ être pris/-e dans un
dilemme

diligent *adj* appliqué/-e

dilute *vtr* diluer (**with** avec)

dim ① *adj* (a) ⟨*room*⟩ sombre
(b) ⟨*light*⟩ faible; **to grow** ~ baisser
(c) ⟨*outline*⟩ vague
(d) ⟨*memory*⟩ vague (*before n*)
(e) (colloq) (stupid) bouché/-e (colloq)
② *vtr* baisser ⟨*light, headlights*⟩; mettre
[qch] en veilleuse ⟨*lamp*⟩

dime *n* (US) ⟨pièce *f* de⟩ dix cents *mpl*
IDIOMS they're a ~ **a dozen** (colloq) on en
trouve à la pelle (colloq)

dimension *n* dimension *f*

-dimensional *combining form* **three**~ à
trois dimensions

dime store *n* (US) bazar *m*

diminish *vtr*, *vi* diminuer

dimple *n* fossette *f*

din *n* vacarme *m*

dine *vi* dîner

diner *n* (a) (person) dîneur/-euse *m/f*
(b) (US) (restaurant) café-restaurant *m*

dinghy *n* (a) (*also* **sailing** ~) dériveur *m*
(b) (inflatable) canot *m*

dingy *adj* ⟨*colour*⟩ défraîchi/-e; ⟨*place*⟩
minable

dining car *n* wagon-restaurant *m*

dining room *n* (in house) salle *f* à manger;
(in hotel) salle *f* de restaurant

dinner *n* (a) dîner *m*; **to go out to** ~ dîner
dehors; **to have** ~ dîner
(b) (banquet) dîner *m* (**for** en l'honneur de)

dinner hour *n* (GB Sch) heure *f* du
déjeuner

dinner jacket, **DJ** *n* smoking *m*

dinner party *n* dîner *m*

dinnertime *n* heure *f* du dîner

dinosaur *n* dinosaure *m*

dip ① *n* (a) (in ground, road) creux *m*
(b) (bathe) baignade *f*
(c) (in prices, rate, sales) (mouvement *m* de)
baisse *f* (**in** dans)
(d) (Culin) sauce *f*
② *vtr* (a) tremper (**in**, **into** dans)
(b) (GB) (Aut) baisser ⟨*headlights*⟩; ~**ped**
headlights codes *mpl*
③ *vi* (a) ⟨*bird, plane*⟩ piquer
(b) ⟨*land, road*⟩ être en pente

(c) to ~ into puiser dans ⟨savings⟩; parcourir ⟨novel⟩

diploma n diplôme m (in en)

diplomacy n diplomatie f

diplomat n diplomate mf

diplomatic adj diplomatique; to be ~ avoir du tact

dipstick n jauge f de niveau d'huile

direct ① adj (gen) direct/-e; ⟨person⟩ franc/ franche
② adv directement; to fly ~ prendre un vol direct
③ vtr (a) (address, aim) adresser ⟨appeal, criticism⟩ (at à; against contre); cibler ⟨campaign⟩ (at sur); orienter ⟨effort, resource⟩ (to, towards vers)
(b) (control) diriger ⟨company, project⟩; régler ⟨traffic⟩
(c) diriger ⟨attack, light⟩ (at vers)
(d) réaliser ⟨film, programme⟩; mettre [qch] en scène ⟨play⟩; diriger ⟨actor, opera⟩
(e) (show route) to ~ sb to sth indiquer le chemin de qch à qn
④ vi (in cinema, radio, TV) faire de la réalisation; (in theatre) faire de la mise en scène

direct debit n prélèvement m automatique

direction ① n direction f; in the right/ wrong ~ dans la bonne/mauvaise direction; to go in the opposite ~ aller en sens inverse; from all ~s de tous les côtés
② directions n pl (a) (for route) indications fpl; to ask for ~s demander son chemin (from à)
(b) (for use) instructions fpl (as to, about sur); ~s for use mode m d'emploi

directly adv (a) ⟨connect, challenge, go⟩ directement; ⟨point⟩ droit; ⟨above⟩ juste
(b) (at once) ~ after aussitôt après; ~ before juste avant
(c) (very soon) d'ici peu
(d) (frankly) ⟨speak⟩ franchement

direct mail n mailing m, publipostage m

director n (a) (of company) (sole) directeur/-trice m/f; (on board) administrateur/-trice m/f
(b) (of play, film) metteur m en scène; (of orchestra) chef m d'orchestre; (of choir) chef m des chœurs

directory n (a) (also **telephone ~**) annuaire m
(b) (for business use) répertoire m d'adresses; street ~ répertoire m des rues
(c) (Comput) répertoire m

directory assistance n (US), **directory enquiries** n pl (GB) (service m des) renseignements mpl

direct speech n style m direct

dirt n (a) (on clothing, in room) saleté f; (on body, cooker) crasse f; (in carpet, engine, filter) saletés fpl
(b) (soil) terre f; (mud) boue f

dirt track n chemin m de terre battue

dirty ① adj (a) ⟨face, clothing, street⟩ sale; ⟨work⟩ salissant/-e; to get ~ se salir; to get sth ~ salir qch
(b) ⟨needle⟩ qui a déjà servi; ⟨wound⟩ infecté/-e
(c) (colloq) ⟨book, joke⟩ cochon/-onne (colloq); ⟨mind⟩ mal tourné/-e
(d) (colloq) ⟨trick⟩ sale (before n)
② vtr salir
IDIOMS to give sb a ~ look (colloq) regarder qn d'un sale œil

disability n infirmité f; **mental/physical ~** handicap m mental/physique

disable vtr (a) ⟨accident⟩ rendre [qn] infirme
(b) immobiliser ⟨machine⟩
(c) (Comput) désactiver

disabled ① n **the ~** les handicapés mpl
② adj handicapé/-e

disabled access n voie f d'accès pour handicapés

disadvantage n inconvénient m; **to be at a ~** être désavantagé/-e

disadvantaged adj défavorisé/-e

disagree vi (a) ne pas être d'accord (with avec; on, about sur); **we often ~** nous avons souvent des avis différents
(b) ⟨facts, accounts, result⟩ être en désaccord (with avec)
(c) **to ~ with sb** ⟨food⟩ ne pas réussir à qn

disagreeable adj désagréable

disagreement n (a) (difference of opinion) désaccord m (about, on sur)
(b) (argument) différend m (about, over sur)

disallow vtr (a) (Sport) refuser ⟨goal⟩
(b) (gen, Law) rejeter ⟨claim, decision⟩

disappear vi disparaître

disappearance n disparition f (of de)

disappoint vtr décevoir

disappointed adj déçu/-e (about, with sth par qch)

disappointing adj décevant/-e

disappointment n déception f; **to be a ~ to sb** décevoir qn

disapproval n désapprobation f (of de)

disapprove vi **to ~ of** désapprouver ⟨person, lifestyle⟩; être contre ⟨smoking⟩

disapproving adj désapprobateur/-trice

disarm vtr, vi désarmer

disarmament n désarmement m

disaster n catastrophe f; (long-term) désastre m

disaster area n région f sinistrée; (figurative) catastrophe f

disaster fund n fonds m de soutien

disaster movie n film m catastrophe

disaster victim n sinistré/-e m/f

disastrous adj désastreux/-euse

disbelief n incrédulité f

disc, disk (US) n (a) (gen, Mus) disque m
(b) identity ~ plaque f d'identité; tax ~ vignette f (automobile)

discard *vtr* **(a)** (get rid of) se débarrasser de ⟨*possessions*⟩; mettre [qch] au rebut ⟨*furniture*⟩
(b) (drop) abandonner ⟨*plan, policy*⟩; laisser tomber ⟨*person*⟩

discerning *adj* perspicace

discharge ⓵ *n* **(a)** (of patient) renvoi *m* au foyer
(b) (of gas, smoke) émission *f*; (of liquid) écoulement *m*; (of waste) déversement *m*
(c) (from eye, wound) sécrétions *fpl*
⓶ *vtr* **(a)** renvoyer ⟨*patient*⟩; décharger ⟨*accused*⟩; **to be ~d from hospital** être autorisé/-e à quitter l'hôpital; **to be ~d from the army** être libéré/-e de l'armée
(b) renvoyer ⟨*employee*⟩
(c) émettre ⟨*gas*⟩; déverser ⟨*sewage*⟩
(d) (Med) **to ~ pus** suppurer

discipline ⓵ *n* discipline *f*
⓶ *vtr* **(a)** (control) discipliner
(b) (punish) punir

disciplined *adj* discipliné/-e

disclaim *vtr* nier

disclaimer *n* démenti *m*

disclose *vtr* révéler ⟨*information*⟩

disclosure *n* révélation *f* (**of** de)

disco *n* discothèque *f*

discomfort *n* **(a)** (physical) sensation *f* pénible
(b) (embarrassment) sentiment *m* de gêne

disconcerting *adj* (worrying) troublant/-e; (unnerving) déconcertant/-e

disconnect *vtr* débrancher ⟨*pipe, fridge*⟩; couper ⟨*telephone*⟩; décrocher ⟨*carriage*⟩

discontent *n* mécontentement *m*

discontented *adj* mécontent/-e

discontinue *vtr* supprimer ⟨*service*⟩; arrêter ⟨*production*⟩; cesser ⟨*visits*⟩

discount ⓵ *n* remise *f* (**on** sur); **to give sb a ~** faire une remise à qn
⓶ *vtr* écarter ⟨*idea, possibility*⟩; ne pas tenir compte de ⟨*advice, report*⟩

discount store *n* solderie *f*

discourage *vtr* décourager

discover *vtr* découvrir (**that** que)

discovery *n* découverte *f*

discredit *vtr* discréditer ⟨*person, organization*⟩; mettre en doute ⟨*report, theory*⟩

discreet *adj* discret/-ète

discrepancy *n* divergence *f*

discretion *n* discrétion *f*; **to use one's ~** agir à sa discrétion

discriminate *vi* **(a)** (act with bias) établir une discrimination (**against** envers; **in favour of** en faveur de)
(b) (distinguish) **to ~ between** faire une *or* la distinction entre

discrimination *n* discrimination *f*

discus *n* disque *m*

discuss *vtr* (talk about) discuter de; (in writing) examiner

discussion *n* discussion *f*; (in public) débat *m*

disdainful *adj* dédaigneux/-euse

disease *n* maladie *f*

disembark *vtr, vi* débarquer

disenchanted *adj* désabusé/-e

disengage *vtr* dégager (**from** de)

disfigure *vtr* défigurer

disgrace ⓵ *n* honte *f*; **to be in ~** (officially) être en disgrâce
⓶ *vtr* déshonorer ⟨*team, family*⟩

disgraceful *adj* scandaleux/-euse

disguise ⓵ *n* déguisement *m*; **in ~** déguisé/-e
⓶ *vtr* déguiser ⟨*person, voice*⟩; camoufler ⟨*blemish*⟩; cacher ⟨*emotion, fact*⟩

disgust ⓵ *n* (physical) dégoût *m*; (moral) écœurement *m* (**at** devant)
⓶ *vtr* (physically) dégoûter; (morally) écœurer

disgusting *adj* (physically) répugnant/-e; (morally) écœurant/-e

dish *n* **(a)** plat *m*; **to do the ~es** faire la vaisselle
(b) (*also* **satellite ~**) antenne *f* parabolique
■ **dish out** distribuer ⟨*advice, compliments, money*⟩; servir ⟨*food*⟩

dishcloth *n* (for washing) lavette *f*; (for drying) torchon *m* (à vaisselle)

dishevelled *adj* ⟨*person*⟩ débraillé/-e; ⟨*hair*⟩ décoiffé/-e; ⟨*clothes*⟩ en désordre

dishonest *adj* malhonnête

dishonesty *n* (financial) malhonnêteté *f*; (moral) mauvaise foi *f*

dishonour (GB), **dishonor** (US) *n* déshonneur *m*

dishtowel *n* torchon *m*

dishwasher *n* (machine) lave-vaisselle *m inv*; (person) plongeur/-euse *m/f*

disillusioned *adj* désabusé/-e; **to be ~ with** perdre ses illusions sur

disinfect *vtr* désinfecter

disinfectant *n* désinfectant *m*

disintegrate *vi* se désagréger

disinterested *adj* impartial/-e

disk *n* **(a)** (Comput) disque *m*
(b) (US) = DISC

disk drive (unit) *n* unité *f* de disques

dislike ⓵ *n* aversion *f* (**for** pour); **to take a ~ to sb** prendre qn en aversion
⓶ *vtr* ne pas aimer (**doing** faire)

dislocate *vtr* **to ~ one's shoulder** se démettre l'épaule

dislodge *vtr* déplacer ⟨*rock, tile, obstacle*⟩

disloyal *adj* déloyal/-e (**to** envers)

dismal *adj* **(a)** ⟨*place, sight*⟩ lugubre
(b) (colloq) ⟨*failure, attempt*⟩ lamentable

dismantle *vtr* **(a)** démonter ⟨*construction*⟩
(b) démanteler ⟨*organization*⟩

dismay *n* consternation *f* (**at** devant)

dismiss *vtr* **(a)** écarter ⟨*idea, suggestion*⟩; exclure ⟨*possibility*⟩　⋯⋗

(b) chasser ⟨*thought, worry*⟩

(c) licencier ⟨*employee*⟩; démettre [qn] de ses fonctions ⟨*director, official*⟩

(d) (end interview with) congédier ⟨*person*⟩; (send out) ⟨*teacher*⟩ laisser sortir ⟨*class*⟩

(e) (Law) **the case was ⁓ed** il y a eu non-lieu

dismissal *n* (of employee) licenciement *m*; (of manager, minister) destitution *f*

dismissive *adj* dédaigneux/-euse

disobedient *adj* désobéissant/-e

disobey ⑴ *vtr* désobéir à ⟨*person*⟩; enfreindre ⟨*law*⟩
⑵ *vi* ⟨*person*⟩ désobéir

disorder *n* **(a)** (lack of order) désordre *m*
(b) (disturbances) émeutes *fpl*
(c) (Med) (malfunction) troubles *mpl*; (disease) maladie *f*

disorganized *adj* désorganisé/-e

disorientate *vtr* désorienter

disown *vtr* renier ⟨*person*⟩; désavouer ⟨*document*⟩

dispassionate *adj* (impartial) objectif/-ive (**about** au sujet de)

dispatch ⑴ *n* (report) dépêche *f*
⑵ *vtr* envoyer ⟨*person*⟩ (**to** à); expédier ⟨*letter, parcel*⟩ (**to** à)

dispel *vtr* dissiper ⟨*doubt, fear, myth*⟩

dispensary *n* (GB) (in hospital) pharmacie *f*; (in chemist's) officine *f*

dispense *vtr* **(a)** ⟨*machine*⟩ distribuer ⟨*drinks, money*⟩
(b) ⟨*chemist*⟩ préparer ⟨*medicine, prescription*⟩
(c) (exempt) dispenser (**from sth** de qch; **from doing** de faire)
■ **dispense with (a)** se passer de ⟨*services, formalities*⟩
(b) abandonner ⟨*policy*⟩
(c) (make unnecessary) rendre inutile

dispenser *n* distributeur *m*

disperse ⑴ *vtr* disperser ⟨*crowd, fumes*⟩
⑵ *vi* **(a)** ⟨*crowd*⟩ se disperser
(b) ⟨*mist*⟩ se dissiper

displaced person *n* personne *f* déplacée

display ⑴ *n* **(a)** (in shop) étalage *m*; (of furniture, vehicles) exposition *f*; **window ⁓** vitrine *f*; **to be on ⁓** être exposé/-e
(b) (demonstration) (of art, craft) démonstration *f*; (of dance, sport) exhibition *f*; **air ⁓** fête *f* aéronautique
(c) (of emotion) démonstration *f*; (of strength) déploiement *m*; (of wealth) étalage *m*
(d) (Aut, Comput) écran *m*
⑵ *vtr* **(a)** (show, set out) afficher ⟨*information, poster*⟩; exposer ⟨*object*⟩
(b) (reveal) faire preuve de ⟨*intelligence, interest, skill*⟩; révéler ⟨*emotion, vice, virtue*⟩
(c) (flaunt) faire étalage de ⟨*beauty, knowledge, wealth*⟩; exhiber ⟨*legs, chest*⟩

displeased *adj* mécontent/-e (**with, at** de)

disposable *adj* **(a)** (throwaway) jetable
(b) (available) disponible

disposal *n* **(a)** (of waste product) élimination *f*; **for ⁓** à jeter

(b) (of company, property) vente *f*
(c) to be at sb's ⁓ être à la disposition de qn

dispose *v* ■ **dispose of (a)** se débarrasser de ⟨*body, rubbish*⟩; détruire ⟨*evidence*⟩; désarmer ⟨*bomb*⟩
(b) écouler ⟨*stock*⟩; vendre ⟨*car, shares*⟩

disproportionate *adj* disproportionné/-e (**to** par rapport à)

disprove *vtr* réfuter

dispute ⑴ *n* **(a)** (quarrel) (between individuals) dispute *f*; (between groups) conflit *m* (**over, about** à propos de)
(b) (controversy) controverse *f* (**over, about** sur)
⑵ *vtr* **(a)** contester ⟨*claim, figures*⟩
(b) se disputer ⟨*property, title*⟩

disqualify *vtr* **(a)** (gen) exclure; **to ⁓ sb from doing** interdire à qn de faire
(b) (Sport) disqualifier
(c) (GB) (Aut) **to ⁓ sb from driving** retirer le permis de conduire à qn

disregard ⑴ *n* (for problem, person) indifférence *f* (**for sth** à qch; **for sb** envers qn); (for danger, life, law) mépris *m* (**for** de)
⑵ *vtr* **(a)** ne pas tenir compte de ⟨*problem, evidence, remark*⟩; fermer les yeux sur ⟨*fault*⟩; mépriser ⟨*danger*⟩
(b) ne pas respecter ⟨*law, instruction*⟩

disrepair *n* délabrement *m*; **to fall into ⁓** se délabrer

disreputable *adj* ⟨*person*⟩ peu recommandable; ⟨*place*⟩ mal famé/-e

disrespect *n* manque *m* de respect (**for** envers)

disrespectful *adj* ⟨*person*⟩ irrespectueux/-euse (**to, towards** envers)

disrupt *vtr* perturber ⟨*traffic, trade, meeting*⟩; bouleverser ⟨*lifestyle, schedule, routine*⟩; interrompre ⟨*power supply*⟩

disruption *n* (disorder) perturbations *fpl*; (of schedule) bouleversement *m*

disruptive *adj* perturbateur/-trice

dissatisfaction *n* mécontentement *m*

dissatisfied *adj* mécontent/-e (**with** de)

dissect *vtr* disséquer

dissertation *n* (GB Univ) mémoire *m* (**on** sur)

dissident *n, adj* dissident/-e (*m/f*)

dissimilar *adj* dissemblable; **⁓ to** différent/-e de

dissolve ⑴ *vtr* **(a)** ⟨*acid, water*⟩ dissoudre ⟨*solid, grease*⟩
(b) faire dissoudre ⟨*tablet, powder*⟩ (**in** dans)
(c) dissoudre ⟨*assembly, parliament, partnership*⟩
⑵ *vi* **(a)** ⟨*tablet*⟩ se dissoudre (**in** dans; **into** en)
(b) ⟨*hope*⟩ s'évanouir; ⟨*outline, image*⟩ disparaître
(c) to ⁓ into tears fondre en larmes

dissuade *vtr* dissuader (**from doing** de faire)

distance *n* distance *f* (**between** entre; **from**

distance learning n enseignement m à distance

distant adj (a) (remote) éloigné/-e
(b) (faint) ⟨memory, prospect⟩ lointain/-e
(c) (cool) ⟨person⟩ distant/-e

distaste n dégoût m

distinct adj (gen) distinct/-e (from de); ⟨resemblance, preference, progress⟩ net/nette (before n); ⟨advantage⟩ indéniable

distinction n (a) (gen) distinction f
(b) (Univ) mention f très bien

distinctive adj caractéristique (of de)

distinguish vtr distinguer (from de); to be ∼ed by se caractériser par

distinguished adj (a) (elegant) distingué/-e
(b) (famous) éminent/-e

distinguishing adj distinctif/-ive

distort vtr déformer

distract vtr distraire; to ∼ sb from doing empêcher qn de faire

distracting adj gênant/-e

distraction n (a) (from concentration) distraction f
(b) (diversion) diversion f

distraught adj éperdu/-e

distress 1 n (a) (emotional) désarroi m; to cause sb ∼ faire de la peine à qn
(b) (physical) souffrance f
(c) ⟨ship⟩ in ∼ en détresse
2 vtr faire de la peine à ⟨person⟩; (stronger) bouleverser ⟨person⟩ (to do de faire)

distressed adj (upset) peiné/-e (at, by par); (stronger) bouleversé/-e (at, by par)

distressing adj ⟨case, event, idea⟩ pénible; ⟨news⟩ navrant/-e; ⟨sight⟩ affligeant/-e

distribute vtr (a) (share out) distribuer ⟨films, supplies, money⟩ (to à; among entre)
(b) (spread out) répartir ⟨load, tax burden⟩

distribution n distribution f

distributor n distributeur m (for sth de qch)

district n (in country) région f; (in city) quartier m; (administrative) district m

district attorney n (US) représentant m du ministère public

distrust vtr se méfier de

disturb vtr (a) (interrupt) déranger ⟨person⟩; troubler ⟨silence, sleep⟩
(b) (upset) troubler ⟨person⟩; (concern) inquiéter ⟨person⟩

disturbance n (a) (interruption, inconvenience) dérangement m
(b) (riot) troubles mpl; (fight) altercation f

disturbed adj (a) ⟨sleep⟩ agité/-e
(b) ⟨child⟩ perturbé/-e

disturbing adj ⟨portrayal⟩ troublant/-e; ⟨book, film⟩ perturbant/-e; ⟨report, increase⟩ inquiétant/-e

disused adj désaffecté/-e

ditch 1 n fossé m
2 vtr (colloq) laisser tomber ⟨friend⟩; abandonner ⟨idea, vehicle⟩; plaquer (colloq) ⟨girlfriend, boyfriend⟩

dither vi tergiverser (about, over sur)

ditto adv idem

dive 1 n (a) (by swimmer) plongeon m
(b) (of plane, bird) piqué m
2 vi (a) ⟨person⟩ plonger (off, from de; down to jusqu'à)
(b) (as hobby) faire de la plongée

diver n plongeur/-euse m/f; (deep-sea) scaphandrier m

diverge vi diverger; to ∼ from s'écarter de

diverse adj (varied) divers/-e; (different) différent/-e

diversify vi se diversifier

diversion n (a) (distraction) diversion f (from à)
(b) (of river, money) détournement m
(c) (of traffic) déviation f

diversity n diversité f

divert vtr (a) détourner ⟨water⟩; dévier ⟨traffic⟩; dérouter ⟨flight⟩ (to sur); détourner ⟨funds⟩ (to au profit de)
(b) (distract) détourner

divide 1 vtr (a) (also ∼ up) partager ⟨food, money, time, work⟩
(b) (separate) séparer (from de)
(c) (split) diviser ⟨friends, group⟩
(d) (in mathematics) diviser (by par)
2 vi ⟨road⟩ bifurquer; ⟨river, train⟩ se séparer en deux; ⟨group⟩ (into two) se séparer en deux; ⟨cell, organism⟩ se diviser

dividend n dividende m

dividing line n ligne f de démarcation

diving n (from board) plongeon m; (under sea) plongée f sous-marine

diving board n plongeoir m

diving suit n scaphandre m

division n (gen) division f

divisive adj ⟨policy⟩ qui sème la discorde; to be socially ∼ créer des inégalités sociales

divorce 1 n divorce m
2 vtr to ∼ sb divorcer de or d'avec qn; they're ∼d ils ont divorcé; she's ∼d elle est divorcée

divorcee n divorcé/-e m/f

DIY n (GB) (abbr = **do-it-yourself**) bricolage m

dizzy adj ⟨height⟩ vertigineux/-euse; to make sb ∼ donner le vertige à qn; to feel ∼ avoir la tête qui tourne

DJ n (abbr = **disc jockey**) DJ m/f

DNA n (abbr = **deoxyribonucleic acid**) ADN m

do 1 v aux (a) (gen) ∼ you like Mozart? est-ce que tu aimes Mozart?, aimes-tu Mozart?; I don't smoke je ne fume pas; don't shut the door ne ferme pas la porte; ∼ sit down asseyez-vous; I ∼ like your dress; j'aime beaucoup ta robe; he lives in London, ⋯⟩

doesn't he? il habite à Londres, n'est-ce pas?; **Lola didn't phone, did she?** Lola n'a pas téléphoné par hasard?; **don't ~ that!** ne fais pas ça!; **he said he'd tell her and he did** il a dit qu'il le lui dirait et il l'a fait; **so/neither does he** lui aussi/non plus

(b) (in short answers) **'I love peaches'—'so ~ I'** 'j'adore les pêches'—'moi aussi'; **'who wrote it?'—'I did'** 'qui l'a écrit?'—'moi'; **'shall I tell him?'—'no don't'** 'est-ce que je le lui dis?'—'non'; **'he knows the President'—'does he?'** il connait le Président'—'vraiment?'; **'Tim didn't say that' — 'yes he did'** 'Tim n'a pas dit ça' — 'si'

2 *vtr* **(a)** (gen) faire; **to ~ the cooking/one's homework** faire la cuisine/ses devoirs; **to ~ sth again** refaire qch; **to ~ sb's hair** coiffer qn; **to ~ one's teeth** se brosser les dents; **what have you done to your hair?** qu'est-ce que vous avez fait à vos cheveux?; **what has he done with the newspaper?** qu'est-ce qu'il a fait du journal?; **to ~ 60** ⟨*car, driver*⟩ faire du 60 à l'heure

(b) (colloq) (cheat) **we've been done** on s'est fait avoir; **to ~ sb out of £5** refaire (colloq) qn de 5 livres sterling

3 *vi* **(a)** (behave) faire; **as you're told** (by me) fais ce que je te dis; (by others) fais ce qu'on te dit

(b) (serve purpose) faire l'affaire; **that box will ~** cette boîte fera l'affaire

(c) (be acceptable) **this really won't ~!** ⟨*of situation, attitude*⟩ ça ne peut pas continuer comme ça!; (of work) c'est franchement mauvais!

(d) (be enough) ⟨*amount of money*⟩ suffire

(e) (get on) ⟨*person*⟩ s'en sortir; ⟨*business*⟩ marcher

(f) (in health) **mother and baby are both ~ing well** la mère et l'enfant se portent bien; **the patient is ~ing well** le malade est en bonne voie

IDIOMS **how ~ you do** enchanté; **well done!** bravo!; **it doesn't ~ to be** ce n'est pas une bonne chose d'être; **it was all I could ~ not to laugh** je me suis retenu pour ne pas rire; **she does nothing but moan** elle ne fait que se plaindre

■ **do away with** se débarrasser de
■ **do up (a)** (fasten) nouer ⟨*laces*⟩; remonter ⟨*zip*⟩; **~ up your buttons** boutonne-toi
  (b) (wrap) faire ⟨*parcel*⟩
  (c) (renovate) restaurer ⟨*house*⟩
■ **do with (a) what's it (got) to ~ with you?** en quoi est-ce que ça te regarde?; **it has nothing to ~ with you** cela ne vous concerne pas
  (b) (tolerate) supporter
  (c) (need) **I could ~ with a holiday** j'aurais bien besoin de partir en vacances
  (d) (finish) **it's all over and done with** c'est bien fini
■ **do without** se passer de ⟨*person, advice*⟩

dock **1** *n* **(a)** (in port) dock *m*; (for repairing ship) cale *f*
  (b) (US) (wharf) appontement *m*
  (c) (GB) (Law) banc *m* des accusés

2 *vi* arriver au port

dockworker *n* docker *m*

dockyard *n* chantier *m* naval

doctor **1** *n* **(a)** (Med) médecin *m*, docteur *m*
  (b) (Univ) docteur *m*
  2 *vtr* frelater ⟨*food, wine*⟩; falsifier ⟨*figures*⟩; altérer ⟨*document*⟩

doctorate *n* doctorat *m*

docudrama *n* docudrame *m*

document *n* document *m*

documentary *n* documentaire *m* (**about**, **on** sur)

dodge **1** *n* (GB) (colloq) (trick) combine *f* (colloq)
  2 *vtr* esquiver ⟨*bullet, blow, question*⟩

dodgem (car) *n* (GB) auto *f* tamponneuse

dodgy *adj* (colloq) (untrustworthy) louche (colloq); (risky) ⟨*decision, plan*⟩ risqué/-e; ⟨*situation, moment*⟩ délicat/-e

dog *n* **(a)** chien *m*; (female) chienne *f*
  (b) (male fox, wolf) mâle *m*
  IDIOMS **to go to the ~s** ⟨*company, country*⟩ aller à vau-l'eau

dog collar *n* **(a)** collier *m* de chien
  (b) (clerical) col *m* romain

dog-eared *adj* écorné/-e

dogged *adj* ⟨*attempt*⟩ obstiné/-e; ⟨*person, refusal*⟩ tenace; ⟨*resistance*⟩ opiniâtre

doghouse *n* (US) niche *f* (à chien)
  IDIOMS **to be in the ~** être tombé/-e en disgrâce

dogmatic *adj* dogmatique (**about** sur)

dog paddle *n* nage *f* à la manière d'un chien

dogsbody *n* (GB) (colloq) bonne *f* à tout faire

doh *n* (Mus) do *m*, ut *m*

doing *n* **this is her ~** c'est son ouvrage; **it takes some ~!** ce n'est pas facile du tout!

dole *n* (GB) (colloq) allocation *f* de chômage; **on the ~** au chômage
■ **dole out** (colloq) distribuer

doll *n* poupée *f*

dollar *n* dollar *m*

dollar bill *n* billet *m* d'un dollar

dolphin *n* dauphin *m*

domain *n* domaine *m* (**of** de)

dome *n* dôme *m*

domestic *adj* **(a)** ⟨*market, flight*⟩ intérieur/-e; ⟨*crisis, issue*⟩ de politique intérieure
  (b) ⟨*life, harmony*⟩ familial/-e; ⟨*dispute*⟩ conjugal/-e; ⟨*violence*⟩ dans la famille

domestic appliance *n* appareil *m* électroménager

domesticate *vtr* domestiquer

dominant *adj* dominant/-e

dominate *vtr, vi* dominer

domineering *adj* autoritaire

domino *n* domino *m*; **to play ~es** jouer aux dominos

donate *vtr* faire don de (**to** à)

donation *n* don *m* (**of** de; **à** to)

done **1** *adj* ⟨*food*⟩ cuit/-e; **well ~** bien cuit/-e

2 *excl* (deal) marché conclu!

IDIOMS **it's not the ~ thing** ça ne se fait pas

donkey *n* âne *m*

donor *n* (**a**) (of organ) donneur/-euse *m/f* (**b**) (of money) donateur/-trice *m/f*

donor card *n* carte *f* de donneur d'organes

doodle *vi* gribouiller

doom *n* (of person) perte *f*; (of country) catastrophe *f*

doomed *adj* condamné/-e; **to be ~ to failure** être voué/-e à l'échec

door *n* porte *f* (**to** de); (in car, train) porte *f*, portière *f*; **behind closed ~s** à huis clos

doorbell *n* sonnette *f*

doorman *n* portier *m*

doormat *n* paillasson *m*

doorstep *n* pas *m* de porte

door-to-door *adj* ⟨*canvassing*⟩ à domicile; **~ selling** porte à porte *m inv*

doorway *n* (**a**) (frame) embrasure *f* (**b**) (entrance) porte *f*, entrée *f*

dope **1** *n* (colloq) (**a**) cannabis *m* (**b**) (fool) imbécile *mf* (colloq)

2 *vtr* (Sport) doper ⟨*horse, athlete*⟩; (gen) droguer ⟨*person*⟩

dope test *n* (Sport) contrôle *m* antidopage

dormant *adj* (**a**) ⟨*emotion, talent*⟩ latent/-e (**b**) ⟨*volcano*⟩ en repos

dormitory *n* (**a**) (GB) dortoir *m* (**b**) (US Univ) résidence *f*, foyer *m*

dormitory town *n* ville *f* dortoir

dormouse *n* muscardin *m*

dose *n* dose *f* (**of** de); **a ~ of flu** une bonne grippe

dot *n* (gen) point *m*; (on fabric) pois *m*

IDIOMS **at ten on the ~** à dix heures pile

dot-com **1** *n* (also **~ company**) société *f* Internet *or* virtuelle, société *f* dot-com

2 *adj* ⟨*shares*⟩ des sociétés Internet *or* virtuelles; ⟨*millionaire*⟩ du commerce électronique

dote *vi* **to ~ on sb/sth** adorer qn/qch

dotted line *n* pointillé *m*

double **1** *n* (**a**) (drink) double *m* (**b**) (of person) sosie *m*; (in film, play) doublure *f*

2 **doubles** *n pl* double *m*; **mixed ~s** double mixte

3 *adj* double; **with a ~ 'n'** avec deux 'n'; **two ~ four (244)** deux cent quarante-quatre

4 *adv* (**a**) **~ the amount** deux fois plus (**b**) **to see ~** voir double (**c**) ⟨*fold, bend*⟩ en deux

5 *vtr* doubler ⟨*amount, dose*⟩; multiplier [qch] par deux ⟨*number*⟩

6 *vi* (**a**) ⟨*sales, prices, salaries*⟩ doubler (**b**) **to ~ for sb** (actor) doubler qn (**c**) **the sofa ~s as a bed** le canapé fait aussi lit

IDIOMS **on** *or* **at the ~** au plus vite

■ **double back** rebrousser chemin

double act *n* duo *m*

double-barrelled name *n* (GB) ≈ nom *m* à particule

double bass *n* contrebasse *f*

double bed *n* lit *m* double, grand lit *m*

double-breasted *adj* ⟨*jacket*⟩ croisé/-e

double-check *vtr* vérifier [qch] à nouveau

double chin *n* double menton *m*

double-click *vi* double-cliquer

double cream *n* (GB) ≈ crème *f* fraîche

double-cross *vtr* (colloq) doubler, trahir ⟨*person*⟩

double-decker *n* (GB) (bus) autobus *m* à impériale *or* à deux étages

double door *n* porte *f* à deux battants

double Dutch *n* (colloq) baragouinage *m* (colloq)

double glazing *n* double vitrage *m*

double-park *vi* se garer en double file

double room *n* chambre *f* pour deux personnes

double standard *n* **to have ~s** faire deux poids deux mesures

double take *n* **to do a ~** avoir une réaction à retardement

double vision *n* **to have ~** voir double

double yellow line(s) *n* (*pl*) (GB Aut) *marquage au sol interdisant le stationnement*

doubt **1** *n* doute *m*; **there is no ~ (that)** il ne fait aucun doute que; **to have no ~ (that)** être certain/-e que; **to be in ~** ⟨*person*⟩ être dans le doute; ⟨*outcome*⟩ être incertain/-e; **if** *or* **when in ~** dans le doute; **without (a) ~** sans aucun doute

2 *vtr* douter de ⟨*fact, ability, honesty, person*⟩; **I ~ it!** j'en doute!; **I ~ if he'll come** je doute qu'il vienne

doubtful *adj* (**a**) (unsure) incertain/-e (**b**) ⟨*character, activity, taste*⟩ douteux/-euse

dough *n* (Culin) pâte *f*

doughnut, donut (US) *n* beignet *m*

douse, dowse *vtr* éteindre ⟨*fire*⟩; tremper ⟨*person*⟩; **to ~ sth with petrol** arroser qch d'essence

dove *n* colombe *f*

Dover *pr n* Douvres

dowdy *adj* ⟨*person*⟩ mal fagoté/-e; ⟨*clothes*⟩ sans chic

down¹

■ **Note** When used to indicate vague direction, *down* often has no explicit translation in French: *to go down to London* = aller à Londres; *down in Brighton* = à Brighton.

– For examples and further usages, see the entry below.

1 *adv* (**a**) **to go** *or* **come ~** descendre; **to fall ~** tomber; **to sit ~ on the floor** s'asseoir par terre; **to pull ~ a blind** baisser un store; **~ below** en bas; **the telephone lines are ~** ⋯❖

les lignes téléphoniques sont coupées; face ~ ⟨fall⟩ face contre terre; ⟨lie⟩ à plat ventre; (in water) le visage dans l'eau
(b) (lower) profits are well ~ on last year's les bénéfices sont nettement inférieurs à ceux de l'année dernière; **to get one's weight ~** maigrir; **I'm ~ to my last cigarette** il ne me reste plus qu'une cigarette
(c) (Sport) **to be two sets ~** ⟨tennis player⟩ perdre par deux sets
(d) (as deposit) **to pay £40 ~** payer 40 livres sterling comptant
2 prep **to go ~ the street** descendre la rue; **to run ~ the hill** descendre la colline en courant; **to go ~ town** aller en ville; **they live ~ the road** ils habitent un peu plus loin dans la rue
3 adj **(a)** (colloq) **to feel ~** être déprimé/-e
(b) ⟨escalator⟩ qui descend
(c) ⟨computer⟩ en panne
IDIOMS **it's ~ to you to do it** c'est à toi de le faire; **~ with tyrants!** à bas les tyrans!

down² n duvet m

down-and-out n clochard/-e m/f

downbeat adj **(a)** (pessimistic) pessimiste
(b) (laidback) décontracté/-e

downfall n chute f; **drink proved to be his ~** c'est la boisson qui a causé sa perte

downhearted adj abattu/-e

downhill adv **to go ~** ⟨person, vehicle⟩ descendre; **he's going ~** (declining) il est sur le déclin

downhill skiing n ski m de piste

download vtr (Comput) télécharger

downmarket adj ⟨products⟩ bas de gamme inv; ⟨area⟩ populaire; ⟨newspaper, programme⟩ grand public inv

down payment n acompte m

downplay vtr minimiser l'importance de

downpour n averse f

downright **1** adj ⟨insult⟩ véritable (before n); ⟨refusal⟩ catégorique; ⟨liar⟩ fieffé/-e (before n)
2 adv ⟨stupid, rude⟩ carrément

downsize vi réduire les effectifs

Down's syndrome n trisomie f 21

downstairs **1** adj ⟨room⟩ en bas; (on ground-floor) du rez-de-chaussée; **the ~ flat** (GB) or **apartment** (US) l'appartement du rez-de-chaussée
2 adv en bas; **to go** or **come ~** descendre (l'escalier)

downstream adj, adv en aval (of de); **to go ~** descendre le courant

down-to-earth adj pratique; **she's very ~** (practical) elle a les pieds sur terre; (unpretentious) elle est très simple

downtown adj (US) ⟨store, hotel⟩ du centre ville

downtrodden adj tyrannisé/-e

downturn n (in economy, career) déclin m (in de); (in demand, profits) chute f (in de).

down under adv (colloq) en Australie

downward **1** adj ⟨movement⟩ vers le bas; **~ trend** (Econ) tendance f à la baisse
2 adv = DOWNWARDS

downwards adv (also **downward**) ⟨look⟩ vers le bas; **to slope ~** descendre en pente (**to** vers)

doze vi somnoler
▪ **doze off** (momentarily) s'assoupir; (to sleep) s'endormir

dozen n **(a)** (twelve) douzaine f; **a ~ eggs** une douzaine d'œufs; **£1 a ~** une livre sterling la douzaine
(b) (several) **~s of** des dizaines de ⟨people, things, times⟩

drab adj terne

draft **1** n **(a)** (of letter, speech) brouillon m; (of novel, play) ébauche f; (of contract, law) avant-projet m
(b) (on bank) traite f (**on** sur)
(c) (US) (conscription) service m militaire
(d) (US) = DRAUGHT
2 vtr **(a)** faire le brouillon de ⟨letter, speech⟩; rédiger ⟨contract, law⟩
(b) (US) (conscript) incorporer (**into** dans)
(c) (GB) (transfer) détacher (**to** auprès de; **from** de)
▪ **draft in** (GB) faire venir, amener ⟨police, troops⟩

draft dodger n (US Mil) insoumis m

draftsman (US) = DRAUGHTSMAN

drag **1** n **(a)** (colloq) **what a ~!** quelle barbe! (colloq)
(b) ⟨person⟩ **in ~** en travesti
2 adj **(a)** ⟨artist⟩ de spectacle de travestis
(b) ⟨racing⟩ de dragsters
3 vtr **(a)** (trail) traîner; (pull) tirer ⟨boat, sledge⟩; **to ~ sth along the ground** traîner qch par terre; **to ~ one's feet** traîner les pieds; (figurative) faire preuve de mauvaise volonté (**on** quant à); **don't ~ my mother into this** ne mêle pas ma mère à ça
(b) (draguer) ⟨river, lake⟩
(c) (Comput) glisser
4 vi **(a)** ⟨hours, days⟩ traîner; ⟨story, plot⟩ traîner en longueur
(b) (trail) **to ~ in** ⟨hem, belt⟩ traîner dans ⟨mud⟩
(c) **to ~ on** tirer une bouffée de ⟨cigarette⟩
▪ **drag on** traîner en longueur

drag and drop n glisser-lâcher m

drain **1** n **(a)** (in street) canalisation f; (in building) canalisation f d'évacuation; (pipe) descente f d'eau; (ditch) fossé m d'écoulement
(b) (of people, skills, money) hémorragie f; **to be a ~ on sb's resources** épuiser les ressources de qn
2 vtr **(a)** drainer ⟨land⟩
(b) épuiser ⟨resources⟩
(c) vider ⟨glass⟩
(d) (Culin) égoutter ⟨pasta, vegetables⟩
3 vi **(a)** ⟨liquid⟩ s'écouler (**out of, from** de; **into** dans)
(b) ⟨dishes, food⟩ s'égoutter

drainage n (of land) drainage m; (system) tout-à-l'égout m inv

draining board n égouttoir m

drainpipe n descente f

drake n canard m (mâle)

drama n (genre) théâtre m; (acting, directing) art m dramatique; (play, dramatic event) drame m; TV/radio ~ dramatique f; **to make a ~ out of sth** faire tout un drame de qch

dramatic adj ‹art, effect, event› dramatique; ‹change, landscape› spectaculaire; ‹entrance› théâtral/-e

dramatist n auteur m dramatique

dramatize vtr (a) (for stage) adapter [qch] à la scène; (for screen) adapter [qch] à l'écran; (for radio) adapter [qch] pour la radio

(b) (make dramatic) donner un caractère dramatique à; (excessively) dramatiser

drape 1 n (US) rideau m

2 vtr draper (**in, with** de)

drastic adj ‹policy, measure› draconien/-ienne; ‹reduction, remedy› drastique; ‹effect› catastrophique; ‹change› radical/-e

drastically adv ‹change, reduce› radicalement; ‹reduce, limit› sévèrement

draught (GB), **draft** (US) n (a) (cold air) courant m d'air

(b) **on ~** ‹beer› à la pression

draughts n (GB) jeu m de dames; **to play ~** jouer aux dames

draughtsman (GB), **draftsman** (US) n dessinateur/-trice m/f

draughty (GB), **drafty** (US) adj plein/-e de courants d'air

draw 1 n (a) (in lottery) tirage m (au sort)

(b) (Sport) match m nul; **it was a ~** (in race) ils sont arrivés ex aequo

2 vtr (a) faire ‹picture, plan›; dessiner ‹person, object›; tracer ‹line›

(b) (pull) ‹animal, engine› tirer

(c) tirer ‹conclusion› (**from** de)

(d) (attract) attirer ‹crowd› (**to** vers); susciter ‹reaction›; **to ~ sb into** mêler qn à ‹conversation›; entraîner qn dans ‹argument, battle›

(e) retirer ‹money› (**from** de); tirer ‹cheque› (**on** sur); toucher ‹wages, pension›

(f) (in lottery) tirer [qch] au sort ‹ticket›

(g) sortir ‹sword, knife›; **to ~ a gun on sb** sortir un pistolet et le braquer sur qn

3 vi (a) (make picture) dessiner

(b) **to ~ ahead** (**of sb/sth**) (in race) gagner du terrain (sur qn/qch); (in contest, election) prendre de l'avance (sur qn/qch); **to ~ alongside** ‹boat› accoster; **to ~ near** ‹time› approcher; **to ~ level** se retrouver au même niveau

(c) (in match) faire match nul

IDIOMS **to ~ the line** fixer des limites; **to ~ the line at doing** se refuser à faire

■ **draw away** (move off) s'éloigner (**from** de); (move ahead) prendre de l'avance (**from** sur)

■ **draw in:** ¶ **~ in** (a) ‹days, nights› raccourcir

(b) ‹bus› arriver; ‹train› entrer en gare

¶ **~ [sth] in** rentrer ‹stomach, claws›

■ **draw out:** ¶ **~ out** ‹train, bus› partir; **the train drew out of the station** le train a quitté la gare

¶ **~ [sth] out (a)** (remove) tirer ‹purse, knife› (**of** de); retirer ‹nail, cork› (**of** de)

(b) (withdraw) retirer ‹money›

(c) (prolong) faire durer

¶ **~ [sb] out** faire sortir [qn] de sa coquille

■ **draw up (a)** établir ‹contract›; dresser, établir ‹list, report›

(b) approcher ‹chair› (**to** de)

drawback n inconvénient m

drawer n tiroir m

drawing n dessin m

drawing board n planche f à dessin

drawing pin n punaise f

drawing room n salon m

drawl n voix f traînante

drawn adj (a) **to look ~** avoir les traits tirés

(b) ‹game, match› nul/nulle

dread vtr appréhender (**doing** de faire); (stronger) redouter (**doing** de faire)

dreadful adj épouvantable, affreux/-euse

dreadfully adv ‹disappointed› terriblement; ‹suffer› affreusement; ‹behave› abominablement; **I'm ~ sorry** je suis navré

dream 1 n rêve m

2 adj ‹house, car, vacation› de rêve

3 vtr rêver (**that** que)

4 vi rêver; **he dreamt about or of sth/doing** il a rêvé de qch/qu'il faisait; **I wouldn't ~ of selling the house** il ne me viendrait jamais à l'esprit de vendre la maison

■ **dream up** concevoir ‹idea›; imaginer ‹character, plot›

dreamer n (a) (inattentive person) rêveur/-euse m/f

(b) (idealist) idéaliste mf

dreary adj ‹weather, landscape, life› morne; ‹person› ennuyeux/-euse

dredge vtr draguer ‹river›

dregs n pl (of wine) lie f; (of coffee) marc m

drench vtr (in rain, sweat) tremper (**in** de)

dress 1 n (a) (garment) robe f

(b) (clothes) tenue f; **formal ~** tenue habillée

2 vtr (a) habiller ‹person›; **to get ~ed** s'habiller; **to be ~ed in** être vêtu/-e de

(b) assaisonner ‹salad›; préparer ‹meat, fish›

(c) panser ‹wound›

■ **dress up** (smartly) s'habiller; (in fancy dress) se déguiser (**as** en)

dress circle n premier balcon m

dresser n (a) **to be a stylish ~** s'habiller avec chic

(b) (for dishes) buffet m

(c) (US) (for clothes) commode-coiffeuse f

dressing n (a) (Med) pansement m

(b) (sauce) assaisonnement m

(c) (US) (stuffing) farce f

dressing gown n robe f de chambre

dressing room n loge f

dressing table n coiffeuse f

dressmaker n couturière f

dress rehearsal n (répétition f) générale f

dress sense n to have ∼ s'habiller avec goût

dribble ⊡ n (of liquid) filet m; (of saliva) bave f

⊡ vi **(a)** ⟨liquid⟩ dégouliner (**on, onto** sur; **from** de); ⟨person⟩ baver

(b) (Sport) dribler

dried adj ⟨fruit, herb⟩ sec/sèche; ⟨flower, vegetable⟩ séché/-e; ⟨milk, egg⟩ en poudre

drier n séchoir m

drift ⊡ n **(a)** the ∼ of the current le sens du courant

(b) (of snow) congère f; (of leaves) tas m

(c) (meaning) sens m (général)

⊡ vi **(a)** ⟨balloon⟩ voler à la dérive; ⟨smoke, fog⟩ flotter

(b) ⟨snow⟩ former des congères fpl; ⟨leaves⟩ s'amonceler

(c) to ∼ **through life** errer sans but dans la vie

■ **drift apart** ⟨friends⟩ se perdre de vue; ⟨lovers⟩ se détacher progressivement l'un de l'autre

driftwood n bois m flotté

drill ⊡ n **(a)** (for wood, masonry) perceuse f; (for oil) trépan m; (for mining) foreuse f; (for teeth) roulette f

(b) (Mil) exercice m

(c) fire ∼ exercice m d'évacuation en cas d'incendie

⊡ vtr **(a)** percer ⟨hole, metal⟩; passer la roulette à ⟨tooth⟩

(b) (Mil) entraîner ⟨soldiers⟩

⊡ vi **(a)** (in wood, masonry) percer un trou (**into** dans); to ∼ **for sth** faire des forages pour trouver qch

(b) (Mil) ⟨soldiers⟩ faire de l'exercice

drink ⊡ n boisson f; to have a ∼ boire quelque chose; (alcoholic) prendre un verre

⊡ vtr boire (**from** dans)

⊡ vi boire (**from** dans); **don't** ∼ **and drive** ne conduisez pas si vous avez bu

drinkable adj (safe) potable; (nice) buvable

drink-driving n (GB) conduite f en état d'ivresse

drinking water n eau f potable

drip ⊡ n **(a)** (drop) goutte f (qui tombe)

(b) (GB) (Med) to be on a ∼ être sous perfusion

⊡ vi **(a)** ⟨liquid⟩ tomber goutte à goutte; to ∼ **from** or **off** dégouliner de

(b) ⟨tap, branches⟩ goutter; ⟨washing⟩ s'égoutter

drive ⊡ n **(a)** to go for a ∼ aller faire un tour (en voiture); it's a 40 km ∼ il y a 40 km de route

(b) (campaign) campagne f (**against** contre; **for, towards** pour; to do pour faire)

(c) (motivation) dynamisme m

(d) (Comput) entraînement m de disques

(e) (Aut) transmission f

(f) (also ∼**way**) allée f

(g) (Sport) drive m

⊡ vtr **(a)** conduire ⟨vehicle, passenger⟩; piloter ⟨racing car⟩; **I** ∼ **15 km every day** je fais 15 km en voiture chaque jour; to ∼ **sth into** rentrer qch dans ⟨garage, space⟩

(b) (compel) pousser ⟨person⟩ (**to do** à faire)

(c) (power, propel) actionner ⟨engine, pump⟩

(d) to ∼ **a nail through sth** enfoncer un clou dans qch

⊡ vi conduire; to ∼ **along** rouler; to ∼ **to work** aller au travail en voiture; to ∼ **into** entrer dans ⟨car park⟩; rentrer dans ⟨tree⟩

■ **drive back (a)** repousser ⟨people, animals⟩

(b) ramener ⟨passenger⟩

drive-by shooting n attaque f criminelle (exécutée d'une voiture en marche)

driver n **(a)** conducteur/-trice m/f; ∼s (motorists) automobilistes mfpl

(b) (of taxi) chauffeur m

driver's license n (US) permis m de conduire

driving ⊡ n conduite f

⊡ adj ⟨rain⟩ battant/-e; ⟨wind, hail⟩ cinglant/-e

driving force n (person) force f agissante (**behind** de); (money, ambition) moteur m (**behind** de)

driving instructor n moniteur/-trice m/f d'auto-école

driving lesson n leçon f de conduite

driving licence n (GB) permis m de conduire

driving school n auto-école f

driving seat n place f du conducteur

IDIOMS to be in the ∼ être aux commandes

driving test n examen m du permis de conduire; to take/pass one's ∼ passer/réussir son permis (de conduire)

drizzle ⊡ n bruine f

⊡ vi bruiner

drone n **(a)** (of engine) ronronnement m; (of insects) bourdonnement m

(b) (Zool) faux bourdon m

drool vi baver; to ∼ **over sb/sth** s'extasier sur qn/qch

droop vi ⟨eyelids, head, shoulders⟩ tomber; ⟨plant⟩ commencer à se faner

drop ⊡ n **(a)** (of liquid) goutte f

(b) (decrease) baisse f (in de); a 5% ∼ **in sth** une baisse de 5% de qch

(c) (fall) there's a ∼ **of 100 m** il y a un dénivelé de 100 m; a steep ∼ **on either side** une pente abrupte de chaque côté; a sheer ∼ un à-pic

(d) (delivery) (from aircraft) largage m

⊡ vtr **(a)** (by accident) laisser tomber; (on purpose) lâcher

(b) ⟨aircraft⟩ parachuter ⟨person, supplies⟩; larguer ⟨bomb⟩

(c) to ∼ **off** déposer ⟨person, object⟩

(d) (lower) baisser ⟨eyes, voice, level, price⟩

(e) to ∼ **a hint about sth** faire allusion à qch; to ∼ **sb a line** envoyer un mot à qn

(f) laisser tomber ⟨*friend, school subject*⟩; renoncer à ⟨*habit, idea*⟩

3 *vi* **(a)** (fall) ⟨*object*⟩ tomber; ⟨*person*⟩ (deliberately) se laisser tomber; (by accident) tomber; **the plane ~ped to an altitude of 1,000 m** l'avion est descendu à une altitude de 1 000 m

(b) the cliff ~s into the sea la falaise tombe dans la mer

(c) (decrease) baisser; **to ~ (from sth) to sth** tomber (de qch) à qch

'IDIOMS **a ~ in the ocean** une goutte d'eau dans la mer

■ **drop in** passer; **to ~ in on sb** passer voir qn

■ **drop off (a)** (fall off) tomber

(b) ~ off (to sleep) s'endormir

(c) (decrease) diminuer

■ **drop out (a)** (fall out) tomber **(of** de)

(b) (from race) se désister; (from project) se retirer; (from school, university) abandonner ses études; (from society) se marginaliser

drop-dead *adv* (colloq) **~ gorgeous** super beau/belle (colloq)

drop-down menu *n* menu *m* déroulant

dropout *n* marginal/-e *m*/*f*

droppings *n pl* (of mouse, sheep) crottes *fpl*; (of horse) crottin *m*; (of bird) fiente *f*

drop shot *n* (Sport) amorti *m*

drought *n* sécheresse *f*

drown **1** *vtr* **(a)** noyer ⟨*person, animal*⟩

(b) (*also* **~ out**) couvrir ⟨*sound*⟩

2 *vi* se noyer

IDIOMS **to ~ one's sorrows** noyer son chagrin dans l'alcool

drowning *n* noyade *f*

drowsy *adj* à moitié endormi/-e; **to feel ~** avoir envie de dormir

drug **1** *n* **(a)** (Med) médicament *m*; **to be on ~s** prendre des médicaments

(b) (narcotic) drogue *f*; **to be on** *or* **to take ~s** (gen) se droguer; ⟨*athlete*⟩ se doper

2 *vtr* administrer des somnifères à ⟨*person*⟩

drug abuse *n* consommation *f* de stupéfiants

drug addict *n* toxicomane *mf*

drug addiction *n* toxicomanie *f*

drugged *adj* ⟨*person*⟩ drogué/-e; ⟨*drink*⟩ additionné/-e d'un narcotique

drug habit *n* accoutumance *f* à la drogue

drug mule *n* mule *f*

drugs raid *n* opération *f* antidrogue

drugstore *n* (US) drugstore *m*

drug-taking *n* usage *m* de stupéfiants; (in sport) dopage *m*.

drug test *n* (Sport) contrôle *m* antidopage

drug user *n* toxicomane *mf*

drum **1** *n* **(a)** (Mus) tambour *m*

(b) (barrel) bidon *m*; (larger) baril *m*

2 drums *n pl* batterie *f*; **to play ~s** jouer de la batterie

3 *vtr* **to ~ one's fingers** tambouriner des doigts **(on** sur); **to ~ sth into sb** enfoncer qch dans le crâne de qn (colloq)

■ **drum up** trouver ⟨*business*⟩; racoler ⟨*customers*⟩

drummer *n* (in army) tambour *m*; (jazz or pop) batteur *m*; (classical) percussionniste *mf*

drumstick *n* **(a)** (Mus) baguette *f* de tambour

(b) (of chicken, turkey) pilon *m*

drunk **1** *n* (*also* **drunkard**) ivrogne *m*

2 *adj* ivre; **to get ~** s'enivrer **(on** de)

drunken *adj* ⟨*person*⟩ ivre; ⟨*party*⟩ bien arrosé/-e; ⟨*sleep*⟩ éthylique; ⟨*state*⟩ d'ivresse

dry **1** *adj* **(a)** sec/sèche; **to keep sth ~** tenir qch au sec; **on ~ land** sur la terre ferme; **a ~ day** un jour sans pluie

(b) ⟨*wit, person, remark*⟩ pince-sans-rire *inv*; ⟨*book*⟩ aride

2 *vtr* faire sécher ⟨*clothes, washing*⟩; sécher ⟨*meat, produce*⟩; **to ~ the dishes** essuyer la vaisselle; **to ~ one's hands** se sécher les mains

3 *vi* ⟨*clothes, washing*⟩ sécher

■ **dry out (a)** ⟨*cloth*⟩ sécher; ⟨*plant*⟩ se dessécher

(b) (colloq) ⟨*alcoholic*⟩ se faire désintoxiquer

■ **dry up**: ¶ **~ up (a)** ⟨*river, well*⟩ s'assécher

(b) (run out) se tarir

(c) (dry the dishes) essuyer la vaisselle

¶ **~ [sth] up** essuyer ⟨*dishes*⟩

dry-clean *vtr* **to have sth ~ed** faire nettoyer qch (chez le teinturier)

dry-cleaner's *n* teinturerie *f*

dryer *n* séchoir *m*

DTP *n* (*abbr* = **desktop publishing**) PAO *f*

dual *adj* double

dual carriageway *n* (GB) route *f* à quatre voies

dual nationality *n* double nationalité *f*

dub *vtr* (into foreign language) doubler **(into** en); **~bed film** film doublé

dubious *adj* ⟨*reputation, answer*⟩ douteux/-euse; ⟨*claim*⟩ suspect/-e

duchess *n* duchesse *f*

duck **1** *n* canard *m*

2 *vtr* **(a) to ~ one's head** baisser vivement la tête

(b) (dodge) esquiver ⟨*blow*⟩

(c) se dérober de ⟨*responsibility*⟩

3 *vi* baisser vivement la tête; ⟨*boxer*⟩ esquiver un coup; **to ~ behind** se cacher derrière

duckling *n* caneton *m*

duct *n* **(a)** (for air, water) conduit *m*; (for wiring) canalisation *f*

(b) (Anat, Med) conduit *m*

dud *adj* (colloq) ⟨*banknote*⟩ faux/fausse (*before n*); ⟨*cheque*⟩ en bois (colloq); ⟨*book, movie*⟩ nul/nulle (colloq)

due **1** *n* **I must give her her ~, she...** il faut lui rendre cette justice, elle...

2 *adj* **(a)** (payable) **to be/fall ~** arriver/venir à échéance; **the rent is ~ on the 6th** le loyer doit être payé le 6; **the balance ~** le solde dû ⋯⊱

(b) (owed) **the respect ∼ to him** le respect auquel il a droit, le respect qu'on lui doit

(c) we are ∼ (for) a wage increase soon nos salaires doivent bientôt être augmentés

(d) after ∼ consideration après mûre réflexion; **in ∼ course** (at the proper time) en temps voulu; (later) plus tard

(e) to be ∼ to do devoir faire; **to be ∼ (in)** ⟨train, bus⟩ être attendu/-e; ⟨person⟩ devoir arriver

3 adv **to face ∼ north** ⟨building⟩ être orienté/-e plein nord; **to go ∼ south** aller droit vers le sud

4 due to phr en raison de; **to be ∼ to** ⟨delay, cancellation⟩ être dû/due à; **∼ to unforeseen circumstances** pour des raisons indépendantes de notre volonté

dues n pl (for membership) cotisation f; (for import, taxes) droits mpl

duet n duo m

duffel bag n sac m (de) marin

duffel coat n duffle-coat m

duke n duc m

dull **1** adj **(a)** ⟨person, book⟩ ennuyeux/-euse; ⟨life, journey⟩ monotone; ⟨appearance⟩ triste; ⟨weather⟩ maussade **(b)** ⟨eye, colour, complexion⟩ terne **2** vtr ternir ⟨shine⟩; émousser ⟨blade, pain⟩

duly adv (in proper fashion) dûment; (as expected, as arranged) comme prévu

dumb adj **(a)** muet/muette; **to be struck ∼** rester muet/muette (**with** de)
(b) (colloq) (stupid) ⟨person⟩ bête; ⟨question, idea⟩ idiot/-e

dumb down vtr abaisser le niveau intellectuel de ⟨course, programme⟩

dumbfounded adj abasourdi/-e

dummy **1** n **(a)** (model) mannequin m **(b)** (GB) (for baby) tétine f **2** adj faux/fausse

dummy run n (trial) essai m

dump **1** n **(a)** (for rubbish) décharge f publique
(b) (Mil) **arms ∼** dépôt m d'armes
(c) (colloq) (town, village) trou m (colloq); (house) baraque f (colloq) minable
2 vtr **(a)** jeter ⟨refuse⟩; ensevelir ⟨nuclear waste⟩; déverser ⟨sewage⟩
(b) (colloq) plaquer (colloq) ⟨boyfriend⟩; se débarasser de ⟨car⟩
IDIOMS to be down in the ∼s (colloq) avoir le cafard (colloq)

dumper (truck), dump truck n tombereau m

dunce n cancre m (**at, in** en)

dune n dune f

dung n (for manure) fumier m

dungarees n pl (fashionwear) salopette f; (workwear) bleu m de travail

Dunkirk pr n Dunkerque

duo n duo m

duplicate **1** n (of document) double m (**of** de); (of painting, cassette) copie f

2 adj **(a)** ⟨cheque, receipt⟩ en duplicata; **a ∼ key** un double de clé
(b) (in two parts) ⟨form, invoice⟩ en deux exemplaires
3 vtr **(a)** (copy) faire un double de ⟨document⟩; copier ⟨painting, cassette⟩
(b) (photocopy) photocopier

durable adj ⟨material⟩ résistant/-e; ⟨equipment⟩ solide; ⟨friendship, tradition⟩ durable

duration n durée f

duress n **under ∼** sous la contrainte

during prep pendant, au cours de

dusk n nuit f tombante, crépuscule m; **at ∼** à la nuit tombante

dust **1** n poussière f
2 vtr épousseter ⟨furniture⟩; saupoudrer ⟨cake⟩ (**with** de, avec)

dustbin n (GB) poubelle f

dust cover n (on book) jaquette f; (on furniture) housse f (de protection)

duster n chiffon m (à poussière)

dustman n (GB) éboueur m

dustpan n pelle f (à poussière)

dusty adj poussiéreux/-euse

Dutch **1** n **(a)** (people) **the ∼** les Néerlandais mpl
(b) (language) néerlandais m
2 adj (gen) néerlandais/-e; ⟨embassy⟩ des Pays-Bas
IDIOMS to go ∼ (colloq) payer chacun sa part; **to go ∼ with sb** (colloq) faire fifty-fifty avec qn (colloq)

duty n **(a)** (obligation) devoir m (**to** envers); **in the course of ∼** (Mil) en service; (gen) dans l'exercice de ses fonctions
(b) (task) fonction f; **to take up one's duties** prendre ses fonctions
(c) (work) service m; **to be on/off ∼** (Mil, Med) être/ne pas être de service; (Sch) être/ne pas être de surveillance
(d) (tax) taxe f; **customs duties** droits mpl de douane

duty-free adj, adv hors taxe(s)

duvet n (GB) couette f

duvet cover n housse f de couette

DVD n (abbr = **digital video disc**) DVD m

dwarf n, adj nain/naine (m/f)

dwell v ■ **dwell on** (talk about) s'étendre sur; (think about) s'attarder sur

dwindle vi diminuer

dye **1** n teinture f
2 vtr teindre; **to ∼ sth red** teindre qch en rouge; **to ∼ one's hair** se teindre les cheveux

dying adj ⟨person, animal⟩ mourant/-e; ⟨art⟩ en voie de disparition

dyke n **(a)** (on coast) digue f; (beside ditch) remblai m
(b) (GB) (ditch) fossé m

dynamic adj dynamique

dynamite n dynamite f

dynamo n **(a)** dynamo f

(b) (colloq) **he's a real ~** il déborde d'énergie
dysentery n dysenterie f
dysfunctional adj dysfonctionnel/-elle

dyslexia n dyslexie f
dyslexic n, adj dyslexique (mf)

Ee

e, **E** n **(a)** (letter) e, E m
(b) E (Mus) mi m
(c) E (drug) ecstasy m

each **1** det ⟨person, group, object⟩ chaque
inv; **~ morning** chaque matin, tous les
matins; **~ one** chacun/-e
2 pron chacun/-e m/f; **~ of you** chacun/-e
de vous, chacun/-e d'entre vous; **oranges at
30p ~** des oranges à 30 pence (la) pièce

each other pron
■ Note each other is very often translated by
using a reflexive pronoun (nous, vous, se, s').

(also **one another**) **they know ~** ils se
connaissent; **to help ~** s'entraider; **kept
apart from ~** séparés l'un de l'autre

eager adj ⟨person, acceptance⟩
enthousiaste; ⟨face⟩ où se lit l'enthousiasme;
⟨student⟩ plein d'enthousiasme; **~ to do**
(keen) désireux/-euse de faire; (impatient)
pressé/-e de faire; **~ for sth** avide de qch; **to
be ~ to please** chercher à faire plaisir

eagle n aigle m

ear n **(a)** oreille f
(b) (of wheat, corn) épi m
IDIOMS **to play it by ~** improviser

earache n **to have ~ (GB)** or **an ~** avoir
une otite

eardrum n tympan m

earl n comte m

early **1** adj **(a)** (one of the first) ⟨years,
novels⟩ premier/-ière (before n); **~ man** les
premiers hommes
(b) ⟨delivery⟩ rapide; ⟨vegetable, fruit⟩
précoce; **to have an ~ lunch/night** déjeuner/
se coucher tôt; **in ~ childhood** dans la petite
or première enfance; **at an ~ age** à un très
jeune âge; **to be in one's ~ thirties** avoir
entre 30 et 35 ans; **at the earliest** au plus tôt;
in the ~ spring au début du printemps; **in
the ~ afternoon** en début d'après-midi
2 adv **(a)** tôt; **to get up ~** se lever tôt or de
bonne heure; **it's too ~** il est trop tôt; **as I
said earlier** comme je l'ai déjà dit
(b) (sooner than expected) en avance; **I'm a bit
~** je suis un peu en avance

early retirement n retraite f anticipée

earmark vtr désigner ⟨person, money, site⟩

earn vtr **(a)** ⟨person⟩ gagner ⟨money⟩;
⟨investment⟩ rapporter ⟨interest⟩; **to ~ a** or
one's living gagner sa vie

(b) to ~ sb's respect se faire respecter de
qn

earner n salarié/-e m/f

earnest **1** n **in ~** ⟨speak⟩ sérieusement;
⟨begin⟩ vraiment, pour de bon
2 adj ⟨person⟩ sérieux/-ieuse; ⟨wish⟩
sincère

earning power n capacité f de gain

earnings n pl (of person) salaire m, revenu
m (**from** de); (of company) gains mpl (**from** de);
(from shares) (taux m de) rendement m

earphones n pl (over ears) casque m; (in
ears) écouteurs mpl

earring n boucle f d'oreille

earth **1** n **(a)** terre f
(b) (colloq) **how/where/who on ~…?**
comment/où/qui donc or diable (colloq)…?;
nothing on ~ would persuade me to come je
ne viendrais pour rien au monde
2 vtr (GB) mettre [qch] à la terre

earthenware n faïence f

earthquake n tremblement m de terre

earth tremor n secousse f sismique

earwig n perce-oreille m

ease **1** n **(a)** (lack of difficulty) facilité f
(b) to feel/to be at ~ se sentir/être à l'aise;
to put sb's mind at ~ rassurer qn (**about** à
propos de)
2 vtr **(a)** atténuer ⟨pain, tension, pressure⟩;
réduire ⟨congestion⟩; diminuer ⟨burden⟩
(b) faciliter ⟨communication, transition⟩
(c) to ~ sth into introduire qch
délicatement dans
3 vi ⟨tension, pain, pressure⟩ s'atténuer;
⟨rain⟩ diminuer
■ **ease off** ⟨business⟩ ralentir; ⟨demand⟩ se
réduire; ⟨traffic, rain⟩ diminuer; ⟨person⟩
relâcher son effort
■ **ease up** ⟨tense person, storm⟩ se calmer;
⟨authorities⟩ relâcher la discipline; **to ~ up
on sb/on sth** être moins sévère envers qn/
pour qch

easel n chevalet m

easily adv facilement; **it's ~ the best** c'est
de loin le meilleur; **she could ~ die** elle
pourrait bien mourir

east **1** n **(a)** (compass direction) est m
(b) the East (Orient) l'Orient m; (part of country)
l'Est m
2 adj (gen) est inv; ⟨wind⟩ d'est ⋯∤

3 adv ⟨move⟩ vers l'est; ⟨live, lie⟩ à l'est (**of** de)

Easter **1** n Pâques m; **at** ~ à Pâques; **Happy** ~ Joyeuses Pâques
2 adj ⟨Sunday, egg⟩ de Pâques

eastern adj (a) ⟨coast⟩ est inv; ⟨town, accent⟩ de l'est; **Eastern Europe** l'Europe de l'Est; ~ **France** l'est de la France
(b) (also **Eastern**) (oriental) oriental/-e

East Timor pr n Timor m oriental

easy **1** adj (a) ⟨job, question, life, victim⟩ facile; **it's** ~ **to do** c'est facile à faire; **it's** ~ **to make a mistake** il est facile de se tromper; **it isn't** ~ **to do** ce n'est pas facile à faire; **it isn't** ~ **to park** il n'est pas facile de se garer; **to make it** or **things easier** faciliter les choses (**for** pour)
(b) (relaxed) ⟨smile, grace⟩ décontracté/-e; ⟨style⟩ plein/-e d'aisance; **at an** ~ **pace** d'un pas tranquille
(c) (colloq) **I'm** ~ ça m'est égal
2 adv (a) **to take it** or **things** ~ ne pas s'en faire
(b) (colloq) **to go** ~ **on** or **with** y aller doucement avec

easygoing adj ⟨person⟩ accommodant/-e; ⟨manner, attitude⟩ souple

easy terms n pl facilités fpl de paiement

eat **1** vtr manger ⟨food⟩; prendre ⟨meal⟩
2 vi manger
■ **eat out** aller au restaurant

eating disorder n trouble m du comportement alimentaire

eating habits n pl habitudes fpl alimentaires

eavesdrop vi écouter aux portes

ebb **1** n reflux m
2 vi ⟨tide⟩ descendre; ⟨enthusiasm⟩ décliner

ebony n (a) (wood) ébène f
(b) (colour) noir m d'ébène

EC n (abbr = **European Community**) CE f

e-cash n argent m électronique, argent m virtuel

eccentric n, adj excentrique (mf)

ECG n (abbr = **electrocardiogram**) ECG m

echo **1** n écho m
2 vtr (a) répercuter ⟨sound⟩
(b) reprendre ⟨ideas, opinions⟩
3 vi retentir, résonner

eclipse **1** n éclipse f (**of** de)
2 vtr éclipser

eco-friendly adj qui ne nuit pas à l'environnement

ecological adj écologique

ecologist n, adj écologiste (mf)

ecology n écologie f

e-commerce n commerce m électronique

economic adj (gen) économique; (profitable) rentable

economical adj ⟨person⟩ économe; ⟨machine, method⟩ économique

economics n (science) économie f; (subject of study) sciences fpl économiques; (financial aspects) aspects mpl économiques (**of** de)

economist n économiste mf

economize vtr, vi économiser

economy n économie f

economy class n classe f économique

economy drive n campagne f de restriction

eco-warrior n éco-guerrier/-ière m/f

ecstasy n (a) extase f
(b) (drug) ecstasy m

ecu, ECU n (abbr = **European Currency Unit**) écu m, ÉCU m

eczema n eczéma m

Eden pr n Éden m, paradis m terrestre

edge **1** n (a) (outer limit) bord m; (of wood, clearing) lisière f; **the film had us on the** ~ **of our seats** le film nous a tenus en haleine
(b) (of blade) tranchant m
(c) (of book, plank) tranche f
(d) **to be on** ~ ⟨person⟩ être énervé/-e
2 vi **to** ~ **forward** avancer doucement; **to** ~ **towards** s'approcher à petits pas de

edgeways, edgewise adv ⟨move⟩ latéralement; ⟨lay, put⟩ sur le côté
IDIOMS **I can't get a word in** ~ je n'arrive pas à placer un mot

edible adj comestible

Edinburgh pr n Édimbourg

edit vtr (a) (in publishing) éditer
(b) (cut) couper ⟨text, version⟩
(c) monter ⟨film, programme⟩

edition n édition f

editor n (of newspaper) rédacteur/-trice m/f en chef (**of** de); (of book, manuscript) correcteur/-trice m/f; (of writer, works, anthology) éditeur/-trice m/f; (of film) monteur/-euse m/f

editorial **1** n éditorial m (**on** sur)
2 adj (a) (in journalism) de la rédaction, rédactionnel/-elle
(b) (in publishing) éditorial/-e

educate vtr (a) ⟨teacher⟩ instruire; ⟨parent⟩ assurer l'instruction de; **to be** ~**d in Paris** faire ses études à Paris
(b) informer ⟨public⟩ (**about, in** sur)

educated adj ⟨person, classes⟩ instruit/-e; ⟨accent⟩ élégant/-e

education n (a) éducation f, instruction f; **health** ~ hygiène f
(b) (formal schooling) études fpl; **to have had a university** or **college** ~ avoir fait des études supérieures
(c) (national system) enseignement m

educational adj (a) ⟨establishment⟩ d'enseignement
(b) ⟨game, programme⟩ éducatif/-ive; ⟨talk⟩ instructif/-ive

EEC n (abbr = **European Economic Community**) CEE f

eel n anguille f

eerie adj ⟨silence, place⟩ étrange et inquiétant/-e

effect **1** *n* (a) effet *m* (of de; on sur); to take ~ ⟨*price increases*⟩ prendre effet; ⟨*pills, anaesthetic*⟩ commencer à agir; **to come into** ~ ⟨*law, rate*⟩ entrer en vigueur; **she dresses like that for** ~ elle s'habille comme ça pour faire de l'effet
(b) (repercussions) répercussions *fpl* (of de; on sur)
2 effects *n pl* effets *mpl*
3 *vtr* effectuer ⟨*repair, sale, change*⟩
4 in effect *phr* en fait, en réalité
effective *adj* efficace
effectively *adv* (a) (efficiently) efficacement
(b) (in effect) en fait, en réalité
effeminate *adj* efféminé/-e
efficiency *n* (of person, method, organization) efficacité *f* (**in doing** à faire); (of machine) rendement *m*
efficient *adj* (a) ⟨*person, management*⟩ efficace (**at doing** pour ce qui est de faire)
(b) ⟨*machine*⟩ économique
effort *n* effort *m*; **to make the** ~ faire l'effort; **to spare no** ~ ne pas ménager ses efforts; **to be worth the** ~ en valoir la peine; **it is an** ~ **to do** il est pénible de faire
EFL *n* (*abbr* = **English as a Foreign Language**) anglais *m* langue étrangère
eg (*abbr* = **exempli gratia**) par ex
egalitarian *adj* égalitaire
egg *n* œuf *m*
■ **egg on** pousser ⟨*person*⟩
eggcup *n* coquetier *m*
eggplant *n* (US) aubergine *f*
egg white *n* blanc *m* d'œuf
egg yolk *n* jaune *m* d'œuf
ego *n* (a) amour-propre *m*; **it boosted his** ~ ça lui a redonné confiance en lui-même
(b) (in psychology) moi *m*, ego *m*
egoism *n* égoïsme *m*
egoist *n* égoïste *mf*
egotist *n* égotiste *mf*
Egypt *pr n* Égypte *f*
eiderdown *n* édredon *m*
eight *n, pron, det* huit (*m*) *inv*
eighteen *n, pron, det* dix-huit (*m*) *inv*
eighteenth **1** *n* (a) (in order) dix-huitième *mf*
(b) (of month) dix-huit *m inv*
(c) (fraction) dix-huitième *m*
2 *adj, adv* dix-huitième
eighth **1** *n* (a) (in order) huitième *mf*
(b) (of month) huit *m inv*
(c) (fraction) huitième *m*
2 *adj, adv* huitième
eighties *n pl* (a) (era) **the** ~ les années *fpl* quatre-vingt
(b) (age) **to be in one's** ~ avoir entre quatre-vingts et quatre-vingt-dix ans
eightieth *n, adj, adv* quatre-vingtième (*mf*)
eighty *n, pron, det* quatre-vingts (*m*)
eighty-one *n, pron, det* quatre-vingt-un (*m*)

Éire *pr n* Éire *f*, République *f* d'Irlande
either **1** *pron, quantif* (a) (one or other) l'un/-e ou l'autre; **take** ~ (**of them**) prends l'un/-e ou l'autre; **I don't like** ~ (**of them**) je n'aime ni l'un/-e ni l'autre; **'which book do you want?'—'**~**'** 'quel livre veux-tu?'—'n'importe'
(b) (both) ~ **of the two is possible** les deux sont possibles
2 *det* (a) (one or the other) n'importe lequel/laquelle; **take** ~ **road** prenez n'importe laquelle des deux routes; **I can't see** ~ **child** je ne vois aucun des deux enfants
(b) (both) **in** ~ **case** dans un cas comme dans l'autre; ~ **way, it will be difficult** de toute manière, ce sera difficile
3 *adv* non plus; **I can't do it** ~ je ne peux pas le faire non plus
4 *conj* (a) (as alternatives) ~...**or**... soit...soit..., (ou)...ou...
(b) (in the negative) **I wouldn't believe** ~ **Patrick or Emily** je ne croirais ni Patrick ni Emily
eject **1** *vtr* (a) ⟨*machine, system*⟩ rejeter ⟨*waste*⟩; ⟨*volcano*⟩ cracher ⟨*lava*⟩
(b) faire sortir ⟨*cassette*⟩
(c) expulser ⟨*troublemaker*⟩
2 *vi* ⟨*pilot*⟩ s'éjecter
eject button *n* touche *f* d'éjection
eke *v* ■ **eke out** faire durer ⟨*income, supplies*⟩ (**by** à force de; **by doing** en faisant); **to** ~ **out a living** essayer de joindre les deux bouts
elaborate **1** *adj* ⟨*excuse*⟩ compliqué/-e; ⟨*network, plan*⟩ complexe; ⟨*design*⟩ travaillé/-e; ⟨*painting, sculpture*⟩ ouvragé/-e
2 *vtr* élaborer ⟨*theory*⟩
3 *vi* entrer dans les détails; **to** ~ **on** s'étendre sur ⟨*proposal*⟩; développer ⟨*remark*⟩
elapse *vi* s'écouler
elastic *n, adj* élastique (*m*)
elasticated *adj* élastique
elastic band *n* élastique *m*
elated *adj* transporté/-e de joie
elbow *n* coude *m*
elbow grease *n* huile *f* de coude (colloq)
elbowroom *n* (room to move) espace *m* vital; (figurative) marge *f* de manœuvre
elder **1** *n* (a) (older person) aîné/-e *m/f*; (of tribe, group) ancien *m*
(b) (tree) sureau *m*
2 *adj* aîné/-e; **the** ~ **girl** l'aînée *f*, la fille aînée
elderly **1** *n* **the** ~ les personnes *fpl* âgées
2 *adj* ⟨*person, population*⟩ âgé/-e
eldest **1** *n* aîné/-e *m/f*
2 *adj* aîné/-e; **the** ~ **child** l'aîné/-e
elect *vtr* (a) (by vote) élire (**from, from among** parmi)
(b) (choose) choisir (**to do** de faire)
election *n* élection *f*, scrutin *m*; **to win an** ~ gagner aux élections

e

election campaign n campagne f électorale

electoral adj électoral/-e

electorate n électorat m, électeurs mpl

electric adj électrique

electrical adj électrique

electric blanket n couverture f chauffante

electrician n électricien/-ienne m/f

electricity n électricité f; **to turn off/on the ~** couper/rétablir le courant (électrique)

electric shock n décharge f électrique

electrify vtr (a) électrifier ⟨railway⟩ (b) électriser ⟨audience⟩

electrocute vtr électrocuter

electronic adj électronique

electronic engineer n électronicien/-ienne m/f

electronic organizer n ordinateur m de poche

electronic publishing n éditique f

electronics n électronique f

electronic tagging n marquage m électronique (des criminels)

elegant adj ⟨person, clothes, gesture⟩ élégant/-e; ⟨manners⟩ distingué/-e; ⟨restaurant⟩ chic

element n (a) élément m; **an ~ of luck** une part de chance (b) (in heater, kettle) résistance f

elementary adj (a) (basic) élémentaire (b) ⟨school⟩ primaire; ⟨teacher⟩ de primaire

elephant n éléphant m

elevate vtr élever (**to** au rang de)

elevated adj ⟨language, rank, site⟩ élevé/-e; ⟨railway, canal⟩ surélevé/-e

elevator n (a) (US) (lift) ascenseur m (b) (hoist) élévateur m

eleven n, pron, det onze (m) inv

eleventh [1] n (a) (in order) onzième mf (b) (of month) onze m inv (c) (fraction) onzième m [2] adj, adv onzième

elf n lutin m

eligible adj **to be ~ for** avoir droit à ⟨allowance, benefit, membership⟩; **to be ~ to do** être en droit de faire

eliminate vtr (gen) éliminer; écarter ⟨suspect⟩

elimination n élimination f; **by a process of ~** en procédant par élimination

élite [1] n élite f [2] adj ⟨group, minority⟩ élitaire; ⟨restaurant, club⟩ réservé/-e à l'élite; ⟨squad⟩ d'élite

elm n orme m

elongated adj allongé/-e

elope vi s'enfuir (**with** avec)

eloquent adj éloquent/-e

else [1] adv d'autre; **somebody/nothing ~** quelqu'un/rien d'autre; **something ~** autre chose; **somewhere** or **someplace** (US) **~** ailleurs; **how ~ can we do it?** comment le faire autrement?; **what ~ would you like?** qu'est-ce que tu voudrais d'autre? [2] **or else** phr sinon

elsewhere adv ailleurs

elusive adj ⟨person, animal, happiness⟩ insaisissable; ⟨prize, victory⟩ hors d'atteinte

emaciated adj ⟨person, feature⟩ émacié/-e; ⟨limb, body⟩ décharné/-e; ⟨animal⟩ étique

e-mail, email [1] n (medium) e-mail m, courrier m électronique; (item of mail) e-mail m, message m électronique [2] vtr envoyer un e-mail à ⟨person⟩; envoyer [qch] par e-mail ⟨document⟩

e-mail address n adresse f électronique

emancipate vtr émanciper

emancipation n émancipation f

embalm vtr embaumer

embankment n (a) (for railway, road) remblai m (b) (by river) quai m, digue f

embargo n embargo m

embark vi (a) (on ship) s'embarquer (**for** pour) (b) **to ~ on** entreprendre ⟨journey⟩; se lancer dans ⟨career, process, project⟩

embarkation n embarquement m

embarrass vtr plonger [qn] dans l'embarras; **to be/to feel ~ed** être/se sentir gêné/-e

embarrassing adj embarrassant/-e

embarrassment n confusion f, gêne f (**about, at** devant); **to my ~** à ma grande confusion

embassy n ambassade f

embers n pl braises fpl

embezzle vtr détourner ⟨funds⟩ (**from** de)

emblem n emblème m

embody vtr incarner ⟨virtue, evil, ideal⟩

embrace [1] n étreinte f [2] vtr (a) (hug) étreindre (b) (include) comprendre [3] vi s'étreindre

embroider [1] vtr (a) broder (**with** de) (b) embellir ⟨story, truth⟩ [2] vi broder, faire de la broderie

embroidery n broderie f

embryo n embryon m

emerald n (a) (stone) émeraude f (b) (colour) émeraude m

emerge vi (a) ⟨person, animal⟩ sortir (**from** de) (b) ⟨problem, result⟩ se faire jour; ⟨pattern⟩ se dégager; ⟨truth⟩ apparaître

emergency [1] n (gen) cas m d'urgence; (Med) urgence f; **in an ~**, **in case of ~** en cas d'urgence; **it's an ~** c'est urgent [2] adj ⟨plan, repairs, call, stop⟩ d'urgence; ⟨brakes, vehicle⟩ de secours

emergency exit n sortie f de secours

emergency landing n atterrissage m d'urgence

emergency services n pl (police)

≈ police *f* secours; (ambulance) service *m* d'aide médicale d'urgence; (fire brigade) (sapeurs-)pompiers *mpl*

emergency worker *n* secouriste *mf*

emigrant *n* (about to leave) émigrant/-e *m/f*; (settled elsewhere) émigré/-e *m/f*

emigrate *vi* émigrer

emission *n* émission *f* (**from** provenant de)

emit *vtr* émettre

emoticon *n* (Comput) émoticône *f*, smiley *m* (colloq)

emotion *n* émotion *f*

emotional *adj* ⟨*problem*⟩ émotif/-ive; ⟨*reaction*⟩ émotionnel/-elle; ⟨*tie, response*⟩ affectif/-ive; ⟨*speech*⟩ passionné/-e; **to feel ~** être ému/-e (**about** par); **she's rather ~** elle est assez émotive

emotionally *adv* ⟨*speak, react*⟩ avec émotion; **~ deprived** privé/-e d'affection; **~ disturbed** caractériel/-ielle

emotive *adj* ⟨*issue*⟩ qui soulève les passions; ⟨*word*⟩ chargé/-e de connotations

empathize *vi* **to ~ with** s'identifier à ⟨*person*⟩

emperor *n* empereur *m*

emphasis *n* accent *m*; **to lay** *or* **put the ~ on sth** mettre l'accent sur qch

emphasize *vtr* mettre l'accent sur ⟨*policy, need*⟩; mettre [qch] en valeur ⟨*eyes*⟩

emphatic *adj* ⟨*statement*⟩ catégorique; ⟨*voice, manner*⟩ énergique; **to be ~ about** insister sur

empire *n* empire *m*

employ *vtr* (a) employer ⟨*person, company*⟩ (**as** en qualité de); **to be ~ed** avoir un emploi
(b) (use) utiliser ⟨*machine, tool*⟩; employer ⟨*tactics, technique*⟩; recourir à ⟨*measures*⟩

employable *adj* capable de faire un travail

employee *n* salarié/-e *m/f*

employer *n* employeur/-euse *m/f*

employment *n* travail *m*, emploi *m*

employment agency *n* bureau *m* de recrutement

empower *vtr* (legally) **to ~ sb to do** autoriser qn à faire; (politically) donner à qn le pouvoir de faire

empress *n* impératrice *f*

empty ⓵ *adj* (a) ⟨*street*⟩ désert/-e; ⟨*desk*⟩ libre; ⟨*container*⟩ vide; ⟨*page*⟩ vierge
(b) ⟨*promise, threat*⟩ en l'air; ⟨*gesture*⟩ vide de sens; ⟨*life*⟩ vide
⓶ *vtr, vi* = EMPTY OUT
■ **empty out**: ¶ **~ out** ⟨*building, container*⟩ se vider; ⟨*contents*⟩ se répandre; ¶ **~ [sth] out** vider ⟨*container, drawer*⟩; verser ⟨*liquid*⟩

empty-handed *adj* ⟨*arrive, leave*⟩ les mains vides; ⟨*return*⟩ bredouille *inv*

emulate *vtr* imiter

emulsion *n* émulsion *f*

enable *vtr* (a) **to ~ sb to do** permettre à qn de faire
(b) faciliter ⟨*growth*⟩; favoriser ⟨*learning*⟩

enamel *n* émail *m*

enchant *vtr* enchanter

enchanting *adj* enchanteur/-eresse

encircle *vtr* ⟨*troops, police*⟩ encercler; ⟨*fence, wall*⟩ entourer; ⟨*belt, bracelet*⟩ enserrer

enclose *vtr* (a) (gen) entourer (**with, by** de); (with fence, wall) clôturer (**with, by** avec)
(b) (in letter) joindre (**with, in** à); **please find ~d a cheque for £10** veuillez trouver ci-joint un chèque de dix livres sterling

enclosure *n* (a) (for animals) enclos *m*; (for racehorses) paddock *m*; (for officials) enceinte *f*
(b) (fence) clôture *f*

encompass *vtr* inclure, comprendre

encore ⓵ *n* bis *m*; **to play an ~** jouer un bis
⓶ *excl* **~!** bis!

encounter ⓵ *n* (gen) rencontre *f* (**with** avec); (Mil) affrontement *m*
⓶ *vtr* rencontrer ⟨*opponent, resistance, problem*⟩; essuyer ⟨*setback*⟩; croiser ⟨*person*⟩

encourage *vtr* (a) encourager (**to do** à faire)
(b) stimuler ⟨*investment*⟩; favoriser ⟨*growth*⟩

encouragement *n* encouragement *m*

encouraging *adj* encourageant/-e

encroach *vi* **to ~ on** ⟨*person*⟩ empiéter sur; ⟨*sea, vegetation*⟩ gagner du terrain sur ⟨*land*⟩

encrypt *vtr* crypter

encyclop(a)edia *n* encyclopédie *f*

end ⓵ *n* (a) (final part) fin *f*; **'The End'** 'Fin'; **to put an ~ to sth** mettre fin à qch; **to come to an ~** se terminer; **in the ~ I went home** finalement je suis rentré chez moi; **for days on ~** pendant des jours et des jours
(b) (extremity) bout *m*, extrémité *f*; **at the ~ of, on the ~ of** au bout de; **at the ~ of the garden** au fond du jardin; **the third from the ~** le/la troisième avant la fin; **to stand sth on (its) ~** mettre qch debout
(c) (aim) but *m*; **to this ~** dans ce but; **a means to an ~** un moyen d'arriver à ses fins
(d) (Sport) **to change ~s** changer de côté
⓶ *vtr* mettre fin à; **to ~ sth with** terminer qch par; **to ~ it all** en finir avec la vie
⓷ *vi* ⟨*day, book*⟩ se terminer (**in, with** par); ⟨*contract, agreement*⟩ expirer
■ **end up** finir par devenir ⟨*president*⟩; finir par être ⟨*rich*⟩; **to ~ up doing** finir par faire

endanger *vtr* mettre [qch] en danger ⟨*health, life*⟩; compromettre ⟨*career, prospects*⟩

endangered species *n* espèce *f* menacée

endearing *adj* ⟨*person, habit*⟩ attachant/-e; ⟨*smile*⟩ engageant/-e

endeavour, endeavor (US) ⓵ *n* tentative *f* (**to do** de faire) ⋯⋙

2 *vtr* **to ~ to do** (do one's best) faire tout son possible pour faire; (find a means) trouver un moyen de faire

ending *n* fin *f*, dénouement *m*

endive *n* (GB) chicorée *f*; (US) endive *f*

endless *adj* ⟨patience, choice⟩ infini/-e; ⟨supply⟩ inépuisable; ⟨list, search, meeting⟩ interminable

endorse *vtr* donner son aval à ⟨policy⟩; appuyer ⟨decision⟩; approuver ⟨product⟩; endosser ⟨cheque⟩

endow *vtr* doter (**with** de)

end result *n* résultat *m* final

endurance *n* endurance *f*

endure **1** *vtr* endurer ⟨hardship⟩; supporter ⟨behaviour, person⟩; subir ⟨attack, defeat⟩
2 *vi* durer

enemy **1** *n* ennemi/-e *m/f*
2 *adj* ⟨forces, aircraft, territory⟩ ennemi/-e; ⟨agent⟩ de l'ennemi

energetic *adj* énergique

energy *n* énergie *f*

energy policy *n* politique *f* énergétique

energy-saving *adj* qui permet de faire des économies d'énergie

enforce *vtr* appliquer ⟨rule, policy⟩; faire respecter ⟨law, court order⟩

engage **1** *vtr* **(a) to be ~d in** se livrer à ⟨activity⟩; **to ~ sb in conversation** engager la conversation avec qn
(b) passer ⟨gear⟩; **to ~ the clutch** embrayer
2 *vi* **to ~ in** se livrer à ⟨activity⟩; se lancer dans ⟨research⟩

engaged *adj* **(a) to be ~** être fiancé/-e (**to** à); **to get ~** se fiancer (**to** à)
(b) ⟨WC, phone⟩ occupé/-e

engaged tone *n* (GB) tonalité *f* 'occupé'

engagement *n* **(a)** (appointment) rendez-vous *m* inv
(b) (before marriage) fiançailles *fpl*

engagement ring *n* bague *f* de fiançailles

engine *n* **(a)** (gen) moteur *m*; (in ship) machines *fpl*
(b) locomotive *f*; **steam ~** locomotive à vapeur

engine driver *n* mécanicien *m*

engineer **1** *n* (graduate) ingénieur *m*; (in factory) mécanicien *m* monteur; (repairer) technicien *m*; (on ship) mécanicien *m*
2 *vtr* **(a)** (plot) manigancer
(b) (build) construire

engineering *n* ingénierie *f*; **civil ~** génie *m* civil

England *pr n* Angleterre *f*

English **1** *n* **(a)** (people) **the ~** les Anglais
(b) (language) anglais *m*
2 *adj* ⟨language, food⟩ anglais/-e; ⟨lesson, teacher⟩ d'anglais; ⟨ambassador, embassy⟩ d'Angleterre

English Channel *pr n* **the ~** la Manche

Englishman *n* Anglais *m*

English-speaking *adj* anglophone

Englishwoman *n* Anglaise *f*

engrave *vtr* graver

engraving *n* gravure *f*

engrossed *adj* **to be ~ in** être absorbé/-e par, être plongé/-e dans

engulf *vtr* engloutir

enhance *vtr* améliorer ⟨prospects, status⟩; mettre [qch] en valeur ⟨appearance, qualities⟩

enigma *n* énigme *f*

enigmatic *adj* énigmatique

enjoy **1** *vtr* **(a)** aimer (doing faire); **I didn't ~ the party** je ne me suis pas amusé/-e à la soirée
(b) (have) jouir de ⟨good health, popularity⟩
2 *v refl* **to ~ oneself** s'amuser

enjoyable *adj* agréable

enjoyment *n* plaisir *m*

enlarge **1** *vtr* agrandir
2 *vi* **(a)** ⟨pupil, pores⟩ se dilater; ⟨tonsils⟩ enfler
(b) to ~ on s'étendre sur ⟨subject⟩; développer ⟨idea⟩

enlighten *vtr* éclairer (**on** sur)

enlightening *adj* instructif/-ive

enlightenment *n* (edification) instruction *f*; (clarification) éclaircissement *m*; **the (Age of) Enlightenment** le Siècle des lumières

enlist **1** *vtr* recruter; **to ~ sb's help** s'assurer l'aide de qn
2 *vi* s'enrôler, s'engager

enmity *n* inimitié *f* (**towards** envers)

enormity *n* énormité *f*

enormous *adj* (gen) énorme; ⟨effort⟩ prodigieux/-ieuse

enough

■ **Note** When *enough* is used as a pronoun and if the sentence does not specify what it is enough of, the pronoun *en*, meaning *of it/of them*, must be added before the verb in French: *will there be enough?* = est-ce qu'il y en aura assez?

1 *pron, quantif* assez; **have you had ~ to eat?** avez-vous assez mangé?; **more than ~** largement assez; **is that ~?** ça suffit?; **I've had ~ of him** j'en ai assez de lui
2 *adv* assez; **curiously ~,...** aussi bizarre que cela puisse paraître...
3 *det* assez de; **have you got ~ chairs?** avez-vous assez de chaises?

enquire **1** *vtr* demander
2 *vi* se renseigner (**about** sur); **to ~ after sb** demander des nouvelles de qn

enquiring *adj* ⟨look, voice⟩ interrogateur/-trice; ⟨mind⟩ curieux/-ieuse

enquiry *n* demande *f* de renseignements; **to make enquiries** demander des renseignements (**about** sur); ▶ INQUIRY

enrage *vtr* rendre [qn] furieux/-ieuse

enrich *vtr* enrichir

enrol, enroll (US) ① *vtr* (gen) inscrire; (Mil) enrôler
② *vi* (gen) s'inscrire (**in, on** à); (Mil) s'engager (**in** dans)

enrolment, enrollment (US) *n* (gen) inscription *f* (**in, on** à); (Mil) enrôlement *m*

ensuing *adj* ⟨*period*⟩ qui suivit; ⟨*event*⟩ qui s'ensuivit

en suite *adj* attenant/-e

ensure *vtr* garantir; **to ~ that...** s'assurer que...

entail *vtr* impliquer ⟨*travel, work*⟩; entraîner ⟨*expense*⟩; nécessiter ⟨*effort*⟩

enter ① *vtr* (a) entrer dans ⟨*room, house, phase, period, profession, army*⟩; participer à ⟨*race, competition*⟩; entrer à ⟨*parliament*⟩; **to ~ sb's mind** *or* **head** venir à l'idée *or* à l'esprit de qn
(b) engager ⟨*horse*⟩ (**for** dans); présenter ⟨*poem, picture*⟩ (**for** à)
(c) inscrire ⟨*figure, fact*⟩ (**in** dans); (in diary) noter ⟨*appointment*⟩ (**in** dans); (in computer) entrer ⟨*data*⟩
② *vi* (a) (come in) entrer
(b) **to ~ for** s'inscrire à ⟨*exam*⟩; s'inscrire pour ⟨*race*⟩
■ **enter into** entrer en ⟨*conversation*⟩; entamer ⟨*negotiations*⟩; passer ⟨*contract*⟩

enterprise *n* (a) (gen) entreprise *f*
(b) (initiative) esprit *m* d'initiative

enterprising *adj* ⟨*person*⟩ entreprenant/-e; ⟨*plan*⟩ audacieux/-ieuse

entertain ① *vtr* (a) (keep amused) divertir; (make laugh) amuser; (keep occupied) distraire, occuper
(b) (play host to) recevoir ⟨*guests*⟩
(c) entretenir ⟨*idea*⟩; nourrir ⟨*doubt, ambition, illusion*⟩
② *vi* recevoir

entertainer *n* (comic) comique *mf*; (performer, raconteur) amuseur/-euse *m/f*

entertaining ① *adj* divertissant/-e
② *n* **they do a lot of ~** ils reçoivent beaucoup

entertainment *n* (a) divertissement *m*, distractions *fpl*
(b) (event) spectacle *m*

entertainment industry *n* industrie *f* du spectacle

enthusiasm *n* enthousiasme *m* (**for** pour)

enthusiast *n* (for sport, DIY) passionné/-e *m/f*; (for music, composer) fervent/-e *m/f*

enthusiastic *adj* (gen) enthousiaste; ⟨*discussion*⟩ exalté/-e; ⟨*worker, gardener*⟩ passionné/-e

entice *vtr* (with offer, charms, prospects) attirer; (with food, money) appâter

entire *adj* entier/-ière; **the ~ family** toute la famille, la famille entière

entirely *adv* ⟨*destroy, escape*⟩ entièrement; ⟨*different, unnecessary*⟩ complètement

entirety *n* ensemble *m*, totalité *f*

entitle *vtr* **to ~ sb to sth** donner droit à qch à qn; **to be ~d to sth** avoir droit à qch; **to be ~d to do** avoir le droit de faire

entitlement *n* droit *m*

entity *n* entité *f*

entrance ① *n* (gen) entrée *f*; **to gain ~ to** être admis/-e à *or* dans ⟨*club, university*⟩
② *vtr* transporter, ravir

entrance examination *n* (GB) (Sch, Univ) examen *m* d'entrée; (for civil service) concours *m* d'entrée

entrance fee *n* droit *m* d'entrée

entrance hall *n* (in house) vestibule *m*; (in public building) hall *m*

entrance requirements *n pl* diplômes *mpl* requis

entrant *n* (in competition) participant/-e *m/f*; (in exam) candidat/-e *m/f*

entreat *vtr* implorer, supplier (**to do** de faire)

entreaty *n* prière *f*, supplication *f*

entrepreneur *n* entrepreneur/-euse *m/f*

entrust *vtr* confier; **to ~ sb with sth, to ~ sth to sb** confier qch à qn

entry *n* (a) (gen) entrée *f*; **to gain ~ to** *or* **into** s'introduire dans ⟨*building*⟩; accéder à ⟨*computer file*⟩; **'no ~'** (on door) 'défense d'entrer'; (in one way street) 'sens interdit'
(b) (in diary) note *f*; (in ledger) écriture *f*
(c) (for competition) œuvre *f* présentée à un concours

entry form *n* (for membership) fiche *f* d'inscription; (for competition) bulletin *m* de participation

entry phone *n* interphone *m*

envelope *n* enveloppe *f*

envious *adj* envieux/-ieuse; **to be ~ of sb/sth** envier qn/qch

environment *n* (physical, cultural) environnement *m*; (social) milieu *m*

environmental *adj* ⟨*conditions, changes*⟩ du milieu; ⟨*concern, issue*⟩ lié/-e à l'environnement, écologique; ⟨*protection, pollution*⟩ de l'environnement; **~ disaster** catastrophe *f* écologique

environmental health *n* hygiène *f* publique

environmentally *adv* **~ safe, ~ sound** qui ne nuit pas à l'environnement; **~ friendly product** produit qui respecte l'environnement

environmental studies *n pl* (GB Sch) études *fpl* géographiques et biologiques de l'environnement

envisage *vtr* (anticipate) prévoir (**doing** de faire); (visualize) envisager (**doing** de faire)

envoy *n* envoyé/-e *m/f*

envy ① *n* envie *f*; (long-term) jalousie *f*
② *vtr* **to ~ sb sth** envier qch à qn

enzyme *n* enzyme *f*

epic ① *n* (gen) épopée *f*; (film) film *m* à grand spectacle; (novel) roman-fleuve *m*
② *adj* épique

epidemic ① n épidémie f
② adj épidémique

epidural n péridurale f

epilepsy n épilepsie f

epileptic n, adj épileptique (mf)

episode n épisode m

epitome n épitomé m; **the ~ of kindness** la bonté incarnée

epitomize vtr personnifier, incarner

epoch n époque f

equal ① n égal/-e m/f
② adj (a) égal/-e (**to** à); **~ opportunities/ rights** égalité f des chances/des droits
(b) **to be ~ to** être à la hauteur de ⟨task⟩
③ adv ⟨finish⟩ à égalité
④ vtr égaler

equality n égalité f; **~ of opportunity** égalité des chances

equalize vi égaliser

equally adv ⟨divide, share⟩ en parts égales; **~ difficult** tout aussi difficile; **~, we might say that...** de même, on pourrait dire que...

equate vtr (identify) assimiler (**with, to** à); (compare) comparer (**with, to** à)

equation n équation f

equator n équateur m

equilibrium n équilibre m

equip vtr équiper (**for** pour; **with** de)

equipment n (gen) équipement m; (office, electrical, photographic) matériel m; **a piece** or **item of ~** un article

equivalent ① n équivalent m
② adj équivalent/-e

era n (in history, geology) ère f; (in politics, fashion) époque f

eradicate vtr éliminer ⟨poverty, crime⟩; éradiquer ⟨disease⟩

erase vtr effacer

eraser n (rubber) gomme f; (for blackboard) brosse f feutrée

erect ① adj ⟨posture⟩ droit/-e; ⟨tail, ears⟩ dressé/-e
② vtr ériger ⟨building⟩; monter ⟨scaffolding, tent, screen⟩

erection n (gen) érection f; (of building) construction f; (edifice) édifice m

ermine n hermine f

erode vtr éroder ⟨rock, metal⟩; saper ⟨confidence⟩

erosion n érosion f

erotic adj érotique

err vi (a) (make mistake) faire erreur
(b) **to ~ on the side of caution** pécher par excès de prudence

errand n commission f, course f; **to run an ~ for sb** aller faire une commission pour qn

erratic adj ⟨behaviour, person, driver⟩ imprévisible; ⟨moods⟩ changeant/-e

error n (in spelling, grammar, typing) faute f; (in calculation, on computer) erreur f

erupt vi (a) ⟨volcano⟩ entrer en éruption
(b) ⟨violence⟩ éclater

eruption n (of volcano) éruption f; (of violence, anger) explosion f

escalate vi ⟨conflict, violence⟩ s'intensifier; ⟨prices⟩ monter en flèche; ⟨unemployment⟩ augmenter rapidement

escalator n escalier m mécanique, escalator® m

escapade n frasque f

escape ① n fuite f, évasion f (**from** de; **to** vers); **to have a narrow** or **lucky ~** l'échapper belle
② vtr échapper à
③ vi (a) ⟨person⟩ s'enfuir, s'évader (**from** de); ⟨animal⟩ s'échapper (**from** de); (figurative) s'évader; **to ~ with one's life** s'en sortir vivant
(b) (leak) fuir

escape clause n clause f dérogatoire

escape key n touche f d'échappement

escape route n (in case of fire etc) plan m d'évacuation; (for fugitives) itinéraire m d'évasion

escapism n évasion f (du réel)

escort ① n (a) (for security) escorte f; **police ~** escorte de police
(b) (companion) compagnon/compagne m/f
(c) (in agency) hôtesse f; **~ agency** agence f d'hôtesses
② vtr (a) (for security) escorter; **to ~ sb in/out** faire entrer/sortir qn sous escorte
(b) (to a function) accompagner; (home) raccompagner

especially adv (a) (above all) surtout, en particulier; **him ~** lui en particulier; **~ as it's so hot** d'autant plus qu'il fait si chaud
(b) (on purpose) exprès, spécialement
(c) (unusually) particulièrement

espresso n express m inv

essay n (a) (Sch) rédaction f (**on, about** sur); (extended) dissertation f (**on** sur)
(b) (literary) essai m (**on** sur)

essence n essence f

essential ① n **a car is not an ~** une voiture n'est pas indispensable; **the ~s** l'essentiel m
② adj ⟨role, feature, element⟩ essentiel/-ielle; ⟨ingredient, reading⟩ indispensable; ⟨difference⟩ fondamental/-e; **it is ~ that we agree** il est indispensable que nous soyons d'accord

essentially adv essentiellement

essential oil n huile f essentielle

establish vtr (gen) établir; fonder ⟨company⟩

establishment n (a) (gen) établissement m
(b) (shop, business) maison f
(c) **the Establishment** l'ordre m établi

estate n (a) (stately home and park) domaine m, propriété f
(b) = HOUSING ESTATE
(c) (assets) biens mpl
(d) (GB) (also **~ car**) break m

estate agency n (GB) agence f
immobilière

estate agent n (GB) agent m immobilier

esteem n estime f

estimate **1** n (a) estimation f
(b) (quote for client) devis m
2 vtr évaluer ⟨value, size, distance⟩; **to ∼
that** estimer que
3 **estimated** pp adj ⟨cost, figure⟩
approximatif/-ive; **an ∼d 300 people** environ
300 personnes

Estonia pr n Estonie f

estranged adj **∼ from sb** séparé/-e de qn;
her ∼ husband son mari dont elle est
séparée

etc adv (written abbr = **et cetera**) etc

etching n eau-forte f

eternal adj ⟨life⟩ éternel/-elle; ⟨chatter,
optimist⟩ perpétuel/-elle

ethical adj ⟨problem, objection⟩ moral/-e;
⟨investment, theory⟩ éthique

ethics n (code) moralité f; **professional ∼**
déontologie f

ethnic adj ethnique

ethnic cleansing n purification f
ethnique

ethnic minority n minorité f ethnique

etiquette n (a) (social) bienséance f,
étiquette f
(b) (professional, diplomatic) protocole m

euphemism n euphémisme m

euphoria n euphorie f

Euro- pref euro-

eurocheque n Eurochèque m

Eurocrat n eurocrate mf

Euro-MP n député m européen

Europe pr n Europe f

European **1** n Européen/-éenne m/f
2 adj européen/-éenne

European Commission n
Commission f européenne

European Monetary System, **EMS**
n système m monétaire européen, SME m

European Monetary Union, **EMU** n
Union f monétaire européenne

European Union, **EU** n Union f
européenne, UE f

eurosceptic n eurosceptique mf

euthanasia n euthanasie f

evacuate vtr évacuer

evacuee n évacué/-e m/f

evade vtr esquiver ⟨blow⟩; éluder
⟨question, problem⟩

evaluate vtr évaluer

evaluation n évaluation f

evaporate vi ⟨liquid⟩ s'évaporer

evaporated milk n lait m condensé non
sucré

evasion n (of responsibility) dérobade f (of à);
tax ∼ évasion f fiscale

evasive adj ⟨answer⟩ évasif/-ive; ⟨look⟩
fuyant/-e

eve n veille f; **on the ∼ of** à la veille de

even¹ **1** adv (a) (gen) même; **he didn't ∼
try** il n'a même pas essayé; **don't tell anyone,
not ∼ Bob** ne dis rien à personne, pas
même à Bob; **∼ if/when** même si/quand
(b) (with comparative) encore; **∼ colder** encore
plus froid
2 **even so** phr quand même
3 **even though** phr bien que
(+ subjunctive)

even² adj ⟨surface, voice, temper⟩ égal/-e;
⟨teeth, hemline⟩ régulier/-ière; ⟨temperature⟩
constant/-e; ⟨number⟩ pair/-e; **to get ∼ with
sb** rendre à qn la monnaie de sa pièce

evening n soir m; (with emphasis on duration)
soirée f; **in the ∼** le soir; **all ∼** toute la
soirée; **every ∼** tous les soirs

evening class n cours m du soir

evening dress n (formal clothes) tenue f de
soirée

event n (a) événement m
(b) (eventuality) cas m; **in the ∼ of a fire** en
cas d'incendie; **in any ∼** de toute façon
(c) (in athletics) épreuve f

eventful adj mouvementé/-e

eventually adv finalement; **to do sth ∼**
finir par faire qch

ever **1** adv (a) jamais; **no-one will ∼ forget**
personne n'oubliera jamais; **hardly ∼**
rarement, presque jamais; **has he ∼ lived
abroad?** est-ce qu'il a déjà vécu à
l'étranger?; **do you ∼ make mistakes?** est-ce
qu'il t'arrive de te tromper?; **he's happier
than he's ∼ been** il n'a jamais été aussi
heureux; **more beautiful than ∼** plus beau/
belle que jamais
(b) (always) toujours; **as cheerful as ∼**
toujours aussi gai; **the same as ∼** toujours
le même; **they lived happily ∼ after** ils
vécurent toujours heureux
2 **ever since** phr depuis; **∼ since we
arrived** depuis notre arrivée

evergreen n arbre m à feuilles
persistantes

everlasting adj éternel/-elle

every **1** det (a) (each) chaque; **∼ time**
chaque fois; **∼ house in the street** toutes les
maisons de la rue; **I've read ∼ one of her
books** j'ai lu tous ses livres
(b) (emphatic) **there is ∼ chance that you'll
have a place** il y a toutes les chances que tu
aies une place; **to have ∼ right to complain**
avoir tous les droits de se plaindre
(c) (indicating frequency) **∼ day** tous les jours;
∼ Thursday tous les jeudis; **once ∼ few
days** tous les deux ou trois jours
2 **every other** phr **∼ other day** tous les
deux jours; **∼ other Sunday** un dimanche
sur deux
IDIOMS **∼ now and then**, **∼ so often** de
temps en temps

everybody pron (also **everyone**) tout le
monde

everyday *adj* ⟨*life*⟩ quotidien/·ienne; ⟨*clothes*⟩ de tous les jours; **in ~ use** d'usage courant

everyone = EVERYBODY

everything *pron* tout

everywhere *adv* partout

evict *vtr* expulser (**from** de)

eviction *n* expulsion *f*

evidence *n* (a) (proof) preuves *fpl* (**that** que; **of**, **for** de; **against** contre)
(b) (testimony) témoignage *m* (**from** de); **to give ~** témoigner, déposer (**for sb** en faveur de qn; **against sb** contre qn)
(c) (trace) trace *f* (**of** de)

evident *adj* manifeste

evidently *adv* (a) (apparently) apparemment
(b) (patently) manifestement

evil **1** *n* mal *m*
2 *adj* ⟨*person, forces*⟩ malfaisant/·e; ⟨*act*⟩ diabolique; ⟨*spirit*⟩ maléfique; ⟨*smell*⟩ nauséabond/·e

evolution *n* évolution *f* (**from** à partir de)

evolve *vi* évoluer

ewe *n* brebis *f*

ex- *pref* ex-, ancien/·ienne (*before n*)

exact *adj* exact/·e; **to be (more) ~** plus précisément

exactly *adv* exactement

exaggerate *vtr*, *vi* exagérer

exaggeration *n* exagération *f*

exam *n* examen *m*

examination *n* examen *m* (**in** de); **French ~** examen *m* de français; **to take/pass an ~** passer/réussir un examen; **to have an ~** (Med) passer un examen médical

examination paper *n* sujets *mpl* d'examen

examine *vtr* examiner

examiner *n* examinateur/·trice *m/f*

example *n* exemple *m*; **for ~** par exemple; **to set a good ~** donner l'exemple; **to make an ~ of sb** punir qn pour l'exemple

excavate **1** *vtr* fouiller ⟨*site*⟩; creuser ⟨*tunnel*⟩
2 *vi* faire des fouilles

exceed *vtr* dépasser (**by** de)

excel *vi* exceller (**at**, **in** en; **at** *or* **in doing** à faire)

excellent *adj* excellent/·e

except **1** *prep* sauf; **everybody ~ Lisa** tout le monde sauf Lisa, tout le monde à l'exception de *or* excepté Lisa; **who could have done it ~ him?** qui aurait pu le faire sinon lui?
2 except for *phr* à part, à l'exception de

exception *n* (a) exception *f* (**for** pour); **with the ~ of** à l'exception de
(b) **to take ~ to** prendre [qch] comme une insulte

exceptional *adj* exceptionnel/·elle

excess **1** *n* excès *m* (**of** de)
2 *adj* **~ weight** excès *m* de poids; **~ baggage** excédent *m* de bagages

excessive *adj* excessif/·ive

exchange **1** *n* (a) échange *m*; **in ~** en échange (**for** de); **~ visit** voyage *m* d'échange
(b) (in banking) change *m*; **the ~ rate** le taux de change
(c) (*also* **telephone ~**) central *m* (téléphonique)
2 *vtr* échanger (**for** contre; **with** avec)

exchange control *n* contrôle *m* des changes

Exchange Rate Mechanism, ERM *n* système *m* monétaire européen

Exchequer *pr n* (GB) **the ~** l'Échiquier *m*, le ministère des finances

excite *vtr* exciter

excited *adj* (gen) excité/·e; ⟨*voice, conversation*⟩ animé/·e

excitement *n* excitation *f*

exciting *adj* passionnant/·e

exclaim *vtr* s'exclamer

exclamation mark, exclamation point (US) *n* point *m* d'exclamation

exclude *vtr* exclure (**from** de)

excluding *prep* à l'exclusion de; **~ VAT** TVA non comprise

exclusion zone *n* zone *f* interdite

exclusive **1** *n* (report) exclusivité *f*
2 *adj* (a) ⟨*club*⟩ fermé/·e; ⟨*hotel*⟩ de luxe; ⟨*district*⟩ huppé/·e
(b) ⟨*story, rights*⟩ exclusif/·ive; ⟨*interview*⟩ en exclusivité; **~ of meals** les repas non compris

excruciating *adj* ⟨*pain*⟩ atroce

excursion *n* (organized) excursion *f*

excuse **1** *n* excuse *f* (**for sth** à qch; **for doing** pour faire; **to do** pour faire); **to make ~s** trouver des excuses; **an ~ to leave early** un bon prétexte pour partir tôt; **there's no ~ for such behaviour** ce genre de conduite est inexcusable
2 *vtr* (a) excuser ⟨*person*⟩ (**for doing** de faire, d'avoir fait); **~ me!** (apology) excusez-moi!, pardon!; (beginning an enquiry) excusez-moi; (pardon) pardon?
(b) (exempt) dispenser (**from sth** de qch; **from doing** de faire)

ex-directory *adj* sur la liste rouge

execute *vtr* exécuter

execution *n* exécution *f*

executioner *n* bourreau *m*

executive **1** *n* (a) cadre *m*; **sales ~** cadre *m* commercial
(b) (committee) exécutif *m*, comité *m* exécutif; **party ~** bureau *m* du parti
2 *adj* (a) ⟨*post*⟩ de cadre
(b) ⟨*power*⟩ exécutif/·ive

exemplify *vtr* illustrer, exemplifier

exempt **1** *adj* exempt/·e (**from** de)
2 *vtr* exempter (**from** de)

exemption *n* exemption *f*; (from exam) dispense *f*

exercise **1** *n* exercice *m*

2 *vtr* (a) exercer ‹*body*›; faire travailler ‹*limb, muscles*›
(b) faire preuve de ‹*control, restraint*›; exercer ‹*power, right*›
3 *vi* faire de l'exercice

exercise bike *n* (at home) vélo *m* d'appartement; (in gym) vélo *m* d'entraînement

exercise book *n* cahier *m*

exert *vtr* exercer ‹*pressure, influence*› (on sur); to ~ oneself se fatiguer

exhale *vi* ‹*person*› expirer

exhaust **1** *n* (a) (*also* ~ **pipe**) pot *m* d'échappement
(b) (*also* ~ **fumes**) gaz *mpl* d'échappement
2 *vtr* épuiser; ~ed épuisé/-e

exhaustion *n* épuisement *m*

exhibit **1** *n* (a) œuvre *f* exposée
(b) (US) (exhibition) exposition *f*
2 *vtr* exposer ‹*work of art*›; manifester ‹*preference, sign*›

exhibition *n* exposition *f*; art ~ exposition; to make an ~ of oneself se donner en spectacle

exhibition centre (GB), **exhibition center** (US) *n* palais *m* des expositions

exhilarating *adj* ‹*game*› stimulant/-e; ‹*experience*› exaltant/-e; ‹*speed*› enivrant/-e

exile **1** *n* (a) (person) exilé/-e *m/f*
(b) (expulsion) exil *m* (from de); in ~ en exil
2 *vtr* exiler (de from)

exist *vi* exister

existence *n* existence *f* (of de)

existing *adj* ‹*laws, order*› existant/-e; ‹*policy, management*› actuel/-elle

exit **1** *n* sortie *f*; 'no ~' 'interdit'
2 *vi* sortir

exodus *n* exode *m*

exotic *adj* exotique

expand **1** *vtr* développer ‹*business, network, range*›; élargir ‹*horizon, knowledge*›; étendre ‹*empire*›; gonfler ‹*lungs*›
2 *vi* ‹*business, sector, town*› se développer; ‹*economy*› être en expansion; ‹*metal*› se dilater

expanse *n* étendue *f*

expansion *n* développement *m* (in de; into dans); (of economy) expansion *f*; (of population) accroissement *m*

expatriate *n, adj* expatrié/-e (*m/f*)

expect **1** *vtr* (a) s'attendre à ‹*event, victory, defeat, trouble*›; to ~ the worst s'attendre au pire; to ~ sb to do s'attendre à ce que qn fasse; I ~ (that) I'll lose je m'attends à perdre; more than ~ed plus que prévu
(b) s'attendre à ‹*sympathy, help*› (from de la part de)
(c) attendre ‹*baby, guest*›
(d) (require) demander, attendre ‹*hard work*› (from de); I ~ you to be punctual je vous demande d'être ponctuel
(e) (GB) (suppose) I ~ so je pense que oui; I ~ he's tired il doit être fatigué

2 *vi* (a) to ~ to do s'attendre à faire
(b) (require) I ~ to see you there je compte bien vous y voir
(c) (be pregnant) to be ~ing attendre un enfant

expectant *adj* (a) ‹*look*› plein d'attente
(b) ‹*mother*› futur/-e (before n)

expectation *n* (a) (prediction) prévision *f*; against all ~(s) à l'encontre des prévisions générales
(b) (hope) aspiration *f*, attente *f*; to live up to sb's ~s répondre à l'attente de qn

expedient *adj* (a) (appropriate) opportun/-e
(b) (advantageous) politique

expedition *n* expédition *f*; to go on an ~ partir en expédition

expel *vtr* (gen) expulser; renvoyer ‹*pupil*›

expenditure *n* dépense *f*

expense **1** *n* (a) (cost) frais *mpl*; (money spent) dépense *f*; at one's own ~ à ses propres frais; to go to great ~ dépenser beaucoup d'argent (to do pour faire); to spare no ~ ne pas regarder à la dépense
(b) at the ~ of au détriment de ‹*health, public, safety*›; at sb's ~ ‹*laugh, joke*› aux dépens de qn
2 **expenses** *n pl* frais *mpl*

expense account *n* frais *mpl* de représentation

expensive *adj* (gen) cher/chère; ‹*holiday, mistake*› coûteux/-euse; ‹*taste*› de luxe

experience **1** *n* expérience *f*
2 *vtr* connaître ‹*loss, problem*›; éprouver ‹*emotion*›

experienced *adj* (gen) expérimenté/-e; ‹*eye*› entraîné/-e

experiment **1** *n* expérience *f* (in en; on sur)
2 *vi* expérimenter, faire des essais

experimental *adj* expérimental/-e

experimentation *n* expériences *fpl*

expert **1** *n* spécialiste *mf* (in en, de), expert *m* (in en)
2 *adj* ‹*opinion, advice*› autorisé/-e; ‹*witness*› expert/-e; ‹*eye*› exercé/-e; an ~ **cook** un cordon bleu

expertise *n* compétences *fpl*; (very specialized) expertise *f* (in dans le domaine de)

expire *vi* ‹*deadline, offer*› expirer; ‹*period*› arriver à terme; my passport has ~d mon passeport est périmé

expiry date *n* (of credit card, permit) date *f* d'expiration

explain *vtr* expliquer (that que; to à)

explanation *n* explication *f* (of de; for à)

explicit *adj* explicite

explode **1** *vtr* (a) faire exploser ‹*bomb*›
(b) pulvériser ‹*theory, rumour, myth*›
2 *vi* (gen) exploser; ‹*boiler, building, ship*› sauter

exploit **1** *n* exploit *m*
2 *vtr* exploiter

exploitation *n* exploitation *f*

explore **1** *vtr* explorer

···⟫

2 *vi* to go exploring partir en exploration

explorer *n* explorateur/-trice *m/f*

explosion *n* explosion *f*

explosive **1** *n* explosif *m*
2 *adj* ⟨*device, force*⟩ explosif/-ive; ⟨*substance*⟩ explosible

export **1** *n* (process) exportation *f* (of de); (product) produit *m* d'exportation
2 *vtr, vi* exporter

exporter *n* exportateur/-trice *m/f* (of de)

expose *vtr* (a) exposer (to à)
(b) (make public) révéler ⟨*identity*⟩; dénoncer ⟨*person, scandal*⟩
(c) to ~ oneself commettre un outrage à la pudeur

exposure *n* (a) (of secret, crime) révélation *f*
(b) (to light, sun, radiation) exposition *f* (to à)
(c) to die of ~ mourir de froid
(d) (*also* ~ **time**) temps *m* de pose
(e) (picture) pose *f*

express **1** *n* rapide *m*
2 *adj* ⟨*letter, parcel*⟩ exprès; ⟨*delivery, train*⟩ rapide
3 *adv* to send sth ~ envoyer qch en exprès
4 *vtr* exprimer; to ~ oneself s'exprimer

expression *n* expression *f*

expressive *adj* expressif/-ive

exquisite *adj* exquis/-e

extend **1** *vtr* (a) agrandir ⟨*house*⟩; prolonger ⟨*runway*⟩; élargir ⟨*range*⟩; ~ed **family** famille *f* étendue
(b) prolonger ⟨*visit, visa*⟩
(c) étendre ⟨*arm, leg*⟩; tendre ⟨*hand*⟩
2 *vi* s'étendre (**as far as** jusqu'à; **from** de)

extension *n* (a) (on cable, table) rallonge *f*; (to house) addition *f*
(b) (phone) poste *m* supplémentaire; ~ (**number**) (numéro *m* de) poste *m*
(c) (of deadline) délai *m* supplémentaire

extension lead *n* rallonge *f*

extensive *adj* (a) ⟨*network*⟩ vaste (before n); ⟨*list*⟩ long/longue (before n); ⟨*tests*⟩ approfondi/-e; ⟨*changes*⟩ important/-e
(b) ⟨*damage, loss*⟩ grave, considérable; ⟨*burns*⟩ grave

extent *n* (a) (of area, problem, power) étendue *f*; (of damage) ampleur *f*
(b) (degree) mesure *f*; to a certain/great ~ dans une certaine/large mesure

exterior **1** *n* extérieur *m* (of de)
2 *adj* extérieur/-e (to à)

exterminate *vtr* éliminer ⟨*vermin*⟩; exterminer ⟨*people, race*⟩

external *adj* (gen) extérieur/-e (to à); ⟨*surface, injury, examiner*⟩ externe

extinct *adj* ⟨*species*⟩ disparu/-e; ⟨*volcano*⟩ éteint/-e; to become ~ ⟨*species, animal, plant*⟩ disparaître

extinguish *vtr* éteindre ⟨*fire, cigarette*⟩

extinguisher *n* extincteur *m*

extra **1** *n* (a) (feature) option *f*; the sunroof is an ~ le toit ouvrant est en option
(b) (actor) figurant/-e *m/f*

2 *adj* supplémentaire; an ~ £1,000 1 000 livres sterling de plus
3 *adv* ~ careful encore plus prudent (que d'habitude); you have to pay ~ il faut payer un supplément

extra charge *n* supplément *m*

extract **1** *n* extrait *m* (from de)
2 *vtr* (a) extraire (from de)
(b) arracher ⟨*promise*⟩ (from à)

extra-curricular *adj* parascolaire

extraordinary *adj* extraordinaire

extraterrestrial *n, adj* extraterrestre (*mf*)

extra time *n* (in sport) prolongation *f*; to go into ~ jouer les prolongations

extravagance *n* (a) (trait) prodigalité *f*
(b) (luxury) luxe *m*

extravagant *adj* (a) ⟨*person*⟩ dépensier/-ière; ⟨*way of life*⟩ dispendieux/-ieuse; to be ~ with sth gaspiller qch
(b) (luxurious) luxueux/-euse

extra virgin olive oil *n* huile *f* d'olive extra vierge

extreme **1** *n* extrême *m*; to go to ~s pousser les choses à l'extrême
2 *adj* (gen) extrême; ⟨*view, measure, reaction*⟩ extrémiste

extremely *adv* extrêmement

extreme sports *n pl* sports *mpl* extrêmes

extremism *n* extrémisme *m*

extrovert *n, adj* extraverti/-e (*m/f*)

eye **1** *n* (a) œil *m*; with blue ~s aux yeux bleus; in front of *or* before your (very) ~s sous vos yeux; to keep an ~ on sb/sth surveiller qn/qch; to have one's ~ on (watch) surveiller ⟨*person*⟩; (want) avoir envie de ⟨*house*⟩; viser ⟨*job*⟩; to catch sb's ~ attirer l'attention de qn; as far as the ~ can see à perte de vue; to have an ~ for avoir le sens de ⟨*detail*⟩
(b) (of needle) chas *m*
2 *vtr* regarder
IDIOMS an ~ for an ~ œil pour œil; to make ~s at sb faire les yeux doux à qn; to see ~ to ~ with sb (about sth) partager le point de vue de qn (au sujet de qch)

eyeball *n* globe *m* oculaire

eyebrow *n* sourcil *m*

eyebrow pencil *n* crayon *m* à sourcils

eye-catching *adj* ⟨*design, poster*⟩ attrayant/-e; ⟨*advertisement, headline*⟩ accrocheur/-euse

eyedrops *n pl* gouttes *fpl* pour les yeux

eyelash *n* cil *m*

eyelid *n* paupière *f*

eye liner *n* eye-liner *m*

eye shadow *n* fard *m* à paupières

eyesight *n* vue *f*

eye test *n* examen *m* de la vue

eyewitness *n* témoin *m* oculaire

e-zine *n* magazine *m* électronique, e-zine *m*

Ff

f, F *n* **(a)** (letter) f, F *m*
(b) F (Mus) fa *m*

fable *n* fable *f*

fabric *n* **(a)** (cloth) tissu *m*
(b) (of building) structure *f*; **the ~ of society** le tissu social

fabricate *vtr* **(a)** inventer [qch] de toutes pièces ⟨*story, evidence*⟩
(b) fabriquer ⟨*document*⟩

fabric softener *n* assouplissant *m*

fabulous *adj* **(a)** fabuleux/-euse
(b) (colloq) (wonderful) sensationnel/-elle (colloq)

façade, facade *n* façade *f* (of de)

face **1** *n* **(a)** (of person) visage *m*, figure *f*; (of animal) face *f*; **to slam the door/laugh in sb's ~** claquer la porte/rire au nez de qn; **to pull** *or* **make a ~** faire une grimace; (in disgust) faire la grimace
(b) to lose ~ perdre la face; **to save ~** sauver la face
(c) (of clock, watch) cadran *m*; (of coin) côté *m*; (of planet) surface *f*; (of cliff, mountain) face *f*; (of playing card) face *f*; **~ up/down** à l'endroit/l'envers
2 *vtr* **(a)** (look towards) ⟨*person*⟩ faire face à; ⟨*building, room*⟩ donner sur; **to ~ south** ⟨*person*⟩ regarder au sud; ⟨*building*⟩ être orienté/-e au sud
(b) se trouver face à ⟨*challenge, crisis*⟩; se trouver menacé/-e de ⟨*defeat, redundancy*⟩; affronter ⟨*rival, team*⟩; **to be ~d with** se trouver confronté/-e à ⟨*problem, decision*⟩
(c) (acknowledge) **~ the facts, you're finished!** regarde la réalité en face, tu es fini!; **let's ~ it, nobody's perfect** admettons-le, personne n'est parfait
(d) (tolerate prospect) **I can't ~ doing** je n'ai pas le courage de faire; **he couldn't ~ the thought of eating** l'idée de manger lui était insupportable
(e) revêtir ⟨*façade, wall*⟩ (**with** de)
3 in the face of *phr* **(a)** en dépit de ⟨*difficulties*⟩
(b) face à, devant ⟨*opposition, enemy, danger*⟩
4 face to face *adv* ⟨*be seated*⟩ face à face; **to come ~ to ~ with** se retrouver face à; **to talk to sb ~ to ~** parler à qn en personne
■ **face up to** faire face à ⟨*problem, responsibilities*⟩

faceless *adj* anonyme

face-lift *n* lifting *m*; **to have a ~** se faire faire un lifting; **to give [sth] a ~** rénover ⟨*building*⟩; réaménager ⟨*town centre*⟩

facet *n* facette *f*

facetious *adj* ⟨*remark*⟩ facétieux/-ieuse; ⟨*person*⟩ farceur/-euse

face-to-face **1** *adj* **a ~ discussion, a ~ meeting** un face-à-face *inv*
2 face to face *adv* ⟨*be seated*⟩ face à face; **to come ~ with** se retrouver face à; **to meet sb ~** rencontrer qn en face-à-face

face value *n* (of coin) valeur *f* nominale; **to take [sth] at ~** prendre [qch] au pied de la lettre; **to take sb at ~** juger qn sur les apparences

facilitate *vtr* faciliter ⟨*progress, talks*⟩; favoriser ⟨*development*⟩

facility **1** *n* **(a)** (building) complexe *m*, installation *f*
(b) (ease) facilité *f*
(c) (feature) fonction *f*
2 facilities *n pl* **(a)** (equipment) équipement *m*; (infrastructure) infrastructure *f*; **facilities for the disabled** installations *fpl* pour les handicapés; **parking facilities** parking *m*

facsimile *n* (gen) fac-similé *m*; (sculpture) reproduction *f*

fact *n* fait *m*; **~s and figures** les faits et les chiffres; **to know for a ~ that** savoir de source sûre que; **due to the ~ that** étant donné que; **in ~, as a matter of ~** en fait; **to be based on ~** être fondé/-e sur des faits réels
IDIOMS **to know the ~s of life** savoir comment les enfants viennent au monde; **the (hard) ~s of life** les réalités de la vie

fact-finding *adj* ⟨*mission, tour*⟩ d'information

faction *n* (group) faction *f*

factor *n* facteur *m*; **common ~** point *m* commun; (in mathematics) facteur commun; **protection ~** indice *m* de protection

factory *n* usine *f*

factory farming *n* élevage *m* industriel

factory shop *n* magasin *m* d'usine

factory worker *n* ouvrier/-ière *m/f* (d'usine)

fact sheet *n* bulletin *m* d'informations

factual *adj* ⟨*evidence*⟩ factuel/-elle; ⟨*account, description*⟩ basé/-e sur les faits; **~ programme** reportage *m*

faculty *n* **(a)** (ability) faculté *f* (**for** de)
(b) (GB Univ) faculté *f*
(c) (US) (Univ, Sch) (staff) corps *m* enseignant

fad *n* **(a)** (craze) engouement *m* (**for** pour)
(b) (whim) (petite) manie *f*

fade **1** *vtr* décolorer
2 *vi* ⟨*fabric*⟩ se décolorer, se défraîchir; ⟨*colour*⟩ passer; ⟨*lettering, smile, memory*⟩ s'effacer; ⟨*flowers*⟩ se faner; ⟨*image*⟩ s'estomper; ⟨*sound*⟩ s'affaiblir; ⟨*interest, excitement*⟩ s'évanouir; ⟨*hearing, light*⟩ baisser ···⟫

■ **fade away** ⟨sound⟩ s'éteindre; ⟨sick person⟩ dépérir

faded adj ⟨clothing⟩ décoloré/-e; ⟨jeans⟩ délavé/-e; ⟨photo⟩ jauni/-e; ⟨flower⟩ fané/-e

faeces, feces (US) n pl matières fpl fécales

fail ⓵ n (in exam) échec m
⓶ vtr (a) échouer à ⟨exam, driving test⟩; échouer en ⟨subject⟩; coller (colloq) ⟨candidate, pupil⟩
(b) (omit) to ~ to do manquer de faire; to ~ to mention that... omettre de signaler que...
(c) (be unable) to ~ to do ne pas réussir à faire
(d) ⟨person⟩ laisser tomber ⟨friend⟩; ⟨courage, attempt⟩ manquer à ⟨person⟩; ⟨memory⟩ faire défaut à ⟨person⟩
⓷ vi (a) (not succeed) ne pas réussir; ⟨exam candidate, attempt, plan⟩ échouer; ⟨crop⟩ être mauvais/-e; if all else ~s en dernier recours
(b) ⟨eyesight, hearing, light⟩ baisser; ⟨health⟩ décliner
(c) ⟨brakes⟩ lâcher; ⟨power⟩ être coupé/-e; ⟨heart⟩ lâcher
⓸ **without fail** phr ⟨arrive, do⟩ sans faute; ⟨happen⟩ à coup sûr

failing ⓵ n défaut m
⓶ prep ~ that, ~ this sinon

failure n (a) (lack of success) échec m (in à)
(b) ⟨person⟩ raté/-e m/f⟨colloq); (venture or event) échec m
(c) (of engine, machine) panne f
(d) (Med) défaillance f
(e) (omission) ~ to comply with the rules non-respect m de la réglementation; ~ to pay non-paiement m

faint ⓵ adj (a) ⟨smell, accent, breeze⟩ léger/-ère; ⟨sound, voice, protest⟩ faible; ⟨markings⟩ à peine visible; ⟨recollection⟩ vague; I haven't the ~est idea je n'en ai pas la moindre idée
(b) to feel ~ se sentir mal, défaillir
⓶ vi s'évanouir (from sous l'effet de)

fainthearted n the ~ (cowardly) les timorés mpl; (over-sensitive) les natures fpl sensibles

fair ⓵ n (funfair, market) foire f; (for charity) kermesse f; trade ~ foire commerciale
⓶ adj (a) ⟨just⟩ ⟨arrangement, person, trial, wage⟩ équitable (to pour); ⟨comment, decision, point⟩ valable; it's only ~ that she should be first ce n'est que justice qu'elle soit la première; it isn't ~ ce n'est pas juste
(b) (quite good) assez bon/bonne
(c) a ~ number of un bon nombre de; the house was a ~ size la maison était de bonne taille
(d) ⟨weather⟩ beau/belle (before n); ⟨wind⟩ favorable
(e) ⟨hair⟩ blond/-e; ⟨complexion⟩ clair/-e
(f) with her own ~ hands de ses blanches mains; the ~ sex le beau sexe
⓷ adv ⟨play⟩ franc jeu
IDIOMS to win ~ and square remporter une victoire indiscutable

fairground n champ m de foire

fair-haired adj blond/-e

fairly adv (a) (quite, rather) assez; ⟨sure⟩ pratiquement
(b) (justly) ⟨obtain, win⟩ honnêtement

fair-minded adj impartial/-e

fairness n (a) (of person) équité f; (of judgment) impartialité f; in all ~ en toute justice
(b) (of complexion) blancheur f; (of hair) blondeur f

fair play n to have a sense of ~ jouer franc jeu, être fair-play; to ensure ~ faire respecter les règles du jeu

fairy n fée f

fairy story, fairy tale n conte m de fées

faith n (a) (confidence) confiance f; I have no ~ in her elle ne m'inspire pas confiance; in good ~ en toute bonne foi
(b) (belief) foi f (in en); the Muslim ~ la foi musulmane

faithful ⓵ n the ~ les fidèles mpl
⓶ adj fidèle (to à)

faithfully adv fidèlement; yours ~ (in letter) veuillez agréer, Monsieur/Madame, mes/nos salutations distinguées

faith healer n guérisseur m

faith healing n guérison f par la foi

fake ⓵ n (a) (jewel, work of art, note) faux m
(b) (person) imposteur m
⓶ adj faux/fausse (before n)
⓷ vtr contrefaire ⟨signature, document⟩; falsifier ⟨results⟩; feindre ⟨emotion, illness⟩
⓸ vi faire semblant

falcon n faucon m

Falklands pr n pl (also **Falkland Islands**) the ~ les îles fpl Malouines

fall ⓵ n (a) (gen) chute f (from de); (in wrestling) tombé m
(b) (decrease) baisse f (in de); (more drastic) chute f (in de)
(c) (in pitch) descente f
(d) (of government) chute f; (of monarchy) renversement m
(e) (US) (autumn) automne m
⓶ **falls** n pl chutes fpl
⓷ vi (a) (gen) tomber (from, off, out of de; into dans); to ~ 10 metres tomber de 10 mètres; to ~ down tomber dans ⟨hole, stairs⟩; to ~ on or to the floor or the ground tomber par terre; to ~ at sb's feet se jeter aux pieds de qn; to ~ from power tomber
(b) ⟨quality, standard, level⟩ diminuer; ⟨temperature, price, production, number⟩ baisser (by de); to ~ to/from descendre à/de
■ **fall apart** (a) ⟨bike, table⟩ être délabré/-e; ⟨shoes⟩ être usé/-e; ⟨car, house⟩ tomber en ruine
(b) ⟨country⟩ se désagréger; ⟨person⟩ craquer (colloq)
■ **fall back** reculer; (Mil) se replier
■ **fall back on** avoir recours à ⟨savings, parents⟩
■ **fall behind** prendre du retard; to ~

behind with (GB) *or* in (US) prendre du retard dans ⟨*work, project*⟩; être en retard pour ⟨*payments, rent*⟩

■ **fall down (a)** ⟨*person, poster*⟩ tomber; ⟨*tent, scaffolding*⟩ s'effondrer

(b) (GB) ⟨*argument, comparison*⟩ faiblir

■ **fall for**: ¶ ~ **for** [sth] se laisser prendre à ⟨*trick, story*⟩; ¶ ~ **for** [sb] tomber amoureux/-euse de

■ **fall in (a)** ⟨*walls, roof*⟩ s'écrouler, s'effondrer

(b) ⟨*soldiers*⟩ former les rangs

■ **fall off (a)** ⟨*person, hat, label*⟩ tomber

(b) ⟨*attendance, sales, output*⟩ diminuer; ⟨*quality*⟩ baisser; ⟨*support*⟩ retomber

■ **fall open** ⟨*book*⟩ tomber ouvert/-e; ⟨*robe*⟩ s'entrebâiller

■ **fall out (a)** tomber; **his hair is ~ing out** il perd ses cheveux

(b) (quarrel) se brouiller (**over** à propos de; **with** avec)

■ **fall over**: ¶ ~ **over** ⟨*person*⟩ tomber (par terre); ⟨*object*⟩ se renverser; ¶ ~ **over** [sth] trébucher sur ⟨*object*⟩

■ **fall through** ⟨*plans, deal*⟩ échouer

fallacy *n* erreur *f*

fallible *adj* faillible

fallout *n* retombées *fpl*

false *adj* faux/fausse

false alarm *n* fausse alerte *f*

false bottom *n* (in bag, box) double fond *m*

falsely *adv* **(a)** (wrongly) faussement; (mistakenly) à tort

(b) ⟨*smile, laugh*⟩ avec affectation

false pretences *n pl* **on** *or* **under ~** en utilisant un subterfuge; (by an action) par des moyens frauduleux

false start *n* faux départ *m*

false teeth *n pl* dentier *m*

falsify *vtr* falsifier

falsity *n* fausseté *f*

falter *vi* **(a)** ⟨*person, courage*⟩ faiblir

(b) (when speaking) ⟨*person*⟩ bafouiller; ⟨*voice*⟩ trembloter

(c) (when walking) ⟨*person*⟩ chanceler; ⟨*footstep*⟩ hésiter

faltering *adj* ⟨*economy, demand*⟩ en déclin; ⟨*voice*⟩ hésitant/-e

fame *n* renommée *f* (**as** en tant que); **~ and fortune** la gloire et la fortune

familiar *adj* familier/-ière (**to** à); **her face looked ~ to me** son visage m'était familier; **that name sounds ~** ce nom me dit quelque chose; **it's a ~ story** c'est un scénario connu; **to be ~ with sth** connaître qch

familiarity *n* familiarité *f* (**with** avec)

familiarize ① *vtr* **to ~ sb with** familiariser qn avec

② *v refl* **to ~ oneself with** se familiariser avec ⟨*system, work*⟩; s'habituer à ⟨*person, place*⟩

family *n* famille *f*; **this must run in the ~** ça doit être de famille

family name *n* nom *m* de famille

family planning *n* planning *m* familial

family tree *n* arbre *m* généalogique

family unit *n* cellule *f* familiale

famine *n* famine *f*

famished *adj* (colloq) **I'm ~** je meurs de faim

famous *adj* (gen) célèbre (**for** pour); ⟨*school, university*⟩ réputé/-e (**for** pour)

fan ① *n* **(a)** (of jazz) mordu/-e *m/f* (colloq); (of star, actor) fan *m/f* (colloq); (Sport) supporter *m*

(b) (for cooling) (mechanical) ventilateur *m*; (hand-held) éventail *m*

② *vtr* attiser ⟨*fire*⟩; **to ~ one's face** s'éventer le visage

■ **fan out**: ¶ ~ **out** ⟨*police, troops*⟩ se déployer (en éventail); ¶ ~ [sth] **out** ouvrir [qch] en éventail ⟨*cards, papers*⟩

fanatic *n* fanatique *mf*

fanaticism *n* fanatisme *m*

fan belt *n* courroie *f* de ventilateur

fancy ① *n* **(a)** (liking) **to take sb's ~** ⟨*object*⟩ faire envie à qn; **to take a ~ to sb** s'attacher à qn; (sexually) (GB) s'enticher de qn

(b) (whim) caprice *m*; **as the ~ takes me** comme ça me prend

(c) (fantasy) imagination *f*; **a flight of ~** une lubie

② *adj* ⟨*equipment*⟩ sophistiqué/-e; ⟨*food, hotel, restaurant*⟩ de luxe; ⟨*paper, box*⟩ fantaisie *inv*; ⟨*clothes*⟩ chic

③ *vtr* **(a)** (colloq) (want) avoir (bien) envie de ⟨*food, drink, object*⟩; **what do you ~ for lunch?** qu'est-ce qui te plairait pour le déjeuner?

(b) (GB) (colloq) **she fancies him** elle s'est entichée de lui

(c) **~ seeing you here!** (colloq) tiens donc, toi ici?

(d) (Sport) voir ⟨qn/qch⟩ gagnant ⟨*athlete, horse*⟩

fancy dress *n* (GB) déguisement *m*; **in ~** déguisé/-e

fancy dress party *n* bal *m* costumé

fang *n* (of dog, wolf) croc *m*; (of snake) crochet *m* (à venin)

fan mail *n* lettres *fpl* envoyées par des admirateurs

fantasize *vi* fantasmer (**about** sur); **to ~ about doing** rêver de faire

fantastic *adj* **(a)** (colloq) (wonderful) merveilleux/-euse, super *inv* (colloq)

(b) (unrealistic) ⟨*story*⟩ invraisemblable

(c) (colloq) (huge) ⟨*profit*⟩ fabuleux/-euse; ⟨*speed, increase*⟩ vertigineux/-euse

(d) (magical) fantastique

fantasy *n* **(a)** (dream) rêve *m*; (in psychology) fantasme *m*

(b) (fiction) fantastique *m*

fanzine *n* magazine *m* des fans, fanzine *m*

FAQ *n* (abbr = **frequently asked questions**) FAQ *f*, foire *f* aux questions

far ① *adv* **(a)** (in space) loin; **~ off, ~ away** au loin; **is it ~ to York?** est-ce que York est ···⊱

loin d'ici?; **how ~ is it to Leeds?** combien y a-t-il (de kilomètres) jusqu'à Leeds?; **how ~ is Glasgow from London?** Glasgow est à quelle distance de Londres?; **as ~ as** jusqu'à
(b) (in time) **as ~ back as 1965** déjà en 1965; **as ~ back as he can remember** d'aussi loin qu'il s'en souvienne; **the holidays are not ~ off** c'est bientôt les vacances
(c) (very much) bien; **~ better** bien mieux; **~ too fast** bien trop vite
(d) how ~ have they got? où en sont-ils?; **as ~ as possible** autant que possible, dans la mesure du possible; **as ~ as we know** pour autant que nous le sachions; **as ~ as I am concerned** quant à moi
(e) to go too ~ aller trop loin; **to push sb too ~** pousser qn à bout
2 *adj* **(a) the ~ north/south (of)** l'extrême nord/sud (de); **the ~ east/west (of)** tout à fait à l'est/l'ouest (de)
(b) autre; **at the ~ end of the room** à l'autre bout de la pièce; **on the ~ side of the wall** de l'autre côté du mur
(c) (of party) **the ~ right/left** l'extrême droite/gauche
3 by far *phr* de loin
4 far from *phr* loin de; **~ from satisfied** loin d'être satisfait/-e
5 so far *phr* **(a)** (up till now) jusqu'ici, jusqu'à présent; **so ~, so good** pour l'instant tout va bien
(b) (up to a point) **you can only trust him so ~** tu ne peux pas lui faire entièrement confiance
IDIOMS **not to be ~ off** *or* **out** *or* **wrong** ne pas être loin du compte; **~ and wide** partout; **to be a ~ cry from** être bien loin de; **she will go ~** elle ira loin; **this wine won't go very ~** on ne va pas aller loin avec ce vin

faraway *adj* lointain/-e

farce *n* farce *f*

farcical *adj* ridicule

fare *n* (on bus, underground) prix *m* du ticket; (on train, plane) prix du billet; **half/full ~** demi-/plein tarif *m*

Far East *pr n* Extrême-Orient *m*

farewell *n* adieu *m*

far-fetched *adj* tiré/-e par les cheveux (colloq)

farm **1** *n* ferme *f*
2 *vtr* cultiver, exploiter ⟨*land*⟩
■ **farm out**: **~ out [sth]** sous-traiter ⟨*work*⟩ (**to** à)

farmer *n* (gen) fermier *m*; (in official terminology) agriculteur *m*; (arable) cultivateur *m*; **pig ~** éleveur *m* de porcs

farming *n* (profession) agriculture *f*; (of land) exploitation *f*; **sheep ~** élevage *m* de moutons

farmyard *n* cour *f* de ferme

far-off *adj* lointain/-e

far-reaching *adj* ⟨*effect*⟩ considérable; ⟨*change, reform*⟩ radical/-e; ⟨*plan, proposal*⟩ d'une portée considérable

far-sighted *adj* **(a)** (prudent) ⟨*person, policy*⟩ prévoyant/-e
(b) (US) ⟨*person*⟩ presbyte

farther *adj, adv* = FURTHER 1A,B 2B

farthest = FURTHEST

fascinate *vtr* (interest) passionner; (stronger) fasciner

fascinating *adj* ⟨*book, discussion*⟩ passionnant/-e; ⟨*person*⟩ fascinant/-e

fascination *n* passion *f* (**with, for** pour)

fascism *n* fascisme *m*

fascist *n, adj* fasciste (*mf*)

fashion **1** *n* **(a)** mode *f* (**for** de); **in ~** à la mode; **to go out of ~** se démoder, passer de mode; **to be all the ~** faire fureur
(b) (manner) façon *f*, manière *f*; **after a ~** plus ou moins bien
2 *vtr* façonner ⟨*clay, wood*⟩ (**into** en); fabriquer ⟨*object*⟩ (**out of, from** de)

fashionable *adj* ⟨*clothes*⟩ à la mode (**among, with** parmi); ⟨*resort, restaurant*⟩ chic (**among, with** parmi)

fashion designer *n* modéliste *mf*; (world-famous) grand couturier *m*

fashion house *n* maison *f* de couture

fashion model *n* mannequin *m*

fashion show *n* présentation *f* de collection

fast **1** *n* jeûne *m*
2 *adj* **(a)** rapide; **to be a ~ reader/runner** lire/courir vite
(b) (ahead of time) **my watch is ~** ma montre avance; **you're five minutes ~** ta montre avance de cinq minutes
3 *adv* **(a)** vite, rapidement; **how ~ can you run?** est-ce que tu cours vite?
(b) ⟨*hold*⟩ ferme; ⟨*stuck*⟩ bel et bien; ⟨*shut*⟩ bien; **to be ~ asleep** dormir à poings fermés

fasten **1** *vtr* **(a)** fermer ⟨*lid, case*⟩; attacher ⟨*belt, necklace*⟩; boutonner ⟨*coat*⟩
(b) fixer ⟨*notice, shelf*⟩ (**to** à; **onto** sur); attacher ⟨*lead, rope*⟩ (**to** à)
2 *vi* ⟨*box*⟩ se fermer; ⟨*necklace, skirt*⟩ s'attacher

fastener *n* (gen) attache *f*; (hook) agrafe *f*; (clasp) fermoir *m*

fast food *n* restauration *f* rapide

fast food restaurant *n* fast-food *m*, restovite *m*

fast-forward **1** *n* avance *f* rapide
2 *vtr* faire avancer rapidement ⟨*tape*⟩

fast-growing *adj* en pleine expansion

fast lane *n* voie *f* de dépassement

fast track **1** *n* promotion *f* accélérée
2 fast-track *vtr* former [qn] de façon accélérée

fat **1** *n* **(a)** (in diet) matières *fpl* grasses; **animal ~s** graisses *fpl* animales
(b) (on meat) gras *m*
(c) (for cooking) matière *f* grasse
(d) (in body) graisse *f*
2 *adj* **(a)** ⟨*person, animal, body, bottom*⟩ gros/grosse (*before n*); **to get ~** grossir

(b) ⟨*wallet*⟩ rebondi/-e; ⟨*envelope, file, magazine*⟩ épais/épaisse

(c) ⟨*profit, cheque*⟩ gros/grosse (*before n*)

fatal *adj* ⟨*accident, injury*⟩ mortel/-elle (**to** pour); ⟨*flaw, mistake*⟩ fatal/-e; ⟨*decision*⟩ funeste; ⟨*day, hour*⟩ fatidique

fatalist *n* fataliste *mf*

fatality *n* (person killed) mort *m*

fatally *adv* **(a)** ⟨*wounded*⟩ mortellement **(b)** ⟨*flawed*⟩ irrémédiablement

fate *n* sort *m*

fateful *adj* ⟨*decision*⟩ fatal/-e; ⟨*day*⟩ fatidique

fat-free *adj* sans matières grasses

father **1** *n* père *m* **2** *vtr* engendrer ⟨*child*⟩

Father Christmas *n* (GB) le père Noël

father-in-law *n* beau-père *m*

fatherly *adj* paternel/-elle

fathom **1** *n* brasse *f* anglaise (= *1.83 m*) **2** *vtr* (*also* ~ **out** (GB)) comprendre

fatigue *n* **(a)** (of person) épuisement *m* **(b)** metal ~ fatigue *f* du métal **(c)** (US) (Mil) corvée *f*

fatten *vtr* (*also* ~ **up**) engraisser ⟨*animal*⟩; faire grossir ⟨*person*⟩

fattening *adj* ⟨*food, drink*⟩ qui fait grossir

fatty *adj* ⟨*tissue, deposit*⟩ graisseux/-euse; ⟨*food, meat*⟩ gras/grasse

fatuous *adj* stupide

faucet *n* (US) robinet *m*

fault **1** *n* **(a)** (flaw) défaut *m* (**in** dans); **he's always finding** ~ il trouve toujours quelque chose à redire **(b)** (responsibility) faute *f*; **to be sb's** ~ être (de) la faute de qn; **it's my own** ~ c'est de ma faute **(c)** (in tennis) ~! faute! **(d)** (in earth) faille *f* **2** *vtr* prendre [qn/qch] en défaut; **it cannot be** ~**ed** c'est irréprochable

faultless *adj* ⟨*performance, manners*⟩ impeccable; ⟨*taste*⟩ irréprochable

faulty *adj* ⟨*wiring, machine*⟩ défectueux/-euse

fauna *n* faune *f*

faux pas *n* impair *m*

favour (GB), **favor** (US) **1** *n* **(a)** (kindness) service *m*; **to do sb a** ~ rendre service à qn; **to return a** *or* **the** ~ rendre la pareille **(b)** **to be in sb's** ~ ⟨*situation*⟩ être avantageux/-euse pour qn; ⟨*financial rates, wind*⟩ être favorable à qn **(c)** **to win/lose** ~ **with sb** s'attirer/perdre les bonnes grâces de qn **2** *vtr* **(a)** (prefer) être pour ⟨*method, solution*⟩; être partisan de ⟨*political party*⟩ **(b)** (benefit) ⟨*circumstances*⟩ favoriser ⟨*person*⟩; ⟨*law*⟩ privilégier ⟨*person*⟩ **3** **in favour of** *phr* **(a)** (on the side of) en faveur de; **to be in** ~ **of sb/sth** être pour qn/qch

(b) (to the advantage of) **to work in sb's** ~ avantager qn; **to decide in sb's** ~ (Law) donner gain de cause à qn

(c) (out of preference for) ⟨*reject*⟩ au profit de

favourable (GB), **favorable** (US) *adj* ⟨*conditions, impression, reply*⟩ favorable (**to** à); ⟨*result, sign*⟩ bon/bonne (*before n*)

favourably (GB), **favorably** (US) *adv* ⟨*speak, write*⟩ en termes favorables; ⟨*look on*⟩ d'un œil favorable; **to compare** ~ **with sth** soutenir la comparaison avec qch

favourite (GB), **favorite** (US) **1** *n* (gen) préféré/-e *m/f*; (Sport) favori/-ite *m/f* **2** *adj* préféré/-e, favori/-ite

favouritism (GB), **favoritism** (US) *n* favoritisme *m*

fawn **1** *n* (Zool) faon *m* **2** *vtr* **to** ~ **on sb** flagorner qn

fax **1** *n* **(a)** (*also* ~ **message**) télécopie *f*, fax *m* **(b)** (*also* ~ **machine**) télécopieur *m*, fax *m* **2** *vtr* télécopier, faxer ⟨*document*⟩; envoyer une télécopie *or* un fax à ⟨*person*⟩

fax number *n* numéro *m* de télécopie *or* de fax

faze *vtr* (colloq) dérouter

fear **1** *n* **(a)** (fright) peur *f* **(b)** (apprehension) crainte *f* (**for** pour) **(c)** (possibility) **there's no** ~ **of him** *or* **his being late** il n'y a pas de danger qu'il soit en retard **2** *vtr* craindre; **to** ~ **the worst** craindre le pire, s'attendre au pire **3** *vi* **to** ~ **for sb/sth** craindre pour qn/qch

fearless *adj* sans peur, intrépide

feasible *adj* **(a)** ⟨*project*⟩ réalisable **(b)** ⟨*excuse, explanation*⟩ plausible

feast **1** *n* (meal) festin *m*; (religious) fête *f* **2** *vi* se régaler (**on** de)

feat *n* exploit *m*; **it was no mean** ~ cela n'a pas été une mince affaire; **a** ~ **of engineering** une prouesse technologique

feather *n* plume *f*

feature **1** *n* **(a)** (distinctive characteristic) trait *m*, caractéristique *f* **(b)** (aspect) aspect *m*, côté *m* **(c)** (of face) trait *m* **(d)** (of car, computer, product) accessoire *m* **(e)** (report) (in paper) article *m* de fond (**on** sur); (on TV, radio) reportage *m* (**on** sur) **2** *vtr* ⟨*film, magazine*⟩ présenter ⟨*story, star*⟩; ⟨*advert, poster*⟩ représenter ⟨*person*⟩ **3** *vi* **(a)** (figure) figurer **(b)** ⟨*performer*⟩ jouer (**in** dans)

feature film *n* long métrage *m*

February *n* février *m*

federal *adj* fédéral/-e

federation *n* fédération *f*

fed up *adj* (colloq) **to be** ~ en avoir marre (colloq) (**of** de)

fee *n* **(a)** (for service) honoraires *mpl*; **school** ~**s** frais *mpl* de scolarité **(b)** (for admission) droit *m* d'entrée; (for membership) cotisation *f*

feeble *adj* (gen) faible; *‹excuse›* peu convaincant/-e; *‹joke, attempt›* médiocre

feed ① *n* (for animals) ration *f* de nourriture; (for baby) (breast) tétée *f*; (bottle) biberon *m* ② *vtr* (a) nourrir *‹animal, plant, person›* (on de); donner à manger à *‹pet›*; ravitailler *‹army›*
(b) (supply) alimenter *‹machine›*; mettre des pièces dans *‹meter›*; faire passer *‹ball›* (to à); to ~ sth into mettre *or* introduire qch dans

feedback *n* (a) (from people) remarques *fpl* (on sur; from de la part de)
(b) (on hi-fi) réaction *f* parasite

feeding bottle *n* biberon *m*

feel ① *n* (a) (atmosphere) atmosphère *f*
(b) (sensation) sensation *f*
(c) to get the ~ of se faire à *‹controls, system›*; to have a ~ for language bien savoir manier la langue
② *vtr* (a) éprouver *‹affection, desire, pride›*; ressentir *‹hostility, obligation, effects›*
(b) (believe) to ~ (that) estimer que
(c) sentir *‹blow, draught, heat›*; ressentir *‹ache, stiffness, effects›*
(d) (touch) tâter *‹washing, cloth›*; palper *‹patient, shoulder, parcel›*; to ~ one's way avancer à tâtons; (figurative) tâter le terrain
(e) avoir conscience de *‹presence, tension›*
③ *vi* (a) se sentir *‹sad, happy, nervous, safe, ill, tired›*; être *‹sure, surprised›*; avoir l'impression d'être *‹trapped, betrayed›*; to ~ afraid/ashamed avoir peur/honte; to ~ hot/thirsty avoir chaud/soif; to ~ as if *or* as though avoir l'impression que; she isn't ~ing herself today elle n'est pas dans son assiette aujourd'hui (colloq)
(b) (seem) être *‹cold, smooth›*; avoir l'air *‹eerie›*; it ~s odd ça fait drôle; it ~s like (a) Sunday on se croirait un dimanche
(c) (want) to ~ like sth avoir envie de qch; I ~ like a drink je prendrais bien un verre
(d) to ~ (around *or* about) in fouiller dans *‹bag, pocket, drawer›*; to ~ along tâtonner le long de *‹edge, wall›*
■ **feel for:** ¶ ~ (around) for [sth] chercher [qch] à tâtons; ¶ ~ for [sb] plaindre
■ **feel up to:** ¶ ~ up to (doing) sth se sentir d'attaque (colloq) *or* assez bien pour (faire) qch

feelgood *adj* optimiste; to play on the ~ factor essayer de créer un sentiment de bien-être

feeling *n* (a) (emotion) sentiment *m*; to hurt sb's ~s blesser qn
(b) (opinion, belief) sentiment *m*; ~s are running high les esprits s'échauffent
(c) (sensitivity) sensibilité *f*; to speak with great ~ parler avec beaucoup de passion
(d) (impression) impression *f*; I had a ~ you'd say that je sentais que tu allais dire ça; I've got a bad ~ about this j'ai le pressentiment que cela va mal se passer
(e) (physical sensation) sensation *f*; a dizzy ~ une sensation de vertige

fee-paying *adj* *‹school›* payant/-e

feign *vtr* feindre *‹innocence, surprise›*; simuler *‹illness, sleep›*

fell ① *n* montagne *f*
② *vtr* abattre *‹tree›*; assommer *‹person›*
IDIOMS in one ~ swoop d'un seul coup

fellow ① *n* (a) (colloq) (man) type *m* (colloq), homme *m*
(b) (of society, association) membre *m* (of de)
(c) (GB) (lecturer) membre *m* (du corps enseignant) d'un collège universitaire
(d) (US) (researcher) universitaire *mf* titulaire d'une bourse de recherche
② *adj* her ~ teachers ses collègues professeurs; a ~ Englishman un compatriote anglais

fellowship *n* (a) (companionship) camaraderie *f*
(b) (association) association *f*

felony *n* crime *m*

felt *n* feutre *m*

felt-tip (pen) *n* feutre *m*

female ① *n* (a) (Bot, Zool) femelle *f*
(b) (woman) femme *f*
② *adj* (a) (Bot, Zool) femelle; ~ rabbit lapine *f*
(b) *‹population, role›* féminin/-e; *‹voice›* de femme; ~ student étudiante *f*
(c) *‹plug, socket›* femelle

feminine ① *n* féminin *m*
② *adj* féminin/-e

feminist *n, adj* féministe (*mf*)

fence ① *n* (a) clôture *f*
(b) (in showjumping) obstacle *m*; (in horseracing) haie *f*
② *vtr* clôturer *‹area, garden›*
IDIOMS to sit on the ~ ne pas prendre position

fencing *n* escrime *f*

fend *vi* to ~ for oneself se débrouiller (tout seul/toute seule)
■ **fend off** repousser *‹attacker›*; parer *‹blow›*; écarter *‹question›*

fender *n* (a) (for fire) garde-cendre *m*
(b) (US) (Aut) aile *f*

fennel *n* fenouil *m*

fern *n* fougère *f*

ferocious *adj* *‹animal›* féroce; *‹attack›* sauvage; *‹heat›* accablant/-e

ferret *n* furet *m*
■ **ferret about** fureter, fouiller (in dans)

ferry ① *n* (long-distance) ferry *m*; (over short distances) bac *m*
② *vtr* transporter *‹passenger, goods›*

fertile *adj* *‹land, imagination›* fertile; *‹human, animal, egg›* fécond/-e

fertility treatment *n* traitement *m* contre la stérilité

fertilize *vtr* fertiliser *‹land›*; féconder *‹animal, plant, egg›*

fertilizer *n* engrais *m*

fervent *adj* *‹admirer›* fervent/-e

fester *vi* *‹wound, sore›* suppurer

festival *n* (gen) fête *f*; (arts event) festival *m*

festivity *n* réjouissance *f*

fetch *vtr* (a) aller chercher; ~! (to dog) rapporte!
(b) ⟨goods⟩ rapporter; **to ~ a good price** rapporter un bon prix; **these vases can ~ up to £600** le prix de ces vases peut atteindre 600 livres sterling

fetching *adj* ravissant/-e

fête *n* (church, village) kermesse *f* (paroissiale)

fetus (US) = FOETUS

feud ⓵ *n* querelle *f*
⓶ *vi* se quereller

feudal *adj* féodal/-e

fever *n* fièvre *f*; **to have a ~** avoir de la fièvre; **gold ~** la fièvre de l'or

feverish *adj* ⟨person, eyes⟩ fiévreux/-euse; ⟨dreams⟩ délirant/-e; ⟨excitement, activity⟩ fébrile

fever pitch *n* **to bring a crowd to ~** déchaîner une foule; **our excitement had reached ~** notre excitation était à son comble

few

■ **Note** When *a few* is used as a pronoun and if the sentence does not specify what it refers to, the pronoun *en* (= of them) must be added before the verb in French: *there were only a few* = il n'y en avait que quelques-uns/quelques-unes.

⓵ *det* (a) (not many) peu de; ~ **visitors/letters** peu de visiteurs/lettres
(b) (couple of) **every ~ days** tous les deux ou trois jours; **the first ~ weeks** les premières semaines
⓶ *pron, quantif* peu; ~ **of us succeeded** peu d'entre nous ont réussi
⓷ **a few** *det, quantif, pron* (a) (as determiner, quantifier) quelques; **a ~ people** quelques personnes; **quite a ~ people** pas mal (colloq) de gens, un bon nombre de personnes; **a ~ of the soldiers** quelques soldats; **a ~ of us** un certain nombre d'entre nous
(b) (as pronoun) quelques-uns/quelques-unes; **I would like a ~ more** j'en voudrais quelques-uns/quelques-unes de plus; **I only need a ~** il ne m'en faut que quelques-uns/quelques-unes
IDIOMS **they are ~ and far between** ils sont rarissimes

fewer ⓵ *det* moins de; ~ **and ~ pupils** de moins en moins d'élèves
⓶ *pron* moins; ~ **than 50 people** moins de 50 personnes; **no ~ than** pas moins de

fewest *det* le moins de

fiancé *n* fiancé *m*

fiancée *n* fiancée *f*

fibre (GB), **fiber** (US) *n* (a) (gen) fibre *f*
(b) (in diet) fibres *fpl*

fibreglass (GB), **fiberglass** (US) *n* fibres *fpl* de verre

fibre optic (GB), **fiber optic** (US) *adj* ⟨cable⟩ à fibres optiques; ⟨link⟩ par fibres optiques

fickle *adj* ⟨lover, friend⟩ inconstant/-e; ⟨fate, public opinion⟩ changeant/-e; ⟨weather⟩ capricieux/-ieuse

fiction *n* (a) (genre) le roman
(b) (invention) fiction *f*

fictional *adj* ⟨character, event⟩ imaginaire

fictionalize *vtr* romancer

fictitious *adj* (a) (false) ⟨name, address⟩ fictif/-ive
(b) (imaginary) imaginaire

fiddle ⓵ *vtr* (colloq) falsifier ⟨tax return, figures⟩
⓶ *vi* (a) (fidget) **to ~ with sth** tripoter qch
(b) (adjust) **to ~ with** tourner ⟨knobs, controls⟩

fidelity *n* fidélité *f* (**of** de; **to** à)

fidget *vi* ne pas tenir en place

field ⓵ *n* (a) (gen) champ *m* (**of** de); (sports ground) terrain *m*; **football ~** terrain de football
(b) (of knowledge) domaine *m* (**of** de)
⓶ *adj* (a) ⟨hospital⟩ de campagne
(b) ⟨test, study⟩ sur le terrain; ⟨work⟩ de terrain

field day *n* (a) (school trip) sortie *f* (éducative)
(b) (US) (sports day) journée *f* sportive
IDIOMS **to have a ~** (gen) s'amuser comme un fou/une folle; ⟨press, critics⟩ jubiler; (make money) ⟨shopkeepers⟩ faire d'excellentes affaires

field trip *n* (one day) sortie *f* éducative; (longer) voyage *m* d'études

fieldwork *n* travail *m* de terrain

fierce *adj* ⟨animal, expression, person⟩ féroce; ⟨battle, storm⟩ violent/-e; ⟨competition⟩ acharné/-e; ⟨flames, heat⟩ intense

fiercely *adv* ⟨oppose⟩ avec acharnement; ⟨fight⟩ sauvagement; ⟨shout⟩ violemment; ⟨burn⟩ avec intensité; ⟨competitive, critical⟩ extrêmement; ⟨determined, loyal⟩ farouchement

fifteen *n, pron, det* quinze (*m*) *inv*

fifteenth ⓵ *n* (a) (in order) quinzième *mf*
(b) (of month) quinze *m inv*
(c) (fraction) quinzième *m*
⓶ *adj, adv* quinzième

fifth ⓵ *n* (a) (in order) cinquième *mf*
(b) (of month) cinq *m*
(c) (fraction) cinquième *m*
⓶ *adj, adv* cinquième

fifties *n pl* (a) (era) **the ~** les années *fpl* cinquante
(b) (age) **to be in one's ~** avoir entre cinquante et soixante ans

fiftieth *n, adj, adv* cinquantième (*mf*)

fifty *n, pron, det* cinquante (*m*) *inv*

fifty-fifty ⓵ *adj* **to have a ~ chance** avoir une chance sur deux (**of doing** de faire)
⓶ *adv* **to share sth ~** partager qch moitié-moitié; **to go ~** faire moitié-moitié

fig *n* figue *f*

fight ⓵ *n* (a) (gen) bagarre *f* (**between** ⋯⟶

entre; **over** pour); (Mil) bataille f (**between** entre; **for** pour); (in boxing) combat m (**between** entre)
(b) (struggle) lutte f (**against** contre; **for** pour; **to do** pour faire)
(c) (argument) dispute f (**over** au sujet de; **with** avec)
2 vtr **(a)** se battre contre ‹person›
(b) (disease, opponent, emotion, proposal); combattre ‹fire›; mener ‹campaign, war› (**against** contre); **to ~ one's way through** se frayer un passage dans ‹crowd›
3 vi **(a)** (gen, Mil) se battre
(b) (campaign) lutter
(c) (argue) se quereller (**over** à propos de)
■ **fight back**: ¶ **~ back** se défendre; ¶ **~ back** [sth] refréner ‹tears, fear, anger›
■ **fight off**: ¶ **~ off** [sth], **~** [sth] **off** se libérer de ‹attacker›; repousser ‹attack›; ¶ **~ off** [sth] lutter contre ‹illness›; rejeter ‹criticism, proposal›

fighter n **(a)** (Sport) boxeur m
(b) (determined person) lutteur/-euse m/f
(c) (also **~ plane**) avion m de chasse

fighting 1 n (gen) bagarre f; (Mil) combat m
2 adj **(a)** ‹unit, force› de combat
(b) ‹talk› agressif/-ive

fighting chance n **to have a ~** avoir de bonnes chances

fighting fit adj **to be ~** être en pleine forme

figment n **a ~ of your imagination** un produit de ton imagination

figurative adj figuré/-e

figure 1 n **(a)** chiffre m; **a four-~ number** un nombre de quatre chiffres; **in double ~s** à deux chiffres
(b) (person) personnage m; **well-known ~** personnalité f célèbre; **father ~** image f du père
(c) (body shape) ligne f; **to lose one's ~** prendre de l'embonpoint
(d) (diagram, shape) figure f
2 vi (appear) figurer (**in** dans)
■ **figure out** trouver ‹answer, reason›; **to ~ out who/why** arriver à comprendre qui/pourquoi

figurehead n (symbolic leader) représentant/-e m/f nominal/-e; (of ship) figure f de proue

figure of speech n figure f de rhétorique

figure skating n patinage m artistique

file 1 n **(a)** (for papers) (gen) dossier m; (cardboard) chemise f; (binder) classeur m
(b) (record) dossier m (**on** sur)
(c) (Comput) fichier m
(d) (tool) lime f
(e) **in single ~** en file indienne
2 vtr **(a)** classer ‹invoice, letter, record› (**under** sous)
(b) déposer ‹application, complaint› (**with** auprès de); **to ~ a lawsuit** (**against sb**) intenter or faire un procès (à qn)

(c) limer ‹wood, metal›; **to ~ one's nails** se limer les ongles
3 vi **they ~d into/out of the classroom** ils sont entrés dans/sortis de la salle l'un après l'autre

file cabinet (US), **filing cabinet** n classeur m à tiroirs

fill 1 vtr **(a)** remplir ‹container, page› (**with** de); garnir ‹cushion, pie, sandwich› (**with** de); ‹dentist› plomber ‹tooth, cavity›
(b) ‹crowd, sound› remplir ‹room, street›; ‹smoke, protesters› envahir ‹building, room›; occuper ‹time, day, hours›; ‹emotion, thought› remplir ‹mind, person›
(c) boucher ‹crack, hole, void› (**with** avec)
(d) répondre à ‹need›
(e) ‹company, university› pourvoir ‹post, vacancy›
(f) ‹applicant› occuper ‹post, vacancy›
(g) ‹wind› gonfler ‹sail›
2 vi se remplir (**with** de)
■ **fill in**: **to ~ in for sb** remplacer qn; ¶ **~** [sth] **in** remplir ‹form›; donner ‹detail, name, date›; ¶ **~** [sb] **in** mettre [qn] au courant (**on** de)
■ **fill out**: ¶ **~ out** ‹person› prendre du poids; ‹face› s'arrondir; ¶ **~** [sth] **out** remplir ‹form›; faire ‹prescription›
■ **fill up**: ¶ **~ up** ‹bath, theatre, bus› se remplir (**with** de); ¶ **~** [sth] **up** remplir ‹kettle, box, room› (**with** de)

filler n **(a)** (for car body) mastic m; (for wall) reboucheur m
(b) (TV show) bouche-trou m

fillet 1 n filet m; **~ steak** filet m de bœuf
2 vtr enlever les arêtes de, fileter ‹fish›

filling 1 n **(a)** (of sandwich, baked potato) garniture f; (for peppers, meat) farce f
(b) (for tooth) plombage m
2 adj ‹food, dish› bourratif/-ive (colloq)

filling station n station-service f

film 1 n **(a)** (movie) film m
(b) (for camera) pellicule f
(c) (layer) pellicule f
2 vtr filmer
3 vi tourner

film fan n cinéphile mf

film festival n festival m de cinéma

film industry n industrie f cinématographique

filming n tournage m

film set n plateau m de tournage

film star n vedette f de cinéma

film studio n studio m de cinéma

filter 1 n filtre m
2 vtr filtrer ‹liquid, gas›; faire passer ‹coffee›
3 vi **to ~ into** ‹light, sound, water› pénétrer dans ‹area›

filth n **(a)** (dirt) crasse f
(b) (vulgarity) obscénités fpl; (swearing) grossièretés fpl

filthy adj **(a)** (dirty) crasseux/-euse; (revolting) répugnant/-e

627

fin ⋯⟶ fire exit ⋯⋯

(b) ⟨*language*⟩ ordurier/-ière; ⟨*mind*⟩ mal tourné/-e
(c) (GB) ⟨*look*⟩ noir/-e
fin *n* (of fish, seal) nageoire *f*; (of shark) aileron *m*
final [1] *n* (Sport) finale *f*
[2] *adj* **(a)** (last) dernier/-ière
(b) ⟨*decision*⟩ définitif/-ive; ⟨*result*⟩ final/-e
finale *n* finale *f*
finalist *n* finaliste *mf*
finalize *vtr* conclure ⟨*contract*⟩; arrêter ⟨*plan, details*⟩; faire la dernière mise au point de ⟨*article*⟩; fixer ⟨*timetable, route*⟩
finally *adv* **(a)** (eventually) finalement, enfin
(b) (lastly) finalement, pour finir
(c) (definitively) définitivement
finals *n pl* (GB) (Univ) examens *mpl* de fin d'études; (US) (Univ) examens *mpl* de fin de semestre
finance [1] *n* **(a)** (gen) finance *f*
(b) (funds) fonds *mpl* (**for** pour; **from** auprès de)
[2] *vtr* financer ⟨*project*⟩
finance company *n* société *f* de financement
finances *n pl* situation *f* financière
financial *adj* financier/-ière
financial year *n* (GB) exercice *m*, année *f* budgétaire
find [1] *n* **(a)** (gen) découverte *f*
(b) (good buy) trouvaille *f*
[2] *vtr* **(a)** trouver; **I can't ~ my keys** je ne trouve pas mes clés; **I couldn't ~ the time** je n'ai pas eu le temps
(b) (experience) éprouver ⟨*pleasure, satisfaction*⟩ (**in** dans)
(c) (Law) **to ~ that** conclure que; **to ~ sb guilty** déclarer qn coupable
■ **find out**: ¶ ~ **out** se renseigner; **if he ever ~s out** si jamais il l'apprend; ¶ ~ **[sth] out** découvrir ⟨*fact, answer, name, cause, truth*⟩; ~ **out who/why/where** trouver qui/pourquoi/où; ¶ ~ **out about [sth] (a)** (learn by chance) découvrir ⟨*plan, affair, breakage*⟩
(b) (research) faire des recherches sur ⟨*subject*⟩
findings *n pl* conclusions *fpl*
fine [1] *n* (gen) amende *f*; (for traffic offence) contravention *f*
[2] *adj* **(a)** (very good) excellent/-e
(b) (satisfactory) bon/bonne (*before n*); **that's ~** très bien; **'~, thanks'** 'très bien, merci'
(c) (nice) ⟨*weather, day*⟩ beau/belle (*before n*)
(d) (delicate) fin/-e
(e) (subtle) ⟨*adjustment, detail, distinction*⟩ subtil/-e
(f) (refined) ⟨*lady, clothes*⟩ beau/belle (*before n*)
(g) (commendable) ⟨*person*⟩ merveilleux/-euse
[3] *adv* ⟨*get along, come along, do*⟩ très bien
[4] *vtr* (gen) condamner [qn] à une amende; (for traffic offence) donner une contravention à
fine art *n* beaux-arts *mpl*
IDIOMS **she's got cheating down to a ~** elle est passée maître dans l'art de tricher

fine-tune *vtr* ajuster
finger [1] *n* doigt *m*
[2] *vtr* toucher ⟨*fruit, goods*⟩; tripoter (colloq) ⟨*necklace*⟩
IDIOMS **to keep one's ~s crossed** croiser les doigts (**for sb** pour qn)
finger-nail *n* ongle *m*
fingerprint *n* empreinte *f* digitale
fingertip *n* bout *m* du doigt
finicky *adj* ⟨*person*⟩ difficile (**about** pour); ⟨*job, task*⟩ minutieux/-ieuse
finish [1] *n* **(a)** (end) fin *f*
(b) (Sport) arrivée *f*
(c) (of wood, car) finition *f*; (of fabric, leather) apprêt *m*
[2] *vtr* **(a)** finir, terminer ⟨*chapter, sentence, task*⟩; terminer, achever ⟨*building, novel*⟩; **to ~ doing** finir de faire
(b) (leave) finir ⟨*work, school*⟩
(c) (consume) finir ⟨*cigarette, drink, meal*⟩
(d) (put an end to) briser ⟨*career*⟩
[3] *vi* (gen) finir; ⟨*speaker*⟩ finir de parler; ⟨*conference, programme, term*⟩ finir, se terminer; ⟨*holidays*⟩ se terminer
■ **finish off** finir, terminer ⟨*letter, meal, task*⟩
■ **finish up**: ¶ ~ **up** finir; ¶ ~ **[sth] up** finir ⟨*milk, paint, cake*⟩
finishing line (GB), **finish line** (US) *n* ligne *f* d'arrivée
finishing touch *n* **to put the ~(es) to sth** mettre la dernière main à qch
finite *adj* (gen) fini/-e; ⟨*resources*⟩ limité/-e
Finland *pr n* Finlande *f*
Finn *n* Finlandais/-e *m/f*
Finnish [1] *n* (language) finnois *m*
[2] *adj* **(a)** ⟨*culture, food, politics*⟩ finlandais/-e; ⟨*ambassador, embassy*⟩ de Finlande
(b) ⟨*grammar*⟩ finnois/-e; ⟨*teacher, lesson*⟩ de finnois
fir *n* (*also* ~ **tree**) sapin *m*
fire [1] *n* **(a)** (gen) feu *m*; **to set ~ to sth** mettre le feu à qch; **to be on ~** être en feu; **to catch ~** prendre feu; **to sit by the ~** s'asseoir près du feu *or* au coin du feu
(b) (blaze) incendie *m*; **to start a ~** provoquer un incendie
(c) to open ~ on sb ouvrir le feu sur qn
[2] *excl* **(a)** (raising alarm) au feu!
(b) (Mil) feu!
[3] *vtr* **(a)** décharger ⟨*gun, weapon*⟩; tirer ⟨*shot*⟩; lancer ⟨*arrow, missile*⟩; **to ~ questions at sb** bombarder qn de questions
(b) (dismiss) renvoyer, virer (colloq) ⟨*person*⟩
[4] *vi* tirer (**at, on** sur)
fire alarm *n* alarme *f* incendie
firearm *n* arme *f* à feu
firebomb [1] *n* bombe *f* incendiaire
[2] *vtr* incendier ⟨*building*⟩
fire brigade *n* pompiers *mpl*
fire engine *n* voiture *f* de pompiers
fire escape *n* escalier *m* de secours
fire exit *n* sortie *f* de secours

fire extinguisher n extincteur m

firefighter n pompier m

fireguard n pare-étincelles m inv

fireman n pompier m

fireplace n cheminée f

fireproof adj ⟨door, clothing⟩ ignifugé/-e

fire service n (sapeurs-)pompiers mpl

fire station n caserne f de pompiers

firewood n bois m à brûler

firework n feu m d'artifice

firing n (of guns) tir m

firing line n to be in the ~ (Mil) être dans la ligne de tir; (under attack) faire l'objet de violentes critiques

firing squad n peloton m d'exécution

firm ① n entreprise f, société f
② adj (a) ⟨mattress, fruit, handshake⟩ ferme
(b) ⟨basis, grasp⟩ solide
(c) ⟨offer, intention, refusal⟩ ferme; ⟨evidence⟩ concret/-ète
(d) ⟨person, leadership⟩ ferme (with sb avec qn)
③ adv to stand ~ tenir bon

first ① n (a) (gen) premier/-ière m/f ⟨to do à faire⟩
(b) (of month) premier m inv; the ~ of May le premier mai
(c) (GB) (Univ) (also ~-class honours degree) ≈ licence f avec mention très bien
② adj premier/-ière (before n); the ~ three pages les trois premières pages; at ~ glance or sight à première vue; I'll ring ~ thing in the morning je vous appellerai en tout début de matinée
③ adv (a) ⟨arrive, leave⟩ le premier/la première; women and children ~ les femmes et les enfants d'abord; to come ~ ⟨contestant⟩ terminer premier/première (in à); ⟨career, family⟩ passer avant tout
(b) (to begin with) d'abord; ~ of all tout d'abord
(c) (for the first time) pour la première fois; I ~ met him in Paris je l'ai rencontré pour la première fois à Paris
④ at first phr au début
IDIOMS ~ things ~ chaque chose en son temps

first aid n (a) (treatment) premiers soins mpl
(b) (as skill) secourisme m

first-aid kit n trousse f de secours

first class adj (a) ⟨hotel, ticket⟩ de première (classe)
(b) ⟨stamp, mail⟩ (au) tarif rapide
(c) (GB) ⟨degree⟩ avec mention très bien
(d) (excellent) excellent/-e

first cousin n (male) cousin m germain; (female) cousine f germaine

first floor n (GB) premier étage m; (US) rez-de-chaussée m

first form n (GB) (Sch) (classe f de) sixième f

first grade n (US Sch) cours m préparatoire

firsthand adj, adv de première main

firstly adv premièrement

first name n prénom m

first night n première f

first-rate adj excellent/-e

first-time buyer n personne f qui achète sa première maison

fish ① n poisson m
② vi pêcher; to ~ for trout pêcher la truite; to ~ for compliments rechercher les compliments
■ **fish out**: ~ out [sth] (a) (from bag, pocket) sortir
(b) (from water) repêcher

fish and chips n poisson m frit avec des frites

fish and chip shop n (GB) friterie f

fishbowl n bocal m (à poissons)

fisherman n pêcheur m

fishing n pêche f; to go ~ aller à la pêche

fishing boat n bateau m de pêche

fishing rod n canne f à pêche

fish market n halle f aux poissons

fishmonger n (GB) poissonnier/-ière m/f; ~'s (shop) poissonnerie f

fishnet adj ⟨stockings⟩ à résille

fish tank n aquarium m

fishy adj (a) ⟨smell, taste⟩ de poisson
(b) (colloq) (suspect) louche (colloq)

fist n poing m

fit ① n (a) (Med) crise f, attaque f
(b) (of anger, passion, panic) accès m; ~ of coughing quinte f de toux; to have sb in ~s (colloq) donner le fou rire à qn
(c) (of garment) to be a good ~ être à la bonne taille; to be a tight ~ être juste
② adj (a) ⟨person⟩ (in trim) en forme; (not ill) en bonne santé; to get ~ retrouver la forme
(b) to be ~ for (worthy of) être digne de ⟨person, hero, king⟩; (capable of) être capable de faire ⟨job⟩; not ~ for human consumption impropre à la consommation; to see or think ~ to do juger bon de faire; to be in no ~ state to do ne pas être en état de faire
③ vtr (a) ⟨garment⟩ être à la taille de; ⟨shoe⟩ être à la pointure de; ⟨key⟩ aller dans ⟨lock⟩; aller dans ⟨envelope⟩
(b) to ~ sth in or into trouver de la place pour qch dans ⟨room, house, car⟩
(c) (install) mettre [qch] en place ⟨lock, door, kitchen, shower⟩
(d) correspondre à ⟨description, requirements⟩
④ vi (a) ⟨garment⟩ être à ma/ta/sa taille, aller; ⟨shoes⟩ être à ma/ta/sa pointure, aller; ⟨key, lid, sheet⟩ aller
(b) ⟨toys, books⟩ tenir (into dans); will the table ~ in that corner? y a-t-il de la place pour la table dans ce coin?
(c) to ~ with correspondre à ⟨story, facts⟩
IDIOMS in ~s and starts par à-coups
■ **fit in**: ¶ ~ in (a) ⟨key, object⟩ aller; will you all ~ in? (into car, room) est-ce qu'il y a de la place pour vous tous?
(b) (figurative) ⟨person⟩ s'intégrer (with à); I'll

~ in with your plans j'accorderai mes projets avec les vôtres
¶ ~ [sb/sth] in caser ⟨objects⟩; caser ⟨game, meeting⟩; trouver le temps pour voir ⟨patient, colleague⟩

fitness n (physical) forme f

fitted adj ⟨wardrobe⟩ encastré/-e; ⟨kitchen⟩ intégré/-e

fitted carpet n moquette f

fitting ⓵ n (a) (part) installation f
(b) (for clothes, hearing aid) essayage m
⓶ adj ⟨description⟩ adéquat/-e; ⟨memorial, testament⟩ qui convient

fitting room n salon m d'essayage

five n, pron, det cinq (m) inv

five-a-side n (also ~ **football**) football m à cinq (joueurs)

fix ⓵ n (a) (difficulty) to be in a ~ être dans le pétrin (colloq)
(b) (colloq) (dose of drugs) shoot m (colloq)
⓶ vtr (a) fixer ⟨date, venue, price, limit⟩; déterminer ⟨position⟩
(b) arranger ⟨meeting, visit⟩; préparer ⟨drink, meal⟩; to ~ one's hair se donner un coup de peigne; how are we ~ed for time/money? qu'est-ce qu'on a comme temps/argent (colloq)?
(c) (mend) réparer
(d) fixer ⟨handle, shelf⟩ (on sur; to à)
(e) fixer ⟨attention⟩ (on sur); tourner ⟨thoughts⟩ (on vers)
(f) (colloq) truquer ⟨contest, election⟩
⓷ fixed pp adj ⟨gaze, income, price⟩ fixe; ⟨expression⟩ figé/-e; ⟨menu⟩ à prix fixe
■ **fix up** organiser ⟨holiday, meeting⟩; décider de ⟨date⟩

fixed-term contract n contrat m à durée déterminée

fixture n (a) installation f; ~s and fittings équipements mpl
(b) (Sport) rencontre f

fizzle v ■ **fizzle out** ⟨interest, romance⟩ s'éteindre; ⟨campaign, project⟩ faire fiasco; ⟨story⟩ se terminer en queue de poisson

fizzy adj gazeux/-euse

flabby adj ⟨skin, muscle⟩ flasque; ⟨person⟩ aux chairs flasques

flag ⓵ n drapeau m
⓶ vi ⟨interest⟩ faiblir; ⟨strength⟩ baisser; ⟨conversation⟩ languir; ⟨athlete⟩ flancher (colloq)
■ **flag down** faire signe de s'arrêter à ⟨person⟩; héler ⟨taxi⟩

flagpole n mât m

flagrant adj flagrant/-e

flagstone n dalle f

flair n (a) (talent) don; to have a ~ for être doué/-e pour ⟨languages⟩
(b) (style) classe f

flake ⓵ n (of snow) flocon m
⓶ vi (also ~ **off**) ⟨paint, varnish⟩ s'écailler; ⟨plaster, stone⟩ s'effriter; ⟨skin⟩ peler

flamboyant adj ⟨person⟩ haut/-e en couleur; ⟨lifestyle⟩ exubérant/-e; ⟨colour, clothes⟩ voyant/-e; ⟨gesture⟩ extravagant/-e

flame n flamme f; in ~s en flammes; to go up in ~s s'enflammer; to burst into ~s s'embraser

flamer n (Internet) auteur m d'un message injurieux

flaming ⓵ n (Internet) envoi m de messages injurieux
⓶ adj (a) ⟨vehicle, building⟩ en flammes
(b) ⟨row⟩ violent/-e

flamingo n flamant m (rose)

flammable adj inflammable

flan n (savoury) quiche f, tarte f; (sweet) tarte f

flank ⓵ n flanc m
⓶ vtr to be ~ed by ⟨person⟩ être flanqué/-e par; ⟨place⟩ être bordé/-e par

flannel n (a) (wool) flanelle f; (cotton) pilou m
(b) (GB) (also **face ~**) ≈ gant m de toilette

flap ⓵ n (a) (on pocket, envelope, tent) rabat m; (on table) abattant m
(b) (of wings) battement m
⓶ vtr the bird ~ped its wings l'oiseau battait des ailes
⓷ vi ⟨wing⟩ battre; ⟨sail, flag⟩ claquer; ⟨clothes⟩ voleter

flare ⓵ n (a) (on runway) balise f lumineuse; (distress signal) fusée f (de détresse); (Mil) (on target) fusée f éclairante
(b) (of match, lighter) lueur f
⓶ vi (a) ⟨firework, match⟩ jeter une brève lueur
(b) ⟨skirt⟩ s'évaser; ⟨nostrils⟩ se dilater
■ **flare up** (a) ⟨fire⟩ s'embraser
(b) ⟨violence⟩ éclater; ⟨person⟩ s'emporter
(c) ⟨illness⟩ réapparaître; ⟨pain⟩ se réveiller

flares n pl pantalon m à pattes d'éléphant

flash ⓵ n (a) (of torch, headlights) lueur f soudaine; (of jewels, metal) éclat m; a ~ of lightning un éclair
(b) in or like a ~ en un clin d'œil
(c) (on camera) flash m
⓶ vtr (a) to ~ one's headlights (at) faire un appel de phares (à)
(b) lancer ⟨look, smile⟩ (at à)
(c) (transmit) faire apparaître ⟨message⟩
(d) (colloq) (show) ⟨person⟩ montrer [qch] rapidement ⟨card, money⟩
(e) (also ~ **about**, ~ **around**) exhiber ⟨credit card⟩; étaler ⟨money⟩
⓷ vi ⟨light⟩ clignoter; ⟨eyes⟩ lancer des éclairs; to ~ on and off clignoter
■ **flash by, flash past** ⟨person, bird⟩ passer comme un éclair; ⟨landscape⟩ défiler

flashback n (a) (in film) flash-back m (to à)
(b) (memory) souvenir m

flashing adj ⟨light, sign⟩ clignotant/-e

flash light n lampe f de poche

flashy adj (colloq) ⟨car, dress, tie⟩ tape-à-l'œil inv; ⟨jewellery⟩ clinquant/-e

flask n thermos® f or m inv; (hip) ~ flasque f

flat [1] n (a) (GB) appartement m; **one-bedroom ~** deux pièces m inv
(b) **the ~** le plat de ⟨hand, sword⟩
[2] adj (a) (gen) plat/-e; ⟨nose, face⟩ aplati/-e
(b) ⟨tyre, ball⟩ dégonflé/-e; **to have a ~ tyre** avoir un pneu à plat
(c) ⟨refusal, denial⟩ catégorique
(d) ⟨fare, fee⟩ forfaitaire; ⟨charge, rate⟩ fixe
(e) ⟨beer⟩ éventé/-e
(f) (GB) ⟨car battery⟩ à plat; ⟨battery⟩ usé/-e
(g) (Mus) ⟨note⟩ bémol inv; ⟨voice, instrument⟩ faux/fausse
[3] adv (a) ⟨lay, lie⟩ à plat; **~ on one's back** sur le dos
(b) **in 10 minutes ~** en 10 minutes pile
(c) ⟨sing⟩ faux
IDIOMS **to fall ~** ⟨joke⟩ tomber à plat; ⟨party⟩ tourner court; ⟨plan⟩ tomber à l'eau

flatmate n (GB) colocataire mf

flat out adv (colloq) ⟨drive⟩ à fond de train; ⟨work⟩ d'arrache-pied

flat rate [1] n taux m fixe
[2] **flat-rate** adj ⟨fee, tax⟩ forfaitaire

flatten [1] vtr (a) ⟨rain⟩ coucher ⟨crops, grass⟩; abattre ⟨fence⟩; ⟨bombing⟩ raser ⟨building⟩
(b) (smooth out) aplanir ⟨surface⟩; aplatir ⟨metal⟩
(c) (crush) écraser ⟨fruit, object⟩
[2] v refl **to ~ oneself** s'aplatir (**against** contre)

flatter vtr flatter (**on** sur)

flattering adj flatteur/-euse

flattery n flatterie f

flaunt vtr étaler ⟨wealth⟩; faire étalage de ⟨charms, knowledge⟩

flavour (GB), **flavor** (US) [1] n goût m; (subtler) saveur f; **full of ~** savoureux/-euse
[2] vtr (gen) donner du goût à; (add specific taste) parfumer (**with** à)

flavouring (GB), **flavoring** (US) n (for sweet taste) parfum m; (for meat, fish) assaisonnement m

flaw n défaut m

flawed adj défectueux/-euse

flea n puce f

flea market n marché m aux puces

fleck [1] n (of colour, light) tache f; (of foam) flocon m; (of blood, paint) petite tache f; (of dust) particule f
[2] vtr **~ed with** ⟨fabric⟩ moucheté/-e de ⟨colour⟩

fledg(e)ling n oisillon m

flee vtr, vi fuir

fleece n toison f; **~-lined** fourré/-e

fleet n (a) (of ships) flotte f; (of small vessels) flottille f
(b) (of vehicles) (on road) convoi m

fleeting adj ⟨memory, pleasure⟩ fugace; ⟨moment⟩ bref/brève (before n); ⟨glance⟩ rapide

Flemish [1] n (a) **the ~** les Flamands mpl
(b) (language) flamand m
[2] adj flamand/-e

flesh n chair f

fleshy adj charnu/-e

flex [1] n (GB) fil m
[2] vtr faire jouer ⟨muscle⟩; fléchir ⟨limb⟩

flexibility n souplesse f, flexibilité f

flexible adj (a) ⟨arrangement, plan⟩ flexible
(b) ⟨person⟩ souple (**about** en ce qui concerne)

flexitime n horaire m flexible or souple

flick [1] n (with finger) chiquenaude f; (with whip, cloth) petit coup m
[2] vtr (a) (with finger) donner une chiquenaude à; (with tail, cloth) donner un petit coup à; **he ~ed his ash on the floor** il a fait tomber sa cendre par terre
(b) appuyer sur ⟨switch⟩

flicker vi ⟨fire, light⟩ vaciller, trembloter; ⟨image⟩ clignoter; ⟨eye, eyelid⟩ cligner
■ **flick through** feuilleter ⟨book⟩

flick knife n (GB) couteau m à cran d'arrêt

flight n (a) (gen) vol m (**to** vers; **from** de); **we took the next ~** (out) nous avons pris l'avion suivant
(b) (escape) fuite f (**from** devant); **to take ~** prendre la fuite
(c) **a ~ of steps** une volée de marches; **six ~s** (of stairs) six étages
(d) **a ~ of fancy** une invention

flight attendant n (male) steward m; (female) hôtesse f de l'air

flight bag n bagage m à main

flight path n route f de vol

flimsy adj ⟨fabric⟩ léger/-ère; ⟨structure⟩ peu solide; ⟨excuse⟩ piètre (before n); ⟨evidence⟩ mince

flinch vi tressaillir; **without ~ing** sans broncher; **to ~ from doing** hésiter à faire

fling [1] n (a) (colloq) (spree) bon temps m
(b) (affair) aventure f
[2] vtr lancer
[3] v refl **to ~ oneself** se jeter (**across** en travers de; **over** par dessus)
■ **fling away: ~** [sth] **away** jeter qch
■ **fling open:** ouvrir [qch] brusquement ⟨door⟩; ouvrir [qch] tout grand ⟨window⟩

flint n (a) (rock) silex m
(b) (in lighter) pierre f à briquet

flip [1] n (somersault) tour m
[2] vtr (a) lancer ⟨coin⟩; faire sauter ⟨pancake⟩
(b) basculer ⟨switch⟩
■ **flip through** feuilleter ⟨book⟩

flipchart n tableau m de conférence, paperboard m

flip-flop n (a) (sandal) tong f
(b) (US) (about-face) volte-face f inv

flippant adj ⟨remark, person⟩ désinvolte; ⟨tone, attitude⟩ cavalier/-ière

flipper n (a) (Zool) nageoire f
(b) (for swimmer) palme f

flirt [1] n flirteur/-euse m/f
[2] vi flirter; **to ~ with** flirter avec ⟨person⟩; jouer avec ⟨danger⟩; caresser ⟨idea⟩

flirtatious *adj* charmeur/-euse, dragueur/-euse (colloq derogatory)

flit *vi* (a) (also ∼ **about**) ⟨bird, moth⟩ voleter; ⟨person⟩ aller d'un pas léger
(b) **a look of panic ∼ted across his face** une expression de panique lui traversa le visage

float **1** *n* (a) (on net) flotteur *m*; (on line) bouchon *m*
(b) (GB) (swimmer's aid) planche *f*; (US) (life jacket) gilet *m* de sauvetage
(c) (carnival vehicle) char *m*
2 *vtr* (a) ⟨person⟩ faire flotter ⟨boat, logs⟩
(b) émettre ⟨shares, loan⟩; lancer [qch] en Bourse ⟨company⟩; laisser flotter ⟨currency⟩
3 *vi* (a) flotter; **to ∼ on one's back** ⟨swimmer⟩ faire la planche; **the boat was ∼ing out to sea** le bateau voguait vers le large; **to ∼ up into the air** s'envoler
(b) ⟨currency⟩ flotter
■ **float off** ⟨boat⟩ dériver; ⟨balloon⟩ s'envoler

floating *adj* (a) ⟨bridge⟩ flottant/-e
(b) ⟨population⟩ instable

floating voter *n* électeur *m* indécis

flock **1** *n* (of sheep, goats) troupeau *m*; (of birds) volée *f*
2 *vi* ⟨animals, people⟩ affluer (**around** autour de; **into** dans); **to ∼ together** ⟨people⟩ s'assembler; ⟨animals⟩ se rassembler

flog *vtr* (beat) flageller

flood **1** *n* (a) inondation *f*
(b) **a ∼ of** un flot de ⟨people, memories⟩; un déluge de ⟨letters, complaints⟩; **to be in ∼s of tears** verser des torrents de larmes
2 *vtr* (a) inonder ⟨area⟩; faire déborder ⟨river⟩
(b) ⟨light⟩ inonder
(c) inonder ⟨market⟩ (**with** de)
(d) (Aut) noyer ⟨engine⟩
3 *vi* (a) ⟨river⟩ déborder
(b) **to ∼ into sth** ⟨light⟩ inonder qch; ⟨people⟩ envahir qch; **to ∼ over sb** ⟨emotion⟩ envahir qn

floodgate *n* vanne *f*

floodlight **1** *n* projecteur *m*; **under ∼s** (Sport) en nocturne
2 *vtr* illuminer ⟨building⟩; éclairer ⟨stage⟩

floor **1** *n* (a) (of room) (wooden) plancher *m*, parquet *m*; (stone) sol *m*; (of car, lift) plancher *m*; **dance ∼** piste *f* de danse; **on the ∼** par terre
(b) (of stock exchange) parquet *m*; (of debating chamber) auditoire *m*; (of factory) atelier *m*
(c) (storey) étage *m*; **on the first ∼** (GB) au premier étage; (US) au rez-de-chaussée
2 *vtr* (a) terrasser ⟨attacker, boxer⟩
(b) ⟨question⟩ décontenancer ⟨candidate⟩
IDIOMS **to wipe the ∼ with sb** battre qn à plates coutures

floorboard *n* latte *f*, planche *f*

floor cloth *n* serpillière *f*

floor show *n* spectacle *m* ⟨de cabaret⟩

flop **1** *n* (colloq) (failure) fiasco *m* (colloq)
2 *vi* (a) **to ∼ (down)** s'effondrer

(b) (colloq) ⟨play, film⟩ faire un four (colloq); ⟨project, venture⟩ être un fiasco (colloq)

floppy *adj* ⟨ears⟩ pendant/-e; ⟨hat⟩ à bords tombants

floppy disk *n* disquette *f*

flora *n* flore *f*

floral *adj* ⟨design, fabric⟩ à fleurs; ⟨arrangement⟩ floral/-e

Florida *pr n* Floride *f*

florist *n* (person) fleuriste *mf*; (shop) fleuriste *m*

floss *n* fil *m* dentaire

flotsam *n* ∼ **and jetsam** épaves *fpl*

flounce **1** *n* (frill) volant *m*
2 *vi* **to ∼ in/off** entrer/partir dans un mouvement d'indignation

flounder *vi* (a) ⟨animal, person⟩ se débattre (**in** dans)
(b) (falter) ⟨speaker⟩ bredouiller; ⟨economy⟩ stagner; ⟨career, company⟩ piétiner

flour *n* farine *f*

flourish **1** *n* (a) (gesture) geste *m* théâtral; **with a ∼** ⟨do⟩ de façon théâtrale
(b) (in style) fioriture *f*
2 *vtr* brandir ⟨ticket, document⟩
3 *vi* prospérer

flourishing *adj* ⟨garden, industry⟩ florissant/-e; ⟨business, town⟩ prospère

flout *vtr* se moquer de ⟨convention, rules⟩

flow **1** *n* (a) (of liquid) écoulement *m*; (of blood, electricity, water) circulation *f*; (of refugees, words) flot *m*; (of information) circulation *f*; **in full ∼** ⟨speaker⟩ en plein discours; **traffic ∼** circulation *f*
(b) (of tide) flux *m*
2 *vi* (a) ⟨liquid⟩ couler (**into** dans); **the river ∼s into the sea** le fleuve se jette dans la mer
(b) ⟨conversation, words⟩ couler; ⟨wine, beer⟩ couler à flots
(c) ⟨blood, electricity⟩ circuler (**through, round** dans)
(d) ⟨hair, dress⟩ flotter

flowchart *n* organigramme *m*

flower **1** *n* fleur *f*; **to be in ∼** être en fleur
2 *vi* (a) ⟨flower, tree⟩ fleurir
(b) ⟨love, person⟩ s'épanouir

flower arranging *n* décoration *f* florale

flower bed *n* parterre *m* de fleurs

flowering **1** *n* floraison *f* (**of** de)
2 *adj* (producing blooms) à fleurs; (in bloom) en fleurs

flower pot *n* pot *m* de fleurs

flower shop *n* fleuriste *m*

flowery *adj* ⟨design⟩ à fleurs; ⟨language, speech⟩ fleuri/-e

flu *n* grippe *f*

fluctuate *vi* fluctuer (**between** entre)

flue *n* (of chimney) conduit *m*; (of stove, boiler) tuyau *m*

fluency *n* aisance *f*

fluent *adj* (a) her French is ~ elle parle couramment français; **in ~ English** dans un anglais parfait
(b) ⟨*speech*⟩ éloquent/-e; ⟨*style*⟩ coulant/-e

fluently *adv* couramment

fluff ⟨1⟩ *n* (on clothes) peluche *f*; (on carpet) poussière *f*; (under furniture) mouton *m*, flocon *m* de poussière
⟨2⟩ *vtr* (a) (*also* ~ **up**) hérisser ⟨*feathers*⟩; faire bouffer ⟨*hair*⟩
(b) (colloq) rater ⟨*cue*, *exam*⟩

fluffy *adj* (a) ⟨*toy*⟩ en peluche; ⟨*hair*⟩ bouffant/-e
(b) (light) ⟨*mixture*⟩ léger/-ère; ⟨*egg white*, *rice*⟩ moelleux/-euse

fluid *n*, *adj* fluide (*m*)

fluid ounce *n* once *f* liquide
((GB) = *0.028* T*l*; (US) = *0.030* l)

fluke *n* coup *m* de veine (colloq); **by a** (**sheer**) ~ (tout à fait) par hasard

fluorescent *adj* fluorescent/-e

fluoride *n* fluorure *m*

flurry *n* (a) (gust) rafale *f*
(b) (bustle) agitation *f* soudaine; **a ~ of activity** un tourbillon d'activité
(c) (of complaints, enquiries) vague *f*

flush ⟨1⟩ *n* (a) (blush) rougeur *f*
(b) (surge) **a ~ of** un élan de ⟨*pleasure*, *pride*⟩; un accès de ⟨*anger*, *shame*⟩
(c) (of toilet) chasse *f* d'eau
⟨2⟩ *vtr* **to ~ the toilet** tirer la chasse (d'eau); **to ~ sth down the toilet** faire partir qch dans les toilettes
⟨3⟩ *vi* (a) (redden) rougir (**with** de)
(b) **the toilet doesn't ~** la chasse d'eau ne fonctionne pas
■ **flush out** débusquer ⟨*sniper*, *spy*⟩; **to ~ sb/sth out of** faire sortir qn/qch de ⟨*shelter*⟩

flushed *adj* (a) ⟨*cheeks*⟩ rouge (**with** de); **to be ~** avoir les joues rouges
(b) **~ with** rayonnant/-e de ⟨*pride*⟩

fluster ⟨1⟩ *n* agitation *f*
⟨2⟩ *vtr* énerver; **to look ~ed** avoir l'air énervé

flute *n* flûte *f*

flutter ⟨1⟩ *n* (of wings, lashes) battement *m*
⟨2⟩ *vtr* (a) **the bird ~ed its wings** l'oiseau battait des ailes
(b) agiter ⟨*fan*, *handkerchief*⟩; **to ~ one's eyelashes** battre des cils
⟨3⟩ *vi* (a) **the bird's wings ~ed** l'oiseau battit des ailes
(b) ⟨*flag*⟩ flotter; ⟨*clothes*, *curtains*⟩ s'agiter; ⟨*eyelids*, *lashes*⟩ battre
(c) (*also* ~ **down**) ⟨*leaves*⟩ tomber en voltigeant
(d) ⟨*heart*⟩ palpiter (**with** de); ⟨*pulse*⟩ battre faiblement

flux *n* (**in a state of**) ~ dans un état de perpétuel changement

fly ⟨1⟩ *n* mouche *f*
⟨2⟩ **flies** *n pl* (of trousers) braguette *f*
⟨3⟩ *vtr* (a) piloter ⟨*aircraft*, *balloon*⟩; faire voler ⟨*kite*⟩

(b) (transport) emmener [qn] par avion ⟨*person*⟩
(c) ⟨*bird*, *aircraft*⟩ parcourir ⟨*distance*⟩
(d) ⟨*ship*⟩ arborer ⟨*flag*⟩
⟨4⟩ *vi* (a) ⟨*bird*, *insect*, *aircraft*, *kite*⟩ voler; **to ~ over** *or* **across sth** survoler qch
(b) ⟨*passenger*⟩ voyager en avion, prendre l'avion; ⟨*pilot*⟩ piloter, voler; **to ~ from Rome to Athens** aller de Rome à Athènes en avion
(c) ⟨*sparks*, *insults*⟩ voler; **to ~ open** s'ouvrir brusquement; **to go ~ing** (colloq) ⟨*person*⟩ faire un vol plané; ⟨*object*⟩ valdinguer (colloq); **to ~ into a rage** se mettre en colère
(d) (*also* ~ **past**, ~ **by**) ⟨*time*, *holidays*⟩ passer très vite, filer (colloq)
(e) ⟨*flag*, *scarf*, *hair*⟩ flotter; **to ~ in the wind** flotter au vent
■ **fly away** s'envoler

fly-by-night *adj* ⟨*company*⟩ douteux/-euse; ⟨*person*⟩ irresponsable

fly-drive *adj* avec formule avion plus voiture

flying ⟨1⟩ *n* **to be afraid of ~** avoir peur de l'avion
⟨2⟩ *adj* (a) ⟨*insect*, *machine*⟩ volant/-e; ⟨*object*, *broken glass*⟩ qui vole; **to take a ~ leap** sauter avec élan
(b) ⟨*visit*⟩ éclair *inv*
IDIOMS **with ~ colours** ⟨*pass*⟩ haut la main; **to get off to a ~ start** prendre un très bon départ

fly-on-the-wall *adj* ⟨*film*⟩ pris/-e sur le vif

flyover *n* (a) (GB) pont *m* routier
(b) (US) (aerial display) défilé *m* aérien

fly spray *n* bombe *f* insecticide

FM *n* (*abbr* = **frequency modulation**) FM *f*

foal *n* poulain *m*

foam ⟨1⟩ *n* (a) (on sea, from mouth) écume *f*; (on drinks) mousse *f*
(b) (chemical) mousse *f*
(c) (*also* ~ **rubber**) mousse *f*
⟨2⟩ *vi* (a) (*also* ~ **up**) ⟨*beer*⟩ mousser; ⟨*sea*⟩ se couvrir d'écume; **to ~ at the mouth** écumer; (figurative) écumer de rage
(b) ⟨*horse*⟩ suer

foam bath *n* bain *m* moussant

fob *n* (pocket) gousset *m*; (chain) chaîne *f*
■ **fob off** se débarrasser de ⟨*enquirer*, *customer*⟩; rejeter ⟨*enquiry*⟩

focal point *n* (a) (in optics) foyer *m*
(b) (of village, building) point *m* de convergence (**of** de; **for** pour)
(c) (main concern) point *m* central

focus ⟨1⟩ *n* (a) (focal point) foyer *m*; **in ~** au point; **to go out of ~** ⟨*device*⟩ se dérégler; ⟨*image*⟩ devenir flou
(b) (device on lens) mise *f* au point
(c) (of attention, interest) centre *m*
(d) (emphasis) accent *m*
⟨2⟩ *vtr* (a) concentrer ⟨*ray*⟩ (**on** sur); fixer ⟨*eyes*⟩ (**on** sur)

(b) mettre [qch] au point, régler ⟨lens, camera⟩

3 vi to ~ on ⟨photographer⟩ cadrer sur; ⟨eyes, attention⟩ se fixer sur; ⟨report⟩ se concentrer sur

4 focused pp adj ⟨person⟩ déterminé/-e

fodder n fourrage m

foe n ennemi/-e m/f

foetus, fetus (US) n fœtus m

fog **1** n brouillard m
2 vtr (also ~ up) ⟨steam⟩ embuer ⟨glass⟩; ⟨light⟩ voiler ⟨film⟩

foggy adj ⟨day, weather⟩ brumeux/-euse; it's ~ il y a du brouillard

foghorn n corne f de brume

foible n petite manie f

foil **1** n papier m d'aluminium; silver ~ papier argenté
2 vtr contrecarrer ⟨person⟩; déjouer ⟨attempt⟩

foist vtr to ~ sth on sb repasser qch à qn

fold **1** n (a) (in fabric, paper, skin) pli m
(b) (for sheep) parc m
2 vtr (a) plier ⟨paper, shirt, chair⟩; replier ⟨wings⟩
(b) croiser ⟨arms⟩; joindre ⟨hands⟩
3 vi (a) ⟨chair⟩ se plier
(b) (fail) ⟨play⟩ quitter l'affiche; ⟨company⟩ fermer
IDIOMS to return to the ~ rentrer au bercail
■ **fold back** rabattre ⟨shutters, sheet, sleeve⟩
■ **fold in** incorporer ⟨sugar, flour⟩
■ **fold up** plier ⟨newspaper, chair⟩

folder n (a) (for papers) chemise f
(b) (for artwork) carton m

folding adj ⟨bed, table, chair⟩ pliant/-e; ⟨door⟩ en accordéon

foliage n feuillage m

folk **1** n (people) gens mpl
2 adj (a) (traditional) ⟨tale, song⟩ folklorique
(b) (modern) ⟨music⟩ folk inv
(c) ⟨hero⟩ populaire

folklore n folklore m

follow **1** vtr (gen) suivre; poursuivre ⟨career⟩; ~ed by suivi/-e de
2 vi (a) suivre; to ~ in sb's footsteps suivre les traces de qn; there's ice cream to ~ ensuite il y a de la glace; the results were as ~s les résultats ont été les suivants
(b) (understand) suivre; I don't ~ je ne suis pas
(c) it ~s that il s'ensuit que
■ **follow through** mener [qch] à terme ⟨project⟩; aller jusqu'au bout de ⟨idea⟩
■ **follow up** donner suite à ⟨letter, threat, offer⟩ (with par); suivre ⟨story, lead⟩

follower n (a) (of thinker, artist) disciple m; (of political leader) partisan/-e m/f
(b) (of team) supporter m

following **1** n (of religion, cult) adeptes mfpl; (of party, political figure) partisans/-anes mpl/fpl; (of soap opera, show) public m; (of sports team) supporters mpl
2 adj suivant/-e
3 prep suite à, à la suite de

follow-up **1** n (a) (film, record, single, programme) suite f (to à)
(b) (of patient, socialwork case) suivi m
2 adj (a) (supplementary) ⟨work⟩ de suivi; ⟨check⟩ de contrôle; ⟨discussion, article⟩ complémentaire; ⟨letter⟩ de rappel
(b) (of patient, ex-inmate) ⟨visit⟩ de contrôle

folly n folie f

fond adj (a) ⟨embrace, farewell⟩ affectueux/-euse; ⟨eyes, smile⟩ tendre; ~ memories de très bons souvenirs
(b) ⟨wish, ambition⟩ cher/chère
(c) to be ~ of sb aimer beaucoup qn; to be ~ of sth aimer qch

fondle vtr caresser

food n nourriture f, alimentation f; frozen ~ aliments surgelés; Chinese ~ la cuisine chinoise; that's ~ for thought ça donne à réfléchir

food aid n aide f alimentaire

foodie n (colloq) amateur m de bonne bouffe (colloq)

food poisoning n intoxication f alimentaire

food processor n robot m ménager

foodstuff n denrée f alimentaire

fool **1** n (a) idiot/-e m/f (to do de faire); you stupid ~! (colloq) espèce d'idiot/-e!; to make sb look a ~ faire passer qn pour un/-e idiot/-e; to act the ~ faire l'imbécile
(b) (jester) fou m
2 vtr tromper, duper

foolhardy adj téméraire

foolish adj (a) ⟨person⟩ bête (to do de faire)
(b) ⟨grin, expression⟩ stupide; to feel ~ se sentir ridicule
(c) ⟨decision, question, remark⟩ idiot/-e

foolproof adj (a) ⟨method, plan⟩ infaillible
(b) ⟨machine⟩ d'utilisation très simple

foot **1** n (a) (of person) pied m; (of animal) patte f; (of sock, chair) pied m; on ~ à pied; from head to ~ de la tête aux pieds; to put one's ~ down faire acte d'autorité; (Aut) accélérer
(b) (measurement) pied m (= 0.3048 m)
(c) (of mountain) pied m (of de); at the ~ of au pied de ⟨bed⟩; à la fin de ⟨list, letter⟩; en bas de ⟨page, stairs⟩
2 vtr to ~ the bill payer la facture (for de, pour)
IDIOMS to be under sb's feet être dans les jambes de qn; rushed off one's feet débordé/-e; to put one's ~ in it (colloq) faire une gaffe; to stand on one's own two feet se débrouiller tout seul/toute seule

footage n film m, pellicule f; some ~ of des images de

foot and mouth (disease) n fièvre f aphteuse

football **1** n (a) (game) (GB) football m; (US) football m américain
(b) (ball) ballon m de football

footballer n (GB) joueur/-euse m/f de football

foot brake n (Aut) frein m (à pied)

footbridge n passerelle f

foothold n prise f (de pied); **to gain a ~** ⟨company⟩ prendre pied; ⟨ideology⟩ s'imposer

footing n (a) (basis) **on a firm ~** sur une base solide; **to be on an equal ~ with sb** être sur un pied d'égalité avec qn (b) (grip for feet) **to lose one's ~** perdre pied

footlights n pl rampe f

footloose adj libre comme l'air

footnote n note f de bas de page

foot passenger n passager m sans véhicule

footpath n (in countryside) sentier m; (in town) trottoir m

footprint n empreinte f (de pied)

footstep n pas m

footstool n repose-pied m

footwear n chaussures fpl

for prep (a) (gen) pour; **~ sb** pour qn; **he cooked dinner ~ us** il nous a préparé à manger; **what's it ~?** c'est pour quoi faire?, ça sert à quoi?; **to go ~ a swim** aller nager; **that's ~ us to decide** c'est à nous de décider; **she's the person ~ the job** elle est la personne qu'il faut pour le travail; **the reason ~ doing** la raison pour laquelle on fait; **if it weren't ~ her...** sans elle...; **'~ sale'** 'à vendre'; **it is impossible ~ me to stay** il m'est impossible de rester (b) ⟨work, play⟩ pour; ⟨MP⟩ de; **the minister ~ education** le ministre de l'éducation (c) (on behalf of) pour; **to be pleased ~ sb** être content/e pour qn; **say hello to him ~ me** dis-lui bonjour de ma part (d) (in time expressions) (with a completed action in the past) pendant; (with an incomplete action started in the past) depuis; (with a future time) pour; **I waited ~ two hours** j'ai attendu pendant deux heures; **I have/had been waiting for an hour** j'attends/j'attendais depuis une heure; **I'm going to Tokyo ~ five weeks** je vais à Tokyo pour cinq semaines; **the best show I've seen ~ years** le meilleur spectacle que j'aie vu depuis des années; **we've been together ~ two years** ça fait deux ans que nous sommes ensemble; **she's off to Paris ~ the weekend** elle va à Paris pour le week-end; **to stay ~ a year** rester un an; **to be away ~ a year** être absent/e pendant un an; **I was in Paris ~ two weeks** j'ai passé deux semaines à Paris; **the car won't be ready ~ another six weeks** la voiture ne sera pas prête avant six semaines; **it's time ~ bed** c'est l'heure d'aller au lit (e) (indicating distance) pendant; **to drive ~ miles** rouler pendant des kilomètres; **the last shop ~ 30 miles** le dernier magasin avant 50 kilomètres (f) (indicating cost, value) pour; **it was sold ~ £100** ça s'est vendu (pour) 100 livres sterling; **a cheque ~ £20** un chèque de 20 livres sterling

(g) (in favour of) **to be ~** être pour ⟨peace, divorce⟩; **the argument ~ recycling** l'argument en faveur du recyclage (h) **T ~ Tom** T comme Tom; **what's the French ~ 'boot'?** comment dit-on 'boot' en français? (i) **~ one thing... and ~ another...** premièrement... et deuxièmement...; **I, ~ one, agree with her** en tout cas moi, je suis d'accord avec elle

forbid vtr défendre, interdire; **to ~ sb to do** défendre or interdire à qn de faire; **to ~ sb sth** défendre or interdire qch à qn; **God ~!** Dieu m'en/l'en etc garde!

forbidden adj ⟨subject, fruit⟩ défendu/-e; ⟨place⟩ interdit/-e; **smoking is ~** il est interdit de fumer

forbidding adj ⟨building⟩ intimidant/-e; ⟨landscape⟩ inhospitalier/-ière; ⟨expression⟩ rébarbatif/-ive

force ⟨1⟩ n force f; **by ~** par la force; **the police ~** la police; **a ~ 10 gale** un vent de force 10 ⟨2⟩ **forces** n pl (also **armed ~s**) **the ~s** les forces fpl armées ⟨3⟩ vtr forcer ⟨to do to faire⟩ ⟨4⟩ **in force** phr (a) (in large numbers) en force (b) ⟨law, prices, ban⟩ en vigueur ∎ **force on:** **~ [sth] on sb** imposer [qch] à qn, forcer qn à accepter [qch]

forced adj ⟨smile, landing⟩ forcé/-e; ⟨conversation⟩ peu naturel/-elle

force-feed vtr gaver ⟨animal, bird⟩; alimenter [qn] de force ⟨person⟩

forceful adj ⟨person, behaviour⟩ énergique; ⟨attack, speech⟩ vigoureux/-euse

ford ⟨1⟩ n gué m ⟨2⟩ vtr **to ~ a river** passer une rivière à gué

fore n **to the ~** en vue, en avant; **to come to the ~** ⟨person, issue⟩ s'imposer à l'attention; ⟨quality⟩ ressortir

forearm n avant-bras m inv

foreboding n pressentiment m

forecast ⟨1⟩ n (a) (also **weather ~**) météo f, bulletin m météorologique (b) (outlook) (gen) pronostics mpl; (Econ) prévisions fpl ⟨2⟩ vtr prévoir ⟨that que⟩

forecaster n (a) (of weather) spécialiste mf de la météorologie (b) (economic) conjoncturiste mf

forecourt n (of shop) parking m; (of garage) aire f de stationnement; (of station) cour f de la gare

forefinger n index m

forefront n **at** or **in the ~ of** à la pointe de ⟨change, research, debate⟩; **au premier plan de** ⟨campaign, struggle⟩

foregone adj **it is a ~ conclusion** c'est couru d'avance

foreground n premier plan m

forehand n (Sport) coup m droit

forehead n front m

foreign adj (a) ⟨country, imports, policy⟩ étranger/-ère; ⟨market⟩ extérieur/-e; ⟨trade, travel⟩ à l'étranger
(b) (alien) ⟨concept⟩ étranger/-ère (to à)

foreign affairs n pl affaires fpl étrangères

foreign body n corps m étranger

foreign correspondent n correspondant/-e m/f à l'étranger

foreigner n étranger/-ère m/f

foreign exchange n devises fpl

foreign exchange market n marché m des changes

foreign minister, foreign secretary (GB) n ministre m des Affaires étrangères

Foreign Office, FO n (GB) ministère m des Affaires étrangères

foreman n (a) (supervisor) contremaître m
(b) (Law) président m (d'un jury)

foremost 1 adj premier/-ière (before n), plus grand
2 adv first and ~ avant tout

forename n prénom m

forensic evidence n résultats mpl des expertises médico-légales

forensic science n médecine f légale

forensic scientist n médecin m légiste

forensic tests n pl expertises fpl médico-légales

forerunner n (person) précurseur m; (institution, invention, model) ancêtre m

foresee vtr prévoir

foreseeable adj prévisible

foreshadow vtr annoncer

foresight n prévoyance f (to do de faire)

foreskin n prépuce m

forest n forêt f

forester n forestier/-ière m/f

forest fire n incendie m de forêt

forestry n (science) sylviculture f; (industry) exploitation f des forêts

foretaste n avant-goût m (of de)

foretell vtr prédire

forever adv pour toujours; **to go on ~** ⟨pain, noise, journey⟩ durer une éternité; **the desert seemed to go on ~** le désert semblait ne pas avoir de limites; **she is ~ complaining** elle est toujours en train de se plaindre

foreword n avant-propos m inv

forfeit 1 n gage m
2 vtr perdre ⟨right, liberty⟩

forge 1 n forge f
2 vtr (a) forger ⟨metal⟩
(b) contrefaire ⟨banknotes, signature⟩; **a ~d passport** un faux passeport
(c) forger ⟨alliance⟩; établir ⟨identity, link⟩
3 vi **to ~ ahead** accélérer; **to ~ ahead with** aller de l'avant dans ⟨plan⟩

forger n (of documents) faussaire m; (of artefacts) contrefacteur/-trice m/f; (of money) faux-monnayeur m

forgery n contrefaçon f

forget 1 vtr oublier (**that** que; **to do de** faire)
2 vi oublier

■ **forget about** oublier

forgetful adj distrait/-e

forget-me-not n myosotis m

forgive vtr pardonner à ⟨person⟩; pardonner ⟨act, remark⟩; **to ~ sb sth** pardonner qch à qn; **to ~ sb for doing** pardonner à qn d'avoir fait

forgiveness n pardon m

forgo vtr renoncer à

fork 1 n (a) (for eating) fourchette f
(b) (tool) fourche f
(c) (in river, on bicycle) fourche f; (in railway) embranchement m; (in road) bifurcation f
2 vi (also ~ **off**) bifurquer

■ **fork out** (colloq) casquer (colloq) (**for** pour)

forked lightning n éclair m ramifié

forklift truck n (GB) (also **forklift** (US)) chariot m élévateur à fourche

forlorn adj (a) (sad) ⟨appearance⟩ malheureux/-euse
(b) (desperate) ⟨attempt⟩ désespéré/-e

form 1 n (a) (gen) forme f; **in the ~ of** sous forme de; **to be in good ~** être en bonne or pleine forme; **it is bad ~ (to do)** cela ne se fait pas (de faire); **as a matter of ~** pour la forme
(b) (document) formulaire m; **blank ~** formulaire vierge
(c) (GB) (Sch) classe f; **in the first ~** ≈ en sixième
2 vtr (a) former ⟨queue, circle, barrier⟩ (**from** avec); nouer ⟨friendship, relationship⟩; **to ~ part of** faire partie de
(b) se faire ⟨impression, opinion⟩
(c) former ⟨personality, tastes, ideas, attitudes⟩
3 vi se former

formal adj (a) (official) ⟨agreement, complaint, invitation⟩ officiel/-ielle
(b) (not casual) ⟨language⟩ soutenu/-e; ⟨occasion⟩ solennel/-elle; ⟨manner⟩ cérémonieux/-ieuse; ⟨clothing⟩ habillé/-e
(c) ⟨training⟩ professionnel/-elle; ⟨qualification⟩ reconnu/-e

formal dress n tenue f de soirée

formality n (a) (legal or social convention) formalité f
(b) (of occasion, manner) solennité f; (of language) caractère m soutenu

formally adv (a) (officially) officiellement
(b) (not casually) cérémonieusement

format 1 n format m
2 vtr (Comput) formater

formation n formation f

former 1 n **the ~** (singular noun) celui-là/celle-là m/f; (plural noun) ceux-là/celles-là mpl/fpl
2 adj (a) ⟨era, life⟩ antérieur/-e; ⟨size, state⟩ initial/-e, original/-e; **he's a shadow of his ~ self** il n'est plus que l'ombre de lui-même ····❯

(b) ⟨leader, husband, champion⟩ ancien/-ienne (before n)

(c) (first of two) premier/-ière (before n)

formerly adv autrefois

formidable adj **(a)** (intimidating) redoutable

(b) (awe-inspiring) impressionnant/-e

formula n **(a)** formule f (for de; for doing pour faire)

(b) (baby milk) lait m en poudre

fort n fort m

forte n to be sb's ∼ être le fort de qn

forth adv from this day ∼ à partir d'aujourd'hui; from that day ∼ à dater de ce jour; ▶ BACK, SO

forthcoming adj **(a)** ⟨event, book⟩ prochain/-e (before n)

(b) she wasn't very ∼ about it elle était peu disposée à en parler

forthright adj direct/-e

forties n pl **(a)** (era) the ∼ les années fpl quarante

(b) (age) to be in one's ∼ avoir entre quarante et cinquante ans

fortieth n, adj, adv quarantième (mf)

fortified adj ⟨place⟩ fortifié/-e; ∼ wine vin m doux; ∼ with vitamins vitaminé/-e

fortify vtr fortifier

fortnight n (GB) quinze jours mpl; the first ∼ in August la première quinzaine d'août

fortnightly adj ⟨meeting, visit⟩ qui a lieu toutes les deux semaines; ⟨magazine⟩ publié/-e toutes les deux semaines

fortunate adj heureux/-euse

fortunately adv heureusement

fortune n **(a)** fortune f; to make a ∼ faire fortune

(b) to have the good ∼ to do avoir la chance or le bonheur de faire

(c) to tell sb's ∼ dire la bonne aventure à qn

fortune-teller n diseur/-euse m/f de bonne aventure

forty n, pron, det quarante (m) inv

forward **1** n (Sport) avant m

2 adj **(a)** (bold) effronté/-e

(b) (towards the front) ⟨movement⟩ en avant; to be too far ∼ ⟨seat⟩ être trop en avant

(c) (advanced) avancé/-e; he's no further ∼ il n'est pas plus avancé

3 adv (also **forwards**) to step ∼ faire un pas en avant; to fall ∼ tomber en avant; to go or walk ∼ avancer; to move sth ∼ avancer qch; a way ∼ une solution

4 vtr **(a)** expédier ⟨goods⟩; envoyer ⟨parcel⟩

(b) (send on) faire suivre, réexpédier ⟨mail⟩

forwarding address n nouvelle adresse f (pour faire suivre le courrier)

forward-looking adj ⟨company, person⟩ tourné/-e vers l'avenir

forward planning n planification f à long terme

forwards = FORWARD 3

fossil n fossile m

fossil fuel n combustible m fossile

foster **1** adj ⟨child, parent⟩ adoptif/-ive

2 vtr **(a)** (encourage) encourager ⟨attitude⟩; promouvoir ⟨activity⟩

(b) prendre [qn] en placement ⟨child⟩

foster family n famille f de placement

foster home n foyer m de placement

foul **1** n (Sport) faute f (by de; on sur)

2 adj **(a)** ⟨smell, air⟩ fétide; ⟨taste⟩ infect/-e

(b) ⟨weather, day⟩ épouvantable; to be in a ∼ mood être d'une humeur massacrante (colloq); to have a ∼ temper avoir un sale caractère

(c) ⟨language⟩ ordurier/-ière

3 adv to taste ∼ avoir un goût infect

4 vtr **(a)** polluer ⟨environment⟩; souiller ⟨pavement⟩

(b) (Sport) commettre une faute contre ⟨player⟩

foul-mouthed adj grossier/-ière

foul play n acte m criminel; (in sport) jeu m irrégulier

foul-up n (colloq) cafouillage m (colloq)

found vtr fonder (on sur)

foundation n **(a)** (founding) fondation f

(b) ∼s (of building) fondations fpl

(c) (also ∼ **cream**) fond m de teint

foundation course n (GB Univ) année f de préparation à des études supérieures

founder n fondateur/-trice m/f

foundry n fonderie f

fountain n fontaine f

fountain pen n stylo m (à encre)

four n, pron, det quatre (m) inv
IDIOMS on all ∼s à quatre pattes

four-by-four n quatre-quatre m inv

four-letter word n mot m grossier

four-star **1** n (GB) (also ∼ **petrol**) super(carburant) m

2 adj ⟨hotel, restaurant⟩ quatre étoiles

fourteen n, pron, det quatorze (m) inv

fourteenth **1** n **(a)** (in order) quatorzième mf

(b) (of month) quatorze m inv

(c) (fraction) quatorzième m

2 adj, adv quatorzième

fourth **1** n **(a)** (in order) quatrième mf

(b) (of month) quatre m inv

(c) (fraction) quatrième m

(d) (also ∼ **gear**) (Aut) quatrième f

2 adj, adv quatrième

four-wheel drive (vehicle) n quatre-quatre m inv

fowl n volaille f

fox n renard m

foxhound n fox-hound m

fox hunting n chasse f au renard

fraction n fraction f (of de)

fracture **1** n fracture f

2 vtr fracturer ⟨bone, rock⟩

3 vi ⟨bone⟩ se fracturer

fragile adj fragile

fragment n (of rock, manuscript) fragment m; (of glass, china) morceau m

fragrance n parfum m
fragrant adj odorant/-e
frail adj ⟨person⟩ frêle; ⟨health, hope⟩ précaire
frame [1] n (a) (of building, boat, roof) charpente f; (of car) châssis m; (of bicycle, racquet) cadre m; (of bed) sommier m; (of tent) armature f
(b) (of picture, window) cadre m; (of door) encadrement m
(c) (body) corps m
[2] **frames** n pl (of spectacles) monture f
[3] vtr (a) encadrer ⟨picture, face⟩
(b) formuler ⟨question⟩
frame of mind n état m d'esprit; **to be in the right/wrong ~ for doing** être/ne pas être d'humeur à faire
framework n structure f; (figurative) cadre m
franc n franc m
France pr n France f
franchise n (a) (right to vote) droit m de vote
(b) (commercial) franchise f
francophile n, adj francophile (mf)
frank adj franc/franche
Frankfurt pr n Francfort
frankly adv franchement
frantic adj (a) ⟨activity⟩ frénétique
(b) ⟨effort, search⟩ désespéré/-e; **to be ~ with worry** être fou/folle d'inquiétude
frantically adv (a) (wildly) frénétiquement
(b) (desperately) désespérément
fraternal adj fraternel/-elle
fraternity n fraternité f
fraud n fraude f
fraudulent adj ⟨practice, use⟩ frauduleux/-euse; ⟨signature, cheque⟩ falsifié/-e; ⟨earnings⟩ illicite
fraught adj ⟨situation, atmosphere⟩ tendu/-e; ⟨person⟩ accablé/-e (with de); **to be ~ with** être lourd/-e de ⟨danger, difficulty⟩
fray vi ⟨material, rope⟩ s'effilocher
frayed adj ⟨nerves⟩ à bout; **tempers were ~** les gens s'énervaient
frazzle n (colloq) **to burn sth to a ~** calciner qch; **to be worn to a ~** être lessivé/-e (colloq)
freak [1] n (a) (strange person) original/-e m/f
(b) (at circus) phénomène m; **~ show** exhibition f de monstres
(c) (unusual occurrence) aberration f; **a ~ of nature** une bizarrerie de la nature
(d) (colloq) (enthusiast) mordu/-e m/f (colloq), fana mf (colloq)
[2] adj ⟨accident, storm⟩ exceptionnel/-elle
■ **freak out** (colloq) (get angry) piquer une crise (colloq); (go mad) flipper (colloq)
freckle n tache f de rousseur
free [1] adj (a) (gen) libre; **to be ~ to do** être libre de faire; **to set [sb/sth] ~** libérer ⟨person⟩; rendre la liberté à ⟨animal⟩
(b) (also **~ of charge**) gratuit/-e; **'admission ~'** 'entrée gratuite'

(c) **to be ~ with** être prodigue de ⟨advice⟩; **to be very ~ with money** dépenser sans compter
[2] adv (a) ⟨run, roam⟩ librement, en toute liberté; **to go ~** ⟨hostage⟩ être libéré/-e; ⟨criminal⟩ circuler en toute liberté
(b) (without paying) gratuitement
[3] vtr (a) (gen) libérer; (from wreckage) dégager
(b) débloquer ⟨money, resources⟩
[4] **-free** combining form **smoke/sugar-~** sans fumée/sucre; **interest-~** sans intérêt
[5] **for free** phr gratuitement
IDIOMS **to have a ~ hand** avoir carte blanche (in pour); **to be a ~ agent** pouvoir agir à sa guise; **~ and easy** décontracté/-e
freebee, freebie n (colloq) (free gift) cadeau m; (newspaper) journal m gratuit; (trip) voyage m gratuit
freedom n liberté f (to do de faire); **~ of the press** liberté de la presse; **~ of information** libre accès m à l'information
freedom fighter n combattant m de la liberté
freefall n chute f libre
Freefone® n (also **Freephone**®) numéro m vert d'appel gratuit
free-for-all n mêlée f générale
free gift n cadeau m
free kick n coup m franc
freelance [1] n (also **freelancer**) free-lance mf
[2] adv ⟨work⟩ en free-lance
freely adv (gen) librement; ⟨spend, give⟩ sans compter; ⟨admit⟩ volontiers
free market n (also **~ economy**) économie f de marché
Freephone® = FREEFONE ®
freepost n (GB) port m payé
free-range adj ⟨chicken⟩ élevé/-e en plein air; ⟨eggs⟩ de poules élevées en plein air
free speech n liberté f d'expression
freestyle n (in swimming) nage f libre; (in skiing) figures fpl libres; (in wrestling) lutte f libre
free trade n libre-échange m
freeware n freeware m, graticiel m
freeway n (US) autoroute f
free will n libre arbitre m; **of one's (own) ~** de plein gré
freeze [1] n (a) (in weather) gelées fpl
(b) (Econ) gel m (on de)
[2] vtr (a) congeler ⟨food⟩; ⟨cold weather⟩ geler ⟨liquid, pipes⟩
(b) (Econ) bloquer, geler ⟨prices, wages, assets⟩
(c) (anaesthetize) insensibiliser ⟨gum, skin⟩
[3] vi (a) ⟨water, pipes⟩ geler; ⟨food⟩ se congeler
(b) (feel cold) geler; **to be freezing to death** mourir de froid
(c) (not move) ⟨person, blood, smile⟩ se figer
[4] v impers geler
freeze-dried adj lyophilisé/-e

freeze frame *n* arrêt *m* sur image

freezer *n* congélateur *m*

freezer compartment *n* freezer *m*

freezing ① *n* zéro *m*; **below** ~ en-dessous de zéro

② *adj* **I'm** ~ je suis gelé; **it's** ~ **in here** on gèle ici

freezing cold *adj* ⟨*room, wind*⟩ glacial/-e; ⟨*water*⟩ glacé/-e

freight *n* (a) (goods) fret *m*, marchandises *fpl*

(b) (transport system) transport *m*

(c) (cost) (frais *mpl* de) port *m*

freighter *n* (a) (ship) cargo *m*

(b) (plane) avion-cargo *m*

French ① *n* (a) (people) the ~ les Français *mpl*

(b) (language) français *m*

② *adj* ⟨*culture, food, politics*⟩ français/-e; ⟨*teacher, lesson*⟩ de français; ⟨*ambassador, embassy*⟩ de France

French fries *n pl* frites *fpl*

Frenchman *n* Français *m*

French-speaking *adj* francophone

French toast *n* pain *m* perdu

French window *n* porte-fenêtre *f*

Frenchwoman *n* Française *f*

frenetic *adj* ⟨*activity*⟩ frénétique; ⟨*lifestyle*⟩ trépidant/-e

frenzied *adj* ⟨*activity*⟩ frénétique; ⟨*attempt*⟩ désespéré/-e

frenzy *n* frénésie *f*, délire *m*

frequency *n* fréquence *f* (of de)

frequent *adj* (a) (common) ⟨*expression*⟩ courant/-e

(b) (happening often) fréquent/-e; **to make** ~ **use of sth** se servir souvent *or* fréquemment de qch

frequently *adv* souvent, fréquemment

fresco *n* fresque *f*

fresh *adj* (a) frais/fraîche; **to smell** ~ avoir une odeur fraîche; ~ **orange juice** jus d'orange pressée; **while it is still** ~ **in your mind** tant que tu l'as tout frais à l'esprit

(b) ⟨*evidence, attempt*⟩ nouveau/-elle (*before n*); ⟨*linen*⟩ propre; **to make a** ~ **start** prendre un nouveau départ

(c) ⟨*approach, outlook*⟩ (tout) nouveau/ (toute) nouvelle (*before n*)

(d) **to feel** *or* **be** ~ ⟨*person*⟩ être plein/-e d'entrain

(e) (colloq) (cheeky) impertinent/-e; **to be** ~ **with sb** être un peu familier/-ière avec qn

fresh air *n* air *m* frais; **to get some** ~ prendre l'air, s'oxygéner

freshen *v* ■ **freshen up** faire un brin de toilette

freshly *adv* fraîchement; ~ **ironed/washed** qui vient d'être repassé/lavé

fresh water *n* eau *f* douce

fret *vi* (a) (be anxious) s'inquiéter (**over, about** pour, au sujet de)

(b) (cry) pleurer

Freudian slip *n* lapsus *m*

friction *n* (a) (rubbing) frottement *m*

(b) (conflict) conflits *mpl* (**between** entre); **to cause** ~ être cause de friction

Friday *n* vendredi *m*

fridge *n* (GB) frigo *m* (colloq), réfrigérateur *m*

fridge-freezer *n* réfrigérateur-congélateur *m*

friend *n* ami/-e *m/f* (of de); **to make** ~s se faire des amis; **to make** ~s **with sb** devenir ami/-e *m/f* avec qn

friendly ① *adj* ⟨*person, attitude, argument, match*⟩ amical/-e; ⟨*animal*⟩ affectueux/-euse; ⟨*government, nation*⟩ ami (*after n*); **to be** ~ **with sb** être ami/-e *m/f* avec qn

② **-friendly** *combining form* **environment-**~ qui ne nuit pas à l'environnement; **user-**~ d'utilisation facile, convivial/-e

friendly fire *n* (Mil) feu *m* allié

friendship *n* amitié *f*

fright *n* peur *f*; **to take** ~ prendre peur, s'effrayer; **to give sb a** ~ faire peur à qn, effrayer qn

frighten *vtr* faire peur à, effrayer

frightened *adj* **to be** ~ avoir peur (**of** de; **to do** de faire)

frightening *adj* effrayant/-e

frightful *adj* (a) (inducing horror) abominable, épouvantable

(b) (colloq) (bad) ⟨*prospect, mistake*⟩ terrible; ⟨*headache*⟩ affreux/-euse

frill *n* (on dress) volant *m*; (on shirt) jabot *m*

fringe *n* (a) (b) frange *f*; **on the** ~s **of society** en marge de la société

(b) (in theatre) the ~ théâtre *m* alternatif

fringe benefits *n pl* avantages *mpl* sociaux *or* en nature

frisk *vtr* fouiller ⟨*person*⟩

fritter *n* beignet *m*

■ **fritter away** gaspiller ⟨*time, money*⟩

frivolous *adj* frivole

frizzy *adj* ⟨*hair*⟩ crépu/-e

frog *n* grenouille *f*

IDIOMS **to have a** ~ **in one's throat** avoir un chat dans la gorge

frogman *n* homme-grenouille *m*

frogs' legs *n pl* cuisses *fpl* de grenouille

from *prep*

■ Note *from* is often translated by *de*: *from Rome* = *de Rome*; *from the sea* = *de la mer*.

– Remember that *de* + *le* always becomes *du* (*from the office* = *du bureau*), and *de* + *les* always becomes *des* (*from the United States* = *des États-Unis*).

– For examples and particular usages, see the entry below.

(a) de; **where is he** ~? d'où est-il?, d'où vient-il?; **she comes** ~ **Oxford** elle vient d'Oxford; **paper** ~ **Denmark** du papier provenant du Danemark; **a flight** ~ **Nice** un vol en provenance de Nice; **a friend** ~ **Chicago** un ami (qui vient) de Chicago; **a**

colleague ∼ Japan un collègue japonais; **a man ∼ the council** un homme qui travaille pour le conseil municipal; **a letter ∼ Tim** une lettre (de la part) de Tim; **who is it ∼?** c'est de la part de qui?; **alcohol can be made ∼ a wide range of products** on peut faire de l'alcool à partir de produits très variés; **10 km ∼ the sea** à 10 km de la mer; **15 years ∼ now** dans 15 ans, d'ici 15 ans
(b) ∼ ... to... de ... à...; **the journey ∼ A to B** le voyage de A à B; **the road ∼ A to B** la route qui va de A à B; **open ∼ 2 pm to 5 pm** ouvert de 14 à 17 heures; ∼ **June to August** du mois de juin au mois d'août; **to rise ∼ 10 to 17%** passer de 10 à 17%; ∼ **start to finish** du début à la fin; **everything ∼ paperclips to wigs** tout, des trombones aux perruques; ∼ **day to day** de jour en jour
(c) (starting from) à partir de; ∼ **today/May** à partir d'aujourd'hui/du mois de mai; **wine ∼ £5 a bottle** du vin à partir de 5 livres sterling la bouteille; ∼ **then on** dès lors; ∼ **the age of 8** depuis l'âge de 8 ans
(d) (based on) ∼ **a short story** d'après un conte; **to speak** ∼ **experience** parler d'expérience
(e) (among) **to choose** or **pick** ∼ choisir parmi
(f) (in mathematics) **10** ∼ **27 leaves 17** 27 moins 10 égale 17
(g) (because of) **I know her** ∼ **work** je la connais car on travaille ensemble; ∼ **what I saw/he said** d'après ce que j'ai vu/ce qu'il a dit

front ⃞1 n **(a)** (of house) façade f; (of shop) devanture f; (of cupboard, box, sweater, building) devant m; (of book) couverture f; (of card, coin, banknote) recto m; (of car, boat) avant m; (of fabric) endroit m; **to button at the ∼** se boutonner sur le devant; **on the ∼ of the envelope** au recto de l'enveloppe
(b) (of train, queue) tête f; (of auditorium) premier rang m; **at the ∼ of the line** en tête de la file; **to sit at the ∼ of the class** s'asseoir au premier rang de la classe; **I'll sit in the ∼** je vais m'asseoir devant; **at the ∼ of the coach** à l'avant du car
(c) (GB) (promenade) front m de mer, bord m de mer; **on the sea** ∼ au bord de la mer
(d) (Mil) front m
(e) (in weather) front m
(f) (façade) façade f; **it's just a** ∼ ce n'est qu'une façade
⃞2 adj (entrance) côté rue; (garden, window) de devant; (bedroom) qui donne sur la rue; (wheel) avant; (seat) (in cinema) au premier rang; (in vehicle) de devant; (leg, paw, tooth) de devant; (view) (before n); (view) de face
⃞3 vtr **(a)** (colloq) être à la tête de (band)
(b) présenter (TV show)
⃞4 vi **to** ∼ **onto** (GB) or **on** (US) donner sur
⃞5 **in front** phr (walk) devant; **the car in** ∼ la voiture de devant; **the people in** ∼ les gens qui sont devant; **to be in** ∼ (in race) être en tête; **I'm 30 points in** ∼ j'ai 30 points d'avance
⃞6 **in front of** phr devant

front bench n (GB Pol) (seats) rangs mpl du gouvernement
front door n porte f d'entrée
frontier n frontière f
front line n **(a)** (Mil) front m
(b) (exposed position) **to be in the** ∼ être en première ligne
front page ⃞1 n première page f
⃞2 **front-page** adj (picture, story) à la une (colloq); **the** ∼ **headlines** les gros titres, la manchette
frost n gel m
frostbite n gelures fpl
frosted adj (nail varnish) nacré/-e; (glass) dépoli/-e, opaque
frosty adj **(a)** (morning) glacial/-e; (windscreen) couvert/-e de givre; **it was a** ∼ **night** il gelait cette nuit-là
(b) (unfriendly) glacial/-e
froth n (on beer, champagne) mousse f; (on water) écume f; (around mouth) écume f
frown vi froncer les sourcils; **to** ∼ **at sb** regarder qn en fronçant les sourcils
■ **frown on, frown upon** désapprouver, critiquer
frozen adj **(a)** (food) congelé/-e
(b) (lake, pipe, ground) gelé/-e; **I'm** ∼ je suis gelé; **to be** ∼ **stiff** être transi/-e de froid
fruit n fruit m; **a piece of** ∼ un fruit
fruit cake n cake m
fruition n to come to ∼ se réaliser; **to bring sth to** ∼ réaliser qch
fruit juice n jus m de fruits
fruit machine n machine f à sous
fruit salad n salade f de fruits
fruity adj (wine, fragrance) fruité/-e
frustrate vtr frustrer (person); réduire [qch] à néant (effort); contrarier (plan); entraver (attempt)
frustrated adj frustré/-e
frustrating adj **(a)** (irritating) énervant/-e
(b) (unsatisfactory) frustrant/-e
frustration n frustration f (at, with quant à)
fry ⃞1 vtr faire frire
⃞2 **fried** pp adj fried fish poisson m frit; **fried food** friture f; **fried eggs** œufs mpl au plat; **fried potatoes** pommes fpl de terre sautées
frying pan n (GB) poêle f (à frire)
fuel ⃞1 n (for heating) combustible m; (for car, plane) carburant m
⃞2 vtr **(a)** alimenter (engine)
(b) ravitailler (plane)
(c) aggraver (tension); attiser (hatred)
fuel tank n (of car) réservoir m
fugitive n fugitif/-ive m/f, fuyard/-e m/f
fulfil (GB), **fulfill** (US) vtr **(a)** réaliser (ambition); répondre à (desire, need); **to feel** ∼**led** se sentir comblé/-e
(b) remplir (duty, conditions, contract)
fulfilment (GB), **fulfillment** (US) n **(a)** (satisfaction) épanouissement m ····∻

(b) the ~ of la réalisation de ⟨ambition, need⟩

full ⟨1⟩ adj (a) (gen) plein/-e (of de); ⟨hotel, flight, car park⟩ complet/-ète; ⟨theatre⟩ comble; **I'm ~ (up)** je n'en peux plus
(b) (busy) ⟨day, week⟩ chargé/-e, bien rempli/-e; **a very ~ life** une vie très remplie
(c) (complete) ⟨name, breakfast, story⟩ complet/-ète; ⟨price, control⟩ total/-e; ⟨responsibility⟩ entier/-ière; ⟨support⟩ inconditionnel/-elle
(d) ⟨member⟩ à part entière
(e) ⟨employment, bloom⟩ plein/-e (before n); **at ~ volume** à plein volume; **at ~ speed** à toute vitesse; **to get ~ marks** (GB) obtenir la note maximale
(f) (for emphasis) ⟨hour, kilo, month⟩ bon/bonne (before n)
(g) (rounded) ⟨cheeks⟩ rond/-e; ⟨figure⟩ fort/-e; ⟨skirt, sleeve⟩ ample
⟨2⟩ adv **to know ~ well that** savoir fort bien que; **with the heating up ~** avec le chauffage à fond
⟨3⟩ **in full** phr ⟨pay⟩ intégralement; **to write sth in ~** écrire qch en toutes lettres

full blast adv (colloq) **the TV was on (at) ~** la télé marchait à pleins tubes (colloq)

full-blown adj (a) ⟨disease⟩ déclaré/-e; ⟨epidemic⟩ extensif/-ive
(b) ⟨crisis, war⟩ à grande échelle

full board n (in hotel) pension f complète

full-cream milk n (GB) lait m entier

full-length adj ⟨coat, curtain⟩ long/longue; ⟨mirror⟩ en pied; **a ~ film** un long métrage

full moon n pleine lune f

full name n nom m et prénom m

full price adj, adv au prix fort

full-scale adj (a) ⟨drawing⟩ grandeur f nature
(b) ⟨investigation⟩ approfondi/-e
(c) ⟨alert⟩ général/-e; ⟨crisis⟩ généralisé/-e

full-size(d) adj grand format inv

full stop n (GB) point m

full time ⟨1⟩ n (Sport) fin m du match
⟨2⟩ **full-time** adj (a) (Sport) ⟨score⟩ final/-e
(b) ⟨job, student⟩ à plein temps
⟨3⟩ adv ⟨study, work⟩ à plein temps

fully adv (a) ⟨understand⟩ très bien; ⟨recover⟩ complètement; ⟨dressed⟩ entièrement; ⟨awake, developed⟩ complètement; **to be ~ qualified** avoir obtenu tous ses diplômes
(b) ⟨open⟩ à fond; **~ booked** complet/-ète

fully-fledged adj ⟨member⟩ à part entière; ⟨lawyer⟩ diplômé/-e

fumble vtr mal attraper ⟨ball⟩
■ **fumble about** (in dark) tâtonner (**to do** pour faire); **to ~ about in** fouiller dans ⟨bag⟩

fume vi (a) ⟨chemical, mixture⟩ fumer
(b) (colloq) **to be fuming** être furibond/-e (colloq)

fumes n pl émanations fpl; **petrol ~** (GB), **gas ~** (US) vapeurs fpl d'essence

fun n plaisir m, amusement m; **to have ~**

s'amuser (**doing** en faisant; **with** avec); **windsurfing is ~** c'est amusant de faire de la planche à voile; **for ~** pour s'amuser; **she is great ~ to be with** on s'amuse beaucoup avec elle
IDIOMS to make ~ of or **poke ~ at sb/sth** se moquer de qn/qch

function ⟨1⟩ n (a) (gen) fonction f
(b) (reception) réception f; (ceremony) cérémonie f (officielle)
⟨2⟩ vi (a) (work properly) fonctionner
(b) **to ~ as** ⟨object⟩ faire fonction de, servir de; ⟨person⟩ jouer le rôle de

functional adj (a) (in working order) opérationnel/-elle
(b) ⟨furniture, design⟩ fonctionnel/-elle

function key n touche f de fonction

fund ⟨1⟩ n fonds m; **relief ~** caisse f de secours; **disaster ~** collecte f en faveur des sinistrés
⟨2⟩ **funds** n pl fonds mpl, capitaux mpl; **to be in ~s** avoir de l'argent
⟨3⟩ vtr financer ⟨company, project⟩

fundamental adj ⟨issue⟩ fondamental/-e; ⟨error, importance⟩ capital/-e; ⟨concern⟩ principal/-e

fundamentalist n, adj (gen) fondamentaliste (mf); (religious) intégriste (mf)

funding n financement m

fund-raising n collecte f de fonds

funeral n enterrement m, obsèques fpl (formal)

funeral home (US), **funeral parlour** n entreprise f de pompes funèbres

fun fair n fête f foraine

fungus n (a) (mushroom) champignon m
(b) (mould) moisissure f

fun-loving adj ⟨person⟩ qui aime s'amuser

funnel n (a) (for liquids) entonnoir m
(b) (on ship) cheminée f

funny adj (amusing) drôle, amusant/-e; (odd) bizarre; **to feel ~** (colloq) se sentir tout/-e chose (colloq)

fur ⟨1⟩ n (of animal) poils mpl; (for garment) fourrure f
⟨2⟩ adj ⟨collar, coat⟩ de fourrure

furious adj (a) furieux/-ieuse (**with, at** contre); **he's ~ about it** cela l'a rendu furieux
(b) ⟨debate, struggle⟩ acharné/-e; ⟨storm⟩ déchaîné/-e; **at a ~ rate** à un rythme effréné

furnace n (boiler) chaudière f; (in foundry) fourneau m; (for forging) four m

furnish vtr meubler ⟨room, apartment⟩

furnishings n pl ameublement m

furniture n mobilier m, meubles mpl; **a piece of ~** un meuble

furry adj ⟨toy⟩ en peluche; ⟨kitten⟩ au poil touffu

further ⟨1⟩ adv (a) (gen) (also **farther**) plus loin (**than** que); **how much ~ is it?** c'est

encore loin?; ~ **back/forward** plus en arrière/en avant; ~ **away** *or* **off** plus loin; ~ **on** encore plus loin
(b) (in time) (*also* **farther**) ~ **back than 1964** avant 1964; **we must look** ~ **ahead** nous devons regarder plus vers l'avenir
(c) I haven't read ~ **than page twenty** je n'ai pas lu au-delà de la page vingt; **prices fell (even)** ~ les prix ont baissé encore plus
2 *adj* **(a)** (additional) **a** ~ **500 people** 500 personnes de plus; ~ **changes** d'autres changements; **without** ~ **delay** sans plus attendre
(b) (*also* **farther**) ⟨*side, end*⟩ autre
3 *vtr* augmenter ⟨*chances*⟩; faire avancer ⟨*career, plan*⟩; servir ⟨*cause*⟩
further education *n* (GB Univ) ≈ enseignement *m* professionnel
furthest (*also* **farthest**) **1** *adj* le plus éloigné/la plus éloignée
2 *adv* (*also* **farthest**) le plus loin
furtive *adj* ⟨*glance, movement*⟩ furtif/-ive; ⟨*behaviour*⟩ suspect/-e
fury *n* fureur *f*; **to be in a** ~ être en fureur
fuse, fuze (US) **1** *n* fusible *m*; **to blow a** ~ faire sauter un fusible; (get angry) piquer une crise (colloq)
2 *vtr* **(a)** (GB) **to** ~ **the lights** faire sauter les plombs
(b) (join) fondre [qch] ensemble ⟨*metals*⟩
fuse box *n* boîte *f* à fusibles

fuselage *n* fuselage *m*
fuse wire *n* fusible *m*
fuss **1** *n* **(a)** (agitation) remue-ménage *m inv*; **to make a** ~ faire des histoires; **to make a** ~ **about sth** faire toute une histoire à propos de qch
(b) to kick up a ~ **about sth** (colloq) piquer une crise à propos de qch (colloq)
(c) (attention) **to make a** ~ **of** être aux petits soins avec *or* pour ⟨*person*⟩; caresser ⟨*animal*⟩
2 *vi* **(a)** (worry) se faire du souci (**about** pour)
(b) (show attention) **to** ~ **over sb** (colloq) être aux petits soins avec *or* pour qn
fussy *adj* **to be** ~ **about one's food/about details** être maniaque sur la nourriture/sur les détails
futile *adj* **(a)** (vain) vain/-e
(b) (inane) futile
future **1** *n* **(a)** avenir *m*; **in the** ~ dans l'avenir; **in** ~ à l'avenir
(b) (*also* ~ **tense**) futur *m*
2 *adj* ⟨*generation, developments, investment, earnings*⟩ futur/-e; ⟨*prospects*⟩ d'avenir; ⟨*queen, king*⟩ futur/-e (*before n*); **at some** ~ **date** à une date ultérieure
fuze (US) = FUSE
fuzzy *adj* **(a)** ⟨*hair, beard*⟩ crépu/-e
(b) ⟨*image*⟩ flou/-e; ⟨*idea, mind*⟩ confus/-e

g

Gg

g, G *n* **(a)** (letter) g, G *m*
(b) G (Mus) sol *m*
(c) g (*written abbr* = **gram**) g
gab: *n* (colloq)
IDIOMS **to have the gift of the** ~ (colloq) avoir du bagou(t) (colloq)
gadget *n* gadget *m*
gaffe *n* bévue *f*
gag **1** *n* **(a)** (on mouth) bâillon *m*
(b) (colloq) (joke) blague *f* (colloq)
2 *vtr* bâillonner ⟨*person*⟩
3 *vi* avoir un haut-le-cœur
gage (US) = GAUGE
gain **1** *n* **(a)** (financial) gain *m*, profit *m*
(b) (increase) augmentation *f* (**in de**)
(c) (advantage) gain *m*; (advances) progrès *m* (**in de**)
2 *vtr* **(a)** (gen) gagner; acquérir ⟨*experience*⟩ (**from de**); obtenir ⟨*advantage*⟩ (**from grâce à**); **we have nothing to** ~ nous n'avons rien à gagner
(b) to ~ **speed** prendre de la vitesse *or* de l'élan; **to** ~ **weight** prendre du poids

3 *vi* **(a)** (increase) **to** ~ **in popularity** gagner en popularité; **to** ~ **in value** prendre de la valeur
(b) (profit) **she hasn't** ~**ed by it** cela ne lui a rien rapporté
■ **gain on** rattraper ⟨*person, vehicle*⟩
galaxy *n* galaxie *f*
gale *n* vent *m* violent
gallery *n* **(a)** (gen) galerie *f*
(b) (art) ~ musée *m* (d'art)
(c) (in theatre) dernier balcon *m*
Gallic *adj* (French) français/-e
galling *adj* vexant/-e
gallon *n* gallon *m* ((GB) = *4.546 l*; (US) = *3.785 l*)
gallop **1** *n* galop *m*
2 *vi* galoper
galore *adv* ⟨*prizes, bargains*⟩ à profusion; ⟨*drinks, sandwiches*⟩ à volonté, à gogo (colloq)
galvanize *vtr* galvaniser ⟨*group, community*⟩; relancer ⟨*campaign*⟩; **to** ~ **sb into doing** pousser qn à faire
gambit *n* **(a)** tactique *f*

⋯⃗

(b) (in chess) gambit *m*

gamble ⊞ *n* pari *m*; **it's a ~** c'est risqué
⊠ *vtr* **(a)** jouer ⟨*money*⟩
(b) (figurative) miser (**on** sur)
⊡ *vi* (at cards, on shares) jouer; (on horses)
parier; (figurative) miser (**on** sur)

gambler *n* joueur/-euse *m/f*

gambling *n* jeu *m* (d'argent)

game ⊞ *n* **(a)** jeu *m*; **to play a ~** jouer à un
jeu; **to have a ~ of** faire une partie de
(b) (match) match *m* (**of** de); (in tennis) jeu *m*
(c) (Culin) gibier *m*
⊠ **games** *n pl* **(a)** (GB) (Sch) sport *m*
(b) (*also* **Games**) (sporting event) Jeux *mpl*
IDIOMS **to give the ~ away** vendre la mèche

gamekeeper *n* garde-chasse *m*

game plan *n* stratégie *f*

game reserve *n* (for hunting) réserve *f* de
chasse; (for protection) réserve *f* naturelle

games console *n* console *f* de jeux
vidéo

game show *n* jeu *m* télévisé

games room *n* salle *f* de jeux

games software *n* logiciel *m* de jeux,
ludiciel *m*

gaming *n* on-line ~ jeux *mpl* en ligne

gaming zone *n* (on Internet) salle *f* de jeux
en ligne

gammon *n* jambon *m*

gang *n* **(a)** (of criminals) gang *m*; (of youths,
friends) bande *f*
(b) (of workmen, prisoners) équipe *f*
■ **gang up** se coaliser (**on, against** contre)

gangland *n* ≈ le Milieu

gang leader *n* chef *m* de bande

gang-rape *n* viol *m* collectif

gangster *n* gangster *m*

gangway *n* **(a)** (to ship) passerelle *f*
(b) (GB) (in bus, cinema) allée *f*

gap *n* **(a)** (gen) trou *m* (**in** dans); (between
planks, curtains) interstice *m* (**in** entre); (between
cars) espace *m* (**in** entre); (in cloud) trouée *f* (**in**
dans)
(b) (of time) intervalle *m*; (in conversation)
silence *m*
(c) (discrepancy) écart *m* (**between** entre); **a
15-year age ~** une différence d'âge de 15 ans
(d) (in knowledge) lacune *f* (**in** dans)
(e) (in market) créneau *m*

gape *vi* **(a)** (stare) rester bouche bée; **to ~ at
sb/sth** regarder qn/qch bouche bée
(b) to ~ open ⟨*chasm*⟩ s'ouvrir tout grand;
⟨*wound*⟩ être béant/-e; ⟨*garment*⟩ bâiller

gaping *adj* ⟨*person*⟩ bouche bée; ⟨*wound,
hole*⟩ béant/-e

gap year *n*: année d'interruption des
études entre le lycée et l'université

garage *n* garage *m*

garbage *n* **(a)** (US) (refuse) ordures *fpl*
(b) (nonsense) âneries *fpl*, bêtises *fpl*

garbage can *n* (US) poubelle *f*

garbage truck *n* (US) camion *m* des
éboueurs

garbled *adj* ⟨*account, instructions*⟩
'confus/-e

garden ⊞ *n* jardin *m*
⊠ *vi* jardiner, faire du jardinage

garden centre (GB), **garden center**
(US) *n* jardinerie *f*

gardener *n* jardinier/-ière *m/f*

gardening *n* jardinage *m*

gargle *vi* se gargariser (**with** avec)

garish *adj* tape-à-l'œil *inv*

garland *n* guirlande *f*

garlic *n* ail *m*

garment *n* vêtement *m*

garnish ⊞ *n* garniture *f*
⊠ *vtr* garnir (**with** de)

garter *n* **(a)** (for stocking) jarretière *f*; (for
socks) fixe-chaussette *m*
(b) (US) (suspender) jarretelle *f*

gas ⊞ *n* **(a)** (fuel) gaz *m*
(b) (anaesthetic) anesthésie *f*
(c) (US) (petrol) essence *f*
⊠ *vtr* gazer

gas chamber *n* chambre *f* à gaz

gas cooker *n* cuisinière *f* à gaz

gas fire *n* (appareil *m* de) chauffage *m* à
gaz

gash ⊞ *n* entaille *f*
⊠ *vtr* entailler

gas mask *n* masque *m* à gaz

gasoline *n* (US) essence *f*

gas oven *n* four *m* à gaz

gasp ⊞ *n* halètement *m*
⊠ *vi* **(a)** (for air) haleter
(b) to ~ (in amazement) avoir le souffle
coupé (par la surprise)

gas pedal *n* (US) accélérateur *m*

gas station *n* (US) station-service *f*

gastro-enteritis *n* gastro-entérite *f*

gate *n* (of field, level crossing) barrière *f*; (in
town, prison, airport, garden) porte *f*; (of courtyard,
palace) portail *m*; **at the ~** à l'entrée

gatecrash *vtr* (colloq) (without paying)
resquiller (colloq) à; (without invitation) se pointer
(colloq) sans invitation à

gatecrasher *n* (colloq) (at concert)
resquilleur/-euse *m/f*; (at party) intrus/-e *m/f*

gather ⊞ *n* (in garment) fronce *f*
⊠ *vtr* **(a)** cueillir ⟨*fruit, flowers*⟩; ramasser
⟨*fallen fruit, wood*⟩; recueillir ⟨*information*⟩;
rassembler ⟨*courage, strength*⟩; **to ~ speed**
prendre de la vitesse
(b) to ~ that... déduire que...; **I ~ (that)** he
was there d'après ce que j'ai compris il était
là
(c) (in sewing) faire des fronces à
⊡ *vi* ⟨*people, crowd*⟩ se rassembler; ⟨*family*⟩
se réunir; ⟨*clouds*⟩ s'amonceler

gathering *n* réunion *f*; **social/family ~**
réunion entre amis/de famille

gaudy *adj* tape-à-l'œil *inv*

gauge, gage (US) ⊞ *n* **(a)** (of gun, screw)
calibre *m*; (of metal, wire) épaisseur *f*
(b) (of railway) écartement *m* (des voies)

(c) (measuring instrument) jauge *f*; **fuel** ∼ jauge d'essence
　②　*vtr* **(a)** mesurer ⟨*diameter*⟩; jauger ⟨*distance, quantity*⟩; calibrer ⟨*gun*⟩
　(b) évaluer ⟨*mood, reaction*⟩

gaunt *adj* décharné/-e

gauze *n* (fabric) gaze *f*; (wire) grillage *m*

gay ①　*n* homosexuel/-elle *m/f*, gay *mf*
　②　*adj* **(a)** homosexuel/-elle
　(b) (happy) gai/-e; ⟨*laughter*⟩ joyeux/-euse

Gaza strip *pr n* bande *f* de Gaza

gaze ①　*n* regard *m*
　②　*vi* **to** ∼ **at sb/sth** regarder qn/qch; (in wonder) contempler qn/qch

GCSE *n* (*abbr* = **General Certificate of Secondary Education**) certificat *m* d'études secondaires

gear *n* **(a)** (equipment) matériel *m*
　(b) (clothes) fringues *fpl* (colloq); **football** ∼ tenue *f* de football
　(c) (Aut) vitesse *f*; **to be in third** ∼ être en troisième; **to put a car in** ∼ passer la vitesse; **you're not in** ∼ tu es au point mort
　■ **gear up** se préparer; **to be** ∼**ed up** être prêt/-e **(for** pour)

gearbox *n* boîte *f* de vitesses

gearstick (GB), **gearshift** (US) *n* levier *m* de vitesses

gear wheel *n* pignon *m*

gel ①　*n* gel *m*
　②　*vi* **(a)** (Culin) prendre
　(b) (figurative) prendre forme

gem *n* (jewel) pierre *f* précieuse

Gemini *n* Gémeaux *mpl*

gender *n* **(a)** (of word) genre *m*
　(b) (of person, animal) sexe *m*

gene *n* gène *m*

genealogy *n* généalogie *f*

gene library *n* génothèque *f*

gene pool *n* patrimoine *m* héréditaire

general ①　*n* général *m*
　②　*adj* général/-e
　③　**in general** *phr* (usually) en général; (overall) dans l'ensemble.

general election *n* élections *fpl* législatives.

generalization *n* généralisation *f* (**about** sur)

generalize *vtr, vi* généraliser (**about** à propos de)

general knowledge *n* culture *f* générale

generally *adv* **(a)** (usually) en général, généralement; ∼ **speaking...** en règle générale...
　(b) (overall) **the quality is** ∼ **good** dans l'ensemble la qualité est bonne
　(c) ⟨*talk*⟩ d'une manière générale

general practitioner, **GP** *n* (médecin *m*) généraliste *m*

general public *n* (grand) public *m*

general-purpose *adj* à usages multiples

general strike *n* grève *f* générale

generate *vtr* produire ⟨*power, heat, income, waste*⟩; créer ⟨*employment*⟩; susciter ⟨*interest, tension, ideas*⟩; entraîner ⟨*profit, publicity*⟩

generation *n* **(a)** génération *f*; **the younger/older** ∼ la jeune/l'ancienne génération
　(b) (of electricity, data) production *f*

generation gap *n* fossé *m* des générations

generator *n* (of electricity) générateur *m*; (in hospital, on farm) groupe *m* électrogène

generosity *n* générosité *f*

generous *adj* (gen) généreux/-euse; ⟨*size*⟩ grand/-e (*before n*); ⟨*hem*⟩ bon/bonne (*before n*)

gene therapy *n* thérapie *f* génique

genetic *adj* génétique

genetically modified, **GM** *adj* génétiquement modifié/-e

genetic engineering *n* génie *m* génétique

genetic fingerprinting *n* empreintes *fpl* génétiques

genetics *n* génétique *f*

genetic testing *n* tests *mpl* de dépistage génétique

Geneva *pr n* Genève

genial *adj* cordial/-e

genitals *n pl* organes *mpl* génitaux

genius *n* génie *m*

genome *n* génome *m*

gentle *adj* (gen) doux/douce; ⟨*hint, reminder*⟩ discret/-ète; ⟨*pressure, touch, breeze*⟩ léger/-ère; ⟨*exercise*⟩ modéré/-e

gentleman *n* **(a)** (man) monsieur *m*
　(b) (well-bred) gentleman *m*

gently *adv* (gen) doucement; ⟨*treat, cleanse*⟩ avec douceur; ⟨*cook*⟩ à feu doux; ⟨*speak*⟩ gentiment; **to break the news** ∼ annoncer la nouvelle avec ménagement

gents *n pl* (toilets) toilettes *fpl*; (on sign) 'Messieurs'

genuine *adj* ⟨*reason, motive*⟩ vrai/-e (*before n*); ⟨*work of art*⟩ authentique; ⟨*jewel, substance*⟩ véritable; ⟨*person, effort, interest*⟩ sincère; ⟨*buyer*⟩ sérieux/-ieuse

genuinely *adv* (really and truly) vraiment; (in reality) réellement

geography *n* géographie *f*

geology *n* géologie *f*

geometry *n* géométrie *f*

gerbil *n* gerbille *f*

geriatric *adj* ⟨*hospital, ward*⟩ gériatrique

germ *n* **(a)** (microbe) microbe *m*
　(b) (seed) germe *m*

German ①　*n* **(a)** (person) Allemand/-e *m/f*
　(b) (language) allemand *m*
　②　*adj* ⟨*custom, food*⟩ allemand/-e; ⟨*ambassador, embassy*⟩ d'Allemagne; ⟨*teacher, course*⟩ d'allemand

German measles *n* rubéole *f*

Germany *pr n* Allemagne *f*

germinate ① *vtr* faire germer
② *vi* germer

germ warfare *n* guerre *f* bactériologique

gesticulate *vi* gesticuler

gesture ① *n* geste *m* (of de)
② *vi* faire un geste; **to ~ at** *or* **towards sth** désigner qch d'un geste; **to ~ to sb** faire signe à qn

get

■ **Note** This much-used verb has no multi-purpose equivalent in French and therefore is very often translated by choosing a synonym: *to get lunch = to prepare lunch = préparer le déjeuner*.

– When *get* is used to express the idea that a job is not by you but by somebody else (*to get a room painted*), *faire* is used in French followed by an infinitive (*faire repeindre une pièce*).

– When *get* has the meaning of *become* and is followed by an adjective (*to get rich*), *devenir* is sometimes useful but check the appropriate entry (RICH) as a single verb often suffices (*s'enrichir*).

– The phrasal verbs (*get around, get down, get on* etc) are listed separately at the end of the entry GET.

– For examples and further uses of *get* see the entry below .

① *vtr* **(a)** (receive) recevoir ⟨*letter, grant*⟩; recevoir, percevoir ⟨*salary, pension*⟩; capter ⟨*channel*⟩
(b) (inherit) **to ~ sth from sb** hériter qch de qn ⟨*article, money*⟩; tenir qch de qn ⟨*trait*⟩
(c) (obtain) obtenir ⟨*permission, divorce*⟩; trouver ⟨*job*⟩
(d) (buy) acheter ⟨*item, newspaper*⟩ (**from** chez); avoir ⟨*ticket*⟩; **to ~ sb sth, to ~ sth for sb** (as gift) acheter qch à qn
(e) (acquire) se faire ⟨*reputation*⟩
(f) (achieve) obtenir ⟨*grade*⟩
(g) (fetch) chercher ⟨*person, help*⟩; **to ~ sb sth, to ~ sth for sb** aller chercher qch pour qn
(h) (move) **to ~ sb/sth downstairs** faire descendre qn/qch
(i) (help progress) **this is ~ting us nowhere** ça ne nous avance à rien; **where will that ~ you?** à quoi ça t'avancera?
(j) (deal with) **I'll ~ it** (of phone) je réponds; (of doorbell) j'y vais
(k) (prepare) préparer ⟨*breakfast, lunch*⟩
(l) (take hold of) attraper ⟨*person*⟩ (**by** par)
(m) (colloq) (oblige to give) **to ~ sth out of sb** faire sortir qch à qn ⟨*money*⟩; obtenir qch de qn ⟨*truth*⟩
(n) (contract) attraper ⟨*cold, disease*⟩; **he got measles from his sister** sa sœur lui a passé la rougeole
(o) (catch) prendre ⟨*bus, train*⟩
(p) (have) **to have got** avoir ⟨*object, money, friend*⟩; **I've got a headache** j'ai mal à la tête; **to ~ the idea that** se mettre dans la tête que
(q) **to ~ a surprise** être surpris/-e; **to ~ a shock** avoir un choc; **to ~ a bang on the head** recevoir un coup sur la tête

(r) (as punishment) prendre ⟨*five years*⟩; avoir ⟨*fine*⟩
(s) (understand, hear) comprendre
(t) (colloq) (annoy) **what ~s me is...** ce qui m'agace c'est que...
(u) **to ~ to like sb** finir par apprécier qn; **how did you ~ to hear of...?** comment avez-vous entendu parler de...?; **we got to know them last year** on a fait leur connaissance l'année dernière
(v) (have opportunity) **to ~ to do** avoir l'occasion de faire, pouvoir faire
(w) (must) **to have got to do** devoir faire ⟨*homework, chore*⟩; **it's got to be done** il faut le faire; **you've got to realize that...** il faut que tu te rendes compte que...
(x) (make) **to ~ sb to pay** faire payer qn; **to ~ sb to tell the truth** faire dire la vérité à qn
(y) (ask) **to ~ sb to wash the dishes** demander à qn de faire la vaisselle
(z) **to ~ the car repaired** faire réparer la voiture; **to ~ one's hair cut** se faire couper les cheveux; **to ~ the car going** faire démarrer la voiture; **to ~ one's socks wet** mouiller ses chaussettes; **to ~ one's finger trapped** se coincer le doigt; **to ~ a dress made** se faire faire une robe
② *vi* **(a)** (become) devenir ⟨*suspicious, old*⟩; **it's ~ting late** il se fait tard
(b) (forming passive) **to ~ killed** se faire tuer; **to ~ hurt** être blessé/-e
(c) (become involved in) **to ~ into** (colloq) se mettre à ⟨*hobby*⟩; commencer dans ⟨*profession*⟩; **to ~ into a fight** se battre
(d) (arrive) **to ~ there** arriver; **to ~ to the airport** arriver à l'aéroport; **how did you ~ here?** comment est-ce que tu es venu?; **where did you ~ to?** où est-ce que tu étais passé?
(e) (progress) **I'm ~ting nowhere with this essay** je n'avance pas dans cette dissertation; **now we're ~ting somewhere** il y a du progrès
(f) (put on) **to ~ into** mettre, enfiler ⟨*pyjamas*⟩

■ **get about (a)** (move) se déplacer
(b) (travel) voyager

■ **get across (a)** traverser ⟨*river, road*⟩
(b) faire passer ⟨*message*⟩ (**to** à)

■ **get ahead** (make progress) progresser

■ **get along (a)** **how are you ~ting along?** (in job, school) comment ça se passe?
(b) ⟨*people*⟩ bien s'entendre (**with** avec)

■ **get around**: ¶ **~ around (a)** = GET ABOUT
(b) (manage to do) **she'll ~ around to visiting us eventually** elle va bien finir par venir nous voir; **I haven't got around to it yet** je n'ai pas encore eu le temps de m'en occuper;
¶ **~ around [sth]** contourner ⟨*problem, law*⟩

■ **get at** (colloq) **(a)** (reach) atteindre ⟨*object*⟩; découvrir ⟨*truth*⟩
(b) (criticize) être après ⟨*person*⟩
(c) (insinuate) **what are you ~ting at?** où est-ce que tu veux en venir?

■ **get away (a)** (leave) partir
(b) (escape) s'échapper

(c) to ~ away with a crime échapper à la justice; **you won't ~ away with it!** tu ne vas pas t'en tirer comme ça!

■ **get away from** (a) quitter ⟨place⟩; échapper à ⟨person⟩
(b) **there's no ~ting away from it** on ne peut pas le nier

■ **get back**: ¶ ~ **back** (a) (return) rentrer; (after short time) revenir
(b) (move backwards) reculer
¶ ~ **back to** [sth] (a) (return to) rentrer à ⟨house, city⟩; revenir à ⟨office, point⟩; **when we ~ back to London** à notre retour à Londres; **to ~ back to sleep** se rendormir; **to ~ back to normal** redevenir normal
(b) (return to earlier stage) revenir à ⟨main topic, former point⟩; ¶ ~ **back to** [sb] revenir à; **I'll ~ back to you** (on phone) je vous rappelle
¶ ~ [sth] **back** (regain) récupérer ⟨lost object⟩; reprendre ⟨strength⟩; **she got her money back** elle a été remboursée

■ **get by** (a) (pass) passer
(b) (survive) s'en sortir (**on, with** avec)

■ **get down**
¶ ~ **down** (a) (descend) descendre (**from, out of** de)
(b) (on floor) se coucher; (crouch) se baisser; **to ~ down on one's knees** s'agenouiller
(c) **to ~ down to** se mettre à ⟨work⟩; **to ~ down to doing** se mettre à faire; ¶ ~ **down** [sth] descendre ⟨slope⟩; ¶ ~ [sth] **down** (from height) descendre
¶ ~ [sb] **down** (colloq) (depress) déprimer

■ **get in**: ¶ ~ **in** (a) (to building) entrer; (to vehicle) monter
(b) (return home) rentrer
(c) (arrive) arriver
(d) (penetrate) pénétrer
(e) ⟨party⟩ passer; ⟨candidate⟩ être élu/-e
(f) (Sch, Univ) ⟨applicant⟩ être admis/-e
¶ ~ [sth] **in** (buy) acheter

■ **get into** (a) (enter) entrer dans ⟨building⟩; monter dans ⟨vehicle⟩
(b) (as member) devenir membre de; (as student) être admis/-e à
(c) (squeeze into) rentrer dans ⟨garment, size⟩

■ **get off**: ¶ ~ **off** (a) (from bus) descendre (**at** à)
(b) (start on journey) partir
(c) (leave work) finir
(d) (colloq) (escape punishment) s'en tirer (**with** avec)
(e) **to ~ off to a good start** prendre un bon départ; **to ~ off to sleep** s'endormir
¶ ~ **off** [sth] (a) descendre de ⟨wall, bus⟩
(b) s'écarter de ⟨subject⟩
¶ ~ [sth] **off** (remove) enlever

■ **get on**: ¶ ~ **on** (a) (climb aboard) monter
(b) (GB) (like each other) bien s'entendre
(c) (fare) **how did you ~ on?** comment est-ce que ça s'est passé?; **how are you ~ting on?** comment est-ce que tu t'en sors?
(d) (GB) (approach) **he's ~ting on for 40** il approche des quarante ans; **it's ~ting on for midnight** il est presque minuit

¶ ~ **on** [sth] monter dans ⟨vehicle⟩
¶ ~ [sth] **on** mettre ⟨garment, lid⟩; monter ⟨tyre⟩

■ **get on with**: ¶ **to ~ on with one's work** continuer à travailler ¶ **to ~ on with** [sb] (GB) s'entendre avec ⟨person⟩

■ **get out**: ¶ ~ **out** (a) (exit) sortir (**through, by** par); ~ **out!** va-t'en!
(b) (alight) descendre
(c) ⟨prisoner⟩ être libéré/-e
(d) ⟨news⟩ être révélé/-e
¶ ~ [sth] **out** (a) (take out) sortir (**of** de)
(b) retirer ⟨cork⟩
(c) enlever ⟨stain⟩
(d) emprunter ⟨library book⟩

■ **get out of** (a) sortir de ⟨building⟩; descendre de ⟨vehicle⟩; être libéré/-e de ⟨prison⟩; quitter ⟨profession⟩
(b) **to ~ out of doing** s'arranger pour ne pas faire; **I'll try to ~ out of it** j'essaierai de me libérer
(c) perdre ⟨habit⟩
(d) **what do you ~ out of your job?** qu'est-ce que ton travail t'apporte?; **what will you ~ out of it?** qu'est-ce que vous en retirerez?

■ **get over** (a) traverser ⟨stream, bridge⟩; passer au-dessus de ⟨wall⟩
(b) se remettre de ⟨illness, shock⟩; **I can't ~ over it** (amazed) je n'en reviens pas
(c) surmonter ⟨problem⟩; **to ~ sth over with** en finir avec qch

■ **get round** (GB): ¶ ~ **round** = GET AROUND;
¶ ~ **round** [sb] (colloq) persuader [qn]

■ **get through**: ¶ ~ **through** (a) (squeeze through) passer
(b) **to ~ through to sb** (on phone) avoir qn au téléphone; (make oneself understood) se faire comprendre
(c) ⟨news, supplies⟩ arriver
(d) ⟨examinee⟩ réussir
¶ ~ **through** [sth] (a) terminer ⟨book⟩; finir ⟨meal, task⟩; réussir à ⟨exam⟩
(b) (use) manger ⟨food⟩; dépenser ⟨money⟩

■ **get together**: ¶ ~ **together** se réunir (**about, over** pour discuter de); ¶ ~ [sb/sth] **together** réunir ⟨people⟩; former ⟨company⟩

■ **get up**: ¶ ~ **up** (a) (from bed, chair) se lever (**from** de)
(b) (on ledge, wall) monter
(c) ⟨storm⟩ se préparer; ⟨wind⟩ se lever
(d) **what did you ~ up to?** (enjoyment) qu'est-ce que tu as fait de beau?; (mischief) qu'est-ce que tu as fabriqué? (colloq)
¶ ~ **up** [sth] (a) arriver en haut de ⟨hill, ladder⟩
(b) augmenter ⟨speed⟩

get-together n réunion f (entre amis).

ghastly adj horrible.

gherkin n cornichon m.

ghetto n ghetto m.

ghetto blaster n (colloq) (gros) radiocassette m portable.

ghost n fantôme m.

giant ⎡1⎤ n géant m.
⎡2⎤ adj géant/-e.

gibberish n charabia m.

giddy *adj* **(a)** to feel ~ avoir la tête qui
tourne
(b) ⟨*height, speed*⟩ vertigineux/-euse

gift *n* **(a)** (present) cadeau *m* (to à); **to give sb
a ~** faire *or* offrir un cadeau à qn
(b) (donation) don *m*
(c) (talent) don *m*; **to have a ~ for doing** avoir
le don de faire; **to have the ~ of the gab**
avoir du bagou(t) (colloq)

gifted *adj* doué/-e

gift shop *n* magasin *m* de cadeaux

gift token, **gift voucher** *n* (GB)
chèque-cadeau *m*

gift wrap *n* papier *m* cadeau

gig *n* (colloq) concert *m* de rock

gigantic *adj* gigantesque

giggle ⟦1⟧ *n* petit rire *m*; **to get the ~s**
attraper le fou rire
⟦2⟧ *vi* rire

gilt ⟦1⟧ *n* dorure *f*
⟦2⟧ *adj* ⟨*frame, paint*⟩ doré/-e

gimmick *n* (scheme) truc *m* (colloq); (object)
gadget *m*

gin *n* gin *m*; **~ and tonic** gin tonic *m*

ginger *n* **(a)** (Bot, Culin) gingembre *m*
(b) (colour) roux *m*

ginger-haired *adj* roux/rousse

girl *n* **(a)** (child) fille *f*; (teenager) jeune fille *f*;
baby ~ petite fille *f*, bébé *m*; **little ~** petite
fille *f*, fillette *f*
(b) (daughter) fille *f*

girlfriend *n* (female friend) amie *f*; (sweetheart)
(petite) amie *f*

girl guide (GB) , **girl scout** (US) *n*
éclaireuse *f*

giro *n* (GB) (system) système *m* de virement
bancaire; (cheque) mandat *m*

gist *n* essentiel *m* (of de)

give ⟦1⟧ *n* élasticité *f*
⟦2⟧ *vtr* (gen) donner (to à); transmettre
⟨*message*⟩ (to à); transmettre, passer ⟨*illness*⟩
(to à); laisser ⟨*seat*⟩ (to à); accorder ⟨*grant*⟩
(to à); faire ⟨*injection, massage*⟩ (to à); faire
⟨*speech*⟩; **to ~ sb sth** donner qch à qn;
(politely, as a gift) offrir qch à qn; **to ~ sb
pleasure** faire plaisir à qn; **~ him my best
(wishes)** transmets-lui mes amitiés; **she gave
him a drink** elle lui a donné à boire; **to ~ sb
enough room** laisser suffisamment de place à
qn
⟦3⟧ *vi* ⟨*mattress, sofa*⟩ s'affaisser; ⟨*shelf,
floorboard*⟩ fléchir; ⟨*branch*⟩ ployer
IDIOMS: **~ or take an inch (or two)** à quelques
centimètres près; **to ~ and take** faire des
concessions; **to ~ as good as one gets**
rendre coup pour coup; **to ~ it all one's got**
(colloq) (y) mettre le paquet

■ **give away**: ¶ **~ [sth] away (a)** donner
⟨*item, sample*⟩
(b) révéler ⟨*secret*⟩
(c) laisser échapper ⟨*match, goal, advantage*⟩
(to au bénéfice de)

¶ **~ [sb] away (a)** (betray) ⟨*expression,
fingerprints*⟩ trahir; ⟨*person*⟩ dénoncer (to à);
to ~ oneself away se trahir
(b) (in marriage) conduire ⟨qn⟩ à l'autel
■ **give back** rendre (to à)
■ **give in**: ¶ **~ in (a)** (yield) céder (to à)
(b) (stop trying) abandonner; **I ~ in—tell me!** je
donne ma langue au chat (colloq)—dis-le-moi!
¶ **~ [sth] in** rendre ⟨*work*⟩; remettre ⟨*ticket,
key*⟩
■ **give off** émettre ⟨*signal, radiation, light*⟩;
dégager ⟨*heat, fumes*⟩
■ **give out**: ¶ **~ out** ⟨*strength*⟩ s'épuiser;
⟨*engine*⟩ tomber en panne; ¶ **~ [sth] out**
(distribute) distribuer (to à)
■ **give up**: ¶ **~ up** abandonner; **to ~ up on**
laisser tomber ⟨*diet, crossword, pupil,
patient*⟩; ne plus compter sur ⟨*friend,
partner*⟩
¶ **~ up [sth] (a)** renoncer à ⟨*habit, title,
claim*⟩; sacrifier ⟨*free time*⟩; quitter ⟨*job*⟩; **to
~ up smoking/drinking** cesser de fumer/de
boire
(b) abandonner ⟨*search, hope, struggle*⟩;
renoncer à ⟨*idea*⟩
(c) céder ⟨*seat, territory*⟩
¶ **~ [sb] up (a)** (hand over) livrer (to à); **to ~
oneself up** se livrer (to à)
(b) laisser tomber ⟨*lover*⟩
■ **give way (a)** (collapse) s'effondrer; ⟨*fence,
cable*⟩ céder; **his legs gave way** ses jambes se
sont dérobées sous lui
(b) (GB) (when driving) céder le passage (to à)
(c) (yield) céder; **to ~ way to** faire place à

give-and-take *n* concessions *fpl*
mutuelles

giveaway *n* **to be a ~** être
révélateur/-trice

given ⟦1⟧ *adj* **(a)** ⟨*point, level, number*⟩
donné/-e; ⟨*volume, length*⟩ déterminé/-e; **at
any ~ moment** à n'importe quel moment
(b) **to be ~ to sth/to doing** avoir tendance à
qch/à faire; **I am not ~ to doing** je n'ai pas
l'habitude de faire
⟦2⟧ *prep* **(a)** (in view of) ~ **(the fact) that** étant
donné que
(b) (with) avec ⟨*training, proper care*⟩

given name *n* prénom *m*

glad *adj* content/-e, heureux/-euse (about de;
that que; to do faire); **he was only too ~
to help me** il ne demandait qu'à m'aider

gladly *adv* (willingly) volontiers; (with pleasure)
avec plaisir

glamorize *vtr* peindre [qn/qch] sous de
belles couleurs

glamorous *adj* ⟨*person, image, look*⟩
séduisant/-e; ⟨*older person*⟩ élégant/-e; ⟨*dress*⟩
splendide; ⟨*occasion*⟩ brillant/-e; ⟨*job*⟩
prestigieux/-ieuse

glamour, glamor (US) *n* (of person)
séduction *f*; (of job) prestige *m*; (of travel, cars)
fascination *f*

glance ⟦1⟧ *n* coup *m* d'œil
⟦2⟧ *vi* **to ~ at** jeter un coup d'œil à; **to ~
around the room** parcourir la pièce du
regard

■ **glance off** ⟨*bullet, stone*⟩ ricocher sur *or* contre

glancing *adj* ⟨*blow, kick*⟩ oblique

gland *n* glande *f*; **to have swollen** ∼**s** avoir des ganglions

glandular fever *n* mononucléose *f* infectieuse

glare [1] *n* (a) (angry look) regard *m* furieux
(b) (from lights) lumière *f* éblouissante
[2] *vi* ⟨*person*⟩ lancer un regard furieux (**at** à)

glaring *adj* (a) ⟨*mistake, injustice*⟩ flagrant/-e
(b) ⟨*light*⟩ éblouissant/-e

glass [1] *n* (a) (material) verre *m*; **wine** ∼ verre à vin; **a** ∼ **of wine** un verre de vin
(b) (mirror) miroir *m*
[2] *adj* ⟨*bottle, shelf*⟩ en verre; ⟨*door*⟩ vitré/-e
[3] **glasses** *n pl* lunettes *fpl*

glass ceiling *n*: niveau professionnel que la discrimination empêche certains groupes sociaux de dépasser

glassy-eyed *adj* (from drink, illness) aux yeux vitreux; (hostile) au regard glacial

glaze [1] *n* (a) (on pottery) vernis *m*
(b) (Culin) nappage *m*; (icing) glaçage *m*
[2] *vtr* (a) vernisser ⟨*pottery*⟩
(b) (Culin) glacer

glazed *adj* ⟨*door*⟩ vitré/-e; **to have a** ∼ **look in one's eyes** avoir les yeux vitreux

gleam [1] *n* (of light) lueur *f*; (of sunshine) rayon *m*; (of gold, polished surface) reflet *m*
[2] *vi* ⟨*light*⟩ luire; ⟨*knife, leather, surface*⟩ reluire; ⟨*eyes*⟩ briller

gleaming *adj* (a) ⟨*eyes, light*⟩ brillant/-e; ⟨*leather, surface*⟩ reluisant/-e
(b) (clean) étincelant/-e (de propreté)

glide *vi* ⟨*skater, boat*⟩ glisser (**on, over** sur); (in air) planer

glider *n* planeur *m*

gliding *n* vol *m* à voile

glimpse [1] *n* (a) vision *f* fugitive (**of** de); **to catch a** ∼ **of sth** entrevoir qch
(b) (insight) aperçu *m* (**of, at** de)
[2] *vtr* entrevoir

glisten *vi* ⟨*eyes, hair, surface*⟩ luire; ⟨*water*⟩ scintiller

glitch *n* (colloq) (gen) pépin *m* (colloq); (Comput) problème *m* technique

glitter [1] *n* (a) (substance) paillettes *fpl*
(b) (sparkle) éclat *m*
[2] *vi* scintiller

gloat *vi* jubiler (**at, over** à l'idée de)

global *adj* (a) (world-wide) mondial/-e
(b) (comprehensive) global/-e

global warming *n* réchauffement *m* de la planète

globe *n* (a) **the** ∼ le globe
(b) (model) globe *m* terrestre

gloom *n* (a) (darkness) obscurité *f*
(b) (despondency) morosité *f* (**about, over** à propos de)

gloomy *adj* (a) (dark) sombre

(b) ⟨*expression, person, voice*⟩ lugubre; ⟨*weather*⟩ morose; ⟨*news, outlook*⟩ déprimant/-e

glorify *vtr* glorifier

glorious *adj* (a) ⟨*view, weather*⟩ magnifique; ⟨*holiday*⟩ merveilleux/-euse
(b) (illustrious) glorieux/-ieuse

glory [1] *n* (a) (honour) gloire *f*
(b) (splendour) splendeur *f*
[2] *vi* **to** ∼ **in** être très fier/fière de

gloss *n* (a) (shine) lustre *m*
(b) (paint) laque *f*

■ **gloss over** (pass rapidly over) glisser sur; (hide) dissimuler

glossary *n* glossaire *m*

glossy *adj* ⟨*hair, material*⟩ luisant/-e; ⟨*photograph*⟩ brillant/-e; ⟨*brochure*⟩ luxueux/-euse

glossy magazine *n* magazine *m* illustré (de luxe)

glove *n* gant *m*

glove compartment *n* boîte *f* à gants

glow [1] *n* (a) (from fire) rougeoiement *m*; (of candle) lueur *f*
(b) (of complexion) éclat *m*
[2] *vi* (a) ⟨*metal, embers*⟩ rougeoyer; ⟨*lamp, cigarette*⟩ luire
(b) **to** ∼ **with health** resplendir de santé; **to** ∼ **with pride** rayonner de fierté

glower *vi* lancer des regards noirs (**at** à)

glowing *adj* (a) ⟨*ember*⟩ rougeoyant/-e; ⟨*face, cheeks*⟩ (from exercise) rouge; (from pleasure) radieux/-ieuse
(b) ⟨*account, terms*⟩ élogieux/-ieuse

glue [1] *n* colle *f*
[2] *vtr* coller; **to** ∼ **sth on** *or* **down** coller qch
[3] **glued** (colloq) *pp adj* **to be** ∼**d to the TV** être collé/-e devant la télé (colloq); **to be** ∼**d to the spot** être cloué/-e sur place

glue sniffer *n* sniffeur/-euse *m/f* (colloq) de colle

glue-sniffing *n* inhalation *f* de colle

glut *n* surabondance *f*, excès *m*

glutton *n* glouton/-onne *m/f*

glycerin(e) *n* glycérine *f*

GMT *n* (*abbr* = **Greenwich Mean Time**) TU

gnash *vtr* **to** ∼ **one's teeth** grincer des dents

gnaw [1] *vtr* ronger ⟨*bone, wood*⟩
[2] *vi* (a) **to** ∼ **at** *or* **on sth** ronger qch
(b) **to** ∼ **at sb** ⟨*hunger, remorse, pain*⟩ tenailler qn

GNP *n* (abbr = **gross national product**) PNB *m*

GNVQ *n* (*abbr* = **General National Vocational Qualification**) ≈ baccalauréat *m* professionnel

go
─────────────────
■ **Note As an intransitive verb**
– *go* as a simple intransitive verb is translated ⋯▸

by *aller*: *where are you going?* = où vas-tu?;
Sasha went to London last week = Sasha est
allé à Londres la semaine dernière.
– Note that *aller* conjugates with *être* in
compound tenses. For the conjugation of *aller*,
see the French verb tables.
– The verb *go* produces a great many phrasal
verbs (*go up, go down, go out, go back* etc.).
Many of these are translated by a single verb in
French (*monter, descendre, sortir, retourner* etc.).
The phrasal verbs are listed separately at the
end of the entry GO.

As an auxiliary verb
– When *go* is used as an auxiliary to show
intention, it is also translated by *aller*: *I'm going
to buy a car* = je vais acheter une voiture; *I was
going to talk to you about it* = j'allais t'en parler.

1 *vi* **(a)** aller (from de; to à, en); **to ~ to
Paris/to California** aller à Paris/en Californie;
to ~ to town/to the country aller en ville/à la
campagne; **they went home** ils sont rentrés
chez eux; **to ~ on holiday** partir en
vacances; **to ~ for a drink** aller prendre un
verre; **~ and ask her** va lui demander; **to ~
to school/work** aller à l'école/au travail; **to
~ to the doctor's** aller chez le médecin; **let's
~, let's get ~ing** allons-y
(b) (leave) partir; **I'm ~ing** je m'en vais
(c) (become) to **~ red** rougir; **to ~ white**
blanchir; **to ~ mad** devenir fou/folle
(d) to ~ unnoticed passer inaperçu/-e; **the
question went unanswered** la question est
restée sans réponse; **to ~ free** être libéré/-e
(e) (become impaired) **his memory is going** il
perd la mémoire; **my voice is going** je n'ai
plus de voix; **the battery is going** la pile est
presque à plat
(f) (of time) passer, s'écouler
(g) (operate, function) ⟨*vehicle, machine, clock*⟩
marcher, fonctionner; **to get [sth] going**
mettre [qch] en marche; **to keep going**
⟨*business*⟩ se maintenir; ⟨*machine*⟩ continuer
à marcher; ⟨*person*⟩ continuer
(h) (belong, be placed) aller; **where do these
plates ~?** où vont ces assiettes?; **it won't ~
into the box** ça ne rentre pas dans la boîte;
five into four won't ~ quatre n'est pas
divisible par cinq
(i) (be about to) **to be going to do** aller faire;
it's going to snow il va neiger
(j) (turn out) passer; **how did the party ~?**
comment s'est passée la soirée?; **it went well/
badly** ça s'est bien/mal passé
(k) (make sound, perform action or movement) (gen)
faire; ⟨*bell, alarm*⟩ sonner; **she went like this
with her fingers** elle a fait comme ça avec ses
doigts
(l) (take one's turn) **you ~ next** c'est ton tour
après, c'est à toi après; **you ~ first** après
vous
(m) (match) **those two colours don't ~
together** ces deux couleurs ne vont pas
ensemble
2 *vtr* faire ⟨*distance, number of miles*⟩
3 *n* (GB) (turn) tour *m*; (try) essai *m*; **whose ~
is it?** à qui le tour?; (in game) à qui de jouer?

4 **to go** *phr* **there are three days/pages to
~** il reste encore trois jours/pages
IDIOMS **to make a ~ of sth** réussir qch; **she's
always on the ~** elle n'arrête jamais; **in one
~** d'un seul coup; **it goes without saying that**
il va sans dire que; **as the saying goes**
comme dit le proverbe; **anything goes** tout
est permis
■ **go about** s'attaquer à ⟨*task*⟩; **to ~ about
one's business** vaquer à ses occupations
■ **go ahead** ⟨*event*⟩ avoir lieu; **~ ahead!**
vas-y! **they are going ahead with the project**
ils ont décidé de mettre le projet en route
■ **go along** aller; **to make sth up as one
goes along** inventer qch au fur et à mesure
■ **go along with** être d'accord avec ⟨*person,
view*⟩; accepter ⟨*plan*⟩
■ **go around** (a) se promener, circuler; **they
~ around everywhere together** ils vont
partout ensemble
(b) ⟨*rumour*⟩ courir
■ **go away** partir; **~ away!** va-t-en!
■ **go back (a)** (return) retourner; (turn back)
rebrousser chemin; **to ~ back to sleep** se
rendormir; **to ~ back to work** se remettre au
travail
(b) (date back) remonter (to à)
(c) (revert) revenir (to à)
■ **go back on** revenir sur ⟨*promise,
decision*⟩
■ **go by**: ¶ **~ by** ⟨*person*⟩ passer; **as time goes
by** avec le temps; ¶ **~ by** ⟨*sth*⟩ juger d'après
⟨*appearances*⟩, **to ~ by the rules** suivre le
règlement
■ **go down**: ¶ **~ down (a)** (descend) (gen)
descendre; ⟨*sun*⟩ se coucher; **to ~ down on
one's knees** se mettre à genoux
(b) to ~ down well/badly être bien/mal
reçu/-e
(c) ⟨*price, temperature, standard*⟩ baisser
(d) ⟨*swelling*⟩ désenfler; ⟨*tyre*⟩ se dégonfler
(e) (Comput) tomber en panne
¶ **~ down [sth]** descendre ⟨*hill*⟩
■ **go for**: ¶ **~ for [sb/sth] (a)** (colloq) (be keen
on) aimer
(b) (apply to) **the same goes for him!** c'est
valable pour lui aussi!
¶ **~ for [sb] (a)** (attack) attaquer
(b) he has a lot going for him il a beaucoup
de choses pour lui
¶ **~ for [sth] (a)** essayer d'obtenir ⟨*honour,
victory*⟩; **she's going for the world record** elle
vise le record mondial; **~ for it!** (colloq) vas-y,
fonce! (colloq)
(b) (choose) choisir, prendre
■ **go in (a)** (enter) entrer; (go back in) rentrer
(b) ⟨*troops*⟩ attaquer
(c) ⟨*sun*⟩ se cacher
■ **go in for (a)** (be keen on) aimer
(b) s'inscrire à ⟨*exam, competition*⟩
■ **go into (a)** (enter) entrer dans ⟨*building*⟩;
se lancer dans ⟨*business, profession*⟩
(b) (examine) étudier ⟨*question*⟩
■ **go off**: ¶ **~ off (a)** ⟨*bomb*⟩ exploser
(b) ⟨*alarm clock*⟩ sonner; ⟨*fire alarm*⟩ se
déclencher
(c) ⟨*person*⟩ partir, s'en aller

(d) (GB) ⟨*milk, cream*⟩ tourner; ⟨*meat*⟩ s'avarier; ⟨*butter*⟩ rancir; ⟨*performer, athlete*⟩ perdre sa forme

(e) ⟨*lights, heating*⟩ s'éteindre

(f) (happen, take place) **the concert went off very well** le concert s'est très bien passé

¶ ~ **off** [sb/sth] (GB) n'aimer plus

■ **go on:** ¶ ~ **on (a)** (happen) se passer; **how long has this been going on?** depuis combien de temps est-ce que ça dure?

(b) (continue on one's way) poursuivre son chemin

(c) (continue) continuer; **the list goes on and on** la liste est infinie

(d) (of time) (elapse) **as time went on, they...** avec le temps, ils...; **as the evening went on** au fur et à mesure que la soirée avançait

(e) to ~ on about sth ne pas arrêter de parler de qch

(f) (proceed) passer; **let's ~ on to the next item** passons au point suivant; **he went on to say that...** puis il a dit que...

(g) ⟨*heating, lights*⟩ s'allumer

(h) ⟨*actor*⟩ entrer en scène

¶ ~ **on** [sth] se fonder sur ⟨*evidence, information*⟩; **that's all we've got to ~ on** c'est tout ce que nous savons avec certitude

■ **go on at** s'en prendre à ⟨*person*⟩

■ **go out (a)** (leave, depart) sortir; **to ~ out for a drink** aller prendre un verre

(b) to ~ out with sb sortir avec qn

(c) ⟨*tide*⟩ descendre

(d) ⟨*fire, light*⟩ s'éteindre

■ **go over**

¶ ~ **over** (cross over) aller (**to** vers)

¶ ~ **over** [sth] **(a)** passer [qch] en revue ⟨*details, facts*⟩; vérifier ⟨*accounts, figures*⟩; relire ⟨*article*⟩

(b) (exceed) dépasser ⟨*limit, sum*⟩

■ **go round** (GB): ¶ ~ **round (a)** ⟨*wheel*⟩ tourner

(b) to ~ round to see sb aller voir qn

(c) ⟨*rumour*⟩ circuler

(d) (make detour) faire un détour

¶ ~ **round** [sth] faire le tour de ⟨*shops, house, museum*⟩

■ **go through:** ¶ ~ **through** ⟨*law*⟩ passer; ⟨*business deal*⟩ être conclu/-e

¶ ~ **through** [sth] **(a)** endurer, subir ⟨*experience*⟩; passer par ⟨*stage, phase*⟩; **she's gone through a lot** elle a beaucoup souffert

(b) (check) examiner

(c) (search) fouiller ⟨*belongings*⟩

(d) (perform) remplir ⟨*formalities*⟩

(e) (use up) dépenser ⟨*money*⟩; consommer ⟨*food, drink*⟩

■ **go through with** réaliser ⟨*plan*⟩; **I can't ~ through with it** je ne peux pas le faire

■ **go under** couler

■ **go up:** ¶ ~ **up (a)** (ascend) monter; **to ~ up to bed** monter se coucher

(b) ⟨*price, temperature*⟩ monter; ⟨*figures*⟩ augmenter; ⟨*curtain*⟩ se lever (**on** sur)

¶ ~ **up** [sth] monter, gravir ⟨*hill*⟩

■ **go without:** ¶ ~ **without** s'en passer

¶ ~ **without** [sth] se passer de

go-ahead *n* (colloq) **to give sb the ~** donner le feu vert à qn; **to get the ~** recevoir le feu vert

goal *n* but *m*

goalkeeper *n* gardien *m* de but

goalpost *n* poteau *m* de but

goat *n* chèvre *f*

gobble **1** *vtr* (*also* ~ **down**, ~ **up**) engloutir

2 *vi* ⟨*turkey*⟩ glouglouter

gobbledygook *n* (colloq) charabia *m* (colloq)

go-between *n* intermédiaire *mf*

gobsmacked *adj* (GB) (colloq) estomaqué/-e (colloq)

god *n* dieu *m*; **God** Dieu *m*

godchild *n* filleul/-e *m/f*

goddaughter *n* filleule *f*

goddess *n* déesse *f*

godfather *n* parrain *m*

godmother *n* marraine *f*

godparent *n* parrain/marraine *m/f*; **the ~s** le parrain et la marraine

godsend *n* aubaine *f*

godson *n* filleul *m*

goggles *n pl* lunettes *fpl*; (for swimming) lunettes *fpl* de plongée

going **1** *n* **(a)** (departure) départ *m*

(b) (progress) **that's good ~!** c'est rapide!; **it was slow ~** (on journey) ça a été long; (at work) ça n'avançait pas vite; **to be heavy ~** ⟨*book*⟩ être difficile à lire; ⟨*work, conversation*⟩ être laborieux/-ieuse

(c) when the **~ gets tough** quand les choses vont mal; **she finds her new job hard ~** elle trouve que son nouveau travail est difficile; **they got out while the ~ was good** ils s'en sont tirés (colloq) avant qu'il ne soit trop tard

2 *adj* **(a)** ⟨*price*⟩ actuel/-elle, en cours; **the ~ rate** le tarif en vigueur

(b) ⟨*concern*⟩ affaire *f* qui marche

(c) it's the best model ~ c'est le meilleur modèle sur le marché

goings-on *n pl* (colloq) (events) événements *mpl*; (activities) activités *fpl*; (behaviour) conduite *f*

go-kart *n* kart *m*

gold **1** *n* or *m*

2 *adj* ⟨*jewellery, tooth*⟩ en or; ⟨*coin, ingot, ore, wire*⟩ d'or

IDIOMS as good as ~ sage comme une image; **to be worth one's weight in ~** valoir son pesant d'or

gold dust *n* poudre *f* d'or; **to be like ~** être une denrée rare

golden *adj* **(a)** (made of gold) en or, d'or

(b) (gold coloured) doré/-e, d'or; **~ hair** cheveux *mpl* blonds dorés

(c) ⟨*age, days*⟩ d'or; **a ~ opportunity** une occasion en or

golden handshake *n* prime *f* de départ

golden rule *n* règle *f* d'or

goldfish *n* poisson *m* rouge

gold medal n médaille f d'or

gold mine n mine f d'or

gold-plated adj plaqué/-e or

gold rush n ruée f vers l'or

goldsmith n orfèvre m

golf n golf m; **to play** ~ faire du golf

golf club n (place) club m de golf; (stick) crosse f de golf

golf course n (terrain m de) golf m

golfer n joueur/-euse m/f de golf, golfeur/-euse m/f

gone adj (a) (departed) parti/-e; (dead) disparu/-e

(b) (past) **it's** ~ **six o'clock** il est six heures passées

gong n gong m

good ⊞ n (a) (virtue) bien m; ~ **and evil** le bien et le mal; **to be up to no** ~ (colloq) mijoter qch (colloq); **to come to no** ~ mal tourner

(b) (benefit) bien m; **it'll do you** ~ ça te fera du bien; **it didn't do my migraine any** ~ ça n'a pas arrangé ma migraine

(c) (use) **it's no** ~ **crying** ça ne sert à rien de pleurer; **what** ~ **would it do me?** à quoi cela me servirait-il?

⊡ adj (a) (gen) bon/bonne (before n); **it's a** ~ **film** c'est un bon film; **it was a** ~ **party** c'était une soirée réussie; **the** ~ **weather** le beau temps; **she's a** ~ **swimmer** elle nage bien; **to be** ~ **at** être bon/bonne en ‹Latin, physics›; être bon/bonne à ‹badminton, chess›; **to be** ~ **with** savoir comment s'y prendre avec ‹children, animals›; aimer ‹figures›; **to have a** ~ **time** s'amuser; **it's** ~ **to see you again** je suis content de vous revoir; **I don't feel too** ~ je ne me sens pas très bien; **the** ~ **thing is that...** ce qui est bien c'est que...; **to taste** ~ avoir bon goût; **to smell** ~ sentir bon; **we had a** ~ **laugh** on a bien ri; **to wait/walk for a** ~ **hour** attendre/marcher une bonne heure

(b) (well-behaved) ‹child, dog› sage; **be** ~! sois sage!

(c) (high quality) ‹hotel› bon/bonne (before n); ‹coat, china› beau/belle (before n); ‹degree› avec mention

(d) (kind) ‹person› gentil/-ille; (virtuous) ‹man, life› vertueux/-euse; **to do sb a** ~ **turn** rendre service à qn; **would you be** ~ **enough to do** auriez-vous la gentillesse de faire

(e) (beneficial) **to be** ~ **for** faire du bien à ‹person, plant›; être bon/bonne pour ‹health, business, morale›

(f) (fortunate) **it's a** ~ **job** or **thing (that)** heureusement que; **it's a** ~ **job** or **thing too!** tant mieux!; ▶ BETTER, BEST

③ excl (expressing pleasure, satisfaction) c'est bien!; (with relief) tant mieux!; (to encourage, approve) très bien!

④ **as good as** phr quasiment; **to be as** ~ **as new** être comme neuf/neuve

⑤ **for good** phr pour toujours

IDIOMS ~ **for you!** bravo!; **it's too** ~ **to be true** c'est trop beau pour être vrai

good afternoon phr bonjour

goodbye phr au revoir

good evening phr bonsoir

good-for-nothing n bon/bonne m/f à rien

good-humoured (GB), **good-humored** (US) adj ‹crowd, discussion› détendu/-e; ‹rivalry› amical/-e; ‹remark, smile› plaisant/-e; **to be** ~ ‹person› avoir bon caractère

good-looking adj beau/belle (before n)

good morning phr bonjour

good-natured adj ‹person› agréable; ‹animal› placide

goodness ⊞ n (a) (quality, virtue) bonté f (b) (nourishment) **to be full of** ~ être plein/-e de bonnes choses

⊡ excl (also ~ **gracious!**) mon Dieu!

IDIOMS **for** ~**' sake!** pour l'amour de Dieu!

goodnight phr bonne nuit

goods n pl articles mpl, marchandise f

goods train n (GB) train m de marchandises

goodwill n (a) (kindness) bonne volonté f (b) (of business) clientèle f

goose n oie f

gooseberry n groseille f à maquereau

IDIOMS **to be** a or **play** ~ tenir la chandelle

goose pimples n pl chair f de poule

gorge ⊞ n gorge f

⊡ v refl **to** ~ **oneself** se gaver (on de)

gorgeous adj (a) (colloq) ‹food, scenery› formidable (colloq); ‹kitten, baby› adorable; ‹weather, day, person› splendide (b) (sumptuous) somptueux/-euse

gorilla n gorille m

gorse n ajoncs mpl

gory adj sanglant/-e

gosh excl (colloq) ça alors! (colloq)

go-slow n (GB) grève f perlée

gospel n Évangile m

gospel music n gospel m

gossip ⊞ n (a) (malicious) commérages mpl (about sur); (not malicious) nouvelles fpl (about sur)

(b) (person) commère f

⊡ vi bavarder; (more maliciously) faire des commérages (about sur)

gossip column n échos mpl

got: to have got phr (a) **to have** ~ avoir (b) **I've** ~ **to go** il faut que j'y aille

gourd n (a) (container) gourde f (b) (fruit) calebasse f

gout n goutte f

govern ⊞ vtr (a) gouverner ‹country, state, city›; administrer ‹colony, province› (b) (control) régir ‹use, conduct, treatment› (c) (determine) déterminer ‹decision›; régler ‹flow, speed›

⊡ vi ‹parliament, president› gouverner

governess n gouvernante f

governing adj ‹party› au pouvoir; ‹class› dirigeant/-e; **the** ~ **principle** l'idée directrice

government [1] *n* gouvernement *m*; (the state) l'État *m*; **in ~** au pouvoir [2] *adj* ⟨*minister, plan*⟩ du gouvernement; ⟨*department, majority, policy*⟩ gouvernemental/-e; ⟨*expenditure, borrowing*⟩ de l'État; ⟨*funds*⟩ public/-ique

governmental *adj* gouvernemental/-e

governor *n* (of state, colony, bank) gouverneur *m*; (of prison) directeur *m*; (of school) membre *m* du conseil d'établissement

gown *n* (dress) robe *f*; (of judge, academic) toge *f*; (of surgeon) blouse *f*

GP *n* (*abbr* = **general practitioner**) (médecin *m*) généraliste *mf*

grab [1] *vtr* empoigner ⟨*money, object*⟩; saisir ⟨*arm, person, opportunity*⟩; **to ~ hold of** se saisir de [2] *vi* **to ~ at** se jeter sur

grace *n* (a) (gen) grâce *f*; **sb's saving ~** ce qui sauve qn (b) **to give sb two days' ~** accorder un délai de deux jours à qn (c) (prayer) (before meal) bénédicité *m*; (after meal) grâces *fpl* IDIOMS **to be full of airs and ~s** prendre des airs

graceful *adj* ⟨*dancer, movement*⟩ gracieux/-ieuse; ⟨*person*⟩ élégant/-e

grade [1] *n* (a) (quality) qualité *f*; **high-/low-~** de qualité supérieure/inférieure (b) (mark) note *f* (**in** en) (c) (rank) échelon *m* (d) (US) (class) classe *f* [2] *vtr* (by quality) classer (**according to** selon); (by size) calibrer (**according to** selon)

grade school *n* (US) école *f* primaire

gradient *n* pente *f*, inclinaison *f*

gradual *adj* (a) ⟨*change, increase*⟩ progressif/-ive (b) ⟨*slope*⟩ doux/douce

gradually *adv* (slowly) peu à peu; (by degrees) progressivement

graduate [1] *n* diplômé/-e *m/f* [2] *vi* (a) terminer ses études (**at** *or* **from** à); (US) (Sch) ≈ finir le lycée (b) (progress) **to ~ (from sth) to** passer (de qch) à

graduate training scheme *n* programme *m* de formation professionnelle pour étudiants diplômés

graduation *n* (*also* **~ ceremony**) (cérémonie *f* de) remise *f* des diplômes

graffiti *n* graffiti *mpl*

graffiti artist *n* tagger *m*

graft [1] *n* greffe *f*; **skin ~** greffe de la peau [2] *vtr* greffer (**onto** sur)

grain *n* (a) (of rice, wheat, sand, salt) grain *m* (b) (crops) céréales *fpl* (c) (figurative) (of truth, comfort) brin *m* (d) (in wood, stone) veines *fpl*; (in leather, paper, fabric) grain *m* IDIOMS **it goes against the ~** c'est contre tous mes/nos/leurs principes

gram(me) *n* gramme *m*

grammar *n* grammaire *f*

grammar school *n* (GB) ≈ lycée *m* (à recrutement sélectif)

grammatical *adj* (a) ⟨*error*⟩ de grammaire (b) (correct) grammaticalement correct

granary *n* grenier *m*

granary bread *n* pain *m* aux céréales

grand *adj* ⟨*building, ceremony*⟩ grandiose; **on a ~ scale** à très grande échelle; **the Grand Canyon** le Grand Cañon *m*; **to play the ~ lady** jouer à la grande dame

grandchild *n* (girl) petite-fille *f*; (boy) petit-fils *m*; **his grandchildren** ses petits-enfants *mpl*

granddaughter *n* petite-fille *f*

grandeur *n* (of scenery) majesté *f*; (of building) caractère *m* grandiose

grandfather *n* grand-père *m*

grandfather clock *n* horloge *f* comtoise

grandma *n* (colloq) mémé *f* (colloq), mamy *f* (colloq), mamie *f* (colloq)

grandmother *n* grand-mère *f*

grandpa *n* (colloq) pépé *m* (colloq), papy *m* (colloq), papi *m* (colloq)

grandparents *n pl* grands-parents *mpl*

grand piano *n* piano *m* à queue

grand slam *n* grand chelem *m*

grandson *n* petit-fils *m*

grandstand *n* tribune *f*

grand total *n* total *m*

granite *n* granit(e) *m*

granny *n* (colloq) mémé *f* (colloq)

grant [1] *n* (gen) subvention *f*; (for study) bourse *f* [2] *vtr* (a) accorder ⟨*permission*⟩; accéder à ⟨*request*⟩ (b) **to ~ sb [sth]** accorder [qch] à qn ⟨*interview, leave, visa*⟩; concéder [qch] à qn ⟨*citizenship*⟩ (c) **to ~ that** reconnaître que IDIOMS **to take sth for ~ed** considérer qch comme allant de soi; **he takes his mother for ~ed** il croit que sa mère est à son service

granulated *adj* ⟨*sugar*⟩ cristallisé/-e

granule *n* (of sugar, salt) grain *m*; (of coffee) granulé *m*

grape *n* grain *m* de raisin; **a bunch of ~s** une grappe de raisin

grapefruit *n* pamplemousse *m*

grapeseed oil *n* huile *f* de pépins de raisin

grapevine *n* (in vineyard) pied *m* de vigne; (in greenhouse, garden) vigne *f* IDIOMS **to hear sth on the ~** apprendre qch par le téléphone arabe

graph *n* graphique *m*

graphic *adj* (a) ⟨*art, display, technique*⟩ graphique (b) ⟨*account*⟩ (pleasantly described) vivant/-e; (gory) cru/-e

graphic design *n* graphisme *m*

graphic designer n graphiste mf
graphics n pl **(a)** (on screen) visualisation f graphique
(b) computer ~ infographie f
(c) (in film, TV) images fpl; (in book) illustrations fpl
graphics card n carte f graphique
graphics interface n interface f graphique
graph paper n papier m millimétré
grasp ⟦1⟧ n **(a)** (hold, grip) prise f
(b) (understanding) maîtrise f
⟦2⟧ vtr **(a)** empoigner ⟨rope, hand⟩; saisir ⟨opportunity⟩
(b) (comprehend) saisir, comprendre
⟦3⟧ vi **to** ~ **at** tenter de saisir
grasping adj cupide
grass n herbe f; (lawn) pelouse f
IDIOMS **the** ~ **is greener (on the other side of the fence)** on croit toujours que c'est mieux ailleurs
grass court n court m en gazon
grasshopper n sauterelle f
grassroots ⟦1⟧ n pl **the** ~ le peuple
⟦2⟧ adj ⟨movement⟩ populaire; ⟨support⟩ de base
grate ⟦1⟧ n grille f de foyer
⟦2⟧ vtr râper ⟨carrot, cheese⟩
⟦3⟧ vi **(a)** ⟨metal object⟩ grincer (on sur)
(b) (annoy) agacer; **that** ~**s** ça m'agace
grateful adj reconnaissant/-e (to à; for de)
grater n râpe f
gratify vtr faire plaisir à ⟨person⟩; satisfaire ⟨desire⟩; **to be gratified** être satisfait/-e
grating ⟦1⟧ n (bars) grille f
⟦2⟧ adj ⟨noise⟩ grinçant/-e; ⟨voice⟩ désagréable
gratitude n reconnaissance f (**to, towards** envers; for de)
gratuitous adj gratuit/-e
grave ⟦1⟧ n tombe f
⟦2⟧ adj **(a)** ⟨illness⟩ grave; ⟨risk⟩ sérieux/-ieuse; ⟨danger⟩ grand/-e (before n)
(b) (solemn) sérieux/-ieuse
gravel n (coarse) graviers mpl; (fine) gravillons mpl
gravestone n pierre f tombale
graveyard n cimetière m
gravitate vi **to** ~ **to(wards)** graviter vers
gravity n **(a)** pesanteur f; **centre of** ~ centre m de gravité
(b) (of situation) gravité f
gravy n sauce f (au jus de rôti)
gravy boat n saucière f
gray (US) = GREY
graze ⟦1⟧ n écorchure f
⟦2⟧ vtr **(a)** **to** ~ **one's knee** s'écorcher le genou (on, against sur)
(b) (touch lightly) frôler
⟦3⟧ vi ⟨sheep⟩ brouter; ⟨cow⟩ paître
grease ⟦1⟧ n graisse f
⟦2⟧ vtr graisser
greasy adj ⟨hair, skin, food⟩ gras/grasse; ⟨overalls⟩ graisseux/-euse

great adj **(a)** (gen) grand/-e (before n); ⟨number, increase⟩ important/-e; ⟨heat⟩ fort/-e (before n); **a** ~ **deal (of)** beaucoup (de); **with** ~ **difficulty** avec beaucoup de mal
(b) (colloq) ⟨book, party, weather⟩ génial/-e (colloq), formidable (colloq); ⟨opportunity⟩ formidable (colloq); **to feel** ~ se sentir en pleine forme; ~! génial!
great aunt n grand-tante f
great big adj (très) grand/-e (before n), énorme
Great Britain pr n Grande-Bretagne f
great grandchild n (girl) arrière-petite-fille f; (garçon) arrière-petit-fils m
great grandfather n arrière-grand-père m
great grandmother n arrière-grand-mère f
great-great grandchild n (girl) arrière-arrière-petite-fille f; (boy) arrière-arrière-petit-fils m
greatly adv ⟨admire, regret⟩ beaucoup, énormément; ⟨surprised, distressed⟩ très, extrêmement; ⟨improved, changed⟩ considérablement
greatness n (of achievement) importance f; (of person) grandeur f
great uncle n grand-oncle m
Greece pr n Grèce f
greed n **(a)** (for money, power) avidité f (**for** de)
(b) (also **greediness**) (for food) gourmandise f
greedy adj **(a)** (for food) gourmand/-e; (stronger) goulu/-e; ⟨look⟩ avide; **a** ~ **pig** (colloq) un goinfre (colloq)
(b) (for money, power) avide (**for** de)
Greek ⟦1⟧ n **(a)** (person) Grec/Grecque m/f
(b) (language) grec m
⟦2⟧ adj ⟨government, island⟩ grec/grecque; ⟨embassy⟩ de Grèce
IDIOMS **it's all** ~ **to me** c'est du chinois pour moi
green ⟦1⟧ n **(a)** (colour) vert m
(b) village ~ terrain m communal
(c) (in bowling) boulingrin m; (in golf) green m
(d) (person) écologiste mf; **the Greens** les Verts
⟦2⟧ **greens** n pl (GB) légumes mpl verts
⟦3⟧ adj **(a)** (in colour) vert/-e
(b) ⟨countryside⟩ verdoyant/-e
(c) (colloq) (naïve) naïf/naïve
(d) (inexperienced) novice
(e) ⟨policies, candidate, issues⟩ écologiste; ⟨product⟩ écologique
green card n **(a)** (driving insurance) carte f verte (internationale)
(b) (US) (residence and work permit) carte f de séjour
greenery n verdure f
greenfield site n terrain m vert
greengrocer n marchand m de fruits et légumes

greenhouse n serre f

greenhouse effect n effet m de serre

Greenland pr n Groenland m

greet vtr (a) (say hello to) saluer
(b) to be ~ed with or by provoquer ⟨dismay, amusement⟩

greeting **1** n salutation f
2 greetings n pl Christmas ~s vœux mpl de Noël; Season's ~s meilleurs vœux

greetings card (GB), **greeting card** (US) n carte f de vœux

grey (GB), **gray** (US) **1** n gris m
2 adj (a) (in colour) gris/-e
(b) (grey-haired) to go or turn ~ grisonner
(c) (dull) ⟨existence, day⟩ morne; ⟨person, town⟩ terne

grey area n zone f floue

grey-haired adj aux cheveux gris

greyhound n lévrier m

grid n (a) grille f
(b) (GB) (network) réseau m

gridlock n embouteillage m, bouchon m

grief n chagrin m
IDIOMS to come to ~ ⟨person⟩ (have an accident) avoir un accident; (fail) échouer; ⟨business⟩ péricliter; **good ~!** mon Dieu!

grief-stricken adj accablé/-e de douleur

grievance n griefs mpl (against contre)

grieve vi to ~ for or over pleurer ⟨person⟩

grievous bodily harm, **GBH** n (Law) coups mpl et blessures fpl

grill **1** n gril m
2 vtr (a) faire griller ⟨meat, fish⟩
(b) (colloq) (interrogate) mettre [qn] sur la sellette (colloq)

grille n (gen) grille f; (on car) calandre f

grim adj (a) ⟨news, town, future⟩ sinistre; ⟨sight, conditions⟩ effroyable; ⟨reality⟩ dur/-e
(b) ⟨struggle⟩ acharné/-e; ⟨resolve⟩ terrible
(c) ⟨face⟩ grave

grimace **1** n grimace f (of de)
2 vi (involuntary) faire une grimace (with, in de); (pull a face) faire la grimace

grime n (of city) saleté f; (on object, person) crasse f

grimy adj ⟨city⟩ noir/-e; ⟨hands, window⟩ crasseux/-euse

grin **1** n sourire m
2 vi sourire (at à; with de)

grind **1** n (colloq) boulot m (colloq) or travail m monotone
2 vtr moudre ⟨corn, coffee beans⟩; écraser ⟨grain⟩; hacher ⟨meat⟩; to ~ one's teeth grincer des dents
3 vi ⟨machine⟩ grincer; to ~ to a halt ⟨machine⟩ s'arrêter; ⟨vehicle⟩ s'arrêter avec un grincement de freins; ⟨factory, production⟩ s'immobiliser

grindstone n meule f or pierre f à aiguiser
IDIOMS to keep or have one's nose to the ~ travailler sans relâche

grip **1** n (a) prise f (on sur)

(b) to lose one's ~ on reality perdre contact avec la réalité; to come to ~s with sth en venir aux prises avec qch; **get a ~ on yourself!** ressaisis-toi!
(c) (of tyre) adhérence f
2 vtr (a) (grab) agripper; (hold) serrer
(b) ⟨tyres⟩ adhérer à ⟨road⟩; ⟨shoes⟩ accrocher à ⟨ground⟩
(c) (captivate) captiver

gripping adj captivant/-e

grisly adj ⟨story, sight⟩ horrible; ⟨remains⟩ macabre

gristle n cartilage m

grit **1** n (a) (on lens) grains mpl de poussière; (sandy dirt) grains mpl de sable
(b) (GB) (for roads) sable m
2 vtr (GB) sabler ⟨road⟩
IDIOMS to ~ one's teeth serrer les dents

grizzly n (also ~ **bear**) grizzli m

groan **1** n (of pain, despair) gémissement m; (of disgust, protest) grognement m
2 vi (in pain) gémir; (in disgust, protest) grogner

grocer n (person) épicier/-ière m/f; ~'s (shop) épicerie f

groceries n pl provisions fpl

grocery n (also ~ **shop** (GB), ~ **store**) épicerie f

groggy adj groggy; to feel ~ avoir les jambes en coton (colloq)

groin n aine f

groom **1** n (a) (bridegroom) the ~ le jeune marié
(b) (for horse) palefrenier/-ière m/f
2 vtr (a) panser ⟨horse⟩
(b) to ~ sb for préparer qn à ⟨exam, career⟩

groove n (gen) rainure f; (on record) sillon m; (on screw) fente f

grope **1** vtr (colloq) (sexually) tripoter (colloq)
2 vi to ~ for sth chercher qch à tâtons

gross **1** n grosse f
2 adj (a) ⟨income, profit⟩ brut/-e
(b) ⟨error, exaggeration⟩ grossier/-ière; ⟨abuse, inequality⟩ choquant/-e; ⟨injustice⟩ flagrant/-e
(c) ⟨behaviour⟩ vulgaire; ⟨language⟩ cru/-e
(d) (colloq) (revolting) dégoûtant/-e
(e) (colloq) (obese) obèse
3 vtr ⟨business, company⟩ faire un bénéfice brut de

grossly adv ⟨misleading, irresponsible⟩ extrêmement; ⟨underpaid⟩ scandaleusement; ~ **overweight** obèse

gross national product, **GNP** n produit m national brut, PNB m

grotesque n, adj grotesque (m)

grotto n grotte f

grotty adj (colloq) minable (colloq); to feel ~ se sentir tout chose (colloq)

ground **1** n (a) sol m, terre f; on the ~ par terre; above ~ en surface; below ~ sous terre
(b) (area, territory) terrain m; a piece of ~ un terrain
(c) (sportsground) terrain m ⋯∲

2 **grounds** *n pl* **(a)** (garden) parc *m* **(of** de)
(b) (reasons) ~s for sth motifs *mpl* de qch;
~s for doing motifs pour faire; **on the** ~s
that en raison du fait que
3 *pp adj* ⟨coffee, pepper⟩ moulu/-e
4 *vtr* **(a)** immobiliser ⟨aircraft⟩
(b) ⟨ship⟩ **to be** ~ed s'échouer
IDIOMS to gain ~ gagner du terrain (**on,**
over sur); **to hold one's** ~ tenir bon; **to go to**
~ se terrer; **that suits me down to the** ~ ça
me convient parfaitement

ground floor *n* rez-de-chaussée *m inv*; **on**
the ~ au rez-de-chaussée

grounding *n* bases *fpl* (**in** en, de)

groundnut oil *n* huile *f* d'arachide

ground rules *n pl* grands principes *mpl*;
to change the ~ modifier les règles du jeu

groundsheet *n* tapis *m* de sol

ground troops *n pl* troupes *fpl* terrestres

groundwork *n* travail *m* préparatoire (**for**
à)

group **1** *n* groupe *m*; **in** ~s en groupes
2 *vtr* grouper
3 *vi* ~ **together** ⟨people⟩ se grouper

group booking *n* réservation *f* de groupe

group therapy *n* thérapie *f* de groupe

group work *n* travail *m* en groupes

grouse *n* tétras *m*

grove *n* bosquet *m*; **lemon** ~ verger *m* de
citronniers

grovel *vi* ramper (**to, before** devant)

grow **1** *vtr* **(a)** cultiver ⟨plant, crop⟩
(b) laisser pousser ⟨beard, nails⟩; **to** ~ **5 cm**
⟨person⟩ grandir de 5 cm; ⟨plant⟩ pousser de
5 cm
2 *vi* **(a)** ⟨person⟩ grandir (**by** de); ⟨plant,
hair⟩ pousser (**by** de)
(b) ⟨population, tension⟩ augmenter (**by** de);
⟨company, economy⟩ se développer;
⟨opposition, support, problem⟩ devenir plus
important; ⟨crisis⟩ s'aggraver
(c) devenir ⟨hotter, stronger⟩; **to** ~ **old**
vieillir; **to** ~ **impatient** s'impatienter; **I grew**
to like him j'ai appris à l'aimer
■ **grow apart** s'éloigner l'un de l'autre
■ **grow on: it** ~s **on you** on finit par l'aimer;
he's ~**ing on me** je commence à le trouver
plus sympathique
■ **grow out of (a) he's grown out of his suit**
son costume est devenu trop petit pour lui
(b) he'll ~ **out of it** (of habit) ça lui passera
■ **grow up** (gen) grandir; (become mature)
devenir adulte; **when I** ~ **up** quand je serai
grand

grower *n* (of fruit) producteur/-trice *m/f*; (of
crops) cultivateur/-trice *m/f*

growl **1** *n* grondement *m*
2 *vi* ⟨dog⟩ gronder

grown-up **1** *n* adulte *mf*, grande personne
f
2 *adj* adulte

growth *n* **(a)** (gen) croissance *f* (**in, of** de);

(of hair, nails) pousse *f*; (of economy) expansion *f*
(**in, of** de); (in numbers, productivity)
augmentation *f* (**in** de)
(b) (tumour) grosseur *f*, tumeur *f*

growth area *n* secteur *m* en expansion

growth industry *n* industrie *f* en
expansion

growth rate *n* taux *m* de croissance

grubby *adj* malpropre

grudge **1** *n* **to bear sb a** ~ en vouloir à qn
2 *vtr* **to** ~ **sb their success** en vouloir à qn
de sa réussite; **to** ~ **doing** rechigner à faire

grudgingly *adv* ⟨admit⟩ avec réticence

gruelling, grueling (US) *adj*
exténuant/-e

gruesome *adj* horrible

gruff *adj* bourru/-e

grumble *vi* ⟨person⟩ ronchonner (**at** sb
après qn; **to** auprès de); **to** ~ **about** se
plaindre de

grumpy *adj* grincheux/-euse

grunge *n* (colloq) (dirt) crasse *f*; (style) grunge
m

grunt **1** *n* grognement *m*
2 *vi* grogner

G-string *n* (garment) string *m*

guarantee **1** *n* garantie *f*
2 *vtr* garantir

guard **1** *n* **(a)** (for person) surveillant/-e *m/f*;
(for place, object, at prison) gardien/-ienne *m/f*;
(soldier) garde *m*
(b) (military duty) garde *f*, surveillance *f*; **to be**
on ~ être de garde
(c) to catch sb off ~ prendre qn au
dépourvu
(d) (GB) (on train) chef *m* de train
2 *vtr* **(a)** (protect) surveiller ⟨place, object⟩;
protéger ⟨person⟩
(b) surveiller ⟨hostage, prisoner⟩
(c) garder ⟨secret⟩

guard dog *n* chien *m* de garde

guarded *adj* circonspect/-e (**about** à propos
de)

guardian *n* **(a)** (gen) gardien/-ienne *m/f* (**of**
de)
(b) (of child) tuteur/-trice *m/f*

guardian angel *n* ange *m* gardien

Guernsey *pr n* Guernesey *f*

guerrilla *n* guérillero *m*

guerrilla war *n* guérilla *f*

guess **1** *n* supposition *f*, conjecture *f*; **at a**
(rough) ~ **I would say that...** au hasard je
dirais que...; **it's anybody's** ~! les paris sont
ouverts!
2 *vtr* **(a)** deviner; ~ **what!** tu sais quoi!
(colloq)
(b) (suppose) supposer
3 *vi* deviner; **to keep sb** ~**ing** ne pas
satisfaire la curiosité de qn

guesswork *n* conjecture *f*

guest *n* (in one's home) invité/-e *m/f*; (at hotel)
client/-e *m/f*; **be my** ~! je vous en prie!

guesthouse *n* pension *f* de famille

guest room n chambre f d'amis

guestworker n travailleur immigré/ travailleuse immigrée m/f

guidance n conseils mpl (**from** de)

guide [1] n (a) (person, book) guide m (**to** de)
(b) (idea) indication f; **as a rough ~** à titre d'indication
(c) (also **Girl Guide**) guide f
[2] vtr guider (**to** vers)

guide book n guide m

guide dog n chien m d'aveugle

guided tour n visite f guidée

guideline n (rough guide) indication f; (in political context) directive f; (advice) conseils mpl

guild n (medieval) guilde f; (modern) association f

guillotine n (a) guillotine f
(b) (for paper) massicot m

guilt n culpabilité f

guilty adj coupable; **to feel ~** culpabiliser; **to feel ~ about** se sentir coupable vis-à-vis de

guinea-pig n (a) (Zool) cochon m d'Inde
(b) (in experiment) cobaye m

guitar n guitare f

guitarist n guitariste mf

gulch n (US) ravin m

gulf n (a) golfe m; **the Gulf** la région f du Golfe
(b) (figurative) fossé m (**between** qui sépare)

Gulf States pr n pl the **~** (in Middle East) les États mpl du Golfe

Gulf War pr n guerre f du Golfe

gull n mouette f

gullible adj crédule

gully n ravin m

gulp [1] n (of liquid) gorgée f, goulée f; (of air) bouffée f, goulée f; (of food) bouchée f
[2] vtr (also **~ down**) engloutir ⟨food, drink⟩
[3] vi avoir la gorge serrée

gum n (a) (in mouth) gencive f
(b) (also **chewing ~**) chewing-gum m
(c) (adhesive) colle f; (resin) gomme f

gun n (weapon) arme f à feu; (revolver) revolver m; (rifle) fusil m; (cannon) canon m; **to fire a ~** tirer
IDIOMS **to jump the ~** agir prématurément; **to stick to one's ~s** (colloq) s'accrocher (colloq)

■ **gun down** abattre, descendre

gunfire n (from hand-held gun) coups mpl de feu; (from artillery) fusillade f

gun laws n pl législation f sur les armes à feu

gun licence n permis m de port d'armes

gunman n homme m armé

gunpoint n **to hold sb up at ~** tenir qn sous la menace d'une arme

gunpowder n poudre f

gunshot n coup m de feu

gunshot wound n blessure f par balle

gurgle [1] n (of water) gargouillement m; (of baby) gazouillis m
[2] vi ⟨water⟩ gargouiller; ⟨baby⟩ gazouiller

guru n gourou m

gush vi jaillir

gust n rafale f

gusto n **with ~** avec enthousiasme

gut [1] n (colloq) bide m (colloq)
[2] adj ⟨feeling, reaction⟩ viscéral/-e, instinctif/-ive
[3] vtr ⟨fire⟩ ravager ⟨building⟩

guts n pl (colloq) (a) (of human) tripes fpl (colloq); (of animal) entrailles fpl
(b) (courage) cran m (colloq)

gutsy adj (colloq) (spirited) fougueux/-euse; (brave) courageux/-euse

gutter n (on roof) gouttière f; (in street) caniveau m

gutter press n presse f à sensation

guy n (colloq) type m (colloq); **a good/bad ~** (in films) un bon/méchant

Guy Fawkes Day n (GB) le 5 novembre (anniversaire de la Conspiration des Poudres)

guzzle vtr (colloq) engloutir

gym n (a) (abbr = **gymnasium**) salle f de gym (colloq), gymnase m
(b) (abbr = **gymnastics**) gym f (colloq)

gymnasium n gymnase m

gymnast n gymnaste mf

gymnastics n pl gymnastique f

gym shoe n tennis f

gynaecologist (GB), **gynecologist** (US) n gynécologue mf

gypsy n (gen) bohémien/-ienne m/f; (Central European) tzigane mf; (Spanish) gitan/-e m/f

H h

h, **H** *n* h, H *m*

habit *n* (a) habitude *f*; **to get into/out of the** ~ **of doing** prendre/perdre l'habitude de faire; **out of** ~ par habitude
(b) (addiction) accoutumance *f*
(c) (of monk, nun) habit *m*

habitable *adj* habitable

habitat *n* habitat *m*

habit-forming *adj* **to be** ~ créer une accoutumance

habitual *adj* ⟨behaviour, reaction⟩ habituel/-elle; ⟨drinker, smoker, liar⟩ invétéré/-e

habitual offender *n* récidiviste *mf*

hack ① *n* (colloq) (writer) écrivaillon *m*; (journalist) journaliste *m/f* qui fait la rubrique des chiens écrasés
② *vtr* tailler dans ⟨bushes⟩ (with à coups de); **to** ~ **sb/sth to pieces** tailler qn/qch en pièces
③ *vi* (a) **to** ~ **through sth** tailler dans qch
(b) (Comput) (colloq) pirater (colloq); **to** ~ **into** s'introduire dans ⟨system⟩

hacker *n* (computer) ~ pirate *m* informatique

hacking *n* (Comput) piratage *m* (colloq) informatique

hackles *n pl* (on dog) poils *mpl* du cou; **the dog's** ~ **began to rise** le chien se hérissait

hackneyed *adj* ⟨joke⟩ éculé/-e; ⟨subject⟩ rebattu/-e; ~ **phrase** cliché *m*

haddock *n* églefin *m*

haemophilia (GB), **hemophilia** (US) *n* hémophilie *f*

haemophiliac (GB), **hemophiliac** (US) *n*, *adj* hémophile ⟨mf⟩

haemorrhage (GB), **hemorrhage** (US)
① *n* hémorragie *f*
② *vi* faire une hémorragie

haemorrhoids (GB), **hemorrhoids** (US) *n pl* hémorroïdes *fpl*

haggard *adj* ⟨appearance, person⟩ exténué/-e; ⟨face, expression⟩ défait/-e

haggle *vi* marchander; **to** ~ **over sth** discuter du prix de qch

Hague *pr n* **The** ~ La Haye

hail ① *n* grêle *f*
② *vtr* (a) héler ⟨person, taxi, ship⟩
(b) (praise) **to** ~ **sb as** acclamer qn comme; **to** ~ **sth as sth** saluer qch comme qch
③ *v impers* grêler

hailstone *n* grêlon *m*

hailstorm *n* averse *f* de grêle

hair *n* (a) (on head) cheveux *mpl*; (on body)

poils *mpl*; (of animal) poil *m*; **to have one's** ~ **done** se faire coiffer; **long-**~**ed** ⟨person⟩ aux cheveux longs; ⟨animal⟩ à poil long
(b) (individually) (on head) cheveu *m*; (on body) poil *m*

IDIOMS **to split** ~**s** couper les cheveux en quatre

hairband *n* bandeau *m*

hairbrush *n* brosse *f* à cheveux

haircut *n* coupe *f* (de cheveux)

hairdo *n* (colloq) coiffure *f*

hairdresser *n* coiffeur/-euse *m/f*

hairdrier *n* (hand-held) sèche-cheveux *m inv*; (hood) casque *m*

hair gel *n* gel *m* coiffant

hairgrip *n* (GB) pince *f* à cheveux

hairpin bend *n* virage *m* en épingle à cheveux

hair-raising *adj* ⟨adventure, tale⟩ à vous faire dresser les cheveux sur la tête

hair remover *n* crème *f* dépilatoire

hair-slide *n* (GB) barrette *f*

hairspray *n* laque *f*

hairstyle *n* coiffure *f*

hairy *adj* poilu/-e

halal *adj* ⟨meat⟩ hallal *inv*

half ① *n* (a) moitié *f*; **to cut sth in** ~ couper qch en deux
(b) (fraction) demi *m*; **four and a** ~ quatre et demi
(c) (GB) (colloq) (half pint) demi-pinte *f*
② *adj* ~ **an hour** une demi-heure; **a** ~**-litre**, ~ **a litre** un demi-litre; **two and a** ~ **cups** deux tasses et demie
③ *pron* (a) la moitié *f*; ~ **of the students** la moitié des étudiants
(b) (in time) demi/-e *m/f*; **an hour and a** ~ une heure et demie; ~ **past two** (GB) deux heures et demie
④ *adv* à moitié; **to** ~ **close sth** fermer qch à moitié; **it's** ~ **the price** c'est moitié moins cher; **I** ~ **expected it** je m'y attendais plus ou moins

IDIOMS **to go halves with sb** partager avec qn

halfback *n* (Sport) demi *m*

half-board *n* demi-pension *f*

half-brother *n* demi-frère *m*

half day *n* demi-journée *f*

half fare *n* demi-tarif *m*

half-hearted *adj* peu enthousiaste

half-heartedly *adv* sans conviction

half hour *n* demi-heure *f*; **on the** ~ à la demie

half-mast *n* **at** ~ en berne

half-moon *n* (a) demi-lune *f*

(b) (of fingernail) lunule f

half price adv, adj à moitié prix

half-sister n demi-sœur f

half term n (GB Sch) vacances fpl de la mi-trimestre

half-time n (Sport) mi-temps f; **at** ∼ à la mi-temps

halfway adv **(a)** à mi-chemin (**between** entre; **to de**); ∼ **up** or **down** à mi-hauteur de ⟨stairs, tree⟩; ∼ **down the page** à mi-page
(b) (in time) ∼ **through** au milieu

halfway house n (rehabilitation centre) centre m de réadaptation

hall n **(a)** (in house) entrée f; (in hotel, airport) hall m; (for public events) (grande) salle f
(b) (country house) manoir m

hallelujah excl alléluia!

hallmark [1] n **(a)** (GB) (on metal) poinçon m
(b) (typical feature) caractéristique f
[2] vtr poinçonner; **to be** ∼**ed** porter un poinçon

hall of residence n résidence f universitaire

Halloween n: la veille de la Toussaint

hallucinate vi avoir des hallucinations

hallucination n hallucination f

hallway n entrée f

halo n **(a)** auréole f
(b) (in astronomy) halo m

halt [1] n (stop) arrêt m; **to come to a** ∼ ⟨vehicle, troops⟩ s'arrêter; ⟨work⟩ être interrompu/-e; **to call a** ∼ **to sth** mettre fin à qch
[2] vtr arrêter
[3] vi s'arrêter

halterneck n, adj dos (m inv) nu

halve [1] vtr réduire [qch] de moitié ⟨number, rate⟩; couper [qch] en deux ⟨carrot, cake⟩
[2] vi ⟨number, rate, time⟩ diminuer de moitié

ham n jambon m

hamburger n **(a)** (burger) hamburger m
(b) (US) (ground beef) pâté m de viande

hammer [1] n marteau m
[2] vtr **(a)** marteler ⟨metal, table⟩; **to** ∼ **sth into** enfoncer qch dans ⟨wall, fence⟩
(b) to ∼ **sth into sb** faire entrer qch dans la tête de qn; **to** ∼ **home a message** bien faire comprendre un message
(c) (colloq) (defeat) battre [qn] à plates coutures
[3] vi (pound) tambouriner (**on, at** contre)
■ **hammer out**: ∼ **out** [sth], ∼ [sth] **out** (negotiate) parvenir à [qch] après maintes discussions ⟨agreement, policy, formula⟩

hamper [1] n panier m à pique-nique
[2] vtr entraver ⟨movement, career, progress⟩

hamster n hamster m

hamstring n tendon m du jarret

hand [1] n **(a)** main f; **he had a pencil in his** ∼ il avait un crayon à la main; **to hold sb's** ∼ tenir qn par la main; **to make sth by** ∼

faire qch à la main; **the letter was delivered by** ∼ la lettre a été remise en mains propres; **to give sb a (helping)** ∼ donner un coup de main à qn; **to have sth to** ∼ avoir qch sous la main; **to be on** ∼ ⟨person⟩ être disponible; **to get out of** ∼ devenir incontrôlable; **to take sb/sth in** ∼ prendre qn/qch en main ⟨situation, person⟩
(b) (cards) jeu m
(c) (worker) ouvrier/-ière m/f; (crew member) membre m de l'équipage
(d) (on clock, dial) aiguille f
(e) on the one ∼..., **on the other** ∼... d'une part..., d'autre part...
[2] vtr **to** ∼ **sth to sb** donner qch à qn
[3] **hand in hand** phr ⟨run, walk⟩ la main dans la main; **to go** ∼ **in** ∼ aller de pair (**with** avec)
[4] **out of hand** phr ⟨reject⟩ d'emblée
IDIOMS **to have one's** ∼**s full** avoir assez à faire; **to try one's** ∼ **at sth** s'essayer à; **to know sth like the back of one's** ∼ connaître qch comme sa poche
■ **hand down** passer ⟨object, clothes⟩ (**to sb** à qn); transmettre ⟨property⟩
■ **hand in** remettre ⟨form⟩ (**to** à); rendre ⟨homework, keys⟩
■ **hand out** distribuer ⟨food, leaflets⟩
■ **hand over**: ¶ ∼ **over to** [sb] passer l'antenne à ⟨reporter⟩; passer la main à ⟨deputy, successor⟩; ¶ ∼ [sth] **over** rendre ⟨weapon⟩; céder ⟨business⟩; remettre ⟨keys, money⟩; ¶ ∼ [sb] **over** livrer ⟨prisoner⟩

handbag n sac m à main

hand baggage n bagages mpl à main

handball n (Sport) handball m

handbook n manuel m; (technical) livret m technique

handbrake n frein m à main

handcuffs n pl menottes fpl

handful n **(a)** (fistful) poignée f
(b) (of people) poignée f; (of buildings, objects) petit nombre m
(c) (colloq) **to be a** ∼ être épuisant/-e

handgun n arme f de poing

hand-held adj ⟨camera⟩ de reportage; ⟨tool⟩ à main; ⟨device⟩ portatif/-ive; ⟨computer⟩ de poche

handicap [1] n handicap m
[2] vtr handicaper

handicapped adj ⟨person⟩ handicapé/-e; **mentally/physically** ∼ **children** des enfants handicapés mentaux/physiques

handicrafts n pl (Sch) travaux mpl manuels

handiwork n ouvrage m

handkerchief n mouchoir m

handle [1] n (on door, drawer, bag) poignée f; (on bucket, cup, basket) anse f; (on frying pan) queue f; (on saucepan, cutlery, hammer, spade) manche m; (on wheelbarrow, pump) bras m
[2] vtr **(a)** manipuler ⟨explosives, food⟩; manier ⟨gun⟩; '∼ **with care**' 'fragile'

···❖

h

(b) (manage) manier ⟨*horse*⟩; manœuvrer ⟨*car*⟩; **to know how to ~ children** savoir s'y prendre avec les enfants
(c) (deal with) faire face à ⟨*crisis*⟩; supporter ⟨*stress*⟩; ⟨*department, lawyer*⟩ s'occuper de ⟨*enquiries, case*⟩

handlebars *n pl* guidon *m*

handling *n* (a) (holding, touching) (of food, waste) manipulation *f*; (of tool, weapon) maniement *m*;
(b) (way of dealing) **her ~ of the theme** sa façon de traiter le thème; **their ~ of the economy** leur gestion de l'économie

handling charge *n* (a) (for goods) frais *mpl* de manutention
(b) (administrative) frais *mpl* administratifs

hand luggage *n* bagages *mpl* à main

handmade *adj* fait/-e à la main

handout *n* (a) (charitable) don *m*
(b) (leaflet) prospectus *m*

handpick *vtr* (a) cueillir [qch] à la main ⟨*grapes*⟩
(b) trier [qn] sur le volet ⟨*staff*⟩

handshake *n* poignée *f* de main

handsome *adj* beau/belle (*before n*)

hands-on *adj* ⟨*experience, manager*⟩ de terrain; ⟨*control*⟩ direct/-e; ⟨*approach*⟩ pragmatique

handstand *n* (Sport) équilibre *m*

handwriting *n* écriture *f*

handwritten *adj* manuscrit/-e

handy *adj* ⟨*book, skill*⟩ utile; ⟨*tool, pocket, size*⟩ pratique; ⟨*shop*⟩ bien situé/-e; **to keep/ have [sth] ~** garder/avoir [qch] sous la main ⟨*keys, passport*⟩

handyman *n* bricoleur *m*

hang [1] *n* **to get the ~ of sth** (colloq) piger qch (colloq)
[2] *vtr* (a) (from hook, coat hanger) accrocher (**from** à; **by** par; **on** à); (from string, rope) suspendre (**from** à); (peg up) étendre ⟨*washing*⟩ (**on** sur)
(b) poser ⟨*wallpaper*⟩
(c) pendre ⟨*criminal, victim*⟩
[3] *vi* (a) (on hook) être accroché/-e; (from height) être suspendu/-e; (on washing line) être étendu/-e
(b) ⟨*arm, leg*⟩ pendre
(c) ⟨*curtain, garment*⟩ tomber
(d) ⟨*person*⟩ être pendu/-e (**for** pour)
[4] *v refl* **to ~ oneself** se pendre (**from** à)
■ **hang around** (colloq) (a) (*also* **~ about**) (wait) attendre; (aimlessly) traîner
(b) **to ~ around with sb** passer son temps avec qn
■ **hang back** (in fear) rester derrière; (figurative) être réticent/-e
■ **hang down** (gen) pendre; ⟨*hem*⟩ être défait/-e
■ **hang on:** ¶ **~ on** (a) (hold on) **to ~ on (to sth)** s'accrocher (à qch)
(b) (colloq) (wait) attendre
(c) (colloq) (survive) tenir (colloq); **~ on in there!** (colloq) tiens bon!
¶ **~ on [sth]** (depend on) dépendre de

■ **hang out:** ¶ **~ out** (a) (protrude) dépasser
(b) (colloq) (live) crécher (colloq)
(c) (colloq) (sit around) traîner (colloq)
¶ **~ [sth] out** étendre ⟨*washing*⟩; sortir ⟨*flag*⟩
■ **hang up:** ¶ **~ up** (on phone) raccrocher; **to ~ up on sb** raccrocher au nez de qn
¶ **~ [sth] up** (on hook) accrocher; (on hanger) suspendre; (on line) étendre

hangar *n* hangar *m*

hanger-on *n* (colloq) parasite *m*

hang-glider *n* deltaplane *m*

hanging *n* (a) (of person) pendaison *f*
(b) (curtain) rideau *m*; (on wall) tenture *f*

hangover *n* (from drink) gueule *f* de bois (colloq)

hang-up *n* (colloq) complexe *m*, problème *m*

hanker *vi* **to ~ after** *or* **for sth** rêver de qch

hanky, hankie (colloq) *n* mouchoir *m*

haphazard *adj* peu méthodique

happen *vi* (a) (occur) arriver, se passer, se produire; **what's ~ing?** qu'est-ce qui se passe?; **to ~ again** se reproduire; **whatever ~s** quoi qu'il arrive
(b) (occur by chance) **if you ~ to see her, say hello** si par hasard tu la vois, salue-la de ma part; **as it ~ed, the weather that day was bad** il s'est trouvé qu'il faisait mauvais ce jour-là

happily *adv* (a) (cheerfully) joyeusement; **a ~ married man** un mari heureux; **they all lived ~ ever after** ils vécurent heureux jusqu'à la fin de leurs jours
(b) (willingly) ⟨*admit*⟩ volontiers
(c) (luckily) heureusement

happiness *n* bonheur *m*

happy *adj* (a) heureux/-euse (**about** de; **that** que + *subjunctive*); **to be ~ with sth** être satisfait/-e de qch; **to keep a child ~** amuser un enfant; **to be ~ to do** être heureux/-euse de faire
(b) (in greetings) **Happy Birthday!** Bon anniversaire!; **Happy Christmas!** Joyeux Noël!; **Happy New Year!** Bonne année!

happy ending *n* heureux dénouement *m*

happy medium *n* juste milieu *m*

harangue *vtr* (about politics) haranguer; (moralize) sermonner

harass [1] *vtr* harceler
[2] **harassed** *pp adj* excédé/-e

harbour (GB), **harbor** (US) [1] *n* port *m*
[2] *vtr* nourrir ⟨*suspicion, illusion*⟩; receler ⟨*criminal*⟩

hard [1] *adj* (a) (firm) dur/-e; **to go ~** durcir
(b) (difficult) ⟨*problem, question, task*⟩ dur/-e, difficile; ⟨*choice, decision, life*⟩ difficile; **it's ~ to do** c'est dur *or* difficile à faire; **to find it ~ to do** avoir du mal à faire; **it was ~ work** ça a été dur *or* difficile; **to be a ~ worker** être travailleur/-euse
(c) (severe) ⟨*person, look, words*⟩ dur/-e, sévère; ⟨*blow*⟩ dur/-e, terrible; ⟨*winter*⟩ rude; **to be ~ on sb** ⟨*person*⟩ être dur/-e envers qn; **~ luck!** pas de chance!; **no ~ feelings!** sans rancune!
(d) ⟨*evidence, fact*⟩ solide

(e) ⟨*liquor*⟩ fort/-e; ⟨*drug*⟩ dur/-e

(f) ⟨*water*⟩ dur/-e, calcaire

2 *adv* ⟨*push, hit, cry*⟩ fort; ⟨*work*⟩ dur; ⟨*study, think*⟩ sérieusement; ⟨*look, listen*⟩ attentivement; **to try ∼** (mentally) faire beaucoup d'efforts; (physically) essayer de toutes ses forces

hard and fast *adj* ⟨*rule, distinction*⟩ absolu/-e

hardback (book) *n* livre *m* relié

hardboard *n* aggloméré *m*

hard-boiled egg *n* œuf *m* dur

hard copy *n* (Comput) tirage *m*

hard core **1** *n* (group, demonstrators) noyau *m* dur

2 hard-core *adj* **(a)** (established) ⟨*supporter, opponent, protest*⟩ irréductible

(b) (extreme) ⟨*pornography, video*⟩ hard *inv* (colloq)

hard court *n* court *m* en dur

hard disk *n* disque *m* dur

hard-earned *adj* ⟨*cash*⟩ durement gagné/-e

harden **1** *vtr* **(a)** (faire) durcir ⟨*glue, wax*⟩

(b) endurcir ⟨*person*⟩ (**to** à); durcir ⟨*attitude*⟩; **to ∼ one's heart** s'endurcir (**to** à)

2 *vi* **(a)** ⟨*glue, wax, skin*⟩ durcir

(b) ⟨*voice, stance*⟩ se durcir

hardened *adj* ⟨*criminal*⟩ endurci/-e; ⟨*drinker*⟩ invétéré/-e

hard hat *n* (helmet) casque *m*; (for riding) bombe *f*

hard-hearted *adj* insensible

hard-hitting *adj* ⟨*speech, criticism*⟩ musclé/-e; ⟨*report*⟩ très critique

hard labour (GB), **hard labor** (US) *n* travaux *mpl* forcés

hardliner *n* jusqu'au-boutiste *mf*; (political) partisan/-e *m/f* de la ligne dure

hardly *adv* **(a)** (barely) ⟨*begin, know, see*⟩ à peine; **∼ had they set off when** à peine étaient-ils partis que

(b) (not really) **one can ∼ expect that** on ne peut guère s'attendre à ce que; **it's ∼ likely** c'est peu probable; **it's ∼ surprising** ce n'est guère étonnant; **I can ∼ believe it!** j'ai peine à le croire!

(c) **∼ any/ever/anybody** presque pas/jamais/personne; **he ∼ ever writes** il n'écrit presque jamais

hard of hearing *adj* **to be ∼** entendre mal

hard-pressed, **hard-pushed** *adj* en difficulté; (for time) pressé/-e; **to be ∼ to do** avoir du mal à faire

hardship *n* **(a)** (difficulty) détresse *f*; (poverty) privations *fpl*

(b) (ordeal) épreuve *f*

hard shoulder *n* bande *f* d'arrêt d'urgence

hard up *adj* (colloq) fauché/-e (colloq)

hardware *n* **(a)** (gen) articles *mpl* de quincaillerie

(b) (Comput) matériel *m* (informatique)

(c) (Mil) équipement *m*

hardware shop, **hardware store** *n* quincaillerie *f*

hard-working *adj* travailleur/-euse

hardy *adj* ⟨*person*⟩ robuste; ⟨*plant*⟩ résistant/-e

hare *n* lièvre *m*

haricot *n* (GB) (*also* **∼ bean**) (dried) haricot *m* blanc; (fresh) haricot *m* vert

harm **1** *n* mal *m*; **to do sb ∼** faire du mal à qn; **to do ∼ to sth** endommager qch; **out of ∼'s way** en sûreté

2 *vtr* faire du mal à ⟨*person*⟩; endommager ⟨*crops, lungs*⟩; nuire à ⟨*population*⟩

harmful *adj* ⟨*chemical, ray*⟩ nocif/-ive; ⟨*behaviour, gossip*⟩ nuisible (**to** pour)

harmless *adj* **(a)** ⟨*chemical, virus*⟩ inoffensif/-ive (**to** pour); ⟨*growth*⟩ bénin/bénigne

(b) ⟨*person*⟩ inoffensif/-ive; ⟨*fun, joke*⟩ innocent/-e

harmonica *n* harmonica *m*

harmonious *adj* harmonieux/-ieuse

harmonize **1** *vtr* harmoniser

2 *vi* jouer en harmonie (**with** avec)

harmony *n* harmonie *f*

harness **1** *n* harnais *m*

2 *vtr* **(a)** harnacher ⟨*horse*⟩

(b) (attach) atteler ⟨*animal*⟩ (**to** à)

(c) exploiter ⟨*power, energy*⟩

harp *n* harpe *f*

■ **harp on** (colloq) rabâcher (colloq) toujours la même chose sur ⟨*issue, event*⟩

harpoon *n* harpon *m*

harrowing *adj* ⟨*experience*⟩ atroce; ⟨*film, image*⟩ déchirant/-e

harsh *adj* **(a)** ⟨*punishment, measures*⟩ sévère; ⟨*tone, regime, person*⟩ dur/-e; ⟨*conditions*⟩ difficile

(b) ⟨*light, colour*⟩ cru/-e; ⟨*sound*⟩ rude, dur/-e à l'oreille

harshly *adv* ⟨*treat, speak*⟩ durement; ⟨*punish*⟩ sévèrement

harvest **1** *n* (of wheat, fruit) récolte *f*; (of grapes) vendange *f*

2 *vtr* moissonner ⟨*corn*⟩; récolter ⟨*vegetables*⟩; cueillir ⟨*fruit*⟩; vendanger ⟨*grapes*⟩

has-been *n* (colloq) homme fini/femme finie *m/f*

hassle (colloq) **1** *n* complications *fpl*; **it was a real ∼** c'était enquiquinant (colloq)

2 *vtr* talonner (**about** à propos de)

haste *n* hâte *f*; **to act in ∼** agir à la hâte

hasten **1** *vtr* accélérer ⟨*destruction*⟩; précipiter ⟨*departure, death, decline*⟩

2 *vi* se hâter; **to ∼ to do** s'empresser de faire

hasty *adj* ⟨*talks, marriage, departure*⟩ précipité/-e; ⟨*meal*⟩ rapide; ⟨*note*⟩ écrit/-e à la hâte; ⟨*decision*⟩ inconsidéré/-e; ⟨*conclusion*⟩ hâtif/-ive

hat *n* chapeau *m*

h

hatch ❶ n (a) (on aircraft) panneau m mobile; (in boat) écoutille f; (in car) portière f
(b) (also **serving** ~) passe-plats m inv
❷ vtr (a) faire éclore ⟨eggs⟩
(b) tramer ⟨plot, scheme⟩
❸ vi ⟨chicks, fish eggs⟩ éclore

hatchback n voiture f avec hayon

hatchet n hachette f

hate ❶ n haine f
❷ vtr (a) (dislike) détester; (violently) haïr
(b) (not enjoy) avoir horreur de ⟨sport, food⟩; to ~ **doing** avoir horreur de faire
(c) (in apology) to ~ **to do** être désolé/-e de faire

hate mail n lettres fpl d'injures

hatred n haine f (**of** de; **for** pour)

hat trick n triplé m

haughty adj ⟨person⟩ hautain/-e; ⟨manner⟩ altier/-ière

haul ❶ n (a) (taken by criminals) butin m
(b) (found by police, customs) saisie f; **arms** ~ saisie d'armes
(c) **it's a long** ~ la route est longue
(d) (of fish) pêche f
❷ vtr (drag) tirer

haulage n (a) (transport) transport m routier
(b) (cost) frais mpl de transport

haunch n hanche f

haunt ❶ n lieu m de prédilection
❷ vtr hanter

haunted adj ⟨house⟩ hanté/-e; ⟨face, look⟩ tourmenté/-e

haunting adj (gen) lancinant/-e; ⟨memory⟩ obsédant/-e

have ❶ vtr (a) (possess) avoir; **she has (got) a dog** elle a un chien; **I haven't (got) enough time** je n'ai pas assez de temps
(b) (with noun object) to ~ **a wash** se laver; to ~ **a sandwich** manger un sandwich; to ~ **a whisky** boire un whisky; to ~ **a cigarette** fumer une cigarette; to ~ **breakfast** prendre le petit déjeuner; to ~ **lunch** déjeuner; **I had some more cake** j'ai repris du gâteau
(c) (receive, get) recevoir ⟨letter⟩; **I've had no news from him** je n'ai pas eu de nouvelles de lui; **to let sb** ~ **sth** donner qch à qn
(d) (hold) faire ⟨party⟩; tenir ⟨meeting⟩; organiser ⟨competition, exhibition⟩; avoir ⟨conversation⟩
(e) (exert, exhibit) avoir ⟨effect, influence⟩; avoir ⟨courage, courtesy⟩ (**to do** de faire)
(f) (spend) passer; to ~ **a nice day** passer une journée agréable; to ~ **a good time** bien s'amuser; to ~ **a hard time** traverser une période difficile; to ~ **a good holiday** (GB) or **vacation** (US) passer de bonnes vacances
(g) (also ~ **got**) to ~ **sth to do** avoir qch à faire; **I've got letters to write** j'ai du courrier à faire; **I've got a lot of work to do** j'ai beaucoup de travail
(h) (suffer) avoir; to ~ **(the) flu/a heart attack** avoir la grippe/une crise cardiaque; to ~ **toothache** avoir mal aux dents; **he had his**

car stolen il s'est fait voler sa voiture; **she has had her windows broken** on lui a cassé ses vitres
(i) to ~ **the car fixed** faire réparer la voiture; to ~ **the house painted** faire peindre la maison; to ~ **one's hair cut** se faire couper les cheveux; to ~ **an injection** se faire faire une piqûre
(j) (cause to become) **she had them completely baffled** elle les a complètement déroutés; **I had it finished by 5 o'clock** je l'avais fini avant 5 heures
(k) (allow) tolérer; **I won't** ~ **this kind of behaviour!** je ne tolérerai pas ce comportement!
(l) (give birth to) ⟨woman⟩ avoir ⟨child⟩; ⟨animal⟩ mettre bas, avoir ⟨young⟩
❷ modal aux (must) **I** ~ **to leave** il faut que je parte, je dois partir; **something has (got) to be done** il faut faire quelque chose; **you don't** ~ **to leave so early** tu n'as pas besoin de or tu n'es pas obligé de partir si tôt
❸ v aux (a) avoir; (with movement and reflexive verbs) être; **she has lost her bag** elle a perdu son sac; **she has already left** elle est déjà partie; **he has hurt himself** il s'est blessé; **having finished his breakfast, he went out** après avoir fini son petit déjeuner, il est sorti
(b) (in tags, short answers) **you've seen the film, haven't you?** tu as vu le film, n'est-ce pas?; **you haven't seen the film,** ~ **you?** tu n'as pas vu le film?; **you haven't seen my bag,** ~ **you?** tu n'as pas vu mon sac, par hasard?; '~ **you seen him?'—'yes, I** ~**!** 'est-ce que tu l'as vu?'—'oui'; **'you've never met him'—'yes I** ~**!'** 'tu ne l'as jamais rencontré'—'mais si!'
(c) (if) **had I known, I wouldn't have bought it** si j'avais su, je ne l'aurais pas acheté
IDIOMS **I've had it (up to here) with...** (colloq) j'en ai marre de... (colloq); **to** ~ **it in for sb** (colloq) avoir qn dans le collimateur (colloq); **she doesn't** ~ **it in her to do** elle est incapable de faire; **to** ~ **it out with sb** s'expliquer avec qn; **the** ~**s and the** ~**-nots** les riches et les pauvres
■ **have on** (a) porter ⟨coat, skirt⟩; **he had (got) nothing on** il n'avait rien sur lui
(b) to ~ **sth on** (be busy) avoir qch de prévu
(c) to ~ **sb on** (colloq) faire marcher qn (colloq)

haven n (a) (safe place) refuge m (**for** pour)
(b) (harbour) port m

havoc n dévastation f; to wreak ~ provoquer des dégâts; (figurative) tout mettre sens dessus dessous

Hawaii pr n Hawaï m

hawk n faucon m

hawthorn n aubépine f

hay n foin m

hay fever n rhume m des foins

haystack n meule f de foin
IDIOMS **it is/was like looking for a needle in a** ~ autant chercher une aiguille dans une botte de foin

haywire adj (colloq) (a) (faulty) **to go ~** ⟨plan⟩ dérailler; ⟨machinery⟩ se détraquer
(b) (crazy) détraqué/-e (colloq)

hazard 1 n risque m (**to** pour); **a health ~** un risque pour la santé
2 vtr hasarder ⟨opinion, guess⟩

hazardous adj dangereux/-euse

haze n (mist) brume f; (of smoke, dust) nuage m

hazel 1 n noisetier m
2 adj ⟨eyes⟩ (couleur de) noisette inv

hazelnut n noisette f

hazy adj ⟨weather, morning⟩ brumeux/-euse; ⟨sunshine⟩ voilé/-e; ⟨idea, memory⟩ vague (before n)

he pron il; (emphatic) lui; **~'s seen us** il nous a vus; **there ~ is** le voilà; **she lives in Oxford but ~ doesn't** elle habite Oxford mais lui non; **~'s a genius** c'est un génie; **~ and I** lui et moi

head 1 n (a) (gen) tête f; **from ~ to foot** or **toe** de la tête aux pieds; **to stand on one's ~** faire le poirier; **£10 a ~** or **per ~** 10 livres sterling par personne
(b) (of family, church) chef m; (of organization) responsable mf, directeur/-trice m/f; **~ of State** chef d'État
2 **heads** n pl (of coin) face f; **'~s or tails?'** 'pile ou face?'
3 adj (a) ⟨injury⟩ à la tête
(b) (chief) ⟨cashier, cook, gardener⟩ en chef
4 vtr (a) être en tête de ⟨list, queue⟩; être à la tête de ⟨firm, team⟩; mener ⟨expedition, inquiry⟩
(b) **~ed writing paper** papier m à lettres à en-tête
(c) (steer) diriger ⟨vehicle⟩ (**towards** vers)
(d) (Sport) **to ~ the ball** faire une tête
5 vi **where was the train ~ed** or **~ing?** où allait le train?; **to ~ home** rentrer; **he's ~ing this way!** il vient par ici!
IDIOMS **to go to sb's ~** monter à la tête de qn; **to keep/lose one's ~** garder/perdre son sang-froid; **off the top of one's ~** ⟨say, answer⟩ sans réfléchir
■ **head for** (a) se diriger vers ⟨place⟩
(b) courir à ⟨defeat⟩; courir vers ⟨trouble⟩

headache n mal m de tête; **to have a ~** avoir mal à la tête

headband n bandeau m

headbutt vtr donner un coup de tête à

head cold n rhume m de cerveau

headdress n (of feathers) coiffure f; (of lace) coiffe f

header n (a) (colloq) (dive) **to take a ~** piquer une tête (colloq)
(b) (in sport) tête f

headfirst adv ⟨fall, plunge⟩ la tête la première; ⟨rush into⟩ tête baissée

head-hunt vtr (seek to recruit) (chercher à) recruter

head-hunter n chasseur m de têtes

heading n (of article, column) titre m; (of subject area, topic) rubrique f; (on notepaper, letter) en-tête m

headlamp, **headlight** n (of car) phare m

headline n (in paper) gros titre m; **to hit the ~s** faire la une (colloq); **the front-page ~** la manchette; **the news ~s** les grands titres (de l'actualité)

headlong 1 adj **a ~ dash** une ruée
2 adv ⟨fall⟩ la tête la première; ⟨run⟩ à toute vitesse

head office n siège m social

head-on adj ⟨crash, collision⟩ de front

headphones n pl casque m

headquarters n pl (gen) siège m social; (Mil) quartier m général

head rest n (gen) appui-tête m; (Aut) repose-tête m inv

head start n **to have a ~** avoir une longueur d'avance (**over** sur)

headstone n pierre f tombale

headstrong adj ⟨person⟩ têtu/-e; ⟨attitude⟩ obstiné/-e

head teacher n directeur/-trice m/f

headway n **to make ~** avancer, faire des progrès

heady adj ⟨wine, mixture⟩ capiteux/-euse; ⟨perfume⟩ entêtant/-e; ⟨experience⟩ grisant/-e

heal 1 vtr guérir ⟨person, injury⟩
2 vi ⟨wound, cut⟩ se cicatriser; **the fracture has ~ed** l'os s'est ressoudé

healer n guérisseur/-euse m/f

healing 1 n guérison f
2 adj ⟨power⟩ curatif/-ive; ⟨effect⟩ salutaire; **the ~ process** le rétablissement

health n santé f; **in good/bad ~** en bonne/mauvaise santé; **here's to your ~!** à votre santé!

health club n club m de remise en forme

health farm n: établissement pour cures d'amaigrissement, de rajeunissement

health food n aliments mpl naturels, aliments mpl diététiques

healthily adv sainement

health insurance n assurance f maladie

Health Service n (a) (GB) (for public) services mpl de santé
(b) (US) (Univ) infirmerie f

healthy adj ⟨person, dog⟩ en bonne santé; ⟨livestock, plant, lifestyle, diet⟩ sain/-e; ⟨air⟩ salutaire; ⟨appetite⟩ robuste; ⟨economy⟩ sain/-e; ⟨profit⟩ excellent/-e

heap 1 n (a) (pile) tas m
(b) (colloq) **~s of** plein de
2 vtr (a) (pile) entasser
(b) **to ~ sth on sb** couvrir qn de qch ⟨praise⟩; accabler qn de qch ⟨scorn⟩

heaped adj **a ~ spoonful** une bonne cuillerée

hear 1 vtr (a) (gen) entendre; **to make oneself heard** se faire entendre; (figurative) faire entendre sa voix
(b) apprendre ⟨news, rumour⟩
(c) (listen to) écouter ⟨lecture, broadcast⟩; ⟨judge⟩ entendre ⟨case, evidence⟩

⋯›

2 *vi* entendre; **to ~ about** entendre parler de
IDIOMS **~! ~!** bravo!
■ **hear from** avoir des nouvelles de ⟨person⟩
■ **hear of** entendre parler de; **I won't ~ of it!** il n'en est pas question!

hearing *n* (a) (sense) ouïe *f*, audition *f*; **his ~ is not very good** il n'a pas l'oreille très fine
(b) (before court) audience *f*

hearing aid *n* prothèse *f* auditive

hearing-impaired *adj* malentendant/-e

hearsay *n* ouï-dire *m inv*, on-dit *m inv*

hearse *n* corbillard *m*

heart *n* (a) (gen) cœur *m*; **by ~** ⟨learn, know⟩ par cœur; **to take sth to ~** prendre qch à cœur; **right in the ~ of London** en plein cœur de Londres; **the ~ of the matter** le fond du problème
(b) (in cards) **~(s)** cœur *m*
IDIOMS **to have one's ~ set on sth** vouloir qch à tout prix; **to take/lose ~** prendre/perdre courage

heartache *n* chagrin *m*

heart attack *n* crise *f* cardiaque, infarctus *m*

heartbeat *n* battement *m* de cœur

heartbreaking *adj* ⟨sight, story⟩ navrant/-e; ⟨cry, appeal⟩ déchirant/-e

heartbroken *adj* **to be ~** avoir le cœur brisé

heart disease *n* maladies *fpl* cardiaques

heartening *adj* encourageant/-e

heart failure *n* arrêt *m* du cœur

heartfelt *adj* sincère

hearth *n* foyer *m*; **~ rug** petit tapis *m*

heartless *adj* ⟨person⟩ sans cœur; ⟨attitude, treatment⟩ cruel/-elle

heartthrob *n* (colloq) idole *f*

heart-to-heart *n* **to have a ~ (with sb)** parler à cœur ouvert (avec qn)

heart transplant *n* greffe *f* du cœur

hearty *adj* ⟨welcome, greeting⟩ cordial/-e; ⟨person⟩ jovial/-e; ⟨laugh⟩ franc/franche; ⟨appetite⟩ solide; ⟨approval⟩ chaleureux/-euse

heat **1** *n* (a) chaleur *f*; **in this ~** par cette chaleur; **in the ~ of the moment** dans le feu de l'action
(b) (Sport) (round) épreuve *f* éliminatoire; (in athletics) série *f*
(c) (Zool) **to be on** *or* **in ~** être en chaleur
2 *vtr* chauffer ⟨house, pool⟩; faire chauffer ⟨food, oven⟩
■ **heat up** faire chauffer ⟨food⟩; (reheat) faire réchauffer

heated *adj* (a) ⟨water, pool⟩ chauffé/-e
(b) ⟨debate, argument⟩ animé/-e

heater *n* appareil *m* de chauffage

heathen *n, adj* (irreligious) païen/-ïenne (*m/f*); (uncivilized) barbare (*mf*)

heather *n* bruyère *f*

heating *n* chauffage *m*

heat stroke *n* coup *m* de chaleur (*avec collapsus*)

heatwave *n* vague *f* de chaleur

heave **1** *vtr* (lift) hisser; (pull) traîner péniblement; (throw) lancer (at sur); **to ~ a sigh** pousser un soupir
2 *vi* (a) ⟨sea, ground⟩ se soulever et s'abaisser
(b) (pull) tirer de toutes ses forces
(c) (retch) avoir un haut-le-cœur; (vomit) vomir

heaven *n* ciel *m*, paradis *m*; **thank ~(s)!** Dieu soit loué!; **good ~s!** grands dieux!

heavenly *adj* (a) ⟨choir, body⟩ céleste; ⟨peace⟩ divin/-e
(b) (colloq) (wonderful) divin/-e

heavily *adv* (a) ⟨lean, fall⟩ lourdement; ⟨sleep, sigh⟩ profondément; ⟨breathe⟩ (noisily) bruyamment; (with difficulty) péniblement; **~ underlined** souligné/-e d'un gros trait
(b) ⟨rain⟩ très fort; ⟨snow, invest, smoke, drink, rely⟩ beaucoup; ⟨bleed⟩ abondamment; ⟨taxed, armed⟩ fortement

heavy *adj* (gen) lourd/-e; ⟨shoes, frame⟩ gros/grosse (before *n*); ⟨line, features⟩ épais/épaisse; ⟨blow, fighting⟩ violent/-e; ⟨rain, frost, perfume, accent⟩ fort/-e; ⟨snow⟩ abondant/-e; ⟨traffic⟩ dense; ⟨gunfire⟩ nourri/-e; ⟨bleeding⟩ abondant/-e; ⟨sentence, fine⟩ sévère; ⟨cold⟩ gros/grosse (before *n*); **with a ~ heart** le cœur gros; **to be a ~ sleeper** avoir le sommeil lourd; **to be a ~ drinker** boire beaucoup

heavy-handed *adj* maladroit/-e

heavy metal *n* hard rock *m*

heavyweight *n* (a) (boxer) poids *m* lourd
(b) (figurative) (colloq) grosse légume *f* (colloq)

Hebrew **1** *n* (a) (person) Hébreu *m*
(b) (language) hébreu *m*
2 *adj* ⟨language⟩ hébraïque; ⟨person⟩ hébreu/hébraïque

heckle **1** *vtr* interpeller
2 *vi* chahuter

hectic *adj* ⟨activity⟩ intense; ⟨day, life, schedule⟩ mouvementé/-e

hedge **1** *n* haie *f*
2 *vi* se dérober
IDIOMS **to ~ one's bets** se couvrir

hedgehog *n* hérisson *m*

hedgerow *n* haie *f*

heed **1** *n* **to take ~ of sb** tenir compte de ce que dit qn; **to take ~ of sth** tenir compte de qch
2 *vtr* tenir compte de ⟨warning, advice⟩

heel *n* talon *m*
IDIOMS **to fall head over ~s in love with sb** tomber éperdument amoureux de qn; **to be hot on sb's ~s** talonner qn

heel bar *n* talon-minute *m*

hefty *adj* ⟨person⟩ costaud (colloq); ⟨object⟩ pesant/-e; ⟨blow⟩ puissant/-e; ⟨sum⟩ considérable

heifer *n* génisse *f*

height *n* (a) (of person) taille *f*; (of table, tower, tree) hauteur *f*

(b) (of plane) altitude *f*; **to be scared of ∼s** avoir le vertige

(c) (peak) **at the ∼ of the season** en pleine saison; **at the ∼ of** au plus fort de ⟨*storm, crisis*⟩; **the ∼ of** le comble de ⟨*luxury, stupidity, cheek*⟩; **to be the ∼ of fashion** être le dernier cri

heighten ⟨1⟩ *vtr* intensifier ⟨*emotion*⟩; augmenter ⟨*tension, suspense*⟩; accentuer ⟨*effect*⟩
⟨2⟩ *vi* ⟨*tension*⟩ monter

heir *n* héritier/-ière *m/f* (**to** de)

heiress *n* héritière *f*

heirloom *n* héritage *m*; **a family ∼** un objet de famille

helicopter *n* hélicoptère *m*

hell *n* **(a)** enfer *m*; **to make sb's life ∼** rendre la vie infernale à qn
(b) (colloq) **a ∼ of a shock** un choc terrible; **a ∼ of a lot worse** nettement pire; **oh, what the ∼!** tant pis!; **why the ∼...?** pourquoi ..., bon Dieu? (colloq); **what the ∼ is he doing?** qu'est-ce qu'il fait, bon Dieu? (colloq)
IDIOMS **for the ∼ of it** (colloq) par plaisir; **to raise ∼** (colloq) faire une scène (**with sb** à qn)

hello *excl* **(a)** (greeting) bonjour!; (on the phone) allô!
(b) (in surprise) tiens!

helm *n* barre *f*; **at the ∼** à la barre

helmet *n* casque *m*

help ⟨1⟩ *n* aide *f*; (in emergency) secours *m*; **with the ∼ of** à l'aide de ⟨*stick, knife*⟩; avec l'aide de ⟨*person*⟩; **it's/she's a (great) ∼** ça/ elle aide beaucoup; **to cry for ∼** appeler au secours
⟨2⟩ *excl* au secours!
⟨3⟩ *vtr* **(a)** (help to do) aider (à faire); (more urgently) secourir; **to ∼ each other** s'entraider; **to ∼ sb across** aider qn à traverser
(b) (serve) **to ∼ sb to** servir ⟨qch⟩ à qn ⟨*food, wine*⟩; **to ∼ oneself** se servir
(c) (prevent) **I couldn't ∼ laughing** je n'ai pas pu m'empêcher de rire; **it can't be ∼ed!** on n'y peut rien!; **he can't ∼ being stupid!** ce n'est pas de sa faute s'il est stupide!
⟨4⟩ *vi* aider; **he never ∼s with the housework** il n'aide jamais à faire le ménage; **this map doesn't ∼ much** cette carte n'est pas d'un grand secours
■ **help out**: ¶ **∼ out** aider, donner un coup de main (colloq); ¶ **∼ [sb] out** aider, donner un coup de main à (colloq); (financially) dépanner (colloq)

help desk *n* service *m* d'assistance technique téléphonique

helper *n* aide *mf*, assistant/-e *m/f*; (for handicapped person) aide *f* sociale

helpful *adj* ⟨*person*⟩ serviable; ⟨*advice, suggestion*⟩ utile

helping *n* portion *f*

helpless *adj* **(a)** (powerless) ⟨*person*⟩ impuissant/-e; (because of infirmity, disability) impotent/-e
(b) (defenceless) ⟨*person*⟩ sans défense

helpline *n* service *m* d'assistance (téléphonique)

hem *n* ourlet *m*
■ **hem in** cerner ⟨*person*⟩

hemisphere *n* hémisphère *m*

hemp *n* chanvre *m*

hen *n* (chicken) poule *f*; (female bird) femelle *f*

hence *adv* **(a)** (for this reason) (before noun) d'où; (before adjective) donc
(b) (from now on) d'ici

henchman *n* acolyte *m*

henna *n* henné *m*

hen night *n* soirée *f* passée entre femmes (*avant le mariage de l'une d'elles*)

hen-pecked *adj* **∼ husband** mari *m* mené par le bout du nez

hepatitis *n* hépatite *f*

her

■ Note In French determiners agree in gender and number with the noun that follows. So *her*, when used as a determiner, is translated by *son* + masculine singular noun (son chien), by *sa* + feminine singular noun (sa maison) BUT by *son* + feminine noun beginning with a vowel or mute 'h' (son assiette) and by *ses* + plural noun (ses enfants).
– When *her* is stressed, *à elle* is added after the noun: HER house = sa maison à elle.

⟨1⟩ *pron* **(a)** (direct object) la, l'; (indirect object) lui; **I saw ∼** je l'ai vue; **he gave ∼ the book** il lui a donné le livre; **catch ∼** attrape-la!; **give it to ∼** donne-le-lui
(b) (after preposition, to be) elle; **it's for ∼** c'est pour elle; **it's ∼** c'est elle
⟨2⟩ *det* son/sa/ses

herald ⟨1⟩ *n* héraut *m*
⟨2⟩ *vtr* (also **∼ in**) annoncer

heraldry *n* héraldique *f*

herb *n* herbe *f*; **mixed ∼s** ≈ herbes de Provence

herbal tea *n* tisane *f*, infusion *f*

herd ⟨1⟩ *n* troupeau *m*
⟨2⟩ *vtr* rassembler ⟨*animals*⟩; **to ∼ people into a room** conduire des gens dans une pièce
IDIOMS **to follow the ∼** être un mouton de Panurge

here *adv*

■ Note When *here* is used to indicate the location of an object, a point etc close to the speaker, it is generally translated by *ici*: come and sit here = viens t'asseoir ici.
– When the location is not so clearly defined, *là* is the usual translation: he's not here at the moment = il n'est pas là pour l'instant.
– *voici* is used to translate *here is* and *here are* when the speaker is drawing attention to an object, a place, a person etc physically close to him or her.
– For examples and particular usages, see the entry below.

(a) ici; **near ∼** près d'ici; **come over ∼** ⋯⊹

venez par ici; **~ and there** par endroits; **~ they are/she comes!** les/la voici!; **~ are my keys** voici mes clés; **~ you are** tiens, tenez
(b) (indicating presence, arrival) **she's not ~ right now** elle n'est pas là pour le moment; **~ we are at last** nous voilà enfin; **we get off ~** c'est là qu'on descend; **now that summer's ~** maintenant que c'est l'été; **~'s our chance** voilà notre chance
IDIOMS **~'s to our success!** à notre succès!; **~'s to you!** à la tienne!

hereabout (US), **hereabouts** (GB) *adv* par ici

hereafter ① *n* **the ~** l'au-delà *m*
② *adv* (Law) ci-après

here and now *n* **the ~** (present) le présent

hereby *adv* par la présente

hereditary *adj* héréditaire

heresy *n* hérésie *f*

heritage *n* patrimoine *m*

hermit *n* ermite *m*

hernia *n* hernie *f*

hero *n* héros *m*

heroic *adj* héroïque

heroin *n* héroïne *f*

heroin addict *n* héroïnomane *mf*

heroine *n* héroïne *f*

heroism *n* héroïsme *m*

heron *n* héron *m*

hero-worship ① *n* culte *m* du héros, adulation *f*
② *vtr* aduler

herring *n* hareng *m*

hers *pron*

■ Note In French, possessive pronouns reflect the gender and number of the noun they are standing for; *hers* is translated by *le sien, la sienne, les siens, les siennes*, according to what is being referred to.

my car is red but ~ is blue ma voiture est rouge mais la sienne est bleue; **the green pen is ~** le stylo vert est à elle; **which house is ~?** laquelle est sa maison?; **I'm a friend of ~** c'est une amie à moi; **it's not ~** ce n'est pas à elle

herself *pron* **(a)** (reflexive) se, s'; **she's hurt ~** elle s'est blessée
(b) (after preposition) elle, elle-même; **for ~** pour elle, pour elle-même; **(all) by ~** toute seule
(c) (emphatic) elle-même; **she made it ~** elle l'a fait elle-même
(d) she's not ~ today elle n'est pas dans son assiette aujourd'hui

hesitant *adj* hésitant/-e; **to be ~ about doing** hésiter à faire

hesitate *vi* hésiter (over sur; to do à faire)

hesitation *n* hésitation *f*

heterosexual *n*, *adj* hétérosexuel/-elle (*m/f*)

hexagon *n* hexagone *m*

hey *excl* (colloq) (call for attention) hé!, eh!; (in protest) dis donc!

heyday *n* (gen) âge *m* d'or; (of person) beaux jours *mpl*

HGV *n* (GB) (*abbr* = **heavy goods vehicle**) PL *m*, poids *m* lourd

hi *excl* (colloq) salut! (colloq)

hibernate *vi* hiberner

hiccup, **hiccough** *n* **(a)** hoquet *m*; **to have (the) ~s** avoir le hoquet
(b) (setback) anicroche *f*

hidden *adj* caché/-e

hide ① *n* (skin) peau *f*; (leather) cuir *m*
② *vtr* cacher ⟨object, person⟩ (from à); dissimuler ⟨feeling⟩ (from à)
③ *vi* se cacher

hide and seek (GB), **hide-and-go-seek** (US) *n* cache-cache *m inv*

hideaway *n* retraite *f*

hideous *adj* ⟨person, monster, object⟩ hideux/-euse; ⟨noise⟩ affreux/-euse

hiding *n* **(a) to go into ~** se cacher; **to come out of ~** sortir de sa cachette
(b) (beating) correction *f*

hiding place *n* cachette *f*

hierarchy *n* hiérarchie *f*

hieroglyph, **hieroglyphic** *n* hiéroglyphe *m*

hi-fi *n* **(a)** (set of equipment) chaîne *f* hi-fi *inv*
(b) (*abbr* = **high fidelity**) hi-fi *f inv*

high ① *n* **(a) to reach a new ~** atteindre son niveau le plus élevé
(b) (colloq) **to be on a ~** être en pleine euphorie
② *adj* **(a)** (gen) haut/-e; **how ~ is the cliff?** quelle est la hauteur de la falaise?; **it is 50 m ~** ça fait 50 m de haut
(b) ⟨number, price, volume⟩ élevé/-e; ⟨wind⟩ violent/-e; ⟨hope⟩ grand/-e (before n); **at ~ speed** à grande vitesse; **to have a ~ temperature** avoir de la fièvre; **~ in** riche en ⟨fat, iron⟩
(c) ⟨quality, standard, rank⟩ supérieur/-e; **friends in ~ places** des amis haut placés
(d) ⟨ideal, principle⟩ noble
(e) ⟨pitch, voice⟩ aigu/aiguë; ⟨note⟩ haut/-e
(f) (colloq) (on drug) défoncé/-e (colloq); (happy) ivre de joie
③ *adv* haut

highbrow *n*, *adj* intellectuel/-elle (*m/f*)

high chair *n* chaise *f* de bébé

high-class *adj* ⟨hotel, shop, car⟩ de luxe; ⟨goods⟩ de première qualité; ⟨area⟩ de grand standing

high court *n* cour *f* suprême

high-definition TV, **HDTV** *n* télévision *f* à haute définition

higher education *n* enseignement *m* supérieur

high fashion *n* haute couture *f*

high-flier *n* jeune loup *m*

high-handed *adj* despotique

high heels *n pl* hauts talons *mpl*

high jump *n* (Sport) saut *m* en hauteur

Highlands *pr n pl* Highlands *mpl*, Hautes-Terres *fpl* (d'Écosse)

highlight ① *n* (a) (in hair) (natural) reflet *m*; (artificial) mèche *f*
(b) (of match, event) point *m* culminant; (of year, evening) point *m* fort
② **highlights** *n pl* (on radio, TV) résumé *m*
③ *vtr* (a) (with pen) surligner
(b) (emphasize) mettre l'accent sur

highlighter *n* (pen) surligneur *m*

highly *adv* ⟨*dangerous, intelligent*⟩ extrêmement; ⟨*unlikely*⟩ fort peu probable; **to think ∼ of sb** penser beaucoup de bien de qn

highly-paid *adj* très bien payé/-e

highly-strung *adj* très tendu/-e

Highness *n* His *or* Her (**Royal**) ∼ Son Altesse *f*

high-pitched *adj* ⟨*voice, sound*⟩ aigu/ aiguë

high point *n* point *m* culminant

high-powered *adj* ⟨*car, engine*⟩ de grande puissance; ⟨*person*⟩ dynamique; ⟨*job*⟩ de haute responsabilité

high-profile *adj* ⟨*politician, group*⟩ bien en vue; ⟨*visit*⟩ qui fait beaucoup de bruit

high-ranking *adj* de haut rang

high rise (building) *n* tour *f* (d'habitation)

high school *n* (US Sch) ≈ lycée *m*; (GB Sch) établissement *m* secondaire

high-speed *adj* ⟨*train*⟩ à grande vitesse

high street (GB) *n* (*also* **High Street**) (in town) rue *f* principale; (in village) grand-rue *f*

high-street shop *n* boutique *f* appartenant à une chaîne

high street spending *n* dépenses *fpl* de consommation courante

high-tech *adj* ⟨*industry*⟩ de pointe; ⟨*equipment, car*⟩ ultramoderne

high tide *n* marée *f* haute

highway *n* (GB) route *f* nationale; (US) autoroute *f*

Highway Code *n* (GB) Code *m* de la Route

hijack *vtr* détourner ⟨*plane*⟩

hijacker *n* (of plane) pirate *m* (de l'air); (of bus, truck) pirate *m* (de la route)

hijacking *n* détournement *m*

hike ① *n* randonnée *f*; **to go on a ∼** faire une randonnée
② *vtr* (*also* **∼ up**) augmenter ⟨*rate, price*⟩

hiker *n* randonneur/-euse *m/f*

hiking *n* randonnée *f*

hilarious *adj* désopilant/-e, hilarant/-e

hill *n* colline *f*; (hillside) coteau *m*; (incline) pente *f*, côte *f*

hillside *n* **on the ∼** à flanc de coteau

hilltop *n* sommet *m* de colline

hilly *adj* vallonné/-e

him *pron* (a) (direct object) le, l'; (indirect object) lui; **I know ∼** je le connais; **catch ∼!** attrape-le!; **I gave ∼ the book** je lui ai donné le livre; **phone ∼!** téléphone-lui!
(b) (after preposition, to be) lui; **it's for ∼** c'est pour lui; **it's ∼** c'est lui

Himalayas *pr n pl* **the ∼** (les montagnes *fpl* de) l'Himalaya *m*

himself *pron* (a) (reflexive) se, s'; **he's hurt ∼** il s'est blessé
(b) (after preposition) lui, lui-même; **for ∼** pour lui, pour lui-même; (all) **by ∼** tout seul
(c) (emphatic) lui-même; **he made it ∼** il l'a fait lui-même
(d) **he's not ∼ today** il n'est pas dans son assiette aujourd'hui

hinder *vtr* entraver ⟨*development, career*⟩; freiner ⟨*progress, efforts*⟩

hind legs *n pl* pattes *fpl* de derrière

hindrance *n* entrave *f*; **to be a ∼ to sb/ sth** gêner qn/qch

hindsight *n* **with (the benefit of) ∼** avec le recul, rétrospectivement

Hindu ① *n* Hindou/-e *m/f*
② *adj* hindou/-e

hinge ① *n* charnière *f*; (lift-off) gond *m*
② *vi* **to ∼ on** dépendre de

hint ① *n* (a) (remark) allusion *f* (**about** à); **to drop ∼s** faire des allusions
(b) (clue) indication *f*; (piece of advice) conseil *m*
(c) (of spice, accent) pointe *f*; (of colour) touche *f*; (of smile) ébauche *f*; (of irony) soupçon *m*
② *vtr* **to ∼ that** laisser entendre que (**to** à)
③ *vi* faire des allusions; **to ∼ at** faire allusion à

hip ① *n* hanche *f*
② *adj* (colloq) ⟨*person*⟩ branché/-e
③ *excl* **∼ ∼ hurrah!** hip hip hip hourra!

hippie, hippy *n, adj* hippie (*mf*)

hippopotamus, hippo *n* hippopotame *m*

hire ① *n* location *f*; **for ∼** ⟨*boat, skis*⟩ à louer; ⟨*taxi*⟩ libre
② *vtr* louer ⟨*equipment, vehicle*⟩; engager ⟨*person*⟩

hire purchase, HP *n* achat *m* à crédit; **on ∼** à crédit

his

■ Note In French determiners agree in gender and number with the noun that follows. So *his*, when used as a determiner, is translated by *son* + masculine singular noun (son chien), by *sa* + feminine singular noun (sa maison) BUT by *son* + feminine noun beginning with a vowel or mute 'h' (son assiette) and by *ses* + plural noun (ses enfants).
– When *his* is stressed, *à lui* is added after the noun: HIS *house* = sa maison à lui.
– In French possessive pronouns reflect the gender and number of the noun they are standing for. When used as a possessive ⋯∴

pronoun, his is translated by le sien, la sienne, les siens or les siennes according to what is being referred to.

1 det son/sa/ses
2 pron **all the drawings were good but ~ was the best** tous les dessins étaient bons mais le sien était le meilleur; **the blue car is ~** la voiture bleue est à lui; **it's not ~** ce n'est pas à lui; **which house is ~?** laquelle est sa maison?; **I'm a colleague of ~** je suis un/-e de ses collègues

hiss **1** n sifflement m
2 vi ⟨person, steam, snake⟩ siffler; ⟨cat⟩ cracher; ⟨fat⟩ grésiller

historian n historien/-ienne m/f

historic(al) adj historique

history n (a) histoire f; **to make ~** entrer dans l'histoire
(b) (past experience) antécédents mpl; **to have a ~ of violence** avoir un passé violent

hit **1** n (a) (blow, stroke) coup m
(b) (success) ⟨play, film⟩ succès m; ⟨record⟩ tube m (colloq); **to be a big ~** avoir un succès fou
(c) (Comput) (visit to Website) hit m (colloq), visite f (à un site Web); (occurences in search) occurence f
2 vtr (a) (strike) frapper ⟨person, ball⟩; **to ~ one's head on sth** se cogner la tête contre qch
(b) atteindre ⟨target, enemy⟩
(c) (collide with) heurter ⟨wall⟩; ⟨vehicle⟩ renverser ⟨person⟩
(d) (affect adversely) affecter, toucher
(e) (reach) arriver à ⟨motorway⟩; rencontrer ⟨traffic, bad weather⟩; ⟨figures, weight⟩ atteindre ⟨level⟩
IDIOMS **to ~ it off with sb** bien s'entendre avec qn
■ **hit back**: ¶ **~ [sb] back** rendre un coup à; ¶ **~ [sth] back** renvoyer ⟨ball⟩

hit-and-run adj ⟨accident⟩ où le chauffeur a pris la fuite

hitch **1** n problème m, pépin m (colloq)
2 vtr (a) attacher ⟨trailer⟩ (**to** à)
(b) (colloq) **to ~ a lift** faire du stop (colloq)
3 vi (colloq) faire du stop (colloq)

hitchhike vi faire du stop (colloq); **to ~ to Paris** aller à Paris en stop (colloq)

hitchhiker n auto-stoppeur/-euse m/f

hitchhiking n auto-stop m

hit man n tueur m à gages

hit parade n palmarès m, hit-parade m

hit single n tube m (colloq)

HIV n (abbr = **human immunodeficiency virus**) (virus m) VIH m; **~ positive** séropositif/-ive; **~ negative** séronégatif/-ive

hive n ruche f; **a ~ of activity** une vraie ruche

hoard **1** n (of treasure) trésor m; (of provisions) provisions fpl; (of miser) magot m (colloq)
2 vtr amasser ⟨objects, money, food⟩

hoarding n (GB) (a) (billboard) panneau m publicitaire
(b) (fence) palissade f

hoarse adj ⟨voice⟩ rauque; **to be ~** être enroué/-e

hoax **1** n canular m
2 adj ⟨call, warning⟩ bidon inv (colloq)

hob n (on cooker) table f de cuisson

hobble vi boitiller

hobby n passe-temps m inv

hockey n (GB) hockey m; (US) hockey m sur glace; **~ stick** crosse f de hockey

hoe **1** n houe f, binette f
2 vtr biner ⟨ground⟩; sarcler ⟨flower beds⟩

hog **1** n (US) (pig) porc m, verrat m
2 vtr (colloq) monopoliser
IDIOMS **to go the whole ~** (colloq) (be extravagant) faire les choses en grand; (go to extremes) aller jusqu'au bout

hoist vtr hisser ⟨flag, sail, heavy object⟩

hold **1** n (a) (grasp) prise f; **to get ~ of** attraper ⟨rope, handle⟩
(b) **to get ~ of** se procurer ⟨book, ticket⟩; découvrir ⟨information⟩
(c) **to get ~ of sb** (contact) joindre qn; (find) trouver qn
(d) (control) emprise f (**on, over** sur); **to have a ~ on or over sb** avoir de l'emprise sur qn; **to get a ~ of oneself** se reprendre
(e) **to put a call on ~** mettre un appel en attente
(f) (in plane) soute f; (on boat) cale f
2 vtr (a) tenir; **to ~ sth in one's hand** tenir qch à la main ⟨brush, pencil⟩; (enclosed) tenir qch dans la main ⟨coin, sweet⟩; **to ~ sb (in one's arms)** serrer qn dans ses bras; **to ~ sth in place** maintenir qch en place
(b) organiser ⟨meeting, competition, reception⟩; célébrer ⟨church service⟩; mener ⟨inquiry⟩; faire passer ⟨interview⟩
(c) (contain) ⟨drawer, box, case⟩ contenir ⟨objects, possessions⟩
(d) avoir ⟨opinion, belief⟩
(e) (keep against will) détenir ⟨person⟩; **to ~ sb hostage** garder qn en otage
(f) détenir, avoir ⟨power, record⟩; être titulaire de ⟨degree⟩
(g) **to ~ sb's attention** retenir l'attention de qn; **to ~ sb responsible** tenir qn pour responsable
(h) (defend successfully) tenir ⟨territory, city⟩; conserver ⟨title, seat⟩; **to ~ one's own** bien se défendre
(i) (on phone) **can you ~ the line please?** ne quittez pas s'il vous plaît
3 vi (a) ⟨bridge, dam, rope⟩ tenir
(b) ⟨weather⟩ se maintenir; ⟨luck⟩ durer
(c) (on phone) patienter
(d) **~ still!** tiens-toi tranquille!
■ **hold against**: **to ~ sth against sb** reprocher qch à qn
■ **hold back**: ¶ **~ back** se retenir (**from doing** de faire)
¶ **~ [sb/sth] back (a)** contenir ⟨water, crowd, anger⟩; retenir ⟨tears, person⟩
(b) entraver ⟨development⟩
■ **hold down (a)** tenir, maîtriser ⟨person⟩
(b) garder ⟨job⟩

■ **hold on** (a) (wait) attendre; '~ on...' (on phone) 'ne quittez pas...'
(b) (grip) s'accrocher; '~ **on (tight)!'** 'tiens-toi (bien)!'
■ **hold on to** s'agripper à ⟨*branch, rope, person*⟩; (to prevent from falling) retenir ⟨*person*⟩; serrer ⟨*object, purse*⟩
■ **hold out:** ¶ ~ **out** tenir bon; **to ~ out against** tenir bon devant ⟨*threat, changes*⟩ ¶ ~ **[sth] out** tendre ⟨*hand*⟩ (to à)
■ **hold to:** ~ **sb to [sth]** faire tenir [qch] à qn ⟨*promise*⟩
■ **hold up** (a) (support) soutenir ⟨*shelf*⟩; tenir ⟨*trousers*⟩
(b) (raise) lever; **to ~ one's hand up** lever la main
(c) (delay) retarder ⟨*person, flight*⟩; ralentir ⟨*production, traffic*⟩
(d) (rob) attaquer

holdall n fourre-tout m, sac m

holder n (of passport, degree, post, account) titulaire mf; (of ticket, record) détenteur/-trice m/f; (of title) tenant/-e m/f

hold-up n (a) (delay) retard m; (on road) embouteillage m, bouchon m
(b) (robbery) hold-up m

hole n (a) (gen) trou m
(b) (GB) (in tooth) cavité f
(c) (of fox, rabbit) terrier m

hole-in-the-wall n (colloq) distributeur m automatique de billets de banque

holiday n (a) (GB) (vacation) vacances fpl; **to go on ~** partir en vacances
(b) (GB) (time off work) congé m
(c) (public, bank) jour m férié

holiday home n résidence f secondaire

holiday job n (in summer) job m (colloq) d'été

holidaymaker n (GB) vacancier/-ière m/f

holiday resort n lieu m de villégiature

Holland pr n Hollande f, Pays-Bas mpl

hollow ① n creux m
② adj ⟨*object, cheeks*⟩ creux/creuse; ⟨*words*⟩ faux/fausse, vain/-e; **a ~ laugh** un rire forcé; **to sound ~** sonner faux

holly n houx m

holocaust n holocauste m; **the Holocaust** l'Holocauste m

hologram n hologramme m

holster n étui m de revolver

holy adj (gen) saint/-e; ⟨*water*⟩ bénit/-e

Holy Bible n Sainte Bible f

Holy Land pr n Terre f Sainte

Holy Spirit n Saint-Esprit m

homage n hommage m; **to pay ~ to** rendre hommage à

home ① n (a) (house) maison f; (country) pays m natal; (institution) foyer m désuni; **to leave ~** quitter la maison
(b) (institution) maison f; **to put sb in a ~** mettre qn dans un établissement spécialisé
(c) (Sport) **to play at ~** jouer à domicile
② adj (a) ⟨*life*⟩ de famille; ⟨*comforts*⟩ du foyer

(b) ⟨*market, affairs*⟩ intérieur/-e; ⟨*news*⟩ national/-e
(c) (Sport) ⟨*match, win*⟩ à domicile; ⟨*team*⟩ qui reçoit
③ adv (a) ⟨*come, go*⟩ (to house) à la maison, chez soi; (to country) dans son pays
(b) **to bring sth ~ to sb** faire comprendre or voir qch à qn; **to strike ~** toucher juste
④ at home phr (a) ⟨*be, work, stay*⟩ à la maison, chez soi
(b) (Sport) ⟨*play*⟩ à domicile
(c) (at ease) ⟨*feel*⟩ à l'aise (**with** avec); **make yourself at ~** fais comme chez toi

home address n adresse f personnelle

home cooking n bonne cuisine f familiale

home economics n (Sch) cours m d'économie domestique

home help n (GB) aide f familiale

homeland n pays m d'origine, patrie f

homeless n the ~ les sans-abri mpl

homely adj (a) (GB) (cosy, welcoming) accueillant/-e
(b) (GB) (unpretentious) simple
(c) (US) (plain) ⟨*person*⟩ sans attraits

homemade adj fait/-e maison, maison inv

Home Office n ministère m de l'Intérieur

homeopathic adj homéopathique

home owner n propriétaire mf

home page n page f d'accueil

home rule n gouvernement m autonome

Home Secretary n Ministre m de l'Intérieur

home shopping n téléachat m

homesick adj **to be ~** (for country) avoir le mal du pays

home town n ville f natale

home video n vidéo f d'amateur

homeward adv **to travel ~(s)** rentrer; **to be ~ bound** être sur le chemin de retour

homework n (a) (Sch) devoirs mpl
(b) (research) **to do some ~ on** faire quelques recherches au sujet de

homeworker n travailleur/-euse m/f à domicile

homeworking n travail m à domicile

homicidal adj homicide

homicide n (a) (murder) homicide m
(b) (person) meurtrier/-ière m/f

homogenous adj homogène

homosexual n, adj homosexuel/-elle (m/f)

homosexuality n homosexualité f

honest adj ⟨*answer, account*⟩ sincère; ⟨*person*⟩ (truthful, trustworthy) honnête; (frank) franc/franche; **to be ~ with sb** être franc/franche avec qn; **to be ~, I don't care** à dire vrai, ça m'est égal

honestly adv (a) (truthfully) honnêtement
(b) (really) vraiment
(c) (sincerely) franchement

h

honesty n honnêteté f

honey n (a) miel m
(b) (colloq) (dear) chéri/-e m/f

honeycomb n (in hive) rayon m de miel; (for sale) gâteau m de miel

honeymoon n lune f de miel; **to go on** ∼ partir en voyage de noces

honeysuckle n chèvrefeuille m

Hong Kong pr n Hongkong m

honk vtr **to** ∼ **one's horn** donner un coup de klaxon®

honor (US) = HONOUR

honorable (US) = HONOURABLE

honorary adj honoraire

honour (GB), **honor** (US) ① n (a) honneur m; **in** ∼ **of** en l'honneur de
(b) (in titles) **Your Honour** Votre Honneur
② vtr honorer ⟨person, cheque, contract⟩; tenir ⟨promise, commitment⟩

honourable (GB), **honorable** (US) adj (gen) honorable; ⟨person, intention⟩ honnête

honours degree n: licence réservée aux meilleurs étudiants

hood n (a) (of coat) capuchon m; (balaclava) cagoule f
(b) (on cooker) hotte f
(c) (GB) (on car, pram) capote f
(d) (US Aut) (bonnet) capot m
(e) (US) (colloq) (gangster) truand m

hoof n sabot m

hook ① n (a) (on wall, for picture) crochet m
(b) (on fishing line) hameçon m
(c) (fastener) agrafe f; ∼**s and eyes** agrafes fpl
(d) **to take the phone off the** ∼ décrocher le téléphone
(e) (in boxing) crochet m; **left** ∼ crochet du gauche
② vtr accrocher (**on, onto** à)
IDIOMS **to get sb off the** ∼ tirer qn d'affaire

hooked adj (a) ⟨nose, beak⟩ crochu/-e
(b) **to be** ∼ **on** se camer (colloq) à ⟨drugs⟩; être mordu/-e (colloq) de ⟨films, computer games⟩

hooligan n vandale m, voyou m; **soccer** ∼ hooligan m

hoop n (ring) cerceau m; (in croquet) arceau m

hooray excl hourra!

hoot ① n (of owl) (h)ululement m; (of car) coup m de klaxon®
② vtr **to** ∼ **one's horn** donner un coup de klaxon®
③ vi ⟨owl⟩ (h)ululer; ⟨car⟩ klaxonner; ⟨person, crowd⟩ (derisively) huer; **to** ∼ **with laughter** éclater de rire

hoover vtr (GB) **to** ∼ **a room** passer l'aspirateur dans une pièce

Hoover® n (GB) aspirateur m

hop ① n (of frog, rabbit, child) bond m; (of bird) sautillement m
② **hops** n pl houblon m
③ vi ⟨person⟩ sauter; (on one leg) sauter à cloche-pied; ⟨bird⟩ sautiller; **to** ∼ **into bed/off a bus** sauter dans son lit/d'un bus

hope ① n espoir m; (of de); **to raise sb's** ∼**s**

faire naître l'espoir chez qn; **to give up** ∼ abandonner tout espoir; **to have no** ∼ **of sth** n'avoir aucune chance de qch
② vtr espérer (**that** que); **to** ∼ **to do** espérer faire; **I (do)** ∼ **so/not** j'espère (bien) que oui/que non
③ vi espérer; **to** ∼ **for a reward** espérer avoir une récompense; **let's** ∼ **for the best** espérons que tout se passera bien

hopeful adj ⟨person, expression⟩ plein/-e d'espoir; ⟨attitude, mood⟩ optimiste; ⟨sign, situation⟩ encourageant/-e

hopefully adv (a) (with luck) avec un peu de chance
(b) (with hope) ⟨say⟩ avec optimisme

hopeless adj (a) ⟨attempt, case, struggle⟩ désespéré/-e; **it's** ∼**!** inutile!
(b) (colloq) (incompetent) nul/nulle (colloq)

hopelessness n (a) (despair) désespoir m
(b) (futility) futilité f (of faire)

hopscotch n marelle f

horizon n horizon m; **on the** ∼ à l'horizon; (figurative) en vue

horizontal adj horizontal/-e

hormone n hormone f

hormone replacement therapy, HRT n hormonothérapie f substitutive

horn n (a) (of animal, snail) corne f
(b) (Mus) cor m
(c) (of car) klaxon® m; (of ship) sirène f

hornet n frelon m

horoscope n horoscope m

horrendous adj épouvantable

horrible adj (a) (unpleasant) ⟨place, clothes, smell⟩ affreux/-euse; ⟨weather, food, person⟩ épouvantable; **to be** ∼ **to sb** être méchant/-e avec qn
(b) (shocking) ⟨death, crime⟩ horrible

horrid adj affreux/-euse

horrific adj atroce

horrify vtr horrifier

horrifying adj ⟨experience, sight⟩ horrifiant/-e; ⟨behaviour⟩ effroyable

horror n horreur f (at devant); **to have a** ∼ **of sth/of doing** avoir horreur de qch/de faire

horror film n film m d'épouvante

horror story n histoire f d'épouvante

horse n cheval m
IDIOMS **from the** ∼**'s mouth** de source sûre
■ **horse about, horse around** chahuter

horseback n **on** ∼ à cheval

horseback riding n (US) équitation f

horse chestnut n (tree) marronnier m (d'Inde); (fruit) marron m (d'Inde)

horsefly n taon m

horsepower n puissance f (en chevaux)

horse race n course f de chevaux

horseracing n courses fpl de chevaux, courses fpl hippiques

horseradish sauce n sauce f au raifort

horseriding n équitation f

horseshoe n fer m à cheval

horseshow *n* concours *m* hippique

horticulture *n* horticulture *f*

hose, hosepipe (GB) *n* (gen) tuyau *m*; (for garden) tuyau *m* d'arrosage; (**fire**) ∼ lance *f* à incendie

hospice *n* établissement *m* de soins palliatifs

hospitable *adj* hospitalier/-ière (**to** envers)

hospital *n* hôpital *m*; **to be taken to** ∼ être hospitalisé/-e; **in** ∼ à l'hôpital

hospitality *n* hospitalité *f*

hospitalize *vtr* hospitaliser

host 1 *n* (**a**) (gen) hôte *m*
(**b**) (on radio, TV) animateur/-trice *m/f*
(**c**) (multitude) foule *f* (**of** de)
2 *vtr* organiser ⟨party⟩; animer ⟨show⟩

hostage *n* otage *m*; **to hold sb** ∼ garder qn en otage

host country *n* pays *m* hôte *or* d'accueil

hostel *n* (for workers, refugees) foyer *m*; (**youth**) ∼ auberge *f* de jeunesse

hostess *n* hôtesse *f*

hostile *adj* hostile (**to** à)

hostility *n* hostilité *f* (**towards** à l'égard de)

hot *adj* (**a**) (gen) chaud/-e; **it's** ∼ **here** il fait chaud ici; **to be** *or* **feel** ∼ ⟨person⟩ avoir chaud; **to go** ∼ **and cold** (with fever) être fiévreux/-euse; (with fear) avoir des sueurs froides
(**b**) (Culin) ⟨mustard, spice⟩ fort/-e; ⟨sauce, dish⟩ épicé/-e
(**c**) **to be** ∼ **on sb's trail** être sur les talons de qn

hot air balloon *n* montgolfière *f*

hotbed *n* foyer *m* (**of** de)

hot dog *n* hot dog *m*

hotel *n* hôtel *m*

hotelier, hotelkeeper *n* (GB) hôtelier/-ière *m/f*

hot-headed *adj* ⟨person⟩ impétueux/-euse

hotline *n* (**a**) (for orders, tickets) ligne *f* ouverte, permanence *f* téléphonique
(**b**) (Mil, Pol) téléphone *m* rouge

hotplate *n* plaque *f* de cuisson

hot seat *n*
IDIOMS **to be in the** ∼ être sur la sellette

hotshot *n* gros bonnet *m* (colloq)

hot spot *n* (colloq) (**a**) (trouble spot) point *m* chaud
(**b**) (sunny country) pays *m* chaud

hot-tempered *adj* colérique

hot water bottle *n* bouillotte *f*

hound 1 *n* chien *m* de chasse
2 *vtr* harceler, traquer ⟨person⟩
■ **hound out** chasser (**of** de)

hour *n* heure *f*; **£10 per** ∼ 10 livres sterling (de) l'heure; **to be paid by the** ∼ être payé/-e à l'heure; **60 km an hour** 60 km à l'heure; **in the early** ∼**s** au petit matin

hourly 1 *adj* horaire
2 *adv* ⟨arrive, phone⟩ toutes les heures

house 1 *n* (**a**) (gen) maison *f*; **at my/his** ∼ chez moi/lui; **to go to sb's** ∼ aller chez qn; **on the** ∼ aux frais de la maison
(**b**) (in theatre) (audience) assistance *f*; (auditorium) salle *f*; (performance) séance *f*
(**c**) (music) house music *f*
2 *vtr* loger ⟨person⟩; abriter ⟨collection⟩

houseboat *n* péniche *f* aménagée

housebound *adj* confiné/-e chez soi

house call *n* visite *f* à domicile

household 1 *n* maison *f*; (in survey) ménage *m*; **head of the** ∼ chef *m* de famille
2 *adj* ⟨expenses⟩ du ménage; ⟨chore⟩ ménager/-ère

household appliance *n* appareil *m* électroménager

householder *n* (**a**) (occupier) occupant/-e *m/f*
(**b**) (owner) propriétaire *mf*

household name *n* **he's a** ∼ il est célèbre

house husband *n* homme *m* au foyer

housekeeper *n* gouvernante *f*

housekeeping *n* (money) argent *m* du ménage

House of Commons *n* (GB) Chambre *f* des communes

House of Lords *n* (GB) Chambre *f* des lords, Chambre *f* haute

House of Representatives *n* (US) Chambre *f* des représentants

houseplant *n* plante *f* d'intérieur

house-proud *adj* fier/fière de son intérieur

Houses of Parliament *n pl* (GB) Parlement *m* Britannique

house-to-house *adj* ⟨search⟩ de maison en maison

house-trained *adj* (GB) propre

house-warming (party) *n* pendaison *f* de crémaillère

housewife *n* femme *f* au foyer; ménagère *f*

housework *n* travaux *mpl* ménagers; **to do the** ∼ faire le ménage

housing *n* logements *mpl*

housing estate *n* (GB) cité *f*

hover *vi* ⟨eagle⟩ planer; ⟨helicopter⟩ faire du surplace; **to** ∼ **around sb/sth** tourner autour de qn/qch

hovercraft *n* aéroglisseur *m*

how 1 *adv* (**a**) (gen) comment ∼ **are you?** comment allez-vous?; ∼**'s your brother?** comment va ton frère?; ∼ **are things?** comment ça va?; ∼ **do you do!** enchanté!; **to know** ∼ **to do** savoir faire
(**b**) (in number, quantity questions) ∼ **much is this?** combien ça coûte?; ∼ **much do you weigh?** combien pèses-tu?; ∼ **many people?** combien de personnes?; ∼ **many times** combien de fois?; ∼ **long will it take?** combien de temps cela va-t-il prendre?; ∼ **tall are you?** combien mesures-tu?; ∼ **far is** ⋯⋗

it? c'est à quelle distance?; ~ **old is she?** quel âge a-t-elle?; ~ **soon can you get here?** dans combien de temps peux-tu être ici?
(c) (in exclamations) ~ **wonderful/awful!** c'est fantastique/affreux!; ~ **clever of you!** comme c'est intelligent de ta part!
2 (colloq) **how come** *phr* ~ **come?** pourquoi?; ~ **come you always get the best place?** comment ça se fait que tu aies toujours la meilleure place?

however 1 *conj* (nevertheless) toutefois, cependant
2 *adv* (no matter how) ~ **hard I try, I can't** j'ai beau essayer, je n'y arrive pas; ~ **difficult the task is** aussi difficile que soit la tâche; ~ **small she may be** si petite soit-elle; ~ **much it costs** quel qu'en soit le prix; ~ **long it takes** quel que soit le temps que ça prendra; ~ **you like** comme tu veux

howl 1 *n* hurlement *m*
2 *vi* hurler

HQ *n* (Mil) (abbr = **headquarters**) QG *m*

HTML *n* (abbr = **HyperText Markup Language**) HTML *m*

hub *n* (of wheel) moyeu *m*; (figurative) centre *m*

hubcap *n* enjoliveur *m*

huddle *vi* **to ~ around** se presser autour de ⟨fire, radio⟩; **to ~ together** se serrer les uns contre les autres

hue *n* **(a)** (colour) couleur *f*, teinte *f*
(b) ~ **and cry** tollé *m*

huff (colloq) 1 *n* **in a ~** vexé/-e
2 *vi* souffler

hug 1 *n* étreinte *f*; **to give sb a ~** serrer qn dans ses bras
2 *vtr* **(a)** (embrace) serrer [qn] dans ses bras
(b) **to ~ the coast/kerb** serrer la côte/le trottoir

huge *adj* ⟨object, garden, city, country⟩ immense; ⟨person, animal⟩ gigantesque; ⟨appetite, success⟩ énorme; ⟨debts, sum⟩ gros/ grosse (before *n*)

hugely *adv* **(a)** (emphatic) extrêmement
(b) ⟨increase, vary⟩ considérablement; ⟨enjoy⟩ énormément

hull *n* (of ship, plane) coque *f*; (of tank) carcasse *f*

hum 1 *n* (of insect, traffic, voices) bourdonnement *m*; (of machinery) ronronnement *m*
2 *vi* ⟨person⟩ fredonner; ⟨insect, aircraft⟩ bourdonner; ⟨machine⟩ ronronner

human 1 *n* humain *m*
2 *adj* ⟨body, behaviour⟩ humain/-e; ⟨characteristic, rights⟩ de l'homme

human being *n* être *m* humain

humane *adj* ⟨person⟩ humain/-e; ⟨act⟩ d'humanité

human interest story *n* histoire *f* vécue

humanitarian *adj* humanitaire

humanity *n* humanité *f*

human nature *n* nature *f* humaine

human resources manager *n* responsable *mf* de la gestion des ressources humaines

humble *adj* (gen) modeste; ⟨person⟩ humble

humid *adj* ⟨climate⟩ humide; ⟨weather⟩ lourd/-e

humidity *n* humidité *f*

humiliate *vtr* humilier

humiliating *adj* humiliant/-e

humiliation *n* humiliation *f*

humorous *adj* **(a)** ⟨story, book⟩ humoristique
(b) ⟨person, look⟩ plein/-e d'humour

humour (GB), **humor** (US) 1 *n* **(a)** (wit) humour *m*; **a good sense of ~** le sens de l'humour
(b) (mood) humeur *f*; **to be in good/bad ~** être de bonne/mauvaise humeur
2 *vtr* amadouer ⟨person⟩

hump *n* bosse *f*

hunch 1 *n* intuition *f*
2 *vtr* **to ~ one's shoulders** rentrer les épaules

hunched *adj* ⟨back, figure⟩ voûté/-e; ⟨shoulders⟩ rentré/-e

hundred 1 *n* cent *m*; **two ~** deux cents; **two ~ and one** deux cent un; **in nineteen ~** en mille neuf cents; **in nineteen ~ and three** en mille neuf cent trois; ~**s of times** des centaines de fois
2 *pron, det* cent; **two ~ francs** deux cents francs; **two ~ and five francs** deux cent cinq francs; **about a ~ people** une centaine de personnes

hundredth *n, adj, adv* centième (*mf*)

hundredweight *n* (GB) = *50.80 kg*; (US) = *45.36 kg*

Hungarian 1 *n* **(a)** (person) Hongrois/-e *m/f*
(b) (language) hongrois *m*
2 *adj* hongrois/-e

Hungary *pr n* Hongrie *f*

hunger *n* faim *f*

hunger strike *n* grève *f* de la faim

hung-over *adj* (colloq) **to be ~** avoir la gueule de bois (colloq)

hungry *adj* **to be ~** avoir faim; **to make sb ~** donner faim à qn; ~ **for** assoiffé/-e de ⟨success, power⟩

hunk *n* **(a)** (of bread, cheese) gros morceau *m*
(b) (colloq) (man) beau mec *m* (colloq)

hunt 1 *n* **(a)** (for animals) chasse *f* (**for** à)
(b) (search) recherche *f* (**for** de)
2 *vtr* rechercher ⟨person⟩; chasser ⟨animal⟩
3 *vi* **(a)** (for prey) chasser
(b) (search) **to ~ for sth** chercher [qch] partout ⟨object, person⟩

hunter *n* (person) chasseur/-euse *m/f*

hunting *n* chasse *f* (**of** à); **to go ~** aller à la chasse

hunt saboteur *n* opposant/-e *m/f* à la chasse au renard

hurdle *n* **(a)** (Sport) haie *f*

(b) (obstacle) obstacle *m*

hurl *vtr* **(a)** (throw) lancer (**at** sur)
(b) (shout) **to ~ insults at sb** accabler qn
d'injures

hurrah, **hurray** *n, excl* hourra (*m*)

hurricane *n* ouragan *m*

hurry ⟦1⟧ *n* hâte *f*, empressement *m*; **to be in
a ~** être pressé/-e (**to do** de faire); **to leave
in a ~** partir à la hâte
⟦2⟧ *vtr* terminer [qch] à la hâte ⟨*meal, task*⟩;
bousculer ⟨*person*⟩
⟦3⟧ *vi* se dépêcher (**over doing** de faire); **to ~
out** sortir précipitamment
■ **hurry up** se dépêcher; **~ up!** dépêche-toi!

hurt ⟦1⟧ *adj* (gen) blessé/-e; **to feel ~** être
peiné/-e
⟦2⟧ *vtr* **(a)** (injure) **to ~ oneself** se blesser, se
faire mal; **to ~ one's back** se blesser *or* se
faire mal au dos
(b) (cause pain to) faire mal à; **you're ~ing my
arm** vous me faites mal au bras
(c) (emotionally) blesser; (offend) froisser; **to ~
sb's feelings** blesser quelqu'un
⟦3⟧ *vi* **(a)** (be painful) faire mal; **my throat ~s**
j'ai mal à la gorge
(b) (emotionally) blesser

hurtful *adj* blessant/-e

hurtle *vi* **to ~ down sth** dévaler qch; **to ~
along a road** foncer sur une route

husband *n* mari *m*; (on form) époux *m*

hush ⟦1⟧ *n* silence *m*
⟦2⟧ *excl* chut!
■ **hush up**: ¶ ~ [sth] **up** étouffer ⟨*affair*⟩
¶ ~ [sb] **up** faire taire ⟨*person*⟩

hush-hush *adj* (colloq) très
confidentiel/-ielle

hustle ⟦1⟧ *n* ~ **(and bustle)** (lively)
effervescence *f*; (tiring) agitation *f*
⟦2⟧ *vtr* pousser, bousculer ⟨*person*⟩

hut *n* (gen) cabane *f*; (dwelling) hutte *f*; (on
beach) cabine *f* (de plage)

hutch *n* (for rabbits) clapier *m*

hydrant *n* (*also* **fire ~**) bouche *f*
d'incendie

hydraulic *adj* hydraulique

hydroelectricity *n* hydroélectricité *f*

hydrofoil *n* **(a)** (craft) hydroptère *m*
(b) (foil) aile *f* portante

hydrogen *n* hydrogène *m*

hyena *n* hyène *f*

hygiene *n* hygiène *f*

hygienic *adj* hygiénique

hymn *n* cantique *m*

hype *n* (colloq) battage *m* publicitaire
■ **hype up** faire du battage pour ⟨*film, star,
book*⟩; gonfler ⟨*story*⟩

hyper *adj* (colloq) surexcité/-e

hyperactive *adj* hyperactif/-ive

hyperlink *n* lien *m* (hypertext)

hypermarket *n* (GB) hypermarché *m*

hypertext *n* hypertext *m*

hyperventilate *vi* être en
hyperventilation

hyphen *n* trait *m* d'union

hypnosis *n* hypnose *f*

hypnotherapy *n* hypnothérapie *f*

hypnotist *n* hypnotiseur *m*

hypnotize *vtr* hypnotiser

hypoallergenic *adj* hypoallergénique

hypocrisy *n* hypocrisie *f*

hypocrite *n* hypocrite *mf*

hypocritical *adj* hypocrite

hypodermic *adj* hypodermique

hypothermia *n* hypothermie *f*

hypothesis *n* hypothèse *f*

hysteria *n* hystérie *f*

hysterical *adj* **(a)** ⟨*person, behaviour*⟩
hystérique
(b) (colloq) (funny) délirant/-e

hysterics *n* **(a)** (fit) crise *f* de nerfs; **to
have ~** avoir une crise de nerfs
(b) (laughter) **to be in ~** rire aux larmes

I i

i, **I¹** *n* i, I *m*

I² *pron* je, j'; **I am called Frances** je m'appelle
Frances; **I closed the door** j'ai fermé la
porte; **he's a student but I'm not** il est
étudiant mais moi pas; **he and I went to the
cinema** lui et moi sommes allés au cinéma

ice ⟦1⟧ *n* glace *f*; (on roads) verglas *m*; (in drink)
glaçons *mpl*
⟦2⟧ *vtr* glacer ⟨*cake*⟩
⟦3⟧ **iced** *pp adj* ⟨*water*⟩ avec des glaçons;
~d tea thé glacé
■ **ice over** ⟨*windscreen, river*⟩ se couvrir de
glace

iceberg *n* iceberg *m*

icebox *n* **(a)** (GB) (freezer compartment)
freezer *m*
(b) (US) (fridge) réfrigérateur *m*

ice-cold *adj* glacé/-e

ice cream *n* glace *f*

ice-cube *n* glaçon *m*

ice hockey *n* hockey *m* sur glace

Iceland *pr n* Islande *f*

Icelandic ⟦1⟧ *n* (language) islandais *m*
⟦2⟧ *adj* ⟨*people, customs*⟩ islandais/-e

ice rink n patinoire f
ice-skate [1] n patin m à glace
[2] vi faire du patin m à glace
ice-skating n patinage m sur glace
icicle n stalactite f (de glace)
icing n glaçage m
icing sugar n (GB) sucre m glace
icon n icône f
iconize vtr (Comput) iconiser
icy adj (a) ⟨road⟩ verglacé/-e
(b) ⟨wind⟩ glacial/-e; ⟨hands⟩ glacé/-e
(c) ⟨look, reception⟩ glacial/-e
ID n pièce f d'identité
ID card n carte f d'identité
idea n idée f (about, on sur); I have no ~ je
n'ai aucune idée; to have no ~ why/how ne
pas savoir pourquoi/comment; I've an ~ that
he might be lying j'ai dans l'idée qu'il ment
ideal [1] n idéal m
[2] adj idéal/-e
idealism n idéalisme m
idealist n idéaliste mf
idealistic adj idéaliste
idealize vtr idéaliser
ideally adv (a) (preferably) ~, the tests
should be free l'idéal serait que les examens
soient gratuits; ~, we'd like to stay l'idéal
pour nous, ce serait de rester
(b) (perfectly) ~ situated idéalement situé/-e
identical adj identique (to, with à)
identical twin n vrai jumeau/vraie
jumelle m/f
identification n (a) identification f (with
à)
(b) (proof of identity) pièce f d'identité
identify [1] vtr identifier (as comme étant;
to à); (pick out) distinguer; to ~ sb/sth with
sb/sth identifier qn/qch à qn/qch
[2] vi to ~ with s'identifier à
identikit n (also **Identikit®**)
portrait-robot m
identity n identité f
identity bracelet n gourmette f
identity card n carte f d'identité
identity parade n (GB) séance f
d'identification
ideological adj idéologique
ideology n idéologie f
idiom n (a) (phrase) idiome m
(b) (language) (of speakers) parler m; (of theatre,
sport) langue f; (of music) style m
idiomatic adj idiomatique
idiosyncrasy n particularité f
idiosyncratic adj particulier/-ière
idiot n idiot/-e m/f
idiotic adj bête
idle [1] adj (a) (lazy) ⟨person⟩ paresseux/-euse
(b) ⟨boast, threat⟩ vain/-e; ⟨curiosity⟩
oiseux/-euse; ⟨chatter⟩ inutile
(c) (without occupation) ⟨person⟩ oisif/-ive; ⟨day,
hour, moment⟩ de loisir
(d) ⟨dock, mine⟩ à l'arrêt; ⟨machine⟩ arrêté/-e

[2] vi ⟨engine⟩ tourner au ralenti
■ **idle away** passer [qch] à ne rien faire
⟨day, time⟩
idol n idole f
idolize vtr adorer ⟨friend, parent⟩; idolâtrer
⟨star⟩
idyllic adj idyllique
ie (abbr = **that is**) c-à-d
if [1] conj (a) si; ~ I won a lot of money, I
would travel si je gagnais beaucoup d'argent,
je voyagerais; ~ I had known, I would have
told you si j'avais su, je te l'aurais dit; ~ I
were you, I... (moi) à ta place, je...; ~ not
sinon; I wonder ~ they will come je me
demande s'ils vont venir; do you mind ~ I
smoke? cela vous dérange si je fume?; what
~ he died? et s'il mourait?
(b) (although) bien que; it's a good shop, ~ a
little expensive c'est un bon magasin, bien
qu'un peu cher
[2] **if only** phr (a) (I wish) si seulement; ~
only I had known! si (seulement) j'avais su!
(b) ~ only because (of) ne serait-ce qu'à
cause de; ~ only for a moment ne serait-ce
que pour un instant
iffy adj (colloq) (dubious) suspect/-e
igloo n igloo m, iglou m
ignite [1] vtr faire exploser ⟨fuel⟩;
enflammer ⟨material⟩
[2] vi ⟨petrol, gas⟩ s'enflammer; ⟨rubbish,
timber⟩ prendre feu
ignition n (a) (system) allumage m
(b) (also ~ **switch**) contact m
ignition key n clé f de contact
ignorance n ignorance f
ignorant adj (of a subject) ignorant/-e;
(uneducated) inculte; to be ~ about tout
ignorer de ⟨subject⟩; to be ~ of ignorer
⟨possibilities⟩
ignore vtr ignorer ⟨person⟩; ne pas relever
⟨mistake, remark⟩; ne pas tenir compte de
⟨feeling, fact⟩; ne pas suivre ⟨advice⟩; se
désintéresser complètement de ⟨problem⟩
ill [1] n mal m; to wish sb ~ souhaiter du
mal à qn
[2] adj malade; I feel ~ je ne me sens pas
bien; to be taken ~, to fall ~ tomber malade
[3] adv he is ~ suited to the post il n'est
guère fait pour ce poste; to speak ~ of sb
dire du mal de qn
ill at ease adj gêné/-e, mal à l'aise
illegal [1] n (US) immigrant/-e m/f
clandestin/-e
[2] adj (gen) illégal/-e; ⟨parking⟩ illicite;
⟨immigrant⟩ clandestin/-e; (Sport)
irrégulier/-ière
illegally adv illégalement
illegible adj illisible
illegitimate adj illégitime
ill-equipped adj mal équipé/-e
ill-fitting adj ⟨garment, shoe⟩ qui va mal
ill-health n mauvaise santé f
illicit adj illicite
ill-informed adj mal informé/-e

illiterate *n, adj* analphabète (*mf*)
illness *n* maladie *f*
illogical *adj* illogique
ill-treatment *n* mauvais traitements *mpl*
illuminate *vtr* éclairer
illuminated *adj* ⟨*sign*⟩ lumineux/-euse
illumination *n* (lighting) éclairage *m*
illuminations *n pl* (GB) illuminations *fpl*
illusion *n* illusion *f*; to have no ∼s about sth ne pas se faire d'illusions sur qch; to be *or* to labour under the ∼ that s'imaginer que
illustrate *vtr* illustrer
illustration *n* illustration *f*
illustrator *n* illustrateur/-trice *m/f*
ill will *n* rancune *f*
image *n* (gen) image *f*; (of company, personality) image *f* de marque; he is the (spitting) ∼ of you c'est toi tout craché
image-conscious *adj* conscient/-e de son image de marque
image maker *n* professionnel/-elle *m/f* de l'image de marque
image processing *n* traitement *m* de l'image
imagery *n* images *fpl*
imaginary *adj* imaginaire
imagination *n* imagination *f*
imaginative *adj* ⟨*person, performance*⟩ plein d'imagination; ⟨*mind*⟩ imaginatif/-ive; ⟨*solution, device*⟩ ingénieux/-ieuse
imagine *vtr* (a) (visualize, picture) (s')imaginer; to ∼ being rich/king s'imaginer riche/roi; you must have ∼d it ce doit être un effet de ton imagination
(b) (suppose) supposer, imaginer (that que)
imbalance *n* déséquilibre *m*
imbecile *n, adj* imbécile (*mf*)
imitate *vtr* imiter
imitation [1] *n* imitation *f*
[2] *adj* ⟨*snow*⟩ artificiel/-ielle; ∼ **fur** imitation *f* fourrure; ∼ **jewel** faux bijou *m*; ∼ **leather** similicuir *m*
imitator *n* imitateur/-trice *m/f*
immaculate *adj* ⟨*dress, manners*⟩ impeccable; ⟨*performance*⟩ parfait/-e
immaterial *adj* (a) (unimportant) sans importance
(b) (intangible) immatériel/-ielle
immature *adj* (a) ⟨*plant*⟩ qui n'est pas arrivé à maturité
(b) (childish) immature; don't be so ∼! ne te conduis pas comme un enfant!
immediate *adj* (a) ⟨*effect, reaction*⟩ immédiat/-e; ⟨*thought*⟩ premier/-ière (*before n*)
(b) ⟨*concern, goal*⟩ premier/-ière (*before n*); ⟨*problem, crisis*⟩ urgent/-e
(c) ⟨*vicinity*⟩ immédiat/-e; his ∼ **family** ses proches; in the ∼ **future** dans l'avenir proche
immediately *adv* immédiatement; ∼ **after/before** juste avant/après
immense *adj* immense

immerse *vtr* plonger (in dans)
immersion course *n* (GB) cours *m* avec immersion linguistique
immigrant *n, adj* (recent) immigrant/-e (*m/f*); (established) immigré/-e (*m/f*)
immigration *n* immigration *f*; ∼ **laws** lois *fpl* sur l'immigration
immigration control *n* (system) contrôle *m* de l'immigration
imminent *adj* imminent/-e
immobile *adj* immobile
immobilize *vtr* paralyser ⟨*traffic, organization*⟩; immobiliser ⟨*engine, patient, limb*⟩
immobilizer *n* système *m* antidémarrage
immoral *adj* immoral/-e
immorality *n* immoralité *f*
immortal *n, adj* immortel/-elle (*m/f*)
immortality *n* immortalité *f*
immortalize *vtr* immortaliser
immune *adj* (a) (Med) ⟨*person*⟩ immunisé/-e (to contre); ⟨*reaction, system*⟩ immunitaire
(b) (oblivious) ∼ **to** insensible à
(c) to be ∼ **from** être à l'abri de ⟨*attack, arrest*⟩; être exempté/-e de ⟨*tax*⟩
immunity *n* immunité *f* (to, against contre)
immunize *vtr* immuniser
impact *n* (a) (effect) impact *m* (on sur); to make an ∼ faire de l'effet
(b) (of hammer, vehicle) choc *m*; (of bomb, bullet) impact *m*; on ∼ au moment de l'impact
impair *vtr* affecter ⟨*performance*⟩; diminuer ⟨*ability*⟩; affaiblir ⟨*hearing, vision*⟩; détériorer ⟨*health*⟩
impaired *adj* ⟨*hearing, vision*⟩ affaibli/-e; his speech is ∼ il a des problèmes d'élocution
impart *vtr* (a) transmettre ⟨*knowledge, enthusiasm*⟩ (to à); communiquer ⟨*information*⟩ (to à)
(b) donner ⟨*atmosphere*⟩
impartial *adj* ⟨*advice, judge*⟩ impartial/-e; ⟨*account*⟩ objectif/-ive
impassable *adj* ⟨*obstacle*⟩ infranchissable; ⟨*road*⟩ impraticable
impassive *adj* impassible
impatience *n* (a) (eagerness) impatience *f* (to do de faire)
(b) (irritation) agacement *m* (with à l'égard de; at devant)
impatient *adj* (a) (eager) ⟨*person*⟩ impatient/-e; ⟨*gesture, tone*⟩ d'impatience; to be ∼ **to do** être impatient/-e *or* avoir hâte de faire
(b) (irritable) agacé/-e (at par); to be/get ∼ **with sb** s'impatienter contre qn
impeach *vtr* mettre [qn] en accusation
impeccable *adj* ⟨*behaviour*⟩ irréprochable; ⟨*appearance*⟩ impeccable
impede *vtr* entraver
impending *adj* imminent/-e

impenetrable *adj* impénétrable

imperative ⓵ *n* impératif *m*
⓶ *adj* ⟨need⟩ urgent/-e; ⟨tone⟩ impérieux/-ieuse

imperceptible *adj* imperceptible

imperfect ⓵ *n* imparfait *m*
⓶ *adj* ⟨goods⟩ défectueux/-euse; ⟨logic, knowledge⟩ imparfait/-e; **the ~ tense** l'imparfait *m*

imperial *adj* (a) (gen) impérial/-e
(b) (GB) ⟨measure⟩ conforme aux normes britanniques

imperious *adj* impérieux/-ieuse

impersonal *adj* impersonnel/-elle

impersonate *vtr* (imitate) imiter; (pretend to be) se faire passer pour ⟨police officer⟩

impersonator *n* imitateur/-trice *m/f*

impertinent *adj* impertinent/-e (**to** envers)

impervious *adj* (to charm, suffering) indifférent/-e (**to** à); (to demands) imperméable (**to** à)

impetuous *adj* ⟨person⟩ impétueux/-euse; ⟨action⟩ impulsif/-ive

impetus *n* (a) impulsion *f* (**to** à)
(b) (momentum) élan *m*; **to gain/lose ~** prendre/perdre de l'élan

impinge *vi* **to ~ on** (restrict) empiéter sur; (affect) affecter

implacable *adj* implacable

implant ⓵ *n* implant *m*
⓶ *vtr* implanter (**in** dans)

implausible *adj* peu plausible

implement ⓵ *n* (gen) instrument *m*; (tool) outil *m*; **farm ~s** outillage *m* agricole
⓶ *vtr* exécuter ⟨contract, decision, idea⟩; mettre [qch] en application ⟨law⟩

implementation *n* (of contract, idea) exécution *f*; (of law, policy) mise *f* en application; (Comput) implémentation *f*

implicate *vtr* impliquer (**in** dans)

implication *n* (a) (possible consequence) implication *f*
(b) (suggestion) insinuation *f*

implicit *adj* (a) (implied) implicite (**in** dans)
(b) ⟨faith, trust⟩ absolu/-e

imply *vtr* (a) ⟨person⟩ (insinuate) insinuer (**that** que); (make known) laisser entendre (**that** que)
(b) (mean) ⟨argument⟩ impliquer; ⟨term, word⟩ laisser supposer (**that** que)

impolite *adj* impoli/-e (**to** envers)

import ⓵ *n* importation *f*
⓶ *vtr* importer (**from** de; **to** en)

importance *n* importance *f*

important *adj* important/-e; **it is ~ that** il est important que (+ *subjunctive*); **his children are very ~ to him** ses enfants comptent beaucoup pour lui

importer *n* importateur/-trice *m/f*

impose ⓵ *vtr* imposer ⟨embargo, rule⟩ (**on sb** à qn; **on sth** sur qch); infliger ⟨sanction⟩

(**on** à); **to ~ a fine on sb** frapper qn d'une amende; **to ~ a tax on tobacco** imposer le tabac
⓶ *vi* s'imposer; **to ~ on sb's kindness** abuser de la bonté de qn

imposing *adj* ⟨person⟩ imposant/-e; ⟨sight⟩ impressionnant/-e

impossible ⓵ *n* **the ~** l'impossible *m*
⓶ *adj* impossible; **to make it ~ for sb to do** mettre qn dans l'impossibilité de faire

impotent *adj* impuissant/-e

impound *vtr* emmener [qch] à la fourrière ⟨vehicle⟩; confisquer ⟨goods⟩

impractical *adj* ⟨suggestion, idea⟩ peu réaliste; **to be ~** ⟨person⟩ manquer d'esprit pratique

imprecise *adj* imprécis/-e

impress ⓵ *vtr* (a) impressionner ⟨person⟩ (**with** par; **by doing** en faisant); **they were ~ed** ça leur a fait bonne impression
(b) **to ~ sth (up)on sb** faire bien comprendre qch à qn
⓶ *vi* faire bonne impression

impression *n* (a) (gen) impression *f*; **to be under** *or* **have the ~ that** avoir l'impression que; **to make a good/bad ~** faire bonne/mauvaise impression (**on** sur)
(b) (imitation) imitation *f*; **to do ~s** faire des imitations

impressionable *adj* influençable

impressive *adj* (gen) impressionnant/-e; ⟨building, sight⟩ imposant/-e

imprint ⓵ *n* empreinte *f*
⓶ *vtr* (a) (fix) graver (**on** dans)
(b) (print) imprimer (**on** sur)

imprison *vtr* emprisonner

imprisonment *n* emprisonnement *m*

improbable *adj* (unlikely to happen) improbable; (unlikely to be true) invraisemblable

impromptu *adj* impromptu/-e

improper *adj* (dishonest) irrégulier/-ière; (indecent) indécent/-e; (incorrect) impropre, abusif/-ive

improve ⓵ *vtr* (gen) améliorer; augmenter ⟨chances⟩; **to ~ one's mind** se cultiver (l'esprit)
⓶ *vi* (a) s'améliorer
(b) **to ~ on** améliorer ⟨score⟩; renchérir sur ⟨offer⟩

improvement *n* (a) amélioration *f* (**in, of, to** de); **the new edition is an ~ on the old one** la nouvelle édition est bien meilleure que l'ancienne
(b) (in house) aménagement *m*; **home ~s** aménagements *mpl* du domicile

improvise ⓵ *vtr* improviser; **an ~d table** une table de fortune
⓶ *vi* improviser

impudent *adj* insolent/-e, impudent/-e

impulse *n* impulsion *f*; **to have a sudden ~ to do** avoir une envie soudaine de faire; **on (an) ~** sur un coup de tête

impulse buy *n* achat *m* d'impulsion

impulsive *adj* (spontaneous) spontané/-e;
(rash) impulsif/-ive

impure *adj* impur/-e

in [1] *prep* (a) (inside) dans; ∼ **the box** dans la
boîte; ∼ **the newspaper** dans le journal; ∼
the school/town dans l'école/la ville; ∼
school/town à l'école/en ville; ∼ **the
country(side)** à la campagne; ∼ **the photo**
sur la photo; **chicken** ∼ **a white wine sauce**
du poulet à la sauce au vin blanc; ∼ **Rome** à
Rome; ∼ **France/Spain** en France/Espagne;
∼ **Canada/the United States** au Canada/aux
États-Unis
(b) (showing occupation, activity) dans; ∼
insurance dans les assurances; **to be** ∼
politics faire de la politique; **to be** ∼ **the
team** faire partie de l'équipe
(c) (present in) chez; **it's rare** ∼ **cats** c'est rare
chez les chats; **he hasn't got it** ∼ **him to
succeed** il n'est pas fait pour réussir
(d) (showing manner, medium) en; ∼ **Greek** en
grec; ∼ **B flat** en si bémol; ∼ **a skirt** en jupe;
dressed ∼ **black** habillé/-e en noir; ∼
pencil/ink au crayon/à l'encre; **to speak** ∼ **a
whisper** chuchoter; ∼ **pairs** par deux; ∼ **a
circle** en cercle; ∼ **the rain** sous la pluie
(e) (as regards) **rich** ∼ **minerals** riche en
minéraux; **deaf** ∼ **one ear** sourd/-e d'une
oreille; **10 cm** ∼ **length** 10 cm de long
(f) (because of) dans; ∼ **his hurry** dans sa
précipitation; ∼ **the confusion** dans la mêlée
(g) (with present participle) en; ∼ **accepting** en
acceptant; ∼ **doing so** en faisant cela
(h) (with superlatives) de; **the tallest tower** ∼
the world la plus grande tour du monde
(i) (in ratios) **a gradient of 1** ∼ **4** une pente de
25%; **a tax of 20 pence** ∼ **the pound** une
taxe de 20 pence par livre sterling; **to have a
one** ∼ **five chance** avoir une chance sur
cinq
(j) (with numbers) **she's** ∼ **her twenties** elle a
entre vingt et trente ans; **to cut sth** ∼ **three**
couper qch en trois; **the temperature was** ∼
the thirties il faisait dans les trente degrés
(k) (during) ∼ **May** en mai; ∼ **1963** en 1963; ∼
summer en été; ∼ **the night** pendant la nuit;
∼ **the morning(s)** le matin; **at four** ∼ **the
morning** à quatre heures du matin; ∼ **the
twenties** dans les années 20
(l) (within) ∼ **ten minutes** en dix minutes; **I'll
be back** ∼ **half an hour** je serai de retour
dans une demi-heure
(m) (for) depuis; **it hasn't rained** ∼ **weeks** il
n'a pas plu depuis des semaines
[2] *adv* (a) **to come** ∼ entrer; **to run** ∼
entrer en courant; **to ask** *or* **invite sb** ∼
faire entrer qn
(b) (at home) **to be** ∼ être là; **to stay** ∼ rester
à la maison
(c) (arrived) **the train is** ∼ le train est en gare;
the ferry is ∼ le ferry est à quai
(d) **the tide is** ∼ c'est marée haute
(e) (Sport) **the ball is** ∼ la balle est bonne
(f) (in supply) **we don't have any** ∼ nous n'en
avons pas en stock; **to get some beer** ∼ aller
chercher de la bière

[3] *adj* (colloq) **to be** ∼, **to be the** ∼ **thing** être
à la mode
[4] **in and out** *phr* **to come** ∼ **and out**
entrer et sortir; **to weave** ∼ **and out of** se
faufiler entre ⟨*traffic, tables*⟩
IDIOMS **he's** ∼ **for a shock/surprise** il va
avoir un choc/être surpris

inability *n* incapacité *f* (**to do** de faire)

inaccessible *adj* (out of reach)
inaccessible; (hard to understand) peu
accessible (**to** à)

inaccuracy *n* (a) (of report, estimate)
inexactitude *f*
(b) (error) inexactitude *f*

inaccurate *adj* inexact/-e

inactive *adj* inactif/-ive

inadequate *adj* insuffisant/-e (**for** pour)

inadvisable *adj* inopportun/-e, à
déconseiller

inane *adj* ⟨person, conversation⟩ idiot/-e;
⟨programme⟩ débile (colloq)

inanimate *adj* inanimé/-e

inappropriate *adj* (a) ⟨behaviour⟩
inconvenant/-e, peu convenable; ⟨remark⟩
inopportun/-e
(b) ⟨advice, word⟩ qui n'est pas approprié

inarticulate *adj* (a) **to be** ∼ ne pas
savoir s'exprimer
(b) ⟨mumble⟩ inarticulé/-e; ⟨speech⟩
inintelligible

inasmuch: **inasmuch as** *phr* (insofar as)
dans la mesure où; (seeing as) vu que

inattentive *adj* ⟨pupil⟩ inattentif/-ive

inaudible *adj* inaudible

inauguration *n* (of exhibition) inauguration
f; (of president) investiture *f*

in-between *adj* intermédiaire

inbuilt *adj* intrinsèque

incapable *adj* incapable (**of doing** de
faire)

incapacitate *vtr* ⟨accident, illness⟩
immobiliser

incendiary device *n* engin *m*
incendiaire

incense *n* encens *m*

incensed *adj* outré/-e (**at** de; **by** par)

incentive *n* (a) **to give sb the** ∼ **to do**
donner envie à qn de faire; **there is no** ∼ **for
people to save** rien n'incite les gens à faire
des économies
(b) (also **cash** ∼) prime *f*

incentive scheme *n* système *m* de
primes d'encouragement

incessant *adj* incessant/-e

incessantly *adv* sans cesse

incest *n* inceste *m*

incestuous *adj* incestueux/-euse

inch *n* (a) pouce *m* (= 2.54 cm)
(b) ∼ **by** ∼ petit à petit; **to come within an**
∼ **of winning** passer à deux doigts de la
victoire

incidence *n* the ~ of la fréquence de ⟨*thefts, deaths*⟩; **high/low** ~ **of sth** taux élevé/ faible de qch

incident *n* incident *m*

incidental *adj* ⟨*detail, remark*⟩ secondaire

incidentally *adv* (by the way) à propos; (by chance) par la même occasion

incident room *n* bureau *m* des enquêteurs

incinerate *vtr* incinérer

incite *vtr* **to** ~ **violence** inciter à la violence; **to** ~ **sb to do** pousser *or* inciter qn à faire

inclination *n* inclination *f*

incline ⊥ *vtr* (a) incliner ⟨*head*⟩
(b) **to be** ~**d to do** avoir tendance à faire; **if you feel so** ~**d** si l'envie vous en prend
② *vi* (a) (tend) **to** ~ **to** *or* **towards** tendre vers
(b) ⟨*road, tower*⟩ s'incliner

include *vtr* inclure, comprendre; **all the ministers, Blanc** ~**d** tous les ministres, Blanc inclu; **breakfast is** ~**d in the price** le petit déjeuner est compris

including *prep* (y) compris; **£50** ~ **VAT** 50 livres sterling TVA comprise; ~ **service** service compris; ~ **July** y compris juillet; **not** ~ **July** sans compter juillet

inclusive *adj* inclus/-e; ⟨*price*⟩ forfaitaire; **all-**~ tout compris

incoherent *adj* incohérent/-e

income *n* revenus *mpl*, revenu *m*

income bracket *n* tranche *f* de revenu

income tax *n* impôt *m* sur le revenu

incoming *adj* ⟨*call, mail*⟩ qui vient de l'extérieur; ⟨*government*⟩ nouveau/-elle; ⟨*tide*⟩ montant/-e

incomparable *adj* sans pareil/-eille

incompatible *adj* incompatible

incompetent *adj* ⟨*doctor, government*⟩ incompétent/-e; ⟨*work, performance*⟩ mauvais/-e (*before n*)

incomplete *adj* (a) ⟨*work, building*⟩ inachevé/-e
(b) ⟨*set*⟩ incomplet/-ète

incomprehensible *adj* ⟨*reason*⟩ incompréhensible; ⟨*speech*⟩ inintelligible

inconceivable *adj* inconcevable

inconclusive *adj* ⟨*meeting*⟩ sans conclusion véritable; ⟨*evidence*⟩ peu concluant/-e

incongruous *adj* ⟨*sight*⟩ déconcertant/-e; ⟨*appearance*⟩ surprenant/-e

inconsiderate *adj* ⟨*person*⟩ peu attentif/-ive à autrui; ⟨*remark*⟩ maladroit/-e; **to be** ~ **towards sb** manquer d'égards envers qn

inconsistent *adj* ⟨*work*⟩ inégal/-e; ⟨*behaviour*⟩ changeant/-e; ⟨*argument*⟩ incohérent/-e; ⟨*attitude*⟩ inconsistant/-e; **to be** ~ **with** être en contradiction avec

inconspicuous *adj* ⟨*person*⟩ qui passe inaperçu/-e; ⟨*place, clothing*⟩ discret/-ète

inconvenience ⊥ *n* (a) (trouble) dérangement *m*; **to put sb to great** ~ causer beaucoup de dérangement à qn
(b) (disadvantage) inconvénient *m*
② *vtr* déranger

inconvenient *adj* ⟨*location, arrangement*⟩ incommode; ⟨*time*⟩ inopportun/-e

incorporate *vtr* (a) (make part of) incorporer (**into** dans)
(b) (contain) comporter
(c) **Smith and Brown Incorporated** Smith et Brown SA

incorrect *adj* incorrect/-e (**to do** de faire)

incorrigible *adj* incorrigible

increase ⊥ *n* (a) (in amount) augmentation *f* (**in, of** de); **a 5%** ~ une augmentation de 5%
(b) (in degree) accroissement *m*; **to be on the** ~ être en progression
② *vtr* augmenter (**by** de; **to** jusqu'à)
③ *vi* augmenter (**by** de); **to** ~ **in value** prendre de la valeur; **to** ~ **in size** s'agrandir

increased *adj* ⟨*demand, risk*⟩ accru/-e

increasing *adj* ⟨*number*⟩ croissant/-e

increasingly *adv* de plus en plus

incredible *adj* incroyable

incredulous *adj* incrédule

incriminating *adj* ⟨*statement, document*⟩ compromettant/-e; ⟨*evidence*⟩ incriminant/-e

incubator *n* (for child) couveuse *f*; (for eggs, bacteria) incubateur *m*

incur *vtr* contracter ⟨*debts*⟩; subir ⟨*loss*⟩; encourir ⟨*expense, risk, wrath*⟩

incurable *adj* (a) ⟨*disease*⟩ incurable
(b) ⟨*optimist, romantic*⟩ incorrigible

incursion *n* (gen) intrusion *f*; (Mil) incursion *f*

indebted *adj* **to be** ~ **to sb** (under an obligation) être redevable à qn; (grateful) être reconnaissant/-e à qn

indecent *adj* (a) (improper) indécent/-e
(b) (unreasonable) ⟨*haste*⟩ malséant/-e

indecent assault *n* attentat *m* à la pudeur

indecent exposure *n* outrage *m* public à la pudeur

indecisive *adj* (gen) indécis/-e (**about** quant à); ⟨*battle, election*⟩ peu concluant/-e

indeed *adv* (a) (certainly) en effet, effectivement; **yes** ~! bien sûr que oui!; '~ **you can**' 'bien sûr que oui'
(b) (in fact) en fait
(c) (for emphasis) vraiment; **that was praise** ~ c'était vraiment un compliment; **thank you very much** ~ merci mille fois

indefinite *adj* (a) (vague) vague
(b) ⟨*period, delay*⟩ illimité/-e; ⟨*number*⟩ indéterminé/-e
(c) **the** ~ **article** l'article *m* indéfini

indefinitely *adv* ⟨*continue, stay*⟩ indéfiniment; ⟨*postpone, ban*⟩ pour une durée indéterminée

indelible *adj* ⟨*ink, mark*⟩ indélébile; ⟨*impression*⟩ ineffaçable

independence *n* indépendance *f*

Independence Day *n* (US) fête *f* de l'Indépendance

independent *adj* indépendant/-e (**of** de)

in-depth ⓵ *adj* ⟨*analysis, study*⟩ approfondi/-e; ⟨*guide*⟩ détaillé/-e
⓶ **in depth** *adv* ⟨*examine, study*⟩ en détail

indescribable *adj* ⟨*chaos, noise*⟩ indescriptible; ⟨*pleasure, beauty*⟩ inexprimable

indestructible *adj* indestructible

index *n* (a) (of book) index *m inv*
(b) (catalogue) catalogue *m*; **card** ~ fichier *m*
(c) (Econ) indice *m*

index card *n* fiche *f*

index finger *n* index *m inv*

index-linked *adj* indexé/-e

India *pr n* Inde *f*

Indian ⓵ *n* (a) (from India) Indien/-ienne *m/f*
(b) (Native American) Indien/-ienne *m/f* d'Amérique
⓶ *adj* (a) (of India) indien/-ienne
(b) (Native American) indien/-ienne, amérindien/-ienne

Indian Ocean *pr n* **the** ~ l'océan *m* Indien

Indian summer *n* été *m* de la Saint Martin

indicate ⓵ *vtr* indiquer (**that** que; **with** de)
⓶ *vi* ⟨*driver*⟩ mettre son clignotant; ⟨*cyclist*⟩ faire signe

indication *n* indication *f*, indice *m*

indicative ⓵ *n* (in grammar) indicatif *m*
⓶ *adj* **to be** ~ **of** montrer

indicator *n* (a) (pointer) aiguille *f*
(b) (board) tableau *m*
(c) (on car) clignotant *m*

indict *vtr* inculper

indictment *n* (a) (Law) acte *m* d'accusation
(b) (criticism) mise *f* en accusation

indie *adj* (colloq) (Mus) indépendant/-e

indifference *n* indifférence *f*

indifferent *adj* (a) (uninterested) indifférent/-e (**to, as to** à)
(b) (mediocre) médiocre

indigenous *adj* indigène (**to** à)

indigestion *n* indigestion *f*; **to have** ~ avoir des brûlures d'estomac

indignant *adj* indigné/-e (**at** de; **about**, **over** par)

indigo *n, adj* indigo (*m*) *inv*

indirect *adj* indirect/-e

indirectly *adv* indirectement

indirect speech *n* discours *m* indirect

indiscreet *adj* indiscret/-ète

indiscretion *n* (lack of discretion) manque *m* de discrétion; (act) indiscrétion *f*

indiscriminate *adj* (a) (random) sans distinction
(b) ⟨*person*⟩ sans discernement

indispensable *adj* indispensable

indisputable *adj* ⟨*champion*⟩ indiscuté/-e; ⟨*fact*⟩ indiscutable

indistinct *adj* ⟨*sound, markings*⟩ indistinct/-e; ⟨*memory*⟩ confus/-e; ⟨*photograph*⟩ flou/-e

individual ⓵ *n* individu *m*
⓶ *adj* (a) ⟨*effort, freedom, portion*⟩ individuel/-elle; ⟨*comfort, attitude*⟩ personnel/-elle; ⟨*tuition*⟩ particulier/-ière
(b) (separate) **each** ~ **article** chaque article (individuellement)
(c) (idiosyncratic) particulier/-ière

individuality *n* individualité *f*

individually *adv* (personally, in person) individuellement; (one at a time) séparément

indoctrinate *vtr* endoctriner

Indonesia *pr n* Indonésie *f*

indoor *adj* ⟨*pool, court*⟩ couvert/-e; ⟨*lavatory*⟩ à l'intérieur; ⟨*photography, shoes*⟩ d'intérieur; ⟨*sports facilities*⟩ en salle

indoors *adv* à l'intérieur, dans la maison; ~ **and outdoors** dedans et dehors; **to go** ~ rentrer

induce *vtr* (a) (persuade) persuader (**to do** de faire); (stronger) inciter (**to** à; **to do** à faire)
(b) (bring about) provoquer

induction course *n* stage *m* d'introduction

induction loop *n* boucle *f* magnétique

indulge ⓵ *vtr* (a) céder à ⟨*whim, desire*⟩
(b) gâter ⟨*child*⟩; céder à ⟨*adult*⟩
⓶ *vi* **to** ~ **in** se livrer à ⟨*speculation*⟩; se complaire dans ⟨*nostalgia*⟩; se laisser tenter par ⟨*food*⟩
⓷ *v refl* **to** ~ **oneself** se faire plaisir

indulgence *n* (a) (tolerance) indulgence *f* (**towards** envers; **for** pour)
(b) ~ **in food** gourmandise *f*; **it's my one** ~ c'est mon péché mignon

indulgent *adj* indulgent/-e (**to, towards** pour, envers)

industrial *adj* (gen) industriel/-ielle; ⟨*accident*⟩ du travail

industrial action *n* (GB) (strike) grève *f*

industrial estate *n* zone *f* industrielle

industrialize *vtr* industrialiser

industrial relations *n pl* relations *fpl* entre les patrons et les ouvriers

industrial waste *n* déchets *mpl* industriels

industrious *adj* diligent/-e

industry *n* (a) industrie *f*; **the oil** ~ l'industrie du pétrole
(b) (diligence) zèle *m* (au travail)

inedible *adj* ⟨*meal*⟩ immangeable; ⟨*plants*⟩ non comestible

ineffective *adj* inefficace

ineffectual *adj* ⟨*person*⟩ incapable; ⟨*policy*⟩ inefficace; ⟨*attempt*⟩ infructueux/-euse

inefficiency *n* (lack of organization) manque ⸬

m d'organisation; (incompetence) incompétence *f*; (of machine, method) inefficacité *f*

inefficient *adj* (disorganized) mal organisé/-e; (incompetent) incompétent/-e; (not effective) inefficace

ineligible *adj* to be ~ (for job) ne pas remplir les conditions pour poser sa candidature (**for** à); (for election) être inéligible; (for pension, benefit) ne pas avoir droit (**for** à)

inequality *n* inégalité *f*

inert *adj* inerte

inertia *n* inertie *f*

inevitable *adj* inévitable (**that** que + *subjunctive*)

inexcusable *adj* inexcusable (**that** que + *subjunctive*)

inexhaustible *adj* inépuisable

inexpensive *adj* pas cher/chère

inexperienced *adj* inexpérimenté/-e

inexplicable *adj* inexplicable

infallible *adj* infaillible

infamous *adj* ⟨person⟩ tristement célèbre; ⟨crime⟩ infâme

infancy *n* (a) petite enfance *f* (b) (figurative) débuts *mpl*; **in its** ~ à ses débuts

infant *n* (baby) bébé *m*; (child) petit enfant *m*

infantry *n* infanterie *f*, fantassins *mpl*

infant school *n* ≈ école *f* maternelle

infatuated *adj* **to be** ~ **with** être entiché/-e de

infatuation *n* engouement *m* (**with** pour)

infect *vtr* contaminer ⟨person, blood, food⟩; infecter ⟨wound⟩

infection *n* infection *f*

infectious *adj* (a) ⟨disease⟩ infectieux/-ieuse; ⟨person⟩ contagieux/-ieuse (b) ⟨laughter⟩ communicatif/-ive

infer *vtr* déduire

inferior ⊞ *n* inférieur/-e *m/f* ⊡ *adj* (a) ⟨goods, work⟩ de qualité inférieure (b) ⟨position⟩ inférieur/-e; **to make sb feel** ~ donner un sentiment d'infériorité à qn

inferiority *n* infériorité *f* (**to** vis-à-vis de)

inferiority complex *n* complexe *m* d'infériorité

inferno *n* brasier *m*

infertile *adj* ⟨land⟩ infertile; ⟨person⟩ stérile

infertility *n* stérilité *f*

infest *vtr* infester (**with** de)

infidelity *n* infidélité *f*

infighting *n* conflits *mpl* internes

infiltrate *vtr* infiltrer ⟨organization, group⟩

infinite *adj* infini/-e

infinitely *adv* infiniment

infinitive *n* infinitif *m*; **in the** ~ à l'infinitif

infinity *n* infini *m*

infirmary *n* (a) (hospital) hôpital *m* (b) (in school, prison) infirmerie *f*

inflamed *adj* (Med) enflammé/-e

inflammable *adj* inflammable

inflammation *n* inflammation *f*

inflatable *adj* ⟨mattress, dinghy⟩ pneumatique; ⟨toy⟩ gonflable

inflate *vtr* gonfler ⟨tyre, dinghy⟩

inflation *n* inflation *f*

inflexible *adj* (a) ⟨person, attitude⟩ inflexible; ⟨system⟩ rigide (b) ⟨material⟩ rigide

inflict *vtr* infliger ⟨pain, presence, defeat⟩ (**on** à); causer ⟨damage⟩ (**on** à)

influence ⊞ *n* influence *f*; **to be** or **have an** ~ **on** avoir une influence sur; **to drive while under the** ~ **of alcohol** conduire en état d'ébriété ⊡ *vtr* influencer ⟨person⟩ (**in** dans); influer sur ⟨decision, choice, result⟩; **to be** ~**d by sb/ sth** se laisser influencer par qn/qch

influential *adj* influent/-e

influenza *n* grippe *f*

influx *n* afflux *m*

info *n* (colloq) renseignements *mpl*, tuyaux *mpl* (colloq)

inform ⊞ *vtr* informer, avertir (**of, about** de; **that** du fait que); **to keep sb** ~**ed** tenir qn informé/-e or au courant (**of, as to** de) ⊡ *vi* **to** ~ **on** or **against** dénoncer

informal *adj* (a) ⟨person⟩ sans façons; ⟨manner, style⟩ simple; ⟨language⟩ familier/-ière; ⟨clothes⟩ de tous les jours (b) ⟨visit⟩ privé/-e; ⟨invitation⟩ verbal/-e; ⟨discussion, interview⟩ informel/-elle

information *n* (a) renseignements *mpl*, informations *fpl* (**on, about** sur); **a piece of** ~ un renseignement, une information (b) (US) (service *m* des) renseignements *mpl*

information desk, information office *n* bureau *m* des renseignements

information pack *n* documentation *f*

information superhighway *n* autoroutes *fpl* de l'information

information technology, IT *n* informatique *f*

informative *adj* instructif/-ive

informer *n* indicateur/-trice *m/f*

infrared *adj* infrarouge

infrastructure *n* infrastructure *f*

infringe ⊞ *vtr* enfreindre ⟨rule⟩; ne pas respecter ⟨rights⟩ ⊡ *vi* **to** ~ **on** or **upon** empiéter sur ⟨rights⟩

infringement *n* (of rule) infraction *f* (**of** à); (of rights) violation *f*

infuriating *adj* exaspérant/-e

ingenious *adj* ingénieux/-ieuse, astucieux/-ieuse

ingenuity *n* ingéniosité *f*

ingenuous *adj* ingénu/-e, candide

ingot *n* lingot *m*

ingrained *adj* ⟨dirt⟩ bien incrusté/-e; ⟨habit, hatred⟩ enraciné/-e

ingratitude *n* ingratitude *f*

ingredient *n* (Culin) ingrédient *m*; (figurative) élément *m* (**of** de)

inhabit *vtr* (a) habiter ⟨house, region, planet⟩
(b) vivre dans ⟨fantasy world⟩

inhabitant *n* habitant/-e *m/f*

inhale ⟨1⟩ *vtr* aspirer, inhaler
⟨2⟩ *vi* (breathe in) inspirer; (smoke) avaler la fumée

inhaler *n* inhalateur *m*

inherent *adj* inhérent/-e (**to** à)

inherit *vtr* hériter de ⟨money, property, title⟩; **to ~ sth from sb** hériter qch de qn

inheritance *n* héritage *m*; **to come into an ~** faire un héritage

inhibit *vtr* inhiber ⟨person, reaction⟩; entraver ⟨activity, progress⟩

inhibited *adj* inhibé/-e, refoulé/-e

inhibition *n* inhibition *f*; **to get rid of one's ~s** se libérer de ses inhibitions

inhospitable *adj* inhospitalier/-ière

in-house *adj* interne

inhuman *adj* inhumain/-e

inhumanity *n* inhumanité *f* (**to** envers)

initial ⟨1⟩ *n* initiale *f*
⟨2⟩ *adj* initial/-e; **~ letter** initiale *f*
⟨3⟩ *vtr* parapher, parafer

initially *adv* au départ

initiate ⟨1⟩ *n* initié/-e *m/f*
⟨2⟩ *vtr* (a) mettre en œuvre ⟨project, reform⟩; amorcer ⟨talks⟩; entamer, engager ⟨proceedings⟩
(b) (teach) **to ~ sb into** initier qn à

initiative *n* initiative *f*; **on one's own ~** de son propre chef

inject *vtr* injecter ⟨vaccine⟩ (**into** dans); **to ~ sb (with sth)** faire une injection *or* une piqûre (de qch) à qn

injection *n* (a) (Med) piqûre *f*
(b) (Tech) injection *f*

injure *vtr* (a) blesser ⟨person⟩; **to ~ one's hand** se blesser la main
(b) nuire à, compromettre ⟨health, reputation⟩

injured ⟨1⟩ *n* **the ~** les blessés *mpl*
⟨2⟩ *adj* (a) (gen) blessé/-e
(b) (Law) **the ~ party** la partie lésée

injury *n* blessure *f*; **head injuries** blessures à la tête

injury time *n* (Sport) arrêts *mpl* de jeu

injustice *n* injustice *f*

ink *n* encre *f*; **in ~** à l'encre

inkjet printer *n* imprimante *f* à jet d'encre

inkling *n* petite idée *f*; **to have an ~ that** avoir idée que

inland ⟨1⟩ *adj* intérieur/-e
⟨2⟩ *adv* ⟨travel, lie⟩ à l'intérieur des terres

Inland Revenue *n* (GB) service *m* des impôts britannique

in-laws *n pl* (parents) beaux-parents *mpl*; (other relatives) belle-famille *f*, parents *mpl* par alliance

inmate *n* (of mental hospital) interné/-e *m/f*; (of prison) détenu/-e *m/f*

inn *n* (a) (hotel) auberge *f*
(b) (pub) pub *m*

inner *adj* intérieur/-e

inner city ⟨1⟩ **the ~** les quartiers *mpl* déshérités
⟨2⟩ **inner-city** *n* ⟨problems⟩ des quartiers déshérités; ⟨area⟩ déshérité/-e

innermost *adj* **sb's ~ thoughts** les pensées les plus intimes de qn

innocence *n* innocence *f*

innocent *n, adj* innocent/-e (*m/f*)

innovation *n* innovation *f*

innovative *adj* innovateur/-trice

innovator *n* innovateur/-trice *m/f*

innuendo *n* (veiled slights) insinuations *fpl*; (sexual references) allusions *fpl* grivoises

inoculation *n* vaccination *f*, inoculation *f*

inoffensive *adj* inoffensif/-ive

in-patient *n* malade *mf* hospitalisé/-e

input *n* (a) (of money) apport *m*; (of energy) alimentation *f* (**of** en)
(b) (contribution) contribution *f*
(c) (Comput) (data) données *fpl* d'entrée *or* à traiter

inquest *n* enquête *f* (**on, into** sur)

inquire = ENQUIRE

inquiry *n* enquête *f* (**into** sur); **murder ~** enquête criminelle; ▶ ENQUIRE

inquisitive *adj* curieux/-ieuse

insane *adj* (gen) fou/folle; (Law) aliéné/-e

insanitary *adj* insalubre, malsain/-e

insanity *n* (gen) folie *f*; (Law) aliénation *f* mentale

insatiable *adj* insatiable

inscription *n* inscription *f*

insect *n* insecte *m*; **~ bite** piqûre *f* d'insecte

insecticide *n, adj* insecticide (*m*)

insect repellent *n* insectifuge *m*, produit *m* anti-insecte

insecure *adj* (a) ⟨person⟩ qui manque d'assurance
(b) ⟨job⟩ précaire; ⟨investment⟩ risqué/-e

insecurity *n* (a) (psychological) manque *m* d'assurance
(b) (of position, situation) insécurité *f*

insensitive *adj* ⟨person⟩ (tactless) sans tact; (unfeeling) insensible (**to** à); ⟨remark⟩ indélicat/-e

inseparable *adj* inséparable (**from** de)

insert *vtr* insérer (**in** dans)

inside ⟨1⟩ *n* intérieur *m*; **to overtake on the ~** (in Europe, US) doubler à droite; (in GB, Australia) doubler à gauche; **people on the ~** les gens qui sont dans la place
⟨2⟩ *prep* (also (US) **~ of**) (a) à l'intérieur de; **~ the box** à l'intérieur de *or* dans la boîte; **to be ~ (the house)** être à l'intérieur (de la maison)
(b) (under) **~ (of) an hour** en moins d'une heure
⟨3⟩ *adj* (a) ⟨cover, pocket⟩ intérieur/-e; ⟨toilet⟩ à l'intérieur ···>

(b) ⟨*information*⟩ de première main
(c) the ~ **lane** (of road) (in Europe, US) la voie de droite; (in GB, Australia) la voie de gauche; (of athletics track) le couloir intérieur
4 *adv* (indoors) à l'intérieur; (in a container) à l'intérieur, dedans; **she's ~** elle est à l'intérieur; **to look ~** regarder à l'intérieur *or* dedans; **to go** *or* **come ~** entrer; **to bring sth ~** rentrer ⟨*chairs*⟩
5 **inside out** *phr* à l'envers; **to turn sth ~ out** retourner qch; **to know sb/sth ~ out** connaître qn/qch à fond
insider dealing *n* délit *m* d'initié
insides *n pl* (colloq) (of human) intestin *m*, estomac *m*, boyaux *mpl* (colloq)
insight *n* **(a)** (glimpse, understanding) aperçu *m*, idée *f* (into de)
(b) (intuition) perspicacité *f*, intuition *f*
insignificant *adj* ⟨*cost, difference*⟩ négligeable; ⟨*person, detail*⟩ insignifiant/-e
insincere *adj* peu sincère; **to be ~** manquer de sincérité
insinuate *vtr* insinuer (**that** que)
insinuation *n* insinuation *f*
insipid *adj* fade
insist **1** *vtr* **(a)** (demand) insister (**that** pour que)
(b) (maintain) affirmer (**that** que)
2 *vi* insister; **to ~ on** exiger ⟨*punctuality, silence*⟩; **to ~ on doing** vouloir à tout prix faire, tenir à faire
insistent *adj* **to be ~** insister (**about** sur; **that** pour que + *subjunctive*)
insofar: insofar as *phr* ~ **as** dans la mesure où
insole *n* semelle *f* (intérieure)
insolent *adj* insolent/-e
insomnia *n* insomnie *f*
inspect *vtr* examiner [qch] de près ⟨*document, product*⟩; contrôler, vérifier ⟨*accounts*⟩; inspecter ⟨*school, factory, pitch, wiring*⟩; contrôler ⟨*passport, ticket, baggage*⟩
inspection *n* (gen) inspection *f*; (of ticket, passport) contrôle *m*; **on closer ~** en y regardant de plus près
inspector *n* **(a)** (gen) inspecteur/-trice *m/f*
(b) (GB) **police ~** inspecteur *m* de police
(c) (GB) (on bus) contrôleur/-euse *m/f*
inspiration *n* inspiration *f* (**for** pour)
inspire *vtr* inspirer; **to be ~d by sth** s'inspirer de qch
inspired *adj* ⟨*person*⟩ inspiré/-e; ⟨*idea*⟩ lumineux/-euse; **an ~ guess** une heureuse inspiration
inspiring *adj* ⟨*person, speech*⟩ enthousiasmant/-e; ⟨*thought*⟩ exaltant/-e
instal(l) *vtr* **(a)** installer ⟨*equipment, software*⟩; poser ⟨*windows*⟩
(b) **to ~ sb in office** installer qn
installation *n* installation *f*
instalment (GB), **installment** (US) *n* versement *m* partiel; **in ~s** en plusieurs versements
instance *n* exemple *m*; **for ~** par exemple

instant **1** *n* instant *m*; **come here this ~!** viens ici tout de suite!
2 *adj* ⟨*access, effect, rapport, success*⟩ immédiat/-e; ⟨*solution*⟩ instantané/-e
(b) ⟨*coffee, soup*⟩ instantané/-e
instant camera *n* polaroïd® *m*
instantly *adv* immédiatement
instead **1** *adv* we didn't go home—we went to the park ~ au lieu de rentrer nous sommes allés au parc; **let's take a taxi ~** prenons plutôt un taxi; **I was going to phone but wrote ~** j'allais téléphoner mais finalement j'ai écrit; **her son went ~** son fils y est allé à sa place
2 **instead of** *phr* ~ **of sth/of doing** au lieu de qch/de faire; **use oil ~ of butter** utilisez de l'huile à la place du beurre; **~ of sb** à la place de qn
instep *n* cou-de-pied *m*
instigate *vtr* lancer ⟨*attack*⟩; engager ⟨*proceedings*⟩
instil (GB), **instill** (US) *vtr* inculquer ⟨*attitude*⟩ (**in** à); donner ⟨*confidence*⟩ (**in** à)
instinct *n* instinct *m* (**for** de)
instinctive *adj* instinctif/-ive
institute **1** *n* institut *m*
2 *vtr* instituer
institution *n* **(a)** (gen) institution *f*; **financial ~** organisme *m* financier
(b) (home, hospital) établissement *m* spécialisé
institutionalize *vtr* **(a)** (place in care) placer [qn] dans un établissement spécialisé; (in mental hospital) interner
(b) (establish officially) institutionnaliser; **~d** ⟨*racism, violence*⟩ institutionnalisé/-e
instruct *vtr* **(a)** **to ~ sb to do** donner l'ordre à qn de faire; **to be ~ed to do** recevoir l'ordre de faire
(b) (teach) instruire; **to ~ sb in** enseigner [qch] à qn ⟨*subject*⟩
instruction *n* instruction *f*; **~s for use** mode *m* d'emploi
instruction book *n* livret *m* de l'utilisateur
instructor *n* **(a)** (in sports, driving) moniteur/-trice *m/f* (**in** de); (military) instructeur *m*
(b) (US) professeur *m*
instrument *n* instrument *m*; **to play an ~** jouer d'un instrument
instrumental **1** *n* instrumental *m*
2 *adj* **(a)** **to be ~ in sth/in doing** contribuer à qch/à faire
(b) (Mus) instrumental/-e
instrument panel *n* tableau *m* de bord
insufficient *adj* there are ~ **copies** il n'y a pas assez d'exemplaires; **to be ~ for** être insuffisant/-e pour
insulate *vtr* isoler ⟨*roof, room, wire*⟩
insulation *n* isolation *f*
insulin *n* insuline *f*
insult **1** *n* insulte *f*
2 *vtr* insulter

insurance n assurance f (**against** contre; **for** pour); **to take out ~ against sth** s'assurer contre qch

insurance policy n (police f d')assurance f

insure vtr assurer (**against** contre)

intact adj intact/-e

intake n (a) (consumption) consommation f (b) (Sch, Univ) (admissions) admissions fpl (c) **an ~ of breath** une inspiration f

intangible adj insaisissable

integral adj intégral/-e; ⟨part⟩ intégrant/-e; **~ to** intrinsèque à

integrate ① vtr (a) (incorporate, absorb) intégrer (**into** dans; **with** à) (b) (combine) combiner ⟨systems⟩ ② vi ⟨person⟩ s'intégrer (**with** à; **into** dans)

integration n intégration f (**with** à)

integrity n intégrité f

intellect n (a) (mental capacity) intelligence f (b) (person) esprit m

intellectual n, adj intellectuel/-elle (m/f)

intelligence n (a) intelligence f (**to do** de faire) (b) (gen, Mil) (information) renseignements mpl (c) (Mil) (secret service) services mpl de renseignements

intelligent adj intelligent/-e

intelligible adj intelligible (**to** à)

intend vtr vouloir; **to ~ to do, to ~ doing** avoir l'intention de faire; **to be ~ed for** être destiné-e à ⟨person⟩; être prévu/-e pour ⟨purpose⟩

intense adj (a) (gen) intense (b) ⟨person⟩ sérieux/-ieuse

intensify ① vtr intensifier ② vi s'intensifier

intensive adj intensif/-ive

intensive care n **in ~** en réanimation

intensive care unit n service m de soins intensifs

intent adj ⟨person, expression⟩ absorbé/-e; **~ on doing** résolu/-e à faire IDIOMS **to all ~s and purposes** quasiment, en fait

intention n intention f (**to do, of doing** de faire)

intentional adj intentionnel/-elle

intentionally adv intentionnellement, exprès

interact vi ⟨two factors, phenomena⟩ agir l'un sur l'autre; ⟨people⟩ communiquer; (Comput) dialoguer

interactive adj interactif/-ive

intercept vtr intercepter

interchange ① n (a) (road junction) échangeur m (b) (exchange) échange m ② vtr échanger

interchangeable adj interchangeable

intercom n interphone® m

intercourse n rapports mpl (sexuels)

interest ① n (a) (gen) intérêt m (**in** pour);

to hold sb's ~ retenir l'attention de qn; **it's in your (own) ~(s) to do** il est dans ton intérêt de faire; **to have sb's best ~s at heart** vouloir le bien de qn (b) (hobby) centre m d'intérêt (c) (on loan, from investment) intérêts mpl (**on** de) ② vtr intéresser (**in** à)

interested adj ⟨expression, onlooker⟩ intéressé/-e; **to be ~ in** s'intéresser à ⟨subject, activity⟩; **I am ~ in doing** ça m'intéresse de faire

interest-free adj sans intérêt

interesting adj intéressant/-e

interest rate n taux m d'intérêt

interface ① n interface f ② vtr connecter, relier

interfere vi (a) **to ~ in** se mêler de ⟨affairs⟩; **she never ~s** elle ne se mêle jamais de ce qui ne la regarde pas (b) (intervene) intervenir (c) **to ~ with** ⟨person⟩ toucher, traficoter (colloq) ⟨machine⟩ (d) **to ~ with** ⟨activity⟩ empiéter sur ⟨family life⟩

interference n (on radio) parasites mpl

interfering adj ⟨person⟩ envahissant/-e

interim ① n **in the ~** entre-temps ② adj ⟨arrangement, government⟩ provisoire; ⟨post, employee⟩ intérimaire

interior ① n (a) intérieur m (b) **Secretary/Department of the Interior** (US) ministre m/ministère m de l'Intérieur ② adj intérieur/-e

interior decorator n décorateur/-trice m/f

interlink vtr **to be ~ed** être lié/-e (**with** à)

interlock vi ⟨pipes⟩ s'emboîter; ⟨mechanisms⟩ s'enclencher; ⟨fingers⟩ s'entrelacer

interlude n (interval) intervalle m; (during play, concert) entracte m

intermediary n, adj intermédiaire (mf)

intermediate adj (a) (gen) intermédiaire (b) (Sch) ⟨course⟩ de niveau moyen; ⟨level⟩ moyen/-enne

intermission n entracte m

intern ① n (US) (a) (Med) interne mf (b) (gen) stagiaire mf ② vtr (Mil) interner

internal adj (a) (gen) interne (b) (within country) intérieur/-e

international adj international/-e

internationally adv ⟨known, respected⟩ dans le monde entier

internee n interné/-e m/f

Internet n Internet m; **on the ~** sur Internet

Internet access n accès m Internet

Internet kiosk n borne f d'accès public à Internet

Internet service provider, **ISP** n fournisseur m d'accès Internet

Internet user n internaute mf
interpret ① vtr interpréter (**as** comme)
② vi faire l'interprète
interpreter n interprète mf
interrogate vtr interroger
interrogation n interrogatoire m
interrogative n interrogatif m; **in the** ~ à
la forme interrogative
interrupt vtr, vi interrompre
interruption n interruption f
intersect ① vtr croiser
② vi ‹roads› se croiser; **to** ~ **with** croiser
intersection n intersection f
interstate n (US) (also ~ **highway**)
autoroute f (inter-États)
interval n (a) intervalle m; **at regular** ~s à
intervalles réguliers; **at four-hourly** ~s
toutes les quatre heures; **at 100 metre** ~s à
100 mètres d'intervalle
(b) (GB) (in theatre) entracte m
intervene vi intervenir (**on behalf of** en
faveur de)
intervention n intervention f (**on behalf
of** en faveur de)
interview ① n (a) (also **job** ~) entretien
m
(b) (in newspaper) interview f
② vtr (a) faire passer un entretien à
‹candidate›
(b) ‹journalist› interviewer ‹celebrity›;
‹police› interroger ‹suspect›
interviewee n (a) (for job) candidat/-e m/f
(b) (on TV, radio) personne f interviewée
interviewer n (a) (for job) personne f
faisant passer l'entretien
(b) (on radio, TV, in press) intervieweur/-euse
m/f
interwar adj **the** ~ **years**
l'entre-deux-guerres m
intestine n intestin m
intimacy n intimité f
intimate adj (a) (gen) intime; **to be on** ~
terms with sb être intime avec qn
(b) ‹knowledge› approfondi/-e
intimidate vtr intimider
intimidating adj ‹behaviour, person›
intimidant/-e; ‹obstacle, sight, size›
impressionnant/-e; ‹prospect› redoutable
into prep (a) ‹put, go, disappear› dans
‹place›; **to run** ~ **a wall** rentrer dans un mur;
to bang ~ **sb/sth** heurter qn/qch; **to go** ~
town/~ **the office** aller en ville/au bureau; **to
get** ~ **a car** monter dans une voiture; **to get**
~ **bed** se mettre au lit
(b) ‹transform› en; **to change dollars** ~
francs changer des dollars en francs; **to
translate sth** ~ **French** traduire qch en
français
(c) **to continue** ~ **the 18th century** continuer
jusqu'au XVIIIe siècle; **well** ~ **the afternoon**
jusque tard dans l'après-midi
(d) (colloq) (keen on) **to be** ~ **sth** être fana de
qch (colloq); **to be** ~ **drugs** se droguer

(e) (in division) **8** ~ **24 goes 3 times** or **is 3** 24
divisé par 8 égale 3
intolerable adj intolérable, insupportable
intolerance n intolérance f (**of, towards**
vis-à-vis de; **to** à)
intolerant adj intolérant/-e (**of, towards**
vis-à-vis de; **with** envers)
intoxicated adj ivre
intoxicating adj ‹drink› alcoolisé/-e;
‹effect, substance› toxique
intranet n intranet m
intransitive adj intransitif/-ive
intravenous adj intraveineux/-euse
intravenous drug user n usager m de
drogues par voie intraveineuse
in-tray n corbeille f arrivée
intrepid adj intrépide
intricate adj ‹mechanism, pattern, plot›
compliqué/-e; ‹problem› complexe
intrigue ① n intrigue f
② vtr intriguer; **she was** ~d **by his story**
son histoire l'intriguait
intriguing adj ‹person, smile› fascinant/-e;
‹story› curieux/-ieuse, intéressant/-e
introduce vtr (a) présenter ‹person› (**as**
comme; **to** à); **may I** ~ **my son?** je vous
présente mon fils; **to** ~ **sb to** initier qn à
‹painting, drugs›
(b) introduire ‹law, reform, word, product,
change› (**in, into** dans)
(c) (on TV, radio) présenter ‹programme›
introduction n (a) (of person) présentation
f; **letter of** ~ lettre de recommandation
(b) (of liquid, system, law) introduction f (**into**
dans)
(c) (to speech, book) introduction f
introductory adj (a) ‹speech, paragraph›
préliminaire; ‹course› d'initiation
(b) ‹offer› de lancement
introvert n introverti/-e m/f
intrude vi (a) **to** ~ **in** s'immiscer dans
‹affairs, conversation›
(b) **to** ~ **on** (on sb's privacy) être importun/-e
intruder n intrus/-e m/f
intrusive adj ‹question, cameras›
indiscret/-ète; ‹phone call, presence›
importun/-e
intuition n intuition f (**about** concernant)
intuitive adj intuitif/-ive
inundate vtr inonder ‹land›; submerger
‹organization, market›
invade vtr envahir
invader n envahisseur/-euse m/f
invalid ① n (sick person) malade mf; (disabled
person) infirme mf
② adj ‹claim, passport› pas valable;
‹contract, marriage› nul/nulle
invaluable adj ‹assistance, experience›
inestimable; ‹person, service› précieux/-ieuse
invasion n invasion f; ~ **of (sb's) privacy**
atteinte f à la vie privée (de qn)
invent vtr inventer
invention n invention f

inventive *adj* inventif/-ive

inventor *n* inventeur/-trice *m/f*

inventory *n* (a) inventaire *m*
(b) (US) stock *m*

inverted commas *n pl* (GB) guillemets *mpl*; in ∼ entre guillemets

invest ① *vtr* investir, placer ⟨*money*⟩; consacrer ⟨*time, energy*⟩ (in à)
② *vi* (a) investir; to ∼ in shares placer son argent en valeurs
(b) (buy) to ∼ in sth s'acheter qch

investigate *vtr* (a) enquêter sur ⟨*crime, case*⟩; faire une enquête sur ⟨*person*⟩
(b) (study) examiner ⟨*possibility, report*⟩

investigation *n* (a) (inquiry) enquête *f* (of, into sur)
(b) (of accounts, reports) vérification *f*

investment *n* (financial) investissement *m*, placement *m*

investment manager *n* gérant/-e *m/f* de porte-feuille

investor *n* investisseur/-euse *m/f* (in dans); (in shares) actionnaire *mf*

invigilate *vtr* surveiller ⟨*examination*⟩

invisible *adj* invisible

invisible ink *n* encre *f* sympathique

invitation *n* invitation *f*

invitation card *n* carton *m* (d'invitation)

invite *vtr* inviter ⟨*person*⟩; to ∼ sb for a drink inviter qn à prendre un verre; to ∼ sb in inviter qn à entrer; to ∼ sb over *or* round (to one's house) inviter qn chez soi

inviting *adj* ⟨*room*⟩ accueillant/-e; ⟨*meal*⟩ appétissant/-e; ⟨*prospect*⟩ alléchant/-e

invoice ① *n* facture *f*
② *vtr* envoyer une facture à ⟨*customer*⟩; to ∼ sb for sth facturer qch à qn

involve *vtr* (a) (entail) impliquer, nécessiter ⟨*effort, travel*⟩; entraîner ⟨*problems*⟩
(b) (cause to participate) faire participer ⟨*person*⟩ (in à); to be ∼d in participer à, être engagé/-e dans ⟨*business, project*⟩; être mêlé/-e à ⟨*scandal, robbery*⟩
(c) (affect) concerner, impliquer ⟨*person, animal, vehicle*⟩
(d) (engross) to get ∼d in se laisser prendre par, se plonger dans ⟨*film, book, work*⟩
(e) to get ∼d with sb avoir une liaison avec qn

involved *adj* (a) (complicated) ⟨*explanation*⟩ compliqué/-e
(b) ⟨*person, group*⟩ (implicated) impliqué/-e; (affected) concerné/-e
(c) (necessary) ⟨*effort*⟩ à fournir; because of the expense ∼ à cause de la dépense que cela entraîne

involvement *n* (a) (in activity, task) participation *f* (in à); (in enterprise, politics) engagement *m* (in dans)
(b) (with group) liens *mpl*; (with person) relations *fpl*

inward ① *adj* ⟨*satisfaction*⟩ personnel/-elle; ⟨*relief, calm*⟩ intérieur/-e

② *adv* (also **inwards**) ⟨*open, move, grow*⟩ vers l'intérieur

inward-looking *adj* replié/-e sur soi-même

inwards = INWARD 2

in-your-face *adj* (colloq) agressif/-ive

iodine *n* (element) iode *m*; (antiseptic) teinture *f* d'iode

IOU *n* reconnaissance *f* de dette

IQ *n* (*abbr* = **intelligence quotient**) QI *m*

Iran *pr n* Iran *m*

Iraq *pr n* Iraq *m*

irate *adj* furieux/-ieuse (about au sujet de)

Ireland *pr n* Irlande *f*

Irish ① *n* (a) (people) the ∼ les Irlandais *mpl*
(b) (language) irlandais *m*
② *adj* irlandais/-e

Irishman *n* Irlandais *m*

Irish Republic *pr n* République *f* d'Irlande

Irish sea *pr n* mer *f* d'Irlande

Irishwoman *n* Irlandaise *f*

iron ① *n* (a) (metal) fer *m*; scrap ∼ ferraille *f*
(b) (for clothes) fer *m* (à repasser)
② *vtr* repasser ⟨*clothes*⟩

ironic(al) *adj* ironique

ironing *n* repassage *m*

ironing board *n* planche *f* à repasser

ironmonger *n* quincaillier/-ière *m/f*; ∼'s (shop) quincaillerie *f*

irony *n* ironie *f*

irrational *adj* ⟨*behaviour*⟩ irrationnel/-elle; ⟨*fear, hostility*⟩ sans fondement; he's rather ∼ il n'est pas très raisonnable

irregular *adj* (a) irrégulier/-ière
(b) (US) ⟨*merchandise*⟩ de second choix

irregularity *n* irrégularité *f*

irrelevant *adj* (a) ⟨*remark*⟩ hors de propos; ⟨*fact*⟩ qui n'est pas pertinent; ⟨*question*⟩ sans rapport avec le sujet
(b) (unimportant) the money's ∼ ce n'est pas l'argent qui compte

irreligious *adj* irréligieux/-ieuse

irreparable *adj* irréparable

irreplaceable *adj* irremplaçable

irrepressible *adj* ⟨*high spirits*⟩ irrépressible; ⟨*person*⟩ infatigable

irresistible *adj* irrésistible

irrespective: irrespective of *phr* sans tenir compte de ⟨*age, class*⟩; sans distinction de ⟨*race*⟩

irresponsible *adj* irresponsable

irreversible *adj* ⟨*process, decision*⟩ irréversible; ⟨*disease*⟩ incurable

irritable *adj* irritable

irritable bowel syndrome *n* colopathie *f* fonctionnelle

irritate *vtr* irriter

irritating *adj* irritant/-e
Islam *n* Islam *m*
Islamic *adj* islamique
island *n* (a) île *f*; (small) îlot *m*
(b) (also **traffic** ∼) refuge *m*
islander *n* insulaire *mf*, habitant/-e *m/f* d'une île (*or* de l'île)
Isle of Man *pr n* île *f* de Man
isolate *vtr* isoler (**from** de)
isolation *n* isolement *m*
Israel *pr n* Israël (*never with article*)
Israeli ⟦1⟧ *n* Israélien/-ienne *m/f*
⟦2⟧ *adj* israélien/-ienne
issue ⟦1⟧ *n* (a) problème *m*, question *f*; **to make an** ∼ **(out) of** faire une histoire de; **at** ∼ en question
(b) (of stamps, shares) émission *f*; (of book) publication *f*
(c) (journal, magazine) numéro *m*; **back** ∼ vieux numéro *m*
⟦2⟧ *vtr* (a) (allocate) distribuer; **to** ∼ **sb with sth** fournir qch à qn
(b) délivrer ⟨*declaration*⟩; émettre ⟨*order, warning*⟩
(c) émettre ⟨*stamps, shares*⟩; publier ⟨*book*⟩
it *pron* (a) (subject pronoun) il, elle; **'where is the chair?'** — **'it's in the kitchen'** 'où est la chaise?' — 'elle est dans la cuisine'; **it's a good film** c'est un bon film
(b) (object pronoun) le, la, l'; **I want** ∼ je le/la veux
(c) (after a preposition) **about/from/of** ∼ en; **in/to** ∼ y; **I've heard about** ∼ j'en ai entendu parler; **he went to** ∼ il y est allé
(d) (in questions) **who is** ∼? qui est-ce?, qui c'est? (colloq); **where is** ∼? (of object) où est-il/elle?; (of place) où est-ce?, où est-ce que c'est?, c'est où? (colloq); **what is** ∼? (of object, noise) qu'est-ce que c'est?, c'est quoi? (colloq); (what's happening?) qu'est-ce qui se passe?; (what is the matter?) qu'est-ce qu'il y a?
(e) (impersonal uses) **it's raining/snowing** il pleut/neige; ∼ **is easy to learn English** il est facile d'apprendre l'anglais; ∼ **doesn't matter** ça ne fait rien; **it's time to eat** c'est l'heure de manger; **it's me** c'est moi

IT *n* (*abbr* = **information technology**) informatique *f*
Italian ⟦1⟧ *n* (a) (person) Italien/-ienne *m/f*
(b) (language) italien *m*
⟦2⟧ *adj* (gen) italien/-ienne; ⟨*embassy*⟩ d'Italie
italics *n pl* italique *m*; **in** ∼ en italique
Italy *pr n* Italie *f*
itch ⟦1⟧ *n* démangeaison *f*
⟦2⟧ *vi* avoir des démangeaisons; **my back is** ∼**ing** j'ai le dos qui me démange; **these socks make me** ∼ ces chaussettes me grattent
itchy *adj* (colloq) **I feel** ∼ **all over** ça me gratte partout
IDIOMS **to have** ∼ **feet** (colloq) avoir la bougeotte (colloq)
item *n* (a) article *m*; ∼**s of clothing** vêtements *mpl*; **news** ∼ article *m*
(b) (on agenda) point *m*
itemize *vtr* détailler; ∼**d bill** facture *f* le détaillée
itinerary *n* itinéraire *m*
its *det* son/sa/ses

■ Note In French determiners agree in number and gender with the noun that follows. *its* is translated by *son* + *masculine noun*: *its nose* = son nez; by *sa* + *feminine noun*: *its tail* = sa queue; BUT by *son* + *feminine noun beginning with a vowel or mute 'h'*: *its ear* = son oreille; and by *ses* + *plural noun*: *its ears* = ses oreilles.

itself *pron* (a) (reflexive) se, s'; **the cat hurt** ∼ le chat s'est fait mal
(b) (emphatic) lui-même/elle-même; **the house** ∼ **was pretty** la maison elle-même était jolie; **he was kindness** ∼ c'était la bonté même *or* personnifiée
(c) (after prepositions) **the heating comes on by** ∼ le chauffage se met en marche tout seul; **learning French is not difficult in** ∼ l'apprentissage du français n'est pas difficile en soi
IVF *n* (*abbr*= **in vitro fertilization**) fécondation *f* in vitro
ivory *n*, *adj* ivoire (*m*)
ivy *n* lierre *m*

Jj

j, **J** *n* j, J *m*
jab ⟦1⟧ *n* (a) (GB) (vaccination) vaccin *m*; (injection) piqûre *f*
(b) (in boxing) direct *m*
⟦2⟧ *vtr* **to** ∼ **sth into sth** planter qch dans qch
jabber *vi* (chatter) jacasser; (in foreign language) baragouiner
jack *n* (a) (for car) cric *m*
(b) (in cards) valet *m* (**of** de)

(c) (in bowls) cochonnet *m*
IDIOMS **to be a** ∼ **of all trades** être un/-e touche-à-tout *inv*
■ **jack in** (GB) (colloq): ∼ **in [sth]**, ∼ **[sth] in** plaquer (colloq), laisser tomber ⟨*job*⟩
jackal *n* chacal *m*
jackdaw *n* choucas *m*
jacket *n* (a) (garment) veste *f*; (man's) veste *f*, veston *m*

(b) (also **dust** ~) jaquette f
(c) (US) (of record) pochette f
jacket potato n pomme f de terre en robe des champs (au four)
jack-in-the-box n diable m à ressort
jackknife vi ⟨lorry⟩ se mettre en portefeuille
jackpot n to hit the ~ (win prize) gagner le gros lot; (have great success) faire un tabac (colloq)
jade n **(a)** (stone) jade m
(b) (also ~ **green**) vert m jade
jaded adj **(a)** (exhausted) fatigué/-e
(b) (bored) ⟨person, palate⟩ blasé/-e
jagged adj ⟨rock, cliff⟩ déchiqueté/-e; ⟨tooth, blade⟩ ébréché/-e; ⟨knife, saw⟩ dentelé/-e
jail ⟨1⟩ n prison f
⟨2⟩ vtr mettre [qn] en prison
jam ⟨1⟩ n **(a)** confiture f; **apricot** ~ confiture d'abricots
(b) (of traffic) embouteillage m
(c) (in machine, system) blocage m
(d) (colloq) (difficulty) pétrin m (colloq); **to be in a** ~ être dans le pétrin (colloq)
(e) (also ~ **session**) bœuf m (colloq), jam-session f
⟨2⟩ vtr **(a)** **to** ~ **one's foot on the brake** freiner à bloc
(b) (wedge) coincer; **the key's** ~med la clé s'est coincée
(c) (block) enrayer ⟨mechanism⟩; coincer ⟨lock, door, system⟩
(d) (also ~ **up**) (crowd) encombrer; **cars** ~med (up) **the roads** les routes étaient embouteillées
(e) (cause interference in) brouiller ⟨frequency⟩
⟨3⟩ vi **(a)** ⟨mechanism⟩ s'enrayer; ⟨lock, door⟩ se coincer
(b) (Mus) improviser
Jamaica pr n Jamaïque f
jam-packed adj bondé/-e; **to be** ~ **with sth** être bourré/-e de qch
jangle ⟨1⟩ n (of bells, pots) tintement m; (of keys) cliquetis m
⟨2⟩ vi ⟨bells⟩ tinter; ⟨bangles, keys⟩ cliqueter
janitor n (US) gardien m
January n janvier m
Japan pr n Japon m
Japanese ⟨1⟩ n **(a)** (person) Japonais/-e m/f
(b) (language) japonais m
⟨2⟩ adj ⟨culture, food, politics⟩ japonais/-e; ⟨teacher, lesson⟩ de japonais; ⟨ambassador, embassy⟩ du Japon
jar ⟨1⟩ n **(a)** pot m; (large) bocal m; (earthenware) jarre f
(b) (jolt) secousse f, choc m
⟨2⟩ vtr **(a)** ébranler, secouer; **to** ~ **one's shoulder** se cogner l'épaule
(b) (US) **to** ~ **sb into action** pousser qn à agir
⟨3⟩ vi **(a)** ⟨music, voice⟩ rendre un son discordant; **to** ~ **on sb's nerves** agacer qn
(b) (clash) ⟨colours⟩ jurer; ⟨note⟩ sonner faux

jargon n jargon m
jasmine n jasmin m
jaundice n jaunisse f
jaundiced adj (cynical) négatif/-ive
javelin n javelot m
jaw n mâchoire f
jawbone n mâchoire f
jawline n menton m
jay n geai m
jazz ⟨1⟩ n jazz m
⟨2⟩ adj ⟨musician, singer⟩ de jazz; ~ **band** jazz-band m
IDIOMS and all that ~ (colloq) et tout le bataclan (colloq)
■ **jazz up** (colloq) rajeunir ⟨dress⟩; égayer ⟨room⟩
jazzy adj **(a)** ⟨colour⟩ voyant/-e; ⟨pattern, dress⟩ bariolé/-e
(b) ⟨music⟩ jazzy inv
jealous adj jaloux/-ouse (of de); **to make sb** ~ rendre qn jaloux
jealousy n jalousie f
jeans n pl jean m; **a pair of** ~ un jean
Jeep® n jeep® f
jeer ⟨1⟩ n huée f
⟨2⟩ vtr huer
⟨3⟩ vi se moquer; **to** ~ **at sb** ⟨crowd⟩ huer qn; ⟨individual⟩ railler qn
jeering n huées fpl
jellied adj en aspic; ~ **eels** anguilles fpl en gelée
Jell-o® n (US) gelée f de fruits
jelly n **(a)** (savoury) gelée f; (sweet) gelée f de fruits
(b) (jam) gelée f
jellyfish n méduse f
jeopardize vtr compromettre ⟨career, plans⟩; mettre [qch] en péril ⟨lives, troops⟩
jeopardy n **in** ~ en péril, menacé/-e
jerk ⟨1⟩ n **(a)** (jolt) (of vehicle) secousse f; (of muscle, limb) tressaillement m, (petit) mouvement m brusque; **with a** ~ **of his head** d'un brusque mouvement de la tête
(b) (colloq) (idiot) abruti m
⟨2⟩ vtr tirer brusquement ⟨object⟩
⟨3⟩ vi ⟨person, limb, muscle⟩ tressaillir
jerky ⟨1⟩ n (US) (also **beef** ~) bœuf m séché
⟨2⟩ adj ⟨movement⟩ saccadé/-e; ⟨style, phrase⟩ haché/-e
jersey n **(a)** (sweater) pull-over m
(b) (for sports) maillot m
(c) (fabric) jersey m
Jersey pr n Jersey f
Jerusalem pr n Jérusalem
jest ⟨1⟩ n plaisanterie f; **in** ~ pour plaisanter
⟨2⟩ vi plaisanter
jester n bouffon m
Jesuit n, adj jésuite (m)
Jesus ⟨1⟩ pr n Jésus; ~ **Christ** Jésus-Christ
⟨2⟩ excl (slang) ~ (**Christ**)! nom de Dieu! (colloq)

jet **1** n (a) (also ~ **plane**) jet m, avion m à réaction
(b) (of water, flame) jet m
(c) (on hob) brûleur m; (of engine) gicleur m
(d) (stone) jais m
2 vi to ~ off to s'envoler pour

jet black adj de jais inv

jet engine n moteur m à réaction, réacteur m

jetfoil n hydroglisseur m

jetlag n décalage m horaire

jetlagged adj to be ~ souffrir du décalage horaire

jet setter n to be a ~ faire partie du jet-set

jet-skiing n jet-ski m

jettison vtr (from ship) jeter [qch] par-dessus bord; (from plane) larguer

jetty n (of stone) jetée f; (of wood) appontement m

Jew n juif/juive m/f

jewel n (a) (gem) pierre f précieuse; (piece of jewellery) bijou m; (in watch) rubis m
(b) (person) perle f; (town, object) joyau m

jeweller (GB), **jeweler** (US) n (person) bijoutier/-ière m/f; ~'s (shop) bijouterie f

jewellery (GB), **jewelry** (US) n (gen) bijoux mpl; (in shop, workshop) bijouterie f; a piece of ~ un bijou

Jewish adj juif/juive

jib n (a) (sail) foc m
(b) (of crane) flèche f

jibe n moquerie f

jiffy n in a ~ en un clin d'œil

Jiffy bag® n enveloppe f matelassée

jig n gigue f

jiggle **1** vtr agiter
2 vi (also ~ **about**, ~ **around**) gigoter; (impatiently) se trémousser

jigsaw n (a) (also ~ **puzzle**) puzzle m
(b) (saw) scie f sauteuse

jilt vtr abandonner, plaquer (colloq)

jingle **1** n (a) (of bells) tintement m; (of keys) cliquetis m
(b) (verse) ritournelle f; (for advert) refrain m publicitaire, sonal m
2 vi (keys, coins) cliqueter

jingoist n, adj chauvin/-e (m/f)

jinx n (a) (curse) sort m; to put a ~ on jeter un sort à; there's a ~ on me j'ai la poisse (colloq)
(b) (unlucky person, object) it's a ~ ça porte la poisse

jitters n pl to have the ~ (person, stock market) être nerveux/-euse; (actor) avoir le trac

job **1** n (a) (employment) emploi m; (post) poste m; to get a ~ trouver un emploi; a teaching ~ un poste d'enseignant; what's her ~? qu'est-ce qu'elle fait (comme travail)?
(b) (role) fonction f; it's my ~ to do c'est à moi de faire
(c) (duty) travail m; she's only doing her ~ elle fait son travail
(d) (task) travail m; to find a ~ for sb to do trouver du travail pour qn
(e) (assignment) tâche f
(f) to make a good ~ of sth faire du bon travail avec qch
(g) (colloq) quite a ~ toute une affaire (colloq) (to do, doing de faire)
2 adj (advert, offer) d'emploi; (pages) des emplois
IDIOMS that'll do the ~ ça fera l'affaire

job centre n (GB) bureau m des services nationaux de l'emploi

job creation scheme n (GB) plan m pour la création d'emplois

job description n description f de poste

job-hunting n chasse f à l'emploi

jobless n the ~ les sans-emplois mpl

jobshare n poste m partagé

job sharing n partage m de poste

jockey n jockey m

jockey shorts n pl (US) slip m (d'homme)

jockstrap n (colloq) suspensoir m

jodhpurs n pl jodhpurs mpl

jog **1** n (a) (with elbow) coup m de coude
(b) at a ~ au petit trot (colloq)
(c) (Sport) to go for a ~ aller faire un jogging
(d) (US) (in road) coude m
2 vtr (with elbow) donner un coup de coude à; to ~ sb's memory rafraîchir la mémoire de qn
3 vi to go ~ging faire du jogging

jogger n joggeur/-euse m/f

jogging n jogging m

join **1** n raccord m
2 vtr (a) devenir membre de (organization, team); adhérer à (club); s'inscrire à (library); entrer dans (firm); s'engager dans (army); to ~ a union se syndiquer
(b) se mettre dans (queue)
(c) (meet up with) rejoindre (person); may I ~ you? (sit down) puis-je me joindre à vous?
(d) (connect) réunir, joindre (ends, pieces); assembler (parts); relier (points, towns) (to à)
(e) (road) rejoindre (motorway); (river) se jeter dans (sea)
3 vi (a) (become member) (of party, club) adhérer; (of group, class) s'inscrire
(b) (pieces) se joindre; (wires) se raccorder; (roads) se rejoindre
■ **join in:** ¶ ~ in participer; ¶ ~ in [sth] participer à (talks, game); prendre part à (strike, demonstration, bidding); to ~ in the fun se joindre à la fête
■ **join up**
¶ ~ up (a) (enlist) s'engager
(b) (meet up) (people) se retrouver; (roads, tracks) se rejoindre
¶ ~ [sth] up relier (characters, dots)

joiner n menuisier/-ière m/f

joint **1** n (a) (Anat) articulation f; to be out of ~ (shoulder) être déboîté/-e

(b) (in carpentry) assemblage *m*; (in metalwork) joint *m*
(c) (of meat) rôti *m*
(d) (colloq) (place) endroit *m*; (café) boui-boui *m* (colloq)
(e) (colloq) (cannabis) joint *m* (colloq)
2 *adj* ⟨action⟩ collectif/-ive; ⟨programme, session⟩ mixte; ⟨measures, procedure⟩ commun/-e; ⟨winner⟩ ex aequo *inv*; ⟨talks⟩ multilatéral/-e

joint account *n* compte *m* joint

joint effort *n* collaboration *f*

joint honours *n pl* (GB Univ) licence *f* combinée

jointly *adv* conjointement; **to be ~ owned by** être la copropriété de

joint owner *n* copropriétaire *mf*

joint venture *n* **(a)** (Econ) coentreprise *f*
(b) (gen) projet *m* en commun

joke **1** *n* **(a)** plaisanterie *f*, blague *f* (colloq) (about sur); **to tell a ~** raconter une blague; **to play a ~ on sb** jouer un tour à qn; **it's no ~ doing** ce n'est pas facile de faire
(b) (person) guignol *m*; (event, situation) farce *f*
2 *vi* plaisanter, blaguer (colloq); **you must be joking!** tu veux rire!

joker *n* **(a)** (prankster) farceur/-euse *m/f*
(b) (in cards) joker *m*

jolly **1** *adj* ⟨person⟩ enjoué/-e; ⟨tune⟩ joyeux/-euse
2 *vtr* **to ~ sb along** amadouer qn

jolt **1** *n* **(a)** (jerk) secousse *f*
(b) (shock) choc *m*
2 *vtr* secouer ⟨passenger⟩
3 *vi* ⟨vehicle⟩ cahoter

Jordan *pr n* (country) Jordanie *f*

jostle *vi* se bousculer (**for** pour; **to do** pour faire)

jot *v* ■ **jot down** noter ⟨ideas, names⟩

journal *n* **(a)** (diary) journal *m*
(b) (periodical) revue *f*; (newspaper) journal *m*

journalism *n* journalisme *m*

journalist *n* journaliste *mf*

journey *n* (long) voyage *m*; (short or habitual) trajet *m*; **bus ~** trajet en bus; **to go on a ~** partir en voyage

jowl *n* (jaw) mâchoire *f*; (fleshy fold) bajoue *f*

joy *n* **(a)** (delight) joie *f* (**at** devant)
(b) (pleasure) plaisir *m*; **the ~ of doing** le plaisir de faire
IDIOMS to be full of the ~s of spring être en pleine forme

joyrider *n* jeune chauffard *m* en voiture volée

joyriding *n* rodéo *m* à la voiture volée

joystick *n* (in plane) manche *m* à balai; (for video game) manette *f*

jubilant *adj* ⟨person⟩ exultant/-e; ⟨crowd⟩ en liesse; ⟨expression, mood⟩ réjoui/-e

jubilee *n* jubilé *m*

Judaism *n* judaïsme *m*

judge **1** *n* **(a)** (in court) juge *m*

(b) (at competition) (gen) membre *m* du jury; (Sport) juge *m*
(c) **to be a good ~ of character** savoir juger les gens
2 *vtr* **(a)** juger ⟨person⟩
(b) faire partie du jury de ⟨show, competition⟩
(c) estimer ⟨distance, age⟩; prévoir ⟨outcome, reaction⟩
(d) (consider) juger, estimer
3 *vi* juger; **judging by** *or* **from...** à en juger d'après...

judgment, judgement *n* jugement *m*

judicial *adj* (gen) judiciaire; ⟨decision⟩ jurisprudentiel/-ielle

judiciary *n* **(a)** (system of courts) système *m* judiciaire
(b) (judges) magistrature *f*

judo *n* judo *m*

jug *n* **(a)** (GB) (earthenware) pichet *m*; (pot-bellied) cruche *f*; (glass) carafe *f*; (for cream, milk, water) pot *m*
(b) (US) (flagon) cruche *f*

juggernaut *n* (GB) poids *m* lourd

juggle *vi* jongler (**with** avec)

juggler *n* jongleur/-euse *m/f*

jugular *n, adj* jugulaire *(f)*

juice *n* **(a)** (from fruit, meat) jus *m*; **fruit ~** jus de fruit
(b) (sap) suc *m*
(c) **gastric ~s** sucs digestifs *or* gastriques

juicy *adj* **(a)** ⟨fruit⟩ juteux/-euse
(b) (colloq) ⟨story⟩ croustillant/-e

jukebox *n* juke-box *m*

July *n* juillet *m*

jumble *n* **(a)** (of papers, objects) tas *m*; (of ideas) fouillis *m*; (of words) fatras *m*
(b) (GB) (items for sale) bric-à-brac *m*, vieux objets *mpl*
■ **jumble up** mélanger ⟨letters, shapes⟩

jumble sale *n* (GB) vente *f* de charité

jumbo *n* (also **~ jet**) gros-porteur *m*

jump **1** *n* **(a)** (leap) saut *m*, bond *m*; **parachute ~** saut en parachute
(b) (in horse race) obstacle *m*
(c) (in price, wages) bond *m* (**in** dans)
2 *vtr* **(a)** sauter ⟨obstacle, ditch⟩
(b) **to ~ the lights** (colloq) griller le feu (rouge); **to ~ the queue** passer devant tout le monde
(c) **to ~ ship** ne pas rejoindre son bâtiment
3 *vi* **(a)** (leap) sauter; **to ~ across** *or* **over sth** franchir qch d'un bond; **to ~ up and down** sautiller; (in anger) trépigner de colère
(b) (start in surprise) sursauter
(c) ⟨prices, rate⟩ monter en flèche
(d) **to ~ at** sauter sur ⟨opportunity⟩; accepter [qch] avec enthousiasme ⟨offer⟩
■ **jump back** ⟨person⟩ faire un bond en arrière; ⟨lever⟩ lâcher brusquement
■ **jump down** ⟨person⟩ sauter (**from** de)
■ **jump on**: ¶ **~ on [sth]** sauter dans ⟨bus, train⟩; sauter sur ⟨bicycle, horse⟩; ¶ **~ on [sb]** sauter sur qn

■ **jump out** ⟨*person*⟩ sauter; **to ~ out of** sauter par ⟨*window*⟩; sauter de ⟨*bed, train*⟩

■ **jump up** ⟨*person*⟩ se lever d'un bond

jumper n (a) (GB) (sweater) pull m, pull-over m

(b) (US) (pinafore) robe f chasuble

jump leads n pl câbles mpl de démarrage

jump-start vtr faire démarrer [qch] avec des câbles ⟨*car*⟩

jump suit n combinaison f

jumpy adj (colloq) ⟨*person*⟩ nerveux/-euse; ⟨*market*⟩ instable

junction n (a) (of two roads) carrefour m; (on motorway) échangeur m

(b) (of railway lines) nœud m ferroviaire; (station) gare f de jonction

June n juin m

jungle n jungle f

junior ① n (a) (younger person) cadet/-ette m/f

(b) (low-ranking worker) subalterne mf

(c) (GB) (Sch) élève mf du primaire

(d) (US) (Univ) ≈ étudiant/-e m/f de premier cycle; (in high school) ≈ élève mf de première

② adj (a) ⟨*colleague, rank, position*⟩ subalterne

(b) (Sport) ⟨*race, team*⟩ des cadets; ⟨*player*⟩ jeune

(c) (also **Junior**) Mortimer ~ Mortimer fils or junior

junior high school n (US) ≈ collège m

junior minister n secrétaire m d'État

junior school n (GB) école f (primaire)

junk n (a) (rubbish) camelote f (colloq)

(b) (second-hand) bric-à-brac m

(c) (boat) jonque f

junk food n nourriture f industrielle

junkie n (colloq) drogué/-e m/f

junk mail n prospectus mpl

junk shop n boutique f de bric-à-brac

junkyard n (for scrap) dépotoir m; (for old cars) cimetière f de voitures

junta n junte f

Jupiter pr n Jupiter f

jurisdiction n (a) (gen) compétence f (over sur)

(b) (Law) juridiction f (over sur)

juror n juré m

jury n jury m

jury box n banc m des jurés

jury duty (US), **jury service** (GB) n to do ~ faire partie d'un jury

just¹ ① adv (a) to have ~ done venir (juste) de faire; he had only ~ left il venait tout juste de partir

(b) (immediately) juste; ~ before/after juste avant/après

(c) (slightly) ~ over/under 20 kg un peu plus/moins de 20 kg

(d) (only, merely) juste; ~ for fun juste pour rire; ~ two days ago il y a juste deux jours; he's ~ a child ce n'est qu'un enfant

(e) (purposely) exprès; he did it ~ to annoy us il l'a fait exprès pour nous embêter

(f) (barely) tout juste; ~ **on time** tout juste à l'heure; he's ~ 20 il a tout juste 20 ans; **I** (only) ~ **caught the train** j'ai eu le train de justesse

(g) (simply) tout simplement; ~ **tell the truth** dis la vérité, tout simplement; **she** ~ **won't listen** elle ne veut tout simplement pas écouter; '~ **a moment**' 'un instant'

(h) (exactly) exactement; **that's** ~ **what I want** c'est exactement ce que je veux; **it's** ~ **right** c'est parfait; **she looks** ~ **like her father** c'est son père tout craché (colloq); **it's** ~ **like him to forget** c'est bien de lui d'oublier

(i) (possibly) **it might** or **could** ~ **be true** il se peut que ce soit vrai

(j) (at this or that very moment) **to be** ~ **doing** être en train de faire; **to be** ~ **about to do** être sur le point de faire; **he was** ~ **leaving** il partait

(k) (positively, totally) vraiment; **that's** ~ **wonderful** c'est vraiment merveilleux

(l) (in requests) **if you could** ~ **hold this box** si vous pouvez tenir cette boîte

(m) (equally) ~ **as big as...** (tout) aussi grand que...

(n) (with imperative) donc; ~ **you dare!** essaie donc voir!; ~ **imagine!** imagine donc!

② **just about** phr presque; ~ **about everything** à peu près tout; **I can** ~ **about see it** je peux tout juste le voir

③ **just as** phr ~ **as he came** juste au moment où il est arrivé

④ **just now** phr en ce moment; **I saw him** ~ **now** je viens juste de le voir

just² adj ⟨*person, decision*⟩ juste; ⟨*demand*⟩ justifié/-e; ⟨*claim, criticism*⟩ légitime

justice n (a) (fairness) justice f; **the portrait doesn't do her** ~ le portrait ne l'avantage pas

(b) (the law) justice f; **to bring sb to** ~ traduire qn en justice

Justice Department n (US) ministère m de la justice

Justice of the Peace n juge m de paix

justifiable adj (that is justified) légitime; (that can be justified) justifiable

justification n raison f; **to have some** ~ **for doing** avoir des raisons de faire

justified adj justifié/-e; **to feel** ~ **in doing** se sentir en droit de faire

justify vtr justifier

jut vi (also ~ **out**) ⟨*cliffs*⟩ avancer en saillie (into dans); ⟨*balcony*⟩ faire saillie (over sur)

juvenile n (gen) jeune mf; (Law) mineur/-e m/f

juvenile delinquency n délinquance f juvénile

juvenile delinquent n jeune délinquant/-e m/f

juvenile offender n délinquant/-e m/f mineur/-e

juxtapose vtr juxtaposer (with à)

K k

k, **K** *n* k, K *m*
kale *n* (*also* **curly ~**) chou *m* frisé
kaleidoscope *n* kaléidoscope *m*
kangaroo *n* kangourou *m*
karaoke *n* karaoké *m*
karate *n* karaté *m*
Kashmir *pr n* Cachemire *m*
kayak *n* kayak *m*
kebab *n* (*also* **shish ~**) chiche-kebab *m*
kedgeree *n* (GB) pilaf *m* de poisson
keel *n* quille *f*
■ **keel over** ⟨*boat*⟩ chavirer
keen *adj* **(a)** (eager) ⟨*artist, footballer, supporter*⟩ enthousiaste; ⟨*student*⟩ assidu/-e;
to be ~ on tenir à ⟨*plan, project*⟩; être chaud/-e pour (colloq) ⟨*idea*⟩; être passionné/-e de ⟨*activity*⟩; to be ~ on doing *or* to do tenir à faire
(b) ⟨*appetite, interest*⟩ vif/vive; ⟨*eye, intelligence*⟩ vif/vive; ⟨*sight*⟩ perçant/-e; ⟨*hearing, sense of smell*⟩ fin/-e
(c) ⟨*competition*⟩ intense
keep ⟨**1**⟩ *n* **(a)** pension *f*; to pay for one's ~ payer une pension
(b) (tower) donjon *m*
⟨**2**⟩ *vtr* **(a)** (retain) garder ⟨*receipt, money, letter, seat*⟩; to ~ sb/sth clean garder qn/qch propre; to ~ sth warm garder qch au chaud; to ~ sb warm protéger qn du froid; to ~ sb waiting faire attendre qn; to ~ sb talking retenir qn; to ~ an engine running laisser un moteur en marche
(b) (detain) retenir; I won't ~ you a minute je n'en ai pas pour longtemps
(c) tenir ⟨*shop*⟩; élever ⟨*chickens*⟩
(d) (sustain) to ~ [sth] going entretenir ⟨*conversation, fire*⟩; maintenir ⟨*tradition*⟩; I'll make you a sandwich to ~ you going je te ferai un sandwich pour que tu tiennes le coup
(e) (store) mettre, ranger; where do you ~ your cups? où rangez-vous vos tasses?
(f) (support) faire vivre, entretenir ⟨*family*⟩
(g) tenir ⟨*accounts, diary*⟩
(h) to ~ sth from sb taire *or* cacher qch à qn; to ~ sth to oneself garder qch pour soi
(i) (prevent) to ~ sb from doing empêcher qn de faire
(j) tenir ⟨*promise*⟩; garder ⟨*secret*⟩; se rendre à ⟨*appointment*⟩
(k) (Mus) to ~ time battre la mesure
⟨**3**⟩ *vi* **(a)** (continue) to ~ doing continuer à *or* de faire, ne pas arrêter de faire; to ~ going ⟨*person*⟩ continuer
(b) (remain) to ~ out of the rain se protéger de la pluie; to ~ warm se protéger du froid; to ~ calm rester calme; to ~ silent garder le silence

(c) ⟨*food*⟩ se conserver, se garder
(d) ⟨*news, business*⟩ attendre
(e) 'how are you ~ing?' 'comment allez-vous?'; she's ~ing well elle va bien
⟨**4**⟩ *v refl* to ~ oneself to oneself ne pas être sociable
⟨**5**⟩ **for keeps** *phr* pour de bon, pour toujours
■ **keep away**: ¶ ~ away ne pas s'approcher (from de); ¶ ~ [sth/sb] away empêcher [qch/qn] de s'approcher
■ **keep back**: ¶ ~ back ne pas s'approcher (from de)
¶ ~ [sb/sth] back **(a)** empêcher [qn] de s'approcher ⟨*crowd*⟩ (from de); ⟨*dam*⟩ retenir ⟨*water*⟩
(b) (retain) garder ⟨*money*⟩; conserver ⟨*food*⟩
■ **keep down** ¶ ~ [sth] down, ~ down [sth] limiter ⟨*number, speed, inflation*⟩; limiter l'augmentation de ⟨*prices, unemployment*⟩; ~ your voice down! baisse la voix!
■ **keep off**: ¶ ~ off [sth] **(a)** ne pas marcher sur ⟨*grass*⟩
(b) éviter ⟨*alcohol*⟩; s'abstenir de parler de ⟨*subject*⟩
¶ ~ [sth] off éloigner ⟨*insects*⟩; this plastic sheet will ~ the rain off cette housse en plastique protège de la pluie
■ **keep on**: ¶ ~ on doing continuer à faire; to ~ on about ne pas arrêter de parler de; to ~ on at sb harceler qn (to do pour qu'il fasse); ¶ ~ [sb] on garder
■ **keep out**: ¶ ~ out of [sth] **(a)** ne pas entrer dans ⟨*house*⟩; '~ out!' 'défense d'entrer'
(b) rester à l'abri de ⟨*sun, danger*⟩
(c) ne pas se mêler de ⟨*argument*⟩; to ~ out of sb's way (not hinder) ne pas gêner qn; (avoid seeing) éviter qn
¶ ~ [sb/sth] out ne pas laisser entrer ⟨*person, animal*⟩
■ **keep to** ne pas s'écarter de ⟨*road*⟩; respecter, s'en tenir à ⟨*facts*⟩; respecter ⟨*law, rules*⟩
■ **keep up**: ¶ ~ up ⟨*car, runner, person*⟩ suivre; ¶ ~ [sth] up **(a)** tenir ⟨*trousers*⟩
(b) continuer ⟨*attack, studies*⟩; entretenir ⟨*correspondence, friendship*⟩; maintenir ⟨*membership, tradition, pace*⟩; ¶ ~ [sb] up ⟨*noise*⟩ empêcher [qn] de dormir
■ **keep up with (a)** aller aussi vite que ⟨*person*⟩; suivre ⟨*class*⟩; ⟨*wages*⟩ suivre ⟨*inflation*⟩; faire face à ⟨*demand*⟩
(b) suivre ⟨*fashion, developments*⟩

keeper *n* (curator) conservateur/-trice *m/f*; (guard) gardien/-ienne *m/f*

keep fit *n* gymnastique *f* d'entretien

keeping n (a) (custody) **in sb's ∼** à la garde de qn; **to put sb/sth in sb's ∼** confier qn/qch à qn
(b) (conformity) **in ∼ with** conforme à ⟨law, tradition⟩; **to be in ∼ with** correspondre à ⟨image, character⟩; s'harmoniser avec ⟨surroundings⟩

keg n (for liquid) fût m; (for gunpowder) baril m

kennel n (a) (GB) (for dog) niche f
(b) (establishment) chenil m

Kenya pr n Kenya m; **in ∼** au Kenya

kerb n (GB) bord m du trottoir

kernel n (of nut, fruitstone) amande f

kerosene, kerosine n (a) (US) (paraffin) pétrole m (lampant)
(b) (fuel) kérosène m

kestrel n (faucon m) crécerelle f

kettle n bouilloire f; **to put the ∼ on** mettre l'eau à chauffer

kettledrum n timbale f

key ① n (a) (lit) clé f; **a front-door ∼** une clé de maison; **a set or bunch of ∼s** un jeu de clés; **under lock and ∼** sous clé; **radiator ∼** clavette f à radiateur
(b) (on computer, piano) touche f; (on oboe, flute) clé f
(c) (vital clue) clé f, secret m (**to** de)
(d) (on map) légende f; (to abbreviations, symbols) liste f; (for code) clé f
(e) (to test, riddle) solutions fpl; (Sch) corrigé m
(f) (Mus) ton m, tonalité f; **to sing in/off ∼** chanter juste/faux
② adj ⟨figure, role⟩ clé; ⟨point⟩ capital/-e
③ vtr (a) (also ∼ **in**) saisir ⟨data⟩
(b) (adapt) adapter (**to** à)

keyboard n clavier m

keyboards n pl synthétiseur m

keyed-up adj (excited) excité/-e; (tense) tendu/-e

keyhole n trou m de serrure

keyhole surgery n chirurgie f endoscopique

keynote speech n discours m programme

key-ring n porte-clés m inv

keyword n mot m clé

khaki adj kaki inv

kibbutz n kibboutz m

kick ① n (a) (of person, horse) coup m de pied; (of donkey, cow) coup m de sabot; (of swimmer) battement m de pieds; (of footballer) tir m
(b) (colloq) (thrill) **to get a ∼ out of doing** prendre plaisir à faire
(c) (of firearm) recul m
② vtr (once) ⟨person⟩ donner un coup de pied à ⟨person⟩; donner un coup de pied dans ⟨door, ball, tin can⟩; ⟨horse⟩ botter ⟨person⟩; ⟨donkey, cow⟩ donner un coup de sabot à ⟨person⟩; (repeatedly) ⟨person⟩ donner des coups de pied à ⟨person⟩; donner des coups de pieds dans ⟨object⟩; **to ∼ sb on the leg**

⟨person, horse⟩ donner à qn un coup de pied à la jambe; ⟨donkey, cow⟩ donner à qn un coup de sabot dans la jambe
③ vi ⟨person⟩ (once) donner un coup de pied; (repeatedly) donner des coups de pied; ⟨swimmer⟩ faire des battements de pieds; ⟨cow⟩ ruer; ⟨horse⟩ botter
IDIOMS **to ∼ the habit** (colloq) (of drug addiction) décrocher (colloq); (of smoking) arrêter de fumer; **I could have ∼ed myself** je me serais donné des claques (colloq)
■ **kick around, kick about** donner des coups de pied dans, s'amuser avec ⟨ball⟩
■ **kick off** (a) (Sport) donner le coup d'envoi
(b) (colloq) (start) commencer
■ **kick out:** ¶ **∼ out** ⟨animal⟩ ruer; ¶ **∼ [sb] out** (colloq) virer (colloq)

kick-off n (Sport) coup m d'envoi

kick-start ① n (also ∼**-starter**) kick m
② vtr (a) faire démarrer [qch] au pied ⟨motorbike⟩
(b) relancer ⟨economy⟩

kid ① n (a) (colloq) (child) enfant mf, gosse mf (colloq); (youth) gamin/-e m/f (colloq)
(b) (young goat) chevreau/-ette m/f
(c) (goatskin) chevreau m
② vtr (colloq) charrier (colloq) (**about** à propos de)
③ vi (colloq) rigoler (colloq); **no ∼ding!** sans blague! (colloq)
④ v refl (colloq) **to ∼ oneself** se faire des illusions

kidnap vtr enlever

kidnapper n ravisseur/-euse m/f

kidnapping n enlèvement m

kidney n (a) (Anat) rein m
(b) (Culin) rognon m

kidney bean n haricot m rouge

kidney machine n rein m artificiel; **to be on a ∼** être sous dialyse

kill ① n mise f à mort
② vtr (a) tuer ⟨person, animal⟩; **they ∼ed each other** ils se sont entre-tués; **even if it ∼s me!** (colloq) même si je dois y laisser ma peau! (colloq); **my feet are ∼ing me** (colloq) j'ai mal aux pieds
(b) mettre fin à, étouffer ⟨rumour⟩; ⟨editor⟩ supprimer ⟨story⟩
(c) faire disparaître ⟨pain⟩; ôter ⟨appetite⟩
(d) (spend) **to ∼ time** tuer le temps (**by doing** en faisant)
③ vi ⟨person, animal, drug⟩ tuer
④ v refl **to ∼ oneself** se suicider

killer n (person) meurtrier m; (animal) tueur/-euse m/f; **heroin is a ∼** l'héroïne tue

killer whale n épaulard m

killing n (of individual) meurtre m (**of** de); (of animal) mise f à mort (**of** de)

killjoy n rabat-joie mf inv

kiln n four m

kilo n kilo m

kilobyte, KB n kilo-octet m, Ko m

kilogram(me) n kilogramme m

kilometre (GB), **kilometer** (US) *n* kilomètre *m*

kilowatt *n* kilowatt *m*

kind **1** *n* (a) (sort, type) sorte *f*, genre *m*, type *m*; this ~ of person ce genre de personne; all ~s of people toutes sortes de personnes; what ~ of dog is it? qu'est-ce que c'est comme chien?; what ~ of person is she? comment est-elle?, quel genre de personne est-ce?; this is one of a ~ il/elle est unique en son genre
(b) (in vague descriptions) a ~ of une sorte de; I heard a ~ of rattling noise j'ai entendu comme un cliquetis
(c) (classified type) espèce *f*, genre *m*; one's own ~ les gens de son espèce
2 *adj* ⟨person, gesture, words⟩ gentil/-ille; ⟨act⟩ bon/bonne (before *n*); to be ~ to sb être gentil/-ille avec qn; to be ~ to animals bien traiter les animaux; that's very ~ of you c'est très gentil *or* aimable de votre part; would you be ~ enough to pass me the salt? auriez-vous l'amabilité de me passer le sel?
3 in kind *phr* ⟨pay⟩ en nature
4 kind of *phr* (colloq) he's ~ of cute il est plutôt mignon; I ~ of like him en fait, je l'aime bien; 'is it interesting?'—'~ of' 'est-ce que c'est intéressant?'—'assez'

kindergarten *n* jardin *m* d'enfants

kind-hearted *adj* ⟨person⟩ de cœur

kindle *vtr* (a) allumer ⟨fire⟩
(b) attiser ⟨desire, passion⟩; susciter ⟨interest⟩

kindly **1** *adj* ⟨person⟩ gentil/-ille; ⟨smile⟩ bienveillant/-e
2 *adv* (a) (in a kind way) avec gentillesse; to speak ~ of sb dire du bien de qn
(b) (obligingly) gentiment; would you ~ do/refrain from doing auriez-vous l'amabilité de faire/de ne pas faire
(c) (favourably) to take ~ to apprécier

kindness *n* gentillesse *f*, bonté *f*

kindred spirit *n* âme *f* sœur

kinetics *n* cinétique *f*

king *n* (a) (monarch) roi *m*; King Charles le roi Charles
(b) (in chess, cards) roi *m*; (in draughts, checkers) dame *f*

kingdom *n* (a) (country) royaume *m*
(b) (Bot, Zool) règne *m*; the animal ~ le règne animal

kingfisher *n* martin-pêcheur *m*

king-size(d) *adj* ⟨packet⟩ géant/-e; ⟨portion, garden⟩ énorme; ~ bed grand lit *m*; ~ cigarettes cigarettes *fpl* extra-longues

kink *n* (in rope, tube) nœud *m*; the hosepipe has a ~ in it le tuyau d'arrosage est tordu

kiosk *n* (a) (stand) kiosque *m*
(b) (GB) (phone box) cabine *f*

kipper *n* (GB) hareng *m* fumé et salé, kipper *m*

kiss **1** *n* baiser *m*; to give sb a ~ embrasser qn, donner un baiser à qn
2 *vtr* embrasser, donner un baiser à ⟨person⟩; to ~ sb on embrasser qn sur ⟨cheek, lips⟩; we ~ed each other nous nous sommes embrassés
3 *vi* s'embrasser

kiss of life *n* (GB) bouche-à-bouche *m inv*; to give sb the ~ faire le bouche-à-bouche à qn

kit *n* (a) (implements) trousse *f*
(b) (gear, clothes) affaires *fpl*; football ~ affaires de football
(c) (for assembly) kit *m*
(d) (Mil) paquetage *m*
■ **kit out** (GB) équiper (with de)

kitbag *n* (for sport) sac *m* de sport; (for travel) sac *m* de voyage; (Mil) sac *m* de soldat

kitchen *n* cuisine *f*

kitchen foil *n* papier *m* d'aluminium

kitchen roll *n* essuie-tout *m inv*

kitchen sink *n* évier *m*

kitchen unit *n* élément *m* de cuisine

kite *n* cerf-volant *m*; to fly a ~ faire voler un cerf-volant

kitten *n* chaton *m*

kitty *n* cagnotte *f*

kiwi fruit *n* kiwi *m*

kleptomaniac *n*, *adj* kleptomane (*mf*)

knack *n* (a) (dexterity) tour *m* de main (of doing pour faire); to get the ~ attraper le tour de main; to lose the ~ perdre la main
(b) (talent) don *m* (for doing de faire)

knapsack *n* sac *m* à dos

knave *n* (in cards) valet *m*

knead *vtr* pétrir ⟨dough⟩; masser ⟨flesh⟩

knee **1** *n* genou *m*; on (one's) hands and ~s à quatre pattes
2 *vtr* donner un coup de genou à ⟨person⟩
IDIOMS to go weak at the ~s avoir les jambes qui flageolent

kneecap *n* rotule *f*

knee-deep *adj* the water was ~ l'eau arrivait aux genoux

kneel *vi* (also ~ down) se mettre à genoux; (in prayer) s'agenouiller; to be ~ing être à genoux

knee-length *adj* ⟨skirt⟩ qui s'arrête au genou; ⟨boots⟩ haut/-e; ⟨socks⟩ long/longue

knickers *n pl* (GB) petite culotte *f*

knick-knack *n* bibelot *m*

knife **1** *n* couteau *m*
2 *vtr* donner un coup de couteau à; to be ~d recevoir un coup de couteau

knife-edge *n* to be (living) on a ~ ⟨person⟩ être au bord de l'abîme

knife-point *n* at ~ sous la menace d'un couteau

knight **1** *n* (gen) chevalier *m*; (in chess) cavalier *m*
2 *vtr* (GB) anoblir ⟨person⟩ (for pour)

knighthood *n* titre *m* de chevalier

knit **1** *vtr* tricoter ⟨sweater, hat⟩; ~ted en tricot
2 *vi* (a) tricoter
(b) ⟨broken bones⟩ se souder

knitting *n* tricot *m*

knitwear *n* tricots *mpl*

knob *n* **(a)** (of door) bouton *m*; (on bannister) boule *f*

(b) (control button) bouton *m*

knobbly (GB), **knobby** (US) *adj* ⟨fingers⟩ noueux/-euse; ⟨knees⟩ saillant/-e

knock **1** *n* **(a)** (blow) coup *m* (**on** sur; **with** de); **a ~ at the door** un coup à la porte; **~! ~!** toc! toc!

(b) (setback) coup *m*; **to take a ~** en prendre un coup

2 *vtr* **(a)** (strike) cogner ⟨object⟩; **to ~ one's head on sth** se cogner la tête contre qch; **to ~ sb unconscious** assommer qn; **to ~ sth off** *or* **out of sth** faire tomber qch de qch

(b) (colloq) (criticize) dénigrer

3 *vi* **(a)** ⟨branch, engine, object⟩ cogner (**on**, **against** contre); ⟨person⟩ frapper (**at**, **on** à)

(b) (collide) **to ~ into** *or* **against sth** heurter qch

■ **knock down (a)** (deliberately) jeter [qn] à terre ⟨person⟩; défoncer ⟨door⟩; démolir ⟨building⟩; (accidentally) renverser ⟨person, object⟩; abattre ⟨fence⟩

(b) ⟨buyer⟩ faire baisser ⟨price⟩; ⟨seller⟩ baisser ⟨price⟩

■ **knock off**: ¶ **~ off** (colloq) arrêter de travailler

¶ **~ [sb/sth] off**, **~ off [sb/sth] (a)** (cause to fall) faire tomber ⟨person, object⟩

(b) (colloq) (reduce) **to ~ £10 off the price of sth** réduire le prix de qch de 10 livres

(c) (colloq) **~ it off!** ça suffit!

■ **knock out (a)** casser ⟨tooth⟩

(b) (make unconscious) ⟨person, blow⟩ assommer; ⟨drug⟩ endormir; ⟨boxer⟩ mettre [qn] au tapis ⟨opponent⟩

(c) (Sport) éliminer ⟨opponent, team⟩

■ **knock over** renverser ⟨person, object⟩

knockdown *adj* ⟨price⟩ sacrifié/-e

knocker *n* heurtoir *m*

knocking *n* (at door) coups *mpl*; (in engine) cognement *m*

knock-kneed *adj* cagneux/-euse

knock-on effect *n* implications *fpl*

knock-out **1** *n* (in boxing) knock-out *m*

2 *adj* **(a)** (Sport) ⟨competition⟩ avec tours éliminatoires

(b) (colloq) ⟨pills⟩ sédatif/-ive

knot **1** *n* **(a)** nœud *m*; **to tie a ~** faire un nœud; **to tie sth in a ~** nouer qch

(b) (in wood) nœud *m*

(c) (group) petit groupe *m* (**of** de)

2 *vtr* nouer (**together** ensemble)

know **1** *vtr* (gen) savoir; (be acquainted or familiar with) connaître ⟨place, person, way⟩; **to ~ why/how** savoir pourquoi/comment; **to ~ how to do** savoir faire; **to ~ sb by sight** connaître qn de vue; **to get to ~ sb** faire connaissance avec qn; **he ~s all about it** il est au courant; **I knew it!** j'en étais sûr!

2 *vi* savoir; **as you ~** comme vous le savez; **to ~ about** (have information) être au courant de ⟨event⟩; (have skill) s'y connaître en ⟨computing, engines⟩; **to ~ of** (from experience) connaître; (from information) avoir entendu parler de; **to let sb ~ of** *or* **about** tenir qn au courant de

IDIOMS to be in the ~ (colloq) être bien informé/-e

know-all *n* (GB) (colloq) je-sais-tout *mf inv*

know-how *n* (colloq) savoir-faire *m inv*

knowing *adj* ⟨look, smile⟩ entendu/-e

knowledge *n* **(a)** (awareness) connaissance *f*; **to my ~** à ma connaissance; **without sb's ~** à l'insu de qn

(b) (factual wisdom) connaissances *fpl*; (of specific field) connaissance *f*; **technical ~** connaissances techniques

knowledgeable *adj* ⟨person⟩ savant/-e; **to be ~ about** s'y connaître en ⟨subject⟩

known *adj* ⟨authority, danger⟩ reconnu/-e; ⟨cure⟩ connu/-e

knuckle *n* **(a)** (of person) jointure *f*, articulation *f*

(b) (Culin) (of lamb, mutton) manche *m* de gigot; (of pork, veal) jarret *m*

■ **knuckle down** (colloq) s'y mettre (sérieusement)

knuckle-duster *n* coup-de-poing *m* américain

koala (bear) *n* koala *m*

Koran *n* Coran *m*

Korea *pr n* Corée *f*

kosher *adj* **(a)** ⟨food, restaurant⟩ casher

(b) (colloq) (not illegal) **it's ~** c'est réglo (colloq)

Kosovan **1** *n* Kosovar/-e *m/f*

2 *adj* kosovar/-e

Kosovo *pr n* Kosovo *m*

Kurd *n* Kurde *mf*

Kurdish *adj* kurde

Kurdistan *pr n* Kurdistan *m*

Kuwait *pr n* Koweït *m*

Ll

l, L *n* l, L *m*

lab *n* labo *m* (colloq)

lab coat *n* blouse *f* blanche

label ❶ *n* **(a)** (on clothing, jar) étiquette *f*
(b) (*also* **record** ∼) label *m*
(c) (Comput) label *m*
❷ *vtr* **(a)** étiqueter ⟨*clothing, jar*⟩
(b) classer, étiqueter (derogatory) ⟨*person*⟩ (**as** comme)

labor (US) = LABOUR

laboratory *n* laboratoire *m*

laborer (US) = LABOURER

labor union *n* (US) syndicat *m*

labour (GB), **labor** (US) ❶ *n* **(a)** (work) travail *m*
(b) (*also* ∼ **force**) main-d'œuvre *f*
(c) (Med) accouchement *m*; **to be in** ∼ être en train d'accoucher
❷ *vi* travailler (dur) (**at** à; **on** sur; **to do** pour faire)
IDIOMS **to** ∼ **the point** insister lourdement

Labour ❶ *n* (GB) parti *m* travailliste
❷ *adj* travailliste

labourer (GB), **laborer** (US) *n* ouvrier/-ière *m/f* du bâtiment

Labour Party *n* (GB) parti *m* travailliste

labour-saving *adj* ⟨*feature, system*⟩ qui facilite le travail; ∼ **device** appareil *m* ménager

labyrinth *n* labyrinthe *m*, dédale *m*

lace ❶ *n* **(a)** (fabric) dentelle *f*
(b) (on shoe, boot, dress) lacet *m*; (on tent) cordon *m*
❷ *vtr* **(a)** lacer ⟨*shoes*⟩
(b) **to** ∼ **a drink with sth** mettre qch dans une boisson

lace-up (shoe) *n* chaussure *f* à lacet

lack ❶ *n* manque *m* (**of** de); **through** ∼ **of** par manque de
❷ *vtr* manquer de
❸ *vi* **to be** ∼**ing** manquer; **to be** ∼**ing in** manquer de

lacklustre (GB), **lackluster** (US) *adj* terne

lacquer *n* **(a)** (for hair) laque *f*
(b) (varnish) laque *f*

lacy *adj* en *or* de dentelle

lad *n* (colloq) (boy) garçon *m*

ladder ❶ *n* **(a)** (for climbing) échelle *f*
(b) (GB) (in stockings) échelle *f*, maille *f* filée
❷ *vtr, vi* filer

laddish *adj* (colloq) macho *inv* (colloq)

ladle *n* (Culin) louche *f*

lady ❶ *n* **(a)** (woman) dame *f*; **ladies and gentlemen** mesdames et messieurs; **a little old** ∼ une petite vieille; **she's a real** ∼ elle est très distinguée
(b) (in titles) **Lady Churchill** Lady Churchill
❷ **ladies** *n pl* toilettes *fpl*; (on sign) 'Dames'

ladybird *n* coccinelle *f*

ladylike *adj* ⟨*behaviour*⟩ distingué/-e

lag ❶ *n* (*also* **time** ∼) décalage *m*
❷ *vtr* calorifuger ⟨*pipe, tank*⟩; isoler ⟨*roof*⟩
■ **lag behind**: ¶ ∼ **behind** ⟨*person, prices*⟩ être à la traîne; ¶ ∼ **behind** [**sb/sth**] traîner derrière ⟨*person*⟩; être en retard sur ⟨*rival, product*⟩

lager *n* bière *f* blonde

lager lout *n* (GB) voyou *m* ⟨*qui se soûle à la bière*⟩

lagoon *n* lagune *f*

laidback *adj* (colloq) décontracté/-e

laid up *adj* **to be** ∼ être alité/-e

lake *n* lac *m*

lamb *n* agneau *m*; **leg of** ∼ gigot *m* d'agneau

lamb's wool *n* laine *f* d'agneau, lambswool *m*

lame *adj* boiteux/-euse

lament ❶ *n* lamentation *f*
❷ *vtr* se lamenter sur ⟨*fate, misfortune*⟩

lamentable *adj* déplorable

laminated *adj* ⟨*plastic*⟩ stratifié/-e; ⟨*wood*⟩ contreplaqué/-e; ⟨*card*⟩ plastifié/-e

lamp *n* lampe *f*

lamppost *n* réverbère *m*

lampshade *n* abat-jour *m*

lance *vtr* percer ⟨*boil, abscess*⟩

land ❶ *n* **(a)** (terrain, property) terrain *m*; (very large) terres *fpl*
(b) (farmland) terre *f*
(c) (country) pays *m*
(d) (not sea) terre *f*; **dry** ∼ terre ferme; **to reach** ∼ toucher terre; **by** ∼ par voie de terre
❷ *vtr* **(a)** ⟨*pilot*⟩ poser ⟨*aircraft*⟩; faire atterrir ⟨*space capsule*⟩
(b) prendre ⟨*fish*⟩
(c) (colloq) décrocher (colloq) ⟨*job, contract, prize*⟩
(d) (colloq) **to be** ∼**ed with sb/sth** se retrouver avec qn/qch sur les bras
❸ *vi* **(a)** ⟨*aircraft, passenger*⟩ atterrir
(b) ⟨*ship*⟩ accoster
(c) ⟨*person, animal, object*⟩ atterrir; ⟨*ball*⟩ toucher le sol; **most of the paint** ∼**ed on me** presque toute la peinture m'est tombée dessus

landing *n* **(a)** (at turn of stairs) palier *m*; (storey) étage *m*   ···⟫

(b) (from boat) (of people) débarquement *m*; (of cargo) déchargement *m*

(c) (by plane) atterrissage *m* (on sur)

landing card *n* carte *f* de débarquement

landing gear *n* train *m* d'atterrissage

landing strip *n* piste *f* d'atterrissage

landlady *n* (owner) propriétaire *f*; (live-in) logeuse *f*; (of pub) patronne *f*

landlord *n* (owner) propriétaire *m*; (live-in) logeur *m*; (of pub) patron *m*

landmark *n* (for bearings) point *m* de repère; (major step) étape *f* importante

land mine *n* mine *f* antipersonnel

landowner *n* propriétaire *mf* foncier/-ière

landscape *n* paysage *m*

landscape gardener *n* jardinier/-ière *m/f* paysagiste

landslide *n* **(a)** glissement *m* de terrain

(b) (*also* ∼ **victory**) victoire *f* écrasante

lane *n* **(a)** (in country) chemin *m*, petite route *f*; (in town) ruelle *f*

(b) (of road) voie *f*, file *f*; (air, sea) couloir *m*; (Sport) couloir *m*

language *n* **(a)** (system in general) langage *m*

(b) (of a particular nation) langue *f*; **the French** ∼ la langue française

(c) (of a particular group, style) langage *m*; **legal** ∼ langage juridique; **bad** *or* **foul** ∼ langage grossier

(d) (Comput) langage *m*

language barrier *n* obstacle *m* *or* barrière *f* de la langue

language laboratory, language lab *n* laboratoire *m* de langues

languish *vi* (remain neglected) ⟨*person*⟩ languir; ⟨*object*⟩ traîner

lank *adj* ⟨*hair*⟩ plat/-e

lantern *n* lanterne *f*

lap *n* **(a)** (of person) genoux *mpl*; **in one's** ∼ sur les genoux

(b) (Sport) (of track) tour *m* de piste; (of racecourse) tour *m* de circuit

IDIOMS **in the** ∼ **of luxury** dans le plus grand luxe

■ **lap up (a)** laper ⟨*milk, water*⟩

(b) boire [qch] comme du petit lait ⟨*compliment, flattery*⟩

lap belt *n* ceinture *f* ventrale

lapel *n* revers *m*

lapse **1** *n* **(a)** (slip) défaillance *f*; **a** ∼ **in concentration** un relâchement de l'attention

(b) (interval) intervalle *m*, laps *m* de temps

2 *vi* **(a)** ⟨*contract, membership*⟩ expirer; ⟨*insurance*⟩ prendre fin

(b) **to** ∼ **into** se mettre à parler ⟨*jargon, German*⟩; tomber dans ⟨*coma*⟩; prendre ⟨*bad habits*⟩

laptop *n* (*also* ∼ **computer**) portable *m*

lard *n* saindoux *m*

larder *n* garde-manger *m* *inv*

large **1** *adj* **(a)** (gen) grand/-e (*before n*);

⟨*appetite, piece, person, nose*⟩ gros/grosse (*before n*); ⟨*amount*⟩ important/-e; ⟨*crowd, family*⟩ nombreux/-euse

2 **at large** *phr* **(a)** ⟨*prisoner, criminal*⟩ en liberté

(b) ⟨*society, population*⟩ en général, dans son ensemble

IDIOMS **by and** ∼ en général

large-scale *adj* à grande échelle

lark *n* **(a)** (Zool) alouette *f*

(b) (colloq) (fun) **for a** ∼ pour rigoler (colloq)

laryngitis *n* laryngite *f*

larynx *n* larynx *m*

lasagne *n* lasagnes *fpl*

laser **1** *n* laser *m*

2 *adj* ⟨*beam, disc*⟩ laser *inv*; ⟨*printer*⟩ à laser

laser treatment *n* thérapie *f* au laser

lash **1** *n* **(a)** (eyelash) cil *m*

(b) (whipstroke) coup *m* de fouet

2 *vtr* fouetter ⟨*person, animal*⟩; ⟨*rain*⟩ cingler ⟨*windows*⟩

■ **lash out** ⟨*person*⟩ devenir violent/-e; **to** ∼ **out at sb** (physically) frapper qn; (verbally) invectiver qn

last **1** *pron* **the** ∼ le dernier/la dernière *m/f* (**to do** à faire); **the** ∼ **but one** l'avant-dernier/-ière; **the night before** ∼ (evening) avant-hier soir; (night) la nuit d'avant-hier; **the week before** ∼ il y a deux semaines

2 *adj* dernier/-ière (*before n*); ∼ **week/year** la semaine/l'année dernière; ∼ **Christmas** à Noël l'an dernier; **over the** ∼ **ten years** durant ces dix dernières années; ∼ **night** (evening) hier soir; (night-time) la nuit dernière

3 *adv* **(a)** **to come in** ∼ ⟨*runner, racing car*⟩ arriver en dernier; **the girls left** ∼ les filles sont parties les dernières; **to leave sth till** ∼ s'occuper de qch en dernier (lieu); ∼ **of all** en dernier lieu

(b) **she was** ∼ **here in 1976** la dernière fois qu'elle est venue ici, c'était en 1976

4 *vi* **(a)** durer; **it's too good to** ∼! c'est trop beau pour que ça dure!; **he won't** ∼ **long here** il ne tiendra pas longtemps ici

(b) ⟨*fabric*⟩ faire de l'usage; ⟨*perishables*⟩ se conserver

5 **at last** *adv* enfin

last-ditch *adj* ⟨*attempt, stand*⟩ désespéré/-e, ultime

lasting *adj* ⟨*effect, impression*⟩ durable; ⟨*relationship*⟩ sérieux/-ieuse

lastly *adv* enfin, finalement

last-minute *adj* de dernière minute

last name *n* nom *m* de famille

last rites *n pl* derniers sacrements *mpl*

latch *n* (fastening) loquet *m*; (spring lock) serrure *f* (de sûreté)

■ **latch on to** (colloq) s'accrocher à ⟨*object, person*⟩; exploiter ⟨*idea*⟩

late **1** *adj* **(a)** ⟨*arrival*⟩ tardif/-ive; **to be** ∼ **(for sth)** être en retard (pour qch); **to make**

sb ~ retarder qn; **to be ~ with the rent** payer son loyer avec du retard; **dinner will be a bit ~** le dîner sera retardé

(b) ⟨*hour, supper, date*⟩ tardif/-ive; **to have a ~ night** (aller) se coucher tard; **to be in one's ~ fifties** approcher de la soixantaine; **in ~ January** (à la) fin janvier; **in the ~ 50s** à la fin des années 50

(c) (deceased) feu/-e (formal); **my ~ wife** ma pauvre femme

2 *adv* **(a)** ⟨*arrive, start, finish*⟩ en retard; **to be running ~** ⟨*person*⟩ être en retard; ⟨*train, bus*⟩ avoir du retard; **to start three months ~** commencer avec trois mois de retard

(b) ⟨*get up, open, close*⟩ tard; ⟨*marry*⟩ sur le tard; **~ last night/in the evening** tard hier soir/dans la soirée

latecomer *n* retardataire *mf*

late developer *n* **to be a ~** ⟨*child*⟩ être lent/-e

lately *adv* ces derniers temps

late-night *adj* ⟨*film*⟩ dernier/-ière (*before n*); ⟨*session*⟩ en nocturne; **it's ~ shopping on Thursdays** les magasins restent ouverts tard le jeudi

later **1** *adj* ⟨*date*⟩ ultérieur/-e; ⟨*model, novel*⟩ postérieur/-e

2 *adv* plus tard; **~ on** plus tard; **six months ~** six mois après; **to leave no ~ than 6 am** partir au plus tard à 6 heures; **see you ~!** à tout à l'heure!

latest **1** *adj* dernier/-ière (*before n*)

2 at the latest *phr* au plus tard

latex *n* latex *m*

lathe *n* tour *m*

lather *n* mousse *f*

Latin **1** *n* (language) latin *m*

2 *adj* latin/-e

Latin America *pr n* Amérique *f* latine

Latin American *adj* latino-américain/-e

latitude *n* latitude *f*

latter *n* **the ~** ce dernier/cette dernière *m/f*; ces derniers/ces dernières *mpl/fpl*

Latvia *pr n* Lettonie *f*

laugh **1** *n* rire *m*; **to like a good ~** aimer bien rire; **to get a ~** faire rire; **for a ~** (colloq) pour rigoler (colloq)

2 *vi* rire (**about, over** de); **to ~ at sb/sth** rire de qn/qch; **the children ~ed at the clown** le clown a fait rire les enfants; **he's afraid of being ~ed at** il a peur qu'on se moque de lui

■ **laugh off** choisir de rire de ⟨*criticism, insult*⟩

laughable *adj* ridicule

laughing stock *n* risée *f*

laughter *n* rires *mpl*

launch **1** *n* **(a)** (for patrolling) vedette *f*; (for pleasure) bateau *m* de plaisance

(b) (of new boat, rocket) lancement *m*; (of lifeboat) mise *f* à l'eau; (of campaign, product) lancement *m*

2 *vtr* **(a)** mettre [qch] à l'eau ⟨*dinghy, lifeboat*⟩; lancer ⟨*new ship, missile, rocket*⟩

(b) (start) lancer ⟨*campaign, career, product*⟩; ouvrir ⟨*investigation*⟩

launch pad, **launching pad** *n* aire *f* de lancement

launder *vtr* **(a)** laver ⟨*clothes*⟩

(b) blanchir ⟨*money*⟩

launderette (GB), **laundromat** (US) *n* laverie *f* automatique

laundry *n* **(a)** (place) (commercial) blanchisserie *f*; (in hotel, house) laverie *f*

(b) (linen) linge *m*; **to do the ~** faire la lessive

laurel *n* laurier *m*

lava *n* lave *f*

lavatory *n* toilettes *fpl*

lavender *n* lavande *f*

lavish **1** *adj* ⟨*party, lifestyle*⟩ somptueux/-euse

2 *vtr* prodiguer ⟨*money, affection*⟩ (**on** à)

lavishly *adv* ⟨*decorated*⟩ luxueusement; ⟨*spend*⟩ sans compter; ⟨*entertain*⟩ généreusement

law *n* **(a)** (gen) loi *f*; **to obey/break the ~** respecter/enfreindre la loi; **to be against the ~** être interdit/-e; **by ~** conformément à la loi

(b) (Univ) droit *m*; **to study ~** faire son droit

law-abiding *adj* respectueux/-euse des lois

law and order *n* ordre *m* public

law court *n* tribunal *m*

law firm *n* cabinet *m* d'avocats

lawful *adj* ⟨*owner, strike*⟩ légal/-e; ⟨*conduct*⟩ licite; ⟨*wife, husband*⟩ légitime

lawless *adj* ⟨*society*⟩ anarchique; ⟨*area, town*⟩ tombé/-e dans l'anarchie

lawn *n* pelouse *f*

lawnmower *n* tondeuse *f* (à gazon)

law school *n* faculté *f* de droit

lawsuit *n* procès *m*

lawyer *n* (who practises law) avocat/-e *m/f*; (expert in law) juriste *mf*

lax *adj* relâché/-e

laxative *n* laxatif *m*

lay **1** *adj* **(a)** (non-specialist) **~ person** profane *mf*

(b) ⟨*preacher, member*⟩ laïque

2 *vtr* **(a)** (place) poser ⟨*object, card*⟩ (**in** dans; **on** sur); (spread out) étaler ⟨*rug, newspaper*⟩ (**on** sur); (arrange) disposer (**on** sur); **to ~ the table (for)** mettre la table (pour)

(b) (prepare) préparer ⟨*plan, trail*⟩; poser ⟨*basis, foundation*⟩; tendre ⟨*trap*⟩

(c) (Zool) pondre ⟨*egg*⟩

3 *vi* ⟨*bird*⟩ pondre

■ **lay down (a)** coucher ⟨*baby, patient*⟩; étaler ⟨*rug, cards*⟩; poser ⟨*book, implement*⟩; déposer ⟨*weapon*⟩

(b) to ~ down one's life for sacrifier sa vie pour

(c) établir ⟨*rule*⟩; poser ⟨*condition*⟩

■ **lay off** (temporarily) mettre [qn] en chômage technique; (permanently) licencier ····❯

■ **lay on** prévoir ⟨*meal, transport*⟩; organiser ⟨*trip*⟩

■ **lay out (a)** disposer ⟨*goods, food*⟩; étaler ⟨*map, garment, fabric*⟩
(b) concevoir ⟨*building, advert*⟩; mettre [qch] en page ⟨*letter*⟩; monter ⟨*page*⟩

layabout *n* (colloq) fainéant/-e *m/f* (colloq)

lay-by *n* (GB) aire *f* de repos

layer ⟦1⟧ *n* couche *f*
⟦2⟧ *vtr* **(a)** couper [qch] en dégradé ⟨*hair*⟩
(b) disposer [qch] en couches ⟨*cheese, potatoes*⟩

layman *n* profane *m*

lay-off *n* (permanent) licenciement *m*; (temporary) mise *f* en chômage technique

layout *n* (of page, book, computer screen) mise *f* en page; (of advert, article) présentation *f*; (of building) agencement *m*; (of town) plan *m*; (of garden) dessin *m*

laze *vi* (*also* ∼ **about**, ∼ **around**) paresser

lazily *adv* ⟨*move, wonder*⟩ nonchalamment; ⟨*lie, float*⟩ mollement; ⟨*flow, bob*⟩ doucement

laziness *n* paresse *f*

lazy *adj* ⟨*person*⟩ paresseux/-euse; ⟨*day, holiday*⟩ paisible; ⟨*movement, pace*⟩ lent/-e

lead¹ ⟦1⟧ *n* **(a)** to be in the ∼ être en tête; to go into the ∼ passer en tête
(b) (initiative) to take the ∼ prendre l'initiative; to follow sb's ∼ suivre l'exemple de qn
(c) (clue) piste *f*
(d) (leading role) rôle *m* principal
(e) (wire) fil *m*
(f) (GB) (for dog) laisse *f*
⟦2⟧ *adj* ⟨*guitarist*⟩ premier/-ière (*before n*); ⟨*role, singer*⟩ principal/-e
⟦3⟧ *vtr* **(a)** (guide, escort) mener, conduire ⟨*person*⟩ (**to sth** à qch; **to sb** auprès de qn); **to ∼ sb away** éloigner qn (**from** de)
(b) (bring) ⟨*path, sign*⟩ mener (**to** à)
(c) (cause) **to ∼ sb to do** amener qn à faire
(d) mener ⟨*army, team, attack, strike*⟩; diriger ⟨*orchestra, research*⟩
(e) (conduct, have) mener ⟨*active life*⟩; **to ∼ a life of luxury** vivre dans le luxe
⟦4⟧ *vi* **(a)** **to ∼ to** ⟨*path*⟩ mener à; ⟨*door*⟩ s'ouvrir sur; ⟨*exit, trapdoor*⟩ donner accès à
(b) (result in) **to ∼ to** entraîner ⟨*complication, discovery, accident*⟩
(c) ⟨*runner, car, company*⟩ être en tête; ⟨*team, side*⟩ mener; **to ∼ by 15 seconds** avoir 15 secondes d'avance
(d) (in walk) aller devant; (in action, discussion) prendre l'initiative; (in dancing) conduire
■ **lead up to (a)** (precede) précéder ⟨*event*⟩
(b) (build up to) amener ⟨*topic*⟩

lead² *n* plomb *m*; (in pencil) mine *f*

leaded petrol (GB), **leaded gasoline** (US) *n* essence *f* au plomb

leader *n* **(a)** (of nation) chef *m* d'État, dirigeant/-e *m/f*; (of gang) chef *m*; (of party) leader *m*; (of trade union) secrétaire *mf*; (of strike, movement) meneur/-euse *m/f*

(b) (in competition) premier/-ière *m/f*; (horse) cheval *m* de tête; (in market, field) leader *m*

leadership *n* dirigeants *mpl*, direction *f*; **under the ∼ of** sous la direction de

leadership contest, leadership election *n* (Pol) élection *f* à la direction du parti

leadership qualities *n pl* qualités *fpl* de leader

lead-free *adj* sans plomb

leading *adj* **(a)** ⟨*lawyer, politician*⟩ éminent/-e, important/-e; ⟨*company, bank*⟩ important/-e; ⟨*brand*⟩ dominant/-e
(b) ⟨*role*⟩ (main) majeur/-e; (in theatre) principal/-e
(c) (Sport) ⟨*driver, car*⟩ en tête de course; ⟨*team*⟩ en tête du classement

leading edge ⟦1⟧ *n* **at the ∼ of** à la pointe de ⟨*technology*⟩
⟦2⟧ **leading-edge** *adj* ⟨*technology*⟩ de pointe

lead story *n* histoire *f* à la une (colloq)

leaf *n* **(a)** (of plant) feuille *f*
(b) (of book) page *f*
IDIOMS **to turn over a new ∼** tourner la page
■ **leaf through** feuilleter ⟨*papers, book*⟩

leaflet *n* (gen) dépliant *m*; (advertising) prospectus *m*

league *n* **(a)** (alliance) ligue *f*; **to be in ∼ with sb** être de mèche avec qn (colloq)
(b) (GB) (Sport) (competition) championnat *m*; (association) ligue *f*
(c) **they're not in the same ∼** ils ne sont pas comparables

league table *n* classement *m*

leak ⟦1⟧ *n* fuite *f*
⟦2⟧ *vtr* divulguer ⟨*information, document*⟩
⟦3⟧ *vi* **(a)** ⟨*container, roof*⟩ fuir; ⟨*boat*⟩ faire eau
(b) ⟨*liquid, gas*⟩ s'échapper (**from** de)

leaky *adj* ⟨*container, pipe*⟩ qui fuit; ⟨*boat*⟩ qui prend l'eau

lean ⟦1⟧ *adj* **(a)** ⟨*body, face*⟩ mince; ⟨*meat*⟩ maigre
(b) ⟨*year, times*⟩ difficile
⟦2⟧ *vtr* appuyer (**against** contre)
⟦3⟧ *vi* ⟨*wall, building*⟩ pencher; **to ∼ against sth** ⟨*bicycle, ladder*⟩ être appuyé/-e contre qch; ⟨*person*⟩ s'appuyer à qch; (with back) s'adosser à qch; **to ∼ out of the window** se pencher par la fenêtre
■ **lean back** se pencher en arrière
■ **lean forward** se pencher en avant
■ **lean on:** ¶ ∼ **on** [sth] s'appuyer sur ⟨*stick*⟩; s'accouder à ⟨*windowsill*⟩; ¶ ∼ **on** [sb] (as support) s'appuyer sur ⟨*person*⟩; (depend on) compter sur ⟨*person*⟩; (pressurize) faire pression sur ⟨*person*⟩
■ **lean over:** ∼ **over** [sth] se pencher par-dessus [qch]

leap ⟦1⟧ *n* **(a)** (jump) saut *m*, bond *m*
(b) (step in process) bond *m* (en avant)
(c) (in price) bond *m* (**in** dans)
⟦2⟧ *vi* **(a)** ⟨*person, animal*⟩ bondir, sauter; **to**

~ **to one's feet, to** ~ **up** se lever d'un bond;
to ~ **across** or **over sth** franchir qch d'un
bond
(b) ⟨*heart*⟩ bondir (**with** de)
(c) (*also* ~ **up**) ⟨*price, profit*⟩ grimper (**by**
de)
■ **leap at:** ~ **at** [**sth**] sauter sur ⟨*chance,
offer*⟩
■ **leap up (a)** (jump to one's feet) bondir sur
ses pieds
(b) ⟨*price, rate*⟩ grimper

leapfrog *n* saute-mouton *m*

leap year *n* année *f* bissextile

learn ⊡ *vtr* (gen) apprendre; acquérir
⟨*skills*⟩ (**from** de); **to** ~ (**how**) **to do**
apprendre à faire; **to** ~ **that** apprendre que
⊡ *vi* apprendre; **to** ~ **about sth** apprendre
qch; **to** ~ **from one's mistakes** tirer la leçon
de ses erreurs

learned *adj* ⟨*person, book*⟩ érudit/-e;
⟨*journal*⟩ spécialisé/-e; ⟨*society*⟩ savant/-e

learner *n* (beginner) débutant/-e *m/f*; **to be a
fast/slow** ~ apprendre/ne pas apprendre
vite

learner driver *n* élève *mf* d'auto-école

learning *n* **(a)** (knowledge) érudition *f*
(b) (process) apprentissage *m*

learning difficulties *n pl* (of
schoolchildren) difficultés *fpl* scolaires; (of
adults) difficultés *fpl* d'apprentissage

lease ⊡ *n* bail *m*
⊡ *vtr* louer [qch] à bail ⟨*house*⟩; louer ⟨*car*⟩

leaseholder *n* locataire *mf* à bail

leash *n* laisse *f*

leasing ⊡ *n* (by company) crédit-bail *m*; (by
individual) location *f* avec option d'achat
⊡ *adj* ⟨*company, scheme*⟩ de leasing

least ⊡ *det* **the** ~ le moins de; (in negative
constructions) le or la moindre; **they have the**
~ **money** ce sont eux qui ont le moins
d'argent; **I haven't the** ~ **idea** je n'en ai pas
la moindre idée
⊡ *pron* **the** ~ le moins; **we have the** ~ c'est
nous qui en avons le moins; **it was the** ~ **I
could do!** c'est la moindre des choses!
⊡ *adv* **(a)** (with adjective or noun) **the** ~ le/la
moins; (with plural noun) les moins; **the** ~
wealthy families les familles les moins riches
(b) (with verbs) le moins *inv*; **I like that one
(the)** ~ c'est celui-là que j'aime le moins;
nobody liked it, ~ **of all John** personne ne
l'aimait, John encore moins que les autres
⊡ **at least** *phr* (at the minimum) au moins;
(qualifying statement) du moins; **she's at** ~ **40**
elle a au moins 40 ans; **they could at** ~ **have
phoned!** ils auraient au moins pu
téléphoner!; **he's gone to bed—at** ~ **I think
so** il est allé se coucher—du moins, je pense
⊡ **in the least** *phr* **not in the** ~ pas du
tout
IDIOMS **last but not** ~, **last but by no means**
~ enfin et surtout

leather ⊡ *n* cuir *m*
⊡ *adj* ⟨*garment, object*⟩ de cuir, en cuir

leave ⊡ *n* congé *m*; **three days'** ~ trois
jours de congé
⊡ *vtr* **(a)** (depart from) partir de ⟨*house,
station etc*⟩; (more permanently) quitter
⟨*country, city etc*⟩; (go out of) sortir de ⟨*room,
building*⟩; **he left home early** il est parti tôt
de chez lui; **to** ~ **school** quitter l'école
(b) (forget) oublier ⟨*child, object*⟩
(c) quitter ⟨*partner*⟩
(d) laisser ⟨*instructions, tip*⟩ (**for** pour; **with**
à); **to** ~ **sb sth** laisser qch à qn; **to** ~ **sb/sth
in sb's care** confier qn/qch à qn
(e) laisser ⟨*food, drink, gap*⟩; **to** ~ **sth lying
around** laisser traîner qch; **to** ~ **sth tidy**
laisser qch en ordre
(f) to ~ **sth to sb** laisser [qch] à qn ⟨*job,
task*⟩; **to** ~ **it (up) to sb to do** laisser à qn le
soin de faire; **to** ~ **sb to it** laisser qn se
débrouiller; ~ **it to** or **with me** je m'en
occupe
(g) ⟨*oil, wine*⟩ faire ⟨*stain*⟩; ⟨*cup, plate*⟩
laisser ⟨*stain, mark*⟩
(h) (postpone) laisser ⟨*task, homework*⟩; ~ **it
till tomorrow** laisse ça pour demain
(i) (bequeath) léguer (**to sb** à qn)
⊡ *vi* partir (**for** pour)
■ **leave behind (a)** (go faster than) distancer
⟨*person, competitor*⟩; **to be** or **get left behind**
(physically) se faire distancer; (intellectually) ne
pas suivre; (in business) ⟨*country, company*⟩ se
laisser distancer
(b) ⟨*traveller*⟩ laisser [qch] derrière soi
⟨*town, country*⟩; ⟨*person*⟩ quitter ⟨*family,
husband*⟩; en finir avec ⟨*past*⟩
(c) (forget) oublier, laisser ⟨*object, child,
animal*⟩
■ **leave out (a)** (accidentally) oublier ⟨*word,
ingredient, person*⟩; (deliberately) omettre
⟨*name, fact*⟩; ne pas mettre ⟨*ingredient,
object*⟩; tenir [qn] à l'écart ⟨*person*⟩; **to** ~ **sb
out of** exclure qn de ⟨*group*⟩
(b) (outdoors) laisser [qch] dehors

leaving ⊡ *n* départ *m*
⊡ *adj* ⟨*party, present*⟩ d'adieu

Lebanon *pr n* **(the)** ~ (le) Liban *m*

lecherous *adj* lubrique

lectern *n* (in church) lutrin *m*; (for lecture
notes) pupitre *m*

lecture ⊡ *n* conférence *f* (**on** sur); (GB)
(Univ) cours *m* magistral (**on** sur)
⊡ *vtr* **(a)** (GB) (Univ) donner des cours à
⟨*class*⟩
(b) (scold) faire la leçon à ⟨*person*⟩
⊡ *vi* **(a)** (gen) donner une conférence (**on**
sur)
(b) (GB) (Univ) **to** ~ **in sth** enseigner qch (à
l'université)

lecture notes *n pl* notes *fpl* de cours

lecturer *n* **(a)** (speaker) conférencier/-ière
m/f
(b) (GB) (Univ) enseignant/-e *m/f* (du
supérieur)
(c) (US) (Univ) ≈ chargé *m* de cours

lecture theatre *n* amphithéâtre *m*

ledge *n* **(a)** (shelf) rebord *m*
(b) (on mountain) saillie *f* (rocheuse)

ledger n registre m de comptabilité, grand livre m

leech n sangsue f

leek n poireau m

leer vi to ∼ at sb/sth lorgner qn/qch (colloq)

leeway n liberté f de manœuvre

left ① n gauche f; on the ∼ sur la gauche; (politically) à gauche
② adj (a) ⟨eye, hand, shoe⟩ gauche
(b) (remaining) to be ∼ rester; there are/we have five minutes ∼ il reste/il nous reste cinq minutes; I've got one ∼ il m'en reste un
③ adv ⟨go, look, turn⟩ à gauche

left-hand adj ⟨side⟩ de gauche

left-hand drive n voiture f avec la conduite à gauche

left-handed adj gaucher/-ère

left-luggage (office) n (GB) consigne f

left-luggage lockers n pl consigne f automatique

leftovers n pl restes mpl

left wing ① n the ∼ la gauche f
② **left-wing** adj ⟨attitude⟩ de gauche; they are very ∼ ils sont très à gauche

leg n (a) (of person, horse) jambe f; (of other animal) patte f
(b) (of furniture) pied m
(c) (Culin) (of lamb) gigot m; (of poultry, pork, frog) cuisse f
(d) (of trousers) jambe f
(e) (of journey, race) étape f
IDIOMS to pull sb's ∼ faire marcher qn

legacy n (a) (Law) legs m
(b) (figurative) héritage m; (of war) séquelles fpl

legal adj (a) ⟨document, system⟩ juridique; ⟨costs⟩ de justice; to take ∼ advice consulter un avocat
(b) ⟨heir, right, separation⟩ légal/-e; ⟨owner, claim⟩ légitime

legal action n to take ∼ against sb intenter un procès à qn

legal aid n aide f juridique

legal holiday n (US) jour m férié

legalize vtr légaliser

legally adv ⟨valid, void⟩ juridiquement; this contract is ∼ binding ce contrat vous engage; ⟨act⟩ légalement

legal proceedings n pl poursuites fpl judiciaires

legal tender n monnaie f légale

legend n légende f (of de)

legendary adj légendaire

leggings n pl (for baby) collant m; (for woman) caleçon m

legible adj lisible

legislation n législation f

legitimate adj (a) (justifiable) ⟨action, question, request⟩ légitime; ⟨excuse⟩ valable
(b) (lawful) ⟨organization⟩ régulier/-ière; ⟨child, heir, owner⟩ légitime

legitimize vtr (legalize) légaliser; (justify) justifier

leisure ① n loisirs mpl; to do sth at (one's) ∼ prendre son temps pour faire qch
② adj ⟨centre, facilities⟩ de loisirs

leisure time n loisirs mpl, temps m libre

leisure wear n vêtements mpl de sport

lemon n (fruit) citron m

lemonade n (fizzy) limonade f; (still) citronnade f; (US) (fresh) citron m pressé

lemon juice n jus m de citron; (GB) (drink) citron m pressé

lemon tea n thé m au citron

lemon tree n citronnier m

lend vtr (a) (loan) prêter ⟨object, money⟩; to ∼ sb sth, to ∼ sth to sb prêter qch à qn; to ∼ a hand donner un coup de main
(b) (give) conférer ⟨quality, credibility⟩ (to à); prêter ⟨support⟩; to ∼ weight to sth donner du poids à qch

lender n prêteur/-euse m/f

lending n prêt m

length ① n (a) longueur f; what ∼ is the plank? de quelle longueur est la planche?; to be 50 cm in ∼ faire 50 cm de long
(b) (of book, film, list) longueur f; (of event, prison sentence) durée f; ∼ of time temps m
(c) (of string, carpet, wood) morceau m; (of fabric) ≈ métrage m; (of pipe, track) tronçon m; dress ∼ hauteur f de robe
(d) (Sport) longueur f
② **at length** phr longuement
IDIOMS to go to great ∼s to do se donner beaucoup de mal pour faire

lengthen ① vtr rallonger ⟨garment⟩ (by de, par); prolonger ⟨shelf, road⟩ (by de, par); prolonger ⟨stay⟩
② vi ⟨queue, list⟩ s'allonger; ⟨days⟩ rallonger

lengthy adj long/longue

lenient adj ⟨person⟩ indulgent/-e (with pour); ⟨punishment⟩ léger/-ère

lens n (in optical instruments) lentille f; (in spectacles) verre m; (in camera) objectif m; (contact) lentille f

lens cap n bouchon m d'objectif

Lent n carême m

lentil n lentille f

Leo pr n Lion m

leopard n léopard m

leotard n justaucorps m inv

leper n lépreux/-euse m/f

leprosy n lèpre f

lesbian n lesbienne f

less ① det moins; ∼ beer moins de bière; I have ∼ money than him j'ai moins d'argent que lui
② pron moins; I have ∼ than you j'en ai moins que toi; ∼ than 10 moins de dix; in ∼ than three hours en moins de trois heures; even ∼ encore moins
③ adv moins; I read ∼ these days je lis moins à présent; the more I see him, the ∼ I like him plus je le vois, moins je l'aime
④ prep moins; ∼ 15% discount moins 15% de remise; ∼ tax avant impôts
⑤ **less and less** phr de moins en moins

lessen *vtr* diminuer ⟨*influence, feelings*⟩; réduire ⟨*cost*⟩; atténuer ⟨*impact, pain*⟩

lesser ⟦1⟧ *adj* moindre; **to a ~ extent** à un moindre degré
⟦2⟧ *adv* moins; **~ known** moins connu

lesson *n* cours *m*, leçon *f*; **Spanish ~** cours d'espagnol; **driving ~** leçon de conduite; **I'm going to teach him a ~!** je vais lui donner une bonne leçon!

let[1]

■ *Note* When *let* is used with another verb to make a suggestion (*let's do it at once*), the first person plural of the appropriate verb can generally be used to express this in French: *faisons-le tout de suite*. (Note that the verb alone translates *let us do* and no pronoun appears in French.)
– In the spoken language, however, French speakers will use the much more colloquial *on* + *present tense* or *si on* + *imperfect tense*:
– *let's go!* = allons-y or on y va!; *let's go to the cinema tonight* = si on allait au cinéma ce soir?
– These translations can also be used for suggestions in the negative:
– *let's not take* or *don't let's take the bus—let's walk* = on ne prend pas le bus, on y va à pied *or* ne prenons pas le bus, allons-y à pied.
– When *let* is used to mean *allow*, it is generally translated by the verb *laisser*. For more examples and particular usages, see the entry below.

vtr **(a)** (in suggestions, commands) **~'s get out of here!** sortons d'ici!; **~'s not** *or* **don't ~'s** (GB) **talk about that!** n'en parlons pas!
(b) (allow) **to ~ sb do** laisser qn faire; **~ me explain** laisse-moi t'expliquer; **don't ~ it get you down** ne te laisse pas abattre; **she wanted to go but they wouldn't ~ her** elle voulait y aller mais ils ne l'ont pas laissée faire; **to ~ one's hair grow** se laisser pousser les cheveux

■ **let down**: ¶ **~ [sb] down (a)** (disappoint) laisser tomber [qn]; **to feel let down** être déçu/-e
(b) (embarrass) faire honte à [qn]
¶ **~ [sth] down (a)** (GB) dégonfler ⟨*tyre*⟩
(b) rallonger ⟨*garment*⟩

■ **let go**: ¶ **~ go** lâcher prise; **to ~ go of sb/ sth** lâcher qn/qch
¶ **~ [sb] go (a)** relâcher ⟨*prisoner*⟩
(b) lâcher ⟨*person, arm*⟩
(c) licencier ⟨*employee*⟩
(d) to ~ oneself go se laisser aller; ¶ **~ [sth] go** lâcher ⟨*rope, bar*⟩

■ **let in**: ¶ **~ [sth] in** ⟨*roof, window*⟩ laisser passer ⟨*rain*⟩; ⟨*shoes*⟩ prendre ⟨*water*⟩; ⟨*curtains*⟩ laisser passer ⟨*light*⟩
¶ **~ [sb] in (a)** (show in) faire entrer; (admit) laisser entrer
(b) to ~ oneself in for aller au devant de ⟨*trouble*⟩

■ **let off**: ¶ **~ off [sth]** tirer ⟨*fireworks*⟩; faire exploser ⟨*bomb*⟩; faire partir ⟨*gun*⟩
¶ **~ [sb] off (a)** (excuse) **to ~ sb off** dispenser qn de ⟨*homework*⟩

(b) (leave unpunished) ne pas punir ⟨*culprit*⟩
■ **let out**: ¶ **~ out** (US) ⟨*school*⟩ finir (at à); ¶ **~ out [sth] (a)** laisser échapper ⟨*cry*⟩; **to ~ out a roar** beugler
(b) (GB) (reveal) révéler (that que); ¶ **~ [sth] out (a)** faire sortir ⟨*animal*⟩; donner libre cours à ⟨*anger*⟩
(b) élargir ⟨*waistband*⟩
¶ **~ [sb] out** laisser sortir ⟨*prisoner*⟩ (of de); faire sortir ⟨*pupils, employees*⟩ (of de)
■ **let up** ⟨*rain, wind*⟩ se calmer; ⟨*pressure*⟩ s'arrêter; ⟨*heat*⟩ diminuer

let[2] *vtr* (*also* **~ out** (GB)) louer (to à); **'to ~'** 'à louer'

letdown *n* déception *f*

lethal *adj* ⟨*substance, gas, dose*⟩ mortel/-elle; ⟨*weapon*⟩ meurtrier/-ière

lethargic *adj* léthargique; (lazy) apathique; **to feel ~** se sentir engourdi/-e

letter *n* **(a)** lettre *f* (**to** pour; **from** de)
(b) (of alphabet) lettre *f*

letter bomb *n* lettre *f* piégée

letter box *n* boîte *f* à lettres

letterhead *n* en-tête *m*

letters page *n* courrier *m* des lecteurs

lettuce *n* salade *f*, laitue *f*

letup *n* accalmie *f*; (respite) pause *f*

leuk(a)emia *n* leucémie *f*

level ⟦1⟧ *n* **(a)** (gen) niveau *m*; **to be on the same ~ as sb** être du même niveau que qn; **at street ~** au niveau de la rue
(b) (of unemployment, illiteracy) taux *m*; (of spending) montant *m*; (of satisfaction, anxiety) degré *m*
(c) (in hierarchy) échelon *m*
⟦2⟧ *adj* **(a)** ⟨*shelf, floor*⟩ droit/-e; ⟨*table*⟩ horizontal/-e
(b) ⟨*ground, surface, land*⟩ plat/-e
(c) (Culin) ⟨*teaspoonful*⟩ ras/-e
(d) to be ~ ⟨*shoulders, windows*⟩ être à la même hauteur; ⟨*floor, building*⟩ être au même niveau; **~ with the ground** au ras du sol
(e) to remain ~ ⟨*figures*⟩ rester stable
⟦3⟧ *adv* **to draw ~** arriver à la même hauteur (**with** que)
⟦4⟧ *vtr* **(a)** (destroy) raser ⟨*village*⟩
(b) lancer ⟨*accusation*⟩ (at contre); adresser ⟨*criticism*⟩ (at à); braquer ⟨*gun*⟩ (at sur)
(c) aplanir ⟨*ground, surface*⟩
IDIOMS **to be ~-pegging** être à égalité; **to ~ with sb** être honnête avec qn
■ **level off** ⟨*prices, curve*⟩ se stabiliser

level crossing *n* passage *m* à niveau

level-headed *adj* sensé/-e

lever *n* (Aut, Tech) levier *m*; (small) manette *f*

levy ⟦1⟧ *n* taxe *f*, impôt *m*
⟦2⟧ *vtr* prélever ⟨*tax, duty*⟩; imposer ⟨*fine*⟩

lewd *adj* ⟨*joke, gesture, remark*⟩ obscène; ⟨*person*⟩ lubrique

liability ⟦1⟧ *n* **(a)** (Law) responsabilité *f*
(b) (drawback) handicap *m*
⟦2⟧ **liabilities** *n pl* passif *m*, dettes *fpl*

liable adj (a) (likely) to be ~ to do risquer de faire; **it's ~ to rain** il risque de pleuvoir, il se peut qu'il pleuve
(b) (legally subject) to be ~ to être passible de ‹fine›; to be ~ for tax ‹person, company› être imposable; ‹goods› être soumis/-e à l'impôt

liaise vi travailler en liaison (**with** avec)

liaison n liaison f

liar n menteur/-euse m/f

libel [1] n diffamation f
[2] vtr diffamer

libellous (GB), **libelous** (US) adj diffamatoire

liberal [1] n libéral/-e m/f
[2] adj (a) (politically) libéral/-e
(b) ‹amount› généreux/-euse; ‹person› prodigue (**with** de)

Liberal n libéral/-e m/f

Liberal Democrat n (GB) libéral-démocrate mf

liberalism n libéralisme m

liberalize vtr libéraliser

liberate [1] vtr libérer (**from** de)
[2] **liberated** pp adj ‹lifestyle, woman› libéré/-e
[3] **liberating** pres p adj libérateur/-trice

liberation n libération f (**from** de); **women's ~** libération de la femme

liberty n liberté f

Libra n Balance f

librarian n bibliothécaire mf

library n bibliothèque f; **public ~** bibliothèque municipale; **mobile ~** (GB) bibliobus m

lice n pl poux mpl

licence (GB), **license** (US) n (a) (for trading) licence f
(b) (to drive, fish) permis m; (for TV) redevance f; to lose one's (driving) ~ se faire retirer son permis (de conduire)
(c) (freedom) licence f

licence number n (of car) numéro m minéralogique or d'immatriculation

licence plate n plaque f minéralogique or d'immatriculation

license [1] n (US) = LICENCE
[2] vtr (a) (authorize) autoriser (**to do** à faire)
(b) faire immatriculer ‹vehicle›

licensed adj (a) ‹restaurant› qui a une licence de débit de boissons
(b) ‹dealer, firm, taxi› agréé/-e; ‹pilot› breveté/-e; ‹vehicle› en règle

licensing laws n pl (GB) lois fpl réglementant la vente des boissons alcoolisées

lick [1] n (a) coup m de langue
(b) a ~ of paint un petit coup de peinture
[2] vtr (a) lécher; to ~ one's lips se lécher les babines
(b) (colloq) écraser ‹team, opponent›; to get ~ed se faire écraser
IDIOMS to ~ one's wounds panser ses blessures

licorice (US) = LIQUORICE

lid n (a) (cover) couvercle m
(b) (eyelid) paupière f

lie [1] n mensonge m; to tell a ~ mentir
[2] vi (a) (tell falsehood) mentir (**to sb** à qn; **about** à propos de); he ~d about her il a menti à son propos
(b) ‹person, animal› (action) s'allonger; (state) être allongé/-e; ‹objects› être couché/-e; he was lying on the bed il était allongé sur le lit; to ~ on one's back s'allonger sur le dos; ~ still ne bougez pas; here ~s John Brown ci-gît John Brown
(c) (be situated) être; (remain) rester; to ~ open ‹book› être ouvert/-e; that's where our future ~s c'est là qu'est notre avenir; to ~ before sb ‹life, career› s'ouvrir devant qn; what ~s ahead? qu'est-ce qui nous attend?; the house lay empty for years la maison est restée vide pendant des années
(d) (can be found) résider; their interests ~ elsewhere leurs intérêts résident ailleurs; to ~ in ‹cause, secret, talent› résider dans; ‹popularity, strength, fault› venir de; the responsibility ~s with them ce sont eux qui sont responsables
IDIOMS to ~ low garder un profil bas; to take it lying down (colloq) se laisser faire
■ **lie around** traîner; to leave sth lying around laisser traîner qch
■ **lie down** (briefly) s'allonger; (for longer period) se coucher

lie detector n détecteur m de mensonge

lie-in n to have a ~ faire la grasse matinée

lieu [1] in lieu adv phr one week's holiday in ~ une semaine de vacances pour compenser
[2] in lieu of prep phr à la place de

life n (a) (gen) vie f; that's ~! c'est la vie!; the first time in my ~ la première fois de ma vie; a job for ~ un emploi à vie; a friend for ~ un ami pour la vie; for the rest of one's ~ pour le restant de ses jours; full of ~ plein/-e de vie; to come to ~ ‹shy person› sortir de sa réserve; ‹fictional character› prendre vie; ‹party› s'animer
(b) (of machine, product) durée f
(c) (Law) to serve ~ être emprisonné/-e à vie; to sentence sb to ~ condamner qn à perpétuité
IDIOMS to have the time of one's ~ s'amuser comme un fou/une folle

lifebelt n bouée f de sauvetage

lifeboat n canot m de sauvetage

life drawing n dessin m d'après modèle

life-expectancy n espérance f de vie; (of product) durée f probable

lifeguard n surveillant/-e m/f de baignade

life imprisonment n réclusion f à perpétuité

life insurance n assurance-vie f

lifejacket n gilet m de sauvetage

lifeless adj ‹body, object› inanimé/-e; ‹performance› peu vivant/-e; ‹voice› éteint/-e

lifelike adj très ressemblant/-e

lifeline n bouée f de sauvetage

lifelong adj ⟨friendship, fear⟩ de toute une vie; **to have had a ~ ambition to do** avoir toujours rêvé de faire

lifesaving n (gen) sauvetage m; (Med) secourisme m

life sentence n condamnation f à perpétuité

life-size adj grandeur nature inv

life span n durée f de vie

life story n vie f

lifestyle n style m de vie

life-support machine n **to be on a ~** être sous assistance respiratoire

lifetime n vie f; **in her ~** de son vivant; **the chance of a ~** une chance unique; **to seem like a ~** sembler une éternité

lift **1** n (a) (GB) (elevator) ascenseur m; (for goods) monte-charge m inv
(b) (ride) **she asked me for a ~** elle m'a demandé de la conduire; **can I give you a ~?** je peux te déposer quelque part?
(c) (colloq) (boost) **to give sb a ~** remonter le moral à qn
2 vtr (a) (pick up) soulever ⟨object, person⟩; **to ~ sth out of the box** sortir qch de la boîte
(b) (raise) lever ⟨arm, head⟩
(c) (remove) lever ⟨ban, sanctions⟩
(d) (boost) **to ~ sb's spirits** remonter le moral à qn
(e) (colloq) (steal) piquer (colloq) (**from** dans)
3 vi ⟨bad mood, headache⟩ disparaître; ⟨fog⟩ se dissiper
■ **lift off**: ¶ ~ **off** ⟨rocket⟩ décoller; ⟨top, cover⟩ s'enlever; ¶ ~ **[sth] off** enlever ⟨cover, lid⟩
■ **lift up** soulever ⟨book, suitcase, lid⟩; lever ⟨head, veil, eyes⟩; relever ⟨jumper, coat⟩

lift-off n lancement m

ligament n ligament m

light **1** n (a) (brightness) lumière f; **against the ~** à contre-jour
(b) (in building, machine) lumière f; (in street) réverbère m; (on ship) feu m; (on dashboard) voyant m (lumineux)
(c) (Aut) (headlight) phare m; (rearlight) feu m arrière; (inside car) veilleuse f
(d) (flame) **to set ~ to** mettre le feu à; **have you got a ~?** tu as du feu?
(e) (aspect) jour m; **to see sth in a different ~** voir qch sous un jour différent
(f) **to come to** or **be brought to ~** être découvert/-e
2 lights n pl (traffic) **~s** feu m, feux mpl; **the ~s are red** le feu est au rouge
3 adj (a) (bright) **to get** or **grow ~er** ⟨sky⟩ s'éclaircir; **while it's still ~** pendant qu'il fait encore jour
(b) ⟨colour, wood, skin⟩ clair/-e; **~ blue** bleu clair inv
(c) ⟨material, wind, clothing, meal⟩ léger/-ère; ⟨rain⟩ fin/-e; ⟨drinker⟩ modéré/-e; **to be a ~ sleeper** avoir le sommeil léger
(d) ⟨knock, footsteps⟩ léger/-ère
(e) ⟨work⟩ peu fatigant/-e; ⟨exercise⟩ léger/-ère

(f) ⟨music⟩ léger/-ère; **a bit of ~ relief** un peu de divertissement; **some ~ reading** quelque chose de facile à lire
4 vtr (a) allumer ⟨oven, cigarette, fire⟩; enflammer ⟨paper⟩; craquer ⟨match⟩
(b) ⟨torch, lamp⟩ éclairer
■ **light up** ⟨lamp⟩ s'allumer; ⟨face⟩ s'éclairer; ⟨eyes⟩ briller de joie

light bulb n ampoule f

lighten **1** vtr éclaircir ⟨colour, hair, skin⟩; détendre ⟨atmosphere⟩
2 vi ⟨sky, hair⟩ s'éclaircir; ⟨atmosphere⟩ se détendre

light entertainment n variétés fpl

lighter n (for smokers) briquet m; (for gas cooker) allume-gaz m inv

lighter fuel n (gas) gaz m à briquet; (liquid) essence f à briquet

light-hearted adj ⟨person⟩ enjoué/-e; ⟨book⟩ humoristique

lighthouse n phare m

lighting n éclairage m

lightly adv (a) ⟨touch, kiss, season⟩ légèrement
(b) ⟨undertake, dismiss⟩ à la légère
(c) **to get off ~** s'en tirer à bon compte

lightning **1** n (in sky) éclairs mpl; (striking sth) foudre f; **a flash of ~** un éclair; **struck by ~** frappé/-e par la foudre
2 adj ⟨visit, raid⟩ éclair inv

light switch n interrupteur m

lightweight adj ⟨garment⟩ léger/-ère; ⟨champion⟩ des poids légers

light year n année-lumière f

like¹ **1** prep (a) (gen) comme; **to be ~ sb/sth** être comme qn/qch; **to look ~** ressembler à; **big cities ~ London** les grandes villes comme Londres or telles que Londres; **you know what she's ~!** tu sais comment elle est!; **it was just ~ a fairytale!** on aurait dit un conte de fée!; **it looks ~ rain** on dirait qu'il va pleuvoir; **what's it ~?** c'est comment?; **what was the weather ~?** quel temps faisait-il?
(b) (typical of) **it's not ~ her to be late** ça ne lui ressemble pas or ce n'est pas son genre d'être en retard; **that's just ~ him!** c'est bien (de) lui!
2 conj (a) (in the same way as) comme; **~ they used to** comme ils le faisaient autrefois
(b) (colloq) (as if) comme si; **he acts ~ he owns the place** il se conduit comme s'il était chez lui
3 n **fires, floods and the ~** les incendies, les inondations et autres catastrophes de ce genre; **she won't speak to the ~s of us!** (colloq) elle refuse de parler à des gens comme nous!

like² vtr (a) aimer bien ⟨person⟩; aimer (bien) ⟨artist, food, music, style⟩; **to ~ doing** or **to do** aimer (bien) faire; **to ~ A best** préférer A; **how do you ~ living in London?** ça te plaît de vivre à Londres?; **she doesn't ~ to be kept waiting** elle n'aime pas qu'on la fasse attendre

(b) (wish) vouloir, aimer; **I would ~ a ticket** je voudrais un billet; **I would ~ to do** je voudrais *or* j'aimerais faire; **would you ~ to come to dinner?** voudriez-vous venir dîner?; **we'd ~ her to come** nous voudrions *or* aimerions qu'elle vienne; **if you ~** si tu veux; **you can do what you ~** tu peux faire ce que tu veux

likeable *adj* ⟨person⟩ sympathique; ⟨novel, music⟩ agréable

likelihood *n* probabilité *f*, chances *fpl*; **in all ~** selon toute probabilité

likely *adj* **(a)** (probable) probable; ⟨explanation⟩ plausible; **prices are ~ to rise** les prix risquent d'augmenter; **it is** *or* **seems ~ that she'll come** il est probable qu'elle viendra; **it is hardly ~ that she'll come** il y a peu de chances qu'elle vienne; **a ~ story!** à d'autres! (colloq)
(b) (promising) ⟨candidate⟩ prometteur/-euse

like-minded *adj* du même avis

liken *vtr* comparer (**to** à)

likeness *n* **(a)** (similarity) ressemblance *f*; **family ~** air *m* de famille
(b) (picture) **to be a good ~** être ressemblant/-e

likewise *adv* (similarly) également, de même; (also) aussi, de même

liking *n* **to take a ~ to sb** se prendre d'affection pour qn; **to be to sb's ~** plaire à qn

lilac *n, adj* lilas (*m*) *inv*

lily *n* lys *m inv*

lily of the valley *n* muguet *m*

limb *n* **(a)** (arm, leg) membre *m*
(b) (of tree) branche *f* (maîtresse)

limber *v* ■ **limber up** s'échauffer

limbo *n* **(a)** (state) les limbes *mpl*; **to be in ~** être dans les limbes
(b) (dance) limbo *m*

lime *n* **(a)** (calcium) chaux *f*
(b) (fruit) citron *m* vert
(c) (*also ~* **tree**) tilleul *m*

lime green *n, adj* citron (*m*) vert *inv*

lime juice *n* jus *m* de citron vert

limelight *n* vedette *f*; **to be in the ~** tenir la vedette

limestone *n* calcaire *m*

limit ① *n* limite *f*; **within ~s** dans une certaine limite; **to push sb to the ~** pousser qn à bout
② *vtr* limiter (**to** à)

limitation *n* **(a)** (restriction) restriction *f* (**on** à)
(b) (shortcoming) limite *f*; **to know one's (own) ~s** connaître ses propres limites

limited *adj* limité/-e

limited company *n* (GB) société *f* anonyme

limousine *n* limousine *f*

limp ① *n* **to have a ~** boiter
② *adj* mou/molle
③ *vi* boiter; **to ~ in/away** entrer/s'éloigner en boitant

linchpin *n* (essential element) **the ~ of** ⟨person⟩ le pilier de; ⟨principle⟩ la base de

line ① *n* **(a)** (gen, Sport) ligne *f*; (shorter, thicker) trait *m*; (in drawing) trait *m*; **a straight ~** une ligne droite
(b) (of people, cars) file *f*; (of trees) rangée *f*; **to stand** *or* **wait in ~** faire la queue
(c) (on face) ride *f*
(d) (rope) corde *f*; (for fishing) ligne *f*; **to put the washing on the ~** étendre le linge
(e) (electric cable) ligne *f* (électrique)
(f) (phone connection) ligne *f*; **at the other end of the ~** au bout du fil; **the ~ went dead** la ligne a été coupée
(g) (rail route) ligne *f* (**between** entre); (rails) voie *f*
(h) (shipping company, airline) compagnie *f*
(i) (in genealogy) lignée *f*
(j) (in prose) ligne *f*; (in poetry) vers *m*; **to learn one's ~s** ⟨actor⟩ apprendre son texte
(k) **to fall into ~ with** s'aligner sur; **to bring sb into ~** ramener qn dans le rang; **to keep sb in ~** tenir qn en main
(l) (stance) **the official ~** la position officielle; **to take a firm ~ with sb** se montrer ferme avec qn
(m) (type of product) gamme *f*
(n) (Mil) **enemy ~s** lignes *fpl* ennemies
② *vtr* doubler ⟨garment⟩ (**with** avec); tapisser ⟨shelf⟩ (**with** de); border ⟨route⟩
③ **in line with** *phr* en accord avec ⟨policy, trend⟩; **to increase in ~ with** augmenter proportionnellement à
■ **line up**: ¶ **~ up** (side by side) se mettre en rang; (one behind the other) se mettre en file
¶ **~ [sth] up (a)** (align) aligner (**with** sur)
(b) sélectionner ⟨team⟩

lined *adj* ⟨face⟩ ridé/-e; ⟨paper⟩ ligné/-e; ⟨curtains⟩ doublé/-e

line manager *n* responsable opérationnel/-elle *m/f*

linen *n* **(a)** (fabric) lin *m*
(b) (household) linge *m* de maison; (underwear) linge *m* de corps

linen basket *n* panier *m* à linge sale

linen cupboard (GB), **linen closet** (US) *n* armoire *f* à linge

line of fire *n* ligne *f* de tir

line of work *n* métier *m*

liner *n* paquebot *m* de grande ligne

linesman *n* (GB) (in tennis) juge *m* de ligne; (in football, hockey) juge *m* de touche

line-up *n* (Sport) équipe *f*; (personnel, pop group) groupe *m*

linger *vi* **(a)** ⟨person⟩ s'attarder; ⟨gaze⟩ s'attarder (**on** sur)
(b) ⟨memory, smell⟩ persister
(c) ⟨doubt, suspicion⟩ subsister

lingerie *n* lingerie *f*

linguist *n* linguiste *mf*

linguistic *adj* linguistique

linguistics *n* linguistique *f*

lining *n* doublure *f*

link ① *n* **(a)** (in chain) maillon *m*
(b) (connection by rail, road) liaison *f*

(c) (between facts, events) rapport *m* (**between** entre); (between people) lien *m* (**with** avec)
(d) (tie) relation *f*, lien *m* (**with** avec; **between** entre)
(e) (in TV, radio, computing) liaison *f*
2 *vtr* **(a)** ⟨*road, cable*⟩ relier ⟨*places, objects*⟩; **to ~ A to B** or **A and B** relier A à B; **to ~ arms** ⟨*people*⟩ se donner le bras
(b) to ~ sth to or **with** lier qch à ⟨*inflation*⟩; établir un lien entre qch et ⟨*fact, crime, illness*⟩
(c) connecter ⟨*terminals*⟩
(d) (in TV, radio) établir une liaison entre ⟨*places*⟩ (**by** par)
3 linked *pp adj* ⟨*circles, symbols*⟩ entrelacé/-e; ⟨*issues, problems*⟩ lié/-e
■ **link up**: ¶ ~ **up** ⟨*firms*⟩ s'associer; **to ~ up with** s'associer avec ⟨*college, firm*⟩; ¶ ~ **[sth] up** relier

link road *n* route *f* de raccordement
link-up *n* **(a)** (on TV, radio) liaison *f*
(b) (collaboration) association *f*
lino *n* lino *m*
lint *n* tissu *m* ouaté
lion *n* lion *m*
lion cub *n* lionceau *m*
lioness *n* lionne *f*
lip *n* **(a)** lèvre *f*
(b) (of jug) bec *m*
liposuction *n* liposuccion *f*
lip-read *vi* lire sur les lèvres de quelqu'un
lipsalve *n* baume *m* pour les lèvres
lip service *n* **to pay ~ to feminism** se dire féministe pour la forme
lipstick *n* rouge *m* à lèvres
liqueur *n* liqueur *f*
liquid *n*, *adj* liquide (*m*)
liquidate *vtr* liquider
liquidation *n* liquidation *f*
liquidizer *n* (GB Culin) mixeur *m*
liquor *n* alcool *m*
liquorice, licorice (US) *n* **(a)** (plant) réglisse *f*
(b) (substance) réglisse *m*
liquor store *n* (US) magasin *m* de vins et spiritueux
Lisbon *pr n* Lisbonne
lisp *n* zézaiement *m*; **to have a ~** zézayer
list **1** *n* liste *f* (**of** de)
2 *vtr* **(a)** (gen) faire la liste de ⟨*objects, people*⟩; **to be ~ed in a directory** être repris/-e dans un répertoire
(b) (Comput) lister
3 *vi* ⟨*vessel*⟩ donner de la bande
4 listed *pp adj* (GB) ⟨*building*⟩ classé; ⟨*company*⟩ coté/-e en Bourse
listen *vi* écouter; **to ~ to sb/sth** écouter qn/qch; **to ~ to reason** écouter la voix de la raison; **to ~ (out) for** guetter
■ **listen in** écouter (par indiscrétion)
listener *n* **(a) to be a good ~** savoir écouter
(b) (to radio) auditeur/-trice *m/f*

listeria *n* (bacteria) listéria *f*; (illness) listériose *f*
listing **1** *n* **(a)** inscription *f* (**in** dans); **Stock Exchange ~** liste *f* des sociétés cotées en Bourse
(b) (Comput) listing *m*
2 listings *n pl* pages *fpl* d'informations
listless *adj* ⟨*person*⟩ apathique
list price *n* prix *m* au catalogue
literacy *n* (in a population) taux *m* d'alphabétisation
literal *adj* **(a)** ⟨*meaning*⟩ littéral/-e
(b) ⟨*translation*⟩ mot à mot
literally *adv* ⟨*mean*⟩ littéralement; ⟨*translate*⟩ mot à mot; **to take sth ~** prendre qch au pied de la lettre; (quite) **~ bel et bien**
literary *adj* littéraire
literary criticism *n* critique *f* littéraire
literate *adj* **(a)** (able to read and write) **to be ~** savoir lire et écrire
(b) (cultured) ⟨*person*⟩ cultivé/-e
literature *n* **(a)** littérature *f*; **a work of ~** une œuvre littéraire
(b) (pamphlets, brochures) documentation *f*
lithe *adj* leste
Lithuania *pr n* Lituanie *f*
litigation *n* litiges *mpl*
litre, liter (US) *n* litre *m*
litter **1** *n* **(a)** (rubbish) détritus *mpl*; (substantial) ordures *fpl*; (paper) papiers *mpl*
(b) (of young) portée *f*; **to have a ~** mettre bas
(c) (for pet tray) litière *f*
2 *vtr* **to be ~ed with** ⟨*ground*⟩ être jonché/-e de
litter bin *n* poubelle *f*
little

■ **Note** When *a little* is used as a pronoun and if the sentence does not specify what it refers to, the pronoun *en* (= *of it*) must be added before the verb: *I have a little left* = il m'en reste un peu.

---

1 *adj* **(a)** (small) petit/-e (*before n*)
(b) (not much) peu de; **~ chance** peu de chances; **very ~ damage** très peu de dégâts; **there's so ~ time** il y a si peu de temps
2 *pron* **a ~ un peu; I only ate a ~** je n'en ai mangé qu'un peu; **he remembers very ~** il ne se souvient pas bien; **there's ~ I can do** je ne peux pas faire grand-chose; **to do as ~ as possible** en faire le moins possible; **~ or nothing** quasiment rien
3 *adv* **(a)** (not much) peu; **I go there very ~** j'y vais très peu; **the next results were ~ better** les résultats suivants étaient à peine meilleurs; **~ more than an hour ago** il y a à peine plus d'une heure
(b) (not at all) **~ did they know that** ils étaient bien loin de se douter que
4 a little (bit) *phr* un peu; **a ~ (bit) anxious** un peu inquiet/-iète; **a ~ less/more** un peu moins/plus; **stay a ~ longer** reste encore un peu ⋯➧

5 **as little as** *phr* **for as** ∼ **as 10 dollars a day** pour seulement 10 dollars par jour; **as** ∼ **as £60** juste 60 livres sterling
IDIOMS ∼ **by** ∼ petit à petit

little finger *n* petit doigt *m*, auriculaire *m*
IDIOMS **to wrap** *or* **twist sb around one's** ∼ mener qn par le bout du nez

live¹ *vi* **(a)** (gen) vivre; **as long as I** ∼... tant que je vivrai...; **to** ∼ **to regret sth** en venir à regretter qch; **long** ∼ **democracy!** vive la démocratie!; **to** ∼ **on** *or* **off** vivre de ⟨*fruit, charity*⟩; vivre sur ⟨*wage*⟩
(b) (dwell) ⟨*person*⟩ vivre, habiter (**with** avec); ⟨*animal*⟩ vivre; **they** ∼ **at number 7** ils habitent au numéro 7; **to** ∼ **in** vivre dans, habiter ⟨*house, apartment*⟩; **easy to** ∼ **with** facile à vivre
(c) (put up with) **to** ∼ **with** accepter ⟨*situation*⟩; supporter ⟨*decor*⟩
IDIOMS **to** ∼ **it up** (colloq) mener la grande vie
■ **live in** ⟨*maid*⟩ être logé/-e et nourri/-e
■ **live on** ⟨*reputation, tradition*⟩ se perpétuer
■ **live up to** ⟨*person*⟩ répondre à ⟨*expectations*⟩; être à la hauteur de ⟨*reputation*⟩

live² **1** *adj* **(a)** (alive) vivant/-e
(b) ⟨*broadcast*⟩ en direct; ⟨*performance*⟩ sur scène; ⟨*album*⟩ enregistré/-e en public; **before a** ∼ **audience** devant un public
(c) ⟨*cable*⟩ sous tension
2 *adv* ⟨*appear, broadcast*⟩ en direct

live-in *adj* ⟨*maid, nanny*⟩ qui est logé/-e et nourri/-e; **to have a** ∼ **lover** vivre en concubinage

livelihood *n* gagne-pain *m*

lively *adj* **(a)** ⟨*person*⟩ plein/-e d'entrain; ⟨*place, atmosphere, conversation*⟩ animé/-e
(b) (fast) ⟨*pace*⟩ vif/vive; ⟨*music, dance*⟩ entraînant/-e

liven *v* ■ **liven up:** ¶ ∼ **up** s'animer; ¶ ∼ [sth] **up** animer ⟨*event*⟩

liver *n* foie *m*

livery *n* **(a)** (uniform) livrée *f*
(b) (boarding horses) **at** ∼ en pension

livestock *n* bétail *m*

live wire *n* boute-en-train *m inv*

livid *adj* **(a)** (furious) furieux/-ieuse
(b) (in colour) ⟨*face, scar*⟩ livide

living **1** *n* **(a)** vie *f*; **to work for a** ∼ travailler pour gagner sa vie; **what do you do for a** ∼**?** qu'est-ce que vous faites dans la vie?
(b) (lifestyle) vie *f*; **easy** ∼ une vie facile
2 *adj* vivant/-e; **within** ∼ **memory** de mémoire d'homme

living conditions *n pl* conditions *fpl* de vie

living expenses *n pl* frais *mpl* de subsistance

living room *n* salle *f* de séjour, salon *m*

living standards *n pl* niveau *m* de vie

living together *n* cohabitation *f*

living will *n*: déclaration écrite (de l'interessé) refusant l'acharnement thérapeutique

lizard *n* lézard *m*

llama *n* lama *m*

load **1** *n* **(a)** (gen) charge *f*; (on vehicle, animal) chargement *m*; (on ship, plane) cargaison *f*; (figurative) fardeau *m*; **three (lorry-)**∼**s of sand** trois camions de sable
(b) (colloq) (a lot) **a (whole)** ∼ **of people** des tas (colloq) de gens; **that's a** ∼ **of nonsense** (colloq) c'est vraiment n'importe quoi (colloq)
2 **loads** *n pl* (colloq) ∼**s of** (+ plural nouns) des tas (colloq) de; ∼**s of times** plein de *or* des tas (colloq) de fois; **we've got** ∼**s of time** nous avons tout notre temps; ∼**s of work** un travail fou (colloq)
3 *vtr* **(a)** (gen) charger ⟨*vehicle, gun*⟩ (**with** de); mettre un film dans ⟨*camera*⟩
(b) (Comput) charger ⟨*program*⟩
(c) **to** ∼ **sb with** combler qn de ⟨*presents, honours*⟩

loaded *adj* **(a)** ⟨*tray, lorry, gun*⟩ chargé/-e (**with** de)
(b) (colloq) (rich) bourré/-e de fric (colloq)
(c) ⟨*question*⟩ tendancieux/-ieuse

loaf *n* pain *m*; **a** ∼ **of bread** un pain
■ **loaf about**, **loaf around** traînasser

loafer *n* **(a)** (shoe) mocassin *m*
(b) (idler) flemmard/-e *m/f* (colloq)

loan **1** *n* (when borrowing) emprunt *m*; (when lending) prêt *m*; **to be on** ∼ être prêté/-e (**to** à)
2 *vtr* (*also* ∼ **out**) prêter (**to** à)

loan shark *n* (colloq) usurier/-ière *m/f*

loath *adj* **to be** ∼ **to do** répugner à faire

loathe *vtr* détester (**doing** faire)

loathing *n* lobbying *m*

loathsome *adj* répugnant/-e

lobby **1** *n* **(a)** (of hotel) hall *m*; (of theatre) lobby *m*
(b) (*also* ∼ **group**) lobby *m*
2 *vi* faire pression (**for** pour obtenir)

lobbying *n* lobbying *m*

lobe *n* lobe *m*

lobster *n* homard *m*

local **1** *n* **(a)** **the** ∼**s** les gens *mpl* du coin
(b) (pub) pub *m* du coin
2 *adj* (gen) local/-e; ⟨*library, shop*⟩ du quartier; ⟨*radio, news*⟩ régional/-e

local anaesthetic *n* anesthésique *m* local

local authority *n* (GB) autorités *fpl* locales

local call *n* communication *f* téléphonique locale

local election *n* élection *f* locale

local government *n* administration *f* locale

locality *n* **(a)** (neighbourhood) voisinage *m*
(b) (place) endroit *m*

localized *adj* localisé/-e

locate *vtr* **(a)** (find) retrouver ⟨*object*⟩; localiser ⟨*fault*⟩
(b) (position) situer ⟨*site*⟩

location *n* endroit *m*; on ~ ⟨*filmed*⟩ en extérieur

lock ⓵ *n* (a) (with key) serrure *f*; (with bolt) verrou *m*; **under ~ and key** sous clé
(b) (of hair) mèche *f*
(c) (on canal) écluse *f*
(d) (Comput) verrouillage *m*
⓶ *vtr* fermer [qch] à clé
⓷ *vi* (a) ⟨*door, drawer*⟩ fermer à clé
(b) ⟨*steering wheel*⟩ se bloquer
■ **lock in** enfermer ⟨*person*⟩; **to ~ oneself in** s'enfermer
■ **lock out**: ~ **sb out** enfermer qn dehors; **to ~ oneself out** s'enfermer dehors
■ **lock together** ⟨*components, pieces*⟩ s'emboîter
■ **lock up**: ¶ ~ **up** fermer; ¶ ~ [**sth**] **up** fermer [qch] à clé ⟨*house*⟩; ¶ ~ [**sb**] **up** enfermer ⟨*hostage*⟩; mettre [qn] sous les verrous ⟨*killer*⟩

locker *n* casier *m*, vestiaire *m*

locker room *n* vestiaire *m*

locket *n* médaillon *m*

locksmith *n* serrurier *m*

locomotive *n* locomotive *f*

locum *n* (GB) remplaçant/-e *m/f*

lodge ⓵ *n* (small house) pavillon *m*; (for gatekeeper) loge *f* (du gardien)
⓶ *vtr* **to ~ an appeal** faire appel; **to ~ a complaint** porter plainte; **to ~ a protest** protester
⓷ *vi* (a) ⟨*person*⟩ loger (**with** chez)
(b) ⟨*bullet*⟩ se loger; ⟨*small object*⟩ se coincer

lodger *n* (room only) locataire *mf*; (with meals) pensionnaire *mf*

lodgings *n pl* logement *m*

loft *n* (a) (attic) grenier *m*
(b) (US) (apartment) loft *m*

loft conversion *n* aménagement *m* de grenier

log ⓵ *n* (a) (of wood) rondin *m*; (for burning) bûche *f*
(b) (of ship) journal *m* de bord; (of plane) carnet *m* de vol
⓶ *vtr* (a) (record) noter
(b) (*also* ~ **up**) avoir à son actif ⟨*miles*⟩
IDIOMS **to sleep like a ~** dormir comme une souche
■ **log in, log on** (Comput) ouvrir une session, se connecter
■ **log off, log out** (Comput) clore une session, se déconnecter

log book *n* (of car) ≈ carte *f* grise; (written record) registre *m*

log cabin *n* cabane *f* en rondins

log fire *n* feu *m* de bois

loggerheads *n pl* **to be at ~** être en désaccord (**with** avec)

logic *n* logique *f*

logical *adj* logique

logistics *n* logistique *f*

logo *n* logo *m*

log-off *n* fin *f* de connexion

log-on *n* début *m* de connexion

loin *n* (Culin) (GB) ≈ côtes *fpl* premières; (US) ≈ filet *m*

loiter *vi* (idly) traîner; (pleasurably) flâner; (suspiciously) rôder

loll *vi* ⟨*person*⟩ se prélasser; ⟨*head*⟩ tomber; ⟨*tongue*⟩ pendre

lollipop *n* sucette *f*

London *pr n* Londres

Londoner *n* Londonien/-ienne *m/f*

lone *adj* solitaire

loneliness *n* (of person) solitude *f*; (of place) isolement *m*

lonely *adj* ⟨*person*⟩ seul/-e; ⟨*life*⟩ solitaire; ⟨*place*⟩ isolé/-e

lonely hearts' column *n* petites annonces *fpl* (de rencontre)

loner *n* solitaire *mf*

lonesome *adj* (US) solitaire

long ⓵ *adj* (gen) long/longue; ⟨*delay*⟩ important/-e; ⟨*grass*⟩ haut/-e; **to be 20 minutes ~** durer 20 minutes; **to be 20 metres ~** avoir *or* faire 20 mètres de long; **to get ~er** ⟨*days, list, queue*⟩ s'allonger; ⟨*grass, hair*⟩ pousser; **she's been away a ~ time** elle est restée longtemps absente; **it's been a ~ time since...** ça fait longtemps que...; **to take a ~ time** ⟨*person*⟩ être lent/-e; ⟨*task*⟩ prendre longtemps; **a ~ way off** loin; **we've come a ~ way** nous avons fait beaucoup de chemin
⓶ *adv* (a) (a long time) longtemps; **I won't be ~** je n'en ai pas pour longtemps; **how ~ will you be?** tu en as pour combien de temps?; **how ~ did it take him?** il lui a fallu combien de temps?; **how ~ is the interval?** combien de temps dure l'entracte?; **I haven't got ~** je n'ai pas beaucoup de temps; **~er than he thought** plus de temps qu'il ne pensait; **before ~** (in past) peu après; (in future) dans peu de temps; **not for ~** pas longtemps; **~ after** longtemps après; **not ~ after** peu après; **~ ago** il y a longtemps; **~ before** bien avant; **he's no ~er head** il n'est plus chef; **I can't stay any ~er** je ne peux pas rester plus longtemps
(b) (for a long time) depuis longtemps; **those days are ~ gone** ce temps-là n'est plus
⓷ *vi* **to ~ for sth** avoir très envie de qch; **to ~ to do** rêver de faire
⓸ **as long as** *phr* (provided) du moment que (+ *indicative*), pourvu que (+ *subjunctive*)
IDIOMS **~ time no see!** (colloq) ça fait une paye (colloq) qu'on ne s'est pas vus!; **so ~!** (colloq) salut!

long-awaited *adj* longtemps attendu/-e

long-distance *adj* ⟨*runner*⟩ de fond; ⟨*telephone call*⟩ (within the country) interurbain/-e; (abroad) international/-e; **~ lorry driver** (GB) routier *m*

long-haired *adj* ⟨*person*⟩ aux cheveux longs; ⟨*animal*⟩ à poil long

longhand *n* **in ~** écrit/-e à la main

long-haul *adj* ⟨*flight, aircraft*⟩ long-courrier *inv*

l

longing n (a) (glance) grand désir m (for de; to do de faire)
(b) (nostalgia) nostalgie f (for de)

longitude n longitude f

long jump n (GB) saut m en longueur

long-life adj ⟨milk⟩ longue conservation inv; ⟨battery⟩ longue durée inv

long-range adj ⟨missile⟩ (à) longue portée; ⟨forecast⟩ à long terme

long-sighted adj presbyte

long-standing adj de longue date

long term ① n in the ~ à long terme ② **long-term** adj, adv à long terme

long-time adj de longue date

long-wave n grandes ondes fpl

long-winded adj verbeux/-euse

loo n (GB) (colloq) vécés mpl (colloq), toilettes fpl

look ① n (a) (glance) coup m d'œil; **to have** or **take a ~ at sth** jeter un coup d'œil à or sur qch; **to have** or **take a good ~ at** regarder [qch] de près; **to have a ~ inside/ behind sth** regarder à l'intérieur de/derrière qch; **to have a ~ round** faire un tour dans ⟨park, town⟩
(b) (search) **to have a (good) ~** (bien) chercher
(c) (expression) regard m; **a ~ of sadness** un regard triste; **from the ~ on his face...** à son expression...
(d) (appearance) (of person) air m; (of building, scenery) aspect m
② **looks** n pl **~s aren't everything** il n'y a pas que la beauté qui compte; **he's losing his ~s** il n'est pas aussi beau qu'autrefois
③ vi (a) regarder (into dans; over par-dessus); **to ~ away** détourner le regard or les yeux; **to ~ out of the window** regarder par la fenêtre
(b) (search) chercher, regarder
(c) (appear, seem) avoir l'air, paraître; **you ~ cold** tu as l'air d'avoir froid; **he ~s young for his age** il fait jeune pour son âge; **that makes you ~ younger** ça te rajeunit; **the picture will ~ good in the study** le tableau ira bien dans le bureau; **it doesn't ~ right** ça ne va pas; **things are ~ing good** les choses se présentent bien; **to ~ like sb/sth** ressembler à qn/qch; **what does the house ~ like?** comment est la maison?; **it ~s like rain** on dirait qu'il va pleuvoir
④ vtr (a) (gaze, stare) regarder; **to ~ sb in the eye** regarder qn dans les yeux
(b) (appear) **to ~ one's age** faire son âge; **she's 40 but she doesn't ~ it** elle a 40 ans mais elle ne les fait pas; **to ~ one's best** être à son avantage

■ **look after** soigner ⟨patient⟩; garder ⟨child⟩; s'occuper de ⟨customer, plant, finances, shop⟩; surveiller ⟨class, luggage⟩; entretenir ⟨car⟩

■ **look around**: ¶ ~ around (a) (glance) regarder autour de soi
(b) **to ~ around for sb/sth** chercher qn/qch

(c) (in town) faire un tour
¶ ~ around [sth] visiter ⟨church, town⟩

■ **look at** (a) regarder; (briefly) jeter un coup d'œil sur
(b) (examine) examiner ⟨patient⟩; jeter un coup d'œil à ⟨car⟩; étudier ⟨problem, options⟩
(c) (see, view) voir ⟨life, situation⟩; envisager ⟨problem⟩

■ **look back** (a) (turn around) se retourner (at pour regarder)
(b) **to ~ back on** se tourner sur ⟨past⟩; repenser à ⟨experience⟩; **~ing back on it** rétrospectivement

■ **look down**: ¶ ~ down (from a height) regarder en bas
¶ ~ down on [sb/sth] (a) regarder [qch] d'en haut
(b) (condescendingly) mépriser

■ **look for** chercher ⟨person, object⟩

■ **look forward to** attendre [qch] avec impatience; **she's ~ing forward to going on holiday** elle a hâte de partir en vacances; **I ~ forward to hearing from you** (in letter) j'espère avoir bientôt de tes nouvelles; (formal) dans l'attente de votre réponse, je vous prie d'agréer mes sincères salutations

■ **look into** examiner ⟨matter⟩

■ **look on**: ¶ ~ on (watch) regarder; (be present) assister à; ¶ ~ on [sb/sth] considérer ⟨person, event⟩ (as comme; with avec)

■ **look out**: ¶ ~ out (take care) faire attention (for à); (be wary) se méfier (for de); **~ out!** attention!; ¶ ~ out for [sb/sth] guetter ⟨person⟩; être à l'affût de ⟨bargain, new talent⟩

■ **look round**: ¶ ~ round (look behind) se retourner; (look about) regarder autour de soi; ¶ ~ round [sth] visiter ⟨town⟩; **to ~ round the shops** faire les magasins

■ **look through**: ¶ ~ through [sth] (a) parcourir ⟨report⟩; feuilleter ⟨magazine⟩
(b) fouiller dans ⟨belongings⟩
¶ ~ through [sb] faire semblant de ne pas voir

■ **look to** (a) (rely on) compter sur [qn/qch]
(b) (turn to) se tourner vers ⟨future, friends⟩

■ **look up**: ¶ ~ up (raise eyes) lever les yeux (from de); (raise head) lever la tête; **things are ~ing up for us** les choses s'arrangent pour nous
¶ ~ [sb/sth] up (a) chercher ⟨phone number, price⟩ (in dans)
(b) passer voir ⟨acquaintance⟩
¶ ~ up to [sb] admirer ⟨person⟩

look-alike n sosie m

look-in n (GB) **to get a ~** avoir sa chance; **to give sb a ~** donner sa chance à qn

look-out n (a) **to be on the ~ for** rechercher ⟨stolen vehicle⟩; être à l'affût de ⟨bargain, new talent⟩; guetter ⟨visitor⟩
(b) (place) poste m d'observation

loom ① n métier m à tisser
② vi (a) (also ~ **up**) surgir (out of de; over au-dessus de)
(b) ⟨war, crisis⟩ menacer; ⟨exam, interview⟩ être imminent/-e; **to ~ large** ⟨issue⟩ peser lourd

loony *adj* (colloq) farfelu/-e (colloq)

loop ⓵ *n* (gen, Comput) boucle *f*
⓶ *vtr* nouer
⓷ *vi* ‹*road, path*› faire une boucle

loophole *n* lacune *f*

loose *adj* (a) ‹*knot, screw*› desserré/-e;
‹*handle, tooth*› branlant/-e; ‹*button*› qui se
découd; ‹*thread*› décousu/-e; **to hang ~**
‹*hair*› être dénoué/-e; **~ connection** faux
contact
(b) ‹*free*› **to break ~** ‹*animal*› s'échapper
(from de); **to cut sb ~** détacher qn; **to let ~**
libérer ‹*animal, prisoner*›
(c) ‹*page*› détaché/-e; **~ change** petite
monnaie
(d) ‹*jacket, trousers*› ample; ‹*collar*› lâche
(e) ‹*link, weave*› lâche
(f) ‹*translation, interpretation*› assez libre;
‹*wording*› imprécis/-e; ‹*connection,
guideline*› vague; ‹*style*› relâché/-e
(g) ‹*morals*› dissolu/-e
IDIOMS **to be at a ~ end** (GB), **to be at ~
ends** (US) ne pas trop savoir quoi faire

loosely *adv* (a) ‹*hold, wind, wrap*› sans
serrer; **his clothes hung ~ on him** il flottait
dans ses vêtements
(b) ‹*connected, organized*› de façon souple
(c) ‹*translate, describe*› assez librement

loosely knit *adj* ‹*group, structure*› peu
uni/-e

loosen *vtr* desserrer ‹*belt, strap, collar*›;
dégager ‹*nail, post*›; relâcher ‹*grip, rope,
control*›; dénouer ‹*hair*›
■ **loosen up** (a) (sport) s'échauffer
(b) (relax) se détendre

loot ⓵ *n* butin *m*
⓶ *vtr* piller ‹*shops*›

looter *n* pillard/-e *m/f*

lopsided *adj* ‹*object, smile*› de travers;
‹*argument, view*› irrationnel/-elle

lord *n* (a) (ruler) seigneur *m* (of de)
(b) (peer) lord *m*; **the (House of) Lords** la
Chambre des Lords; **my Lord** (to noble)
Monsieur le comte/duc etc
IDIOMS **to ~ it over sb** (colloq) regarder qn
de haut

Lord *n* (a) (in prayers) Seigneur *m*
(b) (colloq) (in exclamations) **good ~!** grand
Dieu!

Lord Mayor *n* lord-maire *m*

lordship *n* (*also* **Lordship**) **your/his ~** (of
noble) Monsieur; (of judge) Monsieur le Juge

lorry *n* (GB) camion *m*

lorry driver *n* (GB) routier *m*, chauffeur
m de poids lourd

lose ⓵ *vtr* (a) (gen) perdre; **to ~ one's way**
se perdre; **to ~ interest in sth** se
désintéresser de qch
(b) ‹*clock*› retarder de ‹*minutes, seconds*›
(c) (get rid of) semer (colloq) ‹*pursuer*›
⓶ *vi* (a) (gen) perdre
(b) ‹*clock*› retarder
■ **lose out** être perdant/-e

loser *n* (gen, Sport) perdant/-e *m/f*

loss *n* perte *f* (of de); **to be at a ~** (puzzled)
être perplexe; (helpless) être perdu/-e

lost *adj* (a) ‹*person, animal*› perdu/-e; **to get
~** ‹*person, animal*› se perdre; ‹*object*›
s'égarer; **get ~!** (colloq) fiche le camp! (colloq)
(b) ‹*opportunity*› manqué/-e; ‹*cause*›
perdu/-e; ‹*civilization*› disparu/-e; **to be ~
on sb** passer au-dessus de la tête de qn; **to
be ~ for words** être interloqué/-e; **to be ~ in**
être plongé/-e dans ‹*book, thought*›

lost and found *n* objets *mpl* trouvés

lost property *n* (GB) objets *mpl* trouvés

lot¹ ⓵ *pron* (a) (great deal) **a ~** beaucoup; **he
spent a ~** il a beaucoup dépensé, il a
dépensé beaucoup d'argent; **to mean a ~ to
sb** avoir beaucoup d'importance pour qn
(b) (colloq) **the ~** (le) tout
⓶ *quantif* **a ~ of money/time** beaucoup
d'argent/de temps; **I see a ~ of him** je le
vois beaucoup
⓷ **lots** *quantif, pron* (colloq) **~s (and ~s) of**
des tas (colloq) de, beaucoup de; **~s of things**
des tas (colloq) de choses
⓸ **a lot** *adv* beaucoup; **he's a ~ better/
worse** il va beaucoup mieux/plus mal; **this
happens quite a ~** cela arrive très souvent

lot² *n* (a) (destiny) sort *m*; (quality of life)
condition *f*
(b) (US) parcelle *f* (de terrain)
(c) (at auction) lot *m*
(d) **to draw ~s** tirer au sort
(e) (batch) fournée *f*

lotion *n* lotion *f*

lottery *n* loterie *f*

loud ⓵ *adj* (a) ‹*music, voice*› fort/-e; ‹*noise,
scream*› grand/-e (*before n*); ‹*comment,
laugh*› bruyant/-e; ‹*applause*› vif/vive
(b) ‹*colour*› criard/-e; ‹*person, behaviour*›
exubérant/-e
⓶ *adv* fort; **out ~** à voix haute

loudly *adv* ‹*knock, talk*› bruyamment;
‹*scream*› fort; ‹*protest*› vivement

loudspeaker *n* (for announcements)
haut-parleur *m*; (for hi-fi) enceinte *f*

lounge *n* (a) (in house, hotel) salon *m*
(b) (in airport) **departure ~** salle *f*
d'embarquement
(c) (US) (*also* **cocktail ~**) bar *m*
■ **lounge about**, **lounge around**
paresser

lousy *adj* minable (colloq); **a ~ trick** un sale
tour

lout *n* malotru *m* (colloq)

loutish *adj* ‹*person*› grossier/-ière;
‹*behaviour*› de voyou

louvred (GB), **louvered** (US) *adj* ‹*doors*›
à lamelles

lovable *adj* ‹*person*› sympathique; ‹*child*›
adorable

love ⓵ *n* (a) amour *m*; **to be/fall in ~** être/
tomber amoureux/-euse (with de); **to make ~**
faire l'amour; **Andy sends his ~** Andy
t'embrasse; **with ~ from Bob**, **~ Bob**
affectueusement, Bob   ···›

l

(b) (GB) (term of affection) mon chéri/ma chérie *m/f*
(c) (in tennis) zéro *m*
2 *vtr* aimer; **to ~ each other** s'aimer; **to ~ doing** *or* **to do** aimer beaucoup faire; **'I'd ~ to!'** 'avec plaisir!'
IDIOMS **~ at first sight** le coup de foudre

love affair *n* liaison *f* (**with** avec; **between** entre)

love-life *n* vie *f* amoureuse

lovely *adj* **(a)** (beautiful) ⟨colour, garden, woman⟩ beau/belle (*before n*), joli/-e (*before n*); **to look ~** ⟨child, dress⟩ être ravissant/-e
(b) (pleasant) ⟨letter, person⟩ charmant/-e; ⟨meal, smell⟩ délicieux/-ieuse; ⟨idea, surprise⟩ bon/bonne (*before n*); ⟨present, weather⟩ magnifique

lover *n* **(a)** (male) amant *m*; (female) maîtresse *f*; **they are ~s** ils sont amants
(b) (person in love) amoureux/-euse *m/f*
(c) (enthusiast) amateur *m*; **jazz ~** amateur de jazz

loving *adj* (gen) tendre; ⟨care⟩ affectueux/-euse

low **1** *n* **(a)** (in weather) dépression *f*
(b) to be at *or* **have hit an all-time ~** être au plus bas
2 *adj* **(a)** (gen) bas/basse; ⟨speed⟩ réduit/-e; ⟨number, table⟩ faible (*before n*); ⟨battery⟩ presque à plat *inv*; **in a ~ voice** tout bas; **to be ~ on staff** manquer de personnel; **to be ~ in sugar** contenir peu de sucre
(b) ⟨mark, quality⟩ mauvais/-e (*before n*)
(c) (depressed) déprimé/-e
(d) ⟨behaviour⟩ ignoble
3 *adv* **(a)** ⟨aim⟩ bas; ⟨bend⟩ très bas; ⟨fly⟩ à basse altitude
(b) (in importance) **it's very ~ (down) on the list** c'est tout à fait secondaire
(c) ⟨speak, sing⟩ bas; **to turn [sth] down ~** baisser ⟨heating, light⟩
4 *vi* ⟨cow⟩ meugler

low-alcohol *adj* peu alcoolisé/-e

lowbrow *adj* ⟨person⟩ peu intellectuel/-elle

low-budget *adj* à petit budget

low-calorie *adj* ⟨diet⟩ hypocalorique; ⟨food⟩ à faible teneur en calories

low-cost *adj* économique, bon marché

low-cut *adj* décolleté/-e

low-down *adj* (colloq) tuyau *m* (colloq)

lower **1** *adj* inférieur/-e
2 *vtr* **(a)** baisser ⟨barrier, curtain, flag⟩; abaisser ⟨ceiling⟩; **to ~ sb/sth** descendre qn/qch (**into** dans; **onto** sur)
(b) (reduce) réduire ⟨prices, standards⟩; réduire ⟨pressure, temperature⟩; abaisser ⟨age limit⟩; **to ~ one's voice** baisser la voix
(c) affaler ⟨sail⟩
3 *v refl* **to ~ oneself (a)** s'abaisser
(b) to ~ oneself into s'asseoir précautionneusement dans ⟨bath, armchair⟩

lower class *n* **the ~(es)** la classe ouvrière

lower sixth *n* (GB Sch) ≈ classe *f* de première; **to be in the ~** ≈ être en première

low-fat *adj* ⟨diet⟩ sans matières grasses; ⟨cheese⟩ allégé/-e; ⟨milk⟩ écrémé/-e

low-income *adj* ⟨family⟩ à faible revenue; ⟨bracket⟩ des bas salaires

low-key *adj* ⟨approach⟩ discret/-ète; ⟨meeting, talks⟩ informel/-elle

low-level *adj* ⟨bombing⟩ à basse altitude; ⟨talks⟩ informel/-elle; ⟨radiation⟩ faible

low-lying *adj* à basse altitude

low-paid *adj* ⟨job⟩ faiblement rémunéré/-e; ⟨worker⟩ peu rémunéré/-e

low-priced *adj* à bas prix

low-profile *adj* discret/-ète

low-quality *adj* de qualité inférieure

low-risk *adj* à risque limité

low season *n* basse saison *f*

low-tech *adj* traditionnel/-elle

low tide *n* marée *f* basse

loyal *adj* ⟨friend⟩ loyal/-e (**to** envers); ⟨customer⟩ fidèle (**to** à)

loyalty *n* loyauté *f* (**to, towards** envers)

loyalty card *n* carte *f* de fidélité

lozenge *n* pastille *f*

LP *n* (disque *m*) 33 tours *m*

L-plate *n* (GB Aut) plaque *f* d'élève conducteur débutant accompagné

Ltd (GB) (*abbr* = **limited (liability)**) ≈ SARL

lubricant *n* lubrifiant *m*

lucid *adj* **(a)** (clear) clair/-e
(b) (sane) ⟨person⟩ lucide; ⟨moment⟩ de lucidité

luck *n* chance *f*; **good ~** chance *f*; **bad ~** malchance *f*; **to bring sb good/bad ~** porter bonheur/malheur à qn; **it's good ~** ça porte bonheur; **bad** *or* **hard ~!** pas de chance!; **good ~!** bonne chance!; **to be in/out of ~** avoir de la/ne pas avoir de chance

luckily *adv* heureusement (**for** pour)

lucky *adj* **(a)** (fortunate) **to be ~** avoir de la chance
(b) ⟨charm, colour, number⟩ porte-bonheur *inv*; **it's my ~ day!** c'est mon jour de chance!

lucrative *adj* lucratif/-ive

ludicrous *adj* grotesque

luggage *n* bagages *mpl*

luggage rack *n* porte-bagages *m inv*

lukewarm *adj* tiède

lull **1** *n* (in storm, fighting) accalmie *f*; (in conversation) pause *f*
2 *vtr* **to ~ sb to sleep** endormir qn en le berçant; **to ~ sb into thinking that...** faire croire à qn que...; **to be ~ed into a false sense of security** se laisser aller à un sentiment de sécurité trompeur

lullaby *n* berceuse *f*

lumber **1** *n* (US) bois *m* de construction
2 *vtr* (GB) (colloq) **to get** *or* **be ~ed with sb/sth** se retrouver avec qn/qch sur les bras
3 *vi* (*also* **~ along**) avancer d'un pas lourd; ⟨vehicle⟩ avancer péniblement

lumberjack *n* bûcheron/-onne *m/f*

luminous *adj* lumineux/-euse
lump ①*n* **(a)** (gen) morceau *m*; (of soil, clay) motte *f*; (in sauce) grumeau *m*
(b) (on body) (from knock) bosse *f* (**on** sur)
(c) (tumour) grosseur *f* (**in**, **on** à)
②*vtr* to ~ **X and Y together** mettre X et Y dans le même panier (colloq)
IDIOMS **to have a** ~ **in one's throat** avoir la gorge serrée
lump sum *n* versement *m* unique
lunar *adj* ⟨landscape⟩ lunaire; ⟨eclipse⟩ de lune; ⟨landing⟩ sur la lune
lunatic *n* fou/folle *m/f*
lunch *n* déjeuner *m*; **to have** ~ déjeuner; **to take sb out for** ~ emmener qn déjeuner au restaurant; **to close for** ~ fermer le midi
lunchbox *n* boîte *f* à sandwichs
lunchbreak *n* pause-déjeuner *f*
luncheon voucher, **LV** *n* ticket-repas *m*, ticket-restaurant® *m*
lunch hour *n* heure *f* du déjeuner
lunchtime *n* heure *f* du déjeuner
lung *n* poumon *m*
lunge *vi* bondir (**at** vers; **forward** en avant)
lurch *vi* ⟨person, vehicle⟩ tanguer; **to** ~ **forward** ⟨car⟩ faire un bond en avant
IDIOMS **to leave sb in the** ~ abandonner qn
lure ①*n* **(a)** (attraction) attrait *m* (**of** de)
(b) (in hunting) leurre *m*
②*vtr* attirer (**into** dans; **with** avec); **they** ~**d him out of his house** ils ont réussi à le faire sortir de chez lui par la ruse

lurid *adj* **(a)** ⟨colour⟩ criard/-e
(b) ⟨detail, past⟩ épouvantable
lurk *vi* **he was** ~**ing in the bushes** il était tapi dans les buissons; **to** ~ **in the garden** rôder dans le jardin
luscious *adj* ⟨food⟩ succulent/-e; ⟨woman⟩ pulpeux/-euse
lush *adj* ⟨vegetation⟩ luxuriant/-e; ⟨hotel, surroundings⟩ luxueux/-euse
lust ①*n* **(a)** désir *m*; (deadly sin) luxure *f*
(b) (for power, blood) soif *f* (**for** de)
②*vi* **to** ~ **for** *or* **after sb/sth** convoiter qn/qch
luvvy *n* (colloq) acteur/-trice *m/f* prétentieux/-ieuse
Luxembourg *pr n* Luxembourg *m*
luxurious *adj* ⟨apartment, lifestyle⟩ de luxe (*never after v*); **his apartment is** ~ son appartement est luxueux
luxury ①*n* luxe *m*
②*adj* ⟨hotel, product, holiday⟩ de luxe
lychee *n* litchi *m*
lying *n* mensonges *mpl*
lynch *vtr* lyncher
lynch mob *n* lyncheurs *mpl*
lyrical *adj* lyrique; **to wax** ~ (**about sth**) disserter avec lyrisme (sur qch)
lyrics *n pl* paroles *fpl*
lyric-writer *n* parolier/-ière *m/f*

Mm

m, M *n* m, M *m*
MA *n* (*abbr* = **Master of Arts**) diplôme *m* supérieur de lettres
macabre *adj* macabre
macaroni *n* macaronis *mpl*
mace *n* **(a)** (spice) macis *m*
(b) (ceremonial staff) masse *f*
Macedonia *pr n* Macédoine *f*
machete *n* machette *f*
machine *n* machine *f*; **sewing** ~ **machine** à coudre; **by** ~ à la machine
machine gun *n* mitrailleuse *f*
machine-readable *adj* ⟨data⟩ directement exploitable; ⟨passport⟩ vérifiable par ordinateur
machinery *n* **(a)** (equipment) machines *fpl*; (working parts) mécanisme *m*, rouages *mpl*; **a piece of** ~ une machine
(b) (figurative) dispositifs *mpl*
macho *adj* macho (colloq)
mackerel *n* maquereau *m*

mackintosh, macintosh *n* imperméable *m*
mad *adj* **(a)** ⟨person⟩ fou/folle (**with** de); ⟨dog⟩ enragé/-e; ⟨idea, scheme⟩ insensé/-e; **to go** ~ devenir fou/folle; **to drive sb** ~ rendre qn fou
(b) (colloq) (angry) furieux/-ieuse; **to be** ~ **at** *or* **with sb** être très en colère contre qn; **to go** ~ se mettre dans une colère folle
(c) (colloq) (enthusiastic) ~ **about** *or* **on** fou/folle de (colloq) ⟨person, hobby⟩
(d) ⟨panic⟩ infernal/-e; **the audience went** ~ le public s'est déchaîné
IDIOMS **to work like** ~ travailler comme un fou/une folle
madam *n* madame *f*; **Dear Madam** (in letter) Madame
mad cow disease *n* maladie *f* de la vache folle
maddening *adj* ⟨person⟩ énervant/-e; ⟨delay, situation⟩ exaspérant/-e
made *adj* **a** ~ **man** un homme qui a réussi; ⋯⋮

he's got it ∼ (colloq) (sure to succeed) sa réussite est assurée; (has succeeded) il n'a plus à s'en faire

Madeira pr n Madère

made-to-measure adj ⟨garment⟩ fait/-e sur mesure

made-up adj **(a)** (wearing make-up) maquillé/-e
(b) ⟨story⟩ fabriqué/-e

madly adv **(a)** (frantically) frénétiquement
(b) ⟨jealous⟩ follement; ∼ **in love (with sb)** follement or éperdument amoureux/-euse (de qn)

madman n (colloq) fou m (colloq), malade m (colloq)

madness n folie f; **it is** ∼ **to do** c'est de la folie de faire

Mafia n **the** ∼ la Mafia

magazine n **(a)** revue f; (mainly photos) magazine m; **fashion** ∼ magazine de mode; **women's** ∼ journal m féminin
(b) (on radio, TV) magazine m
(c) (of gun, camera) magasin m

maggot n (in fruit) ver m; (for fishing) asticot m

magic **1** n magie f
2 adj magique

magical adj magique

magic carpet n tapis m volant

magician n (wizard) magicien m; (entertainer) illusionniste m

magistrate n magistrat m

magistrate's court n ≈ tribunal m de police

magnanimous adj magnanime

magnate n magnat m; **oil** ∼ magnat du pétrole

magnesium n magnésium m

magnet n aimant m; (figurative) pôle m d'attraction (**for** pour)

magnetic adj **(a)** ⟨rod⟩ aimanté/-e; ⟨field, force, storm⟩ magnétique
(b) ⟨appeal⟩ irrésistible; **to have a** ∼ **personality** avoir du charisme

magnetism n magnétisme m

magnificent adj magnifique

magnify vtr grossir

magnifying glass n loupe f

magnitude n ampleur f (**of** de)

magnolia n **(a)** (also ∼ **tree**) magnolia m
(b) (colour) crème m

magpie n pie f

mahogany n acajou m

maid n (in house) bonne f; (in hotel) femme f de chambre

maiden **1** n jeune fille f
2 adj ⟨flight, voyage, speech⟩ inaugural/-e

maiden name n nom m de jeune fille

mail **1** n **(a)** (postal service) poste f; **by** ∼ par la poste
(b) (letters) courrier m
(c) (e-mail) courrier m électronique
2 vtr envoyer, expédier ⟨letter, parcel⟩ (**to** à)

mailbox n (for posting) boîte f aux lettres; (for delivery) boîte f à lettres; (for e-mail) boîte f aux lettres électronique

mailing n (for advertising) publipostage m, mailing m

mailing list n fichier-clientèle m

mailman n (US) facteur m

mail order **1** n **to buy (by)** ∼ acheter par correspondance
2 adj ⟨business, goods⟩ de vente f par correspondance

maim vtr estropier

main **1** n **(a)** (pipe) canalisation f
(b) **the** ∼**s** (of electricity) secteur m; (of water, gas) le réseau de distribution; (of sewage) le réseau d'évacuation
2 adj principal/-e

main course n plat m principal

mainframe n (also ∼ **computer**) ordinateur m central

mainland n territoire m continental; **on the** ∼ sur le continent

main line **1** n grande ligne f
2 adj ⟨station⟩ de grande ligne
3 mainline vi (colloq) se piquer

mainly adv surtout, essentiellement

main road n (in country) route f principale; (in town) grande rue f

mainstream **1** n courant m dominant
2 adj **(a)** (conventional) traditionnel/-elle
(b) ∼ **jazz** jazz mainstream

maintain vtr **(a)** (keep steady) maintenir
(b) subvenir aux besoins de ⟨family⟩; entretenir ⟨army, house, property⟩
(c) continuer à affirmer ⟨innocence⟩; **to** ∼ **that** soutenir que

maintenance n **(a)** (upkeep) entretien m (**of** de)
(b) (GB) (Law) (alimony) pension f alimentaire

maisonette n duplex m

maize n maïs m

majestic adj majestueux/-euse

majesty n **(a)** (grandeur) majesté f
(b) **His/Her Majesty** sa Majesté

major **1** n **(a)** (Mil) commandant m
(b) (US) (Univ) matière f principale
(c) (Mus) ton m majeur
2 adj **(a)** ⟨event⟩ important/-e; ⟨role⟩ majeur/-e; ⟨significance⟩ capital/-e; **a** ∼ **operation,** ∼ **surgery** une grosse opération
(b) (main) principal/-e
(c) (Mus) majeur/-e; **in a** ∼ **key** en majeur
3 vi (US) (Univ) **to** ∼ **in** se spécialiser en

Majorca pr n Majorque f; **in** ∼ à Majorque

majority n majorité f (**of** de); **to be in a** or **the** ∼ être en majorité

make **1** n marque f
2 vtr **(a)** (gen) faire; **to** ∼ **the bed** faire le lit; **to** ∼ **a noise** faire du bruit; **to** ∼ **a rule** établir une règle; **to** ∼ **room/the time (for sth)** trouver de la place/du temps (pour qch); **to** ∼ **friends/enemies** se faire des amis/des ennemis; **to** ∼ **oneself understood** se faire comprendre; **it's made (out) of gold** c'est en

or; **made in France** fabriqué en France; **he was made treasurer** on l'a fait trésorier; **to ~ a habit/an issue of sth** faire de qch une habitude/une affaire; **it's been made into a film** on en a fait *or* tiré un film; **three and three ~ six** trois et trois font six
(b) (with adjective) **to ~ sb happy/ill** rendre qn heureux/malade; **to ~ sb hungry** donner faim à qn; **to ~ sth better/bigger/worse** améliorer/agrandir/aggraver qch
(c) (with infinitive) **to ~ sb cry** faire pleurer qn; **I made her smile** je l'ai fait sourire; **to ~ sb pay the bill** faire payer l'addition à qn; **to ~ sb wait** faire attendre qn; **they made me do it** ils m'ont obligé *or* forcé; **it ~s her voice sound funny** ça lui donne une drôle de voix
(d) (earn) gagner ⟨*salary*⟩; **to ~ a living** gagner sa vie; **to ~ a profit** réaliser des bénéfices; **to ~ a loss** subir des pertes
(e) (reach) arriver jusqu'à ⟨*place, position*⟩; atteindre ⟨*ranking, level*⟩; **we'll never ~ it** nous n'y arriverons jamais; **to ~ the front page** faire la une
(f) (estimate, say) **what time do you ~ it?** quelle heure as-tu?; **I ~ it five o'clock** il est cinq heures à ma montre; **let's ~ it five dollars** disons cinq dollars; **can we ~ it a bit later?** peut-on dire un peu plus tard?; **what do you ~ of it?** qu'en dis-tu?
(g) (cause success of) assurer la réussite de ⟨*holiday, meal*⟩; **it really made my day** ça m'a rendu heureux pour la journée
IDIOMS **to ~ it** (colloq) (in career, life) y arriver; (to party, meeting) réussir à venir; **I can't ~ it** je ne peux pas venir
■ **make do** faire avec; **to ~ do with** se contenter de qch
■ **make for (a)** (head for) se diriger vers
(b) (help create) permettre, assurer
■ **make good**: ¶ **~ good** réussir
¶ **~ good [sth] (a)** réparer ⟨*damage, omission*⟩; rattraper ⟨*lost time*⟩; combler ⟨*deficit*⟩
(b) tenir ⟨*promise*⟩
■ **make out**: ¶ **~ out** affirmer, prétendre (**that** que); ¶ **~ [sb/sth] out (a)** (see, distinguish) distinguer
(b) (claim) **to ~ sth out to be easy/difficult** prétendre que qch est facile/difficile
(c) (understand) comprendre (if si); **I can't ~ him out** je n'arrive pas à le comprendre
(d) (write out) faire, rédiger; **to ~ out a cheque to sb** faire un chèque à qn; **it is made out to X** il est à l'ordre de X
■ **make up**: ¶ **~ up (a)** (after quarrel) se réconcilier (**with** avec)
(b) to ~ up for rattraper ⟨*lost time, lost sleep*⟩; compenser ⟨*personal loss*⟩
¶ **~ [sth] up (a)** inventer ⟨*story, excuse*⟩
(b) (prepare) faire ⟨*parcel, garment, bed*⟩; préparer ⟨*prescription*⟩
(c) (constitute) faire; **to be made up of** être fait/-e *or* composé/-e de
(d) (compensate for) rattraper ⟨*loss, time*⟩; combler ⟨*deficit*⟩

make-believe *n* fantaisie *f*
makeover *n* transformation *f*

maker *n* (of clothes, food, appliance) fabricant *m*; (of cars, aircraft) constructeur *m*
makeshift *adj* improvisé/-e
make-up *n* **(a)** maquillage *m*; **to put on one's ~** se maquiller
(b) (character) caractère *m*
make-up bag *n* trousse *f* de maquillage
make-up remover *n* démaquillant *m*
making *n* (of film, programme) réalisation *f*; (of product) fabrication *f*; (of clothes) confection *f*; **his problems are of his own ~** ses ennuis sont de sa faute;
IDIOMS **to have all the ~s of** avoir tout pour faire
maladjusted *adj* inadapté/-e
malaria *n* paludisme *m*
Malaysia *pr n* Malaisie *f*
male ⓵ *n* **(a)** (animal) mâle *m*
(b) (man) homme *m*
⓶ *adj* **(a)** ⟨*plant, animal*⟩ mâle
(b) ⟨*population, role, trait*⟩ masculin/-e; ⟨*company*⟩ des hommes; **a ~ voice** une voix d'homme; **~ student** étudiant *m*
(c) ⟨*plug, socket*⟩ mâle
male chauvinism *n* machisme *m*
male chauvinist *n* phallocrate *m*
male model *n* mannequin *m* homme *or* masculin
malevolent *adj* malveillant/-e
malformed *adj* ⟨*limb, nose*⟩ difforme; ⟨*organ*⟩ malformé/-e
malfunction ⓵ *n* **(a)** (poor operation) mauvais fonctionnement *m*
(b) (breakdown) défaillance *f*
⓶ *vi* mal fonctionner
malice *n* méchanceté *f* (**towards** à)
malicious *adj* ⟨*comment, person*⟩ malveillant/-e; ⟨*act*⟩ méchant/-e; ⟨*lie*⟩ calomnieux/-ieuse
malign *vtr* calomnier
malignant *adj* **(a)** ⟨*look*⟩ malveillant/-e; ⟨*person*⟩ malfaisant/-e
(b) (Med) malin/-igne
mall *n* **(a)** (shopping arcade) (in town) galerie *f* marchande; (in suburbs) (US) centre *m* commercial
(b) (US) (street) rue *f* piétonne
mallet *n* maillet *m*
malnutrition *n* sous-alimentation *f*
malpractice *n* **(a)** (gen, Law) malversations *fpl*
(b) (US) (Med) erreur *f* médicale
malt *n* **(a)** (grain) malt *m*
(b) (whisky) whisky *m* pur malt
(c) (US) (malted milk) lait *m* malté
Malta *pr n* Malte *f*
maltreat *vtr* maltraiter
mammal *n* mammifère *m*
mammoth ⓵ *n* mammouth *m*
⓶ *adj* ⟨*task*⟩ gigantesque; ⟨*organization*⟩ géant/-e

man ⟨1⟩ n (a) homme m; **an old ~** un
vieillard; **~ to ~** d'homme à homme; **~ and
wife** mari et femme
(b) (mankind) l'humanité f
(c) (in chess) pièce f; (in draughts) pion m
⟨2⟩ vtr (a) tenir ⟨switchboard, desk⟩
(b) armer [qch] en hommes ⟨ship⟩
IDIOMS **every ~ for himself** chacun pour soi

manage ⟨1⟩ vtr (a) **to ~ to do** réussir à
faire, se débrouiller (colloq) pour faire
(b) diriger ⟨project, finances, organization⟩;
gérer ⟨business, shop, hotel, estate⟩; gérer
⟨money, time⟩
(c) (handle) savoir s'y prendre avec ⟨person,
animal⟩; manier ⟨tool, boat⟩
⟨2⟩ vi se débrouiller

manageable adj ⟨size, car⟩ maniable;
⟨problem⟩ maîtrisable; ⟨person, animal⟩
docile

management n (a) (system, field) gestion f;
bad ~ mauvaise gestion
(b) (managers) direction f; **top ~** la haute
direction; **the ~ team** l'équipe dirigeante

management consultant n conseiller
m en gestion

management trainee n apprenti
manager m

manager n (of firm, bank) directeur/-trice
m/f; (of shop) gérant/-e m/f; (of farm)
exploitant/-e m/f; (of project) responsable mf,
directeur/-trice m/f; (in show business)
directeur/-trice m/f artistique; (Sport)
manager m

manageress n (of firm, bank) directrice f;
(of shop, hotel) gérante f; (of project) responsable
f, directrice f; (in show business) directrice f
artistique

managerial adj ⟨experience⟩ en gestion;
⟨decision⟩ de la direction; **~ staff** les cadres
mpl

managing director, MD n
directeur/-trice m/f général/-e

mandarin n (a) (fruit) mandarine f; (tree)
mandarinier m
(b) (person) mandarin m

mandate n (authority) autorité f; (Pol)
mandat m

mane n crinière f

manger n mangeoire f

mangle vtr mutiler ⟨body⟩; broyer ⟨vehicle⟩

mango n (fruit) mangue f

mangrove n palétuvier m, manglier m

mangy adj ⟨dog⟩ galeux/-euse

manhandle vtr malmener, maltraiter

manhole n regard m

manhood n (a) âge m d'homme
(b) (masculinity) masculinité f

mania n manie f

maniac n (a) (colloq) fou/folle m/f
(b) (in psychology) maniaque mf

manic adj (a) (manic-depressive)
maniaco-dépressif/-ive; (obsessive)
obsessionnel/-elle
(b) (figurative) ⟨activity, behaviour⟩ frénétique

manicure ⟨1⟩ n manucure f
⟨2⟩ vtr **to ~ one's nails** se faire les ongles

manifest ⟨1⟩ adj manifeste, évident/-e
⟨2⟩ vtr manifester

manifesto n manifeste m, programme m

manipulate vtr manipuler

manipulative adj manipulateur/-trice

mankind n humanité f

manly adj viril/-e

man-made adj ⟨fibre, fabric⟩ synthétique;
⟨lake⟩ artificiel/-ielle; ⟨tools⟩ fait/-e à la main

manner ⟨1⟩ n (a) (way, method) manière f,
façon f; **in this ~** de cette manière or façon;
in a ~ of speaking pour ainsi dire
(b) (way of behaving) attitude f; **she has an
aggressive ~** elle a une attitude agressive
(c) (sort, kind) sorte f, genre m (of de)
⟨2⟩ **manners** n pl (a) manières fpl; **to have
good/bad ~s** avoir de bonnes/mauvaises
manières; **it's bad ~s to do** il est mal élevé
de faire
(b) (customs) mœurs fpl

mannerism n (habit) particularité f; (quirk)
manie f

manoeuvre (GB), **maneuver** (US) ⟨1⟩ n
manœuvre f
⟨2⟩ vtr (a) manœuvrer ⟨vehicle, object⟩
(b) (figurative) manœuvrer ⟨person⟩; faire
dévier ⟨discussion⟩ (**to** vers)
⟨3⟩ vi manœuvrer

manor n (also **~ house**) manoir m

manpower n main-d'œuvre f

mansion n (in countryside) demeure f; (in
town) hôtel m particulier

manslaughter n homicide m
involontaire

mantelpiece n (manteau m de) cheminée
f

manual ⟨1⟩ n manuel m
⟨2⟩ adj ⟨labour, worker⟩ manuel/-elle;
⟨gearbox, typewriter⟩ mécanique

manufacture ⟨1⟩ n (gen) fabrication f; (of
clothes) confection f; (of cars) construction f
⟨2⟩ vtr (gen) fabriquer; construire ⟨cars⟩

manufacturer n (gen) fabricant m (**of** de);
(of cars) constructeur m

manure n fumier m; **horse ~** crottin m de
cheval

manuscript n manuscrit m

many ⟨1⟩ det beaucoup de, un grand nombre
de; **~ people** beaucoup de gens, un grand
nombre de personnes; **~ times** de
nombreuses fois, bien des fois; **for ~ years**
pendant de nombreuses années; **how ~
people/times?** combien de personnes/fois?;
too ~ trop de; **I have as ~ books as you (do)**
j'ai autant de livres que toi; **so ~** tant de
⟨2⟩ pron, quantif beaucoup; **not ~** pas
beaucoup; **too ~** trop; **how ~?** combien?; **as
~ as you like** autant que tu veux; **I didn't
know there were so ~** je ne savais pas qu'il
y en avait autant; **~ (of them) were killed**
beaucoup d'entre eux ont été tués

many-sided adj à multiples facettes

map *n* carte *f* (**of** de); (of town, underground) plan *m* (**of** de); **street** ∼ plan des rues
■ **map out** élaborer, mettre [qch] au point ⟨*plans, strategy*⟩; tracer ⟨*future*⟩

maple *n* érable *m*

mar *vtr* gâcher

marathon ⓵ *n* marathon *m*
⓶ *adj* (a) (Sport) ∼ **runner** marathonien/-ienne *m/f*
(b) (massive) -marathon; **a** ∼ **session** une séance-marathon

marble *n* (a) (stone) marbre *m*
(b) (Games) bille *f*; **to play** ∼**s** jouer aux billes

march ⓵ *n* marche *f*
⓶ *vi* (a) (Mil) marcher au pas; **to** ∼ (**for**) 40 **km** faire une marche de 40 km; **forward** ∼! en avant, marche!
(b) (in protest) manifester (**against** contre; **for** pour)
(c) **to** ∼ **along** (walk briskly) marcher d'un pas vif; **to** ∼ **in** (angrily) entrer l'air furieux; **she** ∼**ed up to his desk** elle s'est dirigée droit sur son bureau

March *n* mars *m*

marcher *n* (in demonstration) manifestant/-e *m/f*; (in procession) marcheur/-euse *m/f*

mare *n* (horse) jument *f*; (donkey) ânesse *f*

margarine *n* margarine *f*

margin *n* marge *f*; **by a narrow** ∼ de justesse, de peu

marginal *adj* marginal/-e

marginalize *vtr* marginaliser

marigold *n* souci *m*

marijuana *n* marijuana *f*

marinade *vtr* (*also* **marinate**) faire mariner

marine ⓵ *n* (a) (soldier) fusilier *m* marin; **the Marines** les marines *mpl*
(b) (navy) **the merchant** ∼ la marine marchande
⓶ *adj* ⟨*mammal, biology*⟩ marin/-e; ⟨*explorer, life*⟩ sous-marin/-e; ⟨*insurance, law*⟩ maritime

marital *adj* conjugal/-e

marital status *n* situation *f* de famille

marjoram *n* marjolaine *f*

mark ⓵ *n* (a) (gen) marque *f*; (stain) tache *f*
(b) **as a** ∼ **of** en signe de ⟨*esteem, respect*⟩
(c) (Sch, Univ) note *f*
(d) **the high-tide** ∼ le maximum de la marée haute; **at gas** ∼ **7** à thermostat 7
(e) (Sport) **on your** ∼**s!** à vos marques!
(f) (*also* **Deutschmark**) deutschmark *m*
⓶ *vtr* (a) (gen) marquer; (stain) tacher
(b) ⟨*arrow, sign, label*⟩ indiquer ⟨*position, road*⟩
(c) (Sch, Univ) corriger; **to** ∼ **sb absent** noter qn absent
(d) (Sport) marquer
⓷ *vi* (a) ⟨*teacher*⟩ faire des corrections
(b) (stain) se tacher
(c) (Sport) marquer

IDIOMS ∼ **my words** crois-moi; **to** ∼ **time** (Mil) marquer le pas; (figurative) (wait) attendre; (wait for right moment) attendre le bon moment

marked *adj* (a) ⟨*difference, increase, contrast*⟩ marqué/-e, net/nette (*before n*); ⟨*accent*⟩ prononcé/-e
(b) **he's a** ∼ **man** on en veut à sa vie

marker *n* (a) (pen) marqueur *m*
(b) (tag) repère *m*

market ⓵ *n* (a) (gen, Econ) marché *m*
(b) (stock market) Bourse *f*
⓶ *vtr* (a) (sell) commercialiser, vendre
(b) (promote) lancer *or* mettre [qch] sur le marché

market day *n* jour *m* du marché

market economy *n* économie *f* de marché

market forces *n pl* forces *fpl* du marché

market gardening *n* culture *f* maraîchère

marketing *n* (a) (field) marketing *m*, mercatique *f*
(b) (department) service *m* de marketing

marketing strategy *n* stratégie *f* commerciale

market leader *n* (product) produit *m* vedette; (company) leader *m* du marché

marketplace *n* place *f* du marché

market research *n* étude *f* de marché

market town *n* bourg *m*

market trader *n* vendeur/-euse *m/f* sur un marché

market value *n* valeur *f* marchande

markings *n pl* (on animal) taches *fpl*; (on aircraft) marques *fpl*; **road** ∼ signalisation *f* horizontale

marksman *n* tireur *m* d'élite

marmalade *n* confiture *f or* marmelade *f* d'oranges

maroon ⓵ *n* bordeaux *m*
⓶ *vtr* **to be** ∼**ed on an island** être bloqué/-e sur une île; **the** ∼**ed sailors** les naufragés

marquee *n* (a) (GB) (tent) grande tente *f*; (of circus) chapiteau *m*
(b) (US) (canopy) (grand) auvent *m*

marriage *n* mariage *m* (**to** avec)

marriage certificate *n* extrait *m* d'acte de mariage

married *adj* ⟨*person*⟩ marié/-e (**to** à); ⟨*life*⟩ conjugal/-e; ∼ **couple** couple *m*

marrow *n* (a) (in bone) moelle *f*
(b) (GB) (vegetable) courge *f*; **baby** ∼ (GB) courgette *f*

marrowbone *n* os *m* à moelle

marry ⓵ *vtr* se marier avec, épouser ⟨*fiancé(e)*⟩; ⟨*priest*⟩ marier ⟨*couple*⟩; **to get married** se marier (**to** avec); **will you** ∼ **me?** veux-tu m'épouser?
⓶ *vi* se marier

Mars *pr n* Mars *f*

marsh *n* (*also* **marshland**) (terrain) marécage *m*; (region) marais *m*

marshal ⓵ *n* (a) (Mil) maréchal *m* ⋯⋗

(b) (at rally, ceremony) membre *m* du service d'ordre

(c) (US) (in fire service) capitaine *m* des pompiers

2 *vtr* rassembler

martial *adj* ‹art, law› martial/-e; ‹spirit› guerrier/-ière

martyr **1** *n* martyr/-e *m/f*
2 *vtr* martyriser

martyrdom *n* martyre *m*

marvel **1** *n* merveille *f*
2 *vi* s'étonner (**at** de), être émerveillé/-e (**at** par)

marvellous (GB), **marvelous** (US) *adj* merveilleux/-euse; **that's ∼!** c'est formidable!

marzipan *n* pâte *f* d'amandes

mascot *n* mascotte *f*; **lucky ∼** porte-bonheur *m inv*

masculine *adj* masculin/-e

masculinity *n* masculinité *f*

mash **1** *n* (for animals) pâtée *f*
2 *vtr* (also ∼ **up**) écraser

mashed potatoes *n pl* purée *f* de pommes de terre

mask **1** *n* masque *m*; (for eyes only) loup *m*
2 *vtr* masquer

masking tape *n* ruban *m* adhésif

masochist *n, adj* masochiste (*mf*)

mason *n* **(a)** (in building) maçon *m*
(b) Mason (also **Free∼**) franc-maçon *m*

masonry *n* maçonnerie *f*

masquerade **1** *n* bal *m* masqué; (figurative) mascarade *f*
2 *vi* **to ∼ as sb/sth** se faire passer pour qn/qch

mass **1** *n* **(a)** masse *f* (**of** de); (of people) foule *f* (**of** de); (of details) quantité *f* (**of** de)
(b) (in church) messe *f*
2 **masses** *n pl* **(a)** **the ∼es** les masses *fpl*
(b) (GB) (colloq) **∼es of work** beaucoup *or* plein (colloq) de travail; **∼es of people** des tas (colloq) de gens
3 *adj* ‹audience, movement, meeting, tourism› de masse; ‹exodus, protest, unemployment› massif/-ive; **∼ hysteria** hystérie *f* collective
4 *vi* ‹troops› se regrouper; ‹bees› se masser; ‹clouds› s'amonceler

massacre **1** *n* massacre *m*
2 *vtr* massacrer

massage **1** *n* massage *m*
2 *vtr* masser

mass grave *n* charnier *m*

massive *adj* (gen) énorme; ‹increase, cut› massif/-ive

mass-marketing *n* commercialisation *f* massive

mass media *n* (mass) médias *mpl*

mass murderer *n* auteur *m* d'un massacre

mass production *n* fabrication *f* en série

mast *n* (on ship, for flags) mât *m*; (for aerial) pylône *m*

master **1** *n* **(a)** (gen) maître *m*
(b) (Sch) (primary) maître *m*, instituteur *m*; (secondary) professeur *m*; (GB Univ) (of college) principal *m*
(c) (also ∼ **copy**) original *m*
2 *adj* ‹chef, craftsman› maître (*before n*); ‹spy› professionnel/-elle
3 *vtr* **(a)** maîtriser ‹subject›; posséder ‹art, skill›
(b) dominer ‹feelings›; surmonter ‹phobia›

master key *n* passe-partout *m inv*

masterly *adj* magistral/-e

mastermind **1** *n* cerveau *m* (**of, behind** de)
2 *vtr* organiser ‹robbery, event›

Master of Arts *n* diplôme *m* supérieur de lettres

master of ceremonies *n* (in cabaret) animateur/-trice *m/f*; (at banquet) maître *m* des cérémonies

Master of Science *n* diplôme *m* supérieur en sciences

masterpiece *n* chef-d'œuvre *m*

master plan *n* plan *m* d'ensemble

master's (degree) *n* ≈ maîtrise (**in** de)

mastery *n* maîtrise *f* (**of** de)

mat **1** *n* **(a)** (on floor) (petit) tapis *m*; (for wiping feet) paillasson *m*
(b) (on table) dessous-de-plat *m inv*; **place ∼** set *m* de table
2 *vi* ‹hair› s'emmêler; ‹wool› se feutrer; ‹fibres› s'enchevêtrer

match **1** *n* **(a)** (Sport) match *m*
(b) (matchstick) allumette *f*
(c) **to be a ∼ for sb** être un adversaire à la mesure de qn; **to be no ∼ for sb** être trop faible pour qn
2 *vtr* **(a)** (gen) correspondre à; ‹colour, bag› être assorti/-e à; **to ∼ (up) the names to the photos** trouver les noms qui correspondent aux photos
(b) (equal) égaler ‹record, achievements›
3 *vi* ‹colours, clothes, curtains› être assortis/-ies; ‹components› aller ensemble; **with gloves to ∼** avec des gants assortis

matchbox *n* boîte *f* d'allumettes

match point *n* balle *f* de match

matchstick *n* allumette *f*

mate **1** *n* **(a)** (GB) (colloq) (friend) copain *m* (colloq); (at work, school) camarade *mf*
(b) (Zool) (male) mâle *m*; (female) femelle *f*
(c) (assistant) aide *mf*
(d) (in navy) second *m*
2 *vtr* **(a)** accoupler ‹animal› (**with** à *or* avec)
(b) (in chess) faire mat
3 *vi* ‹animal› s'accoupler (**with** à, avec)

material **1** *n* **(a)** (substance) (gen) matière *f*, substance *f*; (Tech) matériau *m*; **waste ∼** déchets *mpl*
(b) (fabric) tissu *m*, étoffe *f*
(c) (written matter) documentation *f*; **teaching ∼** matériel *m* pédagogique; **reading ∼** lecture *f*

(d) (potential) étoffe f; **she is star** ~ elle a l'étoffe d'une vedette
[2] **materials** n pl (equipment) matériel m; **cleaning** ~s produits mpl d'entretien; **building** ~s matériaux de construction
[3] adj matériel/-ielle

materialistic adj matérialiste

materialize vi **(a)** ⟨hope, offer, plan, threat⟩ se concrétiser; ⟨event, situation⟩ se réaliser; ⟨idea⟩ prendre forme
(b) (appear) ⟨person, object⟩ surgir; ⟨spirit⟩ se matérialiser

maternal adj maternel/-elle **(towards** avec)

maternity n maternité f

maternity leave n congé m de maternité

maternity unit n service m d'obstétrique

maternity ward n maternité f

math n (US) (colloq) math fpl (colloq)

mathematical adj mathématique

mathematician n mathématicien/-ienne m/f

mathematics n mathématiques fpl

maths n (GB) (colloq) maths fpl (colloq)

matinée n matinée f

mating season n saison f des amours

matriculate vi ⟨student⟩ s'inscrire

matrimony n mariage m

matrix n matrice f

matron n **(a)** (GB) (in hospital) infirmière f en chef; (in school) infirmière f
(b) (of nursing home) directrice f
(c) (US) (warder) gardienne f

matt (GB), **matte** (US) adj ⟨paint⟩ mat/-e; ⟨photograph⟩ sur papier mat

matter [1] n **(a)** (affair) affaire f; (requiring solution) problème m; (on agenda) point m; **it will be no easy** a ~ for the police un problème qui relève de la police; **that's another** ~ c'est une autre histoire; **the fact of the** ~ **is that** la vérité est que
(b) (question) question f; **a** ~ **of** une question de ⟨opinion, principle, taste⟩; **a** ~ **of life and death** une question de vie ou de mort
(c) (trouble) **is anything the** ~? y a-t-il un problème?; **what's the** ~? qu'est-ce qu'il y a?; **what's the** ~ **with Louise?** qu'est-ce qu'elle a, Louise?; **there's something the** ~ **with my car** ma voiture a un problème
(d) (substance) matière f; **vegetable** ~ matière végétale
(e) printed ~ imprimés mpl; **advertising** ~ publicité f; **reading** ~ lecture f; **subject** ~ contenu m
(f) (Med) (pus) pus m
[2] vi **être** important/-e; **it doesn't** ~ ça ne fait rien; **it doesn't** ~ **whether he comes or not** peu importe qu'il vienne ou pas
IDIOMS **as a** ~ **of course** automatiquement;

as a ~ **of fact** en fait; **for that** ~ d'ailleurs; **no** ~ **how late it is** peu importe l'heure; **no** ~ **what (happens)** quoi qu'il arrive; **and to make** ~s **worse** et pour ne rien arranger

matter-of-fact adj ⟨voice, tone⟩ détaché/-e; ⟨person⟩ terre à terre

mattress n matelas m

mature [1] adj **(a)** ⟨plant, animal⟩ adulte
(b) ⟨person⟩ mûr/-e; ⟨attitude, reader⟩ adulte
(c) ⟨hard cheese⟩ fort/-e; ⟨soft cheese⟩ affiné/-e; ⟨whisky⟩ vieux/vieille
[2] vi **(a)** (physically) ⟨person, animal⟩ devenir adulte
(b) (psychologically) ⟨person⟩ mûrir
(c) ⟨wine⟩ vieillir; ⟨cheese⟩ s'affiner
(d) ⟨policy⟩ arriver à échéance

mature student n personne f qui reprend des études (après un temps au foyer ou dans la vie active)

maul vtr ⟨animal⟩ lacérer

mauve n, adj mauve (m)

maverick n, adj nonconformiste (mf)

maxim n maxime f

maximize vtr maximiser ⟨profit, sales⟩; (Comput) agrandir

maximum [1] n maximum m
[2] adj maximum (inv)

maximum security prison n prison f de haute surveillance

may modal aux **(a)** (expressing possibility) **it** ~ **rain** il pleuvra peut-être, il se peut qu'il pleuve; **she** ~ **not have seen him** elle ne l'a peut-être pas vu; **'are you going to accept?'—'I** ~**'** 'tu vas accepter'—'peut-être'; **he** ~ **not come** il risque de ne pas venir; **be that as it** ~ quoi qu'il en soit; **come what** ~ advienne que pourra
(b) (expressing permission) **you** ~ **sit down** vous pouvez vous asseoir; ~ **I come in?** puis-je entrer?
(c) (wish) ~ **he rest in peace** qu'il repose en paix

May n mai m

maybe adv peut-être; ~ **they'll arrive early** peut-être qu'ils arriveront tôt

mayday n (distress signal) mayday m

May Day n premier mai m, fête f du travail

mayhem n (chaos) désordre m; (violence) grabuge m (colloq)

mayor n maire m

mayoress n (wife of mayor) femme f du maire; (lady mayor) mairesse f

maze n (puzzle, in gardens) labyrinthe m; (of streets, corridors) dédale m

MBA n (abbr = **Master of Business Administration**) ≈ maîtrise f de gestion

MC n (abbr = **Master of Ceremonies**) (in cabaret) animateur/-trice m/f; (at banquet) maître m des cérémonies

me pron **(a)** me, m'; **she knows** ~ elle me connaît; **he loves** ~ il m'aime ···⊱

(b) (in imperatives, after prepositions and to be) moi; **give it to ~!** donne-le-moi!; **it's for ~** c'est pour moi; **it's ~** c'est moi

ME n (abbr = **myalgic encephalomyelitis**) encéphalomyélite f myalgique

meadow n **(a)** (field) pré m
(b) (also **~land**) prés mpl, prairies fpl
(c) (also **water ~**) prairie f inondable

meagre (GB), **meager** (US) adj maigre (before n)

meal n **(a)** repas m; **to go out for a ~** aller (manger) au restaurant
(b) (from grain) farine f

mean ① n moyenne f
② adj **(a)** ⟨person⟩ avare, radin/-e (colloq); **he's ~ with money** il est près de ses sous
(b) (unkind, vicious) méchant/-e (**to** avec); **a ~ trick** un sale tour
(c) (average) ⟨weight, age⟩ moyen/-enne
(d) that's no ~ feat! ce n'est pas un mince exploit!
③ vtr **(a)** ⟨word, phrase, symbol⟩ signifier, vouloir dire; ⟨sign⟩ vouloir dire; **the name ~s nothing to me** ce nom ne me dit rien
(b) (intend) **to ~ to do** avoir l'intention de faire; **to be meant for sb** être destiné/-e à qn; **I didn't ~ to do it** je ne l'ai pas fait exprès; **she meant no offence** elle ne pensait pas à mal; **he doesn't ~ you any harm** il ne te veut aucun mal; **to ~ well** avoir de bonnes intentions; **he ~s what he says** (he is sincere) il est sérieux; (he is menacing) il ne plaisante pas; **without ~ing to** par inadvertance
(c) (entail) ⟨strike, law⟩ entraîner ⟨shortages, changes⟩
(d) (intend to say) vouloir dire; **what do you ~ by that remark?** qu'est-ce que tu veux dire par là?; **I know what you ~** je comprends
(e) (money) **~s a lot to him** l'argent compte beaucoup pour lui; **your friendship ~s a lot to me** ton amitié est très importante pour moi
(f) (be destined) **to be meant to do** être destiné/-e à faire; **it was meant to be** or **happen** cela devait arriver; **they were meant for each other** ils étaient faits l'un pour l'autre
(g) (be supposed to be) **he's meant to be/to be doing it** il est censé être/faire

meander vi ⟨river, road⟩ serpenter

meaning n (of word, remark, action, life) sens m; (of symbol, film, dream) signification f

meaningful adj **(a)** (significant) ⟨word, statement, result⟩ significatif/-ive
(b) (profound) ⟨relationship, comment, lyrics⟩ sérieux/-ieuse; ⟨experience⟩ riche
(c) (eloquent) ⟨look, smile⟩ entendu/-e; ⟨gesture⟩ significatif/-ive

meaningless adj **(a)** ⟨word, phrase⟩ dépourvu/-e de sens
(b) (pointless) ⟨act, sacrifice⟩ futile, vain/-e; ⟨violence⟩ insensé/-e

means ① n moyen m (**of doing** de faire); **a ~ of** un moyen de ⟨communication, transport⟩; **by ~ of** au moyen de; **yes, by all ~** oui, certainement; **it is by no ~ certain** c'est loin d'être sûr
② n pl moyens mpl, revenus mpl; **to live within one's ~** vivre selon ses moyens

means test n enquête f sur les ressources

meantime adv (**in the**) **~** pendant ce temps; **for the ~** pour le moment

meanwhile adv **(a)** (during this time) pendant ce temps
(b) (until then) en attendant
(c) (since then) entre-temps

measles n rougeole f

measure ① n **(a)** (gen) mesure f; **to take ~s** prendre des mesures; **weights and ~s** les poids et mesures mpl
(b) (measuring device) instrument m de mesure
② vtr **(a)** mesurer; **to ~ four by five metres** mesurer quatre mètres sur cinq
(b) (compare) **to ~ sth against** comparer qch à
IDIOMS **for good ~** pour faire bonne mesure
■ **measure out** mesurer ⟨land, flour, liquid⟩; doser ⟨medicine⟩
■ **measure up** ⟨person⟩ avoir les qualités requises; **to ~ up to** être à la hauteur de ⟨expectations⟩; soutenir la comparaison avec ⟨achievement⟩

measurement n **(a)** (of room, object) dimension f
(b) (of person) **to take sb's ~s** prendre les mensurations de qn; **chest ~** tour m de poitrine; **leg ~** longueur f de jambe

measuring jug n verre m gradué

meat n viande f; **crab ~** chair f de crabe

meat-eater n (animal) carnivore m; (person) **they're not great ~s** ils ne mangent pas beaucoup de viande

meaty adj **(a)** ⟨flavour, smell⟩ de viande
(b) ⟨article, book⟩ substantiel/-ielle
(c) ⟨person, hand⟩ épais/-aisse

Mecca pr n La Mecque

mechanic n mécanicien/-ienne m/f

mechanical adj mécanique

mechanical engineering n construction f mécanique

mechanics n pl **(a)** (field) mécanique f
(b) (workings) mécanisme m

mechanism n mécanisme m (**of** de)

mechanization n mécanisation f

medal n médaille f; **gold ~** médaille d'or

medallion n médaillon m

medallist (GB), **medalist** (US) n médaillé/-e m/f; **gold ~** médaillé/-e m/f d'or

meddle vi **to ~ in** se mêler de ⟨affairs⟩; **to ~ with** toucher à ⟨property⟩

media ① n médias mpl
② adj ⟨coverage, image, personality⟩ médiatique; ⟨power, reaction, report⟩ des médias

median (strip) n (US) terre-plein m central

media studies n pl communication f et journalisme m

mediate ⒈ *vtr* négocier ⟨*settlement, peace*⟩ ⒉ *vi* ⟨*person*⟩ arbitrer; **to ~ in/between** servir de médiateur dans/entre

mediator *n* médiateur/-trice *m/f*

medical ⒈ *n* (in school, army, for job) visite *f* médicale; (private) examen *m* médical ⒉ *adj* médical/-e

medical insurance *n* assurance-maladie *f*

medical student *n* étudiant/-e *m/f* en médecine

medicated *adj* (gen) médical/-e; ⟨*shampoo*⟩ traitant/-e

medication *n* médicaments *mpl*

medicinal *adj* ⟨*property, use*⟩ thérapeutique; ⟨*herb*⟩ médicinal/-e

medicine *n* (a) (field) médecine *f* (b) (drug) médicament *m* (**for** pour)

medicine cabinet, **medicine cupboard** *n* armoire *f* à pharmacie

medicine man *n* sorcier *m* guérisseur

medieval *adj* médiéval/-e

mediocre *adj* médiocre

mediocrity *n* (a) (state) médiocrité *f* (b) (person) médiocre *mf*

meditate *vtr, vi* méditer

Mediterranean ⒈ *pr n* (a) **the ~** (**sea**) la (mer) Méditerranée (b) (region) **the ~** les pays méditerranéens ⒉ *adj* méditerranéen/-éenne

medium ⒈ *n* (a) (means) moyen *m* (b) **to find** *or* **strike a happy ~** trouver le juste milieu (c) (spiritualist) médium *m* ⒉ *adj* moyen/-enne

medium-dry *adj* ⟨*drink*⟩ demi-sec

medium-rare *adj* ⟨*meat*⟩ à point

medium-sized *adj* de taille moyenne

medley *n* (a) (Mus) pot-pourri *m* (**of** de) (b) (mixture) mélange *m*

meek *adj* docile

meet ⒈ *n* (a) (Sport) rencontre *f* (sportive); **track ~** (US) rencontre *f* d'athlétisme (b) (GB) (in hunting) rendez-vous *m* de chasseurs ⒉ *vtr* (a) rencontrer ⟨*person, team, enemy*⟩ (b) (make acquaintance of) faire la connaissance de ⟨*person*⟩; **have you met each other?** vous vous connaissez? (c) (await) attendre; (fetch) chercher; **she went to ~ them** elle est allée les attendre *or* chercher; **to ~ sb off** (GB) *or* **at** (US) **the plane** attendre qn à l'aéroport (d) répondre à, satisfaire à ⟨*criteria, standards, needs*⟩; payer ⟨*bills, costs*⟩; couvrir ⟨*debts*⟩; faire face à ⟨*obligations, commitments*⟩; remplir ⟨*conditions*⟩ (e) se montrer à la hauteur de ⟨*challenge*⟩ ⒊ *vi* (a) ⟨*people, teams*⟩ se rencontrer; ⟨*committee, parliament*⟩ se réunir; **to ~ again** ⟨*people*⟩ se revoir (b) (by appointment) ⟨*people*⟩ se retrouver (c) (make acquaintance) ⟨*people*⟩ se connaître

(d) ⟨*lips, roads*⟩ se rencontrer; **their eyes met** leurs regards se croisèrent **IDIOMS to make ends ~** joindre les deux bouts

■ **meet up** (colloq) se retrouver; **to ~ up with** (colloq) retrouver ⟨*friend*⟩

■ **meet with**: ¶ **~ with [sb]** rencontrer ⟨*person, delegation*⟩; ¶ **~ with [sth]** rencontrer ⟨*opposition, success, suspicion*⟩; être accueilli/-e avec ⟨*approval*⟩; subir ⟨*failure*⟩

meeting *n* (a) (official) réunion *f*; **in a ~** en réunion (b) (informal) rencontre *f* (c) (GB) (Sport) **athletics ~** rencontre *f* d'athlétisme; **race ~** réunion *f* de courses

meeting-place *n* (lieu *m* de) rendez-vous *m*

meeting point *n* point *m* de rencontre

megabyte, **MB** *n* mégaoctet *m*, Mo *m*

megalomaniac *n, adj* mégalomane (*mf*)

megaphone *n* porte-voix *m inv*

megastore *n* mégastore *m*

melancholy ⒈ *n* mélancolie *f* ⒉ *adj* ⟨*person*⟩ mélancolique; ⟨*music, occasion*⟩ triste

mellow ⒈ *adj* (a) ⟨*wine*⟩ moelleux/-euse; ⟨*flavour*⟩ suave; ⟨*tone*⟩ mélodieux/-ieuse (b) ⟨*person*⟩ détendu/-e; ⟨*atmosphere*⟩ serein/-e ⒉ *vtr* ⟨*experience*⟩ assagir ⟨*person*⟩ ⒊ *vi* ⟨*person, behaviour*⟩ s'assagir

melodrama *n* mélodrame *m*

melodramatic *adj* mélodramatique

melody *n* mélodie *f*

melon *n* melon *m*

melt ⒈ *vtr* (a) faire fondre ⟨*snow, plastic, butter*⟩ (b) attendrir ⟨*heart*⟩ ⒉ *vi* (a) fondre; **to ~ in your mouth** fondre dans la bouche (b) **to ~ into** se fondre dans ⟨*crowd*⟩

meltdown *n* fusion *f* du cœur d'un réacteur

melting point *n* point *m* de fusion

member *n* (a) membre *m*; **to be a ~ of** faire partie de ⟨*group*⟩; être membre de ⟨*club, committee*⟩; **~ of staff** (gen) employé/-e *m/f*; (Sch, Univ) enseignant/-e *m/f*; **~ of the public** (in street) passant/-e *m/f*; (in theatre, cinema) spectateur/-trice *m/f*; **~ state** état *m* membre (b) (*also* **Member**) (of parliament) député *m* (c) (limb) membre *m*

Member of Congress, **MC** *n* (US) membre *m* du Congrès

Member of Parliament, **MP** *n* (GB) député *m* (**for** de)

Member of the European Parliament, **MEP** *n* (GB) député *m* au Parlement européen

membership *n* (a) (of club, organization) adhésion *f* (**of** à) (b) (fee) cotisation *f*

⸱⸱⸱⟩

m

(c) (members) membres *mpl*

membrane *n* membrane *f*

memento *n* souvenir *m* (of de)

memo *n* note *f* de service

memoirs *n pl* mémoires *mpl*

memo pad *n* bloc-notes *m*

memorable *adj* ⟨event⟩ mémorable;
⟨person, quality⟩ inoubliable

memorial ⓵ *n* mémorial *m* (to à)
⓶ *adj* commémoratif/-ive

memorize *vtr* apprendre [qch] par cœur

memory *n* (a) mémoire *f*; from ∼ de
mémoire; to have a good ∼ for faces être
physionomiste; in (loving) ∼ of à la mémoire
de
(b) (recollection) souvenir *m*; childhood
memories souvenirs d'enfance

menace ⓵ *n* menace *f*
⓶ *vtr* menacer (with de, avec)

menacing *adj* menaçant/-e

mend ⓵ *n* to be on the ∼ ⟨person⟩ être en
voie de guérison; ⟨economy⟩ reprendre
⓶ *vtr* réparer ⟨object, road⟩; (stitch)
raccommoder; (darn) repriser; (add patch)
rapiécer; that won't ∼ matters ça
n'arrangera pas les choses
⓷ *vi* ⟨injury⟩ guérir; ⟨person⟩ se rétablir
IDIOMS to ∼ one's ways s'amender

menial *adj* ⟨job⟩ subalterne; ⟨attitude⟩
servile; ∼ tasks basses besognes

meningitis *n* méningite *f*

menopause *n* ménopause *f*

men's room *n* (US) toilettes *fpl* pour
hommes

menstruation *n* menstruation *f*

menswear *n* prêt-à-porter *m* pour
hommes

mental *adj* (gen) mental/-e; ⟨ability, effort,
energy⟩ intellectuel/-elle; ⟨hospital,
institution⟩ psychiatrique

mental block *n* blocage *m* psychologique

mentality *n* mentalité *f*

mentally *adv* (a) ∼ handicapped
handicapé/-e mental; the ∼ ill les malades
mentaux
(b) ∼ exhausted surmené/-e
intellectuellement

mentholated *adj* au menthol

mention ⓵ *n* mention *f* (of de); it got a ∼
on the radio on en a parlé à la radio
⓶ *vtr* (a) faire mention de ⟨person, topic,
fact⟩; please don't ∼ my name ne
mentionnez pas mon nom; to ∼ sb/sth to sb
parler de qn/qch à qn; not to ∼ sans parler
de; without ∼ing any names sans nommer
personne; don't ∼ it! je vous en prie!, je t'en
prie!
(b) (acknowledge) citer ⟨name⟩

menu *n* menu *m*

menu bar *n* barre *f* de menu

MEP *n* (GB) (*abbr* = **Member of the
European Parliament**) député *m* au
Parlement européen

mercenary ⓵ *n* mercenaire *mf*
⓶ *adj* ⟨person⟩ intéressé/-e

merchandise *n* marchandises *fpl*

merchant *n* (selling in bulk) négociant *m*;
(selling small quantities) marchand *m*

merchant bank *n* (GB) banque *f*
d'affaires

merchant banker *n* cadre *m* d'une
banque d'affaires

merchant navy (GB), **merchant
marine** (US) *n* marine *f* marchande

merciful *adj* (a) ⟨person⟩ clément/-e (to,
towards envers); ⟨act⟩ charitable
(b) ⟨occurrence⟩ heureux/-euse; a ∼ release
une délivrance

merciless *adj* ⟨ruler, criticism⟩
impitoyable (to, towards envers); ⟨heat⟩
implacable

mercury ⓵ *n* mercure *m*
⓶ **Mercury** *pr n* Mercure *f*

mercy *n* clémence *f*; to have ∼ on sb avoir
pitié de qn; to beg for ∼ demander grâce; at
the ∼ of à la merci de

mercy killing *n* (a) euthanasie *f*
(b) (act) acte *m* d'euthanasie

mere *adj* (a) ⟨coincidence, nonsense⟩ pur/-e
(before n); ⟨formality⟩ simple (before n); he's
a ∼ child ce n'est qu'un enfant; the beach is
a ∼ 2 km from here la plage n'est qu'à 2 km
d'ici
(b) (very) ⟨idea⟩ simple (before n); the ∼ sight
of her makes me nervous rien que de la voir,
ça rend nerveux

merely *adv* simplement, seulement

merge ⓵ *vtr* (a) to ∼ sth with fusionner
qch avec ⟨company, group⟩
(b) mélanger ⟨colours, designs⟩
⓶ *vi* (a) (also ∼ **together**) ⟨companies,
departments⟩ fusionner (with avec; ⟨roads,
rivers⟩ se rejoindre
(b) ⟨colours, sounds⟩ se confondre

merger *n* fusion *f*

meringue *n* meringue *f*

merit ⓵ *n* mérite *m*
⓶ *vtr* mériter

mermaid *n* sirène *f*

merrily *adv* (a) (happily) joyeusement
(b) (unconcernedly) avec insouciance

merry *adj* (a) (happy) joyeux/-euse, gai/-e;
Merry Christmas! joyeux Noël!
(b) (colloq) (tipsy) éméché/-e

merry-go-round *n* manège *m*

mesh ⓵ *n* (a) (netting) (of string) filet *m*; (of
metal) grillage *m*
(b) (net) mailles *fpl*
⓶ *vi* (Tech) ⟨cogs⟩ s'engrener; to ∼ with
s'emboîter dans

mesmerize ⓵ *vtr* hypnotiser
⓶ **mesmerized** *pp adj* fasciné/-e,
médusé/-e

mess ⓵ *n* (a) désordre *m*; what a ∼! quel
désordre!, quelle pagaille! (colloq); to make a
∼ ⟨person⟩ mettre du désordre; this report is
a ∼! ce rapport est fait n'importe comment!;

to make a ~ **on the carpet** salir la moquette;
to make a ~ **of the job** massacrer (colloq) le
travail
(b) (Mil) cantine f
2 vi (colloq) **(a) to** ~ **with** toucher à ⟨drugs⟩
(b) don't ~ **with him** évite-le; **don't** ~ **with
me** ne me cherche pas
■ **mess about** (colloq), **mess around**
(colloq): ¶ ~ **around** faire l'imbécile; ¶ ~ **[sb]
around** (colloq) traiter qn par-dessus la jambe
(colloq), prendre qn pour un imbécile
■ **mess up** (colloq): ¶ ~ **up** (US) faire
l'imbécile
¶ ~ **[sth] up (a)** semer la pagaille dans
⟨papers⟩; mettre du désordre dans ⟨kitchen⟩
(b) (ruin) louper (colloq) ⟨exam⟩; gâcher
⟨chances, life⟩; ¶ ~ **[sb] up** ⟨drugs, alcohol⟩
détruire; ⟨experience⟩ faire perdre les
pédales à qn (colloq)
message n message m (**about** au sujet de)
message window n (Comput) feuille f de
message
messaging n messagerie f électronique
messenger n messager/-ère m/f; (for hotel,
company) garçon m de courses, coursier/-ière
m/f
messy adj **(a)** ⟨house⟩ en désordre;
⟨appearance⟩ négligé/-e; ⟨handwriting⟩ peu
soigné/-e
(b) ⟨work, job⟩ salissant/-e; **he's a ~ eater** il
mange comme un cochon
(c) ⟨lawsuit⟩ compliqué/-e; **a ~ business**
une sale affaire
metal 1 n métal m
2 adj en métal
metallic adj ⟨substance⟩ métallique;
⟨paint, finish⟩ métallisé/-e; ⟨taste⟩ de métal
metaphor n métaphore f
mete v ■ **mete out** infliger ⟨punishment⟩;
rendre ⟨justice⟩
meteor n météore m
meteorite n météorite f
meter 1 n **(a)** compteur m; **gas ~**
compteur de gaz
(b) (also **parking ~**) parcmètre m
(c) (US) = METRE
2 vtr mesurer la consommation de
⟨electricity, gas⟩
method n **(a)** (of teaching, contraception,
training) méthode f (**for doing** pour faire); (of
payment, treatment, production) mode m (**of** de)
(b) (orderliness) méthode f
methodical adj méthodique
Methodist n, adj méthodiste (mf)
methylated spirit(s) n alcool m à
brûler
meticulous adj méticuleux/-euse
metre (GB), **meter** (US) n mètre m
metric adj métrique
metropolitan adj **(a)** ⟨area, population⟩
urbain/-e; **~ New York** l'agglomération de
New York
(b) **~ France** la France métropolitaine

mettle n courage m; **to be on one's ~** être
sur la sellette; **to put sb on his ~** amener qn
à montrer de quoi il est capable
Mexico pr n Mexique m
miaow 1 n miaou m
2 vi miauler
microbe n microbe m
microchip n puce f, circuit m intégré
microcosm n microcosme m
microfilm n microfilm m
microlighting n ULM m, ultra léger m
motorisé
microphone n microphone m
microscope n microscope m
microwave 1 n ~ (oven) four m à
micro-ondes
2 vtr passer ⟨qch⟩ au four à micro-ondes
mid- pref **in the ~20th century** au milieu du
vingtième siècle; **~afternoon** milieu m de
l'après-midi; (in) **~May** (à la) mi-mai; **he's in
his ~forties** il a environ quarante-cinq ans
midair 1 adj ⟨collision⟩ en plein vol
2 **in midair** phr (in mid-flight) en plein vol;
(in the air) en l'air
midday n midi m
middle 1 n **(a)** milieu m; **in the ~ of** au
milieu de; **in the ~ of May** à la mi-mai; **to be
in the ~ of doing** être en train de faire; **to
split [sth] down the ~** partager ⟨qch⟩ en
deux ⟨bill, work⟩; diviser ⟨qch⟩ en deux
⟨group, opinion⟩; **in the ~ of nowhere** en
pleine brousse (colloq)
(b) (waist) taille f
2 adj ⟨door, shelf⟩ du milieu; ⟨size,
difficulty⟩ moyen/-enne; **there must be a ~
way** il doit y avoir une solution
intermédiaire
middle-aged adj ⟨person⟩ d'âge mûr;
⟨outlook, view⟩ vieux jeu inv
Middle Ages n pl **the ~** le Moyen Âge
middle class 1 n classe f moyenne
2 **middle-class** adj ⟨person⟩ de la classe
moyenne; ⟨attitude, view⟩ bourgeois/-e
Middle East pr n Moyen-Orient m
middle-eastern adj du Moyen-Orient
middleman n intermédiaire m
middle-size(d) adj de taille moyenne
middleweight n poids m moyen
middling adj moyen/-enne; **fair to ~** pas
trop mal
midfield n milieu m du terrain
midge n moucheron m
midget n nain/-e m/f
midnight n minuit m
midriff n ventre m
midst n **in the ~ of** au beau milieu de; **in
the ~ of change/war** en plein changement/
pleine guerre; **in our ~** parmi nous
midsummer n milieu m de l'été
Midsummer('s) Day n la Saint-Jean
midtown n (US) centre-ville m
midway 1 n (US) attractions fpl foraines ····⊱

m

2 adj ⟨post, position⟩ de mi-course; ⟨stage, point⟩ de mi-parcours

3 adv ~ **between/along** à mi-chemin entre/ le long de; ~ **through** au milieu de

midweek **1** adj de milieu de semaine
2 adv en milieu de semaine

midwife n sage-femme f; **male** ~ homme m sage-femme

midwinter n milieu m de l'hiver

might¹ modal aux **(a)** (expressing possibility) peut-être; **'will you come?'—'I** ~' 'tu viendras?'—'peut-être'; **she** ~ **not have heard the news** elle n'a peut-être pas entendu la nouvelle; **I** ~ **lose my job** je risque de perdre mon travail
(b) (expressing annoyance) **you** ~ **have been killed!** tu aurais pu te faire tuer!; **I** ~ **have known!** j'aurais dû m'en douter!
(c) **I thought it** ~ **rain** j'ai pensé qu'il risquait de pleuvoir; **I thought you** ~ **say that** je m'attendais à ce que tu dises ça; **he said you** ~ **be hurt** il a dit que tu serais peut-être blessé
(d) ~ **I make a suggestion?** puis-je me permettre de faire une suggestion?; **it** ~ **be better to wait** ce serait peut-être mieux d'attendre

might² n **(a)** (power) puissance f
(b) (physical strength) force f; **with all his** ~ de toutes ses forces

mighty adj puissant/-e

migrant **1** n (person) migrant/-e m/f; (bird) oiseau m migrateur; (animal) animal m migrateur
2 adj ⟨labour⟩ saisonnier/-ière; ⟨bird, animal⟩ migrateur/-trice

migrate vi **(a)** ⟨person⟩ émigrer
(b) ⟨bird, animal⟩ migrer

mike n (colloq) micro m (colloq)

mild adj **(a)** ⟨surprise⟩ léger/-ère; ⟨interest, irritation⟩ modéré/-e
(b) ⟨weather, winter⟩ doux/douce; ⟨climate⟩ tempéré/-e
(c) ⟨beer, taste, tobacco⟩ léger/-ère; ⟨cheese⟩ doux/douce; ⟨curry⟩ peu épicé/-e
(d) ⟨soap, detergent⟩ doux/douce
(e) ⟨infection⟩ bénin/-igne; ⟨attack, sedative⟩ léger/-ère
(f) ⟨person, voice⟩ doux/douce

mildew n moisissure f

mile n **(a)** mile m (= 1,609 m); **it's 50** ~**s away** ≈ c'est à 80 kilomètres d'ici
(b) **to walk for** ~**s** marcher pendant des kilomètres; **it's** ~**s away!** c'est au bout du monde; **to be** ~**s away** (daydreaming) être complètement ailleurs; ~**s from anywhere** loin de tout; **to stand out a** ~ sauter aux yeux

mileage n **(a)** nombre m de miles
(b) (done by car) kilométrage m
(c) (miles per gallon) consommation f

milestone n borne f (milliaire); (figurative) étape f importante

militant **1** n (activist) agitateur/-trice m/f
2 adj militant/-e

militarize vtr militariser; ~**d zone** zone f militarisée

military **1** n **the** ~ (army) l'armée f; (soldiers) les militaires mpl
2 adj militaire

military service n service m militaire

militia n milice f

milk **1** n lait m; **powdered** ~ lait en poudre; **full cream** ~ lait entier; **skimmed** ~ lait écrémé
2 vtr **(a)** traire ⟨cow⟩
(b) (exploit) exploiter ⟨situation, system⟩; **to** ~ **sb dry** saigner qn à blanc

milk chocolate n chocolat m au lait

milkman n laitier m

milkshake n milkshake m

milky adj **(a)** ⟨drink⟩ au lait
(b) ⟨skin, liquid, colour⟩ laiteux/-euse

Milky Way pr n Voie f lactée

mill **1** n **(a)** moulin m; **water/pepper** ~ moulin à eau/à poivre
(b) (factory) fabrique f; **steel** ~ aciérie f
2 vtr moudre ⟨flour, pepper⟩

millenium bug n bogue m de l'an 2000

millennium n millénaire m

milligram(me) n milligramme m

millimetre (GB), **millimeter** (US) n millimètre m

million **1** n million m; ~**s of** des millions de
2 adj **a** ~ **people/pounds** un million de personnes/de livres

millionaire n millionnaire mf

milometer n (GB) ≈ compteur m kilométrique

mime **1** n mime m; ~ **show** pantomime f
2 vtr, vi mimer

mime artist n mime mf

mimic **1** n imitateur/-trice m/f
2 vtr imiter

mince **1** n (GB) viande f hachée; **beef** ~ bœuf m haché
2 vtr hacher ⟨meat⟩

mind **1** n **(a)** esprit m; **peace of** ~ tranquillité d'esprit; **it's all in the** ~ c'est tout dans la tête (colloq); **to cross sb's** ~ venir à l'esprit de qn; **to have something on one's** ~ être préoccupé/-e; **to set sb's** ~ **at rest** rassurer qn; **nothing could be further from my** ~ loin de moi cette pensée; **to make sb's** ~ **off sth** distraire qn de qch; **my** ~**'s a blank** j'ai un trou de mémoire; **I can't get him out of my** ~ je n'arrive pas à l'oublier; **are you out of your** ~? (colloq) tu es fou/folle? (colloq)
(b) (brain) intelligence f; **with the** ~ **of a two-year-old** avec l'intelligence d'un enfant de deux ans
(c) (opinion) avis m; **to my** ~ à mon avis; **to make up one's** ~ **about/to do** se décider à propos de/à faire; **to change one's** ~ **about sth** changer d'avis sur qch; **to keep an open**

~ **about sth** réserver son jugement sur qch;
to know one's own ~ avoir des idées bien à
soi; **to speak one's** ~ dire ce qu'on a à dire
2 *vtr* **(a)** surveiller ⟨*manners, language*⟩;
faire attention à ⟨*hazard*⟩
(b) I don't ~ ça m'est égal, ça ne me
dérange pas; **I don't** ~ **the cold** le froid ne
me dérange pas; **I don't** ~ **cats, but I prefer
dogs** je n'ai rien contre les chats, mais je
préfère les chiens; **will they** ~ **us being late?**
est-ce qu'ils seront fâchés si nous sommes
en retard?; **would you** ~ **keeping my seat for
me?** est-ce que ça vous ennuierait de garder
ma place?; **I wouldn't** ~ **a glass of wine** je
prendrais volontiers un verre de vin; **if you
don't** ~ si cela ne vous fait rien; **never** ~
(don't worry) ne t'en fais pas; (it doesn't matter)
peu importe; **he can't afford an apartment,
never** ~ **a big house** il ne peut pas se
permettre un appartement encore moins
une grande maison
(c) s'occuper de ⟨*animal, children*⟩; tenir
⟨*shop*⟩
3 in mind *phr* **I have something in** ~ **for
this evening** j'ai une idée pour ce soir; **to
bear sth in** ~ (remember) ne pas oublier qch;
(take into account) prendre qch en compte
IDIOMS **to read sb's** ~ lire dans les pensées
de qn; **to see sth in one's** ~'s **eye** imaginer
qch; **to have a** ~ **of one's own** savoir ce
qu'on veut

mind-blowing *adj* (colloq)
époustouflant/-e (colloq)

mind-boggling *adj* (colloq) stupéfiant/-e

mindless *adj* ⟨*person, programme*⟩ bête;
⟨*work*⟩ abrutissant/-e; ⟨*vandalism*⟩
gratuit/-e; ⟨*task*⟩ machinal/-e

mine¹ *pron*

■ Note In French, possessive pronouns reflect
the gender and number of the noun they are
standing for. So *mine* is translated by *le mien, la
mienne, les miens, les miennes,* according to
what is being referred to.

his car is red but ~ **is blue** sa voiture est
rouge mais la mienne est bleue; **which**
(glass) **is** ~? lequel (de ces verres) est le
mien *or* est à moi?; **his children are older
than** ~ ses enfants sont plus âgés que les
miens; **the blue car is** ~ la voiture bleue est
à moi; **she's a friend of** ~ c'est une amie à
moi; **it's not** ~ ce n'est pas à moi

mine² **1** *n* mine *f*
2 *vtr* **(a)** extraire ⟨*gems, mineral*⟩; exploiter
⟨*area*⟩
(b) (Mil) miner ⟨*area*⟩

minefield *n* champ *m* de mines; (figurative)
terrain *m* miné

miner *n* mineur *m*

mineral **1** *n* (substance, class) minéral *m*;
(for extraction) minerai *m*
2 *adj* minéral/-e; ~ **ore** minerai *m*

mineral water *n* eau *f* minérale

mingle *vi* **(a) to** ~ **with** se mêler à ⟨*crowd,
guests*⟩

(b) ⟨*sounds*⟩ se confondre (**with** à); ⟨*smells,
feelings*⟩ se mêler (**with** à)

miniature **1** *n* miniature *f*
2 *adj* (gen) miniature; ⟨*dog, horse*⟩ nain/-e

minicab *n* (GB) taxi *m* (non agréé)

minidisc *n* minidisque *m*

minimalist *adj* minimaliste

minimum **1** *n* minimum *m* (**of** de)
2 *adj* minimum, minimal/-e

mining **1** *n* exploitation *f* minière
2 *adj* ⟨*industry, town*⟩ minier/-ière;
⟨*accident*⟩ de mine

mini-skirt *n* mini-jupe *f*

minister **1** *n* **(a)** (GB) ministre *m*; ~ **of** *or*
for Defence, Defence ~ ministre de la
Défense
(b) (clergyman) ministre *m* du culte
2 *vi* **to** ~ donner des soins à ⟨*person*⟩; **to**
~ **to sb's needs** pourvoir aux besoins de qn

minister of state *n* (GB) ministre *m*
délégué

ministry *n* (GB) ministère *m*

mink *n* vison *m*

minor **1** *n* (Law) mineur/-e *m/f*
2 *adj* (gen, Mus) mineur/-e; ⟨*injury, burn*⟩
léger/-ère; ~ **road** route secondaire

minority *n* minorité *f*; **to be in the** ~ être
en minorité

minstrel *n* ménestrel *m*

mint **1** *n* **(a)** (herb) menthe *f*
(b) (sweet) bonbon *m* à la menthe
(c) (for coins) hôtel *m* des Monnaies
2 *adj* **in** ~ **condition** à l'état neuf
3 *vtr* **(a)** frapper ⟨*coin*⟩
(b) forger ⟨*word, expression*⟩

minuet *n* menuet *m*

minus **1** *n* **(a)** (in mathematics) moins *m*
(b) (drawback) inconvénient *m*
2 *adj* ⟨*symbol, button*⟩ moins; ⟨*number,
quantity, value*⟩ négatif/-ive; ~ **sign** signe
moins
3 *prep* **(a)** moins; **what is 20** ~ **8?** combien
font 20 moins 8?; **it is** ~ **15** (degrees) il fait
moins 15 (degrés)
(b) (without) sans

minuscule *adj* minuscule

minute¹ **1** *n* minute *f*; **five** ~**s past ten**
dix heures cinq; **it's five** ~**s' walk away** c'est
à cinq minutes à pied; **the** ~ **I heard the
news** dès que j'ai appris la nouvelle; **any** ~
now d'une minute à l'autre; **at the last** ~ à
la dernière minute
2 **minutes** *n pl* compte-rendu *m*

minute² *adj* ⟨*particle*⟩ minuscule;
⟨*quantity*⟩ infime; ⟨*risk, variation*⟩ minime

minute hand *n* aiguille *f* des minutes

miracle *n* miracle *m*; **to work** *or* **perform**
~**s** faire des miracles

miraculous *adj* **(a)** ⟨*escape, recovery*⟩
miraculeux/-euse
(b) ⟨*speed, strength*⟩ prodigieux/-ieuse

mirror **1** *n* **(a)** (gen) miroir *m*, glace *f*; (Aut)
rétroviseur *m*
(b) (figurative) reflet *m*

2 *vtr* refléter; **to be ~ed in** se refléter dans

mirth *n* (laughter) hilarité *f*; (joy) joie *f*

misapprehension *n* malentendu *m*, erreur *f*; **to be (labouring) under a ~** se tromper

misappropriate *vtr* détourner ⟨*funds*⟩

misbehave *vi* ⟨*child*⟩ se tenir mal; ⟨*adult*⟩ se conduire mal

miscalculation *n* erreur *f* de calcul; (figurative) mauvais calcul *m*

miscarriage *n* **(a)** (Med) fausse couche *f*; **to have a ~** faire une fausse couche **(b)** (Law) **a ~ of justice** une grave erreur judiciaire

miscellaneous *adj* divers/-e

mischief *n* espièglerie *f*; **to get into** *or* **make ~** faire des bêtises; **he's up to ~** il prépare quelque chose; **to be full of ~** être espiègle; **it keeps them out of ~** ça les occupe

mischievous *adj* ⟨*child, comedy, humour*⟩ espiègle; ⟨*smile, eyes*⟩ malicieux/-ieuse

misconception *n* idée *f* fausse

misdemeanour, misdemeanor (US) *n* délit *m*

miser *n* avare *mf*

miserable *adj* **(a)** ⟨*person, event, expression*⟩ malheureux/-euse; ⟨*thoughts*⟩ noir/-e; ⟨*weather*⟩ sale (*before n*); **to feel ~** avoir le cafard **(b)** ⟨*amount*⟩ misérable; ⟨*wage, life*⟩ de misère; ⟨*attempt, failure, performance*⟩ lamentable

miserly *adj* ⟨*person*⟩ avare; ⟨*amount*⟩ maigre

misery *n* **(a)** (unhappiness) souffrance *f*; (gloom) abattement *m*; **to make sb's life a ~** faire de la vie de qn un enfer **(b)** (misfortune) **the miseries of unemployment** le chômage et son cortège de misères **(c)** (GB) (colloq) (child) pleurnicheur/-euse *m/f*; (adult) rabat-joie *m inv*

misfire *vi* **(a)** ⟨*gun, rocket*⟩ faire long feu; ⟨*engine*⟩ avoir des ratés **(b)** ⟨*plan, joke*⟩ tomber à plat

misfit *n* marginal/-e *m/f*

misfortune *n* (unfortunate event) malheur *m*; (bad luck) malchance *f*

misgiving *n* crainte *f*; **to have ~s about sth** avoir des craintes quant à qch; **to have ~s about sb** avoir des doutes au sujet de qn

misguided *adj* ⟨*strategy, attempt*⟩ peu judicieux/-ieuse; ⟨*person*⟩ malavisé/-e

mishandle *vtr* **(a)** mal conduire ⟨*operation, meeting*⟩; mal s'y prendre avec ⟨*person*⟩ **(b)** (roughly) manier ⟨*qch*⟩ sans précaution ⟨*object*⟩; malmener ⟨*person, animal*⟩

mishap *n* incident *m*

mishear *vtr* mal entendre

misinform *vtr* mal renseigner

misinterpret *vtr* mal interpréter

misinterpretation *n* interprétation *f* erronée

misjudge *vtr* mal évaluer ⟨*speed, distance*⟩; mal calculer ⟨*shot*⟩; mal juger ⟨*person*⟩

mislay *vtr* égarer

mislead *vtr* (deliberately) tromper; (unintentionally) induire [qn] en erreur

misleading *adj* ⟨*impression, title, information*⟩ trompeur/-euse; ⟨*claim, statement, advertising*⟩ mensonger/-ère

mismanage *vtr* mal diriger ⟨*firm, project*⟩; mal gérer ⟨*finances*⟩

misplace *vtr* égarer

misprint *n* coquille *f*, faute *f* typographique

mispronounce *vtr* mal prononcer

misread *vtr* (read wrongly) mal lire; (misinterpret) mal interpréter ⟨*actions*⟩

misrepresent *vtr* présenter [qn] sous un faux jour ⟨*person*⟩; déformer ⟨*views, facts*⟩

misrepresentation *n* (of facts) déformation *f*

miss **1** *n* **(a)** (in game) coup *m* manqué *or* raté **(b)** **to give [sth] a ~** (colloq) ne pas aller à ⟨*film, lecture*⟩; se passer de ⟨*dish, drink, meal*⟩ **2** *vtr* **(a)** manquer ⟨*target*⟩ **(b)** rater ⟨*bus, plane, event, meeting*⟩; laisser passer ⟨*chance*⟩; **I ~ed the train by five minutes** j'ai raté le train de cinq minutes **(c)** ne pas saisir ⟨*joke, remark*⟩ **(d)** sauter ⟨*line, class*⟩; manquer ⟨*school*⟩ **(e)** (avoid) échapper à ⟨*death, injury*⟩; éviter ⟨*traffic, bad weather, rush hour*⟩; **he just ~ed being caught** il a failli être pris **(f)** **I ~ you** tu me manques; **he ~ed Paris** Paris lui manquait; **I'll ~ coming to the office** le bureau va me manquer **3** *vi* **(a)** (Games, Sport, Mil) rater son coup; **~ed! raté! (b)** ⟨*engine*⟩ avoir des ratés ■ **miss out**: ¶ **~ out** être lésé/-e; ¶ **~ out on** [sth] laisser passer, louper (colloq); ¶ **~ [sb/sth] out** sauter ⟨*line, verse*⟩; omettre ⟨*fact, point, person*⟩

Miss *n* Mademoiselle *f*; (written abbreviation) Mlle

misshapen *adj* ⟨*leg*⟩ difforme; ⟨*object*⟩ déformé/-e

missile *n* **(a)** (Mil) missile *m* **(b)** (rock, bottle) projectile *m*

missing *adj* **to be ~** manquer; **to go ~** ⟨*person, object*⟩ disparaître; **the ~ jewels/child** les bijoux disparus/l'enfant disparu; **there are two books ~** il manque deux livres

mission *n* mission *f*

missionary *n* missionnaire *mf*

mist *n* brume *f* ■ **mist over, mist up** ⟨*lens, window*⟩ s'embuer

mistake **1** *n* (gen) erreur *f*; (in text, spelling, typing) faute *f*; **to make a ~** se tromper; **by ~** par erreur

2 *vtr* **(a) to ~ sth for sth else** prendre qch pour qch d'autre; **to ~ sb for sb else** confondre qn avec qn d'autre
(b) mal interpréter ⟨*meaning*⟩

mistaken *adj* **(a) to be ~** avoir tort; **he was ~ in thinking it was over** il avait tort de croire que c'était fini
(b) ⟨*enthusiasm, generosity*⟩ mal placé/-e

mistletoe *n* gui *m*

mistranslation *n* erreur *f* de traduction

mistreat *vtr* maltraiter

mistress *n* maîtresse *f*

mistrust **1** *n* méfiance *f* (**of** à l'égard de)
2 *vtr* se méfier de

misty *adj* ⟨*conditions, morning*⟩ brumeux/-euse; ⟨*lens, window*⟩ embué/-e; ⟨*photo*⟩ flou/-e

misunderstand *vtr* mal comprendre; (completely) ne pas comprendre

misunderstanding *n* malentendu *m*

misunderstood *adj* **to feel ~** se sentir incompris/-e

misuse **1** *n* (of equipment) mauvais usage *m*; (of word) usage *m* impropre; (of power, authority) abus *m*
2 *vtr* faire mauvais usage de ⟨*equipment*⟩; mal employer ⟨*word, resources*⟩; abuser de ⟨*authority*⟩

mitigate *vtr* atténuer ⟨*effects, distress, sentence*⟩; réduire ⟨*risks*⟩; minimiser ⟨*loss*⟩

mitre (GB), **miter** (US) *n* mitre *f*

mitten *n* moufle *f*

mix **1** *n* **(a)** (gen) mélange *m*
(b) (Mus) mixage *m*, mix *m*
2 *vtr* **(a)** (gen) mélanger (**with** avec; **and** à)
(b) préparer ⟨*drink*⟩; malaxer ⟨*cement, paste*⟩
(c) (Mus) mixer
3 *vi* **(a)** (*also* **~ together**) se mélanger (**with** avec, à)
(b) (socialize) être sociable; **to ~ with** fréquenter
■ **mix up (a)** (confuse) confondre; **to get two things/people ~ed up** confondre deux choses/personnes
(b) (jumble up) mélanger, mêler ⟨*papers, photos*⟩
(c) to get ~ed up in se trouver mêlé/-e à

mixed *adj* **(a)** ⟨*collection, programme, diet*⟩ varié/-e; ⟨*nuts, sweets*⟩ assorti/-e; ⟨*salad*⟩ composé/-e; ⟨*group, community*⟩ (socially, in age) mélangé/-e; (racially) d'origines diverses; **of ~ blood** de sang mêlé
(b) (for both sexes) mixte
(c) ⟨*reaction, feelings, reception*⟩ mitigé/-e

mixed ability *adj* (Sch) ⟨*class, teaching*⟩ sans niveau

mixed race *n* **of ~** métis/-isse

mixer *n* **(a)** (Culin) batteur *m* électrique
(b) (drink) boisson *f* nonalcoolisée

mixing *n* (combining) mélange *m*; (Mus) mixage *m*

mixture *n* mélange *m* (**of** de)

mix-up *n* confusion *f* (**over** sur)

moan **1** *n* **(a)** (noise) gémissement *m*
(b) (colloq) (complaint) plainte *f* (**about** au sujet de)
2 *vi* **(a)** (groan) gémir (**with** de)
(b) (colloq) (complain) râler (colloq) (**about** contre)

moat *n* douve *f*

mob **1** *n* foule *f* (**of** de)
2 *vtr* assaillir ⟨*person*⟩; envahir ⟨*place*⟩

mobile **1** *n* mobile *m*
2 *adj* **(a)** ⟨*object, population*⟩ mobile; ⟨*canteen*⟩ ambulant/-e
(b) to be ~ (able to walk) pouvoir marcher; (able to travel) pouvoir se déplacer

mobile phone *n* téléphone *m* portable, portable *m*

mobilization *n* mobilisation *f*

mobilize *vtr, vi* mobiliser

mocha *n* **(a)** (coffee) moka *m*
(b) (flavour) arôme *m* de café et de chocolat

mock **1** *n* (GB Sch) examen *m* blanc
2 *adj* **(a)** ⟨*suede, ivory*⟩ faux/fausse (*before n*); **~ leather** similicuir *m*
(b) (feigned) simulé/-e; **in ~ terror** en feignant la terreur
3 *vtr* se moquer de ⟨*person, efforts, beliefs*⟩
4 *vi* ⟨*person*⟩ se moquer

mockery *n* moquerie *f*

mod con *n* (GB) confort *m* (moderne)

mode *n* mode *m*

model **1** *n* **(a)** (of car, appliance, garment) modèle *m*
(b) (person) (artist's) modèle *m*; (fashion) mannequin *m*
(c) (scale model) maquette *f*
(d) (perfect example) modèle *m* (**of** de)
2 *adj* **(a)** ⟨*railway, soldier, village*⟩ miniature; ⟨*aeroplane, boat, car*⟩ modèle réduit
(b) ⟨*husband, student, prison*⟩ modèle
3 *vtr* **(a)** modeler ⟨*clay, wax*⟩
(b) ⟨*fashion model*⟩ présenter ⟨*garment*⟩
4 *vi* **(a)** ⟨*artist's model*⟩ poser
(b) ⟨*fashion model*⟩ travailler comme mannequin

modelling (GB), **modeling** (US) *n* **(a)** (of clothes) **to take up ~** devenir mannequin; **have you done any ~?** as-tu déjà travaillé comme mannequin?
(b) (Comput) modélisation *f*

modem *n* modem *m*

moderate **1** *adj* **(a)** (not extreme) modéré/-e (**in** dans)
(b) ⟨*success, income*⟩ moyen/-enne
2 *vtr* modérer
3 *vi* se modérer

moderation *n* modération *f* (**in** dans); **in ~** avec modération

modern *adj* moderne; **the ~ world** le monde contemporain

modernize *vtr* moderniser

modern languages *n pl* langues *fpl* vivantes

m

modest adj (a) modeste (about au sujet de)
(b) ⟨gift, aim⟩ modeste; ⟨sum, salary⟩ modique

modesty n modestie f

modify vtr modifier

modular adj modulaire

module n module m

mogul n magnat m

Mohammed, Mahomet pr n Mahomet

moist adj ⟨soil⟩ humide; ⟨cake⟩ moelleux/-euse; ⟨hands⟩ moite; ⟨skin⟩ bien hydraté/-e

moisten vtr humecter

moisture n humidité f

moisturizer n (lotion) lait m hydratant; (cream) crème f hydratante

molar n, adj molaire (f)

mold (US) = MOULD

mole n (a) (Zool) taupe f
(b) (on skin) grain m de beauté

molecule n molécule f

molest vtr agresser [qn] sexuellement

mollycoddle vtr dorloter

molt (US) = MOULT

molten adj en fusion

moment n (a) (instant) instant m; in a ~ dans un instant; at any ~ à tout instant
(b) (point in time) moment m; at the ~ en ce moment; at the right ~ au bon moment

momentarily adv (a) (for an instant) momentanément
(b) (US) (very soon) dans un instant; (at any moment) d'un moment à l'autre

momentary adj passager/-ère

momentous adj capital/-e

momentum n (gen) élan m; (in physics) vitesse f

monarch n monarque m

monarchy n monarchie f

monastery n monastère m

Monday n lundi m

monetary union n union f monétaire

money n argent m; to make ~ ⟨person⟩ gagner de l'argent; ⟨business, project⟩ rapporter de l'argent
IDIOMS to get one's ~'s worth, to get a good run for one's ~ en avoir pour son argent; your ~ or your life! la bourse ou la vie!

money belt n ceinture f porte-monnaie

moneybox n tirelire f

moneylender n prêteur/-euse m/f

moneymaker n (product) article m qui rapporte beaucoup; (activity) activité f lucrative

money order, MO n mandat m postal

mongrel n (chien m) bâtard m

monitor ① n (Comput, Med) moniteur m
② vtr (a) surveiller ⟨results, patient, breathing⟩
(b) être à l'écoute de ⟨broadcast⟩

monk n moine m

monkey n (a) (Zool) singe m

(b) (colloq) (rascal) galopin m (colloq)

monochrome adj ⟨film⟩ en noir et blanc; ⟨colour scheme⟩ monochrome

monogamous adj monogame

monogamy n monogamie f

monologue, monolog (US) n monologue m

monopolize vtr (a) détenir le monopole de ⟨market, supply⟩
(b) (figurative) monopoliser

monopoly n monopole m

monoski vi faire du monoski

monotonous adj monotone

monotony n monotonie f

monsoon n mousson f

monster n monstre m

monstrous adj (a) (ugly) monstrueux/-euse; ⟨building⟩ hideux/-euse
(b) (huge) énorme

month n mois m; in two ~s, in two ~s' time dans deux mois; every other ~ tous les deux mois; in the ~ of June au mois de juin

monthly ① n (journal) mensuel m
② adj mensuel/-elle; ~ instalment mensualité f
③ adv ⟨pay, earn⟩ au mois; ⟨happen, visit, publish⟩ tous les mois

Montreal pr n Montréal

monument n monument m

moo vi meugler

mood n (a) (humour) humeur f; in a good/bad ~ de bonne/mauvaise humeur; to be in the ~ for doing avoir envie de faire; to be in no ~ for doing ne pas être d'humeur à faire
(b) (bad temper) saute f d'humeur; to be in a ~ être de mauvaise humeur

mood swing n saute f d'humeur

moody adj (a) (unpredictable) d'humeur changeante, lunatique
(b) (sulky) de mauvaise humeur

moon n lune f
IDIOMS to be over the ~ être aux anges; once in a blue ~ tous les trente-six du mois (colloq); the man in the ~ le visage de la Lune

moonlight ① n clair m de lune
② vi travailler au noir

moonlit adj éclairé/-e par la lune; a ~ night une nuit de lune

moor ① n lande f
② vtr amarrer ⟨boat⟩
③ vi ⟨boat⟩ mouiller

moorings n pl amarres fpl

moorland n lande f

moose n (Canadian) orignal m; (European) élan m

mop ① n (a) (of cotton) balai m à franges; (of sponge) balai m éponge
(b) ~ of hair crinière f (colloq)
② vtr (a) laver [qch] à grande eau ⟨floor⟩
(b) to ~ one's face/brow s'éponger le visage/le front
∎ **mop up** éponger ⟨milk, wine⟩

mope vi se morfondre

■ **mope about**, **mope around** traîner (comme une âme en peine)

moped n vélomoteur m

moral ⟨1⟩ n morale f
⟨2⟩ **morals** n pl moralité f
⟨3⟩ adj moral/-e

morale n moral m

morality n moralité f

moral majority n majorité f bien-pensante

morbid adj morbide

more ⟨1⟩ adv (a) (comparative) plus (than que); ∼ **expensive** plus cher/chère; ∼ **easily** plus facilement
(b) (to a greater extent) plus, davantage; **you must rest** ∼ il faut que tu te reposes davantage; **he is all the** ∼ **angry because** il est d'autant plus en colère que
(c) (longer) **I don't work there any** ∼ je n'y travaille plus
(d) (again) **once** ∼ une fois de plus, encore une fois
(e) (else) **nothing** ∼ rien de plus; **something** ∼ autre chose
⟨2⟩ det plus de; **I have** ∼ **money than him** j'ai plus d'argent que lui; **some** ∼ **books** quelques livres de plus; **there's no** ∼ **bread** il n'y a plus de pain; **have some** ∼ **beer!** reprenez de la bière!
⟨3⟩ pron, quantif (a) (larger amount or number) plus; **it costs** ∼ il/elle coûte plus cher (than que); **he eats** ∼ **than you** il mange plus que toi
(b) (additional amount) davantage; (additional number) plus; **I need** ∼ **of them** il m'en faut plus; **I need** ∼ **of it** il m'en faut davantage
⟨4⟩ **more and more** phr de plus en plus; ∼ **and** ∼ **work** de plus en plus de travail
⟨5⟩ **more or less** phr plus ou moins
⟨6⟩ **more than** phr (a) (greater amount or number) plus de; ∼ **than 20 people** plus de 20 personnes; ∼ **than half** plus de la moitié; ∼ **than enough** plus qu'assez
(b) (extremely) ∼ **than generous** plus que généreux

moreover adv de plus, qui plus est

morning ⟨1⟩ n matin m; (with emphasis on duration) matinée f; **in the** ∼ le matin; **on Monday** ∼s le lundi matin; (on) **Monday** ∼ lundi matin; **later this** ∼ plus tard dans la matinée; **yesterday/tomorrow** ∼ hier/demain matin
⟨2⟩ excl (good) ∼! bonjour!

morning-after pill n pilule f du lendemain

Morocco pr n Maroc m

Morse (code) n morse m; **in** ∼ en morse

morsel n morceau m

mortal n, adj mortel/-elle (m/f)

mortality n mortalité f

mortar n mortier m

mortgage n emprunt-logement m (**on** pour)

mortgage rate n taux m de l'emprunt-logement

mortuary n morgue f

mosaic n mosaïque f

Moscow pr n Moscou

Moslem = **MUSLIM**

mosque n mosquée f

mosquito n moustique m

mosquito repellent n anti-moustique m

moss n mousse f

most

■ **Note** When used to form the superlative of adjectives, *most* is translated by *le plus* or *la plus* depending on the gender of the noun and by *les plus* with plural noun: *the most beautiful woman in the room* = la plus belle femme de la pièce; *the most expensive hotel in Paris* = l'hôtel le plus cher de Paris; *the most difficult problems* = les problèmes les plus difficiles. For examples and further uses, see the entry below.

⟨1⟩ det (a) (the majority of) la plupart de; ∼ **people** la plupart des gens
(b) (in superlatives) le plus de; **she got the** ∼ **votes** c'est elle qui a obtenu le plus de voix
⟨2⟩ pron (a) (the greatest number) la plupart (of de); (the largest part) la plus grande partie (of de); ∼ **of the time** la plupart du temps; ∼ **of us** la plupart d'entre nous; **for** ∼ **of the day** pendant la plus grande partie de la journée; ∼ **of the bread** presque tout le pain
(b) (all) **the** ∼ **you can expect is...** tout ce que tu peux espérer c'est...
(c) (in superlatives) le plus; **John has got the** ∼ c'est John qui en a le plus
⟨3⟩ adv (a) (in superlatives) **the** ∼ **beautiful château in France** le plus beau château de France; ∼ **easily** le plus facilement
(b) (very) très, extrêmement; ∼ **encouraging** très or extrêmement encourageant; ∼ **probably** très vraisemblablement
(c) (more than all the rest) le plus; **what annoyed him** ∼ (**of all**) **was** ce qui l'ennuyait le plus c'était que
⟨4⟩ **at (the) most** phr au maximum, au plus
⟨5⟩ **for the most part** phr (most of them) pour la plupart; (most of the time) la plupart du temps; (chiefly) surtout, essentiellement
⟨6⟩ **most of all** phr par-dessus tout
IDIOMS **to make the** ∼ **of** tirer le meilleur parti de ⟨situation, resources, abilities⟩; profiter de ⟨opportunity, good weather⟩

mostly adv (a) (chiefly) surtout, essentiellement; (most of them) pour la plupart
(b) (most of the time) la plupart du temps

MOT n (GB) (also ∼ **test**) contrôle m technique des véhicules

moth n papillon m de nuit; (in clothes) mite f

mother ⟨1⟩ n mère f
⟨2⟩ vtr (coddle) dorloter

motherboard n carte f mère

motherhood n maternité f

mother-in-law n belle-mère f

motherly adj maternel/-elle

mother-of-pearl n nacre f

Mother's Day n fête f des Mères

mother tongue n langue f maternelle

motion ⬚1 n (a) mouvement m; **to set [sth] in ~** mettre [qch] en marche ‹machine›; mettre [qch] en route ‹plan›; déclencher ‹chain of events›
(b) (proposal) motion f
⬚2 vi **to ~ to sb (to do)** faire signe à qn (de faire)

motionless adj immobile

motivate vtr motiver ‹person›

motivated adj (a) ‹person, pupil› motivé/-e
(b) **politically/racially ~** ‹act› politique/raciste

motivation n motivation f

motive n (gen) motif m (**for, behind** de); (for crime) mobile m (**for** de)

motley adj ‹crowd, gathering› bigarré/-e; ‹collection› hétéroclite

motor ⬚1 n moteur m
⬚2 adj (a) ‹vehicle› automobile; ‹show› de l'automobile
(b) ‹mower› à moteur

motorbike n moto f

motorboat n canot m automobile

motorcycle n motocyclette f

motorcyclist n motocycliste mf

motor home n auto-caravane f

motorist n automobiliste mf

motor racing n course f automobile

motorway n (GB) autoroute f

mottled adj ‹skin, paper› marbré/-e; ‹hands› tacheté/-e

motto n devise f

mould (GB), **mold** (US) ⬚1 n (a) (Culin, figurative) moule m
(b) (fungi) moisissure f
⬚2 vtr modeler ‹plastic, clay, shape›; façonner ‹character, opinions› (**into** pour en faire)

mouldy (GB), **moldy** (US) adj moisi/-e; **to go ~** moisir

moult (GB), **molt** (US) vi ‹cat, dog› perdre ses poils; ‹bird› muer

mound n (a) (hillock) tertre m
(b) (heap) monceau m (**of** de)

mount ⬚1 vtr (a) monter sur ‹platform, horse›
(b) monter ‹jewel, picture, exhibit›
(c) organiser ‹demonstration›
⬚2 vi (a) ‹person, staircase› monter (**to** jusqu'à)
(b) ‹number, toll› augmenter; ‹concern› grandir
(c) (on horse) se mettre en selle

mountain n montagne f

mountain bike n vélo m tout-terrain, VTT m

mountaineer n alpiniste mf

mountaineering n alpinisme m

mountainous adj montagneux/-euse

mountain top n cime f

mourn ⬚1 vtr pleurer ‹person, death›
⬚2 vi ‹person› porter le deuil; **to ~ for sb/sth** pleurer qn/qch

mourning n deuil m

mouse n (Comput, Zool) souris f

mousemat n tapis m de souris

mouse pointer n pointeur m de la souris

moustache, **mustache** (US) n moustache f

mouth ⬚1 n (a) (of human, horse) bouche f; (of other animal) gueule f
(b) (of cave, tunnel) entrée f; (of river) embouchure f; (of volcano) bouche f
⬚2 vtr articuler silencieusement
IDIOMS **by word of ~** de bouche à oreille

mouthful n (of food) bouchée f; (of liquid) gorgée f

mouth organ n harmonica m

mouth-to-mouth resuscitation n bouche-à-bouche m inv

mouthwash n eau f dentifrice

mouth-watering adj appétissant/-e

move ⬚1 n (a) (movement) mouvement m; (gesture) geste m
(b) (of residence) déménagement m; (of company) transfert m
(c) (in game) coup m; **it's your ~** c'est ton tour
(d) (step, act) manœuvre f; **a good/bad ~** une bonne/mauvaise idée; **to make the first ~** faire le premier pas
⬚2 vtr (a) déplacer ‹game piece, cursor, car, furniture›; transporter ‹patient, army›; **to ~ sth (out of the way)** enlever qch
(b) ‹person› bouger ‹limb, head›; ‹wind, mechanism› faire bouger ‹leaf, wheel›
(c) (relocate) muter ‹staff›; transférer ‹office›; **to ~ house** déménager
(d) (affect) émouvoir; **to be deeply ~d** être très ému/-e
⬚3 vi (a) (stir) bouger; ‹lips› remuer
(b) (travel) ‹vehicle› rouler; ‹person› avancer; ‹procession, army› être en marche; **to ~ back** reculer; **to ~ forward** s'avancer; **to ~ away** s'éloigner
(c) (change home, location) déménager; **to ~ to the countryside/to Japan** s'installer à la campagne/au Japon
(d) (change job) être muté/-e
(e) (act) agir
IDIOMS **to get a ~ on** (colloq) se dépêcher
▪ **move about**, **move around** ‹person› (fidget) remuer; (move home) déménager
▪ **move along**: ¶ **~ along** (stop loitering) circuler; (proceed) avancer; (squeeze up) se pousser; ¶ **~ [sb/sth] along** faire circuler ‹onlookers, crowd›
▪ **move away** s'éloigner; (move house) déménager
▪ **move in** (a) (to house) emménager; **to ~ in with** s'installer avec ‹friend, lover›
(b) (advance, attack) s'avancer (**on** sur)

■ **move on** ⟨person, traveller⟩ se mettre en route; ⟨vehicle⟩ repartir; **to ~ on to** passer à ⟨next item⟩

■ **move out** (of house) déménager; **to ~ out of** quitter

■ **move over** se pousser

■ **move up (a)** (make room) se pousser
(b) (be promoted) être promu/-e

movement n mouvement m; (of hand, arm) geste m

movie ① n film m
② **movies** n pl **the ~s** le cinéma

movie camera n caméra f

movie star n vedette f de cinéma

movie theater n (US) cinéma m

moving adj (a) ⟨vehicle⟩ en marche; ⟨parts, target⟩ mobile; ⟨staircase, walkway⟩ roulant/-e
(b) ⟨scene, speech⟩ émouvant/-e

mow vtr tondre ⟨grass, lawn⟩

mower n tondeuse f à gazon

MP n (GB) (abbr = **Member of Parliament**) député m (**for** de)

Mr n M., Monsieur

Mrs n Mme, Madame

Ms n ≈ Mme

MSc n (abbr = **Master of Science**) diplôme m supérieur en sciences

much ① adv beaucoup; **~ more/less** beaucoup plus/moins; **~ smaller** beaucoup plus petit; **I don't read ~** je ne lis pas beaucoup; **we'd ~ rather stay here** nous préférerions de beaucoup rester ici; **does it hurt ~?** est-ce que ça fait très mal?; **we don't go out ~** nous ne sortons pas beaucoup or souvent; **it's ~ the same** c'est à peu près pareil (**as** que); **too ~** trop; **very ~** beaucoup; **thank you very ~** merci beaucoup; **as ~** autant (**as** que); **they hated each other as ~ as ever** ils se détestaient toujours autant
② pron beaucoup; **do you have ~ left?** est-ce qu'il vous en reste beaucoup?; **we didn't eat ~** nous n'avons pas mangé grand-chose; **I don't see ~ of them now** je ne les vois plus beaucoup maintenant; **so ~** tellement, tant; **we'd eaten so ~ that** nous avions tellement mangé que; **too ~** trop; **it costs too ~** c'est trop cher; **twice as ~** deux fois plus; **as ~ as possible** autant que possible; **how ~?** combien?; **it's not or nothing ~** ce n'est pas grand-chose; **he's not ~ to look at** il n'est pas très beau
③ det beaucoup de; **I haven't got ~ time** je n'ai pas beaucoup de temps; **she didn't speak ~ English** elle ne connaissait que quelques mots d'anglais; **too ~ money** trop d'argent; **don't use so ~ salt** ne mets pas tant de sel; **we paid twice as ~** nous avons payé deux fois plus; **how ~ time have we got left?** combien de temps nous reste-t-il?
④ **much as** phr bien que (+ subjunctive)
⑤ **so much as** phr without **so ~ as an apology** sans même s'excuser; **if you so ~ as move** si tu fais le moindre mouvement

muck n saletés fpl; (mud) boue f

■ **muck about**, **muck around** (colloq): ¶ **~ about** (fool about) faire l'imbécile; **to ~ about with** traficoter (colloq) ⟨appliance⟩; toucher à ⟨object⟩; ¶ **~ [sb] about** se ficher de (colloq) qn

■ **muck in** mettre la main à la pâte (colloq)

mud n boue f

muddle n (a) (mess) pagaille (colloq)
(b) (mix-up) malentendu m (**over** à propos de)
(c) **to get into a ~** ⟨person⟩ s'embrouiller

■ **muddle up**: ¶ **~ [sth] up** (disorder) semer la pagaille (colloq) dans; ¶ **~ [sb] up** embrouiller les idées de; ¶ **to get [sth] ~d up** s'embrouiller dans ⟨dates, names⟩

muddled adj confus/-e

muddy adj ⟨hand⟩ couvert/-e de boue; ⟨shoe, garment⟩ crotté/-e; ⟨road, water⟩ boueux/-euse; ⟨green, yellow⟩ terne

mudguard n garde-boue m inv

muffle vtr assourdir ⟨bell, drum⟩

mug ① n (a) grande tasse f
(b) (GB) (fool) poire f (colloq); **it's a ~'s game** c'est un attrape-nigaud
② vtr agresser; **to be ~ged** se faire agresser

mugger n agresseur m

mugging n (attack) agression f; (crime) agressions fpl

muggy adj ⟨room, day⟩ étouffant/-e; ⟨weather⟩ lourd/-e

Muhammad pr n Mahomet

mule n mulet m, mule f
IDIOMS **as stubborn as a ~** têtu/-e comme une mule

mull v ■ **mull over** retourner [qch] dans sa tête

mulled wine n vin m chaud

multicultural adj multiculturel/-elle

multidisciplinary adj pluridisciplinaire

multi-ethnic adj multi-ethnique

multi-function adj multifonctions inv

multigym n appareil m de musculation

multilateral adj multilatéral/-e

multimedia n, adj multimédia (m) inv

multinational adj multinational/-e

multiple n, adj multiple (m)

multiple choice adj à choix multiple

multiple sclerosis, **MS** n sclérose f en plaques

multiplex n (Cinema) complexe m multi-salles

multiply ① vtr multiplier (**by** par)
② vi se multiplier

multipurpose adj ⟨tool, gadget⟩ à usages multiples; ⟨area, organization⟩ polyvalent/-e

multipurpose vehicle, **MPV** n monospace m

multi-racial adj multiracial/-e

multistorey adj (GB) ⟨car park⟩ à niveaux multiples; ⟨building⟩ à étages

multitrack adj multipiste inv

multitude n multitude f

m

mum, Mum n (GB) (colloq) maman f
IDIOMS to keep ~ ne pas piper mot

mumble vtr, vi marmonner

mumbo jumbo n (colloq) charabia m
(colloq)

mummy n (a) (colloq) (also **Mummy**)
maman f
(b) (embalmed body) momie f

mumps n oreillons mpl

munch vtr ⟨person⟩ mâcher; ⟨animal⟩
mâchonner

mundane adj terre-à-terre, quelconque

municipal adj municipal/-e

mural n (wall painting) peinture f murale; (in
cave) peinture f rupestre

murder ⓵ n meurtre m
⓶ vtr assassiner
IDIOMS to get away with ~ exercer ses
talents en toute impunité

murderer n assassin m, meurtrier m

murderess n meurtrière f

murderous adj ⟨look⟩ assassin/-e; ⟨deeds,
thoughts⟩ meurtrier/-ière

murky adj (a) ⟨light, water, colour⟩ glauque
(b) ⟨past⟩ trouble

murmur ⓵ n murmure m (of de)
⓶ vtr, vi murmurer

muscle n muscle m
■ **muscle in** (colloq) s'imposer (on dans)

muscle strain n élongation f

muscular adj ⟨disease, tissue⟩ musculaire;
⟨person, body, limbs⟩ musclé/-e

museum n musée m

mushroom n (a) (Bot, Culin) champignon m
(b) (colour) beige m rosé

music n musique f

musical ⓵ n comédie f musicale
⓶ adj (a) ⟨person⟩ musicien/-ienne
(b) ⟨voice, laughter⟩ mélodieux/-ieuse; ⟨score⟩
musical/-e

musical instrument n instrument m
de musique

musician n musicien/-ienne m/f

music video n clip m (vidéo)

musk n musc m

Muslim (also **Moslem**) ⓵ n Musulman/-e
m/f
⓶ adj musulman/-e

mussel n moule f

must ⓵ modal aux (a) (expressing obligation) I
~ go je dois partir, il faut que je parte; he ~
sit the exam in June il faut qu'il passe
l'examen au mois de juin; you ~ check your
rear-view mirror first il faut regarder dans le
rétroviseur d'abord; I ~ say I was impressed
je dois dire que j'ai été impressionné; we
mustn't tell anyone il ne faut en parler à
personne, nous ne devons en parler à
personne

(b) (making deductions) they ~ really detest
each other ils doivent vraiment se détester;
it ~ be pleasant living there ça doit être
agréable de vivre là-bas; he ~ have been
surprised il a dû être surpris
⓶ n it's a ~ c'est indispensable; this film is
a ~ ce film est à voir or à ne pas rater; a
visit to the Louvre is a ~ une visite au
Louvre s'impose

mustache (US) = MOUSTACHE

mustard n moutarde f

muster vtr (also ~ up) rassembler
⟨troops⟩; rallier ⟨support⟩; trouver ⟨energy,
enthusiasm⟩
IDIOMS to pass ~ être acceptable

musty adj to smell ~ sentir le moisi or le
renfermé

mute adj muet/-ette

mutilate vtr mutiler

mutiny n mutinerie f

mutter vtr, vi marmonner

mutton n mouton m

mutual adj (a) (reciprocal) réciproque; the
feeling is ~ c'est réciproque
(b) ⟨friend, interests⟩ commun/-e; ⟨consent⟩
mutuel/-elle; by ~ agreement d'un commun
accord

mutual aid n entraide f

my

■ Note In French, determiners agree in gender
and number with the noun that follows. So my is
translated by mon + masculine singular noun
(mon chien), ma + feminine singular noun (ma
maison) BUT by mon + feminine noun beginning
with a vowel or mute 'h' (mon assiette) and by
mes + plural noun (mes enfants).
– When my is stressed, à moi is added after the
noun: MY house = ma maison à moi.

⓵ det mon/ma/mes
⓶ excl ~ ~! ça alors!

myself pron (a) (reflexive) me, m'; I've hurt
~ je me suis fait mal
(b) (emphatic) moi-même; I saw it ~ je l'ai vu
moi-même; (all) by ~ tout seul/toute seule
(c) (after prepositions) moi, moi-même; I feel
proud of ~ je suis fier de moi
(d) (expressions) I'm not much of a dog-lover
~ personnellement je n'aime pas trop les
chiens; I'm not ~ today je ne suis pas dans
mon assiette aujourd'hui

mysterious adj mystérieux/-ieuse

mystery n (a) mystère m
(b) (book) roman m policier

mystify vtr laisser [qn] perplexe

myth n mythe m

mythology n mythologie f

Nn

n, N n n, N m
naff adj (GB) (colloq) ringard/-e (colloq)
nag vtr enquiquiner (colloq) (**about** au sujet de)
nagging adj (a) his ∼ wife sa mégère de femme
(b) ⟨pain, doubt⟩ tenace
nail 1 n (a) (on finger, toe) ongle m
(b) (Tech) clou m
2 vtr clouer
■ **nail down**: ¶ ∼ [sth] down clouer; ¶ ∼ [sb] down coincer (colloq) ⟨person⟩
nail-biting adj ⟨match, finish⟩ palpitant/-e; ⟨wait⟩ angoissant/-e
nailbrush n brosse f à ongles
nail file n lime f à ongles
nail varnish n vernis m à ongles
nail varnish remover n dissolvant m
naïve adj naïf/naïve
naked adj nu/-e
name 1 n (a) (gen) nom m; (of book, film) titre m; **first** ∼ prénom m; **my** ∼ **is Louis** je m'appelle Louis
(b) (reputation) réputation f
(c) (insult) **to call sb** ∼s injurier qn
2 vtr (a) (call) appeler ⟨person, area⟩; baptiser ⟨boat⟩; **they** ∼d **her after** (GB) or **for** (US) **her mother** ils l'ont appelée comme sa mère; **a boy** ∼d **Pascal** un garçon nommé Pascal
(b) (cite) citer; ∼ **three American States** citez trois États américains
(c) révéler ⟨sources⟩; révéler l'identité de ⟨suspect⟩; **to** ∼ ∼s donner des noms
(d) (state) indiquer ⟨place, time⟩; fixer ⟨price, terms⟩
name-drop vi citer des gens célèbres (qu'on prétend connaître)
namely adv à savoir
namesake n homonyme m
nanny n (GB) bonne f d'enfants
nanny goat n chèvre f
nap 1 n petit somme m; **afternoon** ∼ sieste f
2 vi sommeiller
nape n nuque f; **the** ∼ **of the neck** la nuque
napkin n serviette f (de table)
nappy n (GB) couche f (de bébé)
narcotic 1 n (soporific) narcotique m; (illegal drug) stupéfiant m
2 adj narcotique
narked adj (colloq) en rogne (colloq), en boule (colloq)
narration n récit m, narration f
narrative 1 n (account) récit m; (storytelling) narration f

2 adj ⟨prose, poem⟩ narratif/-ive; ⟨skill, talent⟩ de conteur
narrator n narrateur/-trice m/f
narrow 1 adj (gen) étroit/-e; ⟨views⟩ étriqué/-e; ⟨majority, margin⟩ faible (before n); **to have a** ∼ **lead** avoir une légère avance; **to have a** ∼ **escape** l'échapper belle
2 vtr (a) (limit) limiter (**to** à); **to** ∼ **the gap** réduire l'écart
(b) rétrécir ⟨road, path, arteries⟩; **to** ∼ **one's eyes** plisser les yeux
3 vi (gen) se rétrécir; ⟨gap, margin⟩ se réduire (**to** à)
■ **narrow down** réduire ⟨numbers, list, choice⟩ (**to** à); limiter ⟨investigation, research⟩ (**to** à)
narrowly adv (barely) de justesse
narrow-minded adj borné/-e
nasal adj ⟨vowel⟩ nasal/-e; ⟨accent, voice⟩ nasillard/-e
nasal spray n nébuliseur m (pour le nez)
nasty adj (a) ⟨person, expression, remark⟩ méchant/-e; ⟨experience, surprise, feeling, task⟩ désagréable; ⟨habit, smell, taste⟩ mauvais/-e (before n); ⟨trick⟩ sale (before n); ⟨cut, bruise⟩ vilain/-e (before n); ⟨accident⟩ grave
(b) (ugly) affreux/-euse
nation n nation f; (people) peuple m
national 1 n ressortissant/-e m/f
2 adj national/-e; **the** ∼ **press** (GB) les grands quotidiens mpl
national anthem n hymne m national
National Curriculum n (GB) programme m scolaire national
National Front n (GB) parti britannique d'extrême droite
National Health Service, NHS n (GB) services mpl de santé britanniques, ≈ Sécurité f Sociale
National Insurance, NI n (GB) sécurité f sociale britannique; ∼ **number** numéro m de sécurité sociale
nationalism n nationalisme m
nationality n nationalité f
nationalize vtr nationaliser ⟨industry⟩
nationwide 1 adj ⟨appeal, coverage, strike⟩ sur l'ensemble du territoire; ⟨campaign⟩ national/-e; ⟨survey, poll⟩ à l'échelle nationale
2 adv dans tout le pays
native 1 n autochtone mf; **to be a** ∼ **of** être originaire de
2 adj (a) ⟨land⟩ natal/-e; ⟨tongue⟩ maternel/-elle; ∼ **German speaker** personne f de langue maternelle allemande
(b) ⟨flora, fauna, peoples⟩ indigène

n

Native American n, adj
amérindien/-ienne (m/f)

Nativity n nativité f

NATO n (abbr = **North Atlantic Treaty Organization**) OTAN f

natural adj (a) (gen) naturel/-elle
(b) ⟨gift, talent⟩ inné-e; ⟨artist, storyteller⟩ né/-e
(c) (unaffected) simple, naturel/-elle

naturalize vtr naturaliser ⟨person⟩; **to be ~d** se faire naturaliser

naturally adv (a) (obviously, of course) naturellement
(b) (by nature) de nature; **politeness comes ~ to him** il est d'un naturel poli
(c) ⟨behave, smile, speak⟩ avec naturel

nature n nature f; **let ~ take its course** laissez faire la nature; **it's not in her ~ to be aggressive** elle n'est pas agressive de nature; **it is in the ~ of things** il est dans l'ordre des choses

nature conservancy n protection f de la nature

nature reserve n réserve f naturelle

nature trail n sentier m écologique

naughty adj (a) (disobedient) vilain/-e
(b) (rude) ⟨joke, picture, story⟩ coquin/-e

nausea n nausée f

nauseating adj écœurant/-e

nauseous adj ⟨taste, smell⟩ écœurant/-e; **to feel ~** avoir la nausée

nautical adj nautique

naval adj ⟨battle, forces, base⟩ naval/-e; ⟨officer, recruit, uniform, affairs⟩ de la marine

naval ring n piercing m au nombril

nave n nef f

navel n nombril m

navigate [1] vtr (a) parcourir ⟨seas⟩
(b) piloter ⟨plane⟩; gouverner ⟨ship⟩
[2] vi (in vessel, plane) naviguer; (in rally) faire le copilote; (on journey) tenir la carte

navigation n navigation f

navigator n (in vessel, plane) navigateur/-trice m/f; (in car) copilote mf

navy [1] n (a) (fleet) flotte f; (fighting force) marine f
(b) (also ~ **blue**) bleu m marine
[2] adj (also ~ **blue**) bleu marine inv

Nazi n, adj nazi/-e (m/f)

near [1] adv (a) (close) près; **to live quite ~** habiter tout près; **to move ~er** s'approcher davantage (**to** de); **to bring sth ~er** approcher qch
(b) (nearly) **as ~ perfect as it could be** aussi proche de la perfection que possible; **nowhere ~ finished** loin d'être fini
[2] prep (a) près de; **~ here** près d'ici; **~ the beginning of the article** presque au début de l'article; **he's no ~er (making) a decision** il n'est pas plus décidé
(b) (in time) **~er the time** quand la date approchera; **it's getting ~ Christmas** Noël approche

[3] adj proche; **in the ~ future** dans un avenir proche; **the ~est shops** les magasins les plus proches
[4] vtr approcher de; **to ~ completion** toucher à sa fin
[5] **near enough** phr à peu près
[6] **near to** phr (a) (in space) près de; **~er to** plus près de
(b) (on point of) au bord de ⟨tears, collapse⟩
(c) **to come ~ to doing** faillir faire

nearby [1] adj ⟨person⟩ qui se trouve/trouvait etc à proximité; ⟨town, village⟩ d'à côté
[2] adv tout près; ⟨park, stand, wait⟩ à proximité

nearly adv presque; **I very ~ gave up** j'ai bien failli abandonner; **not ~ as talented as** loin d'être aussi doué que

near miss n **to have a ~** ⟨planes⟩ frôler la collision; ⟨cars⟩ faillir se percuter

near-sighted adj myope

neat [1] adj (a) ⟨person⟩ (in habits) ordonné/-e; (in appearance) soigné/-e; ⟨room, house, desk⟩ bien rangé/-e; ⟨garden, handwriting⟩ soigné/-e
(b) ⟨explanation, solution⟩ habile
(c) ⟨figure⟩ bien fait/-e; ⟨features⟩ régulier/-ière
(d) ⟨alcohol, spirits⟩ sans eau
[2] adv ⟨drink whisky⟩ sec, sans eau

neatly adv (a) (tidily) ⟨dress, fold, arrange⟩ avec soin; ⟨write⟩ proprement
(b) (perfectly) ⟨illustrate, summarize⟩ parfaitement; ⟨link⟩ habilement

necessarily adv (definitely) forcément; (of necessity) nécessairement; **not ~** pas forcément

necessary adj (gen) nécessaire; ⟨qualification⟩ requis/-e; **if ~, as ~** si besoin est; **it is ~ for him to do** il faut qu'il fasse

necessitate vtr nécessiter

necessity n (a) (need) nécessité f; **from ~** par nécessité; **the ~ for** le besoin de
(b) (essential item) **to be an absolute ~** être indispensable

neck n (a) (of person) cou m; (of horse, donkey) encolure f
(b) (collar) col m; (neckline) encolure f
(c) (of bottle, vase, womb) col m
IDIOMS **to be ~ and ~** être à égalité; **to stick one's ~ out** (colloq) prendre des risques

necklace n collier m

neckline n encolure f

necktie n (US) cravate f

nectar n nectar m

nectarine n nectarine f, brugnon m

need [1] modal aux **you needn't finish it today** tu n'es pas obligé de le finir aujourd'hui; **~ he reply?** est-ce qu'il faut qu'il réponde?, est-ce qu'il doit répondre?; **I needn't have hurried** ce n'était pas la peine de me dépêcher, ce n'était pas la peine que je me dépêche
[2] vtr (a) (require) **to ~ sth/to do** avoir besoin de qch/de faire; **more money is ~ed**

nous avons besoin de plus d'argent;
everything you ~ tout ce qu'il vous faut;
everything you ~ to know about computers
tout ce que vous devez savoir sur les
ordinateurs
(b) (have to) **you'll ~ to work hard** il va
falloir que tu travailles dur; **he didn't ~ to
ask permission** il n'était pas obligé de
demander la permission; **something ~ed to
be done** il fallait faire quelque chose
③ *n* **(a)** (necessity) nécessité *f* (**for** de); **I can't
see the ~ for it** je n'en vois pas la nécessité;
to feel the ~ to do éprouver le besoin de
faire; **there's no ~ to wait** inutile d'attendre;
there's no ~ to worry ce n'est pas la peine
de s'inquiéter; **there's no ~, I've done it**
inutile, c'est fait; **if ~ be** s'il le faut, si
nécessaire
(b) (want, requirement) besoin *m* (**for** de); **to be
in ~ of sth** avoir besoin de qch
(c) (poverty) **to be in ~** être dans le besoin

needle ① *n* aiguille *f*
② *vtr* harceler
IDIOMS to have pins and ~s avoir des
fourmis

needless *adj* ⟨anxiety, suffering⟩ inutile;
⟨intrusion, intervention⟩ inopportun/-e

needlework *n* couture *f*

needy *adj* ⟨person⟩ nécessiteux/-euse;
⟨sector, area⟩ sans ressources

negate *vtr* (cancel out) réduire [qch] à néant

negative ① *n* **(a)** (of photo) négatif *m*
(b) (in grammar) négation *f*; **in the ~** à la
forme négative
② *adj* (gen) négatif/-ive; ⟨effect, influence⟩
néfaste

neglect ① *n* **(a)** (of person) négligence *f*; (of
building, garden) manque *m* d'entretien; (of
health, appearance) manque *m* de soin
(b) (lack of interest) indifférence *f* (**of** à l'égard
de)
② *vtr* **(a)** ne pas s'occuper de ⟨person, dog,
plant⟩; ne pas entretenir ⟨garden, house⟩;
négliger ⟨health, friend, work⟩
(b) (fail) **to ~ to do** négliger de faire

neglected *adj* (gen) négligé/-e; ⟨garden,
building⟩ mal entretenu/-e; **to feel ~** se
sentir délaissé/-e

negligence *n* négligence *f*

negligent *adj* ⟨person, procedure⟩
négligent/-e; ⟨air, manner⟩ nonchalant/-e

negligible *adj* négligeable

negotiable *adj* **(a)** ⟨rate, terms⟩
négociable
(b) ⟨road, pass⟩ praticable; ⟨obstacle⟩
franchissable

negotiate ① *vtr* **(a)** (in business, diplomacy)
négocier
(b) négocier ⟨bend⟩; franchir ⟨obstacle⟩
② *vi* négocier (**with** avec; **for** pour obtenir)
③ **negotiated** *pp adj* ⟨settlement, peace⟩
négocié/-e

negotiation *n* négociation *f*; **to be under
~** être en cours de négociations

negotiator *n* négociateur/-trice *m/f*

neigh *vi* hennir

neighbour (GB), **neighbor** (US) *n*
voisin/-e *m/f*

neighbourhood (GB), **neighborhood**
(US) *n* **(a)** (district) quartier *m*
(b) (vicinity) **in the ~** dans le voisinage

neighbouring (GB), **neighboring** (US)
adj voisin/-e

neither ① *conj* **I have ~ the time nor the
money** je n'ai ni le temps ni l'argent; **~ tea,
nor milk** ni (le) thé, ni (le) lait; **'I can't
sleep'—'~ can I'** 'je n'arrive pas à dormir'—
'moi non plus'
② *det* aucun/-e des deux; **~ book is suitable**
aucun des deux livres ne convient; **~ girl
replied** aucune des deux filles n'a répondu
③ *pron, quantif* ni l'un/-e ni l'autre *m/f*; **~
of them came** ni l'un ni l'autre n'est venu

neon ① *n* néon *m*
② *adj* ⟨light, sign⟩ au néon; ⟨atom⟩ de néon

nephew *n* neveu *m*

Neptune *pr n* (planet) Neptune *f*

nerve ① *n* **(a)** (Anat) nerf *m*; (Bot) nervure *f*
(b) (courage) courage *m*; **to lose one's ~**
perdre son courage
(c) (colloq) (cheek) culot *m* (colloq); **you've got
a ~!** tu as un sacré culot! (colloq)
② **nerves** *n pl* (gen) nerfs *mpl*; (stage fright)
trac *m* (colloq); **to get on sb's ~s** taper sur
les nerfs de qn

nerve-(w)racking *adj* angoissant/-e

nervous *adj* **(a)** ⟨person⟩ (fearful) timide;
(anxious) angoissé/-e; (highly strung)
nerveux/-euse; ⟨smile, laugh, habit⟩
nerveux/-euse; **to be ~ about doing** avoir
peur de faire; **to feel ~** (apprehensive) être
angoissé/-e; (before performance) avoir le trac
(colloq); (afraid) avoir peur; (ill at ease) se sentir
mal à l'aise
(b) (Anat, Med) nerveux/-euse

nervous breakdown *n* dépression *f*
nerveuse

nervously *adv* nerveusement

nervous wreck *n* (colloq) boule *f* de nerfs
(colloq)

nest ① *n* **(a)** (of bird, animal) nid *m*
(b) **~ of tables** tables *fpl* gigognes
② *vi* ⟨bird⟩ faire son nid

nest egg *n* magot *m* (colloq)

nestle *vi* **(a)** ⟨person, animal⟩ se blottir
(**against** contre; **under** sous)
(b) ⟨village, house⟩ être niché/-e

net ① *n* (gen) filet *m*; (in football) filets *mpl*
② *adj* (also **nett**) (gen) net/nette; ⟨loss⟩ sec/
sèche
③ *vtr* **(a)** prendre [qch] au filet ⟨fish⟩
(b) (financially) ⟨person⟩ faire un bénéfice de;
⟨sale, export, deal⟩ rapporter

Net *n* Net *m*

netball *n*: sport d'équipe proche du basket
joué par les femmes

net curtain *n* voilage *m*

Netherlands *pr n* **the ~** les Pays-Bas
mpl, la Hollande

netiquette n netiquette f

netspeak n jargon m Internet

netting n (of rope) filet m; (of metal, plastic) grillage m; (fabric) voile m

nettle n (also **stinging** ~) ortie f

network [1] n réseau m (of de)
[2] vtr (Comput) interconnecter
[3] vi tisser un réseau de relations

networking n (a) (Comput) interconnexion f
(b) (establishing contacts) ~ **is important** c'est important d'avoir des contacts

network television n (US) chaîne f nationale

neurosis n névrose f

neurotic adj névrosé/-e

neuter [1] n neutre m
[2] adj neutre
[3] vtr châtrer ⟨animal⟩

neutral [1] n (Aut) **in/into** ~ au point mort
[2] adj neutre (**about** en ce qui concerne)

neutrality n neutralité f

neutralize vtr neutraliser

never adv (a) (not ever) **I** ~ **go to London** je ne vais jamais à Londres; **she** ~ **says anything** elle ne dit jamais rien; **it's now or** ~ c'est le moment ou jamais; ~ **again** plus jamais; ~ **lie to me again!** ne me mens plus jamais!
(b) (emphatic negative) **he** ~ **said a word** il n'a rien dit; **I** ~ **knew that** je ne le savais pas; **he** ~ **so much as apologized** il ne s'est même pas excusé

never-ending adj interminable

nevertheless adv (a) (all the same) quand même
(b) (nonetheless) pourtant, néanmoins

new adj nouveau/-elle (before n); (brand new) neuf/neuve; **I bought a** ~ **computer** (to replace old one) j'ai acheté un nouvel ordinateur; (a brand new model) j'ai acheté un ordinateur neuf; **as good as** ~ comme neuf; **to be** ~ **to** ne pas être habitué/-e à ⟨job, way of life⟩; **we're** ~ **to the area** nous sommes nouveaux venus dans la région

New Age adj ⟨music, traveller⟩ New Age inv

newborn adj nouveau-né/-née

newcomer n (in place, job, club) nouveau venu/nouvelle venue m/f; (in sport, theatre, cinema) nouveau/-elle m/f

newfound adj tout nouveau/toute nouvelle

new look [1] n nouveau style m
[2] **new-look** adj ⟨product⟩ nouvelle version inv; ⟨car, team⟩ nouveau/-elle (before n); ⟨edition, show⟩ remanié/-e

newly adv ⟨arrived, built, formed, qualified⟩ nouvellement; ⟨washed⟩ fraîchement

newlyweds n pl jeunes mariés mpl

news n (a) nouvelle(s) f(pl); **a piece of** ~ une nouvelle; (in newspaper) une information; **have you heard the** ~? tu connais la nouvelle?
(b) (on radio, TV) **the** ~ les informations fpl, le journal m

news agency n agence f de presse

newsagent's n (GB) magasin m de journaux

news bulletin (GB), **newscast** (US) n bulletin m d'information

newscaster n présentateur/-trice m/f des informations

news conference n conférence f de presse

newsdealer n (US) marchand m de journaux

news editor n rédacteur/-trice m/f

newsgroup n forum m de discussion

news headlines n pl (on TV) titres mpl de l'actualité

news item n sujet m d'actualité

newsletter n bulletin m

newspaper n journal m

newsreader n (GB) présentateur/-trice m/f des informations

newsreel n actualités fpl

newsstand n kiosque m à journaux

New Year n le nouvel an m; **to see in the** ~ fêter la Saint-Sylvestre; **Happy** ~! bonne année!

New Year's day (GB), **New Year's** (US) n le jour m de l'an

New Year's Eve n la Saint-Sylvestre

New Zealand pr n Nouvelle-Zélande f

next

■ Note When next is used as an adjective, it is generally translated by prochain when referring to something which is still to come or happen and by suivant when it generally means following: I'll be 40 next year = j'aurai 40 ans l'année prochaine; the next year, he went to Spain = l'année suivante il est allé en Espagne.
– For examples and further usages see the entry below.

[1] pron **from one minute to the** ~ d'un instant à l'autre; **the week after** ~ dans deux semaines
[2] adj (a) prochain/-e, suivant/-e; **get the** ~ **train** prenez le prochain train; **he got on the** ~ **train** il a pris le train suivant; '~!' 'au suivant!'; '**you're** ~' 'c'est à vous'; **the** ~ **size (up)** la taille au-dessus; ~ **Thursday** jeudi prochain; **he's due to arrive in the** ~ **10 minutes** il devrait arriver d'ici 10 minutes; **this time** ~ **week** dans une semaine; **the** ~ **day** le lendemain
(b) ⟨room, street⟩ voisin/-e; ⟨building, house⟩ voisin/-e, d'à côté
[3] adv (a) (afterwards) ensuite, après; **what happened** ~? que s'est-il passé ensuite?
(b) (on a future occasion) **when I** ~ **go there** la prochaine fois que j'irai
(c) (in order) **the** ~ **tallest is Patrick** ensuite c'est Patrick qui est le plus grand
[4] **next to** phr (a) (almost) presque; ~ **to impossible** presque impossible; **to get sth for**

~ to nothing avoir qch pour quasiment rien; **in ~ to no time it was over** en un rien de temps c'était fini

(b) (beside, close to) à côté de; **two seats ~ to each other** deux sièges l'un à côté de l'autre; **to wear silk ~ to the skin** porter de la soie à même la peau

next door ① *adj* (*also* **next-door**) d'à côté
② *adv* ⟨*live, move in*⟩ à côté

next-door neighbour *n* voisin/-e *m/f* (d'à côté)

next of kin *n* **to be sb's ~** être le parent le plus proche de qn

nib *n* plume *f*

nibble *vi* ⟨*animal*⟩ mordiller; ⟨*person*⟩ grignoter

nice *adj* **(a)** ⟨*drive, holiday, place*⟩ agréable; ⟨*house, picture, outfit, weather*⟩ beau/belle (*before n*); **did you have a ~ time?** tu t'es bien amusé?; **~ to have met you** ravi d'avoir fait votre connaissance; **have a ~ day!** bonne journée!; **you look very ~** tu es très chic
(b) (tasty) bon/bonne (*before n*); **to taste ~** avoir bon goût
(c) ⟨*person*⟩ sympathique; **to be ~ to sb** être gentil/-ille avec qn
(d) ⟨*neighbourhood, school*⟩ comme il faut *inv*; **it is not ~ to tell lies** ce n'est pas bien de mentir
IDIOMS **~ one!** (in admiration) bravo!; (ironic) il ne manquait plus que ça!

nice-looking *adj* beau/belle (*before n*)

nicely *adv* **(a)** (kindly) gentiment
(b) (attractively) agréablement
(c) (politely) poliment
(d) (satisfactorily) bien; **that'll do ~** cela fera l'affaire

niche *n* (recess) niche *f*; (figurative) place *f*; (in the market) créneau *m*

niche market *n* marché *m* spécialisé

nick ① *n* encoche *f* (in dans)
② *vtr* **(a)** (cut) faire une entaille dans
(b) (GB) (colloq) (steal) piquer (colloq)
③ *vtr* (arrest) pincer (colloq)
IDIOMS **just in the ~ of time** juste à temps

nickel *n* **(a)** (US) pièce *f* de cinq cents
(b) (metal) nickel *m*

nickname ① *n* surnom *m*
② *vtr* surnommer

nicotine *n* nicotine *f*

nicotine patch *n* patch *m* à la nicotine

niece *n* nièce *f*

niggle (colloq) ① *n* (complaint) remarque *f*; **I've a ~ at the back of my mind** il y a quelque chose qui me travaille
② *vtr* (irritate) tracasser

niggling *adj* ⟨*doubt, worry*⟩ insidieux/-ieuse

night *n* nuit *f*; (before going to bed) soir *m*; **at ~** la nuit; **all ~ long** toute la nuit; **late at ~** tard le soir; **he arrived last ~** il est arrivé hier soir; **I slept badly last ~** j'ai mal dormi

cette nuit *or* la nuit dernière; **the ~ before last** avant-hier soir; **on Tuesday ~s** le mardi soir; **to get an early ~** se coucher tôt; **a ~ at the opera** une soirée à l'opéra

nightclub *n* boîte *f* de nuit

nightclubbing *n* **to go ~** aller en boîte (colloq)

nightdress *n* chemise *f* de nuit

nightingale *n* rossignol *m*

nightlife *n* vie *f* nocturne

nightmare *n* cauchemar *m*; **to have a ~** faire un cauchemar

night school *n* cours *mpl* du soir

night shelter *n* asile *m* de nuit

night shift *n* (period) **to be/work on the ~** être/travailler de nuit; (workers) équipe *f* de nuit

nightshirt *n* chemise *f* de nuit (d'homme)

night spot *n* (colloq) boîte *f* de nuit

night-time *n* nuit *f*; **at ~** la nuit

night watchman *n* veilleur *m* de nuit

nil *n* (gen) néant *m*; (Sport) zéro *m*

Nile *pr n* Nil *m*

nimble *adj* ⟨*person*⟩ agile; ⟨*fingers*⟩ habile

nine *n, pron, det* neuf (*m*) *inv*

nineteen *n, pron, det* dix-neuf (*m*) *inv*
IDIOMS **to talk ~ to the dozen** parler à n'en plus finir

nineteenth ① *n* **(a)** (in order) dix-neuvième *mf*
(b) (of month) dix-neuf *m inv*
(c) (fraction) dix-neuvième *m*
② *adj, adv* dix-neuvième

nineties *n pl* **(a)** (era) **the ~** les années *fpl* quatre-vingt-dix
(b) (age) **to be in one's ~** avoir entre quatre-vingt-dix et cent ans

ninetieth *n, adj, adv* quatre-vingt-dixième (*mf*)

nine-to-five *adj* ⟨*job, routine*⟩ de bureau

ninety *n, pron, det* quatre-vingt-dix (*m*) *inv*

ninth ① *n* **(a)** (in order) neuvième *mf*
(b) (of month) neuf *m inv*
(c) (fraction) neuvième *m*
② *adj, adv* neuvième

nip ① *n* (pinch) pincement *m*; (bite) morsure *f*; **there's a ~ in the air** il fait frisquet (colloq)
② *vtr* (pinch) pincer; (bite) donner un petit coup de dent à; (playfully) mordiller
③ *vi* (bite) mordre; (playfully) mordiller

nipple *n* mamelon *m*

nippy *adj* (colloq) **(a)** (cold) **it's a bit ~** il fait frisquet (colloq)
(b) (quick) ⟨*person*⟩ vif/vive; ⟨*car*⟩ rapide

nit *n* (egg) lente *f*; (larva) larve *f* de pou

nit-pick *vi* chercher la petite bête (colloq), pinailler (colloq)

nitrogen *n* azote *m*

nitty-gritty *n* (colloq) **to get down to the ~** passer aux choses sérieuses

no ① *particle* non; **~ thanks** non merci
② *det* **(a)** (none, not any) aucun/-e; **to have ~** ⋯❖

money ne pas avoir d'argent; she has ∼
talent elle n'a aucun talent; of ∼ interest
sans intérêt
(b) (prohibiting) ∼ **smoking** défense de fumer;
∼ **parking** stationnement interdit; ∼ **talking!**
silence!
(c) (for emphasis) he's ∼ **expert** ce n'est certes
pas un expert; this is ∼ **time to cry** ce n'est
pas le moment de pleurer
(d) (hardly any) in ∼ **time** en un rien de temps
3 *adv* it's ∼ **further/easier** ce n'est pas plus
loin/facile; I ∼ **longer work there** je n'y
travaille plus; ∼ **later than Wednesday** pas
plus tard que mercredi

no., No. (written abbr = **number**) n°

nobility *n* noblesse *f*

noble *n, adj* noble (*m*)

nobody **1** *pron* (also **no-one**) personne;
∼ **saw her** personne ne l'a vue; **there was** ∼
in the car il n'y avait personne dans la
voiture; **I heard** ∼ je n'ai entendu personne;
∼ **but me** personne sauf moi
2 *n* to be a ∼ être insignifiant/-e

nocturnal *adj* nocturne

nod **1** *n* she gave him a ∼ elle lui a fait un
signe de (la) tête; (as greeting) elle l'a salué
d'un signe de tête; (indicating assent) elle a fait
oui de la tête
2 *vtr* to ∼ **one's head** faire un signe de tête;
(to indicate assent) hocher la tête
3 *vi* faire un signe de tête (**to** à); (in assent)
faire oui de la tête

no-go area *n* quartier *m* chaud (*où la
police etc ne s'aventure plus*)

no-hoper *n* (colloq) raté/-e *m/f* (colloq)

noise *n* bruit *m*; (shouting) tapage *m*; to make
a ∼ faire du bruit

noisy *adj* ⟨person, place⟩ bruyant/-e;
⟨meeting, protest⟩ tumultueux/-euse

nomad *n* nomade *mf*

nominal *adj* (gen) nominal/-e; ⟨fee, sum⟩
minime; ⟨fine⟩ symbolique

nominate *vtr* **(a)** (propose) proposer; to ∼
sb for a prize sélectionner qn pour un prix
(b) (appoint) nommer (**to sth** à qch); to ∼ **sb**
(**as**) **chairman** nommer qn président

nomination *n* (as candidate) proposition *f*
de candidat; (for award) sélection *f*;
(appointment) nomination *f* (**to** à)

nominative *n, adj* nominatif (*m*)

nonaddictive *adj* qui ne crée pas de
dépendance

nonalcoholic *adj* non alcoolisé/-e

nonbeliever *n* non-croyant/-e *m/f*

nonchalant *adj* nonchalant/-e

noncommittal *adj* évasif/-ive

noncompliance *n* (with standards)
non-conformité *f* (**with** à); (with orders)
non-obéissance *f* (**with** à)

nonconformist *n, adj* non conformiste

noncooperation *n* refus *m* de
coopération

nondenominational *adj* ⟨church⟩
œcuménique; ⟨school⟩ laïque

nondescript *adj* ⟨person, clothes⟩
insignifiant/-e; ⟨building⟩ quelconque

none *pron* **(a)** (not any) aucun/-e *m/f*; ∼ **of**
us/them aucun de nous/d'entre eux; ∼ **of the**
wine was French il n'y avait aucun vin
français; ∼ **of the milk had been drunk** on
n'avait pas touché au lait; ∼ **of the bread**
was fresh tout le pain était rassis; **we have**
∼ **left** nous n'en avons pas; **there's** ∼ **left** il n'y
en a plus; ∼ **of it was true** il n'y avait rien
de vrai
(b) (nobody) personne; ∼ **but him** personne
sauf lui

nonentity *n* (person) personne *f*
insignifiante

nonessentials *n pl* (objects) accessoires
mpl; (details) accessoire *m sg*

nonetheless *adv* pourtant, néanmoins

nonexistent *adj* inexistant/-e

nonfiction *n* œuvres *fpl* non fictionnelles

no-nonsense *adj* ⟨manner, attitude,
policy⟩ direct/-e; ⟨person⟩ franc/franche

nonplussed *adj* perplexe

non-profitmaking *adj* ⟨organization⟩ à
but non lucratif

nonresident *n* non-résident/-e *m/f*

nonsense *n* (foolishness) absurdités *fpl*; to
talk/write ∼ dire/écrire n'importe quoi; ∼!
balivernes! *fpl*; **I won't stand for this** ∼ j'en
ai assez de ces bêtises

nonsmoker *n* non-fumeur/-euse *m/f*

non-smoking *adj* non fumeur *inv*

nonstarter *n* to be a ∼ ⟨plan, idea⟩ être
voué/-e à l'échec

nonstick *adj* antiadhésif/-ive

nonstop **1** *adj* ⟨journey⟩ sans arrêt; ⟨train,
flight⟩ direct/-e; ⟨noise⟩ incessant/-e
2 *adv* ⟨work, talk, drive, argue⟩ sans arrêt;
⟨fly⟩ sans escale

non-taxable *adj* non imposable

noodles *n pl* nouilles *fpl*

nook *n* coin *m*; **every** ∼ **and cranny** tous les
coins et recoins

noon *n* midi *m*; **at 12** ∼ à midi

no-one = NOBODY 1

noose *n* (loop) nœud *m* coulant; (for hanging)
corde *f*

nor *conj* ∼ **do I** moi non plus; ∼ **can he** lui
non plus; **he was not a cruel man,** ∼ **a mean**
one il n'était ni cruel, ni méchant; **she**
hasn't written, ∼ **has she telephoned** elle n'a
pas écrit, et elle n'a pas téléphoné non plus

norm *n* norme *f* (**for** pour; **to do** de faire)

normal **1** *n* normale *f*; **above/below** ∼
au-dessus/en dessous de la norme
2 *adj* (gen) normal/-e; ⟨place, time⟩
habituel/-elle

normality *n* normalité *f*

normally *adv* normalement

Normandy *pr n* Normandie *f*

north **1** *n* **(a)** (compass direction) nord *m*
(b) (part of world, country) **the North** le Nord

2 adj (gen) nord inv; ⟨wind⟩ du nord; **in ~ London** dans le nord de Londres
3 adv ⟨move⟩ vers le nord; ⟨lie, live⟩ au nord (**of** de)

North Africa pr n Afrique f du Nord

North America pr n Amérique f du Nord

northeast **1** n nord-est m
2 adj ⟨coast, side⟩ nord-est inv; ⟨wind⟩ de nord-est
3 adv ⟨move⟩ vers le nord-est; ⟨lie, live⟩ au nord-est

northern adj ⟨coast⟩ nord inv; ⟨town, accent⟩ du nord; ⟨hemisphere⟩ Nord inv; **~ England** le nord de l'Angleterre

Northern Ireland pr n Irlande f du Nord

North Pole pr n pôle m Nord

North Sea pr n the **~** la mer du Nord

northwest **1** n nord-ouest m
2 adj ⟨coast⟩ nord-ouest inv; ⟨wind⟩ de nord-ouest
3 adv ⟨move⟩ vers le nord-ouest; ⟨lie, live⟩ au nord-ouest

Norway pr n Norvège f

Norwegian **1** n (a) (person) Norvégien/-ienne m/f
(b) (language) norvégien m
2 adj norvégien/-ienne

nose n nez m
IDIOMS **to look down one's ~ at sb/sth** prendre qn/qch de haut; **to turn one's ~ up at sth** faire le dégoûté/la dégoûtée devant qch; **to poke** or **stick one's ~ into sth** (colloq) fourrer son nez dans qch (colloq)
■ **nose about, nose around** fouiner (**in** dans)

nosebleed n saignement m de nez

nose-dive n piqué m; **to go into a ~** ⟨plane⟩ faire un piqué; (figurative) chuter

nose ring n piercing m au nez

nostalgia n nostalgie f

nostalgic adj nostalgique

nostril n (of person) narine f; (of horse) naseau m

nosy adj (colloq) fouineur/-euse (colloq)

not **1** adv (a) (with a verb) ne…pas; **she isn't at home** elle n'est pas chez elle; **we won't need a car** nous n'aurons pas besoin d'une voiture; **hasn't he seen it?** il ne l'a pas vu alors?; **I hope ~** j'espère que non; **certainly ~** sûrement pas; **~ only** or **just** non seulement; **whether it rains or ~** qu'il pleuve ou non; **why ~?** pourquoi pas?; **~ everyone likes it** ça ne plaît pas à tout le monde; **it's ~ every day that** ce n'est pas tous les jours que; **~ a sound was heard** on n'entendait pas un bruit; **~ bad** pas mal
(b) (in question tags) **she's English, isn't she?** elle est anglaise, n'est-ce pas?; **he likes fish doesn't he?** il aime le poisson, n'est-ce pas?
2 not at all phr (in no way) pas du tout; (responding to thanks) de rien
3 not that phr **~ that I know of** pas

(autant) que je sache; **if she refuses, ~ that she will…** si elle refuse, je ne dis pas qu'elle le fera…

notable adj ⟨person⟩ remarquable; ⟨event, success, difference⟩ notable

notably adv (in particular) notamment; (markedly) remarquablement

notch **1** n entaille f
2 vtr encocher ⟨stick⟩
■ **notch up** (colloq) remporter ⟨point, prize⟩

note **1** n (a) (gen) note f; (short letter) mot m; **to take ~ of** prendre note de
(b) (Mus) (sound, symbol) note f; (piano key) touche f
(c) (bank) **~** billet m
2 vtr noter
3 of note phr ⟨person⟩ éminent/-e, réputé/-e; ⟨development⟩ digne d'intérêt
IDIOMS **to compare ~s** échanger ses impressions (**with** avec)
■ **note down** noter

notebook n carnet m

notebook pc n ordinateur m portable

noted adj ⟨intellectual, criminal⟩ célèbre; **to be ~ for** être réputé/-e pour

notepad n bloc-notes m

notepaper n papier m à lettres

noteworthy adj remarquable

nothing

■ **Note** When *nothing* is used alone as a reply to a question in English, it is translated by *rien*: 'what are you doing?'—'nothing' = 'que fais-tu?'—'rien'.
– *nothing* as a pronoun, when it is the subject of a verb, is translated by *rien ne* (+ verb or, in compound tenses, + auxiliary verb): *nothing changes* = rien ne change; *nothing has changed* = rien n'a changé.
– *nothing* as a pronoun, when it is the object of a verb, is translated by *ne…rien*; *ne* comes before the verb, and before the auxiliary in compound tenses, and *rien* comes after the verb or auxiliary: *I see nothing* = je ne vois rien; *I saw nothing* = je n'ai rien vu.
– When *ne rien* is used with an infinitive, the two words are not separated: *I prefer to say nothing* = je préfère ne rien dire.
– For more examples and particular usages, see the entry below.

1 pron **I knew ~ about it** je n'en savais rien; **we can do ~ (about it)** nous n'y pouvons rien; **~ much** pas grand-chose; **~ else** rien d'autre; **I had ~ to do with it!** je n'y étais pour rien!; **it's ~ to do with us** ça ne nous regarde pas; **to stop at ~** ne reculer devant rien (to do pour faire); **he means ~ to me** il n'est rien pour moi; **the names meant ~ to him** les noms ne lui disaient rien; **for ~** (for free) gratuitement; (pointlessly) pour rien
2 adv **it is ~ like as difficult as** c'est loin d'être aussi difficile que; **she is** or **looks ~ like her sister** elle ne ressemble pas du tout à sa sœur
3 nothing but phr **he's ~ but a coward** ⋯⋮➔

ce n'est qu'un lâche; **they've done ~ but moan** (colloq) ils n'ont fait que râler (colloq); **it's caused me ~ but trouble** ça ne m'a valu que des ennuis

notice ① *n* (a) (written sign) pancarte *f*; (advertisement) annonce *f*; (announcing birth, marriage, death) avis *m*
(b) (attention) attention *f*; **to take ~** faire attention (**of à**); **to take no ~ (of)** ne pas faire attention (à)
(c) (notification) préavis *m*; **one month's ~** un mois de préavis; **until further ~** jusqu'à nouvel ordre; **at short ~** à la dernière minute; **to give in one's ~** donner sa démission
② *vtr* remarquer ⟨absence, mark⟩; **to get oneself ~d** se faire remarquer

noticeable *adj* visible

noticeboard *n* panneau *m* d'affichage

notification *n* notification *f*; (in newspaper) avis *m*; **to receive ~ that** être avisé/-e que

notify *vtr* notifier; **to ~ sb of** aviser qn de ⟨result, incident⟩; avertir qn de ⟨intention⟩; informer qn de ⟨birth, death⟩

notion *n* (a) (idea) idée *f*
(b) (understanding) notion *f*

notorious *adj* ⟨criminal, organization⟩ notoire; ⟨district⟩ mal famé/-e; ⟨case⟩ tristement célèbre

notoriously *adv* notoirement; **they're ~ unreliable** il est bien connu qu'on ne peut pas compter sur eux

notwithstanding ① *adv* néanmoins
② *prep* (in spite of) en dépit de; (excepted) exception faite de

nought *n* zéro *m*

noun *n* nom *m*, substantif *m*

nourish *vtr* nourrir (**with** avec; **on** de)

nourishment *n* nourriture *f*

novel ① *n* roman *m*
② *adj* original/-e

novelist *n* romancier/-ière *m/f*

novelty *n* nouveauté *f* (**of doing** de faire)

November *n* novembre *m*

novice *n* débutant/-e *m/f*; (in religious order) novice *mf*

now ① *conj* **~ (that)** maintenant que
② *adv* (a) maintenant; **do it ~** fais-le maintenant; **right ~** tout de suite; **any time ~** d'un moment à l'autre; **(every) ~ and then** or **again** de temps en temps
(b) (with preposition) **you should have phoned him before ~** tu aurais dû lui téléphoner avant; **before** or **until ~** jusqu'à présent; **he should be finished by ~** il devrait avoir déjà fini; **between ~ and next Friday** d'ici vendredi prochain; **between ~ and then** d'ici là; **from ~ on(wards)** dorénavant
(c) (in the past) **it was ~ 4 pm** il était alors 16 heures; **by ~ it was too late** à ce moment-là, il était trop tard
(d) **~ there's a man I can trust!** ah! voilà un

homme en qui on peut avoir confiance!; **careful ~!** attention!; **~ then, let's get back to work** bon, reprenons le travail

nowadays *adv* (these days) de nos jours; (now) actuellement

nowhere ① *adv* nulle part; **I've got ~ else to go** je n'ai nulle part où aller; **there's ~ to sit down** il n'y a pas d'endroit pour s'asseoir; **all this talk is getting us ~** tout ce bavardage ne nous avance à rien; **flattery will get you ~!** tu n'arriveras à rien en me flattant
② **nowhere near** *phr* loin de; **~ near sufficient** loin d'être suffisant/-e

noxious *adj* nocif/-ive

nozzle *n* (of hose, pipe) ajutage *m*; (of hoover) suceur *m*; (for icing) douille *f*

nuance *n* nuance *f*

nuclear *adj* nucléaire

nuclear bomb *n* bombe *f* atomique

nuclear deterrent *n* force *f* de dissuasion nucléaire

nuclear energy, nuclear power *n* énergie *f* nucléaire or atomique

nuclear power station *n* centrale *f* nucléaire

nuclear waste *n* déchets *mpl* nucléaires

nucleus *n* noyau *m*

nude ① *n* nu/-e *m/f*; **in the ~** nu/-e
② *adj* ⟨person⟩ nu/-e

nudge *vtr* (push) pousser du coude; (accidentally) heurter; (brush against) frôler

nudist *n*, *adj* nudiste (*mf*)

nugget *n* pépite *f*

nuisance *n* (gen) embêtement *m*; (Law) nuisance *f*; **what a ~!** que c'est agaçant!

nuisance call *n* appel *m* anonyme

null *adj* (Law) **~ and void** nul et non avenu

nullify *vtr* invalider, annuler

numb ① *adj* (a) (from cold) engourdi/-e (**with** par); (from anaesthetic) insensible; **to go ~** s'engourdir
(b) (figurative) hébété/-e (**with** par)
② *vtr* ⟨cold⟩ engourdir; (Med) insensibiliser; **to ~ the pain** endormir la douleur

number ① *n* (a) (gen) nombre *m*; (written figure) chiffre *m*; **a three-figure ~** un nombre à trois chiffres; **a ~ of** un certain nombre de
(b) (of bus, house, page, telephone) numéro *m*; **a wrong ~** un faux numéro
(c) (by performer) (act) numéro *m*; (song) chanson *f*
② *vtr* (a) (allocate number to) numéroter
(b) (amount to, include) compter
IDIOMS **his days are ~ed** ses jours sont comptés; **to look after ~ one** penser avant tout à son propre intérêt

numberplate *n* (GB) plaque *f* minéralogique or d'immatriculation

numeracy *n* aptitude *f* au calcul

numeral *n* chiffre *m*

numerical *adj* numérique

numerous *adj* nombreux/-euse

nun *n* religieuse *f*, bonne sœur *f*

nurse [1] n (a) (Med) infirmier/-ière m/f;
male ∼ infirmier m
(b) = NURSEMAID
[2] vtr (a) soigner ⟨person, cold⟩
(b) allaiter ⟨baby⟩
(c) nourrir ⟨grievance, hope⟩

nursemaid n nurse f, bonne f d'enfants

nursery n (a) (also day ∼) crèche f; (in
hotel, shop) garderie f
(b) (room) chambre f d'enfants
(c) (for plants) pépinière f

nursery rhyme n comptine f

nursery school n école f maternelle

nursing n profession f d'infirmier/-ière

nursing home n (a) (old people's) maison f
de retraite; (convalescent) maison f de repos
(b) (GB) (maternity) clinique f obstétrique

nurture vtr (a) élever ⟨child⟩; soigner
⟨plant⟩
(b) nourrir ⟨hope, feeling, talent⟩

nut n (a) (walnut) noix f; (hazel) noisette f;
(almond) amande f; (peanut) cacahuète f

(b) (Tech) écrou m

nutcracker n casse-noisettes m inv

nutmeg n noix f de muscade

nutrition n (process) nutrition f,
alimentation f; (science) diététique f

nutritional adj ⟨value⟩ nutritif/-ive;
⟨composition, information⟩ nutritionnel/-elle

nutritious adj nourrissant/-e

nutshell n (a) coquille f de noix or
noisette
(b) (figurative) in a ∼ en un mot

nuzzle vtr frotter son nez contre
∎ **nuzzle up**: to ∼ up against or to sb se
blottir contre qn

NVQ n (abbr = **National Vocational
Qualification**) qualification f nationale
professionnelle (obtenue par formation
continue ou initiale)

nylon n nylon® m

nymph n nymphe f

Oo

o, O n (a) (letter) o, O m
(b) O (spoken number) zéro

oaf n (clumsy) balourd/-e m/f; (loutish) mufle m

oak [1] n chêne m
[2] adj de or en chêne

OAP n (GB) (abbr = **old age pensioner**)
retraité/-e m/f

oar n rame f

oasis n (in desert) oasis f; (figurative) havre m

oat n ∼s avoine f
IDIOMS to sow one's wild ∼s jeter sa
gourme

oath n (a) serment m; under ∼, on ∼ (GB)
sous serment
(b) (swearword) juron m

oatmeal n (a) (cereal) farine f d'avoine
(b) (US) (porridge) bouillie f d'avoine

obedience n obéissance f (to à)

obedient adj obéissant/-e

obese adj obèse

obesity n obésité f

obey [1] vtr obéir à ⟨person, instinct⟩; se
conformer à ⟨instructions, law⟩
[2] vi ⟨person⟩ obéir

obituary n (also ∼ notice) nécrologie f

object [1] n (a) (item) objet m
(b) (goal) but m (of de)
(c) (focus) to be the ∼ of être l'objet de
(d) (in grammar) complément m d'objet
[2] vtr objecter (that que)
[3] vi soulever des objections; to ∼ to

protester contre ⟨attitude, comment⟩; to ∼ to
doing se refuser à faire; I ∼ to their
behaviour je trouve leur comportement
inadmissible

objection n objection f (to à; from de la
part de); I've no ∼(s) je n'y vois pas
d'inconvénient

objectionable adj ⟨remark⟩
désobligeant/-e; ⟨behaviour, language⟩
choquant/-e; ⟨person⟩ insupportable

objective [1] n objectif m
[2] adj objectif/-ive, impartial/-e

objectively adv objectivement

obligation n (a) (duty) devoir m (towards,
to envers); to be under (an) ∼ to do être
obligé/-e de faire
(b) (commitment) obligation f (to envers; to do
de faire)
(c) (debt) dette f

obligatory adj obligatoire (to do de faire)

oblige vtr (a) (compel) obliger (to do à faire)
(b) (be helpful) rendre service à
(c) to be ∼d to sb être reconnaissant/-e à
qn (for de)

obliging adj serviable

obliterate vtr effacer ⟨trace, word,
memory⟩; anéantir ⟨landmark, city⟩

oblivion n oubli m

oblivious adj (unaware) inconscient/-e; to
be ∼ of or to ne pas être conscient/-e de

oblong [1] n rectangle m
[2] adj oblong/oblongue, rectangulaire

O

obnoxious *adj* odieux/-ieuse, exécrable

obscene *adj* obscène

obscure ①*adj* obscur/-e; (indistinct) vague
②*vtr* obscurcir ⟨*truth*⟩; cacher ⟨*view*⟩; **to ~
the issue** embrouiller la question

observant *adj* observateur/-trice

observation *n* observation *f* (of de); **to
keep sb/sth under ~** surveiller qn/qch

observe *vtr* (a) (see, notice) observer (**that**
que)
(b) ⟨*doctor, police*⟩ surveiller
(c) (remark) faire observer (**that** que)
(d) observer ⟨*law, custom*⟩

observer *n* observateur/-trice *m/f* (**of** de)

obsess *vtr* obséder

obsession *n* obsession *f*

obsessive *adj* ⟨*person*⟩ maniaque;
⟨*neurosis*⟩ obsessionnel/-elle; ⟨*thought*⟩
obsédant/-e

obsolescence *n* (gen) désuétude *f*;
built-in ~ obsolescence *f* planifiée

obsolete *adj* ⟨*technology*⟩ dépassé/-e;
⟨*custom, idea*⟩ démodé/-e; ⟨*word*⟩ désuet/-ète

obstacle *n* obstacle *m*; **to be an ~** faire
obstacle (**to** à)

obstacle course *n* (Mil) parcours *m* du
combattant; (figurative) course *f* d'obstacles

obstacle race *n* course *f* d'obstacles

obstetrician *n* obstétricien-ienne *m/f*

obstinate *adj* ⟨*person*⟩ têtu/-e (**about** en ce
qui concerne); ⟨*behaviour, silence, effort*⟩
obstiné/-e; ⟨*resistance*⟩ acharné/-e

obstruct *vtr* cacher ⟨*view*⟩; bloquer ⟨*road*⟩;
gêner ⟨*traffic, person, progress*⟩; faire
obstruction à ⟨*player*⟩; entraver le cours de
⟨*justice*⟩

obstruction *n* (a) (to traffic, progress)
obstacle *m*; (in pipe) bouchon *m*
(b) (in sport) obstruction *f*

obtain *vtr* obtenir

obtrusive *adj* ⟨*noise*⟩ gênant/-e; ⟨*person,
behaviour*⟩ importun/-e

obtuse *adj* ⟨*person*⟩ obtus/-e; ⟨*remark*⟩
stupide

obvious ①*n* **to state the ~** enfoncer les
portes ouvertes
②*adj* évident/-e (**to** pour)

obviously ①*adv* manifestement; **she ~
needs help** il est évident qu'elle a besoin
d'aide; **he's ~ lying** il est clair qu'il ment
②*excl* bien sûr!, évidemment!

occasion *n* occasion *f*; **on one ~** une fois;
to rise to the ~ se montrer à la hauteur des
circonstances; **on special ~s** dans les
grandes occasions

occasional *adj* ⟨*event*⟩ qui a lieu de temps
en temps; **the ~ letter** une lettre de temps en
temps

occasionally *adv* de temps à autre; **very
~** très rarement

occult *n* **the ~** les sciences *fpl* occultes

occupant *n* (a) (of building, bed) occupant/-e
m/f

(b) (of vehicle) passager/-ère *m/f*

occupation *n* (a) (Mil) occupation *f* (**de** of)
(b) (trade) métier *m*; (profession) profession *f*
(c) (activity) occupation *f*

occupational *adj* ⟨*accident*⟩ du travail;
⟨*risk*⟩ du métier; ⟨*safety*⟩ au travail

occupational hazard *n* **it's an ~** ça
fait partie des risques du métier

occupier *n* occupant/-e *m/f*

occupy *vtr* occuper; **to keep oneself
occupied** s'occuper (**by doing** en faisant)

occur *vi* (a) (happen) se produire
(b) (be present) se trouver
(c) **the idea ~red to me that...** l'idée m'est
venue à l'esprit que...; **it didn't ~ to me** ça
ne m'est pas venu à l'idée

occurrence *n* (a) (event) fait *m*; **to be a
rare ~** se produire rarement
(b) (instance) occurrence *f*
(c) (of disease, phenomenon) cas *m*

ocean *n* océan *m*

o'clock *adv* **at one ~** à une heure; **it's two
~** il est deux heures

octagon *n* octogone *m*

octave *n* octave *f*

October *n* octobre *m*

octopus *n* (a) (Zool) pieuvre *f*
(b) (Culin) poulpe *m*

OD *n, vi* (colloq) = OVERDOSE

odd ①*adj* (a) (strange, unusual) ⟨*person,
object, occurrence*⟩ bizarre
(b) ⟨*socks, gloves*⟩ dépareillés
(c) (miscellaneous) **some ~ bits of cloth**
quelques bouts de tissu
(d) ⟨*number*⟩ impair/-e
(e) **to be the ~ one out** ⟨*person, animal,
plant*⟩ être l'exception *f*; ⟨*drawing, word*⟩
être l'intrus *m*; (when selecting team) ⟨*person*⟩
être sans partenaire
②**-odd** *combining form* **sixty-~ people/
years** une soixantaine de personnes/d'années

oddity *n* (odd thing) bizarrerie *f*; (person)
excentrique *mf*

odd job *n* (for money) petit boulot *m*; **~s** (in
house, garden) petits travaux *mpl*

odd-job man *n* homme *m* à tout faire

odds *n pl* (a) (in betting) cote *f* (**on** sur)
(b) (chance, likelihood) chances *fpl*; **the ~ are
against his winning** il y a peu de chances
qu'il gagne; **to win against the ~** gagner
contre toute attente
IDIOMS **at ~** (in dispute) être en conflit;
(inconsistent) en contradiction (**with** avec)

odds and ends *n pl* (GB) bricoles *fpl*
(colloq)

odour (GB), **odor** (US) *n* odeur *f*

of *prep*

▪ **Note** In almost all its uses, the preposition *of* is
translated by *de*. For exceptions, see the entry
below.
– Remember that *de* + *le* always becomes *du*
and that *de* + *les* always becomes *des*.
– When *of it* or *of them* are used for something

already referred to, they are translated by en: *there's a lot of it* = il y en a beaucoup; *there are several of them* = il y en a plusieurs.
– Note, however, the following expressions used when referring to people: *there are six of them* = ils sont six; *there were several of them* = ils étaient plusieurs.

(a) (in most uses) de; **the leg ~ the table** le pied de la table
(b) (made of) en; **a ring (made) ~ gold** une bague en or
(c) **a friend ~ mine** un ami à moi; **that's kind ~ you** c'est très gentil de votre part *or* à vous; **some ~ us/them** quelques-uns d'entre nous/d'entre eux

off ⓵ *adv* (a) (leaving) **to be ~** partir, s'en aller; **it's time you were ~** il est temps que tu partes; **I'm ~** je m'en vais
(b) (at a distance) **to be 30 metres ~** être à 30 mètres; **some way ~** assez loin
(c) (ahead in time) **Easter is a month ~** Pâques est dans un mois; **the exam is still several months ~** l'examen n'aura pas lieu avant plusieurs mois
⓶ *adj* (a) (free) **Tuesday's my day ~** je ne travaille pas le mardi; **to have the morning ~** avoir la matinée libre
(b) (turned off) **to be ~** ⟨*water, gas*⟩ être coupé/-e; ⟨*tap*⟩ être fermé/-e; ⟨*light, TV*⟩ être éteint/-e
(c) (cancelled) ⟨*match, party*⟩ annulé/-e
(d) (removed) **the lid is ~** il n'y a pas de couvercle; **with her make-up ~** sans maquillage; **25% ~** 25% de remise
(e) (colloq) (bad) **to be ~** ⟨*food*⟩ être avarié/-e; ⟨*milk*⟩ avoir tourné/-e
⓷ *prep* (a) (also **just ~**) juste à côté de ⟨*kitchen*⟩; **~ the west coast** au large de la côte ouest; **just ~ the path** tout près du sentier
(b) **it is ~ the point** là n'est pas la question
(c) (colloq) **to be ~ one's food** ne pas avoir d'appétit
IDIOMS to feel a bit ~ (colloq) ne pas être dans son assiette (colloq); **to have an ~ day** ne pas être dans un de ses bons jours

off-centre (GB), **off-center** (US) *adj* décentré/-e
off-chance *n* **just on the ~** au cas où
off-colour *adj* (colloq) (unwell) patraque (colloq)
offence (GB), **offense** (US) *n* (a) (crime) délit *m*
(b) (insult) **to cause ~ to sb** offenser qn; **to take ~ (at)** s'offenser (de)
(c) (Mil) offensive *f*
offend ⓵ *vtr* offenser ⟨*person*⟩
⓶ *vi* commettre une infraction (**against** à)
offender *n* (a) (Law) délinquant/-e *m/f*
(b) (culprit) coupable *mf*
offensive ⓵ *n* (Mil, Sport) offensive *f*
⓶ *adj* ⟨*remark*⟩ injurieux/-ieuse (**to** pour); ⟨*behaviour*⟩ insultant/-e; ⟨*language*⟩ grossier/-ière

offer ⓵ *n* (a) offre *f* (**to do** de faire); **job ~** offre d'emploi
(b) (of goods) **to be on special ~** être en promotion
⓶ *vtr* (gen) offrir; donner ⟨*advice, explanation, information*⟩; émettre ⟨*opinion*⟩; proposer ⟨*service*⟩; **to ~ sb sth** offrir qch à qn; **to ~ to do** se proposer pour faire
⓷ *vi* se proposer
offering *n* (gift) cadeau *m*; (sacrifice) offrande *f*
offhand ⓵ *adj* désinvolte
⓶ *adv* **~, I don't know** comme ça au pied levé je ne sais pas
office *n* (a) (place) bureau *m*
(b) (position) fonction *f*, charge *f*; **public ~** fonctions *fpl* officielles; **to hold ~** ⟨*president, mayor*⟩ être en fonction; ⟨*political party*⟩ être au pouvoir
office block, office building *n* (GB) immeuble *m* de bureaux
officer *n* (a) (in army, navy) officier *m*
(b) (also **police ~**) policier *m*
office worker *n* employé/-e *m/f* de bureau
official ⓵ *n* fonctionnaire *mf*; (of party, union) officiel/-ielle *m/f*; (at town hall) employé/-e *m/f*
⓶ *adj* officiel/-ielle
offing *n* **in the ~** en perspective
off-key *adj* faux/fausse
off-licence *n* (GB) magasin *m* de vins et de spiritueux
off-limits *adj* interdit/-e
off-line *adj* (Comput) (not on the Internet) hors ligne; ⟨*processing*⟩ en différé
off-load *vtr* (get rid of) écouler ⟨*goods*⟩; **to ~ the blame onto sb** rejeter la responsabilité sur qn
off-message *adj* (Pol) **to be ~** être en désaccord avec la politique gouvernementale
off-peak *adj* ⟨*electricity*⟩ au tarif de nuit; ⟨*travel*⟩ en période creuse; ⟨*call*⟩ au tarif réduit
off-putting *adj* (GB) ⟨*manner*⟩ peu engageant/-e; **it was very ~** c'était déroutant
off-road *vi* rouler en tout terrain
off-road vehicle *n* véhicule *m* tout terrain
off-season *adj* ⟨*cruise, holiday*⟩ hors saison
offset *vtr* compenser (**by** par); **to ~ sth against sth** mettre qch et qch en balance
offshore *adj* ⟨*waters*⟩ du large; ⟨*fishing*⟩ au large; ⟨*oil rig*⟩ offshore *inv*
offside ⓵ *n* (GB) côté *m* conducteur
⓶ *adj* (a) (GB) ⟨*lane*⟩ (in France) de gauche; (in UK) de droite
(b) (Sport) hors jeu *inv*
offspring *n* progéniture *f*
offstage *adj, adv* dans les coulisses
off-the-cuff *adj* ⟨*remark, speech*⟩ impromptu/-e

off-the-peg *adj* ⟨*garment*⟩ de prêt-à-porter

off-the-shelf *adj* ⟨*goods*⟩ disponible en magasin; ⟨*software*⟩ fixe

off-the-wall *adj* (colloq) loufoque (colloq)

off-white *adj* blanc cassé *inv*

often *adv* souvent; **as ~ as not, more ~ than not** le plus souvent; **how ~ do you meet?** vous vous voyez tous les combien?; **once too ~** une fois de trop; **every so ~** de temps en temps

oh *excl* oh!; **~ dear!** oh là là!; **~ (really)?** ah bon?

oil ⒈ *n* (gen) huile *f*; (petroleum) pétrole *m*; **crude ~** pétrole brut; **engine ~** huile de moteur; **heating ~** fioul *m*
⒉ *vtr* huiler

oil change *n* vidange *f*

oilcloth *n* toile *f* cirée

oil field *n* champ *m* pétrolifère

oil painting *n* peinture *f* à l'huile

oil refinery *n* raffinerie *f* de pétrole

oil rig *n* (offshore) plate-forme *f* pétrolière offshore; (on land) tour *f* de forage

oilseed rape *n* colza *m*

oilskins *n pl* (GB) ciré *m*

oil slick *n* marée *f* noire

oil well *n* puits *m* de pétrole

oily *adj* ⟨*cloth, food, hair*⟩ gras/grasse; ⟨*dressing, substance*⟩ huileux/-euse

ointment *n* pommade *f*

okay, OK (colloq) ⒈ *n* **to give sb/sth the ~** donner le feu vert à qn/qch
⒉ *adj* **it's ~ by me** ça ne me dérange pas; **is it ~ if...?** est-ce que ça va si...?; **he's ~** (nice) il est sympa (colloq); **to feel ~** aller bien; **I'm ~** ça va; **'how was the match?'—'~'** 'comment as-tu trouvé le match?'—'pas mal'
⒊ *adv* ⟨*cope, work out*⟩ (assez) bien
⒋ *particle* **(a)** (giving agreement) d'accord
(b) (introducing topic) bien

old *adj* **(a)** ⟨*person*⟩ vieux/vieille (*before n*), âgé/-e; ⟨*object, tradition, song*⟩ vieux/vieille (*before n*); **an ~ man** un vieil homme, un vieillard; **an ~ woman** une vieille femme, une vieille; **to get ~** vieillir; **how ~ are you?** quel âge as-tu?; **I'm ten years ~** j'ai dix ans; **a six-year-~ boy** un garçon (âgé) de six ans; **my ~er brother** mon frère aîné; **I'm the ~est** c'est moi l'aîné/-e
(b) (former, previous) ⟨*address, school, job, system*⟩ ancien/-ienne (*before n*); **in the ~ days** autrefois

■ **Note** The irregular form *vieil* of the adjective *vieux/vieille* is used before masculine nouns beginning with a vowel or a mute 'h'.

old age *n* vieillesse *f*

old-age pensioner, OAP *n* (GB) retraité/-e *m/f*

old-fashioned *adj* ⟨*person, ways*⟩ vieux jeu *inv*; ⟨*idea, attitude, garment, machine*⟩ démodé/-e

old people's home *n* maison *f* de retraite

old wives' tale *n* conte *m* de bonne femme

olive ⒈ *n* **(a)** (fruit) olive *f*
(b) (*also* **~ tree**) olivier *m*
⒉ *adj* ⟨*dress, eyes*⟩ vert olive *inv*; ⟨*complexion*⟩ olivâtre

olive green *n, adj* vert (*m*) olive *inv*

olive oil *n* huile *f* d'olive

Olympics *n pl* (*also* **Olympic Games**) jeux *mpl* Olympiques

ombudsman *n* médiateur *m*

omelette *n* omelette *f*

omen *n* présage *m*

ominous *adj* ⟨*cloud*⟩ menaçant/-e; ⟨*news*⟩ inquiétant/-e; ⟨*sign*⟩ de mauvais augure

omission *n* omission *f*

omit *vtr* omettre (**from** de; **to do** de faire)

omnipotent *adj* omnipotent/-e

omnipresent *adj* omniprésent/-e

on ⒈ *prep* **(a)** (position) sur ⟨*table, coast, motorway*⟩; **~ the beach** sur la plage; **~ top of the piano** sur le piano; **~ the floor** par terre; **there's a stain ~ it** il y a une tache dessus; **to live ~ Park Avenue** habiter Park Avenue; **a studio flat ~ Avenue Montaigne** un studio avenue Montaigne; **the paintings ~ the wall** les tableaux qui sont au mur; **I've got no small change ~ me** je n'ai pas de monnaie sur moi; **to have a smile ~ one's face** sourire; **to hang sth ~ a nail** accrocher qch à un clou; **~ a string** au bout d'une ficelle
(b) (about, on the subject of) sur; **~ Africa** sur l'Afrique
(c) **to be ~** faire partie de ⟨*team*⟩; être membre de ⟨*committee*⟩
(d) (in expressions of time) **~ 22 February** le 22 février; **~ Friday** vendredi; **~ Saturdays** le samedi; **~ my birthday** le jour de mon anniversaire; **~ sunny days** quand il fait beau
(e) (immediately after) **~ his arrival** à son arrivée; **~ hearing the truth she...** quand elle a appris la vérité, elle...
(f) (taking) **to be ~ steroids** prendre des stéroïdes; **to be ~ drugs** se droguer
(g) (powered by) **to run ~ batteries** fonctionner sur piles; **to run ~ electricity** marcher à l'électricité
(h) (indicating a medium) **~ TV** à la télé; **~ the news** aux informations; **~ video** en vidéo; **~ drums** à la batterie
(i) (earning) **to be ~ £20,000 a year** gagner 20 000 livres sterling par an; **to be ~ a low income** avoir un bas salaire
(j) (paid for by) **it's ~ me** je t'invite
(k) (indicating transport) **to travel ~ the bus** voyager en bus; **~ the plane** dans l'avion; **to be ~ one's bike** être à vélo; **to leave ~ the first train** prendre le premier train
⒉ *adj* **(a)** **while the meeting is ~** pendant la réunion; **I've got a lot ~** je suis très occupé; **the news is ~ in 10 minutes** les informations sont dans 10 minutes; **what's ~?** (on TV)

qu'est-ce qu'il y a à la télé?; (at the cinema, theatre) qu'est-ce qu'on joue?; **there's nothing ∼** il n'y a rien de bien
(b) to be ∼ ‹TV, oven, light› être allumé/-e; ‹dishwasher, radio› marcher; ‹tap› être ouvert/-e; **the power is ∼** il y a du courant
(c) to be ∼ ‹lid› être mis/-e
3 *adv* **(a) to have nothing ∼** être nu/-e; **to have make-up ∼** être maquillé/-e; **with slippers ∼** en pantoufles
(b) from that day ∼ à partir de ce jour-là; **20 years ∼** 20 ans plus tard; **to walk ∼** continuer à marcher; **to go to Paris then ∼ to Marseilles** aller à Paris et de là à Marseille; **a little further ∼** un peu plus loin
4 on and off *phr* de temps en temps
5 on and on *phr* **to go ∼ and ∼** ‹speaker› parler pendant des heures; ‹speech› durer des heures; **to go ∼ and ∼ about** ne pas arrêter de parler de
IDIOMS it's just *or* **simply not ∼** (GB) (out of the question) c'est hors de question; (not the done thing) ça ne se fait pas; (unacceptable) c'est inadmissible

on-board *adj* (in-car) embarqué/-e

once **1** *n* **just this ∼** pour cette fois; **for ∼** pour une fois
2 *adv* **(a)** (one time) une fois; **∼ and for all** une (bonne) fois pour toutes; **∼ too often** une fois de trop; **∼ a day** une fois par jour
(b) (formerly) autrefois; **∼ upon a time there was a king** il était une fois un roi
3 *conj* une fois que, dès que
4 at once *phr* **(a)** (immediately) tout de suite; **all at ∼** tout d'un coup
(b) (simultaneously) à la fois

once-over *n* (colloq) **to give sth the ∼** jeter un rapide coup d'œil à qch; **to give sb the ∼** évaluer qn au premier coup d'œil

oncoming *adj* ‹car, vehicle› venant en sens inverse

one **1** *det* **(a)** (single) un/une; **∼ car** une voiture; **∼ dog** un chien; **to raise ∼ hand** lever la main
(b) (unique, sole) seul/-e (before n); **my ∼ vice** mon seul vice; **my ∼ and only tie** ma seule et unique cravate; **the ∼ and only Edith Piaf** l'incomparable Edith Piaf
(c) (same) même; **at ∼ and the same time** en même temps
2 *pron* **(a)** (indefinite) un/une *m/f*; **can you lend me ∼?** tu peux m'en prêter un/une?; **∼ of them** (person) l'un d'eux/l'une d'elles; (thing) l'un/l'une *m/f*
(b) (impersonal) (as subject) on; (as object) vous; **∼ never knows** on ne sait jamais
(c) (demonstrative) **the grey ∼** le gris/la grise; **this ∼** celui-ci/celle-ci; **which ∼?** lequel/ laquelle?; **that's the ∼** c'est celui-ci/celle-là; **he's/she's the ∼ who** c'est lui/elle qui
(e) **∼-fifty** (in sterling) une livre cinquante
3 *n* (number) un *m*; (referring to feminine) une *f*; **∼ o'clock** une heure; **in ∼s and twos** par petits groupes
4 one by one *phr* un par un/une par une
IDIOMS to be ∼ up on sb (colloq) avoir un

avantage sur qn; **to go ∼ better than sb** faire mieux que qn; **I for ∼ think that** pour ma part je crois que

one another *pron* (also **each other**)

■ **Note** one another is very often translated by using a reflexive pronoun (nous, vous, se, s').

they love ∼ ils s'aiment; **to help ∼** s'entraider; **to worry about ∼** s'inquiéter l'un pour l'autre; **kept apart from ∼** séparés l'un de l'autre

one-off *adj* (GB) ‹experiment› unique; ‹event, payment› exceptionnel/-elle

one-parent family *n* famille *f* monoparentale

one-piece *adj* **∼ swimsuit** maillot *m* de bain une pièce

one's *det* son/sa/ses; **∼ books/friends** ses livres/amis; **to wash ∼ hands** se laver les mains; **to do ∼ best** faire de son mieux

oneself *pron* **(a)** (reflexive) se, s'; **to wash/ cut ∼** se laver/couper
(b) (for emphasis) soi-même
(c) (after prepositions) soi; **sure of ∼** sûr/-e de soi; **(all) by ∼** tout seul/toute seule

one-sided *adj* ‹account› partial/-e; ‹contest› inégal/-e; ‹deal› inéquitable

one-time *adj* ancien/-ienne (before n)

one-to-one *adj* ‹talk› en tête à tête; **∼ meeting** tête-à-tête *m inv*; **∼ tuition** cours *mpl* particuliers

one-way *adj* **(a)** ‹traffic› à sens unique; **∼ street** sens *m* unique
(b) **∼ ticket** aller *m* simple

ongoing *adj* ‹process› continu/-e; ‹battle, story› continuel/-elle

onion *n* oignon *m*

on-line *adj* (Comput) (on the Internet) en ligne; ‹mode› connecté/-e; ‹data processing› en direct

onlooker *n* spectateur/-trice *m/f*

only **1** *conj* mais, seulement; **I'd go ∼ I'm too old** j'irais bien mais je suis trop vieux
2 *adj* seul/-e; **∼ child** enfant unique
3 *adv* **(a)** (exclusively) **∼ in Italy can one...** il n'y a qu'en Italie que l'on peut...; **∼ time will tell** seul l'avenir nous le dira; **'men ∼'** 'réservé aux hommes'
(b) (in expressions of time) **∼ yesterday** pas plus tard qu'hier; **it seems like ∼ yesterday** j'ai l'impression que c'était hier
(c) (merely) **you ∼ had to ask** tu n'avais qu'à demander; **it's ∼ fair** ce n'est que justice; **he ∼ grazed his knees** il s'est juste égratigné les genoux; **∼ half the money** juste la moitié de l'argent
4 only just *phr* **(a)** (very recently) **to have ∼ just done** venir juste de faire
(b) (barely) **∼ just wide enough** juste assez large; **∼ just** (narrowly) de justesse
5 only too *phr* **∼ too well** trop bien; **∼ too pleased** trop content/-e

on-message *adj* (Pol) **to be ∼** être en accord avec la politique gouvernementale

o.n.o. (GB) ⟨*abbr* = **or nearest offer**⟩ à débattre

on-screen *adj* sur l'écran

onset *n* début *m* (**of** de)

onside *adj, adv* en jeu

on-site *adj* sur place

onslaught *n* attaque *f* (**on** contre)

on-target earnings, **OTE** *n pl* '∼ £40,000' 'salaire plus commission pouvant atteindre 40 000 livres sterling'

on-the-job *adj* ⟨*training*⟩ sur le lieu de travail

on the spot *adv* ⟨*decide*⟩ sur-le-champ; ⟨*killed*⟩ sur le coup; **to be** ∼ être sur place

onto *prep* (*also* **on to**) sur
IDIOMS **to be** ∼ **something** (colloq) être sur une piste

onus *n* obligation *f*; **the** ∼ **is on sb to do it** il incombe à qn de faire

onward ① *adj* ∼ **flight** correspondance *f* (**to** à destination de)
② *adv* = ONWARDS

onwards *adv* (*also* **onward**) **to carry** ∼ continuer; **from now** ∼ à partir d'aujourd'hui; **from that day** ∼ à dater de ce jour

ooze ① *vtr* **the wound** ∼**d blood** du sang suintait de la blessure
② *vi* **to** ∼ **with** ⟨*person*⟩ rayonner de ⟨*charm, sexuality*⟩

opal *n* opale *f*

opaque *adj* opaque

open ① *n* **in the** ∼ (outside) dehors, en plein air; **to bring sth out into the** ∼ mettre qch au grand jour
② *adj* (a) (gen) ouvert/-e; **to be half** ∼ ⟨*door*⟩ être entrouvert/-e; **the** ∼ **air** le plein air; **in** ∼ **country** en rase campagne; **on** ∼ **ground** sur un terrain découvert; **the** ∼ **road** la grand-route; **the** ∼ **sea** la haute mer
(b) (not covered) ⟨*car, carriage*⟩ découvert/-e, décapoté/-e
(c) ∼ **to** exposé/-e à ⟨*air, wind, elements*⟩; ∼ **to attack** exposé/-e à l'attaque; **to lay oneself** ∼ **to criticism** s'exposer (ouvertement) à la critique
(d) ⟨*access, competition*⟩ ouvert/-e à tous; ⟨*meeting*⟩ public/-ique
(e) (candid) ⟨*person*⟩ franc/franche (**about** à propos de)
(f) (blatant) ⟨*hostility, contempt*⟩ non dissimulé/-e
(g) **to leave the date** ∼ laisser la date en suspens; **to keep an** ∼ **mind** réserver son jugement
③ *vtr* (gen) ouvrir; entamer ⟨*discussions*⟩
④ *vi* (a) ⟨*door, flower, curtain*⟩ s'ouvrir; **to** ∼ **onto sth** ⟨*door, window*⟩ donner sur qch
(b) ⟨*shop, bar*⟩ ouvrir; ⟨*meeting, play*⟩ commencer (**with** par)
(c) ⟨*film*⟩ sortir (sur les écrans)
■ **open up**: ¶ ∼ **up** (a) ⟨*shop, branch*⟩ ouvrir
(b) ⟨*gap*⟩ se creuser
(c) (figurative) ⟨*person*⟩ se confier
¶ ∼ [sth] **up** ouvrir

open-air *adj* ⟨*pool, stage*⟩ en plein air

open day *n* journée *f* portes ouvertes

opener *n* (for bottles) décapsuleur *m*; (for cans) ouvre-boîte *m*

open-heart surgery *n* (operation) opération *f* à cœur ouvert

opening ① *n* (a) (start) début *m*
(b) (of exhibition, shop) ouverture *f*; (of play, film) première *f*
(c) (gap) trouée *f*
(d) (opportunity) occasion *f* (**to do** de faire); (in market) débouché *m* (**for** pour); (for job) poste *m*
② *adj* ⟨*scene, move*⟩ premier/-ière (**before** *n*); ⟨*remarks*⟩ préliminaire; ⟨*ceremony*⟩ d'inauguration

opening hours *n pl* heures *fpl* d'ouverture

open learning *n*: formule d'enseignement à distance ou dans un centre ouvert à tous

open market *n* marché *m* libre

open-minded *adj* **to be** ∼ avoir l'esprit ouvert

open-necked *adj* ⟨*shirt*⟩ à col ouvert

open-plan *adj* ⟨*office*⟩ paysagé/-e

open ticket *n* billet *m* ouvert

Open University, **OU** *n* (GB Univ) *système d'enseignement universitaire par correspondance ouvert à tous*

opera *n* opéra *m*

opera glasses *n* jumelles *fpl* de théâtre

opera house *n* opéra *m*

operate ① *vtr* (a) faire marcher ⟨*appliance, vehicle*⟩
(b) (practise) pratiquer ⟨*policy, system*⟩
(c) (manage) gérer
② *vi* (a) (do business) opérer
(b) (function) marcher
(c) (run) ⟨*service*⟩ fonctionner
(d) (Med) opérer; **to** ∼ **on** opérer ⟨*person*⟩; **to** ∼ **on sb's leg** opérer qn à la jambe

operating instructions *n pl* mode *m* d'emploi

operating room (US), **operating theatre** (GB) *n* salle *f* d'opération

operating system *n* système *m* d'exploitation

operation *n* (a) (gen, Med) opération *f*; **to have a heart** ∼ se faire opérer du cœur
(b) **to be in** ∼ ⟨*plan*⟩ être en vigueur; ⟨*machine*⟩ fonctionner; ⟨*oil rig, mine*⟩ être en exploitation

operational *adj* (a) (ready to operate) opérationnel/-elle
(b) ⟨*budget, costs*⟩ d'exploitation

operative ① *n* (worker) employé/-e *m/f*
② *adj* en vigueur

operator *n* (a) (on telephone) standardiste *mf*
(b) (of radio, computer) opérateur *m*
(c) **he's a smooth** ∼ il sait s'y prendre

opinion *n* opinion *f* (**about** de), avis *m*

(about, on sur**); to have a high/low ~ of
sb/sth** avoir une bonne/mauvaise opinion
de qn/qch; **in my ~** à mon avis

opinionated adj **to be ~** avoir des avis
sur tout

opinion poll n sondage m d'opinion

opponent n (in contest) adversaire mf; (of
regime) opposant/-e m/f **(of** à)

opportune adj ⟨moment⟩ opportun/-e

opportunist n, adj opportuniste (mf)

opportunity n occasion f **(for** de); **to take
the ~ to do** profiter de l'occasion pour faire

oppose ① vtr s'opposer à ⟨plan, bill⟩; **to
be ~d to sth/to doing** être contre qch/contre
l'idée de faire
  ② **opposing** pres p adj ⟨party, team⟩
  adverse; ⟨view, style⟩ opposé/-e
  ③ **as opposed to** phr par opposition à

opposite ① n contraire m **(to, of** de)
  ② adj (gen) opposé/-e; ⟨building⟩ d'en face;
  ⟨page⟩ ci-contre; ⟨effect⟩ inverse; **at ~ ends
  of** aux deux bouts de ⟨table, street⟩
  ③ adv en face; **directly ~** juste en face
  ④ prep en face de ⟨building, park, person⟩

opposite number n (gen) homologue m;
(Sport) adversaire mf

opposition n opposition f **(to** à); **the
Opposition** (in politics) l'opposition f

oppress vtr opprimer ⟨people, nation⟩

oppressive adj **(a)** ⟨law⟩ oppressif/-ive
  (b) ⟨heat, atmosphere⟩ oppressant/-e

opt vi **to ~ for sth** opter pour qch; **to ~ to
do** choisir de faire
  ■ **opt out** décider de ne pas participer **(of** à)

optical adj optique

optical illusion n illusion f d'optique

optician n (selling glasses) opticien/-ienne
m/f; (eye specialist) (GB) optométriste mf

optimism n optimisme m

optimist n optimiste mf

optimistic adj optimiste **(about** quant à)

optimize vtr optimiser

optimum n, adj optimum (m)

option n option f **(to do** de faire); **to have
the ~ of doing** pouvoir choisir de faire; **I
didn't have much ~** je n'avais guère le choix

optional adj facultatif/-ive; **~ extras**
accessoires mpl en option

or conj **(a)** (gen) ou; **black ~ white?** noir ou
blanc?; **either here ~ at Dave's** soit ici soit
chez Dave; **whether he likes it ~ not** que
cela lui plaise ou non; **in a week ~ so** dans
huit jours environ; **~ should I say** ou bien
devrais-je dire
  (b) (linking alternatives in the negative) **I can't
  come today ~ tomorrow** je ne peux venir ni
  aujourd'hui ni demain; **without food ~
  lodgings** sans nourriture ni abri
  (c) (otherwise) sinon, autrement

oral ① n oral m
  ② adj ⟨examination, communication,
  contraceptive⟩ oral/-e; ⟨medicine⟩ par voie
  orale

orange ① n **(a)** (fruit) orange f
  (b) (colour) orange m
  ② adj orange inv

orange juice n jus m d'orange

orbit ① n orbite f
  ② vtr décrire une orbite autour de ⟨sun,
  planet⟩

orchard n verger m

orchestra n orchestre m

orchestrate vtr orchestrer

orchid n orchidée f

ordain vtr **(a)** (decree) décréter **(that** que)
  (b) ordonner ⟨priest⟩

ordeal n épreuve f

order ① n **(a)** (gen) ordre m; **in alphabetical
  ~** dans l'ordre alphabétique; **to restore ~**
  rétablir l'ordre
  (b) (command) ordre m **(to do** de faire); **to be
  under ~s to do** avoir (l')ordre de faire
  (c) (in shop, restaurant) commande f
  (d) (operational state) **in working ~** en état de
  marche; **to be out of ~** ⟨phone line⟩ être en
  dérangement; ⟨lift, machine⟩ être en panne
  (e) (all right) **in ~** ⟨documents⟩ en règle; **that
  remark was way out of ~** cette remarque
  était tout à fait déplacée
  (f) (also **religious ~**) ordre m
  ② vtr **(a)** (command) ordonner; **to ~ sb to do**
  ordonner à qn de faire
  (b) commander ⟨goods, meal⟩; réserver
  ⟨taxi⟩ **(for** pour)
  ③ vi ⟨diner, customer⟩ commander
  ④ **in order that** phr (with the same subject)
  afin de (+ infinitive), pour (+ infinitive);
  (when subject of verb changes) afin que
  (+ subjunctive), pour que (+ subjunctive)
  ⑤ **in order to** phr pour, afin de
  ■ **order about, order around: to ~
  people around** donner des ordres

order form n bon m or bulletin m de
commande

orderly ① n (medical) aide-soignant/-e m/f
  ② adj ⟨queue⟩ ordonné/-e; ⟨pattern, row⟩
  régulier/-ière; ⟨mind, system⟩ méthodique;
  ⟨crowd, demonstration⟩ calme

ordinary ① n **to be out of the ~** sortir de
l'ordinaire
  ② adj **(a)** (normal) ⟨family, life, person⟩
  ordinaire; ⟨clothes⟩ de tous les jours
  (b) (average) ⟨consumer, family⟩ moyen/-enne
  (c) (uninspiring) quelconque (derogatory)

ore n minerai m; **iron ~** minerai de fer

organ n **(a)** (gen) organe m
  (b) (Mus) orgue m

organ donor n donneur/-euse m/f
d'organes

organic adj ⟨substance, development⟩
organique; ⟨produce, farming⟩ biologique

organism n organisme m

organization n **(a)** (group) organisation f;
(government) organisme m; (voluntary)
association f
  (b) (arrangement) organisation f **(of** de)

o

organize *vtr* organiser ⟨*event, time, life*⟩; ranger ⟨*books, papers*⟩

organized crime *n* grand banditisme *m*

organizer *n* (a) (person) organisateur/-trice *m/f*
(b) (*also* **personal** ~) (agenda *m*) organisateur *m*; **electronic** ~ agenda électronique

organ transplant *n* transplantation *f* d'organe

orgy *n* orgie *f*

orient ① *n* the Orient l'Orient *m*
② *vtr* (*also* **orientate**) orienter (**towards** vers)

oriental *adj* (gen) oriental/-e; ⟨*appearance, eyes*⟩ d'Oriental; ⟨*carpet*⟩ d'Orient

orienteering *n* course *f* d'orientation

origin *n* origine *f*

original ① *n* original *m*
② *adj* (a) (gen) original/-e
(b) (initial) ⟨*inhabitant, owner*⟩ premier/-ière (*before n*); ⟨*question, site*⟩ originel/-elle

originality *n* originalité *f*

originally *adv* (a) (initially) au départ
(b) (in the first place) à l'origine

originate *vi* ⟨*custom, style, tradition*⟩ voir le jour; ⟨*fire*⟩ se déclarer; **to** ~ **from** ⟨*goods*⟩ provenir de

originator *n* (a) (of idea, rumour) auteur *m*
(b) (of invention, system) créateur/-trice *m/f*

ornament *n* (a) (trinket) bibelot *m*
(b) (ornamentation) ornement *m*

ornamental *adj* ⟨*plant*⟩ ornemental/-e; ⟨*lake*⟩ d'agrément; ⟨*motif*⟩ décoratif/-ive

ornate *adj* richement orné/-e

ornithology *n* ornithologie *f*

orphan *n* orphelin/-e *m/f*

orphanage *n* orphelinat *m*

orthodox *adj* orthodoxe

orthopaedic (GB), **orthopedic** (US) *adj* orthopédique

ostentatious *adj* ostentatoire

osteopath *n* ostéopathe *mf*

ostracize *vtr* ostraciser

ostrich *n* autruche *f*

other ① *adj* autre; **the** ~ **one** l'autre; **the** ~ **25** les 25 autres; ~ **people** les autres; **he was going the** ~ **way** il allait dans la direction opposée; **the** ~ **day** l'autre jour; **every** ~ **year** tous les deux ans; **every** ~ **Saturday** un samedi sur deux
② *pron* **the** ~**s** les autres; ~**s** (as subject) d'autres; (as object) les autres; **one after the** ~ l'un après l'autre; **someone or** ~ quelqu'un; **some book or** ~ un livre, je ne sais plus lequel; **somehow or** ~ d'une manière ou d'une autre
③ **other than** *phr* ~ **than that** à part ça; **nobody knows** ~ **than you** tu es le seul à le savoir

otherwise ① *adv* autrement; **no woman, married or** ~ aucune femme, mariée ou non

② *conj* sinon; **it's quite safe,** ~ **I wouldn't do it** ce n'est pas dangereux du tout, sinon je ne le ferais pas

otter *n* loutre *f*

ouch *excl* aïe!

ought *modal aux* **I** ~ **to do/to have done** je devrais/j'aurais dû faire; **that** ~ **to fix it** ça devrait arranger les choses; **oughtn't we to ask?** ne croyez-vous pas que nous devrions demander?; **we** ~ **to say something** nous devrions dire quelque chose; **someone** ~ **to have accompanied her** quelqu'un aurait dû l'accompagner

ounce *n* once *f* (= 28.35 g)

our *det* notre/nos

■ Note In French, determiners agree in gender and number with the noun that follows. So *our* is translated by *notre* + masculine or feminine singular noun (notre chien, notre maison) and *nos* + plural noun (nos enfants).
– When *our* is stressed, *à nous* is added after the noun: OUR house = notre maison à nous.

ours *pron*

■ Note In French, possessive pronouns reflect the number and gender of the noun they are standing for. Thus *ours* is translated by *le nôtre, la nôtre* or *les nôtres* according to what is being referred to.

their children are older than ~ leurs enfants sont plus âgés que les nôtres; **which tickets are** ~? lesquels de ces billets sont les nôtres *or* à nous?; **a friend of** ~ un ami à nous; **the blue car is** ~ la voiture bleue est à nous; **it's not** ~ ce n'est pas à nous

ourselves *pron* (a) (reflexive) nous; **we've hurt** ~ nous nous sommes fait mal
(b) (emphatic) nous-mêmes; **we did it** ~ nous l'avons fait nous-mêmes
(c) (after prepositions) **for** ~ pour nous, pour nous-mêmes; (all) **by** ~ tout seuls/toutes seules

out

■ Note When *out* is used as an adverb meaning *outside*, it often adds little to the sense of the phrase: they're out in the garden = they're in the garden. In such cases *out* will not usually be translated: ils sont dans le jardin.

① *vtr* révéler l'homosexualité de ⟨*person*⟩
② *adv* (a) (outside) dehors; **to stay** ~ **in the rain** rester (dehors) sous la pluie; ~ **there** dehors
(b) **to go** *or* **walk** ~ sortir; **I couldn't find my way** ~ je ne trouvais pas la sortie; **when the tide is** ~ à marée basse; **further** ~ plus loin; **to invite sb** ~ **to dinner** inviter qn au restaurant
(c) (absent) **to be** ~ être sorti/-e
(d) **to be** ~ ⟨*book, exam results*⟩ être publié/-e
(e) **to be** ~ ⟨*sun, moon, stars*⟩ briller
(f) **to be** ~ ⟨*fire, light*⟩ être éteint/-e
(g) (Sport) **to be** ~ ⟨*player*⟩ être éliminé/-e; '~!' (of ball) 'out!'

(h) (over) **before the week is** ∼ avant la fin
de la semaine
(i) (colloq) **to be** ∼ **to do** être bien décidé/-e à
faire; **he's just** ∼ **for what he can get** c'est
l'intérêt qui le guide
3 out of *phr* **(a) to go** *or* **walk** *or* **come** ∼
of sortir de; **to jump** ∼ **of the window** sauter
par la fenêtre; **to take sth** ∼ **of one's bag**
prendre qch dans son sac
(b) (expressing ratio) sur; **two** ∼ **of every three**
deux sur trois
(c) ‹*reach, sight*›; en dehors de
‹*city*›; à l'abri de ‹*sun*›
(d) to be (right) ∼ **of** ne plus avoir de ‹*item*›
IDIOMS **to be** ∼ **of it** (colloq) être dans les
vapes (colloq)

out-and-out *adj* ‹*villain, liar*› fieffé/-e;
‹*supporter*› pur/-e et dur/-e; ‹*success, failure*›
total/-e

outback *n* **the** ∼ la brousse (australienne)

outboard motor *n* moteur *m* hors-bord

outbreak *n* (of war) début *m*; (of violence,
spots) éruption *f*; (of disease) déclaration *f*

outbuilding *n* dépendance *f*

outburst *n* accès *m*

outcast *n* exclu/-e *m/f*

outcome *n* résultat *m*

outcry *n* tollé *m* (**about, against** contre)

outdated *adj* ‹*idea, practice, theory*›
dépassé/-e; ‹*clothing*› démodé/-e

outdo *vtr* surpasser

outdoor *adj* ‹*life, activity, sport*› de plein
air; ‹*restaurant*› en plein air

outdoors *adv* ‹*sit, work, play*› dehors;
‹*live*› en plein air; ‹*sleep*› à la belle étoile; **to
go** ∼ sortir

outer *adj* **(a)** (outside) extérieur/-e
(b) ‹*limit*› extrême

outer space *n* espace *m*
(extra-atmosphérique)

outfit *n* tenue *f*

outgoing *adj* **(a)** (sociable) ouvert/-e et
sociable
(b) ‹*government*› sortant/-e

outgoings *n pl* (GB) sorties *fpl* (de fonds)

outgrow *vtr* **(a)** (grow too big for) devenir
trop grand pour
(b) (grow too old for) se lasser de [qch] avec le
temps; **he'll** ∼ **it** ça lui passera

outlandish *adj* bizarre

outlast *vtr* durer plus longtemps que

outlaw **1** *n* hors-la-loi *m inv*
2 *vtr* déclarer illégal/-e ‹*practice,
organization*›

outlay *n* dépenses *fpl* (**on** en)

outlet *n* **(a)** (for gas, air, water) tuyau *m* de
sortie
(b) retail ∼ point *m* de vente
(c) (for emotion, talent) exutoire *m*
(d) (US) (socket) prise *f* de courant

outline **1** *n* **(a)** (silhouette) contour *m*
(b) (of plan, policy) grandes lignes *fpl*; (of essay)
plan *m*

2 *vtr* exposer brièvement ‹*aims, plan,
reasons*›

outlive *vtr* survivre à ‹*person*›

outlook *n* **(a)** (attitude) vue *f*
(b) (prospects) perspectives *fpl*

outlying *adj* (away from city centre)
excentré/-e; (remote) isolé/-e

outnumber *vtr* être plus nombreux/-euses
que

out-of-body experience *n* **to have an**
∼ faire une projection hors du corps

out-of-date *adj* ‹*ticket, passport*›
périmé/-e; ‹*concept*› dépassé/-e

outpatient *n* malade *mf* externe; ∼**s'**
department service *m* de consultation

outpost *n* avant-poste *m*

output *n* (yield) rendement *m*; (of factory)
production *f*

outrage **1** *n* **(a)** (anger) indignation *f* (**at**
devant)
(b) (atrocity) atrocité *f*
(c) (scandal) scandale *m*
2 *vtr* scandaliser ‹*public*›

outrageous *adj* scandaleux/-euse;
‹*remark*› outrancier/-ière

outright **1** *adj* ‹*control, majority*›
absolu/-e; ‹*ban*› catégorique; ‹*victory,
winner*› incontesté/-e
2 *adv* (gen) catégoriquement; ‹*killed*› sur le
coup

outset *n* **at the** ∼ au début; **from the** ∼ dès
le début

outside **1** *n* **(a)** extérieur *m*; **on the** ∼ à
l'extérieur
(b) (maximum) **at the** ∼ au maximum
2 *adj* extérieur/-e; ∼ **lane** (in GB) voie *f* de
droite; (in US, Europe) voie *f* de gauche; (on
athletics track) couloir *m* extérieur; **an** ∼
chance une faible chance
3 *adv* dehors
4 *prep* (*also* ∼ **of**) **(a)** en dehors de ‹*city*›;
de l'autre côté de ‹*boundary*›; à l'extérieur
de ‹*building*›
(b) (in front of) devant ‹*house, shop*›

outsider *n* **(a)** (in community) étranger/-ère
m/f
(b) (Sport) outsider *m*

outsize *adj* ‹*clothes*› grande taille

outskirts *n pl* périphérie *f*

outsource *vtr* sous-traiter

outsourcing *n* sous-traitance *f*

outspoken *adj* **to be** ∼ parler sans
détour

outstanding *adj* **(a)** (praiseworthy)
remarquable
(b) (striking) frappant/-e
(c) ‹*bill*› impayé/-e; ‹*work*› inachevé/-e; ∼
debts créances *fpl* à recouvrer

outstay *vtr* **to** ∼ **one's welcome**
s'éterniser

outstretched *adj* ‹*hand, arm*› tendu/-e;
‹*wings*› déployé/-e

outstrip *vtr* dépasser ‹*person*›; excéder
‹*production, demand*›

O

outward [1] adj ⟨appearance, sign⟩
extérieur/-e; ⟨calm⟩ apparent/-e; ~ **journey**
aller m
[2] adv (also **outwards**) vers l'extérieur

outwardly adv (apparently) en apparence

outwards = OUTWARD 2

outweigh vtr l'emporter sur

outwit vtr être plus futé/-e que ⟨person⟩

outworker n travailleur/-euse m/f à
domicile

oval n, adj ovale (m)

ovary n ovaire m

ovation n ovation f; **to give sb a standing**
~ se lever pour ovationner qn

oven n four m

oven glove n manique f

over

■ Note over is often used with another
preposition (to, in, on) without altering
the meaning. In this case over is usually not
translated in French: to be over in France = être
en France; to swim over to sb = nager vers qn.

[1] prep (a) par-dessus; **he jumped** ~ il a
sauté par-dessus; **to wear a sweater** ~ **one's
shirt** porter un pull par-dessus sa chemise; **a
bridge** ~ **the Thames** un pont sur la Tamise
(b) (across) **it's just** ~ **the road** c'est juste de
l'autre côté de la rue; ~ **here/there** par ici/
là; **come** ~ **here!** viens (par) ici!
(c) (above) au-dessus de; **they live** ~ **the shop**
ils habitent au-dessus de la boutique;
children ~ **six** les enfants de plus de six ans;
temperatures ~ **40°** des températures
supérieures à or au-dessus de 40°
(d) (in the course of) ~ **the weekend** pendant
le week-end; ~ **the last few days** au cours de
ces derniers jours; ~ **the years** avec le
temps; ~ **Christmas** à Noël
(e) **to be** ~ s'être remis/-e de ⟨illness,
operation⟩; **to be** ~ **the worst** avoir passé le
pire
(f) (by means of) ~ **the phone** par téléphone;
~ **the radio** à la radio
(g) (everywhere) **all** ~ **the house** partout dans
la maison
[2] adj, adv (a) (finished) **to be** ~ ⟨term,
meeting⟩ être terminé/-e; ⟨war⟩ être fini/-e
(b) (more) **children of six and** ~ les enfants
de plus de six ans
(c) **to invite** or **ask sb** ~ inviter qn; **we had
them** ~ **on Sunday** ils sont venus dimanche
(d) (on radio, TV) ~ **to you** à vous; **now** ~ **to
our Paris studios** nous passons l'antenne à
nos studios de Paris
(e) (showing repetition) **five times** ~ cinq fois de
suite; **to start all** ~ **again** recommencer à
zéro; **I had to do it** ~ (US) j'ai dû
recommencer; **I've told you** ~ **and** ~
(again)... je t'ai dit je ne sais combien de
fois...

overact vi en faire trop

overall [1] n (GB) (coat-type) blouse f; (child's)
tablier m

[2] **overalls** n pl (GB) combinaison f; (US)
salopette f
[3] adj ⟨cost⟩ global/-e; ⟨improvement⟩
général/-e; ⟨effect⟩ d'ensemble; ⟨majority⟩
absolu/-e
[4] adv (a) (in total) en tout
(b) (in general) dans l'ensemble

overawe vtr intimider

overbalance vi ⟨person⟩ perdre
l'équilibre; ⟨pile of objects⟩ s'écrouler

overboard adv par-dessus bord, à l'eau

overbook vtr, vi surréserver

overcast adj ⟨sky⟩ couvert/-e

overcharge vtr faire payer trop cher à

overcoat n pardessus m

overcome [1] vtr battre ⟨opponent⟩;
vaincre ⟨enemy⟩; surmonter ⟨dislike, fear⟩; **to
be** ~ **with despair** succomber au désespoir
[2] vi triompher

overcook vtr trop cuire

overcrowded adj ⟨train, room⟩ bondé/-e;
⟨city⟩ surpeuplé/-e; ⟨class⟩ surchargé/-e

overcrowding n (in city, institution)
surpeuplement m; (in transport)
surencombrement m; ~ **in classrooms** les
classes surchargées

overdo vtr **to** ~ **it** (when describing) exagérer;
(when performing) forcer la note (colloq); (when
working) en faire trop

overdose, OD [1] n (large dose) surdose f;
(lethal dose) (of medicine) dose f mortelle; (of
drugs) overdose f; **to take an** ~ absorber une
dose excessive de médicaments
[2] vi (on medicine) prendre une dose mortelle
de médicaments; (on drugs) faire une overdose

overdraft n découvert m

overdrawn adj à découvert

overdressed adj trop habillé/-e

overdrive n **to go into** ~ ⟨person⟩ s'activer
intensivement

overdue adj ⟨baby, work⟩ en retard (**by**
de); ⟨bill⟩ impayé/-e; **this measure is long** ~
cette mesure aurait dû être prise il y a
longtemps

overeat vi manger à l'excès

overestimate vtr surestimer

overexcited adj surexcité/-e

overflow [1] vtr ⟨river⟩ inonder ⟨banks⟩
[2] vi déborder (**into** dans; **with** de)

overgrown adj ⟨garden⟩ envahi/-e par la
végétation

overhaul [1] n (of machine) révision f; (of
system) restructuration f
[2] vtr réviser ⟨car, machine⟩; restructurer
⟨system⟩

overhead [1] adj ⟨cable, railway⟩
aérien/-ienne
[2] adv (a) (in sky) dans le ciel
(b) (above sb's head) au-dessus de ma/sa etc
tête

overhead projector n rétroprojecteur
m

overheads n pl frais mpl généraux

overhear *vtr* entendre par hasard
overheat *vi* ⟨*car, equipment*⟩ chauffer
overindulge *vi* faire des excès
overjoyed *adj* fou/folle de joie (**at** devant)
overkill *n* (excess publicity) matraquage *m*
overland ① *adj* ⟨*route*⟩ terrestre;
⟨*journey*⟩ par route
② *adv* par route
overlap *vi* se chevaucher
overleaf *adv* au verso
overload *vtr* surcharger (**with** de)
overlook *vtr* (a) ⟨*building, window*⟩
donner sur
(b) (miss) ne pas voir ⟨*detail, error*⟩; **to ~ the
fact that** négliger le fait que
(c) (ignore) ignorer ⟨*effect, need*⟩
overnight ① *adj* (a) ⟨*journey, train*⟩ de
nuit; ⟨*stop*⟩ pour une nuit
(b) ⟨*success*⟩ immédiat/-e
② *adv* (a) **to stay ~** passer la nuit
(b) ⟨*change, disappear, transform*⟩ du jour
au lendemain
overnight bag *n* petit sac *m* de voyage
overpopulated *adj* surpeuplé/-e
overpower *vtr* (a) maîtriser ⟨*thief*⟩;
vaincre ⟨*army*⟩
(b) ⟨*smell, smoke*⟩ accabler
overpowering *adj* ⟨*person*⟩
intimidant/-e; ⟨*desire, urge*⟩ irrésistible;
⟨*heat*⟩ accablant/-e; ⟨*smell*⟩ irrespirable
overpriced *adj* **it's ~** c'est trop cher pour
ce que c'est
overqualified *adj* surqualifié/-e
overrated *adj* ⟨*person, work*⟩ surfait/-e
overreact *vi* réagir de façon excessive
override *vtr* l'emporter sur
⟨*consideration*⟩; passer outre à ⟨*decision*⟩
overriding *adj* ⟨*importance*⟩ primordial/-e;
⟨*priority*⟩ numéro un
overrule *vtr* **to be ~d** ⟨*decision*⟩ être
annulé/-e
overrun *vtr* (a) (invade) envahir ⟨*country,
site*⟩
(b) (exceed) dépasser ⟨*time, budget*⟩
overseas ① *adj* (a) ⟨*student, investor*⟩
étranger/-ère
(b) ⟨*trade, market*⟩ extérieur/-e
② *adv* à l'étranger
overshadow *vtr* éclipser ⟨*achievement*⟩
oversight *n* erreur *f*; **due to an ~** par
inadvertance
oversimplify *vtr* simplifier [qch] à l'excès
oversleep *vi* se réveiller trop tard
overspend *vi* trop dépenser
overstay *vtr* **to ~ one's visa** dépasser la
limite de validité de son visa
overstep *vtr* dépasser ⟨*bounds*⟩; **to ~ the
mark** aller trop loin
overt *adj* évident/-e, manifeste

overtake *vtr, vi* dépasser
over-the-top, OTT *adj* (colloq)
outrancier/-ière; **to go over the top** aller
trop loin
overthrow *vtr* renverser ⟨*government,
system*⟩
overtime ① *n* heures *fpl* supplémentaires
② *adv* **to work ~** ⟨*person*⟩ faire des heures
supplémentaires
overtone *n* sous-entendu *m*, connotation *f*
overture *n* ouverture *f*
overturn ① *vtr* (a) renverser ⟨*car, chair*⟩;
faire chavirer ⟨*boat*⟩
(b) faire annuler ⟨*decision, sentence*⟩
② *vi* ⟨*car, chair*⟩ se renverser; ⟨*boat*⟩
chavirer
overweight *adj* (a) ⟨*person*⟩ trop gros/
grosse
(b) ⟨*suitcase*⟩ trop lourd/-e
overwhelm ① *vtr* (a) ⟨*wave, avalanche*⟩
submerger; ⟨*enemy*⟩ écraser
(b) ⟨*shame, grief*⟩ accabler
② **overwhelmed** *pp adj* (with letters, offers,
kindness) submergé/-e (**with, by** de); (with
shame, work) accablé/-e (**with, by** de); (by sight,
experience) ébloui/-e (**by** par)
overwhelming *adj* ⟨*defeat, victory,
majority*⟩ écrasant/-e; ⟨*desire*⟩ irrésistible;
⟨*heat, sorrow*⟩ accablant/-e; ⟨*support*⟩
massif/-ive
overwork *vi* se surmener
overworked *adj* surmené/-e
owe *vtr* devoir; **to ~ sth to sb** devoir qch à
qn
owing ① *adj* à payer, dû/-e
② **owing to** *phr* en raison de
owl *n* hibou *m*; (with tufted ears) chouette *f*
own ① *adj* propre; **her ~ car** sa propre
voiture
② *pron* **my ~** le mien, la mienne; **his/her ~**
le sien, la sienne; **he has a room of his ~** il
a sa propre chambre *or* une chambre à lui;
a house of our (very) ~ une maison (bien) à
nous
③ *vtr* avoir ⟨*car, house, dog*⟩; **she ~s three
shops** elle est propriétaire de trois
magasins; **who ~s that house?** à qui est
cette maison?
IDIOMS **to get one's ~ back** se venger (**on
sb** de qn); **on one's ~** tout seul/toute seule
■ **own up** avouer
owner *n* propriétaire *mf*; **car ~**
automobiliste *mf*; **home ~** propriétaire *mf*
ownership *n* propriété *f*; (of land)
possession *f*
ox *n* bœuf *m*
oxygen *n* oxygène *m*
oyster *n* huitre *f*
ozone *n* ozone *m*
ozone layer *n* couche *f* d'ozone

Pp

p, **P** n p, P m

PA n (abbr = **personal assistant**) secrétaire mf de direction

pace 1 n (step) pas m; (rate) rythme m; (speed) vitesse f; **at a fast/slow ~** vite/lentement; **at walking ~** au pas
2 vi **to ~ up and down** faire les cent pas; **to ~ up and down** arpenter ⟨cage, room⟩

pacemaker n (a) (Med) stimulateur m cardiaque
(b) (athlete) lièvre m

Pacific pr n **the ~** le Pacifique; **the ~ Ocean** l'océan Pacifique

pacifist n, adj pacifiste (mf)

pacify vtr apaiser ⟨person⟩; pacifier ⟨country⟩

pack 1 n (a) (box) paquet m; (large box) boîte f; (bag) sachet m
(b) (group) bande f; (of hounds) meute f; **a ~ of lies** un tissu de mensonges
(c) (in rugby) pack m
(d) (of cards) jeu m de cartes
(e) (backpack) sac m à dos
2 vtr (a) (in suitcase) mettre [qch] dans une valise ⟨clothes⟩; (in box, crate) emballer ⟨ornaments, books⟩
(b) emballer ⟨box, crate⟩; **to ~ one's suitcase** faire sa valise
(c) ⟨crowd⟩ remplir complètement ⟨church, theatre⟩
(d) tasser ⟨snow, earth⟩
3 vi (a) ⟨person⟩ faire ses valises
(b) **to ~ into** ⟨crowd⟩ s'entasser dans ⟨place⟩
■ **pack up**: ¶ **~ up** (a) ⟨person⟩ faire ses valises
(b) (colloq) (break down) ⟨TV, machine⟩ se détraquer (colloq); ⟨car⟩ tomber en panne
¶ **~ [sth] up, ~ up [sth]** (in boxes, crates) emballer

package 1 n (a) (parcel) paquet m, colis m
(b) (of proposals, measures, aid) ensemble m (of de)
(c) (Comput) progiciel m
2 vtr conditionner, emballer

package deal n offre f globale

package holiday (GB), **package tour** n voyage m organisé

packaging n conditionnement m

packed adj comble; **~ with** plein/-e de

packed lunch n panier-repas m

packet n (gen) paquet m; (sachet) sachet m

packing n (a) (packaging) emballage m
(b) **to do one's ~** faire ses valises

pact n pacte m

pad 1 n (a) (of paper) bloc m
(b) (for leg) jambière f
(c) (of paw) coussinet m; (of finger) pulpe f

(d) (also **launch ~**) rampe f de lancement
2 vtr rembourrer ⟨chair, shoulders, jacket⟩ (with avec); capitonner ⟨walls⟩
3 vi **to ~ along/around** avancer/aller et venir à pas feutrés
■ **pad out** étoffer, délayer ⟨essay, speech⟩

padded envelope n enveloppe f matelassée

padding n (stuffing) rembourrage m

paddle 1 n (a) (oar) pagaie f
(b) **to go for a ~** faire trempette f
2 vi (a) (row) pagayer
(b) (wade) patauger
(c) ⟨duck, swan⟩ barboter

paddling pool n (public) pataugeoire f; (inflatable) piscine f gonflable

padlock 1 n (on door) cadenas m; (for bicycle) antivol m
2 vtr cadenasser ⟨door, gate⟩; mettre un antivol à ⟨bicycle⟩

paediatrician (GB), **pediatrician** (US) n pédiatre mf

paedophile (GB), **pedophile** (US) n pédophile mf

pagan n, adj païen/païenne (m/f)

page 1 n (a) (in book) page f; **on ~ two** à la page deux
(b) (attendant) groom m; (US) coursier m
2 vtr (on pager) rechercher; (over loudspeaker) faire appeler

pageant n (play) reconstitution f historique; (carnival) fête f à thème historique

pageboy n (at wedding) garçon m d'honneur

pager n récepteur m d'appel

paid adj ⟨work, job⟩ rémunéré/-e; ⟨holiday⟩ payé/-e; **~ assassin** tueur m à gages

pain 1 n (a) douleur f; **to be in ~** souffrir; **period ~s** règles fpl douloureuses
(b) (colloq) (annoying person, thing) **he's/it's a ~** il est/c'est enquiquinant (colloq); **he's a ~ in the neck** (colloq) il est casse-pieds (colloq)
2 **pains** n pl **to be at ~s to do** prendre grand soin de faire; **to take great ~s over** or **with sth** se donner beaucoup de mal pour qch

painful adj douloureux/-euse; ⟨lesson, memory⟩ pénible

painkiller n analgésique m

painless adj (a) (pain-free) indolore
(b) (trouble-free) sans peine

painstaking adj minutieux/-ieuse

paint 1 n peinture f
2 **paints** n pl couleurs fpl
3 vtr (a) (gen) peindre; peindre le portrait de ⟨person⟩; **to ~ one's nails** se vernir les ongles
(b) (depict) dépeindre

4 *vi* peindre
paintbox *n* boîte *f* de couleurs
paintbrush *n* pinceau *m*
painter *n* peintre *m*
painting *n* (a) (activity, art form) peinture *f*
(b) (work of art) tableau *m*; (unframed) toile *f*;
(of person) portrait *m*
(c) (decorating) peintures *fpl*
pair *n* (a) (gen) paire *f*; to be one of a ∼
faire partie d'une paire; in ∼s ⟨*work*⟩ en
groupes de deux; a ∼ of scissors une paire
de ciseaux; a ∼ of trousers un pantalon
(b) (couple) couple *m*
∎ **pair off** (as a couple) se mettre ensemble;
(for temporary purposes) se mettre par deux
∎ **pair up** ⟨*dancers, lovers*⟩ former un
couple; ⟨*competitors*⟩ faire équipe
paisley *n* tissu *m* à motifs cachemire
pajamas (US) = PYJAMAS
Pakistan *pr n* Pakistan *m*
Pakistani **1** *n* Pakistanais/-e *m/f*
2 *adj* pakistanais/-e
palace *n* palais *m*
palatable *n* ⟨*food*⟩ savoureux/-euse;
⟨*solution, idea*⟩ acceptable
palate *n* palais *m*
pale **1** *adj* (gen) pâle; ⟨*light, dawn*⟩
blafard/-e; **to turn** or **go** ∼ pâlir
2 *vi* pâlir; **to** ∼ **into insignificance** devenir
dérisoire
Palestine *pr n* Palestine *f*
Palestinian **1** *n* Palestinien/-ienne *m/f*
2 *adj* palestinien/-ienne
palette *n* palette *f*
pallet *n* (for loading) palette *f*
pallid *adj* ⟨*skin, light*⟩ blafard/-e
palm *n* (a) paume *f*; **in the** ∼ **of one's hand**
dans le creux de la main; **he read my** ∼ il
m'a lu les lignes de la main
(b) (also ∼ **tree**) palmier *m*
(c) (also ∼ **leaf**) palme *f*
∎ **palm off** (colloq): **to** ∼ **sth off** faire passer
qch (as pour); **to** ∼ **sth off on sb, to** ∼ **sb**
off with sth refiler (colloq) qch à qn
Palm Sunday *n* dimanche *m* des
Rameaux
palmtop *n* (also ∼ **computer**)
ordinateur *m* de poche
palpable *adj* ⟨*fear, tension*⟩ palpable; ⟨*lie,
error, nonsense*⟩ manifeste
palpitate *vi* palpiter (with de)
paltry *adj* ⟨*sum*⟩ dérisoire; ⟨*excuse*⟩ piètre
(before *n*)
pamper *vtr* choyer ⟨*person, pet*⟩
pamphlet *n* brochure *f*; (political) tract *m*
pan **1** *n* (saucepan) casserole *f*
2 *vtr* (a) (colloq) (criticize) éreinter
(b) (in photography) faire un panoramique de
pancake *n* crêpe *f*
pancake day *n* mardi *m* gras
pandemonium *n* tohu-bohu *m*
pander *vi* **to** ∼ **to** céder aux exigences de
⟨*person*⟩; flatter ⟨*whim*⟩

pane *n* vitre *f*, carreau *m*; **a** ∼ **of glass** une
vitre, un carreau
panel *n* (a) (of experts, judges) commission *f*;
(on discussion programme) invités *mpl*; (on quiz
show) jury *m*
(b) (section of wall) panneau *m*
(c) (of instruments, switches) tableau *m*
pang *n* (a) (emotional) serrement *m* de cœur;
a ∼ **of jealousy** une pointe de jalousie
(b) ∼s **of hunger** crampes *fpl* d'estomac
panhandler *n* (US) (colloq) mendiant/-e *m/f*
panic **1** *n* panique *f*, affolement *m*
2 *vtr* affoler ⟨*person, animal*⟩; semer la
panique dans ⟨*crowd*⟩
3 *vi* s'affoler
panic buying *n* achats *mpl* par crainte
de la pénurie
panic-stricken *adj* pris/-e de panique
panorama *n* panorama *m*
pansy *n* pensée *f*
pant *vi* haleter
panther *n* (a) (leopard) panthère *f*
(b) (US) (puma) puma *m*
pantomime *n* (GB) spectacle *m* pour
enfants
pantry *n* garde-manger *m inv*
pants *n pl* (a) (US) (trousers) pantalon *m*
(b) (GB) (underwear) slip *m*
panty hose *n* (US) collant *m*
panty-liner *n* protège-slip *m*
paper **1** *n* (a) (for writing, drawing) papier *m*;
a piece of ∼ (scrap) un bout de papier; (clean
sheet) une feuille (de papier); (for wrapping) un
morceau de papier; **writing/tissue** ∼ papier
à lettres/de soie
(b) (also **wall**∼) papier *m* peint
(c) (newspaper) journal *m*
(d) article *m* (on sur); (lecture)
communication *f* (on sur)
(e) (exam) épreuve *f* (on de)
2 papers *n pl* (documents) papiers *mpl*
3 *adj* ⟨*bag, hat, handkerchief, napkin*⟩ en
papier; ⟨*plate, cup*⟩ en carton
4 *vtr* tapisser ⟨*room, wall*⟩
paperback *n* livre *m* de poche
paperclip *n* trombone *m*
paper knife *n* coupe-papier *m inv*
paper round *n* **he does a** ∼ il livre des
journaux
paper shop *n* marchand *m* de journaux
paper towel *n* essuie-tout *m inv*
paperweight *n* presse-papier *m inv*
paperwork *n* (administration) travail *m*
administratif; (documentation) documents *mpl*
par *n* (a) **to be on a** ∼ **with** ⟨*performance*⟩
être comparable à; ⟨*person*⟩ être l'égal/-e de;
to be up to ∼ être à la hauteur; **to be below**
or **under** ∼ ⟨*performance*⟩ être en dessous de
la moyenne; ⟨*person*⟩ ne pas se sentir en
forme
(b) (in golf) par *m*
parachute **1** *n* parachute *m*
2 *vi* descendre en parachute

parachute drop n parachutage m

parachute jump n saut m en parachute

parachuting n parachutisme m

parade [1] n (a) (procession) parade f
(b) (Mil) défilé m
[2] vtr (display) faire étalage de
[3] vi défiler (**through** dans); to ~ **up and down** ‹soldier, model› défiler; ‹child› parader

parade ground n champ m de manœuvres

paradise n paradis m; **in** ~ au paradis

paradox n paradoxe m

paradoxical adj paradoxal/-e

paraffin n (a) (GB) (fuel) pétrole m
(b) (also ~ **wax**) paraffine f

paragliding n parapente m

paragon n modèle m (**of** de)

paragraph n paragraphe m

parallel [1] n (a) (gen) parallèle m
(b) (in mathematics) parallèle f
[2] adj (a) (gen) parallèle (**to, with** à)
(b) (similar) analogue (**to, with** à)
[3] adv ~ **to,** ~ **with** parallèlement à

paralyse (GB), **paralyze** (US) vtr paralyser

paralysis n paralysie f

paramedic n auxiliaire mf médical/-e

parameter n paramètre m

paramilitary [1] n membre m d'une organisation paramilitaire
[2] adj paramilitaire

paramount adj **to be** ~, **to be of** ~ **importance** être d'une importance capitale

paranoid adj (Med) paranoïde; (gen) paranoïaque (**about** au sujet de)

paraphernalia n attirail m

paraphrase vtr paraphraser

parascending n parachutisme m ascensionnel

parasite n parasite m

paratrooper n parachutiste m

parcel n paquet m, colis m
IDIOMS **to be part and** ~ **of** faire partie intégrante de
■ **parcel up:** ~ **up** [sth], ~ [sth] **up** emballer

parcel bomb n colis m piégé

parched adj (a) (dry) desséché/-e
(b) (thirsty) **to be** ~ mourir de soif

parchment n (document) parchemin m; (paper) papier-parchemin m

pardon [1] n (a) (gen) pardon m
(b) (Law) (also **free** ~) grâce f
[2] excl (what?) pardon?; (sorry!) pardon!
[3] vtr (a) (gen) pardonner; ~ **me!** pardon!
(b) (Law) gracier ‹criminal›

parent n parent m

parental adj des parents, parental/-e

parent company n maison f mère

parenthood n (fatherhood) paternité f; (motherhood) maternité f

parenting n éducation f des enfants

parents' evening n réunion f pour les parents d'élèves

Paris pr n Paris

parish n (a) (gen) paroisse f
(b) (GB) (administrative) commune f

Parisian [1] n Parisien/-ienne m/f
[2] adj parisien/-ienne

park [1] n (a) (public garden) jardin m public, parc m
(b) (estate) parc m
[2] vtr garer ‹car›
[3] vi ‹driver› se garer
[4] **parked** pp adj en stationnement

park-and-ride n parking m relais

parking n stationnement m; '**No** ~' 'stationnement interdit'

parking lot n (US) parking m

parking meter n parcmètre m

parking place, parking space n place f

parking ticket n (fine) contravention f, PV m (colloq)

parliament n parlement m

parliamentary adj parlementaire

parlour (GB), **parlor** (US) n petit salon m

parody [1] n parodie f
[2] vtr parodier ‹person, style›

parole n liberté f conditionnelle; **on** ~ en liberté conditionnelle

parrot n perroquet m

parry vtr (a) (Sport) parer
(b) éluder ‹question›

parsley n persil m

parsnip n panais m

part [1] n (a) (of whole) partie f; (of country) région f; **to be** (a) ~ **of** faire partie de; **that's the best/hardest** ~ c'est ça le meilleur/le plus dur; **for the most** ~ dans l'ensemble
(b) (Tech) (component) pièce f; **spare** ~**s** pièces détachées
(c) (of serial) épisode m
(d) (role) rôle m (**in** dans); **to take** ~ participer (**in** à)
(e) (actor's role) rôle m (**of** de)
(f) (measure) mesure f
(g) (behalf) **on the** ~ **of** de la part de; **for my** ~ pour ma part
(h) (US) (in hair) raie f
[2] adv en partie; ~ **French,** ~ **Chinese** moitié français, moitié Chinois
[3] vtr séparer ‹two people›; écarter ‹legs›; entrouvrir ‹lips, curtains›; **to** ~ **one's hair** se faire une raie
[4] vi (a) (split up) se séparer; **to** ~ **from sb** quitter qn
(b) ‹crowd, clouds› s'ouvrir
■ **part with** se séparer de ‹object›; **to** ~ **with money** débourser

part exchange n (GB) reprise f; **to take sth in** ~ reprendre qch

partial adj (a) (not complete) partiel/-ielle
(b) (biased) partial/-e
(c) (fond) **to be** ~ **to** avoir un faible pour

partially sighted n the ~ les malvoyants mpl

participant n participant/-e m/f (in à)

participate vi participer (in à)

participation n participation f (in à)

participle n participe m

particle n particule f

particular ⨡ adj (a) (gen) particulier/-ière; **for no ~ reason** sans raison particulière
(b) (fussy) méticuleux/-euse; **to be ~ about** être exigeant/-e sur ⟨cleanliness, punctuality⟩; prendre grand soin de ⟨appearance⟩; être difficile pour ⟨food⟩
⨢ **in particular** phr en particulier

particularly adv (a) (in particular) en particulier
(b) (especially) spécialement

particulars n pl (information) détails mpl; (name, address) coordonnées fpl

parting n (a) séparation f
(b) (GB) (in hair) raie f

partisan n (gen, Mil) partisan m

partition ⨡ n (a) (in room, house) cloison f
(b) (of country) partition f
⨢ vtr (a) cloisonner ⟨area, room⟩
(b) diviser ⟨country⟩

partly adv en partie

partner n (a) (professional) associé/-e m/f (in dans)
(b) (economic, political, sporting) partenaire m
(c) (married) époux/-se m/f; (unmarried) partenaire m/f

partnership n association f; **to go into ~ with** s'associer à

part of speech n partie f du discours

part-time adj, adv à temps partiel

party n (a) (social event) fête f; (in evening) soirée f; (formal) réception f; **to have a ~** faire une fête; **birthday ~** (fête d')anniversaire m; **children's ~** goûter m d'enfants
(b) (group) groupe m; (Mil) détachement m; **rescue ~** équipe f de secouristes
(c) (in politics) parti m
(d) (Law) partie f

party dress n robe f de soirée; (for child) belle robe f

party line n (a) **the ~** la ligne du parti
(b) (phone line) ligne f commune

party political broadcast n: émission dans laquelle un parti expose sa politique

pass ⨡ n (a) (permit) laisser-passer m inv; (for journalists) coupe-file m inv; **travel ~** carte f d'abonnement
(b) (Sch, Univ) (in exam) moyenne f (in en); **to get a ~** être reçu/-e
(c) (Sport) (in ball games) passe f; (in fencing) botte f
(d) (in mountains) col m
⨢ vtr (a) (gen) passer ⟨plate, ball, time⟩
(b) passer ⟨checkpoint, customs⟩; passer

devant ⟨building, area⟩; dépasser ⟨vehicle, level, expectation⟩; **to ~ sb in the street** croiser qn dans la rue
(c) ⟨person⟩ réussir ⟨test, exam⟩; ⟨car, machine⟩ passer [qch] (avec succès) ⟨test⟩
(d) adopter ⟨bill, motion⟩
(e) admettre ⟨candidate⟩
(f) prononcer ⟨sentence⟩
⨤ vi (a) passer; (in exam) réussir
IDIOMS **to make a ~ at sb** faire du plat (colloq) à qn
■ **pass around, pass round** faire circuler ⟨document, photos⟩; faire passer ⟨food, plates⟩
■ **pass away** décéder
■ **pass by** ⟨procession⟩ défiler; ⟨person⟩ passer
■ **pass down** transmettre (from de; to à)
■ **pass off** faire passer ⟨person, incident⟩ (as pour)
■ **pass on** transmettre ⟨condolences, message⟩; passer ⟨clothes, cold⟩ (to à)
■ **pass out** (faint) perdre connaissance; (fall drunk) tomber ivre mort
■ **pass through** traverser

passable adj (a) ⟨standard, quality⟩ passable; ⟨knowledge, performance⟩ assez bon/bonne
(b) ⟨road⟩ praticable; ⟨river⟩ franchissable

passage n (a) (gen) passage
(b) (also ~way) (indoors) corridor m
(c) (journey) traversée f

passenger n (in car, plane, ship) passager/-ère m/f; (in train, bus, on underground) voyageur/-euse m/f

passerby n passant/-e m/f

passing adj (a) ⟨motorist, policeman⟩ qui passe/qui passait
(b) ⟨whim⟩ passager/-ère
(c) ⟨reference⟩ en passant inv
(d) ⟨resemblance⟩ vague (before n)

passion n passion f

passionate adj passionné/-e

passive ⨡ n the ~ le passif, la voix passive
⨢ adj passif/-ive

passkey n passe m

pass mark n moyenne f

Passover n Pâque f juive

passport n passeport m

password n mot m de passe

past ⨡ n passé m; **in the ~** dans le passé
⨢ adj (a) (preceding) ⟨weeks, months⟩ dernier/-ière (before n); **in the ~ two years** dans les deux dernières années; **during the ~ few days** ces derniers jours
(b) (former) ⟨times, problems, experience⟩ passé/-e; ⟨president⟩ ancien/-ienne (before n); ⟨government⟩ précédent/-e; **in times ~** autrefois, jadis
(c) **summer is ~** l'été est fini; **that's all ~** c'est du passé
⨤ prep (a) **to walk** or **go ~ sb/sth** passer devant qn/qch; **to drive ~ sth** passer devant qch (en voiture) ⋯▸

(b) (in time) **it's ~ 6** il est 6 heures passées; **twenty ~ two** deux heures vingt; **half ~ two** deux heures et demie; **he is ~ 70** il a 70 ans passés
(c) (beyond) après; **~ the church** après l'église; **to be ~ caring** ne plus s'en faire
4 *adv* **to go** *or* **walk ~** passer
IDIOMS **to be ~ it** (colloq) avoir passé l'âge; **to be ~ its best** ⟨*food*⟩ être un peu avancé/-e; ⟨*wine*⟩ être un peu éventé/-e; **I wouldn't put it ~ him (to do)** ça ne m'étonnerait pas de lui (qu'il fasse)

pasta *n* pâtes *fpl* (alimentaires)

paste **1** *n* **(a)** (glue) colle *f*
(b) (mixture) pâte *f*
(c) (Culin) (fish, meat) pâté *m*; (vegetable) purée *f*
2 *vtr* (gen, Comput) coller (**onto** sur; **into** dans; **together** ensemble)

pastel **1** *n* pastel *m*
2 *adj* ⟨*colour, pink, shade*⟩ pastel *inv*

pasteurize *vtr* pasteuriser

pastime *n* passe-temps *m inv*

pastor *n* pasteur *m*

pastoral *n* pastoral/-e; ⟨*role, work*⟩ de conseiller/-ère

pastrami *n* bœuf *m* fumé

pastry *n* **(a)** (mixture) pâte *f*
(b) (cake) pâtisserie *f*

past tense *n* passé *m*

pasture *n* pré *m*, pâturage *m*

pat **1** *n* **(a)** (gentle tap) petite tape *f*
(b) (of butter) noix *f*
2 *vtr* tapoter ⟨*hand*⟩; caresser ⟨*dog*⟩
IDIOMS **to have sth off** (GB) *or* **down ~** connaître qch par cœur

patch **1** *n* **(a)** (in clothes) pièce *f*; (on tyre) rustine® *f*; (on eye) bandeau *m*
(b) (of snow, ice) plaque *f*; (of damp, rust, sunlight) tache *f*; (of fog) nappe *f*; (of blue sky) coin *m*
(c) (area of ground) zone *f*; (for planting) carré *m*; **a ~ of grass** un coin d'herbe
(d) (GB) (colloq) (territory) territoire *m*
(e) (colloq) (period) période *f*
2 *vtr* rapiécer ⟨*hole, trousers*⟩; réparer ⟨*tyre*⟩
■ **patch up**: ¶ **~ up [sth]**, **~ [sth] up** soigner ⟨*person*⟩; rapiécer ⟨*hole, trousers*⟩; réparer ⟨*ceiling, tyre*⟩; (fig) rafistoler (colloq) ⟨*marriage*⟩; ¶ **~ up [sth]** résoudre ⟨*differences*⟩

patchy *adj* ⟨*colour, essay, quality*⟩ inégal/-e; ⟨*knowledge*⟩ incomplet/-ète; **~ cloud** nuages *mpl* épars

paté *n* pâté *m*; **salmon ~** terrine *f* de saumon

patent **1** *n* brevet *m* (**for, on** pour)
2 *adj* (obvious) manifeste
3 *vtr* faire breveter

patent leather *n* (cuir *m*) verni *m*

paternal *adj* paternel/-elle

paternity *n* paternité *f*

paternity leave *n* congé *m* de paternité

path *n* **(a)** (track) (*also* **~way**) chemin *m*; (narrower) sentier *m*; (in garden) allée *f*

(b) (course) (of projectile, vehicle, sun) trajectoire *f*; (of river) cours *m*; (of hurricane) itinéraire *m*
(c) (option) voie *f*

pathetic *adj* **(a)** (moving) pathétique
(b) (inadequate) misérable
(c) (colloq) (awful) lamentable

pathological *adj* ⟨*fear, hatred*⟩ pathologique; ⟨*jealousy*⟩ maladif/-ive

pathology *n* pathologie *f*

patience *n* **(a)** patience *f* (**with** avec)
(b) (card game) réussite *f*

patient **1** *n* patient/-e *m/f*
2 *adj* patient (**with** avec)

patiently *adv* avec patience, patiemment

patio *n* **(a)** (terrace) terrasse *f*
(b) (courtyard) patio *m*

patio doors *n pl* porte-fenêtre *f*

patriot *n* patriote *mf*

patriotic *adj* ⟨*mood, song*⟩ patriotique; ⟨*person*⟩ patriote

patriotism *n* patriotisme *m*

patrol **1** *n* patrouille *f*
2 *vtr, vi* patrouiller

patrol boat, **patrol vessel** *n* patrouilleur *m*

patrol car *n* voiture *f* de police

patron *n* **(a)** (of artist) mécène *m*; (of person) protecteur/-trice *m/f*; (of charity) bienfaiteur/-trice *m/f*
(b) (client) client/-e *m/f* (**of** de)

patronage *n* (support) patronage *m*; **~ of the arts** mécénat *m*

patronize *vtr* **(a)** traiter [qn] avec condescendance ⟨*person*⟩
(b) fréquenter ⟨*restaurant, cinema*⟩

patronizing *adj* condescendant/-e

patron saint *n* saint/-e *m/f* patron/-onne

patter **1** *n* **(a)** (of rain) crépitement *m*; **~ of footsteps** bruit *m* de pas rapides et légers
(b) (talk) baratin *m*
2 *vi* ⟨*child, mouse*⟩ trottiner; ⟨*rain*⟩ crépiter

pattern *n* **(a)** (design) dessin *m*, motif *m*
(b) (of behaviour) mode *m*; **weather ~s** tendances *fpl* climatiques
(c) (in dressmaking) patron *m*; (in knitting) modèle *m*
(d) (model, example) modèle *m*

patterned *adj* ⟨*fabric*⟩ à motifs

paunch *n* ventre *m*

pauper *n* indigent/-e *m/f*

pause **1** *n* **(a)** (silence) silence *m*
(b) (break) pause *f*
(c) (stoppage) interruption *f*
2 *vi* **(a)** (stop speaking) marquer une pause
(b) (stop) s'arrêter; **to ~ in** interrompre ⟨*activity*⟩; **to ~ for thought** faire une pause pour réfléchir
(c) (hesitate) hésiter

pave *vtr* paver (**with** de); **to ~ the way for sb/sth** ouvrir la voie à qn/qch

pavement *n* **(a)** (GB) (footpath) trottoir *m*
(b) (US) (roadway) chaussée *f*

pavement café *n* café *m* avec terrasse

pavilion n pavillon m

paving slab, **paving stone** n dalle f

paw ⓵ n patte f
⓶ vtr **to ~ the ground** ⟨horse⟩ piaffer; ⟨bull⟩ frapper le sol du sabot

pawn ⓵ n pion m
⓶ vtr mettre [qch] au mont-de-piété

pawnbroker n prêteur/-euse m/f sur gages

pawnshop n mont-de-piété m

pay ⓵ n salaire m
⓶ vtr (a) payer (for pour); **to ~ cash** payer comptant; **to ~ sth into** verser qch sur ⟨account⟩; **all expenses paid** tous frais payés
(b) ⟨account⟩ rapporter ⟨interest⟩
(c) (give) **to ~ attention to** faire attention à; **to ~ a tribute to sb** rendre hommage à qn; **to ~ sb a compliment** faire des compliments à qn; **to ~ sb a visit** rendre visite à qn
(d) (benefit) **it would ~ him to do** il y gagnerait à faire; **it doesn't ~ to do** cela ne sert à rien de faire
⓷ vi (a) ⟨person⟩ payer; **to ~ for sth** payer qch; **you have to ~ to get in** l'entrée est payante; **to ~ one's own way** payer sa part; **the work doesn't ~ very well** le travail est mal payé
(b) ⟨business⟩ rapporter; ⟨activity⟩ payer; **to ~ for itself** ⟨business, purchase⟩ s'amortir
■ **pay back** rembourser ⟨person, money⟩
■ **pay in** (GB) déposer ⟨cheque, sum⟩
■ **pay off:** ¶ **~ off** être payant/-e
¶ **~ [sb] off** (a) (dismiss) congédier ⟨worker⟩
(b) (bribe) acheter le silence de ⟨person⟩; ¶ **~ [sth] off** rembourser ⟨debt⟩
■ **pay up** (colloq) **~ up** payer

payable adj (a) (gen) payable
(b) **to make a cheque ~ to** faire un chèque à l'ordre de

pay cheque (GB), **pay check** (US) n chèque m de paie

payday n jour m de paie

payee n bénéficiaire mf

payment n (gen) paiement m; (in settlement) règlement m; (into account, of instalments) versement m; **monthly ~** mensualité f

pay-packet n enveloppe f de paie

pay phone n téléphone m public

payslip n bulletin m de salaire

pay television n télévision f à péage

pc, PC n (abbr = **personal computer**) ordinateur m (personnel), PC m

PE n (abbr = **physical education**) éducation f physique

pea n pois m

peace n paix f; **to keep the ~** (between countries, individuals) maintenir la paix; (in town) ⟨police⟩ maintenir l'ordre public; **I need a bit of ~ and quiet** j'ai besoin d'un peu de calme; **to find ~ of mind** trouver la paix

peaceful adj (a) (tranquil) paisible
(b) (without conflict) pacifique

peacefully adv (a) ⟨sleep⟩ paisiblement
(b) (without violence) pacifiquement

peace-keeping forces n pl forces fpl de maintien de la paix

peacemaker n (Pol) artisan m de la paix; (in family) conciliateur m

peace process n processus m de paix

peace talks n pl pourparlers mpl de paix

peacetime n temps m de paix

peach n pêche f

peacock n paon m

peak ⓵ n (a) (of mountain) pic m (of de)
(b) (of cap) visière f
(c) (of inflation, demand, price) maximum m (in dans; of de); (on a graph) sommet m
(d) (of career, empire) apogée m (of de); (of fitness, form) meilleur m (of de); **in the ~ of condition** en excellente santé; **to be past its** or **one's ~** avoir fait son temps
⓶ adj ⟨figure, level, price⟩ maximum; ⟨fitness⟩ meilleur/-e
⓷ vi culminer (at à)

peaked adj (a) ⟨cap, hat⟩ à visière; ⟨roof⟩ pointu/-e
(b) (US) pâlot/-otte

peak period n période f de pointe

peak rate n (for phone calls) tarif m rouge

peak time n (on TV) heures fpl de grande écoute; (for switchboard, traffic) heures fpl de pointe

peaky adj (colloq) pâlot/-otte

peal n (of bells) carillonnement m; (of thunder) grondement m; **~s of laughter** éclats mpl de rire

peanut n (nut) cacahuète f; (plant) arachide f

peanut butter n beurre m de cacahuètes

pear n poire f

pearl ⓵ n perle f
⓶ adj ⟨necklace, brooch⟩ de perles; ⟨button⟩ en nacre

pear tree n poirier m

peasant n paysan/-anne m/f

peat n tourbe f

pebble n caillou m; (on beach) galet m

pecan n noix f de pecan

peck ⓵ n (a) (from bird) coup m de bec
(b) (colloq) **to give sb a ~ (on the cheek)** faire une bise à qn
⓶ vtr ⟨bird⟩ picorer ⟨food⟩; donner un coup de bec à ⟨person, animal⟩
⓷ vi (a) ⟨bird⟩ **to ~ at** picorer ⟨food⟩
(b) (colloq) **to ~ at one's food** ⟨person⟩ chipoter

pecking order n ordre m hiérarchique

peckish adj (colloq) **to be ~** avoir un petit creux (colloq)

pectorals n pl (also **pecs** (colloq)) pectoraux mpl

peculiar adj (a) (odd) bizarre
(b) **to be ~ to** être particulier/-ière à or propre à

peculiarity n (a) (feature) particularité f
(b) (strangeness) bizarrerie f

pedal ⓵ n pédale f

⋯⟶

2 *vi* pédaler

pedal bin *n* (GB) poubelle *f* à pédale

pedal boat *n* pédalo® *m*

pedantic *adj* pédant/-e

peddle *vtr* colporter ‹*wares, ideas*›; **to ~ drugs** revendre de la drogue

peddler *n* (street vendor) colporteur *m*; **drug ~** trafiquant *m*

pedestal *n* socle *m*, piédestal *m*; **to put sb on a ~** mettre qn sur un piédestal

pedestrian **1** *n* piéton *m*
2 *adj* ‹*street, area*› piétonnier/-ière, piéton/-onne

pedestrian crossing *n* passage *m* pour piétons, passage *m* clouté

pedestrian precinct *n* (GB) zone *f* piétonne

pediatrician (US) = PAEDIATRICIAN

pedicure *n* **to have a ~** se faire soigner les pieds

pedigree **1** *n* **(a)** (of animal) pedigree *m*; (of person) ascendance *f*
(b) (purebred animal) animal *m* avec pedigree
2 *adj* ‹*animal*› de pure race

pee *n* (colloq) pipi *m* (colloq); **to have a ~** faire pipi (colloq)

peek *n* **to have a ~ at** jeter un coup d'œil furtif à

peel **1** *n* (gen) peau *f*; (of citrus fruit) écorce *f*; (of onion) pelure *f*; (peelings) épluchures *fpl*
2 *vtr* éplucher ‹*vegetable, fruit*›; décortiquer ‹*prawn*›; écorcer ‹*stick*›
3 *vi* ‹*skin*› peler; ‹*fruit, vegetable*› s'éplucher

■ **peel off**: ¶ **~ off** ‹*label*› se détacher; ‹*paint*› s'écailler; ‹*paper*› se décoller; ¶ **~ [sth] off** enlever ‹*clothing, label*›

peeler *n* économe *m*

peelings *n pl* épluchures *fpl*

peep **1** *n* **to have a ~ at sth** jeter un coup d'œil à qch; (furtively) regarder qch à la dérobée
2 *vi* **(a)** jeter un coup d'œil (**over** par-dessus; **through** par); **to ~ at sb/sth** jeter un coup d'œil à qn/qch; (furtively) regarder qn/qch furtivement
(b) ‹*chick*› pépier

peephole *n* (in fence) trou *m*; (in door) judas *m*

peer **1** *n* **(a)** (equal) (in status) pair *m*; (in profession) collègue *m/f*
(b) (contemporary) (adult) personne *f* de la même génération; (child) enfant *mf* du même âge
(c) (GB) (*also* **~ of the realm**) pair *m*
2 *vi* **to ~ at** scruter, regarder attentivement

peerage *n* (GB Pol) pairie *f*; **to be given a ~** être anobli/-e

peer group *n* **(a)** (of same status) pairs *mpl*
(b) (contemporaries) (adults) personnes *fpl* de la même génération; (children) enfants *mpl* du même âge

peer group pressure *n* pression *f* du groupe

peg *n* **(a)** (hook) patère *f*
(b) (GB) (*also* **clothes ~**) pince *f* à linge
(c) (of tent) piquet *m*
(d) (in carpentry) cheville *f*

pejorative *adj* péjoratif/-ive

Peking *pr n* Pékin

pelican *n* pélican *m*

pellet *n* **(a)** (of paper, wax, mud) boulette *f*
(b) (of shot) plomb *m*

pelmet *n* cantonnière *f*

pelt **1** *n* (fur) fourrure *f*; (hide) peau *f*
2 *vtr* bombarder (**with sth** de qch)
3 *vi* **(a)** (*also* **~ down**) ‹*rain*› tomber à verse
(b) (run) **to ~ along** courir à toutes jambes

pelvis *n* bassin *m*, pelvis *m*

pen *n* **(a)** (for writing) stylo *m*
(b) (for animals) parc *m*, enclos *m*

penal *n* ‹*law, code, system*› pénal/-e; ‹*colony, institution*› pénitentiaire

penalize *vtr* pénaliser

penalty *n* **(a)** (punishment) peine *f*, pénalité *f*; (fine) amende *f*
(b) (figurative) prix *m* (**for** de)
(c) (in soccer) penalty *m*; (in rugby) pénalité *f*

pence (GB) ▶ PENNY

pencil *n* crayon *m*; **in ~** au crayon
■ **pencil in**: **~ [sth] in**, **~ in [sth]** écrire [qch] au crayon; **let's ~ in the second of May** disons le deux mai pour l'instant

pencil case *n* trousse *f* (à crayons)

pencil sharpener *n* taille-crayon *m*

pendant *n* (on necklace) pendentif *m*

pending **1** *adj* **(a)** ‹*case*› en instance; ‹*matter*› en souffrance
(b) (imminent) imminent/-e
2 *prep* en attendant

pendulum *n* pendule *m*, balancier *m*

penetrate *vtr* pénétrer; percer ‹*cloud, silence, defences*›; traverser ‹*wall*›; ‹*spy*› infiltrer ‹*organization*›

penetrating *adj* ‹*cold, eyes, question*› pénétrant/-e; ‹*sound, voice*› perçant/-e

pen friend *n* correspondant/-e *m/f*

penguin *n* pingouin *m*, manchot *m*

penicillin *n* pénicilline *f*

peninsula *n* péninsule *f*

penis *n* pénis *m*

penitent *n*, *adj* pénitent/-e (*m/f*)

penitentiary *n* (US) prison *f*

penknife *n* canif *m*

pennant *n* **(a)** (flag) fanion *m*; (on boat) flamme *f*
(b) (US Sport) championnat *m*

penniless *adj* sans le sou, sans ressources

penny *n* **(a)** (GB) penny *m*; **a five pence** *or* **five p piece** une pièce de cinq pence; **a 25p stamp** un timbre-poste à 25 pence
(b) (US) cent *m*
IDIOMS **the ~ dropped** (colloq) ça a fait tilt (colloq); **not to have a ~ to one's name** être sans le sou

pension n (from state) pension f; (from employer) retraite f

pensioner n retraité/-e m/f

pension scheme n plan m de retraite

pentagon n (a) pentagone m
(b) the Pentagon (US) le Pentagone m

Pentecost n Pentecôte f

penthouse n appartement m de grand standing

pent-up adj ⟨energy, frustration⟩ contenu/-e; ⟨feelings⟩ réprimé/-e

penultimate adj avant-dernier/-ière

people ⊡ n (nation) peuple m
② n pl (a) (in general) gens mpl; (specified or counted) personnes fpl; old ∼ les personnes âgées; they're nice ∼ ce sont des gens sympathiques; there were a lot of ∼ il y avait beaucoup de monde; other ∼'s property le bien des autres
(b) (of a town) habitants mpl; (of a country) peuple m
(c) (citizens) the ∼ le peuple

■ Note gens is masculine plural and never countable. When counting people, you must use *personnes* rather than *gens*: three people = trois personnes.
– When used with gens, some adjectives such as vieux, bon, mauvais, petit, vilain placed before gens take the feminine form: les vieilles gens.

people carrier n monospace m

pep v ■ pep up remettre [qn] d'aplomb ⟨person⟩; animer ⟨party, team⟩

pepper n (a) (spice) poivre m
(b) (vegetable) poivron m

peppercorn n grain m de poivre

pepper mill n moulin m à poivre

peppermint n (a) (sweet) pastille f de menthe
(b) (plant) menthe f poivrée

pepper pot, pepper shaker n poivrier m

pep talk n (colloq) laïus m (colloq) d'encouragement

per prep par; ∼ annum par an; ∼ head par tête or personne; 80 km ∼ hour 80 km à l'heure; £5 ∼ hour 5 livres sterling (de) l'heure; as ∼ your instructions conformément à vos instructions

per capita adj, adv par personne

perceive vtr percevoir

per cent n, adv pour cent (m)

percentage n pourcentage m

perceptible adj perceptible (to à)

perception n (a) (by senses) perception f
(b) (view) my ∼ of him l'idée que je me fais de lui
(c) (insight) perspicacité f

perceptive adj ⟨person⟩ perspicace; ⟨analysis⟩ fin/-e; ⟨article⟩ intelligent/-e

perch ⊡ n (a) (gen) perchoir m
(b) (fish) perche f
② vi se percher (on sur)

percolator n cafetière f à pression

percussion n (Mus) percussions fpl

perennial adj (a) perpétuel/-elle
(b) ⟨plant⟩ vivace

perfect ⊡ n parfait m; in the ∼ au parfait
② adj (gen) parfait/-e (for pour); ⟨moment, name, place, partner, solution⟩ idéal/-e (for pour); ⟨hostess⟩ exemplaire
③ vtr perfectionner

perfection n perfection f (of de)

perfectionist n, adj perfectionniste (mf)

perfectly adv (a) (totally) ⟨clear, happy⟩ tout à fait
(b) (very well) ⟨fit, illustrate⟩ parfaitement

perforate vtr perforer

perform ⊡ vtr (a) exécuter ⟨task⟩; accomplir ⟨duties⟩; procéder à ⟨operation⟩
(b) jouer ⟨play⟩; chanter ⟨song⟩; exécuter ⟨dance, trick⟩
(c) célébrer ⟨ceremony⟩
② vi (a) ⟨actor, musician⟩ jouer
(b) to ∼ well/badly ⟨team⟩ bien/mal jouer; ⟨interviewee⟩ faire bonne/mauvaise impression; ⟨exam candidate, company⟩ avoir de bons/de mauvais résultats

performance n (a) (rendition) interprétation f (of de)
(b) (concert, show, play) représentation f (of de); to put on a ∼ of Hamlet donner une représentation d'Hamlet
(c) (of team, sportsman) performance f (in à)
(d) (of duties) exercice m (of de); (of task) exécution f (of de)
(e) (of car, engine) performances fpl

performance artist n artiste mf de performances

performance indicators n pl tableau m de bord

performer n artiste mf

performing arts n pl arts mpl scéniques

perfume ⊡ n parfum m
② vtr parfumer

perhaps adv peut-être; ∼ she's forgotten elle a peut-être oublié

peril n péril m, danger m

perimeter n périmètre m

period ⊡ n (a) (gen) période f; (era) époque f
(b) (US) (full stop) point m
(c) (menstruation) règles fpl
(d) (Sch) (lesson) cours m, leçon f; to have a free ∼ ≈ avoir une heure de libre
② adj (of a certain era) ⟨costume, furniture⟩ d'époque

periodical n, adj périodique (m)

peripheral adj ⟨vision, suburb⟩ périphérique; ⟨issue, investment⟩ annexe

periphery n périphérie f; to remain on the ∼ of rester à l'écart de ⟨event, movement⟩

periscope n périscope m

perish vi (a) (die) périr (from de)
(b) ⟨food⟩ se gâter; ⟨rubber⟩ se détériorer

perishables n pl denrées fpl périssables

p

perjure v refl to ~ oneself faire un faux témoignage

perjury n faux témoignage m

perk n (colloq) avantage m

■ **perk up** ⟨person⟩ se ragaillardir; ⟨business, life, plant⟩ reprendre

perky adj guilleret/-ette

perm n permanente f; to have a ~ se faire faire une permanente

permanent [1] n (US) permanente f
[2] adj permanent/-e

permanently adv ⟨happy, tired⟩ en permanence; ⟨employed, disabled⟩ de façon permanente; ⟨close, emigrate, settle⟩ définitivement

permeate vtr (a) ⟨liquid, gas⟩ s'infiltrer dans; ⟨odour⟩ pénétrer dans
(b) ⟨ideas⟩ imprégner

permissible adj ⟨level, conduct⟩ admissible; ⟨error⟩ acceptable

permission n permission f; (official) autorisation f; to get ~ to do obtenir la permission or l'autorisation de faire

permissive adj permissif/-ive

permit [1] n (a) permis m; work ~ permis m de travail;
(b) (US Aut) permis m (de conduire)
[2] vtr permettre; to ~ sb to do permettre à qn de faire; smoking is not ~ted il est interdit de fumer
[3] vi permettre

pernickety adj (colloq) (a) (detail-conscious) pointilleux/-euse (about sur)
(b) (choosy) tatillon/-onne (about quant à)

peroxide blonde n blonde f décolorée

perpendicular adj perpendiculaire

perpetrate vtr perpétrer ⟨deed, fraud⟩; monter ⟨hoax⟩

perpetrator n auteur m (of de)

perpetual adj ⟨meetings, longing, turmoil⟩ perpétuel/-elle; ⟨darkness, stench⟩ permanent/-e

perpetuate vtr perpétuer

perplexed adj perplexe

persecute vtr persécuter

persecution n persécution f

perseverance n persévérance f

persevere vi persévérer (with, at dans)

persist vi persister (in dans; in doing à faire)

persistence n persévérance f

persistent adj (a) (persevering) persévérant/-e; (obstinate) obstiné/-e (in dans)
(b) ⟨rain, denial⟩ persistant/-e; ⟨enquiries, noise, pressure⟩ continuel/-elle; ⟨illness, fears, idea⟩ tenace

persistent offender n récidiviste mf

person n personne f; in ~ en personne; to have sth about one's ~ avoir qch sur soi

personable adj ⟨person⟩ qui présente bien

personal [1] n (US) petite annonce f personnelle
[2] adj ⟨opinion, life, call, matter⟩

personnel/-elle; ⟨safety, choice, income, insurance⟩ individuel/-elle; ⟨service⟩ personnalisé/-e; to make a ~ appearance venir en personne (at à)

personal ad n petite annonce f personnelle

personal column n petites annonces fpl personnelles

personality n personnalité f

personal loan n emprunt m; (by bank etc) prêt m personnel

personally adv personnellement

personal organizer n ≈ agenda m

personal property n biens mpl personnels

personal stereo n baladeur m

personify vtr incarner ⟨ideal⟩

personnel n (a) (staff, troops) personnel m
(b) (department) service m du personnel

perspective n perspective f; to keep things in ~ garder un sens de la mesure; to put things into ~ relativiser les choses

perspex® n plexiglas® m

perspiration n (a) (sweat) sueur f
(b) (sweating) transpiration f

perspire vi transpirer

persuade vtr (a) (influence) persuader; to ~ sb to do persuader qn de faire
(b) (convince) convaincre (of de; that que)

persuasion n (a) (persuading) persuasion f
(b) (religion) confession f
(c) (political views) conviction f

persuasive adj ⟨person⟩ persuasif/-ive; ⟨argument, evidence⟩ convaincant/-e

pert adj ⟨person, manner⟩ espiègle; ⟨hat, nose⟩ coquin/-e

pertinent adj pertinent/-e

perturb vtr perturber

perturbing adj troublant/-e

pervade vtr imprégner

perverse adj (a) (twisted) ⟨person⟩ retors/-e; ⟨desire⟩ pervers/-e
(b) (contrary) ⟨refusal, attempt, attitude⟩ illogique; to take a ~ pleasure in doing prendre un malin plaisir à faire

perversion n (a) (deviation) perversion f
(b) (of facts, justice) travestissement m

pervert [1] n pervers/-e m/f
[2] vtr (a) (corrupt) corrompre
(b) (misrepresent) travestir ⟨truth⟩; dénaturer ⟨meaning⟩; to ~ the course of justice entraver l'action de la justice

perverted adj (deviant) pervers/-e; (distorted) ⟨idea⟩ tordu/-e

pessimism n pessimisme m

pessimist n pessimiste mf

pessimistic adj pessimiste

pest n (a) (animal) animal m nuisible; (insect) insecte m nuisible
(b) (colloq) (person) enquiquineur/-euse m/f (colloq)

pester vtr harceler

pesticide n pesticide m

pet [1] n **(a)** (animal) animal m de compagnie
(b) (favourite) chouchou/chouchoute m/f
(colloq)
[2] adj **(a)** (favourite) favori/-ite
(b) ~ **dog** chien
[3] vtr caresser (animal)
[4] vi (people) échanger des caresses

petal n pétale m

peter v ▪ **peter out** (conversation) tarir;
(supplies) s'épuiser

pet food n aliments mpl pour chiens et
chats

pet hate (GB) n bête f noire

petition [1] n pétition f
[2] vtr adresser une pétition à (person, body)
[3] vi to ~ **for divorce** demander le divorce

pet name n petit nom m

pet project n enfant m chéri ((figurative))

petrified adj pétrifié/-e

petrol (GB) n essence f; **to fill up with** ~
faire le plein (d'essence)

petrol can n bidon m à essence

petroleum n pétrole m

petrol station n (GB) station f d'essence

pet shop (GB), **pet store** (US) n
animalerie f

petticoat n (full slip) combinaison m; (half
slip) jupon m

petty adj (person, squabble) mesquin/-e;
(detail) insignifiant/-e

petty cash n petite caisse f

petty crime n petite délinquance f

petty officer n ≈ maître m

petty theft n larcin m

pew n banc m (d'église)

pewter n étain m

PGCE n (abbr = **postgraduate
certificate in education**) diplôme m de
spécialisation dans l'enseignement

pharmaceutical adj pharmaceutique

pharmacist n pharmacien/-ienne m/f

pharmacy n pharmacie f

phase [1] n phase f; **it's just a** ~ (he's/
they're going through) ça lui/leur passera
[2] vtr échelonner (**over** sur)
▪ **phase in** introduire [qch]
progressivement
▪ **phase out** supprimer [qch] peu à peu

PhD n (abbr = **Doctor of Philosophy**)
doctorat m

pheasant n faisan/-e m/f

phenomenal adj phénoménal/-e

phenomenon n phénomène m

phew excl (in relief) ouf!; (when too hot) pff!

philanthropist n philanthrope mf

philistine n béotien/-ienne m/f

philosopher n philosophe mf

philosophic(al) adj **(a)** (knowledge,
question) philosophique
(b) (calm, stoical) philosophe (**about** à propos
de)

philosophy n philosophie f

phobia n phobie f

phone [1] n téléphone m; **to be on the** ~ (be
talking) être au téléphone (**to sb** avec qn); (be
subscriber) avoir le téléphone
[2] vtr (also ~ **up**) passer un coup de fil à
(colloq), téléphoner à, appeler
[3] vi (also ~ **up**) téléphoner; **to** ~ **for a taxi**
appeler un taxi

phone book n annuaire m (téléphonique)

phone booth, **phone box** (GB) n
cabine f téléphonique

phone call n coup m de fil (colloq); (more
formal) communication f (téléphonique)

phone card n (GB) télécarte f

phone-in n émission f à ligne ouverte

phone link n liaison f téléphonique

phone number n numéro m de
téléphone

phoney (colloq) [1] n **(a)** (affected person)
poseur/-euse m/f
(b) (impostor) charlatan m
[2] adj (address, accent) faux/fausse (before
n); (company, excuse) bidon inv (colloq);
(emotion) simulé/-e

phoney war n **the** ~ la drôle de guerre

phosphates n pl phosphates mpl

photo = PHOTOGRAPH 1

photo album n album m de photos

photo booth n photomaton® m

photo-call n séance f de photos

photocopier n photocopieuse f

photocopy [1] n photocopie f
[2] vtr photocopier

photogenic adj photogénique

photograph [1] n (also **photo**) photo f; **in
the** ~ sur la photo; **to take a** ~ **of sb/sth**
prendre qn/qch en photo
[2] vtr photographier, prendre [qn/qch] en
photo

photographer n photographe mf

photography n photographie f

photo opportunity n séance f de photos

photo session n séance f de photos

phrase [1] n expression f
[2] vtr formuler (question, speech)

phrasebook n manuel m de conversation

physical [1] n (colloq) (check-up) bilan m de
santé
[2] adj physique

physical fitness n forme f physique

physically handicapped adj **to be** ~
être handicapé/-e m/f physique

physicist n physicien/-ienne m/f

physics n physique f

physiology n physiologie f

physiotherapy n kinésithérapie f

physique n physique m

pianist n pianiste mf

piano n piano m

pick [1] n **(a)** (tool) pioche f, pic m; (of
climber) piolet m

p

(b) (choice) choix *m*; **to have one's ~ of** avoir le choix parmi; **take your ~** choisis
(c) the ~ of the bunch (singular) le meilleur/la meilleure du lot
2 *vtr* **(a)** (choose) choisir ⟨**from** parmi⟩; (in sport) sélectionner ⟨*player*⟩ ⟨**from** parmi⟩; **to ~ a fight** chercher à se bagarrer (colloq) ⟨**with** avec⟩; (quarrel) chercher querelle ⟨**with** à⟩
(b) to ~ one's way through avancer avec précaution parmi ⟨*rubble, litter*⟩
(c) cueillir ⟨*fruit, flowers*⟩
(d) gratter ⟨*spot, scab*⟩; **to ~ sth from** *or* **off** enlever qch de; **to ~ one's teeth/nose** se curer les dents/le nez
3 *vi* choisir
■ **pick at (a)** ⟨*person*⟩ manger [qch] du bout des dents ⟨*food*⟩; gratter ⟨*spot, scab*⟩
(b) ⟨*bird*⟩ picorer ⟨*crumbs*⟩
■ **pick on** harceler, s'en prendre à ⟨*person*⟩
■ **pick out (a)** (select) choisir; (single out) repérer
(b) distinguer ⟨*landmark*⟩; reconnaître ⟨*person in photo*⟩; repérer ⟨*person in crowd*⟩
■ **pick up: ¶ ~ up** ⟨*business*⟩ reprendre; ⟨*weather, health*⟩ s'améliorer; ⟨*ill person*⟩ se rétablir
¶ ~ [sb/sth] up (a) (lift up) ramasser ⟨*object, litter, toys*⟩; relever ⟨*person*⟩; **to ~ up the receiver** décrocher le téléphone; **to ~ oneself up** se relever
(b) prendre ⟨*passenger, cargo*⟩; passer prendre ⟨*ticket, keys*⟩; prendre, acheter ⟨*milk, paper*⟩; **could you ~ me up?** est-ce que tu peux venir me chercher?
(c) apprendre ⟨*language*⟩; prendre ⟨*habit, accent*⟩; développer ⟨*skill*⟩; **you'll soon ~ it up** tu t'y mettras vite
(d) trouver ⟨*trail, scent*⟩; ⟨*radar*⟩ détecter la présence de ⟨*aircraft, person, object*⟩; ⟨*radio receiver*⟩ capter ⟨*signal*⟩
(e) gagner ⟨*point*⟩; acquérir ⟨*reputation*⟩; **to ~ up speed** prendre de la vitesse
(f) (resume) reprendre ⟨*conversation, career*⟩
(g) ramasser ⟨*partner, prostitute*⟩
pickaxe (GB), **pickax** (US) *n* pioche *f*
picket 1 *n* piquet *m* (de grève)
2 *vtr* installer un piquet de grève aux portes de ⟨*factory*⟩
picking 1 *n* (of crop) cueillette *f*
2 pickings *n pl* (rewards) gains *mpl*
pickle 1 *n* **(a)** (preserves) conserves *fpl* au vinaigre
(b) (gherkin) cornichon *m*
2 *vtr* (in vinegar) conserver [qch] dans du vinaigre
IDIOMS to be in a ~ être dans le pétrin (colloq)
pick-me-up *n* remontant *m*
pickpocket *n* voleur *m* à la tire
pickup truck *n* (GB) pick-up *m inv*
picnic *n* pique-nique *m*; **to go for** *or* **on a ~** aller faire un pique-nique, pique-niquer
picture 1 *n* **(a)** (painting) peinture *f*, tableau *m*; (drawing) dessin *m*; (in book) illustration *f*; (in mind) image *f*
(b) (description) description *f*

(c) (snapshot) photo *f*, photographie *f*
(d) I get the ~ je vois; **to put sb in the ~** mettre qn au courant
(e) (film) film *m*
(f) (on TV screen) image *f*
2 *vtr* s'imaginer
picture card *n* figure *f* ⟨*carte*⟩
picture frame *n* cadre *m*
picture hook *n* crochet *m* (à tableaux)
picturesque *adj* pittoresque
pie *n* tourte *f*; **meat ~** tourte à la viande
piece *n* **(a)** (gen) morceau *m*; (of string, ribbon) bout *m*; **a ~ of furniture** un meuble; **a ~ of luggage** une valise; **a ~ of advice** un conseil; **a ~ of information** un renseignement; **a ~ of luck** un coup de chance; **£20 a ~** 20 livres sterling pièce; **to fall to ~s** ⟨*object*⟩ tomber en morceaux; ⟨*argument*⟩ s'effondrer; **to go to ~s** (from shock) s'effondrer; (emotionally) craquer (colloq); (in interview) paniquer complètement
(b) (of jigsaw, machine, model) pièce *f*; **to take sth to ~s** démonter qch
(c) (article) article *m* ⟨**on** sur⟩
(d) (coin) **a 50p ~** une pièce de 50 pence
(e) (in chess) pièce *f*
IDIOMS to give sb a ~ of one's mind dire ses quatre vérités à qn
■ **piece together: ~ [sth] together, ~ together [sth]** reconstituer ⟨*vase, letter*⟩; assembler ⟨*puzzle*⟩; reconstituer ⟨*facts*⟩
piecemeal 1 *adj* (random) fragmentaire; (at different times) irrégulier/-ière
2 *adv* petit à petit
pie chart *n* diagramme *m* circulaire sectorisé, camembert *m* (colloq)
pier *n* (at seaside) jetée *f* (sur pilotis); (landing stage) embarcadère *f*
pierce *vtr* (make hole in) percer; (penetrate) transpercer
piercing *adj* ⟨*scream, eyes*⟩ perçant/-e; ⟨*light*⟩ intense; ⟨*wind*⟩ glacial/-e, pénétrant/-e
pig *n* **(a)** (animal) porc *m*, cochon *m*
(b) (colloq) ⟨*person*⟩ (greedy) goinfre *m* (colloq); (dirty) cochon/-onne *m/f* (colloq); (nasty) sale type *m* (colloq)
■ **pig out** (colloq) se goinfrer (colloq), s'empiffrer (colloq) ⟨**on** de⟩
pigeon *n* pigeon *m*
pigeonhole (GB) **1** *n* casier *m*
2 *vtr* étiqueter, cataloguer
pigeon-toed *adj* **to be ~** marcher les pieds en dedans
piggyback (ride) *n* **to give sb a ~** porter qn sur son dos *or* sur ses épaules
piggy bank *n* tirelire *f*
pigheaded *adj* entêté/-e, obstiné/-e
piglet *n* porcelet *m*, petit cochon *m*
pigment *n* pigment *m*
pigpen (US) = PIGSTY
pigskin *n* peau *f* de porc
pigsty, pigpen (US) *n* porcherie *f*
pigtail *n* natte *f*
pike *n* (fish) brochet *m*

pile 1 *n* (a) (heap) tas *m* (of de); (stack) pile *f* (of de); **in a ~** en tas *or* en pile
(b) (of fabric, carpet) poil *m*
(c) (colloq) **~s of** des tas (colloq) de ⟨*books, letters*⟩; **~s of money** plein d'argent (colloq)
2 **piles** *n pl* hémorroïdes *fpl*
3 *vtr* entasser (**on** sur; **into** dans)
■ **pile up** ⟨*debts, problems, work*⟩ s'accumuler

pileup *n* carambolage *m*

pilfer 1 *vtr* dérober (**from** dans)
2 *vi* commettre des larcins

pilgrim *n* pèlerin *m* (**to** de)

pilgrimage *n* pèlerinage *m*

pill *n* (a) (gen) comprimé *m*, cachet *m*
(b) (contraceptive) **the ~** la pilule

pillage *vtr, vi* piller

pillar *n* pilier *m*

pillar box *n* (GB) boîte *f* aux lettres

pillion 1 *n* (also **~ seat**) siège *m* de passager
2 *adv* **to ride ~** monter en croupe

pillow *n* oreiller *m*

pillowcase *n* taie *f* d'oreiller

pilot 1 *n* pilote *m*
2 *adj* (a) ⟨*project, study*⟩ pilote; ⟨*series*⟩ expérimental/-e
(b) ⟨*error*⟩ de pilotage

pilot light *n* veilleuse *f*; (electric) voyant *m* lumineux

pilot scheme *n* projet-pilote *m*

pimp *n* proxénète *m*

pimple *n* bouton *m*

pimply *adj* boutonneux/-euse

pin 1 *n* (a) (for cloth, paper) épingle *f*
(b) **three-~ plug** prise *f* à trois fiches
(c) (for wood, metal) goujon *m*
(d) (Med) broche *f*
(e) (brooch) barrette *f*
2 *vtr* (a) épingler ⟨*dress, hem, curtain*⟩ (**to** à)
(b) (trap) **to ~ sb to** coincer qn contre ⟨*wall, floor*⟩
(c) (colloq) **to ~ sth on sb** mettre qch sur le dos de qn ⟨*theft*⟩
■ **pin down**: ¶ **~ [sb] down** (a) (physically) immobiliser (**to** à)
(b) (figurative) coincer; **to ~ sb down to a definite date** arriver à fixer une date ferme avec qn
¶ **~ [sth] down** identifier ⟨*concept, feeling*⟩
■ **pin up** accrocher ⟨*poster, notice*⟩ (**on** à)

PIN (number) *n* (*abbr* = **personal identification number**) code *m* confidentiel (pour carte bancaire)

pinafore *n* (a) (apron) tablier *m*
(b) (dress) robe-chasuble *f*

pinball *n* flipper *m*

pincers *n pl* tenailles *fpl*

pinch 1 *n* (a) pincement *m*; **to give sb a ~** pincer qn
(b) (of salt, spice) pincée *f*
2 *vtr* (a) (on arm, leg) pincer
(b) ⟨*shoe*⟩ serrer

(c) (colloq) (steal) faucher (colloq) (**from** à)
3 *vi* ⟨*shoe*⟩ serrer
IDIOMS **to feel the ~** avoir de la peine à joindre les deux bouts

pine 1 *n* pin *m*
2 *adj* ⟨*furniture*⟩ en pin
3 *vi* ⟨*person*⟩ languir (**for** après); ⟨*animal*⟩ s'ennuyer (**for** de)

pineapple *n* ananas *m*

pinecone *n* pomme *f* de pin

ping-pong® *n* ping-pong® *m*

pink 1 *n* (a) (colour) rose *m*
(b) (flower) œillet *m* mignardise
2 *adj* rose; **to go** *or* **turn ~** rosir; (blush) rougir (**with** de)

pinnacle *n* (a) (on building) pinacle *m*
(b) (of rock) cime *f* (**of** de)
(c) (figurative) apogée *m* (**of** de)

pinpoint *vtr* indiquer ⟨*problem, causes, location, site*⟩; déterminer ⟨*time*⟩

pinstripe(d) *adj* ⟨*fabric, suit*⟩ à fines rayures

pint *n* pinte *f* ((GB) = *0.57 l*, (US) = *0.47 l*); **a ~ of milk** ≈ un demi-litre de lait; **a ~ (of beer)** un demi

pinup *n* (woman) pin-up *f* (colloq); (poster of star) affiche *f* de vedette; (star) idole *f*

pioneer 1 *n* pionnier *m* (**of, in** de)
2 *vtr* **to ~ the use of** être le premier/la première à utiliser

pious *adj* pieux/pieuse

pip *n* (a) (seed) pépin *m*
(b) (on radio) top *m*
IDIOMS **to be ~ped at** *or* **to the post** se faire souffler la victoire

pipe 1 *n* (a) (for gas, water) tuyau *m*; (underground) conduite *f*
(b) (smoker's) pipe *f*
2 **pipes** *n pl* (Mus) cornemuse *f*
3 *vtr* **water is ~d across/to** l'eau est acheminée par canalisation à travers/jusqu'à
■ **pipe down** (colloq) faire moins de bruit
■ **pipe up** ⟨*voice*⟩ se faire entendre

pipe-dream *n* chimère *f*

pipeline *n* oléoduc *m*; **to be in the ~** être prévu/-e

piping hot *adj* fumant/-e

pique *n* dépit *m*; **a fit of ~** un accès de dépit

pirate 1 *n* pirate *m*
2 *adj* ⟨*video, tape, radio*⟩ pirate (*after n*); ⟨*ship*⟩ de pirates
3 *vtr* pirater ⟨*tape, video, software*⟩

pirouette *n* pirouette *f*

Pisa *pr n* Pise

Pisces *n* Poissons *mpl*

pistol *n* pistolet *m*

piston *n* piston *m*

pit 1 *n* (a) (in ground, in garage) fosse *f*; **gravel ~** carrière *f* de gravier
(b) (mine) mine *f*
(c) (in theatre) parterre *m*; **orchestra ~** fosse *f* d'orchestre ⋯▸

p

(d) (US) (in fruit) noyau m

2 *vtr* to ~ sb against opposer qn à ⟨*opponent*⟩; to ~ one's wits against sb se mesurer à qn

IDIOMS it's the ~s! (colloq) c'est l'horreur!

pit bull terrier n pit bull m

pitch **1** n (a) (sportsground) terrain m; football ~ terrain de foot(ball)
(b) (of note, voice) hauteur f; (in music) ton m;
(c) (highest point) comble m
(d) (sales talk) boniment m
(e) (for street trader) emplacement m

2 *vtr* (a) (throw) jeter ⟨*into* dans⟩; (Sport) lancer
(b) adapter ⟨*campaign, speech*⟩ ⟨*at* à⟩
(c) ⟨*singer*⟩ trouver ⟨*note*⟩
(d) planter ⟨*tent*⟩; to ~ camp établir un camp

3 *vi* (a) ⟨*boat*⟩ tanguer
(b) (US) (in baseball) lancer (la balle)

■ **pitch in** (colloq) (eat) attaquer (colloq); (help) donner un coup de main (colloq)

pitch-black adj tout/-e noir/-e

pitcher n (a) (jug) cruche f
(b) (US Sport) lanceur m

pitchfork n fourche f

pitfall n écueil m (of de)

pith n (a) (of fruit) peau f blanche
(b) (of plant) moelle f

pitiful adj ⟨*cry, sight*⟩ pitoyable; ⟨*state*⟩ lamentable; ⟨*amount*⟩ ridicule

pitiless adj impitoyable

pittance n to live on/earn a ~ vivre avec/ gagner trois fois rien

pity **1** n (a) (compassion) pitié f (for pour); out of ~ par pitié; to take ~ on sb avoir pitié de qn
(b) (shame) dommage m; what a ~! quel dommage!

2 *vtr* plaindre

pivot **1** *vtr* faire pivoter ⟨*lever*⟩; orienter ⟨*lamp*⟩

2 *vi* (a) ⟨*lamp, device*⟩ pivoter (on sur)
(b) (figurative) ⟨*outcome, success*⟩ reposer (on sur)

pixel n pixel m

pizza n pizza f

placard n (at protest march) pancarte f; (on wall) affiche f

place **1** n (a) (location, position) endroit m; in ~s ⟨*hilly, damaged, worn*⟩ par endroits; ~ of birth/work lieu m de naissance/travail; ~ of residence domicile m; to be in the right ~ at the right time être là où il faut quand il le faut; to lose/find one's ~ (in book) perdre/ retrouver sa page; (in paragraph, speech) perdre/retrouver le fil; all over the ~ (everywhere) partout
(b) (home) at Isabelle's ~ chez Isabelle; your ~ or mine? chez toi ou chez moi?
(c) (on bus, at table, in queue) place f
(d) (on team, with firm, on course) place f (on dans, as comme)
(e) (in competition, race) place f; to finish in first ~ terminer premier/-ière or à la première

place; in the first ~ (firstly, when listing) premièrement; (most importantly, most notably) tout d'abord, pour commencer
(f) (correct position) everything is in its ~ tout est bien à sa place; to hold sth in ~ maintenir qch en place; in ~ ⟨*law, system, scheme*⟩ en place; to put sb in his/her ~ remettre qn à sa place
(g) (personal level or position) it's not my ~ to do ce n'est pas à moi de faire; in his ~ à sa place
(h) (moment) moment m; in ~s ⟨*funny, boring, silly*⟩ par moments

2 *vtr* (a) (gen) placer
(b) passer ⟨*order*⟩; to place a bet parier (on sur)
(c) (in competition, exam) classer
(d) (identify) situer ⟨*person*⟩; reconnaître ⟨*accent*⟩

3 **out of place** phr déplacé/-e; to look out of ~ ⟨*building, person*⟩ détonner

place mat n set m de table

placement n (also **work** ~) stage m

place-name n nom m de lieu

placid adj placide

plagiarize *vtr*, *vi* plagier

plague **1** n (a) (bubonic) peste f
(b) (epidemic) épidémie f
(c) (of ants, locusts) invasion f
(d) (figurative) plaie f

2 *vtr* (a) to be ~d by être en proie à ⟨*doubts, difficulties*⟩
(b) (harass) harceler

plaice n plie f, carrelet m

plaid adj écossais/-e

plain **1** n plaine f

2 adj (a) (simple) simple
(b) (of one colour) uni/-e; ⟨*envelope*⟩ sans inscription; a ~ blue dress une robe toute bleue
(c) ⟨*woman*⟩ quelconque
(d) (obvious) évident/-e, clair/-e; it's ~ to see ça saute aux yeux
(e) ⟨*common sense*⟩ simple (before n); ⟨*ignorance*⟩ pur/-e et simple (after n)
(f) ⟨*yoghurt, rice*⟩ nature inv

plain chocolate n choclat m à croquer

plain clothes adj ⟨*policeman*⟩ en civil

plainly adv (a) (obviously) manifestement
(b) ⟨*see, remember*⟩ clairement
(c) ⟨*speak*⟩ franchement
(d) ⟨*dress, eat*⟩ simplement; ⟨*furnished*⟩ sobrement

plait n natte f

plan **1** n (gen) plan m; (definite aim) projet m (for de; to do pour faire); to go according to ~ se passer comme prévu

2 *vtr* (a) (prepare, organize) planifier ⟨*future*⟩; organiser, préparer ⟨*timetable, meeting, expedition*⟩; organiser ⟨*day*⟩; faire un plan de ⟨*career*⟩; faire le plan de ⟨*essay, book*⟩; préméditer ⟨*crime*⟩
(b) (intend, propose) projeter ⟨*visit, trip*⟩; to ~ to do projeter de faire
(c) (design) concevoir

3 *vi* prévoir; **to ∼ for sth** prévoir qch; **to ∼ on doing** compter faire
■ **plan ahead** (vaguely) faire des projets; (look, think ahead) prévoir

plane *n* **(a)** (aircraft) avion *m*
(b) (in geometry) plan *m*
(c) (tool) rabot *m*
(d) (*also* **∼ tree**) platane *m*

planet *n* planète *f*

plank *n* planche *f*

planner *n* planificateur/-trice *m/f*; (in town planning) urbaniste *mf*

planning *n* **(a)** (of industry, economy, work) planification *f*; (of holiday, party) organisation *f*
(b) (in town) urbanisme *m*; (out of town) aménagement *m* du territoire

planning permission *n* permis *m* de construire

plant **1** *n* **(a)** (Bot) plante *f*
(b) (factory) usine *f*
2 *vtr* **(a)** planter (*seed, bulb, tree*)
(b) placer (*bomb, spy*); **to ∼ drugs on sb** cacher de la drogue sur qn pour l'incriminer
3 *v refl* **to ∼ oneself between/in front of** se planter entre/devant

plantation *n* plantation *f*

plaque *n* **(a)** (on wall, monument) plaque *f*
(b) (on teeth) plaque *f* dentaire

plaster **1** *n* **(a)** (gen) plâtre *m*
(b) (GB) (*also* **sticking ∼**) sparadrap *m*
2 *vtr* **(a)** faire les plâtres de (*house*)
(b) (cover) couvrir (**with** de)

plaster cast *n* plâtre *m*

plasterer *n* plâtrier *m*

plastic **1** *n* plastique *m*; (credit cards) cartes *fpl* de crédit
2 *adj* (*bag, toys, container*) en plastique

plastic surgeon *n* chirurgien *m* esthétique

plastic surgery *n* chirurgie *f* plastique

plate **1** **(a)** (dish) (for eating) assiette *f*; (for serving) plat *m*
(b) (sheet of metal) plaque *f*, tôle *f*
(c) (numberplate) plaque *f* minéralogique
(d) (illustration) planche *f*
(e) (in dentistry) dentier *m*
(f) (in earth's crust) plaque *f*
2 **-plated** *combining form* gold/silver-**∼d** plaqué/-e or/argent

plate glass *n* verre *m* à vitre

platform *n* **(a)** (for performance) estrade *f*; (at public meeting) tribune *f*
(b) (in scaffolding) plate-forme *f*
(c) (in politics) plate-forme *f* électorale
(d) (at station) quai *m*
(e) (Comput) plate-forme *f*

platform shoes *n pl* chaussures *fpl* à plateforme

platinum *n* platine *m*

platinum blonde *n* blonde *f* platine *or* platinée

platonic *adj* platonique

platoon *n* (of soldiers, police, firemen) section *f*; (in cavalry) peloton *m*

platter *n* (dish) plat *m*

plausible *adj* plausible, vraisemblable

play **1** *n* **(a)** (in theatre) pièce *f* (**about** sur)
(b) (recreation) jeu *m*
(c) (Sport) (game) partie *f*; **out of ∼/in ∼** (*ball*) hors jeu/en jeu
(d) (movement, interaction) jeu *m*; **to come into ∼** entrer en jeu; **a ∼ on words** un jeu de mots
2 *vtr* **(a)** jouer à (*game, cards*); jouer (*card*); **to ∼ hide and seek** jouer à cache-cache; **to ∼ a joke on sb** jouer un tour à qn
(b) jouer de (*instrument*); jouer (*tune, symphony, chord*); jouer à (*venue*)
(c) (in theatre) interpréter, jouer (*role*)
(d) mettre (*tape, video, CD*)
3 *vi* jouer
IDIOMS **to ∼ for time** essayer de gagner du temps
■ **play along: to ∼ along with sb** entrer dans le jeu de qn
■ **play down:** minimiser (*effects, disaster*)
■ **play out: ∼ out [sth]** vivre (*fantasy*)
■ **play up** (colloq) (*computer, person*) faire des siennes (colloq)

play-acting *n* comédie *f*, simagrées *fpl*

playboy *n* playboy *m*

player *n* (in sport, music) joueur/-euse *m/f*; (actor) comédien/-ienne *m/f*; **tennis ∼** joueur/-euse *m/f* de tennis

playful *adj* (*remark*) taquin/-e; (*child, kitten*) joueur/-euse

playground *n* cour *f* de récréation

playgroup *n* ≈ halte-garderie *f*

playhouse *n* théâtre *m*

playing card *n* carte *f* à jouer

playing field *n* terrain *m* de sport

play-off *n* (GB) prolongation *f*; (US) match *m* crucial

playroom *n* salle *f* de jeux

playschool *n* ≈ halte-garderie *f*

plaything *n* jouet *m*

playtime *n* récréation *f*

playwright *n* auteur *m* dramatique

plaza *n* **(a)** (square) place *f*; **shopping ∼** centre *m* commercial
(b) (US) péage *m*

plc, PLC *n* (GB) (*abbr* = **public limited company**) SA

plea *n* **(a)** (gen) appel *m* (**for** à); (for money, food) demande *f* (**for** de)
(b) (Law) **to enter a ∼ of guilty/not guilty** plaider coupable/non coupable

plead **1** *vtr* plaider
2 *vi* **(a)** **to ∼ with sb** supplier qn
(b) (Law) plaider

pleasant *adj* agréable

please **1** *adv* s'il vous plaît; (informally) s'il te plaît; **'may I?'—'∼ do'** 'je peux?'—'oui, je vous en prie' ···✦

P

2 *vtr* faire plaisir à ⟨*person*⟩; **she is hard to ~** elle est difficile (à contenter)

3 *vi* plaire; **do as you ~** fais comme il te plaira, fais comme tu veux

pleased *adj* content/-e (**that** que + *subjunctive*; **about, at** de; **with** de); **to look ~ with oneself** avoir l'air content de soi; **I am ~ to announce that...** j'ai le plaisir d'annoncer que...; **~ to meet you** enchanté

pleasing *adj* ⟨*appearance, colour, voice*⟩ agréable; ⟨*manner, personality*⟩ avenant/-e; ⟨*effect, result*⟩ heureux/-euse

pleasurable *adj* agréable

pleasure *n* plaisir *m* (**of** de; **of doing** de faire); **for ~** par plaisir; **my ~** (replying to request for help) avec plaisir; (replying to thanks) je vous en prie

pleat *n* pli *m*

pleated *adj* ⟨*skirt*⟩ plissé/-e; ⟨*trousers*⟩ à plis (*after n*)

pledge **1** *n* (a) (promise) promesse *f*
(b) (money promised to charity) promesse *f* de don
2 *vtr* promettre ⟨*allegiance, aid, support*⟩ (**to** à); **to ~ one's word** donner sa parole

plentiful *adj* abondant/-e

plenty *quantif, pron* **~ of** beaucoup de; **~ to do** beaucoup à faire

pliable *adj* ⟨*twig, plastic*⟩ flexible; ⟨*person*⟩ malléable

pliers *n pl* pinces *fpl*; **a pair of ~s** des pinces

plight *n* (a) (dilemma) situation *f* désespérée
(b) (suffering) détresse *f*

plimsoll *n* (GB) chaussure *f* de tennis

plod *v* ■ **plod along** ⟨*walk*⟩ avancer d'un pas lent
■ **plod away** ⟨*work*⟩ travailler ferme, bosser (colloq)

plodder *n* bûcheur/-euse *m/f* (colloq)

plonk (colloq) **1** *n* (wine) vin *m* ordinaire, pinard *m* (slang)
2 *vtr* (*also* **~ down**) planter ⟨*plate, bottle, box*⟩ (**on** sur)

plot **1** *n* (a) (conspiracy) complot *m*
(b) (of novel, film, play) intrigue *f*
(c) **~ of land** parcelle *f* de terre; **a vegetable ~** un carré de légumes
(d) (building site) terrain *m* à bâtir
2 *vtr* (a) (plan) comploter ⟨*murder, attack, return*⟩; fomenter ⟨*revolution*⟩
(b) (chart) relever [qch] sur une carte ⟨*course*⟩
(c) (on graph) tracer [qch] point par point ⟨*curve, graph*⟩
3 *vi* conspirer (**against** contre)

plough (GB), **plow** (US) **1** *n* charrue *f*
2 *vtr* (a) labourer ⟨*land, field*⟩; creuser ⟨*furrow*⟩
(b) (invest) **to ~ money into** investir beaucoup d'argent dans ⟨*project, company*⟩
■ **plough back**: **~** [sth] **back, ~ back** [sth] réinvestir ⟨*profits, money*⟩ (**into** dans)
■ **plough through** avancer péniblement dans ⟨*mud, snow*⟩; ramer sur (colloq) ⟨*book*⟩

ploy *n* stratagème *m* (**to do** pour faire)

pluck **1** *n* courage *m*, cran *m* (colloq)
2 *vtr* (a) cueillir ⟨*flower, fruit*⟩
(b) plumer ⟨*chicken*⟩
(c) (in music) pincer ⟨*strings*⟩; pincer les cordes de ⟨*guitar*⟩
(d) **to ~ one's eyebrows** s'épiler les sourcils
IDIOMS **to ~ up one's courage** prendre son courage à deux mains

plucky *adj* courageux/-euse

plug **1** *n* (a) (on appliance) prise *f* (de courant)
(b) (in bath, sink) bonde *f*
(c) (*also* **spark ~**) bougie *f*
(d) (in advertising) pub *f* (colloq), publicité *f* (**for** pour)
2 *vtr* (a) boucher ⟨*hole*⟩ (**with** avec)
(b) (colloq) (promote) faire de la publicité pour ⟨*book, show, product*⟩
(c) **to ~ sth into** brancher qch à
■ **plug in**: ¶ **~ in** se brancher; ¶ **~** [sth] **in** brancher ⟨*appliance*⟩

plug and play *n* plug and play *m* (**on branche et ça marche**)

plughole *n* (GB) bonde *f*

plum **1** *n* prune *f*
2 *adj* (a) (colour) prune *inv*
(b) (colloq) **to get a ~ job** décrocher un boulot en or (colloq)

plumb **1** *adv* (a) (US) (colloq) ⟨*crazy*⟩ complètement
(b) (colloq) **~ in the middle** en plein milieu
2 *vtr* sonder ⟨*depths*⟩; **to ~ the depths of** toucher le fond de ⟨*despair, misery*⟩

plumber *n* plombier *m*

plumbing *n* plomberie *f*

plummet *vi* chuter, dégringoler (colloq)

plump *adj* ⟨*person, arm, leg*⟩ potelé/-e; ⟨*cheek, face*⟩ rond/-e, plein/-e

plunge **1** *vtr* plonger (**into** dans)
2 *vi* ⟨*road, cliff, waterfall*⟩ plonger; ⟨*bird, plane*⟩ piquer; ⟨*person*⟩ (dive) plonger; (fall) tomber (**from** de); ⟨*rate, value*⟩ chuter
IDIOMS **to take the ~** se jeter à l'eau

plunger *n* ventouse *f*

plural **1** *n* pluriel *m*; **in the ~** au pluriel
2 *adj* ⟨*noun, adjective*⟩ au pluriel; ⟨*form, ending*⟩ du pluriel

plus **1** *n* avantage *m*
2 *adj* **the ~ side** le côté positif; **50 ~** plus de 50; **the 65-~ age group** les personnes qui ont 65 ans et plus
3 *prep* plus; **15 ~ 12** 15 plus 12
4 *conj* et; **bedroom ~ bathroom** chambre et salle de bains

plus-fours *n pl* culotte *f* de golf

plus sign *n* signe *m* plus

Pluto *pr n* (planet) Pluton *f*

plutonium *n* plutonium *m*

ply **1** *vtr* (a) vendre ⟨*wares*⟩; **to ~ one's trade** exercer son métier
(b) **to ~ sb with food/drink** ne cesser de remplir l'assiette/le verre de qn

2 *vi* ⟨*boat, bus*⟩ faire la navette (**between** entre)

plywood *n* contreplaqué *m*

pm *adv* (*abbr* = **post meridiem**) two ∼ deux heures de l'après-midi; **nine** ∼ neuf heures du soir

pneumatic drill *n* marteau *m* piqueur

pneumonia *n* pneumonie *f*

poach **1** *vtr* (a) chasser [qch] illégalement ⟨*game*⟩
(b) (Culin) faire pocher
2 *vi* braconner

poacher *n* braconnier *m*

PO Box *n* boîte *f* postale

pocket **1** *n* (a) (in garment) poche *f*
(b) (in billiards) bourse *f*
2 *adj* ⟨*diary, dictionary, edition*⟩ de poche
3 *vtr* empocher

pocketbook *n* (US) (wallet) portefeuille *m*; (handbag) sac *m* à main

pocketknife *n* couteau *m* de poche

pocket money *n* argent *m* de poche

podgy *adj* (colloq) grassouillet/-ette

podium *n* (for speaker, conductor) estrade *f*; (for winner) podium *m*

poem *n* poème *m*

poet *n* poète *m*

poetic *adj* poétique

poetry *n* poésie *f*; **to write/read** ∼ écrire/ lire des poèmes

poignant *adj* poignant/-e

point **1** *n* (a) (of knife, needle, pencil) pointe *f*
(b) (location, position on scale) point *m*; (less specific) endroit *m*
(c) (extent, degree) point *m*; **up to a** ∼ jusqu'à un certain point
(d) (moment) (precise) moment *m*; (stage) stade *m*; **to be on the** ∼ **of doing** être sur le point de faire; **at this** ∼ **in her career** à ce stade(-là) de sa carrière; **at some** ∼ **in the future** plus tard; **at one** ∼ à un moment donné
(e) (question, idea) point *m*; **to make the** ∼ **that** faire remarquer que; **you've made your** ∼ vous vous êtes exprimé; **to make a** ∼ **of doing** (as matter of pride) mettre un point d'honneur à faire; (do deliberately) faire exprès
(f) (central idea) point *m* essentiel; **to come straight to the** ∼ aller droit au fait; **to keep** *or* **stick to the** ∼ rester dans le sujet; **to miss the** ∼ ne pas comprendre; **that's beside the** ∼ là n'est pas la question; **to get the** ∼ comprendre; **that's not the** ∼ il ne s'agit pas de cela
(g) (purpose) objet *m*; **what's the** ∼ **of doing...?** à quoi bon faire...?; **there's no** ∼ **in doing** ça ne sert à rien de faire; **I don't see the** ∼ **of doing** je ne vois pas l'intérêt de faire
(h) (feature, characteristic) point *m*, côté *m*; **her strong** ∼ son point fort
(i) (in scoring) point *m*; **match** ∼ (in tennis) balle *f* de match
(j) (decimal point) virgule *f*

(k) (headland) pointe *f*
2 *vtr* (a) (aim, direct) **to** ∼ **sth at sb** braquer qch sur qn ⟨*camera, gun*⟩; **to** ∼ **one's finger at sb** montrer qn du doigt
(b) (show) **to** ∼ **the way to** indiquer la direction de
(c) (in ballet, gym) **to** ∼ **one's toes** faire des pointes
3 *vi* (a) (indicate) indiquer *or* montrer (du doigt); **to** ∼ **at sb/sth** montrer qn/qch du doigt
(b) ⟨*signpost, arrow, compass*⟩ indiquer; **to be** ∼**ing at sb** ⟨*gun, camera*⟩ être braqué/-e sur qn
■ **point out** montrer ⟨*place, person*⟩ (to à); faire remarquer ⟨*fact, discrepancy*⟩

point-blank *adv* (a) ⟨*shoot*⟩ à bout portant
(b) ⟨*refuse, deny*⟩ catégoriquement

pointed *adj* (a) ⟨*hat, stick, chin*⟩ pointu/-e
(b) ⟨*remark*⟩ qui vise quelqu'un

pointer *n* (a) (piece of information) indication *f*
(b) (on projector screen) flèche *f*
(c) (Comput) pointeur *m*

pointless *adj* ⟨*request, activity*⟩ absurde; **it's** ∼ **to do/for me to do** ça ne sert à rien de faire/que je fasse

point of view *n* point *m* de vue

poise *n* (a) (confidence) assurance *f*
(b) (physical elegance) aisance *f*

poised *adj* (a) (self-possessed) plein/-e d'assurance
(b) (elegant) plein/-e d'aisance
(c) (on the point of) **to be** ∼ **to do** être sur le point de faire

poison **1** *n* poison *m*
2 *vtr* empoisonner ⟨*person, environment, relationship*⟩; ⟨*fumes*⟩ intoxiquer ⟨*person*⟩

poisoning *n* empoisonnement *m*

poisonous *adj* (a) ⟨*chemicals, gas*⟩ toxique; ⟨*mushroom, berry*⟩ vénéneux/-euse; ⟨*snake, insect, bite*⟩ venimeux/-euse
(b) ⟨*rumour, propaganda*⟩ pernicieux/-ieuse

poke *vtr* (a) (jab, prod) pousser ⟨qn⟩ du bout du doigt ⟨*person*⟩; donner un coup dans ⟨*pile, substance*⟩; tisonner ⟨*fire*⟩
(b) (push, put) **to** ∼ **sth into** enfoncer qch dans ⟨*hole, pot*⟩; **to** ∼ **one's head out of the window** passer la tête par la fenêtre
■ **poke around, poke about** farfouiller (in dans)
■ **poke out**: ¶ ∼ **out** ⟨*elbow, toe, blade*⟩ dépasser; ¶ ∼ **out [sth]**, ∼ **[sth] out** sortir ⟨*head, nose, tongue*⟩

poker *n* (a) (for fire) tisonnier *m*
(b) (cardgame) poker *m*
IDIOMS (as) **stiff as a** ∼ raide comme la justice

poker-faced *adj* ⟨*person*⟩ impassible

Poland *pr n* Pologne *f*

polar *adj* polaire

pole *n* (a) (stick) perche *f*; (for tent, flag) mât *m*; (for skiing) bâton *m*
(b) (of earth's axis) pôle *m*

Pole n Polonais/-e m/f
pole star n étoile f polaire
pole vault n saut m à la perche
police ⨯1⨯ n (a) (police force) the ∼ la police
(b) (policemen) policiers mpl
⨯2⨯ vtr maintenir l'ordre dans ⟨area⟩
police constable, PC n agent m de
police
Police Department, PD n (US)
services mpl de police (d'une ville)
police force n police f
policeman n agent m de police
police officer n policier m
police station n poste m de police;
(larger) commissariat m
policewoman n femme f policier
policing n (a) (maintaining law and order)
maintien m de l'ordre
(b) (of demonstration, match) organisation f du
service d'ordre
(c) (of measures) contrôle m de l'application
policy n (a) (plan, rule) politique f (on sur)
(b) (in insurance) (cover) contrat m; (document)
police f
policyholder n assuré/-e m/f
policy unit n comité m de conseillers
politiques
polio n poliomyélite f
polish ⨯1⨯ n (a) (for wood, floor) cire f; (for
shoes) cirage m; (for brass, silver) pâte f à polir;
(for car) lustre m
(b) (shiny surface) éclat m
(c) (of manner, performance) élégance f
⨯2⨯ vtr (a) cirer ⟨shoes, furniture⟩; astiquer
⟨leather, car, glass, brass⟩; polir ⟨stone⟩
(b) (refine) soigner ⟨performance, image⟩;
affiner ⟨style⟩
■ **polish off** (colloq) expédier (colloq) ⟨food,
job⟩
Polish ⨯1⨯ n (language) polonais m
⨯2⨯ adj polonais/-e
polished adj (a) ⟨surface, wood⟩ poli/-e;
⟨floor, shoes⟩ ciré/-e
(b) ⟨manner⟩ raffiné/-e
(c) ⟨performance⟩ (bien) rodé/-e
polite adj poli/-e (to avec)
politeness n politesse f
political adj politique
politically correct, PC adj
politiquement correct/-e
political prisoner n prisonnier/-ière m/f
politique
politician n homme/femme m/f politique
politicize vtr politiser
politics n (a) (gen) politique f
(b) (subject) sciences fpl politiques
(c) (views) opinions fpl politiques
poll ⨯1⨯ n (a) (vote casting) scrutin m, vote m;
(election) élections fpl; **to go to the** ∼**s** se
rendre aux urnes
(b) (survey) sondage m (on sur)
⨯2⨯ vtr (a) obtenir ⟨votes⟩
(b) (canvass) interroger ⟨group⟩

pollen n pollen m
polling booth n isoloir m
polling day n jour m des élections
polling station n bureau m de vote
poll tax n (GB) ≈ impôts mpl locaux
pollutant n polluant m
pollute vtr polluer
polluter n pollueur/-euse m/f
pollution n pollution f
polo n polo m
polo neck n (GB) col m roulé
poltergeist n esprit m frappeur
poly ⨯1⨯ n (GB) (colloq) abbr = POLYTECHNIC
⨯2⨯ **poly+** pref poly-
polystyrene n polystyrène m
polytechnic n (GB) (also **poly**)
établissement m d'enseignement supérieur
polythene n (GB) polyéthylène m
pomegranate n grenade f
pompom, pompon n pompon m
pompous adj ⟨person⟩ plein/-e de
suffisance; ⟨air, speech, style⟩ pompeux/-euse
pond n (large) étang m; (smaller) mare f; (in
garden) bassin m
ponder vi réfléchir (on à); (more deeply)
méditer (on sur)
pontiff n pontife m
pontoon n (a) (pier) ponton m
(b) (GB) (Games) vingt-et-un m
pony n poney m
ponytail n queue f de cheval
poodle n caniche m
pool ⨯1⨯ n (a) (pond) étang m; (artificial) bassin
m
(b) (also **swimming** ∼) piscine f
(c) (of water, light) flaque f; **a** ∼ **of blood** une
mare de sang
(d) (kitty) cagnotte f; (in cards) mises fpl
(e) (of money, resources) pool m; (of ideas,
experience) réservoir m
(f) (billiards) billard m américain
⨯2⨯ **pools** n pl (GB) (also **football** ∼**s**) ≈
loto m sportif
⨯3⨯ vtr mettre [qch] en commun
pool table n table f de billard américain
poor adj (a) ⟨person, country⟩ pauvre (in en)
(b) ⟨quality, work, planning, weather,
visibility⟩ mauvais/-e (before n); ⟨attendance⟩
faible
(c) (deserving pity) pauvre (before n); ∼ **you!**
mon/ma pauvre!
(d) ⟨attempt, excuse⟩ piètre (before n)
poorly adv (a) ⟨live, dress, dressed⟩
pauvrement
(b) ⟨written, lit, paid⟩ mal
pop ⨯1⨯ n (a) (sound) pan m; **to go** ∼ faire
pan
(b) (colloq) (drink) soda m
(c) (music) musique f pop
⨯2⨯ adj ⟨concert, group, music, song⟩ pop;
⟨record, singer⟩ de pop
⨯3⨯ vtr (a) faire éclater ⟨balloon, bubble⟩
(b) faire sauter ⟨cork⟩

(c) (colloq) (put) **to ~ sth in(to)** mettre qch dans ⟨*oven, cupboard, mouth*⟩

4 *vi* **(a)** ⟨*balloon*⟩ éclater; ⟨*cork, buttons*⟩ sauter

(b) ⟨*ears*⟩ se déboucher brusquement; **her eyes were ~ping out of her head** les yeux lui sortaient de la tête

(c) (GB) (colloq) (go) **to ~ into town/the bank** faire un saut (colloq) en ville/à la banque

■ **pop in** (GB) (colloq) passer

■ **pop out** (GB) (colloq) sortir

■ **pop round, pop over** (GB) passer

pope *n* pape *m*; **Pope Paul VI** le Pape Paul VI

poplar *n* peuplier *m*

poppy *n* pavot *m*; **wild ~** coquelicot *m*

pop sock *n* mi-bas *m*

popular *adj* **(a)** ⟨*actor, politician*⟩ populaire (**with, among** parmi); ⟨*hobby, sport*⟩ répandu/-e (**with, among** chez); ⟨*food, dish*⟩ prisé/-e (**with, among** par); ⟨*product, resort, colour, design*⟩ en vogue (**with, among** chez); **John is very ~** John a beaucoup d'amis

(b) (of or for the people) ⟨*music, movement, press*⟩ populaire; ⟨*entertainment*⟩ grand public *inv*; ⟨*science, history*⟩ de vulgarisation

popularity *n* popularité *f* (**of** de; **with** auprès de)

popularize *vtr* (make fashionable) généraliser; (make accessible) vulgariser

population *n* population *f*

pop-up menu *n* menu *m* déroulant

porcelain *n* porcelaine *f*

porch *n* **(a)** (of house, church) porche *m*

(b) (US) (veranda) véranda *f*

porcupine *n* porc-épic *m*

pore *n* pore *m*

■ **pore over** être plongé/-e dans ⟨*book*⟩; étudier soigneusement ⟨*map*⟩

pork *n* (viande *f* de) porc *m*

pornographic *adj* pornographique

pornography *n* pornographie *f*

porpoise *n* marsouin *m*

porridge *n* porridge *m* (*bouillie de flocons d'avoine*)

port *n* **(a)** (harbour) port *m*; **in ~** au port; **~ of call** escale *f*; (figurative) arrêt *m*

(b) (drink) porto *m*

(c) (Comput) port *m*

portable *adj* portable

porter *n* **(a)** (in station, airport, hotel) porteur *m*; (in hospital) brancardier *m*

(b) (GB) (doorman) (of hotel) portier *m*; (of apartment block) gardien/-ienne *m/f*

(c) (US) (steward) employé *m* des wagons-lits

portfolio *n* **(a)** (case) porte-documents *m* *inv*; (for drawings) carton *m* (à dessins)

(b) (sample) portfolio *m*

(c) (in politics, finance) portefeuille *m*

porthole *n* hublot *m*

portion *n* **(a)** (of house, machine, document, country) partie *f* (**of** de)

(b) (share) (of money, blame) part *f* (**of** de)

(c) (at meal) portion *f*

portrait *n* portrait *m*

portray *vtr* **(a)** (depict) décrire ⟨*place, era, event*⟩; présenter ⟨*person, situation*⟩

(b) ⟨*actor*⟩ interpréter ⟨*character*⟩

(c) ⟨*artist*⟩ peindre ⟨*person*⟩; ⟨*picture, artist*⟩ représenter ⟨*scene*⟩

Portugal *pr n* Portugal *m*

Portuguese **1** *n* **(a)** (person) Portugais/-e *m/f*

(b) (language) portugais *m*

2 *adj* portugais/-e

pose **1** *vtr* poser ⟨*problem*⟩ (**for** pour); présenter ⟨*challenge*⟩ (**to** à); représenter ⟨*threat, risk*⟩ (**to** pour); soulever ⟨*question*⟩ (**about** de)

2 *vi* **(a)** ⟨*artist's model*⟩ poser; ⟨*performer*⟩ prendre des poses

(b) **to ~ as** se faire passer pour

(c) (posture) frimer (colloq)

poser *n* (colloq) **(a)** (person) frimeur/-euse *m/f* (colloq)

(b) (puzzle) colle *f* (colloq)

posh *adj* (colloq) ⟨*person*⟩ huppé/-e (colloq); ⟨*house, area, clothes, car*⟩ chic; ⟨*voice*⟩ distingué/-e

position **1** *n* **(a)** (gen) position *f*; **to be in ~** (in place) être en place; (ready) être prêt/-e

(b) (situation, state) situation *f*; **to be in a ~ to do** être en mesure de faire

(c) (Sport) poste *m*; **what ~ does he play?** quel est son poste?

(d) (job) poste *m*

2 *vtr* poster ⟨*policemen, soldiers*⟩; disposer ⟨*object*⟩

positive *adj* **(a)** (affirmative) ⟨*answer, reaction, result*⟩ positif/-ive

(b) (optimistic) ⟨*message, person, feeling, tone*⟩ positif/-ive

(c) (constructive) ⟨*contribution, effect, progress*⟩ positif/-ive; ⟨*advantage, good*⟩ réel/réelle (*before n*)

(d) (sure) ⟨*identification, proof*⟩ formel/-elle; ⟨*fact*⟩ indéniable; **to be ~** être sûr/-e (**about** de; **that** que)

(e) (forceful) ⟨*action*⟩ catégorique

(f) (in mathematics, science) positif/-ive

(g) (extreme) ⟨*pleasure*⟩ pur/-e (*before n*); ⟨*disgrace, outrage, genius*⟩ véritable (*before n*)

positive discrimination *n* mesures *fpl* antidiscriminatoires

possess *vtr* **(a)** posséder ⟨*property, weapon, proof, charm*⟩; avoir ⟨*power, advantage*⟩; (illegally) détenir ⟨*arms, drugs*⟩

(b) (take control of) ⟨*anger, fury*⟩ s'emparer de ⟨*person*⟩; ⟨*devil*⟩ posséder ⟨*person*⟩; **what ~ed you to do that?** qu'est-ce qui t'a pris de faire ça?

possession **1** *n* **(a)** (gen) possession *f*

(b) (Law) (illegal) détention *f* (**of** de)

2 **possessions** *n pl* biens *mpl*

possessive **1** *n* (in grammar) possessif *m*

2 *adj* possessif/-ive (**towards** à l'égard de; **with** avec)

p

possibility n (a) (chance, prospect)
possibilité f
(b) (eventuality) éventualité f

possible adj possible; **he did as much as
~** il a fait tout son possible; **as far as ~**
dans la mesure du possible; **as quickly as ~**
le plus vite possible; **as soon as ~** dès que
possible

possibly adv (a) (maybe) peut-être
(b) (for emphasis) **how could they ~
understand?** comment donc pourraient-ils
comprendre?; **we can't ~ afford it** nous n'en
avons absolument pas les moyens

post 1 n (a) (job) poste m (**as, of** de); **to
hold a ~** occuper un poste
(b) (GB) (postal system) poste f; (letters)
courrier m; (delivery) distribution f; **by return
of ~** par retour du courrier; **it was lost in
the ~** cela s'est égaré dans le courrier
(c) (Mil) poste m
(d) (pole) poteau m
2 **post-** pref post-; **in ~-1992 Europe** dans
l'Europe d'après 1992
3 vtr (a) (GB) (send by post) poster, expédier
[qch] (par la poste); (put in letterbox) mettre
[qch] à la poste
(b) (stick up) afficher ‹notice, poster›;
annoncer ‹details, results›
(c) (gen, Mil) (send abroad) affecter (**to** à)
(d) (station) poster ‹guard, sentry›

postage n affranchissement m; **including
~ and packing** frais mpl d'expédition inclus;
~ free franc de port

postal adj ‹charges, district› postal/-e;
‹application› par la poste

postal order, **PO** n (GB) mandat m (**for**
de)

postbox n (GB) boîte f aux lettres

postcard n carte f postale

post code n (GB) code m postal

postdate vtr postdater

poster n (for information) affiche f; (decorative)
poster m

posterity n postérité f

poster paint n gouache f

postgraduate 1 n ≈ étudiant/-e m/f de
troisième cycle
2 adj ≈ de troisième cycle

posthumous adj posthume

postman n facteur m

postmark n cachet m de la poste

post-mortem n autopsie f

post-natal adj post-natal/-e

post office, **PO** n poste f

postpone vtr reporter, remettre (**until** à;
for de)

postscript n (in letter) post-scriptum m inv
(**to** à); (to book) postface f (**to** à)

posture 1 n (a) (pose) posture f; (figurative)
(stance) position f
(b) (bearing) maintien m; **to have good/bad ~**
se tenir bien/mal
2 vi poser, prendre des poses

post-viral (fatigue) syndrome n
encéphalomyélite f myalgique

postwar adj d'après-guerre

pot 1 n (a) (container) pot m
(b) (teapot) théière f; (coffee pot) cafetière f
(c) **~s and pans** casseroles fpl
(d) (piece of pottery) poterie f
2 vtr (a) mettre [qch] en pot ‹jam›
(b) (in billiards) blouser ‹ball›
(c) mettre [qch] en pot ‹plant›
3 **potted** pp adj (a) ‹plant› en pot
(b) ‹biography, history› bref/brève (**before** n)
IDIOMS **to go to ~** (colloq) ‹person› se laisser
aller; ‹situation› aller à vau-l'eau; **to take ~
luck (for meal)** (GB) manger à la fortune du
pot; (gen) prendre ce que l'on trouve

potassium n potassium m

potato n pomme f de terre

potato chips (US), **potato crisps**
(GB) n pl chips fpl

potato peeler n épluche-légumes m inv

pot belly n bedaine f

potent adj (a) ‹symbol, drug› puissant/-e;
‹drink› fort/-e
(b) (sexually) viril/-e

potential 1 n potentiel m (**as** en tant que;
for de); **the ~ to do** les qualités fpl
nécessaires pour faire; **to fulfil one's ~**
montrer de quoi on est capable
2 adj ‹buyer, danger, energy, market, victim›
potentiel/-ielle; ‹champion, rival› en
puissance; ‹investor› éventuel/-elle

pothole n fondrière f, nid m de poule

potholing n (GB) spéléologie f

pot plant n plante f d'appartement

potter n potier m
■ **potter about**, **potter around** (GB) (do
odd jobs) bricoler (colloq); (go about daily chores)
suivre son petit train-train (colloq)

pottery n poterie f

potting compost n terreau m

potty (colloq) 1 n pot m (d'enfant)
2 adj (GB) ‹person› dingue (colloq); ‹idea›
farfelu/-e (colloq); **to be ~ about** être toqué/-e
de (colloq)

pouch n (a) (bag) petit sac m; (for tobacco)
blague f (à tabac); (for ammunition) étui m (à
munitions)
(b) (of marsupials) poche f ventrale

poultry n (birds) volailles fpl; (meat) volaille f

pounce vi bondir; **to ~ on** ‹animal› bondir
sur ‹prey, object›; ‹person› se jeter sur
‹victim›

pound 1 n (a) (weight measurement) livre f
(= 453.6 g); **two ~s of apples** ≈ un kilo de
pommes
(b) (unit of currency) livre f
(c) (for dogs, cars) fourrière f
2 vtr (a) (Culin) piler ‹spices, grain›; aplatir
‹meat›
(b) ‹waves› battre ‹shore›
(c) ‹artillery› pilonner ‹city›
3 vi (a) **to ~ on** marteler ‹door, wall›
(b) ‹heart› battre

(c) to ~ up/down the stairs monter/
descendre l'escalier d'un pas lourd
(d) my head is ~ing j'ai l'impression que
ma tête va éclater
pour 1 vtr (a) verser ⟨liquid⟩; couler
⟨cement, metal, wax⟩
(b) (also ~ out) servir ⟨drink⟩
(c) to ~ money into investir des sommes
énormes dans
2 vi (a) ⟨liquid⟩ couler (à flots); to ~ into
⟨water, liquid⟩ couler dans; ⟨smoke, fumes⟩
se répandre dans; ⟨light⟩ inonder ⟨room⟩;
tears ~ed down her face les larmes
ruisselaient sur son visage
(b) to ~ into ⟨people⟩ affluer dans; to ~ out
of ⟨people, cars⟩ sortir en grand nombre de
3 v impers it's ~ing (with rain) il pleut à
verse
■ **pour away** vider
■ **pour in** ⟨people⟩ affluer; ⟨letters, money⟩
pleuvoir; ⟨water⟩ entrer à flots
■ **pour out**: ¶ ~ out ⟨liquid, smoke, crowd⟩
se déverser; ⟨people⟩ sortir en grand nombre
¶ ~ [sth] out (a) verser, servir ⟨coffee, wine⟩
(b) rejeter ⟨fumes, sewage⟩; to ~ out one's
troubles or heart to sb s'épancher auprès de
qn
pout vi faire la moue
poverty n pauvreté f; (more severe) misère f
poverty line n seuil m de pauvreté
poverty-stricken adj dans la misère
POW n (abbr = **prisoner of war**)
prisonnier/-ière m/f de guerre
powder 1 n poudre f
2 vtr to ~ one's face se poudrer le visage
powdered adj ⟨egg, milk, coffee⟩ en
poudre
powdery adj ⟨snow⟩ poudreux/-euse;
⟨stone⟩ friable
power 1 n (a) (control) pouvoir m; to be in/
come to ~ être/accéder au pouvoir; to be in
sb's ~ être à la merci de qn
(b) (influence) influence f (over sur)
(c) (capability) pouvoir m; to do everything in
one's ~ faire tout ce qui est en son pouvoir
(to do pour faire)
(d) (also ~s) (authority) attributions fpl
(e) (physical force) (of person, explosion) force f;
(of storm) violence f
(f) (Tech) énergie f; (current) courant m; to
switch on the ~ mettre le courant
(g) (of vehicle, plane) puissance f; to be
running at full/half ~ fonctionner à plein/
mi-régime
(h) (in mathematics) 6 to the ~ of 3 6
puissance 3
(i) (country) puissance f
2 adj ⟨drill, cable⟩ électrique; ⟨brakes⟩
assisté/-e
3 vtr faire marcher ⟨engine⟩; propulser
⟨plane, boat⟩
IDIOMS to do sb a ~ of good faire à qn un
bien fou; the ~s that be les autorités
powerboat n hors-bord m inv
power cut n coupure f de courant

powerful adj ⟨person, engine, computer⟩
puissant/-e; ⟨smell, emotion, voice,
government⟩ fort/-e; ⟨argument⟩ solide
powerless adj impuissant/-e (against face
à); to be ~ to do ne pas pouvoir faire
power line n ligne f à haute tension
power of attorney n procuration f
power plant (US), **power station** n
centrale f (électrique)
power sharing n partage m du pouvoir
power steering n direction f assistée
power user n (Comput) utilisateur/-trice
mf avancé/-e
PR n (a) (abbr = **public relations**)
relations fpl publiques
(b) abbr = PROPORTIONAL REPRESENTATION
practical 1 n (exam) épreuve f pratique;
(lesson) travaux mpl pratiques
2 adj (a) (gen) pratique
(b) ⟨plan⟩ réalisable
practicality n (a) (of person) esprit m
pratique; (of equipment) facilité f d'utilisation
(b) (of scheme, idea, project) aspect m pratique
practical joke n farce f
practically adv (a) (almost) pratiquement
(b) (in practical way) d'une manière pratique
practice 1 n (a) (exercises) exercices mpl;
(experience) entraînement m; to have had ~
in or at sth/in or at doing sth avoir déjà fait
qch; to be out of ~ être rouillé/-e (colloq)
(b) (for sport) entraînement m; (for music,
drama) répétition f
(c) (procedure) pratique f, usage m; it's
standard ~ to do il est d'usage de faire;
business ~ usage en affaires
(d) (habit) habitude f
(e) (custom) coutume f
(f) (business of doctor, lawyer) cabinet m
(g) (not theory) pratique f; in ~ en pratique
2 adj ⟨game, match⟩ d'essai; ⟨flight⟩
d'entraînement
3 vtr, vi (US) = PRACTISE
IDIOMS ~ makes perfect c'est en forgeant
qu'on devient forgeron (Proverb)
practise (GB), **practice** (US) 1 vtr (a)
travailler ⟨song, speech, French⟩; s'exercer à
⟨movement, shot⟩; répéter ⟨play⟩; to ~ the
piano travailler le piano; to ~ doing or how
to do s'entraîner à faire
(b) (use) pratiquer ⟨restraint, kindness⟩;
utiliser ⟨method⟩
(c) exercer ⟨profession⟩
(d) (observe) pratiquer ⟨custom, religion⟩
2 vi (a) (at instrument) s'exercer; (for sports)
s'entraîner; (for play, concert) répéter
(b) (work) exercer; to ~ as exercer la
profession de ⟨doctor, lawyer⟩
practising (GB), **practicing** (US) adj
⟨Christian, Muslim⟩ pratiquant/-e; ⟨doctor,
lawyer⟩ en exercice; ⟨homosexual⟩ actif/-ive
pragmatic adj pragmatique
pragmatist n pragmatiste mf
prairie n plaine f (herbeuse)
praise 1 n éloges mpl, louanges fpl ⸱⸱⸱⟶

2 *vtr* **(a)** faire l'éloge de ⟨*person, book*⟩ **(as en tant que)**
(b) louer ⟨*God*⟩ **(for pour)**
praiseworthy *adj* digne d'éloges
pram *n* (GB) landau *m*
prance *vi* ⟨*horse*⟩ caracoler; ⟨*person*⟩ sautiller
prank *n* farce *f*
prattle *vi* bavarder; ⟨*children*⟩ babiller; **to ~ on about sth** parler de qch à n'en plus finir
prawn *n* crevette *f* rose, bouquet *m*
pray *vi* prier **(for pour)**
prayer *n* prière *f*; **to say one's ~s** faire sa prière
preach **1** *vtr* prêcher **(to à)**
2 *vi* prêcher **(to à)**; (figurative) sermonner
IDIOMS **to practise what one ~es** prêcher d'exemple
preacher *n* prédicateur *m*; ⟨*clergyman*⟩ pasteur *m*
prearrange *vtr* fixer [qch] à l'avance
precarious *adj* précaire
precaution *n* précaution *f* **(against contre)**
precautionary *adj* préventif/-ive
precede *vtr* précéder
precedence *n* **(a)** (in importance) priorité *f* **(over sur)**
(b) (in rank) préséance *f* **(over sur)**
precedent *n* précédent *m*; **to set a ~** créer un précédent
preceding *adj* précédent/-e
precinct *n* **(a)** (GB) (*also* **shopping ~**) quartier *m* commerçant
(b) (GB) (*also* **pedestrian ~**) zone *f* piétonne
(c) (US) (administrative district) circonscription *f*
precious *adj* **(a)** (valuable) précieux/-ieuse
(b) (held dear) ⟨*person*⟩ cher/chère **(to à)**
(c) (affected) précieux/-ieuse, affecté/-e
precipice *n* précipice *m*
précis *n* résumé *m*
precise *adj* **(a)** (exact) précis/-e
(b) ⟨*person, mind*⟩ méticuleux/-euse
precisely *adv* **(a)** (exactly) exactement, précisément; **at ten o'clock ~** à dix heures précises
(b) (accurately) ⟨*describe, record*⟩ avec précision
precision *n* précision *f*
preclude *vtr* exclure ⟨*possibility*⟩; empêcher ⟨*action*⟩
precocious *adj* précoce
preconceived *adj* préconçu/-e
preconception *n* opinion *f* préconçue
precondition *n* condition *f* requise
precursor *n* (person) précurseur *m*; (sign) signe *m* avant-coureur
predate *vtr* antidater ⟨*cheque*⟩; ⟨*discovery, building*⟩ être antérieur/-e à
predator *n* prédateur *m*
predecessor *n* prédécesseur *m*

predetermine *vtr* déterminer d'avance
predicament *n* situation *f* difficile
predict *vtr* prédire
predictable *adj* prévisible
prediction *n* prédiction *f* **(that selon laquelle)**
predispose *vtr* prédisposer
predominant *adj* prédominant/-e
predominantly *adv* principalement
predominate *vi* prédominer
pre-eminent *adj* éminent/-e
pre-empt *vtr* **(a)** anticiper ⟨*question, decision, move*⟩; devancer ⟨*person*⟩
(b) (thwart) contrecarrer ⟨*action, plan*⟩
pre-emptive *adj* préventif/-ive
preen *v refl* **to ~ oneself** ⟨*bird*⟩ se lisser les plumes; ⟨*person*⟩ se pomponner
prefab *n* (bâtiment *m*) préfabriqué *m*
preface *n* (to book) préface *f*; (to speech) préambule *m*
prefect *n* (GB) (Sch) élève *m/f* chargé/-e de la surveillance
prefer *vtr* **(a)** (like better) préférer, aimer mieux; **I ~ painting to drawing** je préfère la peinture au dessin; **to ~ it if** aimer mieux que (+ *subjunctive*)
(b) (Law) **to ~ charges** ⟨*police*⟩ déférer [qn] au parquet
preferable *adj* préférable **(to à)**
preferably *adv* de préférence
preference *n* préférence *f* **(for pour)**
preferential *adj* préférentiel/-ielle
prefigure *vtr* ⟨*event*⟩ préfigurer; ⟨*person*⟩ être le précurseur de
prefix *n* préfixe *m*
pregnancy *n* (gen) grossesse *f*; (Zool) gestation *f*
pregnant *adj* (gen) enceinte; (Zool) pleine; **to get sb ~** (colloq) faire un enfant à qn (colloq)
preheat *vtr* préchauffer ⟨*oven*⟩
prehistoric *adj* préhistorique
prejudice **1** *n* préjugé *m*; **racial/political ~** préjugés raciaux/en matière de politique
2 *vtr* **(a)** (bias) influencer; **to ~ sb against/in favour of** prévenir qn contre/en faveur de
(b) porter préjudice à ⟨*claim, case*⟩; léser ⟨*person*⟩; compromettre ⟨*chances*⟩
prejudiced *adj* ⟨*person*⟩ plein/-e de préjugés; ⟨*account*⟩ partial/-e; ⟨*opinion*⟩ préconçu/-e
preliminary **1** *n* **(a)** (gen) **as a ~ to** en prélude à
(b) (Sport) épreuve *f* éliminatoire
2 **preliminaries** *n pl* préliminaires *mpl* **(to à)**
3 *adj* préliminaire
prelude *n* prélude *m* **(to à)**
premarital *adj* avant le mariage
premature *adj* ⟨*baby, action*⟩ prématuré/-e; ⟨*ejaculation, menopause*⟩ précoce

premeditate *vtr* préméditer

premier ☐1☐ *n* premier ministre *m*
☐2☐ *adj* premier/-ière ⟨*before n*⟩

première ☐1☐ *n* première *f*
☐2☐ *vtr* donner [qch] en première ⟨*film, play*⟩

premises *n pl* locaux *mpl*; **on the ~** sur place; **off the ~** à l'extérieur; **to leave the ~** quitter les lieux

premium *n* (a) (extra payment) supplément *m*
(b) (on stock exchange) prime *f* d'émission
(c) (in insurance) prime *f* (d'assurance)
(d) **to be at a ~** valoir de l'or; **to set a** ⟨**high**⟩ **~ on sth** mettre qch au (tout) premier plan

premium bond (GB) *n* obligation *f* à lots

premonition *n* prémonition *f*

prenatal *adj* prénatal/-e

preoccupation *n* préoccupation *f*

preoccupied *adj* préoccupé/-e

preoccupy *vtr* préoccuper

prepaid *adj* payé/-e d'avance; **~ envelope** enveloppe *f* affranchie pour la réponse

preparation *n* préparation *f*; **~s** préparatifs *mpl*; **in ~ for sth** en vue de qch

preparatory *adj* ⟨*training, course, drawing*⟩ préparatoire; ⟨*meeting, report, investigations*⟩ préliminaire

preparatory school *n* (a) (GB) école *f* primaire privée
(b) (US) lycée *m* privé

prepare ☐1☐ *vtr* préparer; **to ~ to do** se préparer à faire; **to ~ sb for** préparer qn à
☐2☐ *vi* **to ~ for** se préparer à ⟨*trip, talks, exam, war*⟩; se préparer pour ⟨*party, ceremony, game*⟩; **to ~ oneself** se préparer

prepared *adj* (a) (willing) **to be ~ to do** être prêt/-e à faire
(b) (ready) **to be ~ for** être prêt/-e pour ⟨*event*⟩; **to come ~** venir bien préparé/-e; **to be ~ for the worst** s'attendre au pire

preposition *n* préposition *f*

preposterous *adj* grotesque

prerequisite *n* (a) (gen) préalable *m* (of de; for à)
(b) (US) (Univ) unité *f* de valeur

prerogative *n* (official) prérogative *f*; (personal) droit *m*

preschool ☐1☐ *n* (US) école *f* maternelle
☐2☐ *adj* préscolaire

prescribe *vtr* (a) (Med, figurative) prescrire (for sb à qn; for sth pour qch)
(b) imposer ⟨*rule*⟩

prescription *n* ordonnance *f*; **repeat ~** ordonnance renouvelable

prescription charges *n pl* frais *mpl* d'ordonnance

presence *n* présence *f*

presence of mind *n* présence *f* d'esprit

present ☐1☐ *n* (a) (gift) cadeau *m*; **to give sb a ~** offrir un cadeau à qn
(b) **the ~** le présent; **for the ~** pour le moment, pour l'instant
(c) (also **~ tense**) présent *m*

☐2☐ *adj* (a) (attending) présent/-e; **to be ~ at** assister à
(b) (current) actuel/-elle; **up to the ~ day** jusqu'à ce jour
☐3☐ *vtr* (a) (gen) présenter; offrir ⟨*chance, opportunity*⟩; **to be ~ed with a choice** se trouver face à un choix
(b) remettre ⟨*prize, certificate*⟩ (to à)
☐4☐ *v refl* **to ~ oneself** se présenter; **to ~ itself** ⟨*opportunity, thought*⟩ se présenter
☐5☐ **at present** *phr* (at this moment) en ce moment; (nowadays) actuellement

presentable *adj* présentable

presentation *n* (a) (gen) présentation *f*
(b) (talk) exposé *m*
(c) (of gift, award) remise *f* (of de)
(d) (portrayal) représentation *f*

present-day *adj* actuel/-elle

presenter *n* présentateur/-trice *m/f*

presently *adv* (currently) à présent; (soon, in future) bientôt

present perfect *n* passé *m* composé

preservation *n* (of building, wildlife, peace) préservation *f* (of de); (of food) conservation *f* (of de); (of life) protection *f* (of de)

preservative *n* (for food) agent *m* de conservation; (for wood) revêtement *m* (protecteur)

preserve ☐1☐ *n* (a) (Culin) (jam) confiture *f*; (pickle) conserve *f*
(b) (territory) chasse *f* gardée (of de)
☐2☐ *vtr* (a) (save) préserver ⟨*land, building, tradition*⟩ (for pour); entretenir ⟨*wood, leather, painting*⟩
(b) (maintain) préserver ⟨*peace, standards, rights*⟩; maintenir ⟨*order*⟩; garder ⟨*humour, dignity, health*⟩
(c) conserver ⟨*food*⟩

preset *vtr* régler (à l'avance) ⟨*timer, cooker*⟩; programmer ⟨*video*⟩

preside *vi* présider; **to ~ at sth** présider qch; **to ~ over** présider ⟨*conference, committee*⟩

presidency *n* présidence *f*

president *n* (a) président/-e *m/f*; **to run for ~** être candidat/-e à la présidence
(b) (US) (managing director) président-directeur *m* général

presidential *adj* présidentiel/-ielle

press ☐1☐ *n* (a) **the ~, the Press** la presse *f*; **to get a good/bad ~** avoir bonne/mauvaise presse
(b) (also **printing ~**) presse *f*
(c) (device for flattening) presse *f*
☐2☐ *vtr* (a) (push) appuyer sur; **to ~ sth in** enfoncer qch; **to ~ one's nose against sth** coller son nez contre qch
(b) (squeeze) presser ⟨*fruit, flower*⟩; serrer ⟨*arm, hand, person*⟩
(c) (iron) repasser ⟨*clothes*⟩
(d) (urge) faire pression sur ⟨*person*⟩; mettre [qch] en avant ⟨*issue*⟩; **to ~ sb to do** presser qn de faire; **to ~ a point** insister
☐3☐ *vi* (a) **to ~ (down)** appuyer

(b) ⟨crowd, person⟩ se presser (**forward** vers l'avant)

4 v refl **to ~ oneself against** se plaquer contre ⟨wall⟩; se presser contre ⟨person⟩

■ **press for** faire pression pour obtenir ⟨change, release⟩; **to be ~ed for** ne pas avoir beaucoup de ⟨time, cash⟩

■ **press on** continuer; **to ~ on with** faire avancer ⟨reform, plan⟩

press agency n agence f de presse

press conference n conférence f de presse

pressing adj (a) (urgent) urgent/-e (b) ⟨invitation⟩ pressant/-e

press release n communiqué m de presse

press-stud n (GB) (bouton-)pression m

press-up n pompe f (colloq)

pressure n (a) (gen) pression f; **to put ~ on sb** faire pression sur qn; **to do sth under ~** faire qch sous la contrainte (b) (of traffic, tourists) flux m

pressure cooker n cocotte-minute® f

pressure group n groupe m de pression

pressurize vtr (a) pressuriser ⟨cabin, suit, gas⟩ (b) faire pression sur ⟨person⟩; **he was ~d into going on** a fait pression sur lui pour qu'il y aille

prestige n prestige m

prestigious adj prestigieux/-ieuse

presumably adv sans doute

presume vtr (a) (suppose) supposer, présumer (b) (dare) **to ~ to do** se permettre de faire

presumptuous adj présomptueux/-euse, arrogant/-e

presuppose vtr présupposer (**that** que)

pre-tax adj avant impôts inv

pretence (GB), **pretense** (US) n faux-semblant m; **to make a ~ of sth** feindre qch; **to make a ~ of doing** faire semblant de faire

pretend **1** vtr **to ~ that** faire comme si; **to ~ to do** faire semblant de faire **2** vi faire semblant

pretension n prétention f

pretentious adj prétentieux/-ieuse

preterite n prétérit

pretext n prétexte m

pretty **1** adj joli/-e; **it was not a ~ sight** ce n'était pas beau à voir **2** adv (colloq) (very) vraiment; (fairly) assez; **~ good** pas mal du tout

prevail vi (a) (win) prévaloir (**against** contre) (b) (be common) prédominer

■ **prevail upon** persuader ⟨person⟩

prevailing adj ⟨attitude, style⟩ qui prévaut; ⟨rate⟩ en vigueur; ⟨wind⟩ dominant/-e

prevalent adj (a) (widespread) répandu/-e (b) (ruling) qui prévaut

prevaricate vi se dérober

prevent vtr prévenir ⟨fire, illness, violence⟩; éviter ⟨conflict, disaster, damage⟩; faire obstacle à ⟨marriage⟩; **to ~ sb from doing** empêcher qn de faire

preventable adj évitable

prevention n prévention f; **crime ~** lutte f contre la délinquance

preventive adj préventif/-ive

preview n (of film, play) avant-première f

previous adj précédent/-e; (further back in time) antérieur/-e

previously adv (before) auparavant, avant; (already) déjà

prewar adj d'avant-guerre inv

prey n proie f

■ **prey on** (a) (hunt) chasser (b) (worry) **to ~ on sb's mind** préoccuper qn (c) (exploit) exploiter ⟨fears, worries⟩

price **1** n (a) (cost) prix m; **to go up in ~** augmenter; **to pay a high ~ for sth** payer qch cher; **at any ~** à tout prix (b) (value) valeur f; **to put a ~ on** évaluer ⟨object, antique⟩ **2** vtr fixer le prix de (**at** à)

price cut n baisse f du prix

price freeze n blocage m des prix

priceless adj (a) (extremely valuable) inestimable (b) (colloq) (amusing) impayable (colloq)

price list n (in shop, catalogue) liste f des prix; (in bar, restaurant) tarif m

price rise n hausse f des prix

price tag n (label) étiquette f

price war n guerre f des prix

prick **1** n (of needle) piqûre f **2** vtr piquer; **to ~ one's finger** se piquer le doigt **3** vi piquer

■ **prick up**: **to ~ up one's ears** ⟨person⟩ dresser l'oreille; **the dog ~ed up its ears** le chien a dressé les oreilles

prickle **1** n (of hedgehog, plant) piquant m **2** vi ⟨hairs⟩ se hérisser (**with** de)

prickly adj (a) ⟨bush, leaf⟩ épineux/-euse; ⟨animal⟩ armé/-e de piquants; ⟨thorn⟩ piquant/-e (b) (itchy) qui gratte (c) (colloq) (touchy) irritable (**about** à propos de)

pride **1** n (a) fierté f; **to take ~ in** être fier/fière de ⟨ability, achievement⟩; soigner ⟨appearance, work⟩; **to be sb's ~ and joy** être la (grande) fierté de qn (b) (self-respect) amour-propre m; (excessive) orgueil m (c) (of lions) troupe f **2** v refl **to ~ oneself on sth/on doing** être fier/fière de qch/de faire IDIOMS **to have ~ of place** occuper la place d'honneur

priest n prêtre m; **parish ~** curé m

priesthood n (calling) prêtrise f; **to enter the ~** entrer dans les ordres

prig n bégueule mf

prim *adj* (also ~ **and proper**) ⟨*person, manner, appearance*⟩ guindé/-e; ⟨*expression*⟩ pincé/-e; ⟨*voice*⟩ affecté/-e; ⟨*clothing*⟩ très convenable

primarily *adv* (chiefly) essentiellement; (originally) à l'origine

primary ⟦1⟧ *n* (US) (also ~ **election**) primaire *f*
⟦2⟧ *adj* (a) (main) principal/-e; ⟨*sense, meaning, stage*⟩ premier/-ière; **of ~ importance** de première importance
(b) (Sch) ⟨*teaching, education*⟩ primaire
(c) ⟨*industry, products*⟩ de base

primary colour (GB), **primary color** (US) *n* couleur *f* primaire

primary school *n* école *f* primaire

primary (school) teacher *n* (GB) instituteur/-trice *m/f*

primate *n* (a) (mammal) primate *m*
(b) (archbishop) primat *m* (of de)

prime ⟦1⟧ *n* **in one's ~** (professionally) à son apogée; (physically) dans la fleur de l'âge; **in its ~** à son apogée; **to be past its ~** avoir connu des jours meilleurs
⟦2⟧ *adj* (a) (chief) principal/-e; ⟨*importance*⟩ primordial/-e
(b) (good quality) ⟨*site*⟩ de premier ordre; ⟨*meat, cuts*⟩ de premier choix; **of ~ quality** de première qualité
(c) (classic) ⟨*example*⟩ excellent/-e (before n)
⟦3⟧ *vtr* (a) (brief) préparer; **to ~ sb about** mettre qn au courant de; **to ~ sb to say** souffler à qn de dire
(b) (Mil, Tech) amorcer

prime minister, PM *n* Premier ministre *m*

prime mover *n* (person) promoteur/-trice *m/f*

prime number *n* nombre *m* premier

prime time *n* heures *fpl* de grande écoute *m*

primeval *adj* primitif/-ive

primitive ⟦1⟧ *n* primitif *m*
⟦2⟧ *adj* primitif/-ive

primrose *n* primevère *f* (jaune)

prince *n* prince *m*

princess *n* princesse *f*

principal ⟦1⟧ *n* (of senior school) proviseur *m*; (of junior school, college) directeur/-trice *m/f*
⟦2⟧ *adj* principal/-e

principle *n* principe *m*; **in ~** en principe; **on ~** par principe

print ⟦1⟧ *n* (a) (typeface) caractères *mpl*; **the small** *or* **fine ~** les détails; **in ~** disponible en librairie; **out of ~** épuisé/-e
(b) (etching) estampe *f*; (engraving) gravure *f*
(c) (of photo) épreuve *f*
(d) (of finger, hand, foot) empreinte *f*; (of tyre) trace *f*
(e) (fabric) tissu *m* imprimé
⟦2⟧ *vtr* (a) imprimer ⟨*book, banknote, pattern, design*⟩
(b) (publish) publier
(c) faire développer ⟨*photos*⟩

(d) (write) écrire [qch] en script

■ **print off** tirer ⟨*copies*⟩

■ **print out** imprimer

printer *n* (person, firm) imprimeur *m*; (machine) imprimante *f*

printout *n* sortie *f* sur imprimante; (perforated) listing *m*

print-preview *vtr* prévisualiser

prior ⟦1⟧ *adj* (a) (previous) préalable; **~ notice** préavis *m*
(b) (more important) prioritaire
⟦2⟧ **prior to** *phr* avant

priority *n* priorité *f*

priory *n* prieuré *m*

prise *v* ■ **prise apart** séparer ⟨*layers, people*⟩

■ **prise off** enlever [qch] en forçant ⟨*lid*⟩

■ **prise open** ouvrir [qch] en forçant ⟨*door*⟩

prism *n* prisme *m*

prison *n* prison *f*; **to put sb in ~** emprisonner qn

prison camp *n* camp *m* de prisonniers

prisoner *n* prisonnier/-ière *m/f*; (in jail) détenu/-e *m/f*

prison officer *n* surveillant/-e *m/f* de prison

prison sentence *n* peine *f* de prison

pristine *adj* immaculé/-e

privacy *n* (a) (private life) vie *f* privée; **to invade sb's ~** s'immiscer dans la vie privée de qn
(b) (solitude) intimité *f* (of de)

private ⟦1⟧ *n* simple soldat *m*
⟦2⟧ *adj* (a) ⟨*property, vehicle, meeting, life*⟩ privé/-e; ⟨*letter, phone call*⟩ personnel/-elle; ⟨*sale*⟩ de particulier à particulier; ⟨*place*⟩ tranquille; **room with ~ bath** chambre avec salle de bains particulière; **a ~ joke** une plaisanterie pour initiés
(b) ⟨*sector, education, school, hospital*⟩ privé/-e; ⟨*accommodation, lesson*⟩ particulier/-ière
⟦3⟧ **in private** *phr* en privé

private eye *n* (colloq) détective *m* privé

privately *adv* (a) (in private) en privé
(b) (not in public sector) dans le privé; **~-owned** privé/-e

privatization *n* privatisation *f*

privatize *vtr* privatiser

privilege *n* privilège *m*

privileged *adj* ⟨*minority, life*⟩ privilégié/-e; ⟨*information*⟩ confidentiel/-ielle

prize ⟦1⟧ *n* (a) (award) prix *m*; (in lottery) lot *m*; **first ~** premier prix; (in lottery) gros lot
(b) (valued object) trésor *m*; (reward for effort) récompense *f*
⟦2⟧ *adj* (a) ⟨*vegetable, bull*⟩ primé/-e; ⟨*pupil*⟩ hors-pair *inv*
(b) ⟨*possession*⟩ précieux/-ieuse
(c) ⟨*idiot, example*⟩ parfait/-e (before n)

prize draw *n* (for charity) tombola *f*; (for advertising) tirage *m* au sort

prize-giving *n* remise *f* des prix

prize money n argent m du prix

prizewinner n (in lottery) gagnant/-e m/f; (of award) lauréat/-e m/f

pro ⓵ n (a) (colloq) (professional) pro mf (colloq) (b) (advantage) the ∼s and cons le pour et le contre; the ∼s and cons of sth les avantages et les inconvénients de qch
⓶ prep (colloq) (in favour of) pour

proactive adj ⟨approach, role⟩ dynamique

probability n (of desirable event) chances fpl; (of unwelcome event) risques mpl

probable adj probable

probably adv probablement

probation n (a) (for adult) sursis m avec mise à l'épreuve; (for juvenile) mise f en liberté surveillée
(b) (trial period) période f d'essai

probationary adj (trial) ⟨period, year⟩ d'essai; (training) ⟨period⟩ probatoire

probation officer n (for juveniles) délégué/-e m/f à la liberté surveillée; (for adults) agent m de probation

probe ⓵ n (a) (investigation) enquête f
(b) (instrument) sonde f
⓶ vtr (Med, Tech) sonder (**with** avec)

probing adj ⟨look⟩ inquisiteur/-trice; ⟨question⟩ pénétrant/-e; ⟨examination⟩ très poussé-e

problem ⓵ n problème m
⓶ adj ⟨child⟩ difficile; ⟨family⟩ à problèmes

problematic(al) adj problématique

problem page n courrier m du cœur

procedure n procédure f

proceed vi (a) (set about) procéder; (continue) poursuivre; to ∼ with poursuivre
(b) (be in progress) ⟨project, work⟩ avancer; ⟨interview, talks, trial⟩ se poursuivre
(c) ⟨person, road⟩ continuer; ⟨vehicle⟩ avancer

proceedings n pl (a) (meeting) réunion f; (ceremony) cérémonie f; (discussion) débats mpl
(b) (Law) poursuites fpl

proceeds n pl (of sale) produit m; (of event) recette f

process ⓵ n (a) (gen) processus m (**of** de); to be in the ∼ of doing être en train de faire; in the ∼ en même temps
(b) (method) procédé m
⓶ vtr (a) traiter ⟨applications, data⟩
(b) traiter ⟨raw materials, chemical, waste⟩
(c) développer ⟨film⟩
(d) (Culin) (mix) mixer; (chop) hacher

processing n traitement m; the food ∼ industry l'industrie alimentaire

procession n (of demonstration, carnival) défilé m; (formal) cortège m; (religious) procession f

processor n (Comput) unité f centrale

proclaim vtr proclamer (**that** que)

proclamation n proclamation f

procrastinate vi atermoyer

procure vtr procurer; to ∼ sth for sb procurer qch à qn; to ∼ sth for oneself se procurer qch

prod ⓵ n (a) (poke) petit coup m
(b) (colloq) (reminder) to give sb a ∼ secouer (colloq) qn
⓶ vtr (also ∼ **at**) (with foot, instrument, stick) donner des petits coups à; (with finger) toucher

prodigy n prodige m

produce ⓵ n produits mpl
⓶ vtr (a) (cause) produire ⟨result, effect⟩; provoquer ⟨reaction, change⟩
(b) ⟨region, farmer, company⟩ produire (**from** à partir de); ⟨worker, machine⟩ fabriquer
(c) (generate) produire ⟨heat, sound, energy⟩; rapporter ⟨profits⟩
(d) (present) produire ⟨passport, report⟩; fournir ⟨evidence, argument, example⟩; to ∼ sth from sortir qch de ⟨pocket, bag⟩
(e) produire ⟨show, film⟩; (GB) mettre [qch] en scène ⟨play⟩
(f) (put together) préparer ⟨meal⟩; mettre au point ⟨timetable, package, solution⟩; éditer ⟨brochure, guide⟩

producer n (a) (of produce) producteur m; (of machinery, goods) fabricant m
(b) (of film) producteur/-trice m/f; (GB) (of play) metteur m en scène

product n produit m

production n (a) (of crop, foodstuffs, metal) production f (**of** de); (of machinery, furniture, cars) fabrication (**of** de)
(b) (output) production f
(c) (of film, opera) production f (**of** de); (of play) mise f en scène (**of** de)

production line n chaîne f de fabrication

productive adj ⟨factory, land, day⟩ productif/-ive; ⟨system, method, use⟩ efficace; ⟨discussion⟩ fructueux/-euse

productivity n productivité f

profane adj (a) (blasphemous) impie
(b) (secular) profane

profession n profession f

professional ⓵ n professionnel/-elle m/f
⓶ adj professionnel/-elle

professionalism n (of person, organization) professionnalisme m; (of performance, work) (haute) qualité f

professionally adv (a) (expertly) ⟨designed⟩ par un professionnel
(b) (in work situation) dans un cadre professionnel
(c) ⟨play sport⟩ en professionnel/-elle; he sings ∼ il est chanteur professionnel
(d) (to a high standard) de manière professionnelle

professor n (a) (Univ) (chair holder) professeur m d'Université
(b) (US Univ) (teacher) professeur m

proficiency n (practical) compétence f (**in**, **at** en); (academic) niveau m (**in** en)

proficient adj compétent/-e

profile n (of face) profil m; (of body)

silhouette f; **in** ∼ de profil; **to have/maintain a high** ∼ occuper/rester sur le devant de la scène

profiling n (gen, Med) typage m

profit ① n (a) bénéfice m, profit m; **gross/ net** ∼ bénéfice brut/net
(b) (figurative) profit m
② vtr profiter à ⟨person, group⟩
③ vi **to** ∼ **by** or **from sth** tirer profit de qch

profitable adj rentable; (figurative) fructueux/-euse

profit margin n marge f bénéficiaire

profit sharing n intéressement m des salariés aux bénéfices

profound adj profond/-e

profuse adj ⟨praise, thanks⟩ profus/-e; ⟨bleeding⟩ abondant/-e

profusely adv ⟨sweat, bleed⟩ abondamment; **to apologize** ∼ se confondre en excuses

prognosis n (a) (Med) pronostic m (**on, about** sur)
(b) (prediction) pronostics mpl

program ① n (a) (Comput) programme m
(b) (US) (on radio, TV) émission f
② vtr, vi programmer (**to do** pour faire)

programme (GB), **program** (US) ① n
(a) (broadcast) émission f (**about** sur)
(b) (schedule) programme m
(c) (for play, opera) programme m
② vtr programmer ⟨machine⟩ (**to do** pour faire)

programmer n programmeur/-euse m/f

progress ① n (a) (advances) progrès m; **to make** ∼ ⟨person⟩ faire des progrès
(b) (of person, inquiry) progression f; (of talks, disease, career) évolution f; **to be in** ∼ ⟨discussions, exam⟩ être en cours
② vi progresser

progression n (a) (evolution) évolution f
(b) (improvement) progression f
(c) (series) suite f

progressive adj (a) (gen) progressif/-ive
(b) (forward-looking) ⟨person, policy⟩ progressiste; ⟨school⟩ parallèle

progress report n (on construction work) rapport m sur l'état des travaux; (on project) rapport m sur l'état du projet; (on patient) bulletin m de santé

prohibit vtr interdire; **to** ∼ **sb from doing** interdire à qn de faire

prohibition n interdiction f (**on, against** de)

prohibitive adj prohibitif/-ive

project ① n (a) (scheme) projet m (**to do** pour faire)
(b) (Sch) dossier m (**on** sur); (Univ) mémoire m (**on** sur); **research** ∼ programme m de recherches
(c) (US) (state housing) (large) ≈ cité f HLM; (small) ≈ lotissement m HLM
② vtr (a) envoyer ⟨missile⟩; faire porter ⟨voice⟩
(b) projeter ⟨guilt, anxiety⟩ (**onto** sur)

(c) (estimate) prévoir
(d) projeter ⟨image, slides⟩

projecting adj saillant/-e

projector n projecteur m

pro-life adj contre l'avortement

proliferate vi proliférer

prolific adj (gen) prolifique; ⟨decade⟩ fécond/-e; ⟨growth⟩ rapide

prologue n prologue m (**to** de)

prolong vtr prolonger

promenade n (path) promenade f; (by sea) front m de mer

prominent adj (a) ⟨figure, campaigner⟩ très en vue; ⟨artist⟩ éminent/-e; **to play a** ∼ **part in sth** jouer un rôle de premier plan dans qch
(b) ⟨place, feature⟩ proéminent/-e; ⟨ridge, cheekbone⟩ saillant/-e; ⟨eye⟩ exorbité/-e

promiscuity n (sexual) vagabondage m sexuel

promiscuous adj ⟨person⟩ aux mœurs légères

promise ① n promesse f; **to break one's** ∼ manquer à sa promesse; **she shows great** ∼ elle promet beaucoup
② vtr **to** ∼ **to do** promettre de faire; **to** ∼ **sb sth** promettre qch à qn
③ vi promettre; **do you** ∼? c'est promis?

promising adj ⟨situation, result, future⟩ prometteur/-euse; ⟨artist, candidate⟩ qui promet

promote vtr (a) (in rank) promouvoir (**to** à)
(b) (advertise) faire de la publicité pour; (market) promouvoir
(c) (encourage) promouvoir
(d) (GB) (in football) **to be** ∼**d from the fourth to the third division** passer de quatrième en troisième division

promotion n promotion f

promotional video n vidéo f publicitaire

prompt ① adj rapide; **to be** ∼ **to do** être prompt/-e à faire
② vtr (a) provoquer ⟨reaction, decision⟩; susciter ⟨concern, comment⟩; **to** ∼ **sb to do** inciter qn à faire
(b) (remind) souffler à ⟨actor⟩

prompter n (a) (in theatre) souffleur/-euse m/f
(b) (US) (teleprompter) téléprompteur m

promptly adv (a) (immediately) immédiatement
(b) (without delay) rapidement
(c) (punctually) à l'heure; ∼ **at six o'clock** à six heures précises

prone adj (a) **to be** ∼ **to** être sujet/-ette à ⟨colds⟩; être enclin/-e à ⟨depression⟩
(b) **to lie** ∼ être allongé/-e face contre terre

pronoun n pronom m

pronounce vtr prononcer
■ **pronounce on** se prononcer sur ⟨case, matter⟩

pronounced adj ⟨accent, tendency⟩ prononcé/-e; ⟨change, increase⟩ marqué/-e

pronunciation n prononciation f
proof n (a) (evidence) preuve f; ~ **of identity** pièce f d'identité
(b) (in printing, photography) épreuve f
(c) (of alcohol) **to be 70%** ~ ≈ titrer 40° d'alcool
proof of purchase n justificatif m d'achat
proofread vtr corriger les épreuves de
prop 1 n étai m
2 **props** n pl accessoires mpl
3 vtr (a) (also ~ **up**) étayer
(b) **to ~ sb/sth against sth** appuyer qn/qch contre qch
propaganda n propagande f
propagate vi se propager
propel vtr propulser
propeller n hélice f
proper adj (a) (right) ⟨term, spelling⟩ correct/-e; ⟨order, tool, response⟩ bon/bonne (before n); ⟨clothing⟩ qu'il faut; **everything is in the ~ place** tout est à sa place
(b) (adequate) ⟨recognition, facilities⟩ convenable; ⟨education, training⟩ bon/bonne (before n); ⟨care⟩ requis/-e
(c) (respectable) ⟨person⟩ correct/-e; ⟨upbringing⟩ convenable
(d) (real, full) ⟨doctor, holiday, job⟩ vrai/-e (before n)
(e) (actual) **in the village** ~ dans le village même
properly adv (a) (correctly) correctement
(b) (fully) complètement; **I didn't have time to thank you** ~ je n'ai pas eu le temps de vous remercier
(c) (adequately) convenablement
proper name, proper noun n nom m propre
property n (a) (belongings) propriété f, biens mpl
(b) (real estate) biens mpl immobiliers
(c) (house) propriété f
(d) (characteristic) propriété f
property developer n promoteur m immobilier
property owner n propriétaire mf
prophecy n prophétie f
prophet n prophète m
proportion 1 n (a) (of group, population) proportion f (of de); (of income, profit, work) part f (of de)
(b) (ratio) proportion f
(c) (harmony) **out of/in** ~ hors de/en proportion
(d) (perspective) **to get sth out of all** ~ faire tout un drame de qch; **to be out of all** ~ être tout à fait disproportionné/-e (**to** par rapport à)
2 **proportions** n pl dimensions fpl
proportional adj proportionnel/-elle
proportional representation, PR n représentation f proportionnelle
proposal n (a) (suggestion) proposition f
(b) (of marriage) demande f en mariage

propose 1 vtr proposer ⟨course of action, solution⟩; présenter ⟨motion⟩
2 vi faire sa demande en mariage (**to** à)
3 **proposed** pp adj ⟨action, reform⟩ envisagé/-e
proposition 1 n (a) (suggestion) proposition f
(b) (assertion) assertion f
2 vtr faire une proposition à ⟨person⟩
proprietor n propriétaire mf (**of** de)
propriety n (a) (politeness) correction f
(b) (morality) décence f
proscribe vtr proscrire
prose n (a) prose f
(b) (GB) (translation) thème m
prosecute 1 vtr poursuivre [qn] en justice
2 vi engager des poursuites
prosecution n (Law) (a) (accusation) poursuites fpl (judiciaires)
(b) **the** ~ le/les plaignant/-s; (state, Crown) le ministère public
prosecutor n (Law) procureur m
prospect 1 n (a) (hope) espoir m, chance f
(b) (outlook) perspective f
2 **prospects** n pl perspectives fpl
prospective adj ⟨buyer, candidate⟩ potentiel/-ielle; ⟨husband, wife⟩ futur/-e (before n)
prospectus n brochure f
prosper vi prospérer
prosperity n prospérité f
prosperous adj prospère
prostate n (also ~ **gland**) prostate f
prostitute 1 n prostituée f; **male** ~ prostitué m
2 vtr prostituer ⟨person, talent⟩
prostitution n prostitution f
prostrate adj **to lie** ~ être allongé/-e de tout son long; ~ **with grief** accablé/-e de chagrin
protagonist n protagoniste mf
protect vtr (gen) protéger (**against** contre; **from** de, contre); défendre ⟨consumer, interests⟩ (**against** contre)
protection n protection f
protection factor n indice m de protection
protection racket n racket m
protective adj protecteur/-trice
protein n protéine f
protest 1 n (a) protestation f; **in** ~ en signe de protestation
(b) (demonstration) manifestation f
2 vtr (a) **to** ~ **that** protester que; **to** ~ **one's innocence** protester de son innocence
(b) (US) (complain about) protester contre (**to** auprès de)
3 vi (a) (complain) protester
(b) (demonstrate) manifester (**against** contre)
Protestant n, adj protestant/-e (m/f)
protester n manifestant/-e m/f
protocol n protocole m

prototype n prototype m (of de)

protrude vi (gen) dépasser; ⟨teeth⟩ avancer

protruding adj ⟨rock⟩ en saillie; ⟨eyes⟩ globuleux/-euse; ⟨ears⟩ décollé/-e; ⟨ribs⟩ saillant/-e; ⟨chin⟩ en avant

proud adj (a) fier/fière (of de); ⟨owner⟩ heureux/-euse (before n)
(b) ⟨day, moment⟩ grand/-e (before n)

prove ☐1 vtr prouver; (by demonstration) démontrer; to ~ a point montrer qu'on a raison
☐2 vi to ~ to be s'avérer être
☐3 v refl to ~ oneself faire ses preuves; to ~ oneself (to be) se révéler

proverb n proverbe m

provide vtr (a) (supply) fournir ⟨opportunity, evidence, jobs, meals⟩ (for à); apporter ⟨answer, support⟩ (for à); assurer ⟨service, access, training, shelter⟩ (for à)
(b) ⟨clause, law⟩ prévoir (that que)
■ **provide for** (a) envisager ⟨eventuality, expenses⟩
(b) subvenir aux besoins de ⟨family⟩; to be well ~d for être à l'abri du besoin

provided, providing conj (also ~ that) à condition que (+ subjunctive)

province n province f; in the ~s en province

provincial adj (a) ⟨newspaper, town⟩ de province; ⟨life⟩ provincial/-e
(b) (narrow) provincial/-e

provision ☐1 n (a) (of goods, equipment) fourniture f (of de; to à); (of service) prestation f; ~ of food/supplies approvisionnement m (to de)
(b) (for future) dispositions fpl
(c) (in agreement) clause f; (in bill, act) disposition f
☐2 **provisions** n pl (supplies) provisions fpl

provisional adj provisoire

provocative adj (a) ⟨dress, remark⟩ provocant/-e
(b) ⟨book⟩ qui fait réfléchir

provoke vtr (a) (annoy) provoquer
(b) (cause) susciter ⟨anger, complaints⟩; provoquer ⟨laughter, reaction⟩

prow n proue f

prowess n (a) (skill) prouesses fpl
(b) (bravery) vaillance f

prowl ☐1 vtr to ~ the streets rôder dans les rues
☐2 vi ⟨animal, person⟩ rôder

proximity n proximité f

proxy n (a) (person) mandataire mf
(b) by ~ par procuration

prudent adj prudent/-e

prudish adj pudibond/-e, prude

prune ☐1 n (Culin) pruneau m
☐2 vtr (cut back) tailler; (thin out) élaguer

pry vi to ~ into mettre son nez dans

PS n (abbr = **postscriptum**) PS m

psalm n psaume m

pseudonym n pseudonyme m

psych v ■ **psych up** (colloq): to ~ oneself up se préparer (psychologiquement) (for pour)

psychiatric adj psychiatrique

psychiatrist n psychiatre mf

psychiatry n psychiatrie f

psychic n médium m, voyant/-e m/f

psychoanalysis n psychanalyse f

psychological adj psychologique

psychologist n psychologue mf

psychology n psychologie f

psychopath n psychopathe mf

psychotherapist n psychothérapeute mf

PTO (abbr = **please turn over**) TSVP

pub n (GB) pub m

puberty n puberté f

public ☐1 n the ~ le public
☐2 adj (gen) public/-ique; ⟨library, amenity⟩ municipal/-e; ⟨duty, spirit⟩ civique; to be in the ~ eye occuper le devant de la scène
☐3 **in public** phr en public

public address (system) n (système m de) sonorisation f

public assistance n (US) aide f sociale

publication n publication f

public company n société f anonyme par actions

public convenience n (GB) toilettes fpl

public holiday n (GB) jour m férié

publicity n publicité f; to attract ~ attirer l'attention des médias

publicity campaign n (to sell product) campagne f publicitaire; (to raise social issue) campagne f de sensibilisation

publicity stunt n coup m publicitaire

publicize vtr (a) attirer l'attention du public sur ⟨issue, problem⟩
(b) rendre [qch] public ⟨information, facts⟩
(c) faire de la publicité pour ⟨show⟩

publicly adv publiquement

public opinion n opinion f publique

public prosecutor n procureur m général

public relations, PR n relations fpl publiques

public school n (GB) école f privée; (US) école f publique

public sector n secteur m public

public transport n transports mpl en commun

publish vtr publier ⟨book, letter, guide⟩; éditer ⟨newspaper, magazine⟩

publisher n (person) éditeur/-trice m/f; (also **publishing house**) maison f d'édition

publishing n édition f

pudding n (a) (GB) (dessert course) dessert m
(b) (cooked dish) pudding m ⸱ ⸱ ⸱⟶

p

(c) (GB) (sausage) **black/white** ~ boudin *m* noir/blanc

puddle *n* flaque *f*

puff ⟦1⟧ *n* (of air, smoke, steam) bouffée *f*; (of breath) souffle *m*
⟦2⟧ *vtr* tirer sur ⟨*pipe*⟩
⟦3⟧ *vi* **(a)** to ~ at tirer des bouffées de ⟨*cigarette, pipe*⟩
(b) (pant) souffler
■ **puff out (a)** gonfler ⟨*cheeks*⟩; ⟨*bird*⟩ hérisser ⟨*feathers*⟩
(b) to ~ out smoke lancer des bouffées de fumée
■ **puff up**: ¶ ~ up ⟨*feathers*⟩ se hérisser; ⟨*eye*⟩ devenir bouffi/-e; ⟨*rice*⟩ gonfler; ¶ ~ [*sth*] up hérisser ⟨*feathers, fur*⟩; **~ed up with pride** rempli/-e d'orgueil

puff pastry *n* pâte *f* feuilletée

puffy *adj* bouffi/-e

pull ⟦1⟧ *n* **(a)** (tug) coup *m*; **to give sth a ~** tirer sur qch
(b) (attraction) force *f*; (figurative) attrait *m* (of de)
(c) (colloq) (influence) influence *f* (over, with sur)
⟦2⟧ *vtr* **(a)** (gen) tirer; tirer sur ⟨*cord, rope*⟩; **to ~ sb/sth through** faire passer qn/qch par ⟨*hole, window*⟩; **to ~ sth out of** tirer qch de ⟨*pocket, drawer*⟩; **to ~ sb out of** retirer qn de ⟨*wreckage*⟩; sortir qn de ⟨*river*⟩
(b) (colloq) sortir ⟨*gun, knife*⟩; **to ~ a gun on sb** menacer qn avec un pistolet
(c) appuyer sur ⟨*trigger*⟩
(d) se faire une élongation à ⟨*muscle*⟩
(e) to ~ a face faire la grimace
⟦3⟧ *vi* tirer (at, on sur)
■ **pull apart (a)** (dismantle) démonter
(b) (destroy) ⟨*child*⟩ mettre en pièces; ⟨*animal*⟩ déchiqueter
■ **pull away**: ¶ ~ away ⟨*car*⟩ démarrer; ¶ ~ [*sb/sth*] away éloigner ⟨*person*⟩; retirer ⟨*hand*⟩; **to ~ sb/sth away from** écarter qn/qch de ⟨*window, wall*⟩
■ **pull back (a)** ⟨*troops*⟩ se retirer (**from** de)
(b) ⟨*car, person*⟩ reculer
■ **pull down** démolir ⟨*building*⟩; baisser ⟨*blind, trousers*⟩
■ **pull in** ⟨*car, bus, driver*⟩ s'arrêter
■ **pull off (a)** ôter ⟨*coat, sweater*⟩; enlever ⟨*shoes, lid, sticker*⟩
(b) conclure ⟨*deal*⟩; réaliser ⟨*feat*⟩
■ **pull out**: ¶ ~ out **(a)** ⟨*car, truck*⟩ déboîter; **to ~ out of sth** quitter qch ⟨*station, drive*⟩
(b) ⟨*troops, participants*⟩ se retirer (**of** de)
¶ ~ [*sth*] out **(a)** extraire ⟨*tooth*⟩; enlever ⟨*splinter*⟩; arracher ⟨*weeds*⟩
(b) (from pocket) sortir
■ **pull over** ¶ ~ over ⟨*motorist, car*⟩ s'arrêter (sur le côté); ¶ ~ [*sb/sth*] over ⟨*police*⟩ forcer ⟨qn/qch⟩ à se ranger sur le côté
■ **pull through** ⟨*accident victim*⟩ s'en tirer
■ **pull together**: ¶ ~ together faire un effort; ¶ ~ **oneself together** se ressaisir
■ **pull up**: ¶ ~ up s'arrêter
¶ ~ up [*sth*], ~ [*sth*] up **(a)** (uproot) arracher

(b) lever ⟨*anchor*⟩; remonter ⟨*trousers, socks*⟩; prendre ⟨*chair*⟩
¶ ~ [*sb*] up **(a)** (lift) hisser
(b) (reprimand) réprimander
(c) arrêter ⟨*driver*⟩

pull-down menu *n* (Comput) menu *m* déroulant

pulley *n* poulie *f*

pullover *n* pull-over *m*

pulp ⟦1⟧ *n* (soft centre) pulpe *f*; (crushed mass) pâte *f*
⟦2⟧ *vtr* écraser ⟨*fruit, vegetable*⟩; réduire [qch] en pâte ⟨*wood, cloth*⟩; mettre [qch] au pilon ⟨*newspapers, books*⟩

pulp fiction *n* littérature *f* de gare

pulpit *n* chaire *f*

pulse *n* pouls *m*

pulse rate *n* pouls *m*

pulverize *vtr* pulvériser

pump ⟦1⟧ *n* **(a)** (for air) pompe *f*; **bicycle ~** pompe à vélo
(b) (plimsoll) chaussure *f* de sport; (GB) (flat shoe) ballerine *f*; (US) (shoe with heel) chaussure *f* à talon
⟦2⟧ *vtr* **(a)** pomper ⟨*air, gas, water*⟩ (**out of** de)
(b) (colloq) (question) cuisiner (colloq) ⟨*person*⟩
(c) (Med) to ~ sb's stomach faire un lavage d'estomac à qn
⟦3⟧ *vi* ⟨*heart*⟩ battre violemment
■ **pump up** gonfler ⟨*tyre, air bed*⟩

pumpkin *n* citrouille *f*

pun *n* jeu *m* de mots, calembour *m*

punch ⟦1⟧ *n* **(a)** (blow) coup *m* de poing
(b) (of style, performance) énergie *f*
(c) (drink) punch *m*
⟦2⟧ *vtr* **(a)** donner un coup de poing à ⟨*person*⟩; **to ~ sb in the face** donner un coup de poing dans la figure de qn
(b) perforer ⟨*cards, tape*⟩; (manually) poinçonner ⟨*ticket*⟩

Punch-and-Judy show *n* ≈ (spectacle *m* de) guignol *m*

punchbag *n* (GB) sac *m* de sable

punch line *n* chute *f*

punch-up *n* (GB) (colloq) bagarre *f*

punctual *adj* ponctuel/-elle

punctually *adv* ⟨*start, arrive, leave*⟩ à l'heure

punctuation *n* ponctuation *f*

punctuation mark *n* signe *m* de ponctuation

puncture ⟦1⟧ *n* crevaison *f*; **we had a ~ on the way** on a crevé en chemin
⟦2⟧ *vtr* crever ⟨*tyre, balloon, air bed*⟩; **to ~ a lung** se perforer un poumon

puncture (repair) kit *n* boîte *f* de rustines®

pundit *n* expert/-e *m/f*

pungent *adj* ⟨*flavour*⟩ relevé/-e; ⟨*smell*⟩ fort/-e; ⟨*gas, smoke*⟩ âcre

punish *vtr* punir

punishment ···▷ put ····

punishment *n* punition *f*; (stronger) châtiment *m*

punitive *adj* punitif/-ive

punk **1** *n* (a) (music) punk *m* **(b)** (punk rocker) punk *mf* **(c)** (US) (colloq) voyou *m* **2** *adj* punk *inv*

punnet *n* (GB) barquette *f*

punt *n* (a) (boat) barque *f* (à fond plat) **(b)** (Irish pound) livre *f* irlandaise

puny *adj* ⟨person, body⟩ chétif/-ive

pup *n* (a) (*also* **puppy**) chiot *m* **(b)** (seal, otter) petit *m*

pupil *n* (a) (Sch) élève *mf* **(b)** (in eye) pupille *f*

puppet *n* marionnette *f*

purchase **1** *n* achat *m* **2** *vtr* acheter

purchasing power *n* pouvoir *m* d'achat

pure *adj* pur/-e

puree *n* purée *f*

purely *adv* purement

purge **1** *n* purge *f* **2** *vtr* purger ⟨party, system⟩ (**of** de); expier ⟨sin⟩

purify *vtr* (gen) purifier; épurer ⟨water, chemical⟩

purist *n, adj* puriste (*mf*)

purity *n* pureté *f*

purple **1** *n* violet *m* **2** *adj* (bluish) violet/-ette; (reddish) pourpre

purpose **1** *n* (a) (aim) but *m*; **for the ∼ of doing** dans le but de faire **(b)** (*also* **strength of ∼**) résolution *f* **2** **on ∼** *phr* exprès

purposely *adv* exprès, intentionnellement

purpose-made *adj* fait/-e spécialement (for pour)

purr **1** *n* (of cat, engine) ronronnement *m* **2** *vi* ⟨cat, engine⟩ ronronner

purse *n* (for money) porte-monnaie *m inv*; (US) (handbag) sac *m* à main **IDIOMS to hold the ∼-strings** tenir les cordons de la bourse

purser *n* commissaire *m* de bord

pursue *vtr* (a) (chase) poursuivre **(b)** poursuivre ⟨aim, ambition, studies⟩; mener ⟨policy⟩; se livrer à ⟨occupation, interest⟩; **to ∼ a career** faire carrière (**in** dans)

pursuer *n* poursuivant/-e *m/f*

pursuit *n* (a) poursuite *f*; **in ∼ of** à la poursuite de; **in hot ∼** à vos/ses etc trousses **(b)** (hobby) passe-temps *m inv*; **artistic ∼s** activités *fpl* artistiques

push **1** *n* poussée *f*; **to give sb/sth a ∼** pousser qn/qch **2** *vtr* (a) pousser ⟨person, car, pram⟩; appuyer sur ⟨button, switch⟩; **to ∼ sb/sth away** repousser qn/qch; **she ∼ed him down**

the stairs elle l'a poussé dans l'escalier; **to ∼ sb aside** écarter qn; **to ∼ sb too far** pousser qn à bout **(b)** (colloq) (promote) promouvoir ⟨policy, theory⟩ **(c)** (colloq) (sell) vendre ⟨drugs⟩ **3** *vi* pousser; **to ∼ past sb** bousculer qn **IDIOMS at a ∼** (GB) (colloq) s'il le faut; **to ∼ one's luck** aller un peu trop loin

■ **push around** (colloq) (bully) bousculer ⟨person⟩

■ **push for** faire pression en faveur de ⟨reform⟩

■ **push in**: ¶ **∼ in** resquiller; ¶ **∼ [sth] in** enfoncer ⟨button, door, window⟩

■ **push over**: ¶ **∼ over!** (colloq) pousse-toi!; ¶ **∼ [sb/sth] over** renverser ⟨person, table, car⟩

■ **push through** faire voter ⟨bill, legislation⟩; faire passer ⟨deal⟩

push-button *adj* ⟨telephone⟩ à touches

pushchair *n* (GB) poussette *f*

pusher *n* (colloq) (*also* **drug ∼**) revendeur/-euse *m/f* de drogue

push-start *vtr* pousser [qch] pour le/la faire démarrer ⟨vehicle⟩

push-up *n* (Sport) pompe *f* (colloq)

pushy *adj* (colloq) (ambitious) arriviste; **she's very ∼** (assertive) elle s'impose

put *vtr* (a) (place) mettre ⟨object, person⟩ (**in** dans; **on** sur); **to ∼ sth through** glisser qch dans ⟨letterbox⟩; **to ∼ sb through** envoyer qn à ⟨university⟩; faire passer qn par ⟨ordeal⟩; faire passer [qch] à qn ⟨test⟩; **to ∼ one's hand to** porter la main à ⟨mouth⟩ **(b)** (devote, invest) **to ∼ money/energy into sth** investir de l'argent/son énergie dans qch; **to ∼ a lot into** s'engager à fond pour ⟨work, project⟩; sacrifier beaucoup à ⟨marriage⟩ **(c) to ∼ money towards** donner de l'argent pour ⟨gift⟩; **∼ it towards some new clothes** sers-t'en pour acheter des vêtements; **to ∼ tax on sth** taxer qch **(d)** (express) **to ∼ it bluntly** pour parler franchement; **let me ∼ it another way** laissez-moi m'exprimer différemment **IDIOMS I wouldn't ∼ it past him!** ça ne m'étonnerait pas de lui!

■ **put across** communiquer ⟨idea, case⟩

■ **put away** (a) (tidy away) ranger **(b)** (save) mettre [qch] de côté **(c)** (colloq) avaler ⟨food⟩; descendre (colloq) ⟨drink⟩

■ **put back** (a) (return) remettre; **to ∼ sth back where it belongs** remettre qch à sa place **(b)** remettre ⟨meeting⟩ (**to** à; **until** jusqu'à); repousser ⟨date⟩ **(c)** retarder ⟨clock, watch⟩

■ **put down**: ¶ **∼ [sth] down** (a) poser ⟨object⟩ **(b)** réprimer ⟨rebellion⟩ **(c)** (write down) mettre (par écrit) **(d) to ∼ sth down to** mettre qch sur le compte de; **to ∼ sth down to the fact that** imputer qch au fait que ····▷

(e) (by injection) piquer ⟨*animal*⟩
(f) **to ~ down a deposit** verser des arrhes; **to ~ £50 down on sth** verser 50 livres sterling d'arrhes sur qch
¶ **~ [sb] down** (a) déposer ⟨*passenger*⟩
(b) (colloq) (humiliate) rabaisser
■ **put forward** (a) (propose) avancer ⟨*theory, name*⟩; soumettre ⟨*plan*⟩; présenter la candidature de ⟨*person*⟩
(b) (in time) avancer ⟨*meeting, date, clock*⟩ ⟨by de; to à⟩
■ **put in**: ¶ **~ in** (a) ⟨*ship*⟩ faire escale ⟨at à; to dans⟩
(b) **to ~ in for** postuler pour ⟨*job, promotion, rise*⟩; demander ⟨*transfer*⟩
¶ **~ [sth] in** (a) installer ⟨*heating, units*⟩
(b) (make) faire ⟨*request, claim*⟩; **to ~ in an appearance** faire une apparition
(c) passer ⟨*time*⟩
(d) (insert) mettre
■ **put off**: ¶ **~ [sth] off** (a) (delay, defer) remettre [qch] ⟨à plus tard⟩
(b) (turn off) éteindre ⟨*light, radio*⟩
¶ **~ [sb] off** (a) décommander ⟨*guest*⟩; dissuader ⟨*person*⟩; **to be easily put off** se décourager facilement
(b) (repel) ⟨*appearance, smell*⟩ dégoûter; ⟨*manner, person*⟩ déconcerter
■ **put on** (a) mettre ⟨*garment, make-up*⟩
(b) allumer ⟨*light, heating*⟩; mettre ⟨*record, music*⟩; **to ~ the kettle on** mettre de l'eau à chauffer
(c) prendre ⟨*weight, kilo*⟩
(d) (produce) monter ⟨*play, exhibition*⟩
(e) (adopt) prendre ⟨*accent, expression*⟩; **he's ~ting it on** il fait semblant
■ **put out** (a) (extend) tendre ⟨*hand*⟩; **to ~ out one's tongue** tirer la langue
(b) éteindre ⟨*fire, cigarette*⟩
(c) sortir ⟨*bin, garbage*⟩; faire sortir ⟨*cat*⟩
(d) diffuser ⟨*warning, statement*⟩
(e) mettre ⟨*food, towels*⟩

(f) (dislocate) se démettre ⟨*shoulder*⟩
(g) (inconvenience) déranger ⟨*person*⟩; (annoy) contrarier ⟨*person*⟩
■ **put through** (a) (implement) faire passer ⟨*bill, reform*⟩
(b) passer ⟨*caller*⟩ ⟨to à⟩
■ **put together** (a) (assemble) assembler ⟨*pieces, parts*⟩; **to ~ sth back together** reconstituer qch
(b) (place together) mettre ensemble
(c) établir ⟨*list*⟩; faire ⟨*film, programme*⟩
(d) construire ⟨*argument*⟩
■ **put up**: ¶ **~ up [sth]** opposer ⟨*resistance*⟩; **to ~ up a fight** combattre
¶ **~ [sth] up** (a) hisser ⟨*flag, sail*⟩; relever ⟨*hair*⟩; **to ~ up one's hand** lever la main
(b) mettre ⟨*sign, plaque*⟩; afficher ⟨*list*⟩
(c) dresser ⟨*fence, tent*⟩
(d) augmenter ⟨*rent, prices, tax*⟩; faire monter ⟨*temperature*⟩
(e) (provide) fournir ⟨*money*⟩
¶ **~ [sb] up** (a) (lodge) héberger
(b) **to ~ sb up to sth** pousser qn à qch
■ **put up with** supporter ⟨*person, situation*⟩

put-down *n* remarque *f* humiliante

putty *n* mastic *m*

puzzle ① *n* (a) (mystery) mystère *m*
(b) (game) casse-tête *m inv*
② *vtr* déconcerter

puzzle book *n* livre *m* de jeux

puzzled *adj* perplexe

PVC *n* (*abbr* = **polyvinyl chloride**) PVC *m*

pygmy *n* pygmée *mf*

pyjamas (GB), **pajamas** (US) *n pl* pyjama *m*; **a pair of ~** un pyjama

pylon *n* pylône *m*

pyramid *n* pyramide *f*

python *n* python *m*

Qq

q, Q *n* q, Q *m*
quack ① *n* (a) (of duck) coin-coin *m inv*
(b) (GB) (colloq) (doctor) toubib *m* (colloq)
(c) (impostor) charlatan *m*
② *vi* cancaner
quadrangle *n* (a) (shape) quadrilatère *m*
(b) (courtyard) cour *f* carrée
quadruple ① *n, adj* quadruple (*m*)
② *vtr, vi* quadrupler
quadruplet *n* quadruplé/-e *m/f*
quagmire *n* bourbier *m*
quail ① *n* caille *f*; **~'s egg** œuf *m* de caille
② *vi* trembler
quaint *adj* (a) (pretty) pittoresque

(b) (old-world) au charme vieillot
(c) (odd) bizarre
quake *vi* trembler
qualification *n* (a) (diploma, degree) diplôme *m* (in en); (experience, skills) qualification *f*
(b) (restriction) restriction *f*; **without ~** sans réserves
qualified *adj* (a) (for job) (having diploma) diplômé/-e; (having experience, skills) qualifié/-e
(b) (competent) (having authority) qualifié/-e (**to do** pour faire); (having knowledge) compétent/-e (**to do** pour faire)
(c) (modified) nuancé/-e, mitigé/-e

qualifier *n* (contestant) qualifié/-e *m/f*; (match) éliminatoire *f*

qualify ① *vtr* (a) (modify) nuancer ‹approval, opinion›; préciser ‹statement, remark›
(b) (entitle) to ～ sb to do donner à qn le droit de faire
② *vi* (a) (get diploma, degree) obtenir son diplôme (as de, en)
(b) (be eligible) remplir les conditions (requises); to ～ for avoir droit à ‹membership, legal aid›; to ～ to do avoir le droit de faire
(c) (Sport) se qualifier

qualitative *adj* qualitatif/-ive

quality ① *n* qualité *f*
② *adj* de qualité

quality control *n* contrôle *m* de qualité

qualm *n* scrupule *m*

quandary *n* embarras *m*; (serious) dilemme *m*

quantifiable *adj* facile à évaluer

quantify *vtr* quantifier

quantitative *adj* quantitatif/-ive

quantity *n* quantité *f*; in ～ en grande quantité

quantity surveyor *n* métreur *m*

quantum leap *n* saut *m* quantique; (figurative) bond *m* prodigieux

quarantine ① *n* quarantaine *f*; in ～ en quarantaine
② *vtr* mettre [qn/qch] en quarantaine

quarrel ① *n* dispute *f* (**between** entre; **over** au sujet de); **to have a** ～ se disputer
② *vi* (a) (argue) se disputer
(b) (sever relations) se brouiller
(c) **to** ～ **with** contester ‹claim, idea›; se plaindre de ‹price, verdict›

quarrelling (GB), **quarreling** (US) *n* disputes *fpl*

quarrelsome *adj* ‹person› querelleur/-euse; ‹remark› agressif/-ive

quarry ① *n* (a) (in ground) carrière *f*
(b) (prey) proie *f*; (in hunting) gibier *m*
② *vtr* extraire ‹stone›

quarry tile *n* carreau *m* de terre cuite

quart *n* (GB) = 1.136 l, (US) = 0.946 l

quarter ① *n* (a) (one fourth) quart *m*; **in** ～ **of an hour** dans un quart d'heure
(b) (three months) trimestre *m*
(c) (district) quartier *m*
② **quarters** *n pl* (Mil) quartiers *mpl*; (gen) logement *m*
③ *pron* (a) (25%) quart *m*; **only a** ～ **passed** seul le quart a réussi
(b) (in time phrases) **at (a)** ～ **to 11** (GB), **at a** ～ **of 11** (US) à onze heures moins le quart; **an hour and a** ～ une heure et quart
④ *adj* **a** ～ **century** un quart de siècle
⑤ *adv* **a** ～ **full** au quart plein; ～ **the price** quatre fois moins cher
⑥ *vtr* couper [qch] en quatre ‹cake, apple›
⑦ **at close quarters** *phr* de près

quarterfinal *n* quart *m* de finale

quarterly ① *adj* trimestriel/-ielle
② *adv* tous les trois mois

quartermaster *n* (in army) intendant *m*; (in navy) maître *m* de timonerie

quartet *n* quatuor *m*; **jazz** ～ quartette *m*

quartz *n* quartz *m*

quash *vtr* rejeter ‹proposal›; réprimer ‹rebellion›

quasi(-) *pref* quasi (+ adj), quasi- (+ n)

quaver ① *n* (a) (GB) (Mus) croche *f*
(b) (trembling) tremblement *m* (in dans)
② *vi* trembloter

quay *n* quai *m*; **on the** ～ sur le quai

quayside *n* quai *m*

queasiness *n* nausée *f*

queasy *adj* **to be** or **feel** ～ avoir mal au cœur

Quebec *pr n* Québec *m*; **in** ～ (city) à Québec; (province) au Québec

queen *n* (a) (gen) reine *f*
(b) (in cards) dame *f*

queen bee *n* reine *f* des abeilles

queen mother *n* Reine mère *f*

Queen's Counsel, QC *n* (GB) (Law) avocat *m* éminent

queer *adj* (a) (strange) étrange, bizarre
(b) (suspicious) louche, suspect

quell *vtr* étouffer ‹anger, anxiety, revolt›

quench *vtr* étancher ‹thirst›; étouffer ‹desire›

querulous *adj* grincheux/-euse

query ① *n* question *f* (**about** au sujet de); **a** ～ **from sb** une question venant de qn
② *vtr* mettre en doute; **to** ～ **whether** demander si

quest *n* quête *f*; **the** ～ **for sb/sth** la recherche de qn/qch

question ① *n* (a) (gen) question *f* (**about** sur); **to ask sb a** ～ poser une question à qn; **it's a** ～ **of doing** il s'agit de faire; **that's another** ～ c'est une autre affaire; **there was never any** ～ **of you paying** il n'a jamais été question que tu paies; **the person in** ～ la personne en question; **it's out of the** ～ **for him to leave** il est hors de question qu'il parte
(b) (doubt) doute *m*; **to call sth into** ～ mettre qch en doute; **it's open to** ～ cela se discute
② *vtr* (a) (interrogate) questionner ‹suspect, politician›
(b) (cast doubt upon) mettre en doute ‹tactics, methods›

questionable *adj* (a) (debatable) discutable
(b) (dubious) douteux/-euse

questioner *n* interrogateur/-trice *m/f*

questioning *n* (of person) interrogation *f*; **to bring sb in for** ～ amener qn pour interrogatoire

question mark *n* point *m* d'interrogation

questionnaire *n* questionnaire *m* (**on** sur)

q

queue ① n (GB) (of people) queue *f*, file *f*
(d'attente); (of vehicles) file *f*; **to stand in a ~**
faire la queue; **to join the ~** ⟨person⟩ se
mettre à la queue; ⟨car⟩ se mettre dans la
file; **to jump the ~** (colloq) passer avant son
tour
② vi (also ~ **up**) ⟨people⟩ faire la queue (**for**
pour); ⟨taxis⟩ attendre en ligne

queue-jump vi resquiller, passer avant
son tour

quibble vi chicaner (**about, over** sur)

quick ① n **to bite one's nails to the ~** se
ronger les ongles jusqu'au sang
② adj (a) (speedy) ⟨pace, reply, profit, meal⟩
rapide; ⟨storm, shower⟩ bref/brève (*before* n);
to have a ~ coffee prendre un café en
vitesse; **to have a ~ wash** faire une toilette
rapide; **she's a ~ worker** elle travaille vite;
the ~est way to do le meilleur moyen de
faire; **to make a ~ recovery** se rétablir vite;
be ~ (about it)! dépêche-toi!
(b) (clever) ⟨child, student⟩ vif/vive d'esprit
(c) (prompt) ⟨reaction⟩ vif/vive; **to be a ~
learner** apprendre vite
③ adv ~! vite!; ~ **as a flash** avec la rapidité
de l'éclair
IDIOMS **to cut** *or* **sting sb to the ~** piquer qn
au vif

quicken ① vtr accélérer ⟨pace⟩; stimuler
⟨interest⟩
② vi ⟨pace⟩ s'accélérer; ⟨anger⟩ s'intensifier

quick-fire adj rapide

quicklime n chaux *f* vive

quickly adv (rapidly) vite, rapidement;
(without delay) sans tarder; (**come**) ~! (viens)
vite!

quick march n (Mil) ≈ pas *m* cadencé

quicksand n sables *mpl* mouvants;
(figurative) bourbier *m*

quicksilver n mercure *m*

quick-tempered adj coléreux/-euse

quick time n (US) marche *f* rapide

quid n (GB) (colloq) livre *f* (sterling)

quiet ① n (a) (silence) silence *m*
(b) (peace) tranquillité *f*
(c) (colloq) (secret) **on the ~** discrètement
② adj (a) (silent) ⟨church, person, room⟩
silencieux/-ieuse; **to keep ~** garder le
silence; **to go ~** se taire; **to keep sb ~** faire
taire ⟨dog, child⟩; **be ~** (stop talking) tais-toi;
(make no noise) ne fais pas de bruit
(b) (not noisy) ⟨voice⟩ bas/basse; ⟨engine⟩
silencieux/-ieuse; ⟨music⟩ doux/douce; **in a ~
voice** à voix basse; **to keep the children ~**
⟨activity⟩ tenir les enfants tranquilles
(c) (discreet) discret/-ète; **to have a ~ word
with sb** prendre qn à part pour lui parler
(d) (calm) ⟨village, holiday, night, life⟩
tranquille
(e) ⟨meal⟩ intime; ⟨wedding⟩ célébré/-e dans
l'intimité
(f) (secret) **to keep [sth] ~** ne pas divulguer
⟨plans⟩; garder [qch] secret/-ète ⟨engagement⟩

quieten vtr (a) (calm) calmer ⟨person,
animal⟩

(b) (silence) faire taire ⟨critics, children⟩
■ **quieten down**: ¶ ~ **down** (a) (become
calm) ⟨person, activity⟩ se calmer
(b) (fall silent) se taire
¶ ~ **[sb/sth] down** (a) (calm) calmer
(b) (silence) faire taire

quietly adv (a) (not noisily) ⟨move⟩ sans
bruit; ⟨cough, speak⟩ doucement
(b) (silently) ⟨play, read, sit⟩ en silence
(c) (calmly) calmement

quietness n (a) (silence) silence *m*
(b) (of voice) faiblesse *f*
(c) (of place) tranquillité *f*

quiff n (GB) (on forehead) toupet *m*; (on top of
head) houppe *f*

quill n (a) (feather) penne *f*; (stem of feather)
tuyau *m* de plume
(b) (on porcupine) piquant *m*
(c) (also ~ **pen**) plume *f* d'oie

quilt ① n (a) (GB) (duvet) couette *f*
(b) (bed cover) dessus *m* de lit
② vtr matelasser

quinine n quinine *f*

quintuplet n quintuplé/-e *m/f*

quip ① n trait *m* d'esprit
② vi plaisanter

quirk n (of person) excentricité *f*; (of fate,
nature) caprice *m*

quit ① vtr démissionner de ⟨job⟩; quitter
⟨place, person, profession⟩
② vi (a) (give up) arrêter (**doing** de faire)
(b) (resign) démissionner

quite adv (a) (completely) ⟨new, ready,
understand⟩ tout à fait; ⟨alone, empty,
exhausted⟩ complètement; ⟨impossible⟩
totalement; ⟨extraordinary⟩ vraiment; **I ~
agree** je suis tout à fait d'accord; **you're ~
right** vous avez entièrement raison; **it's ~ all
right** c'est sans importance; **are you ~ sure?**
en êtes-vous certain?; ~ **clearly** (see) très
clairement
(b) (exactly) **not ~** pas exactement; **I don't ~
know** je ne sais pas du tout
(c) (rather) ⟨big, easily, often⟩ assez; **it's ~
small** ce n'est pas très grand; **it's ~ warm
today** il fait bon aujourd'hui; **it's ~ likely
that** il est très probable que; **I ~ like Chinese
food** j'aime assez la cuisine chinoise; ~ **a
few** un bon nombre de ⟨people, examples⟩; ~
a lot of money pas mal d'argent; **I've thought
about it ~ a bit** j'y ai pas mal réfléchi
(d) (as intensifier) ~ **simply** tout simplement;
~ **a difference** une différence considérable;
that will be ~ a change for you ce sera un
grand changement pour toi; **she's ~ a
woman!** quelle femme!
(e) (expressing agreement) ~ (**so**) c'est sûr

quits adj (colloq) **to be ~** être quitte (**with**
sb envers qn)

quiver ① n (a) (trembling) tremblement *m*
(b) (for arrows) carquois *m*
② vi ⟨voice, lip, animal⟩ trembler (**with** de);
⟨leaves⟩ frémir; ⟨flame⟩ vaciller

q

quiz 1 n (a) (game) jeu m de questions-réponses, quiz m; (written, in magazine) questionnaire m (**about** sur)
(b) (US Sch) interrogation f
2 vtr questionner (**about** au sujet de)
quiz game, **quiz show** n jeu m de questions-réponses
quizzical adj interrogateur/-trice
quota n (a) (prescribed number, amount) quota m (**of**, **for** de)
(b) (share) part f (**of** de); (officially allocated) quote-part f
quotation n (a) (quote) citation f
(b) (estimate) devis m
quotation marks n pl (also **quotes**) guillemets mpl; **in ∼** entre guillemets
quote 1 n (a) (quotation) citation f (**from** de)
(b) (statement to journalist) déclaration f
(c) (estimate) devis m
2 **quotes** n pl = QUOTATION MARKS
3 vtr (a) citer ⟨person, passage, proverb⟩; rapporter ⟨words⟩; rappeler ⟨reference number⟩; **she was ∼d as saying that...** elle aurait dit que...
(b) (state) indiquer ⟨price, figure⟩; **they ∼d us £200** dans leur devis, ils ont demandé £200 sterling
(c) (on stock exchange) coter ⟨share, price⟩ (**at** à)
(d) (in betting) **to be ∼d 6 to 1** être coté/-e entre 6 et 1
4 vi (from text, author) faire des citations; **to ∼ from Keats** citer Keats

Rr

r, **R** n r, R m
rabbi n rabbin m
rabbit n lapin m
rabid adj (a) (with rabies) enragé/-e
(b) (fanatical) fanatique
rabies n rage f
race 1 n (a) (gen, Sport) course f; **to have a ∼** faire la course
(b) (ethnic group) race f
2 vtr faire la course avec ⟨person, car, horse⟩ (**to** jusqu'à)
3 vi (a) (gen, Sport) courir; **to ∼ in/away** entrer/partir en courant
(b) (hurry) se dépêcher (**to do** de faire)
(c) ⟨heart⟩ battre précipitamment; ⟨engine⟩ s'emballer
racehorse n cheval m de course
racer n (bike) vélo m de course
race relations n pl relations fpl inter-raciales
racetrack n (for horses) champ m de courses; (for cars) circuit m; (for dogs, cycles) piste f
racial adj racial/-e
racing n courses fpl
racing car n voiture f de course
racing cyclist n coureur/-euse m/f cycliste
racing driver n coureur/-euse m/f automobile
racism n racisme m
racist n, adj raciste (mf)
rack 1 n (a) (for plates) égouttoir m; (for clothes) portant m; (for bottles) casier m
(b) = ROOF RACK
(c) (torture) chevalet m
2 vtr **∼ed with** torturé/-e par ⟨guilt⟩
IDIOMS **to ∼ one's brains** se creuser la cervelle (colloq)
racket n (a) (Sport) (also **racquet**) raquette f
(b) (colloq) (noise) vacarme m
(c) (swindle) escroquerie f
racketeering n racket m
racquetball n (US) ≈ squash m
racy adj (a) (lively) plein/-e de verve
(b) (risqué) osé/-e
radar n radar m
radiant adj radieux/-ieuse
radiate vtr (a) rayonner de ⟨happiness⟩; déborder de ⟨confidence⟩
(b) émettre ⟨heat⟩
radiation n (medical, nuclear) radiation f; (rays) radiations fpl
radiation exposure n irradiation f
radiation sickness n maladie f des rayons
radiator n radiateur m
radical n, adj radical/-e (m/f)
radio 1 n radio f; **on the ∼** à la radio
2 adj ⟨signal⟩ radio inv; ⟨programme⟩ de radio
3 vtr **to ∼ sth (to sb)** communiquer qch par radio (à qn)
4 vi **to ∼ for help** appeler au secours par radio
radioactive adj radioactif/-ive
radio alarm n radio-réveil m
radio announcer n speaker/-erine m/f
radio cassette (recorder) n radiocassette f
radiology n radiologie f

r

radio station n (channel) station f de radio; (installation) station f émettrice

radiotherapy n radiothérapie f

radish n radis m

radius n rayon m

raffle n tombola f

raft n radeau m

rafter n chevron m

rag n **(a)** (cloth) chiffon m
(b) (colloq) (newspaper) torchon m (colloq)

rage ①n **(a)** rage f, colère f; **to fly into a ~** entrer dans une colère noire
(b) (colloq) **to be (all) the ~** faire fureur
②vi **(a)** ⟨storm, battle⟩ faire rage
(b) ⟨person⟩ tempêter (**at, against** contre)

ragged adj **(a)** ⟨garment⟩ en loques; ⟨cuff, collar⟩ effiloché/-e; ⟨person⟩ dépenaillé/-e
(b) ⟨outline⟩ déchiqueté/-e

raging adj **(a)** ⟨passion, argument⟩ violent/-e; ⟨thirst, pain⟩ atroce; **a ~ toothache** une rage de dents
(b) ⟨blizzard, sea⟩ déchaîné/-e

rags n pl loques fpl; **in ~** en haillons

raid ①n raid m (**on** sur); (on bank) hold-up m (**on** de); (by police, customs) rafle f (**on** dans)
②vtr ⟨military⟩ faire un raid sur; ⟨police⟩ faire une rafle dans; ⟨criminals⟩ attaquer ⟨bank⟩

raider n **(a)** (thief) pillard m
(b) (also **corporate ~**) raider m

rail n **(a)** (on balcony) balustrade f; (on tower) garde-fou m; (handrail) rampe f
(b) (for curtains) tringle f
(c) (for train) rail m; **by ~** par chemin de fer

railing n (also **~s**) grille f

railroad n (US) **(a)** (network) chemin m de fer
(b) (also **~ track**) voie f ferrée

railroad car n (US) wagon m

railway n (GB) **(a)** (network) chemin m de fer
(b) (also **~ line**) ligne f de chemin de fer
(c) (also **~ track**) voie f ferrée

railway carriage n (GB) wagon m

railway station n (GB) gare f

rain ①n pluie f; **in the ~** sous la pluie
②v impers pleuvoir; **it's ~ing (hard)** il pleut (à verse)

rainbow n arc-en-ciel m

raincoat n imperméable m

raindrop n goutte f de pluie

rainfall n niveau m de précipitations

rain forest n forêt f tropicale

rainy adj ⟨afternoon, climate⟩ pluvieux/-ieuse

rainy season n saison f des pluies

raise ①n (US) (pay rise) augmentation f
②vtr **(a)** (lift) lever ⟨baton, barrier, curtain⟩; hisser ⟨flag⟩; soulever ⟨lid⟩; renflouer ⟨sunken ship⟩; **to ~ one's hand/head** lever la main/tête
(b) (increase) augmenter ⟨price, offer, salary⟩ (**from** de; **to** à); élever ⟨standard⟩; reculer ⟨age limit⟩; **to ~ one's voice** (to be heard)

parler plus fort; (in anger) hausser le ton; **to ~ the bidding** (in gambling) monter la mise; (at auction) monter l'enchère
(c) (cause) faire naître ⟨fears⟩; soulever ⟨dust⟩
(d) (mention) soulever ⟨issue, objection⟩
(e) (bring up) élever ⟨child, family⟩
(f) (breed) élever ⟨livestock⟩
(g) (find) trouver ⟨capital⟩
(h) (collect) lever ⟨tax⟩; ⟨person⟩ collecter ⟨money⟩
(i) (end) lever ⟨ban⟩
(j) (give) **to ~ the alarm** donner l'alarme

raised adj ⟨platform, jetty⟩ surélevé/-e; **~ voices** des éclats de voix

raisin n raisin m sec

rake ①n râteau m
②vtr ratisser ⟨grass, leaves⟩
■ **rake up**: **~ up** [sth], **~** [sth] **up** ressusciter ⟨grievance⟩; remuer ⟨past⟩

rally ①n **(a)** (meeting) rassemblement m
(b) (race) rallye m
(c) (in tennis) échange m
②vtr rassembler ⟨support, troops⟩
③vi **(a)** ⟨people⟩ se rallier (**to** à)
(b) (recover) ⟨patient⟩ se rétablir

rallying call n cri m de ralliement

ram ①n bélier m
②vtr **(a)** (crash into) rentrer dans, heurter
(b) (push) enfoncer

RAM n (Comput) (abbr = **random access memory**) RAM f

ramble n randonnée f, balade f
■ **ramble on** discourir (**about** sur)

rambler n randonneur/-euse m/f

rambling adj **(a)** ⟨house⟩ plein/-e de coins et de recoins
(b) ⟨talk, article⟩ décousu/-e

ramification n ramification f

ramp n rampe f; (GB) (to slow traffic) ralentisseur m; (up to plane) passerelle f; (US) (slip road) bretelle f

rampage n **to be** or **go on the ~** tout saccager

rampant adj ⟨crime, disease⟩ endémique

rampart n rempart m

ram raid ①n casse f à la voiture bélier
②vtr dévaliser [qch] à l'aide d'une voiture bélier

ramshackle adj délabré/-e

ranch n ranch m

rancid adj rance; **to go ~** rancir

random adj (fait/-e) au hasard

range ①n **(a)** (of prices, products) gamme f; (of activities) éventail m, choix m; (of radar, weapon) portée f (**of** de)
(b) (US) (prairie) prairie f
(c) (of mountains) chaîne f
(d) (stove) (wood) fourneau m
(e) (also **shooting ~**) champ m de tir
②vi **(a)** (vary) varier (**between** entre)
(b) (cover) **to ~ over sth** couvrir qch

ranger n garde-forestier m

rank ① n (a) (gen) rang m; (in military, police) grade m; **to break ~s** ⟨soldiers⟩ rompre les rangs; **to close ~s** serrer les rangs
(b) taxi ~ station f de taxis
② adj (a) ⟨outsider, beginner⟩ complet/-ète
(b) ⟨odour⟩ fétide
③ vtr classer (**among** parmi)
④ vi se classer (**among** parmi)

rank and file n the ~ la base f

ranking n classement m

rankle vi it still ~s je ne l'ai pas encore digéré (colloq)

ransack vtr fouiller ⟨drawer⟩ (**for** pour trouver); mettre [qch] à sac ⟨house⟩

ransom n rançon f; **to hold sb to** (GB) or **for** (US) ~ garder qn en otage

rant vi déclamer; **to ~ and rave** tempêter

rap ① n (a) (tap) coup m sec
(b) (music) rap m
② vtr frapper sur ⟨table, door⟩

rape ① n (a) (attack) viol m
(b) (plant) colza m
② vtr violer

rapid adj rapide

rapidly adv rapidement

rapids n pl rapides mpl

rapist n violeur m

rapper n (Mus) rappeur/-euse m/f

rapport n bons rapports mpl

rapture n ravissement m; **to go into ~s about sth** s'extasier sur qch

rapturous adj ⟨delight⟩ extasié/-e; ⟨applause⟩ frénétique

rare adj (a) (uncommon) rare
(b) ⟨steak⟩ saignant/-e

rarely adv rarement

raring adj **to be ~ to do** être très impatient/-e de faire; **to be ~ to go** piaffer d'impatience

rarity n (a) **to be a ~** ⟨occurrence⟩ être rare; ⟨plant⟩ être une plante rare; ⟨collector's item⟩ être une pièce rare
(b) (rareness) rareté f

rascal n coquin/-e m/f

rash ① n (a) (on skin) rougeurs fpl
(b) (figurative) vague f (**of** de)
② adj irréfléchi/-e

rasher n tranche f

raspberry n framboise f

rasping adj ⟨voice, sound⟩ râpeux/-euse

rat n rat m

rate ① n (a) (speed) rythme m; **at this ~** (figurative) à ce train-là
(b) (level) taux m; **the interest ~** le taux d'intérêt
(c) (charge, fee) tarif m
(d) (in foreign exchange) cours m
② **rates** n pl (GB) impôts mpl locaux; **business ~s** ≈ taxe f professionnelle
③ vtr (a) (classify) **to ~ sb as sth** considérer qn comme qch; **to ~ sb among** classer qn parmi
(b) estimer ⟨honesty, friendship, person⟩

IDIOMS **at any ~** en tout cas

ratepayer n (GB) contribuable mf

rather adv (a) plutôt (**than** que); **I ~ like him** je le trouve plutôt sympathique; **it's ~ like an apple** ça ressemble un peu à une pomme
(b) (preferably) **I would** (much) **~ do** je préférerais (de loin) faire (**than do** que faire); **I'd ~ not** j'aimerais mieux pas

ratify vtr ratifier

rating n cote f

ratings n pl indice m d'écoute, audimat® m

ratio n proportion f, rapport m

ration ① n ration f
② vtr rationner ⟨food⟩ (**to** à); limiter la ration de ⟨person⟩ (**to** à)

rational adj ⟨approach, argument⟩ rationnel/-elle; ⟨person⟩ sensé/-e

rationale n (a) (reasons) raisons fpl (**for**; **for doing** de faire)
(b) (logic) logique f (**behind** de)

rationalize vtr (a) (justify) justifier
(b) (GB) (streamline) rationaliser

rationing n rationnement m

rat race n foire f d'empoigne

rat run n: petite rue servant de raccourci

rattle ① n (a) (of bottles, cutlery, chains) cliquetis m; (of window, engine) vibrations fpl
(b) (baby's) hochet m
② vtr ⟨wind⟩ faire vibrer ⟨window⟩; ⟨person⟩ s'acharner sur ⟨handle⟩
③ vi ⟨bottles, cutlery, chains⟩ s'entrechoquer; ⟨window⟩ vibrer

rattlesnake n serpent m à sonnette, crotale m

raucous adj ⟨laugh⟩ éraillé/-e; ⟨person⟩ bruyant/-e

raunchy adj (colloq) ⟨performer, voice, song⟩ torride

ravage vtr ravager

rave ① n (GB) (colloq) (party) bringue f (colloq) (branchée)
② adj (colloq) ⟨review⟩ dithyrambique
③ vi (enthusiastically) parler avec enthousiasme (**about** de); (when fevered) délirer

ravenous adj ⟨animal⟩ vorace; **to be ~** avoir une faim de loup

ravine n ravin m

raving adj (fanatical) enragé/-e; **a ~ lunatic** un fou furieux/une folle furieuse

ravioli n ravioli mpl

ravishing adj ravissant/-e

raw adj (a) ⟨food⟩ cru/-e; ⟨rubber, sugar, data⟩ brut/-e; ⟨sewage⟩ non traité/-e
(b) (without skin) ⟨patch⟩ à vif
(c) (cold) ⟨weather⟩ froid/-e et humide
(d) (inexperienced) inexpérimenté/-e
IDIOMS **to get a ~ deal** (colloq) être défavorisé/-e

raw material n matière f première

ray n rayon m; **a ~ of** une lueur de ⟨hope⟩

r

raze *vtr* raser

razor *n* rasoir *m*

razor blade *n* lame *f* de rasoir

re¹ *n* (Mus) ré *m*

re² *prep* (*abbr* = **with reference to**) (about) au sujet de; (in letterhead) 'objet'

RE *n* (Sch) (*abbr* = **Religious Education**) éducation *f* religieuse

reach ▮1▮ *n* portée *f*; **out of** ~ hors de portée; **within (arm's)** ~ à portée de (la) main; **within easy** ~ ⟨*place*⟩ tout près ▮2▮ *vtr* (a) atteindre ⟨*place, person, object, switch*⟩; ⟨*sound, news, letter*⟩ parvenir à ⟨*person, place*⟩
(b) (come to) arriver à ⟨*decision, understanding*⟩; **to** ~ **a verdict** (Law) rendre un verdict
(c) toucher ⟨*audience, market*⟩
(d) (in height, length) arriver à ⟨*floor, ceiling*⟩ ▮3▮ *vi* (a) **to** ~ **up/down** lever/baisser le bras; **to** ~ **out** tendre le bras
(b) (extend) **to** ~ (**up/down**) **to** arriver jusqu'à

reaches *n pl* **the upper/lower** ~ (of river) la partie supérieure/inférieure

react *vi* réagir (**to** à; **against** contre)

reaction *n* réaction *f*

reactionary *n, adj* réactionnaire (*mf*)

reactor *n* réacteur *m*

read ▮1▮ *vtr* (a) (gen) lire; **to** ~ **sb's mind** lire dans les pensées de qn
(b) (at university) faire des études de ⟨*history, French*⟩
(c) relever ⟨*meter*⟩ ▮2▮ *vi* lire (**to sb** à qn)
■ **read out** lire [qch] à haute voix
■ **read up: to** ~ **up on sth/sb** étudier qch/qn à fond

readable *adj* (a) (legible) lisible
(b) (enjoyable) agréable à lire

reader *n* lecteur/-trice *m/f*

readily *adv* (a) (willingly) sans hésiter
(b) (easily) facilement

reading *n* (a) lecture *f*
(b) (on meter) relevé *m* (**on** de); (on instrument) indication *f* (**on** de)
(c) (interpretation) interprétation *f* (**of** de)

reading glasses *n pl* lunettes *fpl* (pour lire)

reading list *n* liste *f* d'ouvrages recommandés

readjust ▮1▮ *vtr* régler [qch] de nouveau ▮2▮ *vi* ⟨*person*⟩ se réadapter (**to** à)

readvertise *vtr* refaire paraître une annonce pour ⟨*post, item*⟩

ready *adj* (a) (prepared) prêt/-e (**for** pour; **to do** à faire); **to get** ~ se préparer; **to get sth** ~ préparer qch; ~, **steady, go** à vos marques, prêts, partez!
(b) (willing) prêt/-e (**to do** à faire)

ready-made *adj* ⟨*clothes*⟩ de confection; ⟨*excuse*⟩ tout/-e fait/-e

ready-to-wear *adj* ⟨*garment*⟩ prêt-à-porter

real *adj* (a) (not imaginary) véritable, réel/ réelle; **in** ~ **life** dans la réalité
(b) (genuine) ⟨*diamond, flower, leather*⟩ vrai/-e (*before n*), authentique
(c) (proper) ⟨*holiday, rest*⟩ véritable, vrai/-e (*before n*)
(d) (for emphasis) ⟨*charmer, pleasure*⟩ vrai/-e (*before n*)

real estate *n* (a) (property) biens *mpl* immobiliers
(b) (US) (profession) immobilier *m*

realism *n* réalisme *m*

realist *n, adj* réaliste (*mf*)

realistic *adj* réaliste

reality *n* réalité *f* (**of** de)

realization *n* prise *f* de conscience

realize *vtr* (a) se rendre compte de; **to** ~ **that** se rendre compte que; **to make sb** ~ **sth** faire comprendre qch à qn
(b) réaliser ⟨*idea, dream, goal*⟩; **to** ~ **one's potential** développer ses capacités

reallocate *vtr* réattribuer

really ▮1▮ *adv* (a) (gen) vraiment
(b) (in actual fact) en fait, réellement; ~? (expressing disbelief) c'est vrai? ▮2▮ *excl* (*also* **well** ~) franchement!

real time *n* (Comput) temps *m* réel

reap *vtr* (a) moissonner ⟨*corn*⟩
(b) récolter ⟨*benefits*⟩

reappear *vi* reparaître

reappearance *n* réapparition *f*

reapply *vi* reposer sa candidature (**for** à)

reappraise *vtr* réexaminer ⟨*question*⟩; réévaluer ⟨*writer, work*⟩

rear ▮1▮ *n* (a) (of building, car, room) arrière *m*; (of procession, train) queue *f*
(b) (of person) derrière *m* (colloq) ▮2▮ *adj* (a) ⟨*door, garden*⟩ de derrière
(b) (of car) ⟨*light, seat, wheel*⟩ arrière *inv* ▮3▮ *vtr* élever ⟨*child, animals*⟩; cultiver ⟨*plants*⟩ ▮4▮ *vi* (*also* ~ **up**) ⟨*horse*⟩ se cabrer

rearmament *n* réarmement *m*

rearrange *vtr* réaménager ⟨*room*⟩; modifier ⟨*plans*⟩; changer ⟨*appointment*⟩

rear-view mirror *n* rétroviseur *m*

reason ▮1▮ *n* (a) (cause) raison *f* (**for, behind** de); **for no (good)** ~ sans raison valable; **to have** ~ **to do** avoir des raisons de faire; **the** ~ **why...** la raison pour laquelle...; **I'll tell you the** ~ **why** je vais te *or* vous dire pourquoi; **to have every** ~ **to do** avoir tout lieu de faire; **with good** ~ à juste titre
(b) (common sense) raison *f*; **to listen to** *or* **see** ~ entendre raison; **it stands to** ~ **that** il va sans dire que; **within** ~ dans la limite du raisonnable ▮2▮ *vi* **to** ~ **with sb** raisonner qn

reasonable *adj* (a) (sensible) raisonnable
(b) (moderately good) convenable

reasonably *adv* (a) (sensibly) raisonnablement
(b) (rather) assez

reasoning *n* raisonnement *m*

reassert *vtr* réaffirmer ⟨*authority, claim*⟩

reassess *vtr* réexaminer, reconsidérer

reassurance *n* **(a)** (comfort) réconfort *m*
(b) (guarantee) garantie *f*

reassure *vtr* rassurer ⟨*person*⟩ (about sur)

reassuring *adj* rassurant/-e

rebate *n* remboursement *m*

rebel ⟨1⟩ *n* rebelle *mf*
⟨2⟩ *vi* se rebeller

rebellion *n* rébellion *f*, révolte *f*

rebellious *adj* rebelle, insoumis/-e

rebuff ⟨1⟩ *n* rebuffade *f*
⟨2⟩ *vtr* rabrouer ⟨*person*⟩; repousser
⟨*advances*⟩

rebuild *vtr* reconstruire

rebuke ⟨1⟩ *n* réprimande *f*
⟨2⟩ *vtr* réprimander (for pour)

rebut *vtr* réfuter

recall ⟨1⟩ *n* (memory) mémoire *f*
⟨2⟩ *vtr* **(a)** (remember) se souvenir de
(b) (summon back) rappeler

recapitulate *vtr, vi* récapituler

recapture *vtr* recapturer ⟨*prisoner,
animal*⟩; reprendre ⟨*town*⟩; recréer ⟨*period,
atmosphere*⟩

recede *vi* (gen) s'éloigner; ⟨*hope, memory*⟩
s'estomper

receding *adj* ⟨*chin*⟩ fuyant/-e; **he has a ∼
hairline** son front se dégarnit

receipt ⟨1⟩ *n* (a) reçu *m*, récépissé *m* (for
pour); (from till) ticket *m* de caisse
(b) (act of receiving) réception *f*
⟨2⟩ **receipts** *n pl* (takings) recette *f* (from de)

receive ⟨1⟩ *vtr* **(a)** (gen) recevoir; receler
⟨*stolen goods*⟩
(b) (greet) accueillir, recevoir ⟨*visitor,
proposal, play*⟩ (with avec); **to be well ∼d**
être bien reçu/-e
⟨2⟩ **received** *pp adj* ⟨*ideas, opinions*⟩
reçu/-e

receiver *n* **(a)** (telephone) combiné *m*
(b) (radio or TV) (poste *m*) récepteur *m*

receivership *n* (GB) **to go into ∼** être
placé/-e sous administration judiciaire

receiving *n* (crime) recel *m*

recent *adj* ⟨*event, change, arrival, film*⟩
récent/-e; ⟨*acquaintance, development*⟩
nouveau/-elle (*before n*); **in ∼ years** au cours
des dernières années

recently *adv* récemment; **until ∼** jusqu'à
ces derniers temps

reception *n* **(a)** (*also* ∼ **desk**) réception
f
(b) (gathering) réception *f* (for sb en l'honneur
de qn; for sth à l'occasion de qch)
(c) (welcome) accueil *m* (for de)
(d) (on radio, TV) réception *f* (on sur)

receptionist *n* réceptionniste *mf*

receptive *adj* réceptif/-ive (to à)

recess *n* **(a)** (in parliament) (holiday) vacances
fpl
(b) (US) (break) (in school) récréation *f*; (during
meeting) pause *f*

(c) (alcove) alcôve *f*, recoin *m*

recession *n* récession *f*

recharge *vtr* recharger

rechargeable *adj* rechargeable

recipe *n* recette *f* (for de)

recipient *n* (of letter) destinataire *mf*; (of
benefits, aid, cheque) bénéficiaire *mf*; (of prize,
award) lauréat/-e *m/f*

reciprocal *adj* réciproque

reciprocate ⟨1⟩ *vtr* retourner
⟨*compliment*⟩; payer [qch] de retour ⟨*love*⟩;
rendre ⟨*affection*⟩
⟨2⟩ *vi* rendre la pareille

recital *n* récital *m*

recite *vtr, vi* réciter

reckless *adj* imprudent/-e

recklessly *adv* ⟨*act*⟩ avec imprudence;
⟨*promise, spend*⟩ de manière inconsciente

reckon *vtr* **(a)** (judge) considérer (that que)
(b) (colloq) (think) **to ∼ (that)** croire que
(c) (calculate) calculer ⟨*amount*⟩
■ **reckon on** (colloq): ¶ **∼ on [sb/sth]**
compter sur; ¶ **∼ on doing** compter faire
■ **reckon with** compter avec

reckoning *n* (estimation) estimation *f*;
(accurate calculation) calculs *mpl*

reclaim *vtr* **(a)** reconquérir ⟨*coastal land*⟩;
assécher ⟨*marsh*⟩; défricher ⟨*forest*⟩;
récupérer ⟨*glass, metal*⟩
(b) récupérer ⟨*deposit, money*⟩

reclaimable *adj* ⟨*waste product*⟩
récupérable

recline *vi* ⟨*person*⟩ s'allonger; ⟨*seat*⟩
s'incliner

reclining *adj* **(a)** ⟨*figure*⟩ allongé/-e
(b) ⟨*seat*⟩ inclinable; ⟨*chair*⟩ réglable

recluse *n* reclus/-e *m/f*

recognition *n* reconnaissance *f*; **in ∼ of**
en reconnaissance de

recognizable *adj* reconnaissable

recognize *vtr* reconnaître (by à)

recoil *vi* reculer (from devant)

recollect ⟨1⟩ *vtr* se souvenir de, se
rappeler
⟨2⟩ *vi* se souvenir

recollection *n* souvenir *m*

recommend *vtr* **(a)** (commend)
recommander
(b) (advise) conseiller, recommander

recommendation *n* recommandation *f*;
to give sb a ∼ recommander qn

recommended reading *n* livres *mpl*
conseillés *or* recommandés

recompense *n* **(a)** (reward) récompense *f*
(for de)
(b) (compensation) dédommagement *m* (for
pour)

reconcile *vtr* **(a)** réconcilier ⟨*people*⟩
(b) concilier ⟨*attitudes, views*⟩
(c) to become ∼d to sth se résigner à qch

reconnaissance *n* reconnaissance *f*

reconnoitre (GB), **reconnoiter** (US) ⋯⟶
⟨1⟩ *vtr* reconnaître

r

2 *vi* faire une reconnaissance

reconsider 1 *vtr* réexaminer
2 *vi* réfléchir

reconstruct *vtr* (a) (rebuild) reconstruire ⟨*building*⟩
(b) ⟨*police*⟩ faire une reconstitution de ⟨*crime*⟩

reconstruction *n* (a) (of building) reconstruction *f*
(b) (of crime) reconstitution *f*

record 1 *n* (a) (of events) compte-rendu *m*; (of official proceedings) procès-verbal *m*; **to keep a ∼ of sth** noter qch; **to say sth off the ∼** dire qch en privé; **to set the ∼ straight** mettre les choses au clair
(b) (data) ∼**s** (historical, public) archives *fpl*; (personal, administrative) dossier *m*
(c) (history) (of individual) passé *m*; (of organization, group) réputation *f*
(d) (*also* **criminal ∼**) casier *m* judiciaire
(e) (Mus) disque *m*
(f) (of athlete) record *m* (**for, in** de)
2 *adj* (a) ⟨*company, label*⟩ de disques
(b) ⟨*sales, time*⟩ record (*after n*); **to be at a ∼ high/low** être à son niveau le plus haut/bas
3 *vtr* (a) (note) noter ⟨*detail, idea, opinion*⟩
(b) (on disc, tape) enregistrer
(c) ⟨*instrument*⟩ enregistrer ⟨*temperature, rainfall*⟩

record book *n* livre *m* des records

recorded *adj* (on tape) enregistré/-e; (documented) ⟨*case, sighting*⟩ connu/-e

recorded delivery *n* (GB) **to send sth ∼** envoyer qch en recommandé

recorder *n* (Mus) flûte *f* à bec

record-holder *n* recordman/ recordwoman *m/f*

recording *n* enregistrement *m*

record player *n* tourne-disque *m*

recourse *n* recours *m* (**to** à)

recover 1 *vtr* (a) retrouver, récupérer ⟨*money, vehicle*⟩; récupérer ⟨*territory*⟩; (from water) repêcher, retrouver ⟨*body, wreck*⟩; **to ∼ one's strength** reprendre des forces
(b) (recoup) réparer, compenser ⟨*losses*⟩
2 *vi* (a) (from illness) se remettre (**from** de); (from defeat) se ressaisir (**from** après)
(b) ⟨*economy*⟩ se redresser

recovery *n* (a) (getting better) rétablissement *m*, guérison *f*
(b) (of economy, company, market) reprise *f*
(c) (getting back) (of vehicle) rapatriement *m*; (of money) récupération *f*

recovery vehicle *n* camion *m* de dépannage

recreate *vtr* recréer

recreation *n* (a) (leisure) loisirs *mpl*
(b) (playtime) récréation *f*

recreational drug *n*: drogue que l'on prend de façon occasionnelle

recreational vehicle, RV *n* camping-car *m*

recrimination *n* récrimination *f*

recruit 1 *n* recrue *f*

2 *vtr* recruter (**from** dans)

recruiting officer *n* officier *m* recruteur

recruitment *n* recrutement *m*

rectangle *n* rectangle *m*

rectangular *adj* rectangulaire

rectify *vtr* rectifier

rector *n* pasteur *m*

recuperate *vi* se rétablir (**from** de), récupérer

recur *vi* ⟨*event, error*⟩ se reproduire; ⟨*illness*⟩ réapparaître; ⟨*theme*⟩ revenir

recurrence *n* (of illness) récurrence *f*; (of symptom) réapparition *f*

recurrent *adj* récurrent/-e

recycle *vtr* recycler ⟨*paper, waste*⟩

recycling *n* recyclage *m*

red 1 *n* (a) (colour) rouge *m*; **in ∼** en rouge
(b) **to be in the ∼** ⟨*person, account*⟩ être à découvert; ⟨*company*⟩ être en déficit
2 *adj* rouge (**with** de); ⟨*hair*⟩ roux/rousse; **to go** *or* **turn ∼** rougir
IDIOMS **to be caught ∼-handed** être pris/-e la main dans le sac (colloq)

red alert *n* alerte *f* rouge

Red Cross *n* Croix-Rouge *f*

redcurrant *n* groseille *f*

redden *vtr, vi* rougir

redecorate *vtr* repeindre et retapisser, refaire

redeem *vtr* (a) retirer ⟨*pawned goods*⟩; rembourser ⟨*debt*⟩
(b) racheter ⟨*sinner*⟩; **her one ∼ing feature is...** ce qui la rachète, c'est...

redeploy *vtr* redéployer ⟨*troops*⟩; réaffecter ⟨*staff*⟩

redevelop *vtr* réaménager ⟨*site, town*⟩

red-faced *adj* (embarrassed) penaud/-e

redhead *n* roux/rousse *m/f*

red herring *n* faux problème *m*

red-hot *adj* ⟨*metal, coal*⟩ chauffé/-e au rouge

redial 1 *vtr* refaire ⟨*number*⟩
2 *vi* recomposer le numéro

redial facility *n* rappel *m* du dernier numéro composé

redirect *vtr* canaliser ⟨*resources*⟩; dévier ⟨*traffic*⟩; réexpédier ⟨*mail*⟩

rediscover *vtr* redécouvrir

red light area *n* quartier *m* chaud

redo *vtr* refaire

red pepper *n* poivron *m* rouge

redress *vtr* **to ∼ the balance** rétablir l'équilibre

red tape *n* paperasserie *f*

reduce *vtr* (a) réduire ⟨*inflation, number, pressure, sentence*⟩ (**by** de); baisser ⟨*prices, temperature*⟩; **to ∼ speed** ralentir; **to ∼ sb to tears** faire pleurer qn; **to be ∼d to begging** en être réduit/-e à la mendicité
(b) (in cooking) faire réduire ⟨*sauce, stock*⟩

reduction *n* **(a)** (in inflation, pressure, number) réduction *f* (**in** de); (of weight, size) diminution *f* (**in** de)
(b) (discount) réduction *f*, rabais *m*
redundancy *n* **(a)** (unemployment) chômage *m*
(b) (dismissal) licenciement *m*
redundant *adj* **(a)** (GB) (dismissed) licencié/-e; (out of work) au chômage; **to be made ∼** être licencié/-e
(b) (not needed) superflu/-e
reed *n* **(a)** (plant) roseau *m*
(b) (Mus) anche *f*
reef *n* récif *m*, écueil *m*
reek *vi* **to ∼ (of sth)** puer (qch)
reel 1 *n* bobine *f*; (for fishing) moulinet *m*
2 *vi* (sway) (person) tituber; **the blow sent him ∼ing** le coup l'a projeté en arrière
■ **reel off** débiter (list, names)
re-elect *vtr* réélire
re-emerge *vi* (person, sun) réapparaître; (problem) resurgir
re-examine *vtr* réexaminer
refectory *n* réfectoire *m*
refer 1 *vtr* renvoyer (task, problem) (**to** à); **to ∼ sb to** (person) envoyer qn à (department)
2 *vi* **(a)** (allude to) **to ∼ to** parler de, faire allusion à (person, topic, event)
(b) (relate, apply) **to ∼ to** (number, date, term) se rapporter à
(c) (consult) **to ∼ to** consulter (notes, article)
referee 1 *n* **(a)** arbitre *m*
(b) (GB) (giving job reference) personne *f* pouvant fournir des références
2 *vtr*, *vi* arbitrer
reference 1 *n* **(a)** (allusion) référence *f* (**to** à), allusion *f* (**to** à)
(b) (consultation) **without ∼ to sb/sth** sans consulter qn/qch; **for future ∼** pour information
(c) (in book, letter) référence *f*
(d) (testimonial) références *fpl*
2 **with reference to** *phr* **with ∼ to your letter** suite à votre lettre
reference book *n* ouvrage *m* de référence
reference number *n* numéro *m* de référence
referendum *n* référendum *m*
referral *n* (of matter, problem) renvoi *m* (**to** à)
refill 1 *n* (for ballpoint, lighter, perfume) recharge *f*
2 *vtr* recharger (pen, lighter); remplir [qch] à nouveau (glass, bottle)
refine *vtr* **(a)** raffiner (oil, sugar)
(b) (improve) peaufiner (theory)
refined *adj* raffiné/-e
refinement *n* (elegance) raffinement *m*
refinery *n* raffinerie *f*
reflect 1 *vtr* refléter (image); **to be ∼ed in sth** se refléter dans qch
(b) renvoyer, réfléchir (light, heat)
(c) (think) se dire

2 *vi* **(a)** (think) réfléchir (**on, upon** à)
(b) **to ∼ well/badly on sb** faire honneur/du tort à qn
reflection *n* **(a)** (image) reflet *m* (**of** de), image *f* (**of** de)
(b) (thought) réflexion *f*; **on ∼** à la réflexion
reflector *n* (on vehicle) catadioptre *m*
reflex 1 *n* réflexe *m*
2 *adj* réflexe; **a ∼ action** un réflexe
reflexive verb *n* verbe *m* pronominal réfléchi
reform 1 *n* réforme *f*
2 *vtr* réformer
reformation *n* réforme *f*; **the Reformation** la Réforme
refrain 1 *n* refrain *m*
2 *vi* se retenir; **to ∼ from doing** s'abstenir de faire
refresh *vtr* (bath, drink) rafraîchir; (rest) reposer; **to ∼ sb's memory** rafraîchir la mémoire à qn
refresher course *n* cours *m* de recyclage
refreshing *adj* (drink, shower) rafraîchissant/-e; (rest) réparateur/-trice
refreshments *n pl* (drinks) rafraîchissements *mpl*; **light ∼** repas *m* léger
refrigerate *vtr* frigorifier
refrigerator *n* réfrigérateur *m*, frigidaire® *m*
refuel *vi* se ravitailler en carburant
refuge *n* **(a)** (shelter, protection) refuge *m* (**from** contre); **to take ∼ from** s'abriter de (storm)
(b) (hostel) foyer *m*
refugee *n* réfugié/-e *m/f*
refugee camp *n* camp *m* de réfugiés
refund 1 *n* remboursement *m*
2 *vtr* rembourser
refurbish *vtr* rénover
refusal *n* refus *m* (**to do** de faire); (to application) réponse *f* négative
refuse¹ 1 *vtr* refuser (**to do** de faire)
2 *vi* refuser
refuse² *n* (GB) (household) ordures *fpl*; (industrial) déchets *mpl*; (garden) déchets *mpl* de jardinage
refuse collector *n* (GB) éboueur *m*
refute *vtr* réfuter
regain *vtr* retrouver (health, strength, sight, composure); reconquérir (power, seat); reprendre (lead, control); **to ∼ consciousness** reprendre connaissance
regal *adj* royal/-e
regale *vtr* régaler (**with** de)
regalia *n pl* insignes *mpl*
regard 1 *n* **(a)** (consideration) égard *m*; **out of ∼ for** par égard pour
(b) (esteem) estime *f* (**for** pour); **to hold sb/sth in high ∼** avoir beaucoup d'estime pour qn/qch ···⟶

r

(c) with *or* in ~ to en ce qui concerne; **in this ~** à cet égard
2 *vtr* considérer (**as comme**)

regarding *prep* concernant

regardless 1 *prep* **~ of** sans tenir compte de
2 *adv* malgré tout

regards *n pl* amitiés *fpl*; **give them my ~** transmettez-leur mes amitiés

regatta *n* régate *f*

regent *n* régent/-e *m/f*

reggae *n* reggae *m*

regime, **régime** *n* régime *m*

regiment *n* régiment *m*

region *n* région *f*; **(somewhere) in the ~ of £300** environ 300 livres sterling

regional *adj* régional/-e

register 1 *n* registre *m*; (at school) cahier *m* des absences
2 *vtr* **(a)** déclarer ⟨birth, death⟩; faire immatriculer ⟨vehicle⟩; faire enregistrer ⟨luggage, company⟩; déposer ⟨trademark, complaint⟩
(b) ⟨instrument⟩ indiquer ⟨speed, temperature⟩; ⟨person⟩ exprimer ⟨anger, disapproval⟩
(c) envoyer [qch] en recommandé ⟨letter⟩
3 *vi* (for course, school, to vote) s'inscrire; (at hotel) se présenter

registered *adj* **(a)** ⟨voter⟩ inscrit/-e; ⟨vehicle, student⟩ immatriculé/-e; ⟨charity⟩ ≈ agréé/-e
(b) ⟨letter⟩ recommandé/-e; **by ~ post** en recommandé

registered trademark *n* marque *m* déposée

registrar *n* **(a)** (GB) (gen) officier *m* d'état civil; (medical) adjoint *m*
(b) (academic) responsable *mf* du bureau de la scolarité

registration *n* (of person) inscription *f*; (of trademark, patent) dépôt *m*; (of birth, death, marriage) déclaration *f*

registration number *n* numéro *m* d'immatriculation

registry office *n* (GB) bureau *m* de l'état civil; **to get married in a ~** se marier civilement

regress *vi* régresser (**to** au stade de)

regret 1 *n* regret *m* (**about** à propos de); **to have no ~s about doing** ne pas regretter d'avoir fait
2 *vtr* regretter (**that** que + *subjunctive*); **to ~ doing** regretter d'avoir fait; **I ~ to inform you that** j'ai le regret de vous informer que

regretfully *adv* à regret

regrettable *adj* regrettable (**that** que + *subjunctive*)

regular 1 *n* **(a)** (client, visitor) habitué/-e *m/f*
(b) (US) (petrol) ordinaire *m*
2 *adj* **(a)** (gen) régulier/-ière; **to take ~ exercise** faire de l'exercice régulièrement
(b) (usual) ⟨activity, customer, visitor⟩ habituel/-elle; ⟨viewer, listener⟩ fidèle

(c) ⟨army, soldier⟩ de métier

regularity *n* régularité *f*

regularly *adv* régulièrement

regulate *vtr* **(a)** (gen, Econ) réguler
(b) (adjust) régler ⟨mechanism⟩

regulation 1 *n* **(a)** (gen) règlement *m*; (for safety, fire) consigne *f*; **under the (new) ~s** selon la (nouvelle) réglementation; **against the ~s** contraire au règlement *or* aux normes
(b) (controlling) réglementation *f*
2 *adj* ⟨width, length, uniform⟩ réglementaire

regurgitate *vtr* régurgiter; (figurative) ressortir

rehabilitate *vtr* réinsérer ⟨handicapped person, ex-prisoner⟩; réhabiliter ⟨addict, area⟩

rehabilitation centre (GB), **rehabilitation center** (US) *n* (for the handicapped) centre *m* de rééducation; (for addicts etc) centre *m* de réinsertion

rehearsal *n* répétition *f* (**of** de)

rehearse 1 *vtr* répéter ⟨scene⟩; préparer ⟨speech, excuse⟩
2 *vi* répéter (**for** pour)

reheat *vtr* réchauffer

rehouse *vtr* reloger

reign 1 *n* règne *m*
2 *vi* régner (**over** sur)

reimburse *vtr* rembourser

rein *n* rêne *f*

reincarnation *n* réincarnation *f*

reindeer *n* renne *m*

reinforce *vtr* renforcer

reinforced concrete *n* béton *m* armé

reinforcement *n* (support) renfort *m*; **~s** (Mil) renforts

reinstate *vtr* réintégrer ⟨employee⟩

reiterate *vtr* réitérer

reject 1 *n* marchandise *f* de deuxième choix
2 *vtr* rejeter ⟨advice, application, person, transplant⟩; refuser ⟨candidate, manuscript⟩; démentir ⟨claim, suggestion⟩

rejection *n* (gen) rejet *m*; (of candidate, manuscript) refus *m*

rejection letter *n* lettre *f* de refus

rejoice *vi* se réjouir (**at, over** de)

rejuvenate *vtr* rajeunir

rekindle *vtr* ranimer

relapse 1 *n* rechute *f*
2 *vi* (Med) rechuter; (gen) **to ~ into** retomber dans

relate 1 *vtr* **(a)** (connect) faire le rapprochement entre
(b) (recount) raconter ⟨story⟩ (**to** à)
2 *vi* **to ~ to** (have connection) se rapporter à; (communicate) s'entendre avec

related *adj* **(a)** ⟨person⟩ apparenté/-e (**by, through** par; **to** à)
(b) (connected) ⟨area, idea, incident⟩ lié/-e (**to** à); **drug-~** lié/-e à la drogue

relation 1 n (a) (relative) parent/-e m/f; **my
~s** ma famille
(b) (connection) rapport m
2 **relations** n pl (dealings) relations fpl
(with avec)
relationship n (a) (between people)
relations fpl; (with colleagues) rapports mpl
(b) (connection) rapport m (**to, with** avec)
relative 1 n parent/-e m/f; **my ~s** ma
famille
2 adj (a) (gen) relatif/-ive
(b) (respective) respectif/-ive
relatively adv relativement; **~ speaking**
toutes proportions gardées
relax 1 vtr décontracter (muscle);
assouplir (restrictions, discipline); détendre
(body); relâcher (efforts, grip, concentration)
2 vi (a) (person) se détendre
(b) (grip) se relâcher; (jaw, muscle) se
décontracter
relaxation n (a) (of person) détente f
(b) (of restrictions, discipline) assouplissement m
(in de)
relaxed adj détendu/-e, décontracté/-e
relaxing adj (atmosphere, activity)
délassant/-e; (vacation) reposant/-e
relay 1 n (a) (of workers) équipe f (de relais)
(b) (also ~ **race**) course f de relais
2 vtr transmettre (message) (**to** à)
release 1 n (a) (liberation) libération f
(b) (relief) soulagement m
(c) (for press) communiqué m
(d) (of film) sortie f
(e) (film, video, record) (also **new ~**)
nouveauté f
2 vtr (a) libérer (prisoner); dégager
(accident victim); relâcher (animal); **to ~ sb
from** dégager qn de (promise)
(b) faire jouer (catch, clasp); déclencher
(shutter); desserrer (handbrake); larguer
(bomb)
(c) (let go) lâcher (object, arm, hand)
(d) faire sortir (film, record)
relegate vtr (a) reléguer (person, object)
(**to** à)
(b) (GB) (Sport) reléguer (**to** en)
relegation n relégation f
relent vi céder
relentless adj (pressure) implacable;
(noise, activity) incessant/-e; (attack)
acharné/-e
relevant adj (a) (issue, facts, point)
pertinent/-e; (information) utile; **to be ~ to**
avoir rapport à
(b) (appropriate) (chapter) correspondant/-e;
(period) en question
reliable adj (friend, witness) digne de
confiance, fiable; (employee, firm)
sérieux/-ieuse; (car, memory, account) fiable;
(information, source) sûr/-e
reliant adj **to be ~ on** être dépendant/-e de
relic n relique f
relief n (a) (from pain, distress) soulagement
m
(b) (aid) aide f, secours m

(c) (in sculpture, geography) relief m
relief agency n organisation f
humanitaire
relief fund n fonds m de secours
relief supplies n pl secours mpl
relief work n travail m humanitaire
relief worker n secouriste mf
relieve vtr (a) soulager (pain, suffering,
tension); dissiper (boredom); remédier à
(poverty, famine); **to be ~d** être soulagé/-e
(b) **to ~ sb of** débarrasser qn de (coat, bag);
soulager qn de (burden)
(c) (help) secourir (troops, population)
(d) relever (worker, sentry)
religion n religion f
religious adj (gen) religieux/-ieuse;
(person) croyant/-e; (war) de religion
relinquish vtr renoncer à (claim, right)
(to in faveur de); céder (task, power) (**to** à)
relish 1 n (a) **with ~** (eat, drink) avec un
plaisir évident
(b) (Culin) condiment m
2 vtr savourer (food); se réjouir de
(prospect)
relocate 1 vtr muter
2 vi (company) déménager; (employee) être
muté/-e
reluctance n réticence f (**to do** à faire)
reluctant adj (person) peu enthousiaste;
to be ~ to do être peu disposé/-e à faire
reluctantly adv à contrecœur
rely vi (a) (be dependent) **to ~ on** dépendre
de (person, aid, industry); reposer sur
(method, technology, exports)
(b) (count) **to ~ on sb/sth** compter sur
qn/qch (**to do** pour faire)
remain vi rester; **to ~ silent** garder le
silence
remainder n reste m (**of** de)
remains n pl restes mpl
remand 1 n **on ~** (in custody) en détention
provisoire; (on bail) en liberté sous caution
2 vtr **to be ~ed in custody** être placé/-e en
détention provisoire
remand centre n (GB) centre m de
détention (provisoire)
remark 1 n remarque f
2 vtr (a) (comment) faire remarquer (**that**
que; **to** à)
(b) (notice) remarquer (**that** que)
remarkable adj remarquable
remarry vi se remarier
remedial adj (Sch) (class) de rattrapage
remedy 1 n remède m (**for** à, contre)
2 vtr remédier à
remember 1 vtr (a) (recall) se souvenir
de, se rappeler (fact, name, place, event); se
souvenir de (person); **to ~ doing** se rappeler
avoir fait, se souvenir d'avoir fait
(b) (not forget) **to ~ to do** penser à faire, ne
pas oublier de faire
2 vi se souvenir

r

remind *vtr* rappeler; **to ~ sb of sb/sth** rappeler qn/qch à qn; **to ~ sb to do** rappeler à qn de faire

reminder *n* rappel *m* (of de; that du fait que)

reminisce *vi* évoquer ses souvenirs (about de)

reminiscent *adj* **to be ~ of sb/sth** faire penser à qn/qch

remiss *adj* négligent/-e

remission *n* **(a)** (of sentence, debt) remise *f* **(b)** (Med) rémission *f*

remit *n* attributions *fpl*

remnant *n* (gen) reste *m*; (of building, past) vestige *m*; (of fabric) coupon *m*

remorse *n* remords *m* (for de)

remote *adj* **(a)** ⟨area, village⟩ isolé/-e; ⟨ancestor, country⟩ éloigné/-e **(b)** (aloof) ⟨person⟩ distant/-e **(c)** (slight) ⟨chance⟩ vague, infime

remote control *n* télécommande *f*

remote-controlled *adj* télécommandé/-e

remotely *adv* ⟨resemble⟩ vaguement; **he's not ~ interested** ça ne l'intéresse pas du tout

removal *n* **(a)** (of furniture, parcel, rubbish) enlèvement *m*; (Med) ablation *f*; **stain ~** détachage *m* **(b)** (change of home) déménagement *m* (from de; to à)

remove *vtr* **(a)** (gen, Med) enlever (from de); enlever, ôter ⟨clothes, shoes⟩; supprimer ⟨threat⟩; chasser ⟨doubt⟩; **cousin once ~d** cousin au deuxième degré **(b)** **to ~ sb from office** démettre qn de ses fonctions

remover *n* déménageur *m*

remuneration *n* rémunération *f*

Renaissance *n* **the ~** la Renaissance

render *vtr* rendre

rendezvous ① *n* rendez-vous *m inv* ② *vi* **to ~ with sb** rejoindre qn

renegade *n* renégat/-e *m/f*

renew ① *vtr* (gen) renouveler; renouer ⟨acquaintance⟩; raviver ⟨courage⟩; faire prolonger ⟨library book⟩

renewal *n* (of contract, passport) renouvellement *m*; (of hostilities) reprise *f*, (of interest) regain *m*

renewed *adj* ⟨interest, optimism⟩ accru/-e; ⟨attack, call⟩ renouvelé/-e

renounce *vtr* (gen) renoncer à; renier ⟨faith, friend⟩

renovate *vtr* rénover ⟨building⟩

renovation *n* rénovation *f*; **~s** travaux *mpl* de rénovation

renowned *adj* célèbre (for pour)

rent ① *n* loyer *m*; **for ~** à louer ② *vtr* louer

rental *n* (of car, premises, equipment) location *f*; (of phone line) abonnement *m*

rent boy *n* jeune prostitué *m*

reoffend *vi* récidiver

reopen *vtr, vi* rouvrir

reorganize *vtr* réorganiser

rep *n* représentant/-e *m/f* (de commerce)

repair ① *n* réparation *f*; **to be (damaged) beyond ~** ne pas être réparable; **to be in good/bad ~** être en bon/mauvais état ② *vtr* réparer

repairman *n* réparateur *m*

repatriate *vtr* rapatrier

repatriation *n* rapatriement *m*

repay *vtr* rembourser ⟨person, sum⟩; rendre ⟨hospitality, favour⟩

repayment *n* remboursement *m* (on de)

repeal ① *n* abrogation *f* (of de) ② *vtr* abroger

repeat ① *n* (gen) répétition *f*; (on radio, TV) rediffusion *f*; (Mus) reprise *f* ② *vtr* (gen) répéter; (Sch) redoubler ⟨year⟩; rediffuser ⟨programme⟩

repeated *adj* ⟨warnings, requests, attempts⟩ répété/-e; ⟨setbacks⟩ successif/-ive

repeatedly *adv* plusieurs fois, à plusieurs reprises

repel *vtr* repousser

repellent *adj* repoussant/-e

repent *vi* se repentir

repercussion *n* répercussion *f*

repertoire *n* répertoire *m*

repetition *n* répétition *f*

repetitive *adj* répétitif/-ive

repetitive strain injury, RSI *n* microtraumatismes *mpl* répétés

replace *vtr* **(a)** (put back) remettre ⟨lid, cork⟩; remettre [qch] à sa place ⟨book, ornament⟩ **(b)** (provide replacement for) remplacer (with par)

replacement *n* **(a)** (person) remplaçant/-e *m/f* (for de) **(b)** (act) remplacement *m* **(c)** (spare part) pièce *f* de rechange

replay ① *n* (Sport) match *m* rejoué ② *vtr* rejouer

replenish *vtr* reconstituer ⟨stocks⟩

replica *n* réplique *f*, copie *f* (of de)

reply ① *n* réponse *f* ② *vtr, vi* répondre

report ① *n* **(a)** (written account) rapport *m* (on sur); (verbal account, minutes) compte-rendu *m*; (in media) communiqué *m*; (longer) reportage *m* **(b)** (GB) (Sch) (also **school ~**) bulletin *m* scolaire; (US) (Sch) (review) critique *f* ② *vtr* **(a)** signaler ⟨fact, event, theft, accident⟩; **to ~ sth to sb** transmettre qch à qn ⟨result, decision, news⟩ **(b)** (make complaint about) signaler ⟨person⟩; se plaindre de ⟨noise⟩ ③ *vi* **(a)** **to ~ on** faire un compte-rendu sur ⟨talks, progress⟩; ⟨reporter⟩ faire un reportage sur ⟨events⟩; ⟨committee, group⟩ faire un rapport sur **(b)** (present oneself) se présenter; **to ~ for duty** prendre son service

(c) to ~ être sous les ordres (directs) de ⟨*manager, superior*⟩

report card *n* (US) bulletin *m* scolaire

reporter *n* journaliste *mf*, reporter *mf*

repose *n* repos *m*; **in ~** au repos

repossess *vtr* ⟨*bank*⟩ saisir ⟨*house*⟩; ⟨*creditor*⟩ reprendre possession de ⟨*property*⟩

repossession *n* saisie *f* immobilière

reprehensible *adj* répréhensible

represent *vtr* **(a)** (gen) représenter
(b) (present) présenter ⟨*person, event*⟩ **(as** comme)

representation *n* **(a)** représentation *f* **(of** de; **by** par)
(b) to make ~s to sb faire des démarches *fpl* auprès de qn

representative ⒈ *n* **(a)** représentant/-e *m/f*
(b) (US) (politician) député *m*
⒉ *adj* représentatif/-ive **(of** de), typique **(of** de)

repress *vtr* réprimer ⟨*reaction, smile*⟩; refouler ⟨*feelings*⟩

reprieve ⒈ *n* **(a)** (Law) remise *f* de peine
(b) (delay) sursis *m*
(c) (respite) répit *m*
⒉ *vtr* accorder une remise de peine à ⟨*prisoner*⟩

reprimand ⒈ *n* réprimande *f*
⒉ *vtr* réprimander

reprisal *n* représailles *fpl*

reproach ⒈ *n* reproche *m*; **beyond ~** irréprochable
⒉ *vtr* reprocher à ⟨*person*⟩; **to ~ sb with** *or* **for sth** reprocher qch à qn

reprocessing plant *n* (*also* **nuclear ~**) usine *f* de retraitement (des déchets nucléaires)

reproduce ⒈ *vtr* reproduire
⒉ *vi* se reproduire

reproduction *n* reproduction *f*

reproduction furniture *n* meubles *mpl* de style

reproductive *adj* reproducteur/-trice

reproof *n* réprimande *f*

reprove *vtr* réprimander **(for doing** de faire)

reptile *n* reptile *m*

republic *n* république *f*

republican ⒈ *n* républicain/-e *m/f*; **Republican** (US) Républicain/-e *m/f*
⒉ *adj* (*also* **Republican**) républicain/-e

repudiate *vtr* rejeter

repugnant *adj* répugnant/-e

repulse *vtr* repousser

repulsion *n* répulsion *f*

repulsive *adj* repoussant/-e

reputable *adj* de bonne réputation

reputation *n* réputation *f* **(as** de)

repute *n* **of ~** réputé/-e

reputed *adj* (gen) réputé/-e; (Law) putatif/-ive; **he is ~ to be very rich** à ce que l'on dit il serait très riche

request ⒈ *n* **(a)** demande *f* **(for** de; **to** à), requête *f* **(for** de; **to** à); **on ~** sur demande
(b) (on radio) dédicace *f*
⒉ *vtr* demander **(from** à); **to ~ sb to do** demander à qn de faire

require *vtr* **(a)** (need) avoir besoin de
(b) (necessitate) ⟨*job, situation*⟩ exiger ⟨*funds, qualifications*⟩; **to be ~d to do** être tenu/-e de faire

requirement *n* **(a)** (need) besoin *m*
(b) (condition) condition *f*
(c) (obligation) obligation *f* **(to do** de faire)
(d) (US) (Univ) matière *f* obligatoire

requisite *adj* exigé/-e, requis/-e

requisition *vtr* réquisitionner

reschedule *vtr* (change time) changer l'heure de; (change date) changer la date de

rescue ⒈ *n* **(a)** (aid) secours *m*; **to come/ go to sb's ~** venir/aller au secours de qn; **to come to the ~** venir à la rescousse
(b) (operation) sauvetage *m* **(of** de)
⒉ *vtr* **(a)** (save) sauver
(b) (aid) porter secours à
(c) (release) libérer

rescue worker *n* secouriste *mf*

research ⒈ *n* recherche *f* **(into, on** sur)
⒉ *vtr* faire des recherches sur ⟨*topic*⟩; préparer ⟨*book, article*⟩

research and development, **R&D** *n* recherche-développement *f*, recherche *f* et développement *m*

researcher *n* chercheur/-euse *m/f*; (in TV) documentaliste *mf*

resemblance *n* ressemblance *f* **(between** entre; **to** avec)

resemble *vtr* ressembler à; **to ~ each other** se ressembler

resent *vtr* en vouloir à ⟨*person*⟩ **(for doing** d'avoir fait); ne pas aimer ⟨*tone*⟩

resentful *adj* plein/-e de ressentiment **(of** sb envers qn)

resentment *n* ressentiment *m*

reservation *n* **(a)** (doubt) réserve *f*; **without ~** sans réserve; **to have ~s about sth** avoir des doutes sur qch
(b) (booking) réservation *f*
(c) (US) (Indian) ~ réserve *f* (indienne)

reservation desk *n* bureau *m* des réservations

reserve ⒈ *n* **(a)** (stock) réserve *f*; **to keep sth in ~** tenir qch en réserve
(b) (reticence) réserve *f*
(c) (Mil) **the ~(s)** la réserve
(d) (Sport) remplaçant *m/f*
(e) réserve *f*; **wildlife ~** réserve naturelle
⒉ *vtr* réserver

reserved *adj* réservé/-e

reservoir *n* réservoir *m*

reset *vtr* régler ⟨*machine*⟩; remettre [qch] à l'heure ⟨*clock*⟩

reshuffle *n* remaniement *m*

reside *vi* résider, habiter (**with** avec)
residence *n* résidence *f*
residence permit *n* permis *m* de séjour
resident [1] *n* (gen) résident/-e *m/f*; (of street) riverain/-e *m/f*; (of guest house) pensionnaire *mf*
[2] *adj* ⟨*population*⟩ local/-e; ⟨*staff, tutor*⟩ à demeure
residential *adj* ⟨*area*⟩ résidentiel/-ielle; ⟨*staff*⟩ à demeure; ⟨*course*⟩ en internat; **to be in ∼ care** être pris en charge par une institution
residue *n* résidu *m* (**of** de)
resign [1] *vtr* démissionner de ⟨*post, job*⟩
[2] *vi* démissionner (**as** du poste de; **from** de)
[3] *v refl* **to ∼ oneself** se résigner (**to** à)
resignation *n* (a) (from post) démission *f* (**from** de; **as** du poste de)
(b) (patience) résignation *f*
resigned *adj* résigné/-e (**to** à)
resilient *adj* (morally) déterminé/-e; (physically) résistant/-e
resin *n* résine *f*
resist [1] *vtr* résister à
[2] *vi* résister
resistance *n* résistance *f* (**to** à)
Resistance *n* **the ∼** la Résistance
resistance fighter *n* résistant/-e *m/f*
resistant *adj* (a) heat-∼ résistant/-e à la chaleur; water-∼ imperméable
(b) (opposed) ∼ **to** réfractaire à
resit *vtr* (GB) repasser ⟨*exam, test*⟩
reskill *vtr* recycler
resolute *adj* ⟨*person*⟩ résolu/-e
resolution *n* résolution *f*; **to make a ∼ to do** prendre la résolution de faire
resolve [1] *n* détermination *f*
[2] *vtr* (a) (gen) résoudre
(b) (decide) **to ∼ that** décider que; **to ∼ to do** résoudre de faire
resonant *adj* ⟨*voice*⟩ sonore
resort [1] *n* (a) recours *m*; **as a last ∼** en dernier recours
(b) seaside ∼ station *f* balnéaire; **ski ∼** station *f* de ski
[2] *vi* **to ∼ to** recourir à
resound *vi* (a) ⟨*noise*⟩ retentir (**through** dans)
(b) ⟨*place*⟩ retentir (**with** de)
resounding *adj* ⟨*cheers*⟩ retentissant/-e; ⟨*success*⟩ éclatant/-e
resource *n* ressource *f*
resource centre (GB), **resource center** (US) *n* centre *m* de documentation
resourceful *adj* plein/-e de ressources, débrouillard/-e (colloq)
respect [1] *n* (a) (gen) respect *m*; **out of ∼** par respect (**for** pour); **with (all due) ∼** sauf votre respect; **with ∼ to** par rapport à
(b) (aspect) égard *m*; **in many ∼s** à bien des égards
[2] **respects** *n pl* respects *mpl*; **to pay one's ∼s to sb** présenter ses respects à qn

[3] *vtr* respecter
respectable *adj* (a) ⟨*person, family*⟩ respectable
(b) (adequate) ⟨*amount*⟩ respectable; ⟨*performance*⟩ honorable
respectful *adj* respectueux/-euse
respective *adj* respectif/-ive
respiration *n* respiration *f*
respirator *n* respirateur *m*
respiratory *adj* respiratoire
respite *n* répit *m* (**from** dans)
respond *vi* (a) (answer) répondre (**to** à; **with** par)
(b) (react) réagir (**to** à)
response *n* (a) (answer) réponse *f* (**to** à); **in ∼ to** en réponse à
(b) (reaction) réaction *f* (**to** à; **from** de)
responsibility *n* responsabilité *f* (**for** de); **to take ∼ for sth** prendre la responsabilité de qch
responsible *adj* (a) (to blame) responsable (**for** de)
(b) (in charge) ∼ **for doing** chargé/-e de faire
(c) (trustworthy) responsable
(d) ⟨*job*⟩ à responsabilités
responsive *adj* réceptif/-ive
rest [1] *n* (a) (remainder) **the ∼** le reste (**of** de); **for the ∼ of my life** pour le restant de mes jours
(b) (other people) **the ∼ (of them)** les autres
(c) (repose) repos *m*; (break) pause *f*; **to have a ∼** se reposer
[2] *vtr* (a) (lean) **to ∼ sth on** appuyer qch sur
(b) reposer ⟨*legs*⟩; ne pas utiliser ⟨*injured limb*⟩
[3] *vi* (a) se reposer; **to ∼ easy** être tranquille; **to let the matter ∼** en rester là
(b) (be supported) **to ∼ on** reposer sur
(c) **to ∼ on** ⟨*decision*⟩ reposer sur ⟨*assumption*⟩
■ **rest with**: ∼ **with** [sb/sth] être entre les mains de
restart *vtr* (a) reprendre ⟨*talks*⟩
(b) remettre [qch] en marche ⟨*engine*⟩
restaurant *n* restaurant *m*
restaurant car *n* (GB) wagon-restaurant *m*
restaurant owner *n* restaurateur/-trice *m/f*
restful *adj* ⟨*holiday*⟩ reposant/-e; ⟨*place*⟩ paisible
restless *adj* ⟨*person*⟩ nerveux/-euse; ⟨*patient, sleep*⟩ agité/-e
restock *vtr* regarnir ⟨*shelf*⟩ (**with** en); réapprovisionner ⟨*shop*⟩ (**with** en)
restoration *n* restauration *f*
restore *vtr* (a) restituer ⟨*property*⟩ (**to** à)
(b) rétablir ⟨*health, peace, monarchy*⟩; rendre ⟨*faculty*⟩; **to ∼ sb to power** ramener qn au pouvoir
(c) (repair) restaurer
restrain [1] *vtr* retenir ⟨*person*⟩; contenir ⟨*crowd*⟩; maîtriser ⟨*animal*⟩
[2] *v refl* **to ∼ oneself** se retenir

restrained adj ‹manner› calme; ‹reaction› modéré/-e; ‹person› posé/-e

restraint n (a) (moderation) modération f (b) (restriction) restriction f; **wage ~** contrôle m des salaires (c) (constraint) contrainte f

restrict vtr limiter ‹activity, choice, growth› (**to** à); restreindre ‹freedom›; réserver ‹access, membership› (**to** à)

restricted adj ‹growth, movement› limité/-e; ‹document› confidentiel/-ielle; ‹parking› réglementé/-e

restriction n limitation f

re-string vtr changer les cordes de ‹guitar›; recorder ‹racket›; renfiler ‹necklace›

rest room n (US) toilettes fpl

result ① n résultat m (**of** de); **as a ~ of** à la suite de; **as a ~** en conséquence ② vi résulter; **to ~ in** avoir pour résultat

resume vtr, vi reprendre

résumé n (a) (summary) résumé m (b) (US) (CV) curriculum vitae m inv

resumption n reprise f (**of** de)

resurface ① vtr refaire (la surface de) ‹road› ② vi ‹submarine› faire surface; ‹person› refaire surface

resurrect vtr ressusciter

resurrection n résurrection f; **the Resurrection** la Résurrection

resuscitate vtr (Med) réanimer

resuscitation n réanimation f

retail ① n vente f au détail ② adv au détail ③ vi **to ~ at** se vendre au détail à

retailer n détaillant m

retail price n prix m de détail

retail sales n pl ventes fpl au détail

retail trade n commerce m de détail

retain vtr garder ‹control, identity›; conserver ‹heat, title›; retenir ‹water, fact›

retaliate vi réagir

retaliation n représailles fpl (**for** de)

retarded adj retardé/-e

retch vi avoir des haut-le-cœur

rethink n to have a **~** y repenser

reticent adj réticent/-e; **to be ~ about sth** être discret/-ète sur qch

retina n rétine f

retinue n escorte f

retire vi (a) (from work) prendre sa retraite (b) (withdraw) se retirer (**from** de)

retired adj retraité/-e

retirement n retraite f

retirement age n âge m de la retraite

retirement home n maison f de retraite

retiring adj (shy) réservé/-e

retort ① n riposte f ② vtr rétorquer (**that** que)

retrace vtr **to ~ one's steps** revenir sur ses pas

retract ① vtr rétracter ‹statement, claws›; escamoter ‹landing gear› ② vi ‹landing gear› s'escamoter

retrain ① vtr recycler ‹staff› ② vi ‹person› se recycler

retraining n recyclage m

retreat ① n retraite f ② vi ‹person› se retirer (**into** dans; **from** de); ‹army› se replier (**to** sur); ‹flood water› reculer; **to ~ into a dream world** se réfugier dans un monde imaginaire

retrial n nouveau procès m

retrieve vtr récupérer ‹object›; redresser ‹situation›; extraire ‹data›

retrograde adj rétrograde

retrospect: **in retrospect** phr rétrospectivement

retrospective ① n (also **~ exhibition** or **~ show**) rétrospective f ② adj (a) (gen) rétrospectif/-ive (b) (Law) rétroactif/-ive

return ① n (a) (gen) retour m (**to** à; **from** de; **of** de); **by ~ of post** par retour du courrier (b) (on investment) rendement m (**on** de) ② vtr (a) (give back) rendre; (pay back) rembourser; **to ~ sb's call** rappeler qn (b) (bring back) rapporter (**to** à) (c) (put back) remettre (d) (send back) renvoyer; '**~ to sender**' 'retour à l'expéditeur' (e) (reciprocate) répondre à ‹love› (f) (Mil) riposter à ‹fire› (g) (Law) prononcer ‹verdict› (h) rapporter ‹profit› ③ vi (a) (come back) revenir (**from** de); retourner (**to** à); (get back from abroad) rentrer (**from** de); (get back home) rentrer chez soi (b) (resume) **to ~** reprendre ‹activity›; **to ~ to power** revenir au pouvoir (c) (recur) ‹symptom, doubt› réapparaître ④ **in return** phr en échange (**for** de) IDIOMS **many happy ~s!** bon anniversaire!

return fare n prix m d'un billet aller-retour

return flight n vol m de retour

return ticket n billet m aller-retour

return trip n retour m

reunification n réunification f

reunion n réunion f

reunite vtr réunir ‹family›; réunifier ‹party›

reuse vtr réutiliser

rev vtr (colloq) monter le régime de ‹engine›

revalue vtr réévaluer

revamp vtr rajeunir ‹image›; réorganiser ‹company›; retaper (colloq) ‹building›

reveal vtr révéler ‹truth, plan›; dévoiler ‹plan›; **to ~ sth to sb** révéler qch à qn

revealing adj (a) ‹remark› révélateur/-trice (b) ‹blouse› décolleté/-e

r

revel *vi* to ~ in sth/in doing se délecter de qch/à faire

revelation *n* révélation *f*

revenge ① *n* vengeance *f*; to get one's ~ se venger (**for** de; **on** sur)
② *v refl* to ~ oneself se venger

revenue *n* revenus *mpl*

reverberate *vi* résonner (**with** de; **through** dans, par); (figurative) se propager

revere *vtr* révérer

reverence *n* profond respect *m*

Reverend *n* (a) (Protestant) pasteur *m*
(b) (as title) the ~ Jones le révérend Jones; ~ Mother Révérende Mère

reverent *adj* ⟨hush⟩ religieux/-ieuse; ⟨expression⟩ de respect

reverie *n* rêverie *f*

reversal *n* (of policy, roles) renversement *m*; (of order, trend) inversion *f*; (of fortune) revers *m*

reverse ① *n* (a) (opposite) the ~ le contraire
(b) (back) the ~ (of coin) le revers; (of banknote) le verso; (of fabric) l'envers *m*
(c) (Aut) (*also* ~ **gear**) marche *f* arrière
② *adj* (a) ⟨effect⟩ contraire; **in** ~ **order** ⟨answer questions⟩ en commençant par le dernier/la dernière; ⟨list⟩ en commençant par la fin
(b) (Aut) ~ **gear** marche *f* arrière
③ *vtr* inverser ⟨trend, process⟩; renverser ⟨roles⟩; faire rouler [qch] en marche arrière ⟨car⟩; **to** ~ **the charges** appeler en PCV
④ *vi* ⟨driver⟩ faire marche arrière
⑤ **in reverse** *phr* en sens inverse

reverse charge call *n* appel *m* en PCV

reversible *adj* réversible

revert *vi* to ~ to reprendre ⟨habit, name⟩; redevenir ⟨wilderness⟩

review ① *n* (a) (reconsideration) révision *f* (of de); (report) rapport *m* (of sur)
(b) (of book, film) critique *f* (of de)
(c) (magazine) revue *f*
(d) (Mil) revue *f*
(e) (US) (Sch, Univ) révision *f*
② *vtr* (a) reconsidérer ⟨situation⟩; réviser ⟨attitude, policy⟩; passer [qch] en revue ⟨troops⟩
(b) faire la critique de ⟨book, film⟩
(c) (US) (Sch, Univ) réviser

reviewer *n* critique *m*

revise ① *vtr* (a) (alter) réviser, modifier ⟨estimate, figures⟩; **to** ~ **one's opinion of sb/sth** réviser son jugement sur qn/qc
(b) (GB) (for exam) réviser ⟨subject⟩
(c) (correct) revoir, réviser ⟨text⟩
② *vi* (GB) ⟨student⟩ réviser

revision *n* révision *f*

revitalize *vtr* revitaliser

revival *n* (of economy) reprise *f*; (of interest) regain *m*; (of custom, language) renouveau *m*

revive ① *vtr* (a) ranimer ⟨person⟩
(b) raviver ⟨custom⟩; ranimer ⟨interest, hopes⟩; relancer ⟨movement, fashion⟩; revigorer ⟨economy⟩

② *vi* (a) ⟨person⟩ reprendre connaissance
(b) ⟨economy⟩ reprendre

revoke *vtr* révoquer ⟨will⟩; annuler ⟨decision⟩

revolt ① *n* révolte *f* (**against** contre)
② *vtr* dégoûter, révolter
③ *vi* se révolter (**against** contre)

revolting *adj* (a) (physically) répugnant/-e; (morally) révoltant/-e
(b) (colloq) ⟨food⟩ infect/-e; ⟨person⟩ affreux/-euse

revolution *n* (a) révolution *f* (**in** dans)
(b) (Aut, Tech) tour *m*

revolutionary *n, adj* révolutionnaire (*mf*)

revolutionize *vtr* révolutionner

revolve *vi* (a) (turn) tourner (**around** autour de)
(b) **to** ~ **around** (be focused on) être axé/-e sur

revolving *adj* ⟨chair⟩ pivotant/-e; ⟨stage⟩ tournant/-e; ~ **door** porte *f* à tambour

revue *n* revue *f*

revulsion *n* dégoût *m*

reward ① *n* récompense *f*; **a £50** ~ 50 livres sterling de récompense
② *vtr* récompenser (**for** de, pour)

rewarding *adj* ⟨experience⟩ enrichissant/-e; ⟨job⟩ gratifiant/-e

rewind *vtr* rembobiner ⟨tape, film⟩

rewind button *n* bouton *m* de retour en arrière

rewire *vtr* refaire l'installation électrique de ⟨building⟩

reword *vtr* reformuler

rework *vtr* retravailler ⟨theme, metal⟩

rewrite *vtr* ré(é)crire ⟨story, history⟩

rhapsody *n* rhapsodie *f*

rhetoric *n* rhétorique *f*

rhetorical *adj* rhétorique

rheumatism *n* rhumatisme *m*

Rhine *pr n* Rhin *m*

rhinoceros *n* rhinocéros *m*

rhubarb *n* rhubarbe *f*

rhyme ① *n* (a) (gen) rime *f*
(b) (poem) vers *mpl*; (children's) comptine *f*
② *vi* rimer (**with** avec)

rhythm *n* rythme *m*

rhythmic(al) *adj* rythmique

rib *n* (a) (Anat, Culin) côte *f*
(b) (in umbrella) baleine *f*; (in plane, building) nervure *f*

ribbon *n* ruban *m*

rib cage *n* cage *f* thoracique

rice *n* riz *m*

rich ① *n* the ~ les riches *mpl*
② *adj* riche; **to grow** *or* **get** ~ s'enrichir; **to make sb** ~ enrichir qn

riches *n pl* richesses *fpl*

richness *n* richesse *f*

rickety *adj* branlant/-e

rickshaw *n* pousse-pousse *m inv*

ricochet *vi* ricocher (**off** sur)

rid 1 *vtr* to ~ sb/sth of débarrasser qn/qch de
2 *pp adj* to get ~ of se débarrasser de ‹old car, guests›; éliminer ‹poverty›

riddance *n*
IDIOMS **good ~ (to bad rubbish)!** bon débarras! (colloq)

riddle 1 *n* (a) (puzzle) devinette *f*
(b) (mystery) énigme *f*
2 *vtr* to be ~d with être criblé/-e de ‹bullets›; être rongé/-e par ‹disease, guilt›

ride 1 *n* (a) (in vehicle, on bike) trajet *m* (in, on en, à); (for pleasure) tour *m*, promenade *f*; to go for a ~ aller faire un tour; to give sb a ~ (US) emmener qn (en voiture)
(b) (on horse) promenade *f* à cheval
2 *vtr* (a) rouler à ‹bike›; to ~ a horse monter à cheval; can you ~ a bike? sais-tu faire du vélo?
(b) (US) prendre ‹bus, subway›; parcourir ‹range›
(c) chevaucher ‹wave›
3 *vi* (go horse-riding) faire du cheval; to ~ in or on prendre ‹bus›
IDIOMS to take sb for a ~ (colloq) rouler qn (colloq)

■ **ride out** surmonter ‹crisis›; survivre à ‹recession›; to ~ out the storm surmonter la crise

■ **ride up** (a) ‹rider› s'approcher (to de)
(b) ‹skirt› remonter

rider *n* (a) (on horse) cavalier/-ière *m/f*; (on motorbike) motocycliste *mf*; (on bike) cycliste *mf*
(b) (to document) annexe *f*

ridge *n* (a) (along mountain top) arête *f*, crête *f*
(b) (on rock, metal surface) strie *f*; (in ploughed land) crête *f*
(c) (on roof) faîte *m*, faîtage *m*

ridicule 1 *n* ridicule *m*
2 *vtr* tourner [qn/qch] en ridicule

ridiculous *adj* ridicule

riding *n* équitation *f*; to go ~ faire de l'équitation

riding school *n* centre *m* équestre

rife *adj* to be ~ être répandu/-e

riffraff *n* populace *f*

rifle 1 *n* (firearm) fusil *m*
2 *vtr* vider ‹wallet, safe›
■ **rifle through** fouiller dans

rift *n* (a) (disagreement) désaccord *m*; (permanent) rupture *f*
(b) (in rock) fissure *f*; (in clouds) trouée *f*

rig 1 *n* (for oil) (on land) tour *f* de forage; (offshore) plate-forme *f* pétrolière offshore
2 *vtr* truquer ‹election, result›
■ **rig up** installer ‹equipment›; improviser ‹clothes line, shelter›

rigging *n* (a) (on ship) gréement *m*
(b) (of election, competition, result) truquage *m*

right 1 *n* (a) (side, direction) droite *f*; on or to your ~ à votre droite
(b) (in politics) (*also* **Right**) the ~ la droite
(c) (morally) bien *m*; ~ and wrong le bien et le mal

(d) (just claim) droit *m*; to have a ~ to sth avoir droit à qch; civil ~s droits civils
2 *adj* (a) (not left) droit/-e, de droite
(b) (morally) bien; (fair) juste; it is only ~ and proper ce n'est que justice; to do the ~ thing faire ce qu'il faut
(c) (correct) ‹choice, direction, size, answer› bon/bonne (*before n*); ‹word› juste; ‹time› exact/-e; to be ~ ‹person› avoir raison; ‹answer› être juste
(d) (suitable) qui convient; the ~ person for the job la personne qu'il faut pour le poste; to be in the ~ place at the ~ time être là où il faut au bon moment
(e) (in good order) the engine isn't quite ~ le moteur ne fonctionne pas très bien; I don't feel quite ~ these days je ne me sens pas très bien ces jours-ci
(f) to put *or* set ~ corriger ‹mistake›; réparer ‹injustice›; arranger ‹situation›; réparer ‹machine›
(g) ‹angle› droit/-e; at ~ angles to à angle droit avec, perpendiculaire à
3 *adv* (a) (not left) à droite; to turn/look ~ tourner/regarder à droite
(b) (directly) droit, directement; it's ~ in front of you c'est droit *or* juste devant toi; I'll be ~ back je reviens tout de suite
(c) (exactly) ~ in the middle of the room en plein milieu de la pièce; ~ now (immediately) tout de suite; (US) (at this point in time) en ce moment
(d) (correctly) juste, comme il faut; you're not doing it ~ tu ne fais pas ça comme il faut; to guess ~ deviner juste
(e) (completely) tout; go ~ back to the beginning revenez tout au début; ~ at the bottom tout au fond; to turn the central heating ~ up mettre le chauffage central à fond
(f) (very well) bon; ~, let's have a look bon, voyons ça
4 *vtr* redresser
IDIOMS **by ~s** normalement, en principe

right angle *n* angle *m* droit

right away *adv* tout de suite

righteous *adj* vertueux/-euse

rightful *adj* légitime

right-hand *adj* du côté droit; on the ~ side sur la droite

right-hand drive *n* conduite *f* à droite

right-handed *adv* ‹person› droitier/-ière; ‹blow› du droit

right-hand man *n* bras *m* droit

rightly *adv* (a) (accurately) correctement
(b) (justifiably) à juste titre; ~ or wrongly à tort ou à raison
(c) (with certainty) au juste; I don't ~ know je ne sais pas au juste

right-of-centre *adj* (Pol) centre-droite *inv*

right of way *n* (a) (Aut) priorité *f*
(b) (over land) droit *m* de passage; 'no ~' 'entrée *f* interdite'

r

right-on adj (colloq) they're very ~ (colloq) ils s'appliquent à être idéologiquement corrects sur tout

right-thinking adj bien-pensant/-e

right wing **1** n the ~ la droite

2 **right-wing** adj ⟨attitude⟩ de droite; they are very ~ ils sont très à droite

rigid adj ⟨rules, person, material⟩ rigide; ⟨controls, timetable⟩ strict/-e

rigidly adv ⟨oppose⟩ fermement; ⟨control⟩ rigoureusement; ⟨stick to, apply⟩ strictement

rigorous adj rigoureux/-euse

rigour (GB), **rigor** (US) n rigueur f

rim n bord m; (on wheel) jante f

rind n (a) (on cheese) croûte f; (on bacon) couenne f
(b) (on fruit) peau f

ring **1** n (a) anneau m; (with stone) bague f; a diamond ~ une bague de diamants; a wedding ~ une alliance
(b) (circle) cercle m; to have ~s under one's eyes avoir les yeux cernés
(c) (at door) coup m de sonnette; (of phone) sonnerie f
(d) (in circus) piste f; (in boxing) ring m
(e) (of smugglers, spies) réseau m
(f) (on cooker) (electric) plaque f; (gas) brûleur m
2 vtr (a) sonner ⟨church bells⟩; to ~ the doorbell or bell sonner
(b) (GB) (also ~ up) appeler
3 vi (a) ⟨bell, phone, person⟩ sonner; the doorbell rang on a sonné à la porte
(b) ⟨footsteps, laughter⟩ résonner; to ~ true sonner vrai
(c) (GB) (phone) téléphoner; to ~ for appeler ⟨taxi⟩

■ **ring off** (GB) raccrocher

■ **ring out** ⟨voice, cry⟩ retentir; ⟨bells⟩ sonner

ring binder n classeur m à anneaux

ringing n (a) (of bell, alarm) sonnerie f
(b) (in ears) bourdonnement m

ringleader n meneur/-euse m/f

ringlet n anglaise f

ringroad n (GB) périphérique m

rinse **1** n rinçage m
2 vtr rincer; (wash) laver

riot **1** n (a) émeute f, révolte f; prison ~ mutinerie f
(b) a ~ of une profusion de ⟨colours⟩
2 vi ⟨crowd, demonstrators⟩ se soulever; ⟨prisoners⟩ se mutiner
IDIOMS to run ~ ⟨crowd⟩ se déchaîner; ⟨imagination⟩ se débrider; ⟨plant⟩ proliférer

rioter n émeutier/-ière m/f; (in prison) mutin m

riot gear n tenue f antiémeutes

rioting n émeutes fpl, bagarres fpl

riot police n forces fpl antiémeutes

rip **1** vtr déchirer; to ~ sth out arracher qch
2 vi ⟨fabric⟩ se déchirer

■ **rip off**: ¶ ~ off [sth], ~ [sth] off (a) arracher ⟨garment, roof⟩

(b) (colloq) (steal) rafler (colloq) ⟨idea, design⟩
¶ ~ [sb] off (colloq) arnaquer (slang)

■ **rip through**: ~ through [sth] ⟨bomb blast⟩ défoncer ⟨building⟩

RIP abbr qu'il/elle repose en paix

ripe adj ⟨fruit⟩ mûr/-e; ⟨cheese⟩ fait/-e

ripen **1** vtr mûrir ⟨fruit⟩; affiner ⟨cheese⟩
2 vi ⟨fruit⟩ mûrir; ⟨cheese⟩ se faire

rip-off n (colloq) arnaque f (slang)

ripple **1** n ondulation f
2 vi (a) ⟨water⟩ se rider; (making noise) clapoter
(b) ⟨hair, corn⟩ onduler; ⟨muscles⟩ saillir

rise **1** n (a) (increase) augmentation f (in de); (in prices, pressure) hausse f (in de); (in temperature) élévation f (in de)
(b) (of person) ascension f; (of empire) essor m
(c) (slope) montée f
2 vi (a) ⟨water, tension⟩ monter; ⟨price, temperature⟩ augmenter; ⟨voice⟩ devenir plus fort/-e; ⟨hopes⟩ grandir
(b) (get up) ⟨person⟩ se lever; (after falling) se relever; to ~ from the dead ressusciter; to ~ to the occasion se montrer à la hauteur
(c) ⟨road⟩ monter; ⟨cliff⟩ s'élever
(d) ⟨sun, moon⟩ se lever
(e) ⟨dough⟩ lever
IDIOMS to give ~ to donner lieu à ⟨rumours⟩; causer ⟨problem⟩

rising **1** n soulèvement m
2 adj (gen) en hausse; ⟨tension⟩ grandissant/-e; ⟨sun, moon⟩ levant/-e

risk **1** n risque m; to run a ~ courir un risque; to take ~s prendre des risques; at ~ menacé/-e
2 vtr risquer; to ~ doing courir le risque de faire

risky adj ⟨decision, undertaking⟩ risqué/-e; ⟨share, investment⟩ à risques

risqué adj osé/-e

rite n rite m

ritual **1** n rituel m, rites mpl
2 adj rituel/-elle

rival **1** n (person) rival/-e m/f; (company) concurrent/-e m/f
2 adj ⟨team, business⟩ rival/-e; ⟨claim⟩ opposé/-e
3 vtr rivaliser avec (in de)

rivalry n rivalité f (between entre)

river n (flowing into sea) fleuve m; (tributary) rivière f

riverbank n berge f; along the ~ le long de la rivière

riverside **1** n berges fpl
2 adj ⟨pub⟩ au bord de la rivière

rivet **1** n rivet m
2 vtr (a) (Tech) riveter
(b) to be ~ed by être captivé/-e par; to be ~ed to the spot être cloué/-e sur place

riveting adj fascinant/-e

Riviera n the Italian ~ la Riviera; the French ~ la Côte d'Azur

road n (a) route f; the ~ to Leeds la route de Leeds

(b) (street) rue f
(c) (figurative) voie f (to de); **to be on the right ∼** être sur la bonne voie
roadblock n barrage m routier
road hump n ralentisseur m
road rage n violence f au volant
roadshow n (play, show) spectacle m de tournée; (publicity tour) tour m promotionnel
roadside n bord m de la route
roadsign n panneau m de signalisation
road tax disc n vignette f
roadworks n pl travaux mpl (routiers)
roadworthy adj en état de rouler
roam vtr parcourir ⟨countryside⟩; faire le tour de ⟨shops⟩; traîner dans ⟨streets⟩
■ **roam around** ⟨person⟩ vadrouiller (colloq)
roar ⟨1⟩ n (of lion) rugissement m; (of person) hurlement m; (of engine) vrombissement m; (of traffic) grondement m; **a ∼ of laughter** un éclat de rire
⟨2⟩ vi ⟨lion⟩ rugir; ⟨person⟩ hurler; ⟨sea, wind⟩ mugir; ⟨fire⟩ ronfler; ⟨engine⟩ vrombir
roaring adj **(a)** ⟨engine, traffic⟩ grondant/-e; **a ∼ fire** une belle flambée
(b) ⟨success⟩ fou/folle
roast ⟨1⟩ n (Culin) rôti m; (US) barbecue m
⟨2⟩ adj ⟨meat, potatoes⟩ rôti/-e; **∼ beef** rôti m de bœuf, rosbif m
⟨3⟩ vtr rôtir ⟨meat, potatoes⟩; (faire) griller ⟨chestnuts⟩; torréfier ⟨coffee beans⟩
rob vtr voler ⟨person⟩; dévaliser ⟨bank, train⟩; **to ∼ sb of sth** voler qch à qn; (figurative) priver qn de qch
robber n voleur/-euse m/f
robbery n vol m
robe n robe f
robin n (also **∼ redbreast**) rouge-gorge m
robot n robot m
robust adj robuste
rock ⟨1⟩ n **(a)** (substance) roche f; **solid ∼** roche dure
(b) (boulder) rocher m
(c) (also **∼ music**) rock m
⟨2⟩ vtr **(a)** balancer ⟨cradle⟩; bercer ⟨baby, boat⟩
(b) ⟨tremor⟩ secouer ⟨town⟩; ⟨scandal⟩ ébranler ⟨government⟩
⟨3⟩ vi ⟨person⟩ se balancer; **to ∼ back and forth** se balancer d'avant en arrière
IDIOMS on the **∼s** ⟨drink⟩ avec des glaçons; **to be on the ∼s** ⟨marriage⟩ aller à vau-l'eau
rock and roll n (also **rock'n'roll**) rock and roll m
rock bottom n to hit **∼** toucher le fond
rock climber n varappeur/-euse m/f
rock climbing n varappe f
rockery n (GB) rocaille f
rocket ⟨1⟩ n **(a)** (gen, Mil) fusée f
(b) (salad) roquette f
⟨2⟩ vi ⟨price, profit⟩ monter en flèche
rock face n paroi f rocheuse
rockfall n chute f de pierres

rocking chair n fauteuil m à bascule
rocking horse n cheval m à bascule
rock star n rock-star f
rocky adj **(a)** ⟨beach, path, road⟩ rocailleux/-euse; ⟨coast⟩ rocheux/-euse
(b) ⟨relationship, period⟩ difficile; ⟨business⟩ précaire
Rocky Mountains pr n pl (also **Rockies**) the **∼** les montagnes fpl Rocheuses
rod n **(a)** (gen, Tech) tige f; **curtain/stair ∼** tringle f à rideaux/de marche
(b) (for punishment) baguette f
(c) (for fishing) canne f à pêche
rodent n rongeur m
roe n œufs mpl (de poisson)
roe deer n (male) chevreuil m; (female) chevrette f
rogue n **(a)** (rascal) coquin m
(b) (animal) solitaire m
role n rôle m (of de); **title ∼** rôle-titre m
role model n modèle m
role-play n (Sch) jeu m de rôle; (for therapy) psychodrame m
roll ⟨1⟩ n **(a)** (of paper, cloth) rouleau m; (of banknotes) liasse f; (of flesh) bourrelet m; **a ∼ of film** une pellicule
(b) (bread) petit pain m; **cheese ∼** sandwich m au fromage
(c) (of dice) lancer m
(d) (register) liste f; **to call the ∼** faire l'appel
⟨2⟩ vtr **(a)** (gen) rouler; faire rouler ⟨dice⟩; **to ∼ sth into a ball** faire une boulette de ⟨paper⟩; faire une boule de ⟨clay, dough⟩
(b) étirer ⟨dough⟩
⟨3⟩ vi **(a)** ⟨person, animal⟩ rouler (onto sur); ⟨car, plane⟩ faire un tonneau; ⟨ship⟩ tanguer
(b) ⟨thunder⟩ gronder; ⟨drum⟩ rouler
(c) ⟨camera, press⟩ tourner
■ **roll about** (GB), **roll around** ⟨animal, person⟩ se rouler; ⟨marbles, tins⟩ rouler
■ **roll down** baisser ⟨blind, sleeve⟩
■ **roll over** se retourner
■ **roll up** enrouler ⟨rug, poster⟩; **to ∼ up one's sleeves** retrousser ses manches
roller n **(a)** (gen) rouleau m
(b) (curler) bigoudi m
rollerblade ⟨1⟩ n patin m en ligne
⟨2⟩ vi faire du patin en ligne
roller blind n store m
roller coaster n montagnes fpl russes
roller-skate n patin m à roulettes
roller-skating n patinage m à roulettes; **to go ∼** faire du patin à roulettes
rolling pin n rouleau m à pâtisserie
rollneck n col m roulé
ROM n (abbr = **read-only memory**) ROM f, mémoire f morte
Roman ⟨1⟩ n Romain/-e m/f
⟨2⟩ adj romain/-e
Roman Catholic n, adj catholique (mf)
romance n **(a)** (of era, place) charme m; (of travel) côté m romantique ⋯⋗

r

(b) (love affair) histoire *f* d'amour; (love) amour *m*

(c) (novel) roman *m* d'amour; (film) film *m* d'amour

Romania *pr n* Roumanie *f*

Romanian **1** *n* **(a)** (person) Roumain/-e *m/f*

(b) (language) roumain *m*

2 *adj* roumain/-e

romantic **1** *n* romantique *mf*

2 *adj* **(a)** (setting, story, person) romantique

(b) (attachment) sentimental/-e

(c) (novel, film) d'amour

romantic fiction *n* (genre) romans *mpl* d'amour

romanticize *vtr* idéaliser

Romany *n* Tzigane *mf*, Romani *mf*

romp **1** *n* ébats *mpl*

2 *vi* s'ébattre

rompers *n pl* (also **romper suit**) barboteuse *f*

roof *n* **(a)** (on building) toit *m*

(b) (Anat) the ~ of the mouth la voûte du palais

IDIOMS **to go through** *or* **hit the ~** (colloq) (person) sauter au plafond (colloq); (prices) battre tous les records

roof rack *n* galerie *f*

rooftop *n* toit *m*

rook *n* **(a)** (bird) (corbeau *m*) freux *m*

(b) (in chess) tour *f*

room **1** *n* **(a)** pièce *f*; (bedroom) chambre *f*; (for working) bureau *m*; (for meetings, teaching, operating) salle *f*

(b) (space) place *f*; **to make ~** faire de la place

2 *vi* (US) loger (**with** chez)

roommate *n* **(a)** (in same room) camarade *mf* de chambre

(b) (US) (flatmate) compagnon/compagne *m/f* d'appartement

room service *n* service *m* de chambre

room temperature *n* température *f* ambiante; **at ~** (wine) chambré/-e

roomy *adj* (car, house) spacieux/-ieuse; (garment) ample; (bag, cupboard) grand/-e (before n)

roost **1** *n* perchoir *m*

2 *vi* (in trees) percher (pour la nuit); (in attic) se nicher

IDIOMS **to rule the ~** faire la loi

rooster *n* coq *m*

root **1** *n* **(a)** racine *f*; **to take ~** (plant) prendre racine; (idea, value) s'établir; (industry) s'implanter

(b) (of problem) fond *m*; (of evil) origine *f*

2 *vtr* **to be ~ed in** être ancré/-e dans; **deeply-~ed** bien enraciné/-e; **~ed to the spot** figé/-e sur place

■ **root around, root about** fouiller (in dans)

■ **root out** traquer (corruption); déloger (person)

rootless *adj* sans racines

rope **1** *n* (gen, Sport) corde *f*; (of pearls) rang *m*

2 *vtr* attacher (victim, animal) (**to** à); encorder (climber)

IDIOMS **to know the ~s** connaître les ficelles (colloq)

■ **rope in** (colloq) : ~ **[sb] in**, ~ **in [sb]** (to help with task) embaucher (colloq)

rope ladder *n* échelle *f* de corde

rosary *n* (prayer) rosaire *m*; (beads) chapelet *m*

rose *n* rose *f*

rosebud *n* bouton *m* de rose

rose bush *n* rosier *m*

rosemary *n* romarin *m*

rose-tinted *adj*

IDIOMS **to see the world through ~ spectacles** voir la vie en rose

rosette *n* (for winner) cocarde *f*

roster *n* (also **duty ~**) tableau *m* de service

rostrum *n* estrade *f*

rosy *adj* (cheek, light) rose; **to paint a ~ picture** peindre un tableau favorable

rot **1** *n* pourriture *f*

2 *vtr* pourrir

3 *vi* (also ~ **away**) pourrir

rota *n* (GB) tableau *m* de service

rotary *adj* rotatif/-ive

rotate **1** *vtr* faire tourner (blade)

2 *vi* (blade, handle, wings) tourner

rotation *n* rotation *f*

rote *n* **by ~** par cœur

rotten *adj* **(a)** (produce) pourri/-e; (teeth) gâté/-e; (smell) de pourriture

(b) (corrupt) pourri/-e (colloq)

(c) (colloq) (bad) (weather) pourri/-e; (cook, driver) exécrable

rouble *n* rouble *m*

rough **1** *adj* **(a)** (material) rêche; (hand, skin, surface, rock) rugueux/-euse; (terrain) cahoteux/-euse

(b) (person, behaviour, sport) brutal/-e, violent/-e; (landing) brutal/-e; (area) dur/-e

(c) (description, map) sommaire; (figure, idea, estimate) approximatif/-ive

(d) (difficult) dur, difficile; **a ~ time** une période difficile

(e) (crude) grossier/-ière

(f) (harsh) (voice, taste, wine) âpre

(g) (stormy) (sea, crossing) agité/-e

2 *adv* **to sleep ~** dormir à la dure

IDIOMS **to ~ it** vivre à la dure

roughage *n* fibres *fpl*

rough-and-ready *adj* (person, manner) fruste; (conditions) rudimentaire; (method, system) sommaire

roughen *vtr* rendre [qch] rêche *or* rugueux

roughly *adv* **(a)** (calculate) grossièrement; ~ **speaking** en gros; ~ **10%** à peu près 10%

(b) (treat, hit) brutalement

(c) (make) grossièrement

rough paper *n* feuille *f* de brouillon

roulette n roulette f

round 1 adv (GB) **(a)** all ~ tout autour;
whisky all ~! du whisky pour tout le
monde!; **to go all the way** ~ faire tout le
tour; **to go** ~ **and** ~ tourner en rond
(b) (to place, home) **to go** ~ **to sb's house**
passer chez qn; **to ask sb** ~ dire à qn de
passer à la maison; **to invite sb** ~ **for lunch**
inviter qn à déjeuner (chez soi)
(c) all year ~ toute l'année; **this time** ~
cette fois-ci
2 prep (GB) **(a)** autour de ⟨table⟩; **to sit** ~
the fire s'asseoir au coin du feu
(b) to go ~ **the corner** tourner au coin de la
rue; **just** ~ **the corner** tout près; **to go** ~ **an
obstacle** contourner un obstacle
(c) her sister took us ~ Oxford sa sœur
nous a fait visiter Oxford; **to go** ~ **the
shops** faire les magasins
3 n **(a)** (of competition) manche f; (of golf,
cards) partie f; (in boxing) round m; (in
showjumping) parcours m; (in election) tour m;
(of talks) série f; **a** ~ **of drinks** une tournée; **a**
~ **of ammunition** une cartouche; **a** ~ **of
applause** une salve d'applaudissements; **a** ~
of toast un toast
(b) to do one's ~**s** ⟨postman, milkman⟩
faire sa tournée; ⟨doctor⟩ visiter ses
malades; ⟨guard⟩ faire sa ronde; **to go** or **do
the** ~**s** ⟨rumour, flu⟩ circuler
(c) (shape) rondelle f
4 adj **(a)** rond/-e; **in** ~ **figures, that's £100**
si on arrondit, ça fait 100 livres sterling; **a**
~ **dozen** une douzaine exactement
(b) to have ~ **shoulders** avoir le dos voûté;
5 vtr contourner ⟨headland⟩; **to** ~ **the
corner** tourner au coin; **to** ~ **a bend** prendre
un virage
6 **round about** phr **(a)** (approximately) à
peu près, environ
(b) (vicinity) **the people** ~ **about** les gens des
environs

■ **round off (a)** finir ⟨meal, evening⟩ **(with**
par); conclure ⟨speech⟩
(b) arrondir ⟨corner, figure⟩

■ **round on** (GB): ~ **on** [sb] attaquer
violemment; **she** ~**ed on me** elle m'est
tombée dessus (colloq)

■ **round up (a)** regrouper ⟨people⟩;
rassembler ⟨livestock⟩
(b) arrondir [qch] au chiffre supérieur
⟨figure⟩

roundabout 1 n (GB) (in fairground)
manège m; (in playground) tourniquet m; (for
traffic) rond-point m
2 adj **to come by a** ~ **way** faire un détour;
by ~ **means** par des moyens détournés; **a** ~
way of saying une façon détournée de dire

rounders n (GB) ≈ baseball m

round-neck(ed) sweater n pull-over
m ras-de-cou inv

round-the-clock adj 24 heures sur 24

round-the-world adj autour du monde

round trip n aller-retour m

roundup n **(a)** (herding) rassemblement m
(of de)

(b) (by police) rafle f

rouse vtr réveiller ⟨person⟩; susciter
⟨anger, interest⟩

rousing adj ⟨speech⟩ galvanisant/-e;
⟨music⟩ exaltant/-e

rout 1 n déroute f, défaite f
2 vtr (Mil) mettre en déroute; (figurative)
battre à plates coutures

route 1 n chemin m, itinéraire m; (in
shipping) route f; (in aviation) ligne f; (figurative)
(to power) voie f (**to** de); **bus** ~ ligne
d'autobus
2 vtr expédier, acheminer ⟨goods⟩

routine 1 n **(a)** routine f
(b) (act) numéro m
2 adj **(a)** ⟨enquiry, matter⟩ de routine
(b) (uninspiring) routinier/-ière

routinely adv **(a)** ⟨check, review⟩
systématiquement
(b) ⟨tortured, abused⟩ régulièrement

row¹ 1 n **(a)** (of people, plants, stitches) rang
m (of de); (of houses, seats, books) rangée f (of
de)
(b) (succession) **six times in a** ~ six fois de
suite; **the third week in a** ~ la troisième
semaine d'affilée
2 vtr **to** ~ **a boat up the river** remonter la
rivière à la rame
3 vi (gen) ramer; (Sport) faire de l'aviron; **to**
~ **across** traverser [qch] à la rame ⟨lake⟩

row² 1 n **(a)** (quarrel) dispute f (**about** à
propos de); (public) querelle f; **to have a** ~
with se disputer avec
(b) (noise) tapage m
2 vi se disputer (**with** avec; **about, over** à
propos de)

rowboat n (US) bateau m à rames

rowdy adj (noisy) tapageur/-euse; (in class)
chahuteur/-euse

rowing n aviron m

rowing boat n (GB) bateau m à rames

royal adj royal/-e

royal blue n, adj bleu (m) roi inv

Royal Highness n His ~ Son Altesse f
royale; Your ~ Votre Altesse f

royalty n **(a)** (persons) membres mpl d'une
famille royale
(b) (to author, musician) droits mpl d'auteur;
(on patent) royalties fpl

rub 1 n **(a)** (massage) friction f
(b) (polish) coup m de chiffon
2 vtr se frotter ⟨chin, eyes⟩; frotter ⟨stain,
surface⟩; frictionner ⟨sb's back⟩; **to** ~ **sth
into the skin** faire pénétrer qch dans la peau
3 vi frotter
IDIOMS **to** ~ **sb up the wrong way** prendre
qn à rebrousse-poil (colloq)

■ **rub out** (erase) effacer

■ **rub in**: ~ [sth] **in**, ~ **in** [sth] faire pénétrer
⟨lotion⟩; **there's no need to** ~ **it in!** (colloq)
inutile d'en rajouter! (colloq)

rubber 1 n **(a)** (substance) caoutchouc m
(b) (GB) (eraser) gomme f
2 adj de or en caoutchouc

r

rubber band n élastique m

rubber glove n gant m en or de caoutchouc

rubber plant n caoutchouc m

rubber stamp n tampon m

rubber tree n hévéa m

rubbish ① n (a) (refuse) déchets mpl; (domestic) ordures fpl; (on site) gravats mpl
(b) (inferior goods) camelote f (colloq); **this book is ~!** (colloq) ce livre est nul! (colloq)
(c) (nonsense) bêtises fpl
② vtr (GB) descendre [qn/qch] en flammes

rubbish bin n (GB) poubelle f

rubbish dump n (GB) décharge f (publique)

rubbish heap n tas m d'ordures

rubble n (after explosion) décombres mpl; (on site) gravats mpl

ruby ① n (a) (gem) rubis m
(b) (also ~ **red**) rouge m rubis
② adj (a) ⟨liquid, lips⟩ vermeil/-eille; ~ **wedding** noces fpl de vermeil
(b) ⟨bracelet, necklace⟩ de rubis

rucksack n sac m à dos

rudder n (on boat) gouvernail m; (on plane) gouverne f

ruddy adj ⟨cheeks⟩ coloré/-e

rude adj (a) (impolite) ⟨comment⟩ impoli/-e; ⟨person⟩ mal élevé/-e; **to be ~ to sb** être impoli/-e envers qn
(b) (indecent) ⟨joke⟩ grossier/-ière; **a ~ word** un gros mot

rudimentary adj rudimentaire

rudiments n pl rudiments mpl (**of** de)

rueful adj ⟨smile, thought⟩ triste

ruff n (of lace) fraise f; (of fur, feathers) collier m

ruffle ① n (at sleeve) manchette f; (at neck) ruche f; (on shirt front) jabot m
② vtr (a) ébouriffer ⟨hair, fur⟩; hérisser ⟨feathers⟩; rider ⟨water⟩
(b) (disconcert) énerver; (upset) froisser

rug n (a) tapis m; (by bed) descente f de lit
(b) (GB) (blanket) couverture f

rugby n rugby m

rugby league n rugby m à 13

rugby union n rugby m à 15

rugged adj (a) ⟨landscape⟩ accidenté/-e; ⟨coastline⟩ déchiqueté/-e
(b) ⟨man, features⟩ rude

ruin ① n ruine f
② vtr (a) ruiner ⟨economy, career⟩; **to ~ one's eyesight** s'abîmer la vue
(b) gâcher ⟨holiday, meal⟩; abîmer ⟨clothes⟩
IDIOMS **to go to rack and ~** se délabrer

ruined adj (a) (derelict) en ruines
(b) (spoilt) ⟨holiday, meal⟩ gâché/-e; ⟨clothes, furniture⟩ abîmé/-e; ⟨reputation⟩ ruiné/-e; (financially) ruiné/-e

rule ① n (a) (of game, language) règle f; (of school, organization) règlement m; **against the**

~**s** contraire aux règles or au règlement (**to do de** faire); ~**s and regulations** réglementation f; **as a ~** généralement
(b) (authority) domination f, gouvernement m
(c) (for measuring) règle f
② vtr (a) ⟨ruler, law⟩ gouverner; ⟨monarch⟩ régner sur; ⟨party⟩ diriger; ⟨army⟩ commander
(b) ⟨factor⟩ dicter ⟨strategy⟩; **to be ~d by** ⟨person⟩ être mené/-e par ⟨passions, spouse⟩
(c) (draw) faire, tirer ⟨line⟩
(d) ⟨court, umpire⟩ **to ~ that** décréter que
③ vi (a) ⟨monarch, anarchy⟩ régner
(b) ⟨court, umpire⟩ statuer
■ **rule out** (a) exclure ⟨possibility, candidate⟩ (**of** de); **to ~ out doing** exclure de faire
(b) interdire ⟨activity⟩

ruler n (a) (leader) dirigeant/-e m/f
(b) (measure) règle f

ruling ① n décision f
② adj (a) (in power) dirigeant/-e
(b) (dominant) dominant/-e

rum n rhum m

rumble ① n (of thunder, artillery, trucks) grondement m; (of stomach) gargouillement m
② vi ⟨thunder, artillery⟩ gronder; ⟨stomach⟩ gargouiller

ruminate vi (a) (think) **to ~ on** or **about** ruminer sur
(b) (Zool) ruminer

rummage vi fouiller (**through** dans)

rummy n rami m

rumour (GB), **rumor** (US) n rumeur f, bruit m

rumoured (GB), **rumored** (US) adj **it is ~ that** il paraît que, on dit que

rump n (a) (also ~ **steak**) rumsteck m
(b) (of animal) croupe f

rumple vtr ébouriffer ⟨hair⟩; froisser ⟨clothes, sheets, papers⟩

run ① n (a) course f; **a two-mile ~** une course de deux miles; **to go for a ~** aller courir; **to break into a ~** se mettre à courir
(b) (flight) **on the ~** en fuite; **to make a ~ for it** fuir, s'enfuir
(c) (series) (of successes, failures) série f; (in printing) tirage m; **to have a ~ of luck** être en veine
(d) (trip, route) trajet m
(e) (in cricket, baseball) point m
(f) (for rabbit, chickens) enclos m
(g) (in tights) échelle f
(h) (for skiing) piste f
(i) (in cards) suite f
② vtr (a) courir ⟨distance, marathon⟩; **to ~ a race** faire une course
(b) (drive) **to ~ sb to the station** conduire qn à la gare
(c) (pass, move) **to ~ one's hand over** passer la main sur; **to ~ one's eye(s) over** parcourir rapidement
(d) (manage) diriger; **a well-/badly-run organization** une organisation bien/mal dirigée
(e) (operate) faire fonctionner ⟨machine⟩; faire

tourner ⟨*motor*⟩; exécuter ⟨*program*⟩; entretenir ⟨*car*⟩; **to ~ tests on** effectuer des tests sur
(f) (organize, offer) organiser ⟨*competition, course*⟩; mettre [qch] en place ⟨*bus service*⟩
(g) faire couler ⟨*bath*⟩; ouvrir ⟨*tap*⟩
(h) (enter) faire courir ⟨*horse*⟩; présenter ⟨*candidate*⟩
3 *vi* **(a)** (of person, animal) courir; **to ~ across/down sth** traverser/descendre qch en courant; **to ~ for the bus** courir pour attraper le bus; **to come ~ning** accourir **(towards** vers)
(b) (flee) fuir, s'enfuir; **to ~ for one's life** s'enfuir pour sauver sa peau (colloq)
(c) (colloq) (rush off) filer (colloq)
(d) (function) ⟨*machine*⟩ marcher; **to leave the engine ~ning** laisser tourner le moteur
(e) (continue, last) ⟨*contract, lease*⟩ être valide
(f) ⟨*play, musical*⟩ tenir l'affiche **(for** pendant)
(g) (pass) **to ~ past/through** ⟨*road, frontier, path*⟩ passer/traverser; **to ~ (from) east to west** aller d'est en ouest
(h) (move) ⟨*sledge*⟩ glisser; ⟨*curtain*⟩ coulisser
(i) ⟨*bus, train*⟩ circuler
(j) (flow) couler; **tears ran down his face** les larmes coulaient sur son visage; **my nose is ~ning** j'ai le nez qui coule
(k) ⟨*dye, garment*⟩ déteindre; ⟨*make-up*⟩ couler
(l) (as candidate) se présenter; **to ~ for president** être candidat/-e à la présidence
IDIOMS in the long ~ à long terme; **in the short ~** à brève échéance
■ **run about**, **run around** courir
■ **run away:** ¶ **~ away** s'enfuir; **to ~ away from home** ⟨*child*⟩ faire une fugue
¶ **~ away with [sb/sth] (a)** (flee) partir avec
(b) rafler (colloq) ⟨*prize, title*⟩
■ **run down:** ¶ **~ down** ⟨*battery*⟩ se décharger; ⟨*watch*⟩ retarder
¶ **~ [sb/sth] down (a)** (in vehicle) renverser
(b) réduire ⟨*production, defences*⟩; user ⟨*battery*⟩
(c) (disparage) dénigrer
■ **run into (a)** heurter, rentrer dans (colloq) ⟨*car, wall*⟩
(b) (encounter) rencontrer ⟨*person, difficulty*⟩
(c) (amount to) s'élever à ⟨*hundreds, millions*⟩
■ **run off** partir en courant
■ **run out:** ¶ **~ out (a)** ⟨*supplies, oil*⟩ s'épuiser; **time is ~ning out** le temps manque
(b) ⟨*pen, machine*⟩ être vide
(c) ⟨*contract, passport*⟩ expirer
¶ **~ out of** ne plus avoir de ⟨*petrol, time, money, ideas*⟩; **to be ~ning out of** n'avoir presque plus de ⟨*petrol, time, money, ideas*⟩
■ **run over** (in vehicle) (injure) renverser; (kill) écraser
■ **run through** parcourir ⟨*list, article*⟩; répéter ⟨*scene, speech*⟩
■ **run up** accumuler ⟨*debt*⟩
■ **run up against** se heurter à ⟨*difficulty*⟩

runaway *adj* ⟨*teenager*⟩ fugueur/-euse; ⟨*slave*⟩ fugitif/-ive; ⟨*horse*⟩ emballé/-e
rundown *n* récapitulatif *m* **(on** de)
run-down *adj* **(a)** (exhausted) fatigué/-e, à plat (colloq)
(b) (shabby) décrépit/-e
rung *n* **(a)** (of ladder) barreau *m*
(b) (in hierarchy) échelon *m*
run-in *n* (colloq) prise *f* de bec (colloq)
runner *n* **(a)** (person, animal) coureur *m*
(b) (horse) partant/-e *m/f*
(c) (messenger) estafette *f*
(d) (for door, seat) glissière *f*; (for drawer) coulisseau *m*; (on sled) patin *m*
(e) (on stairs) chemin *m* d'escalier
runner bean *n* (GB) haricot *m* d'Espagne
runner up *n* second/-e *m/f* **(to** après)
running **1** *n* **(a)** (sport, exercise) course *f* à pied
(b) (management) direction *f* **(of** de)
2 *adj* **(a)** ⟨*water*⟩ courant/-e; ⟨*tap*⟩ ouvert/-e
(b) **five days ~** cinq jours de suite
IDIOMS to be in/out of the ~ être/ne plus être dans la course **(for** pour)
running battle *n* éternel conflit *m*
running commentary *n* commentaire *m* ininterrompu
running total *n* total *m* cumulé
runny *adj* ⟨*jam, sauce*⟩ liquide; ⟨*butter*⟩ fondu/-e; ⟨*omelette*⟩ baveux/-euse; **to have a ~ nose** avoir le nez qui coule
run-of-the-mill *adj* ordinaire, banal/-e
runt *n* **(a)** (of litter) le plus faible *m* de la portée
(b) (weakling) avorton *m*
run-up *n* **(a)** (for a jump) course *f* d'élan; **to take a ~** prendre son élan pour sauter
(b) (preceding period) **the ~ to** la dernière ligne droite avant
runway *n* piste *f* d'aviation
rupee *n* roupie *f*
rupture *n* rupture *f*
rural *adj* (country) rural/-e; (pastoral) champêtre
ruse *n* stratagème *m*
rush **1** *n* **(a)** (surge) ruée *f* **(to do** pour faire); **to make a ~ for sth** ⟨*crowd*⟩ se ruer vers qch; ⟨*individual*⟩ se précipiter vers qch
(b) (hurry) **to be in a ~** être pressé/-e **(to do** de faire); **to leave in a ~** partir en vitesse
(c) (of liquid, adrenalin) montée *f*; (of air) bouffée *f*
(d) (plant) jonc *m*
2 *vtr* **(a)** **to ~ sth to** envoyer qch d'urgence à; **to be ~ed to the hospital** être emmené/-e d'urgence à l'hôpital
(b) expédier ⟨*task, speech*⟩
(c) (hurry) bousculer ⟨*person*⟩
(d) (charge at) sauter sur ⟨*person*⟩; prendre d'assaut ⟨*building*⟩
3 *vi* ⟨*person*⟩ (hurry) se dépêcher **(to do de** faire); (rush forward) se précipiter **(to do** pour ···⟶

r

faire); to ~ out of the room se précipiter hors de la pièce; to ~ down the stairs/past descendre l'escalier/passer à toute vitesse
■ **rush into**: ¶ to ~ into marriage/a purchase se marier/acheter sans prendre le temps de réfléchir; ¶ ~ [sb] into doing bousculer [qn] pour qu'il/elle fasse
■ **rush out**: ¶ ~ out sortir en vitesse
■ **rush through**: ¶ ~ through [sth] expédier ⟨task⟩; ¶ ~ [sth] through adopter en vitesse ⟨legislation⟩; traiter en priorité ⟨order, application⟩

rushed adj ⟨attempt, letter⟩ expédié/-e

rush hour n heures fpl de pointe

rusk n biscuit m pour bébés

russet adj roussâtre

Russia pr n Russie f

Russian ① n (a) (person) Russe mf (b) (language) russe m ② adj ⟨culture, food, politics⟩ russe; ⟨teacher, lesson⟩ de russe; ⟨embassy⟩ de Russie

rust ① n rouille f ② vtr rouiller ⟨metal⟩ ③ vi ⟨metal⟩ se rouiller

rustic adj rustique

rustle ① n (of paper, dry leaves) froissement m; (of leaves, silk) bruissement m ② vtr froisser ⟨papers⟩

rusty adj rouillé/-e

rut n (a) (in ground) ornière f (b) (routine) be in a ~ être enlisé/-e dans la routine (c) (Zool) the ~ le rut

ruthless adj impitoyable (in dans)

RV n (US) (abbr = **recreational vehicle**) camping-car m, autocaravane f

Rwanda pr n Rwanda m

rye n (a) (cereal) seigle m (b) (US) (also ~ **whiskey**) whisky m à base de seigle

rye bread n pain m de seigle

Ss

s, S n s, S m

sabbath n (also **Sabbath**) (Jewish) sabbat m; (Christian) jour m du seigneur

sabbatical n congé m sabbatique

sabotage ① n sabotage m ② vtr saboter

saboteur n saboteur/-euse m/f

sabre, saber (US) n sabre m

sachet n sachet m

sack ① n (a) sac m (b) to get the ~ (colloq) se faire mettre à la porte (colloq) ② vtr (a) (colloq) mettre [qn] à la porte (colloq) ⟨employee⟩ (b) mettre [qch] à sac ⟨town⟩

sacrament n sacrement m

sacred adj sacré/-e (to pour)

sacrifice ① n sacrifice m (to à; of de) ② vtr (a) (gen) sacrifier (to à) (b) (to the gods) offrir [qch] en sacrifice (to à) ③ v refl to ~ oneself se sacrifier (for pour)

sacrilege n sacrilège m

sacrosanct adj sacro-saint/-e

sad adj triste (that que + subjunctive); it makes me ~ cela me rend triste

sadden vtr attrister

saddle ① n selle f ② vtr (a) seller ⟨horse⟩ (b) to ~ sb with mettre [qch] sur les bras de qn ⟨responsibility, task⟩

saddle bag n sacoche f

sadist n sadique mf

sadistic adj sadique

sadness n tristesse f

sae n abbr = STAMPED ADDRESSED ENVELOPE

safari n safari m

safari park n parc m zoologique (où les animaux vivent en semi-liberté)

safe ① n coffre-fort m ② adj (a) (after ordeal, risk) ⟨person⟩ sain et sauf/saine et sauve; ⟨object⟩ intact/-e; ~ and sound sain et sauf/saine et sauve (b) (free from threat, harm) to be ~ ⟨person⟩ être en sécurité; ⟨document, valuables⟩ être en lieu sûr; ⟨company, job, reputation⟩ ne pas être menacé/-e; is the bike ~ here? est-ce qu'on peut laisser le vélo ici sans risque?; have a ~ journey! bon voyage! (c) (risk-free) ⟨toy, level, method⟩ sans danger; ⟨place, vehicle⟩ sûr/-e; ⟨structure, building⟩ solide; it's not ~ c'est dangereux (d) (prudent) ⟨investment⟩ sûr/-e; ⟨choice⟩ prudent/-e (e) (reliable) to be in ~ hands être en bonnes mains IDIOMS better ~ than sorry! mieux vaut prévenir que guérir!; just to be on the ~ side simplement par précaution

safe bet n it's a ~ c'est quelque chose de sûr

safe-conduct n laissez-passer m inv

safe-deposit box n coffre m (à la banque)

safeguard ① n garantie f (for pour; against contre) ② vtr protéger (against, from contre)

safe house n refuge m
safekeeping n in sb's ~ à la garde de
qn
safely adv (a) ⟨come back⟩ (of person) sans
encombre; (of parcel, goods) sans dommage; (of
plane) ⟨land, take off⟩ sans problème; I
arrived ~ je suis bien arrivé
(b) we can ~ assume that… nous pouvons
être certains que…
(c) ⟨locked, hidden⟩ bien
safe sex n rapports mpl sexuels sans
risque
safety n sécurité f; in ~ en (toute)
sécurité; to reach ~ parvenir en lieu sûr
safety belt n ceinture f de sécurité
safety net n filet m (de protection);
(figurative) filet m de sécurité
safety pin n épingle f de sûreté
sag vi (a) ⟨beam, mattress⟩ s'affaisser; ⟨tent,
rope⟩ ne pas être bien tendu/-e
(b) ⟨breasts⟩ pendre; ⟨flesh⟩ être flasque
saga n saga f
sage n (a) (herb) sauge f
(b) (wise person) sage m
Sagittarius n Sagittaire m
Sahara pr n Sahara m; the ~ desert le
désert du Sahara
sail ⟨1⟩ n (a) (of boat) voile f; to set sail
prendre la mer; a ship in full ~ un navire
toutes voiles dehors
(b) (of windmill) aile f
⟨2⟩ vtr (a) piloter ⟨ship, yacht⟩
(b) traverser [qch] en bateau ⟨ocean,
channel⟩
⟨3⟩ vi (a) ⟨person⟩ voyager en bateau; to ~
around the world faire le tour du monde en
bateau
(b) ⟨ship⟩ to ~ across traverser ⟨ocean⟩; the
boat ~s at 10 am le bateau part à 10 h
(c) (as hobby) to go ~ing faire de la voile
■ **sail through** gagner [qch] facilement
⟨match⟩; to ~ through an exam réussir un
examen les doigts dans le nez (colloq)
sailboard n planche f à voile
sailboarder n véliplanchiste mf
sailboat n (US) bateau m à voiles
sailing n voile f
sailing boat n bateau m à voiles
sailing ship n voilier m
sailor n marin m
saint n saint/-e m/f; **Saint Mark** saint Marc
sake n (a) for the ~ of clarity pour la
clarté; for the ~ of argument à titre
d'exemple; to kill for the ~ of killing tuer
pour le plaisir de tuer; for old times' ~ en
souvenir du bon vieux temps
(b) (benefit) for the ~ of sb, for sb's ~ par
égard pour qn; for God's/heaven's ~! pour
l'amour de Dieu/du ciel!
salad n salade f; ham ~ salade au jambon
salad bar n buffet m de crudités
salad bowl n saladier m
salad dressing n sauce f pour salade

salami n saucisson m sec
salary n salaire m
sale n (a) (gen) vente f (of de; to à); for sale
à vendre; on ~ (GB) en vente
(b) (at cut prices) solde f; the sales les soldes;
in the ~(s) (GB), on ~ (US) en solde
sale price n prix m soldé
sales assistant n (GB) vendeur/-euse
m/f
sales executive n cadre m commercial
salesman n (rep) représentant m; (in shop)
vendeur m
sales pitch n baratin m (colloq)
publicitaire
sales rep, sales representative n
représentant/-e m/f
saleswoman n (rep) représentante f; (in
shop) vendeuse f
saliva n salive f
salivate vi saliver
sallow adj cireux/-euse
salmon n saumon m
salmonella n salmonelle f
salon n salon m
saloon n (a) (GB) (also ~ car) berline f
(b) (US) saloon m, bar m
(c) (on boat) salon m
salt ⟨1⟩ n sel m
⟨2⟩ vtr saler ⟨meat, fish, road, path⟩
saltcellar n salière f
salty adj ⟨water, food, flavour⟩ salé/-e
salutary adj salutaire
salute ⟨1⟩ n salut m
⟨2⟩ vtr, vi saluer
salvage ⟨1⟩ n (a) (rescue) sauvetage m (of
de)
(b) (goods rescued) biens mpl récupérés
⟨2⟩ vtr (a) sauver ⟨cargo, materials,
belongings⟩ (from de); effectuer le sauvetage
de ⟨ship⟩
(b) sauver ⟨marriage, reputation, game⟩
(c) (for recycling) récupérer ⟨metal, paper⟩
salvation n salut m
Salvation Army n Armée f du Salut
salve ⟨1⟩ n baume m
⟨2⟩ vtr to ~ one's conscience soulager sa
conscience
Samaritan n the Good ~ le bon
Samaritain; the ~s les Samaritains mpl
same ⟨1⟩ adj même (as que); to be the ~
être le/la même; to look the ~ être
pareil/-eille; to be the ~ as sth être comme
qch; it amounts or comes to the ~ thing cela
revient au même; it's all the ~ to me ça
m'est complètement égal; if it's all the ~ to
you si ça ne te fait rien; at the ~ time en
même temps; to remain or stay the ~ ne pas
changer
⟨2⟩ **the same** pron la même chose (as que);
I'll have the ~ je prendrai la même chose; to
do the ~ as sb faire comme qn; the ~ to
you! (in greeting) à toi aussi, à toi de même!;
(of insult) toi-même! (colloq) ⋯⋗

S

3 the same adv ⟨act, dress⟩ de la même façon; **to feel the ~ as sb** penser comme qn
IDIOMS **all the ~...**, **just the ~,...** tout de même,...; **thanks all the ~** merci quand même

same-day adj ⟨service⟩ effectué/-e dans la journée

sample **1** n **(a)** (of product, fabric) échantillon m
(b) (for analysis) prélèvement m
2 vtr **(a)** (taste) goûter (à) ⟨food, wine⟩
(b) (test) essayer ⟨products⟩; sonder ⟨opinion, market⟩

sanatorium (GB), **sanitarium** (US) n sanatorium m

sanctimonious adj supérieur/-e

sanction **1** n sanction f; **to impose ~s** prendre des sanctions
2 vtr (permit) autoriser; (approve) sanctionner

sanctity n sainteté f

sanctuary n **(a)** (safe place) refuge m
(b) (holy place) sanctuaire m
(c) (for wildlife) réserve f; (for mistreated pets) refuge m

sand **1** n sable m
2 vtr **(a)** (also **~ down**) poncer ⟨floor⟩; frotter [qch] au papier de verre ⟨woodwork⟩
(b) sabler ⟨icy road⟩

sandal n sandale f

sand castle n château m de sable

sand dune n dune f

sandpaper **1** n papier m de verre
2 vtr poncer

sandpit n (quarry) sablière f; (for children) bac m à sable

sandstone n grès m

sandwich **1** n sandwich m; **cucumber ~** sandwich au concombre
2 vtr **to be ~ed between** ⟨car, building, person⟩ être pris/-e en sandwich entre

sandwich bar n sandwich bar m

sandwich course n (GB) cours m avec stage pratique

sandy adj **(a)** ⟨beach⟩ de sable; ⟨path, soil⟩ sablonneux/-euse
(b) ⟨hair⟩ blond roux inv; ⟨colour⟩ sable inv (after n)

sane adj **(a)** ⟨person⟩ sain/-e d'esprit
(b) ⟨policy, judgment⟩ sensé/-e

sanitarium (US) = SANATORIUM

sanitary adj **(a)** ⟨engineer, installations⟩ sanitaire
(b) (hygienic) hygiénique; (clean) propre

sanitary towel (GB), **sanitary napkin** (US) n serviette f hygiénique or périodique

sanitation n installations fpl sanitaires

sanity n équilibre m mental

Santa (Claus) pr n le père Noël

sap **1** n sève f
2 vtr saper ⟨strength, courage, confidence⟩

sapling n jeune arbre m

sapphire n **(a)** (stone) saphir m

(b) (colour) bleu m saphir

sarcasm n sarcasme m

sarcastic adj sarcastique

sardine n sardine f

Sardinia pr n Sardaigne f

sardonic adj ⟨laugh, look⟩ sardonique; ⟨person, remark⟩ acerbe

SAS n (GB) (abbr = **Special Air Service**) commandos mpl britanniques aéroportés

sash n (round waist) large ceinture f; (ceremonial) écharpe f

Satan pr n Satan

satanic adj ⟨rites⟩ satanique; ⟨pride, smile⟩ démoniaque

satchel n cartable m (à bandoulière)

satellite n satellite m

satellite dish n antenne f parabolique

satellite TV n télévision f par satellite

satin **1** n satin m
2 adj ⟨garment, shoe⟩ de satin; **with a ~ finish** satiné/-e

satire n satire f (**on** sur)

satiric(al) adj satirique

satirize vtr faire la satire de

satisfaction n satisfaction f

satisfactory adj satisfaisant/-e

satisfied adj **(a)** (pleased) satisfait/-e (**with, about** de)
(b) (convinced) convaincu/-e (**by** par; **that** que)

satisfy vtr **(a)** satisfaire ⟨person, need, desires, curiosity⟩; assouvir ⟨hunger⟩
(b) (persuade) convaincre ⟨person, public opinion⟩ (**that** que)
(c) (meet) satisfaire à ⟨demand, requirements, conditions⟩

satisfying adj **(a)** ⟨meal⟩ substantiel/-ielle
(b) ⟨job⟩ qui apporte de la satisfaction
(c) ⟨result, progress⟩ satisfaisant/-e

saturate vtr saturer (**with** de)

saturated adj (wet) ⟨person, clothes⟩ trempé/-e; ⟨ground⟩ détrempé/-e

saturation point n point m de saturation; **to reach ~** arriver à saturation

Saturday n samedi m; **he has a ~ job** il a un petit boulot (colloq) le samedi

Saturn pr n (planet) Saturne f

sauce n sauce f

saucepan n casserole f

saucer n soucoupe f

Saudi Arabia pr n Arabie f saoudite

sauna n sauna m

saunter vi (also **~ along**) marcher d'un pas nonchalant; **to ~ off** s'éloigner d'un pas nonchalant

sausage n saucisse f

sausage roll n feuilleté m à la chair à saucisse

savage **1** n sauvage mf
2 adj **(a)** (gen) féroce; ⟨blow, beating⟩ violent/-e; ⟨attack⟩ sauvage; ⟨criticism⟩ virulent/-e
3 vtr ⟨dog⟩ attaquer [qn/qch] sauvagement; ⟨lion⟩ déchiqueter

S

save [1] n (Sport) arrêt m de but
[2] vtr (a) (rescue) sauver (from de); to ~ sb's life sauver la vie à qn
(b) (put by, keep) mettre [qch] de côté ⟨money, food⟩ (to do pour faire); garder ⟨goods, documents⟩ (for pour); sauvegarder ⟨data, file⟩; to have money ~d avoir de l'argent de côté; to ~ sth for sb, to ~ sb sth garder qch pour qn
(c) (economize on) économiser ⟨money⟩ (by doing en faisant); gagner ⟨time, space⟩ (by doing en faisant); to ~ one's energy ménager ses forces; you'll ~ money vous ferez des économies; to ~ sb/sth (from) having to do éviter à qn/qch de faire
(d) (Sport) arrêter
[3] vi (a) (put money by) = SAVE UP
(b) (economize) économiser, faire des économies; to ~ on faire des économies de ⟨energy, paper⟩
■ **save up** faire des économies; to ~ up for mettre de l'argent de côté pour s'acheter ⟨car, house⟩; mettre de l'argent de côté pour s'offrir ⟨holiday⟩

saver n épargnant/-e m/f

saving grace n bon côté m; it's his ~ c'est ce qui le sauve

savings n pl économies fpl

savings account n (GB) compte m d'épargne; (US) compte m rémunéré

savings bank n caisse f d'épargne

saviour (GB), **savior** (US) n sauveur m

savour (GB), **savor** (US) [1] n saveur f
[2] vtr savourer

savoury (GB), **savory** (US) adj (not sweet) salé/-e; (appetizing) appétissant/-e

saw [1] n scie f
[2] vtr scier; to ~ through/down/off scier

sawdust n sciure f (de bois)

sawn-off shotgun n (GB) fusil m à canon scié

saxophone n saxophone m

say [1] n to have one's ~ dire ce qu'on a à dire (on sur); to have a ~/no ~ in sth avoir/ne pas avoir son mot à dire sur qch; to have no ~ in the matter ne pas avoir voix au chapitre
[2] vtr (a) (gen) dire (to à); 'hello,' he said 'bonjour,' dit-il; to ~ (that) dire que; they ~ she's very rich, she is said to be very rich on dit qu'elle est très riche; to ~ sth about sb/sth dire qch au sujet de qn/qch; to ~ sth to oneself se dire qch; let's ~ no more about it n'en parlons plus; it goes without ~ing that il va sans dire que; that is to ~ c'est-à-dire; let's ~ there are 20 mettons or supposons qu'il y en ait 20; how high would you ~ it is? à ton avis, quelle en est la hauteur?; I'd ~ she was about 25 je lui donnerais environ 25 ans
(b) ⟨sign, clock, dial, gauge⟩ indiquer
[3] vi stop when I ~ arrête quand je te le dirai; he wouldn't ~ il n'a pas voulu le dire
IDIOMS it ~s a lot for sb/sth c'est tout à l'honneur de qn/qch; there's a lot to be said

for that method cette méthode est très intéressante à bien des égards; when all is said and done tout compte fait, en fin de compte

saying n dicton m

scab n croûte f

scaffolding n échafaudage m

scald vtr ébouillanter

scalding adj brûlant/-e

scale [1] n (a) (gen) échelle f; pay ~, salary ~ échelle des salaires; on a ~ of 1 to 10 sur une échelle allant de 1 à 10
(b) (extent) (of disaster, success, violence) étendue f (of de); (of defeat, recession, task) ampleur f (of de); (of activity, operation) envergure f (of de)
(c) (on ruler, gauge) graduation f
(d) (for weighing) balance f
(e) (Mus) gamme f
(f) (on fish, insect) écaille f
[2] **scales** n pl balance f
[3] vtr (a) escalader ⟨wall, mountain⟩
(b) écailler ⟨fish⟩
■ **scale down**: ~ [sth] down, ~ down [sth] réduire l'échelle de ⟨drawing⟩; réduire ⟨activity⟩

scale drawing n dessin m à l'échelle

scale model n maquette f à l'échelle

scallop, scollop n coquille f Saint-Jacques

scalp [1] n cuir m chevelu
[2] vtr scalper

scam n (colloq) escroquerie f

scamper vi to ~ about or around ⟨child, dog⟩ gambader; ⟨mouse⟩ trottiner

scan [1] n (Med) (CAT) scanner m; (ultrasound) échographie f
[2] vtr (a) lire rapidement ⟨page, newspaper⟩
(b) (examine) scruter ⟨face, horizon⟩
(c) ⟨beam of light, radar⟩ balayer
(d) (Med) faire un scanner de ⟨organ⟩

scandal n scandale m

scandalize vtr scandaliser

scandalous adj scandaleux/-euse

Scandinavia pr n Scandinavie f

scanner n (Comput, Med) scanner m; (for bar codes) lecteur m optique

scanty adj ⟨meal, supply⟩ maigre (before n); ⟨information⟩ sommaire; ⟨knowledge⟩ rudimentaire; ⟨swimsuit⟩ minuscule

scapegoat n bouc m émissaire (for de)

scar [1] n cicatrice f; (on face from knife) balafre f
[2] vtr marquer; (on face with knife) balafrer; to ~ sb for life laisser à qn une cicatrice permanente; (figurative) marquer qn pour la vie

scarce adj rare; to become ~ se faire rare

scarcely adv à peine; ~ anybody believes it presque personne ne le croit

scare [1] n (a) peur f; to give sb a ~ faire peur à qn
(b) (alert) alerte f; bomb ~ alerte à la bombe
[2] vtr faire peur à

S

■ **scare away**, **scare off** faire fuir ⟨*animal, attacker*⟩; (figurative) dissuader

scarecrow n épouvantail m

scared adj ⟨*animal, person*⟩ effrayé/-e; ⟨*look*⟩ apeuré/-e; **to be** or **feel ~** avoir peur; **to be ~ stiff** (colloq) avoir une peur bleue (colloq)

scaremongering n alarmisme m

scarf n (long) écharpe f; (square) foulard m

scarlet n, adj écarlate (f)

scarlet fever n scarlatine f

scary adj (colloq) qui fait peur

scathing adj ⟨*remark, tone, wit*⟩ cinglant/-e; ⟨*criticism*⟩ virulent/-e

scatter ⟨1⟩ vtr (a) (*also* **~ around**, **~ about**) répandre ⟨*seeds, earth*⟩; éparpiller ⟨*books, papers, clothes*⟩
(b) disperser ⟨*crowd, herd*⟩
⟨2⟩ vi ⟨*people, animals, birds*⟩ se disperser

scatter-brained adj ⟨*person*⟩ étourdi/-e; ⟨*idea*⟩ farfelu/-e (colloq)

scattered adj ⟨*houses, trees, population, clouds*⟩ épars/-e; ⟨*books, litter*⟩ éparpillé/-e; ⟨*support, resistance*⟩ clairsemé/-e

scatty adj (colloq) (GB) étourdi/-e

scavenge vi **to ~ for food** ⟨*bird, animal*⟩ chercher de la nourriture

scavenger n (a) (animal) charognard m
(b) (person) (for food) faiseur m de poubelles; (for objects) récupérateur m

scenario n (gen) cas m de figure; (of film, play) scénario m

scene n (a) (gen) scène f; **behind the ~s** dans les coulisses fpl; **you need a change of ~** tu as besoin de changer de décor
(b) (of crime, accident) lieu m; **at** or **on the ~** sur les lieux
(c) (image, sight) image f
(d) (view) vue f

scenery n (a) (landscape) paysage m
(b) (in theatre) décors mpl

scent ⟨1⟩ n (a) (smell) odeur f
(b) (perfume) parfum m
(c) (of animal) fumet m; (in hunting) piste f
⟨2⟩ vtr (a) flairer ⟨*prey, animal*⟩
(b) pressentir ⟨*danger, trouble*⟩
(c) (perfume) parfumer ⟨*air*⟩

sceptic (GB), **skeptic** (US) n sceptique mf

sceptical (GB), **skeptical** (US) adj sceptique

scepticism (GB), **skepticism** (US) n scepticisme m

schedule ⟨1⟩ n (a) (of work, events) programme m; (timetable) horaire m; **to be ahead of/behind ~** être en avance/en retard; **to arrive on/ahead of ~** ⟨*bus, train, plane*⟩ arriver à l'heure/en avance
(b) (list) liste f
⟨2⟩ vtr (plan) prévoir; (arrange) programmer

scheduled flight n vol m régulier

scheme ⟨1⟩ n (a) projet m, plan m (**to do**, **for doing** pour faire); **pension ~** régime m de retraite

(b) (plot) combine f (**to do** pour faire)
⟨2⟩ vi comploter

scheming n machinations fpl

schizophrenic adj schizophrénique

scholar n érudit/-e m/f

scholarship n bourse f (**to** pour)

school ⟨1⟩ n (a) école f; **at ~** à l'école
(b) (US) (university) université f
(c) (of fish) banc m
⟨2⟩ adj ⟨*holiday, outing, trip, uniform, year*⟩ scolaire

schoolbag n sac m de classe

schoolboy n (pupil) élève m; (primary) écolier m; (secondary) collégien m

schoolchild n écolier/-ière m/f

school fees n pl frais mpl de scolarité

schoolfriend n camarade mf de classe

schoolgirl n (pupil) élève f; (primary) écolière f; (secondary) collégienne f

schooling n scolarité f

school-leaver n (GB) jeune mf ayant fini sa scolarité

school leaving age n âge m de fin de scolarité

school lunch n repas m de la cantine scolaire

school report (GB), **school report card** (US) n bulletin m scolaire

schoolteacher n enseignant/-e m/f; (primary) instituteur/-trice m/f; (secondary) professeur m

schoolwork n travail m de classe

science ⟨1⟩ n science f; **to study ~** étudier les sciences
⟨2⟩ adj ⟨*exam, subject*⟩ scientifique; ⟨*teacher, textbook*⟩ de sciences

science fiction n science-fiction f

scientific adj scientifique

scientist n scientifique mf

scissors n pl ciseaux mpl

scoff ⟨1⟩ vtr (GB) (colloq) (eat) engloutir (colloq), bouffer (colloq)
⟨2⟩ vi se moquer (**at** de)

scold vtr gronder (**for doing** pour avoir fait)

scoop ⟨1⟩ n (a) (for measuring) mesure f
(b) (of ice cream) boule f
(c) (in journalism) exclusivité f
⟨2⟩ vtr (colloq) décrocher (colloq) ⟨*prize, sum of money, story*⟩

scooter n (a) (child's) trottinette f
(b) (motorized) scooter m

scope n (a) (opportunity) possibilité f (**for** de)
(b) (of inquiry, report, book) portée f; (of plan) envergure f
(c) (of person) compétences fpl

scorch ⟨1⟩ n (also **~ mark**) légère brûlure f
⟨2⟩ vtr ⟨*fire*⟩ brûler; ⟨*sun*⟩ dessécher ⟨*grass, trees*⟩; griller ⟨*lawn*⟩; roussir ⟨*fabric*⟩

scorching adj (colloq) (also **~ hot**) ⟨*day*⟩ torride; ⟨*weather*⟩ caniculaire

score ⓵ n (a) (Sport) score m; (in cards) marque f; **to keep (the) ~** marquer les points; (in cards) tenir la marque
(b) (in exam, test) note f, résultat m
(c) (Mus) (written music) partition f; (for film) musique f (de film)
(d) (twenty) **a ~** vingt m, une vingtaine f
(e) **on this** or **that ~** à ce sujet
⓶ vtr (a) marquer ⟨goal, point⟩; reporter ⟨victory, success⟩; **to ~ 9 out of 10** avoir 9 sur 10
(b) (cut) entailler
⓷ vi (gain point) marquer un point; (obtain goal) marquer un but
IDIOMS to settle a ~ régler ses comptes

scoreboard n tableau m d'affichage

scorn ⓵ n mépris m (**for** pour)
⓶ vtr (despise) mépriser; (reject) accueillir avec mépris ⟨claim, suggestion⟩

scornful adj méprisant/-e

Scorpio n Scorpion m

Scot n Écossais/-e m/f

Scotch ⓵ n (also **~ whisky**) whisky m, scotch m
⓶ adj écossais/-e

Scotch tape® n (US) scotch® m

scot-free adj **to get off ~** (unpunished) s'en tirer sans être inquiété/-e; (unharmed) s'en sortir indemne

Scotland pr n Écosse f

Scottish adj écossais/-e

scour vtr (a) (scrub) récurer
(b) (search) parcourir ⟨area, list⟩ (**for** à la recherche de)

scourer n tampon m à récurer

scourge n fléau m

scout n (a) (also **boy ~**) scout m
(b) (Mil) éclaireur m
(c) (also **talent ~**) découvreur/-euse m/f de nouveaux talents
■ **scout around** explorer; **to ~ around for sth** rechercher qch

scowl ⓵ n air m renfrogné
⓶ vi prendre un air renfrogné

scramble ⓵ n (a) (rush) course f (**for** pour; **to do** pour faire)
(b) (climb) escalade f
⓶ vtr brouiller ⟨signal⟩
⓷ vi (a) **to ~ up** escalader; **to ~ down** dégringoler

scrambled egg n (also **~s** pl) œufs mpl brouillés

scrambling n (sport) motocross m

scrap ⓵ n (a) (of paper, cloth) petit morceau m; (of news, information) fragment m
(b) (old iron) ferraille f
⓶ **scraps** n pl (of food) restes mpl; (from butcher's) déchets mpl
⓷ vtr (a) (colloq) abandonner ⟨idea, plan, system⟩
(b) détruire ⟨aircraft, equipment⟩

scrapbook n album m

scrap dealer n ferrailleur m

scrape ⓵ n **to get into a ~** (colloq) s'attirer des ennuis
⓶ vtr (a) (clean) gratter ⟨vegetables, shoes⟩
(b) érafler ⟨car, paintwork, furniture⟩; **to ~ one's knees** s'écorcher les genoux
⓷ vi **to ~ against sth** (rub) frotter contre qch; (scratch) érafler qch
■ **scrape by** (financially) s'en sortir à peine; (in situation) s'en tirer de justesse
■ **scrape in** (to university, class) entrer de justesse
■ **scrape out:** ¶ **~ out [sth], ~ [sth] out** nettoyer [qch] en grattant ⟨saucepan⟩
■ **scrape through:** ¶ **~ through** s'en tirer de justesse; ¶ **~ through [sth]** réussir de justesse à ⟨exam, test⟩

scrap heap n **to be thrown on the ~** être mis/-e au rebut

scrap iron, scrap metal n ferraille f

scrap paper n papier m brouillon

scrap yard n chantier m de ferraille, casse f

scratch ⓵ n (a) (on skin) égratignure f; (from a claw, fingernail) griffure f
(b) (on metal, furniture) éraflure f; (on record, glass) rayure f
(c) (sound) grattement m
(d) (colloq) **he/his work is not up to ~** il/son travail n'est pas à la hauteur
(e) **to start from ~** partir de zéro
⓶ vtr (a) **to ~ one's initials on sth** graver ses initiales sur qch
(b) ⟨cat, person⟩ griffer ⟨person⟩; ⟨thorns, rose bush⟩ égratigner ⟨person⟩; érafler ⟨car, wood⟩; rayer ⟨record⟩; ⟨cat⟩ se faire les griffes sur ⟨furniture⟩; ⟨person⟩ **to ~ sb's eyes out** arracher les yeux à quelqu'un
(c) **to ~ sb's back** gratter le dos de qn
⓷ vi se gratter

scratch card n jeu m de grattage

scrawl ⓵ n gribouillage m
⓶ vtr, vi gribouiller

scrawny adj ⟨person, animal⟩ décharné/-e

scream ⓵ n (of person, animal) cri m (perçant); (stronger) hurlement m; (of brakes) grincement m; (of tyres) crissement m
⓶ vtr crier
⓷ vi crier; (stronger) hurler

screech ⓵ n (of person, animal) cri m strident; (of tyres) crissement m
⓶ vi ⟨person, animal⟩ pousser un cri strident; ⟨tyres⟩ crisser

screen ⓵ n (a) (on TV, VDU, at cinema) écran m
(b) (furniture) paravent m
(c) (US) (in door) grille f
⓶ vtr (a) (at cinema) projeter; (on TV) diffuser
(b) (conceal) cacher; (protect) protéger (**from** de)
(c) (test) examiner le cas de ⟨applicants, candidates⟩; contrôler ⟨baggage⟩; **to ~ sb for cancer** faire passer à qn des tests de dépistage du cancer

screening n (a) (showing) projection f; (on TV) diffusion f ····⋗

(b) (of patients) examens *mpl* de dépistage
(c) (vetting) filtrage *m*

screenplay *n* scénario *m*

screen saver *n* économiseur *m* d'écran

screenwriter *n* scénariste *mf*

screw ⓵ *n* vis *f*
⓶ *vtr* visser (**into** dans; **onto** sur)
■ **screw up (a)** froisser ⟨*piece of paper, material*⟩; **to ~ up one's eyes** plisser les yeux; **to ~ up one's face** faire la grimace
(b) (colloq) faire foirer (colloq) ⟨*plan, task*⟩

screwdriver *n* **(a)** (tool) tournevis *m*
(b) (cocktail) vodka-orange *f*

scribble *vtr*, *vi* griffonner, gribouiller

scrimp *vi* économiser; **to ~ and save** se priver de tout

script *n* **(a)** (for film, radio, TV) script *m*; (for play) texte *m*
(b) (GB) (Sch, Univ) copie *f* (d'examen)

scripture *n* (*also* **Holy Scripture, Holy Scriptures**) (Christian) Ecritures *fpl*; (other) textes *mpl* sacrés

scriptwriter *n* scénariste *mf*

scroll *n* rouleau *m*
■ **scroll down**: ¶ ~ **down** ⟨*person*⟩ faire défiler de haut en bas; ¶ ~ **down** [sth] faire défiler [qch] de haut en bas ⟨*document*⟩
■ **scroll up**: ¶ ~ **up** ⟨*person*⟩ faire défiler de bas en haut; ¶ ~ **up** [sth] faire défiler [qch] de bas en haut ⟨*document*⟩

scroll bar *n* barre *f* de défilement

scrounge *vtr* (colloq) **to ~ sth off sb** piquer (colloq) qch à qn ⟨*cigarette*⟩; taper (colloq) qn de ⟨*money*⟩

scrounger *n* (colloq) parasite *m*

scrub ⓵ *n* **(a)** (clean) **to give sth a (good) ~** (bien) nettoyer qch
(b) (Bot) broussailles *fpl*
⓶ *vtr* frotter ⟨*back, clothes*⟩; récurer ⟨*pan, floor*⟩; nettoyer ⟨*vegetable*⟩; **to ~ one's nails** se brosser les ongles
■ **scrub up** ⟨*doctor*⟩ se stériliser les mains

scrubbing brush, scrub brush (US) *n* brosse *f* de ménage

scruff *n* **by the ~ of the neck** par la peau du cou

scruffy *adj* ⟨*clothes, person*⟩ dépenaillé/-e; ⟨*flat, town*⟩ délabré/-e

scrum, scrummage *n* (in rugby) mêlée *f*

scrunchie *n* chouchou *m*

scruple *n* scrupule *m* (**about** vis-à-vis de)

scrupulous *adj* scrupuleux/-euse

scrutinize *vtr* scruter ⟨*face, motives*⟩; examiner [qch] minutieusement ⟨*document, plan*⟩; vérifier ⟨*accounts, votes*⟩

scrutiny *n* examen *m*

scuba diving *n* plongée *f* sous-marine

scuff ⓵ *n* (*also* **~ mark**) (on floor, furniture) rayure *f*; (on leather) éraflure *f*
⓶ *vtr* érafler ⟨*shoes*⟩; rayer ⟨*floor, furniture*⟩

scuffle *n* bagarre *f*

sculpt *vtr*, *vi* sculpter

sculptor *n* sculpteur *m*

sculpture *n* sculpture *f*

scum *n* **(a)** (on pond) écume *f*
(b) (on liquid) mousse *f*
(c) **they're the ~ of the earth** c'est de la racaille

scuttle ⓵ *vtr* **(a)** saborder ⟨*ship*⟩
(b) faire échouer ⟨*talks, project*⟩
⓶ *vi* **to ~ away** *or* **off** filer

scythe *n* faux *f inv*

sea ⓵ *n* mer *f*; **beside** *or* **by the ~** au bord de la mer; **the open ~** le large; **by ~** ⟨*travel*⟩ en bateau; ⟨*send*⟩ par bateau
⓶ *adj* ⟨*air, breeze*⟩ marin/-e; ⟨*bird, water*⟩ de mer; ⟨*crossing, voyage*⟩ par mer; ⟨*battle*⟩ naval/-e; ⟨*power*⟩ maritime

seafood *n* fruits *mpl* de mer

seafront *n* front *m* de mer

seagull *n* mouette *f*

sea horse *n* hippocampe *m*

seal ⓵ *n* **(a)** (Zool) phoque *m*
(b) (stamp) sceau *m*
(c) (on container) plomb *m*; (on package, letter) cachet *m*; (on door) scellés *mpl*
⓶ *vtr* **(a)** cacheter ⟨*document*⟩
(b) fermer, cacheter ⟨*envelope*⟩
(c) fermer [qch] hermétiquement ⟨*jar, tin*⟩; rendre [qch] étanche ⟨*window frame*⟩
(d) sceller ⟨*alliance, friendship*⟩ (**with** par); **to ~ sb's fate** décider du sort de qn
■ **seal off** isoler ⟨*ward*⟩; boucler ⟨*area, building*⟩; barrer ⟨*street*⟩

sea lion *n* lion *m* de mer

seam *n* (of garment) couture *f*

seamless *adj* ⟨*transition*⟩ sans heurts; ⟨*process, whole*⟩ continu/-e

seaplane *n* hydravion *m*

search ⓵ *n* **(a)** (for person, object) recherches *fpl* (**for sb/sth** pour retrouver qn/qch); **in ~ of** à la recherche de
(b) (of place) fouille *f* (**of** de)
(c) (Comput) recherche *f*
⓶ *vtr* **(a)** fouiller ⟨*area, building*⟩; fouiller dans ⟨*cupboard, drawer, memory*⟩
(b) examiner (attentivement) ⟨*map, records*⟩
⓷ *vi* **(a)** chercher; **to ~ for** *or* **after sb/sth** chercher qn/qch; **to ~ through** fouiller dans ⟨*cupboard, bag*⟩; examiner ⟨*records, file*⟩
(b) (Comput) **to ~ for** rechercher ⟨*data, file*⟩
■ **search out**: ~ [sb/sth] **out**, ~ **out** [sb/sth] découvrir

search engine *n* moteur *m* de recherche

searching *adj* ⟨*look, question*⟩ pénétrant/-e

searchlight *n* projecteur *m*

search party *n* équipe *f* de secours

search warrant *n* mandat *m* de perquisition

sea salt *n* sel *m* de mer

seashell *n* coquillage *m*

seashore *n* (part of coast) littoral *m*; (beach) plage *f*

seasick *adj* **to feel ~** avoir le mal de mer

seaside ⓵ *n* **the ~** le bord de la mer
⓶ *adj* ⟨*hotel*⟩ en bord de mer; ⟨*town*⟩ maritime; **~ resort** station *f* balnéaire

season [1] *n* saison *f*; **strawberries are in/ out of** ∼ c'est/ce n'est pas la saison des fraises; **the holiday** ∼ la période des vacances; **Season's greetings!** Joyeuses fêtes!
[2] *vtr* (with spices) relever; (with condiments) assaisonner

seasonal *adj* ⟨work, change⟩ saisonnier/-ière; ⟨fruit, produce⟩ de saison

seasoned *adj* ⟨soldier⟩ aguerri/-e; ⟨traveller⟩ grand/-e (*before n*); ⟨campaigner, performer⟩ expérimenté/-e; ⟨dish⟩ assaisonné/-e; **highly** ∼ relevé/-e, épicé/-e

seasoning *n* assaisonnement *m*

season ticket *n* (for travel) carte *f* d'abonnement; (for theatre, matches) abonnement *m*

seat [1] *n* (a) (chair) siège *m*; (bench-type) banquette *f*
(b) (place) place *f*; **take** *or* **have a** ∼ asseyez-vous; **to book a** ∼ réserver une place
(c) (of trousers) fond *m*
[2] *vtr* (a) placer ⟨person⟩
(b) **the car** ∼**s five** c'est une voiture à cinq places; **the table** ∼**s six** c'est une table de six couverts

seatbelt *n* ceinture *f* (de sécurité)

-seater *combining form* **a two**∼ (plane) un avion *m* à deux places; (car) un coupé; (sofa) un (canapé) deux places

seating *n* places *fpl* assises; **I'll organize the** ∼ je placerai les gens

sea urchin *n* oursin *m*

sea view *n* vue *f* sur la mer

seaweed *n* algue *f* marine

seaworthy *adj* en état de naviguer

secateurs *n pl* (GB) sécateur *m*

secluded *adj* retiré/-e

seclusion *n* isolement *m* (**from** à l'écart de)

second [1] *n* (a) (in order) deuxième *mf*, second/-e *m/f*
(b) (unit of time) seconde *f*; (instant) instant *m*
(c) (of month) deux *m inv*
(d) (Aut) (*also* ∼ **gear**) deuxième *f*, seconde *f*
(e) (defective article) article *m* qui a un défaut
(f) (*also* ∼**-class honours degree**) (GB) (Univ) ≈ licence *f* avec mention bien
[2] *adj* deuxième, second/-e; **to have a** ∼ **helping** (**of sth**) reprendre (de qch); **to have a** ∼ **chance to do sth** avoir une nouvelle chance de faire
[3] *adv* (in second place) deuxième; **to come** *or* **finish** ∼ arriver deuxième; **the** ∼ **biggest building** le deuxième bâtiment de par sa grandeur
(b) (*also* **secondly**) deuxièmement
[4] *vtr* (in debate) appuyer ⟨proposal⟩
IDIOMS **to be** ∼ **nature** être automatique; **to be** ∼ **to none** être sans pareil; **on** ∼ **thoughts** à la réflexion; **to have** ∼ **thoughts** avoir quelques hésitations *or* doutes

secondary *adj* secondaire

secondary school *n* ≈ école *f* secondaire

second class [1] *adv* ⟨travel⟩ en deuxième classe; ⟨send⟩ au tarif lent
[2] **second-class** *adj*
(a) ⟨post, stamp⟩ au tarif lent
(b) ⟨carriage, ticket⟩ de deuxième classe
(c) (second-rate) de qualité inférieure

second hand [1] *n* (on watch, clock) trotteuse *f*
[2] **second-hand** *adj* ⟨clothes, car⟩ d'occasion; ⟨news, information⟩ de seconde main
[3] *adv* ⟨buy⟩ d'occasion; ⟨find out, hear⟩ indirectement

secondly *adv* deuxièmement

second name *n* (surname) nom *m* de famille; (second forename) deuxième prénom *m*

second-rate *adj* de second ordre

seconds *n pl* (colloq) rab *m* (colloq)

secrecy *n* secret *m*

secret [1] *n* secret *m*; **to tell sb a** ∼ confier un secret à qn
[2] *adj* secret/-ète
[3] **in secret** *phr* en secret

secretarial *adj* ⟨skills, work⟩ de secrétaire; ⟨college⟩ de secrétariat

secretary *n* (a) (assistant) secrétaire *mf* (**to sb** de qn)
(b) **Foreign Secretary** (GB), **Secretary of State** (US) ministre *m* des Affaires étrangères

secretive *adj* ⟨person, organization⟩ secret/-ète; **to be** ∼ **about sth** faire un mystère de qch

secretly *adv* secrètement

secret weapon *n* arme *f* secrète

sect *n* secte *f*

section *n* (a) (of train, aircraft, town, book) partie *f*; (of pipe, tunnel, road) tronçon *m*; (of object, kit) élément *m*; (of fruit) quartier *m*; (of population) tranche *f*
(b) (of company, department) service *m*; (of library, shop) rayon *m*
(c) (of act, bill, report) article *m*; (of newspaper) rubrique *f*

sector *n* secteur *m*

secular *adj* ⟨politics, society, education⟩ laïque; ⟨belief, music⟩ profane

secure [1] *adj* (a) ⟨job, marriage, income⟩ stable; ⟨basis, base⟩ solide
(b) ⟨hiding place⟩ sûr/-e
(c) ⟨padlock, knot⟩ solide; ⟨structure, ladder⟩ stable; ⟨rope⟩ bien attaché/-e; ⟨door, window⟩ bien fermé/-e
(d) **to feel** ∼ se sentir en sécurité
[2] *vtr* (a) obtenir ⟨promise, release, right, victory⟩
(b) bien attacher ⟨rope⟩; bien fermer ⟨door, window⟩; stabiliser ⟨ladder⟩
(c) protéger ⟨house⟩; assurer ⟨position, future⟩
(d) garantir ⟨loan, debt⟩ (**against, on** sur)

secure unit *n* (in children's home) section ⋯⟶

S

surveillée dans une maison de rééducation; (in psychiatric hospital) quartier *m* de haute sécurité

securities *n pl* titres *mpl*

security ⓵ *n* (a) sécurité *f*; **job ~** sécurité de l'emploi; **national ~** sûreté *f* de l'État
(b) (guarantee) garantie *f* (**on** sur)
⓶ *adj* ⟨*camera, check, measures*⟩ de sécurité; ⟨*firm, staff*⟩ de surveillance

security guard *n* garde *m* sécurité, vigile *m*

security leak *n* fuite *f* (*d'information*)

sedate ⓵ *adj* ⟨*person*⟩ posé/-e; ⟨*lifestyle, pace*⟩ tranquille
⓶ *vtr* mettre [qn] sous calmants ⟨*patient*⟩

sedation *n* sédation *f*; **under ~** sous calmants

sedative *n* sédatif *m*, calmant *m*

seduce *vtr* séduire

seductive *adj* ⟨*person*⟩ séduisant/-e; ⟨*smile*⟩ aguicheur/-euse

see ⓵ *vtr* (a) voir; **can you ~ him?** est-ce que tu le vois?; **I can't ~ him** je ne le vois pas; **to ~ the sights** faire du tourisme; **~ you next week!** à la semaine prochaine!; **to ~ sb as** considérer qn comme ⟨*friend, hero*⟩; **it remains to be seen whether** *or* **if** il reste à voir si
(b) (make sure) **to ~ (to it) that** veiller à ce que (+ *subjunctive*); **~ (to it) that the children are in bed by nine** veillez à ce que les enfants soient couchés à neuf heures
(c) (accompany) **to ~ sb to the station** accompagner qn à la gare; **to ~ sb home** raccompagner qn chez lui/elle
⓶ *vi* voir; **I can't ~** je ne vois rien; **I'll go and ~** je vais voir; **we'll just have to wait and ~** il ne nous reste plus qu'à attendre; **let's ~, let me ~** voyons (un peu)
■ **see off: to ~ sb off** dire au revoir à qn
■ **see out: to ~ sb out** raccompagner qn à la porte
■ **see through:** ¶ **~ through [sth]** déceler ⟨*deception, lie*⟩; ¶ **~ through [sb]** percer [qn] à jour; ¶ **~ [sth] through** mener [qch] à bonne fin
■ **see to** s'occuper de ⟨*arrangements*⟩

seed *n* (a) (gen) graine *f*; (fruit pip) pépin *m*; (for sowing) semences *fpl*; **to go to ~** ⟨*plant*⟩ monter en graine; ⟨*person*⟩ se ramollir; ⟨*organization, country*⟩ être en déclin
(b) (Sport) tête *f* de série

seedling *n* plant *m*

seedy *adj* ⟨*person*⟩ louche; ⟨*area, club*⟩ mal famé/-e

seek *vtr* (a) chercher ⟨*agreement, refuge, solution*⟩; demander ⟨*advice, help, permission*⟩
(b) ⟨*police, employer*⟩ rechercher ⟨*person*⟩
■ **seek out** aller chercher, dénicher

seem *vi* sembler; **it ~s that** il semble que (+ *subjunctive*); **it ~s to me that** il me semble que (+ *indicative*); **he ~s happy/disappointed**

il a l'air heureux/déçu; **it ~s odd (to me)** ça (me) paraît bizarre; **he ~s to be looking for someone** on dirait qu'il cherche quelqu'un

seep *vi* suinter; **to ~ away** s'écouler; **to ~ through sth** ⟨*water, gas*⟩ s'infiltrer à travers qch; ⟨*light*⟩ filtrer à travers qch

seesaw ⓵ *n* tapecul *m*
⓶ *vi* ⟨*price, rate*⟩ osciller

seethe *vi* (a) **to ~ with rage** bouillir de colère; **he was seething** il était furibond
(b) (teem) grouiller; **the streets were seething with tourists** les rues grouillaient de touristes

see-through *adj* transparent/-e

segment *n* segment *m*; (of orange) quartier *m*

segregate *vtr* (a) (separate) séparer (**from** de)
(b) (isolate) isoler (**from** de)

segregated *adj* ⟨*education, society*⟩ ségrégationniste; ⟨*area, school*⟩ où la ségrégation raciale (*or* religieuse) est en vigueur

segregation *n* ségrégation *f* (**from** de)

seize *vtr* (a) saisir; **to ~ hold of** se saisir de ⟨*person*⟩; s'emparer de ⟨*object*⟩
(b) s'emparer de ⟨*territory, prisoner, power*⟩; prendre ⟨*control*⟩
■ **seize up** ⟨*engine*⟩ se gripper; ⟨*limb*⟩ se bloquer

seizure *n* (a) (of territory, power) prise *f*; (of arms, drugs, property) saisie *f*
(b) (Med) attaque *f*

seldom *adv* rarement

select ⓵ *adj* ⟨*group*⟩ privilégié/-e; ⟨*hotel*⟩ chic, sélect/-e; ⟨*area*⟩ chic, cossu/-e
⓶ *vtr* sélectionner (**from, from among** parmi)

selection *n* sélection *f*

selective *adj* ⟨*memory, recruitment*⟩ sélectif/-ive; ⟨*admission, education*⟩ basé/-e sur la sélection; ⟨*account*⟩ tendancieux/-ieuse

self *n* moi *m*; **he's back to his old ~ again** il est redevenu lui-même

self-addressed envelope, SAE *n* enveloppe *f* à mon/votre etc adresse

self-adhesive *adj* autocollant/-e

self-assembly *adj* en kit

self-assured *adj* plein/-e d'assurance

self-catering *adj* ⟨*flat*⟩ avec cuisine; **~ holiday** vacances *fpl* en location

self-centred (GB), **self-centered** (US) *adj* égocentrique

self-confessed *adj* avoué/-e

self-confidence *n* assurance *f*

self-confident *adj* ⟨*person*⟩ sûr/-e de soi; ⟨*attitude*⟩ plein/-e d'assurance

self-conscious *adj* (a) (shy) timide; **to be ~ about sth/about doing** être gêné/-e par qch/de faire
(b) ⟨*style*⟩ conscient/-e

self-contained *adj* ⟨*flat*⟩ indépendant/-e

self-control *n* sang-froid *m*

s

self-defence (GB), **self-defense** (US) *n* (gen) autodéfense *f*; (Law) légitime défense *f*

self-destructive *adj* autodestructeur/-trice

self-determination *n* autodétermination *f*

self-disciplined *adj* autodiscipliné/-e

self-effacing *adj* effacé/-e

self-employed *adj* indépendant/-e; **to be ~** travailler à son compte

self-esteem *n* amour-propre *m*

self-evident *adj* évident/-e

self-explanatory *adj* explicite

self-expression *n* expression *f* de soi/de lui-même etc

self-governing *adj* autonome

self-image *n* image *f* de soi-même/de lui-même etc

self-important *adj* suffisant/-e

self-induced *adj* auto-infligé/-e

self-indulgent *adj* complaisant/-e

self-interested *adj* intéressé/-e

selfish *adj* égoïste (**to do** de faire)

selfishness *n* égoïsme *m*

selfless *adj* ⟨*person*⟩ dévoué/-e; ⟨*devotion*⟩ désintéressé/-e

self-pity *n* apitoiement *m* sur soi-même

self-portrait *n* autoportrait *m*

self-raising flour (GB), **self-rising flour** (US) *n* farine *f* à gâteau

self-reliant *adj* autosuffisant/-e

self-respect *n* respect *m* de soi

self-respecting *adj* ⟨*teacher, journalist, comedian*⟩ qui se respecte

self-righteous *adj* satisfait/-e de soi-même

self-rule *n* autonomie *f*

self-sacrifice *n* abnégation *f*

self-satisfied *adj* satisfait/-e de soi-même

self-service **1** *n* libre-service *m*
2 *adj* ⟨*cafeteria*⟩ en libre-service

self-sufficient *adj* autosuffisant/-e

self-taught *adj* autodidacte

sell **1** *vtr* (a) vendre; **to ~ sth to sb, to ~ sb sth** vendre qch à qn; **to ~ sth for £5** vendre qch 5 livres sterling
(b) (promote sale of) faire vendre
(c) faire accepter ⟨*idea, image, policy, party*⟩
2 *vi* (a) ⟨*person, shop, dealer*⟩ vendre (**to sb** à qn)
(b) ⟨*goods, product, house, book*⟩ se vendre
■ **sell off**: **~ [sth] off, ~ off [sth]** liquider; (in sale) solder
■ **sell out** (a) ⟨*merchandise*⟩ se vendre; **we've sold out of tickets** tous les billets ont été vendus; **we've sold out** nous avons tout vendu; **the play has sold out** la pièce affiche complet
(b) (colloq) (betray one's principles) retourner sa veste (colloq)

sell-by date *n* date *f* limite de vente

seller's market *n* marché *m* à la hausse

selling **1** *n* vente *f*
2 *adj* ⟨*price*⟩ de vente

Sellotape® **1** *n* scotch® *m*
2 sellotape *vtr* scotcher

sellout **1** *n* **the show was a ~** le spectacle affichait complet
2 *adj* ⟨*performance*⟩ à guichets fermés

semen *n* sperme *m*

semester *n* (US) semestre *m*

semiautomatic *n, adj* semi-automatique (*m*)

semibreve *n* (GB) (Mus) ronde *f*

semicircle *n* demi-cercle *m*

semicolon *n* point-virgule *m*

semiconscious *adj* à peine conscient/-e

semidarkness *n* pénombre *f*, demi-jour *m*

semi-detached (house) *n* maison *f* jumelée

semifinal *n* demi-finale *f*

semifinalist *n* demi-finaliste *mf*

seminar *n* séminaire *m* (**on** sur)

semi-skimmed *adj* ⟨*milk*⟩ demi-écrémé/-e

senate *n* sénat *m*

senator *n* sénateur *m* (**for** de)

send *vtr* (a) envoyer; **to ~ sth to sb, to ~ sb sth** envoyer qch à qn; **to ~ sb home** (from school, work) renvoyer qn chez lui/elle; **to ~ sb to prison** mettre qn en prison; **~ her my love!** embrasse-la de ma part; **~ them my regards** transmettez-leur mes amitiés
(b) **to ~ shivers down sb's spine** donner froid dans le dos à qn; **to ~ sb to sleep** endormir qn; **it sent him into fits of laughter** ça l'a fait éclater de rire
IDIOMS **to ~ sb packing** (colloq) envoyer balader qn (colloq)
■ **send away**: **¶ ~ away for [sth]** commander [qch] par correspondance; **¶ ~ [sb/sth] away** faire partir; **to ~ an appliance away to be mended** envoyer un appareil chez le fabricant pour le faire réparer
■ **send for** appeler ⟨*doctor, plumber*⟩; demander ⟨*reinforcements*⟩
■ **send in** envoyer ⟨*letter, form, troops*⟩; faire entrer ⟨*visitor*⟩; **to ~ in one's application** poser sa candidature
■ **send off**: **¶ ~ off for [sth]** commander [qch] par correspondance; **¶ ~ [sth] off** envoyer, expédier ⟨*letter*⟩; **¶ ~ [sb] off** (Sport) expulser
■ **send on** expédier [qch] à l'avance ⟨*baggage*⟩; faire suivre ⟨*letter, parcel*⟩
■ **send out** (a) émettre ⟨*light, heat*⟩
(b) faire sortir ⟨*pupil*⟩
■ **send up** (GB) (colloq) (parody) parodier

sender *n* expéditeur/-trice *m/f*

send-off *n* adieux *mpl*

send-up *n* (GB) (colloq) parodie *f*

senile *adj* sénile

senile dementia *n* démence *f* sénile

S

senior [1] n (a) (gen) aîné/-e m/f; **to be sb's ~** être plus âgé/-e que qn
(b) (GB) (Sch) élève mf dans les grandes classes; (US) (Sch) élève mf de terminale
[2] adj (a) (older) ⟨person⟩ plus âgé/-e
(b) ⟨civil servant⟩ haut/-e (before n); ⟨partner⟩ principal/-e; ⟨officer, job, post⟩ supérieur/-e

senior citizen n personne f du troisième âge

senior high school n (US Sch) ≈ lycée m

seniority n (in years) âge m; (in rank) statut m supérieur; (in years of service) ancienneté f

senior management n direction f

senior school n lycée m

sensation n sensation f; **to cause** or **create a ~** faire sensation

sensational adj sensationnel/-elle

sensationalist adj ⟨headline, story, writer⟩ à sensation

sensationalize vtr faire un reportage à sensation sur ⟨event, story⟩

sense [1] n (a) (faculty, ability) sens m; **a ~ of humour/direction** le sens de l'humour/de l'orientation; **~ of hearing** ouïe f; **~ of sight** vue f; **~ of smell** odorat m; **~ of taste** goût m; **~ of touch** toucher m; **to lose all ~ of time** perdre toute notion du temps
(b) (feeling) sens m; **a ~ of identity** un sentiment d'identité; **a ~ of purpose** le sentiment d'avoir un but
(c) (common) ~ bon sens m; **to have the ~ to do** avoir le bon sens de faire
(d) (meaning) sens m; (reason) **there's no ~ in doing** cela ne sert à rien de faire; **to make ~ of sth** comprendre qch; **I can't make ~ of this article** je ne comprends rien à cet article; **to make ~** ⟨sentence, film⟩ avoir un sens
[2] **senses** n pl **to come to one's senses** revenir à la raison
[3] vtr (a) deviner (that que); **to ~ danger** sentir un danger
(b) ⟨machine⟩ détecter
IDIOMS **to see ~** entendre raison; **to talk ~** dire des choses sensées

senseless adj (a) ⟨violence⟩ gratuit/-e; ⟨discussion⟩ absurde; ⟨act, waste⟩ insensé/-e
(b) **to knock sb ~** faire perdre connaissance à qn

sensible adj ⟨person, attitude⟩ raisonnable; ⟨decision, solution⟩ judicieux/-ieuse; ⟨garment⟩ pratique; ⟨diet⟩ intelligent/-e

sensitive adj (a) (gen) sensible (to à)
(b) ⟨person⟩ (easily hurt) sensible, susceptible (to à)
(c) ⟨situation⟩ délicat/-e; ⟨issue⟩ difficile; ⟨information⟩ confidentiel/-ielle

sensitivity n sensibilité f (to à)

sensor n détecteur m

sensual adj sensuel/-elle

sentence [1] n (a) (Law) peine f; **to serve a ~** purger une peine
(b) (in grammar) phrase f

[2] vtr condamner (**to** à; **to do** à faire; **for** pour)

sentiment n (a) (feeling) sentiment m (**for** pour; **towards** envers)
(b) (opinion) opinion f

sentimental adj sentimental/-e

sentry n sentinelle f

separate [1] adj (a) (independent, apart) ⟨piece, section⟩ à part; **she has a ~ room** elle a une chambre à part; **the flat is ~ from the rest of the house** l'appartement est indépendant du reste de la maison; **keep the knives ~** rangez les couteaux séparément; **keep the knives ~ from the forks** séparez les couteaux des fourchettes
(b) (different) ⟨sections, problems⟩ différent/-e; ⟨organizations, agreements⟩ distinct/-e; **they have ~ rooms** ils ont chacun leur chambre; **they asked for ~ bills** (in restaurant) ils ont demandé chacun leur addition
[2] vtr (a) séparer (**from** de)
(b) (sort out) répartir ⟨people⟩; trier ⟨objects, produce⟩
[3] vi se séparer (**from** de)

separately adv séparément

separates n pl (garments) coordonnés mpl

separation n séparation f (**from** de)

separatist n, adj séparatiste (mf)

September n septembre m

septic adj infecté/-e; **to go** or **turn ~** s'infecter

septic tank n fosse f septique

sequel n suite f (**to** à)

sequence n (a) (series) série f
(b) (order) ordre m; **in ~** dans l'ordre
(c) (in film) séquence f

Serbia pr n Serbie f

Serb, Serbian [1] n Serbe mf
[2] adj serbe

serene adj serein/-e

sergeant n (a) (GB) (Mil) sergent m
(b) (US) (Mil) caporal-chef m
(c) (in police) ≈ brigadier m

serial n feuilleton m; **TV ~** feuilleton télévisé

serialize vtr adapter [qch] en feuilleton

serial killer n tueur m en série

serial number n numéro m de série

series n série f; **a drama ~** une série de fiction

serious adj ⟨person, expression, discussion, offer⟩ sérieux/-ieuse; ⟨accident, crime, crisis, problem⟩ grave; ⟨literature, actor⟩ de qualité; ⟨attempt, concern⟩ réel/réelle; **to be ~ about sth** prendre qch au sérieux; **to be ~ about doing** avoir vraiment l'intention de faire

seriously adv (a) ⟨speak, think⟩ sérieusement; **to take sb/sth ~** prendre qn/qch au sérieux
(b) ⟨ill, injured⟩ gravement; ⟨underestimate⟩ vraiment

seriousness n (a) (of person, film, study) sérieux m; (of tone, occasion, reply) gravité f; **in all ~** sérieusement

(b) (of illness, problem, situation) gravité f

sermon n sermon m

serrated adj dentelé/-e; **~ knife**
couteau-scie m

serum n sérum m

servant n domestique mf

serve ⃞1 n (Sport) service m
⃞2 vtr **(a)** servir ⟨country, cause, public⟩;
travailler au service de ⟨employer, family⟩
(b) servir ⟨customer, guest, meal, dish⟩; **to ~
sb with sth** servir qch à qn
(c) (provide facility) ⟨power station, reservoir⟩
alimenter; ⟨public transport, library,
hospital⟩ desservir
(d) (satisfy) servir ⟨interests⟩; satisfaire
⟨needs⟩
(e) to ~ a purpose être utile; **to ~ the** or
sb's purpose faire l'affaire
(f) purger ⟨prison sentence⟩
(g) (Law) délivrer ⟨injunction⟩ (**on sb** à qn);
to ~ a summons on sb citer qn à
comparaître
(h) (Sport) servir
⃞3 vi **(a)** (in shop) servir; (at table) faire le
service
(b) to ~ on être membre de ⟨committee,
jury⟩
(c) to ~ as sth servir de qch
(d) (Mil) servir (**as** comme; **under** sous)
(e) (Sport) servir (**for** pour); **Bruno to ~** au
service, Bruno
IDIOMS **it ~s you right!** ça t'apprendra!

server n (Sport, Comput) serveur m

service ⃞1 n **(a)** (gen) service m; (accident
and) **emergency ~** service des urgences; **'out
of ~'** (on machine) 'en panne'
(b) (overhaul) révision f
(c) (ceremony) office m; **Sunday ~** office du
dimanche; **marriage ~** cérémonie f nuptiale
⃞2 **services** n pl **(a)** (also **~ area**) aire m
de services
(b) (Mil) **the Services** les armées f pl
⃞3 vtr faire la révision de ⟨vehicle⟩;
entretenir ⟨machine, boiler⟩; **to have one's
car ~d** faire réviser sa voiture

service centre (GB), **service
center** (US) n centre m de service
après-vente

service charge n **(a)** (in restaurant)
service m; **what is the ~?** le service est de
combien?
(b) (in banking) frais mpl de gestion de
compte

service engineer n technicien m de
maintenance

serviceman n militaire m

service provider n fournisseur m
d'accès

service station n station-service f

servicewoman n femme f soldat

serving n portion f

serving dish n plat m (de service)

serving spoon n cuillère f de service

session n **(a)** (gen) séance f
(b) (of parliament) session f

(c) (US) (Sch) (term) trimestre m; (period of
lessons) cours mpl

set ⃞1 n **(a)** (of keys, tools) jeu m; (of golf clubs,
chairs) série f; (of cutlery) service m; (of rules,
instructions, tests) série f; **a new ~ of clothes**
des vêtements neufs; **they're sold in ~s of
10** ils sont vendus par lots de 10; **a ~ of
fingerprints** des empreintes digitales; **a ~ of
traffic lights** des feux mpl (de signalisation);
a chess ~ un jeu d'échecs; **a ~ of false
teeth** un dentier
(b) (Sport) (in tennis) set m
(c) TV or **television ~** poste m de télévision
(d) (scenery) (for play) décor m; (for film) plateau
m
(e) (GB) (Sch) groupe m
(f) (hair-do) mise f en plis
⃞2 adj **(a)** ⟨pattern, procedure, rule, task⟩
bien déterminé/-e; ⟨time, price⟩ fixe; ⟨menu⟩
à prix fixe; **~ phrase** expression f consacrée;
to be ~ in one's ways avoir ses habitudes
(b) ⟨expression, smile⟩ figé/-e
(c) (Sch, Univ) ⟨text⟩ au programme
(d) (ready) prêt/-e (**for** pour; **to do** à faire)
(e) to be (dead) ~ against sth/doing être
tout à fait contre qch/l'idée de faire; **to be ~
on doing** tenir absolument à faire
(f) ⟨jam, jelly, honey⟩ épais/épaisse; ⟨cement⟩
dur/-e; ⟨yoghurt⟩ ferme
⃞3 vtr **(a)** (place) placer ⟨object⟩ (**on** sur);
monter ⟨gem⟩ (**in** dans); **a house ~ among
the trees** une maison située au milieu des
arbres; **to ~ the record straight** mettre les
choses au point; **his eyes are ~ very close
together** ses yeux sont très rapprochés
(b) mettre ⟨table⟩; tendre ⟨trap⟩
(c) fixer ⟨date, deadline, price, target⟩; lancer
⟨fashion, trend⟩; donner ⟨tone⟩; établir
⟨precedent, record⟩; **to ~ a good/bad
example to sb** montrer le bon/mauvais
exemple à qn; **to ~ one's sights on** viser
(d) mettre [qch] à l'heure ⟨clock⟩; mettre
⟨alarm clock, burglar alarm⟩
(e) (start) **to ~ sth going** mettre qch en
marche ⟨machine⟩; **to ~ sb laughing/
thinking** faire rire/réfléchir qn
(f) donner ⟨homework, essay⟩; **to ~ an exam**
préparer les sujets d'examen
(g) (in fiction, film) situer; **the film is ~ in
Munich** le film se passe à Munich
(h) to ~ sth to music mettre qch en
musique
(i) (Med) immobiliser ⟨broken bone⟩
(j) to have one's hair ~ se faire faire une
mise en plis
⃞4 vi **(a)** ⟨sun⟩ se coucher
(b) ⟨jam, concrete⟩ prendre; ⟨glue⟩ sécher
(c) (Med) ⟨fracture⟩ se ressouder
■ **set about** se mettre à ⟨work⟩; **to ~ about
(the job** or **task of) doing** commencer à faire
■ **set apart** distinguer (**from** de)
■ **set aside** réserver ⟨area, room, time⟩ (**for**
pour); mettre [qch] de côté ⟨money, stock⟩
■ **set back**: ¶ **~ back [sth]**, **~ [sth] back**
(delay) retarder; ¶ **~ [sb] back** (colloq) coûter
les yeux de la tête à ⟨colloq⟩ ····⋗

S

■ **set down**: ~ **down [sth]**, ~ **[sth] down (a)**
(establish) fixer ⟨conditions⟩
(b) (record) enregistrer ⟨fact⟩

■ **set in** ⟨infection⟩ se déclarer; ⟨depression⟩
s'installer

■ **set off**: ¶ ~ **off** partir (for pour); **to** ~ **off
on a journey** partir en voyage
¶ ~ **[sth] off (a)** faire partir ⟨firework⟩; faire
exploser ⟨bomb⟩; déclencher ⟨riot, panic,
alarm⟩
(b) (enhance) mettre [qch] en valeur
⟨garment⟩
(c) to ~ **sth off against profits/debts** déduire
qch des bénéfices/des dettes; ¶ ~ **[sb] off**
faire pleurer ⟨baby⟩; **she laughed and that** ~
me off elle a ri et ça m'a fait rire à mon tour

■ **set on**: ¶ ~ **on [sb]** attaquer qn; ¶ ~ **[sth]
on sb** lâcher [qch] contre qn ⟨dog⟩

■ **set out**: ¶ ~ **out** se mettre en route (for
pour; **to do** pour faire); **to** ~ **out to do**
⟨person⟩ entreprendre de faire
¶ ~ **[sth] out (a)** disposer ⟨goods, chairs,
food⟩; préparer ⟨board game⟩
(b) présenter ⟨ideas, proposals⟩; formuler
⟨objections, terms⟩

■ **set up**: ¶ **to** ~ **up on one's own** s'établir à
son compte; **to** ~ **up in business** monter une
affaire
¶ ~ **[sth] up (a)** monter ⟨stand, stall⟩;
assembler ⟨equipment, easel⟩; ériger
⟨roadblock⟩; **to** ~ **up home** s'installer
(b) préparer ⟨experiment⟩; (Sport) préparer
⟨goal, try⟩
(c) créer ⟨business, company⟩; implanter
⟨factory⟩; former ⟨support group, charity⟩;
constituer ⟨committee⟩
(d) organiser ⟨meeting⟩; mettre [qch] en
place ⟨procedures⟩; ¶ ~ **[sb] up (a) she** ~ **her
son up (in business)** elle a aidé son fils à s'installer comme jardinier
(b) that deal has ~ **her up for life** grâce à ce
contrat elle n'aura plus à se soucier de rien
(c) (GB) (colloq) ⟨police⟩ tendre un piège à
⟨criminal⟩; ⟨friend⟩ monter un coup contre
⟨person⟩

setback n revers m (for pour)

settee n canapé m

setting n **(a)** (location) cadre m
(b) (in jewellery) monture f
(c) (position on dial) position f (de réglage)

setting-up n (of scheme, business) création f;
(of factory) implantation f

settle 1 vtr **(a)** installer ⟨person, animal⟩
(b) calmer ⟨stomach, nerves⟩
(c) régler ⟨matter, business, dispute⟩; mettre
fin à ⟨conflict, strike⟩; régler, résoudre
⟨problem⟩; décider ⟨match⟩; **that's** ~d voilà
qui est réglé
(d) fixer ⟨arrangements, price⟩
(e) to ~ **one's affairs** mettre de l'ordre dans
ses affaires
(f) régler ⟨bill, debt, claim⟩
2 vi **(a)** ⟨dust⟩ se déposer; ⟨bird, insect⟩ se
poser
(b) (in new home) s'installer
(c) ⟨contents, ground⟩ se tasser

(d) ⟨weather⟩ se mettre au beau fixe
(e) (Law) régler; **to** ~ **out of court** parvenir à
un règlement à l'amiable

■ **settle down (a)** (get comfortable) s'installer
(on sur; in dans)
(b) (calm down) ⟨person⟩ se calmer
(c) (marry) se ranger

■ **settle for**: ~ **for sth** se contenter de qch

■ **settle in (a)** (move in) s'installer
(b) (become acclimatized) s'adapter

■ **settle up** (pay) payer

settlement n **(a)** (agreement) accord m
(b) (Law) règlement m
(c) (dwellings) village m; (colonial) territoire m

set-top box n décodeur m

seven n, pron, det sept (m) inv

seventeen n, pron, det dix-sept (m) inv

seventeenth 1 n **(a)** (in order)
dix-septième mf
(b) (of month) dix-sept m inv
(c) (fraction) dix-septième m
2 adj, adv dix-septième

seventh 1 n **(a)** (in order) septième mf
(b) (of month) sept m inv
(c) (fraction) septième m
2 adj, adv septième

seventies n pl **(a)** (era) the ~ les années
fpl soixante-dix
(b) (age) **to be in one's** ~ avoir plus de
soixante-dix ans

seventieth n, adj, adv soixante-dixième
(mf)

seventy n, pron, det soixante-dix (m) inv

sever vtr **(a)** sectionner ⟨limb, artery⟩;
couper ⟨rope, branch⟩
(b) rompre ⟨link, relations⟩; couper
⟨communications⟩

several 1 quantif ~ **of you/us** plusieurs
d'entre vous/d'entre nous
2 det plusieurs; ~ **books** plusieurs livres

severe adj **(a)** ⟨problem, damage, shortage,
injury, depression, shock⟩ grave; ⟨weather,
cold, winter⟩ rigoureux/-euse
(b) (harsh) sévère (with sb avec qn)
(c) ⟨haircut, clothes⟩ austère

severely adv ⟨damage⟩ sévèrement; ⟨affect,
shock⟩ durement; ⟨disabled⟩ gravement;
⟨injured⟩ grièvement; ⟨beat⟩ violemment

severity n (of problem, illness) gravité f; (of
punishment, treatment) sévérité f; (of climate)
rigueur f

sew 1 vtr coudre
2 vi coudre, faire de la couture

■ **sew up** recoudre ⟨hole, tear⟩; faire ⟨seam⟩;
(re)coudre ⟨wound⟩

sewage n eaux fpl usées

sewer n égout m

sewing n (activity) couture f; (piece of work)
ouvrage m

sewing machine n machine f à coudre

sex 1 n **(a)** (gender) sexe m; **the opposite** ~
le sexe opposé
(b) (intercourse) (one act) rapport m sexuel;
(repeated) rapports mpl sexuels

2 *adj* sexuel/-elle

sex change n to have a ~ changer de sexe

sex discrimination n discrimination f sexuelle

sex education n éducation f sexuelle

sexism n sexisme m

sexist n, adj sexiste (mf)

sex object n objet m érotique

sex offender n délinquant/-e m/f sexuel/-elle

sexual adj sexuel/-elle

sexual abuse n violence f sexuelle

sexual harassment n harcèlement m sexuel

sexuality n sexualité f

sexually transmitted disease, STD n maladie f sexuellement transmissible, MST f

sexy adj (colloq) ⟨person, clothing⟩ sexy inv (colloq); ⟨book⟩ érotique

shabby adj ⟨person⟩ habillé/-e de façon miteuse; ⟨room, furnishings, clothing⟩ miteux/-euse; ⟨treatment⟩ mesquin/-e

shack n cabane f

shade **1** n (a) (shadow) ombre f; **in the** ~ à l'ombre (**of** de)
(b) (of colour) ton m
(c) (also **lamp** ~) abat-jour m inv
(d) (US) (also **window** ~) store m
2 vtr donner de l'ombre à; **to** ~ **one's eyes** (with one's hand) s'abriter les yeux de la main
IDIOMS **to put sb in the** ~ éclipser qn; **to put sth in the** ~ surpasser or surclasser qch

shadow **1** n ombre f; **to have** ~**s under one's eyes** avoir les yeux cernés
2 vtr filer ⟨person⟩

shadow cabinet n (GB) cabinet m fantôme

shadowy adj (dark) sombre; (indistinct) ⟨outline⟩ flou/-e; ⟨form⟩ indistinct/-e

shady adj (a) ⟨place⟩ ombragé/-e
(b) ⟨deal, businessman⟩ véreux/-euse

shaft n (a) (of tool) manche m; (of arrow) tige f; (in machine) axe m
(b) (passage, vent) puits m
(c) ~ **of light** rai m; ~ **of lightning** éclair m

shaggy adj ⟨hair, beard, eyebrows⟩ en broussailles; ⟨animal⟩ poilu/-e

shake **1** n (a) **to give sb/sth a** ~ secouer qn/qch
(b) (also **milk-**~) milk-shake m
2 vtr (a) (gen) secouer; **to** ~ **one's head** (in dismay) hocher la tête; (to say no) faire non de la tête; **to** ~ **hands with sb, to** ~ **sb's hand** serrer la main de qn, donner une poignée de main à qn
(b) ébranler ⟨confidence, faith, resolve⟩; ⟨event, disaster⟩ secouer ⟨person⟩
3 vi (a) trembler; **to** ~ **with** trembler de ⟨fear, cold, emotion⟩; se tordre de ⟨laughter⟩
(b) (shake hands) **'let's** ~ **on it!' '**serrons-nous la main!'

■ **shake off** se débarrasser de ⟨cold, depression, habit, person⟩; se défaire de ⟨feeling⟩

■ **shake up** (a) agiter ⟨bottle, mixture⟩
(b) ⟨experience, news⟩ secouer ⟨person⟩

shaken adj (shocked) choqué/-e

shake-up n réorganisation f; (Pol) remaniement m

shaky adj (a) ⟨chair, ladder⟩ branlant/-e; **I feel a bit** ~ je me sens un peu flageolant
(b) ⟨relationship, position⟩ instable; ⟨evidence, argument⟩ peu solide; ⟨knowledge, memory⟩ peu sûr/-e; ⟨regime⟩ chancelant/-e; **my French is a bit** ~ mon français est un peu hésitant

shall modal aux (a) (in future tense) **I** ~ or **I'll see you tomorrow** je vous verrai demain; **we** ~ **not** or **shan't have a reply before Friday** nous n'aurons pas de réponse avant vendredi
(b) (in suggestions) ~ **I set the table?** est-ce que je mets la table?; ~ **we go to the cinema tonight?** et si on allait au cinéma ce soir?; **let's buy some peaches,** ~ **we?** et si on achetait des pêches?

shallot n (a) (GB) échalote f
(b) (US) cive f

shallow adj ⟨container, water, grave⟩ peu profond/-e; ⟨breathing, character, response⟩ superficiel/-ielle

shallows n pl bas-fonds mpl

sham **1** n (a) (person) imposteur m
(b) **it's (all) a** ~ c'est de la comédie
2 adj ⟨event⟩ prétendu/-e (before n); ⟨object, building, idea⟩ factice; ⟨activity, emotion⟩ feint/-e
3 vi faire semblant

shambles n (colloq) pagaille f (colloq)

shame **1** n (a) (gen) honte f
(b) **it's a (real) shame** c'est (vraiment) dommage; **it was a** ~ **(that) she lost** c'est dommage qu'elle ait perdu
2 vtr (a) (embarrass) faire honte à
(b) (disgrace) déshonorer (**by doing** en faisant)

shameful adj honteux/-euse

shameless adj ⟨person⟩ éhonté/-e; ⟨attitude⟩ effronté/-e; ⟨negligence⟩ scandaleux/-euse

shampoo **1** n shampooing m
2 vtr faire shampooing à; **to** ~ **one's hair** se faire un shampooing

shamrock n trèfle m

shandy, shandygaff (US) n panaché m

shantytown n bidonville m

shape **1** n forme f; **a square** ~ une forme carrée; **what** ~ **is the room?** quelle forme a la pièce?; **to take** ~ prendre forme; **to be in/ out of** ~ ⟨person⟩ être/ne pas être en forme; **to get in** ~ se mettre en forme; **to knock sth into** ~ mettre qch au point ⟨project, idea, essay⟩
2 vtr (a) modeler ⟨clay⟩; sculpter ⟨wood⟩
(b) ⟨person, event⟩ déterminer ⟨future, idea⟩; modeler ⟨character⟩ ⋯▸

S

■ **shape up (a)** (develop) ⟨person⟩ s'en sortir **(b)** (meet expectations) être à la hauteur

-shaped *combining form* star-/V-~ en forme d'étoile/de V

shapeless *adj* sans forme, informe

shapely *adj* ⟨woman⟩ bien fait/-e; ⟨ankle⟩ fin/-e; ⟨leg⟩ bien galbé/-e

share 1 *n* **(a)** part *f* (of de); **to pay one's (fair)** ~ payer sa part
(b) (in stock market) action *f*
2 *vtr* partager **(with** avec**); we ~ an interest in animals** nous aimons tous les deux les animaux
3 *vi* **to ~ in** prendre part à

■ **share out** (amongst selves) partager ⟨food⟩; (amongst others) répartir ⟨food⟩ **(among, between** entre**)**

shared *adj* ⟨house, interest⟩ partagé/-e; ⟨facilities⟩ commun/-e

shareholder *n* actionnaire *mf*

share option scheme *n* plan *m* de participation par achat d'actions

shareware *n* shareware *m*, logiciel *m* contributif

shark *n* requin *m*

sharp 1 *adj* **(a)** ⟨razor⟩ tranchant/-e; ⟨edge⟩ coupant/-e; ⟨blade, scissors, knife⟩ bien aiguisé/-e
(b) ⟨tooth, fingernail, end, needle⟩ pointu/-e; ⟨pencil⟩ bien taillé/-e; ⟨features⟩ anguleux/-euse
(c) ⟨angle⟩ aigu/aiguë; ⟨bend⟩ brusque; ⟨drop, incline⟩ fort/-e; ⟨fall, rise⟩ brusque, brutal/-e
(d) ⟨taste, smell⟩ âcre; ⟨fruit⟩ acide
(e) ⟨pain, cold⟩ vif/vive; ⟨cry⟩ aigu/aiguë; ⟨blow⟩ sévère; ⟨frost⟩ intense
(f) ⟨tongue⟩ acéré/-e; ⟨tone⟩ acerbe
(g) ⟨person, mind⟩ vif/vive; ⟨eyesight⟩ perçant/-e
(h) ⟨businessman⟩ malin/-igne; ~ **operator** filou *m*
(i) ⟨image⟩ net/nette; ⟨contrast⟩ prononcé/-e
(j) (Mus) ⟨note⟩ dièse *inv*; (too high) aigu/aiguë
2 *adv* **(a)** ⟨stop⟩ net; **to turn** ~ **left** tourner brusquement vers la gauche
(b) (colloq) **at 9 o'clock** ~ à neuf heures pile (colloq)
(c) (Mus) ⟨sing, play⟩ trop haut

sharpen *vtr* aiguiser, affûter ⟨blade, scissors⟩; tailler ⟨pencil⟩

sharpener *n* taille-crayon *m*

sharply *adv* **(a)** ⟨turn, rise, fall⟩ brusquement, brutalement
(b) ⟨speak⟩ d'un ton brusque

shatter 1 *vtr* fracasser ⟨window, glass⟩; rompre ⟨peace, silence⟩; briser ⟨hope⟩; démolir ⟨nerves⟩
2 *vi* ⟨window, glass⟩ voler en éclats

shattered *adj* **(a)** ⟨dream⟩ brisé/-e; ⟨life, confidence⟩ anéanti/-e
(b) ⟨person⟩ (devastated) effondré/-e; (tired) (colloq) crevé/-e (colloq), épuisé/-e

shave 1 *n* **to have a** ~ se raser

2 *vtr* ⟨barber⟩ raser ⟨person⟩; **to ~ one's beard off** se raser la barbe; **to ~ one's legs** se raser les jambes
3 *vi* se raser

IDIOMS **that was a close** ~! je l'ai/il l'a etc échappé belle!

shaver *n* (also **electric** ~) rasoir *m* électrique

shaving 1 *n* **(a)** (action) rasage *m*
(b) ~**s** (of wood, metal) copeaux *mpl*
2 *adj* ⟨cream, foam⟩ à raser

shaving brush *n* blaireau *m*

shaving mirror *n* petit miroir *m*

shawl *n* châle *m*

she *pron* elle; ~**'s not at home** elle n'est pas chez elle; **here** ~ **is** la voici; **there** ~ **is** la voilà; ~**'s a beautiful woman** c'est une belle femme

sheaf *n* (of corn, flowers) gerbe *f*; (of papers) liasse *f*

shear *vtr* tondre ⟨grass, sheep⟩

shears *n pl* **(a)** (for garden) cisaille *f*
(b) (for sheep) tondeuse *f*

shed 1 *n* (in garden) remise *f*, abri *m*; (at factory site, port) hangar *m*
2 *vtr* **(a)** verser ⟨tears⟩; perdre ⟨leaves, weight, antlers⟩; ⟨lorry⟩ déverser ⟨load⟩; verser ⟨blood⟩; **to ~ skin** muer
(b) répandre ⟨light, happiness⟩

sheep *n* mouton *m*; (ewe) brebis *f*; **black** ~ brebis *f* galeuse

sheep dog *n* chien *m* de berger

sheepish *adj* penaud/-e

sheepskin *n* peau *f* de mouton

sheer *adj* **(a)** ⟨boredom, hypocrisy, stupidity⟩ pur/-e (before *n*)
(b) ⟨cliff⟩ à pic
(c) ⟨fabric⟩ léger/-ère, fin/-e; ⟨stockings⟩ extra-fin/-e

sheet *n* **(a)** (of paper, stamps) feuille *f*; (of metal, glass) plaque *f*
(b) (for bed) drap *m*; **dust** ~ housse *f*
(c) **fact** ~ bulletin *m* d'informations
(d) (of ice) couche *f*; (of flame) rideau *m*

sheet lightning *n* éclair *m* en nappe

sheet metal *n* tôle *f*

sheik *n* cheik *m*

shelf *n* **(a)** étagère *f*; (in oven) plaque *f*; (in shop, fridge) rayon *m*; **(a set of) shelves** une étagère
(b) (in rock, ice) corniche *f*

shelf-life *n* (of product) durée *f* de conservation; (of technology, pop music) durée *f* de vie

shell 1 *n* **(a)** (of egg, nut, snail) coquille *f*; (of crab, tortoise, shrimp) carapace *f*; **sea** ~ coquillage *m*; **to come out of one's** ~ sortir de sa coquille
(b) (bomb) obus *m*; (cartridge) cartouche *f*
(c) (of building) carcasse *f*
2 *vtr* **(a)** (Mil) pilonner ⟨town, installation⟩
(b) (Culin) écosser ⟨peas⟩; décortiquer ⟨prawn, nut⟩

■ **shell out** (colloq): ~ **out** [sth] débourser ⟨*sum*⟩ (**for** pour)

shellfish *n pl* (a) (Zool) crùstacés *mpl*; (mussels, oysters) coquillages *mpl*
(b) (Culin) fruits *mpl* de mer

shelter ⟦1⟧ *n* (a) (change) abri *m*; **to take** ~ **from** s'abriter de ⟨*weather*⟩
(b) (for homeless) refuge *m* (**for** pour); (for refugees) asile *m*
⟦2⟧ *vtr* (a) (against weather) abriter (**from**, **against** de); (from truth) protéger (**from** de)
(b) donner refuge *or* asile à ⟨*refugee*, *criminal*⟩
⟦3⟧ *vi* se mettre à l'abri; **to** ~ **from the storm** s'abriter de l'orage

sheltered accommodation *n* foyer-résidence *m*

shelving *n* (at home) étagères *fpl*; (in shop) rayons *mpl*

shepherd *n* berger *m*

shepherd's pie *n* hachis *m* Parmentier

sheriff *n* shérif *m*

sherry *n* xérès *m*, sherry *m*

shield ⟦1⟧ *n* (a) (Mil) bouclier *m*
(b) (on machine) écran *m* de protection; (around gun) pare-balles *m inv*
(c) (US) (policeman's badge) insigne *m*
⟦2⟧ *vtr* protéger; **to** ~ **one's eyes** se protéger les yeux

shift ⟦1⟧ *n* (a) (change) changement *m* (**in** de), modification *f* (**in** de)
(b) (at work) période *f* de travail; (group of workers) équipe *f*; **to work an eight-hour** ~ faire les trois-huit
⟦2⟧ *vtr* (a) déplacer ⟨*furniture*, *vehicle*⟩; bouger, remuer ⟨*arm*⟩; changer ⟨*theatre scenery*⟩
(b) faire partir, enlever ⟨*stain*, *dirt*⟩
(c) rejeter ⟨*blame*, *responsibility*⟩ (**onto** sur); **to** ~ **attention away from a problem** détourner l'attention d'un problème
(d) (US Aut) **to** ~ **gear** changer de vitesse
⟦3⟧ *vi* (*also* ~ **about**) ⟨*load*⟩ bouger; **to** ~ **from one foot to the other** se dandiner d'un pied sur l'autre

shift key *n* touche *f* de majuscule

shiftless *adj* paresseux/-euse, apathique

shift work *n* travail *m* posté

shifty *adj* louche, sournois/-e

shimmer *vi* (a) ⟨*jewels*, *water*⟩ scintiller; ⟨*silk*⟩ chatoyer
(b) (in heat) ⟨*landscape*⟩ vibrer

shin, shinbone *n* tibia *m*

shine ⟦1⟧ *n* lustre *m*
⟦2⟧ *vtr* (a) braquer ⟨*headlights*, *spotlight*, *torch*⟩ (**on** sur)
(b) faire reluire ⟨*silver*⟩; cirer ⟨*shoes*⟩
⟦3⟧ *vi* (a) ⟨*hair*, *light*, *sun*⟩ briller; ⟨*brass*, *floor*⟩ reluire; **the light is shining in my eyes** j'ai la lumière dans les yeux
(b) ⟨*eyes*⟩ briller (**with** de); ⟨*face*⟩ rayonner (**with** de)
(c) (excel) briller; **to** ~ **at** être brillant/-e en ⟨*science*, *languages*⟩

IDIOMS to take a ~ **to sb** (colloq) s'enticher de qn (colloq)

■ **shine through** ⟨*talent*⟩ éclater au grand jour

shingle ⟦1⟧ *n* (a) (on beach) galets *mpl*
(b) (on roof) bardeau *m*
⟦2⟧ **shingles** *n pl* (Med) zona *m*

shining *adj* (a) ⟨*hair*, *metal*, *eyes*⟩ brillant/-e
(b) ⟨*face*⟩ radieux/-ieuse
(c) ⟨*example*⟩ parfait/-e (*before n*)

shiny *adj* (a) ⟨*metal*, *surface*, *hair*⟩ brillant/-e
(b) ⟨*shoes*, *wood*⟩ bien ciré/-e

ship ⟦1⟧ *n* navire *m*; (smaller) bateau *m*; **passenger** ~ paquebot *m*
⟦2⟧ *vtr* transporter [qch] par mer

shipment *n* cargaison *f*

ship owner *n* armateur *m*

shipping *n* navigation *f*, trafic *m* maritime

shipping company *n* compagnie *f* maritime

shipwreck ⟦1⟧ *n* (event) naufrage *m*; (ship) épave *f*
⟦2⟧ *vtr* **to be** ~**ed** faire naufrage; **a** ~**ed sailor** un marin naufragé

shipyard *n* chantier *m* naval

shirk *vtr* esquiver ⟨*task*, *duty*⟩; fuir ⟨*responsibility*⟩

shirt *n* (man's) chemise *f*; (woman's) chemisier *m*; (for sport) maillot *m*

shirt-sleeve *n* manche *f* de chemise; **in one's** ~**s** en manches de chemise

shirty *adj* (GB) (colloq) **to get** ~ prendre la mouche (colloq)

shit *excl* (slang) merde! (slang)

shiver ⟦1⟧ *n* frisson *m*; **to give sb the** ~**s** donner froid dans le dos à qn
⟦2⟧ *vi* (with cold) grelotter (**with** de); (with fear) frémir (**with** de); (with disgust) frissonner (**with** de)

shoal *n* (of fish) banc *m*

shock ⟦1⟧ *n* (a) choc *m*; **to get** *or* **have a** ~ avoir un choc; **to give sb a** ~ faire un choc à qn; **to be in** ~ être en état de choc
(b) (electrical) décharge *f*; **to get a** ~ prendre une décharge
(c) (of collision) choc *m*; (of explosion) souffle *m*
(d) **a** ~ **of red hair** une tignasse rousse
⟦2⟧ *vtr* (distress) consterner; (scandalize) choquer

shock absorber *n* amortisseur *m*

shocking *adj* ⟨*sight*⟩ consternant/-e; ⟨*news*⟩ choquant/-e

shock wave *n* remous *mpl*; **to send** ~**s through the stock market** provoquer des remous à la Bourse

shoddy *adj* ⟨*product*⟩ de mauvaise qualité; ⟨*work*⟩ mal fait/-e

shoe ⟦1⟧ *n* chaussure *f*; (for horse) fer *m*
⟦2⟧ *vtr* ferrer ⟨*horse*⟩

shoelace *n* lacet *m* de chaussure

shoe polish *n* cirage *m*

S

shoe shop n magasin m de chaussures

shoe size n pointure f

shoestring n (US) lacet m de chaussure
IDIOMS **on a ~** (colloq) avec peu de moyens

shoo vtr (also **~ away**) chasser

shoot [1] n (Bot) pousse f
[2] vtr (a) tirer ‹bullet, arrow› (**at** sur); lancer ‹missile› (**at** sur)
(b) tirer sur ‹person, animal›; (kill) abattre ‹person, animal›; **she shot him in the leg** elle lui a tiré dans la jambe; **to ~ sb dead** abattre qn; **to ~ oneself** se tirer une balle
(c) **to ~ questions at sb** bombarder qn de questions
(d) (film) tourner ‹film, scene›; prendre [qch] (en photo) ‹subject›
(e) mettre ‹bolt›
(f) **to ~ the rapids** franchir les rapides
(g) (US) jouer à ‹pool›
[3] vi (a) tirer (**at** sur)
(b) **to ~ forward** s'élancer à toute vitesse; **the car shot past** la voiture est passée en trombe
(c) (Sport) tirer, shooter
■ **shoot down** abattre, descendre (colloq) ‹plane, pilot›
■ **shoot up**: ¶ ‹flames, spray› jaillir; ‹prices, profits› monter en flèche; ¶ **~ up [sth]**, **~ [sth] up** (inject) (colloq) se shooter à (colloq) ‹heroin›

shooting [1] n (a) (killing) meurtre m (par arme à feu)
(b) (shots) coups mpl de feu, fusillade f
[2] adj ‹pain› lancinant/-e

shooting range n stand m de tir

shooting star n étoile f filante

shoot-out n (colloq) fusillade f

shop [1] n (a) magasin m; (small, fashionable) boutique f; **to go to the ~s** aller faire les courses
(b) (US) (in department store) rayon m
(c) (workshop) atelier m
[2] vi **to go ~ping** aller faire des courses; (browse) aller faire les magasins
IDIOMS **to talk ~** parler boutique
■ **shop around** (compare prices) faire le tour des magasins (**for** pour trouver); (compare courses, services etc) bien chercher

shopaholic n (colloq) accro mf (colloq) du shopping

shop assistant n (GB) vendeur/-euse m/f

shopkeeper n commerçant/-e m/f

shoplifter n voleur/-euse m/f à l'étalage

shoplifting n vol m à l'étalage

shopping n courses fpl

shopping bag n sac m à provisions

shopping centre (GB), **shopping mall** (US) n centre m commercial

shopping trolley n caddie® m

shop-soiled adj ‹garment› sali/-e

shop steward n représentant/-e m/f syndical/-e

shop window n vitrine f

shore n (of sea) côte f, rivage m; (of lake) rive f; **on ~** à terre

short [1] n (a) (drink) alcool m fort
(b) (film) court métrage m
[2] **shorts** n pl short m; (underwear) caleçon m
[3] adj (a) ‹stay, memory, period› court/-e (before n); ‹course› de courte durée; ‹conversation, speech, chapter› bref/brève (before n); **the days are getting ~er** les jours diminuent or raccourcissent
(b) ‹hair, dress, distance, stick› court/-e (before n)
(c) ‹person› petit/-e (before n)
(d) **to be in ~ supply** être difficile à trouver; **time is getting ~** le temps presse
(e) (lacking) **he is ~ of sth** il lui manque qch; **to be ~ on** ‹person› manquer de ‹talent, tact›; **to run ~ of** manquer de ‹clothes, money, food›
(f) **Tom is ~ for Thomas** Tom est le diminutif de Thomas
(g) (abrupt) **to be ~ with sb** être brusque avec qn
(h) ‹pastry› brisé/-e
[4] adv ‹stop› net; **to stop ~ of doing** se retenir pour ne pas faire
[5] **in short** phr bref
[6] **short of** phr **~ of doing** à moins de faire
IDIOMS **to sell oneself ~** se sous-estimer; **to make ~ work of sth/sb** expédier qch/qn

shortage n pénurie f, manque m (**of** de)

shortbread, **shortcake** n sablé m

short-change vtr ne pas rendre toute sa monnaie à

short circuit [1] n court-circuit m
[2] **short-circuit** vtr court-circuiter
[3] **short-circuit** vi faire court-circuit

shortcomings n pl points mpl faibles

shortcut n raccourci m

shorten [1] vtr abréger ‹visit, life›; raccourcir ‹garment, talk›; réduire ‹time, list›
[2] vi ‹days› diminuer

shortfall n (in budget, accounts) déficit m; (in earnings, exports) manque m

shorthand n sténographie f, sténo f (colloq)

shorthand-typist n sténo-dactylo f

shortlist [1] n liste f des candidats sélectionnés
[2] vtr sélectionner ‹applicant› (**for** pour)

short-lived adj **to be ~** ne pas durer longtemps

shortly adv (a) ‹return› bientôt; ‹be published› prochainement
(b) **~ after(wards)/before** peu (de temps) après/avant
(c) (crossly) sèchement

shortsighted adj (a) myope
(b) (figurative) ‹person› peu clairvoyant/-e; ‹policy, decision› à courte vue

short-sleeved adj à manches courtes

short-staffed *adj* to be ~ manquer de personnel

short story *n* nouvelle *f*

short term ⓵ *n* in the ~ dans l'immédiat
⓶ **short-term** *adj* à court terme

shortwave *n* ondes *fpl* courtes

shot ⓵ *n* (a) (from gun) coup *m* (de feu)
(b) (Sport) (in tennis, golf, cricket) coup *m*; (in football) tir *m*
(c) (snapshot) photo *f* (of de)
(d) (in film-making) plan *m* (of de); action ~ scène *f* d'action
(e) (injection) piqûre *f* (of de)
(f) to have a ~ at doing essayer de faire
(g) (person) a good ~ un bon tireur
⓶ *adj* ⟨silk⟩ changeant/-e

shotgun *n* fusil *m*

shot put *n* (Sport) lancer *m* de poids

should *modal aux* (a) ~ I call the doctor? est-ce que je devrais faire venir le médecin?; why shouldn't I do it? pourquoi est-ce que je ne le ferais pas?; she ~ learn to drive elle devrait apprendre à conduire; shouldn't you be at school? tu ne devrais pas être à l'école?
(b) it shouldn't be difficult ça ne devrait pas être difficile; she ~ have been here hours ago elle devrait être ici déjà arriver il y a plusieurs heures déjà; it shouldn't have cost so much ça n'aurait pas dû coûter si cher
(c) I ~ think she's about 40 à mon avis, elle doit avoir à peu près 40 ans; I shouldn't be surprised cela ne m'étonnerait pas
(d) ~ you require any further information, please contact… si vous souhaitez plus de renseignements, adressez-vous à…
(e) I ~ think so! je l'espère!; I ~ think not! j'espère bien que non!; how ~ I know? comment veux-tu que je le sache?; flowers? you shouldn't have! des fleurs? il ne fallait pas!

shoulder ⓵ *n* épaule *f*
⓶ *vtr* se charger de ⟨burden, expense, task⟩; endosser ⟨responsibility⟩
IDIOMS to rub ~s with sb côtoyer qn

shoulder blade *n* omoplate *f*

shoulder-length *adj* ⟨hair⟩ mi-long/-ue

shoulder pad *n* épaulette *f*

shout ⓵ *n* cri *m* (of de)
⓶ *vtr* crier; (stronger) hurler
⓷ *vi* crier; to ~ at sb crier après qn; he was ~ing to me il me criait quelque chose
■ **shout out** pousser un cri

shouting *n* cris *mpl*

shove (colloq) ⓵ *n* to give sb/sth a ~ pousser qn/qch
⓶ *vtr* (a) (push) pousser (against contre); to ~ sth into sth fourrer qch dans qch
(b) (jostle) bousculer ⟨person⟩
⓷ *vi* pousser
■ **shove up** (colloq) se pousser

shovel ⓵ *n* pelle *f*
⓶ *vtr* enlever [qch] à la pelle ⟨leaves, snow⟩ (off de)

show ⓵ *n* (a) spectacle *m*; (in cinema) séance *f*; (on radio, TV) émission *f*; (of slides) projection *f*
(b) (exhibition) exposition *f*; (of cars, boats) salon *m*; (of fashion) défilé *m*; flower/dog ~ exposition florale/canine
(c) (of feelings) semblant *m* (of de); (of strength) démonstration *f* (of de); (of wealth) étalage *m* (of de); he made a ~ of concern il a affiché sa sollicitude; to be just for ~ être de l'esbroufe (colloq)
⓶ *vtr* (a) montrer ⟨person, object, photo, feelings⟩ (to à); présenter ⟨ticket⟩ (to à); ⟨TV channel, cinema⟩ passer ⟨film⟩; ⟨garment⟩ laisser voir ⟨underclothes, stain⟩; indiquer ⟨time, direction⟩; to ~ sb sth montrer qch à qn; that carpet ~s the dirt cette moquette est salissante
(b) (exhibit) présenter ⟨animal⟩; exposer ⟨flower, vegetables⟩
(c) (prove) démontrer ⟨truth, guilt⟩
(d) to ~ sb to their seat placer qn; to ~ sb to their room accompagner qn à sa chambre; to ~ sb to the door reconduire qn
⓷ *vi* (a) ⟨stain, label⟩ se voir; ⟨emotion⟩ se voir; (in eyes) se lire
(b) ⟨film⟩ passer
IDIOMS to have nothing to ~ for sth ne rien avoir tiré de qch
■ **show in**: ¶ ~ [sb] in faire entrer
■ **show off**: ¶ ~ off (colloq) faire le fier/la fière; ¶ ~ [sb/sth] off faire admirer ⟨skill⟩; exhiber ⟨baby, car⟩
■ **show out**: ¶ ~ [sb] out accompagner [qn] à la porte
■ **show round**: ¶ ~ [sb] round faire visiter
■ **show up**: ¶ ~ up (colloq) (arrive) se montrer (colloq); ¶ ~ up [sth] révéler ⟨fault, mark⟩; ¶ ~ [sb] up faire honte à ⟨person⟩

show business *n* industrie *f* du spectacle

showcase *n* (for paintings, ideas) vitrine *f*; (for new artist etc) tremplin *m*

showdown *n* confrontation *f*

shower ⓵ *n* (a) douche *f*; to have a ~ prendre une douche
(b) (of rain) averse *f*
⓶ *vtr* (a) to ~ sb with sth couvrir qn de ⟨gifts, compliments, praise⟩
⓷ *vi* ⟨person⟩ prendre une douche

show house *n* maison-témoin *f*

showjumping *n* saut *m* d'obstacles

show-off *n* (colloq) m'as-tu-vu *mf inv* (colloq)

show of hands *n* vote *m* à mains levées

showroom *n* exposition *f*; to look at cars in a ~ regarder les voitures exposées

shrapnel *n* éclats *mpl* d'obus

shred ⓵ *n* (a) (of paper, fabric) lambeau *m*
(b) (of evidence, truth) parcelle *f*
⓶ *vtr* déchiqueter ⟨paper⟩; râper ⟨vegetables⟩

shredder *n* (for paper) déchiqueteuse *f*

shrewd *adj* ⟨person⟩ habile; ⟨move, investment⟩ astucieux/-ieuse

S

shriek ① n (a) (of pain, fear) cri m perçant, hurlement m; (of delight) cri m; ~s of laughter éclats mpl de rire
(b) (of bird) cri m
② vi crier, hurler (**in, with** de)

shrill adj ⟨voice, cry, laugh⟩ perçant/-e; ⟨whistle, tone⟩ strident/-e

shrimp n crevette f grise

shrine n (a) (place) lieu m de pèlerinage
(b) (building) chapelle f
(c) (tomb) tombeau m

shrink ① vtr faire rétrécir ⟨fabric⟩; contracter ⟨wood⟩
② vi (a) ⟨fabric⟩ rétrécir; ⟨timber⟩ se contracter; ⟨dough, meat⟩ réduire; ⟨sales⟩ être en recul; ⟨resources⟩ s'amenuiser; ⟨old person, body⟩ se tasser
(b) to ~ from se dérober devant ⟨conflict, responsibility⟩; to ~ from doing hésiter à faire

shrinking adj ⟨population, market⟩ en baisse; ⟨audience⟩ qui s'amenuise

shrink-wrap vtr emballer [qch] sous film plastique

shrivel ① vtr ⟨sun, heat⟩ flétrir ⟨skin⟩; dessécher ⟨plant, leaf⟩
② vi (also ~ **up**) ⟨fruit, vegetable⟩ se ratatiner; ⟨skin⟩ se flétrir; ⟨plant, meat⟩ se dessécher

shroud ① n linceul m
② vtr envelopper (**in** dans)

Shrove Tuesday n mardi m gras

shrub n arbuste m

shrubbery n massif m d'arbustes

shrug ① n haussement m d'épaules
② vtr to ~ one's shoulders hausser les épaules
■ **shrug off** ignorer ⟨problem, rumour⟩

shudder ① n (a) (of person) frisson m (**of** de)
(b) (of vehicle) secousse f
② vi (a) ⟨person⟩ frissonner (**with** de)
(b) ⟨vehicle⟩ to ~ **to a halt** avoir quelques soubresauts et s'arrêter

shuffle vtr (a) battre ⟨cards⟩
(b) brasser ⟨papers⟩
(c) to ~ one's feet traîner les pieds

shun vtr fuir ⟨people, publicity, temptation⟩; dédaigner ⟨work⟩

shunt ① vtr aiguiller ⟨wagon, engine⟩ (**into** sur)
② vi ⟨train⟩ changer de voie

shut ① adj fermé/-e; **her eyes were** ~ elle avait les yeux fermés; **to slam the door** ~ claquer la porte (pour bien la fermer); **to keep one's mouth** (colloq) ~ se taire
② vtr fermer
③ vi (a) ⟨door, book, box, mouth⟩ se fermer
(b) ⟨office, factory⟩ fermer
■ **shut down**: ¶ ~ **down** ⟨business⟩ fermer; ⟨machinery⟩ s'arrêter; ¶ ~ [sth] **down** fermer ⟨business⟩; arrêter ⟨machinery⟩
■ **shut in**: ~ [sb/sth] **in** enfermer
■ **shut off**: ~ [sth] **off**, ~ **off** [sth] couper ⟨supply, motor⟩

■ **shut out** (a) laisser [qn/qch] dehors ⟨animal, person⟩; éliminer ⟨noise⟩; **to be** ~ **out** être à la porte
(b) empêcher [qch] d'entrer ⟨light⟩
■ **shut up**: ¶ ~ **up** (colloq) se taire (**about** au sujet de)
¶ ~ [sb] **up** (a) (colloq) (silence) faire taire ⟨person⟩
(b) (confine) enfermer ⟨person, animal⟩ (**in** dans)
¶ ~ [sth] **up**, ~ **up** [sth] fermer ⟨house⟩

shutdown n fermeture f

shutter n (a) (wooden, metal) volet m; (on shop front) store m
(b) (on camera) obturateur m

shuttle ① n (a) navette f
(b) (also ~**cock**) volant m
② vtr transporter ⟨passengers⟩

shuttle service n service m de navette

shy ① adj ⟨person⟩ timide (**with, of** avec); ⟨animal⟩ farouche (**with, of** avec)
② vi ⟨horse⟩ faire un écart (**at** devant)
■ **shy away** se tenir à l'écart (**from** de)

Siberia pr n Sibérie f

sibling n frère/sœur m/f

Sicily pr n Sicile f

sick adj (a) (ill) malade; **worried** ~ malade d'inquiétude
(b) (nauseous) **to be** ~ vomir; **to feel** ~ avoir mal au cœur
(c) ⟨joke, mind⟩ malsain/-e
(d) (disgusted) écœuré/-e, dégoûté/-e
(e) (colloq) **to be** ~ **of** sb/sth en avoir assez or marre (colloq) de qn/qch

sick bay n infirmerie f

sick building syndrome n syndrome m causé par un milieu de travail insalubre

sicken ① vtr (disgust) écœurer
② vi to be ~**ing for sth** couver qch

sickening adj ⟨sight⟩ qui soulève le cœur; ⟨smell, cruelty⟩ écœurant/-e

sick leave n congé m de maladie

sickly adj (a) ⟨person, plant⟩ chétif/-ive
(b) ⟨smell, taste⟩ écœurant/-e; ⟨colour⟩ fadasse; ~ **sweet** douceâtre

sickness n (a) (illness) maladie f
(b) (nausea) nausée f; **bouts of** ~ vomissements mpl

sick note n (colloq) (for school) mot m d'excuse; (for work) certificat m médical

sickpay n indemnité f de maladie

sickroom n infirmerie f

side ① n (a) (gen) côté m; (of animal's body, hill) flanc m; (of lake, road) bord m; **on one's/its** ~ sur le côté; ~ **by** ~ côte à côte; **at** or **by the** ~ **of** au bord de ⟨lake, road⟩; à côté de ⟨building⟩
(b) **to take** ~s prendre position; **to change** ~s changer de camp
(c) (Sport) (team) équipe f
② adj ⟨door, window, entrance, view⟩ latéral/-e
③ **on the side** phr **with salad on the** ~

avec de la salade; **to work on the ∼** (in addition) travailler à côté; (illegally) travailler au noir

■ **side with** se mettre du côté de ⟨person⟩

sideboard n buffet m

sideboards (GB), **sideburns** n pl pattes fpl

side effect n (of drug) effet m secondaire; (of action) répercussion f

side impact bars n pl (Aut) renforts mpl latéraux

sideline n (a) as a ∼ comme à-côté
(b) (Sport) ligne f de touche; **on the ∼s** sur la touche

sidelong adj ⟨look⟩ oblique

side plate n petite assiette f

side saddle adv en amazone

side show n attraction f

sidestep vtr éviter ⟨opponent⟩; éluder ⟨issue⟩

side street n petite rue f

side stroke n brasse f indienne

sidetrack vtr fourvoyer ⟨person⟩; **to get ∼ed** se fourvoyer

sidewalk n (US) trottoir m

sideways **1** adj ⟨look, glance⟩ de travers
2 adv ⟨move⟩ latéralement; ⟨look at⟩ de travers

siding n voie f de garage

siege n siège m; **to lay ∼ to sth** assiéger qch

siesta n sieste f; **to have a ∼** faire la sieste

sieve **1** n (for draining) passoire f; (for sifting) tamis m
2 vtr tamiser ⟨flour⟩

sift vtr (a) tamiser, passer [qch] au tamis ⟨flour⟩
(b) passer [qch] au crible ⟨information⟩

■ **sift through** trier ⟨applications⟩; fouiller (dans) ⟨ashes⟩

sigh **1** n soupir m
2 vi soupirer, pousser un soupir; **to ∼ with relief** pousser un soupir de soulagement

sight **1** n (a) vue f; **at first ∼** à première vue; **to catch ∼ of sb/sth** apercevoir qn/qch; **to lose ∼ of sb/sth** perdre qn/qch de vue; **I can't stand the ∼ of him!** je ne peux pas le voir (colloq) (en peinture)!; **to be in ∼** ⟨land, border⟩ être en vue; ⟨peace, freedom⟩ être proche; **to be out of ∼** être caché/-e; **don't let her out of your ∼!** ne la quitte pas des yeux!
(b) (scene) spectacle m; **it was not a pretty ∼!** ce n'était pas beau à voir!
2 sights n pl (a) attractions fpl touristiques (**of** de); **to see the ∼s** faire du tourisme
(b) (on rifle, telescope) viseur m
(c) **to set one's ∼s on sth** viser qch

sightseeing n tourisme m; **to go ∼** faire du tourisme

sightseer n touriste mf

sign **1** n (a) (gen) signe m; **the pound ∼** le symbole de la livre sterling

(b) (road sign) panneau m (**for** pour); (smaller) pancarte f; (outside shop) enseigne f
2 vtr, vi signer

■ **sign on** (a) (GB) (for benefit) pointer au chômage
(b) (for course) s'inscrire (**for** à, dans)

■ **sign up** (a) (in forces) s'engager
(b) (for course) s'inscrire (**for** à, dans)

signal **1** n signal m (**for** de)
2 vtr **to ∼ (to sb) that** faire signe (à qn) que
3 vi (a) (gesture) faire des signes
(b) (in car) mettre son clignotant

signature n signature f

signature tune n indicatif m

significance n (a) (importance) importance f
(b) (meaning) signification f

significant adj ⟨amount, impact⟩ considérable; ⟨event, role⟩ important/-e; ⟨name⟩ significatif/-ive

signify vtr indiquer

sign language n code m or langage m gestuel

signpost n panneau m indicateur

Sikh n, adj sikh (mf)

silence **1** n silence m; **in ∼** en silence
2 vtr faire taire

silencer n silencieux m

silent adj (a) silencieux/-ieuse; **to be ∼** se taire
(b) ⟨disapproval, prayer⟩ muet/muette
(c) ⟨film⟩ muet/muette

silhouette n silhouette f

silicon chip n puce f électronique

silk n soie f

silky adj soyeux/-euse

sill n (of window) (interior) rebord m; (exterior) appui m

silly **1** adj ⟨person⟩ idiot/-e; ⟨question, game⟩ stupide; ⟨behaviour, clothes⟩ ridicule
2 adv **to drink oneself ∼** s'abrutir d'alcool; **to bore sb ∼** assommer qn

silo n silo m

silt n limon m, vase f

silver **1** n (a) (metal, colour) argent m
(b) (silverware) argenterie f
(c) (medal) médaille f d'argent
2 adj ⟨ring, coin⟩ en argent

silver birch n bouleau m argenté

silver foil n (GB) papier m d'aluminium

silverware n argenterie f

similar adj similaire, analogue; **∼ to** analogue à, comparable à

similarity n ressemblance f (**to, with** avec)

similarly adv de la même façon

simmer vi (a) ⟨soup⟩ cuire à feu doux, mijoter; ⟨water⟩ frémir
(b) ⟨person⟩ bouillonner (**with** de); ⟨revolt, violence⟩ couver

simple adj (a) (gen) simple; ⟨dress, style⟩ sobre ⋯∶

S

(b) (dimwitted) simplet/-ette (colloq), simple d'esprit

simplicity n simplicité f

simplify vtr simplifier

simplistic adj simpliste

simply adv **(a)** ⟨write, dress, live⟩ simplement, avec simplicité; **to put it ~... en deux mots... (b)** (merely) simplement

simulate vtr (feign) simuler ⟨anger, illness⟩; affecter ⟨interest⟩; (reproduce) simuler

simulator n simulateur m

simultaneous adj simultané/-e

sin **1** n péché m, crime m
2 vi pécher (**against** contre)

since **1** prep depuis; **I haven't seen him ~ then** je ne l'ai pas vu depuis; **I haven't been feeling well ~ Monday** je ne me sens pas bien depuis lundi; **I had been waiting ~ 9 o'clock** j'attendais depuis 9 heures
2 conj **(a)** (from the time when) depuis que; **~ he's been away** depuis qu' il est absent; **ever ~ I married him** depuis que nous nous sommes mariés, depuis notre mariage; **I've known him ~ I was 12** je le connais depuis que j'ai 12 ans or depuis l'âge de 12 ans; **it's 10 years ~ we last met** cela fait 10 ans que nous ne nous sommes pas revus
(b) (because) comme; **~ you're so clever, do it yourself!** puisque tu es tellement malin, fais-le toi-même!
3 adv **she has ~ qualified** depuis elle a obtenu son diplôme; **I haven't phoned her ~** je ne lui ai pas téléphoné depuis

sincere adj sincère

sincerely adv sincèrement; **Yours ~, Sincerely yours** (US) Veuillez agréer, Monsieur/Madame, l'expression de mes sentiments les meilleurs

sincerity n sincérité f

sinew n tendon m

sing **1** vtr chanter; **to ~ sb's praises** chanter les louanges de qn
2 vi chanter

Singapore pr n Singapour f

singe vtr brûler [qch] légèrement ⟨hair, clothing⟩; (with iron) roussir ⟨clothes⟩

singer n chanteur/-euse m/f

singing n chant m

single **1** n **(a)** (also **~ ticket**) aller m simple
(b) (also **~ room**) chambre f pour une personne
(c) (record) 45 tours m
2 adj **(a)** (sole) seul/-e (before n)
(b) (for one) ⟨sheet, bed, person⟩ pour une personne
(c) (unmarried) célibataire
(d) **every ~ day** tous les jours sans exception; **every ~ one of those people** chacune de ces personnes
■ **single out** choisir ⟨person⟩

single cream n ≈ crème f fraîche liquide

single currency n monnaie f unique

single file adv en file indienne

single-handed(ly) adv tout seul/toute seule

single market n marché m unique

single-minded adj tenace, résolu/-e

single mother n mère f qui élève ses enfants seule

single-parent adj ⟨family⟩ monoparental/-e

singles n pl (Sport) **the women's/men's ~** le simple dames/messieurs

singles bar n bar m de rencontres pour célibataires

singles charts n pl palmarès m des 45 tours

single-sex adj non mixte

singlet n (GB) **(a)** (Sport) maillot m
(b) (vest) maillot m de corps

singular **1** n singulier m
2 adj singulier/-ière

sinister adj sinistre

sink **1** n (in kitchen) évier m; (in bathroom) lavabo m
2 vtr **(a)** couler ⟨ship⟩
(b) forer ⟨oil well, shaft⟩; creuser ⟨foundations⟩; enfoncer ⟨post, pillar⟩ (**into** dans); **the dog sank its teeth into my arm** le chien a planté ses crocs dans mon bras
3 vi **(a)** ⟨ship, object, person⟩ couler
(b) ⟨sun⟩ baisser; ⟨cake⟩ redescendre; **to ~ to the floor** s'effondrer; **to ~ into a chair** s'affaler dans un fauteuil; **to ~ into a deep sleep** sombrer dans un profond sommeil
(c) ⟨building, wall⟩ s'effondrer; **to ~ into** s'enfoncer dans ⟨mud⟩; sombrer dans ⟨anarchy, obscurity⟩
■ **sink in** ⟨news⟩ faire son chemin

sinner n pécheur/-eresse m/f

sinus n sinus m inv

sip **1** n petite gorgée f
2 vtr boire [qch] à petites gorgées

siphon **1** n siphon m
2 vtr (also **~ off**) siphonner ⟨petrol, water⟩

sir n **(a)** Monsieur m; **Dear Sir** Monsieur
(b) (GB) (in titles) **Sir James** Sir James

siren n sirène f

sirloin n aloyau m

sister n **(a)** (gen) sœur f
(b) (GB) (nurse) infirmière f chef

sister-in-law n belle-sœur f

sit **1** vtr (GB) se présenter à, passer ⟨exam⟩
2 vi **(a)** s'asseoir (**at** à; **in** dans; **on** sur); **to be sitting** être assis/-e; **to ~ still** se tenir tranquille
(b) ⟨committee, court⟩ siéger
(c) **to ~ on** faire partie de ⟨committee, jury⟩
(d) ⟨hen⟩ **to ~ on** couver ⟨eggs⟩
■ **sit about**, **sit around** rester assis à ne rien faire
■ **sit down** s'asseoir (**at** à; **in** dans; **on** sur)
■ **sit in** ⟨observer⟩ assister (**on** à)
■ **sit up** se redresser; **to be ~ing up** être assis/-e; **~ up straight!** tiens-toi droit!

sitcom n (colloq) sitcom m

site *n* (a) (*also* **building ∼**) (before building) terrain *m*; (during building) chantier *m*
(b) (for tent) emplacement *m*; **caravan ∼** (GB) terrain *m* de caravaning
(c) (archaeological) site *m*

sitting *n* (a) (session) séance *f*
(b) (in canteen) service *m*

sitting room *n* salon *m*

sitting target *n* cible *f* facile

situate *vtr* situer; **to be ∼d** être situé/-e, se trouver

situation *n* situation *f*

sit-ups *n pl* abdominaux *mpl*

six *n, pron, det* six (*m*) *inv*

sixteen *n, pron, det* seize (*m*) *inv*

sixteenth ⊡ *n* (a) (in order) seizième *mf*
(b) (of month) seize *m inv*
(c) (fraction) seizième *m*
⊡ *adj, adv* seizième

sixth ⊡ *n* (a) (in order) sixième *mf*
(b) (of month) six *m inv*
(c) (fraction) sixième *m*
⊡ *adj, adv* sixième

sixth form (GB) (Sch) *n* (lower) ≈ classes *fpl* de première; (upper) ≈ classes *fpl* de terminale

sixth form college *n* (GB) lycée *m* (*n'ayant que des classes de première et terminale*)

sixth sense *n* sixième sens *m*

sixties *n pl* (a) **the ∼** les années *fpl* soixante
(b) **to be in one's ∼** avoir entre soixante et soixante-dix ans

sixtieth *n, adj, adv* soixantième (*mf*)

sixty *n, pron, det* soixante (*m*) *inv*

size *n* (of person, paper, clothes) taille *f*; (of container, room, building, region) grandeur *f*; (of apple, egg, book, parcel) grosseur *f*; (of carpet, bed, machine) dimensions *fpl*; (of population, audience) importance *f*; (of class, company) effectif *m*; (of shoes, gloves) pointure *f*
IDIOMS **to cut sb down to ∼** remettre qn à sa place, rabattre le caquet à qn (colloq)
■ **size up** se faire une opinion de 〈*person*〉; évaluer 〈*situation*〉; mesurer 〈*problem*〉

sizeable *adj* 〈*amount*〉 assez important/-e; 〈*house, field, town*〉 assez grand/-e

sizzle *vi* grésiller

skate ⊡ *n* (a) (ice) patin *m* à glace; (roller) patin *m* à roulettes
(b) (fish) raie *f*
⊡ *vi* patiner (**on, along** sur)

skateboard *n* skateboard *m*, planche *f* à roulettes

skateboarder *n* skateur/-euse *m/f*

skater *n* patineur/-euse *m/f*

skating *n* patinage *m*

skating rink *n* (ice) patinoire *f*; (roller-skating) piste *f* de patins à roulettes

skeleton *n* squelette *m*

skeleton key *n* passe-partout *m inv*

skeptic (US) = SCEPTIC

skeptical (US) = SCEPTICAL

skepticism (US) = SCEPTICISM

sketch ⊡ *n* (a) (drawing, draft) esquisse *f*; (hasty outline) croquis *m*; **rough ∼** ébauche *f*
(b) (comic scene) sketch *m*
⊡ *vtr* faire une esquisse de; (hastily) faire un croquis de

sketchbook *n* carnet *m* à croquis

sketchpad *n* bloc *m* à dessin

sketchy *adj* 〈*information, details*〉 insuffisant/-e; 〈*memory*〉 vague

skewer ⊡ *n* (for kebab) brochette *f*; (for joint) broche *f*
⊡ *vtr* embrocher

ski ⊡ *n* ski *m*
⊡ *vi* faire du ski; **to ∼ down a slope** descendre une pente à skis

ski boot *n* chaussure *f* de ski

skid ⊡ *n* dérapage *m*
⊡ *vi* déraper (**on** sur)

skier *n* skieur/-ieuse *m/f*

skiing *n* ski *m*; **to go ∼** faire du ski

skiing holiday *n* vacances *fpl* de neige

ski jumping *n* saut *m* à skis

skilful (GB), **skillful** (US) *adj* habile, adroit/-e

ski lift *n* remontée *f* mécanique

skill ⊡ *n* (a) (intellectual) habileté *f*, adresse *f*; (physical) dextérité *f*
(b) (special ability) (acquired) compétence *f*, capacités *fpl*; (practical) technique *f*
⊡ **skills** *n pl* (training) connaissances *fpl*

skilled *adj* (a) (trained) 〈*labour, work*〉 qualifié/-e
(b) (talented) consommé/-e

skim ⊡ *vtr* (a) (remove cream) écrémer; (remove scum) écumer
(b) 〈*plane, bird*〉 raser, frôler 〈*surface, treetops*〉
(c) **to ∼ stones** faire des ricochets avec des cailloux
⊡ *vi* **to ∼ through** parcourir 〈*book, article*〉; **to ∼ over** passer rapidement sur 〈*event, facts*〉

skim(med) milk *n* lait *m* écrémé

skimp *vi* **to ∼ on** lésiner sur

skimpy *adj* 〈*garment*〉 minuscule; 〈*portion, allowance, income*〉 maigre (*before n*)

skin ⊡ *n* peau *f*; (of onion) pelure *f*
⊡ *vtr* (a) écorcher 〈*animal*〉
(b) **to ∼ one's knee** s'écorcher le genou
IDIOMS **to have a thick ∼** être insensible; **to be** *or* **get soaked to the ∼** être trempé/-e jusqu'aux os (colloq); **by the ∼ of one's teeth** de justesse

skin-deep *adj* superficiel/-ielle

skin diving *n* plongée *f* sous-marine

skinhead *n* (GB) (youth) skin(head) *m*

skinny *adj* (colloq) maigre

skint *adj* (colloq) (GB) fauché/-e (colloq)

skintight *adj* moulant/-e

skip ⊡ *n* (a) (jump) petit bond *m*
(b) (GB) (container) benne *f*

S

2 *vtr* sauter ⟨*page, lunch, school*⟩

3 *vi* (a) (once) bondir; (several times) sautiller
(b) (with rope) sauter à la corde

ski pants *n* fuseau *m* (de ski)

ski pass *n* forfait-skieur *m*

skipper *n* (of ship) capitaine *m*; (of fishing
boat) patron *m*; (of yacht) skipper *m*

skipping rope *n* corde *f* à sauter

ski resort *n* station *f* de ski

skirt **1** *n* jupe *f*
2 *vtr* (a) contourner ⟨*wood, village, city*⟩
(b) esquiver ⟨*problem*⟩

skirting board *n* plinthe *f*

ski slope *n* piste *f*

ski suit *n* combinaison *f* de ski

skittle **1** *n* quille *f*
2 skittles *n pl* (jeu *m* de) quilles *fpl*

skive *vi* (GB) (colloq) (*also* ~ **off**) (shirk) tirer
au flanc (colloq); (be absent) (from school) sécher
l'école (colloq); (from work) ne pas aller au
boulot (colloq)

skulk *vi* rôder; **to** ~ **out/off** sortir/s'éloigner
furtivement

skull *n* crâne *m*

skunk *n* moufette *f*

sky *n* ciel *m*

skydiving *n* parachutisme *m* (en chute
libre)

sky-high *adj* ⟨*prices, rates*⟩ exorbitant/-e

skyjacker *n* (colloq) pirate *m* de l'air

skylight *n* fenêtre *f* à tabatière

skyline *n* (in countryside) ligne *f* d'horizon; (in
city) ligne *f* des toits

skyscraper *n* gratte-ciel *m inv*

slab *n* (of stone, wood, concrete) dalle *f*; (of meat,
cheese, cake) pavé *m*; (of chocolate) tablette *f*

slack **1** *n* (in rope, cable) mou *m*
2 *adj* (a) ⟨*worker*⟩ peu consciencieux/-ieuse;
⟨*work*⟩ peu soigné/-e
(b) ⟨*period*⟩ creux/creuse (*after n*); ⟨*demand,
sales*⟩ faible
(c) ⟨*cable, rope, body*⟩ détendu/-e
3 *vi* ⟨*worker*⟩ se relâcher dans son travail
■ **slack off** ⟨*business, trade*⟩ diminuer;
⟨*rain*⟩ se calmer

slacken **1** *vtr* (a) donner du mou à ⟨*rope*⟩;
lâcher ⟨*reins*⟩
(b) réduire ⟨*pace*⟩
2 *vi* (a) ⟨*rope*⟩ se relâcher
(b) ⟨*activity, pace, speed, business*⟩ ralentir

slalom *n* slalom *m*

slam **1** *vtr* ⟨*person*⟩ claquer ⟨*door*⟩; ⟨*wind*⟩
faire claquer ⟨*door*⟩; **to** ~ **the door in sb's
face** claquer la porte au nez de qn; **to** ~ **the
ball into the net** renvoyer brutalement la
balle dans le filet
2 *vi* ⟨*door*⟩ claquer (**against** contre); **to** ~
shut se refermer en claquant

slander *n* (gen) calomnie *f* (**on** sur); (Law)
diffamation *f* orale

slang *n* argot *m*

slangy *adj* (colloq) argotique

slant **1** *n* (a) (perspective) point *m* de vue
(**on** sur)
(b) (bias) tendance *f*
(c) (slope) pente *f*
2 *vi* ⟨*floor, ground*⟩ être en pente;
⟨*handwriting*⟩ pencher (**to** vers)

slanting *adj* ⟨*roof*⟩ en pente; ~ **eyes** yeux
mpl bridés

slap **1** *n* tape *f* (**on** sur); (stronger) claque *f*
(**on** sur); **a** ~ **in the face** une gifle
2 *vtr* donner une tape à ⟨*person, animal*⟩; **to**
~ **sb in the face** gifler qn

slap bang *adv* (colloq) **he ran** ~ **into the
wall** il s'est cogné en plein dans le mur en
courant; ~ **in the middle (of)** au beau milieu
(de)

slapdash *adj* (colloq) ⟨*person*⟩
brouillon/-onne (colloq); **in a** ~ **way** à la
va-vite

slash **1** *n* (a) (wound) balafre *f* (**on** à)
(b) (in fabric, seat, tyre) lacération *f*; (in painting)
entaille *f*; (in skirt) fente *f*
(c) (in printing) barre *f* oblique
2 *vtr* (a) balafrer ⟨*cheek*⟩; faire une balafre
à ⟨*person*⟩; couper ⟨*throat*⟩; ⟨*knife*⟩ entailler
⟨*face*⟩; **to** ~ **one's wrists** se tailler les veines
(b) taillader ⟨*painting, fabric, tyres*⟩;
trancher ⟨*cord*⟩
(c) (reduce) réduire [qch] (considérablement)
⟨*amount, spending*⟩; sacrifier ⟨*prices*⟩

slat *n* (of shutter, blind) lamelle *f*; (of bench, bed)
lame *f*

slate **1** *n* ardoise *f*
2 *vtr* (a) couvrir [qch] d'ardoises ⟨*roof*⟩
(b) (GB) (colloq) (criticize) taper sur (colloq) (**for**
pour)
IDIOMS **to wipe the** ~ **clean** faire table rase

slaughter **1** *n* (a) (in butchery) abattage *m*
(b) (massacre) massacre *m*, boucherie *f* (colloq)
2 *vtr* (a) abattre ⟨*animal*⟩
(b) massacrer ⟨*people*⟩
(c) (colloq) (defeat) écraser

slaughterhouse *n* abattoir *m*

Slav **1** *n* Slave *mf*
2 *adj* slave

slave **1** *n* esclave *mf*
2 *vi* (*also* ~ **away**) travailler comme un
forçat, trimer (colloq)

slaver *vi* ⟨*person, animal*⟩ baver

slavery *n* esclavage *m*

slaw (US) = COLESLAW

slay *vtr* faire périr ⟨*enemy*⟩; pourfendre
⟨*dragon*⟩

sleaze *n* (colloq) (pornography) pornographie *f*;
(corruption) corruption *f*

sleazy *adj* (colloq) ⟨*club, area, character*⟩
louche; ⟨*story, aspect*⟩ scabreux/-euse; ⟨*café,
hotel*⟩ borgne

sled, sledge (GB) **1** *n* luge *f*; (sleigh)
traîneau *m*
2 *vi* faire de la luge

sledgehammer *n* masse *f*

sleek *adj* (a) ⟨*hair*⟩ lisse et brillant/-e;
⟨*animal*⟩ au poil lisse et brillant

S

(b) ⟨*shape*⟩ élégant/-e; ⟨*figure*⟩ mince et harmonieux/-ieuse

sleep ① *n* sommeil *m*; **to go to ~** s'endormir; **to go back to ~** se rendormir; **to send** *or* **put sb to ~** endormir qn; **to have a ~** dormir; **my leg has gone to ~** (colloq) j'ai la jambe engourdie; **to put an animal to ~** faire piquer un animal

② *vi* dormir; **to ~ at a friend's house** coucher chez un ami

IDIOMS **to ~ like a log** *or* **top** dormir comme une souche *or* un loir

■ **sleep in** (stay in bed late) faire la grasse matinée; (oversleep) dormir trop tard

■ **sleep on: to ~ on a decision** attendre le lendemain pour prendre une décision

sleeping bag *n* sac *m* de couchage

sleeping car *n* voiture-lit *f*, wagon-lit *m*

sleeping pill *n* somnifère *m*

sleepless *adj* **to have a ~ night** passer une nuit blanche

sleepover *n* she's having a ~ elle invite des amies à coucher chez elle

sleepwalk *vi* marcher en dormant, être somnambule

sleepy *adj* ⟨*voice, village*⟩ endormi/-e, somnolent/-e; **to feel** *or* **be ~** avoir envie de dormir, avoir sommeil; **to make sb ~** ⟨*fresh air*⟩ donner envie de dormir à qn; ⟨*wine*⟩ endormir qn, assoupir qn

sleet *n* neige *f* fondue

sleeve *n* **(a)** (of garment) manche *f*
(b) (of record) pochette *f*
(c) (Tech) (inner) chemise *f*; (outer) gaine *f*
IDIOMS **to have something up one's ~** avoir quelque chose en réserve

sleeveless *adj* sans manches

sleigh *n* traîneau *m*

sleight of hand *n* **(a)** (dexterity) dextérité *f*
(b) (trick) tour *m* de passe-passe

slender *adj* **(a)** ⟨*person*⟩ mince; ⟨*waist*⟩ fin/-e
(b) ⟨*income, means*⟩ modeste, maigre (*before n*)

sleuth *n* limier *m*, détective *m*

slew *vi* ⟨*vehicle*⟩ déraper; ⟨*mast*⟩ pivoter

slice ① *n* **(a)** (of bread, meat) tranche *f*; (of cheese) morceau *m*; (of pie, tart) part *m*; (of lemon, cucumber, sausage) rondelle *f*
(b) (of profits) part *f*; (of territory, population) partie *f*
(c) (utensil) spatule *f*
② *vtr* **(a)** couper [qch] (en tranches) ⟨*loaf, roast*⟩; couper [qch] en rondelles ⟨*lemon, cucumber*⟩
(b) fendre ⟨*air*⟩
(c) (Sport) slicer, couper ⟨*ball*⟩
③ *vi* **to ~ through** fendre ⟨*water, air*⟩; trancher ⟨*timber, rope, meat*⟩

sliced bread *n* pain *m* en tranches

slice of life *n* tranche *f* de vie

slick ① *n* (*also* **oil ~**) (on water) nappe *f* de pétrole; (on shore) marée *f* noire

② *adj* **(a)** ⟨*production*⟩ habile; ⟨*operation*⟩ mené/-e rondement
(b) (superficial) qui a un éclat plutôt superficiel
(c) ⟨*person*⟩ roublard/-e (colloq); ⟨*answer*⟩ astucieux/-ieuse; ⟨*excuse*⟩ facile
(d) (US) (slippery) ⟨*road, surface*⟩ glissant/-e; ⟨*hair*⟩ lissé/-e

slide ① *n* **(a)** (in playground) toboggan *m*
(b) (photographic) diapositive *f*
(c) (microscope plate) lame *f* porte-objet
(d) (GB) (*also* **hair ~**) barrette *f*
(e) (decline) baisse *f* (**in** de)
② *vtr* faire glisser
③ *vi* **(a)** ⟨*car, person*⟩ glisser, partir en glissade (**into** dans; **on** sur); **to ~ in and out** ⟨*drawer*⟩ coulisser
(b) ⟨*prices, shares*⟩ baisser

slide projector *n* projecteur *m* de diapositives

slide rule (GB), **slide ruler** (US) *n* règle *f* à calcul

slide show *n* (at exhibition) diaporama *m*; (at lecture, at home) séance *f* de projection

sliding *adj* ⟨*door*⟩ coulissant/-e; ⟨*roof*⟩ ouvrant/-e

sliding scale *n* échelle *f* mobile

slight ① *n* affront *m* (**on** à; **from** de la part de)
② *adj* **(a)** (gen) léger/-ère (*before n*); ⟨*risk, danger*⟩ faible (*before n*); ⟨*pause, hesitation*⟩ petit/-e (*before n*); **not to have the ~est difficulty** ne pas avoir la moindre difficulté
(b) (in build) mince
③ *vtr* **(a)** (offend) offenser; (stronger) humilier
(b) (US) (underestimate) sous-estimer

slightly *adv* ⟨*fall, change*⟩ légèrement; ⟨*different, more, less*⟩ un peu

slim ① *adj* ⟨*person, figure*⟩ mince; ⟨*ankle, leg*⟩ fin/-e, mince; ⟨*watch, calculator*⟩ plat/-e
② *vi* (GB) maigrir; **I'm ~ming** je fais un régime amaigrissant

slime *n* dépôt *m* gluant *or* visqueux; (of slug, snail) bave *f*

sling ① *n* **(a)** (Med) écharpe *f*
(b) (for carrying baby) porte-bébé *m*; (for carrying load) élingue *f*
② *vtr* lancer ⟨*object, insult*⟩ (**at** à)

slip ① *n* **(a)** (error) erreur *f*; **~ of the tongue** lapsus *m*
(b) (receipt) reçu *m*; (for salary) bulletin *m*; **~ of paper** bout *m* de papier
(c) (stumble) faux pas *m*
(d) (petticoat) (full) combinaison *f*; (half) jupon *m*
② *vtr* **(a)** (gen) glisser (**into** dans); **she ~ped the shirt over her head** (put on) elle a enfilé sa chemise; (take off) elle a retiré sa chemise
(b) ⟨*dog*⟩ se dégager de ⟨*leash*⟩; ⟨*boat*⟩ filer ⟨*moorings*⟩; **it had ~ped my mind** j'avais complètement oublié (que); **to let ~ a remark** laisser échapper une remarque
(c) (Med) **to ~ a disc** se déplacer une vertèbre

⋯⋗

⓷ *vi* **(a)** to ~ **into** passer ⟨*dress, costume*⟩; tomber dans ⟨*coma*⟩
(b) to ~ **into/out of** se glisser dans/hors de ⟨*room, building*⟩
(c) ⟨*person, vehicle*⟩ glisser (**on** sur; **off** de); ⟨*knife, razor, pen*⟩ glisser, déraper; to ~ **through sb's fingers** ⟨*money, opportunity*⟩ filer entre les doigts de qn
(d) (Aut) ⟨*clutch*⟩ patiner

slipknot *n* nœud *m* coulant
slip-on (shoe) *n* mocassin *m*
slipped disc *n* hernie *f* discale
slipper *n* pantoufle *f*
slippery *adj* glissant/-e
slip road *n* bretelle *f* d'accès
slipshod *adj* ⟨*person*⟩ négligent/-e; ⟨*appearance, work*⟩ négligé/-e, peu soigné/-e
slip-up *n* (colloq) bourde *f* (colloq)
slit ⓵ *n* fente *f* (**in** dans)
⓶ *adj* ⟨*eyes*⟩ bridé/-e; ⟨*skirt*⟩ fendu/-e
⓷ *vtr* (on purpose) faire une fente dans; (by accident) déchirer; to ~ **sb's throat** égorger qn; to ~ **one's wrists** s'ouvrir les veines
slither *vi* glisser
sliver *n* (of glass) éclat *m*; (of food) mince tranche *f*
slob *n* (colloq) (lazy) flemmard/-e *m/f* (colloq)
slog *vi* (colloq) (*also* ~ **away**) travailler dur, bosser (colloq)
slogan *n* slogan *m*
slop ⓵ *vtr* renverser ⟨*liquid*⟩
⓶ *vi* (*also* ~ **over**) ⟨*liquid*⟩ déborder
slope ⓵ *n* pente *f*
⓶ *vi* être en pente (**towards** vers); ⟨*writing*⟩ pencher (**to** vers)
sloping *adj* ⟨*ground, roof*⟩ en pente; ⟨*ceiling*⟩ incliné/-e; ⟨*writing*⟩ penché/-e
sloppy *adj* **(a)** (colloq) ⟨*appearance*⟩ débraillé/-e; ⟨*work*⟩ peu soigné/-e
(b) (colloq) (over-emotional) sentimental/-e
slot ⓵ *n* **(a)** (for coin, ticket) fente *f*; (for letters) ouverture *f*; (groove) rainure *f*
(b) (in timetable, schedule) créneau *m*
⓶ *vtr* to ~ **sth into a machine** insérer qch dans une machine
⓷ *vi* to ~ **into sth** ⟨*coin, piece*⟩ s'insérer dans qch; to ~ **into place** *or* **position** s'encastrer
■ **slot together** s'emboîter
sloth *n* (Zool) paresseux *m*
slot machine *n* (game) machine *f* à sous; (vending machine) distributeur *m* automatique
slouch *vi* être avachi/-e
Slovakia *pr n* Slovaquie *f*
Slovenia *pr n* Slovénie *f*
slovenly *adj* négligé/-e
slow ⓵ *adj* **(a)** (gen) lent/-e;
(b) ⟨*business, market*⟩ stagnant/-e
(c) (dull-witted) lent/-e (d'esprit)
(d) to be ~ ⟨*clock, watch*⟩ retarder; **to be 10 minutes** ~ retarder de 10 minutes
⓶ *adv* lentement

⓷ *vtr, vi* (*also* ~ **down**) ralentir
slowly *adv* lentement
slow motion *n* ralenti *m*; **in** ~ au ralenti
slow-moving *adj* lent/-e
sludge *n* **(a)** (*also* **sewage** ~) eaux *fpl* usées
(b) (mud) vase *f*
slug *n* limace *f*
sluggish *adj* **(a)** ⟨*person, animal*⟩ léthargique; ⟨*circulation*⟩ lent/-e
(b) ⟨*market, trade*⟩ qui stagne
sluice *n* **(a)** (*also* ~ **gate**) vanne *f*
(b) (*also* ~**way**) canal *m*
slum *n* **(a)** (area) quartier *m* pauvre
(b) (dwelling) taudis *m*
slumber ⓵ *n* sommeil *m*
⓶ *vi* sommeiller
slump ⓵ *n* (in trade, prices) effondrement *m* (**in** de)
⓶ *vi* **(a)** ⟨*demand, trade, price*⟩ chuter (**from** de; **to** à; **by** de); ⟨*economy, market*⟩ s'effondrer; ⟨*popularity*⟩ être en forte baisse
(b) ⟨*person, body*⟩ s'affaler (colloq)
slur ⓵ *n* **(a)** (in speech) marmonnement *m*
(b) (Mus) liaison *f*
(c) (aspersion) calomnie *f*
⓶ *vi* avoir du mal à articuler
⓷ **slurred** *pp adj* ⟨*voice, speech*⟩ inarticulé/-e
slush *n* neige *f* fondue
slush fund *n* caisse *f* noire
sly *adj* ⟨*person, animal*⟩ rusé/-e; ⟨*remark, smile*⟩ entendu/-e
IDIOMS on the ~ en douce (colloq), en cachette
smack ⓵ *n* claque *f*; (on face) gifle *f*
⓶ *vtr* (on face) gifler ⟨*person*⟩; taper ⟨*object*⟩ (**on** sur; **against** contre); **she** ~**ed him on the bottom** elle lui a donné une tape sur les fesses
⓷ *vi* to ~ **of** sentir
small ⓵ *n* **the** ~ **of the back** le creux du dos
⓶ *adj* **(a)** (gen) petit/-e (*before n*); ⟨*quantity, amount*⟩ faible (*before n*)
(b) to feel ~ être dans ses petits souliers (colloq); **to make sb feel** *or* **look** ~ humilier qn
⓷ *adv* ⟨*write*⟩ petit
small ad *n* (GB) petite annonce *f*
small change *n* petite monnaie *f*
small talk *n* banalités *fpl*; **to make** ~ faire la conversation
smart ⓵ *adj* **(a)** (elegant) ⟨*person, clothes*⟩ élégant/-e; ⟨*restaurant, hotel, street*⟩ chic
(b) (clever) malin/-e
(c) ⟨*blow*⟩ vif/vive; ⟨*rebuke*⟩ cinglant/-e; **to walk at a** ~ **pace** marcher à vive allure
(d) (Comput) intelligent/-e
⓶ *vi* ⟨*cut, cheeks*⟩ brûler; **his eyes were** ~**ing from the smoke** la fumée lui brûlait les yeux
smart bomb *n* bombe *f* intelligente
smart card *n* carte *f* à puce

smarten *v* ▪ **smarten up** embellir ⟨*room*⟩; **to ~ oneself up** se faire beau

smash ①*n* (a) (colloq) (*also* **~-up**) (accident) collision *f*
(b) (colloq) (*also* **~ hit**) tube *m* (colloq)
(c) (in tennis) smash *m*
(d) (sound) fracas *m*
②*vtr* (a) briser ⟨*glass, door, car*⟩; (more violently) fracasser
(b) démanteler ⟨*drugs ring, gang*⟩
(c) (Sport) **to ~ the ball** faire un smash
③*vi* se briser, se fracasser

smashing *adj* (GB) (colloq) formidable (colloq)

smattering *n* notions *fpl* (**of** de); **to have a ~ of Russian** avoir quelques connaissances en russe

smear ①*n* (a) (spot) tache *f*; (streak) traînée *f*
(b) (defamation) propos *m* diffamatoire
(c) (Med) (*also* **~ test**) frottis *m*
②*vtr* faire des taches sur ⟨*glass, window*⟩; **her face was ~ed with jam** elle avait le visage barbouillé de confiture
(b) (spread) étaler ⟨*butter, paint*⟩; appliquer ⟨*lotion*⟩ (**on** sur)
③*vi* ⟨*ink, paint*⟩ s'étaler; ⟨*lipstick, make-up*⟩ couler

smell ①*n* (a) odeur *f*
(b) (sense) odorat *m*
②*vtr* ⟨*person*⟩ sentir; ⟨*animal*⟩ renifler, sentir; **I can ~ burning** ça sent le brûlé
③*vi* sentir; **that ~s nice/horrible** ça sent bon/très mauvais; **to ~ of sth** sentir qch

smelling salts *n pl* sels *mpl*

smelly *adj* malodorant/-e, qui sent mauvais

smile ①*n* sourire *m*
②*vi* sourire (**at sb** à qn)
▪ **smile on**: **~ on** [*sb/sth*] ⟨*fortune, weather*⟩ sourire à; ⟨*person*⟩ être favorable à

smiley *n* (colloq) souriant *m*, smiley *m* (colloq)

smirk ①*n* (self-satisfied) petit sourire *m* satisfait; (knowing) sourire *m* en coin
②*vi* (in a self-satisfied way) avoir un petit sourire satisfait; (knowingly) avoir un sourire en coin

smithereens *n pl* **in ~** en mille morceaux; **to smash sth to ~** faire voler qch en éclats

smock *n* blouse *f*, sarrau *m*

smog *n* smog *m*

smoke ①*n* fumée *f*
②*vtr* fumer
③*vi* fumer

smoke alarm *n* détecteur *m* de fumée

smoked *adj* fumé/e

smoker *n* fumeur/-euse *m/f*

smoke screen *n* (Mil) écran *m* de fumée; (figurative) diversion *f*

smoking ①*n* **~ and drinking** le tabac et l'alcool; **to give up ~** arrêter de fumer; '**no ~**' 'défense de fumer'
②*adj* ⟨*compartment, section*⟩ fumeurs (*after n*)

smoking-related *adj* ⟨*disease*⟩ associé/-e au tabac

smoky *adj* ⟨*room*⟩ enfumé/-e; ⟨*cheese, bacon*⟩ fumé/-e

smooth ①*adj* (a) ⟨*stone, surface, skin, fabric*⟩ lisse; ⟨*curve, breathing*⟩ régulier/-ière; ⟨*sauce*⟩ homogène; ⟨*crossing, flight*⟩ sans heurts; ⟨*movement*⟩ aisé/-e
(b) ⟨*taste, wine, whisky*⟩ moelleux/-euse
(c) ⟨*suave*⟩ ⟨*person*⟩ mielleux/-euse; ⟨*manners, appearance*⟩ onctueux/-euse; **to be a ~ talker** être enjôleur/-euse
②*vtr* (a) (flatten out) lisser; (get creases out) défroisser
(b) faciliter ⟨*transition, path*⟩
▪ **smooth over**: ¶ **~ over** [*sth*] atténuer ⟨*differences*⟩; aplanir ⟨*difficulties, problems*⟩; **to ~ things over** arranger les choses

smooth-running *adj* ⟨*organization, event*⟩ qui marche bien

smother *vtr* étouffer

smoulder (GB), **smolder** (US) *vi* (a) ⟨*cigarette, fire*⟩ se consumer
(b) ⟨*hatred, jealousy*⟩ couver; **to ~ with** être consumé/-e de

smudge ①*n* trace *f*
②*vtr* étaler ⟨*make-up, print, ink, paint*⟩; faire des traces sur ⟨*paper, paintwork*⟩
③*vi* ⟨*make-up, print, ink, paint*⟩ s'étaler

smug *adj* suffisant/-e

smuggle *vtr* faire du trafic de ⟨*arms, drugs*⟩; faire passer [*qch*] en contrebande ⟨*watches, alcohol, cigarettes*⟩; **to ~ sb/sth in** faire entrer qn/qch clandestinement

smuggler *n* contrebandier/-ière *m/f*; **drug/arms ~** passeur/-euse *m/f* de drogue/ d'armes

smuggling *n* contrebande *f*; **drug/arms ~** trafic *m* de drogue/d'armes

smutty *adj* (a) (crude) grivois/-e
(b) (dirty) ⟨*face*⟩ noir/-e; ⟨*mark*⟩ noirâtre

snack ①*n* (a) (small meal) repas *m* léger; (instead of meal) casse-croûte *m inv*
(b) (crisps, peanuts) **~s** amuse-gueule *m inv*
②*vi* grignoter, manger légèrement

snag *n* (a) (hitch) inconvénient *m* (**in** de)
(b) (tear) accroc *m* (**in** à)

snail *n* escargot *m*

snail mail *n* (colloq) courrier *m* postal

snake *n* serpent *m*

snap ①*n* (a) (of branch) craquement *m*; (of fingers, elastic) claquement *m*
(b) (colloq) (photograph) photo *f*
(c) (game) ≈ bataille *f*
②*adj* ⟨*decision, judgment, vote*⟩ rapide
③*vtr* (a) faire claquer ⟨*fingers, jaws, elastic*⟩
(b) (break) (faire) casser net
(c) (say crossly) dire [*qch*] hargneusement
④*vi* (a) (break) se casser
(b) (speak sharply) parler hargneusement
▪ **snap at** (a) (speak sharply) parler sèchement à ····⊹

(b) ⟨dog⟩ essayer de mordre
■ **snap up** sauter sur ⟨bargain⟩
snappy adj ⟨rhythm, reply⟩ rapide; ⟨advertisement⟩ accrocheur/-euse
snapshot n photo f
snare ⟨1⟩ n piège m
⟨2⟩ vtr prendre [qn/qch] au piège
snarl vi ⟨animal⟩ gronder férocement; ⟨person⟩ grogner
snarl-up n (in traffic) embouteillage m; (in distribution network) blocage m
snatch ⟨1⟩ n **(a)** (of conversation) bribe f; (of tune) quelques notes fpl
(b) (theft) vol m
⟨2⟩ vtr **(a)** (grab) attraper ⟨book, key⟩; **to ~ sth from sb** arracher qch à qn
(b) (colloq) (steal) voler ⟨handbag⟩ (**from** à)
sneak vi **to ~ in/out** entrer/sortir furtivement; **to ~ up on sb/sth** s'approcher sans bruit de qn/qch
sneaker n (US) basket f, (chaussure f de) tennis f
sneaking adj ⟨suspicion⟩ vague
sneaky adj sournois/-e
sneer ⟨1⟩ n sourire m méprisant
⟨2⟩ vi sourire avec mépris
sneeze ⟨1⟩ n éternuement m
⟨2⟩ vi éternuer
snide adj sournois/-e
sniff ⟨1⟩ n reniflement m
⟨2⟩ vtr ⟨dog⟩ flairer; ⟨person⟩ sentir ⟨food⟩; inhaler ⟨glue, cocaine⟩
⟨3⟩ vi renifler
snigger ⟨1⟩ n ricanement m
⟨2⟩ vi ricaner
snip vtr découper (à petits coups de ciseaux) ⟨fabric, paper⟩; tailler ⟨hedge⟩
■ **snip off** couper
sniper n tireur m embusqué
snippet n (of conversation, information) bribes f; (of text, fabric, music) fragment m
snivel vi pleurnicher
snob n snob mf
snobbery n snobisme m
snobbish adj snob
snooker ⟨1⟩ n (game) snooker m
⟨2⟩ vtr **(a)** (Sport, figurative) coincer ⟨player, person⟩
(b) (US) (deceive) avoir (colloq) ⟨person⟩
snoop (colloq) ⟨1⟩ n fouineur/-euse m/f
⟨2⟩ vi fouiner, fureter
snooze (colloq) ⟨1⟩ n petit somme m
⟨2⟩ vi sommeiller
snore ⟨1⟩ n ronflement m
⟨2⟩ vi ronfler
snorkel n tuba m
snorkelling n plongée f avec tuba
snort ⟨1⟩ vi ⟨person, pig⟩ grogner; ⟨horse, bull⟩ s'ébrouer
⟨2⟩ vtr sniffer ⟨drugs⟩
snout n museau m; (of pig) groin m
snow ⟨1⟩ n neige f
⟨2⟩ v impers neiger; **it's ~ing** il neige

snowball ⟨1⟩ n boule f de neige
⟨2⟩ vi faire boule de neige
snowboard ⟨1⟩ n surf m des neiges
⟨2⟩ vi faire du surf des neiges
snowdrift n congère f
snowdrop n perce-neige m inv
snowfall n chute f de neige
snowflake n flocon m de neige
snowman n bonhomme m de neige
snow mobile n motoneige f
snow plough (GB), **snow plow** (US) n chasse-neige m inv
snow shoe n raquette f
snub ⟨1⟩ n rebuffade f
⟨2⟩ vtr rembarrer
snub-nosed adj au nez retroussé
snuff n tabac m à priser
snug adj ⟨bed, room⟩ douillet/-ette; ⟨coat⟩ chaud/-e
snuggle vi se blottir
so ⟨1⟩ adv **(a)** (to such an extent) si, tellement; **~ happy/quickly** si or tellement heureux/ vite; **~ much noise/many things** tant de bruit/de choses
(b) (in such a way) **~ arranged/worded that** organisé/rédigé d'une telle façon que; **and ~ on and ~ forth** et ainsi de suite; **~ be it!** soit!
(c) (thus) ainsi; (therefore) donc; **~ that's the reason** voilà donc pourquoi; **~ you're going are you?** alors tu y vas?
(d) (true) **is that ~?** c'est vrai?; **if (that's) ~** si c'est vrai
(e) (also) aussi; **~ is she** elle aussi; **~ do I** moi aussi
(f) (colloq) (thereabouts) environ; **20 or ~** environ 20
(g) (other uses) **I think/don't think ~** je crois/ ne crois pas; **I'm afraid ~** j'ai bien peur que oui or si; **~ it would appear** c'est ce qu'il semble; **~ to speak** si je puis dire; **I told you ~** je te l'avais bien dit; **~ I see** je le vois bien; **who says ~?** qui dit ça?; **only more ~** mais encore plus; **he dived and as he did ~...** il a plongé et en le faisant...; **'it's broken'—'~ it is'** 'c'est cassé'—'je le vois bien!'; **~ (what)?** et alors?
⟨2⟩ **so (that)** phr (in order that) pour que (+ subjunctive)
⟨3⟩ **so as** phr pour; **~ as to attract attention** pour attirer l'attention
⟨4⟩ **so much** phr tellement; **she worries ~ much** elle s'inquiète tellement; **she taught me ~ much** elle m'a tant appris; **thank you ~ much** merci beaucoup
IDIOMS **~ much the better** tant mieux; **~ ~** comme ci comme ça
soak ⟨1⟩ vtr **(a)** ⟨rain⟩ tremper ⟨person, clothes⟩
(b) ⟨person⟩ faire tremper ⟨clothes, foods⟩
⟨2⟩ vi **(a)** ⟨clothes, foods⟩ tremper
(b) ⟨liquid⟩ **to ~ into** être absorbé/-e par; **to ~ through** traverser
■ **soak up**: ¶ **~ [sth] up, ~ up [sth]**

absorber; ¶ ∼ up [sth] s'imprégner de ⟨atmosphere⟩; **to ∼ up the sun** faire le plein (colloq) de soleil

soaked adj trempé/-e; **to be ∼ through** or **∼ to the skin** être trempé/-e jusqu'aux os

soaking adj trempé/-e

soap n savon m; **a bar of ∼** un savon

soap opera n feuilleton m

soap powder n lessive f (en poudre)

soar vi (a) ⟨ball⟩ filer; ⟨bird, plane⟩ prendre son essor
(b) (glide) planer
(c) ⟨price, temperature, costs⟩ monter en flèche; ⟨hopes⟩ grandir considérablement
(d) ⟨tower, cliffs⟩ se dresser

soaring adj ⟨inflation, demand⟩ en forte progression; ⟨prices, temperatures⟩ en forte hausse

sob [1] n sanglot m
[2] vi sangloter

sober [1] adj (a) **I'm ∼** (not drunk) je n'ai pas bu d'alcool; (in protest) je ne suis pas ivre
(b) (no longer drunk) dessoûlé/-e
(c) (serious) ⟨person⟩ sérieux/-ieuse; ⟨mood⟩ grave
(d) ⟨colour, suit⟩ sobre
[2] vtr ⟨news, reprimand⟩ calmer
■ **sober up** dessoûler

sob story n (colloq) mélo m (colloq)

soccer n football m

sociable adj ⟨person⟩ sociable; ⟨evening⟩ agréable

social adj (a) (gen) social/-e
(b) ⟨call, visit⟩ amical/-e

social climber n (still rising) arriviste mf; (at his/her peak) parvenu/-e mf

social club n club m

social gathering n réunion f entre amis

socialism n socialisme m

socialist n, adj (also **Socialist**) socialiste (mf)

socialite n mondain/-e m/f

socialize vi rencontrer des gens; **to ∼ with sb** fréquenter qn

social life n (of person) vie f sociale; (of town) vie f culturelle

social science n science f sociale

social security n aide f sociale; **to be on ∼** recevoir l'aide sociale

Social Services n pl (GB) services mpl sociaux

social work n travail m social

social worker n travailleur/-euse m/f social/-e

society n (a) (gen) société f
(b) (club) société f; (for social contact) association f
(c) (also **high ∼**) haute société f

sociologist n sociologue mf

sociology n sociologie f

sock n chaussette f

socket n (a) (for plug) prise f (de courant); (for bulb) douille f
(b) (of joint) cavité f articulaire; (of eye) orbite f

soda n (a) (chemical) soude f
(b) (also **washing ∼**) soude f ménagère
(c) (also **∼ water**) eau f de seltz; **whisky and ∼** whisky m soda
(d) (also **∼ pop**) (US) soda m

sodden adj ⟨towel, clothing⟩ trempé/-e; ⟨ground⟩ détrempé/-e

sofa n canapé m

sofa bed n canapé-lit m

soft adj (a) (gen) doux/douce; ⟨ground⟩ meuble; ⟨bed, cushion⟩ moelleux/-euse; ⟨brush, hair⟩ souple; ⟨dough, butter⟩ mou/ molle; ⟨impact, touch⟩ léger/-ère; ⟨eyes, heart⟩ tendre; ⟨fold⟩ souple
(b) (lenient) ⟨parent, teacher⟩ (trop) indulgent/-e

soft cheese n fromage m à pâte molle

soft drink n boisson f non alcoolisée

soft drug n drogue f douce

soften [1] vtr (a) adoucir ⟨skin, water, light, outline⟩; ramollir ⟨butter⟩
(b) atténuer ⟨blow, shock, pain⟩
[2] vi (a) ⟨light, outline, music, colour⟩ s'adoucir; ⟨skin⟩ devenir plus doux; ⟨substance⟩ se ramollir
(b) ⟨person⟩ s'assouplir (**towards sb** vis-à-vis de qn)
■ **soften up**: ¶ ∼ up amollir; ¶ ∼ [sb] up affaiblir ⟨enemy, opponent⟩; attendrir ⟨customer⟩

softly adv ⟨speak, touch, blow⟩ doucement; ⟨fall⟩ en douceur

soft option n **to take the ∼** choisir la facilité

soft porn n (colloq) soft m (colloq)

soft spot n (colloq) **to have a ∼ for sb** avoir un faible (colloq) pour qn

soft-top n décapotable f

soft touch n (colloq) poire f (colloq)

soft toy n peluche f

software n logiciel m

software house n fabricant m de logiciels

software package n progiciel m

software piracy n piratage m de logiciels

soggy adj ⟨ground⟩ détrempé/-e; ⟨food⟩ ramolli/-e

soil [1] n sol m, terre f
[2] vtr salir

soiled adj (a) (dirty) sali/-e
(b) (also **shop-∼**) vendu/-e avec défaut

solace [1] n (feeling of comfort) consolation f; (source of comfort) réconfort m
[2] vtr consoler (**for** de)

solar adj solaire

solar eclipse n éclipse f de soleil

solar power n énergie f solaire

solder vtr, vi souder (**onto, to** à)

S

soldier *n* soldat *m*
■ **soldier on** persévérer malgré tout
sole [1] *n* (a) (fish) sole *f*
(b) (of foot) plante *f*; (of shoe, sock) semelle *f*
[2] *adj* (a) (single) seul/-e ⟨*before n*⟩, unique ⟨*before n*⟩
(b) ⟨*agent, right*⟩ exclusif/-ive; ⟨*trader*⟩ indépendant
solely *adv* (wholly) entièrement; (exclusively) uniquement
solemn *adj* ⟨*occasion, person, voice*⟩ solennel/-elle; ⟨*duty, warning*⟩ formel/-elle
solicit [1] *vtr* solliciter ⟨*information, help, money, votes*⟩; rechercher ⟨*business, investment, orders*⟩
[2] *vi* ⟨*prostitute*⟩ racoler
soliciting *n* racolage *m*
solicitor *n* (GB) (for documents, oaths) ≈ notaire *m*; (for court and police work) ≈ avocat/-e *m/f*
solid [1] *n* solide *m*
[2] *adj* (a) (gen) solide; **to go** *or* **become** ∼ se solidifier
(b) ⟨*gold, marble*⟩ massif/-ive; **the gate was made of** ∼ **steel** le portail était tout en acier; **cut through** ∼ **rock** tailler dans la roche
(c) ⟨*crowd*⟩ compact/-e; ⟨*line*⟩ continu/-e; **five** ∼ **days, five days** ∼ cinq jours entiers
(d) ⟨*advice, worker*⟩ sérieux/-ieuse; ⟨*investment*⟩ sûr/-e
[3] *adv* ⟨*freeze*⟩ complètement; **to be packed** ∼ ⟨*hall*⟩ être bondé/-e; **the play is booked** ∼ la pièce affiche complet
solidarity *n* solidarité *f*
solidify [1] *vtr* solidifier
[2] *vi* ⟨*liquid*⟩ se solidifier; ⟨*honey, oil*⟩ se figer
solitary *adj* (a) (unaccompanied) ⟨*occupation, walker*⟩ solitaire
(b) (lonely) ⟨*person*⟩ très seul/-e; ⟨*farm, village*⟩ isolé/-e
(c) (single) seul/-e
solitary confinement *n* isolement *m* cellulaire
solo [1] *n* solo *m*
[2] *adj, adv* en solo
soloist *n* soliste *mf*
solstice *n* solstice *m*
soluble *adj* soluble
solution *n* solution *f*
solve *vtr* résoudre ⟨*equation, problem*⟩; élucider ⟨*crime*⟩; trouver la solution de ⟨*mystery*⟩; trouver la solution à ⟨*clue, crossword*⟩; trouver une solution à ⟨*crisis, poverty, unemployment*⟩
solvent [1] *n* solvant *m*
[2] *adj* (in funds) solvable
sombre (GB), **somber** (US) *adj* sombre
some

■ **Note** When *some* is used to mean an unspecified amount of something, it is translated by *du, de l'* (before a vowel or mute 'h'), *de la* or *des* according to the gender and number of the noun that follows: *I'd like some bread* = je

voudrais du pain; *have some water* = prenez de l'eau; *we've bought some beer* = nous avons acheté de la bière; *they've bought some peaches* = ils ont acheté des pêches.
— But note that when a plural noun is preceded by an adjective in French, *some* is translated by *de* alone: *some pretty dresses* = de jolies robes.
— When *some* is used as a pronoun, it is translated by *en* which is placed before the verb in French: *would you like some?* = est-ce que vous en voulez?; *I've got some* = j'en ai.
— For further examples, see the entry below.

[1] *det* (a) (an unspecified amount or number) du/ de l'/de la/des; ∼ **old socks** des vieilles chaussettes; ∼ **red socks** des chaussettes rouges; **I need** ∼ **help** j'ai besoin d'aide
(b) (certain) certain/-e ⟨*before n*⟩; ∼ **people say that** certaines personnes disent que; **to** ∼ **extent** dans une certaine mesure
(c) (a considerable amount or number) **his suggestion was greeted with** ∼ **hostility** sa suggestion a été accueillie avec hostilité; **it will take** ∼ **doing** ça ne va pas être facile à faire; **we stayed there for** ∼ **time** nous sommes restés là assez longtemps
(d) (a little, a slight) **the meeting did have** ∼ **effect** la réunion a eu un certain effet; **you must have** ∼ **idea where the house is** tu dois avoir une idée de l'endroit où se trouve la maison
(e) (an unknown) **he's doing** ∼ **course** il suit des cours; **a car of** ∼ **sort,** ∼ **sort of car** une voiture quelconque
[2] *pron, quantif* (a) (an unspecified amount or number) en; **he took** ∼ **of it/of them** il en a pris un peu/quelques-uns; **(do) have** ∼**!** servez-vous!
(b) (certain ones) certain/-e; ∼ **(of them) are blue** certains sont bleus; ∼ **(of them) arrived early** certains d'entre eux sont arrivés tôt
[3] *adv* (a) (approximately) environ; ∼ **20 people** environ 20 personnes
(b) (US) (colloq) un peu

somebody *pron* (also **someone**) quelqu'un; ∼ **famous** quelqu'un de célèbre

somehow *adv* (a) (also ∼ **or other**) (of future action) d'une manière ou d'une autre; (of past action) je ne sais comment; **we'll get there** ∼ on y arrivera d'une manière ou d'une autre; **we managed it** ∼ nous avons réussi je ne sais comment
(b) (for some reason) ∼ **it doesn't seem very important** en fait, ça ne semble pas très important

someone = SOMEBODY

somersault [1] *n* (of gymnast) roulade *f*; (of child) galipette *f*; (accidental) culbute *f*
[2] *vi* ⟨*gymnast*⟩ faire une roulade; ⟨*vehicle*⟩ faire un tonneau

something [1] *pron* quelque chose; ∼ **interesting** quelque chose d'intéressant; ∼ **to do** quelque chose à faire; **there's** ∼ **wrong** il y a un problème; ∼ **or other** quelque chose; **in nineteen-sixty-**∼ en mille neuf cent soixante et quelques; **she's gone shopping or** ~ elle est allée faire les courses ou quelque chose comme ça

2 something of *phr* **she is** ~ **of an expert on...** elle est assez experte en...; **it was** ~ **of a surprise** c'était assez étonnant

sometime *adv* **we'll have to do it** ~ il va falloir qu'on le fasse un jour ou l'autre; **I'll tell you about it** ~ je te raconterai ça un de ces jours; **I'll phone you** ~ **next week** je te téléphonerai dans le courant de la semaine prochaine

sometimes *adv* parfois, quelquefois

somewhat *adv* (with adjective) plutôt; (with verb, adverb) un peu

somewhere *adv* (some place) quelque part; ~ **hot** un endroit chaud; ~ **or other** je ne sais où; ~ **between 50 and 100 people** entre 50 et 100 personnes

son *n* fils *m*

sonata *n* sonate *f*

song *n* chanson *f*; (of bird) chant *m*

songwriter *n* (of words) parolier/-ière *m/f*; (of words and music) auteur-compositeur *m* de chansons

sonic *adj* sonore

sonic boom *n* bang *m*

son-in-law *n* gendre *m*

sonnet *n* sonnet *m*

soon *adv* **(a)** (in a short time) bientôt; **see you** ~**!** à bientôt!
(b) (quickly) vite
(c) (early) tôt; **the** ~**er the better** le plus tôt sera le mieux; **as** ~ **as possible** dès que possible; **as** ~ **as you can** dès que tu pourras; **as** ~ **as he has finished** dès qu'il aura fini; ~**er or later** tôt ou tard
(d) (not long) ~ **afterwards** peu après; **no** ~**er had I finished than...** j'avais à peine fini que...

soot *n* suie *f*

soothe *vtr* calmer ⟨*pain, nerves, person*⟩; apaiser ⟨*sunburn*⟩

soothing *adj* ⟨*music, voice*⟩ apaisant/-e; ⟨*cream, effect*⟩ calmant/-e; ⟨*words*⟩ rassurant/-e

sophisticated *adj* **(a)** ⟨*person*⟩ (cultured) raffiné/-e; (affected) sophistiqué/-e; (elegant) chic; ⟨*restaurant*⟩ chic
(b) ⟨*taste*⟩ raffiné/-e; ⟨*civilization*⟩ évolué/-e
(c) ⟨*equipment, technology*⟩ sophistiqué/-e

soporific *adj* soporifique

soprano *n* (person) soprano *mf*; (voice, instrument) soprano *m*

sorcerer *n* sorcier *m*

sordid *adj* sordide

sore **1** *n* plaie *f*
2 *n* **(a)** ⟨*eyes, gums*⟩ irrité/-e; ⟨*muscle, arm, foot*⟩ endolori/-e; **to have a** ~ **throat** avoir mal à la gorge
(b) ⟨*subject, point*⟩ délicat/-e

sorrow *n* chagrin *m*

sorrowful *adj* ⟨*look*⟩ affligé/-e; ⟨*voice*⟩ triste

sorry **1** *adj* **(a)** désolé/-e; **I'm terribly** ~ je suis vraiment désolé, je suis navré; **I'm** ~ **I'm late** je suis désolé d'être en retard; **to be** ~ **about sth** s'excuser de qch; **to say** ~ s'excuser; **to be** ~ **to do** regretter de faire
(b) (pitying) **to be** *or* **feel** ~ **for sb** plaindre qn; **to feel** ~ **for oneself** s'apitoyer sur soi-même
(c) ⟨*state, sight, business*⟩ triste; ⟨*person*⟩ minable
2 *excl* **(a)** (apologizing) pardon!, désolé!
(b) (pardon) ~? pardon?

sort **1** *n* sorte *f*, genre *m*; **books, records— that** ~ **of thing** des livres, des disques, ce genre de choses; **I'm not that** ~ **of person** ce n'est pas mon genre; **some** ~ **of computer** une sorte d'ordinateur
2 *vtr* classer ⟨*data, files, stamps*⟩; trier ⟨*letters, apples, potatoes*⟩; **to** ~ **books into piles** ranger des livres en piles
3 of sorts, of a sort *phr* **a duck of** ~**s** *or* **of a** ~ une sorte de canard; **progress of** ~**s** un semblant de progrès
4 sort of *phr* (colloq) ~ **of cute** plutôt mignon/-onne; **I** ~ **of understand** je comprends plus ou moins; ~ **of blue-green** dans les bleu-vert; **it just** ~ **of happened** c'est arrivé comme ça
IDIOMS to be *or* **feel out of** ~**s** (ill) ne pas être dans son assiette; (grumpy) être de mauvais poil (colloq); **it takes all** ~**s (to make a world)** il faut de tout pour faire un monde
■ **sort out (a)** régler ⟨*problem, matter*⟩
(b) s'occuper de ⟨*details, arrangements*⟩; **I'll** ~ **it out** je m'en occuperai
(c) ranger ⟨*cupboard, desk*⟩; classer ⟨*files, documents*⟩; mettre de l'ordre dans ⟨*finances, affairs*⟩; clarifier ⟨*ideas*⟩
(d) trier ⟨*photos, clothes*⟩

sort code *n* code *m* d'agence

SOS *n* SOS *m*

so-so (colloq) **1** *adj* moyen/-enne
2 *adv* comme ci comme ça (colloq)

sought-after *adj* ⟨*person, skill*⟩ demandé/-e, recherché/-e; ⟨*job, brand, area*⟩ prisé/-e

soul *n* **(a)** (gen) âme *f*
(b) (*also* ~ **music**) soul *m*

soul-destroying *adj* abrutissant/-e

soul mate *n* âme *f* sœur

soul-searching *n* débat *m* intérieur

sound **1** *n* **(a)** (gen) son *m*; (noise) bruit *m* (of de); **to turn the** ~ **up/down** augmenter/baisser le volume; **the** ~ **of voices** un bruit de voix; **a grating** *or* **rasping** ~ un grincement; **without a** ~ sans bruit
(b) (figurative) **by the** ~ **of it, we're in for a rough crossing** d'après ce qu'on a dit, la traversée va être mauvaise
(c) (Med) sonde *f*
(d) (strait) détroit *m*
2 *adj* **(a)** ⟨*heart, constitution*⟩ solide; ⟨*health*⟩ bon/bonne (*before n*); **to be of** ~ **mind** être sain/-e d'esprit ⋯⟶

S

(b) ⟨basis, argument⟩ solide; ⟨judgment⟩
sain/-e; ⟨advice, investment⟩ bon/bonne
(before n), sûr/-e
⌐3⌐ vtr faire retentir ⟨siren, foghorn⟩; **to ~**
one's horn klaxonner; **to ~ the alarm** sonner
l'alarme
⌐4⌐ vi **(a)** (seem) sembler; **it ~s as if he's**
really in trouble il semble qu'il ait vraiment
des ennuis; **it ~s like it might be dangerous**
ça a l'air dangereux; **to ~ boring** paraître
ennuyeux; **it ~s like a flute** on dirait une
flûte
(b) ⟨alarm, buzzer, bugle⟩ sonner
⌐5⌐ adv **to be ~ asleep** dormir à poings
fermés
■ **sound out** sonder, interroger ⟨person⟩
sound barrier n mur m du son
sound bite n: bref extrait d'une interview
enregistrée
sound card n (Comput) carte f son
sound effect n effet m sonore
soundly adv ⟨sleep⟩ à poings fermés;
⟨defeat⟩ à plates coutures
soundproof adj insonorisé/-e
sound system n (hi-fi) stéréo f (colloq); (for
disco etc) sono f (colloq)
soundtrack n (of film) bande f sonore; (on
record) bande f originale
soup n soupe f, potage m
soup kitchen n soupe f populaire
soup plate n assiette f creuse
soupspoon n cuillère f à soupe
sour ⌐1⌐ adj **(a)** aigre; **to go ~** ⟨milk⟩
tourner
(b) (bad-tempered) revêche
⌐2⌐ vtr gâter ⟨relations, atmosphere⟩
source n source f; **at ~** à la source; **~ of**
source f de ⟨anxiety, resentment, satisfaction⟩;
cause f de ⟨problem, error, infection,
pollution⟩
sourdough n (US) levain m
south ⌐1⌐ n **(a)** (compass direction) sud m
(b) (part of world, country) **the South** le Sud
⌐2⌐ adj (gen) sud; ⟨wind⟩ du sud; **in ~**
London dans le sud de Londres
⌐3⌐ adv ⟨move⟩ vers le sud; ⟨lie, live⟩ au sud
(of de)
South Africa pr n Afrique f du Sud
South America pr n Amérique f du Sud
southeast ⌐1⌐ n sud-est m
⌐2⌐ adj ⟨coast, side⟩ sud-est inv; ⟨wind⟩ de
sud-est
⌐3⌐ adv ⟨move⟩ vers le sud-est; ⟨lie, live⟩ au
sud-est
southern adj ⟨coast⟩ sud inv; ⟨town,
accent⟩ du sud; ⟨hemisphere⟩ Sud inv; **~**
England le sud de l'Angleterre
South Pole pr n pôle m Sud
southwest ⌐1⌐ n sud-ouest m
⌐2⌐ adj ⟨coast⟩ sud-ouest inv; ⟨wind⟩ de
sud-ouest
⌐3⌐ adv ⟨move⟩ vers le sud-ouest; ⟨lie, live⟩ au
sud-ouest
souvenir n souvenir m

sovereign ⌐1⌐ n **(a)** (monarch) souverain/-e
m/f
(b) (coin) souverain m
⌐2⌐ adj souverain/-e (after n)
sovereignty n souveraineté f
Soviet Union pr n Union f soviétique
sow[1] n truie f
sow[2] vtr **(a)** semer ⟨seeds, corn⟩
(b) ensemencer ⟨field, garden⟩ (**with** de)
(c) (figurative) semer
soya n soja m
soya sauce, soy sauce n sauce f soja
spa n **(a)** (town) station f thermale
(b) (US) (health club) club m de remise en
forme
space ⌐1⌐ n **(a)** (also **outer ~**) espace m
(b) (room) place f, espace m
(c) (gap) espace m (**between** entre); (on form)
case f
(d) (interval of time) intervalle m; **in the ~ of**
five minutes en l'espace de cinq minutes
(e) (area of land) espace m; **open ~s** espaces
libres
⌐2⌐ adj ⟨programme, rocket⟩ spatial/-e
⌐3⌐ vtr espacer
■ **space out** espacer ⟨words, objects⟩;
échelonner ⟨payments⟩
space-bar n barre f d'espacement
spaced out adj (colloq) **he's completely ~**
(colloq) il plane (colloq) complètement
spaceship n vaisseau m spatial
space station n station f orbitale
spacesuit n combinaison f spatiale
spacing n espacement m; (of payments)
échelonnement m; **in single/double ~** en
simple/double interligne
spacious adj spacieux/-ieuse
spade n **(a)** (implement) bêche f, pelle f
(b) (in cards) pique m
spaghetti n spaghetti mpl inv
Spain pr n Espagne f
spamming n (Internet) envoi m de
publicités à l'ensemble des connectés
span ⌐1⌐ n **(a)** (of time) durée f
(b) (of bridge) travée f; ⟨wing⟩~ envergure f
⌐2⌐ vtr **(a)** ⟨bridge, arch⟩ enjamber
(b) (figurative) s'étendre sur
Spaniard n Espagnol/-e m/f
spaniel n épagneul m
Spanish ⌐1⌐ n **(a)** (people) **the ~** les
Espagnols mpl
(b) (language) espagnol m
⌐2⌐ adj (gen) espagnol/-e; ⟨teacher, lesson⟩
d'espagnol; ⟨embassy⟩ d'Espagne
spank vtr donner une fessée à
spanner n (GB) clé f (de serrage)
spar vi ⟨boxers⟩ échanger des coups
spare ⌐1⌐ n (part) pièce f de rechange; (wheel)
roue f de secours
⌐2⌐ adj **(a)** ⟨cash⟩ restant/-e; ⟨seat⟩ disponible;
⟨copy⟩ en plus; **I've got a ~ ticket** j'ai un
ticket en trop; **a ~ moment** un moment de
libre

(b) ⟨part⟩ de rechange; ⟨wheel⟩ de secours
(c) ⟨person, build⟩ élancé/-e
3 vtr **(a)** to have sth to ~ avoir qch de disponible; **to catch the train with five minutes to** ~ prendre le train avec cinq minutes d'avance; **can you** ~ **a minute?** as-tu un moment?
(b) (treat leniently) épargner; **to** ~ **sb sth** épargner qch à qn
(c) (manage without) se passer de ⟨person⟩
IDIOMS **to** ~ **no effort** faire tout son possible

spare part n pièce f de rechange
spare room n chambre f d'amis
spare time n loisirs mpl
spare tyre (GB), **spare tire** (US) n pneu m de rechange
sparingly adv ⟨use, add⟩ en petite quantité
spark **1** n étincelle f
2 vtr (also ~ **off**) provoquer ⟨reaction, panic⟩; être à l'origine de ⟨friendship, affair⟩
sparkle **1** n scintillement m; (in eye) éclair m
2 vi ⟨flame, light⟩ étinceler; ⟨jewel, frost, metal, water⟩ scintiller; ⟨eyes⟩ briller; ⟨drink⟩ pétiller
sparkler n cierge m magique
sparkling adj **(a)** ⟨eyes⟩ brillant/-e
(b) ⟨wit⟩ plein/-e de brio
(c) ⟨drink⟩ pétillant/-e
spark plug n bougie f
sparrow n moineau m
sparse adj clairsemé/-e
sparsely adv peu; ~ **wooded** peu boisé/-e; ~ **populated** à faible population
spasm n (of pain) spasme m (**of** de); (of panic, rage) accès m (**of** de)
spate n **(a) in full** ~ (GB) ⟨river⟩ en pleine crue; ⟨person⟩ en plein discours
(b) a ~ **of** une série de ⟨incidents⟩
spatula n spatule f
speak **1** vtr **(a)** parler ⟨language⟩; **can you** ~ **English?** parlez-vous (l')anglais?
(b) ⟨truth⟩; prononcer ⟨word, name⟩; **to** ~ **one's mind** dire ce qu'on pense
2 vi parler (**to, with** à; **about, of** de); **who's** ~**ing?** (on phone) qui est à l'appareil?; **(this is) Eileen** ~**ing** c'est Eileen; **generally** ~**ing** en règle générale; **roughly** ~**ing** en gros; **strictly** ~**ing** à proprement parler
■ **speak out** se prononcer
■ **speak up (a)** (louder) parler plus fort
(b) (dare to speak) intervenir
speaker n **(a)** (person talking) personne f qui parle; (public speaker) orateur/-trice m/f
(b) a French ~ un/-e francophone; **a Russian** ~ un/-e russophone
(c) (on stereo system) haut-parleur m
-speaking combining form **English-/French-**~ anglophone/francophone; **Welsh-**~ ⟨person⟩ qui parle le gallois
spear n lance f
spearhead vtr mener ⟨campaign, revolt, reform⟩

spearmint n menthe f verte
special adj (gen) spécial/-e; ⟨case, reason, treatment⟩ particulier/-ière; ⟨friend⟩ très cher/chère
special effect n effet m spécial
specialist n spécialiste m/f (**in** de)
speciality (GB), **specialty** (US) n spécialité f
specialize vi se spécialiser
specially adv **(a)** (specially) spécialement; **I made it** ~ **for you** je l'ai fait exprès pour toi
(b) (particularly) particulièrement; ⟨like, enjoy⟩ surtout
special needs n pl (Sch) difficultés fpl d'apprentissage scolaire
special school n établissement m médico-éducatif pour enfants handicapés
species n espèce f
specific adj précis/-e
specifically adv **(a)** (specially) spécialement
(b) (explicitly) explicitement
(c) (in particular) en particulier
specify **1** vtr stipuler; ⟨person⟩ préciser
2 specified pp adj ⟨amount, date, day⟩ spécifié/-e
specimen n (of rock, urine, handwriting) échantillon m; (of blood, tissue) prélèvement; (of species, plant) spécimen m
speck n (of dust, soot) grain m; (of dirt, mud, blood) petite tache f; (of light) point m
spectacle **1** n spectacle m
2 spectacles n pl lunettes fpl
spectacular adj spectaculaire
spectator n spectateur/-trice m/f
spectre (GB), **specter** (US) n spectre m
spectrum n **(a)** (of colours) spectre m
(b) (range) gamme f
speculate **1** vtr **to** ~ **that** supposer que
2 vi spéculer (**on** sur; **about** à propos de)
speculation n **(a)** (conjecture) spéculations fpl
(b) (financial) spéculation f (**in** sur)
speech n **(a)** discours m (**on** sur; **about** à propos de); **to give a** ~ faire un discours
(b) (faculty) parole f
(c) (language) langage m
speech day n (GB) (Sch) (jour m de la) distribution f des prix
speech impediment n défaut m d'élocution
speechless adj muet/-ette (**with** de); **to be** ~ **with** rester muet de; **I was** ~ **at the news** la nouvelle m'a laissé sans voix
speed **1** n **(a)** vitesse f; (of response, reaction) rapidité f; **at top** ~ à toute vitesse;
(b) (colloq) (drug) amphétamines fpl
2 vtr hâter ⟨process, recovery⟩
3 vi **(a)** to ~ **along** ⟨driver, car⟩ rouler à toute allure; **to** ~ **away** s'eloigner à toute allure
(b) (drive too fast) conduire trop vite ···◊

S

■ **speed up:** ¶ ∼ up ⟨*walker*⟩ aller plus vite; ⟨*athlete, driver, car*⟩ accélérer; ⟨*worker*⟩ travailler plus vite; ¶ ∼ [sth] up accélérer

speedboat n hors-bord m

speed camera n ≈ cinémomètre m

speed hump n ralentisseur m

speeding n excès m de vitesse

speed limit n limitation f de vitesse

speedometer n compteur m (de vitesse)

spell ①️ n (a) (period) moment m, période f; sunny ∼ éclaircie f
(b) (magic words) formule f magique; **to be under a** ∼ être envoûté/-e; **to cast** *or* **put a** ∼ **on sb** jeter un sort à qn; **to be under sb's** ∼ être sous le charme de qn
②️ vtr (a) écrire ⟨*word*⟩
(b) signifier ⟨*danger, disaster*⟩
③️ vi **he can't/can** ∼ il a une mauvaise/ bonne orthographe

■ **spell out (a)** épeler ⟨*word*⟩
(b) (explain) expliquer [qch] clairement

spellbound adj envoûté/-e (by par)

spellcheck vtr effectuer une correction orthographique sur ⟨*document*⟩

spellchecker n correcteur m orthographique.

spelling n orthographe f

spend ①️ vtr (a) dépenser ⟨*money, salary*⟩ (on en)
(b) passer ⟨*time*⟩ (**doing** à faire)
②️ vi dépenser

spending cut n réduction f des dépenses; (Pol) restriction f budgétaire

spending power n pouvoir m d'achat

spending spree n folie f (colloq) (de dépense); **to go on a** ∼ faire des folies (colloq)

spendthrift adj ⟨*person*⟩ dépensier/-ière

sperm n sperme m

sperm donor n donneur m de sperme

spew vtr vomir

sphere n (a) (shape) sphère f
(b) (field) domaine m (of de); ∼ **of influence** sphère f d'influence

spherical adj sphérique

spice n (Culin) épice f; (figurative) piment m

spick-and-span adj impeccable

spicy adj (a) ⟨*food*⟩ épicé/-e
(b) ⟨*detail*⟩ croustillant/-e

spider n araignée f

spiderweb n (US) toile f d'araignée

spike ①️ n pointe f
②️ vtr (colloq) corser ⟨*drink*⟩ (**with** de)

spiky adj ⟨*hair*⟩ en brosse inv; ⟨*branch*⟩ piquant/-e; ⟨*object*⟩ acéré/-e

spill ①️ vtr renverser ⟨*drink*⟩ (on, over sur)
②️ vi se répandre (**onto** sur; **into** dans)
■ **spill over** déborder; **to** ∼ **over into** dégénérer en ⟨*looting, hostility*⟩

spin ①️ n (a) (of wheel) tour m; (of dancer, skater) pirouette f
(b) **to go into a** ∼ ⟨*plane*⟩ descendre en vrille
(c) **to go for a** ∼ (in car) aller faire un tour

②️ vtr (a) lancer ⟨*top*⟩; faire tourner ⟨*globe, wheel*⟩
(b) filer ⟨*wool, thread*⟩
(c) ⟨*spider*⟩ tisser ⟨*web*⟩
③️ vi tourner; ⟨*weathercock, top*⟩ tournoyer; ⟨*dancer*⟩ pirouetter; **my head is** ∼**ning** j'ai la tête qui tourne

■ **spin out** prolonger ⟨*visit*⟩; faire traîner [qch] en longueur ⟨*speech*⟩; faire durer ⟨*work, money*⟩

■ **spin round:** ¶ ∼ round ⟨*person*⟩ se retourner rapidement; ⟨*dancer, skater*⟩ pirouetter; ⟨*car*⟩ faire un tête-à-queue; ¶ ∼ [sb/sth] round faire tourner ⟨*wheel*⟩

spinach n (Culin) épinards mpl

spinal cord n moelle f épinière

spindly adj grêle

spin doctor n (Pol) consultant m en communication attaché à un parti politique

spin-drier, spin dryer n essoreuse f

spine n (a) (Anat) colonne f vertébrale
(b) (on hedgehog, cactus) piquant m
(c) (of book) dos m

spineless adj mou/molle

spin-off n (a) (incidental benefit) retombée f favorable
(b) (by-product) sous-produit m

spinster n célibataire f; (derogatory) vieille fille f

spiral ①️ n spirale f
②️ adj ⟨*structure*⟩ en spirale
③️ vi ⟨*prices, costs*⟩ monter en flèche
④️ **spiralling** (GB), **spiraling** (US) pres p adj qui monte en flèche

spiral staircase n escalier m en colimaçon

spire n flèche f

spirit ①️ n (a) (gen) esprit m
(b) (courage, determination) courage m
②️ **spirits** n pl (a) (alcohol) spiritueux mpl
(b) **to be in good** ∼**s** être de bonne humeur; **to be in high** ∼**s** être d'excellente humeur; **to keep one's** ∼**s up** garder le moral

spirited adj ⟨*horse, debate, reply*⟩ fougueux/-euse; ⟨*attack, defence*⟩ vif/vive

spirit level n niveau m à bulle

spiritual ①️ n spiritual m
②️ adj spirituel/-elle

spit ①️ n (a) (saliva) salive f
(b) (Culin) broche f
②️ vtr ⟨*person*⟩ cracher; ⟨*pan*⟩ projeter ⟨*oil*⟩
③️ vi ⟨*cat, person*⟩ cracher (**at, on** sur); ⟨*oil, sausage*⟩ grésiller; ⟨*logs, fire*⟩ crépiter
④️ v impers **it's** ∼**ting (with rain)** il bruine
IDIOMS to be the ∼**ting image of sb** être le portrait tout craché de qn

spite ①️ n rancune f
②️ vtr faire du mal à; (less strong) embêter
③️ **in spite of** phr malgré; **in** ∼ **of the fact that** bien que

spiteful adj ⟨*person*⟩ rancunier/-ière; ⟨*remark*⟩ méchant/-e

splash ①️ n (a) (sound) plouf m

(b) (of mud) tache *f*; (of water, oil) éclaboussure *f*; (of colour) touche *f*; (of tonic, soda) goutte *f*
2 *vtr* éclabousser; **to ~ water on to one's face** s'asperger le visage d'eau
3 *vi* faire des éclaboussures
■ **splash out** (colloq) faire des folies; **to ~ out on sth** faire la folie de s'offrir qch

splay *vtr* écarter ⟨*feet, fingers*⟩

spleen *n* (Anat) rate *f*

splendid *adj* splendide; ⟨*idea, holiday, performance*⟩ merveilleux/-euse

splendour (GB), **splendor** (US) *n* splendeur *f*

splice *vtr* coller ⟨*tape, film*⟩; épisser ⟨*ends of rope*⟩

splint *n* (for injury) attelle *f*

splinter **1** *n* éclat *m*
2 *vi* ⟨*glass, windscreen*⟩ se briser; ⟨*wood*⟩ se fendre; ⟨*alliance*⟩ se scinder

splinter group *n* groupe *m* dissident

split **1** *n* (a) (in fabric) déchirure *f*; (in rock, wood) fissure *f*
(b) (in party, alliance) scission *f* (**in** de)
2 **splits** *n pl* **to do the ~s** faire le grand écart
3 *adj* ⟨*fabric*⟩ déchiré/-e; ⟨*seam*⟩ défait/-e; ⟨*log, lip*⟩ fendu/-e
4 *vtr* (a) fendre ⟨*log, rock*⟩ (**in, into** en); déchirer ⟨*garment*⟩
(b) diviser ⟨*party*⟩
(c) (share) partager (**between** entre)
5 *vi* (a) ⟨*wood, log, rock*⟩ se fendre (**in , into** en); ⟨*fabric, garment*⟩ se déchirer
(b) ⟨*party*⟩ se diviser
■ **split up**: ¶ **~ up** ⟨*couple, band*⟩ se séparer; ¶ **~ [sth] up** diviser (**into** en)

split second *n* fraction *f* de seconde

splutter *vi* ⟨*person*⟩ bafouiller; ⟨*fire, fat*⟩ grésiller

spoil **1** *vtr* (a) (mar) gâcher ⟨*event, view, game*⟩; gâter ⟨*place, taste, effect*⟩; **to ~ sth for sb** gâcher qch à qn
(b) (ruin) abîmer ⟨*garment, crops*⟩
(c) (pamper) gâter ⟨*child, pet*⟩
2 *vi* ⟨*product, foodstuff*⟩ s'abîmer

spoiled, spoilt (GB) *adj* ⟨*child, dog*⟩ gâté/-e; **a ~ brat** (colloq) un gamin pourri (colloq)

spoiler *n* (Aut) becquet *m*

spoils *n pl* (of war) butin *m* (**of** de)

spoilsport *n* (colloq) **to be a ~** être un rabat-joie

spoke *n* rayon *m*

spokesman *n* porte-parole *m inv*

spokeswoman *n* porte-parole *m inv*

sponge **1** *n* (a) éponge *f*
(b) (also ~ **cake**) génoise *f*
2 *vtr* éponger ⟨*material, stain, face*⟩
3 *vi* (colloq) **to ~ off** *or* **on** vivre sur le dos de ⟨*family, state*⟩

sponge bag *n* trousse *f* de toilette

sponsor **1** *n* (a) (advertiser, backer) sponsor *m*
(b) (patron) mécène *m*

2 *vtr* sponsoriser ⟨*event, team*⟩; financer ⟨*student*⟩; parrainer ⟨*child*⟩

sponsorship *n* sponsorat *m*

spontaneous *adj* spontané/-e

spontaneously *adv* spontanément

spoof *n* (colloq) (parody) parodie *f* (**on** de)

spooky *adj* (colloq) ⟨*house, atmosphere*⟩ sinistre; ⟨*story*⟩ qui fait froid dans le dos

spool *n* bobine *f*

spoon *n* cuillère *f*; (teaspoon) petite cuillère *f*

spoonful *n* cuillerée *f*, cuillère *f*

sporadic *adj* sporadique

sport *n* (a) sport *m*
(b) **he's a good ~** (good loser) il est beau joueur

sporting *adj* (a) ⟨*fixture, event*⟩ sportif/-ive
(b) (fair, generous) généreux/-euse; **to have a ~ chance of doing** avoir de bonnes chances de faire

sports car *n* voiture *f* de sport

sports centre (GB), **~s center** (US) *n* centre *m* sportif

sports club *n* club *m* sportif

sports ground *n* (large) stade *m*; (in school, club) terrain *m* de sports

sports jacket *n* (GB) veste *f* en tweed

sportsman *n* sportif *m*

sports star *n* vedette *f* sportive

sportswear *n* vêtements *mpl* de sport

sportswoman *n* sportive *f*

sporty *adj* (colloq) sportif/-ive

spot **1** *n* (a) (on animal) tache *f*; (on fabric) pois *m*; (on dice, domino) point *m*
(b) (stain) tache *f*
(c) (pimple) bouton *m*
(d) (place) endroit *m*; **on the ~** sur place; **to decide on the ~** décider sur-le-champ
(e) (colloq) (small amount) **a ~ of** un peu de
(f) (colloq) **to be in a (tight) ~** être dans une situation embêtante
2 *vtr* (a) apercevoir ⟨*person*⟩; repérer ⟨*difference, mistake*⟩
(b) (stain) tacher

spot check *n* contrôle *m* surprise

spotless *adj* impeccable

spotlight *n* (a) (light) projecteur *m*; (in home) spot *m*
(b) (focus of attention) **to be in** *or* **under the ~** ⟨*person*⟩ être sur la sellette; **the ~ is on Aids** le sida fait la une; **to turn** *or* **put the ~ on sb/sth** attirer l'attention sur qn/qch

spotted *adj* ⟨*fabric*⟩ à pois; ⟨*fur, dog*⟩ tacheté/-e

spotty *adj* (pimply) ⟨*skin*⟩ boutonneux/-euse; **he's very ~** il est plein de boutons; (patterned) à pois (*after n*)

spouse *n* époux/épouse *m/f*

spout **1** *n* (of kettle, teapot) bec *m* verseur
2 *vtr* (a) (spurt) faire jaillir ⟨*water*⟩
(b) (recite) débiter ⟨*poetry, statistics*⟩
3 *vi* ⟨*liquid*⟩ jaillir (**from, out of** de)

sprain **1** *n* entorse *f*

2 *vtr* to ~ one's ankle se faire une entorse à la cheville; (less severely) se fouler la cheville

sprawl **1** *n* (of suburbs, buildings) étendue *f*
2 *vi* s'étaler

spray **1** *n* **(a)** (seawater) embruns *mpl*; (other) nuages *mpl* de (fines) gouttelettes **(b)** (container) (for perfume) vaporisateur *m*; (can) bombe *f*; (for inhalant, throat, nose) pulvérisateur *m* **(c)** (of flowers) (bunch) gerbe *f*; (single branch) rameau *m*
2 *vtr* **(a)** vaporiser ⟨*liquid*⟩; asperger ⟨*person*⟩ (with de); to ~ sth onto sth (onto fire) projeter qch sur qch ⟨*foam, water*⟩; (onto surface, flowers) vaporiser qch sur qch ⟨*paint, water*⟩

spray can *n* bombe *f*, aérosol *m*

spread **1** *n* **(a)** (of disease, drugs) propagation *f*; (of news, information) diffusion *f* **(b)** (Culin) pâte *f* à tartiner
2 *vtr* **(a)** (unfold) étaler, étendre ⟨*cloth, newspaper, map*⟩ (on, over sur); ⟨*bird*⟩ déployer ⟨*wings*⟩ **(b)** étaler ⟨*butter, jam, glue*⟩ (on, over sur) **(c)** (distribute) disperser ⟨*troops*⟩; répartir ⟨*workload, responsibility*⟩ **(d)** (also ~ **out**) étaler, échelonner ⟨*payments, meetings*⟩ (over sur) **(e)** propager ⟨*disease, fire*⟩; semer ⟨*confusion, panic*⟩; faire circuler ⟨*rumour, story*⟩
3 *vi* **(a)** ⟨*butter, jam, glue*⟩ s'étaler **(b)** ⟨*forest, drought*⟩ s'étendre (over sur); ⟨*disease, fear, fire*⟩ se propager; ⟨*rumour, story*⟩ circuler; ⟨*stain, damp*⟩ s'étaler
■ **spread out**: ¶ ~ out ⟨*group*⟩ se disperser (over sur); ⟨*wings, tail*⟩ se déployer; ¶ ~ [sth] out étaler, étendre ⟨*cloth, map, rug*⟩ (on, over sur)

spread-eagled *adj* bras et jambes écartés

spreadsheet *n* tableur *m*

spree *n* to go on a ~ (drinking) faire la bringue (colloq); to go on a shopping ~ aller faire des folies dans les magasins

sprig *n* (of holly) petite branche *f*; (of parsley) brin *m*

sprightly *adj* alerte, gaillard

spring **1** *n* **(a)** (season) printemps *m*; in ~ au printemps **(b)** (of wire) ressort *m* **(c)** (leap) bond *m* **(d)** (water source) source *f*
2 *vtr* **(a)** déclencher ⟨*trap, lock*⟩ **(b)** to ~ a leak ⟨*tank, barrel*⟩ commencer à fuir **(c)** to ~ [sth] on sb annoncer [qch] de but en blanc à qn ⟨*news, plan*⟩
3 *vi* **(a)** (jump) bondir (onto sur) **(b)** (originate) to ~ from venir de
■ **spring up** ⟨*new building*⟩ apparaître

spring-clean *vtr* nettoyer [qch] de fond en comble ⟨*house*⟩

spring onion *n* (GB) ciboule *f*

springtime *n* printemps *m*

springy *adj* ⟨*mattress, seat*⟩ élastique

sprinkle *vtr* to ~ sth with saupoudrer qch de ⟨*salt, sugar*⟩; parsemer qch de ⟨*herbs*⟩; to ~ sth with water humecter qch

sprinkler *n* **(a)** (for lawn) arroseur *m* **(b)** (to extinguish fires) diffuseur *m*

sprint **1** *n* (race) sprint *m*, course *f* de vitesse
2 *vi* (in athletics) sprinter; (to catch bus) courir (à toute vitesse)

sprout **1** *n* (also **Brussels** ~) chou *m* de Bruxelles
2 *vi* ⟨*seed, shoot*⟩ germer; ⟨*grass, weeds*⟩ pousser

spruce **1** *n* (also ~ **tree**) épicéa *m*
2 *adj* ⟨*person*⟩ soigné/-e; ⟨*house, garden*⟩ bien tenu/-e
■ **spruce up** astiquer ⟨*house*⟩; nettoyer ⟨*garden*⟩; to ~ oneself up se faire beau/belle

spry *adj* alerte, leste

spun *adj* ⟨*glass, gold, sugar*⟩ filé/-e

spur **1** *n* **(a)** (for horse) éperon *m*; (figurative) aiguillon *m* **(b)** (of rock) contrefort *m*
2 *vtr* (also ~ **on**) éperonner ⟨*horse*⟩; aiguillonner ⟨*person*⟩; to ~ sb to do inciter qn à faire
IDIOMS on the ~ of the moment sur une impulsion

spurn *vtr* refuser [qch] (avec mépris)

spurt **1** *n* **(a)** (gush) (of water, oil, blood) giclée *f*; (of flame) jaillissement *m* **(b)** (of activity) regain *m*; (of energy) sursaut *m*; (in growth) poussée *f*; to put on a ~ ⟨*runner, cyclist*⟩ pousser une pointe de vitesse
2 *vi* (also ~ **out**) jaillir (from, out of de)

spy **1** *n* espion/-ionne *m/f*
2 *vtr* remarquer, discerner ⟨*figure, object*⟩
3 *vi* to ~ on sb/sth espionner qn/qch

spying *n* espionnage *m*

squabble *vi* se disputer, se chamailler (colloq)

squad *n* (Mil) escouade *f*; (Sport) sélection *f*

squad car *n* voiture *f* de police

squadron *n* escadron *m*

squalid *adj* sordide

squall *n* (wind) bourrasque *f*, rafale *f* (of de); (at sea) grain *m*

squalor *n* (filth) saleté *f* repoussante; (wretchedness) misère *f* (noire)

squander *vtr* gaspiller

square **1** *n* **(a)** (shape) carré *m* **(b)** (in town) place *f* **(c)** (in game, crossword) case *f*; (of glass, linoleum) carreau *m* **(d)** (colloq) (person) ringard/-e *m/f* (colloq)
2 *adj* **(a)** (in shape) carré/-e; four ~ metres quatre mètres carrés **(b)** (quits) to be ~ ⟨*people*⟩ être quitte
3 *vtr* **(a)** to ~ one's shoulders redresser les épaules **(b)** (settle) régler ⟨*account, debt*⟩
IDIOMS to go back to ~ one retourner à la case départ

■ **square up** (settle accounts) régler ses comptes

square bracket n crochet m; **in ~s** entre crochets

square root n racine f carrée

squash [1] n (a) (sport) squash m
(b) (drink) sirop m
(c) (vegetable) courge f
[2] vtr écraser

■ **squash up** (colloq) se serrer (**against** contre)

squat [1] adj ⟨person, structure, object⟩ trapu/-e
[2] vi (a) (crouch) s'accroupir
(b) **to ~ in** squatter ⟨building⟩

squatter n squatter m

squawk vi ⟨hen⟩ pousser des gloussements; ⟨duck, parrot⟩ pousser des cris rauques

squeak [1] n (of door, wheel, chalk) grincement m; (of mouse, soft toy) couinement m; (of furniture, shoes) craquement m
[2] vi ⟨door, wheel, chalk⟩ grincer; ⟨mouse, soft toy⟩ couiner; ⟨shoes, furniture⟩ craquer (**on** sur)

squeaky adj ⟨voice⟩ aigu/aiguë; ⟨gate, hinge, wheel⟩ grinçant/-e

squeal vi ⟨person, animal⟩ pousser des cris aigus

squeamish adj impressionnable, sensible

squeeze [1] n (a) (on credit, finances) resserrement m (**on** de)
(b) (colloq) (crush) **it will be a tight ~** ce sera un peu juste
[2] vtr (a) presser ⟨lemon, bottle, tube⟩; serrer ⟨arm, hand⟩; appuyer sur ⟨trigger⟩; percer ⟨spot⟩; **to ~ water out of** essorer, tordre ⟨cloth⟩
(b) (figurative) réussir à obtenir ⟨money⟩ (**out of** de); **to ~ the truth out of sb** arracher la vérité à qn
(c) (fit) **to ~ sth into sth** entasser qch dans qch

■ **squeeze in**: ¶ **~ in** ⟨person⟩ se glisser; ¶ **~ [sb] in** ⟨doctor etc⟩ faire passer [qn] entre deux rendez-vous

■ **squeeze past** ⟨car, person⟩ passer

squelch vi ⟨water, mud⟩ glouglouter; **to ~ along** avancer en pataugeant

squid n calmar m, encornet m

squiggle n gribouillis m

squint [1] n strabisme m; **to have a ~** loucher
[2] vi (a) (look) plisser les yeux
(b) (have eye condition) loucher

squire n ≈ châtelain m

squirm vi (wriggle) se tortiller; ⟨person⟩ (in pain) se tordre; (with embarrassment) être très mal à l'aise

squirrel n écureuil m

squirt [1] vtr faire gicler ⟨liquid⟩
[2] vi ⟨liquid⟩ jaillir (**from, out of** de)

stab [1] n (a) (act) coup m de couteau; **a ~ in the back** (figurative) un coup en traître
(b) (of pain) élancement m (**of** de)
[2] vtr poignarder ⟨person⟩

stabbing n agression f au couteau

stability n stabilité f

stabilize [1] vtr stabiliser
[2] vi se stabiliser

stable [1] n écurie f; **riding ~s** manège m
[2] adj (a) (steady) stable
(b) (psychologically) équilibré/-e

stack [1] n (pile) pile f; (of hay, straw) meule f
[2] vtr (a) (also ~ **up**) (pile) empiler
(b) (fill) remplir ⟨shelves⟩
(c) mettre [qch] en attente ⟨planes, calls⟩

stadium n stade m

staff n (of company) personnel m; (of a school, college) personnel m enseignant

staff meeting n réunion f du personnel enseignant

staff room n salle f des professeurs

stag n cerf m

stage [1] n (a) (phase) (of illness, career, life) stade m (**of, in** de); (of project, process, plan) phase f (**of, in** de); (of journey, negotiations) étape f (**of, in** de)
(b) (raised platform) estrade f; (in theatre) scène f
[2] vtr (a) (organize) organiser ⟨event, rebellion, strike⟩
(b) (fake) simuler ⟨quarrel, scene⟩
(c) (in theatre) monter ⟨play⟩

stagecoach n diligence f

stage fright n trac m

stage-manager n régisseur/-euse m/f

stagger [1] vtr (a) (astonish) stupéfier, abasourdir
(b) (échelonner) ⟨holidays, payments⟩
[2] vi (from weakness) chanceler; (drunkenly) tituber

staggering adj ⟨amount, increase⟩ prodigieux/-ieuse; ⟨news⟩ renversant/-e; ⟨achievement, contrast⟩ stupéfiant/-e; ⟨success⟩ étourdissant/-e

stagnant adj stagnant/-e

stagnate vi stagner

stag night, **stag party** n soirée f pour enterrer une vie de garçon

staid adj guindé/-e

stain [1] n (a) (mark) tache f
(b) (dye) teinture f
[2] vtr (a) (soil) tacher ⟨clothes, carpet, table⟩
(b) teindre ⟨wood⟩

stained glass n verre m coloré

stained glass window n vitrail m

stainless steel n acier m inoxydable

stain remover n détachant m

stair [1] n (step) marche f (d'escalier)
[2] **stairs** n pl **the ~s** l'escalier m; **to fall down the ~s** tomber dans l'escalier

staircase, **stairway** n escalier m

stake [1] n (a) (amount risked) enjeu m; **to be at ~** être en jeu
(b) (investment) participation f (**in** dans)
(c) (post) pieu m

⋯▸

2 *vtr* miser ⟨*money, property*⟩; risquer ⟨*reputation*⟩

■ **stake out**: ~ out [sth], ~ [sth] out surveiller ⟨*place*⟩

stale *adj* ⟨*bread, cake*⟩ rassis/-e; ⟨*beer*⟩ éventé/-e; ⟨*smell*⟩ de renfermé; ⟨*ideas*⟩ éculé/-e

stalemate *n* **(a)** (in chess) pat *m*
(b) (deadlock) impasse *f*

stalk **1** *n* (on plant, flower) tige *f*; (of leaf, apple) queue *f*; (of mushroom) pied *m*
2 *vtr* ⟨*hunter, murderer*⟩ traquer ⟨*prey, victim*⟩; ⟨*animal*⟩ chasser ⟨*prey*⟩

stall **1** *n* **(a)** (at market, fair) stand *m*
(b) (in stable) stalle *f*
2 **stalls** *n pl* (GB) orchestre *m*
3 *vtr* caler ⟨*engine, car*⟩
4 *vi* **(a)** ⟨*car*⟩ caler
(b) (play for time) temporiser

stallholder *n* marchand/-e *m/f*

stallion *n* étalon *m*

stalwart *adj* loyal/-e

stamina *n* résistance *f*, endurance *f*

stammer **1** *n* bégaiement *m*
2 *vi* bégayer

stamp **1** *n* **(a)** (for envelope) timbre *m*
(b) (on passport, document) cachet *m*
(c) (marker) (rubber) tampon *m*; (metal) cachet *m*
2 *vtr* **(a)** apposer [qch] au tampon ⟨*date, name*⟩ (on sur); tamponner ⟨*ticket, book*⟩; viser ⟨*document, passport*⟩
(b) to ~ one's foot (in anger) taper du pied
3 *vi* ⟨*horse*⟩ piaffer; to ~ on écraser (du pied) ⟨*toy, foot*⟩; piétiner ⟨*soil, ground*⟩

stamp-collecting *n* philatélie *f*

stamped addressed envelope, sae *n* enveloppe *f* timbrée à votre/son etc adresse

stampede **1** *n* débandade *f*
2 *vi* s'enfuir (pris d'affolement)

stance *n* position *f*

stand **1** *n* **(a)** (support, frame) support *m*; (for coats) portemanteau *m*
(b) (stall) (in market) éventaire *m*; (kiosk) kiosque *m*; (at exhibition, trade fair) stand *m*
(c) (in stadium) tribunes *fpl*
(d) (witness box) barre *f*
(e) (stance) to take a ~ on sth prendre position sur qch
(f) (to make) a last ~ (livrer) une dernière bataille
2 *vtr* **(a)** (place) mettre ⟨*person, object*⟩ (against contre; in dans; on sur)
(b) (bear) supporter ⟨*cold, weight*⟩; tolérer ⟨*nonsense, bad behaviour*⟩; I can't ~ him je ne peux pas le supporter *or* le sentir; I can't ~ this town je déteste cette ville; I can't ~ doing je déteste faire
(c) (colloq) to ~ sb a drink payer un verre à qn
(d) to ~ trial passer en jugement
3 *vi* **(a)** (*also* ~ up) se lever
(b) (be upright) ⟨*person*⟩ se tenir debout; ⟨*object*⟩ tenir debout; to remain ~ing rester debout
(c) ⟨*building, village*⟩ se trouver, être
(d) (step) to ~ on marcher sur ⟨*insect, foot*⟩
(e) (be) as things ~... étant donné l'état actuel des choses...; the total ~s at 300 le total est de 300; to ~ in sb's way (figurative) faire obstacle à qn
(f) (remain valid) ⟨*offer, agreement*⟩ rester valable
(g) (be a candidate) se présenter (as comme); to ~ for election se présenter aux élections

■ **stand back** ⟨*person, crowd*⟩ reculer (from de); (figurative) prendre du recul (from par rapport à)

■ **stand by**: ¶ ~ by ⟨*doctor, army*⟩ être prêt/-e à intervenir; ¶ ~ by [sb/sth] soutenir ⟨*person*⟩; s'en tenir à ⟨*principles, decision*⟩

■ **stand down** démissionner

■ **stand for (a)** (represent) représenter; ⟨*initials*⟩ vouloir dire
(b) (tolerate) tolérer

■ **stand in**: to ~ in for sb remplacer qn

■ **stand out** ⟨*person*⟩ sortir de l'ordinaire; ⟨*work, ability*⟩ être remarquable

■ **stand up**: ¶ ~ up **(a)** (rise) se lever
(b) (stay upright) se tenir debout
(c) ⟨*theory, story*⟩ tenir debout
(d) to ~ up to tenir tête à ⟨*person*⟩
(e) to ~ up for défendre ⟨*person, rights*⟩
¶ ~ [sth] up redresser ⟨*object*⟩
¶ ~ [sb] up (colloq) poser un lapin à (colloq)

standard **1** *n* **(a)** (level) niveau *m*; not to be up to ~ ne pas avoir le niveau requis
(b) (official specification) norme *f* (for de)
(c) (banner) étendard *m*
2 *adj* ⟨*size, rate, pay*⟩ standard *inv*; ⟨*procedure*⟩ habituel/-elle; ⟨*image*⟩ traditionnel/-elle; it's ~ practice c'est l'usage

Standard Assessment Task *n* (GB) (Sch) test *m* d'aptitude scolaire (*par tranches d'âge*)

standardize *vtr* normaliser, standardiser

standard lamp *n* (GB) lampadaire *m*

standard of living *n* niveau *m* de vie

standby *n* (person) remplaçant/-e *m/f*; to be on ~ ⟨*army, emergency services*⟩ être prêt/-e à intervenir; (for airline ticket) être en stand-by

stand-in *n* remplaçant/-e *m/f*

standing **1** *n* **(a)** (reputation) réputation *f*, rang *m* (among parmi; with chez)
(b) (length of time) of long ~ de longue date
2 *adj* **(a)** ⟨*army, committee, force*⟩ actif/-ive
(b) ⟨*invitation*⟩ permanent/-e

standing charge *n* frais *mpl* d'abonnement *m*

standing order *n* virement *m* automatique

stand-off *n* (US) impasse *f*

standpoint *n* point *m* de vue

standstill *n* to be at a ~ ⟨*traffic*⟩ être à l'arrêt; ⟨*factory, port*⟩ être au point mort;

⟨*work*⟩ être arrêté/e; ⟨*talks*⟩ être arrivé/-e à une impasse; **to come to a ~** ⟨*person, car*⟩ s'arrêter

stand-up ① *n* (*also* **~ comedy**) one man show *m* comique
② *adj* **~ comedian** comique *mf*

Stanley knife® *n* cutter *m*

staple ① *n* (a) (for paper) agrafe *f*
(b) (basic food) aliment *m* de base
② *adj* ⟨*product, food, diet*⟩ de base
③ *vtr* agrafer (**to** à; **onto** sur)

stapler *n* agrafeuse *f*

star ① *n* (a) (in sky) étoile *f*
(b) (celebrity) vedette *f*, star *f*
(c) (asterisk) astérisque *m*
(d) (ranking) **a three-~** hotel un hôtel (à) trois étoiles
② *vi* ⟨*actor*⟩ jouer le rôle principal (**in** dans)
③ *vtr* ⟨*film, play*⟩ avoir [qn] pour vedette ⟨*actor*⟩

starch *n* (a) (carbohydrate) féculents *mpl*
(b) (for clothes) amidon *m*

stardom *n* célébrité *f*; **to rise to ~** devenir une vedette

stare ① *n* regard *m* fixe
② *vi* **to ~ at sb/sth** regarder fixement qn/qch

starfish *n* étoile *f* de mer

stark *adj* ⟨*landscape*⟩ désolé/-e; ⟨*room, decor*⟩ nu/-e; **in ~ contrast to** en opposition totale avec
IDIOMS **~ naked** tout/-e nu/-e

starry *adj* ⟨*night, sky*⟩ étoilé/-e

starry-eyed *adj* ébloui/-e (**about** par)

star sign *n* signe *m* astrologique

star-studded *adj* avec de nombreuses vedettes

start ① *n* (a) (beginning) début *m*
(b) (in sport) (advantage) avantage *m*; (in time, distance) avance *f*; (departure line) ligne *f* de départ
(c) (movement) **with a ~** en sursaut
② *vtr* (a) (begin) commencer; entamer ⟨*bottle, packet*⟩; **to ~ doing** commencer à faire
(b) (cause, initiate) déclencher ⟨*quarrel, war*⟩; lancer ⟨*fashion, rumour*⟩
(c) faire démarrer ⟨*car*⟩; mettre [qch] en marche ⟨*machine*⟩
③ *vi* (a) (begin) commencer (**by doing** par faire); **to ~ again** recommencer
(b) ⟨*car, engine, machine*⟩ démarrer
(c) (depart) partir
(d) (jump nervously) sursauter (**in** de)
④ **to start with** *phr* (a) (firstly) d'abord, premièrement
(b) (at first) au début
■ **start off**: ¶ **~ off** (a) (set off) ⟨*train, bus*⟩ démarrer; ⟨*person*⟩ partir
(b) (begin) ⟨*person*⟩ commencer; ⟨*business, employee*⟩ débuter (**as** comme; **in** dans)
¶ **~ [sth] off** (a) commencer ⟨*visit, talk*⟩ (**with** par)
(b) mettre [qch] en marche ⟨*machine*⟩
■ **start out** (on journey) partir

■ **start over** (US) recommencer (à zéro)

■ **start up**: ¶ **~ up** ⟨*engine*⟩ démarrer; ¶ **~ [sth]** up faire démarrer ⟨*car*⟩; ouvrir ⟨*shop*⟩; créer ⟨*business*⟩

starter *n* (a) (of race) starter *m*
(b) (on menu) hors-d'œuvre *m inv*
IDIOMS **for ~s** (colloq) pour commencer

startle *vtr* (a) (take aback) surprendre
(b) (alarm) effrayer

startling *adj* saisissant/-e

starvation *n* famine *f*; **to die of ~** mourir de faim

starve ① *vtr* affamer; (figurative) priver (**of** de); **to ~ oneself** se sous-alimenter
② *vi* mourir de faim; **to be ~d of** être en mal de ⟨*company, conversation*⟩

starving *adj* (hungry) **to be ~** mourir de faim; (hunger-stricken) affamé/-e

state ① *n* (a) état *m*; **he's not in a fit ~ to drive** il n'est pas en état de conduire
(b) (government, nation) (*also* **State**) État *m*
② **States** *n pl* **the States** les États-Unis *mpl*
③ *adj* ⟨*school, sector*⟩ public/-ique; ⟨*enterprise, pension*⟩ d'État; ⟨*subsidy*⟩ de l'État
(b) ⟨*occasion*⟩ d'apparat; ⟨*visit*⟩ officiel/-ielle
④ *vtr* (a) (declare) exposer ⟨*fact, opinion*⟩; indiquer ⟨*age, income*⟩; **to ~ that** ⟨*person*⟩ déclarer que
(b) (specify) spécifier ⟨*amount, time, terms*⟩; exprimer ⟨*preference*⟩
IDIOMS **to be in a ~** être dans tous ses états

State Department *n* (US) ministère *m* des Affaires étrangères

state-funded *adj* subventionné/-e par l'État

stateless *adj* apatride

stately *adj* imposant/-e

stately home *n* (GB) château *m*

statement *n* (a) déclaration *f*; (official) communiqué *m*
(b) (*also* **bank ~**) relevé *m* de compte

state of the art *adj* ⟨*equipment*⟩ ultramoderne; ⟨*technology*⟩ de pointe

statesman *n* homme *m* d'État

static ① *n* (a) (*also* **~ electricity**) électricité *f* statique
(b) (interference) parasites *mpl*
② *adj* (a) (stationary) ⟨*image*⟩ fixe; ⟨*traffic*⟩ bloqué/-e
(b) (stable) ⟨*population, prices*⟩ stationnaire

station ① *n* (a) (*also* **railway ~**) (GB) gare *f*
(b) (radio, TV) station *f*
(c) (*also* **police ~**) commissariat *m*; (small) poste *m* de police
② *vtr* poster ⟨*officer, guard*⟩; stationner ⟨*troops*⟩

stationary *adj* immobile, à l'arrêt

stationer *n* (*also* **~'s**) papeterie *f*

stationery *n* fournitures *fpl* de bureau; (writing paper) papier *m* à lettres

station wagon *n* (US) break *m*

S

statistic n statistique f; **~s show that...** d'après les statistiques...

statistical adj statistique

statue n statue f

stature n **(a)** (height) taille f
(b) (status) envergure f

status n **(a)** (position) position f
(b) (prestige) prestige m
(c) (legal, professional) statut m **(as de)**; **financial ~** situation f financière

status quo n statu quo m

status symbol n signe m de prestige

statute n texte m de loi; **by ~** par la loi

statutory adj légal/-e

staunch adj ⟨supporter, defence⟩ loyal/-e; ⟨Catholic, communist⟩ fervent/-e

stave n (Mus) portée f
■ **stave off** tromper ⟨hunger, fatigue⟩; écarter ⟨threat⟩

stay ☐ n **(a)** (visit) séjour m
(b) **~ of execution** sursis m
☐ vi **(a)** (remain) rester; **to ~ for lunch** rester (à) déjeuner
(b) (have accommodation) loger; **to ~ in a hotel/ with a friend** loger à l'hôtel/chez un ami; **to ~ overnight** passer la nuit
(c) (visit) passer quelques jours **(with chez)**
■ **stay in** rester à la maison
■ **stay out**: **to ~ out late/all night** rentrer tard/ne pas rentrer de la nuit; **to ~ out of trouble** éviter les ennuis
■ **stay up (a)** (waiting for sb) veiller
(b) (as habit) se coucher tard
(c) (not fall down) tenir

staying-power n endurance f

steadfast adj tenace

steadily adv **(a)** (gradually) progressivement
(b) ⟨work, rain⟩ sans interruption

steady ☐ adj **(a)** (continual) ⟨stream, increase⟩ constant/-e; ⟨rain⟩ incessant/-e; ⟨breathing, progress⟩ régulier/-ière
(b) (stable) stable; **to hold** [sth] **~** bien tenir ⟨ladder⟩
(c) ⟨voice, hand⟩ ferme; ⟨gaze⟩ calme
(d) (reliable) ⟨job⟩ stable; ⟨relationship⟩ durable
☐ vtr **to ~ one's nerves** se calmer les nerfs

steak n (of beef) steak m; (of fish) darne f

steal ☐ vtr voler **(from sb** à qn)
☐ vi **(a)** (thieve) voler
(b) (creep) **to ~ into/out of a room** entrer/ quitter une pièce subrepticement

stealing n vol m

stealthy adj ⟨step, glance⟩ furtif/-ive

steam ☐ n vapeur f
☐ vtr faire cuire [qch] à la vapeur ⟨vegetables⟩
☐ vi fumer, dégager de la vapeur
IDIOMS **to run out of ~** s'essouffler; **to let off ~** décompresser
■ **steam up** ⟨window, glasses⟩ s'embuer

steam engine n locomotive f à vapeur

steamer n (boat) (bateau m à) vapeur m

steamroller n rouleau m compresseur

steamy adj **(a)** ⟨window⟩ embué/-e; ⟨climate⟩ chaud/-e et humide
(b) (colloq) (erotic) torride

steel ☐ n acier m
☐ v refl **to ~ oneself** s'armer de courage

steelworks, steelyard n installations fpl sidérurgiques

steep ☐ adj **(a)** ⟨slope, stairs⟩ raide; ⟨street, path⟩ escarpé/-e; ⟨roof⟩ en pente raide
(b) (sharp) ⟨rise, fall⟩ fort/-e **(before n)**
(c) (colloq) ⟨price⟩ exorbitant/-e
☐ vtr **to ~ sth in** faire tremper qch dans

steeple n (tower) clocher m; (spire) flèche f

steer ☐ n (animal) bouvillon m
☐ vtr **(a)** piloter ⟨ship, car⟩
(b) (guide) diriger ⟨person⟩
☐ vi (in car) piloter; (in boat) gouverner
IDIOMS **to ~ clear of sb/sth** se tenir à l'écart de qn/qch

steering lock n blocage m de direction

steering wheel n volant m

stem ☐ n **(a)** (of flower, leaf) tige f; (of fruit) queue f
(b) (of glass) pied m
☐ vtr arrêter ⟨flow⟩; enrayer ⟨advance, tide⟩
☐ vi **to ~ from** provenir de

stencil ☐ n pochoir m
☐ vtr décorer [qch] au pochoir ⟨fabric, surface⟩

stenography n (US) sténographie f

step ☐ n **(a)** (pace) pas m
(b) (measure) mesure f; **to take ~s** prendre des mesures
(c) (stage) étape f **(in dans)**
(d) (stair) marche f; **~s** (small ladder) escabeau m
☐ vi marcher **(in dans; on sur)**; **to ~ into** entrer dans ⟨lift⟩; monter dans ⟨dinghy⟩; **to ~ off** descendre de ⟨pavement⟩; **to ~ over** enjamber ⟨fence⟩
IDIOMS **one ~ at a time** chaque chose en son temps
■ **step back** (figurative) prendre du recul **(from** par rapport à)
■ **step down** se retirer; (as electoral candidate) se désister
■ **step in** intervenir **(and do pour faire)**
■ **step up** accroître ⟨production⟩; intensifier ⟨campaign⟩

step aerobics n step m

stepbrother n demi-frère m

step-by-step ☐ adj ⟨guide⟩ complet/-ète
☐ **step by step** adv ⟨explain⟩ étape par étape

stepchild n beau-fils/belle-fille m/f

stepdaughter n belle-fille f

stepfather n beau-père m

stepladder n escabeau m

stepmother n belle-mère f

stepping stone n pierre f de gué; (figurative) tremplin m

stepsister n demi-sœur f

stepson n beau-fils m

stereo n **(a)** (sound) stéréo f; **in ~** en stéréo

(b) (*also* ~ **system**) chaîne *f* stéréo; **personal** ~ baladeur *m*

stereotype *n* stéréotype *m*

sterile *adj* stérile

sterilize *vtr* stériliser

sterling *n* livre *f* sterling *inv*

stern 1 *n* (of ship) poupe *f*
2 *adj* sévère

steroid *n* stéroïde *m*

stew 1 *n* ragoût *m*
2 *vtr* cuire [qch] en ragoût ⟨*meat*⟩; faire cuire ⟨*fruit*⟩; ~ed apples compote *f* de pommes

steward *n* (on plane, ship) steward *m*; (of club) intendant/-e *m/f*; (at races) organisateur *m*

stewardess *n* (on plane) hôtesse *f* (de l'air)

stick 1 *n* (a) (of wood, chalk, dynamite) bâton *m*
(b) (*also* **walking** ~) canne *f*
(c) (in hockey) crosse *f*
2 *vtr* (a) to ~ sth into sth planter qch dans qch
(b) (colloq) (put) mettre
(c) (fix in place) coller ⟨*poster, stamp*⟩ (**on** sur; **to** à)
3 *vi* (a) the thorn stuck in my finger l'épine m'est restée dans le doigt
(b) ⟨*stamp, glue*⟩ coller; to ~ to the pan ⟨*sauce, rice*⟩ attacher
(c) ⟨*drawer, door, lift*⟩ se coincer
(d) (remain) rester; to ~ in sb's mind rester gravé dans la mémoire de qn
■ **stick at:** ~ at [sth] persévérer dans ⟨*task*⟩
■ **stick out:** ¶ ~ out ⟨*nail, sharp object*⟩ dépasser (**of** de); his ears ~ out il a les oreilles décollées; ¶ ~ [sth] out: to ~ out one's hand/foot tendre la main/le pied; to ~ one's tongue out tirer la langue
■ **stick to** (a) (keep to) s'en tenir à ⟨*facts, point*⟩; maintenir ⟨*story, version*⟩
(b) (follow) suivre ⟨*river, road*⟩
■ **stick together** (a) ⟨*pages*⟩ se coller
(b) (colloq) (be loyal) être solidaires
(c) (colloq) (not separate) rester ensemble
■ **stick up** (project) se dresser; to ~ up for sb défendre qn

sticker *n* autocollant *m*

sticking plaster *n* pansement *m* adhésif, sparadrap *m*

sticky *n* (a) ⟨*floor, fingers*⟩ poisseux/-euse; ⟨*label*⟩ adhésif/-ive
(b) (sweaty) ⟨*hand, palm*⟩ moite

sticky tape *n* (colloq) Scotch® *m*, ruban *m* adhésif

stiff 1 *adj* (a) raide; (after sport, sleeping badly) courbaturé/-e; ~ neck torticolis *m*; to have ~ legs (after sport) avoir des courbatures dans les jambes
(b) ⟨*lever, handle*⟩ dur/-e à manier
(c) ⟨*manner, style*⟩ compassé/-e
(d) (tough) ⟨*sentence*⟩ sévère; ⟨*exam, climb*⟩ difficile; ⟨*competition*⟩ rude
(e) (high) ⟨*charge, fine*⟩ élevé/-e

(f) a ~ drink un remontant
2 *adv* (colloq) to bore sb ~ ennuyer qn à mourir; to be scared ~ avoir une peur bleue

stiffen 1 *vtr* renforcer ⟨*card*⟩; empeser ⟨*fabric*⟩
2 *vi* (a) ⟨*person*⟩ se raidir
(b) ⟨*egg white*⟩ devenir ferme; ⟨*mixture*⟩ prendre de la consistance

stifle *vtr* étouffer

stigma *n* stigmate *m*

stigmatize *vtr* stigmatiser

stile *n* échalier *m*

stiletto *n* (*also* ~ **heel**) (shoe, heel) talon *m* aiguille

still¹ *adv* (a) encore, toujours; he's ~ as crazy as ever! il est toujours aussi fou!; they're ~ in town ils sont encore en ville
(b) (referring to the future) encore; I have four exams ~ to go j'ai encore quatre examens à passer
(c) (nevertheless) quand même
(d) (with comparatives) encore; better/worse ~ encore mieux/pire

still² 1 *n* (a) (for making alcohol) alambic *m*
(b) (photograph) photo *f* de plateau
2 *adj* (a) (motionless) ⟨*air, water*⟩ calme; ⟨*hand, person*⟩ immobile
(b) (peaceful) ⟨*countryside, streets*⟩ tranquille
(c) ⟨*drink*⟩ non gazeux/-euse
3 *adv* ⟨*lie, stay*⟩ immobile; to sit ~ se tenir tranquille; to stand ~ ne pas bouger

still life *n* nature *f* morte

stilted *adj* guindé/-e

stimulant *n* stimulant *m* (**to** de)

stimulate *vtr* stimuler

stimulating *adj* stimulant/-e

stimulus *n* (a) (physical) stimulus *m*
(b) (boost) impulsion *f*
(c) (incentive) stimulant *m*

sting 1 *n* (a) (part of insect) aiguillon *m*
(b) (result of being stung) piqûre *f*
2 *vtr* (a) ⟨*insect*⟩ piquer
(b) ⟨*wind*⟩ cingler
3 *vi* (gen) piquer; ⟨*cut*⟩ cuire

stingy *adj* radin/-e (colloq)

stink 1 *n* (mauvaise) odeur *f*
2 *vi* puer

stint 1 *n* to do a three-year ~ travailler trois ans
2 *vi* to ~ on lésiner sur ⟨*drink, presents*⟩

stipulate *vtr* stipuler (**that** que)

stir 1 *n* to cause (quite) a ~ faire sensation
2 *vtr* (a) remuer ⟨*liquid, sauce*⟩; mélanger ⟨*paint, powder*⟩; to ~ sth into sth incorporer qch à qch
(b) ⟨*breeze*⟩ agiter ⟨*leaves, papers*⟩
3 *vi* (a) ⟨*leaves, papers*⟩ trembler; ⟨*curtains*⟩ remuer
(b) (budge) bouger
■ **stir up** provoquer ⟨*trouble*⟩; attiser ⟨*hatred, unrest*⟩; exciter ⟨*crowd*⟩

stir-fry 1 *n* sauté *m*

2 *vtr* faire sauter ⟨*beef, vegetable*⟩

stirring *adj* ⟨*story*⟩ passionnant/-e; ⟨*music, speech*⟩ enthousiasmant/-e

stirrup *n* étrier *m*

stitch **1** *n* (a) (in sewing, embroidery) point *m*; (in knitting, crochet) maille *f*
(b) (in wound) point *m* de suture
(c) (pain) point *m* de côté
2 *vtr* coudre (**to, onto** à); recoudre ⟨*wound*⟩

stoat *n* hermine *f*

stock **1** *n* (a) (supply) stock *m*; **we're out of ∼** nous n'en avons plus
(b) (descent) souche *f*, origine *f*
(c) (Culin) bouillon *m*
(d) (livestock) bétail *m*
2 **stocks** *n pl* (a) (GB) (in finance) valeurs *fpl*, titres *mpl*; **∼s and shares** valeurs *fpl* mobilières
(b) (US) actions *fpl*
(c) **the ∼s** le pilori
3 *adj* ⟨*size*⟩ courant/-e; ⟨*answer*⟩ classique; ⟨*character*⟩ stéréotypé/-e
4 *vtr* (a) (sell) avoir, vendre
(b) remplir ⟨*fridge*⟩; garnir ⟨*shelves*⟩; approvisionner ⟨*shop*⟩
IDIOMS **to take ∼** faire le point (**of** sur)
■ **stock up** s'approvisionner (**with, on** en)

stockbroker *n* agent *m* de change

stock-cube *n* bouillon-cube® *m*

stock exchange *n* **the ∼** la Bourse

Stockholm *pr n* Stockholm

stocking *n* bas *m*

stock market *n* (a) (stock exchange) Bourse *f* (des valeurs)
(b) (prices, trading activity) marché *m* (des valeurs)

stockpile *vtr* stocker ⟨*weapons*⟩; faire des stocks de ⟨*food, goods*⟩

stock room *n* magasin *m*

stock-still *adv* **to stand ∼** rester cloué/-e sur place

stocktaking *n* inventaire *m*

stocky *adj* trapu/-e

stodgy *adj* ⟨*food*⟩ bourratif/-ive

stoical *adj* stoïque

stoke *vtr* (also **∼ up**) alimenter ⟨*fire, furnace*⟩

stolid *adj* ⟨*person, character*⟩ flegmatique

stomach **1** *n* estomac *m*; (belly) ventre *m*
2 *vtr* supporter ⟨*person, attitude*⟩

stomach ache *n* **to have (a) ∼** avoir mal au ventre

stone **1** *n* (a) pierre *f*; (pebble) caillou *m*
(b) (in fruit) noyau *m*
(c) (GB) (weight) = *6.35 kg*
2 *vtr* dénoyauter ⟨*peach*⟩

Stone Age *n* âge *m* de pierre

stone circle *n* enceinte *f* de monolithes, cromlech *m*

stone-cold *adj* glacé/-e.

stone mason *n* tailleur *m* de pierre

stonewall *vi* faire de l'obstruction

stone-washed *adj* délavé/-e

stony *adj* (a) (rocky) pierreux/-euse
(b) ⟨*look, silence*⟩ glacial/-e

stool *n* tabouret *m*

stoop **1** *n* **to have a ∼** avoir le dos voûté
2 *vi* être voûté/-e; (bend down) se baisser; **to ∼ so low as to do** s'abaisser jusqu'à faire

stop **1** *n* (a) (gen) arrêt *m*; **to come to a ∼** ⟨*vehicle, work, progress*⟩ s'arrêter; **to put a ∼ to** mettre fin à
(b) (in telegram) stop *m*
2 *vtr* (a) (cease) arrêter; (temporarily) interrompre ⟨*activity*⟩; **to ∼ doing** arrêter de faire
(b) (prevent) empêcher; **to ∼ sb (from) doing** empêcher qn de faire
(c) supprimer ⟨*allowance*⟩; **to ∼ a cheque** faire opposition à un chèque
(d) (plug) boucher ⟨*gap, hole, bottle*⟩
3 *vi* (a) s'arrêter
(b) (stay) rester; **to ∼ for dinner** rester dîner; **I can't ∼** je n'ai vraiment pas le temps
4 *v refl* **to ∼ oneself** se retenir
■ **stop off** (on journey) faire un arrêt
■ **stop up**: **∼ [sth] up, ∼ up [sth]** boucher ⟨*hole*⟩

stopgap *n* bouche-trou *m*

stop-off *n* (quick break) arrêt *m*; (longer) halte *f*

stopover *n* escale *f*

stoppage *n* (strike) arrêt *m* de travail

stopper *n* (for flask, jar) bouchon *m*

stop sign *n* (panneau *m* de) stop *m*

stopwatch *n* chronomètre *m*

storage **1** *n* (of food, fuel) stockage *m* (**of** de); **to be in ∼** ⟨*furniture*⟩ être au garde-meuble
2 *adj* ⟨*space*⟩ de rangement

storage heater *n* radiateur *m* électrique à accumulation

store **1** *n* (a) (shop) magasin *m*; (smaller) boutique *f*
(b) (supply) provision *f*
(c) (place) (for food, fuel) réserve *f*; (for furniture) garde-meuble *m*
(d) **what does the future have in ∼ for us?** qu'est-ce que l'avenir nous réserve?
2 *vtr* (a) conserver ⟨*food, information*⟩; ranger ⟨*furniture*⟩
(b) (Comput) mémoriser ⟨*data*⟩

storekeeper *n* (US) commerçant/-e *m/f*

storeroom *n* (in house, school, office) réserve *f*; (in factory, shop) magasin *m*

storey (GB), **story** (US) *n* étage *m*; **on the third ∼** (GB) au troisième étage; (US) au quatrième étage

stork *n* cigogne *f*

storm **1** *n* tempête *f*; (thunderstorm) orage *m*
2 *vtr* prendre [qch] d'assaut ⟨*citadel, prison*⟩
3 *vi* **he ∼ed off in a temper** il est parti furibond

stormy *adj* orageux/-euse; **∼ scenes** éclats *mpl*

story *n* **(a)** (gen) histoire *f* (about, of de); **a true ~** une histoire vécue; **a ghost ~** une histoire de fantômes
(b) (in newspaper) article *m* (on, about sur)
(c) (rumour) rumeur *f* (about sur); **the ~ goes that** on raconte que
(d) (US) (floor) étage *m*
storybook *n* livre *m* de contes
storyteller *n* conteur/-euse *m/f*
stout *adj* **(a)** (fat) corpulent/-e
(b) (strong) ⟨wall⟩ épais/-aisse
stove *n* **(a)** (cooker) cuisinière *f*
(b) (heater) poêle *m*
stow *vtr* ranger ⟨baggage⟩
stowaway *n* passager/-ère *m/f* clandestin/-e
straddle *vtr* enfourcher ⟨horse, bike⟩; s'asseoir à califourchon sur ⟨chair⟩
straggle *vi* **(a)** ⟨houses, villages⟩ être disséminé/-e le long de
(b) (dawdle) traîner
straggler *n* traînard/-e *m/f*
straggly *adj* ⟨hair, beard⟩ en désordre
straight **1** *adj* **(a)** ⟨line, nose, road⟩ droit/-e; ⟨hair⟩ raide; **in a ~ line** en ligne droite
(b) (level, upright) bien droit/-e; **the picture isn't ~** le tableau est de travers
(c) (tidy, in order) en ordre
(d) (clear) **to get sth ~** comprendre qch; **to set the record ~** mettre les choses au clair
(e) (honest, direct) ⟨person⟩ honnête, droit/-e; ⟨answer, question⟩ clair/-e; **to be ~ with sb** jouer franc-jeu avec qn
(f) ⟨choice⟩ simple
(g) ⟨spirits, drink⟩ sec, sans eau
(h) ⟨actor, role⟩ sérieux/-ieuse
2 *adv* **(a)** droit; **stand up ~!** tenez-vous droit!; **to go/keep ~ ahead** aller/continuer tout droit; **to look ~ ahead** regarder droit devant soi
(b) (without delay) directement; **to go ~ back to Paris** rentrer directement à Paris
(c) (frankly) tout net; **I'll tell you ~** (colloq) je vous le dirai tout net; **~ out** carrément
(d) (neat) ⟨drink⟩ sec, sans eau
IDIOMS **to keep a ~ face** garder son sérieux
straightaway *adv* tout de suite
straighten *vtr* tendre ⟨arm, leg⟩; redresser ⟨picture, teeth⟩; ajuster ⟨tie, hat⟩; défriser ⟨hair⟩
■ **straighten out**: **to ~ things out** (resolve) arranger les choses
■ **straighten up**: ¶ **~ up** ⟨person⟩ se redresser; ¶ **~ [sth] up** (tidy) ranger ⟨objects, room⟩
straightforward *adj* ⟨answer, person⟩ franc/franche; ⟨account⟩ simple
straight-laced *adj* collet-monté *inv*
strain **1** *n* **(a)** (force) effort *m* (on sur)
(b) (pressure) (on person) stress *m*; (in relations) tension *f*
(c) (of virus, bacteria) souche *f*
2 *vtr* **(a)** **to ~ one's eyes** (to see) plisser les yeux; **to ~ one's ears** tendre l'oreille

(b) (try) mettre [qch] à rude épreuve ⟨patience⟩
(c) (injure) **to ~ a muscle** se froisser un muscle; **to ~ one's eyes** se fatiguer les yeux; **to ~ one's back** se faire un tour de reins
(d) (sieve) passer ⟨sauce⟩; égoutter ⟨vegetables, pasta, rice⟩
3 *vi* **to ~ at** tirer sur ⟨leash, rope⟩
strained *adj* (tense) tendu/-e; (injured) ⟨muscle⟩ froissé/-e
strainer *n* passoire *f*
strait *n* détroit *m*
IDIOMS **to be in dire ~s** être aux abois
straitjacket *n* camisole *f* de force
strand **1** *n* (gen) fil *m*; (of hair) mèche *f*
2 *vtr* **to be ~ed** être bloqué/-e; **to leave sb ~ed** laisser qn en rade (colloq)
strange *adj* **(a)** (unfamiliar) inconnu/-e; **a ~ man** un inconnu
(b) (odd) bizarre; **it is ~ (that)** il est bizarre que (+ subjunctive)
strangely *adv* ⟨behave, react⟩ d'une façon étrange; ⟨quiet, empty⟩ étrangement; **~ enough,...** chose étrange,...
stranger *n* (from elsewhere) étranger/-ère *m/f*; (unknown person) inconnu/-e *m/f*
strangle *vtr* étrangler
stranglehold *n* (control) mainmise *f*
strap **1** *n* (on shoe) bride *f*; (on case, harness) courroie *f*; (on watch) bracelet *m*; (on handbag) bandoulière *f*; (on dress, bra) bretelle *f*
2 *vtr* attacher (to à)
strapless *adj* sans bretelles
strapped *adj* (colloq) **to be ~ for** être à court de ⟨cash, staff⟩
strapping *adj* costaud/-e
stratagem *n* stratagème *m*
strategic *adj* stratégique
strategy *n* stratégie *f*
straw *n* paille *f*
IDIOMS **to clutch at ~s** se raccrocher à n'importe quoi; **the last ~** la goutte qui fait déborder le vase
strawberry **1** *n* fraise *f*; **strawberries and cream** fraises à la crème
2 *adj* ⟨tart⟩ aux fraises; ⟨ice cream⟩ à la fraise; ⟨jam⟩ de fraises
straw poll *n* sondage *m* non-officiel
stray **1** *n* (dog) chien *m* errant; (cat) chat *m* vagabond
2 *adj* ⟨dog⟩ errant/-e; ⟨cat⟩ vagabond/-e; ⟨bullet⟩ perdu/-e; ⟨tourist⟩ isolé/-e
3 *vi* **(a)** (wander) s'égarer; **to ~ from the road** s'écarter de la route
(b) ⟨eyes, mind⟩ errer
streak **1** *n* **(a)** (in character) côté *m*
(b) (period) **a winning/losing ~** une bonne/ mauvaise passe
(c) (of paint) traînée *f*; **~ of lightning** éclair *m*
(d) (in hair) mèche *f*
2 *vtr* **(a)** strier ⟨sea, sky⟩
(b) **to get one's hair ~ed** se faire faire des mèches

S

3 vi to ~ **past** passer comme une flèche

streaky bacon n (GB) bacon m entrelardé

stream **1** n (a) (brook) ruisseau m
(b) a ~ **of** un flot de ⟨traffic, questions⟩; a ~ **of abuse** un torrent d'insultes
2 vi (a) (flow) ruisseler; **sunlight was ~ing into the room** le soleil entrait à flots dans la pièce; **people ~ed out of the theatre** un flot de gens sortait du théâtre
(b) ⟨banners, hair⟩ to ~ **in the wind** flotter au vent
(c) ⟨eyes, nose⟩ couler

streamer n (of paper) banderole f

streamline vtr (a) (in design) caréner
(b) (make more efficient) rationaliser ⟨distribution, production⟩
(c) (cut) dégraisser ⟨company⟩

streamlined adj (a) ⟨cooker, furniture⟩ aux lignes modernes; ⟨hull, body⟩ caréné/-e
(b) ⟨production, system⟩ simplifié/-e

street n rue f; **in** or **on the** ~ dans la rue

street cred n (colloq) **to have** ~ être dans le coup (colloq)

streetlamp n (old gas-lamp) réverbère m; (modern) lampadaire m

street market n marché m en plein air

street plan n indicateur m des rues

street value n valeur f à la revente

streetwise adj (colloq) dégourdi/-e (colloq)

strength n (of wind, person, government, bond, argument) force f; (of lens, magnet, voice, army) puissance f; (of structure, equipment) solidité f; (of material) résistance f; (of feeling) intensité f

strengthen vtr renforcer ⟨building, argument, love, position⟩; consolider ⟨bond, links⟩; affirmer ⟨power, role⟩; fortifier ⟨muscles⟩; raffermir ⟨dollar⟩

strenuous adj ⟨exercise⟩ énergique; ⟨activity, job⟩ ardu/-e

stress **1** n (a) (nervous) tension f, stress m; **mental** ~ tension nerveuse; **to be under** ~ être stressé/-e
(b) (emphasis) accent m (on sur); **to lay** ~ **on** insister sur ⟨fact, problem⟩
(c) (in physics) effort m
(d) (in pronouncing) accent m
2 vtr mettre l'accent sur, insister sur; **to** ~ **the importance of sth** souligner l'importance de qch; **to** ~ **(that)** souligner que
■ **stress out** (colloq) ~ **[sb]** out stresser [qn]

stressed adj (a) (also ~ **out**) stressé/-e
(b) ⟨syllable⟩ accentué/-e

stressful adj stressant/-e

stretch **1** n (a) (of road, track) tronçon m; (of coastline, river) partie f
(b) (of water, countryside) étendue f
(c) (period) période f; **to work for 12 hours at a** ~ travailler 12 heures d'affilée
2 adj ⟨cover, fabric, waist⟩ extensible
3 vtr (a) (extend) tendre ⟨rope, net⟩; étirer ⟨arms, legs⟩; **to** ~ **one's legs** (figurative) se dégourdir les jambes
(b) étirer ⟨elastic⟩; élargir ⟨shoe⟩

(c) déformer ⟨truth⟩
(d) utiliser [qch] au maximum ⟨budget, resources⟩
4 vi (a) ⟨person⟩ s'étirer
(b) ⟨road, track⟩ s'étaler (**for, over** sur); ⟨beach, moor⟩ s'étendre (**for** sur)
(c) ⟨elastic⟩ s'étendre; ⟨shoe⟩ s'élargir
■ **stretch out**: ¶ ~ **out** s'étendre; ¶ ~ **[sth] out** tendre ⟨hand, foot⟩ (**towards** vers); étendre ⟨arm, leg⟩; étaler ⟨nets, sheet⟩

stretcher n brancard m

strew vtr éparpiller ⟨litter, paper⟩ (**on** sur); ~n **with** jonché/-e de

stricken adj (a) ⟨face⟩ affligé/-e; ⟨area⟩ sinistré/-e; ~ **by** frappé/-e de ⟨illness⟩; pris/-e de ⟨fear⟩; accablé/-e de ⟨guilt⟩
(b) ⟨plane, ship⟩ en détresse

strict adj ⟨person⟩ strict/-e (**about** sur); ⟨view⟩ rigide; ⟨silence⟩ absolu/-e; ⟨Methodist, Catholic⟩ de stricte observance; **in** ~ **confidence** à titre strictement confidentiel; **in** ~ **secrecy** dans le plus grand secret

strictly adv (a) ⟨treat⟩ avec sévérité
(b) ⟨confidential, prohibited⟩ strictement; ~ **speaking** à proprement parler

stride **1** n enjambée f
2 vi to ~ **out/in** sortir/entrer à grands pas; **to** ~ **across sth** enjamber qch
IDIOMS **to take sth in one's** ~ prendre qch calmement

strife n conflits mpl

strike **1** n (a) grève f; **on** ~ en grève
(b) (attack) attaque f
2 vtr (a) (hit) frapper ⟨person, vessel⟩; heurter ⟨rock, tree, pedestrian⟩; **he struck his head on the table** il s'est cogné la tête contre la table; **to be struck by lightning** être frappé/-e par la foudre
(b) (afflict) frapper ⟨area, people⟩
(c) ⟨idea, thought⟩ venir à l'esprit de ⟨person⟩; ⟨resemblance⟩ frapper; **to** ~ **sb as odd** paraître étrange à qn
(d) (colloq) (find) tomber sur (colloq) ⟨oil, gold⟩
(e) (achieve) conclure ⟨deal, bargain⟩; **to** ~ **a balance** trouver le juste milieu (**between** entre)
(f) frotter ⟨match⟩
(g) ⟨clock⟩ sonner
3 vi (a) (gen) frapper
(b) ⟨workers⟩ faire (la) grève
■ **strike down** terrasser ⟨person⟩
■ **strike off**: ¶ ~ **[sth] off, ~ off [sth]** (delete) rayer; ¶ ~ **[sb] off** radier ⟨doctor⟩; ¶ ~ **[sb/sth] off sth** rayer [qn/qch] de ⟨list⟩
■ **strike out**: ¶ ~ **out** (hit out) frapper; **to** ~ **out at** attaquer ⟨adversary⟩; s'en prendre à ⟨critics⟩; ¶ ~ **[sth] out** rayer
■ **strike up** ⟨orchestra⟩ commencer à jouer; **to** ~ **up a conversation with** engager la conversation avec; **to** ~ **up a friendship with** se lier d'amitié avec

strikebreaker n briseur/-euse m/f de grève

strikebreaking n retour m au travail

strike force n force f d'intervention

s

striker n (a) (person on strike) gréviste mf
(b) (in football) attaquant/-e m/f

striking adj ⟨person⟩ (good-looking) beau/
belle (before n); ⟨design, contrast⟩ frappant/-e

string ① n (a) (twine) ficelle f; a piece of ∼
un bout de ficelle
(b) (on bow, racket) corde f; (on puppet) fil m
(c) (series) a ∼ of un défilé de ⟨visitors⟩; une
succession de ⟨successes, awards⟩
(d) (set) ∼ of pearls collier m de perles
② **strings** n pl (Mus) the ∼s les cordes fpl
③ vtr enfiler ⟨beads, pearls⟩ (on sur)
IDIOMS to pull ∼s (colloq) faire jouer le
piston (colloq)
■ **string along** (GB) (colloq): ¶ ∼ along
suivre ¶ ∼ [sb] along mener qn en bateau
(colloq)
■ **string together** aligner ⟨words⟩

string bean n haricot m à écosser

stringed instrument n instrument m
à cordes

stringent adj rigoureux/-euse

strip ① n bande f (of de)
② vtr (a) déshabiller ⟨person⟩; vider ⟨house,
room⟩; défaire ⟨bed⟩; to ∼ sb of dépouiller
qn de ⟨belongings, rights⟩
(b) (remove paint from) décaper
(c) (dismantle) démonter
③ vi se déshabiller

strip cartoon n bande f dessinée

stripe n (a) (on fabric, wallpaper) rayure f
(b) (on animal) (isolated) rayure f; (one of many)
zébrure f

striped adj rayé/-e

strip lighting n éclairage m au néon m

stripper n strip-teaseur/-euse m/f

strive vi s'efforcer (to do de faire)

stroke ① n (a) (gen) coup m; at a single ∼
d'un seul coup; a ∼ of luck un coup de
chance; a ∼ of genius un trait de génie
(b) (in swimming) mouvement m des bras;
(particular style) nage f
(c) (of pen) trait m; (of brush) touche f
(d) (Med) congestion f cérébrale
② vtr caresser

stroll ① n promenade f, tour m
② vi se promener, flâner

stroller n (US) (pushchair) poussette f

strong adj (a) (powerful) ⟨arm, person,
current, wind⟩ fort/-e; ⟨army, swimmer,
country⟩ puissant/-e
(b) ⟨heart, fabric, table⟩ solide; ⟨candidate,
argument⟩ de poids
(c) ⟨tea, medicine, glue⟩ fort/-e; ⟨coffee⟩
serré/-e
(d) ⟨smell, taste⟩ fort/-e
(e) ⟨desire, feeling⟩ profond/-e
(f) ⟨chance, possibility⟩ fort/-e (before n)
IDIOMS to be still going ∼ ⟨person⟩ se porter
toujours très bien; ⟨relationship⟩ aller
toujours bien; it's not my ∼ point ce n'est
pas mon fort

strongbox n coffre-fort m

stronghold n forteresse f; (figurative) fief m

strongly adv (a) ⟨oppose, advise⟩
vivement; ⟨protest, deny⟩ énergiquement;
⟨suspect⟩ fortement; ⟨believe⟩ fermement; I
feel ∼ about this c'est quelque chose qui me
tient à cœur
(b) (solidly) solidement

strongroom n chambre f forte

strong-willed adj obstiné/-e

structural damage n dégâts mpl
matériels

structure ① n (a) (organization) structure f
(b) (building) construction f
② vtr structurer ⟨argument, essay, novel⟩;
organiser ⟨day, life⟩

struggle ① n (gen) lutte f; (scuffle) rixe f
② vi (a) (put up a fight) se débattre (to do
pour faire); (tussle, scuffle) se battre
(b) (try hard) lutter (to do pour faire; for
pour)

struggling adj ⟨writer, artist⟩ qui essaie
de percer

strum vtr (carelessly) gratter ⟨guitar, tune⟩;
(gently) jouer doucement de ⟨guitar⟩

strung out adj (colloq) to be ∼ on être
accro (colloq) à ⟨drug⟩; to be ∼ (from drugs)
être en état de manque

strut ① n montant m
② vi (also ∼ about, ∼ around) se
pavaner

stub ① n (of pencil) bout m; (of cheque, ticket)
talon m; (of cigarette) mégot m
② vtr to ∼ one's toe se cogner l'orteil
■ **stub out** écraser ⟨cigarette⟩

stubble n (a) (straw) chaume m
(b) (beard) barbe f de plusieurs jours

stubborn adj ⟨person, animal⟩ entêté/-e;
⟨behaviour⟩ obstiné/-e; ⟨refusal⟩ opiniâtre;
⟨stain⟩ rebelle

stuck adj (a) (jammed, trapped) coincé/-e; to
get ∼ in rester coincé/-e dans ⟨lift⟩; s'enliser
dans ⟨mud⟩
(b) to be ∼ for an answer ne pas savoir quoi
répondre

stuck-up adj (colloq) bêcheur/-euse (colloq)

stud n (a) (on jacket) clou m; (on door) clou m
à grosse tête; (on boot) crampon m
(b) (stallion) étalon m; (horse farm) haras m
(c) (earring) clou m d'oreille

student n étudiant/-e m/f

student grant n bourse f d'études

student ID card n carte f d'étudiant

student nurse n élève mf infirmier/-ière

student teacher n enseignant/-e m/f
stagiaire

student union n (building) maison f des
étudiants

studio n (gen) studio m; (of painter) atelier m

studious adj studieux/-ieuse

study ① n (a) (work, research) étude f (of, on
de)
(b) (room) bureau m
② **studies** n pl études fpl; **computer
studies** informatique f; **social studies**
sciences fpl humaines

⋯✧

3 adj ‹leave, group, visit› d'étude; ~ **trip** voyage m d'études

4 vtr étudier

5 vi faire ses études

study aid n outil m pédagogique (destiné à l'élève)

stuff 1 n (things) choses fpl, trucs mpl (colloq); (personal belongings) affaires fpl; (rubbish, junk) bazar m (colloq); (substance) truc m (colloq)

2 vtr (a) rembourrer ‹cushion› (with de); bourrer ‹suitcase, room› (with de)

(b) (shove) fourrer (colloq) (in, into dans)

(c) (Culin) farcir ‹turkey, chicken›

(d) empailler ‹dead animal, bird›

stuffed adj ‹turkey, chicken› farci/-e; ‹toy animal› en peluche; ‹bird, fox› empaillé/-e

stuffing n (a) (Culin) farce f

(b) (of furniture, pillow) rembourrage m

stuffy adj (a) (airless) étouffant/-e

(b) (staid) guindé/-e

stumble vi (a) (trip) trébucher (**against** contre; **on, over** sur)

(b) (in speech) hésiter

■ **stumble across** tomber par hasard sur ‹rare find›

stumbling block n obstacle m

stump 1 n (of tree) souche f; (of candle, pencil, cigar) bout m; (of tooth) chicot m; (part of limb, tail) moignon m

2 vtr (colloq) **to be ~ed by sth** être en peine d'expliquer qch; **I'm ~ed!** (in quiz) je sèche! (colloq); (nonplussed) aucune idée!

■ **stump up** (GB) (colloq) débourser (**for** pour)

stun vtr (a) (daze) assommer

(b) (amaze) stupéfier

stunned adj (a) (dazed) assommé/-e

(b) (amazed) ‹person› stupéfait/-e; ‹silence› figé/-e

stunning adj (beautiful) sensationnel/-elle

stunt 1 n (a) (for attention) coup m organisé, truc m (colloq)

(b) (in film) cascade f

2 vtr empêcher ‹development›; nuire à ‹plant growth›

stunted adj rabougri/-e

stuntman n cascadeur m

stupefying adj stupéfiant/-e

stupendous adj prodigieux/-ieuse

stupid adj bête, stupide; **I've done something ~** j'ai fait une bêtise

stupidity n bêtise f

stupor n stupeur f; **in a drunken ~** hébété/-e par l'alcool

sturdy adj robuste, solide

stutter vtr, vi bégayer

St Valentine's Day n la Saint-Valentin

sty n (a) (for pigs) porcherie f

(b) (also **stye**) orgelet m

style 1 n (a) (manner) style m

(b) (elegance) classe f; **to do things in ~** faire les choses en grand

(c) (design) (of car, clothing) modèle m; (of house) type m

(d) (fashion) mode f

2 vtr couper ‹hair›

styling 1 n (a) (design) conception f

(b) (in hairdressing) coupe f

2 adj ‹gel, mousse, product› coiffant/-e

stylish adj ‹car, coat, person› élégant/-e; ‹resort, restaurant› chic

stylist n (a) (hairdresser) coiffeur/-euse m/f

(b) (designer) concepteur/-trice m/f

stylistic adj stylistique

stylus n pointe f de lecture

suave adj ‹person› mielleux/-euse

subconscious 1 n the ~ le subconscient

2 adj inconscient/-e

subcontinent n sous-continent m

subcontract vtr sous-traiter (**out to** à)

subcontractor n sous-traitant m

subdivide vtr subdiviser

subdue vtr soumettre ‹people, nation›

subdued adj ‹person› silencieux/-ieuse; ‹excitement› contenu/-e; ‹lighting› tamisé/-e

subheading n sous-titre m

subject 1 n (a) (topic) sujet m; **to change the ~** parler d'autre chose

(b) (at school, college) matière f; (for research, study) sujet m

(c) **to be the ~ of an inquiry** faire l'objet d'une enquête

(d) (citizen) sujet/-ette m/f

2 adj (a) (liable) **to be ~ to** être sujet/-ette à ‹flooding, fits›; être passible de ‹tax›

(b) (dependent) **to be ~ to** dépendre de ‹approval›; être soumis/-e à ‹law›

3 vtr **to ~ sb to sth** faire subir qch à qn

subject heading n sujet m

subjective adj subjectif/-ive

subjugate vtr subjuguer ‹country, people›

subjunctive n subjonctif m

sublet vtr, vi sous-louer

sublime adj ‹beauty, genius› sublime; ‹indifference› suprême

subliminal adj subliminal/-e

submachine gun n mitraillette f

submarine n sous-marin m

submerge vtr ‹sea, flood› submerger; ‹person› immerger (in dans)

submission n soumission f (to à)

submissive adj ‹person› soumis/-e; ‹behaviour› docile

submit 1 vtr soumettre ‹report, plan, script› (to à); présenter ‹bill, application›

2 vi se soumettre; **to ~ to** subir ‹indignity, injustice›; céder à ‹will, demand›

subnormal adj ‹person› arriéré/-e

subordinate n, adj subalterne (mf)

subpoena vtr assigner [qn] à comparaître

subscribe vi (a) **to ~ to** partager ‹view, values›

(b) **to ~ to** être abonné/-e à ‹magazine›

subscriber n abonné/-e m/f (to de)

subscription n abonnement m (to à)

subsequent *adj* (in past) ultérieur/-e; (in future) à venir

subsequently *adv* par la suite

subservient *adj* servile (**to** envers)

subside *vi* (a) ⟨*storm, wind, noise*⟩ s'apaiser; ⟨*emotion*⟩ se calmer; ⟨*fever, excitement*⟩ retomber
(b) ⟨*building, land*⟩ s'affaisser

subsidiary **1** *n* (*also* ~ **company**) filiale *f*
2 *adj* secondaire (**to** par rapport à)

subsidize *vtr* subventionner

subsidy *n* subvention *f* (**to, for** à)

subsist *vi* subsister

subsistence *n* subsistance *f*

subsistence level *n* niveau *m* minimum pour vivre

substance *n* (a) (gen) substance *f*
(b) (of argument, talks) essentiel *m*; (of claim, accusation) fondement *m*

substance abuse *n* abus *m* de substances toxiques

substandard *adj* de qualité inférieure

substantial *adj* (a) (considerable) considérable; ⟨*sum, quantity*⟩ important/-e; ⟨*meal*⟩ substantiel/-ielle
(b) (solid) ⟨*proof, lock*⟩ solide

substantiate *vtr* justifier ⟨*allegation*⟩; appuyer [qch] par des preuves ⟨*statement*⟩

substitute **1** *n* (a) (person) remplaçant/-e *m/f*
(b) (product, substance) succédané *m*
2 *vtr* substituer (**for** à)

subtitle *n* sous-titre *m*

subtitled *adj* sous-titré/-e

subtle *adj* (gen) subtil/-e; ⟨*change*⟩ imperceptible; ⟨*hint*⟩ voilé/-e; ⟨*lighting*⟩ tamisé/-e

subtlety *n* subtilité *f*

subtotal *n* sous-total *m*

subtract *vtr* soustraire (**from** de)

subtraction *n* soustraction *f*

suburb **1** *n* banlieue *f*; inner ~ faubourg *m*
2 **suburbs** *n pl* **the** ~**s** la banlieue

suburban *adj* ⟨*street, shop, train*⟩ de banlieue; (US) ⟨*shopping mall*⟩ à l'extérieur de la ville

suburbia *n* banlieue *f*

subversive **1** *n* élément *m* subversif
2 *adj* subversif/-ive

subway *n* (a) (GB) (for pedestrians) passage *m* souterrain
(b) (US) (underground railway) métro *m*

sub-zero *adj* inférieur/-e à zéro

succeed **1** *vtr* succéder à ⟨*person*⟩
2 *vi* réussir; **to** ~ **in doing** réussir à faire

succeeding *adj* qui suit, suivant/-e

success *n* succès *m*, réussite *f*; **to be a** ~ ⟨*party*⟩ être réussi/-e; ⟨*film, person*⟩ avoir du succès

successful *adj* ⟨*attempt, operation*⟩ réussi/-e; ⟨*plan, campaign*⟩ couronné/-e de

succès; ⟨*film, book, writer*⟩ (profitable) à succès; (well regarded) apprécié/-e; ⟨*businessman*⟩ prospère; ⟨*career*⟩ brillant/-e; **to be** ~ réussir (**in doing** à faire)

successfully *adv* avec succès

succession *n* (a) (sequence) série *f* (**of** de); **in** ~ de suite; **in close** ~ coup sur coup
(b) (inheriting) succession *f* (**to** à)

successive *adj* successif/-ive; ⟨*day, week*⟩ consécutif/-ive

successor *n* successeur *m*

success rate *n* taux *m* de réussite

success story *n* réussite *f*

succinct *adj* succinct/-e

succulent *adj* succulent/-e

succumb *vi* succomber (**to** à)

such **1** *det* tel/telle; (similar) pareil/-eille; ~ **a situation** une telle situation; **in** ~ **a situation** dans une situation pareille; **some** ~ **remark** quelque chose comme ça; **there's no** ~ **thing** ça n'existe pas; **you'll do no** ~ **thing!** il n'en est pas question!; **in** ~ **a way that** d'une telle façon que; ~ **money as I have** le peu d'argent *or* tout l'argent que j'ai
2 *adv* (with adjectives) si, tellement; (with nouns) tel/telle; **in** ~ **a persuasive way** d'une façon si convaincante; ~ **a nice boy!** un garçon si gentil!; ~ **good quality** une telle qualité; **I hadn't seen** ~ **a good film for years** je n'avais pas vu un aussi bon film depuis des années; ~ **a lot of problems** tant de problèmes; **there were (ever** (colloq)) ~ **a lot of people** il y avait beaucoup de monde
3 **such as** *phr* comme, tel/telle que; **a house** ~ **as this** une maison comme celle-ci; **a person** ~ **as her** une personne comme elle; **have you** ~ **a thing as a screwdriver?** auriez-vous un tournevis par hasard?

such and such *det* tel/telle; **on** ~ **a topic** sur tel ou tel sujet

suck **1** *vtr* sucer ⟨*thumb, fruit, lollipop, pencil*⟩; (drink in) aspirer ⟨*liquid, air*⟩
2 *vi* **to** ~ **at** sucer; **to** ~ **on** tirer sur ⟨*pipe*⟩
■ **suck up:** ¶ ~ **up** (colloq) faire de la lèche (colloq); **to** ~ **up to sb** cirer les pompes à qn (colloq); ¶ ~ **[sth] up** pomper ⟨*liquid*⟩; aspirer ⟨*dirt*⟩

sucker *n* (a) (colloq) (dupe) bonne poire *f* (colloq)
(b) (on plant) surgeon *m*
(c) (pad) ventouse *f*

suction *n* succion *f*

suction pad *n* ventouse *f*

sudden *adj* (gen) soudain/-e; ⟨*movement*⟩ brusque; **all of a** ~ tout à coup

sudden death play-off *n*: penalties *pour départager deux équipes*

suddenly *adv* ⟨*die, grow pale*⟩ subitement; ⟨*happen*⟩ tout à coup

suds *n pl* (*also* **soap** ~) (foam) mousse *f* (de savon); (soapy water) eau *f* savonneuse

sue **1** *vtr* intenter un procès à; **to** ~ **sb for** ⋯⟡

S

divorce demander le divorce à qn; **to ∼ sb for damages** réclamer à qn des dommages-intérêts

[2] *vi* intenter un procès

suede [1] *n* daim *m*

[2] *adj* ⟨*shoe, glove*⟩ en daim

suffer [1] *vtr* subir ⟨*loss, consequences, defeat*⟩; **to ∼ a heart attack** avoir une crise cardiaque

[2] *vi* (a) souffrir; **to ∼ from** souffrir de ⟨*rheumatism, heat*⟩; avoir ⟨*headache, high blood pressure, cold*⟩; **to ∼ from depression** être dépressif/-ive

(b) (do badly) ⟨*company, profits*⟩ souffrir; ⟨*health, quality, work*⟩ s'en ressentir

sufferer *n* victime *f*; **leukemia ∼s** les leucémiques *mpl*

suffering [1] *n* souffrances *fpl* (**of** de)

[2] *adj* souffrant/-e

sufficient *adj* suffisamment de, assez de; **to be ∼** suffire

sufficiently *adv* suffisamment, assez

suffocate [1] *vtr* ⟨*smoke, fumes*⟩ asphyxier; ⟨*person, anger*⟩ étouffer

[2] *vi* (a) (by smoke, fumes) être asphyxié/-e; (by pillow) être étouffé/-e

(b) (figurative) suffoquer

suffocating *adj* ⟨*smoke*⟩ asphyxiant/-e; ⟨*atmosphere, heat*⟩ étouffant/-e

suffrage *n* (right) droit *m* de vote; (system) suffrage *m*

sugar *n* sucre *m*; **brown ∼** sucre *m* roux

sugar beet *n* betterave *f* à sucre

sugar cane *n* canne *f* à sucre

sugar-free *adj* sans sucre

sugar lump *n* morceau *m* de sucre

suggest *vtr* suggérer; **they ∼ed that I (should) leave** ils m'ont suggéré de partir

suggestion *n* (a) (gen) suggestion *f*; **at sb's ∼** sur le conseil de qn

(b) (hint) soupçon *m* (**of** de); (of smile) pointe *f*

suggestive *adj* suggestif/-ive

suicidal *adj* suicidaire

suicide *n* (action) suicide *m*; (person) suicidé/-e *m/f*; **to commit ∼** se suicider

suit [1] *n* (a) (man's) costume *m*; (woman's) tailleur *m*; **a ∼ of armour** une armure (complète)

(b) (lawsuit) procès *m*

(c) (in cards) couleur *f*

[2] *vtr* (a) ⟨*colour, outfit*⟩ aller à ⟨*person*⟩

(b) ⟨*date, climate, arrangement*⟩ convenir à

[3] *vi* convenir

[4] *v refl* **to ∼ oneself** faire comme on veut

suitable *adj* ⟨*accommodation, clothing, employment*⟩ adéquat/-e; ⟨*candidate*⟩ apte; ⟨*gift, gesture*⟩ approprié/-e; ⟨*moment*⟩ opportun/-e; **to be ∼ for** convenir à ⟨*person*⟩; bien se prêter à ⟨*climate, activity, occasion*⟩

suitably *adv* convenablement

suitcase *n* valise *f*

suite *n* (a) (gen) suite *f*

(b) (furniture) mobilier *m*

suited *adj* **to be ∼ to** ⟨*place, clothes*⟩ être commode pour; ⟨*game, style*⟩ convenir à; ⟨*person*⟩ être fait/-e pour

sulk *vi* bouder (**about, over** à cause de)

sulky *adj* boudeur/-euse; **to look ∼** faire la tête

sullen *adj* ⟨*person, expression*⟩ renfrogné/-e; ⟨*day, sky, mood*⟩ maussade

sulphur (GB), **sulfur** (US) *n* soufre *m*

sulphuric acid *n* acide *m* sulfurique

sultana *n* (Culin) raisin *m* de Smyrne

sultry *adj* (a) ⟨*day*⟩ étouffant/-e; ⟨*weather*⟩ lourd/-e

(b) ⟨*look, smile*⟩ sensuel/-elle

sum *n* (a) (of money) somme *f*

(b) (calculation) calcul *m*

■ **sum up**: ¶ **∼ up** récapituler; ¶ **∼ up [sth]** résumer

summarize *vtr* résumer ⟨*book, problem*⟩; récapituler ⟨*argument, speech*⟩

summary *n* résumé *m*

summer [1] *n* été *m*; **in ∼** en été

[2] *adj* ⟨*evening, resort, clothes*⟩ d'été

summer camp *n* (US) colonie *f* de vacances

summer holiday (GB), **summer vacation** (US) *n* (gen) vacances *fpl* (d'été); (Sch, Univ) grandes vacances *fpl*

summerhouse *n* pavillon *m* (de jardin)

summer school *n* université *f* d'été

summertime *n* été *m*

summit *n* sommet *m*

summon *vtr* (a) (gen) faire venir

(b) (Law) citer

■ **summon up** rassembler ⟨*energy, strength*⟩ (**to do** pour faire)

summons [1] *n* (a) (Law) citation *f*

(b) (gen) injonction *f* (**from** de; **to** à)

[2] *vtr* citer (**to** à; **to do** à faire; **for** pour)

sumptuous *adj* somptueux/-euse

sum total *n* (of money) montant *m* total; (of achievements) ensemble *m*

sun *n* soleil *m*; **in the ∼** au soleil

sunbathe *vi* se faire bronzer

sunbed *n* (lounger) chaise *f* longue; (with sunlamp) lit *m* solaire

sun block *n* crème *f* écran total

sunburn *n* coup *m* de soleil

sunburned, **sunburnt** *adj* (burnt) brûlé/-e par le soleil; (tanned) (GB) bronzé/-e; **to get ∼** attraper un coup de soleil

Sunday *n* dimanche *m*

Sunday best *n* (dressed) **in one's ∼** endimanché/-e

Sunday trading *n* commerce *m* dominical

sundial *n* cadran *m* solaire

sundress *n* robe *f* bain de soleil

sundries *n pl* articles *mpl* divers

sundry *adj* divers/-e; (**to) all and ∼** (à) tout le monde

sunflower *n* tournesol *m*

sunglasses *n pl* lunettes *fpl* de soleil
sun hat *n* chapeau *m* de soleil
sunken *adj* (a) ⟨*treasure, wreck*⟩ immergé/-e
(b) ⟨*cheek*⟩ creux/creuse; ⟨*eye*⟩ cave
(c) ⟨*bath*⟩ encastré/-e; ⟨*garden*⟩ en contrebas
sunlamp *n* lampe *f* à bronzer
sunlight *n* lumière *f* du soleil
sunny *adj* (a) ensoleillé/-e; **it's going to be ~** il va faire (du) soleil
(b) ⟨*child, temperament*⟩ enjoué/-e
sunrise *n* lever *m* du soleil
sunroof *n* toit *m* ouvrant
sunset *n* coucher *m* du soleil
sunshade *n* parasol *m*
sunshield *n* pare-soleil *m inv*
sunshine *n* soleil *m*
sunstroke *n* insolation *f*
suntan *n* bronzage *m*; **to get a ~** bronzer
suntan lotion *n* lotion *f* solaire
suntanned *adj* bronzé/-e
suntan oil *n* huile *f* solaire
super *adj, excl* (colloq) formidable
superb *adj* superbe
supercilious *adj* dédaigneux/-euse
superficial *adj* superficiel/-ielle
superfluous *adj* superflu/-e
superimpose *vtr* superposer (**on** à)
superintendent *n* (a) (supervisor) responsable *mf*
(b) (*also* **police ~**) ≈ commissaire *m* de police
(c) (US) (for apartments) concierge *mf*
(d) (US) (*also* **school ~**) inspecteur/-trice *m/f*
superior ▮1▮ *n* supérieur/-e *m/f*
▮2▮ *adj* (a) supérieur/-e (**to** à; **in** en); ⟨*product*⟩ de qualité supérieure
(b) (condescending) condescendant/-e
superiority *n* supériorité *f*
superlative ▮1▮ *n* superlatif *m*
▮2▮ *adj* ⟨*performance, service*⟩ superbe
superman *n* surhomme *m*
supermarket *n* supermarché *m*
supermodel *n* top model *m*
supernatural ▮1▮ *n* surnaturel *m*
▮2▮ *adj* surnaturel/-elle
superpower *n* superpuissance *f*
supersede *vtr* remplacer
supersonic *adj* supersonique
superstar *n* superstar *f*
superstition *n* superstition *f*
superstitious *adj* superstitieux/-ieuse
superstore *n* (large supermarket) hypermarché *m*; (specialist shop) grande surface *f*
supervise *vtr* superviser ⟨*activity, staff*⟩; surveiller ⟨*child, patient*⟩
supervision *n* (a) (of staff, work) supervision *f*
(b) (of child, patient) surveillance *f*

supervisor *n* (a) (for staff) responsable *m*
(b) (GB) (for thesis) directeur/-trice *m/f* de thèse
(c) (US Sch) directeur/-trice *m/f* d'études
supper *n* (evening meal) dîner *m*; (late snack) collation *f* (du soir); (after a show) souper *m*; **the Last Supper** la Cène *f*
supple *adj* souple
supplement ▮1▮ *n* (a) (fee) supplément *m*
(b) (to diet, income) complément *m* (**to** à)
(c) (in newspaper) supplément *m*
▮2▮ *vtr* compléter ⟨*diet, resources, training*⟩ (**with** de); augmenter ⟨*income, staff*⟩ (**with** de)
supplementary *adj* supplémentaire
supplier *n* fournisseur *m* (**of, to** de)
supply ▮1▮ *n* (a) (stock) réserves *fpl*; **in short ~** difficile à obtenir; **to get in a ~ of sth** s'approvisionner en qch
(b) (source) (of fuel, gas, oxygen) alimentation *f*; (of food) approvisionnement *m*; (of equipment) fourniture *f*
▮2▮ **supplies** *n pl* (a) (equipment) réserves *fpl*; **food supplies** ravitaillement *m*
(b) (for office) fournitures *fpl*
▮3▮ *vtr* (provide) fournir (**to, for** à); approvisionner ⟨*factory, company*⟩ (**with** en); (with fuel, food) ravitailler ⟨*town, area*⟩ (**with** en)
supply and demand *n* l'offre *f* et la demande
supply teacher *n* (GB) suppléant/-e *m/f*
support ▮1▮ *n* (a) (moral, financial, political) soutien *m*, appui *m*; **to give sb/sth (one's) ~** apporter son soutien à qn/qch; **means of ~** (financial) moyens *mpl* de subsistance
(b) (physical, for weight) support *m*
(c) (person) soutien *m*; **to be a ~ to sb** aider qn
▮2▮ *vtr* (a) (morally, financially) soutenir ⟨*person, cause, organization, currency*⟩; donner à ⟨*charity*⟩
(b) (physically) supporter ⟨*weight*⟩; soutenir ⟨*person*⟩
(c) confirmer ⟨*argument, theory*⟩
(d) (maintain) ⟨*breadwinner, farm*⟩ subvenir aux besoins de
supporter *n* (gen) partisan *m*; (Sport) supporter *m*; (of political party) sympathisant/-e *m/f*
support group *n* groupe *m* de soutien
supporting *adj* **~ actor/actress** second rôle masculin/féminin; **the ~ cast** les seconds rôles *mpl*
supportive *adj* ⟨*person, organization*⟩ d'un grand secours; ⟨*role, network*⟩ de soutien
suppose *vtr* (a) (assume) supposer (**that** que); **I ~ so/not** je suppose que oui/non
(b) (think) **to ~ (that)** penser *or* croire que
supposed *adj* **to be ~ to do/be** être censé/-e faire/être; **it's ~ to be a good hotel** il paraît que c'est un bon hôtel
supposing *conj* **~ (that) he says no?** et s'il dit non?; **~ your income is X** supposons que ton revenu soit de X

S

suppress *vtr* supprimer ⟨*evidence, information*⟩; réprimer ⟨*smile, urge, rebellion*⟩; étouffer ⟨*scandal, yawn*⟩; dissimuler ⟨*truth*⟩

supreme *adj* suprême

surcharge *n* supplément *m*

sure ⓵ *adj* (gen) sûr/-e (about, of de); I'm not ~ when he's coming je ne sais pas trop quand il viendra; we'll be there tomorrow for ~! on y sera demain sans faute!; nobody knows for ~ personne ne (le) sait au juste; to make ~ that (ascertain) s'assurer que; (ensure) faire en sorte que; he's ~ to fail il va sûrement échouer; to be ~ of oneself être sûr/-e de soi
⓶ *adv* '~!' (of course) 'bien sûr!'; ~ enough effectivement

sure-fire *adj* (colloq) garanti/-e

sure-footed *adj* agile

surely *adv* sûrement, certainement

surf ⓵ *n* (waves) vagues *fpl* (déferlantes); (foam) écume *f*
⓶ *vtr* to ~ the Internet naviguer *or* surfer sur Internet
⓷ *vi* (a) (Sport) faire du surf
(b) (Comput) naviguer *or* surfer sur Internet

surface ⓵ *n* (a) surface *f*; on the ~ (of liquid) à la surface; (of solid) sur la surface
(b) (of solid, cube) côté *m*
(c) (worktop) plan *m* de travail
⓶ *vi* (a) ⟨*person, object*⟩ remonter à la surface; ⟨*submarine*⟩ faire surface
(b) ⟨*problem*⟩ se manifester

surface area *n* superficie *f*

surfboard *n* planche *f* de surf

surfer *n* (a) (on water) surfeur/-euse *m/f*
(b) (Comput) internaute *mf*

surfing *n* surf *m*

surge ⓵ *n* (a) (of water, blood, energy) montée *f* (of de); (of anger, desire) accès *m* (of de)
(b) (in prices, unemployment) hausse *f* (in de); (in demand) accroissement *m* (in de)
⓶ *vi* (a) ⟨*water, waves*⟩ déferler; ⟨*blood, energy, emotion*⟩ monter; to ~ forward ⟨*crowd*⟩ s'élancer en avant
(b) ⟨*prices, demand*⟩ monter en flèche

surgeon *n* chirurgien *m*

surgery *n* (a) (operation) chirurgie *f*; to have ~ se faire opérer
(b) (GB) (Med) (premises) cabinet *m*

surgical *adj* ⟨*instrument*⟩ chirurgical/-e; ⟨*boot, stocking*⟩ orthopédique

surgical spirit *n* alcool *m* (à 90 degrés)

surly *adj* revêche

surname *n* nom *m* de famille

surpass ⓵ *vtr* surpasser (in en); dépasser ⟨*expectations*⟩
⓶ *v refl* to ~ oneself se surpasser

surplus ⓵ *n* surplus *m*; (in business) excédent *m*
⓶ *adj* (gen) en trop; (in business) excédentaire

surprise ⓵ *n* surprise *f*; to take sb by ~ (gen) prendre qn au dépourvu; (Mil) surprendre qn

⓶ *vtr* (a) surprendre, étonner; it ~d them that no-one came ils ont été surpris que personne ne vienne
(b) surprendre ⟨*intruder*⟩; attaquer [qch] par surprise ⟨*garrison*⟩

surprised *adj* étonné/-e; I'm not ~ ça ne m'étonne pas

surprising *adj* étonnant/-e, surprenant/-e

surprisingly *adv* ⟨*well, quickly*⟩ étonnamment; ~ frank d'une franchise étonnante

surreal *adj* surréaliste

surrealist *n, adj* surréaliste (*mf*)

surrender ⓵ *n* (a) (of army) capitulation *f* (to devant); (of soldier, town) reddition *f* (to à)
(b) (of territory, rights) abandon *m* (to à); (of weapons, document) remise *f* (to à)
⓶ *vtr* (a) livrer ⟨*town*⟩ (to à); céder ⟨*weapons*⟩ (to à)
(b) racheter ⟨*insurance policy*⟩; rendre ⟨*passport*⟩ (to à)
⓷ *vi* ⟨*army, soldier*⟩ se rendre (to à); ⟨*country*⟩ capituler (to devant)

surrogate ⓵ *n* substitut *m* (for de)
⓶ *adj* de substitution

surrogate mother *n* mère *f* porteuse

surround *vtr* (gen) entourer; ⟨*police*⟩ encercler ⟨*building*⟩; cerner ⟨*person*⟩

surrounding *adj* environnant/-e; the ~ area les environs *mpl*

surroundings *n pl* cadre *m*; (of town) environs *mpl*; natural ~ milieu *m* naturel

surveillance *n* surveillance *f*

survey ⓵ *n* (a) (of trends, prices) enquête *f* (of sur); (by questioning people) sondage *m*; (study) étude *f* (of de)
(b) (GB) (of house) expertise *f* (on de)
(c) (of land) étude *f* topographique; (map) levé *m* topographique
⓶ *vtr* (a) faire une étude de ⟨*market, trends*⟩
(b) (GB) faire une expertise de ⟨*house*⟩
(c) faire l'étude topographique de ⟨*area*⟩
(d) contempler ⟨*scene, landscape*⟩

surveyor *n* (a) (GB) (in housebuying) expert *m* (en immobilier)
(b) (for map-making) topographe *mf*

survival *n* (of person, animal) survie *f* (of de); (of custom, belief) survivance *f* (of de)

survive ⓵ *vtr* (a) survivre à ⟨*winter, heart attack*⟩; réchapper de ⟨*accident*⟩; surmonter ⟨*crisis*⟩
(b) survivre à ⟨*person*⟩
⓶ *vi* survivre; to ~ on sth vivre de qch

surviving *adj* survivant/-e

survivor *n* (a) (of accident, attack) rescapé/-e *m/f*
(b) (Law) survivant/-e *m/f*

susceptible *adj* sensible (to à)

suspect ⓵ *n* suspect/-e *m/f*
⓶ *adj* suspect/-e
⓷ *vtr* (a) (believe) soupçonner ⟨*murder, plot*⟩; to ~ that penser que
(b) (doubt) douter de ⟨*truth, motives*⟩
(c) (have under suspicion) soupçonner ⟨*person*⟩

suspend *vtr* **(a)** (gen) suspendre
(b) exclure [qn] temporairement *‹pupil›*
(**from** de)
suspended sentence *n* condamnation
f avec sursis
suspender belt *n* (GB) porte-jarretelles
m inv
suspenders *n pl* **(a)** (GB) (for stockings)
jarretelles *fpl*
(b) (US) (braces) bretelles *fpl*
suspense *n* (in film, novel) suspense *m*; **to
leave sb in ~** laisser qn dans l'expectative
suspension *n* **(a)** (gen, Aut) suspension *f*
(b) (of pupil) exclusion *f* temporaire
suspicion *n* méfiance *f* (**of** de); **to arouse
~** éveiller des soupçons; **to have ~s about
sb/sth** avoir des doutes *mpl* sur qn/qch
suspicious *adj* **(a)** (wary) méfiant/-e; **to be
~ of sth** se méfier de qch
(b) *‹person, object›* suspect/-e; *‹behaviour,
activity›* louche
sustain *vtr* **(a)** (maintain) maintenir
‹interest, success›
(b) (Mus) soutenir *‹note›*
(c) (support) soutenir; (physically) donner des
forces à; **to ~ life** rendre la vie possible
(d) recevoir *‹injury, burn›*; éprouver *‹loss›*
sustainable *adj ‹development, forestry›*
durable; *‹resource›* renouvelable; *‹growth›*
viable
sustenance *n* nourriture *f*
swab *n* (Med) tampon *m*
swagger *vi* **(a)** (walk) se pavaner
(b) (boast) fanfaronner
swallow ¹ *n* **(a)** (bird) hirondelle *f*
(b) (gulp) gorgée *f*
² *vtr* **(a)** (eat) avaler
(b) ravaler *‹pride›*
(c) (colloq) (believe) avaler (colloq)
³ *vi* avaler; (nervously) avaler sa salive
swamp ¹ *n* marais *m*, marécage *m*
² *vtr* inonder
swan *n* cygne *m*
swap (colloq) ¹ *n* échange *m*
² *vtr* échanger; **to ~ sth for sth** échanger
qch contre qch; **to ~ places** changer de
place
swarm ¹ *n* (of bees) essaim *m*; (of flies)
nuée *f*
² *vi ‹bees›* essaimer; **to be ~ing with**
grouiller de *‹people, maggots›*
swarthy *adj* basané/-e
swastika *n* croix *f* gammée, svastika *m*
swat *vtr* écraser *‹fly, wasp›* (**with** avec)
sway ¹ *n* **to hold ~** avoir une grande
influence; **to hold ~ over** dominer
² *vtr* **(a)** (influence) influencer
(b) (rock) osciller
³ *vi ‹tree, bridge›* osciller; *‹person›*
chanceler; (to music) se balancer
swear ¹ *vtr* jurer (**to do** de faire); **to ~ sb
to secrecy** faire jurer le secret à qn
² *vi* **(a)** (curse) jurer

(b) (attest) **to ~ to having done** jurer avoir
fait
■ **swear by** (colloq) **~ by [sth/sb]** ne jurer
que par *‹remedy, expert›*
■ **swear in: ~ in [sb], ~ [sb] in** faire prêter
serment à
swearing *n* jurons *mpl*
swearword *n* juron *m*, gros mot *m*
sweat ① *n* sueur *f*; **to break out into a ~**
se mettre à suer; **to be in a cold ~ about sth**
avoir des sueurs froides à l'idée de qch
② **sweats** *n pl* (US) survêtement *m*
③ *vi ‹person, horse›* transpirer, suer;
‹hands, feet, cheese› transpirer
sweatband *n* bandeau *m*
sweater *n* pull *m*
sweat pants *n pl* (US) pantalon *m* de
survêtement
sweatshirt *n* sweatshirt *m*
sweatshop *n* atelier *m* où on exploite le
personnel
sweaty *adj ‹person›* en sueur; *‹hand,
palm›* moite
swede *n* (GB) rutabaga *m*
Swede *n* Suédois/-e *m/f*
Sweden *pr n* Suède *f*
Swedish ① *n* (language) suédois *m*
② *adj* suédois/-e
sweep ① *n* **(a)** **to give sth a ~** donner un
coup de balai à qch
(b) (movement) **with a ~ of his arm** d'un
grand geste du bras
(c) (of land, woods) étendue *f*
(d) (*also* **chimney ~**) ramoneur *m*
② *vtr* **(a)** balayer *‹floor, path›*; ramoner
‹chimney›
(b) (push) **to ~ sth off the table** faire tomber
qch de la table (d'un grand geste de la
main); **to ~ sb off his/her feet** (figurative) faire
perdre la tête à qn
(c) *‹beam, searchlight›* balayer
③ *vi* **(a)** (clean) balayer
(b) **to ~ in/out** (majestically) entrer/sortir
majestueusement
■ **sweep aside** écarter *‹person, objection›*
■ **sweep up** balayer
sweeping *adj* **(a)** *‹change, review›*
radical/-e
(b) **~ generalization** généralisation *f* à
l'emporte-pièce
sweet ① *n* (GB) **(a)** (candy) bonbon *m*
(b) (dessert) dessert *m*
② *adj* **(a)** (gen) doux/douce; *‹food, tea, taste›*
sucré/-e; **to have a ~ tooth** aimer les
sucreries
(b) (kind) *‹person›* gentil/-ille
(c) (cute) *‹baby, cottage›* mignon/-onne
③ *adv* **to taste ~** avoir un goût sucré; **to
smell ~** sentir bon
sweet-and-sour *adj* aigre-doux/-douce
sweetcorn *n* maïs *m*
sweeten *vtr* **(a)** (Culin) sucrer (**with** avec)
(b) rendre [qch] plus tentant *‹offer›*
■ **sweeten up** amadouer *‹person›*

sweetener n (a) (in food) édulcorant m
(b) (colloq) (bribe) incitation f; (illegal)
pot-de-vin m

sweetheart n (boyfriend) petit ami m;
(girlfriend) petite amie f

sweetly adv ⟨say, smile⟩ gentiment

sweet potato n patate f douce

sweet-talk vtr (colloq) baratiner (colloq)

swell ① n (of waves, sea) houle f
② vtr gonfler ⟨crowd, funds⟩; grossir ⟨river⟩
③ vi ⟨balloon, tyre, stomach⟩ se gonfler;
⟨wood⟩ gonfler; ⟨ankle, gland⟩ enfler; ⟨river⟩
grossir; ⟨crowd⟩ s'accroître

swelling n (on limb, skin) enflure f; (on head)
bosse f

sweltering adj (colloq) torride

swerve vi faire un écart; to ∼ off the road
sortir de la route

swift ① n martinet m
② adj rapide, prompt/-e

swill n pâtée f (des porcs)

swim ① n baignade f; to go for a ∼ (in sea,
river) aller se baigner; (in pool) aller à la
piscine
② vtr nager ⟨distance, stroke⟩
③ vi (a) nager; to ∼ across sth traverser
qch à la nage
(b) to be ∼ming in baigner dans ⟨sauce, oil⟩
(c) ⟨scene, room⟩ tourner

swimmer n nageur/-euse m/f

swimming n natation f

swimming costume n (GB) maillot m
de bain

swimming pool n piscine f

swimming trunks n pl slip m de bain

swimsuit n maillot m de bain

swindle ① n escroquerie f
② vtr escroquer; to ∼ sb out of sth
escroquer qch à qn

swindler n escroc m

swing ① n (a) (of pendulum, needle)
oscillation f; (of hips, body) balancement m
(b) (in public opinion) revirement m (in de); (in
prices, economy) fluctuation f (in de); (in mood)
saute f (in de)
(c) (in playground) balançoire f
② vtr (to and fro) balancer; to ∼ sb round and
round faire tournoyer qn
③ vi (a) (to and fro) se balancer; ⟨pendulum⟩
osciller
(b) to ∼ open s'ouvrir; the car swung into
the drive la voiture s'est engagée dans l'allée;
to ∼ around ⟨person⟩ se retourner
(brusquement)
(c) (change) to ∼ from optimism to despair
passer de l'optimisme au désespoir; the party
swung towards the left le parti a basculé
vers la gauche
IDIOMS to get into the ∼ of things (colloq) se
mettre dans le bain (colloq); to be in full ∼
battre son plein (colloq)

swing door (GB), **swinging door** (US)
n porte f battante

swipe card n carte f à piste magnétique

swirl vi tourbillonner

Swiss ① n Suisse mf
② adj suisse; ⟨embassy⟩ de Suisse

switch ① n (a) (change) changement m (in
de)
(b) (for light) interrupteur m; (on radio,
appliance) bouton m
② vtr (a) reporter ⟨attention⟩ (to sur); to ∼
flights changer de vol
(b) intervertir ⟨objects, roles⟩; I've ∼ed the
furniture round j'ai changé la disposition des
meubles
③ vi changer
■ **switch off** éteindre ⟨appliance, light,
engine⟩; couper ⟨supply⟩
■ **switch on** allumer ⟨appliance, light,
engine⟩
■ **switch over** (on TV) changer de chaîne

switchboard n standard m

switchboard operator n standardiste
mf

switchover n passage m (from de; to à)

Switzerland pr n Suisse f

swivel vtr faire pivoter ⟨chair, camera⟩;
tourner ⟨head, body⟩
■ **swivel round** pivoter

swivel chair, **swivel seat** n fauteuil
m tournant, chaise f tournante

swollen adj ⟨ankle, gland⟩ enflé/-e; ⟨eyes⟩
gonflé/-e; ⟨river⟩ en crue

swoop vi ⟨bird, bat, plane⟩ plonger; to
∼ down descendre en piqué; to ∼ down on
fondre sur
(b) ⟨police, raider⟩ faire une descente

sword n épée f

swordfish n espadon m

sworn adj (a) ⟨statement⟩ fait/-e sous
serment
(b) ⟨enemy⟩ juré/-e; ⟨ally⟩ pour la vie

swot (colloq) ① n bûcheur/-euse m/f (colloq)
② vi bûcher (colloq)

sycamore n (also ∼ **tree**) sycomore m

syllable n syllabe f

syllabus n programme m

symbol n symbole m (of, for de)

symbolic adj symbolique (of de)

symbolism n symbolisme m

symbolize vtr symboliser (by par)

symmetric(al) adj symétrique

sympathetic adj (compassionate)
compatissant/-e (to, towards envers);
(understanding) compréhensif/-ive; (kindly)
gentil/-ille; (well disposed) bien disposé/-e (to,
towards à l'égard de)

sympathize vi (a) témoigner de la
sympathie (with à); I ∼ with you in your grief
je compatis à votre douleur
(b) (support) to ∼ with souscrire à ⟨aims,
views⟩

sympathizer n sympathisant/-e m/f (of
de)

sympathy n (a) (compassion) compassion f
(b) (solidarity) solidarité f

S

symphony *n* symphonie *f*
symphony orchestra *n* orchestre *m* symphonique
symptom *n* symptôme *m*
synagogue *n* synagogue *f*
synchronize *vtr* synchroniser
syndicate *n* (gen) syndicat *m*; (of companies) consortium *m*
syndrome *n* syndrome *m*
synonymous *adj* synonyme (**with** de)
synopsis *n* (of play) synopsis *m*; (of book) résumé *m*
syntax *n* syntaxe *f*
synthesis *n* synthèse *f*
synthesizer *n* synthétiseur *m*
synthetic *adj* synthétique

syringe ① *n* seringue *f*
② *vtr* **to have one's ears ~d** se faire déboucher les oreilles (avec une seringue)

syrup *n* sirop *m*

system *n* système *m* (**for doing, to do** pour faire); **road ~** réseau *m* routier; **reproductive ~** appareil *m* reproducteur; **to get sth out of one's ~** oublier qch

systematic *adj* (a) (efficient) méthodique (b) (deliberate) systématique

systematically *adv* ⟨work, list⟩ méthodiquement; ⟨arrange, destroy⟩ systématiquement

systems analyst *n* analyste *mf* (de) systèmes

Tt

t, T *n* t, T *m*
tab *n* (a) (loop) attache *f*
(b) (on can) languette *f*
(c) (label) étiquette *f*
IDIOMS **to keep ~s on sb** (colloq) tenir qn à l'œil (colloq)
tabby (cat) *n* chat/chatte *m/f* tigré/-e
table ① *n* (a) table *f*; **to set the ~** mettre le couvert
(b) (list) table *f*, tableau *m*
② *vtr* (a) (GB) (present) présenter
(b) (US) (postpone) ajourner
tablecloth *n* nappe *f*
table manners *n pl* **to have good/bad ~** savoir/ne pas savoir se tenir à table
table mat *n* (under plate) set *m* de table; (under serving-dish) dessous-de-plat *m inv*
tablespoon *n* (a) (object) cuillère *f* de service
(b) (also **~ful**) cuillerée *f* à soupe
tablet *n* comprimé *m* (**for** pour)
table tennis *n* tennis *m* de table, ping-pong® *m*
tabloid ① *n* tabloïde *m*; **the ~s** la presse populaire
② *adj* ⟨journalism, press⟩ populaire
taboo *n, adj* tabou (*m*)
tacit *adj* tacite
tack ① *n* (a) (nail) clou *m*
(b) (US) (drawing pin) punaise *f*
(c) (Naut) bordée *f*
(d) (tactic) tactique *f*
② *vtr* (a) (nail) **to ~ sth to** clouer qch à
(b) (in sewing) bâtir
③ *vi* ⟨sailor⟩ faire une bordée; ⟨yacht⟩ louvoyer

■ **tack on**: **~ [sth] on, ~ on [sth]** ajouter [qch] après coup ⟨clause, ending, building⟩ (**to** à)
tackle ① *n* (a) (in soccer, hockey) tacle *m*; (in rugby, American football) plaquage *m*
(b) (for fishing) articles *mpl* de pêche
(c) (on ship) gréement *m*; (for lifting) palan *m*
② *vtr* (a) s'attaquer à ⟨task, problem⟩
(b) (confront) **to ~ sb about** parler à qn de
(c) (in soccer, hockey) tacler; (in rugby, American football) plaquer
tacky *adj* (a) (sticky) collant/-e
(b) (colloq) (cheap) tocard/-e (colloq)
tact *n* tact *m*
tactful *adj* ⟨person, letter⟩ plein/-e de tact; ⟨enquiry⟩ discret/-ète
tactical *adj* tactique; **~ voting** vote *m* utile
tactics *n pl* tactique *f*
tactless *adj* ⟨person, question, suggestion⟩ indélicat/-e; **to be ~** ⟨person, remark⟩ manquer de tact
tadpole *n* têtard *m*
tag *n* (label) étiquette *f*; (on cat, dog) plaque *f*; (on file) onglet *m*
■ **tag along** suivre
tail *n* queue *f*
■ **tail off** (a) ⟨figures, demand⟩ diminuer
(b) ⟨voice⟩ s'éteindre
tailback *n* bouchon *m*
tailgate *n* hayon *m*
tail-off *n* diminution *f*
tailor ① *n* tailleur *m*
② *vtr* **to ~ sth to** adapter qch à ⟨needs, person⟩
tailor-made *adj* ⟨garment⟩ fait/-e sur mesure; (figurative) conçu/-e spécialement

t

tails n pl **(a)** (tailcoat) habit m
(b) (of coin) pile f; **heads or ∼?** pile ou face?

tainted adj ⟨food⟩ avarié/-e; ⟨water, air⟩
pollué/-e **(with** par); ⟨reputation⟩ entaché/-e

take **1** n (in film-making) prise f (de vues);
(Mus) enregistrement m

2 vtr **(a)** (gen) prendre; **he took the book off
the shelf** il a pris le livre sur l'étagère; **she
took a chocolate from the box** elle a pris un
chocolat dans la boîte; **he took a pen out of
his pocket** il a sorti un stylo de sa poche; **to
∼ an exam** passer un examen; **to ∼ a shower**
prendre une douche; **to ∼ sb/sth seriously**
prendre qn/qch au sérieux
(b) (carry with one) emporter, prendre ⟨object⟩;
(carry to a place) emporter, porter ⟨object⟩; **to
∼ sb sth, to ∼ sth to sb** apporter qch à qn;
he took his umbrella with him il a emporté
son parapluie; **to ∼ a letter to the post office**
porter une lettre à la poste; **to ∼ the car to
the garage** emmener la voiture au garage; **to
∼ sth upstairs/downstairs** monter/descendre
qch
(c) (accompany, lead) emmener ⟨person⟩; **to ∼
sb to** ⟨bus⟩ conduire qn à ⟨place⟩; ⟨road⟩
conduire or mener qn à ⟨place⟩; **I'll ∼ you to
your room** je vais vous conduire à votre
chambre; **he took her home** il l'a
raccompagnée; **to ∼ a dog/a child for a walk**
promener un chien/emmener un enfant faire
une promenade
(d) (accept) ⟨person⟩ accepter ⟨job, bribe⟩;
⟨shop⟩ accepter ⟨credit card, cheque⟩; ⟨person⟩
supporter ⟨pain, criticism⟩; **she can't ∼ a
joke** elle ne comprend pas la plaisanterie; **I
can't ∼ any more!** je n'en peux plus!
(e) (require) demander, exiger ⟨patience, skill,
courage⟩; **it ∼s patience to do il** faut de la
patience pour faire; **it ∼s three hours to get
there** il faut trois heures pour y aller; **it
won't ∼ long** ça ne prendra pas longtemps; **it
took her ten minutes to repair it** elle a mis
dix minutes pour le réparer; **to have what it
∼s** avoir tout ce qu'il faut **(to do** pour faire)
(f) (assume) **I ∼ it that** je suppose que
(g) (hold) ⟨hall, bus⟩ pouvoir contenir ⟨50
people⟩; ⟨tank, container⟩ avoir une capacité
de ⟨quantity⟩
(h) (wear) **what size do you ∼?** (in clothes)
quelle taille faites-vous?; (in shoes) quelle
pointure faites-vous?; **I ∼ a size 10** (in clothes)
je m'habille en 36; **I ∼ a size 5** (in shoes) je
chausse du 38
(i) (subtract) soustraire ⟨number, quantity⟩
(from de)

3 vi ⟨drug⟩ faire effet; ⟨dye, plant⟩ prendre
IDIOMS that's my last offer, ∼ it or leave it!
c'est ma dernière proposition, c'est à
prendre ou à laisser!; **to ∼ a lot out of sb**
fatiguer beaucoup qn
■ **take aback** interloquer; **to be ∼n aback**
rester interloqué/-e
■ **take after** tenir de ⟨person⟩
■ **take apart** démonter ⟨car, machine⟩
■ **take away (a)** (carry away) emporter
(b) (remove) enlever ⟨object⟩; emmener
⟨person⟩

(c) (subtract) soustraire ⟨number⟩; **that doesn't
∼ anything away from his achievement** ça
n'enlève rien à ce qu'il a accompli
■ **take back (a)** (to shop) rapporter ⟨goods⟩
(b) retirer ⟨statement, words⟩
(c) (accompany) ramener ⟨person⟩
(d) (accept again) reprendre
■ **take down (a)** enlever ⟨picture, curtains⟩;
démonter ⟨tent, scaffolding⟩
(b) noter ⟨name, details⟩
■ **take hold** ⟨disease, epidemic⟩ s'installer;
⟨idea, ideology⟩ se répandre; **to ∼ hold of**
prendre ⟨object, hand⟩
■ **take in (a)** (deceive) tromper; **I wasn't taken
in by him** je ne me suis pas laissé prendre à
son jeu
(b) recueillir ⟨refugee⟩; prendre ⟨lodger⟩
(c) (understand) saisir, comprendre ⟨situation⟩
(d) (observe) noter ⟨detail⟩
(e) (encompass) inclure
(f) (absorb) absorber ⟨nutrients, oxygen⟩
(g) ⟨boat⟩ prendre ⟨water⟩
(h) (in sewing) reprendre ⟨garment⟩
■ **take off: ¶ ∼ off (a)** ⟨plane⟩ décoller
(b) ⟨idea, fashion⟩ prendre
¶ ∼ [sth] off (a) to ∼ £10 off (the price)
réduire le prix de 10 livres sterling
(b) to ∼ two days off prendre deux jours de
congé
¶ ∼ off [sth] enlever ⟨clothing, shoes, lid⟩
¶ ∼ [sb] off (colloq) (imitate) imiter ⟨person⟩
■ **take on (a)** (employ) embaucher ⟨staff,
worker⟩
(b) jouer contre ⟨team, player⟩; (fight) se
battre contre ⟨person⟩
(c) (accept) prendre ⟨responsibilities, work⟩
■ **take out: ¶ ∼ [sth] out (a)** sortir ⟨object⟩
(from, of de); extraire ⟨tooth⟩; enlever
⟨appendix⟩; retirer ⟨money⟩
(b) to ∼ [sth] out on sb passer [qch] sur qn
⟨anger, frustration⟩; **to ∼ it out on sb** s'en
prendre à qn
¶ ∼ [sb] out sortir avec ⟨person⟩; **to ∼ sb out
to dinner** emmener qn dîner
■ **take over: ¶ ∼ over (a)** ⟨army, faction⟩
prendre le pouvoir
(b) (be successor) ⟨person⟩ prendre la suite; **to
∼ over from** remplacer ⟨predecessor⟩
¶ ∼ over [sth] prendre le contrôle de ⟨town,
region⟩; reprendre ⟨business⟩
■ **take part** prendre part; **to ∼ part in**
participer à
■ **take place** avoir lieu
■ **take to (a)** se prendre de sympathie pour
⟨person⟩
(b) (begin) **to ∼ to doing** se mettre à faire
(c) (go) se réfugier dans ⟨forest, hills⟩; **to ∼
to the streets** descendre dans la rue
■ **take up: ¶ to ∼ up with** s'attacher à
⟨person, group⟩
¶ ∼ up [sth] (a) (lift) enlever ⟨carpet,
pavement⟩
(b) (start) se mettre à ⟨golf, guitar⟩; prendre
⟨job⟩; **to ∼ up one's duties** entrer dans ses
fonctions
(c) (continue) reprendre ⟨story, cry, refrain⟩

(d) (accept) accepter ⟨*offer, invitation*⟩; relever ⟨*challenge*⟩
(e) to ∼ **sth up with sb** soulever [qch] avec qn ⟨*matter*⟩
(f) (occupy) prendre ⟨*space, time, energy*⟩
(g) prendre ⟨*position, stance*⟩
(h) (shorten) raccourcir ⟨*skirt, curtains*⟩
¶ ∼ **sb up on (a)** reprendre qn sur ⟨*point, assertion*⟩
(b) to ∼ **sb up on an offer** accepter l'offre de qn

take-away *n* (GB) **(a)** (meal) repas *m* à emporter
(b) (restaurant) restaurant *m* qui fait des plats à emporter

take-home pay *n* salaire *m* net

taken *adj* **(a)** to be ∼ ⟨*seat, room*⟩ être occupé/-e
(b) (impressed) **to be ∼ with** être emballé/-e (colloq) par ⟨*idea, person*⟩

take-off *n* **(a)** (by plane) décollage *m*
(b) (colloq) (imitation) imitation *f* (**of** de)

take-out *adj* (US) ⟨*food*⟩ à emporter

takeover *n* (of company) rachat *m*; (of political power) prise *f* de pouvoir

takeover bid *n* offre *f* publique d'achat, OPA *f*

taker *n* preneur/-euse *m/f*

takings *n pl* recette *f*

talc, talcum (powder) *n* talc *m*

tale *n* (story) histoire *f*; (fantasy story) conte *m*; (narrative, account) récit *m*

talent *n* talent *m*

talent contest *n* concours *m* de jeunes talents *or* d'amateurs

talented *adj* doué/-e, talentueux/-euse

talisman *n* talisman *m*

talk ① *n* **(a)** (talking, gossip) propos *mpl*; **they are the ∼ of the town** on ne parle que d'eux
(b) (conversation) conversation *f*, discussion *f*
(c) (speech) exposé *m* (**about, on** sur); (more informal) causerie *f*
② **talks** *n pl* négociations *fpl*; (political) pourparlers *mpl*; **peace ∼** pourparlers de paix
③ *vtr* parler; **to ∼ business** parler affaires; **to ∼ nonsense** raconter n'importe quoi; **to ∼ sb into/out of doing** persuader/dissuader qn de faire; **he ∼ed his way out of it** il s'en est tiré grâce à son bagout (colloq)
④ *vi* parler; (gossip) bavarder; **to ∼ to oneself** parler tout seul/toute seule

talkative *adj* bavard/-e

talking ① *n* **I'll do the ∼** c'est moi qui parlerai; **'no ∼!'** 'silence!'
② *adj* ⟨*bird, doll*⟩ qui parle

talking book *n* livre *m* enregistré (à l'usage des non-voyants)

talking-to *n* réprimande *f*

talk show *n* talk-show *m*

tall *adj* ⟨*person*⟩ grand/-e; ⟨*building, tree, chimney*⟩ haut/-e; **he's six feet ∼** ≈ il mesure un mètre quatre-vingts; **to grow ∼er** grandir

tally ① *n* compte *m*
② *vi* concorder

tambourine *n* tambourin *m*

tame ① *adj* **(a)** ⟨*animal*⟩ apprivoisé/-e
(b) ⟨*story, party*⟩ sage; ⟨*reform*⟩ timide
② *vtr* **(a)** apprivoiser ⟨*bird, wild animal*⟩; dompter ⟨*lion, tiger*⟩
(b) soumettre ⟨*person*⟩

tamper *vi* **to ∼ with** tripoter ⟨*machinery, lock*⟩; trafiquer ⟨*accounts, evidence*⟩

tampon *n* tampon *m*

tan ① *n* **(a)** (*also* **sun∼**) bronzage *m*
(b) (colour) fauve *m*
② *adj* fauve
③ *vtr* **(a)** bronzer ⟨*skin*⟩
(b) tanner ⟨*animal hide*⟩
④ *vi* ⟨*skin, person*⟩ bronzer

tandem *n* tandem *m*; **in ∼** en tandem

tang *n* (taste) goût *m* acidulé; (smell) odeur *f* piquante

tangent *n* tangente *f*; **to go off on a ∼** partir dans une digression

tangerine *n* tangerine *f*

tangible *adj* tangible

tangle ① *n* (of hair, string, wires) enchevêtrement *m*; (of clothes, sheets) fouillis *m*
② *vi* ⟨*hair, string, cable*⟩ s'emmêler
■ **tangle up**: ¶ ∼ **up** s'embrouiller; ¶ **to get ∼d up** ⟨*hair, string, wires*⟩ s'emmêler

tangy *adj* acidulé/-e

tank *n* **(a)** (gen, Aut) réservoir *m*; (for oil) cuve *f*; (for water) citerne *f*; (for fish) aquarium *m*
(b) (Mil) char *m* (de combat)

tankard *n* chope *f*

tanker *n* **(a)** (ship) navire-citerne *m*; **oil ∼** pétrolier *m*
(b) (lorry) camion-citerne *m*

tanned *adj* (*also* **sun∼**) bronzé/-e

Tannoy® *n* (GB) **the ∼** le système de haut-parleurs

tantalizing *adj* ⟨*suggestion*⟩ tentant/-e; ⟨*possibility*⟩ séduisant/-e; ⟨*glimpse*⟩ excitant/-e

tantamount *adj* **to be ∼ to** équivaloir à, être équivalent/-e à

tantrum *n* crise *f* de colère; **to throw a ∼** piquer une crise (colloq)

tap ① *n* **(a)** (for water, gas) robinet *m*
(b) (blow) petit coup *m*
② *vtr* **(a)** (knock) taper (doucement); (repeatedly) tapoter
(b) mettre [qch] sur écoute ⟨*telephone*⟩
(c) inciser ⟨*rubber tree*⟩; exploiter ⟨*resources*⟩
■ **tap in:** ∼ [sth] **in**, ∼ **in** [sth] enfoncer ⟨*nail*⟩; taper ⟨*information, number*⟩

tap dance *n* (*also* ∼ **dancing**) claquettes *fpl*

tape ① *n* **(a)** bande *f* (magnétique); (cassette) cassette *f*; (video) cassette *f* vidéo; (recording) enregistrement *m*
(b) (*also* **adhesive ∼**) scotch® *m*

⋯✦

2 *vtr* (a) (record) enregistrer
(b) (stick) to ~ sth to coller qch à ⟨*surface, door*⟩

tape deck *n* platine *f* cassette

tape measure *n* mètre *m* ruban

taper *vi* ⟨*sleeve, trouser leg*⟩ se resserrer; ⟨*column, spire*⟩ s'effiler

tape recorder *n* magnétophone *m*

tapestry *n* tapisserie *f*

tapeworm *n* ver *m* solitaire, ténia *m*

tap water *n* eau *f* du robinet

tar *n* goudron *m*; (on roads) bitume *m*.

target **1** *n* (a) (in archery, shooting) cible *f*; (Mil) objectif *f*
(b) (butt) cible *f*; to be the ~ of abuse être insulté/-e
(c) (goal) objectif *m*
2 *adj* ⟨*date, figure*⟩ prévu/-e; ⟨*audience, group*⟩ visé/-e, ciblé/-e
3 *vtr* (a) diriger ⟨*weapon, missile*⟩; prendre [qch] pour cible ⟨*city, site*⟩
(b) (in marketing) viser ⟨*group, sector*⟩

target language *n* langue *f* cible

tariff *n* (a) (price list) tarif *m*
(b) (customs duty) droit *m* de douane

tarmac *n* (a) (*also* **Tarmac**®) macadam *m*
(b) (GB) (of airfield) piste *f*

tarnish **1** *vtr* ternir
2 *vi* se ternir

tarpaulin *n* (material) toile *f* de bâche; (sheet) bâche *f*

tarragon *n* estragon *m*

tart *n* (small) tartelette *f*; (large) tarte *f*
■ **tart up** (GB) (colloq): ¶ ~ [sth] up, ~ up [sth] retaper (colloq) ⟨*house, room*⟩; ¶ ~ oneself up se pomponner (colloq)

tartan *adj* écossais/-e

task *n* tâche *f*; a hard ~ une lourde tâche

task bar *n* barre *f* de tâches

task force *n* (Mil) corps *m* expéditionnaire; (committee) groupe *m* de travail

taskmaster *n* tyran *m*; to be a hard ~ être très exigeant/-e

tassel *n* gland *m*

taste **1** *n* (a) (gen) goût *m*; that's a matter of ~ ça dépend des goûts; to be in bad ~ être de mauvais goût
(b) (brief experience) expérience *f*; (foretaste) avant-goût *m*
2 *vtr* (a) (try) goûter ⟨*food, drink*⟩
(b) I can ~ the brandy in this coffee je sens le (goût du) cognac dans ce café
(c) (experience) goûter à ⟨*freedom, success*⟩
3 *vi* to ~ sweet avoir un goût sucré; to ~ horrible avoir mauvais goût; to ~ like sth avoir le goût de qch; to ~ of avoir un goût de

taste bud *n* papille *f* gustative

tasteful *adj* de bon goût

tasteless *adj* (a) ⟨*remark, joke*⟩ de mauvais goût
(b) ⟨*food, drink*⟩ insipide

tasty *adj* ⟨*food*⟩ succulent/-e

tatters *n pl* to be in ~ ⟨*clothing*⟩ être en lambeaux; ⟨*career, reputation*⟩ être en ruines

tattoo **1** *n* tatouage *m*
2 *vtr* tatouer (on sur)

tatty *adj* (colloq) ⟨*carpet, garment*⟩ miteux/-euse; ⟨*book, shoes*⟩ en mauvais état

taunt *vtr* railler ⟨*person*⟩

Taurus *n* Taureau *m*

taut *adj* tendu/-e

tauten **1** *vtr* tendre
2 *vi* se tendre

tax **1** *n* (on goods, services, property) taxe *f*; (on income, profits) impôt *m*
2 *vtr* (a) imposer ⟨*earnings, person*⟩; taxer ⟨*luxury goods*⟩
(b) mettre [qch] à l'épreuve ⟨*patience*⟩

taxation *n* (a) (imposition of taxes) imposition *f*
(b) (revenue from taxes) impôts *mpl*

tax bracket *n* tranche *f* d'imposition du revenu

tax collector *n* percepteur *m*

tax disc *n* vignette *f* (automobile)

tax evasion *n* fraude *f* fiscale

tax exile *n*: *personne qui s'est expatriée pour raisons fiscales*

tax-free *adj* exempt/-e d'impôt

tax haven *n* paradis *m* fiscal

taxi *n* taxi *m*; by ~ en taxi

taxing *adj* épuisant/-e

taxi rank (GB), **taxi stand** *n* station *f* de taxis

tax office *n* perception *f*

taxpayer *n* contribuable *mf*

tax return *n* (a) (form) feuille *f* d'impôts
(b) (declaration) déclaration *f* de revenus

TB *n* (*abbr* = **tuberculosis**) tuberculose *f*

tea *n* (a) (drink) thé *m*
(b) (GB) (afternoon meal) thé *m*; (for children) goûter *m*; (evening meal) dîner *m*

tea bag *n* sachet *m* de thé

tea break *n* (GB) pause-café *f*

teach **1** *vtr* enseigner à ⟨*children, adults*⟩; enseigner ⟨*subject*⟩; to ~ sb enseigner [qch] à qn ⟨*academic subject*⟩; apprendre [qch] à qn ⟨*practical skill*⟩; to ~ school (US) être instituteur/-trice; to ~ sb a lesson ⟨*person*⟩ donner une bonne leçon à qn; ⟨*experience*⟩ servir de leçon à qn
2 *vi* enseigner

teacher *n* (in general) enseignant/-e *m/f*; (secondary) professeur *m*; (primary) instituteur/-trice *m/f*; (special needs) éducateur/-trice *m/f*

teacher training *n* formation *f* pédagogique

teaching **1** *n* enseignement *m*
2 *adj* ⟨*post*⟩ d'enseignant; ⟨*method, qualification*⟩ pédagogique; ⟨*staff*⟩ enseignant/-e

teaching hospital *n* centre *m* hospitalo-universitaire, CHU *m*

teacup *n* tasse *f* à thé

teak n teck m

team n équipe f

team member n équipier/-ière m/f

team spirit n esprit m d'équipe

teamwork n collaboration f

teapot n théière f

tear¹ [1] n (gen) accroc m; (Med) déchirure f [2] vtr déchirer ‹garment, paper›; **to ~ sth out of** arracher qch de ‹book, notepad› [3] vi (a) (rip) se déchirer (b) (rush) **to ~ out/off** sortir/partir en trombe

■ **tear apart** (a) mettre [qch] en pièces ‹prey›; déchirer ‹country› (b) (separate) séparer (c) (colloq) (criticize) descendre [qn] en flammes

■ **tear off** (carefully) détacher; (violently) arracher

■ **tear open** ouvrir [qch] en le/la déchirant

■ **tear out** détacher ‹coupon, cheque›; arracher ‹page›

■ **tear up** déchirer ‹letter, document›

tear² n larme f; **to burst into ~s** fondre en larmes

tearful adj ‹person, face› en larmes; ‹voice› larmoyant/-e

tear gas n gaz m lacrymogène

tease vtr taquiner ‹person› (**about** à propos de); tourmenter ‹animal›

teasing n taquineries fpl

teaspoon n petite cuillère f, cuillère f à café

teaspoonful n cuillerée f à café

teat n (a) (of cow, goat, ewe) trayon m (b) (GB) (on baby's bottle) tétine f

teatime n l'heure f du thé

tea towel n (GB) torchon m (à vaisselle)

technical adj technique

technical college n institut m d'enseignement technique

technical drawing n dessin m industriel

technical hitch n incident m technique

technicality n (a) (technical detail) détail m technique (**of** de) (b) (minor detail) point m de détail (c) (technical nature) technicité f

technically adv (a) (strictly speaking) théoriquement (b) (technologically) techniquement

technician n technicien/-ienne m/f

technique n technique f

techno [1] n techno f [2] adj techno inv

technological adj technologique

technology n technologie f; **information ~** informatique f

teddy n (also **~ bear**) ours m en peluche

tedious adj ennuyeux/-euse

teem vi **to be ~ing with** grouiller de ‹people›

teenage adj ‹son, daughter› qui est adolescent/-e; ‹singer, player› jeune (before n); ‹fashion› des adolescents

teenager n jeune mf, adolescent/-e m/f

teens n pl adolescence f; **to be in one's ~** être adolescent/-e

tee-shirt n tee-shirt, T-shirt m

teeter vi vaciller

teethe vi faire ses dents

teething troubles n pl difficultés fpl initiales

teetotal adj **I'm ~** je ne bois jamais d'alcool

teetotaller (GB), **teetotaler** (US) n personne f qui ne boit jamais d'alcool

TEFL n (abbr = **Teaching of English as a Foreign Language**) enseignement m de l'anglais langue étrangère

telecommunications n pl télécommunications fpl

telecommuting n télétravail m

teleconference n téléconférence f

telecottaging n télétravail m

telegram n télégramme m

telegraph [1] n télégraphe m [2] vtr télégraphier

telegraph pole n poteau m télégraphique

telemarketer n téléprospecteur/-trice m/f

telemarketing n télémarketing m

telepathy n télépathie f

telephone [1] n téléphone m; **to be on the ~** (connected) avoir le téléphone; (talking) être au téléphone [2] vtr téléphoner à ‹person›; téléphoner ‹instructions›; **to ~ France** appeler la France [3] vi appeler, téléphoner

telephone banking n transactions fpl bancaires télématiques

telephone booth, **telephone box** (GB) n cabine f téléphonique

telephone call n appel m téléphonique

telephone directory n annuaire m (du téléphone)

telephone number n numéro m de téléphone

telephone operator n standardiste mf

telephonist n (GB) standardiste mf

telephoto lens n téléobjectif m

telesales n télévente f

telescope n télescope m

teleshopping n téléachat m

teletext n télétexte m

televise vtr téléviser

television n (a) (medium) télévision f; **on ~** à la télévision (b) (set) téléviseur m

television licence n redevance f télévision

television programme n émission f de télévision

t

television set n téléviseur m, poste m de télévision

teleworking n télétravail m

telex ① n télex m
② vtr télexer

tell ① vtr (a) (gen) dire; raconter ⟨joke, story⟩; prédire ⟨future⟩; **to ~ sb about sth** parler de qch à qn; **to ~ sb to do** dire à qn de faire; **to ~ sb how to do/what to do** expliquer à qn comment faire/ce qu'il faut faire; **to ~ the time** ⟨clock⟩ indiquer or marquer l'heure; ⟨person⟩ lire l'heure; **can you ~ me the time please?** peux-tu me dire l'heure (qu'il est), s'il te plaît?; **I was told that** on m'a dit que; **I told you so!** je te l'avais bien dit!
(b) (deduce) **you can ~ (that) he's lying** on voit bien qu'il ment; **I can ~ (that) he's disappointed** je sais qu'il est déçu
(c) (distinguish) distinguer; **can you ~ the difference?** est-ce que vous voyez la différence?; **how can you ~ them apart?** comment peut-on les distinguer l'un de l'autre?
② vi (a) (reveal secret) **don't ~!** ne le répète pas!
(b) (know) savoir; **as far as I can ~** pour autant que je sache; **how can you ~?** comment le sais-tu?
(c) (show effect) **her age is beginning to ~** elle commence à faire son âge
■ **tell off** réprimander ⟨person⟩
■ **tell on** (a) dénoncer ⟨person⟩ (to à)
(b) **the strain is beginning to ~ on him** on commence à voir sur lui les effets de la fatigue

telling adj ⟨remark, omission⟩ révélateur/-trice

tell-tale ① n rapporteur/-euse m/f
② adj ⟨sign⟩ révélateur/-trice

telly n (GB) (colloq) télé f (colloq)

temp (GB) (colloq) ① n intérimaire mf
② vi travailler comme intérimaire

temper ① n (a) (mood) humeur f; **to be in a good/bad ~** être de bonne/mauvaise humeur
(b) **to be in a ~** être en colère; **to lose one's ~** se mettre en colère (with contre)
(c) (nature) caractère m
② vtr (a) (moderate) tempérer
(b) tremper ⟨steel⟩

temperament n (a) (nature) tempérament m
(b) (excitability) humeur f

temperamental adj (volatile) capricieux/-ieuse

temperate adj ⟨climate, zone⟩ tempéré/-e; ⟨person, habit⟩ modéré/-e

temperature n température f; **to have a ~** avoir de la température or de la fièvre

temper tantrum n caprice m

tempest n tempête f

tempestuous adj turbulent/-e

template n gabarit m; (Comput) modèle m

temple n (a) (building) temple m
(b) (Anat) tempe f

temporarily adv (for a limited time) temporairement; (provisionally) provisoirement

temporary adj ⟨job, contract⟩ temporaire; ⟨manager, secretary⟩ intérimaire; ⟨arrangement, accommodation⟩ provisoire

tempt vtr tenter; **to be ~ed to do** être tenté/-e de faire

temptation n tentation f

tempting adj ⟨offer⟩ alléchant/-e; ⟨food, smell⟩ appétissant/-e; ⟨idea⟩ tentant/-e

ten n, pron, det dix (m) inv

tenacious adj tenace

tenancy n location f

tenant n locataire mf

tend ① vtr soigner ⟨patient⟩; entretenir ⟨garden⟩; s'occuper de ⟨stall, store⟩
② vi **to ~ to do** avoir tendance à faire

tendency n tendance f (**to do** à faire)

tender ① n soumission f
② adj (a) ⟨meat⟩ tendre
(b) ⟨kiss, love, smile⟩ tendre
(c) ⟨bruise, skin⟩ sensible
③ présenter ⟨apology, fare⟩; donner ⟨resignation⟩

tendon n tendon m

tendril n vrille f

tenement n immeuble m ancien

tenner n (GB) (colloq) (note) billet m de dix livres

tennis n tennis m

tennis court n court m de tennis, tennis m inv

tenor n (Mus) ténor m

tenpin bowling (GB), **tenpins** (US) n bowling m (à dix quilles)

tense ① n temps m; **the present ~** le présent; **in the past ~** au passé
② adj ⟨person, atmosphere, conversation⟩ tendu/-e; ⟨moment⟩ de tension; **to make sb ~** rendre qn nerveux
③ vtr tendre ⟨muscle⟩; raidir ⟨body⟩
■ **tense up** ⟨person⟩ se crisper

tension n (a) (gen, Tech) tension f
(b) (suspense) suspense m

tent n tente f

tentacle n tentacule m

tentative adj ⟨smile, suggestion⟩ timide; ⟨conclusion, offer⟩ provisoire

tenterhooks n pl
IDIOMS **to be on ~** être sur des charbons ardents; **to keep sb on ~** faire languir qn

tenth ① n (a) (in order) dixième mf
(b) (of month) dix m inv
(c) (fraction) dixième m
② adj, adv dixième

tenuous adj ⟨link⟩ ténu/-e; ⟨distinction, theory⟩ mince

tepid adj tiède

term ① n (a) (period of time) (gen) période f, terme m; (Sch, Univ) trimestre m; **autumn/spring/summer ~** (Sch, Univ) premier/

deuxième/troisième trimestre **the president's first ~ of office** le premier mandat du président
(b) (word, phrase) terme *m*
2 terms *n pl* **(a)** (conditions) termes *mpl*; (of financial arrangement) conditions *fpl* de paiement
(b) to come to ~s with assumer ‹*identity, past, disability*›; accepter ‹*death, defeat, failure*›; affronter ‹*issue*›
(c) (relations) termes *mpl*; **to be on good ~s with** être en bons termes avec
3 *vtr* appeler, nommer
4 in terms of *phr* du point de vue de, sur le plan de
terminal 1 *n* **(a)** (at station) terminus *m*; (in airport) aérogare *f*; **ferry ~** gare *f* maritime
(b) (Comput) terminal *m*
(c) (for electricity) borne *f*
2 *adj* ‹*stage*› terminal/-e; ‹*illness*› (incurable) incurable; (at final stage) en phase terminale
terminate 1 *vtr* mettre fin à ‹*meeting, phase, relationship*›; résilier ‹*contract*›; annuler ‹*agreement*›; interrompre ‹*pregnancy*›
2 *vi* se terminer
termination *n* **(a)** (of contract) résiliation *f*; (of service) interruption *f*
(b) (Med) interruption *f* de grossesse
terminology *n* terminologie *f*
terminus *n* (GB) terminus *m*
terrace 1 *n* **(a)** (patio) terrasse *f*
(b) (row of houses) alignement *m* de maisons
2 terraces *n pl* (GB) (in stadium) gradins *mpl*
terrace(d) house *n* maison *f* (*située dans un alignement de maisons identiques et contiguës*)
terracotta (a) (earthenware) terre *f* cuite
(b) (colour) ocre brun *m*
terrain *n* terrain *m*
terrible *adj* **(a)** ‹*pain, noise, sight*› épouvantable; ‹*accident, fight*› terrible; ‹*mistake*› grave
(b) (colloq) ‹*food, weather*› affreux/-euse
terribly *adv* **(a)** (very) ‹*pleased, obvious*› très; ‹*clever*› extrêmement; **I'm ~ sorry** je suis navré
(b) (badly) ‹*suffer*› horriblement; ‹*sing, drive*› affreusement mal
terrific *adj* **(a)** (huge) ‹*amount*› énorme; ‹*noise*› épouvantable; ‹*speed*› fou/folle; ‹*accident, shock*› terrible
(b) (colloq) (wonderful) formidable
terrifically *adv* extrêmement
terrified *adj* terrifié/-e; **to be ~ of** avoir une peur folle de
terrify *vtr* terrifier
terrifying *adj* (frightening) terrifiant/-e; (alarming) effroyable
territorial *adj* territorial/-e
territory *n* territoire *m*; (figurative) domaine *m*
terror 1 *n* terreur *f*

2 *adj* ‹*tactic*› d'intimidation; **a ~ campaign** une vague terroriste
terrorism *n* terrorisme *m*
terrorist *n* terroriste *mf*
terrorize *vtr* terroriser
terry *n* (also **~ towelling** (GB), **~ cloth** (US)) tissu *m* éponge
terse *adj* ‹*style*› succinct/-e; ‹*person, statement*› laconique
tertiary *adj* ‹*sector*› tertiaire; ‹*education*› supérieur/-e
test 1 *n* **(a)** (gen) test *m*; (Sch, Univ) (written) contrôle *m*; (oral) épreuve *f* orale; **to put sb/sth to the ~** mettre qn/qch à l'épreuve
(b) (of equipment, machine, new model) essai *m*
(c) (Med) (of blood, urine) analyse *f*; (of organ) examen *m*; (to detect virus, cancer) test *m* de dépistage; **to have a blood ~** se faire faire une analyse de sang
(d) (Aut) (also **driving ~**) examen *m* du permis de conduire
2 *vtr* **(a)** (gen) évaluer ‹*intelligence, efficiency*›; (Sch) (in classroom) interroger (**on** en); (at exam time) contrôler
(b) (new model, product) essayer; (Med) analyser ‹*blood, sample*›; expérimenter ‹*new drug*›; **to have one's eyes ~ed** se faire faire un examen des yeux
(c) mettre [qch] à l'épreuve ‹*strength, patience*›
testament *n* **(a)** (proof) témoignage *m*; **to be a ~ to sth** témoigner de qch
(b) the Old/the New Testament l'Ancien/le Nouveau Testament
test ban *n* interdiction *f* d'essais nucléaires
test case *n* procès *m* qui fait jurisprudence
test-drive *vtr* faire un essai de route à, essayer
testicle *n* testicule *m*
testify 1 *vtr* témoigner (**that** que)
2 *vi* témoigner; **to ~ to** témoigner de
testimony *n* témoignage *m*, déposition *f*
testing *n* (of drug, cosmetic) expérimentation *f*; (of blood, water etc) analyse *f*; (Sch) contrôles *mpl*
test paper *n* (Sch) interrogation *f* écrite
test tube *n* éprouvette *f*
test-tube baby *n* bébé-éprouvette *m*
tetanus *n* tétanos *m*
tether *vtr* attacher (**to** à)
IDIOMS **to be at the end of one's ~** être au bout du rouleau (colloq)
text *n* texte *m*
textbook 1 *n* manuel *m* (**about**, **on** sur) .
2 *adj* ‹*case*› exemplaire; ‹*example*› parfait/-e
textile *n* textile *m*
texture *n* texture *f*
Thames *pr n* **the (river) ~** la Tamise

than 1 *prep* (a) (in comparisons) que; **he's taller ~ me** il est plus grand que moi; **he has more ~ me** il en a plus que moi (b) (expressing quantity, degree, value) de; **more/less ~ 100** plus/moins de 100; **more ~ half** plus de la moitié; **temperatures lower ~ 30 degrees** des températures de moins de 30 degrés 2 *conj* (a) (in comparisons) que; **he's older ~ I am** il est plus âgé que moi; **it took us longer ~ we expected** ça nous a pris plus de temps que prévu (b) (expressing preferences) **I'd sooner** *or* **rather go to Rome ~ go to Venice** je préférerais aller à Rome que d'aller à Venise, j'aimerais mieux aller à Rome qu'à Venise (c) (when) **hardly** *or* **no sooner had he left ~ the phone rang** à peine était-il parti que le téléphone a sonné (d) (US) **to be different ~ sth** être différent/-e de qch

thank *vtr* remercier ⟨*person*⟩; **~ God!** Dieu merci!

thankful *adj* (grateful) reconnaissant/-e; (relieved) soulagé/-e

thankfully *adv* (a) (luckily) heureusement (b) (with relief) avec soulagement; (with gratitude) avec gratitude

thankless *adj* ⟨*task, person*⟩ ingrat/-e

thanks 1 *n pl* remerciements *mpl*; **with ~** avec mes/nos remerciements 2 *adv* (colloq) merci; **~ a lot** merci beaucoup; **no ~** non merci 3 **thanks to** *phr* grâce à

Thanksgiving (Day) *n* (US) jour *m* d'Action de Grâces

thank you 1 *n* (*also* **thank-you, thankyou**) merci *m*; **to say ~ to sb** dire merci à qn 2 *adj* ⟨*letter, gift*⟩ de remerciement 3 *adv* merci; **~ for coming** merci d'être venu; **~ very much** merci beaucoup

that

■ Note **As a determiner**
– In French, determiners agree in gender and number with the noun that follows; *that* is translated by *ce* + masculine singular noun (*ce monsieur*), by *cet* + masculine singular noun beginning with a vowel or mute 'h' (*cet arbre, cet homme*) and by *cette* + feminine singular noun (*cette femme*). The plural form *those* is translated by *ces*.
– Note, however, that the above translations are also used for the English *this* (plural *these*). So when it is necessary to insist on *that* as opposed to others of the same sort *-là* is added to the noun: *I prefer* THAT *version* = je préfère cette version-là.
As a pronoun (*meaning that one*)
– In French, pronouns reflect the gender and number of the noun they are standing for. So *that* (meaning *that one*) is translated by *celui-là* for a masculine noun, *celle-là* for a feminine

noun; *those* (meaning *those ones*) is translated by *ceux-là* for a masculine plural noun and *celles-là* for a feminine plural noun.

1 *det* /cet/cette/ces; **~ chair** cette chaise; **those chairs** ces chaises; **at ~ moment** à ce moment-là; **at ~ time** à cette époque-là; **you can't do it ~ way** tu ne peux pas le faire comme ça; **he went ~ way** il est allé par là; **~ lazy son of yours** ton paresseux de fils 2 *dem pron* (a) (that one) celui-/celle-/ceux-/celles-là (b) (that thing, that person) **what's ~?** qu'est-ce que c'est que ça?; **who's ~?** qui est-ce?; (on phone) qui est à l'appareil?; **is ~ Françoise?** c'est Françoise?; **who told you ~?** qui t'a dit ça?; **~'s how he did it** c'est comme ça qu'il l'a fait; **what did he mean by ~?** qu'est-ce qu'il entendait par là?; **~'s the kitchen** ça, c'est la cuisine 3 *rel pron* (a) (as subject) qui; (as object) que; **the day ~ she arrived** le jour où elle est arrivée (b) (with a preposition) lequel, laquelle, lesquels, lesquelles; **the chair ~ I was sitting on** la chaise sur laquelle j'étais assis (c) (with prepositions translated by à) auquel, à laquelle, auxquels, auxquelles, **the girls ~ I was talking to** les filles auxquelles je parlais (d) (with prepositions translated by *de*) dont; **the people ~ I've talked about** les personnes dont j'ai parlé 4 *conj* que; **he said ~ he had finished** il a dit qu'il avait fini 5 *adv* **it's about ~ thick** c'est à peu près épais comme ça; **I can't do ~ much work in one day** je ne peux pas faire autant de travail dans une journée; **he can't swim ~ far** il ne peut pas nager aussi loin IDIOMS **~ is (to say)…** c'est-à-dire…; **~'s it!** (that's right) c'est ça!; (that's enough) ça suffit!; **I don't want to see you again and ~'s ~!** je ne veux pas te revoir point final!

thatched cottage *n* chaumière *f*

thatched roof *n* toit *m* de chaume

thaw 1 *n* dégel *m* 2 *vtr* faire fondre ⟨*ice, snow*⟩; décongeler ⟨*frozen food*⟩ 3 *vi* (a) ⟨*snow*⟩ fondre; ⟨*ground, frozen food*⟩ dégeler (b) (figurative) se détendre

the *det* le/la/l'/les

■ Note In French, determiners agree in gender and number with the noun that follows. So *the* is translated by *le* or *l'* + masculine singular noun (*le chien, l'ami*), by *la* or *l'* + feminine singular noun (*la chaise, l'amie*) and by *les* + plural noun (*les chaussures*).
– When *the* is used with a preposition that translates by *de* in French *de* + *le* + masculine singular noun = *du* (*du fromage*) and *de* + *les* + plural noun = *des* (*des crayons*).
– When *the* is used with a preposition that translates by *à* in French *à* + *le* + masculine singular noun = *au* (*au cinéma*) and *à* + *les* + plural noun = *aux* (*aux enfants*).

two chapters of ∼ book deux chapitres du livre; I met them at ∼ supermarket je les ai rencontrés au supermarché; ∼ French les Français; ∼ wounded les blessés; she buys only ∼ best elle n'achète que ce qu'il y a de mieux; ∼ more I learn ∼ less I understand plus j'apprends moins je comprends; ∼ longer he waits ∼ harder it will be plus il attendra plus ce sera difficile; ∼ sooner ∼ better le plus tôt sera le mieux; ∼ fastest train le train le plus rapide; ∼ prettiest house in the village la plus jolie maison du village; THE book of the year le meilleur livre de l'année; do you mean THE Charlie Parker? tu veux dire le célèbre Charlie Parker?; Charles ∼ First Charles 1er or Premier; ∼ Smiths les Smith

theatre, **theater** (US) n (a) théâtre m; **to go to the** ∼ aller au théâtre
(b) (US) (cinema) cinéma m

theatregoer n amateur mf de théâtre

theatrical adj théâtral/-e; ⟨group⟩ de théâtre

theft n vol m (of de)

their det leur/leurs

■ **Note** In French, determiners agree in gender and number with the noun that follows. So *their* is translated by *leur* + masculine or feminine singular noun (*leur chien, leur maison*) and by *leurs* + plural noun (*leurs enfants*).
− When *their* is stressed, *à eux* is added after the noun: THEIR house = leur maison à eux.

theirs pron

■ **Note** In French, possessive pronouns reflect the gender and number of the noun they are standing for; *theirs* is translated by *le leur, la leur, les leurs*, according to what is being referred to.

my car is red but ∼ is blue ma voiture est rouge mais la leur est bleue; my children are older than ∼ mes enfants sont plus âgés que les leurs; which house is ∼? c'est laquelle leur maison?; the money wasn't ∼ to give away ils or elles n'avaient pas à donner cet argent

them pron (a) (direct object) les; I've seen ∼ je les ai vus; catch ∼! attrape-les!; don't eat ∼! ne les mange pas!
(b) (indirect object) leur; I gave it to ∼ je le leur ai donné; write to ∼! écris-leur!
(c) (with prepositions, with être) eux, elles; with ∼ avec eux/elles; it's ∼ c'est eux/elles both of ∼ tous/toutes les deux; both of ∼ work in London ils/elles travaillent à Londres tous/toutes les deux; some of ∼ quelques-uns d'entre eux/quelques-unes d'entre elles

theme n thème m

theme park n parc m d'attractions (à thème)

theme song, **theme tune** n (of film) musique f; (of radio, TV programme) indicatif m

themselves pron

■ **Note** When used as a reflexive pronoun, direct and indirect, *themselves* is translated by *se* (or *s'* before a vowel or mute 'h').
− When used for emphasis, the translation is *eux-mêmes* in the masculine and *elles-mêmes* in the feminine: they did it themselves = ils l'ont fait eux-mêmes or elles l'ont fait elles-mêmes.
− After a preposition, the translation is *eux* or *elles* or *eux-mêmes* or *elles-mêmes*: they bought the painting for themselves = (masculine or mixed gender) ils ont acheté le tableau pour eux or pour eux-mêmes; (feminine gender) elles ont acheté le tableau pour elles or pour elles-mêmes.

(a) (reflexive) se, s'; they washed ∼ ils se sont lavés
(b) (emphatic) eux-mêmes/elles-mêmes
(c) (after preposition) eux/elles, eux-mêmes/elles-mêmes; (all) by ∼ tout seuls/toutes seules

then adv (a) (at that time) alors, à ce moment-là; (implying more distant past) en ce temps-là; I was working in Oxford ∼ je travaillais alors à Oxford; since ∼ depuis
(b) (afterwards, next) puis, ensuite
(c) (in that case, so) alors
(d) (therefore) donc
(e) (in addition, besides) puis, aussi

thence adv de là

theology n théologie f

theorem n théorème m

theoretical adj théorique

theoretically adv théoriquement; ∼ speaking en théorie

theory n théorie f; in ∼ en théorie

therapeutic adj thérapeutique

therapist n thérapeute mf

therapy n thérapie f

there

■ **Note** *there* is generally translated by *là* after prepositions (*near there* = près de là) and when emphasizing the location of an object/a point etc visible to the speaker: put them there = mettez-les là.
− *voilà* is used to draw attention to a visible place/object/person: *there's my watch* = voilà ma montre, whereas *il y a* is used for generalizations: *there's a village nearby* = il y a un village tout près.
− *there*, when unstressed with verbs such as *aller* and *être*, is translated by *y*: we went there last year = nous y sommes allés l'année dernière, but not where emphasis is made: *it was there that we went last year* = c'est là que nous sommes allés l'année dernière.
− For examples of the above and further uses, see the entry below.

1 pron ∼ is/are il y a; ∼ isn't any room il n'y a pas de place; ∼ are many reasons il y a beaucoup de raisons; ∼ are two il y en a deux; ∼ is some left il en reste; ∼ seems to be il semble y avoir
2 adv (a) là; up to ∼, down to ∼ jusque là; ···❖

put it in ~ mettez-le là-dedans; **stand ~**
mettez-vous là; **go over ~** va là-bas; **will she
be ~ now?** est-ce qu'elle y est maintenant?
(b) (to draw attention) (to person, activity) voilà; **~
you are** (seeing somebody arrive) vous voilà;
(giving object) tenez, voilà; (that's done) et voilà;
~'s a bus coming voilà un bus; **that
paragraph ~** ce paragraphe
3 *excl* ~ ~! allez! allez!; **~, I told you!** voilà,
je te l'avais bien dit!; **~, you've woken the
baby!** c'est malin, tu as réveillé le bébé!
4 there again *phr* (on the other hand) d'un
autre côté

thereabouts (GB), **thereabout** (US)
adv **(a)** (in the vicinity) par là
(b) (roughly) **100 dollars or ~** 100 dollars
environ

thereby *conj* ainsi

therefore *adv* donc, par conséquent

thermal *adj* thermique; ⟨*spring*⟩
thermal/-e; ⟨*garment*⟩ en thermolactyl®

thermal imaging *n* thermographie *f*

thermometer *n* thermomètre *m*

Thermos® *n* (*also* ~ **flask**) bouteille *f*
thermos®

thermostat *n* thermostat *m*

thesaurus *n* dictionnaire *m* analogique

these ▶ THIS

thesis *n* **(a)** (Univ) (doctoral) thèse *f*; (master's)
mémoire *m*
(b) (theory) thèse *f*

they *pron*

■ Note *they* is translated by *ils* (masculine) or
elles (feminine). For a group of people or things
of mixed gender, *ils* is always used. The
emphatic form is *eux* (masculine) or *elles*
(feminine).

~ have already gone (masculine or mixed) ils
sont déjà partis; (feminine) elles sont déjà
parties; **here ~ are!** les voici!; **there ~ are!**
les voilà!

thick **1** *adj* **(a)** (gen) épais/épaisse; ⟨*forest,
vegetation, fog*⟩ dense, épais/épaisse; **to be 6
cm ~** faire 6 cm d'épaisseur
(b) (colloq) (stupid) bête
2 *adv* **don't spread the butter on too ~** ne
mets pas trop de beurre; **the snow lay ~ on
the ground** il y avait une épaisse couche de
neige sur le sol
IDIOMS **to be in the ~ of** être au beau milieu
de

thicken **1** *vtr* épaissir
2 *vi* s'épaissir; ⟨*voice*⟩ s'enrouer

thicket *n* fourré *m*

thickly *adv* ⟨*spread*⟩ en une couche épaisse;
⟨*cut*⟩ en morceaux épais

thickness *n* épaisseur *f*

thickset *adj* trapu/-e

thick-skinned *adj* insensible

thief *n* voleur/-euse *m/f*

thieve *vtr, vi* voler

thigh *n* cuisse *f*

thimble *n* dé *m* à coudre

thin **1** *adj* **(a)** ⟨*nose, lips, wall*⟩ mince; ⟨*line,
stripe, wire, paper*⟩ fin/-e; ⟨*slice, layer*⟩ fin/-e,
mince; ⟨*fabric, mist*⟩ léger/-ère
(b) ⟨*mixture*⟩ liquide; ⟨*soup, sauce*⟩ clair/-e
(c) ⟨*person, body*⟩ maigre; **to get ~** maigrir
(d) to wear ~ ⟨*joke, excuse*⟩ être usé/-e
2 *vtr* diluer ⟨*paint*⟩; allonger ⟨*sauce, soup*⟩
3 *vi* (*also* ~ **out**) ⟨*crowd*⟩ se disperser;
⟨*hair*⟩ se clairsemer

thing **1** *n* **(a)** (object) chose *f*, truc *m* (colloq);
(action, task, event) chose *f*; **the best ~** (to do)
would be to go and see her le mieux serait
d'aller la voir; **I couldn't hear a ~** (that) **he
said** je n'ai rien entendu de ce qu'il a dit; **the
~ is,** (that)... ce qu'il y a, c'est que...; **the
only ~ is,...** la seule chose, c'est que...
(b) (person, animal) **she's a pretty little ~** c'est
une jolie petite fille; **you lucky ~!** (colloq)
veinard/-e! (colloq)
2 things *n pl* **(a)** (personal belongings,
equipment) affaires *fpl*
(b) (situation, circumstances, matters) les choses
fpl; **how are ~s with you?** comment ça va?;
all ~s considered tout compte fait
IDIOMS **for one ~... (and) for another ~...**
premièrement... et deuxièmement...; **I must
be seeing ~s!** je dois avoir des visions!

think **1** *vtr* **(a)** (believe) croire, penser; **I ~
so** je crois; **I don't ~ so** je ne crois pas; **what
do you ~ it will cost?** combien ça va coûter
à ton avis?
(b) (imagine) imaginer, croire
(c) (have opinion) **to ~ a lot/not much of**
penser/ne pas penser beaucoup de bien de;
what do you ~ of him? que penses-tu de lui?
2 *vi* **(a)** penser; (carefully) réfléchir; **to ~
about** *or* **of sb/sth** penser à qn/qch; **I'll have
to ~ about it** il faudra que j'y réfléchisse; **to
~ hard** bien réfléchir; **to be ~ing of doing**
envisager de faire; **to ~ about doing** penser
à faire
(b) (consider) **to ~ of sb as** considérer qn
comme
(c) (remember) **to ~ of** se rappeler
■ **think again** (reflect more) se repencher sur
la question; (change mind) changer d'avis
■ **think ahead** bien réfléchir (à l'avance)
■ **think back** se reporter en arrière (**to** à)
■ **think over**: ~ **over [sth]**, ~ **[sth] over**
réfléchir à
■ **think through** bien réfléchir à ⟨*proposal,
action*⟩; faire le tour de ⟨*problem, question*⟩

thinking *n* (reflection) réflexion *f*; **current ~**
is that la tendance actuelle de l'opinion est
que; **to my way of ~** à mon avis

think-tank *n* groupe *m* de réflexion

thinly *adv* ⟨*slice*⟩ en tranches fines; ⟨*spread*⟩
en couche mince; ~ **disguised** à peine
déguisé/-e

thinner *n* diluant *m*

third **1** *n* **(a)** (in order) troisième *mf*
(b) (of month) trois *m inv*
(c) (fraction) tiers *m*
(d) (*also* ~-**class honours degree**) (GB
Univ) ≈ licence *f* avec mention passable
(e) (*also* ~ **gear**) (Aut) troisième *f*

2 *adj* troisième
3 *adv* (a) ⟨*come, finish*⟩ troisième
(b) (*also* **thirdly**) troisièmement
third-class *adj* de troisième classe
third degree *n* (colloq) **to give sb the ~**
⟨*parent, teacher*⟩ soumettre qn à une
interrogation
third party *n* tiers *m*
Third Way *n* (GB Pol) troisième voie *f*
Third World *n* tiers-monde *m*
thirst *n* soif *f* (**for** de)
thirsty *adj* assoiffé/-e; **to be ~** avoir soif;
to make sb ~ donner soif à qn
thirteen *n, pron, det* treize (*m*) *inv*
thirteenth **1** *n* (a) (in order) treizième *mf*
(b) (of month) treize *m inv*
(c) (fraction) treizième *m*
2 *adj, adv* treizième
thirties *n pl* (a) (era) **the ~** les années *fpl*
trente
(b) (age) **to be in one's ~** avoir entre trente
et quarante ans
thirtieth **1** *n* (a) (in order) trentième *mf*
(b) (of month) trente *m inv*
(c) (fraction) trentième *m*
2 *adj, adv* trentième
thirty *n, pron, det* trente (*m*) *inv*
thirty-first **1** *n* (of month) trente et un *m*
2 *adj* trente et unième
thirty something *n*: jeune cadre de plus
de trente ans qui s'installe, fonde une famille,
etc

this

■ Note **As a determiner**
– In French, determiners agree in gender and
number with the noun that follows; *this* is
translated by *ce* + masculine singular noun (*ce
monsieur*) BUT by *cet* + masculine singular noun
beginning with a vowel or mute 'h' (*cet arbre,
cet homme*) and by *cette* + feminine singular
noun (*cette femme*). The plural form *these* is
translated by *ces* (*ces livres, ces histoires*).
– Note, however, that the above translations are
also used for the English *that* (*plural those*). So
when it is necessary to insist on *this* as opposed
to another or others of the same sort, the
adverbial tag *-ci* (*this one here*) is added to the
noun: *I prefer* THIS *version* = je préfère cette
version-ci.
As a pronoun (*meaning this one*)
– In French, pronouns reflect the gender and
number of the noun they are standing for. So
this (*meaning this one*) is translated by *celui-ci*
for a masculine noun, *celle-ci* for a feminine
noun; *those* (*meaning those ones*) is translated
by *ceux-ci* for a masculine plural noun, *celles-ci*
for a feminine plural noun: *of all the dresses this
is the prettiest one* = de toutes les robes celle-ci
est la plus jolie.
– For other uses of *this*, see the entry below.

1 *det* **~ paper** ce papier; **~ lamp** cette
lampe; **do it ~ way** not that way fais-le
comme ça et pas comme ça
2 *pron* **what's ~?** qu'est-ce que c'est?;

who's ~? qui est-ce?; (on telephone) qui est à
l'appareil?; **whose is ~?** à qui appartient
ceci?; **~ is the dining room** voici la salle à
manger; **~ is my sister Moira** (introduction)
voici ma sœur Moira; (on photo) c'est ma
sœur, Moira; **~ is not the right one** ce n'est
pas le bon; **who did ~?** qui a fait ça?; **~ is
what happens when** voilà ce qui se passe
quand
3 *adv* **it's ~ big** c'est grand comme ça
IDIOMS **to talk about ~ and that** parler de
tout et de rien
thistle *n* chardon *m*
thong *n* (a) (on whip) lanière *f*
(b) (on shoe, garment) lacet *m*
(c) (underwear) string *m* ficelle
thorn *n* épine *f*
thorough *adj* (a) (detailed) ⟨*analysis,
knowledge*⟩ approfondi/-e; ⟨*search, work*⟩
minutieux/-ieuse
(b) (meticulous) minutieux/-ieuse
thoroughbred **1** *n* pur-sang *m*
2 *adj* de pure race
thoroughfare *n* rue *f*; **'no ~'** 'passage
interdit'
thoroughly *adv* (a) (meticulously) ⟨*clean,
examine, read*⟩ à fond; ⟨*check, search*⟩
minutieusement
(b) (completely) ⟨*clean, reliable, dangerous*⟩
tout à fait; ⟨*agree*⟩ parfaitement;
⟨*recommend*⟩ chaleureusement
those ▶ THAT
though **1** *conj* bien que (+ *subjunctive*); **a
foolish ~ courageous act** un acte stupide
quoique courageux
2 *adv* quand même, pourtant; **it's very
expensive, ~** c'est très cher, pourtant
thought *n* (a) (idea) idée *f*, pensée *f*
(b) (reflection) pensée *f*; **deep in ~** plongé
dans ses pensées
(c) (consideration) considération *f*; **to give ~ to
sth** considérer qch
thoughtful *adj* (a) (reflective) pensif/-ive
(b) (considerate) ⟨*person, gesture*⟩
prévenant/-e; ⟨*letter*⟩ gentil/-ille
thoughtless *adj* irréfléchi/-e
thought-out *adj* **well/badly ~** bien/mal
conçu/-e
thought-provoking *adj* qui fait
réfléchir
thousand *n, pron, det* mille *m inv*; **a ~
and two** mille deux; **about a ~** un millier;
four ~ pounds quatre mille livres sterling;
~s of des milliers de
thousandth *n, adj, adv* millième (*mf*)
thrash *vtr* (a) (whip) rouer [qn] de coups
(b) (Mil, Sport) (colloq) écraser
■ **thrash about, thrash around** se
débattre
■ **thrash out** venir à bout de ⟨*problem*⟩;
réussir à élaborer ⟨*plan*⟩
thrashing *n* raclée *f*
thread **1** *n* (a) (for sewing) fil *m*
(b) (of screw) filetage *m*   ···ϟ

t

(c) (of story, argument) fil *m*
2 *vtr* enfiler ⟨*bead, needle*⟩

threadbare *adj* usé/-e jusqu'à la corde

threat *n* menace *f* (**to** pour)

threaten **1** *vtr* menacer; **to ~ to do** ⟨*person*⟩ menacer de faire; ⟨*event, thing*⟩ risquer de faire; **to be ~ed with extinction** risquer de disparaître
2 *vi* menacer

three *n, pron, det* trois (*m*) *inv*

three-dimensional *adj* en trois dimensions

threefold **1** *adj* triple
2 *adv* triplement; **to increase ~** tripler

three-piece suit *n* (costume *m*) trois-pièces *m inv*

three-piece suite *n* salon *m* trois pièces

three-quarters *n* trois-quarts *mpl*; **~ of an hour** trois-quarts d'heure

thresh *vtr* battre

threshold *n* seuil *m*

thrift *n* économie *f*

thrifty *adj* ⟨*person*⟩ économe (**in** dans)

thrill **1** *n* **(a)** (sensation) frisson *m*
(b) (pleasure) plaisir *m*
2 *vtr* transporter [qn] de joie
3 *vi* frissonner (**at, to** à)

thrilled *adj* ravi/-e; **~ed with** enchanté/-e de

thriller *n* thriller *m*

thrilling *adj* ⟨*adventure, match, story*⟩ palpitant/-e; ⟨*concert, moment, sensation*⟩ exaltant/-e

thrive *vi* ⟨*person*⟩ se porter bien; ⟨*plant*⟩ pousser bien; ⟨*business, community*⟩ prospérer

thriving *adj* ⟨*business, community*⟩ florissant/-e; ⟨*plant, animal*⟩ en pleine santé

throat *n* gorge *f*; **to have a sore ~** avoir mal à la gorge

throb *vi* **(a)** ⟨*heart, pulse*⟩ battre; **my head is ~bing** ça me lance dans la tête
(b) ⟨*motor*⟩ vibrer; ⟨*music, building*⟩ résonner

throbbing *adj* ⟨*pain, ache, music*⟩ lancinant/-e

throne *n* trône *m*

throng **1** *n* foule *f* (**of** de)
2 *vtr* envahir ⟨*street, town*⟩

throttle *n* (accelerator) accélérateur *m*

through **1** *prep* **(a)** (from one side to the other) à travers; **the nail went right ~ the wall** le clou a traversé le mur
(b) (via, by way of) **to go ~ the town centre** passer par le centre-ville; **to look ~** regarder avec ⟨*telescope*⟩; regarder par ⟨*hole, window*⟩; **it was ~ her that I got this job** c'est par son intermédiaire que j'ai eu ce travail
(c) (past) **to go ~** brûler ⟨*red light*⟩; **to get** *or* **go ~** passer à travers ⟨*barricade*⟩; passer ⟨*customs*⟩; **she's been ~ a lot** elle en a vu des vertes et des pas mûres (colloq)

(d) (because of) **~ carelessness** par négligence; **~ illness** pour cause de maladie
(e) (until the end of) **all** *or* **right ~ the day** toute la journée
(f) (up to and including) jusqu'à; **from Friday ~ to Sunday** de vendredi jusqu'à dimanche
2 *adj* **(a)** ⟨*train, ticket, route*⟩ direct/-e; ⟨*freight*⟩ à forfait; **'no ~ road'** 'voie sans issue'
(b) (successful) **to be ~ to the next round** être sélectionné/-e pour le deuxième tour
(c) (colloq) (finished) fini/-e; **are you ~ with the paper?** as-tu fini de lire le journal?
3 *adv* **the water went ~** l'eau est passée à travers; **to let sb ~** laisser passer qn; **to read sth right ~** lire qch jusqu'au bout
4 **through and through** *phr* English **~ and ~** anglais jusqu'au bout des ongles

throughout **1** *prep* **(a)** (all over) **~ France** dans toute la France; **~ the world** dans le monde entier
(b) (for the duration of) tout au long de; **~ his life** toute sa vie; **~ history** à travers l'histoire
2 *adv* (in every part) partout; (the whole time) tout le temps

throughway *n* (US) voie *f* rapide *or* express

throw **1** *n* (in football) touche *f*; (of javelin) lancer *m*; (in judo, wrestling) jeté *m*; (of dice) coup *m*
2 *vtr* **(a)** (with careful aim) lancer; (downwards) jeter; (with violence) projeter; **to ~ sth at sb** lancer qch à qn; **to ~ a six** (in dice) faire un six
(b) ⟨*horse*⟩ désarçonner ⟨*rider*⟩
(c) lancer ⟨*punch*⟩; jeter ⟨*glance*⟩; projeter ⟨*light, shadow*⟩ (**on** sur)
(d) (disconcert) désarçonner
(e) **to ~ a party** faire une fête (colloq)
(f) (in pottery) tourner
3 *vi* lancer

■ **throw away** jeter ⟨*paper, old clothes*⟩; gâcher ⟨*chance, life*⟩
■ **throw back** rejeter ⟨*fish*⟩; relancer ⟨*ball*⟩
■ **throw in: ~ [sth], ~ [sth] in** (give free) faire cadeau de; (add) ajouter
■ **throw out (a)** jeter ⟨*rubbish*⟩; expulser ⟨*person*⟩ (**of** de)
(b) rejeter ⟨*application, decision*⟩
■ **throw together: ¶ ~ [sb] together** réunir ⟨*people*⟩; ¶ **~ [sth] together** improviser
■ **throw up: ¶ ~ up** (colloq) vomir **~ [sth] up**
(a) lever ⟨*arms, hands*⟩; lancer ⟨*ball*⟩
(b) (colloq) (abandon) laisser tomber ⟨*job*⟩

throwaway *adj* (discardable) jetable; ⟨*society*⟩ de consommation; ⟨*remark*⟩ désinvolte

throwback *n* survivance *f* (**to** de)

thrush *n* (Zool) grive *f*

thrust **1** *n* **(a)** (gen, Mil, Tech) poussée *f*; **sword ~** coup *m* d'épée
(b) (of argument) portée *f*
2 *vtr* **to ~ sth towards** *or* **at sb** mettre brusquement qch sous le nez de qn; **to ~ sth into sth** enfoncer qch dans qch

thud ⟦1⟧ *n* bruit *m* sourd
⟦2⟧ *vi* faire un bruit sourd

thug *n* voyou *m*

thumb ⟦1⟧ *n* pouce *m*
⟦2⟧ *vtr* (a) (*also* ~ **through**) feuilleter ⟨*book, magazine*⟩
(b) (colloq) to ~ **a lift** faire du stop (colloq)
IDIOMS to be under sb's ~ être sous la domination de qn

thumbs down *n* (colloq) to give sb/sth the ~ rejeter qn/qch; **to get the** ~ être rejeté/-e

thumbs up *n* (colloq) to give sb/sth the ~ (approve) approuver qn/qch; **start the car when I give you the** ~ démarre quand je te fais signe

thumbtack *n* punaise *f*

thump ⟦1⟧ *n* (a) (blow) (grand) coup *m*
(b) (sound) bruit *m* sourd
⟦2⟧ *vtr* taper sur; **he** ~ed **me** il m'a tapé dessus
⟦3⟧ *vi* ⟨*heart*⟩ battre violemment; ⟨*music, rhythm*⟩ résonner

thunder ⟦1⟧ *n* (a) tonnerre *m*; **a peal of** ~ un roulement de tonnerre
(b) (of hooves) fracas *m*; (of applause) tonnerre *m*
⟦2⟧ *v impers* tonner

thunderbolt *n* foudre *f*

thunderclap *n* coup *m* de tonnerre

thunderstorm *n* orage *m*

thunderstruck *adj* abasourdi/-e

Thursday *n* jeudi *m*

thus *adv* ainsi; ~ **far** jusqu'à présent

thwart *vtr* contrarier ⟨*plan*⟩; contrecarrer les desseins de ⟨*person*⟩

thyme *n* thym *m*

thyroid *n* (*also* ~ **gland**) thyroïde *f*

tiara *n* (woman's) diadème *m*; (Pope's) tiare *f*

Tibet *pr n* Tibet *m*

tick ⟦1⟧ *n* (a) (of clock) tic-tac *m*
(b) (mark) coche *f*
(c) (Zool) tique *f*
⟦2⟧ *vtr* cocher ⟨*box, name, answer*⟩
⟦3⟧ *vi* ⟨*bomb, clock, watch*⟩ faire tic-tac
■ **tick off** cocher ⟨*name, item*⟩

ticket *n* (a) (for plane, train, cinema, exhibition) billet *m* (**for** pour); (for bus, underground, cloakroom, left-luggage) ticket *m*; (for library) carte *f*; (label) étiquette *f*
(b) (Aut) (colloq) (for fine) PV *m* (colloq)
(c) (US) (of political party) liste *f* (électorale)

ticket office *n* (office) bureau *m* de vente (des billets); (booth) guichet *m*

tickle ⟦1⟧ *n* chatouillement *m*
⟦2⟧ *vtr* (a) ⟨*person, feather*⟩ chatouiller; ⟨*wool, garment*⟩ gratter
(b) (colloq) (gratify) chatouiller ⟨*palate, vanity*⟩
(c) (amuse) amuser
⟦3⟧ *vi* chatouiller

tidal wave *n* raz-de-marée *m inv*

tide *n* marée *f*; (figurative) (of emotion) vague *f*; (of events) cours *m*

tidy ⟦1⟧ *adj* (a) ⟨*house, room, desk*⟩ bien

rangé/-e; ⟨*garden, work, appearance*⟩ soigné/-e; ⟨*habits, person*⟩ ordonné/-e; ⟨*hair*⟩ bien coiffé/-e
(b) (colloq) ⟨*amount*⟩ beau/belle (*before n*)
⟦2⟧ *vtr, vi* = TIDY UP
■ **tidy up:** ¶ ~ **up** faire du rangement; **to** ~ **up after** ranger derrière ⟨*person*⟩; ¶ ~ **up** [sth] ranger ⟨*house, room, objects*⟩; arranger ⟨*appearance, hair*⟩

tie ⟦1⟧ *n* (a) (piece of clothing) cravate *f*
(b) (bond) lien *m*
(c) (constraint) contrainte *f*
(d) (draw) match *m* nul
⟦2⟧ *vtr* (a) attacher ⟨*label, animal*⟩ (**to** à); ligoter ⟨*hands*⟩; ficeler ⟨*parcel*⟩ (**with** avec); nouer ⟨*scarf, cravate*⟩; attacher ⟨*laces*⟩; **to** ~ **a knot in sth** faire un nœud à qch
(b) (link) associer (**to** à)
(c) **to be** ~**d to** être rivé/-e à ⟨*job*⟩; être cloué/-e à (colloq) ⟨*house*⟩
⟦3⟧ *vi* (a) (fasten) s'attacher
(b) (draw) (in match) faire match nul; (in race) être ex aequo; (in vote) obtenir le même nombre de voix
■ **tie back** nouer [qch] derrière ⟨*hair*⟩
■ **tie down: she feels** ~**d down** elle se sent coincée (colloq); **he doesn't want to be** ~**d down** il ne veut pas perdre sa liberté; **to** ~ **sb down to sth** (limit) imposer qch à qn
■ **tie in with** concorder avec ⟨*fact, event*⟩
■ **tie up** (a) ligoter ⟨*prisoner*⟩; ficeler ⟨*parcel*⟩; attacher ⟨*animal*⟩
(b) (freeze) immobiliser ⟨*capital*⟩
(c) **to be** ~**d up** (busy) être pris/-e
(d) (finalize) conclure ⟨*deal*⟩; **to** ~ **up the loose ends** régler les derniers détails

tie break(er) *n* (in tennis) tie-break *m*; (in quiz) question *f* subsidiaire

tier *n* (of cake, sandwich) étage *m*; (of system) niveau *m*; (of seating) gradin *m*

tiff *n* (petite) querelle *f*

tiger *n* tigre *m*

tight ⟦1⟧ *adj* (a) ⟨*grip*⟩ ferme; ⟨*knot*⟩ serré/-e; ⟨*rope, voice*⟩ tendu/-e
(b) ⟨*space*⟩ étroit/-e; ⟨*clothing*⟩ serré/-e; (closefitting) ⟨*jacket, shirt*⟩ ajusté/-e; **my shoes are too** ~ mes chaussures me serrent
(c) (strict) ⟨*security, deadline*⟩ strict/-e; ⟨*budget, credit, schedule*⟩ serré/-e
⟦2⟧ *adv* ⟨*hold, grip*⟩ fermement; **hold** ~!; **sit** ~! ne bouge pas!

tighten ⟦1⟧ *vtr* serrer ⟨*lid, screw*⟩; resserrer ⟨*grip*⟩; renforcer ⟨*security, restrictions*⟩
⟦2⟧ *vi* ⟨*lips*⟩ se serrer; ⟨*muscle*⟩ se contracter

tight-fisted *adj* (colloq) radin/-e (colloq)

tight-fitting *adj* ajusté/-e

tight-knit *adj* uni/-e

tightly *adv* ⟨*grasp, hold*⟩ fermement; ⟨*embrace*⟩ bien fort; ⟨*fastened*⟩ bien

tightrope *n* corde *f* raide

tightrope walker *n* funambule *mf*

tights *n pl* (GB) collant *m*

tile ⟦1⟧ *n* (for roof) tuile *f*; (for floor, wall) carreau *m*   ⋯▶

2 *vtr* poser des tuiles sur ⟨*roof*⟩; carreler ⟨*floor, wall*⟩

till¹ = UNTIL

till² *n* caisse *f*

tiller *n* barre *f*

till receipt *n* ticket *m* (de caisse)

tilt **1** *vtr* pencher ⟨*table, sunshade*⟩; incliner ⟨*head*⟩; rabattre ⟨*hat, cap*⟩
2 *vi* (slant) pencher

timber *n* (for building) bois *m* (de construction); (trees) arbres *mpl*; (beam) poutre *f*

time **1** *n* (a) temps *m*; **as ∼ goes/went by** avec le temps; **you've got plenty of ∼** tu as tout ton temps; **a long ∼** longtemps; **a long ∼ ago** il y a longtemps; **in five days' ∼** dans cinq jours
(b) (hour of the day, night) heure *f*; **what ∼ is it?, what's the ∼?** quelle heure est-il?; **10 am French ∼** 10 heures, heure française; **this ∼ last week** il y a exactement huit jours; **on ∼** à l'heure; **the train ∼s** les horaires *mpl* des trains; **it's ∼ for bed** c'est l'heure d'aller au lit; **it's ∼ we started** il est temps de commencer; **about ∼ too!** ce n'est pas trop tôt!; **in ∼ for Christmas** à temps pour Noël
(c) (era, epoch) époque *f*; **at the ∼** à l'époque; **in former ∼s** autrefois; **it's just like old ∼s** c'est comme au bon vieux temps
(d) (moment) moment *m*; **at ∼s** par moments; **at the right ∼** au bon moment; **this is no ∼ for jokes** ce n'est pas le moment de plaisanter; **at all ∼s** à tout moment; **any ∼ now** d'un moment à l'autre; **by the ∼ I finished the letter the post had gone** le temps de finir ma lettre et le courrier était parti; **some ∼ next month** dans le courant du mois prochain; **for the ∼ being** pour le moment
(e) (occasion) fois *f*; **nine ∼s out of ten** neuf fois sur dix; **three ∼s a month** trois fois par mois; **three at a ∼** trois à la fois; **from ∼ to ∼** de temps en temps
(f) (experience) **to have a hard ∼ doing** avoir du mal à faire; **he's having a hard ∼** il traverse une période difficile; **we had a good ∼ on** s'est bien amusés
(g) (Mus) mesure *f*
(h) **ten ∼s longer/stronger** dix fois plus long/plus fort; **eight ∼s as much** huit fois autant
(i) (in mathematics) fois *f*
2 *vtr* (a) (schedule) prévoir ⟨*holiday, visit, attack*⟩; fixer ⟨*appointment, meeting*⟩
(b) (judge) calculer ⟨*blow, shot*⟩
(c) chronométrer ⟨*athlete, cyclist*⟩
IDIOMS **all in good ∼** chaque chose en son temps; **only ∼ will tell** l'avenir nous le dira; **to have ∼ on one's hands** (for brief period) avoir du temps devant soi; (longer) avoir beaucoup de temps libre

time bomb *n* bombe *f* à retardement

time-consuming *adj* qui prend du temps

time difference *n* décalage *m* horaire

time-frame *n* (period envisaged) calendrier *m*; (period allocated) délai *m*

timeless *adj* éternel/-elle

time-limit *n* (a) (deadline) date *f* limite
(b) (maximum duration) durée *f* maximum

timely *adj* opportun/-e

time off *n* (leave) congé *m*; (free time) temps *m* libre

timer *n* (on light) minuterie *f*; (for cooking) minuteur *m*

timeshare *n* (house) maison *f* en multipropriété; (apartment) appartement *m* en multipropriété

time-sheet *n* feuille *f* de présence

timespan *n* durée *f*

timetable **1** *n* (Sch) emploi *m* du temps; (for plans, negotiations) calendrier *m*; (for buses, trains) horaire *m*
2 *vtr* fixer l'heure de ⟨*class*⟩; fixer la date de ⟨*meeting*⟩

time zone *n* fuseau *m* horaire

timid *adj* timide; ⟨*animal*⟩ craintif/-ive

timing *n* (a) (gen) **the ∼ of the announcement was unfortunate** le moment choisi pour la déclaration était inopportun
(b) (Aut) réglage *m* de l'allumage
(c) (Mus) sens *m* du rythme

tin *n* (a) (metal) étain *m*
(b) (GB) (can) boîte *f* (de conserve)
(c) (for biscuits, cake) boîte *f*; (for paint) pot *m*; (for baking) moule *m*; (for roasting) plat *m* (à rôtir)

tin can *n* boîte *f* en fer-blanc

tin foil *n* papier *m* (d')aluminium

tinge **1** *n* nuance *f*
2 *vtr* teinter (with de)

tingle **1** *n* (physical) picotement *m*; (psychological) frisson *m*
2 *vi* (physically) picoter; (psychologically) frissonner

tinker *vi* **to ∼ with** bricoler ⟨*car*⟩; faire des retouches à ⟨*document*⟩

tinkle **1** *n* tintement *m*
2 *vi* tinter

tinned *adj* ⟨*meat, fruit*⟩ en boîte, en conserve

tinny *adj* ⟨*sound*⟩ grêle; (badly made) de camelote (colloq)

tin opener *n* (GB) ouvre-boîtes *m inv*

tinsel *n* guirlandes *fpl*

tint *n* (trace) nuance *f*; (pale colour) teinte *f*; (hair colour) shampooing *m* colorant

tinted *adj* ⟨*glass, spectacles*⟩ fumé/-e; ⟨*hair*⟩ teint/-e

tiny *adj* tout/-e petit/-e

tip **1** *n* (a) (of stick, sword, pen, shoe, spire) pointe *f*; (of branch, leaf, shoot, tail, feather) extrémité *f*; (of finger, nose, tongue) bout *m*
(b) (gratuity) pourboire *m*
(c) (practical hint) truc *m* (colloq), conseil *m*; (in betting) tuyau *m* (colloq)
2 *vtr* (a) (tilt) incliner; (pour) verser; (dump) déverser ⟨*waste, rubbish*⟩

(b) (predict) **to ~ sb/sth to win** prédire que qn/qch va gagner
(c) donner un pourboire à ⟨*waiter, driver*⟩
3 *vi* (tilt) s'incliner
■ **tip off**: **~ off [sb]**, **~ [sb] off** avertir
■ **tip over** faire basculer ⟨*chair*⟩; renverser ⟨*bucket, pile*⟩

tip-off *n* dénonciation *f*

tiptoe **1** *n* **on ~** sur la pointe des pieds
2 *vi* marcher sur la pointe des pieds

tire **1** *n* (US) pneu *m*
2 *vtr* fatiguer
3 *vi* **(a)** (get tired) se fatiguer
(b) (get bored) **to ~ of** se lasser de
■ **tire out** épuiser ⟨*person*⟩; **to be ~d out** être éreinté/-e

tired *adj* **(a)** (weary) ⟨*person, face, legs*⟩ fatigué/-e; ⟨*voice*⟩ las/lasse
(b) (bored) **to be ~ of sth/of doing** en avoir assez de qch/de faire; **to grow ~ of sth/of doing** se lasser de qch/de faire

tiredness *n* fatigue *f*

tireless *adj* ⟨*person*⟩ inlassable, infatigable; ⟨*efforts*⟩ constant/-e

tiresome *adj* ⟨*person, habit*⟩ agaçant/-e; ⟨*problem, duty*⟩ fastidieux/-ieuse

tiring *adj* fatigant/-e (**to do** de faire)

tissue *n* **(a)** (handkerchief) mouchoir *m* en papier
(b) (*also* **~ paper**) papier *m* de soie
(c) (Anat, Bot) tissu *m*

tit *n* (Zool) mésange *f*
IDIOMS **~ for tat** un prêté pour un rendu

titbit *n* (GB) (of food) gâterie *f*; (of gossip) cancan *m* (colloq)

title **1** *n* titre *m*
2 **titles** *n pl* (in film) générique *m*
3 *vtr* intituler ⟨*book, play*⟩

title bar *n* barre *f* de titre

titleholder *n* tenant/-e *m/f* du titre

title role *n* rôle *m* titre

titter **1** *n* ricanement *m*
2 *vi* ricaner

tizzy *n* (colloq) **to be in a ~** être dans tous ses états

to

■ **Note** Remember that when *to* is translated by *à* then *à* + *le* = *au* and *à* + *les* = *aux*.

1 *infinitive particle* **(a)** (expressing purpose) pour; **to do sth ~ impress one's friends** faire qch pour impressionner ses amis
(b) (linking consecutive acts) **he looked up ~ see...** en levant les yeux, il a vu...
(c) (after superlatives) à; **the youngest ~ do** le *or* la plus jeune à faire
(d) (avoiding repetition of verb) **'did you go?'**— **'no I promised not ~'** 'tu y es allé?'—'non j'avais promis de ne pas le faire'; **'are you staying?'—'I want ~ but...'** 'tu restes?'— 'j'aimerais bien mais...'
(e) (following impersonal verb) **it is difficult ~ do** il est difficile de faire; **it's difficult ~**

understand c'est difficile à comprendre; **it's easy ~ read her writing** il est facile de lire son écriture
2 *prep* **(a)** (in direction of) à ⟨*shops, school*⟩; (with purpose of visiting) chez ⟨*doctor's*⟩; (towards) vers; **she's gone ~ Mary's** elle est partie chez Mary; **~ Paris** à Paris; **~ Spain** en Espagne; **~ town** en ville; **the road ~ the village** la route qui mène au village; **turned ~ the wall** tourné vers le mur
(b) (up to) jusqu'à; **~ the end/this day** jusqu'à la fin/ce jour
(c) (in telling time) **ten (minutes) ~ three** trois heures moins dix; **it's five ~** il est moins cinq
(d) (introducing direct or indirect object) ⟨*give, offer*⟩ à; (*to* + personal pronoun) me/te/lui/ nous/vous/leur; **give the book ~ Sophie** donne le livre à Sophie; **be nice ~ your brother** sois gentil avec ton frère; **~ me it's just a minor problem** pour moi ce n'est qu'un problème mineur; **she gave it ~ them/ him** elle le leur/lui a donné
(e) (in toasts, dedications) à; **~ prosperity** à la prospérité; **~ our dear son** (on tombstone) à notre cher fils
(f) (in accordance with) **is it ~ your taste?** c'est à ton goût?; **to dance ~ the music** danser sur la musique
(g) (in relationships, comparisons) **to win by three goals ~ two** gagner par trois buts à deux; **next door ~ the school** à côté de l'école
(h) (showing accuracy) **three weeks ~ the day** trois semaines jour pour jour; **~ scale** à l'échelle
(i) (showing reason) **to invite sb ~ dinner** inviter qn à dîner; **~ this end** à cette fin
(j) (belonging to) de; **the key ~ the safe** la clé du coffre; **a room ~ myself** une chambre pour moi tout seul; **personal assistant ~ the director** assistant du directeur
(k) ⟨*tied*⟩ à; ⟨*pinned*⟩ à ⟨*noticeboard*⟩; sur ⟨*lapel, dress*⟩
(l) (showing reaction) à; **~ his surprise/dismay** à sa grande surprise/consternation

toad *n* crapaud *m*

toadstool *n* champignon *m* vénéneux

to and fro *adv* ⟨*swing*⟩ d'avant en arrière; **to go ~** ⟨*person*⟩ aller et venir

toast **1** *n* **(a)** (bread) toast *m*; **a slice of ~** un toast
(b) (drink) toast *m*; **to drink a ~** lever son verre
2 *vtr* **(a)** faire griller ⟨*bread*⟩
(b) porter un toast à ⟨*person, success*⟩

toaster *n* grille-pain *m inv*

tobacco *n* tabac *m*

toboggan *n* luge *f*, toboggan *m*

today **1** *n* aujourd'hui *m*; **~ is Monday** (aujourd'hui) nous sommes lundi
2 *adv* aujourd'hui; (nowadays) de nos jours; **~ week** dans une semaine aujourd'hui; **a week ago ~** il y a une semaine aujourd'hui; **~ later** plus tard dans la journée

toddler *n* très jeune enfant *m*

toe n (a) (Anat) orteil m; **big/little ~** gros/petit orteil
(b) (of sock, shoe) bout m
IDIOMS **to ~ the line** marcher droit; **from top to ~** de la tête aux pieds

toehold n (in climbing) prise f; **to get** or **gain a ~ in** s'introduire dans ⟨market, organization⟩

toffee n caramel m (au beurre)

together [1] adv (a) ensemble; **to get back ~ again** se remettre ensemble; **to be close ~** être rapprochés/-es; **she's cleverer than all the rest of them put ~** elle est plus intelligente que tous les autres réunis; **they belong ~** ⟨objects⟩ ils vont ensemble; ⟨people⟩ ils sont faits l'un pour l'autre; **the talks brought the two sides closer ~** les négociations ont rapproché les deux parties
(b) (at the same time) à la fois
[2] **together with** phr (as well as) ainsi que; (in the company of) avec
IDIOMS **to get one's act ~** s'organiser

togetherness n (in team, friendship) camaraderie f; (in family, couple) intimité f

toil [1] n labeur m
[2] vi (a) (also **toil away**) (work) peiner
(b) (struggle) **to ~ up the hill** monter péniblement la côte

toilet n toilettes fpl; **public ~(s)** toilettes publiques

toilet bag n trousse f de toilette

toilet paper, **toilet tissue** n papier m hygiénique

toiletries n pl articles mpl de toilette

toilet roll n (roll) rouleau m de papier toilette; (tissue) papier m toilette

token [1] n (a) (for machine, phone) jeton m
(b) (voucher) bon m; **book/record ~** chèque-cadeau m pour livre/pour disque
(c) (symbol) témoignage m **as a ~ of** en signe de
[2] adj symbolique; **to make a ~ gesture** faire un geste pour la forme

tolerable adj (bearable) tolérable; (adequate) acceptable

tolerance n (gen, Med) tolérance f

tolerant adj tolérant/-e

tolerate vtr (permit) tolérer; (put up with) supporter

toll [1] n (a) (death) ~ nombre m de victimes (**from** de)
(b) (levy) (on road, bridge) péage m
(c) (of bell) son m; (for funeral) glas m
[2] vtr, vi sonner

toll call n (US) communication f interurbaine

tomato [1] n tomate f
[2] adj ⟨puree⟩ de tomate; ⟨juice, salad⟩ de tomates; ⟨soup⟩ à la tomate

tomato sauce n sauce f tomate

tomb n tombeau m

tomboy n garçon m manqué

tombstone n pierre f tombale

tomcat n matou m

tomorrow [1] n demain m; **I'll do it by ~** je le ferai d'ici demain
[2] adv demain; **see you ~!** à demain!; ~ **week** demain en huit; **a week ago ~** il y aura une semaine demain

tomorrow afternoon n, adv demain après-midi

tomorrow evening n, adv demain soir

tomorrow morning n, adv demain matin

ton n (a) (in weight) (GB) (also **gross ~** or **long ~**) tonne f britannique (= 1.016 kg); (US) (also **net ~** or **short ~**) tonne f américaine (= 907 kg); **metric ~** tonne f
(b) (colloq) (a lot) ~**s of** des tas de (colloq) ⟨food, paper, bands⟩

tone [1] n (a) (gen) ton m; **his ~ of voice** son ton; **to set the ~** donner le ton à (**for** à)
(b) (Mus) timbre m; (on phone) tonalité f
(c) (of muscle) tonus m
[2] vtr (also ~ **up**) tonifier ⟨body, muscles⟩
[3] vi (also ~**in**) (blend) ⟨colours⟩ s'harmoniser
■ **tone down** atténuer ⟨colours, criticism⟩; adoucir le ton de ⟨letter, statement⟩

tone-deaf adj **to be ~** ne pas avoir l'oreille musicale

tongs n pl (for coal) pincettes fpl; (in laboratory, for sugar) pince f

tongue n (a) (gen) langue f; **to stick one's ~ out at sb** tirer la langue à qn; **to lose one's ~** (figurative) avaler sa langue
(b) (on shoe) languette f
IDIOMS **I have his name on the tip of my ~** j'ai son nom sur le bout de la langue; **a slip of the ~** un lapsus

tongue-in-cheek adj, adv au deuxième degré

tongue stud n piercing m de la langue

tongue-tied adj muet/-ette

tongue-twister n phrase f difficile à dire

tonic n (a) (also ~ **water**) eau f tonique; **a gin and ~** un gin tonic
(b) (Med) remontant m

tonight [1] n ce soir
[2] adv (this evening) ce soir; (after bedtime) cette nuit

tonne n tonne f

tonsil n amygdale f; **to have one's ~s out** se faire opérer des amygdales

tonsillitis n amygdalite f

too adv (a) (also) aussi; **have you been to India ~?** (like me) est-ce que toi aussi tu es allé en Inde?; (as well as other countries) est-ce que tu es allé en Inde aussi?
(b) (excessively) trop; ~ **big** trop grand/-e; ~ **many/~ few people** trop de/trop peu de gens; **I ate ~ much** j'ai trop mangé; **you're ~ kind!** vous êtes trop aimable!; **I'm not ~ sure about that** je n'en suis pas si sûr

tool n outil m

tool bar n barre f d'outils

toolbox n boîte f à outils

tool kit n trousse f à outils

tooth n dent f
toothache n mal m de dents; **to have ~**
(GB) or **a ~** avoir mal aux dents
toothbrush n brosse f à dents
toothpaste n dentifrice m
toothpick n cure-dents m inv
top ⊞ n (a) (of page, ladder, stairs, wall) haut
m; (of list) tête f; (of mountain, hill) sommet m;
(of garden, field) (autre) bout m; (of vegetable)
fane f; (of box, cake) dessus m; (surface) surface
f; **at the ~ of** en haut de ⟨page, stairs, street,
scale⟩; au sommet de ⟨hill⟩; en tête de ⟨list⟩;
at the ~ of the building au dernier étage de
l'immeuble; **at the ~ of the table** à la place
d'honneur; **to be at the ~ of the agenda** être
une priorité
(b) (highest position) **to aim for the ~** viser
haut; **to get to** or **make it to the ~** réussir;
to be ~ of the class être le premier/la
première de la classe; **to be ~ of the bill** être
la tête d'affiche
(c) (cap, lid) (of pen) capuchon m; (of bottle)
bouchon m; (with serrated edge) capsule f; (of
paint-tin, saucepan) couvercle m
(d) (item of clothing) haut m
(e) (toy) toupie f
⊡ adj **(a)** (highest) ⟨step, storey⟩ dernier/-ière
(before n); ⟨bunk⟩ de haut; ⟨button, shelf⟩ du
haut; ⟨layer, lip⟩ supérieur/-e; ⟨speed⟩
maximum; ⟨concern, priority⟩ majeur/-e; **in
the ~ left-hand corner** en haut à gauche; **to
get ~ marks** (Sch) avoir dix sur dix or vingt
sur vingt
(b) (furthest away) ⟨field, house⟩ du bout
(c) (leading) ⟨adviser, politician⟩ de haut
niveau; ⟨job⟩ élevé/-e; ⟨wine, restaurant⟩
haut/-e de gamme
⊟ vtr **(a)** être en tête de ⟨charts, polls⟩
(b) (exceed) dépasser ⟨sum, figure⟩
(c) (finish off) compléter (**with** par); (Culin)
recouvrir ⟨cake⟩
⊠ **on top of** phr **(a)** (on) sur ⟨cupboard,
fridge, layer⟩
(b) (in addition to) en plus de ⟨salary,
workload⟩
IDIOMS **on ~ of all this, to ~ it all**
par-dessus le marché (colloq); **from ~ to
bottom** de fond en comble; **to be over the ~,
to be OTT** (colloq) ⟨behaviour, reaction⟩ être
exagéré/-e; **to feel on ~ of the world** être
aux anges; **to shout at the ~ of one's voice**
crier à tue-tête
■ **top up** remplir (à nouveau) ⟨tank, glass⟩

topaz n topaze f
top hat n haut-de-forme m
top-heavy adj lourd/-e du haut
topic n (of conversation, conference) sujet m; (of
essay, research) thème m
topical adj d'actualité
topless adj ⟨model⟩ aux seins nus
top-level adj ⟨talks, negotiations⟩ au plus
haut niveau
top management n (haute) direction f
top-of-the-range adj haut de gamme
inv

topping n (of jam, cream) nappage m
topple ⊞ vtr renverser
⊡ vi (sway) ⟨vase, pile of books⟩ vaciller; (fall)
(also ~ **over**) ⟨vase, person⟩ basculer; ⟨pile
of books⟩ s'effondrer
top-ranking adj important/-e
top secret adj ultrasecret/-ète
topsy-turvy adj, adv (colloq) sens dessus
dessous
torch n **(a)** (GB) (flashlight) lampe f de poche
(b) (burning) flambeau m, torche f
torment ⊞ n supplice m
⊡ vtr tourmenter
tormentor n persécuteur/-trice m/f
torn adj déchiré/-e
tornado n tornade f
torpedo n torpille f
torrent n torrent m; (figurative) flot m
torrential adj torrentiel/-ielle
torrid adj torride
torso n torse m
tortoise n tortue f
tortoiseshell n (shell) écaille f
tortuous adj tortueux/-euse
torture ⊞ n torture f; (figurative) supplice m
⊡ vtr torturer; (figurative) tourmenter
Tory n (GB) Tory mf, conservateur/-trice
m/f
toss ⊞ n **(a)** (throw) jet m; **a ~ of the head**
un mouvement brusque de la tête
(b) to decide sth on the ~ of a coin décider
qch à pile ou face
⊡ vtr **(a)** (throw) lancer ⟨ball, stick, dice⟩;
faire sauter ⟨pancake⟩; tourner ⟨salad⟩; **to ~
a coin** jouer à pile ou face
(b) ⟨animal⟩ secouer ⟨head, mane⟩; **to ~
one's head** ⟨person⟩ rejeter la tête en arrière
(c) ⟨horse⟩ désarçonner ⟨rider⟩
(d) ⟨wind⟩ agiter ⟨branches, leaves⟩
⊟ vi **(a)** ⟨person⟩ se retourner; **I ~ed and
turned all night** je me suis tourné et
retourné toute la nuit
(b) (flip a coin) tirer à pile ou face; **to ~ for
first turn** tirer le premier tour à pile ou face
■ **toss off** (colloq): **~** [sth] **off, ~ off** [sth]
expédier
■ **toss out**: ¶ **~** [sth] **out, ~ out** [sth] jeter
⟨newspaper, empty bottles⟩; ¶ **~** [sb] **out**
éjecter (**from** de)
tot n **(a)** (colloq) (toddler) tout/-e petit/-e enfant
m/f
(b) (GB) (of whisky, rum) petite dose f
total ⊞ n total m; **in ~** au total
⊡ adj **(a)** ⟨cost, amount, profit⟩ total/-e
(b) (complete) ⟨effect⟩ global/-e; ⟨disaster,
eclipse⟩ total/-e; ⟨ignorance⟩ complet/-ète
⊟ vtr **(a)** (add up) additionner ⟨figures⟩
(b) ⟨bill⟩ se monter à ⟨sum⟩
totalitarian n, adj totalitaire (mf)
totally adv ⟨blind, deaf⟩ complètement;
⟨unacceptable, convinced⟩ totalement; ⟨agree,
change, new, different⟩ entièrement
totem n (pole) totem m; (symbol) symbole m

totter *vi* ⟨*person, regime, government*⟩ chanceler; ⟨*drunk person*⟩ tituber; ⟨*baby*⟩ trébucher; ⟨*pile of books, building*⟩ chanceler

touch ① *n* (a) contact *m* (physique); **the ~ of her hand** le contact de sa main
(b) (sense) toucher *m*
(c) (style, skill) (of artist, writer) touche *f*; (of musician) toucher *m*; **to lose one's ~** perdre la main; **that's a clever ~**! ça, c'est génial!
(d) (little) **a ~** un petit peu
(e) (communication) **to get/stay in ~ with** se mettre/rester en contact avec; **he's out of ~ with reality** il est déconnecté de la réalité
(f) (Sport) touche *f*
② *vtr* (a) toucher; (interfere with) toucher à; **to ~ sb on the shoulder** toucher l'épaule de qn; **I never ~ alcohol** je ne prends jamais d'alcool
(b) (affect) toucher; (adversely) affecter; (as matter of concern) concerner; **we were most ~ed** nous avons été très touchés
③ *vi* se toucher
IDIOMS **to be a soft ~** (colloq) être un pigeon (colloq); **it's ~ and go whether he'll make it through the night** il risque fort de ne pas passer la nuit
■ **touch down** (a) ⟨*plane*⟩ atterrir
(b) (Sport) (in rugby) marquer un essai
■ **touch (up)on** effleurer ⟨*topic*⟩

touchdown *n* (a) (by plane) atterrissage *m*
(b) (Sport) essai *m*

touched *adj* (a) (emotionally) touché/-e
(b) (colloq) (mad) dérangé/-e (colloq)

touching *adj* touchant/-e

touch line *n* ligne *f* de touche

touchpad *n* tablette *f* tactile

touch screen *n* écran *m* tactile

touch-tone *adj* ⟨*telephone*⟩ à touches

touch-type *vi* taper au toucher

touchy *adj* susceptible (**about** sur la question de)

tough ① *adj* (a) ⟨*businessman*⟩ coriace; ⟨*criminal*⟩ endurci/-e; ⟨*policy, measure, law*⟩ sévère; ⟨*opposition, competition*⟩ rude; **a ~ guy** un dur (colloq)
(b) (difficult) difficile
(c) (robust) ⟨*person, animal*⟩ robuste; ⟨*plant, material*⟩ résistant/-e
(d) ⟨*meat*⟩ coriace
(e) (rough) ⟨*area, school*⟩ dur/-e
② *excl* (colloq) tant pis pour toi!

toughen *vtr* (a) renforcer ⟨*leather, plastic*⟩; tremper ⟨*glass, steel*⟩; durcir ⟨*skin*⟩
(b) (*also* **~ up**) endurcir ⟨*person*⟩; renforcer ⟨*law*⟩

toupee *n* postiche *m*

tour ① *n* (a) (of country) circuit *m*; (of city) tour *m*; (of building) visite *f*; (trip in bus) excursion *f*
(b) (by team, band, theatre company) tournée *f*
② *vtr* (a) visiter ⟨*building, country, gallery*⟩
(b) ⟨*band, team*⟩ être en tournée en ⟨*country*⟩; ⟨*theatre production*⟩ tourner en ⟨*country*⟩
③ *vi* ⟨*orchestra, play, team*⟩ être en tournée

touring *n* (a) (by tourist) tourisme *m*
(b) (by team, theatre company, band) tournée *f*

tourism *n* tourisme *m*

tourist *n* touriste *mf*

tourist class *n* (on flight) classe *f* touriste

tourist (information) office *n* (in town) syndicat *m* d'initiative; (national organization) office *m* du tourisme

tourist trap *n* piège *m* à touristes

touristy *adj* (colloq) envahi/-e par les touristes

tournament *n* tournoi *m*

tousle *vtr* ébouriffer ⟨*hair*⟩

tousled *adj* ⟨*hair*⟩ ébouriffé/-e; ⟨*person, appearance*⟩ débraillé/-e

tout *n* (a) (GB) (selling tickets) revendeur *m* de billets au marché noir
(b) (soliciting custom) racoleur/-euse *m/f*
(c) (racing) vendeur *m* de tuyaux

tow ① *n* (Aut) **to be on ~** être en remorque
② *vtr* remorquer, tracter ⟨*trailer, caravan*⟩
■ **tow away**: **~ away** [sth], **~** [sth] **away** ⟨*police*⟩ emmener [qch] à la fourrière; ⟨*recovery service*⟩ remorquer

toward(s) *prep*
■ **Note** When *towards* is used to talk about direction or position, it is generally translated by *vers*: she ran toward(s) him = elle a couru vers lui.
– When *toward(s)* is used to mean *in relation to*, it is translated by *envers*: his attitude toward(s) his parents = son attitude envers ses parents.
For further examples, see the entry below.

(a) vers; **~ the east** vers l'est; **he was standing with his back ~ me** il me tournait le dos; **~ evening** vers le soir; **~ the end of** vers la fin de ⟨*month, life*⟩
(b) envers; **to be friendly/hostile ~ sb** se montrer cordial/hostile envers qn
(c) (as contribution) **the money will go ~ a new car** l'argent servira à payer une nouvelle voiture

towel *n* serviette *f* (de toilette)

towelling *n* (cloth) tissu *m* éponge

tower ① *n* (a) (structure) tour *f*
(b) (Comput) boîtier *m* vertical, tour *f*
② *vi* **to ~ above** *or* **over** dominer
IDIOMS **to be a ~ of strength** être solide comme un roc

tower block *n* (GB) tour *f* (d'habitation)

towering *adj* imposant/-e

town *n* ville *f*; **to go into ~** aller en ville
IDIOMS **to go to ~ on** on ne pas lésiner sur ⟨*decor, catering*⟩; exploiter [qch] à fond ⟨*story, scandal*⟩; **he's the talk of the ~** on ne parle que de lui

town-and-country planning *n* aménagement *m* du territoire

town centre (GB), **town center** (US) *n* centre-ville *m*

town council *n* (GB) conseil *m* municipal

town hall *n* mairie *f*

town house n petite maison f en centre ville; (mansion) hôtel m particulier

town planning n (GB) urbanisme m

township n commune f; (in South Africa) township m

towpath n chemin m de halage

tow truck n dépanneuse f

toxic adj toxique

toxin n toxine f

toy ⓵ n jouet m
⓶ vi to ~ with jouer avec ⟨object, feelings⟩; caresser ⟨idea⟩; to ~ with one's food chipoter

toy boy n (colloq) (GB) gigolo m

toyshop n magasin m de jouets

trace ⓵ n trace f
⓶ vtr (a) (locate) retrouver ⟨person, weapon, car⟩; dépister ⟨fault⟩; déterminer ⟨cause⟩; **the call was ~d to a London number** on a pu établir que le coup de téléphone venait d'un numéro à Londres
(b) (also ~ **back**) faire remonter ⟨origins, ancestry⟩ (to à)
(c) (draw) tracer; (copy) décalquer ⟨map, outline⟩

tracing paper n papier-calque m

track ⓵ n (a) (print) (of animal, person, vehicle) traces fpl
(b) (course, trajectory) (of person) trace f; (of missile, aircraft, storm) trajectoire f; **to keep ~ of** ⟨person⟩ se tenir au courant de ⟨developments, events⟩; suivre le fil de ⟨conversation⟩; ⟨police⟩ suivre les mouvements de ⟨criminal⟩; **to lose ~ of** perdre de vue ⟨friend⟩; perdre la trace de ⟨document, aircraft, suspect⟩; perdre le fil de ⟨conversation⟩; **to lose ~ of (the) time** perdre la notion du temps
(c) (path, road) sentier m, chemin m; (Sport) piste f
(d) (railtrack) voie f ferrée; (US) (platform) quai m; **to leave the ~(s)** ⟨train⟩ dérailler
(e) (on record, tape, CD) morceau m
(f) (of tank, tractor) chenille f
(g) (US Sch) (stream) groupe m de niveau
⓶ vtr suivre la trace de ⟨person, animal⟩; suivre la trajectoire de ⟨rocket, plane⟩
■ **track down** retrouver ⟨person, object⟩

tracker ball n boule f de commande

tracker dog n chien m policier

track record n **to have a good ~** avoir de bons antécédents

track shoe n chaussure f de course à pointes

tracksuit n survêtement m

tract n (a) (of land) étendue f
(b) (pamphlet) pamphlet m

tractor n tracteur m

trade ⓵ n (a) (activity) commerce m; **to do a good ~** faire de bonnes affaires
(b) (sector of industry) industrie f
(c) (profession) (manual) métier m; (intellectual) profession f; **by ~** de métier
⓶ vtr échanger (**for** contre)

③ vi faire du commerce
■ **trade in**: he ~d in his old car for a new one on lui a repris sa vieille voiture et il en a acheté une nouvelle

trade fair n salon m

trade-in n reprise f (d'un article usagé à l'achat d'un article neuf)

trademark n marque f déposée

trade name n nom m (de marque)

trade-off n compromis m

trader n (a) (shopkeeper, stallholder) commerçant/-e m/f
(b) (at stock exchange) opérateur/-trice m/f (en Bourse)

tradesman's entrance n entrée f de service

Trades Union Congress, TUC n (GB) Confédération f des syndicats (britanniques)

trade union n syndicat m

trade union member n syndiqué/-e m/f

trading n (a) (business) commerce m
(b) (at stock exchange) transactions fpl (boursières)

trading estate n zone f industrielle

tradition n tradition f

traditional adj traditionnel/-elle

traditionalist n, adj traditionaliste (mf)

traffic ⓵ n (a) (on road) circulation f; (air, sea, rail) trafic m
(b) (in drugs, arms, slaves, goods) trafic m (**in** de)
⓶ vi to ~ **in** faire du trafic de ⟨drugs, arms, stolen goods⟩

traffic calming n mesures fpl pour ralentir la circulation

traffic jam n embouteillage m

trafficker n trafiquant/-e m/f (**in** de)

traffic lights n pl feux mpl (de signalisation)

traffic warden n (GB) contractuel/-elle m/f

tragedy n tragédie f

tragic adj tragique

trail ⓵ n (a) (path) chemin m, piste f
(b) (of blood, dust, slime) traînée f, trace f
(c) (trace) trace f, piste f
⓶ vtr (a) (follow) ⟨animal, person⟩ suivre la piste de; ⟨car⟩ suivre
(b) (drag) traîner
③ vi (a) ⟨skirt, scarf⟩ traîner; ⟨plant⟩ pendre
(b) (shuffle) to ~ **in/out** entrer/sortir en traînant les pieds
(c) (lag) traîner; **our team were ~ing by 3 goals to 1** notre équipe avait un retard de 2 buts

trail bike n moto f tout terrain

trail blazer n pionnier/-ière m/f

trailer n (a) (vehicle, boat) remorque f
(b) (US) (caravan) caravane f
(c) (for film) bande-annonce f

trailer park n (US) terrain m de caravaning

train [1] n (a) (means of transport) train m; (underground) rame f; **a ~ to Paris** un train pour Paris; **to go to Paris by ~** aller à Paris en train
(b) (succession) (of events) série f; **my ~ of thought** le fil de mes pensées
(c) (procession) (of animals, vehicles, people) file f; (of mourners) cortège m
(d) (of dress) traîne f
[2] vtr (a) former ⟨staff, worker, musician⟩; entraîner ⟨athlete, player⟩; dresser ⟨circus animal, dog⟩
(b) (aim) braquer ⟨gun, binoculars⟩ (on sur)
[3] vi (a) (for profession) être formé/-e, étudier; **he's ~ing to be/he ~ed as a doctor** il suit/il a reçu une formation de docteur
(b) (Sport) s'entraîner

trained adj ⟨staff⟩ qualifié/-e; ⟨professional⟩ diplômé/-e; ⟨voice, eye, ear⟩ exercé/-e; ⟨singer, actor⟩ professionnel/-elle; ⟨animal⟩ dressé/-e

trainee n stagiaire mf

trainer n (a) (of athlete, horse) entraîneur/-euse m/f; (of circus animal, dogs) dresseur/-euse m/f
(b) (GB) (shoe) (high) basket f; (low) tennis m

training n (a) (gen) formation f; (less specialized) apprentissage m
(b) (Mil, Sport) entraînement m

training college n (GB) école f professionnelle; (for teachers) centre m de formation pédagogique

training course n stage m de formation

train spotter n passionné/-e m/f de trains

trait n trait m

traitor n traître/traîtresse m/f (**to** à)

tram n (GB) tramway m

tramp n (rural) vagabond m; (urban) clochard/-e m/f

trample vtr piétiner

trampoline n trampoline m

trance n transe f; (figurative) état m second; **to go into a ~** entrer en transe

tranquil adj tranquille

tranquillizer, tranquilizer (US) n tranquillisant m

transaction n transaction f

transatlantic adj ⟨crossing, flight⟩ transatlantique; ⟨accent⟩ d'outre-atlantique inv

transcend vtr (gen) transcender; (surpass) surpasser

transcribe vtr transcrire

transcript n (a) (copy) transcription f
(b) (US) (Sch) duplicata m de livret scolaire

transfer [1] n (a) (gen) transfert m; (of property, debt) cession f; (of funds) virement m; (of employee) mutation f
(b) (GB) (on skin, china, paper) décalcomanie f; (on T-shirt) transfert m
[2] vtr (a) transférer ⟨data, baggage⟩; virer ⟨money⟩; céder ⟨property, power⟩; reporter ⟨allegiance, support⟩; **I'm ~ring you to reception** je vous passe la réception
(b) (relocate) transférer ⟨office, prisoner, player⟩; muter ⟨employee⟩
[3] vi (a) ⟨player, passenger⟩ être transféré/-e; ⟨employee⟩ être muté/-e
(b) ⟨traveller⟩ changer d'avion

transferable adj (gen) transmissible; (in finance) négociable

transfer passenger n passager/-ère m/f en transit

transferred charge call n appel m en PCV

transfixed adj (fascinated) fasciné/-e; (horrified) paralysé/-e d'horreur

transform vtr transformer

transformation n transformation f

transformer n transformateur m

transfusion n transfusion f

transgenic adj transgénique

transient adj ⟨phase⟩ transitoire; ⟨emotion, beauty⟩ éphémère; ⟨population⟩ de passage

transistor n transistor m

transit n transit m; **in ~** en transit

transition n transition f

transitional adj ⟨arrangement, measure⟩ transitoire; ⟨period⟩ de transition

transitive adj transitif/-ive

translate [1] vtr traduire
[2] vi (a) ⟨person⟩ traduire
(b) ⟨word, phrase, text⟩ se traduire

translation n traduction f; (school exercise) version f

translator n traducteur/-trice m/f

transmission n transmission f

transmit [1] vtr transmettre
[2] vi émettre

transmitter n (in radio, TV) émetteur m; (in telecommunications) capsule f microphonique

transparency n (slide) diapositive f; (for overhead projector) transparent m

transparent adj transparent/-e

transplant [1] n (operation) transplantation f; (organ, tissue transplanted) transplant m
[2] vtr transplanter

transport [1] n (also **transportation** (US)) transport m; **air/road ~** transport aérien/par route; **to travel by public ~** utiliser les transports en commun
[2] vtr transporter

transportation n transport m

transpose vtr transposer

transsexual n, adj transsexuel/-elle (m/f)

transvestite n travesti/-e m/f

trap [1] n (a) (snare) piège m
(b) (vehicle) cabriolet m
[2] vtr (a) (snare) prendre [qn/qch] au piège
(b) (catch) coincer ⟨person, finger⟩; retenir ⟨heat⟩

trapdoor n trappe f

trash n (a) (US) (refuse) (in streets) déchets mpl; (from household) ordures fpl

(b) (colloq) (low-grade goods) camelote *f* (colloq)
(c) (colloq) (nonsense) âneries *fpl*; **the film is (absolute)** ∼ le film est (complètement) nul (colloq)

trashcan *n* (US) poubelle *f*

trashy *adj* (colloq) ⟨novel, film⟩ nul/nulle (colloq) ⟨goods⟩ de pacotille

trauma *n* traumatisme *m*

traumatic *adj* (psychologically) traumatisant/-e; (Med) traumatique

traumatize *vtr* traumatiser

travel ⊡ *n* voyages *mpl*; **foreign** ∼ voyages à l'étranger
⊡ *vtr* parcourir ⟨country, road, distance⟩
⊡ *vi* **(a)** (journey) voyager; **he** ∼**s widely** il voyage beaucoup; **to** ∼ **abroad/to Brazil** aller à l'étranger/au Brésil
(b) (move) ⟨person, object, plane, boat⟩ aller; ⟨car, train⟩ aller, rouler; ⟨light, sound⟩ se propager; **to** ∼ **back in time** remonter le temps
(c) to ∼ **well** ⟨cheese, wine⟩ supporter le transport

travel agency *n* agence *f* de voyages

travel agent *n* agent *m* de voyages

travel card *n* carte *f* de transport

travel insurance *n* assurance *f* voyage

traveller (GB), **traveler** (US) *n* **(a)** (voyager) voyageur/-euse *m/f*
(b) (GB) (gypsy) nomade *mf*

traveller's cheque (GB), **traveler's check** (US) *n* chèque-voyage *m*

travelling (GB), **traveling** (US) ⊡ *n* (touring) voyages *mpl*; (on single occasion) voyage *m*; **to go** ∼ partir en voyage; **the job involves** ∼ le poste exige des déplacements
⊡ *adj* **(a)** ⟨actor, company, circus⟩ itinérant/-e
(b) ⟨companion, rug⟩ de voyage; ⟨conditions⟩ (on road) de route
(c) ⟨allowance, expenses⟩ de déplacement

travelling salesman *n* voyageur *m* de commerce

travel-sick *adj* **to be** or **get** ∼ souffrir du mal des transports

trawler *n* chalutier *m*

tray *n* plateau *m*

treacherous *adj* traître/traîtresse

treachery *n* traîtrise *f*

treacle *n* (GB) (black) mélasse *f*; (golden syrup) mélasse *f* raffinée

tread ⊡ *n* (of tyre) (pattern) sculptures *fpl*; (outer surface) chape *f*
⊡ *vtr* fouler ⟨street, path, area⟩; **to** ∼ **water** nager sur place
⊡ *vi* marcher; **to** ∼ **on** (walk) marcher sur; (squash) piétiner; **to** ∼ **carefully** être prudent/-e

treason *n* trahison *f*; **high** ∼ haute trahison

treasure ⊡ *n* trésor *m*
⊡ *vtr* **(a)** (cherish) chérir ⟨person, gift⟩
(b) (prize) tenir beaucoup à ⟨friendship⟩

treasurer *n* **(a)** (on committee) trésorier/-ière *m/f*
(b) (US) (in company) directeur *m* financier

Treasury *n* (also ∼ **Department**) ministère *m* des finances

treat ⊡ *n* (pleasure) (petit) plaisir *m*; (food) gâterie *f*; **I took them to the museum as a** ∼ je les ai emmenés au musée pour leur faire plaisir; **it's my** ∼ (colloq) c'est moi qui paie
⊡ *vtr* **(a)** (gen, Med) traiter; **to** ∼ **sb well/ badly** bien traiter/maltraiter qn; **to** ∼ **sb/sth with care** prendre soin de qn/qch; **they** ∼ **the house like a hotel** ils prennent la maison pour un hôtel
(b) (pay for) **to** ∼ **sb to sth** payer or offrir qch à qn; **to** ∼ **oneself to** s'offrir ⟨holiday, hairdo⟩

treatment *n* traitement *m*

treaty *n* traité *m*

treble ⊡ *adj* triple
⊡ *vtr*, *vi* tripler

tree *n* arbre *m*; **an apple/a cherry** ∼ un pommier/un cerisier

tree stump *n* souche *f*

treetop *n* cime *f* (d'un arbre)

tree trunk *n* tronc *m* d'arbre

trek ⊡ *n* (long journey) randonnée *f*; (laborious) randonnée *f* pénible
⊡ *vi* **to** ∼ **across** traverser péniblement ⟨desert⟩

trekking *n* **to go** ∼ faire de la randonnée pédestre

tremble *vi* trembler

tremendous *adj* ⟨effort, improvement, amount⟩ énorme; ⟨pleasure⟩ immense; ⟨storm, explosion⟩ violent/-e; ⟨success⟩ fou/ folle (colloq)

tremor *n* **(a)** (in voice) tremblement *m*
(b) (in earthquake) secousse *f*

trench *n* tranchée *f*

trench coat *n* imperméable *m*, trench-coat *m*

trend *n* **(a)** (tendency) tendance *f*
(b) (fashion) mode *f*; **to set a new** ∼ lancer une nouvelle mode

trendsetter *n* innovateur/-trice *m/f*; **to be a** ∼ lancer des modes

trendy *adj* (colloq) branché/-e (colloq)

trespass *vi* s'introduire illégalement; **'no** ∼**ing'** 'défense d'entrer'

trespasser *n* intrus/-e *m/f*

trial ⊡ *n* **(a)** (Law) procès *m*; **to go on** ∼, **to stand** ∼ passer en jugement
(b) (test) (of machine, vehicle) essai *m*; (of drug, new product) test *m*; **on** ∼ à l'essai; **by** ∼ **and error** ⟨learn⟩ par l'expérience; ⟨proceed⟩ par tâtonnements
(c) (Sport) épreuve *f*
(d) (trouble) épreuve *f*; (less strong) difficulté *f*
⊡ *adj* ⟨period, separation⟩ d'essai; **on a** ∼ **basis** à titre expérimental

trial run *n* essai *m*; **to take a car for a** ∼ essayer une voiture

triangle *n* triangle *m*

t

tribe n tribu f

tribunal n tribunal m

tributary n affluent m

tribute n hommage m; **to pay ~ to** rendre hommage à; **floral ~** (spray) gerbe f, (wreath) couronne f

trick ① n (a) (to deceive) tour m, combine f; **to play a ~ on sb** jouer un tour à qn; **a ~ of the light** un effet de lumière

(b) (by magician, conjurer, dog) tour m; **to do a ~** faire un tour

(c) (knack, secret) astuce f

(d) (in cards) pli m; **to take** or **win a ~** faire un pli

② adj ⟨photo, shot⟩ truqué/-e

③ vtr duper, rouler (colloq); **to ~ sb into doing sth** amener qn à faire qch par la ruse IDIOMS **the ~s of the trade** les ficelles du métier; **that'll do the ~** ça fera l'affaire

trickle ① n (of liquid) filet m; (of powder, sand) écoulement m; (of investment, orders) petite quantité f; (of people) petit nombre m

② vi **to ~ down** dégouliner le long de ⟨pane, wall⟩; **to ~ into** ⟨liquid⟩ s'écouler dans ⟨container⟩; ⟨people⟩ s'infiltrer dans ⟨country, organization⟩

∎ **trickle away** ⟨water⟩ s'écouler lentement; ⟨people⟩ s'éloigner lentement

trick question n question f piège

tricky adj (a) ⟨decision, task⟩ difficile; ⟨problem⟩ épineux/-euse; ⟨situation⟩ délicat/-e

(b) (wily) malin/-igne

tricycle n (cycle) tricycle m

trifle ① n (a) (GB) (Culin) ≈ diplomate m

(b) (triviality) bagatelle f

② vi **to ~ with** jouer avec ⟨feelings, affections⟩; **to ~ with sb** traiter qn à la légère

trifling adj ⟨sum, cost, detail⟩ insignifiant/-e

trigger n (a) (on gun) gâchette f

(b) (on machine) manette f

∎ **trigger off** déclencher

trilogy n trilogie f

trim ① n (a) (of hair) coupe f d'entretien

(b) (good condition) **to keep oneself in ~** se maintenir en bonne forme physique

② adj ⟨garden⟩ soigné/-e; ⟨boat, house⟩ bien tenu/-e; ⟨figure⟩ svelte; ⟨waist⟩ fin/-e

③ vtr (a) (cut) couper ⟨hair, grass, material⟩; tailler ⟨beard, hedge⟩

(b) (reduce) réduire (by de)

(c) (Culin) dégraisser ⟨meat⟩

(d) (decorate) décorer ⟨tree, furniture⟩; border ⟨dress, handkerchief⟩

trimming n (on clothing) garniture f; **~s** (Culin) (with dish) accompagnements mpl traditionnels

trinket n babiole f

trio n trio m (of de)

trip ① n (a) (journey) (abroad) voyage m; (excursion) excursion f; **business ~** voyage d'affaires

(b) (colloq) trip m (colloq)

② vtr (also **~ over, ~ up**) faire trébucher; (with foot) faire un croche-pied à

③ vi (a) (also **~ over, ~ up**) (stumble) trébucher, faire un faux pas; **to ~ on** or **over** trébucher sur ⟨step, rock⟩; se prendre les pieds dans ⟨scarf, rope⟩

(b) (walk lightly) **to ~ along** ⟨child⟩ gambader; ⟨adult⟩ marcher d'un pas léger

triple adj triple

triplet n (child) triplé/-e m/f

triplicate: in ~ phr en trois exemplaires

tripod n trépied m

triumph ① n triomphe m

② vi triompher (over de)

triumphant adj ⟨person, team⟩ triomphant/-e; ⟨return, success⟩ triomphal/-e

trivia n pl futilités fpl

trivial adj ⟨matter, scale, film⟩ insignifiant/-e; ⟨error, offence⟩ léger/-ère (before n); ⟨conversation, argument, person⟩ futile

trivialize vtr banaliser; minimiser ⟨role⟩

trolley n (a) (GB) (for food, drinks, luggage, shopping) chariot m

(b) (US) tramway m

trolley bus n trolleybus m

trolley car n tramway m, tram m

troop n troupe f

trooper n (a) (Mil) homme m de troupe

(b) (US) (policeman) policier m

trophy n trophée m

tropic n tropique m; **in the ~s** sous les tropiques

tropical adj tropical/-e

trot ① n trot m; **at a ~** au trot

② vi ⟨animal, rider⟩ trotter; ⟨person⟩ courir, trotter; ⟨child⟩ trottiner

IDIOMS **on the ~** (colloq) (one after the other) coup sur coup; (continuously) d'affilée

∎ **trot out** (colloq): **~ out [sth]** débiter ⟨excuse, explanation⟩

trouble ① n (a) (problems) problèmes mpl; (personal) ennuis mpl; (difficulties) difficultés fpl; **to be in** or **get into ~** ⟨person⟩ avoir des ennuis; ⟨company⟩ avoir des difficultés; **to get sb into ~** créer des ennuis à qn; **back ~** mal m de dos; **what's the ~?** qu'est-ce qui ne va pas?; **to have ~ doing** avoir du mal à faire; **to get sb out of ~** tirer qn d'affaire

(b) (effort, inconvenience) peine f; **it's not worth the ~** cela n'en vaut pas la peine; **to take the ~ to do, to go to the ~ of doing** se donner la peine de faire; **to save sb the ~ of doing** épargner à qn la peine de faire; **to go to a lot of ~** se donner beaucoup de mal

② **troubles** n pl soucis mpl; **money ~s** problèmes mpl d'argent

③ vtr (a) (disturb, inconvenience) déranger ⟨person⟩; **may** or **could I ~ you to do?** puis-je vous demander de faire?

(b) (bother) **to be ~d by** être incommodé/-e par ⟨cough, pain⟩

(c) (worry) tracasser ⟨person⟩; **don't let that ~ you** ne te tracasse pas pour cela

troubled adj ‹person, expression›
soucieux/-ieuse; ‹mind› inquiet/-iète; ‹sleep,
times, area› agité/-e

troublefree adj sans problèmes

troublemaker n fauteur/-trice m/f de
troubles

troubleshooter n consultant/-e m/f en
gestion des entreprises

troublesome adj ‹person›
ennuyeux/-euse; ‹problem› gênant/-e;
‹cough, pain› désagréable

trouble spot n point m chaud

trough n (a) (for drinking) abreuvoir m; (for
animal feed) auge f
(b) (between waves, hills, on graph) creux m
(c) (in weather) zone f dépressionnaire

trousers n pl pantalon m; **short** ~ culotte
f courte

trout n truite f

trowel n (a) (for cement) truelle f
(b) (for gardening) déplantoir m

truancy n absentéisme m

truant n to play ~ faire l'école
buissonnière

truce n trêve f

truck n (a) (lorry) camion m
(b) (rail wagon) wagon m de marchandises

truck driver, trucker (colloq) n routier
m

trudge vi marcher d'un pas lourd; **to** ~
through the snow marcher péniblement
dans la neige

true ①adj (a) (based on fact, not a lie) ‹news,
fact, story› vrai/-e; (from real life) ‹story›
vécu/-e
(b) (real, genuine) vrai/-e (before n); ‹identity,
age› véritable (before n); **to come** ~ se
réaliser
(c) (heartfelt, sincere) ‹feeling, understanding›
sincère; ~ **love** le véritable amour
(d) (accurate) ‹copy› conforme; ‹assessment›
correct, juste
(e) (faithful, loyal) fidèle; (**to** à)
(f) (Mus) ‹note, instrument› juste
②adv ‹aim, fire› juste

true-life adj ‹adventure, story› vécu/-e

truffle n truffe f

truly adv (a) (gen) vraiment; **well and** ~ bel
et bien
(b) (in letter) yours ~ je vous prie d'agréer
l'expression de mes sentiments distingués
(formal)

trump n atout m
IDIOMS to come up ~s sauver la situation

trumped-up adj ‹charge› forgé/-e de
toutes pièces

trumpet n (a) (instrument, player) trompette f
(b) (elephant call) barrissement m
IDIOMS to blow one's own ~ vanter ses
propres mérites

trumpeter n trompettiste mf

truncheon n matraque f

trunk n (a) (of tree, body) tronc m
(b) (of elephant) trompe f

(c) (for travel) malle f
(d) (US) (car boot) coffre m

trunks n pl slip m de bain

truss n (Med) bandage m herniaire
■ **truss up** brider, trousser ‹chicken›;
ligoter ‹person›

trust ①n (a) (faith) confiance f; **to put one's**
~ **in** se fier à
(b) (Law) (arrangement) fidéicommis m;
(property involved) propriété f fiduciaire
②vtr (a) (believe) se fier à ‹person,
judgment›
(b) (rely on) faire confiance à
(c) (entrust) **to** ~ **sb with sth** confier qch à qn
③vi **to** ~ **in** faire confiance à ‹person›;
croire en ‹God, fortune›; **to** ~ **to luck** se fier
au hasard
④v refl **to** ~ **oneself to do** être sûr de
pouvoir faire

trust company n société f fiduciaire

trusted adj ‹friend› fidèle

trusted third party, TTP n tierce
partie f de confiance, TPC f

trustee n (a) (who administers property in trust)
fiduciaire m
(b) (of company) administrateur/-trice m/f (of
de)

trust fund n fonds m en fidéicommis

trusting adj ‹person› qui fait facilement
confiance aux gens

trustworthy adj ‹staff, firm›
sérieux/-ieuse; ‹friend, lover› digne de
confiance

truth n (real facts) the ~ la vérité; **there is
some** ~ **in it** il y a du vrai dans cela

truthful adj ‹person› honnête; ‹account,
version› vrai/-e

try ①n (a) (attempt) essai m; **to have a** ~
essayer (**at doing** de faire)
(b) (Sport) essai m
②vtr (a) (attempt) essayer de répondre à
‹exam question›; **to** ~ **doing** or **to do** essayer
de faire; **to** ~ **hard to do** faire de gros efforts
pour faire; **to** ~ **one's best to do** faire tout
son possible pour faire
(b) (test out) essayer ‹tool, product, method,
activity›; prendre [qn] à l'essai ‹person›;
‹thief› essayer d'ouvrir ‹door, window›;
tourner ‹door knob›; **to** ~ **one's hand at sth**
s'essayer à qch
(c) (taste) goûter ‹food›
(d) (consult) demander à ‹person›; consulter
‹book›; ~ **the library** demandez à la
bibliothèque
(e) (subject to stress) **to** ~ **sb's patience**
pousser qn à bout
(f) (Law) juger ‹case, criminal›
③vi essayer; **to** ~ **again** (to perform task)
recommencer; (to see somebody) repasser; (to
phone) rappeler; **to** ~ **for** essayer d'obtenir
‹loan, university place›; essayer de battre
‹world record›; essayer d'avoir ‹baby›; **keep**
~**ing!** essaie encore!
■ **try on** essayer ‹hat, dress›
■ **try out**: ~ [sth] **out**, ~ **out** [sth] essayer

trying adj ⟨person⟩ pénible; ⟨experience⟩ éprouvant/-e

T-shirt n T-shirt m

tub n (a) (for flowers, water) bac m; (of ice cream, pâté) pot m
(b) (US) (bath) baignoire f

tubby adj (colloq) grassouillet/-ette (colloq)

tube n (a) (cylinder, container) tube m
(b) (GB) (colloq) **the ∼** le métro (londonien)
(c) (US) (colloq) (TV) télé f (colloq)
(d) (in TV set) tube m cathodique
(e) (in tyre) chambre f à air

tuberculosis n tuberculose f

tuck ⟨1⟩ n (in sewing) pli m
⟨2⟩ vtr (put) glisser; **to ∼ one's shirt into one's trousers** rentrer sa chemise dans son pantalon
■ **tuck away** (put away) ranger; (hide) cacher; **the house was ∼ed away in the wood** la maison se cachait or était cachée dans le bois
■ **tuck in** rentrer ⟨garment, shirt⟩; border ⟨bedclothes, person⟩

Tuesday n mardi m

tuft n touffe f

tug ⟨1⟩ n (a) (pull) secousse f; **to give sth a ∼** tirer sur qch
(b) (also **tug boat**) remorqueur m
⟨2⟩ vtr (pull) tirer
⟨3⟩ vi **to ∼ at** or **on** tirer sur ⟨rope, hair⟩

tug-of-love n: lutte entre les parents pour la garde de l'enfant

tug-of-war n (Sport) gagne-terrain m

tuition n cours mpl

tuition fees n pl frais mpl pédagogiques

tulip n tulipe f

tumble ⟨1⟩ n (a) (fall) chute f; **to take a ∼** ⟨person⟩ faire une chute
(b) (of clown, acrobat) culbute f
⟨2⟩ vi (a) (fall) ⟨person, object⟩ tomber (off, out of de)
(b) ⟨price, share, currency⟩ chuter
(c) ⟨clown, acrobat, child⟩ faire des culbutes
■ **tumble down** ⟨wall, building⟩ s'écrouler

tumble-drier, **tumble-dryer** n sèche-linge m inv

tumble-dry vtr sécher (en machine)

tumbler n verre m droit

tummy n (colloq) ventre m

tumour (GB), **tumor** (US) n tumeur f

tumult n (a) (noise) tumulte m
(b) (disorder) agitation f

tuna n (also **∼ fish**) thon m

tune ⟨1⟩ n air m; **to be in/out of ∼** ⟨instrument⟩ être/ne pas être en accord; **to sing in/out of ∼** chanter juste/faux
⟨2⟩ vtr accorder ⟨musical instrument⟩; régler ⟨engine, radio, TV⟩
■ **tune in**: ¶ **∼ in** mettre la radio; **to ∼ in to** se mettre à l'écoute de ⟨programme⟩; régler sur ⟨channel⟩; ¶ **∼ [sth] in** régler (to sur)

tunic n (for gym) tunique f; (for nurse, schoolgirl) blouse f; (for soldier) vareuse f

tuning fork n diapason m

tunnel ⟨1⟩ n tunnel m
⟨2⟩ vtr, vi creuser

tunnel vision n **to have ∼** (figurative) avoir des œillères

turbine n turbine f

turbo n (engine) turbo m; (car) turbo f

turbocharged adj turbo inv

turbot n turbot m

turbulent adj (a) ⟨water⟩ agité/-e
(b) ⟨times, situation⟩ agité/-e; ⟨career, history⟩ mouvementé/-e; ⟨passions, character, faction⟩ turbulent/-e

tureen n soupière f

turf ⟨1⟩ n (grass) gazon m; (peat) tourbe f
⟨2⟩ vtr gazonner ⟨lawn, pitch⟩
■ **turf out**: **∼ out [sb/sth]**, **∼ [sb/sth] out** virer (colloq)

Turk n Turc/Turque m/f

turkey n (a) (bird) dinde f
(b) (US) (colloq) (flop) bide m (colloq); (bad film) navet m (colloq)

Turkey pr n Turquie f

Turkish ⟨1⟩ n (language) turc m
⟨2⟩ adj turc/turque

Turkish delight n loukoum m

turmoil n désarroi m

turn ⟨1⟩ n (a) (in games, sequence) tour m; **whose ∼ is it?** c'est à qui le tour?; **to be sb's ∼ to do** être le tour de qn de faire; **to take ∼s at sleeping, to take it in ∼s to sleep** dormir à tour de rôle; **by ∼s** tour à tour; **to speak out of ∼** commettre un impair
(b) (circular movement) tour m; **to give sth a ∼** tourner qch; **to do a ∼** ⟨dancer⟩ faire un tour
(c) (in vehicle) virage m; **to make** or **do a left/right ∼** tourner à gauche/à droite
(d) (bend, side road) tournant m, virage m; **take the next right ∼, take the next ∼ on the right** prenez la prochaine (rue) à droite
(e) (change, development) tournure f; **to take a ∼ for the better** ⟨things, events, situation⟩ prendre une meilleure tournure; **to take a ∼ for the worse** ⟨situation⟩ se dégrader; ⟨health⟩ s'aggraver
(f) (GB) (colloq) (attack) crise f; **a dizzy ∼** un vertige; **it gave me quite a ∼, it gave me a nasty ∼** ça m'a fait un coup (colloq)
(g) (act) numéro m
⟨2⟩ vtr (a) (rotate) tourner ⟨wheel, handle⟩; serrer ⟨screw⟩; ⟨mechanism⟩ faire tourner ⟨cog, wheel⟩
(b) (turn over, reverse) retourner ⟨mattress, soil, steak, collar⟩; tourner ⟨page⟩; **it ∼s my stomach** ça me soulève le cœur
(c) (change direction of) tourner ⟨chair, head, face, car⟩
(d) (focus direction of) **to ∼ [sth] on sb** braquer [qch] sur qn ⟨gun, hose, torch⟩
(e) (transform) **to ∼ sth white/black** blanchir/noircir qch; **to ∼ sth opaque** rendre qch opaque; **to ∼ sth into** transformer qch en ⟨office, car park, desert⟩; **to ∼ a book into a**

film adapter un livre pour le cinéma; **to ~ sb into** ⟨magician⟩ changer qn en ⟨frog⟩; ⟨experience⟩ faire de qn ⟨extrovert, maniac⟩ **(f)** (deflect) détourner ⟨person, conversation⟩ **(towards** vers; **from** de)
(g) (colloq) (pass the age of) **he has ~ed 50** il a 50 ans passés; **she has just ~ed 30** elle vient d'avoir 30 ans
(h) (on lathe) tourner ⟨wood, piece⟩
3 vi **(a)** (change direction) ⟨person, car, plane, road⟩ tourner; ⟨ship⟩ virer; **to ~ down** or **into** tourner dans ⟨street, alley⟩; **to ~ towards** tourner en direction de ⟨village, mountains⟩
(b) (reverse direction) ⟨person, vehicle⟩ faire demi-tour; ⟨tide⟩ changer; ⟨luck⟩ tourner
(c) (revolve) ⟨key, wheel, planet⟩ tourner; ⟨person⟩ se tourner
(d) (hinge) **to ~ on** ⟨argument⟩ tourner autour de ⟨point, issue⟩; ⟨outcome⟩ dépendre de ⟨factor⟩
(e) (spin round angrily) **to ~ on sb** ⟨dog⟩ attaquer qn; ⟨person⟩ se retourner contre qn
(f) (resort to) **to ~ to** se tourner vers ⟨person, religion⟩; **to ~ to drink/drugs** se mettre à boire/se droguer; **I don't know where to ~** je ne sais plus où donner de la tête (colloq)
(g) (change) **to ~ into** ⟨person, tadpole⟩ se transformer en ⟨frog⟩; ⟨sofa⟩ se transformer en ⟨bed⟩; ⟨situation, evening⟩ tourner à ⟨farce, disaster⟩; **to ~ to** ⟨substance⟩ se changer en ⟨ice, gold⟩; ⟨fear, surprise⟩ faire place à ⟨horror, relief⟩
(h) (become by transformation) devenir ⟨pale, cloudy, green⟩; **to ~ white/black/red** blanchir/noircir/rougir; **the weather is ~ing cold/warm** le temps se rafraîchit/se réchauffe
(i) (go sour) ⟨milk⟩ tourner
(j) ⟨trees, leaves⟩ jaunir
4 **in turn** phr ⟨answer, speak⟩ à tour de rôle; **she spoke to each of us in ~** elle nous a parlé chacun à notre tour
IDIOMS to do sb a good ~ rendre un service à qn

■ **turn against**: ¶ **~ against** [sb/sth] se retourner contre; ¶ **~** [sb] **against** retourner [qn] contre

■ **turn around**: ¶ **~ around (a)** (to face other way) ⟨person⟩ se retourner; ⟨bus, vehicle⟩ faire demi-tour
(b) (revolve, rotate) ⟨object, windmill, dancer⟩ tourner
¶ **~** [sth] **around** tourner [qch] dans l'autre sens ⟨object⟩

■ **turn aside** se détourner **(from** de)

■ **turn away**: ¶ **~ away** se détourner; ¶ **~** [sb] **away** refuser ⟨spectator, applicant⟩; ne pas laisser entrer ⟨salesman, caller⟩

■ **turn back**: ¶ **~ back (a)** (on foot) rebrousser chemin; (in vehicle) faire demi-tour; **there's no ~ing back** il n'est pas question de revenir en arrière
(b) (in book) revenir
¶ **~** [sth] **back** reculer ⟨dial, clock⟩
¶ **~** [sb] **back** refouler ⟨people, vehicles⟩

■ **turn down (a)** (reduce) baisser ⟨volume, radio, gas⟩
(b) (fold over) rabattre ⟨sheet, collar⟩; retourner ⟨corner of page⟩
(c) (refuse) refuser ⟨person, request⟩; rejeter ⟨offer, suggestion⟩

■ **turn off**: ¶ **~ off (a)** ⟨driver, walker⟩ tourner
(b) ⟨motor, fan⟩ s'arrêter
¶ **~** [sth] **off (a)** éteindre ⟨light, oven, TV, radio⟩; fermer ⟨tap⟩; couper ⟨water, gas, engine⟩
(b) (leave) quitter ⟨road⟩
¶ **~** [sb] **off** (colloq) rebuter

■ **turn on (a)** allumer ⟨light, oven, TV, radio, gas⟩; ouvrir ⟨tap⟩
(b) (colloq) exciter ⟨person⟩

■ **turn out**: ¶ **~ out (a)** (be eventually) **to ~ out well/badly** bien/mal se terminer; **it depends how things ~ out** cela dépend de la façon dont les choses vont tourner; **to ~ out to be wrong/easy** se révéler faux/facile; **it ~s out that they know each other already** il se trouve qu'ils se connaissent déjà
(b) (come out) ⟨crowd, people⟩ venir
¶ **~** [sth] **out (a)** (turn off) éteindre ⟨light⟩
(b) (empty) vider ⟨pocket, bag⟩; (Culin) démouler ⟨mousse⟩
(c) (produce) fabriquer ⟨goods⟩; former ⟨scientists, graduates⟩
¶ **~** [sb] **out** (evict) mettre [qn] à la porte

■ **turn over**: ¶ **~ over (a)** (roll over) ⟨person, vehicle⟩ se retourner
(b) (turn page) tourner la page
(c) ⟨engine⟩ se mettre en marche
¶ **~** [sb/sth] **over (a)** (turn) tourner ⟨page, paper⟩; retourner ⟨card, object, mattress, soil, patient⟩
(b) (hand over) remettre ⟨object, money, find, papers⟩; livrer ⟨person⟩ **(to** à); remettre la succession de ⟨company⟩

■ **turn round** (GB) = TURN AROUND

■ **turn up**: ¶ **~ up (a)** (arrive, show up) arriver, se pointer (colloq); **don't worry—it will ~ up** ne t'inquiète pas—tu finiras par le retrouver
(b) (present itself) ⟨opportunity, job⟩ se présenter
(c) (point up) ⟨corner, edge⟩ être relevé/-e
¶ **~** [sth] **up (a)** (increase, intensify) augmenter ⟨heating, volume, gas⟩; mettre [qch] plus fort ⟨TV, radio, music⟩
(b) (point up) relever ⟨collar⟩

turnaround n (in attitude) revirement m; (of fortune) revirement m (**in** de); (for the better) redressement m (**in** de)

turning n (GB) (in road) virage m

turning point n tournant m (**in, of** de)

turnip n navet m

turnoff n **(a)** (in road) embranchement m
(b) (colloq) (person) **to be a real ~** être vraiment repoussant/-e

turn of mind n tournure f d'esprit

turn of phrase n (expression) expression f

turnout n (to vote, strike, demonstrate) taux m ⋯⫶

de participation; **there was a magnificent ∼ for the parade** beaucoup de gens sont venus voir le défilé

turnover n **(a)** (of company) chiffre m d'affaires
(b) (of stock) rotation f; (of staff) taux m de renouvellement

turnpike n (tollgate) barrière f de péage; (US) (toll expressway) autoroute f à péage

turnstile n (gate) tourniquet m; (to count number of visitors) compteur m pour entrées

turntable n (on record player) platine f

turnup n (GB) (of trousers) revers m

turpentine, **turps** (colloq) n térébenthine f

turret n tourelle f

turtle n (GB) tortue f marine; (US) tortue f

turtle dove n tourterelle f

turtleneck (sweater) n pull-over m à col cheminée

Tuscany pr n Toscane f

tusk n défense f

tussle n empoignade f **(for** pour)

tutor n **(a)** (private teacher) professeur m particulier
(b) (GB Univ) chargé/-e m/f de travaux dirigés
(c) (US Univ) assistant/-e m/f

tutorial n (Univ) (group) classe f de travaux dirigés; (private) cours m privé

tuxedo n (US) smoking m

TV n (colloq) (abbr = **television**) télé f (colloq)

TV dinner n plateau m télé

TV screen n écran m télé

twang n (of string, wire) vibration f; (of tone) ton m nasillard

tweak vtr tordre ‹ear, nose›; tirer ‹hair, moustache›

tweezers n pl pincettes fpl; (for eyebrows) pince f à épiler

twelfth ❶ n **(a)** (in order) douzième mf
(b) (of month) douze m inv
(c) (fraction) douzième m
❷ adj, adv douzième

twelve n, pron, det douze (m) inv

twenties n pl **(a)** (era) **the ∼** les années fpl vingt
(b) (age) **to be in one's ∼** avoir entre vingt et trente ans

twentieth ❶ n **(a)** (in order) vingtième mf
(b) (of month) vingt m
(c) (fraction) vingtième m
❷ adj, adv vingtième

twenty n, pron, det vingt (m) inv

twice adv deux fois; **∼ a day** or **daily** deux fois par jour; **she's ∼ his age** elle a le double de son âge; **∼ as much**, **∼ as many** deux fois plus

twiddle vtr tripoter; **to ∼ one's thumbs** se tourner les pouces

twig n brindille f

twilight n crépuscule m

twilight zone n zone f d'ombre

twin ❶ n jumeau/-elle m/f
❷ adj **(a)** ‹brother, sister› jumeau/-elle
(b) ‹masts, propellers, beds› jumeaux/-elles (after n); ‹speakers› jumelés
❸ vtr jumeler ‹town› **(with** avec)

twine n ficelle f

twinge n (of pain) élancement m; (of conscience, doubt) accès m; (of jealousy) pointe f

twinkle vi ‹light, star, jewel› scintiller; ‹eyes› pétiller

twin town n ville f jumelle

twirl ❶ n tournoiement m
❷ vtr faire tournoyer ‹baton, partner›; entortiller ‹ribbon, vine›
❸ vi ‹dancer› tournoyer; **to ∼ round** (turn round) se retourner brusquement

twist ❶ n **(a)** (in rope, cord, wool) tortillon m; (in road) zigzag m; (in river) coude m
(b) (in play, story) coup m de théâtre; (in events) rebondissement m
(c) (small amount) (of yarn, thread, hair) torsade f; **a ∼ of lemon** une tranche de citron
❷ vtr **(a)** (turn) tourner ‹knob, handle›; (open) dévisser ‹cap, lid›; (close) visser ‹cap, lid›; **he ∼ed around in his chair** il s'est retourné dans son fauteuil
(b) (wind) enrouler; **to ∼ threads together** torsader des fils
(c) (bend, distort) tordre ‹metal, rod, branch›; déformer ‹words, facts, meaning›; **his face was ∼ed with pain** son visage était tordu de douleur
(d) (injure) **to ∼ one's ankle/wrist** se tordre le bras/le poignet; **to ∼ one's neck** attraper un torticolis
❸ vi **(a)** ‹person› **to ∼ round** (turn round) se retourner
(b) ‹rope, flex, coil› s'entortiller; **to ∼ and turn** ‹road, path› serpenter

twisted adj ‹wire, metal› tordu/-e; ‹cord› entortillé/-e; ‹ankle, wrist› tordu/-e; ‹sense of humour› malsain/-e

twit n (colloq) idiot/-e m/f

twitch ❶ n **(a)** (tic) tic m
(b) (spasm) soubresaut m
❷ vtr tirer sur [qch] d'un coup sec ‹fabric, curtain›
❸ vi ‹person› avoir des tics; ‹mouth› trembler; ‹eye› cligner nerveusement; ‹limb, muscle› tressauter

twitchy adj agité/-e

twitter vi ‹bird› gazouiller

two n, det, pron deux (m) inv; **in ∼s and threes** par deux ou trois, deux ou trois à la fois; **to break sth in ∼** casser qch en deux
IDIOMS **to be in ∼ minds about doing** hésiter à faire; **to put ∼ and ∼ together** faire le rapprochement

two-faced adj hypocrite, fourbe

twofold ❶ adj double
❷ adv doublement; **to increase ∼** doubler

two-piece n (also **∼ suit**) (woman's) tailleur m; (man's) costume m (deux-pièces)

two-seater n (car) voiture f à deux places; (plane) avion m à deux places

two-tier adj ⟨society, health service⟩ à deux vitesses

two-time vtr (colloq) être infidèle envers, tromper ⟨partner⟩

two-way adj ⟨street⟩ à double sens; ⟨traffic⟩ dans les deux sens; ⟨communication, exchange⟩ bilatéral/-e

two-way mirror n glace f sans tain

two-way radio n émetteur-récepteur m

tycoon n magnat m

type ① n (a) (variety, kind) type m, genre m (of de)
(b) (in printing) caractères mpl
② vtr taper (à la machine) ⟨word, letter⟩; a ~d letter une lettre dactylographiée
③ vi taper (à la machine)

typecast vtr cataloguer ⟨person⟩

typeface n police f (de caractères)

typewriter n machine f à écrire

typhoid n typhoïde f

typhoon n typhon m

typical adj ⟨case, example, day, village⟩ typique; ⟨generosity, compassion⟩ caractéristique; it's ~ of him to be late cela ne m'étonne pas de lui qu'il soit en retard

typically adv ⟨react, behave⟩ (of person) comme à mon/ton etc habitude; ~ English ⟨place, behaviour⟩ typiquement anglais; she's ~ English c'est l'Anglaise type

typify vtr ⟨feature, behaviour⟩ caractériser; ⟨person, institution⟩ être le type même de

typing n dactylo f

typist n dactylo mf

typographic(al) adj typographique

typography n typographie f

tyrannize vtr tyranniser

tyranny n tyrannie f (over sur)

tyrant n tyran m

tyre (GB), **tire** (US) n pneu m; spare ~ (for car) pneu m de rechange; (fat) bourrelet m

tyre pressure n pression f des pneus

U u

u, U n u, U m

udder n pis m

UFO n (abbr = **unidentified flying object**) ovni m inv

ugly adj (a) ⟨person, building⟩ laid/-e
(b) ⟨situation⟩ dangereux/-euse

UK pr n (abbr = **United Kingdom**) Royaume-Uni m

Ukraine pr n the ~ l'Ukraine f

ulcer n ulcère m

ulterior adj without any ~ motive sans arrière-pensée

ultimate ① n the ~ in le nec plus ultra de ⟨comfort, luxury⟩
② adj ⟨result, destination⟩ final/-e; ⟨sacrifice⟩ ultime (before n)

ultimately adv en fin de compte, au bout du compte

ultimatum n ultimatum m

ultramarine n, adj outremer (m) inv

ultrasound n ultrasons mpl

ultrasound scan n échographie f

ultraviolet adj ultraviolet/-ette

umbilical cord n cordon m ombilical

umbrella n parapluie m

umpire n arbitre m

UN n (abbr = **United Nations**) the ~ l'ONU f

unable adj to be ~ to do (lacking means or opportunity) ne pas pouvoir faire; (lacking knowledge or skill) ne pas savoir faire; (incapable, not qualified) être incapable de faire

unabridged adj intégral/-e

unacceptable adj ⟨proposal⟩ inacceptable; ⟨behaviour⟩ inadmissible

unaccompanied adj (a) ⟨child, baggage⟩ non accompagné/-e; ⟨man, woman⟩ seul/-e
(b) (Mus) sans accompagnement

unaccounted adj to be ~ for (gen) être introuvable; two of the crew are still ~ for deux membres de l'équipage sont toujours portés disparus

unaccustomed adj to be ~ to sth/to doing ne pas avoir l'habitude de qch/de faire

unaffected adj (a) to be ~ ne pas être affecté/-e (by par)
(b) (natural) tout simple

unafraid adj ⟨person⟩ sans peur

unaided adv ⟨stand, sit, walk⟩ sans aide

unambiguous adj sans équivoque

unanimous adj unanime

unanimously adv ⟨agree, condemn⟩ unanimement; ⟨vote⟩ à l'unanimité

unannounced adv ⟨arrive, call⟩ sans prévenir

unanswered adj ⟨letter, question⟩ resté/-e sans réponse

unappetizing adj peu appétissant/-e

unappreciative adj ⟨person, audience⟩ ingrat/-e

unapproachable adj inaccessible

u

unarmed adj ⟨person⟩ non armé/-e; ⟨combat⟩ sans armes

unashamedly adv ouvertement

unasked adv ⟨come, attend⟩ sans être invité/-e; **to do sth** ∼ faire qch spontanément

unassuming adj modeste

unattached adj (a) ⟨part, element⟩ détaché/-e

(b) (single) ⟨person⟩ célibataire

unattainable adj inaccessible

unattractive adj ⟨person⟩ peu attirant/-e; ⟨proposition⟩ peu intéressant/-e (**to** pour)

unauthorized adj fait/-e sans autorisation

unavailable adj **to be** ∼ ⟨person⟩ ne pas être disponible

unavoidable adj inévitable

unaware adj (a) (not informed) **to be** ∼ **that** ignorer que

(b) (not conscious) **to be** ∼ **of sth** ne pas être conscient/-e de qch

unawares adv **to catch** or **take sb** ∼ prendre qn au dépourvu

unbearable adj insupportable

unbeatable adj imbattable

unbeknown adv ∼ **to sb** à l'insu de qn

unbelievable adj incroyable

unbending adj inflexible

unbias(s)ed adj impartial/-e

unblock vtr déboucher ⟨pipe, sink⟩

unborn adj ⟨child⟩ à naître; **her** ∼ **child** l'enfant qu'elle porte/portait etc

unbreakable adj incassable

unbroken adj (a) ⟨sequence, silence, view⟩ ininterrompu/-e

(b) ⟨pottery⟩ intact/-e

unbuckle vtr déboucler ⟨belt⟩; défaire la boucle de ⟨shoe⟩

unbutton vtr déboutonner

uncalled-for adj ⟨remark⟩ déplacé/-e

uncanny adj ⟨resemblance⟩ étrange; ⟨accuracy⟩ étonnant/-e; ⟨silence⟩ troublant/-e

uncaring adj ⟨world⟩ indifférent/-e

uncertain [1] adj (a) (unsure) incertain/-e; **to be** ∼ **about** ne pas être certain/-e de

(b) (changeable) ⟨temper⟩ instable; ⟨weather⟩ variable

[2] **in no** ∼ **terms** phr ⟨state⟩ en termes on ne peut plus clairs

uncertainty n incertitude f

unchallenged adj incontesté/-e; **to go** ∼ ⟨statement, decision⟩ ne pas être récusé/-e

unchanged adj inchangé/-e

uncharacteristic adj ⟨generosity⟩ peu habituel/-elle; **it was** ∼ **of him to...** ce n'est pas son genre de...

uncharitable adj peu charitable

unchecked adv de manière incontrôlée

uncivilized adj (a) (inhumane) ⟨treatment, conditions⟩ inhumain/-e

(b) (uncouth, rude) grossier/-ière

(c) (barbarous) ⟨people, nation⟩ non civilisé/-e

uncle n oncle m

unclear adj (a) ⟨motive, reason⟩ peu clair/-e; **it is** ∼ **how/whether...** on ne sait pas très bien comment/si...

(b) ⟨instructions, voice⟩ pas clair/-e; ⟨answer⟩ peu clair/-e; ⟨handwriting⟩ difficile à lire

uncomfortable adj (a) ⟨shoes, garment, seat⟩ inconfortable; ⟨journey, heat⟩ pénible; **you look** ∼ **in that chair** tu n'as pas l'air à l'aise dans ce fauteuil

(b) ⟨feeling, silence, situation⟩ pénible; **to make sb** (**feel**) ∼ mettre qn mal à l'aise

uncommon adj rare

uncommunicative adj peu communicatif/-ive

uncomplimentary adj peu flatteur/-euse

uncompromising adj intransigeant/-e

unconcerned adj (uninterested) indifférent/-e (**with** à); (not caring) insouciant/-e; (untroubled) imperturbable

unconditional adj ⟨obedience, support, love⟩ inconditionnel/-elle; ⟨offer, surrender⟩ sans condition

unconfirmed adj non confirmé/-e

unconnected adj ⟨incidents, facts⟩ sans lien entre eux/elles; **to be** ∼ **with** ⟨event, fact⟩ n'avoir aucun rapport avec; ⟨person⟩ n'avoir aucun lien avec

unconscious [1] n **the** ∼ l'inconscient m

[2] adj (a) (insensible) sans connaissance; **to knock sb** ∼ assommer qn

(b) (unaware) **to be** ∼ **of sth** ne pas être conscient/-e de qch

(c) ⟨bias, hostility⟩ inconscient/-e

unconstitutional adj inconstitutionnel/-elle

uncontested adj ⟨leader, fact⟩ incontesté/-e; ⟨seat⟩ non disputé/-e

uncontrollable adj ⟨emotion⟩ incontrôlable; ⟨tears⟩ qu'on ne peut retenir

uncontrollably adv ⟨laugh, sob⟩ sans pouvoir se contrôler

unconventional adj peu conventionnel/-elle

unconvincing adj peu convaincant/-e

uncooked adj non cuit/-e

uncooperative adj peu coopératif/-ive

uncoordinated adj ⟨efforts, service⟩ désordonné/-e; **to be** ∼ ⟨person⟩ manquer de coordination

uncouth adj ⟨person⟩ grossier/-ière; ⟨accent⟩ peu raffiné/-e

uncover vtr dévoiler ⟨scandal⟩; découvrir ⟨evidence, body⟩

uncritical adj peu critique

unctuous adj onctueux/-euse, mielleux/-euse

uncut adj (a) ⟨film, version⟩ intégral/-e

(b) ⟨gem⟩ non taillé/-e

undamaged adj ⟨crops⟩ non endommagé/-e; ⟨building, reputation⟩ intact/-e

u

undecided adj ⟨person⟩ indécis/-e; ⟨outcome⟩ incertain/-e

undemanding adj ⟨task⟩ peu fatigant/-e; ⟨person⟩ peu exigeant/-e

undemocratic adj antidémocratique

undemonstrative adj peu démonstratif/-ive

undeniable adj indéniable

under **1** prep (a) sous; ~ **the bed** sous le lit; ~ **it** en dessous; **it's** ~ **there** c'est là-dessous; ~ **letter D** sous la lettre D
(b) (less than) ~ **£10** moins de 10 livres sterling; **children** ~ **five** les enfants de moins de cinq ans or au-dessous de cinq ans; **a number** ~ **ten** un nombre inférieur à dix; **temperatures** ~ **10°C** des températures inférieures à or au-dessous de 10°C
(c) (according to) ~ **the law** selon la loi
(d) (subordinate to) sous; **I have 50 people** ~ **me** j'ai 50 employés sous mes ordres
2 adv (a) ⟨crawl, sit, hide⟩ en dessous; **to go** ~ ⟨diver, swimmer⟩ disparaître sous l'eau
(b) (less) moins; **£10 and** ~ 10 livres sterling et moins; **children of six and** ~ des enfants de six ans et au-dessous
(c) (anaesthetized) **to put sb** ~ endormir qn

underachieve vi (Sch) ne pas obtenir les résultats dont on est capable

underachiever n (Sch) sous-performant/-e m/f

underage adj ~ **drinking** la consommation d'alcool par les mineurs; **to be** ~ être mineur/-e

undercarriage n train m d'atterrissage

underclass n classe f sous-prolétariat

underclothes n pl sous-vêtements mpl

undercoat n couche f de fond

undercooked adj pas assez cuit/-e; **the meat is** ~ la viande n'est pas assez cuite

undercover adj ⟨activity, group⟩ clandestin/-e; ⟨agent⟩ secret/-ète

undercurrent n (in water) courant m profond; (in sea) courant m sous-marin; (figurative) courant m sous-jacent

undercut vtr concurrencer ⟨prices⟩

underdeveloped adj ⟨country⟩ sous-développé/-e; ⟨negative⟩ pas assez développé/-e

underdog n (in society) opprimé/-e m/f; (in game, contest) perdant/-e m/f

underdone adj ⟨food⟩ pas assez cuit/-e; ⟨steak⟩ (GB) saignant/-e

underestimate vtr sous-estimer

underexpose vtr sous-exposer

underfed adj sous-alimenté/-e

underfoot adv sous les pieds; **the ground was wet** ~ le sol était humide

underfunded adj insuffisamment financé/-e

undergo vtr subir ⟨change, test, operation⟩; suivre ⟨treatment, training⟩; **to** ~ **surgery** subir une intervention chirurgicale

undergraduate n étudiant/-e m/f

underground **1** n (a) (GB) (subway) métro m; **on the** ~ dans le métro
(b) **the** ~ (political) la clandestinité; (artistic) l'underground m
2 adj (a) (below ground) souterrain/-e
(b) (secret) clandestin/-e
(c) (artistic) underground inv
3 adv (a) (below ground) sous terre
(b) (secretly) **to go** ~ passer dans la clandestinité

underground train n rame f (de métro)

undergrowth n sous-bois m

underhand adj (also **underhanded** (US)) ⟨person, method⟩ sournois/-e; ~ **dealings** magouilles fpl (colloq)

underline vtr souligner

underling n subordonné/-e m/f

underlying adj ⟨problem⟩ sous-jacent/-e

undermine vtr saper ⟨foundations, authority, efforts⟩; ébranler ⟨confidence, position⟩

underneath **1** n dessous m
2 adv dessous, en dessous
3 prep sous, au-dessous de; **from** ~ **a pile of books** de dessous une pile de livres

undernourished adj sous-alimenté/-e

underpants n pl slip m; **a pair of** ~ un slip

underpass n (for traffic) voie f inférieure; (for pedestrians) passage m souterrain

underpay vtr sous-payer ⟨employee⟩

underprivileged adj défavorisé/-e

underrate vtr sous-estimer

under-secretary n (also ~ **of state**) (GB) sous-secrétaire mf d'État

undersell **1** vtr vendre moins cher que ⟨competitor⟩
2 v refl **to** ~ **oneself** se dévaloriser

undershirt n (US) maillot m de corps

understaffed adj **to be** ~ manquer de personnel

understand **1** vtr (a) (gen) comprendre; **to make oneself understood** se faire comprendre
(b) (believe) **to** ~ **that** croire que
2 vi comprendre (**about** à propos de)

understandable adj compréhensible; **it's** ~ ça se comprend

understandably adv naturellement

understanding **1** n (a) (grasp of subject, issue) compréhension f
(b) (arrangement) entente f (**about** sur; **between** entre)
(c) (sympathy) compréhension f
(d) (powers of reason) entendement m
2 adj ⟨tone⟩ bienveillant/-e; ⟨person⟩ compréhensif/-ive

understatement n litote f

understudy n doublure f (**to** de)

undertake vtr (a) entreprendre ⟨search, study, trip⟩; se charger de ⟨mission, offensive⟩ ····>

u

(b) to ∼ to do s'engager à faire

undertaker n (person) entrepreneur m de pompes funèbres; (company) entreprise f de pompes funèbres

undertaking n **(a)** (venture) entreprise f **(b)** (promise) garantie f

under-the-counter adj ‹goods, trade› illicite; ‹payment› sous le manteau

undertone n **(a)** (low voice) voix f basse **(b)** (hint) nuance f

undervalue vtr **(a)** (financially) sous-évaluer **(b)** sous-estimer ‹person, quality›

underwater ① adj ‹cable, exploration› sous-marin/-e; ‹lighting› sous l'eau ② adv sous l'eau

underway adj to get ∼ ‹vehicle› se mettre en route; ‹season› commencer

underwear n sous-vêtements mpl

underweight adj trop maigre

underworld n milieu m, pègre f

undesirable adj ‹aspect, habit, result› indésirable; ‹influence› néfaste; ‹friend› peu recommandable

undetected adv ‹break in, listen› sans être aperçu/-e; to go ∼ ‹person› rester inaperçu/-e; ‹cancer› rester non décelé/-e; ‹crime› rester non découvert/-e

undeterred adj to be ∼ by sb/sth ne pas se laisser démonter par qn/qch

undeveloped adj ‹person, organ, idea› non développé/-e; ‹land› inexploité/-e; ‹country› sous-développé/-e

undignified adj indigne

undisciplined adj indiscipliné/-e

undiscovered adj ‹secret› non révélé/-e; ‹land› inexploré/-e; ‹crime, document› non découvert/-e

undiscriminating adj sans discernement

undisguised adj non déguisé/-e

undisputed adj incontesté/-e

undisturbed adj ‹sleep› paisible, tranquille; to leave sb/sth ∼ ne pas déranger qn/qch

undivided adj to give sb one's ∼ attention accorder à qn toute son attention

undo vtr **(a)** défaire ‹button, lock›; ouvrir ‹parcel› **(b)** annuler ‹good, effort›

undone adj défait/-e; to come ∼ ‹parcel, button› se défaire

undoubtedly adv indubitablement

undress ① vtr déshabiller ② vi se déshabiller

undrinkable adj (unpleasant) imbuvable; (dangerous) non potable

undue adj excessif/-ive

unduly adv ‹optimistic, surprised› excessivement; ‹neglect, worry› outre mesure

unearthly adj ‹light, landscape› surnaturel/-elle; ‹cry, silence› étrange; at an ∼ hour à une heure indue

uneasily adv **(a)** (anxiously) avec inquiétude

(b) (uncomfortably) avec gêne

uneasiness n (worry) appréhension f (about au sujet de); (dissatisfaction) malaise m

uneasy adj **(a)** ‹person› inquiet/-iète (about, at au sujet de); ‹conscience› pas tranquille **(b)** ‹compromise› difficile; ‹peace› boiteux/-euse; ‹silence› gêné/-e **(c)** ‹sleep› agité/-e

uneconomical adj (wasteful) pas économique; (not profitable) pas rentable

uneducated adj **(a)** ‹person› sans instruction **(b)** ‹person, speech› inculte; ‹accent, tastes› commun/-e

unemotional adj ‹person› impassible; ‹account, reunion› froid/-e

unemployed ① n the ∼ les chômeurs mpl ② adj au chômage, sans emploi

unemployment n chômage m

unemployment benefit (GB), **unemployment compensation** (US) n allocations fpl de chômage

unemployment rate n taux m de chômage

unenthusiastic adj peu enthousiaste

unenviable adj peu enviable

unequal adj ‹amounts, contest, pay› inégal/-e

unequivocal adj ‹person, declaration› explicite; ‹answer, support› sans équivoque

unethical adj (gen) contraire à la morale; (Med) contraire à la déontologie

uneven adj ‹hem, teeth› irrégulier/-ière; ‹contest, surface› inégal/-e

uneventful adj ‹day, life, career› ordinaire; ‹journey, period› sans histoires

unexciting adj sans intérêt

unexpected adj ‹arrival, success› imprévu/-e; ‹ally, outcome› inattendu/-e; ‹death› inopiné/-e

unexpectedly adv ‹happen› à l'improviste; ‹large, small, fast› étonnamment

unexplored adj inexploré/-e

unfailing adj ‹support› fidèle; ‹optimism› à toute épreuve; ‹efforts› constant/-e

unfair adj injuste (to, on envers; to do de faire); ‹play, tactics› irrégulier/-ière; ‹trading› frauduleux/-euse

unfair dismissal n licenciement m abusif

unfairness n injustice f

unfaithful adj infidèle (to à)

unfamiliar adj **(a)** ‹face, name, place› inconnu/-e (to à); ‹concept, feeling, situation› inhabituel/-elle (to à) **(b)** to be ∼ with sth ne pas connaître qch

unfashionable adj qui n'est pas à la mode

unfasten vtr défaire ‹clothing, button›; ouvrir ‹bag›

unfavourable *adj* défavorable

unfinished *adj* ⟨work⟩ inachevé/-e; **to have ∼ business** avoir des choses à régler

unfit *adj* (a) (out of condition) qui n'est pas en forme
(b) ⟨housing⟩ inadéquat/-e; ⟨pitch, road⟩ impraticable (**for** à); **∼ for human consumption** impropre à la consommation humaine

unflattering *adj* peu flatteur/-euse

unfold **1** *vtr* déplier ⟨paper, map, deck, chair⟩; déployer ⟨wings⟩; décroiser ⟨arms⟩
2 *vi* (a) ⟨leaf⟩ s'ouvrir
(b) ⟨scene⟩ se dérouler; ⟨mystery⟩ se dévoiler

unforeseeable *adj* imprévisible

unforeseen *adj* imprévu/-e

unforgettable *adj* inoubliable

unforgivable *adj* impardonnable

unforgiving *adj* impitoyable

unfortunate *adj* (a) (pitiable) malheureux/-euse
(b) (regrettable) ⟨incident, choice⟩ malencontreux/-euse; ⟨remark⟩ fâcheux/-euse
(c) (unlucky) malchanceux/-euse

unfortunately *adv* malheureusement

unfounded *adj* sans fondement

unfriendly *adj* ⟨person, attitude, reception⟩ peu amical/-e; ⟨place⟩ inhospitalier/-ière

unfulfilled *adj* ⟨ambition⟩ non réalisé/-e; ⟨desire, need⟩ inassouvi/-e; **to feel ∼** se sentir insatisfait/-e

unfurnished *adj* non meublé/-e

ungracious *adj* désobligeant/-e (**of** de la part de)

ungrammatical *adj* incorrect/-e

ungrateful *adj* ingrat/-e (**of** de la part de; **towards** envers)

unhappily *adv* (a) (miserably) d'un air malheureux
(b) (unfortunately) malheureusement
(c) (inappropriately) malencontreusement

unhappiness *n* (a) (misery) tristesse *f*
(b) (dissatisfaction) mécontentement *m*

unhappy *adj* (a) ⟨person, childhood, situation⟩ malheureux/-euse; ⟨face, occasion⟩ triste
(b) (dissatisfied) mécontent/-e; **to be ∼ with sth** ne pas être satisfait/-e de qch
(c) (concerned) inquiet/-iète

unharmed *adj* ⟨person⟩ indemne; ⟨object⟩ intact/-e

unhealthy *adj* (a) ⟨person⟩ maladif/-ive; ⟨diet⟩ malsain/-e; ⟨conditions⟩ insalubre
(b) (unwholesome) malsain/-e

unheard-of *adj* (a) (shocking) inouï/-e
(b) ⟨price⟩ record; ⟨actor⟩ inconnu/-e

unheeded *adj* **to go ∼** ⟨warning, plea⟩ rester vain/-e

unhelpful *adj* ⟨employee⟩ peu serviable; ⟨attitude⟩ peu obligeant/-e

unhindered *adj* **∼ by** sans être entravé/-e par ⟨rules⟩; sans être encombré/-e par ⟨luggage⟩

unhook *vtr* dégrafer ⟨skirt⟩; décrocher ⟨picture⟩ (**from** de)

unhurried *adj* ⟨person⟩ posé/-e; ⟨pace, meal⟩ tranquille

unhygienic *adj* ⟨conditions⟩ insalubre; ⟨way, method⟩ peu hygiénique

unidentified *adj* non identifié/-e

unification *n* unification *f* (**of** de)

uniform **1** *n* uniforme *m*
2 *adj* identique; ⟨temperature⟩ constant/-e

unify *vtr* unifier

unilateral *adj* unilatéral/-e

unimaginative *adj* ⟨style⟩ sans originalité; **to be ∼** manquer d'imagination

unimpeded *adj* ⟨access, influx⟩ libre

unimportant *adj* sans importance

unimpressed *adj* **to be ∼ by** être peu impressionné/-e par ⟨person, performance⟩; n'être guère convaincu/-e par ⟨argument⟩

uninhabitable *adj* inhabitable

uninhabited *adj* inhabité/-e

uninhibited *adj* ⟨person⟩ sans complexes (**about** en ce qui concerne)

uninitiated *n* **the ∼** les profanes

uninjured *adj* indemne

uninspired *adj* ⟨approach⟩ terne; ⟨performance⟩ honnête; **to be ∼** ⟨person⟩ manquer d'inspiration; ⟨strategy⟩ manquer d'imagination

unintelligible *adj* incompréhensible

unintended *adj* ⟨slur, irony⟩ involontaire; ⟨consequence⟩ non voulu/-e

unintentional *adj* involontaire

uninterested *adj* indifférent/-e (**in** à)

uninteresting *adj* sans intérêt

uninvited *adj* ⟨attentions⟩ non sollicité/-e; ⟨remark⟩ gratuit/-e; **∼ guest** intrus/-e *m/f*

uninviting *adj* ⟨place⟩ rébarbatif/-ive; ⟨food⟩ peu appétissant/-e

union *n* (a) (also **trade ∼**) syndicat *m*
(b) (uniting) union *f*; (marriage) union *f*, mariage *m*

Unionist *n, adj* unioniste (*mf*)

Union Jack *n* drapeau *m* du Royaume-Uni

unique *adj* (a) (sole) unique; **to be ∼ to** être particulier/-ière à
(b) (remarkable) unique, exceptionnel/-elle

unisex *adj* unisexe

unison *n* **in ∼** à l'unisson

unit *n* (a) (gen) unité *f*
(b) (group) groupe *m*; (in army, police) unité *f*
(c) (department) (gen, Med) service *m*
(d) (piece of furniture) élément *m*

unite **1** *vtr* unir (**with** à)
2 *vi* s'unir (**with** à)

united *adj* ⟨group, front⟩ uni/-e (**in** dans); ⟨effort⟩ conjoint/-e

United Kingdom *pr n* Royaume-Uni *m*

u

United Nations (Organization) n (Organisation f des) Nations fpl unies

United States (of America) pr n États-Unis mpl (d'Amérique)

unit trust n ≈ société f d'investissement à capital variable, SICAV f

unity n unité f

universal adj ⟨acclaim, reaction⟩ général/-e; ⟨education⟩ pour tous; ⟨principle, truth⟩ universel/-elle

universally adv ⟨believed⟩ par tous, universellement; ⟨known, loved⟩ de tous

universe n univers m

university n université f

unjust adj injuste (**to** envers)

unjustified adj injustifié/-e

unkempt adj ⟨appearance⟩ négligé/-e; ⟨hair⟩ ébouriffé/-e; ⟨beard⟩ peu soigné/-e

unkind adj ⟨person, thought, act⟩ pas très gentil/-ille; ⟨remark⟩ désobligeant/-e; **to be ~ to sb** (by deed) ne pas être gentil avec qn; (verbally) être méchant/-e avec qn

unknown ① n (a) **the ~** l'inconnu m (b) (person) inconnu/-e m/f ② adj inconnu/-e

unlace vtr délacer

unlawful adj ⟨activity⟩ illégal/-e; ⟨detention⟩ arbitraire; **~ killing** meurtre m

unlawfully adv illégalement

unleaded petrol (GB), **unleaded gasoline** (US) n essence f sans plomb

unleavened adj sans levain

unless conj à moins que (+ subjunctive), à moins de (+ infinitive); **he won't come ~ you invite him** il ne viendra pas à moins que tu (ne) l'invites; **she can't take the job ~ she finds a nanny** elle ne peut pas accepter le poste à moins de trouver une nourrice

unlike prep (a) (in contrast to) contrairement à, à la différence de; **~ me, he...** contrairement à moi, il... (b) (different from) différent/-e de (c) (uncharacteristic of) **it's ~ her (to be so rude)** ça ne lui ressemble pas (d'être aussi impolie)

unlikely adj (a) (unexpected) improbable, peu probable; **it is ~ that** il est peu probable que (+ subjunctive) (b) ⟨partner, choice, situation⟩ inattendu/-e (c) ⟨story⟩ invraisemblable

unlimited adj illimité/-e; ⟨access⟩ libre (before n)

unlined adj (a) ⟨garment, curtain⟩ sans doublure (b) ⟨paper⟩ non réglé

unload ① vtr (a) décharger ⟨goods, vessel, gun, camera⟩ (b) (get rid of) se décharger de ⟨feelings⟩ (on(to) sur); se débarrasser de ⟨goods⟩ ② vi ⟨truck, ship⟩ décharger

unlock vtr ouvrir ⟨door⟩; **to be ~ed** ne pas être fermé/-e à clé

unluckily adv malheureusement (**for** pour)

unlucky adj (a) ⟨person⟩ malchanceux/-euse; ⟨event⟩ malencontreux/-euse; ⟨day⟩ de malchance (b) ⟨number, colour⟩ néfaste, maléfique; **it's ~ to do** ça porte malheur de faire

unmade adj ⟨bed⟩ défait/-e

unmanageable adj ⟨child, dog⟩ difficile; ⟨system⟩ ingérable; ⟨hair⟩ rebelle

unmarried adj célibataire

unmistakable adj (a) (recognizable) caractéristique (**of** de) (b) (unambiguous) sans ambiguïté (c) (marked) net/nette

unmotivated adj ⟨act⟩ gratuit/-e; ⟨person⟩ non motivé/-e

unmoved adj (unconcerned) indifférent/-e (**by** à); (emotionally) insensible (**by** à)

unnamed adj (name not divulged) ⟨company, source⟩ dont le nom n'a pas été divulgué; (without name) **as yet ~** encore à la recherche d'un nom

unnatural adj (a) (odd) anormal/-e; **it is ~ that** ce n'est pas normal que (+ subjunctive) (b) ⟨style, laugh⟩ affecté/-e (c) ⟨silence, colour⟩ insolite

unnecessarily adv inutilement

unnecessary adj (a) (not needed) inutile; **it is ~ to do** il est inutile de faire; **it is ~ for you to do** il est inutile que tu fasses (b) (uncalled for) déplacé/-e

unnerve vtr déconcerter, rendre [qn] nerveux/-euse

unnoticed adj inaperçu/-e

unobstructed adj ⟨view, exit, road⟩ dégagé/-e

unobtainable adj ⟨supplies⟩ impossible à se procurer; ⟨number⟩ impossible à obtenir

unobtrusive adj ⟨person⟩ effacé/-e; ⟨site, object, noise⟩ discret/-ète

unoccupied adj ⟨house, shop⟩ inoccupé/-e; ⟨seat⟩ libre

unofficial adj ⟨figure⟩ officieux/-ieuse; ⟨candidate⟩ indépendant/-e; ⟨strike⟩ sauvage

unorthodox adj peu orthodoxe

unpack vtr défaire ⟨suitcase⟩; déballer ⟨belongings⟩

unpaid adj ⟨bill, tax⟩ impayé/-e; ⟨debt⟩ non acquitté/-e; ⟨work⟩ non rémunéré/-e; **~ leave** congé m sans solde

unpalatable adj (a) ⟨truth, statistic⟩ inconfortable; ⟨advice⟩ dur/-e à avaler (b) ⟨food⟩ qui n'a pas bon goût

unparalleled adj (a) ⟨strength, luxury⟩ sans égal; ⟨success⟩ hors pair (b) (unprecedented) sans précédent

unpasteurized adj ⟨milk⟩ cru/-e; ⟨cheese⟩ au lait cru

unperturbed adj imperturbable

unplanned adj ⟨stoppage, increase⟩ imprévu/-e; ⟨pregnancy, baby⟩ non prévu/-e

unpleasant adj désagréable

unpleasantness n (a) (of odour, experience, remark) caractère m désagréable

(b) (bad feeling) dissensions *fpl* **(between** entre)

unplug *vtr* débrancher ‹appliance›; déboucher ‹sink›

unpopular *adj* impopulaire

unprecedented *adj* sans précédent

unpredictable *adj* ‹event› imprévisible; ‹weather› incertain/-e; **he's ∼** on ne sait jamais à quoi s'attendre avec lui

unpremeditated *adj* non prémédité/-e

unprepared *adj* **(a)** ‹person› pas préparé/-e **(for** pour)
(b) ‹speech› improvisé/-e; ‹translation› non préparé/-e

unprepossessing *adj* peu avenant/-e

unpretentious *adj* sans prétention

unproductive *adj* improductif/-ive

unprofessional *adj* peu professionnel/-elle

unprofitable *adj* non rentable

unprotected *adj* ‹person, sex, area› sans protection **(from** contre)

unprovoked *adj* ‹attack, aggression› délibéré/-e

unqualified *adj* **(a)** ‹person› non qualifié/-e
(b) ‹support, respect› inconditionnel/-elle; ‹success› grand/-e **(before** n)

unquestionable *adj* incontestable

unravel ①*vtr* défaire ‹knitting›; démêler ‹thread, mystery›
②*vi* ‹knitting› se défaire; ‹mystery, thread› se démêler; ‹plot› se dénouer

unreal *adj* **(a)** (not real) irréel/-éelle
(b) (colloq) (unbelievable) incroyable

unrealistic *adj* irréaliste, peu réaliste

unreasonable *adj* **(a)** ‹behaviour, expectation› qui n'est pas raisonnable; **he's being very ∼ about it** il n'est vraiment pas raisonnable
(b) ‹price, demand› excessif/-ive

unrecognizable *adj* méconnaissable

unrelated *adj* **(a)** (not connected) sans rapport **(to** avec)
(b) (as family) **to be ∼** ne pas avoir de lien de parenté

unrelenting *adj* ‹heat, stare, person› implacable; ‹pursuit, zeal› acharné/-e

unreliable *adj* ‹evidence› douteux/-euse; ‹method, employee› peu sûr/-e; ‹equipment› peu fiable; **she's very ∼** on ne peut pas compter sur elle

unrepentant *adj* impénitent/-e

unrequited *adj* ‹love› sans retour

unresolved *adj* irrésolu/-e

unrest *n* **(a)** (dissatisfaction) malaise *m*
(b) (agitation) troubles *mpl*

unrestricted *adj* ‹access› libre **(before** n); ‹power› illimité/-e

unrewarding *adj* (unfulfilling) peu gratifiant/-e; (thankless) ingrat/-e

unripe *adj* ‹fruit› pas mûr/-e

unrivalled *adj* sans égal

unroll *vtr* dérouler

unruffled *adj* **(a)** (calm) imperturbable
(b) ‹hair› lisse

unruly *adj* indiscipliné/-e

unsafe *adj* **(a)** ‹environment› malsain/-e; ‹drinking water› non potable; ‹goods, working conditions› dangereux/-euse
(b) (threatened) **to feel ∼** ne pas se sentir en sécurité

unsaid *adj* **to leave sth ∼** passer qch sous silence

unsatisfactory *adj* insatisfaisant/-e

unsatisfied *adj* ‹person› insatisfait/-e; ‹need› inassouvi/-e

unsatisfying *adj* peu satisfaisant/-e

unsavoury (GB), **unsavory** (US) *adj* ‹individual› louche, répugnant/-e

unscathed *adj* indemne

unscheduled *adj* ‹appearance, speech› surprise **(after** n); ‹flight› supplémentaire; ‹stop› qui n'a pas été prévu

unscrew *vtr* dévisser

unscrupulous *adj* ‹person› sans scrupules; ‹tactic› peu scrupuleux/-euse

unseat *vtr* désarçonner ‹rider›

unseen *adv* ‹escape, slip away› sans être vu/-e

unselfconscious *adj* **(a)** (natural) naturel/-elle
(b) (uninhibited) sans complexes

unselfish *adj* ‹person› qui pense aux autres; ‹act› désintéressé/-e

unsentimental *adj* ‹account, film› qui ne donne pas dans la sensiblerie; ‹person› qui ne fait pas de sentiment

unsettled *adj* **(a)** ‹weather, climate› instable; ‹person› perturbé/-e
(b) ‹account› impayé/-e

unsettling *adj* ‹question, experience› troublant/-e; ‹work of art› dérangeant/-e

unshaken *adj* ‹person› imperturbable **(by** devant); ‹belief› inébranlable

unshaven *adj* pas rasé/-e

unskilled *adj* ‹worker, labour› non qualifié/-e; ‹job, work› qui n'exige pas de qualification professionnelle

unsociable *adj* peu sociable

unsocial *adj* **to work ∼ hours** travailler en dehors des heures normales

unsolicited *adj* non sollicité/-e

unsophisticated *adj* ‹person› sans façons; ‹mind› simple; ‹analysis› simpliste

unspeakable *adj* **(a)** (dreadful) ‹pain, sorrow› inexprimable; ‹act› innommable
(b) (inexpressible) ‹joy› indescriptible

unspoiled, unspoilt *adj* ‹landscape, town› préservé/-e intact

unspoken *adj* **(a)** (secret) inexprimé/-e
(b) (implicit) tacite

unstable *adj* instable

unsteady *adj* ‹steps, legs, voice› ⋯⋗

u

chancelant/-e; ⟨*ladder*⟩ instable; ⟨*hand*⟩
tremblant/-e; **to be ∼ on one's feet** marcher
de façon mal assurée

unstoppable *adj* ⟨*force, momentum*⟩
irrésistible; ⟨*athlete, leader*⟩ imbattable

unstuck *adj* **to come ∼** ⟨*stamp*⟩ se
décoller; ⟨*person*⟩ connaître un échec

unsubstantiated *adj* non corroboré/-e

unsuccessful *adj* **(a)** ⟨*attempt,
campaign*⟩ infructueux/-euse; ⟨*novel, film*⟩
sans succès; ⟨*effort, search*⟩ vain/-e; **to be ∼**
⟨*attempt*⟩ échouer
(b) ⟨*candidate*⟩ (for job) malchanceux/-euse; (in
election) malheureux/-euse; ⟨*businessperson*⟩
malchanceux/-euse; ⟨*artist*⟩ inconnu/-e; **to be
∼ in doing** ne pas réussir à faire

unsuccessfully *adv* ⟨*try*⟩ en vain;
⟨*challenge, bid*⟩ sans succès

unsuitable *adj* ⟨*location, clothing,
accommodation, time*⟩ inapproprié/-e;
⟨*moment*⟩ inopportun/-e; **to be ∼** ne pas
convenir (**for sb** à qn); **to be ∼ for a job** ne
pas convenir pour un travail

unsupervised *adj* ⟨*activity*⟩ non
encadré/-e; ⟨*child*⟩ laissé/-e sans surveillance

unsure *adj* peu sûr/-e (**of** de); **to be ∼
about how/why/where** ne pas savoir très
bien comment/pourquoi/où; **to be ∼ of
oneself** manquer de confiance en soi

unsuspecting *adj* ⟨*person*⟩ naïf/-ïve;
⟨*public*⟩ non averti/-e

unsweetened *adj* sans sucre, non
sucré/-e

unsympathetic *adj* **(a)** (uncaring) ⟨*person,
attitude, tone*⟩ peu compatissant/-e
(b) (unattractive) ⟨*person, character*⟩
antipathique

untaxed *adj* ⟨*goods*⟩ non taxé/-e; ⟨*car*⟩ sans
vignette

untenable *adj* ⟨*position*⟩ intenable; ⟨*claim,
argument*⟩ indéfendable

unthinkable *adj* impensable

untidily *adv* ⟨*scattered, strewn*⟩ en
désordre; **∼ dressed** habillé/-e de façon
débraillée

untidy *adj* ⟨*person*⟩ (in habits) désordonné/-e;
(in appearance) peu soigné/-e; ⟨*habits, clothes*⟩
négligé/-e; ⟨*room*⟩ en désordre

untie *vtr* défaire, dénouer ⟨*knot, rope, laces*⟩;
défaire ⟨*parcel*⟩; délier ⟨*hands, hostage*⟩

until (*also* **till**)

■ **Note** When used as a preposition in positive
sentences, *until* is translated by *jusqu'à*: *they're
staying until Monday* = ils restent jusqu'à lundi.
– Remember that *jusqu'à* + *le* becomes *jusqu'au*
and *jusqu'à* + *les* becomes *jusqu'aux*: *until the
right moment* = jusqu'au bon moment; *until the
exams* = jusqu'aux examens.
– In negative sentences, *not until* is translated
by *ne...pas avant*: *I can't see you until Friday* =
je ne peux pas vous voir avant vendredi.
– When used as a conjunction in positive
sentences, *until* is translated by *jusqu'à ce que* +

subjunctive: *we'll stay here until Maya comes
back* = nous resterons ici jusqu'à ce que Maya
revienne.
– In negative sentences where the two verbs
have different subjects, *not until* is translated by
ne...pas avant que + *subjunctive*: *we won't leave
until Maya comes back* = nous ne partirons pas
avant que Maya revienne.
– In negative sentences where the two verbs
have the same subject, *not until* is translated by
pas avant de + *infinitive*: *we won't leave until
we've seen Claire* = nous ne partirons pas avant
d'avoir vu Claire.
– For more examples and particular usages, see
the entry below.

1 *prep* jusqu'à; (after negative verb) avant; **∼
Tuesday** jusqu'à mardi; **∼ the sixties**
jusqu'aux années soixante; **∼ now** jusqu'à
présent; **∼ then** jusqu'à ce moment-là,
jusque-là; (up) **∼ 1901** jusqu'en *or* jusqu'à
1901; **valid (up) ∼ April 2006** valable jusqu'en
avril 2006; **to work from Monday ∼ Saturday**
travailler du lundi au samedi
2 *conj* jusqu'à ce que (+ *subjunctive*); (in
negative constructions) avant que (+ *subjunctive*),
avant de (+ *infinitive*); **we'll stay ∼ a solution
is reached** nous resterons jusqu'à ce que
nous trouvions une solution; **let's watch TV
∼ he's ready** regardons la télévision en
attendant qu'il soit prêt; **I'll wait ∼ I get back**
j'attendrai d'être rentré (**before doing** pour
faire); **she waited ∼ they were alone** elle a
attendu qu'ils soient seuls

untimely *adj* ⟨*arrival, announcement*⟩
inopportun/-e; ⟨*death*⟩ prématuré/-e

untold *adj* (not quantifiable); **∼ millions** des
millions et des millions; **∼ damage**
d'énormes dégâts; (endless) ⟨*misery, joy*⟩
indicible

untrained *adj* ⟨*worker*⟩ sans formation;
⟨*eye*⟩ inexercé/-e; **to be ∼** n'avoir aucune
formation

untranslatable *adj* intraduisible (**into**
en)

untroubled *adj* ⟨*face, life*⟩ paisible; **to be
∼** (by news) ne pas être troublé/-e (**by** par)

untrue *adj* faux/fausse

untrustworthy *adj* ⟨*information*⟩
douteux/-euse; ⟨*person*⟩ indigne de confiance

unused¹ *adj* **to be ∼ to sth/to doing** ne pas
être habitué/-e à qch/à faire

unused² *adj* ⟨*machine, building*⟩
inutilisé/-e; ⟨*stamp*⟩ neuf/neuve

unusual *adj* ⟨*colour, animal, flower*⟩ peu
commun/-e; ⟨*feature, occurrence, skill*⟩ peu
commun/-e, inhabituel/-elle; ⟨*dish, dress,
person*⟩ original/-e; **it is ∼ to find/see** il est
rare de trouver/voir; **there's nothing ∼
about it** cela n'a rien d'extraordinaire

unusually *adv* exceptionnellement

unwanted *adj* ⟨*goods, produce*⟩
superflu/-e; ⟨*pet*⟩ abandonné/-e; ⟨*visitor*⟩
indésirable; ⟨*child*⟩ non souhaité/-e; **to feel ∼**
se sentir de trop

unwarranted *adj* injustifié/-e

unwary *n* the ∼ les imprudents *mpl*

unwelcome *adj* ⟨visitor, interruption⟩ importun/-e; ⟨news⟩ fâcheux/-euse

unwell *adj* souffrant/-e; **he is feeling** ∼ il ne se sent pas très bien

unwilling *adj* ⟨attention, departure⟩ forcé/-e; **he is** ∼ **to do it** il n'est pas disposé à le faire; (stronger) il ne veut pas le faire

unwillingness *n* réticence *f* (**to do** à faire)

unwind **1** *vtr* dérouler ⟨cable, bandage, scarf⟩

2 *vi* (a) ⟨tape, cable, scarf⟩ se dérouler
(b) (relax) se relaxer

unwise *adj* ⟨choice, loan, decision⟩ peu judicieux/-ieuse; ⟨person⟩ imprudent/-e

unwisely *adv* imprudemment

unwittingly *adv* (innocently) innocemment; (without wanting to) involontairement

unworthy *adj* indigne (**of** de)

unwrap *vtr* déballer ⟨parcel⟩

unwritten *adj* ⟨rule, agreement⟩ tacite

unzip *vtr* (a) (open) défaire la fermeture à glissière de ⟨garment, bag⟩
(b) (Comput) dézipper, décomprimer

up **1** *adj* (a) (out of bed) **she's** ∼ elle est levée; **we were** ∼ **very late last night** nous nous sommes couchés très tard hier soir; **they were** ∼ **all night** ils ont veillé toute la nuit; **I was still** ∼ **at 2 am** j'étais toujours debout à 2 heures du matin
(b) (higher in amount, level) **sales are** ∼ **(by 10%)** les ventes ont augmenté (de 10%); **numbers of students are** ∼ le nombre d'étudiants est en hausse
(c) (colloq) (wrong) **what's** ∼? qu'est-ce qui se passe?; **what's** ∼ **with him?** qu'est-ce qu'il a?
(d) (erected, affixed) **the notice is** ∼ **on the board** l'annonce est affichée sur le panneau; **is the tent** ∼? est-ce que la tente est déjà montée?; **he had his hand** ∼ **for five minutes** il a gardé la main levée pendant cinq minutes
(e) (open) **the blinds were** ∼ les stores étaient levés; **when the lever is** ∼ **the machine is off** si le levier est vers le haut la machine est arrêtée
(f) (finished) **'time's** ∼**!'** 'c'est l'heure!'; **when the four days were** ∼ à la fin des quatre jours
(g) (facing upwards) **'this side** ∼**'** 'haut'; **she was floating face** ∼ elle flottait sur le dos
(h) (pinned up) **her hair was** ∼ elle avait les cheveux relevés

2 *adv* (a) ∼ **here/there** là-haut; ∼ **on the wardrobe** sur l'armoire; ∼ **in the tree/the clouds** dans l'arbre/les nuages; ∼ **in London** à Londres; ∼ **to/in Scotland** en Écosse; ∼ **North** au Nord; **four floors** ∼ **from here** quatre étages au-dessus; **on the second shelf** ∼ sur la deuxième étagère en partant du bas
(b) (ahead) d'avance; **to be four points** ∼ **(on sb)** avoir quatre points d'avance (sur qn)

(c) (upwards) **T-shirts from £2** ∼ des T-shirts à partir de deux livres

3 *prep* ∼ **the tree** dans l'arbre; **the library is** ∼ **the stairs** la bibliothèque se trouve en haut de l'escalier; **he ran** ∼ **the stairs** il a monté l'escalier en courant; **he lives just** ∼ **the road** il habite juste à côté; **to walk/drive** ∼ **the road** remonter la rue; **he put it** ∼ **his sleeve** il l'a mis dans sa manche

4 **up above** *phr* au-dessus; ∼ **above sth** au-dessus de qch

5 **up against** *phr* contre ⟨wall⟩; **to come** ∼ **against** rencontrer ⟨opposition⟩

6 **up and about** *phr* debout; **to be** ∼ **and about again** être de nouveau sur pied

7 **up and down** *phr* (a) (to and fro) **to walk** ∼ **and down** aller et venir, faire les cent pas
(b) (throughout) ∼ **and down the country** dans tout le pays

8 **up to** *phr* (a) (to particular level) jusqu'à; ∼ **to here/there** jusqu'ici/jusque là
(b) (as many as) jusqu'à, près de; ∼ **to 20 people/50 dollars** jusqu'à 20 personnes/50 dollars
(c) (until) jusqu'à; ∼ **to 1964** jusqu'en 1964; ∼ **to 10.30 pm** jusqu'à 22 h 30; ∼ **to now** jusqu'à maintenant
(d) **I'm not** ∼ **to it** (not capable) je n'en suis pas capable; (not well enough) je n'en ai pas la force; (can't face it) je n'en ai pas le courage
(e) **it's** ∼ **to him to do** c'est à lui de faire; **it's** ∼ **to you!** c'est à toi de décider!
(f) (doing) **what is he** ∼ **to?** qu'est-ce qu'il fait?; **they're** ∼ **to something** ils mijotent quelque chose (colloq)
IDIOMS **to be one** ∼ **on sb** faire mieux que qn; **to be (well)** ∼ **on** s'y connaître en ⟨art, history⟩; être au courant de ⟨news⟩; **the** ∼**s and downs** les hauts et les bas (**of** de)

up and coming *adj* prometteur/-euse

upbeat *adj* optimiste

upbringing *n* éducation *f*

update *vtr* (a) (revise) mettre *or* remettre [qch] à jour ⟨database, information⟩; actualiser ⟨price, value⟩
(b) (modernize) moderniser
(c) (inform) mettre [qn] au courant (**on** de)

upfront *adj* (colloq) (a) (frank) franc/franche
(b) ⟨money⟩ payé/-e d'avance

upgrade **1** *n* (new version) nouvelle version *f*, mise *f* à jour; (in tourism) surclassement *m*
2 *vtr* (a) (modernize) moderniser; (improve) améliorer
(b) (Comput) améliorer ⟨software, hardware⟩
(c) (raise) promouvoir ⟨person⟩; revaloriser ⟨job⟩

upheaval *n* (a) (disturbance) bouleversement *m*
(b) (instability) (political, emotional) bouleversements *mpl*; (physical) remue-ménage *m inv*

uphill **1** *adj* (a) ⟨road⟩ qui monte; ∼ **slope** côte *f*, montée *f*
(b) ⟨task⟩ difficile
2 *adv* **to go/walk** ∼ monter

uphold vtr soutenir ⟨right⟩; faire respecter ⟨law⟩; confirmer ⟨decision⟩

upholstery n (a) (covering) revêtement m (b) (stuffing) rembourrage m

upkeep n (a) (of property) entretien m (of de) (b) (cost) frais mpl d'entretien

uplifting adj tonique

upload vtr to ~ sth to a server télécharger qch vers un serveur

upmarket adj ⟨car, hotel⟩ haut de gamme; ⟨area⟩ riche

upon prep (a) (on) sur (b) (linking two nouns) thousands ~ thousands of people des milliers et des milliers de personnes

upper ① n (of shoe) empeigne f ② adj (a) ⟨shelf, cupboard⟩ du haut; ⟨floor, deck, lip⟩ supérieur/-e; ⟨teeth⟩ du haut (b) (in rank, scale) supérieur/-e (c) the ~ limit la limite maximale (on de) IDIOMS to have/get the ~ hand avoir/ prendre le dessus

upper case adj ~ letters (lettres fpl) majuscules fpl

upper class n (pl ~es) the ~, the ~es l'aristocratie f et la haute bourgeoisie

uppermost adj (a) (highest) ⟨branch⟩ le plus haut/la plus haute; (in rank) ⟨echelon⟩ le plus élevé/la plus élevée (b) to be ~ in sb's mind être au premier plan des préoccupations de qn

upper sixth n (GB) (Sch) ≈ (classe f) terminale f

upright ① adj (a) (physically) droit/-e; to stay ~ ⟨person⟩ rester debout (b) (morally) droit/-e ② adv to stand ~ se tenir droit; to sit ~ (action) se redresser

uprising n soulèvement m (against contre)

uproar n (noise) tumulte m; (protest) protestations fpl

uproot vtr déraciner

upset ① n (a) (surprise, setback) revers m (b) (upheaval) bouleversement m (c) (distress) peine f (d) to have a stomach ~ avoir l'estomac détraqué ② adj to be or feel ~ (distressed) être très affecté/-e; (annoyed) être contrarié/-e; to get ~ (angry) se fâcher (about pour); (distressed) se tracasser (about pour) ③ vtr (a) (distress) ⟨sight, news⟩ bouleverser; ⟨person⟩ faire de la peine à (b) (annoy) contrarier (c) bouleverser ⟨plan⟩; déjouer ⟨calculations⟩ (d) (destabilize) rompre ⟨balance⟩ (e) (Med) rendre [qn] malade ⟨person⟩; perturber ⟨digestion⟩

upsetting adj (distressing) navrant/-e; (annoying) contrariant/-e

upside down ① adj à l'envers ② adv à l'envers; to turn the house ~ mettre la maison sens dessus dessous

upstage vtr éclipser

upstairs ① n haut m ② adj ⟨room⟩ du haut; an ~ bedroom une chambre à l'étage ③ adv en haut; to go ~ monter (l'escalier)

upstart n, adj arriviste (mf)

upstream adv ⟨travel⟩ vers l'amont; ~ from here en amont d'ici

uptake n IDIOMS to be quick/slow on the ~ (colloq) comprendre/ne pas comprendre vite

uptight adj (colloq) (a) (tense) tendu/-e (b) (inhibited) coincé/-e (colloq)

up-to-date adj (a) ⟨music, clothes⟩ à la mode; ⟨equipment⟩ moderne (b) ⟨records, timetable⟩ à jour; ⟨information⟩ récent/-e (c) (informed) ⟨person⟩ au courant (with de)

up-to-the-minute adj ⟨information⟩ dernier/-ière

upward ① adj ⟨push, movement⟩ vers le haut; ⟨path, road⟩ qui monte; ⟨trend⟩ à la hausse ② adv (also **upwards**) ⟨look, point⟩ vers le haut; to go or move ~ monter; from £10 ~ à partir de 10 livres sterling

upwardly mobile adj en pleine ascension sociale

upwards = UPWARD 2

uranium n uranium m

Uranus pr n Uranus f

urban adj urbain/-e

urban planning n urbanisme m

urban sprawl n mitage m

urchin n gamin m

Urdu n urdu m

urge ① n forte envie f, désir m (to do de faire) ② vtr conseiller vivement, préconiser ⟨caution, restraint, resistance⟩; to ~ sb to do conseiller vivement à qn de faire; (stronger) pousser qn à faire

urgency n (of situation, appeal, request) urgence f; (of voice, tone) insistance f; a matter of ~ une affaire urgente

urgent adj (a) (pressing) ⟨case, need⟩ urgent/-e, pressant/-e; ⟨message, demand⟩ urgent/-e; ⟨meeting, measures⟩ d'urgence (b) ⟨request, tone⟩ insistant/-e

urgently adv ⟨request⟩ d'urgence; ⟨plead⟩ instamment

urinal n (place) urinoir m; (fixture) urinal m

urinate vi uriner

urine n urine f

URL n (abbr = **Unified Resource Locator**) adresse f URL

urn n urne f

us pron nous; she knows ~ elle nous connaît; both of ~ tous/toutes les deux; every single one of ~ chacun/-e d'entre nous; some of ~ quelques-uns/-unes d'entre nous; she's one of ~ elle est des nôtres

US pr n (abbr = **United States**) USA mpl

USA *pr n* (*abbr* = **United States of America**) USA *mpl*

use ① *n* (a) (act of using) (of substance, object, machine) emploi *m*, utilisation *f* (of de); (of word, expression) emploi *m*, usage *m* (of de); **for the ~** of à l'usage de ⟨*customer, staff*⟩; **for my own ~** pour mon usage personnel; **to make ~ of sth** utiliser qch; **to put sth to good ~** tirer parti de qch; **while the machine is in ~** lorsque la machine est en service *or* en fonctionnement; **to have the ~ of** avoir l'usage de ⟨*house, car, kitchen*⟩; avoir la jouissance de ⟨*garden*⟩; **to lose the ~ of one's legs** perdre l'usage de ses jambes (b) (way of using) (of resource, object, material) utilisation *f*; (of term) emploi *m*; **to have no further ~ for sb/sth** ne plus avoir besoin de qn/qch (c) (usefulness) **to be of ~** être utile (to à); **to be (of) no ~** ⟨*object*⟩ ne servir à rien; ⟨*person*⟩ n'être bon/bonne à rien; **what's the ~ of crying?** à quoi bon pleurer?; **it's no ~ (he won't listen)** c'est inutile (il n'écoutera pas)
② *vtr* (a) se servir de, utiliser ⟨*object, car, room, money*⟩; employer ⟨*method, word*⟩; profiter de, saisir ⟨*opportunity*⟩; faire jouer ⟨*influence*⟩; avoir recours à ⟨*blackmail*⟩; utiliser ⟨*knowledge, talent*⟩; **to ~ sb/sth as** se servir de qn/qch comme; **to ~ sth to do** se servir de qch pour faire (b) (consume) consommer ⟨*fuel, food*⟩; utiliser ⟨*water, leftovers*⟩ (c) (exploit) se servir de ⟨*person*⟩
③ **used** *pp adj* ⟨*car*⟩ d'occasion; ⟨*envelope*⟩ qui a déjà servi
■ **use up** finir ⟨*food*⟩; dépenser ⟨*money*⟩; épuiser ⟨*supplies*⟩

used
■ **Note** To translate *used to do*, use the imperfect tense in French: *he used to live in York* = il habitait York.
– To emphasize a contrast between past and present, you can use *avant*: *I used to love sport* = avant, j'adorais le sport.

① *modal aux* **I ~ to read a lot** je lisais beaucoup; **she ~ to smoke, didn't she?** elle fumait avant, non?; **she doesn't smoke now, but she ~ to** elle ne fume plus maintenant, mais elle fumait avant; **there ~ to be a pub here** il y avait un pub ici (dans le temps)
② *adj* **to be ~ to sth** avoir l'habitude de qch, être habitué/-e à qch; **to get ~ to** s'habituer à; **I'm not ~ to it** je n'ai pas l'habitude; **you'll get ~ to it** tu t'y habitueras

useful *adj* utile

useless *adj* (a) (not helpful) inutile (b) (not able to be used) inutilisable (c) (colloq) (incompetent) incapable, nul/nulle (colloq)

user *n* (of public service) usager *m*; (of product, machine) utilisateur/-trice *m/f*

user-friendly *adj* (Comput) convivial/-e; (gen) facile à utiliser

user group *n* groupe *m* d'utilisateurs

usher *vtr* conduire, escorter; **to ~ sb in/out** faire entrer/sortir qn

usherette *n* ouvreuse *f*

USSR *pr n* (*abbr* = **Union of Soviet Socialist Republics**) URSS *f*

usual *adj* (gen) habituel/-elle; ⟨*word, term*⟩ usuel/-elle; **it is ~ for sb to do** c'est normal pour qn de faire; **it is ~ to do** il est d'usage de faire; **as ~** comme d'habitude; **more/less than ~** plus/moins que d'habitude

usually *adv* d'habitude, normalement

utensil *n* ustensile *m*

uterus *n* utérus *m*

utility ① *n* (a) (usefulness) utilité *f* (b) (*also* **public ~**) (service) service *m* public
② **utilities** *n pl* (US) factures *fpl*

utility company *n* société *f* chargée d'assurer un service public

utmost ① *n* **to do** *or* **try one's ~ to do** faire tout son possible pour faire; **to the ~ of one's abilities** au maximum de ses capacités
② *adj* ⟨*caution, ease, secrecy*⟩ le plus grand/la plus grande (*before n*); ⟨*limit*⟩ extrême; **it is of the ~ importance that** il est extrêmement important que (+ *subjunctive*)

Utopia *n* utopie *f*

utter ① *adj* ⟨*disaster, boredom, despair*⟩ total/-e; ⟨*honesty, sincerity*⟩ absolu/-e; ⟨*fool, stranger*⟩ parfait/-e (*before n*)
② *vtr* prononcer ⟨*word, curse*⟩; pousser ⟨*cry*⟩; émettre ⟨*sound*⟩

utterly *adv* complètement; ⟨*condemn*⟩ avec vigueur

U-turn *n* demi-tour *m*; (figurative) volte-face *f inv*

UV *adj* (*abbr* = **ultraviolet**) ⟨*light, ray, radiation*⟩ ultraviolet/-ette

Vv

v, V *n* **(a)** (letter) v, V *m*
(b) v (*abbr* = **versus**) contre
vacancy *n* **(a)** (room) 'vacancies' 'chambres
libres'; 'no vacancies' 'complet'
(b) (unfilled job) poste *m* à pourvoir, poste *m*
vacant
vacant *adj* **(a)** ⟨*flat, room, seat*⟩ libre,
disponible; ⟨*office, land*⟩ inoccupé/-e
(b) ⟨*job, post*⟩ vacant/-e, à pourvoir
(c) ⟨*look, stare*⟩ absent/-e; ⟨*expression*⟩ vide
vacant possession *n* jouissance *f*
immédiate
vacate *vtr* quitter ⟨*house, premises, job*⟩
vacation *n* vacances *fpl*; **on** ∼ en vacances
vacationer *n* (US) vacancier/-ière *m/f*
vaccinate *vtr* vacciner (**against** contre)
vaccination *n* vaccination *f* (**against**
contre)
vaccine *n* vaccin *m* (**against** contre)
vacillate *vi* hésiter
vacuum ⏹1 *n* **(a)** (gen) vide *m*
(b) (*also* ∼ **cleaner**) aspirateur *m*
⏹2 *vtr* passer [qch] à l'aspirateur ⟨*carpet*⟩;
passer l'aspirateur dans ⟨*room*⟩
vacuum pack *vtr* emballer [qch] sous
vide
vagrant *n, adj* vagabond/-e (*m/f*)
vague *adj* **(a)** (gen) vague; **to be** ∼ **about**
rester vague sur *or* évasif/-ive au sujet de
⟨*plans, past*⟩
(b) (distracted) ⟨*person, expression*⟩ distrait/-e
vaguely *adv* **(a)** (gen) vaguement
(b) (distractedly) ⟨*smile, gaze*⟩ d'un air distrait
or vague
vain ⏹1 *adj* **(a)** (conceited) vaniteux/-euse,
vain/-e (*after n*)
(b) (futile) ⟨*attempt, promise, hope*⟩ vain/-e
(*before n*)
⏹2 **in vain** *phr* en vain
valentine card *n* carte *f* de la
Saint-Valentin
Valentine('s) Day *n* la Saint-Valentin
valet *n* **(a)** (employee) valet *m* de chambre
(b) (US) (rack) valet *m* de nuit
valet parking *n* service *m* de voiturier
valiant *adj* ⟨*soldier*⟩ vaillant/-e; ⟨*attempt*⟩
courageux/-euse
valid *adj* **(a)** ⟨*passport, licence*⟩ valide;
⟨*ticket, offer*⟩ valable (**for** pour)
(b) ⟨*argument, excuse*⟩ valable; ⟨*complaint*⟩
fondé/-e; ⟨*point, comment*⟩ pertinent/-e
validate *vtr* **(a)** prouver le bien-fondé de
⟨*claim, theory*⟩
(b) valider ⟨*document, passport*⟩
valley *n* vallée *f*; (small) vallon *m*
valour (GB), **valor** (US) *n* bravoure *f*

valuable *adj* **(a)** ⟨*object, asset*⟩ de valeur;
to be ∼ avoir de la valeur; **a very** ∼ **ring** une
bague de grande valeur
(b) ⟨*advice, information, lesson, member*⟩
précieux/-ieuse
valuables *n pl* objets *mpl* de valeur
valuation *n* (of house, land, company)
évaluation *f*; (of antique, art) expertise *f*; **to
have a** ∼ **done on sth** faire évaluer qch
value ⏹1 *n* valeur *f*; **novelty** ∼ caractère
nouveau; **to be good** ∼ avoir un bon rapport
qualité-prix; **to get** ∼ **for money** en avoir
pour son argent
⏹2 *vtr* **(a)** évaluer ⟨*house, asset, company*⟩ (**at**
à); expertiser ⟨*antique, jewel, painting*⟩
(b) (appreciate) apprécier ⟨*person, friendship,
opinion, help*⟩; tenir à ⟨*independence, life*⟩
value pack *n* lot *m* économique
valve *n* **(a)** (in machine, engine) soupape *f*; (on
tyre, football) valve *f*
(b) (Anat) valvule *f*
van *n* **(a)** (small, for deliveries) fourgonnette *f*,
camionnette *f*; (larger, for removals) fourgon *m*
(b) (US) (camper) auto-caravane *f*,
camping-car *m*
vandal *n* vandale *mf*
vandalism *n* vandalisme *m*
vandalize *vtr* vandaliser
van driver *n* chauffeur *m* de camionnette
vanguard *n* avant-garde *f*; **in the** ∼ à
l'avant-garde
vanilla *n* vanille *f*
vanish *vi* disparaître (**from** de); **to** ∼ **into
thin air** se volatiliser
vanity *n* vanité *f*
vantage point *n* point *m* de vue, position
f élevée
vaporizer *n* vaporisateur *m*
vapour (GB), **vapor** (US) *n* vapeur *f*
vapour trail *n* traînée *f* de condensation,
traînée *f* d'avion
variable *n, adj* variable (*f*)
variance *n* **to be at** ∼ **with** ne pas
concorder avec ⟨*evidence, facts*⟩
variant *n* variante *f* (**of** de; **on** par rapport
à)
variation *n* **(a)** (change) variation *f*,
différence *f* (**in, of** de)
(b) (new version) variante *f* (**of** de); (in music)
variation *f* (**on** sur)
varied *adj* varié/-e
variety *n* **(a)** (diversity, range) variété *f* (**in, of**
de); **for a** ∼ **of reasons** pour diverses
raisons; **a** ∼ **of sizes/colours** un grand choix
de tailles/de coloris
(b) (type) type *m*; (of plant) variété *f*

variety show *n* spectacle de variétés

various *adj* (a) (different) différents/-es (*before n*)
(b) (several) divers/-es

varnish ① *n* vernis *m*
② *vtr* vernir ‹*woodwork*›; **to ~ one's nails** se vernir les ongles

vary ① *vtr* varier ‹*menu, programme*›; faire varier ‹*temperature*›; changer de ‹*method, pace, route*›
② *vi* varier (**with, according to** selon); **it varies from one town to another** cela varie d'une ville à l'autre

varying *adj* variable

vase *n* vase *m*; **flower ~** vase à fleurs

vast *adj* (a) ‹*amount, sum, improvement, difference*› énorme; **the ~ majority** la très grande majorité
(b) ‹*room, area, plain*› vaste (*before n*), immense

vat *n* cuve *f*; **beer/wine ~** cuve à bière/vin

VAT *n* (GB) (*abbr* = **value-added tax**) TVA *f*, taxe *f* à la valeur ajoutée

Vatican *pr n* Vatican *m*; **~ City** cité *f* du Vatican

vault ① *n* (a) (roof) voûte *f*
(b) (*also* **~s**) (of house, for wine) cave *f*; (of bank) chambre *f* forte; (for safe-deposit boxes) salle *f* des coffres
② *vtr* sauter par-dessus ‹*fence, bar*›
③ *vi* sauter (**over** par-dessus)

VCR *n* (*abbr* = **video cassette recorder**) magnétoscope *m*

VD *n* (*abbr* = **venereal disease**) MST *f*

VDU *n* (*abbr* = **visual display unit**) écran *m* de visualisation

veal *n* veau *m*

veer *vi* ‹*ship*› virer; (*also* **~ off**) ‹*person, road*› tourner; **to ~ off course** dévier de sa route

vegan *n, adj* végétalien/-ienne (*m/f*)

veganism *n* végétalisme *m*

vegeburger® ▶ VEGGIE BURGER

vegetable ① *n* légume *m*
② *adj* ‹*soup, patch*› de légumes; ‹*fat, oil*› végétal/-e; **~ garden** potager *m*

vegetarian *n, adj* végétarien/-ienne (*m/f*)

vegetarianism *n* végétarisme *m*

vegetate *vi* végéter

vegetation *n* végétation *f*

veggie burger *n* croquette *f* pour végétariens

vehement *adj* véhément/-e

vehicle *n* véhicule *m*

veil ① *n* (gen, figurative) voile *m*; (on hat) voilette *f*
② *vtr* ‹*mist, cloud*› voiler

veiled *adj* voilé/-e

vein *n* (blood vessel) veine *f*; (on insect wing, leaf) nervure *f*; (in cheese) veinure *f*; (of ore) veine *f*

velocity *n* vélocité *f*

velour(s) *n* velours *m*

velvet *n* velours *m*; **crushed ~** velours frappé

velvety *adj* velouté/-e

vending machine *n* distributeur *m* automatique

vendor *n* (a) (in street, kiosk) marchand/-e *m/f*
(b) (as opposed to buyer) vendeur/-euse *m/f*

veneer *n* placage *m*; (figurative) vernis *m*

venereal disease *n* maladie *f* vénérienne

venetian blind *n* store *m* vénitien

Venezuela *pr n* Venezuela *m*

vengeance *n* vengeance *f*; **with a ~** de plus belle

Venice *pr n* Venise

venison *n* (viande *f* de) chevreuil *m*

venom *n* venim *m*

venomous *adj* venimeux/-euse

vent ① *n* (outlet for gas, pressure) bouche *f*, conduit *m*; **air ~** bouche d'aération; **to give ~ to** décharger ‹*anger, feelings*›
② *vtr* décharger ‹*anger, frustration*› (**on** sur)

ventilate *vtr* aérer ‹*room*›

ventilation *n* (a) (gen) aération *f*, ventilation *f*
(b) (of patient) ventilation *f* artificielle

ventilator *n* (for patient) respirateur *m* artificiel

ventriloquist *n* ventriloque *mf*

venture ① *n* (a) (undertaking) aventure *f*, entreprise *f*; **a commercial ~** une entreprise commerciale
(b) (experiment) essai *m*
② *vtr* hasarder ‹*opinion, suggestion*›; **to ~ to do** se risquer à faire
③ *vi* **to ~ into** s'aventurer dans ‹*place, street, city*›; **to ~ out(doors)** s'aventurer dehors

venture capital *n* capital-risque *m*

venue *n* lieu *m*

Venus *pr n* Vénus *f*

verb *n* verbe *m*

verbal *adj* verbal/-e

verbatim ① *adj* ‹*report, account*› textuel/-elle
② *adv* ‹*describe, record*› mot pour mot

verbose *adj* verbeux/-euse

verdict *n* (a) (Law) verdict *m*; **a ~ of guilty/not guilty** un verdict positif/négatif
(b) (figurative) (opinion) verdict *m*; **well, what's the ~?** (colloq) eh bien, qu'est-ce que tu en penses?

verge *n* (a) (GB) (by road) accotement *m*, bas-côté *m*
(b) (brink) **on the ~ of** au bord de ‹*tears*›; au seuil de ‹*adolescence, death*›; **on the ~ of doing** sur le point de faire
■ **verge on** friser ‹*panic, stupidity, contempt*›

verification *n* vérification *f*

verify *vtr* vérifier

V

vermicelli *n* vermicelles *mpl*

vermilion *n, adj* vermillon (*m*) *inv*

vermin *n* (a) (rodents) animaux *mpl* nuisibles

(b) (lice, insects) vermine *f*

verruca *n* verrue *f* plantaire

versatile *adj* (a) ⟨person⟩ plein/-e de ressources, aux talents divers (*after n*); ⟨mind⟩ souple

(b) ⟨vehicle⟩ polyvalent/-e; ⟨equipment⟩ à usages multiples

verse *n* (a) (poems) poésie *f*

(b) (form) vers *mpl*; **in ~** en vers

(c) (part of poem) strophe *f*; (of song) couplet *m*

version *n* version *f* (**of** de)

versus *prep* contre

vertebra *n* vertèbre *f*

vertebrate *n* vertébré *m*

vertical *adj* vertical/-e; **a ~ drop** un à-pic

vertigo *n* vertige *m*; **to get ~** avoir le vertige

verve *n* brio *m*, verve *f*

very ① *adj* (a) (actual) même (*after n*); **this ~ second** immédiatement

(b) (ideal) **the ~ person I need** exactement la personne qu'il me faut

(c) (ultimate) tout/-e; **from the ~ beginning** depuis le tout début; **at the ~ front** tout devant; **on the ~ edge** à l'extrême bord

(d) (mere) ⟨mention, thought, word⟩ seul/-e (*before n*); **the ~ idea!** quelle idée!

② *adv* (a) (extremely) très; **I'm ~ sorry** je suis vraiment désolé; **~ well** très bien; **that's all ~ well but who's going to pay for it?** c'est bien beau, tout ça, mais qui va payer?; **~ much** beaucoup; **I didn't eat ~ much** je n'ai pas mangé grand-chose

(b) (absolutely) **the ~ best/worst thing** de loin la meilleure/pire chose; **at the ~ latest** au plus tard; **at the ~ least** tout au moins; **the ~ next day** le lendemain même; **a car of your ~ own** ta propre voiture

vessel *n* (a) (ship) vaisseau *m*

(b) (Anat) **blood ~** vaisseau *m* sanguin

(c) (container) vase *m*

vest *n* (a) (underwear) maillot *m* de corps

(b) (for sport, fashion) débardeur *m*

(c) (US) (waistcoat) gilet *m*

vested interest *n* **to have a ~** être personnellement intéressé/-e (**in** dans)

vestige *n* vestige *m*

vet ① *n* (a) (*abbr* = **veterinary surgeon**) vétérinaire *mf*

(b) (US) (colloq) (Mil) ancien combattant *m*, vétéran *m*

② *vtr* mener une enquête approfondie sur ⟨person⟩; passer [qch] en revue ⟨plan⟩; approuver ⟨publication⟩

veteran ① *n* vétéran *m*

② *adj* ⟨sportsman, politician⟩ chevronné/-e

veterinarian *n* (US) vétérinaire *mf*

veterinary surgeon *n* vétérinaire *mf*

veterinary surgery *n* clinique *f* vétérinaire

veto ① *n* (a) (practice) veto *m*

(b) (right) droit *m* de veto (**over, on** sur)

② *vtr* mettre *or* opposer son veto à

vetting *n* contrôle *m*

vex *vtr* (annoy) contrarier; (worry) tracasser

vexed *adj* (a) (annoyed) mécontent/-e (**with** de)

(b) ⟨question, issue⟩ épineux/-euse

VHF *n* (*abbr* = **very high frequency**) VHF

via *prep* (a) (by way of) (on ticket, timetable) via; (other contexts) en passant par; **we came ~ Paris** nous sommes venus en passant par Paris

(b) (by means of) par

viability *n* (of company) viabilité *f*; (of project, idea) validité *f*

viable *adj* ⟨company, government, farm⟩ viable; ⟨project, idea, plan⟩ réalisable, valable

viaduct *n* viaduc *m*

vibrant *adj* ⟨person, place, personality⟩ plein/-e de vie; ⟨colour⟩ éclatant/-e

vibrate *vi* vibrer (**with** de)

vibration *n* vibration *f*

vicar *n* pasteur *m*

vicarage *n* presbytère *m*

vicarious *adj* ⟨pleasure⟩ indirect/-e

vice *n* (a) vice *m*; (amusing weakness) faiblesse *f*

(b) (*also* **vise** (US)) (tool) étau *m*

vice-captain *n* capitaine *m* en second

vice-chancellor *n* président/-e *m/f* d'Université

vice-president *n* vice-président/-e *m/f*

vice squad *n* brigade *f* des mœurs

vicinity *n* voisinage *m*; **in the (immediate) ~ of Oxford** à proximité (immédiate) d'Oxford

vicious *adj* ⟨animal⟩ malfaisant/-e; ⟨speech, attack⟩ brutal/-e; ⟨rumour, person, lie⟩ malveillant/-e

vicious circle *n* cercle *m* vicieux

victim *n* victime *f*

victimization *n* persécution *f*

victimize *vtr* persécuter

victor *n* vainqueur *m*

Victorian *adj* victorien/-ienne

victorious *adj* victorieux/-ieuse (**over** sur)

victory *n* victoire *f*

video ① *n* (a) (*also* **~ recorder**) magnétoscope *m*

(b) (*also* **~ cassette**) cassette *f* vidéo; **on ~** en vidéo

(c) (*also* **~ film**) vidéo *f*

② *adj* vidéo (*inv*)

③ *vtr* (a) (from TV) enregistrer [qch]

(b) (on camcorder) filmer [qch] en vidéo

video camera *n* caméra *f* vidéo

video card *n* (Comput) carte *f* vidéo

video clip *n* (from film) extrait *m*; (Mus) clip *m*

videoconference n vidéoconférence f

videoconferencing n vidéoconférence f

videodisc n vidéodisque m

video game n jeu m vidéo

video jock n (colloq) vidéo jockey mf

video nasty n vidéo f représentant des violences véritables

videophone n vidéophone m, visiophone m

video shop (GB), **video store** (US) n vidéoclub m

videotape n bande f vidéo

vie vi rivaliser (**with** avec; **for** pour; **to do** pour faire)

Vienna pr n Vienne

view 1 n (a) (gen) vue f; **in (full)** ∼ **of sb** devant qn or sous les yeux de qn; **to disappear from** ∼ disparaître
(b) (personal opinion, attitude) avis m, opinion f; **point of** ∼ point m de vue; **in his** ∼ à son avis
2 vtr (a) (consider) considérer; (envisage) envisager
(b) (look at) voir ⟨scene, building, collection, exhibition⟩; visiter ⟨house, castle⟩; regarder ⟨programme⟩
(c) (Comput) visualiser
3 **in view of** phr (considering) vu, étant donné
4 **with a view to** phr **with a** ∼ **to doing** en vue de faire, afin de faire

viewer n (a) (of TV) téléspectateur/-trice m/f
(b) (of property) visiteur/-euse m/f
(c) (on camera) visionneuse f

viewfinder n viseur m

viewing 1 n (of exhibition, house) visite f; (of film) projection f; (of new range) présentation f
2 adj ⟨habits, preferences⟩ des téléspectateurs; ∼ **figures** taux m d'écoute

viewpoint n (all contexts) point m de vue

vigil n (gen) veille f; (by sickbed) veillée f; (by demonstrators) manifestation f silencieuse

vigilant adj vigilant/-e

vigilante n membre m d'un groupe d'autodéfense

vigorous adj vigoureux/-euse

vigour (GB), **vigor** (US) n vigueur f

vile adj ⟨smell⟩ infect/-e; ⟨weather⟩ abominable; ⟨place, colour⟩ horrible; ⟨mood⟩ exécrable

villa n (in town) pavillon m; (in country, for holiday) villa f

village n village m

village green n terrain m communal

village hall n salle f des fêtes

villager n villageois/-e m/f

villain n (in book, film) méchant m; (child) coquin/-e m/f; (criminal) bandit m

vindicate vtr justifier

vindictive adj vindicatif/-ive

vindictiveness n esprit m de vengeance

vine n (a) (grapevine) vigne f
(b) (climbing plant) plante f grimpante

vinegar n vinaigre m

vineyard n vignoble m

vintage 1 n (wine) millésime m
2 adj (a) ⟨wine, champagne⟩ millésimé/-e; ⟨port⟩ vieux/vieille
(b) ⟨comedy⟩ classique

vintage car n voiture f d'époque

vinyl 1 n vinyle m
2 adj en vinyle; ⟨paint⟩ vinylique

viola n (violon m) alto m

violate vtr (a) violer ⟨law, agreement, rights⟩
(b) profaner ⟨sacred place⟩; troubler ⟨peace⟩

violation n violation f; **traffic** ∼ infraction f au code de la route

violence n violence f

violent adj (a) ⟨crime, behaviour, film, storm, emotion⟩ violent/-e
(b) ⟨contrast⟩ brutal/-e
(c) ⟨colour⟩ criard/-e

violently adv ⟨attack, react, shake⟩ violemment; ⟨brake, swerve⟩ brusquement

violet 1 n (a) (flower) violette f
(b) (colour) violet m
2 adj violet/-ette

violin n violon m

violinist n violoniste mf

VIP (abbr = **very important person**)
1 n personnalité f (en vue)
2 adj ⟨area, lounge⟩ réservé/-e aux personnalités; ∼ **guest** hôte mf de marque; **to give sb (the)** ∼ **treatment** recevoir qn en hôte de marque

viper n vipère f

virgin n, adj vierge (f)

Virgo n Vierge f

virile adj viril/-e

virtual adj (a) (gen) quasi-total/-e; **he was a** ∼ **prisoner** il était pratiquement prisonnier
(b) (Comput) virtuel/-elle

virtually adv pratiquement, presque; **it's** ∼ **impossible** c'est quasiment (colloq) impossible

virtual reality n réalité f virtuelle

virtue 1 n (a) (goodness) vertu f
(b) (advantage) avantage m
2 **by virtue of** phr en raison de

virtuoso n virtuose mf (**of** de)

virtuous adj vertueux/-euse

virus n virus m

virus checker n logiciel m antivirus

visa n visa m; **tourist** ∼ visa de touriste

vis-à-vis prep (in relation to) par rapport à; (concerning) en ce qui concerne

visibility n visibilité f

visible adj (a) (able to be seen) visible; **clearly** ∼ bien visible
(b) (concrete) ⟨improvement, sign⟩ évident/-e

visibly adv ⟨moved, shocked⟩ manifestement

V

vision n (a) (idea, mental picture, hallucination) vision f
(b) (ability to see) vue f
(c) (foresight) sagacité f

visionary n, adj visionnaire (mf)

visit ☐1 n (gen) visite f; (stay) séjour m; a state ~ une visite officielle; to pay a ~ to sb, to pay sb a ~ aller voir qn; (more formal) rendre visite à qn
☐2 vtr (a) to ~ Paris (see) visiter Paris; (stay) faire un séjour à Paris, aller passer quelques jours à Paris; to ~ sb (call) aller voir qn; (more formal) rendre visite à qn; (stay with) aller (passer quelques jours) chez qn
(b) (US) to ~ with sb aller voir qn

visiting card n (US) carte f de visite

visiting hours n pl heures fpl de visite

visitor n (a) (caller) invité/-e m/f
(b) (tourist) visiteur/-euse m/f

visitor centre n centre m d'accueil et d'information des visiteurs

visitors' book n (in exhibition) livre m d'or; (in hotel) registre m

visor n visière f

vista n panorama m; (figurative) perspective f

visual adj visuel/-elle

visual aid n support m visuel

visual arts n pl arts mpl plastiques

visualize vtr (a) (picture) s'imaginer
(b) (envisage) envisager

visually impaired n the ~ les malvoyants mpl

vital adj (a) (essential) (gen) primordial/-e; (match, point, support, factor) décisif/-ive; (service, help) indispensable; (treatment, organ, force) vital/-e; of ~ importance d'une importance capitale
(b) (person) plein/-e de vie

vitality n vitalité f

vitally adv (important) extrêmement; (needed) absolument

vital statistics n (of woman) mensurations fpl

vitamin n vitamine f

viva ☐1 n oral m
☐2 excl vive!

vivacious adj plein/-e de vivacité

vivid adj (a) (bright) (colour, light) vif/vive
(b) (graphic) (imagination) vif/vive; (memory, picture) (très) net/nette; (dream, impression, description) frappant/-e

vividly adv (describe, illustrate) de façon très vivante; (remember, recall) très bien

vivisection n vivisection f

vixen n (a) (fox) renarde f
(b) (woman) mégère f

viz adv (abbr = **videlicet**) à savoir

V-neck n (a) (neck) encolure f en V
(b) (sweater) pull m en V

vocabulary n vocabulaire m

vocal adj (a) (concerning speech) vocal/-e
(b) (vociferous) (person) qui se fait entendre

vocalist n chanteur/-euse m/f (dans un groupe pop)

vocals n pl chant m; to do the backing ~ faire les chœurs

vocation n vocation f

vocational adj professionnel/-elle

vocational course n stage m de formation professionnelle

vociferous adj (person, protest) véhément/-e

vogue n vogue f (for de)

voice ☐1 n voix f; in a loud ~ à haute voix; in a low ~ à voix basse; in a cross ~ d'une voix irritée; to have lost one's ~ (when ill) être aphone; at the top of one's ~ à tue-tête
☐2 vtr exprimer (concern, grievance)

voicemail n messagerie f vocale

voice-over n voix-off f

voice recognition n reconnaissance f vocale

void ☐1 n vide m; to fill the ~ combler le vide
☐2 adj (a) (Law) (contract, agreement) nul/nulle; (cheque) annulé/-e
(b) (empty) vide; ~ of dépourvu/-e de

volatile adj (situation) explosif/-ive; (person) lunatique; (market, exchange rate) instable

volcano n volcan m

volley ☐1 n (a) (in tennis) volée f
(b) (of gunfire) salve f (of de)
(c) (series) a ~ of un feu roulant de (questions); une bordée de (insults, oaths)
☐2 vtr (in tennis) prendre [qch] de volée (ball)
☐3 vi (in tennis) jouer à la volée

volleyball n volley(-ball) m

volt n volt m

voltage n tension f

volume n (a) (gen) volume m (of de); (of container) capacité f
(b) (book) volume m; (part of set) tome m

volume control n (bouton m de) réglage m du volume

voluntarily adv de plein gré, volontairement

voluntary adj (a) (gen) volontaire
(b) (unpaid) bénévole

voluntary redundancy n départ m volontaire

volunteer ☐1 n (a) (offering to do sth) volontaire mf
(b) (unpaid worker) bénévole mf
☐2 vtr (a) (offer) offrir; to ~ to do offrir de faire, se porter volontaire pour faire
(b) fournir [qch] spontanément (information)
☐3 vi (a) se porter volontaire (for pour)
(b) (as soldier) s'engager comme volontaire

voluptuous adj voluptueux/-euse

vomit ☐1 n vomi m
☐2 vtr, vi vomir

voodoo n vaudou m

voracious adj vorace

vortex n tourbillon m

vote 1 n (a) (gen) vote m
(b) (franchise) **the ~** le droit de vote
2 vtr **(a)** (gen) voter; **to ~ sb into/out of office** élire/ne pas réélire qn
(b) (colloq) (propose) proposer
3 vi voter (on sur; **for sb** pour qn; **against** contre); **let's ~ on it** mettons-le aux voix; **to ~ to strike** voter la grève
vote of confidence n vote m de confiance (**in** en)
vote of thanks n discours m de remerciement
voter n électeur/-trice m/f
voting n scrutin m
voting age n majorité f électorale
vouch v ■ **vouch for (a)** (informally) répondre de ⟨person⟩; témoigner de ⟨fact⟩
(b) (officially) se porter garant de
voucher n bon m

vow 1 n (religious) vœu m; (of honour) serment m; **marriage** or **wedding ~s** promesses fpl du mariage
2 vtr faire vœu de ⟨love, revenge, allegiance⟩; **to ~ to do** jurer de faire
vowel n voyelle f
voyage n voyage m
V-sign n (a) (victory sign) V m de la victoire
(b) (GB) (offensive gesture) geste m obscène
VSO n (abbr = **Voluntary Service Overseas**) coopération f civile
vulgar adj **(a)** (tasteless) ⟨furniture, clothes⟩ de mauvais goût; ⟨taste⟩ douteux/-euse; ⟨person⟩ vulgaire
(b) (rude) grossier/-ière
vulnerable adj vulnérable (**to** à)
vulture n vautour m

Ww

w, W n w, W m
wad n (a) (of banknotes, paper) liasse f (**of** de)
(b) (of cotton wool, padding) boule f (**of** de)
waddle vi ⟨duck, person⟩ se dandiner
wade vi (a) (in water) **to ~ into the water** entrer dans l'eau; **to ~ ashore** marcher dans l'eau jusqu'au rivage; **to ~ across** traverser à gué
(b) he was wading through 'War and Peace' il lisait 'Guerre et Paix', mais ça avançait lentement
waders n pl cuissardes fpl
wafer n (Culin) gaufrette f
wafer-thin adj ⟨slice⟩ ultrafin/-e
waffle 1 n (a) (Culin) gaufre f
(b) (colloq) (empty words) verbiage m
2 vi (colloq) (also **~ on**) (speaking) bavasser (colloq); (writing) faire du remplissage
waft vi **to ~ towards** flotter vers; **to ~ up** monter
wag 1 vtr remuer ⟨tail⟩
2 vi ⟨tail⟩ remuer, frétiller; **tongues will ~** ça va faire jaser
wage 1 n (also **~s** pl) salaire m
2 vtr mener ⟨campaign⟩; **to ~ (a) war against sb/sth** faire la guerre contre qn/qch
wage earner n (a) (person earning a wage) salarié/-e m/f (hebdomadaire)
(b) (breadwinner) soutien m de famille
wage packet n (a) (envelope) enveloppe f de paie
(b) (money) paie f
wager n pari m; **to make** or **lay a ~** parier, faire un pari
wage slip n feuille f de paie

waggon (GB), **wagon** n (a) (horse-drawn) chariot m
(b) (GB) (on rail) wagon m (de marchandises)
IDIOMS to be on the ~ (colloq) être au régime sec
wail 1 n (of person) gémissement m; (of siren) hurlement m; (of musical instrument) son m plaintif
2 vi ⟨person, wind⟩ gémir; ⟨siren⟩ hurler; ⟨music⟩ pleurer
waist n taille f
waistband n ceinture f
waistcoat n (GB) gilet m
waistline n taille f
waist measurement n tour m de taille
wait 1 n attente f; **an hour's ~** une heure d'attente
2 vtr **(a)** attendre ⟨one's turn⟩
(b) (US) **to ~ table** servir à table
3 vi attendre; **to keep sb ~ing** faire attendre qn; **to ~ for sb/sth** attendre qn/qch; **to ~ for sb/sth to do** attendre que qn/qch fasse; **to ~ to do** attendre de faire; **I can't ~ to do** j'ai hâte de faire; (stronger) je meurs d'impatience de faire; **you'll have to ~ and see** attends et tu verras
IDIOMS to lie in ~ for sb guetter qn
■ **wait around, wait about** (GB) attendre
■ **wait behind** attendre un peu; **to ~ behind for sb** attendre qn
■ **wait on** servir ⟨person⟩; **to ~ on sb hand and foot** être aux petits soins pour qn
■ **wait up (a)** (stay awake) veiller; **to ~ up for sb** veiller jusqu'au retour de qn
(b) (US) **~ up!** attends!

W

waiter *n* serveur *m*; '~!' 'monsieur!'

waiting game *n* **to play a** ~ attendre son heure; (in politics) faire de l'attentisme

waiting list *n* liste *f* d'attente

waiting room *n* salle *f* d'attente

waitress *n* serveuse *f*; '~!' 'madame!','mademoiselle!'

waive *vtr* déroger à ⟨rule⟩; renoncer à ⟨claim, right⟩; supprimer ⟨fee⟩

wake ⓵ *vtr* réveiller; **to** ~ **sb from a dream** tirer qn d'un rêve
⓶ *vi* se réveiller
■ **wake up**: ¶ ~ **up** se réveiller; ~ **up!** réveille-toi!; (to reality) ouvre les yeux!; ¶ ~ **[sb] up** réveiller

wake-up call *n* réveil *m* téléphoné

Wales *pr n* pays *m* de Galles

walk ⓵ *n* (a) promenade *f*; (shorter) tour *m*; (hike) randonnée *f*; **it's about ten minutes'** ~ c'est à environ dix minutes à pied; **to go for a** ~ (aller) faire une promenade
(b) (gait) démarche *f*
(c) (pace) pas *m*
(d) (path) allée *f*
(e) (Sport) épreuve *f* de marche
⓶ *vtr* (a) faire [qch] à pied ⟨distance, path, road⟩
(b) conduire ⟨horse⟩; promener ⟨dog⟩; **to** ~ **sb home** raccompagner qn chez lui/elle
⓷ *vi* (in general) marcher; (for pleasure) se promener; (not run) aller au pas; (not ride or drive) aller à pied; **it's not very far, let's** ~ ce n'est pas très loin, allons-y à pied; **he** ~**ed up/down the road** il a remonté/descendu la rue (à pied)

■ **Note** *à pied* is often omitted with movement verbs if we already know that the person is on foot. If it is surprising or ambiguous, *à pied* should be included.

■ **walk around**: ¶ ~ **around** se promener; (aimlessly) traîner; ¶ ~ **around [sth]** (to and fro) faire un tour dans; (make circuit of) faire le tour de
■ **walk away** (a) s'éloigner (**from** de)
(b) (refuse to face) **to** ~ **away from** se désintéresser de ⟨problem⟩
(c) (survive unscathed) sortir indemne (**from** de)
(d) (win easily) **to** ~ **away with** gagner [qch] haut la main ⟨game, tournament⟩; remporter [qch] haut la main ⟨election⟩; décrocher ⟨prize, honour⟩
■ **walk back** revenir sur ses pas (**to** jusqu'à); **we** ~**ed back** (**home**) nous sommes rentrés à pied
■ **walk in** entrer; **I'd just** ~**ed in when** je venais à peine d'entrer quand
■ **walk into**: ~ **into [sth]** (a) (enter) entrer dans
(b) tomber dans ⟨trap⟩; se fourrer dans ⟨tricky situation⟩
(c) (bump into) rentrer dans ⟨door, person⟩
■ **walk off**: ¶ ~ **off** (a) partir brusquement
(b) (colloq) **to** ~ **off with sth** (innocently) partir

avec qch; (as theft) filer (colloq) avec qch
¶ ~ **[sth] off** se promener pour faire passer ⟨hangover, large meal⟩
■ **walk out** (a) sortir (**of** de)
(b) (desert) partir; **to** ~ **out on** laisser tomber (colloq) ⟨lover⟩; rompre ⟨contract, undertaking⟩
(c) (as protest) partir en signe de protestation; (on strike) se mettre en grève
■ **walk over**: ¶ ~ **over** s'approcher (**to** de)
¶ ~ **over [sb]** (colloq) (a) (defeat) battre [qn] à plates coutures
(b) (humiliate) marcher sur les pieds de
■ **walk round**: ¶ ~ **round** faire le tour; ¶ ~ **round [sth]** (round edge of) faire le tour de; (visit) visiter ⟨town⟩
■ **walk through**: traverser ⟨house, forest⟩; passer ⟨door⟩; parcourir ⟨streets⟩; marcher dans ⟨snow, mud, grass⟩
■ **walk up**: **to** ~ **up to** s'approcher de

walker *n* (for pleasure) promeneur/-euse *m/f*; (for exercise) marcheur/-euse *m/f*

walkie-talkie *n* talkie-walkie *m*

walking *n* (for pleasure) promenades *fpl* à pied; (for exercise) marche *f* à pied

walking boots *n pl* chaussures *fpl* de marche

walking distance *n* **to be within** ~ être à quelques minutes de marche (**of** de)

walking pace *n* pas *m*; **at a** ~ au pas

walking stick *n* canne *f*

walkman® *n* walkman® *m*, baladeur *m*

walkout *n* (strike) grève *f* surprise

walkover *n* victoire *f* facile (**for** pour)

walkway *n* allée *f*

wall *n* (a) (construction) mur *m*
(b) (of cave, tunnel) paroi *f*
(c) (Anat) paroi *f*

wall chart *n* affiche *f*

walled *adj* ⟨city⟩ fortifié/-e; ⟨garden⟩ clos/-e

wallet *n* (for notes) portefeuille *m*; (for documents) porte-documents *m inv*

wallflower *n* giroflée *f* jaune
IDIOMS to be a ~ faire tapisserie

wall light *n* applique *f* murale

wall-mounted *adj* fixé/-e au mur

wallow *vi* **to** ~ **in** se vautrer dans ⟨mud, luxury⟩; se complaire dans ⟨self-pity, nostalgia⟩

wallpaper ⓵ *n* (a) (for walls) papier *m* peint
(b) (Comput) fond *m* d'écran
⓶ *vtr* tapisser ⟨room⟩

walnut *n* (a) (nut) noix *f*
(b) (tree, wood) noyer *m*

walrus *n* morse *m*

waltz ⓵ *n* valse *f*
⓶ *vi* danser la valse (**with** avec)

wand *n* baguette *f*

wander ⓵ *vtr* parcourir; **to** ~ **the streets** traîner dans la rue
⓶ *vi* (a) (walk, stroll) se promener; **to** ~ **around town** se balader en ville

(b) (stray) errer; **to ~ away** or **off** s'éloigner **(from de)**

(c) ⟨*eyes, hands*⟩ errer **(over** sur⟩; ⟨*attention*⟩ se relâcher; **her mind is ~ing** elle divague
■ **wander about**, **wander around** (stroll) se balader; (when lost) errer

wane *vi* ⟨*moon*⟩ décroître; ⟨*enthusiasm, popularity*⟩ diminuer

wangle (colloq) **1** *n* combine *f* (colloq)
2 *vtr* soutirer ⟨*money, promise*⟩; se débrouiller pour avoir ⟨*leave*⟩; **to ~ sth for sb** se débrouiller pour faire avoir qch à qn

wannabe(e) *n* (colloq): *personne qui rêve d'être célèbre*

want **1** *n* **(a)** (need) besoin *m*
(b) (lack) défaut *m*; **for ~ of** à défaut or faute de; **it's not for ~ of trying** ce n'est pas faute d'avoir essayé
2 *vtr* **(a)** (desire) vouloir; **I ~** (as general statement) je veux; (would like) je voudrais; (am seeking) je souhaite; **I don't ~ to** je n'en ai pas envie; (flat refusal) je ne veux pas; **to ~ to do** vouloir faire; **to ~ sb to do** vouloir que qn fasse
(b) (colloq) (need) avoir besoin de
(c) (require presence of) demander; **if anyone ~s me** si quelqu'un me demande; **you're ~ed on the phone** on vous demande au téléphone; **to be ~ed by the police** être recherché/-e par la police
3 *vi* **to ~ for** manquer de

wanting *adj* **to be ~** faire défaut; **to be ~ in** manquer de; **to be found ~** s'avérer décevant/-e

wanton *adj* ⟨*cruelty, damage, waste*⟩ gratuit/-e; ⟨*disregard*⟩ délibéré/-e

war *n* guerre *f*; **in the ~** à la guerre; **to wage ~ on** faire la guerre contre; (figurative) mener une lutte contre

ward *n* **(a)** (in hospital) (unit) service *m*; (room) unité *f*; (separate building) pavillon *m*; **maternity ~** service de maternité; **hospital ~** salle *f* d'hôpital
(b) (electoral) circonscription *f* électorale
(c) (also **~ of court**) (Law) pupille *m*
■ **ward off** chasser ⟨*evil, predator*⟩; faire taire ⟨*accusations, criticism*⟩; écarter ⟨*attack, threat*⟩; éviter ⟨*disaster*⟩

warden *n* (of institution, college) directeur/-trice *m/f*; (of park, estate) gardien/-ienne *m/f*

warder *n* (GB) gardien/-ienne *m/f*

wardrobe *n* **(a)** (furniture) armoire *f*
(b) (set of clothes) garde-robe *f*; (for theatre) costumes *mpl*

warehouse *n* entrepôt *m*

wares *n pl* marchandise *f*, marchandises *fpl*

warfare *n* guerre *f*

war game *n* jeu *m* de stratégie (militaire)

warhead *n* ogive *f*

warlike *adj* ⟨*people*⟩ guerrier/-ière; ⟨*mood, words*⟩ belliqueux/-euse

warm **1** *adj* **(a)** ⟨*place, food, temperature, water, day, clothing*⟩ chaud/-e; **to be ~** ⟨*person*⟩ avoir chaud; **it's ~** il fait bon or chaud
(b) (affectionate) ⟨*person, atmosphere, welcome*⟩ chaleureux/-euse; ⟨*admiration, support*⟩ enthousiaste
(c) ⟨*colour*⟩ chaud/-e
2 *vtr* chauffer ⟨*plate, food, water*⟩; réchauffer ⟨*implement, bed*⟩; **to ~ oneself** se réchauffer; **to ~ one's hands** se réchauffer les mains
3 *vi* ⟨*food, liquid, object*⟩ chauffer
■ **warm to**, **warm towards** se prendre de sympathie pour ⟨*person*⟩; se faire à ⟨*idea*⟩; prendre goût à ⟨*task*⟩
■ **warm up**: ¶ **~ up (a)** ⟨*person, room, house*⟩ se réchauffer; ⟨*food, liquid, engine*⟩ chauffer
(b) (become lively) s'animer
(c) ⟨*athlete*⟩ s'échauffer; ⟨*singer*⟩ s'échauffer la voix; ⟨*orchestra, musician*⟩ se préparer
¶ **~ [sth] up** réchauffer ⟨*room, bed, person*⟩; faire réchauffer ⟨*food*⟩

warm-hearted *adj* chaleureux/-euse

warmly *adv* ⟨*smile, thank, recommend*⟩ chaleureusement; ⟨*speak, praise*⟩ avec enthousiasme

warmth *n* chaleur *f*

warm-up *n* échauffement *m*

warn **1** *vtr* avertir, prévenir; **to ~ sb about** or **against sth** mettre qn en garde contre qch; **to ~ sb to do** conseiller or dire à qn de faire; **to ~ sb not to do** déconseiller à qn de faire
2 *vi* **to ~ of sth** annoncer qch

warning *n* avertissement *m*; (by an authority) avis *m*; (by light, siren) alerte *f*; **to give sb ~** avertir qn (**of** de); **advance ~** préavis *m*; **health ~** mise en garde; **flood ~** avis de crue

warning light *n* voyant *m* lumineux

warning shot *n* coup *m* de semonce

warning sign *n* (on road) panneau *m* d'avertissement; (of illness, stress) signe *m* annonciateur

warning triangle *n* (Aut) triangle *m* de présignalisation

warp **1** *vtr* **(a)** déformer ⟨*metal, wood, record*⟩
(b) pervertir ⟨*mind, personality*⟩
2 *vi* se déformer

warped *adj* **(a)** ⟨*metal, wood, record*⟩ déformé/-e
(b) ⟨*mind, humour*⟩ tordu/-e; ⟨*personality, sexuality*⟩ perverti/-e; ⟨*account, view*⟩ faussé/-e

warplane *n* avion *m* militaire

warrant **1** *n* (Law) mandat *m*
2 *vtr* justifier ⟨*action, measure*⟩

warranty *n* garantie *f*

warren *n* **(a)** (rabbits') garenne *f*
(b) (building, maze of streets) labyrinthe *m*

warring *adj* en conflit

warrior *n* guerrier/-ière *m/f*

W

Warsaw *pr n* Varsovie

warship *n* navire *m* de guerre

wart *n* verrue *f*

wartime *n* **in** ~ en temps de guerre

war-torn *adj* déchiré/-e par la guerre

war veteran *n* ancien combattant *m*

wary *adj* **(a)** (cautious) prudent/-e; **to be** ~ montrer de la circonspection (**of** vis-à-vis de); **to be** ~ **of doing** hésiter à faire **(b)** (distrustful) méfiant/-e; **to be** ~ se méfier (**of** de)

wash ①1 *n* **(a)** (clean) **to have a** ~ se laver; **to give [sth] a** ~ laver ⟨*window, floor*⟩; nettoyer ⟨*object*⟩; lessiver ⟨*paintwork, walls*⟩; **to give [sb] a** ~ débarbouiller ⟨*child*⟩ **(b)** (laundry process) lavage *m*; **weekly** ~ lessive *f* hebdomadaire; **in the** ~ (about to be cleaned) au sale; (being cleaned) au lavage **(c)** (from boat) remous *m* ②2 *vtr* laver ⟨*person, clothes, floor*⟩; nettoyer ⟨*object, wound*⟩; lessiver ⟨*paintwork, surface*⟩; **to get** ~**ed** se laver; **to** ~ **one's hands/face** se laver les mains/le visage; **to** ~ **the dishes** faire la vaisselle ③3 *vi* **(a)** ⟨*person*⟩ se laver, faire sa toilette; ⟨*animal*⟩ faire sa toilette **(b)** (do laundry) faire la lessive

■ **wash away** emporter ⟨*structure, debris, person*⟩

■ **wash up**: ¶ ~ **up (a)** (GB) (do dishes) faire la vaisselle **(b)** (US) (clean oneself) faire un brin de toilette (colloq) ¶ ~ **[sth] up (a)** (clean) laver ⟨*plate*⟩; nettoyer ⟨*pan*⟩ **(b)** ⟨*tide*⟩ rejeter ⟨*debris*⟩

washable *adj* lavable

washbasin *n* lavabo *m*

washbowl *n* (US) lavabo *m*

washcloth *n* (US) lavette *f*

washed-out *adj* **(a)** (faded) délavé/-e **(b)** (tired) épuisé/-e, lessivé/-e (colloq)

washed-up *adj* (colloq) fichu/-e (colloq)

washer *n* (Tech) (as seal) joint *m*

washer-dryer *n* lave-linge/sèche-linge *m inv*

washing *n* (laundry) (to be cleaned) linge *m* sale; (when clean) linge *m*; **to do the** ~ faire la lessive

washing line *n* corde *f* à linge

washing machine *n* machine *f* à laver

washing powder *n* (GB) lessive *f* (en poudre)

washing-up *n* (GB) vaisselle *f*

washing-up liquid *n* (GB) liquide *m* (à) vaisselle

washout *n* **(a)** (colloq) (project, system) fiasco *m* **(b)** (colloq) (person) nullité *f* (colloq) **(c)** (game, camp) fiasco *m* dû à la pluie

washroom *n* toilettes *fpl*

wash-stand *n* (US) lavabo *m*

wasp *n* guêpe *f*

waspish *adj* acerbe

wastage *n* **(a)** (of money, resources, talent) gaspillage *m*; (of heat, energy) déperdition *f* **(b)** (*also* **natural** ~) élimination *f* naturelle

waste ①1 *n* **(a)** (of food, money, energy) gaspillage *m* (**of** de); (of time) perte *f* (**of** de); **a** ~ **of effort** un effort inutile; **that car is such a** ~ **of money!** cette voiture, c'est vraiment de l'argent jeté par les fenêtres!; **to let sth go to** ~ gaspiller qch **(b)** (detritus) (*also* **wastes** (US)) déchets *mpl* (**from** de) ②2 **wastes** *n pl* **(a)** (wilderness) étendues *fpl* sauvages **(b)** (US) = WASTE 1B ③3 *adj* **(a)** ⟨*heat, energy*⟩ gaspillé/-e; ⟨*water*⟩ usé/-e; ~ **materials** déchets *mpl* **(b)** ⟨*land*⟩ inculte **(c)** **to lay** ~ **to** dévaster ④4 *vtr* **(a)** (squander) gaspiller ⟨*food, resources, energy, money, talents*⟩; perdre ⟨*time, opportunity*⟩; user ⟨*strength*⟩ **(b)** (make thinner) décharner; (make weaker) atrophier

wastebasket *n* corbeille *f* à papier

wastebin *n* (GB) (for paper) corbeille *f* à papier; (for rubbish) poubelle *f*

wasted *adj* **(a)** ⟨*effort, life, vote*⟩ inutile; ⟨*energy, years*⟩ gaspillé/-e **(b)** (fleshless) ⟨*body, limb*⟩ décharné/-e; (weak) ⟨*body, limb*⟩ atrophié/-e

waste disposal *n* traitement *m* des déchets

waste disposal unit *n* (GB) broyeur *m* d'ordures

wasteful *adj* ⟨*product, machine*⟩ qui consomme beaucoup; ⟨*method, process*⟩ peu économique; ⟨*person*⟩ gaspilleur/-euse

wasteland *n* (urban) terrain *m* vague; (rural) terre *f* à l'abandon

wastepaper *n* papier *m* or papiers *mpl* à jeter

wastepaper basket, **wastepaper bin** (GB) *n* corbeille *f* à papier

waste pipe *n* tuyau *m* de vidange

wasting *adj* ⟨*disease*⟩ débilitant/-e

watch ①1 *n* **(a)** (timepiece) montre *f* **(b)** (surveillance) surveillance *f* (**on** sur); **to keep** ~ monter la garde; **to keep (a)** ~ **on sb/sth** surveiller qn/qch ②2 *vtr* **(a)** (look at) regarder; (observe) observer **(b)** (monitor) suivre ⟨*career, development*⟩; surveiller ⟨*situation*⟩ **(c)** (keep under surveillance) surveiller ⟨*person, movements*⟩ **(d)** (pay attention to) faire attention à ⟨*obstacle, dangerous object, money*⟩; surveiller ⟨*language, manners, weight*⟩; **to** ~ **one's step** (figurative) faire attention **(e)** (look after) garder ⟨*person, property*⟩ ③3 *vi* regarder (**from** de)

■ **watch for** guetter ⟨*person, chance*⟩; surveiller l'apparition de ⟨*symptom*⟩

■ **watch out** (be careful) faire attention (**for** à); (keep watch) guetter; ~ **out!** attention!

■ **watch over** veiller sur ⟨*person*⟩; veiller à ⟨*interests, rights, welfare*⟩

watchable *adj* qui se laisse regarder

watchband *n* (US) bracelet *m* de montre

watchdog *n* **(a)** (dog) chien *m* de garde **(b)** (organization) organisme *m* de surveillance

watchmaker *n* horloger/-ère *m/f*

watchman *n* (guard) gardien *m*

watch strap *n* bracelet *m* de montre

watchword *n* slogan *m*

water ① *n* eau *f*
② *vtr* arroser ⟨*lawn, plant*⟩; irriguer ⟨*crop, field*⟩; abreuver ⟨*livestock*⟩
③ *vi* the smell of cooking makes my mouth ∼ l'odeur de cuisine me fait venir l'eau à la bouche; **the smoke made her eyes ∼** la fumée l'a fait pleurer

■ **water down (a)** couper [qch] d'eau ⟨*beer, wine*⟩; diluer ⟨*syrup*⟩
(b) atténuer ⟨*effect, plans, policy*⟩; édulcorer ⟨*description, story*⟩

water bed *n* matelas *m* d'eau

water bird *n* oiseau *m* aquatique

water birth *n* accouchement *m* aquatique

water bottle *n* (for cyclist) bidon *m*

water cannon *n* canon *m* à eau

watercolour (GB), **watercolor** (US) *n* (paint) peinture *f* pour aquarelle; (painting) aquarelle *f*

watercress *n* cresson *m* (de fontaine)

waterfall *n* cascade *f*

water filter *n* filtre *m* à eau

waterfront *n* (on harbour) front *m* de mer; (by lakeside, riverside) bord *m* de l'eau

water-heater *n* chauffe-eau *m inv*

watering can *n* arrosoir *m*

water jump *n* rivière *f*

water level *n* niveau *m* d'eau

water lily *n* nénuphar *m*

waterlogged *adj* ⟨*ground, pitch*⟩ détrempé/-e

water main *n* canalisation *f* d'eau

watermark *n* (of sea) laisse *f*; (of river) ligne *f* des hautes eaux; (on paper) filigrane *m*

watermelon *n* pastèque *f*

water power *n* énergie *f* hydraulique

waterproof *adj* ⟨*coat*⟩ imperméable; ⟨*make-up*⟩ résistant/-e à l'eau

waterproofs *n pl* vêtements *mpl* imperméables

water-resistant *adj* qui résiste à l'eau

water-ski ① *n* ski *m* nautique
② *vi* faire du ski nautique

water-skiing *n* ski *m* nautique

water slide *n* toboggan *m* de piscine

water sport *n* sport *m* nautique

water supply *n* (in an area) approvisionnement *m* en eau; (to a building) alimentation *f* en eau

watertight *adj* **(a)** ⟨*container, seal*⟩ étanche

(b) ⟨*argument, case*⟩ incontestable; ⟨*alibi*⟩ irréfutable

water tower *n* château *m* d'eau

water trough *n* abreuvoir *m*

waterway *n* voie *f* navigable

water wings *n pl* bracelets *mpl* de natation

watery *adj* **(a)** ⟨*sauce, paint*⟩ trop liquide; ⟨*coffee*⟩ trop léger/-ère
(b) ⟨*colour, smile*⟩ pâle

watt *n* watt *m*

wave ① *n* **(a)** (of hand) signe *m* (de la main)
(b) (of water) vague *f*; **to make ∼s** ⟨*wind*⟩ faire des vagues; (cause a stir) faire du bruit; (cause trouble) créer des histoires (colloq)
(c) (outbreak, surge) vague *f* (**of** de)
(d) (of light, radio) onde *f*
(e) (in hair) cran *m*
② *vtr* **(a)** agiter ⟨*flag, ticket, banknote*⟩; brandir ⟨*umbrella, stick, gun*⟩
(b) to ∼ goodbye to sb faire au revoir de la main à qn
③ *vi* **(a)** (with hand) **to ∼ to** *or* **at sb** saluer qn de la main
(b) ⟨*branches*⟩ être agité/-e par le vent; ⟨*corn*⟩ ondoyer; ⟨*flag*⟩ flotter au vent

wave band *n* bande *f* de fréquence

wavelength *n* (on radio) longueur *f* d'onde
IDIOMS **to be on the same ∼ as sb** être sur la même longueur d'onde que qn

waver *vi* **(a)** (weaken) ⟨*person*⟩ vaciller; ⟨*courage, love*⟩ faiblir; ⟨*voice*⟩ trembler
(b) (hesitate) hésiter (**between** entre; **over** sur)

wavy *adj* ⟨*hair, line*⟩ ondulé/-e

wax ① *n* (for candle, seal) cire *f*; (for skis) fart *m*; (in ear) cérumen *m*
② *vtr* **(a)** cirer ⟨*floor*⟩; lustrer ⟨*car*⟩; farter ⟨*ski*⟩
(b) (depilate) épiler [qch] à la cire ⟨*legs*⟩
③ *vi* ⟨*moon*⟩ croître

waxed jacket *n* ciré *m*

wax paper *n* papier *m* paraffin

waxwork *n* personnage *m* en cire

waxworks *n* musée *m* de cire

waxy *adj* cireux/-euse

way ① *n* **(a)** (route, road) chemin *m* (**from** de; **to** à); **the quickest ∼ to town** le chemin le plus court pour aller en ville; **to ask the ∼ to the station** demander le chemin pour aller à la gare; **there is no ∼ around the problem** il n'y a pas moyen de contourner le problème; **on the ∼ back** sur le chemin du retour; **on the ∼ back from the meeting** en revenant de la réunion; **the ∼ in** l'entrée (**to** de); **the ∼ out** la sortie (**of** de); **a ∼ out of our difficulties** un moyen de nous sortir de nos difficultés; **the ∼ up** la montée; **on the ∼** en route; **to be out of sb's ∼** ⟨*place*⟩ ne pas être sur le chemin de qn; **don't go out of your ∼ to do** ne te donne pas de mal pour faire; **out of the ∼** (isolated) isolé/-e; (unusual) extraordinaire; **by ∼ of** (via) en passant par; **to make one's ∼ towards** se diriger vers; **to** ⋯⋙

W

make one's ~ along avancer le long de; **to make one's own ~ there** y aller par ses propres moyens

(b) (direction) direction *f*, sens *m*; **which ~ did he go?** dans quelle direction est-il parti?; **he went that ~** il est parti par là; **come this ~** suivez-moi, venez par ici; **'this ~ up'** 'haut'; **to look the other ~** (to see) regarder de l'autre côté; (to avoid seeing unpleasant thing) détourner les yeux; (to ignore wrongdoing) fermer les yeux; **the other ~ up** dans l'autre sens; **the right ~ up** dans le bon sens; **the wrong ~ up** à l'envers; **to turn sth the other ~ around** retourner qch; **I didn't ask her, it was the other ~ around** ce n'est pas moi qui le lui ai demandé, c'est l'inverse; **the wrong/right ~ around** dans le mauvais/bon sens

(c) (space in front, projected route) passage *m*; **to be in sb's ~** empêcher qn de passer; **to be in the ~** gêner le passage; **to get out of the ~** s'écarter (du chemin); **to get out of sb's ~** laisser passer qn; **to keep out of the ~** rester à l'écart; **to keep out of sb's ~** éviter qn; **to make ~** s'écarter; **to make ~ for sb/sth** faire place à qn/qch

(d) (distance) distance *f*; **it's a long ~** c'est loin (**to** jusqu'à); **to go all the ~ to China** aller jusqu'en Chine

(e) (manner) façon *f*, manière *f*; **do it this/that ~** fais-le comme ceci/cela; **to do another ~** faire autrement; **the French ~** à la française; **to write sth the right/wrong ~** écrire qch bien/mal; **try to see it my ~** mets-toi à ma place; **in his/her/its own ~** à sa façon; **to have a ~ with words** savoir manier les mots; **to have a ~ with children** savoir s'y prendre avec les enfants; **a ~ of doing** (method) une façon *or* manière de faire; (means) un moyen de faire; **I like the ~ he dresses** j'aime la façon dont il s'habille; **either ~, she's wrong** de toute façon, elle a tort; **one ~ or another** d'une façon ou d'une autre; **I don't care one ~ or the other** ça m'est égal; **you can't have it both ~s** on ne peut pas avoir le beurre et l'argent du beurre; **no ~!** (colloq) pas question! (colloq); **~ of life** mode de vie

(f) (respect, aspect) sens *m*; **in a ~ it's sad** en un sens c'est triste; **in a ~ that's true** dans une certaine mesure c'est vrai; **in many ~s** à bien des égards; **in some ~s** à certains égards; **in no ~, not in any ~** aucunement

(g) (custom, manner) coutume *f*, manière *f*; **that's the modern ~** c'est ce qui se fait de nos jours; **I know all her little ~s** je connais toutes ses petites habitudes; **that's just his ~** il est comme ça; **it's the ~ of the world** c'est la vie

(h) (will, desire) **to get one's ~, to have one's own ~** faire à son idée; **she likes (to have) her own ~** elle aime n'en faire qu'à sa tête; **if I had my ~** si cela ne tenait qu'à moi; **have it your (own) ~** comme tu voudras

2 *adv* **we went ~ over budget** le budget a été largement dépassé; **to be ~ out** (in guess, estimate) être loin du compte; **that's ~ out of order** je trouve ça un peu fort

3 **by the way** *phr* en passant; **by the ~,...** à propos,...; **what time is it, by the ~?** quelle heure est-il, au fait?

waylay *vtr* ⟨*attacker*⟩ attaquer; ⟨*beggar, friend*⟩ arrêter, harponner (colloq)

waymark *n* balise *f*

way-out *adj* (colloq) excentrique

wayside *n*
IDIOMS to fall by the ~ (stray morally) quitter le droit chemin; (fail, not stay the course) abandonner en cours de route; (be cancelled, fall through) tomber à l'eau

wayward *adj* ⟨*person, nature*⟩ difficile; ⟨*husband, wife*⟩ volage

we *pron* nous

■ **Note** In standard French, *we* is translated by *nous* but in informal French, *on* is frequently used: *we're going to the cinema* = nous allons au cinéma *or more informally* on va au cinéma.
– *on* is also used in correct French to refer to a large, vaguely defined group: *we shouldn't lie to our children* = on ne devrait pas mentir à ses enfants.

~ saw her yesterday nous l'avons vue hier; **~ left at six** nous sommes partis à six heures; (informal) on est partis (colloq) à six heures; **~ Scots like the sun** nous autres Écossais, nous aimons le soleil; **WE didn't say that** nous, nous n'avons pas dit cela; (informal) nous, on n'a pas dit ça (colloq); **~ all make mistakes** tout le monde peut se tromper

weak *adj* **(a)** ⟨*person, animal, muscle, limb*⟩ faible; ⟨*health, ankle, heart, nerves*⟩ fragile; ⟨*stomach*⟩ délicat/-e; ⟨*intellect*⟩ médiocre; ⟨*chin*⟩ fuyant/-e; **to be ~ with** *or* **from hunger** être affaibli/-e par la faim; **to grow** *or* **become ~(er)** ⟨*person*⟩ s'affaiblir; ⟨*pulse, heartbeat*⟩ faiblir
(b) ⟨*beam, support*⟩ peu solide; ⟨*structure*⟩ fragile
(c) (lacking authority, strength) ⟨*government, team, pupil, president*⟩ faible; ⟨*parent, teacher*⟩ (not firm) qui manque de fermeté; (poor) piètre (before n); ⟨*plot*⟩ mince; ⟨*actor, protest, excuse, argument*⟩ peu convaincant/-e; **~ link** *or* **spot** point m faible
(d) (faint) ⟨*light, current, concentration, sound*⟩ faible; ⟨*tea, coffee*⟩ léger/-ère
(e) ⟨*economy, dollar*⟩ faible (**against** par rapport à)

weaken **1** *vtr* **(a)** (through illness, damage) affaiblir ⟨*person, heart, structure*⟩; diminuer ⟨*resistance*⟩; rendre [qch] moins solide ⟨*joint, bank, wall*⟩
(b) (undermine) nuire à l'autorité de ⟨*government, president*⟩; affaiblir ⟨*team, company, authority, defence*⟩; amoindrir ⟨*argument, power*⟩; nuire à ⟨*morale*⟩
(c) (dilute) diluer
2 *vi* **(a)** (physically) s'affaiblir
(b) ⟨*government, resolve*⟩ fléchir; ⟨*support, alliance*⟩ se relâcher
(c) (Econ) ⟨*economy, currency*⟩ être en baisse

weakling *n* (physically) gringalet *m*; (morally) mauviette *f*

weakness n (a) (weak point) point m faible
(b) (liking) faible m (for pour)
(c) (physical, moral) faiblesse f
(d) (lack of authority) faiblesse f; (of evidence, position) fragilité f
(e) (of light, current, sound) faiblesse f; (of tea, solution) légèreté f
(f) (of economy, currency) faiblesse f

weak-willed adj to be ~ manquer de
fermeté

wealth n (a) (possessions) fortune f
(b) (state) richesse f
(c) (large amount) a ~ of une mine de
⟨information⟩; une profusion de ⟨detail⟩;
énormément de ⟨experience, talent⟩

wealthy adj riche

wean vtr sevrer ⟨baby⟩; to ~ sb away from
or off sth détourner qn de qch

weapon n arme f

weaponry n matériel m de guerre

wear ⟨1⟩ n (a) (clothing) children's/sports ~
vêtements mpl pour enfants/de sport
(b) (use) for everyday ~ de tous les jours; for
summer ~ pour l'été
(c) (damage) usure f (on de); ~ and tear
usure f; to be the worse for ~ (drunk) être
ivre; (tired) être épuisé/-e
⟨2⟩ vtr (a) (be dressed in) porter; to ~ blue
s'habiller en bleu; to ~ one's hair long/short
avoir les cheveux longs/courts
(b) (put on, use) mettre; I haven't got a thing
to ~ je n'ai rien à me mettre; to ~ make-up
se maquiller
(c) (display) he wore a puzzled frown il
fronçait les sourcils d'un air perplexe
(d) (damage by use) user; to ~ a hole in
trouer ⟨garment, sheet⟩
⟨3⟩ vi ⟨carpet, shoes⟩ s'user; my patience is
~ing thin je commence à être à bout de
patience
■ **wear away** ⟨inscription⟩ s'effacer; ⟨tread,
cliff, façade⟩ s'user
■ **wear down**: ¶ ~ down s'user; to be worn
down être usé/-e; ¶ ~ [sth] down user
⟨steps⟩; saper ⟨resistance, resolve⟩; ¶ ~ [sb]
down épuiser
■ **wear off** (a) ⟨drug, effect⟩ se dissiper;
⟨sensation⟩ passer
(b) (come off) s'effacer
■ **wear out**: ¶ ~ out s'user; ¶ ~ [sth] out
user; ¶ ~ [sb] out épuiser
■ **wear through** ⟨elbow, trousers⟩ se
trouer; ⟨sole, metal, fabric⟩ se percer

weariness n lassitude f

wearing adj (exhausting) fatigant/-e; (irritating)
pénible

weary ⟨1⟩ adj ⟨person, smile, sigh, voice⟩
las/lasse; ⟨eyes, limbs, mind⟩ fatigué/-e; to
grow ~ se lasser (of de; of doing de faire)
⟨2⟩ vi se lasser (of de; of doing de faire)

weasel n (a) (Zool) belette f
(b) (sly person) sournois/-e m/f

weather ⟨1⟩ n temps m; what's the ~ like?
quel temps fait-il?; the ~ here is hot il fait

chaud ici; in hot/cold ~ quand il fait chaud/
froid; ~ permitting si le temps le permet; in
all ~s par tous les temps
⟨2⟩ vtr survivre à ⟨crisis, upheaval⟩; to ~ the
storm (figurative) surmonter la crise
IDIOMS to be under the ~ ne pas se sentir
bien

weatherbeaten adj ⟨face⟩ hâlé/-e;
⟨rocks, landscape⟩ battu/-e par les vents

weathercock n girouette f

weather forecast n bulletin m
météorologique

weather forecaster n (on TV)
présentateur/-trice m/f de la météo;
(specialist) météorologue mf, météorologiste
mf

weatherproof adj ⟨garment, shoe⟩
imperméable; ⟨shelter, door⟩ étanche

weave ⟨1⟩ vtr (a) tisser ⟨rug, fabric⟩
(b) tresser ⟨cane, basket, wreath⟩
⟨2⟩ vi to ~ in and out se faufiler (of entre);
to ~ towards sth (drunk) s'approcher en
titubant de qch

weaving n tissage m

web n (a) (also **spider's** ~) toile f
(d'araignée)
(b) (network) a ~ of un réseau de ⟨ropes,
lines⟩; a ~ of lies un tissu de mensonges

Web n Web m, Toile f

webbing n (material) sangles fpl

Web cam n Webcam f

web foot n patte f palmée

Webmaster n Webmestre m, Webmaster
m

Web page n page f Web

Web server n serveur m Web

Website n site m Web

Web space n espace m Web

wed n the newly ~s les jeunes mariés mpl

wedding n mariage m; a church ~ un
mariage religieux

wedding anniversary n anniversaire
m de mariage

wedding day n jour m des noces

wedding dress, **wedding gown** n
robe f de mariée

wedding reception n repas m de
mariage

wedding ring n alliance f

wedge ⟨1⟩ n (a) (to insert in rock, wood) coin
m; (to hold sth in position) cale f; (in rock climbing)
piton m
(b) (of cake, pie, cheese) morceau m
⟨2⟩ vtr (a) to ~ sth in place caler qch; to ~ a
door open caler une porte pour la tenir
ouverte
(b) (jam) to ~ sth into enfoncer qch dans; to
be ~d between être coincé/-e entre
IDIOMS that's the thin end of the ~ c'est le
commencement de la fin

Wednesday n mercredi m

wee vi (GB) (colloq) faire pipi

W

weed 1 *n* mauvaise herbe *f*; (in water)
herbes *fpl* aquatiques
2 *vtr, vi* désherber
■ **weed out**: ¶ ~ [sb] out, ~ out [sb] (gen)
éliminer; se débarrasser de ⟨employee⟩; ¶ ~
[sth] out, ~ out [sth] se débarrasser de
⟨stock, items⟩

weedkiller *n* désherbant *m*, herbicide *m*

weedy *adj* (colloq) ⟨person, build⟩ malingre;
⟨character, personality⟩ faible

week *n* semaine *f*; **last/next** ~ la semaine
dernière/prochaine; **this** ~ cette semaine;
the ~ **before last** il y a deux semaines; **the** ~
after next dans deux semaines; **every other** ~
tous les quinze jours; **twice a** ~ deux fois
par semaine; ~ **in** ~ **out** toutes les semaines;
a ~ **today/on Monday** (GB), **today/Monday** ~
aujourd'hui/lundi en huit; **a** ~ **yesterday**
(GB), **a** ~ **from yesterday** (US) il y a eu huit
jours *or* une semaine hier; **in three** ~s' **time**
dans trois semaines; **the working** *or* **work**
(US) ~ la semaine de travail

weekday *n* jour *m* de (la) semaine; **on** ~s
en semaine

weekend *n* week-end *m*; **at the** ~ (GB), **on
the** ~ (US) pendant le week-end; **at** ~s (GB),
on ~s (US) le week-end

weekend bag *n* petit sac *m* de voyage

weekend cottage *n* résidence *f*
secondaire

weekly 1 *n* (newspaper) journal *m*
hebdomadaire; (magazine) (revue *f*)
hebdomadaire *m*
2 *adj* hebdomadaire; **on a** ~ **basis** à la
semaine
3 *adv* ⟨pay⟩ à la semaine; ⟨meet, visit⟩ une
fois par semaine

weep *vi* (a) (cry) pleurer (**over** sur)
(b) (ooze) suinter

weepy *adj* ⟨mood, film⟩ larmoyant/-e; **to
feel** ~ avoir envie de pleurer

weigh 1 *vtr* (a) (on scales) peser; **to** ~ **10
kilos** peser 10 kilos; **how much** *or* **what do
you** ~? combien pèses-tu?; **to** ~ **oneself** se
peser
(b) (assess) évaluer ⟨arguments, advantages,
options⟩; peser ⟨consequences, risks, words⟩
2 *vi* **to** ~ **on sb** peser sur qn; **to** ~ **on sb's
mind** préoccuper qn
■ **weigh down**: ¶ ~ **down on** [sb/sth] peser
sur; ¶ ~ [sb/sth] **down** surcharger ⟨vehicle,
boat⟩; faire plier ⟨branches⟩; ⟨responsibility,
debt⟩ accabler; **to be** ~ed **down with** crouler
sous le poids de ⟨luggage⟩; être accablé/-e de
⟨worry, guilt⟩
■ **weigh in** ⟨boxer, wrestler⟩ se faire peser;
⟨jockey⟩ aller au pesage
■ **weigh out** peser ⟨ingredients, quantity⟩
■ **weigh up** évaluer ⟨prospects, situation⟩;
juger ⟨person⟩; mettre [qch] en balance
⟨options, benefits, risks⟩

weighing machine *n* (for people) balance
f; (for luggage, freight) bascule *f*

weight 1 *n* poids *m*; **to put on/lose** ~
prendre/perdre du poids

2 *vtr* lester ⟨net, arrow⟩
IDIOMS not to carry much ~ ne pas peser
lourd (**with** pour); **to be a** ~ **off one's mind**
être un grand soulagement; **to pull one's** ~
faire sa part de travail; **to throw one's** ~
about *or* **around** faire l'important/-e *m/f*

weightlessness *n* (in space) apesanteur *f*

weight-lifter *n* haltérophile *m*

weight-lifting *n* haltérophilie *f*

weight problem *n* problème *m* de poids

weight training *n* musculation *f* (en
salle)

weighty *adj* (a) (serious) de grand poids
(b) (heavy) lourd/-e

weir *n* barrage *m*

weird *adj* (strange) bizarre; (eerie)
mystérieux/-ieuse

welcome 1 *n* accueil *m*; **to give sb a
warm** ~ faire un accueil chaleureux à qn
2 *adj* (a) bienvenu/-e; **to be** ~ être le
bienvenu/la bienvenue *m/f*; **to make sb** ~ (on
arrival) réserver un bon accueil à qn
(b) 'thanks'—'you're ~' 'merci'—'de rien'
3 *excl* (to respected guest) soyez le bienvenu/la
bienvenue *m/f* chez nous!; (greeting friend)
entre donc!; ~ **back!**, ~ **home!** je suis
content que tu sois de retour!
4 *vtr* accueillir ⟨person⟩; se réjouir de
⟨news, decision, change⟩; être heureux/-euse
de recevoir ⟨contribution⟩; accueillir
favorablement ⟨initiative, move⟩

welcoming *adj* ⟨atmosphere, person⟩
accueillant/-e; ⟨ceremony, committee⟩
d'accueil

weld *vtr* (also ~ **together**) souder; **to** ~
sth on *or* **to** souder qch à

welfare 1 *n* (a) (well-being) bien-être *m inv*;
(interest) intérêt *m*
(b) (state assistance) assistance *f* sociale;
(money) aide *f* sociale
2 *adj* ⟨system⟩ de protection sociale; (US)
⟨meal⟩ gratuit/-e

welfare benefit *n* prestation *f* sociale

welfare services *n pl* services *mpl*
sociaux

welfare spending *n* dépenses *fpl*
sociales

welfare state *n* (as concept)
État-providence *m*; (stressing state assistance)
protection *f* sociale

well¹ 1 *adj* bien; **to feel** ~ se sentir bien;
are you ~? vous allez bien?, tu vas bien?;
she's not ~ **enough to travel** elle n'est pas en
état de voyager; **to get** ~ se rétablir; **that's
all very** ~, **but** tout ça c'est bien beau, mais;
it would be just as ~ **to check** il vaudrait
mieux vérifier; **it would be as** ~ **for you not
to get involved** tu ferais mieux de ne pas t'en
mêler; **the flight was delayed, which was just
as** ~ le vol a été retardé, ce qui n'était pas
plus mal
2 *adv* bien; **to do** ~ **at school** être bon/
bonne élève; **mother and baby are both doing**
~ la mère et l'enfant se portent bien; **the
operation went** ~ l'opération s'est bien

passée; **~ done!** bravo!; **you may ~ be right**
il se pourrait bien que tu aies raison; **we
may as ~ go home** on ferait aussi bien de
rentrer; **it was ~ worth waiting for** ça valait
vraiment la peine d'attendre; **to wish sb ~**
souhaiter beaucoup de chance à qn
3 *excl* **(a)** (expressing astonishment) eh bien!;
(expressing indignation, disgust) ça alors!;
(expressing disappointment) tant pis!; (qualifying
statement) enfin; **~, you may be right** après
tout, tu as peut-être raison; **~, that's too
bad** c'est vraiment dommage; **~ then, what's
the problem?** alors, quel est le problème?;
very ~ then très bien
4 as well *phr* aussi
5 as well as *phr* aussi bien que; **they
have a house in the country as ~ as an
apartment in Paris** ils ont à la fois une
maison à la campagne et un appartement à
Paris
IDIOMS **to be ~ in with sb** (colloq) être bien
avec qn (colloq); **to be ~ up in sth** s'y
connaître en qch; **to leave ~ alone** (GB) *or* **~
enough alone** (US) ne pas s'en mêler

well² *n* (sunk in ground) puits *m*; (pool) source
f

well-balanced *adj* équilibré/-e
well-behaved *adj* ⟨child⟩ sage; ⟨dog⟩
bien dressé/-e
well-being *n* bien-être *m inv*
well-defined *adj* ⟨outline⟩ net/nette; ⟨role,
boundary⟩ bien défini/-e
well-disposed *adj* **to be ~ towards** être
bien disposé/-e envers ⟨person⟩; être
favorable à ⟨regime, idea, policy⟩
well done *adj* ⟨steak⟩ bien cuit/-e; ⟨task⟩
bien fait/-e
well-educated *adj* (having a good
education) instruit/-e; (cultured) cultivé/-e
well-heeled *adj* (colloq) riche
well-informed *adj* bien informé/-e
(**about** sur); **he's very ~** il est très au
courant de l'actualité
wellington (boot) *n* (GB) botte *f* de
caoutchouc
well-kept *adj* ⟨house, garden, village⟩ bien
entretenu/-e
well-known *adj* ⟨person, place⟩ célèbre; **to
be ~ to sb** être connu/-e de qn; **it is ~ that,
it is a ~ fact that** il est bien connu que
well-liked *adj* très apprécié/-e
well-made *adj* bien fait/-e
well-meaning *adj* ⟨person⟩ bien
intentionné/-e; ⟨advice⟩ qui part d'une bonne
intention
well-meant *adj* **his offer was ~** sa
proposition partait d'une bonne intention
well-off **1** *n* **the ~** les gens *mpl* aisés; **the
less ~** les plus défavorisés *mpl*
2 *adj* (wealthy) aisé/-e; **to be ~ for** avoir
beaucoup de ⟨space, provisions⟩
well-read *adj* cultivé/-e
well-respected *adj* très respecté/-e

well-rounded *adj* ⟨education,
programme⟩ complet/-ète; ⟨individual⟩ qui a
reçu une éducation complète
well-thought-out *adj* bien élaboré/-e
well-timed *adj* qui tombe/tombait à
point; **that was well timed!** (of entrance,
phonecall etc) c'est bien tombé!
well-to-do *adj* aisé/-e
well-wisher *n* personne *f* qui veut
témoigner sa sympathie
well-worn *adj* ⟨carpet, garment⟩ élimé/-e;
⟨steps⟩ usé/-e; ⟨joke⟩ rebattu/-e
Welsh **1** *n* **(a)** (people) **the ~** les Gallois
mpl
(b) (language) gallois *m*
2 *adj* gallois/-e
welt *n* (on skin) marque *f* (de coup)
welterweight *n* poids *m* welter
west **1** *n* **(a)** (compass direction) ouest *m*
(b) the West l'Occident *m*, l'Ouest *m*; (part of
country) l'Ouest *m*; (political entity) l'Occident *m*
2 *adj* (gen) ouest *inv*; ⟨wind⟩ d'ouest
3 *adv* ⟨move⟩ vers l'ouest; ⟨lie, live⟩ à
l'ouest (**of** de)
West Bank *pr n* Cisjordanie *f*.
western **1** *n* (film) western *m*
2 *adj* **(a)** ⟨coast⟩ ouest *inv*; ⟨town, accent⟩
de l'ouest; **~ France** l'ouest de la France
(b) (Pol) occidental/-e
westerner *n* Occidental/-e *m/f*
westernize *vtr* occidentaliser; **to become
~d** s'occidentaliser
west-facing *adj* exposé/-e à l'ouest
West Indian **1** *n* Antillais/-e *m/f*
2 *adj* antillais/-e
West Indies *pr n pl* Antilles *fpl*
wet **1** *adj* **(a)** (damp) ⟨hair, clothes, grass,
surface⟩ mouillé/-e; **to get ~** se faire
mouiller; **to get one's feet ~** se mouiller les
pieds; **to get the floor ~** tremper le sol; **~
through** trempé/-e
(b) (freshly applied) ⟨cement, varnish⟩ humide;
'~ paint' 'peinture fraîche'
(c) (rainy) ⟨weather, day, night⟩
pluvieux/-ieuse; ⟨season⟩ des pluies; **when
it's ~** quand il pleut
(d) (GB) ⟨person⟩ qui manque de caractère
2 *vtr* **(a)** mouiller ⟨floor, object, clothes⟩
(b) to ~ one's pants/the bed ⟨adult⟩
mouiller sa culotte/le lit; ⟨child⟩ faire pipi
dans sa culotte/dans son lit
wet blanket *n* (colloq) rabat-joie *mf inv*
wet-look *adj* luisant/-e
wet suit *n* combinaison *f* de plongée
whack **1** *n* (blow) (grand) coup *m*
2 *excl* paf!
3 *vtr* **(a)** (hit) battre ⟨person, animal⟩;
frapper ⟨ball⟩
(b) (GB) (colloq) (defeat) piler (colloq)
whacked *adj* (colloq) (tired) vanné/-e (colloq)
whacky *adj* (colloq) ⟨person⟩ dingue (colloq);
⟨sense of humour⟩ farfelu/-e (colloq)
whale **1** *n* **(a)** (Zool) baleine *f* ⋯✣

W

(b) (colloq) **to have a ~ of a time** s'amuser comme un fou

2 *vtr* (US) (colloq) (thrash) donner une raclée à (colloq)

whaling *n* pêche *f* à la baleine

wharf *n* quai *m*

what

■ Note **As a pronoun**
— When used in questions as an object pronoun *what* is translated by *qu'est-ce que* (*qu'est-ce qu'* in front of a vowel or mute 'h'): *what did you say?* qu'est-ce que tu as dit? Alternatively you can use *que* (*qu'* before a vowel or mute 'h'), but note that subject and verb are reversed and a hyphen is inserted before a pronoun: *what did you say?* qu'as-tu dit?
— As a subject pronoun in questions *what is* translated by *qu'est-ce qui*: *what is happening?* qu'est-ce qui se passe? Alternatively *que* can be used and the subject and verb are reversed and the subject becomes *il*: *what is happening?* que se passe-t-il?
— When *what* is used to introduce a clause it is translated by *ce que* (*ce qu'*) as the object of the verb: *I don't know what you want* je ne sais pas ce que tu veux. As the subject of the verb it is translated by *ce qui*: *what matters is that...* ce qui compte c'est que...

1 *pron* **with ~?** avec quoi?; **and ~ else?** et quoi d'autre?; **~ for?** (why) pourquoi?; (about what) à propos de quoi?; **~'s the matter?** qu'est-ce qu'il y a?; **~'s her telephone number?** quel est son numéro de téléphone?; **~'s that button for?** à quoi sert ce bouton?; **~'s it like?** comment c'est?; **do ~ you want** fais ce que tu veux; **take ~ you need** prends ce dont tu as besoin; **~ I need is** ce dont j'ai besoin c'est; **and ~'s more** et en plus; **and ~'s worse** et en plus; **he did ~?** il a fait quoi?; **George ~?** George comment?

2 *det* quel/quelle/quels/quelles; **do you know ~ train he took?** est-ce que tu sais quel train il a pris?; **~ a nice dress/car!** quelle belle robe/voiture!; **~ a strange thing to do!** quelle drôle d'idée!; **~ use is that?** à quoi ça sert?; **~ money he earns he spends** tout ce qu'il gagne, il le dépense; **~ few friends she had** les quelques amis qu'elle avait

3 **what about** *phr* **(a)** (to draw attention) **~ about the children?** et les enfants (alors)?
(b) (to make suggestion) **~ about a meal out?** et si on dînait au restaurant?; **~ about Tuesday?** qu'est-ce que tu dirais de mardi?

4 **what if** *phr* et si; **~ if I bring the dessert?** et si j'apportais le dessert?

5 *excl* quoi!, comment!

IDIOMS **~ with one thing and another** avec ceci et cela

what-d'yer-call-it *n* (colloq) machin *m* (colloq)

whatever **1** *pron* **(a)** (that which) (as subject) ce qui; (as object) ce que; **to do ~ one can** faire ce qu'on peut

(b) (anything that) (as subject) tout ce qui; (as object) tout ce que; **do ~ you like** fais tout ce que tu veux; **~ you say** (as you like) tout ce qui vous plaira

(c) (no matter what) quoi que (+ *subjunctive*); **~ happens** quoi qu'il arrive; **~ she says, ignore it** quoi qu'elle dise n'en tiens pas compte; **~ it costs it doesn't matter** quel que soit le prix, ça n'a pas d'importance

(d) (what on earth) (as subject) qu'est-ce qui; (as object) qu'est-ce que; **~'s that?** qu'est-ce c'est que ça?

2 *det* **(a)** (any) **they eat ~ food they can get** ils mangent tout ce qu'ils trouvent à manger
(b) (no matter what) **~ their arguments** quels que soient leurs arguments; **~ the reason** quelle que soit la raison; **for ~ reason** pour je ne sais quelle raison

3 *adv* (*also* **whatsoever**) **to have no idea ~** ne pas avoir la moindre idée; '**any petrol?**'—'**none**' '~' 'il y a de l'essence?'—'pas du tout'

what's-her-name *n* (colloq) Machin *m* (colloq)

what's-his-name *n* (colloq) Machin *m* (colloq)

wheat *n* blé *m*

wheat germ *n* germe *m* de blé

wheatmeal *n* farine *f* complète

wheedle *vtr* **to ~ sth out of sb** soutirer qch à qn par la cajolerie

wheel **1** *n* **(a)** (on vehicle) roue *f*; (on trolley, piece of furniture) roulette *f*
(b) (for steering) (in vehicle) volant *m*; (on boat) roue *f* (de gouvernail); **to be at** *or* **behind the ~** être au volant
(c) (in watch, mechanism, machine) rouage *m*
(d) (for pottery) tour *m*

2 *vtr* pousser ⟨bicycle, barrow⟩; **they ~ed me into the operating theatre** ils m'ont emmené dans la salle d'opération sur un chariot

3 *vi* (*also* **~ round**) ⟨person, regiment⟩ faire demi-tour; ⟨car, motorbike⟩ braquer fortement; ⟨ship⟩ virer de bord

IDIOMS **to ~ and deal** magouiller (colloq)

wheelbarrow *n* brouette *f*

wheelchair *n* fauteuil *m* roulant

wheelclamp *n* (Aut) sabot *m* de Denver

wheeler dealer *n* (colloq) magouilleur/-euse *m/f* (colloq)

wheelie bin *n* poubelle *f* à roulettes

wheeze *vi* avoir la respiration sifflante

wheezy *adj* ⟨voice, cough⟩ rauque; **to have a ~ chest** avoir la respiration sifflante

when

■ Note *When* in questions is usually translated by *quand*.
— Note that there are three ways of asking questions using *quand*: *when did she leave?* = quand est-ce qu'elle est partie?, elle est partie quand?, quand est-elle partie?
— When talking about future time, *quand* will be used with the future tense of the verb: *tell him when you see him* = dis-lui quand tu le verras.

1 *adv* **(a)** (in questions) quand; **~ are we leaving?** quand est-ce qu'on part?; **~ is the concert?** c'est quand le concert?; **I wonder ~ the film starts** je me demande à quelle heure commence le film; **say ~** dis-moi stop
(b) (whenever) quand; **he's only happy ~ he's moaning** il n'est content que quand il rouspète; **~ I eat ice cream, I feel ill** quand *or* chaque fois que je mange de la glace, j'ai mal au cœur
2 *rel pron* où; **the week ~ it all happened** la semaine où tout cela s'est produit; **there are times ~ it's too stressful** il y a des moments où c'est trop stressant
3 *conj* **(a)** (expressing time) quand; **~ he was at school** quand il était à l'école, lorsqu'il était à l'école; **~ I am 18** quand j'aurai 18 ans; **~ he arrives, I'll let you know** quand il arrivera *or* dès qu'il arrivera, je te le dirai
(b) (expressing contrast) alors que; **why buy their products ~ ours are cheaper?** pourquoi acheter leurs produits alors que les nôtres sont moins chers?
4 *pron* quand; **until/since ~?** jusqu'à/depuis quand?; **1982, that's ~ I was born** 1982, c'est l'année où je suis né; **that's ~ I found out** c'est à ce moment-là que j'ai su

whenever *adv* **(a)** (no matter when) **~ you want** quand tu veux; **I'll come ~ it is convenient** je viendrai quand cela vous arrangera
(b) (every time that) chaque fois que; **~ I see a black cat, I make a wish** chaque fois que je vois un chat noir, je fais un vœu

where

■ **Note** *where* in questions is usually translated by *où*: *where are the plates?* = où sont les assiettes?; *I don't know where the plates are* = je ne sais pas où sont les assiettes; *do you know where he is?* = est-ce que tu sais où il est?; *do you know where Paul is?* = est-ce que tu sais où est Paul?

– Note that *où + est-ce que* does not require a change in word order: *where did you see her?* = où est-ce que tu l'as vue?

1 *adv* où; **~ is my coat?** où est mon manteau?; **~ do you work?** où est-ce que vous travaillez; **ask him ~ he went** demande-lui où il est allé; **do you know ~ she's going?** est-ce tu sais où elle va?; **sit ~ you like** asseyez-vous où vous voulez; **it's cold ~ we live** il fait froid là où nous habitons; **~ necessary** si nécessaire; **~ possible** dans la mesure du possible
2 *pron* **from ~?** d'où?; **that's ~ I fell** c'est là que je suis tombé; **that is ~ he is mistaken** c'est là qu'il se trompe

whereabouts *n pl* do you know his **~?** savez-vous où il est?

whereas *conj* **she likes dogs ~ I prefer cats** elle aime les chiens mais moi je préfère les chats; **he chose to stay quiet ~ I would have complained** il a choisi de ne rien dire alors que moi je me serais sûrement plaint

whereby *conj* **a system ~ all staff will carry identification** un système qui prévoit que tous les membres du personnel auront une carte

wherever *adv* **(a)** (in questions) **~ has he got to?** où est-ce qu'il a bien pu passer?
(b) (anywhere) **~ she goes I'll go** où qu'elle aille, j'irai; **~ you want** où tu veux; **we'll meet ~'s convenient for you** nous nous retrouverons là où ça t'arrange
(c) (whenever) **~ necessary** quand c'est nécessaire; **~ possible** dans la mesure du possible

whet *vtr* **to ~ the appetite** stimuler l'appétit; **the books ~ted his appetite for travel** les livres lui donnèrent envie de voyager

whether *conj*

■ **Note** When *whether* is used to mean *if*, it is translated by *si*: *I wonder whether she got my letter* = je me demande si elle a reçu ma lettre.
– In *whether...or not* sentences, *whether* is translated by *que* and the verb that follows is in the subjunctive.

(a) (when outcome is uncertain) si; **I wasn't sure ~ to answer or not** je ne savais pas s'il fallait répondre; **can you check ~ it's cooked?** est-ce que tu peux vérifier si c'est cuit?
(b) (no matter if) **you're coming ~ you like it or not!** tu viendras que cela te plaise ou non!; **~ you have children or not, this book should interest you** que vous ayez des enfants ou non, ce livre devrait vous intéresser

whew *excl* (in relief) ouf!; (in hot weather) pff!; (in surprise) hein!

which **1** *pron* **(a)** (in questions) lequel/laquelle/lesquels/lesquelles; **there are three peaches, ~ do you want?** il y a trois pêches, laquelle veux-tu?; **show her ~ you mean** montre-lui celui/celle etc dont tu parles; **I don't mind ~** ça m'est égal; **can you tell ~ is ~?** peux-tu les distinguer?
(b) (relative pronoun) (as subject) qui; (as object) que; (with a preposition) lequel/laquelle/lesquels/lesquelles; (with a preposition translated by *de*) dont; **the book ~ is on the table** le livre qui est sur la table; **the book ~ I am reading** le livre que je lis; **the contract ~ he's spoken about** le contrat dont il a parlé; **~ reminds me...** ce qui me fait penser que...
(c) (with a superlative adjective) quel/quelle/quels/quelles; **~ is the biggest?** (masculine objects) quel est le plus gros?
2 *det* quel/quelle/quels/quelles; **~ books?** quels livres?; **she asked me ~ coach was leaving first** elle m'a demandé lequel des cars allait partir le premier; **~ one of the children...?** lequel *or* laquelle des enfants...?; **you may wish to join, in ~ case...** vous voulez peut-être vous inscrire, auquel cas...

whichever **1** *pron* **(a)** (the one that) (as subject) celui *m* qui, celle *f* qui; (as object) celui *m* que, celle *f* que; **'which restaurant?'—'~ is nearest'** 'quel ⋯▷

restaurant?'—'celui qui est le plus proche';
come at 2 or 2.30, ~ suits you best viens à
14 h ou 14 h 30, comme cela te convient le
mieux

(b) (no matter which one) (as subject) quel *m* que
soit celui qui, quelle *f* que soit celle qui; (as
object) quel *m* que soit celui que, quelle *f* que
soit celle que; **'do you want the big piece or
the small piece?'**—'~' 'est-ce que tu veux le
gros ou le petit morceau?'—'n'importe'

2 *det* **(a)** (the one that) **let's go to ~ station is
nearest** allons à la gare la plus proche

(b) (no matter which) **I'll be happy ~ horse wins**
quel que soit le cheval qui gagne je serai
content

whiff *n* (of perfume, food) odeur *f*; (of smoke,
garlic) bouffée *f*

while **1** *conj* (*also* **whilst**) **(a)** (during the
time that) pendant que; **he made a sandwich ~
I phoned** il s'est fait un sandwich pendant
que je téléphonais; **~ in Spain, I visited
Madrid** pendant que j'étais en Espagne, j'ai
visité Madrid; **I fell asleep ~ watching TV** je
me suis endormi en regardant la télé; **close
the door ~ you're at it** ferme la porte
pendant que tu y es

(b) (although) bien que (+ *subjunctive*),
quoique (+ *subjunctive*)

(c) (whereas) alors que, tandis que; **she likes
dogs ~ I prefer cats** elle aime les chiens
mais moi je préfère les chats

2 *n* **a ~ ago** il y a quelque temps; **a ~ later**
quelque temps plus tard; **for a good ~**
pendant longtemps; **a short ~ ago** il y a peu
de temps; **it will take a ~** cela va prendre un
certain temps; **after a (short) ~** au bout d'un
moment; **once in a ~** de temps en temps

■ **while away** tuer ⟨*time*⟩ **(doing, by doing**
en faisant)

whilst = WHILE 1

whim *n* caprice *m*; **on a ~** sur un coup de
tête

whimper **1** *n* gémissement *m* (**of** de)

2 *vi* **(a)** ⟨*person, animal*⟩ gémir

(b) (whinge) ⟨*person*⟩ pleurnicher

whimsical *adj* ⟨*person*⟩ fantasque; ⟨*play,
tale, manner, idea*⟩ saugrenu/-e

whine *vi* (complain) se plaindre (**about** de);
(snivel) pleurnicher; ⟨*dog*⟩ gémir

whinge *vi* (colloq) râler

whining **1** *n* (complaints) jérémiades *fpl*; (of
dog) gémissements *mpl*

2 *adj* ⟨*voice*⟩ geignard/-e; ⟨*child*⟩
pleurnicheur/-euse

whinny *vi* ⟨*horse*⟩ hennir doucement

whip **1** *n* **(a)** (for punishment) fouet *m*; (for
horse) cravache *f*

(b) (Culin) mousse *f*

2 *vtr* **(a)** (beat) fouetter

(b) (Culin) fouetter ⟨*cream*⟩; battre [qch] en
neige ⟨*egg whites*⟩

(c) (colloq) **to ~ sth out** sortir qch
brusquement; (remove quickly) **he ~ped the
plates off the table** il a prestement retiré les
assiettes de la table; **I ~ped the key out of**

his hand je lui ai arraché la clé des mains;
to ~ the crowd up into a frenzy mettre la
foule en délire

whiplash injury *n* (Med) coup *m* du lapin

whip-round *n* (GB) (colloq) collecte *f*

whirl **1** *n* **(a)** (of activity, excitement) tourbillon
m (**of** de)

(b) (spiral motif) spirale *f*

2 *vi* ⟨*dancer*⟩ tournoyer; ⟨*blade, propeller*⟩
tourner; ⟨*snowflakes, dust, thoughts*⟩
tourbillonner

IDIOMS **to give sth a ~** (colloq) essayer qch

■ **whirl round** ⟨*person*⟩ se retourner
brusquement; ⟨*blade, clock hand*⟩ tourner
brusquement

whirlpool *n* tourbillon *m*

whirlpool bath *n* bain *m* bouillonnant.

whirlwind *n* tourbillon *m*

whirr *vi* ⟨*motor*⟩ vrombir; ⟨*camera, fan*⟩
tourner; ⟨*insect*⟩ bourdonner; ⟨*wings*⟩ bruire

whisk **1** *n* (*also* **egg ~**) (manual) fouet *m*;
(electric) batteur *m*

2 *vtr* **(a)** (Culin) battre

(b) (transport quickly) **he was ~ed off to meet
the president** on l'a emmené sur le champ
rencontrer le président; **she was ~ed off to
hospital** elle a été emmenée d'urgence à
l'hôpital

whisker **1** *n* (of animal) poil *m* de
moustache

2 **whiskers** *n pl* (of animal) moustaches *fpl*;
(of man) (beard) barbe *f*; (moustache) moustache
f

whisper **1** *n* chuchotement *m*; **to speak in
a ~ or in ~s** parler à voix basse

2 *vtr* chuchoter (**to** à); **to ~ sth to sb**
chuchoter qch à qn; **'she's asleep,' he ~ed**
'elle dort', dit-il en chuchotant

3 *vi* chuchoter; **to ~ to sb** parler à voix
basse à qn

whistle **1** *n* **(a)** (object) sifflet *m*; **to blow
the or one's ~** donner un coup de sifflet

(b) (sound) (through mouth) sifflement *m*; (by
referee) coup *m* de sifflet; (of bird, train)
sifflement *m*

2 *vtr* siffler; (casually) siffloter

3 *vi* siffler; **to ~ at sb/sth** siffler qn/qch; **to
~ for** siffler ⟨*dog*⟩

IDIOMS **to blow the ~ on sb** dénoncer qn

white **1** *n* **(a)** (gen) blanc *m*

(b) (*also* **White**) (Caucasian) Blanc/Blanche
m/f

(c) (in chess, draughts) blancs *mpl*

2 *adj* **(a)** blanc/blanche; **bright ~ teeth**
dents d'un blanc éclatant; **to go or turn ~**
devenir blanc, blanchir; **to paint sth ~**
peindre qch en blanc

(b) ⟨*race, child, skin*⟩ blanc/blanche; ⟨*area*⟩
habité/-e par des Blancs; ⟨*culture, prejudice*⟩
des Blancs; **a ~ man/woman** un Blanc/une
Blanche

(c) (pale) pâle (**with** de); **to go or turn ~** pâlir
(**with** de)

whitebait *n* (raw) blanchaille *f*; (fried) petite
friture *f*

whiteboard *n* tableau *m* blanc

white coffee *n* (at home) café *m* au lait; (in café) (café *m*) crème *m*

white-collar *adj* ⟨job, work⟩ d'employé de bureau; ⟨staff⟩ de bureau; ∼ **worker** col *m* blanc, employé/-e *m/f* de bureau

white elephant *n* **(a)** (item, knicknack) bibelot *m*
(b) (public project) réalisation *f* coûteuse et peu rentable

white goods *n pl* (appliances) gros électro-ménager *m*

white horses *n pl* (waves) moutons *mpl*

White House *n* the ∼ la Maison Blanche

white-knuckle ride *n* tour *m* de manège qui fait peur

white lie *n* pieux mensonge *m*

whitener *n* **(a)** (for clothes) agent *m* blanchissant
(b) (for shoes) produit *m* pour blanchir
(c) (for coffee, tea) succédané *m* de lait en poudre

whiteness *n* blancheur *f*

white spirit *n* white-spirit *m*

whitewash ⓵ *n* **(a)** (for walls) lait *m* de chaux
(b) (figurative) (cover-up) mise *f* en scène
⓶ *vtr* **(a)** blanchir [qch] à la chaux ⟨wall⟩
(b) (also ∼ **over**) blanchir ⟨facts⟩

white water *n* eau *f* vive

white water rafting *n* rafting *m* en eau vive

white wedding *n* mariage *m* en blanc

Whitsun *n* (also **Whitsuntide**) Pentecôte *f*

Whit Sunday *n* Pentecôte *f*

whittle *vtr* tailler [qch] au couteau; **to ∼ sth away** *or* **down** réduire qch (**to** à)

whizz *vi* **to ∼ by** *or* **past** ⟨arrow, bullet⟩ passer en sifflant; ⟨car⟩ passer à toute allure; ⟨person⟩ passer rapidement

whizz-kid *n* (colloq) jeune prodige *m*

who *pron*

■ Note Note that there are three ways of asking questions using *qui* as the object of the verb: *who did he call?* = qui est-ce qu'il a appelé?, qui a-t-il appelé?, il a appelé qui?

(a) (in questions) (as subject) qui (est-ce qui); (as object) qui (est-ce que); (after prepositions) qui; ∼ **knows the answer?** qui connaît la réponse?; ∼**'s going to be there?** qui sera là?; ∼ **did you invite?** qui est-ce que tu as invité?, qui as-tu invité?; ∼ **was she with?** avec qui était-elle?; ∼ **did you buy it for?** pour qui l'as-tu acheté?; ∼ **did you get it from?** qui te l'a donné?
(b) (relative) (as subject) qui; (as object) que; (after prepositions) qui; **his friend,** ∼ **lives in Paris** son ami, qui habite Paris; **his friend** ∼ **he sees once a week** l'ami qu'il voit une fois par semaine

(c) (whoever) **bring** ∼ **you like** tu peux amener qui tu veux; ∼ **do you think you are?** tu te prends pour qui?

whodun(n)it *n* polar *m* (colloq), roman *m* policier

whoever *pron* **(a)** (the one that) ∼ **wins the election** celui ou celle qui gagnera les élections
(b) (anyone that) (as subject) quiconque; (as object) qui; ∼ **saw the accident should contact us** quiconque a assisté à l'accident devrait nous contacter; **invite** ∼ **you like** invite qui tu veux
(c) (no matter who) ∼ **you are** qui que vous soyez

whole ⓵ *n* **(a)** (total unit) tout *m*; **as a** ∼ (not in separate parts) en entier; (overall) dans l'ensemble
(b) (all) **the** ∼ **of** tout/-e; **the** ∼ **of the weekend/August** tout le week-end/mois d'août; **the** ∼ **of London is talking about it** tout Londres en parle; **nearly the** ∼ **of Berlin was destroyed** Berlin a été presque entièrement détruit
⓶ *adj* **(a)** (entire) tout/-e, entier/-ière; (more emphatic) tout entier/-ière; **a** ∼ **hour** une heure entière; **a** ∼ **day** toute une journée; **for three** ∼ **weeks** pendant trois semaines entières; **his** ∼ **life** toute sa vie, sa vie entière; **the** ∼ **truth** toute la vérité; **the most beautiful city in the** ∼ **world** la plus belle ville du monde
(b) (emphatic use) **a** ∼ **new way of life** un mode de vie complètement différent; **that's the** ∼ **point of the exercise** c'est tout l'intérêt de l'exercice
(c) (intact) intact/-e
⓷ *adv* ⟨swallow, cook⟩ tout entier
⓸ **on the whole** *phr* dans l'ensemble

wholefood *n* (GB) produits *mpl* biologiques

wholehearted *adj* ⟨approval, support⟩ sans réserve; **to be in** ∼ **agreement with** être en accord total avec

wholeheartedly *adv* sans réserve

wholemeal *adj* (also **wholewheat**) complet/-ète

whole milk *n* lait *m* entier

wholesale ⓵ *adj* **(a)** ⟨business⟩ de gros
(b) (large-scale) ⟨destruction⟩ total/-e; ⟨acceptance, rejection⟩ en bloc; ⟨attack⟩ sur tous les fronts
⓶ *adv* **(a)** ⟨buy, sell⟩ en gros
(b) ⟨accept, reject⟩ en bloc

wholesaler *n* grossiste *mf*, marchand/-e *m/f* en gros

wholesome *adj* **(a)** (healthy) sain/-e
(b) (decent) ⟨person, appearance⟩ bien propre; ⟨entertainment⟩ innocent/-e

wholewheat = WHOLEMEAL

wholly *adv* entièrement, tout à fait

whom *pron* **(a)** (in questions) qui (est-ce que); (after prepositions) qui; ∼ **did she meet?** qui ····⊱

a-t-elle rencontré?, qui est-ce qu'elle a rencontré?; **to ~ are you referring?** à qui est-ce que vous faites allusion?
(b) (relative) que; (after prepositions) qui; **the person to ~/of ~ I spoke** la personne à qui/dont j'ai parlé

whooping cough n coqueluche f

whopper n (colloq) (large thing) monstre m

whopping adj (colloq) (also ~ **great**) monstre (colloq)

whorl n (of cream, chocolate) spirale f; (on fingerprint) volute f; (shell pattern) spire f; (of petals) verticille m

whose ⒈ pron (a) (in questions) à qui; ~ **is this?** à qui est ceci?
(b) (relative) dont; **the boy ~ dog was killed** le garçon dont le chien a été tué; **the man ~ daughter he was married to** l'homme dont il avait épousé la fille
⒉ det ~ **pen is that?** à qui est ce stylo?; **do you know ~ car was stolen?** est-ce que tu sais à qui appartenait la voiture volée?; ~ **coat did you take?** tu as pris le manteau de qui?

why

■ **Note** Note that there are three ways of asking questions using *why*:
– *why did you go?* = pourquoi est-ce que tu y es allé?, pourquoi y es-tu allé?, tu y es allé pourquoi?

⒈ adv **(a)** (in questions) pourquoi; ~ **do you ask?** pourquoi est-ce que tu me poses la question?, pourquoi me poses-tu la question?; ~ **bother?** pourquoi se tracasser?; ~ **the delay?** pourquoi ce retard?; ~ **not?** pourquoi pas?; **'tell them'—'~ should I?'** 'dis-le-leur'—'et pourquoi (est-ce que je devrais le faire)?'
(b) (making suggestions) pourquoi; ~ **don't we go away for the weekend?** pourquoi ne pas partir quelque part pour le week-end?; ~ **don't I invite them for dinner?** et si je les invitais à manger?
⒉ conj pour ça; **that is ~ they came** c'est pour ça qu'ils sont venus; **I need to know the reason ~** j'ai besoin de savoir pourquoi

wick n mèche f

wicked adj **(a)** (evil) ⟨person⟩ méchant/-e; ⟨heart, deed⟩ cruel/-elle; ⟨plot⟩ pernicieux/-ieuse; ⟨intention⟩ mauvais/-e (before n)
(b) ⟨grin, humour⟩ malicieux/-ieuse; ⟨thoughts⟩ pervers/-e
(c) (vicious) ⟨wind⟩ méchant/-e; ⟨weapon⟩ redoutable; **to have a ~ tongue** être mauvaise langue

wicker ⒈ n (also **wickerwork**) osier m
⒉ adj ⟨basket, furniture⟩ en osier

wide ⒈ adj **(a)** (broad) ⟨river, opening, mouth⟩ large; ⟨margin⟩ grand/-e; **how ~ is your garden?** quelle est la largeur de votre jardin?; **it's 30 cm ~** il fait 30 cm de large; **the river is 1 km across at its ~st** le fleuve

fait *or* atteint 1 km à son point le plus large; **her eyes were ~ with fear** ses yeux étaient agrandis par la peur
(b) (immense) ⟨ocean, desert, expanse⟩ vaste (before n)
(c) (extensive) ⟨variety, choice⟩ grand/-e (before n); **a ~ range of opinions** une grande variété d'opinions; **a ~ range of products** une vaste gamme de produits
(d) (Sport) ⟨ball, shot⟩ perdu/-e
⒉ adv **to open one's eyes ~** ouvrir grand les yeux; **to open the door/window ~** ouvrir la porte/la fenêtre en grand; **his eyes are (set) ~ apart** il a les yeux très écartés; **his legs were ~ apart** il avait les jambes écartées; **to be ~ of the mark** ⟨ball, dart⟩ être à côté; ⟨guess⟩ être loin de la vérité

wide-angle lens n objectif m à grand angle

wide awake adj complètement éveillé/-e

wide-eyed adj **(a)** (with surprise, fear) **he was ~** il ouvrait de grands yeux; ~ **with fear/surprise** les yeux écarquillés de peur/surprise; **she stared/listened ~** elle regardait/écoutait les yeux écarquillés
(b) (naïve) ⟨person, innocence⟩ ingénu/-e

widely adv **(a)** (commonly) ⟨accepted, used⟩ largement; **this product is now ~ available** on trouve maintenant ce produit partout
(b) ⟨spaced, planted⟩ à de grands intervalles; ⟨travel, differ, vary⟩ beaucoup

widely-read adj ⟨student⟩ qui a beaucoup lu; ⟨author⟩ très lu/-e

widen ⒈ vtr élargir ⟨road, gap⟩; étendre ⟨powers⟩; **this has ~ed their lead in the opinion polls** ceci a renforcé leur position dominante dans les sondages
⒉ vi s'élargir

widening adj ⟨division⟩ de plus en plus grand/-e; ⟨gap⟩ qui s'élargit de plus en plus

wide open adj **(a)** ⟨door, window, eyes, mouth⟩ grand/-e ouvert/-e
(b) **the race is ~** l'issue de la course est indécise

wide-ranging adj ⟨reforms⟩ de grande envergure; ⟨interests⟩ très variés

wide screen n grand écran m

wide-screen TV n téléviseur m à grand écran

widespread adj ⟨epidemic⟩ généralisé/-e; ⟨devastation⟩ étendu/-e; ⟨belief⟩ très répandu/-e

widow ⒈ n veuve f
⒉ vtr **to be ~ed** devenir veuf/veuve m/f

widower n veuf m

width n **(a)** largeur f; **it is 30 metres in ~** il fait *or* mesure 30 mètres de large
(b) (of fabric) lé m

wield vtr **(a)** brandir ⟨weapon, tool⟩
(b) exercer ⟨power⟩ (over sur)

wife n femme f; (more formally) épouse f; **the baker's/farmer's ~** la boulangère/la fermière

wig n (whole head) perruque f; (partial) postiche m

w

wiggle (colloq) ⟨1⟩ *n* a ~ **of the hips** un roulement des hanches
⟨2⟩ *vtr* faire bouger ⟨*tooth, wedged object*⟩; **to ~ one's hips** rouler les hanches; **to ~ one's fingers/toes** remuer les doigts/orteils
⟨3⟩ *vi* ⟨*snake, worm*⟩ se tortiller

wild ⟨1⟩ *n* **in the ~** ⟨*conditions, life*⟩ en liberté; **to grow in the ~** pousser à l'état sauvage; **the call of the ~** l'appel de la nature
⟨2⟩ *adj* **(a)** ⟨*animal, plant*⟩ sauvage; **the pony is still quite ~** le poney est encore assez farouche
(b) ⟨*landscape*⟩ sauvage
(c) ⟨*wind*⟩ violent/-e; ⟨*sea*⟩ agité/-e; **it was a ~ night** c'était une nuit de tempête
(d) ⟨*party, laughter, person*⟩ fou/folle; ⟨*imagination*⟩ délirant/-e; ⟨*applause*⟩ déchaîné/-e; **to go ~** se déchaîner
(e) (colloq) (furious) furieux/-ieuse; **he'll go** *or* **be ~!** ça va le mettre hors de lui!
(f) (colloq) (enthusiastic) **to be ~ about** être un/une fana (colloq) de; **I'm not ~ about him/it** il/ça ne m'emballe pas (colloq) pas
(g) (outlandish) ⟨*idea, plan*⟩ fou/folle; ⟨*claim, promise, accusation*⟩ extravagant/-e; ⟨*story*⟩ farfelu/-e (colloq)
⟨3⟩ *adv* ⟨*grow*⟩ à l'état sauvage; **the garden had run ~** le jardin était devenu une vraie jungle; **those children are allowed to run ~!** on permet à ces enfants de faire n'importe quoi!; **to let one's imagination run ~** laisser libre cours à son imagination

wild boar *n* sanglier *m*

wilderness *n* étendue *f* sauvage et désolée

wild-eyed *adj* au regard égaré

wildfire *n* **to spread like ~** se répandre comme une traînée de poudre

wild flower *n* fleur *f* des champs, fleur *f* sauvage

wild-goose chase *n* **it turned out to be a ~** ça n'a abouti à rien; **to lead sb on a ~** mettre qn sur une mauvaise piste

wildlife *n* (animals) faune *f*; (animals and plants) faune *f* et flore *f*

wildlife park, wildlife reserve, wildlife sanctuary *n* réserve *f* naturelle

wildly *adv* **(a)** ⟨*invest, spend, talk*⟩ de façon insensée; ⟨*fire, shoot*⟩ au hasard; **to hit out/run ~** envoyer des coups/courir dans tous les sens
(b) ⟨*wave, gesture*⟩ de manière très agitée; ⟨*applaud*⟩ à tout rompre; **to fluctuate ~** subir des fluctuations violentes; **to beat ~** ⟨*heart*⟩ battre à tout rompre
(c) ⟨*enthusiastic, optimistic*⟩ extrêmement

wilds *n pl* **to live in the ~ of Arizona** habiter au fin fond de l'Arizona

Wild West *n* Far West *m*

wilful (GB), **willful** (US) *adj* **(a)** ⟨*person, behaviour*⟩ volontaire
(b) ⟨*damage, disobedience*⟩ délibéré/-e

wilfully (GB), **willfully** (US) *adv* **(a)** (in headstrong way) obstinément
(b) (deliberately) délibérément

will¹ ⟨1⟩ *modal aux* **(a)** (expressing the future) **I'll see you tomorrow** je te verrai demain; **it won't rain** il ne pleuvra pas; **~ there be many people?** est-ce qu'il y aura beaucoup de monde?; **they'll come tomorrow** ils vont venir demain; **what ~ you do now?** qu'est-ce que tu vas faire maintenant?
(b) (expressing willingness or intention) **~ you help me?** est-ce que tu m'aideras?; **we won't stay too long** nous ne resterons pas trop longtemps; **he won't cooperate** il ne veut pas coopérer
(c) (in requests, commands) **~ you pass the salt please?** est-ce que tu peux me passer le sel s'il te plaît; **~ you please be quiet!** est-ce que tu vas te taire?; **wait a minute, ~ you!** attends un peu!
(d) (in invitations) **~ you have some tea?** est-ce que vous voulez du thé?; **won't you join us for dinner?** est-ce que tu veux dîner avec nous?; **what ~ you have to drink?** qu'est-ce que tu prends?
(e) (in assumptions) **he'll be about 30 now** il doit avoir 30 ans maintenant; **you'll be tired, I expect** tu dois être fatigué je suppose
(f) (indicating sth predictable or customary) **they ~ ask for a deposit** ils demandent une caution; **these things ~ happen** ce sont des choses qui arrivent; **you ~ keep contradicting her!** il faut toujours que tu la contredises!
(g) (in short answers and tag questions) **you'll come again, won't you?** tu reviendras, n'est-ce pas?; **you won't forget, ~ you?** tu n'oublieras pas, n'est-ce pas?; **that'll be cheaper, won't it?** ça sera moins cher, non?; **'they won't be ready'—'yes, they ~'** 'ils ne seront pas prêts'—'(bien sûr que) si'; **'~ you call me?'—'yes, I ~'** 'est-ce que tu me téléphoneras?'—'bien sûr que oui'; **'she'll be furious'—'no, she won't!'** 'elle sera furieuse'—'bien sûr que non!'; **'I'll do it'—'no you won't!'** 'je le ferai'—'il n'en est pas question!'
⟨2⟩ *vtr* **(a)** (urge mentally) **to ~ sb to do** supplier mentalement qn de faire; **to ~ sb to live** prier pour que qn vive
(b) (wish, desire) vouloir
(c) (Law) léguer (**to** à)

will² ⟨1⟩ *n* **(a)** volonté *f* (**to do** de faire); **to have a ~ of one's own** n'en faire qu'à sa tête; **against my ~** contre mon gré; **to do with a ~** faire de bon cœur; **to lose the ~ to live** ne plus avoir envie de vivre
(b) (Law) testament *m*; **to leave sb sth in one's ~** léguer qch à qn
⟨2⟩ **at will** *phr* ⟨*select, take*⟩ à volonté; **they can wander about at ~** ils peuvent se promener comme ils veulent

willing *adj* **(a)** (prepared) **to be ~ to do** être prêt/-e à faire
(b) (eager) ⟨*pupil, helper*⟩ de bonne volonté; ⟨*slave*⟩ consentant/-e; ⟨*recruit, victim*⟩ volontaire; **to show ~** faire preuve de bonne volonté

W

willingly *adv* ⟨*accept, help*⟩ volontiers; ⟨*work*⟩ avec bonne volonté

willingness *n* (readiness) volonté *f* (**to do** de faire)

willow *n* (*also* ∼ **tree**) saule *m*

will power *n* volonté *f* (**to do** de faire)

willy-nilly *adv* (a) (regardless of choice) bon gré mal gré
(b) (haphazardly) au hasard

wilt *vi* (a) ⟨*plant, flower*⟩ se faner
(b) ⟨*person*⟩ (from heat, fatigue) se sentir faible; (at daunting prospect) perdre courage

wimp *n* (colloq) (ineffectual) lavette *f* (colloq); (fearful) poule *f* mouillée (colloq)

win ⊡ *n* victoire *f* (**over** sur)
⊡ *vtr* (a) gagner ⟨*match, bet, battle, money*⟩; remporter ⟨*election*⟩
(b) (acquire) obtenir ⟨*delay, reprieve*⟩; gagner ⟨*friendship, heart*⟩; s'attirer ⟨*sympathy*⟩; s'acquérir ⟨*support*⟩ (of de); **to** ∼ **sb's love/ respect** se faire aimer/respecter de qn
⊡ *vi* gagner; **to** ∼ **against sb** l'emporter sur qn

■ **win back**: ¶ ∼ [sth] **back**, ∼ **back** [sth] récupérer ⟨*support, votes*⟩ (**from sb** sur qn); regagner ⟨*affection, respect*⟩; reprendre ⟨*prize, territory*⟩ (**from** à)

■ **win over, win round** convaincre ⟨*person*⟩

wince ⊡ *n* grimace *f*
⊡ *vi* grimacer, faire une grimace

winch ⊡ *n* treuil *m*
⊡ *vtr* **to** ∼ **sth down/up** descendre/hisser qch au treuil

wind¹ ⊡ *n* (a) vent *m*; **the** ∼ **is blowing** il y a du vent; **which way is the** ∼ **blowing?** d'où vient le vent?
(b) (breath) **to knock the** ∼ **out of sb** couper le souffle à qn; **to get one's** ∼ reprendre souffle
(c) (flatulence) vents *mpl*; **to break** ∼ lâcher un vent
⊡ *vtr* (a) (make breathless) ⟨*blow, punch*⟩ couper la respiration à; ⟨*climb*⟩ essouffler
(b) faire faire son rot à ⟨*baby*⟩

wind² ⊡ *vtr* (a) (coil up) enrouler ⟨*hair, rope, wire*⟩ (**on, onto** sur; **round** autour de)
(b) (*also* ∼ **up**) remonter ⟨*clock, toy*⟩
(c) donner un tour de ⟨*handle*⟩
(d) **to** ∼ **its way** ⟨*procession, road, river*⟩ serpenter
⊡ *vi* ⟨*road, river*⟩ serpenter (**along** le long de); ⟨*stairs*⟩ tourner

■ **wind down**: ¶ ∼ **down** (a) ⟨*organization*⟩ réduire ses activités; ⟨*activity, production*⟩ toucher à sa fin; ⟨*person*⟩ se détendre
(b) ⟨*clockwork*⟩ être sur le point de s'arrêter
¶ ∼ [sth] **down** (a) baisser ⟨*car window*⟩
(b) mettre fin à ⟨*activity, organization*⟩

■ **wind up**: ¶ ∼ **up** (a) (finish) ⟨*event*⟩ se terminer (**with** par); ⟨*speaker*⟩ conclure
(b) (colloq) (end up) finir, se retrouver
¶ ∼ [sth] **up** (a) liquider ⟨*business*⟩; mettre fin à ⟨*debate, meeting, project*⟩

(b) remonter ⟨*clock, car window*⟩
¶ ∼ [sb] **up** (a) (tease) faire marcher ⟨*person*⟩
(b) (make tense) énerver

wind chimes *n pl* carillon *m* éolien

wind energy *n* énergie *f* éolienne

windfall *n* fruit *m* tombé par terre; (figurative) aubaine *f*

windfall profit *n* profit *m* inattendu

winding *adj* ⟨*road, river*⟩ sinueux/-euse; ⟨*stairs*⟩ en spirale

wind instrument *n* instrument *m* à vent

windmill *n* moulin *m* à vent

window *n* (a) (of house) fenêtre *f*; (of shop, public building) vitrine *f*; (of vehicle) (gen) vitre *f*; (of plane) hublot *m*; (stained glass) vitrail *m*; **to look out of** *or* **through the** ∼ regarder par la fenêtre
(b) (for service at bank or post office) guichet *m*

window blind *n* store *m*

window box *n* jardinière *f*

window cleaner *n* laveur/-euse *m/f* de carreaux

window display *n* vitrine *f*

window ledge *n* appui *m* de fenêtre

windowpane *n* carreau *m*

window seat *n* (a) (in room) banquette *f*
(b) (in plane, bus, train) place *f* côté vitre

window-shopping *n* **to go** ∼ faire du lèche-vitrines *m inv* (colloq)

windowsill *n* rebord *m* de fenêtre

windpipe *n* trachée-artère *f*

windpower *n* énergie *f* éolienne

windscreen (GB), **windshield** (US) *n* pare-brise *m inv*

windscreen wiper *n* (GB) essuie-glace *m inv*

windshield (US) = WINDSCREEN

windsurf *vi* faire de la planche à voile

windsurfer *n* (person) véliplanchiste *mf*; (board) planche *f* à voile

windswept *adj* venteux/-euse

windy *adj* ⟨*place*⟩ venteux/-euse; ⟨*day*⟩ de vent; **it was very** ∼ il faisait beaucoup de vent

wine *n* (a) (drink) vin *m*
(b) (colour) lie-de-vin *m*

wine bar *n* bar *m* à vin

wine box *n* ≈ cubitainer® *m*

wine cellar *n* cave *f*

wine glass *n* verre *m* à vin

wine grower *n* viticulteur/-trice *m/f*

wine growing ⊡ *n* viticulture *f*
⊡ *adj* ⟨*region*⟩ vinicole

wine list *n* carte *f* des vins

wine rack *n* casier *m* à bouteilles

wine shop *n* marchand *m* de vin

wine tasting *n* dégustation *f* de vins

wine vinegar *n* vinaigre *m* de vin

wine waiter *n* sommelier/-ière *m/f*

wing ⊡ *n* aile *f*

2 wings n pl (in theatre) **the ~s** les coulisses fpl; **to be waiting in the ~s** (figurative) attendre son heure

winger n (GB) (colloq) ailier m

wing nut n écrou m à oreilles

wink 1 n clin m d'œil; **we didn't get a ~ of sleep all night** nous n'avons pas fermé l'œil de la nuit
2 vi cligner de l'œil; **to ~ at sb** faire un clin d'œil à qn

winner n (a) (victor) gagnant/-e m/f
(b) (success) **to be a ~** ⟨film, book, song⟩ avoir un gros succès

winning adj (a) (victorious) gagnant/-e
(b) ⟨smile⟩ engageant/-e; **to have ~ ways** avoir du charme

winning post n poteau m d'arrivée

winnings n pl gains mpl

winning streak n **to be on a ~** être dans une bonne période

winter 1 n hiver m; **in ~** en hiver
2 adj ⟨sports, clothes, weather⟩ d'hiver
3 vi passer l'hiver

wintertime n hiver m

wipe 1 n (a) **to give sth a ~** (clean, dust) donner un coup de chiffon à qch; (dry) essuyer qch
(b) (for face, baby) lingette f
2 vtr essuyer ⟨table, glass⟩ (on sur; with avec); **to ~ one's hands/feet** s'essuyer les mains/les pieds; **to ~ one's nose** se moucher; **to ~ a baby's bottom** essuyer (les fesses d')un bébé; **to ~ the dishes** essuyer la vaisselle
■ **wipe away** essuyer ⟨tears, sweat⟩; faire partir ⟨dirt, mark⟩
■ **wipe out** (a) nettoyer ⟨container, cupboard⟩
(b) annuler ⟨inflation⟩; anéantir ⟨species, enemy, population⟩
■ **wipe up:** ¶ **~ up** essuyer la vaisselle; ¶ **~ [sth] up** essuyer

wipe-clean adj facile à nettoyer

wire 1 n (a) fil m; **electric/telephone ~** fil électrique/téléphonique
(b) (US) (telegram) télégramme m
2 vtr (a) **to ~ a house** installer l'électricité dans une maison; **to ~ a plug/a lamp** connecter une prise/une lampe
(b) (telegraph) télégraphier à ⟨person⟩; télégraphier ⟨money⟩

wiring n (in house) installation f électrique; (in appliance) circuit m (électrique)

wiry adj (a) ⟨person, body⟩ mince et nerveux/-euse
(b) ⟨hair⟩ rêche

wisdom n sagesse f

wisdom tooth n dent f de sagesse

wise 1 adj ⟨person, words, precaution, saying⟩ sage; ⟨choice, investment⟩ judicieux/-ieuse; ⟨smile, nod⟩ avisé/-e; **a ~ man** un sage; **a ~ move** une décision judicieuse; **to be none the ~r** (understand no better) ne pas être plus avancé/-e; (not realize) ne s'apercevoir de rien

2 -wise combining form (a) (direction) dans le sens de; **length-~** dans le sens de la longueur
(b) (with regard to) pour ce qui est de; **work-~** pour ce qui est du travail

wisecrack n vanne f (colloq)

wise guy n (colloq) gros malin m (colloq)

wisely adv judicieusement

wish 1 n (a) (request) souhait m (for de); **to make a ~** faire un vœu; **her ~ came true** son souhait s'est réalisé
(b) (desire) désir m (for de; **to do** de faire); **to go against sb's ~es** aller contre la volonté de qn
2 **wishes** n pl vœux mpl; **good** or **best ~es** meilleurs vœux; (ending letter) bien amicalement; **best ~es on your birthday** meilleurs vœux pour votre anniversaire; **please give him my best ~es** je vous prie de lui faire toutes mes amitiés
3 vtr (a) (expressing longing) **I ~ he were here/had been here** si seulement il était ici/ avait été ici; **he ~ed he had written** il regrettait de ne pas avoir écrit
(b) (express congratulations, greetings) souhaiter; **I ~ you good luck/a happy birthday** je vous souhaite bonne chance/un bon anniversaire; **I ~ him well** je souhaite que tout aille bien pour lui
(c) (want) souhaiter, désirer
4 vi (a) (desire) vouloir; **just as you ~** comme vous voudrez
(b) (make a wish) faire un vœu

wishful thinking n **that's ~** c'est prendre ses désirs pour des réalités

wishy-washy adj (colloq) ⟨colour⟩ délavé/-e; ⟨person⟩ incolore et inodore (colloq)

wisp n (of hair) mèche f; (of straw) brin m; (of smoke, cloud) volute f

wispy adj ⟨hair, beard⟩ fin/-e; ⟨cloud, smoke⟩ léger/-ère

wisteria n glycine f

wistful adj (sad) mélancolique; (nostalgic) nostalgique

wit 1 n (a) (sense of humour) esprit m
(b) (witty person) personne f spirituelle
2 **to wit** phr à savoir

witch n sorcière f

witchcraft n sorcellerie f

witch doctor n shaman m

witch-hunt n chasse f aux sorcières

with prep (a) (gen) avec; **a meeting ~ sb** une réunion avec qn; **to hit sb ~ sth** frapper qn avec qch; **~ difficulty/pleasure** avec difficulté/plaisir; **to be patient ~ sb** être patient/-e avec qn; **delighted ~ sth** ravi/-e de qch; **to travel ~ sb** voyager avec qn; **to live ~ sb** (in one's own house) vivre avec qn; (in their house) vivre chez qn; **I'll be ~ you in a second** je suis à vous dans un instant; **take your umbrella ~ you** emporte ton parapluie; **bring the books back ~ you** rapporte les livres
(b) (in descriptions) à; avec; de; **a girl ~ black hair** une fille aux cheveux noirs; **the boy ~** ⋯▸

W

the broken leg le garçon à la jambe cassée; **a boy ~ a broken leg** un garçon avec une jambe cassée; **a TV ~ remote control** une télévision avec télécommande; **furnished ~ antiques** meublé/-e avec des meubles anciens; **covered ~ mud** couvert/-e de boue; **to lie ~ one's eyes closed** être allongé/-e les yeux fermés; **to stand ~ one's arms folded** se tenir les bras croisés; **filled ~ sth** rempli/-e de qch
(c) (according to) **to increase ~ time** augmenter avec le temps; **to vary ~ the temperature** varier selon la température
(d) (owning, bringing) **passengers ~ tickets** les passagers munis de billets; **people ~ qualifications** les gens qualifiés; **somebody ~ your experience** quelqu'un qui a ton expérience; **have you got the report ~ you?** est-ce que tu as (amené) le rapport?
(e) (as regards) **how are things ~ you?** comment ça va?; **what's up ~ you?** qu'est-ce que tu as?; **what do you want ~ another car?** qu'est-ce que tu veux faire d'une deuxième voiture?
(f) (because of) **sick ~ worry** malade d'inquiétude; **he can see better ~ his glasses on** il voit mieux avec ses lunettes; **I can't do it ~ you watching** je ne peux pas le faire si tu me regardes
(g) (suffering from) **people ~ Aids/leukemia** les personnes atteintes du sida/de leucémie; **to be ill ~ flu** avoir la grippe
(h) (employed by, customer of) **a reporter ~ the Gazette** un journaliste de la Gazette; **he's ~ the UN** il travaille pour l'ONU; **I'm ~ Chemco** je travaille chez Chemco; **we're ~ the National Bank** nous sommes à la National Bank
(i) (in the same direction as) **to sail ~ the wind** naviguer dans le sens du vent; **to drift ~ the tide** dériver avec le courant

withdraw ① *vtr* retirer ⟨*hand, money, application, permission, troops*⟩; renoncer à, retirer ⟨*claim*⟩; rétracter ⟨*accusation, statement*⟩
② *vi* **(a)** (gen) se retirer (**from** de)
(b) (psychologically) se replier sur soi-même

withdrawal *n* **(a)** (of money, troops) retrait *m* (**of, from** de)
(b) (psychological reaction) repli *m* sur soi
(c) (of drug addict) état *m* de manque

withdrawal symptoms *n pl* symptômes *mpl* de manque; **to be suffering from ~** être en état de manque

withdrawn *adj* ⟨*person*⟩ renfermé/-e, replié/-e sur soi-même

wither ① *vtr* flétrir
② *vi* se flétrir

withering *adj* ⟨*look*⟩ plein/-e de mépris; ⟨*contempt, comment*⟩ cinglant/-e

withhold *vtr* différer ⟨*payment*⟩; retenir ⟨*tax, grant, rent*⟩; refuser ⟨*consent, permission*⟩; ne pas divulguer ⟨*information*⟩

within ① *prep* **(a)** (inside) **~ the city walls**

dans l'enceinte de la ville; **~ the party** au sein du parti; **it's a play ~ a play** c'est une pièce dans la pièce
(b) (in expressions of time) **I'll do it ~ the hour** je le ferai en moins d'une heure; **15 burglaries ~ a month** 15 cambriolages en (moins d')un mois; **they died ~ a week of each other** ils sont morts à une semaine d'intervalle
(c) (not more than) **to be ~ several metres of sth** être à quelques mètres seulement de qch; **it's accurate to ~ a millimetre** c'est exact au millimètre près
(d) **to live ~ one's income** vivre selon ses moyens
② *adv* à l'intérieur; **from ~** de l'intérieur

without ① *prep* sans; **~ a key** sans clé; **~ any money** sans argent; **she left ~ it** elle est partie sans; **they left ~ me** ils sont partis sans moi; **~ looking** sans regarder; **it goes ~ saying** cela va de soi
② *adv* à l'extérieur; **from ~** de l'extérieur

withstand *vtr* résister à

witness ① *n* **(a)** (gen, Law) (person) témoin *m*; **she was a ~ to the accident** elle a été témoin de l'accident; **~ for the prosecution/the defence** témoin à charge/à décharge
(b) (testimony) témoignage *m*; **to be** *or* **bear ~ to sth** témoigner de qch
② *vtr* **(a)** (see) être témoin de, assister à ⟨*incident, attack*⟩
(b) servir de témoin lors de la signature de ⟨*will, treaty*⟩; être témoin à ⟨*marriage*⟩

witness box (GB), **witness stand** (US) *n* barre *f* des témoins

wits *n pl* (intelligence) intelligence *f*; (presence of mind) présence *f* d'esprit; **to collect** *or* **gather one's ~** rassembler ses esprits; **to frighten sb out of their ~** faire une peur épouvantable à qn; **to live by one's ~** vivre d'expédients; **a battle of ~** une joute verbale
IDIOMS **to be at one's ~ end** ne plus savoir quoi faire

witticism *n* bon mot *m*

witty *adj* spirituel/-elle

wizard *n* **(a)** (magician) magicien *m*
(b) (expert) **to be a ~ at chess/computing** être un as (colloq) aux échecs/en informatique

wizened *adj* ratatiné/-e

wobble *vi* ⟨*table, chair*⟩ branler; ⟨*pile of books, plates*⟩ osciller; ⟨*jelly*⟩ trembloter; ⟨*person*⟩ (on bicycle) osciller; (on ladder, tightrope) chanceler

wobbly *adj* ⟨*table, chair*⟩ bancal/-e; ⟨*tooth*⟩ branlant/-e

woe *n* malheur *m*; **a tale of ~** une histoire pathétique

wolf *n* loup *m*; **she-~** louve *f*
IDIOMS **to cry ~** crier au loup

wolf-whistle ① *n* sifflement *m*
② *vi* siffler

woman *n* femme *f*; **a ~ Prime Minister** une femme premier ministre; **he's always criticizing women drivers** il est toujours en train de critiquer les femmes au volant

woman friend *n* amie *f*

womanizer *n* coureur *m* (de jupons)

womb *n* (Anat) utérus *m*

women's refuge *n* foyer *m* pour femmes battues

women's studies *n pl* études *fpl* féministes

wonder ⟦1⟧ *n* (a) (miracle) merveille *f*; **to do** *or* **work** ∼s faire des merveilles (**for** pour; **with** avec); (**it's) no** ∼ **that he's late** (ce n'est) pas étonnant qu'il soit en retard
(b) (amazement) émerveillement *m*
⟦2⟧ *vtr* (ask oneself) se demander; **I** ∼ **how/why/whether** je me demande comment/pourquoi/si; (as polite request) **I** ∼ **if you could help me?** pourriez-vous m'aider?; **it makes you** ∼ cela donne à penser; **it makes you** ∼ **why** c'est à se demander pourquoi
⟦3⟧ *vi* (a) (think) ∼ **about sth/about doing sth** penser à qch/à faire qch
(b) (be surprised) **to** ∼ **at sth** s'étonner de qch; (admiringly) s'émerveiller de qch

wonderful *adj* ⟨book, film, meal, experience, holiday⟩ merveilleux/-euse; ⟨musician, teacher⟩ excellent/-e

wonderfully *adv* ⟨funny, exciting, clever⟩ très; ⟨work, cope, drive⟩ admirablement

wonky *adj* (colloq) (crooked) de traviole (colloq); (wobbly) ⟨furniture⟩ bancal/-e

wont *adj* **to be** ∼ **to do** avoir coutume de faire; **as is his/their** ∼ comme à son/leur habitude

woo *vtr* courtiser

wood ⟦1⟧ *n* bois *m*
⟦2⟧ **woods** *n pl* bois *mpl*
⟦3⟧ *adj* ⟨fire, smoke⟩ de bois; ∼ **floor** plancher *m*
IDIOMS **touch** ∼! (GB), **knock on** ∼! (US) touchons du bois!; **we are not out of the** ∼ **yet** on n'est pas encore sorti de l'auberge

wooden *adj* (a) ⟨furniture, object, house⟩ en bois; ⟨leg, spoon⟩ de bois
(b) ⟨expression⟩ figé/-e

woodland *n* bois *m*

woodpecker *n* pic *m*

wood pigeon *n* pigeon *m* ramier

woodwind *n pl* bois *mpl*

woodwork *n* (a) (carpentry) menuiserie *f*
(b) (doors, windows) boiseries *fpl*

woodworm *n* ver *m* du bois

wool *n* laine *f*; **pure (new)** ∼ pure laine (vierge).
IDIOMS **to pull the** ∼ **over sb's eyes** duper qn

woollen (GB), **woolen** (US) ⟦1⟧ *n* (garment) lainage *m*
⟦2⟧ *adj* ⟨garment⟩ de laine

woolly (GB), **wooly** (US) ⟦1⟧ *n* (colloq) lainage *m*
⟦2⟧ *adj* (a) ⟨garment⟩ de laine; ⟨animal coat, hair⟩ laineux/-euse; ⟨cloud⟩ cotonneux/-euse
(b) ⟨thinking⟩ flou/-e

word ⟦1⟧ *n* (a) mot *m*; **to have the last** ∼ avoir le dernier mot; **I couldn't get a** ∼ **in** je n'ai pas pu placer un mot; **in other** ∼s en d'autres termes; **a** ∼ **of warning** un avertissement; **a** ∼ **of advice** un conseil; **too sad for** ∼s trop triste; **I believed every** ∼ **he said** je croyais tout ce qu'il me disait; **I mean every** ∼ **of it** je pense ce que je dis; **a man of few** ∼s un homme peu loquace; **not a** ∼ **to anybody** pas un mot à qui que ce soit; **I don't believe a** ∼ **of it** je n'en crois pas un mot
(b) (information) nouvelles *fpl* (**about** concernant); **there is no** ∼ **of the missing climbers** on est sans nouvelles des alpinistes disparus; ∼ **got out that...** la nouvelle a transpiré que...; **to bring/send** ∼ **that** annoncer/faire savoir que
(c) (promise, affirmation) parole *f*; **he gave me his** ∼ il m'a donné sa parole; **to keep/break one's** ∼ tenir/ne pas tenir parole; **to take sb's** ∼ **for it** croire qn sur parole; **take my** ∼ **for it!** crois-moi!
(d) (rumour) ∼ **has it that he's a millionaire** on dit qu'il est millionnaire; ∼ **got around that...** le bruit a couru que...
(e) (command) ordre *m*; **to give the** ∼ **to do** donner l'ordre de faire
⟦2⟧ **words** *n pl* (of play) texte *m*; (of song) paroles *fpl*
⟦3⟧ *vtr* formuler ⟨reply, letter, statement⟩
IDIOMS **my** ∼! (in surprise) ma parole!; **right from the** ∼ **go** dès le départ; **to have a** ∼ **with sb about sth** parler à qn à propos de qch; **to have** ∼s **with sb** s'accrocher avec qn; **to put in a good** ∼ **for sb** glisser un mot en faveur de qn

word for word *adv* ⟨copy, translate⟩ mot à mot; ⟨repeat⟩ mot pour mot

wording *n* formulation *f*

wordlist *n* liste *f* de mots

word-of-mouth ⟦1⟧ *adj* verbal/-e
⟦2⟧ **by word of mouth** *phr* verbalement

word processing, WP *n* traitement *m* de texte

word processor *n* machine *f* à traitement de texte

work ⟦1⟧ *n* (a) (physical or mental activity) travail *m* (**on** sur); **it was hard** ∼ **doing** ça a été dur de faire; **to be hard at** ∼ travailler dur; **it's thirsty** ∼ ça donne soif
(b) (occupation) travail *m*; **to be in** ∼ avoir du travail *or* un emploi; **place of** ∼ lieu *m* de travail; **to be off** ∼ (on vacation) être en congé; **to be off** ∼ **with flu** être en arrêt de travail parce qu'on a la grippe; **to be out of** ∼ être au chômage
(c) (place of employment) **to go to** ∼ aller au travail
(d) (building, construction) travaux *mpl* (**on** sur)
(e) (essay, report) travail *m*; (artwork, novel, sculpture) œuvre *f* (**by** de); (study) ouvrage *m* (**by** de; **on** sur); (research) recherches *fpl* (**on** sur); **a** ∼ **of reference** un ouvrage de référence; **a** ∼ **of fiction** une œuvre de fiction; **the** ∼s **of Racine** l'œuvre *m* de Racine; **this attack is the** ∼ **of professionals** l'attaque est l'œuvre de professionnels ⋯⋯⟶

W

2 works n pl **(a)** (factory) usine f
(b) (building work) travaux mpl
(c) (colloq) (everything) **the (full** or **whole) ~s** toute la panoplie (colloq)
3 vtr **(a)** (drive) **to ~ sb hard** surmener qn
(b) (labour) **to ~ days/nights** travailler de jour/de nuit; **to ~ a 40 hour week** faire la semaine de 40 heures; **he ~ed his way through college** il a travaillé pour payer ses études
(c) (operate) se servir de ‹computer, machine›
(d) (exploit commercially) exploiter ‹mine, seam›
(e) (bring about) **to ~ wonders** or **miracles** faire des merveilles
(f) (use to one's advantage) **to ~ the system** exploiter le système
(g) (fashion) travailler ‹clay, metal›
(h) (manoeuvre) **to ~ sth into** introduire qch dans ‹slot, hole›; **to ~ a lever up and down** actionner un levier
(i) (exercise) faire travailler ‹muscles›
(j) (move) **to ~ one's way through** se frayer un passage à travers ‹crowd›; **to ~ one's way along** avancer le long de ‹ledge, windowsill›; **to ~ one's hands free** se libérer les mains; **it ~ed its way loose, it ~ed itself loose** cela s'est desserré peu à peu
4 vi **(a)** (do a job) travailler (**doing** à faire); **to ~ for a living** gagner sa vie
(b) (strive) lutter (**against** contre; **for** pour; **to do** pour faire); **to ~ towards** aller vers ‹solution›; s'acheminer vers ‹compromise›; négocier ‹agreement›
(c) (function) fonctionner; **to ~ on electricity** marcher or fonctionner à l'électricité; **the washing machine isn't ~ing** la machine à laver est en panne
(d) (act, operate) **it doesn't** or **things don't ~ like that** ça ne marche pas comme ça; **to ~ in sb's favour** tourner à l'avantage de qn; **to ~ against sb** jouer en la défaveur de qn
(e) (be successful) ‹treatment› avoir de l'effet; ‹detergent, drug› agir (**against** contre; **on** sur); ‹plan› réussir; ‹argument, theory› tenir debout; **flattery won't ~ with me** la flatterie ne marche pas avec moi
IDIOMS **to ~ one's way up** gravir tous les échelons; **to ~ one's way up the company** faire son chemin dans l'entreprise

■ **work in**: **~ in [sth], ~ [sth] in (a)** glisser ‹joke›; mentionner ‹fact, name›
(b) ((Culin)) incorporer

■ **work off (a)** (remove) retirer ‹lid›
(b) (repay) travailler pour rembourser ‹loan, debt›
(c) (get rid of) se débarrasser de ‹excess weight›; dépenser ‹excess energy›; passer ‹anger, frustration›

■ **work on**: **¶ ~ on** continuer à travailler; **¶ ~ on [sb]** travailler (colloq) ‹person›; **¶ ~ on [sth]** travailler à ‹book, report›; travailler sur ‹project›; s'occuper de ‹case, problem›; chercher ‹cure, solution›; examiner ‹idea, theory›

■ **work out**: **¶ ~ out (a)** (exercise) s'entraîner
(b) (go according to plan) marcher

(c) (add up) **to ~ out at** (GB) or **to** (US) s'élever à
¶ ~ [sth] out (a) (calculate) calculer ‹amount›
(b) (solve) trouver ‹answer, reason, culprit›; résoudre ‹problem›; comprendre ‹clue›
(c) (devise) concevoir ‹plan, scheme›; trouver ‹route›
¶ ~ [sb] out comprendre ‹person›

■ **work up**: **¶ ~ up [sth]** développer ‹interest›; accroître ‹support›; **to ~ up the courage to do** trouver le courage de faire; **to ~ up some enthusiasm for** s'enthousiasmer pour; **to ~ up an appetite** s'ouvrir l'appétit
¶ ~ up to [sth] se préparer à ‹confrontation, announcement›
¶ ~ [sb] up (a) (excite) exciter ‹child, crowd›
(b) (annoy) **to get ~ed up, to ~ oneself up** s'énerver

workable adj **(a)** ‹idea, plan, suggestion› réalisable; ‹system› pratique; ‹arrangement, compromise› possible
(b) ‹land, mine› exploitable; ‹cement› maniable

workaholic n (colloq) bourreau m de travail

workbook n (blank) cahier m; (with exercises) livre m d'exercices

worker n (in manual job) ouvrier/-ière m/f; (in white-collar job) employé/-e m/f

work experience n stage m

workforce n (in industry) main-d'œuvre f; (in service sector) effectifs mpl

working adj **(a)** ‹parent, woman› qui travaille; ‹conditions, environment, methods› de travail; ‹population, life› actif/-ive; ‹breakfast, lunch, day› de travail; **during ~ hours** (in office) pendant les heures de bureau; (in shop) pendant les heures d'ouverture
(b) (provisional) ‹document› de travail; ‹definition, title› provisoire
(c) (functional) ‹model› qui fonctionne; ‹farm, mine› en exploitation; **in full ~ order** en parfait état de marche

working class **1** n classe f ouvrière; **the ~es** les classes fpl laborieuses
2 working-class adj ‹area, background, family, life› ouvrier/-ière; ‹culture, London› prolétarien/-ienne; ‹person› de la classe ouvrière

workings n pl rouages mpl
workload n charge f de travail
workman n ouvrier m
workmanship n **a carpenter famous for sound ~** un menuisier connu pour la qualité de son travail; **furniture of the finest ~** des meubles d'une belle facture; **a piece of poor** or **shoddy ~** du travail mal fait or bâclé
workmate n collègue mf de travail
work of art n œuvre f d'art
workout n séance f de mise en forme
workpack n fiches fpl de travail
work permit n permis m de travail
workplace n lieu m de travail
work-sharing n partage m du travail

worksheet *n* (Sch) feuille *f* de questions

workshop *n* atelier *m*

work station *n* poste *m* de travail

worktop *n* plan *m* de travail

work-to-rule *n* grève *f* du zèle

world ① *n* monde *m*; **throughout the ~** dans le monde entier; **to go round the ~** faire le tour du monde; **the biggest in the ~** le plus grand du monde; **more than anything in the ~** plus que tout au monde; **to go up in the ~** faire du chemin; **to go down in the ~** déchoir; **the Eastern/Western ~** les pays de l'Est/occidentaux; **the ancient ~** l'antiquité; **he lives in a ~ of his own** il vit dans un monde à part
② *adj* ⟨events, market, leader, politics, rights, scale⟩ mondial/-e; ⟨record, tour, championship⟩ du monde; ⟨cruise⟩ autour du monde
IDIOMS **to be on top of the ~** être aux anges; **to get the best of both ~s** gagner sur les deux tableaux; **a man/woman of the ~** un homme/une femme d'expérience; **out of this ~** extraordinaire; **there's a ~ of difference** il y a une différence énorme; **it did him the** *or* **a ~ of good** ça lui a fait énormément de bien; **to think the ~ of sb** penser le plus grand bien de qn; **what/ where/who in the ~?** que/où/qui etc diable?; **~s apart** diamétralement opposé

world-class *adj* de niveau mondial

World Cup *n* Coupe *f* du Monde

World Fair *n* Exposition *f* universelle

world-famous *adj* mondialement connu/-e

world leader *n* **(a)** (politician) chef *m* d'État
(b) (athlete) meilleur/-e *m/f* du monde; (company) leader *m* mondial

worldly *adj* **(a)** (not spiritual) matériel/-ielle
(b) (experienced) ⟨person⟩ avisé/-e, qui a de l'expérience

worldly-wise *adj* avisé/-e, qui a de l'expérience

world music *n* musiques *fpl* du monde

world power *n* puissance *f* mondiale

worldview *n* vision *f* du monde

world war *n* guerre *f* mondiale; **the First/ Second World War** la Première/Seconde Guerre mondiale

world-wide ① *adj* mondial/-e
② *adv* dans le monde entier

World Wide Web *n* Toile *f* mondiale, Web *m*

worm *n* ver *m*

worn *adj* ⟨carpet, clothing, shoe, tyre⟩ usé/-e; ⟨stone⟩ abîmé/-e; ⟨tread⟩ lisse

worn-out *adj* **(a)** ⟨carpet, brake⟩ complètement usé/-e
(b) ⟨person⟩ épuisé/-e

worried *adj* ⟨person, face⟩ inquiet/-iète; **to be ~ about sb/sth** se faire du souci *or* s'inquiéter pour qn/qch; **I'm ~ (that) he might get lost** j'ai peur qu'il ne se perde

worrier *n* anxieux/-ieuse *m/f*

worry ① *n* **(a)** (anxiety) soucis *mpl* (**about, over** à propos de)
(b) (problem) souci *m* (**about, over** au sujet de)
② *vtr* **(a)** (concern) inquiéter; **I ~ that he won't come** j'ai peur qu'il ne vienne pas; **it worried him that he couldn't find the keys** ça l'a inquiété de ne pas trouver les clés
(b) (bother) ennuyer; **would it ~ you if I opened the window?** est-ce que ça vous ennuierait que j'ouvre la fenêtre?
(c) ⟨dog⟩ harceler ⟨sheep⟩
③ *vi* (be anxious) s'inquiéter; **to ~ about** *or* **over sb/sth** s'inquiéter *or* se faire du souci pour qn/qch; **don't ~!** ne t'inquiète pas!; **there's nothing to ~ about** il n'y a pas lieu de s'inquiéter
④ *v refl* **to ~ oneself** s'inquiéter, se faire du souci (**about sb** au sujet de qn; **about sth** à propos de qch); **to ~ oneself sick over sth** se ronger les sangs (colloq) au sujet de qch
■ **worry at** ⟨dog⟩ mordiller, jouer avec ⟨toy⟩; ⟨person⟩ retourner [qch] dans tous les sens ⟨problem⟩

worry beads *n pl* chapelet *m* antistress

worrying *adj* inquiétant/-e

worse ① *adj* pire (**than** que); **to get ~** ⟨pressure, noise⟩ augmenter; ⟨conditions, weather⟩ empirer; ⟨illness, conflict⟩ s'aggraver; **he's getting ~** (in health) il va plus mal; **the cough is getting ~** la toux empire; **to feel ~** (more ill) se sentir plus malade; (more unhappy) aller moins bien; **and what is ~** et le pire, c'est que; **and to make matters ~**, he lied et pour ne rien arranger, il a menti
② *n* **there is ~ to come** ce n'est pas encore le pire; **to change for the ~** empirer
③ *adv* ⟨play, sing⟩ moins bien (**than** que); **to behave ~** se conduire plus mal; **she could do ~ than follow his example** ce ne serait pas si mal si elle suivait son exemple

worsen ① *vtr* aggraver ⟨situation, problem⟩
② *vi* ⟨condition, health, weather, situation⟩ se détériorer; ⟨problem, crisis, shortage, flooding⟩ s'aggraver

worsening ① *n* aggravation *f* (**of** de)
② *adj* ⟨situation⟩ en voie de détérioration; ⟨problem, shortage⟩ en voie d'aggravation

worse off *adj* **(a)** (less wealthy) **to be ~** avoir moins d'argent (**than** que); **I'm £10 a week ~** j'ai dix livres de moins par semaine
(b) (in a worse situation) **to be ~** être dans une situation pire

worship ① *n* **(a)** (religious devotion) culte *m*; **sun/ancestor ~** culte du soleil/des ancêtres; **place of ~** lieu *m* de culte
(b) (veneration) vénération *f*
② **Worship** *pr n* (GB) **Your Worship** (to judge) Monsieur le juge; (to mayor) Monsieur le maire
③ *vtr* **(a)** (venerate) vénérer ⟨God, Buddha⟩; (give praise) rendre hommage à ┈┈╬

(b) adorer, avoir un culte pour ⟨*person*⟩; avoir le culte de ⟨*money, success*⟩
④ *vi* pratiquer sa religion

worshipper *n* fidèle *mf*

worst ① *n* **(a)** (most difficult, unpleasant) **the ~** le/la pire *m/f*; **if the ~ came to the ~** (in serious circumstances) dans le pire des cas; (involving fatality) si le pire devait arriver
(b) (most negative trait) **to bring out the ~ in sb** mettre à jour ce qu'il y a de plus mauvais chez qn
(c) (of the lowest standard, quality) **the ~** le plus mauvais/la plus mauvaise *m/f*; **he's one of the ~** c'est un des plus mauvais; **to be the ~ at French** être le plus mauvais en français
② *adj* **(a)** (most unsatisfactory, unpleasant) pire, plus mauvais/-e; **the ~ book I've ever read** le plus mauvais livre que j'aie jamais lu; **the ~ thing about the film is...** ce qu'il y a de pire dans le film c'est...
(b) (most serious) plus grave; **one of the ~ recessions** une des crises les plus graves
③ *adv* **the children suffer (the) ~** ce sont les enfants qui souffrent le plus; **they were (the) ~ hit by the strike** ce sont eux qui ont été les plus touchés par la grève; **~ of all,...** le pire de tout, c'est que...

worth ① *n* **(a)** (quantity) **five pounds' ~ of sth** pour cinq livres de qch; **thousands of pounds' ~ of damage** des milliers de livres de dégâts; **a week's ~ of supplies** une semaine de provisions; **to get one's money's ~** en avoir pour son argent
(b) (value) valeur *f*; **of great ~** de grande valeur; **of no ~** sans valeur
② *adj* **(a)** (of financial value) **to be ~ sth** valoir qch; **how much is it ~?** combien cela vaut-il?; **the pound was ~ 10 francs then** à l'époque, la livre valait 10 francs
(b) (of abstract value) **to be ~ sth** valoir qch; **to be ~ it** (en) valoir la peine; **the book isn't ~ reading** le livre ne vaut pas la peine d'être lu; **that's ~ knowing** cela est bon à savoir; **those little pleasures that make life ~ living** ces petits plaisirs qui rendent la vie agréable
IDIOMS **for all one is ~** de toutes ses forces; **for what it's ~** pour ce que cela vaut; **to be ~ sb's while** valoir le coup

worthless *adj* sans valeur; **he's ~** c'est un bon à rien

worthwhile *adj* ⟨*discussion, undertaking, visit*⟩ qui en vaut la peine; ⟨*career, project*⟩ intéressant/-e; **to be ~ doing** valoir la peine de faire

worthy *adj* **(a)** (deserving) **to be ~ of sth** mériter qch, être digne de qch; **~ of note** digne d'intérêt; **to be ~ of doing** ⟨*person*⟩ être digne de faire
(b) (admirable) ⟨*cause*⟩ noble; ⟨*citizen, friend*⟩ digne

would *modal aux* **(a)** (expressing the conditional) **it ~ be nice if everyone were there, wouldn't it?** ce serait bien si tout le monde était là, n'est-ce pas?; **if he had more money, he'd buy a car** s'il avait plus d'argent il achèterait une voiture; **we ~ have missed the train if we had left later** si nous étions partis plus tard, nous aurions raté le train; **we wouldn't have succeeded without him** nous n'aurions pas réussi sans lui
(b) (in indirect statements or questions) **we thought he'd forget** nous pensions qu'il oublierait; **did she say she ~ be coming?** est-ce qu'elle a dit qu'elle viendrait?; **I wish he ~ be quiet!** il ne pourrait pas se taire!
(c) (expressing willingness to act) **she wouldn't listen to me** elle ne voulait pas m'écouter; **he wouldn't do a thing to help us** il n'a rien voulu faire pour nous aider; **they asked me to leave but I wouldn't** ils m'ont demandé de partir mais j'ai refusé; **of course you ~ contradict him!** bien sûr il a fallu que tu le contredises!
(d) (in requests) **~ you give her the message?** est-ce que vous voulez bien lui transmettre le message?; **switch off the radio, ~ you?** éteins la radio, tu veux bien?; **~ you excuse me for a moment?** excusez-moi un instant
(e) (expressing one's wishes) **you like something to eat?** désirez-vous *or* voulez-vous manger quelque chose?; **I ~ like a beer** je voudrais une bière; **we ~ like to stay another night** nous aimerions rester une nuit de plus; **she'd have liked to stay here** elle aurait aimé rester ici; **I wouldn't mind another slice of cake** je prendrais bien un autre morceau de gâteau
(f) (offering advice) **if I were you, I wouldn't say anything** à ta place, je ne dirais rien; **it ~ be better to write** il vaudrait mieux écrire; **it ~ be a good idea to wait** ce serait une bonne idée d'attendre; **you ~ do well to check the timetable** tu ferais bien de vérifier l'horaire
(g) (in assumptions) **I ~ have been 12** je devais avoir 12 ans; **it ~ have been about midday** il devait être à peu près midi
(h) (used to) **she ~ talk for hours** elle parlait pendant des heures

would-be *adj* **(a)** (desirous of being) **~ emigrants/investors** personnes *or* ceux qui désirent émigrer/investir
(b) (so-called) **~ intellectuals** les soi-disant intellectuels
(c) (having intended to be) **the ~ thieves were arrested** les voleurs ont été arrêtés avant qu'ils aient pu passer à l'acte

wound ① *n* **(a)** (injury) blessure *f*; (cut) plaie *f*; **bullet ~** blessure par balle; **knife ~** coup *m* de couteau; **a ~ to** *or* **in the head** une blessure à la tête
(b) (figurative) blessure *f*
② *vtr* blesser
IDIOMS **to lick one's ~s** panser ses blessures; **to rub salt into the ~** remuer le couteau dans la plaie

wounded ① *n* **the ~** les blessés/blessées *m/f*
② *adj* blessé/-e; **~ in the arm** blessé au bras

wrangle ① *n* querelle *f*
② *vi* se quereller (**over, about** sur, à propos de; **with** avec)

wrap ① *n* (shawl) châle *m*; (stole) étole *f*

917

2 *vtr* (in paper) emballer (**in** dans); (in blanket, garment) envelopper (**in** dans); **to be ~ped in** être emmitouflé/-e dans ⟨*blanket*⟩; être enveloppé/-e dans ⟨*newspaper*⟩; être enveloppé/-e de ⟨*mystery*⟩
IDIOMS **to keep sth/to be under ~s** garder qch/être secret/-ète
■ **wrap up**: ¶ **~ up** se couvrir; **~ up well** or **warm!** couvre-toi bien!
¶ **~ [sth] up (a)** faire ⟨*parcel*⟩; envelopper ⟨*gift, purchase*⟩; emballer ⟨*rubbish*⟩
(b) to be ~ped up in ne s'occuper que de ⟨*person, child*⟩; être absorbé/-e dans ⟨*activity, work*⟩; **they are completely ~ped up in each other** ils ne vivent que l'un pour l'autre
(c) dissimuler ⟨*meaning, facts, ideas*⟩ (**in** derrière)
wraparound *adj* ⟨*window, windscreen*⟩ panoramique; ⟨*skirt*⟩ portefeuille
wraparound sunglasses *n pl* lunettes *fpl* de soleil enveloppantes
wrap-over *adj* ⟨*skirt*⟩ portefeuille; ⟨*dress*⟩ croisé/-e
wrapper *n* (of sweet) papier *m*
wrapping *n* emballage *m*
wrapping paper *n* (brown) papier *m* d'emballage; (decorative) papier *m* cadeau
wreak *vtr* assouvir ⟨*revenge*⟩ (**on** sur); **to ~ havoc** or **damage** infliger des dégâts; **to ~ havoc** or **damage on sth** dévaster qch
wreath *n* couronne *f*; **to lay a ~** déposer une gerbe
wreck **1** *n* **(a)** (car, plane) (crashed) épave *f*; (burnt out) carcasse *f*
(b) (sunken ship) épave *f*
(c) (person) épave *f*
2 *vtr* **(a)** ⟨*explosion, fire, vandals*⟩ dévaster ⟨*building, machinery*⟩; ⟨*person, driver, impact*⟩ détruire ⟨*vehicle*⟩
(b) ruiner ⟨*career, chances, health, life, marriage*⟩; gâcher ⟨*holiday, weekend*⟩
wreckage *n* **(a)** (of plane, car, ship) épave *f*; (of building) décombres *mpl*
(b) (of hopes, plans) naufrage *m*
wrecked *adj* **(a)** ⟨*car, plane*⟩ accidenté/-e; ⟨*ship*⟩ naufragé/-e; ⟨*building*⟩ démoli/-e
(b) ⟨*life, career, marriage*⟩ ruiné/-e
wren *n* roitelet *m*
wrench **1** *n* **(a)** (tool) tourne-à-gauche *m inv*
(b) (emotional upheaval) déchirement *m*
2 *vtr* tirer violemment sur ⟨*handle*⟩; **to ~ one's ankle/knee** se tordre la cheville/le genou; **to ~ sth from sb** arracher qch à qn; **to ~ sth away from sth** arracher qch de qch
wrestle **1** *vtr* **to ~ sb for sth** lutter contre qn pour qch; **to ~ sb to the ground** terrasser qn
2 *vi* **(a)** (Sport) faire du catch
(b) (struggle) **to ~ with** se débattre avec ⟨*person, problem, homework, conscience*⟩; se battre avec ⟨*controls, zip, suitcase*⟩; lutter contre ⟨*temptation*⟩
wrestler *n* catcheur/-euse *m/f*
wrestling *n* catch *m*

wretched *adj* ⟨*person*⟩ infortuné/-e; ⟨*existence, appearance, conditions*⟩ misérable; ⟨*weather*⟩ affreux/-euse; ⟨*accommodation*⟩ minable; ⟨*amount*⟩ dérisoire
wriggle **1** *vtr* **to ~ one's toes/fingers** remuer les orteils/doigts; **to ~ one's way out of sth** se sortir de qch
2 *vi* ⟨*person*⟩ s'agiter, gigoter; ⟨*snake, worm*⟩ se tortiller; ⟨*fish*⟩ frétiller; **to ~ out of** se défiler devant ⟨*duty, task*⟩
wring *vtr* **(a)** (*also* **~ out**) essorer ⟨*clothes, cloth*⟩
(b) (extract) arracher ⟨*confession, money*⟩ (**from, out of** à)
(c) (twist) **to ~ sb's/sth's neck** tordre le cou à qn/qch; **to ~ one's hands** se tordre les mains; (figurative) se lamenter
wrinkle **1** *n* (on skin) ride *f*; (in fabric) pli *m*
2 *vtr* **(a)** rider ⟨*skin*⟩; **to ~ one's nose** faire la grimace (**at** devant)
(b) froisser ⟨*fabric*⟩
3 *vi* ⟨*skin*⟩ se rider; ⟨*fabric*⟩ se froisser; ⟨*wallpaper*⟩ gondoler
wrist *n* poignet *m*
wristband *n* (for tennis, on sleeve) poignet *m*
wristwatch *n* montre-bracelet *f*
writ *n* assignation *f* (**for** pour); **to issue** or **serve a ~ against sb, to serve sb with a ~** assigner qn en justice
write **1** *vtr* **(a)** écrire ⟨*letter, poem, novel*⟩ (**to** à); composer ⟨*song, symphony*⟩; rédiger ⟨*business letter, article, report, prescription*⟩; faire ⟨*cheque*⟩; écrire ⟨*software, program*⟩; élaborer ⟨*legislation*⟩; **he wrote me a cheque for £100** il m'a fait un chèque de 100 livres sterling; **I wrote home** j'ai écrit à ma famille
(b) (US) écrire à ⟨*person*⟩
2 *vi* écrire (**to sb** à qn)
■ **write back** répondre (**to** à)
■ **write down** noter ⟨*details, name*⟩; mettre [qch] par écrit ⟨*ideas, suggestions*⟩; consigner [qch] par écrit ⟨*information, findings*⟩
■ **write off**: ¶ **~ off** écrire une lettre (**to** à); **to ~ off for** écrire pour demander
¶ **~ [sb/sth] off (a)** (wreck) bousiller complètement (colloq) ⟨*car*⟩
(b) (in bookkeeping) passer [qch] aux pertes et profits ⟨*bad debt, loss*⟩; amortir ⟨*capital*⟩
(c) (end) annuler ⟨*debt, project, operation*⟩
■ **write out (a)** (put down on paper) écrire
(b) (copy) copier
write-off *n* **(a)** (US) (in taxation) somme *f* déductible de la déclaration des revenus
(b) (wreck) épave *f*
writer *n* (author) (professional) écrivain *m*; (nonprofessional) auteur *m*
writer's block *n* l'angoisse *f* de la page blanche
write-up *n* **(a)** (review) critique *f*
(b) (account) rapport *m* (**of** sur)
writhe *vi* (*also* **~ about, ~ around**) se tortiller; **to ~ in agony** se tordre de douleur
writing *n* **(a)** (activity) **~ is her life** écrire, c'est sa vie ····▷

W

(b) (handwriting) écriture *f*; **his ~ is poor/good** il écrit mal/bien
(c) (words and letters) écriture *f*; **to put sth in ~** mettre qch par écrit
(d) (literature) littérature *f*
writing pad *n* bloc *m* de papier à lettres
writing paper *n* papier *m* à lettres
writing table *n* bureau *m*
written *adj* ⟨reply, guarantee, proof⟩ écrit/-e; **he failed the ~ paper** il a échoué à l'écrit; **~ evidence** *or* **proof** (Law) preuves *fpl* écrites; **the ~ word** l'écriture
wrong **1** *n* **(a)** (evil) mal *m*
(b) (injustice) tort *m*; **to right a ~** réparer un tort
2 *adj* **(a)** (incorrect) faux/fausse (*before n*); (ill-chosen) mauvais/-e (*before n*); **he took the ~ key** il a pris la mauvaise clé; **it's the ~ glue for the purpose** ce n'est pas la colle qu'il faut; **to go the ~ way** se tromper de chemin; **I dialled the ~ number** je me suis trompé de numéro, j'ai fait un faux *or* mauvais numéro; **you've got the ~ number** vous faites erreur
(b) (reprehensible, unjust) **it is ~ to cheat** c'est mal de tricher; **she hasn't done anything ~** elle n'a rien fait de mal; **it was ~ of me to do** je n'aurais pas dû faire; **it is ~ that** c'est injuste que; **there's nothing ~ with** *or* **in sth** il n'y a pas de mal à qch; **(so) what's ~ with that?** où est le mal?
(c) (mistaken) **to be ~** ⟨person⟩ avoir tort, se tromper; **to be ~ about** se tromper sur; **she was ~ about him** elle s'est trompée sur son compte; **to prove sb ~** donner tort à qn

(d) (not as it should be) **there is something (badly) ~** il y a quelque chose qui ne va pas (du tout); **there's something ~ with this computer** il y a un problème avec cet ordinateur; **the wording is all ~** la formulation ne va pas du tout; **what's ~ with your arm?** qu'est-ce que tu as au bras?; **what's ~ with you?** (to person suffering) qu'est-ce que tu as?; (to person behaving oddly) qu'est-ce qui t'arrive?; **your clock is ~** votre pendule n'est pas à l'heure
3 *adv* **to get** [sth] **~** se tromper de ⟨date, time, details⟩; se tromper dans ⟨calculations⟩; **I think you've got it ~** je pense que tu te trompes; **to go ~** ⟨person⟩ se tromper; ⟨machine⟩ ne plus marcher
4 *vtr* faire du tort à ⟨person, family⟩
IDIOMS **to be in the ~** être mas mon/ton etc tort; **to get on the ~ side of sb** se faire mal voir de qn; **to go down the ~ way** ⟨food, drink⟩ passer de travers
wrongdoer *n* malfaiteur *m*
wrongfoot *vtr* (Sport) prendre [qn] à contre-pied; (figurative) prendre [qn] au dépourvu
wrongly *adv* mal; **he concluded, ~, that...** il a conclu, à tort, que...; **rightly or ~** à tort ou à raison
wrought *adj* ⟨silver, gold⟩ travaillé/-e
wrought iron *n* fer *m* forgé
wry *adj* ⟨smile, look, humour⟩ narquois/-e; **to have a ~ sense of humour** être pince-sans-rire

Xx

x, **X** *n* **(a)** (letter) x, X *m*
(b) (standing for number, name) **for x people** pour x personnes; **Ms X** Mme X; **X marks the spot** l'endroit est marqué d'une croix
(c) (kisses ending letter) grosses bises
X-certificate *adj* ⟨film⟩ interdit/-e aux moins de 18 ans
xenophobia *n* xénophobie *f*
xerox® *vtr* photocopier

Xmas *n* Noël *m*
X-rated *adj* ⟨film, video⟩ interdit/-e aux moins de 18 ans
X-ray **1** *n* **(a)** (ray) rayon *m* X
(b) (photo) radiographie *f*, radio *f* (colloq); **to have an ~** se faire radiographier; **to give sb an ~** faire une radiographie à qn
2 *vtr* radiographier
X-ray unit *n* service *m* de radiologie

Yy

y, Y *n* y, Y *m*

yacht *n* yacht *m*

yachting *n* yachting *m*; **to go ~** faire du yachting

yachtsman *n* yachtman *m*

yahoo **1** *n* abruti/-e *m* (colloq)
2 *excl* hourra!

yak *n* yack *m*

Yale lock® *n* serrure *f* de sûreté

yam *n* igname *f*

yank **1** *n* coup *m* sec; **to give sth a ~** tirer qch d'un coup sec
2 *vtr* tirer ⟨*person, rope*⟩
■ **yank out** arracher

Yank *n* yankee *mf*

Yankee *n* yankee *m*

yap **1** *n* jappement *m*
2 *vi* ⟨*dog*⟩ japper (**at** après)

yapping **1** *n* jappements *mpl*
2 *adj* ⟨*dog*⟩ jappeur/-euse

yard *n* **(a)** yard *m* (= 0.9144 m)
(b) (of house, farm, prison, hospital) cour *f*
(c) (US) (garden) jardin *m*
(d) (for storage) dépôt *m*; (for construction) chantier *m*; **builder's ~** dépôt *m* de matériaux de construction

yardarm *n* bout *m* de vergue

yardstick *n* (figurative) critères *mpl*

yarn *n* **(a)** (fibre) fibre *f* textile; (wool) laine *f*
(b) (tale) histoire *f*; **to spin a ~** raconter des histoires

yashmak *n* voile *m* islamique

yawn **1** *n* bâillement *m*; **to give a ~** bâiller
2 *vi* **(a)** ⟨*person*⟩ bâiller
(b) ⟨*abyss, chasm*⟩ béer

yeah *particle* (colloq) ouais (colloq), oui; **oh ~?** vraiment?

year **1** *n* **(a)** (period of time) an *m*; (with emphasis on duration) année *f*; **in the ~ 1789/2000** en 1789/l'an 2000; **two ~s ago** il y a deux ans; **all (the) ~ round** toute l'année; **every ~** tous les ans; **over the ~s** au cours des ans *or* des années; **the ~ before last** il y a deux ans; **every ~** tous les ans; **they have been living in Paris for ~s** ils habitent Paris depuis des années; **for the first time in ~s** pour la première fois depuis des années; **it's a ~ since I heard from him** je n'ai plus de ses nouvelles depuis un an; **they lived in Paris for ~s** ils ont habité Paris pendant des années; **to earn £30,000 a ~** gagner 30 000 livres sterling par an
(b) (indicating age) **to be 19 ~s old** *or* **19 ~s of age** avoir 19 ans; **a two-~-old child** un enfant de deux ans

(c) (pupil) **first/second-~** ≈ élève *mf* de sixième/cinquième
2 **years** (colloq) *n pl* (a long time) **that would take ~s!** ça prendrait une éternité!; **it's ~s since we last met!** ça fait un siècle qu'on ne s'est pas vus!
IDIOMS **this job has put ~s on me!** ce travail m'a vieilli de 10 ans!

yearbook *n* **(a)** (directory) annuaire *m*
(b) (US) album *m* de promotion

yearlong *adj* ⟨*stay, course, absence*⟩ d'un an, d'une année

yearly **1** *adj* ⟨*visit, account, income*⟩ annuel/-elle
2 *adv* annuellement

yearn *vi* **(a)** **to ~ for** désirer (avoir) ⟨*child*⟩; aspirer à ⟨*freedom, unity*⟩; attendre ⟨*season, event*⟩; **to ~ to do** avoir très envie de faire
(b) (miss) **she ~s for her son** son fils lui manque terriblement

yearning **1** *n* désir *m* ardent (**for** de; **to do** de faire)
2 **yearnings** *n pl* aspirations *fpl*
3 *adj* ⟨*expression*⟩ plein/-e de désir

year out *n*: année d'interruption des études entre le lycée et l'université.

year tutor *n*: professeur responsable de toutes les classes d'un même niveau

yeast *n* levure *f*

yell **1** *n* (shout) cri *m*; (of rage, pain) hurlement *m*
2 *vtr* crier ⟨*warning*⟩; (louder) hurler ⟨*insults*⟩
3 *vi* crier; **to ~ at sb** crier après qn

yelling *n* cris *mpl*

yellow **1** *n* jaune *m*
2 *adj* **(a)** (in colour) jaune; **to go** *or* **turn ~** jaunir
(b) (colloq) (cowardly) trouillard/-e (colloq)
3 *vi* jaunir

yellow-belly *n* (colloq) trouillard/-e *m/f* (colloq)

yellow card *n* (Sport) carton *m* jaune

yellowish *adj* tirant sur le jaune; (unpleasantly) jaunâtre

Yellow Pages® *n pl* pages *fpl* jaunes

yelp **1** *n* glapissement *m*
2 *vi* glapir

Yemen *pr n* Yémen *m*

yen *n* **(a)** (currency) yen *m*
(b) (colloq) (craving) **to have a ~ for sth/to do** avoir grande envie de qch/de faire

yeoman *n* (*also* **~ farmer**) franc tenancier *m*

yeoman of the guard *n* (GB) membre *m* de la garde royale

yep, **yup** *particle* (colloq) (US) ouais (colloq), oui

yes *particle* oui; (in reply to negative question) si

■ Note *yes* is translated by *oui*, except when used in reply to a negative question in which case the translation is *si* or, more emphatically, *mais si*: *'did you see him?'—'yes (I did)'* = 'est-ce que tu l'as vu?'—'oui (je l'ai vu)'; *'you're not hungry, are you?'—'yes I am'* = 'tu n'as pas faim?'—'si (j'ai faim)'.

– Note that there are no direct equivalents in French for tag questions and short replies such as *yes I did, yes I am*.

– For some suggestions on how to translate these, see DO.

yes-man *n* (colloq) lèche-bottes *m inv*

yesterday ① *n* hier *m*; ∼'s **newspaper** le journal d'hier; ∼ **was a sad day for all of us** la journée d'hier a été triste pour nous tous; ∼ **was the fifth of April** hier nous étions le cinq avril; **the day before** ∼ avant-hier ② *adv* hier; **only** ∼ pas plus tard qu'hier; **all day** ∼ toute la journée d'hier

yesterday afternoon *n*, *adv* hier après-midi

yesterday evening *n*, *adv* hier soir

yesterday morning *n*, *adv* hier matin

yesteryear *n* temps *m* jadis; **the fashions of** ∼ la mode d'antan *or* du temps jadis

yes-vote *n* oui *m*

yet ① *conj* pourtant ② *adv* (a) (up till now, so far) encore; (in questions) déjà; (with superlatives) jusqu'ici; **it's not ready** ∼ ce n'est pas encore prêt; **has he arrived** ∼? est-il (déjà) arrivé?; **not** ∼ pas encore, pas pour l'instant; **it's the best** ∼ jusqu'ici, c'est le meilleur (b) (*also* **just** ∼) tout de suite, encore; **don't start** ∼ ne commence pas tout de suite (c) (still) encore; **they may** ∼ **come** ils pourraient encore arriver; **he'll finish it** ∼ il va le finir; **he won't come for hours** ∼ il ne viendra pas avant quelques heures (d) (even, still) encore; ∼ **more cars** encore plus de voitures; ∼ **another attack** encore une autre attaque; ∼ **again** encore une fois

yew *n* (*also* ∼ **tree**) if *m*

Y-fronts *n pl* (GB) slip *m* ouvert

YHA *n* (GB) (*abbr* = **Youth Hostels Association**) association *f* des auberges de jeunesse

yield ① *n* rendement *m* ② *vtr* (a) (produce) produire (b) (provide) donner, fournir 〈*result, meaning*〉; fournir 〈*clue*〉 (c) (surrender) céder (to à); **to** ∼ **ground** (figurative) céder du terrain ③ *vi* (a) (to person, temptation, pressure, threats) céder (**to** à) (b) (under weight, physical pressure) céder (**under** sous) (c) (be superseded) **to** ∼ **to** 〈*technology, phenomenon*〉 céder le pas à (d) (US) (driving) céder le passage

yob, **yobbo** *n* (GB) (colloq) loubard *m* (colloq), voyou *m*

yodel *vi* jodler, iodler

yoga *n* yoga *m*

yoghurt *n* yaourt *m*, yoghourt *m*

yo-heave-ho *excl* oh! hisse!

yoke ① *n* joug *m* ② *vtr* (*also* ∼ **up**) atteler

yokel *n* péquenaud/-e *m/f* (colloq), plouc *mf* (colloq)

yolk *n* jaune *m* (d'œuf)

yonks *n pl* (colloq) **I haven't seen him for** ∼ ça fait une éternité que je ne l'ai pas vu

you *pron*

■ Note In French *you* has two forms: *tu* and *vous*. The usual word to use to anyone you do not know very well is *vous*, also called the polite form: *can I help you?* est-ce que je peux vous aider? The more informal *tu* (plural *vous*) is used between close friends and family members, within groups of children and young people and by adults when talking to children: *there's a biscuit for you* il y a un biscuit pour toi. If in doubt, use the *vous* form.

(a) (subject) tu, vous; (object) te, t', vous YOU **would never do that**
(b) (with preposition, for emphasis) toi, vous; (polite) vous, **vous ne feriez jamais cela**; (informal) toi, **tu ne ferais jamais ça**; ∼ **English** vous autres Anglais; ∼ **idiot!** (colloq) espèce d'imbécile! (colloq); ∼ **two can stay** vous deux, vous pouvez rester
(c) (as indefinite pronoun) (subject) on; (object, indirect object) vous, te; ∼ **never know!** on ne sait jamais!; **it makes** ∼ **sleepy** ça fait dormir

you-know-what *pron* (colloq) vous-savez-quoi, tu-sais-quoi

you-know-who *pron* (colloq) qui-vous-savez, qui-tu-sais

young ① *n* (a) (young people) **the** ∼ les jeunes *mpl*, la jeunesse *f* (b) (animal's offspring) petits *mpl* ② *adj* (not very old) jeune; **to be** ∼ **at heart** avoir l'esprit jeune; **she is ten years** ∼**er than him** elle a dix ans de moins que lui; **I feel ten years** ∼**er** j'ai l'impression d'avoir rajeuni de dix ans; ∼ **lady** jeune femme *f*; ∼ **people** jeunes gens *mpl*; ∼ **person** jeune *m*; **the** ∼**er generation** la jeune génération; **her** ∼**er brother** son frère cadet; **I'm not as** ∼ **as I used to be** je n'ai plus 20 ans

young blood *n* sang *m* neuf

youngish *adj* assez jeune

young-looking *adj* **to be** ∼ faire (très) jeune

young offender *n* délinquant/-e *m/f*

young professional *n* jeune salarié/-e *m/f*

youngster *n* (a) (young person) jeune *m* (b) (child) enfant *mf*

your

■ Note For a full note on the use of the *vous* and *tu* forms in French, see the entry YOU.

– In French, determiners agree in gender and number with the noun that follows: *your* + masculine singular noun = *ton, votre* (*your dog* ton/votre chien); *your* + feminine singular noun = *ta, votre* (*your house* ta/votre maison); *your* + plural noun = *tes, vos* (*your parents* tes/vos parents).

(a) *det* votre/vos; (more informally) ton/ta/tes
(b) (used impersonally) son, sa, ses; **you buy ~ tickets at the door** on prend ses billets à l'entrée; **smoking is bad for ~ health** le tabac est mauvais pour la santé
(c) (for emphasis) à vous, à toi; YOUR house votre maison à vous, ta maison à toi

yours *pron*

■ **Note** For a full note on the use of the *vous* and *tu* forms in French, see the note for the entry YOU.
– In French, possessive pronouns reflect the gender and number of the noun they are standing for. When *yours* is referring to only one person, it is translated by *le vôtre, la vôtre, les vôtres* or, more informally, *le tien, la tienne, les tiens, les tiennes.* When *yours* is referring to more than one person, it is translated by *le vôtre, la vôtre, les vôtres.*

my car is red but ~ is blue ma voiture est rouge mais la vôtre *or* la tienne est bleue; **her children are older than ~** ses enfants sont plus âgés que les vôtres *or* les tiens; **which house is ~?** votre *or* ta maison c'est laquelle?; **he's a colleague of ~** c'est un de vos *or* tes collègues; **it's not ~** ce n'est pas à vous *or* à toi; **the money wasn't ~ to give away** vous n'aviez pas à donner cet argent

yourself *pron*

■ **Note** For a full note on the use of the *vous* and *tu* forms in French, see the entry YOU.
– When used as a reflexive pronoun, direct and indirect, *yourself* is translated by *vous* or familiarly *te* (or *t'* before a vowel or mute 'h'): *you've hurt yourself* = vous vous êtes fait mal *or* tu t'es fait mal.
– In imperatives, the translation is *vous* or *toi:* *help yourself* = servez-vous *or* sers-toi. (Note the hyphens.)
– When used for emphasis, the translation is *vous-même* or *toi-même: you yourself don't know* = vous ne savez pas vous-même *or* tu ne sais pas toi-même.

(a) (reflexive) vous, te, t'; **have you hurt ~?** est-ce que tu t'es fait mal?
(b) (in imperatives) vous, toi
(c) (emphatic) vous-même, toi-même; **you ~ said that...** vous avez dit vous-même que..., tu as dit toi-même que...
(d) (after prepositions) vous, vous-même, toi, toi-même
(e) (expressions) **(all) by ~** tout seul/toute seule; **you're not ~ today** tu n'as pas l'air dans ton assiette aujourd'hui

yourselves *pron*

■ **Note**
– When used as a reflexive pronoun, direct and indirect, *yourselves* is translated by *vous: help yourselves* = servez-vous.
– When used for emphasis, the translation is *vous-mêmes: do it yourselves* = faites-le vous-mêmes.

(a) (reflexive) vous
(b) (emphatic) vous-mêmes
(c) (after prepositions) vous, vous-mêmes; **all by ~** tous seuls/toutes seules

youth *n* **(a)** (young man) jeune homme *m*; **a gang of ~s** une bande de jeunes gens
(b) (period, state of being young) jeunesse *f*; **because of his ~** à cause de son jeune âge
(c) (young people) jeunes *mpl*

youth club *n* centre *m* de jeunes

youthful *adj* **(a)** (young) jeune
(b) (typical of youth) **his ~ looks** son air jeune

youth hostel *n* auberge *f* de jeunesse

youth hostelling *n* logement *m* en auberge de jeunesse

youth work *n* travail *m* social auprès des jeunes

youth worker *n* éducateur/-trice *m/f*

yowl *vi* ⟨person, dog⟩ hurler; ⟨cat⟩ miauler; ⟨baby⟩ brailler

yoyo *n* yo-yo *m*

yuck *excl* (GB) (colloq) berk (colloq)!

yucky *adj* (GB) (colloq) dégoûtant/-e

Yugoslavia *pr n* Yougoslavie *f*

Yule log *n* bûche *f* de Noël

yummy (colloq) **1** *adj* délicieux/-ieuse
2 *excl* miam-miam (colloq)

yuppie *n* **1** jeune cadre *m* dynamique
2 *adj* ⟨image, style, fashion⟩ de jeune cadre dynamique

y

Zz

z, Z n z, Z m

zany adj loufoque (colloq)

zap (colloq) **1** excl paf!
2 vtr **(a)** (destroy) détruire ⟨town⟩; tuer ⟨person, animal⟩
(b) (fire at) tirer sur ⟨person⟩
(c) (delete from computer screen) supprimer
3 vi **to ~ into town/a shop** faire un saut (colloq) en ville/dans un magasin; **to ~ from channel to channel** zapper (colloq)

zapper n (colloq) (TV remote control) télécommande f

zeal n **(a)** (fanaticism) zèle m; (religious) ferveur f
(b) (enthusiasm) ardeur f, zèle m

zealot n fanatique mf

zebra n zèbre m

zebra crossing n (GB) passage m (protégé) pour piétons

zenith n (figurative) apogée m

zero **1** n zéro m
2 adj ⟨altitude, growth, inflation, voltage⟩ zéro inv; ⟨confidence, interest, involvement, development⟩ nul/nulle; **sub-~ temperatures** des températures en dessous de zéro
■ **zero in: to ~ in on** [sth] (Mil) viser ⟨target⟩; (figurative) cerner ⟨problem⟩; foncer droit sur ⟨person⟩; repérer ⟨place⟩

zero hour n heure f H

zest n (enthusiasm) entrain m; **his ~ for life** sa joie de vivre

zigzag **1** n zigzag m
2 adj ⟨design, pattern⟩ à zigzags; ⟨route, road⟩ en zigzag
3 vi ⟨person, vehicle, road⟩ zigzaguer; ⟨river, path⟩ serpenter; **to ~ up/down** monter/descendre en zigzag

zilch n (colloq) que dalle (slang)

zimmer® n déambulateur m

zing n (colloq) (energy) entrain m

zip **1** n **(a)** (also **~ fastener, zipper** (US)) fermeture f à glissière, fermeture f éclair®; **to do up/undo a ~** tirer/défaire une fermeture à glissière
(b) (colloq) (energy) tonus m
(c) (US) (also **~ code**) code m postal
2 vtr **(a)** (close) **to ~ sth shut** fermer qch en tirant la fermeture à glissière
(b) (Comput) zipper, comprimer
3 vi (colloq) **to ~ along, to ~ past** filer à toute allure; **to ~ past sb/sth** dépasser qn/qch à toute allure
■ **zip through** (colloq): **to ~ through a book** lire un livre en diagonale (colloq)
■ **zip up**: ¶ **~ up** ⟨garment, bag⟩ se fermer par une fermeture à glissière; ¶ **~** [sth] **up** remonter la fermeture à glissière de qch

zipper (US) = ZIP 1A

zip pocket n poche f à fermeture à glissière

zodiac n zodiaque m

zombie n zombi(e) m; (figurative) abruti/-e m/f (colloq)

zone **1** n zone f
2 vtr (divide) diviser [qch] en zones

zonked adj (colloq) (also **zonked out**) (tired) crevé/-e (colloq)

zoo n zoo m

zoo keeper n gardien/-ienne m/f de zoo

zoologist n zoologue mf, zoologiste mf

zoology n zoologie f

zoom **1** n (also **~ lens**) zoom m
2 vi **(a)** (colloq) (move quickly) **to ~ past** passer en trombe; **to ~ around** passer à toute vitesse dans; **he's ~ed off to Paris** il a foncé (colloq) à Paris
(b) (colloq) (rocket) ⟨prices, profits⟩ monter en flèche

zucchini n (US) courgette f

z

Grammar Reference

French verbs

Standard verb endings

	-er	-ir	-r, -re		-er	-ir	-r, -re

Indicative Present

		-er	-ir	-r, -re
Singular	1	-e	-is	-s *or* -e
	2	-es	-is	-s *or* -es
	3	-e	-it	-t *or* -e
Plural	1	-ons	-(iss)ons	-ons
	2	-ez	-(iss)ez	-ez
	3	-ent	-(iss)ent	-ent

Subjunctive Present

		-er	-ir	-r, -re
Singular	1	-e	-(iss)e	-e
	2	-es	-(iss)es	-es
	3	-e	-(iss)e	-e
Plural	1	-ions	-(iss)ions	-ions
	2	-iez	-(iss)iez	-iez
	3	-ent	-(iss)ent	-ent

Indicative Imperfect

		-er	-ir	-r, -re
Singular	1	-ais	-(iss)ais	-ais
	2	-ais	-(iss)ais	-ais
	3	-ait	-(iss)ait	-ait
Plural	1	-ions	-(iss)ions	-ions
	2	-iez	-(iss)iez	-iez
	3	-aient	-(iss)aient	-aient

Subjunctive Imperfect

		-er	-ir	-r, -re
Singular	1	-asse	-sse	-sse
	2	-asses	-sses	-sses
	3	-ât	-it	-it *or* -ût
Plural	1	-assions	-ssions	-ssions
	2	-assiez	-ssiez	-ssiez
	3	-assent	-issent	-ssent

Indicative Past historic

		-er	-ir	-r, -re
Singular	1	-ai	-is	-s
	2	-as	-is	-s
	3	-a	-it	-t
Plural	1	-âmes	-îmes	-mes
	2	-âtes	-îtes	-tes
	3	-èrent	-irent	-rent

Imperative Present

		-er	-ir	-r, -re
Singular	1			
	2			
	3	-e	-s	-s
Plural	1	-ons	-(iss)ons	-ons
	2	-ez	-(iss)ez	-ez

Indicative Future

		-er	-ir	-r, -re
Singular	1	-erai	-rai	-rai
	2	-eras	-ras	-ras
	3	-era	-ra	-ra
Plural	1	-erons	-rons	-rons
	2	-erez	-rez	-rez
	3	-eront	-ront	-ront

Conditional Present

		-er	-ir	-r, -re
Singular	1	-erais	-rais	-rais
	2	-erais	-rais	-rais
	3	-erait	-rait	-rait
Plural	1	-erions	-rions	-rions
	2	-eriez	-riez	-riez
	3	-eraient	-raient	-raient

Infinitive

	-er	-ir	-r, -re
Present	-er	-ir	-r *or* -re

Participle

	-er	-ir	-r, -re
Present	-ant	-(iss)ant	-ant
Past	-é	-i	-i *or* -u

1 aimer

Indicative

Present

j'	aime
tu	aimes
il	aime
nous	aimons
vous	aimez
ils	aiment

Imperfect

j'	aimais
tu	aimais
il	aimait
nous	aimions
vous	aimiez
ils	aimaient

Past historic

j'	aimai
tu	aimas
il	aima
nous	aimâmes
vous	aimâtes
ils	aimèrent

Future

j'	aimerai
tu	aimeras
il	aimera
nous	aimerons
vous	aimerez
ils	aimeront

Perfect

j'	ai	aimé
tu	as	aimé
il	a	aimé
nous	avons	aimé
vous	avez	aimé
ils	ont	aimé

Pluperfect

j'	avais	aimé
tu	avais	aimé
il	avait	aimé
nous	avions	aimé
vous	aviez	aimé
ils	avaient	aimé

Imperative

Present aime
aimons
aimez

Past aie aimé
ayons aimé
ayez aimé

Subjunctive

Present

(que) j'	aime
(que) tu	aimes
(qu')il	aime
(que) nous	aimions
(que) vous	aimiez
(qu')ils	aiment

Perfect

(que) j'	aie	aimé
(que) tu	aies	aimé
(qu')il	ait	aimé
(que) nous	ayons	aimé
(que) vous	ayez	aimé
(qu')ils	aient	aimé

Pluperfect

(que) j'	eusse	aimé
(que) tu	eusses	aimé
(qu')il	eût	aimé
(que) nous	eussions aimé
(que) vous	eussiez	aimé
(qu')ils	eussent	aimé

Conditional

Present

j'	aimerais
tu	aimerais
il	aimerait
nous	aimerions
vous	aimeriez
ils	aimeraient

Past I

j'	aurais	aimé
tu	aurais	aimé
il	aurait	aimé
nous	aurions	aimé
vous	auriez	aimé
ils	auraient	aimé

Participle

Present aimant

Past aimé, -e
ayant aimé

Infinitive

Present aimer

Past avoir aimé

2 plier

Indicative

Present

je	plie
tu	plies
il	plie
nous	plions
vous	pliez
ils	plient

Imperfect

je	pliais
tu	pliais
il	pliait
nous	pliions
vous	pliiez
ils	pliaient

Past historic

je	pliai
tu	plias
il	plia
nous	pliâmes
vous	pliâtes
ils	plièrent

Future

je	plierai
tu	plieras
il	pliera
nous	plierons
vous	plierez
ils	plieront

Perfect

j'	ai	plié
tu	as	plié
il	a	plié
nous	avons	plié
vous	avez	plié
ils	ont	plié

Pluperfect

j'	avais	plié
tu	avais	plié
il	avait	plié
nous	avions	plié
vous	aviez	plié
ils	avaient	plié

Imperative

Present plie
plions
pliez

Past aie plié
ayons plié
ayez plié

Subjunctive

Present

(que) je	plie
(que) tu	plies
(qu')il	plie
(que) nous	pliions
(que) vous	pliiez
(qu')ils	plient

Perfect

(que) j'	aie	plié
(que) tu	aies	plié
(qu')il	ait	plié
(que) nous	ayons	plié
(que) vous	ayez	plié
(qu')ils	aient	plié

Pluperfect

(que) j'	eusse	plié
(que) tu	eusses	plié
(qu')il	eût	plié
(que) nous	eussions plié
(que) vous	eussiez	plié
(qu')ils	eussent	plié

Conditional

Present

je	plierais
tu	plierais
il	plierait
nous	plierions
vous	plieriez
ils	plieraient

Past I

j'	aurais	plié
tu	aurais	plié
il	aurait	plié
nous	aurions	plié
vous	auriez	plié
ils	auraient	plié

Participle

Present pliant

Past plié, -e
ayant plié

Infinitive

Present plier

Past avoir plié

3 finir

Indicative

Present

je	fin**is**
tu	fin**is**
il	fin**it**
nous	fin**issons**
vous	fin**issez**
ils	fin**issent**

Imperfect

je	fin**issais**
tu	fin**issais**
il	fin**issait**
nous	fin**issions**
vous	fin**issiez**
ils	fin**issaient**

Past historic

je	fin**is**
tu	fin**is**
il	fin**it**
nous	fin**îmes**
vous	fin**îtes**
ils	fin**irent**

Future

je	fin**irai**
tu	fin**iras**
il	fin**ira**
nous	fin**irons**
vous	fin**irez**
ils	fin**iront**

Perfect

j'	ai	fin**i**
tu	as	fin**i**
il	a	fin**i**
nous	avons	fin**i**
vous	avez	fin**i**
ils	ont	fin**i**

Pluperfect

j'	avais	fin**i**
tu	avais	fin**i**
il	avait	fin**i**
nous	avions	fin**i**
vous	aviez	fin**i**
ils	avaient	fin**i**

Imperative

Present

	fin**is**
	fin**issons**
	fin**issez**

Past

aie	fin**i**
ayons	fin**i**
ayez	fin**i**

Subjunctive

Present

(que) je	fin**isse**	
(que) tu	fin**isses**	
(qu')il	fin**isse**	
(que) nous	fin**issions**	
(que) vous	fin**issiez**	
(qu')ils	fin**issent**	

Perfect

(que) j'	aie	fin**i**
(que) tu	aies	fin**i**
(qu')il	ait	fin**i**
(que) nous	ayons	fin**i**
(que) vous	ayez	fin**i**
(qu')ils	aient	fin**i**

Pluperfect

(que) j'	eusse	fin**i**
(que) tu	eusses	fin**i**
(qu')il	eût	fin**i**
(que) nous	eussions	fin**i**
(que) vous	eussiez	fin**i**
(qu')ils	eussent	fin**i**

Conditional

Present

je	fin**irais**
tu	fin**irais**
il	fin**irait**
nous	fin**irions**
vous	fin**iriez**
ils	fin**iraient**

Past I

j'	aurais	fin**i**
tu	aurais	fin**i**
il	aurait	fin**i**
nous	aurions	fin**i**
vous	auriez	fin**i**
ils	auraient	fin**i**

Participle

Present fin**issant**

Past	fin**i**, -e
	ayant fin**i**

Infinitive

Present fin**ir**

Past avoir fin**i**

4 offrir

Indicative

Present

j'	offre
tu	offr**es**
il	offre
nous	offr**ons**
vous	offr**ez**
ils	offr**ent**

Imperfect

j'	offr**ais**
tu	offr**ais**
il	offr**ait**
nous	offr**ions**
vous	offr**iez**
ils	offr**aient**

Past historic

j'	offr**is**
tu	offr**is**
il	offr**it**
nous	offr**îmes**
vous	offr**îtes**
ils	offr**irent**

Future

j'	offr**irai**
tu	offr**iras**
il	offr**ira**
nous	offr**irons**
vous	offr**irez**
ils	offr**iront**

Perfect

j'	ai	offert
tu	as	offert
il	a	offert
nous	avons	offert
vous	avez	offert
ils	ont	offert

Pluperfect

j'	avais	offert
tu	avais	offert
il	avait	offert
nous	avions	offert
vous	aviez	offert
ils	avaient	offert

Imperative

Present

	offre
	offr**ons**
	offr**ez**

Past

aie	offert
ayons	offert
ayez	offert

Subjunctive

Present

(que) j'	offr**e**
(que) tu	offr**es**
(qu')il	offr**e**
(que) nous	offr**ions**
(que) vous	offr**iez**
(qu')ils	offr**ent**

Perfect

(que) j'	aie	offert
(que) tu	aies	offert
(qu')il	ait	offert
(que) nous	ayons	offert
(que) vous	ayez	offert
(qu')ils	aient	offert

Pluperfect

(que) j'	eusse	offert
(que) tu	eusses	offert
(qu')il	eût	offert
(que) nous	eussions	offert
(que) vous	eussiez	offert
(qu')ils	eussent	offert

Conditional

Present

j'	offr**irais**
tu	offr**irais**
il	offr**irait**
nous	offr**irions**
vous	offr**iriez**
ils	offr**iraient**

Past I

j'	aurais	offert
tu	aurais	offert
il	aurait	offert
nous	aurions	offert
vous	auriez	offert
ils	auraient	offert

Participle

Present offr**ant**

Past	offert, -e
	ayant offert

Infinitive

Present offr**ir**

Past avoir offert

5 recevoir

Indicative

Present

je	reçois
tu	reçois
il	reçoit
nous	recevons
vous	recevez
ils	reçoivent

Imperfect

je	recevais
tu	recevais
il	recevait
nous	recevions
vous	receviez
ils	recevaient

Past historic

je	reçus
tu	reçus
il	reçut
nous	reçûmes
vous	reçûtes
ils	reçurent

Future

je	recevrai
tu	recevras
il	recevra
nous	recevrons
vous	recevrez
ils	recevront

Perfect

j'	ai	reçu
tu	as	reçu
il	a	reçu
nous	avons	reçu
vous	avez	reçu
ils	ont	reçu

Pluperfect

j'	avais	reçu
tu	avais	reçu
il	avait	reçu
nous	avions	reçu
vous	aviez	reçu
ils	avaient	reçu

Imperative

Present reçois
recevons
recevez

Past aie reçu
ayons reçu
ayez reçu

Subjunctive

Present

(que) je	reçoive
(que) tu	reçoives
(qu')il	reçoive
(que) nous	recevions
(que) vous	receviez
(qu')ils	reçoivent

Perfect

(que) j'	aie	reçu
(que) tu	aies	reçu
(qu')il	ait	reçu
(que) nous	ayons	reçu
(que) vous	ayez	reçu
(qu')ils	aient	reçu

Pluperfect

(que) j'	eusse	reçu
(que) tu	eusses	reçu
(qu')il	eût	reçu
(que) nous	eussions	reçu
(que) vous	eussiez	reçu
(qu')ils	eussent	reçu

Conditional

Present

je	recevrais
tu	recevrais
il	recevrait
nous	recevrions
vous	recevriez
ils	recevraient

Past I

j'	aurais	reçu
tu	aurais	reçu
il	aurait	reçu
nous	aurions	reçu
vous	auriez	reçu
ils	auraient	reçu

Participle

Present recevant

Past reçu, -e
ayant reçu

Infinitive

Present recevoir

Past avoir reçu

6 rendre

Indicative

Present

je	rends
tu	rends
il	rend
nous	rendons
vous	rendez
ils	rendent

Imperfect

je	rendais
tu	rendais
il	rendait
nous	rendions
vous	rendiez
ils	rendaient

Past historic

je	rendis
tu	rendis
il	rendit
nous	rendîmes
vous	rendîtes
ils	rendirent

Future

je	rendrai
tu	rendras
il	rendra
nous	rendrons
vous	rendrez
ils	rendront

Perfect

j'	ai	rendu
tu	as	rendu
il	a	rendu
nous	avons	rendu
vous	avez	rendu
ils	ont	rendu

Pluperfect

j'	avais	rendu
tu	avais	rendu
il	avait	rendu
nous	avions	rendu
vous	aviez	rendu
ils	avaient	rendu

Imperative

Present rends
rendons
rendez

Past aie rendu
ayons rendu
ayez rendu

Subjunctive

Present

(que) je	rende
(que) tu	rendes
(qu')il	rende
(que) nous	rendions
(que) vous	rendiez
(qu')ils	rendent

Perfect

(que) j'	aie	rendu
(que) tu	aies	rendu
(qu')il	ait	rendu
(que) nous	ayons	rendu
(que) vous	ayez	rendu
(qu')ils	aient	rendu

Pluperfect

(que) j'	eusse	rendu
(que) tu	eusses	rendu
(qu')il	eût	rendu
(que) nous	eussions	rendu
(que) vous	eussiez	rendu
(qu')ils	eussent	rendu

Conditional

Present

je	rendrais
tu	rendrais
il	rendrait
nous	rendrions
vous	rendriez
ils	rendraient

Past I

j'	aurais	rendu
tu	aurais	rendu
il	aurait	rendu
nous	aurions	rendu
vous	auriez	rendu
ils	auraient	rendu

Participle

Present rendant

Past rendu, -e
ayant rendu

Infinitive

Present rendre

Past avoir rendu

7 être

Indicative

Present

je	suis
tu	es
il	est
nous	sommes
vous	êtes
ils	sont

Imperfect

j'	étais
tu	étais
il	était
nous	étions
vous	étiez
ils	étaient

Past historic

je	fus
tu	fus
il	fut
nous	fûmes
vous	fûtes
ils	furent

Future

je	serai
tu	seras
il	sera
nous	serons
vous	serez
ils	seront

Perfect

j'	ai	été
tu	as	été
il	a	été
nous	avons	été
vous	avez	été
ils	ont	été

Pluperfect

j'	avais	été
tu	avais	été
il	avait	été
nous	avions	été
vous	aviez	été
ils	avaient	été

Imperative

Present

	sois
	soyons
	soyez

Past

aie	été
ayons	été
ayez	été

Subjunctive

Present

(que) je	sois
(que) tu	sois
(qu')il	soit
(que) nous	soyons
(que) vous	soyez
(qu')ils	soient

Perfect

(que) j'	aie	été
(que) tu	aies	été
(qu')il	ait	été
(que) nous	ayons	été
(que) vous	ayez	été
(qu')ils	aient	été

Pluperfect

(que) j'	eusse	été
(que) tu	eusses	été
(qu')il	eût	été
(que) nous	eussions	été
(que) vous	eussiez	été
(qu')ils	eussent	été

Conditional

Present

je	serais
tu	serais
il	serait
nous	serions
vous	seriez
ils	seraient

Past I

j'	aurais	été
tu	aurais	été
il	aurait	été
nous	aurions	été
vous	auriez	été
ils	auraient	été

Participle

Present étant

Past été (invariable)
ayant été

Infinitive

Present être

Past avoir été

8 avoir

Indicative

Present

j'	ai
tu	as
il	a
nous	avons
vous	avez
ils	ont

Imperfect

j'	avais
tu	avais
il	avait
nous	avions
vous	aviez
ils	avaient

Past historic

j'	eus
tu	eus
il	eut
nous	eûmes
vous	eûtes
ils	eurent

Future

j'	aurai
tu	auras
il	aura
nous	aurons
vous	aurez
ils	auront

Perfect

j'	ai	eu
tu	as	eu
il	a	eu
nous	avons	eu
vous	avez	eu
ils	ont	eu

Pluperfect

j'	avais	eu
tu	avais	eu
il	avait	eu
nous	avions	eu
vous	aviez	eu
ils	avaient	eu

Imperative

Present

	aie
	ayons
	ayez

Past

aie	eu
ayons	eu
ayez	eu

Subjunctive

Present

(que) j'	aie
(que) tu	aie
(qu')il	ait
(que) nous	ayons
(que) vous	ayez
(qu')ils	aient

Perfect

(que) j'	aie	eu
(que) tu	aies	eu
(qu')il	ait	eu
(que) nous	ayons	eu
(que) vous	ayez	eu
(qu')ils	aient	eu

Pluperfect

(que) j'	eusse	eu
(que) tu	eusses	eu
(qu')il	eût	eu
(que) nous	eussions	eu
(que) vous	eussiez	eu
(qu')ils	eussent	eu

Conditional

Present

j'	aurais
tu	aurais
il	aurait
nous	aurions
vous	auriez
ils	auraient

Past I

j'	aurais	eu
tu	aurais	eu
il	aurait	eu
nous	aurions	eu
vous	auriez	eu
ils	auraient	eu

Participle

Present ayant

Past eu, -e
ayant eu

Infinitive

Present avoir

Past avoir eu

9 aller

Indicative

Present

je	vais
tu	vas
il	va
nous	allons
vous	allez
ils	vont

Imperfect

j'	allais
tu	allais
il	allait
nous	allions
vous	alliez
ils	allaient

Past historic

j'	allai
tu	allas
il	alla
nous	allâmes
vous	allâtes
ils	allèrent

Future

j'	irai
tu	iras
il	ira
nous	irons
vous	irez
ils	iront

Perfect

je	suis	allé
tu	es	allé
il	est	allé
nous	sommes	allés
vous	êtes	allés
ils	sont	allés

Pluperfect

j'	étais	allé
tu	étais	allé
il	était	allé
nous	étions	allés
vous	étiez	allés
ils	étaient	allés

Imperative

Present

	va
	allons
	allez

Past

	sois	allé
	soyons	allés
	soyez	allés

Subjunctive

Present

(que) j'	aille
(que) tu	ailles
(qu')il	aille
(que) nous	allions
(que) vous	alliez
(qu')ils	aillent

Perfect

(que) je	sois	allé
(que) tu	sois	allé
(qu')il	soit	allé
(que) nous	soyons	allés
(que) vous	soyez	allés
(qu')ils	soient	allés

Pluperfect

(que) je	fusse	allé
(que) tu	fusses	allé
(qu')il	fût	allé
(que) nous	fussions	allés
(que) vous	fussiez	allés
(qu')ils	fussent	allés

Conditional

Present

j'	irais
tu	irais
il	irait
nous	irions
vous	iriez
ils	iraient

Past I

je	serais	allé
tu	serais	allé
il	serait	allé
nous	serions	allés
vous	seriez	allés
ils	seraient	allés

Participle

Present allant

Past allé, -e

étant allé

Infinitive

Present aller

Past être allé

10 faire

Indicative

Present

je	fais
tu	fais
il	fait
nous	faisons
vous	faites
ils	font

Imperfect

je	faisais
tu	faisais
il	faisait
nous	faisions
vous	faisiez
ils	faisaient

Past historic

je	fis
tu	fis
il	fit
nous	fîmes
vous	fîtes
ils	firent

Future

je	ferai
tu	feras
il	fera
nous	ferons
vous	ferez
ils	feront

Perfect

j'	ai	fait
tu	as	fait
il	a	fait
nous	avons	fait
vous	avez	fait
ils	ont	fait

Pluperfect

j'	avais	fait
tu	avais	fait
il	avait	fait
nous	avions	fait
vous	aviez	fait
ils	avaient	fait

Imperative

Present

	fais
	faisons
	faites

Past

	aie	fait
	ayons	fait
	ayez	fait

Subjunctive

Present

(que) je	fasse
(que) tu	fasses
(qu')il	fasse
(que) nous	fassions
(que) vous	fassiez
(qu')ils	fassent

Perfect

(que) j'	aie	fait
(que) tu	aies	fait
(qu')il	ait	fait
(que) nous	ayons	fait
(que) vous	ayez	fait
(qu')ils	aient	fait

Pluperfect

(que) j'	eusse	fait
(que) tu	eusses	fait
(qu')il	eût	fait
(que) nous	eussions	fait
(que) vous	eussiez	fait
(qu')ils	eussent	fait

Conditional

Present

je	ferais
tu	ferais
il	ferait
nous	ferions
vous	feriez
ils	feraient

Past I

j'	aurais	fait
tu	aurais	fait
il	aurait	fait
nous	aurions	fait
vous	auriez	fait
ils	auraient	fait

Participle

Present faisant

Past fait, -e

ayant fait

Infinitive

Present faire

Past avoir fait

Infinitive		Indicative			
	Rules	Present	Imperfect	Past Historic	Future
11 créer	*always* é	je crée, -es, -e, -ent nous créons, -ez	je créais …	je créai …	je créerai …
12 placer	c	je place, -es, -e, -ez, -ent	nous placions, -iez	ils placèrent	je placerai …
	ç *before* a *and* o	nous plaçons	je plaçais, -ais, -ait, -aient	je plaçai, -as, -a, -âmes, -âtes	
13 manger	g	je mange, -es, -e, -ez, -ent	nous mangions, -iez	ils mangèrent	je mangerai …
	ge *before* a *and* o	nous mangeons	je mangeais, -eais, -eait, -eaient	je mangeai, -as, -a, -âmes, -âtes	
14 céder	è *before silent final syllable*	je cède, -es, -e, -ent			
	é	nous cédons, -ez	je cédais …	je cédai …	je céderai …
15 assiéger	è *before silent final syllable*	j'assiège, -es, -e, -ent			
	ge *before* a *and* o	nous assiégeons	j'assiégeais, -eais, -eait, -eaient	j'assiégeai	
	é *before silent syllable*				j'assiégerai …
16 lever	è *before silent syllable*	je lève, -es, -e, -ent			je lèverai …
	e	nous levons, -ez	je levais …	je levai …	
17 geler	è *before silent syllable*	je gèle, -es, -e, -ent			je gèlerai …
	e	nous gelons, -ez	je gelais …	je gelai …	
18 acheter	è *before silent syllable*	j'achète, -es, -e, -ent			j'achèterai …
	e	nous achetons, -ez	j'achetais …	j'achetai …	
19 appeler	ll *before mute* e	j'appelle, -es, -e, -ent			j'appellerai …
	l	nous appelons, -ez	j'appelais …	j'appelai …	
20 jeter	tt *before mute* e	je jette, -es, -e, -ent			je jetterai …
	t	nous jetons, -ez	je jetais …	je jetai …	
21 payer	i *before mute* e	je paie, -es, -e, -ent			je paierai …
	or y	je paye, -es, -e, -ent nous payons, -ez	je payais …	je payai …	je payerai …

Conditional	Subjunctive	Imperative	Participle		
Present	Present		Present	Past	
je créerais ...	que je crée ...	crée	créant	créé, -e	**11**
		créons, -ez			
je placerais ...	que je place ...	place, -ez		placé, -e	**12**
		plaçons	plaçant		
je mangerais ...	que je mange ...	mange, -ez		mangé, -e	**13**
		mangeons	mangeant		
	que je cède, -es, -e, -ent	cède			**14**
je céderais ...	que nous cédions, -iez	cédons, -ez	cédant	cédé, -e	
	que j'assiège ...	assiège			**15**
j'assiégerais ...	que nous assiégions , -iez	assiégeons	assiégeant	assiégé, -e	
je lèverais ...	que je lève, -es, -e, -ent	lève			**16**
	que nous levions, -iez	levons, -ez	levant	levé, -e	
je gèlerais ...	que je gèle, -es, -e, -ent	gèle			**17**
	que nous gelions, -iez	gelons, -ez	gelant	gelé, -e	
j'achèterais ...	que j'achète, -es, -e, -ent	achète			**18**
	que nous achetions, -iez	achetons, -ez	achetant	acheté, -e	
j'appellerais ...	que j'appelle, -es, -e, -ent	appelle			**19**
	que nous appelions, -iez	appelons, -ez	appelant	appelé, -e	
je jetterais ...	que je jette, -es, -e, -ent	jette			**20**
	que nous jetions, -iez	jetons, -ez	jetant	jeté, -e	
je paierais ...	que je paie, -es, -e, -ent	paie			**21**
je payerais ...	que je paye, -es, -e, -ent	paye			
	que nous payions, -iez	payons, -ez	payant	payé, -e	

French verbs

Infinitive	Rules	Indicative			
		Present	Imperfect	Past Historic	Future
22 essuyer	i *before mute* e	j'essuie, -es, -e, -ent			j'essuierai ...
	y	nous essuyons, -ez	j'essuyais ...	j'essuyai ...	
23 employer	i *before mute* e	j'emploie, -es, -e, -ent			j'emploierai ...
	y	nous employons, -ez	j'employais ...	j'employai ...	
24 envoyer	i *before mute* e	j'envoie, -es, -e, -ent			
	y	nous envoyons, -ez	j'envoyais ...	j'envoyai ...	
	err				j'enverrai ...
25 haïr	i	je hais, -s, -t			
	ï	ns haïssons, -ez, -ent	je haïssais ...	je haïs ... (haïmes, haïtes)	je haïrai ...
26 courir		je cours ...	je courais ...	je courus ...	je courrai ...
27 cueillir		je cueille, -es, -e, nous cueillons ...	je cueillais ...	je cueillis ...	je cueillerai ...
28 assaillir		j'assaille, -es, -e, nous assaillons, -ez, -ent	j'assaillais ...	j'assaillis ...	j'assaillirai ...
29 fuir	i *before consonants and* e	je fuis, -s, -t, -ent		je fuis ...	je fuirai ...
	y *before* a, ez, i, o	nous fuyons, -ez	je fuyais ...		
30 partir	*without* t	je pars ...			
	with t	il part ...	je partais ...	je partis ...	je partirai ...
31 bouillir	ou	je bous, s, t			
	ouill	nous bouillons ...	je bouillais ...	je bouillis ...	je bouillirai ...
32 couvrir		je couvre, -es, -e, nous couvrons ...	je couvrais ...	je couvris ...	je couvrirai ...
33 vêtir		je vêts ...	je vêtais ...	je vêtis ...	je vêtirai ...
34 mourir	eur	je meurs, -s, -t, -ent			
	our	nous mourons, -ez	je mourais ...	je mourus ...	je mourrai ...
35 acquérir	quier	j'acquiers, -s, -t, -ièrent			
	quer	nous acquérons, -ez	j'acquérais ...		j'acquerrai ...
	qu			j'acquis ...	

· ·

Conditional Present	Subjunctive Present	Imperative	Participle Present	Past	
j'essuierais …	que j'essuie, -es, -e, -ent	essuie			22
	que nous essuyions, -iez	essuyons, -ez	essuyant	essuyé, e	
j'emploierais …	que j'emploie, -es, -e, -ent	emploie			23
	que nous employions, -iez	employons, -ez	employant	employé, -e	
	que j'envoie, -es, -e, -ent	envoie			24
	que nous envoyions, -iez	envoyons, -ez	envoyant	envoyé, -e	
j'enverrais …					
		hais			25
je haïrais …	que je haïsse, qu'il haïsse	haïssons, haïssez	haïssant	haï, -e	
je courrais …	que je coure …	cours, courons, -ez	courant	couru, -e	26
je cueillerais …		cueille			27
	que je cueille …	cueillons, -ez	cueillant	cueilli, -e	
j'assaillirais …	que j'assaille …	assaille assaillons, -ez	assaillant	assailli, -e	28
je fuirais …	que je fuie, -es, -e, -ent	fuis		fui, -e	29
	que nous fuyions, -iez	fuyons, -ez	fuyant		
		pars			30
je partirais …	que je parte …	partons, -ez	partant	parti, -e	
		bous			31
je bouillirais …	que je bouille …	bouillons, -ez	bouillant	bouilli, -e	
	que je couvre; -es, -e, -ent	couvre			32
je couvrirais …	que nous couvrions …	couvrons, -ez	couvrant	couvert, -e	
je vêtirais …	que je vête …	vêts vêtons, vêtez	vêtant	vêtu, -e	33
	que je meure …	meurs		mort, -e	34
je mourrais …		mourons, -ez	mourant		
	que j'acquière, -es, -e, -ent	acquiers			35
j'acquerrais …	que nous acquérions, -iez	acquérons, -ez	acquérant		
				acquis, -e	

Infinitive		Indicative			
	Rules	**Present**	**Imperfect**	**Past Historic**	**Future**
36 venir	i	je viens, -s, -t, -nent		je vins ... ils vinrent	je viendrai ...
	e	nous venons, -ez	je venais ...		
37 gésir	Defective	je gis, tu gis, il gît, nous gisons, -ez, -ent	je gisais ...		
38 ouïr	Archaic	j'ois ... nous oyons ...	j'oyais ...	j'ouïs ...	j'ouïrai ...
39 pleuvoir		il pleut ils pleuvent	il pleuvait ils pleuvaient	il plut ils plurent	il pleuvra ils pleuvront
40 pourvoir	i	je pourvois, -s, -t, -ent			je pourvoirai ...
	y	nous pourvoyons, -ez	je pourvoyais ...		
	u			je pourvus ...	
41 asseoir	ie	j'assieds, -ds, -d			j'assiérai ...
	ey	nous asseyons, -ez, -ent	j'asseyais ...		
	i			j'assis ...	
asseoir (oi/oy replace ie/ey)	oi	j'assois, -s, -t, -ent			j'assoirai ...
	oy	nous assoyons, -ez	j'assoyais ...		
42 prévoir	oi	je prévois, -s, -t, -ent			je prévoirai ...
	oy	nous prévoyons, -ez	je prévoyais ...		
	i/u			je prévis ...	
43 mouvoir	eu	je meus, -s, -t, -vent			
	ou	nous mouvons, -ez	je mouvais ...		je mouvrai ...
	u			je mus, -s, -t, -(û)mes, -(û)tes, -rent	
44 devoir	û in the past participle masc. sing.	je dois, -s, -t -vent		je dus ...	
		nous devons, -ez	je devais ...		je devrai ...
45 valoir	au, aille	je vaux, -x, -t			je vaudrai ...
	al	nous valons, -ez, -ent	je valais ...	je valus ...	
prévaloir					

Conditional Present	Subjunctive Present	Imperative	Participle Present	Past	
je viendrais …	que je vienne, -es, -e, -ent	viens			**36**
	que nous venions, -iez	venons, -ez	venant	venu, -e	
			gisant		**37**
j'ouïrais …	que j'oie …	ois		ouï, -e	**38**
	que nous oyions …	oyons, -ez	oyant		
il pleuvrait ils pleuvraient	qu'il pleuve qu'ils pleuvent		pleuvant	plu	**39**
je pourvoirais …	que je pourvoie, -es, -e, -ent	pourvois			**40**
	que nous pourvoyions, -iez	pourvoyons, -ez	pourvoyant		
				pourvu, -e	
j'assiérais …		assieds			**41**
	que j' asseye …	asseyons, -ez	asséyant		
	que nous asseyions …			assis, -e	
j'assoirais …	que j'assoie, -es, -e, -ent	assois			
	que nous assoyions, -iez	assoyons, -ez	assoyant		
je prévoirais …	que je prévoie, -es, -e, -ent	prévois			**42**
	que ns prévoyions, -iez	prévoyons, -ez	prévoyant		
				prévu, -e	
	que je meuve, -es, -e, -ent	meus			**43**
je mouvrais …	que nous mouvions, -iez	mouvons, -ez	mouvant		
				mû, mue	
	que je doive, -es, -e, -ent	dois		dû, due	**44**
je devrais …	que nous devions, -iez	devons, -ez	devant		
je vaudrais …	que je vaille, -es, -e, -ent	vaux			**45**
	que nous valions, -iez	valons, -ez	valant	valu, -e	
	que je prévale, -es, -e				

Infinitive		Indicative			
	Rules	Present	Imperfect	Past Historic	Future
46 voir	oi	je vois, -s, -t, -ent			
	oy	nous voyons, -ez	je voyais …		
	i/e/u			je vis …	je verrai …
47 savoir	5 forms	je sais, -s, -t, nous savons, -ez, -ent	je savais …	je sus …	je saurai …
48 vouloir	veu/veuil	je veux, -x, -t, veulent			
	voul/voudr	nous voulons, -ez	je voulais …	je voulus …	je voudrai …
49 pouvoir	eu/u(i)	je peux, -x, -t, peuvent		je pus …	
	ouv/our	nous pouvons, -ez	je pouvais …		je pourrai …
50 falloir	*Impersonal*	il faut	il fallait	il fallut	il faudra
51 déchoir	choir *and* échoir *are defective*	je déchois, -s, -t, -ent			
		nous déchoyons, -ez	je déchoyais …	je déchus …	je décherrai …
52 prendre	prend	je prends, -ds, -d			je prendrai …
	pren	nous prenons, -ez ils prennent	je prenais …		
	pri(s)			je pris …	
53 rompre		je romps, -ps, -pt, nous rompons …	je rompais …	je rompis …	je romprai …
54 craindre	ain/aind	je crains, -s, -t			je craindrai …
	aign	nous craignons, -ez, -ent	je craignais …	je craignis …	
55 peindre	ein	je peins, -s, -t			je peindrai …
	eign	nous peignons, -ez, -ent	je peignais …	je peignis …	
56 joindre	oin/oind	je joins, -s, -t			je joindrai …
	oign	nous joignons, -ez, -ent	je joignais …	je joignis …	
57 vaincre	ainc	je vaincs, -cs, -c			je vaincrai …
	ainqu	nous vainquons, -ez, -ent	je vainquais …	je vainquis …	
58 traire	i	je trais, -s, -t, -ent		(obsolete)	je trairai …
	y	nous trayons, -ez	je trayais …		

Conditional	Subjunctive	Imperative	Participle		
Present	Present		Present	Past	
	que je voie, -es, -e, -ent	vois			46
	que nous voyions, -iez	voyons, -ez	voyant		
je verrais ...				vu, -e	
je saurais ...	que je sache ...	sache, -ons, -ez	sachant	su, -e	47
	que je veuille, -es, -e, -ent	veux (veuille)			48
je voudrais ...	que nous voulions, -iez	voulons, -ez (veuillez)	voulant	voulu, -e	
	que je puisse ...	(obsolete)		pu	49
je pourrais ...			pouvant		
il faudrait	qu'il faille	(no form)	(obsolete)	fallu	50
	que je déchoie, -es, -e, -ent	déchois	(no form but échéant)		51
je décherrais ...	que nous déchoyions, -iez	déchoyons, -ez		déchu, -e	
je prendrais ...		prends			52
	que je prenne ...	prenons, -ez	prenant		
				pris, -e	
je romprais ...	que je rompe ...	romps -pons, -pez	rompant	rompu, -e	53
je craindrais ...		crains		craint, -e	54
	que je craigne ...	craignons, -ez	craignant		
je peindrais ...		peins		peint, -e	55
	que je peigne ...	peignons, -ez	peignant		
je joindrais ...		joins		joint, -e	56
	que je joigne ...	joignons, -ez	joignant		
je vaincrais ...		vaincs		vaincu, -e	57
	que je vainque ...	vainquons, -ez	vainquant		
je trairais ...	que je traie, -es, -e, -ent	trais		trait, -e	58
	que nous trayions,	trayons, -ez	trayant		

Infinitive	Rules	Indicative Present	Imperfect	Past Historic	Future
59 plaire	ai	je plais, tu plais, il plaît (but il tait) nous plaisons ...	je plaisais ...		je plairai ...
	u			je plus ...	
60 mettre	met	je mets, nous mettons	je mettais ...		je mettrai ...
	mis			je mis ...	
61 battre	t	je bats, -ts, -t			
	tt	nous battons ...	je battais ...	je battis ...	je battrai ...
62 suivre	ui	je suis, -s, -t			
	uiv	nous suivons ...	je suivais ...	je suivis ...	je suivrai ...
63 vivre	vi/viv	je vis, -s, -t, nous vivons ...	je vivais ...		je vivrai ...
	véc			je vécus ...	
64 suffire		je suffis, -s, -t, nous suffisons ...	je suffisais ...	je suffis ...	je suffirai ...
65 médire		je médis, -s, -t, nous médisons, vous médisez (but vous dites, redites)	je médisais ...	je médis ...	je médirai ...
66 lire	i	je lis, -s, -t			je lirai ...
	is	nous lisons, -ez, -ent	je lisais ...		
	u			je lus ...	
67 écrire	i	j'écris, -s, -t			j'écrirai ...
	iv	nous écrivons, -ez, -ent	j'écrivais ...	j'écrivis ...	
68 rire		je ris, -s, -t, nous rions ...	je riais ... nous riions, -iez	je ris ... nous rîmes ...	je rirai ...
69 conduire		je conduis ...	je conduisais ...	je conduisis...	je conduirai ...
70 boire	oi	je bois, -s, -t, -vent			je boirai ...
	u(v)	nous buvons, -ez	je buvais ...	je bus ...	
71 croire	oi	je crois, -s, -t, ils croient			je croirai ...
	oy	nous croyons, -ez	je croyais ...		
	u			je crus ...	

. . . .

Conditional Present	Subjunctive Present	Imperative	Participle Present	Past	
je plairais …	que je plaise …	plais plaisons, -ez	plaisant		59
				plu	
je mettrais …	que je mette …	mets mettons, -ez	mettant		60
				mis, -e	
		bats			61
je battrais …	que je batte …	battons, -ez	battant	battu, -e	
		suis			62
je suivrais …	que je suive …	suivons, -ez	suivant	suivi, -e	
je vivrais …	que je vive …	vis vivons, -ez	vivant		63
				vécu, -e	
je suffirais …	que je suffise …	suffis suffisons, -ez	suffisant	suffi (but confit, déconfit, frit, circoncis)	64
je médirais …	que je médise … que nous médisions, -iez	médis médisons médisez (but dites, redites)	médisant	médit	65
je lirais …		lis			66
	que je lise …	lisons, -ez	lisant		
				lu, -e	
j'écrirais …		écris		écrit, -e	67
	que j'écrive …	écrivons, -ez	écrivant		
je rirais …	que je rie …	ris, rions, riez	riant	ri	68
	que nous riions, -iez				
je conduirais …	que je conduise …	conduis conduisons, -ez	conduisant	conduit, -e (but lui, nui)	69
je boirais …	que je boive, -es, -e, -ent	bois			70
	que nous buvions, -iez	buvons, -ez	buvant	bu, -e	
je croirais …	que je croie …	crois			71
		croyons, -ez	croyant		
				cru, -e	

French verbs

Infinitive		Indicative			
	Rules	Present	Imperfect	Past Historic	Future
72 croître	oî	je croîs, -s, -t			je croîtrai …
	oiss	nous croissons, -ez, -ent	je croissais …		
	û			je crûs …	
73 connaître		je connais, -s, -ssons, -ssez, -ssent	je connaissais …	je connus …	
	î before t	il connaît			je connaîtrai …
74 naître	î before t naisse	je nais, nais, naît nous naissons, -ez, -ent	je naissais …		je naîtrai …
	naqu			je naquis …	
75 résoudre	ou/oudr ol/olv	je résous, -s, -t nous résolvons, -ez, -ent	je résolvais …	(absoudre and dissoudre have no past historic)	je résoudrai…
	olu			je résolus …	
76 coudre	oud	je couds, -ds, -d			je coudrai …
	ous	nous cousons, -ez, -ent	je cousais …	je cousis …	
77 moudre	moud	je mouds, -ds, -d			je moudrai …
	moul	nous moulons, -ez, -ent	je moulais …	je moulus …	
78 conclure		je conclus, -s, -t, nous concluons, -ez, -ent	je concluais …	je conclus …	je conclurai …
79 clore	Defective	je clos, -os, -ôt ils closent	(obsolete)	(obsolete)	je clorai …
80 maudire		je maudis, -s, -t nous maudissons, -ez, -ent	je maudissais …	je maudis …	je maudirai …

Conditional Present	Subjunctive Present	Imperative	Participle Present	Past	
je croîtrais...		croîs			72
	que je croisse ...	croissons, -ez	croissant		
				crû, crue (but accru, -e)	
	que je connaisse ...	connais, -ssons, -ssez	connaissant	connu, -e	73
je connaîtrais ...					
		nais		né, -e	74
je naîtrais ...					
	que je naisse ...	naissons, -ez	naissant		
je résoudrais ...		résous		(absous, -oute; dissous, -oute)	75
	que je résolve ...	résolvons, -ez	résolvant		
				résolu, -e	
je coudrais ...		couds			76
	que je couse ...	cousons, -ez	cousant	cousu, -e	
je moudrais ...		mouds			77
	que je moule ...	moulons, -ez	moulant	moulu, -e	
je conclurais ...	que je conclue ...	conclus concluons, -ez	concluant	conclu, -e (but inclus, -e)	78
je clorais ...	que je close ...	clos	closant	clos, -e	79
je maudirais ...	que je maudisse ... qu'il maudisse	maudis -ssons, -ssez	maudissant	maudit, -e	80

Glossary of grammatical terms

Abbreviation A shortened form of a word or phrase made by leaving out some letters or by using only the initial letter of each word: etc., DNA

Active In the active form the subject of the verb performs the action: **she whistled = elle a sifflé**

Adjective A word describing a noun: **a** *red* **pencil = un crayon** *rouge*

Adverb A word that describes or changes the meaning of a verb, an adjective, or another adverb: **he drives** *fast* **= il conduit** *vite*; *fairly* **often =** *assez* **souvent**

Article The definite article, **the = le, la, l', les**, and indefinite article, **a/an = un, une**, are used in front of a noun

Attributive An adjective or noun is attributive when it is used directly before a noun: **the** *big* **dog = le** *grand* **chien;** *birthday* **card = carte d'anniversaire**

Auxiliary verb One of the verbs used to form the perfect, pluperfect, and future perfect tenses. In French the auxiliary verbs are **avoir** and **être**: **I have read the letter – j'***ai* **lu la lettre; he had already gone = il** *était* **déjà parti**

Cardinal number A whole number representing a quantity: **one, two, three = un/une, deux, trois**

Clause A self-contained section of a sentence that contains a subject and a verb

Collective noun A noun that is singular in form but refers to a group of persons or things, e.g. **royalty, grain**

Collocate A word that regularly occurs with another; in French **livre** is a typical collocate of the verb **lire**

Comparative The form of an adjective or adverb for comparing two or more nouns or pronouns, often using **more, less** or **as (plus, moins, aussi): smaller = plus petit; more frequently = plus fréquemment; as intelligent = aussi intelligent**

Compound adjective An adjective formed from two separate words : **tout-puissant = all-powerful; nord-américain = North American**

Compound noun A noun formed from two or more separate words: **porte-clés = keyring**

Conditional tense A tense of a verb that expresses what might happen if something else occurred: **I would invite them = je les inviterais**

Conjugation Variation of the form of a verb to show tense, person, mood, etc.

Conjunction A word used to link clauses: **and = et, because = parce que**

Definite article: **the = le, la, l', les**

Demonstrative pronoun A pronoun indicating the person or thing referred to: *this one* **is cheaper =** *celui-ci* **est moins cher**

Determiner A word that comes before a noun to show how it is being used: **the = le, la, l', les; some = du/de l'/de la/des; my = mon/ma/mes**

Direct object the noun or pronoun directly affected by the verb: **she ate** *the apple* **= elle a mangé** *la pomme*

Direct speech A speaker's actual words or the use of these in writing

Elliptical Having a word or words omitted, especially where the sense can be guessed from the context

Ending Letters added to the stem of verbs, as well as to nouns and adjectives, according to tense, number, gender

Exclamation A sound, word, or remark expressing a strong feeling such as anger, fear, or joy: **ouch! = aïe!**

Feminine One of the two noun genders in French: **la femme = the woman; la carte = the card**

Future tense The tense of a verb that refers to something that will happen in the future: **I will go = j'irai**

Gender One of the two groups of nouns in French: masculine and feminine

Imperative A form of a verb that expresses a command: **hurry up! = dépêche-toi!**

Imperfect tense The tense of a verb that refers to an uncompleted or a habitual action in the past: **I went there every day = j'y allais tous les jours**

Impersonal verb A verb used in English only with 'it' and in French only with 'il': **it is raining = il pleut**

Indefinite article: **a/an = un, une**

Ordinal numbers§

1st	1er‡	premier (*fem.* première)	30th	30e	trentième
2nd	2e	second *or* deuxième	31st	31e	trente et unième
3rd	3e	troisième	40th	40e	quarantième
4th	4e	quatrième	50th	50e	cinquantième
5th	5e	cinquième	60th	60e	soixantième
6th	6e	sixième	70th	70e	soixante-dixième
7th	7e	septième	71st	71e	soixante et onzième
8th	8e	huitième	72nd	72e	soixante-douzième
9th	9e	neuvième	73rd	73e	soixante-treizième
10th	10e	dixième	74th	74e	soixante-quatorzième
11th	11e	onzième	75th	75e	soixante-quinzième
12th	12e	douzième	79th	79e	soixante-dix-neuvième
13th	13e	treizième	80th	80e	quatre-vingtième
14th	14e	quatorzième	81st	81e	quatre-vingt-unième
15th	15e	quinzième	90th	90e	quatre-vingt-dixième
16th	16e	seizième	91st	91e	quatre-vingt-onzième
17th	17e	dix-septième	99th	99e	quatre-vingt-dix-neuvième
18th	18e	dix-huitième	100th	100e	centième
19th	19e	dix-neuvième	101st	101e	cent et unième
20th	20e	vingtième	102nd	102e	cent-deuxième
21st	21e	vingt et unième	200th	200e	deux centième
22nd	22e	vingt-deuxième	1,000th	1 000e	millième
23rd	23e	vingt-troisième	2,000th	2 000e	deux millième
24th	24e	vingt-quatrième	1,000,000th	1 000 000e	millionième
25th	25e	vingt-cinquième			

…English, French makes nouns by adding …finite article:

… =le premier (*or* la
première, *or* les premiers
m pl or les premières *f pl*)

…d …..= le second (*or* la seconde etc)

…ree ….= les trois premiers *or* les
trois premières

…ench word order in:

…hest ..= le troisième
…e   pays le plus
          riche du monde

…en in the following examples:

…...........= il y en a six
….......= j'en ai cent

…hen the thing you are
…t expressed (the French
…of them are six, I of them
…. However, **en** is not
…ct is specified:

…..= il y a six pommes

§ All the ordinal numbers in French behave
like ordinary adjectives and take normal
plural endings where appropriate.

‡ This is the masculine form; the feminine is
1re and the plural **1ers** (*m*) or **1res** (*f*). All
the other abbreviations of ordinal numbers
are invariable.

Decimals in French

Note that French uses a comma where English
has a decimal point.

written as	spoken as
0,25	zéro virgule vingt-cinq
0,05	zéro virgule zéro cinq
3,45	trois virgule quarante-cinq
8,195	huit virgule cent quatre-vingt-quinze

Indefinite pronoun A pronoun that does
not identify a specific person or object: **one =
on; something = quelque chose**

Indicative form The form of a verb used
when making a statement of fact or asking
questions of fact: **we like animals = nous
aimons les animaux**

Indirect object The noun or pronoun
indirectly affected by the verb, at which the
direct object is aimed: **she gave *him* the key =
elle *lui* a donné la clé**

Indirect speech A report of what
someone has said which does not reproduce
the exact words

Infinitive The basic part of a verb: **to play
= jouer**

Inflect To change the ending or form of a
word to show its tense or its grammatical
relation to other words: **donne** and **donnez** are
inflected forms of the verb **donner**

Interrogative pronoun A pronoun that
asks a question: **who? = qui?**

Intransitive verb A verb that does not
have a direct object: **he died yesterday = il est
mort hier**

Invariable adjective An adjective that
has the same form in the feminine as the
masculine, as French **ivoire, transmanche**

Invariable noun A noun that has the
same form in the plural as the singular, as.
English **sheep, species**, French **précis,
rabais**

Irregular verb A verb that does not follow
one of the set patterns and has its own
individual forms, e.g. English **to be**, French
être

Masculine One of the two noun genders in
French: **le garçon = the boy; le livre = the
book**

Modal verb A verb that is used with
another verb to express permission,
obligation, possibility, such as **might, should**.
The French modal verbs are **devoir, pouvoir,
savoir, vouloir, falloir**

Negative Expressing refusal or denial:
**there aren't any = il n'y en a pas; he won't
go = il ne veut pas partir**

Noun A word that names a person or thing

Number The state of being either singular
or plural

Object The word or group of words which is
immediately affected by the action indicated
by the verb, as **livre** in **il a lu le livre**, or
voiture in **elle lave la voiture**

Ordinal number A number that shows
the position of a person or thing in a series:
**the *third* time = la *troisième* fois, the *fourth*
door on the left = la *quatrième* porte à
gauche**

Part of speech A grammatical term for
the function of a word; noun, verb, adjective,
etc., are parts of speech

Passive In the passive form the subject of
the verb experiences the action rather than
performs it: **he was punished = il a été puni**

Past participle The part of a verb used to
form past tenses: **she had *gone* = elle était
*partie***

Perfect tense The tense of a verb that
refers to an action that has taken place in a
period of time that includes the present: **I have
already eaten = j'ai déjà mangé; my bike
has been stolen = on m'a volé mon vélo**

Person Any of the three groups of personal
pronouns and forms taken by verbs. In the
singular the **first person** (e.g. **I/je**) refers to
the person speaking; **the second person** (e.g.
you/tu) refers to the person spoken to; the
third person (e.g. **he, she it/il, elle**) refers to
the person spoken about. The corresponding
plural forms are **we/nous, you/vous,
they/ils, elles**

Personal pronoun A pronoun that refers
to a person or thing

Phrasal verb A verb in English combined
with a preposition or an adverb to have a
particular meaning: **run away = se sauver**

Phrase A self-contained section of a
sentence that does not contain a full verb

Pluperfect tense The tense of a verb
that refers to something that happened before a
particular point in the past: **when I arrived,
he *had* already *left* = quand je suis arrivé,
il *était* déjà *parti***

Plural Of nouns, etc., referring to more than
one: **the children = les enfants**

Possessive adjective An adjective
that shows possession, belonging to someone
or something: **my = mon/ma/mes**

Possessive pronoun a pronoun that
shows possession, belonging to someone or
something: **mine = le mien/la mienne/les
miens/les miennes**

Postpositive Placed after the word to
which it relates, as **in stock** in the phrase
items in stock

Predicative An adjective is predicative
when it comes after a verb such as **be** or
become in English, or after **être** or **devenir** in
French: **she is beautiful = elle est belle**

Prefix A group of letters added to the beginning of a word to change its meaning, e.g. anti-, ultra-, non-

Preposition A word that stands in front of a noun or pronoun, usually indicating movement, position or time: *on the chair* = *sur la chaise*; *towards the car* = *vers la voiture*

Present participle The part of a verb in English that ends in –ing; the corresponding ending in French is -ant

Present tense The tense of a verb that refers to something happening now: **I make** = **je fais**

Pronoun A word that stands instead of a noun: **he** = **il, she** = **elle, mine** = **le mien/la mienne/les miens/les miennes**

Proper noun A name of a person, place, institution etc. written with a capital letter at the start; **France, the Alps, Madeleine, l'Europe** are all proper nouns

Reflexive pronoun A pronoun that goes with a reflexive verb: in French **me, te, se, nous, vous, se**

Reflexive verb a verb whose object is the same as its subject. In French it is used with a reflexive pronoun and conjugated with **être**: **you should wash yourself** = **tu devrais te laver**

Regular verb A verb that follows a set pattern in its different forms

Relative pronoun A pronoun that introduces a subordinate clause, relating to a person or thing mentioned in the main clause: **the book** *which* **I chose** = **le livre** *que* **j'ai choisi**

Reported speech Another name for **Indirect speech**

Sentence A sequence of words, with a subject and a verb, that can stand on their own to make a statement, ask a question, or give a command

Singular Of nouns, etc., referring to just one: **the tree** = **l'arbre**

Stem The part of a verb to which endings are added; **donn-** is the stem of **donner**

Subject In a clause or sentence, the noun or pronoun that causes the action of the verb: *he* **caught the ball** = *il* **a attrapé le ballon**

Subjunctive A verb form that is used to express doubt or uncertainty in English. It is more widely used in French, particularly after certain conjunctions and with verbs of wishing, fearing, ordering, forbidding followed by **que**: **I want you to be good** = **je veux que tu sois sage; you may be right** = **il est possible que tu aies raison**

Subordinate clause A clause which adds information to the main clause of a sentence, but cannot function as a sentence by itself, e.g. **when it rang** in **she answered the phone when it rang**

Suffix A group of letters joined to the end of a word to form another word, as –**eur** in **grandeur** or –**able** in **véritable**

Superlative The form of an adjective or adverb that makes it the 'most' or 'least': **the** *biggest* **house** = **la plus grande maison; the** *cheapest* **CD** = **le CD** *le moins cher*

Tense The form of a verb that tells when the action takes place: present, future, imperfect, perfect, pluperfect are all tenses

Transitive verb A verb that is used with a direct object: **I wrote the letter** = **j'ai écrit la lettre**

Verb A word or group of words that describes an action: **the children are playing** = **les enfants jouent**

Numbers

Cardinal numbers

0	zéro*	16	seize	90	quatre-vingt-dix	1 200 mille** deux cen...
1	un†	17	dix-sept	91	quatre-vingt-onze	2 000 deux mille††
2	deux	18	dix-huit	92	quatre-vingt-douze	1 0000 dix mille
3	trois	19	dix-neuf	99	quatre-vingt-dix-neuf	100 000 cent mill...
4	quatre	20	vingt	101	cent un†	100 200 cent d...
5	cinq	21	vingt et un	102	cent deux	1 000 000 un...
6	six	22	vingt-deux	110	cent dix	1 264 932 u...
7	sept	30	trente	187	cent quatre-vingt-	deux cen...
8	huit	40	quarante		sept	quatre ...
9	neuf	50	cinquante	200	deux cents	trente-...
10	dix	60	soixante	250	deux cent◊	1 000 ...
11	onze	70	soixante-dix		cinquante	mill...
12	douze	71	soixante et onze	1 000	mille∞	1 00...
13	treize	80	quatre-vingts§	1 001	mille un†	b...
14	quatorze	81	quatre-vingt-un¶	1 002	mille deux	
15	quinze	82	quatre-vingt-deux	1 020	mille vingt	

* In English *0* may be called *nought, zero* or even *nothing*; French is always *zéro*: **a nought** = **un zéro.**

† **one** is **une** in French when it agrees with a feminine noun, so **un crayon** but **une table, une des tables, vingt et une tables**, etc.

§ Note that when *80* is used as a page number it has no **s**: **page eighty** = **page quatre-vingt.**

¶ **vingt** has no **s** when it is in the middle of a number. The only exception to this rule is when *quatre-vingts* is followed by *millions, milliards* or *billions*, eg **quatre-vingts millions, quatre-vingts billions** etc.

◊ **cent** does not take an **s** when it is in the middle of a number. The only exception to this rule is when it is followed by *millions, milliards* or *billions*, eg **trois cents millions, six cents billions** etc. It has a normal plural when it modifies other nouns: **200 inhabitants** = **deux cents habitants.**

∞ Where English wou... has simply a space... be used, e.g. **1.000**... separation in da... hundreds: **in 19**...

** In dates, the s... **mille,** i.e. **en**... However, wh... thousands,... **en l'an m**...

†† **mille** is...

‡ The Fr... **billio**... full t... **mill**... **d'h**... fi...

Like ...
the de...
the firs...

the secon...
the first t...

Note the F...
the third ric...
country in th...
world

Use of en

Note the use of...
there are six ...
I've got a hundre...

en must be used w...
talking about is n...
says literally there...
have a hundred etc...
needed when the ob...
there are six apples ...

Approximate numbers

When you want to say 'about ...', remember the French ending -*aine*:

about ten ....= une dizaine

about ten books ......= une dizaine de livres

about fifteen ....= une quinzaine

about fifteen people ...= une quinzaine de personnes

Similarly *une trentaine, une quarantaine, une cinquantaine, une soixantaine* and *une centaine* (and *une douzaine* means *a dozen*). For other numbers, use *environ* (*about*):

about thirty-five ......= environ trente-cinq

hundreds of books ...= des centaines de livres

thousands of books ...= des milliers de livres

I've got thousands ....= j'en ai des milliers

Percentages in French

written as	spoken as
25%	vingt-cinq pour cent
50%	cinquante pour cent
100%	cent pour cent
200%	deux cents pour cent
365%	trois cent soixante pour cent
4,25%	quatre virgule vingt-cinq pour cent

Fractions in French

in figures	in words
$1/2$	un demi*
$1/3$	un tiers
$1/4$	un quart
$1/5$	un cinquième
$1/6$	un sixième
$1/7$	un septième
$1/8$	un huitième
$1/9$	un neuvième
$1/10$	un dixième
$1/11$	un onzième
$1/12$	un douzième (*etc*)

* Note that **half**, when not a fraction, is translated by the noun **moitié** or the adjective **demi**; see the dictionary entry.

Phrases

numbers up to ten ....= les nombres jusqu'à dix

to count up to ten ....= compter jusqu'à dix

almost ten ....= presque dix

less than ten ....= moins de dix

more than ten ....= plus de dix

all ten of them ......= tous les dix

all ten boys ....= les dix garçons

my last ten pounds ...= mes dix dernières livres

the next twelve weeks ..= les douze prochaines semaines

the other two ....= les deux autres

the last four ....= les quatre derniers

Calculations in French

$10 + 3 = 13$ ......dix et trois font *or* égalent treize

$10 - 3 = 7$ ....trois ôté de dix il reste sept *or* dix moins trois égale sept

$10 \times 3 = 30$ ......dix fois trois égalent trente

$30 : 3 = 10$ ......($30 \div 3 = 10$) trente divisé par trois égale dix

5^2 ....cinq au carré

5^3 ....cinq puissance trois

$\sqrt{12}$ ....racine carrée de douze

in figures	in words
$2/3$	deux tiers†
$2/5$	deux cinquièmes
$3/4$	trois quarts
$3/5$	trois cinquièmes (etc)
$1\,1/2$	un et demi
$1\,1/3$	un (et) un tiers
$1\,1/4$	un et quart
$1\,1/5$	un (et) un cinquième
$5\,2/3$	cinq (et) deux tiers
$5\,3/4$	cinq (et) trois quarts

† Note the use of **les** and **d'entre** when these fractions are used about a group of people or things: **two-thirds of them = les deux tiers d'entre eux**.

Weights and measures

Weight/Le poids

1,000 milligrams (mg) . . . . = 1 gram (g) . . . . = 15.43 grains
1 000* milligrammes (mg) . . . . = 1 gramme (g)

1,000 grams . . . . = 1 kilogram (kg) . . . . = 2.205 pounds
1 000 grammes. = 1 kilogramme (kg)

1,000 kilograms . . . . = 1 tonne (t) . . . . = 19.684 hundredweight
1 000 kilogrammes. . . . . = 1 tonne (t)

                           1 ounce (oz.) . . . . = 28.35g†

16 ounces . . . . = 1 pound (lb.) . . . . = 0.454 kg

14 pounds . . . . = 1 stone (st.) . . . . = 6.35 kg

112 pounds . . . . = 1 hundredweight . . . . = 50.8 kg

20 hundredweight . . . . = 1 ton (t.) . . . . = 1,016.05 kg

* Where English would have a comma, French has a space.

† Note that French uses a comma where English has a decimal point.

Length/Les mesures de longueur

10 millimetres (mm) . . . . = 1 centimetre (cm) . . . . = 0.394 inch
10 millimètres (mm) . . . . = 1 centimètre (cm)

100 centimetres . . . . = 1 metre (m) . . . . = 39.4 inches/1.094 yards
100 centimètres . . . . = 1 mètre (m)

1,000 metres. . . . . = 1 kilometre (km). . . . . = 0.6214 mile ≈ 5/8 mile
1 000 mètres. . . . . = 1 kilomètre (km)

                           1 inch (in.) . . . . = 25.4 mm

12 inches. . . . . = 1 foot (ft.) . . . . = 30.48 cm

3 feet . . . . = 1 yard (yd.) . . . . = 0.914 m

220 yards. . . . . = 1 furlong . . . . = 201.17 m

8 furlongs . . . . = 1 mile (m.) . . . . = 1.609 km

1,760 yards . . . . = 1 mile (m.) . . . . = 1.609 km

Weights and Measures

Square measure/La superficie

100 square metres (sq. m) . . . . = 1 are . . . . = 0.025 acre
100 mètres carrés (m²) . . . . = *1 are (a)*

100 ares . . . . = 1 hectare (ha) . . . . = 2.471 acres
100 ares . . . . = *1 hectare (ha)*

100 hectares . . . . = 1 square kilometre (sq. km) . . . = 0.386 square miles
100 hectares . . . . = *1 kilomètre carré (km²)*

1 square inch . . . . = 6.452 cm²

144 square inches . . . . = 1 square foot . . . . = 929.03 cm²

9 square feet . . . . = 1 square yard . . . . = 0.836 m²

4,840 square yards . . . . = 1 acre . . . . = 0.405 ha

640 acres . . . . = 1 square mile . . . . = 2.59 km²/259 ha

Cubic Measure/Le volume

1 cubic centimetre (cc) . . . . = 0.06 cubic inches
1 centimètre cube (cm³)

1,000,000 cubic centimetres . . . . = 1 cubic metre (cu. m) . . . . = 35.714 cubic feet/
1 000 000 centimètres cubes . . . . = *1 mètre cube (m³)*   1.307 cubic yards

1 cubic inch . . . . = 16.4 cm³

1,728 cubic inches . . . . = 1 cubic foot . . . . = 0.028 m³

27 cubic feet . . . . = 1 cubic yard . . . . = 0.764 m³

Capacity/La capacité

10 millilitres (ml) . . . . = 1 centilitre (cl)
10 millilitres (ml) . . . . = *1 centilitre (cl)*

100 centilitres . . . . = 1 litre (l) . . . . = 1.76 pints (2.1 US pints)/
100 centilitres . . . . = *1 litre (l)*   0.22 gallons (0.264 US gallons)

4 gills . . . . = 1 pint (pt.) . . . . = 0.568 l
                                                        (1.201 US pints)

2 pints . . . . = 1 quart (qt.) . . . . = 1.136 l
                                                        (1.201 US quarts)

4 quarts . . . . = 1 gallon (gal.) . . . . = 4.546 l
                                                        (1.201 US gallons)

Also available from Oxford University Press

Concise Oxford-Hachette French Dictionary
Over 175,000 words and phrases, and 270,000 translations
0-19-860242-1

Oxford French Cartoon-strip Vocabulary Builder
Claire Bretécher's cartoons, plus all the short-cuts to
sounding really French
0-19-860267-7

Oxford French Verbpack
0-19-860338-X

Oxford French Wordpack
0-19-860335-5

Oxford French Grammar
0-19-860341-X